THE GOOD PUB GUIDE

2016

HOBGOBLIN

WYCHWOOD BREWERY

SINCE 1983

I'm bringing taste to the nation with my Legendary Ruby & my Guilt Edged Golden Beer. So...

WYCH bREW arE YOU?

BORN OUT OF CHARACTER
www.wychwood.co.uk

GOLD
WYCHWOOD BREWERY
GUILT EDGED GOLDEN BEER
4.2% vol
HOBGOBLIN

HOBGOBLIN
WYCHWOOD BREWERY
4.5% vol
Traditionally Crafted Legendary Ruby Beer

The Good Pub Guide 2016

Edited by Fiona Stapley

Associate Editor: Patrick Stapley
Editorial Research: Fiona Wright

Founded by Alisdair Aird in 1982

EBURY PRESS
LONDON

Please send reports on pubs to:

The Good Pub Guide
FREEPOST RTJR-ZCYZ-RJZT, Perrymans Lane, Etchingham TN19 7DN

or **feedback@goodguides.com**

or visit our website: **www.thegoodpubguide.co.uk**

If you would like to advertise in the next edition of *The Good Pub Guide*,
please email **goodpubguide@tbs-ltd.co.uk**

10 9 8 7 6 5 4 3 2 1

Published in 2015 by Ebury Press, an imprint of Ebury Publishing

Ebury Press, an imprint of Ebury Publishing
20 Vauxhall Bridge Road,
London, SW1V 2SA

Text © Ebury Publishing 2015
Maps © PerroGraphics 2015
Fiona Stapley has asserted her right to be identified as the author of this Work
in accordance with the Copyright, Designs and Patents Act 1988

www.eburypublishing.co.uk

Penguin Random House is committed to a sustainable future for
our business, our readers and our planet. This book is made from
Forest Stewardship Council® certified paper.

To buy books by your favourite authors and register for offers,
visit www.randomhouse.co.uk

Typeset from authors' files by Jerry Goldie Graphic Design
Project manager and copy editor Cath Phillips
Proofreader Tamsin Shelton

Printed and bound in Great Britain by Clays Ltd, St Ives PLC

ISBN 9781785030321

Contents

·PIPERS·
CRISP Co
— MADE BY FARMERS —

Great Crisps, Great Beer,

Great Pub

Introduction & The Good Pub Guide Awards 2016

In the early 1980s, Alisdair Aird had a brainwave. He decided to write a book about the best pubs in Britain. After some research and asking everyone he knew for their favourite pubs, he travelled the country with a portable typewriter on his lap and reams of paper – and *The Good Pub Guide* was published in 1982. It quickly became an annual bestseller and thousands of people began writing in about their best pubs and taverns; they continue to do so, more than 30 years on. The first edition I helped Alisdair with was in 1986 and we've worked together in happy cahoots since then, finding wonderful new pubs every year. This is the 2016 edition of *The Good Pub Guide* – and the first without Alisdair, who has now retired from full-time work. Little will change: ideals and values remain the same, as will anonymous inspections and the inclusion of what we think are the best pubs in the country.

Are children a problem in pubs?

Most pubs in this book welcome children and certainly our readers very much enjoy being able to go to a pub as a family treat. But while most children behave well, a persistent small number spoil things for everyone else.

Times have changed. When I was a child, my father had to leave me outside in the car with a bag of crisps to keep me happy while he popped in for his pint. Then, 30 years ago, when I first worked on the *Guide*, in came the dreaded Family Room, that unloved and characterless back room that families were banished to. These days, the era of children being seen but not heard has been consigned to history – and quite right too.

But now that almost all pubs warmly welcome children throughout, the few problem families, whose children run riot, stick out like the proverbial sore thumb. We get more complaints from readers about unruly children than anything else, with comments such as: 'Why are there undisciplined children who are allowed to run around unchecked, or screaming babies who aren't taken outside to calm down?' 'My peaceful lunch by the fire with a pint was totally ruined by a child running around whooping and tripping up staff – and when asked to quieten down by the landlord, he faced abuse from over-protective parents – ridiculous!'

It's a delicate situation for publicans who have to try to please everyone, but this quote from a landlady is apt: 'My pub is not suitable for noisy or badly behaved children, but charming ones are warmly welcomed.' A technique adopted by many pubs is to seat families together in one room where possible and those hoping for a quiet meal in another, and to have age and time restrictions in the evening – that way, everyone understands the rules and can relax and enjoy themselves.

Of course, many businesses target the children's market with great skill and effectiveness, offering ball pits, well equipped play areas, high chairs with balloons attached, colourful menus with crayons – and perhaps parents with particularly boisterous children should head first for these establishments.

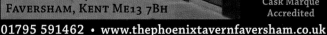

The pubs in this book aim to cater to all ages; as one top publican said, 'There is nothing more pleasant than a large family group out for Sunday lunch, with all generations present – including well behaved children.' Another suggests that if you treat children maturely and not as 'special cases' – by encouraging them to have small helpings of adult food rather than having a children's menu thrust at them, and providing free wi-fi so they can sit quietly and chat on social media or play games – then they will respond in kind.

In truth, any parent would be being a little dishonest if they did not admit to looking forward to handing their kids to granny and grandpa for the evening so they could go out for a relaxed meal. By definition, this requires the exclusion (or very good behaviour) of the children of others. The boot is now on the other foot!

Younger landlords helping pub fortunes

More than one in seven of Britain's pubs are now being run by licensees aged between 25 and 35. This is a big change: a jump of almost a quarter in that age group in just the last three years. Not deterred by what has been a difficult time for the industry and rejecting often uninspiring office jobs for the chance to run their own business, a new generation of publicans is bringing fresh enthusiasm to the licensed trade. In turn, this is drawing in younger customers, curious to see what might be different. The interest in craft beers is booming and the niche spirit trade is burgeoning, with small companies springing up across the country producing artisan gin, vodka and whisky.

These new, younger landlords and landladies are absolutely in tune with such trends, and with today's fitter, leaner mood and the demands for fair-priced healthy food. They take enormous care to source their produce as locally as possible, using free-range and organic ingredients and personally visiting the people who produce it for them. Many are growing their own vegetables and fruit and even rearing animals. Mark and Kerry Vernon, who took over the Tram in Eardisley, Herefordshire, are typical of this new generation. When they started, Kerry says, they were 'pretty naive' and lacked experience, but they had new ideas and bags of energy – and through sheer hard work they've turned the Tram into what we consider one of that county's best pubs.

Drinks: the search for fair prices and top quality

Our national survey of beer prices shows a huge 82p-a-pint difference in the price of a pint of ale between Herefordshire, the cheapest area, and London, the most expensive. How does your area rank? Here are the details, in average price order:

Bargain beer
Herefordshire, Yorkshire, Derbyshire, Worcestershire, Cumbria, Shropshire, Nottinghamshire, Northumbria

Fair-priced beer
Wales, Lancashire, Cornwall, Northamptonshire, Staffordshire, Gloucestershire, Cheshire, Somerset, Leicestershire

Average-priced beer
Essex, Cambridgeshire, Lincolnshire, Devon, Norfolk, Warwickshire, Bedfordshire, Dorset, Wiltshire, Suffolk, Hampshire, Scotland, Hertfordshire, Oxfordshire

Expensive beer
Buckinghamshire, Kent, Surrey, Isle of Wight, Sussex, Berkshire, Scottish Islands

Rip-off beer
London

Harveys in Lewes, East Sussex was founded in 1790 and has been run by the same family for eight generations. They operate across the South-east selling carefully crafted regular and seasonal ales to their own 48 pubs and to well over 500 other outlets. Every Tuesday they deliver beer around Lewes by dray cart. For their multi-award-winning real ales, **Harveys** is our **Brewery of the Year 2016**.

In this edition, there are 328 pubs deemed outstanding in the quality, and often the range, of beers they sell – each gets a Beer Award. This year's Top Ten Beer Pubs are the **Bhurtpore** in Aston and **Mill** in Chester (Cheshire), **Watermill** at Ings (Cumbria), **Fat Cat** in Norwich (Norfolk), **Malt Shovel** in Northampton (Northamptonshire), **Fat Cat** in Ipswich (Suffolk), **Red Lion** in Cricklade (Wiltshire), **Kelham Island**

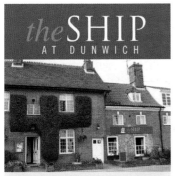

Tavern in Sheffield (Yorkshire), **Nags Head** in Malvern (Worcestershire) and **Clachaig** at Glencoe (Scotland). With an exceptionally knowledgeable landlord who keeps 32 well kept ales at any one time, the **Fat Cat** in Norwich is **Beer Pub of the Year 2016**.

You typically save yourself 48p a pint if you drink at one of the 21 own-brew pubs in this edition. Our Top Ten Own-Brew Pubs are the **Brewery Tap** in Peterborough (Cambridgeshire), **Beer Hall at Hawkshead Brewery** in Staveley, **Drunken Duck** near Hawkshead and **Watermill** at Ings (Cumbria), **Old Poets Corner** in Ashover (Derbyshire), **Church Inn** at Uppermill (Lancashire), **Grainstore** in Oakham (Leicestershire & Rutland), **Dipton Mill Inn** in Diptonmill (Northumbria), **Gribble** at Oving (Sussex) and **Weighbridge Brewhouse** in Swindon (Wiltshire). For its ten excellent Oakham ales, the **Grainstore** in Oakham is our **Own-Brew Pub of the Year 2016**.

Over 370 pubs hold a Wine Award, with many offering an outstanding choice by the glass. Our Top Ten Wine Pubs are the **Old Bridge Hotel** in Huntingdon (Cambridgeshire), **Drunken Duck** near Hawkshead (Cumbria), **Nobody Inn** at Doddiscombsleigh (Devon), **Yew Tree** at Clifford's Mesne (Gloucestershire), **Inn at Whitewell**, Whitewell (Lancashire), **Olive Branch** in Clipsham (Leicestershire & Rutland), **Woods** in Dulverton (Somerset), **The Inn West End** in West End (Surrey), **Crown** at Roecliffe (Yorkshire) and **Griffin** at Felinfach (Wales). With an extraordinary choice of 400 wines (they'll open any of them just for a glass), **Woods** in Dulverton wins again and is **Wine Pub of the Year 2016**.

Of the many pubs that stock a fantastic collection of malt whiskies, our Top Ten Whisky Pubs are the **Old Harkers Arms** in Chester (Cheshire), **Nobody Inn** at Doddiscombsleigh (Devon), **Red Fox** at Thornton Hough and **Old Hall** at Worsley (Lancashire), **Greyhound** at Bessels Leigh (Oxfordshire), **Old Orchard** on the outskirts of west London and **Clachaig** at Glencoe, **Bow Bar** in Edinburgh, **Bon Accord** in Glasgow and **Sligachan Hotel** at Sligachan on the Isle of Skye (Scotland). With over 400 malts to choose from, the **Sligachan Hotel** on the Isle of Skye is **Whisky Pub of the Year 2016.**

The Epicurean Collection encompasses pubs across the south of Britain – each carefully chosen to be close to beautiful countryside and each in fine old buildings of character. And although under the umbrella of a company, the pubs are run

Ridley Inns

Characterful, family-run pubs with great food

The Cock

Old Uckfield Road (A26), Near Ringmer, BN8 5RX

Food served 7 days a week lunchtime and evening and all day Sunday.

Large Garden and Sun Terrace
Log Fire in Winter
Roasts served all day Sunday
Open all day on Bank Holidays
Vegetarian Menu always available (5 choices)
Real Ales incl. Harveys and other locally sour
micro breweries
Home Cooked Food – something for every ta
diet and budget!

tel: 01273 812040
www.cockpub.co.uk

The Highlands In

Eastbourne Road, Ridgewood, Uckfield, TN22 5SP

Food served 7 days a week lunchtime and evening and all day Sunday until 6.30pm

Sports Bar showing all BT and Sky Sports
fixtures with special Sports Bar menu
Formal Restaurant area with seating for 120
covers and separate Restaurant Bar Area
Real Ales incl. Harveys and other locally sour
micro breweries
Extensive selection of wines by the glass
Large Sun Trap Garden with al fresco Dining
Live music every Sunday night

tel: 01825 762989
www.highlandsinn.co.uk

individually by their landlords, and their chefs are in charge of creating their own menus. They all have a gently civilised but friendly, easy-going atmosphere, well trained, courteous staff and offer a thoughtful choice of drinks and first class food. We've been delighted with all the pubs we've visited this year. The **Epicurean Collection** is our **Pub Group of the Year 2016**.

The best pubs in town and country

It's heartening that there are still so many unpretentious and unchanging pubs, and it was difficult to whittle the list down to just ten. But our top examples are the **White Lion** in Barthomley (Cheshire), **Barley Mow** at Kirk Ireton (Derbyshire), **Rugglestone** at Widecombe (Devon), **Digby Tap** in Sherborne and **Square & Compass** at Worth Matravers (Dorset), **Viper** at Mill Green (Essex), **Harrow** in Steep (Hampshire), **Three Horseshoes** in Warham (Norfolk), **Crown & Trumpet** in Broadway (Worcestershire) and **Old Point House** in Angle (Wales). The **White Lion** in Barthomley is **Unspoilt Pub of the Year 2016**.

Well run town pubs are just as popular for morning coffee for shoppers as they are for fairly priced food and drink for regulars.

And if a genuine welcome extends to all, then they deserve special praise. Our Top Ten Town Pubs this year are the **Punter** in Cambridge (Cambridgeshire), **Old Harkers Arms** in Chester (Cheshire), **Eight Bells** in Chipping Campden and **Old Spot** in Dursley (Gloucestershire), **Wykeham Arms** in Winchester (Hampshire), **Wharf** in Manchester (Lancashire), **Old Green Tree** in Bath (Somerset), **Old Joint Stock** in Birmingham (Warwickshire), **Kays Bar** in Edinburgh (Scotland) and **Olde Mitre** in central London. **The Wykeham Arms**, located close to Winchester's lovely cathedral, is **Town Pub of the Year 2016**.

A fine country pub conjures up images of roaring log fires, beams and flagstones, heart-warming food and drink and good surrounding walks. Our Top Ten Country Pubs are the **White Horse** in Hedgerley (Buckinghamshire), **Pheasant** at Burwardsley (Cheshire), **Duke of York** in Iddesleigh (Devon), **Brace of Pheasants** in Plush (Dorset), **English Partridge** at Bighton and **Royal Oak** at Fritham (Hampshire), **Cottage of Content** at Carey (Herefordshire), **Malet Arms** at Newton Tony (Wiltshire), **Fleece** in Bretforton (Worcestershire) and **Harp** at Old Radnor (Wales). **The Fleece** at Bretforton with its charming rooms and interesting history is **Country Pub of the Year 2016**.

A weekend away

Staying in an inn for those few precious days away is a growing trend – so much so, that many pubs with a spare room or two upstairs or an outbuilding that can be converted are opening up well equipped and character bedrooms. One-third of the Main Entries in this book now hold one of our Stay Awards. Our Top Ten Inns are the **New Inn** at Coleford (Devon), **New Inn** in Cerne Abbas (Dorset), **Kings Head** in Bledington (Gloucestershire), **Wellington Arms** in Baughurst (Hampshire), **Inn at Whitewell** at Whitewell (Lancashire), **Lord Crewe Arms** in Blanchland (Northumbria), **Luttrell Arms** in Dunster (Somerset), **Cat** in West Hoathly (Sussex), **Blue Lion** in East Witton (Yorkshire) and **Griffin** at Felinfach (Wales). The lovely, individually furnished and thoughtfully equipped bedrooms (some with fireplaces and four-posters) in a 15th-c hotel with stunning medieval features make the **Luttrell Arms** in Dunster **Inn of the Year 2016**.

The search for value and taste

Searching for value is easy, but searching for fair prices and interesting food is more challenging. With the cost of raw materials ever rising, it becomes more and more difficult for chefs to hold down prices. The Top Ten Value pubs are the **Drake Manor** in Buckland Monachorum (Devon), **Digby Tap** in Sherborne and **Green Man** in Wimborne Minster (Dorset), **Yew Tree** at Lower Wield (Hampshire), **Ring o' Bells** at Lathom (Lancashire), **Queens Head** at Kirkby la Thorpe (Lincolnshire), **Dipton Mill** at Diptonmill (Northumbria), **Queen Victoria** at Priddy (Somerset), **Lord Nelson** in Southwold (Suffolk) and **Crown & Trumpet** in Broadway (Worcestershire). As well as offering real value, it's a gem of a pub: the **Crown & Trumpet** in Broadway is **Value Pub of the Year 2016**.

To win one of our Food Awards, pubs have to offer outstanding meals – in fact, many easily outclass restaurants in their vicinity. The quality of the cooking relies on chefs spending much time and effort sourcing the best local, seasonal produce and building up good working relationships with farmers, game-keepers and growers. More and more pubs now grow their own fruit, vegetables and herbs, rear livestock and keep bees and chickens. This year's Top Ten Dining Pubs are the **Treby Arms** in Sparkwell (Devon), **Wellington Arms** in Baughurst (Hampshire), **Stagg** in Titley (Herefordshire), **Plough** in Kingham (Oxfordshire), **Assheton Arms** in Downham (Lancashire), **Red Lion** in Stathern (Leicestershire & Rutland), **Lord Poulett Arms** in Hinton St George (Somerset), **Horse Guards** in Tillington (Sussex), **Pipe & Glass** in South Dalton (Yorkshire) and **Bunch of Grapes** in Pontypridd (Wales). As well as offering exceptional food, they brew their own beer, stock a wide range of other interesting drinks and provide a friendly, informal atmosphere – the **Bunch of Grapes** in Pontypridd is **Dining Pub of the Year 2016**.

Pub of the year

Our new finds for this year's Guide are as wide-ranging as ever, from smart hotels with lively bars through first class dining pubs to town taverns with quirky character. The Top Ten New Pubs are the **Pointer** in Brill (Buckinghamshire), **White Lion** in Barthomley (Cheshire), **Rusty Bike** in Exeter (Devon), **Anchor** in Chideock (Dorset), **Porch House** in Stow-on-the-Wold and **Royal Oak** in Tetbury (Gloucestershire), **Barley Mow** in Barley and **Derby Arms** in Longridge (Lancashire), **White**

Horse in Baston (Lincolnshire) and **Jolly Fisherman** in Craster (Northumbria). The beautifully restored old **Porch House** in Stow-on-the-Wold is **New Pub of the Year 2016**.

A professional landlord or landlady are worth their weight in gold – they can turn what might otherwise be an ordinary pub into a true gem. Our Top Ten Licensees are **Alex Clarke** who owns both the Black Bull in Balsham and the Red Lion at Hinxton (Cambridgeshire), **Simon** and **Sally Jackson** of the Horse & Groom in Upper Oddington (Gloucestershire), **Kathryn Horton** of the Ostrich in Newland (Gloucestershire), **Mary Holmes** of the Sun in Bentworth, **Hassan Matini** of the Trooper in Petersfield and **Tim Gray** of the Yew Tree in Lower Wield (Hampshire), **Mark** and **Kerry Vernon** of the Tram in Eardisley (Herefordshire), **Peter** and **Veryan Graham** of the George in Croscombe (Somerset), the **Mainey family** of the Crown in Roecliffe and **Valerie Sails** and **Eric Broadwith** of the Grantley Arms in Grantley (Yorkshire). For her warmth of character and generosity of spirit, **Kathryn Horton** of the Ostrich in Newland is **Landlady of the Year 2016**.

To compete in the Pub of the Year category, a pub has to have unanimous enthusiasm from our readers on all aspects of its business – it has to be at the top of its game. Our Top Ten Pubs are listed below in county order. For ten years, brothers Will and Tom Greenstock have been at the helm of the first class and excellent all-rounder the **Horse & Groom** in Bourton-on-the-Hill. This is our **Pub of the Year 2016**.

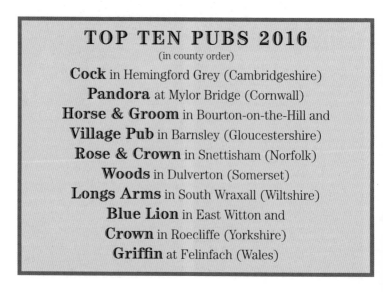

TOP TEN PUBS 2016
(in county order)
Cock in Hemingford Grey (Cambridgeshire)
Pandora at Mylor Bridge (Cornwall)
Horse & Groom in Bourton-on-the-Hill and
Village Pub in Barnsley (Gloucestershire)
Rose & Crown in Snettisham (Norfolk)
Woods in Dulverton (Somerset)
Longs Arms in South Wraxall (Wiltshire)
Blue Lion in East Witton and
Crown in Roecliffe (Yorkshire)
Griffin at Felinfach (Wales)

VIEW FROM THE FRONT

Crafty does it

By **Jonny Garrett**

Beer is changing. While the beards may remain, the cliché of flat, warm British beer is dead. A new guard of young and exciting breweries is springing up, located across the UK and producing everything from classic bitters to barrel-aged IPAs.

It's a job in itself just to keep up with them, so, as professional beer drinkers, we've made it our job to do just that. What started as a blurry idea in our local pub has become an obsession. In fact, beer has become a lifestyle – we drink it, brew it, match food with it, even cook with it.

Beer is the greatest drink on earth because its possibilities are endless. The four ingredients used to make it – water, malt, hops and yeast – come in numerous varieties, which means no batch, let alone style, of beer is identical. It's this variation, and the resulting gorgeous flavours, that great breweries use to their advantage. From sour beers to hop bombs, champagne lagers to whisky-aged porters, no other drink has so many guises.

> Beer is the greatest drink on earth because its possibilities are endless

We've drunk our way around Britain to find the country's best breweries, sipping at pub firesides in Cumbria, brushing elbows at festivals in Manchester, relaxing on picnic benches in Welsh gardens, and drinking at tap rooms in south London. We've found some fantastic new breweries and pubs along the way, but also found that some of the old masters are easily keeping up.

A great beer needs to be many things: unique and exciting, while also staying true to a brewing tradition that is hundreds of years old – this is the essence of craft beer.

Here are our ten favourite British beers, and the magical places where we've drunk them.

BrewDog 5am Saint
Our go-to red ale from the Scottish brewery that helped to kick-start the UK beer revival. Sweet and malty but never cloying, with a satisfying fizz and bitter finish.
BrewDog, Aberdeen, Scotland

Beavertown Gamma Ray

Loved by beer nerds and casual drinkers alike, Beavertown Brewery always hits the mark. Gamma Ray puts many US pale ales to shame – gorgeous aromas of mango and passion fruit, then a bitter finish that leaves you gasping for more.

Port Street Beer House, Manchester, Lancashire

St Austell Admiral's Ale

One word sums up this underrated and beautiful strong bitter – fruitcake. Raisins and spices race up from the glass, billowing out like sails. Drinking it for the first time while looking out over Charlestown Harbour in Cornwall is a memory we will remember fondly for ever.

Rashleigh Arms, Charlestown, Cornwall

Oakham Citra

A testament to new-world hops, and one of the first examples of them being used in the UK. Citra is a citrusy and tangy flower, but adds lots of bitterness too, something Oakham has balanced perfectly with sweet, clean malts.

Southampton Arms, Highgate Road, London, NW5

Brains Black Mountain
A modern twist on a dark beer, packed with sweet pale malts and lots of citrusy hops. Lighter than you'd expect but loaded with coffee, chocolate and pithy fruits – and brewed in collaboration with us!
Goat Major, Cardiff, Wales

Coniston Bluebird Bitter
A light and refreshing British bitter, showing why oldies are goldies and proving that you don't need a mountain of hops to make a truly astonishing beer. Balanced and moreish, with just a bit of pithy bitterness to round it out.
Black Bull, Coniston, Cumbria

Ilkley Siberia
Taking a Belgian-style spiced saison and making it their own with a hint of rhubarb, this Yorkshire cask brewery is brilliant at breathing new life into old recipes.
Rake, Winchester Walk, London, SE1

Thornbridge Jaipur
One of the best IPAs ever made. Quite a claim, given the style was invented in colonial times to survive the journey to India. Hoppy and bittersweet, yet clean and light as many lagers.
Pivni, York, Yorkshire

Meantime London Porter
Porter is named after the dock workers who loved it. This beer is based on a centuries-old recipe and brewed in Greenwich – hence Meantime. With its chocolate and liquorice aroma and hint of dark fruits, it's the perfect fireside beer.
Stag, Fleet Road, London, NW3

Siren Limoncello IPA
Proof of the power of beer. A modern IPA inspired by limoncello, with plenty of lemon juice and zest added. Sweet and sour with a little bitterness at the end, it fills the whole mouth with flavour. The barrel-aged version, Whiskey Sour, is possibly even better.
Old Fountain, Baldwin Street, London, EC1

Jonny Garrett and Brad Evans The Craft Beer Boys are the brains behind the **Craft Beer Channe**l (www.youtube.com/thecraftbeerchannel), which is dedicated to all good beer, from British bitters to US palate-smashers and everything in between. Find Jonny and Brad on YouTube for weekly adventures tracking down the world's best beers, brewing with their favourite breweries, and cooking delicious food to go with the beer.

Three cheers! It's English!

By **Jonica Fox**

The pleasure and excitement of drinking a delicious English or Welsh wine reverberates back 2,000 years. You can almost feel the heartbeat of invading Romans, bringing their wines and vines, founding the first English vineyards – doing such a good job of it, in fact, that by 1 AD Rome was legislating to protect local production by limiting the import of English wines.

So what happened between then and now? Political, economic, social and climatic changes, with a significant dash of passion and determination.

Home went the Romans leaving vineyards as far north as Suffolk and Northamptonshire. Then the Normans arrived, discovering English vineyards still in production and adding a dash of French expertise. In 1085 the Domesday Book recorded 42 flourishing vineyards: 30 private and 12 church estates (though experts believe there were more). Centuries unfolded; monasteries and abbeys took over. For a long time you could measure English wine production on a 'barrel per monk' basis.

Then came climate change: cold winds, actual and metaphorical, blew about the vines with the start of the Little Ice Age (bringing frost fairs to the River Thames and starvation winters) and the Dissolution of the Monasteries under Henry VIII. Both were real blows. And yet, in the 1660s, Samuel Pepys was describing red wine from Walthamstow as 'very good'. (Essex still produces some excellent wines today.) About the same time, Christopher Merrett used technical advances in English glass bottle-making to invent bottle-fermented sparkling wine – a technique made famous by Dom Pérignon who Ðbottled stars – in champagne from 1695.

Experimentation breeds success

Vines continued to be planted, from Wales to the Wash, including Hampton Court's 'Great Vine' in 1769, the world's largest vine – which still produces 600lbs of grapes every year.

The combination of Victorian tariff reforms (which cut import duty on wine by 83 per cent) and the devastating loss of life and skills in World War I ended centuries of English winemaking. The post-war revival was initially founded on eccentric passion and German vines, as they seemed most likely to thrive in the 20th-century English climate.

Then came a turning point: English vineyards started to experiment. The noble grapes (champagne varieties) and other new cultivars replaced the old German ones; pinot noir, pinot meunier and chardonnay for sparkling wines, and new cultivars such as bacchus and rondo for lovely still whites and reds. English sparkling wines led the way, winning golds in world-class competitions, beating champagnes, cavas and proseccos in the process. Nowadays, locally produced still wines are award-winners too.

Today, you can enjoy English and Welsh wines across the country and visit vineyards from Kent to Cornwall, Cardiff to Cardigan, even as far north as Holmfirth, Yorkshire – the village used, appropriately enough, to film the TV sitcom *Last of the Summer Wine*.

As you browse the pages of *The Good Pub Guide*, you'll find many echoes of our English wine heritage – travelling down Vine Street or up Grape Hill, and stopping off at the Vine Inn, the Grapevine, the Old Vine or the Contented Vine. As with English wine today, there's much to enjoy.

Jonica Fox and her husband Gerard run **Sussex Vineyards** (www.sussexvineyards.com), producing English sparkling wines from their two vineyards. Planted with champagne grapes, the vineyards lie either side of the historic High Weald village of Mayfield in East Sussex. **Favourite local pubs** Middle House (Mayfield) and Mark Cross Inn (Mark Cross), both in Sussex.

Make mine a homebrew

By **James Morton**

A strange thing is happening. As old pubs continue to close, new breweries are burgeoning. As demand diminishes, the number of suppliers swells.

It might seem illogical, but I see this as a necessary development in the British taste for beer. It's sad that pubs are closing, but there is a hard truth that the headlines avoid: those that are abandoned, for the most part deserve to be. Their proprietors are stuck in the past, refusing to keep up with the only demand that matters. Quality.

> No longer will punters accept badly kept cask ales from breweries run by people with no care for their product

No longer will punters accept badly kept cask ales from breweries run by people with no care for their product. We're so much more educated now about beer and flavour: we're importing bottles and kegs from all over the world and every last molecule of flavour created from the hops, malt, yeast and water makes it to our taste buds. My mind, at least, has been blown.

Blown, mostly, by beer from the west coast of the USA. Hoppy, strong, fizzy, with slap-you-in-the-face drinkability. The imaginations of brewers at Sierra Nevada, Russian River and similar outfits have fundamentally altered the British beer landscape.

Now, the first beer made by nearly every new UK brewery is a US-style hoppy pale ale of some sort. Most are average, but on a level above any bitter produced by the local microbrewery of a decade ago. The real and brilliant truth, though, is that you can make beer better than any of them at home.

Share and share alike

The brewing community, both professional and amateur, is a kind one. We share beer and we share recipes. If you're partial to a particular beer, go online – you'll probably find the recipe. If not, email the brewer and they'll probably tell you. And maybe even send you a case of beer too. You can use these recipes to brew your favourite beer for a fraction of the price – but of the same, or better, quality. If you don't believe me, try it. Home brewing isn't what it once was – forget cans of sticky syrup, plastic buckets and exploding bottles – it's a way for people to get the freshest, highest-quality beers to share with their friends.

Professional brewers used to be factory workers or scientists or business entrepreneurs. Now, I guarantee, the owner of every new brewery in the UK started out as a home brewer who loved their craft. They just realised how easy it was – a professional set-up is simply a scaled replica of a homebrew set-up. A bank loan and you're banging.

To get started at home, all you need is a big stockpot and a large cloth bag – I made the latter from some voile curtains from John Lewis and got my pot for less than a tenner off eBay. If you've got an old brewing kit abandoned in a shed or cupboard somewhere, you've already got everything you need to make beer that's as good as the best in the world. All the ingredients, as well as a vibrant and helpful community, are freely available online. Get brewing!

James Morton was runner-up in the BBC's *The Great British Bake Off* in 2012 and is the author of *Brilliant Breads* (Ebury, 2013) and *How Baking Works* (Ebury, 2015).
Favourite pub Belle, Great Western Road, Glasgow – for its ambience, open fires and high prevalence of dogs.

The softly softly approach

By **Steve Carter**

'Ill have the usual'. A phrase so often associated with a trip down the pub, but these days is there really something as simple and uniform as a typical tipple? With a fifth of adults in the UK now claiming to not drink alcohol, according to National Statistics,[1] gone are the days when customers conform to the stereotypes of Al Murray's 'Pub Landlord', ordering a 'pint for the fella and a glass of white wine for the lady'.

Premium, not-from-concentrate, nothing added, nothing taken away fruit juices look, taste and say something so different

Today, soft drinks play an increasingly important role within the pub sector, spurred on by popular initiatives such as #dryjanuary and heightened consumer-health awareness; they represent a business-boosting category not to be ignored. Sales of soft drinks contributed nearly £3bn to the pub and club sector in 2014, nearly twice that of sales of cider and over £750m more than sales of wines and champagne.[2]

But do we currently give our 'non-drinking' customers enough credence? Even the phrase so often used to describe them implies they are slightly less important than their alcohol-drinking partners.

Those pubs and bars tapping into the growing customer demand for exciting soft drinks are the ones reaping the rewards from this expanding sector. A move away from only promoting and serving 'the usual' and instead presenting a range of premium brands is as important within soft drinks as it is for beers, wines

[1] Adult Drinking Habits in Great Britain 2013, Office of National Statistics
[2] Britvic Soft Drinks Review 2015

Discover an Individual Inn.
...Individually Different

and spirits. Our 'non-drinking' drinking patrons can no longer be simply quenched with a reconstituted OJ from the carton or a syrup-pumped carbonate. Tastes are more sophisticated, health choices more apparent and lifestyle references more poignant.

Not all soft drinks are the same. Premium, not-from-concentrate, nothing added, nothing taken away fruit juices look, taste and say something so different from their mainstream made-from-concentrate counterparts. They tap into consumers' appetite for provenance, quality and superiority and help pub owners put their soft drinks on a pedestal that will in turn help boost sales and drive profits.

Pub owners need to think creatively about soft drinks, understand what their audience is looking for and excite and inspire through the drinks they stock and sell. New or nostalgic flavours, standout packaging and point of sale and innovative product lines all help to capture the imagination of those opting to avoid alcohol. Mocktails can offer a more imaginative approach and are a great means of promoting sales of premium soft drinks. They provide an ideal opportunity for pub and bar owners to create a signature portfolio of non-alcoholic drinks or align with category brand-leaders who can suggest recipes and offer supporting point of sale material.

So get behind the search for more of an 'atypical tipple', embrace the evolving soft drinks generation and enjoy your 'unusual' at the bar.

Unusual Suspects: Mocktail Recipes

Apple & Elderflower Fizz

Fill a highball glass with ice. Add Frobishers Apple Juice (250ml), lemon juice (20ml) and elderflower cordial (20ml). Top with soda water and stir. Serve garnished with a sprig of mint.

Cranberry Caboose

Muddle half a lime in a highball glass. Add ice and pour in Frobishers Cranberry Juice (250ml). Top with lemonade and stir. Drizzle grenadine (1 tsp) through the centre. Garnish with lemon and lime wedges and serve.

Steve Carter began his career straight from university at Grand Met Brewing, and has worked within the drinks business ever since. He held senior positions at First Drinks and Taunton Cider before moving to premium fruit juice brand **Frobishers** in 2009, where he is sales and marketing director.

Favourite pub Horseshoe, Ebbesbourne Wake, Wiltshire.

Spirited beginnings

By **Fairfax Hall** and **Sam Galsworthy**

When we opened our little blue doors on to our beautiful copper still, Prudence, in Chiswick in 2009, we were the first to do so in London for nearly two centuries. Nobody in living memory had been granted a licence to distil in small batches, the traditional way – not, in fact, since the 1820s. With the real sense of a mission to restore gin to its former glory in the city where it earned its name, and as pioneers of the capital's craft distilling revival, we had 200 years of history to live up to. And it was in west London that we fell in love with the Princess Victoria pub – a charming and quintessential gin palace in all regards, it's our neighbourhood delight.

We truly believe in spirits created properly, without shortcuts or compromises made to generate volume. It's this philosophy that set us apart then, and continues to set us apart now. We make all our gin on three beautiful copper stills (since we launched, Prudence has gained two sisters) at our own distillery, and regularly welcome guests to see us at work. To us, distilling on copper is critical because it purifies and cleanses the spirit, making it smooth, round and eminently sippable.

> Distilling on copper is critical because it purifies and cleanses the spirit, making it smooth, round and eminently sippable

The other thing that's critical to our craft is that we never ever make gin using a concentrate (or two-shot) method. Not many people know about this, but most gins are produced this way. It's a different process and on a different scale. What we make in a year, bigger distilleries produce in a morning. Instead, we follow the one-shot process: we put the right amount of botanicals into the still, with the right amount of spirit, and only blend the heart cut that we capture with water before it goes into the bottle. Our master distiller, Jared Brown, is an unrivalled drinks historian; he took inspiration from history for our London Dry Gin recipe. It uses ten classic botanicals that, when combined with our uncompromising standards, produces a quint-essential London dry gin. Juniper-driven with light citrus notes, it has a nice long, dry finish and is of truly outstanding quality.

Fairfax and Sam are childhood friends who set up the **Sipsmith** distillery (www.sipsmith.com) to bring classic London dry gin, made the way it used to be – the way it should be – back to the city where it all began.
Favourite pub Princess Victoria, Uxbridge Road, London W12

What is a Good Pub?

We hear about possible new entries for this *Guide* from our many thousands of correspondents who tell us about the pubs they visit – by post, by email at feedback@goodguides.com or via our website, www. thegoodpubguide.co.uk. These might be places they visit regularly (and it's their continued approval that reassures us about keeping a pub as a full entry for another year) or pubs they have discovered on their travels and that we, perhaps, know nothing about. And it's from these new discoveries that we create a shortlist to be considered for possible inclusion as new Main Entries.

What marks a pub out for special attention could be an out-of-the-ordinary choice of drinks – a wide range of real ales (perhaps even brewed by the pub itself), several hundred whiskies, a remarkable wine list, interesting spirits from small distillers or proper farm ciders and perries. It could be delicious food (often outclassing most restaurants in the area) or meals that are remarkable value. Perhaps, as a place to stay, it's special in some way, with lovely bedrooms and obliging service. Maybe it's the building itself (from centuries-old parts of monasteries to extravagant Victorian gin-palaces), or its surroundings (lovely countryside or attractive waterside).

Most important of all is the pub's atmosphere. You should feel welcomed and at home, and that the landlord or landlady is genuinely pleased to see you. After all, a good publican can make or break a pub. It follows from this that a great many ordinary local pubs, perfectly good in their own right, don't earn a place in the *Guide*. What makes them attractive to their regular customers could make strangers feel slightly left out.

Another key point is that there's not necessarily any link between charm and luxury. A basic unspoilt tavern may be worth travelling miles to find, while an overly smart refurbished dining pub may not be worth crossing the street for.

The pubs featured as Main Entries do pay a fee, which helps to cover the *Guide's* production costs. But no pub can gain an entry simply by paying a fee. Only pubs that have been inspected anonymously, and approved by us, are invited to join.

Using the *Guide*

The Counties

England has been split alphabetically into counties. Each chapter starts by picking out the pubs that are currently doing best in the area, or are specially attractive for one reason or another.

The county boundaries we use are those for the administrative counties (not the old traditional counties, which were changed back in 1976). We have left the new unitary authorities within the counties that they formed part of until their creation in the most recent local government reorganisation. Metropolitan areas have been included in the counties around them – for example, Merseyside in Lancashire. And occasionally we have grouped counties together – for example, Rutland with Leicestershire, and Durham with Northumberland to make Northumbria. If in doubt, check the Contents pages.

Scotland, Wales and London have each been covered in single chapters. Pubs are listed alphabetically (except in London, which is split into Central, East, North, South and West), under the name of the town or village where they are. If the village is so small that you might not find it on a road map, we've listed it under the name of the nearest sizeable village or town. The maps use the same town and village names, and additionally include a few big cities that don't have any listed pubs – for orientation.

We list pubs in their true county, not their postal county. Just once or twice, when the village itself is in one county but the pub is just over the border in the next-door county, we have used the village county, not the pub one.

Stars ★

Really outstanding pubs are awarded a star, and in one case two: these are the aristocrats among pubs. The stars do NOT signify extra luxury or specially good food – in fact, some of the pubs that appeal most distinctively and strongly are decidedly basic in terms of food and surroundings. The detailed description of each pub shows what its particular appeal is, and this is what the stars refer to.

Food Award ⊙

Pubs where food is really outstanding.

Stay Award ⇒

Pubs that are good as places to stay at (obviously, you can't expect the same level of luxury at £60 a head as you'd get for £100 a head). Pubs with bedrooms are marked on the maps as a square.

Wine Award ♀
Pubs with particularly enjoyable wines by the glass – often a good range.

Beer Award 🍺
Pubs where the quality of the beer is quite exceptional, or pubs that keep a particularly interesting range of beers in good condition.

Value Award £
This distinguishes pubs that offer really good value food. In all the award-winning pubs, you will find an interesting choice at under £10.

Recommenders
At the end of each Main Entry we include the names of readers who have recently recommended that pub (unless they've asked us not to use their names).

Important note: the description of the pub and the comments on it are our own and not the recommenders'.

Also Worth a Visit
The Also Worth a Visit section at the end of each county chapter includes brief descriptions of pubs that have been recommended by readers in the year before the *Guide* goes to print and that we feel are worthy of inclusion – many of them, indeed, as good in their way as the featured pubs (these are picked out by a star). We have inspected and approved nearly half of these ourselves. All the others are recommended by our reader-reporters. The descriptions of these other pubs, written by us, usually reflect the experience of several different people.

The pubs in Also Worth a Visit may become featured entries in future editions. So do please help us know which are hot prospects for our inspection programme (and which are not!), by reporting on them. There are report forms at the back of the *Guide*, or you can email us at feedback@goodguides.com, or write to us at

The Good Pub Guide, FREEPOST RTJR-ZCYZ-RJZT,
Perrymans Lane, Etchingham TN19 7DN.

Locating Pubs
To help readers who use digital mapping systems we include a postcode for every pub. Pubs outside London are given a British Grid four-figure map reference. Where a pub is exceptionally difficult to find, we include a six-figure reference in the directions. The Map number (Main Entries only) refers to the maps at the back of the *Guide*.

Motorway Pubs
If a pub is within four or five miles of a motorway junction we give special directions for finding it from the motorway. The Special

Interest Lists at the end of the book include a list of these pubs, motorway by motorway.

Prices and Other Factual Details

The *Guide* went to press during the summer of 2015, after each pub was sent a checking sheet to get up-to-date food, drink and bedroom prices and other factual information. By the summer of 2016 prices are bound to have increased, but if you find a significantly different price please let us know.

Breweries or independent chains to which pubs are 'tied' are named at the beginning of the italic-print rubric after each Main Entry. That generally means the pub has to get most if not all its drinks from that brewery or chain. If the brewery is not an independent one but just part of a combine, we name the combine in brackets. When the pub is tied, we have spelled out whether the landlord is a tenant, has the pub on a lease, or is a manager. Tenants and leaseholders of breweries generally have considerably greater freedom to do things their own way, and in particular are allowed to buy drinks including a beer from sources other than their tied brewery.

Free houses are pubs not tied to a brewery. In theory they can shop around, but in practice many free houses have loans from the big brewers, on terms that bind them to sell those breweries' beers. So don't be too surprised to find that so-called free houses may be stocking a range of beers restricted to those from a single brewery.

Real ale is used by us to mean beer that has been maturing naturally in its cask. We do not count as real ale beer that has been pasteurised or filtered to remove its natural yeasts.

Other drinks. We've also looked out particularly for pubs doing enterprising non-alcoholic drinks (including good tea or coffee), interesting spirits (especially malt whiskies), country wines, freshly squeezed juices and good farm ciders.

Bar food usually refers to what is sold in the bar; we do not describe menus that are restricted to a separate restaurant. If we know that a pub serves sandwiches, we say so – if you don't see them mentioned, assume you can't get them. Food listed is an example of the sort of thing you'd find served in the bar on a normal day.

Children. If we don't mention children at all, assume that they are not welcome. All but one or two pubs allow children in their garden if they have one. 'Children welcome' means the pub has told us that it lets them in with no special restrictions. In other cases, we report exactly what arrangements pubs say they make for children. However, we have to note that in readers' experience some pubs make restrictions that they haven't told us about (children only if eating, for example). If you come across this, please let us know, so that we can clarify with the pub concerned for the next edition. The absence of any reference to children in an Also Worth a Visit entry means we don't know either way. Children's Certificates exist, but in practice children are allowed into some part of most pubs in this *Guide* (there is no legal restriction on the movement of children over 14 in any pub). Children under 16 cannot have alcoholic drinks. Children aged 16 and 17 can drink beer, wine or cider with a meal if it is bought by an adult and they are accompanied by an adult.

Dogs. If Main Entry licensees have told us they allow dogs in their pub or bedrooms, we say so; absence of reference to dogs means dogs are not welcome. If you take a dog into a pub you should have it on a lead. We also mention in the text any pub dogs or cats (or indeed other animals) that we've come across ourselves, or heard about from readers.

Parking. If we know there is a problem with parking, we say so, otherwise assume there is a car park.

Credit cards. We say if a pub does not accept them; some that do may put a surcharge on credit card bills, to cover charges made by the card company. We also say if we know that a pub tries to retain customers' credit cards while they are eating. This is a reprehensible practice, and if a pub tries it on you, please tell them that all banks and card companies frown on it – and please let us know the pub's name, so that we can warn readers in future editions.

Telephone numbers are given for all pubs that are not ex-directory.

Opening hours are for summer; we say if we know of differences in winter, or on particular days of the week. In the country, many pubs may open rather later and close earlier than their details show (if you come across this, please let us know – with details). Pubs are allowed to stay open all day if licensed to do so. However, outside cities many pubs in England and Wales close during the afternoon. We'd be grateful to hear of any differences from the hours we quote.

Bedroom prices normally include full english breakfasts (if available), VAT and any automatic service charge. If we give just one price, it is the total price for two people sharing a double or twin-bedded room for one night. Prices before the '/' are for single occupancy, prices after it for double.

Meal times. Bar food is commonly served from 12-2 and 7-9, at least from Monday to Saturday. We spell out the times if they are significantly different. To be sure of a table it's best to book before you go. Sunday hours vary considerably from pub to pub, so it's advisable to check before you leave.

Disabled access. Deliberately, we do not ask pubs about this, as their answers would not give a reliable picture of how easy access is. Instead, we depend on readers' direct experience. If you are able to give us help about this, we would be particularly grateful for your reports.

Electronic Route Planning

Microsoft® AutoRoute™, a route-finding software package, shows the location of pubs in *The Good Pub Guide* on detailed maps and includes our text entries for those pubs on screen.

Our website (www.thegoodpubguide.co.uk) includes every pub in the *Guide*.

iPhone and iPad

You can search and read *The Good Pub Guide* both on our website (www.thegoodpubguide.co.uk) and as a download on your smartphone or iPad. They contain all the pubs in this *Guide*. You can also write reviews and let us know about undiscovered gems.

There are apps available for iPhone and iPad – and the *Guide* can be downloaded as an eBook to your reader.

Changes during the year – please tell us

Changes are inevitable during the course of the year. Landlords change, and so do their policies. We hope that you will find everything just as we say, but if not please let us know. You can find out how by referring to the Report Forms section at the end of the *Guide*.

Editors' acknowledgements

We could not produce the Guide without the huge help we have from the many thousands of readers who report to us on the pubs they visit, often in great detail. Particular thanks to these greatly valued correspondents: Chris and Angela Buckell, Richard Tilbrook, Tony and Wendy Hobden, George Atkinson, Phil and Jane Hodson, Clive and Fran Dutson, Michael and Jenny Back, Roger and Donna Huggins, Gordon and Margaret Ormondroyd, Peter Meister, Dr W I C Clark, Gerry and Rosemary Dobson, Tracey and Stephen Groves, Paul Humphreys, Michael Doswell, Brian and Anna Marsden, Sara Fulton and Roger Baker, Simon and Mandy King, Ann and Colin Hunt, R K Phillips, John Wooll, Brian Glozier, Liz Bell, Michael Butler, N R White, Steve Whalley, John Pritchard, Mrs Margo Finlay and Jörg Kasprowski, Susan and John Douglas, John Evans, Richard Kennell, Tina and David Woods-Taylor, Taff Thomas, Neil and Angela Huxter, Simon Collett-Jones, Tony and Jill Radnor, Giles and Annie Francis, Derek and Sylvia Stephenson, Ian Herdman, Ian Phillips, David Jackman, Dave Braisted, Roy Hoing, R T and J C Moggridge, Val and Alan Green, Sheila Topham, Stanley and Annie Matthews, John Beeken, Ross Balaam, John and Sylvia Harrop, Guy Vowles, Edward Mirzoeff, Colin and Maggie Fancourt, Mike and Mary Carter, M G Hart, Paul and Sue Merrick, Dr Kevan Tucker, Pat and Tony Martin, Simon Cleasby, Conor McGaughey, GSB, Bob and Margaret Holder, Mike and Wena Stevenson, Theocsbrian, Tom McLean, Brian and Janet Ainscough, David Stewart, Jeremy King, Richard and Penny Gibbs, B and M Kendall, Tony Scott, R L Borthwick, Dr J Barrie Jones, Comus and Sarah Elliott, John and Eleanor Holdsworth, Tom and Jill Jones, David M Smith, Dennis and Doreen Haward, David and Stella Martin, Mr and Mrs P R Thomas, Christian Mole, Mike and Eleanor Anderson, Gerry Price, S G N Bennett, Ray and Winifred Halliday, Robert W Buckle, Hugh Roberts, David and Judy Robison, Nigel and Jean Eames, David Lamb, R C Vincent, Paul A Moore, Roger and Anne Newbury, Stephen Woad, Alistair Forsyth, Mr and Mrs J Watkins, Conrad Freezer, Adrian Johnson, Nigel and Sue Foster, Tony and Maggie Harwood, Pat and Stewart Gordon, Lynda and Trevor Smith, Martin and Alison Stainsby, Chris and Val Ramstedt, Glenwys and Alan Lawrence, David and Sally Frost, M Carr, Hunter and Christine Wright, Eddie Edwards, Bill Adie, JHBS, John Jenkins, Miss B D Picton, Lesley and Peter Barrett, Walter and Susan Rinaldi-Butcher, Peter Hacker, John Allman, Philip Meek, WAH, Roy and Lindsey Fentiman, David Carr, Mr and Mrs D J Nash, Ron Corbett, Peter and Jean Hoare, DF and NF, Martin Day, Richard Stanfield, Robert Watt, Patrick and Daphne Darley, Katharine Cowherd, Pauline Jennings, William and Ann Reid, Steve and Liz Tilley, Wilburoo, Roger and Val Little, Di and Mike Gillam, Peter Flynn, Revd R P Tickle, John and Jennifer Spinks, Dennis Jones, Paul Sayers, Michael Hill, Mrs P Sumner, Barry Collett, Malcolm and Jane Levitt, Steve Bloomfield, David and Carole Newton ,David Crook, Carol and Luke Wilson, Mrs J Ekins-Daukes, B R Merritt, Richard and Judy Winn, Margaret and Peter Staples, Peter Smith and Judith Brown, Mrs Carolyn Dixon, B J Harding, Henry Fryer, Paul Rampton and Julie Harding, Derek Stafford, Paul Fitzpatrick, Mrs P R Sykes, Richard Sumner, Gene and Tony Freemantle, the Dutchman, John Evans, Geoffrey Kemp, Mike and Jayne Bastin, Bernard Stradling MBE, Dr D J and Mrs S C Walker, Roy and Gill Payne, Malcolm and Pauline Pellatt, Dr Matt Burleigh, D and M T Ayres-Regan, George Edwards, R and S Bentley, Quentin and Carol Williamson, Colin McLachlan, Richard Elliott, Richard Cole, PL, V Brogden, David Heath, Christopher and Elise Way, PLC, Howard and Margaret Buchanan, James Anderson, Liz and Brian Barnard, Robert Turnham, P and D Carpenter, Barbara and Peter Kelly, Tim Brogan, J V Dadswell, Philip and Susan Philcox, Graham and Elizabeth Hargreaves, Dr and Mrs J D Abell, W K Wood, Alan and Angela Scouller, Bill Gulliver and Harry Thomson, Mr and Mrs A Dempster, Mr and Mrs D B Lawton, J R Wildon, Alan Cowell, Mick and Moira Brummell, David Field, Robert Wivell and Paul Lucas.

Thanks too to the ladies at The Book Service for their cheerful dedication: Maria Tegerdine, Michele Csaforda, Carol Bryant, Shona Wallace and Kerry Rusch. And particularly to John Holliday of Trade Wind Technology, who built and looks after our all-important database.

Fiona Stapley

ENGLAND

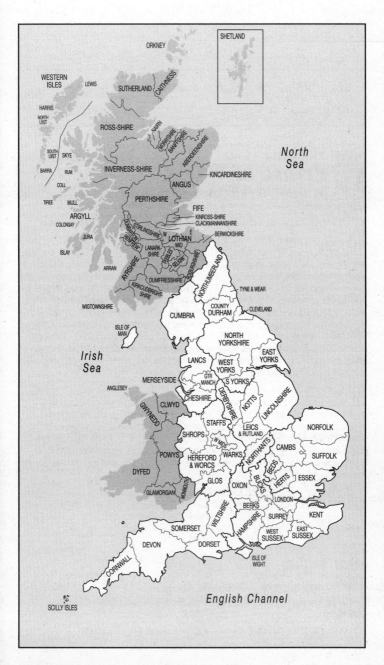

Bedfordshire

KEY	★ Star Pub	🎯 Top Quality Food	🍺 Great Beer
♀ Good Wines	£ Bargain Meals	🛏 Good Bedrooms	🍴 Serves Food

AMPTHILL
TL0338   Map 5
Prince of Wales
(01525) 840504 – www.princeofwales-ampthill.com
Bedford Street (B540 N from central crossroads); MK45 2NB

Civilised with contemporary décor and up-to-date food; bedrooms

It's a pleasant surprise to walk through the doors of this traditional-looking red-brick town house to find a comfortable and stylish interior. Set on two levels, it's more of an open-plan bar-brasserie than a straightforward pub, with good lighting and modern prints on mainly cream walls (dark green and maroon accents at either end). The slightly sunken flagstoned area with a log fire in the exposed brick fireplace leads to a partly ply-panelled dining room with dark leather dining chairs set around a mixed batch of sturdy tables, and there are plenty of church candles and big leather deco-style armchairs and sofas at low tables on wood-strip flooring; background music. Charles Wells Bombardier and Eagle on handpump, plenty of wines by the glass and good coffee. The nicely planted two-level lawn has picnic-sets, with more on a terrace by the car park.

🍴 Quite a choice of food includes lunchtime sandwiches, coconut tempura prawns with sweet chilli sauce, tomato, asparagus and basil tagliatelle, sausages with red onion gravy and mash of the week, Jack Daniels and coke-marinated barbecue ribs with corn on the cob, coleslaw and southern fries, chicken breast wrapped in smoked ham with a tomato, black olive and basil sauce, pork loin with cider jus and apple and blackberry compote, and puddings such as banoffi pie and pineapple and malibu cheesecake. *Benchmark main dish: beef fillet wellington £24.00. Two-course evening meal £18.50.*

Wells & Youngs ~ Lease Richard and Neia Heathorn ~ Real ale ~ Open 11-11 (midnight Fri, Sat); 12-5 (8 in summer) Sun ~ Bar food 12-2.30 (3 weekends), 6.30-9; 7-9.30 Fri, Sat; not Sun evening ~ Restaurant ~ Children welcome ~ Dogs allowed in bar and bedrooms ~ Wi-fi ~ Bedrooms: £55/£70 *Recommended by Pip White, Edward May*

BEDFORD
TL0550   Map 5
Park ♀
(01234) 273929 – www.theparkbedford.co.uk
Corner of Kimbolton Road (B660) and Park Avenue, out past Bedford Hospital; MK40 2PA

Civilised and individual oasis – a great asset for the town

This easy-going pub is open all day, so there's a good, bustling atmosphere and a wide mix of customers dropping in and out. The décor throughout is appealing with thoughtful touches added here and there and you can choose where to sit according to your mood: a more or less conventional bar with heavy beams, panelled dado and leaded lights in big windows, a light and airy conservatory sitting room with easy chairs well spread on a carpet, and an extensive series of softly lit rambling dining areas, carpeted or flagstoned. Charles Wells Bombardier, Eagle IPA and DNA and a guest beer on handpump, inventive bar nibbles and an excellent choice of wines by the glass; background music. The sheltered brick-paved terrace has good timber furniture, some under dark red canopies, and attractive shrub plantings.

Popular food served all day includes lunchtime ciabattas, potted mackerel with cranberry jelly, carpaccio of duck with cauliflower, hazelnut and pickled fennel salad, sharing platters, a pasta and risotto dish of the day, smoked salmon fishcake with bubble and squeak, a poached egg and sorrel cream sauce, pork loin stuffed with spinach in light puff pastry with wild mushroom and port ragoût, corn-fed chicken with parmentier potatoes, beetroot and balsamic syrup and puddings. *Benchmark main dish: Salmon supreme with polenta croutons and tarragon and pea purée £16.50. Two-course evening meal £21.00.*

Little Gems Country Dining Pubs ~ Manager Tyrone Bentham ~ Real ale ~ Open 11.30-11.30 (midnight Fri, Sat); 12-11 Sun ~ Bar food 12-3, 6-10; 12-10 Sat; 12-8 Sun ~ Restaurant ~ Children allowed in one bar and restaurant ~ Dogs allowed in bar ~ Wi-fi ~ Comedy Sun evening every two months *Recommended by Pip White, Harvey Brown*

FLITTON
White Hart ♀
TL0535 Map 5

(01525) 862022 – www.whitehartflitton.co.uk
Village signed off A507; MK45 5EJ

Simply furnished and friendly village pub with bar and dining area, real ales, interesting food and seats in the garden

Nestled between the 13th-c church and Flitton Moor, this is a friendly pub in a quiet village. The minimally decorated front bar has dark leather tub chairs around low tables, contemporary leather and chrome seats at pedestal tables, and Farrow & Ball painted walls. B&T Dragon Slayer and a guest such as Buntingford Twitchell on handpump and 20 wines – as well as champagne and prosecco – by the glass; TV. Steps lead down to a good-sized, simply furnished back dining area with red plush seats and banquettes on dark wooden floorboards. The nice garden has neat shrub borders, and teak seats and tables on a terrace shaded by cedars and weeping willows.

As well as their renowned steaks, the highly thought-of food includes crayfish, prawn and apple cocktail, chicken liver pâté with caramelised onion marmalade, line-caught cod with ratatouille, sesame-crusted chicken breast with teriyaki and orange pak choi, pork belly with apple mash, crackling and cider jus, and puddings such as rum and raisin crème brûlée and lemon, lime and ginger posset; they also offer a two- and three-course set menu (not Sunday, Monday or Friday and Saturday evenings). *Benchmark main dish: aberdeen angus steak with home-made chips £15.95. Two-course evening meal £20.00.*

Free house ~ Licensees Phil and Clare Hale ~ Real ale ~ Open 12-2.30, 6-midnight; 12-3, 6-1am Sat; 12-5 Sun; closed Sun evening, Mon ~ Bar food 12-2, 6.30-9 (9.30 Fri, Sat); 12-2.30 Sun ~ Restaurant ~ Children welcome ~ Dogs allowed in bar ~ Wi-fi
Recommended by Richard and Liz Thorne, Alison and Michael Harper

IRELAND
Black Horse 🖈 ♀

TL1341 Map 5

(01462) 811398 – www.blackhorseireland.com

Off A600 Shefford–Bedford; SG17 5QL

Contemporary décor in old building, impressive food, good wine list and lovely garden with attractive terraces; bedrooms

Attentive, helpful staff welcome you into this 17th-c pub and although it would be a huge shame to miss out on the particularly good food, the bar is warm and relaxing with inglenook fireplaces, beams in low ceilings and timbering – and they do keep a fine range of drinks: Adnams Bitter and Sharps Doom Bar on handpump, 24 wines by the glass, a dozen malt whiskies, Weston's cider and good coffee from the long green-slate bar counter. There are leather armchairs and comfortable wall seating, a mix of elegant wooden and high-backed leather dining chairs around attractive tables on polished oak boards or sandstone flooring, original artwork, and fresh flowers on each table. French windows open from the restaurant on to various terraces with individual furnishings and pretty flowering pots and beds. The comfortable, well equipped bedrooms are across the courtyard in a separate building; continental breakfasts are included and taken in your room. The Birch at Woburn is under the same ownership.

 From seasonally changing menus, the thoughtful choice of excellent food includes lunchtime ciabattas, chicken and tarragon ballotine with piccalilli purée, stilton pâté with roasted beetroot, a pie of the day, wild mushroom and sun-dried tomato pasta with basil sauce, steak burger with toppings, battered onion rings and fries, bream fillets on pea and lemon risotto, local pork steak with spiced apple jam, venison with spiced red cabbage and redcurrant jus, and puddings. *Benchmark main dish: beer-battered fish and chips £13.95. Two-course evening meal £23.00.*

Free house ~ Licensee Darren Campbell ~ Real ale ~ Open 12-3, 6-11; 12-6 Sun; closed Sun evening ~ Bar food 12-2.30, 6.15-9.45; 12-5 Sun ~ Restaurant ~ Children welcome ~ Wi-fi ~ Bedrooms: /£79.95 *Recommended by Martin and Clare Warne, Caroline Prescott*

OAKLEY
Bedford Arms ♀

TL0053 Map 5

(01234) 822280 – www.bedfordarmsoakley.co.uk

High Street; MK43 7RH

16th-c village inn with individual rooms, real ales and wines by the glass, fish and other popular food in two dining rooms and seats in the garden

In each of the interconnected rooms in this updated 16th-c village pub, the contemporary décor is different. The pubbiest part, with a baby grand piano, has straightforward wooden furniture on bare boards, flower prints on the walls, daily papers, a decorative woodburning stove with a flat-screen TV above it, and Charles Wells Bombardier Burning Gold, Reserve The Colonels Choice and Eagle IPA on handpump and 30 wines by the glass; darts. The four cosy, individually decorated rooms leading off the main bar are the nicest places for a drink and chat. One has a large circular pine table (just right for a private party), the second has farmhouse chairs and a cushioned pew beside a small fireplace, the third has ladder-back chairs and shiny tables on ancient floor tiles and the last is very much Victorian in style. The stone-floored dining rooms have tartan-covered seating or wicker chairs and the light, airy conservatory overlooks the pretty garden, where there are seats for warm-weather meals.

▌▌ They specialise in fresh fish with daily dishes displayed on a board, but also serve
lunchtime sandwiches, chicken liver and madeira pâté, beef carpaccio with red
onion and parmesan, home-cooked ham and eggs, stuffed vegetable pancake with a tomato
and cheese glaze, chicken stuffed with soft cheese and garlic on a white bean and pancetta
cassoulet, slow-braised pork belly with apple mash and cider liquor, and puddings.
Benchmark main dish: pie of the day £11.95. Two-course evening meal £23.00.

Wells & Youngs ~ Tenants Tim and Yvonne Walker ~ Real ale ~ Open 12-11 (10.30 Sun) ~
Bar food 12-2.30, 6.15-9.30; 12-4 Sun ~ Restaurant ~ Children welcome ~ Dogs allowed
in bar ~ Wi-fi *Recommended by Harvey Brown, Michael Sargent*

RAVENSDEN
TL0754   Map 5

Horse & Jockey ⓘ☆❘ ♀

(01234) 772319 – www.horseandjockey.info
Village signed off B660 N of Bedford; pub at Church End, off village road; MK44 2RR

Contemporary comfort, with enjoyable food and good range of drinks

Run with care and enthusiasm, this is a friendly place with a good mix of
customers. The refurbished interior is pleasantly modern with a quiet
colour scheme of olive greys and dark red, careful lighting, leather easy chairs
in the bar, a wall of meticulously arranged old local photographs, a rack of
recent *Country Life* issues and daily papers; background music and board
games. Adnams Southwold, Gun Dog Booze Hound, McEwans IPA and a
guest beer on handpump and 20 wines by the glass served by charming staff.
The bright dining room has nice chunky tables and high-backed seats, well
lit prints and a contemporary etched glass screen; it overlooks a sheltered
terrace with smart, up-to-date tables and chairs under cocktail parasols on
decking and a few picnic-sets on the grass beside. The handsome medieval
church with churchyard is further off.

Interesting food includes lunchtime open sandwiches, pheasant and mushroom
terrine with piccalilli, cajun whitebread with tartare sauce, steak burger with
relish and chips, aubergine parmigiana, truffle chicken with bacon, girolles and baby
onions on mash, duck confit with bubble and squeak, braised red cabbage and red
wine jus, catalan fish stew and puddings such as apple and pear cake with cinammon
ice-cream and sticky toffee fig pudding with crème anglaise. *Benchmark main dish:
smoked haddock florentine with poached egg and hollandaise £12.50. Two-course
evening meal £20.00.*

Free house ~ Licensees Darron and Sarah Smith ~ Real ale ~ Open 12-3, 6-11 (midnight
Sat); 12-8 Sun ~ Bar food 12-2, 7-9; 12-6 Sun ~ Restaurant ~ Children welcome ~ Dogs
allowed in bar ~ Wi-fi *Recommended by Michael Sargent, S Holder, Harvey Brown*

SUTTON
TL2247   Map 5

John o' Gaunt ☆❘ ♀

(01767) 260377 – www.johnogauntsutton.co.uk
Off B1040 Biggleswade–Potton; SG19 2NE

Bustling friendly pub run by first class licensees, with smashing food, attractive bars and seats in garden

'It's a real treat to come here,' says one reader with enthusiasm – and many
others agree. And although the good food cooked by the landlord remains
high on everyone's list, this is a proper pub with bar skittles and pétanque
teams, real ale and a friendly, welcoming atmosphere. There are beams and
timbering, red-painted or pretty wallpapered walls, paintings by local artists
(for sale), and fresh flowers and house plants. The gently refurbished bar
has leather seats and sofas around ships' tables on flagstones, an open fire

and stools against the counter where they keep Adnams Broadside and Lighthouse and Woodfordes Wherry on handpump, 12 wines by the glass and local cider; background music. The dining rooms have a new woodburning stove and all sorts of chairs, from elegant high-backed and black-cushioned to dark leather or carved ones around a medley of tables on bare boards. You can sit outside in the well sheltered garden. To reach the pub, you have to drive through a shallow ford by a hump-backed 14th-c packhorse bridge.

The highly enjoyable food includes open sandwiches using home-made focaccia, chicken liver parfait with red onion marmalade, tempura king prawns and salmon with soy, chilli and lime, rump burger with cheddar, tomato chutney and chips, gnocchi with butternut squash, spinach, parmesan and pine nuts, cod fillet with puy lentils, smoked bacon and spinach and puddings such as vanilla panna cotta with pomegranate jelly and bitter chocolate fondant with white chocolate ice-cream. *Benchmark main dish: pie of the day £12.50. Two-course evening meal £19.00.*

Free house ~ Licensees Jago and Jane Hurt ~ Real ale ~ Open 12-3, 6-11; 12-6 Sun; closed Sun evening, all day Mon (except bank holiday lunchtimes) ~ Bar food 12-2, 6.30-9; 12-3 Sun ~ Children welcome ~ Dogs allowed in bar ~ Wi-fi *Recommended by Isobel Mackinlay, David Stewart, Margaret and Roy Randle*

WOBURN   SP9433   Map 4

Birch 🍽 ♀

(01525) 290295 – www.birchwoburn.com

3.5 miles from M1 junction 13; follow Woburn signs via A507 and A4012, right in village then A5130 (Newport Road); MK17 9HX

Bedfordshire Dining Pub of the Year

Well run dining establishment with focus on imaginative food, good wines and attentive service

Our readers enjoy their visits to this family-run, edge-of-town pub – both for a drink and a chat and for a rewarding meal. There are quite a few individually and elegantly furnished linked rooms with contemporary décor and paintwork. The upper dining area has high-backed leather or wooden dining chairs around tables on stripped and polished floorboards, while the lower part is in a light and airy conservatory with a pitched glazed roof, ceramic floor tiles, light coloured furnishings and original artwork and fresh flowers. The bustling bar is similarly furnished and has a few high bar stools against the sleek, smart counter where they serve Adnams Bitter and Sharps Doom Bar on handpump, 15 good wines by the glass, a dozen malt whiskies and quite a few teas and coffees; unobtrusive background music. There are tables out on a sheltered deck, and in summer the front of the pub has masses of flowering hanging baskets and tubs. This is sister pub to the Black Horse at Ireland.

From a seasonally changing menu, the particularly good food includes meat and fish cooked to your specification on an open griddle, plus lunchtime ciabattas, oxtail and apple terrine with poached pear and pickled walnut dressing, potted crab and prawns with pickled vegetables, burger with toppings, onion rings and fries, roasted hake on fresh herb and garlic risotto, confit of pork belly with cauliflower and parmesan purée, haunch of venison on pea, mint, potato and garlic fricassée, and puddings such as cherry and chocolate brownie with poached cherries and calvados parfait with sweet fennel seeds, blackberries and orange sorbet. *Benchmark main dish: griddled bass fillets £14.95. Two-course evening meal £23.00.*

Free house ~ Licensee Mark Campbell ~ Real ale ~ Open 12-3, 6-11; 12-6 Sun ~ Bar food 12-2.30, 6.15-9.45; 12-5 Sun ~ Restaurant ~ Children welcome
Recommended by Michael Sargent, Barbara and Peter Kelly, Richard Kennell, Roy Hoing

Also Worth a Visit in Bedfordshire

Besides the fully inspected pubs, you might like to try these pubs that have been recommended to us and described by readers. Do tell us what you think of them: feedback@goodguides.com

---

AMPTHILL   TL0337
Albion (01525) 634857
Dunstable Street; MK45 2JT Drinkers' pub with up to 12 well kept ales including local B&T and Everards, real ciders and a perry, friendly knowledgeable staff, no food apart from lunchtime rolls; traditional music night second Sat of month; dogs welcome, paved beer garden, open all day.
(Edward May)

BEDFORD   TL0550
d'Parys (01234) 340248
De Parys Avenue; MK40 2UA Recently opened dining pub in former red-brick Victorian hotel; contemporary revamp keeping original features such as parquet floors, stained glass, period fireplaces and sweeping staircase, open-plan drinking area with long wooden tables and benches, some leather button-back sofas, Charles Wells ales and plenty of wines by the glass, cocktails, popular food including weekday set lunch, separate counter serving coffee, ice-cream and sweets, attentive friendly staff; children welcome, outside seating, 14 stylish bedrooms, open (and food) all day.
(Michael Sargent)

BEDFORD   TL0549
Embankment (01234) 261332
The Embankment; MK40 3PD Revamped mock-Tudor hotel (Peach group) adjacent to the river, airy L-shaped front bar with mix of modern furniture on wood floor, pretty blue-tiled fireplace, Charles Wells ales and several wines by the glass, good choice of food from sandwiches and deli boards up, cheerful helpful service, restaurant; background music; children welcome, seats out on front terrace looking across to the Great Ouse, 20 bedrooms (best ones with river views), good breakfast, open all day.
(George Atkinson)

BIDDENHAM   TL0249
Three Tuns (01234) 354847
Off A428; MK40 4BD Refurbished part-thatched village dining pub with bar, lounge and new restaurant extension, good varied menu (not Sun evening, Mon) from traditional favourites and chargrills up, lunchtime and evening set menus (Tues-Fri), extensive wine list, well kept Greene King ales, fast friendly service; spacious garden with picnic-sets, more contemporary furniture on terrace and decked area, open all day. *(Michael Sargent, Susan and Jeremy Arthern)*

BLETSOE   TL0157
★ Falcon (01234) 781222
Rushden Road (A6 N of Bedford); MK44 1QN Refurbished 17th-c building with comfortable opened-up bar, low beams and joists, seating from cushioned wall/window seats to high-backed settles, wood-burner in double-sided fireplace, snug with sofas and old pews, panelled dining room, enjoyable fairly traditional food plus some interesting specials, Charles Wells and a guest ale, decent choice of wines by the glass and good coffee, efficient friendly service; unobtrusive background music, daily papers; decked and paved terrace in lovely big garden down to the Great Ouse, open all day.
(Emma Scofield)

BOLNHURST   TL0858
★ Plough (01234) 376274
Kimbolton Road; MK44 2EX Stylishly converted Tudor building with thriving atmosphere, charming staff and top notch food (must book Sat night), Adnams and a couple of interesting guests, good carefully annotated wine list (including organic vintages) with over a dozen by the glass, home-made summer lemonade and tomato juice, airy dining rooms, log fires; children welcome, dogs in bar, attractive tree-shaded garden with decking overlooking pond, remains of old moat, closed Sun evening, Mon and for two weeks after Christmas.
(Michael Sargent, K Carr-Brion, Ryta Lyndley, Mike Buckingham and others)

BROOM   TL1743
Cock (01767) 314411
High Street; from A1 opposite Biggleswade turn-off, follow 'Old Warden 3, Aerodrome 2' signpost, first left signed Broom; SG18 9NA Unspoilt 19th-c village-green pub, four changing ales tapped from casks by cellar steps off central corridor (no counter), Potton Press cider, traditional food such as steak and kidney pudding, original latch doors linking one quietly cosy little room to the next (four in all), low ceilings, stripped panelling, farmhouse tables and chairs on old tiles, open fires, games room with bar skittles and darts; children and dogs welcome, picnic-sets on terrace by back lawn, open all day. *(Caroline Prescott)*

CARDINGTON   TL0847
Kings Arms (01234) 838533
The Green; off A603 E of Bedford; MK44 3SP Much extended Mitchells & Butlers village dining pub with interestingly furnished linked rooms; easy-going bar with

cushioned wall seats, tub chairs around trestle-style or copper-topped tables, driftwood mirrors, Sharps Doom Bar and a couple of guests from rustic counter, dining room with church chairs and white-painted tables on coir, sepia photographs of airships, good choice of food from light lunches up, more formal room with Victorian furniture, portraits and unusual log-end wallpaper, comfortable end room with leather banquettes and big log fire; background music, TV; well behaved children and dogs welcome, disabled facilities, modern seats on terrace, picnic-sets under willows to one side, open (and food) all day. *(Harvey Brown)*

CLOPHILL
TL0837

Flying Horse (01525) 860293

The Green; MK45 4AD Extended Mitchells & Butlers dining pub on edge of roundabout, split-level beamed bar with log fire in old brick fireplace, comfortable armchairs, tub chairs and cushioned stools around small copper-topped tables on stripped boards, church candles and contemporary woodblock bird paintings, Sharps Doom Bar and a guest, several wines by the glass, enjoyable food including fixed-price weekday deal till 6pm, friendly young staff, open-plan timbered dining area with raised central log fire (huge conical hood), white-painted chairs around pale tables, lower dining area too; children and dogs (in bar) welcome, disabled access, seats under parasols on side terrace and out in front, open (and food) all day. *(Martin Jones)*

CLOPHILL
TL0838

Stone Jug (01525) 860526

N on A6 from A507 roundabout, after 200 metres, second turn on right into backstreet; MK45 4BY Secluded old stone-built local (originally three cottages), cosy and welcoming, with traditional old-fashioned atmosphere, popular good value pubby lunchtime food (not Sun, Mon), friendly service, well kept local ales such as B&T Shefford, various rooms around L-shaped bar, darts in small games extension; background music; children welcome, roadside picnic-sets and pretty little back terrace, open all day Fri-Sun. *(Martin Jones)*

GREAT BARFORD
TL1351

Anchor (01234) 870364

High Street; off A421; MK44 3LF Open-plan pub by medieval arched bridge and church, Charles Wells ales and guests kept well, good sensibly priced food (all day Sat, Sun) from snacks up, river views from main bar, back restaurant (children welcome here); background music; picnic-sets overlooking Great Ouse, three bedrooms, open all day weekends. *(Emma Scofield)*

HARLINGTON
TL0330

Old Sun (01525) 877330

Sundon Road, by Methodist church; LU5 6LS Traditional 18th-c village pub, friendly and relaxed, with up to five well kept ales including Harveys and St Austell, good range of spirits too, reasonably priced home-made food (Tues and Fri evenings, Sun lunchtime), log fires; children and dogs welcome (pub dog is Pip), not good for wheelchairs, garden with play area, open all day. *(Emma Scofield)*

HENLOW
TL1738

Crown (01462) 812433

High Street; SG16 6BS Nicely updated beamed dining pub with good choice of popular food including children's menu, several wines by the glass, well kept Caledonian Flying Scotsman, Courage Directors and a guest, smiley helpful staff, woodburners (one in inglenook); quiet background music, free wi-fi, daily newspapers; terrace and small garden, open (and food) all day. *(Dr W I C Clark)*

HENLOW
TL1738

★**Engineers Arms** (01462) 812284

A6001 S of Biggleswade; High Street; SG16 6AA Traditional 19th-c village pub, up to a dozen changing ales plus good choice of ciders/perries, bottled belgian beers and wines by the glass, helpful knowledgeable staff, limited range of good value snacks, comfortable carpeted front room with old local photographs, bric-a-brac collections and good open fire, smaller tiled inner room and another comfortable carpeted one, beer/cider/country wine festivals, monthly live music, disco and quiz nights; sports TVs, juke box and silenced fruit machine; dogs allowed in bar, plenty of outside seating, open all day (till 1am Fri, Sat). *(George Atkinson)*

HOUGHTON CONQUEST
TL0441

★**Knife & Cleaver** (01234) 930789

Between B530 (old A418) and A6, S of Bedford; MK45 3LA Refurbished and extended 17th-c village dining pub opposite church, good variety of well liked food from separate bar and restaurant menus, extensive choice of wines by the glass including champagne, Charles Wells ales and a guest, friendly helpful staff; free wi-fi; children welcome, no dogs inside, nine chalet bedrooms arranged around courtyard and garden, good breakfast, free charging of electric cars for guests, open all day from 7am (8am weekends), till 8pm Sun. *(Vikki and Matt Wharton)*

KEMPSTON
TL0247

King William IV (01234) 400292

High Street; MK42 7AL Attractive old beamed pub under newish management, enjoyable fairly traditional food from sandwiches/baguettes up, well kept Charles Wells and guests, good-sized bar and restaurant; fruit machine, free wi-fi; children welcome, sheltered terrace and big garden, open (and food) all day. *(S Holder)*

LITTLE GRANSDEN   TL2755

Chequers (01767) 677348
Main Road; SG19 3DW Village local in
same family for over 60 years and retaining
1950s feel; simple bar with coal fire, darts
and framed historical information about the
pub, step down to cosy snug with another fire
and bench seats, comfortable back lounge
with fish tank, interesting range of own-
brewed Son of Sid ales, no food apart from
good fish and chips Fri evening (must book);
open all day Fri, Sat. *(Edward May)*

MAULDEN   TL0538

★ Dog & Badger (01525) 860237
*Clophill Road E of village, towards
A6/A507 junction; MK45 2AD* Attractive
neatly kept bow-windowed cottage, family
run and friendly, with good, well priced
food (booking advised weekends) including
sharing boards, pizzas and grills, set lunch
Mon-Sat and other deals, beams and exposed
brickwork, high stools on bare boards by
carved wooden counter serving Charles Wells
and guests, mix of dining chairs around
wooden tables, double-sided fireplace, steps
down to two carpeted areas and restaurant;
background music, sports TV; children
welcome, tables and smokers' shelter in
front, garden behind with sturdy play area,
open all day Fri-Sun. *(Edward May)*

MAULDEN   TL0537

White Hart (01525) 406118
Ampthill Road; MK45 2DH Modernised
17th-c thatched and low-beamed pub,
good choice of food from pubby choices up,
friendly helpful service, a couple of ales
including Charles Wells and good choice of
wines by the glass, large well divided dining
area; background music, Sun quiz; children
welcome, plenty of tables in sizeable gardens
with pleasant back decking, play area, open
all day. *(Gus Swan)*

NORTHILL   TL1446

★ Crown (01767) 627337
*Ickwell Road; off B658 W of Biggleswade;
SG18 9AA* Prettily situated village pub; cosy
flagstoned bar with copper-topped counter,
heavy low beams and bay window seats,
woodburner here and in restaurant with
modern furniture on light wood floor, steps up
to another dining area with exposed brick and
high ceiling, good brasserie-style food (not
Sun evening) including lunchtime baguettes
and panini, Greene King and guests, plenty of
wines by the glass, good friendly service; soft
background music; children welcome, no dogs
inside, tables out at front and on sheltered
side terrace, more in big back garden with
play area, open all day Fri-Sun. *(Gus Swan)*

ODELL   SP9657

Bell (01234) 720254
*Off A6 S of Rushden, via Sharnbrook;
High Street; MK43 7AS* This popular
thatched Greene King pub was about to
reopen under new management as we went
to press – reports please; several low-beamed
rooms around central servery, mix of old
settles and neat modern furniture, open fires;
big garden backing on to river, handy for
Harrold-Odell Country Park, has been open
all day Fri-Sun. *(Peter Brix)*

RISELEY   TL0462

Fox & Hounds (01234) 709714
*Off A6 from Sharnbrook/Bletsoe
roundabout; High Street, just E of Gold
Street; MK44 1DT* Modernised village pub
dating from the 16th c; low beams, stripped
boards and imposing stone fireplace, Charles
Wells Bombardier and Eagle, steaks cut to
weight and other food, separate dining room;
children and dogs (in bar) welcome, seats
out in front and in back garden with terrace,
open (and food) all day. *(Mrs Margo Finlay,
Jörg Kasprowski, Michael Sargent)*

SALFORD   SP9339

Swan (01908) 281008
*Not far from M1 junction 13 – left off
A5140; MK17 8BD* Popular Edwardian
country dining pub (Peach group), good
choice of well liked food and wine, Sharps
Doom Bar and Cornish Coaster, friendly staff,
updated interior with drinking area to right of
central servery, sofas and leather chairs on
wood floor, restaurant to left with modern
country cottage feel and window view into
kitchen; background music; children welcome,
dogs in bar, seats out on decking, kitchen
garden and own smokehouse, open all day.
(S Holder)

SOULDROP   SP9861

★ Bedford Arms (01234) 781384
*Village signposted off A6 Rushden–
Bedford; High Street; MK44 1EY* Popular
village pub dating from the 17th c, chatty
regulars in cosy low-beamed bar with snug
and alcove, Black Sheep, Greene King IPA
and guests such as Copper Kettle (brewed
just a mile away), Hopping Mad and Phipps,
local ciders and several wines by the glass,
good value generous pubby food (not Sun
evening) in cottagey dining area with more
low beams, broad floorboards and central
fireplace, shelves of china and art for sale,
roomy mansard-ceilinged part with big
inglenook, table skittles, shove-ha'penny
and darts; TV and games machine, free wi-fi;
children and dogs (in bar) welcome, boules
in neat garden, open all day Fri-Sun, closed
Mon; for sale last we heard. *(George Atkinson)*

STAGSDEN   SP9848

Royal George (01234) 823299
High Street; MK43 8SG Village pub
with modern opened-up interior, enjoyable
food including signature wood-fired pizzas
from open kitchen, beers such as Greene
King Abbot and Sharps Doom Bar, friendly
attentive staff, comfortable sofas on wood-

strip flooring, woodburner in brick fireplace; children welcome, small lawn at the back and terrace, local walks, open all day weekends. *(Peter Brix)*

STEPPINGLEY   TL0135
French Horn (01525) 720122
Off A507 just N of Flitwick; Church End; MK45 5AU Comfortable dining pub next to church, linked rooms with stippled beams, standing posts and wall timbers, two inglenooks (one with woodburner), eclectic mix of chesterfields, leather armchairs, cushioned antique dining chairs and other new and old furniture on flagstones or bare boards, Greene King IPA and a changing guest, good range of wines by the glass and malt whiskies, well liked freshly made food (all day weekends) served by friendly staff, elegant dining room; background music, TV, free wi-fi; children and dogs (in bar) welcome, open all day (till 1am Sat). *(Isobel Mackinlay, Caroline Prescott)*

STUDHAM   TL0215
Red Lion (01582) 872530
Church Road; LU6 2QA Character community pub with hands-on landlord, public bar and eating areas filled with pictures and bits and pieces collected over many years, house plants, wood flooring, carpeting and old red and black tiles, open fire, ales such as Adnams, Fullers, Greene King and Timothy Taylors, enjoyable pubby food (not evenings Sun, Mon, Tues); background music; children and dogs welcome, green picnic-sets in front under pretty window boxes, more on side grass, play house, open all day Fri-Sun. *(Gus Swan)*

THURLEIGH   TL0558
Jackal (01234) 771293
High Street; MK44 2DB Friendly part-thatched village pub dating from the 17th c; easy chairs and good fire in tiled-floor bar (where dogs allowed), another fire in comfortable carpeted dining lounge, enjoyable home-made food (not Sun evening) cooked by landlord, well kept Charles Wells ales; background music; seats and pretty hanging baskets/tubs out by road, nice rambling garden behind with chickens, closed Mon. *(Michael Sargent)*

TILSWORTH   SP9824
Anchor (01525) 411404
Just off A5 NW of Dunstable; LU7 9PU Refurbished 19th-c red-brick village pub, three well kept real ales and enjoyable food including good steaks, friendly efficient service, dining conservatory; children welcome, picnic-sets in large garden with play area, open all day. *(Toby Jones)*

TOTTERNHOE   SP9721
Cross Keys (01525) 220434
Off A505 W of A5; Castle Hill Road;

LU6 2DA Restored thatched and timbered two-bar pub below remains of a mott and bailey fort, low beams and cosy furnishings, good straightforward food (not Sun or Mon evenings), well kept ales including Adnams Broadside and Greene King IPA, dining room; big-screen TV; children and dogs welcome, good views from attractive big garden, open all day Thurs-Sun. *(Toby Jones)*

TURVEY   SP9352
★Three Fyshes (01234) 881463
A428 NW of Bedford; Bridge Street, W end of village; MK43 8ER Well maintained early 17th-c beamed pub, big inglenook with woodburner, mix of easy and upright chairs around tables on tiles or ancient flagstones, good home-made food including lunchtime set menu, friendly attentive service, Marstons, Timothy Taylors and a couple of guests, decent choice of wines, extended carpeted side restaurant; background music; dogs welcome in bar, children in eating areas; decking and canopy in charming garden overlooking bridge and mill on the Great Ouse (note the flood marks), car park further along the street, open all day from 9am. *(George Atkinson)*

WESTONING   SP0332
Chequers (01525) 712967
Park Road (A5120 N of M1 junction 12); MK45 5LA Refurbished thatched village pub with enjoyable food including good value set lunch and other deals, Adnams and Greene King ales, good choice of wines by the glass and various teas/coffees, helpful friendly service, low-beamed front bar, good-sized stables restaurant; free wi-fi; children and dogs (in bar) welcome, courtyard tables, open all day from 9am (10am weekends) for breakfast. *(Michael Jones)*

WOBURN   SP9433
Bell (01525) 290280
Bedford Street; MK17 9QJ Small beamed bar area, longer bare-boards dining lounge up steps, pleasant décor and furnishings, decent good value food all day including set menu, friendly helpful service, Greene King ales and good choice of wines by the glass; background music, games; children welcome, back terrace, hotel part across busy road, handy for Woburn Park. *(Mrs Margo Finlay, Jörg Kasprowski, Brian and Jean Hepworth)*

WOOTTON   TL0046
Legstraps (01234) 854112
Keeley Lane; MK43 9HR Refurbished dining pub with enjoyable food from lunchtime sandwiches and deli boards to more upscale choices, changing ales and plenty of wines by the glass including champagne; dogs in bar area, open all day Fri, Sat, till 6pm Sun, closed Mon. *(Toby Jones)*

Berkshire

BRAY
Crown 🍴 🍷

(01628) 621936 – www.thecrownatbray.co.uk

SU9079 Map 2

1.75 miles from M4 junction 9; A308 towards Windsor, then left at Bray signpost on to B3028; High Street; SL6 2AH

Ancient low-beamed pub with knocked-through rooms, enjoyable food, real ales and plenty of outside seating

There is a little bar area in this 16th-c pub with high stools around an equally high table and simple tables and chairs beside an open fire. Locals do drop in for a chat and a drink, but most emphasis is on dining (not surprising given that the owner is Heston Blumenthal). The snug rooms have some panelling, heavy old beams – some so low you may have to mind your head – plenty of timbers at elbow height where walls have been knocked through, a second log fire and neatly upholstered dining chairs and cushioned settles. Courage Best and Directors and a couple of changing guest beers on handpump and around 18 wines by the glass; board games. The covered and heated courtyard has modern slatted chairs and tables and there are plenty of picnic-sets in the large, enclosed back garden; croquet and aunt sally.

🍴 As well as lunchtime sandwiches, the highly rated food includes confit potted duck with cornichons, king prawn cocktail, watercress and caper risotto, fish and chips with home-made tartare sauce, chargrilled rare-breed bavette steak and marrowbone sauce, fillet of scottish salmon with spinach, tomato and shallots, and puddings such as earl grey tea panna cotta with lemon crumble and white chocolate bread and butter pudding; they offer take-away fish and chips and burgers 12-2, 6-9 Mon-Thurs. *Benchmark main dish: burger with pickles and fries £14.95. Two-course evening meal £21.95.*

Scottish Courage ~ Lease David Hyde ~ Real ale ~ Open 11.30-11; 12-10.30 Sun ~ Bar food 12-2.30 (3 Sat), 6-9.30 (10 Fri, Sat); 12-5 Sun ~ Children welcome ~ Dogs allowed in bar ~ Wi-fi *Recommended by Mike Swan, Phoebe Peacock, Simon Collett-Jones*

'Children welcome' means the pub says it lets children inside without any special restriction. If it allows them in, but to restricted areas such as an eating area or family room, we specify this. Places with separate restaurants often let children use them, and hotels usually let children into public areas such as lounges. Some pubs impose an evening time limit – let us know if you find one earlier than 9pm.

BRAY
Hinds Head 🍽 ♈

SU9079 Map 2

(01628) 626151 – www.hindsheadbray.com

High Street; car park opposite (exit rather tricky); SL6 2AB

Berkshire Dining Pub of the Year

Ancient low-beamed pub with knocked-through rooms, enjoyable food, real ales and plenty of outside seating

This is Heston Blumenthal's second pub in the village – and it's a handsome old place. The thoroughly traditional L-shaped bar has dark beams and panelling, polished oak parquet, blazing log fires, red-cushioned built-in wall seats and studded leather carving chairs around small round tables, and latticed windows. High chairs line the counter where they keep beers from local breweries such as Rebellion and Windsor & Eton and a changing guest on handpump, 19 wines by the glass from an extensive list, 18 malt whiskies, and a dozen specialist gins with interesting ways of serving them.

 Good, interesting food includes a hash of snails, raw highland estate venison with horseradish, turnip and shallot dressing, goats cheese royale butternut squash, baby onions and pumpkin velouté, chicken, ham and leek pie, oxtail and kidney pudding, fillet of wild bass with crushed jerusalem artichoke, cider butter sauce and mussels, bone-in sirloin of veal, and puddings such as rhubarb trifle and warm chocolate pudding with marmalade ice-cream; there's also a two- and three-course set menu. *Benchmark main dish: 10oz rare-breed ribeye steak £28.00. Two-course evening meal £25.00.*

Free house ~ Licensee Nabiel El-Nakib ~ Real ale ~ Open 11.30 (12 Mon)-11; 12-7 Sun ~ Bar food 12-2.30, 6.15-9.30; 12-4 Sun ~ Restaurant ~ Children welcome ~ Dogs allowed in bar ~ Wi-fi *Recommended by Colin McLachlan, Andrew Stone*

CHIEVELEY
Crab & Boar ★ ♈ ⇌

SU4574 Map 2

(01635) 247550 – www.crabandboar.com

North Heath, W of village; RG20 8UE

Stylish inn with interconnected bars and dining rooms, a welcoming, easy-going atmosphere, thoughtful choice of drinks, imaginative food and charming staff; seats outside; well equipped bedrooms

Smartly civilised but with a friendly, informal atmosphere and courteous, helpful staff, this attractive inn had just reopened on our visit, after a complete refurbishment. The L-shaped bar is light and airy at one end with tall green leather chairs lining a high shelf, a couple of unusual, equally high tables with garden planter bases, a contemporary chandelier and stools lining the shabby-chic counter where they keep Ramsbury Gold and Ringwood Best on handpump and good wines by the glass. The other end is cosier, with leather armchairs and sofas facing one another across a low table (set with chess pieces) in front of a woodburner in a large fireplace. The first room leading off here is really an extension of the bar (and dogs are allowed here too) with beams and timbering, tartan-upholstered stall seating and leather banquettes, and framed race tickets on the walls. The dining rooms, interconnected by timbering and steps, are decorated with old fishing reels, a large boar's head and photos and prints, with an eclectic mix of attractive chairs and tables on bare floorboards or carpet; an end room is just right for a private party. The garden has elegant metal or teak tables and chairs on gravel and grass; there's also a fountain and an outside bar and basic kitchen. The comfortable, well equipped bedrooms have fine country views and private courtyards and four have their own hot tub.

Extremely good, attractively presented food includes light bites such as moules frites, breaded deep-fried rabbit, pulled pork sliders and potted salmon on toast, plus pressed ham hock with crackling, apples and capers, trout escabeche with fennel, carrot and shallots, roast salmon with crab bisque and sautéed potatoes, fricassée of vegetables with chervil velouté, spatchcocked poussin with grilled hispi cabbage and pomme purée, lobster thermidor, and puddings such as peaches with granola and home-made vanilla ice-cream and custard tart with rhubarb. *Benchmark main dish: pork belly and cheek with alliums, wild garlic and celeriac purée £18.00. Two-course evening meal £25.00.*

Free house ~ Licensees Matt and Katie Beamish ~ Real ale ~ Open 11-11 ~ Bar food 12-2.30, 6-9.30; 12-3, 6-8 Sun ~ Restaurant ~ Children welcome ~ Dogs allowed in bar ~ Wi-fi ~ Bedrooms: /£110 *Recommended by Caroline Prescott, Emma Scofield*

COOKHAM DEAN   SU8785 Map 2

Chequers

(01628) 481232 – www.chequersbrasserie.co.uk
Dean Lane; follow signpost Cookham Dean, Marlow; SL6 9BQ

Friendly, civilised dining pub with neat, comfortable bar and restaurant, airy conservatory, first rate food and three real ales

Spic and span inside and out, this civilised place is popular at any time of year. In warm weather you can sit at picnic-sets under smart green parasols on the front grass, while in winter there are log fires. Helpful, professional staff will make you just as welcome if it's a pint and a chat that you want rather than a full meal – though most customers are here for the imaginative food. The busy little bar has a relaxed atmosphere, comfortable old sofas on flagstones, Rebellion IPA and Smuggler on handpump and ten good wines by the glass. Assorted dining tables on either side of the bar have crisp white linen and fresh flowers; maybe background music. The area on the left, with an open stove in its big brick fireplace, leads back to a conservatory that overlooks the neat sloping lawn.

 As well as a two- and three-course set lunch menu (not Sun), the interesting choice of food includes scotch duck egg with black pudding, red onion jam and balsamic, confit duck terrine with chutney, halloumi with rösti potato, spinach, a poached egg and pesto, beer-battered fish and chips, calves liver, bacon and red wine jus, fillet steak with peppercorn sauce, and puddings such as blueberry cheesecake and sticky toffee pudding with butterscotch sauce. *Benchmark main dish: chicken breast wrapped in parma ham with creamy savoy cabbage and jus £14.95. Two-course evening meal £22.00.*

Free house ~ Licensee Peter Roehrig ~ Real ale ~ Open 12-3, 5.30-11; 12-11 Sat; 12-6 Sun ~ Bar food 12-2.30, 6.30-9.30; 12-5 Sun ~ Children welcome *Recommended by R K Phillips, Harvey Brown, Gus Swan*

FRILSHAM   SU5573 Map 2

Pot Kiln

(01635) 201366 – www.potkiln.org
From Yattendon take turning S, opposite church, follow first Frilsham signpost, but just after crossing motorway go straight on towards Bucklebury, ignoring Frilsham signposted right; pub on right after about half a mile; RG18 0XX

Country dining pub with bustling small bar, local beers, imaginative food and suntrap garden

There's always a good mix of both regulars and visitors in this well run country pub and the friendly, efficient staff keep things running smoothly even when the place is packed. The little bar has West Berkshire Brick Kiln Bitter and Swift Pale Ale and a guest beer on handpump, nine wines by the glass and maybe a couple of ciders. The main bar area has dark wooden tables and chairs on bare boards and a winter log fire, while the extended lounge is open-plan at the back and leads into a large, pretty dining room with a nice jumble of old tables and chairs and an old-looking stone fireplace; darts. It's in an idyllic spot with wide, unobstructed views from seats in a big suntrap garden, and there are plenty of walks in the nearby woods.

Using venison from the local estate plus local crayfish, the well liked food includes ciabatta sandwiches, pigeon salad with artichoke purée, bacon and black pudding, mussels in onions and cider cream, linguine with chanterelle and trumpet mushrooms in cream, beef and fallow deer burger with bacon, aged cheddar and crisp potatoes, coq au vin, plaice with brown shrimps and beurre blanc, and puddings. *Benchmark main dish: pave of fallow deer with crispy shallots, potato purée and peppercorn sauce £21.00. Two-course evening meal £25.00.*

Free house ~ Licensees Tom Dennis and Michael Robinson ~ Real ale ~ Open 12-3, 6-11; 12-11 Sat; 12-9.30 Sun; closed Tues ~ Bar food 12-2.30, 7-9; 12-3.30, 6-8 Sun ~ Restaurant ~ Children welcome ~ Dogs allowed in bar ~ Wi-fi *Recommended by Alistair Forsyth, Pat and Tony Martin*

HARE HATCH
Horse & Groom ♀ ◖
SU8077 Map 2

(0118) 940 3136 – www.brunningandprice.co.uk/horseandgroom
A4 Bath Road W of Maidenhead; RG10 9SB

Spreading pub with attractively refurbished, timbered rooms, friendly staff, enjoyable food, a fine range of drinks and seats outside

For 300 years, this handsome old coaching inn has been a landmark for travellers and there are plenty of signs of great age in the interconnected rooms – and much of interest too: beams and timbering, a pleasing variety of well spread individual tables and chairs on mahogany-stained boards, oriental rugs and some carpet to soften the acoustics, open fires in attractive tiled fireplaces, a profusion of mainly old or antique prints and mirrors, book-lined shelves and house plants. The long bar counter has a splendid choice of drinks served by well trained, courteous staff, including a good changing range of 15 wines by the glass, Brakspears Bitter and Special, Jennings Cocker Hoop, Wychwood Hobgoblin and a changing guest on handpump, Weston's farm cider, lots of spirits including 77 malt whiskies, and several coffees; also several different daily papers. A sheltered back garden has picnic-sets and the front terrace has teak tables and chairs under parasols.

Good, interesting food includes sandwiches, scallops with pancetta, cauliflower purée, tempura samphire and rhubarb purée, rabbit, chicken and pork terrine with candied carrot chutney, moroccan-spiced salmon with lemon and mint crème fraîche and couscous, steak burger with bacon, cheddar, coleslaw and chips, duo of pork (slow-roasted belly and braised cheek) with black pudding mash and cider jus, crispy beef in sweet chilli dressing on oriental leaves with cashews, and puddings such as apple and coconut crumble and chocolate brownie with chocolate sauce. *Benchmark main dish: lamb shoulder with dauphinoise potatoes and rosemary gravy £17.95. Two-course evening meal £21.50.*

Brunning & Price ~ Manager Mark Hider ~ Real ale ~ Open 11.30-11 (10.30 Sun) ~ Bar food 12-10 (9.30 Sun) ~ Well behaved children welcome ~ Dogs allowed in bar ~ Wi-fi *Recommended by John Boothman, D J and P M Taylor*

INKPEN

SU3764   Map 2

Crown & Garter

(01488) 668325 – www.crownandgarter.co.uk

Inkpen Common: Inkpen signposted with Kintbury off A4; in Kintbury turn left into Inkpen Road, then keep on into Inkpen Common; RG17 9QR

Recently refurbished country pub with open fires, modern touches blending with original features, enjoyable food and seats outside; bedrooms

Tucked away down a country lane, this rather fine old brick pub has been recently refurbished. There's a spreading bar area with wooden stools against the counter where they serve West Berkshire Good Old Boy and Mr Chubbs Lunchtime Bitter on handpump and ten wines by the glass; leading off here is a snug with seats by a log fire in a raised brick fireplace. Throughout, an assortment of upholstered dining chairs are grouped around simple tables on pale floorboards, with armchairs here and there, cushioned wall seating, mirrors and modern artwork on contemporary paintwork and wallpaper depicting both bookcases (in the smart restaurant) and old suitcases. The front terrace has seats and tables under parasols. The comfortable bedrooms are in a separate single-storey L-shaped building around an attractive garden. They've also opened a separate bakery and coffee shop (which becomes a private dining space in the evening). Disabled access.

Using seasonal, local produce, the interesting food includes sandwiches, goats cheese mousse with chicory, apple and walnut praline, game pâté with apple and quince chutney, burger with smoked mayonnaise and chips, butternut squash risotto, pork loin with braised spelt, cipollini onions and red cabbage purée, smoked cod with chive sauce and braised lentils, and puddings such as lemon tart with Sipsmith gin and tonic sorbet and ginger parkin pudding with toasted breadcrumb ice-cream and sticky ginger sauce. *Benchmark main dish: bouillabaisse £14.50. Two-course evening meal £21.00.*

Free house ~ Licensee Romilla Arber ~ Real ale ~ Open 12-11; 12-6 Sun; closed Mon and Tues lunchtimes ~ Bar food 12-2.30 (3 Sun), 6.30-9 ~ Restaurant ~ Children welcome ~ Dogs allowed in bar ~ Wi-fi ~ Bedrooms: £100/£120 *Recommended by Mrs Julie Thomas, David and Judy Robison, Mrs P Sumner*

INKPEN

SU3564   Map 2

Swan

(01488) 668326 – www.theswaninn-organics.co.uk

Lower Inkpen; coming from A338 in Hungerford, take Park Street (first left after railway bridge); RG17 9DX

Extended country pub with rambling rooms, traditional décor, real ales and plenty of seats outside; comfortable bedrooms

After a walk in the nearby North Wessex Downs, this much-extended pub is a useful spot for refreshment. It's owned by local, organic beef farmers and you can buy their produce (and ready-made meals and groceries) in the interesting farm shop next door. The rambling beamed rooms have cosy corners, traditional pubby furniture, eclectic bric-a-brac and three log fires, and there's a flagstoned games area plus a cosy restaurant. Butts Jester and Traditional and a changing summer guest on handpump, several wines by the glass and maybe home-made sloe gin; darts, shut the box and board games. The bedrooms are quiet and comfortable. There are picnic-sets on tiered front terraces overlooking a footpath.

The menu, using their organic farm produce, includes sandwiches, home-cured bresaola, chicken liver pâté with chutney, beef and onion pie, burgers with cheese and chips, thai green chicken curry, ricotta and spinach cannelloni, beer-battered cod and chips, a steak of the day with a choice of sauces, and puddings such as chocolate fudge cake with chocolate sauce and apple and blackberry crumble. *Benchmark main dish: beef medallions with gravy in giant yorkshire pudding £14.00. Two-course evening meal £19.00.*

Free house ~ Licensees Mary and Bernard Harris ~ Real ale ~ Open 12-2.30, 6.30-11; 12-11 Sat; 12-10.30 Sun; closed Sun evening in winter ~ Bar food 12-3, 7-9 ~ Restaurant ~ Children welcome ~ Wi-fi ~ Bedrooms: £70/£90 *Recommended by Chris and Angela Buckell, Peter Brix*

KINTBURY SU3866 Map 2

Dundas Arms ♀ ⇌

(01488) 658263 – www.dundasarms.co.uk

Village signposted off A4 Newbury–Hungerford about a mile W of Halfway; Station Road – pub just over hump-back canal bridge, at start of village itself; RG17 9UT

Carefully updated inn with relaxed informal bar, good two-level restaurant, and lovely waterside garden; comfortable bedrooms

This handsome inn between a quiet pool of the River Kennet and the Kennet & Avon Canal was erected early in the 19th c for the canal builders. As well as picnic-sets on decking overlooking the water, the large, pretty back garden (with water on each side) has plenty of well spaced tables on grass among shrubs and trees. This is overlooked by the big windows of the smart two-level restaurant. At the other end is a smallish bar, taking its relaxed informal mood from the cheerful helpful staff. Here there are sporting prints above a high oak dado, neat little cushioned arts-and-crafts chairs around a few stripped or polished tables on broad floorboards, and high chairs by the counter, which serves Tutts Clump farm cider from handpump as well as Ramsbury Gold, Ringwood Best and two or three ales from West Berkshire, and 14 wines by the glass. Between the bar and restaurant is a cosy, tartan-carpeted sitting room with wing chairs and a splendid leather and mahogany settee, daily papers, a good winter log fire flanked by glazed bookcases, and big silhouette portraits on topiary-print wallpaper. Pleasant nearby walks.

 Quite a choice of rewarding food includes pork rillettes with pickled beetroot and toffee apple purée, twice-baked blue cheese soufflé with onion jam, plum tomato and goats cheese tarte tatin, beer-battered fish of the day, hot smoked local pheasant with quince purée and chestnuts, fish pie, 21-day-aged rib-eye steak with triple-cooked chips, and puddings such as banana eton mess and white chocolate and raspberry cheesecake. *Benchmark main dish: burger with toppings, coleslaw and fries £12.85. Two-course evening meal £21.50.*

Free house ~ Licensee Emily Carr ~ Real ale ~ Open 12-11 (10.30 Sun) ~ Bar food 12-3, 6-9; 12-10 Sat; 12-9 Sun ~ Restaurant ~ Children welcome ~ Dogs allowed in bar and bedrooms ~ Wi-fi ~ Bedrooms: £80/£140 *Recommended by Harvey Brown, Neil Allen*

NEWBURY SU4767 Map 2

Newbury ⭐ ♀ ▦

(01635) 49000 – www.thenewburypub.co.uk

Bartholomew Street; RG14 5HB

Lively pub with thoughtful choice of drinks, good food and plenty of bar and dining space

They keep a fantastic choice of drinks in this stylish and cheerful town pub: Two Cocks 1643 Cavalier and 1643 Roundhead, West Berkshire Good Old Boy and a guest from Wickwar on handpump, a farm cider, 20 malt whiskies, around 25 wines by the glass, an extensive cocktail list and a fine range of coffees and teas (including tea grown in Cornwall). The bar has an assortment of wooden dining chairs around sturdy farmhouse and other solid tables on bare boards, comfortable leather sofas, big paintings on pale painted walls, and church candles. Light and airy, the dining rooms have wall benches and church chairs around more rustic tables on more bare boards, and shelves full of cookery books.

 As well as sandwiches, weekend brunches and their own-made ice-cream, chutneys and bread, the highly popular food includes braised octopus with chorizo, tomato and crispy artichoke, garlic Aylesbury snails with pumpkin and salad, brioche burger with bacon jam and fries, crispy pork terrine with black pudding, rémoulade and braised apple, stone bass with saffron shellfish broth and wild mushrooms, steaks cooked in their charcoal oven, and puddings such as banoffi arctic rolls with caramelised banana. *Benchmark main dish: mussels, prawns and scallops in cider and cream £17.50. Two-course evening meal £24.00.*

Free house ~ Licensees Clarke Oldfield and Peter Lumber ~ Real ale ~ Open 12 (10 Sat)-1am; 10am-11pm Sun ~ Bar food 12-3, 5.30-11; 12-4, 6-11 (9 Sun) Sat ~ Restaurant ~ Children welcome ~ Dogs allowed in bar ~ Wi-fi *Recommended by Harvey Brown, Alfie Bayliss, Ian Herdman*

PEASEMORE
Fox

SU4577   Map 2

(01635) 248480 – www.foxatpeasemore.co.uk
4 miles from M4 junction 13, via Chieveley: keep on through Chieveley to Peasemore, turning left into Hillgreen Lane at small sign to Fox Inn; village also signposted from B4494 Newbury–Wantage; RG20 7JN

Friendly downland pub on top form under its expert licensees

Always deservedly busy and much enjoyed by our readers, this is a cheerful pub run by top-class licensees. The long bare-boards bar has strategically placed high-backed settles, comfort guaranteed by plenty of colourful cushions, a warm woodburning stove in a stripped brick chimneybreast, and for real sybarites two luxuriously carpeted end areas, one with velour tub armchairs. Friendly, efficient black-clad staff serve Ridgeside Black Night, West Berkshire Good Old Boy and White Horse Dragon Hill on handpump, 15 wines by the glass and summer farm cider; background music. This is downland horse-training country, and a couple of picnic-table sets at the front look out to the rolling fields beyond the quiet country lane – on a clear day as far as the Hampshire border hills some 20 miles south; there are more on a smallish sheltered back terrace.

Good country cooking includes sandwiches, tempura prawns, smoked salmon and timbale of prawns, baked portobello mushroom filled with wild mushrooms and pine nuts in tomato sauce, a pie of the day, chicken with cheese wrapped in bacon with creamy brandy and wild mushroom sauce, lamb shank in red wine, rosemary and garlic, salmon and haddock fishcake with chips, and puddings such as vanilla cheesecake with berry coulis and chocolate brownie with chocolate sauce. *Benchmark main dish: beef wellington with port and stilton sauce £19.50. Two-course evening meal £25.00.*

Free house ~ Licensees Philip and Lauren Davison ~ Real ale ~ Open 12-3, 6-11; 12-11 (8 Sun) Sat; closed Mon, Tues evening ~ Bar food 12-2.30, 6-9; 12-9 Sat; 12-5 Sun ~ Restaurant ~ Children welcome ~ Dogs allowed in bar ~ Wi-fi *Recommended by Ian Herdman, Harvey Brown*

RUSCOMBE
Royal Oak

SU7976   Map 2

(0118) 934 5190 – www.burattas.co.uk

Ruscombe Lane (B3024 just E of Twyford); RG10 9JN

Wide choice of popular food at welcoming pub with interesting furnishings and paintings, local beer and wine

There's something for everyone in this well run pub, whether it's just a pint and a chat, a light snack or a full three-course meal – and you'll be warmly welcomed by the friendly, efficient staff, too. The bars are open-plan and carpeted and cleverly laid out so that each area is fairly snug, but it still maintains an overall feel of a lot of people enjoying themselves. A good variety of furniture runs from dark oak tables to big chunky pine ones with mixed seating to match; the two sofas facing each other are popular. Contrasting with the old exposed ceiling joists, mostly unframed modern paintings and prints decorate the walls (painted in cream, white and soft green). Binghams (the brewery is just across the road) Space Hoppy and Twyford Tipple and Fullers London Pride on handpump, 15 wines by the glass (they stock wines from the Stanlake Park Vineyard in the village), several malt whiskies and attentive service. Picnic-sets are ranged around a venerable central hawthorn in the garden behind (where there are ducks and chickens); summer barbecues. The pub (known locally as Buratta's, so don't drive past) is on the Henley Arts Trail. Do visit the landlady's antiques and collectables shop which is open during pub hours.

Reliably good food includes a good range of sandwiches, smoked haddock and spring onion fishcake, chicken liver parfait with chilli butter, sausages and mash with caramelised onion gravy, stilton and bacon burger with chips, mushroom and leek stroganoff, a pie of the week, spicy beef in hoisin and peanut sauce, fresh mackerel with apple and cider sauce, braised shoulder of lamb with mustard mash and rosemary sauce, and puddings. *Benchmark main dish: monkfish wrapped in parma ham with green peppercorn sauce £15.00. Two-course evening meal £22.00.*

Enterprise ~ Lease Jenny and Stefano Buratta ~ Real ale ~ Open 12-3, 6-11; 12-4 Sun; closed Sun and Mon evenings ~ Bar food 12-2.30, 7-9.30; 12-3 Sun ~ Restaurant ~ Children welcome ~ Dogs welcome ~ Wi-fi *Recommended by Paul Humphreys, Emma Scofield, Bill Gulliver and Harry Thomson*

SHEFFORD WOODLANDS
Pheasant

SU3673   Map 2

(01488) 648284 – www.thepheasant-inn.co.uk

Under 0.5 miles from M4 junction 14 – A338 towards Wantage, first left on B4000; RG17 7AA

Bustling bars, a separate dining room, enjoyable food and beer and seats outside; bedrooms

A thoroughly enjoyable pub and consistently popular with our readers. The various interconnecting bar rooms have a mix of elegant wooden dining chairs and settles around all sorts of tables, big mirrors here and there, plenty of horse-related prints, photos and paintings (including a huge mural) – the owners are keen racegoers – and a warm fire in a little brick fireplace. One snug little room, with log-end wallpaper, has armchairs, a cushioned chesterfield and a flat-screen TV. There's also a separate dining room; background music. Ramsbury Gold and two guests such as Two Cocks 1643 Leveller and Upham Punter on handpump and quite a few good wines by the glass. Seats in the garden have attractive views. The comfortable modern bedrooms are in a separate extension, and the continental breakfasts (cooked is also available) are good.

🍴 Highly thought-of food includes lunchtime sandwiches, crispy salt and pepper squid with garlic aioli, ham hock, chicken and pistachio terrine with tomato compote, mushroom, spinach and smoked cheddar cannelloni, calves liver, celeriac and carrot mash and onion jus, cod fritters with onion bhaji, curried chickpeas, chorizo and yoghurt with red peppers, corn-fed chicken stuffed with pork and sage with artichoke, bacon, celeriac purée and red wine sauce, and puddings such as sticky toffee pudding and lemon meringue cheesecake with orange marshmallows. *Benchmark main dish: pork three-ways (loin, crispy belly, shoulder) with apple tart, onion purée and parma ham £16.50. Two-course evening meal £22.00.*

Free house ~ Licensee Rupert Fowler ~ Real ale ~ Open 10am-11pm; 10am-10.30pm Sun ~ Bar food 12-2.30, 6.30-9.30 (6-9 Sun) ~ Children welcome ~ Dogs allowed in bar ~ Wi-fi ~ Bedrooms: /£90 *Recommended by Mr and Mrs P R Thomas, Katharine Cowherd*

SONNING   SU7575   Map 2
Bull 🛏

(0118) 969 3901 ~ www.fullershotels.com
Off B478, by church; village signed off A4 E of Reading; RG4 6UP

Pretty timbered inn in attractive spot near Thames, plenty of character in old-fashioned bars, Fullers beers, friendly staff and good food; bedrooms

In early summer when the wisteria is flowering and the courtyard is full of bright flower tubs, this lovely 16th-c inn looks its best. The two old-fashioned bar rooms have low ceilings and heavy beams, cosy alcoves, leather armchairs and sofas, cushioned antique settles and low wooden chairs on bare boards, and open fireplaces. Fullers Chiswick, HSB, Honey Dew, London Pride and a couple of guests on handpump served by helpful staff, 16 good wines by the glass, cocktails and a farm cider. The dining room has an assortment of wooden chairs and tables, rugs on parquet flooring and shelves of books; TV. The bedrooms are comfortable and well equipped. If you bear left through the ivy-clad churchyard opposite, then turn left along the bank of the River Thames, you come to a very pretty lock. The Thames Valley Park is close by.

🍴 Interesting food includes sandwiches, popcorn tiger prawns with smoked aioli, potted duck with dark cherry compote, sharing platters, sausages with crispy leeks and onion cider gravy, wild and chestnut mushroom cottage or steak and kidney pies, teriyaki salmon with noodles, bean sprouts, peppers and light chilli sauce, pheasant two-ways with mulled wine sauce, whole baked plaice with herb and garlic butter, and puddings such as plum and apple strudel and chocolate brownie with chocolate sauce. *Benchmark main dish: home-made pies £16.00. Two-course evening meal £20.00.*

Fullers ~ Manager Christine Mason ~ Real ale ~ Open 10am-11pm (midnight Sat); 12-10.30 Sun ~ Bar food 10-9.30 ~ Restaurant ~ Children welcome ~ Dogs allowed in bar ~ Wi-fi ~ Tribute acts monthly ~ Bedrooms: /£105 *Recommended by M A Borthwick, Susan and John Douglas, Simon Collett-Jones. Roy Hoing*

Please keep sending us reports. We rely on readers for news of new discoveries, and particularly for news of changes - however slight - at the fully described pubs: feedback@goodguides.com, or (no stamp needed) The Good Pub Guide, FREEPOST RTJR-ZCYZ-RJZT, Perrymans Lane, Etchingham TN19 7DN.

SWALLOWFIELD   SU7364   Map 2
George & Dragon 🌟 ᵧ

(0118) 988 4432 – www.georgeanddragonswallowfield.co.uk

Church Road, towards Farley Hill; RG7 1TJ

Busy country pub with enjoyable bar food, real ales, friendly service and seats outside

A fter enjoying one of the nearby walks (details are given on their website), you can expect a good choice of drinks and interesting food at this comfortable country pub. The long-serving licensees are warmly welcoming and the various interconnected rooms have plenty of character: beams (some quite low) and standing timbers, a happy mix of nice old dining chairs and settles around individual wooden tables, rugs on flagstones, lit candles, a big log fire and country prints on red or bare brick walls; background music. Fullers London Pride, Ringwood Best and Sharps Doom Bar on handpump, quite a few wines by the glass and several gins and whiskies. There are picnic-sets on gravel or paving in the garden.

 Quite a choice of tasty food includes lunchtime ciabattas, chicken liver parfait with fig compote, crab salad with lemon mayonnaise, avocado and chilli and tomato sauce, burger with toppings, guacamole and chips, aubergine filled with mozzarella, pine nuts, pesto and tomato fondue, chicken breast filled with mushroom and chestnut stuffing with red wine jus, calves liver and bacon with caramelised onions, king prawn red thai curry, and puddings such as chocolate brownie with red berries and chocolate sauce and lemon posset. *Benchmark main dish: slow-roasted half shoulder of lamb with garlic mash and rosemary sauce £14.95. Two-course evening meal £21.50.*

Free house ~ Licensee Paul Dailey ~ Real ale ~ Open 12-11 (midnight Sat) ~ Bar food 12-2.30, 7-9.30 (10 Fri, Sat); 12-3, 7-9 Sun ~ Restaurant ~ Children welcome ~ Dogs allowed in bar *Recommended by John Pritchard, Mrs P Sumner, Simon Collett-Jones*

UPPER BASILDON   SU5976   Map 2
Red Lion ᵧ 🍺

(01491) 671234 – www.theredlionupperbasildon.co.uk

Off A329 NW of Pangbourne; Aldworth Road; RG8 8NG

Laid-back country pub with friendly family atmosphere, popular food and a good choice of drinks

T hey are quite relaxed here as to whether you're dropping in for a drink after a walk or hoping to enjoy the tempting food – there's a genuine welcome for all. With pale blue-grey paintwork throughout (even on the beams), the bars have chapel chairs, a few pews and miscellaneous stripped tables on bare floorboards, and a green leather chesterfield and armchair. Courage Directors, Sharps Doom Bar, West Berkshire Good Old Boy and a weekly changing guest on handpump, a dozen wines from an extensive list, and a farm cider. Beyond a double-sided woodburning stove, a pitched-ceiling area has much the same furniture on cord carpet, but a big cut-glass chandelier and large mirror give it a slightly more formal dining feel. The *Independent* and *Racing Post*, occasional background music and regular (usually jazz-related) live music. There are sturdy picnic-sets in the sizeable enclosed garden, and summer barbecues and hog roasts.

🍴 Reliably good food includes lunchtime sandwiches and platters, pork and madeira terrine with tomato and chilli jam, smoked salmon and prawn cocktail, chicken caesar salad, barbecue ribs and coleslaw, beer-battered haddock and chips, pork and leek sausages with onion gravy and parsley mash, burger with toppings and fries, rump

of lamb with white bean, garlic and thyme casserole and red wine gravy, and puddings
such as dark chocolate mousse and banoffi pie. *Benchmark main dish: seafood
platter £16.50. Two-course evening meal £21.00.*

Enterprise ~ Lease Alison Green ~ Real ale ~ Open 11-3, 5-11; 11-11 Sat; 11-10.30 Sun ~
Bar food 12-2.30, 6-9 (9.30 Fri, Sat); 12-3, 6-8.30 Sun ~ Restaurant ~ Children welcome ~
Dogs allowed in bar ~ Wi-fi *Recommended by Belinda Stamp, Neil Allen*

 WHITE WALTHAM   SU8477   Map 2

Beehive

(01628) 822877 – www.thebeehivewhitewaltham.co.uk
Waltham Road (B3024 W of Maidenhead); SL6 3SH

**Attractive village pub with welcoming staff and enjoyable food
and drinks choice; seats outside**

There's a bit more emphasis now on the particularly good food, but that
certainly doesn't mean that those in for a pint and a natter are not made
just as welcome. The atmosphere is bustling and friendly, helped along by the
hospitable landlord and his friendly staff. To the right are several comfortably
spacious areas with leather chairs around sturdy tables, while to the left is a
neat bar brightened up by cheerful scatter cushions on comfortable built-in
wall seats and captain's chairs. Fullers London Pride, Rebellion IPA, Sharps
Doom Bar and a guest beer on handpump, 12 wines by the glass and a good
choice of soft drinks. A brick-built room has glass doors opening on to the
front terrace (the teak seats and picnic-sets here take in the pub's rather fine
topiary). Background music and board games. A good-sized sheltered back
lawn has seats and tables, and the village cricket field is opposite. Disabled
access and facilities.

Good rewarding food from a seasonal menu, cooked by the landlord, includes
lunchtime sandwiches, crab linguine with chilli, lemon and mint, fricassée
of rabbit with dandelion, caramelised shallots and blewit mushrooms, mozzarella,
parmesan and saffron risotto with rocket, confit duck leg with braised lentils and red
wine sauce, grilled cornish sardines, haunch of venison with peppery game sauce, and
puddings such as chocolate fondant with toffee sauce and baked alaska. *Benchmark
main dish: calves liver and bacon £15.95. Two-course evening meal £22.00.*

Enterprise ~ Lease Dominic Chapman ~ Real ale ~ Open 12-3, 5-11; 12-11 Sat; 12-8.30 Sun
~ Bar food 12-2.30, 6.30-9.30; 12-4 (7 in summer) Sun ~ Restaurant ~ Children welcome ~
Dogs allowed in bar ~ Wi-fi ~ Quiz last Thurs of month
*Recommended by John Pritchard, Richard and Liz Thorne, Roger and Donna Huggins, Nigel and
Sue Foster, Susan and John Douglas*

WOOLHAMPTON   SU5766   Map 2

Rowbarge ⭐ ♀ 🍺

(0118) 971 2213 – www.brunningandprice.co.uk/rowbarge
Station Road; RG7 5SH

**Rambling rooms full of interest in canalside pub, six real ales,
good bistro-style food and lots of outside seating**

The setting by the Kennet & Avon Canal is attractive and there are wooden
chairs and tables on a decked terrace and picnic-sets among trees by the
water. Inside, six rambling rooms with beams and timbering are connected
by open doorways and knocked-through walls. The décor is gently themed to
represent the nearby canal with hundreds of prints and photographs (some
of rowing and boats) and oars on the walls, plus old glass and stone bottles
in nooks and crannies, big house plants and fresh flowers, plenty of candles

and several open fires; the many large mirrors create an impression of even more space. Throughout, there are antique dining chairs around various nice old tables, settles, built-in cushioned wall seating, armchairs, a group of high stools around a huge wooden barrel table, and rugs on polished boards, stone tiles or carpeting. Friendly, helpful staff serve Phoenix Brunning & Price Original plus guests such as Butts Barbus Barbus, Itchen Valley Hampshire Rose, Milk Street The Usual, Ramsbury Same Again and Triple fff Altons Pride on handpump, 20 wines by the glass and 60 malt whiskies; background music and board games.

An interesting choice of attractively presented food includes sandwiches, lime and chilli-cured salmon with aromatic vegetables, pigs cheek fritter with black pudding, celeriac purée and parsnip crisps, chicken lyonnaise salad, butternut squash risotto with mozzarella, smoked haddock and salmon fishcakes, venison stew, guinea fowl with bacon, mustard and cream, and puddings such as crème brûlée and bread and butter pudding with apricot sauce. *Benchmark main dish: braised lamb shoulder with dauphinoise potatoes and rosemary gravy £16.95. Two-course evening meal £19.50.*

Brunning & Price ~ Manager Stephen Butt ~ Real ale ~ Open 11-11 (10.30 Sun) ~ Bar food 12-10 (9 Sun) ~ Restaurant ~ Children welcome ~ Dogs allowed in bar ~ Wi-fi
Recommended by John Pritchard, Ron Corbett, Mrs P Sumner

YATTENDON   SU5574   Map 2
Royal Oak 🌟 ♟ 🛏
(01635) 201325 – www.royaloakyattendon.co.uk
The Square; B4009 NE from Newbury; right at Hampstead Norreys, village signed on left; RG18 0UG

Handsome old inn with beamed and panelled rooms, lovely flowers, local beers, imaginative food and seats in pretty garden; comfortable bedrooms

With the West Berkshire brewery actually in the village, the four real ales on handpump in this civilised place are on tip top form; the ten wines by the glass are well chosen. The charming bar rooms have beams and panelling, an appealing mix of wooden dining chairs around interesting tables, some half-panelled wall seating, rugs on quarry tiles or wooden floorboards, plenty of prints on brick, cream or red walls, lovely flower arrangements and four log fires. Under the trellising in the walled back garden are wicker armchairs and tables, and there are picnic-sets under parasols at the front. This is a comfortable place to stay and the light, attractive bedrooms overlook the garden or village square; breakfasts are good. The pub is only ten minutes from Newbury Racecourse and does get pretty busy on race days.

Using the best local produce, the fine food includes sandwiches, devilled ox kidneys on toast, spiced crab cakes with harissa mayonnaise, braised beef with truffle mash, mushrooms and shallots, smoked haddock kedgeree with boiled egg, wild boar sausage toad in the hole with onion gravy, butter-poached organic chicken with stuffed cabbage and bacon and jus, and puddings such as chocolate and Cointreau torte and apple, cranberry and cinnamon crumble; they also offer a two- and three-course set weekday lunch. *Benchmark main dish: rib-eye steak with pepper sauce £25.00. Two-course evening meal £24.00.*

Free house ~ Licensee Rob McGill ~ Real ale ~ Open 11-11; 12-10.30 Sun ~ Bar food 12-2.30 (3 weekends), 6.30-9.30 (9 Sun) ~ Children welcome ~ Dogs welcome ~ Wi-fi ~ Bedrooms: £95/£115 *Recommended by Neil and Angela Huxter, Wendy Breese, Colin McLachlan, Alistair Forsyth*

Also Worth a Visit in Berkshire

Besides the fully inspected pubs, you might like to try these pubs that have been recommended to us and described by readers. Do tell us what you think of them: feedback@goodguides.com

ALDWORTH SU5579

★ **Bell** (01635) 578272

A329 Reading–Wallingford; left on to B4009 at Streatley; RG8 9SE Unspoilt and unchanging (in same family for over 250 years), simply furnished panelled rooms, beams in ochre ceiling, ancient one-handed clock, woodburner, glass-panelled hatch serving Arkells, West Berkshire and a monthly guest, Upton cider, nice house wines, maybe winter mulled wine, good value rolls, ploughman's and winter soup, traditional pub games, no mobile phones or credit cards; can get busy weekends; well behaved children and dogs welcome, seats in quiet, cottagey garden by village cricket ground, animals in paddock behind pub, maybe Christmas mummers and summer morris, closed Mon (open lunchtime bank holidays). *(Andrew Stone)*

ALDWORTH SU5579

Four Points (01635) 578367

B4009 towards Hampstead Norreys; RG8 9RL Attractive 17th-c thatched roadside pub with low beams, standing timbers and panelling, nice fire in bar with more formal seating area to the left and restaurant at back, good value home-made food (all day weekends) from baguettes up, local Two Cocks and Wadworths 6X, friendly helpful young staff; children welcome, garden over road with play area. *(Andrew Stone)*

ARBORFIELD CROSS SU7667

Bull (0118) 976 2244

On roundabout; RG2 9QD Light open-plan dining pub with most tables set for the good popular food (booking advised), extensive menu including some french dishes, well priced house wines, efficient friendly service; children welcome, picnic-sets in garden, closed Mon, otherwise open all day. *(Paul Humphreys, John Pritchard, Paul Lucas)*

ASHMORE GREEN SU4969

Sun in the Wood (01635) 42377

B4009 (Shaw Road) off A339, right to Kiln Road, left to Stoney Lane; RG18 9HF Refurbished and extended 19th-c dining pub again under new management; enjoyable food (not Sun evening) from stone-baked pizzas and pub favourites up, fixed-price menu lunchtime/early evening, Wadworths ales and several wines by the glass, good coffee too, spacious interior with light open feel; background music; children welcome, dogs in bar, terrace and woodside garden, open all day. *(John Pritchard)*

ASTON SU7884

★ **Flower Pot** (01491) 574721

Off A4130 Henley–Maidenhead at top of Remenham Hill; RG9 3DG Roomy popular country pub with nice local feel, roaring log fire, array of stuffed fish and fishing prints in airy country dining area, enjoyable food from baguettes to fish and game, well kept ales including Brakspears, quick friendly service, snug traditional bar with more fishing memorabilia; very busy with walkers and families at weekends; lots of picnic-sets giving quiet country views from big dog-friendly orchard garden, side field with poultry, Thames nearby, bedrooms. *(Roy Hoing, Susan and John Douglas)*

BARKHAM SU7866

Bull (0118) 976 2816

Barkham Road; RG41 4TL Traditional pub run by friendly thai family, opened-up interior with dining area to one end, half a dozen ales such as Gales, Otter, St Austell and Timothy Taylors, popular food including SE asian choices; Mon quiz; open all day (till 7pm Sun). *(Paul Humphreys, John Pritchard)*

BEENHAM SU5868

Six Bells (0118) 971 3368

The Green; RG7 5NX Comfortable red-brick Victorian village pub with good food including imaginative additions to standard pub menu, West Berkshire Good Old Boy and a couple of guests, friendly owners and staff, two bars with winter fires, dining conservatory; children welcome lunchtime, four bedrooms, closed Mon lunchtime. *(John Pritchard, Richard Tilbrook)*

BURCHETTS GREEN SU8381

Crown (01628) 824079

Side road from A4 after Knowle Green on left, linking to A404; SL6 6QZ Village dining pub with good food cooked by owner-chef (not Mon or lunchtimes except Sun), compact log-fire bar for drinkers and dogs, a couple of interesting changing ales, friendly accommodating service, other areas set for eating, stripped-pine tables on wood floors; children welcome away from bar, picnic-sets out at front, back garden with vegetable patch, good walks nearby. *(Susan and John Douglas)*

BURGHFIELD SU6668

Hatch Gate (0118) 983 2059

The Hatch; RG30 3TH Popular 16th-c beamed pub with Greene King ales and well liked indian food including good value Sun buffet; sports TV; children welcome, garden with play area, open all day weekends. *(Dr and Mrs R E S Tanner)*

CHARVIL   SU7776
Lands End (0118) 934 0700
Lands End Lane/Whistley Mill Lane near Old River ford; RG10 0UE Welcoming 1930s Tudor-style pub with reasonably priced food from good baguettes to blackboard specials, well kept Brakspears and a dozen wines by the glass, efficient accommodating staff, open-plan bar with log fire, separate restaurant, various stuffed fish (good fishing nearby); children welcome, sizeable garden with terrace picnic-sets. *(Paul Humphreys)*

CHEAPSIDE   SU9469
Thatched Tavern (01344) 620874
Off A332/A329, then off B383 at Village Hall sign; SL5 7QG Civilised dining pub with a good deal of character and plenty of room for just a drink; up-to-date often ambitious food (can be pricey) along with more traditional choices, good range of wines by the glass, Fullers London Pride, a beer named for the pub and a guest ale, Weston's cider, big inglenook log fire, low beams and polished flagstones in cottagey core, three smart dining rooms off; children welcome, dogs in bar, tables on terrace and attractive sheltered back lawn, handy for Virginia Water, open all day weekends and busy on race days. *(Susan and John Douglas)*

CHIEVELEY   SU4773
★Olde Red Lion (01635) 248379
Handy for M4 junction 13 via A34 N-bound; Green Lane; RG20 8XB Attractive village pub with friendly landlord and helpful staff, three well kept Arkells beers, nice varied choice of generously served food from good sandwiches and baguettes up, reasonable prices, low-beamed carpeted L-shaped bar with panelling and hunting prints, log fire, extended back restaurant; background music, games machine, TV; wheelchair accessible throughout, small garden, five bedrooms in separate old building, open all day weekends. *(Andrew Stone)*

COMPTON   SU5180
Swan (01635) 579400
High Street; RG20 6NJ New owners for this pub near Newbury Racecourse; cushioned wall seating, high chairs around equally high tables, flagstones, Greene King Morlands Original and Yardbird plus a guest, food has been good, two dining rooms with contemporary wallpaper or pale paintwork, pen and ink cartoons and hunting prints, dark tables on bare boards, log fire, also comfortable end room with sofas; background music, TV, free wi-fi; children and dogs (in bar) welcome, seats in pretty garden, up-to-date bedrooms, open all day weekends. *(Harvey Brown, Caroline Prescott)*

COOKHAM   SU8985
★Bel & the Dragon (01628) 521263
High Street (B4447); SL6 9SQ Smartly updated 15th-c inn; heavy beams, log fires and simple country furnishings in two-room front bar and dining area, hand-painted cartoons on pastel walls, more modern bistro-style back restaurant, helpful friendly staff, good food cooked to order including cheaper lunchtime menu, Rebellion IPA and a local guest, good choice of wines; children welcome, dogs in bar, well tended garden with terrace tables, five bedrooms, Stanley Spencer Gallery almost opposite, open all day. *(Lindy Andrews)*

COOKHAM   SU8985
Ferry (01628) 525123
Sutton Road; SL6 9SN Splendidly placed riverside pub/restaurant with relaxing contemporary décor, wide choice of food all day including sharing plates and fixed-price menu (Mon-Fri 12-6), good service, Sharps Doom Bar and a guest, some interesting lagers, comprehensive wine list and decent coffee, light and airy Thames-view dining areas upstairs and down, sofas and coffee tables by fireplace, small servery in beamed core; background music; children welcome, extensive terrace overlooking river with slipway. *(Ian Phillips, Neil and Angela Huxter)*

COOKHAM   SU8885
★White Oak (01628) 523043
The Pound (B4447); SL6 9QE Bustling pub with emphasis on airy back dining area: three rows of light wood tables in varying sizes, comfortably cushioned or upholstered chairs and brown leather wall banquettes, polished boards, white-framed mirrors on mushroom walls, end french windows, linked front bar with armchairs, other seats on slightly raised platform, cosier areas at each side, interesting well liked food cooked by landlord, Greene King Abbot and good choice of wines, friendly staff; free wi-fi; children welcome, sturdy wooden furniture on sheltered back terrace and steps up to white wirework tables on grass, closed Sun evening, otherwise open all day. *(Alfie Bayliss, Harvey Brown, Simon Collett-Jones)*

COOKHAM DEAN   SU8785
★Jolly Farmer (01628) 482905
Church Road, off Hills Lane; SL6 9PD Traditional pub owned by village consortium; old-fashioned unspoilt bars with open fires, five well kept ales including Brakspears, Courage and Rebellion, local cider (apples from the pub's garden) and decent wines, sensibly priced popular food (not Sun or Mon evenings) from sandwiches up, pleasant staff, good-sized more modern eating area and small dining room, old and new local photographs, pub games; well behaved children and dogs welcome (friendly resident black lab called Czar), tables out in front and

on side terrace, nice garden with play area, open all day. *(Paul Humphreys)*

COOKHAM DEAN   SU8785
Uncle Toms Cabin (01628) 483339
Off A308 Maidenhead–Marlow; Hills Lane, towards Cookham Rise and Cookham; SL6 9NT Welcoming small-roomed local with simple sensitively modernised interior, four well kept mainstream ales and plenty of wines by the glass, good food cooked by owner-chef, low beams, wood floors and sage-green panelling, gleaming horsebrasses, open fire; children in eating areas, dogs in bar, seats out at front and in sheltered sloping back garden, peaceful country setting, closes at 9pm Sun and Mon. *(Susan and John Douglas, Paul Humphreys)*

EAST GARSTON   SU3676
★**Queens Arms** (01488) 648757
3.5 miles from M4 junction 14; A338 and village signposted Gt Shefford; RG17 7ET Friendly pub at the heart of racehorse-training country; opened-up bar with antique prints (many jockeys), wheelbacks around well spaced tables on bare boards, Ramsbury and Sharps Doom Bar, ten wines by the glass and fair choice of whiskies, lighter dining area with more prints, enjoyable food; background music, TV for racing, newspapers including *Racing Post*, free wi-fi; children and dogs (in bar) welcome, seats on sheltered terrace, spacious attractively decorated bedrooms, fly fishing and shooting can be arranged, good surrounding downland walks, open all day. *(Richard Tilbrook)*

EAST ILSLEY   SU4981
★**Crown & Horns** (01635) 281545
Just off A34, about 5 miles N of M4 junction 13; Compton Road; RG20 7LH Civilised Georgian pub in horse-training country, rambling beamed rooms, log fires, enjoyable home-made food from sandwiches, pizzas and pub favourites up including good Sun lunch, five real ales, friendly efficient staff; background music; children, dogs and muddy boots welcome, tables in pretty courtyard, modern bedroom extension, open all day from 10am, busy on Newbury race days. *(R T and J C Moggridge)*

GREAT SHEFFORD   SU3875
Swan (01488) 648271
2 miles from M4 junction 14, A338 towards Wantage (Newbury Road); RG17 7DS Bay-windowed low-ceilinged 18th-c pub under newish management, enjoyable food from traditional favourites and pizzas up, ales such as Sharps Doom Bar and West Berkshire, friendly helpful staff, easy chairs in bar area, nice river-view dining room; quiz second Weds of month; children and dogs welcome, tables on attractive waterside lawn and terrace. *(Lindy Andrews)*

HAMPSTEAD NORREYS   SU5376
White Hart (01635) 202248
Church Street; RG18 0TB Friendly and relaxed low-beamed village pub with three linked rooms, fireside seating and good-sized dining area, enjoyable sensibly priced home-made food from good sandwiches up, a couple of well kept Greene King ales and a guest, well chosen wines, quiz first Sun of the month; children and dogs (in bar) welcome, back terrace and garden, open all day weekends. *(Andrew Stone)*

HARE HATCH   SU8078
Queen Victoria (0118) 940 3122
Blakes Lane; just N of A4 Reading–Maidenhead; RG10 9TA Early 18th-c country pub refurbished under new owner, two low-ceilinged wood floored rooms with small conservatory to one side, ales such as Fullers and Rebellion, good value pubby food from sandwiches up, open fire; seats out in front, open all day weekends. *(Paul Humphreys)*

HENLEY   SU7682
★**Little Angel** (01491) 411008
Remenham Lane (A4130, just over bridge E of Henley); RG9 2LS Civilised dining pub, more or less open-plan but with distinct modernised seating areas, bare boards throughout, little bar with leather cube stools, tub and farmhouse chairs, other parts with mix of dining tables and chairs, artwork on Farrow & Ball paintwork, contemporary food (all day weekends) from sharing plates up, Brakspears ales and several wines by the glass, pleasant attentive service, airy conservatory; background music; well behaved children allowed, dogs in bar, tables on sheltered floodlit back terrace looking over to cricket pitch, open all day. *(Roy Hoing)*

HOLYPORT   SU8977
George (01628) 628317
1.5 miles from M4 junction 8/9, via A308(M)/A330; The Green; SL6 2JL Attractive 16th-c pub on picturesque village green with duck pond, colourful history and plenty of old-world charm, open-plan low-beamed interior, cosy and dimly lit, with nice fireplace, good food from pub favourites up, well kept Fullers London Pride, Rebellion IPA and a guest, nice wines from sound list, friendly helpful service; background music; children and dogs (in bar) welcome, picnic-sets on pretty terrace, open all day Sat, closed Sun evening, no food Mon. *(Paul Humphreys, Simon Collett-Jones)*

HUNGERFORD   SU3368
Plume of Feathers (01488) 682154
High Street; street parking opposite; RG17 0NB This well liked unspoilt pub was up for sale as we went to press – news please; open-plan interior stretching back

from the smallish bow-windowed façade, bare boards and some low beams, open fire at the back, Greene King ales from island bar; small sheltered back courtyard. *(JPC, Mike and Mary Carter, Colin McLachlan, Paul Lucas)*

HUNGERFORD NEWTOWN SU3571
Tally Ho (01488) 682312
A338 just S of M4 junction 14;
RG17 0PP Traditional red-brick beamed pub owned and refurbished by the local community, friendly and welcoming, with good food (not Sun evening) from baguettes to seasonal specials such as pheasant, Hook Norton, Ramsbury, West Berkshire and a guest, log fire; occasional music and quiz nights; children welcome, picnic-sets out in front, open all day. *(Mr Jim Allen)*

HURLEY SU8281
Dew Drop (01628) 315662
Small yellow sign to pub off A4130 just W;
SL6 6RB Old flint and brick pub tucked away in nice rustic setting, friendly new licensees and staff, well liked food from lunchtime sandwiches and pub favourites to more unusual dishes and daily specials, Brakspears and a guest ale, log fire; children and dogs welcome, french windows to terrace, pleasant views from back garden, good local walks, open all day Sat, till 6pm Sun, closed Mon. *(Paul Humphreys)*

HURST SU7973
★ Castle (0118) 934 0034 *Church Hill;*
RG10 0SJ Popular old dining pub still owned by the church opposite; very good well presented food (not Sun evening, Mon) including daily specials, well kept Binghams and local guests, nice wines by the glass (their house wines are particularly good and affordably priced), well trained helpful staff, bar and two restaurant areas, beams, wood floors and old brick nogging, some visible wattle and daub, roaring fire; children welcome, dogs in bar, garden picnic-sets, open all day weekends, closed Mon lunchtime. *(Paul Humphreys, John Pritchard and others)*

HURST SU8074
Green Man (0118) 934 2599
Off A321 just outside village; RG10 0BP Partly 17th-c pub with enjoyable good value food from sandwiches and sharing plates to steaks and blackboard specials, weekday set menu choices too, well kept Brakspears, pleasant attentive service, bar with dark beams and standing timbers, cosy alcoves, wall seats and built-in settles, hot little fire in one fireplace, old iron stove in another, dining area with modern sturdy wooden tables and high-backed chairs on solid oak floor; children and dogs welcome, sheltered terrace, picnic-sets under spreading oak trees in large garden with play area, open (and food) all day weekends. *(Paul Humphreys and others)*

KNOWL HILL SU8178
★ Bird in Hand (01628) 826622
A4, handy for M4 junction 8/9;
RG10 9UP Relaxed, civilised and roomy, with cosy alcoves, heavy beams, panelling and splendid log fire in tartan-carpeted main area, wide choice of popular home-made food (special diets catered for) from baguettes up, four well kept mainly local ales and good choice of other drinks, efficient service, much older side bar, smart restaurant; soft background music, regular events including music and quiz nights, free wi-fi; tables on front terrace and in neat garden, summer weekend barbecues, 22 bedrooms (some in separate block), open (and food) all day. *(Susan and John Douglas, Paul Humphreys)*

KNOWL HILL SU8279
New Inn (01628) 822552
Bath Road (A4); RG10 9UU Revamped family-run roadside inn (was the Old Devil), nice bright interior with black-painted beams, popular italian-based menu (also tapas), good choice of wines, ales such as Binghams, Rebellion and Wychwood; children welcome, verandah above lawned garden, nine bedrooms, open (and food) all day. *(Paul Humphreys)*

LAMBOURN SU3180
Malt Shovel (01488) 73777
Upper Lambourn; signed from B4000; RG17 8QN Décor and customers reflecting racing-stables surroundings, traditional locals' bar, enjoyable home-made food in smart modern dining extension including evening specials, well kept Box Steam and a guest, nice choice of wines by the glass; sports bar with pool, TVs for racing, weekend live music; children welcome, garden and play area, five bedrooms, open all day. *(Michael Sargent)*

LITTLEWICK GREEN SU8379
Cricketers (01628) 822888
Not far from M4 junction 9; A404(M) then left on to A4 – village signed on left; Coronation Road; SL6 3RA Welcoming old-fashioned village pub in charming spot opposite cricket green (can get crowded); well kept Badger ales and good choice of wines by the glass, enjoyable pub food from lunchtime sandwiches and baguettes to specials, traditional interior with three linked rooms, huge clock above brick fireplace; background music, TV, Tues quiz; children and dogs (they have their own) welcome, pretty hanging baskets and a few tables out in front behind picket fence, open all day, closed Mon in winter. *(Paul Humphreys)*

MARSH BENHAM SU4267
Red House (01635) 582017
Off A4 W of Newbury; RG20 8LY Attractive thatched dining pub with good fairly traditional food with a twist from french chef-owner including set menu choices (Mon-Sat till 6.30pm), West Berkshire and a guest ale, lots

of wines by the glass, afternoon tea, roomy flagstoned/wood floor bar with woodburner, refurbished restaurant; background music; children and dogs welcome, terrace and long lawns sloping to water meadows and the River Kennet, open (and food) all day. *(Rob Anderson)*

MIDGHAM SU5566
Coach & Horses (0118) 971 3384
Bath Road (N side); RG7 5UX Comfortable main-road pub with good choice of food from baguettes up including lunchtime offers, cheerful efficient service, Fullers London Pride and West Berkshire Good Old Boy, flagstoned bar with sofa by brick fireplace, steps up to small half-panelled carpeted dining area with country-style furniture, second dining room; children welcome, garden behind, closed Sun evening, Mon. *(John Pritchard)*

MORTIMER SU6564
Horse & Groom (0118) 933 2813
The Street; RG7 3RD Double-fronted Victorian pub next to church, reliable well cooked food from pub favourites up including good daily specials and seasonal game (they list local suppliers), two or three real ales and decent wines by the glass, open fire; children welcome, picnic-sets on side lawn, parking opposite. *(Dr and Mrs R E S Tanner)*

NEWBURY SU4767
Lock Stock & Barrel
(01635) 580550 *Northbrook Street; RG14 1AA* Popular modern pub standing out for its canalside setting, recently refurbished interior with low ceiling, light wood or slate flooring and painted panelling, lots of windows overlooking canal, varied choice of enjoyable sensibly priced food all day from sandwiches up, well kept Fullers/Gales beers, efficient friendly staff; free wi-fi; children welcome, outside seating including suntrap Astroturf roof terrace looking over a series of locks towards handsome church, open till midnight Fri, Sat. *(Rob Anderson)*

PALEY STREET SU8676
★ Royal Oak (01628) 620541
B3024 W; SL6 3JN Attractively modernised and extended 17th-c restauranty pub owned by Sir Michael Parkinson and son Nick; highly regarded british cooking (not cheap) and most here to eat, cheaper set lunch menu Mon-Fri, good service, dining room split by brick pillars and timbering with mix of well spaced wooden tables and leather chairs on bare boards or flagstones, smallish informal beamed bar with woodburner, leather sofas and cricketing prints, Fullers London Pride and wide choice of wines by the glass including champagne; background jazz; children welcome (no pushchairs in restaurant), seats outside among troughs of herbs, closed Sun. *(Tracey and Stephen Groves)*

PANGBOURNE SU6376
Cross Keys (0118) 984 3268
Church Road, opposite church; RG8 7AR 18th-c pub with linked split-level beamed rooms, simple bar on right, neat dining area to the left, two Greene King ales and a guest, enjoyable food from good sandwiches up including lunchtime set menu (Mon-Thurs), friendly helpful young staff; background music; children and dogs welcome, streamside (River Pang) terrace at back with covered seating area, paid daytime parking some way off, open all day. *(N R White, Paul Humphreys)*

READING SU7173
★ Alehouse (0118) 950 8119
Broad Street; RG1 2BH Cheerful no-frills drinkers' pub with eight well kept quickly changing ales and a couple of craft beers, also lots of different bottled beers, farm ciders and perry; small bare-boards bar with raised seating area, hundreds of pump clips on walls and ceiling, corridor to several appealing little panelled rooms, some little more than alcoves, no food; background music, TV; open all day. *(John Pritchard)*

READING SU7272
Jolly Anglers (0118) 376 7823
Kennetside; RG1 3EA Simple two-room pub on River Kennet towpath, originally built for workers at the former Huntley & Palmers biscuit factory; four or more well kept changing ales and up to ten ciders/perries, good value home-made food including vegetarian/vegan choices, piano, original fireplaces, darts and other pub games, open mike night Mon; picnic-sets in back garden up steep steps, open (and food) all day. *(Susan and John Douglas)*

READING SU7174
Moderation (0118) 375 0767
Caversham Road; RG1 8BB Modernised airy Victorian pub with some eastern influences to the décor, enjoyable reasonably priced food including thai/indonesian choices, pleasant prompt service, three well kept changing ales; seats out at front and in enclosed garden behind, open all day. *(Dave Braisted)*

READING SU7073
Nags Head 07765 880137
Russell Street; RG1 7XD Largish mock-Tudor drinkers' pub just outside town centre attracting good mix of customers, a dozen well kept changing ales and 13 real ciders, baguettes and pies, open fire, darts and cribbage; background and occasional live music, TV for major sporting events; beer garden, open all day. *(John Pritchard)*

READING SU7173
★ Sweeney & Todd (0118) 958 6466
Castle Street; RG1 7RD Pie shop with popular bar/restaurant behind (little changed in 30 years), warren of private

period-feel alcoves and other areas on various levels, good home-made food all day including their range of pies such as venison and wild boar, cheery service, small bar with four well kept ales including Wadworths and Adnams, Weston's cider and decent wines; children welcome in restaurant area, open all day (closed Sun evening and bank holidays). *(John Pritchard, Simon Collett-Jones)*

SHINFIELD SU7367
★ **Magpie & Parrot** (0118) 988 4130
2.6 miles from M4 junction 11, via B3270; A327 just SE of Shinfield on Arborfield Road; RG2 9EA Unusual homely little roadside cottage with warm fire, lots of bric-a-brac (miniature and historic bottles, stuffed birds, dozens of model cars, veteran AA badges and automotive instruments) in two cosy spic-and-span bars, Fullers London Pride and local guests from small corner counter, weekday lunchtime snacks and evening fish and chips (Thurs, Fri), hospitable landlady; no credit cards or mobile phones; pub dog (others welcome), seats on back terrace and marquee on immaculate lawn, open 12-7.30, closed Sun evening. *(Anne and Ben Smith)*

SHURLOCK ROW SU8374
★ **Shurlock Inn** (0118) 934 9094
Just off B3018 SE of Twyford; The Street; RG10 0PS Cosy village-owned pub with good food (all day Sun) from pubby choices up, four ales including West Berkshire Mr Chubbs and one from Rebellion, nice house wines, log fire in double-sided fireplace dividing bar and larger dining room, new oak flooring, panelling and one or two old beams; background music; children welcome, dogs in bar, black metal furniture on side and back terraces, garden with picnic-sets under parasols and fenced play area, open all day Fri, Sat, till 9pm Sun. *(Charlotte)*

STANFORD DINGLEY SU5771
Old Boot (0118) 974 4292
Off A340 via Bradfield, coming from A4 just W of M4 junction 12; RG7 6LT Stylish 18th-c pub with old pews, settles, country chairs and polished tables in beamed bar, inglenook log fire, striking pictures, hunting prints and boot ornaments, West Berkshire Good Old Boy and a guest, several wines by the glass and popular food, conservatory-style restaurant; free wi-fi; children and dogs (in bar) welcome, picnic-sets out at front and in large suntrap garden behind with pleasant rural views, lovely village, open all day weekends. *(Harvey Brown, Mike Swan)*

SULHAMSTEAD SU6269
Spring (0118) 930 3440
Bath Road (A4); RG7 5HP Interesting barn conversion reopened 2014 under new management; good variety of popular food from sandwiches up, three real ales including Fullers London Pride and West Berkshire

Good Old Boy, friendly staff, spacious bar with some comfortable seating, balustraded upstairs dining area under raftered ceiling; children welcome, plenty of seats outside, open all day. *(Anne and Ben Smith)*

SUNNINGHILL SU9367
Carpenters Arms (01344) 622763
Upper Village Road; SL5 7AQ Restauranty village pub run by french team, good authentic french country cooking, not cheap but they do offer a reasonably priced set lunch (Mon-Sat), nice wines, Sharps Doom Bar; no children in the evening, terrace tables, open all day and best to book. *(Anne and Ben Smith)*

SUNNINGHILL SU9367
Dog & Partridge (01344) 623204
Upper Village Road; SL5 7AQ Modern feel with emphasis on good home-made food (all day Sun till 7pm), friendly helpful staff, Fullers, Sharps and Windsor & Eton, good range of wines; background and some live music; children and dogs welcome, disabled facilities, sunny courtyard garden with fountain, play area, open all day Fri-Sun, closed Mon. *(Anne and Ben Smith)*

THEALE SU6471
Bull (0118) 930 3478
High Street; RG7 5AH Old modernised and extended inn, large bar with tiled floor and dark half-panelling, carpeted dining area behind with banquettes, enjoyable good value food from pub favourites up delivered by dumb-waiter from upstairs kitchen, three or four well kept Wadworths ales; background and some live music, quiz nights; children and dogs (on leads) welcome, seats outside, open (and food) all day. *(John Pritchard)*

THEALE SU6471
★ **Fox & Hounds** (0118) 930 2295
2 miles from M4 junction 12; follow A4 W, then first left signed for station, over two roundabouts, past station on left, keep in Station Road, over narrow canal bridge to Sheffield Bottom S of town; RG7 4BE Large neatly kept dining pub, friendly and relaxed, with well priced food (not Sun evening) from baguettes and pizzas to blackboard specials, several well kept Wadworths ales, Weston's cider, decent wines and coffee, L-shaped bar with dividers, traditional mix of furniture on carpet or bare boards including area with modern sofas and low tables, two open fires, daily papers; pool and darts, Sun quiz; children and dogs welcome, outside seating at front and sides, lakeside bird reserve opposite, open all day Fri-Sun. *(John Pritchard)*

THEALE SU6168
Winning Hand (0118) 930 2472
A4 W, opposite Sulhamstead turn; handy for M4 junction 12; RG7 5JB Good choice of enjoyable bar and restaurant food

including well priced set menu, friendly
efficient young service, two changing ales and
varied wine list, dining room with stripped-
pine furniture and church candles on brass
or wrought-iron stands, further eating area
with modern furniture on light wood floor
and contemporary artwork; quiet background
music, no dogs; children welcome, tables on
front and back terraces, closed Sun evening,
Mon. *(John Pritchard)*

THREE MILE CROSS   SU7167

Swan (0118) 988 3674

*A33 just S of M4 junction 11; Basingstoke
Road; RG7 1AT* Smallish traditional pub
built in the 17th c and later a posting house,
well kept ales including Fullers London
Pride, Loddon Hoppit and Timothy Taylors
Boltmaker, enjoyable fairly standard home-
made food at reasonable prices, friendly staff,
two beamed bars, inglenook with hanging
black pots, old prints and some impressive
stuffed fish; large well arranged outside
seating area behind (also home to wolfhound
Mr Niall, the London Irish RFC mascot), near
Madejski Stadium and very busy on match
days, open all day weekdays, closed Sun
evening. *(John Pritchard)*

WALTHAM ST LAWRENCE   SU8376

★ **Bell** (0118) 934 1788

*B3024 E of Twyford; The Street;
RG10 0JJ* Welcoming 14th-c village local
with well preserved beamed and timbered
interior, cheerful landlord and chatty
regulars, good home-made blackboard food
(not Sun evening) from bar snacks including
own pork pies up, friendly service, five well
kept predominantly local beers, up to eight
real ciders and plenty of wines by the glass,
good choice of whiskies too, warm log fires,
compact panelled lounge, daily papers;
children and dogs welcome, pretty back
garden with extended terrace and shady trees,
open all day weekends. *(Paul Humphreys)*

WALTHAM ST LAWRENCE   SU8376

Star (0118) 996 0366

Broadmoor Road; RG10 0HY
Welcoming old beamed pub reopened 2014
after refit, enjoyable well priced food (not
Mon), Wadworths ales, dining area up a step,
two open fires; Mon quiz, some live music;
children and dogs welcome, large back garden
with bouncy castle, closed Sun evening, Mon
lunchtime. *(Jill Kay, Paul Humphreys)*

WARGRAVE   SU7878

Bull (0843) 289 1773

*Off A321 Henley–Twyford; High Street;
RG10 8DE* Low-beamed 15th-c coaching
inn, refurbished and well run by hospitable
landlady; main bar with inglenook log fire,
two dining areas (one up steps for families),
enjoyable traditional home-made food from
baguettes up, Brakspears ales and a guest,
friendly helpful staff; background music, free
wi-fi; well behaved dogs welcome, walled

garden behind, four bedrooms, open all day
weekends. *(Paul Humphreys)*

WEST ILSLEY   SU4782

Harrow (01635) 281260

*Signed off A34 at E Ilsley slip road;
RG20 7AR* Appealing and welcoming
country pub in peaceful spot overlooking
cricket pitch and pond, Victorian prints in
deep-coloured knocked-through bar, some
antique furnishings, log fire, good choice of
enjoyable sensibly priced home-made food
(not Sun or Mon evenings), well kept Greene
King ales and nice selection of wines by
the glass, afternoon teas; children in eating
areas, dogs allowed in bar, big garden with
picnic-sets, more seats on pleasant terrace,
handy for Ridgeway walkers, may close early
Sun evening if quiet. *(David and Judy Robison,
Helen and Brian Edgeley, M and GR, John T Ames)*

WINDSOR   SU9676

Carpenters Arms (01753) 863739

Market Street; SL4 1PB Nicholsons pub
rambling around central servery with good
choice of well kept ales and several wines
by the glass, reasonably priced pubby food
from sandwiches up including range of
pies, friendly helpful service, sturdy pub
furnishings and Victorian-style décor with
two pretty fireplaces, family areas up a few
steps, also downstairs beside former tunnel
entrance with suits of armour; background
music, no dogs; tables out on cobbled
pedestrian alley opposite castle, no nearby
parking, handy for Legoland bus stop, open
(and food) all day. *(Simon Collett-Jones, David
M Smith)*

WINDSOR   SU9676

Two Brewers (01753) 855426

Park Street; SL4 1LB In the shadow of
Windsor Castle with three cosy unchanging
bare-board rooms, well kept ales such as
Fullers London Pride, St Austell Tribute and
Sharps Doom Bar, good choice of wines by
the glass, enjoyable freshly made food (not
Fri-Sun evenings) from shortish mid-priced
menu, friendly efficient service, thriving
old-fashioned pub atmosphere, beams and
open fire, enamel signs and posters on walls;
background music, daily papers; no children
inside, dogs welcome, tables and attractive
hanging baskets out by pretty Georgian street
next to Windsor Park's Long Walk, open all
day. *(Richard Stanfield, Nigel and Sue Foster)*

WINDSOR   SU9576

Vansittart Arms (01753) 865988

Vansittart Road; SL4 5DD Friendly
three-room Victorian local with cosy corners
and open fires, well kept Fullers/Gales beers,
enjoyable good value home-made food (all
day weekends); background music, sports
TV, pool, newspapers and free wi-fi; children
and dogs welcome, good-sized beer garden
with heated smokers' area, open all day.
(Andrew Stone)

Buckinghamshire

KEY  ★ Star Pub   🍽 Top Quality Food   🍺 Great Beer

🍷 Good Wines   £ Bargain Meals   🛏 Good Bedrooms   🍴 Serves Food

---

 ADSTOCK   SP7330   Map 4

Old Thatched Inn 🍽 🍺

(01296) 712584 – www.theoldthatchedinn.co.uk

Main Street, off A413; MK18 2JN

Pretty thatched dining pub with keen landlord, friendly staff, five real ales and good food

Our readers consistently enjoy their visits to this well run and pretty thatched dining pub – and staff remain courteous and attentive. The small front bar area has low beams, sofas on flagstones, high bar chairs and an open fire and they keep Fullers London Pride, Goffs Jouster, Hook Norton Hooky Bitter and Lion, and Tring Side Pocket for a Toad on handpump, 15 wines by the glass, a dozen malt whiskies and three ciders. A dining area leads off with more beams and a mix of pale wooden dining chairs around miscellaneous tables on a stripped wooden floor; background music. There's also a modern conservatory restaurant at the back with well spaced tables on bare boards. The sheltered terrace has tables and chairs under a gazebo. This is an attractive village.

🍽 Rewarding food includes pork and shredded ham hock fritters with mustard mayonnaise and pickled vegetables, prawn cocktail, cumberland sausages with bubble and squeak and red wine gravy, chicken, ham and mushroom pie, slow-roasted pork belly with wild boar and garlic sausage, braised red cabbage and cider apple purée, salmon fillet with chorizo and tomato provençale, and puddings such as vanilla crème brûlée with ginger crème fraîche and white chocolate mousse with raspberry jelly; they also offer a two- and three-course weekday set lunch. *Benchmark main dish: duck breast with horseradish potato croquette and roast baby parsnips £16.50. Two-course evening meal £21.25.*

Free house ~ Licensee Andrew Judge ~ Real ale ~ Open 12-11 (midnight Sat, 10.30 Sun) ~ Bar food 12-2.30, 6-9.30; 12-8 Sun ~ Restaurant ~ Well behaved children welcome ~ Dogs allowed in bar ~ Wi-fi *Recommended by George Atkinson, Graham and Carol Parker, Mike and Mary Carter*

 AYLESBURY   SP8113   Map 4

Kings Head 🍺

(01296) 718812 – www.farmersbar.co.uk

Kings Head Passage (off Bourbon Street), also entrance off Temple Street; no nearby parking except for disabled; HP20 2RW

Handsome town centre pub with civilised atmosphere, good local ales (used in the food too) and friendly service

It's such a surprise to come across this rather special 15th-c building tucked away as it is in a modern town centre. The Farmers Bar is just one part – the others being a coffee shop, arts and crafts shop, tourist information office and conference rooms. Three timeless rooms have been restored with careful and unpretentious simplicity: stripped boards, cream walls with little decoration, gentle lighting, a variety of seating including upholstered sofas and armchairs, cushioned high-backed settles and some simple modern pale dining tables and chairs dotted around. Most of the bar tables are of round glass, supported on low cask tops. The neat corner bar has Chiltern Ale, Beechwood Bitter and Black (this is the brewery tap for Chiltern) and a couple of guests on handpump, a dozen wines by the glass, a farm cider and some interesting bottled beers. Service is friendly and there's no background music or machines. The atmospheric medieval cobbled courtyard has teak seats and tables, some beneath a pillared roof; summer barbecues and live events. The place is owned by the National Trust. Disabled access and facilities.

🍴 Served with home-made beer bread, the lunchtime-only food includes sandwiches, salmon and haddock fishcake with citrus mayonnaise, cheese and bacon rarebit, sausage casserole, venison burger with coleslaw and chips, game pie, leek and stilton bread and butter bake, lamb stew with minted dumplings, and puddings such as treacle tart and sticky date and toffee pudding. *Benchmark main dish: cider-glazed ham, free-range egg and chips £8.95.*

Chiltern ~ Manager George Jenkinson ~ Real ale ~ Open 11-11; 12-10.30 Sun ~ Bar food 12-2 (12-3 weekends); not evenings ~ Children welcome away from bar ~ Wi-fi
Recommended by Tony and Wendy Hobden, Graham and Carol Parker

BOVINGDON GREEN
SU8386 Map 2

Royal Oak 🍴🏅 ♀

(01628) 488611 – www.royaloakmarlow.co.uk

0.75 miles N of Marlow, on back road to Frieth signposted off West Street (A4155) in centre; SL7 2JF

Civilised dining pub with nice little bar, a fine choice of wines by the glass, real ales and imaginative food

Although many customers are here to eat, they do keep a fine range of drinks in this little whitewashed pub: Rebellion IPA and Smuggler on handpump, 25 wines by the glass (plus pudding wines), several gins and farm cider. The low-beamed cosy snug, closest to the car park, has three small tables and a woodburning stove in an exposed brick fireplace (with a big pile of logs beside it). Several other attractively decorated areas open off the central bar with half-panelled walls variously painted in pale blue, green or cream (though the dining room ones are red). Throughout, there's a mix of church chairs, stripped wooden tables and chunky wall seats, with rugs on the partly wooden, partly flagstoned floors, co-ordinated cushions and curtains, and a very bright, airy feel. Thoughtful extra touches enhance the tone: a bowl of olives on the bar, carefully laid-out newspapers and fresh flowers or candles on the tables. Board games and background music. A sunny terrace with good solid tables leads to an appealing garden; there's also a smaller side garden, a kitchen herb garden and a pétanque court. Red kites regularly fly over.

🍴 Well executed, modern british food includes sandwiches, goats cheese with basil quinoa, walnuts and local damson vinaigrette, smoked haddock croquette with beetroot remoulade and lemon purée, jerusalem artichoke risotto with roasted chervil root, beetroot jelly and toasted almond dressing, chicken breast with confit potato, charred leeks and chestnut velouté, salmon fillet with bombay-spiced potato cake and coconut curry cream, and puddings such as marshmallow parfait with banana, chocolate and honeycomb and hot chocolate fondant pudding with bay leaf ice-cream. *Benchmark main dish: cornish hake fillet with sautéed gnocchi, puy lentils and bacon £15.75. Two-course evening meal £22.25.*

Salisbury Pubs ~ Manager James Molier ~ Real ale ~ Open 11-11; 12-10.30 Sun ~ Bar food 12-2.30 (3 Sat), 6.30-9.30 (10 Fri, Sat); 12-9 Sun ~ Restaurant ~ Children welcome ~ Dogs allowed in bar ~ Wi-fi *Recommended by Dave Braisted, Richard and Liz Thorne, Brian Glozier, Alistair Forsyth*

BRILL   SP6513   Map 4

Pointer ⭐ ☆ ♀

(01844) 238339 – www.thepointerbrill.co.uk
Church Street; HP18 9RT

● ●
Buckinghamshire Dining Pub of the Year

Carefully restored pub in a pretty village with rewarding food, local ales and interesting furnishings

Unusually, this handsome place is a pub-cum-restaurant-cum-butchery business – all the meat comes from their own livestock herds and neighbouring farms, and you can buy their meat, charcuterie and freshly baked bread in the deli next door. It's very stylishly refurbished with low beams, windsor chairs, elegant armchairs and sofas with brocaded cushions, open fires or woodburners in brick fireplaces and animal hide stools by the counter. A beer named for the pub (from the XT Brewing Company), Vale Best Bitter (brewed in the village) and a couple of guest ales on handpump, a dozen fair-priced wines by the glass, and friendly, attentive staff. The airy and attractive restaurant has antique Ercol chairs around pale oak tables, cushioned window seats, rafters in a high vaulted ceiling and an open kitchen. French windows open on to the sizeable garden. Tolkien is said to have based the village of Bree in *The Lord of the Rings* on this pretty village.

From a well judged menu, the high standards of food includes lunchtime baguettes, charred mackerel with beetroot, salsify and blood orange balsamic vinegar, duck liver parfait with clementine and onion jam, wood-fired pepper omelettes with sheeps milk cheese, tomato preserve and parsley dressing, burger with wholegrain mustard mayonnaise, toppings and fries, beer-battered haddock and chips, rose veal rump with free-range egg and mustard cream, pheasant with apples, prunes and gravy, and puddings such as warm chocolate fondant with passion-fruit sorbet and sticky date pudding with caramelised banana and toffee parfait. *Benchmark main dish: rib-eye steak with béarnaise butter and chips £24.00. Two-course evening meal £23.00.*

Free house ~ Licensees David and Fiona Howden ~ Real ale ~ Open 12-11 (2.30-10.30 Mon); 12-midnight Fri, Sat; 12-10.30 Sun ~ Bar food 12-2.30, 6.30-9 (6.30-10 Fri, Sat); 1-5 Sun; not Sun evening or Mon ~ Restaurant ~ No children after 6.30 unless eating ~ Dogs allowed in bar ~ Wi-fi *Recommended by Alfie Bayliss, Phoebe Peacock, Belinda Stamp*

COLESHILL   SU9594   Map 4

Harte & Magpies

(01494) 726754 – www.magpiespub.com
E of village on A355 Amersham–Beaconsfield, by junction with Magpie Lane; HP7 0LU

Friendly and busy roadside dining pub with enjoyable all-day food, well kept local ales and seats in big garden

They certainly attract a wide mix of customers at this enthusiastically run pub: walkers and their dogs (they keep dog treats in a jar behind the counter), families (there's a children's play area) and those keen on live music and comedy events (see the website for dates). It's a big, open-plan place but the rambling collection of miscellaneous pews, high-backed booths and some quite distinctive tables and chairs and cosy boltholes over to the right give it a pleasantly snug feel. There's a profusion of vigorously patriotic antique prints and candles in bottles, and Scrumpy Jack the self-possessed young labrador. Chiltern Ale and Rebellion Smuggler on handpump and a good choice of other drinks too; service is friendly. Outside, a terrace has picnic-sets by a tree picturesquely draped with wisteria and a big sloping informal garden has more trees and more tables on wood chippings. Plenty of nearby walks.

Usefully served all day starting with breakfast (not Sun), the good food includes lunchtime baguettes, moroccan-spiced lamb koftas with tzatziki, shell-on garlic prawns, various pizzas, spicy tomato and garlic pasta, burger with toppings and chips, gammon with egg and pineapple, beef in ale pie, slow-roast pork belly with bubble and squeak and apple sauce, and puddings such as hot chocolate fondant and sticky toffee pudding. *Benchmark main dish: beer-battered cod and chips £12.50. Two-course evening meal £17.50.*

Free house ~ Licensee Stephen Lever ~ Real ale ~ Open 10am-11pm; 11-10 Sun ~ Bar food 10-9.45; 12-8 Sun ~ Children welcome ~ Dogs welcome ~ Wi-fi ~ Live music and comedy evenings *Recommended by Richard and Liz Thorne, Edward May*

DENHAM
TQ0487 Map 3

Swan ⭐ ♀

(01895) 832085 – www.swaninndenham.co.uk

Village signed from M25 junction 16; UB9 5BH

Double-fronted dining pub in quiet village with interesting furnishings, log fires, fine choice of drinks and large garden

One of the best times to visit this handsome Georgian pub is when the wisteria is flowering in May. But at any time of year, you'll be welcomed by friendly staff into the stylishly furnished bars. There's a nice mix of antique and old-fashioned chairs and solid tables, rich heavily draped curtains, log fires, newspapers to read and fresh flowers. Rebellion IPA and a guest beer on handpump, over 20 wines by the glass (plus pudding wines) and a good choice of vodkas and liqueurs; background music. In warm weather, the extensive back garden is a big draw (it's also floodlit at night) and there are seats and tables on a sheltered terrace, with more on a spacious lawn. It can get busy at weekends, when parking may be tricky.

Using the best local produce, the inventive food includes indian-spiced mussels with coriander flatbread, honey-roast ham hock with soft boiled quail's egg and pea shoot and baby gem salad, chickpea and sweetcorn burger with cucumber pickle and polenta chips, pork tenderloin with cider-braised cabbage and caramelised nectarine jus, seared scallops with butternut squash risotto cake and pumpkin seed pesto, and puddings such as orange panna cotta with rhubarb and ginger shortbread crumb and dark chocolate brownie with caramel clotted cream. *Benchmark main dish: bubble and squeak with oak-smoked bacon, free-range poached egg and hollandaise sauce £11.75. Two-course evening meal £24.00.*

Little Gems Country Dining Pubs ~ Manager Mark Littlewood ~ Real ale ~ Open 11.30-11.30; 12-11 Sun ~ Bar food 12-2.30 (3 Sat), 6-9 (9.30 Fri, Sat); 12-8 Sun ~ Restaurant ~ Children welcome ~ Dogs allowed in bar ~ Wi-fi *Recommended by Alfie Bayliss, Phoebe Peacock*

EASINGTON

SP6810   Map 4

Mole & Chicken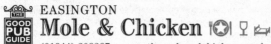

(01844) 208387 – www.themoleandchicken.co.uk

From B4011 in Long Crendon follow Chearsley, Waddesdon signpost into Carters Lane opposite indian restaurant, then turn left into Chilton Road; HP18 9EY

Country views from decking and garden, an inviting interior, real ales and enjoyable food and drink; nice bedrooms

This is a civilised place to stay in cosy and comfortable bedrooms, and the breakfasts are good too. The opened-up interior is arranged so that the different parts seem quite snug and self-contained without being cut off from the relaxed and sociable atmosphere. The heavily beamed bar curves around the serving counter in a sort of S-shape, and there are cream-cushioned farmhouse chairs around oak and pine tables on flagstones or tiles, a couple of dark leather sofas, church candles and good winter log fires. Vale Best Bitter and XT Four on handpump, several wines by the glass and quite a few malt whiskies; background music. At the back of this creeper-clad pub is a raised terrace and decked area with views

 First class food includes breakfasts for non-residents (7.30-9.30am), lunchtime sandwiches, crispy salt and pepper squid with pickled kohlrabi and black garlic, devilled kidneys on toast, onion and balsamic tart with polenta chips, rump burger with cheese, bacon and chips, corn-fed chicken caesar with crispy skin, charred gem lettuce and a poached egg, fresh pasta with braised rabbit and wild mushrooms, confit duck salad with spicy thai herbs and cashews, 28-day dry-aged steaks with a choice of sauces, and puddings such as raspberry crème brûlée and caramelised apple tart with cinnamon ice-cream. *Benchmark main dish: beer-battered fish of the day with chips £13.50. Two-course evening meal £23.50.*

Free house ~ Licensee Steve Bush ~ Real ale ~ Open 7.30am (8 weekends)-11pm ~ Bar food 7.30-9.30am; 12-2.30, 6.30-9.30; 8-9.30am, 12-3.30, 6-9 Sun ~ Children welcome ~ Wi-fi ~ Bedrooms: $85/$110 *Recommended by Richard Kennell, Alfie Bayliss*

FINGEST

SU7791   Map 2

Chequers

(01491) 638335 – www.chequersfingest.com

Off B482 Marlow–Stokenchurch; RG9 6QD

Friendly, spotlessly kept old pub with big garden, real ales and interesting food

Dating from the 15th c, this white-shuttered brick and flint pub is charmingly placed; over the road is a unique Norman twin-roofed church tower – probably the nave of the original church. The unaffected public bar has real country charm, and other neatly kept old-fashioned rooms are warm, cosy and traditional, with large open fires, horsebrasses, pewter tankards, and pub team photographs on the walls. Brakspears Bitter and Special and a guest such as Ringwood Boondoggle on handpump alongside quite a few wines by the glass, several malt whiskies and farm cider; board games and a house cat and dog. French doors from the smart back dining extension open to a terrace (plenty of picnic-sets), which leads on to the big, beautifully tended garden with fine views over the Hambleden Valley. There are plenty of good surrounding walks with quiet pastures sloping up to beechwoods.

Good food includes lunchtime sandwiches, welsh rarebit, asparagus with crispy fried egg and hollandaise, pea and mint linguine, confit chicken salad, sausages with onion rings and mash, whole grilled mackerel with salad, venison with fondant potato and jus, and puddings such as toffee and banana pancake and crème brûlée. *Benchmark main dish: beer-battered fresh fish and chips £14.00. Two-course evening meal £25.30.*

Brakspears ~ Tenants Jaxon and Emma Keedwell ~ Real ale ~ Open 12-3, 5.30-11.15; 12-11.15 Sat; 12-10.30 Sun; closed bank holiday evenings ~ Bar food 12-2 (3 Sat, 4 Sun), 7-9 (9.30 Fri, Sat) ~ Restaurant ~ Children welcome ~ Dogs allowed in bar
Recommended by Ms Caroline Heaney, Isobel Mackinlay, Simon Collett-Jones

FORTY GREEN   SU9291   Map 2

Royal Standard of England 🍺

(01494) 673382 – www.rsoe.co.uk

3.5 miles from M40 junction 2, via A40 to Beaconsfield, then follow sign to Forty Green, off B474 0.75 miles N of New Beaconsfield; keep going through village; HP9 1XT

Full of history and character, fascinating antiques in rambling rooms, and good choice of drinks and food

The rambling rooms in this ancient place (it's been trading for nearly 900 years and the leaflet documenting the pub's history is very interesting) have some fine old features to look out for: huge black ship's timbers, lovely worn floors, carved oak panelling, roaring winter fires with handsomely decorated iron firebacks and cluttered mantelpieces – there's also a massive settle apparently built to fit the curved transom of an Elizabethan ship. Nooks and crannies are filled with a collection of antiques, including rifles, powder-flasks and bugles, ancient pewter and pottery tankards, lots of tarnished brass and copper, needlework samplers and richly coloured stained glass. As well as brewing their own Britannia Pale, they keep six changing guests from other breweries such as Brakspears, Chiltern, Rebellion, Vale and Windsor & Eton; there's also a carefully annotated list of bottled beers and malt whiskies, farm ciders, perry, somerset brandy and around a dozen wines by the glass. You can sit outside in a neatly hedged front rose garden or under the shade of a tree; look out for the red gargoyle on the wall facing the car park. The inn is used regularly for filming television programmes such as *Midsomer Murders*.

🍽 Traditional, hearty food includes lunchtime baguettes (until 5pm), gin-cured gravadlax with beetroot and horseradish sauce, devilled lambs kidneys on fried crouton, gnocchi with artichokes, sun-dried tomatoes and parmesan, sausages and mash with onion gravy, steak and kidney pudding, fish pie, pork belly with bubble and squeak and apple sauce, and puddings such as sticky toffee pudding with caramel sauce and crème brûlée. *Benchmark main dish: beer-battered fish and chips £14.00. Two-course evening meal £20.00.*

Own brew ~ Licensee Matthew O'Keeffe ~ Real ale ~ Open 11-11; 12-10.30 Sun ~ Bar food 12-10 ~ Children welcome ~ Dogs welcome ~ Wi-fi *Recommended by Paul Humphreys, Gordon and Jenny Quick, Richard and Liz Thorne, Tracey and Stephen Groves, D J and P M Taylor, Richard Tilbrook, Roy Hoing, N R White, Susan and John Douglas*

FULMER   SU9985   Map 2

Black Horse ⭐ ♀

(01753) 663183 – www.theblackhorsefulmer.com

Village signposted off A40 in Gerrards Cross, W of its junction with A413; Windmill Road; SL3 6HD

Appealingly reworked dining pub, friendly and relaxed, with enjoyable up-to-date food, exemplary service and pleasant garden; bedrooms

Just head for the church to find this 17th-c pub (once craftsmen's cottages). The building has been gradually extended over the years to form a charming and thoughtfully run country pub with a lot of character. There's a proper bar in the middle and two cosy areas to the left with low black beams, rugs on bare boards, settles and other solid pub furniture and several open log fires. Greene King IPA and London Glory and Timothy Taylors Boltmaker on handpump, 21 wines by the glass and 20 malt whiskies; staff are friendly and efficient even when pushed. Background music, TV. The main area on the right is set for dining and leads to the good-sized suntrap back terrace where there's a summer barbecue bar. The two bedrooms are stylish and well equipped. This is a charming conservation village.

 Popular, interesting food includes sandwiches (until 6pm), prawn and lobster cocktail with bloody mary mayonnaise, bourbon and chipotle sticky ribs with coleslaw, sharing platters, beer-battered haddock and skinny fries, butternut squash and manchego cannelloni with tarragon crème fraîche, calves liver with roast garlic mash, smoked bacon and jus, corn-fed chicken with wild mushroom velouté, bass fillets with crab, asparagus and lemon risotto, and puddings such as white chocolate and raspberry crème brûlée and vanilla cheesecake with blueberry compote. *Benchmark main dish: lamb shank shepherd's pie £16.50. Two-course evening meal £22.50.*

Greene King ~ Lease David Webster ~ Real ale ~ Open 10am-midnight; 12-10.30 Sun ~ Bar food 12-3, 6-9.30 (10 Fri, Sat); 12-7 Sun ~ Restaurant ~ Children welcome ~ Dogs allowed in bar ~ Wi-fi ~ Quiz Mon 8pm Sept-Apr ~ Bedrooms: /£125 *Recommended by M G Hart, Simon Collett-Jones*

GREAT MISSENDEN SP9000 Map 4
Nags Head 🏆 🛏

(01494) 862200 – www.nagsheadbucks.com
Old London Road, E – beyond Abbey; HP16 0DG

Well run and pretty inn with beamed bars, an open fire, a good range of drinks and modern cooking; comfortable bedrooms

Built as three small cottages in the 15th c, this is now a quietly civilised dining pub that Roald Dahl used as his local. There's a low-beamed area on the left, a loftier part on the right, a mix of small pews, dining chairs and tables on carpet, Quentin Blake prints on cream walls and a log fire in a handsome fireplace. Rebellion IPA and a couple of guests such as Malt IPA and Vale Red Kite on handpump from the unusual bar counter (the windows behind face the road), 26 wines by the glass from an extensive list and half a dozen vintage Armagnacs. There's an outside dining area beneath a pergola and seats on the extensive back lawn. The beamed bedrooms are well equipped and comfortable, and the breakfasts are very good. The Roald Dahl Museum & Story Centre is just a stroll away.

 As well as serving breakfasts to non-residents (8-10am), the prettily presented food includes smoked haddock and cheese fishcake with a poached egg and mustard cream, duck liver parfait with pear chutney, artichoke, leek and pea risotto topped with smoked cheese with tomato and basil coulis, wild boar and apple sausages with chive mash and red wine gravy, chicken ballotine with chanterelle mushroom and brandy cream, slow-cooked lamb shank with rosemary jus and glazed onions, and puddings such as apple and rhubarb tart; they also offer a two- and three-course set weekday menu (not Fri evening). *Benchmark main dish: steak and kidney in ale pie £14.95. Two-course evening meal £23.50.*

Free house ~ Licensee Adam Michaels ~ Real ale ~ Open 8am-11pm ~ Bar food 12-2.30, 6.30-9.30; 12-3.30, 6.30-8.30 Sun ~ Children welcome ~ Dogs allowed in bar ~ Wi-fi ~ Bedrooms: £75/£95 *Recommended by Alfie Bayliss, Tracey and Stephen Groves, Toby Jones, Mr and Mrs J Watkins*

HAMBLEDEN   SU7886   Map 2

Stag & Huntsman 🏠

(01491) 571227 – www.thestagandhuntsman.co.uk

Off A4155 Henley–Marlow; RG9 6RP

Friendly inn with chatty bar, plenty of dining space and good food, welcoming staff and country garden; bedrooms

The little bar in this handsome brick and flint pub has the atmosphere of a thriving local with plenty of chatty regulars plus walkers and their dogs: stools against the counter, built-in cushioned wall seating, simple tables and chairs, bare floorboards. Rebellion IPA and Zebedee, Sharps Doom Bar and a guest ale on handpump and several wines by the glass, served by warmly, friendly staff. There's also a sizeable open-plan room with armchairs beside a woodburning stove in a brick fireplace, and a sofa and stools around a polished chest on more boards; this leads into the dining room with all sorts of wooden or high-backed red leather dining chairs around a variety of wooden tables, and hunting prints and other pictures on floral wallpaper. Darts and background music. The bedrooms are warm and comfortable and the breakfasts good. There are seats in the country garden.

 Tasty food includes lunchtime sandwiches (not Sun), chicken liver parfait with chutney, breaded brie with cranberry sauce, thai beef salad with chilli, ginger and roasted peanuts, minted pea and mascarpone risotto, burger with bacon, cheese and chips, beer-battered fish and chips, steaks with peppercorn sauce, and puddings such as white chocolate crème brûlée and glazed lemon tart with lemon sorbet. *Benchmark main dish: roast beef and all the trimmings £14.95. Two-course evening meal £20.00.*

Free house ~ Licensee Jaxon Keedwell ~ Real ale ~ Open 11-11; 12-11 (10.30 Sun) Sat ~ Bar food 12-2.30 (3 Sun), 6-9.30 ~ Restaurant ~ Children welcome ~ Dogs allowed in bar ~ Wi-fi ~ Bedrooms: £100/£120 *Recommended by John Pritchard, Susan and John Douglas, Lindy Andrews*

HEDGERLEY   SU9687   Map 2

White Horse ★ 📖 £

(01753) 643225

2.4 miles from M40 junction 2; at exit roundabout take Slough turn-off following alongside M40; after 1.5 miles turn right at T junction into Village Lane; SL2 3UY

Old-fashioned drinkers' pub with lots of beers tapped straight from the cask, regular beer festivals, home-made lunchtime food and a cheery mix of customers

You'd never believe this delightful and convivial country gem was so close to suburbia as it feels a world away. The cottagey main bar has plenty of unspoilt character, with lots of beams, brasses and exposed brickwork, low wooden tables, standing timbers, jugs, ballcocks and other bric-a-brac, a log fire, and a good few leaflets and notices about village events. A little flagstoned public bar on the left has darts, shove-ha'penny and board games. They keep Rebellion IPA and up to seven daily changing guests, sourced from all over the country and tapped straight from casks kept in a room behind the tiny hatch counter. Their Easter, May, Spring and August bank holiday beer festivals (they can get through about 130 beers during the May event) are highlights of the local calendar. This marvellous range of drinks extends to three farm ciders, still apple juice, a perry, belgian beers, eight wines by the glass, 15 malt whiskies and winter mulled wine. The canopied extension leads out to the garden where there are tables, the occasional barbecue and lots of hanging baskets; a few tables in front of the building overlook the quiet road. Good walks nearby, and the pub is handy for the Church Wood RSPB reserve and popular with walkers and cyclists; it's often crowded at weekends.

🍴 Lunchtime bar food includes good sandwiches, a salad bar with home-cooked quiches and cold meats, changing hot dishes such as soup, sausages and lamb casserole, and proper puddings such as plum sponge and bread and butter pudding. *Benchmark main dish: home-made pies £7.45.*

Free house ~ Licensees Doris Hobbs and Kevin Brooker ~ Real ale ~ Open 11-2.30, 5-11; 11-11 Sat; 12-10.30 Sun ~ Bar food 12-2 (2.30 weekends) ~ Children allowed in canopied extension area ~ Dogs allowed in bar *Recommended by Roy Hoing, N R White, Simon Collett-Jones, Alistair Forsyth, Gus Swan*

LEY HILL
SP9901 Map 4
Swan 🍺

(01494) 783075 – www.swanleyhill.com
Village signposted off A416 in Chesham; HP5 1UT

Charming, old-fashioned pub with friendly licensees, chatty customers, four real ales and quite a choice of popular food

In fine weather, this 16th-c pub looks at its best with picnic-sets among tubs of flowers and hanging baskets at the front and more seats, benches and tables under parasols in the bigger back garden (where they offer full dining service). Inside, the hands-on, friendly licensees keep it all spic and span and there are plenty of original features and a lot of character. The main bar is cosily old-fashioned with black beams (mind your head) and standing timbers, an old range, a log fire, a nice mix of old furniture and a collection of old local photographs. St Austell Tribute, Timothy Taylors Landlord and Tring Side Pocket for a Toad on handpump and several wines by the glass. The dining section is light and airy with a raftered ceiling, cream walls, red and gold curtains and all sorts of old tables and chairs on timber floors. It's worth wandering over to the common (where there's a cricket pitch and a nine-hole golf course) opposite this little timbered inn to turn back and admire the very pretty picture it makes.

🍴 Well liked food includes lunchtime sandwiches, duck liver parfait with port and red onion marmalade, crab cakes with chilli, ginger and coriander, home-cooked honey-roast ham and free-range eggs, mediterranean vegetable tagliatelle, steak and kidney in Guinness pie, seafood pot in creamy wine sauce, chicken with confit potato and a creamy white wine and mushroom sauce, and puddings such as vanilla crème brûlée and sticky toffee and date pudding with toffee sauce. *Benchmark main dish: slow-cooked pork belly with apple purée and red wine jus £14.75. Two-course evening meal £20.50.*

Free house ~ Licensee Nigel Byatt ~ Real ale ~ Open 12-2.30, 5.30-11; 12-4 Sun; closed Sun evening, Mon ~ Bar food 12-2.30 (3 Sun), 6-9 ~ Restaurant ~ Children welcome until 9pm *Recommended by Isobel Mackinlay, John and Penny Wheeler*

LITTLE MARLOW
SU8787 Map 2
Queens Head 🏵

(01628) 482927 – www.marlowslittlesecret.co.uk
Village signposted off A4155 E of Marlow near Kings Head; bear right into Pound Lane cul-de-sac; SL7 3SR

Charmingly tucked-away country pub, with good food and beers, friendly staff and seats in an appealing garden

'**Y**ou'd be hard-pushed to find fault with this smashing pub' and 'this is a hidden treasure,' say our readers about this consistently well run pub. The friendly, unpretentious main bar has simple but comfortable furniture on polished boards and leads back to a sizeable squarish carpeted dining extension with good solid tables. Throughout are old local photographs on cream or maroon walls, panelled dados painted brown or sage, and lighted candles. On the right is a small, quite separate, low-ceilinged public bar with Fullers London Pride and Rebellion IPA and Roasted Nuts on handpump, several wines by the glass, quite a range of whiskies and good coffee; neatly dressed efficient staff and unobtrusive background music. On a summer's day, the garden in front of this pretty tiled cottage is a decided plus, though not large: sheltered and neatly planted, it has teak tables and quite closely arranged picnic-sets, and white-painted metal furniture in a little wickerwork bower.

 First class food includes sandwiches, pulled pork croquette with red cabbage and apple sauce, scallops with black pudding and leek purée, roasted halloumi and sweet potato filo roll with spicy tomato jam, braised beef with spicy potatoes and port jus, salmon fillet with beetroot risotto, venison pudding with truffle mash, and puddings such as pecan tart with bourbon ice-cream and chocolate cheesecake. *Benchmark main dish: beer-battered haddock and chips £10.95. Two-course evening meal £20.00.*

Punch ~ Lease Daniel O'Sullivan ~ Real ale ~ Open 12-11 ~ Bar food 12-2, 7-9 ~ Restaurant ~ Children welcome ~ Wi-fi *Recommended by Simon Collett-Jones, Gerald and Brenda Culliford, Roy Hoing, Alistair Forsyth, Gus Swan*

LITTLE MISSENDEN   SU9298 Map 4
Crown 🍺 £

(01494) 862571 – www.the-crown-little-missenden.co.uk
Crown Lane, SE end of village, which is signposted off A413 W of Amersham; HP7 0RD

Long-serving licensees and pubby feel in little brick cottage, with several real ales and traditional food; attractive garden

For over 90 years, the same friendly family have been running this traditional brick-built local and it remains a favourite with regulars and visitors alike. Kept spic and span, it has old red flooring tiles on the left, oak parquet on the right, built-in wall seats, studded red leatherette chairs and a few small tables and a winter fire. Adnams Bitter, St Austell Tribute and a guest or two such as Rebellion IPA and Vale Gravitas on handpump or tapped from the cask, farm cider, summer Pimms and several malt whiskies; darts and board games. The large attractive sheltered garden behind has picnic-sets and other tables, and there are also seats out in front. Bedrooms are in a converted barn (continental breakfasts in your room only). The interesting church in the pretty village is well worth a visit.

Honest lunchtime-only food (not Sun) includes their famous bucks bite, sandwiches, filled baked potatoes, pasty with beans, field mushrooms stuffed with bacon and brie, and steak and kidney pie. *Benchmark main dish: steak in ale pie £8.95.*

Free house ~ Licensees Trevor and Carolyn How ~ Real ale ~ Open 11-2.30 (3 Sat), 6-11; 12-3, 7-10.30 Sun ~ Bar food 12-2; not Sun ~ Wi-fi ~ Bedrooms: £70/£85 *Recommended by Edward May, Toby Jones, Roy Hoing*

The 🍺 symbol shows pubs that keep their beer unusually well,
have a particularly good range or brew their own.

LONG CRENDON
SP6908   Map 4

Eight Bells 🍺 £

(01844) 208244 – www.8bellspub.com

High Street, off B4011 N of Thame; car park entrance off Chearsley Road, not 'Village roads only'; HP18 9AL

Good beers and sensibly priced seasonal food in nicely traditional village pub with charming garden

This friendly and unchanging old village pub was actually called the Five Bells in 1607 – and only changed its name in 1771 when the church got its eight bells. The little bare-boards bar on the left has Ringwood Best, Tiny Rebel Fubar, XT Four and a guest beer on handpump or tapped from the cask, a dozen wines by the glass and three farm ciders; service is cheerful. A bigger low-ceilinged room on the right has a log fire, daily papers and a pleasantly haphazard mix of tables and simple seats on ancient red and black tiles; one snug little hidey-hole with just three tables is devoted to the local morris men – frequent visitors. Board games, TV and background music. The little back garden is a joy in summer and there are well spaced picnic-sets among a colourful variety of shrubs and flowers; aunt sally. The interesting old village is known to many from TV's *Midsomer Murders*.

 Fairly priced food includes sandwiches, popcorn chicken with barbecue sauce, crispy squid, prawns and whitebait with chilli aioli, eggs poached in chilli sauce with harissa couscous, pickled vegetables and hummus, various pizzas, beef or chicken burgers with toppings, burger sauce and fries, steak and kidney pie, slow-cooked lamb shoulder with chorizo and white bean cassoulet, and puddings such as spotted dick and custard and white chocolate and cardamom parfait. *Benchmark main dish: beer-battered fish and chips £11.50. Two-course evening meal £16.00.*

Free house ~ Licensee Paul Mitchell ~ Real ale ~ Open 12-11 ~ Bar food 12 (10 weekends)-9 ~ Restaurant ~ Children welcome ~ Dogs welcome ~ Wi-fi
Recommended by Brian Glozier, Martin Jones, Peter Brix

MILTON KEYNES
SP8939   Map 4

Swan ♀

(01908) 665240 – www.theswan-mkvillage.co.uk

Broughton Road, Milton Keynes village; MK10 9AH

Plenty of space in well thought-out rooms, contemporary furnishings, open fires in inglenooks, enjoyable food and drink and seats outside

There's plenty of both drinking and dining space in this pretty, thatched pub and the interconnecting rooms have an easy-going yet stylish feel. It's been cleverly done, mixing original features with contemporary furnishings and the beamed main bar area has an open fire in an inglenook fireplace with logs piled up neatly on each side and two plush armchairs in front, several high tables and chairs dotted about, a cushioned wall banquette with scatter cushions, and wooden dining chairs and chunky tables on flagstones. St Austell Proper Job and Youngs Bitter and Bombardier on handpump, 30 wines by the glass, good coffees and courteous service. Leading off to the left is a cosy room with a gas stove, more cushioned banquettes and similar tables and chairs on parquet flooring, bookcase-effect wallpaper and photos of the pub. The spreading, partly beamed restaurant, with views of the open kitchen, has all manner of wooden and pretty fabric-covered dining chairs, cushioned settles and wall seats and a few curved banquettes (creating snug, private areas) on floorboards and a woodburning stove. Doors open on to an outside dining area overlooking the garden where there are seats and picnic-sets on grass.

🍴 Making good use of home-grown herbs, the very good food includes lunchtime sandwiches, guinea fowl ballotine with star anise jus, smoked haddock, salmon and dill fishcake with aioli, sharing platters, pasta with pesto and garlic in a creamy sauce, a pie of the day, grilled gammon with free-range eggs, pineapple pickle and chips, slow-cooked lamb with honey and minted mash, and puddings such as vanilla crème brûlée and sticky toffee pudding with butterscotch sauce. *Benchmark main dish: braised beef with parsnip purée and roasted bone marrow £18.25. Two-course evening meal £22.00.*

Little Gems Country Dining Pubs ~ Manager Harry Wilkins ~ Real ale ~ Open 11-11 (midnight Fri, Sat); 12-10.30 Sun ~ Bar food 12-3, 6-9.30; 12-10 Fri, Sat; 12-8 Sun ~ Restaurant ~ Children welcome but must be well behaved ~ Dogs allowed in bar ~ Wi-fi
Recommended by Toby Jones, Edward May

PENN
Old Queens Head 🎖 ♀
SU9093 Map 4

(01494) 813371 – www.oldqueensheadpenn.co.uk
Hammersley Lane/Church Road, off B474 between Penn and Tylers Green; HP10 8EY

Stylishly updated pub with highly enjoyable food, a good choice of drinks and walks nearby

As the ancient beechwoods of Common or Penn Woods are nearby, walkers and their dogs head to this welcoming dining pub for refreshment; dogs might be offered a biscuit. The open-plan rooms have lots of different areas to sit in, all with different aspects, and are decorated in a stylish mix of contemporary and chintz. There are well spaced tables, a modicum of old prints and comfortably varied seating on flagstones or broad dark boards. Stairs lead up to an attractive (and popular) two-level dining room, partly carpeted, with stripped rafters. The active bar side has Greene King IPA and Old Speckled Hen on handpump, over 20 wines by the glass (plus pudding wines) and a good choice of liqueurs; the turntable-top bar stools let you swivel to face the log fire in the big nearby fireplace. Daily papers and background music. The sunny terrace overlooks the church of St Margaret's and there are picnic-sets on the sheltered L-shaped lawn.

🍴 Interesting food using seasonal produce includes weekday lunchtime sandwiches, lamb koftas with roasted red pepper, coriander and pine nut salad and lime yoghurt, black pudding and pork scotch egg with spiced red onion marmalade, chargrilled aubergine gnocchi with grilled goats cheese and tomato salsa, chicken breast with butternut squash, dauphinoise potatoes and wild mushroom cream, salmon with crispy herb croquettes and tomato and chive dressing, and puddings such as carrot and maple syrup sponge with vanilla mascarpone and toffee popcorn sundae with salted caramel ice-cream. *Benchmark main dish: bacon with bubble and squeak, free-range poached egg and hollandaise £11.75. Two-course evening meal £20.25.*

Little Gems Country Dining Pubs ~ Manager Tina Brown ~ Real ale ~ Open 11.30-11.30 ~ Bar food 12-2.30, 6.30-9.30; 9.30-3, 6.30-10 Sat; 12-9 Sun ~ Restaurant ~ Children welcome ~ Dogs allowed in bar ~ Wi-fi   *Recommended by Richard Kennell, Peter Brix, Phoebe Peacock*

PRESTWOOD
Polecat 🎖 ♀
SP8799 Map 4

(01494) 862253 – www.thepolecatinn.co.uk
170 Wycombe Road (A4128 N of High Wycombe); HP16 0HJ

Enjoyable food, real ales and a chatty atmosphere in several smallish civilised rooms; attractive sizeable garden

The garden of this civilised pub is most attractive, with lots of spring bulbs, colourful summer hanging baskets and tubs and plenty of herbaceous plants; there are picnic-sets under parasols on neat grass out in front beneath a big fairy-lit pear tree, more on a large well kept lawn at the back and a big children's play area. Inside, several smallish rooms, opening off the low-ceilinged bar, have an assortment of tables and chairs, various stuffed birds, stuffed white polecats in one big cabinet, small country pictures, rugs on bare boards or red tiles, and a couple of leather wing chairs by a good open fire. Malt Golden Ale and Prestwoods Best, Rebellion IPA and Roasted Nuts and Vale Red Kite on handpump, 30 wines by the glass and home-made cordials.

Under the new licensee, the good food includes sandwiches, chicken liver and pistachio pâté with apricot chutney, twice-baked stilton soufflé, smoked haddock and spinach fishcakes, greek spinach and feta pie with tomato and basil sauce, wild boar sausages with apple ratatouille and sage mash, chicken curry, beef medallions stuffed with blue cheese, wrapped in bacon with red wine sauce, and puddings such as profiteroles with chocolate sauce and sticky toffee pudding with butterscotch sauce. *Benchmark main dish: pie of the day £11.00. Two-course evening meal £18.00.*

Free house ~ Licensee Philip Whitehouse ~ Real ale ~ Open 11.30-11; 12-6 Sun; 11.30-3, 6.30-11 in winter; closed Sun evening ~ Bar food 12-2, 7-9; 12-3 Sun ~ Restaurant ~ Children welcome ~ Dogs allowed in bar ~ Wi-fi *Recommended by David and Sue Smith, Peter and Jan Humphreys, Tracey and Stephen Groves, Roy Hoing*

SEER GREEN
Jolly Cricketers 🏅◖🍺

SU9691 Map 2

(01494) 676308 – www.thejollycricketers.co.uk
Chalfont Road, opposite the church; HP9 2YG

Bustling and friendly village pub with cricketing paraphernalia, a thoughtful choice of drinks, enjoyable food and seats on a back terrace

With its chatty, welcoming and gently civilised atmosphere, this well run brick pub appeals to both regulars and visitors. The two rooms of the parquet-floored bar are divided by a big chimney, with a woodburning stove in each room, nice cushioned seats in bow windows, a mix of pale farmhouse and antique dining chairs around wooden and painted tables, candles and fresh flowers, and plenty of old cricketing photos, prints and bats on the walls. The stools at the bar are well used by locals, and friendly, helpful staff serve Rebellion IPA and Vale VPA plus three guests on handpump (they hold regular beer festivals), 16 good wines by the glass, 20 malt whiskies and home-made sloe gin and blackberry vodka; big glass jars of nuts and dried fruit behind the bar, board games, TV and background music. The separate restaurant is similarly furnished and has a tiny cushioned settle, teddy bears in cricket gear, a basket of cricket bats and a chandelier over the table by the window. There's a handsome wisteria at the front and picnic-sets on a back terrace; occasional live music.

Highly rewarding food includes sandwiches, devilled crab with melba toast, local rabbit and ham terrine with carrot and vanilla purée, roasted squash with aged feta and quinoa and lovage dressing, beer-battered cod cheek with gribiche sauce, hake with lemon and parsley crust, potato gnocchi and cucumber and butter sauce, rib-eye steak with tarragon and roasted garlic butter and puddings such as apple and hazelnut crumble and Valrhona chocolate brownie with cherries and pistachio ice-cream. *Benchmark main dish: pork belly, local black pudding and coriander potato cake with pak choi and yuzu dressing £15.75. Two-course evening meal £22.00.*

Free house ~ Licensees Amanda and Chris Lillitou ~ Real ale ~ Open 12-11.30 (midnight Fri, Sat); 12-10.30 Sun ~ Bar food 12-2.30 (3 Sat), 6.30-9; 12-7 Sun ~ Restaurant ~ Live music once a month Sun 5.30pm ~ Dogs allowed in bar ~ Wi-fi
Recommended by Tracey and Stephen Groves, Edward May, Roger and Donna Huggins

STOKE MANDEVILLE
SP8310 Map 4

Bell 🌟 ♀

(01296) 612434 – www.bellstokemandeville.co.uk
Lower Road; HP22 5XA

Friendly landlord and staff in extended red-brick Victorian pub, with a fine choice of drinks, interesting food and seats outside

This is an extended red-brick Victorian pub with a bustling but easy-going atmosphere. The interconnected bar and dining areas have flagstones or polished pine floorboards and prints, drawings and maps of local interest and hunting prints on the walls above a dark blue dado. High stools line the counter where they keep Charles Wells Bombardier and Eagle and a guest ale on handpump and 20 wines (including sweet wines) by the glass; there are some equally high stools and tables opposite. Throughout are high-backed cushioned wooden and farmhouse chairs, wall settles with scatter cushions, and rustic benches around a medley of tables, some painted beams, and a woodburning stove; a snug alcove has just one table surrounded by cushioned wall seats. The little side terrace has picnic-sets and there are more on grass beside a weeping birch.

Interesting food includes sandwiches, bubble and squeak with bacon, poached egg and hollandaise, grilled mackerel with quinoa, broccoli and mint crème fraîche, wild mushroom and tarragon risotto with truffle oil, burger with toppings and skinny fries, venison steak with fig tart and redcurrant jus, cod fillet with wholegrain mustard mash and parsley sauce, and puddings such as coconut panna cotta with pineapple and chilli salsa and dark chocolate brownie. *Benchmark main dish: beef bourguignon with thyme dumplings and roast vegetable purée £13.75. Two-course evening meal £20.50.*

Wells & Youngs ~ Lease James Penlington ~ Real ale ~ Open 10am-11pm (10.30pm Sun) ~ Bar food 12-9.30 (8.30 Sun) ~ Restaurant ~ Children welcome ~ Dogs allowed in bar ~ Wi-fi
Recommended by Kate Day, Alexander Attridge, Jerry Scales, Sharon Cottle

THE LEE
SP8904 Map 4

Old Swan

(01494) 837239 – www.theoldswanpub.co.uk
Swan Bottom, back road 0.75 miles N of The Lee; HP16 9NU

Country pub with character bars and dining areas, friendly service, real ales, highly thought-of food and seats in big garden

Tucked away in the Chiltern Hills, this is a 16th-c pub run by a friendly family. There are several attractively furnished linked rooms with heavy beams, flagstones and old quarry tiles, high-backed antique settles and window seats with scatter cushions, little plush stools and straightforward dining chairs around wooden tables and a log fire in an inglenook cooking range. High bar stools line the counter where they keep Chiltern Ale, Sharps Doom Bar and a weekend guest on handpump and several wines by the glass. The big, spreading back garden has picnic-sets and contemporary seating around rustic tables. Good surrounding walks and cycling routes.

🍴 Rewarding food includes baguettes, double-baked cauliflower cheese soufflé with real ale chutney, duck liver, champagne and orange pâté with beetroot relish, panko-breaded fishcake with aioli, honey and mustard-glazed smoked ham hock with a fried duck egg and chips, a pie of the day, mixed seafood linguine in tomato and paprika sauce, calves liver with pancetta, sweet onion mash and beef jus, slow-cooked chicken leg in five spice with stir-fried vegetables and hoisin sauce, and puddings such as white chocolate mousse with a dark chocolate cylinder and crunchy honeycomb and lemon meringue parfait with pistachios and Limoncello; steak night is Tuesday and they also offer a Wednesday evening two- and three-course set menu. *Benchmark main dish: steaks with a choice of potatoes and sauces £19.00. Two-course evening meal £22.00.*

Free house ~ Licensees Phil and Jane Joel ~ Real ale ~ Open 12-3, 6-9; 12-11 Fri, Sat; 12-7 Sun; closed Mon lunchtime ~ Bar food 12-2.30, 7 (6.30 Fri, Sat)-9; 12-3 Sun; not Sun evening, Mon ~ Restaurant ~ Children welcome ~ Dogs allowed in bar ~ Wi-fi
Recommended by Emma Scofield, Peter Pilbeam, Mr and Mrs J Watkins

WOOBURN COMMON

SU9187   Map 2

Chequers ⭐ 🍷 🛏

(01628) 529575 – www.chequers-inn.com
From A4094 N of Maidenhead at junction with A4155 Marlow road keep on A4094 for another 0.75 miles, then at roundabout turn right towards Wooburn Common and into Kiln Lane; if you find yourself in Honey Hill, Hedsor, turn left into Kiln Lane at the top of the hill; OS Sheet 175 map reference 910870; HP10 0JQ

Busy, friendly hotel with a bustling bar, four real ales, bar food and more elaborate dishes in smart restaurant; comfortable bedrooms

Feeling nicely pubby with chatty locals, the friendly bar remains the heart of this place, despite quite an emphasis on the hotel and restaurant side. There are low beams, standing timbers and alcoves, characterful rickety furniture and comfortably lived-in sofas on bare boards, a bright log-effect gas fire, pictures, plates, a two-man saw and tankards. In contrast, the bar to the left, with its dark brown leather sofas at low tables on wooden floors, feels modern and simple; the smart restaurant has high-backed black leather dining chairs around white-clothed tables. Rebellion IPA and Smuggler and St Austell Tribute on handpump, a good sizeable wine list (with a dozen by the glass) and a fair range of malt whiskies and brandies; background music, TV. The spacious garden, set away from the road, has seats around cast-iron tables and summer barbecues.

⭐ A wide choice of highly rewarding food includes sandwiches and wraps, ham hock and black pudding terrine with crispy quail egg and piccalilli, poached conger eel with ricotta gnocchi, pickled grapes and curry cream, cumberland sausage with onion gravy, beer-battered haddock and chips, duck breast and crispy rillettes with mango emulsion, grilled green onion and pomegranate jus, saddle of lamb with crispy belly, goats cheese mash and mint jus, and puddings such as salt caramel ganache with butter brittle, cocoa caviar and Baileys ice-cream; they also offer a two- and three-course set lunch. *Benchmark main dish: burger with toppings, coleslaw and chips £10.95. Two-course evening meal £26.00.*

Free house ~ Licensee Peter Roehrig ~ Real ale ~ Open 11am-12.30pm (midnight Sun) ~ Bar food 12-9.30 ~ Restaurant ~ Children welcome ~ Dogs allowed in bar ~ Wi-fi ~ Bedrooms: £99.50/£107.50 *Recommended by Caroline Prescott, Charlie May, David Greene*

Please let us know what you think of a pub's bedrooms: feedback@goodguides.com or (no stamp needed) The Good Pub Guide, FREEPOST RTJR-ZCYZ-RJZT, Perrymans Lane, Etchingham TN19 7DN.

Also Worth a Visit in Buckinghamshire

Besides the fully inspected pubs, you might like to try these pubs that have been recommended to us and described by readers. Do tell us what you think of them: feedback@goodguides.com

---

AMERSHAM   SU9597

Elephant & Castle (01494) 726410

High Street; HP7 0DT Modernised twin-gabled low-beamed local, good value tasty food from sandwiches to full meals including weekday set menu (lunchtime/early evening), three well kept ales such as Hook Norton Old Hooky from U-shaped counter, quick friendly service, wood burner in large brick fireplace, conservatory; background and some live music; garden behind, children welcome, open all day. *(Quentin and Carol Williamson)*

ASHERIDGE   SP9404

Blue Ball (01494) 758305

Braziers End; HP5 2UX Small country pub with light airy décor, enjoyable good value home-made food (not Sun) from baguettes and baked potatoes up, well kept changing ales such as Fullers London Pride and Charles Wells Bombardier, friendly staff; children welcome till 6pm, good Chilterns walking country, bedrooms, open all day Fri-Sun. *(R Anderson, Mrs P Sumner)*

ASKETT   SP8105

★ **Three Crowns** (01844) 347166

W off A4010 into Letter Box Lane; HP27 9LT Handsome, well run and welcoming pub in small hamlet among the Chiltern Hills; main emphasis on the particularly good interesting food, but also real ales such as Vale from herringbone-brick counter, good wine list, two contemporary-styled beamed dining rooms with mix of high-backed pale wood or black leather chairs around dark wood tables, light flooring, minimal décor; some picnic-sets outside under parasols, pretty front flower beds and baskets, closed Sun evening, Mon. *(Peter and Jan Humphreys, D R Stevenson, Edward Mirzoeff)*

AYLESBURY   SP8212

Broad Leys (01296) 399979

Wendover Road; HP21 9LB Renovated 17th-c dining pub with enjoyable home-made food from sharing plates up, weekday afternoon teas and weekend brunch, friendly service, ales such as Fullers London Pride, Hook Norton and Vale, bar area with beams, stripped brick and flagstones, painted pine tables in bare-boards restaurant beyond; some live music; children welcome, good-sized garden with attractive terrace (summer barbecues), two bedrooms and nearby self-catering cottage, open (and food) all day. *(Susan and Jeremy Arthern)*

BEACONSFIELD   SU9490

Royal Saracens (01494) 674119

1 mile from M40 junction 2; London End (A40); HP9 2JH Striking timbered façade (former coaching inn) with well updated open-plan interior, comfortable chairs around light wood tables, massive beams and timbers in one corner, log fires, welcoming efficient young staff, wide choice of enjoyable food including shared dishes and fixed-price weekday menu (busy at weekends when best to book), well kept ales such as Fullers London Pride and Sharps Doom Bar, quite a few wines by the glass, large back restaurant; attractive sheltered courtyard, open (and food) all day. *(Gordon and Jenny Quick)*

BENNETT END   SU7897

Three Horseshoes (01494) 483273

Horseshoe Road; from Radnage on unclassified road towards Princes Risborough, left into Bennett End Road, then right into Horseshoe Road; HP14 4EB Country pub in lovely quiet spot – seemingly off the beaten track but close to M40; well kept Rebellion IPA and a guest, several wines by the glass and good choice of food including traditional options and cheaper set menus, flagstoned softly lit snug bar with log fire in raised fireplace, original brickwork and bread oven, two further sitting areas, one with long winged settle, the other enclosed by standing timbers, stone-floor dining room with big windows overlooking garden, red telephone box half submerged in duck pond, unspoilt valley beyond; can be busy on warm summer's day; children welcome till 9pm, dogs in bar, six bedrooms (two in garden annexe), closed Sun evening, Mon lunchtime. *(Roy Hoing, Paul Humphreys)*

BLEDLOW RIDGE   SU7997

Boot (01494) 481499

Chinnor Road; HP14 4AW Welcoming village pub with fresh contemporary décor, good food from sandwiches, sharing plates and pub favourites up (best to book weekends), well kept Rebellion, Sharps Doom Bar and a guest, several wines by the glass from extensive list, dining room with exposed rafters and large brick fireplace; background music, TV; children and dogs welcome, terrace and in sizeable lawned garden, open all day Fri, Sat, till 7pm Sun, closed Mon. *(Andrew Stone)*

BOURNE END   SU8987

Bounty (01628) 520056

Cock Marsh, actually across the river along the Cookham towpath, but shortest

walk – still about 0.25 miles – is from Bourne End, over the railway bridge; SL8 5RG Welcoming take-us-as-you-find-us pub tucked away in outstanding setting on bank of the Thames and accessible only by foot or boat; collection of flags on ceiling and jumble of other bits and pieces, well kept Rebellion ales from boat counter, basic standard food including children's meals, back dining area, darts and bar billiards; background music inside and out; dogs and muddy walkers welcome, picnic-sets with parasols on front terrace, play area to right, open all day in summer (may be boat trips), just weekends in winter and closes early if quiet. *(N R White)*

BRADENHAM   SU8297
Red Lion (01494) 562212
A4010, by Walters Ash turn-off; HP14 4HF Welcoming NT-owned pub with small simple bar and good-sized low-beamed dining room, three or four well kept Rebellion ales, enjoyable home-made food from good baguettes up; children, walkers and dogs welcome, picnic-sets on terrace and lawn, pretty village green nearby, closed Sun evening, Mon. *(David Lamb)*

BRILL   SP6514
★ Pheasant (01844) 239370
Windmill Street; off B4011 Bicester–Long Crendon; HP18 9TG More or less open-plan with raftered bar area, leather tub seats in front of woodburner, three well kept ales including Vale and a house beer from Skinners, good food (till 6pm Sun) from changing menu, charming staff, dining areas with high-backed leather or dark wooden chairs, attractively framed prints, books on shelves; background music; children and dogs (in bar) welcome, seats out on raised deck with steps down to garden, fine views over post windmill (one of the oldest in working order), walks from the door, four comfortable bedrooms (two in former bakehouse), good breakfast, open all day. *(Alan Weedon, Neil and Angela Huxter)*

BUCKINGHAM   SP6933
Villiers (01280) 822444
Castle Street; MK18 1BS Pub part of this large comfortable hotel with own courtyard entrance, big inglenook log fire, panelling and stripped masonry in flagstoned bar, beers from Hook Norton and Black Sheep, reliably good food from shortish menu (also set menu choices), competent friendly staff, sofas and armchairs in more formal front lounges, restaurant with two large tropical fish tanks; no dogs; children welcome till 9pm, terrace, tables, 49 bedrooms, open all day. *(Andrew Stone)*

BUTLERS CROSS   SP8407
Russell Arms (01296) 624411
Off A4010 S of Aylesbury, at Nash Lee roundabout; or off A413 in Wendover;

passing station; Chalkshire Road; HP17 0TS Recently refurbished 18th-c beamed pub, a former coaching inn and servants' quarters for nearby Chequers; bar and two dining areas, eclectic mix of stripped wooden tables and chairs, open fire and woodburner in inglenook, well kept local ales along with St Austell Tribute, 17 wines by the glass and good freshly made food, friendly welcoming staff; background music; children and dogs allowed, pretty garden with suntrap terrace, well placed for Chilterns walks, open all day. *(Tracey and Stephen Groves)*

CADSDEN   SP8204
Plough (01844) 343302
Cadsden Road; HP27 0NB Extended former 16th-c coaching inn with airy open-plan bar/dining area, clean and bright, with well spaced pine tables on flagstones, exposed brick and some faux beams, very popular with families and Chilterns ramblers, good choice of real ales, well presented home-made food (not especially cheap), cherry pie festival first Sun in Aug, efficient service; lots of tables in delightful quiet front and back gardens, some woodland seating, pretty spot on Ridgeway path (shoe covers for walkers), bedrooms, open all day weekends (no food Sun evening). *(Roy Hoing)*

CHACKMORE   SP6835
Queens Head (01280) 813004
Main Street; MK18 5JF Comfortable old-fashioned village pub by Stowe Gardens (NT), enjoyable fairly priced food, three well kept ales and good value house wines, nice local feel in bar, small dining room; picnic-sets out in front under parasols, more in back garden. *(Paul Humphreys)*

CHALFONT ST GILES   SU9895
Ivy House (01494) 872184
A413 S; HP8 4RS Old brick and flint beamed coaching inn, enjoyable home-cooked food served by friendly young staff, well kept Fullers ales, decent wines by the glass and over 30 whiskies, L-shaped bar where dogs allowed, lighter flagstoned dining extension; quiz first Thurs of month, free wi-fi; children welcome, some seats out under covered front part by road, pleasant terrace and sloping garden, five comfortable bedrooms, good hearty breakfast, open all day (food all day weekends, till 7pm Sun). *(Tracey and Stephen Groves, V Brogden)*

CHALFONT ST GILES   SU9893
Miltons Head (01494) 872961
Deanway; HP8 4JL Popular little pub/restaurant with good mainly italian food cooked by sardinian landlord, also pizza menu and traditional Sun roasts, reasonable prices and best to book, nice italian wines and coffee, no real ales but Peroni on draught; children and dogs welcome, small side terrace, handy for John Milton's Cottage, closed Sun evening, Mon. *(Andrew Stone)*

CHEARSLEY   SP7110
Bell (01844) 208077
The Green; HP18 0DJ Cosy traditional
thatched and beamed pub on attractive
village green, Fullers beers and good wines
by the glass, enjoyable sensibly priced home-
made food (not Sun or Mon evenings),
efficient friendly service, inglenook with big
woodburner; quiz (first Sun of month), bingo
(first Tues); children in eating area, dogs
welcome, plenty of tables in spacious back
garden with heated terrace and play area.
(Rob Anderson)

CHENIES   TQ0198
Bedford Arms (01923) 283301
*2 miles from M25 junction 18; A404
towards Amersham, then village
signposted on right; Chesham Road;
WD3 6EQ* Popular country-house hotel with
recently modernised knocked-through front
bar, good food here or in more formal oak-
panelled restaurant, friendly helpful staff,
Fullers London Pride, Tring Side Pocket for a
Toad and a guest, decent choice of wines by
the glass; tables on attractive front terrace
and in lovely garden behind with mature
oaks, 18 bedrooms, open all day.
(Richard Kennell)

CHENIES   TQ0298
★ Red Lion (01923) 282722
*2 miles from M25 junction 18; A404
towards Amersham, then village
signposted on right; Chesham Road;
WD3 6ED* Long-serving licensees in
proper village pub with loyal local following,
L-shaped bar with comfortable built-in wall
benches and other seats, old photographs of
village and traction engines, small back snug
and neat dining extension with more modern
décor, well kept Rebellion, Vale, Wadworths
and a guest, ten wines by the glass, popular
food including good Sun roasts, friendly
attentive service; no under-14s, dogs welcome
in bar, pretty hanging baskets and window
boxes, picnic-sets on small side terrace,
good local walks, open (and food) all day
weekends. *(John Boothman, Mrs Margo Finlay,
Jörg Kasprowski, Roy Hoing, Brian Glozier, John
Evans, Richard Kennell)*

CHESHAM   SP9604
Black Horse (01494) 784656
*Vale Road, N off A416 in Chesham;
HP5 3NS* Popular extended black-beamed
country pub under enthusiastic new
management; enjoyable home-made food
including weekday deal, Fullers London Pride
and three guests, several wines by the glass,
good friendly service, inglenook log fire;
fortnightly Mon quiz and maybe some live
music; children, dogs and walkers welcome,
picnic-sets out in front and on back lawn
with play area and heated smokers' shelter,
classic car meetings, closed Mon lunchtime,
otherwise open all day. *(Rob Anderson)*

CHESHAM   SP9501
Queens Head (01494) 778690
Church Street; HP5 1JD Popular well run
Fullers corner pub, two traditional beamed
bars with scrubbed tables and log fires, their
ales and a guest kept well, good thai food
along with modest range of pub staples,
restaurant, friendly staff and chatty locals;
sports TV; children welcome, tables in small
courtyard used by smokers, next to little
River Chess, open all day. *(Tracey and Stephen
Groves)*

COLNBROOK   TQ0277
Ostrich (01753) 682628
*1.25 miles from M4 junction 5 via A4/
B3378, then 'village only' road; High
Street; SL3 0JZ* Spectacular timbered
Elizabethan building (with even longer
gruesome history – tales of over 60 murders!);
contemporary interior with comfortable sofas
on stripped wood and a rather startling red
plastic/stainless steel bar counter, three
well kept ales (one badged for them) and
good choice of wines by the glass including
champagne, enjoyable sensibly priced food
from sandwiches and pub favourites up, good
value set lunch Mon-Sat, efficient friendly
service, attractive restaurant with open fire;
soft background music, comedy and live
music nights upstairs; children welcome,
open all day Sun. *(Nigel and Sue Foster)*

CUBLINGTON   SP8322
Unicorn (01296) 681261
High Street; LU7 0LQ Extended low-
beamed 17th-c pub incorporating the village
post office, popular sensibly priced food from
interesting menu, Sharps, Shepherd Neame,
XT and guests (May, Aug beer festivals),
good friendly service, handsome fireplace
at one end; Mon quiz and some live music;
big enclosed garden behind, open all day.
*(Mr and Mrs D B Lawton, Graham and
Carol Parker)*

CUDDINGTON   SP7311
★ Crown (01844) 292222
*Spurt Street; off A418 Thame–Aylesbury;
HP18 0BB* Convivial thatched cottage with
chatty mix of customers, comfortable pubby
furnishings including cushioned settles in
two low-beamed linked rooms, big inglenook
log fire, well kept Fullers and guests, around
20 wines by the glass, good home-cooked
food (not Sun evening), competent friendly
service, carpeted two-room back dining area
with country-kitchen chairs around nice mix
of tables; children welcome; neat side terrace
with modern garden furniture and planters,
picnic-sets in front. *(Rob Anderson)*

DINTON   SP7610
Seven Stars (01296) 749000
*Signed off A418 Aylesbury–Thame,
near Gibraltar turn-off; Stars Lane;
HP17 8UL* Pretty 17th-c community-

owned pub run by french landlady and well supported locally, inglenook bar, beamed lounge and dining room, a couple of well kept ales (one local), plenty of wines by the glass, good food cooked to order from pub staples up including some french dishes, friendly service; tables in sheltered garden with terrace, pleasant village, open all day weekends. *(Graham and Carol Parker, David Lamb)*

DORNEY   SU9279
Palmer Arms (01628) 666612
2.7 miles from M4 junction 7, via B3026; Village Road; SL4 6QW
Modernised and extended dining pub in attractive conservation village, good popular food (best to book) from snacks and pub favourites to more restauranty dishes, friendly efficient service, Greene King ales, lots of wines by the glass (interesting list) and good coffee, open fires in civilised front bar and back dining room, daily newspapers; background music; children and dogs (in certain areas) welcome, disabled facilities, terrace overlooking mediterranean-feel garden, enclosed play area, nice riverside walks nearby, open (and food) all day. *(I D Barnett)*

DORNEY   SU9279
Pineapple (01628) 662353
Lake End Road: 2.4 miles from M4 junction 7; left on A4 then left on B3026; SL4 6QS Nicely old-fashioned pub handy for Dorney Court (where the first english pineapple was grown in 1661); shiny low Anaglypta ceilings, black-panelled dados, leather chairs around sturdy country tables (one very long, another in big bow window), woodburner and pretty little fireplace, china pineapples and other decorations on shelves in one of three cottagey carpeted linked rooms on left, well kept Fullers London Pride, Sharps Doom Bar and Windsor & Eton Guardsman, over 1,000 varieties of sandwiches in five different fresh breads; background music, games machine; children and dogs welcome, rustic seats on roadside verandah, round picnic-sets in garden, fairy-lit decking under oak tree, some motorway noise, open (and food) all day. *(Jo Garnett)*

EDLESBOROUGH   SW6225
Travellers Rest (01525) 221841
Tring Road; LU6 2EE Popular rurally placed Vintage Inn, their usual food and three well kept mainstream ales such as Sharps Doom Bar, a dozen wines by the glass, good friendly service; children welcome, outside seating, open all day. *(Ross Balaam)*

FLACKWELL HEATH   SU8889
Crooked Billet (01628) 521216
Off A404; Sheepridge Lane; SL7 3SG Steps up to cosily old-fashioned and totally unspoilt 16th-c pub, Brakspears and Charles Wells ales, reasonably priced traditional

lunchtime food, friendly service, eating area spread pleasantly through alcoves, low beams and good open fire; lovely cottagey garden with nice views (beyond road), walks nearby. *(Susan and John Douglas)*

FRIETH   SU7990
Prince Albert (01494) 881683
Off B482 SW of High Wycombe; RG9 6PY Friendly cottagey Chilterns local with low black beams and joists, high-backed settles, big black stove in inglenook and log fire in larger area on right, decent lunchtime food from sandwiches up (also Fri and Sat evenings – they ask you to book on Sat), well kept Brakspears and guests, quiz and folk nights; children and dogs welcome, nicely planted informal side garden with views of woods and fields, good walks, open all day. *(Jo Garnett)*

GAWCOTT   SP6831
Crown (01280) 822322
Hillesden Road; MK18 4JF Welcoming black-beamed village pub, good value popular food including carvery Weds and Sun, well kept ales such as Sharps Doom Bar from herringbone-brick counter, restaurant area; background music, Sky TV, pool; children welcome, long back garden with swings, open all day (no food Sun evening, Mon). *(Jo Garnett)*

GERRARDS CROSS   TQ0089
★Three Oaks (01753) 899016
Austenwood Lane, just NW of junction with Kingsway (B416); SL9 8NL Civilised and relaxed dining pub facing Austenwood Common, welcoming neatly dressed staff, two-room front bar with fireside bookshelves, tartan wing armchairs, sturdy wall settles and comfortable banquettes, well kept Fullers and Rebellion, several wines by the glass, dining part with three linked rooms, popular well thought-of food; soft background music, free wi-fi; children welcome, sturdy wooden tables on flagstoned side terrace, open all day. *(Simon Collett-Jones)*

GREAT BRICKHILL   SP9029
Red Lion (01525) 261715
Ivy Lane; MK17 9AH Roadside village pub under friendly new management, enjoyable food (maybe some nepalese dishes), ales such as Greene King IPA and St Austell Tribute, log fire in small bar, woodburner in restaurant; fabulous views over Buckinghamshire and beyond from walled back lawn. *(Martin Jones)*

GREAT HAMPDEN   SP8401
★Hampden Arms (01494) 488255
W of Great Missenden, off A4128; HP16 9RQ Friendly village pub opposite cricket pitch, good mix of locals and visitors, comfortably furnished rooms (back one more rustic with big woodburner), Fullers

London Pride, Rebellion IPA and a guest, Addlestone's cider and several wines by the glass from small corner bar, reasonably priced pubby food including one or two greek dishes, cheerful efficient service; children and dogs welcome, seats in tree-sheltered garden, good Hampden Common walks. *(David Lamb)*

GREAT KINGSHILL   SU8798
★**Red Lion** (01494) 711262
A4128 N of High Wycombe; HP15 6EB Welcoming village pub with contemporary décor and relaxed informal atmosphere, well cooked brasserie-style food including fixed-price menu (Tues-Sat lunchtime, Tues-Thurs early evening), local beers and good value wine list, 'lobby' and cosy little flagstoned bar with leather tub chairs by log fire, spacious candlelit dining room; well behaved children welcome, closed Sun evening, Mon. *(Tracey and Stephen Groves)*

GREAT MISSENDEN   SP8901
★**Cross Keys** (01494) 865373
High Street; HP16 0AU Friendly and relaxed village pub dating from the 16th c, unspoilt beamed bar divided by standing timbers, traditional furnishings including high-backed settle, log-effect gas fire in huge fireplace, well kept Fullers ales and often an unusual guest, enjoyable fairly priced food from sandwiches and pizzas up, cheerful helpful staff, spacious beamed restaurant; free wi-fi; children and dogs welcome, picnic-sets on back terrace, open all day (food all day Thurs-Sat, till 4pm Sun). *(Martin Jones)*

GROVE   SP9122
★**Grove Lock** (01525) 380940
Pub signed off B488, on left just S of A505 roundabout (S of Leighton Buzzard); LU7 0QU Overlooking Grand Union Canal and usefully open all day; open plan with lofty high-raftered pitched roof in bar, squashy brown leather sofas on oak boards, eclectic mix of tables and chairs including butcher's block tables by bar, big open-standing log fire, steps down to original lock-keeper's cottage (now a three-room restaurant area), enjoyable food from sandwiches to daily specials, Fullers ales and lots of wines by the glass; background music, free wi-fi; children welcome, seats on canopied deck and waterside lawn by Lock 28. *(Martin Jones)*

HADDENHAM   SP7408
Green Dragon (01844) 292331
Village signposted off A418 and A4129, E/NE of Thame; then follow Church End signs into Churchway; HP17 8AA Shuttered 18th-c village dining pub continuing well under present management,

open-plan modernised interior with two log fires, well kept Sharps, Timothy Taylors and a guest, plenty of wines by the glass and enjoyable home-made food (not Sun evening), good friendly staff; children and dogs welcome, big sheltered gravel terrace, picnic-sets in appealing garden, open all day (till 9pm Sun). *(Charlie May)*

HUGHENDEN VALLEY   SU8697
★**Harrow** (01494) 564105
Warrendene Road, off A4128 N of High Wycombe; HP14 4LX Small cheerful brick and flint roadside cottage surrounded by Chilterns walks; traditionally furnished with tiled-floor bar on left, black beams and joists, woodburner in big fireplace, pewter mugs, country pictures and wall seats, similar but bigger right-hand bar with sizeable dining tables on brick floor, carpeted back dining room, tasty pub food (not Sun evening) from sandwiches up including meal deal Mon-Weds, Courage Best, Fullers London Pride and Shepherd Neame Spitfire, friendly staff; Tues quiz; children and dogs welcome, disabled access, plenty of picnic-sets in front with more on back lawn, play area, open all day. *(Charlie May)*

HYDE HEATH   SU9300
Plough (01494) 774408
Off B485 Great Missenden–Chesham; HP6 5RW Small prettily placed pub with traditional bare-boards bar and carpeted dining extension, good value traditional food including walkers' menu, Fullers London Pride, St Austell Tribute and a local beer, real fires; background music, TV; motorbikes welcome, picnic-sets on green opposite, open all day Fri-Sun. *(Roy Hoing)*

ICKFORD   SP6407
Rising Sun (01844) 339238
E of Thame; Worminghall Road; HP18 9JD Pretty thatched local with cosy low-beamed bar, friendly staff and regulars, Adnams, Black Sheep, Hook Norton and a weekly guest, enjoyable reasonably priced home-made food, log fire; children, walkers and dogs welcome, pleasant garden with picnic-sets and play area, handy for Waterperry Gardens, open all day weekends. *(Charlie May)*

IVINGHOE ASTON   SP9518
Village Swan (01525) 220544
Aston; signed from B489 NE of Ivinghoe; LU7 9DP Village-owned pub managed by new dutch couple (the former glitzy décor has gone), traditional beamed interior with open fire, enjoyable home-made food from varied menu including some dutch dishes, three real ales and nice wines by the glass; quiz first Mon of month, free wi-fi; children,

---

If we know a pub has an outdoor play area for children, we mention it.

walkers and dogs welcome, covered outside area and garden, handy for Ivinghoe Beacon and Icknield Way, open all day weekends, closed Mon and weekday lunchtimes. *(Peter Brix)*

LACEY GREEN   SP8200
Black Horse (01844) 345195
Main Road; HP27 0QU Friendly mix of customers in this two-bar beamed country local, popular good value home-made food (not Sun evening, Mon) from baguettes up, breakfast from 9am Tues-Sat, four real ales including Brakspears, nice choice of wines by the glass, quotations written on walls, inglenook woodburner; darts, sports TV; children welcome, picnic-sets in garden with play area and aunt sally, closed Mon lunchtime, open all day Thurs-Sun. *(Paul Humphreys)*

LACEY GREEN   SP8100
Whip (01844) 344060
Pink Road; HP27 0PG Cheery and attractive hilltop local welcoming walkers, mix of simple traditional furnishings in smallish front bar and larger downstairs dining area, popular good value food from sandwiches to daily specials (booking advised weekends), six interesting well kept/priced ales and a couple of proper ciders, beer festivals (May and Sept) with live jazz, good landlord and friendly helpful service; TV, fruit machine; tables in mature sheltered garden looking up to windmill, open all day. *(Peter Brix)*

LITTLE KINGSHILL   SU8999
Full Moon (01494) 862397
Hare Lane; HP16 0EE Picturesque brick and flint village pub with popular well presented food including some unusual choices such as crocodile fillets, well kept Adnams, Fullers London Pride, Charles Wells and a guest, nice wines, friendly helpful service from busy staff, traditional beamed and quarry-tiled bar with open fire, bigger dining room; Thurs quiz; children and dogs welcome, round picnic-sets out at front, lawned garden with swings, good walks. *(Martin Jones)*

LITTLE MARLOW   SU8788
★ Kings Head (01628) 484407
Church Road; A4155 about 2 miles E of Marlow; SL7 3RZ Long, flower-covered local with open-plan bar, low beams, captain's chairs and other traditional seating around dark wood tables, cricketing memorabilia (pitch opposite), log fire, half a dozen well kept ales such as Adnams, Fullers and Rebellion, popular pubby blackboard food from baguettes up (booking advised weekends), free bar nibbles Sun, helpful friendly service, gingham-clothed tables in attractive dining room; big walled garden with modern terrace furniture, open all day. *(Paul Humphreys, Roy Hoing)*

LITTLE MISSENDEN   SU9298
★ Red Lion (01494) 862876
Off A413 Amersham–Great Missenden; HP7 0QZ Unchanging pretty 15th-c cottage with long-serving landlord; small black-beamed bar, plain seats around elm pub tables, piano squashed into big inglenook beside black kitchen range packed with copper pots, kettles and rack of old guns, little country dining room with pheasant décor, well kept Greene King IPA, Marstons Pedigree and Wadworths 6X, fair-priced wines, good coffee, enjoyable inexpensive pubby food and good friendly service; live music Tues and Sat; children welcome, dogs in bar, picnic-sets out in front and on grass behind wall, back garden with little bridge over River Misbourne, some fancy waterfowl, stables farm shop, open all day Fri, Sat. *(Roy Hoing, Susan and John Douglas)*

LITTLEWORTH COMMON   SP9386
Blackwood Arms (01753) 645672
3 miles S of M40 junction 2; Common Lane; SL1 8PP Traditional little 19th-c brick pub (used in the film *My Week with Marilyn*) in lovely spot on edge of beechwoods, sturdy mix of furniture on bare boards, roaring log fire, enjoyable home-made food (not Sun evening) from open sandwiches up, well kept Brakspears and guests, interesting selection of wines, friendly staff; free wi-fi; children and dogs welcome, hitching rail for horses, nice garden with paved area, good local walks, closed Mon, otherwise open all day (till 7pm Sun). *(Alistair Forsyth)*

LUDGERSHALL   SP6617
Bull & Butcher (01844) 238094
Off A41 Aylesbury–Bicester; bear left to The Green; HP18 9NZ Nicely old-fashioned welcoming country pub facing village green, bar with low beams in ochre ceiling, wall bench and simple pub furniture on dark tiles or flagstones, inglenook log fire, back dining room, decent bar food from shortish well priced menu, a couple of changing ales, aunt sally and dominoes teams, quiz (second Sun of month); children welcome, picnic-sets on pleasant front terrace, play area on green, open all day Sun, closed Mon and lunchtime Tues. *(David Lamb)*

MAIDS MORETON   SP7035
Wheatsheaf (01280) 822903
Main Street, just off A413 Towcester–Buckingham; MK18 1QR Attractive 17th-c thatched and low-beamed local smartened up and again under new management; good pubby food and well kept ales such as Tring, Sharps and Skinners, friendly service, bar with bare boards and tiled floors, two inglenooks, conservatory restaurant; seats on front terrace, hatch service for pleasant enclosed back garden. *(George Atkinson)*

MARLOW   SU8587
Britannia (01628) 485066
Little Marlow Road; SL7 1HL Modernised
McMullens pub with nautical theme, their
ales in good condition and decent choice of
wines, all-day food from reasonably priced
menu, friendly attentive staff; free wi-fi;
children welcome, open all day (till midnight
Fri, Sat). *(Cliff Sparkes)*

MARLOW   SU8486
★**Hand & Flowers** (01628) 482277
West Street (A4155); SL7 2BP Restaurant
rather than pub owned by celebrity chef
Tom Kerridge; nice informal atmosphere in
three linked beamed rooms all set for dining,
high-backed leather-seated chairs and brown
suede wall seats around chunky tables,
bare boards or flagstones, fresh flowers and
candles, first class food and professional
service, extension with stools at counter for
dining and drinking plus more set tables,
Greene King, Rebellion and a beer named for
the pub, lots of wines by the glass from good
list and specialist gins; children welcome,
comfortable character bedrooms, Thames
walks nearby, closed Sun evening. *(Tracey
and Stephen Groves, Gerry Price, Susan and John
Douglas)*

MARLOW   SU8586
★**Two Brewers** (01628) 484140
*St Peter Street, first right off Station
Road from double roundabout; SL7 1NQ*
Popular 18th-c red-brick beamed pub
renovated after major fire; good freshly
made food from lunchtime sandwiches up,
Brakspears, Fullers and Rebellion ales, over
20 wines by the glass including champagne,
friendly attentive service, various dining
areas including upstairs room and cellar
restaurant; children welcome, dogs in some
parts, seats outside, open all day (food all day
Sat, till 4pm Sun). *(Martin Jones)*

MARLOW BOTTOM   SU8588
Three Horseshoes (01628) 483109
*Signed from Handy Cross roundabout,
off M40 junction 4; SL7 3RA* Welcoming
much extended former coaching inn tied to
nearby Rebellion, their full range kept well
and served by knowledgeable uniformed
staff, extensive choice of reasonably priced
blackboard food (not Sun evening), good
value wines, beams and log fires, comfortable
traditional furnishings on different levels,
brewery photographs; children and dogs
welcome, big back garden, good walks
nearby, open all day Fri, Sat. *(Rob Anderson)*

MARSWORTH   SP9114
Red Lion (01296) 668366
*Vicarage Road; off B489 Dunstable–
Aylesbury; HP23 4LU* Partly thatched
18th-c pub close to impressive flight of locks
on Grand Union Canal; plain public bar
on right with quarry tiles, straightforward

furniture and small coal fire, Fullers
London Pride and good selection of guests,
traditional food at low prices, friendly
service, raised ceiling area with red leather
stools and sofas, multi-level lounge to left
with comfortable sofas in one part and
various knick-knacks, two-roomed games
area (bar billiards, darts and juke box);
children and dogs welcome, picnic-sets out
in front, back terrace with heated smokers'
gazebo, steps up to sizeable garden, more
seats on village green opposite with old
stocks. *(Susan and John Douglas)*

MOULSOE   SP9141
Carrington Arms (01908) 218050
*1.25 miles from M1 junction 14: A509
N, first right signed Moulsoe; Cranfield
Road; MK16 0HB* Good choice of well liked
food including chargrilled meats and fish
sold by weight from refrigerated display, up
to three changing ales, friendly helpful staff,
elegant open-plan layout; children allowed,
long pretty garden behind with giant chess
set, 16 bedrooms in two adjacent blocks,
open all day. *(Rob Anderson)*

NEWPORT PAGNELL   SP8743
Cannon (01908) 211495
High Street; MK16 8AQ Friendly little
bay-windowed drinkers' pub with interesting
military theme, four well kept reasonably
priced ales, carpeted half-panelled interior
with gas woodburner in central fireplace, live
music and comedy nights in room behind; TV,
juke box; seats out in small backyard, open
all day. *(John and Mary Warner)*

NEWTON LONGVILLE   SP8431
Crooked Billet (01908) 373936
*Off A421 S of Milton Keynes; Westbrook
End; MK17 0DF* Thatched pub under
newish management, good food from
sandwiches and pub favourites up, a beer
badged for them along with Greene King
Abbot and a guest, plenty of wines by the
glass, modernised extended pubby bar, log
fire in dining area; well behaved children
welcome, no dogs, tables out on lawn.
(John and Mary Warner)

OLNEY   SP8851
★**Swan** (01234) 711111
High Street S; MK46 4AA Cosy little pub
with beamed and timbered linked rooms,
good reasonably priced food (not Sun
evening, Mon) from sandwiches up, at least
three well kept changing ales and plenty of
wines by the glass, quick friendly service,
rather close-set pine tables, cheery log
fires, small back bistro dining room (booking
advised); courtyard tables, open all day (Sun
till 6pm). *(S Holder, Gerry and Rosemary Dobson)*

PENN   SU9093
★**Red Lion** (01494) 813107
Elm Road, B474; HP10 8LF Bustling
16th-c pub opposite village pond, various

bar rooms and mix of furniture including cushioned mate's chairs, settles and rustic tables with candlesticks, homely sofas and armchairs, rugs on ancient parquet or old quarry tiles, fantastic collection of British Empire prints and paintings, window sills and mantelpieces crammed with Staffordshire dogs, plates and old bottles, hop-strung beams, woodburner in big fireplace, Aylesbury, Chiltern and Windsor & Eton, real cider, well liked food including daily specials; TV and board games; children and dogs welcome, seats on front terrace, open all day; for sale as we went to press so things may change. *(Paul Humphreys, Tracey and Stephen Groves)*

PENN STREET   SU9295
★ **Hit or Miss**   (01494) 713109
Off A404 SW of Amersham, keep on towards Winchmore Hill; HP7 0PX Traditional pub under friendly licensees, heavily beamed main bar with leather sofas and armchairs on parquet flooring, horsebrasses, open fire, two carpeted rooms with interesting cricket and chair-making memorabilia, more sofas, wheelback and other dining chairs around pine tables, Badger ales (summer beer festival), interesting if not cheap food; background music, free wi-fi; children welcome, dogs in certain areas, picnic-sets on terrace overlooking pub's cricket pitch, open all day. *(Roy Hoing, D R Stevenson)*

PENN STREET   SU9295
Squirrel   (01494) 711291
Off A404 SW of Amersham, opposite the Common; HP7 0PX Friendly sister pub to nearby Hit or Miss, open-plan bar with flagstones, log fire and mix of furniture including comfortable sofas, reasonably priced home-made pubby food from baguettes up (not Sun evening, Mon), good children's meals too, up to five well kept ales such as Rebellion, Tring, Vale and XT, Weston's cider, bric-a-brac and cricketing memorabilia, sweets in traditional glass jars, live acoustic music Fri; covered outside deck with logburner, good play area in big garden with village cricket view, lovely walks, closed Mon lunchtime, otherwise open all day. *(Ross Balaam)*

POUNDON   SP6425
Sow & Pigs   (01869) 277728
Main Street; OX27 9BA Small beamed village local with L-shaped bar, Brakspears ales and maybe a Marstons-related guest, good well priced home-made food (not Sun evening, Tues) from short menu; sports TV;

children and dogs welcome, tables in good-sized back garden, open all day Fri, Sat, till 6pm Sun, from 4pm other days. *(John and Mary Warner)*

PRINCES RISBOROUGH   SP8104
Red Lion   (01844) 344476
Whiteleaf, off A4010; OS Sheet 165 map reference 817043; HP27 0LL Simple comfortably worn-in village pub with welcoming landlady, decent pub food at reasonable prices, well kept Sharps Doom Bar and a couple of guests, log fire, traditional games; children and walkers (no muddy boots) welcome, seats in garden behind, extensive views over to Oxfordshire, charming village, open all day weekends, closed Mon. *(Edward Mirzoeff)*

SKIRMETT   SU7790
★ **Frog**   (01491) 638996
From A4155 NE of Henley take Hambleden turn and keep on; or from B482 Stokenchurch–Marlow take Turville turn and keep on; RG9 6TG Pretty pub in Chilterns countryside; nice public bar with log fire, prints on walls, cushioned sofa and leather-seated stools on wood floor, high chairs by counter, Rebellion IPA, Gales Seafarer and a changing guest,18 wines by the glass including champagne, 24 malt whiskies, two dining rooms in different styles – one light and airy with country kitchen furniture, the other more formal with dark red walls, smarter furniture and candlelight, good interesting food (not always cheap) from baguettes and deli boards up, friendly attentive staff; background music; children welcome, dogs in bar (their black lab is Belle), side gate to lovely garden with unusual five-sided tables, attractive valley views and farmland walks, Chiltern Valley Winery & Brewery nearby, three comfortable bedrooms, closed Sun evening Oct–May. *(Simon Rodway, David Jackman, Paul Humphreys, Tracey and Stephen Groves, Richard Kennell and others)*

STOKE GOLDINGTON   SP8348
★ **Lamb**   (01908) 551233
High Street (B526 Newport Pagnell–Northampton); MK16 8NR Chatty village pub with friendly helpful licensees, up to four interesting changing ales, real ciders and good range of wines, enjoyable generous home-made food (all day Sat, not Sun evening) from baguettes to good value Sun roasts, lounge with log fire and sheep decorations, two small pleasant dining rooms, darts and table skittles in public bar; may be soft background music, TV; children

If a compulsory service charge is mentioned prominently on a menu or accommodation terms, you must pay it if service was satisfactory. If service is really bad, you are legally entitled to refuse to pay some or all of the service charge as compensation for not getting the service you might reasonably have expected.

and dogs welcome, terrace and sheltered garden behind with play equipment, bedrooms in adjacent cottage, closed Mon lunchtime, otherwise open all day (till 7pm Sun). *(Andrew Stone)*

STOKE MANDEVILLE   SP8310
★**Woolpack** (01296) 615970
Risborough Road (A4010 S of Aylesbury); HP22 5UP Thatched Mitchells & Butlers pub with boldly decorated contemporary interior, Brakspears, Purity Pure UBU and Sharps Doom Bar, several wines by the glass, cocktails, good choice of food including set weekday menu (till 6pm), amiable service and relaxed atmosphere; well behaved children allowed, seats in back garden and on the heated front terrace, open (and food) all day. *(Edward Mirzoeff)*

STONE   SP7912
Bugle Horn (01296) 747594
Oxford Road, Hartwell (A418 SW of Aylesbury); HP17 8QP Long 17th-c stone-built former farmhouse (Vintage Inn), comfortable linked rooms with mix of furniture, their usual choice of reasonably priced food including set menu till 5pm, three well kept ales and lots of wines by the glass, log fires, conservatory; children welcome, attractive terrace, lovely trees in big garden with pastures beyond, open (and food) all day. *(Graham and Carol Parker)*

STONY STRATFORD   SP7840
Old George (01908) 562181
High Street; MK11 1AA Attractive beamed and timbered inn dating from the 16th c, enjoyable good value food from sandwiches and wraps up, quick friendly service, real ales such as Marstons, Ringwood and Wychwood, dining room behind; background and some live music, quiz nights; upstairs lavatories; tables in back courtyard, 11 bedrooms, limited nearby parking. *(Rob Anderson)*

TAPLOW   SU9182
Oak & Saw (01628) 604074
Rectory Road; SL6 0ET Open-plan bare-boards local opposite attractive village green, clean and unpretentious, with well kept Brakspears, Fullers London Pride and a guest, tasty fairly priced food (not Sun evening, Mon) from well filled baguettes to dry-aged steaks, helpful friendly service, interesting pictures, central brick fireplace; children and dogs welcome, back terrace and lots of cheerful hanging baskets, closed Mon lunchtime, otherwise open all day. *(Paul Humphreys)*

THE LEE   SP8904
★**Cock & Rabbit** (01494) 837540
Back roads 2.5 miles N of Great Missenden, E of A413; HP16 9LZ Overlooking village green and run by same friendly italian family for over 25 years; much emphasis on their good

italian cooking, also lunchtime baps and Weds evening pasta deal, Greene King, Sharps and a beer named for the pub, plush-seated lounge, cosy dining room and larger restaurant; children welcome, dogs in bar, seats outside on verandah, terraces and lawn, good walks, open all day weekends. *(Roy Hoing)*

TURVILLE   SU7691
★**Bull & Butcher** (01491) 638283
Valley road off A4155 Henley–Marlow at Mill End, past Hambleden and Skirmett; RG9 6QU Popular black and white pub in pretty village (famous as film and TV setting), two traditional low-beamed rooms with inglenooks, wall settles in tiled-floor bar, deep well incorporated into glass-topped table, Brakspears ales kept well and decent wines by the glass, enjoyable traditional food including lunchtime sandwiches, friendly staff; background and some live music; children and dogs welcome, seats by fruit trees in attractive garden, good walks, closed Sun evening in winter otherwise open all day. *(David Tindal, Gordon Neighbour, Susan and John Douglas, Brian Glozier)*

WADDESDON   SP7316
Long Dog (01296) 651320
High Street; HP18 0JF Well renovated village pub with good tapas-style food from open-view kitchen, friendly accommodating service, well kept ales and nice choice of wines by the glass, bar area with open fire; background music, live jazz every other Tues; children and dogs welcome (resident dachshund), tables out front and back, very handy for Waddesdon Manor (NT), open (and food) all day. *(Rob Anderson)*

WEEDON   SP8118
Five Elms (01296) 641439
Stockaway; HP22 4NL Welcoming two-bar cottagey thatched pub, low beams and log fires, ample helpings of good traditional food cooked by landlord (best to book), Tring Side Pocket for a Toad or Skinners Betty Stogs kept well, good reasonably priced wines, old photographs and prints, separate dining room, games such as shove-ha'penny; a few picnic-sets out in front, pretty village, closed Sun evening. *(John and Mary Warner)*

WENDOVER   SP8609
Village Gate (01296) 623884
Aylesbury Road (B4009); HP22 6BA Country dining pub under new ownership; interconnected rooms with contemporary paintwork and furnishings, bar with woodburner in brick fireplace, ales such as St Austell, Tring and Wychwood Hobgoblin, good choice of well liked food from bar snacks and sharing boards to restaurant dishes, other rooms laid for eating with high-backed plush, wooden or leather dining chairs around mix of tables on oak boarding

(some carpeting and stone tiling too), one part with high-raftered ceiling; children welcome, outside seating including roped-off decked area, long-reaching country views, open all day, no food Sun evening. *(John and Mary Warner)*

WESTON UNDERWOOD   SP8650
Cowpers Oak (01234) 711382
Signed off A509 in Olney; High Street; MK46 5JS Wisteria-clad beamed village pub, enjoyable home-cooked food (special diets catered for), Hopping Mad, Woodfordes Wherry and a couple of guests, friendly helpful staff, nice mix of old-fashioned furnishings including pews, painted panelling and some stripped stone, two open fires, restaurant behind; background music, Mon quiz; children and dogs welcome, small suntrap front terrace, more tables on back decking and in big orchard garden, fenced play area, open all day weekends (till 9pm Sun). *(Andrew Stone)*

WINCHMORE HILL   SU9394
Plough (01494) 259757
The Hill; HP7 0PA Village pub/restaurant with italian-influenced food including good pizzas (landlord is from Campania), flagstones, low beams and open fires, linked dining area with polished wood floor, real ales and imported lagers, nice coffee, little shop selling italian wines and other produce; children welcome, tables on terrace and lawn, pleasant walks nearby, open all day from 9.30am for breakfast. *(Andrew Stone)*

WINSLOW   SP7627
Bell (01296) 714091
Market Square; MK18 3AB Fine old coaching inn back under ownership of good former landlord; friendly welcoming staff, reasonably priced food in beamed bar and carvery restaurant, Greene King ales; courtyard tables, character bedrooms. *(Dr W I C Clark)*

Post Office address codings confusingly give the impression that some pubs are in Buckinghamshire, when they're really in Bedfordshire or Berkshire (which is where we list them).

Cambridgeshire

 BALSHAM   TL5850 Map 5

Black Bull 🌟 🍺 🛏

(01223) 893844 – www.blackbull-balsham.co.uk

*Village signposted off A11 SW of Newmarket, and off A1307 in Linton; High Street;
CB21 4DJ*

**Pretty thatched pub with bedroom extension – a good all-rounder –
enjoyable food too**

The restoration of this 16th-c thatched inn has been done with great care,
preserving many original features while updating the décor. The beamed
bar spreads around a central servery where they keep their own-label Red
& Black Ale (from Nethergate) plus Adnams Ghost Ship, Hellhound Dirty
Blond and Woodfordes Wherry on handpump, 12 wines by the glass from
a good list, 15 malt whiskies, draught lager and interesting juices. Dividers
and standing timbers break up the space, which has an open fire (and
leather sofas in front of it), floorboards and low black beams in the front
part; furniture includes small leatherette-seated dining chairs. A restaurant
extension (in a listed barn) has a high-raftered oak panelled roof and a
network of standing posts and steel ties. The front terrace has teak tables
and chairs by a long, pleasantly old-fashioned verandah and there are more
seats in a small sheltered back garden. Smart, comfortable bedrooms are in
a neat single-storey extension. This pub has the same good owners as the
Red Lion at Hinxton.

🌟 The highly thought-of food includes sandwiches, home-cured salmon with
dill and lemon sauce, chicken caesar salad, burger with toppings, garlic
mayonnaise and chips, mushroom cottage pie, duck breast with confit leg and five-spice
sauce, rack of lamb with fondant potato and red wine sauce, baked cod with porcini
mushrooms and julienne of leek and bacon, and puddings such as white chocolate
crème brûlée and cinnamon doughnut with miniature toffee apple, apple purée and
salted caramel. *Benchmark main dish: steak in ale pie £14.00. Two-course evening
meal £20.00.*

Free house ~ Licensee Alex Clarke ~ Real ale ~ Open 7.30am (8.30am weekends)-11pm
(10.30pm Sun) ~ Bar food 12-2, 6.30-9; 12-2.30, 6.30-9.30 Fri, Sat; 12-3, 6.30-8.30 Sun ~
Restaurant ~ Well behaved children welcome ~ Dogs allowed in bar ~ Wi-fi ~ Bedrooms:
£90/£115 *Recommended by Caroline Prescott, Neil Allen, Carol and Barry Craddock*

Bedroom prices are for high summer. Even then you may get reductions for more than
one night, or (outside tourist areas) weekends. Winter special rates are common, and
many inns cut bedroom prices if you have a full evening meal.

BRANDON CREEK
TL6091   Map 5

Ship

(01353) 676228 – www.theshipbrandoncreek.co.uk

A10 Ely–Downham Market; PE38 0PP

Bustling pub in fine riverside spot with plenty of outside seating, cosy snug and busy bar, four ales, good wines by the glass and well liked food

A father and son team run this waterside 17th-c pub, and seats on the terrace and in the riverside garden make the most of its position. It's a friendly place and the carefully modernised bar at the centre of the building has massive stone masonry in the sunken former forge area, a big log fire at one end and a woodburning stove at the other, interesting old fenland photographs and prints, and paintings by local artists. Adnams Southwold, Woodfordes Wherry and a couple of guests such as Cottage Thunderbolt and Star Galaxy on handpump, nine wines by the glass, a dozen gins and farm cider; board games and background music. There's a cosy snug on the left with another open fire and a restaurant overlooking both the Great Ouse and the Little Ouse rivers; they have moorings for visiting boats.

Highly rated, seasonal food includes sandwiches and baguettes, parsnip panna cotta with candied beetroot, wild mushrooms in creamy sauce, chicken caesar salad, butternut and goats cheese risotto, a pie of the day, plaice with bacon and caper butter, rosemary and garlic lamb rump, venison haunch with red wine jus, and puddings such as white chocolate and rhubarb délice and baked yoghurt with cinnamon honey, toffee cherry and cider-poached apple. *Benchmark main dish: beer-battered fish and chips £10.00. Two-course evening meal £19.50.*

Free house ~ Licensee Mark Thomas ~ Real ale ~ Open 12-11 ~ Bar food 12-3, 6-9; 12-9 Sat; 12-8 Sun ~ Restaurant ~ Children welcome ~ Dogs allowed in bar ~ Wi-fi ~ Live music Fri evening *Recommended by Carol and Barry Craddock, Dr Simon Innes*

CAMBRIDGE
TL4459   Map 5

Punter

(01223) 3633221 – www.thepuntercambridge.com

Pound Hill, on corner of A1303 ring road; CB3 0AE

Good enterprising food in relaxed and interestingly furnished surroundings

The rambling and informal linked rooms here have quite a bit of character and are filled with paintings, antique prints and a pleasing choice of seating on old dark floorboards – pews, elderly dining chairs, Lloyd Loom easy chairs. One prized corner is down a few steps, behind a wooden railing. The scrubbed tables feature candles in bottles or assorted candlesticks, and staff are quick and friendly. Adnams Ghost Ship, an ale named for the pub from Oakham, Sharps Doom Bar and a guest ale on handpump and decent wines by the glass; board games and background jazz music. The flagstoned and mainly covered former coachyard has tables and picnic-table sets; beyond is a raftered barn bar, similar in style, with more pictures on its papered walls, a large rug on dark flagstones and a big-screen TV. This is sister pub to the Punter in Oxford.

As well as their bargain £5 lunch dishes, the good, interesting food includes rabbit rillettes with plum chutney, whitebait with cayenne mayonnaise, halloumi with baby spinach, golden beetroot, toasted pine nuts and tahini honey dressing, roast chicken with harissa yoghurt and tabbouleh, burger with toppings and chips, steak or fish pie, and puddings. *Benchmark main dish: venison steak with garlic butter and chips £13.50. Two-course evening meal £18.00.*

Punch ~ Lease Paul Fox ~ Real ale ~ Open 12-midnight (11.30 Sun) ~ Bar food 12-3, 6-10; 12-10 Sat; 12-9 Sun ~ Children welcome ~ Dogs welcome ~ Wi-fi
Recommended by Lindy Andrews, Isobel Mackinlay, Mrs Margo Finlay, Jörg Kasprowski

 DUXFORD   TL4746   Map 5

John Barleycorn 🛏

(01223) 832699 – www.johnbarleycorn.co.uk
Handy for M11 junction 10; right at first roundabout, then left at main village junction; CB22 4PP

Pretty pub with friendly staff, attractive beamed interior, real ales and good wines, enjoyable food and seats on terrace and in garden; bedrooms in converted barn

A t the far end of the village, this early 17th-c building is a charming former coaching inn with a low thatched roof and shuttered windows. Inside, standing timbers and brick pillars create alcoves and different drinking and dining areas: hops on heavy beams and nice old floor tiles, log fires, all manner of seating from rustic blue-painted cushioned settles through white-painted and plain wooden dining chairs to some rather fine antique farmhouse chairs and quite a mix of wooden tables. There's also a lot to look at, including china plates, copper pans, old clocks, a butterchurn, a large stuffed fish and plenty of pictures on blue or pale yellow walls. Greene King Abbot and IPA and guests such as Hook Norton Hooky and Timothy Taylors Landlord on handpump and ten wines by the glass; background music. There are blue-painted picnic-sets beside pretty hanging baskets on the front terrace and more picnic-sets among flowering tubs and shrubs in the back garden. This is a comfortable place to stay. The pub was used by the young airmen of Douglas Bader's Duxford Wing during World War II. The Air Museum is close by.

Enjoyable food includes sandwiches (until 6pm), smoked kipper and scottish whisky pâté, garlic and rosemary-infused baked camembert with red onion marmalade, grazing boards, local sausages and mash with veal jus, honey-roasted butternut squash risotto with halloumi cheese, steak burger with toppings, coleslaw and chips, yellow-fin tuna in lime and coriander and pak choi in a ginger and carrot broth, and puddings. *Benchmark main dish: pie of the day £11.45. Two-course evening meal £17.00.*

Greene King ~ Tenant Nicholas Kersey ~ Real ale ~ Open 11-11 (10.30 Sun) ~ Bar food 12-3, 5-9.30; 12-9.30 Fri, Sat; 12-8 Sun ~ Children welcome ~ Dogs allowed in bar ~ Wi-fi ~ Bedrooms: /£79.50 *Recommended by Gordon and Margaret Ormondroyd, Pat and Stewart Gordon, Lindy Andrews, Charlie May*

 ELTON   TL0894   Map 5

Crown 🕼✪ ♀ 🛏

(01832) 280232 – www.thecrowninn.org
Off B671 S of Wansford (A1/A47), and village signposted off A605 Peterborough–Oundle; Duck Street; PE8 6RQ

Pretty pub in charming village with interesting food, several real ales, well chosen wines and a friendly atmosphere; stylish bedrooms

R un with care by the chef-patron and his friendly staff, this is a lovely golden stone and thatched village pub (follow the brown sign towards Nassington to find it). The softly lit beamed bar has leather and antique dining chairs around a nice mix of chunky tables on bare boards, an open fire in a stone fireplace and good pictures and pubby ornaments on pastel walls. The beamed main dining area has fresh flowers and candles and similar tables and chairs on stripped wooden flooring, and there's a carefully refurbished dining extension too. High bar chairs against the counter are popular with locals, and they keep Golden Crown (brewed for them by Tydd Steam), Grainstore Phipps IPA, Greene King IPA and a guest or two on handpump, well chosen wines by the glass and farm cider; board games, background music and TV. There are tables outside on the front terrace. The bedrooms are smart, comfortable and well equipped and the breakfasts are especially good. Elton Mill and Lock are close by.

Cooked by the landlord, the extremely good food includes sandwiches and baguettes, pork liver and wild mushroom pâté with red onion chutney, cod cheek with crispy fried chorizo, samphire and crab bisque, honey-glazed, home-cooked ham with free-range egg, home-made faggot with bubble and squeak, crispy bacon and shallot jus, rump of lamb with baby vegetables, salsa verde and mint sauce, and puddings such as apple and blackberry pie with apple crumble ice-cream and chocolate brownie with salted caramel sauce. *Benchmark main dish: slow-roasted pork shoulder with crispy bacon hash brown, apple purée and cauliflower cheese £15.95. Two-course evening meal £25.00.*

Free house ~ Licensee Marcus Lamb ~ Real ale ~ Open 12-11 ~ Bar food 12-2 (12-4 bank hols), 7-9 ~ Restaurant ~ Children welcome ~ Dogs allowed in bar ~ Wi-fi ~ Bedrooms: £72/£117 *Recommended by Barry Collett, George Atkinson, Peter and Jean Hoare*

FEN DRAYTON
TL3468   Map 5

Three Tuns

(01954) 230242 – www.the3tuns.co.uk

Off A14 NW of Cambridge at Fenstanton; High Street; CB24 5SJ

Lovely old pub with traditional furnishings in bar and dining room, real ales, tasty food and seats in garden

This is a lovely old building with a lot of history – it may have been the medieval guildhall for the pretty village, and its heavy-set moulded Tudor beams and timbers were certainly built to last. The three rooms are more or less open-plan, with a mix of burgundy cushioned stools, nice old dining chairs and settles in the friendly bar and wooden dining chairs and tables on the red-patterned carpet in the dining room; framed prints of the pub too. Open fires in each room help create a warm and relaxed atmosphere, all helped along by the friendly licensees. Greene King IPA and Old Speckled Hen, Mauldons Bronze Adder and Timothy Taylors Boltmaker on handpump and a dozen wines by the glass. A well tended lawn at the back has seats and tables, a covered dining area and a play area for children.

As well as an OAP weekday lunch deal and a takeaway evening menu (Mon-Thurs), the fairly priced, popular food includes lunchtime sandwiches and wraps, lamb samosas with yoghurt and mint dressing, lemon and pepper scallops with lemon mayonnaise, a pie of the day, chicken balti, vegetable enchiladas with guacamole and sour cream, gammon steak with onion rings, egg or pineapple and chips, tuna steak with lemon and herb butter, and puddings such as crème brûlée or cheesecake of the day. *Benchmark main dish: chicken fajitas £10.25. Two-course evening meal £16.00.*

Greene King ~ Tenants Mr and Mrs Baretto ~ Real ale ~ Open 12-3, 6-11 (12-11 Fri, Sat in summer); 12-4 Sun ~ Bar food 12-2, 6-9 (9.30 Fri, Sat); 12-2 Sun ~ Restaurant ~ Children welcome ~ Dogs allowed in bar ~ Wi-fi *Recommended by Pat and Graham Williamson, B and M Kendall, George Atkinson, Gordon and Margaret Ormondroyd*

GREAT WILBRAHAM

TL5558 Map 5

Carpenters Arms 🍽 ♀ 🍺

(01223) 882093 – www.carpentersarmsgastropub.co.uk

Off A14 or A11 SW of Newmarket, following The Wilbrahams signposts; High Street; CB21 5JD

Inviting village pub with traditional bar, good food in both the bar and back restaurant; nice garden

The low-ceilinged village bar on the right is properly pubby with bar billiards, a woodburning stove in a big inglenook and their own-brewed Crafty Beers Carpenters Cask, Mild Mannered and Sauvignon Blonde on handpump. Also, a carefully chosen wine list (strong on the Roussillon region), copper pots and iron tools, and cushioned pews and simple seats around solid pub tables on floor tiles; background music. Service is spot on: thoughtful, helpful and cheerful. On the left, a small, cosy, carpeted dining area has another big stone fireplace and overflowing bookshelves; this leads through to a sitting area with comfortable sofas and plenty of magazines. The light and airy extended main dining room has country kitchen chairs around chunky tables. A huge honeysuckle swathes the tree in the pretty back courtyard, and, further on, an attractive homely garden, with fruit and vegetables, has round picnic-sets shaded by tall trees.

 Excellent food cooked by the landlady using home-grown and other local produce has french influences: sandwiches and baguettes, country terrine with home-made chutney, warm salad of duck confit with five-spice dressing and mango, pomegranate and spring onion salad, tartiflette (potatoes, onions and bacon baked with cream and reblochon cheese), chicken breast with coriander butter and walnut sauce, beef filled with spicy cocoa sauce and mushroom fricassée, and puddings such as catalan crème brûlée and crumble of the day. *Benchmark main dish: slow-roast pork belly with cinnamon and apple cider sauce and red cabbage £14.50. Two-course evening meal £22.00*

Free house ~ Licensees Rick and Heather Hurley ~ Real ale ~ Open 11.30-3, 6.30-11; 11.30-3 Sun; closed Sun evening, Tues ~ Bar food 12-2.15, 7-9; 12-3 Sun ~ Restaurant ~ Children welcome ~ Wi-fi *Recommended by Steve and Suzanne Griffiths, M and GR, Michael Butler*

HEMINGFORD ABBOTS

TL2870 Map 5

Axe & Compass

(01480) 463605 – www.axeandcompass.co.uk

High Street; village signposted off A14 W of Cambridge; PE28 9AH

Thatched pub in charming village with several linked rooms, a good range of drinks and food served by friendly staff and seats and a play area outside

There's always a happy mix of customers in this bustling, partly 15th-c pub – and plenty of space in the various linked rooms. The simple, beamed public bar has mate's chairs and stools around wooden tables on lovely ancient floor tiles, and an open two-way fireplace (not in use) into the snug next door where there's a woodburning stove. The main room has more beams and standing timbers, tweed tartan-patterned chairs and armchairs and cushioned wall seating around nice old tables on wood floors, local photographs, a TV at each end and stools against the counter where they serve Adnams Lighthouse, Oakham Inferno and Sharps Doom Bar on handpump, 12 wines by the glass and local cider; there's a second woodburner in a small brick fireplace. The long dining room has more photos on green walls and high-backed dark leather dining and other chairs around pale wooden tables. The garden, between the pretty thatched pub and the tall-spired church, has a fenced-off area with play equipment, contemporary seats and tables on the terrace and picnic-sets on grass. Disabled facilities.

From a well thought-out menu the popular food includes sandwiches, nibbles to share, salt and pepper calamari, eggs benedict on toasted brioche, beer-battered cod and chips, sweet potato and chickpea curry, chargrilled thyme and oregano chicken with creamed leeks and hash browns, pork medallions with a mushroom and brandy cream sauce, and puddings such as lemon tart with berry coulis and vanilla cheesecake with white chocolate sauce; they also offer a two- and three-course set weekday lunch. *Benchmark main dish: home-made pies £11.95. Two-course evening meal £18.00.*

Enterprise ~ Lease Emma Tester ~ Real ale ~ Open 12-11 (10 Mon in winter); 12-8 Sun ~ Bar food 12-2.30, 6-9; 12-9 Sat; 12-4 Sun ~ Restaurant ~ Well behaved children welcome ~ Dogs allowed in bar ~ Wi-fi ~ Live music first Fri of month *Recommended by Toby Jones, Kevin Adams*

HEMINGFORD GREY   TL2970   Map 5

Cock ★ ♀ ◧

(01480) 463609 – www.cambscuisine.com/the-cock-hemingford
Village signposted off A14 eastbound, and (via A1096 St Ives road) westbound; High Street; PE28 9BJ

Imaginative food in pretty pub with extensive wine list, four interesting beers, a bustling atmosphere and a smart restaurant

A charming pub for both drinkers and diners, this is in a delightful village on the River Ouse. The bar rooms have white-painted or dark beams and lots of contemporary pale yellow and cream paintwork, fresh flowers and church candles, artworks here and there, and throughout a really attractive mix of old wooden dining chairs, settles and tables. They've sensibly kept the traditional public bar on the left for drinkers only: an open woodburning stove on a raised hearth, bar stools, wall seats and a carver, and steps that lead down to more seating. Brewsters Hophead, Elgoods Cambridge Bitter, Great Oakley Wagtail and Oldershaw Great Expectations on handpump, 18 wines by the glass mainly from the Languedoc-Roussillon region, Calvors (an East Anglian lager) and Cromwell cider (made in the village); they hold a beer festival every August Bank Holiday weekend. In marked contrast, the stylishly simple restaurant on the right – you must book to be sure of a table – is set for dining, with flowers on each table, pale wooden floorboards and another woodburning stove. There are seats and tables among stone troughs and flowers on the terrace and in the neat garden, and pretty hanging baskets. Sister pub is the Tickell Arms in Whittlesford.

Championing the best local produce, the exceptional food includes lunchtime sandwiches, goat and apricot terrine with aubergine and mint chutney, pheasant and squash pithivier with pickled shallots and crispy sage, home-made sausages with a choice of sauces, a daily fresh fish dish such as smoked haddock, leek and mustard fishcakes with roast garlic mayonnaise, chicken supreme stuffed with truffle mousse with mushroom purée, potato terrine and port sauce, and puddings such as Malteser and white chocolate cheesecake with salted caramel and rosewater and vanilla panna cotta with raspberry sorbet; they also offer a two- and three-course weekday set lunch and have a steak and chop night on Tuesdays. *Benchmark main dish: sea bass fillets with dill and lemon potatoes, roast beetroot and carrot butter sauce £17.50. Two-course evening meal £23.00.*

Free house ~ Licensees Oliver Thain and Richard Bradley ~ Real ale ~ Open 11.30-3, 6-11; 11.30-11 Sat; 12-10.30 Sun ~ Bar food 12-2.30, 6.30 (6 Fri, Sat)-9; 12-2.45, 6.30-8.30 Sun ~

Restaurant ~ Children allowed in bar lunchtime only; must be over 5 in evening restaurant ~ Dogs allowed in bar ~ Wi-fi *Recommended by Revd R P Tickle, Gordon and Margaret Ormondroyd*

HINXTON   TL4945 Map 5
Red Lion 🌟 � 🍺 ⇌

(01799) 530601 – www.redlionhinxton.co.uk

2 miles off M11 junction 9 northbound; take first exit off A11, A1301 N, then left turn into village – High Street; a little further from junction 10, via A505 E and A1301 S; CB10 1QY

16th-c pub with friendly staff, interesting bar food, real ales and a big landscaped garden; comfortable bedrooms

With winter open fires and a big, neatly kept garden for warmer weather, this pink-washed old place is perfect at any time of the year. The low-beamed bar has oak chairs and tables on bare boards, two leather chesterfield sofas, an open fire and an old wall clock and a relaxed, friendly atmosphere. Their own-label Red & Black Ale (from the local Nethergate Brewery) plus Adnams Ghost Ship, Woodfordes Wherry and a guest such as Crafty Beers Sauvignon Blonde on handpump, 20 wines by the glass, 15 malt whiskies and first class service. An informal dining area has high-backed settles, and the smart restaurant (with oak rafters and traditional dry peg construction) is decorated with various pictures and assorted clocks. Outside, there are teak tables and chairs on a terrace, picnic-sets on grass, a dovecote and views of the village church; another terrace by the porch has a huge parasol for sunny days. Well equipped, pretty bedrooms are in a separate flint and brick building. The pub is handy for the Imperial War Museum at Duxford. They also own the Black Bull in Balsham just up the road.

🌟 Impressive food includes sandwiches and baguettes, ham mousse with red pepper salsa, smoked venison loin with redcurrant coulis, cherry tomato and basil risotto with parmesan crisp, smoked haddock and salmon fishcake with pomegranate and fennel salad and dill mayonnaise, steak in ale pie, free-range chicken with toasted fennel, jus and sweet potato chips, and puddings such as chocolate and orange tart with mango sorbet and rhubarb crème brûlée. *Benchmark main dish: lamb rump with cumin and coriander puy lentils, curly kale and red wine jus £18.00. Two-course evening meal £20.00.*

Free house ~ Licensee Alex Clarke ~ Real ale ~ Open 7.30am (8.30am weekends)-11pm (10.30pm Sun) ~ Bar food 12-2, 6.30-9; 12-2.30, 6.30-9.30 Fri, Sat; 12-8.30 Sun ~ Restaurant ~ Well behaved children welcome ~ Dogs allowed in bar ~ Wi-fi ~ Bedrooms: £95/£120
Recommended by Mrs Margo Finlay, Jörg Kasprowski, Tom and Ruth Rees, Gerry and Rosemary Dobson

HUNTINGDON   TL2471 Map 5
Old Bridge Hotel 🌟 � ⇌

(01480) 424300 – www.huntsbridge.com

1 High Street; ring road just off B1044 entering from easternmost A14 slip road; PE29 3TQ

Georgian hotel with smartly pubby bar, splendid range of drinks, first class service and excellent food; fine bedrooms

You can pop into this extremely civilised and warmly friendly place at any time of the day for morning coffee, afternoon tea, all-day snacks and an interesting choice of lunch and supper – our readers love it. And while the hotel side clearly dominates, there's a wide mix of customers who very much enjoy the traditional pubby bar. This has a log fire, comfortable sofas and low wooden tables on polished floorboards, and Adnams Bitter, Hart No 1 and Nene Valley Australian Pale on handpump. They also have an exceptional wine list (up to 36 by the glass in the bar) and a wine shop where you can taste a selection of the wines before you buy. Food is available in the big airy Terrace (an indoor room, but with beautifully painted verdant murals suggesting the open air) or in the slightly more formal panelled restaurant. There are seats and tables on the terrace by the Great Ouse, and they have their own landing stage. This is a special place to stay in luxurious bedrooms, some of which overlook the river.

Delicious food includes hot and cold sandwiches, foie gras set in roast onion jam, salmon gravadlax with crab and fennel coleslaw, girolle, leek and camembert puff pastry pie, pork and leek sausages with white onion and mustard sauce, halibut fillet with mussel and garlic risotto and samphire, truffle and honey-glazed gressingham duck breast with fondant potato and turnips cooked in merlot, and puddings such as chocolate tart with white chocolate chip ice-cream and panna cotta with poached rhubarb; the good british cheeseboard is served with quince jelly and home-made biscuits. *Benchmark main dish: aberdeen angus steak ciabatta sandwich with caramelised onions and grain mustard £9.95. Two-course evening meal £26.00.*

Huntsbridge ~ Licensee John Hoskins ~ Real ale ~ Open 11-11 ~ Bar food 12-2, 6.30-10 ~ Restaurant ~ Children welcome ~ Dogs allowed in bar and bedrooms ~ Wi-fi ~ Bedrooms: £99/£180 *Recommended by Michael Sargent, Mrs Margo Finlay, Jörg Kasprowski, Isobel Mackinlay, Lindy Andrews*

KEYSTON

TL0475 Map 5

Pheasant ★○│ ♀

(01832) 710241 – www.thepheasant-keyston.co.uk
Just off A14 SE of Thrapston; brown sign to pub down village loop road, off B663; PE28 0RE

• •
Cambridgeshire Dining Pub of the Year

Good civilised country dining pub with appealing décor and attractive garden

With excellent food and a fine range of ales and wines, this lovely thatched old place is a favourite with numerous customers. The main bar has pitched rafters high above and lower dark beams in side areas, while the central serving area has padded stools along the leather-quilted counter and dark flagstones, with hop bines above the handpumps for Adnams Southwold, Brewsters Hophead and Digfield Fools Nook, and a tempting array of 14 wines by the glass. Nearby are armchairs, a chesterfield, quite a throne of a seat carved in 17th-c style, other comfortable seats around low tables, and a log fire in a lofty fireplace. The rest of the pub is mostly red-carpeted with dining chairs around a variety of polished tables, and large sporting prints – even hunting-scene wallpaper in one part. Lighted candles and tea-lights throughout, and the attentive attitude of neat friendly staff, add to the feeling of well-being. The attractively planted and well kept garden behind has tables on lawn and terrace, and there are picnic-sets in front. This is a quiet farming hamlet.

The landlord cooks the first class food which includes crab linguine with chilli, ginger and mint, hare terrine with burnt orange purée and cranberry sauce, ricotta and spinach tart with fennel and red onion marmalade, free-range pork sausages with leeks and onion purée, salmon with sesame gnocchi, pak choi and wok-fried greens with chilli, corn-fed chicken with truffle mash, celeriac purée, capers and tarragon, and puddings such as pot au chocolat with mascarpone and griottine cherries and lemongrass panna cotta with rhubarb sorbet and pineapple; they also offer a two- and three-course set menu (not Saturday evening, Sunday or Monday). *Benchmark main dish: local venison with roast beetroot, sauerkraut and orange and red wine sauce £18.95. Two-course evening meal £20.00.*

Free house ~ Licensee Simon Cadge ~ Real ale ~ Open 12-3, 6-11; 12-midnight Fri, Sat; 12-5 Sun; closed Sun evening, Mon ~ Bar food 12-2 (2.30 Fri, Sat), 6.30-9.30; 12-3.30 Sun ~ Restaurant ~ Children welcome ~ Dogs allowed in bar ~ Wi-fi *Recommended by Michael Sargent, Alex and Hazel Evans, J F M and M West*

KIMBOLTON
TL0967 Map 5
New Sun 🏅🍷
(01480) 860052 – www.newsuninn.co.uk
High Street; PE28 0HA

Interesting bars and rooms, tapas menu plus other good food, and a pleasant back garden

This interesting and well run old place is on the lovely main street, so customers tend to drop in and out all day from morning coffee onwards. The cosiest room is perhaps the low-beamed front lounge with standing timbers and exposed brickwork, a couple of comfortable armchairs and a sofa beside a log fire, and books on shelves. This leads into a narrower locals' bar with Charles Wells Bombardier and Eagle and a weekly changing guest on handpump, 17 wines by the glass (including champagne and pudding wines) and 11 gins; background music, board games, piano and quiz machine. The traditionally furnished dining room opens off here. The airy conservatory with high-backed leather dining chairs has doors leading to the terrace where there are smart seats and tables under giant umbrellas. Note that some of the nearby parking spaces have a 30-minute limit.

 Consistently enjoyable food includes lunchtime sandwiches and baked potatoes, lots of tapas such as spanish meats with manchego, fried squid with aioli and pork belly nuggets with quince paste, king prawns in garlic and chilli, mushroom and red onion stroganoff, home-cooked ham and free-range eggs, sea bream with squid and chorizo, veal rump with bourguignon sauce, rack of local lamb with wild mushroom casserole and dauphinoise potatoes, and puddings such as vanilla panna cotta with mulled, spiced pear and Malteser cheesecake. *Benchmark main dish: steak and kidney pudding £11.00. Two-course evening meal £18.50.*

Wells & Youngs ~ Lease Stephen and Elaine Rogers ~ Real ale ~ Open 11.30-11; 12-10.30 Sun ~ Bar food 12-2.15 (2.30 Sun), 7-9.30; not Sun or Mon evenings ~ Restaurant ~ Well behaved children welcome away from bar ~ Dogs allowed in bar ~ Wi-fi
Recommended by Mike and Mary Carter, Carol and Barry Craddock

PETERBOROUGH
TL1899 Map 5
Brewery Tap 🍺 £
(01733) 358500 – www.thebrewery-tap.com
Opposite Queensgate car park; PE1 2AA

Fantastic range of real ales including their own brews, popular thai food and a lively, friendly atmosphere

There are claims that this multi-award-winning microbrewery, Oakham Ales (housed in a striking modern conversion of an old labour exchange), is the largest brewpub in Europe. The open-plan contemporary interior has an expanse of light wood and stone floors and blue-painted iron pillars holding up a steel-corded mezzanine level. It's stylishly lit by a giant suspended steel ring with bulbs running around the rim and steel-meshed wall lights. A band of chequered floor tiles traces the path of the long sculpted pale wood bar counter, which is boldly backed by an impressive display of bottles in a ceiling-high wall of wooden cubes. There's also a comfortable downstairs area, a big-screen TV for sporting events, background music and regular live bands and comedy nights. A two-storey glass wall gives fascinating views of the brewery, from which they produce their own Oakham Bishops Farewell, Black Hole Porter, Citra, Inferno, JHB and seasonal ales; also, up to eight guests, quite a few whiskies and several wines by the glass. It gets very busy in the evening.

The thai food remains incredibly popular. As well as set menus and specials, you might find tom yum soup, chicken, beef, pork, prawn, duck and vegetable curries, stir-fried crispy chilli beef, talay pad cha (prawns, squid and mussels with crushed garlic, chilli and ginger), various noodle dishes, all sorts of salads and stir-fries and five kinds of rice. *Benchmark main dish: pad thai noodles £7.50. Two-course evening meal £15.00.*

Own brew ~ Licensee Jessica Loock ~ Real ale ~ Open 12-11 (10.30 Sun) ~ Bar food 12-2.30, 5.30-9.30; 12-10.30 Thurs-Sat; 12-3.30, 5.30-9.30 Sun ~ Restaurant ~ Children welcome during food service times only ~ Dogs allowed in bar ~ Wi-fi *Recommended by Pat and Tony Martin, Martin Jones*

REACH
Dykes End 🍺

TL5666 Map 5

(01638) 743816 – www.dykesend.co.uk
From B1102 follow signpost to Swaffham Prior and Upware; village signposted; CB25 0JD

Candlelit rooms in former farmhouse, enjoyable food and own-brewed beer

For locals, this 17th-c former farmhouse is the heart of their village; for visitors, it's a welcome stop for refreshment after walking nearby Devil's Dyke. It's a pub that remains proud of old-fashioned values such as no background music, games machines, food sachets or paper napkins. A high-backed winged settle screens off the door, and the simply decorated ochre-walled bar has stripped heavy pine tables and pale kitchen chairs on dark boards and a couple of rugs. In a panelled section on the left are a few rather smarter dining tables, and on the right a step leads down to a red-carpeted part with the small red-walled servery and sensibly placed darts at the back; board games. All the tables have lighted candles and there may be a big bowl of flowers to brighten up the serving counter. Adnams Southwold, Mighty Oak Oscar Wilde, Sharps Special Ale and Thwaites Wainwright on handpump alongside a decent wine list, and Old Rosie cider. There are picnic-sets under parasols on the front grass.

Proper home-made food using seasonal produce includes lunchtime sandwiches, ham hock terrine with piccalilli, pear, goats cheese, baby gem and walnut salad, vegetable cassoulet, local sausages with onion gravy, beer-battered haddock and chips, chicken parmigiana, steak-frites, and puddings such as ginger parkin with muscovado sauce and golden syrup crème brûlée. *Benchmark main dish: bouillabaisse £13.95. Two-course evening meal £20.00.*

Free house ~ Licensee George Gibson ~ Real ale ~ Open 12-2.30, 6-11; 12-11 Sat; 12-10.30 Sun; closed Mon lunchtime ~ Bar food 12-1.45, 6.45-8.45; not Sun evening, Mon ~ Restaurant ~ Children allowed but must be well behaved ~ Dogs welcome ~ Wi-fi *Recommended by Hilary and Neil Christopher, Andrew Stone*

STILTON

TL1689   Map 5

Bell ♀ ⇔

(01733) 241066 – www.thebellstilton.co.uk

High Street; village signposted from A1 S of Peterborough; PE7 3RA

Fine coaching inn with several civilised rooms including a residents' bar, popular food, a thoughtful choice of drinks and seats in a very pretty courtyard; bedrooms

Although the left-hand side here is a civilised hotel in a lovely former coaching inn, our readers tend to head for the two neatly kept right-hand bars (which have the most character). There are bow windows, sturdy upright wooden seats on flagstone floors, and a good big log fire in one handsome stone fireplace. The partly stripped walls have big prints of sailing and winter coaching scenes and a giant pair of blacksmith's bellows hangs in the middle of the front bar. Digfield Fools Nook, Grainstore Rutland Panther, Greene King IPA and Old Speckled Hen and Oakham Bishops Farewell on handpump, quite a few malt whiskies and around a dozen wines by the glass; service is helpful and welcoming. Other rooms include a residents' bar, a bistro and a restaurant; background music and TV. Through the fine coach arch is a very pretty sheltered courtyard with tables, and a well that dates from Roman times. The bedrooms mix old-world charm with modern facilities and three are on the ground floor.

Enjoyable food includes stilton pâté with celery chutney, oak-smoked salmon with citrus potato salad, sausages of the day with onion rings and gravy, a changing vegetarian pasta dish, cod on butternut squash risotto with a tomato and basil sauce, chicken with wild mushroom and stilton sauce, beef bourguignon, pork belly with black pudding mash and apple and calvados jus, and puddings such as sticky toffee pudding with clotted cream and lemon tart with blood orange sorbet. *Benchmark main dish: steak burger topped with stilton £13.65. Two-course evening meal £20.00.*

Free house ~ Licensee Liam McGivern ~ Real ale ~ Open 12-2.30, 6-11; 12-midnight Sat; 12-10.30 Sun ~ Bar food 12-2 (2.30 Sat), 6-9.30; 12-3, 6-9 Sun ~ Restaurant ~ Children welcome ~ Wi-fi ~ Bedrooms: £80/£108 *Recommended by Margaret and Peter Staples, Mrs J Kavanagh, Gus Swan, Emma Scofield*

UFFORD

TF0904   Map 5

White Hart ◨ ⇔

(01780) 740250 – www.whitehartufford.co.uk

Main Street; S on to Ufford Road off B1443 at Bainton, then right; PE9 3BH

Lots of interest in bustling pub, plenty of drinking and dining space, interesting food and extensive garden; bedrooms

This is a friendly 17th-c stone pub in a pretty village with three acres of gardens at the back; as well as a sunken dining area with plenty of chairs and tables and picnic-sets on the grass, there are steps up to various quiet corners and lovely flowers and shrubs. Inside, the bar has an easy-going atmosphere, railway memorabilia, farm tools and chamber pots, scatter cushions on leather benches, some nice old chairs and tables, a woodburning stove, exposed stone walls and stools against the counter where they serve Adnams Southwold, Fullers London Pride, Oakham JHB and a guest beer on handpump and several wines by the glass. There's also an elegant beamed restaurant and an airy Orangery. Four of the comfortable bedrooms are in the pub, with two more in a converted cart shed and four new ones in the Old Brewery.

As well as lunchtime baguettes and ciabattas, the popular food includes chicken liver parfait with chutney, prawn and avocado tian with tomato and herb salsa, several platters, honey and mustard-glazed ham and free-range eggs, vegetable risotto with aged parmesan, burger with lots of toppings and chips, lamb shank with redcurrant and thyme jus, salmon fillet with chive butter sauce, duck breast with orange jus and cider-braised red cabbage, and puddings such as chocolate and walnut praline and pineapple upside-down cake with cardamom ice-cream; they also offer a two- and three-course set lunch. *Benchmark main dish: pork and stilton wellington with wholegrain mustard mash and cider cream sauce £14.95. Two-course evening meal £20.00.*

Free house ~ Licensee Sue Olver ~ Real ale ~ Open 9am-11pm ~ Bar food 12-2.30, 6-9.30; 12-3 Sun (maybe till 5 in summer) ~ Restaurant ~ Children welcome ~ Dogs allowed in bar ~ Wi-fi ~ Bedrooms: /£85 *Recommended by Gordon and Margaret Ormondroyd*

WHITTLESFORD TL4648 Map 5

Tickell Arms

(01223) 833025 – www.cambscuisine.com/the-tickell-whittlesford

2.4 miles from M11 junction 10: A505 towards Newmarket, then 2nd turn left signposted Whittlesford; keep on into North Road; CB22 4NZ

Light and refreshing dining pub with good enterprising food and pretty garden

The main emphasis here is on the dining area on the right, reached through an ornate (and rare, says one reader) glazed partition, but there's also a proper L-shaped bar with floor tiles, on the left. This contains three porcelain handpumps from the era of the legendarily autocratic regime of the Wagner-loving former owner Kim Tickell; these are now orphaned and decorate a high 'counter' that's suspended between a pair of ornate cast-iron pillars and lined with bentwood bar stools. Under bowler-hatted lampshades over the counter, neatly dressed and friendly staff serve Brewsters Hophead, Elgoods Cambridge Bitter, Milton Pegasus and Nethergate Old Growler on handpump and a good range of fairly priced wines by the glass including champagne. Tables in the dining room vary from sturdy to massive, with leather-cushioned bentwood and other dining chairs and one dark pew, and fresh minimalist décor in palest buff. This opens into an even lighter limestone-floored conservatory area, partly divided by a very high-backed ribbed-leather banquette. The side terrace has comfortable tables, and the secluded garden beyond has pergolas and a pond. This is sister pub to the Cock in Hemingford Grey.

Inventive food using the best seasonal produce includes lunchtime sandwiches, baked camembert with apple and thyme jam, hazelnut-crusted pigeon with celeriac rémoulade with sultana and pine nut dressing, crispy egg and truffled polenta with shallots, asparagus and broad beans, sausages and mash with caramelised onion gravy, bream fillet with herb gnocchi, chestnut mushrooms, salsify and mushroom sauce, and puddings such as coffee and banana mousse with roasted coffee beans and chilled Calvados rice pudding and pear jelly; steak and chop night is Tuesday and they also offer a two and three-course set weekday lunchtime menu. *Benchmark main dish: lamb with carrots, chive potatoes and red wine sauce £17.00. Two-course evening meal £23.00.*

Free house ~ Licensees Oliver Thain, Richard Bradley and Max Freeman ~ Real ale ~ Open 12-3, 6-11; 12-10.30 Sun ~ Bar food 12-2.30, 6.30-9 (9.30 Fri); 12-3, 6-9.30 Sat; 12-3, 6-8 Sun ~ Restaurant ~ Children must be over 10 in pub and over 5 in restaurant ~ Dogs allowed in bar ~ Wi-fi *Recommended by Hilary and Neil Christopher, Alison and Michael Harper*

Also Worth a Visit in Cambridgeshire

Besides the fully inspected pubs, you might like to try these pubs that have been recommended to us and described by readers. Do tell us what you think of them: feedback@goodguides.com

---

ABBOTS RIPTON   TL2377

Abbots Elm (01487) 773773
B1090; PE28 2PA Open-plan thatched dining pub reconstructed after major fire; good food from bar meals to interesting restaurant dishes, set menus too, extensive choice of wines by the glass including champagne, three well kept ales, good service; children and dogs welcome, three bedrooms, open all day Sat, till 5pm Sun. *(Anne Morton)*

ABINGTON PIGOTTS   TL3044

Pig & Abbot (01763) 853515
High Street; SG8 0SD Welcoming Queen Anne local with two small traditional bars and restaurant, good choice of enjoyable home-cooked food at reasonable prices, friendly efficient staff, well kept Adnams Southwold, Fullers London Pride and guests, beams and log fires; children and dogs welcome, side and back terraces, pretty village with good surrounding walks, open all day weekends – very busy then. *(Charlie May)*

BABRAHAM   TL5150

George (01223) 833800
High Street; just off A1307; CB22 3AG Beamed and timbered dining pub with good food from freshly baked baguettes and pub favourites up, Greene King ales and a guest, several wines by the glass, happy hour Mon-Thurs 5-7pm, bar area with comfortable seating, carpeted restaurant, attentive service, some live music and quiz nights; children welcome, tables in garden with heated terrace, nice setting on quiet road, open (and food) all day from breakfast on. *(Toby Jones)*

BARRINGTON   TL3849

Royal Oak (01223) 870791
Turn off A10 about 3.7 miles SW of M11 junction 11, in Foxton; West Green; CB22 7RZ Rambling thatched Tudor pub with tables out overlooking classic village green, heavy low beams and timbers, mixed furnishings, a beer named for the pub from Greene King along with Adnams, Woodfordes and a local guest, Aspall's and Thatcher's cider, enjoyable food from pub favourites up, good wine list, efficient friendly service, airy dining conservatory; background music, free wi-fi; children welcome, classic car club first Fri of month. *(Anon)*

BOURN   TL3256

★ **Willow Tree** (01954) 719775
High Street, just off B1046 W of Cambridge; CB23 2SQ Light and airy dining pub with relaxed informal atmosphere despite the cut-glass chandeliers, sprinkling of Louis XVI furniture and profusion of silver-plate candlesticks; accomplished restaurant-style cooking (all day Sun till 8pm), Milton and Woodfordes ales, several wines by the glass and inventive cocktails, friendly efficient staff; children welcome, smart tables and chairs on back deck, grassed area beyond car park with fruit trees and huge weeping willow acting as 'pole' for circular tent, open all day. *(Evelyn and Derek Walter, Mrs Margo Finlay, Jörg Kasprowski)*

BOXWORTH   TL3464

Golden Ball (01954) 267397
High Street; CB23 4LY Attractive partly thatched building with contemporary open-plan bar and three-part restaurant in original core, friendly helpful staff, popular food (all day Sun till 8pm) from baguettes through suet puddings and pies to grills, well kept Charles Wells ales including Courage Best, good whisky choice; children welcome, nice garden and heated terrace, pastures behind, 11 quiet bedrooms in adjacent block, open all day. *(John Gibbon)*

BRAMPTON   TL2170

Black Bull (01480) 457201
Church Road; PE28 4PF 16th-c and later with updated low-ceilinged interior, stripped-wood floor and inglenook woodburner in split-level main bar, restaurant area with light wood furniture on tiles, enjoyable well priced food (not Sun evening) including own sausages and pies, four real ales, alcoholic milkshakes, friendly staff; free wi-fi; children welcome and dogs (home-made treats for them), garden play area, open all day (till 9pm Sun). *(Neil Allen)*

BRINKLEY   TL6254

Brinkley Lion (01638) 507936
High Street; CB8 0RA Friendly old country pub with beams and inglenook log fire, enjoyable food (not Sun evening) including tapas, range of pub favourites and daily specials, lunchtime set deal, three beers on tap (maybe a brazilian one), decent wines by the glass; free wi-fi; children and dogs welcome (resident cairnoodle is Waffle), garden tables, open all day weekends. *(David Stewart)*

BROUGHTON   TL2877

★ **Crown** (01487) 824428
Off A141 opposite RAF Wyton; Bridge Road; PE28 3AY Attractively tucked-away mansard-roofed dining pub opposite church, fresh airy décor with country pine tables and chairs on stone floors, some leather bucket

seats and sofa, good well presented food (not Sun evening) from lunchtime sandwiches up, friendly service, real ales such as Church End and Mauldons, restaurant; background music; children and dogs welcome, disabled access and facilities, tables out on big stretch of grass behind, open all day Sun till 8pm. *(Neil Allen)*

BUCKDEN   TL1967
★ **George** (01480) 812300
High Street; PE19 5XA Handsome and stylish Georgian-faced hotel with bustling informal bar, fine fan beamwork, leather and chrome chairs, log fire, Adnams Southwold and a changing guest from chrome-topped counter, lots of wines including champagne by the glass, teas and coffees, popular brasserie with good modern food served by helpful enthusiastic young staff; background music; children and dogs welcome, tables under large parasols on pretty sheltered terrace with box hedging, charming bedrooms, open all day. *(Michael Sargent, J F M and M West, Richard Kennell)*

BUCKDEN   TL1967
Lion (01480) 810313
High Street; PE19 5XA Partly 15th-c coaching inn, black beams and big inglenook log fire in airy bow-windowed entrance bar with plush bucket seats, wing armchairs and sofas, enjoyable food from lunchtime sandwiches up, fine choice of wines, Adnams Southwold and a guest, prompt friendly staff, panelled back restaurant beyond latticed window partition; children welcome, back courtyard, 14 bedrooms, open all day. *(Anne and Ben Smith)*

CAMBRIDGE   TL4458
Anchor (01223) 353554
Silver Street; CB3 9EL Pub/restaurant in beautiful riverside position by punting station, popular with tourists and can get very busy; fine river views from upper dining room and suntrap terrace, five well kept beers and plenty of wines by the glass, good variety of food (fairly priced for the area), friendly service; fortnightly live jazz; children welcome, open all day. *(Dave Braisted)*

CAMBRIDGE   TL4658
★ **Cambridge Blue** (01223) 471680
85 Gwydir Street; CB1 2LG Friendly little backstreet local under newish management; a dozen or more interesting ales (some tapped from the cask – regular festivals), six craft kegs, 200 bottled beers and 35 whiskies, enjoyable well priced food including seasonal specials, all home-made (even ketchup and other sauces), attractive conservatory and extended back bar area with lots of breweriana and old advertising signs; free wi-fi; children and dogs welcome, seats in surprisingly rural-feeling back garden bordering cemetery, open (and food) all day and can get very busy weekends. *(Anne and Ben Smith)*

CAMBRIDGE   TL4558
Cambridge Brew House
(01223) 855185 *King Street; CB1 1LH*
Contemporary open-plan pub visibly brewing its own beers (plenty of guest ales/craft beers on tap too), enjoyable food from open kitchen including british tapas, sharing boards and own-smoked meats and fish, weekend brunch, friendly staff, sports TV in upstairs bar; open (and food) all day. *(Caroline Prescott)*

CAMBRIDGE   TL4459
Castle (01223) 353194
Castle Street; CB3 0AJ Full Adnams range and several interesting guest beers in big airy bare-boards bar, five pleasantly simple rooms, scrubbed tables, wide range of good value pub food from sandwiches up, quick friendly young staff, peaceful upstairs (downstairs can be noisier, with background music); picnic-sets in good walled back courtyard, open all day Fri, Sat. *(Simon Watkins, John Marsh)*

CAMBRIDGE   TL4658
Clarendon Arms (01223) 971015
Clarendon Street; CB1 1JX Backstreet corner local with welcoming helpful landlord; flagstones and bare boards, lots of pictures including local scenes, standard well used furniture, step down to back bar, Greene King and three guests, good locally distilled gin, enjoyable food (not Sun evening, Mon, Tues) from snacks to Sun roasts; dogs welcome, wheelchair access possible with help, seats in sunny back courtyard, open all day. *(Chris and Angela Buckell)*

CAMBRIDGE   TL4657
Devonshire Arms (01223) 316610
Devonshire Road; CB1 2BH Popular and welcoming Milton-tied pub with two cheerful chatty linked bars, their well kept ales and guests, real cider, also great choice of bottled beers, decent wines and a dozen malts, low-priced food from sandwiches and pizzas to steaks, creaky wood floors, mix of furniture including long narrow refectory tables, architectural prints and steam engine pictures, woodburner in back bar; wheelchair access, handy for the station, open all day. *(Chris and Angela Buckell)*

CAMBRIDGE   TL4458
★ **Eagle** (01223) 505020
Benet Street; CB2 3QN
Once the city's most important coaching inn; rambling rooms with two medieval mullioned windows and the remains of possibly medieval wall paintings, two fireplaces dating from around 1600, lovely worn wooden floors and plenty of pine panelling, dark red ceiling left unpainted since World War II to preserve signatures of british and american airmen made with Zippo lighters, candle smoke and lipstick, well kept Greene King ales including Eagle DNA (Crick and Watson announced the

discovery of DNA's structure here in 1953) and two guests, decent choice of enjoyable food served efficiently considering the crowds; children welcome, disabled facilities, heavy wooden seats in attractive cobbled and galleried courtyard, open all day. *(John Wooll, Mrs Sally Scott, Barry Collett, Michael Butler)*

CAMBRIDGE TL4558
Elm Tree (01223) 502632
Orchard Street; CB1 1JT Traditional one-bar backstreet drinkers' pub with welcoming atmosphere, ten well kept ales including B&T and Charles Wells, good range of continental bottled beers, local ciders/perries usually poured from the barrel, friendly knowledgeable staff, no food, nice unspoilt interior with breweriana, some live music; wheelchair access, a few tables out at side, open all day. *(Chris and Angela Buckell)*

CAMBRIDGE TL4559
Fort St George (01223) 354327
Midsummer Common; CB4 1HA Picturesque old pub (reached by foot only) in charming waterside position overlooking ducks, swans, punts and boathouses; extended around old-fashioned Tudor core, good value bar food including traditional Sun lunch, well kept Greene King ales and decent wines, cheery helpful young staff, oars on beams, historic boating photographs, stuffed fish etc; children and dogs welcome, wheelchair access via side door, lots of tables outside. *(Simon Watkins)*

CAMBRIDGE TL4558
★ **Free Press** (01223) 368337
Prospect Row; CB1 1DU Unspoilt little backstreet pub with interesting décor including old newspaper pages and printing memorabilia (was printshop for a local paper); Greene King IPA, Abbot and Mild plus regularly changing guests, 25 malt whiskies, lots of gins and rums, tasty good value food served by friendly staff, log fire, board games; children and dogs (in bar) welcome, wheelchair access, small sheltered paved garden behind, open all day Fri, Sat. *(Roy Shutz)*

CAMBRIDGE TL4657
★ **Kingston Arms** (01223) 319414
Kingston Street; CB1 2NU Victorian backstreet pub with ten well kept interesting ales, over 50 bottled beers, a couple of real ciders and good choice of wines by the glass, enjoyable freshly prepared food including some real bargains, companionably big plain tables and basic seating, thriving chatty atmosphere; free wi-fi; children and dogs welcome, back beer garden (heated and partly covered), open all day Fri-Sun. *(Anon)*

CAMBRIDGE TL4557
Live & Let Live (01223) 460261
Mawson Road; CB1 2EA Popular backstreet pub, friendly and relaxed, with half a dozen well kept ales including

Oakham, proper cider and over 120 rums, snacky food, panelled interior with sturdy varnished tables on bare boards, some steam railway and brewery memorabilia, old gas light fittings, cribbage and dominoes; dogs welcome, disabled access awkward but possible. *(Anon)*

CAMBRIDGE TL4458
Mill (01223) 311829
Mill Lane; CB2 1RX Pleasant refurbished pub in picturesque spot overlooking mill pond where punts can be hired; seven mainly local ales and proper cider, reasonably priced pubby food (all day weekends) including children's choices, Mon quiz; open all day. *(Caroline Prescott)*

CAMBRIDGE TL4458
Mitre (01223) 358403
Bridge Street, opposite St Johns College; CB2 1UF Popular Nicholsons pub close to the river, spacious rambling bar on several levels, their usual good value food cooked well and served all day including fixed-price menu, good selection of well kept ales, farm cider, reasonably priced wines by the glass, good friendly service; background music, free wi-fi; children welcome, disabled access. *(Revd R P Tickle)*

CAMBRIDGE TL4559
★ **Old Spring** (01223) 357228
Ferry Path; car park on Chesterton Road; CB4 1HB Extended Victorian pub, roomy and airy, with smartly old-fashioned scrubbed-wood décor, enjoyable well priced home-made food from pub staples to more enterprising dishes, friendly efficient service, well kept Greene King IPA, Abbot and four guests, plenty of wines by the glass and good coffee, two log fires, bare boards and lots of old pictures, long back conservatory; background music; well behaved children welcome, dogs outside only, disabled facilities, seats out in front and on large heated back terrace, open all day. *(Simon Watkins)*

CAMBRIDGE TL4459
Pickerel (01223) 355068
Magdalene Street, opposite the college; CB3 0AF Nicely old-fashioned former coaching inn close to the river, popular with locals and students (can get crowded evenings – 20% student discount), bars front and back, low beams and some dark panelling, Theakstons, Woodfordes and guests, plenty of wines by the glass, good value Taylor Walker menu, friendly staff; background music, TV, free wi-fi; children welcome, no dogs, wheelchair access with help, heated courtyard, open (and food) all day. *(M and J White)*

CAMBRIDGE TL4458
Pint Shop (01223) 352293
Peas Hill; CB2 3PN Newly revamped former university offices; front bar with

restaurant behind, parquet floors and grey painted walls, simple furnishings and pendant lighting, a dozen craft/cask beers from smaller brewers listed on blackboard, good selection of wines and some 60 gins, unusual food from bar snacks up cooked on charcoal grill, set menu options Mon-Fri, local artwork for sale; handy for the Cambridge Art Theatre and Corn Exchange. *(R Anderson)*

CASTOR   TL1298
★ **Prince of Wales Feathers**
(01733) 380222 *Off A47; PE5 7AL*
Friendly stone-built local with well kept Adnams, Castor, Woodfordes and interesting guests, farm cider and perry too, good value food cooked by landlady (not weekend evenings) including popular Sun roasts, open-plan interior with dining area to the left; Sat live music, Sun quiz, Sky TV, pool (free Thurs); children and dogs welcome, disabled facilities, attractive front terrace and another at the back with large smokers' shelter, open all day, till late weekends. *(Lindy Andrews)*

CONINGTON   TL3266
White Swan (01954) 267251
Sgned off A14 (was A604) Cambridge–Huntingdon; Elsworth Road; CB23 4LN
Quietly placed 18th-c red-brick country pub, ales tapped from the cask such as Adnams, local Cromwell's Cider, reasonably priced pubby food (not evenings Sun-Weds), traditional bar with tiled floor and log fire; children and dogs welcome, big front garden with play area, summer barbecues, closed Mon. *(David Stewart)*

DUXFORD   TL4745
Plough (01223) 833170
St Peters Street; CB22 4RP Popular early 18th-c thatched pub, clean bright and friendly, with enjoyable home-made food from shortish reasonably priced menu, Adnams, Everards and guests kept well, woodburner in brick fireplace; children welcome, handy for IWM Duxford, open all day (no food Sun evening, Mon, Tues lunchtime). *(Gordon and Margaret Ormondroyd)*

ELLINGTON   TL1671
Mermaid (01480) 891106
High Street; PE28 0AB Popular 17th-c village pub recently reopened/restored under new management; imaginative well presented food from owner-chef as well as pub favourites, real ales and decent wines from brick counter, friendly service, beams (some hiding coins left by US airmen), woodburner; garden overlooking church, closed Mon. *(Carol and Barry Craddock)*

ELSWORTH   TL3163
George & Dragon (01954) 267236
Off A14 NW of Cambridge, via Boxworth, or off A428; CB23 8JQ
Neatly kept dining pub with friendly helpful staff and easy-going atmosphere – same group as the Eaton Oak at St Neots and Rose at Stapleford; pleasant panelled main bar with fishy theme opening on left to slightly elevated dining area, woodburner, garden room overlooking attractive terraces, more formal restaurant on right, wide choice of enjoyable food including deals, Greene King ales and a guest, decent wines; steps to lavatories, free wi-fi; children welcome, dogs in bar, open (and food) all day Sun. *(Michael and Jenny Back and others)*

ELTISLEY   TL2759
Eltisley (01480) 880308
The Green; village signposted off A428 Cambridge–St Neots; PE19 6TG Village-green inn with all sorts of rambling areas, grey-painted walls and beams, bare boards and flagstones, leatherette wall seats, curved high-backed settles and easy chairs by cast-iron stove in massive central chimneypiece, food from pub favourites up including good value set lunch, Charles Wells ales and decent wines by the glass, friendly young staff, cosy low-beamed library down some steps, more formal raftered dining room; background music; children and dogs welcome, canopied deck in sheltered back area, six stylish bedrooms in separate block, open all day Sat, closed Sun evening, Mon. *(Michael Sargent, Michael Butler)*

ELTON   TL0893
Black Horse (01832) 281222
Overend; B671 off A605 W of Peterborough and A1(M); PE8 6RU
Honey-stone beamed dining pub, neatly updated and opened up, with enjoyable food from sandwiches and pub favourites to daily specials, Adnams, Digfield and a guest, decent wines and good coffee, friendly staff; children welcome, clean dogs in bar area, terrace and garden with views across to Elton Hall park and village church, open all day. *(Toby Jones)*

ELY   TL5479
Cutter (01353) 662713
Annesdale, off Station Road (or walk S along Riverside Walk from Maltings); CB7 4BN Beautifully placed modernised riverside pub with bar, dining lounge and restaurant, good choice of enjoyable, promptly served food from sandwiches up, well kept Adnams, Sharps, Woodfordes and a guest from boat-shaped counter, nice wines by the glass, decent coffee, good views from window seats and terrace; children welcome, no dogs inside, moorings, open all day from 9am. *(J F M and M West)*

ELY   TL5480
Lamb (01353) 663574
Brook Street (Lynn Road); CB7 4EJ
Good choice of food in popular hotel's panelled lounge bar or restaurant, friendly welcoming staff, Greene King ales and plenty of wines by the glass, decent coffee;

children welcome, close to cathedral, 31 clean comfortable bedrooms, good breakfast. *(Dave Braisted, John Wooll)*

ETTON   TF1406
Golden Pheasant (01733) 252387
Just off B1443 N of Peterborough, signed from near N end of A15 bypass;
PE6 7DA Revamped yellow-brick Georgian farmhouse (a pub since 1964), spacious bare-boards bar with open fire, Greene King, Grainstore, Oakham and a couple of interesting small brewery guests from central counter, decent choice of wines and spirits, good food (not Sun night) including competitively priced weekday set menu (lunchtime/early evening), prompt cheerful service, back panelled restaurant; some live music; children and dogs welcome, big tree-sheltered garden with play area, table tennis and table football in marquee, vintage car meetings, on Green Wheel cycle route, open all day Fri-Sun, closed Mon lunchtime. *(Howard and Margaret Buchanan)*

FOWLMERE   TL4245
★ Chequers (01763) 208558
High Street (B1368); SG8 7SR Popular 16th-c coaching inn with two comfortable downstairs rooms, long cushioned wall seats, dining chairs around dark tables, log fire, good traditional food served by friendly staff, Greene King IPA and two guests, several wines by the glass, attractive upstairs beamed and timbered dining room with interesting moulded plasterwork above one fireplace, spacious conservatory (children welcome here); no dogs inside, terrace and garden with tables under parasols. *(Richard Kennell)*

FOWLMERE   TL4245
Queens Head (01763) 208091
Long Lane; SG8 7SZ Pretty 17th-century beamed and thatched cottage revamped under present management, clean interior with comfortable sofas and chairs, Greene King, Sharps and a guest, reasonably priced pub food including good ploughman's, friendly staff; children welcome, dogs in garden only, handy for IWM Duxford, open all day Fri-Sun. *(Anon)*

GRANTCHESTER   TL4355
★ Blue Ball (01223) 840679
Broadway; CB3 9NQ Character bare-boards local rebuilt 1900 on site of much older pub (cellars still remain), Adnams Southwold and a guest kept in top condition by veteran hands-on landlord (there's a list of previous publicans back to 1767), good log fire, cards and traditional games including shut the box and ring the bull, newspapers and lots of books, live music Thurs; no food or children; dogs welcome, tables on small terrace with lovely views to Grantchester Meadows, good heated smokers' shelter, nice village, open from 2pm (midday weekends). *(Stuart Gideon, Mrs Catherine Simmonds)*

GREAT ABINGTON   TL5348
Three Tuns (01223) 891467
Off A1307 Cambridge–Haverhill, and A11; CB21 6AB Peacefully set 16th-c beamed village pub, low-backed settles on stripped-wood floors, open fires, good authentic thai food (traditional roast on Sun), three well kept changing ales, welcoming landlord and friendly efficient staff; garden picnic-sets, nine well appointed bedrooms in modern block, open all day weekends. *(Mrs Margo Finlay, Jörg Kasprowski)*

GREAT CHISHILL   TL4239
★ Pheasant (01763) 838535
Follow Heydon signpost from B1039 in village; SG8 8SR Popular old split-level flagstoned pub with beams, timbering, open fires and some elaborately carved (though modern) seats and settles, good freshly made food (not Sun evening) using local produce, welcoming friendly staff, two or three ales including one for the pub from Nethergate, good choice of wines by the glass, small dining room (best to book), darts, cribbage, dominoes; no under-14s inside; dogs allowed, charming secluded back garden with small play area, open all day weekends. *(Anne and Ben Smith)*

GREAT GRANSDEN   TL2655
Crown & Cushion (01767) 677214
Off B1046 Cambridge–St Neots; West Street; SG19 3AT Small thatched and beamed local in pretty village, two or three well kept ales such as Adnams and Oakham, authentic indonesian cooking from landlady (Fri evening, Sat, Sun), friendly staff, woodburner in big fireplace; live music; small garden, open all day weekends, closed Mon. *(Toby Jones)*

HARDWICK   TL3758
Blue Lion (01954) 210328
Signed off A428 (was A45) W of Cambridge; Main Street; CB23 7QU Attractive 18th-c dining pub, split-level interior with beams and timbers, leather armchairs by copper-canopied inglenook, good food from landlord-chef in bar and extended dining area with conservatory, friendly efficient young staff, Greene King IPA and guests; children welcome, pretty roadside front garden, more seats on decking and lawn with play area, handy for Wimpole Way walks, open all day (food all day weekends). *(Charlie May)*

HELPSTON   TF1205
Blue Bell (01733) 252394
Woodgate; off B1443; PE6 7ED Extended 17th-c pub refurbished under new owners, four real ales including Fullers London Pride and a house beer from Star, enjoyable food, good friendly service; children and dogs welcome. *(Dr Simon Innes)*

HEYDON TL4339

★ **King William IV** (01763) 838773
Off A505 W of M11 junction 10;
SG8 8PW Rambling dimly lit rooms with
fascinating rustic jumble (ploughshares,
yokes, iron tools, cowbells and so forth) along
with copperware and china in nooks and
crannies, log fire, Fullers, Greene King and
Timothy Taylors ales, good varied choice of
well presented food including proper home-
made pies, helpful staff; background music;
children and dogs (in bar) welcome, teak
furniture on heated terrace and in pretty
garden, four bedrooms in separate building,
open all day weekends. *(Mrs Margo Finlay,
Jörg Kasprowski)*

HISTON TL4363

★ **Red Lion** (01223) 564437
*High Street, off Station Road; 3.7 miles
from M11 junction 1; CB24 9JD*
Impressive choice of draught and bottled
beers along with traditional cider and perry
(festivals Easter/early Sept), ceiling joists in
L-shaped main bar packed with hundreds of
beer mats and pump clips among hop bines
and whisky-water jugs, fine collection of old
brewery advertisements, traditional pub
food with a twist (all day Sat, not Mon, Fri,
Sun evenings), cheerful efficient service,
comfortable brocaded wall seats, matching
mate's chairs and pubby tables, log fires, nice
working antique one-arm bandit, extended
bar on left (well behaved children allowed
here) with darts, TV and huge collection of
beer bottles; mobile phones discouraged, no
dogs inside; disabled access/facilities, picnic-
sets in neat garden, limited parking, open
all day. *(Charlie May)*

LITTLE WILBRAHAM TL5458

★ **Hole in the Wall** (01223) 812282
*High Street; A1303 Newmarket Road to
Stow cum Quy off A14, then left at The
Wilbrahams signpost, then right at Little
Wilbrahams signpost; CB1 5JY*
Tucked-away pub/restaurant with cosy
carpeted ochre-walled bar on right, log fire
in big brick fireplace, 16th-c beams and
timbers, snug little window seats and other
mixed seating around scrubbed kitchen
tables, similar middle room with fire in open
range, rather plusher main dining room with
another fire, really good inventive cooking
including evening tasting menu (set lunch
is more affordable), Fellows ales and guests,
ten wines by the glass and some unusual
soft drinks; well behaved children allowed,
dogs in bar, neat side garden with good teak
furniture and small verandah, interesting
walk to nearby unspoilt Little Wilbraham
Fen, closed Sun evening, all day Mon and for
two weeks in Jan. *(R J Shears)*

MADINGLEY TL3960

Three Horseshoes (01954) 210221
High Street; off A1303 W of Cambridge;

CB23 8AB Civilised thatched restauranty
pub – most customers come here for the
inventive italian-influenced food (not cheap);
there is, though, a small pleasantly relaxed
bar, with simple wooden furniture on bare
boards and open fire (can be a crush at peak
times), two real ales and plenty of wines
by the glass from excellent list, friendly
service, pretty dining conservatory; children
welcome, picnic-sets under parasols in sunny
garden. *(Anon)*

NEEDINGWORTH TL3571

Pike & Eel (01480) 463336
*Pub signed from A1123; Overcote Road;
PE27 4TW* Peacefully placed old riverside
hotel with spacious lawns and small marina;
plush bar opening into room with easy chairs,
sofas and big open fire, restaurant in light
and airy glass-walled block overlooking
water, enjoyable food, ales including Adnams
Broadside and Greene King IPA, decent
wines and coffee, pleasant attentive service;
background music; children welcome, 12
clean simple bedrooms, good breakfast, open
all day. *(Dr Simon Innes)*

NEWTON TL4349

★ **Queens Head** (01223) 870436
*2.5 miles from M11 junction 11; A10
towards Royston, then left on to B1368;
CB22 7PG* Lovely traditional unchanging
pub run by same welcoming family for many
years – lots of loyal customers; peaceful bow-
windowed main bar with crooked beams in
low ceiling, bare wooden benches and seats
built into cream walls, curved high-backed
settle, paintings and big log fire, Adnams ales
tapped from the cask, farm cider and simple
food such as soup and sandwiches, small
carpeted saloon, traditional games including
table skittles, shove-ha'penny and nine men's
morris; no credit cards; children on best
behaviour allowed in games room only, dogs
welcome, seats out in front by vine trellis.
(Neil Allen)

OFFORD D'ARCY TL2166

Horseshoe (01480) 810293
High Street; PE19 5RH Extended former
17th-c coaching house with two bars and
restaurant, emphasis on good food including
popular Sun carvery, friendly service, up to
five changing ales and well chosen wines,
beams and inglenooks; children welcome,
lawned garden with play area, open all day
Fri-Sun. *(Anne and Ben Smith)*

ORWELL TL3650

Chequers (01223) 207840
Town Green Road; SG8 5QL Village
dining pub with good food (not Sun evening)
including popular themed nights, well kept
ales such as Lacons and Sharps Doom Bar,
decent choice of wines by the glass, pleasant
helpful staff; children and dogs (in bar)
welcome, disabled facilities, open all day
Fri-Sun, closed Mon. *(Neil Allen)*

PAMPISFORD   TL4948

★ **Chequers** (01223) 833220
*2.6 miles from M11 junction 10: A505
E, then village and pub signed off; Town
Lane; CB22 4ER* Traditional neatly kept
old pub with friendly licensees, low beams
and comfortable old-fashioned furnishings,
booth seating on pale ceramic tiles in cream-
walled main area, low step down to bare-
boards part with dark pink walls, Greene
King IPA, Woodfordes Wherry and two guests,
good fairly priced food including themed
nights, Sun carvery and OAP lunch Weds,
good friendly service; TV; children and dogs
welcome (their collie is Snoopy), picnic-sets
in prettily planted small garden lit by black
street lamps, parking may be tricky, open all
day (till 4pm Sun). *(D and M T Ayres-Regan,
Roy Hoing)*

PETERBOROUGH   TL1998

★ **Charters** (01733) 315700
Town Bridge, S side; PE1 1FP Interesting
conversion of dutch grain barge moored on
River Nene; sizeable timbered bar on lower
deck with up to a dozen real ales including
Oakham (regular beer festivals), restaurant
above serving good value SE asian food, lots
of wooden tables and pews; background
music, live bands (Fri and Sat after 10.30pm,
Sun from 3.30pm); children welcome till
9pm, dogs in bar, huge riverside garden (gets
packed in fine weather), open all day (till
midnight Fri, Sat). *(Pat and Tony Martin)*

PETERBOROUGH   TL1897

Coalheavers Arms (01733) 565664
Park Street, Woodston; PE2 9BH Friendly
old-fashioned 19th-c flagstoned local, well
kept Milton and guest beers, traditional
cider, good range of continental imports and
malt whiskies, basic snacks; Sun quiz, near
football ground and busy on match days;
pleasant garden, closed lunchtime Mon-Weds,
open all day Fri-Sun. *(Anon)*

PETERBOROUGH   TL1898

Drapers Arms (01733) 847570
Cowgate; PE1 1LZ Roomy open-plan
Wetherspoons in converted draper's, fine
ale range, low-priced promptly served food
all day; can get very busy Fri, Sat evenings;
children welcome, open from 8am. *(Lindy
Andrews)*

SHEPRETH   TL3947

Plough (01763) 290348
*Signed just off A10 S of Cambridge;
High Street; SG8 6PP* Recently reopened
and extensively refurbished red-brick
village pub, decent-sized bar area with vinyl
record and Spitfire theme (IWM Duxford
nearby), Elgoods and a couple of guests,
good selection of other drinks, reasonably
priced food from snacks up, pleasant young
staff; background and some live music,
free wi-fi; children welcome, garden with

covered terrace, open (and food) all day
weekends. *(Anon)*

SPALDWICK   TL1372

George (01480) 890293
*Just off A14 W of Huntingdon;
PE28 0TD* Friendly well run 17th-c village
pub (former coaching inn), sofas in bar,
larger dining area including raftered part,
nice food (till 7pm Sun) from good value
bar snacks up, Timothy Taylors Landlord,
Woodfordes Wherry and a guest, decent
wines by the glass; children and dogs (in bar)
welcome, seats out behind under parasols,
open all day Fri-Sun. *(Dr Simon Innes)*

ST NEOTS   TL1761

Eaton Oak (01480) 219555
*Just off A1, Great North Road/Crosshall
Road; PE19 7DB* Under same ownership
as the George & Dragon at Elsworth and
Rose at Stapleford; wide choice of popular
food including grills, fresh fish and very good
value early evening deal for two (Mon-Thurs),
Charles Wells ales and maybe a guest,
good friendly service, plenty of nooks and
crannies in older part, light airy dining area,
conservatory; free wi-fi; children and dogs (in
bar) welcome, disabled access and facilities,
tables out under parasols, tubs of flowers and
smokers' shelter, nine bedrooms, open all day
(breakfast for non-residents). *(Michael and
Jenny Back and others)*

STAPLEFORD   TL4651

★ **Rose** (01223) 843349
*London Road; M11 junction 11;
CB22 5DG* Comfortable sister pub to the
Eaton Oak at St Neots and George & Dragon
at Elsworth, emphasis on dining and can get
very busy, wide choice of good reasonably
priced food including weekday early-bird
deal, pleasant uniformed staff, Courage
Directors, Youngs Best and Wells Bombardier,
small low-ceilinged lounge with inglenook
woodburner, roomy split-level dining area,
steps up to lavatories, faint background
music; picnic-sets on back grass, open (and
food) all day Sun. *(Michael and Jenny Back)*

STILTON   TL1689

Stilton Cheese (01733) 240546
Signed off A1; North Street; PE7 3RP
Welcoming former coaching inn with wide
range of good food from sandwiches to fish
specials, a couple of ales such as Adnams
and Timothy Taylors Landlord, decent wines,
old interior with roaring log fire in central
bar, four linked dining rooms; no dogs;
children welcome, tables out in back garden
with sheltered deck, six barn-conversion
bedrooms, closed Sun evening and
lunchtimes Mon, Tues. *(M and GR)*

STOW CUM QUY   TL5260

White Swan (01223) 811821
*Off A14 E of Cambridge, via B1102;
CB25 9AB* Cosy 17th-c beamed village

pub-restaurant, five well kept ales including Adnams, Weston's cider, several wines by the glass from good list, local English Spirits range and nice selection of malt whiskies, enjoyable home-made food from bar snacks and pubby choices to more ambitious restaurant dishes, big fireplace, friendly chatty atmosphere; children and dogs welcome, wheelchair access through side door (ramps provided), terrace picnic-sets, handy for Anglesey Abbey (NT), open all day. *(M and GR, Chris and Angela Buckell, Paul Humphreys)*

SUTTON GAULT   TL4279
★ **Anchor** (01353) 778537
Bury Lane off High Street (B1381); CB6 2BD Tucked-away old inn with charming candlelit rooms, emphasis on good inventive food (may be limited space for drinkers at weekends) and a nice place to stay in comfortable bedrooms overlooking the river; Nethergate Growler tapped from the cask and a dozen wines by the glass from thoughtful list, helpful friendly staff, stylishly simple with heavy beams and timbers, antique settles and scrubbed pine tables on gently undulating floors, good lithographs and big prints, two log fires; children welcome, seats outside and you can walk along the high embankment (good bird-watching). *(Mrs Margo Finlay, Jörg Kasprowski, Mr and Mrs P R Thomas, M and GR)*

THORNEY   TL2799
Dog in a Doublet (01733) 202256
B1040 towards Thorney; PE6 0RW Friendly dining pub across from river, good bar food and more upmarket restaurant menu (some produce from own farm), well kept ales, deli counter, beams and open fire; children and dogs (in bar) welcome, handy for Hereward Way walks, four bedrooms and camping, open all day Fri-Sun, closed Mon, Tues lunchtime. *(Janek Skutela)*

THRIPLOW   TL4346
Green Man (01763) 208855
3 miles from M11 junction 10; A505 towards Royston, then first right; Lower Street; SG8 7RJ Little roadside pub owned/refurbished by the village and under welcoming new management, good food from shortish daily changing menu along with blackboard tapas, four well kept ales and decent wines by the glass, efficient friendly service; quiz last Tues of month; children welcome, picnic-sets on small grassy triangle in front, closed Mon, otherwise open (and food) all day (till 7pm Sun). *(Mrs Margo Finlay, Jörg Kasprowski, Alex and Hazel Evans)*

TILBROOK   TL0769
White Horse (01480) 860764
High Street (B645); PE28 0JP Welcoming and relaxed 18th-c pub at edge of village, low-beamed bar with interesting local prints and horsebrasses, dining conservatory, Charles Wells ales, enjoyable reasonably priced food (not Sun evening, Mon) from varied menu including midweek set deal, nice range of coffees, good uniformed service, pub games including table skittles; popular live music first Mon of month, free wi-fi; big garden with play equipment, goats, chickens and ducks, closed Mon lunchtime, otherwise open all day. *(Ryta Lyndley, John Allman)*

WARESLEY   TL2454
Duncombe Arms (01767) 650265
Eltisley Road (B1040, 5 miles S of A428); SG19 3BS Comfortable welcoming old pub, well managed with some emphasis on eating, long main bar with fire at one end, reliably good pub food including specials, well kept Greene King ales, helpful friendly service, back room and restaurant; children welcome, picnic-sets in shrub-sheltered garden. *(Margaret and Roy Randle, Richard Kennell)*

WHITTLESFORD   TL4648
Bees in the Wall (01223) 834289
North Road; handy for M11 junction 10 and IWM Duxford; CB22 4NZ Village-edge local with comfortably worn-in split-level timbered lounge, polished tables and country prints, small tiled public bar with old wall settles, darts, decent good value food (not Sun or Tues evenings) from sandwiches up, well kept Timothy Taylors Landlord and guests, open fires; may be background music, games machine; no dogs, picnic-sets in big paddock-style garden with terrace, bees still in the wall (here since the 1950s), closed Mon. *(Anon)*

WHITTLESFORD   TL4748
Red Lion (01223) 832047
Station Road; CB22 4NL Modernised old coaching inn handy for IWM Duxford; beamed bar with well kept Adnams beers, enjoyable home-made food including Sun carvery, friendly staff, various dining area including glass-roofed atrium, warm fires; tables out on lawn (overlooked by A505), 18 bedrooms, adjacent to station and Duxford Chapel (EH), open (and food) all day. *(P and D Carpenter)*

WOODDITTON   TL6558
Three Blackbirds (01638) 731100
Signed off B1063 at Cheveley; CB8 9SQ Popular two-bar thatched pub, low 17th-c beams, mix of old country furniture on bare boards, pictures and knick-knacks, open fires, good food from deli boards to daily specials, Adnams, Timothy Taylors and changing local guests, plenty of wines by the glass including champagne, restaurant; children welcome, garden picnic-sets, open all day Sun till 7pm. *(Michael and Jenny Back)*

Cheshire

ALDFORD   SJ4259 Map 7
Grosvenor Arms ★ 🔯 ♟ 🍺

(01244) 620228 – www.brunningandprice.co.uk/grosvenorarms

B5130 Chester–Wrexham; CH3 6HJ

Spacious place with impressive range of drinks, wide-ranging imaginative menu, good service, suntrap terrace and garden

For a big pub, this Victorian brick and half-timbered place has a great deal of character. The various rooms have plenty of interest and individuality and a buoyantly chatty atmosphere – and staff are well trained and attentive. Spacious cream-painted areas are sectioned by big knocked-through arches with a variety of floor finishes (wood, quarry tiles, flagstone, black and white tiles) – the richly coloured turkish rugs look well against these natural materials. Good solid pieces of traditional furniture, plenty of pictures and attractive lighting keep it all intimate. A handsomely boarded panelled room has tall bookshelves lining one wall; good selection of board games. Phoenix Brunning & Price Original, Sharps Doom Bar, Snowdonia Gold and Weetwood Eastgate are served from a fine-looking bar counter and they offer 20 wines by the glass, over 80 whiskies and distinctive soft drinks such as peach and elderflower cordial and Willington Fruit Farm pressed apple juice. Lovely on summer evenings, the airy, terracotta-floored conservatory has lots of gigantic low-hanging flowering baskets and chunky pale wood garden furniture. It opens out to a large elegant suntrap terrace and a neat lawn with picnic-sets.

🔯 Contemporary brasserie-style dishes include sandwiches, maple-glazed pork belly with barbecue butter beans and toasted sweetcorn, cauliflower and onion bhaji with mango salsa, mint and yoghurt, smoked haddock kedgeree with a poached egg, steak burger with toppings, coleslaw and chips, steamed lamb and mint pudding with garlic mash, chicken with almond couscous and tomato and chickpea stew, and puddings such as steamed jam sponge with custard and vanilla and ginger cheesecake with blueberry compote. *Benchmark main dish: beef rendang curry £14.75. Two-course evening meal £21.00.*

Brunning & Price ~ Manager Tracey Owen ~ Real ale ~ Open 11-11 (10.30 Sun) ~ Bar food 12-9.30 (10 Fri, Sat; 9 Sun) ~ Children welcome ~ Dogs allowed in bar ~ Wi-fi
Recommended by Stephen Shepherd, Clive Watkin, John and Mary Warner, Nick Sharpe

---

The letters and figures after the name of each town are its Ordnance Survey map reference. *Using the Guide* at the beginning of the book explains how it helps you find a pub, in road atlases or large-scale maps as well as in our own maps.

ALLOSTOCK
SJ7271 Map 7

Three Greyhounds Inn 🏵 ♀

(01565) 723455 – www.thethreegreyhoundsinn.co.uk

4.7 miles from M6 junction 18: A54 E then forking left on B5803 into Holmes Chapel, left at roundabout on to A50 for 2 miles, then left on to B5082 towards Northwich; Holmes Chapel Road; WA16 9JY

Relaxing, civilised and welcoming, with enjoyable food and drink all day

After enjoying a nearby walk or a stroll around Shakerley Mere nature reserve just across the road, this prominent former farmhouse is just the place for refreshment; dogs are welcome in the Brandy Snug and the big garden and they now have a doggy menu. The rooms are interconnected by open doorways and décor throughout is restful: thick rugs on quarry tiles or bare boards, candles and soft lighting, dark grey walls (or interesting woven wooden ones made from old brandy barrels) hung with modern black-on-white prints. There are four open fires, and an appealing variety of wooden dining chairs, cushioned wall seats, little stools and plenty of plump purple scatter cushions around all sorts of tables – do note the one made from giant bellows. A good choice of drinks includes 15 interesting wines by the glass, 50 brandies and three house ales – Almighty Allostock Ale (from Mobberley), Byley Bomber (from Caledonian) and Three Greyhounds Bitter (from Weetwood) plus three quickly changing guests on handpump; unobtrusive background music. Above the old farm barns is a newly restored private dining and party room called the Old Dog House. The big side lawn has picnic-table sets under parasols, with more tables on a decked side verandah with a Perspex roof. The pub is owned by Tim Bird and Mary McLaughlin.

 Inventive food includes sandwiches, sharing plates, mussels in cider, smoked venison loin with beetroot, bitter chocolate jam and pickled onion salad, baked butternut and sage dumplings with red pepper stew and feta, crispy local rabbit and black pudding with pumpkin and smoked almond hash with a fried duck egg, sea trout cured in brandy with sweet pickled cucumber and wasabi crème fraîche, free-range pork belly with maple-roasted plums and cider and cumin lentils, and puddings such as apple, blackberry and cider crumble and dark chocolate and orange brownie; they also serve an interesting range of british cheeses. *Benchmark main dish: burger with toppings, coleslaw and chips £11.95. Two-course evening meal £19.00.*

Free house ~ Licensee James Griffiths ~ Real ale ~ Open 12-11 (midnight Sat); 12-10.30 Sun ~ Bar food 12-9.15 (9.45 Fri, Sat) ~ No under-10s after 7pm ~ Dogs allowed in bar ~ Wi-fi ~ Live music Fri evenings *Recommended by David Heath, Nick Sharpe, John and Mary Warner, Dr and Mrs A K Clarke*

ASTBURY
SJ8461 Map 7

Egerton Arms £ 🛏

(01260) 273946 – www.egertonarms.co.uk

Village signposted off A34 S of Congleton; CW12 4RQ

Friendly and cheery pub with popular bar food, four real ales and large garden; nice bedrooms

This former farmhouse is a popular pub with a good mix of chatty customers, all warmly welcomed by the hands-on, friendly landlord and his attentive staff. The cream-painted rooms are decorated with newspaper cuttings relating to 'Grace' (the landlady's name), the odd piece of armour, shelves of books and quite a few mementoes of the Sandow Brothers (one of whom was the landlady's father) who performed as 'the World's Strongest

Youths'. In summer, dried flowers replace the fire in the big fireplace; background music and TV. Robinsons Dizzy Blonde, Double Hop, Unicorn and a guest beer on handpump, nine wines by the glass, 16 malt whiskies and alcoholic winter warmers. There are picnic-sets on a terrace with more on grass, and a gazebo and children's play area; the village church is opposite and the pub is handy for Little Moreton Hall (National Trust).

🍴 Tasty food at fair prices includes sandwiches and baps, duck pâté, spicy chicken wings, sharing boards, vegetable curry, lasagne, smoked haddock risotto, gammon and eggs, steak and mushroom in ale pudding, lambs liver and onions, bass fillets in tarragon butter, and puddings such as apricot and maple syrup sundae and chocolate and orange cheesecake.; they also offer an OAP two- and three-course set lunch that's remarkable value. *Benchmark main dish: steak and onions braised in ale £10.95. Two-course evening meal £18.00.*

Robinsons ~ Tenants Allen and Grace Smith ~ Real ale ~ Open 11.30-11 (10.30 Sun) ~ Bar food 11.30-2, 6-9; 12-8 Sun ~ Restaurant ~ Children welcome ~ Wi-fi ~ Bedrooms: £60/£70
Recommended by Dr D J and Mrs S C Walker, Roger and Anne Newbury

ASTON
Bhurtpore ★ ♀ 🍺 £

SJ6146 Map 7

(01270) 780917 – www.bhurtpore.co.uk
Off A530 SW of Nantwich; in village follow Wrenbury signpost; CW5 8DQ

Fantastic range of drinks (especially real ales) in warm-hearted pub with some unusual artefacts; big garden

You'll find around 11 real ales, sourced from all over the country, at any one time at this mecca for beer lovers – they get through more than 1,000 different ones in a year – examples include Blackwater End of Days, Coastal Poseidon, Conwy Clogwyn Gold, Hales Chaos Reigns, Ossett Inception, Redwillow Ageless and Salopian Labyrinth. They also stock dozens of unusual bottled beers and fruit beers, a great many bottled ciders and perries and farm cider, over 100 different whiskies, carefully selected soft drinks and 11 wines from a good list; summer beer festival. The pub name commemorates the siege of Bhurtpore (a town in India) during which local landowner Sir Stapleton Cotton (later Viscount Combermere) was commander-in-chief. The connection with India also explains some of the quirky artefacts in the carpeted lounge bar – look out for the sunglasses-wearing turbanned figure behind the counter; also good local period photographs and some attractive furniture in the comfortable public bar; board games, pool, TV and games machine. Weekends tend to be pretty busy.

🍴 As well as their popular half a dozen curries, the tasty food includes sandwiches, baguettes and toasties, chicken liver pâté with cider chutney, ham and free-range eggs, Old Spot cumberland sausages with onion gravy and sweet potato mash, chicken breast with stilton and smoked bacon sauce, seasonal game dishes, and puddings such as rhubarb and apple crumble and chocolate and raspberry brownies. *Benchmark main dish: steak and kidney in ale pie £10.50. Two-course evening meal £16.00.*

Free house ~ Licensee Simon George ~ Real ale ~ Open 12-2.30, 6.30-11.30; 12-midnight Fri, Sat; 12-11 Sun ~ Bar food 12-2, 6.30-9.30; 12-9.30 Sat; 12-9 Sun ~ Restaurant ~ Children welcome ~ Dogs allowed in bar ~ Wi-fi *Recommended by Nick Sharpe, Jo Garnett*

BARTHOMLEY

SJ7752 Map 7

White Lion £

(01270) 882242 – www.whitelionbarthomley.co.uk

M6 junction 16, B5078 N towards Alsager, then Barthomley signed on left; CW2 5PG

Charming 17th-c thatched village tavern with classic period interior, up to half a dozen real ales and good value lunchtime food

If ever there was a perfect respite from the dreary M6, then this timeless and unpretentious pub is it. The bar has a blazing open fire, heavy oak beams dating from Stuart times, attractively moulded black panelling, Cheshire prints on the walls, latticed windows and uneven wobbly old tables. Up some steps, a second room has another welcoming open fire, more oak panelling, a high-backed winged settle and a paraffin lamp hinged to the wall; shove-ha'penny; local societies make good use of a third room. There's Banks's Bitter, Jennings Cocker Hoop and Sneck Lifter, Marstons Burton Bitter and Pedigree and Sunbeam Best Bitter on handpump served by genuinely friendly staff. The gents' are across an open courtyard. In summer, seats on cobbles outside offer views of the attractive old village and the early 15th-c red sandstone church of St Bertiline (where you can learn about the Barthomley massacre).

Very good value food includes sandwiches, baguettes, pizzas, steak in ale pie or cottage pie at lunchtime, with evening choices such as creamy garlic mushrooms, prawn cocktail, sausages and mash with onion gravy, chicken pesto pasta, and puddings such as fruit crumble and bread and butter pudding. *Benchmark main dish: hotpot with red cabbage £6.95. Two-course evening meal £13.25.*

Marstons ~ Tenant Peter Butler ~ Real ale ~ Open 11.30-11 (10.30 Sun) ~ Bar food 12-2 (3 Weds-Sun), 6-9 (Thurs-Sat evenings only) ~ Children welcome away from bar ~ Dogs allowed in bar ~ Wi-fi *Recommended by Dr W I C Clark, Nick Sharpe*

BOSTOCK GREEN

SJ6769 Map 7

Hayhurst Arms ♀ ◖

(01606) 541810 – www.brunningandprice.co.uk/hayhurstarms

London Road, Bostock Green; CW10 9JP

Interesting and cleverly renovated pub with a marvellous selection of drinks, a wide choice of rewarding food, friendly staff and seats outside

Built as Reading Rooms in 1845, this handsome tall pub has been completely refurbished by Brunning & Price, who have also incorporated the former stables and coach house. The long main bar is divided into different dining areas by elegant support pillars; throughout, it's light and airy with big windows, house plants, bookshelves, standard lamps and metal chandeliers, and prints, old photographs and paintings arranged frame-to-frame above wooden dados. The varied dark wooden dining chairs are grouped around tables of all sizes on rugs, quarry tiles, wide floorboards and carpet, and three open fireplaces have big mirrors above them, with hefty leather armchairs to the sides. A couple of cosier rooms lead off. Phoenix Brunning & Price Original, Cheshire Brewhouse DBA and Lindow The Black Lake, Spitting Feathers Thirst Quencher, Weetwood Eastgate Ale and Wincle Lord Lucan on handpump, 15 wines by the glass and a huge choice of malt whiskies; staff are efficient and courteous. The outside terrace has good quality tables and chairs under parasols, and the village green opposite has swings and a play tractor.

🍴 Appealing food from a creative menu includes sandwiches, char siu pork belly with pak choi, radish and pickled ginger salad, red pepper and goats cheese panna cotta with dried cherry tomatoes and artichoke salad, mussels in white wine, cream and garlic, steak and kidney pudding, cumin- and chilli-spiced chicken with roast sweet potatoes and tzatziki salad, fish pie, venison haunch with blackberry jus, and puddings such as hot waffle with toffee apples and crushed meringues with marmalade cream and roasted plums. *Benchmark main dish: braised lamb shoulder with dauphinoise potatoes and rosemary gravy £16.95. Two-course evening meal £19.50.*

Brunning & Price ~ Manager Christopher Beswick ~ Real ale ~ Open 11-11; 12-10.30 Sun ~ Bar food 12-10 (9.30 Sun) ~ Children welcome ~ Dogs allowed in bar ~ Wi-fi
Recommended by Peter Pilbeam, Lindy Andrews

BUNBURY
SJ5658 Map 7

Dysart Arms 🎖️ ♀ 🍺

(01829) 260183 – www.brunningandprice.co.uk/dysart
Bowes Gate Road; village signposted off A51 NW of Nantwich; and from A49 S of Tarporley – coming in this way on northernmost village access road, bear left in village centre; CW6 9PH

Civilised chatty dining pub attractively filled with good furniture in thoughtfully laid-out rooms, with enjoyable food and a lovely garden with pretty views

If you want to bag one of the sturdy wooden tables on the terrace or a picnic-set on the lawn in the neatly kept and slightly elevated garden, you must arrive promptly; the views of the splendid church at the end of this pretty village and the distant Peckforton Hills beyond are lovely. Although the interior has been opened up, the neatly kept rooms still retain a cottagey feel as they ramble around the pleasantly lit central bar. Cream walls keep it light, clean and airy, with deep venetian-red ceilings adding cosiness; each room (some with good winter fires) is nicely furnished with an appealing variety of well spaced sturdy wooden tables and chairs, a couple of tall filled bookcases and just the right amount of carefully chosen bric-a-brac, properly lit pictures and plants. Flooring ranges from red and black tiles to stripped boards and some carpet. Phoenix Brunning & Price Original and Weetwood Best Bitter with guests from breweries such as Big Hand, Pennine and Seren on handpump alongside a good selection of 17 wines by the glass and around 20 malts; background music and board games.

🎖️ Creative, seasonal food includes sandwiches, goats cheese terrine with fig chutney, sea trout on cucumber, spring onion and sesame salad with teriyaki dressing, steak burger with toppings, coleslaw and chips, honey-roast ham with free-range eggs, crab and leek quiche with herb and lemon crumb, twice-cooked pork belly with black pudding stuffing, roast cauliflower purée and pear tarte tatin, warm crispy lamb, olive and feta salad with mint and yoghurt dressing, and puddings such as white and dark chocolate truffle torte and crème brûlée. *Benchmark main dish: beer-battered haddock and chips £12.75. Two-course evening meal £20.00.*

Brunning & Price ~ Manager Kate John ~ Real ale ~ Open 11.30-11; 12-10.30 Sun ~ Bar food 12-9.30 (9 Sun) ~ Children welcome ~ Dogs allowed in bar ~ Wi-fi
Recommended by Claes Mauroy, Edward May, Emma Scofield

If a compulsory service charge is mentioned prominently on a menu or accommodation terms, you must pay it if service was satisfactory. If service is really bad, you are legally entitled to refuse to pay some or all of the service charge as compensation for not getting the service you might reasonably have expected.

BURLEYDAM

SJ6042 Map 7

Combermere Arms 🍴 🍺

(01948) 871223 – www.brunningandprice.co.uk/combermere

A525 Whitchurch–Audlem; SY13 4AT

Roomy and attractive beamed pub successfully mixing a good drinking side with imaginative all-day food

Consistently well run and highly enjoyable, this extended, partly 16th-c pub is a fine all-rounder – and you'll get an equally nice welcome whether you're eating or just in for a drink. The many rambling yet intimate-feeling rooms are attractive and understated; the various nooks and crannies are filled with all sorts of antique cushioned dining chairs around dark wood tables, rugs on wood (some old, some new oak) and stone floors, prints hung frame-to-frame on cream walls, bookshelves, deep red ceilings, panelling and open fires. Phoenix Brunning & Price Original, Cheshire Cat IPA, Joules Slumbering Monk, Salopian Shropshire Gold, Stonehouse Station Bitter and Timothy Taylors Boltmaker on handpump, 100 malt whiskies, 14 wines by the glass from an extensive list and three farm ciders; board games and background music. Outside there are good solid wood tables and picnic-sets in a pretty, well tended garden.

 The up-to-date and interesting food includes sandwiches, scallops with shredded ham bonbons, pea purée and green apple reduction, garlic wild mushrooms on toasted brioche, crab and prawn linguine, pork and apple sausages with onion gravy, thai chicken salad with pak choi, mango and a coconut and lime dressing, braised lamb shoulder with dauphinoise potatoes and rosemary gravy, and puddings such as raspberry bakewell tart and crème brûlée. *Benchmark main dish: crispy beef salad with chilli and cashews £12.95. Two-course evening meal £19.80.*

Brunning & Price ~ Manager Lisa Hares ~ Real ale ~ Open 12-11 (10.30 Sun) ~ Bar food 12-9.30 (10 Thurs-Sat, 9 Sun) ~ Children welcome ~ Dogs allowed in bar ~ Wi-fi
Recommended by Brian and Anna Marsden, John and Mary Warner, Dr and Mrs A K Clarke

BURWARDSLEY

SJ5256 Map 7

Pheasant ★ 🍴 ⏰ 🛏

(01829) 770434 – www.thepheasantinn.co.uk

Higher Burwardsley; signposted from Tattenhall (which itself is signposted off A41 S of Chester) and from Harthill (reached by turning off A534 Nantwich–Holt at the Copper Mine); follow pub's signpost uphill from Post Office; OS Sheet 117 map reference 523566; CH3 9PF

Fantastic views and enjoyable food at this fresh conversion of an old heavily beamed inn; good bedrooms

From the windows in the attractive bar, some of the comfortable bedrooms and the picnic-sets on the terrace, you can enjoy one of the county's most magnificent views right across the Cheshire plains; on a clear day with the telescope you can see as far as the pier head and cathedrals in Liverpool. The attractive low-beamed interior is airy and modern-feeling in parts, and the various separate areas have nice old chairs spread spaciously on wooden floors and a log fire in a huge see-through fireplace. Local Weetwood Best and Eastgate plus guests such as Cheshire Brew Brothers Chester Gold and Cheshire Cat Blonde Ale on handpump, a dozen wines by the glass, ten malt whiskies and local farm cider served by friendly, helpful staff; quiet background music and daily newspapers. There are some lovely surrounding walks and the scenic Sandstone Trail along the Peckforton Hills is nearby. Sister pubs are the Fishpool in Delamere and Bears Paw at Warmingham.

Enjoyable food from an interesting menu includes hot and cold sandwiches (until 6pm), moules marinière, crispy ox cheek with celeriac and horseradish rémoulade, streaky bacon and candied beetroot, sharing boards, pumpkin, parmesan and sage risotto with trompette mushrooms, lime and basil, a pie of the day, smoked bacon chop with fried duck egg and salsa verde, lamb shank with mint and red wine sauce, coq au vin, duck breast with beetroot ketchup, stuffed leg and agen prunes, and puddings such as baked alaska or treacle tart with walnut brittle and candied orange. *Benchmark main dish: beer-battered haddock and chips £13.50. Two-course evening meal £21.00.*

Free house ~ Licensee Andrew Nelson ~ Real ale ~ Open 11-11 (10.30 Sun) ~ Bar food 12-9.30 (10 Fri, Sat; 9 Sun) ~ Restaurant ~ Children welcome ~ Dogs allowed in bar and bedrooms ~ Wi-fi ~ Bedrooms: £75/£85 *Recommended by Claes Mauroy, Hilary and Neil Christopher, Toby Jones*

CHESTER
Albion ★ ◀ £

SJ4066 Map 7

(01244) 340345 – www.albioninnchester.co.uk
Albion Street; CH1 1RQ

Strongly traditional pub with comfortable Edwardian décor and captivating World War I memorabilia; pubby food and good drinks

'A wonderful place,' says a reader with enthusiasm – and we agree. The charming licensees have been running this genuinely friendly, old-fashioned pub for more than 40 years and over this time have amassed an absorbing collection of World War I memorabilia; in fact, this is an officially listed site of four war memorials to soldiers from the Cheshire Regiment. The peaceful rooms are filled with big engravings of men leaving for war and similarly moving prints of wounded veterans, as well as flags, advertisements and so on. There are also leatherette and hoop-backed chairs around cast-iron-framed tables, lamps, an open fire in the Edwardian fireplace and dark floral William Morris wallpaper (designed on the first day of World War I). You might even be lucky enough to hear the vintage 1928 Steck pianola being played; there's an attractive side dining room too. Harviestoun Haggis Hunters Ale and St Austell Tribute on handpump, new world wines, fresh orange juice, organic bottled cider and fruit juice, over 25 malt whiskies and a good selection of rums and gins. Bedrooms are small but comfortable and furnished in keeping with the pub's style (free parking for residents and a bottle of house wine if dining). An attractive way to reach the place is along the city wall, coming down at Newgate/Wolfsgate and walking along Park Street. No children.

The generously served 'trench rations' include club and doorstep sandwiches, corned beef hash with pickled red cabbage, fish pie with cheese topping, boiled gammon and pease pudding with parsley sauce, haggis and tatties, and lambs liver, bacon and onions with cider gravy. *Benchmark main dish: roast turkey and stuffing with cranberry and apple sauce £10.70. Two-course evening meal £15.00.*

Punch ~ Lease Mike and Christina Mercer ~ Real ale ~ No credit cards ~ Open 12-3, 5 (6 Sat)-11; 12-2.30 Sun; closed Sun evening ~ Bar food 12-2, 5-8 (8.30 Sat) ~ Restaurant ~ Dogs allowed in bar ~ Bedrooms: £75/£85 *Recommended by Pat and Tony Martin, Dr J Barrie Jones*

Places with gardens or terraces usually let children sit there –
we note in the text the very few exceptions that don't.

CHESTER
Architect 🏠❄️ ♀ ◀️

SJ4066 Map 7

(01244) 353070 – www.brunningandprice.co.uk/architect

Nicholas Street (A5268); CH1 2NX

Bustling pub by the racecourse with interesting furnishings and décor, attentive staff, a good choice of drinks and super food

With views over Roodee Racecourse (binoculars are provided), this lively establishment is almost two separate places connected by a glass passage. The pubbiest part, with more of a bustling feel, is the garden room where they serve Phoenix Brunning & Price Original and Weetwood Eastgate with guests such as Big Shed Engineers Best, Brimstage Sandpiper Pale, Cheshire Brewhouse Engine Vein and Howard Town Monks Gold on handpump, 18 wines by the glass, 74 whiskies and farm cider. Throughout there are elegant antique dining chairs around a mix of nice old tables on rugs or bare floorboards, hundreds of interesting paintings and prints on green, cream or yellow walls, house plants and flowers on window sills and mantelpieces, and lots of bookcases. Also, open fires, armchairs in front of a woodburning stove or tucked into cosy nooks, candelabra and big mirrors, and a friendly, easy-going atmosphere. Big windows and french doors look over the terrace, where there are plenty of good quality wooden seats and tables under parasols.

 Well presented and very highly rated, the smashing food includes sandwiches, cured salmon with wasabi cream and soy jelly, rabbit and prune faggot with wild mushroom gravy, honey-roast ham with free-range eggs, goats cheese, bulgar wheat and fig salad with sumac-toasted cauliflower, beer-battered haddock and chips, steak in ale pudding, chicken with lemon thyme potato dumplings and tarragon jus, and puddings such as lemon and passion-fruit tart with strawberry coulis and rum sponge with hazelnut and chocolate terrine and orange sauce. *Benchmark main dish: braised lamb shoulder with dauphinoise potatoes £17.75. Two-course evening meal £21.00.*

Brunning & Price ~ Manager Jon Astle-Rowe ~ Real ale ~ Open 10.30am-11pm; 10.30-10.30 Sun ~ Bar food 12-10 (9.30 Sun) ~ Restaurant ~ Children welcome ~ Dogs allowed in bar ~ Wi-fi *Recommended by Wendda and John Knapp, Edward Mirzoeff, Peter Pilbeam*

CHESTER
Mill ◀️ £

SJ4166 Map 7

(01244) 350035 – www.millhotel.com

Milton Street; CH1 3NF

Big hotel with huge range of real ales, good value food and cheery service in sizeable bar

An astonishing range of at least ten (and up to 16) beers are kept on handpump in this smart, modern hotel – and they get through more than 2,000 guests a year. Weetwood Best and Mill Premium (brewed for them by Coach House) are available all the time, with other regulars being from Bank Top, Cheshire, Copper Dragon, Peerless, Rudgate, Salopian, Stonehouse and Titanic; also, a dozen wines by the glass, two farm ciders and 20 malt whiskies. You'll find a real mix of customers in the neatly kept bar which has some exposed brickwork and supporting pillars, local photographs on cream-papered walls, contemporary seats around marble-topped tables on light wooden flooring, and helpful, friendly staff. One comfortable area is reminiscent of a bar on a cruise liner; quiet background music and unobtrusively placed big-screen sports TV. Converted from an old mill, the hotel straddles either side of the Shropshire Union Canal, with a glassed-in bridge connecting the two sections. The bedrooms are comfortable and rather smart.

A wide choice of good food from several different menus includes sandwiches and baguettes, tiger prawns with sweet chilli sauce, stuffed red peppers on couscous, pizzas, vegetable lasagne, chilli con carne, curries, breadcrumbed chicken breast stuffed with brie, leek and pine nuts and creamy tarragon sauce, and puddings such as sherry trifle and raspberry crème brûlée. *Benchmark main dish: steak in ale pie £12.50. Two-course evening meal £18.00.*

Free house ~ Licensee Gordon Vickers ~ Real ale ~ Open 10am-midnight (11pm Sun) ~ Bar food 11.30-11; 12-10 Sun ~ Restaurant ~ Children welcome ~ Wi-fi ~ Live jazz Mon evening ~ Bedrooms: £73/£95 *Recommended by Peter Brix, John Harris, John Wooll*

CHESTER
SJ4166   Map 7
Old Harkers Arms
(01244) 344525 – www.brunningandprice.co.uk/harkers
Russell Street, down steps off City Road where it crosses canal; CH3 5AL

Well run canalside building with a lively atmosphere, fantastic range of drinks and extremely good food

The name for this clever conversion of an early Victorian warehouse is taken from a Mr Harker who once ran a canal-boat chandler's here. And the pub is indeed right by the Shropshire Union Canal – you can watch the boats from the tall windows that run the length of the main bar. The striking industrial interior with its high ceilings is divided into user-friendly spaces by brick pillars. Walls are covered with old prints hung frame-to-frame, there's a wall of bookshelves above a leather banquette at one end, the mixed dark wood furniture is set out in intimate groups on stripped-wood floors, and attractive lamps lend some cosiness; board games. Cheerful staff serve up to nine real ales on handpump including Phoenix Brunning & Price Original, Weetwood Cheshire Cat and half a dozen regularly changing guests such as Facers North Star Porter, Fullers London Pride, Salopian Oracle, Tatton Best and Wincle Lord Lucan; also, 130 malt whiskies, 24 wines from a well described list and six farm ciders.

Enterprising food includes sandwiches, chicken liver pâté with caramelised red onion marmalade, curried crab croquettes with chilli, mango and spring onion salsa, carrot, lentil and mint fritters with red pepper, apricot and giant couscous salad, beef in ale pudding, seared swordfish steak with tomato sauce and charred vegetables, shredded duck salad with oranges, pistachio nuts and pomegranate dressing, and puddings such as iced black forest parfait with boozy cherries and lemon trifle. *Benchmark main dish: braised lamb shoulder with dauphinoise potatoes £16.95. Two-course evening meal £19.00.*

Brunning & Price ~ Manager Paul Jeffery ~ Real ale ~ Open 10.30am-11pm; 12-10.30 Sun ~ Bar food 12-9.30 ~ Children welcome but no babies, toddlers or pushchairs ~ Dogs allowed in bar ~ Wi-fi *Recommended by Wendda and John Knapp, Roger and Anne Newbury, Dr Kevan Tucker*

CHOLMONDELEY
SJ5550   Map 7
Cholmondeley Arms
(01829) 720300 – www.cholmondeleyarms.co.uk
Bickley Moss; A49 5.5 miles N of Whitchurch; SY14 8HN

Imaginatively converted high-ceilinged schoolhouse with a decent range of real ales and wines, well presented food and a sizeable garden; refurbished bedrooms

The bedrooms here (in the old headmaster's house opposite and named after real and fictional teachers) have been refurbished this year with the addition of antique furniture; many of the pictures dotted about actually did belong to former headmasters. The bar rooms, with their lofty ceilings and tall Victorian windows, have a great deal of individuality, and the huge old radiators and school paraphernalia (hockey sticks, tennis rackets, trunks and so forth) are all testament to its former incarnation. Also, armchairs by the fire with a massive stag's head above, big mirrors, all sorts of dining chairs and tables, warmly coloured rugs on bare boards, fresh flowers and church candles; background music. Cholmondeley Best and Headmasters Ale (both Weetwood beers) and three guests such as Salopian Shropshire Gold, Tatton Best and Wincle Waller on handpump, 15 wines by the glass and an amazing range of 250 gins. There's plenty of seating outside on the sizeable lawn, which drifts off into open countryside, and more in front overlooking the quiet road. The pub (owned by Tim Bird and Mary McLaughlin) is handily placed for Cholmondeley Castle Gardens.

Quite a choice of inventive food includes venison, pheasant and rabbit terrine with chutney, field mushrooms with white wine, cream and shallots, spinach, ricotta and pine nut-stuffed aubergine with date, pomegranate and pearl barley salad, wagyu beef burger with treacle-cured bacon, toppings and chips, fish pie with spicy roasted cauliflower, confit duck leg and chorizo with a fried duck egg, and puddings such as milk chocolate brownie with pistachio ice-cream and rum and raisin sponge with custard. *Benchmark main dish: steak and kidney pie £13.95. Two-course evening meal £19.00.*

Free house ~ Licensee Jessica Turner ~ Real ale ~ Open 12-11 (11.30 Sat, 10.30 Sun) ~ Bar food 12-9.15 (9.45 Fri, Sat) ~ No under-10s after 7pm ~ Dogs welcome ~ Wi-fi ~ Live easy-listening music Fri evening monthly ~ Bedrooms: £69.95/£88.95
Recommended by Steve Whalley, Ray and Winifred Halliday, Peter Harrison, Claes Mauroy, Dr and Mrs A K Clarke, R T and J C Moggridge

COTEBROOK
Fox & Barrel

SJ5765   Map 7

(01829) 760529 – www.foxandbarrel.co.uk
A49 NE of Tarporley; CW6 9DZ

Attractive building with stylishly airy décor, an enterprising menu and good wines

Despite the imaginative food, this is no straightforward dining pub and drinkers feel happily at home perched on the high chairs against the counter or on cushioned benches and settles enjoying a chat. Friendly staff serve Caledonian Deuchars IPA, Weetwood Eastgate and a couple of guests such as Black Sheep Golden Sheep and Slaters Top Totty on handpump; they also have a good array of wines including about 20 by the glass. A big log fire dominates the bar, while a larger uncluttered beamed dining area has attractive rugs and an eclectic mix of period tables on polished floorboards, with extensive wall panelling hung with framed old prints. The new front terrace has plenty of smart tables and chairs under parasols; at the back, there are picnic-sets on grass and some nice old fruit trees.

Tempting food from a wide menu includes sandwiches, twice-baked cheshire cheese soufflé, air-dried ham with honey-roast figs and marinated artichokes, honey-glazed gammon with pineapple and egg, wild mushroom and celeriac lasagne, salmon and smoked haddock fishcakes with dill mayonnaise, duck breast with braised faggot, salsify and madeira sauce, game pudding with juniper sauce, and puddings such as crème brûlée with mango compote and chocolate fondant. *Benchmark main dish: beer-battered fish and chips £13.75. Two-course evening meal £21.50.*

Free house ~ Licensee Gary Kidd ~ Real ale ~ Open 12-11 (10.30 Sun) ~ Bar food 12-9.30 (9 Sun) ~ Children welcome ~ Dogs allowed in bar ~ Wi-fi *Recommended by Hilary Forrest, John Harris*

DELAMERE
Fishpool ♀ 🍺   SJ5667   Map 7

(01606) 883277 – www.thefishpoolinn.co.uk

Junction A54/B5152 Chester Road/Fishpool Road, a mile W of A49; CW8 2HP

Something for everyone in extensive, interestingly laid-out pub, with a good range of food and drinks served all day

Both the layout and the décor have been given much thought and style here, and a large, cheerful open section has plenty of snug, cosy areas leading off with unusual and varied furnishings. There's a lofty central area, partly skylit – and full of contented diners – with a row of booths facing the long bar counter, and plenty of other tables with banquettes or overstuffed small armchairs on pale floorboards laid with rugs; then comes a conservatory overlooking picnic-sets on a flagstone terrace, and a lawn beyond. Off on two sides are many rooms with much lower ceilings, some with heavy dark beams, some with bright polychrome tile or intricate parquet flooring, William Morris wallpaper here, dusky paintwork or neat bookshelves there, sofas, armchairs, a fire in an old-fashioned open range, lots of old prints, and some intriguing objects including carved or painted animal skulls. Weetwood Best, Cheshire Cat and Eastgate plus guests such as Woodlands Ash Blonde and Red Squirrel on handpump, 13 wines by the glass and farm cider; unobtrusive background music; upstairs lavatories. Sister pubs are the Pheasant in Burwardsley and the Bears Paw in Warmingham.

Quite a choice of seasonal food includes sandwiches (until 6pm), creamy garlic mushrooms with truffle oil, chicken liver parfait with chutney, tandoori chicken and mango and pawpaw salad with mint crème fraîche, thin-crust pizzas from their wood-fired oven, tiger prawns and monkfish in sweet chilli sauce and stir-fried vegetables, slow-roast pork belly with apricot and sage stuffing, smoked bacon and puy lentils and red wine reduction, lamb shank with redcurrant and rosemary sauce, and puddings such as sticky toffee pudding with banoffi ice-cream and kirsch cherry crème brûlée; they also serve proper weekday afternoon tea. *Benchmark main dish: pie of the day £13.25. Two-course evening meal £22.00.*

Free house ~ Licensee Andrew Nelson ~ Real ale ~ Open 11-11 (10.30 Sun) ~ Bar food 12-9.30; 12-10 Fri, Sat; 12-9 Sun ~ Restaurant ~ Children welcome ~ Dogs allowed in bar ~ Wi-fi *Recommended by Malcolm and Pauline Pellatt, Lindy Andrews*

EATON
Plough 🛏   SJ8765   Map 7

(01260) 280207 – www.theploughinncheshire.com

A536 Congleton–Macclesfield; CW12 2NH

Neat and cosy village pub with up to four interesting beers, bar food and views from big attractive garden; good bedrooms

With friendly, attentive service and good food, this is a bustling village pub with a genuine welcome for visitors too. The carefully converted traditional bar has plenty of beams and exposed brickwork, a couple of snug little alcoves, comfortable armchairs and cushioned wooden wall seats on red patterned carpets, long red curtains, leaded windows and a woodburning stove in the big stone fireplace. Storm Desert Storm, Charles Wells Bombardier plus a couple of guest beers on handpump, ten wines by the glass from a decent list and 20 malt whiskies; background music, board games and occasional TV. Moved here piece by piece from its original home in Wales, the heavily raftered barn at the back makes a striking restaurant. From the big tree-filled back garden there are fine views of the fringes of the Peak District, with picnic-sets on the lawn and seats and tables set for dining on a covered decked terrace with heaters. The appealingly designed bedrooms are in a converted stable block. Dogs are allowed at the management's discretion.

Well liked food includes chicken liver pâté with home-made chutney, moules marinière, chilli con carne, mushroom stroganoff, wild boar sausages with mash, burger with toppings and french fries, steak and kidney pudding, slow-cooked lamb shoulder with minted gravy, and puddings such as fruit crumble and ice-cream sundae with chocolate sauce. *Benchmark main dish: rump steak plus trimmings £12.95. Two-course evening meal £15.00.*

Free house ~ Licensee Thomas Philip McCumesky ~ Real ale ~ Open 12-11 (midnight Sat); 12-10 Sun ~ Bar food 12-2.30, 6-9.30; 12-9.30 Sat; 12-8 Sun ~ Restaurant ~ Children welcome ~ Dogs allowed in bedrooms ~ Wi-fi ~ Bedrooms: £60/£75 *Recommended by Caroline Prescott, John and Mary Warner*

KETTLESHULME
Swan 🎔

SJ9879   Map 7

(01663) 732943

B5470 Macclesfield–Chapel-en-le-Frith, a mile W of Whaley Bridge; SK23 7QU

Charming 16th-c cottagey pub with enjoyable food (especially fish), good beer and an attractive garden

The friendly, courteous staff and enjoyable food in this pretty white cottage come in for warm praise from our readers. The interior is snug and cosy, with latticed windows, very low dark beams hung with big copper jugs and kettles, timbered walls, antique coaching and other prints and maps, ancient oak settles on a turkish carpet and log fires; a new dining room, with an open kitchen on view, has been introduced. Marstons Bitter on handpump with a couple of guest beers from breweries such as Phoenix and Whim, and 12 wines by the glass. The front terrace has teak tables, another two-level terrace has further tables and steamer benches under parasols, and there's a sizeable streamside garden. The pub is handy for walks in the relatively unfrequented north-west part of the Peak District National Park.

A thoughtful choice of interesting food includes sandwiches, rabbit liver and onions on toast, moules marinière, roast vegetable and butternut squash risotto, line-caught wild bass with spicy chorizo, tomato and saffron sauce, red thai chicken with lemongrass and lime leaves, game pie, langoustines with fennel and Pernod topped with a scallop baked in its shell, steaks from their new Josper oven, and puddings such as mulled poached pear with stem ginger ice-cream and chocolate brownie with chocolate sauce. *Benchmark main dish: beer-battered fish and chips £12.50. Two-course evening meal £20.00.*

Free house ~ Licensee Robert Cloughley ~ Real ale ~ Open 12-11 (midnight Sat); 12-10.30 Sun; closed Mon lunchtime ~ Bar food 12-9; 12-4 Sun ~ Restaurant ~ Children welcome ~ Dogs welcome *Recommended by John William Isaacson, Dr Kevan Tucker, Malcolm and Pauline Pellatt, Roger Yates, David Heath*

People named as recommenders after the full entries have told us that the pub should be included. But they have not written the report – we have, after anonymous on-the-spot inspection.

LACH DENNIS
SJ7072 Map 7
Duke of Portland 🏅 ♟
(01606) 46264 – www.dukeofportland.com

Holmes Chapel Road (B5082, off A556 SE of Northwich); CW9 7SY

Good food in stylish upscale dining pub that doesn't neglect the beer side

The carefully prepared food tends to be the main draw at this civilised pub, but you're equally welcome to sink into one of the comfortable leather sofas by the pretty Victorian fireplace to enjoy a relaxing drink. The bar area is decorated in beige, grey and creams, with square leather pouffes opposite sofas, chunky low tables on tartan carpets, an unusual contemporary fireplace and nicely framed prints above a panelled dado. Friendly staff behind the handsomely carved counter serve Banks's Bitter, Jennings Cocker Hoop, Marstons Pedigree and Wychwood Hobgoblin on handpump and several wines by the glass. The main dining room, with its lofty ceiling, sturdy balustrades and big pictures, gives quite a sense of occasion, but keeps a fairly relaxed feel – perhaps because of the friendly mix of styles in the comfortable dining chairs on its floorboards; background music. Outside, a neat terrace has picnic-sets among modernist planters and lovely countryside views.

Rewarding food includes beetroot-cured salmon with potato and dill blini and vodka crème fraîche, slow-cooked brisket with parmesan croquettes and shallot and watercress salad, vegetable linguine, duo of pork belly and hickory smoked ribs with coleslaw, burgers with toppings and a choice of sauces, grilled bass fillet with prawn and lemon butter, lamb tasting plate (mini shepherd's pie, confit of shoulder, cutlet with garlic jus) and puddings. *Benchmark main dish: peppered calves liver with crispy pancetta, tobacco onions and onion gravy £13.50. Two-course evening meal £20.00.*

Marstons ~ Lease Michael Massey ~ Real ale ~ Open 12-11 (midnight Sat); 12-10.30 Sun ~ Bar food 12-9.30 (8 Sun) ~ Restaurant ~ Children welcome ~ Dogs allowed in bar ~ Wi-fi
Recommended by Peter Brix, Nick Sharpe

LOWER PEOVER
SJ7474 Map 7
Bells of Peover 🏅
(01565) 722269 – www.thebellsofpeover.com

Just off B5081; The Cobbles; handy for M6 junction 17; WA16 9PZ

Wisteria-covered pub in pretty setting with real ales and interesting food; lots of seating areas in the garden

This is a lovely old building in a charming spot on a quiet cobbled lane. The various rooms have beams, panelling and open fires that contrast cleverly with contemporary seating ranging from brown leather cushioned wall banquettes to high-backed upholstered or leather dining chairs around an assortment of tables on bare boards; there are prints, paintings and mirrors on the walls. Robinsons Hartleys XB, Dizzy Blonde and Unicorn on handpump and several wines by the glass served by helpful, friendly staff; background music. Seats on the front terrace overlook the black and white 14th-c church, while at the side a spacious lawn beyond the old coachyard spreads down through trees and under rose pergolas to a little stream. No dogs inside.

Using the best local produce, the highly thought-of food includes open lobster and king prawn ravioli with tarragon butter sauce, crispy breaded pancetta with a fried duck egg and fruity fig sauce, aubergine and spinach moussaka with feta bonbons and oregano fries, steak and onion pie with triple-cooked chips, whole baked mackerel with lime and coriander butter, steak burger with toppings and skinny fries, lamb loin and lamb faggot with carrot purée, potato pave and port jus, and puddings such as lemon brûlée tart with raspberry sorbet and sherry trifle with praline cream; they also offer a two- and three-course weekday set menu. *Benchmark main dish: lemongrass and chilli chicken with noodles, pak choi and stir-fried vegetables in a fragrant broth £13.95. Two-course evening meal £20.00.*

Robinsons ~ Manager Joe Lourenco ~ Real ale ~ Open 12-11 ~ Bar food 12-9 (9.30 Fri, Sat; 8 Sun) ~ Restaurant ~ Children welcome ~ Wi-fi *Recommended by Hugh Roberts*

LOWER WITHINGTON   SJ8268   Map 7

Black Swan

(01477) 571770 – www.blackswancheshire.com

Trap Street; SK11 9EQ

Neatly kept and well run pub with character rooms, cottagey décor, enjoyable food and seats outside

It's all very light and airy here – with an easy-going atmosphere and a great deal of individual character too. Several cottage rooms have chesterfield sofas with brightly patterned scatter cushions, wooden and prettily upholstered chairs around scrubbed pine and painted tables, walls of red or green paintwork, bare brick or all kinds of cheerful wallpaper, assorted lighting from hanging floral lampshades to table lamps, and fresh flowers on window sills. Also, open fires, antlers, decorative plates and prints. Friendly staff serve Jennings Cumberland and guests from breweries such as Redwillow and Wincle on handpump, and a dozen wines by the glass. Outside there are green-painted picnic-sets and other seats on a side terrace and beneath a gazebo, and they have a summer pizza oven; boules. A gentle one-hour walk for dogs leads through the fields opposite. This is sister pub to the Swan at Newby Bridge (in Cumbria).

Some sort of good food is enjoyed all day: sandwiches, chorizo scotch egg with saffron aioli, crispy salt and pepper squid with chilli, lime and garlic mayonnaise, sharing boards with home-made flatbread, rotisserie chicken with smoky bourbon and cola barbecue sauce and chips, wild mushroom risotto, ox cheek ragoût with pesto linguine, hake fillet with curried potato, cauliflower rösti and mussel broth, and puddings. *Benchmark main dish: burger with toppings, pickles and french fries £11.95. Two-course evening meal £18.00.*

Free house ~ Licensee Sarah Gibbs ~ Real ale ~ Open 11-11; 10-midnight Fri, Sat; 10-10 Sun ~ Bar food 12-9 ~ Children welcome ~ Dogs allowed in bar ~ Wi-fi
Recommended by Roger and Anne Newbury, Hilary Forrest

MACCLESFIELD   SJ9271   Map 7

Sutton Hall 🍺

(01260) 253211 – www.brunningandprice.co.uk/suttonhall

Leaving Macclesfield southwards on A523, turn left into Byrons Lane signposted 'Langley, Wincle', then just before canal viaduct fork right into Bullocks Lane; OS Sheet 118 map reference 925715; SK11 0HE

Historic building set in attractive grounds, with a fine range of drinks and well trained, courteous staff

Considering this former convent is over 400 years old, it's highly impressive that fine original features have been carefully restored and incorporated into the fabric of an up-to-date pub. The original hall at the heart of the building is especially noteworthy – in particular the entrance space. A charming series of rooms (a bar, a library with books on shelves and a raised open fire and dining areas), some divided by tall oak timbers, are cosy with plenty of character, antique oak panelling, warmly coloured rugs on broad flagstones, bare boards and tiles, lots of pictures placed frame-to-frame, and two more fires. The atmosphere is nicely relaxed and a good range of drinks includes Phoenix Brunning & Price Original, Timothy Taylors Boltmaker, Wincle Lord Lucan and a couple of guests from brewers such as Beartown and Tatton on handpump, 18 wines by the glass from an extensive list and 30 malt whiskies. The pretty gardens have spaciously laid out tables, some on their own little terraces, sloping lawns and fine mature trees.

🍴 A wide choice of food includes sandwiches, potted shrimp and crayfish with pickled cucumber, garlic wild mushrooms on toast with a poached egg, jerk sweet potato and black bean curry on banana bread, pork and chorizo meatballs with peperonata sauce on pasta, asian-spiced duck salad with preserved plums, crisp mushrooms, water chestnuts and cashews, lamb shoulder with dauphinoise potatoes, and puddings such as crème brûlée and dark chocolate cheesecake with rum and raisin syrup. *Benchmark main dish: beer-battered haddock and chips £12.75. Two-course evening meal £20.50.*

Brunning & Price ~ Manager Syd Foster ~ Real ale ~ Open 11-11 (10.30 Sun) ~ Bar food 12-10 (9.30 Sun) ~ Children welcome ~ Dogs allowed in bar ~ Wi-fi
Recommended by John Wooll, Hilary Forrest, Edward May

MARTON
SJ8568   Map 7
Davenport Arms 🍴 £
(01260) 224269 – www.thedavenportarms.co.uk
A34 N of Congleton; SK11 9HF

Handsome pub with welcoming bar, comfortable restaurant, good food and drink, and good-sized sheltered garden

To find this welcoming pub, just head for the 14th-c timbered church opposite (which is worth a visit in its own right). The two linked front bar rooms have a good traditional feel, with comfortably cushioned wall settles, wing armchairs and other hand-picked furnishings on patterned carpet, a woodburning stove, a ticking clock, old prints on the cream walls and colourful jugs hanging from sturdy beams. You can eat (or just have a drink or coffee), and there's also a pleasantly light and airy more formal dining area behind; background music. Courage Directors, Theakstons Black Bull and a couple of guests such as Bollington White Nancy and Moorhouses Pride of Pendle on handpump, ten wines by the glass and friendly, helpful staff. Outside is a terrace with metal garden furniture, a fairy-lit arbour and a timber shelter, well spaced picnic-sets and a set of swings in the garden beyond, and a substantial separate play area. They do take caravans but you must book.

🍴 Good quality food includes lunchtime baguettes and wraps, black pudding, bacon and tomato stack with a poached egg, chilli and garlic king prawn salad with mango and onion salsa, fresh tagliatelle with tomato pesto and parmesan, home-baked ham and eggs, a curry and a pie of the day, full rack of ribs with coleslaw and chips, home-made fishcakes with citrus mayonnaise, braised beef with horseradish mash, and puddings. *Benchmark main dish: beer-battered fish and chips £12.95. Two-course evening meal £18.00.*

Free house ~ Licensees Ron Dalton and Sara Griffith ~ Real ale ~ Open 12-2.30, 6-11; 12-11 Sat; 12-11 Sun; closed Mon lunchtime except bank hols ~ Bar food 12-2.30, 6-9; 12-9 Sat; 12-8 Sun ~ Restaurant ~ Children welcome but not in restaurant after 8pm ~ Wi-fi
Recommended by Dr D J and Mrs S C Walker

MOBBERLEY
Bulls Head 🌟 ⚲ 🍺   SJ7879 Map 7
(01565) 873395 – www.thebullsheadpub.co.uk
Mill Lane; WA16 7HX

Terrific all-rounder with interesting food and drink and plenty of pubby character

There's a fine range of drinks in this especially well run, friendly pub – it's all been kept nice and pubby with just a touch of modernity. Four Weetwood beers (named for the pub) and three local guests from brewers such as Beartown, Tatton and Wincle on handpump (useful tasting notes too), 15 wines by the glass and around 80 whiskies. Several rooms are furnished quite traditionally, with an unpretentious mix of wooden tables, cushioned wall seats and chairs on fine old quarry tiles, black and pale grey walls contrasting well with warming red lampshades, and pink bare-brick walls and pale stripped-timber detailing; also, lots of mirrors, hops, candles, open fires, background music and board games. Dogs get a warm welcome (they're allowed in the snug) with friendly staff dispensing doggie biscuits from a huge jar, and they keep popular walk leaflets. There are seats outside in the big garden. The pub is owned by Tim Bird and Mary McLaughlin.

 Quite a choice of extremely good food includes hot and cold sandwiches, potted duck with red onion and blueberry compote, corned beef hashcake with bacon and a fried local egg, sharing platters, beer-battered haddock and chips, calves liver with bacon and onion gravy, slow-cooked lamb shank with spiced redcurrants and gravy, smoked haddock and salmon fishcakes with dill mayonnaise, and puddings such as chocolate brownie with chocolate sauce and apple crumble with cinnamon ice-cream. *Benchmark main dish: steak in ale pie £13.95. Two-course evening meal £19.00.*

Free house ~ Licensee Barry Lawlor ~ Real ale ~ Open 12-11 (midnight Fri); 12-11.30 Sat; 12-10.30 Sun ~ Bar food 12-9.15 (9.45 Fri, Sat); 12-9 Sun ~ Children welcome but no under-10s after 7pm ~ Dogs allowed in bar ~ Wi-fi ~ Live jazz occasional Sun 2pm
Recommended by Brian and Anna Marsden, Nigel and Sue Foster, Dr and Mrs A K Clarke

MOBBERLEY
Church Inn ★ 🌟 ⚲ 🍺   SJ7980 Map 7
(01565) 873178 – www.churchinnmobberley.co.uk
Brown sign to pub off B5085 on Wilmslow side of village; Church Lane; WA16 7RD

Nicely traditional, friendly country pub with bags of character; good food and drink

Behind this pretty brick building – opposite the village church – is a sunny garden that snakes down to the old bowling green with lovely pastoral views; a side courtyard has extremely sturdy tables and benches. Inside, small snug interconnected rooms have all manner of nice old tables and chairs on wide floorboards, low ceilings, plenty of candlelight and friendly young staff; it's best to book in advance to be sure of a table. The décor in soothing greys and dark green, with some oak-leaf wallpaper, is perked up by a collection of stuffed grouse and their relatives, and a huge variety of pictures; background pop music. Beartown Best Bitter, Mallorys Mobberley Best (George Mallory, lost near Everest's summit in 1924, is remembered in the church with a stained-glass window) and WhirlyBird and Tatton Church Ale-Alujah on handpump, and unusual and rewarding wines, with 15 by the glass; wine tastings can be booked in the upstairs private dining room. They give out a detailed leaflet describing a good four-mile round walk from the pub, passing sister pub the Bulls Head en route. Dogs are welcomed in the bar with not just a tub of snacks on the counter, but maybe even the offer of a meaty 'beer'.

 Rewarding food includes lunchtime sandwiches (not Sun), warm shredded pigeon with chicory and walnut salad and spiced pomegranate dressing, salmon fishcakes with pickled ginger, cucumber and lemon mayonnaise, tarte tatin of caramelised shallots, spinach and goats cheese with pear, frisée and toasted pine nut salad, sharing boards, slow-cooked treacle and ale beef with caramelised onion mash, lamb burger with home-made chips, crisp duck breast with spiced polenta, and puddings such as sticky ginger pudding with whisky sauce and millionaire's shortbread cheesecake; they offer Sunday brunch (10.30-12). *Benchmark main dish: shepherd's pie £13.95. Two-course evening meal £21.00.*

Free house ~ Licensee Simon Umpleby ~ Real ale ~ Open 12-11 (midnight Sat); 12-10.30 Sun ~ Bar food 12-9 (9.30 Fri, Sat); 10.30-8.30 Sun ~ Children welcome but no under-10s after 6pm ~ Dogs allowed in bar ~ Wi-fi *Recommended by Caroline Prescott, Belinda Stamp, Dr and Mrs A K Clarke*

MOTTRAM ST ANDREW   SJ8878 Map 7

Bulls Head 🏅 ♀ 🍺

(01625) 828111 – www.brunningandprice.co.uk/bullshead
A538 Prestbury–Wilmslow; Wilmslow Road/Priest Lane; E side of village; SK10 4QH

Superb country dining pub, a thoughtful range of drinks and interesting food, plenty of character and well trained staff

This makes an excellent retreat at any time of day. And while they do have a bustling bar, perhaps the main emphasis is on the dining areas at the far end. Four levels stack up alongside or above one other, each with a distinctive décor and style, from the informality of a sunken area with rugs on its tiled floor, through a comfortable library/dining room, to another with an upstairs conservatory feel and the last, higher-windowed, with more of a special-occasion atmosphere. The rest of the pub has an appealing and abundant mix of old prints and pictures, comfortable seating in great variety, a coal fire in one room, a blazing woodburning stove in a two-way fireplace dividing two other rooms and an antique black kitchen range in yet another. Phoenix Brunning & Price Original and Wincle Waller with guests such as Merlin Excalibur, Pennine Real Blonde and Timothy Taylors Landlord on handpump, around 20 wines by the glass, a fine range of spirits, and an attractive separate tea and coffee station with pretty blue and white china cups, teapots and jugs. Also, background music, daily papers and board games. There are picnic-sets beneath cocktail parasols on the lawn.

🍽 Excellent food includes sandwiches, indian-spiced lamb koftas with bombay potatoes and mint and cucumber raita, chicken liver pâté with caramelised onion marmalade, meat or vegetarian platters, steak burger with toppings, coleslaw and chips, steak and kidney pudding, pheasant breast bourguignon with rabbit and prune faggot, sumac- and orange-spiced chicken with mixed pepper, giant couscous and harissa courgettes, and puddings such as peach bakewell tart with apricot coulis and strawberry ice-cream and hot waffle with caramelised banana and toffee sauce. *Benchmark main dish: lamb shoulder with dauphinoise potatoes and rosemary gravy £18.95. Two-course evening meal £21.50.*

Brunning & Price ~ Manager Andrew Coverley ~ Real ale ~ Open 10.30am-11pm; 12-10.30 Sun ~ Bar food 12-10 (9.30 Sun) ~ Children welcome ~ Dogs allowed in bar ~ Wi-fi *Recommended by John Wooll, Pat and Tony Martin, Michael Butler, Brian and Anna Marsden, W K Wood*

NETHER ALDERLEY

SJ8576 Map 7

Wizard

(01625) 584000 – www.ainscoughs.co.uk

B5087 Macclesfield Road, opposite Artists Lane; SK10 4UB

Bustling pub with interesting food, real ales, a friendly welcome and relaxed atmosphere

The various rooms here, connected by open doorways, are cleverly done up in a mix of modern rustic and traditional styles. There are beams and open fires, antique dining chairs (some prettily cushioned) and settles around all sorts of tables, rugs on pale floorboards, prints and paintings on contemporary paintwork and decorative items ranging from a grandfather clock to staffordshire dogs and modern lampshades; fresh flowers and plants dotted about. Thwaites Wainwright and a guest from Storm on handpump and quite a few wines by the glass; background music. There are plenty of seats in the sizeable back garden – just right after a walk along Alderley Edge. The pub is part of the Ainscoughs group.

Using local, seasonal produce, the enterprising food includes lunchtime sandwiches, beef carpaccio with truffle oil and beetroot relish, pork and black pudding terrine with pickled cabbage, spinach, feta and ricotta pie, gammon and eggs, chicken with thyme and chestnut mousse, potato rösti and shallot sauce, cod on mashed potato with king prawn and pea cream, and puddings such as vanilla and lemon panna cotta and sticky toffee pudding with toffee sauce. *Benchmark main dish: beer-battered fish and triple-cooked chips £11.95. Two-course evening meal £20.00.*

Free house ~ Licensee Amy Pilley ~ Real ale ~ Open 12-11 (7 Sun) ~ Bar food 12-2.30, 6-9; 12-9 Sat; 12-6 Sun ~ Children welcome ~ Dogs allowed in bar ~ Wi-fi
Recommended by Anne and Ben Smith, John Harris

SANDBACH

SJ7560 Map 7

Old Hall

(01270) 758170 – www.brunningandprice.co.uk/oldhall

1.2 miles from M6 junction 17: A534 – ignore first turn into town and take the second – if you reach the roundabout, double back; CW11 1AL

Glorious mid 17th-c hall-house with impressive original features, plenty of drinking and dining space, six real ales and imaginative food

The room to the left of the entrance hall in this stunning 17th-c manor house has some of the best of the many wonderful original architectural features here. It remains much as it has been for centuries, with a Jacobean fireplace, oak panelling and priest's hole. This leads into the Oak Room, divided by standing timbers into two dining areas with heavy beams, oak flooring and reclaimed panelling. Other rooms in the original building have hefty beams and oak boards, three open fires and a woodburning stove; the cosy snugs are carpeted. The Garden Room is big and bright, with reclaimed quarry tiling and exposed A-frame oak timbering, and opens on to a suntrap back terrace with teak tables and chairs among flowering tubs. Throughout, the walls are covered with countless interesting prints, there's an appealing collection of antique dining chairs and tables of all sizes, and plenty of rugs, bookcases and plants. From the handsome bar counter, efficient and friendly staff serve Phoenix Brunning & Price Original, Redwillow Feckless and Three Tuns XXX with three quickly changing guests on handpump, 16 good wines by the glass, 50 malt whiskies and farm cider; board games. There are picnic-sets in front of the building by rose bushes and clipped box hedging.

Accomplished, attractively presented food includes sandwiches, tiger prawn, crayfish and apple cocktail with pomegranate dressing, crispy duck salad with hoisin, watermelon and chilli cashews, pork and leek sausages with onion gravy, tandoori grilled halloumi with toasted coconut, fresh pineapple, lime and mint salad, sicilian fish stew, steak and kidney pudding, duck breast with duck hash cake and black cherry sauce, and puddings such as crème brûlée and sticky toffee pudding with toffee sauce. *Benchmark main dish: braised lamb shoulder with dauphinoise potatoes and rosemary gravy £16.95. Two-course evening meal £20.00.*

Brunning & Price ~ Manager Chris Button ~ Real ale ~ Open 10.30am-11pm; 9am-11pm (10.30pm Sun) Sat ~ Bar food 12-10; 9am-10pm Sat; 9am-9.30pm Sun ~ Restaurant ~ Children welcome ~ Dogs allowed in bar ~ Wi-fi *Recommended by R T and J C Moggridge, Hugh Roberts, JPC*

SPURSTOW
Yew Tree ★ 🌟 ☲ ◨

SJ5657   Map 7

(01829) 260274 – www.theyewtreebunbury.com
Off A49 S of Tarporley; follow 'Bunbury 1, Haughton 2' signpost into Long Lane; CW6 9RD

Cheshire Dining Pub of the Year

Plenty of individuality, smashing food and drinks and a bouncy atmosphere

With quirky and individual décor, cheerful, friendly staff and a thoughtful choice of both food and drink – this entertaining place is popular with a wide mix of customers. There's a magnificent hunting tapestry and surprisingly angled bright tartans, nicely simple pale grey, off-white and cream surfaces that explode into striking bold wallpaper, and an elegant medley of attractive old tables and chairs. Timorous Beasties' giant bees are papered on to the bar ceiling and a stag's head looms out of the wall above a log fire. And the doors to the loos are quite a puzzle – which of the many knobs and handles actually work?! Heavy Industry Electric Mountain, Moorhouses Black Cat, Rebel Sail Ale, Slaters Bitter and Stonehouse Station Bitter on handpump, 20 malt whiskies, 15 wines by the glass from an interesting list and 20 gins. A more dining-oriented area shares the same feeling of relaxed bonhomie – a favourite table is snugged into a stripped-wood alcove resembling a stable stall; background music. A terrace outside has teak tables, with more on the lawn.

Seasonal, local produce is at the heart of the menu; the seriously good food includes lunchtime sandwiches, salt and pepper squid with romesco sauce, parmesan arancini with cauliflower purée and tea-soaked sultanas, smoked chicken caesar salad with soft-boiled eggs and croutons, a pie of the day, herb-crusted salmon chop with parsley mash and creamed spinach, a trio of lamb (shepherd's pie, grilled rump, confit shoulder) with carrot purée and rosemary jus, and puddings such as banana parfait with toffee sauce and caramelised banana and chocolate and hazelnut pavlova. *Benchmark main dish: fish pie £12.00. Two-course evening meal £20.00.*

Free house ~ Licensees Jon and Lindsay Cox ~ Real ale ~ Open 12-11 (10.30 Sun)) ~ Bar food 12-9.30 (10 Fri, Sat); 12-9 Sun ~ Children welcome ~ Dogs welcome ~ Wi-fi ~ Live music last Fri of month *Recommended by Tim Brogan, Steve Whalley*

Real ale may be served from handpumps, electric pumps (not just the on-off switches used for keg beer) or – common in Scotland – tall taps called founts (pronounced 'fonts') where a separate pump pushes the beer up under air pressure.

SWETTENHAM

SJ7967 Map 7

Swettenham Arms 🍴 ♀

(01477) 571284 – www.swettenhamarms.co.uk

Off A54 Congleton–Holmes Chapel or A535 Chelford–Holmes Chapel; CW12 2LF

Big old country pub in a fine setting with shining brasses, five real ales and tempting food

Our readers enjoy their visits to this carefully run, former nunnery so much that they return again and again. The three interlinked areas are still nicely traditional, with individual furnishings on bare floorboards or a sweep of fitted turkey carpet, dark heavy beams, a polished copper bar, three new woodburning stoves, plenty of shiny brasses and a variety of old prints (military, hunting, old ships, reproduction Old Masters and so forth). Friendly efficient staff serve Tatton Best, Timothy Taylors Landlord, Charles Wells Bombardier and Wincle Waller on handpump, 14 wines by the glass, several malt whiskies and winter mulled wine and cider. Outside, behind the pub, are tables on a lawn that merges into a lovely sunflower and lavender meadow. There are walks in the pretty surrounding countryside and Quinta Arboretum is close by. Do visit the interesting village church which dates in part from the 13th c.

 Using only local, seasonal produce, the very rewarding food includes sandwiches, hand-dived scallops with crispy pancetta, mixed game terrine with pickled sweet chestnuts, tempura scampi with fennel and courgette salad, wild mushroom and butternut squash risotto, chicken and mushroom pie, braised ox cheek with smoked onion mash and bourguignon sauce, and puddings such as chocolate mousse with raspberry yoghurt sorbet and bakewell tart with vanilla ice-cream. *Benchmark main dish: steak and mushroom in ale pie £12.95. Two-course evening meal £18.00.*

Free house ~ Licensees Jim and Frances Cunningham ~ Real ale ~ No credit cards ~ Open 11.30-11 (midnight Sat); 12-10 Sun; 11.30-3.30, 6-11 in winter ~ Bar food 12-9.30; 12-2.30, 6-9.30 in winter ~ Restaurant ~ Children welcome ~ Dogs allowed in bar ~ Wi-fi
Recommended by Hilary Forrest, Mr and Mrs R Shardlow, Robert Wivell

THELWALL

SJ6587 Map 7

Little Manor ♀

(01925) 212070 – www.brunningandprice.co.uk/littlemanor

Bell Lane; WA4 2SX

Restored manor house with plenty of room, lots of interest, well kept ales and tasty bistro-style food; seats outside

There's so much to look at in this big, handsome 17th-c house. The six beamed rooms, connected by open doorways and standing timbers, have been thoughtfully renovated; there are plenty of nooks and crannies too. Flooring ranges from rugs on bare boards through carpeting to some fine old black and white tiles, and there's an appealing variety of antique dining chairs around small, large, circular or square tables, as well as leather armchairs by open fires (note the lovely carved wooden one); background music. Lighting is from metal chandeliers, wall lights and standard lamps, and the décor includes hundreds of intriguing prints and photos, books on shelves and lots of old glass and stone bottles on window sills and mantelpieces; plenty of fresh flowers and house plants too. Phoenix Brunning & Price Original and Coach House Cromwells Best Bitter with guests from Hawkshead, Tatton and Wincle on handpump, around 15 wines by the glass, almost 30 gins and 60 whiskies; the young staff are consistently helpful. In fine weather you can sit at the chunky teak chairs and tables on the terrace; some are under a heated shelter.

🍴 From a seasonal menu, the interesting food includes sandwiches, cider-braised pig cheeks with pork medallion, black pudding fritter, apple crisp and cider jelly, mussels with leek, cider and cream, vegetable curry with cashew nut rice, honey-roast ham with free-range eggs, fish pie, steak burger with toppings, coleslaw and chips, duck breast with sweet potato fondant, tempura vegetables and red wine hoisin sauce, and puddings such as passion-fruit and lime cheesecake with mango and chilli salsa and mango and ginger ice-cream, and bread and butter pudding with apricot sauce. *Benchmark main dish: beer-battered haddock and chips £12.75. Two-course evening meal £18.50.*

Brunning & Price ~ Manager Jill Dowling ~ Real ale ~ Open 11-11; 12-10.30 Sun ~ Bar food 12-10 (9 Sun) ~ Children welcome ~ Dogs allowed in bar ~ Wi-fi
Recommended by David Jackman, R T and J C Moggridge

WARMINGHAM   SJ7161   Map 7
Bears Paw 🍺 🛏

(01270) 526317 – www.thebearspaw.co.uk
School Lane; CW11 3QN

Nicely maintained place with enjoyable food, half a dozen real ales and seats outside; bedrooms

Our readers enjoy staying in the comfortable and well equipped bedrooms here and breakfasts are particularly good. There's a maze of linked rooms with plenty of individual character, but we especially like the two little sitting rooms with panelling, fashionable wallpaper, bookshelves and slouchy leather furniture with plumped-up cushions comfortably arranged by woodburning stoves in magnificent fireplaces; stripped wood flooring and a dado keep it all informal. An eclectic mix of old wooden tables and some nice old carved chairs are well spaced throughout the dining areas, with lofty windows providing a light and airy feel and big pot plants adding freshness. There are stools at the long bar counter where cheerful, efficient staff serve Beartown Ursa Minor and Wojtek, Westwood Best, Wincle Life of Riley and Woodlands Oak Beauty on handpump, a dozen wines by the glass, quite a few malt whiskies and local cider; background music. A small front garden by the car park has seats and tables. This is sister pub to the Pheasant in Burwardsley and the Fishpool at Delamere.

🍴 Using free-range local produce, the reliably good food includes sandwiches (until 6pm), duck liver parfait with red onion marmalade, sizzling tiger prawns with chilli, garlic and basil, several sharing boards, roast sweet potato, spinach and blue cheese or rabbit, leek, mushroom and wholegrain mustard pies, home-smoked chicken and wild mushroom tagliatelle with parmesan, bass with garlic gnocchi, crispy calamari, red wine poached salsify and butter sauce, lamp rump with rosemary potato cake and redcurrant jus, and puddings such as dark chocolate and banana tart and apple and rhubarb pie. *Benchmark main dish: steak in ale pie £12.95. Two-course evening meal £21.00.*

Free house ~ Licensee Andrew Nelson ~ Real ale ~ Open 11-11 (10.30 Sun) ~ Bar food 12-9.30 (10 Fri, Sat); 12-9 Sun ~ Restaurant ~ Children welcome ~ Dogs allowed in bar and bedrooms ~ Wi-fi ~ Bedrooms: £95/£105 *Recommended by David Jackman, William and Ann Reid*

WHITELEY GREEN   SJ9278   Map 7
Windmill 🍷 🍺

(01625) 574222 – www.thewindmill.info
Brown sign to pub off A523 Macclesfield–Poynton, just N of Prestbury; Hole House Lane; SK10 5SJ

Extensive relaxed country dining bar with big sheltered garden and enjoyable food

Middlewood Way (a sort of linear country park) and Macclesfield Canal (Bridge 25) are just a stroll away from this bustling pub. The interior spreads around a big bar counter faced with maroon leather padding, its handpumps serving Sharps Doom Bar and local guests from breweries such as Beartown, Mobberley, Storm and Tatton; also, a dozen wines by the glass served by friendly and helpful staff. Most of the pub is given over to dining tables, mainly in a pleasantly informal, painted base/stripped top style, on bare boards. One area has several leather sofas and fabric-upholstered easy chairs; another by a log fire in a huge brick fireplace has more easy chairs and a squishy suede sofa. Background pop music, daily papers. The pub is up a long quiet lane in deepest leafy Cheshire countryside, and its spreading lawns, surrounded by a belt of young trees, provide plenty of room for well spaced tables and picnic-sets, and even a maze to baffle children.

High-quality food from a changing menu includes sandwiches, home-smoked duck breast with pickled kohlrabi and scorched clementine dressing, chicken livers in brandy sauce on toasted ciabatta, cumberland sausage casserole, falafel cake with curried lentils and raita dip, chicken with sweet potato blini and wild mushroom sauce, bass fillets with moules marinière and kale stew, and puddings such as sticky toffee pudding with butterscotch sauce and dark chocolate fondant with mascarpone ice-cream; steak night is the first Wednesday of the month. *Benchmark main dish: beer-battered haddock and chips £13.00. Two-course evening meal £18.00.*

Mitchells & Butlers ~ Lease Peter Nixon ~ Real ale ~ Open 12-11 (10.30 Sun) ~ Bar food 12-2.30, 5-9.30; 12-9.30 Sat; 12-8 Sun ~ Children welcome ~ Dogs allowed in bar ~ Wi-fi ~ Live music every second and last Fri of month *Recommended by Adam Macintosh, John Wooll*

Also Worth a Visit in Cheshire

Besides the fully inspected pubs, you might like to try these pubs that have been recommended to us and described by readers. Do tell us what you think of them: feedback@goodguides.com

ALLGREAVE   SU9767
Rose & Crown (01260) 227232
A54 Congleton–Buxton; SK11 0BJ
Welcoming roadside pub in remote upland spot with good Dane Valley views and walks; refurbished beamed rooms, wood floors and log fires, good local food from bar and restaurant menus including daily specials, half a dozen well kept ales such as Jennings and Wincle from new wood-clad servery, cheerful attentive service; children and dogs welcome, lawned garden taking in the views, three bedrooms. *(Peter Brix)*

ALPRAHAM   SJ5759
Travellers Rest (01829) 260523
A51 Nantwich–Chester; CW6 9JA
Timeless four-room country local in same friendly family for three generations, well kept Tetleys and Weetwood, leatherette, wicker and Formica, some flock wallpaper, fine old brewery mirrors, darts and dominoes, chatty regulars, no food; may be nesting swallows in the outside gents'; dogs welcome, back bowling green, 'Hat Day' last Sun before

Christmas with locals sporting unusual headgear, eggs for sale, closed weekday lunchtimes. *(Claes Mauroy)*

BARBRIDGE   SJ6156
Barbridge Inn (01270) 528327
Just off A51 N of Nantwich; CW5 6AY
Open-plan family dining pub by lively marina at junction of Shropshire Union and Middlewich canals, enjoyable good value food from sandwiches to steaks served by friendly staff, local Woodlands beers kept well, conservatory; background music, no dogs inside; waterside garden with play area, open (and food) all day. *(Emma Scofield)*

BARTON   SJ4454
★**Cock o' Barton** (01829) 782277
Barton Road (A534 E of Farndon); SY14 7HU Stylish contemporary décor in bright open skylit bar, good choice of well liked up-to-date food (children eat for free Sun), cocktail menu and plenty of wines by the glass, ales such as Spitting Feathers and Stonehouse, neat courteous staff, beamed restaurant areas; background and some

live music; tables in sunken heated inner courtyard with canopies and modern water feature, picnic-sets on back lawn, closed Mon, otherwise open (and food) all day. *(Anon)*

BIRKENHEAD   SJ3386
Refreshment Rooms
(0151) 644 5893 *Bedford Road E; CH42 1LS* Bow-fronted former 19th-c refreshment rooms for the Mersey ferry; three rooms with interesting collection of old photographs and other memorabilia, good selection of mainly local ales such as Liverpool Organic, Peerless and a house beer from Lees (HMS Conway), Rosie's welsh cider and a couple of interesting lagers, good competitively priced home-made food including OAP deal (Mon-Weds) and other set menus, friendly prompt service; quiz Weds, live music last Fri of month, pool; children and dogs welcome, beer garden at back with play area, open (and food) all day. *(Tom and Jill Jones)*

BOLLINGTON   SJ9377
Church House
(01625) 574014 *Church Street; SK10 5PY* Welcoming village pub with good reasonably priced home-made food including OAP menu, efficient friendly service, well kept Adnams, Saltaire and a guest, nice open fire, separate dining room; children and clean dogs welcome, good place to start or end a walk, bedrooms, open all day weekends (food all day Sun). *(Dr D J and Mrs S C Walker)*

BOLLINGTON   SJ9477
Poachers
(01625) 572086 *Mill Lane; SK10 5BU* Stone-built village local prettily set in good walking area, comfortable and welcoming, with good pubby food including bargain lunches, well kept Storm, Weetwood and three guests, daily newspapers; children and dogs welcome, sunny back garden, open (and food) all day Sun, closed Mon lunchtime. *(Edward May)*

BOLLINGTON   SJ9377
Vale
(01625) 575147 *Adlington Road; SK10 5JT* Friendly tap for Bollington Brewery in three converted 19th-c cottages, their full range and a couple of local guests (tasters offered), good range of enjoyable freshly made food, efficient knowledgeable young staff, interesting photos, newspapers and books, roaring fire; picnic-sets out behind overlooking cricket pitch, near Middlewood Way and Macclesfield Canal, open all day Fri-Sun. *(Peter Pilbeam)*

BRERETON GREEN   SJ7764
Bears Head
(01477) 544732 *Handy for M6 junction 17; set back off A50 S of Holmes Chapel; CW11 1RS* Beautiful 17th-c black and white timbered Vintage Inn with civilised linked rooms, low beams, log fires and old-fashioned furniture

on flagstones or bare boards, enjoyable well prepared food served by friendly staff, Sharps Doom Bar, Thwaites Wainwright and a guest; 25 bedrooms in modern Innkeepers Lodge, open (and food) all day. *(Dr D J and Mrs S C Walker)*

BURTONWOOD   SJ5692
Fiddle i'th' Bag (01925) 225442
3 miles from M62 junction 9, signposted from A49 towards Newton-le-Willows; WA5 4BT Eccentric place (not to everyone's taste) crammed with bric-a-brac and memorabilia, three well kept changing ales and enjoyable uncomplicated home-made food (cash only), friendly staff; may be nostalgic background music; children welcome, open all day weekends. *(Anon)*

CHELFORD   SJ8175
★Egerton Arms (01625) 861366
A537 Macclesfield–Knutsford; SK11 9BB Cheerful rambling old village pub, beams and nice mix of furniture including carved settles, wooden porter's chair by grandfather clock, Copper Dragon Golden Pippin, Wells Bombardier and three guests, good food and service, restaurant, steps down to little raftered games area with pool and darts; background music (live jazz last Fri of month), sports TV; children and dogs welcome, picnic-sets on canopied deck, more on grass and toddlers' play area, adjoining deli, open (and food) all day. *(Dr D J and Mrs S C Walker)*

CHESTER   SJ4065
★Bear & Billet (01244) 351002
Lower Bridge Street; CH1 1RU Handsome 17th-c timbered Okells pub with four changing guest ales, belgian and american imports and nice range of wines by the glass, reasonably priced home-made pubby food, interesting features and some attractive furnishings in friendly and comfortable open-plan bar with coal fire, sitting and dining rooms upstairs; sports TVs; children and dogs welcome, pleasant courtyard, open all day. *(Toby Jones)*

CHESTER   SJ4065
Brewery Tap (01244) 340999
Lower Bridge Street; CH1 1RU Tap for Spitting Feathers Brewery in interesting Jacobean building with 18th-c brick façade, steps up to lofty bar (former great hall) serving their well kept ales plus mainly local guests, real cider and good choice of wines, hearty home-made food using local suppliers including produce from Spitting Feathers farm (rare-breed pork); open (and food) all day. *(Roger and Anne Newbury)*

CHESTER   SJ4166
Cellar (01244) 318950
City Road; CH1 3AE Laid-back Canal Quarter bar with four well kept changing ales (cheaper on Mon), craft kegs and good

selection of interesting imported beers, some good value food including burgers, live music Fri and Sat (can get packed), basement bar for private functions; sports TV; closed weekday lunchtimes, open all day weekends (till 2.30am Fri, Sat). *(Toby Jones)*

CHESTER SJ4066

Coach House (01244) 351900

Northgate Street; CH1 2HQ Updated 19th-c coaching inn by town hall and cathedral, comfortable lounge with central bar, Thwaites and a guest, good choice of bottled beers and wines by the glass, enjoyable reasonably priced home-made food from semi-open kitchen, afternoon teas, prompt friendly service; children and dogs welcome, tables out in front, eight bedrooms, open all day from 9am for breakfast. *(Robert W Buckle)*

CHESTER SJ4065

Cross Keys (01244) 344460

Duke Street/Lower Bridge Street; CH1 1RU Small Victorian corner pub with ornate interior, dark panelling, etched mirrors and stained-glass windows, button-back leather wall benches and cast-iron tables on bare boards, open fire, well kept Joules ales and a guest, sensibly priced pubby food (not Mon, Tues), upstairs function room; free wi-fi; seats out in front, open all day. *(Dr Kevan Tucker)*

CHESTER SJ4066

Olde Boot (01244) 314540

Eastgate Row N; CH1 1LQ Lovely 17th-c Rows building, heavy beams, dark woodwork, oak flooring and flagstones, old kitchen range in lounge beyond, settles and oak panelling in upper area, well kept/priced Sam Smiths, cheerful service and bustling atmosphere; no children. *(Edward Mirzoeff)*

CHESTER SJ4066

Pied Bull (01244) 325829

Upper Northgate Street; CH1 2HQ Old beamed and panelled coaching inn with roomy open-plan carpeted bar, good own-brewed ales along with guests, enjoyable fairly priced traditional food from sandwiches and baked potatoes up, friendly staff and locals, imposing stone fireplace with tapestry above, divided inner dining area; background music, games machines; children welcome, handsome Jacobean stairs to 13 bedrooms, open (and food) all day. *(Jo Garnett)*

CHESTER SJ4066

Telfords Warehouse (01244) 390090

Tower Wharf, behind Northgate Street near railway; CH1 4EZ Well kept interesting ales in large converted canal building, fairly priced up-to-date food including good sandwich menu, friendly efficient young staff, bare boards, exposed brickwork and high pitched ceiling, big wall of windows overlooking the water, some old

enamel signs and massive iron winding gear in bar, steps up to heavily beamed area with sofas, artwork and restaurant; late-night live music, bouncers on the door; tables out by canal, open all day (till late Weds-Sun). *(Edward Mirzoeff)*

CHURCH MINSHULL SJ6660

Badger (01270) 522607

B5074 Winsford–Nantwich; handy for Shropshire Union Canal, Middlewich branch; CW5 6DY Refurbished 18th-c coaching inn in pretty village next to church, good imaginative food from sharing boards up (pub favourite too), well kept ales such as Black Sheep, Tatton and Wincle, Thatcher's cider, interesting range of wines and several malt whiskies, friendly helpful staff, bar and spacious lounge leading to back conservatory; children till 6pm, five bedrooms, good breakfast, open (and food) all day. *(Leo and Barbara Lionet, John and Hazel Sarkanen)*

COMBERBACH SJ6477

Spinner & Bergamot (01606) 891307 *Warrington Road; CW9 6AY* Comfortable 18th-c beamed village pub (named after two racehorses), good home-made food including smaller helpings on some main courses, friendly attentive service, well kept Robinsons ales and good wines, pitched-ceiling timber dining extension, two-room carpeted lounge and tiled-floor public bar where dogs allowed, log fires, some Manchester United memorabilia; unobtrusive background music, sports TV, Mon quiz; children welcome, picnic-sets on sloping lawn, lots of flowers, small verandah, bowling green, open all day (food all day Sun). *(Tom and Jill Jones)*

CONGLETON SJ8659

Horseshoe (01260) 272205

Fence Lane, Newbold Astbury, between A34 and A527 S; CW12 3NL Former 18th-c coaching inn set in peaceful countryside; three small carpeted rooms with decorative plates, copper and brass and other knick-knacks (some on delft shelves), mix of seating including plush banquettes and iron-base tables, log fire, well kept predominantly Robinsons ales, popular hearty home-made food at reasonable prices, friendly staff and locals; no dogs; children welcome, rustic garden furniture, adventure play area with tractor, good walks. *(Dr D J and Mrs S C Walker)*

CONGLETON SJ8762

Queens Head (01260) 272546

Park Lane (set down from flyover); CW12 3DE Friendly local by Macclesfield Canal, quaint dark interior with open fire, up to nine well kept ales and good selection of malt whiskies, reasonably priced hearty pub food (not Sun evening), friendly staff, table skittles, darts and pool (free Sun); sports TV, quiz Mon, poker Tues; children and dogs

welcome, steps up from towpath
to nice garden with play area and boules,
three bedrooms, useful for station, open
all day. (Anon)

COTEBROOK   SJ5765
Alvanley Arms (01829) 760200
A49/B5152 N of Tarporley; CW6 9DS
Welcoming roadside coaching inn, 17th-c
behind its Georgian façade, with Robinsons
ales and good value food including midweek
set deal, three beamed rooms, big open fire,
shire horse décor (plenty of tack and pictures
– adjacent stud open in season); background
music; children welcome, garden with large
pond, pleasant walks, seven comfortable
bedrooms. (Malcolm and Pauline Pellatt)

CREWE   SJ7055
Borough Arms (01270) 748189
Earle Street; CW1 2BG Own microbrewery
and lots of changing guest ales, good choice
of continental beers too, friendly staff and
regulars, two small rooms off central bar
and downstairs lounge; occasional sports
TV; picnic-sets on back terrace and lawn,
open all day Fri-Sun, closed lunchtime other
days. (Jo Garnett)

DUNHAM MASSEY   SJ7288
Rope & Anchor (0161) 927 7901
Paddock Lane; WA14 5RP Minimalist feel
with neutral colours throughout and lots of
varnished wood and chrome, swish brasswork
around the bar, light wooden floors with inset
slate tiling, limed tables and bench seating,
mix of armchairs, large log-effect gas fire
behind glass, Lees beers and good range of
wines by the glass, nice food from sandwiches
and pub staples to more upscale dishes,
efficient friendly staff, additional upstairs
dining area; background music; children
welcome, lots of outside seating with heaters
and umbrellas, smokers' shelter, open all
day. (Hilary Forrest)

FADDILEY   SJ5852
★ Thatch (01270) 524223
A534 Wrexham–Nantwich; CW5 8JE
Attractive, thatched, low-beamed and
timbered dining pub carefully extended
from medieval core, open fires, raised room
to right of bar, back barn-style dining room
(children allowed here), well kept ales such
as Salopian and Weetwood, good choice of
enjoyable popular food (booking advised
weekends), friendly helpful service, relaxing
atmosphere; soft background music, free
wi-fi; charming country garden with play
area, open all day weekends, closed Mon and
Tues lunchtimes. (Nick Sharpe)

FRODSHAM   SJ5276
Travellers Rest (01928) 735125
B5152 Frodsham–Kingsley; WA6 6SL
Popular family-run roadside dining pub
with good food from sandwiches and pub
favourites up, well kept Black Sheep,

Marstons and a guest, good selection of
wines, attentive cheerful service; free wi-fi;
children welcome, superb views across Weaver
Valley, open all day (food till 6pm Sun).
(John and Mary Warner)

FULLERS MOOR   SJ4954
Sandstone (01829) 782333
A534; CH3 9JH Light and airy dining pub
with wide choice of good sensibly priced
fresh food from sandwiches and snacks up,
four well kept ales including Stonehouse and
maybe own Sandstone (brewed in Wrexham),
friendly efficient staff, woodburner, dining
conservatory; Tues quiz; children and dogs
(in bar) welcome, spacious garden with
lovely views, handy for Sandstone Trail, open
(and food) all day weekends. (John and Mary
Warner)

GAWSWORTH   SJ8869
★ Harrington Arms (01260) 223325
*Off A536; Congleton Road/Church Lane;
SK11 9RJ* This unspoilt three-storey
building is still part of a working farm; low
17th-c beams, tiled and flagstoned floors,
snug corners and open fires, counter in
narrow space on right serving Robinsons ales,
a guest beer and good selection of wines and
whiskies, several unpretentious rooms off
with old settles and eclectic mix of tables
and chairs, lots of pictures on red or pale
painted walls, well liked hearty food from hot
and cold sandwiches to daily specials, chatty
relaxed atmosphere; background music, free
wi-fi; children and dogs (in bar) welcome,
benches out on small front cobbled area,
more seats in garden overlooking fields, lane
leads to one of Cheshire's prettiest villages,
open all day weekends. (Stuart Paulley,
Dr D J and Mrs S C Walker, Claes Mauroy)

GOOSTREY   SJ7770
Crown (01477) 532128
Off A50 and A535; CW4 8PE Extended
18th-c village pub, beams and open fires,
good choice of enjoyable food with some main
courses available in smaller sizes, friendly
efficient service, well kept ales including
locals such as Tatton and Weetwood, plenty
of wines by the glass; open mike night first
Weds of month; close to Jodrell Bank, open
all day. (Malcolm and Pauline Pellatt)

GRAPPENHALL   SJ6386
★ Parr Arms (01925) 212120
*Near M6 junction 20 – A50 towards
Warrington, left after 1.5 miles; Church
Lane; WA4 3EP* Renovated black-beamed
pub in picture-postcard setting with picnic-
sets out on cobbles by church, more tables
on small canopied back terrace, reasonably
priced food from ciabattas to blackboard
specials, friendly helpful service, well
kept Robinsons from central bar, log fires;
children and dogs welcome, open (and food)
all day. (Hilary Forrest)

GREAT BUDWORTH   SJ6677
George & Dragon (01606) 892650
Signed off A559 NE of Northwich; High Street opposite church; CW9 6HF
Characterful building dating from 1722 (front part is 19th-c) in delightful village; Lees ales kept well and plenty of wines by the glass, welcoming friendly young staff, good choice of enjoyable reasonably priced home-made food from lunchtime sandwiches and baguettes to specials, dark panelled bar with log fire, grandfather clock and leather button-back banquettes, back area more restauranty with wood floors and exposed brickwork, tables around central woodburner, some stuffed animals and hunting memorabilia; children and dogs (in bar) welcome, open (and food) all day. *(Anon)*

HASLINGTON   SJ7356
Hawk (01270) 582181
A534 Crewe–Sandbach; CW1 5RG Cosy old timbered coaching inn with several small rooms including notable oak-panelled back one, beams and open fires, more modern restaurant, Robinsons ales and good value pub food; sports TV, free wi-fi; beer garden with smokers' shelter, open all day. *(Hilary and Neal Christopher)*

HOLLINS GREEN   SJ6991
Black Swan (0161) 222 4444
Just off A57 Manchester–Warrington, 3 miles from M6 junction 21; WA3 6LA Refurbished and extended 17th-c coaching inn, enjoyable fairly traditional food cooked to order, half a dozen changing ales and good choice of wines from reasonably priced list; events such as poker and quiz nights, monthly farmers' market; children welcome, sizeable garden with terrace, duck pond and play area, 14 bedrooms, local walks (leaflets available), open (and food) all day. *(Martin and Patricia Forest)*

KERRIDGE   SJ9276
Lord Clyde (01625) 562123
Clarke Lane, off A523; SK10 5AH Converted from two mid 19th-c stone cottages, main emphasis on food but can just pop in for a drink, first class creative cooking from chef-owner (must book) including tasting menus, also lunchtime sandwiches and ploughman's, well kept ales such as Greene King, Thwaites and Weetwood, efficient friendly service; background music; dogs in bar, good local walks, open all day Fri-Sun, closed Mon lunchtime (no food Sat lunchtime, Sun, Mon lunchtime). *(Lindy Andrews)*

KNUTSFORD   SJ7578
Lord Eldon (01565) 652261
Tatton Street, off A50 at White Bear roundabout; WA16 6AD Old brick-built coaching inn with four comfortable rooms, much bigger inside than it looks, friendly staff and locals, beams, brasses and large open fire, well kept Tetleys and a couple of guests; music and quiz nights; back garden but no car park, handy for Tatton Park, open all day. *(Peter Brix)*

KNUTSFORD   SJ7578
Rose & Crown (01565) 652366
King Street; WA16 6DT Beamed and panelled 17th-c inn with bar and Chophouse restaurant, good food from extensive menu, Mobberley ales along with a beer badged for the pub and guests such as Shepherd Neame Spitfire, plenty of wines by the glass including champagne, good personable service; children welcome, nine bedrooms, open (and food) all day. *(W D Christian)*

LANGLEY   SJ9569
★ Hanging Gate (01260) 252238
Meg Lane, Higher Sutton; SK11 0NG Remote old place close to the moors with wonderful distant views to Liverpool Cathedral and even Snowdonia; three cosy little low-beamed simply furnished rooms, log fires, Hydes and a couple of guests, good choice of wines by the glass and quite a few malt whiskies, food from pub favourites up, board games and books; background music, free wi-fi; children in restaurant only, dogs in bar, sheltered outside seating area, open all day Fri-Sun. *(Dr Kevan Tucker)*

LANGLEY   SJ9471
★ Leather's Smithy (01260) 252313
Off A523 S of Macclesfield; OS Sheet 118 map reference 952715; SK11 0NE Isolated stone-built pub up in fine walking country next to reservoir, well kept Theakstons and two or three guests, lots of whiskies, good food from sandwiches to blackboard specials such as pheasant and wild boar, good welcoming service, beams and log fire, flagstoned bar, carpeted dining areas, interesting local prints and photographs; unobtrusive background music; children welcome, no dogs but muddy boots allowed in bar, picnic-sets in garden behind and on grass opposite, lovely views, open all day weekends. *(Peter Brix)*

LITTLE BOLLINGTON   SJ7387
★ Swan with Two Nicks
(0161) 928 2914 *2 miles from M56 junction 7 – A56 towards Lymm, then first right at Stamford Arms into Park Lane; use A556 to get back on to M56 westbound; WA14 4TJ* Extended village pub full of beams, brass, copper and bric-a-brac, some antique settles and roaring log fire, good choice of enjoyable generously served food from baguettes up, popular Sun lunch (best to book), half a dozen well kept ales including a house beer from Coach House, decent wines and coffee, efficient service; children and dogs welcome, tables outside, attractive hamlet by Dunham Massey (NT) deer park, walks by Bridgewater Canal, open (and food)

all day. *(Gerry and Rosemary Dobson, Hilary Forrest, Brian and Anna Marsden)*

LITTLE BUDWORTH   SJ5867
Cabbage Hall   (01829) 760292
Forest Road (A49); CW6 9ES Restauranty pub (part of the Pesto chain) specialising in good tapas-style (piattini) italian food, drinkers catered for in comfortable bar with ales such as Weetwood and decent wines by the glass, efficient friendly staff; children welcome, garden tables, open (and food) all day. *(Tom and Jill Jones)*

LITTLE BUDWORTH   SJ5965
Egerton Arms   (01829) 760424
Pinfold Lane; CW6 9BS Welcoming 18th-c family-run country pub (Woodward & Falconer), enjoyable home-made food including wood-fired pizzas and range of burgers, a couple of house beers from Conwy and four guests, good selection of bottled beers and interesting cocktails; Sat live music; children and dogs welcome, closed Mon, otherwise open all day. *(Anon)*

LITTLE LEIGH   SJ6076
Holly Bush   (01606) 853196
A49 just S of A533; CW8 4QY Ancient thatched and timbered pub, spotlessly clean, with good choice of enjoyable well priced food including several vegetarian options, charming helpful staff, Tetleys and a couple of mainstream guests, restaurant; children welcome, no dogs inside, wheelchair access, courtyard tables and garden with play area, 14 bedrooms in converted back barn, open all day weekends (food all day Sun). *(Tom and Jill Jones)*

LOWER WHITLEY   SJ6178
Chetwode Arms   (01925) 730203
Just off A49, handy for M56 junction 10; Street Lane; WA4 4EN Rambling low-beamed dining pub dating from the 17th c, good food including range of exotic meats cooked on a hot stone, early-bird deal (before 7pm), welcoming efficient service, solid furnishings all clean and polished, small front bar with warm open fire, four real ales including Adnams, good wines by the glass; well behaved children allowed but best to ask first, limited wheelchair access, bowling green, closed lunchtimes apart from Sun (1-8pm). *(Emma Scofield)*

LYMM   SJ7087
Barn Owl   (01925) 752020
Agden Wharf, Warrington Lane (just off B5159 E); WA13 0SW Comfortably extended popular pub in nice setting by Bridgewater Canal, Thwaites ales and four guests, decent wines by the glass, reasonable choice of good value all-day pub food including OAP deals and Sun carvery, efficient service even when busy, friendly atmosphere; children and dogs welcome, disabled facilities, may

be canal trips, moorings (space for one narrowboat). *(Edward May)*

MACCLESFIELD   SJ9273
Puss in Boots   (01625) 263378
Buxton Road; SK10 1NF Unpretentious Victorian stone pub by bridge over Macclesfield Canal, public bar, lounge and dining area, decent food including good value Sun carvery, Bollington and Greene King ales, hospitable staff; sports TV, games machine, occasional live bands; children welcome, seats in garden and by canal, play area, open all day (till 1am Fri, Sat). *(John Wooll)*

MACCLESFIELD   SJ9173
Waters Green Tavern
(01625) 422653 *Waters Green, opposite station; SK11 6LH* Half a dozen quickly changing mainly northern ales in roomy L-shaped open-plan local, good value home-made lunchtime food (not Sun), friendly staff and regulars, open fire, back pool room, juke box; dogs welcome. *(Edward May)*

MICKLE TRAFFORD   SJ4470
Shrewsbury Arms   (01244) 303262
Warrington Road (A56); CH2 4EB Spacious roadside dining pub divided into several compact areas, one with comfortable leather sofas, beams, flagstones and woodburners in brick fireplaces, decent choice of moderately priced food from sandwiches and stone-baked pizzas up, lunchtime set menu, Black Sheep, Courage Directors and Sharps Doom Bar, friendly obliging staff; background music; children and dogs welcome, tables outside, play area, nice walks nearby, open (and food) all day. *(Chilliski)*

MOBBERLEY   SJ8179
Plough & Flail   (01565) 873537
Off B5085 Knutsford–Alderley Edge; at E end of village turn into Moss Lane, then left into Paddock Hill Lane (look out for small green signs to pub); WA16 7DB Extensive family dining pub tucked down narrow lanes; low-beamed bar with chunky cushioned dining chairs and stripped tables, flagstones and panelled dado, Lees ales and good choice of wines by the glass, wood-floored side area with low sofas, enjoyable food (Sun till 8pm) including daily specials, comfortable airy dining room and conservatory; background music, free wi-fi; teak tables on heated terraces, picnic-sets on neat lawns, play area, open (and food) all day. *(Peter Pilbeam)*

MOULDSWORTH   SJ5170
Goshawk   (01928) 740900
Station Road (B5393); CH3 8AJ Comfortable Woodward & Falconer family dining pub (former station hotel); mix of furniture in extensive series of rooms including small 'library' area, masses of pictures, double-aspect log fire, good

popular food from sandwiches to restauranty dishes, cheerful attentive uniformed staff, half a dozen well kept ales such as Montys, Weetwood and Woodland plus a couple of house beers brewed by Conwy, nice wines by the glass; background music; dogs allowed in bar, disabled facilities, good spot near Delamere Forest with big outdoor space including play area and bowling green, open all day. *(Edward May)*

NANTWICH   SJ6452
★ **Black Lion** (01270) 628711
Welsh Row; CW5 5ED Old black and white building smartened up but keeping beams, timbered brickwork and open fire, good food (not Sun evening, Mon) from short interesting menu, three well kept Weetwood ales and three regularly changing guests, good service, upstairs rooms with old wooden tables and leather sofas on undulating floors; dogs welcome, covered outside seating area, open all day weekends, closed Mon lunchtime. *(Peter Pilbeam)*

NANTWICH   SJ6552
Vine (01270) 619055
Hospital Street; CW5 5RP Fairly straightforward black and white fronted pub dating from the 17th c, modernised interior stretching far back with quiet corners, five well kept ales including Hydes, friendly staff and locals, pubby lunchtime food (maybe evening too by the time you read this), raised seating areas, darts and dominoes; background music, sports TV; children and dogs welcome, small outside seating area behind, open all day till midnight; refurbishment planned as we went to press. *(Anon)*

NESTON   SJ2976
Harp (0151) 336 6980
Quayside, SW of Little Neston; keep on along track at end of Marshlands Road; CH64 0TB Tucked-away little two-room country local with well kept ales including Timothy Taylors, decent choice of bottled beers, wines and some good malt whiskies, enjoyable simple pub food, woodburner in pretty fireplace, pale quarry tiles and simple furnishings, interesting old photographs, hatch servery to lounge; children and dogs allowed, garden behind, picnic-sets up on front grassy bank facing Dee Marshes and Wales, glorious sunsets with wild calls of wading birds, open all day. *(Tony Tollitt)*

PARKGATE   SJ2778
Boathouse (0151) 336 4187
Village signed off A540; CH64 6RN Popular black and white timbered pub (Woodward & Falconer) with attractively refurbished linked rooms, wide choice of good food (booking advised) from snacks up, cheerful attentive staff, well kept changing ales including a couple of house beers from Conwy, several wines by the glass, big conservatory with great views to Wales over silted Dee estuary (RSPB reserve), may be egrets and kestrels. *(Nick Sharpe)*

PARKGATE   SJ2778
Ship (0151) 336 3931
The Parade; CH64 6SA Bow-window estuary views from hotel's refurbished bar, well kept Marstons Pedigree and guests, several wines by the glass and over 50 whiskies, good reasonably priced home-cooked food including daily specials and popular Sun roasts, afternoon tea, good friendly service, log fire; Weds quiz night; children welcome, no dogs inside, a few tables out at front and to the side, 25 bedrooms, open all day. *(John and Gwyn Brignal, Doug Collins)*

PEOVER HEATH   SJ7973
★ **Dog** (01625) 861421
Wellbank Lane; the pub is often listed under Over Peover instead; WA16 8UP Nicely renovated traditional country pub with intimate rooms, good variety of generously served food (all day weekends), five ales including Weetwood, decent choice of wines by the glass and malt whiskies, friendly efficient staff; children welcome, dogs in tap room, picnic-sets out at front and in pretty back garden, can walk from here to the Jodrell Bank Discovery Centre and Arboretum, six bedrooms, open (and food) all day. *(Brian and Anna Marsden, Gerry and Rosemary Dobson, Mr and Mrs R Shardlow)*

POYNTON   SJ9483
Boars Head (01625) 876676
Shrigley Road N, Higher Poynton, off A523; SK12 1TE Welcoming Victorian country pub with good value straightforward home-made food including speciality pies, four well kept ales such as Black Sheep and Jennings, warm woodburner; walkers and dogs welcome, next to Middlewood Way and close to Macclesfield Canal moorings, also handy for Lyme Park (NT), open all day weekends. *(Dr D J and Mrs S C Walker)*

POYNTON   SJ9283
Cask Tavern (01625) 875157
Park Lane; SK12 1RE Busy Bollington pub with five of their well kept ales and a guest, craft beers, real ciders and several wines by the glass including draught prosecco, no food; dogs allowed, open all day Fri-Sun, from 4pm other days. *(Brian and Anna Marsden)*

PRESTBURY   SJ8976
Legh Arms (01625) 829130
A538, village centre; SK10 4DG Smart beamed hotel with divided-up bar and lounge areas, Robinsons ales and decent wines, enjoyable bar food from substantial sandwiches up, more elaborate restaurant choices, efficient friendly staff and lively jolly atmosphere, soft furnishings, ladder-back chairs around solid dark tables, brocaded

bucket seats, stylish french prints and italian engravings, staffordshire dogs on mantelpiece, cosy panelled back part with narrow offshoot, open fire; background music, daily papers; children and dogs welcome, seats on heated terrace, bedrooms, good breakfast, open all day. *(John Wooll)*

SHOCKLACH   SJ4349
Bull (01829) 250335
Off B5069 W of Malpas; SY14 7BL
Welcoming 19th-c village dining pub with refurbished beamed interior, bare boards and flagstones, some hand-painted floor tiles in one part, open fire, good food (all day weekends, not Mon) from lunchtime sandwiches and pub favourites to more elaborate restaurant choices, a beer named for the pub from Marstons and a guest such as Cheshire Brewhouse, decent house wines, garden room; background music, Mon quiz; children and dogs (in bar) welcome, picnic-sets on back terrace, open all day (from 3pm Mon). *(Jill Sparrow)*

STOAK   SJ4273
★**Bunbury Arms** (01244) 301665
Little Stanney Lane; a mile from M53 junction 10, A5117 W then first left; CH2 4HW Big but cosy beamed lounge with antique furniture, pictures and books, small snug, wide choice of enjoyable fairly priced food (all day Sun) from sandwiches and wraps to interesting specials including fresh fish, three good changing ales, extensive wine list, open fires, board games and Mon quiz; can get busy; garden tables (some motorway noise), short walk for Shropshire Canal users (Bridge 136 or 138), also handy for Cheshire Oaks shopping outlet, open all day. *(Tony Tollitt, Roger and Anne Newbury)*

STYAL   SJ8383
Ship (01625) 444888
B5166 near Ringway Airport; SK9 4JE
Refurbished 17th-c pub under same ownership as the Dog at Peover, good food from extensive menu and well kept ales including Dunham Massey and Weetwood, plenty of wines by the glass, friendly helpful service, log fire; children welcome, attractive NT village with good walks on the doorstep, open (and food) all day. *(Dr D J and Mrs S C Walker, Mike and Wena Stevenson)*

WESTON   SJ7352
White Lion (01270) 587011
Not far from M6 junction 16, via A500; CW2 5NA Renovated 17th-c black and white dining inn, low-beamed lounge bar with slate floor, standing timbers and inglenook woodburner, popular food here or in restaurant, cocktail bar, three well

kept ales including Salopian Shropshire Gold, pleasant helpful staff; background music; children in eating areas, lovely garden with bowling green (not owned by the pub), 17 comfortable if dated bedrooms (refurbishment planned), open all day. *(Nick Sharpe)*

WHITEGATE   SJ6268
Plough (01606) 889455
Beauty Bank, Foxwist Green; OS Sheet 118 map reference 624684; off A556 just W of Northwich, or A54 W of Winsford; CW8 2BP Comfortable country pub with bar and extended dining area, wide choice of good home-made food (best to book) from panini and baked potatoes up, cheerful efficient service, four well kept Robinsons ales and plenty of wines by the glass; background music, free wi-fi; no under-14s inside, well behaved dogs allowed in tap room, disabled access, picnic-sets out at front and in back garden, colourful window boxes and hanging baskets, popular walks nearby, open (and food) all day. *(Anon)*

WILDBOARCLOUGH   SJ9868
Crag (01260) 227239
Village signed from A54; bear left at fork, then left at T junction; SK11 0BD
Old stone-built pub in charming little sheltered valley below moors (good walk up Shutlingsloe for great views), enjoyable generously served home-made food including Sun carvery, three well kept local beers, friendly staff, plates on delft shelving, various stuffed animals, open fires; walkers welcome, terrace with covered smokers' shelter. *(Dr Kevan Tucker)*

WILLINGTON   SJ5367
★**Boot** (01829) 751375
Boothsdale, off A54 at Kelsall; CW6 0NH
Attractive hillside dining pub in row of converted cottages, views over Cheshire plain to Wales, popular food from pub staples to daily specials, local Weetwood ales and decent choice of wines and malt whiskies, friendly staff, small opened-up unpretentiously furnished rooms, lots of original features, woodburner, extension with french windows overlooking garden; well behaved children welcome (no pushchairs), dogs outside only, picnic-sets on raised suntrap terrace, open all day. *(Hilary and Neal Christopher)*

WILMSLOW   SJ8282
Honey Bee (01625) 526511
Altrincham Road, Styal; SK9 4LT Large red-brick Vintage Inn (former retirement home) with several linked rooms around central bar, well kept Sharps Doom Bar,

---

Half pints: by law, a pub should not charge more for half a pint than half the price of a full pint, unless it shows that half-pint price on its price list.

Thwaites Wainwright and a guest, their usual choice of enjoyable food including popular Sun roasts, open fires; children welcome, no dogs inside, terrace and garden seating, open all day. *(Michael Butler)*

WILMSLOW   SJ8379
Horse & Jockey (01625) 582158
Gravel Lane; SK9 6EG Recently refurbished red-brick Victorian pub, enjoyable good value food (all day weekends, till 7.30pm Sun) cooked by owner-chef from pub favourites up, ales such as Black Sheep, Jennings, Marstons and Robinsons, friendly service; children and dogs welcome, open all day. *(Anon)*

WINCLE   SJ9665
★ ## Ship (01260) 227217
Village signposted off A54 Congleton–Buxton; SK11 0QE Friendly 16th-c stone-built country pub under newish management; bare-boards bar leading to carpeted dining room, old stables area with flagstones, beams, woodburner and open fire, good generously served food (not Sun evening) from varied menu, three Lees ales and several wines by the glass, quick attentive service; children and dogs welcome, tables in small side garden, good Dane Valley walks, open all day. *(Anon)*

WRENBURY   SJ5947
★ ## Dusty Miller (01270) 780537
Cholmondeley Road; village signed from A530 Nantwich–Whitchurch; CW5 8HG Well converted 19th-c corn mill with fine canal views from gravel terrace and series of tall glazed arches in bar, spacious modern feel, comfortably furnished with tapestried banquettes, oak settles and wheelback chairs around rustic tables, quarry-tiled area by bar with oak settle and refectory table, old lift hoist up under the rafters, four Robinsons beers, farm cider and enjoyable generously served food (all day weekends), good friendly service; background music; children and dogs welcome, closed Mon, otherwise open all day. *(Lindy Andrews)*

Cornwall

KEY   ★ Star Pub   🍽 Top Quality Food   🍺 Great Beer
🍷 Good Wines   £ Bargain Meals   🛏 Good Bedrooms   🍴 Serves Food

BLISLAND   SX1073   Map 1

Blisland Inn 🍺 £
(01208) 850739
Village signposted off A30 and B3266 NE of Bodmin; PL30 4JF

A fine choice of real ales, beer-related memorabilia, friendly staff, pubby food and seats outside

Beside a pretty, tree-lined village green, this traditional, firmly old-fashioned pub is run by a genuinely welcoming landlord. Every inch of the beams and ceiling is covered with beer badges (or their particularly wide-ranging collection of mugs), and the walls are similarly filled with beer-related posters and the like. Tapped from the cask or on handpump, the ales include two named for the pub by Sharps – Blisland Special and Bulldog – as well as quickly changing beers from local breweries such as Atlantic, Bude, Cottage, Padstow and Skinners; also, farm cider, fruit wines and real apple juice. Service is good. The carpeted lounge has several barometers on the walls, toby jugs on beams and a few standing timbers, while the family room has pool, table skittles, euchre, cribbage and dominoes; background music. Plenty of picnic-sets outside. The popular Camel Trail cycle path is close by – though the hill up to Blisland is pretty steep. As with many pubs in this area, the approach by car involves negotiating several single-track roads.

🍴 Honest, home-cooked food includes baps (the crab is said to be good), whitebait, ham and eggs, sausage and mash, leek and mushroom bake, moroccan-style lamb, and puddings such as apple crumble and sticky toffee pudding. *Benchmark main dish: steak in ale pie £9.00. Two-course evening meal £15.50.*

Free house ~ Licensees Gary and Margaret Marshall ~ Real ale ~ Open 11.30-11.30 (midnight Sat); 12-10.30 Sun ~ Bar food 12-2, 6.30-9; not Sun evening ~ Restaurant ~ Children in family room only ~ Dogs welcome ~ Live music every second Sat
Recommended by John and Bernadette Elliott, R J Herd

BOSCASTLE   SX0991   Map 1

Cobweb
(01840) 250278 – http://cobwebinn.com
B3263, just E of harbour; PL35 0HE

Plenty of interest in cheerful pub, several real ales and friendly staff

'Worth a Main Entry on all counts,' says one reader with enthusiasm – and many others agree (as do we). The two interesting bars have quite a mix of seats (from settles and carved chairs to more pubby furniture), heavy beams hung with hundreds of bottles and jugs, lots of pictures of bygone years, and cosy log fires. They keep four real ales such as St Austell Proper Job and Tribute, Sharps Doom Bar and a guest beer on handpump and a local cider, and the atmosphere is cheerful and bustling, especially at peak times; games machine, darts, juke box and pool. The restaurant is upstairs. There are picnic-sets and benches outside – some under cover. A self-catering apartment is for rent.

🍴 Traditional food at fair prices includes sandwiches, deep-fried whitebait, gammon and egg, beer-battered fish and chips, meat or vegetarian lasagne, mixed grill, steak, and puddings such as a crumble or cheesecake. *Benchmark main dish: steak in ale pie £9.80. Two-course evening meal £15.50.*

Free house ~ Licensees Ivor and Adrian Bright ~ Real ale ~ Open 10.30am-11pm (midnight Sat) ~ Bar food 11.30-2.30, 6-9.30 ~ Restaurant ~ Children welcome ~ Dogs allowed in bar
Recommended by John and Bernadette Elliott, Roy and Lindsey Fentiman

CADGWITH
SW7214   Map 1
Cadgwith Cove Inn

(01326) 290513 – www.cadgwithcoveinn.com
Down very narrow lane off A3083 S of Helston; no nearby parking; TR12 7JX

Traditionally furnished bars, real ales, all-day food and fine coastal walks; bedrooms

This friendly little pub is in a fishing cove with lovely coastal walks in either direction. The two front rooms have bench seating and tables on parquet flooring, a log fire, lots of local photographs and memorabilia such as naval hat ribands, fancy knotwork and compass binnacles; some of the dark beams have blue spliced rope hand-holds. Otter Bitter, Sharps Doom Bar, Skinners Betty Stogs and a guest from Atlantic on handpump; background music, darts, board games, euchre, TV and Monday evening quiz. A back bar has a huge and colourful fish mural. Seats on the good-sized front terrace look down to the fish sheds by the bay, and the comfortable, newly refurbished bedrooms overlook the sea. It's best to park at the top of the village and wander down through the thatched cottages, but it's quite a steep hike back up again. They have a Kellys ice-cream parlour in the back bar.

🍴 Using fish caught in the bay and offering morning coffee and afternoon teas, the food includes sandwiches, pasties, moules marinière, a daily vegetarian choice, crab salad, burger with toppings, chips and red pepper mayonnaise, poussin with pea purée and blackened onions, a whole fish of the day, daily specials, and puddings such as poached pear in amaretto sauce and chocolate and orange sponge with chocolate sauce. *Benchmark main dish: beer-battered fish and chips £11.70. Two-course evening meal £19.00.*

Punch ~ Lease Garry and Helen Holmes ~ Real ale ~ Open 11.30am-midnight ~ Bar food 12-3, 6-9 ~ Restaurant ~ Children welcome ~ Dogs welcome ~ Wi-fi ~ Folk night Tues, local singers Fri ~ Bedrooms: $40/$97 *Recommended by Adrian Johnson, David Eberlin, Barry Collett*

CONSTANTINE
SW7328   Map 1
Trengilly Wartha 🍷 🛏

(01326) 340332 – www.trengilly.co.uk
Nancenoy; A3083 S of Helston, signposted Gweek near RNAS Culdrose, then fork right after Gweek; OS Sheet 204 map reference 731282; TR11 5RP

Well run inn surrounded by big gardens with a friendly welcome for all, an easy-going atmosphere and popular food and drink; bedrooms

Despite being tucked away down country lanes, this well run inn has plenty of customers. There's a genuine welcome from the courteous licensees and their charming staff and the long, low-beamed main bar has a sociable feel (especially in the evening when locals drop in). There are all sorts of tables and chairs, a woodburning stove, cricket team photos on the walls, Greene King Abbot, Penzance Potion No 9 and Skinners Pennycomequick on handpump, up to 20 wines by the glass, 50 malt whiskies and quite a choice of gins and rums. Leading off the bar is the conservatory family room and there's also a cosy bistro. The six acres of gardens are well worth a wander and offer plenty of seats and picnic-sets under large parasols. The cottagey bedrooms are comfortable and the breakfasts very good; plenty of surrounding walks.

High quality food includes chicken liver pâté with home-made chutney, crab pot, wild mushroom and cheese risotto, thai pork burger with chilli mayonnaise, chicken and leek pie, guinea fowl with chorizo sauce, haddock in a creamy crab sauce, duck with chilli plum sauce, local sirloin steak and puddings. *Benchmark main dish: local mussels in white wine, cream and garlic £12.80. Two-course evening meal £21.50.*

Free house ~ Licensees Will and Lisa Lea ~ Real ale ~ Open 11 (12 Sun)-3.15, 6-11 ~ Bar food 12-2.15, 6.30-9.30 ~ Restaurant ~ Children welcome away from bar area ~ Dogs allowed in bar and bedrooms ~ Wi-fi ~ Live music Weds evening ~ Bedrooms: £60/£84
Recommended by Chris and Angela Buckell, Colin McKerrow, Alison Ball, Ian Walton, Maureen Wood

DEVORAN
Old Quay

SW7938 Map 1

(01872) 863142 – www.theoldquayinn.co.uk
Devoran from new Carnon Cross roundabout A39 Truro–Falmouth, left on old road, right at mini roundabout; TR3 6NE

Light and airy bar rooms in friendly pub with four real ales, good wine and imaginative food and seats on pretty back terraces; bedrooms

This is an enjoyable pub to spend a couple of hours in, and you can be sure of a warm welcome from the cheerful staff and friendly locals. The roomy bar has an interesting 'woodburner' set halfway up one wall, a cushioned window seat, wall settles and a few bar stools around just three tables on stripped boards, and bar chairs by the counter. They keep Bass, Otter Bitter, Sharps Doom Bar, Skinners Betty Stogs and a guest such as Wychwood Hobgoblin on handpump and good wines by the glass; you can buy their own jams and chutneys. Off to the left is an airy room with pictures by local artists (for sale) on white walls, built-in, cushioned wall seating, plush stools and a couple of big tables on the dark slate floor. To the other side of the bar is another light room with more settles and farmhouse chairs, attractive blue and white striped cushions and more sailing photographs; darts and board games. As well as benches outside at the front looking down through the trees to the water, there's a series of snug little back terraces with picnic-sets and chairs and tables. Nearby parking is limited unless you arrive early. There is wheelchair access through a side door. The pub is next to the coast-to-coast Portreath to Devoran Mineral Tramway cycle path.

Using the best local produce, the tempting food includes lunchtime sandwiches, prawn cocktail, chicken liver pâté with onion relish, cola and honey home-roasted ham with a free-range egg, moules marinière, beef, chicken and vegetarian burgers with toppings, onion rings and chips, dill, tumeric and beer-battered fish and chips, ham fritters with cheese fondue and onion chutney, hake with spinach, fine beans and a poached egg, and puddings such as white chocolate and lime tart and crème brûlée. *Benchmark main dish: smoked haddock and mussel risotto £12.50. Two-course evening meal £18.00.*

Punch ~ Tenants John and Hannah Calland ~ Real ale ~ Open 11-11 ~ Bar food 12-3, 6-9 ~ Restaurant ~ Children welcome ~ Dogs allowed in bar ~ Wi-fi ~ Bedrooms: £58.50/£75
Recommended by Chris and Angela Buckell, Ian Herdman, David Crook, Richard Tilbrook

GURNARDS HEAD
SW4337 Map 1
Gurnards Head Hotel 🍽 ♀ 🛏
(01736) 796928 – www.gurnardshead.co.uk
B3306 Zennor–St Just; TR26 3DE

Interesting inn close to the sea, with lots of wines by the glass, good inventive food and fine surrounding walks; comfortable bedrooms

Just 500 metres from the Atlantic and in rugged National Trust countryside, this is a civilised but informal inn that's usefully open all day. The bar rooms are painted in bold, strong colours and there are paintings by local artists, open fires and all manner of wooden dining chairs and tables on stripped boards. St Austell Tribute, Skinners Betty Stogs and a guest on handpump, 14 wines by the glass or carafe and a couple of ciders; background music, darts and board games. The large back garden has plenty of seats. Bedrooms are comfortable and have views of the rugged moors or the sea. This is under the same ownership as the Old Coastguard in Mousehole (also in Cornwall) and the Griffin at Felinfach (in Wales).

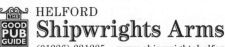 From a short, seasonal menu, the highly rewarding food includes blue cheese panna cotta with pickled walnut, apple and cider caramel, coffee pigeon with celeriac rémoulade, prunes and walnuts, pasta with spinach, wild mushroom and earl grey smoked cherry tomatoes, rolled hake with olive gnocchi, parma ham, almonds and romesco, duck breast with carrot, orange, braised chicory and pomegranate, venison stew, and puddings such as treacle tart with maple and pecan ice-cream and vanilla panna cotta with blood orange. *Benchmark main dish: pork belly, brawn, charred leeks and butternut squash and date and five-spice sauce £16.95. Two-course evening meal £22.00.*

Free house ~ Licensees Charles and Edmund Inkin ~ Real ale ~ Open 10am-11pm ~ Bar food 12-2.30, 6-9.30 ~ Restaurant ~ Children welcome ~ Dogs allowed in bar and bedrooms ~ Wi-fi ~ Bedrooms: £90/£115 *Recommended by J D and A P, Stephen Shepherd, J R Wildon, Chris and Val Ramstedt, Sally Melling, Peter Brix*

HELFORD
SW7526 Map 1
Shipwrights Arms
(01326) 231235 – www.shipwrightshelford.co.uk
Off B3293 SE of Helston, via Mawgan; TR12 6JX

17th-c waterside inn with seats on terraces dropping down to the creek, cheerfully decorated bars, winter fire, friendly service and tasty food

This thatched pub is an idyllic spot in fine weather. The terraces that drop down to the water's edge give a lovely view of the beautiful wooded creek (at its best at high tide), and seats on various levels (the ones at the top are covered) make the most of this; it's very much first come, first served, so do arrive early. Good surrounding walks – including a long-distance coast path that goes right past the door. Inside, there's quite a nautical theme, with navigation lamps, models of ships, paintings of fishing boats, drawings of fish and shellfish and even the odd figurehead; plenty of blue paintwork and blue patterned wallpaper add to the seaside feel. Painted high-backed dining chairs with attractive seats, leather wall banquettes and scatter cushions on window seats are grouped around wooden tables of varying sizes. Stools line the counter where they keep St Austell Tribute and a guest ale on handpump, several wines by the glass and good rums; a winter open fire.

 Popular food includes sandwiches, breaded local brie with sweet beetroot chutney, house-smoked fish chowder, ham and eggs, portobello mushroom with goats cheese and salad, megrim sole with pepper and tomato sauce, chicken breast with butternut squash, ginger, lemongrass and sun-dried tomato sauce, home-made monkfish scampi with chips, and puddings such as lime and lemon cheesecake and sticky toffee pudding. *Benchmark main dish: beer-battered fish and chips £11.00. Two-course evening meal £19.50.*

Free house ~ Licensees David and Vicky Harford ~ Real ale ~ Open 11-11 ~ Bar food 12-9 ~ Restaurant ~ Children welcome ~ Dogs welcome ~ Wi-fi ~ Live jazz Sun lunchtime
Recommended by Alfie Bayliss, Harvey Brown

HELFORD PASSAGE   SW7626   Map 1

Ferryboat

(01326) 250625 – www.thewrightbrothers.co.uk
Signed from B3291; TR11 5LB

Old pub by sandy beach, extremely popular in fine weather, with pubby food and St Austell ales

This 300-year-old pub is in a charming location, and in summer there's a ferry from Helford village across the water. You can book seats on the terrace in advance – they're much prized in warm weather as they overlook a sandy beach – and also hire small boats and arrange fishing trips. It's not huge inside, with just one bar room: farmhouse and blue-painted kitchen chairs and built-in cushioned wall seats around stripped wooden tables on grey slates, and mirrors above a woodburning stove. An arched doorway leads to a games room with pool, darts, board games and a leather sofa. St Austell Proper Job, Tribute and a guest on handpump, a dozen wines by the glass and farm cider. The walk down from the car park is quite steep.

 Some sort of food is available all day: sandwiches, treacle-cured smoked salmon with crème fraîche, local crab rarebit with pickled vegetables, pumpkin, shallot and brie tart, cheeseburger with coleslaw and chips, sausages with mustard mash and onion gravy, moules marinière, and puddings such as pear and almond tart and sticky toffee pudding. *Benchmark main dish: beer-battered haddock and chips £12.00. Two-course evening meal £19.00.*

St Austell ~ Tenant Ben Wright ~ Real ale ~ Open 11-11 ~ Bar food 12-3, 6-9.30 ~ Children welcome ~ Dogs allowed in bar ~ Wi-fi ~ Live bands Fri and Sun evenings
Recommended by Edward May, Belinda May, Richard Tilbrook

HELSTON   SW6522   Map 1

Halzephron ♀ 🛏

(01326) 240406 – www.halzephron-inn.co.uk
Gunwalloe, village about 4 miles S but not marked on many road maps; look for brown sign on A3083 alongside perimeter fence of RNAS Culdrose; TR12 7QB

Bustling pub in lovely spot with tasty bar food, local beers and good nearby walks; bedrooms

Our readers have been coming to this popular inn for many years and, despite changes here and there, still very much enjoy their visits; the coast walks in both directions are lovely. The neatly kept bar and dining areas have an informal, friendly atmosphere, comfortable seating, a warm winter fire in the woodburning stove, Sharps Doom Bar, Skinners Betty Stogs and a guest such as Brains Bitter on handpump, nine wines by the glass, 41 malt whiskies and summer farm cider. The dining gallery seats up to 30 people; darts and board games. Picnic-sets outside look across National Trust fields and countryside. Gunwalloe fishing cove is just 300 metres away and Church Cove with its sandy beach is nearby.

Popular food includes sandwiches, crab cakes with sweet chilli sauce, baked camembert with garlic and redcurrant jelly, local ham and free-range eggs, butternut squash and leek crumble, white crab meat salad or thermidor, steak in ale pie, duck breast with apricot and brandy jus and savoury cabbage, free-range chicken with grain mustard, sweet peppers and cashew nuts on rice, calves liver and bacon in a rich red wine sauce and puddings. *Benchmark main dish: pork medallions and black pudding in creamy garlic and rosemary sauce £12.95. Two-course evening meal £20.00.*

Free house ~ Licensee Claire Murray ~ Real ale ~ Open 11-11; 12-10.30 Sun ~ Bar food 12-2, 7-9 ~ Restaurant ~ Children welcome ~ Dogs allowed in bar and bedrooms ~ Wi-fi ~ Bedrooms: £55/£94 *Recommended by Toby Jones, Martin Jones*

LANLIVERY
SX0759 Map 1

Crown 🛏

(01208) 872707 – www.wagtailinns.com
Signposted off A390 Lostwithiel–St Austell (tricky to find from other directions); PL30 5BT

Chatty atmosphere in nice old pub, traditional rooms and well liked food and drink; bedrooms

This is one of Cornwall's oldest pubs and is said, in part, to date from the 12th c. The main bar has a log fire in a huge fireplace, traditional settles on big flagstones, some cushioned farmhouse chairs, church and other wooden chairs around all sorts of tables, old yachting photographs, and beams in boarded ceilings. Harbour Amber, Skinners Betty Stogs and a changing guest on handpump and several wines by the glass. A couple of other rooms are similarly furnished (including a dining conservatory) and there's another open fire. The porch has a huge lit-up well with a glass top and the quiet, pretty garden has picnic-sets. Bedrooms (in separate buildings) are comfortable and overlook the garden; breakfasts are good. The Eden Project is ten minutes away by car.

Tasty food includes sandwiches, crab au gratin, garlic mushrooms, various pizzas, walnut and blue cheese tart, crab salad, burger with toppings and fries, chicken in mushroom and brandy sauce, seafood pasta, pork steak in honey and mustard sauce, and puddings such as key lime pie and chocolate brownie. *Benchmark main dish: beer-battered cod and chips £10.95. Two-course evening meal £17.50.*

Wagtail Inns ~ Licensee Nigel Wakeham ~ Real ale ~ Open 11.30-11; 12-10.30 Sun ~ Bar food 12-2.30, 6-9 ~ Restaurant ~ Children welcome away from bar ~ Dogs allowed in bar and bedrooms ~ Wi-fi ~ Bedrooms: /£70 *Recommended by Richard Stanfield, Wendy Breese*

LOSTWITHIEL
SX1059 Map 1

Globe ♀ 🍺

(01208) 872501 – www.globeinn.com
North Street (close to medieval bridge); PL22 0EG

Unassuming bar in traditional local, interesting food and drinks and friendly staff; suntrap back courtyard with outside heaters

There's always a good mix of both regulars and visitors in this popular town pub with a warm welcome for all. The unassuming bar, which is long and on the narrow side, has a mix of pubby tables and seats, local photographs on pale green plank panelling at one end and nice, mainly local prints (for sale) on canary yellow walls above a coal-effect stove at the snug inner end; there's also a small red-walled front alcove. The ornately carved bar counter, with comfortable chrome and leatherette stools, dispenses Sharps Doom Bar, Skinners Betty Stogs and a changing guest on handpump, 11 reasonably priced wines by the glass, 20 malt whiskies and two local ciders; background music, darts and board games and TV. The sheltered back courtyard is not large but has some attractive and unusual plants, and is a real suntrap (with an extendable awning and outside heaters). You can park in several of the nearby streets or the (free) town car park. The 13th-c church is worth a look and the ancient river bridge, a few metres away, is lovely.

High quality food includes chicken liver pâté, prawn cocktail, pasta carbonara, lentil roast with red onion, mushroom and port sauce, a choice of pies, moroccan-style lamb burger with minted yoghurt dressing, barbecue ribs with coleslaw and chips, fresh mackerel fillets on mediterranean vegeteables, a curry of the day, duck with port and redcurrant sauce, and puddings such as key lime pie and bread and butter pudding. *Benchmark main dish: bass fillets with red pesto, wrapped in parma ham £16.95. Two-course evening meal £19.50.*

Free house ~ Licensee William Erwin ~ Real ale ~ Open 12-11 (midnight Fri, Sat) ~ Bar food 12-2, 6.30-9 ~ Restaurant ~ Children welcome but no pushchairs in restaurant ~ Dogs allowed in bar ~ Wi-fi ~ Live music Fri, quiz Sun ~ Bedrooms: /£70
Recommended by Stephen Shepherd, Peter Salmon, John Marsh, R K Phillips

MORWENSTOW   SS2015   Map 1

Bush 🛏

(01288) 331242 – www.thebushinnmorwenstow.com
Signed off A39 N of Kilkhampton; Crosstown; EX23 9SR

Ancient pub in fine spot, character bar, several dining rooms and outside dining huts and well liked food; bedrooms

For those enjoying the marvellous surrounding walks (good nearby surfing beaches too), some kind of well liked food is served all day in this former smugglers' inn. The character bar has traditional pubby furniture on big flagstones, a woodburner in a large stone fireplace, horse tack and copper knick-knacks, St Austell HSD and Tribute and a guest from a local brewery on handpump, eight wines by the glass, several whiskies and farm cider; background music, games machine, darts and board games. One beamed dining room has tall pale wooden dining chairs and tables on bare boards, small prints on cream-painted walls, fresh flowers and another woodburning stove; a second has big windows overlooking the picnic-sets and heated dining huts. The neat bedrooms have lovely views and breakfasts are served until 11am; the courtyard room allows dogs.

The highly thought-of food includes doorstep sandwiches and ciabatta rolls, chicken liver and pork pâté, smoked mackerel salad, ham and free-range eggs, beer-battered fish of the day, smoked salmon, pea and asparagus frittata, beef or vegetarian burger and chips, duck leg confit with smoked bacon and tomato cassoulet, and puddings such as sticky toffee pudding and lemon and raspberry posset. *Benchmark main dish: mussels in white wine and cream £12.00. Two-course evening meal £15.50.*

Free house ~ Licensees Colin and Gill Fletcher ~ Real ale ~ Open 12-11 ~ Bar food 12-9; 12-3, 5-8 (9 Weds-Sat) in winter ~ Restaurant ~ Children welcome ~ Dogs allowed in bar and bedrooms ~ Wi-fi ~ Live music first Sat evening of month ~ Bedrooms: £65/£90
Recommended by Toby Jones, Edward May, Ryta Lyndley, David Crook

MOUSEHOLE
SW4726   Map 1

Old Coastguard 🌟 ♀ 🛏

(01736) 731222 – www.oldcoastguardhotel.co.uk
The Parade (edge of village, Newlyn coast road); TR19 6PR

Lovely position for carefully refurbished inn, a civilised, friendly atmosphere, character furnishings, a good choice of wines and first rate food; bedrooms with sea views

In fine weather, this edge-of-village inn really comes into its own with seats on the terrace looking over the sea to St Michael's Mount and the Lizard – and a path in the garden, with its tropical palms and dracaena, leading down to rock pools below. The comfortable bedrooms have the same view. The bar rooms have boldly coloured walls hung with paintings of sailing boats and local scenes, stripped floorboards and an atmosphere of informal but civilised comfort. The Upper Deck houses the bar and the restaurant, with a nice mix of antique dining chairs around oak and distressed pine tables, lamps on big barrel tables and chairs to either side of the log fire, topped by a vast bressumer beam. Harbour Amber, Rebel Sail Ale and St Austell Tribute on handpump, 14 wines by the glass or carafe, a farm cider and a good choice of soft drinks. The Lower Deck has glass windows running the length of the building, several deep sofas and armchairs, and shelves of books and games; background music. This is sister pub to the Gurnards Head (also Cornwall) and the Griffin at Felinfach (Wales).

 As well as their value two- and three-course set lunch (not Sun), the impressive food includes crab, tarragon mayonnaise and fennel salad, ham hock terrine with apple chutney, celeriac risotto with roasted pear, local blue cheese and walnuts, slow-cooked beef with bubble and squeak, greens and a fried egg, monkfish with mustard pomme purée, pancetta, clams and garlic, lamb shoulder with crisp sweetbreads, leeks and turnips, and puddings such as white chocolate panna cotta with cherry jam and banana cake with prunes and malted milk ice-cream. *Benchmark main dish: fish stew with fennel and aioli £12.50. Two-course evening meal £22.00.*

Free house ~ Licensees Charles and Edmund Inkin ~ Real ale ~ Open 8am-11.30pm ~ Bar food 12.30 (12 Sun)-2.30, 6.30-9 ~ Restaurant ~ Children welcome ~ Dogs allowed in bar and bedrooms ~ Wi-fi ~ Occasional live music Sun ~ Bedrooms: £100/£145
Recommended by Alison Ball, Ian Walton, Peter Andrews, Geoff and Linda Payne, Martin Jones, Toby Jones

MOUSEHOLE
SW4626   Map 1

Ship 🛏

(01736) 731234 – www.shipinnmousehole.co.uk
Harbourside; TR19 6QX

Bustling harbourside local in pretty village; bedrooms

In the heart of a lovely village and just across the road from the harbour, this cheerful pub has a good mix of customers. The opened-up main bar has black beams and panelling, built-in wooden wall benches and stools around low tables, sailors' fancy ropework, granite flagstones and a cosy open fire. St Austell Cornish Best, HSD, Trelawny and Tribute on handpump, several wines by the glass and maybe background music. The bedrooms are above the pub or in the cottage next door and some overlook the water. It's best to park at the top of the village and walk down (traffic can be a bit of a nightmare in summer). The elaborate harbour lights at Christmas are well worth a visit.

Reasonably priced food includes sandwiches, field mushrooms filled with blue cheese and garlic, salt and pepper squid, vegetable chilli, cheeseburger with onion rings and chips, local white crab meat salad, chicken with bacon, cheese and barbecue sauce, scampi with lime mayonnaise, and puddings. *Benchmark main dish: fresh fish of the day £10.95. Two-course evening meal £17.50.*

St Austell ~ Manager Melanie Matthews ~ Real ale ~ Open 11-11; 11-10.30 Sun ~ Bar food 12-2.30, 6-8.30 ~ Restaurant ~ Children welcome ~ Dogs allowed in bar and bedrooms ~ Wi-fi ~ Bedrooms: /£120 *Recommended by Alan Johnson, Charlie May, Toby Jones*

MYLOR BRIDGE
Pandora ♀

SW8137 Map 1

(01326) 372678 – www.pandorainn.com

Restronguet Passage: from A39 in Penryn, take turning signposted Mylor Church, Mylor Bridge, Flushing and go straight through Mylor Bridge following Restronguet Passage signs; or from A39 further N, at or near Perranarworthal, take turning signposted Mylor, Restronguet, then follow Restronguet Weir signs, but turn left downhill at Restronguet Passage sign; TR11 5ST

Beautifully placed waterside inn with lots of atmosphere in beamed and flagstoned rooms, and all-day food

On a quiet warm day at high tide with a seat on the long floating jetty in front of this medieval thatched pub, you can forget the troubles of the world for a while: it's idyllic. But you must arrive early to bag a seat outside or in, as they only take bookings for the upstairs restaurant. There's a back cabin bar with pale farmhouse chairs, high-backed settles and a model galleon in a big glass cabinet. Several other rambling, interconnecting rooms have low beams, beautifully polished big flagstones, cosy alcoves, cushioned built-in wall seats and pubby tables and chairs, three large log fires in high hearths (to protect them against tidal floods) and maps, yacht pictures, oars and ship's wheels; church candles help with the lighting. St Austell HSD, Proper Job, Trelawny and Tribute on handpump, 17 wines by the glass and 18 malt whiskies served by friendly, efficient staff. Upstairs, the attractive dining room has exposed oak vaulting, dark tables and chairs on pale oak flooring and large brass bells and lanterns. Because of the pub's popularity, parking is extremely difficult at peak times; wheelchair access.

As well as morning coffee and summer afternoon cream teas, some sort of good food is offered all day: sandwiches (until 5pm), shellfish marinière, pork rillettes with date chutney, sharing tapas board, burger with toppings and coleslaw, own-made sausages with caramelised onion gravy, honey-glazed root vegetable tarte tatin with beetroot, dauphinoise potatoes and roasted fennel cream, beer-battered daily fresh fish and chips, pork cutlet with boulangère potato, black pudding and quince and red wine jus, and puddings such as banana split and caramelised vanilla crème brûlée. *Benchmark main dish: fish pie in Pernod cream sauce £13.00. Two-course evening meal £20.00.*

St Austell ~ Tenant John Milan ~ Real ale ~ Open 10.30am-11pm ~ Bar food 10.30-9.30 ~ Restaurant ~ Children welcome away from bar area ~ Dogs allowed in bar ~ Wi-fi *Recommended by Chris and Angela Buckell, Mick and Moira Brummell, John and Bernadette Elliott, Colin McKerrow, David Eberlin, John Marsh, Mr and Mrs J Watkins, Richard Tilbrook*

PENZANCE
SW4730 Map 1

Turks Head

(01736) 363093 – www.turksheadpenzance.co.uk

At top of main street, by big domed building turn left down Chapel Street; TR18 4AF

Cheerfully run pub with a good, bustling atmosphere and popular food and beer

This is just as a town pub should be – well run, cheerful and friendly, with a good mix of customers. The bar has old flat irons, jugs and so forth hanging from the beams, pottery above the wood-effect panelling, wall seats and tables and a couple of elbow-rests around central pillars; background music. Sharps Doom Bar, Skinners Betty Stogs and guests such as Greene King Abbot and Wadworths 6X on handpump, a dozen wines by the glass and 12 malt whiskies. The suntrap back garden has big urns of flowers. There's been a Turks Head here for over 700 years – though most of the original building was destroyed by a Spanish raiding party in the 16th c.

Well thought-of food cooked by a *MasterChef* semi-finalist includes lunchtime sandwiches, creamy seafood chowder, panko-breadcrumbed king prawns with soy, lime and sweet chilli, steak, spicy lamb or bean burgers with toppings and chips, seafood pie, lambs liver with bacon, celeriac mash and red wine and onion gravy, local sausages with mustard mash, and puddings. *Benchmark main dish: braised pork cheeks, pea purée, black pudding mash and cider jus £10.95. Two-course evening meal £16.60.*

Punch ~ Lease Jonathan and Helen Gibbard ~ Real ale ~ Open 11.30am-midnight; 12-midnight Sun ~ Bar food 12-2.30, 6-10 (9.30 in winter) ~ Restaurant ~ Children welcome ~ Dogs allowed in bar ~ Wi-fi *Recommended by Alan Johnson, Alison Ball, Ian Walton, Andrew Stone*

PERRANUTHNOE
SW5329 Map 1

Victoria 🔶

(01736) 710309 – www.victoriainn-penzance.co.uk

Signed off A394 Penzance–Helston; TR20 9NP

Carefully furnished inn close to Mount's Bay beaches, friendly welcome, local beers, interesting fresh food and seats in pretty garden; bedrooms

Just a minute from the South West Coast Path and just over a mile from the beaches of Mount's Bay, this bustling inn is under enthusiastic new owners since it was last in these pages. The L-shaped bar has various cosy corners, exposed joists, a woodburning stove and an attractive array of dining chairs around wooden tables on oak flooring. The restaurant is separate. Cornish Crown Honeyfuggle, Sharps Doom Bar and Skinners Keel Over on handpump and several wines by the glass; background music. The pub spaniel is called Monty. The pretty tiered garden has seats and tables, and the bedrooms are light and airy.

Using the best seasonal, local produce, the imaginative food includes lunchtime sandwiches, crab with aioli, salsa vegetables, gazpacho and croutons, duck liver pâté with port jelly and pickled vegetables, crispy basil and cheese arancini with roasted tomatoes and herb oil, pork sausages with black pudding and bubble and squeak, megrim sole with herbs, anchovies and pesto sauce, garlic-roasted chicken with girolle and parmesan risotto and truffle oil, and puddings such as white chocolate and mascarpone mousse with chocolate sorbet and sticky ginger pudding with apple compote, toffee sauce and milk ice-cream. *Benchmark main dish: pork belly, black pudding and pork cheek with bubble and squeak, bacon and cabbage and apple sauce £15.00. Two-course evening meal £20.50.*

Free house ~ Licensee Nik Boyle ~ Real ale ~ Open 12-midnight; 12-6 Sun ~ Bar food 12-2.30, 6.15-9; 12-4.30 Sun ~ Restaurant ~ Children welcome ~ Dogs allowed in bar ~ Wi-fi ~ Bedrooms: /£75 *Recommended by Brian and Anna Marsden, Alison Ball, Ian Walton, Di and Mike Gillam, Ross Balaam*

PERRANWELL STATION
SW7739 Map 1

Royal Oak

(01872) 863175 – www.theroyaloakperranwellstation.co.uk
Village signposted off A393 Redruth–Falmouth and A39 Falmouth–Truro; TR3 7PX

Welcoming and relaxed pub, with well liked food and real ales

You'll usually find a group of locals chatting at the bar in this small traditional village pub – always a good sign – and there's a welcome for all. The carpeted bar, with a relaxed atmosphere, has horsebrasses on black beams and paintings by local artists on the walls, and rambles around beyond a big stone fireplace to a snug room, behind which more candle-lit tables can be found. St Austell Proper Job, Sharps Doom Bar, Skinners Lushingtons and a guest ale such as Purple Moose Madogs Ale on handpump, as well as good wines by the glass and farm cider. There are picnic-sets in front and more seats in the garden, and the pub is surrounded by walks and cycle paths in attractive countryside.

Tasty food includes sandwiches, baguettes, scallops with chorizo, sherry and cream, whole baked goats cheese with red onion marmalade, mushroom stroganoff, a trio of local fish meunière, duck leg confit with tomato and red onion reduction, steaks with a choice of sauces, and puddings. *Benchmark main dish: crab bake £13.75. Two-course evening meal £19.00.*

Free house ~ Licensees Tim Cairns and Lizzie Archer ~ Real ale ~ Open 11-3.30, 6-midnight; 11-midnight Sat; 12-11.30 Sun ~ Bar food 12-2.30, 6.30-9.30 ~ Children welcome ~ Dogs allowed in bar ~ Wi-fi *Recommended by Tom and Jill Jones, John Marsh*

PHILLEIGH
SW8739 Map 1

Roseland

(01872) 580254 – www.roselandinn.co.uk
Between A3078 and B3289, NE of St Mawes just E of King Harry Ferry; TR2 5NB

Character bars and back dining room in attractive pub, local ales, good food and seats on pretty front terrace

As this pretty pub is so close to the King Harry Ferry and Trelissick Gardens (National Trust), there are plenty of visitors at peak times, so it's best to book a table in advance. The two character bar rooms (one with flagstones, the other carpeted) have farmhouse and other dining chairs and built-in red cushioned seats, a woodburning stove, old photographs, brass spoons and horsebrasses, and some giant beetles and butterflies in glass cases. The tiny lower area is liked by regulars and there's a popular back restaurant too. Skinners Betty Stogs, Sharps Doom Bar and a guest beer on handpump and several decent wines by the glass; staff are friendly and helpful. There are seats on a pretty paved front courtyard.

Well liked food includes lunchtime sandwiches, scallops with herb butter, parma ham and asparagus with raspberry vinaigrette, sharing tapas boards, wild mushroom risotto, ham and mushroom tagliatelle, sausages with onion gravy, beer-battered fish and chips, game hotpot, rib-eye steak, and puddings such as their take on eton mess (amaretti biscuits with chocolate, meringue and espresso cream) and sticky toffee pudding with butterscotch sauce. *Benchmark main dish: bass with smoked salmon and crayfish risotto £15.95. Two-course evening meal £20.50.*

Punch ~ Tenant Philip Heslip ~ Real ale ~ Open 11-3, 5-11 ~ Bar food 12-2.30, 6-9 ~ Restaurant ~ Children welcome ~ Dogs allowed in bar ~ Wi-fi
Recommended by Chris and Angela Buckell, R and S Bentley

POLKERRIS

SX0952 Map 1

Rashleigh

(01726) 813991 – www.therashleighinnpolkerris.co.uk
Signposted off A3082 Fowey–St Austell; PL24 2TL

Lovely beachside spot with heaters on sizeable sun terrace, five real ales and quite a choice of food

In warm weather, the front terrace here is marvellous. There are seats under a big awning, outside heaters and wonderful views towards the far side of St Austell and Mevagissey bays; a fine beach with restored jetty is just a few steps away. Inside, the cosy bar has comfortably cushioned chairs around dark wooden tables at the front, and similar furnishings, local photographs and a winter log fire at the back. Otter Bitter, Skinners Betty Stogs, Timothy Taylors Landlord and a guest such as Bath Gem on handpump, several wines by the glass, two farm ciders and organic soft drinks. All the tables in the restaurant have a sea view. There's plenty of parking in either the pub's own car park or the large village one. The local section of the South West Coast Path is renowned for its striking scenery.

As well as daily fresh fish and shellfish and afternoon snacks, the good food includes sandwiches and ciabattas, whole baked camembert with garlic and rosemary and real ale chutney, crab cakes with sweet chilli sauce, red onion, chickpea and rocket curry, steak in ale pie, trio of local sausages with caramelised onion gravy, moroccan-style lamb tagine, griddled tuna steak with stir-fried vegetables, moules marinière, and puddings such as pina colada tart and chocolate fudge cake. *Benchmark main dish: beer-battered cod and chips £9.95. Two-course evening meal £16.00.*

Free house ~ Licensees Jon and Samantha Spode ~ Real ale ~ Open 11-11 ~ Bar food 12-3, 6-9 ~ Restaurant ~ Children welcome ~ Dogs allowed in bar *Recommended by Robert Turnham, Richard Tilbrook, R K Phillips*

POLPERRO

SX2050 Map 1

Blue Peter ⚓ £

(01503) 272743 – www.thebluepeter.co.uk
Quay Road; PL13 2QZ

Friendly pub overlooking pretty harbour with a good mix of customers, fishing paraphernalia and local paintings, real ales and carefully prepared food

Thankfully, not much changes in this small harbourside pub – which is just how its regular visitors and our readers like it. The cosy low-beamed bar has a chatty, relaxed atmosphere, traditional furnishings that include a small winged settle and a polished pew, wooden flooring, fishing regalia, photographs and pictures by local artists, lots of candles and a solid wood bar counter: St Austell Tribute and guests from local breweries such as Bays, Cornish Crown and Harbour on handpump. One window seat looks down on the harbour, while another looks out past rocks to the sea; families must use the upstairs room. Background music and board games. There are a few seats outside on the terrace and more in an amphitheatre-style area upstairs. The pub gets crowded at peak times. Usefully, they have a cash machine (there's no bank in the village).

Good food at fair prices includes sandwiches (the crab is popular), chicken liver pâté, beef in ale pie, fishcakes of the day, honey-roasted ham and egg, beer-battered fresh fish and chips, a pasta dish of the day, rib-eye steaks, and puddings such as crème brûlée and fruit crumble; they also offer breakfasts from 9am in season. *Benchmark main dish: seafood platter £17.25. Two-course evening meal £17.00.*

Free house ~ Licensees Steve and Caroline Steadman ~ Real ale ~ Open 10am-11pm; 10am-10.30pm Sun ~ Bar food 12-3, 6-9; all day in summer peak season ~ Restaurant ~ Children in upstairs family room only ~ Dogs allowed in bar ~ Wi-fi ~ Live music Fri and Sat evenings in summer *Recommended by Richard Tilbrook, Barry Collett, Edward May*

PORT ISAAC   SX0080   Map 1
Port Gaverne Inn 🛏

(01208) 880244 – www.portgavernehotel.co.uk
Port Gaverne signposted from Port Isaac and from B3314 E of Pendoggett; PL29 3SQ

Bustling small hotel near the sea with a proper bar and real ales, well liked food in several dining areas and seats in the garden; bedrooms

Our readers very much enjoy staying in this 17th-c inn and the individually furnished and comfortable rooms have much character; the stairs up to most of them are fairly steep, but staff will carry your luggage. The bar is full of lively chat – especially in the evenings – and there are low beams, flagstones and carpeting, some exposed stone and a big log fire; the lounge has some interesting old local photographs. You can eat in the bar or in the Captain's Cabin – a little room where everything is shrunk to scale (old oak chest, model sailing ship, even the prints on the white stone walls). St Austell Proper Job and Tribute, Skinners Betty Stogs and Timothy Taylors Landlord on handpump, a decent choice of wines and several whiskies. There are seats and tables under parasols at the front, with more in the terraced garden, and splendid clifftop walks all around.

As well as a two- and three-course set lunch, the reliably good food includes lunchtime sandwiches and afternoon cream teas, chicken liver brûlée with fig chutney, scallops with black pudding and apple cider cream, ham hock with duck eggs and mustard cream, cod in crisp cornflake batter with triple-cooked chips, vegetarian risotto, rare-breed beef and venison burger with toppings and sweet pickles, lobster thermidor, and puddings such as apple tarte tatin with caramel milk sorbet and banana parfait with candied lime and lime curd. *Benchmark main dish: fish pie £15.95. Two-course evening meal £21.50.*

Free house ~ Licensee Jackie Barnard ~ Real ale ~ Open 12-2.30, 5-10; 11-10 Sat, Sun ~ Bar food 12-2, 7-9 ~ Restaurant ~ Children welcome ~ Dogs welcome ~ Wi-fi ~ Bedrooms: £95/£150 *Recommended by John and Bernadette Elliott, Phil and Helen Holt, John T Ames, Mrs A W Johns*

PORTHLEVEN   SW6225   Map 1
Ship

(01326) 564204 – www.theshipinncornwall.co.uk
Mount Pleasant Road (harbour) off B3304; TR13 9JS

Friendly harbourside pub with fantastic views, pubby furnishings, real ales and tasty food and seats on terrace

Try to arrive early enough at this old fishermen's pub to bag a window seat in the bar, then watch the sea birds and boats in the harbour just metres away (it's interestingly floodlit at night); the candlelit dining room shares the same view. There are open fires in stone fireplaces, cushioned settles, mate's chairs and other wooden dining chairs around all sorts of tables on floorboards or flagstones, banknotes and beer mats on the ceilings and walls, various lamps and pennants and a bustling atmosphere. Sharps Cornish Coaster and Doom Bar, Skinners Porthleven and Rebel Bal Maiden on handpump; background music. They also have a cosy, traditionally furnished and separate function room. Seats in the terraced garden look over the water.

Good quality food includes sandwiches, crab cakes with pesto dressing, field mushrooms stuffed with cheese, various platters, beef, chicken or bean burgers with toppings and fries, crab salad, mussels with garlic mayonnaise and frites, rump steak with potato wedges, and puddings such as treacle tart and apple crumble. *Benchmark main dish: fish pie £11.95. Two-course evening meal £16.00.*

Free house ~ Licensee Oliver Waite ~ Real ale ~ Open 11-11 ~ Bar food 12-2, 6.30-9 ~ Well behaved children welcome ~ Dogs allowed in bar ~ Wi-fi *Recommended by Geoff and Linda Payne, Alan Johnson, Clifford Blakemore*

PORTHTOWAN   SW6948 Map 1
Blue
(01209) 890329 – www.blue-bar.co.uk
Beach Road, East Cliff; car park (fee in season) advised; TR4 8AW

Informal, busy bar (certainly not a traditional pub) right by a stunning beach, with modern food and wide choice of drinks

There's a real mix of cheerful customers in this bustling bar – most of them straight off the wonderful beach next door. They all pile in here throughout the day and the atmosphere is easy and informal; big picture windows look across the terrace to the huge expanse of sand and sea. The front bays have built-in pine seats, while the rest of the large room has wicker and white chairs around pale tables on grey-painted floorboards, cream or orange walls, several bar stools and plenty of standing space around the counter; ceiling fans, some big ferny plants and fairly quiet background music. St Austell Tribute, Sharps Doom Bar and Skinners Betty Stogs on handpump, several wines by the glass, cocktails and shots, and all kinds of coffees, hot chocolates and teas.

Usefully serving food all day from 10am (their Fri-Sun brunches are popular), there are daily specials plus nachos with cheese, sour cream and guacamole, various sharing platters, beef, chicken or vegetarian burgers with toppings and rustic chips, beer-battered fish, steaks, and puddings such as waffles with clotted cream ice-cream and sticky toffee pudding. *Benchmark main dish: mussels in white wine, cream and garlic £13.50. Two-course evening meal £16.00.*

Free house ~ Licensees Tara Roberts and Luke Morris ~ Real ale ~ Open 10am-11pm (10pm Sun) ~ Bar food 10-9 ~ Children welcome ~ Dogs allowed in bar ~ Wi-fi ~ Acoustic music Sat evening, comedy night monthly *Recommended by Edward May, Toby Jones, Tom and Jill Jones*

ST IVES   SW5441 Map 1
Queens
(01736) 796468 – www.queenshotelstives.com
High Street; TR26 1RR

Bustling inn just back from the harbour with a spacious bar, open fire, real ales and tasty food; light bedrooms

With good food, local ales and regular live music, it's not surprising that this late Georgian inn is so popular with both regulars and visitors.

The spreading open-plan bar has a relaxed atmosphere, a happy mish-mash of wooden chairs around scrubbed tables on bare floorboards, tartan banquettes on either side of the Victorian fireplace, a wall of barometers above a leather chesterfield sofa and some brown leather armchairs; fresh flowers and candles on tables and on the mantelpiece above the open fire. Red-painted bar chairs line the white marble-topped counter where they serve St Austell Cornish Best, HSD, Proper Job and Tribute on handpump, ten wines by the glass, a good choice of spirits and farm cider; background music and TV for sports events. The attractive bedrooms are airy and simply furnished with cornish artwork on the walls and some period furniture. The window boxes and hanging baskets are quite a sight in summer.

Enjoyable food includes lunchtime sandwiches, tempura tiger prawns with pickled cucumber and fennel, venison with a poached duck egg, herb salad and truffle oil, burger with toppings and chips, chicken with chorizo and dauphinoise potatoes, beer-battered fish and chips, pork belly with hogs pudding, smoked bacon potato cake and caramelised apple, and puddings such as chocolate brownie with butterscotch ice-cream and apple crumble with marmalade ice-cream. *Benchmark main dish: braised lamb shoulder with aubergines, tomatoes and capers £13.00. Two-course evening meal £19.50.*

St Austell ~ Tenant Neythan Hayes ~ Real ale ~ Open 11-11 ~ Bar food 12-2.30, 6-9; 12-3, 6-8; not Sun evening in winter ~ Children welcome ~ Dogs allowed in bar ~ Wi-fi ~ Live music summer Sat evenings ~ Bedrooms: £69/£79 *Recommended by Hilary and Neil Christopher, Peter Brix*

ST MERRYN
SW8874   Map 1

Cornish Arms

(01841) 532700 – www.rickstein.com/eat-with-us/the-cornish-arms
Churchtown (B3276 towards Padstow); PL28 8ND

Busy roadside pub, liked by locals and visitors, with bar and dining rooms, real ales, good pubby food, friendly service and seats outside

In the summer, this roadside pub gets quite packed with holidaymakers, so our readers tend to enjoy their visits more out of season. The main door leads into a sizeable informal area with a pool table and plenty of cushioned wall seating; to the left, a light, airy dining room overlooks the terrace. There's an unusual modern upright woodburner (with tightly packed logs on each side), photographs of the sea and former games teams, and pale wooden dining chairs around tables on quarry tiles. This leads to two more linked rooms with ceiling joists; the first has pubby furniture on huge flagstones, while the end room has more cushioned wall seating, contemporary seats and tables and parquet flooring. St Austell Proper Job, Trelawny and a guest ale on handpump, 17 wines by the glass, a farm cider, friendly service, background music and TV. The window boxes are pretty and there are picnic-sets on a side terrace – with more on grass.

Good quality traditional food includes sandwiches, field mushrooms with parmesan and aioli, ham hock terrine with piccalilli, ham and egg, aubergine with tomato, taleggio and parmesan, sausages with mash and gravy, burger with cheese, chipotle relish and chips, grilled hake and chips, and puddings such as apple and blackberry pie and orange parfait; they may offer a two-course fish menu on Fri evenings. *Benchmark main dish: pint of prawns £12.95. Two-course evening meal £18.00.*

St Austell ~ Tenant Siebe Richards ~ Real ale ~ Open 11.30-11 ~ Bar food 12-3, 5.30-9.30; 12-7 Sun ~ Children welcome ~ Dogs welcome ~ Wi-fi *Recommended by Alison Ball, Ian Walton, Chris and Val Ramstedt*

ST TUDY
St Tudy Inn 🎯 ♀

SX0676 Map 1

(01208) 850656 – www.sttudyinn.com

Off A391 near Wadebridge; PL30 3NN

Refurbished pub with several bars and dining rooms, good wines by the glass, enjoyable food and seats outside

With particularly good food cooked by the new landlady and a warm welcome for all their customers, it's not surprising that this attractive village pub is doing so well. The main bar has a leather armchair beside the log fire in a raised fireplace (fairy lights on the bressumer beam), beer cask seats, chairs and cushioned window seats by a mix of tables on floor slates and stools against the wooden counter where they keep Padstow May Day and Sharps Doom Bar on handpump, a dozen wines by the glass and a couple of ciders. The dining rooms are relaxed and informal, with a mix of dark farmhouse, wheelback and elegant wooden chairs and tables on bare boards or rugs, a second fireplace, fresh flowers and candlelight; background music. As we went to press, they were working on the garden – though there are picnic-sets beneath parasols at the front.

Using the best local produce, the well liked food includes sandwiches, garlic mushrooms on sourdough, scallops with thyme and garlic, caramelised onion tarte tatin, burger with toppings and fries, lamb tagine with spices, apricots and coriander, steak and kidney pie, lemon sole with herb dressing, and puddings such as treacle tart and raspberry meringue roulade. *Benchmark main dish: beer-battered gurnard and chips £13.00. Two-course evening meal £21.00.*

Free house ~ Licensee Emily Scott ~ Real ale ~ Open 12-midnight (11 Sun); closed Mon ~ Bar food 12-2.30, 6-9 ~ Restaurant ~ Children welcome ~ Dogs allowed in bar ~ Wi-fi
Recommended by Caroline Prescott, Lindy Andrews

TREBURLEY
Springer Spaniel 🎯 ♀

SX3477 Map 1

(01579) 370424 – www.thespringerspaniel.co.uk

A388 Callington–Launceston; PL15 9NS

Cornwall Dining Pub of the Year

Cosy, friendly pub with highly popular, first class food, friendly staff and an easy-going atmosphere

Given that the food is pretty special, most customers are here to dine. But locals do drop in for a pint and a chat, dogs are welcome (there's a water bowl and a jar of dog biscuits by the door) and the atmosphere is easy-going and friendly. The small beamed bar has antlers and a few copper pans on an exposed stone wall above a woodburning stove, books on shelves, pictures of springer spaniels, a rather fine high-backed settle and other country kitchen chairs and tables and old parquet flooring. A little dining room has more bookcases, candles and similar tables and chairs, and stairs lead up to the main restaurant; a second woodburner is set into a slate wall with a stag's head above it. Otter Bright and St Austells Tribute on handpump and ten good wines by the glass (including sparkling); background music. Outside in the small enclosed, paved garden are picnic-sets.

Particularly good food includes salt and pepper crispy squid with lemon mayonnaise, pigeon wellington with mushroom purée, spicy onion scotch egg with roasted sweet potato purée and chickpeas, burger with barbecue pulled pork and fries, steak and venison pudding, roast sirloin with bone marrow crumble and herb-crusted tomato, and puddings such as dark chocolate and hazelnut mousse and lemon posset with meringue. *Benchmark main dish: cocoa-marinated venison £21.95. Two-course evening meal £22.00.*

Free house ~ Licensees Anton and Clare Piotrowski ~ Real ale ~ Open 12-11; closed Mon ~ Bar food 12-3, 6-9; snacks all day ~ Restaurant ~ Children welcome ~ Dogs allowed in bar
Recommended by Isobel Mackinlay, Edward May

 TREVAUNANCE COVE   SW7251   Map 1

Driftwood Spars

(01872) 552428 – www.driftwoodspars.com
Off B3285 in St Agnes; Quay Road; TR5 0RT

Friendly old inn with plenty of history, own-brew beers, a wide range of other drinks and popular food, and beach nearby; bedrooms

There's so much going for this well run pub – its position (just up the lane from a dramatic cove and beach), its ales (including home-brews), its food (good and usefully serving something all day) and its accommodation (attractive, comfortable and overlooking the coast). The bars are timbered with massive ships' spars (the masts of great sailing ships, many of which were wrecked along this coast), and furnishings include dark wooden farmhouse and tub chairs and settles around different sized tables, padded stools by the counter, old ship prints, lots of nautical and wreck memorabilia and woodburning stoves. It's said that an old smugglers' tunnel leads from behind the bar up through the cliff. Seven real ales on handpump might include their own Driftwood Alfie's Revenge, Blonde and Lou's Brew with guests such as St Austell Tribute, Sharps Doom Bar and Skinners Lushington; they hold two beer festivals a year. Also, 25 malt whiskies, ten rums, seven gins and several wines by the glass. There's table football and pool. The modern dining room overlooks the cove and service is friendly and helpful. There are pretty summer hanging baskets and seats in the garden.

Thursday is pie night, Friday is fish and chips with a buy-one-get-one-free deal and there's a winter weekday two-course set menu. Also, lunchtime sandwiches, wraps and platters, ham hock ballotine with ale chutney, potted rabbit with mustard butter, tempura vegetables with thai-style salad, sausage and mash with red onion gravy, fish pie with cheesy mash, lemon and thyme chicken with honey and mustard sauce and bubble and squeak cake, and puddings such as raspberry crème brûlée and an ale plate (ale with chocolate pudding, chocolate mousse and cherry ice-cream). *Benchmark main dish: ale sausages with red onion gravy and mash £9.95. Two-course evening meal £17.00.*

Own brew ~ Licensee Louise Treseder ~ Real ale ~ Open 11-11; 11-10.30 Sun ~ Bar food 12-2.30, 6-9 ~ Restaurant ~ Children welcome ~ Dogs welcome ~ Wi-fi ~ Live music Sat evenings, open mike first and third Sun of month ~ Bedrooms: £64/£90
Recommended by Tracey and Phil Eagles, Edward May

 WADEBRIDGE   SW9972   Map 1

Ship ♀

(01208) 813845 – www.shipinnwadebridge.co.uk
Gonvena Hill, towards Polzeath; PL27 6DF

One of the oldest pubs in town, beams and open fires, carefully refurbished bars, real ales and good, seasonally changing food

There's plenty of nautical memorabilia on rough whitewashed walls above a blue dado in this 16th-c pub and a friendly atmosphere in which to enjoy them. Seating in the bar area ranges from leather button-back wall banquettes to all sorts of wooden dining chairs, stools and window seats topped with scatter cushions plus flagstone or bare board flooring, books on shelves, church candles and open fires; background music and they have a backgammon evening on the first Monday evening of the month. High chairs line the counter, where attentive staff serve Padstow Pride and Sharps Atlantic and Doom Bar on handpump and 14 wines by the glass; of the two dining areas, one has high rafters and brass ship lights. The small decked terrace outside has seats and chairs.

Letting the local produce shine through the often interesting food includes lunchtime sandwiches, mussels with cider and bacon, smoked duck with orange, fennel, Pernod and watercress salad, beef, pulled pork and grilled field mushroom burgers with toppings, coleslaw and fries, smoked haddock fishcakes with lemon mayonnaise, pork belly with green lentils, pancetta and onion sauce, and puddings such as bakewell tart with clotted cream and chocolate brownie with chocolate sauce; burger night is Tuesday and steak evening is Thursday. *Benchmark main dish: hake fillet with olive oil mash, grilled vegetables and gremolata £14.50. Two-course evening meal £20.00.*

Punch ~ Tenants Rupert and Sarah Wilson ~ Real ale ~ Open 12-2.30, 5-11; 12-11 Sun ~ Bar food 12-2 (3 Sun in winter), 5-9 (9.30 Fri, Sat) ~ Children welcome ~ Dogs allowed in bar ~ Wi-fi ~ Live jazz third Sun of month, folk club last Tues of month
Recommended by Jacqui Stevens, Lindy Andrews

WAINHOUSE CORNER
SX1895 Map 1
Old Wainhouse

(01840) 230711 – www.oldwainhouseinn.co.uk
A39; EX23 0BA

Cheerful pub, open all day with friendly staff and a good mix of customers, plenty of seating spaces, real ales and tasty food

Light and airy, the simply furnished but comfortable bedrooms here look out towards the sea and are popular with walkers on the South West Coast Path. The main bar has an easy-going, cheerful atmosphere, an attractive built-in settle, stripped rustic farmhouse chairs and dining chairs around a mix of tables on enormous old flagstones, a large woodburner with stone bottles on the mantelpiece above it, and beams hung with scythes, saws, a horse collar and other tack, spiles, copper pans and brass plates; do note the lovely photograph of a man driving a pig across a bridge. Off here is a simpler room with similar furniture, a pool table and background music. The dining room to the left of the main door has elegant high-backed dining chairs around pale wooden tables, another woodburner and more horse tack. Sharps Cornish Coaster and Doom Bar on handpump and friendly service. Outside, a grass area to one side of the building has picnic-sets.

The menu features top quality local meat, game and fish and includes crab and leek tart, chicken liver parfait with onion jam, beer-battered pollock and chips, blue cheese risotto with spiced walnuts, tarragon-stuffed chicken breast wrapped in parma ham with red wine sauce, and puddings such as crème brûlée and apple and cherry crumble. *Benchmark main dish: sirloin steak with a choice of sauces £18.95. Two-course evening meal £19.50.*

Enterprise ~ Lease Bryony Self ~ Real ale ~ Open 10am-midnight ~ Bar food 10-9 ~ Restaurant ~ Children welcome ~ Dogs welcome ~ Wi-fi ~ Live music first Sun of month ~ Bedrooms: £55/£90 *Recommended by Toby Jones, Peter Brix*

Also Worth a Visit in Cornwall

Besides the fully inspected pubs, you might like to try these pubs that have been recommended to us and described by readers. Do tell us what you think of them: feedback@goodguides.com

ALTARNUN   SX2280
Kings Head (01566) 86241
Five Lanes; PL15 7RX Old mansard-roofed beamed village pub, Greene King Abbot and guests such as Dartmoor and local Penpont, Weston's cider, generous reasonably priced pubby food from sandwiches and baguettes up including popular Sun carvery, carpeted lounge set for dining with big log fire, slate floor restaurant and public bar with another fire, ghost of former landlady Peggy Bray; background music, TV, pool; children and dogs welcome, picnic-sets on front terrace and in small raised garden, four bedrooms, open all day and handy for A30. *(Caroline Prescott)*

ALTARNUN   SX2083
★ Rising Sun (01566) 86636
NW; village signed off A39 just W of A395 junction; PL15 7SN Tucked-away 16th-c pub with traditionally furnished L-shaped main bar, slate flagstones and coal fires, good choice of food including excellent local seafood, Penpont, Skinners and guests, traditional cider, good friendly service; background music, pool; dogs and well behaved children allowed in bar but not restaurant, seats on suntrap terrace and in garden, pétanque, camping field, nice village with beautiful church, open all day weekends. *(John and Bernadette Elliott, Alison Ball, Ian Walton)*

BODINNICK   SX1352
Old Ferry (01726) 870237
Across the water from Fowey; coming by road, to avoid the ferry queue, turn left as you go downhill – car park on left before pub; PL23 1LX Old inn just up from the river with lovely views from terrace, dining room and some of its 12 comfortable bedrooms; traditional bar with nautical memorabilia, old photographs and woodburner, back room hewn into the rock, well kept Sharps ales and at least one guest, nice wines, good food from lunchtime sandwiches up including daily specials and children's menu, friendly french landlord and helpful staff; good circular walks, lane by pub in front of ferry slipway is extremely steep and parking limited, open (and food) all day. *(Giles Smith and Sandra Kiely)*

BODMIN   SX0467
Borough Arms (01208) 73118
Dunmere (A389 NW); PL31 2RD Roomy 19th-c roadside pub refurbished under new management; good value food including daily carvery, St Austell ales, cheerful staff, partly

panelled stripped-stone walls, open fire, side snug and separate dining room; background music; children and dogs (in bar) welcome, picnic-sets out among shady apple trees, play area, on Camel Trail, open (and food) all day. *(Mick and Moira Brummell)*

BOSCASTLE   SX0990
★ Napoleon (01840) 250204
High Street, top of village; PL35 0BD Welcoming 16th-c thick-walled white cottage at top of steep quaint village (fine views halfway up); cosy rooms on different levels, slate floors, oak beams and log fires, interesting Napoleon prints and lots of knick-knacks, good food from daily changing menu in bar areas or small evening restaurant, well kept St Austell tapped from casks, decent wines and coffee, traditional games; background music (live Fri, sing-along Tues), sports TV, free wi-fi; children and dogs welcome, small covered terrace and large sheltered garden, open all day. *(Anon)*

BOSCASTLE   SX0991
Wellington (01840) 250202
Harbour; PL35 0AQ Old hotel's long beamed and carpeted bar, good fairly priced food from varied menu, ales such as Skinners and St Austell kept well, nice coffee, roaring log fire, upstairs gallery area and separate evening restaurant with set menu (not cheap); children welcome, big secluded garden, comfortable bedrooms, open all day. *(Ryta Lyndley)*

BOTALLACK   SW3632
★ Queens Arms (01736) 788318
B3306; TR19 7QG Honest old pub with good home-made food including local seafood, meat sourced within 3 miles, well kept Sharps and Skinners, good friendly service, log fires (one in unusual granite inglenook), dark wood furniture, tin mining and other old local photographs on stripped-stone walls, family extension; dogs welcome, tables out in front and pleasant back garden, wonderful clifftop walks nearby, lodge accommodation, open all day. *(Martin Jones)*

BUDE   SS2006
Brendon Arms (01288) 354542
Falcon Terrace; EX23 8SD Popular pub (particularly in summer) near canal and owned by same family since 1872; two big friendly pubby bars and back family room, well kept ales such as St Austell and Sharps, decent wines by the glass, enjoyable traditional food from sandwiches and baked potatoes up; juke box, sports TV, free wi-fi, pool and darts; dogs allowed in public bar,

disabled access, picnic-sets on front grass, heated smokers' shelter, bedrooms and holiday apartments, good walks nearby, open all day. *(Harvey Brown)*

BUDE   SS2006
Falcon   (01288) 352005
Breakwater Road; EX23 8SD Popular 19th-c hotel overlooking canal, enjoyable good value food in carpeted bar with lots of plush banquettes and fire, good friendly service, well kept St Austell Tribute and a couple of guests, restaurant; free wi-fi; children welcome, attractive well maintained gardens, comfortable bedrooms, good breakfast, open all day in summer, all day weekends winter. *(Ryta Lyndley, Theocsbrian)*

CALSTOCK   SX4368
★Tamar   (01822) 832487
The Quay; PL18 9QA Cheerful relaxed local dating from the 17th c, just opposite the Tamar with its imposing viaduct, dark stripped stone, flagstones, tiles and bare boards, pool room with woodburner, more modern back dining room, good generous straightforward food and summer cream teas, well kept Sharps Doom Bar and other cornish ales, good service from cheery young staff and reasonable prices, some live music; children away from bar and well behaved dogs welcome, nicely furnished terrace, heated smokers' shelter, hilly walk or ferry to Cotehele (NT). *(Ian Herdman)*

CAWSAND   SX4350
Cross Keys   (01752) 822706
The Square; PL10 1PF Welcoming pub in little village square, slate-floored traditional locals' bar with some cask tables, steps up to carpeted dining room with nautical décor, Dartmoor Legend or Wooden Hand plus summer guests, enjoyable home-made food including fish/seafood specials, reasonable prices, friendly helpful service; background music (live Sun afternoon), big TV, free wi-fi; children welcome, towels provided for wet dogs, self-catering apartment, no parking close by, open all day, but closed Mon Jan-Mar. *(Harvey Brown)*

CHAPEL AMBLE   SW9975
Maltsters Arms   (01208) 812473
Off A39 NE of Wadebridge; PL27 6EU Country pub-restaurant with good food including Sun lunchtime carvery, friendly accommodating staff, St Austell Tribute and Sharps Doom Bar, Weston's cider, log fire, beams, painted half-panelling, stripped stone and some slate flagstones, modern back extension, Weds quiz and fortnightly live music; children welcome, seats outside. *(Isobel Mackinlay)*

CHARLESTOWN   SX0351
Harbourside Inn   (01726) 67955
Part of Pier House Hotel; PL25 3NJ Glass-fronted warehouse conversion alongside hotel, great spot looking over classic little harbour and its historic sailing ships, half a dozen ales including Bass, Sharps and Skinners, enjoyable pubby food from good sandwiches up, friendly efficient service; live music Sat night, two sports TVs, pool; interesting film-set conservation village with shipwreck museum, good walks, parking away from pub. *(Stanley and Annie Matthews)*

CHARLESTOWN   SX0351
Rashleigh Arms   (01726) 73635
Quay Road; PL25 3NX Modernised early 19th-c pub with nautical touches, public bar, lounge and dining area, well kept St Austell range, good wine choice and coffee, enjoyable fairly priced food all day including popular Sun carvery, friendly obliging service; background music, fortnightly live bands Fri, trad jazz second Sun of month, free wi-fi; children welcome, dogs in bar, disabled facilities, front terrace and garden with picnic-sets, eight bedrooms (some with sea views), Grade II listed car park (site of old coal storage yards), attractive harbour with tall ships. *(Taff Thomas)*

COMFORD   SW7339
Fox & Hounds   (01209) 820251
Comford; A393/B3298; TR16 6AX Attractive rambling low-beamed pub; stripped stone and painted panelling, high-backed settles and cottagey chairs on flagstones, some comfortable leather seating too, three woodburners, generous helpings of enjoyable fairly traditional food, St Austell ales, newspapers, darts and board games; background music; children and dogs (in bar) welcome, disabled facilities, nice floral displays in front, picnic-sets in back garden, open all day weekends, closed Mon. *(Peter Brix)*

COVERACK   SW7818
Paris   (01326) 280258
The Cove; TR12 6SX Comfortable Edwardian seaside inn above harbour in beautiful fishing village, carpeted L-shaped bar with well kept St Austell ales and Healey's cider, large relaxed dining room with white tablecloths and spectacular bay views, wide choice of interesting if not always cheap food including good fresh fish, Sun lunchtime carvery, helpful cheery service, model of namesake ship (wrecked nearby in 1899), popular Weds quiz; children welcome, more sea views from garden and four bedrooms, limited parking. *(Tom and Jill Jones)*

CRACKINGTON HAVEN   SX1496
★Coombe Barton   (01840) 230345
Off A39 Bude–Camelford; EX23 0JG Much extended old inn in beautiful setting overlooking splendid sandy bay, modernised pubby bar with plenty of room for summer crowds, welcoming young staff, wide range of simple bar food including local fish, popular carvery Sun lunchtime, Sharps, St Austell

and good wine choice, lots of local pictures, surfboard hanging from plank ceiling, big plain family room, restaurant; darts, pool, fruit machines, background music and TV; dogs allowed in bar, side terrace with plenty of tables, roomy bedrooms, good breakfast, open all day in season. *(Theocsbrian)*

CRAFTHOLE   SX3654

⋆**Finnygook** (01503) 230338

B3247, off A374 Torpoint road; PL11 3BQ 15th-c coaching inn with beams and joists in smart bar, long cushioned wall pews and carved cushioned dining chairs around wooden tables on bare boards, central log fire, high chairs and tables near counter serving Bays, Harbour and St Austell, decent choice of wines by the glass, ten malt whiskies and a real cider, record player (bring your own vinyl), dining room with fine views, unusual log-effect gas fire in big cabinet, dining library, enjoyable interesting food and friendly attentive service; live music last Fri of month, free wi-fi; children and dogs welcome, good surrounding walks, bedrooms, closed Mon Oct-Apr, otherwise open all day. *(Susan and Jeremy Arthern, Sharon and John Hancock)*

CREMYLL   SX4553

Edgcumbe Arms (01752) 822294

End of B3247; PL10 1HX Worth knowing for its splendid setting by Plymouth foot-ferry with great Tamar views and picnic-sets out by the water; attractive layout and décor, slate floors, big settles and comfortably old-fashioned furnishings including fireside sofas, old pictures and china, well kept St Austell ales, food from sandwiches up including lunchtime carvery (evenings Fri-Sun), good family room/games area; pay car park some way off; children in eating area, dogs allowed in one bar (most tables here too low to eat at), four bedrooms, open all day. *(Peter Brix)*

CROWS NEST   SX2669

Crows Nest (01579) 345930

Signed off B3264 N of Liskeard; OS Sheet 201 map reference 263692; PL14 5JQ Old-fashioned 17th-c inn with good traditional food and well kept St Austell ales, attractive furnishings under bowed beams, big log fire, chatty locals; children and dogs welcome, picnic-sets on terrace by quiet lane, handy for Bodmin Moor walks, open all day weekends. *(John and Bernadette Elliott)*

CUBERT   SW7857

⋆**Smugglers Den** (01637) 830209

Off A3075 S of Newquay; TR8 5PY Big open-plan 16th-c thatched pub tucked away in small hamlet and under new ownership; good locally sourced food and up to four beers (May pie and ale festival), several wines by the glass, friendly staff, neat ranks of tables, dim lighting, stripped stone and

heavy beam and plank ceilings, west country pictures and seafaring memorabilia, steps down to part with huge inglenook, another step to big side dining room, also a little snug area with woodburner and leather armchairs; background music; children and dogs welcome, small front courtyard, terrace with nice country views, sloping lawn and play area, camping opposite, open all day. *(John Coatsworth)*

DULOE   SX2358

Plough (01503) 262556

B3254 N of Looe; PL14 4PN Popular restauranty pub with three country-chic linked dining rooms all with woodburners, dark polished slate floors, a mix of pews and other seats, good fairly priced locally sourced food (must book weekends) including some imaginative dishes, also lunchtime sandwiches and snacks, reasonably priced wines, well kept St Austell, Sharps and summer guests, friendly service; unobtrusive background music; children and dogs welcome, picnic-sets out by road, open all day Sun. *(Paul Bonner, Mike and Jayne Bastin, Michael and Jenny Virtue)*

EDMONTON   SW9672

⋆**Quarryman** (01208) 816444

Off A39 just W of Wadebridge bypass; PL27 7JA Welcoming busy family-run pub adjoining small separately owned holiday courtyard complex; three-room beamed bar with interesting decorations including old sporting memorabilia, fairly pubby food from shortish menu with good individual dishes such as sizzling steaks and portuguese fish stew, quick friendly service, well kept Otter, Skinners and two guests, seven wines by the glass, no mobile phones or background music; well behaved children and dogs allowed, disabled access (but upstairs lavatories), picnic-sets in front and courtyard behind, self-catering apartment, open all day. *(Caroline Prescott)*

FALMOUTH   SW8132

5 Degrees West (01326) 311288

Grove Place, by harbourside car park; TR11 4AU Modern split-level open-plan bar with mixed furnishings including squashy sofas and low tables on stripped wood floors, log fire in driftwood-effect fireplace, local artwork, enjoyable food from snacks to grills, five real ales, nine ciders and good choice of other drinks, back dining area; background music (live Thurs, Fri), quiz Mon, free wi-fi; children and dogs welcome, disabled facilities, seats out at front and on attractive sheltered back terrace, open (and food) all day. *(Robert Watt)*

FALMOUTH   SW8032

Beerwolf (01326) 618474

Bells Court (opposite Marks & Spencer); TR11 3AZ Stairs up to intriguing old pub-cum-bookshop hidden down little alley in centre of town, good selection of well kept changing beers and ciders, decent coffee, no food but can bring your own, friendly staff and laid-back atmosphere, eclectic mix of furniture on bare boards, raftered ceilings, table tennis and table football; free wi-fi; children welcome, a few picnic-sets outside, open all day. *(Giles and Annie Francis)*

FALMOUTH   SW8132

★ **Chain Locker** (01326) 311085

Custom House Quay; TR11 3HH Busy old-fashioned place in fine spot by inner harbour with window tables and lots more seats outside, good selection of Sharps and Skinners ales, generous food from sandwiches and baguettes to local fish, nooks and crannies, bare boards and masses of nautical bric-a-brac; background music, darts alley, games machine; well behaved children and dogs welcome, self-catering accommodation, pay parking close by, open all day. *(Ken Parry, Ian Herdman, Mick and Moira Brummell, Richard Tilbrook)*

FALMOUTH   SW8132

Front (01326) 212168

Custom House Quay; TR11 3JT Bare-boards drinkers' pub with good changing selection of ales, some tapped from the cask, also foreign beers and ciders/perries, friendly knowledgeable staff, no food but can bring your own (good fish and chip shop above), mix of customers from students to beards; seats outside, open all day. *(Phil and Jane Villiers)*

FALMOUTH   SW8032

Seven Stars (01326) 312111

The Moor (centre); TR11 3QA Quirky 17th-c local, unchanging and unsmart (not to everyone's taste), friendly atmosphere and chatty regulars, no gimmicks, machines or mobile phones, up to six well kept ales tapped from the cask including Bass, Sharps and Skinners, bar snacks (maybe oysters), big key ring collection, quiet back snug; corridor hatch serving roadside courtyard, open all day. *(Anon)*

FLUSHING   SW8033

Seven Stars (01326) 374373

Trefusis Road; TR11 5TY Old-style waterside pub with welcoming local atmosphere, well kept ales and pubby food, coal fire, separate dining room, darts and pool; children and dogs welcome, pavement picnic-sets, great views of Falmouth with foot-ferry across, open all day. *(Richard Tilbrook)*

FOWEY   SX1251

Galleon (01726) 833014

Fore Street; from centre follow car-ferry signs; PL23 1AQ Superb spot by harbour and estuary, good beer range (local/ national) and decent choice of wines, well liked pubby food from extensive reasonably

priced menu, modern décor with lots of solid pine and exposed stone, dining areas off, Sun lunchtime jazz, live bands Fri evening; pool, big-screen TV, quiz machine, free wi-fi; children welcome, disabled facilities, attractive extended waterside terrace and sheltered courtyard with covered heated area, seven bedrooms (two with estuary-view), open all day. *(Ann and Mike Bolton, Ian Herdman)*

FOWEY   SX1251

★ **King of Prussia** (01726) 833694

Town Quay; PL23 1AT Handsome quayside building with roomy neatly kept upstairs bar, bay windows looking over harbour to Polruan, nice choice of enjoyable food from crab sandwiches and tapas boards up, St Austell ales and sensibly priced wines, generally friendly helpful staff, side restaurant; background music, pool, free wi-fi; children and dogs welcome, partly enclosed outside seating area, six pleasant bedrooms (all with views), open all day. *(Monica Shelley, Ann and Mike Bolton)*

FOWEY   SX1251

Lugger (01726) 833435

Fore Street; PL23 1AH Centrally placed St Austell pub with up to three of their ales in top condition, spotless front bar with nautical memorabilia, small back dining area, good mix of locals and visitors (can get busy), enjoyable food including local fish; children welcome, pavement tables, open all day. *(Ann and Mike Bolton, Ian Herdman)*

FOWEY   SX1251

Safe Harbour (01726) 833379

Lostwithiel Street; PL23 1BP Welcoming 19th-c coaching inn set away from main tourist part; lounge/dining area and lower-level regulars' bar, good value home-made food and well kept/priced St Austell ales, old local prints, upstairs overflow dining room; pool, darts, games machine; heated side terrace, seven bedrooms and a self-catering apartment, open all day till midnight. *(Ian Herdman, Ann and Mike Bolton)*

FOWEY   SX1251

★ **Ship** (01726) 832230

Trafalgar Square; PL23 1AZ Bustling unchanging local with log fire and banquettes in tidy bar, lots of yachting prints and nauticalia, well kept St Austell ales, newspapers, steps up to family dining room with big stained-glass window, generous helpings of good sensibly priced food from sandwiches up, pool/darts room; background music, sports TV; dogs allowed, comfortably old-fashioned bedrooms, some oak-panelled. *(Nick Lawless)*

GERRANS   SW8735

Royal Standard (01872) 580271

The Square; TR2 5EB Friendly little local (less touristy than nearby Plume of

Feathers) with narrow doorways linking carpeted rooms, up to three well kept local ales, Sharps cider and Skinners lager, short choice of well chosen wines, enjoyable pub food from sandwiches to local fish, old photographs on white plaster or black boarded walls, brass shell cases and kitchen utensils, woodburner, lakeland terrier called Millie; children welcome away from bar, disabled access, sunny beer garden, opposite interesting 15th-c church (rebuilt in 19th c after fire). *(Chris and Angela Buckell)*

GOLANT   SX1254

★ **Fishermans Arms** (01726) 832453

Fore Street (B3269); PL23 1LN Bustling partly flagstoned small waterside local with lovely views across River Fowey from front bar and terrace, good value generous home-made food including nice crab sandwiches and seafood, efficient friendly service, up to five well kept cornish ales (tasting trays available), good wines by the glass, blazing log fire, interesting pictures; children and dogs welcome, pleasant garden, open all day in summer, all day Fri-Sun winter. *(Charlie May)*

GORRAN CHURCHTOWN   SW9942

Barley Sheaf (01726) 843330

Follow Gorran Haven signs from Mevagissey; PL26 6HN Built in 1837 by local farmer and now owned and extensively refurbished by his great- (x3) grandson; enjoyable home-made food including popular Sun lunch, well kept Sharps Doom Bar and guests, local cider, friendly staff; Tues quiz and some live music; children and dogs welcome, well tended sunny beer garden, open all day summer. *(Nick Lawless, Martin and Sue Radcliffe)*

GRAMPOUND   SW9348

Dolphin (01726) 882435

A390 St Austell–Truro; TR2 4RR Friendly family-run St Austell pub with their well kept ales and decent choice of wines, good generous pub food, two-level bar with black beams and some panelling, polished wood or carpeted floors, pubby furniture with a few high-backed settles, pictures of old Grampound, log fire; darts (they have the UK's first blind team), pool, Thurs quiz; children welcome, dogs in bar, wheelchair access from car park, beer garden, good smokery opposite, handy for Trewithen Gardens, open all day Sat. *(Belinda May)*

GULVAL   SW4831

Coldstreamer (01736) 362072

Centre of village by drinking fountain; TR18 3BB Welcoming place (sister pub to the Dolphin in Penzance) with good food including fresh Newlyn fish, a couple of well kept local ales and guests, traditional bar with woodburner, old photographs and traditional games, restaurant with modern pine furniture on wood floor, local artwork; children welcome, quiet pleasant village very

handy for Trengwainton Gardens (NT) and Scillies heliport, comfortable bedrooms, open all day. *(Toby Jones)*

GUNNISLAKE   SX4371

Tavistock (01822) 832217

Fore Street; PL18 9BN Traditional old family-run inn with welcoming helpful landlord and staff, well kept St Austell Tribute and Sharps Doom Bar, enjoyable food from sandwiches to blackboard specials, carpeted bar with lots of decorative plates, old local pictures, horsebrasses on beams, separate restaurant, woodburners; free wi-fi, TV; dogs welcome, open (and food) all day. *(Hugh Roberts)*

HARROWBARROW   SX4069

Cross House (01579) 350482

Off A390 E of Callington; School Road – towards Metherell; PL17 8BQ Substantial stone building (former farmhouse) with spreading carpeted bar, some booth seating, cushioned wall seats and stools around pub tables, hearty helpings of enjoyable reasonably priced home-made food, well kept St Austell ales and nice wines by the glass, good friendly service, open fire and woodburner, darts area, restaurant; children and dogs (in bar) welcome, disabled facilities, plenty of picnic-sets on good-sized lawn, play area, handy for Cotehele (NT), open all day. *(Belinda May)*

HELSTON   SW6527

★ **Blue Anchor** (01326) 562821

Coinagehall Street; TR13 8EL Many (not all) love this no-nonsense, highly individual, 15th-c thatched pub; quaint rooms off corridor, flagstones, stripped stone, low beams and well worn furniture, family room, traditional games and skittle alley, ancient back brewhouse still producing distinctive and very strong Spingo IPA, Middle and seasonals such as Bragget with honey and herbs, no food but can bring your own (good pasty shop nearby), friendly local atmosphere; regular live music, Mon quiz; back garden with own bar, four bedrooms in house next door, big breakfast, open all day. *(Phil and Jane Hodson)*

HESSENFORD   SX3057

Copley Arms (01503) 240209

A387 Looe–Torpoint; PL11 3HJ Friendly 17th-c village pub with slightly old-fashioned feel, popular with families and passing tourists, enjoyable reasonably priced food from sandwiches to grills in linked carpeted areas, well kept St Austell ales and nice choice of wines, variety of teas and coffee, log fires, tables in cosy booths, one part with sofas and easy chairs, big family room; background and some live music, Thurs quiz; dogs allowed in one area, a few roadside picnic-sets by small River Seaton, fenced play area, five bedrooms, open all day. *(Lindy Andrews)*

HOLYWELL   SW7658
St Pirans (01637) 830205
Holywell Road; TR8 5PP Great location
backing on to dunes and popular with
holidaymakers, friendly helpful staff, well
kept ales such as St Austell and Sharps,
decent wines, enjoyable pub food with
blackboard specials; children and dogs
welcome, tables on large back terrace, open
all day, but closed out of season. *(Alison Ball,
Ian Walton)*

HOLYWELL   SW7658
Treguth (01637) 830248
*Signed from Cubert, SW of Newquay;
TR8 5PP* Ancient whitewashed stone and
thatch pub near big beach, cosy low-beamed
carpeted bar with big stone fireplace,
larger dining room at back, three real ales
and enjoyable home-cooked food, friendly
service; Weds quiz, pool; children and
dogs welcome, handy for campsites and
popular with holidaymakers, open all day
weekends. *(Richard Stanfield)*

KINGSAND   SX4350
Devonport (01752) 822869
The Cleave; PL10 1NF Character pub
with lovely bay views from front bar, three
changing local ales and good choice of
enjoyable well priced food, friendly service,
scrubbed floorboards and Victorian décor,
lots of ship photographs and bric-a-brac,
mix of cast-iron-framed pub furniture with
window seats and pine settles, log fire, back
snug; dogs welcome, tables out by sea wall,
good value bedrooms. *(Charlie May)*

LELANT   SW5436
Old Quay House (01736) 753445
*Griggs Quay, Lelant Saltings; A3047/
B3301 S of village; TR27 6JG* Large
pub in great spot by bird sanctuary estuary;
enjoyable home-made pub food including
Sun carvery, Sharps and Skinners ales, dining
area off well divided open-plan bar, upstairs
restaurant; children and dogs (in bar)
welcome, garden and small roof terrace with
views over saltings, play area, nine motel-type
bedrooms, open all day. *(Toby Jones)*

LELANT   SW5436
Watermill (01736) 757912
Lelant Downs; A3074 S; TR27 6LQ
Mill-conversion family dining pub; working
waterwheel behind with gearing in dark-
beamed central bar opening into brighter
airy front extension, upstairs evening (and
Sun lunchtime) restaurant, Sharps Doom Bar,
Skinners Betty Stogs and a guest, enjoyable
food served by friendly staff; live music Fri,

free wi-fi; dogs welcome, good-sized pretty
streamside garden, open all day.
(Charlie May)

LERRYN   SX1356
Ship (01208) 872374
*Signed off A390 in Lostwithiel; Fore
Street; PL22 0PT* Lovely spot especially
when tide's in; local ales, farm ciders and
good wine and whisky choice, sensibly
priced food served by cheerful staff, huge
woodburner, attractive dining conservatory,
games room with pool, library/internet café
area; free wi-fi; children welcome, dogs on
leads (they have two black labs), picnic-sets
and play area outside, near famous stepping
stones and three well signed waterside walks,
five bedrooms in adjoining building and self-
catering cottage, open all day. *(Nick Lawless)*

LIZARD   SW7012
Top House (01326) 290974
A3083; TR12 7NQ Neat clean pub with
friendly staff and regulars, enjoyable
local food from sandwiches and snacks up
including fresh fish, children's meals and
cream teas, well kept cornish ales, lots
of good local sea pictures, fine shipwreck
relics and serpentine craftwork (note
the handpumps), warm welcoming log
fire; sheltered terrace, eight bedrooms in
adjoining building (three with sea views),
good coastal walks, open all day in summer,
all day weekends in winter. *(Stanley and
Annie Matthews)*

LIZARD   SW7012
Witchball (01326) 290662
Lighthouse Road; TR12 7NJ Small
friendly beamed pub popular with locals,
good food including fresh fish and seafood,
Sun carvery, well kept ales such as Chough,
St Austell and Skinners, cornish cider,
cheerful helpful staff, Sat quiz; children and
dogs welcome, front terrace, open all day
summer, closed winter lunchtimes Mon and
Tues. *(Tom and Jill Jones)*

LOOE   SX2553
Olde Salutation (01503) 262784
Fore Street, East Looe; PL13 1AE
Good welcoming bustle in big squareish
slightly sloping beamed and tiled bar,
reasonably priced straightforward food from
notable crab sandwiches to Sun roasts (no
credit cards), well kept Sharps Doom Bar and
Cornish Orchards cider served by cheerful
staff, red leatherette seats and neat tables,
blazing fire in nice old-fashioned fireplace,
lots of local fishing photographs, side snug
with olde-worlde harbour mural, step down
to simple family room; may be background

Cribbage is a card game using a block of wood with holes for matchsticks or
special pins to score with; regulars in cribbage pubs are usually happy to teach
strangers how to play.

music; dogs welcome, lots of hanging baskets, handy for coast path, forget about parking, open all day. *(William and Ann Reid)*

LUDGVAN   SW5033
★ **White Hart** (01736) 740574
Off A30 Penzance–Hayle at Crowlas;
TR20 8EY Appealing old village pub, friendly and welcoming, with well kept Sharps Doom Bar and a guest tapped from the cask, own summer cider and premium range of spirits, enjoyable blackboard food from pub standards up including good value Sun lunch, small unspoilt beamed rooms with wood and stone floors, nooks and crannies, woodburners; quiz first Weds of month; dogs welcome, beer garden and little decked area at back, interesting church next door, two bedrooms, open all day Fri-Sun.
(R and S Bentley)

MARAZION   SW5130
Godolphin Arms (01736) 888510
West End; TR17 0EN Revamped former coaching inn with wonderful views across to St Michael's Mount, light contemporary décor and modern furnishings, good food from sandwiches and sharing plates up, St Austell and Skinners ales, lots of wines by the glass and good coffee, helpful friendly staff; children welcome, beachside terrace, ten stylish bedrooms (most with sea view, some with balconies), good breakfast, open all day from 8am. *(Anon)*

MARAZION   SW5130
Kings Arms (01736) 710291
The Square; TR17 0AP Old one-bar pub in small square, comfortable and welcoming with warm woodburner, good well presented food (best to book) including local fish from regularly changing menu, well kept St Austell ales, friendly helpful staff; children and dogs welcome, sunny picnic-sets out in front, open all day. *(Alan Johnson)*

MAWGAN   SW7025
Ship (01326) 221240
Churchfield, signed off Higher Lane;
TR12 6AD Former 18th-c courthouse in nice setting near Helford river on the Lizard peninsula; high-ceiling bare-boards bar with woodburner in stone fireplace, end snug, raised eating area, emphasis on good food including local fish/seafood and seasonal game, well kept ales such as Penzance Potion No 9 and St Austell Tribute; well behaved children and dogs welcome, garden with picnic-sets, closed lunchtimes and all day Sun, Mon. *(Clifford Blakemore)*

MAWNAN SMITH   SW7728
Red Lion (01326) 250026
W of Falmouth, off former B3291
Penryn–Gweek; The Square; TR11 5EP
Old thatched and beamed pub with cosy series of dimly lit lived-in rooms including raftered bar, enjoyable food from open-view

kitchen, good fresh fish and other daily specials, friendly helpful service, plenty of wines by the glass and three well kept ales including one named for the pub, good coffee, daily papers, woodburner in huge stone fireplace, dark woodwork, country and marine pictures, plates and bric-a-brac; Tues quiz, background music, TV; children (away from bar) and dogs welcome, disabled access, picnic-sets outside, handy for Glendurgan (NT) and Trebah Gardens, open all day. *(Maureen Wood)*

MENHENIOT   SX2862
Golden Lion (01209) 860332
Top of village by reservoir; TR16 6NW
Tucked-away little stone pub in nice spot by Stithians Reservoir; beamed bar and snug, woodburner, St Austell ales and good selection of wines by the glass, enjoyable generous food (all day weekends) from pub favourites up, friendly staff, restaurant with lake view, folk night third Sat of month; children and dogs welcome, attractive garden with heated shelter, good walks, camping, open (and food) all day weekends. *(Mick and Moira Brummell)*

MEVAGISSEY   SX0144
★ **Fountain** (01726) 842320
Cliff Street, down alley by Post Office;
PL26 6QH Popular low-beamed fishermen's pub, slate floor, some stripped stone and a welcoming coal fire, old local pictures, piano, well kept St Austell ales, good food at reasonable prices including local fish/seafood (particularly good fish stew), friendly staff, back bar with glass-topped pit, small upstairs evening restaurant; children and dogs welcome, pretty frontage with picnic-sets, two bedrooms, open all day in summer.
(Peter Brix)

MEVAGISSEY   SX0144
Ship (01726) 843324
Fore Street, near harbour; PL26 6UQ
16th-c pub with interesting alcove areas in big open-plan bar, low beams and flagstones, nautical décor, woodburner, fairly priced pubby food including good fresh fish, small helpings available, St Austell ales kept well, cheery uniformed staff; background and some live music, games machines, pool; dogs allowed, children welcome in two front rooms, five bedrooms, open all day in summer. *(Anon)*

MINIONS   SX2671
Cheesewring (01579) 362321
Overlooking the Hurlers; PL14 5LE
Homely village pub (claims to be the highest in Cornwall) useful for Bodmin Moor walks, well kept ales including Sharps Doom Bar and good choice of reasonably priced home-made food, lots of brass and ornaments, woodburner, friendly staff and chatty locals; children and dogs welcome, bedrooms, open all day. *(Harvey Brown)*

MITCHELL SW8554
★ **Plume of Feathers**
(01872) 510387/511125 *Off A30*
Bodmin–Redruth, by A3076 junction;
take southwards road then first right;
TR8 5AX 16th-c coaching inn with several
linked bar and dining rooms, appealing
contemporary décor with local artwork on
pastel walls, stripped beams and standing
timbers, painted dados and two open fires,
good food from varied menu including pub
standards, Sharps, Skinners and St Austell,
seveal wines by the glass, impressive
dining conservatory; background music;
children (away from bar) and dogs welcome,
picnic-sets under parasols in well planted
garden areas, comfortable stable-conversion
bedrooms, open all day from 8am. *(Tom
and Jill Jones, Brian and Anna Marsden, Alison
Ball, Ian Walton, Maureen Wood, Chris and Val
Ramstedt)*

MITHIAN SW7450
★ **Miners Arms** (01872) 552375
Off B3285 E of Street Agnes; TR5 0QF
Cosy old stone-built pub with traditional
small rooms and passages, pubby furnishings
and open fires, fine old wall painting of
Elizabeth I in back bar, popular good value
food, Sharps and Skinners ales kept well,
friendly helpful staff; background music,
board games; children welcome, dogs in
some rooms, seats on sheltered front cobbled
forecourt, back terrace and in garden, open
all day. *(Toby Jones)*

MULLION SW6719
Old Inn (01326) 240240
*In small one-way street opposite church
– not down in the cove; TR12 7HN*
Thatched and beamed 16th-c pub with
enjoyable fairly priced home-made food, well
kept St Austell ales and a guest, friendly
helpful staff, narrowish bar with linked
eating areas, big inglenook; TV, pool; children
and dogs welcome, picnic-sets on terrace and
in garden, five bedrooms, open all day (till
midnight Fri, Sat). *(Anon)*

MYLOR BRIDGE SW8036
Lemon Arms (01326) 373666
Lemon Hill; TR11 5NA Popular and
friendly traditional village pub, opened-up
bar area with stripped stone walls and
panelling, well kept St Austell ales, enjoyable
generously served food at fair prices (no
credit cards); children and dogs welcome,
wheelchair access with help, picnic-
sets on back terrace, good coastal walks
nearby. *(Chris and Angela Buckell)*

NEWLYN SW4629
★ **Tolcarne** (01736) 363074
Tolcarne Place; TR18 5PR Traditional
17th-c quayside pub with very good food
(not Mon) cooked by chef-landlord, much
emphasis on local fish/seafood (menu

changes daily) and booking advised, friendly
efficient service, St Austell Tribute, Skinners
Betty Stogs and maybe a local microbrew,
live jazz Sun lunchtime; children and dogs
welcome, terrace (harbour wall cuts off
view), good parking. *(Martin and Anne Muers)*

NEWLYN EAST SW8256
Pheasant (01872) 510237
Churchtown; TR8 5LJ Traditional village
pub in quiet backstreet, friendly and busy,
with enjoyable reasonably priced pubby food
including popular Sun carvery, Dartmoor
and Sharps ales, good service; not far from
Trerice Gardens (NT). *(Stanley and Annie
Matthews)*

NEWQUAY SW8061
Fort (01637) 875700
Fore Street; TR7 1HA Massive recently
built pub in magnificent setting high above
surfing beach and small harbour, decent
food all day from sandwiches, hot baguettes
and baked potatoes up, open-plan areas
well divided by balustrades and surviving
fragments of former harbourmaster's house,
good solid furnishings from country kitchen
to button-back settees, soft lighting, friendly
staff coping well at busy times, full St Austell
range, games part with two pool tables,
excellent indoor children's play area; great
views from long glass-walled side section
and sizeable garden with multi-level terrace
and further play areas, open all day. *(Alan
Johnson, Richard Stanfield, Adrian Johnson)*

NEWQUAY SW8061
Lewinnick Lodge (01637) 878117
*Pentire headland, off Pentire Road;
TR7 1NX* Modern flint-walled bar-
restaurant built into bluff above the sea – big
picture windows for the terrific views; light
and airy bar with wicker seating, spreading
dining areas with contemporary furnishings
on light oak flooring, three or four well kept
ales and several wines by the glass, popular
bistro-style food from shortish menu, good
service and pleasant relaxed atmosphere
even when busy; children and dogs (in
bar) welcome, modern seats and tables on
terraces making most of stunning Atlantic
views, ten bedrooms, open all day; same
management as the Plume of Feathers in
Mitchell. *(Harvey Brown)*

PADSTOW SW9175
★ **Golden Lion** (01841) 532797
Lanadwell Street; PL28 8AN Old inn
dating from the 14th c, cheerful black-
beamed locals' bar and high-raftered back
lounge with plush banquettes, Sharps Doom
Bar, Padstow Windjammer and Tintagel
Castle Gold, reasonably priced simple bar
lunches including good crab sandwiches,
evening steaks and fresh fish, friendly staff,
coal fire and woodburner; pool in family area,
background music, sports TV; dogs welcome,
colourful floral displays at front, terrace

tables, three bedrooms, open all day (no food Sun evening). *(Toby Jones)*

PADSTOW SW9175
Harbour Inn (01841) 533148
Strand Street; PL28 8BU Attractive pub set just back from the harbour and a quieter alternative; long room with nautical bric-a-brac, front area with comfy sofas, woodburner, well kept St Austell ales, enjoyable home-made food including daily specials, good coffee, friendly helpful staff; children and dogs welcome, open all day. *(Charlie May)*

PADSTOW SW9175
London (01841) 532554
Llanadwell Street; PL28 8AN Intimate proper fishermen's local with lots of pictures and nautical memorabilia, mix of tables, chairs and built-in benches, friendly ex-merchant navy landlord, half a dozen well kept St Austell ales and decent choice of malt whiskies, good value bar food including fresh local fish, more evening choice, back dining area (arrive early for a table), two log fires; background and some live music; children and dogs welcome (resident boxer is Pixie), three reasonably priced bedrooms, open all day. *(Tony Tollitt)*

PADSTOW SW9275
Old Custom House (01841) 532359
South Quay; PL28 8BL Large, bright and airy open-plan seaside bar, comfortable and well divided, with rustic décor and cosy corners, beams, exposed brickwork and bare boards, raised sections, big family area and conservatory, good food choice from baguettes up, four local ales including St Austell, efficient service (they swipe your card if running a tab), adjoining fish restaurant; background and live music, TV, machines, pool; good spot by harbour, attractive sea-view bedrooms, open all day and can get very busy. *(Brian and Anna Marsden, Adrian Johnson)*

PELYNT SX2054
★ Jubilee (01503) 220312
B3359 NW of Looe; PL13 2JZ Popular early 17th-c beamed inn with wide range of good locally sourced home-made food (best to book in season), well kept St Austell ales and decent wines by the glass, friendly helpful young staff, spotless interior with interesting Queen Victoria mementoes (pub renamed in 1897 to celebrate her diamond jubilee), some handsome antique furnishings, log fire in big stone fireplace, separate bar with darts, pool and games machine; children and dogs welcome, disabled facilities, large terrace, 11 comfortable bedrooms, open all day weekends. *(Anon)*

PENDOGGETT SX0279
Cornish Arms (01208) 880263
B3314; PL30 3HH Old beamed coaching inn with traditional oak settles on front bar's polished slate floor, good range of St Austell ales, decent wines by the glass and enjoyable food, friendly efficient service, comfortably spaced tables in small carpeted dining room, proper back locals' bar with woodburner and games; provision for children, dogs welcome in bars, disabled access, terrace with distant sea view, bedrooms, open all day. *(R T and J C Moggridge)*

PENELEWEY SW8140
Punch Bowl & Ladle
(01872) 862237 *B3289; TR3 6QY* Thatched dining pub with good home-made food from sandwiches up, helpful chatty service, four St Austell ales, Healey's cider and good wine and whisky selection, black beams, some white-painted stone walls and oak panelling, rustic bric-a-brac and big sofas, steps down to lounge/dining area, restaurant; soft background music, free wi-fi; children (away from bar) and dogs welcome, wheelchair access (not from small side terrace), handy for Trelissick Gardens (NT), open all day. *(Chris and Angela Buckell, Mick and Moira Brummell, PL)*

PENZANCE SW4730
Admiral Benbow (01736) 363448
Chapel Street; TR18 4AF Wonderfully quirky pub, full of atmosphere and packed with interesting nautical paraphernalia, friendly helpful staff, good value above-average food including local fish, well kept cornish ales, cosy corners, fire, downstairs restaurant in captain's cabin style, upper floor with pool table, pleasant view from back room; children and dogs welcome, open all day in summer. *(Tom and Jill Jones)*

PENZANCE SW4730
Crown (01736) 351070
Victoria Square, Bread Street; TR18 2EP Friendly little backstreet corner local with neat bar and snug dining room, own-brewed Cornish Crown beers plus a guest, several wines by the glass, enjoyable good value home-made food (not Mon, Tues, limited menu Sun evening); Mon acoustic music, Tues quiz, board games (beat the landlady at Snatch for a free pint); children and dogs welcome, seats outside, open all day. *(Alfie Bayliss)*

PENZANCE SW4729
★ Dolphin (01736) 364106
Quay Street, opposite harbour after swing-bridge; TR18 4BD Well run old pub (under same ownership as the Coldstreamer at Gulval), enjoyable good value food including fresh fish, up to four well kept St Austell ales and good wines by the glass, roomy bar on different levels, nautical memorabilia, three resident ghosts; pool and juke box; children and dogs welcome, pavement picnic-sets, two bedrooms (harbour views), no car park (public one not

far away), handy for Scillies ferry, open (and food) all day. *(Martin Jones)*

PILLATON   SX3664
★**Weary Friar** (01579) 350238
Off Callington–Landrake back road;
PL12 6QS Tucked-away welcoming 12th-c inn, good generously served food from wide-ranging menu in bar and restaurant (best to book), friendly helpful staff, well kept St Austell and Sharps, farm cider, knocked-together carpeted rooms, dark beams, copper and brass, log fires in stone fireplaces; children welcome, no dogs inside, tables out in front and behind, church next door (Tues evening bell-ringing), 14 bedrooms, open all day. *(Edward May)*

POLGOOTH   SW9950
Polgooth Inn (01726) 74089
Well signed off A390 W of St Austell;
Ricketts Lane; PL26 7DA Welcoming spacious country pub, separate servery for good generous food from sandwiches to daily specials, children's helpings and reasonable prices, well kept St Austell ales and good choice of wines by the glass, eating area around sizeable bar with woodburner, good big family room, live music; fills quickly in summer (handy for nearby caravan parks), no booking after 6.30pm and can be a wait for a table; dogs welcome, steps up to play area, tables out on terrace and grass, Sun summer barbecues, pretty countryside, open all day. *(Isobel Mackinlay)*

POLPERRO   SX2051
Crumplehorn Mill (01503) 272348
Top of village near main car park;
PL13 2RJ Converted mill and farmhouse keeping beams, flagstones and some stripped stone, snug lower bar leading to long main room with cosy end eating area, well kept cornish ales, wide choice of enjoyable good value food from snacks to blackboard specials (booking advised), friendly speedy service, log fire; children and dogs welcome, outside seating and working mill wheel, bedrooms and self-catering apartments, open all day. *(Robert Turnham)*

POLPERRO   SX2050
Three Pilchards (01503) 272233
Quay Road; PL13 2QZ Small low-beamed local behind fish quay, good choice of reasonably priced generous food from baguettes to fresh fish, well kept St Austell Tribute and up to four guests, efficient obliging service even when busy, lots of black woodwork, dim lighting, simple furnishings, open fire in big stone fireplace; children and dogs welcome, picnic-sets on terrace up steep steps, open all day. *(Barry Collett)*

POLRUAN   SX1250
★**Lugger** (01726) 870007
The Quay; back roads off A390 in Lostwithiel, or foot-ferry from Fowey;

PL23 1PA Popular and friendly waterside pub refurbished and doing well under present management; steps up to cosy beamed bar with open fire and woodburner, restaurant on upper level, very good freshly cooked food from bar snacks to daily blackboard specials including local fish, Sun carvery, well kept St Austell ales; children, dogs and muddy boots welcome, good local walks, limited parking, open all day. *(Monica Shelley, Richard Tilbrook, Nick Lawless)*

PORT ISAAC   SW9980
★**Golden Lion** (01208) 880336
Fore Street; PL29 3RB Nicely positioned 17th-c pub with friendly local atmosphere in simply furnished old rooms, bar and snug with open fire, window seats and balcony tables looking down on rocky harbour and lifeboat slip far below, upstairs restaurant, straightforward food including good local fish, St Austell ales, darts and dominoes; background music – live in cellar bar (open mainly weekends), games machine; children and dogs welcome, dramatic cliff walks, open all day. *(Adrian Johnson)*

PORTHALLOW   SW7923
Five Pilchards (01326) 280256
SE of Helston; B3293 to Street Keverne, then village signed; TR12 6PP Sturdy old-fashioned stone-built local in secluded cove right by shingle beach, lots of salvaged nautical gear, interesting shipwreck memorabilia and model boats, woodburner, cornish ales and enjoyable reasonably priced straightforward food including local fish, friendly chatty staff, conservatory; children and dogs welcome, seats out in sheltered yard, bedrooms, open all day Sun (in winter closed Sun evening, Mon lunchtime and all day Tues). *(Fran Ward)*

PORTHLEVEN   SW6325
Atlantic (01326) 562439
Peverell Terrace; TR13 9DZ Friendly buzzy pub in great setting up above harbour, good value tasty food, real ales including Skinners and St Austell from boat-shaped counter, big open-plan lounge with well spaced seating and cosier alcoves, good log fire in granite fireplace, dining room with amazing trompe l'oeil murals; lovely bay views from front terrace, open all day. *(Lindy Andrews)*

PORTHLEVEN   SW6225
Harbour Inn (01326) 573876
Commercial Road; TR13 9JB Large neatly kept pub-hotel in outstanding harbourside setting, well organised friendly service, expansive lounge and bar with impressive dining area off, big public bar with panelling, well kept St Austell ales, good range of pubby food including catch of the day and nice pasties, carvery Wed lunchtime and Sun; unobtrusive background music (live Sat), Thurs quiz, free wi-fi; children welcome,

picnic-sets on big quayside terrace, 15 well equipped bedrooms (some with harbour view), good breakfast, open all day. *(Tom and Jill Jones, Alison Ball, Ian Walton, M J Winterton)*

PORTLOE   SW9339

★**Ship** (01872) 501356

At top of village; TR2 5RA Cheerful traditional local in charming fishing village; L-shaped bar with tankards hanging from beams, nautical bric-a-brac and local memorabilia, an amazing beer bottle collection, straightforward dark pubby chairs and tables on red carpet, St Austell ales, cider/perry and six wines by the glass, popular pubby food; background music, free wi-fi; children and dogs (in bar) welcome, sloping streamside garden across road, clean comfortable bedrooms, beach close by. *(Chris and Angela Buckell, Barry Collett)*

PORTSCATHO   SW8735

Plume of Feathers (01872) 580321

The Square; TR2 5HW Largely stripped-stone coastal village pub with sea-related bric-a-brac and pictures in two comfortable linked areas, also small side bar and separate restaurant, St Austell ales and reasonably priced food; background music, free wi-fi; children, dogs and muddy boots welcome, disabled access (steps to restaurant and gents'), picnic-sets out under awning, lovely coast walks, open all day in summer (and other times if busy). *(Charlie May)*

ROSUDGEON   SW5529

Falmouth Packet (01736) 762240

A394; TR20 9QE Comfortably modernised old pub with bare-stone walls, slate/carpeted floors and open fire, good food using local produce (booking advised), own pickles, relishes etc for sale, well kept Penzance ales and guests, family run with good friendly service, conservatory; children welcome, tables out at front and in garden, self-catering cottage, open all day Fri, till 7pm Sun. *(Edward May)*

RUAN LANIHORNE   SW8942

★**Kings Head** (01872) 501263

Village signed off A3078 St Mawes Road; TR2 5NX Country pub in quiet hamlet with interesting church nearby; relaxed small bar with log fire, Skinners and a guest, maybe farm cider, well liked food especially local fish, dining area to the right divided in two, lots of china cups hanging from ceiling joists, cabinet filled with old bottles, hunting prints and cartoons, separate restaurant to the left; background music; well behaved children allowed in dining areas, dogs in bar only, terrace across road and nice lower beer garden, walks along Fal estuary, in winter closed Sun evening and Mon. *(R and S Bentley, Barry Collett, R K Phillips)*

ST ISSEY   SW9271

Ring o' Bells (01841) 540251

A389 Wadebridge–Padstow; Churchtown; PL27 7QA Traditional slate-clad 18th-c village pub with open fire at one end of beamed bar, pool the other, well kept Courage Best, Sharps Doom Bar and a guest, good choice of wines and whiskies, friendly service, enjoyable sensibly priced local food (own vegetables and pork) in long narrow side dining room, live folk first Sat of month; can get packed in summer; children and dogs welcome, decked courtyard, hanging baskets and tubs, four bedrooms, car park across road, open all day weekends. *(Stephen Green)*

ST IVES   SW5140

Lifeboat (01736) 794123

Wharf Road; TR26 1LF Thriving family-friendly beamed quayside pub, wide choice of good value generously served pubby food, well kept St Austell ales, spacious interior with harbour-view tables and cosier corners, nautical theme including lifeboat pictures, friendly helpful staff, Sept music festival; sports TV, fruit machine, no dogs; disabled access/facilities, open (and food) all day. *(Toby Jones)*

ST IVES   SW5441

Pedn Olva (01736) 796222

The Warren; TR26 2EA Hotel not pub, but has well kept reasonably priced St Austell ales in roomy bar, fine views of sea and Porthminster beach (especially from tables on roof terrace), all-day bar food and separate restaurant, good service; comfortable bedrooms. *(Alan Johnson)*

ST IVES   SW5140

★**Sloop** (01736) 796584

The Wharf; TR26 1LP Busy low-beamed, panelled and flagstoned harbourside pub with bright St Ives School pictures and attractive portrait drawings in front bar, booth seating in back bar, good choice of food from sandwiches and baguettes to lots of fresh local fish, quick friendly service even though busy, well kept ales such as Greene King Old Speckled Hen and Sharps Doom Bar, good coffee; background and live music, TV; children in eating area, beach view from roof terrace and seats out on cobbles, open all day (breakfast from 9am), bedrooms, handy for Tate gallery. *(Alan Johnson, Brian and Anna Marsden, Alison Ball, Ian Walton, Stanley and Annie Matthews)*

ST IVES   SW5140

Union (01736) 796486

Fore Street; TR26 1AB Popular and friendly low-beamed local, roomy but cosy, with good value food from sandwiches to

---

Tipping is not normal for bar meals, and not usually expected.

local fish, well kept Sharps Doom Bar and Weston's Old Rosie cider, decent wines and coffee, small hot fire, leather sofas on carpet, dark woodwork and masses of ship photographs; background music; dogs welcome. *(Alan Johnson)*

ST JUST IN PENWITH   SW3731
Kings Arms (01736) 788545

Market Square; TR19 7HF Three separate carpeted areas, granite walls and beamed and boarded ceilings, open fire and woodburner, shortish menu of good home-made food (not Sun evening), helpful caring service, well kept St Austell ales; background music (live Sun), Weds quiz, TV; children and dogs welcome, tables out in front. *(Alan Johnson)*

ST JUST IN PENWITH   SW3731
★**Star** (01736) 788767

Fore Street; TR19 7LL Low-beamed two-room local with friendly landlord and relaxed informal atmosphere, five well kept St Austell ales, no food (bring your own lunchtime sandwiches or pasties), dimly lit main bar with dark walls covered in flags and photographs, coal fire, darts and euchre, nostalgic juke box, live celtic music Mon, open mike Thurs; tables in attractive backyard with smokers' shelter, open all day. *(Alan Johnson)*

ST KEW   SX0276
★**St Kew Inn** (01208) 841259

Village signposted from A39 NE of Wadebridge; PL30 3HB Popular 15th-c pub with neat beamed bar, stone walls, winged high-backed settles and more traditional furniture on tartan carpeting, all sorts of jugs dotted about, roaring log fire in stone fireplace, three dining areas, St Austell beers from cask and handpump, good choice of well liked food (not Sun evening in winter), friendly attentive service, live music every other Fri; children away from bar and dogs welcome, pretty flowering tubs and baskets outside, picnic-sets in garden over road, open all day in summer. *(J D and A P, Edna Jones)*

ST MAWES   SW8433
★**Rising Sun** (01326) 270233

The Square; TR2 5DJ Light and airy pub across road from harbour wall; relaxed bar on right with end woodburner, sea-view bow window opposite, rugs on stripped wood, a few dining tables, sizeable carpeted left-hand bar with dark wood furniture, well prepared tasty food including good fish and chips served by friendly young staff, well kept St Austell ales and nice wines by the glass, wood-floored conservatory; background music; awkward wheelchair access, picnic-sets on sunny front terrace, comfortable bedrooms, open all day. *(Tom and Jill Jones, John Marsh, Stanley and Annie Matthews, R K Phillips)*

ST MAWES   SW8433
Victory (01326) 270324

Victory Hill; TR2 5DQ Popular pub tucked up from the harbour; slate floor locals' bar on left, carpeted dining area to the right, more formal upstairs restaurant with balcony, well kept Otter, Sharps and Skinners, good food including plenty of local fish, log fires, friendly staff; background music, no wheelchair access; children welcome, one or two picnic-sets outside, two good value bedrooms, open all day. *(Barry Collett)*

ST MAWGAN   SW8765
★**Falcon** (01637) 860225

NE of Newquay, off B3276 or A3059; TR8 4EP Friendly old wisteria-clad pub in quiet village setting opposite church; big fireplace with large stone bottles either side, farmhouse and cushioned wheelback chairs around assorted tables on patterned carpet, antique coaching prints and falcon pictures, a beer named for the pub from Penpont plus guests, well liked food, compact stone-floored dining room; darts, free wi-fi; children (away from bar) and dogs (in bar) welcome, cobbled courtyard and peaceful flower-filled back garden with wishing well, comfortable bedrooms, handy for nearby Newquay Airport, nearby Japanese garden worth a visit, open all day in summer. *(Brian and Anna Marsden, Richard Stanfield, Robert Watt)*

ST MINVER   SW9677
Four Ways (01208) 862384

Churchtown; PL27 6QH Friendly 17th-c village inn run by the same family for almost a century; slate-floored bar with oak beams and open fire, good choice of ales and ciders, reasonably priced home-made food; small enclosed outside seating area, nine bedrooms. *(Adrian Johnson)*

STITHIANS   SW7640
Cornish Arms (01872) 863445

Frogpool, not shown on many road maps but is NE of A393, ie opposite side to Stithians itself; TR4 8RP Unspoilt 18th-c village pub run by brother and sister team (he cooks), long beamed bar with fires either end, cosy snug, good value wholesome food (not Mon) from sandwiches and four types of ploughman's up, local ales and ciders; pool (free Tues), euchre; well behaved children and dogs welcome, closed Mon lunchtime. *(John Marsh)*

TIDEFORD   SX3459
Rod & Line (01752) 851323

Church Road; PL12 5HW Small old-fashioned rustic local set back from road up steps, friendly lively atmosphere, Greene King Abbot and St Austell Tribute kept well, nice food including good fresh fish/seafood from blackboard menu (order at bar), angling theme with rods etc, low-bowed ceiling, settles, good log fire; children and dogs welcome, tables outside, open all day. *(Mark Mincher-Lockett)*

TOWAN CROSS   SW4078
Victory (01209) 890359
Off B3277; TR4 8BN Comfortable roadside local with above-average good value food, four ales including Skinners, helpful staff; pool, euchre and Tues quiz; children and dogs welcome, beer garden, camping, handy for good uncrowded beaches, open all day. *(John Marsh)*

TREBARWITH   SX0586
Mill House (01840) 770200
Signed off B3263 and B3314 SE of Tintagel; PL34 0HD Former 18th-c corn mill wonderfully set in own steep woods above the sea; bar with white-painted beams, Delabole flagstones and mix of furniture including comfortable sofas, light and airy restaurant with pitched ceiling, enjoyable bar food and more upmarket evening restaurant menu, friendly staff, up to four local ales, decent wines by the glass and good coffee; background and live music; children and dogs welcome, sunny terrace and streamside garden, eight bedrooms, open all day. *(Ryta Lyndley)*

TREBARWITH   SX0585
Port William (01840) 770230
Trebarwith Strand; PL34 0HB Lovely seaside setting with glorious views and sunsets, waterside picnic-sets across road and on covered terrace, maritime memorabilia and log fires inside, St Austell ales, enjoyable food from sandwiches and baked potatoes to daily specials (they may ask to swipe a card before you eat); background music; children and dogs welcome, eight well equipped comfortable bedrooms, open all day. *(D B Mines)*

TREEN   SW3923
★Logan Rock (01736) 810495
Just off B3315 Penzance–Lands End; TR19 6LG Low-beamed traditional bar with well kept St Austell ales, tasty food from sandwiches and pasties up, good vegetarian options too, inglenook fire, small back snug with excellent cricket memorabilia (welcoming landlady eminent in county's cricket association), family room (no under-14s in bar); dogs welcome on leads, pretty split-level garden behind with covered area, good coast walks including to Logan Rock itself, handy for Minack Theatre, open all day in season and can get very busy. *(Anon)*

TREGADILLETT   SX2983
★Eliot Arms (01566) 772051
Village signposted off A30 at junction with A395, W end of Launceston bypass; PL15 7EU Creeper-covered with series of small rooms, interesting collections including 72 antique clocks, 700 snuffs and hundreds of horsebrasses, also barometers, old prints and

shelves of books/china, fine mix of furniture on Delabole slate from high-backed settles and chaises longues to more modern seats, open fires, well kept St Austell Tribute, Wadworths 6X and a guest, good value generous food, friendly staff; background music, darts, games machine; children and dogs welcome, outside seating front and back, lovely hanging baskets and tubs, two bedrooms, open all day. *(John and Bernadette Elliott, Peter Salmon)*

TREGONY   SW9244
Kings Arms (01872) 530202
Fore Street (B3287); TR2 5RW Light and airy 16th-c coaching inn, long traditional main bar and two beamed and panelled front dining areas, St Austell ales, Healey's cider/perry and nice wines, good quality reasonably priced pub food using local produce, tea and coffee, prompt service and friendly chatty atmosphere, two fireplaces, one with huge cornish range, pubby furniture on carpet or flagstones, old team photographs, back games room; dogs very welcome and well behaved children, disabled access, tables in pleasant suntrap garden, charming village. *(Chris and Angela Buckell, Phil and Jane Hodson)*

TREMATON   SX3960
Crooked Inn (01752) 848177
Off A38 just W of Saltash; PL12 4RZ Friendly family-run inn down a long drive, open-plan bar with lower lounge leading to a conservatory, beams, straightforward furnishings and log fire, well kept cornish ales and decent wines by the glass, good choice of popular freshly made food from sandwiches to daily specials; children and dogs welcome, terrace overlooking garden and valley, play area, roaming ducks and other animals, 15 bedrooms, open all day. *(John Evans)*

TRURO   SW8244
★Old Ale House (01872) 271122
Quay Street; TR1 2HD Town-centre tap for Skinners brewery, five of their ales (samples offered) plus guests, some from casks behind bar, west country ciders and several wines by the glass including country ones, tasty food from snacks and sharing plates up, good cheerful service, dimly lit beamed bar with engaging mix of furnishings, sawdust on the floor, beer mats on walls and ceiling, some interesting 1920s bric-a-brac, life-size cutout of Betty Stogs, daily newspapers and free monkey nuts, upstairs room with table football; juke box; children (away from bar) and dogs welcome, open all day. *(Alan Johnson, B and M Kendall)*

TRURO   SW8244
White Hart (01872) 277294
New Bridge Street (aka Crab & Ale House); TR1 2AA Compact old city-centre pub with nautical theme, friendly staff and locals, five well kept ales including Greene

King IPA, St Austell Tribute and Sharps Doom Bar, good reasonably priced pub food; background music, disco Sat, quiz Thurs; children welcome, open all day. *(Alan Johnson)*

TYWARDREATH   SX0854
New Inn (01726) 813901
Off A3082; Fore Street; PL24 2QP Welcoming 18th-c local in nice village setting, St Austell ales and guests including Bass tapped from the cask, good food (not Tues) in small back restaurant, friendly relaxed atmosphere; some live music; children and dogs welcome, large secluded garden behind, open all day. *(Anon)*

VERYAN   SW9139
New Inn (01872) 501362
Village signed off A3078; TR2 5QA Comfortable and homely one-bar beamed local, good value food from sandwiches up (can get busy in evening so worth booking), St Austell ales, Healey's cider and decent wines by the glass, friendly attentive service, inglenook woodburner, polished brass and old pictures; background music; dogs and well behaved children welcome, wheelchair access with help, secluded beer garden behind, two bedrooms, interesting partly thatched village not far from nice beach, nearby parking unlikely in summer. *(R K Phillips)*

WATERGATE BAY   SW8464
Beach Hut (01637) 860877
B3276 coast road N of Newquay; TR8 4AA Great views from bustling modern beach bar with customers of all ages, surfing photographs on planked walls, cushioned wicker and cane armchairs around green and orange tables, weathered stripped-wood floor, unusual sloping bleached-board ceiling, big windows and doors opening to glass-fronted deck looking across sand to the sea, simpler end room, three real ales including Skinners, decent wines by the glass and lots of coffees and teas, good modern food served by friendly young staff; background music; dogs welcome in bar, easy wheelchair access, open 8.30am-11pm, 10.30am-5pm in winter. *(Chris and Val Ramstedt)*

WENDRON   SW6731
New Inn (01326) 572683
B3297; TR13 0EA Friendly little 18th-c granite-built country pub, three well kept changing ales and enjoyable reasonably priced home-cooked food; children and dogs welcome, garden behind with valley views. *(Toby Jones)*

ZELAH   SW8151
Hawkins Arms (01872) 540339
A30; TR4 9HU Homely 18th-c stone-built beamed local, well kept Tintagel Castle Gold and one or more guests, tasty well presented food from sandwiches to blackboard

specials, nice coffee, friendly landlord and staff, copper and brass in bar and dining room, woodburner in stone fireplace; children and dogs welcome, back and side terraces. *(Anon)*

ZENNOR   SW4538
★Tinners Arms (01736) 796927
B3306 W of St Ives; TR26 3BY Friendly welcome and good food from ploughman's with three cornish cheeses to fresh local fish, long unspoilt bar with flagstones, granite, stripped pine and real fires each end, back dining room, well kept St Austell and Sharps ales, farm cider, sensibly priced wines and decent coffee, quick service even when busy, nice mix of locals and visitors, Thurs folk night; children, muddy boots and dogs welcome, tables in small suntrap courtyard, lovely peaceful windswept setting near coast path and by church with 15th-c carved mermaid bench, bedrooms in building next door, open all day. *(John Marsh)*

ISLES OF SCILLY

ST AGNES   SV8808
★Turks Head (01720) 422434
The Quay; TR22 0PL One of the UK's most beautifully placed pubs, idyllic sea and island views from garden terrace, can get very busy on fine days, good food from pasties to popular fresh seafood (best to get there early), well kept ales such as Skinners Betty Stogs, proper cider, friendly licensees and good cheerful service; children and dogs welcome, closed in winter, otherwise open all day. *(Michael Butler, Stephen Shepherd)*

ST MARY'S   SV9010
Atlantic Inn (01720) 422323
The Strand; next to but independent from Atlantic Hotel; TR21 0HY Spreading and hospitable dark bar with well kept St Austell ales, pubby food including children's menu, sea-view restaurant, low beams, hanging boat and other nauticalia, mix of locals and tourists – busy evenings, quieter on sunny lunchtimes; darts, pool, games machines, background and live music, free wi-fi; nice raised verandah with wide views over harbour, good bedrooms in adjacent hotel. *(Michael Butler, Neil and Anita Christopher, Stephen Shepherd)*

ST MARY'S   SV9010
Mermaid (01720) 422701
The Bank; TR21 0HY Splendid picture-window views across town beach and harbour from back restaurant extension, unpretentious dimly lit bar with lots of seafaring relics and ceiling flags, stone floor and rough timber, woodburner, steps down to second bar with tiled floor, boat counter and another woodburner, large helpings of enjoyable well priced food including children's choices, Sun carvery,

well kept Ales of Scilly, Sharps and Skinners; background music, pool; children and dogs (in bar) welcome, packed Weds and Fri when the gigs race, open all day. *(Michael Butler)*

ST MARY'S   SV9110
Old Town Inn (01720) 422301
Old Town; TR21 0NN Nice local feel in welcoming light bar and big back dining area, wood floors and panelling, good freshly made food (not Mon-Weds in winter) from daily changing menu, up to four well kept ales including Sharps Doom Bar and a beer badged for the pub, great range of ciders (35 in summer), live music including monthly folk club, cinema in back function room; pool and darts; children and dogs welcome, wheelchair access, tables in garden behind, three courtyard bedrooms, handy for airport, open all day in season (from 5pm weekdays, all day weekends in winter). *(Harvey Brown)*

TRESCO   SV8815
★ New Inn (01720) 423006
New Grimsby; TR24 0QG Handy for ferries and close to the famous gardens; main bar with comfortable old sofas, banquettes, planked partition seating and farmhouse tables and chairs, a few standing timbers, boat pictures, collection of old telescopes and large model yacht, pavilion extension with cheerful yellow walls and plenty of seats on blue-painted floors, Ales of Scilly and Skinners, a dozen good wines by the glass, quite a choice of spirits and several coffees, enjoyable food including daily specials; background music, board games, darts and pool; children and dogs (in bar) welcome, seats on flower-filled sea-view terrace, bedrooms, open all day in summer. *(Michael Butler, Ken Parry, Bernard Stradling, R J Herd)*

Cumbria

AMBLESIDE   NY3704 Map 9
Golden Rule 🍺

(015394) 32257 – www.goldenrule-ambleside.co.uk

Smithy Brow; follow Kirkstone Pass signpost from A591 on N side of town; LA22 9AS

Simple town local with a cosy, relaxed atmosphere and real ales

Despite being an unchanging Lakeland local, there's a genuine welcome for
visitors too (and their well behaved dogs). The bar area has built-in wall
seats around cast-iron-framed tables (one with a local map set into its top),
horsebrasses on black beams, assorted pictures on the walls, a welcoming
winter fire and a relaxed atmosphere. Robinsons Dizzy Blonde, Double Hop,
Hartleys Cumbria Way, XB and Trooper and a couple of guests on handpump
and Weston's cider; they also offer various teas and good coffee all day. A
brass measuring rule hangs above the bar (hence the pub's name). There's
also a back room with TV (not much used), a room on the left with darts and
a games machine, and another room, down a couple of steps on the right,
with lots of seating. The backyard has benches and a covered heated area,
and the window boxes are especially colourful. There's no car park.

🍴 As the scotch eggs and pies run out fast (if they have them), don't assume you will
get something to eat.

Robinsons ~ Tenant John Lockley ~ Real ale ~ Open 10am-midnight ~ Children welcome
away from bar and must leave by 9pm ~ Dogs welcome ~ Wi-fi
Recommended by Chris Johnson, Mike and Eleanor Anderson

AMBLESIDE   NY3703 Map 9
Wateredge Inn 🍷 🛏

(015394) 32332 – www.wateredgehotel.co.uk

Borrans Road, off A591; LA22 0EP

**Lovely lakeside spot for family-run inn, plenty of room both inside
and out, six ales on handpump and enjoyable all day food; comfortable
bedrooms**

You can look over Lake Windermere from many of the stylish, comfortable
bedrooms, from big windows in the bar and from the many seats in
the sizeable garden (which actually runs down to the water's edge). The
modernised bar (originally two 17th-c cottages) has a wide mix of customers,
an easy-going, bustling atmosphere, leather tub chairs around wooden tables
on flagstones and several different areas leading off with similar furniture,
exposed stone or wood-panelled walls and interesting old photographs

and paintings. A cosy and much favoured room has beams and timbering, sofas, armchairs and an open fire. The six real ales on handpump served by friendly, cheerful staff come from breweries such as Barngates, Cumberland, Jennings, Theakstons, Tirril and Watermill and they offer 17 wines by the glass and quite a choice of coffees. Background music and TV. They have their own moorings.

🍴 Some sort of popular food is served all day, including hot and cold sandwiches, whitebait with aioli, chicken liver pâté with spiced fruit chutney, cumberland sausages with red wine and onion gravy, butternut squash, pea and smoked cheese pasta, chicken curry, burger with toppings, onion rings, coleslaw and fries, fish pie, mixed game casserole, and puddings such as chocolate fudge cake and vanilla and raspberry ripple crème brûlée. *Benchmark main dish: lamb hotpot £12.95. Two-course evening meal £18.00.*

Free house ~ Licensee Derek Cowap ~ Real ale ~ Open 11-11 ~ Bar food 12-9 ~ Children welcome ~ Dogs allowed in bar and bedrooms ~ Wi-fi ~ Bedrooms: £55/£104
Recommended by Comus and Sarah Elliott, John Oates, Tina and David Woods-Taylor

BASSENTHWAITE LAKE

NY1930 Map 9

Pheasant ★ 🏵 🍷 🛏

(017687) 76234 – www.the-pheasant.co.uk
Follow Pheasant Inn sign at N end of dual carriageway stretch of A66 by Bassenthwaite Lake; CA13 9YE

Delightful, old-fashioned bar in smart hotel, with enjoyable bar food and a fine range of drinks; comfortable bedrooms

Of course, this is a smart, civilised hotel and most customers are here to enjoy a restaurant meal or as residents – but at its heart is a charming little bar of proper character that's much used by chatty locals. Nicely old-fashioned, it has mellow polished walls, cushioned oak settles, rush-seat chairs and library seats, and hunting prints and photographs. Coniston Bluebird, Cumberland Corby Ale and Hawkshead Bitter on handpump, a dozen good wines by the glass, over 60 malt whiskies and several gins and vodkas, all served by friendly, knowledgeable staff. There's a front bistro, a formal back restaurant overlooking the garden and several comfortable lounges with log fires, beautiful flower arrangements, fine parquet flooring, antiques and plants. The garden has seats and tables and is surrounded by attractive woodland; there are plenty of walks in all directions.

🏵 You can eat in the bar, bistro or lounges at lunchtime, and in the bistro and restaurant only in the evening: lunchtime open sandwiches and baguettes, beetroot-cured salmon gravadlax with beetroot jelly and purée and horseradish cream, red wine-poached pear with goats curd, crisp parma ham and pistachio nuts, beer-battered haddock with triple-cooked chips, chicken and leek pie, wild mushroom risotto, sea trout fillet with watercress and pea velouté, and puddings such as Drambuie panna cotta with berry compote and milk and chocolate mousse with honeycomb ice-cream; they also offer a two- and three-course set lunch. *Benchmark main dish: slow-cooked pork belly £14.00. Two-course evening meal £23.00.*

Free house ~ Licensee Matthew Wylie ~ Real ale ~ Open 11.30-11 ~ Bar food 12-2.30, 6-9 ~ Restaurant ~ Children welcome but must be over 8 in bedrooms ~ Dogs allowed in bar and bedrooms ~ Wi-fi ~ Bedrooms: £95/£110 *Recommended by Martin and Sue Day, Hilary De Lyon and Martin Webster, Robert Wivell, Tina and David Woods-Taylor, Pat and Stewart Gordon*

The details at the end of each featured entry start by saying whether the pub is a free house, or if it belongs to a brewery or pub group (which we name).

BOWLAND BRIDGE   SD4189   Map 9
Hare & Hounds 🌟 ♈ 🛏

(015395) 68333 – www.hareandhoundsbowlandbridge.co.uk

Signed from A5074; LA11 6NN

17th-c inn in quiet spot with a friendly, cheerful landlady, real ales, popular food and fine views; comfortable bedrooms

The comfortable bedrooms in this peacefully set and handsome former coaching inn make a good base for the area – Lake Windermere is just three miles away. It's a genuinely friendly place and the little bar has a log fire, daily papers to read and high chairs by the wooden counter where they serve Hare of the Dog (named for the pub by Tirril) and guests such as Coniston Bluebird and Thwaites Best on handpump, a farm cider from half a mile away, and a dozen wines by the glass. Leading off here, other rooms are appealingly furnished with a mix of interesting dining chairs around all sorts of tables on black slate or old pine-boarded floors, numerous hunting prints on painted or stripped-stone walls, a candlelit moroccan-style lantern in a fireplace with neatly stacked logs to one side, and a relaxed atmosphere; background music and board games. The collie is called Murphy. There are teak tables and chairs under parasols on the front terrace, with more seats in the spacious side garden and fine valley views.

 Good, seasonal country cooking includes lunchtime hot and cold sandwiches, twice-baked cheese soufflé with creamy chive sauce, smoked mackerel and celeriac pâté, fennel, wild mushroom, leek and white wine pie, burger of the day with toppings, beer-battered onion rings and chips, braised local lamb shank with redcurrant and mint gravy, bass on ratatouille with basil pesto cream, and puddings such as lemon posset and spiced rum and raisin crème brûlée; also, pre-ordered breakfasts to non-residents (9-10am). *Benchmark main dish: steak in ale pie £12.95. Two-course evening meal £20.00.*

Free house ~ Licensee Kerry Parsons ~ Real ale ~ Open 12-11 (10.30 Sun) ~ Bar food 12-2, 6-9; all day weekends ~ Children welcome ~ Dogs allowed in bar ~ Wi-fi ~ Bedrooms: /£95
Recommended by David Jackman, Jacqui Stevens, Caroline Prescott, Simon Cleasby

BOWNESS-ON-WINDERMERE   SD4096   Map 9
Hole in t' Wall 🍺

(015394) 43488

Fallbarrow Road, off St Martins Parade; LA23 3DH

Lively and unchanging town local with popular ales and friendly staff

As the town's oldest pub, this is full of character and interest with a cheerful mix of both locals and visitors – all welcomed by the friendly licensees. The split-level rooms have beams, stripped stone and flagstones, lots of country knick-knacks and old pictures, and a splendid log fire beneath a vast slate mantelpiece; the upper room has some noteworthy plasterwork. Robinsons Dizzy Blonde, Hannibals Nectar, Hartleys XB and Unicorn on handpump and 20 malt whiskies; juke box in the bottom bar. The small flagstoned front courtyard has sheltered picnic-sets and outdoor heaters.

🍴 Bar food includes pâté of the day, scampi and chips, a daily curry, fish pie, and puddings such as chocolate sponge and sticky toffee pudding. *Benchmark main dish: steak in ale pie £11.25. Two-course evening meal £18.00.*

Robinsons ~ Tenant Susan Burnet ~ Real ale ~ Open 11-11 (11.30 Fri, Sat); 12-11 Sun ~ Bar food 12-2.30, 6-8.30; 12-8 Fri, Sat; 12-5 Sun ~ Children welcome ~ Live music Fri evening
Recommended by Roger and Donna Huggins, I D Barnett, Simon Cleasby

BRIGSTEER
Wheatsheaf ♀

SD4889   Map 9

(015395) 68938 – www.thewheatsheafbrigsteer.co.uk

Off Brigsteer Brow; LA8 8AN

Bustling pub surrounded by pretty countryside, with interestingly furnished and decorated rooms, a good choice of food and drink, and seats outside; luxury bunkhouse bedrooms

There's plenty of character in the various rooms here and the atmosphere is easy-going and friendly. The bar has a two-way log fire, carved wooden stools against the counter and Bowness Bay Swan Blonde, Hawkshead Bitter, Thwaites Wainwright and Ulverston Lonesome Pine on handpump, 16 wines by the glass and eight malt whiskies. Throughout, an appealing variety of cushioned dining chairs, carved and boxed settles and window seats are set around an array of tables on either flagstones or floorboards, walls with pale-painted woodwork or wallpaper are hung with animal and bird sketches, cartoons or interesting clock faces, and the lighting is both old-fashioned and contemporary. Outside there are seats and tables along the front of the building and picnic-sets on raised terracing. Their Lumley Fee luxury bunkhouse (half a mile up the road) has five ensuite rooms and fine country views; breakfasts are hearty.

Highly thought-of food from a seasonal menu includes nibbles and sandwiches, smoked salmon and mackerel pâté with balsamic syrup, creamy cheese and chilli soufflé, sharing boards, pizzas and flatbreads (they also offer pizzas to take away), cumberland sausages with apple and grain mustard mash and rich gravy, wild mushroom and spinach risotto, spiced lamb burger with cajun-dusted chips, fish pie, and puddings such as lemon posset and sticky toffee pudding; Thursday is curry night. *Benchmark main dish: slow-cooked brisket of beef with chestnut mushroom and bacon gravy £13.50. Two-course evening meal £20.00.*

Individual Inns ~ Managers Nicki Higgs and Tom Roberts ~ Real ale ~ Open 10am-11pm ~ Bar food 12-3, 5.30-9; snacks 3-5.30; 12-7.30 Sun ~ Restaurant ~ Children welcome ~ Dogs allowed in bar ~ Wi-fi ~ Bedrooms: /£70   *Recommended by Ray and Winifred Halliday, Peter Andrews, Kath Edwards, Hugh Roberts, Gordon and Margaret Ormondroyd*

BROUGHTON MILLS
Blacksmiths Arms

SD2190   Map 9

(01229) 716824 – www.theblacksmithsarms.com

Off A593 N of Broughton-in-Furness; LA20 6AX

Friendly little pub with rewarding food, local beers and open fires; fine nearby walks

An inn since 1748 (but a farmhouse before that), this charming little pub is surrounded by quiet countryside. The four small bars have beams, warm log fires, a relaxed, friendly atmosphere and are simply but attractively decorated with straightforward chairs and tables on ancient slate floors. Barngates Cracker, Hawkshead Bitter and Tirril Nameless Ale on handpump, ten wines by the glass and summer farm cider; darts, board games and dominoes. The hanging baskets and tubs of flowers in front of the building are very pretty in summer, and there are seats and tables under parasols on the back terrace.

As well as lunchtime sandwiches, the reliably good food includes confit of shredded duck leg with hoisin sauce, baked goats cheese with rocket, red onion, walnut and sun-dried tomato salad, cumberland sausage with spring onion mash, black pudding and red onion and balsamic gravy, pork tenderloin wrapped in pancetta with chorizo and chickpea casserole and duck fat-roasted potatoes, wild mushroom, cream and parmesan risotto with truffle oil, salmon fillet with fricassée of peas, pancetta and broad beans with mussel sauce, and puddings such as dark chocolate brownie with warm chocolate sauce and lime and ginger crème brûlée; they also offer a two-course set lunch. *Benchmark main dish: braised lamb shoulder with roasted root vegetables and dauphinoise potatoes £13.95. Two-course evening meal £18.50.*

Free house ~ Licensees Mike and Sophie Lane ~ Real ale ~ Open 12-2.30, 5-11; 12-11 Sat, Sun; closed Mon lunchtime ~ Bar food 12-2, 6-9; not Mon ~ Restaurant ~ Children welcome ~ Dogs welcome *Recommended by Jo Garnett, Simon Cleasby*

 CARLETON   NY5329 Map 9

Cross Keys

(01768) 865588 – www.thecrosskeyspenrith.co.uk
A686, off A66 roundabout at Penrith; CA11 8TP

Friendly refurbished pub with several connected seating areas, real ales and popular food

There's quite a bustle of customers in this well run pub – particularly at lunchtime when lovers of the outdoors crowd in (walkers, cyclists and so forth). The beamed main bar has a friendly feel, pubby tables and chairs on light wooden floorboards, modern metal wall lights and pictures on bare stone walls, and Tirril 1823 and a guest such as Charles Wells Bombardier on handpump. Steps lead down to a small area with high bar stools around a high drinking table and then upstairs to the restaurant: a light, airy room with big windows, large wrought-iron candelabras hanging from the vaulted ceiling, solid pale wooden tables and chairs, and doors to a verandah. At the far end of the main bar are yet another couple of small connected bar rooms with darts, games machine, pool, juke box and dominoes; TV and background music. There are fell views from the garden. This is under the same ownership as the Highland Drove in Great Salkeld.

High quality food includes lunchtime sandwiches and hot baguettes, deep-fried rosemary and garlic brie wedges with redcurrant sauce, salmon fishcake with lemon and chive aioli, sharing platters, smoked cheese and chilli polenta with confit tomato and roast beetroot, quite a choice of burgers with toppings and chips, cumberland sausages with mash and gravy, chicken with black pudding and wholegrain mustard sauce, and puddings such as chocolate brownie with chocolate sauce and vanilla crème brûlée; they hold steak nights on Monday and Tuesday. *Benchmark main dish: steak in ale pie £10.95. Two-course evening meal £16.00.*

Free house ~ Licensee Paul Newton ~ Real ale ~ Open 12-3, 5-midnight; 12-1am Sat; 12-midnight Sun ~ Bar food 12-2.30, 6 (5.30 Fri, Sat)-9 (8.30 Sun) ~ Restaurant ~ Children welcome ~ Dogs allowed in bar ~ Wi-fi *Recommended by Kim Skuse, Lindy Andrews*

 CARTMEL   SD3778 Map 7

Kings Arms

(015395) 33246 – www.thekingsarmscartmel.com
The Square; LA11 6QB

Bustling village pub with five real ales and well liked food

The famous priory is just a stone's throw from this 18th-c former coaching inn right in the middle of a historic village. The cosy bars have beams, open log fires, flagstones and wooden floorboards and an attractive range of seats from nice old wooden or leather and brass-studded dining chairs around a mix of wooden tables to comfortable leather armchairs. Hawkshead Bitter, Brodie's Prime, Lakeland Gold and Windermere Pale and a guest beer on handpump served by friendly staff. Seats and picnic-sets out in front face the lovely square; good surrounding walks.

From seasonal menus, the popular food includes sandwiches, game terrine with chutney, crispy duck spring rolls with asian dipping sauce, mushroom, sweet potato and thyme pie, chicken with fennel and dill salad, slow-roast pork belly with black pudding, caramelised apple and mustard sauce, salmon steak with leek and shrimp cream sauce, and puddings such as banoffi pie and sticky toffee pudding with butterscotch sauce. *Benchmark main dish: steak in ale pie £12.95. Two-course evening meal £18.00.*

Enterprise ~ Lease Karen Lyons ~ Real ale ~ Open 10am-midnight (1am Fri, Sat) ~ Bar food 12-10 ~ Restaurant ~ Children welcome ~ Dogs welcome ~ Wi-fi ~ Live bands Fri, Sat evenings *Recommended by Gordon and Margaret Ormondroyd, Simon Cleasby*

CARTMEL FELL SD4189 Map 9
Masons Arms 🌟 ♀ 🍺

(015395) 68486 – www.masonsarmsstrawberrybank.co.uk
Strawberry Bank, a few miles S of Windermere between A592 and A5074; perhaps the simplest way to find the pub is to go uphill W from Bowland Bridge (which is signposted off A5074) towards Newby Bridge and keep right, then left at the staggered crossroads – it's then on your right, below Gummer's How; OS Sheet 97 map reference 413895; LA11 6NW

Stunning views, beamed bar with plenty of character, interesting food and real ales plus many foreign bottled beers; self-catering cottages and apartments

From windows in the pub and from the rustic benches and tables on the heated terrace there are stunning views down over the Winster Valley to the woods below Whitbarrow Scar. Their stylish and comfortable self-catering cottages and apartments share the same fine outlook. The main bar has plenty of character, with low black beams in the bowed ceiling, and country chairs and plain wooden tables on polished flagstones. A small lounge has oak tables and settles to match its fine Jacobean panelling. There's also a plain little room beyond the serving counter with pictures and a fire in an open range, a family room with the atmosphere of an old parlour, and an upstairs dining room; background music and board games. Cumberland Corby Blonde, Cumbrian Legendary Loweswater Gold, Hawkshead Bitter and Thwaites Wainwright on handpump, quite a few foreign bottled beers, 12 wines by the glass, ten malt whiskies and farm cider; service is friendly and helpful.

Impressive food includes lunchtime sandwiches and wraps, thai crab fritters with saffron mayonnaise, spare ribs in sticky sauce, battered fresh haddock and chips, a stew of the day, chicken stuffed with pork, mango and blue cheese with red wine jus, slow-roasted lamb shoulder with smoked garlic and rosemary jus, and puddings such as honeycomb cheesecake and jam roly-poly with custard. *Benchmark main dish: pie of the day £12.95. Two-course evening meal £18.95.*

Individual Inns ~ Managers John and Diane Taylor ~ Real ale ~ Open 11.30-11; 12-10.30 Sun ~ Bar food 12-2.30, 6-9; 12-9 weekends ~ Restaurant ~ Children welcome ~ Dogs allowed in bedrooms ~ Wi-fi *Recommended by Ray and Winifred Halliday, Christian Mole, Gordon and Margaret Ormondroyd*

There are report forms at the back of the book.

CLIFTON   NY5326   Map 9

George & Dragon 🏮 ♟ 🛏

(01768) 865381 – www.georgeanddragonclifton.co.uk

A6; near M6 junction 40; CA10 2ER

Former coaching inn with attractive bars and sizeable restaurant, local ales, well chosen wines, imaginative food and seats outside; smart bedrooms

Our readers love their visits to this carefully restored 18th-c inn, whether for a pint and a bar nibble or an overnight stay in the stylish and comfortable bedrooms (excellent breakfasts too). There's a relaxed reception room with leather chairs around a low table in front of an open fire, bright rugs on flagstones, a table in a private nook to one side of the reception desk (just right for a group of six) and a comfortable bed for Porter, the pub's patterdale terrier. Through wrought-iron gates is the main bar area with additional cheerful rugs on flagstones, assorted wooden farmhouse chairs and tables, grey panelling topped with yellow-painted walls, photographs of the Lowther Estate and of the family with hunting dogs, various sheep and fell pictures and some high bar stools by the panelled bar counter. Cumberland Corby Blonde, Hawkshead Bitter and a changing guest beer on handpump, 20 wines by the glass from a well chosen list and home-made soft drinks. Another room is similarly furnished; background music and TV. The sizeable restaurant to the left of the entrance consists of four open-plan rooms: plenty of old pews and church chairs around tables set for dining, a woodburning stove and a contemporary open kitchen. Outside, there are tables on the decoratively paved front area and in a high-walled enclosed courtyard, and a herb garden.

 Using produce reared and grown on the Lowther Estate to which this inn belongs, the accomplished cooking from an interesting menu includes lunchtime sandwiches, rabbit terrine with pear purée and pickled vegetables, queen scallops with pasta, tomato and basil-infused oil, thai-flavoured tofu with peanut and vegetable stir-fry, hake fillet with lemon and parsley crust and mixed bean, vegetable and tomato casserole, twice-cooked beef rissole with pancetta, wild mushrooms and port wine sauce, and puddings such as lemon posset and sticky toffee pudding with fudge sauce; they also offer a two- and three-course set menu (not Sat evening or Sun lunchtime). *Benchmark main dish: rare-breed burger with relish and chips £12.95. Two-course evening meal £23.00.*

Free house ~ Licensee Charles Lowther ~ Real ale ~ Open 12-midnight ~ Bar food 12-2.30, 6-9 ~ Restaurant ~ Children welcome ~ Dogs allowed in bar and bedrooms ~ Wi-fi ~ Bedrooms: £85/£95 *Recommended by John and Eleanor Holdsworth, Kim Skuse, David Heath, Robert Wivell, Dave Braisted, Lee and Liz Potter, Simon Cleasby*

CONISTON   SD3098   Map 9

Sun 🍺 🛏

(015394) 41248 – www.thesunconiston.com

Signed left off A593 at the bridge; LA21 8HQ

Lovely position for extended old pub with a lively bar, plenty of dining space, real ales, well liked food and seats outside; comfortable bedrooms

The cheerful bar with its good mix of customers (often with their dogs) is at the heart of this dramatically set 16th-c inn. There are beams and timbers, exposed stone walls, flagstones and a Victorian-style range. Also, cask seats, old settles and cast-iron-framed tables and quite a few Donald

Campbell photographs (this was his HQ during his final attempt on the world water-speed record). A fine range of up to eight real ales on handpump might include Barngates Red Bull Terrier, Coniston Bluebird Bitter, Cumbrian Legendary Loweswater Gold, Hawkshead Bitter, Ulverstone Lonesome Pine and guests from breweries such as Beckstones and Wolf; the friendly staff also keep eight wines by the glass and 20 malt whiskies. Above the bar is another room, with extra seating for families and larger groups, and there's also a sizeable side lounge that leads into the dining conservatory; pool, darts and TV. The bedrooms are quiet and comfortable and their fine mountain views are shared by the seats and tables on the terrace and in the big tree-sheltered garden.

Honest, tasty food includes sandwiches, whitebait with dill mayonnaise, breaded brie with cranberry, mushroom stroganoff, chicken with black pudding and wholegrain mustard sauce, cumberland sausages with sweet red cabbage and apple sauce, crispy pork belly with cider gravy, and puddings such as raspberry fool with whisky syrup and bakewell tart. *Benchmark main dish: home-made pies £12.95. Two-course evening meal £17.00.*

Free house ~ Licensee Alan Piper ~ Real ale ~ Open 11-11 ~ Bar food 12-2.30, 5.30-8.30 ~ Restaurant ~ Children welcome ~ Dogs allowed in bar and bedrooms ~ Wi-fi ~ Bedrooms: £45/£70 *Recommended by Caroline Prescott*

CROSTHWAITE
Punch Bowl ⭐ ♀ 🛏
SD4491 Map 9

(015395) 68237 – www.the-punchbowl.co.uk
Village signed off A5074 SE of Windermere; LA8 8HR

Cumbria Dining Pub of the Year

Smart dining pub with a proper bar and several other elegant rooms, real ales, a fine wine list, impressive food and friendly staff; comfortable, stylish bedrooms

'As good as anywhere we've stayed and eaten at in the last five years' – praise indeed from a well travelled reader on this civilised inn. There's a relaxed and nicely uncluttered feel throughout, and the public bar has rafters, a couple of eye-catching rugs on flagstones, bar stools by the slate-topped counter, Barngates Tag Lag and Coniston Bluebird on handpump, 16 wines and two sparkling wines by the glass, 15 malt whiskies and local damson gin. To the right are two linked carpeted and beamed rooms with well spaced country pine furniture of varying sizes, including a big refectory table, and walls that are painted in restrained neutral tones with an attractive assortment of prints; winter log fire, woodburning stove, lots of fresh flowers and daily papers. On the left, the wooden-floored restaurant area (also light, airy and attractive) has comfortable high-backed leather dining chairs; background music. The lovely bedrooms are well equipped and breakfasts are very good. Tables and seats on a terrace are stepped into the hillside and overlook the pretty Lyth Valley.

Delicious food using first class seasonal produce includes open sandwiches using home-made bread, rabbit terrine with celeriac rémoulade, smoked haddock kedgeree with curried mayonnaise and a quail egg, salted pork hash cake with fried duck egg and damson ketchup, calves liver with bacon, onions and smoked potato, cod with mussels, leeks and bacon in cider, daube of beef with garlic mash and roast shallot purée, and puddings such as dark chocolate délice with coffee crumble and peanut butter and caramel cheesecake with banana, honeycomb and lime jelly. *Benchmark main dish: maple-glazed duck with braised red cabbage, dauphinoise potatoes, golden raisins and orange £18.95. Two-course evening meal £25.00.*

Free house ~ Licensees Richard Rose and Lorraine Stanton ~ Real ale ~ Open 12-11 ~ Bar food 12-8.45; 12-4, 5.30-8.45 weekends ~ Restaurant ~ Children welcome ~ Dogs allowed in bar ~ Wi-fi ~ Bedrooms: £95/£130 *Recommended by Richard Tilbrook, Pat and Tony Martin, Peter and Josie Fawcett, Colin McLachlan, Ray and Winifred Halliday, Pat and Graham Williamson, J R Wildon, Simon Cleasby*

 ELTERWATER   NY3204   Map 9
Britannia
(015394) 37210 – www.thebritanniainn.com
Off B5343; LA22 9HP

Much loved inn surrounded by wonderful walks and scenery, with up to seven real ales and well liked food; bedrooms

Being such a smashing pub and right at the heart of the Lake District does mean crowds at peak times, but there's a very relaxed, informal atmosphere, and staff remain friendly and helpful; wonderful walks from the door. The little front bar has beams and a couple of window seats that look across to Elterwater through the trees, while the small back bar is traditionally furnished: thick slate walls, winter coal fires, oak benches, settles, windsor chairs and a big old rocking chair. A couple of beers are named for the pub – Britannia Special (from Coniston) and Britannia Gold (from Eden) – plus Coniston Bluebird and Jennings Neddy Boggle and Sneck Lifter and a couple of guest beers on handpump, and 12 malt whiskies. The lounge is comfortable, and there's also a hall and dining room. Bedrooms are warm and charming. Plenty of seats outside, and visiting dancers (morris, step and garland) in summer.

Some sort of enjoyable food is served all day: hot and cold filled rolls, mackerel, haddock and salmon fishcakes with garlic mayonnaise, grilled haggis with home-made plum jam, cumberland sausages with onion gravy, wild and button mushroom stroganoff with creamy brandy sauce, chicken, ham and leek pie, beer-battered fresh haddock, burger with toppings, red onion marmalade and chips, and puddings such as a brûlée of the day and dark chocolate and mixed berry tart with blackcurrant ice-cream. *Benchmark main dish: braised lamb shoulder in mint and spices with red wine sauce £13.95. Two-course evening meal £19.50.*

Free house ~ Licensee Andrew Parker ~ Real ale ~ Open 10.30am-11pm ~ Bar food 12-5, 6-9 ~ Restaurant ~ Children welcome ~ Dogs allowed in bar and bedrooms ~ Wi-fi ~ Bedrooms: £89/£99 *Recommended by Carol and Barry Craddock, Anne and Ben Smith, Tina and David Woods-Taylor, Brian and Anna Marsden*

GREAT SALKELD   NY5536   Map 10
Highland Drove 🌟
(01768) 898349 – www. highlanddroveinnpenrith.co.uk
B6412, off A686 NE of Penrith; CA11 9NA

Bustling place with a cheerful mix of customers, good food in several dining areas, fair choice of drinks, and fine views from the upstairs verandah; bedrooms

The earliest customers here were scottish drovers walking their cattle from the Highlands to the markets in northern England – now they come from all over the country. The spotlessly kept, chatty main bar has sandstone flooring, stone walls, cushioned wheelback chairs around a mix of tables and an open fire in a raised stone fireplace. The downstairs eating area has more cushioned dining chairs around wooden tables on pale wooden floorboards, stone walls and ceiling joists, and a two-way fire in a raised stone fireplace that separates this room from the coffee lounge with its comfortable leather chairs and sofas. There's also an upstairs restaurant – it's best to book to be sure of a table. A beer named for the pub from Eden, Theakstons Black Bull and a guest ale on handpump, a dozen wines by the glass and 28 malt whiskies; background music, darts, pool and dominoes. The lovely views over the Eden Valley and the Pennines are best enjoyed from seats on the upstairs verandah; there are also seats on the back terrace. This is under the same ownership as the Cross Keys in Carleton.

Quite a choice of good, popular food includes lunchtime sandwiches and rolls (not Sun), ham hock terrine with spiced pear chutney, thai fishcakes with stir-fried red pepper and spring onion noodles and sweet chilli, steak or chicken burgers with toppings and chips, steak in ale pie, gammon with eggs and pineapple, red snapper fillet on mussel and clam minestrone with rouille, venison medallions with game sausage, sweet potato purée and a red wine, redcurrant and thyme sauce, and puddings such as chocolate brownie with chocolate and brandy sauce and raspberry and apple crumble. *Benchmark main dish: rump steak with parsley mash, confit banana shallot, leek and haggis cannelloni and madeira sauce £19.95. Two-course evening meal £20.00.*

Free house ~ Licensees Donald and Paul Newton ~ Real ale ~ Open 12-3, 6-11; 12-midnight Sat; closed Mon lunchtime ~ Bar food 12-2, 6-9 ~ Restaurant ~ Children welcome ~ Dogs allowed in bar ~ Wi-fi ~ Bedrooms: £47.50/£80 *Recommended by Dave Braisted, Kim Skuse*

HAWKSHEAD
Drunken Duck 🌟 ♀ 🍺 🛏

NY3501 Map 9

(015394) 36347 – www.drunkenduckinn.co.uk

Barngates; the pub is signposted from B5286 Hawkshead–Ambleside, opposite the Outgate Inn and from north first right after the wooded caravan site; LA22 0NG

Stylish little bar, several restaurant areas, own-brewed beers and bar meals as well as innovative restaurant choices; stunning views and lovely bedrooms

At its most informal at lunchtime, this is a civilised inn with a small, smart bar and own-brewed real ales. From their Barngates brewery they offer Brathay Gold, Catnap, Cracker, Goodhews Dry Stout, Red Bull Terrier and Tag Lag on handpump – as well as 16 wines by the glass from a fine list, 25 malt whiskies and 16 gins. There's an easy-going atmosphere, leather bar stools by the slate-topped counter, leather club chairs, beams and oak floorboards, photographs, coaching prints and hunting pictures on the walls, and horsebrasses and some kentish hop bines as decoration. The three restaurant areas are elegant, and the beautifully furnished bedrooms get booked up months in advance; some have their own balcony and overlook the garden and tarn. You can sit at the wooden tables and benches on grass opposite the building, from where there are spectacular views across the fells; the numerous spring and summer bulbs are lovely.

Top quality local produce is at the heart of the excellent food: lunchtime sandwiches, gin-cured salmon with cucumber and horseradish, ox cheek, onion broth and horseradish vinegar, a meze board to share, spiced cauliflower heart with spinach, sultanas and onion pakora, steak pie and mash, pork shoulder and cheek with celeriac, braised celery and crackling, cod with smoked potato, capers and leeks, and puddings such as chocolate bar with salted caramel ice-cream and treacle tart with prunes and clotted cream ice-cream. *Benchmark main dish: mutton loin and shoulder with salt-baked parsnip and kale £22.00. Two-course evening meal £27.00.*

Own brew ~ Licensee Steph Barton ~ Real ale ~ Open 11.30-11; 12-10.30 Sun ~ Bar food 12-4, 6.30-9 ~ Restaurant ~ Children welcome ~ Dogs allowed in bar ~ Wi-fi ~ Bedrooms: £78.75/£105 *Recommended by Christian Mole, Carol and Barry Craddock, Colin McLachlan*

INGS

SD4498 Map 9

Watermill

(01539) 821309 – www.lakelandpub.co.uk

Just off A591 E of Windermere; LA8 9PY

Busy, cleverly converted pub with fantastic range of real ales including own brews, and well liked food; bedrooms

With up to 16 beers on handpump, this bustling place gets pretty busy at peak times. Their own brews include Watermill A Bit'er Ruff, Blackbeard, Collie Wobbles, Dogth Vader, Isle of Dogs, Windermere Blonde, Ruff Justice and W'ruff Night, and there are guests such as Coniston Bluebird, Cumbrian Legendary Loweswater Gold, Fell Robust Porter and Unsworths Yard Cartmel Peninsula and Crusader Gold. Also, scrumpy cider, a huge choice of foreign bottled beers and 40 malt whiskies. The building, cleverly converted from a wood mill and joiner's shop, has plenty of character and the bars have an assortment of chairs, padded benches and solid oak tables, bar counters made from old church wood, open fires and interesting photographs and amusing cartoons by a local artist. The spacious lounge bar, in much the same traditional style as the other rooms, has rocking chairs and a big open fire; darts and board games. There are seats in the gardens and lots to do nearby. Dogs may get free biscuits and water. Readers enjoy staying here.

From an extensive menu and served all day, the hearty food includes lunchtime sandwiches, creamy garlic mushrooms, baked camembert with garlic and thyme, vegetable cannelloni, rack of ribs in barbecue sauce, beer-battered fresh haddock and chips, chicken in creamy mustard and rosemary sauce, gammon with free-range egg and pineapple, and puddings such as hot chocolate fudge cake and crème brûlée. *Benchmark main dish: beef in ale pie £10.95. Two-course evening meal £17.50.*

Own brew ~ Licensee Brian Coulthwaite ~ Real ale ~ Open 11-11 (10.30 Sun) ~ Bar food 12-9 ~ Children welcome ~ Dogs allowed in bar and bedrooms ~ Wi-fi ~ Storytelling first Tues of month, folk music third Tues of month ~ Bedrooms: £48/£86
Recommended by David Fowler, Ray and Winifred Halliday, Dennis Jones

LANGDALE

NY2806 Map 9

Old Dungeon Ghyll £

(015394) 37272 – www.odg.co.uk

B5343; LA22 9JY

Straightforward place in lovely position with real ales, traditional food and fine surrounding walks; bedrooms

Full of character and atmosphere, this boisterous place is a real fell-walkers' and climbers' haven. It's right at the heart of the Great Langdale Valley and has plenty of character; the vibe is basic but cosy, so there's no need to remove boots or muddy trousers – you can sit on seats in old cattle stalls by the big warming fire and enjoy the fine choice of six real ales on handpump: Jennings Cumberland, Theakstons Old Peculier, Yates Best Bitter and quickly changing guests such as Cumbrian Legendary Esthwaite, Irwell Works Pleasantly Blue and Pennine Best Bitter. Farm cider and several malt whiskies. It's a good place to stay, with warm bedrooms and highly rated breakfasts. It may get lively on a Saturday night (there's a popular National Trust campsite opposite).

Honest food includes their own bread and cakes, lunchtime sandwiches, pâté of the day, prawn cocktail, beer-battered fish and chips, a pie of the day, spicy chilli con carne, vegetable goulash, gammon and free-range eggs, and puddings. *Benchmark main dish: cumberland sausage with onion gravy and apple sauce £10.45. Two-course evening meal £16.50.*

Free house ~ Licensee Neil Walmsley ~ Real ale ~ Open 11-11 (10.30 Sun) ~ Bar food 12-2, 6-9 ~ Restaurant ~ Children welcome ~ Dogs allowed in bar and bedrooms ~ Wi-fi ~ Live folk music Weds evening ~ Bedrooms: /£106 *Recommended by Comus and Sarah Elliott, Hilary and Neil Christopher*

LEVENS
SD4987 Map 9
Strickland Arms ♀ ◖
(015395) 61010 – www.ainscoughs.co.uk
4 miles from M6 junction 36, via A590; just off A590, by Sizergh Castle gates; LA8 8DZ

Friendly, open-plan pub with popular food, local ales and a fine setting; seats outside

You must book a table in advance as this civilised and well run place is always deservedly busy. It's largely open-plan with a light and airy feel; the bar on the right has oriental rugs on flagstones, a log fire, Black Swan Blonde Ale, Cumberland Corby Blonde, Kirkby Lonsdale Monumental, Thwaites Lancaster Bomber and a guest beer on handpump, several malt whiskies and nine wines by the glass. On the left are polished boards and another log fire, and throughout there's a nice mix of sturdy country furniture, candles on tables, hunting scenes and other old prints on the walls, curtain in heavy fabric and some staffordshire china ornaments. Two of the dining rooms are upstairs; background music and board games. The flagstoned front terrace has plenty of seats; disabled access and facilities. Sizergh Castle, a lovely, partly medieval house with beautiful gardens run by the National Trust, is open in the afternoon (not Friday or Saturday) from April to October. The pub is part of the Ainscoughs group.

Good rustic food includes chicken liver with shallots and madeira, salmon and cod fishcake with ginger and lemon dressing, cumberland sausage with onion cider gravy, a pie of the week, lancashire hotpot, vegetable cottage pie, gammon with free-range egg and pineapple, chicken in wild mushroom sauce, and puddings such as raspberry pavlova and caramel crunch. *Benchmark main dish: wild boar burger £12.50. Two-course evening meal £18.50.*

Free house ~ Licensee Nicola Harrison ~ Real ale ~ Open 12-11 (10.30 Sun) ~ Bar food 12-2.30, 6-9; 12-9 Sat; 12-8.30 Sun ~ Children welcome ~ Dogs welcome ~ Wi-fi *Recommended by W K Wood, Ray and Winifred Halliday, John and Sylvia Harrop, Richard Cox*

LITTLE LANGDALE
NY3103 Map 9
Three Shires ◖ ⇤
(015394) 37215 – www.threeshiresinn.co.uk
From A593 3 miles W of Ambleside take small road signposted The Langdales, Wrynose Pass; then bear left at first fork; LA22 9NZ

Fine valley views from seats on the terrace, local ales, quite a choice of food and comfortable bedrooms

The three shires are the historical counties of Cumberland, Westmorland and Lancashire, which meet at the top of the nearby Wrynose Pass. This is a reliably well run and welcoming inn in a lovely spot, with views over the valley from seats on the terrace to the partly wooded hills below; there are more seats on a neat lawn behind the car park, backed by a small oak wood, and award-winning summer hanging baskets. The comfortably extended back bar has green Lakeland stone and homely red patterned wallpaper, stripped timbers and a stripped beam-and-joist ceiling, antique oak carved settles, country kitchen chairs and stools on big dark slate flagstones, and cumbrian photographs. Bowness Bay Swan Blonde, Coniston Old Man, Cumbria Legendary Loweswater Gold and Hawkshead Red on handpump, over 50 malt whiskies and a decent wine list. The front restaurant has chunky leather dining chairs around solid tables on wood flooring, wine bottle prints on the dark red walls and fresh flowers; a snug leads off here. The residents' lounge has been refurbished. Darts, TV and board games.

🍴 Enjoyable food includes lunchtime sandwiches, baked goats cheese filo parcel with apple relish, grilled smoked salmon with a tian of pickled cucumber and celery and lime sorbet, cumberland sausage with beer-battered onion rings and chips, beef in Guinness pie, spinach, chickpea and sweet potato curry, rump of local lamb with roast vegetable couscous and minted yoghurt dressing, and puddings such as sticky toffee pudding with banoffi ice-cream and vanilla crème brûlée with fruit compote. *Benchmark main dish: local venison and cranberry burger with blue cheese £13.95. Two-course evening meal £20.00.*

Free house ~ Licensee Ian Stephenson ~ Real ale ~ Open 11-10.30 (11 Fri, Sat); 12-10.30 Sun; 11-3; 6-10.30 in winter; closed 3 weeks Jan ~ Bar food 12-2, 6-9; snacks in afternoon ~ Restaurant ~ Children welcome ~ Dogs allowed in bar ~ Wi-fi ~ Bedrooms: /£100
Recommended by Hugh Roberts, Barry Collett, Tina and David Woods-Taylor, Brian and Anna Marsden

LOWESWATER   NY1421   Map 9

Kirkstile Inn 🍺 🛏

(01900) 85219 – www.kirkstile.com

From B5289 follow signs to Loweswater Lake; OS Sheet 89 map reference 140210; CA13 0RU

Lovely location for this well run, popular inn with busy bar, own-brewed beers, good food and friendly welcome; bedrooms

The stunning views of the peaks surrounding this friendly little pub can be enjoyed from picnic-sets on the lawn, from the very attractive covered verandah in front of the building and from the bow windows in one of the rooms off the bar; if you're lucky, you might spot a red squirrel. The bustling main bar has a roaring log fire, a cosy atmosphere, low beams and carpeting, comfortably cushioned small settles and pews, partly stripped stone walls, board games and a slate shove-ha'penny board. As well as their own-brewed Cumbrian Legendary Esthwaite, Langdale and Loweswater Gold, they often keep a guest such as Watermill Collie Wobbles on handpump; nine wines by the glass and 20 malt whiskies. Dogs are allowed only in the bar and not during evening food service. There are marvellous hikes of all levels nearby.

🍴 Popular food includes sandwiches, deep-fried brie with chutney, scotch egg (free-range egg coated in cumberland sausage and black pudding) with roasted red pepper and onion salsa, vegetable teriyaki stir-fry, salmon fillet with chive crushed potatoes and dill and mustard cream, lamb and black pudding stew, beer-battered fish and chips, and puddings such as a fruit crumble and a cheesecake of the day. *Benchmark main dish: steak in ale pie £10.50. Two-course evening meal £18.50.*

Own brew ~ Licensee Roger Humphreys ~ Real ale ~ Open 11-11; 12-11 Sun ~ Bar food 12-2, 6-9; light meals and tea in afternoon ~ Restaurant ~ Children welcome ~ Dogs allowed in bar ~ Bedrooms: £63.50/£103 *Recommended by Martin and Sue Day, Christian Mole, Comus and Sarah Elliott, Margaret and Peter Staples*

LUPTON
Plough ⌾ ♀ ⇌
SO5581   Map 7

(015395) 67700 – www.theploughatlupton.co.uk
A65, near M6 junction 36; LA6 1PJ

**Attractive 18th-c inn with open-plan smart rooms, a good choice
of drinks, interesting food and seats outside; fine bedrooms**

Surrounded by fine walks, this stylish inn makes a good base – and the
bedrooms are attractive, warm and comfortable. There are spreading
open-plan bar rooms with beams, hunting prints and cartoons on grey-
painted walls, rugs on wooden floors, a nice mix of antique dining chairs
and tables, comfortable leather sofas and armchairs in front of a large
woodburning stove, and fresh flowers and daily papers; background music.
High bar stools sit beside the granite-topped bar counter, from where neatly
dressed, friendly staff serve Bowness Bay Swan Blonde, Kirkby Lonsdale
Monumental, Thwaites Wainwright and a couple of guests on handpump,
ten wines by the glass and specialist spirits; board games. There are rustic
wooden tables and chairs under parasols behind a white picket fence, with
more in the back garden.

Imaginative food includes lunchtime sandwiches, seared local duck livers with
whisky cream sauce, mussels poached in cider with smoked bacon, garlic and
parsley, roasted butternut squash and cheese risotto, game sausages with caramelised
onion mash and gravy, free-range chicken with parsley mash and honey-glazed parsnips,
salmon fillet with roasted cauliflower and pak choi, confit pork belly with cider jus,
and puddings such as apple panna cotta with caramel syrup and honeycomb toffee and
white chocolate pistachio cake with pistachio purée and star anise white chocolate
sauce. *Benchmark main dish: beer-battered fresh fish and chips £12.50. Two-course
evening meal £19.00.*

Free house ~ Licensee Paul Spencer ~ Real ale ~ Open 11-11; 12-11 Sun ~ Bar food 12-9 ~
Restaurant ~ Children welcome ~ Dogs allowed in bar and bedrooms ~ Wi-fi ~ Bedrooms:
£85/£120 *Recommended by Kay and Alistair Butler, Ray and Winifred Halliday, Ian Herdman,
Charles North, Hugh Roberts, Pat and Stewart Gordon*

NEAR SAWREY
Tower Bank Arms 🍺 ⇌
SD3795   Map 9

(015394) 36334 – www.towerbankarms.com
B5285 towards the Windermere ferry; LA22 0LF

**Well run pub with several real ales, well thought of bar food,
and a friendly welcome; nice bedrooms**

The bedrooms in this friendly, bustling pub (which backs on to Beatrix
Potter's farm and features in *The Tale of Jemima Puddle-Duck*) have
been refurbished this year; breakfasts remain particularly good. The low-
beamed main bar has plenty of rustic charm, with a rough slate floor, game
and fowl pictures, a grandfather clock, a log fire and fresh flowers; there's
also a separate restaurant. Barngates Cracker Ale and Tag Lag, Cumbrian
Legendary Loweswater Gold and Hawkshead Bitter and Brodie's Prime on
handpump, nine wines by the glass, 15 malt whiskies and four farm ciders;
board games and darts. There are pleasant views of the wooded Claife
Heights from seats in the extended garden.

Generous helpings of tasty food includes lunchtime sandwiches, pigeon breast with
walnut and orange salad, smoked haddock, cheese and spring onion fishcake with
lemon, lime and dill mayonnaise, beer-battered haddock and chips, cumberland sausage

with caramelised red onion gravy, salmon on asparagus, dill and white wine risotto with pesto oil, pork belly with black pudding, cider fondant potato and apple and sage gravy, and puddings such as chocolate orange brownie sundae and sticky toffee pudding. *Benchmark main dish: beef in ale stew £12.75. Two-course evening meal £19.50.*

Free house ~ Licensee Anthony Hutton ~ Real ale ~ Open 11.30-11; 12-10.30 Sun; may close on afternoons if quiet in winter; closed 1 week early Dec, 1 week early Jan ~ Bar food 12-2, 6-9 (8 Mon-Thurs in winter and bank holidays) ~ Restaurant ~ Children welcome ~ Dogs allowed in bar and bedrooms ~ Wi-fi ~ Bedrooms: /£95 *Recommended by Mike Swan, Belinda Stamp*

 NEWBY BRIDGE   SD3686   Map 9
Swan
(015395) 31681 – www.swanhotel.com
Just off A590; LA12 8NB

Riverside hotel with bustling bar, helpful staff serving real ales and wines by the glass, bold fabrics and décor, and seats on a waterside terrace; comfortable bedrooms

The heart of this extended 17th-c former coaching inn is, as it always has been, the bar, where you'll find locals, hotel guests and boating folk all mingling happily. There are low ceilings, cheerful floral print upholstered dining chairs around scrubbed tables on bare floorboards, window seats, a log fire in a little iron fireplace, pictures and railway posters on the grey-green walls, and stools at the long bar counter. Jennings Cumberland, Cumbrian Legendary Loweswater Gold and a guest beer on handpump, served by smart, friendly staff; background music. Towards the back is another log fire with a sofa and upholstered pouffes around a low table, and a similarly furnished further room; the front snug is cosy. In the main hotel off to the left are two sizeable restaurants (upstairs and downstairs). Original features mix well with the bold fabrics and wallpaper, fresh flowers, nice old pieces of china and modern artwork – it's all been done with a great deal of thought and care. Plenty of pretty iron-work tables and chairs line the riverside terrace. The contemporary bedrooms are comfortable and well equipped, and some overlook the River Leven.

As well as breakfasts, sandwiches and afternoon teas, the interesting food includes chorizo scotch egg with red pepper purée, smoked pork ribs in sticky bourbon and cola sauce, sharing boards, burger with toppings, onion rings and fries, polenta cake with celeriac, confit shallots, crispy goats cheese, a fried egg and tomato fondue, coq au vin, salmon with avocado salsa and gremolata new potatoes, and puddings. *Benchmark main dish: beer-battered fish and chips £13.95. Two-course evening meal £20.00.*

Free house ~ Licensee Sarah Gibbs ~ Real ale ~ Open 10am-11pm ~ Bar food 12-9 ~ Restaurant ~ Children welcome ~ Dogs allowed in bar ~ Wi-fi ~ Bedrooms: /£99 *Recommended by Caroline Prescott, John and Sylvia Harrop*

RAVENSTONEDALE   NY7203   Map 10
Black Swan ⭐ 🍴 🛏
(015396) 23204 – www.blackswanhotel.com
Just off A685 SW of Kirkby Stephen; CA17 4NG

Bustling hotel with thriving bar, several real ales, enjoyable food and good surrounding walks; comfortable bedrooms

The individually decorated bedrooms in this smart and neatly kept Victorian hotel are an enjoyable place to stay – some have disabled access, others are dog friendly – and breakfasts are generous. The popular U-shaped bar has friendly, helpful staff, several original period features, stripped-stone walls, plush stools by the counter, a comfortable newly upholstered tweed banquette, various dining chairs and little stools around a mix of tables and fresh flowers; you can eat here or in two separate restaurants. Black Sheep Ale and Bitter and guests such as Derwent Blonde and Tirril Old Faithful on handpump, eight wines by the glass, more than 30 malt whiskies and a good choice of fruit juices and pressés; background music, TV, darts, board games and newspapers and magazines. There are picnic-sets in the tree-sheltered streamside garden across the road and lots of good walks from the door; they have leaflets describing some routes. They also run the village store, which has café seating outside.

Assured cooking from a seasonal menu includes sandwiches, spicy lamb and rosemary meatballs with chorizo and aubergine sauce, home-cured fine herb salmon gravadlax with beetroot carpaccio and fresh horseradish, steak in ale pie, french onion and smoked cheese tart, sticky lime marmalade chicken with mushroom and onion stuffing and parsley and lime crème fraîche sauce, gammon with a runny scotch egg and chips, peppered lambs liver with bacon and onion cream sauce and black pudding potato cake. *Benchmark main dish: free-range chicken with crispy pancetta, oven-dried tomatoes, charred baby gem and jus £13.50. Two-course evening meal £18.00.*

Free house ~ Licensees Louise and Alan Dinnes ~ Real ale ~ Open 7.30am-midnight (1am Sat) ~ Bar food 12-9 ~ Restaurant ~ Children welcome ~ Dogs allowed in bar and bedrooms ~ Wi-fi ~ Bedrooms: £75/£80 *Recommended by Kim Skuse, Steve and Liz Tilley, Michael Butler*

RAVENSTONEDALE
Kings Head

NY7204 Map 10

(015396) 23050 – www.kings-head.com
Pub visible from A685 W of Kirkby Stephen; CA17 4NH

Riverside inn with beamed bar and adjacent dining room, attractive furnishings, three real ales and interesting food; comfortable bedrooms

Both regulars and visitors are warmly welcomed to this pleasantly opened-up village inn. The beamed bar rooms have lovely big flagstones, assorted rugs, a wing chair by a log fire in a raised fireplace, an attractive array of fine wooden chairs and cushioned settles around various tables, a few prints on grey-painted walls and an old yoke above the double-sided woodburner and bread oven. Cumberland Corby Noir, Jennings Cumberland and Tirril Old Faithful on handpump and eight wines by the glass, served by friendly staff; background music and a games room with pool, darts and local photographs. The dining room is similarly furnished, but with some upholstered chairs on wooden floors, tartan curtains, fresh flowers and a few prints. Bedrooms are comfortable and breakfasts hearty. There are picnic-sets by the river in a nicely fenced-off area, and plenty of good surrounding walks.

Tempting food includes sandwiches, queen scallop and prawn ragoût with parmesan cream, cheese and onion soufflé with chive cream sauce, spiced chickpea and spinach burger with red onion marmalade, smoked haddock with crayfish cream sauce and a poached egg, ballotine of chicken with pearl barley and smoked chicken and tarragon, venison and cranberry pie, and puddings such as baked apple and cinnamon iced parfait with raisin purée and treacle tart with mulled wine syrup and blackberries. *Benchmark main dish: confit pork belly with black pudding potato cake and red wine jus £13.50. Two-course evening meal £20.00.*

Free house ~ Licensee Beverley Fothergill ~ Real ale ~ Open 11-11 (10.30 Sun) ~ Bar food
12-9 ~ Restaurant ~ Children welcome ~ Dogs allowed in bar ~ Wi-fi ~ Bedrooms: £75/£98
Recommended by Carol and Barry Craddock, Rob Anderson

STAVELEY   SD4798   Map 10

Beer Hall at Hawkshead Brewery ◀

(01539) 825260 – www.hawksheadbrewery.co.uk
Staveley Mill Yard, Back Lane; LA8 9LR

**Hawkshead Brewery showcase plus a huge choice of bottled beers,
brewery memorabilia and knowledgeable staff**

Served by friendly, helpful staff, the range of ales in this spacious and
modern glass-fronted building is fantastic. They keep the full range
of Hawkshead Brewery ales and from the 14 handpumps there might be
Bitter, Brodie's Prime, Cumbrian Five Hop, Dry Stone Stout, Lakeland Gold,
Lakeland Lager, Red, Windermere Pale and seasonal beers; regular beer
festivals. Also, an extensive choice of bottled beers and whiskies with an
emphasis on independent producers. The main bar is on two levels with the
lower level dominated by the stainless-steel fermenting vessels. There are
high-backed chairs around light wooden tables, benches beside long tables,
nice dark leather sofas around low tables (all on oak floorboards) and a
couple of walls are almost entirely covered with artistic photos of barley and
hops and the brewing process. You can buy T-shirts, branded glasses and
polypins and there are brewery tours. Parking can be tricky at peak times.

A choice of tapas includes sticky barbecue ribs, sweetcorn and coriander fritters
and wild boar and apple sausages, plus more substantial choices such as yorkshire
pudding filled with beef braised in ale, salmon with pesto dressing and a poached egg,
cheese, onion and potato pie, beer-battered haddock with chips, and puddings such as
trio of cherry bakewell tart, sticky toffee pudding and vanilla ice-cream and 'banofflate'
sundae (chocolate brownie with chocolate sauce and fresh banana and toffee
sauce). *Benchmark main dish: brewers lunch (a slice of pie, sausages, salami, black
pudding, bbq ribs, pickles and chutney) £15.00. Two-course evening meal £18.00.*

Own brew ~ Licensee Alex Brodie ~ Real ale ~ Open 12-6 Mon-Thurs; 12-11 Fri, Sat; 12-8
Sun ~ Bar food 12-3; 12-8 Fri, Sat; 12-6 Sun ~ Children welcome ~ Dogs allowed in bar ~
Wi-fi ~ Live music Sun from 5pm *Recommended by Dennis Jones, Kay and Alistair Butler*

STAVELEY   SD4797   Map 9

Eagle & Child ◀ £ ⇦

(01539) 821320 – www.eaglechildinn.co.uk
Kendal Road; just off A591 Windermere–Kendal; LA8 9LP

**Welcoming inn with warming log fires, a good range of local beers and
enjoyable food; bedrooms**

Even on a dreary day you'll find a cheerful, bustling atmosphere here
and a log fire beneath the impressive mantelbeam. The L-shaped
flagstoned main bar area has plenty of separate sections furnished with
pews, banquettes, bow window seats and high-backed dining chairs around
polished dark tables. Also, police truncheons and walking sticks, some nice
photographs and interesting prints, a delft shelf of bric-a-brac, a few farm
tools and another log fire. The real ales on handpump might be Cumberland
Legendary Loweswater Gold, Yates Bitter and two guests from Barngates and
Village Brewer, and they keep several wines by the glass, 20 malt whiskies

and farm cider; background music, darts and board games. An upstairs barn-themed dining room has its own bar for functions. The bedrooms are comfortable and the breakfasts very generous. There are picnic-sets under cocktail parasols in a sheltered garden by the River Kent, with more on a good-sized back terrace and a second garden behind. This is a lovely spot, with walks along the Dales Way and more that fan out from the recreation ground just across the road.

As well as their Lunch for a Fiver deal (not Sun), the popular food includes moules marinière, chicken liver pâté with chutney, malaysian vegetable curry, fresh beer-battered haddock and chips, moroccan-style lamb with couscous, chicken wrapped in bacon with barbecue and cheese sauce, steak and mushroom in ale pie, gammon with egg and pineapple, and puddings such as hot chocolate fudge cake and apple crumble. *Benchmark main dish: braised lamb shank with red wine jus and creamy mash £12.95. Two-course evening meal £16.00.*

Free house ~ Licensees Richard and Denise Coleman ~ Real ale ~ Open 11-11; 12-10.30 Sun ~ Bar food 12-2.30, 6-9; 12-9 weekends ~ Restaurant ~ Children welcome ~ Dogs allowed in bar ~ Wi-fi ~ Bedrooms: £60/£80 *Recommended by David Jackman, Roger and Donna Huggins, Tina and David Woods-Taylor*

STONETHWAITE
Langstrath 🍴 🛏
NY2513   Map 9

(017687) 77239 – www.thelangstrath.com
Off B5289 S of Derwentwater; CA12 5XG

Civilised little place in lovely spot, traditional food with a modern twist, four real ales, good wines and malt whiskies, and seats outside; bedrooms

The comfortable, warm bedrooms in this civilised and friendly little inn are just right as a base on a walking holiday, and there's a cosy residents' lounge too (in what was the original 16th-c cottage). The neat, simple bar – at its pubbiest at lunchtime – has a welcoming log fire in a big stone fireplace, rustic tables, plain chairs and cushioned wall seats, and walking cartoons and attractive Lakeland mountain photographs on its textured white walls. Four real ales on handpump such as Jennings Cumberland Ale and Cocker Hoop, Keswick Gold and Theakstons Old Peculier, 30 malt whiskies and several wines by the glass; background music and board games. The restaurant has fine views. Outside, a big sycamore shelters several picnic-sets with views up to Eagle Crag. With both the Cumbrian Way and the Coast to Coast path close by, walking is a highly popular activity here.

Good, hearty food includes baguettes and sandwiches (until 4pm), potted local brown shrimps, haggis and black pudding balls with pancetta and brandy apple sauce, honey-glazed ham and free-range eggs, lasagne, burger with tomato relish and chips, pork schnitzel with bubble and squeak and cider gravy, turkey, ham, mushroom and sage pudding, a fresh fish dish of the day, and puddings such as vanilla crème brûlée and white chocolate panna cotta. *Benchmark main dish: steak in ale pie £14.25. Two-course evening meal £19.00.*

Free house ~ Licensees Guy and Jacqui Frazer-Hollins ~ Real ale ~ Open 12-10.30; closed Mon, all Dec, Jan ~ Bar food 12-4, 6-9 ~ Restaurant ~ Children welcome but over-10s only in bedrooms ~ Dogs allowed in bar ~ Wi-fi ~ Bedrooms: £75/£110 *Recommended by Graham and Elizabeth Hargreaves, Tina and David Woods-Taylor, John Jenkins, Martin and Sue Day*

If we know a featured-entry pub does sandwiches, we always say so – if they're not mentioned, you'll have to assume you can't get one.

TALKIN   NY5457   Map 10

Blacksmiths Arms ♀ ⇔

(016977) 3452 – www.blacksmithstalkin.co.uk

Village signposted from B6413 S of Brampton; CA8 1LE

Neatly kept and welcoming pub with tasty bar food, several real ales and fine nearby walks; bedrooms

This actually was a blacksmiths in the 18th c. Today, it's a friendly pub and a quiet and comfortable place to stay – the bedrooms and bathrooms are newly refurbished. Several neatly kept, traditionally furnished bars include a warm lounge on the right with a log fire, upholstered banquettes and wheelback chairs around dark wooden tables on patterned red carpeting, and country prints and other pictures on the walls. The restaurant is to the left and there's also a long lounge opposite the bar, with a step up another room at the back. Black Sheep Best, Hesket Newmarket Skiddaw Special Bitter, Yates Bitter and a guest ale from Yates on handpump, 20 wines by the glass, 30 malt whiskies and local gin and vodka; background music, darts and board games. There are a couple of picnic-sets outside the front door with more in the back garden; good walks in attractive surrounding countryside.

Well thought-of food includes sandwiches, deep-fried brie with cranberry sauce, prawn cocktail, pumpkin and red onion tagine, steak and kidney pie, sweet and sour chicken, cumberland sausage with fried egg, salmon in white wine and creamy parsley and lemon sauce, beef stroganoff, trio of fishcakes with sweet chilli dip, and puddings. *Benchmark main dish: beer-battered haddock and chips £8.95. Two-course evening meal £16.00.*

Free house ~ Licensees Donald and Anne Jackson ~ Real ale ~ Open 12-midnight ~
Bar food 12-2, 6-9 ~ Restaurant ~ Children welcome ~ Wi-fi ~ Bedrooms: £55/£75
Recommended by Dr Kevan Tucker, Carol and Barry Craddock

TIRRIL   NY5026   Map 10

Queens Head

(01768) 863219 – www.queensheadinn.co.uk

B5320, not far from M6 junction 40; CA10 2JF

18th-c Lakeland pub with two bars, real ales, speciality pies, and seats outside; bedrooms

The oldest parts of the main bar (the inn dates from 1719) have original flagstones and floorboards, low beams and black panelling, and there are nice little tables and chairs on either side of the inglenook fireplace (always lit in winter). Another bar to the right of the entrance has pews and chairs around sizeable tables on a wooden floor, and candles in the fireplace, while the back locals' bar has heavy beams and a pool table; there are three dining rooms too. Robinsons Cumbria Way, Dizzy Blonde and Unicorn on handpump and several wines by the glass. Outside, there are picnic-sets at the front, and modern chairs and tables under cover on the back terrace. The hard-working licensees also run the Pie Mill (you can eat their pies here) and the village shop. The pub is very close to several interesting places including Dalemain at Dacre, and Ullswater is nearby.

Food includes up to eight pies, plus sandwiches, creamy garlic mushrooms, vegetable lasagne, honey-roast ham and egg, a curry of the day, braised lamb shoulder in redcurrant gravy, cod topped with king prawns in parsley butter, steaks with trimmings and chips, and puddings such as a fruit pie of the day and sticky toffee pudding. *Benchmark main dish: venison steak with juniper and port sauce £17.20. Two-course evening meal £19.00.*

Robinsons ~ Tenants Margaret and Jim Hodge ~ Real ale ~ Open 11-11 (midnight Sat); 12-10.30 Sun ~ Bar food 12-2.30, 5-8.30 ~ Restaurant ~ Children welcome ~ Dogs allowed in bar and bedrooms ~ Wi-fi ~ Bedrooms: £50/£75 *Recommended by Rosie Fielder, Roger and Donna Huggins, Graham and Elizabeth Hargreaves, Tina and David Woods-Taylor*

ULVERSTON
SD3177 Map 7

Bay Horse ♀ ⇔

(01229) 583972 – www.thebayhorsehotel.co.uk

Canal Foot signposted off A590, then wend your way past the huge Glaxo factory; LA12 9EL

Civilised waterside hotel with lunchtime bar food, three real ales and a fine choice of wines; smart bedrooms

The bar in this civilised and friendly hotel is at its most informal at lunchtime and has a relaxed atmosphere despite its smart furnishings. There are cushioned teak dining chairs, paisley-patterned built-in wall banquettes, glossy hardwood traditional tables, a huge stone horse's head, black beams and props, and numerous horsebrasses. Magazines are dotted about, there's an open fire in the handsomely marbled, grey-slate fireplace and decently reproduced background music; board games. Jennings Cocker Hoop and Cumberland on handpump, 16 wines by the glass (including champagne and prosecco) from a carefully chosen, interesting list and several malt whiskies. The conservatory restaurant has lovely views over Morecambe Bay and there are some seats outside on the terrace. Our readers enjoy staying here and the bedrooms have french windows that open out to a panoramic view of the Leven estuary (the bird life is wonderful); breakfasts are excellent.

Consistently good food includes hot and cold lunchtime sandwiches, button mushrooms in tomato, cream and brandy sauce on a peanut butter crouton, deep-fried chilli prawns with sweet and sour sauce, lamb shank with orange, ginger and red wine, angus steak and kidney pie, breadcrumbed chicken stuffed with cheese and herb pâté with grilled smoked bacon, medallions of minced pork in sweet and sour sauce, and puddings such as dark chocolate and brandy crème brûlée and hazelnut galette with lemon curd and raspberries; in the evening, the emphasis is on the restaurant when they have one sitting (7.30pm) and light snacks only are available in the bar. *Benchmark main dish: fresh crab and salmon fishcakes with white wine and herb cream sauce £15.50. Two-course evening meal £23.00.*

Free house ~ Licensee Robert Lyons ~ Real ale ~ Open 9am-11pm (10.30pm Sun) ~ Bar food 12-4 (2 in the restaurant), 7-8.30 ~ Restaurant ~ Children welcome lunchtime, over-10s only in bedrooms ~ Dogs allowed in bar and bedrooms ~ Wi-fi ~ Bedrooms: £80/£100 *Recommended by W K Wood, Hugh Roberts*

WITHERSLACK
SD4482 Map 10

Derby Arms 🍴⭐ 🍺 ⇔

(015395) 52207 – www.ainscoughs.co.uk

Just off A590; LA11 6RH

Bustling country inn with half a dozen ales, good wines, particularly good food and a friendly welcome; reasonably priced bedrooms

There's plenty to do nearby – Sizergh Castle (National Trust), Levens Hall, and good walks around the Southern Lakes and Dales – and the comfortable, reasonably priced rooms here make a good base. The main bar has lots of sporting prints on pale grey walls, elegant old dining chairs and tables on large rugs over floorboards, some hops above the bar counter, an open fire and an easy-going atmosphere. A fine choice of drinks served by friendly, courteous staff includes up to six real ales on handpump, such as Black Swan Blonde Ale, Blakemere Gold, Cumberland Corby Ale, Kirkby Lonsdale Cherkeby, Thwaites Wainwright and a guest; also, 11 wines by the glass and 22 malt whiskies. A larger room to the right is similarly furnished (with the addition of some cushioned pews) and has numerous political cartoons and local castle prints, a cumbrian scene above another open fire, and alcoves in the back wall full of nice bristol blue glass, ornate plates and staffordshire dogs and figurines. Large windows lighten up the rooms, helped at night by candles in brass candlesticks; background music, TV and pool. There are two additional rooms – one with dark red walls, a red velvet sofa, more sporting prints and a handsome mirror over the fireplace. This is part of the Ainscoughs group.

Interesting food (using beef from their own farm) includes sandwiches, chicken livers in mushroom, smoked bacon and thyme, crispy squid with lemon aioli, cumberland sausage with onion gravy, wild mushroom risotto, fishcake with cheese and spring onion, soft poached egg and chive oil, burger with toppings, coleslaw and chips, corn-fed chicken with tarragon mash and mushroom crème fraîche, a pie of the day, and puddings such as chocolate brownie and crème brûlée with damson and plum ice-cream. *Benchmark main dish: beer-battered haddock and chips £11.95. Two-course evening meal £19.00.*

Free house ~ Licensee Nicola Harrison ~ Real ale ~ Open 12-11 (10.30 Sun) ~ Bar food 12-2.30, 6-9.30; all day weekends ~ Children welcome ~ Dogs allowed in bar and bedrooms ~ Wi-fi ~ Bedrooms: £60/£80 *Recommended by Kay and Alistair Butler, Peter Andrews, Belinda Stamp, Toby Jones*

YANWATH NY5128 Map 9

Gate Inn

(01768) 862386 – www.yanwathgate.com

2.25 miles from M6 junction 40; A66 towards Brough, then right on A6, right on B5320, then follow village signpost; CA10 2LF

Emphasis on imaginative food but with local beers and thoughtfully chosen wines, a pubby atmosphere and a warm welcome from helpful staff

Of course, with such excellent cooking at this civilised and immaculately kept 17th-c pub, most customers are here to dine – but plenty of locals do drop in for a chat. They keep Barngates Pale, Tirril Academy Ale and Yates Cumbrian Ale on handpump; also, a dozen or so good wines by the glass, 12 malt whiskies and Weston's Old Rosie cider. A cosy bar of charming antiquity has country pine and dark wood furniture, lots of brasses on the beams, church candles on all the tables and a woodburning stove in an attractive stone inglenook; staff are courteous and helpful. Two restaurant areas have oak floors, panelled oak walls and heavy beams; background music. There are seats on the terrace and in the garden.

Using the best local, seasonal produce, the accomplished cooking includes weekday open sandwiches, mussels with scrumpy and clotted cream sauce, smoked duck terrine with chicory and walnut salad, beer-battered fresh fish and chips, pork tenderloin with black pudding, haggis and peppercorn sauce, sweet potato, chickpea and butternut squash tagine with apricot and toasted almond couscous, smoked haddock with mild potato and spinach curry and free-range poached egg, and puddings such as toffee apple and calvados 'frushie' with vanilla pod custard and lemon posset. *Benchmark main dish: wild local venison steak with chestnuts, baby beetroot and dauphinoise potatoes £19.95. Two-course evening meal £24.00.*

Free house ~ Licensee David Gordon ~ Real ale ~ Open 12-11 ~ Bar food 12-2.30, 6-9 ~ Restaurant ~ Children welcome ~ Dogs allowed in bar ~ Wi-fi
Recommended by Roger and Donna Huggins, Clifford Blakemore, Dave Braisted, Tina and David Woods-Taylor

Also Worth a Visit in Cumbria

Besides the fully inspected pubs, you might like to try these pubs that have been recommended to us and described by readers. Do tell us what you think of them: feedback@goodguides.com

ALLITHWAITE   SD3876
Pheasant (015395) 32239
B5277; LA11 7RQ Welcoming family-run pub on village outskirts, enjoyable freshly cooked traditional food including good Sun roasts, reasonable prices and various deals, friendly helpful service, Thwaites Original and four other local beers, traditional bar with log fire, two dining areas off, Thurs quiz; children welcome (not in conservatory), dogs in bar, outside tables on deck with Humphrey Head and Morecambe Bay views, open (and food) all day. *(David Cannings, GSB, Mike Stokes)*

ALSTON   NY7146
Angel (01434) 381363
Front Street; CA9 3HU Simple 17th-c inn on steep cobbled street of charming small Pennine market town, mainly local ales and generously served food including daily specials, reasonable prices, timbers, traditional furnishings and open fires, friendly local atmosphere; children and dogs welcome, tables in sheltered back garden, bedrooms. *(Dr Kevan Tucker)*

AMBLESIDE   NY4008
★**Kirkstone Pass Inn** (015394) 33888
A592 N of Troutbeck; LA22 9LQ Lakeland's highest pub, in grand scenery, flagstones, stripped stone and dark beams, lots of old photographs and bric-a-brac, open fires, good value pubby food and changing cumbrian ales, hot drinks, daily papers; soft background music; well behaved children and dogs welcome, tables outside with incredible views to Windermere, bedrooms, bunkhouse and camping field, open all day in summer (till 6pm Sun). *(Anon)*

APPLEBY   NY6819
★**Royal Oak** (01768) 351463
B6542/Bongate; CA16 6UN Attractive old beamed and timbered coaching inn on edge of town, popular generously served food including early-bird and OAP deals, friendly efficient young staff, log fire in panelled bar, lounge with easy chairs and carved settle, traditional snug, restaurant; background music, TV; children and dogs welcome (menus for both), terrace tables, 11 bedrooms and self-catering cottage,

good breakfast, open all day from 8am. *(Mike Swan)*

ARMATHWAITE   NY5046
Dukes Head (016974) 72226
Off A6 S of Carlisle; right at T junction; Front Street; CA4 9PB Eden Valley village inn with enjoyable good value pub food, Black Sheep, Lancaster and a guest, cheerful helpful service, comfortable lounge/dining area divided by central stone fireplace, settles and mix of tables and chairs on carpet or bare boards, some upholstered wall benches, small public bar with pool; background music, free wi-fi; children and dogs welcome, seats on paved area, decking and back lawn, five bedrooms (three ensuite), closed Mon, Tues lunchtimes (Mon-Sat lunchtimes and all day Tues in winter). *(Caroline Prescott)*

ARMATHWAITE   NY5045
★**Fox & Pheasant** (016974) 72400
E of village, over bridge; CA4 9PY Well run friendly old coaching inn with lovely River Eden views, well kept Robinsons ales and decent wines by the glass, good freshly made food, log fire in main beamed and flagstoned bar, converted stables dining area with exposed stone walls and woodburner, also a small more formal Victorian dining room; picnic-sets outside, comfortable bedrooms. *(Anon)*

ASKHAM   NY5123
Punch Bowl (01931) 712443
4.5 miles from M6 junction 40; CA10 2PF Attractive 18th-c village pub with spacious beamed main bar, locals' bar, snug lounge and dining room, open fires, well kept ales such as Copper Dragon, Jennings and Thwaites, decent choice of food from pub standards up, friendly staff; children and dogs welcome, picnic-sets out in front, on edge of green opposite Askham Hall, six bedrooms, open all day. *(Roger and Donna Huggins)*

ASKHAM   NY5123
Queens Head (01931) 712225
Lower Green; off A6 or B5320 S of Penrith; CA10 2PF Traditional 17th-c beamed pub with enjoyable good value home-made food including gluten-free choices and

blackboard specials, well kept beers such as
Black Sheep, friendly staff, banquettes and
other red upholstered seating, dark wood
tables, brasses, old photographs and a couple
of animal's heads, open fires, flagstoned
restaurant, games room with pool and TV;
background music, free wi-fi; children and
dogs welcome, tables out at front and in
pleasant garden, four bedrooms, open (and
food) all day. *(Lindy Andrews)*

BASSENTHWAITE NY2332
Sun (017687) 76439
Off A591 N of Keswick; CA12 4QP
White-rendered 17th-c village pub; rambling
bar with low black beams, blazing winter
fires in two stone fireplaces, built-in wall
seats and heavy wooden tables, two Jennings
ales and a guest, generous food served by
friendly staff, cosy dining room; children and
dogs welcome, terrace with views of the fells
and Skiddaw, open all day weekends, from
4pm other days. *(Annette Nicolle)*

BEETHAM SD4979
Wheatsheaf (015395) 62123
*Village (and inn) signed off A6 S
of Milnthorpe; LA7 7AL* Striking old
building with fine black and white timbered
cornerpiece, handily positioned on the
old road to the Lake District; traditionally
furnished rooms, opened-up lounge with
exposed beams and joists, main bar (behind
on the right) with open fire, two upstairs
dining rooms, residents' lounge, Thwaites
Wainwright and a couple from local Cross
Bay, several wines by the glass and quite
a few malt whiskies, decent choice of food
including deals, friendly service; children
welcome, dogs in bar, plenty of surrounding
walks, pretty 14th-c church opposite, five
bedrooms, open all day. *(S G N Bennett)*

BOOT NY1701
Boot Inn (019467) 23711
*Aka Burnmoor; signed just off the
Wrynose/Hardknott Pass road; CA19 1TG*
Refurbished beamed country inn with three
or more real ales, decent wines and enjoyable
locally sourced home-made food, friendly
helpful staff, log-fire bar, conservatory;
children and dogs welcome (there are
resident dogs), garden with play area, lovely
surroundings and walks, nine bedrooms, big
breakfast, open all day. *(Mike Swan)*

BOOT NY1701
★ Brook House (019467) 23288
*From Ambleside, W of Hardknott Pass;
CA19 1TG* Good views and walks from
this friendly family-run inn, wide choice
of enjoyable often interesting food from
sandwiches up, over 160 whiskies and good
range of well kept ales such as Barngates,
Cumbrian Legendary, Hawkshead and
Yates, Weston's cider or perry, decent wines,
relaxed and comfortable raftered bar with
woodburner and stuffed animals, smaller

plush snug, peaceful separate restaurant;
children and dogs welcome, tables on
flagstoned terrace, eight reasonably priced
bedrooms, good breakfast (for nearby
campers too), mountain weather reports,
excellent drying room, handy for Eskdale
miniature railway terminus, open all
day. *(Hugh Roberts, Kay and Alistair Butler)*

BOOT NY1901
Woolpack (019467) 23230
*Bleabeck, midway between Boot and
Hardknott Pass; CA19 1TH* Last
pub before the Hardknott Pass; warm
welcoming atmosphere with main walkers'
bar and more contemporary café bar, also
an evening restaurant (Fri, Sat), good
home-made food including wood-fired
pizzas, pies, steaks and daily specials, up
to eight well kept ales, real cider and vast
range of vodkas and gins, Apr sausage and
cider festsival, June beer festival; pool
room, some live music; children and dogs
welcome, mountain-view garden with play
area, eight bedrooms, open (and food) all
day. *(Alan Eaves, Sarah Flynn)*

BOUTH SD3285
★ White Hart (01229) 861229
*Village signed off A590 near
Haverthwaite; LA12 8JB* Cheerful
bustling old inn with Lakeland feel, six
changing ales and 25 malt whiskies, popular
generously served food (all day Sun)
including children's menu, good friendly
service, sloping ceilings and floors, old
local photographs, farm tools and stuffed
animals, collection of long-stemmed clay
pipes, two woodburners; background music;
no dogs at mealtimes, seats outside and fine
surrounding walks, playground opposite, five
comfortable bedrooms, open all day.
(Jo Garnett)

BOWNESS-ON-WINDERMERE SD4096
Royal Oak (015394) 43970
Brantfell Road; LA23 3EG Handy for
steamer pier, interconnecting bar, dining
room and big games room, old photographs
and bric-a-brac, open fire, well kept ales such
as Coniston, Jennings, Timothy Taylors and
Tetleys, generous reasonably priced pub food
from baguettes to specials, friendly efficient
service; pool, darts, juke box and quiz
machine; children and dogs welcome, tables
out in front, eight bedrooms, open (and food)
all day. *(Dennis Jones)*

BRAITHWAITE NY2324
Middle Ruddings (017687) 78436
*Middle Ruddings, road running parallel
with A66; CA12 5RY* Welcoming family-
run country inn, good food in bar or carpeted
dining conservatory with Skiddaw views,
friendly attentive service, three well kept
local ales, good choice of bottled beers and
ciders; children and dogs welcome, garden

with terrace picnic-sets, 14 bedrooms, good breakfast, open all day. *(David Heath)*

BRAITHWAITE   NY2323
Royal Oak (017687) 78533
B5292 at top of village; CA12 5SY Buzzy local atmosphere, four well kept Jennings ales and hearty helpings of traditional food (children's servings available), prompt helpful service, well worn-in flagstoned bar, restaurant; background music, TV; no dogs at mealtimes, bedrooms, open all day. *(Michael Butler, Martin and Sue Day, Tina and David Woods-Taylor)*

BROUGHTON-IN-FURNESS   SD2187
Manor Arms (01229) 716286
The Square; LA20 6HY End-of-terrace drinkers' pub on quiet sloping square, up to eight well priced changing ales and good choice of ciders, flagstones and nice bow-window seat in front bar, coal fire in big stone fireplace, old photographs and chiming clocks, limited food such as toasties; pool, free wi-fi; children and dogs allowed, bedrooms, open all day. *(Anon)*

BUTTERMERE   NY1716
Bridge Hotel (017687) 70252
Just off B5289 SW of Keswick; CA13 9UZ Welcoming and popular with walkers, hotel feel but with two traditional comfortable beamed bars (dogs allowed in one), four well kept cumbrian ales and good food, more upmarket menu in evening dining room; free wi-fi; children welcome, fell views from flagstoned terrace, 21 bedrooms and six self-catering apartments, open (and food) all day. *(I D Barnett)*

CARLISLE   NY4056
Kings Head (01228) 533797
Fisher Street (pedestrianised); CA3 8RF Recently refurbished 17th-c split-level pub, lots of beams (some painted), wood and stone floors, friendly bustling atmosphere, Yates and two or three guests, good value food, upstairs dining room; background music, TV; no children or dogs, back courtyard (summer live music) and historical plaque outside explaining why Carlisle is not in the Domesday Book, open all day. *(Dave Braisted)*

CARTMEL   SD3778
Cavendish Arms (015395) 36240
Cavendish Street, off the Square; LA11 6QA Former coaching inn with simply furnished open-plan beamed bar, roaring log fire (even on cooler summer evenings), three or four ales featuring a house beer from Cumberland, several wines by the glass and decent coffee, friendly attentive staff, ample helpings of enjoyable food from shortish menu including lunchtime sandwiches, restaurant; children welcome, dogs in bar, tables out in front and behind by stream, nice village with notable priory church, good walks, ten bedrooms – three more above their shop in the square, open (and food) all day. *(Kay and Alistair Butler, John and Sylvia Harrop)*

CARTMEL   SD3778
Royal Oak (015395) 36259
The Square; LA11 6QB Low-beamed flagstoned local under same management as the Kings Arms next door (see Main Entries); cosy nooks and big log fire, good value food including traditional choices, home-made pizzas, pasta and grills, Thwaites and two changing local guests, welcoming helpful staff; background and weekend live music, two sports TVs; children and dogs welcome, nice big riverside garden with heated terrace, four bedrooms, open all day (till 1am Fri, Sat). *(Kay and Alistair Butler, Simon Cleasby)*

CASTERTON   SD6379
★ Pheasant (015242) 71230
A683; LA6 2RX 18th-c family-run inn with neatly refurbished beamed rooms, good interesting food alongside traditional favourites, three well kept changing local ales and several malt whiskies, welcoming helpful staff, arched and panelled restaurant; background music, free wi-fi; children and dogs welcome, a few roadside seats, more in pleasant garden with Vale of Lune views, near church with notable Pre-Raphaelite stained glass and paintings, ten bedrooms, closed Mon lunchtime, otherwise open all day. *(John and Bridget Dean)*

CASTLE CARROCK   NY5455
Duke of Cumberland
(01228) 670341 *Geltsdale Road; CA8 9LU* Popular village-green pub under friendly family ownership, upholstered wall benches and mix of pubby furniture on slate floor, coal fire, dining area with old farmhouse tables and chairs, a couple of well kept local ales, enjoyable nicely presented pub food at reasonable prices; children welcome, no dogs inside, open all day. *(Dr Kevan Tucker)*

CHAPEL STILE   NY3205
Wainwrights (015394) 38088
B5343; LA22 9JH Popular white-rendered former farmhouse, half a dozen ales including Jennings and plenty of wines by the glass, enjoyable well priced pubby food from good sandwiches up, friendly helpful service,

---

A star symbol before the name of a pub shows exceptional character and appeal. It doesn't mean extra comfort. Even quite a basic pub can win a star, if it's individual enough.

roomy new-feeling bar welcoming walkers and dogs, slate floor and good log fire, other spreading carpeted areas with beams, some half-panelling, cushioned settles and mix of dining chairs around wooden tables, old kitchen range; background music, TV and games machines, Weds quiz; children welcome, terrace picnic-sets, fine views, open (and food) all day. *(G Jennings, Comus and Sarah Elliott)*

COCKERMOUTH   NY1230
1761 (01900) 829282
Market Place; CA13 9NH Handsome old building with shopfront windows, well kept Yates and two local guests, good choice of foreign beers and wines by the glass, real cider, fair-priced interesting light snacks, two (gas) woodburners (one in back room with some ancient stripped brick), slate flagstones by counter on left, bare boards on right, polychrome tiles of a former corridor floor dividing the two, cushioned window seats and a couple of high-backed settles, big Lakeland landscape photographs, traditional pub games; background music, free wi-fi; children and dogs (in bar) welcome, disabled facilities, back courtyard below lawn sloping up to church, open from 3pm. *(Mike Swan)*

COCKERMOUTH   NY1230
Castle Bar 07765 696679
Market Place; CA13 9NQ Renovated 16th-c pub on three floors, beams, timbers and other original features mixing with modern furnishings, five well kept local beers including Cumberland Legendary and Jennings (cheaper 4-7pm Mon-Fri, 12-8.30pm Sun), Weston's cider, good choice of enjoyable food in upstairs dining room or in any of the three ground-floor areas, friendly young staff; sports TV; children and dogs (downstairs) welcome, seats on back tiered terrace, open all day. *(Mike and Eleanor Anderson)*

COCKERMOUTH   NY1231
Trout (01900) 823591
Crown Street; CA13 0EJ Busy comfortably modernised old hotel with well liked food in bar, restaurant or terrace bistro, local ales including Jennings, decent wines by the glass; gardens down to river, 49 bedrooms, open all day. *(Robert Wivell, John Jenkins)*

CONISTON   SD3097
Black Bull (015394) 41335/41668
Yewdale Road (A593); LA21 8DU Bustling 17th-c beamed inn brewing its own good Coniston beers; back area (liked by walkers and their dogs) with slate floor, more comfortable carpeted front part has log fire and Donald Campbell memorabilia, enjoyable food including daily specials, friendly helpful staff, lounge with 'big toe' of Old Man of Coniston (large piece of stone in the wall), restaurant; they may ask to keep a credit card if you run a tab; children welcome,

plenty of seats in former coachyard, 15 bedrooms, open (and food) all day from 8am, parking not easy at peak times. *(Anon)*

CROOK   SD4695
Sun (01539) 821351
B5284 Kendal–Bowness; LA8 8LA End of terrace roadside country pub recently refurbished and under new management; low-beamed bar with dining areas off, ales such as Coniston and Hawkshead, log fire; children and dogs have been welcome, reports please. *(Anon)*

DENT   SD7086
George & Dragon (015396) 25256
Main Street; LA10 5QL Two-bar corner pub in cobbled street, the Dent Brewery tap, with their full range kept well plus real cider and perry, old panelling, partitioned tables and open fire, enjoyable food from snacks up, prompt friendly service, steps down to restaurant, games room with pool and juke box; sports TV; children, walkers and dogs welcome, ten bedrooms, lovely village, open all day. *(Anne and Ben Smith)*

DENT   SD7086
Sun (015396) 25208
Main Street; LA10 5QL Old-fashioned local with five well kept changing ales including Kirkby Lonsdale, generous helpings of tasty pub food, traditional beamed and flagstoned bar with coal fire; live acoustic music, darts and dominoes; children, dogs and muddy boots welcome, four bedrooms, open all day (food all day weekends). *(Chilliski)*

ENNERDALE BRIDGE   NY0716
Fox & Hounds (01946) 861373
High Street; CA23 3AR Popular community-owned pub, smart and clean with flowers on tables, five well kept ales including local Ennerdale and Jennings, tasty reasonably priced home-made food; picnic-sets in streamside garden, three bedrooms, substantial breakfast, handy for walkers on Coast to Coast path, open all day. *(Tina and David Woods-Taylor)*

ENNERDALE BRIDGE   NY0615
Shepherds Arms (01946) 861249
Off A5086 E of Egremont; CA23 3AR Friendly well placed walkers' inn by car-free dale, bar with log fire and woodburner, up to five local beers and good choice of generous home-made food, can provide packed lunches, panelled dining room and conservatory; free wi-fi; children welcome, seats outside by beck, eight bedrooms. *(Michael Byrne)*

ESKDALE GREEN   NY1200
Bower House (01946) 723244
0.5 miles W of Eskdale Green; CA19 1TD Modernised 17th-c stone-built inn extended around beamed core, log fires, four regional

ales including one named for the pub, usual food in bar and biggish restaurant, friendly atmosphere; free wi-fi; children and dogs welcome, nicely tended sheltered garden by cricket field, play area, charming spot with great view of Muncaster Fell, good walks, bedrooms (some in converted barn), open all day. *(Mike Swan)*

ESKDALE GREEN   NY1400

King George IV (01946) 723470

E of village; CA19 1TS Cheerful beamed and flagstoned bar with log fire, good range of well kept ales and over 100 malt whiskies, sensibly priced plentiful pubby food from sandwiches to daily specials, friendly fast service, restaurant, games room with pool; free wi-fi; children and dogs welcome, fine views from garden tables (road nearby), lots of good walks, bedrooms and self-catering, open all day. *(Brian Gower)*

FAR SAWREY   SD3795

Cuckoo Brow (015394) 43425

B5285 N of village; LA22 0LQ Renovated 300-year-old coaching inn, opened-up bar with wood floors and central woodburner, steps down to former stables with tables in stalls, harnesses on rough white walls, even water troughs and mangers, well kept Coniston, Cumbrian Legendary and a couple of local guests, good hearty food served by friendly helpful staff; background music; children, walkers and dogs welcome, seats on nice front lawn, lovely setting, 14 bedrooms, open (and food) all day. *(Lindy Andrews)*

FAUGH   NY5054

String of Horses (01228) 670297

S of village, on left as you go downhill; CA8 9EG Welcoming 17th-c coaching inn with cosy communicating beamed rooms, log fires, oak panelling and some interesting carved furniture, tasty traditional food alongside central american/mexican dishes, well kept local beers and nice house wines, restaurant; free wi-fi; children welcome, a few tables out in front, 11 comfortable bedrooms, good breakfast, closed lunchtimes and all day Mon. *(Anon)*

FOXFIELD   SD2085

★ Prince of Wales (01229) 716238

Opposite station; LA20 6BX Cheery bare-boards pub with half a dozen good changing ales including bargain beers brewed here and at their associated Tigertops Brewery, bottled imports and real cider too, huge helpings of enjoyable home-made food (lots of unusual pasties), good friendly service and character landlord, hot coal fire, pub games including bar billiards, daily papers and beer-related reading matter; children (games for them) and dogs welcome, four reasonably priced bedrooms, open all day Fri-Sun, from mid-afternoon Wed, Thurs, closed Mon, Tues. *(Sarah Flynn)*

GOSFORTH   NY0703

Gosforth Hall (019467) 25322

Off A595 and unclassified road to Wasdale; CA20 1AZ Friendly well run Jacobean inn with interesting history and some recent refurbishment, beamed and carpeted bar (popular with locals), fine plaster coat-of-arms above woodburner, lounge/reception area with huge fireplace, ales such as Hawkshead, Keswick and Yates, enjoyable home-made food including good range of pies, restaurant; TV; nice big side garden, 22 bedrooms (some in new extension), open all day. *(Clifford Blakemore)*

GREAT URSWICK   SD2674

General Burgoyne (01229) 586394

Church Road; LA12 0SZ Flagstoned early 17th-c village pub overlooking small tarn, four cosy rambling rooms with beams and log fires (look for the skull in a cupboard), three Robinsons ales, good creative cooking from landlord-chef along with pub favourites, dining conservatory; children and dogs welcome, picnic-sets out at front, open all day weekends, closed Mon. *(Carol and Barry Craddock)*

GREYSTOKE   NY4430

Boot & Shoe (01768) 483343

By village green, off B5288; CA11 0TP Cosy two-bar 17th-c inn by green in pretty 'Tarzan' village; low ceilings, exposed brickwork and dark wood, good generously served traditional food, well kept Black Sheep and local microbrews, bustling friendly atmosphere, live music; children and dogs welcome, seats out at front and in back garden, on national cycle route, bedrooms, open all day. *(Mike Swan)*

HARTSOP   NY4013

Brotherswater Inn (01768) 482239

A592; CA11 0NZ Walkers' and campers' pub in magnificent setting at the bottom of Kirkstone Pass, local ales including Jennings and good choice of malt whiskies, generous helpings of enjoyable reasonably priced food, friendly staff; free wi-fi; dogs welcome, beautiful fells views from picture windows and terrace tables, six bedrooms, bunkhouse and campsite, open all day (from 8am for breakfast). *(Jo Garnett)*

HAWKSHEAD   SD3598

Kings Arms (015394) 36372

The Square; LA22 0NZ Old inn with low ceilings and traditional pubby furnishings, log fire, local ales such as Cumbrian Legendary and Hawkshead from well stocked bar, good variety of enjoyable food from lunchtime sandwiches to daily specials, quick service, side dining area; background music, free wi-fi; children and dogs welcome, terrace overlooking central square of lovely Elizabethan village, bedrooms, self-catering cottages nearby, free fishing permits for residents, open all day till midnight. *(WAH)*

HAWKSHEAD SD3598
Queens Head (015394) 36271
Main Street; LA22 ONS Timbered pub in charming village, low-ceilinged bar with heavy bowed black beams, red plush wall seats and stools around hefty traditional tables, decorative plates on panelled walls, open fire, snug little room off, several eating areas, Robinsons ales and a guest, good wine and whisky choice, enjoyable bar food and more elaborate evening meals, friendly helpful staff; background music, TV, darts; children and dogs welcome, seats outside and pretty window boxes, 13 bedrooms, open all day. *(B J Harding)*

HAWKSHEAD SD3598
Red Lion (015394) 36213
Main Street; LA22 ONS Friendly old inn with good selection of well kept local ales including Hawkshead, enjoyable traditional home-made food, original panelling and good log fire; dogs very welcome (menu for them), eight bedrooms (some sloping floors), open all day. *(Richard Tilbrook)*

HESKET NEWMARKET NY3438
★Old Crown (016974) 78288
Village signed off B5299 in Caldbeck; CA7 8JG Straightforward cooperative-owned local in attractive village, small bar with bric-a-brac, mountaineering kit and pictures, log fire, own good Hesket Newmarket beers (can book brewery tours), generous helpings of freshly made pub food, reasonable prices and friendly service (can be slow at busy times), dining room and garden room, folk night first Sun of month; juke box, pool and board games; children and dogs welcome, lovely walking country away from Lake District crowds (near Cumbria Way), closed lunchtimes Mon-Thurs (Mon-Tues in school holidays). *(Dr Kevan Tucker, Hilary De Lyon and Martin Webster)*

KENDAL SD5192
Riflemans Arms (01539) 723224
Greenside; LA9 4LD Village-green setting on edge of town, friendly locals and staff, Greene King Abbot and guests, no food, Thurs folk night; children and dogs welcome, closed weekday lunchtimes, open all day weekends. *(Hugh Roberts)*

KESWICK NY2623
Dog & Gun (017687) 73463
Lake Road; off top end of Market Square; CA12 5BT Recently refurbished beamed town pub, button-back leather banquettes, stools and small round tables on light wood flooring, collection of striking mountain photographs, reasonably priced hearty food including signature goulash, half a dozen or so well kept ales (several from Keswick), log fire; children (till 9.30pm) and dogs welcome, open (and food) all day, can get very busy in season. *(Anon)*

KESWICK NY2623
George (017687) 72076
St Johns Street; CA12 5AZ Handsome 17th-c coaching inn with open-plan main bar and attractive traditional dark-panelled side room, old-fashioned settles and modern banquettes under black beams, log fires, daily papers, four Jennings ales and a couple of guests kept well, plenty of wines by the glass, generous home-made food including signature cow pie, prompt friendly service, restaurant; background music, Tues quiz; children welcome in eating areas, dogs in bar, 13 bedrooms, open all day. *(Lindy Andrews)*

KESWICK NY2421
Swinside Inn (017687) 78253
Newlands Valley, just SW; CA12 5UE Friendly pub in peaceful valley setting; carpeted low-beamed bar with upholstered settles and chairs around substantial tables, open fire, three well kept ales such as Black Sheep, Caledonian and Theakstons, decent choice of reasonably priced pubby food, stripped-floor area beyond with woodburner, back games part; background and occasional live music, TV, free wi-fi; children and dogs welcome, tables in garden and on upper and lower terraces giving fine views across to the high crags and fells around Rosedale Pike, six bedrooms, open all day. *(CJJH, Tina and David Woods-Taylor)*

KIRKBY LONSDALE SD6178
Orange Tree (01524) 271716
Fairbank B6254; LA6 2BD Family-run inn acting as tap for Kirkby Lonsdale brewery, well kept guest beers too and good choice of wines, carpeted beamed bar with sporting pictures and old range, enjoyable food in back dining room served by friendly staff; background music, pool and darts; children and dogs welcome, comfortable bedrooms (some in building next door), open all day. *(Mike Swan)*

KIRKBY LONSDALE SD6278
Red Dragon (01524) 271205
Main Street; LA6 2AH Traditional Robinsons inn with their ales kept well and wide choice of generously served home-cooked food, beams and flagstones, matching wooden furniture including a couple of high-backed settles, log fire and woodburner; background music, free wi-fi; children and dogs welcome, eight bedrooms, open (and food) all day. *(Ray and Winifred Halliday)*

KIRKBY LONSDALE SD6178
★Sun (01524) 271965
Market Street (B6254); LA6 2AU Cheerful and busy 17th-c inn with striking good balance between pub and restaurant; unusual-looking building with upper floors supported by three sturdy pillars above pavement, attractive rambling beamed bar with flagstones and stripped oak boards,

pews, armchairs and cosy window seats, big landscapes and country pictures on cream walls, two log fires, comfortable back lounge and modern dining room, good contemporary food (booking advised), well kept Hawkshead, Thwaites and a guest, friendly helpful service; background music; children and dogs welcome, nice bedrooms, no car park, open all day from 9am, closed Mon till 3pm. *(Anne and Ben Smith)*

KIRKOSWALD   NY5641
Fetherston Arms (01768) 898284
The Square; CA10 1DQ Busy old stone inn with cosy bar and various dining areas, enjoyable food at reasonable prices including good home-made pies, interesting range of well kept changing beers, friendly helpful staff; bedrooms, nice Eden Valley village. *(David Heath)*

LANGDALE   NY2906
Sticklebarn (015394) 37356
By car park for Stickle Ghyll; LA22 9JU Glorious views from this roomy and busy Langdale Valley walkers'/climbers' bar owned and run by the NT; up to five well kept changing ales and a real cider, home-made locally sourced food (some meat from next-door farm), mountaineering photographs, two woodburners; background music (live Sat in season); children, dogs and boots welcome, big terrace with inner verandah, outside pizza oven, open (and food) all day, shuts winter at 6pm (9pm weekends). *(Comus and Sarah Elliott)*

LEVENS   SD4885
Hare & Hounds (015395) 60004
Off A590; LA8 8PN Welcoming smartened-up village pub handy for Sizergh Castle (NT), five well kept changing local ales and good home-made pub food including pizzas, partly panelled low-beamed lounge bar, front tap room with coal fire, further room down steps; Weds quiz in winter; children and dogs welcome, good views from front terrace, open all day weekends, closed Mon and till 4pm Tues-Fri. *(Belinda Stamp)*

LORTON   NY1526
★Wheatsheaf (01900) 85199
B5289 Buttermere–Cockermouth; CA13 9UW Friendly local atmosphere in neatly furnished bar with two log fires and vibrant purple walls, affable hard-working landlord, Jennings ales and regular changing guests, several good value wines, popular home-made food (all day Sun) from sandwiches up, curry night Weds (quiz then too), fresh fish Thurs and Fri evenings, smallish restaurant (best to book), good friendly service; children and dogs welcome, tables out behind and campsite, open all day weekends, closed lunchtimes Tues, Weds (Mon-Thurs lunchtimes in winter). *(Caroline Prescott)*

LOWICK GREEN   SD3084
Farmers Arms (01229) 861277
Just off A5092 SE of village; LA12 8DT Stable bar with heavy black beams, huge slate flagstones and log fire, cosy corners, some interesting furniture and pictures in plusher hotel lounge/dining area, tasty reasonably priced food (all day Fri-Sun) from sandwiches and basket meals up, Thwaites Wainwright, Fullers London Pride and three guests, decent choice of wines by the glass, good friendly service; pool and darts, Sky TV, background music, free wi-fi; children and dogs welcome, ten comfortable bedrooms, good breakfast, closed Mon lunchtime, otherwise open all day. *(Derek and Margaret Senior)*

MUNGRISDALE   NY3630
★Mill Inn (017687) 79632
Off A66 Penrith–Keswick, 1 mile W of A5091 Ullswater turn-off; CA11 0XR Part 17th-c pub in fine setting below fells with wonderful surrounding walks, neatly kept bar, log fire in stone fireplace, old millstone built into counter serving Robinsons, Hartleys and a guest beer, traditional dark wood furnishings, hunting pictures on walls, quite a choice of enjoyable food using local produce, separate dining room; darts, winter pool, dominoes; children and dogs welcome, seats in garden by river, six bedrooms, open all day. *(David Jackman, Martin and Sue Day, John Oates, WAH)*

NETHER WASDALE   NY1204
★Strands (01946) 726237
SW of Wast Water; CA20 1ET Lovely spot below the remote high fells around Wast Water, own-brew beers and popular good value food, well cared-for high-beamed main bar with woodburner, smaller public bar with pool, separate dining room, pleasant staff and relaxed friendly atmosphere; background music, maybe a local folk group; children and dogs welcome, neat garden with terrace and belvedere, 14 bedrooms, good breakfast, open all day. *(Carol and Barry Craddock)*

NEWBIGGIN   NY5649
Blue Bell (01768) 896615
B6413; CA8 9DH Tiny L-shaped one-room village pub, friendly and unpretentious, with two local ales and decent pubby food cooked by landlady, fireplace on right with woodburner; storytelling last Thurs of month, darts and pool; good Eden Valley walks, closed weekday lunchtimes. *(Dr Kevan Tucker)*

PENRITH   NY5130
Moo Bar (01768) 606637
King Street; CA11 7AY Bare-boards bar opened 2012 (originally a 19th-c cattle house), ever-changing range of six local ales, craft beers such as BrewDog and over 100 bottled imports, friendly knowledgeable staff and good mix of customers, no food, upstairs

'Udder Room' with sofas and sports TV, Mon folk night; well behaved dogs welcome, open all day. *(Geoff O'Connell)*

PENRUDDOCK   NY4227

Herdwick (01768) 483007

Off A66 Penrith–Keswick; CA11 0QU Renovated 18th-c inn under newish management, well kept Jennings and at least one guest from curved servery, decent wines and enjoyable sensibly priced pubby food, Sun carvery, friendly efficient staff, stripped stone and white paintwork, good log fire, dining room with upper gallery, games room with pool and darts; children and dogs welcome, seats out at back, five good value bedrooms, open (and food) all day weekends. *(Alan Eaves)*

POOLEY BRIDGE   NY4724

Sun (017684) 86205

Centre of village (B5320); CA10 2NN Friendly roadside local in row of whitewashed cottages, well kept Jennings and guests, decent choice of enjoyable fairly traditional food, two bars with steps between (dogs allowed in lower one), restaurant; children welcome, picnic-sets in garden with play fort, nine reasonably priced comfortable bedrooms. *(Steve and Liz Tilley, David Heath)*

RAVENSTONEDALE   NY7401

Fat Lamb (015396) 23242

Crossbank; A683 Sedbergh–Kirkby Stephen; CA17 4LL Isolated inn surrounded by great scenery and lovely walks, pews in comfortable beamed bar with fire in traditional black inglenook range, interesting local photographs and bird plates, propeller from 1930s biplane over servery, friendly helpful staff, wide choice of good proper food from filled baguettes to enjoyable restaurant meals, well kept Black Sheep, decent wines and around 60 malt whiskies; children and dogs welcome, disabled facilities, tables out by nature reserve pastures, 12 bedrooms, open all day. *(Mike Swan)*

ROSTHWAITE   NY2514

Scafell (017687) 77208

B5289 S of Keswick; CA12 5XB Hotel's big tile-floored back bar useful for walkers, weather board and blazing log fire, up to eight well kept ales in season, enjoyable food from sandwiches up, afternoon teas, also cocktail bar/sun lounge and dining room, friendly helpful staff; background music, pool; children and dogs welcome, tables out overlooking beck, 23 bedrooms, open all day. *(Belinda Stamp)*

RULEHOLME   NY5060

Golden Fleece (01228) 573686

Signed off A689; CA6 4NF Hospitable whitewashed inn with series of softly lit linked rooms, good interesting food, a couple of local ales and well priced wine list, friendly attentive service; children

welcome, seven comfortable well equipped bedrooms, hearty cumbrian breakfast, handy for Hadrian's Wall and Carlisle Airport, closed Mon and maybe Tues lunchtime. *(Malcolm Greening, Michael Doswell)*

RYDAL   NY3606

Glen Rothay Hotel (015394) 34500

A591 Ambleside–Grasmere; LA22 9LR Attractive small 17th-c country hotel with up to five well kept changing local ales in back Badger Bar, good choice of enjoyable locally sourced food from sandwiches up, beamed and panelled dining lounge with open fire, restaurant, helpful friendly staff; unusual loos cut into the rock; children, walkers and dogs welcome, tables in pretty garden (resident badgers are fed at dusk), eight comfortable bedrooms, open all day. *(Anon)*

SANDFORD   NY7316

★ Sandford Arms (01768) 351121

Village and pub signposted just off A66 W of Brough; CA16 6NR Neat former 18th-c farmhouse in peaceful village, good food (all day weekends Apr-Oct) from chef-landlord, L-shaped part-carpeted main bar with stripped beams and stonework, well kept ales including a house beer from Tirril, comfortable raised and balustraded eating area, more formal dining room and second flagstoned bar, woodburner; background music; children and dogs welcome, seats in front garden and covered courtyard, four bedrooms, closed Tues and lunchtime Weds. *(Lindy Andrews)*

SANTON BRIDGE   NY1101

Bridge Inn (01946) 726221

Off A595 at Holmrook or Gosforth; CA19 1UX Old inn set in charming riverside spot with fell views, bustling beamed and timbered bar, some booths around stripped-pine tables, log fire, Jennings and other Marstons-related beers, good food from well balanced menu including blackboard specials, Sun carvery, friendly helpful staff, separate dining room and small reception hall with open fire and daily papers; background music, free wi-fi; children and dogs (in bar) welcome, seats outside by quiet road, plenty of walks, 16 bedrooms, open all day from 8am (breakfast for non-residents). *(John and Sylvia Harrop)*

SATTERTHWAITE   SD3392

Eagles Head (01229) 860237

S edge of village; LA12 8LN Pretty and prettily placed on the edge of beautiful Grizedale Forest (visitor centre nearby); low black beams and comfortable furnishings, various odds and ends including antlers, horsebrasses, decorative plates and earthenware, woodburner, ales such as Barngates, Hawkshead and Cumbrian Legendary, enjoyable pubby food, friendly welcoming staff; occasional live music; children, dogs and muddy boots welcome, picnic-sets in attractive tree-shaded courtyard garden with pergola, open all day summer, closed Mon in winter. *(Glenwys and Alan Lawrence)*

SEATHWAITE   SD2295
★ **Newfield Inn** (01229) 716208
Duddon Valley, near Ulpha (not Seathwaite in Borrowdale); LA20 6ED
Friendly 16th-c cottage with good local atmosphere in slate-floored bar, wooden tables and chairs, interesting pictures, woodburner, three changing local beers and good straightforward food, comfortable side room, games room; children and dogs welcome, tables in nice garden with hill views and play area, good walks, two self-catering flats, open all day. *(Anon)*

SEDBERGH   SD6592
Red Lion (015396) 20433
Finkle Street (A683); LA10 5BZ
Cheerful beamed local opposite church, down to earth and comfortable, with good value generous home-made food (meat from next-door butcher), well kept Jennings and other Marstons-related beers, good open fire; quiz and music nights, sports TV, free wi-fi; children welcome, no dogs, open all day weekends when it can get very busy, closed Mon. *(Derek Stafford, John Evans)*

ST BEES   NX9711
Queens (01946) 822287
Main Street; CA27 0DE Friendly 17th-c two-bar pub with well kept Jennings and good reasonably priced home-made food, dining area and conservatory, log fires, Thurs quiz and monthly live music; two-tier garden behind, good walks (Coast to Coast path starts/ends here), 14 bedrooms, good breakfast. *(Frank Gorman)*

THRELKELD   NY3225
★ **Horse & Farrier** (017687) 79688
A66 Penrith–Keswick; CA12 4SQ Popular and welcoming 17th-c inn with linked mainly carpeted rooms (some flagstones), mix of furniture from comfortably padded seats to pubby chairs and wall settles, candlelit tables, beams and open fires, good nicely presented local food such as Morecambe Bay scallops and Penruddock duck, selection of Jennings ales and guests kept well, efficient service, partly stripped-stone restaurant; children welcome, dogs allowed in one part of bar, disabled facilities, a few picnic-sets outside and fine views towards Helvellyn range, walks from the back door, bedrooms, open all day. *(WAH, Martin and Sue Day, Christian Mole, Margaret and Peter Staples, Chris and Val Ramstedt and others)*

TORVER   SD2894
Wilson Arms (01539) 441237
A593; LA21 8BB Old family-run roadside inn, beams, nice log fire and some modern touches, well kept Cumbrian ales and good

locally sourced food cooked to order (greater evening choice) in bar or dining room, friendly service; free wi-fi; children and dogs welcome, hill views (including Old Man of Coniston) from tables outside, deli, seven bedrooms and three holiday cottages, open (and food) all day. *(Mike Swan)*

TROUTBECK   NY4103
Mortal Man (015394) 33193
A592 N of Windermere; Upper Road; LA23 1PL Beamed and partly panelled bar with cosy room off, log fires, well kept local ales including a house beer from Hawkshead, several wines by the glass, well liked food in bar and picture-window restaurant; folk night Sun, quiz Weds, free wi-fi; children and dogs welcome, great views from sunny garden, lovely village, bedrooms, open all day. *(J D O Carter)*

TROUTBECK   NY3827
Troutbeck Inn (017684) 83635
A5091/A66; CA11 0SJ Former railway hotel with small bar, lounge and log-fire restaurant, good food cooked by landlord-chef, a couple of Jennings ales, efficient friendly service; children and dogs (in bar) welcome, seven bedrooms and four self-catering cottages in converted stables, open all day in season. *(Graham and Elizabeth Hargreaves)*

ULDALE   NY2436
Snooty Fox (016973) 71479
Village signed off B5299 W of Caldbeck; CA7 1HA Comfortable two-bar village inn, good-quality home-cooked food (not Weds) using local ingredients, up to four well kept changing ales including one named for the pub, decent selection of whiskies, friendly attentive staff, fox hunting memorabilia; winter pool; children in dining areas, dogs in snug, nice location with garden at back, three bedrooms, closed lunchtimes. *(Annette Nicolle)*

ULVERSTON   SD2878
★ **Farmers Arms** (01229) 584469
Market Place; LA12 7BA Convivial attractively modernised town pub, front bar with comfortable sofas, contemporary wicker chairs and original fireplace, daily newspapers, quickly changing ales and a dozen wines by the glass, good choice of interesting fairly priced food, second bar leading to big raftered dining area (children here only); unobtrusive background music, Thurs quiz; seats on attractive heated front terrace, lots of colourful tubs and hanging baskets, Thurs market day (pub busy then), bedrooms and self-catering cottages, open all day from 9.30am. *(Belinda Stamp)*

UNDERBARROW   SD4692
Punchbowl (01539) 568234
From centre of Kendal at town hall, turn left into Beast Banks signed for

Underbarrow, then follow Underbarrow Road; LA8 8HQ Small friendly open-plan village local, beamed bar with mix of furniture including leather sofas on stone floor, woodburner, Hawkshead and a couple of local guests, good choice of freshly prepared food, mezzanine restaurant; free wi-fi; children and dogs (in bar) welcome, picnic-sets and covered balcony outside, handy for walkers, closed Tues. *(Anon)*

WASDALE HEAD NY1807

Wasdale Head Inn (019467) 26229

NE of Wast Water; CA20 1EX Mountain hotel worth knowing for its stunning fellside setting; roomy walkers' bar with welcoming fire, several local ales and good choice of wines, ample helpings of enjoyable home-made food; residents' bar, lounge and panelled restaurant; children welcome, dogs in bar, nine bedrooms, also nine apartments (six self-catering) in converted barn and camping, open all day. *(Mike Swan)*

WINSTER SD4193

★ Brown Horse (015394) 43443

A5074 S of Windermere; LA23 3NR Refurbished 19th-c coaching inn set in pretty valley; chatty beamed and flagstoned bar with church pews, lovely tall settle and mate's chairs around mix of tables, own-brew Winster Valley ales plus local guests, several wines by the glass and ten malt whiskies, candlelit dining room with medley of painted and antique chairs and tables, old skis, carpet beaters, hunting horns and antlers, popular food; children and dogs (in bar) welcome, seats out at front among flowering tubs, more on raised terrace, contemporary-style bedrooms and self-catering, open all day.

(Hugh Roberts, R T and J C Moggridge)

Derbyshire

KEY ★ Star Pub 🍽️ Top Quality Food 🍺 Great Beer
🍷 Good Wines £ Bargain Meals 🛏️ Good Bedrooms 🍴 Serves Food

ASHOVER SK3462 Map 7

Old Poets Corner 🍺 £ 🛏️

(01246) 590888 – www.oldpoets.co.uk
Butts Road (B6036, off A632 Matlock–Chesterfield); S45 0EW

**A fine range of interesting real ales (some own brew) and ciders in
characterful village pub with enthusiastic owners; hearty, reasonably
priced food; bedrooms**

If you wish to do a tour of their microbrewery, it's best to contact this
cheerful village local in advance. The ales they produce are Ashover Light
Rale, Coffin Lane Stout, Hydro and Poets Tipple – and they keep guests
from breweries such as Abbeydale, Batemans, Blue Monkey, Kelham Island,
Oakham, Roosters, Salopian, Sarah Hughes and Slaters; they hold regular
beer festivals. Also, a terrific choice of eight farm ciders, a dozen fruit wines,
20 malt whiskies and belgian beers. The informal bar has an easy-going
atmosphere and a mix of chairs and pews, while a small room opening off
the bar has a stack of newspapers and vintage comics; background music.
French doors lead to a tiny balcony with a couple of tables. They hold regular
acoustic, folk and blues sessions (posters advertise forthcoming events) as
well as quiz nights, poetry evenings and morris dancers. The bedrooms are
attractive and there's a holiday cottage sleeping up to eight.

🍴 Hearty, honest food includes battered king prawns with chilli dip, creamy garlic
mushrooms, filled baguettes, chilli con carne, a choice of nine local sausages using
free-range meat (you can buy them to take home as well), vegetable lasagne, chicken
wrapped in bacon with cheese and barbecue sauce, beer-battered haddock and chips,
liver and onions with stout gravy, and puddings. *Benchmark main dish: meat and
potato in ale pie £8.25. Two-course evening meal £15.50.*

Own brew ~ Licensees Kim and Jackie Beresford ~ Real ale ~ Open 12-11 ~ Bar food 12-2,
6-9; 12-9.30 Sat; 12-4, 6-9 Sun ~ Restaurant ~ Children welcome away from bar ~ Dogs
allowed in bar and bedrooms ~ Wi-fi ~ Acoustic evenings Tues, Sun; quiz Weds ~
Bedrooms: £55/£80 *Recommended by D B Mines, Peter Pilbeam, John and Mary Warner*

BASLOW SK2572 Map 7

Devonshire Arms 🛏️

(01246) 582551 – www.devonshirearmsbaslow.co.uk
A619; DE45 1SR

**Opened-up and refurbished inn with plenty of space for drinking
and dining, real ales, friendly staff and enjoyable food; bedrooms**

With so much to see and do nearby, the comfortable and attractive bedrooms in this bustling pub make a good base for exploring. Careful refurbishments have opened up the connecting bar and dining areas to blend modern ideas with some original features – and it works well. From the central bar counter with high stools and chairs the various rooms fan out: flagstones and carpeting, large mirrors, portraits and paintings in gilt frames, partitioning and big swagged curtains creating cosy niches, contemporary paintwork and lighting and an easy-going atmosphere helped along by courteous staff. Throughout, seating ranges from upholstered (or wooden) dining and tub chairs, leather chesterfields and button-back leather wall banquettes, big cushioned benches, high chairs around equally high tables and plenty of stools of every description. Hatties, their coffee shop, has pretty tea cups and plates on the walls. Peak Bakewell Best Bitter and Chatsworth Gold and Timothy Taylors Landlord on handpump, and good wines are all available by the glass; background music, TV and board games.

Good, thoughtful cooking using top quality local ingredients includes sandwiches, crispy pork terrine with watermelon, pickled turnip and beetroot, gin-cured salmon with cucumber, radish and wasabi dressing, wild mushroom tagliatelle, sausages with caramelised onion gravy, beer-battered haddock and chips, venison stew, soy-marinated salmon with thai-spiced broth, rice noodles and coconut crisps, and puddings such as crème caramel with sweet wine jelly and raisin purée and sticky toffee pudding with toffee sauce. *Benchmark main dish: beef in ale pie £14.00. Two-course evening meal £17.00.*

Free house ~ Licensee David McHattie ~ Real ale ~ Open 12-11 ~ Bar food 12-9 (8 winter Sun) ~ Children welcome ~ Dogs allowed in bar and bedrooms ~ Wi-fi ~ Bedrooms: /£75
Recommended by Anne and Ben Smith, Neil Allen, Jo Garnett

BRADWELL
Samuel Fox 🛏

SK1782 Map 7

(01433) 621562 ~ www.samuelfox.co.uk
B6049; S33 9JT

Friendly, well run inn in the Hope Valley, real ales and fine food, good service and neat bars; comfortable bedrooms

The comfortable, restful bedrooms here make a very good base for exploring the area and there are some wonderful walks in the surrounding Derbyshire Peak District National Park. It's a neatly kept stone inn with a wide mix of customers in the open-plan bar and interlinked dining rooms; although there's quite an emphasis on the interesting food, regulars do pop in for a pint of local ale and a chat. Red or dogtooth upholstered tub chairs are grouped around tables on striped carpet or wooden flooring, country scenes hang on wallpapered walls above a grey dado, curtains are neatly swagged and there are several open brick fireplaces. Bradfield Farmers Bitter and Pennine Real Blonde handpump, 16 wines by the glass from a good list and a farm cider served by helpful, courteous staff; board games. The neat restaurant is similarly furnished but with red plush dining chairs. At the front of the building white metal seating is built around small ornamental trees and there are some wooden seats too. No dogs inside. Wheelchair access.

Highly thought-of food from an interesting menu that focuses on local produce includes pressed ham hock with salt-baked beetroot and sweet and sour onions, flame-grilled sea trout with roasted fennel and red pepper dressing, ravioli with blue cheese, fried radicchio and cider sauce, pheasant with wild mushrooms, pickled red cabbage and stuffed artichokes, sea bream fillet with charred kale, sweet potatoes and pickled pear sauce, and puddings such as baked chocolate alaska with iced raspberries, or vanilla, rhubarb, earl grey and ginger bread. *Benchmark main dish: braised beef cheeks in red wine sauce £16.50. Two-course evening meal £23.00.*

Free house ~ Licensee John Duckett ~ Real ale ~ Open 6-11; 12-3, 6-11 Fri; 12-11 Sat; 1-8 Sun; closed all Mon and Tues; lunchtimes Weds and Thurs ~ Bar food 6-9 Weds, Thurs; 12-2.30, 6-9 Fri, Sat; 1-8 Sun ~ Restaurant ~ Children welcome ~ Wi-fi ~ Bedrooms: £95/£130 *Recommended by W K Wood, John and Mary Warner*

BRETTON
Barrel
SK2078 Map 7

(01433) 630856 – www.thebarrelinn.co.uk

Signposted from Foolow, which itself is signposted from A623 just E of junction with B6465 to Bakewell; can also be reached from either the B6049 at Great Hucklow, or the B6001 via Abney, from Leadmill just S of Hathersage; S32 5QD

Remote dining pub with traditional décor, popular food and friendly staff; bedrooms

One reader so enjoyed a stay in the comfortable bedrooms here that he's booked a walking holiday using this welcoming pub as a base – the surrounding hikes are excellent. Stubs of massive knocked-through stone walls divide the place into several spic and span areas. The cosy dark oak-beamed bar is charmingly traditional with gleaming copper and brass, a warming fire, patterned carpet, low doorways and stools lined up at the counter. Marstons Pedigree and EPA and Wychwood Hobgoblin on handpump, 28 malt whiskies, a farm cider and wines by the glass, all served by friendly, smartly dressed staff; background radio. The outdoor seats on the front terrace by the road and in a courtyard garden are nicely sheltered from the inevitable breeze at this height (the inn is on the edge of an isolated ridge with unparalleled views).

Tasty food includes sandwiches, chicken liver pâté with a changing chutney, stilton mushrooms, beer-battered fish and chips, a seasonal vegetarian risotto, lambs liver and onions, game pie, and puddings such as bakewell tart or sticky toffee pudding. *Benchmark main dish: steak in ale pie £11.95. Two-course evening meal £20.00.*

Free house ~ Licensee Philip Cone ~ Real ale ~ Open 11-3, 6-11 (may open all day in high summer); 11-11 Sat, Sun ~ Bar food 12-2, 6-9; 12-9 Sat, Sun ~ Well behaved children welcome ~ Wi-fi ~ Bedrooms: /£85 *Recommended by Dennis Jones, Liz and Brian Barnard*

CHELMORTON
Church Inn 🍺 £ 🛏
SK1170 Map 7

(01298) 85319 – www.thechurchinn.co.uk

Village signposted off A5270, between A6 and A515 SE of Buxton; keep on up through village towards church; SK17 9SL

Cosy, convivial, traditional inn beautifully set in High Peak walking country; good value food; bedrooms

Dating from 1742, this warmly friendly inn is quietly set at the end of a road up to the moors. The chatty, low-ceilinged bar has a warming fire and is traditionally furnished with built-in cushioned benches and simple chairs around polished cast-iron-framed tables (a couple still with their squeaky sewing treadles). Shelves of books, Tiffany-style lamps and house plants in the curtained windows, atmospheric Dales photographs and prints, and a coal-effect stove in the stripped-stone end wall all add to the cosy feel.

Abbeydale Moonshine, Adnams Bitter, Marstons Pedigree and guests such as Kelham Island Easy Rider and Thornbridge Jaipur on handpump; darts in a tile-floored games area on the left; TV and board games. The inn is opposite a mainly 18th-c church and is prettily tucked into woodland, with fine views over the village and hills beyond from good teak tables on a two-level terrace. The cottagey bedrooms are comfortable and the breakfasts good.

The fair-priced food includes black pudding fritters with spiced chutney, prawn cocktail, vegetable curry, gammon with egg and pineapple, chicken in stilton sauce, specials such as lamb shank with red wine and rosemary sauce, duck breast with orange and Grand Marnier sauce, pork stroganoff, and puddings. *Benchmark main dish: rabbit pie £12.95. Two-course evening meal £15.00.*

Free house ~ Licensees Julie and Justin Satur ~ Real ale ~ Open 12-3, 6-11; 12-11.30 Sat; 12-11 Sun ~ Bar food 12-2.30, 6-8.30; 12-8.30 Fri-Sun ~ Children welcome ~ Dogs allowed in bar ~ Wi-fi ~ Bedrooms: £55/£80 *Recommended by John Wooll, Mitchell Humphreys, Mr and Mrs R Shardlow, J A Snell, Ann and Tony Bennett-Hughes*

CHINLEY
Old Hall ★ 🍺 🛏

SK0382 Map 7

(01663) 750529 – www.old-hall-inn.co.uk

Village signposted off A6 (very sharp turn) E of New Mills; also off A624 N of Chapel-en-le-Frith; Whitehough Head Lane, off B6062; SK23 6EJ

Charming small Peak District inn with a great range of beers and ciders, good country food and striking ancient dining hall; comfortable bedrooms

With exceptional real ales, good food and plenty to look at in this splendid building, it's not surprising our readers enjoy their visits so much. The warm bar – basically four small friendly rooms opened into a single area tucked behind a massive central chimney – contains open fires, broad flagstones, red patterned carpet, sturdy country tables, a couple of long pews and various other seats including a leather chesterfield and a wing armchair. The dining room is rather grand with a great stone chimney soaring into high eaves, refectory tables on a parquet floor, lovely old mullioned windows and a splendid minstrels' gallery. Marstons Burton Bitter and guests from breweries such as Marble, Peak, Phoenix, Thornbridge and Whim on handpump, as well as interesting lagers on tap, 12 malt whiskies, six cask ciders, a rare range of bottled ciders and (mostly belgian) beers; beer festivals with music are held in late February and September. Also, around a dozen new world wines by the glass and friendly, helpful service. The pretty walled garden has picnic-sets under sycamore trees. Some of the attractive bedrooms look over the garden and there's also a self-catering cottage.

From a wide menu, the good food includes sandwiches, haddock, leek and smoked bacon gratin, confit pork belly on apple salad, sharing platters, home-roasted ham with free-range eggs, cumberland sausages with onion gravy, vegetarian thai green curry, rosemary and mint lamb burger with gruyère, coleslaw and chips, chicken and chorizo cassoulet, and puddings such as blackberry panna cotta and bread and butter pudding with local Hilly Billy ice-cream; they also offer an early-bird menu (not Sat evening or Sun). *Benchmark main dish: steak in ale pudding £12.00. Two-course evening meal £19.50.*

Free house ~ Licensee Daniel Capper ~ Real ale ~ Open 12-midnight ~ Bar food 12-2, 5-9 (9.30 Fri, Sat); 12-7.30 Sun ~ Restaurant ~ Children welcome ~ Dogs allowed in bar ~ Wi-fi ~ Bedrooms: £75/£89 *Recommended by Hawtins, Mike Swan, Brian and Anna Marsden, Ann and Tony Bennett-Hughes*

FENNY BENTLEY
SK1750 Map 7

Coach & Horses

(01335) 350246 – www.coachandhorsesfennybentley.co.uk

A515 N of Ashbourne; DE6 1LB

Cosy former coaching inn with pretty country furnishings, roaring open fires and food all day

The friendly Dawson family welcome both regulars and visitors into their comfortable and very well run former coaching inn. The traditional interior has all the trappings you'd expect of a country pub, from roaring log fires, exposed brick hearths and flagstone floors to black beams hung with pewter mugs, and hand-made pine furniture that includes wall settles with floral-print cushions. There's also a conservatory dining room and a cosy front dining room. Marstons Pedigree and a guest such as Slaters Top Totty on handpump, a couple of farm ciders, eight wines by the glass, and the landlord is knowledgeable about malt whiskies – he stocks around two dozen; quiet background music. A side garden by an elder tree (with views across fields) has seats and tables, and there are more modern tables and chairs under cocktail parasols on a front roadside terrace. It's a short walk from the Tissington Trail, a popular cycling/walking path along a former railway line that is best joined at the nearby picture-book village of Tissington. No dogs inside.

Highly rated food includes sandwiches and baguettes (until 5pm), baked brie and fig tart with port and cranberry compote, a seafood medley, sweet potato, chickpea and vegetable curry, cumberland sausage ring with cranberry and port sauce, chicken wrapped in bacon with tomato and chorizo stuffing on mediterranean vegetables, salmon en croûte with white wine and watercress sauce, rib-eye steak with creamy pepper sauce, and puddings. *Benchmark main dish: 10oz barnsley chop with brandy and shallot jus £15.50. Two-course evening meal £22.00.*

Free house ~ Licensees John and Matthew Dawson ~ Real ale ~ Open 11-11 ~ Bar food 12-9 ~ Restaurant ~ Children welcome ~ Wi-fi *Recommended by P Dawn, Brian BT, Fiona Todd, Jill and Julian Tasker, Dennis Jones, Steve and Suzanne Griffiths, Joy Griffiths, Martin and Sue Day*

GREAT LONGSTONE
SK1971 Map 7

Crispin

(01629) 640237 – www.thecrispingreatlongstone.co.uk

Main Street; village signed from A6020, N of Ashford in the Water; DE45 1TZ

Spotless traditional pub with emphasis on good, fairly priced pubby food; good drinks choice too

At the heart of the Peak District this well established, welcoming pub is surrounded by good walks. Décor throughout is traditional: brass or copper implements, decorative plates, a photo collage of regulars, horsebrasses on the beams in the red ceiling, cushioned built-in wall benches and upholstered chairs and stools around polished tables on red carpet, and a fire. A corner area is snugly partitioned off, and there's a separate, more formal dining room on the right; darts, board games and maybe faint background music. Cheerful staff serve a good choice of wines and whiskies, as well as Robinsons Dizzy Blonde, Double Hop, Trooper, Unicorn and Voodoo Dawn on handpump and Weston's Old Rosie cider. There are picnic-sets out in front (one under a heated canopy), set well back above the quiet lane, and more in the garden.

As well as a very good value OAP weekday two-course menu, the tasty, traditional food includes sandwiches, chicken liver pâté with cumberland sauce, dressed seasonal crab, omelettes, chilli con carne, fish and chips, liver and onions, various curries and puddings. *Benchmark main dish: steak in stout pudding £12.95. Two-course evening meal £35.00.*

Robinsons ~ Tenant Paul Rowlinson ~ Real ale ~ Open 12-3, 6-midnight; 12-11 Sat, Sun ~ Bar food 12-2.30, 6-9 ~ Restaurant ~ Children welcome ~ Dogs welcome ~ Wi-fi
Recommended by Ann and Tony Bennett-Hughes, John and Mary Warner

HASSOP   SK2272   Map 7
Eyre Arms
(01629) 640390 – www.eyrearms.com
B6001 N of Bakewell; DE45 1NS

Comfortable, neatly kept pub with decent food and beer, and pretty views from the garden

In autumn, the creeper covering this 17th-c former farmhouse bursts into spectacular colour – it's quite a sight. Inside, the low-ceilinged beamed rooms are snug and cosy with cheery log fires and traditional furnishings including cushioned oak settles, comfortable plush chairs, a longcase clock, old pictures and lots of brass and copper. The small public bar has an unusual collection of teapots, as well as Black Sheep Ale, Peak Swift Nick and a guest such as Bradfield Farmers Blonde on handpump, eight wines by the glass and 20 malt whiskies; darts, board games and background music. The dining room is dominated by a painting of the Eyre coat of arms above the stone fireplace. In summer, the hanging baskets are lovely and the delightful garden with its gurgling fountain looks straight out to fine Peak District countryside.

Tasty, popular food includes lunchtime sandwiches, deep-fried mushrooms with a garlic dip, prawn cocktail, local trout with almonds, lamb curry with chutneys, rabbit pie, aubergine and mushroom lasagne, chicken with bacon, mushrooms and cheese, duck with orange and Grand Marnier sauce, and puddings such as profiteroles and bakewell pudding. *Benchmark main dish: steak and kidney pie £11.95. Two-course evening meal £18.00.*

Free house ~ Licensees Nick and Lynne Smith ~ Real ale ~ Open 11-3, 6-11; 12-11 Sat; 12-10.30 Sun; closed Mon evenings in winter, two weeks Jan ~ Bar food 12-2.30, 6-9; 12-9 weekends ~ Children welcome ~ Dogs allowed in bar *Recommended by Caroline Prescott, Emma Scofield, Ann and Tony Bennett-Hughes*

HATHERSAGE   SK2380   Map 7
Plough
(01433) 650319 – www.theploughinn-hathersage.co.uk
Leadmill; B6001 towards Bakewell; S32 1BA

Derbyshire Dining Pub of the Year

Comfortable dining pub with good food, beer and wine and seats in the waterside garden; bedrooms

The well equipped beamed bedrooms in a barn conversion make this a good base for exploring the Peak District. The cosy, traditionally furnished rooms have rows of dark wooden chairs and tables (with cruets showing the emphasis on dining) and a long banquette running almost the length of one wall on bright tartan and oriental patterned carpets; also, a big log fire, a woodburning stove and decorative plates on terracotta walls. The neat dining room is slightly more formal. They have a good wine list (with

21 by the glass), 20 malt whiskies, and Black Sheep Best, Bradfield Farmers Blonde and Greene King Old Speckled Hen on handpump; quiet background music. The nine-acre grounds are on the banks of the River Derwent – the pretty garden slopes down to the water – and there's a terrace with wonderful valley views.

 Well presented and very good, the food includes sandwiches, venison carpaccio with beetroot and horseradish purée, seared scallops and slow-roast pork belly with aioli, ravioli of spinach and gorgonzola with butternut squash and sage butter sauce, pizzas with lots of toppings, barbecue ribs with cajun-spiced sweet potato fries and sour cream, saddle of rabbit with braised leg, pancetta and rosemary jus, lamb rump with port jus, king prawns with linguine, chilli, garlic and parsley, and puddings such as chocolate brownie and sticky toffee pudding ice-cream and cinnamon poached pear with lemon panna cotta. *Benchmark main dish: rib-eye steak with a choice of fries £20.00. Two-course evening meal £27.00.*

Free house ~ Licensees Bob, Cynthia and Elliott Emery ~ Real ale ~ Open 11-11; 12-10.30 Sun ~ Bar food 11.30-9.30; 12-8.30 Sun ~ Restaurant ~ Children welcome ~ Dogs welcome ~ Wi-fi ~ Pianist Fri evenings ~ Bedrooms: £80/£105 *Recommended by David Cochrane, Richard Cole, Jill and Julian Tasker, David Carr, Dr Kevan Tucker, Ann and Tony Bennett-Hughes*

HAYFIELD
Lantern Pike
SK0388   Map 7

(01663) 747590 – www.lanternpikeinn.co.uk
Glossop Road (A624 N) at Little Hayfield, just N of Hayfield; SK22 2NG

Relaxing retreat from the surrounding moors of Kinder Scout, with reasonably priced food; bedrooms

The traditional red plush bar in this homely place proudly displays photos of the original *Coronation Street* cast, many of whom were regulars here, along with Tony Warren (the series creator) who based his characters on some of the locals. It's quite possible that the interior hasn't changed much since those days. There's a warm fire, an array of antique clocks and a montage of local photographs. Lancaster Blonde and Timothy Taylors Landlord on handpump; TV and background music. The tables on the stone-walled terrace look over a big-windowed weaver's house towards Lantern Pike hill. Dogs may be allowed in at the licensees' discretion, and if clean; good walks in the Peak District National Park.

Using the best local produce and chalked on boards, the food includes sandwiches, garlic mushrooms, chicken pâté, gammon and egg, vegetable bake, steak and kidney pie, smoked haddock in a creamy fish velouté, chicken chasseur, lambs liver and onions, and puddings such as hot chocolate fudge cake and apple pie. *Benchmark main dish: chilli con carne £9.95. Two-course evening meal £17.00.*

Enterprise ~ Lease Stella and Tom Cuncliffe ~ Real ale ~ Open 12-3, 5-11; 12-11 Sat, Sun; closed Mon lunchtime ~ Bar food 12-2.30, 5-8 (9 Fri); all day weekends ~ Restaurant ~ Children welcome ~ Dogs allowed in bar ~ Wi-fi ~ Bedrooms: £53/£66 *Recommended by Stuart Paulley, Dean Johnson*

HAYFIELD
Royal 🛏
SK0387   Map 7

(01663) 742721 – www.theroyalathayfield.com
Market Street; SK22 2EP

Big, bustling inn with fine panelled rooms, friendly service and thoughtful choice of drinks and food; bedrooms

On fine days, drinkers spill out on to the sunny terrace in front of this traditional stone-built coaching inn – but it's just as popular in winter when the oak-panelled bar and lounge areas have open fires. There's a fine collection of seats from long settles with pretty scatter cushions through elegant upholstered dining chairs to tub chairs and chesterfields, around an assortment of solid tables on rugs and flagstones; house plants, daily papers. Thwaites Original and guests such as Elgoods Goatbusters, Happy Valley Sworn Secret, Rebel Sail Ale and Wood Street Senator on handpump (they hold a beer festival in October), nine wines by the glass and three farm ciders; background music, TV and board games. The bedrooms are spotlessly clean and comfortable and breakfasts are good.

 As well as sandwiches and wraps, the wide choice of food includes chicken and pork pâté with red onion marmalade, prawn and crayfish cocktail, thai green vegetable curry, beef bourguignon with dumplings, a trio of local sausages with wholegrain mustard mash and onion gravy, chicken and mushroom pie, duck breast on stir-fried vegetables with a tangy orange sauce, moroccan-style lamb tagine with rice, and puddings such as chocolate fudge cake and crème brûlée; they also offer a two- and three-course set menu on Friday and Saturday evenings (in the bistro). *Benchmark main dish: roast beef and yorkshire pudding £9.95. Two-course evening meal £15.00.*

Free house ~ Licensees Mark Miller and Lisa Davis ~ Real ale ~ Open 11-11 (11.30 Sat); 12-10.30 Sun ~ Bar food 12-2.30, 6-8.30; 12-9 Sat; 12-7 Sun ~ Restaurant ~ Children welcome ~ Dogs welcome ~ Wi-fi ~ Bedrooms: £60/£80 *Recommended by P Dawn, Carol and Barry Craddock, Hilary and Neil Christopher*

HURDLOW
Royal Oak

SK1265 Map 7

(01298) 83288 – www.peakpub.co.uk
Monyash–Longnor Road, just off A515 S of Buxton; SK17 9QJ

Bustling, carefully renovated pub in rural spot with beamed rooms, friendly staff and tasty, all-day food

A notably friendly welcome is just what tired customers from the High Peak Trail want – plus well kept ales and enjoyable food; the self-catering barn with bunk bedrooms and the campsite are very popular too. The two-roomed beamed bar has an open fire in a stone fireplace, lots of copper kettles, bed warming pans, horsebrasses and country pictures, cushioned wheelback chairs and wall settles around dark tables, and stools against the counter where friendly, helpful staff serve Buxton SPA, Thornbridge Wild Swan and Whim Arbor Light, Hartington Bitter and IPA on handpump, nine wines by the glass and several malt whiskies; background music and board games. The attractive dining room has country dining chairs and wheelbacks and a cushioned pine settle in one corner on bare floorboards, pretty curtains and an open fire. For large groups, there's also a flagstoned cellar room with benches on either side of long tables. The terraced garden has plenty of seats and picnic-sets on the grass.

As well a wide choice of all-day food includes sandwiches, beer-battered crab cakes with tartare sauce, buffalo-style chicken wings with blue cheese dressing, sharing platters, butternut squash, spinach and walnut lasagne, gammon and eggs, thai chicken curry, pork fillet with black pudding mash and Grand Marnier cream sauce, cajun salmon with lemon oil dressing, a big mixed grill, and puddings such as apple and mixed berry crumble and white chocolate cheesecake. *Benchmark main dish: beef and stilton pie £12.50. Two-course evening meal £18.50.*

Free house ~ Licensee Justin Heslop ~ Real ale ~ Open 10am (8.30am weekends)-11pm ~ Bar food 10 (8.30 breakfasts)-9 ~ Children welcome ~ Dogs welcome ~ Wi-fi
Recommended by Brian and Anna Marsden, Emma Scofield

INGLEBY
SK3427 Map 7

John Thompson ◖ £ ⇌

(01332) 862469 – www.johnthompsoninn.com

*NW of Melbourne; turn off A514 at Swarkestone Bridge or in Stanton by Bridge;
can also be reached from Ticknall (or from Repton on B5008); DE73 7HW*

**Own-brew pub that strikes the right balance between attentive
service, roomy comfort and good value lunchtime food**

They've been brewing their own John Thompson brews since 1977
when the brewery opened to celebrate the silver jubilee of HM Queen
Elizabeth II; it's the longest established microbrewery in the country and has
been in every edition of this Guide since it started in 1983. The simple but
comfortable and immaculately kept modernised lounge has ceiling joists,
some old oak settles, button-back leather seats, sturdy oak tables, antique
prints and paintings and a log-effect gas fire; background music. A couple of
smaller, cosier rooms open off; piano, games machine, board games, darts,
TV, and pool in the conservatory. Friendly staff serve some of their own
John Thompson brews, such as JTS XXX, Rich Porter, St Nicks and Summer
Gold, alongside a guest such as Timothy Taylors Landlord. There are lots of
tables by flower beds on the neat lawns or you can sit on the partly covered
terrace, surrounded by pretty countryside. Breakfast is left in your fridge if
you stay in one of the self-catering chalet lodges. Dogs are allowed in the
conservatory.

Honest straightforward food – available lunchtime only – includes sandwiches,
baked potatoes, cheese and broccoli pasta bake, a choice of salads, a carvery, and
puddings such as bread and butter pudding and fruit crumble. *Benchmark main dish:
roast beef carvery £8.95.*

Own brew ~ Licensee Nick Thompson ~ Real ale ~ Open 11-2.30, 6-11; 11-11 Sat; 12-10.30
Sun; closed Mon lunchtime except bank holidays ~ Bar food 12-2 ~ Restaurant ~ Children
until 9pm ~ Dogs allowed in bar ~ Wi-fi *Recommended by Stephen Shepherd, Dr D J and
Mrs S C Walker, Michael Butler, Steve and Suzanne Griffiths, Dennis Jones*

KIRK IRETON
SK2650 Map 7

Barley Mow ◖ ⇌

(01335) 370306

Village signed off B5023 S of Wirksworth; DE6 3JP

**Welcoming old inn that focuses on real ale and conversation;
bedrooms**

Unspoilt and unchanging, this special pub has been welcoming travellers
since 1750 and has been run by a long-serving, kindly landlady for over
30 years. The small main bar is relaxed and pubby with a roaring coal fire,
antique settles on tiles or built into panelling, four slate-topped tables and
shuttered mullioned windows. Another room has built-in cushioned pews
on oak parquet and a small woodburning stove; a third has more pews, low
beams and big landscape prints. In casks behind a modest wooden counter
are five well kept ales, such as Abbeydale Daily Bread, Froth Blowers Piffle
Snonker, Northumberland Bosuns Bitter, Thornbridge Lumford and Whim
Hartington IPA; french wines and farm cider too. There are two pub dogs.
Outside you'll find a good-sized garden, a couple of benches out in front, and
a shop in what used to be the stable. This hilltop village is very pretty and
within walking distance of Carsington Water. Bedrooms are comfortable,
and readers enjoy the good breakfasts served in the stone-flagged kitchen.
Dogs may be allowed in bedrooms if clean, but not at breakfast.

🍴 Very inexpensive lunchtime filled rolls are the only food; the decent evening meals (no choice) are for overnight guests.

Free house ~ Licensee Mary Short ~ Real ale ~ No credit cards ~ Open 12-2, 7-11 (10.30 Sun) ~ Bar food lunchtime rolls only ~ Children welcome ~ Dogs allowed in bar ~ Bedrooms: £45/£65 *Recommended by Edward May, Emma Scofield*

LADYBOWER RESERVOIR   SK1986   Map 7
Ladybower Inn 🍺
(01433) 651241 – www.ladybower-inn.co.uk
A57 Sheffield–Glossop, just E of junction with A6013; S33 0AX

Comfortable, proper pub nestling above reservoir in good walking country; good value bedrooms

The various carpeted areas here are homely with traditional furnishings that take in peach cottagey wallpaper and curtains, little pictures, cast-iron fireplaces, wall banquettes, captain's and country kitchen chairs and the like. The most relaxed place in which to eat is at the end on the right, with leather-padded traditional dining chairs around heavier tables, Lancaster Bomber pictures recalling the Dambusters' practice runs on the reservoir, and a coal-effect fire; unobtrusive background music and darts. Acorn Barnsley, Bradfield Farmers Blonde, Greene King Ruddles County and two guests on handpump, and decent wines by the glass. If you stay in the annexe bedrooms you won't be disturbed by traffic noise – but the road is busy, so crossing from the car park opposite needs care; picnic-sets out in front.

🍴 Usefully served all day, food includes hot and cold sandwiches, potted pheasant with pickled gherkins, prawn and crayfish cocktail, mushroom, spinach and chestnut pasty, gammon and free-range eggs, rabbit and jerusalem artichoke crumble, fresh haddock and chips, free-range chicken with crispy bacon and dauphinoise potatoes, pork belly stuffed with black pudding on sage mash with creamy onion sauce, lamb casserole with baked sweet potato, and puddings. *Benchmark main dish: beef in ale pie £10.50. Two-course evening meal £18.00.*

Free house ~ Licensee Deborah Wilde ~ Real ale ~ Open 10am-11pm ~ Bar food 12-9 ~ Restaurant ~ Children welcome ~ Dogs allowed in bar ~ Wi-fi ~ Bedrooms: £45/£80 *Recommended by Martin and Sue Day, Lindy Andrews*

LADYBOWER RESERVOIR   SK2084   Map 7
Yorkshire Bridge
(01433) 651361 – www.yorkshire-bridge.co.uk
A6013 N of Bamford; S33 0AZ

Just south of the dam, with several real ales, friendly staff, tasty food and fine views; bedrooms

After a walk by the reservoir you'll get a friendly welcome in this pleasantly genteel inn. The cosy bar has a woodburning stove, countless tankards hanging from beams, lots of china plates, photographs and paintings on red walls, horsebrasses and copper items, and red plush dining chairs around a mix of tables on red patterned carpeting. There's lots of space in several other rooms – including a light and airy garden room with fine valley views – with an assortment of seating ranging from wicker and metal to bentwood-style chairs around quite a choice of wooden tables, on carpeting or flagstones, plus many more decorative plates and photos. Friendly staff serve Bombs Gone (named for the pub from Bradfield), Bradfield Farmers Blonde, Kelham Island Easy Rider, Peak Bakewell Best

Bitter and Thornbridge Lord Marples on handpump, and nine wines by the glass. Dogs are allowed in some bedrooms, but not in the bar at mealtimes.

🍴 Generously served food (though you can opt for smaller helpings) includes sandwiches, stilton garlic mushrooms, giant yorkshire pudding with onion sauce and gravy, salad platters (including a huge prawn cocktail), lasagne, steak and kidney pie, haddock and chips, chilli con carne, steaks with a choice of sauces, and puddings. *Benchmark main dish: pot-roast lamb £16.75. Two-course evening meal £20.50.*

Free house ~ Licensee John Illingworth ~ Real ale ~ Open 11-11 (10.30 Sun) ~ Bar food 12-2.30, 5.30-8.30 (9 Fri, Sat); 12-8.30 Sun ~ Children welcome ~ Dogs allowed in bar and bedrooms ~ Wi-fi ~ Bedrooms: £60/£75 *Recommended by Caroline Prescott, Hilary Forrest, Brian and Anna Marsden*

OVER HADDON   SK2066   Map 7
Lathkil 🍺

(01629) 812501 – www.lathkil.co.uk
Village and inn signposted from B5055 just SW of Bakewell; DE45 1JE

Traditional pub well placed for Lathkill Dale with super views, good range of beers and well liked food; warm bedrooms

The same friendly family have been running this unpretentious hotel for 34 years – from father down to daughter. Right at the heart of the Peak District National Park, it's very popular with walkers and cyclists and many use the warm and comfortable bedrooms as a base; breakfasts are hearty. The views are spectacular and can be enjoyed from seats in the walled garden and from windows in the bar. The airy room on the right as you enter has a nice fire in an attractively carved fireplace, old-fashioned settles with upholstered cushions, chairs, black beams, a delft shelf of blue and white plates and some original prints and photographs. On the left, the sunny spacious dining area doubles as an evening restaurant and there's a woodburning stove. Adnams Ghost Ship, Navigation Arctic Blast, Pennine Natural Gold and Storm Bosley Cloud on handpump, a reasonable range of wines (including mulled wine) and a decent selection of malt whiskies; background music, darts, TV and board games. Dogs are welcome, but muddy boots must be left in the lobby.

🍴 Buffet-style lunch includes filled rolls, soup, pâté of the day, lasagne and venison casserole, with evening choices such as smoked duck salad with blackcurrant vinaigrette, whole mini camembert with chutney, sweet potato, spinach and chickpea curry, steak and kidney pie, chicken stuffed with garlic mushrooms with a sweet wine sauce, salmon with chilli and lime butter, mixed grill and puddings such as lemon meringue pie and red and blackcurrant cheesecake with blackcurrant coulis. *Benchmark main dish: beef in ale casserole £10.75. Two-course evening meal £18.25.*

Free house ~ Licensee Alice Grigor-Taylor ~ Real ale ~ Open 11-11; 12-10.30 Sun ~ Bar food 12-2 (2.30 weekends), 6.30-8.30 ~ Restaurant ~ Children welcome but over-10s only in the bar ~ Dogs allowed in bar and bedrooms ~ Wi-fi ~ Bedrooms: £60/£75
Recommended by Kim Skuse, Derek and Sylvia Stephenson, Ann and Tony Bennett-Hughes

> Real ale to us means beer that has matured naturally in its cask – not pressurised or filtered. We name all real ales stocked. We usually name ales preserved under a light blanket of carbon dioxide too, though purists – pointing out that this stops the natural yeasts developing – would disagree (most people, including us, can't tell the difference!)

STANTON IN PEAK

SK2364 Map 7

Flying Childers 🍺 £

(01629) 636333 – www.flyingchilders.com

Village signposted from B6056 S of Bakewell; Main Road; DE4 2LW

Top notch beer and inexpensive simple bar lunches in a warm-hearted, unspoilt pub – a delight

This homely pub evolved from several cottages and is in a beautiful steep stone village overlooking a rich green valley. There's a well tended garden at the back with picnic-sets and more seats out in front. The friendly landlord keeps Charles Wells Bombardier and a couple of guests such as Abbeydale Deception and Storm Bosley Cloud on handpump, and several wines by the glass. The best room in which to enjoy them is the snug little right-hand bar, virtually built for chat, with its dark beam-and-plank ceiling, dark wall settles, single pew, plain tables, a hot coal and log fire, a few team photographs, dominoes and cribbage; background music. There's a bigger, equally unpretentious bar on the right. The surrounding walks are very fine and both walkers and their dogs are warmly welcomed; they keep doggy treats behind the bar.

Lunchtime food cooked by the landlady using some home-grown produce includes filled rolls and toasties, home-made soups and usually weekend dishes such as sausages, liver and bacon and game stews.

Free house ~ Licensees Stuart and Mandy Redfern ~ Real ale ~ No credit cards ~ Open 12-2 (3 weekends), 7-11; closed Mon and Tues lunchtimes ~ Bar food 12-2 ~ Children in lounge bar only ~ Dogs allowed in bar ~ Live acoustic music first Thurs of month
Recommended by Edward May, Caroline Prescott, Ann and Tony Bennett-Hughes

WOOLLEY MOOR

SK3661 Map 7

White Horse ⭐ 🍷 🛏

(01246) 590319 – www.thewhitehorsewoolleymoor.co.uk

Badger Lane, off B6014 Matlock–Clay Cross; DE55 6FG

Attractive old dining pub with good food and drinks in pretty countryside; new bedrooms

Seven new contemporary and very well equipped bedroom suites have been added here with floor-to-ceiling windows providing lovely views over the rolling countryside; each has a private balcony area. It's a neat and uncluttered place: the bar, snug and dining room have wooden dining chairs, tables, leather stools and leather sofas on flagstoned or wooden floors, with a woodburning stove in the bar and an open fire in the dining room, boldly patterned curtains and blinds and little to distract on the cream walls. Peak Bakewell Best Bitter and Chatsworth Gold on handpump and up to a dozen wines by the glass; background music. In the front garden you'll find picnic-sets under parasols on gravel and boules. Ogston Reservoir is just a couple of minutes' drive away.

 Using the best local produce, the highly thought-of food includes ciabattas, crab and prawn ravioli with shellfish bisque, crispy chicken with bacon jam and salted popcorn, aubergine, cherry tomato and confit garlic risotto, chicken with dijon and shallot cream on crushed potatoes, beer-battered cod and chips, barbary duck breast with blackberry jus and dauphinoise potatoes, bass fillets with crayfish and herb linguine, and puddings such as chocolate brownie with chocolate praline ice-cream and lemon tart with clotted cream; they also offer a two- and three-course set menu. *Benchmark main dish: crispy pork belly with spring onion mash and smoked bacon sauce £13.95. Two-course evening meal £20.00.*

Free house ~ Licensees David and Melanie Boulby ~ Real ale ~ Open 12-11; 12-6 Sun; closed
Sun evening, Mon (except bank holidays) ~ Bar food 12-1.45, 6-8.45; 12-4 Sun ~ Restaurant
~ Children welcome ~ Dogs allowed in bedrooms ~ Bedrooms: £139/£149
Recommended by M G Hart, Jo Garnett, Dr Simon Innes

Also Worth a Visit in Derbyshire

Besides the fully inspected pubs, you might like to try these pubs that
have been recommended to us and described by readers. Do tell us what
you think of them: feedback@goodguides.com

ALDERWASLEY SK3153
Bear (01629) 822585
*Left off A6 at Ambergate on to Holly
Lane (turns into Jackass Lane) then
right at end (staggered crossroads);
DE56 2RD* Unspoilt country inn with
beamed cottagey rooms, one with large
glass chandelier over assorted tables and
chairs, another with tartan-covered wall
banquettes and double-sided woodburner,
other décor includes staffordshire china
ornaments, old paintings/engravings and
a grandfather clock, Sharps Doom Bar,
Timothy Taylors Landlord, Thornbridge
Jaipur and guests, several wines by the
glass (decent list) and malt whiskies,
generously served food (all day Fri-Sun);
children and dogs (in bar) welcome, seats
in lovely garden with fine views, decent
bedrooms plus two self-catering cottages,
open all day. *(Stephen Shepherd, Dennis
Jones, Richard Cole)*

ASHFORD IN THE WATER SK1969
★Ashford Arms (01629) 812725
Church Street; DE45 1QB Attractive
18th-c inn set in pretty village, ample
choice of good quality reasonably priced
food including Weds steak night (32oz rump
if you're really peckish), well kept Black
Sheep and two local guests such as Peak,
nice wines, friendly staff, restaurant and
dining conservatory; free wi-fi; children and
dogs welcome, plenty of tables outside, eight
comfortable bedrooms, open all day Sun
(food till 5pm). *(Emma Scofield)*

ASHFORD IN THE WATER SK1969
★Bulls Head (01629) 812931
*Off A6 NW of Bakewell; Church Street
(B6465, off A6020); DE45 1QB*
Traditional 17th-c village pub run by same
family since 1953; cosy two-room beamed
and carpeted bar with fires, one or two
character gothic seats, spindleback and
wheelback chairs around cast-iron-framed
tables, local photographs and country
prints on cream walls, daily papers, three
Robinsons ales and good choice of traditional
food (not Tues evening), friendly efficient
service; background music; children
welcome, dogs in bar, overshoes for walkers,
hardwood tables and benches in front and

in good-sized garden behind with boules and
Jenga. *(Emma Scofield)*

ASTON-UPON-TRENT SK4129
Malt (01332) 792256
*M1 junction 24A on to A50, village
signed left near Shardlow; The Green
(one-way street); DE72 2AA* Comfortably
modernised village pub with enjoyable good
value food (not Sun evening, Mon, Tues), well
kept Bass, Marstons Pedigree, Sharps Doom
Bar and three guests, friendly atmosphere;
TV; children and dogs welcome, back terrace,
open all day. *(Brian and Jean Hepworth)*

BAKEWELL SK2168
Castle Inn (01629) 812103
Bridge Street; DE45 1DU Georgian-
fronted bay-windowed pub (actually dates
from the 16th c) with well kept Greene King
ales and a guest, decent competitively priced
traditional food, three candlelit rooms with
two open fires, flagstones, stripped stone
and lots of pictures, good friendly service;
background music and fruit machine; dogs
welcome, level inside for wheelchairs but
steps at front, tables out by road, gets busy
Mon market day, four bedrooms. *(David Carr)*

BAMFORD SK2083
Anglers Rest (01433) 659317
A6013/Taggs Knoll; S33 0BQ Friendly
community-owned pub with good local beers
and tasty food, café bar and post office;
Weds quiz and some live music including folk;
children, walkers and dogs welcome, open
all day. *(Phil Taylor)*

BASLOW SK2572
Wheatsheaf (01246) 582240
Nether End; DE45 1SR Cheerful
Marstons inn (former coaching house)
with comfortable carpeted interior, popular
reasonably priced pub food including good
children's menu, four well kept ales, prompt
friendly service; free wi-fi; plenty of seats
outside and play area, bedrooms, open all
day. *(Derek and Sylvia Stephenson, John Wooll,
Ms Edna M Jones)*

BEELEY SK2667
★Devonshire Arms (01629) 733259
*B6012, off A6 Matlock–Bakewell;
DE4 2NR* Lovely 18th-c stone inn; original

part with black beams, flagstones, stripped stone and cheerful log fires, contrasting ultra-modern bistro/conservatory, up to six well kept changing ales, several wines by the glass and good range of malt whiskies, imaginative food (not cheap) using local ingredients; background music; children welcome, dogs allowed in bedrooms but not bar, attractive Peak District village near Chatsworth, open all day. *(Stephen Shepherd, Hilary Forrest, David Carr)*

BELPER   SK3349
Bulls Head (01773) 824900
Belper Lane End; DE56 2DL Friendly village local with own Shottle Farm ales (brewed nearby) and enjoyable food including pizza nights and Sun carvery, small simple front bar with beams, flagstones and stripped wood, larger back bar with comfortable sofas and open fire, sizeable dining conservatory; music and quiz evenings; picnic-sets out in front, big lawned garden, open all day weekends, closed weekday lunchtimes. *(Richard Stanfield)*

BIRCHOVER   SK2362
★ Druid (01629) 653836
Off B5056; Main Street; DE4 2BL 17th-c stone pub at edge of village; traditional quarry-tiled bar with open fire, dining areas either side plus more modern downstairs restaurant with wood-strip floor, good varied menu changing regularly including some unusual choices, up to five very well kept ales (tasters offered), Hogan's cider, some live folk and jazz; background music, free wi-fi; children welcome, dogs in bar, tables out in front on two levels, more seats in newly landscaped back garden, good area for walks, Nine Ladies stone circle nearby, open all day. *(Carol and Barry Craddock)*

BIRCHOVER   SK2362
Red Lion (01629) 650363
Main Street; DE4 2BN Friendly early 18th-c stone-built pub with popular good value italian-influenced food (landlord is from Sardinia), also make their own cheese and have a deli next door, Sun carvery, well kept ales (up to five in summer) and four ciders, glass-covered well inside, woodburners; acoustic music session Sun evening; children and dogs welcome, nice rural views from outside seats, popular with walkers, open all day weekends, closed Mon, Tues in winter. *(Anon)*

BONSALL   SK2758
★ Barley Mow (01629) 825685
Off A5012 W of Cromford; The Dale; DE4 2AY Basic one-room stone-built local with friendly colourful atmosphere, beams, pubby furnishings and woodburner, pictures and plenty of bric-a-brac, well kept local ales and real ciders, hearty helpings of food from short daily changing menu (be prepared to share a table), live music Fri and Sat; outside

loos; children and dogs welcome, nice little front terrace, events such as hen racing and world-record-breaking day, popular with UFO enthusiasts, walks from the pub, camping, open all day weekends, closed Mon and lunchtimes Tues-Fri. *(Edward May)*

BONSALL   SK2758
Kings Head (01629) 822703
Yeoman Street; DE4 2AA Welcoming 17th-c stone-built village local with two cosy beamed rooms, pubby furniture including cushioned wall benches, various knick-knacks and china, woodburners, good value home-made food (not Sun or Mon evenings), three Batemans ales; some live music and quiz nights; dogs welcome, seats out at front and in back courtyard, handy for Limestone Way and other walks, closed weekday lunchtimes. *(Richard Stanfield)*

BRACKENFIELD   SK3658
Plough (01629) 534437
A615 Matlock–Alfreton, about a mile NW of Wessington; DE55 6DD Much modernised 16th-c former farmhouse in lovely setting, welcoming three-level beamed bar with cheerful log-effect gas fire, well kept ales and plenty of wines by the glass, good popular food including weekday lunchtime set deal and blackboard specials, appealing lower-level restaurant extension; children welcome, large neatly kept gardens with terrace, closed Mon, otherwise open all day (food till 6pm Sun). *(Mr and Mrs R Shardlow)*

BRASSINGTON   SK2354
★ Olde Gate (01629) 540448
Village signed off B5056 and B5035 NE of Ashbourne; DE4 4HJ Wonderfully unspoilt place – like stepping back in time; mullioned windows, 17th-c kitchen range with gleaming copper pots, a venerable wall clock, rush-seated old chairs and antique settles, beams hung with pewter mugs and shelves lined with Doulton stoneware, panelled Georgian room and, to left of a small hatch-served lobby, a cosy beamed room with stripped panelled settles, scrubbed-top tables and a blazing fire under a huge mantelbeam; Jennings Cumberland and Ringwood Boondoggle, fairly priced food (no credit cards); children and dogs (in bar) welcome, benches in small front yard, garden with tables looking out over pastures, boules, closed Mon, Tues lunchtime, no food Sun evening; landlord leaving last we heard so things may change. *(Ralph Beaumont)*

BUXTON   SK0573
Old Hall (01298) 22841
The Square, almost opposite Opera House; SK17 6BD Large usefully placed historic hotel with bar, wine bar doing good value enjoyable food (all day weekends), various lounges and a more formal restaurant, well kept ales such as Buxton, Sharps and Thornbridge, good choice of

wines by the glass; 38 bedrooms, open all day. *(Brian and Jean Hepworth)*

BUXTON   SK0573

★ **Old Sun** (01298) 23452

High Street; SK17 6HA Charming old building with several cosy and interesting traditional linked areas, well kept Marstons-related ales and good choice of wines by the glass, simple bargain home-made food from good sandwiches up, low beams, bare boards or tiles, soft lighting, old local photographs, open fire; background music and some live acoustic evenings, Sun quiz, no dogs; children till 7pm, roadside garden, open all day. *(Barry Collett, J A Snell, Ann and Tony Bennett-Hughes)*

BUXTON   SK0573

Tap House (01298) 214085

Old Court House, George Street; SK17 6AT Buxton brewery tap with their cask and craft range plus guests, also good selection of bottled beers, wines and spirits, tasty well priced food including some cooked in smoker, various interesting teas and coffees, friendly knowledgeable staff, daily newspapers; children welcome, some outside seating, open all day (till 1am Fri, Sat). *(Michael Mellers)*

BUXWORTH   SK0282

Navigation (01663) 732072

S of village towards Silkhill, off B6062; SK23 7NE Friendly inn by restored canal basin, six well kept ales including Timothy Taylors Landlord and Thwaites Wainwright, good value pubby food from sandwiches up, cheery welcoming staff, linked low-ceilinged rooms, canalia, brassware and old photographs, open fires, games room with pool and darts; background music, Thurs quiz; children allowed away from main bar, dogs in some areas, disabled access, tables on sunken flagstoned terrace, play area, five bedrooms, breakfast 8-11am (non-residents welcome), open all day. *(Edward May)*

CALVER   SK2374

Derwentwater Arms (01433) 639211

In centre, bear left from Main Street into Folds Head; Low Side; S32 3XQ Elevated stone-built village pub under newish licensees, big windows looking down across car park to cricket pitch, good fairly priced pubby food from lunchtime baguettes to daily specials, three well kept ales including Adnams and Peak, friendly helpful service; children, walkers and dogs (in bar) welcome, terraces on slopes below (disabled access from back car park), open all day weekends. *(Brian and Anna Marsden)*

CASTLETON   SK1582

Bulls Head (01433) 620256

Cross Street (A6187); S33 8WH Imposing building spreading through several attractive linked areas, handsome panelling and

pictures, appealing mix of comfortable seating including sofas and easy chairs, heavy drapes and coal fires, well kept Robinsons ales, popular food from sandwiches and hot ciabattas to pub standards and specials, helpful friendly service; background music, no dogs; some roadside picnic-sets, five bedrooms, open (and food) all day. *(Lindy Andrews)*

CASTLETON   SK1482

★ **George** (01433) 620238

Castle Street; S33 8WG Busy but relaxed old pub with flagstoned bar and restaurant, well kept Courage Best and other Charles Wells ales, good choice of malts, enjoyable reasonably priced pub food including range of home-made pies, friendly staff, ancient beams and stripped stone, copper and brass, log fires; children and dogs welcome, tables out at front and behind, castle views, good walks, bedrooms, open all day (food all day Sat, till 6pm Sun). *(Lindy Andrews)*

CASTLETON   SK1583

Olde Cheshire Cheese

(01433) 620330 *How Lane; S33 8WJ* Family-run 17th-c inn with two linked beamed and carpeted areas, cosy and spotless, ales such as Acorn, Bradfield and Peak, good range of reasonably priced wholesome food and decent house wines, quick friendly service, two gas woodburners, lots of photographs, toby jugs, plates and brassware, back dining room where children welcome; background music, free wi-fi; dogs allowed in bar, ten bedrooms, parking across road, open (and food) all day. *(Dennis Jones)*

CASTLETON   SK1582

★ **Olde Nags Head** (01433) 620248

Cross Street (A6187); S33 8WH Small solidly built hotel dating from the 17th c, interesting antique oak furniture and coal fire in civilised beamed and flagstoned bar, adjoining snug with leather sofas, steps down to restaurant, well kept Black Sheep, Sharps Doom Bar and guests, nice coffee and good locally sourced food, friendly helpful staff; live music Sat; children and dogs (in bar) welcome, nine comfortable bedrooms, good breakfast, open all day. *(Steve and Suzanne Griffiths)*

CHESTERFIELD   SK3871

Chesterfield Arms (01246) 236634

Newbold Road (B6051); S41 7PH Friendly 19th-c pub with 12 or more real ales including Everards and three from own microbrewery (regular beer festivals), also craft beers, six ciders and good choice of wines and whiskies, basic snacks along with pie and curry nights, open fire, oak panelling and stripped wood/flagstoned floors, conservatory linking barn room; Wed quiz, monthly live music; outside tables on decking, open all day (from 4pm Mon-Weds). *(P Dawn)*

CHESTERFIELD   SK3671

Manor (01246) 237555

Old Road; near the school; S40 3QT
Converted manor house down tree-lined
drive, bar with tartan-upholstered armchairs
by open fire, high stools around equally high
tables, leather banquettes down one side
creating booths, wood and flagstoned floors
with chequered tiles by servery, ales such
as Brampton and Peak, second room with
tartan wall seating and a wide mix of dining
chairs, good range of food from sandwiches
and sharing plates up including Sun carvery
and themed evenings, friendly staff; quiz and
music nights, fruit machine, TV; children
welcome, tables under big parasols on front
terrace, second terrace by play area, open
all day. *(John and Mary Warner)*

CHESTERFIELD   SK3670

Rose & Crown (01246) 563750

Old Road; S40 2QT Popular Brampton
Brewery pub with their full range plus
Everards and two changing guests, Weston's
cider, enjoyable home-made food (not
weekend evenings) from baguettes up,
helpful staff and hands-on landlord, spacious
traditional refurbishment with leather
banquettes, panelling, carpet or wood floors,
brewery memorabilia and cast-iron Victorian
fireplace, cosy snug area; Tues quiz, trad jazz
first Sun of month, free wi-fi; tables outside,
open all day. *(Trevor Cooper)*

CHINLEY   SK0482

Paper Mill (01663) 750529

Whitehough Head Lane; SK23 6EJ Under
same management as next door Old Hall
(see Main Entries); good selection of
ales, craft kegs such as Thornbridge and
plenty of bottled belgian beers, simple bar
snacks including cheeseboards and mini
ploughman's, also a raclette room (must book
in advance – minimum eight people), good
choice of teas and coffees, friendly helpful
young staff, flagstones, woodburners and
open fire, local artwork for sale; TV for major
sporting events; children, walkers and dogs
welcome, seats out at front and on split-level
back terrace, plenty of good local walks, four
bedrooms, closed weekdays till 5pm, open all
day weekends. *(Sally Barnett, Richard Newman,
Elizabeth Land, Sue Kennerley, James Cadman,
T Matthews)*

CLIFTON   SK1645

Cock (01335) 342654

Cross Side, opposite church; DE6 2GJ
Unpretentious two-bar beamed village local,
comfortable and friendly, with jovial landlord,
enjoyable reasonably priced home-made pub
food from baguettes up, well kept Marstons
Pedigree, Timothy Taylors Landlord and a
couple of guests, decent choice of wines
by the glass, separate dining room, darts,
quiz first Tues of month; children, dogs
and walkers welcome, garden with play

equipment, closed Mon lunchtime.
(Pete and Jan Woods)

COMBS   SK0378

Beehive (01298) 812758

*Village signposted off B5470 W of
Chapel-en-le-Frith; SK23 9UT* Roomy,
neat and comfortable, with emphasis on
good freshly made food (all day Sun) from
baguettes to steaks and interesting specials,
also very good value weekday set menu,
ales including Marstons Pedigree and a
house beer from Wychwood, good choice of
wines by the glass, log fire, heavy beams and
copperware; background music, TV, Tues
quiz; plenty of tables out in front, by lovely
valley tucked away from main road, good
walks, one-bed holiday cottage next door,
open all day. *(John and Mary Warner)*

CRICH   SK3454

Cliff (01773) 852444

Cromford Road, Town End; DE4 5DP
Unpretentious little two-room roadside pub,
well kept ales such as Blue Monkey, Buxton,
Dancing Duck and Sharps, straightforward
reasonably priced food (not weekend
evenings or Mon), welcoming staff and
friendly regulars, two woodburners; maybe
Sun folk night; children and dogs welcome,
great views and walks, handy for National
Tramway Museum, open all day weekends,
closed weekday lunchtimes. *(Anon)*

CROWDECOTE   SK1065

Packhorse (01298) 83618

B5055 W of Bakewell; SK17 0DB Small
three-room 16th-c pub in lovely setting,
welcoming landlord and staff, good
reasonably priced home-made food from
weekday light bites and sandwiches up, four
well kept changing ales, split-level interior
with brick or carpeted floors, stripped-stone
walls, open fire and two woodburners, pool
room; tables out behind, beautiful views and
a popular walking route, closed Mon, Tues.
(Jo Garnett)

DERBY   SK3538

Abbey Inn (01332) 558297

Darley Street; DE22 1DX Former abbey
gatehouse opposite Derwent-side park
(pleasant riverside walk from centre),
massive 15th-c or older stonework remnants,
brick floor, studded oak doors, coal fire in
big inglenook, stone spiral staircase to upper
bar (open weekends and evenings Tues, Fri)
with oak rafters and tapestries, bargain Sam
Smiths and reasonably priced bar food; the
lavatories with their beams, stonework and
tiles are worth a look too; children and dogs
(downstairs) welcome, open all day.
(Jo Garnett)

DERBY   SK3635

Alexandra (01332) 293993

Siddals Road; DE1 2QE Imposing
Victorian pub, popular locally; two simple

rooms with traditional furnishings on bare boards or carpet, railway prints/memorabilia, well kept Castle Rock and several quickly changing microbrewery guests, lots of continental bottled beers with more on tap, snack food such as pork pies and cobs; background music; children and dogs welcome, nicely planted backyard, 1960s locomotive cab in car park, four bedrooms, open all day. *(P Dawn)*

DERBY   SK3535
Babington Arms (01332) 383647
Babington Lane; DE1 1TA Large open-plan Wetherspoons with 16 real ales and four proper ciders, good friendly service, usual well priced food, comfortable seating with steps up to relaxed back area; attractive verandah, open all day from 8am for breakfast. *(Edward May)*

DERBY   SK3536
Brewery Tap (01332) 366283
Derwent Street/Exeter Place; DE1 2ED 19th-c Derby Brewing Co pub (aka Royal Standard) with unusual bowed end, ten ales including five of their own from curved brick counter, lots of bottled imports, decent good value food all day (till 5pm Sun) from sandwiches and baked potatoes up, open-plan bare-boards interior with two high-ceilinged drinking areas, small upstairs room and roof terrace overlooking the Derwent; live music Tues; open all day (till 1am Fri, Sat). *(P Dawn)*

DERBY   SK3635
Brunswick (01332) 290677
Railway Terrace; close to Derby Midland Station; DE1 2RU One of Britain's oldest railwaymen's pubs, up to 16 ales including Everards and selection from own microbrewery, real ciders and good choice of bottled beers, cheap traditional lunchtime food, high-ceilinged panelled bar, snug with coal fire, chatty front parlour, interesting old train photographs and prints; quiz Mon, jazz upstairs Thurs, darts, TV, games machine, free wi-fi; dogs welcome, walled beer garden and side terrace, open all day. *(P Dawn)*

DERBY   SK3435
Exeter Arms (01332) 605323
Exeter Place; DE1 2EU Victorian survivor amid 1930s apartment blocks and car parks; recently extended into next-door cottage, but keeping its traditional character including tiled-floor snug with curved wall benches and polished open range, friendly staff, well kept Dancing Duck, Marstons and two guests, good pubby food with a twist served all day (till 6pm Sun); quiz Mon, summer live music Sat in small garden with outside bar (beer

festivals), open all day (till midnight Fri, Sat). *(P Dawn)*

DERBY   SK3534
Falstaff (01332) 342902
Silver Hill Road, off Normanton Road; DE23 6UJ Big friendly Victorian pub (aka the Folly) brewing its own good value ales, main bar with new slate floor and log-effect gas fire, left-hand bar with games, coal fire and brewery memorabilia in quieter lounge; open all day. *(Richard Stanfield)*

DERBY   SK3436
Five Lamps (01332) 348730
Duffield Road; DE1 3BH Corner pub with opened-up but well divided interior around central servery, wood-strip or carpeted floors, panelling, leather button-back bench seats, small balustraded raised section, a dozen well kept local ales such as Buxton, Everards, Oakham, Peak, Whim and a house beer from Derby, real ciders, decent good value pubby food (not Sun evening); background music, TV, games machines; a few picnic-sets outside, open all day (till midnight Fri, Sat). *(P Dawn)*

DERBY   SK3536
Olde Dolphin (01332) 267711
Queen Street; DE1 3DL Quaint 16th-c timber-framed pub just below cathedral, four small dark unpretentious rooms including appealing snug, big bowed black beams, shiny panelling, opaque leaded windows, lantern lights and coal fires, half a dozen predominantly mainstream ales, reasonably priced bar food and upstairs evening steak restaurant (Thurs-Sat); quiz nights; no under-14s inside, sizeable outside area for drinkers/smokers, open all day. *(P Dawn)*

DERBY   SK3335
Rowditch (01332) 343123
Uttoxeter New Road (A516); DE22 3LL Popular character local with own microbrewery, well kept Marstons Pedigree and guests too, country wines, friendly landlord, attractive small snug on right, coal fire, pianist first and third Sat of month; no children or dogs; pleasant back garden, closed weekday lunchtimes. *(Jo Garnett)*

DERBY   SK3536
Silk Mill (01332) 349160
Full Street; DE1 3AF Refurbished 1920s pub keeping traditional feel, central bar with lounge and skylit dining area off, plush banquettes, cushioned stools and cast-iron-framed tables on wood floors, open fires, one or two quirky touches such as fish wallpaper, a stuffed crocodile and antler chandelier, good choice of real ales and ciders, several

---

Post Office address codings confusingly give the impression that a few pubs are in Derbyshire, when they're really in Cheshire (which is where we list them).

wines by the glass, enjoyable food (all day Sat, till 6pm Sun) from sandwiches and sharing boards up, friendly service; Weds folk night, daily newspapers and free wi-fi; open all day. *(P Dawn)*

DUFFIELD   SK3543
Pattern Makers Arms
(01332) 842844 *Crown Street, off King Street; DE56 4EY* Welcoming Edwardian backstreet local with well kept Bass (from the jug), Marstons, Timothy Taylors and guests, (under-10s eat free Mon-Sat), pubby furniture on wood or carpeted floors, upholstered banquettes, some stained-glass and etched windows, darts, pool and other games, Sun quiz; background music, TV; beer garden behind, open all day Fri-Sun. *(Andrew Bosi)*

EARL STERNDALE   SK0966
★ **Quiet Woman** (01298) 83211
Village signed off B5053 S of Buxton; SK17 0BU Old-fashioned unchanging country local in lovely Peak District countryside, simple beamed interior with plain furniture on quarry tiles, china ornaments and coal fire, well kept Marstons Bitter and guests, own-label bottled beers (available in gift packs), good pork pies, family room with pool, skittles and darts; picnic-sets out in front along with budgies, hens, ducks and donkeys, you can buy free-range eggs, local poetry books and even hay, good hikes across nearby Dove Valley towards Longnor and Hollinsclough, small campsite next door, caravan for hire. *(Barry Collett, Ann and Tony Bennett-Hughes)*

EDALE   SK1285
Old Nags Head (01433) 670291
Off A625 E of Chapel-en-le-Frith; Grindsbrook Booth; S33 7ZD Relaxed well used traditional pub at start of Pennine Way, food from sandwiches up including carvery, four well kept local ales, friendly service, log fire, flagstoned area for booted walkers, airy back family room; TV, pool and darts; dogs welcome, front terrace and garden, two self-catering cottages, closed Mon and Tues out of season, otherwise open all day, can get very busy weekends. *(Emma Scofield)*

EDLASTON   SK1842
Shire Horse (01335) 342714
Off A515 S of Ashbourne, just beside Wyaston; DE6 2DQ Timbered pub with good mix of drinkers and diners in large bar with open fire and separate restaurant/conservatory, friendly helpful staff, popular fairly priced food (not Sun evening) including specials board, Marstons Pedigree and Sharps Doom Bar, good house wines; children and dogs (in bar) welcome, tables out in front and in back garden with terrace, peaceful spot, nice views, open all day Sun. *(Stephen Green, Colin Bateman)*

ELMTON   SK5073
★ **Elm Tree** (01909) 721261
Off B6417 S of Clowne; S80 4LS Softly lit popular country pub doing well under enthusiastic owners, good choice of food all day (till 6pm Sun) from simple inexpensive dishes up, weekday lunchtime set menu, well kept Black Sheep plus one or two guests, wide choice of wines, quick friendly service, stripped stone and panelling, log fire, back barn restaurant (mainly for functions); children and dogs welcome, garden tables, play area, closed Tues. *(Mr and Mrs R Shardlow, Derek and Sylvia Stephenson)*

ELTON   SK2260
★ **Duke of York** (01629) 650367
Village signed off B5056 W of Matlock; Main Street; DE4 2BW Unspoilt local kept spotless by long-serving amiable landlady (here since 1968) and now helped by her nephew; bargain Marstons Burton Bitter, lovely little quarry-tiled back tap room with coal fire in massive fireplace, glazed bar and hatch to corridor, prints and more fires in the two front rooms – one with pool table, the other with darts and dominoes, friendly chatty locals; outside lavatories; children and dogs welcome, charming village, open 8.45pm-11pm and Sun lunchtime, closed Mon, no food. *(Anon)*

FOOLOW   SK1976
★ **Bulls Head** (01433) 630873
Village signposted off A623 Baslow–Tideswell; S32 5QR Friendly pub by green in pretty upland village; simply furnished flagstoned bar with interesting collection of photographs including some saucy Edwardian ones, Black Sheep, Peak and two guests, over 30 malts, good food (all day Sun) with more elaborate evening choices, OAP weekday lunch deal, step down to former stables with high ceiling joists, stripped stone and woodburner, sedate partly panelled dining room with plates on delft shelves; background music (live Fri evening); children, walkers and dogs welcome (resident westies Holly and Jack, and shih tzu Daisy), side picnic-sets with nice views, paths from here out over rolling pasture enclosed by dry stone walls, three refurbished bedrooms, closed Mon. *(Dr Kevan Tucker, Ann and Tony Bennett-Hughes)*

FROGGATT EDGE   SK2476
★ **Chequers** (01433) 630231
A625, off A623 N of Bakewell; S32 3ZJ Roadside country dining pub with opened-up bar and eating areas, cushioned settles, farmhouse and captain's chairs around mix of tables, antique prints, longcase clock and woodburner, well liked interesting food (all day weekends) along with more traditional choices, home-made chutneys and preserves for sale, Bradfield, Peak and a guest ale, eight wines by the glass, friendly helpful

staff; background music; children welcome, no dogs inside, garden with Froggatt Edge up through woods behind, six comfortable clean bedrooms, good breakfast, open all day. *(Stephen Shepherd)*

FROGGATT EDGE   SK2577
Grouse (01433) 630423
Longshaw, off B6054 NE of Froggatt; S11 7TZ Nicely old-fashioned beamed pub in same family since 1965, carpeted front bar with wall benches and other seating, log fire, back bar with coal-effect gas fire, small conservatory, enjoyable hearty home-made food (all day Sun, not Mon evening) from nice sandwiches to blackboard specials, four well kept Marstons-related beers and over 40 malt whiskies, friendly prompt service; children and dogs welcome, terrace seating, lovely views and good moorland walks, open all day weekends. *(Peter Pilbeam)*

GLOSSOP   SK0394
Star (01457) 853072
Howard Street; SK13 7DD Unpretentious corner alehouse opposite station with four well kept changing ales and Weston's Old Rosie cider, no food (you can bring your own), interesting layout including flagstoned tap room with hatch service, old local photographs; background music; resident alsatian Heidi, open all day from 4pm (2pm Thurs, Fri, noon Sat, Sun). *(Emma Scofield)*

HARDWICK HALL   SK4663
★ Hardwick Inn (01246) 850245
Quite handy for M1 junction 29; S44 5QJ Popular golden-stone pub dating from the 15th c at the south gate of park of Hardwick Hall (NT); several linked rooms including proper bar, open fires, fine range of some 220 malt whiskies and plenty of wines by the glass, well kept Black Sheep, Peak, Theakstons and a Brampton ale badged for the pub, generous helpings of good reasonably priced bar food including excellent ploughman's, carvery restaurant, long-serving licensees and efficient friendly staff; unobtrusive background music; children allowed away from bar areas, dogs in one part, tables out at front and in pleasant back garden, open all day. *(Edward Mirzoeff, Derek and Sylvia Stephenson)*

HARTINGTON   SK1260
Charles Cotton (01298) 84229
Market Place; SK17 0AL Popular stone-built hotel in attractive village centre; large comfortable bar-bistro with open fire, enjoyable food from lunchtime sandwiches and snacks up (more restauranty evening choice), up to five ales including local Whim, bottled beers and real cider, nice wines and italian coffee, friendly helpful service, restaurant and summer tearoom; background and some live music; children, walkers and dogs (in bar) welcome, seats out at front

and in small back garden, 17 bedrooms, open all day. *(Peter Pilbeam)*

HARTINGTON   SK1260
Devonshire Arms (01298) 84232
Market Place; SK17 0AL Traditional unpretentious two-bar pub in attractive village, welcoming and cheerful, with good generous home-made food (smaller helpings available), ales such as Marstons Pedigree, log fires; maybe background music; children and dogs welcome, tables out in front facing duck pond, more in small garden, good walks, open (and food) all day weekends. *(Alan Johnson, Steve and Suzanne Griffiths)*

HATHERSAGE   SK2381
★ Scotsmans Pack (01433) 650253
School Lane, off A6187; S32 1BZ Bustling inn equally popular with drinkers and diners; dark panelled rooms with lots of interesting knick-knacks, upholstered gingham stools and dining chairs, cushioned wall seats and assortment of tables, woodburner, five well kept Marstons-related ales, enjoyable food including daily specials board; background music (live first Fri of month), TV, darts; picnic-sets on terrace overlooking trout stream, plenty of surrounding walks, bedrooms, open (and food) all day in summer, all day Fri-Sun in winter. *(Dennis Jones)*

HEAGE   SK3750
Black Boy (01773) 856799
Old Road (B6013); DE56 2BN Village pub-restaurant with welcoming licensees, popular good value food including fish specials in bar and upstairs dining area, a house beer brewed by Marstons and well kept regularly changing guests, upholstered settles, decorative copperware and jugs, open fire; TV for major sports events, no dogs; children welcome, small outside seating area, open all day. *(John Beeken)*

HOGNASTON   SK2350
★ Red Lion (01335) 370396
Off B5035 Ashbourne–Wirksworth; DE6 1PR Traditional 17th-c village inn with open-plan beamed bar, three fires, attractive mix of old tables, curved settles and other seats on ancient flagstones, friendly licensees, enjoyable well presented home-made food from shortish menu in bar and conservatory restaurant, nice wines by the glass, Marstons Pedigree and guests; background music; picnic-sets in field behind, boules, handy for Carsington Water, three good bedrooms, big breakfast. *(Anon)*

HOLBROOK   SK3645
★ Dead Poets (01332) 780301
Chapel Street; village signed off A6 S of Belper; DE56 0TQ Unchanging drinkers' local with up to nine ales including Everards (some served from jugs), real cider and country wines, filled cobs and good value

weekday bar food, simple cottagey décor with beams, stripped-stone walls and broad flagstones, high-backed settles forming booths, big log fire, plenty of tucked-away corners, woodburner in snug, children allowed in back conservatory till 8pm; quiet background music, no credit cards; dogs welcome, seats out at back, open all day Fri-Sun. *(Peter Pilbeam)*

HOPE   SK1783

★**Cheshire Cheese** (01433) 620381

Off A6187, towards Edale; S33 6ZF
16th-c traditional stone inn with snug oak-beamed rooms on different levels, open fires, red carpets or stone floors, straightforward furnishings and gleaming brasses, friendly staff serving up to four ales including Bradfield and Peak, a dozen malts, pubby food from sandwiches up; Weds quiz, folk night first and third Thurs of month; children welcome, dogs allowed in bar, good local walks in the summits of Lose Hill and Win Hill or the cave district around Castleton, four bedrooms, limited parking, open all day weekends in summer, closed Mon.
(John Wooll, Dennis Jones, David Carr)

HORSLEY WOODHOUSE   SK3944

Old Oak (01332) 881299

Main Street (A609 Belper–Ilkeston); DE7 6AW Busy roadside local linked to nearby Bottle Brook and Leadmill microbreweries, their ales and guests plus weekend back bar with another eight well priced beers tapped from the cask, farm ciders, basic snacks (can also bring your own food), beamed rooms with blazing coal fires, chatty friendly atmosphere, occasional live music; children and dogs welcome, hatch to covered courtyard tables, nice views, closed weekday lunchtimes till 4pm, open all day weekends. *(Jo Garnett)*

ILKESTON   SK4742

Dewdrop (0115) 932 9684

Station Street, Ilkeston junction, off A6096; DE7 5TE Large Victorian red-brick corner local in old industrial area, not strong on bar comfort but popular for its well kept beers (up to eight) such as Bobs, Blue Monkey and Oakham, simple bar snacks, back lounge with fire and piano, connecting lobby to front public bar with pool, darts and TV, some Barnes Wallis memorabilia; sheltered outside seating at back, walks by former Nottingham Canal, open all day weekends, closed weekday lunchtimes.
(P Dawn)

ILKESTON   SK4641

Spanish Bar (0115) 930 8666

South Street; DE7 5QJ Busy bar with half a dozen well kept/priced ales, traditional ciders and bottled belgian beers, friendly efficient staff, evening overspill room; Tues quiz night; small back garden and skittle alley, open all day. *(P Dawn)*

LITTLE EATON   SK3641

Queens Head (01332) 986065

Alfreton Road; DE21 5DF Stone-built beamed former coaching inn, well kept Derby Brewery beers plus a couple of guests, enjoyable home-made food from sharing plates up, good service and relaxing atmosphere; occasional live acoustic music; café-style furniture on partly covered terrace, open all day. *(Derek and Sylvia Stephenson)*

LITTLE LONGSTONE   SK1971

Packhorse (01629) 640471

Off A6 NW of Bakewell via Monsal Dale; DE45 1NN Three comfortable linked beamed rooms, pine tables on flagstones, well kept Thornbridge ales and a guest, popular locally sourced food from daily changing blackboard, good value wine list, coal fires; Thurs quiz; children, dogs and hikers welcome (on Monsal Trail), terrace in steep little back garden, open (and food) all day weekends. *(Ann and Tony Bennett-Hughes)*

LITTON   SK1675

Red Lion (01298) 871458

Village signposted off A623, between B6465 and B6049 junctions; also signposted off B6049; SK17 8QU New landlady for this traditional village pub, two linked front rooms with low beams, panelling and open fires, bigger stripped-stone back room, three real ales, enjoyable home-made food from sandwiches to daily specials; dogs allowed, seats and tables in front with more on village green, good walks in nearby Dales, open (and food) all day. *(Alan Johnson, Dennis Jones, Brian and Anna Marsden)*

LULLINGTON   SK2513

Colvile Arms (01827) 373212

Off A444 S of Burton; Main Street; DE12 8EG Popular 18th-c village pub with high-backed settles in simple panelled bar, cosy comfortable beamed lounge, pleasant atmosphere and friendly staff, well kept Bass, Marstons Pedigree and a guest, no food except cobs; soft background music; picnic-sets on small sheltered back lawn, closed lunchtimes apart from Sun. *(Carol and Barry Craddock)*

MAKENEY   SK3544

★**Holly Bush** (01332) 841729

From A6 heading N after Duffield, take first right after crossing River Derwent, then first left; DE56 0RX Down-to-earth two-bar village pub (former farmhouse) with three blazing coal fires (one in old-fashioned range by snug's curved high-backed settle), flagstones, beams, black panelling and tiled floors, lots of brewing advertisements, half a dozen or so well kept changing ales (some brought from cellar in jugs), real cider, cheap food including rolls and pork pies, may be local cheeses for sale, games lobby with hatch service (children allowed here), regular beer festivals; picnic-sets outside, walkers and dogs welcome, open all day. *(Cliff Sparkes)*

MATLOCK SK2960
Thorn Tree (01629) 580295
Jackson Road, Matlock Bank; DE4 3JQ Superb valley views to Riber Castle from this homely 19th-c stone-built local, Bass, Greene King, Timothy Taylors Landlord and four guests, simple well cooked food (Tues-Fri lunchtimes, Sun 5-6.30pm, Weds pie night), friendly staff and regulars; free wi-fi; dogs welcome, closed Mon lunchtime, open all day Fri-Sun. *(Edward May)*

MELBOURNE SK3825
Blue Bell (01332) 865764
Church Street; DE73 8EJ Chatty pub with well kept Shardlow and other local ales, straightforward reasonably priced food, friendly efficient young staff, main bar with sporting theme, snug, restaurant; sports TVs, pool; dogs welcome, terrace tables, nice setting near church and handy for Melbourne Hall, open all day. *(John Beeken)*

MILFORD SK3545
King William IV (01332) 840842
Milford Bridge; DE56 0RR Friendly and relaxing stone-built pub across from the River Derwent; long room with low beams, bare boards and quarry tiles, old settles and a blazing coal fire, well kept Greene King, Sharps, Timothy Taylors and a couple of guests, simple food; music and quiz nights; dogs welcome, three bedrooms, closed weekday lunchtimes, open all day weekends. *(Carol and Barry Craddock)*

MILLERS DALE SK1473
Anglers Rest (01298) 871323
Just down Litton Lane; pub is PH on OS Sheet 119 map reference 142734; SK17 8SN Creeper-clad pub in lovely quiet riverside setting on Monsal Trail, two bars and dining room, log fires, Adnams, Storm and two usually local guests, enjoyable simple food, cheery helpful service, reasonable prices, darts, pool, muddy walkers and dogs (they have their own) in public bar; children welcome, wonderful gorge views and river walks, self-catering apartment, open all day Sat, till 9pm Sun. *(Ann and Tony Bennett-Hughes)*

MILLTOWN SK3562
Nettle (01246) 590462
Fallgate, Littlemoor; S45 0ES Interesting 16th-c family-run pub with small traditional bar and linked areas behind, a couple of well kept Peak ales and good range of enjoyable locally sourced food from bar snacks up, Sun

---

carvery, beams, stone walls, tartan carpets and log fires, restaurant; children and dogs welcome, tables outside, four bedrooms, good breakfast. *(Lee and Liz Potter)*

MONSAL HEAD SK1871
★**Monsal Head Hotel** (01629) 640250
B6465; DE45 1NL Outstanding hilltop location for this friendly inn, cosy stables bar with stripped timber horse-stalls, harness and brassware, cushioned oak pews, farmhouse chairs and benches on flagstones, big open fire, good selection of mainly local ales including one badged for them from Pennine, german bottled beers and several wines by the glass, enjoyable locally sourced food from lunchtime sandwiches up (they may ask to keep your credit card while you eat), elegant restaurant; children (over 3), well behaved dogs and muddy walkers welcome, big garden, stunning views of Monsal Dale with its huge viaduct, seven comfortable bedrooms, open all day till midnight. *(Emma Scofield, Edward May, Kay and Alistair Butler)*

MONYASH SK1566
★**Bulls Head** (01629) 812372
B5055 W of Bakewell; DE45 1JH Rambling stone pub with high-ceilinged rooms, straightforward traditional furnishings including plush stools lined along bar, horse pictures and a shelf of china, log fire, Black Sheep and a couple of guests, restaurant with high-backed dining chairs on heated stone floor, popular fairly traditional food (all day weekends) from sandwiches and baked potatoes up, friendly service, small back room with darts, board games and pool; background music; children and dogs welcome, plenty of picnic-sets under parasols in big garden, gate leading to well equipped public play area, good surrounding walks, open all day Fri-Sun. *(Derek and Sylvia Stephenson)*

MOORWOOD MOOR SK3656
White Hart (01629) 534888
Inns Lane; village signed from South Wingfield; DE55 7NU Cleanly refurbished country inn with good food including deals in bar and restaurant, helpful attentive staff, well kept Sharps Doom Bar, Timothy Taylors Landlord and a couple of local guests; children welcome, ten modern bedrooms, open (and food) all day. *(Derek and Sylvia Stephenson)*

NEW MILLS SJ9886
Fox (0161) 427 1634
Brook Bottom Road; SK22 3AY Tucked-away unmodernised country local at end of single-track road, Robinsons ales and good

---

Though we don't usually mention it in the text, most pubs will now make coffee or tea – it's always worth asking.

value basic food (not Tues evening) including sandwiches, log fire, darts and pool; no credit cards; children and dogs welcome, lots of tables outside, good walking area, open all day Fri-Sun. *(Carol and Barry Craddock)*

NEWTON SOLNEY   SK2825
Brickmakers Arms (01283) 703170
Main Street (B5008 NE of Burton); DE15 0SJ Friendly end-of-terrace beamed village pub owned by Burton Bridge Brewery; their ales kept well and occasional guests, plenty of bottled beers too, no food, two rooms off bar, one with original panelling and delft shelf displaying jugs and plates, pubby furniture, built-in wall seats and open fires, area with piano and books, also a little shop; Mon quiz; tables on terrace, open all day weekends, closed lunchtimes during the week. *(Anon)*

OCKBROOK   SK4236
Royal Oak (01332) 662378
Off B6096 just outside Spondon; Green Lane; DE72 3SE 18th-c village local run by same friendly family since 1953, good value honest food (not weekend evenings) from good lunchtime cobs to steaks, well kept Bass and interesting guest beers, tile-floored tap room, carpeted snug, inner bar with Victorian prints, larger and lighter side room, nice old settle in entrance corridor, open fires, darts and dominoes, some live music; children welcome, dogs in the evening, sheltered cottage garden and cobbled front courtyard, separate play area, open all day weekends. *(Lindy Andrews)*

OSMASTON   SK1943
Shoulder of Mutton (01335) 342371
Off A52 SE of Ashbourne; DE6 1LW Down-to-earth red-brick beamed pub with three well kept ales including Marstons Pedigree, enjoyable generous home-made food, good friendly service, post office and shop; picnic-sets in attractive garden, farmland views, peaceful pretty village with thatched cottages, duck pond and good walks. *(Anon)*

PARWICH   SK1854
★Sycamore (01335) 390212
By church; DE6 1QL Chatty old country pub well run by cheerful welcoming landlady, Robinsons ales and good honest home-made food, log fire in neat traditional back bar, pool in small front hatch-served games room, another room serving as proper village shop; children welcome, tables in front courtyard, picnic-sets on neat side grass, good walks, open all day weekends. *(Carol and Barry Craddock)*

PILSLEY   SK2371
★Devonshire Arms (01246) 583258;
bedroom bookings (01756) 718111
Village signposted off A619 W of Baslow, and pub just below B6048; High Street;

DE45 1UL Civilised little country inn on the Chatsworth Estate; gentle contemporary slant with flagstoned bar and several fairly compact areas off (each with own character), log fires in stone fireplaces, comfortable seating and big modern paintings, four local ales and several wines by the glass, food from lunchtime open sandwiches up using Estate produce; children welcome, a few tables outside, Chatsworth farm shop at the top of lane, bedrooms, open all day. *(Malcolm and Pauline Pellatt)*

REPTON   SK3026
Bulls Head (01283) 704422
High Street; DE65 6GF Lively village pub with interesting décor in various interconnecting bars, beams and pillars, mix of wooden dining chairs, settles and built-in wall seats with scatter cushions, squashy sofas, bare boards, flagstones and log fires, driftwood sculptures, animal hide décor and an arty bull's head, ales from Marstons, Shardlow and Purity, 15 wines by the glass and 20 malt whiskies, popular food including wood-fired pizzas, cheerful staff, upstairs restaurant; background music, free wi-fi; children and dogs (in bar) welcome, sizeable heated terrace with neatly set tables and chairs under big parasols, open (and food) all day. *(Stephen Shepherd)*

RIPLEY   SK3950
Talbot Taphouse (01773) 742626
Butterley Hill; DE5 3LT Full range of local Amber ales and changing guests kept well by knowledgeable landlord, also traditional ciders, draught belgian and bottled beers, long narrow panelled room with comfy chairs, open fire in brick fireplace, bar billiards and table skittles, friendly atmosphere; open all day Fri-Sun, from 5pm other days. *(Jo Garnett)*

ROWSLEY   SK2565
★Peacock (01629) 733518
Bakewell Road; DE4 2EB Civilised small 17th-c country hotel, comfortable seating in spacious modern lounge, inner bar with log fire, bare stone walls and some Robert 'Mouseman' Thompson furniture, good if not cheap food from lunchtime sandwiches to restaurant meals, Peak ales, nice wines and well served coffee, pleasant helpful staff; attractive riverside gardens, trout fishing, 14 good bedrooms. *(Peter Pilbeam)*

SHARDLOW   SK4430
Malt Shovel (01332) 792066
3.5 miles from M1 junction 24, via A6 towards Derby; The Wharf; DE72 2HG Canalside pub in 18th-c former maltings, interesting odd-angled layout with cosy corners, Marstons-related ales, good value tasty home-made food from lunchtime sandwiches and baked potatoes up (evening food Thurs only), quick friendly service, beams, panelling and central open fire; live

music Sun, free wi-fi; dogs welcome, lots of terrace tables by Trent & Mersey Canal, pretty hanging baskets, open all day. *(Anon)*

SHARDLOW   SK4429
Old Crown (01332) 792392
Off A50 just W of M1 junction 24; Cavendish Bridge, E of village; DE72 2HL Good value pub with half a dozen well kept Marstons-related ales and decent choice of malt whiskies, pubby food (not Sun evening, Mon) from sandwiches and baguettes up, beams with masses of jugs and mugs, walls covered with other bric-a-brac and breweriana, big inglenook; quiz Mon, fortnightly live music Tues; children and dogs welcome, garden with play area, open all day. *(Stephen Shepherd)*

SHELDON   SK1768
★**Cock & Pullet** (01629) 814292
Village signed off A6 just W of Ashford; DE45 1QS Charming no-frills village pub with low beams, exposed stonework, flagstones and open fire, cheerful mismatch of furnishings, large collection of clocks and various representations of poultry (some stuffed), well kept Black Sheep, Sharps and Timothy Taylors, good simple food from shortish menu, reasonable prices and nice staff, pool and TV in plainer public bar; quiet background music, no credit cards; children and dogs welcome, seats and water feature on pleasant back terrace, pretty village just off Limestone Way and popular all year with walkers, clean bedrooms, open all day. *(Ann and Tony Bennett-Hughes)*

SHIRLEY   SK2141
Saracens Head (01335) 360330
Church Lane; DE6 3AS Modernised late 18th-c dining pub in attractive village; good range of interesting well presented food from pubby to more expensive restaurant dishes, four Greene King ales, speciality coffees, simple country-style dining furniture and two pretty working art nouveau fireplaces; background music; children and dogs (in bar area) welcome, picnic-sets out in front and on back terrace, self-catering cottage, open all day Sun. *(Carol and Barry Craddock)*

SMISBY   SK3419
Smisby Arms (01530) 412677
Nelsons Square; LE65 2UA Low-beamed village local serving generous helpings of good reasonably priced food, friendly helpful service, two well kept changing ales, bright little dining extension down steps; children welcome, no dogs, a few tables out in front, open all day Sun. *(Edward May)*

STONEDGE   SK3367
Red Lion (01246) 566142
Darley Road (B5057); S45 0LW Revamped bar-bistro (former 17th-c coaching inn) on edge of the Peak District; good attractively presented food from sandwiches

up using local ingredients including own vegetables, real ales and good choice of wines, bare stone walls, flagstones and wood floors, some substantial timbers, lounge area with comfortable seating and open fire; picnic-sets out under parasols at back, 27 bedrooms in adjacent modern hotel, open all day. *(John and Mary Warner)*

SUDBURY   SK1632
Vernon Arms (01283) 585329
Off A50/A515; Main Road; DE6 5HS Rambling 17th-c pub with enjoyable reasonably priced food including good Sun roasts, four Marstons-related ales, friendly service (may slow at busy times), three main rooms with stairs to bar; background music; children welcome, good big garden, handy for Sudbury Hall (NT), open all day. *(Dennis Jones)*

SUTTON CUM DUCKMANTON   SK4371
Arkwright Arms (01246) 232053
A632 Bolsover–Chesterfield; S44 5JG Friendly mock-Tudor pub with bar, pool room (dogs allowed here) and dining room, all with real fires, good choice of well priced food (not Sun evening), up to 16 changing ales, ten real ciders and four perries (beer/cider festivals Easter/Aug bank holidays); TV, games machine; children welcome, seats out at front and on side terrace, attractive hanging baskets, play equipment, open all day. *(Emma Scofield)*

TICKNALL   SK3523
★**Wheel** (01332) 864488
Main Street (A514); DE73 7JZ Stylish contemporary décor in bar and upstairs restaurant, enjoyable interesting home-made food (all day weekends) including daily specials, friendly attentive staff, well kept Marstons Pedigree and a guest; children welcome, no dogs inside, nice outside area with café tables on raised deck, near entrance to Calke Abbey (NT). *(John and Mary Warner)*

TIDESWELL   SK1575
Horse & Jockey (01298) 872211
Queen Street; SK17 8JZ Friendly and relaxed family-run local reworked in old-fashioned style, with beams, flagstones, cushioned wall benches and coal fire in small public bar's traditional open range, bare boards, button-back banquettes and woodburner in lounge, Sharps, Tetleys and a couple of local guests, decent modestly priced food, stripped-stone dining room; children and dogs welcome, five bedrooms, good walks, open all day. *(Derek and Sylvia Stephenson)*

WARDLOW   SK1875
★**Three Stags Heads** (01298) 872268
Wardlow Mires; A623/B6465; SK17 8RW Basic unchanging pub (17th-c longhouse)

of great individuality, flagstoned floors, old country furniture, heating from cast-iron kitchen ranges, old photographs, long-serving plain-talking landlord, locals in favourite corners, well kept Abbeydale ales including house beer Black Lurcher (brewed at a hefty 8% ABV), lots of bottled beers, hearty seasonal food on home-made plates (licensees are potters and have a small gallery), may be free roast chestnuts or cheese on the bar, folk music Sun afternoon; no credit cards or mobile phones; well behaved children and dogs welcome, hill views from front terrace, good walking country, only open Fri evening and all day weekends. *(Dennis Jones, Ann and Tony Bennett-Hughes)*

WHITTINGTON MOOR SK3873
Derby Tup (01246) 454316
Sheffield Road; B6057 just S of A61 roundabout; S41 8LS Popular Castle Rock local redecorated under enthusiastic new landlord; their ales along with Pigeon Fishers (landlord owns the brewery) and several guests, also craft beers, up to seven ciders and good range of other drinks, simple furniture, coal fire and lots of standing room as well as two side snugs, lunchtime sandwiches and snacks (full Sun lunch) and some themed nights; live music including jam sessions first and third Thurs of month; children, walkers and dogs welcome, plans for a roof terrace as we went to press, open all day and can get very busy weekend evenings and on match days. *(P Dawn)*

WILLINGTON SK2928
Dragon (01283) 704795
The Green; DE65 6BP Renovated and extended pub backing on to Trent & Mersey Canal, enjoyable well cooked food (all day Fri-Sun) from sandwiches and sharing boards to pub favourites and grills, Marstons Pedigree, Sharps Doom Bar, Timothy Taylors Landlord and local guests; weekend live music, sports TV, free wi-fi; children welcome, picnic-sets out overlooking canal, moorings, open all day. *(Anon)*

WINSTER SK2460
★**Bowling Green** (01629) 650219
East Bank, by NT Market House; DE4 2DS Traditional old stone pub with good chatty atmosphere, character landlord and welcoming staff, enjoyable reasonably priced home-made food, at least three well kept changing local ales and good selection of whiskies, end log fire, dining area and family conservatory (dogs allowed here too); nice village, good walks, closed Mon, Tues and lunchtimes apart from Sun. *(Ann and Tony Bennett-Hughes)*

WINSTER SK2360
Miners Standard (01629) 650279
Bank Top (B5056 above village); DE4 2DR Simply furnished 17th-c stone local, friendly and relaxed, with bar, snug and restaurant, well kept Brampton, Marstons Pedigree and guests, good value honest pub food, big woodburner, lead-mining photographs and minerals, lots of brass, a backwards clock and ancient well; background music; children (away from bar) and dogs welcome, attractive view from garden, campsite next door, interesting stone-built village below, open all day weekends. *(Jo Garnett)*

WIRKSWORTH SK2854
Royal Oak (01629) 823000
North End; DE4 4FG Friendly old-fashioned little terraced local, five well kept ales including Bass, Timothy Taylors Landlord and Whim Hartington, some bric-a-brac and interesting old photographs, pool room; only open evenings from 8pm and Sun lunchtime. *(Emma Scofield)*

Please tell us if any pub deserves to be upgraded to a featured entry – and why: feedback@goodguides.com, or (no stamp needed) The Good Pub Guide, FREEPOST RTJR-ZCYZ-RJZT, Perrymans Lane, Etchingham TN19 7DN.

Devon

AVONWICK
SX6958 Map 1

Turtley Corn Mill 🍷 🛏

(01364) 646100 – www.turtleycornmill.com

0.5 miles off A38 roundabout at SW end of South Brent bypass; TQ10 9ES

Clever conversion of tall mill house with interestingly furnished areas, local beers, modern bar food and huge garden; bedrooms

Always extremely busy – but the friendly staff cope well with the crowds – this is a carefully converted watermill with a lot of character. The spreading series of linked areas are decorated with some individuality: bookcases, fat church candles and oriental rugs in one area, dark flagstones by the bar, a strategically placed woodburning stove dividing off one part, and a side enclave with a modern pew built in around a really big table. Lighting is good, with plenty of big windows looking out over the grounds, and there's a pleasant array of prints, a history of the mill and framed 78rpm discs on pastel-painted walls, elderly wireless sets and house plants and a mix of comfortable dining chairs around heavy baluster-leg tables. Hanlons Yellow Hammer, Otter Ale, St Austell Tribute and Summerskills Start Point on handpump, nine wines by the glass and around 30 malt whiskies. The extensive garden has plenty of well spaced picnic-sets, a giant chess set and a small lake with interesting ducks.

🍴 Good, brasserie-style food includes breakfast (8.30-11am), chicken and ham terrine with pear chutney, prawn and crayfish cocktail, local sausages with mash and gravy, spinach and ricotta lasagne, chicken skewers with romesco dipping sauce and skinny fries, steak pie, grilled whole lemon sole with caper butter, braised lamb shank, and puddings such as lime and passion-fruit cheesecake and chocolate tart with coffee bean syrup; they also offer a two- and three-course weekday set menu (12-6pm). *Benchmark main dish: beer-battered local haddock and fries £14.25. Two-course evening meal £20.00.*

Free house ~ Licensees Lesley and Bruce Brunning ~ Real ale ~ Open 11-11; 12-10.30 Sun ~ Bar food 8.30am-9.30pm ~ Children welcome ~ Dogs allowed in bar ~ Wi-fi ~ Bedrooms: £99/£110 *Recommended by B J Harding, Lynda and Trevor Smith, Martin and Karen Wake*

BEESANDS
SX8140 Map 1

Cricket 🛏

(01548) 580215 – www.thecricketinn.com

About 3 miles S of A379, from Chillington; in village turn right along foreshore road; TQ7 2EN

Welcoming pub with plenty of fish dishes and real ales; clean, airy bedrooms

They always keep a few tables free here for those who just want a drink and a chat – but (as one reader put it) 'you'd be daft not to eat'. The light, airy décor is new england in style, with dark wood or leather chairs around big, solid light wood tables on stripped-wood flooring by the bar and light brown patterned carpet in the restaurant. Big TV screens at either end roll through old local photographs, sport or the news; the atmosphere is relaxed and locals are chatty and friendly. Otter Ale and Bitter and St Austell Tribute on handpump, 14 wines by the glass and local cider; background music. The cheerful black labrador is called Brewster. There are picnic-sets beside the sea wall (a little bleak but essential protection) with pebbly Start Bay beach just over the other side. The South West Coast Path runs through the village.

🍴 Using crab, scallops and lobster caught in the bay, the changing food includes sandwiches, crab soup, chicken liver parfait with truffled butter and onion marmalade, roasted root vegetables in a blue cheese and walnut cream in a vol au vent case, a pie of the day, beer-battered cod and chips, confit smoked duck with celeriac purée, gratin potatoes and duck jus, skate fillet with spiced butter sauce, and puddings such as chocolate fondant and baked alaska. *Benchmark main dish: seafood pancake £12.50. Two-course evening meal £20.00.*

Heavitree ~ Tenant Nigel Heath ~ Real ale ~ Open 11-11 ~ Bar food 12-2.30, 6-8.30; 12-8.30 high summer ~ Restaurant ~ Children welcome ~ Dogs allowed in bar ~ Wi-fi ~ Bedrooms: /£110 *Recommended by Peter Travis, Jane and Kai Horsburgh, Helen and Brian Edgeley, Richard Tilbrook, Bob and Margaret Holder*

BRAMPFORD SPEKE   SX9298 Map 1

THE GOOD PUB GUIDE

Lazy Toad ⭐

(01392) 841591 – www.thelazytoadinn.co.uk
Off A377 N of Exeter; EX5 5DP

Well run dining pub in pretty village with delicious food, real ales, friendly service and pretty garden; bedrooms

This is a friendly 18th-c inn in a charming village – it's well worth wandering around the thatched cottages. The interconnected bar rooms have beams, standing timbers and slate floors, a comfortable sofa by the open log fire, and cushioned wall settles and high-backed wooden dining chairs around a mix of tables; the cream-painted brick walls are hung with lots of pictures. Hanlons Yellowhammer, Otter Bitter and St Austell Tribute on handpump and several wines by the glass are served by attentive staff; the irish terrier is called Rufus. The courtyard (once used by the local farrier and wheelwright) has green-painted picnic-sets, with more in the walled garden. The comfortable, pretty bedrooms are in the main building and the annexe (one is dog friendly). There are fine walks beside the River Exe and on the Exe Valley Way and Devonshire Heartland Way.

⭐ Highly enjoyable food under the new owners includes sandwiches, lime-cured salmon with horseradish cream, chicken liver parfait with onion marmalade, steak and kidney pudding, blue cheese and hazelnut tortellini with onion purée, crispy fish and chips, chicken breast and leg with fondant potato, and puddings such as banana loaf with peanut butter ice-cream and dark chocolate mousse with candied pistachio nuts. *Benchmark main dish: Sunday roast £12.95. Two-course evening meal £18.00.*

Free house ~ Licensees Harriet and Mike Daly ~ Real ale ~ Open 12-11; 12-5 Sun ~ Bar food 12-2, 7-9 ~ Children welcome but must be over 12 in bedrooms ~ Dogs allowed in bar and bedrooms ~ Wi-fi ~ Bedrooms: £58/£85 *Recommended by Lindy Andrews, Hilary and Neil Christopher, Bob and Margaret Holder*

BRANSCOMBE

SY1888 Map 1

Fountain Head ◗ £

(01297) 680359 – www.fountainheadinn.com

Upper village, above the robust old church; village signposted off A3052 Sidmouth–Seaton, then from Branscombe Square follow road uphill towards Sidmouth and after about a mile turn left after the church; OS Sheet 192 map reference SY188889; EX12 3BG

Old-fashioned and friendly stone pub with own-brewed beers and reasonably priced, well liked food

Handy for coastal walks, this medieval pub is one for lovers of unspoilt and unchanging places. The atmosphere is nicely old-fashioned with no background music, TV or games machines, and the room on the left (formerly a smithy) has forge tools and horseshoes on high oak beams, cushioned pews and mate's chairs and a log fire in the original raised firebed with its tall central chimney. They keep their own-brewed Branscombe Vale Branoc and Summa That plus a changing guest beer on handpump, several wines by the glass and local cider; there's a beer festival in June. On the right, an irregularly shaped, more orthodox snug room has another log fire, a white-painted plank ceiling with an unusual carved ceiling rose, brown-varnished panelled walls and a flagstone and lime ash floor. Local artists' paintings and greeting cards are for sale; darts and board games. You can sit outside on the front loggia and terrace listening to the little stream gurgling beneath the flagstoned path.

Tasty food at reasonable prices includes lunchtime sandwiches, scallops wrapped in bacon with sweet chilli mayonnaise, beer-battered brie wedges with home-made pear and ginger chutney, chicken caesar salad, home-cooked honey-roast ham and eggs, macaroni cheese, creamy fish pie, mustard and demerara-coated leg of lamb with roasted sweet potato, fennel, shallots and red wine dressing and puddings. *Benchmark main dish: beer-battered cod and chips £10.80. Two-course evening meal £20.00.*

Free house~ Licensees Jon Woodley and Teresa Hoare ~ Real ale ~ Open 11-3, 6-11; 12-10.30 Sun ~ Bar food 12-2, 6.30-9 ~ Restaurant ~ Children welcome away from main bar area ~ Dogs allowed in bar ~ Live entertainment Sun evenings in summer
Recommended by Roger and Donna Huggins, Nigel Williams, Revd R P Tickle, John Coatsworth

BRANSCOMBE

SY2088 Map 1

Masons Arms 🛏

(01297) 680300 – www.masonsarms.co.uk

Main Street; signed off A3052 Sidmouth–Seaton, then bear left into village; EX12 3DJ

Rambling low-beamed rooms, woodburning stoves, a fair choice of real ales, popular food and seats on quiet terrace and in garden; cottagey bedrooms

They've added six new bedrooms, and there are more in the pub itself or in converted cottages overlooking the gardens (dogs are allowed in these rooms). The rambling main bar is the heart of the place with comfortable seats and chairs on slate floors, ancient ships' beams, a log fire in a massive hearth, St Austell Proper Job and Tribute and guest beers such as Branscombe Vale Summa That and Otter Bitter on handpump and ten wines by the glass. As there's a good mix of locals and visitors, you can be sure of a cheerful, bustling atmosphere and the licensees offer a warm welcome to all. A second bar also has a slate floor, a fireplace with a two-sided woodburning stove and stripped pine; there are also two dining rooms. A quiet flower-filled front terrace, with thatched-roof tables, extends into a side garden. The sea is just a stroll away and the pretty village is well worth exploring.

🍴 Traditional dishes plus interesting daily specials includes pâté with spiced tomato chutney, crispy squid with sweet chilli sauce, a pie of the day, local sausages with caramelised onions and red wine gravy, mushroom burger with toppings and chunky chips, couscous chicken and salad topped with toasted peanuts, chilli and lime, chargrilled rump steak with herb butter and puddings. *Benchmark main dish: mussels with frites £12.50. Two-course evening meal £19.50.*

St Austell ~ Managers Simon and Alison Ede ~ Real ale ~ Open 11-11; 12-10.30 Sun ~ Bar food 12-2.15, 6.30-9 ~ Restaurant ~ Children welcome in bar area ~ Dogs allowed in bar and bedrooms ~ Wi-fi ~ Bedrooms: /£95 *Recommended by Mr and Mrs J Watkins*

BUCKLAND BREWER   SS4220 Map 1
Coach & Horses
(01237) 451395 – www.coachandhorsesbucklandbrewer.co.uk
Village signposted off A388 S of Monkleigh; OS Sheet 190 map reference 423206; EX39 5LU

Friendly old village pub with a mix of customers, open fires and real ales; good nearby walks

The heavily beamed bar in this thatched old pub (mind your head on some of the beams) has comfortable seats, a handsome antique settle and a woodburning stove in an inglenook; there's also a good log fire in the big stone inglenook of the small lounge. A little back room has darts and pool; the three-legged cat is called Marmite. Long-serving and friendly licensees keep Exmoor Gold, Otter Ale and Sharps Doom Bar on handpump, local farm ciders and several wines by the glass; skittle alley (which doubles as a function room), background music, games machine, darts, pool table and occasional TV for sports. There are picnic-sets on the front terrace and in the side garden. They have a holiday cottage to rent next door. The RHS garden Rosemoor is about five miles away.

🍴 There's quite a choice of curries, as well as sandwiches, deep-fried camembert with jelly, mushrooms baked with stilton, burger with bacon and local cheese, gammon with pineapple or egg, beer-battered fish and chips, steaks with a choice of sauces, and puddings such as fruit crumble and banoffi pie. *Benchmark main dish: steak in Guinness pie £9.95. Two-course evening meal £17.50.*

Free house ~ Licensees Oliver and Nicola Wolfe ~ Real ale ~ Open 12-3, 5.30-midnight; 12-3, 6-10.30 Sun ~ Bar food 12-2, 6.30-9.30 ~ Restaurant ~ Children welcome ~ Dogs allowed in bar ~ Wi-fi *Recommended by Pat and Tony Martin, Bob and Margaret Holder*

BUCKLAND MONACHORUM   SX4968 Map 1
Drake Manor 🍺 £ 🛏
(01822) 853892 – www.drakemanorinn.co.uk
Off A386 via Crapstone, just S of Yelverton roundabout; PL20 7NA

Nice little village pub with snug rooms, popular food, quite a choice of drinks and pretty back garden; bedrooms

Originally built to house workers constructing the nearby church in the 12th century, this bustling pub has been run by the same hands-on landlady for 25 years. The heavily beamed public bar on the left has brocade-cushioned wall seats, prints of the village from 1905 onwards, horse tack and a few ship badges, and a woodburning stove in a very big stone fireplace; a small door leads to a low-beamed cubbyhole. The snug Drakes Bar has beams hung with tiny cups and big brass keys, a woodburning stove in another stone fireplace, horsebrasses and stirrups, and a mix of seats and tables (note the fine stripped-pine high-backed settle with hood). On the right is a small beamed dining room with settles and tables on flagstones. Shove-ha'penny, darts, euchre and board games. Dartmoor Jail Ale, Otter Amber and Sharps Doom Bar on handpump, ten wines by the glass and a dozen malt whiskies. There are picnic-sets in the prettily planted and sheltered back garden and the front floral displays are much admired; morris men perform regularly in summer. The bedrooms are comfortable and they also have an attractive self-catering apartment. Buckland Abbey (National Trust) is close by.

Good, popular food includes lunchtime baguettes, whitebait with chilli mayonnaise, goats cheese salad with basil oil, ham and free-range eggs, rare-breed local sausages with onion gravy, a duo of mediterranean vegetable tarts with feta, beer-battered cod and home-made tartare sauce, chicken with lime and chilli rub and crème fraîche and lime dressing, minted lamb burger with toppings and chips, and puddings. *Benchmark main dish: steak and kidney pie £9.95. Two-course evening meal £15.00.*

Punch ~ Lease Mandy Robinson ~ Real ale ~ Open 11.30-2.30, 6.30-11; 11.30-11.30 Fri, Sat; 12-11 Sun ~ Bar food 11.30-2 (2.30 Fri-Sun), 6.30-9.30 (10 Fri, Sat) ~ Restaurant ~ Children allowed in restaurant and area off main bar ~ Dogs allowed in bar ~ Wi-fi ~ Bedrooms: /£90
Recommended by Stephen Shepherd, Mr and Mrs J Watkins

CHAGFORD   SX7087   Map 1

Three Crowns 🛏

(01647) 433444 – www.threecrowns-chagford.co.uk
High Street; TQ13 8AJ

13th-c thatched inn on the edge of Dartmoor National Park; stylishly refurbished bar and lounges, conservatory restaurant, good food and thoughtful choice of drinks; smart bedrooms

Although this 13th-c former manor house has had a major refurbishment, it's been carefully done to blend the ancient and modern with great care and thought. The bar has leather armchairs and stools in front of a big log fire, built-in panelled wall seats with bright scatter cushions, a few leather tub chairs and pretty curtains with tassled tie-backs. Dartmoor Jail Ale and St Austell Proper Job and Tribute on handpump and several wines by the glass, served by friendly, efficient staff. The dining lounges have all sorts of leather, plush or carved wooden chairs and settles around an assortment of tables, and big gilt-edged mirrors over fireplaces. Throughout these rooms are painted beams, standing timbers, pale flagstones, rugs, exposed stone walls hung with photographs and prints and various copper kettles, pots and warming pans; background music. There's also a conservatory-style dining area with various furnishings; the courtyard has sturdy tables and chairs among box topiary. Bedrooms are stylish, well equipped and comfortable, and breakfasts good and generous. Parking is limited but there's more in a nearby pay-and-display car park.

Interesting food includes lunchtime sandwiches, scotch duck egg with white wine, pear and blue cheese salad, a trio of fishcakes with gribiche sauce, a pie of the day, roasted vegetable and goats cheese tart, mussels with curried cream sauce, corn-fed chicken with barley, kale and red wine sauce, hake fillet with crayfish and chive risotto, and puddings such as treacle tart and hot chocolate fondant; they also offer a high tea menu (12-6 Mon-Fri, you must book in advance). *Benchmark main dish: beer-battered fish and chips £10.50. Two-course evening meal £20.00.*

St Austell ~ Manager Jared Lothian ~ Real ale ~ Open 8am-11pm ~ Bar food 12-2.30, 6-9 ~ Restaurant ~ Children welcome ~ Dogs allowed in bar and bedrooms ~ Wi-fi ~ Bedrooms: £99/£105 *Recommended by Di and Mike Gillam, Gerry Price, Isobel Mackinlay*

COCKWOOD   SX9780   Map 1

Anchor 🍷 🍺

(01626) 890203 – www.anchorinncockwood.com

Off, but visible from, A379 Exeter–Torbay, after Starcross; EX6 8RA

Busy dining pub specialising in seafood (other choices available), with up to six real ales

---

So popular is this well run dining pub that there are queues at the door before opening time. It's in a fine spot fronting the little harbour with its bobbing boats, swans and ducks, and tables on a sheltered verandah overlook the water. As well as an extension made up of mainly reclaimed timber and decorated with over 300 ship emblems, brass and copper lamps and nautical knick-knacks, there are several small, low-ceilinged, rambling rooms with black panelling and good-sized tables in various nooks; the snug has a cheerful winter coal fire. Otter Ale, St Austell Tribute and Tintagel Castle Gold plus a couple of guests such as Dartmoor Dragons Breath and Exe Valley Devon Glory on handpump (beer festivals at Easter and Halloween), ten wines by the glass and 40 malt whiskies; background music, darts, cards and board games.

 A huge range of fish dishes includes 20 ways of serving River Exe mussels and five ways of serving local scallops, as well as sandwiches and baguettes, crab and brandy soup, sharing platters, local sausages with onion gravy, razor clam and chorizo spaghetti, homity pie with home-made coleslaw, a proper fish pie, duck breast on spiced sweet and sour vegetables, surf and turf, and puddings such as lemon cheesecake and chocolate and orange fudge crunch with hazelnuts and cherries. *Benchmark main dish: 28 varieties of mussels £14.95. Two-course evening meal £25.00.*

Heavitree ~ Lease Malcolm and Katherine Protheroe, Scott Hellier ~ Real ale ~ Open 11-11; 11.30-10.30 Sun ~ Bar food 12-10 (9.30 Sun) ~ Restaurant ~ Children welcome if seated and away from bar; no pushchairs ~ Dogs allowed in bar *Recommended by Dr and Mrs J D Abell, Patrick and Daphne Darley*

COLEFORD   SS7701   Map 1

New Inn 🎯 🍷 🛏

(01363) 84242 – www.thenewinncoleford.co.uk

Just off A377 Crediton–Barnstaple; EX17 5BZ

Ancient thatched inn with interestingly furnished areas, well liked food and real ales and welcoming licensees; bedrooms

---

At 600 years old, this warmly friendly place is one of the oldest 'new' inns in the country. The U-shaped building has the servery in the 'angle' with interestingly furnished areas leading off it: ancient and modern settles, cushioned stone wall seats, some character tables (a pheasant worked into the grain of one) and carved dressers and chests. Also, paraffin lamps, antique prints on the white walls, landscape-decorated plates on one beam and pewter tankards on another. Captain, the chatty parrot, may greet you with a 'hello' or even a 'goodbye'. Otter Ale and Sharps Doom Bar on handpump, local cider, 15 wines by the glass and a dozen malt whiskies; background music, darts and board games. There are chairs and tables on decking beneath a pruned willow tree by the babbling stream, and more in a covered dining area. The bedrooms are well equipped and comfortable and the breakfasts particularly good.

🎯 Quite a choice of popular food includes sandwiches and baguettes, sizzling king prawns in garlic butter, cauliflower and cumin fritters with chilli and yoghurt dip, home-cooked ham and egg, local pork sausages with spring onion mash and cider sauce, aubergine, feta, basil and sweet potato moussaka, beer-battered cod and chips, and puddings such as banana, toffee and hazelnut eton mess and chocolate and Baileys cheesecake with chocolate sauce; they also offer a handful of good value, regularly changing main courses called 'bar bowls' – such as mackerel fillet on beetroot and parmesan risotto, confit of duck stir-fry with hoisin noodles, and chilli con carne. *Benchmark main dish: local venison and beef pie with a mustard seed crust £13.95. Two-course evening meal £20.00.*

Free house ~ Licensees Carole and George Cowie ~ Real ale ~ Open 12-3, 6-11 (10.30 Sun) ~ Bar food 12-2, 6.30-9.30 ~ Restaurant ~ Children welcome ~ Dogs allowed in bar ~ Wi-fi ~ Monthly quiz, summer hog roasts and bi-annual sea shanty singers ~ Bedrooms: £69/£89
Recommended by Nick Lawless, Michael Butler, J R Wildon

DALWOOD
ST2400 Map 1
Tuckers Arms 🍽
(01404) 881342 – www.thetuckersarms.co.uk
Village signposted off A35 Axminster–Honiton; keep on past village; EX13 7EG

13th-c thatched inn with friendly, hard-working young licensees, real ales and interesting bar food

Once again there's warm praise from our readers for this pretty thatched longhouse – many come back on a regular basis. The beamed and flagstoned bar has a bustling, friendly atmosphere, traditional furnishings including assorted dining chairs, window seats and wall settles, and a log fire in an inglenook fireplace with numerous horsebrasses on the wall above. The back bar has an enormous collection of miniature bottles and there's also a more formal dining room; lots of copper implements and platters. Branscombe Vale Branoc and Otter Bitter and Amber on handpump, several wines by the glass and up to 20 malt whiskies; background music and a double skittle alley. In summer, the hanging baskets are pretty and there are seats in the garden. Apart from the church, this is the oldest building in the parish.

Highly popular and extremely good food includes mini beetroot and goats cheese calzone, an antipasti plate, grilled chicken salad with melted local blue cheese dressing, burger with spiced tomato chutney, toppings, onion rings and chips, a daily changing fish dish such as crab and king prawn ravioli with a spiced marinara cream, lamb rump with mint jelly and garlic and chive oil, and puddings such as dark chocolate and salted caramel tart and stem ginger and lemon sponge. *Benchmark main dish: crab and mixed seafood chowder £12.95. Two-course evening meal £19.50.*

Free house ~ Licensee Tracey Pearson ~ Real ale ~ Open 11.30-3, 6.30-11.30 ~ Bar food 12-2, 6.30-9 ~ Restaurant ~ Well behaved children in restaurant ~ Dogs allowed in bar ~ Wi-fi ~ Bedrooms: £45/£69.50 *Recommended by Nick Lawless, Patrick and Daphne Darley*

DARTMOUTH
SX8751 Map 1
Royal Castle Hotel ♀ 🛏

(01803) 833033 – www.royalcastle.co.uk
The Quay; TQ6 9PS

350-year-old hotel by the harbour with a genuine mix of customers, real ales and good food; comfortable bedrooms

This 17th-c inn was originally two Tudor merchant houses (although the façade is Regency) and there's a great deal of character and many original features – some of the beams are said to have come from the wreckage of the Spanish Armada. The two ground floor bars are quite different. The traditional Galleon bar (on the right) has a log fire in a Tudor fireplace, some fine antiques and maritime pieces, quite a bit of copper and brass and plenty of chatty locals. The Harbour Bar (to the left of the flagstoned entrance hall) is contemporary in style and rather smart, with a big-screen TV and live acoustic music on Thursday evenings. The more formal restaurant looks over the river; background music. Dartmoor Jail Ale, Otter Amber, Sharps Doom Bar and a guest like Fullers Front Row on handpump, and 28 wines by the glass. Some of the stylish bedrooms overlook the water; dogs, welcome in all rooms, get treats and a toy; they have their own secure parking.

As well as breakfasts from 8am, some kind of good food is offered all day: sandwiches, free-range chicken and ham ballotine with marinated figs, scallops and confit pork belly with apple and vanilla purée, crab salad with citrus dressing, sharing platters, asparagus risotto, a pie of the week, local cumberland sausages with onion gravy, chicken, beef and lamb burgers with toppings, relish and skinny fries, seafood chowder with herb croutons, lamb loin with glazed sweetbreads and carrot and ginger purée, and puddings such as treacle tart and raspberry cheesecake. *Benchmark main dish: beer-battered fresh cod and chips £12.95. Two-course evening meal £20.00.*

Free house ~ Licensees Nigel and Anne Way ~ Real ale ~ Open 8am-11pm (10.30 Sun) ~ Bar food 8am-10pm ~ Restaurant ~ Children welcome ~ Dogs allowed in bar ~ Wi-fi ~ Live acoustic music Thurs evening, jazz Sun afternoon ~ Bedrooms: £120/£175
Recommended by Peter Harrison, Mrs Sally Scott, Richard Tilbrook

DODDISCOMBSLEIGH
SX8586 Map 1

Nobody Inn ♀

(01647) 252394 – www.nobodyinn.co.uk
Off B3193; EX6 7PS

Busy old pub with plenty of character, a fine range of drinks, well liked bar food and friendly staff; bedrooms

An extraordinary range of drinks in this 17th-c inn includes a beer named for the pub from Branscombe Vale and two changing guests such as Cotleigh Old Hooker Still Game and Exe Valley Bitter on handpump, 30 wines by the glass from a list of 200, 270 malt whiskies and three farm ciders. The beamed lounge bar of two character rooms contains handsomely carved antique settles, windsor and wheelback chairs, all sorts of wooden tables, guns and hunting prints in a snug area by one of the big inglenook fireplaces, and fresh flowers; board games. The restaurant is more formal. There are picnic-sets in the pretty garden with views of the surrounding wooded hill pastures. The local church has some of the best medieval stained glass in the west country.

Quite a choice of popular food using local, seasonal produce includes ham hock and madeira-soaked date terrine with madeira syrup, home-smoked salmon with horseradish cream, butternut squash and sage risotto, home-cooked ham and eggs, burger with toppings and french fries, sea bream with a soft herb crust and creamed leeks, venison, spinach and braised shoulder tortellini with parsnip purée, potato and celeriac gratin and juniper jus, and puddings such as chocolate brownie and treacle tart. *Benchmark main dish: steak in ale pie £12.95. Two-course evening meal £20.00.*

Free house ~ Licensee Susan Burdge ~ Real ale ~ Open 11-11; 12-10.30 Sun ~ Bar food 12-2, 6.30-9; 12-3, 7-9 Sun ~ Restaurant ~ Children welcome away from main bar; no under-5s in restaurant ~ Dogs allowed in bar ~ Wi-fi ~ Bedrooms: £65/£99
Recommended by Stephen Shepherd, Martin Jones, Peter Brix

EXETER

SX9293   Map 1

Rusty Bike ◀

(01392) 214440 – www.rustybike-exeter.co.uk

Howell Road; EX4 4LZ

Bustling, quirky pub tucked away in a backstreet, with ales from own-brew sister pub, hearty food and lively atmosphere

A wide mix of customers enjoy this individual backstreet pub – it's been transformed from a run-down tavern into an interesting and lively place with good food, a thoughtful choice of drinks and regular events. The large open-plan bar has bench seating, long wall pews and church chairs around a medley of tables on stripped boards, big modern art pieces on the walls, table football, books piled on to shelves and window sills, and a lovely carved counter where they dispense Fat Pig John Street Ale, Pigmalion and Steamhammer (brewed at their sister pub, the Fat Pig, also in Exeter – see Also Worth a Visit) on handpump, 18 wines by the glass, 80 malt whiskies and farm cider; board games. The Snug is similarly furnished and has a vast, ornate mirror on one wall and there's a separate restaurant with elegant chairs around chunky tables and doors to an outside terrace.

 Using carefully sourced (and sometimes foraged) produce, the enjoyable rustic-style food includes sandwiches, home-cured rare-breed beef carpaccio with capers, smoked salmon with pickled cucumber, beetroot tart with horseradish cream, rare-breed pigs livers, smoked bacon, mustard potatoes and cider gravy, brill fillet with beer-battered onion rings and chips, beef bourguignon and mash, pressed venison haunch with cured fillet, roasted apple, pickled red onion and blackberry vinegar, and puddings such as dark chocolate mousse with orange cream and cinnamon and raspberry eton mess. *Benchmark main dish: pork belly with lentils and bacon £17.50. Two-course evening meal £22.00.*

Free house ~ Licensee Hamish Lothian ~ Real ale ~ Open 5-11 (midnight Sat); closed lunchtimes except Sun ~ Bar food 6-10; 12-7 Sun ~ Restaurant ~ Children welcome until 8pm ~ Dogs welcome ~ Wi-fi *Recommended by Edward May, Alison and Michael Harper*

FROGMORE

SX7742   Map 1

Globe ⇌

(01548) 531351 – www.theglobeinn.co.uk

A379 E of Kingsbridge; TQ7 2NR

Extended and neatly refurbished inn with a bar and several seating and dining areas, real ales and nice wines by the glass, helpful staff, popular food and seats outside; comfortable bedrooms

With light, airy and well equipped bedrooms and generous breakfasts, this white-painted inn is a good base for exploring the area. The neatly kept bar has a double-sided woodburner with horsebrass-decorated stone pillars on either side, another fireplace filled with logs, cushioned settles, chunky farmhouse chairs and built-in wall seating around a mix of tables on wooden flooring, and a copper diving helmet. Attentive staff serve Otter Ale, Skinners Betty Stogs and South Hams Eddystone on handpump and several wines by the glass. The slate-floored games room has a pool table and darts. There's also a comfortable lounge with an open fire, cushioned dining chairs and tables on red carpeting, a big leather sofa, a model yacht and a large yacht painting – spot the clever mural of a log pile. Teak tables and chairs sit on the back terrace, with steps leading up to another level with picnic-sets; the summer window boxes are very pretty.

🍴 Food is all about pubby favourites, such as lunchtime baguettes, deep-fried whitebait with tartare sauce, tiger prawns in garlic and chilli, burger with toppings and chips, cod and chips, pizzas, clam chowder, a curry of the day, daily specials (such as stuffed peppers on couscous with a creamy herb sauce and pork fillet stuffed with figs and blue cheese on apple rösti with honeyed fig dressing) and puddings. *Benchmark main dish: steak in ale pie £10.50. Two-course evening meal £19.00.*

Free house ~ Licensees John and Lynda Horsley ~ Real ale ~ Open 12-11; 12-2.30, 6-11; 12-2.30, 6.30-10.30 Sun in winter; closed Mon lunchtime in winter ~ Bar food 12-2, 6-9 ~ Restaurant ~ Children welcome ~ Dogs allowed in bar and bedrooms ~ Wi-fi ~ Bedrooms: £60/$85 *Recommended by Hilary and Neil Christopher*

GEORGEHAM
SS4639   Map 1

Rock 🌟 🍴 🍷
(01271) 890322 – www.therockinn.biz
Rock Hill, above village; EX33 1JW

Beamed family pub with good food, five real ales, plenty of room inside and out and a relaxed atmosphere

Bustling and friendly, this neat place has a good mix of both drinkers and diners. The sizeable, heavy beamed bar is divided in two by a step. The pubby top part has half-planked walls, an open woodburning stove in a stone fireplace and captain's and farmhouse chairs around wooden tables on quarry tiles; the lower area has panelled wall seats, some built-in settles forming a cosy booth, old local photographs and ancient flat irons. Leading off here is a red-carpeted dining room with attractive black and white photographs of North Devon folk. Friendly young staff serve local Braunton #2 Bitter plus Exmoor Gold, Greene King Abbot, St Austell Tribute and Sharps Doom Bar on handpump and a dozen wines by the glass; background music and board games. The light and airy back dining conservatory has high-backed wooden or modern dining chairs around tables under a vine, with a little terrace beyond. There are picnic-sets at the front by pretty hanging baskets and tubs; wheelchair access.

🌟 High quality food (using meat from home-reared pigs and eggs from their free-range hens) includes lunchtime doorstep sandwiches, prawn and crayfish cocktail, portobello mushrooms on toast with a poached egg, sharing boards, honey-glazed ham and eggs, broccoli and stilton tart, burger with toppings, coleslaw and chips, a proper fish pie, specials (such as line-caught bass with saffron and mussel velouté and slow-braised oxtail faggots with herb mash and caramelised onion gravy) and puddings. *Benchmark main dish: beer-battered cod and chips £10.95. Two-course evening meal £18.00.*

Punch ~ Lease Daniel Craddock ~ Real ale ~ Open 11am-11.30pm (midnight Sat); 12-11.30 Sun ~ Bar food 12-2.30, 6-9; 12-9 Sun; may serve food all day in high summer ~ Restaurant ~ Children welcome ~ Dogs allowed in bar ~ Wi-fi
Recommended by Bob and Margaret Holder, Stephen Shepherd, John Jenkins

HAYTOR VALE
SX7777   Map 1

Rock ★ 🌟 🍷 🛏
(01364) 661305 – www.rock-inn.co.uk
Haytor signposted off B3387 just W of Bovey Tracey, on good moorland road to Widecombe; TQ13 9XP

Civilised Dartmoor inn with lovely food, real ales and seats in pretty garden; comfortable bedrooms

With wonderful walks and plenty to do and see close by, it makes sense to use the smart, beamed bedrooms here (some with garden and some with moor views); breakfasts are excellent. It's a civilised and particularly well run inn and at its most informal at lunchtime. Dartmoor IPA and Jail Ale on handpump, 15 wines (plus champagne and sparkling rosé) by the glass and 16 malt whiskies. The two neatly kept, linked, partly panelled bar rooms have lots of dark wood and red plush, polished antique tables with candles and fresh flowers, old-fashioned prints and decorative plates, and warming winter log fires (the main fireplace has a fine Stuart fireback). There's also a light and spacious dining room in the lower part of the inn and a residents' lounge. The large, pretty garden opposite has some seats, with more on the little terrace next to the pub. You can park at the back of the building.

Delicious, first class food includes lunchtime sandwiches, local mussels in cider, apple and tarragon sauce, duck scotch egg with chilli jam, pumpkin and pine nut ravioli with mustard and sage velouté, venison burger with tomato relish and chips, chicken and wild mushroom risotto, roast monkfish with creamed leeks, chorizo and caramelised salsify, duck breast with a cassoulet of butter beans, lentils and haricot beans in tomato and chorizo, and puddings such as triple-layer chocolate brownie and vanilla panna cotta with plum jelly and lemon sorbet; they also offer a two- and three-course set evening menu. *Benchmark main dish: local rib-eye steak with peppercorn sauce £16.95. Two-course evening meal £20.00.*

Free house ~ Licensee Christopher Graves ~ Real ale ~ Open 11-11; 12-10.30 Sun ~ Bar food 12-2, 7-9 ~ Restaurant ~ Children welcome away from main bar ~ Dogs allowed in bedrooms ~ Wi-fi ~ Bedrooms: £80/£95 *Recommended by Dr and Mrs J D Abell, B J Harding, J R Wildon*

HORNDON
SX5280 Map 1

Elephants Nest 🍺 £ 🛏

(01822) 810273 – www.elephantsnest.co.uk

If coming from Okehampton on A386, turn left at Mary Tavy Inn, then left after about 0.5 miles; pub signposted beside Mary Tavy Inn; then Horndon signposted; on OS Sheet it's named as the New Inn; PL19 9NQ

Isolated old inn with some interesting original features, real ales and changing food; comfortable bedrooms

The charming landlord in this remote old inn – on the lower slopes of Dartmoor with plenty of walks – offers a warm welcome to all. The main bar has lots of beer pump clips on the beams, high bar chairs by the bar counter, Dartmoor Jail Ale, Otter Amber and Palmers IPA on handpump, a couple of farm ciders, several wines by the glass and 15 malt whiskies. Two other rooms have an assortment of wooden dining chairs around a mix of tables, and throughout there are bare stone walls, flagstones, horsebrasses and three woodburning stoves. The spreading, pretty garden (with an area reserved for adults only) has picnic-sets under parasols and looks across dry-stone walls to pastures and rougher moorland above. The bedrooms are attractively furnished and deeply comfortable and the breakfasts especially good.

Enjoyable food using the best local produce (the Value Award is for lunchtime choices) includes lunchtime baguettes, pork terrine with fig relish, portobello mushrooms topped with semi-dried tomatoes and blue cheese, ham and egg, an antipasti plate, burger with red onion marmalade and chips, home-made fish pie, chicken stuffed with taleggio cheese and rosemary, wrapped in pancetta with a creamy sauce, and puddings such as chocolate brownie and mixed fruit crumble. *Benchmark main dish: smoked haddock with welsh rarebit £14.95. Two-course evening meal £21.00.*

Free house ~ Licensee Hugh Cook ~ Real ale ~ Open 12-3, 6.30-11 (10.30 Sun) ~ Bar food 12-2.15, 6.30-9 ~ Restaurant ~ Children welcome away from bar ~ Dogs welcome ~ Bedrooms: £87.50/£97.50 *Recommended by Stephen Shepherd, J R Wildon, Phil and Jane Villiers, Wendy Breese*

IDDESLEIGH   SS5608   Map 1
Duke of York 🛏

(01837) 810253 – www.dukeofyorkdevon.co.uk
B3217 Exbourne–Dolton; EX19 8BG

Unfussy and exceptionally friendly, with simply furnished bars, popular food and a fair choice of drinks; charming bedrooms

This long thatched pub was originally four cottages built for craftsmen rebuilding the church – it dates from the 15th c. The unspoilt bar has plenty of homely character: rocking chairs, cushioned benches built into the wall's black-painted wooden dado, stripped tables and other simple country furnishings, banknotes pinned to beams, and a large open fireplace. Adnams Broadside, Bays Topsail and Teignworthy Neap Tide tapped from the cask and a dozen wines by the glass. It can get pretty cramped at peak times. The dining room has a huge inglenook fireplace. Through a small coach arch is a little back garden with some picnic-sets. Three bedrooms are in the pub, with three more just a minute's walk away. Michael Morpurgo, author of *War Horse*, got the inspiration to write the novel after talking to World War I veteran Wilfred Ellis in front of the fire here almost 30 years ago.

As well as pubby choices listed on boards (sandwiches, local sausages and mash with onion gravy, beer-battered fish and chips), the hearty food includes hot and spicy chicken wings, smoked salmon and dill pâté, haggis with swede and potato cakes and red wine sauce (there's a vegetarian version too), whole brill stuffed with prawns in white wine and parsley sauce, duck breast with orange compote sauce, and puddings. *Benchmark main dish: steak and kidney pudding £12.95. Two-course evening meal £15.00.*

Free house ~ Licensee John Pittam ~ Real ale ~ Open 11-11 (midnight); 12-11 Sun ~ Bar food 12-3, 5.30-9.30 Mon-Weds; all day Thurs-Sun ~ Restaurant ~ Children welcome ~ Dogs allowed in bar and bedrooms ~ Wi-fi ~ Bedrooms: £50/£75
Recommended by S G N Bennett, Mark Flynn, Ron Corbett, John Marsh

KING'S NYMPTON   SS6819   Map 1
Grove ⭐ ♀ 🍺

(01769) 580406 – www.thegroveinn.co.uk
Off B3226 SW of South Molton; EX37 9ST

Thatched 17th-c pub in remote village with local beers, highly rated bar food and cheerful licensees

They keep a thoughtful and very good choice of drinks at this 17th-c thatched pub, including Clearwater Cavalier Ale, Exe Valley Ale and Devon Dawn and Hunters Half Bore on handpump (the particularly friendly landlord tries to source his ales as locally as possible and they hold a beer festival in July), 25 wines (and champagne) by the glass, 65 malt whiskies and local cider. The low-beamed bar has lots of bookmarks hanging from the ceiling, simple pubby furnishings on flagstones, bare stone walls and a winter log fire; darts and board games. There's a self-catering cottage to rent, and the pub is surrounded by quiet rolling and wooded countryside. This is a lovely conservation village.

Using the best local, seasonal produce, the enjoyable hearty food includes sandwiches, a duo of smoked local trout with horseradish cream, chicken liver pâté with toasted brioche, vegetable curry, all-day breakfast, rose veal burger with cheese and chips, steak and kidney pudding with mustard mash (made to order with 24 hours' notice), roasted hake with salsa verde, individual beef wellington, and puddings such as hot chocolate pudding and sea-salt treacle tart. *Benchmark main dish: free-range chicken breast stuffed with blue cheese, parma ham and wild garlic £11.00. Two-course evening meal £16.00.*

Free house ~ Licensees Robert and Deborah Smallbone ~ Real ale ~ Open 12-3, 6-11; 12-4, 7-10 Sun; closed Mon lunchtime except bank holidays ~ Bar food 12-2, 6.45-9; 12-4 Sun ~ Restaurant ~ Well behaved children welcome ~ Dogs allowed in bar ~ Wi-fi
Recommended by Mark Flynn, Mr and Mrs D Mackenzie

KINGSBRIDGE
SX7344 Map 1

Dodbrooke Inn ◧ £
(01548) 852068
Church Street, Dodbrooke (parking some way off); TQ7 1DB

Bustling local with friendly licensees, chatty locals and well thought-of food and drink

Customers of all ages crowd into the traditional bar here to be looked after by the long-serving, hands-on licensees who keep everything running smoothly. It's a small terraced pub in a quiet residential area; the bar has built-in cushioned stall seats and plush cushioned stools around pubby tables, some horse harness, local photographs and china jugs, a log fire and an easy-going atmosphere. Bath Gem, Sharps Doom Bar and a couple of guest beers on handpump, local cider and eight wines by the glass. You can sit in the covered courtyard, which might be candlelit in warm weather.

 Tasty food includes home-made pâté, scallops and bacon, five-bean chilli, chicken in creamy white wine sauce, baked bass with red onions, slow-roast leg of lamb in garlic and red wine, crispy roasted pork belly, popular steaks, and puddings such as lemon tart and sticky toffee pudding. *Benchmark main dish: charcoal-grilled steaks £13.50. Two-course evening meal £18.50.*

Free house ~ Licensees Michael and Jill Dyson ~ Real ale ~ Open 12-2, 5-11; 12-2.30, 7-10.30 Sun; closed Mon-Weds lunchtimes ~ Bar food 12-1.30, 5-8.30; 12-1.30, 7-8.30 Sun ~ Children welcome if over 5 ~ Wi-fi *Recommended by Peter Brix, Edward May*

KINGSKERSWELL
SX8666 Map 1

Bickley Mill 🛏
(01803) 873201 – www.bickleymill.co.uk
Bickley Road, SW of Kingskerswell; TQ12 5LN

Welcoming inn surrounded by lovely countryside with bustling bars, attractive furnishings and enjoyable food and drink; contemporary bedrooms

The friendly young licensees are sure to make you welcome in this former flour mill, and they've decorated the place with style. The rambling beamed rooms have three open fires, rugs on wooden floors, an appealing variety of seating from rustic chairs and tables through settles to sofas piled with cushions, black and white photos or modern art on the stone walls, and an easy-going atmosphere. Bays Devon Dumpling and Topsail on handpump and 14 wines by the glass, served by helpful, courteous staff. Outside, there are seats on a big terrace and a subtropical hillside garden. The restful, well

equipped bedrooms are modern and comfortable, and the breakfasts good.
The surrounding countryside is lovely.

 Rewarding food using meat from local farms includes smoked duck and walnut salad with raspberry vinaigrette, king prawn and crayfish cocktail, home-cooked honey-glazed ham and free-range eggs, roasted red pepper and tomato cannelloni, poached and smoked salmon and dill fishcakes with tartare sauce, trio of lamb cutlets with rosemary potatoes and fresh mint sauce, and puddings such as lavender panna cotta and toffee, pecan nut and banana pudding. *Benchmark main dish: beer-battered haddock and chips £11.45. Two-course evening meal £18.50.*

Free house ~ Licensees Vanessa and James Woodleigh-Smith ~ Real ale ~ Open 11-11; 12-10.30 Sun ~ Bar food 12-2.30, 6-9; 12-3, 6-8 Sun ~ Children welcome ~ Dogs allowed in bar ~ Wi-fi ~ Bedrooms: £75/£90 *Recommended by Mike and Mary Carter*

LUSTLEIGH SX7881 Map 1
Cleave
(01647) 277223 ~ www.thecleavelustleigh.uk.com
Off A382 Bovey Tracey–Moretonhampstead; TQ13 9TJ

Thatched pub in popular beauty spot with a roaring log fire and popular food and drink; pretty summer garden

In clement weather, the sheltered garden here comes into its own – it's got plenty of seats and lots of hanging baskets and flower beds. But this picture-postcard pub is busy at any time of the year, so it's best to arrive early to be sure of a table. The low-ceilinged beamed bar has a roaring log fire, granite walls and attractive antique high-backed settles, cushioned wall seats and wheelback chairs around tables on red patterned carpet. Dartmoor Jail Ale, Otter Ale and Bitter and a guest ale on handpump and several wines by the glass. At the back (formerly the old station waiting room) is a light and airy bistro with pale wooden tables and chairs on a wood-strip floor and candlelight; doors from here open to an outside eating area. This is a lovely village and there are good walks in the surrounding Dartmoor National Park.

 Served all day, the well thought-of food includes baguettes, chicken liver parfait with orange brioche, local mussels, vegetable lasagne, rack of pork ribs in barbecue sauce, seared ox tongue with bubble and squeak and parsley sauce, lamb and chorizo pudding, beef stroganoff, pork in an apple and brandy cream sauce, a fresh fish dish of the day, and puddings such as lemon tart and hot gingerbread with banana ice-cream. *Benchmark main dish: ligurian fish stew £15.95. Two-course evening meal £22.00.*

Heavitree ~ Tenant Ben Whitton ~ Real ale ~ Open 11-11 (9 Sun) ~ Bar food 12-9 (7 Sun) ~ Restaurant ~ Children welcome ~ Dogs allowed in bar ~ Wi-fi
Recommended by Mike and Mary Carter, Caroline Prescott, Alfie Bayliss

MARLDON SX8663 Map 1
Church House ⭐🍴 🍷
(01803) 558279 ~ www.churchhousemarldon.com
Off A380 NW of Paignton; TQ3 1SL

Spreading bar plus several other rooms in this pleasant inn, particularly good food, fine choice of drinks and seats on three terraces

Just head for the church to find this traditional 15th-c pub, a neatly kept and friendly place. The attractively furnished, spreading bar with its woodburning stove has several different areas radiating off the big semicircular bar counter: unusual windows, some beams, dark pine and other nice old dining chairs around solid tables, and yellow leather bar chairs. Leading off here is a cosy little candlelit room with four tables on bare boards, a dark wood dado and stone fireplace. There's also a restaurant with a large stone fireplace and, at the other end of the building, a similarly interesting room, split into two, with a stone floor in one part and a wooden floor (and big woodburning stove) in the other. The old barn holds yet another restaurant, with displays by local artists. St Austell Tribute and Teignworthy Gun Dog and Neap Tide on handpump, 18 wines by the glass, ten malt whiskies and a farm cider; background music. There are picnic-sets on three carefully maintained grassy terraces behind the pub, and the village cricket field is opposite.

 Highly rated food includes sandwiches and baguettes, savoury baklava filled with spinach, feta and pine nuts with a mint yoghurt dressing, ham hock terrine with spiced apple chutney, thai green curry tiger prawns with coconut rice, corn-fed chicken with mushroom mousse and bacon, chive and cream sauce, beer-battered cod and chips, cider-marinated pork loin with black pudding and wholegrain mustard and cream sauce, and puddings such as sticky toffee pudding with toffee sauce and crème brûlée. *Benchmark main dish: shoulder of lamb with redcurrant sauce £16.50. Two-course evening meal £21.00.*

Enterprise ~ Lease Julian Cook ~ Real ale ~ Open 11.30-3, 5.30-11 (11.30 Sat); 12-3, 5.30-10.30 Sun ~ Bar food 12-2, 7-9 ~ Restaurant ~ Children welcome ~ Dogs allowed in bar
Recommended by Mike and Mary Carter, John and Mary Warner, Harvey Brown

MORETONHAMPSTEAD   SX7586 Map 1
Horse 🎇

(01647) 440242 – www.thehorsedartmoor.co.uk
George Street; TQ13 8NF

Attractive mediterranean-style courtyard behind simply furnished town pub, with a good choice of drinks and well liked food

There's always something going on here, from live bands to art shows, and the genuinely friendly landlady and her chef husband remain as enthusiastic as ever. The bar has leather chesterfields and deep armchairs in front of a woodburning stove, all manner of wooden chairs, settles and tables on carpet or wooden floorboards, rustic tools and horse tack alongside military and hunting prints on the walls, and a dresser offering home-made cakes and local cider and juice for sale. There are stools by the green planked counter where they serve Marstons Pedigree, Otter Ale and Shepherd Neame New World Pale Ale on handpump, a dozen wines by the glass, ten malt whiskies, two farm ciders and quite a few coffees. A long light room leads off from here, and there's also a high-ceilinged barn-like back dining room. The sheltered inner courtyard, with metal tables and chairs, is popular in warm weather.

 The popular and interesting food (they smoke and cure pastrami, salt beef and salmon), includes sandwiches and panini, tapas (calamari with lemon aioli, baby chorizo in red wine, battered anchovy beignets, oxtail croquette on warm sherry lentils), moules frites, a choice of lunchtime frittatas, crab linguine with chilli butter, local lamb kofta with feta, mint and lime dressing and cucumber and harissa raita, corn-fed chicken cannelloni with sweetcorn mousse, venison with potato rösti, wild mushrooms and veal jus, and puddings. *Benchmark main dish: thin-crust pizzas £9.95. Two-course evening meal £16.00.*

Free house ~ Licensees Nigel Hoyle and Malene Graulund ~ Real ale ~ Open 12-3.30, 5-midnight; closed Sun lunchtime in winter, Mon lunchtime ~ Bar food 12.30-2.30, 6.30-9 ~

Restaurant ~ Children welcome ~ Dogs allowed in bar ~ Wi-fi ~ Live folk last Mon of month, blues third Thurs of month *Recommended by Isobel Mackinlay, Phoebe Peacock*

POSTBRIDGE   SX6780 Map 1

Warren House

(01822) 880208 – www.warrenhouseinn.co.uk

B3212 0.75 miles NE of Postbridge; PL20 6TA

Straightforward old pub, relaxing for a drink or meal after a Dartmoor hike

For walkers crossing Dartmoor, this isolated pub is a welcome haven. There's a lot of local character and the place is something of a focus for the scattered moorland community. The cosy bar is straightforward, with simple furnishings such as easy chairs and settles beneath the beamed ochre ceiling, old pictures of the inn on partly panelled stone walls and dim lighting (powered by the pub's own generator); one of the open fires is said to have been kept alight since 1845. There's also a family room. Butcombe Haka, Sarah Hughes Dark Ruby Mild, Otter Ale and Summerskills Start Point on handpump, local farm cider and malt whiskies; background music and board games. The picnic-sets on both sides of the road have moorland views.

Honest pubby food includes lunchtime baguettes, rabbit pie, spinach and ricotta cannelloni, cajun chicken and chips, smoked haddock and spring onion fishcakes, gammon and pineapple, breaded king prawns with a garlic dip, local steaks and puddings. *Benchmark main dish: steak in ale pie £12.75. Two-course evening meal £18.50.*

Free house ~ Licensee Peter Parsons ~ Real ale ~ Open 11-11; 12-10.30 Sun; 11-3 Mon, Tues in winter ~ Bar food 12 (11 in winter)-9 (8.30 Sun); 12-2.30 Mon, Tues in winter ~ Restaurant ~ Children in family room only ~ Dogs allowed in bar
Recommended by David Crook, Edward May, Neil Allen

RATTERY   SX7461 Map 1

Church House

(01364) 642220 – www.thechurchhouseinn.co.uk

Village signposted from A385 W of Totnes, and A38 S of Buckfastleigh; TQ10 9LD

A genuine welcome from the friendly landlord in this ancient place plus a good range of drinks, popular bar food and peaceful views

This is one of Britain's oldest pubs, so there's plenty to look at while enjoying a pint – Dartmoor Jail Ale and Legend and St Austell Proper Job are on handpump. Parts of the original building, dating from around 1030, still survive – notably the spiral stone steps behind a little stone doorway on the left. The rooms have plenty of character: massive oak beams and standing timbers in the homely open-plan bar, large fireplaces (one with a cosy nook partitioned around it), traditional pubby chairs and tables on patterned carpet, some window seats and prints and horsebrasses on plain white walls. The dining room is separated by heavy curtains and there's a lounge too. Drinks include 19 malt whiskies and a dozen wines by the glass. The garden has picnic-sets on the large hedged-in lawn and peaceful views of the partly wooded surrounding hills.

Traditional dishes plus daily specials include sandwiches and baguettes, prawn cocktail, deep-fried camembert with cranberry sauce, moussaka, stilton and vegetable crumble, chicken wrapped in smoked bacon in cheese and leek sauce, pork and leek sausages with cheesy mash, steak and kidney pudding, a mixed grill, and puddings such as lemon meringue pie and syrup sponge pudding with custard. *Benchmark main dish: half roast guinea fowl with cherry and port sauce £14.95. Two-course evening meal £19.50.*

Free house ~ Licensee Ray Hardy ~ Real ale ~ Open 11-3, 6-11; 12-3, 6-10.30 Sun ~ Bar food 11.30 (12 Sun)-2, 6.30-9 ~ Restaurant ~ Children welcome ~ Dogs allowed in bar ~ Wi-fi
Recommended by John Evans, Roger and Donna Huggins

SANDFORD   SS8202   Map 1
Lamb 🍺 🛏

(01363) 773676 – www.lambinnsandford.co.uk
The Square; EX17 4LW

16th-c inn with beams and standing timbers, four real ales and decent wines by the glass, very good food and seats in garden; well equipped bedrooms

Bustling and friendly, this charming village pub has an easy-going atmosphere. The beamed bar has a log fire in a stone fireplace with red leather sofas beside it, cushioned window seats, a settle and various dining chairs around a few tables on patterned carpet; towards the back is a handsome carved chest, a table of newspapers and magazines and a noticeboard of local news and adverts. Dartmoor Jail Ale, Exeter Avocet, Otter Bitter and St Austell Tribute on handpump, nine wines by the glass, cocktails, farm cider and 20 malt whiskies. The linked dining area has a woodburning stove, a cushioned wall pew, all manner of nice old wooden dining chairs and tables (each with a church candle) and similarly heavy beams; the landlord's wife created the large animal paintings (also in the bedrooms). There's also a simpler public bar and a skittle alley; the jack russell is called Tiny, the collie, Bob. The informal cobbled garden has fairy lights and simple seats and tables, and there are picnic-sets on grass beyond the hedge. The bedrooms are comfortable, modern and well equipped. Nearby parking is at a premium, but the village car park is just a few minutes' walk up the small lane to the right.

The short choice of interesting food includes sandwiches, duck liver parfait with red onion marmalade, beetroot panna cotta with apple and onion purée, sausages with onion gravy, spelt risotto with jerusalem artichoke and button onions, haddock with a gruyère crust, leek fondue and roasted root vegetables, guinea fowl breast with leg ballotine, potato rösti and choux de bruxelle, and puddings such as fruit crumble with crème anglaise and sticky toffee pudding with toffee sauce; curry night is Sunday. *Benchmark main dish: venison haunch with celeriac and pear tart and port and venison jus £14.50. Two-course evening meal £19.00.*

Free house ~ Licensee Mark Hildyard ~ Real ale ~ Open 9am-11pm; 10.30am-midnight (10.30pm Sun) Sat ~ Bar food 12-2.15, 6-9.15; 12-3, 6-8.30 Sun ~ Restaurant ~ Children welcome ~ Dogs welcome ~ Wi-fi ~ Open mike night last Fri of month ~ Bedrooms: £69/£89
Recommended by Richard and Penny Gibbs

SIDBURY   SY1496   Map 1
Hare & Hounds 🍺

(01404) 41760 – www.hareandhounds-devon.co.uk
3 miles N of Sidbury, at Putts Corner; A375 towards Honiton, crossroads with B3174; EX10 0QQ

Large, well run roadside pub with log fires, beams and attractive layout, popular daily carvery and a big garden

Although this is not a straightforward pub (many customers are here to enjoy the exceptionally popular carvery), they do keep Otter Ale and Bitter and St Austell Tribute tapped from the cask and eight wines by the glass. It's a pretty big place but gets packed at peak times and you should book in advance to be sure of a seat. There are two log fires (and rather unusual wood-framed leather sofas complete with pouffes), heavy beams, fresh flowers, and red plush cushioned dining chairs, window seats and leather sofas around plenty of tables on carpeting or bare boards. The newer dining extension, with a central open fire, leads on to a decked area; the seats here, and the picnic-sets in the big garden, have marvellous views down the Sid Valley to the sea at Sidmouth.

As well as a highly thought-of carvery using the best local meat, they also offer a wide choice of dishes such as sandwiches, baguettes and paninis, prawn cocktail and smoked salmon, garlic mushrooms in cream and sherry, vegetable, chicken or beef burgers with toppings, coleslaw and chips, smoked haddock and broccoli bake, steak and kidney pudding, turkey curry and puddings. *Benchmark main dish: daily carvery £10.35. Two-course evening meal £15.00.*

Heartstone Inns ~ Managers Graham Cole and Lindsey Chun ~ Real ale ~ Open 10am-11pm ~ Bar food 12-9 ~ Children welcome but no under-12s in bar area ~ Dogs allowed in bar ~ Wi-fi *Recommended by John and Susan Miln, Roy Hoing*

SLAPTON

SX8245   Map 1

Tower

(01548) 580216 – www.thetowerinn.com
Off A379 Dartmouth–Kingsbridge; TQ7 2PN

Bustling inn with friendly young owners, beams and log fires, good beers and wines and pretty back garden; bedrooms

In 1347, this atmospheric old place was built to house the men working on the 14th-c chantry (the ivy-covered ruins of which overlook the picnic-sets on the neat lawn in the pretty back garden). The low-ceilinged beamed bar has a relaxed atmosphere, armchairs, low-backed settles and scrubbed oak tables on flagstones or bare boards, open log fires and a genuine core of chatty locals; Butcombe Bitter, Dartmoor Jail Ale, Otter Bitter and St Austell Proper Job on handpump, local cider and several wines by the glass. The comfortable bedrooms are reached via an external stone staircase and the inn makes a good base for exploring the area. The lane up to the pub is very narrow and parking can be tricky at peak times.

With seasonal changing menus and fish from the bay, the food includes sandwiches, crab beignet with crispy seawood and dill dressing, pork rillettes with warm scratchings, trio of pork (belly, cumberland sausage, black pudding, with apple fritter and calvados sauce), hake with french dumplings, crab bisque and braised fennel, butternut squash gnocchi with spinach and parmesan crust, and puddings such as passion-fruit posset with champagne jelly and white chocolate and raspberry cheesecake with raspberry coulis. *Benchmark main dish: cote du boeuf for two £45.00. Two-course evening meal £25.00.*

Free house ~ Licensee Dan Cheshire ~ Real ale ~ Open 12-3, 6-11 (10.30 Sun); closed Sun evening in winter, first two weeks Jan ~ Bar food 12-2.30, 6.30-9.30 ~ Children welcome ~ Dogs allowed in bar and bedrooms ~ Wi-fi ~ Bedrooms: £65/£85
Recommended by Peter Travis, David Gunn, Peter Pilbeam, Alfie Bayliss

We checked prices with the pubs as we went to press in summer 2015.
They should hold until around spring 2016.

SOUTH POOL

SX7740   Map 1

Millbrook 🌟

(01548) 531581 – www.millbrookinnsouthpool.co.uk

Off A379 E of Kingsbridge; TQ7 2RW

Delightful village local by the Salcombe estuary with local ales, very good food and a warm welcome for all

When high tide coincides with meal times, this tiny, easy-going pub gets pretty packed with boating visitors – particularly at weekends. There are several little beamed bars; the main one has a log fire in an inglenook fireplace, a couple of settles and a blanket box on turkey rugs and stools against the counter where they keep Red Rock Drift Wood and South Hams Hopnosis and Wild Blonde on handpump, seven wines by the glass, 18 malt whiskies, a dozen gins and a couple of local farm ciders; daily papers. The dining area to the right has a woodburning stove, settles and wheelback chairs around scrubbed wooden tables, and stone and cream walls decorated with maps, hunting pictures, a barometer and a brass clock. This leads to another small dining area and there's also a simply furnished Top Bar. Seats on the outside terrace overlook the water. An honesty Veg Shed sells fresh vegetables and local sausages and bacon.

 Local, seasonal produce is at the heart of the imaginative food: poached eggs in red wine sauce, snails in garlic and parsley butter, goats cheese tortilla, pork belly with ginger and chilli ketchup, chorizo and sauté potatoes, moules marinière and frites, guinea fowl cassoulet, mackerel ceviche with quenelles of crab on a herby pastry disk with pickled fennel and crispy bacon, and puddings such as vanilla panna cotta with berry coulis and iced white chocolate meringue cake with chocolate sauce; they also offer a two- and three-course menu. *Benchmark main dish: bouillabaise £20.00. Two-course evening meal £25.00.*

Free house ~ Licensees Ian Dent and Diana Hunt ~ Real ale ~ Open 12-11 ~ Bar food 12-2, 7-9 ~ Restaurant ~ Children welcome ~ Dogs allowed in bar ~ Wi-fi
Recommended by Nick Lawless

SOUTH ZEAL

SX6593   Map 1

Oxenham Arms 🛏

(01837) 840244 – www.theoxenhamarms.com

Off A30/A382; EX20 2JT

Wonderful old inn with lots to look at, character bars, four real ales, enjoyable food and big garden; bedrooms

This ancient place, first licensed in 1477, was built to combat the pagan power of the Neolithic standing stone that still forms part of the wall in the room behind the bar (there's actually 20 feet of stone below the floor). The heavily beamed, partly panelled front bar has elegant mullioned windows and Stuart fireplaces, all sorts of chairs and built-in wall seats with scatter cushions around low oak tables on bare floorboards, and bar stools against the counter where friendly staff serve a couple of beers named for the pub – Merry Monk (from Dartmoor) and Oxy Ale (from Red Rock) – plus Hanlons Yellowhammer and Teignworthy Gun Dog on handpump; several wines by the glass, 40 malt whiskies, 20 ports and four farm ciders. A small room has beams, wheelback chairs around polished tables, decorative plates and another open fire. The imposing curved stone steps lead up to the four-acre garden where there are plenty of seats and fine views; there are also seats under parasols out in front. Charles Dickens, snowed up one winter, wrote a lot of *Pickwick Papers* here. You can walk straight from the door on to the moor.

🍴 Quite a choice of rewarding food includes ham hock terrine with home-made piccalilli, prawn and crayfish cocktail, home-cooked honey and mustard glazed ham and eggs, vegetable and chickpea tagine with rosemary, preserved lemons and couscous, lambs liver and bacon with wholegrain mustard mash and caramelised onion gravy, seafood linguine, venison steak with sloe gin and blackcurrant jus, and puddings such as Baileys cheesecake and bread and butter pudding. *Benchmark main dish: steak in ale pie £11.25. Two-course evening meal £19.00.*

Free house ~ Licensees Simon and Lyn Powell ~ Real ale ~ Open 11-11 (10.30 Sun) ~ Bar food 11-9 (8.30 Sun) ~ Restaurant ~ Children welcome ~ Dogs allowed in bar ~ Wi-fi ~ Bedrooms: $85/$95 *Recommended by Ian Herdman, Ron Corbett, David and Stella Martin*

SPARKWELL   SX5857   Map 1

Treby Arms ✪

(01752) 837363 – www.thetrebyarms.co.uk

Off A38 at Smithaleigh, W of Ivybridge, Sparkwell signed from village; PL7 5DD

Devon Dining Pub of the Year

Village pub offering delicious food, real ales, good wines and a friendly welcome

Of course, most customers come to this little village pub to enjoy the excellent food cooked by 2012 *MasterChef* winner Anton Piotrowski – but they do have a bar area used by locals for a pint and a chat and this keeps the atmosphere nicely informal. This little room has stools against the counter, simple wooden dining chairs and tables, a built-in cushioned window seat and a woodburning stove in a stone fireplace with shelves of cookery and guide books piled up on either side. Dartmoor Jail Ale, Otter Ale and St Austell Tribute on handpump, several good wines by the glass from a list with helpful notes, 20 malt whiskies and local cider served by friendly, competent staff. Off to the right is the dining room with another woodburning stove, old glass and stone bottles on the mantelpiece and captain's and wheelback chairs around rustic tables; there's another carpeted dining room upstairs. The sunny front terrace has seats and tables.

🖼️ Highly accomplished food includes lots of bar nibbles (such as potted crab, duck nuggets with brown sauce, ham hock and a fried egg) plus tandoori frogs legs with bombay potato salad, yoghurt and crispy onion, cider and black treacle-glazed pork cheek with celeriac, leek and celery fondue, caramelised cauliflower and truffle risotto with goats cheese bonbons and shiitake mushrooms, line-caught cod in white wine batter with chips, cajun lamb rump with lamb samosa, baby gem, tzatziki and squash purée, and puddings such as warm chocolate with mint ice-cream, pistachios and chocolate crumble, and lemon millefeuille with cream cheese, lemon curd, orange foam and raspberry sorbet; good local cheeses and they also offer a two- and three-course set menu. *Benchmark main dish: herb-rolled venison loin with king oyster mushroom, confit onion and beetroot purée £28.00. Two-course evening meal £31.00.*

Free house ~ Licensees Anton and Clare Piotrowski ~ Real ale ~ Open 12-3, 6-11; 12-11 Sat; 12-10.30 Sun; closed Mon ~ Bar food 12-2, 6-9; 12-9 Fri-Sun ~ Restaurant ~ Children welcome ~ Dogs allowed in bar ~ Wi-fi *Recommended by John Evans, Isobel Mackinlay*

TIPTON ST JOHN
Golden Lion
SY0991   Map 1

(01404) 812881 – www.goldenliontipton.co.uk

Pub signed off B3176 Sidmouth–Ottery St Mary; EX10 0AA

Friendly village pub with three real ales, well liked bar food, a good mix of customers and plenty of seats in the attractive garden

This bustling village pub was once a straightforward railway inn, but now attracts both regulars and diners from further afield. The main bar, split into two, has a comfortable, relaxed atmosphere, as does the back snug. Throughout are paintings by west country artists, art deco prints, Tiffany lamps and, hanging from the beams, hops, copper pots and kettles. A few tables are kept for those just wanting a pint and a chat. Bass and Otter Ale and Bitter on handpump and 14 wines by the glass; maybe background music and cards. There are seats on the terracotta-walled terrace with outside heaters and grapevines and more seats on the grass edged by pretty flowering borders. Dog walkers and smokers may use a verandah.

Popular food includes sandwiches, home-smoked duck salad with onion marmalade, crayfish with lime and garlic mayonnaise, home-cooked ham and egg, moules frites, vegetable lasagne, liver and bacon, duck breast with oriental plum sauce, slow-roasted lamb shank, venison pie, and puddings such as fruit crumble and lemon brioche pudding. *Benchmark main dish: chunky bouillabaise £7.95. Two-course evening meal £20.00.*

Heavitree ~ Tenants François and Michelle Teissier ~ Real ale ~ Open 12-2.30, 6-10 (11 Fri, Sat); closed Sun evening ~ Bar food 12-2, 6.30-8 (8.30 Fri, Sat) ~ Children welcome
Recommended by Edward May, Steve and Claire Harvey

TOPSHAM
Globe
SX968   Map 1

(01392) 873471 – www.theglobetopsham.co.uk

Fore Street; 2 miles from M5 junction 30; EX3 0HR

Thoughtfully refurbished, substantial inn with relaxed bar and dining areas, west country ales and popular food and seats on big terrace; well equipped bedrooms

In the middle of a charming village close to the Exe estuary and nature reserve, this handsome 16th-c former coaching inn has been carefully refurbished in the past couple of years. Original features mix easily with contemporary touches and paintwork, and the atmosphere throughout is easy-going and friendly. The red-painted panelling in the bar is hung with old prints, there's an open fire in a small brick fireplace with logs piled to one side, armchairs in a corner and suede tub and pubby chairs around dark tables on bare floorboards. Another bar has pale-painted panelling, a shelf of old glass bottles, a sizeable cushioned settle and more traditional chairs and tables on tartan carpet and a woodburning stove. The elegant dining room features church candles in huge candlesticks, green paintwork above a grey dado and another open fire. St Austell Proper Job, Trelawny and Tribute on handpump and several wines by the glass served by helpful staff. Outside, the large terrace has plenty of good quality seats and tables under dark parasols. The individually decorated, modern bedrooms are well equipped and comfortable and breakfasts are good.

Helpfully served all day, the food is of a high standard: sandwiches, duck liver and wild mushroom parfait with sherry jelly, local mussels in chilli, tomato and coriander, butternut squash, pine nut and rocket linguine, a changing pie, burger with toppings, pickles and chips, chicken supreme with smoked black pudding mousseline, celeriac rösti and roasted pear, confit pork belly with apple fondant, sage mash and crackling, and puddings. *Benchmark main dish: beer-battered fish and chips £12.50. Two-course evening meal £20.50.*

St Austell ~ Manager Jason Manton ~ Real ale ~ Open 10am-11pm (11.30 Fri, Sat); 10am-10.30pm Sun ~ Bar food 12-9.30 (9 Sun) ~ Children welcome ~ Dogs allowed in bar and bedrooms ~ Wi-fi ~ Bedrooms: /£106 *Recommended by Mike Swan, Toby Jones*

TORQUAY
SX9265   Map 1
Cary Arms 🍷 🛏
(01803) 327110 – www.caryarms.co.uk
Beach Road: off B3199 Babbacombe Road, via Babbacombe Downs Road; turn steeply down near Babbacombe Theatre; TQ1 3LX

Interesting bar in secluded hotel with lovely sea views, plenty of outside seating, enjoyable if not cheap food, real ales and friendly service; bedrooms

The windows in the bar of this charming higgledy-piggledy hotel, the picnic-sets on terraces and the teak chairs and tables on gravel – all offer glorious views over Babbacombe Bay; the rather special boutique-style bedrooms also look over the water. The beamed, grotto-effect bar has rough pink granite walls, alcoves, rustic hobbit-style red leather cushioned chairs around carved wooden tables on slate or bare boards, an open woodburning stove with a ship's wheel above it, and some high bar chairs beside the stone bar counter. Bays Topsail, Hanlons Yellowhammer and Otter Ale on handpump, nine good wines by the glass and two local ciders served by cheerful young staff; a small, glass-enclosed entrance room has large ship lanterns and cleats. Outside, there's a bar, a barbecue and pizza oven and steps that lead down to the quay. They have six mooring spaces and can arrange a water taxi for guests arriving by boat – plus four self-catering cottages. The lane down to the hotel is tortuously steep and not for the faint-hearted.

Using home-grown herbs, making their own fudge, scones, cakes, chutneys and so forth and using the best local producers, the rewarding food includes lunchtime sandwiches, chicken, mushroom and tarragon in creamy white sauce on toasted brioche, seared scallops on spinach purée with chorizo and wild garlic pesto, tomato, chilli and basil pasta topped with mozzarella, burger with home-made tomato relish and fries, crab salad with wholegrain mustard mayonnaise, roasted lamb rump with parmentier potatoes, wild garlic and redcurrant jus, and puddings such as lime and lemon panna cotta and white chocolate and passion-fruit cheesecake with berry coulis. *Benchmark main dish: local battered fish and chips £13.95. Two-course evening meal £22.00.*

Free house ~ Licensee Felicia Crosby ~ Real ale ~ Open 12-11 ~ Bar food 12-3, 6.30-9 ~ Restaurant ~ Children welcome ~ Dogs allowed in bar and bedrooms ~ Wi-fi ~ Bedrooms: £180/£295 *Recommended by K B Ohlson, Hilary and Neil Christopher, Caroline Prescott*

WIDECOMBE
SX7276   Map 1
Rugglestone ◀
(01364) 621327 – www.rugglestoneinn.co.uk
Village at end of B3387; pub just S – turn left at church and NT church house, OS Sheet 191 map reference 720765; TQ13 7TF

Unspoilt local with a couple of bars, cheerful customers, friendly staff, four real ales and traditional pub food

After enjoying one of the wonderful walks in the surrounding Dartmoor National Park, this simple little place makes a perfect pit stop. The unspoilt bar has just four tables, a few window and wall seats, a one-person pew built into the corner by a nice old stone fireplace (with a woodburner) and a good mix of customers. The rudimentary bar counter dispenses Bays Up 'N' Under, Dartmoor Legend, Otter Bitter and a beer named for the pub from Teignworthy tapped from the cask; local farm cider and a decent small wine list. The room on the right is slightly bigger and lighter in feel, with beams, another stone fireplace, stripped-pine tables and a built-in wall bench; there's also a small dining room. To reach the picnic-sets in the garden you have to cross a bridge over a little moorland stream. A holiday cottage is for rent.

Generous helpings of good food includes baps and baguettes, a large pasty, local potted crab, deep-fried brie with redcurrant jelly, home-cooked ham and eggs, steak and stilton pie, roasted vegetable lasagne, spicy meatballs in tomato sauce topped with cheese, smoked trout salad with home-made coleslaw and horseradish sauce, and puddings. *Benchmark main dish: fish pie £10.50. Two-course evening meal £16.50.*

Free house ~ Licensees Richard and Vicki Palmer ~ Real ale ~ Open 11.30-3, 6-11.30 (5-midnight Fri); 11.30am-midnight Sat; 11.30-11 Sun ~ Bar food 12-2, 6.30-9 ~ Restaurant ~ Children allowed away from bar area ~ Dogs welcome
Recommended by John T Ames, John Hammond

WOODBURY SALTERTON
SY0189 Map 1
Diggers Rest
(01395) 232375 – www.diggersrest.co.uk
3.5 miles from M5 junction 30: A3052 towards Sidmouth, village signposted on right about 0.5 miles after Clyst St Mary; also signposted from B3179 SE of Exeter; EX5 1PQ

Bustling village pub with real ales, well liked food and country views from the terraced garden

Easy to find from the M5, this is a thatched former cider house in the middle of a quiet village. It's a friendly place and the main bar has antique furniture, local art on the walls and a cosy seating area by the open fire. The modern extension is light and airy and opens on to the garden. Bays Topsail and Otter Ale and Bitter on handpump; 13 wines by the glass and Weston's cider; service is attentive and efficient. Background music, darts, TV and board games. The window boxes and flowering baskets are pretty, and there are lots of good surrounding walks.

From a changing menu, food includes sandwiches, garlic spare ribs with oriental slaw, lemon and dill fishcakes with garlic mayonnaise, creamed leek and gruyère tart with a soft poached egg, chicken with crispy pancetta, lentils and red wine jus, salmon with curried local mussels and spinach, steak and kidney pie, and puddings such as dark chocolate pot with salted caramel and apple strudel with cinnamon syrup. *Benchmark main dish: burgers with toppings and chips £10.95. Two-course evening meal £19.00.*

Heartstone Inns ~ Licensee Marc Slater ~ Real ale ~ Open 11-3, 5.30-11; 11-11 Sat, Sun ~ Bar food 12-2.15, 6-9 ~ Restaurant ~ Children welcome ~ Dogs allowed in bar ~ Wi-fi ~ Live music, check website for dates *Recommended by M G Hart, John Wooll, John Evans, Katharine Cowherd, Roy Hoing, Roger and Donna Huggins*

Also Worth a Visit in Devon

Besides the fully inspected pubs, you might like to try these pubs that have been recommended to us and described by readers. Do tell us what you think of them: feedback@goodguides.com

ABBOTSKERSWELL   SX8568
Court Farm (01626) 361866
Wilton Way; look for the church tower;
TQ12 5NY Attractive neatly extended
17th-c longhouse tucked away in picturesque
hamlet, various rooms off long beamed and
paved main bar, good mix of furnishings,
well priced popular food from sandwiches to
steaks, lunchtime two-for-one deal weekdays,
friendly helpful staff, several ales including
Bass and Otter, farm cider and decent wines,
woodburners; background music, pool and
darts; children welcome, picnic-sets in pretty
lawned garden, open all day (food all day
Thurs-Sun). *(Isobel Mackinlay)*

APPLEDORE   SS4630
Beaver (01237) 474822
Irsha Street; EX39 1RY Relaxed
harbourside pub with lovely estuary view
from popular raised dining area, well priced
food especially fresh local fish, prompt
friendly service, good choice of west country
ales, farm cider, decent house wines and
great range of whiskies; background and
some live music including jazz, pool in
smaller games room, TV; children and dogs
welcome, disabled access (but no nearby
parking), tables on small sheltered water-
view terrace. *(John T Ames)*

ASHPRINGTON   SX8157
Durant Arms (01803) 732240
Off A381 S of Totnes; TQ9 7UP
Comfortably refurbished 18th-c village inn
under friendly newish family ownership;
enjoyable home-cooked food and three well
kept ales including Otter Amber, slate-floored
bar with stag's head above woodburner, china
on delft shelf, other connecting rooms; vintage
juke box; children, walkers and dogs welcome,
four bedrooms (one in courtyard annexe),
closed Sun evening, Mon. *(Mike Swan)*

ASHPRINGTON   SX8056
Watermans Arms (01803) 732214
Bow Bridge, on Tuckenhay Road;
TQ9 7EG 17th-c creekside inn; beamed and
quarry-tiled main bar area, built-in cushioned
wall seats and wheelbacks around stripped
tables, woodburner, dining room with fishing-
related décor, comfortable area down steps
and front bar with log fire, four Palmers ales
and several wines by the glass, good choice of
traditional food from sandwiches and baked
potatoes up; live music Weds; children and
dogs welcome, seats out by the water (maybe
kingfishers) and in garden, bedrooms (some
in purpose-built annexe), open all day.
(Phoebe Peacock)

AXMOUTH   SY2591
★ **Harbour Inn** (01297) 20371
B3172 Seaton–Axminster; EX12 4AF
Family-run thatched pub by estuary; two
heavily beamed bar rooms with brass-
bound cask seats, settles and all manner of
tables on bare boards, pots hanging in huge
inglenook, lots of model boats and accounts
of shipwrecks, glass balls in nets and a large
turtle shell, more heavy beams in two dining
rooms, snug alcove leading off with nautical
bric-a-brac, Badger ales and several wines by
the glass, good choice of enjoyable food from
sandwiches and deli boards up, pool, skittle
alley; children and dogs (in bar) welcome,
modern furniture on terrace, picnic-sets
on grass, open (and food) all day from
9am. *(Alfie Bayliss)*

AYLESBEARE   SY0490
Halfway (01395) 232273
A3052 Exeter–Sidmouth, junction with
B3180; EX5 2JP Welcoming modernised
roadside dining pub, well cooked food from
fairly priced pub favourites up including good
fresh fish/seafood and other daily specials,
well kept Otter, efficient friendly service,
Dartmoor views from restaurant and raised
outside seating area; children welcome, open
(and food) all day. *(Gene and Tony Freemantle)*

BAMPTON   SS9520
★ **Exeter Inn** (01398) 331345
A396 some way S, at B3227 roundabout;
EX16 9DY Long low roadside pub under
welcoming owners; stone-built with several
updated linked rooms, mainly flagstoned, two
log fires and woodburner, large restaurant,
wide choice of good generous food at sensible
prices including fresh fish, Sun carvery,
friendly efficient service, Cotleigh, Exmoor
and guests tapped from the cask, daily
papers; children and dogs welcome, disabled
facilities, tables out in front, 12 bedrooms,
fairly handy for Knightshayes (NT), open all
day. *(Neil Allen)*

BAMPTON   SS9622
Quarrymans Rest (01398) 331480
Briton Street; EX16 9LN Village pub
under newish hard-working landlord; bustling
beamed and carpeted main bar, leather sofas
in front of inglenook woodburner, dining
chairs and some housekeepers' chairs around
wooden tables, enjoyable home-made food
and four well kept west country ales, steps
up to comfortable stripped-stone dining
room with high-backed leather chairs and
heavy pine tables; pool and games machines;
children and dogs welcome, picnic-sets in

pretty back garden, more seats in front, four bedrooms, open all day. *(S G N Bennett)*

BAMPTON SS9522
Swan (01398) 332248
Station Road; EX16 9NG Popular beamed village inn with spacious bare-boards bar, woodburners in two inglenooks, three changing local beers and good home-made food (not Mon), efficient friendly service; children and dogs welcome, good modern bedrooms, big breakfast, closed Mon lunchtime otherwise open all day. *(Peter Pilbeam)*

BANTHAM SX6643
★**Sloop** (01548) 560489
Off A379/B3197 NW of Kingsbridge; TQ7 3AJ Welcoming 14th-c split-level pub close to fine beach and walks, popular and relaxed, with good mix of customers in black-beamed stripped-stone bar, country tables and chairs on flagstones, blazing woodburner, well kept St Austell and a guest ale, enjoyable food from nice sandwiches to good fresh fish, friendly efficient service, restaurant; background music; children and dogs welcome, seats out at back, five bedrooms, open all day in summer. *(Lynda and Trevor Smith, Peter Travis, Jane and Kai Horsburgh, Theocsbrian, Bob and Margaret Holder)*

BEER ST2289
Anchor (01297) 20386
Fore Street; EX12 3ET Sea-view inn with wide choice of enjoyable food including local fish, Greene King and Otter, good value wines, rambling open-plan layout with old local photographs, large eating area, friendly staff; background music, sports TV, free wi-fi; children well looked after, lots of tables in attractive clifftop garden over road, reasonably priced bedrooms. *(Patrick and Daphne Darley, John Coatsworth, Roger and Donna Huggins)*

BELSTONE SX61293
Tors (01837) 840689
A mile off A30; EX20 1QZ Small Victorian granite pub-hotel in peaceful Dartmoor-edge village, family-run and welcoming, with long carpeted bar divided by settles, well kept ales such as Dartmoor and Sharps, over 50 malt whiskies and good choice of wines, enjoyable well presented food from sandwiches to specials, cheerful prompt service, restaurant; children welcome and dogs (they have their own), disabled access, seats out on nearby grassy area overlooking valley, good walks, bedrooms, open all day in summer. *(Chris and Angela Buckell)*

BERE FERRERS SX4563
Old Plough (01822) 840358
Long dead-end road off B3257 S of Tavistock; PL20 7JL 16th-c pub in secluded River Tavy village, stripped stone and panelling, low beam-and-plank ceilings, slate flagstones and woodburner, enjoyable

good value home-cooked food (decent vegetarian choice), well kept Hunters, Sharps Doom Bar and a couple of guests, real cider, warm local atmosphere, steps down to cosy restaurant; live music; children and dogs welcome, garden overlooking estuary, open all day weekends. *(Peter Pilbeam)*

BERRYNARBOR SS5546
Olde Globe (01271) 882465
Off A399 E of Ilfracombe; EX34 9SG Rambling dimly lit rooms geared to family visitors (cutlasses, swords, shields and rustic oddments), good choice of reasonably priced straightforward food including Sun carvery, Exmoor and St Austell ales, friendly service, ancient walls and flagstones, high-backed oak settles and antique tables, lots of old pictures, open fire and woodburner, more modern family room, play areas inside and out; background and summer live music; dogs welcome, tables on paved front terrace and side lawn, pretty village, open (and food) all day in season from 9am. *(Toby Jones)*

BIDEFORD SS4526
Kings Arms (01237) 475196
The Quay; EX39 2HW Popular old-fashioned 16th-c pub with Victorian harlequin floor tiles in alcovey front bar, friendly staff, well kept west country ales and reasonably priced pubby food, back raised family area; background music; dogs welcome, tables out on pavement, three bedrooms, handy for Lundy ferry, open (and food) all day. *(Neil Allen)*

BISHOP'S TAWTON SS5629
★**Chichester Arms** (01271) 343945
Signed off A377 outside Barnstaple; East Street; EX32 0DQ Friendly 15th-c cob and thatch pub, good generous well priced food from baguettes to fresh local fish and seasonal game, quick obliging service even when crowded, St Austell Tribute, Charles Wells Bombardier and a guest, decent wines, heavy low beams, large stone fireplace, restaurant; children welcome, awkward disabled access but staff very helpful, picnic-sets on front terrace and in back garden, open all day. *(Peter and Jean Hoare)*

BLACKAWTON SX8050
★**Normandy Arms** (01803) 712884
Signposted off A3122 W of Dartmouth; TQ9 7BN Restaurant pub and most here for the very good (if not cheap) food in two main dining areas, high-backed chairs around wooden tables on slate floors, drinkers' area with tub leather chairs and sofas by woodburner, a couple of local ales, good wines by the glass and cocktails; benches out in front and picnic-sets in small garden across lane, pretty village (May worm-charming competition), three bedrooms, closed Sun, Mon and lunchtimes Tues, Weds. *(Hilary and Neil Christopher)*

BRAYFORD   SS7235
★ **Poltimore Arms** (01598) 710381
*Yarde Down; 3 miles towards
Simonsbath; EX36 3HA* Ivy-clad 17th-c
beamed pub – so remote it generates its own
electricity and water is from a spring; good
home-made food including daily specials
(best to book) and two or three changing
ales tapped from the cask, friendly helpful
staff, traditional furnishings, woodburner in
inglenook, two attractive restaurant areas
separated by another woodburner, good
country views; children and dogs welcome,
picnic-sets in side garden, shop and gallery,
open all day. *(Neil Allen)*

BRENDON   SS7547
★ **Rockford Inn** (01598) 741214
*Rockford; Lynton–Simonsbath Road, off
B3223; EX35 6PT* Homely and welcoming
small 17th-c beamed inn surrounded by
fine walks and scenery; neatly linked rooms
with cushioned settles, wall seats and other
straightforward furniture, country prints
and horse tack, open fires, good helpings of
enjoyable well priced pubby food, well kept
Clearwater, Cotleigh and Exmoor tapped
from the cask, farm cider, decent wines by
the glass, lots of pump clips and toby jugs
behind counter; background music, board
games; children and dogs (in bar) welcome,
seats out overlooking East Lyn river, well
appointed bedrooms, open all day (afternoon
break Sun). *(Sheila Topham)*

BRENDON   SS7648
Staghunters (01598) 741222
Leedford Lane; EX35 6PS Idyllically set
family-run hotel with gardens by East Lyn
river, good choice of enjoyable reasonably
priced food, well kept Cotleigh and Exmoor
ales, friendly efficient staff, bar with
woodburner, restaurant; can get very busy,
though quiet out of season; walkers and dogs
welcome, riverside tables, 12 good value
bedrooms. *(Bob and Margaret Holder)*

BRIXHAM   SX9256
Blue Anchor (01803) 859373
Fore Street/King Street; TQ5 8AH
Friendly harbourside local of some character,
plenty of nautical hardware, banquettes
and log fire, up to four well kept ales and
enjoyable generously served food from good
sandwiches up, two small dining rooms – one
a former chapel down steps, interesting
old photographs, regular live music; dogs
welcome, open all day. *(Alison and
Michael Harper)*

BRIXHAM   SX9256
★ **Maritime** (01803) 853535
*King Street (up steps from harbour –
nearby parking virtually non-existent);
TQ5 9TH* Single bar packed with bric-a-
brac, chamber-pots hanging from beams,
hundreds of key fobs, cigarette cards,

pre-war ensigns, toby jugs, mannequins,
astronomical charts, even a binnacle by the
door, friendly long-serving landlady, Bays
Best and Hunters Half Bore and Pheasant
Plucker, over 80 malt whiskies, no food or
credit cards, lively terrier called George and
Mr Tibbs the parrot; background music, small
TV, darts and board games; well behaved
children and dogs allowed, fine views over
harbour, six bedrooms (not ensuite), closed
lunchtime. *(Mrs Sally Scott)*

BROADCLYST   SX9997
New Inn (01392) 461312
Wimple Road; EX5 3BX Friendly
former 17th-c farmhouse with stripped
bricks, boarded ceiling, low doorways and
log fires, well cooked reasonably priced
pubby food, Dartmoor, Hanlons, Otter
and Sharps, good attentive service, small
restaurant, skittle alley; children and dogs
welcome, garden with play area, open all day.
(Philip Kingsbury)

BROADCLYST   SX9897
Red Lion (01392) 461271
B3121, by church; EX5 3EL Refurbished
16th-c pub now under same owners as the
Hunters at Newton Tracey; heavy beams,
flagstones and log fires, St Austell Tribute
and a local guest, enjoyable well priced
traditional food (special diets catered for)
in bar and restaurant, good cheerful service;
children and dogs welcome, picnic-sets out in
front below wisteria, more in small enclosed
garden across quiet lane, nice village and
church, not far from Killerton (NT), open all
day weekends. *(Gene and Tony Freemantle)*

BROADHEMBURY   ST1004
Drewe Arms (01404) 841267
*Off A373 Cullompton–Honiton;
EX14 3NF* Extended partly thatched family-
run pub dating from the 15th c; carved beams
and handsome stone-mullioned windows,
woodburner and open fire, mix of furniture
(some perhaps not matching age of building),
modernised bar area, five local ales and
seven wines by the glass, enjoyable pubby
food (all day weekends), friendly helpful
service, skittle alley; terrace seats, more up
steps on tree-shaded lawn, nice setting near
church in pretty village, open all day.
(Peter Kirkman)

BUCKFAST   SX7467
Abbey Inn (01364) 642343
Buckfast Road, off B3380; TQ11 0EA
Lovely position perched on bank of River
Dart; partly panelled bar with woodburner,
three St Austell ales and Healey's cider,
enjoyable reasonably priced pubby food
from sandwiches and baguettes up, big
dining room with more panelling and river
views; background music; children and dogs
(in bar) welcome, terrace and bedrooms
overlooking the water, open all day.
(B J Harding)

BUDLEIGH SALTERTON   SY0681
Feathers (01395) 442042
High Street; EX9 6LE Old town-centre
inn with bustling local atmosphere in long
beamed bar, well kept St Austell Tribute
and three west country guests, enjoyable
reasonably priced pubby food (not Sun
evening) including specials, more intimate
softly lit dining lounge, friendly staff; Sun
quiz, pool, darts; children and dogs welcome,
four bedrooms, open all day. *(Roger and
Donna Huggins)*

BURGH ISLAND   SX6444
Pilchard (01548) 810514
*300 metres across tidal sands from
Bigbury-on-Sea; walk, or summer sea
tractor if tide's in; TQ7 4BG* Sadly, the
splendid beamed and flagstoned upper
bar with its lanterns and roaring log fire
is reserved for guests at the associated
flamboyantly art deco hotel, but the more
utilitarian lower bar is still worth a visit
for the unbeatable setting high above
the sea swarming below this tidal island;
Sharps, Thwaites and an ale named for the
pub, lunchtime baguettes, Fri curry night;
children and dogs welcome, tables outside,
some down by beach, open all day.
(Caroline Prescott)

BUTTERLEIGH   SS9708
Butterleigh Inn (01884) 855433
Off A396 in Bickleigh; EX15 1PN
Traditional heavy-beamed country pub,
friendly and relaxed with good mix of
customers, enjoyable reasonably priced
pubby food (not Mon, Sun evening)
including Sun carvery, four well kept ales
such as Cotleigh and Otter, good choice of
wines, unspoilt lived-in interior with two
big fireplaces, back dining room; children
welcome, picnic-sets in large garden,
four comfortable bedrooms, closed Mon
lunchtime and winter Sun evening.
(Isobel Mackinlay)

CADELEIGH   SS9107
★Cadeleigh Arms (01884) 855238
*Village signed off A3072 W of junction
with A396 Tiverton–Exeter at Bickleigh;
EX16 8HP* Attractive and friendly old pub
owned by the local community, well kept
Cotleigh, Dartmoor, St Austell and a guest,
fresh locally sourced food (not Sun evening)
from favourites up, carpeted room on left
with bay-window seat and ornamental stove,
flagstoned room to the right has high-backed
settles and log fire in big fireplace, airy
dining room down a couple of steps with
valley views, local artwork, games room
(pool and darts) and skittle alley;
background music; children and dogs
welcome, picnic-sets on gravel terrace with
barbecue, more on gently sloping lawn,
closed Mon lunchtime. *(Mike Swan)*

CALIFORNIA CROSS   SX7053
California (01548) 821449
*Brown sign to pub off A3121 S of A38
junction; PL21 0SG* Neatly modernised
18th-c or older dining pub with beams,
panelling, stripped stone and log fire, wide
choice of enjoyable food from baguettes
to steaks in bar and family area, popular
Sun lunch (best to book), separate evening
restaurant (Weds-Sun) and small snug,
St Austell Tribute, Sharps Doom Bar and a
local guest, farm cider and decent wines by
the glass, good friendly service; background
music; dogs welcome, attractive garden
and back terrace, open all day. *(Bob and
Margaret Holder)*

CHAGFORD   SX7087
Ring o' Bells (01647) 432466
Off A382; TQ13 8AH Welcoming old pub
with beamed and panelled bar, four well
kept ales including Dartmoor, traditional
fairly priced home-made food, good friendly
service, woodburner in big fireplace; some
live music; dogs and well behaved children
welcome, sunny walled garden, nearby
moorland walks, four comfortable bedrooms,
open all day. *(Toby Jones)*

CHALLACOMBE   SS6941
Black Venus (01598) 763251
*B3358 Blackmoor Gate–Simonsbath;
EX31 4TT* Low-beamed 16th-c pub with
friendly helpful staff, two or three well kept
changing ales, Thatcher's cider and decent
wines by the glass, enjoyable fairly priced
food from sandwiches to popular Sun lunch,
pews and comfortable chairs, woodburner
and big fireplace, roomy attractive dining
area, games room with pool and darts; free
wi-fi; children and dogs welcome, garden play
area, lovely countryside and good walks from
the door, open all day in summer. *(Alison and
Michael Harper)*

CHERITON BISHOP   SX7792
★Old Thatch Inn (01647) 24204
Off A30; EX6 6JH Attractive thatched
village with welcoming relaxed atmosphere,
rambling beamed bar separated by big stone
fireplace (woodburner), Otter, Dartmoor
and other well kept local ales, ciders such
as Sandford's, good freshly prepared food
from owner-chef, efficient friendly service,
restaurant; free wi-fi; children and dogs
welcome, nice sheltered garden, two
comfortable clean bedrooms. *(Maureen Wood)*

CHITTLEHAMHOLT   SS6420
★Exeter Inn (01769) 540281
*Off A377 Barnstaple–Crediton, and
B3226 SW of South Molton; EX37 9NS*
Spotless 16th-c thatched coaching inn with
friendly staff and long-serving licensees,
good food (should book weekends) from
sandwiches and traditional choices up, well
kept ales such as Exmoor and Otter (some

tapped from the cask), local ciders and good wine choice, barrel seats by open stove in huge fireplace, beams spotted with hundreds of matchboxes, shelves of old bottles, traditional games, lounge with comfortable seating and woodburner, dining room and barn-style conservatory; background music; children and dogs welcome, gravel terrace, three bedrooms and four self-catering units. *(Mark Flynn)*

CHRISTOW SX8385

★ **Teign House** (01647) 252286
Teign Valley Road (B3193); EX6 7PL
Former farmhouse in country setting, open fire in beamed bar, very good freshly made food from pub favourites up, also an asian menu, friendly helpful staff, up to five well kept local ales, own cider and nice wines, dining room; well behaved children and dogs welcome, garden and camping field, open all day Fri-Sun, may close Mon. *(Mike Swan)*

CHULMLEIGH SS6814

Red Lion (01769) 580384
East Street; EX18 7DD Nicely updated and well divided 17th-c coaching inn, beams and open fires, enjoyable fairly priced food including pasta dishes, pizzas and grills, St Austell, Sharps and a guest, friendly helpful service; children welcome, five bedrooms, open all day Fri-Sun, closed Mon lunchtime. *(Anon)*

CHURCHSTOW SX7145

Church House (01548) 852237
A379 NW of Kingsbridge; TQ7 3QW
Attractive building dating from the 13th c, heavy black beams and stripped stone, enjoyable home-made food including daily specials and popular carvery (Weds-Sat evenings, Sun lunchtime, booking advised), St Austell ales and decent wines, friendly staff, back conservatory with floodlit well; children welcome, dogs in certain areas, tables on big terrace. *(Helen and Brian Edgeley)*

CLAYHIDON ST1615

Half Moon (01823) 680291
On main road through village; EX15 3TJ
Attractive old village pub with warm friendly atmosphere, wide choice of good home-made food from sharing boards up, well kept Otter and a couple of guests, farm cider, good wine list, comfortable bar with inglenook log fire; some live music; children and dogs welcome, picnic-sets in tiered garden over road, valley views, closed Sun evening, Mon. *(Guy Vowles)*

CLAYHIDON ST1817

Merry Harriers (01823) 421270
3 miles from M5 junction 26, A38 Wellington; left at roundabout then right to Ford Street; after a mile turn left, then at hilltop T junction turn left towards Chard – pub is signed from here; EX15 3TR Roadside country pub

under newish management; several small linked carpeted areas with comfortably cushioned pews and farmhouse chairs, woodburner, Exmoor, Otter and a guest ale, traditional food in two beamed dining areas with quarry tiles and lightly timbered white walls, friendly helpful staff; skittle alley; children and dogs welcome, sizeable garden with play equipment, good surrounding walks, open all day Sat, closed Sun evening, Mon. *(Bob and Margaret Holder, Comus and Sarah Elliott, Richard and Patricia Jefferson, William Ruxton)*

CLOVELLY SS3124

Red Lion (01237) 431237
The Quay; EX39 5TF Rambling 18th-c building in lovely position on curving quay below spectacular cliffs, beams, flagstones, log fire and interesting local photographs in character back bar (dogs on leads allowed here), well kept Country Life and Sharps Doom Bar, bar food and upstairs restaurant, efficient service; great views, 11 attractive bedrooms (six more in Sail Loft annexe), own car park for residents and diners, open all day. *(Anon)*

CLYST HYDON ST0201

★ **Five Bells** (01884) 277288
W of village, just off B3176 not far from M5 junction 28; EX15 2NT Thatched and beamed dining pub under same owners as the Jack in the Green at Rockbeare; smartly refurbished interior with several different areas including raised dining part, woodburner in large stone fireplace, really good attractively presented food including weekday set lunch, efficient friendly service, four well kept ales such as Butcombe and Otter, games room with pool and sports TV; children welcome, lovely cottagey garden with profusion of spring and summer flowers, country views. *(Keith Hannaford, Barrie and Anne King, Paul and Sonia Broadgate)*

COCKWOOD SX9780

★ **Ship** (01626) 890373
Off A379 N of Dawlish; EX6 8NU
Comfortable traditional 17th-c pub set back from estuary and harbour – gets very busy in season; good value freshly made food including good fish dishes and puddings, Thurs pie night, OAP lunch deal Fri, Butcombe and Sharps Doom Bar, friendly staff and locals, partitioned beamed bar with big log fire and ancient oven, decorative plates and seafaring memorabilia, small restaurant; background music; children and dogs welcome, nice steep-sided garden. *(Gavin and Helle May)*

COLYTON SY2494

Kingfisher (01297) 552476
Off A35 and A3052 E of Sidmouth; Dolphin Street; EX24 6NA Low-beamed 16th-c village pub with four well kept ales such as Sharps and Skinners, popular

reasonably priced food, stripped stone, plush seats and elm settles, back restaurant, pub games and skittle alley; outside gents'; children and dogs welcome, terrace tables, garden with water feature, boules, open all day. *(Roger and Donna Huggins)*

COMBE MARTIN   SS5846
Pack o' Cards   (01271) 882300
High Street; EX34 OET Unusual 'house of cards' building constructed in the late 17th c to celebrate a substantial gambling win – four floors, 13 rooms and 52 windows; snug bar area and various side rooms, St Austell Tribute, Charles Wells Bombardier and a guest, enjoyable inexpensive pub food including children's choices and good Sun roast, friendly helpful service, restaurant; dogs welcome, pretty riverside garden with play area, six comfortable bedrooms, generous breakfast, open all day.
(Peter Pilbeam)

COMBEINTEIGNHEAD   SX9071
Wild Goose   (01626) 872241
Off unclassified coast road Newton Abbot–Shaldon, up hill in village; TQ12 4RA Rambling 17th-c pub refurbished under friendly new family owners; five west country ales in spacious back beamed lounge, agricultural bits and pieces on the walls, enjoyable freshly made food including daily specials, front bar with big fireplace, more beams, standing timbers and some flagstones, step down to area with another large fireplace, further cosy room with tub chairs; background and fortnightly live music, Sun quiz, TV projector for major sporting events; children and dogs welcome, back garden with nice country views, open all day weekends. *(Isobel Mackinlay)*

COUNTISBURY   SS7449
Blue Ball   (01598) 741263
A39, E of Lynton; EX35 6NE Beautifully set heavy-beamed rambling pub, friendly licensees, good range of generous local food in bar and restaurant, three ales including one badged for them, decent wines and proper ciders, log fires; background music; children, dogs and walkers welcome, views from terrace tables, good nearby cliff walks (pub provides handouts of four circular routes), comfortable bedrooms, open all day. *(Mr and Mrs D J Nash, Lynda and Trevor Smith)*

CREDITON   SS8300
Crediton Inn   (01363) 772882
Mill Street (follow Tiverton sign); EX17 1EZ Small friendly local (the 'Kirton') with long-serving landlady, well kept Hanlons Yellowhammer and up to nine quickly changing guests (Nov beer festival), cheap well prepared weekend food, home-made scotch eggs other times, back games room/skittle alley; free wi-fi; open all day Mon-Sat. *(Mike Swan)*

CROYDE   SS4439
Manor House Inn   (01271) 890241
St Marys Road, off B3231 NW of Braunton; EX33 1PG Friendly family pub with cheerful efficient service, three well kept west country ales, good choice of enjoyable fairly priced food from lunchtime sandwiches to blackboard specials, carvery Weds and Sun, cream teas, restaurant and dining conservatory; background and live music, sports TV, games end, skittle alley; dogs welcome in bar, disabled facilities, attractive terraced garden with good big play area, open all day. *(Pat and Tony Martin)*

CROYDE   SS4439
Thatch   (01271) 890349
B3231 NW of Braunton; Hobbs Hill; EX33 1LZ Lively thatched pub near great surfing beaches (can get packed in summer); rambling and roomy, with beams, open fire, settles and good seating, enjoyable pubby food from sandwiches and baked potatoes up, well kept changing local ales, morning coffee, teas, cheerful young staff, smart restaurant with dressers and lots of china; background and live music (Fri); children in eating areas, tables on flower-filled suntrap terraces, large gardens shared with neighbouring Billy Budds, good play area, simple clean bedrooms and self-catering cottage, open (and food) all day. *(Pat and Tony Martin)*

CULMSTOCK   ST1013
★ Culm Valley   (01884) 840354
B3391, off A38 E of M5 junction 27; EX15 3JJ Friendly 18th-c pub under new ownership (some refurbishment); informal lively atmosphere, bar with hotchpotch of modern and unrenovated furnishings, big fireplace with woodburner, well liked food from varied menu, four changing ales, local cider and plenty of wines by the glass, good service, dining room and small front conservatory, large back room with photos for sale; free wi-fi; children and dogs (in bar) welcome, tables out on raised grassed area (former railway platform) overlooking bridge and River Culm, new covered smokers' area behind, open all day Fri-Sun. *(Guy Vowles)*

DARTINGTON   SX7861
Cott   (01803) 863777
Cott signed off A385 W of Totnes, opposite A384 turn-off; TQ9 6HE Long 14th-c thatched pub with heavy beams, flagstones, nice mix of old furniture and two inglenooks (one with big woodburner), good home-made locally sourced food from traditional choices up in bar and restaurant, three ales including local Hunters and Greene King, Ashridge cider, nice wines by the glass, friendly helpful service, live music Sun; children and dogs welcome, wheelchair access (with help into restaurant), picnic-sets in garden and on pretty terrace, five comfortable bedrooms, open all day. *(John Evans)*

DARTMOUTH   SX8751
★ **Cherub** (01803) 832571
Higher Street; walk along riverfront,
right into Hauley Road and up steps
at end; TQ6 9RB Ancient building
(Dartmouth's oldest) with two heavily
timbered upper floors jutting over the street
and many original interior features, oak
beams, leaded lights, tapestried seats and
big stone fireplace with photo of pub ghost
above, up to six well kept ales including
St Austell in bustling bar, low-ceilinged
upstairs restaurant, good food from pub
favourites to fish specials, efficient friendly
service; background music; children welcome
(no pushchairs), dogs in bar, open all day.
(Richard Tilbrook)

DARTMOUTH   SX8751
Dolphin (01803) 833698
Market Street; TQ6 9QE Interesting
building in picturesque part of town, quirky
and laid-back, with own Bridgetown beer
(brewed in Totnes) and St Austell Tribute,
good food including well priced fish platters,
friendly staff; background and live music;
children and dogs welcome, open all day.
(Hilary and Neil Christopher)

DARTMOUTH   SX8751
Floating Bridge (01803) 832354
Opposite Upper Ferry, use Dart Marina
Hotel car park; Coombe Road (A379);
TQ6 9PQ Bustling quayside pub in lovely
spot, bar with lots of stools by windows
making most of waterside view, black
and white photographs of local boating
scenes, St Austell Tribute, Sharps Doom
Bar and guests, several wines by the
glass, straightforward pub food including
sandwiches, bare-boards dining room with
leather-backed chairs around wooden
tables; children and dogs (in bar) welcome,
pretty window boxes, seats out by the river
looking at busy ferry crossing, more on
sizeable roof terrace, open (and food) all day.
(Peter Harrison, Steve and Liz Tilley, John Harris)

DAWLISH WARREN   SX9778
Mount Pleasant (01626) 863151
Mount Pleasant Road; EX7 0NA
Expansive sea views from large recently
refurbished inn (run by same family for over
30 years), carpeted heavily beamed lounge
and linked rooms, well kept Otter ales, wide
choice of fairly standard home-cooked food
including children's, friendly service and
good mix of customers; skittle alley; terrace
tables, handy for coast path and nature
reserve, bedrooms, open all day. *(Anon)*

DITTISHAM   SX8654
★ **Ferry Boat** (01803) 722368
Manor Street; best to park in village car
park and walk down; TQ6 0EX
Cheerful riverside pub with lively mix of
customers; beamed bar with log fires and
straightforward pubby furniture, lots of
boating bits and pieces, tide times chalked
on wall, flags on ceiling, picture-window
view of River Dart, at least three ales such
as Dorset, Otter and Sharps, a dozen wines
by the glass, good range of tasty home-made
food including pie of the day and various
curries, efficient service; background and
some live music; children and dogs welcome,
moorings for visiting boats on adjacent
pontoon and bell to summon ferry, good
walks, open (and food) all day. *(Ken Parry,*
Lynda and Trevor Smith, Bruce Jamieson, Richard
Tilbrook, Steve and Liz Tilley)

DITTISHAM   SX8654
Red Lion (01803) 722235
The Level; TQ6 0ES Lovely location
looking down over attractive village and River
Dart; welcoming atmosphere, decent food
including daily specials, Dartmoor, Palmers
and a summer guest, good italian coffee and
morning pastries, carpeted bar, restaurant,
open fires; also houses village store, tiny post
office, library and craft shop; children and
dogs welcome, eight bedrooms (some with
river view), open from 8.30am, may shut Weds
and weekend afternoons in winter.
(Bruce Jamieson)

DREWSTEIGNTON   SX7390
Drewe Arms (01647) 281409
Off A30 NW of Moretonhampstead;
EX6 6QN Pretty thatched village pub
under newish management; unspoilt room
on left with basic wooden wall benches,
stools and tables, original serving hatch,
ales such as Dartmoor and Otter from tap
room casks, local cider, enjoyable sensibly
priced pubby food including daily specials,
two dining areas, one with Rayburn and
history of Britain's longest serving landlady
(Mabel Mudge), another with woodburner,
darts and board games, live music and
quiz nights in back Long Room; free wi-fi;
children and dogs welcome, seats under
umbrellas on front terrace and in garden,
pretty flowering tubs and baskets, two
four-poster bedrooms, four bunk rooms,
on Dartmoor Trail and handy for Castle
Drogo (NT), open (and food) all day in
summer. *(Gerry Price, Mr and Mrs J Watkins)*

DUNSFORD   SX8189
Royal Oak (01647) 252256
Signed from Moretonhampstead;
EX6 7DA Friendly comfortably worn-in
village inn, good generous home-made food
at reasonable prices, changing ales such as
Otter and Sharps, local cider, airy lounge
with woodburner and view from sunny dining
bay, simple dining room, steps down to pool
room; background and some live music, quiz
nights; children well looked after, sheltered
tiered garden with play area, various animals
including donkeys, miniature ponies, alpacas
and chipmunks, good value bedrooms in
converted barn. *(Alfie Bayliss)*

EAST ALLINGTON SX7648
Fortescue Arms (01548) 521215
Village signed off A381 Totnes–
Kingsbridge, S of A3122 junction;
TQ9 7RA Pretty family-run village pub;
two-room bar with mix of wooden tables and
chairs on black slate floor, some brewery
memorabilia, three Dartmoor ales and eight
wines by the glass, restaurant with own bar,
high-backed dining chairs around painted
tables, well liked freshly made food including
pizzas, good friendly service; background
and occasional live music, free wi-fi; children
and dogs welcome, seats out at the front
with more on sheltered terrace, open all
day during school holidays (closed Mon and
lunchtimes Tues-Thurs at other times).
(Neil Allen)

EAST BUDLEIGH SY0684
Sir Walter Raleigh (01395) 442510
High Street; EX9 7ED Friendly little
low-beamed 16th-c village local, well kept
changing west country beers and well liked
traditional food, restaurant down step;
children and dogs welcome, parking some
way off, wonderful medieval bench carvings
in nearby church, handy too for Bicton Park
gardens. *(Bertie Yarwood)*

EAST DOWN SS5941
Pyne Arms (01271) 850055
Off A39 Barnstaple–Lynton near
Arlington; EX31 4LX Old pub tucked
away in small hamlet, cosy carpeted bar
with lots of alcoves, woodburner, sensibly
priced traditional food and daily specials,
Exmoor and a guest ale, good choice of wines,
flagstoned area with sofas, conservatory;
background music, free wi-fi; children
and dogs welcome, small enclosed garden,
good walks, handy for Arlington Court
(NT), open all day weekends, closed Mon
lunchtime. *(Neil Allen)*

EAST PRAWLE SX7836
Pigs Nose (01548) 511209
Prawle Green; TQ7 2BY Relaxed and
quirky three-room 16th-c pub, low beams
and flagstones, lots of interesting bric-a-brac
and pictures, mix of old furniture, jars of
wild flowers and candles on tables, open fire,
local ales tapped from the cask, farm ciders
and enjoyable simple pubby food, small
family area with unusual toys, pool, darts and
knitting, friendly dogs (others welcome and
menu for them); unobtrusive background
music, hall for live bands (landlord was
1960s tour manager); tables outside, pleasant
spot on village green, closed Sun evening in
winter. *(Richard Tilbrook)*

EXETER SX9292
Chaucers (01392) 422365
Basement of Tesco Metro, High Street;
EX4 3LR Steps down to this large, dimly
lit olde-worlde-style pub/bistro/wine bar;

beamed low ceiling and timber-framed walls,
wood floors, several levels with booths and
alcoves, comfortable furnishings, Marstons-
related ales and well priced wines (plenty by
the glass), cocktails, good choice of enjoyable
food from snacks to specials, friendly service;
background music, silent games machines,
no under-14s; open all day (till 4pm Sun).
(Anon)

EXETER SX9192
Fat Pig (01392) 437217
John Street; EX1 1BL Popular Victorian
corner pub (same owners as the Rusty
Bike in Howell Road – see Main Entries),
welcoming and relaxed, with focus on dining,
good food from daily changing blackboard
menus using local produce (some from
owner's farm), home-smoked meats, own
ales (brewed in the cellar), real ciders and
good wine choice, light and airy stripped-
pine interior with painted half-panelling
and nice fire, small conservatory-style room,
Mon quiz; tables in heated courtyard, open
all day Sat, till 5pm Sun, closed weekday
lunchtimes. *(Roger and Donna Huggins)*

EXETER SX9292
Georges Meeting House
(01392) 454250 *South Street; EX1 1ED*
Wetherspoons in grand former 18th-c
chapel, bare-boards interior with three-sided
gallery, stained glass and tall pulpit at
one end, good range of real ales from long
counter, their usual good value food; children
welcome, tables in attractive side garden
under parasols, open all day from 8am.
(Roger and Donna Huggins)

EXETER SX9292
★**Hour Glass** (01392) 258722
Melbourne Street; off B3015 Topsham
Road; EX2 4AU Old-fashioned bow-
cornered pub tucked away in surviving
Georgian part above the quay; good inventive
food including vegetarian from shortish
regularly changing menu, up to five well kept
ales (usually one from Otter) and extensive
range of wines and spirits, friendly relaxed
atmosphere, beams, bare boards and mix of
furnishings, assorted pictures on dark red
walls and various odds and ends including
a stuffed badger, open fire in small brick
fireplace; background and live music;
children away from bar and dogs welcome
(resident cats), open all day weekends,
closed Mon lunchtime. *(Roger and Donna*
Huggins)

EXETER SX9193
★**Imperial** (01392) 434050
New North Road (above St David's
Station); EX4 4AH Impressive 19th-c
mansion in own six-acre hillside park with
sweeping drive, various different areas
including two clubby little side bars, fine
old ballroom with elaborate plasterwork
and gilding, light and airy former orangery

with unusual mirrored end wall, interesting pictures, up to 14 real ales, standard good value Wetherspoons menu; popular with students and can get very busy; plenty of picnic-sets in grounds and elegant garden furniture in attractive cobbled courtyard, open all day. *(Roger and Donna Huggins)*

EXETER SX9292

Old Fire House (01392) 277279

New North Road; EX4 4EP Relaxed city-centre pub in Georgian building behind high arched wrought-iron gates, up to ten real ales, several ciders and good choice of bottled beers and wines, bargain food including late evening pizzas, friendly efficient staff, arranged over two floors with dimly lit beamed rooms and simple furniture; background music, live weekends and popular with young crowd (modest admission charge Fri, Sat night); picnic-sets in front courtyard, open all day till late. *(David Crook, Roger and Donna Huggins)*

EXETER SX9292

Prospect (01392) 273152

The Quay; EX2 4AN Early 19th-c pub in good quayside position, well kept ales such as Exmoor, Otter and St Austell, friendly efficient young staff, usual food, plenty of comfortable tables including raised river-view dining area, rather cavernous back part; background and live music; children welcome, tables out by historic ship-canal basin, open (and food) all day. *(Roger and Donna Huggins)*

EXETER SX9292

Well House (01392) 223611

Cathedral Yard (attached to Royal Clarence Hotel); EX1 1HB Splendid position with big windows looking across to cathedral in partly divided open-plan bar, good choice of real ales and ciders (festivals), eight wines by the glass and enjoyable food from hotel's kitchen, quick friendly service, lots of Victorian prints, daily papers, Roman well below (can be viewed by prior arrangement); live music last Sun of month; open all day. *(Michael Butler, Ken Parry, John T Ames)*

EXMINSTER SX9686

★**Turf Hotel** (01392) 833128

From A379 S of village, follow the signs to the Swan's Nest, then continue to end of track, by gates; park and walk right along canal towpath – nearly a mile; EX6 8EE Remote but popular waterside pub reached by 20-minute towpath walk, cycle ride or 60-seater boat from Topsham quay (15-minute trip); several little rooms – end one with slate floor, pine walls, built-in seats and woodburner, simple room along corridor serves Exeter Avocet, Otter Ale and Bitter and Hanlons Yellowhammer, local cider/juices and ten wines by the glass, interesting locally sourced food; background

music, board games; children and dogs welcome, big garden with picnic-sets and popular summer barbecues, arrive early for a seat in good weather, bedrooms, open all day, but closed Jan, Feb. *(Richard and Penny Gibbs, Hilary and Neil Christopher, Peter Kirkman)*

EXMOUTH SX9980

Grapevine (01395) 222208

Victoria Road; EX8 1DL Popular red-brick corner pub (calls itself a pub-bistro), light and spacious with mix of wooden tables and seating, rugs on bare boards, local modern artwork, good range of changing west country ales and bottled imports, tasty well presented food including daily specials and set deal (Mon-Thurs), friendly service and nice relaxed atmosphere; background music, live bands Fri, charity quiz Mon, free wi-fi; children welcome, open all day from 9am, till 4pm Sun. *(Alison and Michael Harper)*

EXMOUTH SY9980

Grove (01395) 272101

Esplanade; EX8 1BJ Roomy high-gabled Victorian pub set back from beach, traditional furnishings, caricatures and local prints, enjoyable pubby food including local fish specials, friendly staff, Charles Wells and guests kept well, decent house wines, attractive fireplace at back, sea views from appealing upstairs dining room and balcony; background music, quiz Thurs; children welcome, picnic-sets in front garden, open all day (food all day weekends). *(PL)*

GEORGEHAM SS4639

Kings Arms (01271) 890240

B3231 (Chapel Street) Croyde–Woolacombe; EX33 1JJ Welcoming comfortably modernised village pub with red walls, slate floors and leather sofas by big woodburner, good freshly cooked food using local ingredients, efficient friendly service, St Austell Tribute and a couple of local guests, good choice of wines, upstairs dining area with tables out on sunny balcony, some traditional pub games; background and live music; children and dogs welcome, small front terrace screened from road, open all day. *(Neil Allen)*

HARBERTON SX7758

★**Church House** (01803) 863707

Off A381 S of Totnes; next to church; TQ9 7SF Ancient village pub under newish licensees, well kept ales including Quercus and a house beer from Hunters, ten wines by the glass, local cider, good fairly priced food (not Sun evening), friendly efficient service, unusually long bar with blackened beams, medieval latticed glass and oak panelling, attractive 17th- and 18th-c pews and settles, woodburner in big inglenook, separate dining room; children and dogs welcome (resident golden retriever), sunny walled back garden, bedrooms, open all day Sun, closed Mon lunchtime. *(Isobel Mackinlay)*

HARTLAND
SS2524
Hart (01237) 441474
The Square; EX39 6BL Old village pub with good freshly made food from interesting varied menu, ales such as Sharps and Skinners, reasonably priced wines, friendly helpful staff, log fire; children and dogs welcome, closed Sun evening, Mon.
(Peter Pilbeam)

HATHERLEIGH
SS5404
George (01837) 811612
A386 N of Okehampton; Market Street; EX20 3JN Completely rebuilt after original 15th-c thatched and timbered pub burnt down on Christmas Eve 2008; old-style interior with lots of reclaimed timbers and other old materials, mix of furniture (some new) on carpet, wood and tiled floors, open fires, enjoyable home-made food including daily specials and Sun carvery, well kept Courage Directors, St Austell Tribute and a guest, decent coffee; 13 bedrooms, open all day. *(John T Ames)*

HEMYOCK
ST1313
Catherine Wheel (01823) 680224
Cornhill; EX15 3RQ Popular and friendly village pub with bar, lounge and restaurant, Otter and Sharps Doom Bar, plenty of wines by the glass and good interesting food (sometimes foraged), fresh flowers on tables, leather sofas by woodburner; darts and pool, function room with skittle alley, Sun quiz; children welcome, closed Mon lunchtime. *(Richard and Patricia Jefferson, Patrick and Daphne Darley, Guy Vowles)*

HOLNE
SX7069
★ Church House (01364) 631208
Signed off B3357 W of Ashburton; TQ13 7SJ Medieval inn in quaint moorland hamlet surrounded by slopes of Dartmoor where *War Horse* was filmed; lower bar with stripped pine panelling and 18th-c curved elm settle, heavy 16th-c oak partition separating it from lounge bar, candles and log fires, ales from Dartmoor and St Austell, real cider, several wines by the glass, hearty food (not Sun evening); background and monthly live music, board games; children and dogs welcome, fine views from the pillared porch, good walks (on Two Moors Way), bedrooms, church with fine medieval rood screen is worth a visit. *(Toby Jones)*

HOLSWORTHY
SS3304
Rydon Inn (01409) 259444
Rydon (A3072 W); EX22 7HU Comfortably extended family-run dining pub, clean and tidy, with enjoyable food and well kept ales such as Otter and Sharps, good friendly service, raftered bar with thatched servery, woodburner in stone fireplace; background music; children and dogs welcome, disabled facilities, views over lake from conservatory and deck, well

tended garden, open all day. *(Alison and Michael Harper)*

HONITON
ST1599
Heathfield (01404) 45321
Walnut Road; EX14 2UG Ancient thatched and beamed pub in contrasting residential area, well run and spacious, with Greene King ales and good value reliable food from varied menu including the Heathfield Whopper (20oz rump steak), Sun carvery, cheerful prompt service, skittle alley; children welcome, seven bedrooms, open all day Fri-Sun. *(Bob and Margaret Holder, Colin McKerrow)*

HONITON
SY1198
★ Holt (01404) 47707
High Street, W end; EX14 1LA Charming little bustling pub run by two brothers, relaxed and informal, with just one room downstairs, chunky tables and chairs on slate flooring, brown leather sofas, a coal-effect woodburner, shelves of books, full range of Otter beers (the family founded the brewery), bigger brighter upstairs dining room with similar furniture on pale floorboards, attractive musician prints, very good tapas and other inventive food, cookery classes and quarterly music festivals; well behaved children welcome, dogs in bar, closed Sun, Mon. *(Michael Butler, Guy Vowles, Revd R P Tickle, Mike and Jayne Bastin, David and Judy Robison and others)*

HOPE COVE
SX6740
Hope & Anchor (01548) 561294
Tucked away by car park; TQ7 3HQ Bustling unpretentious inn, friendly and comfortably unfussy, in lovely seaside spot, good open fire, helpful amiable young staff, good value straightforward food including lots of fish, well kept St Austell Dartmoor and a beer named for the pub, reasonably priced wines, flagstones and bare boards, dining room views to Burgh Island, big separate family room; background music; dogs welcome, sea-view tables out on decking, great coast walks, bedrooms, good breakfast, open all day. *(Peter Travis, Theocsbrian)*

HORNS CROSS
SS3823
★ Hoops (01237) 451222
A39 Clovelly–Bideford, W of village; EX39 5DL Pretty thatched inn with good bustling atmosphere; traditionally furnished bar has china hanging from beams, log fires in sizeable fireplaces and some standing timbers and partitioning, more formal restaurant with attractive mix of tables and chairs, some panelling, exposed stone and another open fire, Hoops Bitter (from Country Life) and Hoops Best and Light (from Forge), over a dozen wines by the glass, enjoyable fairly straightforward food using local suppliers, friendly helpful staff; may be background music; children and dogs welcome, picnic-sets under parasols

in enclosed courtyard, more seats on terrace and in two acres of gardens, well equipped bedrooms, open all day. *(Anon)*

HORSEBRIDGE   SX4074

★ **Royal** (01822) 870214

Off A384 Tavistock–Launceston; PL19 8PJ Dimly lit ancient local with dark half-panelling, log fires, slate floors, scrubbed tables and interesting bric-a-brac, good reasonably priced home-made food including plenty of fish, friendly staff, well kept Dartmoor, St Austell and Skinners poured from the cask, real cider, café-style side room; no children in the evening, picnic-sets on front and side terraces and in big garden, quiet rustic spot by lovely old Tamar bridge, popular with walkers and cyclists.
(Hilary and Neil Christopher)

IDE   SX9090

Huntsman (01392) 272779

High Street; EX2 9RN Welcoming thatched and beamed country pub, tasty sensibly priced home-made food using local suppliers from sandwiches to good value Sun lunch, ales such as Exmoor, Otter and Sharps, friendly attentive service; some live music; children welcome, picnic-sets in pleasant garden. *(Anon)*

IDE   SX8990

Poachers (01392) 273847

3 miles from M5 junction 31, via A30; High Street; EX2 9RW Cosy beamed pub in quaint village, Branscombe Vale Branoc and four changing west country guests from ornate curved wooden bar, enjoyable home-made food, mismatched old chairs and sofas, various pictures and odds and ends, big log fire, restaurant; free wi-fi; dogs welcome (they have a boxer), tables in pleasant garden with barbecue, three comfortable bedrooms, open all day (till late Fri, Sat). *(Anon)*

IDEFORD   SX8977

★ **Royal Oak** (01626) 852274

2 miles off A380; TQ13 0AY Unpretentious little 16th-c thatched and flagstoned village local, friendly helpful service, a couple of changing local ales, generous helpings of tasty well priced food, navy theme including interesting Nelson and Churchill memorabilia, beams, panelling and big open fireplace; children and dogs welcome, tables out at front and by car park over road, closed Mon lunchtime. *(Martin and Ruth Lucas)*

ILFRACOMBE   SS5247

George & Dragon (01271) 863851

Fore Street; EX34 9ED One of the oldest pubs here (14th c) and handy for the harbour, clean and comfortable with friendly local atmosphere, ales such as Exmoor, Sharps and Shepherd Neame, decent wines,

traditional home-made food including local fish, beams, stripped stone and open fireplaces, lots of ornaments etc; background music, Tues quiz, no mobile phones; children and dogs welcome, open all day and can get very busy weekends. *(Dave Braisted)*

ILFRACOMBE   SS5247

Ship & Pilot (01271) 863562

Broad Street, off harbour; EX34 9EE Bright yellow pub near harbour with friendly mix of regulars and visitors, six well kept changing ales (usually have Bass), two proper ciders and a perry, no food apart from rolls, traditional open-plan interior with lots of old photos, darts and juke box, weekend live music; a couple of TVs for sport; tables outside, open all day. *(Neil Allen)*

ILSINGTON   SX7876

Carpenters Arms (01364) 661629

Old Town Hill; TQ13 9RG Unspoilt little 18th-c local next to the church in this quiet village, beams and flagstones, country-style pine furniture, brasses, woodburner, enjoyable generously served home-made food and well kept changing ales, friendly atmosphere, darts; children, well behaved dogs and muddy boots welcome, tables out at front, good walks, no car park, open all day weekends. *(Toby Jones)*

INSTOW   SS4730

Boat House (01271) 861292

Marine Parade; EX39 4JJ Modern high-ceilinged bar-restaurant with huge tidal beach just across lane and views to Appledore, wide choice of good food including plenty of fish/seafood, two well kept local ales and decent wines by the glass, friendly prompt service, lively family bustle; background music; roof terrace. *(David Field)*

KILMINGTON   SY2698

New Inn (01297) 33376

Signed off Gammons Hill; EX13 7SF Traditional thatched pub (originally three 14th-c cottages) redecorated under friendly new licensees; good food and well kept Palmers ales; skittle alley; picnic-sets in large garden with tree-shaded areas. *(Anon)*

KILMINGTON   SY2798

★ **Old Inn** (01297) 32096

A35; EX13 7RB Thatched 16th-c pub, beams and flagstones, welcoming licensees and nice bustling atmosphere, generous helpings of enjoyable good value food using local suppliers, well kept Branscombe Vale, Otter and a guest, good choice of wines, amiable attentive service, small character front bar with traditional games (there's also a skittle alley), back lounge with leather armchairs by inglenook log fire, small restaurant; children welcome, beer gardens. *(Phil and Jane Villiers)*

KINGSBRIDGE   SX7343

Crabshell (01548) 852345

Embankment Road, edge of town;
TQ7 1JZ Great waterside position,
charming when tide is in, with lovely views
from big windows and outside tables,
emphasis on food (generous helpings)
including good fish/seafood, friendly staff,
well kept local Quercus ales, feature open
fire; children welcome, open all day. *(Peter*
Travis, B J Harding)

KINGSTON   SX6347

Dolphin (01548) 810314

Off B3392 S of Modbury (can also be
reached from A379 W of Modbury);
TQ7 4QE Cosy and peaceful 16th-c inn run
by two brothers; knocked-through beamed
rooms with pubby furniture and cushioned
wall seats on red carpeting, open fire and
woodburner in inglenook fireplaces, well
kept ales such as Otter, St Austell, Sharps
and Timothy Taylors, farm cider and decent
wines by the glass; change of chef and menu
much reduced as we went to press; children
and dogs welcome, seats in garden, pretty
tubs and window boxes, quiet village with
several tracks leading down to the sea, three
bedrooms in building across lane, closes
some Sun evenings in winter. *(B J Harding,*
Steve Whalley)

KINGSWEAR   SX8851

★ Ship (01803) 752348

Higher Street; TQ6 0AG Attractive old
beamed local by the church, plenty of
atmosphere and kind cheerful service, well
kept Adnams, Otter, Wadworths and guests
from horseshoe bar, Addlestone's cider
and nice wines, popular food including
good local fish (best views from restaurant
up steps), nautical bric-a-brac and local
photographs, tartan carpets and two log fires;
occasional live music, big-screen sports TV;
dogs welcome, a couple of river-view tables
outside, open all day and busy in summer, all
day Fri-Sun winter. *(Richard Tilbrook)*

LAKE   SX5288

★ Bearslake (01837) 861334

A386 just S of Sourton; EX20 4HQ
Rambling thatch and stone pub (former
longhouse dating from the 13th c), leather
sofas and high bar chairs on crazy-paved
slate floor at one end, three more rooms
with woodburners, toby jugs, farm tools and
traps, stripped stone, well kept ales such as
Otter and Teignworthy, good range of spirits,
decent wines and well liked food, beamed
restaurant; wi-fi through most of the building;
children allowed, large sheltered streamside
garden, Dartmoor walks, six comfortable

bedrooms, generous breakfast, closed Sun
evening, otherwise open all day. *(Isobel*
Mackinlay)

LANDSCOVE   SX7766

Live & Let Live (01803) 762663

SE end of village by Methodist chapel;
TQ13 7LZ Friendly open-plan village local
with decent freshly made food and well
kept ales such as Teignworthy, impressive
collection of miniatures, log fire; children
and dogs welcome, tables on small front deck
and in little orchard across lane, good walks,
closed Mon. *(Anon)*

LEE   SS4846

Grampus (01271) 862906

Signed off B3343/A361 W of Ilfracombe;
EX34 8LR Attractive unpretentious 14th-c
beamed pub, friendly and relaxed, with good
range of well kept ales and local ciders,
reasonably priced traditional food (not Sun
evening), tea room (in season) and shop;
skittles, pool and darts, live music Fri; dogs
very welcome, lots of tables in appealing
sheltered garden, short stroll from sea and
superb coast walks, open all day summer
weekends. *(Eddie Edwards)*

LIFTON   SX3885

★ Arundell Arms (01566) 784666

Fore Street; PL16 0AA Good interesting
lunchtime food in substantial country-
house fishing hotel, warmly welcoming and
individual, with rich décor, nice staff and
sophisticated service, good choice of wines
by the glass, morning coffee and afternoon
tea, restaurant; also adjacent Courthouse bar,
complete with original cells, doing good fairly
priced pubby food (not Mon evening), well
kept St Austell Tribute and Dartmoor Jail;
can arrange fishing tuition – also shooting,
deer-stalking and riding; 21 bedrooms, useful
A30 stop. *(Alison and Michael Harper)*

LITTLEHEMPSTON   SX8162

Pig & Whistle (01803) 863733

Newton Road (A381); TQ9 6LT Large
welcoming former coaching inn, enjoyable
traditional food and ales such as Dartmoor
and Teignworthy, long bar with beams and
stripped stone, extensive dining area; free
wi-fi; children welcome, decked front terrace,
two bedrooms, open all day. *(Anon)*

LITTLEHEMPSTON   SX8162

Tally Ho (01803) 862316

Off A381 NE of Totnes; TQ9 6LY
Old community-owned pub opposite church,
neat and cosy, with low black beams, stripped
stone walls and red carpet, traditional food
from sandwiches to steaks, well kept ales
from Bays, Dartmoor and Hunters, friendly

If you report on a pub that's not a featured entry, please tell us any lunchtimes or
evenings when it doesn't serve bar food.

atmosphere; children welcome, picnic-sets on flower-filled terrace, open all day Sun (food till 6pm), closed Mon. *(Neil Allen)*

LOWER ASHTON   SX8484
Manor Inn (01647) 252304
Ashton signposted off B3193 N of Chudleigh; EX6 7QL Well run country pub under friendly hard-working licensees, good quality sensibly priced food including lunchtime set menu, well kept ales such as Otter and Teignworthy, good choice of wines, open fires in both bars, back restaurant in converted smithy; dogs welcome, disabled access, garden picnic-sets with nice rural outlook, open all day Sun, closed Mon. *(Toby Jones)*

LUPPITT   ST1606
★ Luppitt Inn (01404) 891613
Back roads N of Honiton; EX14 4RT Unspoilt basic farmhouse pub tucked away in lovely countryside, an amazing survivor, with chatty long-serving landlady, tiny room with corner bar and a table, another not much bigger with fireplace, cheap Otter tapped from the cask, intriguing metal puzzles made by a neighbour, no food or music, lavatories across the yard; closed lunchtimes and all day Sun. *(Anon)*

LUTON   SX9076
★ Elizabethan (01626) 775425
Haldon Moor; TQ13 0BL Tucked-away much-altered low-beamed dining pub (once owned by Elizabeth I); wide choice of good well presented food including daily specials and popular Sun lunch, three well kept ales and several reasonably priced wines by the glass, warm friendly service from attentive staff, thriving atmosphere; children welcome, pretty front garden, open all day Sun. *(Peter Pilbeam)*

LYDFORD   SX5184
Castle Inn (01822) 820241
Off A386 Okehampton–Tavistock; EX20 4BH Tudor inn owned by St Austell, friendly helpful staff, traditional twin bars with big slate flagstones, bowed low beams and granite walls, high backed settles and four inglenook log fires, notable stained-glass door, good popular food, restaurant; free wi-fi; children and dogs welcome in certain areas, seats out at front and in sheltered back garden, lovely NT river gorge nearby, eight bedrooms, open all day. *(Peter Pilbeam)*

LYMPSTONE   SX9884
Swan (01395) 272644
The Strand, by station entrance; EX8 5ET Well cared for pub with nice old-fashioned décor, split-level panelled dining area with leather sofas by big fire, good home-made food including local fish, well kept ales such as Otter, Palmers, St Austell and Wadworths, short interesting wine list, welcoming helpful staff, games room with

pool, some live music; children welcome, picnic-sets out at front and smokers' area, popular with cyclists (bike racks provided), open all day. *(Anon)*

LYNMOUTH   SS7249
Rising Sun (01598) 753223
Harbourside; EX35 6EG Wonderful position overlooking harbour; bustling beamed and stripped-stone bar with good fire, four Exmoor ales, popular food from comprehensive menu (emphasis on fish), upmarket hotel side with attractive restaurant; background music; dogs welcome, gardens behind, bedrooms in cottagey old thatched building, parking can be a problem – expensive during the day, sparse at night. *(Lynda and Trevor Smith)*

MEAVY   SX5467
★ Royal Oak (01822) 852944
Off B3212 E of Yelverton; PL20 6PJ Partly 15th-c pub taking its name from the 800-year-old oak on green opposite; heavy beamed L-shaped bar with church pews, red plush banquettes, old agricultural prints and church pictures, smaller locals' bar with flagstones and big open-hearth fireplace, separate dining room, good food served by friendly staff, four well kept ales including Dartmoor, farm ciders, a dozen wines by the glass and several malt whiskies; background music, board games; children and dogs (in bar) welcome, picnic-sets out in front and on green, pretty Dartmoor-edge village, open all day in summer, all day weekends winter. *(Hugh Roberts, Margaret and Peter Staples)*

MERTON   SS5212
Malt Scoop (01805) 603924
New Street; EX20 3EA Thatched former farmhouse (a pub since the early 19th c), renovated interior with original slate floors and inglenook, enjoyable generously served bar food at fair prices, separate restaurant menu (Thurs-Sun), St Austell ales, friendly service; children and dogs welcome, two bedrooms, open all day Fri-Sun. *(Peter Pilbeam)*

MOLLAND   SS8028
London (01769) 550269
Village signed off B3227 E of South Molton; EX36 3NG Proper Exmoor inn at its busiest in the shooting season; two small linked rooms by old-fashioned central servery, local stag-hunting pictures, cushioned benches and plain chairs around rough stripped trestle tables, Exmoor Ale, attractive beamed room on left with famous stag story on wall, panelled dining room on right with big curved settle by fireplace (good hunting and game bird prints), enjoyable home-made food using fresh local produce including seasonal game, small hall with stuffed birds and animals; fine Victorian lavatories; children and dogs welcome,

picnic-sets in cottagey garden, untouched early 18th-c box pews in church next door, two bedrooms. *(Isobel Mackinlay)*

MONKLEIGH   SS4520
Bell (01805) 938285
A388; EX39 5JS Well looked-after thatched and beamed 17th-c village pub, carpeted bar and small restaurant, three real ales including Dartmoor, enjoyable reasonably priced food including daily specials and Sun carvery, friendly staff; background music, darts; children welcome (till 9pm) and dogs (treats for good ones), wheelchair access, garden with raised deck, views and good walks, closed Mon. *(Phil and Jane Hodson)*

MORCHARD BISHOP   SS7607
London Inn (01363) 877222
Signed off A377 Crediton–Barnstaple; EX17 6NW Prettily placed 16th-c village coaching inn, helpful friendly service (mother and daughter licensees), good generous home-made food (best to book weekends), Fullers London Pride and a guest, low-beamed open-plan carpeted bar with woodburner in large fireplace, thriving local atmosphere, small dining room; pool, darts and skittles; children and dogs welcome. *(Anon)*

MORTEHOE   SS4545
Chichester Arms (01271) 870411
Off A361 Ilfracombe–Braunton; EX34 7DU Blue-shuttered former 16th-c vicarage, enjoyable local food including good crab, well kept west country ales, quick friendly service, panelled lounge, dining room and pubby locals' bar with darts and pool, interesting old local photographs; skittle alley and games machines in summer children's room, dogs welcome in bar, tables out in front and in paved side garden, lovely coast walk, open all day. *(Toby Jones)*

NEWTON ABBOT   SX8671
Olde Cider Bar (01626) 354221
East Street; TQ12 2LD Basic old-fashioned cider house with plenty of atmosphere; around 30 interesting reasonably priced ciders (some very strong), a couple of perries, more in bottles, good country wines from the cask too, baguettes, pasties etc, friendly staff, stools made from cask staves, barrel seats and wall benches, flagstones and bare boards; small back games room with bar billiards and machines; terrace tables, open all day; up for sale but business as usual last we heard. *(Toby Jones)*

NEWTON ABBOT   SX8468
Two Mile Oak (01803) 812411
A381 2 miles S, at Denbury/ Kingskerswell crossroads; TQ12 6DF Appealing two-bar beamed coaching inn, black panelling, traditional furnishings and candlelit alcoves, inglenook and

woodburners, well kept Bass, Otter and guests tapped from the cask, nine wines by the glass, enjoyable well priced pubby food from sandwiches and baked potatoes up (special diets catered for), decent coffee, cheerful staff; background music; children and dogs welcome, round picnic-sets on terrace and lawn, open all day. *(Roger and Donna Huggins)*

NEWTON FERRERS   SX5447
Dolphin (01752) 872007
Riverside Road East: Newton Hill off Church Park (B3186) then left; PL8 1AE Shuttered 18th-c pub in attractive setting; L-shaped bar with a few low black beams, pews and benches on slate floors and some white plank panelling, open fire, up to four well kept ales including St Austell, decent wines by the glass, enjoyable traditional food including good fish and chips and daily specials, friendly staff; children and dogs (in bar) welcome, terraces over lane looking down on River Yealm and yachts, open all day in summer when can get packed, parking limited. *(Mrs Carole Baldock)*

NEWTON ST CYRES   SX8798
Beer Engine (01392) 851282
Off A377 towards Thorverton; EX5 5AX Friendly former railway hotel brewing its own beers since the 1980s, wide choice of good home-made food including local fish and popular Sun lunch; children welcome, decked verandah, steps down to garden, open all day. *(Neil Allen)*

NEWTON TRACEY   SS5226
★ Hunters (01271) 858339
B3232 Barnstaple–Torrington; EX31 3PL Extended 15th-c pub with massive low beams and two inglenooks, good reasonably priced freshly made food from pub standards up, well kept St Austell Tribute and Sharps Doom Bar, decent wines, efficient friendly service, skittle alley/ overflow dining area; soft background music; children and dogs welcome, disabled access using ramp, tables on small terrace behind, open all day. *(Theocsbrian)*

NOMANSLAND   SS8313
Mount Pleasant (01884) 860271
B3137 Tiverton–South Molton; EX16 8NN Informal country local with good mix of customers, huge fireplaces in long low-beamed main bar, well kept ales such as Cotleigh, Exmoor and Sharps, several wines by the glass, Weston's cider, good range of freshly cooked food (special diets catered for), friendly attentive service, happy mismatch of simple well worn furniture including comfy old sofa, candles on tables, country pictures, daily papers, cosy dining room (former smithy with original forge), darts in public bar; background music; well behaved children and dogs welcome, picnic-sets in back garden. *(Anon)*

NORTH BOVEY SX7483

★**Ring of Bells** (01647) 440375
*Off A382/B3212 SW of
Moretonhampstead; TQ13 8RB* Bulgy-
walled thatched inn dating from the 13th c,
low beams, flagstones, big log fire, sturdy
rustic tables and winding staircases, good
imaginative local food, well kept St Austell,
Teignworthy and guests, plenty of wines by
the glass from good list, helpful friendly staff,
carpeted dining room and overspill room;
children and dogs (in bar) welcome, garden
by lovely tree-covered village green below
Dartmoor, good walks, five big clean bedrooms,
open all day. *(Alison and Michael Harper)*

NOSS MAYO SX5447

★**Ship** (01752) 872387
*Off A379 via B3186, E of Plymouth;
PL8 1EW* Charming setting overlooking
inlet and visiting boats (can get crowded
in good weather); thick-walled bars with
bare boards and log fires, six well kept west
country beers including local Summerskills,
good choice of wines and malt whiskies,
popular food from wide-ranging menu,
friendly efficient service, lots of local
pictures and charts, books, newspapers and
board games, restaurant upstairs; children
welcome, dogs downstairs, plenty of seats on
heated waterside terrace, parking restricted
at high tide, open (and food) all day. *(Lynda
and Trevor Smith, John Evans)*

OAKFORD SS9121

Red Lion (01398) 351592
Rookery Hill; EX16 9ES Friendly
refurbished 17th-c village coaching inn
(partly rebuilt in Georgian times) under new
management; well kept ales such as Otter,
reasonably priced pubby food including
Thurs OAP lunch deal and Sun carvery till
4pm, woodburner in big inglenook; children,
walkers and dogs welcome, four comfortable
bedrooms, open all day Sun till 8pm, closed
Mon lunchtime. *(Anon)*

PARKHAM SS3821

★**Bell** (01237) 451201
Rectory Lane; EX39 5PL Spotlessly kept
thatched village pub, three communicating
rooms (one on lower level), beams and
standing timbers, woodburner and small
coal fire, pubby furniture on red patterned
carpet, brass, copper and old photographs, a
grandfather clock, model ships and lanterns
hanging above bar serving Exmoor, Otter
and Sharps, a dozen malt whiskies, popular
food; darts, free wi-fi; well behaved children
welcome, dogs in bar, picnic-sets on covered
back terrace with fairy lights, open (and
food) all day Sun. *(Peter Brix)*

PARRACOMBE SS6644

★**Fox & Goose** (01598) 763239
*Off A39 Blackmoor Gate–Lynton;
EX31 4PE* Popular rambling Victorian
pub, hunting and farming memorabilia
and interesting old photographs, well kept
Cotleigh and Exmoor, farm cider, good choice
of wines by the glass, generous well prepared
food from imaginative menu, also freshly
made pizzas, friendly staff, log fire, separate
dining room; children and dogs welcome,
small front verandah, riverside terrace and
garden room, three bedrooms, open all day in
summer. *(Neil Allen)*

PETER TAVY SX5177

★**Peter Tavy Inn** (01822) 810348
*Off A386 near Mary Tavy, N of
Tavistock; PL19 9NN* Old stone village inn
tucked away at end of little lane, bustling
low-beamed bar with high-backed settles on
black flagstones, mullioned windows, good
log fire in big stone fireplace, snug dining
area with carved wooden chairs, hops on
beams and plenty of pictures, up to five well
kept west country ales, Winkleigh's cider,
good wine and malt whisky choice, well
liked food including vegetarian options,
quick friendly service, separate restaurant;
children and dogs welcome, picnic-sets in
pretty garden, peaceful moorland views.
(Helen and Brian Edgeley, Stephen Shepherd)

PLYMOUTH SX4953

Bridge (01752) 403888
Shaw Way, Mount Batten; PL9 9XH
Modern two-storey bar-restaurant with
terrace and balcony overlooking busy
Yacht Haven Marina, enjoyable food from
sandwiches and pub favourites up, nice
choice of wines by the glass, St Austell
Tribute and Sharps Doom Bar, impressive
fish tank upstairs; children welcome, well
behaved dogs downstairs, open all day from
9am for breakfast. *(Peter Brix)*

PLYMOUTH SX4854

China House (01752) 661592
*Sutton Harbour, via Sutton Road off
Exeter Street (A374); PL4 0DW* Attractive
Vintage Inns conversion of Plymouth's oldest
warehouse, lovely marina views, dimly lit and
inviting interior with beams and flagstones,
bare slate and stone walls, two good log fires,
interesting photographs, their usual food
including good value set menu, Butcombe,
St Austell Tribute and a guest, plenty of wines
by the glass; background music; children
welcome, no dogs, good parking and disabled
access/facilities, tables out on waterside
balconies, open (and food) all day.
(Roger and Donna Huggins)

PLYMOUTH SX4854

Dolphin (01752) 660876
Barbican; PL1 2LS Unpretentious chatty
local with good range of well kept cask-
tapped ales including Bass and St Austell,
open fire, Beryl Cook paintings (even one of
the friendly landlord), no food but can bring
your own; dogs welcome, open all day.
(Phoebe Peacock)

PLYMOUTH   SX4555
Lounge (01752) 561330
Stopford Place, Stoke; PL1 4QT
Old-fashioned end-of-terrace panelled local,
cheery landlord and chatty regulars, well
kept Bass and a couple of guests, decent
lunchtime pubby food from baguettes
up; dogs welcome, small enclosed front
garden, open all day weekends, closed Mon
lunchtime, busy on match days. *(Phoebe
Peacock)*

PLYMTREE   ST0502
Blacksmiths Arms (01884) 277474
Near church; EX15 2JU Friendly 19th-c
beamed and carpeted pub with reasonably
priced home-made food (takeaways
available), three well kept changing local
ales and decent choice of wines by the glass;
pool room and skittle alley; children welcome
and dogs (theirs is called Jagermeister),
garden with boules and play area, open
all day Sat, till 4pm Sun, closed weekday
lunchtimes. *(Anon)*

POUNDSGATE   SX7072
Tavistock Inn (01364) 631251
B3357 continuation; TQ13 7NY
Picturesque old pub liked by walkers (plenty
of nearby hikes), beams and other original
features such as narrow-stepped granite
spiral staircase, original flagstones and
ancient log fireplaces, St Austell Tribute,
Sharps Doom Bar and a summer guest,
enjoyable traditional food served by friendly
staff, pub cat; children and dogs welcome,
tables on front terrace and in quiet back
garden, pretty flower boxes, open (and food)
all day in summer. *(Neil Allen)*

PUSEHILL   SS4228
Pig on the Hill (01237) 459222
*Off B3226 near Westward Ho!;
EX39 5AH* Extensively refurbished
restaurnty pub (originally a cowshed); good
choice of fresh well presented food (booking
advised evenings and weekends), friendly
helpful service, Country Life and local guests,
games room with skittle alley; background
music; children and dogs (in bar) welcome,
disabled facilities, good views from terrace
tables and picnic-sets on grass, play area,
boules, open all day. *(Toby Jones)*

RINGMORE   SX6545
Journeys End (01548) 810205
*Signed off B3392 at Pickwick Inn,
St Anns Chapel, near Bigbury; best to
park opposite church; TQ7 4HL* Ancient
village inn with friendly chatty licensees,
character panelled lounge and other linked
rooms, Sharps Doom Bar and local guests
tapped from the cask, farm cider, decent
wines, well executed nicely presented food
from good shortish menu (not Sun evening,
best to book in summer), good value set
lunch, log fires, family dining conservatory

with board games; dogs welcome, pleasant
big terraced garden with boules, attractive
setting near thatched cottages and not far
from the sea, open all day weekends, closed
Mon. *(Tracey and Phil Eagles, Peter Travis,
Sharon and John Hancock)*

ROBOROUGH   SS5717
New Inn (01805) 603247
Off B3217 N of Winkleigh; EX19 8SY
Tucked-away 16th-c thatched village
pub, cheerful and busy, with well kept
Teignworthy and a couple of guests, ten
proper ciders and several wines by the glass,
good variety of enjoyable locally sourced
food, beamed bar with woodburner, tiny back
room leading up to dining room; children and
dogs welcome, seats on sunny front terrace,
open all day Fri-Sun, closed lunchtimes Mon,
Tues. *(Mark Flynn)*

ROCKBEARE   SY0195
★ Jack in the Green (01404) 822240
*Signed from A30 bypass E of Exeter;
EX5 2EE* Neat welcoming dining pub run
well by long-serving owner; flagstoned lounge
bar with comfortable sofas, ales such as
Butcombe, Otter and Sharps, local cider, a
dozen wines by the glass (over 100 by the
bottle), first class food from interesting menu
including excellent puddings, emphasis on
larger dining side with old hunting/shooting
photographs and leather chesterfields
by big woodburner, good friendly service;
background music; well behaved children
welcome, no dogs inside, disabled facilities,
plenty of seats in courtyard, open all day Sun,
closed 25 Dec-5 Jan, quite handy for M5.
*(John Evans, Stephen Shepherd, Mrs J Ekins-
Daukes, David and Helena Johnson, Patrick and
Daphne Darley and others)*

SALCOMBE   SX7439
Fortescue (01548) 842868
*Union Street, end of Fore Street;
TQ8 8BZ* Proper pub with five linked
nautical-theme rooms, enjoyable good value
food including local fish, prompt cheerful
service, well kept ales such as Bass, Courage
and Otter, decent wines, good woodburner,
old local black and white shipping pictures,
big public bar with games, small dining room;
children welcome, courtyard picnic-sets.
(Peter Brix)

SALCOMBE   SX7439
★ Victoria (01548) 842604
Fore Street; TQ8 8BU Attractive 19th-c
pub opposite harbour car park, neat nautical
décor, comfortable furnishings and big open
fires, enjoyable sensibly priced home-
made food, well kept St Austell ales and
decent wines, friendly enthusiastic service,
separate family area; background music;
dogs welcome, large sheltered tiered garden
behind with good play area and chickens,
bedrooms, open all day and can get very busy
at weekends. *(Ken Parry)*

SAMPFORD COURTENAY   SS6300
New Inn   (01837) 82247
B3072 Crediton–Holsworthy; EX20 2TB
Attractive 16th-c thatched restaurant and
bar, nice choice of good interesting food from
landlord-chef at reasonable prices, local ales
and cider, relaxed friendly atmosphere with
candlelit tables, beams and log fires; garden
picnic-sets, picturesque village. *(Mike Swan)*

SAMPFORD PEVERELL   ST0314
Globe   (01884) 821214
*A mile from M5 junction 27, village
signed from Tiverton turn-off; Lower
Town; EX16 7BJ* New management for this
spacious and comfortable village inn backing
on to Grand Western Canal; good pub food
and well kept ales including Sharps Doom
Bar, cosy beamed lounge, back restaurant;
children welcome, disabled facilities,
courtyard and enclosed garden with play
area, six refurbished bedrooms, open (and
food) all day. *(J D O Carter)*

SANDY PARK   SX7189
Sandy Park Inn   (01647) 433267
*A382 Whiddon Down–
Moretonhampstead; TQ13 8JW*
Welcoming little thatched and beamed inn
under new ownership; built-in varnished
wall settles around nice tables, stools by
counter serving Dartmoor, Otter and a
couple of guests, good fairly traditional food
cooked by landlord including fresh fish, small
dining room on left, inner snug; open mike
night third Sun of month; children and dogs
welcome, big garden with fine views, three
comfortable bedrooms, open all day (food till
7pm Sun). *(Anon)*

SCORRITON   SX7068
Tradesmans Arms   (01364) 631206
Main road through village; TQ11 0JB
Welcoming open-plan Dartmoor-edge pub,
tasty well presented local food, Dartmoor,
Otter and guests, friendly service, fresh
flowers and woodburner, wonderful rolling
hill views from conservatory and garden,
Thurs quiz; dogs welcome, bedrooms, open
all day Sun. *(Caroline Prescott)*

SHALDON   SX9372
Clifford Arms   (01626) 872311
Fore Street; TQ14 ODE Attractive 18th-c
open-plan pub on two levels, clean and
bright, with good range of home-made
blackboard food (not mid Jan), up to five
mainly local ales, eight wines by the glass,
low beams and stone walls, wood or carpeted
floors, log fire, live jazz Sun and Mon;
children over 5 welcome, front terrace and
decked area at back with palms, pleasant
seaside village. *(Mike Swan)*

SHALDON   SX9472
London Inn   (01626) 872453
Bank Street/The Green; TQ14 8AW
Popular bustling pub opposite bowling green
in pretty waterside village, ample helpings
of good reasonably priced food using local
suppliers, Otter and St Austell ales, friendly
efficient service; background music, pool;
children and dogs (in bar) welcome, open
all day. *(Toby Jones)*

SHALDON   SX9272
Shipwrights Arms   (01626) 873232
B3195 to Newton Abbot; TQ14 0AQ
Friendly end-of-terrace village pub, two
bars with open fires, well kept ales such as
Hunters, Otter and Teignworthy, enjoyable
food from short menu; live music, free wi-fi;
children and dogs welcome, River Teign
view from walled back terrace, open all day
weekends, closed weekday lunchtimes and
all day Tues. *(Neil Allen)*

SHEBBEAR   SS4309
★ Devils Stone Inn   (01409) 281210
*Off A3072 or A388 NE of Holsworthy;
EX21 5RU* Neatly kept 17th-c beamed
village pub reputed to be one of England's
most haunted; seats in front of open
woodburner, long L-shaped pew and second
smaller one, flagstone floors, St Austell
Tribute and a couple of guests, decent wines,
enjoyable food in dining room across corridor,
plain back games room with pool and darts;
picnic-sets on front terrace and in garden
behind, next to actual Devil's Stone (turned
by villagers on 5 Nov to keep the devil at
bay), eight bedrooms (steep stairs to some),
can arrange fishing and shooting, open all
day weekends. *(Anon)*

SHEEPWASH   SS4806
★ Half Moon   (01409) 231376
*Off A3072 Holsworthy–Hatherleigh at
Highampton; EX21 5NE* Ancient inn
loved by anglers for its 12 miles of River
Torridge fishing (salmon, sea and brown
trout), small tackle shop and rod room with
drying facilities; simply furnished main bar,
lots of beams, log fire in big fireplace, well
kept St Austell, Sharps and a local guest,
several wines by the glass, wide choice of
enjoyable food including blackboard specials,
friendly service, separate extended dining
room, bar billiards; children and dogs
welcome, 13 bedrooms (four in converted
stables), generous breakfast, tiny Dartmoor
village off the beaten track. *(Roy Hoing)*

SIDBURY   SY1391
Red Lion   (01395) 597313
Fore Street, opposite church; EX10 0SD
Small village local in terrace row overlooking

church; recent refurbishment by new owner including new wood flooring and a locally crafted oak servery, enjoyable home-made food in log-fire bar or back dining area, three real ales (usually Branscombe Vale Branoc), friendly helpful staff; well behaved children and dogs welcome, four bedrooms, closed Sun evening, Mon, Tues lunchtime. *(Roger and Donna Huggins)*

SIDFORD   SY1389

★ **Blue Ball** (01395) 514062

A3052 just N of Sidmouth; EX10 9QL Handsome thatched pub in same friendly family for over 100 years; central bar with three main areas each with log fire, pale beams, nice mix of wooden dining chairs around circular tables on patterned carpet, prints, horsebrasses and plenty of bric-a-brac, well kept Bass, Otter, St Austell and Sharps, popular bar food, pleasant attentive service, chatty public bar, board games, darts, skittle alley; background music and games machine; children and dogs welcome, flower-filled garden, terrace and smokers' gazebo, coastal walks close by, bedrooms, open all day from 8am for breakfast. *(Roger and Donna Huggins)*

SIDFORD   SY1390

Rising Sun (01395) 513722

School Street; EX10 9PF Friendly two-bar traditional local, well kept Bass, Branscombe Vale, Otter and a winter guest (guest cider in summer), well priced home-made pubby food, mix of tables and chairs on wood floors, old local photographs on white walls; pool and darts, some live music, silent TV; children welcome away from bar, steep garden behind, parking at nearby Spar (free after 6pm), open all day weekends. *(Roger and Donna Huggins and others)*

SIDMOUTH   ST1287

Anchor (01395) 514129

Old Fore Street; EX10 8LP Welcoming family-run pub popular for its fresh fish and other good value food, well kept Caledonian ales including one named for them, decent choice of wines, good friendly service, large carpeted L-shaped room with nautical pictures, steps down to restaurant; darts; tables out in front, more in back beer garden with stage for live acts, open (and food) all day. *(Roger and Donna Huggins and others)*

SIDMOUTH   SY1287

Dukes (01395) 513320

Esplanade; EX10 8AR More brasserie than pub, but long bar on left has Branscombe Vale and a couple of guests, good food all day specialising in local fish (best to book in the evening), friendly efficient young staff, daily papers, linked areas including conservatory and flagstoned eating area (once a chapel), smart contemporary décor; big-screen TV; children welcome, disabled facilities, prom-view terrace tables, bedrooms in adjoining

Elizabeth Hotel, open all day (may be summer queues). *(Michael Butler, Roger and Donna Huggins)*

SIDMOUTH   SY1287

★ **Swan** (01395) 512849

York Street; EX10 8BY Cheerful old-fashioned town-centre local, well kept Charles Wells and enjoyable good value blackboard food from sandwiches up, friendly helpful staff, lounge bar with interesting pictures and memorabilia, darts and woodburner in bigger light and airy public bar with boarded walls and ceilings, daily newspapers, separate dining area; no under-14s, dogs welcome, flower-filled garden with smokers' area, open all day. *(Roger and Donna Huggins)*

SILVERTON   SS9503

Lamb (01392) 860272

Fore Street; EX5 4HZ Flagstoned local run well by friendly landlord, Exe Valley, Otter and a guest tapped from stillage casks, inexpensive home-made pubby food including specials, separate eating area, skittle alley; handy for Killerton (NT), open all day weekends. *(Alfie Bayliss)*

SLAPTON   SX8245

★ **Queens Arms** (01548) 580800

Sands Road corner, before church; TQ7 2PN Smartly kept one-room village local with welcoming staff and regulars, good straightforward inexpensive food, four ales including Dartmoor and Otter, snug comfortable chairs, roaring log fire, fascinating World War II photos and scrapbooks, dominoes and draughts; children and dogs welcome, lots of tables in lovely suntrap stepped garden. *(Toby Jones)*

SOURTON   SX5390

★ **Highwayman** (01837) 861243

A386, S of junction with A30; EX20 4HN Unique place – a quirky fantasy of dimly lit stonework and flagstone-floored burrows and alcoves, all sorts of things to look at, one room a make-believe sailing galleon; a couple of local ales, proper cider and maybe organic wines, lunchtime sandwiches, home-made pasties and platters (evening food mainly for residents), friendly chatty service; nostalgic background music; children allowed in certain areas, outside fairy-tale pumpkin house and an old-lady-who-lived-in-the-shoe, period bedrooms with four-posters and half-testers, bunkrooms for walkers/cyclists. *(Peter Pilbeam)*

SOUTH BRENT   SX6960

Oak (01364) 72133

Station Road; TQ10 9BE Friendly village pub with well priced traditional and modern food, three well kept local ales and good choice of wines by the glass, welcoming helpful service, comfortable open-plan bar with some leather sofas, restaurant, Weds folk night; children and dogs welcome, small courtyard, five bedrooms, little nearby parking. *(Alison and Michael Harper)*

SPREYTON   SX6996
★**Tom Cobley** (01647) 231314
Dragdown Hill; W out of village; EX17 5AL Fantastic range of drinks including up to 14 real ales (some tapped from the cask), similar number of ciders/perries and quite a selection of malts, engaging landlord and cheerful helpful staff, comfortable little bar with straightforward pubby furnishings, open fire, local photographs and country scenes, honest traditional food in large beamed back dining room; background music; children welcome, dogs in bar, seats out at front by quiet street, more in tree-shaded garden, good value bedrooms (some sharing bathrooms), open till 1am Fri and Sat, closed Mon lunchtime. *(Ian Herdman)*

STAPLE CROSS   ST0320
Staplecross Inn (01398) 361374
Holcombe Rogus–Hockworthy; TA21 0NH Traditional family-run village local, well cooked pubby food including blackboard specials, Otter, St Austell and a guest beer, three linked rooms with quarry tiles, stripped stone, beams and substantial woodburners in big fireplaces; well behaved children and dogs welcome, open all day weekends, from 4pm weekdays, closed Mon. *(Neil Allen)*

STAVERTON   SX7964
★**Sea Trout** (01803) 762274
Village signposted from A384 NW of Totnes; TQ9 6PA Welcoming partly 15th-c inn with good mix of customers, neat rambling beamed lounge with fishing theme, elegant wheelbacks and mix of tables on carpet or wood floors, simple locals' bar with stag's head, horsebrasses and large stuffed fish above woodburner, Palmers ales, good interesting food as well as pub standards, smartly furnished panelled restaurant, conservatory; children and dogs (in bar) welcome, attractive terrace garden behind, well equipped bedrooms, fishing available on nearby River Dart, open all day from 8am. *(Lynda and Trevor Smith, Peter Pilbeam)*

STICKLEPATH   SX6494
★**Devonshire** (01837) 840626
Off A30 at Whiddon Down or Okehampton; EX20 2NW Welcoming old-fashioned 16th-c thatched village local next to Finch Foundry museum (NT); low-beamed slate-floor bar with big log fire, longcase clock and easy-going old furnishings, key collection, sofa in small snug, well kept low-priced ales tapped from the cask, farm cider, good value sandwiches, soup and home-made pasties from the Aga, games room, lively folk night first Sun of month; dogs welcome

(pub has its own), wheelchair access from car park, good walks, bedrooms, open all day Fri, Sat. *(Peter Pilbeam)*

STOKE FLEMING   SX8648
Green Dragon (01803) 770238
Church Street; TQ6 0PX Popular and friendly village pub with yachtsman landlord, well worn-in beamed and flagstoned interior, boat pictures and charts, sleepy dogs and cats, snug with sofas, armchairs, grandfather clock and open fire, well kept ales such as Bass, Otter and Wadworths, Addlestone's and Aspall's ciders, good choice of wines by the glass, enjoyable local food including good fish soup and venison burgers, prompt service; children welcome, tables out on partly covered heated terrace, lovely garden with play area, handy for coast path. *(Richard Tilbrook, Maureen Wood)*

STOKE GABRIEL   SX8457
Church House (01803) 782384
Off A385 just W of junction with A3022; Church Walk; TQ9 6SD Friendly and popular early 14th-c pub; lounge bar with fine medieval beam-and-plank ceiling, black oak partition wall, window seats cut into thick butter-coloured walls, woodburner in huge fireplace, ancient mummified cat, well kept Bass, Sharps Doom Bar and a guest, enjoyable good value food, little locals' bar; background music; Sun quiz; no under-14s, dogs welcome in bar, picnic-sets on small front terrace, old stocks (pub used to incorporate the village courthouse), limited parking, open all day. *(Alfie Bayliss)*

STOKENHAM   SX8042
Church House (01548) 580253
Opposite church, N of A379 towards Torcross; TQ7 2SZ Attractive extended old pub overlooking common, three open-plan areas, low beams, mix of seating on flagstones, lots of knick-knacks, Otter ales and a guest, well liked food from good sandwiches up using local produce, dining conservatory; live music including jazz; children and dogs (in bar) welcome, picnic-sets on lawn with play area, interesting church next door. *(Toby Jones)*

STOKENHAM   SX8042
Tradesmans Arms (01548) 580996
Just off A379 Dartmouth–Kingsbridge; TQ7 2SZ Picturesque partly thatched 14th-c pub overlooking village green, good attractively presented food using local ingredients, sensible wine list and well kept west country beers, traditional low-beamed cottagey interior, log fire, restaurant; children and dogs welcome, nice bedrooms. *(Lynda and Trevor Smith, Nick Lawless, Sam)*

TEIGNMOUTH   SX9372
Olde Jolly Sailor (01626) 772864
Set back from Northumberland Place; TQ14 8DE Town's oldest pub, comfortable

low-ceilinged interior with stripped stone walls, Dartmoor Jail, Sharps Doom Bar and guests, enjoyable pubby food (not Sun evening); live jazz Mon, sports TV, free wi-fi; children and dogs welcome, seats in front courtyard and behind, open all day. *(Roger and Donna Huggins)*

THORVERTON   SS9202
Thorverton Arms (01392) 860205
Village signed off A396 Exeter–Tiverton; EX5 5NS Spacious 16th-c coaching inn with five adjoining areas including log-fire bar and restaurant, good well presented home-made food at reasonable prices, three real ales including Otter, welcoming landlord and efficient friendly staff; pool; children and dogs (in bar) welcome, wisteria-draped terrace and sunny garden, pleasant village, six comfortable bedrooms, nice breakfast. *(Peter Brix)*

TOPSHAM   SX9688
★ Bridge Inn (01392) 873862
2.5 miles from M5 junction 30: Topsham signposted from exit roundabout; in Topsham follow signpost (A376) Exmouth, on the Elmgrove Road, into Bridge Hill; EX3 0QQ Very special old drinkers' pub (16th-c former maltings) in landlady's family for five generations and with up to nine well kept ales; quite unchanging and completely unspoilt with friendly staff and locals, character small rooms and snugs, traditional furniture including a nice high-backed settle, woodburner, the 'bar' is landlady's front parlour (as notice on the door politely reminds customers), simple food, live folk and blues; no background music, mobile phones or credit cards; children and dogs welcome, picnic-sets overlooking weir. *(Roger and Donna Huggins)*

TOPSHAM   SX9687
Lighter (01392) 875439
Fore Street; EX3 0HZ Big busy pub overlooking quay, quickly served food from good sandwiches and light dishes to fresh fish, three Badger ales kept well, nautical décor, old local photographs, panelling and large central log fire, friendly staff, good children's area; games machines, background music; lots of waterside tables (bird views at half tide), handy for antiques centre but little nearby parking. *(Neil Allen)*

TOPSHAM   SX9688
Passage House (01392) 873653
Ferry Road, off main street; EX3 0JN Relaxed 18th-c pub with traditional black-beamed bar and slate-floored lower dining area, good food from sandwiches to local fish, well kept ales and decent wines, friendly service; peaceful terrace looking over moorings and river (lovely at sunset) to nature reserve beyond. *(Peter Andrews)*

TORBRYAN   SX8266
★ Old Church House (01803) 812372
Pub signed off A381; TQ12 5UR Character 13th-c former farmhouse with attractive bar (popular with locals), benches built into fine panelling, settle and other seats by big log fire, Hunters, Skinners, St Austell and a guest, several wines by the glass and around 35 malt whiskies, good variety of well liked tasty food, cheerful helpful staff, discreetly lit lounges, one with a splendid deep Tudor inglenook; background music; dogs welcome, comfortable bedrooms (woodburner in one), good breakfast. *(Michael Butler)*

TORCROSS   SX8242
Start Bay (01548) 580553
A379 S of Dartmouth; TQ7 2TQ More fish and chip restaurant than pub but does sell Bass, Otter, local wine and cider; very much set out for eating and exceptionally busy at peak times with staff coping well, food is enjoyable and sensibly priced; wheelback chairs around dark tables, country pictures, some photographs of storms buffeting the building, winter coal fire, small drinking area by counter, large family room; no dogs during food times, seats outside (highly prized) looking over pebble beach and wildlife lagoon, open all day. *(Peter Brix)*

TORQUAY   SX9166
Crown & Sceptre (01803) 328290
Petitor Road, St Marychurch; TQ1 4QA Friendly two-bar local with six real ales including Butcombe, St Austell and Otter, interesting naval memorabilia and chamber-pot collection, basic good value lunchtime food, snacks any time, regular live music including jazz Tues, folk Fri; children and dogs welcome, two gardens, open all day Fri-Sun. *(Anon)*

TORQUAY   SX9163
Hole in the Wall (01803) 200755
Park Lane, opposite clock tower; TQ1 2AU Ancient two-bar local tucked away near harbour, reasonably priced usual food including good fresh fish, several well kept ales such as Bays, Butcombe, Otter and Sharps, Blackawton cider, smooth cobbled floors, low beams and alcoves, lots of nautical brassware, ship models, old local photographs and chamber-pots, restaurant/function room (band nights); can get very busy weekends; some seats in alley out at front, open all day. *(Mrs Sally Scott, Dr and Mrs A K Clarke)*

TOTNES   SX8060
Albert (01803) 863214
Bridgetown; TQ9 5AD Unpretentious slate-hung pub near the river, small bar and two other rooms, low beams, flagstones, panelling, some old settles and lots of knick-knacks, friendly landlord brewing his

own good Bridgetown ales, real cider and plenty of whiskies, friendly local atmosphere; quiz and music nights, darts, free wi-fi; dogs welcome (Albert is the resident spaniel), paved beer garden behind. *(Toby Jones)*

TOTNES SX7960
Bay Horse (01803) 862088
Cistern Street; TQ9 5SP Welcoming traditional 15th-c two-bar inn, four well kept local ales such as Dartmoor and New Lion, ciders such as Sandford Orchards, simple lunchtime food; background and regular live music including good Sun jazz; children and dogs welcome, nice garden behind, three refurbished bedrooms, good breakfast, open all day. *(Peter Pilbeam)*

TOTNES SX7960
★ **Kingsbridge Inn** (01803) 863324
Leechwell Street; TQ9 5SY Attractive rambling 17th-c pub-restaurant run by two brothers; black beams, timbering and white-painted stone walls, big woodburner, enjoyable fairly traditional food from changing blackboard menu, Butcombe, Otter and nice choice of wines, good friendly service; live music every other Sat, other events such as film and tango nights in upstairs Piano Bar; children and dogs welcome, tables on back deck, closed Sun evening, Mon, but may open all day in summer. *(Bruce Jamieson, Richard Tilbrook, Roger and Donna Huggins)*

TOTNES SX8060
★ **Royal Seven Stars** (01803) 862125
Fore Street, The Plains; TQ9 5DD Good town-centre bar and coffee bar in well run civilised old hotel, friendly and easy-going, with well kept ales and enjoyable generously served food all day from breakfast on, separate brasserie/grill room with adjoining champagne bar; covered and heated tables out in front, river across busy main road, 21 bedrooms. *(Michael and Lynne Gittins)*

TOTNES SX8059
★ **Steam Packet** (01803) 863880
St Peters Quay, on W bank (ie not on Steam Packet Quay); TQ9 5EW Quayside inn with three distinct bar areas, light oak floor, some bare-stone and brick walls, dark half-panelling and delft shelving, squashy leather sofa in one part against wall of books, fireplace at either end, Dartmoor Jail, Sharps Doom Bar and a guest, proper cider and a dozen wines by the glass, popular fairly priced traditional food (all day Sun), friendly staff coping well at busy times, conservatory restaurant; background music, TV, free wi-fi; children and dogs welcome, seats on terrace overlooking River Dart, bedrooms, open all day. *(Mike Swan)*

TUCKENHAY SX8156
★ **Maltsters Arms** (01803) 732350
Ashprington Road, off A381 from Totnes; TQ9 7EQ Popular old pub in lovely quiet spot by wooded Bow Creek, good food from bar snacks to fresh fish specials, well kept Bays and three west country guests, local ciders and great range of wines by the glass, friendly service, creek-view restaurant; free wi-fi; children and dogs welcome, waterside terrace with open-air bar and summer barbecues, pontoon for visiting boats, six well appointed bedrooms, open all day. *(David Gunn)*

UGBOROUGH SX6755
Anchor (01752) 690388
Off A3121; PL21 0NG Light contemporary décor in 17th-c beamed village dining pub; interesting menu including one or two pub favourites (no food Sun evening, Mon), snacks in separate log-fire bar with upholstered bucket chairs and leather sofas on wood floor, ales such as Bass and Sharps Doom Bar from polished stone counter, friendly helpful staff; local artwork for sale, cookery classes; six bedrooms and four cabins, open all day. *(Caroline Prescott)*

UGBOROUGH SX6755
Ship (01752) 892565
Off A3121 SE of Ivybridge; PL21 0NS Friendly dining pub extended from cosy 16th-c flagstoned core, well divided open-plan eating areas a step down from neat bar with woodburner, good home-made food including some interesting blackboard specials (plenty of fish), cheerful efficient service, well kept Palmers, St Austell and a local guest, nice house wines; background music; children welcome, dogs in bar, tables out in front, open all day Fri-Sun in summer. *(John and Susan Miln, Lynda and Trevor Smith, John Evans)*

WEARE GIFFARD SS4722
Cyder Press (01237) 425517
Tavern Gardens; EX39 4QR Welcoming village local with St Austell ales and enjoyable fairly priced home-made food, black beams and timbers, inglenook woodburner; quiz nights and Tues acoustic music; children (till 8.30pm) and dogs welcome, seats outside, beautiful countryside and handy for Tarka Trail, two bedrooms, closed Mon lunchtime. *(Mark Flynn)*

WEMBURY SX5349
Odd Wheel (01752) 863052
Knighton Road; PL9 0JD Modernised village pub with five well kept west country ales, good fairly traditional food from sandwiches and ciabattas up, reasonable

---

If you know a pub is ever open all day, please tell us.

prices including good value set lunch Mon-Fri, friendly helpful service, restaurant, pool and dogs in bar; children welcome, seats out on decking, fenced play area, open (and food) all day weekends. *(Mo and David Trudgill, Hugh Roberts)*

WEMBWORTHY SS6609

★**Lymington Arms** (01837) 83572

Lama Cross; EX18 7SA Large early 19th-c beamed dining pub in pleasant country setting, wide choice of reliably good food including some interesting specials, good service from character landlady and friendly staff, well kept Sharps Doom Bar and a west country guest, Winkleigh's farm cider, decent wines, comfortably plush seating and red tablecloths in partly stripped-stone bar, big back restaurant; children welcome, picnic-sets outside, closed Sun evening, Mon and Tues (and may shut early if quiet). *(Mike Swan)*

WESTON ST1400

★**Otter** (01404) 42594

Off A373, or A30 at W end of Honiton bypass; EX14 3NZ Big busy family pub with heavy low beams, enjoyable good value food (best to book) from light dishes up including lots of vegetarian options, good Sun carvery, OAP specials and other deals, cheerful helpful staff, well kept Cotleigh and Otter ales, good log fire; background music; disabled access, picnic-sets on big lawn leading to River Otter, play area, open all day. *(Bob and Margaret Holder, Robert Watt)*

WHIMPLE SY0497

New Fountain (01404) 822350

Off A30 Exeter–Honiton; Church Road; EX5 2TA Unassuming two-bar beamed village pub with friendly local atmosphere, good inexpensive home-made food (not Mon lunchtime) from short unfussy menu, well kept Teignworthy and a guest, woodburner; well behaved dogs welcome, some outside seating, local heritage centre in car park (open Weds, Sat); changing hands as we went to press, but expected to stay much the same. *(Michael and Lynne Gittins)*

WONSON SX6789

★**Northmore Arms** (01647) 231428

Between Throwleigh and Gidleigh; EX20 2JA Far from smart and a favourite with those who take to its idiosyncratic style (not all do); two simple old-fashioned rooms,

log fire and woodburner, low beams and stripped stone, well kept ales such as Dartmoor tapped from the cask, farm cider and decent house wines, good honest home-made food (all day Mon-Sat), darts and board games; children and dogs welcome, picnic-sets outside, beautiful remote walking country, closed Sun evening. *(Isobel Mackinlay)*

WOOLACOMBE SS4543

Red Barn (01271) 870264

Barton Road/Challacombe Hill Road; EX34 7DF Popular modern seaside bar-restaurant looking out on superb beach, food all day from sandwiches and ciabattas up, well kept St Austell and guest ales, efficient staff coping well when busy, surfing pictures and memorabilia; live music; children and dogs welcome. *(Eddie Edwards)*

YEALMPTON SX5851

Rose & Crown (01752) 880223

A379 Kingsbridge–Plymouth; PL8 2EB Central bar counter, all dark wood and heavy brass, leather-seated stools and mix of furnishings on stripped-wood floors, emphasis on popular bar and restaurant food including lunchtime/early evening set menu (not available Sun or Mon evening), friendly efficient service even at busy times, three St Austell ales, quite a few wines by the glass and decent coffee; children welcome, dogs in bar, tables in walled garden with pond, also a lawned area, open (and food) all day. *(John Evans)*

LUNDY

LUNDY SS1344

★**Marisco** (01271) 870870

Get there by ferry (Bideford and Ilfracombe) or helicopter (Hartland Point); EX39 2LY One of England's most isolated pubs – yet surprisingly busy most nights, great setting, steep trudge up from landing stage, galleried interior with lifebelts and shipwreck salvage, open fire, two St Austell ales named for the island and its spring water on tap, Weston's cider and reasonably priced house wines, good basic food using Lundy produce and lots of fresh seafood, friendly staff, books and games; no mobile phones; children welcome, tables outside, souvenir shop doubling as general store for the island's few residents, open (and food) all day from breakfast on. *(Anon)*

Dorset

KEY  Star Pub   Top Quality Food   Great Beer

Good Wines   £ Bargain Meals   Good Bedrooms   Serves Food

ASKERSWELL
SY5393   Map 2

Spyway £ 🛏

(01308) 485250 – www.spyway-inn.co.uk

Off A35 Bridport–Dorchester; DT2 9EP

Extremely popular family-run inn with a genuine welcome, unspoilt décor, real ales, well liked food and fine views; bedrooms

Once our readers have discovered this country inn, they tend to return on a regular basis – often staying overnight in the comfortable bedrooms with views over the garden; breakfasts are excellent. The unspoilt little rooms are cosily filled with old-fashioned high-backed settles, cushioned wall and window seats and some tub chairs. Old photos of the pub and rustic scenes are displayed on the walls and jugs hang from the beams; the warm Rayburn is a bonus on chilly days. Otter Ale and Bitter and a guest such as Butcombe on handpump, ten wines by the glass and farm cider are served by friendly staff. The dining area has old oak beams and timber uprights, red-cushioned dining chairs around dark tables on patterned carpet, horse tack and horsebrasses on the walls, and a woodburning stove. Two smaller rooms lead off from here. There are marvellous views of the downs and coast from seats on the back terrace and in the garden, and a small children's play area. The pub's steep lane continues up Eggardon Hill, one of the highest points in the region.

Enjoyable food using local produce includes pigeon and smoked bacon salad, mozzarella fritters with sweet chilli dip, red thai vegetable curry, lambs liver with onions and bacon, chicken breast stuffed with haggis with a whisky cream sauce, pork belly with cider sauce, bass fillets with sauté potatoes, and puddings such as crème brûlée and sticky toffee pudding. *Benchmark main dish: steak in ale pie £11.25. Two-course evening meal £16.00.*

Free house ~ Licensee Tim Wilkes ~ Real ale ~ Open 12-3, 6-11 ~ Bar food 12-3, 6-9 ~ Restaurant ~ Children welcome ~ Wi-fi ~ Bedrooms: £50/£80 *Recommended by Dru and Louisa Marshall, Pete Flower, B and M Kendall, Katharine Cowherd, Comus and Sarah Elliott, Tom and Jill Jones, Dennis and Doreen Haward*

BRIDPORT
SY4692   Map 1

Stable

(01308) 426876 – www.thestabledorset.co.uk

At the back of the Bull Hotel; DT6 3LF

Lots of draught ciders and perry, freshly made pizzas and friendly, helpful service in big, buzzy place

Customers of all ages love this lively cider and pizza bar tucked away behind the Bull Hotel on the High Street. The lofty barn-like room is rustic in design: rough planked walls and ceiling, some big steel columns, two long rows of pale wooden tables flanked by wide benches, hefty wooden candlesticks holding fat candles, and steps up to a raised end area with cushioned red wall benches and brass-studded red leather dining chairs around a few tables. They have St Austell Proper Job on handpump, over 80 varieties of cider (plus plenty of bottled cider) and six wines by the glass. It's the easy-going, young-at-heart atmosphere, and music to match, that pulls it all together. An upstairs room (not always open) is similar in style. There are sister operations in Bath and Bristol (Somerset), Falmouth and Fistral Beach (both in Cornwall) and Poole and Weymouth (both in Dorset).

As well as a dozen excellent pizzas made from scratch, the popular food includes pies (such as spicy lamb with chickpeas and chorizo; ham hock and pea and pumpkin; spinach and feta), interesting hearty salads and puddings such as apple crumble and chocolate brownie with clotted cream ice-cream. *Benchmark main dish: pizzas £11.00. Two-course evening meal £15.00.*

Free house ~ Licensees Nikki and Richard Cooper ~ Real ale ~ Open 5-11 (all day during school holidays); 12-11 Sat, Sun ~ Bar food 5-9.30; 12-9.30 weekends ~ Children welcome ~ Dogs allowed in bar ~ Wi-fi *Recommended by Pete Flower, Edward May*

BUCKHORN WESTON   ST7524   Map 2
Stapleton Arms 🌟 ☆ ♀ 🛏

(01963) 370396 – www.thestapletonarms.com
Church Hill; off A30 Shaftesbury–Sherborne via Kington Magna; SP8 5HS

Handsome old building with a sizeable, civilised bar and separate dining room, good choice of real ales and wines by the glass, enjoyable food and friendly service; bedrooms

After a lovely surrounding walk (they can provide boots, maps and picnics), this civilised yet informal inn is just the place to head for. You can sit outside at elegant metal tables and chairs on York flagstones and gravel at the front – or in the charming back garden. Inside, the large bar has several different seating areas with dark slate flagstones or bare boards, church candles and big vases of flowers. To the left, leather or pink hessian sofas face one another across a low table in front of a log fire in a fine stone fireplace, some high stools are grouped around an equally high shelf, and a circular corner table comes with chapel chairs. A squashy leather sofa in the centre, with a big trunk as a table, seems a much prized place to sit, while off to the right is a long L-shaped wall seat with sizeable cushions, as well as farmhouse and more chapel chairs around wooden tables. Modern art adorns the dark red walls. Friendly staff serve Butcombe Bitter, Keystone Gold Hill and Plain Sheep Dip on handpump, 32 wines by the glass, farm cider and 16 malt whiskies. The separate restaurant (with shutters and carpet) has big candles in the fireplace and in glass jars on the window sills, walls painted blue or mushroom, and elegant Victorian-style dining chairs around dark tables. The well equipped bedrooms are both antique and contemporary in style and breakfasts are highly praised. Wincanton Racecourse is nearby.

From a seasonal and thoughtful menu, the highly enjoyable food includes lunchtime sandwiches, smoked mackerel and horseradish tartare with yoghurt, carrot and courgette pickle, mushroom ragoût on rye with fried duck egg, pheasant with pea purée, croquette potato and sage cream sauce, chicken, leek and smoked bacon pie, pork belly with black pudding, bream fillets with chorizo crushed potatoes and crayfish aioli, and puddings such as chocolate and Baileys soufflé with orange spiced ice-cream and new york cheesecake. *Benchmark main dish: steak burger with toppings and triple-cooked chips £12.00. Two-course evening meal £21.00.*

Free house ~ Licensee Victoria Reeves ~ Real ale ~ Open 11-3, 6-11; 11-11 Sat; 12-11 Sun ~ Bar food 12-3, 6-10 ~ Restaurant ~ Children welcome ~ Dogs allowed in bar ~ Wi-fi ~ Bedrooms: £70/£90 *Recommended by Mr Yeldahn, Mr and Mrs J Watkins*

 CERNE ABBAS ST6601 Map 2

New Inn

(01300) 341274 – www.thenewinncerneabbas.co.uk
Long Street; DT2 7JF

Dorset Dining Pub of the Year

Carefully refurbished former coaching inn with character bar and two dining rooms, friendly licensees, local ales and inventive food; fine bedrooms

This is a special place to stay and the smart, well equipped bedrooms are found in both the charming 16th-c main building and the converted stable-block. The friendly, hands-on licensees and their helpful staff are genuinely welcoming and throughout there's a great deal of character and original features – including lovely mullioned windows and heavy oak beams. The bar has a solid oak counter, an attractive mix of old dining tables and chairs on slate or polished wooden floors, settles built into various nooks and crannies, and a woodburner in the opened-up Yorkstone fireplace. Palmers Copper, Dorset Gold and IPA on handpump, a dozen wines by the glass, ten malt whiskies and local cider. The two dining rooms are furnished in a similar style. There are seats on the terrace and picnic-sets beneath mature fruit trees or parasols in the back garden. You can walk from the attractive stone-built village to the prehistoric Cerne Abbas Giant chalk carving and on to other nearby villages.

Seriously good food includes sandwiches, twice-baked local crab soufflé, terrine of confit duck and foie gras with rhubarb chutney, ham terrine and fried eggs, leek and parmesan risotto with a poached egg, lunchtime burger with pickles and triple-cooked chips, line-caught cod with crispy potatoes, marinated peppers and lemon jam, truffle-roasted chicken breast with crushed carrots and madeira cream, and puddings such as coffee crème brûlée and raspberry and white chocolate alaska with nougatine. *Benchmark main dish: slow-roast pork belly with champ mash, red cabbage and apple £15.95. Two-course evening meal £23.00.*

Palmers ~ Tenant Jeremy Lee ~ Real ale ~ Open 12-3, 6-11 (10.30 Sun in winter) ~ Bar food 12-2, 7-9 (8.30 Sun) ~ Children welcome ~ Dogs allowed in bar ~ Wi-fi ~ Bedrooms: £85/£95 *Recommended by Alan Johnson, M G Hart, Michael Doswell, Richard Tilbrook, Patrick and Daphne Darley, John and Sarah Perry, Andrew Reed, J R Wildon, Dr Martin Owton, Mrs P Sumner*

 **CHIDEOCK** SY4191 Map 1

Anchor

(01297) 489215 – www.theanchorinnseatown.co.uk
Off A35 from Chideock; DT6 6JU

Stunning beach position for carefully renovated inn, lots of character, well kept ales and popular food and seats on front terrace; light, airy bedrooms

The setting here is outstanding with the extensively but thoughtfully refurbished inn overlooking the beach, sea and cliffs; the terrace makes the most of this with good quality seats, stools and tables under parasols. Inside, plenty of original character has been kept in the three smallish, light rooms: padded wall seating, nice old wooden chairs and stools around scrubbed tables on bare boards, a couple of woodburning stoves (one under a huge bressumer beam), tilley lamps, model ships and lots of historic photographs of the pub, the area and locals. From the wood-panelled bar they serve Palmers 200, Best, Copper and Dorset Gold on handpump, seven wines by the glass and cocktails; background music. The attractive, airy bedrooms are decorated with nautical touches using driftwood and ropework and take in the fine views. Lovely walks along the Dorset Coast Path. You can park for free in front of the pub, or across the road for £2 (refundable against a spend of £20 or more in the pub).

Highly rated food includes ciabatta sandwiches, sticky paprika, honey and sesame seed ribs with peanut and red cabbage salad and chilli lime dressing, sharing platters, sausages with mustard mash and red wine gravy, spiced squash, roast vegetable and chickpea stew with herby polenta and salsa verde, smoked haddock and salmon gratin topped with chilli breadcrumbs, specials such as whole megrim sole with chorizo and anchovy butter, chicken with wild mushroom and goats cheese sauce and crispy prosciutto, and puddings. *Benchmark main dish: beer-battered fish and chips £11.95. Two-course evening meal £20.00.*

Palmers ~ Tenant Paul Wiscombe ~ Real ale ~ Open 10am (9am weekends)-11pm ~ Bar food 12-9; 12-2.30, 6-9 weekdays in winter ~ Children welcome ~ Dogs allowed in bar ~ Wi-fi ~ Bedrooms: £105/£120 *Recommended by Paul Humphreys, Dru and Louisa Marshall, Pete Flower, Martin and Sue Radcliffe, Lucy Ryan, Sheila Topham*

CHIDEOCK
George

SY4292 Map 1

(01297) 489419 – www.georgeinnchideock.co.uk
A35 Bridport–Lyme Regis; DT6 6JD

Comfortably traditional local with a thriving atmosphere and well liked food and drink

A welcome break from the busy A35, this heavily thatched old village inn is a bustling place with a good mix of customers. The cosy, low-ceilinged, carpeted bar is nicely traditional, with Palmers 200, Copper and IPA on handpump, six wines by the glass and farm cider, warm log fires, and brassware and pewter tankards hanging from dark beams. There are wooden pews and long built-in tongue-and-groove banquettes, cream walls hung with old tools and high shelves of bottles, plates and mugs; background music, TV, bar billiards, darts and board games. The garden room opens on to a pretty walled garden with a terrace and a much used wood-fired oven.

Using free-range meat and other local produce, the popular food relies on daily specials such as potted crab on toast, mushroom, leek and goats cheese risotto, chicken with leeks and smoked bacon sauce, and bream fillets topped with herby crab sauce; the short à la carte menu includes sandwiches, home-made chorizo scotch egg, home-cooked ham and free-range eggs and beer-battered fish or burgers with toppings, both with chips, and puddings. *Benchmark main dish: beer-battered fish and chips £10.50. Two-course evening meal £16.50.*

Palmers ~ Tenants Mr and Mrs Steve Smith ~ Real ale ~ Open 12-3, 6-11 ~ Bar food 12-2.30, 6-9.30 ~ Restaurant ~ Children welcome but not in snug bar ~ Dogs allowed in bar ~ Wi-fi ~ Live music Weds and Sat evenings in summer *Recommended by Brian and Anna Marsden, Paul Humphreys, Pete Flower*

CHURCH KNOWLE
SY9381 Map 2

New Inn ♀

(01929) 480357 – www.newinn-churchknowle.co.uk

Village signed off A351 N of Corfe Castle; BH20 5NQ

Partly thatched former farmhouse with plenty of seating in various rooms, open fires, a thoughtful choice of drinks, good food and a friendly landlord

After a visit to the nearby ruins of Corfe Castle, this cheerful pub is just the place for refreshment. The connected character bar rooms have so much of interest: brass and copper measuring jugs, bed warmers, pots and pans, horsebrasses, elderly board games and books, stone jars, china plates, a glass cabinet filled with household items from years ago, tilley lamps, the odd mangle and set of scales, a coastguard flag and an old diver's helmet. The main bar has an open fire in a stone fireplace, high-backed black leather dining chairs and cushioned wall settles around heavy rustic tables on red-patterned carpet and quite a few stools against the counter; board games. Dorset Jurassic, Sharps Doom Bar and a changing guest ale on handpump, six wines by the glass and farm cider; there's a wine shack from which you can choose your own wines, and also a wide choice of teas, coffees and local soft drinks. The dining room leads off here; it has similar furnishings, a serving counter with hot plates, two fireplaces (one with church candles, the other with a stove) and a dark red dado. Outside are picnic-sets on the lawn. They have a campsite.

 The food has an emphasis on local fish and shellfish, such as fresh crab soup, scallops in garlic butter, mixed seafood and prawn curry, and local mussels, sardines and lobster; non-fishy choices include lunchtime sandwiches, chicken liver parfait with red onion marmalade, crispy duck on honey and soy-dressed salad, gammon and free-range eggs, steak in ale pie, moussaka, lambs liver and bacon, and puddings such as chocolate and Grand Marnier mousse and vanilla and passion-fruit panna cotta with a berry compote. *Benchmark main dish: roast of the day £10.50. Two-course evening meal £19.00.*

Punch ~ Tenants Maurice and Rosemary Estop ~ Real ale ~ Open 11-3, 6-11; 12-3.30, 6-11 Sat, Sun ~ Bar food 12-2.15, 6 (5 in summer holidays)-9.15 ~ Restaurant ~ Children welcome ~ Wi-fi *Recommended by Wendy Breese, Eddie Edwards, R Halliday, Peter Pilbeam*

CRANBORNE
SU0513 Map 2

Inn at Cranborne ⇦

(01725) 551249 – www.theinnatcranborne.co.uk

Wimborne Street (B3078 N of Wimborne); BH21 5PP

Neatly refurbished old inn with bustling friendly atmosphere in bars and dining areas, good choice of drinks, highly rated food and seats outside; comfortable bedrooms

Thomas Hardy visited this bustling inn while writing *Tess of the D'Urbervilles*. Obviously it's much changed since then and the carefully refurbished, rambling bars have heavy beams, open doorways and the odd standing timber, and a chatty, relaxed atmosphere. The main bar area, divided into two by a partition, is our favourite place to sit: grey-planked and tartan-cushioned built-in wall seats lined with big scatter cushions and assorted chairs (farmhouse, wheelback, ladderback) on parquet flooring, flagstones or rugs, nightlights on each table and a woodburner in the inglenook fireplace, with George the pub dog's bed beside it. Badger First Gold and Hopping Hare on handpump and several wines by the glass served by friendly, helpful staff; background music, TV, darts and board games. The dining areas lead back from here, with similar furnishings and a little brick fireplace piled with logs; there's also a second bar with white-painted or wooden furniture and another woodburning stove. Plenty of coaching prints on grey walls above a darker grey dado, and church candles. Outside, you'll find benches, seats and tables on neat gravel. The comfortable, well equipped bedrooms are individually furnished and the breakfasts very good.

Using their own-grown plus other top quality local produce, the interesting food includes lunchtime open sandwiches, treacle-cured salmon with piccalilli, pork pâté with red onion chutney, all-day breakfast, butternut squash, sage and parmesan risotto, wild boar and apple sausages with parmesan mash, spiced roast onions and red wine gravy, smoked pressed ham hock, free-range eggs and triple-cooked chips, duck breast with leg faggot and date sauce, and puddings such as dark chocolate mousse with orange curd, poppyseed sponge, honeycomb and chocolate oil and quince and pear nut crumble with sauce anglaise. *Benchmark main dish: slow-cooked beef cheeks with potatoes of the day and red wine jus £11.50. Two-course evening meal £19.50.*

Badger ~ Tenant Jane Gould ~ Real ale ~ Open 11-11 (10 Sun) ~ Bar food 12-2, 6-9; 12-2.30, 6-9.30 (9 Sun) Fri, Sat ~ Restaurant (evening only) ~ Children welcome ~ Dogs welcome ~ Wi-fi ~ Live music last Fri of month ~ Bedrooms: £75/£99 *Recommended by Ian Malone, Peter Brix*

EVERSHOT
ST5704   Map 2

Acorn ♀ 🛏

(01935) 83228 – www.acorn-inn.co.uk
Off A37 S of Yeovil; DT2 0JW

A 400-year-old inn in a pretty village, plenty of character in several rooms, log fires and knick-knacks, and friendly licensees; bedrooms

Very much the heart of the community but with a warm welcome for visitors too, this bustling inn is immortalised as the Sow & Acorn in Thomas Hardy's *Tess of the D'Urbervilles*. The public bar has a log fire, lots of beer mats on beams, big flagstones and high chairs against the counter where they serve Bath Gem and Cheddar Gorge Best on handpump, 39 wines by the glass and 100 malt whiskies; dogs are looked after with a bowl of water and biscuits behind the bar. A second bar has comfortable beige leather wall banquettes and little stools around tables set with fresh flowers, and a turkish rug on nice old quarry tiles. This leads to a bistro-style dining room with ladderback chairs around red gingham and beige-clothed tables; the slightly more formal restaurant is similarly furnished. There's also a comfortable lounge with armchairs, board games, shelves of books and a skittle alley. Throughout are open fires, wood panelling, pretty knick-knacks, all manner of copper and brass items, water jugs, wall prints and photographs; background music, TV and darts. The walled garden has picnic-sets under a fine beech tree. Each of the attractive bedrooms is individually decorated and has a Thomas Hardy theme; numerous nearby walks.

Quite a choice of rewarding food using seasonal local produce includes sandwiches, pressed confit of rabbit and smoked bacon with tomato and onion chutney and a fried quail's egg, brixham crab and dill fishcakes on sweetcorn purée with mango and coriander salsa, bubble and squeak potato cake topped with roasted vegetables and blue cheese with pesto and balsamic reduction, trio of pork (braised cheek, slow-roasted belly, loin) with bubble and squeak, apple purée and port reduction, guinea fowl breast stuffed with brie and rocket on sweet potato purée and crispy shallots, and puddings such as caramelised rhubarb and custard with a shot of rhubarb vodka and chocolate and chilli tart with lime sorbet and crème fraîche. *Benchmark main dish: beer-battered fish and triple-cooked chips £13.00. Two-course evening meal £21.00.*

Free house ~ Licensee Alex Mackenzie ~ Real ale ~ Open 11-11; 12-10.30 Sun ~ Bar food 12-2, 7-9 ~ Restaurant ~ Children welcome ~ Dogs allowed in bar and bedrooms ~ Wi-fi ~ Bedrooms: £89/£110 *Recommended by Alan Johnson, Nick Sharpe, Charlie May*

FARNHAM
ST9515 Map 2

Museum

(01725) 516261 – www.museuminn.co.uk

Village signposted off A354 Blandford Forum–Salisbury; DT11 8DE

Partly thatched and rather smart inn with appealing rooms, inventive modern cooking, real ales and fine wines, and seats outside; lovely bedrooms

This is a lovely place to stay, with four luxurious rooms in the 17th-c pub itself and four more in the converted stables; they also have a large, self-catering thatched cottage. Despite the emphasis on overnight guests and on the excellent food, the proper little bar remains its beating heart. There are beams, flagstones, a big inglenook fireplace, quite an assortment of dining chairs around plain or painted wooden tables, and bar stools against the counter where friendly, helpful staff serve Isle of Purbeck Best, Ringwood Best and a guest from Waylands Sixpenny 6D on handpump, several wines by the glass, a dozen malt whiskies and farm cider. Leading off here is a simply but attractively furnished dining room with cushioned window seats, a long dark leather button-back wall seat, similar chairs and tables on bare floorboards and quite a few photographs on the patterned wallpaper; there's also a quiet lounge with armchairs around a low table in front of an open fire, books on shelves and board games. A terrace has cushioned seats and tables under parasols.

 Excellent food using the best local produce (the chef makes his own bread and cheese and catches local game) includes moules marinière, ham hock terrine with red onion chutney, aubergine and feta schnitzel on red pepper coulis, chicken kiev with slaw and chips, rare-breed steak in ale pie, slow-roast pork belly with champ mash and apple sauce, fish pie, pheasant in cider with cabbage and bacon, and puddings such as lemon tart with berry compote and crème brûlée. *Benchmark main dish: somerset cheese soufflé £13.95. Two-course evening meal £21.00.*

Free house ~ Real ale ~ Open 12-11 ~ Bar food 12-3, 6.30-9.30 ~ Restaurant (Fri and Sat evenings, Sun lunch only) ~ Children welcome ~ Dogs welcome ~ Wi-fi ~ Bedrooms: £80/£90 *Recommended by Charlie May, Peter Brix*

KINGSTON
SY9579 Map 2

Scott Arms

(01929) 480270 – www.thescottarms.com

West Street (B3069); BH20 5LH

Wonderful views from a large garden, rambling character rooms, real ales and interesting food and an easy-going atmosphere; bedrooms

From the big, attractive garden with its rustic-style seating there are magnificent views of Corfe Castle and the Purbeck Hills, and the creeper-covered pub is a fine spot to relax after enjoying one of the area's many good walks. A new outside kitchen has been opened with a jerk shack for caribbean-style food (the landlady is jamaican). The bar areas and more formal dining room are on several levels, with stripped stone and brickwork, flagstones and bare boards, beams and high rafters, seats ranging from sofas and easy chairs through all manner of wooden chairs around tables of varying sizes, and open fires; stairs lead up from the bar to a small minstrel's gallery-like area with sofas facing one another across a table. The two bedrooms are attractively decorated; there's a self-catering apartment too.

 As well as jamaican specialities such as ackee, saltfish, plantain and lime oil, mutton or vegetarian curries and jerk chicken (best to phone ahead to check these are on), the popular food includes field mushrooms stuffed with blue cheese, prawn cocktail, sharing boards, ham and free-range eggs, moroccan-style vegetable stew, bangers and mash with stockpot gravy, burger with toppings, onion marmalade and chips, fresh local crab, and puddings such as warm chocolate brownie and eton mess. *Benchmark main dish: beer-battered fish and chips £12.95. Two-course evening meal £19.00.*

Greene King~ Lease Ian, Simon and Cynthia Coppack ~ Real ale ~ Open 11-11 ~ Bar food 12-2.30 (2.45 weekends), 6-8.30 ~ Children welcome ~ Dogs allowed in bar ~ Wi-fi ~ Bedrooms: £90/£105 *Recommended by Eddie Edwards, Jo Garnett, Gus Swan*

MIDDLEMARSH   ST6607 Map 2
Hunters Moon 🛏
(01963) 210966 – www.hunters-moon.org.uk
A352 Sherborne–Dorchester; DT9 5QN

Plenty of bric-a-brac in several linked areas, reasonably priced food and quite a choice of drinks; comfortable bedrooms

You can be sure of a genuine welcome from the hands-on licensees and their cheerful staff in this busy former coaching inn. The traditional beamed bar rooms are cosily filled with a great variety of tables and chairs on red patterned carpet, an array of ornamentation from horsebrasses up, and lighting in the form of converted oil lamps; the atmosphere is properly pubby. Booths are formed by some attractively cushioned settles, walls are of exposed brick, stone and some panelling and there are three log fires (one in a capacious inglenook); background music, children's books and toys and board games. Butcombe Bitter and a couple of guests such as Black Sheep and Wells Bombardier Burning Gold on handpump, farm cider and 16 wines by the glass. A neat lawn has picnic-sets, including some circular ones.

 Good food includes half a pint of prawns, baked brie wrapped in filo pastry with cranberry compote, sharing platters, smoked salmon and pea pasta, various pizzas, beef, chicken or mushroom burgers with toppings, onion rings and chips, local faggots, mash and onion gravy, a curry of the week, slow-roasted lamb shank in garlic and rosemary sauce, a mixed grill and puddings. *Benchmark main dish: beer-battered cod and chips £11.50. Two-course evening meal £19.00.*

Enterprise ~ Lease Dean and Emma Mortimer ~ Real ale ~ Open 10.30-2.30, 6 (5 Fri)-11; 10.30am-11pm Sat, Sun ~ Bar food 12-2, 6-9; all day weekends ~ Children welcome ~ Dogs welcome ~ Wi-fi ~ Bedrooms: £65/£75 *Recommended by Gene and Tony Freemantle, Peter Brix, Dr Simon Innes*

MUDEFORD   SZ1792 Map 2
Ship in Distress
(01202) 485123 – www.ship-in-distress.co.uk
Stanpit; off B3059 at roundabout; BH23 3NA

Wide choice of fish dishes, quirky nautical décor and friendly staff in a cheerful cottage pub

Within walking distance of the harbour, this 300-year-old former smugglers' pub is full of amusing seaside-themed paraphernalia. There's an aquarium, model boats, the odd piratical figure, brightly painted fish cutouts swimming across the walls, rope fancywork, brassware, lanterns and oars; darts, games machine, board games, big screen TV, background music and a winter woodburning stove. As well as several boat pictures, the room on the right has tables with masses of snapshots (under the glass tabletops) of locals caught up in various waterside japes. Ringwood Best and a guest or two such as Dartmoor Jail Ale and Sharps Doom Bar on handpump, alongside several wines by the glass. A spreading and bustling two-room restaurant area has a fish tank, contemporary works by local artists (for sale) and a light-hearted mural giving the impression of a window opening on to a sunny boating scene. There are seats and tables on the suntrap back terrace and a covered heated area for chilly evenings.

Fresh fish and shellfish from local fishermen features strongly: cockles, whelks, scallops, mussels, crab, whole lemon sole, bass and so forth. They also offer sandwiches and baguettes, duck and orange pâté, cottage pie, gammon and egg, and puddings such as lemon posset and crème brûlée; a two-course set lunch is available Tues-Thurs. *Benchmark main dish: fruits de mer platter £25.00. Two-course evening meal £22.00.*

Punch ~ Lease Maggie Wheeler ~ Real ale ~ Open 11am-midnight (11pm Sun) ~ Bar food 12-2 (2.30 weekends), 6.30-9 ~ Restaurant ~ Children welcome ~ Dogs allowed in bar ~ Wi-fi ~ Bingo Weds evening *Recommended by Katharine Cowherd, Alfie Bayliss*

NETTLECOMBE SY5195 Map 2
Marquis of Lorne 🍺

(01308) 485236 – www.themarquisoflorne.co.uk
Off A3066 Bridport–Beaminster, via West Milton; DT6 3SY

Attractive country pub with enjoyable food and drink, friendly licensees and seats in big garden; bedrooms

Eggardon Hill, one of Dorset's most spectacular Iron Age hill forts with views over the coast and surrounding countryside, is within walking distance of this former farmhouse; the countryside here is particularly lovely. The comfortable, bustling main bar has a log fire, mahogany panelling, old prints and photographs and neatly matching chairs and tables. Two dining areas lead off, the smaller of which has another log fire. The wooden-floored snug (liked by locals) has board games, table skittles and background music, and they keep Palmers Copper, Dorset Gold and IPA on handpump, with ten wines by the glass from a decent list. The big mature garden is just the place to be in warm weather with its pretty herbaceous borders, picnic-sets under apple trees and a rustic-style play area.

Using home-grown seasonal produce, the highly rated food includes duck liver pâté with spiced pears, scallops and black pudding with garlic and parsley cream, mustard and brown sugar baked ham and eggs, vegetarian lasagne, lambs liver and bacon, sticky beef with indonesian-style salad, grilled bass with creamed prawn velouté, and puddings such as triple-chocolate cheesecake and brioche bread and butter pudding. *Benchmark main dish: slow-roasted pork belly with apple sauce £14.00. Two-course evening meal £20.50.*

Palmers ~ Tenants Stephen and Tracey Brady ~ Real ale ~ Open 12-2.30, 6-11 ~ Bar food 12-2, 6-9 ~ Restaurant ~ Children welcome ~ Dogs allowed in bar ~ Wi-fi ~ Bedrooms: £80/£90 *Recommended by Dr D J and Mrs S C Walker, Colin McLachlan*

The 🍺 symbol shows pubs that keep their beer unusually well,
have a particularly good range or brew their own.

PLUSH
ST7102 Map 2

Brace of Pheasants 🏅 ♀ ⇌

(01300) 348357 – www.braceofpheasants.co.uk

Village signposted from B3143 N of Dorchester at Piddletrenthide; DT2 7RQ

16th-c thatched pub with friendly service, three real ales, lots of wines by the glass, generously served food and decent garden; comfortable bedrooms

Consistently well run and much enjoyed by its many customers, this 16th-c inn remains on top form. The beamed bar has a bustling, friendly atmosphere, windsor chairs around good solid tables on patterned carpeting, a few standing timbers, a huge heavy-beamed inglenook at one end with cosy seating inside, and a good warming log fire at the other. Flack Manor Double Drop and Ringwood Best are tapped from the cask by the helpful licensees, and they offer a fine choice of wines with 18 by the glass, and two proper farm ciders. A decent-sized garden includes a terrace and a lawn sloping up towards a rockery. Attractively fitted out and comfortable, the bedrooms are in a converted bowling alley; each has a little outdoor terrace. The pub is well placed for walks – an attractive bridleway behind the building leads to the left of the woods and over to Church Hill.

 Rewarding food (they list their suppliers on menus) includes sandwiches, beer-battered pigeon strips with red onion marmalade, home-cured gravadlax with sweet pickled cucumber, goats cheese salad with beetroot and walnuts, lambs kidneys in mustard cream sauce, trio of wild boar and apple sausages with onion gravy, confit duck leg with madeira and seville orange sauce and root vegetable gratin, venison steak with port and redcurrant sauce, and puddings such as spotted dick and custard and sticky toffee pudding with caramel sauce. *Benchmark main dish: beer-battered fish and chips £12.95. Two-course evening meal £22.00.*

Free house ~ Licensees Phil and Carol Bennett ~ Real ale ~ Open 12-3, 7-11 (10.30 Sun) ~ Bar food 12-2, 7-9 ~ Children welcome ~ Dogs allowed in bar ~ Wi-fi ~ Bedrooms: $105/$115
Recommended by David and Stella Martin, Alan Johnson, Phil Bryant, Barry Collett, David and Carole Newton, PLC

SHERBORNE
ST6316 Map 2

Digby Tap ◖ £

(01935) 813148 – www.digbytap.co.uk

Cooks Lane; park in Digby Road and walk round corner; DT9 3NS

Regularly changing ales in simple alehouse, open all day with very inexpensive beer and food

Delightfully unpretentious with no frills whatsoever, this old-fashioned town tavern remains much loved by customers of all ages and from every walk of life. There's a lively, chatty and warmly welcoming atmosphere, unbelievably good value food and a fine range of ales: Cottage Golden Arrow, Otter Bitter, Plain Sheep Dip and Yeovil Star Gazer on handpump. Also, several wines by the glass and a choice of malt whiskies. The straightforward flagstoned bar, with its cosy corners, is full of understated character; the small games room has a pool table and a quiz machine, and there's also a TV room; mobile phones are banned. Beautiful Sherborne Abbey is just a stroll away.

🍴 Generous helpings of incredibly good value, straightforward food – lunchtime only – include sandwiches and toasties, three-egg omelettes, sausages with free-range eggs, burgers and specials such as sausage casserole, fish pie and a mixed grill. *Benchmark main dish: ham, egg and chips £5.00.*

Free house ~ Licensees Oliver Wilson and Nick Whigham ~ Real ale ~ No credit cards ~
Open 11-11; 12-11 Sun ~ Bar food 12-2; not Sun ~ Children welcome before 6pm ~
Dogs allowed in bar ~ Wi-fi *Recommended by Tony and Wendy Hobden, Edward May*

SHROTON
ST8512   Map 2
Cricketers

(01258) 860421 – www.thecricketersshroton.co.uk

Off A350 N of Blandford (village also called Iwerne Courtney); follow signs; DT11 8QD

**Country pub with real ales, well liked food and pretty garden;
nice views and walks nearby**

It's the warmth of the welcome from the friendly licensees and their staff
that really stands out here – you immediately feel at home. The bright,
divided bar has a woodburning stove in a stone fireplace, cushioned high-
backed windsor and ladderback chairs in one area and black leather ones in
another, all sorts of tables, a settle with scatter cushions, and red and cream
walls decorated with cricket bats and photos of cricket teams; there's also a
cosy little alcove and a spreading dining area towards the back. Butcombe
Bitter, Otter Amber and Salisbury English Ale on handpump (they hold a
beer festival on the early May Bank Holiday weekend) and several wines by
the glass; background music. At the front of the building are some circular
picnic-sets and a secluded and pretty back garden has more seats on a
terrace and a lawn. Walks up to the Iron Age ramparts on the summit reveal
terrific views, and the pub sits on the Wessex Ridgeway; walkers must leave
muddy boots outside.

As well as lunchtime baguettes, the popular food includes garlic mushrooms on
toast with a poached egg, whitebait with tartare sauce, sausages with bacon and
butter bean cassoulet, black bean and vegetable chilli, a pie of the day, lambs liver and
bacon with onion gravy, pork, prune and apple meatballs with cider sauce, ox cheek with
horseradish and orange dumplings, and puddings such as steamed ginger pudding with
ginger ice-cream and toffee sauce and salted caramel crème brûlée. *Benchmark main
dish: pie of the day £11.50. Two-course evening meal £19.50.*

Heartstone Inns ~ Licensees Joe and Sally Grieves ~ Real ale ~ Open 12-3, 6-11; 12-11 Sun
~ Bar food 12-2.30, 6.30-9; no food Sun evening Sept-May ~ Children welcome ~ Wi-fi
Recommended by Michael and Sheila Hawkins, Paul Denny

TARRANT MONKTON
ST9408   Map 2
Langton Arms ⭐ 🍺 🛏

(01258) 830225 – www.thelangtonarms.co.uk

Village signposted from A354, then head for church; DT11 8RX

**Charming thatched pub with friendly staff, real ales, good food, plenty
of dining space and seats outside; bedrooms**

Readers happily return to this bustling thatched pub on a regular basis
and it's attractively placed next to the church in a pretty Dorset village.
The bars have a few beams, high-backed tartan dining chairs around wooden
tables on carpeting, a cushioned window seat, a few high chairs against
the light oak counter and Flack Manor Double Drop and a guest such as
Butcombe Best on handpump, ten wines by the glass, ten malt whiskies
and a farm cider. The two connected, beamed dining rooms, furnished with
cushioned wooden chairs around white-clothed tables, lead into a light and
airy conservatory; country prints, dried flower arrangements, background
music, TV and board games. In fine weather, you can sit out in front or at
teak tables in the flower-filled back garden; there's also a well equipped

children's play area. The comfortable bedrooms occupy brick buildings around the attractive courtyard, with four in a neighbouring cottage.

 Using home-grown and other local, seasonal produce and beef from their own farm, the high quality food includes sandwiches, chicken liver parfait with plum chutney, camembert fondue with red onion relish and croutons, sharing platters, twice-baked cheese soufflé, venison sausages with apple mash and onion gravy, thai green chicken curry, bass fillets with white wine velouté, steaks with a choice of sauces, and puddings such as sticky toffee pudding with butterscotch sauce and crème brûlée. *Benchmark main dish: steak in port and red wine pie £15.50. Two-course evening meal £22.00.*

Free house ~ Licensee Barbara Cossins ~ Real ale ~ Open 11am-midnight; 12-midnight Sun ~ Bar food 12-2.30, 6-9.30 (10 Fri); all day weekends ~ Restaurant ~ Children welcome ~ Dogs allowed in bar and bedrooms ~ Wi-fi ~ Bedrooms: £70/£90 *Recommended by Steve Whalley, David and Carole Newton, Colin McLachlan, Tony and Rosemary Swainson*

TRENT
Rose & Crown 🌟 🛏
ST5818 Map 2

(01935) 850776 – www.roseandcrowntrent.co.uk
Opposite the church; DT9 4SL

Character thatched pub with a friendly licensee, cosy rooms, open fires, a good choice of drinks and well thought-of food; bedrooms

In a pretty rural spot opposite a lovely church, this is a charming inn with a good mix of both locals and visitors. The cosy little bar on the right has big, comfortable sofas and stools around a low table in front of an open fire, fresh flowers and candlelight. The bar opposite is furnished with nice old wooden tables and chairs on quarry tiles, and stools against the counter where they serve Wadworths 6X, IPA and Horizon and guests such as St Austell Proper Job and a beer from Hop Kettle on handpump, and 14 wines by the glass; board games. Two other connected rooms have similar wooden tables and chairs, settles and pews, a grandfather clock, pewter tankards and more fireplaces. Throughout are all sorts of pictures, including Stuart prints commemorating the fact that Charles II sought refuge in this village after the Battle of Worcester. The simply furnished back dining room leads to the garden with seats and tables and fine views (and sunsets); there are some picnic-sets at the front. The pretty bedrooms are in a converted byre.

 Impressive food includes lunchtime sandwiches, mussels in cider and cream, chicken liver parfait with onion marmalade, mustard-glazed ham and free-range eggs, confit fennel tarte tatin with creamy blue cheese and pickled walnuts, hake with brown shrimp butter and saffron potatoes, venison with salsify, braised beetroots, foie gras-stuffed prune and bubble and squeak cake, and puddings such as coffee and date pudding with malted chocolate mousse, lemon mascarpone and coffee syrup and fruit crumble. *Benchmark main dish: steak with peppercorn sauce and chips £17.00. Two-course evening meal £21.00.*

Wadworths ~ Tenant Nick Lamb ~ Real ale ~ Open 11-11 ~ Bar food 12-2.30, 6-9 ~ Children welcome ~ Dogs welcome ~ Wi-fi ~ Bedrooms: £65/£85 *Recommended by Gene and Tony Freemantle, J R Wildon, Martin and Anne Terry*

WEST BAY
West Bay 🌟 🛏
SY4690 Map 1

(01308) 422157 – www.thewestbayhotel.co.uk
Station Road; DT6 4EW

Relaxed seaside inn with emphasis on seafood; bedrooms

The daily fresh fish specials are a highlight here – the fish is landed at the busy little harbour just a stroll away. The fairly simple front part of the building, with bare boards, a coal-effect gas fire and a mix of sea and nostalgic prints, is separated by an island servery from the cosier carpeted dining area, which has more of a country kitchen feel; background music and board games. Though its spaciousness means it never feels crowded, booking is essential in season. Palmers 200, Best, Copper, Dorset Gold and a seasonal guest are served on handpump alongside good house wines (including eight by the glass) and several malt whiskies. There are tables in a small side garden and more in the large main garden. Several local teams meet to play in the pub's 100-year-old skittle alley. Bedrooms are quiet and comfortable.

 Highly enjoyable food includes freshly caught crab, lobster, scallops, sole and skate plus sandwiches and baguettes, fishcakes with sweet chilli aioli, mussels served several different ways, home-cooked honey-roast ham and free-range eggs, wild mushroom stroganoff, free-range chicken wrapped in smoked bacon with chorizo, sun-blush tomato and spring onion sauce, slow-cooked pork belly with sage, black pudding and cider jus, gilt-head bream with oriental stir-fried vegetables, and puddings. *Benchmark main dish: whole grilled fresh fish of the day £16.95. Two-course evening meal £21.00.*

Palmers ~ Tenant Samuel Good ~ Real ale ~ Open 12-11 (midnight Sat, 10 Sun); 12-3, 6-11 Nov-Mar in winter ~ Bar food 12-2 (3 weekends), 6-9 (8 Sun) ~ Children welcome till 8pm ~ Dogs allowed in bar ~ Wi-fi ~ Bedrooms: £85/£115 *Recommended by Charlie May, Phil Bryant, Comus and Sarah Elliott, Steve and Liz Tilley*

WEST STOUR
ST7822 Map 2

Ship 🏅 ♀ 🛏

(01747) 838640 – www.shipinn-dorset.com
A30 W of Shaftesbury; SP8 5RP

Civilised and pleasantly updated roadside dining inn, offering a wide range of food and ales; bedrooms

Being a country pub and close to the Stour Valley Way, walkers and their good-natured dogs are welcomed by the convivial hands-on landlord. The neatly kept rooms include a smallish but airy bar on the left with cream décor, a mix of chunky farmhouse furniture on dark boards and big sash windows that look beyond the road and car park to rolling pastures. The smaller flagstoned public bar has a good log fire and low ceilings. Butcombe Bitter, Hook Norton Hooky and Otter Amber on handpump, 14 wines by the glass and four farm ciders. During their summer beer festival they showcase a dozen beers and ten ciders, all from the west country. On the right, two carpeted dining rooms with stripped pine dado, stone walls and shutters are similarly furnished in a pleasantly informal style, and have some attractive contemporary cow prints; TV, numerous board games and background music. The bedlington terriers are called Douglas and Toby. Bedrooms are attractive and comfortable and you'll get pastoral views and a particularly good and hearty breakfast.

 As well as a two- and three-course set menu (not weekends), the highly enjoyable food includes lunchtime sandwiches, devilled kidneys with toasted brioche and balsamic drizzle, twice-baked gruyère, roasted pepper and dill soufflé, bison burger with toppings and fries, rabbit and smoked bacon hotpot in cider and grain mustard gravy, broccoli, leek and pea cream pasta with pine nuts and parmesan crisps, ginger beer-battered cod with chunky chips, pistachio-stuffed pork fillet with pear cream sauce and black pudding and bubble and squeak, and puddings. *Benchmark main dish:*

*posh fish pie (scallops, tiger prawns, salmon, smoked haddock and capers) £14.95.
Two-course evening meal £21.00.*

Free house ~ Licensee Gavin Griggs ~ Real ale ~ Open 12-3, 6-11.30 (midnight Sat); 12-11
Sun ~ Bar food 12-2.30, 6-9; not Sun evening ~ Restaurant ~ Well behaved children in
restaurant and lounge ~ Dogs allowed in bar ~ Wi-fi ~ Bedrooms: £60/£90
Recommended by Hugh Roberts, Peter Brix, Lindy Andrews

WEYMOUTH   SY6878   Map 2

Red Lion ✦ £

(01305) 786940 – www.theredlionweymouth.co.uk
Hope Square; DT4 8TR

**Bustling place with sunny terrace, a smashing range of drinks,
tasty food and lots to look at**

With a cheerful, lively atmosphere, a genuinely warm welcome and
a fine range of drinks, it's not surprising this handsome Victorian pub
is so busy. The refurbished bare-boards interior, kept cosy with candles,
has all manner of wooden chairs and tables, cushioned wall seats, some
unusual high, maroon-cushioned benches beside equally high tables, the
odd armchair here and there, numerous pictures and artefacts relating to
the lifeboat crews and their boats (this is the closest pub to Weymouth RNLI)
and other bric-a-brac on stripped brick walls. Some nice contemporary
touches include the woven timber wall and loads of mirrors wittily
overlapped. Dorset Jurassic, Hop Back Summer Lightning, Lifeboat Bitter
(named for the pub, brewed by Otter), Red Lion Bitter (also named for the
pub, from Dorset) and Sharps Doom Bar on handpump, over 80 rums (they
have a rum 'bible' to explain them) and 12 wines by the glass; service is
helpful and friendly. Also, daily papers, board games and background music.
There are plenty of seats outside that stay warmed by the sun well into the
evening. The pub is owned by Tim Bird and Mary McLaughlin – who also own
the Three Greyhounds in Allostock, Cholmondeley Arms at Cholmondeley
and Bulls Head and Church Inn in Mobberley (all in Cheshire).

As well as their popular sharing seafood boards, the highly thought-of food
includes filled baps, crispy salt and pepper whitebait, baked camembert with
ale chutney, burger with toppings, chips and tomato and caramelised onion chutney,
butternut squash, cranberry and blue cheese or steak in ale pies, barbecue pork ribs
with sweetcorn hash cake, smoked haddock fishcakes, and puddings such as chocolate
brownie and strawberry shortbread cheesecake; the Value Award is for the handful
of dishes under £10. *Benchmark main dish: fish pie £11.95. Two-course evening
meal £17.00.*

Free house ~ Licensee Brian McLaughlin ~ Real ale ~ Open 11-11 (midnight Fri, Sat);
12-10.30 Sun; 12-10.30 (11 Fri, Sat) Mon-Thurs in winter ~ Bar food 12-9; 12-3, 6-9 Oct-Mar
~ Children welcome until 7pm ~ Wi-fi ~ Live music outside summer Suns 2pm
Recommended by B and M Kendall, Phil and Jane Villiers, Edward May

WIMBORNE MINSTER   SZ0199   Map 2

Green Man ✦ £

(01202) 881021 – www.greenmanwimborne.com
Victoria Road, at junction with West Street (B3082/B3073); BH21 1EN

Cosy, warm-hearted town pub with simple food at bargain prices

In summer, the award-winning flowering tubs, hanging baskets and
window boxes here are quite amazing and there are more on the heated

back terrace. But at any time of the year this is a smashing town pub with a genuinely friendly landlord and a good mix of customers popping in and out all day. The four small linked areas have maroon plush banquettes and polished dark pub tables, copper and brass ornaments, red walls, Wadworths 6X, IPA and Swordfish on handpump and a farm cider. One room has a log fire in a sizeable brick fireplace, another has a coal-effect gas fire, and there are two dart boards, a silenced games machine, background music and TV; the Barn houses a pool table. Their little border terrier is called Cooper.

🍴 Incredible value, the traditional food includes sandwiches, toasties and jumbo rolls, thai-style fishcakes, a full english breakfast, beef or vegetable burgers with chips, lasagne, fish with fries and lamb shank with red wine and rosemary sauce; their Sunday roast deal includes a pudding. *Benchmark main dish: Sunday roast £7.95.*

Wadworths ~ Tenant Andrew Kiff ~ Real ale ~ Open 10am-11.30pm (midnight Sat) ~ Bar food 10-2 ~ Restaurant ~ Children welcome until 7.30pm ~ Dogs allowed in bar ~ Wi-fi ~ Live music Fri-Sun evenings *Recommended by B and M Kendall, Alfie Bayliss*

WORTH MATRAVERS   SY9777 Map 2
Square & Compass ★ ◖

(01929) 439229 – www.squareandcompasspub.co.uk
At fork of both roads signposted to village from B3069; BH19 3LF

Unchanging country tavern with masses of character, in the same family for many years; lovely sea views and fine nearby walks

For those who love honest, basic and quite unchanging places, this is a gem – and it's been run by the Newman family for more than a century. The simple offerings are not to everyone's taste, and to this day there's no bar counter. Cottage Wessex Pride, Palmers Copper, Flowerpots Goodens Gold, Yeovil Ruby and up to ten ciders are tapped from a row of casks and passed through two serving hatches to customers in the drinking corridor; also, a dozen malt whiskies. A couple of unspoilt rooms have straightforward furniture on flagstones, a woodburning stove and a loyal crowd of friendly locals; darts and shove-ha'penny. From the benches of local stone out in front there's a fantastic view over the village rooftops down to the sea. There may be free-roaming chickens and other birds clucking around and the small (free) museum exhibits local fossils and artefacts, mostly collected by the friendly current landlord and his father. Wonderful walks lead to some exciting switchback sections of the coast path above St Aldhelm's Head and Chapman's Pool – you'll need to park in the public car park (£2 honesty box) 100 metres along the Corfe Castle road.

🍴 Bar food is limited to home-made pasties and pies.

Free house ~ Licensees Charlie Newman and Kevin Hunt ~ Real ale ~ No credit cards ~ Open 12-11; 12-3, 6-11 Mon-Thurs in winter ~ Bar food all day ~ Children welcome ~ Dogs welcome ~ Live music Fri and Sat evenings, Sun lunchtime *Recommended by Alan Johnson, Robert Watt, Ian Phillips, David and Stella Martin, Wendy Breese, Eddie Edwards, Phil and Jane Villiers, Michael Sargent, Peter Meister, David and Judy Robison*

A star after the name of a pub shows exceptional quality. It means most people (after reading the report to see just why the star has been won) would think a special trip worthwhile.

Also Worth a Visit in Dorset

Besides the fully inspected pubs, you might like to try these pubs that have been recommended to us and described by readers. Do tell us what you think of them: feedback@goodguides.com

BISHOP'S CAUNDLE   ST6913
White Hart (01963) 23301
A3030 SE of Sherborne; DT9 5ND Smallish 17th-c roadside pub with reworked carpeted interior, dark beams, panelling, stripped stone and log fire, good well presented food from varied menu including daily specials, Sharps Doom Bar and local guests, restaurant; skittle alley; children and dogs welcome, country views from garden, closed Sun evening, Mon. *(David and Stella Martin)*

BOURNEMOUTH   SZ1092
Cricketers Arms (01202) 551589
Windham Road; BH1 4RN Well preserved Victorian pub near station, separate public and lounge bars, lots of dark wood, etched windows and stained glass, tiled fireplaces, Fullers London Pride and two quickly changing guests, food weekend lunchtimes only; fortnightly Mon folk night; children and dogs welcome, picnic-sets out in front, open all day. *(Gus Swan)*

BOURNEMOUTH   SZ0891
Goat & Tricycle (01202) 314220
West Hill Road; BH2 5PF Interesting two-level rambling Edwardian local (two former pubs knocked together); Wadworths ales and guests from pillared bar's impressive rank of ten handpumps, real cider, reasonably priced pubby food, friendly staff; background music, Sun quiz, free wi-fi; no under-18s, dogs welcome, good disabled access, part-covered yard, open (and food) all day. *(Gus Swan)*

BOURTON   ST7731
★ **White Lion** (01747) 840866
High Street, off old A303 E of Wincanton; SP8 5AT Popular 18th-c low-beamed dining pub with welcoming landlord and friendly young staff, three smallish opened-up rooms creating one well divided space, big flagstones, some stripped stone and half-panelling, bow-window seats and fine inglenook log fire, good well priced food here or in large restaurant, Otter and couple of west country guests, Rich's and Thatcher's cider, nice wines; children and dogs welcome, picnic-sets on back paved area and raised lawn, three bedrooms, good breakfast, open all day Fri-Sun. *(Edward Mirzoeff, Martin and Karen Wake, Colin and Maggie Fancourt)*

BRIDPORT   SY4692
Bull (01308) 422878
East Street B3162; DT6 3LF Bustling former Georgian coaching inn, comfortable armchairs in front of open fire in reception, second fire in bar with dark turquoise wall banquettes and white-painted dining chairs around dark tables, flowers and candlelight, a couple of beers from Otter, good wines by the glass and ten malt whiskies, informal dining room with similar furnishings, popular food from good sandwiches up, cosy cocktail bar tucked away upstairs; free wi-fi; children and dogs (in bar) welcome, sheltered back courtyard and separate cider and pizza Stable bar (see Main Entries), 19 comfortable bedrooms, good breakfast, open all day from 8am. *(Dr D J and Mrs S C Walker, Michael Sargent, Comus and Sarah Elliott, Steve and Liz Tilley)*

BRIDPORT   SY4692
George (01308) 423187
South Street; DT6 3NQ Relaxed cheerful town pub refurbished under present welcoming licensees, enjoyable modern pub food from open kitchen, well kept Palmers and good choice of wines by the glass, efficient friendly service; children welcome, disabled facilities, open all day, from 10am market days (Weds, Sat) for popular brunch. *(Martin and Sue Radcliffe)*

BRIDPORT   SY4692
Ropemakers (01308) 421255
West Street; DT6 3QP Welcoming town-centre pub, long and rambling, with lots of pictures and memorabilia, well kept Palmers ales and good value home-made food from nice sandwiches up, regular live music and other events; courtyard tables behind, open all day except Sun evening. *(Val and Alan Green, Comus and Sarah Elliott)*

BRIDPORT   SY4692
Tiger (01308) 427543
Barrack Street, off South Street; DT6 3LY Cheerful and attractive open-plan Victorian beamed pub with well kept Sharps Doom Bar and three guests, real ciders, no food except breakfast for residents, skittle alley, darts; sports TV; seats in heated courtyard, five bedrooms, open all day. *(Michael and Lynne Gittins, Comus and Sarah Elliott)*

BURTON BRADSTOCK   SY4889
Anchor (01308) 897228
B3157 SE of Bridport; DT6 4QF Cheerful helpful staff in pricey but good seafood restaurant, other food including nice local steaks, village pub section too with blackboard choices from baguettes up, ales such as Dorset, St Austell and Sharps, decent wines by the glass and several malt whiskies, table skittles, live music second Sun of month; children and dogs (in bar) welcome,

two bedrooms, open all day Fri-Sun. *(Paul Humphreys, Comus and Sarah Elliott)*

BURTON BRADSTOCK   SY4889
Three Horseshoes   (01308) 897259
Mill Street; DT6 4QZ Traditional thatched pub handy for nearby sandy beach; pubby furniture on patterned carpet, brocaded built-in wall seats, one table made from an old bed complete with headrest, old photographs of the pub, horsebrasses and open woodburner, neat small dining room, Palmers ales and popular straightforward food; background music; children and dogs (in bar) welcome, picnic-sets on back grass and a few seats out in front, open all day in summer. *(B and M Kendall)*

CHARMOUTH   SY3693
Royal Oak   (01297) 560277
Off A3052/A35 E of Lyme Regis; The Street; DT6 6PE Three-room split-level village local, popular and friendly, with enjoyable good value food and well kept Palmers ales, good service; quiz and music nights; children and dogs welcome, open all day weekends. *(Caroline Prescott)*

CHEDINGTON   ST4805
Winyards Gap   (01935) 891244
A356 Dorchester–Crewkerne; DT8 3HY Attractive dining pub surrounded by NT land with spectacular view over Parrett Valley and into Somerset; enjoyable food from sandwiches to daily specials, also Sun carvery and good value OAP weekday lunch, four well kept changing ales, local ciders, bar with woodburner, steps down to restaurant, skittle alley/dining room; children and dogs welcome (they have a st bernard), tables on front lawn under parasols, good walks, open all day. *(Dr Simon Innes)*

CHETNOLE   ST6008
★ Chetnole Inn   (01935) 872337
Village signed off A37 S of Yeovil; DT9 6NU Attractive inn under new management; hop-strung beams, huge flagstones and country kitchen décor, well kept Sharps Doom Bar and guests, woodburner and comfortable leather sofa in snug (dogs allowed here), pale wood tables on stripped boards in dining room with log fire, well liked food from lunchtime snacks up, friendly efficient staff; picnic-sets out in front and in delightful back garden, three bedrooms overlooking old church, open all day weekends. *(M G Hart, Ian Malone)*

CHILD OKEFORD   ST8213
★ Saxon   (01258) 860310
Signed off A350 Blandford–Shaftesbury and A357 Blandford–Sherborne; Gold Hill; DT11 8HD Welcoming 17th-c village pub, quietly clubby snug bar with log fire, two dining rooms, Butcombe, Ringwood and guests, nice choice of wines, well liked reasonably priced home-made food including

good Sun roast, efficient service; children and dogs (in bar) welcome, attractive back garden, good walks on neolithic Hambledon Hill, four comfortable bedrooms. *(Robert Watt)*

CHRISTCHURCH   SZ1593
Rising Sun   (01202) 486122
Purewell; BH23 1EJ Comfortably updated old pub specialising in authentic thai food, Flack Manor and Sharps Doom Bar from L-shaped bar, good choice of wines by the glass, pleasant helpful young staff; terrace with palms and black rattan-style furniture under large umbrellas. *(Gus Swan)*

CORFE CASTLE   SY9681
Castle Inn   (01929) 480208
East Street; BH20 5EE Welcoming little two-room pub mentioned in Hardy's *The Hand of Ethelberta*, well liked fairly priced food using local supplies including popular Fri fish night, good service, up to three ales such as Dorset, Ringwood and Sharps, heavy black beams, exposed stone walls, flagstones and open fire; children welcome, back terrace and big sunny garden with mature trees, steam train views, open all day. *(Robert Watt)*

CORFE CASTLE   SY9681
Fox   (01929) 480449
West Street; BH20 5HD Old-fashioned take-us-as-you-find-us stone-built local (not everyone's cup of tea); ales tapped from the cask and generous reasonably priced home-made food, good log fire in early medieval stone fireplace, glassed-over well in second bar; dogs but not children allowed, informal castle-view garden. *(Gus Swan)*

CORFE CASTLE   SY9682
Greyhound   (01929) 480205
A351; The Square; BH20 5EZ Bustling picturesque old pub in centre of this tourist village, three small low-ceilinged panelled rooms, steps and corridors, well kept ales such as Palmers, Ringwood and Sharps, local cider, good choice of food from sandwiches, light dishes and pizzas up, highish prices, traditional games including Purbeck longboard shove-ha'penny, family room; background and weekend live music; dogs welcome, garden with large decked area, great views of castle and countryside, pretty courtyard opening on to castle bridge, open all day weekends and in summer. *(Dr D J and Mrs S C Walker, Mrs Sally Scott, Eddie Edwards)*

CORFE MULLEN   SY9798
Coventry Arms   (01258) 857284
Mill Street (A31 W of Wimborne); BH21 3RH Modernised 15th-c roadside pub with bar and four dining rooms, low ceilings, eclectic mix of furniture on flagstones or wood flooring, large central open fire, Ringwood, Timothy Taylors Landlord and one or two cask-tapped guests, well liked fairly priced food from open kitchen, friendly

helpful staff; background and occasional live music; children and dogs welcome, riverside garden with terrace, open all day. *(Katharine Cowherd, Peter Salmon)*

DEWLISH   SY7798
Oak (01258) 837352
Off A354 Dorchester–Blandford Forum; DT2 7ND Welcoming red-brick village pub, two or three well kept local ales and enjoyable good value food including specials, friendly helpful service, woodburner and open fire in bar, small dining room; winter quiz; children welcome, good-sized garden behind, two bedrooms and self-catering cottage. *(PJ)*

DORCHESTER   SY6990
★ Blue Raddle (01305) 267762
Church Street, near central short-stay car park; DT1 1JN Cheery pubby atmosphere in long carpeted and partly panelled bar, well kept Branscombe Vale, Dartmoor, St Austell and guests, local ciders, good wines and coffee, enjoyable simple home-made lunchtime food (not Sun, Mon, Tues), evenings Thurs-Sat only, coal-effect gas fires; background and live folk music (Weds fortnightly), no children; dogs welcome, good disabled access apart from one step, closed Mon lunchtime. *(Comus and Sarah Elliott, Steve and Liz Tilley)*

DORCHESTER   SY6990
Kings Arms (01305) 265353
High East Street; DT1 1HF Georgian hotel's comfortably furnished carpeted bar, beamed section and open fire, Ringwood Best, Wychwood Hobgoblin and a guest, decent wines, enjoyable fairly pubby food from panini to daily specials, restaurant; children welcome, close associations with Nelson and Hardy's *The Mayor of Casterbridge*, 37 bedrooms, closed Sun lunchtime. *(Val and Alan Green)*

EAST CHALDON   SY7983
Sailors Return (01305) 854441
Village signposted from A352 Wareham–Dorchester; from village green, follow Dorchester, Weymouth signpost; note that the village is also known as Chaldon Herring; OS sheet 194 map reference 790834; DT2 8DN Thatched village pub under new management; five real ales such as Palmers, Otter and Ringwood, enjoyable food from short menu including fresh local fish, Weds pie night, flagstoned bar and various dining areas; children and dogs welcome (there's a friendly pub dog), picnic-sets out at front and in side garden, useful for coast path, open all day summer (all day weekends winter). *(Dr Simon Innes)*

EAST LULWORTH   SY8581
Weld Arms (01929) 400211
B3070 SW of Wareham; BH20 5QQ Thatched 17th-c cottage-row pub, civilised log-fire bar with sofas, ales such as Palmers and Sharps, Weston's cider and some nice wines by the glass, well liked home-made food from lunchtime sandwiches and baguettes up, friendly helpful service, two dining rooms; children and dogs welcome, picnic-sets out in big back garden with play area, open all day. *(R Halliday)*

EAST MORDEN   SY9194
★ Cock & Bottle (01929) 459238
B3075 W of Poole; BH20 7DL Popular extended dining pub with wide choice of good if not cheap food (best to book), well kept Badger ales and nice selection of wines by the glass, efficient cheerful service; children and dogs allowed in certain areas, outside seating and pleasant pastoral outlook, closed Sun evening. *(David and Carole Newton)*

EAST STOUR   ST8123
Kings Arms (01747) 838325
A30, 2 miles E of village; The Common; SP8 5NB Extended dining pub with popular food from scottish landlord-chef including bargain lunch menu and all-day Sun carvery (best to book), mainly west country ales, decent wines and good selection of malt whiskies, friendly efficient staff, open fire in bar, airy dining area with light wood furniture, scottish pictures and Burns quotes; gentle background music; children welcome, dogs in bar, good disabled access, picnic-sets in big garden, bluebell walks nearby, three bedrooms, open all day weekends. *(Roy Hoing)*

FERNDOWN   SZ0697
Kings Arms (01202) 577490
Ringwood Road; BH22 9AA Recently refurbished restaurant pub with well liked food including good steaks, early-bird deal (Mon-Thurs 4.30-6.30pm), three real ales including Ringwood Best and good selection of wines by the glass, friendly helpful staff; children welcome, rattan-style furniture on part-covered terrace, open (and food) all day. *(Peter Grant)*

FONTMELL MAGNA   ST8616
★ Fontmell (01747) 811441
A350 S of Shaftesbury; SP7 0PA Imposing dining pub with rooms, much emphasis on the enterprising modern cooking, but also some more straightforward dishes, good wine list, local ales including a house beer (Mallyshag) from Keystone, small bar area with stripy stools, comfy sofas and easy

---

Virtually all pubs in this book sell wine by the glass. We mention wines if they are a cut above the average.

chairs, some bold colours, restaurant with shelves of books and wine bottles, windows overlooking fast-flowing stream that runs under the building; garden across road with two wood-fired pizza ovens, six comfortable well appointed bedrooms, open all day in summer, closed Mon and Tues lunchtimes in winter. *(Peter Brix)*

HIGHCLIFFE   SZ2193
Galleon (01425) 279855
Lymington Road; BH23 5EA Contemporary interior with leather sofas, light wood floors and open fires, good choice of well prepared food from snacks and pub favourites up including daily specials, local ales such as Ringwood, good service, conservatory opening on to terrace and sunny garden; background music – live most weekends, Tues quiz; children welcome, play area and summer barbecues, open all day (till midnight Fri, Sat). *(David and Sally Frost)*

HINTON ST MARY   ST7816
White Horse (01258) 472723
Just off B3092 a mile N of Sturminster; DT10 1NA Welcoming traditional old village pub, good food from fairly short changing menu cooked by landlord-chef (best to book), well kept ales such as Sharps Doom Bar and decent house wines, unusual inglenook fireplace in cheerful bar, extended dining room; children, walkers and dogs welcome (pub dog is Pepper), picnic-sets in small well maintained garden, attractive setting, open all day weekends. *(Peter Brix)*

HURN   SZ1397
Avon Causeway (01202) 482714
Village signed off A338, then follow Avon, Sopley, Mutchams sign; BH23 6AS Roomy comfortable hotel/dining pub, enjoyable food from well filled baguettes and pub favourites up, well kept Wadworths ales, helpful staff, interesting railway decorations and pullman-coach restaurant (used for functions) by former 1870s station platform; children and dogs welcome, disabled access, nice garden (some road noise) with play area, 12 good value bedrooms, near Bournemouth Airport (2 weeks free parking if you stay before or after you fly), open all day. *(Gus Swan)*

IBBERTON   ST7807
Crown (01258) 817448
Village W of Blandford Forum; DT11 0EN Traditional village dining pub, flagstones, toby jugs and comfortable seats by inglenook woodburner, back eating area, ales such as Butcombe and Palmers from brick-faced bar, local cider, enjoyable freshly made food at a reasonable price, friendly helpful staff; dogs on leads in bar and in lovely garden, beautiful spot under Bulbarrow Hill, good walks, closed Mon (also Tues lunchtime and Sun evening in winter). *(Anon)*

LANGTON MATRAVERS   SY9978
Kings Arms (01929) 422979
High Street; BH19 3HA Friendly old-fashioned village local under newish enthusiastic landlord; ancient flagstoned corridor to bar, simple rooms off, one with a fine local marble fireplace, well kept ever-changing ales and enjoyable good value pubby food, cheerful helpful staff, splendid antique Purbeck longboard for shove-ha'penny; children and dogs welcome, sunny picnic-sets outside, good walks including to Dancing Ledge, open (and food) all day. *(Jo Garnett)*

LYME REGIS   SY3391
Cobb Arms (01297) 443242
Marine Parade, Monmouth Beach; DT7 3JF Spacious place with well kept Palmers ales, decent wines and good choice of reasonably priced freshly cooked food (gluten-free options available), cream teas, quick service, a couple of sofas, ship pictures and marine fish tank, open fire; pool, juke box, TVs; children and dogs welcome, disabled access (one step up from road), tables on small back terrace, next to harbour, beach and coastal walk, three bedrooms, open all day. *(Mrs Sally Scott, Sheila Topham, Roger and Donna Huggins)*

LYME REGIS   SY3391
★Harbour Inn (01297) 442299
Marine Parade; DT7 3JF More eating than pubby with thriving family atmosphere, friendly busy staff and generally very well liked food from lunchtime sandwiches to local fish (not cheap, booking advised in season), good choice of wines by the glass, well kept Otter and St Austell, tea and coffee, clean-cut modern décor keeping original flagstones and stone walls (lively acoustic), paintings for sale, sea views from front windows; background music; dogs welcome, disabled access from street, verandah tables. *(Caroline Prescott)*

LYME REGIS   SY3492
★Pilot Boat (01297) 443157
Bridge Street; DT7 3QA Popular all-day family food place near waterfront, modernised interior neatly cared for by long-serving licensees, wide choice of good sensibly priced food cooked to order including local fish, nice crab sandwiches, well kept Palmers ales and several wines by the glass, efficient friendly service, plenty of tables in cheery nautically themed areas; skittle alley; dogs welcome on the lead, terrace tables. *(B and M Kendall, Mrs P Sumner)*

LYME REGIS   SY3391
Royal Standard (01297) 442637
Marine Parade, The Cobb; DT7 3JF Right on broadest part of beach, properly pubby bar with log fire, fine built-in stripped

high settles, local photographs and even old-fashioned ring-up tills, quieter eating area with stripped brick and pine, well kept Palmers ales, uncomplicated food from lunchtime sandwiches and baked potatoes up, friendly helpful service; darts, prominent pool table, background and some live music, free wi-fi; children and dogs welcome, good-sized suntrap courtyard with own servery and harbour views, open all day from 10am and gets very busy in season. *(Dru and Louisa Marshall, Roger and Donna Huggins)*

LYME REGIS   SY3492
Volunteer (01297) 442214
Top of Broad Street (A3052 towards Exeter); DT7 3QE Cosy old-fashioned pub with long low-ceilinged bar, nice mix of customers (can get crowded), a well kept house beer from Branscombe tapped from the cask and two west country guests, enjoyable modestly priced food in dining lounge (children allowed here), friendly young staff, roaring fires; dogs welcome, open all day. *(Caroline Prescott)*

LYTCHETT MINSTER   SY9693
★ St Peters Finger (01202) 622275
Dorchester Road; BH16 6JE Well run two-part beamed roadhouse with cheerful efficient staff, popular sensibly priced food from sandwiches and baguettes up, small helpings available, Badger ales and several wines by the glass, welcoming end log fire, homely mix of furnishings in different sections giving cosy feel despite its size; tables on big part-covered terrace, open (and food) all day. *(M G Hart)*

MANSTON   ST8116
Plough (01258) 472484
B3091 Shaftesbury–Sturminster Newton, just N; DT10 1HB Welcoming good-sized traditional country pub, five real ales including Butcombe, Palmers and Sharps, enjoyable fairly priced standard food, beams, richly decorated plasterwork, ceilings and bar front, red patterned carpets, dining conservatory; Fri live music; garden and adjacent caravan site, open all day, till 8pm Sun. *(Alfie Bayliss)*

MARNHULL   ST7719
Blackmore Vale (01258) 820701
Burton Street, via Church Hill off B3092; DT10 1JJ Welcoming old stone-built village pub, good freshly made traditional food from landlord-chef including two-course 'smaller appetites' lunch (Mon-Sat), three Badger ales, good choice of reasonably priced wines, pleasantly opened-up beamed and flagstoned dining bar with woodburner, more flagstones

and oak flooring in cosy smaller bar with log fire; background music; children, walkers and dogs welcome, garden tables, open all day Sun. *(Anon)*

MARNHULL   ST7818
Crown (01258) 820224
About 3 miles N of Sturminster Newton; Crown Road; DT10 1LN Partly thatched inn dating from the 16th c (the Pure Drop Inn in Hardy's *Tess of the D'Urbervilles*); linked rooms with oak beams, huge flagstones or bare boards, log fire in big stone hearth in oldest part, more modern furnishings and carpet elsewhere, Badger ales and enjoyable food, good friendly service, restaurant; children welcome, peaceful enclosed garden, bedrooms, open all day weekends. *(Nick Sharpe)*

MARTINSTOWN   SY6488
Brewers Arms (01305) 889361
Burnside (B3159); DT2 9LB Friendly family-run village pub, good reasonably fairly priced home-made food from lunchtime baguettes to specials, Tues curry night, Palmers Copper and Sharps Doom Bar, restaurant; regular live music, Weds quiz; children and dogs welcome, garden picnic-sets, good local walks, two bedrooms, closed Sun evening, Mon. *(Gus Swan)*

MELBURY OSMOND   ST58707
Rest & Welcome (01935) 83248
Yeovil Road (A37); DT2 0NF Newish management at this friendly two-bar roadside pub (the Sheaf of Arrows in Hardy's 'Interlopers at the Knap'), enjoyable home-made food and three mainly local ales, pubby furniture on carpet, some beams, woodburner, back skittle alley; background music; children and dogs welcome, nice garden with play area, open all day. *(Lindy Andrews)*

MELPLASH   SY4897
Half Moon (01308) 488321
A3066 Bridport–Beaminster; DT6 3UD Landlord-chef who built a strong reputaion for his creative cooking has left this thatched and shuttered roadside pub – reports please; beams, log fire, pubby furnishings on patterned carpet, hunting horns and country-style pictures, Palmers ales; picnic-sets in mature back garden. *(Anon)*

MILTON ABBAS   ST8001
Hambro Arms (01258) 880233
Signed off A354 SW of Blandford; DT11 0BP Nicely updated pub in beautiful late 18th-c thatched landscaped village, two beamed bars and restaurant, well kept ales

---

The letters and figures after the name of each town are its Ordnance Survey map reference. *Using the Guide* at the beginning of the book explains how it helps you find a pub, in road atlases or large-scale maps as well as in our own maps.

such as Dorset Piddle, Ringwood and Sharps Doom Bar, good food from ciabattas and panini up, prompt friendly service; children welcome, dogs in bar, tables on front terrace, four bedrooms, open all day weekends, closed Mon (early Oct-end Mar). *(Robert Watt)*

MOTCOMBE   ST8426
Coppleridge (01747) 851980
Signed from The Street, follow to Mere/ Gillingham; SP7 9HW Welcoming country inn set in former 18th-c farmhouse, traditional bar and various dining rooms, good home-made food from sandwiches/ ciabattas up, steak night Thurs, ales such as Butcombe and decent wines, friendly helpful staff; children welcome, dogs in bar and garden room, ten spacious courtyard bedrooms, 15-acre grounds with play area and two tennis courts, open all day. *(Peter Brix)*

NORDEN HEATH   SY94834
Halfway (01929) 480402
A351 Wareham–Corfe Castle; BH20 5DU Cosily laid-out partly thatched 16th-c pub, Badger beers, good wines by the glass and enjoyable food including children's and vegetarian choices, front rooms with flagstones, stripped stone and woodburners, snug little side area, pitched-ceiling back room; dogs welcome, picnic-sets on paved terrace and lawn, good nearby walks, open (and food) all day. *(Wendy Breese)*

OSMINGTON MILLS   SY7381
★**Smugglers** (01305) 833125
Off A353 NE of Weymouth; DT3 6HF Bustling old partly thatched family-oriented inn, well extended, with cosy dimly lit timber-divided areas, woodburners, old local pictures, Badger ales, guests beers and several wines by the glass, good food from well priced menu, friendly staff coping well at busy times; picnic sets on crazy paving by little stream, thatched summer bar, play area, lovely views from car park (parking charge refunded at bar), useful for coast path, four bedrooms, open (and food) all day. *(Michael Hill)*

PAMPHILL   ST9900
★**Vine** (01202) 882259
Off B3082 on NW edge of Wimborne: turn on to Cowgrove Hill at Cowgrove sign, then left up Vine Hill; BH21 4EE Simple old-fashioned place run by same family for three generations and part of Kingston Lacy estate (NT); two tiny bars with coal-effect gas fire, handful of tables and seats on lino, local photographs and notices on painted panelling, narrow wooden stairs up to room with darts, a couple of real ales, local cider and foreign bottled beers, lunchtime bar snacks; quiet background music, no credit cards, outside lavatories;

children (away from bar) and dogs welcome, verandah with grapevine, sheltered gravel terrace and grassy area. *(Peter Brix)*

PIDDLEHINTON   SY7197
Thimble (01300) 348270
High Street (B3143); DT2 7TD Partly thatched pub with two handsome fireplaces and deep glassed-over well in low-beamed carpeted core, enjoyable freshly made food from sandwiches (home-baked bread) and one or two pub favourites up, friendly if not always speedy service, well kept Palmers ales; background music, free wi-fi; children and dogs welcome, disabled facilities, garden with stream and little bridge, closed Mon. *(Robert Watt)*

POOLE   SZ0391
Cow (01202) 723155
Station Road, Ashley Cross, Parkstone; beside Parkstone Station; BH14 8UD Interesting open-plan pub with airy bistro bar, squashy sofas, leather seating cubes and low tables on stripped-wood floors, open fire in exposed brick fireplace, good food from sandwiches and sharing boards through pub favourites to grills, Greene King and four mainly local guests, also craft beers such as BrewDog and a dozen wines by the glass, friendly welcoming staff; background music (live Thurs), Mon quiz, TV for major sports events, free wi-fi; children and dogs welcome, enclosed heated terrace, open (and food) all day, can get very busy. *(Jo Garnett)*

POOLE   SZ0190
Poole Arms (01202) 673450
Town Quay; BH15 1HJ 17th-c waterfront pub looking across harbour to Brownsea Island, good fresh fish/seafood at fair prices, well kept Ringwood, one comfortably old-fashioned room with boarded ceiling and nautical prints, good friendly service; outside gents'; no children, picnic-sets in front of the handsome green-tiled façade, almost next door to the Portsmouth Hoy. *(David M Smith)*

POOLE   SZ0090
Portsmouth Hoy (01202) 673517
The Quay; BH15 1HJ Harbourside pub with views to Brownsea Island, old-world atmosphere with dark wood, beams and bare boards, good food including fresh fish, well kept Badger ales, friendly service; children welcome, outside tables shared with the Poole Arms, open all day. *(Anon)*

POOLE   SZ0090
Rope & Anchor (01202) 675677
Sarum Street; BH15 1JW Recently refurbished spit-level Wadworths pub next to Poole Museum; good food including fresh fish, well kept beers and nice wines by the glass, friendly accommodating staff;

If we know a pub has an outdoor play area for children, we mention it.

background music, daily papers; dogs welcome, seats on back terrace, open (and food) all day. *(Dave Braisted)*

PORTLAND   SY6873
Cove House (01305) 820895
Follow Chiswell signposts – is at NW corner of Portland; DT5 1AW Low-beamed 18th-c pub in superb position, effectively built into the sea defences just above the end of Chesil Beach, great views from three-room bar's bay windows, Sharps Doom Bar and other well kept beers, pubby food (all day weekends) including nice crab sandwiches; background music, Mon quiz, steep steps down to gents'; children welcome, dogs in bar, tables out by seawall, open all day. *(Jo Garnett)*

POWERSTOCK   SY5196
★ **Three Horseshoes** (01308) 485328
Off A3066 Beaminster–Bridport via West Milton; DT6 3TF Tucked-away pub surrounded by good walks; cheerful cosy bar with flagstones and stripped panelling, windsor and mate's chairs around assorted tables, Palmers ales and eight wines by the glass, nice food cooked by landlord, slightly more formal dining room with local paintings for sale; background music, board games; children and dogs (in bar) welcome, picnic-sets on back terrace with garden and country views, two comfortable bedrooms, closed Mon lunchtime. *(Dr D J and Mrs S C Walker, B and M Kendall, Comus and Sarah Elliott)*

PUDDLETOWN   SY7594
Blue Vinney (01305) 848228
The Moor; DT2 8TE Large modernised village pub with beamed oak-floor bar and restaurant, nice variety of popular well presented food (not Sun evening) from lunchtime baguettes up, well kept Sharps, Youngs and a beer named for the pub, friendly young staff; children welcome, terrace overlooking garden with play area, open all day Fri-Sun. *(Michael Doswell)*

PUNCKNOWLE   SY5388
Crown 01308 897711
Off B3157 Bridport–Abbotsbury; DT2 9BN 16th-c thatched inn with enjoyable pubby food from sandwiches and snacks up including pizzas and children's meals, Palmers ales and good choice of wines by the glass, inglenook log fires each end of low-beamed stripped-stone lounge, steps up to public bar with books and another log fire, small shop selling local produce including freshly baked bread; dogs welcome, disabled facilities, valley views from peaceful pretty back garden, good walks, one bedroom, open all day. *(Comus and Sarah Elliott)*

SANDFORD ORCAS   ST6220
★ **Mitre** (01963) 220271
Off B3148 and B3145 N of Sherborne; DT9 4RU Thriving tucked-away country

---

local with welcoming long-serving licensees, three well kept changing ales, ciders such as Bridge Farm, wholesome home-made food (not Mon) from good soup and sandwiches up, flagstones, log fires and fresh flowers, small bar and larger pleasantly homely dining area; occasional open mike nights; children welcome and dogs (theirs are Finlay and Freya), pretty back garden with terrace, good local walks (on Macmillan Way and Monarch's Way), closed Mon lunchtime. *(Edward May)*

SHAPWICK   ST9301
Anchor (01258) 857269
Off A350 Blandford–Poole; West Street; DT11 9LB Welcoming red-brick Victorian pub owned by village consortium; popular freshly made food (booking advised) including good value set deal Mon-Thurs, ales such as Palmers, Ringwood and Sharps, real cider, good service, scrubbed pine tables on wood floors, pastel walls and open fires; children welcome, tables out in front, more in attractive garden with terrace behind, handy for Kingston Lacy (NT). *(Colin and Maggie Fancourt)*

SHAVE CROSS   SY4198
Shave Cross Inn (01308) 868358
On back lane Bridport–Marshwood, signposted locally; OS Sheet 193 map reference 415980; DT6 6HW Former medieval monks' lodging; small character timbered and flagstoned bar with huge inglenook, Branscombe ales including one badged for the pub, farm ciders and vintage rums, attractive restaurant with grandfather clock, pricey caribbean-influenced food (also more traditional bar menu), pleasant staff, ancient skittle alley with pool, darts and a juke box; background music; children and dogs welcome, sheltered pretty garden with thatched wishing well, carp pool and play area, seven recently built boutique bedrooms, helipad, Mon. *(Paul Humphreys)*

SPETISBURY   ST9102
Woodpecker (01258) 452658
A350 SE of Blandford; High Street; DT11 9DJ Popular village pub with welcoming chatty landlord, comfortable open-plan interior, good choice of affordably priced home-made food (not Sun, Mon evenings), at least four well kept changing ales along with ciders/perries, bar billiards; seats out in small front garden. *(M and GR)*

STOBOROUGH   SY9286
Kings Arms (01929) 552705
B3075 S of Wareham; Corfe Road opposite petrol station; BH20 5AB Part-thatched 17th-c village pub, well kept Purbeck, Ringwood and three guests, sizeable helpings of enjoyable pubby food plus specials in bar and restaurant, friendly chatty staff; live music Sat; children and dogs welcome, disabled access, views over

marshes to River Frome from terrace tables, open all day weekends. *(M G Hart)*

STOKE ABBOTT   ST4500
★ **New Inn** (01308) 868333
Off B3162 and B3163 2 miles W of Beaminster; DT8 3JW New welcoming owners for this 17th-c thatched pub, good home-cooked food including daily specials, well kept Palmers ales, woodburner in big inglenook, beams, brasses and copper, some handsome panelling, flagstoned dining room; children and dogs (in bar) welcome, wheelchair access, two attractive gardens, unspoilt quiet thatched village with good surrounding walks, street fair third Sat in July, closed Sun evening, Mon. *(Dr Simon Innes)*

STOURPAINE   ST8609
White Horse (01258) 453535
Shaston Road; A350 NW of Blandford; DT11 8TA Traditional country local extended from early 18th-c core (originally two cottages), popular food from landlord-chef including deals, good friendly service, well kept Badger ales and sensible wine list, open-plan layout with scrubbed pine tables on bare boards, woodburners, games part with pool, post office and shop; well behaved children welcome, dogs in bar, seats out at front and on back deck, open all day weekends. *(Robert Watt)*

STOURTON CAUNDLE   ST7115
★ **Trooper** (01963) 362405
Village signed off A30 E of Milborne Port; DT10 2JW Pretty little stone-built pub in lovely village setting, friendly staff and atmosphere, good simple food and well kept changing beers including own microbrews, reasonable prices, spotless tiny low-ceilinged bar, stripped-stone dining room, darts, dominoes and shove-ha'penny, skittle alley; background and some live music (folk and jazz), sports TV, outside gents'; children and dogs welcome, a few picnic-sets out in front, pleasant side garden with play area, camping, closed Mon lunchtime. *(Emma Scofield)*

STRATTON   SY6593
Saxon Arms (01305) 260020
Off A37 NW of Dorchester; The Square; DT2 9WG Traditional (though recently built) flint-and-thatch local, open-plan, bright and spacious with light oak tables and comfortable settles on flagstones or carpet, open fire, well kept Ringwood, Timothy Taylors Landlord and two guests, good value wines, tasty generous food including good choice of specials and winter lunchtime set deal (Mon-Thurs), large comfortable dining section on right; background

music, traditional games; children and dogs welcome, terrace tables overlooking village green, open (and food) all day Fri-Sun. *(Anon)*

STUDLAND   SZ0382
Bankes Arms (01929) 450225
Off B3351, Isle of Purbeck; Manor Road; BH19 3AU Very popular spot above fine beach, outstanding country, sea and cliff views from huge garden over road with lots of seating; comfortably basic big bar with raised drinking area, beams, flagstones and good log fire, well kept changing ales including own Isle of Purbeck, local cider, nice wines by the glass and enjoyable freshly made food, efficient service, darts and pool in side area; background music, machines, sports TV; over-8s and dogs welcome, just off coast path and can get very busy on summer weekends, parking complicated (NT car park), good-sized comfortable bedrooms, open (and food) all day. *(Peter Brix)*

STURMINSTER MARSHALL   SY9499
Black Horse (01258) 857217
A350; BH21 4AQ Welcoming roadside country pub with enjoyable good value food from nice sandwiches up, Badger ales, long comfortable beamed and panelled bar; children welcome, no dogs, closed Sun evening. *(Gus Swan)*

STURMINSTER MARSHALL   SY9500
Red Lion (01258) 857319
Opposite church; off A350 Blandford–Poole; BH21 4BU Attractive village pub opposite handsome church, bustling local atmosphere, wide variety of enjoyable food including good value set menu (Tues-Thurs, Sun evening), special diets catered for, well kept Badger ales and nice wines, roomy U-shaped bar with log fire, good-sized dining room in former skittle alley; background music; children and dogs welcome, disabled access, back garden with wicker furniture and picnic-sets, open all day Sun, closed Mon. *(Jo Garnett)*

STURMINSTER NEWTON   ST7813
Bull (01258) 472435
A357, S of centre; DT10 2BS Refurbished thatched and beamed 16th-c riverside pub, Badger ales and enjoyable home-made food; children welcome, roadside picnic-sets, more in secluded back garden, open all day weekends. *(Anon)*

SUTTON POYNTZ   SY7083
Springhead (01305) 832117
Off A353 NE of Weymouth; Sutton Road; DT3 6LW Appealingly placed village pub, good well presented home-cooked food from

---

We include some hotels with a good bar that offers facilities comparable to those of a pub.

lunchtime sandwiches/panini up, well kept Greene King Abbot, St Austell Proper Job and Sharps Doom Bar, open-plan beamed bar with light blue half-panelling, stripped pine boards and some high rustic tables, woodburner in painted brick fireplace, light airy dining room with mix of chairs around country pine tables, large mirror and a couple of animal heads; background music, TV; children and dogs welcome, wheelchair access, lovely spot opposite willow stream, play area in big back garden, walks to White Horse Hill and Dorset Coast Path, open (and food) all day. (D W Stokes)

TARRANT KEYNSTON   ST9204
True Lovers Knot   (01258) 452209
B3082 Blandford–Wimborne; DT11 9JG
Neatly kept corner pub with modernised largely carpeted bar, some beams and flagstones, woodburner, uncluttered dining extension, enjoyable food (plenty of gluten-free choices) from traditional dishes up including good Sun carvery, weekday OAP lunch deal, Badger ales, decent wines by the glass; children and dogs welcome, picnic-sets in big garden overlooking fields, four well equipped bedrooms, good breakfast, campsite. (Lindy Andrews)

THREE LEGGED CROSS   SU0905
Three Legged Cross   (01202) 826052
Ringwood Road, towards Ashley Heath and A31; BH21 6RE Picturesque thatched Vintage Inn, long and low, with pleasant rambling layout, their usual reasonably priced food and some interesting specials, ales such as Ringwood, decent wines; children welcome, lots of tables on attractive terrace and front lawn by fish pond, handy for Moors Valley Country Park, open all day. (David Cannings)

TOLPUDDLE   SY7994
Martyrs   (01305) 848249
Former A35 W of Bere Regis; DT2 7ES
Village dining pub built in the 1920s, enjoyable home-made food including Sun carvery, two or three Badger ales, friendly accommodating staff, opened-up bare-boards interior; background music; children welcome, good disabled access, small front terrace and garden behind, open (and food) all day. (Mrs P Sumner)

UPLODERS   SY5093
Crown   (01308) 485356
Signed off A35 E of Bridport; DT6 4NU
Stone-built village corner pub, log fires, dark low beams, flagstones and mix of old furniture including stripped pine, grandfather clock, good fairly traditional home-made food using local suppliers, Palmers ales; background music; children and dogs welcome, tables in attractive two-tier garden, closed Mon. (Dru and Louisa Marshall)

UPWEY   SY6785
Old Ship   (01305) 812522
Off A354; Ridgeway; DT3 5QQ
Traditional 17th-c beamed pub (features in Hardy's *Under the Greenwood Tree*), alcoves and log fires, well kept Ringwood and a couple of guests, enjoyable sensibly priced food from baguettes to blackboard specials, pleasant helpful staff; skittle alley; children and dogs (theirs is Lucy) welcome, picnic-sets in garden with terrace, interesting walks nearby, open all day Fri, Sat. (M G Hart)

WAREHAM   SY9287
Kings Arms   (01929) 552503
North Street (A351, N end of town); BH20 4AD Traditional stone and thatch town local, well kept Ringwood and guests, decent good value pubby food, friendly staff, back serving counter and two bars off flagstoned central corridor, beams and inglenook, darts; live music at weekends; children and dogs welcome, garden behind with picnic-sets, open all day. (Adrian Johnson)

WAREHAM   SY9287
Old Granary   (01929) 552010
The Quay; BH20 4LP Fine old brick building in good riverside position – can get very busy; emphasis on dining but two small beamed rooms by main door for drinkers, enjoyable fairly standard food, well kept Badger ales and good wines by the glass, friendly efficient young staff, airy dining room with leather high-backed chairs and pews around pale wood tables, brick walls and new oak standing timbers, two further rooms with big photographs of the pub, woodburners; quiet background music; children welcome, seats out overlooking water and on covered roof terrace, boats for hire over bridge, limited nearby parking, open all day from 9am (10am Sun). (Adrian Johnson)

WAREHAM   SY9287
Quay Inn   (01929) 552735
The Quay; BH20 4LP Comfortable 18th-c inn in great spot by the water, enjoyable food including pubby favourites and cook-your-own meat on a hot stone, Tues steak night offer, friendly attentive service, well kept Otter, Isle of Purbeck and Ringwood, reasonably priced wine list, open fires; weekend live music; children welcome, terrace area and picnic-sets out on quay, boat trips, bedrooms, parking nearby can be difficult, market day Sat, open all day in summer. (Edward May)

WAREHAM FOREST   SY9089
★ Silent Woman   (01929) 552909
Wareham–Bere Regis; Bere Road; BH20 7PA Long neatly kept dining pub divided by doorways and standing timbers, good variety of enjoyable carefully prepared food including daily specials, Badger ales

kept well and plenty of wines by the glass, traditional furnishings, farm tools and stripped masonry; background music; no children inside, dogs welcome, wheelchair access, plenty of picnic-sets outside including a covered area, walks nearby, so best to check it's open. *(M G Hart, Glenwys and Alan Lawrence)*

WAYTOWN SY4797

Hare & Hounds (01308) 488203

Between B3162 and A3066 N of Bridport; DT6 5LQ Attractive 18th-c country local up and down steps, friendly staff and regulars, well kept Palmers tapped from the cask, local cider, enjoyable good value food generously served including popular Sun lunch, open fire, two small cottagey rooms and pretty dining room; children and dogs welcome (there's a pub dog and treats on the bar), lovely Brit Valley views from sizeable well maintained garden, play area, occasional barbecues and live music. *(Sancha Butcher)*

WEST BEXINGTON SY5386

Manor Hotel (01308) 897660

Off B3157 SE of Bridport; Beach Road; DT2 9DF Relaxing quietly set hotel with long history and fine sea views; good choice of enjoyable food in beamed cellar bar, flagstoned restaurant or Victorian-style conservatory, well kept Otter, Thatcher's cider and several wines by the glass, friendly owners; children welcome, dogs on leads (not in restaurant), charming well kept garden, close to Chesil Beach, 13 bedrooms. *(Emma Scofield)*

WEST LULWORTH SY8280

Castle Inn (01929) 400311

B3070 SW of Wareham; BH20 5RN Pretty 16th-c thatched inn in lovely spot near Lulworth Cove, good walks and lots of summer visitors; beamed flagstoned bar with well kept changing local ales, 12 ciders/perries, pubby food, maze of booth seating divided by ledges, cosy more modern-feeling lounge bar, pleasant restaurant; background music; children and particularly dogs welcome, front terrace, long attractive garden behind on several levels, 12 bedrooms, open (and food) all day. *(Nick Sharpe)*

WEST LULWORTH SY8280

Lulworth Cove (01929) 400333

Main Road; BH20 5RQ Modernised inn with good range of enjoyable reasonably priced food, well kept Badger ales and several wines by the glass, helpful friendly service, seaside theme bar with bare boards and painted panelling; free wi-fi; children and dogs welcome, picnic-sets on sizeable terrace, short stroll down to cove, 12 bedrooms (some with sea-view balcony), open (and food) all day. *(Pete Coates, Comus and Sarah Elliott)*

WEST PARLEY SZ0898

Curlew (01202) 594811

Christchurch Road; BH22 8SQ Upmarket Vintage Inn in early 19th-c farmhouse; beamed areas around central bar, mixed furnishings, candlelit tables and two log fires, emphasis on enjoyable food including good value fixed-price menu (till 5pm), well kept Ringwood, St Austell and a guest, good choice of wines, friendly courteous staff; unobtrusive background music, TV; picnic-sets in front garden, open all day. *(David and Sally Frost)*

WEST STAFFORD SY7289

Wise Man (01305) 261970

Sgned off A352 Dorchester–Wareham; DT2 8AG 16th-c thatched and beamed pub near Hardy's Cottage (NT), open-plan interior with flagstone and wood floors, good well priced food from lunchtime ciabattas up including some interesting choices, Sun carvery, Butcombe, Timothy Taylors and a couple of guests from central bar, good choice of wines by the glass, friendly attentive staff; children and dogs welcome, disabled facilities, plenty of seats outside, lovely walks nearby, open all day weekends. *(Anon)*

WEYMOUTH SY6778

Boot 07809 440772

High West Street; DT4 8JH Friendly unspoilt old local near the harbour; beams, bare boards, panelling, hooded stone-mullioned windows and coal fires, cosy gently sloping snug, ten well kept ales including Ringwood and other Marstons-related beers, real cider and good selection of malt whiskies, no food apart from pork pies and pickled eggs; live music Tues, quiz Weds; free wi-fi; disabled access, pavement tables, open all day. *(Gus Swan)*

WEYMOUTH SY6779

Handmade Pie & Ale House (01305) 459342 *Queen Street; DT4 7HZ* Friendly and relaxed place opposite the station, wide range of good home-made pies plus other food, six well kept changing ales and plenty of ciders; open (and food) all day. *(Victoria)*

WEYMOUTH SY6878

Nothe Tavern (01305) 839255

Barrack Road; DT4 8TZ Roomy and comfortable 19th-c pub near Nothe Fort, wide range of popular food including fresh local fish and good Sun carvery, friendly efficient service, two well kept Ringwood ales and a guest, decent wines and good choice of malt whiskies, lots of dark wood, whisky-water jugs on ceiling, interesting prints and photographs, restaurant with distant harbour glimpses; may be quiet background music; children and dogs welcome, more views from terrace, open all day weekends. *(D J and P M Taylor)*

WEYMOUTH   SY6778
Ship (01305) 773879
Custom House Quay; DT4 8BE Neatly
modernised and extended waterfront pub
with several nautical-theme open-plan levels,
well kept Badger ales from long bar, several
wines by the glass, enjoyable good value
usual food (upstairs only in the evening)
from sandwiches and baguettes up, friendly
helpful staff; unobtrusive background music;
dogs welcome in bar (biscuits for them),
wheelchair access downstairs, some quayside
seating and pleasant back terrace, open all
day. *(Gus Swan)*

WIMBORNE MINSTER   SU0100
★ ## Olive Branch (01202) 884686
*East Borough, just off Hanham Road
(B3073, just E of its junction with
B3078); BH21 1PF* Major recent
refurbishment for this handsome townhouse,
spacious interior with various dining areas,
one with beams and view into kitchen,
another more canteen-like with long tables
and benches, relaxed atmosphere, Badger
ales in comfortable bar with woodburner;
plenty of tables outside, good car park,
open all day from 8am (9am Sun). *(Richard
Tilbrook, Michael Butler, Roger and Donna
Huggins)*

WIMBORNE ST GILES   SU0212
Bull (01725) 517300
Off B3078 N of Wimborne; BH21 5NF
Refurbished open-plan Edwardian dining
inn, good if not particularly cheap food
using fresh local ingredients (organic
where possible), also a weekday set menu
(lunchtime/early evening), fine choice of
wines by the glass, Badger ales, good friendly
service, conservatory overlooking neatly kept
garden; children and dogs welcome, five
stylish bedrooms, open all day. *(Anon)*

WINKTON   SZ1696
Fishermans Haunt (01202) 477283
B3347 N of Christchurch; BH23 7AS
Comfortable big-windowed riverside inn on
fringes of New Forest, four well kept Fullers/
Gales beers and good range of other drinks,
enjoyable food using local produce such as
venison, good helpful service, two log fires,
restaurant views of River Avon; background
music; children and dogs (in bar) welcome,
disabled facilities, tables among shrubs
in quiet back garden, heaters in covered
area, 12 bedrooms, good breakfast, open
all day. *(David and Sally Frost, Paul Rampton,
Julie Harding)*

WINTERBORNE
STICKLAND   ST8304
Crown (01258) 881042
North Street; DT11 0NJ Refurbished
thatched village pub, two rooms separated
by servery, smaller one with inglenook
woodburner, high-backed settle and dark
tables and chairs on patterned carpet, the
other with low beams more tables and chairs
and darts, well kept Ringwood and guests,
a local cider and enjoyable traditional food
from sandwiches and light dishes up, prompt
cheerful service; live music Fri monthly, quiz
second Tues of month, free wi-fi; children and
dogs welcome, pretty back terrace and steps
up to lawned area with village view, open all
day Fri-Sun. *(Michael Doswell, Marina Reece)*

Post Office address codings confusingly give the impression that some pubs are in
Dorset, when they're really in Somerset (which is where we list them).

Essex

KEY ★ Star Pub 🌟 Top Quality Food 🍺 Great Beer
🍷 Good Wines £ Bargain Meals 🛏 Good Bedrooms 🍴 Serves Food

 ARKESDEN   TL4834   Map 5

Axe & Compasses 🍷

(01799) 550272 – www.axeandcompasses.co.uk
Off B1038; CB11 4EX

Comfortable, thatched pub with Greene King beers and decent food; seats outside

---

Although this rambling thatched pub is always busy, the pleasant licensees and their staff create a relaxed, welcoming atmosphere. The oldest part (dating from the 17th c) has low-slung ceilings, original floor tiles, upholstered tartan chairs, cushioned wall seats and settles around polished tables, a woodburner in a brick fireplace, and stools against the counter on wooden flooring; darts. The smart, neat dining room has high-backed leather or elegant wooden chairs around pale tables on more floorboards, with photos of the pub and local area on pale walls. Greene King IPA and Old Speckled Hen and a changing guest beer on handpump, a very good wine list (with 15 by the glass) and around two dozen malt whiskies. There's a side terrace with seats and tables and pretty hanging baskets, and some benches at the front. This is a particularly lovely village.

🍴 Tasty food includes lunchtime sandwiches, king scallops with mushrooms, white wine and cream, feta cheese filo parcels with a sweet cherry tomato dressing, vegetarian risotto, lamb kebabs with greek salad, salmon and smoked haddock fishcakes with dill and lemon butter sauce, chicken, leek and bacon crumble, beef stew with dumplings, duck breast on pak choi with ginger and lemongrass sauce, and puddings. *Benchmark main dish: steak, kidney and mushroom pie £13.95. Two-course evening meal £23.00.*

Greene King ~ Tenants Themis and Diane Christou ~ Real ale ~ Open 11.30-2.30, 6-11; 12-3, 6-10 Sun ~ Bar food 12-2 (2.30 Sun), 6.30-9; not Sun evening in winter ~ Restaurant ~ Children welcome ~ Dogs allowed in bar *Recommended by Martin Jones, David Jackson, Mrs P J Pearce*

AYTHORPE RODING   TL5915   Map 5

Axe & Compasses 🍺

(01279) 876648 – www.theaxeandcompasses.co.uk
B184 S of Dunmow; CM6 1PP

Appealing free house with a nice balance of eating and drinking, and a friendly welcome

---

Packed full of customers at any time, this is an attractive weatherboarded pub with popular food, quiz and music events. Everything is warm, cosy and neatly kept – there are bent old beams and timbers in stripped red-brick walls, comfortable bar chairs at the counter, leatherette settles, stools and dark country chairs around a few pub tables on pale boards and turkish rugs. The original part (on the left) has a two-way fireplace marking off a snug little raftered dining area, which has sentimental prints on dark masonry and a big open-faced clock. Adnams Broadside and Ghost Ship, Sharps Doom Bar and a guest ale on handpump or tapped from the cask, 13 wines by the glass and up to three Weston's farm ciders; background music and board games. The small back garden has stylish modern tables and chairs, and there are views across fields to a windmill.

As well as serving breakfast (9-11.30am), the wide choice of good food includes sandwiches, chicken liver pâté with red onion marmalade, prawn and crayfish cocktail, pies such as rabbit, pork and cider, feta, spinach and sweet potato and steak in ale, toad in the hole with gravy, lamb tagine with herby couscous, thai fish curry, and puddings such as white chocolate and cherry cheesecake and Baileys crème brûlée with a cappuccino smoothie shot. *Benchmark main dish: beer-battered fish and chips £10.95. Two-course evening meal £18.00.*

Free house ~ Licensee David Hunt ~ Real ale ~ Open 9am-11pm (10.30 Sun) ~ Bar food 9-2.30, 6-9; 9-9 (8 Sun) Sat ~ Restaurant ~ Children welcome ~ Dogs allowed in bar ~ Wi-fi
Recommended by N R White, Mrs Margo Finlay, Jörg Kasprowski, Evelyn and Derek Walter, Tina and David Woods-Taylor

DUNMOW
TL6222   Map 5
Angel & Harp
(01371) 859259 – www.angelandharp.co.uk
Church Road, Church End; B1057 signposted to Finchingfield/The Bardfields, off B184 N of town; CM6 2AD

Comfortable and relaxing, a good place to drop in any time of day

You must book in advance to be sure of a table here – especially at weekends (when it's very popular with families). The interconnected rooms ramble about through standing timbers and doorways and there's a good choice of seating from armchairs, sofas and banquettes to more upright dining chairs – or, for a very pubby feel, the bar stools along each side of the free-standing zinc 'counter' that spans two uprights. The low-ceilinged main area has a substantial brick fireplace and some fine old floor tiles as well as carpet. Adnams Explorer, Nethergate IPA and a guest from Mauldons or Mighty Oak on handpump and eight wines by the glass; good coffee too. The atmosphere is friendly and informal and staff are neatly dressed and helpful; background music. Up a few steps, an interesting raftered room has Perspex chairs around one huge table. A glass wall gives tables in an attractive L-shaped extension a view over the flagstoned courtyard with its wishing fountain, cushioned metal chairs under big canopies and picnic-table sets on the grass beyond.

Some sort of food is served all day, starting with breakfast at 9am: sandwiches, meze and deli boards, ham and free-range egg, barbecue ribs with coleslaw, honey-roast butternut squash, mushroom and chestnut risotto, several pizzas and burgers, chicken wrapped in parma ham with creamy mushroom sauce, steak in ale pie, salmon fillet with crayfish and chive cream, and puddings such as crème brûlée and chocolate brownie with chocolate sauce. *Benchmark main dish: beer-battered cod and chips £11.95. Two-course evening meal £19.50.*

Free house ~ Licensee David Hunt ~ Real ale ~ Open 9am-11pm (10pm Sun) ~ Bar food 9am-9.30pm (8 Sun) ~ Restaurant ~ Children welcome ~ Dogs allowed in bar ~ Wi-fi
Recommended by Tina and David Woods-Taylor, Ruth May

FEERING
TL8720 Map 5

Sun £

(01376) 570442 – www.suninnfeering.co.uk

Just off A12 Kelvedon bypass; Feering Hill (B1024 just W of Feering proper); CO5 9NH

Striking 16th-c pub with six real ales, well liked food and pleasant garden

---

Throughout this timbered and jettied pub (gently refurbished this year) are handsomely carved black beams and timbers galore, and attractive wildflower murals in a frieze above the central timber divider. The spreading slate-floored bar is relaxed, unpretentious and civilised, with two big woodburning stoves – one in the huge central inglenook fireplace, another by an antique winged settle on the left. Half a dozen ales on handpump include Shepherd Neame Bishops Finger, Master Brew Bitter, Spitfire and Whitstable Bay Pale, plus a couple of guest beers, and summer and winter beer festivals; also, 11 wines by the glass and ten malt whiskies served by cheerful staff. Daily papers and board games. A brick-paved back courtyard has tables, heaters and a shelter; in the garden beyond tall trees shade green picnic-sets.

Tasty food includes sandwiches, baguettes and panini, smoked salmon, apple and celeriac rémoulade, chicken, coriander and chilli cakes with pickled asian-style cucumber, butternut squash, pear and gorgonzola tart, beer-battered fresh haddock and chips, burger with toppings and onion rings, spanish-style fish and mussel stew, herb-crusted rack of lamb with red wine jus, and puddings such as steamed rhubarb sponge with crème anglaise and chocolate and banana brioche stack with chocolate chip ice-cream. *Benchmark main dish: beef, mushroom and stilton pie £10.95. Two-course evening meal £15.00.*

Shepherd Neame ~ Tenant Andy Howard ~ Real ale ~ Open 12-3, 5.30-11; 12-midnight Sat; 12-10.30 Sun ~ Bar food 12-2.30, 6-9 (9.30 Fri, Sat); 12-8 Sun ~ Children welcome away from bar ~ Dogs welcome ~ Wi-fi *Recommended by Edward Mirzoeff, N R White*

FULLER STREET
TL7416 Map 5

Square & Compasses

(01245) 361477 – www.thesquareandcompasses.co.uk

Back road Great Leighs–Hatfield Peverel; CM3 2BB

Neatly kept country pub, handy for walks, with two woodburning stoves, four ales and enjoyable food

---

This smashing pub is, not surprisingly, always packed to the rafters – and our readers love it; you'll need to book a table in advance. It's gently civilised and well looked after and the dining room features shelves of bottles and decanters against timbered walls, and an appealing variety of dining chairs around dark wooden tables set with linen napkins, on carpeting. The L-shaped beamed bar has two woodburning stoves in inglenook fireplaces, and friendly staff serve Adnams Lighthouse, Farmers Ales A Drop of Nelsons Blood, Mighty Oak Maldon Gold and Wibblers Dengie IPA tapped from the cask, Weston's cider and 18 wines by the glass; there's a small extension for walkers and dogs. Background jazz. The tables out in front on decking offer gentle country views, and the Essex Way long-distance footpath is nearby.

Food is good and uses local, seasonal produce: sandwiches, scallops with pea purée and truffle oil, mini pigeon and haggis pie, home-cooked ham and free-range eggs, fennel and carrot cheesecake with parsnip crisp and potato salad, beer-battered fish of the day, garlic and thyme lamb on rosemary crushed potatoes with red wine sauce, stuffed pheasant wrapped in bacon with wild mushrooms and game sauce, and puddings such as rhubarb crumble tart and chocolate and almond praline torte with amaretto sauce and blueberry compote. *Benchmark main dish: steak in ale pie £11.95. Two-course evening meal £20.50.*

Free house ~ Licensee Victor Roome ~ Real ale ~ Open 11.30-11; 12-midnight Sat; 12-11.30 Sun ~ Bar food 12-2 (2.30 Sat), 6.30-9.30; 12-6 Sun ~ Restaurant ~ Well behaved children welcome ~ Dogs allowed in bar *Recommended by Evelyn and Derek Walter, N R White, Mrs Margo Finlay, Jörg Kasprowski*

 FYFIELD   TL5706   Map 5

Queens Head

(01277) 899231 – www.thequeensheadfyfield.co.uk
Corner of B184 and Queen Street; CM5 0RY

Friendly old pub with seats in riverside garden, a good choice of drinks and highly thought-of food

In a small village, this 15th-c pub is friendly, easy-going and usefully open all day at weekends. The compact, low-beamed, L-shaped bar has exposed timbers, pretty lamps on nice sturdy elm tables and comfortable seating from wall banquettes to attractive, unusual high-backed chairs, some in a snug little side booth. In summer, two facing fireplaces have church candles instead of a fire. Adnams Broadside and Southwold and Crouch Vale Brewers Gold on handpump and several good wines by the glass; background music. The upstairs restaurant is more formal. On sunny days, it's best to arrive early to bag a seat in the prettily planted back garden that runs down to the sleepy River Roding.

Attractively presented and interesting, the food includes seared scallop with parma ham crumb, saffron baby onions, pea velouté and herb emulsion, crispy quail with sour tamarind and tempura baby vegetables, tomato and taleggio arancini with onion, tomato and garlic sauce, duo of lamb (shepherd's pie and rump) with butter bean casserole and mint oil, cod with curried mussels and sauté spinach, and puddings such as salted caramel tart with walnut praline and marshmallow and baked new york cheesecake with red berry compote. *Benchmark main dish: pork belly with salt and pepper cuttlefish, sweet pepper and chilli salsa and cauliflower purée £18.95. Two-course evening meal £25.00.*

Free house ~ Licensee Daniel Lamprecht ~ Real ale ~ Open 12-3.30, 6-11; 12-11 Sat; 12-10.30 Sun; closed Mon ~ Bar food 12-2.30 (4 Sat), 6.30-9.30; 12-6 Sun ~ Restaurant ~ Children welcome away from bar ~ Wi-fi ~ Folk music monthly (best to phone) *Recommended by Mrs Margo Finlay, Jörg Kasprowski*

GOLDHANGER   TL9008   Map 5

Chequers

(01621) 788203 – www.thechequersgoldhanger.co.uk
Church Street; off B1026 E of Heybridge; CM9 8AS

Cheerful and neatly kept pub with six real ales, traditional furnishings, friendly staff and tasty food

The reliably good food and half a dozen real ales keep customers coming back on a regular basis to this well run village pub. The nice old corridor with its red and black floor tiles leads to six rambling rooms, including a spacious lounge with dark beams, black panelling and a huge sash window overlooking the graveyard, a traditional dining room with bare boards and carpeting and a games room with bar billiards; woodburning stove, open fires, TV and background music. Adnams Ghost Ship, Crouch Vale Brewers Gold, Sharps Doom Bar, Youngs Bitter and guests such as Camerons Strongarm and York Centurions Ghost Ale on handpump; they also hold spring and autumn beer festivals. Also, 16 wines by the glass, ten malt whiskies and several farm ciders. There are picnic-sets under umbrellas in the courtyard with its grapevine. Next door is a fine old church.

The popular food includes sandwiches, garlic and rosemary-coated brie with onion chutney, spicy crispy whitebait with tartare sauce, ham and free-range eggs, aubergine, butternut squash and walnut bake, lamb and mint pudding, crispy lemon and herb chicken with coleslaw, barbecue sauce and chips, smoked haddock and spring onion fishcakes with horseradish dip, steak in stout pie, and puddings such as chocolate pot and lemon meringue pie. *Benchmark main dish: beer-battered cod and chips £11.25. Two-course evening meal £18.20.*

Punch ~ Lease Philip Glover and Dominic Davies ~ Real ale ~ Open 11-11; 12-11 Sun ~ Bar food 12-3, 6.30-9; not Sun evening or Mon bank holiday evening ~ Restaurant ~ Children welcome except in tap room ~ Dogs allowed in bar ~ Wi-fi *Recommended by Caroline Prescott, John and Mary Warner*

HATFIELD BROAD OAK
Dukes Head ♀

TL5416   Map 5

(01279) 718598 – www.thedukeshead.co.uk
B183 Hatfield Heath–Takeley; High Street; CM22 7HH

Relaxed, well run dining pub with enjoyable food in an attractive layout of nicely linked separate areas

After a walk in nearby Hatfield Forest (National Trust), head to this friendly pub for refreshment; Sam and Zac the pub dogs welcome other canines and there are always dog biscuits behind the bar. Rambling around the central woodburner and side servery are various cosy seating areas: good solid wooden dining chairs around a variety of chunky stripped tables, with a comfortable group of armchairs and a sofa at one end, and a slightly more formal area at the back on the right. Cheerful prints on the wall and some magenta panels in the mostly cream décor make for a buoyant mood. Greene King IPA, Sharps Doom Bar, Timothy Taylors Landlord and a guest such as Purity Mad Goose on handpump and 30 wines by the glass from a good list, served by cheerful staff; background music and board games. The back garden, with its sheltered terrace, has chairs around teak tables under cocktail parasols, and chickens at the end; also, picnic-sets in the front corner of the building, which has some nice pargeting.

Served all day at weekends, the interesting food includes venison and field mushroom kebab with chilli jam and onion seed flatbread, crispy salt and pepper calamari, spicy halloumi fritters with pomegranate tabbouleh, spiced aubergine and tomato ragoût with coriander yoghurt, beer-battered haddock with triple-cooked chips, sausages of the day with shallot and thyme gravy, veal escalope with a fried egg, polenta chips and sherry jus, and puddings such as chocolate and macadamia nut brownie with chocolate fudge sauce and pineapple tarte tatin with pistachio and coconut cheesecake and pecan brittle. *Benchmark main dish: king prawn spaghetti £13.25. Two-course evening meal £19.95.*

Enterprise ~ Lease Liz Flodman ~ Real ale ~ Open 11.30-11; 10.30-11 (10.30 Sun) Sat ~ Bar food 12-2.30, 6-9.30 (10 Fri); all day weekends ~ Restaurant ~ Children welcome ~ Dogs allowed in bar ~ Wi-fi *Recommended by Grahame Brooks, Isobel Mackinlay, Harvey Brown*

You can send reports directly to us at feedback@goodguides.com

HORNDON-ON-THE-HILL

TQ6783 Map 3

Bell 🏅 ☉ ⧉ 🛏

(01375) 642463 – www.bell-inn.co.uk

M25 junction 30 into A13, then left after 7 miles on to B1007, village signposted from here; SS17 8LD

••

Essex Dining Pub of the Year

Lovely historic pub with fine food and a very good range of drinks; attractive bedrooms

The same friendly family have run this lovely old inn for more than 75 years and it remains a fine place to drink, eat and stay. The heavily beamed, panelled bar maintains a strongly pubby appearance with high-backed antique settles and benches, rugs on flagstones and highly polished oak floorboards, and an open log fire. Look out for the curious collection of ossified hot cross buns hanging along a beam in the saloon bar. The first was put there in 1906 to mark the day (a Good Friday) that Jack Turnell became licensee; the tradition continues to this day, with the oldest available person in the village hanging the bun each year. The timbered restaurant has numerous old copper pots and pans hanging from beams. An impressive range of drinks includes Greene King IPA, Sharps Doom Bar and guests such as Brains SA and Sharps Atlantic on handpump, and over 100 well chosen wines (14 by the glass). Two giant umbrellas cover the courtyard, which is very pretty in summer with its hanging baskets. This is a lovely place to stay, with individually styled, thoughtfully equipped rooms of all sizes – and good breakfasts.

⭐ Accomplished food using some home-grown and other local, seasonal produce includes lunchtime sandwiches, mosaic of smoked haddock, crayfish, mackerel and salmon with saffron potato salad and jerusalem artichoke cream, chicken and tarragon ballotine with devilled chicken livers and curried mayonnaise, onion tarte tatin with poached duck egg, tempura of spring onion, chard and hazelnut brown butter, garlic-roasted corn-fed chicken on puy lentils, pancetta and button mushrooms, and puddings such as milk chocolate ganache doughnuts on crushed honeycomb with hot white chocolate sauce and shortbread tart with amaretti parfait, red wine poached pear and frosted blackberries. *Benchmark main dish: calves liver with smoked bacon and bubble and squeak £14.10. Two-course evening meal £24.95.*

Free house ~ Licensee John Vereker ~ Real ale ~ Open 11-11; 12-10.30 Sun ~ Bar food 12-2, 6.30 (6 Sat)-9.45; 12-2.30, 7-9.45 Sun ~ Restaurant ~ Children welcome ~ Dogs allowed in bar and bedrooms ~ Wi-fi ~ Bedrooms: /£90 *Recommended by N R White, Mrs Margo Finlay, Jörg Kasprowski, John and Enid*

LITTLE WALDEN

TL5441 Map 5

Crown ⧉ £

(01799) 522475 – www.thecrownlittlewalden.co.uk

B1052 N of Saffron Walden; CB10 1XA

Bustling 18th-c cottage pub with a warming log fire, hearty food and bedrooms

Although this particularly well run and thoroughly enjoyable pub is very much the hub of the community, the friendly, helpful landlord and his courteous staff are careful to make sure visitors feel welcome too. The low-ceilinged rooms have a cosy, chatty atmosphere and traditional furnishings, with book-room-red walls, floral curtains, bare boards, navy carpeting, cosy warm fires and an unusual walk-through fireplace. A higgledy-piggledy mix of chairs ranges from high-backed pews to little cushioned armchairs spaced around a good variety of closely arranged tables, mostly big, some stripped. The small red-tiled room on the right has two small tables. Three changing beers, including Adnams Broadside and Southwold, Greene King Abbot or Woodfordes Wherry, are tapped straight from casks racked up behind the bar; TV, disabled access. Tables on the terrace have views over the surrounding tranquil countryside. Our readers love staying overnight here and the breakfasts are excellent.

 Good, popular food includes lunchtime sandwiches and baguettes, crayfish cocktail, chicken liver pâté, honey-roast ham and egg, wild mushroom stroganoff, moussaka, chicken and leek pie, beer-battered fish and chips, pork fillet in cajun sauce, prawn curry, and puddings such as eton mess and treacle pudding. *Benchmark main dish: steak and mushroom pie £9.95. Two-course evening meal £16.00.*

Free house ~ Licensee Colin Hayling ~ Real ale ~ Open 11.30-2.30 (3 Sat), 6-11; 12-10.30 Sun ~ Bar food 12-2, 6.30-9; 12-3 Sun; not Mon evening ~ Restaurant ~ Children welcome ~ Dogs allowed in bar and bedrooms ~ Wi-fi ~ Live jazz Weds evenings ~ Bedrooms: /£75
Recommended by Mrs Margo Finlay, Jörg Kasprowski, Nick Clare, Sara Fulton, Roger Baker, Roger and Donna Huggins, Dave Braisted, Adrian Johnson, David Twitchett

LITTLE WALTHAM
White Hart
TL7013   Map 5

THE GOOD PUB GUIDE

(01245) 360205 – www.whitehartessex.co.uk
The Street; CM3 3NY

Busy, popular all-day pub with tasty food, several real ales, modern furnishings and helpful staff; seats in garden

Open all day, for breakfast (9-11.30am), coffee and cakes (you can buy cakes to take away too) and lunch and supper, this bustling and handsome old place is in a little village just north of Chelmsford. It's notably well run and there's a wide mix of customers popping in and out – all welcomed by the friendly staff. Completely refurbished in a contemporary style, the open-plan rooms have wooden floors, tartan carpet and black slates, seating that ranges from woven cane chairs (topped with a fur) through upholstered wall banquettes and cushioned window seats to dogtooth upholstered armchairs and wooden dining chairs, pale tables of varying sizes, and fireplaces (some piled high with logs). There are splashes of bright colour from walls, lampshades and flowering plants, and décor that takes in metal deer heads, antler chandeliers, mirrors, church candles in tall glass lanterns and heavily swagged curtains or window blinds. Adnams Ghost Ship, Nethergate IPA and guests such as Bishop Nick Heresy, Cottage Golden Arrow and Wibblers Apprentice on handpump, good wines by the glass and Weston's Old Rosie cider. The garden has cheerfully coloured metal chairs and equally colourful parasols, modern rattan-style seating and picnic-sets on flagstones or on grass.

As well as several 2-for-1 offers, the wide choice of popular food includes sandwiches, chicken liver pâté with red onion chutney, prawn and crayfish cocktail, sausages with onion gravy, vegetarian or beef burgers with toppings and chips, chicken breast wrapped in parma ham with creamy mushroom sauce, a fish platter, rack of baby back barbecue ribs with coleslaw and chips, salmon with a crayfish and chive cream and crispy leeks, and puddings such as jam roly-poly and custard and Baileys crème brûlée with a café latte smoothie shot. *Benchmark main dish: beer-battered cod and chips £11.95. Two-course evening meal £17.00.*

Free house ~ Licensee Alessandra Hunt ~ Real ale ~ Open 9am-11pm (11.30 Sat); 9am-10.30pm Sun ~ Bar food 9am-9.30pm (8 Sun) ~ Children welcome ~ Dogs allowed in bar ~ Wi-fi *Recommended by Tina and David Woods-Taylor, Lindy Andrews*

LITTLEY GREEN

TL6917   Map 5

Compasses ◀

(01245) 362308 – www.compasseslittleygreen.co.uk

Village signposted off B1417 Felsted road in Hartoft End (opposite former Ridleys Brewery), about a mile N of junction with B1008 (former A130); CM3 1BU

Charming brick tavern – a prime example of what is now an all too rare breed; bedrooms

The bar here is a companionable place and the choice of drinks is second to none: Bishop Nick Ridleys Rite (brewed in Felsted by the landlord's brother) as well as Adnams Southwold, Skinners Betty Stogs, Tyne Bank Single Blonde and two weekend guest ales, all tapped from casks in a back cellar; in summer and at Christmas they hold beer festivals featuring dozens of beers, alongside festivities that may include vintage ploughing in the field opposite. Also, Fosseway and Tumpy Ground farm ciders, perries from Cornish Orchards and Gwynt y Ddraig and eight wines by the glass. The bar has very traditional brown-painted panelling and wall benches, plain chairs and tables on quarry tiles, with chat and laughter rather than piped music. There's a piano, darts and board games in one side room, and decorative mugs hanging from beams in another. There are picnic-sets out on the sheltered side grass and the garden behind, with a couple of long tables on the front cobbles by the quiet lane. Bedrooms are in a small newish block.

A big blackboard shows the day's range of huffers: big rolls with a hearty range of hot or cold fillings. They also serve ploughman's, baked potatoes, and a few sensibly priced dishes such as soup, chicken liver pâté, beer-battered fish and chips, gammon and egg, chicken curry, scampi and rib-eye steak. *Benchmark main dish: huffers £9.00. Two-course evening meal £14.50.*

Free house ~ Licensee Jocelyn Ridley ~ Real ale ~ Open 12-3, 5.30-11.30; 12-11.30 Thurs-Sun ~ Bar food 12-2.30 (4 Sat, 5 Sun), 7-9.30 ~ Children welcome ~ Dogs welcome ~ Wi-fi ~ Live folk music every third Mon ~ Bedrooms: /£90 *Recommended by David Jackson*

MARGARETTING TYE

TL6801   Map 5

White Hart ◀ £ ⇐

(01277) 840478 – www.thewhitehart.uk.com

From B1002 (just S of A12/A414 junction) follow Maldon Road for 1.3 miles, then turn right immediately after river bridge, into Swan Lane, keeping on for 0.7 miles; The Tye; CM4 9JX

Cheery pub with a fine choice of ales, good food, plenty of customers and a family garden; bedrooms

An impressive range of six real ales are tapped straight from the cask here: Adnams Southwold and Broadside, Mighty Oak IPA and Oscar Wilde and a couple of guests such as Colchester Metropolis and Skinners Betty Stogs; they hold beer festivals in July and November. Also, a german wheat beer, interesting bottled beers, quite a range of spirits and winter mulled wine. It's a particularly well run pub and always busy with a good mix of customers, and the open-plan but cottagey rooms have walls and wainscoting painted in chalky traditional colours that match well with the dark timbers and mix of old wooden chairs and tables; a stuffed deer head is mounted on the chimney breast above a woodburning stove. The neat carpeted back conservatory is similar in style, and the front lobby has a bookcase of charity paperbacks. Darts, board games and background music. There are plenty of picnic-sets out on grass and terracing around the pub, with a sturdy play area, a fenced duck pond and views across the fields; lovely sunsets.

🍴 Highly thought-of food includes lunchtime sandwiches, malaysian chicken strips with raita, smoked mackerel pâté with pickled cucumber, ham and free-range eggs, goats cheese and asparagus tart, beef, pork and chorizo burger with toppings and chips, calves liver and bacon, slow-braised pork belly and barbecued pork ribs with coleslaw and chips, seafood gratin, and puddings such as apple and rhubarb crumble and hot chocolate fudge cake. *Benchmark main dish: steak in ale pie £10.95. Two-course evening meal £17.50.*

Free house ~ Licensee Elizabeth Haines ~ Real ale ~ Open 11.30-3.30, 5.30-midnight; 11.30-midnight Sat; 12-midnight Sun; 11.30-3.30, 6-11 weekdays in winter ~ Bar food 12-2.30 (3.30 Sat), 6-9 (9.30 Fri, Sat); 12-7.30 Sun; not Mon evening ~ Restaurant ~ Well behaved children welcome ~ Dogs allowed in bar ~ Wi-fi ~ Bedrooms: /£80 *Recommended by George Atkinson, John Boothman, Mrs Margo Finlay, Jörg Kasprowski, David Jackson, David Twitchett*

MILL GREEN
TL6401 Map 5

Viper 🍺 £

(01277) 352010

The Common; from Fryerning (which is signposted off N-bound A12 Ingatestone bypass) follow Writtle signposts; CM4 0PT

Delightfully unpretentious, with local ales, simple pub food and no modern intrusions

The cottage garden at this quiet old-fashioned country local is a mass of colour in summer with the pub almost hidden by overflowing hanging baskets and window boxes; the lawn has some seats and tables. Inside, the cosy, unchanging rooms have spindleback and country kitchen chairs and tapestried wall seats around neat little old tables, and a log fire. The fairly basic parquet-floored tap room is more simply furnished with traditional wooden wall seats and a coal fire; beyond is another room with country kitchen chairs and sensibly placed darts. As well as a couple of beers named for the pub, there might be Viper (named for the pub from Nethergate), Jake the Snake (named for them from Mighty Oak), Animal Big Bang, Canterbury Nitro Engenius and Mighty Oak Oscar Wilde on handpump, plus Weston's scrumpy and perry. Live bands play at their Easter and August beer festivals, and morris dancers sometimes appear outside. The pub cat is called Millie and the west highland terrier, Jimmy. There are plenty of walkers, cyclists and families, particularly at weekends.

🍴 Simple lunchtime-only food includes sandwiches, baked potatoes, pâté with toast, cottage pie, sausages with beans and gravy, chicken curry, beef stew with dumplings, and puddings such as spotted dick with custard and apple crumble. *Benchmark main dish: steak in ale pie £7.50.*

Free house ~ Licensee Donna Torris ~ Real ale ~ Open 12-3, 6-11; 12-11 Sat; 12-10.30 Sun ~ Bar food 12-2 (3 weekends) ~ Children allowed at one end of bar ~ Dogs allowed in bar ~ Wi-fi *Recommended by Mike Swan, Charlie May, David Twitchett*

SAFFRON WALDEN
TL5338 Map 5

Eight Bells 🍷

(01799) 522790 – www.8bells-pub.co.uk

Bridge Street; B184 towards Cambridge; CB10 1BU

Beautiful bar and dining rooms with much character, helpful courteous staff, enjoyable food and drink, and seats in the garden

As this handsomely timbered black and white Tudor inn is handy for Audley End (English Heritage) and close to some good walks, it's particularly popular at lunchtimes. The open-plan, beamed bar area has leather armchairs, chesterfield sofas and old wooden settles on bare floorboards, a coal-effect gas fire in a brick fireplace and interesting old photographs; St Austell Tribute, Sharps Doom Bar and Woodfordes Wherry on handpump, ten wines by the glass and several malt whiskies. Staff are friendly and the atmosphere is relaxed and gently civilised. The back dining part is in a splendidly raftered and timbered barn with modern dark wood furniture and upholstered wall banquettes, a woodburning stove built into a log-effect end wall and display cabinets with old books, candlesticks and so forth; background music. There are seats and tables outside and a raised decked area.

🍴 A thoughtful choice of good food using local, seasonal produce includes sandwiches, poussin breast and leg with orange, juniper, dates and chicory, onion and gorgonzola tartlet with slow-roasted tomatoes, grazing boards, smoked haddock, pea and broad bean risotto, burger with toppings and skinny fries, lamb with sweetbreads, shank tortellini, mushrooms and mustard seeds, pork tenderloin with braised short ribs, ibérico ham, rhubarb chutney and black pepper jus, battered fish of the day with chips, and puddings such as lime cheesecake with mango and chilli jelly and sticky toffee pudding with butterscotch sauce and salted caramel ice-cream. *Benchmark main dish: rare-breed sausages with caramelised red onion gravy £12.50. Two-course evening meal £20.00.*

Cozy Pubs ~ Licensee Leanne Langman ~ Real ale ~ Open 10am-11pm (midnight Sat); 10am-10.30pm Sun ~ Bar food 12-10; 12-6 Sun ~ Restaurant ~ Children welcome ~ Dogs allowed in bar ~ Wi-fi *Recommended by Hilary and Neil Christopher, Andrew Stone*

SOUTH HANNINGFIELD
TQ7497 Map 5

Old Windmill 🏅 ♀

(01268) 712280 – www.brunningandprice.co.uk/oldwindmill
Off A130 S of Chelmsford; CM3 8HT

Extensive, invitingly converted pub with interesting food and a good range of drinks

Thanks to the appealing food and wide choice of drinks, there's always an abundance of chatty, cheerful customers here. Cosy, rambling areas are created by a forest of stripped standing timbers and open doorways and there's an agreeable mix of highly polished old tables and chairs, frame-to-frame pictures on cream walls, woodburning stoves and homely pot plants. Deep green or dark red dado and a few old rugs dotted on the glowing wood floors provide splashes of colour; other areas are more subdued with beige carpeting. Phoenix Brunning & Price Original and five guests such as Adnams Broadside, Crouch Vale Essex Boys Best Bitter, Ilkley Mary Jane, Mighty Oak IPA and Oscar Wilde on handpump, with a dozen wines by the glass, 70 malt whiskies and a good range of spirits; background music. A back terrace has tables and chairs under parasols and there are picnic-sets on the lawn, and a few more seats out in front.

⭐ From a brasserie-style menu, the reliably good food includes sandwiches (until 5pm), basil panna cotta with tomato salad and black olive tapenade, smoked salmon and prawn tian with crab mayonnaise, stilton and leek potato cakes with pear and fig chutney and apple, walnut and chicory salad, pork and leek sausages with onion gravy, steak burger with toppings, coleslaw and chips, cumin and chilli-spiced chicken with roast sweet potatoes and tzatziki, and puddings such as chocolate and honeycomb brownie with white chocolate ice-cream and crème brûlée. *Benchmark main dish: slow-roasted lamb shoulder with mint gravy and dauphinoise potatoes £16.95. Two-course evening meal £21.00.*

Brunning & Price ~ Manager Nick Clark ~ Real ale ~ Open 11.30-11; 12-10.30 Sun ~
Bar food 12-10 (9.30 Sun) ~ Restaurant ~ Children welcome ~ Dogs allowed in bar ~ Wi-fi
Recommended by David Jackman, John Boothman, N R White, David Twitchett

STOCK   TQ6999 Map 5
Hoop
(01277) 841137 – www.thehoop.co.uk
B1007; from A12 Chelmsford bypass take Galleywood, Billericay turn-off; CM4 9BD

**Happy weatherboarded pub with interesting beers, nice food
and a large garden**

They've held an end of May beer festival here for many years and feature
100 real ales, 80 ciders, a hog roast and a barbecue. On a regular basis
there's Adnams Southwold and guests from Crouch Vale, Harveys and
Sharps on handpump and local wines too. The open-plan bar has beams
and standing timbers (hinting at the original layout when it was once three
weavers' cottages), pubby tables and chairs and a happy bustle of cheery
locals and visitors. The dining room up in the timbered eaves is a fine room
with an open fire in a big brick-walled fireplace, napery and elegant high-
backed wooden chairs on bare boards. Prettily bordered with flowers, the
large sheltered back garden has picnic-sets and a covered seating area.
Parking is limited, so it's worth arriving early.

Quite a choice of food includes sandwiches, prawn and crab cocktail, potted rabbit
with waldorf salad, a vegetarian pasta dish of the day, beef and mushroom in
ale pie, beer-battered fish of the day with chips, lamb rump with black olive caramel,
spiced carrots and potato terrine, wild bass with vegetables à la grecque and orange
and thyme broth, seafood linguine, and puddings such as apple strudel with cinnamon
ice-cream and lemon drizzle cake with lemon sorbet and mascarpone; curry night
is Monday. *Benchmark main dish: toad in the hole £10.50. Two-course evening
meal £16.00.*

Free house ~ Licensee Michelle Corrigan ~ Real ale ~ Open 11-11; 12-10.30 Sun ~ Bar food
12-2.30, 6-9; 12-9.30 Sat; 12-3 Sun ~ Restaurant ~ Children welcome on left-hand side of bar
~ Dogs allowed in bar ~ Wi-fi *Recommended by Edward Mirzoeff, John and Enid*

WENDENS AMBO   TL5136 Map 5
Bell
(01799) 540382
B1039 W of village; CB11 4JY

**Chatty local with lots going on, good ales and ciders, pubby food
and big garden**

In warm weather, the three-acre garden here really comes into its own with
seats under parasols on the paved terrace, a pond leading to the River
Uttle, a woodland walk and a children's timber playground. Inside, there's
an easy-going atmosphere with lively banter from the friendly locals and a
genuine welcome for all from the cheerful landlord. The cottagey, bustling
bars have low ceilings, brasses on ancient timbers, wheelback chairs at neat
tables, a winter log fire and Growler Hound Dog and Priory Mild, Oakham
JHB and Woodfordes Wherry on handpump, farm cider and perry, and
several wines by the glass.

Well liked food includes sandwiches, prawn cocktail, ardennes pâté and toast,
mushroom, chestnut and red bean casserole, ham or local sausages with free-range
eggs and chips, thai green chicken curry, duck in cherry sauce, moroccan-style lamb

tagine, and puddings such as apple and blackberry crumble and treacle sponge pudding; as we went to press they were installing a wood-fired pizza oven. *Benchmark main dish: steak and mushroom in ale pie £9.95. Two-course evening meal £16.50.*

Free house ~ Licensee Simon Holland ~ Real ale ~ Open 12-2.30, 5-10.30 (5-10 Mon); 12-11 Fri, Sat; 12-10 Sun; closed Mon lunchtime except bank holidays ~ Bar food 12-2 (3 Sat, 4 Sun), 6-9; not Sun evening, Mon ~ Restaurant ~ Children welcome ~ Dogs welcome ~ Wi-fi
Recommended by Mrs Margo Finlay, Jörg Kasprowski, Tony Hobden

Also Worth a Visit in Essex

Besides the fully inspected pubs, you might like to try these pubs that have been recommended to us and described by readers. Do tell us what you think of them: feedback@goodguides.com

ARDLEIGH   TM0429
★ **Wooden Fender** (01206) 230466
A137 towards Colchester; CO7 7PA
Pleasantly extended and furnished old pub with friendly attentive service, beams and log fires, good freshly made food from light dishes and sharing plates to daily specials, Greene King and guests, decent wines; children welcome in large dining area, dogs in bar, good-sized garden with play area, open all day Sat, till 9pm Sun. *(David and Gill Carrington)*

ASHDON   TL5842
Rose & Crown (01799) 584337
Back road Saffron Walden–Haverhill, junction with back road to Radwinter; CB10 2HB Refurbished 17th-c beamed pub again under new management; Woodfordes, Lacons and three guests, enjoyable fairly priced traditional food including one or two specials, friendly helpful service; children and dogs welcome, tables in raised garden, open all day Sat, till 7pm Sun. *(Harvey Brown)*

BELCHAMP ST PAUL   TL7942
Half Moon (01787) 277402
Cole Green; CO10 7DP Thatched 16th-c pub overlooking green, popular reasonably priced home-made food (not Sun evening), well kept Greene King IPA and guests, decent wines by the glass, friendly staff, snug beamed interior with log fire, restaurant, Aug beer/music festival; children welcome, no dogs inside, tables out in front and in back garden, open all day weekends. *(Anon)*

BIRCHANGER   TL5122
★ **Three Willows** (01279) 815913
Under a mile from M11 junction 8: A120 towards Bishop's Stortford, then almost immediately right to Birchanger Village; don't be waylaid earlier by the Birchanger Services signpost; CM23 5QR Welcoming dining pub feeling nicely tucked away – some modernisation by present owners; spacious carpeted bar with lots of cricketing memorabilia, Greene King ales, well furnished smaller lounge bar, good range

of popular fairly traditional food including plenty of fresh fish; children welcome, dogs allowed in bar, picnic-sets out in front and on lawn behind (some motorway and Stansted Airport noise), good play area, closed Sun evening. *(Mrs Margo Finlay, Jörg Kasprowski and others)*

BLACKMORE END   TL7430
Bull (01371) 851740
Off A131 via Bocking Church Street and Beazley End; towards Wethersfield; CM7 4DD Tucked-away village dining pub dating from the 15th c, well restored opened-up interior with beams, stone or wood floors and back-to-back woodburners in central brick fireplace, enjoyable food from pub favourites up, OAP set lunch Weds, Adnams and a couple of guests, decent wines; some live music; children welcome, no dogs inside, tables in side garden and maybe summer barbecues, open all day (till midnight Fri, Sat). *(J B and M E Benson)*

BOREHAM   TL7409
Lion (01245) 394900
Main Road; CM3 3JA Stylish bistro-bar with rooms, good well presented and affordably priced food (order at bar) from snacks to daily specials, several wines by the glass, bottled beers and well kept ales including one named for them, efficient friendly staff, conservatory; children welcome, no dogs, open all day. *(Tina and David Woods-Taylor)*

BROXTED   TL5726
Prince of Wales (01279) 850256
Brick End; CM6 2BJ Village pub encircled by roads, comfortable and welcoming, with enjoyable fairly priced pubby food including bargain weekday deal till 5pm, five well kept ales such as Bishop Nicks, Greene King and Saffron, decent wine choice, split-level beamed bar, connecting room with woodburners, conservatory; children welcome, a few picnic-sets out at front, window boxes and hanging baskets, beer garden behind, closed Mon, otherwise open all day. *(Christopher Ensor)*

BULMER TYE   TL8438
★**Bulmer Fox** (01787) 312277
A131 S of Sudbury; CO10 7EB Popular
pub-bistro with good fairly priced food from
varied menu, neatly laid tables with forms to
write your order (can also order at the bar),
Adnams and Greene King IPA, help-yourself
water fountain, friendly well trained staff,
bare boards with one or two 'rugs' painted
on them, pastel colours and lively acoustics,
quieter side room and intimate central snug,
home-made chutneys, preserves etc for sale;
children welcome, sheltered back terrace
with arbour. *(Mrs Carolyn Dixon)*

BURNHAM-ON-CROUCH   TQ9495
★**White Harte** (01621) 782106
The Quay; CM0 8AS Cosy old-fashioned
17th-c hotel on water's edge with views from
garden of yacht-filled River Crouch; partly
carpeted bars with down-to-earth charm,
assorted nautical bric-a-brac and hardware,
other traditionally furnished high-ceilinged
rooms with sea pictures on brown panelled or
stripped brick walls, cushioned seats around
oak tables, enormous winter log fire, well
kept Adnams and Crouch Vale, enjoyable food
and friendly efficient service; children and
dogs welcome, bedrooms, good breakfast,
open all day. *(John and Mary Warner)*

CASTLE HEDINGHAM   TL7835
Bell (01787) 460350
St James Street B1058; CO9 3EJ Beamed
and timbered three-bar pub dating from the
15th c, unpretentious and unspoilt (well run
by same family for over 45 years), Adnams,
Mighty Oak and guests served from the
cask (July and Nov beer festivals), popular
pubby food and turkish specials; background
and Fri live music (lunchtime jazz last
Sun of month); dogs welcome, children
away from public bar, garden with hops,
handy for Hedingham Castle, open all day
Fri-Sun. *(Anon)*

CASTLE HEDINGHAM   TL7835
Wheatsheaf (01787) 469939
Top end of Queen Street; CO9 3EX
Friendly 15th-c local under new
management; Bishop Nicks Heresy, Fullers
London Pride, Greene King IPA and Sharps
Doom Bar, enjoyable lunchtime (and Thurs-
Sat evening) food including Sat tapas and
good value Sun roasts, moulded beams (some
with floral carvings), quarry tiles, inglenook
woodburner, steps up to carpeted dining
area; open all day. *(Dr W I C Clark)*

CHELMSFORD   TL7006
Queens Head (01245) 265181
Lower Anchor Street; CM2 0AS Lively
well run Victorian corner local with very
well kept Crouch Vale beers and interesting
guests, summer farm cider and good value
wines, friendly staff, bargain food weekday
lunchtimes from baguettes up, bare boards

and winter log fires; Weds quiz; dogs
welcome, picnic-sets in colourful courtyard,
handy for county cricket ground, open all day.
(Lindy Andrews)

CHRISHALL   TL4439
Red Cow (01763) 838792
*High Street; off B1039 Wendens Ambo–
Great Chishill; SG8 8RN* Popular 16th-c
thatched pub with lots of atmosphere;
timbers, low beams, wood floors and log
fires, one half laid for dining, enjoyable food
(not Sun evening) from simple bar meals
up including Tues-Thurs evening deals, well
kept ales such as Adnams and Greene King,
Aspall's cider and several wines by the glass,
weekend afternoon teas, cookery classes;
some live music; children and dogs welcome,
nice garden and handy for Icknield Way
walkers, old adjacent barn for functions,
open all day weekends, closed Mon.
(R Anderson, Mrs Margo Finlay, Jörg Kasprowski)

CLAVERING   TL4832
★**Cricketers** (01799) 550442
B1038 Newport–Buntingford; CB11 4QT
Busy dining pub with plenty of old-fashioned
charm, inventive food and signed cookbooks
by Jamie Oliver (his parents own it); main
area with very low beams and big open
fireplace, bays of deep purple button-backed
banquettes and padded leather dining chairs
on dark floorboards, split-level back part with
carpeted dining areas and some big copper
and brass pans on dark beams and timbers,
three Adnams beers and 19 wines by the
glass; background music, free wi-fi; children
welcome, attractive front terrace with wicker-
look seats around teak tables, bedrooms,
handy for Stansted Airport, open all day from
7am, food all day Sun. *(Peter Rozée, Mrs Margo
Finlay, Jörg Kasprowski, M and GR)*

COGGESHALL   TL8224
★**Compasses** (01376) 561322
*Pattiswick, signed off A120 W;
CM77 8BG* More country restaurant than
pub with enjoyable well presented food
using local produce from light lunches up,
also weekday set deals and children's meals,
Adnams, Woodfordes and maybe local Bishop
Nicks, good wine choice, cheerful attentive
young staff, neatly comfortable spacious
beamed bars, barn restaurant; some live
music; plenty of lawn and orchard tables,
rolling farmland beyond, open all day.
(John and Mary Warner)

COLCHESTER   TM9824
Hospital Arms (01206) 542398
*Crouch Street (opposite hospital);
CO3 3HA* Friendly pub with several small
linked areas, good selection of well kept
Adnams ales and guests, tasty inexpensive
lunchtime food, quick cheerful service;
games machines; children till 6pm and dogs
welcome, beer garden behind, open all day
and can get crowded. *(Harvey Brown)*

COLNE ENGAINE   TL8530
Five Bells   (01787) 224166
*Signed off A1124 (was A604) in Earls
Colne; Mill Lane; CO6 2HY* Welcoming
and popular village pub with list of landlords
back to 1579, good home-made food using
local produce, own-baked bread, six well
kept changing ales including Adnams (Nov
festival), friendly efficient service, bare
boards or carpeted floors, woodburners,
old photographs, high-raftered dining area
(former slaughterhouse), public bar with
pool and sports TV, some live music; free
wi-fi; children, walkers and dogs welcome,
disabled facilities, attractive front terrace
with gentle Colne Valley views, open (and
food) all day. *(Mrs Margo Finlay, Jörg
Kasprowski)*

COOPERSALE STREET   TL4701
★Theydon Oak   (01992) 572618
*Off B172 E of Theydon Bois; or follow
Hobbs Cross Open Farm brown sign off
B1393 at N end of Epping; CM16 7QJ*
Attractive old weatherboarded dining pub,
very popular for its good food (all day Sun till
7pm) from pubby choices up including Mon
evening deal, a house beer from Dominion
and five changing guests, friendly prompt
service, beams and masses of brass, copper
and old brewery mirrors, two woodburners;
background music, no dogs inside; children
welcome, tables on side terrace and in
fenced garden with small stream, lots of
hanging baskets, separate play area, open
all day. *(Gordon Neighbour, Brian Glozier)*

DANBURY   TL7705
Griffin   (01245) 222905
A414, top of Danbury Hill; CM3 4DH
Renovated 16th-c pub with well divided
interior, beams and some carved woodwork,
mix of new and old furniture on wood,
stone or carpeted floors, log fires, enjoyable
food from pub standards, deli boards and
pizzas up, changing real ales and nice
choice of wines by the glass, friendly if
not always speedy service; background
music; children welcome, terrace seating,
views. *(John Boothman)*

DEDHAM   TM0533
★Sun   (01206) 323351
High Street (B2109); CO7 6DF Stylish
old Tudor coaching inn opposite church; good
italian-influenced food using seasonal local
produce, also cheaper set menu (not Fri, Sat
or Sun lunchtime), must book at peak times,
impressive wine selection (over 20 by the
glass), well kept Adnams, Crouch Vale and
two guests, Aspall's cider, friendly efficient
young staff, historic panelled interior with
high carved beams, handsome furnishings
and splendid fireplaces; background music,
TV; children and dogs (in bar) welcome,
picnic-sets on quiet back lawn with mature
trees and view of church, characterful

panelled bedrooms, good Flatford Mill walk,
open all day. *(N R White, Kay and Alistair Butler)*

DUTON HILL   TL6026
Three Horseshoes   (01371) 870681
*Off B184 Dunmow–Thaxted, 3 miles N of
Dunmow; CM6 2DX* Friendly traditional
village local, well kept Mighty Oak and a
couple of guests (late May Bank Holiday
beer festival), central fire, aged armchairs
by fireplace in homely left-hand parlour, lots
of interesting memorabilia, darts and pool
in small public bar, no food, folk club third
Thurs of month; dogs welcome, old enamel
signs out at front, garden with pond and
nice views, closed lunchtimes Mon-Thurs.
(Ruth May)

EDNEY COMMON   TL6504
Green Man   (01245) 248076
Highwood Road; CM1 3QE Comfortable
country pub-restaurant, good well presented
food from interesting changing menu cooked
by chef-owners, extensive wine list (several
by the glass), a couple of real ales, friendly
attentive staff, carpeted interior with black
beams and timbers; tables out at front and in
garden, closed Sun evening, Mon. *(Phil and
Jane Hodson)*

EPPING FOREST   TL4501
Forest Gate   (01992) 572312
Bell Common; CM16 4DZ Large friendly
open-plan pub dating from the 17th c and
run by the same family for over 50 years;
beams, flagstones and panelling, well kept
Adnams, Nethergate and guests from brick-
faced bar, some basic food; dogs welcome,
tables on front lawn, popular with walkers,
bedrooms and adjacent rather upmarket
restaurant. *(Ruth May)*

FINCHINGFIELD   TL6832
Fox   (01371) 810151
The Green; CM7 4JX Pargeted 16th-c
building with spacious beamed bar, exposed
brickwork and central fireplace, patterned
carpet, floor tiles by counter serving four
real ales including Adnams and Nethergate,
good choice of wines by the glass, popular
freshly made food (not Sun evening) from
sandwiches and pub favourites up, afternoon
tea, pleasant staff; background and some live
music (may be Thurs jazz); children and dogs
welcome, picnic-sets in front overlooking
village duck pond, open all day. *(Lois Dyer,
David Twitchett)*

FINGRINGHOE   TM0220
Whalebone   (01206) 729307
*Off A134 just S of Colchester centre,
or B1025; CO5 7BG* Old pub geared
for dining, airy country-chic rooms with
cream-painted tables on oak floors, fresh
flowers and log fire, good local food (not Sun
evening) from interestingly varied menu,
nice sandwiches too, well kept beers such as
Adnams, friendly helpful staff, barn function

room; background music; children and dogs welcome, charming back garden with peaceful valley view, front terrace, handy for Fingringhoe Wick nature reserve, open all day weekends. *(N R White)*

FYFIELD TL5707

Black Bull (01277) 899225
Dunmow Road (B184), N end of village; CM5 0NN Traditional pub serving generous helpings of enjoyable food including good fresh fish and popular Sun roasts (they do takeaways), Fullers London Pride and Greene King IPA, friendly staff, heavy low beams and standing timbers in comfortably opened-up pubby bar and country-style dining area, open fire; background music; tables in back garden by car park, ten bedrooms in adjacent building, open all day Sun till 9pm. *(Richard Kennell)*

GESTINGTHORPE TL8138

★**Pheasant** (01787) 461196
Off B1058; CO9 3AU Civilised country pub with old-fashioned character in small opened-up beamed rooms, settles and mix of other furniture on bare boards, books and china platters on shelves, woodburners in nice brick fireplaces, Adnams Southwold, a house beer from Woodfordes and an occasional guest, nine wines by the glass, good food using some home-grown produce; children and dogs (in bar) welcome, seats outside under parasols with views over fields, five stylish bedrooms, open all day (may close Mon if quiet), shut first two weeks Jan. *(Mrs Margo Finlay, Jörg Kasprowski, Walter and Susan Rinaldi-Butcher)*

GREAT CHESTERFORD TL5142

Crown & Thistle (01799) 530278
1.5 miles from M11 junction 9A; pub signposted off B184, in High Street; CB10 1PL Landlord at this traditional village pub (a previous Main Entry) was leaving as we went to press – news/reports please; substantial building with decorative plasterwork inside and out, particularly around the early 16th-c inglenook, long handsomely proportioned dining room with striking photographic mural of the village, low-ceilinged carpeted area by bar serving ales such as Buntingford, Milton and Woodfordes, food and service have been good; suntrap back courtyard with picnic-sets, may close Sun evening. *(David Jackman, Mrs Margo Finlay, Jörg Kasprowski)*

GREAT HENNY TL8738

Henny Swan (01787) 267953
Henny Street; CO10 7LS Welcoming dining pub in great location on the River

Stour; recent redecoration by new licensees to bar, lounge and restaurant, open fires, Adnams, Sharps and a guest such as Nethergate, plenty of wines by the glass, good food from interesting menu including tapas, lunchtime sandwiches too, friendly efficient service; background music; children welcome, terrace and waterside garden, open (and food) all day. *(Charlie May)*

HASTINGWOOD TL4807

★**Rainbow & Dove** (01279) 415419
0.5 miles from M11 junction 7; CM17 9JX Pleasantly traditional low-beamed pub with three small rooms, built-in cushioned wall seats and mate's chairs around pubby tables, stripped stone and cream or green paintwork, golfing memorabilia, woodburner in original fireplace, three or four changing ales, good choice of wines by the glass and enjoyable fairly priced food, friendly licensees and staff; background music, darts; children and dogs welcome, tables out under parasols, country views, closed Sun and Mon evenings. *(Anon)*

HATFIELD HEATH TL5115

Thatchers (01279) 730270
Stortford Road (A1005); CM22 7DU Thatched and weatherboarded 16th-c dining pub at end of large green, good popular food (best to book weekends) from varied menu, well kept Greene King IPA, St Austell Tribute and two guests from long counter, several wines by the glass, woodburners, beams, some copper and brass and old local photographs; background music; children in back dining area, no dogs inside, tables out in front behind picket fence, open all day weekends (food till 7pm Sun).
(Harvey Brown)

HENHAM TL5428

Cock (01279) 850347
Church End; CM22 6AN Welcoming old timbered place striking good balance between community local and dining pub, nice choice of well priced home-made food (not Sun evening), four ales including Greene King, Saffron (brewed in the village) and Sharps, decent wines, good open fires, restaurant with leather-backed chairs on wood floor, sports TV in snug; children welcome, dogs in bar, seats out at front and in tree-shaded garden behind, open all day Fri-Sun. *(Lindy Andrews)*

HERONGATE TQ6491

★**Olde Dog** (01277) 810337
Billericay Road, off A128 Brentwood–Grays at big sign for Boars Head; CM13 3SD Welcoming weatherboarded

---

Please tell us if any pub deserves to be upgraded to a featured entry – and why: feedback@goodguides.com, or (no stamp needed) The Good Pub Guide, FREEPOST RTJR-ZCYZ-RJZT, Perrymans Lane, Etchingham TN19 7DN.

country pub dating from the 16th c, long attractive dark-beamed bar and separate dining areas, exposed brickwork and uneven floors, well kept Greene King, a house beer from Crouch Vale and guests tapped from the cask, popular food (all day Sat, till 7pm Sun), friendly staff; pleasant front terrace and neat sheltered side garden, open all day. *(A N Bance)*

HOWLETT END   TL5834
White Hart   (01799) 599030
Thaxted Road (B184 SE of Saffron Walden); CB10 2UZ Comfortable pub-restaurant with two smartly set modern dining rooms either side of small tiled-floor bar, good food from sandwiches and light dishes up, Greene King IPA and local guests, nice choice of wines, friendly helpful service; children welcome, terrace and big garden, quiet spot, closed Sun evening, Mon. *(Isobel Mackinlay)*

LANGHAM   TM0232
Shepherd   (01206) 272711
Moor Road/High Street; CO4 5NR Refurbished 1920s village pub, L-shaped bar with areas off, wood floors and painted half-panelling, large OS map covering one wall, comfortable sofas, woodburner, two Adnams beers and a guest such as Maldon, plenty of wines by the glass and good selection of other drinks, enjoyable varied choice of food (not Sun, Mon evenings) including set menu, good friendly service; quiz first Tues of month, film nights; children and dogs (in bar) welcome, side garden, open all day (till 9pm Sun). *(Malcolm Greening)*

LEIGH-ON-SEA   TQ8385
★ Crooked Billet   (01702) 480289
High Street; SS9 2EP Homely old pub with waterfront views from big bay windows, packed on busy summer days when service can be frantic but friendly, well kept Adnams, Nicholsons, Sharps and changing guests including seasonals, enjoyable standard Nicholsons menu, log fires, beams, panelled dado and bare boards, local fishing pictures and bric-a-brac; background music; children allowed if eating but no under-21s after 6pm, side garden and terrace, seawall seating over road shared with Osborne's good shellfish stall (plastic glasses for outside), pay-and-display parking by flyover, open all day. *(George Atkinson, David Jackson, N R White)*

LITTLE BRAXTED   TL8413
Green Man   (01621) 891659
Kelvedon Road; signed off B1389; OS Sheet 168 map reference 848133; CM8 3LB Village pub refurbished by new owners, modern décor with old beams and log fires, good food (till 6pm Sun) from traditional choices up, Greene King ales and a guest, Aspall's cider, friendly attentive staff; children welcome, picnic-sets out at front and in pleasant sheltered garden with ducks. *(Tina and David Woods-Taylor)*

LITTLE BROMLEY   TM1028
Haywain   (01206) 390004
Bentley Road; CO11 2PL Welcoming family-run 18th-c pub popular with locals and visitors, carpeted interior with various cosy areas leading off from main bar, beams, exposed brickwork and open fires, well kept Adnams Southwold and three regional guests, generous helpings of enjoyable home-made food (booking recommended evenings/weekends), good friendly service; closed Sun evening, all Mon, Tues lunchtime. *(Anon)*

LOUGHTON   TQ4296
Victoria   (020) 8508 1779
Smarts Lane; IG10 4BP Welcoming flower-decked Victorian local with enjoyable home-made pubby food (large helpings), good range of fairly mainstream beers including Adnams and Greene King, chatty panelled bare-boards bar with small raised end dining area; children and dogs welcome, pleasant neatly kept front garden, Epping Forest walks. *(Harvey Brown)*

MALDON   TL8407
★ Blue Boar   (01621) 855888
Silver Street; car park behind; CM9 4QE Quirky cross between coaching inn and antiques or auction showroom, most showy in the main building's lounge and dining room, interesting antique furnishings and pictures also in the separate smallish dark-timbered bar and its spectacular raftered upper room, good Farmers ales brewed at the back, also Adnams Southwold and a guest, enjoyable food from bar snacks to daily specials, friendly helpful staff; tables outside, 28 bedrooms (some with four-posters, some perhaps in need of refurbishment), good breakfast, car park fee refunded at bar, open all day. *(Lindy Andrews)*

MATCHING GREEN   TL5310
Chequers   (01279) 731276
Off Downhall Road; CM17 0PZ Red-brick Victorian pub/restaurant in picturesque village, not particularly cheap but very enjoyable traditional and mediterranean-style food from good lunchtime ciabattas up, also fixed-price weekday lunch, vegetarian menu and children's choices, friendly helpful staff dressed in black, nice wines from comprehensive list, well kept Greene King IPA; background music and occasional cabaret/tribute nights; disabled facilities, quiet spot overlooking large green, good local walks, open all Fri-Sun, closed Mon. *(Tina and David Woods-Taylor, Roger and Pauline Pearce)*

MATCHING TYE   TL5111
Fox   (01279) 731335
The Green; CM17 0QS Long 18th-c village pub opposite tiny green, decent range of popular well priced food including good Sun roast, Greene King IPA, Shepherd Neame Spitfire and a guest, welcoming service,

various areas including beamed restaurant and raftered barn room, comfortable dark wood furniture, brasses, woodburners; live music and quiz nights, TV; children welcome, 12 bedrooms. *(Mrs Margo Finlay, Jörg Kasprowski)*

MESSING   TL8919
Old Crown   (01621) 815575
Signed off B1022 and B1023; Lodge Road; CO5 9TU Attractive late 17th-c village pub with good interesting food (not Sun evening) from light lunches up, well kept Adnams, cheerful helpful staff; shop/deli behind, near fine church, open all day. *(Steve and Irene Homer)*

MILL GREEN   TL6301
Cricketers   (01277) 352400
Mill Green Road; CM4 0JD Welcoming 19th-c country pub with beams and interesting cricketing memorabilia, good food (not Sun, Mon evenings) from sandwiches and pubby choices up including daily specials, two Greene King ales and a guest, decent wines, restaurant; children welcome, tables on front terrace behind white picket fence, more in tree-shaded garden behind, open all day Sun. *(Mrs Margo Finlay, Jörg Kasprowski)*

MISTLEY   TM1131
★Thorn   (01206) 392821
High Street (B1352 E of Manningtree); CO11 1HE Popular for American chef-landlady's good food (especially seafood), but there's also a friendly all-day welcome if you just want a drink or coffee; high black beams give a clue to the building's age (Matthew Hopkins, the notorious 17th-c witchfinder general, based himself here), décor, though, is crisply up to date – comfortable basketweave chairs and mixed dining tables on terracotta tiles around horseshoe bar, cream walls above sage dado, colourful modern artwork, end brick fireplace with woodburner, newspapers and magazines; cookery classes; front terrace tables looking across to Robert Adam's swan fountain, interesting waterside village, ten comfortable bedrooms. *(Kay and Alistair Butler)*

MOUNT BURES   TL9031
★Thatchers Arms   (01787) 227460
Off B1508; CO8 5AT Well run modernised pub with good local food cooked to order, meal deals Tues-Fri, three or four well kept ales including Adnams Southwold and Crouch Vale Brewers Gold, cheerful efficient staff; background music; children and dogs welcome, plenty of picnic-sets out behind, peaceful Stour Valley views, closed

Mon, otherwise open all day (food all day weekends). *(N R White)*

NORTH SHOEBURY   TQ9286
Angel   (01702) 589600
Parsons Corner; SS3 8UD Conversion of timbered and partly thatched former post office, Greene King, Woodfordes and a couple of guests, good popular food including daily specials, panelling and exposed brickwork, woodburner, tartan-carpeted restaurant where children allowed; background music; dogs welcome in bar, disabled facilities, open all day weekends. *(B J Harding)*

ORSETT   TQ6483
Dog & Partridge   (01375) 891377
A128 S of Bulphan; RM16 3HU Roadside pub with good straightforward food and well kept beers, friendly helpful staff; large garden with duck pond, open all day. *(Tina and David Woods-Taylor)*

PAGLESHAM   TQ9492
Plough & Sail   (01702) 258242
East End; SS4 2EQ Relaxed 17th-c weatherboarded dining pub in pretty spot, popular fairly traditional food at affordable prices, friendly service, well kept changing ales, local cider and decent house wines, low beams and big log fires, pine tables, lots of brasses and pictures, traditional games; background music; children welcome, front picnic-sets and attractive side garden, open all day Sun. *(Mrs Margo Finlay, Jörg Kasprowski)*

PAGLESHAM   TQ9293
★Punchbowl   (01702) 258376
Church End; SS4 2DP Weatherboarded 16th-c former sailmaker's loft with low beams and stripped brickwork, pews, barrel chairs and lots of brass, local pictures, lower room laid for dining, Adnams Southwold, Sharps Doom Bar and a couple of guests such as Bishop Nicks, popular fairly priced food including good OAP menu (Tues, Thurs), friendly attentive staff, cribbage and darts; background music; children usually welcome if eating but check first, no dogs inside, picnic-sets in front by lane, open (and food) all day Sun. *(George Atkinson)*

PELDON   TL9916
Plough   (01206) 735808
Lower Road; CO5 7QR Cosy and welcoming little white weatherboarded village pub, good choice of well liked generous food, Greene King and a guest such as Sharps Doom Bar, friendly accommodating service, beams and log fire; children and dogs welcome, open all day Sun. *(David Jackson)*

A few pubs try to make you leave a credit card at the bar, as a sort of deposit if you order food. This is a bad practice, and the banks and credit card firms warn you not to let your card go like this.

PELDON   TM0015

★ **Rose** (01206) 735248
*B1025 Colchester–Mersea (do not turn
left to Peldon village); CO5 7QJ* Friendly
old inn with dark bowed beams, standing
timbers and little leaded-light windows,
some antique mahogany and padded leather
wall banquettes, arched brick fireplace,
Adnams, Greene King and Woodfordes,
several wines by glass and enjoyable food
(not Sun evening), cosy restaurant and smart
airy garden room; children welcome away
from bar, plenty of seats in spacious garden
with pretty pond, comfortable country-
style bedrooms, open all day (till 7pm Sun
in winter). *(Mike Swan, Charlie May, Dave
Braisted)*

PENTLOW   TL8146

Pinkuah Arms (01787) 280857
Pinkuah Lane; CO10 7JW Recent
contemporary refurbishment for this
beamed country pub (aka Pinkers), well
liked food (not Sun evening, Mon) from pub
favourites to more restauranty dishes, good
value lunchtime set menu and other deals,
Adnams, Greene King, Timothy Taylors and
Woodfordes, friendly efficient service; quiz
last Tues of month; children and dogs (in
bar) welcome, garden and terrace with
modern furniture, open all day. *(Adele
Summers, Alan Black)*

PURLEIGH   TL8401

Bell (01621) 828348
*Off B1010 E of Danbury, by church
at top of hill; CM3 6QJ* Cosy rambling
beamed and timbered pub with fine views
over the marshes and Blackwater estuary;
bare boards, hops and brasses, inglenook
log fire, well kept ales such as Adnams and
Mighty Oak, plenty of wines by the glass
(some local), good sensibly priced home-
made food including specials, friendly staff;
cinema in adjoining barn; children welcome,
picnic-sets on side grass, good walks (on
St Peter's Way), closed Sun evening, Mon.
(Giles and Annie Francis)

RICKLING GREEN   TL5129

Cricketers Arms (01799) 543210
*Just off B1383 N of Stansted Mountfichet;
CB11 3YG* Brick-built beamed dining
pub under same management as the Eight
Bells in Saffron Walden (see Main Entries);
enjoyable food from reasonably priced varied
menu, good selection of wines and cheerful
attentive staff, split-level modernised
interior; children welcome, nice position
opposite cricket green (they can provide
hampers), ten bedrooms. *(Charles Gysin)*

RIDGEWELL   TL7341

Kings Head (01440) 788331
A1017 Haverhill–Halstead; CO9 4RU
Recently refurbished 15th-c village pub,
beams and inglenook log fires, four well kept

changing ales, five ciders/perries and decent
selection of wines, good sensibly priced
home-cooked food from interestingly varied
menu, friendly staff; well behaved children
and dogs welcome, garden tables, open all
day Sat, till 9pm Sun closed Mon, Tues (no
food Weds lunchtime, Sun evening). *(Adele
Summers, Alan Black)*

RIDGEWELL   TL7340

White Horse (01440) 785532
*Mill Road (A1017 Haverhill–Halstead);
CO9 4SG* Comfortable beamed village pub
with four well kept changing ales (some
tapped from the cask), real ciders and decent
wines by the glass, good generous food
including lunchtime set menu (Weds-Sat),
friendly service; background music, free wi-fi;
well behaved children welcome, no dogs,
tables out on terrace, modern bedroom block
with good disabled access, closed lunchtimes
Mon and Tues, otherwise open all day.
(Mike Swan)

ROMFORD   TQ5088

Mawney Arms (01708) 761162
Mawney Road; RM7 7HT Popular open-
plan Ember Inn with refurbished restaurant
and bar areas, good value all-day food,
changing ales, Sun quiz; garden behind, open
all day. *(Robert Lester)*

ROXWELL   TL6508

Hare (01245) 248788
*Bishops Stortford Road (A1060);
CM1 4LU* Refurbished open-plan pub
(Pie & Pint Inns); Golden Crust ales (brewed
by Brentwood) and guests such as Adnams
and Timothy Taylors, plenty of wines by the
glass, good choice of traditional food with
smaller helpings available, teas, coffee and
home-made cakes, friendly attentive service,
some timbers and log fire; children welcome,
no dogs inside, terrace and garden with
stream, farmland views, open all day.
(John and Mary Warner)

SAFFRON WALDEN   TL5438

Old English Gentleman
(01799) 523595 *Gold Street; CB10 1EJ*
Busy 19th-c red-brick town-centre pub,
bare boards, panelling and log fires, plenty
of inviting nooks and crannies, well kept
Adnams Southwold, Woodfordes Wherry and
a couple of guests, plenty of wines by the
glass including champagne, good choice of
enjoyable lunchtime food from sandwiches
and deli boards up; background music;
part-covered heated terrace with modern
furniture, open all day (till 1am Fri, Sat).
(Alcuin Bramerton)

SOUTHMINSTER   TQ9699

Station Arms (01621) 772225
Station Road; CM0 7EW Popular
weatherboarded local with unpretentious
L-shaped bar, bare boards and panelling,
friendly chatty atmosphere, well kept

Adnams Southwold and several guests, beer festivals (Jan, May), live blues and folk nights; back courtyard, open all day Sat from 2pm. *(Mike Swan)*

STAPLEFORD TAWNEY   TL5001
★ **Mole Trap**   (01992) 522394
Tawney Common; signed off A113 N of M25 overpass – keep on; OS Sheet 167 map reference 500013; CM16 7PU
Popular unpretentious little country pub, carpeted beamed bar (mind your head as you go in) with brocaded wall seats and plain pub tables, steps down to similar area, warming fires, well kept Fullers London Pride and changing guests, reasonably priced down-to-earth food (not Sun and Mon evenings), cheery swift service; no credit cards, quiet background radio; children welcome away from bar, small dogs allowed at quiet times, beer garden with rural views. *(George Atkinson, David Jackson, David Twitchett)*

STEEPLE BUMPSTEAD   TL6841
Fox & Hounds   (01440) 731810
Chapel Street; CB9 7DQ Welcoming 15th-c beamed village pub, popular home-made food (booking advised) from varied menu including good value Mon evening two-course deal, well kept Greene King IPA and three quickly changing guests, several wines by the glass, good friendly service, small restaurant with pine furniture, log fire; some seats out in front behind picket fence, more on little terrace behind, open all day Fri-Sun (no food Sun evening). *(Adele Summers, Alan Black)*

STISTED   TL7923
Dolphin   (01376) 321143
A120 E of Braintree, by village turn; CM77 8EU Old mansard-roofed roadside pub with cheerful heavily beamed and timbered bar, well liked home-cooked food including set menu choices, Greene King ales tapped from the cask, brasses, antlers and lots of small prints, log fire, bright extended eating area on left; background music; children and dogs welcome, seats out at front and in pretty back garden with covered area, views over fields, open (and food) all day. *(Harvey Brown)*

STOCK   TQ6998
Bakers Arms   (01277) 840423
Common Road, just off B1007 Chelmsford–Billericay; CM4 9NF Popular open-plan beamed pub with good home-made food including some mediterranean influences, friendly attentive service, ales such as Crouch Vale, Adnams and Greene King, airy dining room with

french windows to enclosed terrace, more seats out at front and in side garden; children welcome, open all day (food all day Fri-Sun). *(John and Enid)*

STOW MARIES   TQ8399
★ **Prince of Wales**   (01621) 828971
B1012 between South Woodham Ferrers and Cold Norton Posters; CM3 6SA Cheery atmosphere in several little low-ceilinged unspoilt rooms, bare boards and log fires, conservatory dining area, half a dozen widely sourced ales, bottled and draught belgian beers including fruit ones, enjoyable food (all day Sun) with some interesting specials, home-made pizzas (winter Thurs) from Victorian baker's oven, live jazz (third Fri of month); children in family room, terrace and garden tables, summer Sun barbecues, good bedrooms in converted stable, open all day. *(N R White, David Heath)*

TAKELEY   TL5421
Green Man   (01279) 879181
The Street; CM22 6QU Small well renovated village pub, ales such as Sharps and Charles Wells, nice wines by the glass and good well presented food, also coffee shop serving lovely cakes; free wi-fi; children and dogs welcome, handy for Hatfield Forest (NT) and Stansted Airport, five bedrooms, open all day. *(Mrs Margo Finlay, Jörg Kasprowski)*

TENDRING   TM1523
Cherry Tree   (01255) 830340
Off A120 E of Colchester; B1035 junction with Crow Lane, E of village centre; CO16 9AP Extended heavy-beamed red-brick dining pub, good food (not Sun evening, booking advised weekends) including daily specials and set lunch (Tues-Sat), helpful friendly staff, high-backed black leather chairs around compact pub tables on broad polished boards, open fire, comfortable chairs by counter serving Adnams, Greene King and good value wines by the glass, two areas set with white linen; children welcome, disabled facilities, teak tables under parasols on sheltered back terrace, more tables on lawn behind tall hedge, closed Mon. *(N R White)*

THEYDON BOIS   TQ4599
Queen Victoria   (01992) 812392
Coppice Row (B172); CM16 7ES Nice spot set back from green, cosy beamed and carpeted traditional lounge, roaring log fire, local pictures and mug collection, two further bars and end restaurant, popular good value food including children's menu, McMullen

---

Please keep sending us reports. We rely on readers for news of new discoveries, and particularly for news of changes – however slight – at the fully described pubs: feedback@goodguides.com, or (no stamp needed) The Good Pub Guide, FREEPOST RTJR-ZCYZ-RJZT, Perrymans Lane, Etchingham TN19 7DN.

ales and decent house wines, friendly efficient young staff; background music; dogs welcome, picnic-sets on well laid-out front terrace, open all day. *(Robert Lester, N R White)*

UPSHIRE   TL4100
Horseshoes   (01992) 712745
Horseshoe Hill, E of Waltham Abbey; EN9 3SN Welcoming Victorian pub with small bar area and dining room, good freshly made food (not Sun evening, Mon) from chef-landlord with some emphasis on fish, well kept McMullen and guests, friendly helpful staff; children and dogs (in bar) welcome, garden overlooking Lea Valley, more tables out in front, good walks, open all day. *(David Jackson)*

WICKHAM St PAUL   TL8336
★**Victory**   (01787) 269364
SW of Sudbury; The Green; CO9 2PT Attractive and spacious old dining pub, varied choice of good freshly made food (not Sun evening), OAP lunch deal Tues-Fri, friendly efficient service, Adnams and guests from brick-fronted bar, beams and timbers, leather sofas and armchairs, inglenook woodburner; background music, pool and darts; children welcome, neat garden overlooking village cricket green, open all day Fri-Sun, closed Mon lunchtime. *(Adele Summers, Alan Black)*

WIDDINGTON   TL5331
★**Fleur de Lys**   (01799) 543280
Signed off B1383 N of Stansted; CB11 3SG Welcoming unpretentious low-beamed and timbered village pub, enjoyable locally sourced food (not Sun evening, Mon, Tues evening) in bar and dining room from sandwiches to very good (if pricey) steaks, set lunch deal Weds, Thurs (cheaper for over-60s), well kept Adnams, Sharps and two guests chosen by regulars, decent wines, dim lighting, tiled and wood floors, inglenook log fire; pool and other games in back bar; dogs welcome, picnic-sets in pretty garden, open all day Fri-Sun, closed Mon lunchtime. *(Mrs Margo Finlay, Jörg Kasprowski)*

WIVENHOE   TM0321
Black Buoy   (01206) 822425
Off A133; CO7 9BS Refurbished village pub owned by local consortium; open-plan partly timbered bare-boards bar, well kept ales such as Colchester, Mighty Oak and Red Fox, a craft keg, Aspall's cider and several wines by the glass, good sensibly priced home-made food (not Sun evening) from lunchtime sandwiches to daily specials, cheerful service, open fires, upper dining area glimpsing river over roofs; well behaved children and dogs in certain areas, terrace seating, two bedrooms, open all day. *(Anon)*

Gloucestershire

ASHLEWORTH   SO8125 Map 4

Queens Arms 🎯 🍷 🍺

(01452) 700395 – www.queensarmsashleworth.co.uk

Village signposted off A417 at Hartpury; GL19 4HT

Neatly kept pub with friendly licensees, a civilised bar, highly rated food, thoughtful wines and sunny courtyard

Our readers always enjoy their visits to this particularly well run village inn – the same hard-working, hands-on south african licensees have been here for over 17 years. It's all kept spic and span, and the friendly, civilised main bar has an appealing variety of farmhouse and brocaded dining chairs around big oak and mahogany tables on green carpet, and numerous pictures and paintings on the faintly patterned wallpaper and washed red ochre walls; at night, it's softly lit by fringed wall lamps and candles. A little art gallery displays work by local artists. Donnington BB, Ludlow Gold and a summer guest on handpump, 15 wines by the glass including south african ones, 22 malt whiskies, winter mulled wine and summer home-made lemonade; background music. The friendly pub cat is called Talulah. The sunny courtyard has cast-iron chairs and tables and lovely flower beds in summer; two perfectly clipped mushroom-shaped yews dominate the front of the building. Wheelchair access.

🎯 Good, popular food includes baguettes, pork and duck liver terrine, moules marinière, spinach and mushroom crêpes with neapolitan sauce, steak and kidney pie, tomato bredie (a south african speciality: spiced lamb stew), calves liver and bacon with onion mash and sage and port sauce, crispy duck with orange and grand marnier sauce, crab-stuffed red snapper with a chilli, ginger and garlic dressing, mixed grill, and puddings such as banoffi pie and triple chocolate brownie. *Benchmark main dish: sirloin steak with a choice of sauces £15.95. Two-course evening meal £19.00.*

Free house ~ Licensees Tony and Gill Burreddu ~ Real ale ~ Open 12-3, 7-11; 12-3 Sun; closed Sun evening, Mon ~ Bar food 12-2, 7-9 ~ Restaurant ~ Well behaved children allowed
Recommended by P and J Shapley, Bernard Stradling, Mark Sykes

BARNSLEY   SP0705 Map 4

Village Pub 🎯 🍷 🛏

(01285) 740421 – www.thevillagepub.co.uk

B4425 Cirencester–Burford; GL7 5EF

Bustling pub with comfortable communicating rooms, first class food and a good choice of drinks, and seats in the back courtyard; individually decorated bedrooms

With consistently excellent food and a genuine welcome for customers of all ages, this lovely country pub remains a favourite with our readers. The low-ceilinged bar rooms are smart and contemporary with pale paintwork, flagstones and oak floorboards, heavy swagged curtains, plush chairs, stools and window settles around polished candlelit tables, three open fireplaces and country magazines and newspapers, and – being at the heart of the village – a cheerful crowd of regulars. Hook Norton Old Hooky and Sharps Doom Bar on handpump, an extensive wine list with a dozen by the glass and farm cider. The sheltered back courtyard has solid wooden furniture under parasols, outdoor heaters and its own servery. This is an extremely comfortable and civilised place to stay and the breakfasts are especially good.

 Making impressive use of local, seasonal produce, the rewarding food includes twice-baked cheese soufflé, home-smoked pigeon breast with fresh figs, watercress and hazelnuts, a board of english charcuterie with cheese and pickles, smoked haddock fishcakes with a poached egg, spinach and lemon butter sauce, chicken kiev with baked mushrooms, slow-cooked pork belly with roasted squash and caper sauce, chargrilled calves liver with champ and bacon, and puddings such as chocolate st emilion and plum, apple and hazelnut cobbler. *Benchmark main dish: rare-breed beef burger with bacon jam, toppings and chips £14.00. Two-course evening meal £22.50.*

Free house ~ Licensee Michael Mella ~ Real ale ~ Open 11-11 ~ Bar food 12-2.30 (3 Sat), 7-9.30 (10 Fri, Sat); 12-9 Sun ~ Children welcome ~ Dogs allowed in bar and bedrooms ~ Wi-fi ~ Bedrooms: £105/£165 *Recommended by Tracey and Stephen Groves, Steve and Liz Tilley, Richard Cole, Alan and Angela Scouller, Wilburoo, Richard Tilbrook*

BLAISDON
Red Hart ◀

SO7016 Map 4

(01452) 830477 – www.redhartinn.co.uk
Village signposted off A4136 just SW of junction with A40 W of Gloucester; OS Sheet 162 map reference 703169; GL17 0AH

Village pub with interesting bric-a-brac in attractive rooms, popular bar food and several real ales

There's a lot to look at in this bustling pub – both in the flagstoned main bar and in the attractive beamed and carpeted restaurant on the right: woodworking and farming hand tools on magnolia walls and hanging from beams, old photographs of prize-winning farm stock and a framed valuation inventory of the pub in 1903, a deer's head, lots of books and pot plants and some interesting prints. Also, cushioned wall and window seats and traditional pub tables set with candles. Four real ales from breweries such as Bespoke, Cotswold Spring, Otter and Wye Valley on handpump, ten wines by the glass and local cider; background music and board games. On the left, you'll find additional dining space for families. The summer window boxes at the front of the building are very pretty and there are picnic-sets on the terrace and in the garden and a children's play area; the lower part has a smoking shelter and barbecue area. Wheelchair access. The little church above the village is worth a visit.

Well liked food includes sandwiches, prawn cocktail, pear, stilton and walnut tart, ham, egg and bubble and squeak, steak in ale pie, sausage and mash with onion gravy, thai-style cod cakes with sweet chilli sauce, spiced chicken breast with moroccan-style vegetable couscous, duck breast with red wine sauce and boulangère potatoes, mixed grill, and puddings. *Benchmark main dish: slow-roast pork belly £13.50. Two-course evening meal £18.00.*

Free house ~ Licensee Sharon Hookings ~ Real ale ~ Open 12-2.30 (3 weekends), 6-11; 12-4, 7-11 Sun ~ Bar food 12-2, 7-9 ~ Restaurant ~ Children welcome ~ Dogs allowed in bar ~ Wi-fi *Recommended by R T and J C Moggridge, Chris and Val Ramstedt, Chris and Angela Buckell*

BLEDINGTON   SP2422 Map 4
Kings Head 🔯 ♀ 🍺 🛏

(01608) 658365 – www.kingsheadinn.net

B4450 The Green; OX7 6XQ

Beams and atmospheric furnishings in 16th-c inn, super wines by the glass, real ales and delicious food; smart bedrooms

This former cider house is a lovely place to stay, and the setting – opposite the green in a tranquil village – is very pretty. The main bar is the beating heart of the place and is full of ancient beams and other atmospheric furnishings (high-backed wooden settles, gate-leg or pedestal tables) and has a warming log fire in a stone inglenook; sporting memorabilia of rugby, racing, cricket and hunting. To the left, a drinking area has built-in wall benches, stools and dining chairs around wooden tables, rugs on bare boards and a woodburning stove. Hook Norton Best and guests from breweries such as Butcombe, Flying Monk and Wye Valley on handpump, a super wine list with ten by the glass and 20 malt whiskies; background music. There are seats out in front and rattan-style armchairs around tables in the lovely back courtyard garden with its pagoda; maybe free-ranging bantams and ducks. The same first class licensees also run the Swan at Swinbrook (in Oxfordshire).

Using local, free-range and organic produce, the imaginative food includes lunchtime open sandwiches, treacle-smoked salmon caesar salad, rabbit and guinea fowl terrine with pickled wild mushrooms, lamb burger with feta, paprika and mint, bloody mary ketchup and skinny chips, pork belly with bubble and squeak, cauliflower purée, baby onions and port juices, teriyaki salmon fillet with sweetcorn salsa, horseradish potato purée and wasabi, and puddings such as rhubarb, blackberry sorbet, honey and thyme panna cotta and sherbert, and chocolate ale cake with malt cream. *Benchmark main dish: chilli cheeseburger with harissa mayonnaise and chips £14.00. Two-course evening meal £23.00.*

Free house ~ Licensees Nicola and Archie Orr-Ewing ~ Real ale ~ Open 11.30-11 ~ Bar food 12-2, 6.30-9 ~ Restaurant ~ Children welcome ~ Dogs allowed in bar ~ Wi-fi ~ Bedrooms: £80/£100 *Recommended by Richard Tilbrook, Liz Bell, Bernard Stradling, Richard Cole, Mike and Mary Carter, Jamie and Sue May, Alun and Jennifer Evans*

BOURTON-ON-THE-HILL   SP1732 Map 4
Horse & Groom 🔯 ♀ 🛏

(01386) 700413 – www.horseandgroom.info

A44 W of Moreton-in-Marsh; GL56 9AQ

Gloucestershire Dining Pub of the Year

Handsome Georgian inn with a fine range of drinks, excellent food, friendly staff and lovely views from seats outside; smart bedrooms

'A consistently reliable favourite' and 'everything here is as lovely as ever' are just two comments from readers on this particularly well run, honey-coloured stone inn. The pubby bar is light, airy and simply furnished with a pleasing mix of farmhouse and other wooden chairs, settles, cushioned wall and window seats and tables on bare boards, a woodburning stove in a stone fireplace, Goffs Jouster and guests such as

Hook Norton Lion and Wickwar Coopers WPA on handpump, 22 wines by the glass, local Hogan's farm cider and locally brewed lagers from the Cotswold Brewing Company. There are plenty of original features throughout; board games. Dining areas spread off from here – again, with a very attractive variety of dining chairs and rustic tables, rugs here and there, snug little corners, an open fire and horse paintings and prints on pale-painted or exposed stone walls. The large back garden has lots of seats under parasols and fine countryside views. This is a special place to stay, with individually styled, well equipped bedrooms and good breakfasts. It's best to arrive early to be sure of a space in the smallish car park. Batsford Arboretum is not far away.

The first class, imaginative food (suppliers are named on the menu) is cooked by one of the landlords: hand-picked crab with shaved fennel, cucumber and watercress salad and chilli and lemon dressing, home-cured salt beef with roasted beetroot, soft quail eggs and horseradish cream, rare-breed pork and chorizo meatballs in tomato and rosemary sauce on linguine, roast squash, spinach, cauliflower and chickpea-stuffed pancake with moroccan-spiced sauce, guinea fowl breast with duxelle stuffing and tarragon cream sauce, and puddings such as espresso crème brûlée and chocolate panna cotta with hazelnut biscotti. *Benchmark main dish: beer-battered cod with minted pea purée £13.75. Two-course evening meal £20.00.*

Free house ~ Licensee Tom Greenstock ~ Real ale ~ Open 11-2.30 (3 Sat), 6-11; 12-3.30 Sun; closed Sun evening except bank holiday weekends ~ Bar food 12-2, 7-9 (9.30 Fri, Sat); 12-2.30 Sun ~ Restaurant ~ Children welcome ~ Wi-fi ~ Bedrooms: £80/£120
Recommended by J R Wildon, Richard Tilbrook, P and J Shapley, David Bird, Michael Sargent, John Jenkins

BROCKHAMPTON

SP0322   Map 4

Craven Arms

(01242) 820410 – www.thecravenarms.co.uk
Village signposted off A436 Andoversford–Naunton – look out for inn sign at head of lane in village; can also be reached from A40 Andoversford–Cheltenham via Whittington and Syreford; GL54 5XQ

Friendly village pub with tasty bar food, real ales and seats in a big garden

This is a very well cared for and attractive 16th-c country pub and the convivial landlord and his attentive staff offer all their customers a genuine welcome. The character bars have low beams, roughly coursed thick stone walls and some tiled flooring; although it's largely been opened out to give a sizeable eating area off the smaller bar servery, there's a feeling of several communicating rooms. The furniture is mainly pine, with comfortable leather sofas, wall settles and tub chairs; also, gin traps, various stuffed animal trophies and a woodburning stove. Otter Bitter, Butcombe Legless Bob (named for the landlord, with 20p per pint going to Diabetes UK) and Stroud Budding on handpump, eight wines by the glass and a farm cider; board games. The large garden has plenty of seats and the views are lovely; good surrounding walks. They plan on opening bedrooms.

As well as their interesting barbecue-style 'hot rock' meat and fish choices with all sorts of sauces and dips, the highly thought-of food includes mussels in creamy white wine and chilli, chicken liver parfait with truffle butter and onion marmalade, local ham and free-range eggs, fresh beer-battered haddock and chips, rare-breed sausages and mash with gravy, spiced squash, spinach and ricotta crumble, steak in ale pie, slow-roast lamb with red wine jus, and puddings. *Benchmark main dish: chicken in a basket with chipotle sauce £12.00. Two-course evening meal £18.00.*

Free house ~ Licensees Barbara and Bob Price ~ Real ale ~ Open 12-3, 6-11; 12-11 Sat; 12-5 Sun; closed Sun evening, Mon ~ Bar food 12-2 (2.30 Sat), 6.30-9; 12.30-3.30 Sun ~ Restaurant ~ Children welcome ~ Dogs allowed in bar ~ Wi-fi *Recommended by Mrs Jo Rees, Tom McLean, Richard Tilbrook*

CHELTENHAM

SO9624   Map 4

Royal Oak ♀ ◀

(01242) 522344 – www.royal-oak-prestbury.co.uk

Off B4348 just N; The Burgage, Prestbury; GL52 3DL

Cheerful pub with popular food, several real ales and wine by the glass, and seats in the sheltered garden

As this very well run and friendly pub is open all day – and close to the town – amiable locals and visitors drop in and out regularly. There's an informal, bustling atmosphere and the congenial low-beamed bar has fresh flowers and polished brasses, a comfortable mix of seating including chapel chairs on parquet flooring, some interesting pictures on the ochre walls and a woodburning stove in a stone fireplace. Dark Star Hophead, Purity Mad Goose, Thornbridge Jaipur, Timothy Taylors Landlord and Wye Valley HPA on handpump and several wines by the glass; efficient, helpful service. Dining room tables are nicely spaced so that you don't feel crowded, and the skittle alley doubles as a function room; they hold a lot of fun events such as beer, sausage, cider and cheese festivals. There are seats and tables under canopies on the heated terrace and in a sheltered garden. Sister pub is the Gloucester Old Spot in Coombe Hill.

Enjoyable food includes lunchtime doorstep sandwiches, twice-baked celeriac and stilton soufflé, devilled lambs kidneys on toast, ham, egg and beef tomato, local game sausages with colcannon mash and onion gravy, wild mushroom cobbler with garlic, spinach and cheddar dumplings, steak burger with gruyère, sweet red onion relish and chips, mesquite barbecue butterflied chicken with sweet potato mash and tomato and oregano sauce, lamb shank casserole with red wine, rosemary and root vegetables, and puddings. *Benchmark main dish: slow-roast pork belly with mustard parsnip cream and roast onion and thyme sauce £14.00. Two-course evening meal £21.00.*

Free house ~ Licensees Simon and Kate Daws ~ Real ale ~ Open 11-11; 12-10.30 Sun ~ Bar food 12-2, 6-9; 12-8 Sun ~ Restaurant ~ Children welcome in dining room and before 7pm in bar ~ Wi-fi *Recommended by Michael Sargent, R C Vincent, Ian Herdman, M G Hart, Gordon and Jenny Quick*

CHIPPING CAMPDEN

SP1539   Map 4

Eight Bells ◀ 🛏

(01386) 840371 – www.eightbellsinn.co.uk

Church Street (one-way – entrance off B4035); GL55 6JG

Lovely inn with massive timbers and beams, log fires, quite a choice of bar food, real ales and seats in a large terraced garden; bedrooms

An impressive range of drinks, good food and a bustling, cheerful atmosphere keep this handsome old inn full of happy customers; it's best to book a table in advance. The candlelit bars have heavy oak beams, massive timber supports and stripped-stone walls with cushioned pews, sofas and solid dark wood furniture on broad flagstones, and log fires in up to three restored stone fireplaces. A glass panel in the dining room floor reveals the passage from the church by which Roman Catholic priests could escape from the Roundheads. Hook Norton Hooky, Goffs Jouster, Purity Pure

UBU and Wye Valley HPA on handpump from the fine oak bar counter, seven wines by the glass and two farm ciders; background music and board games. There's a large terraced garden with plenty of seats, and striking views of the almshouses and church. Attractive and comfortable bedrooms and highly thought-of breakfasts. The pub is handy for the Cotswold Way walk which leads to Bath.

 Changing with the seasons, the choice of good food includes lunchtime ciabatta sandwiches (not Sun), butterflied sardines with rustic tomato sauce, chicken liver parfait with home-made chutney, spinach and sun-dried tomato risotto with crispy leeks, pork and leek sausages with apple mash and cider and wholegrain mustard sauce, beer-battered cod with skin-on chips, creamy chicken curry, and puddings such as white chocolate cheesecake with dark chocolate drizzle and apple and cinnamon sponge pudding. *Benchmark main dish: beer-battered fish and chips £13.50. Two-course evening meal £20.00.*

Free house ~ Licensee Neil Hargreaves ~ Real ale ~ Open 12-11 (10.30 Sun) ~ Bar food 12-2, 6.30-9; 12-2.30, 6.30-9.30 Fri, Sat; 12-9 Sun ~ Restaurant ~ Well behaved children welcome in dining room but not in bar after 7pm; must be over 6 in bedrooms ~ Dogs allowed in bar ~ Wi-fi ~ Bedrooms: £75/£115 *Recommended by Michael Sargent, Sharon and John Hancock, Richard Tilbrook, W M Lien*

CIRENCESTER
Fleece

SP0202   Map 4

(01285) 658507 – www.thefleececirencester.co.uk

Market Place; GL7 2NZ

Carefully renovated inn with plenty of room in various bars and lounges, courteous staff, enjoyable food and drink and seats on terrace; character bedrooms

The comfortable, attractive and well equipped bedrooms (some with much character) in this 17th-c inn make a good base for exploring the lovely town and surrounding countryside; breakfasts are hearty. There's plenty of room in the various bars, lounges and airy dining areas, all different in style. Wheelback and mate's chairs and high bar stools and tables around the counter, wicker tub and high-backed yellow or orange dining chairs around an assortment of wooden tables, shelves of glassware and pottery, and french windows that open on to the terrace where there are white metal tables and chairs under parasols. Throughout, there are bare floorboards, contemporary pale paintwork, plenty of prints and fresh flowers and good lighting. Efficient, courteous staff serve Thwaites Lancaster Bomber and Wainwright and a couple of guests from Cotswold Lion and Flying Monk on handpump, several wines by the glass and good coffees and teas.

Seasonal and local (where possible) produce is used for the all-day food: sandwiches and afternoon tea (until 6pm), chicken and duck liver pâté with sweet wine jelly, tiger prawn tempura with fresh lime and sweet chilli dip, sharing deli boards, roasted butternut squash risotto with crispy sage, rare-breed pork sausages with apple and cider chutney and caramelised onion gravy, various burgers with toppings and battered onion rings, fresh fish of the day with salsa verde, and puddings such as banana, toffee and pecan sundae and chocolate and hazelnut brownie. *Benchmark main dish: beer-battered fish and chips £13.50. Two-course evening meal £19.00.*

Free house ~ Licensee Paul Hodgkinson ~ Real ale ~ Open 10.30am-11pm (10.30 Sun) ~ Bar food 12-9.30 (9 Sun) ~ Restaurant ~ Children welcome ~ Dogs allowed in bar and bedrooms ~ Wi-fi ~ Bedrooms: /£109 *Recommended by Richard Tilbrook, Edward May, Lindy Andrews, Jo Garnett*

CLIFFORD'S MESNE   SO6922   Map 4

Yew Tree 🌟 ♈ ◧

(01531) 820719 – www.yewtreeinn.com

From A40 W of Huntley, turn off at 'May Hill 1, Clifford's Mesne 2.5' signpost –
pub eventually signed up steep narrow lane on left; Clifford's Mesne also signposted
off B4216 S of Newent – pub then signed on right; GL18 1JS

Unusual dining pub nicely tucked away on slopes of May Hill,
with inventive food and fantastic choice of drinks

With excellent food and a wonderful choice of wines, this interesting place remains charming and gently civilised. The smallish two-room beamed bar has an attractive mix of small settles, a pew and character chairs around various tables including some antique ones, rugs on an unusual stone floor and a warm woodburning stove. Up a few steps is a more formal carpeted dining room and, beyond, a sofa by a big log fire; newspapers and maybe background music. The remarkable range of provincial french wines from small producers are served by glass (three sizes), 500ml jug and bottle – and there's a seating area in the small informal wine shop. If you buy a bottle with your meal, the mark-up is £6, which is excellent value especially at the top end. Sharps Own, Wickwar Gold and Wye Valley HPA on handpump, local farm cider and perry, 22 gins and good value winter mulled wine and cider; service is prompt and genial. The teak tables on the side terrace are best placed for the views; steps lead down to a sturdy play area.

 Delicious food includes lunchtime sandwiches, hot crab pot, smoked duck and pomegranate salad, nut roast with rich tomato sauce, wild duck and pork cassoulet, teriyaki salmon with pak choi and crispy ginger, pheasant with home-made pheasant sausage, parsnip purée and warm bacon dressing, their speciality seafood skillet, and puddings such as lime posset and ginger sponge with warm chocolate fudge sauce; on Weds-Sat lunchtimes they offer light lunches and smaller helpings for under £10. *Benchmark main dish: beef wellington £19.00. Two-course evening meal £22.00.*

Free house ~ Licensees Mr and Mrs Philip Todd ~ Real ale ~ Open 12-2.30, 6-11; 12-5 Sun; closed Sun evening, Mon, Tues lunchtime ~ Bar food 12-2, 6-9; 12-4 Sun ~ Children welcome ~ Dogs welcome ~ Wi-fi *Recommended by Guy Vowles, Chris and Angela Buckell, Mike and Mary Carter, R T and J C Moggridge*

COOMBE HILL   SO8926   Map 4

Gloucester Old Spot ★ ◧

(01242) 680321 – www.thegloucesteroldspot.co.uk

A mile from M5 junction 10 (access only from southbound/to northbound
carriageways); A4019 towards A38 Gloucester–Tewkesbury; GL51 9SY

The country local comes of age – a model for today's country pubs

If you're on the busy M5 (in either direction) and fancy a break, head for this bustling and cheerful country pub. The quarry-tiled beamed bar has chapel chairs and other seats around assorted tables (including one in a bow-windowed alcove) and opens into a lighter, partly panelled area with cushioned settles and stripped kitchen tables. Purity Mad Goose, Timothy Taylors Landlord and Wye Valley Butty Bach on handpump, seven decent wines by the glass and farm cider and perry – all served by young, friendly staff. Decoration is in unobtrusive good taste, with winter log fires. A handsome separate dining room has similar country furniture, high stripped-brick walls, dark flagstones and candlelight. Outside, there are chunky benches and tables under parasols on a terrace, with some oak barrel tables on brickwork and pretty flowers in vintage buckets and baskets; heaters for cooler weather. This is sister pub to the Royal Oak in Prestbury, near Cheltenham.

 Good, enjoyable food includes lunchtime crusty cobs, chicken liver parfait with plum and madeira chutney, pigeon and venison faggot with parsnip purée, blackberries and port dressing, twice-baked smoked haddock and gruyère soufflé with a poached egg and salsa verde, spiced pork and chorizo burger with guacamole, cheddar, asian slaw and chips, coq au vin with welsh rarebit crouton, seafood crêpe with mornay sauce, 28-day dry-aged steaks with sauces, and puddings; they also offer a two-course set lunch. *Benchmark main dish: slow-roast pork belly, garlic sausage, black pudding, cheek croquette, cassoulet sauce £14.95. Two-course evening meal £22.00.*

Free house ~ Licensee Simon Daws ~ Real ale ~ Open 10am-11pm (10 Sun) ~ Bar food 12-2, 6-9; 12-8 Sun ~ Restaurant ~ Children welcome ~ Dogs allowed in bar ~ Wi-fi
Recommended by M G Hart, Patrick and Daphne Darley, Dr and Mrs A K Clarke, Chris and Val Ramstedt

COWLEY
SO9714 Map 4
Green Dragon 🏅💻
(01242) 870271 – www.green-dragon-inn.co.uk
Off A435 S of Cheltenham at Elkstone, Cockleford sign; OS Sheet 163 map reference 970142; GL53 9NW

17th-c inn with character bars, separate restaurant, popular food, real ales and seats on terraces; well appointed bedrooms

So busy is this attractive and well run stone-fronted pub that you must book ahead to guarantee a table. The two beamed bars have plenty of character and a cosy, nicely old-fashioned feel, with big flagstones and wooden floorboards, candlelit tables and winter log fires in two stone fireplaces; staff are consistently friendly and helpful. Hook Norton Hooky, Sharps Doom Bar and guests such as Butcombe Bitter and St Austell Tribute on handpump, nine wines by the glass and 11 malt whiskies; background music. The furniture and the bar itself in the upper Mouse Bar were made by Robert Thompson – little mice run over the hand-carved tables, chairs and mantelpiece; there's also a small upstairs restaurant and a separate skittle alley. Bedrooms are comfortable and well appointed and breakfasts generous. There are seats outside on terraces and this is good walking country.

 Good food includes lunchtime sandwiches, smoked salmon tartare with dill crème fraîche, warm chicken liver and bacon salad with quail eggs and croutons, burger with toppings, caramelised onion and tomato chutney and fries, mushroom ravioli with pesto cream sauce, steak and kidney pudding, cajun salmon with jalapeno and pea risotto, beef bourguignon, and puddings such as banoffi pie and crème brûlée. *Benchmark main dish: roasted duck breast with plum and ginger sauce £16.95. Two-course evening meal £24.00.*

Buccaneer Holdings ~ Managers Simon and Nicky Haly ~ Real ale ~ Open 11-11; 12-10.30 Sun ~ Bar food 12-2.30 (3 Sat), 6-10; 12-3.30, 6-9 Sun ~ Restaurant ~ Children welcome ~ Dogs allowed in bar ~ Wi-fi ~ Bedrooms: /£105 *Recommended by Roy Shutz, Richard Tilbrook, Tom McLean, Chris and Val Ramstedt, Brian Glozier*

DURSLEY
ST7598 Map 4
Old Spot 🍺
(01453) 542870 – www.oldspotinn.co.uk
Hill Road; by bus station; GL11 4JQ

Unassuming and cheery town pub with a fine range of ales, regular beer festivals and good value lunchtime food

A splendid choice of drinks in this bustling town local includes up to eight real ales, 40 malt whiskies, three farm ciders, half a dozen wines by the glass and speciality spirits. On handpump, the beers include Otter Bitter and Uley Old Ric as regulars with guests that include Bespoke Round Robin, Plain Inncognito and Raw Citra Pale Ale; they hold a couple of annual beer festivals. The front door opens into a deep-pink small room with stools on shiny quarry tiles beside a pine-boarded bar counter, and old enamel beer signs on the walls and ceiling; there's a profusion of porcine paraphernalia. A small room leads off on the left and the little wood-floored room to the right has a stone fireplace. A step goes down to a cosy Victorian tiled snug and (to the right) a meeting room. The heated and covered garden has seats. Wheelchair access. Sister pub is the Old Badger in Eastington.

Tasty lunchtime-only food includes doorstep sandwiches (the soup-and-sandwich deal is popular), chicken liver pâté with onion chutney, trio of local sausages with onion gravy, spinach, walnut and sage cannelloni, burger with toppings, coleslaw and potato wedges, moroccan-style lamb tagine with couscous, salmon and smoked haddock fishcakes, and puddings such as blueberry cheesecake and a seasonal crumble. *Benchmark main dish: pie of the day £10.95.*

Free house ~ Licensee Ellie Sainty ~ Real ale ~ Open 11-11; 12-11 Sun ~ Bar food 12-6 (4 Sun); no evening meals ~ Children welcome away from bar area before 9pm ~ Dogs allowed in bar ~ Wi-fi *Recommended by Michael Snelgrove, PL, Mike Swan, Martin Jones*

EASTINGTON
Old Badger 🍺

SO7705   Map 4

(01453) 822892 – www.oldbadgerinn.co.uk
Alkerton Road, a mile from M5 junction 13; GL10 3AT

Friendly, traditionally furnished pub with plenty to look at, five real ales, tasty food and seats in attractive garden

Just two minutes from the busy M5, this is a friendly pub with an informal, easy-going feel. The split-level connected rooms feature two open fires and are traditionally furnished with built-in planked and cushioned wall seats, settles and farmhouse chairs around all sorts of tables on quarry tiles and floorboards. There are stone bottles, bookshelves, breweriana on red or cream walls, and even a stuffed badger. Sarah Hughes Dark Ruby Mild, Marstons Pedigree New World, Moles Tap, Uley Bitter and Wye Valley HPA on handpump, ten wines by the glass, a dozen malt whiskies and farm cider, served by helpful, smiling staff. The nicely landscaped garden has benches and picnic-sets on the terrace, lawn and under a covered gazebo; the flowering tubs and window boxes are pretty. Sister pub is the Old Spot in Dursley.

Tasty food includes lunchtime sandwiches, several tapas (from crispy whitebait through chicken satay with peanut sauce to mini breaded brie with chilli jam), vegetarian moussaka, smoked haddock and salmon fishcakes with crayfish and chive sauce, chicken stuffed with truffle and wild mushroom duxelle with shoe-string potatoes, burgers with toppings and chips, slow-cooked beef short rib with gremolata, and puddings such as white chocolate and mango tart and caramelised pineapple sponge pudding. *Benchmark main dish: pie of the day £10.95. Two-course evening meal £17.00.*

Free house ~ Licensees Ellie Sainty and Julie Gilborson ~ Real ale ~ Open 12-11; 12-9 Sun in winter ~ Bar food 12-2.30, 6-9; 12-4 Sun ~ Children welcome away from bar area ~ Dogs welcome ~ Wi-fi ~ Live music monthly Sat *Recommended by Michael Snelgrove, Alison and Michael Harper, John Harris, Clive and Fran Dutson*

FORD

SP0829 Map 4

Plough 🍺 🛏

(01386) 584215 – www.theploughinnatford.co.uk

B4077 Stow–Alderton; GL54 5RU

**16th-c inn in horse-racing country with a bustling atmosphere,
first class service, good food and well kept beer; bedrooms**

As this honey-coloured stone pub is opposite a well known racehorse
trainer's yard, many of the customers belong to the racing fraternity.
But visitors are just as warmly welcomed by the hands-on landlord and his
courteous staff, and the atmosphere is easy-going and chatty. The beamed
and stripped-stone bar has racing prints and photos, old settles and benches
around big tables on uneven flagstones, oak tables in a snug alcove, and open
fires and woodburning stoves. Darts, TV (for the races) and background
music. Donnington BB and SBA on handpump, seven wines by the glass
and a dozen malt whiskies. There are picnic-sets under parasols and pretty
hanging baskets at the front, and a large back garden with a children's play
fort. Bedrooms are comfortable (the quietest ones are away from the pub)
and there are views of the gallops. It gets packed on race days. Cotswold
Farm Park is nearby.

🍴 Using local meat and game, the popular food includes baguettes, scallops with
chorizo and lemon oil, confit of local pigeon and gressingham duck in tomato,
pepper and white bean casserole, honey and mustard-glazed ham with free-range eggs,
vegetarian wellington with wild mushroom sauce, a pie of the day, chicken curry, a fish
dish of the day, twice-roasted pork belly with black pudding fritter and cider gravy, and
puddings such as sticky toffee pudding and a seasonal crumble. *Benchmark main dish:
half a roast gressingham duck with bubble and squeak and orange sauce £16.95.
Two-course evening meal £18.50.*

Donnington ~ Tenant Craig Brown ~ Real ale ~ Open 9.30am-11pm ~ Bar food 12-2, 6-9; all
day Fri-Sun ~ Restaurant ~ Children welcome ~ Dogs welcome ~ Wi-fi ~ Bedrooms: $60/$80
Recommended by Richard Tilbrook, Mike and Mary Carter, Guy Vowles, Chris and Val Ramstedt

 GLOUCESTER

SO8318 Map 4

Café René 🍺

(01452) 309340 – www.caferene.co.uk

*Southgate Street; best to park in Blackfriars car park (Ladybellegate Street) and walk
through passageway – pub entrance is just across road; GL1 1TP*

**Unusual and interestingly placed bar with good value food all day,
and good choice of drinks**

This interesting bar, dating from the 17th c, is reached via a flagstoned
passageway beside the partly Norman church of St Mary de Crypt. There's
some stripped brick and timbering plus an internal floodlit well with water
trickling down into its depths, and a very subterranean feel – no windows,
black beams, dim lighting. The long bar counter is made of dozens of big
casks, and they keep five changing real ales tapped from the cask, from
breweries such as Elgoods, Goffs, Kennet & Avon, Kinver and Wychwood,
plus farm ciders and a good choice of wines by the glass (decoration consists
mainly of great banks of empty wine bottles); service remains friendly and
efficient even when really pushed. One antique panelled high-backed settle
joins the usual pub tables and wheelback chairs on carpet, and there's a
sizeable dining area. Well reproduced background music, a silenced games
machine and big-screen TV. There are picnic-sets under parasols out by the
churchyard. They hold a popular rhythm and blues festival at the end of July.

🍴 Good food – served all day – includes lunchtime sandwiches and wraps, garlic mushrooms in white wine and cream, prawn cocktail, a trio of sausages with wholegrain mustard mash and red onion gravy, fresh tagliatelle with tomato, cream cheese and basil sauce, beer-battered cod and chips, steak in ale pie, caribbean curried lamb, popular chargrilled dishes such as baby back ribs in barbecue sauce and cajun chicken, and puddings such as strawberry and champagne roulade and sticky toffee pudding. *Benchmark main dish: burgers with toppings, choice of potatoes and home-made salsa £8.50. Two-course evening meal £13.00.*

Free house ~ Licensee Paul Soden ~ Real ale ~ Open 11am–midnight (later Fri, Sat) ~ Bar food 12-10 ~ Restaurant ~ Wi-fi ~ Live music Weds, Fri evenings
Recommended by Chris and Angela Buckell, R T and J C Moggridge

GRETTON   SP0130   Map 4

Royal Oak 🍺

(01242) 604999 – www.royaloakgretton.co.uk
Off B4077 E of Tewkesbury; GL54 5EP

Golden-stone pub with light, airy rooms, open fires, six real ales, popular food and friendly atmosphere; good surrounding walks

Our readers enjoy their visits to this carefully refurbished pub – particularly in warm weather as the seats on the flower-filled back terrace have fine views over the village and across the valley to Dumbleton Hills and the Malverns; as well as a neat lawn, there's a children's play area and a bookable tennis court. Inside, it's light and airy with an easy-going atmosphere. The bar rooms have white-painted kitchen chairs and leather tub chairs around pale wood-topped tables on bare boards or flagstones, scatter cushions on settles, open fires and old Bugatti photographs and farm tools on pale walls above grey dados. The dining room and conservatory are stylish with high-backed chairs around big, chunky tables, antlers on one wall, a big central woodburning stove, candelabras and evening candlelight; background music. Box Steam Chuffin' Ale, Brakspears Oxford Gold, Cotswold Spring Stunner, Jennings Cocker Hoop, Ramsbury Gold and Wye Valley HPA on handpump, 14 wines by the glass and summer farm cider. Bantams roam freely, and in summer the steam trains from the Great Western Railway run along the bottom of the garden. Wheelchair access to bar, but not to the raised dining room.

🍴 Good, popular and attractively presented food includes sandwiches, a charcuterie platter, oriental shredded duck stir-fry with pancakes and a plum and hoisin sauce, a pie of the day, gnocchi with spinach, tomatoes, basil pesto and goats cheese, burgers such as spicy chicken with piri-piri mayonnaise, toppings and fries, confit of rare-breed pork with tarragon mash and cider cream sauce, barnsley lamb chop with minted red wine jus, and puddings such as lime and chocolate cheesecake and sticky toffee pudding with caramel sauce. *Benchmark main dish: beer-battered haddock and chips £12.00. Two-course evening meal £18.00.*

Free house ~ Licensee Rob Owen ~ Real ale ~ Open 10am–11pm ~ Bar food 12-2.30, 6-9; 12-8 Sun ~ Restaurant ~ Children welcome ~ Dogs allowed in bar
Recommended by Theocsbrian, R T and J C Moggridge, Chris and Angela Buckell

KILCOT   SO6925   Map 4

Kilcot Inn 🛏️

(01989) 720707 – www.kilcotinn.com
2.3 miles from M50 junction 3; B4221 towards Newent; GL18 1NG

Attractively reworked small country inn, kind staff, enjoyable local food and drink; bedrooms

The hard-working landlord and his courteous staff will make you most welcome in this carefully restored inn. The open-plan bar and dining areas have stripped beams, bare boards and dark flagstones, sunny bay-window seats, homely armchairs by one of the two warm woodburning stoves, tables with padded dining chairs, and daily papers. Stools line the brick counter where they keep four draught ciders and perry (with more by the bottle), as well as Marstons EPA and Wye Valley Butty Bach on handpump, 20 malt whiskies, local wine and organic fruit juice; TV and maybe background music. The front terrace has picnic-sets under cocktail parasols, with more out behind. This is a nice place to stay with light, airy, comfortable bedrooms; breakfasts are good with local bacon and free-range eggs. There's a smart shed for bicycles.

Enjoyable food using local, seasonal produce includes lunchtime sandwiches, chicken liver parfait with red onion chutney, spiced yoghurt chicken skewers with cucumber and mint dip, spinach and ricotta lasagne, a pie of the day, cider-battered fish and chips, saddle of rabbit with pistachio stuffing, potato rösti and rabbit sauce, beef bourguignon, and puddings such as dark chocolate and cognac torte with banana ice-cream and lime and lemon cheesecake with calvados glaze. *Benchmark main dish: slow-roast pork belly with smoked bacon, leek-stuffed potato skins and cider sauce £13.25. Two-course evening meal £19.50.*

Free house ~ Licensee Mark Lawrence ~ Real ale ~ Open 9am-11pm; best to phone for reduced Sunday openings Jan/Feb ~ Bar food 12-2.30, 6-9 (9.30 Thurs-Sat); 12-3 Sun ~ Restaurant ~ Children welcome ~ Dogs allowed in bar ~ Wi-fi ~ Bedrooms: £75/£85
Recommended by Mike Swan, Emma Scofield, R T and J C Moggridge, Mike and Mary Carter, Richard Kennell

LEIGHTERTON
Royal Oak 🕮 ♀

ST8290   Map 2

(01666) 890250 – www.royaloakleighterton.co.uk
Village signposted off A46 S of Nailsworth; GL8 8UN

Handsome country pub elegantly refurbished, with good choice of drinks, imaginative food and kind staff

Coming here is an all-round good experience. As one reader put it: 'a lovely pub in a smashing spot with a friendly landlord and good food to boot.' The rambling bar has plenty of nice touches, from the pair of log fireplaces facing each other (you have to look twice to be sure it's not a mirror) to the splendid heavy low-loading antique trolley holding the daily papers. Part parquet, part broad boards, with some stripped stone and some pastel paintwork, and carefully chosen furniture from stylish strung-seat dining chairs to soft sofas. Bath Gem and Butcombe Rare Breed on handpump, ten interesting wines by the glass and farm cider; background music. A sheltered side courtyard has teak and metal tables and chairs. Good disabled access. The pub is handy for Westonbirt Arboretum and walks near the quiet village.

Top quality food using the best local, seasonal produce includes lunchtime sandwiches, pigeon, ham hock and foie gras terrine with pear chutney, smoked salmon with fennel and lemon coleslaw, cauliflower, squash and chickpea tagine with pistachio and prune couscous and mint yoghurt, venison sausages with braised radicchio, pearl barley, pancetta and juniper hollandaise, duck breast with truffled savoy cabbage and fondant potato, and puddings such as quince and hazelnut crumble with bay leaf anglaise and white chocolate parfait with orange and honeycomb; they also offer a two- and three-course set menu. *Benchmark main dish: roast lamb rump with caponata and crispy polenta £16.00. Two-course evening meal £20.00.*

Free house ~ Licensees Paul and Antonia Whitbread ~ Real ale ~ Open 12-3, 6-11; 12-11 Sat; 12-9 Sun; closed Mon ~ Bar food 12-2, 6-9; 12-2.30, 6-9.30 Sat; 12-3 Sun; no food Sun evening except bank holidays ~ Restaurant ~ Children welcome ~ Dogs allowed in bar ~ Wi-fi
Recommended by Tom and Ruth Rees, Michael Doswell

LOWER SLAUGHTER

SP1622   Map 4

Slaughters Country Inn ♀ ⇌

(01451) 822143 – www.theslaughtersinn.co.uk
Village signposted off A429 Bourton-on-the-Water to Stow-on-the-Wold; GL54 2HS

Comfortable streamside inn in beautiful Cotswold village, enjoyable country food, real ales and attractive dining bar; bedrooms

The comfortable, stylish rooms in this extended stone-built inn make a fine base for exploring the area; some are in the main house and some across the courtyard. The spreading bar has a good mix of locals and visitors in several low-beamed linked rooms, plus well spaced tables on polished flagstones and a variety of seats from simple chairs to soft sofas. Log fires, medieval-motif curtains for the mullioned windows, shelves of board games, a few carefully placed landscapes or stuffed fish on cream or puce walls add up to understated refinement – and what really sets the style of the place is the thoroughly professional and efficient service. There's Brakspears and Wychwood Hobgoblin on handpump, and a dozen good wines by the glass. The smart evening restaurant looks over a sweep of lawn and the sheep pasture beyond. The terraces have tables and chairs under parasols and the little River Eye flows slowly along the front of the building.

Good, interesting food includes sandwiches, devilled cornish sardines with new potato and chive salad, chicken caesar salad, burger with cheese, fries and spiced tomato relish, a pie of the day, potato gnocchi with goats cheese and a herb crumb, cornish day-boat fish pie, and puddings such as sticky toffee pudding with toffee sauce and griottine cherry clafoutis and toasted almond ice-cream. *Benchmark main dish: beer-battered fish and chips £13.50. Two-course evening meal £24.00.*

Free house ~ Licensee Stuart Hodges ~ Real ale ~ Open 11-11 ~ Bar food 12-3, 6.30-9; afternoon tea 3-5.30 ~ Restaurant ~ Children welcome ~ Dogs allowed in bar and bedrooms ~ Wi-fi ~ Bedrooms: £95/£105   *Recommended by Richard Tilbrook, David Fowler, R K Phillips*

MORETON-IN-MARSH

SP1729   Map 4

Coach & Horses ◀

(01451) 830208 – www.coachandhorsesganborough.co.uk
Ganborough (on A424 about 2.5 miles N); GL56 0QZ

Well run country pub with a warm welcome, neatly kept rooms, local ale and traditional food

As this well looked-after country pub is so close to Donningtons Brewery, the BB and SBA on handpump are particularly well kept; nine wines by the glass too. It's a friendly place with a warm welcome from all. The bar has a winter log fire in a central chimneypiece, cushioned settles on flagstones, fish prints on the wall (the landlord is a keen fisherman, and Albert the huge stuffed pike was caught by his great-great-grandfather) and magazines; Pennell is the black labrador. Steps lead up to the stone-walled dining room with smart red high-backed chairs around pale wooden tables on carpet. The skittle alley doubles as a function room, and they still hope to add a conservatory; background music and darts. The big garden has wooden benches, summer parasols and a decked area. A new play area has a slide, sandpits and chalkboards for children; giant Jenga.

Using local, seasonal produce, the well thought-of food includes lunchtime sandwiches, chicken liver pâté with red onion marmalade, toasted goats cheese on a herb croûte, beer-battered haddock and chips, rare-breed sausage with wholegrain mustard mash and red onion gravy, rabbit pie, slow-cooked pork belly with dauphinoise potatoes, and puddings such as a crumble of the day and belgian chocolate torte; curry night is the first Tuesday of the month. *Benchmark main dish: steak in ale pie £12.95. Two-course evening meal £19.50.*

Donnington ~ Tenants Jonathan and Jane Kerr ~ Real ale ~ Open 12-3, 5.30-11; 12-9 Sun; closed Mon, winter Tues ~ Bar food 12-2, 6-9; 12-3 (2.30 winter) Sun ~ Restaurant ~ Children welcome ~ Dogs allowed in bar *Recommended by Edward May, Christian Mole*

NAILSWORTH
Weighbridge
ST8699 Map 4

(01453) 832520 – www.weighbridgeinn.co.uk
B4014 towards Tetbury; GL6 9AL

Super two-in-one pies served in cosy old-fashioned bar rooms, a fine choice of drinks, friendly service and a sheltered garden

A former landlord here also used to operate the nearby weighbridge – hence the pub's name. Our readers continue to enjoy their regular visits, particularly for the friendly welcome and their famous two-in-one pies. The relaxed bar has three cosily old-fashioned rooms with open fires, stripped-stone walls and antique settles, country chairs and window seats. The black-beamed ceiling of the lounge bar is thickly festooned with black ironware – sheep shears, gin traps, lamps and a large collection of keys, many from the old Longfords Mill opposite the pub. Upstairs is a raftered hayloft with an engaging mix of rustic tables. No noisy games machines or background music. Uley Old Spot, Wadworths 6X and a couple of guest beers such as Black Sheep and Cotswold Spring Codrington Best on handpump, 18 wines (and champagne and prosecco) by the glass, farm cider, 12 malt whiskies and 20 gins. A sheltered landscaped garden at the back has picnic-sets under umbrellas. Good disabled access and facilities.

The two-in-one pies (also available for home baking) come in a divided bowl – one half contains the filling of your choice (perhaps steak, kidney and stout, salmon in cream sauce, or root vegetables with beans and pulses in tomato sauce) with a pastry topping, the other half with home-made cauliflower cheese (or broccoli mornay or root vegetables). Also, lunchtime baguettes, a charcuterie board, omelettes and frittata, burger with toppings, coleslaw and fries, gammon with a duck egg and pineapple, cottage pie, and puddings such as orange and chocolate bread and butter pudding and crème brûlée. *Benchmark main dish: two-in-one pies £12.40. Two-course evening meal £17.50.*

Free house ~ Licensee Howard Parker ~ Real ale ~ Open 12-11 (10.30 Sun) ~ Bar food 12-9.30 ~ Restaurant ~ Children allowed away from the bars ~ Dogs welcome ~ Wi-fi
Recommended by Michael Snelgrove, Tom and Ruth Rees

NETHER WESTCOTE
Feathered Nest ★ 🌟 ♀ 🛏
SP2220 Map 4

(01993) 833030 – www.thefeatherednestinn.co.uk
Off A424 Burford to Stow-on-the-Wold; OX7 6SD

Caring service, a happy atmosphere, attractive surroundings and beautifully presented, inventive food and drink; lovely bedrooms

Of course, many customers are here for the exceptional restaurant food from a highly creative kitchen – but there is a companiable bar with three real ales and a few pubby dining choices too. This softly lit, largely stripped-stone bar has real saddles as bar stools (some of the country's best racehorse trainers live locally), a carved settle among other carefully chosen seats, dark flagstones and low beams. They have 26 wines by the glass from an impressive list, and the ales on handpump might include Cotswold Spring Codrington Codger, Purity Pure UBU and a guest beer; service is exemplary. The bar opens into an ochre-walled high-raftered room with deeply comfortable sofas by a vast log fire; background music and TV. Two attractively decorated dining rooms, both on two levels, have a pleasing mix of antique tables in varying sizes, and a lively, up-to-date atmosphere. A flagstoned terrace and heated shelter have teak tables and wicker armchairs, and a spreading lawn bounded by floodlit trees has groups of rustic seats, with the Evenlode Valley beyond. This is a lovely place to stay, in individually decorated, well equipped rooms, and breakfasts are delicious.

The imaginative and beautifully presented restaurant choices include haddock with scotch egg, red lentil dahl, chilli and coriander, pigeon with pastrami, red cabbage, celeriac, apple and flatbread, stone bass with pearl millet in squid ink, sea purslane and langoustine bisque, and pheasant with cep gnocchi, butternut squash, bacon and cumberland jelly. There are also more modest bar dishes such as chicken liver parfait with granola and pear chutney, a ham board with soft-boiled egg, pickles, chutneys and home-made bread, darne of hake with caper butter and sauté potatoes, and puddings such as sticky toffee pudding with lemon curd, pecans and clotted cream, and burnt cream with strawberries, vanilla and sorrel. *Benchmark main dish: burger with toppings, tomato relish and skinny chips £16.00. Two-course evening meal £25.00.*

Free house ~ Licensee Amanda Timmer ~ Real ale ~ Open 11.30-11 (8 Sun); closed Mon except bank holidays ~ Bar food 12-2.30, 6.30-9.30; 12-3.30 Sun; not Sun evening except bank holidays) ~ Restaurant ~ Children welcome but must be over 12 in bedrooms ~ Dogs allowed in bar ~ Wi-fi ~ Bedrooms: £150/£180 *Recommended by Martin and Karen Wake, Liz Bell, Bernard Stradling, Christian Mole*

NEWLAND
Ostrich 🏅 🍷 🍺

SO5509   Map 4

(01594) 833260 – www.theostrichinn.com

Off B4228 in Coleford; or can be reached from the A466 in Redbrook, by turn-off at the England–Wales border – keep bearing right; GL16 8NP

Super range of beers in welcoming country pub, with spacious bar, open fire and good interesting food

With a genuine welcome from the charming landlady and her helpful staff, and a roaring log fire, this partly 13th-c pub is just the place to head for on a cold day. There's a fine choice of real ales on handpump too, from breweries such as Bath, Otter, RHC, Wye Valley and a couple of changing guests. Also, several wines by the glass and a couple of farm ciders; newspapers to read, perhaps quiet background jazz and board games. The low-ceilinged bar is spacious but cosily traditional, with a chatty, relaxed atmosphere, creaky floors, window shutters, candles in bottles on the tables, miners' lamps on uneven walls, and comfortable furnishings that include cushioned window seats, wall settles and rod-backed country kitchen chairs. The walled garden has picnic-sets, with more out in front, and the pub is popular with walkers and their dogs; Alfie the pub lurcher (now 17) might be there to greet them. The church, known as the Cathedral of the Forest, is worth a visit.

Highly enjoyable food includes rabbit rillettes with rosemary jelly, duck and foie gras terrine with kumquat marmalade, steak in ale or wild mushroom pie, fresh smoked haddock with cream, egg and horseradish topped with dauphinoise potatoes, guinea fowl with calvados, smoked pancetta and sage cream sauce on potato rösti, stone bass fillet with chorizo, clam and saffron risotto, and puddings. *Benchmark main dish: salmon and spinach fishcakes with parsley sauce £12.50. Two-course evening meal £18.00.*

Free house ~ Licensee Kathryn Horton ~ Real ale ~ Open 12-3, 6.30-11; 12-3, 6-midnight Sat; 12-4, 6.30-10.30 Sun ~ Bar food 12-2.30, 6.30 (6 Sat)-9.30 ~ Restaurant ~ Children welcome ~ Dogs allowed in bar ~ Wi-fi *Recommended by Gordon and Ann Robinson, Miss B D Picton*

NORTH CERNEY   SP0208   Map 4
Bathurst Arms ♀ ⇔
(01285) 832150 – www.bathurstarms.com
A435 Cirencester–Cheltenham; GL7 7BZ

Bustling inn with beamed bar, open fires, real ales and wines by the glass and interesting food; comfortable bedrooms

New licensees have taken over this handsome 17th-c inn and have carried out some refurbishments. The heart of the place remains the original beamed and panelled bar with its convivial atmosphere, flagstones, attractive medley of old tables and chairs, old-fashioned window seats and a fireplace at each end – one is huge and houses an open woodburner. An oak-floored room off here has country tables and winged high-backed settles forming a few booths; background music, TV and board games. The restaurant has another woodburning stove. Hook Norton Bitter, Ramsbury Gold and a changing guest beer on handpump and 23 good wines by the glass. The garden has the River Chun running through it, picnic-sets and plenty of shrubs. Bedrooms are comfortable and breakfasts good. Cerney House Gardens are worth a visit and there are lots of surrounding walks in lovely countryside.

Good food includes lunchtime sandwiches, duck leg and foie gras terrine with caramelised figs, roasted beetroot, horseradish and rosemary risotto, trio of local sausages with wholegrain mustard mash and red onion gravy, moules frites, creamy chicken and mushroom pasta, beer-battered fish and chips, rump steak with béarnaise sauce, and puddings such as vanilla panna cotta with poached pear and raspberry coulis and dark chocolate fondant with white chocolate ice-cream. *Benchmark main dish: burger with toppings and chips £12.00. Two-course evening meal £20.00.*

Free house ~ Licensees Graeme and Anita Brister ~ Real ale ~ Open 11-11 (10.30 Sun) ~ Bar food 12-3, 6-9 (9.30 Fri); 12-9.30 Sat; 12-4 Sun ~ Restaurant ~ Children welcome ~ Dogs allowed in bar and bedrooms ~ Wi-fi ~ Bedrooms: £75/£85 *Recommended by Lisa Kehoe, Giles and Annie Francis, Neil and Anita Christopher, Richard and Patricia Jefferson, Richard Tilbrook, W M Lien, Dennis and Doreen Haward, R T and J C Moggridge*

NORTHLEACH   SP1114   Map 4
Wheatsheaf ⍾◎ ♀ ⇔
(01451) 860244 – www.cotswoldswheatsheaf.com
West End; the inn is on your left as you come in following the sign off A429, just SW of the junction with A40; GL54 3EZ

Attractive stone inn with contemporary food, real ales, candles, fresh flowers and a relaxed atmosphere; stylish bedrooms

This is a lovely little town with a fine old market square – and this civilised former coaching inn fits in very nicely. Bustling and friendly, it has a cheerful mix of customers who pop in and out all day. The airy, big-windowed, linked rooms have high ceilings, antique and contemporary artwork, church candles and fresh flowers, an attractive mix of dining chairs, big leather button-back settles and stools around wooden tables, flagstones in the central bar, wooden floors laid with turkish rugs in the airy dining rooms, and three open fires. Ales on handpump come from Bath, Barnsley, Otter and Sharps and they keep a dozen wines by the glass from a fantastic list of around 300 and local cider; background music, TV and board games. There are seats in the pretty back garden and they can arrange fishing on the River Coln. The comfortable bedrooms are individually styled and breakfast highly rated. Dogs are genuinely welcomed – they even keep a jar of pigs' ears behind the bar for them.

 From a seasonal menu, the highly rewarding, all-day food includes breakfasts for non-residents (8-10am), twice-baked cheddar soufflé with spinach and grain mustard, devilled kidneys on toast, jerusalem artichoke risotto with parmesan, beer-battered whiting with fries, pigeon pie with pearl onions, calves liver with tomato sauce, anchovies, capers and crispy sage, saffron cod with clams, smoked aubergine and romano peppers, and puddings such as white chocolate mousse with berry compote and sticky toffee pudding with honey and ginger ice-cream. *Benchmark main dish: whole lemon sole with lemon and caper butter £20.00. Two-course evening meal £21.00.*

Free house ~ Licensees Sam and Georgina Pearman ~ Real ale ~ Open 8am-11pm ~ Bar food 12-3, 6-10.30; 12-4, 6-10 Sun ~ Children welcome ~ Dogs allowed in bar and bedrooms ~ Wi-fi ~ Bedrooms: £130/£150 *Recommended by Richard Tilbrook, Tony and Rachel Schendel, Guy Vowles, Fiona Smith, Tracey and Stephen Groves, Alan and Angela Scouller, Dave Braisted*

OAKRIDGE LYNCH

SO9103 Map 4

Butchers Arms

(01285) 760371 – www.butchersarmsoakridge.com

Off Eastcombe–Bisley Road E of Stroud; GL6 7NZ

Bustling country pub with nice old bars and dining room, real ales, food cooked by the landlady and seats in a big garden

In a small village surrounded by lovely countryside and good walks, this well run 18th-c pub has picnic-sets and other seats and tables in a big garden overlooking a valley. Inside, it's relaxed and friendly and the beamed bar has an open fire in a big stone fireplace with large copper pans to each side, an attractive medley of chapel and other country chairs around tables of various sizes on wooden floorboards, and modern art on exposed stone walls. Stools line the central counter where they keep Wadworths 6X, Horizon and IPA on handpump and several wines by the glass. The dining room is similarly furnished, with hunting prints and old photos on pale walls above a grey dado, a longcase clock and stone bottles on window sills. They have a self-catering cottage next to the pub.

Cooked by the landlady, the highly thought-of food includes lunchtime sandwiches, thai fishcakes with chilli sauce, pork and chicken terrine with apple chutney, moules frites, cottage pie, spaghetti carbonara, stilton and leek sausage with onion gravy, chicken with spicy tomato sauce and sauté potatoes, 28-day-aged irish steaks with a choice of sauces, and puddings such as chocolate brownie and lemon tart. *Benchmark main dish: irish beef burger with toppings, coleslaw and fries £9.95. Two-course evening meal £18.75.*

Wadworths ~ Tenants Philip and Alison McLaughlin ~ Real ale ~ Open 12-3, 6-11; 12-11 Sat, Sun; closed Mon except bank holidays ~ Bar food 12-2, 6-9; not Sun evening, Mon ~ Restaurant ~ Children welcome away from main bar ~ Dogs allowed in bar ~ Wi-fi
Recommended by Andrew Stone, Rob Anderson, David and Stella Martin

OLDBURY-ON-SEVERN   ST6092 Map 2

Anchor ♀ ◀ £

(01454) 413331 – www.anchorinnoldbury.co.uk

Village signposted from B4061; BS35 1QA

**Friendly country pub with tasty bar food, a fine choice of drinks
and a pretty garden with hanging baskets; bedrooms**

A fine choice of drinks in this well run, very popular village pub includes
real ales on handpump such as Bass, Butcombe Bitter, St Austell Proper
Job and Trelawny, a dozen wines by the glass, three farm ciders and around
80 malt whiskies with helpful tasting notes; service from cheerful staff is
good. The neatly kept lounge has modern beams and stonework, a variety
of tables including an attractive oval oak gate-leg, cushioned window seats,
winged seats against the wall, oil paintings by a local artist and a big log fire.
The bar has old photographs and farming and fishing bric-a-brac on the walls.
Diners can eat in the lounge, the bar area or in the dining room at the back
(good for larger groups); the menu is the same everywhere. The garden is
pretty in summer, when the hanging baskets and window boxes are lovely;
boules. Wheelchair access and a disabled lavatory. You can walk to the River
Severn and along numerous footpaths and bridleways; nearby St Arilda's
church is interesting, on an odd little knoll, with wild flowers among the
gravestones (the primroses and daffodils make quite a show in spring).

Enjoyable food includes lunchtime ciabattas, crayfish mayonnaise, deep-fried
camembert with berry sauce, butternut squash, red onion and cranberry tagine,
home-baked ham with bubble and squeak and free-range eggs, lamb curry, chicken with
rösti potato, cognac, mushroom and parsley sauce, smoked haddock and salmon pie, and
puddings such as warm lemon polenta cake with lemon syrup and crème brûlée; they
also offer a two- and three-course set menu (not Fri evening, all Sat or lunch Sun).
Benchmark main dish: home-made pies £9.95. Two-course evening meal £13.50.

Free house ~ Licensees Michael Dowdeswell and Mark Sorrell ~ Real ale ~ Open 11.30-
2.30, 6-11; 11.30am-midnight Fri, Sat; 12-11 Sun ~ Bar food 12-2 (2.30 Sat, 3 Sun), 6-9 ~
Restaurant ~ Children in dining room only ~ Dogs allowed in bar ~ Bedrooms: £45/£75
Recommended by Chris and Angela Buckell, Caroline Prescott, Chris and Val Ramstedt

SHEEPSCOMBE   SO8910 Map 4

Butchers Arms £

(01452) 812113 – www.butchers-arms.co.uk

*Village signed off B4070 NE of Stroud; or A46 N of Painswick (but narrow lanes);
GL6 7RH*

**Refurbished and extended country pub with open fire and
woodburner, plenty to look at, several real ales and enjoyable food;
fine views**

They've carefully extended the bar and restaurant in this bustling country
pub without losing any of its character. One half of the bar has parquet
flooring, the other has old quarry tiles – as well as a woodburning stove,
farmhouse chairs and stools around scrubbed tables, two big bay windows
with cushioned seats, low beams clad with horsebrasses, delft shelves lined
with china, brass and copper cups, lamps, blow torches and even a pitchfork,
and walls hung with photos of the village and surrounding area, and hunting
prints. Leading off here is a new high-ceilinged room with fine exposed-stone
walls hung with maps of local walks (there are many) and wheelback and
mate's chairs around tables on bare boards. The more formal restaurant is
carpeted and has an open log fire. Otter Bitter, Prescott Hill Climb and Wye

Valley Butty Bach on handpump, several wines by the glass and Weston's cider and perry; daily papers, darts, chess, cribbage and draughts. The view over the lovely surrounding steep beechwood valley is terrific, and the seats outside make the most of it. The area was apparently once a hunting ground for Henry VIII.

 Reliably good food includes lunchtime sandwiches, chicken liver pâté with plum and apple chutney, tempura king prawns with sweet chilli dip, sharing platters, butternut squash, leek and thyme risotto topped with goats cheese, ham and free-range eggs, real ale and cumberland sausages with grain mustard mash and onion gravy, a pie of the week, daily specials and puddings. *Benchmark main dish: burger with toppings and fries £10.50. Two-course evening meal £16.50.*

Free house ~ Licensees Mark and Sharon Tallents ~ Real ale ~ Open 11.30-3, 6.30-11; 11.30-11.30 Sat; 12-10.30 Sun ~ Bar food 12-2.30, 6.30-9.30; all day Sat; 12-6 Sun ~ Restaurant ~ Children welcome ~ Dogs allowed in bar ~ Wi-fi *Recommended by Mr and Mrs J Gittins, Neil and Anita Christopher, Guy Vowles, M G Hart, R T and J C Moggridge*

SOUTHROP
Swan ⭐ ♀
SP2003 Map 4

(01367) 850205 – www.theswanatsouthrop.co.uk
Off A361 Lechlade–Burford; GL7 3NU

Creeper-covered pub with proper village bar, two dining rooms, imaginative food and a fine choice of drinks

The food in this creeper-covered 17th-c inn is so popular and so very good that you must book ahead to be sure of a table. But this is no straightforward dining pub – there's a chatty bar with a bustling, informal atmosphere, stools against the counter, simple tables and chairs and drinks that include Bath Gem, Hook Norton Hooky and Sharps Doom Bar on handpump and 15 wines by the glass from a carefully chosen list. The low-ceilinged front dining rooms have open fires, all manner of tweed-upholstered dining chairs around a nice mix of old tables, cushions on settles, rugs on flagstones, nightlights, candles and lots of fresh flowers. There's a skittle alley, and tables in the sheltered back garden. They have self-catering cottages to let. This is a very attractive village-green setting and the surrounding walks are lovely.

 Using home-grown salads and vegetables and other top quality local, seasonal produce, the creative food includes lunchtime sandwiches, mackerel with miso, pea shoots, sesame and cucumber, game terrine with quince jelly, scotch egg with wild garlic and goats cheese ravioli and skinny chips, asian beef salad with chilli, coriander, sesame, hazelnuts and nam jim sauce, pork fillet wrapped in prosciutto with saffron risotto, and puddings such as rhubarb crème brûlée and sticky toffee pudding. *Benchmark main dish: burger with toppings and chips £12.50. Two-course evening meal £24.00.*

Free house ~ Licensee Dominic Abbott ~ Real ale ~ Open 12-3, 6-11; 12-11 Sat (12-3, 6-11 in winter); 12-4 Sun; ~ Bar food 12-2.30 (3 weekends), 6-9 (9.30 Fri, Sat) ~ Restaurant ~ Children welcome ~ Dogs welcome ~ Wi-fi *Recommended by Mike and Mary Carter, Tracey and Stephen Groves, Alun and Jennifer Evans*

STANTON
Mount ⭐
SP0634 Map 4

(01386) 584316 – www.themountinn.co.uk
Village signposted off B4632 SW of Broadway; keep on past village on no-through road uphill, bear left; WR12 7NE

Bustling pub in a lovely spot with fine views, friendly licensees and good, popular food

There are such lovely walks (on the Cotswold Way National Trail and the new Wyche Way) around this friendly 17th-c pub that, at lunchtime in particular, there are several walkers and maybe their dogs (they keep dog biscuits behind the bar). In warm weather, you can sit on the terrace and enjoy the fantastic view over the honey-coloured stone house and the Vale of Evesham towards the welsh mountains; more seats in the peaceful garden and also boules. Inside, the bars have low ceilings, heavy beams and flagstones and a big log fire in an inglenook fireplace. The restaurant's large picture windows make the most of the view. Donnington BB and SBA on handpump served by cheerful staff, and a good choice of wines by the glass; darts, board games.

 Good, popular food includes lunchtime baguettes, chicken liver parfait with red onion marmalade, a plate of cured meats and manchego with quince jelly, mushroom stroganoff, gloucester old spot sausages with cheddar mash and rich jus, gammon and free-range eggs, sirloin steak with café de paris butter, and puddings such as apple crumble and chocolate brownie. *Benchmark main dish: beer-battered fish and chips £12.50. Two-course evening meal £20.00.*

Donnington ~ Tenants Karl and Pip Baston ~ Real ale ~ Open 12-3, 6-11; 12-11 Sat, Sun (12-3, 6-11 in winter); closed Sun evening, Mon in winter ~ Bar food 12-2, 6-9 ~ Restaurant ~ Well behaved children welcome ~ Dogs welcome ~ Wi-fi
Recommended by Guy Vowles, Richard Tilbrook, M G Hart, S Holder

STOW-ON-THE-WOLD   SP1925   Map 4

Porch House 🍽️⭐🍷🛏️

(01451) 870048 – www.porch-house.co.uk
Digbeth Street; GL54 1BN

Lovely old inn with much character, carefully refurbished bars and dining areas, friendly, courteous staff and a fine choice of drinks and food; comfortable bedrooms

In a lovely small town, this is an appealing pub that, although mainly 17th-c, has some striking features and parts of great antiquity, including thousand-year-old timbers (there was some sort of inn on the site in 947). It's been beautifully restored, creating plenty of space for both drinking and dining with beams (some hop-draped), big flagstones or bare floorboards, exposed stone walls and open fireplaces. The bar areas have all sorts of cushioned wooden and upholstered chairs, little stools and settles with scatter cushions around myriad tables, church candles and lanterns, books on shelves and stone bottles on window sills and two woodburning stoves; the cosy snug is similarly furnished but has sofas and armchairs too. Brakspears Bitter and Oxford Gold, Ringwood Boondoggle and Revisionist Canadian Red on handpump, good wines by the glass, home-brewed ginger ale and home-made lemonade. There's a dining room with upholstered, tall-backed chairs (some are strikingly blue-cushioned), and also a conservatory. The atmosphere throughout is informal and gently civilised. A raised terrace has rattan chairs and cushioned wall benches around rustic tables intermingled with more contemporary seats. Bedrooms are individually designed and stylish and breakfasts particularly good.

🍽️ Enjoyable food using local, seasonal produce includes lunchtime sandwiches, ham hock terrine with quail egg and tarragon, treacle-cured salmon with toasted soda bread, butternut squash and cheese gratin with a mushroom crust, burger with chorizo, cheddar, corn relish and skin-on chips, guinea fowl breast with confit leg, bacon, chestnuts and parsnips, grilled chicken with béarnaise or pepper sauce, slow-roasted tomato and chips, salmon fillet with roasted fennel and caper vinaigrette, and puddings such as chocolate brownie with toffee sauce and apple and berry crumble. *Benchmark main dish: local venison haunch on lentils with braised beetroot and red wine sauce £17.50. Two-course evening meal £21.00.*

Free house ~ Licensee Alex Davenport-Jones ~ Real ale ~ Open 8am-midnight (1am Sat); 8am-10.30pm Sun ~ Bar food 12-3, 6.30-9.30; 12-4, 6.30-8.30 Sun ~ Restaurant ~ Children welcome ~ Dogs allowed in bar and bedrooms ~ Wi-fi ~ Bedrooms: /£99
Recommended by Belinda Stamp, Nick Sharpe

TETBURY   ST8494 Map 4
Gumstool
(01666) 890391 – www.calcotmanor.co.uk
Part of Calcot Manor Hotel; A4135 W of town, just E of junction with A46; GL8 8YJ

Civilised bar with relaxed atmosphere, super choice of drinks and enjoyable food; bedrooms

Our readers continue to enjoy very much their visits to this bar-brasserie (which is attached to the very smart Calcot Manor Hotel); of course, it isn't a traditional pub, but it does keep up to four real ales on handpump and the atmosphere is informal and relaxed. The stylish layout is cleverly divided to give a feeling of intimacy without losing the overall sense of contented bustle: flagstones, elegant wooden dining chairs and tables, well chosen pictures and drawings on mushroom-coloured walls, and leather tub armchairs and stools in front of the big log fire. Butcombe Bitter, Hook Norton Hooky and Sharps Doom Bar on handpump, two dozen interesting wines by the glass and several malt whiskies; background music. Westonbirt Arboretum is not far away.

Given the civilised setting, the prices are fair and the food is first class: twice-baked arbroath smokie and montgomery cheddar cheese soufflé, baked scallops with spinach, prosciutto and mornay sauce, local sausages with red onion jam, corn-fed chicken with rösti potatoes and mushrooms, gurnard with brown shrimps, tomatoes and spinach, duck breast with carrot purée, braised fennel and promegranate, and puddings such as white chocolate mousse with bitter chocolate tuile and coconut and vanilla rice pudding with candied pineapple. *Benchmark main dish: rare-breed burger £15.00. Two-course evening meal £24.00.*

Free house ~ Licensees Paul Sadler and Richard Ball ~ Real ale ~ Open 11-11 ~ Bar food 12-2 (2.30 Sat), 6-9.30; 12-4, 6-9 Sun ~ Children welcome ~ Dogs allowed in bedrooms ~ Wi-fi ~ Bedrooms: /£280 *Recommended by KC, Bernard Stradling, Mr and Mrs P R Thomas, Dr and Mrs A K Clarke*

TETBURY   ST8993 Map 4
Royal Oak
(01666) 500021 – www.theroyaloaktetbury.co.uk
Cirencester Road; GL8 8EY

Golden-stone former coaching inn with a good mix of locals and visitors, a rambling bar, upstairs dining room and seats outside; bedrooms

The renovations to this lovely 18th-c building have been done with great care and thought, and original features blend easily with up-to-date touches. But what stands out most to visitors is the genuine welcome from the helpful, courteous staff and the easy-going, friendly atmosphere – this extends to families and dogs too. The open-plan, rambling bar has a roaring log fire at one end, several snug areas, green leather padded built-in wall seats, stools and a variety of chairs around dark tables on wide floorboards, elbow tables dotted here and there, and a handsome carved counter where they serve Bath Gem, Milk Street Zig Zag, Moor So'Hop, Severn Vale Dursley Steam Bitter and Stroud Tom Long on handpump, ten wines by the glass, a farm cider, interesting spirits and a good choice of tea and coffee; the pretty piano does get used. The beamed and timbered dining room is upstairs with a fine raftered ceiling, dark polished furniture on more wide floorboards, creamy yellow paintwork and candlelight. Outside there are picnic-sets under parasols on terraces and a lawn. The bedrooms – spotlessly kept and full of character – are across a cobbled courtyard, and breakfasts highly thought of and generous. You can walk from the doorstep into the woods.

Well presented and extremely good, the food includes lunchtime sandwiches, pheasant, pistachio and venison terrine wrapped in streaky bacon with celeriac remoulade, smoked fish and spring onion boudain with sweetcorn purée and port reduction, chopped salad with warm chicken, crispy bacon, free-range egg, avocado and shaved parmesan, porcini mushroom and herb burger with seeded coleslaw and fries, beer-battered fish of the day with home-made tartare sauce, and puddings such as ginger sponge with caramel sauce and peanut butter tart with peanut brittle. *Benchmark main dish: rare-breed burger with toppings, coleslaw and fries £10.00. Two-course evening meal £19.00.*

Free house ~ Licensees Kate Lewis and Chris York ~ Real ale ~ Open 11-11 (11.30 Fri, Sat); 12-11 Sun ~ Bar food 12-2.30, 5-9.30; 12-5 Sun ~ Restaurant ~ Children welcome until 8pm (unless in restaurant) ~ Dogs allowed in bar and bedrooms ~ Wi-fi ~ Live music Sun (best to phone) ~ Bedrooms: £75/£85 *Recommended by Caroline Prescott, Edward May, Nick Sharpe*

UPPER ODDINGTON   SP2225   Map 4
Horse & Groom ★ ⊚ ♀

(01451) 830584 – www.horseandgroom.uk.com
Village signposted from A436 E of Stow-on-the-Wold; GL56 0XH

Pretty 16th-c Cotswold inn with enterprising food, plenty of wines by the glass, local beers and comfortable, character bars; lovely bedrooms

All aspects of this very well run pub are praised by our readers – particularly the genuine welcome from the hands-on, helpful landlord, Mr Jackson. The bar has pale polished flagstones, a handsome antique oak box settle among other more modern seats, some nice armchairs at one end, oak beams in the ochre ceiling, stripped-stone walls and a log fire in the inglenook fireplace; the comfortable lounge is similarly furnished. Cotswold Lion Best in Show, Prescott Hill Climb and Wye Valley Bitter on handpump, 25 wines (including champagne and sweet wines) by the glass, 20 malt whiskies and gin, vodka, lager and cider from the local Cotswold Brewing Company. There are seats and tables under green parasols on the terrace and in the pretty garden. Some of the individually styled, different sized bedrooms are in the main house, some are in the 'cottage'; first class breakfasts.

Making everything in-house using local, seasonal produce, the interesting food includes sandwiches and ciabattas, lemon potato pancake with smoked salmon and a poached egg, confit duck spring roll with tamarind dipping sauce, rare-breed sausages with wholegrain mustard mash and red onion marmalade gravy, roast butternut squash, wild mushroom and spinach risotto, lamb chump with honey-roast parsnips, fondant potato and thyme jus, and puddings such as pistachio parfait with berry compote and orange and cinnamon crème brûlée. *Benchmark main dish: pie of the day £15.00. Two-course evening meal £23.00.*

Free house ~ Licensees Simon and Sally Jackson ~ Real ale ~ Open 12-3, 5.30-11; 12-3, 6.30-10.30 Sun ~ Bar food 12-2, 6.30 (7 Sun)-9 ~ Children welcome ~ Dogs allowed in bar ~ Wi-fi ~ Bedrooms: £85/£110 *Recommended by Richard Tilbrook, Michael Doswell, Katharine Cowherd, Theocsbrian, Bernard Stradling, R L Borthwick*

WESTON SUBEDGE   SP1241   Map 4

Seagrave Arms 🏠 ⚓ 🛏

(01386) 840192 – www.seagravearms.co.uk

B4632; GL55 6QH

Handsome stone inn with several little bars and dining rooms, charming hands-on owner, friendly staff and impressive food; contemporary bedrooms

Being close to the Cotswold Way, this golden-stone Georgian country inn is popular with walkers and their dogs – especially at lunchtime. There's a cosy little bar with a chatty atmosphere, an open fire, ancient flagstones, half-panelled walls and padded window seats, Hook Norton Lion and Ringwood Boondoggle on handpump and 14 wines (plus prosecco and champagne) by the glass, served by helpful, friendly staff; background music, TV and board games. The two dining rooms have an appealing variety of wooden chairs and tables on floorboards. Outside, there are wicker chairs and tables on neat gravel at the front of the building and more seats in the back garden. Most of the well equipped, modern bedrooms are in the main house, with others in the converted stables; breakfasts are good and hearty.

Cooked by the landlord using sustainable local produce, with a sensibly short menu supplemented by daily specials, the rewarding food includes lunchtime sandwiches, foie gras with rhubarb, granola and mustard seeds, sea bream fillet, tartare, oyster, cucumber and nasturtium, pearl barley and spelt risotto with butternut squash, nuts and crispy rice, corn-fed chicken with mushrooms, peas, truffle and smoked almonds, pigeon with salt-baked jerusalem artichoke, smoked bacon, apple and a spring roll, and puddings such as banana sticky toffee pudding with salted butterscotch and popcorn ice-cream and crème brûlée doughnut. *Benchmark main dish: 28-day-aged scotch short rib with smoked garlic and chips £19.00. Two-course evening meal £20.00.*

Free house ~ Licensees Hannah Brown and Newstead Sawyer ~ Real ale ~ Open 12-11; 12-9 Sun ~ Bar food 12-2.30, 6-9.30; 12-9.30 Sat; 12-8 Sun ~ Restaurant ~ Children welcome ~ Dogs allowed in bar and bedrooms ~ Wi-fi ~ Bedrooms: £70/£105
Recommended by Nick Sharpe, Alison and Michael Harper

Also Worth a Visit in Gloucestershire

Besides the fully inspected pubs, you might like to try these pubs that have been recommended to us and described by readers. Do tell us what you think of them: feedback@goodguides.com

ALDERTON   SP9933

Gardeners Arms (01242) 620257
Beckford Road, off B4077 Tewkesbury–Stow; GL20 8NL Attractive thatched Tudor pub with enjoyable pubby food from lunchtime sandwiches up, breakfast from 9.30am, good welcoming service, Sharps Doom Bar and two or three well kept guests, decent wines by the glass, various modernised areas, one featuring an old well, log fire; live music Fri, monthly quiz; children welcome, dogs allowed in some parts, tables on sheltered terrace, good-sized garden with boules, open (and food) all day Sun. *(Emma Scofield)*

ALDSWORTH
SP1510

Sherborne Arms (01451) 844346

B4425 Burford–Cirencester; GL54 3RB
Rural pub (former 17th-c farmhouse) set
down from the road and run by same family
since 1984; enjoyable good value home-made
food including signature lamb and apricot
casserole, three real ales, proper cider,
beams, stripped stone and log fire, smallish
bar and big dining area, conservatory, games/
function room; background music; children
and dogs welcome, disabled access, pleasant
front garden with smokers' shelter, closed
Sun evening, Mon. *(Alan and Angela Scouller)*

AMBERLEY
SO8401

Amberley Inn (01453) 872565

*Steeply off A46 Stroud–Nailsworth –
gentler approach from N Nailsworth;
GL5 5AF* Popular well located old stone inn
with beautiful views and good local walks,
two comfortable bars, snug and more formal
restaurant, well kept Stroud ales, enjoyable
locally sourced food from bar snacks up
(special diets catered for), friendly helpful
staff; surcharge if paying by credit card;
children and dogs welcome, side terrace and
back garden, 11 bedrooms. *(Neil and Anita
Christopher)*

AMPNEY CRUCIS
SP0701

Crown of Crucis (01285) 851806

A417 E of Cirencester; GL7 5RS
Modernised roadside inn with spacious
split-level bar, beams and log fires, good
choice of food including competitively priced
dish of the day (weekday lunchtimes), a
beer named for them from Wickwar and a
guest, decent house wines, pleasant efficient
service; children and dogs welcome, disabled
facilities, lots of tables out on grass by
car park, quiet modern bedrooms around
courtyard, good breakfast, cricket pitch over
stream, open all day. *(R K Phillips, Neil and
Anita Christopher, R L Borthwick)*

ASHLEWORTH QUAY
SO8125

Boat (01452) 700272

*Ashleworth signposted off A417 N of
Gloucester; quay signed from village;
GL19 4HZ* Unpretentious tiny alehouse
reopened under friendly new licensees;
front flagstoned parlour with built-in settle
by scrubbed deal table, old-fashioned
kitchen range, elderly fireside chairs, mats
on flagstones, cribbage and dominoes, back
quarry-tiled dining room with fireplace,
cosy snug, up to ten mostly local ales and
around eight ciders, pubby food from rolls
up; children, dogs and muddy boots welcome,
tricky for wheelchairs (but staff willing to
help), sunny crazy-paved front courtyard,
more seats at side of building, River Severn
moorings, open all day summer, closed Mon
and Weds lunchtime in winter. *(Edward May)*

AUST
ST5788

Boars Head (01454) 632278

*0.5 miles from M48 junction 1,
off Avonmouth Road; BS35 4AX*
16th-c village pub handy for the 'old' Severn
bridge, Marstons-related ales and decent
house wines, well priced food including
deals, good friendly service, linked rooms
and alcoves, beams, some stripped stone
and huge log fire, old prints and bric-a-brac;
background music, free wi-fi; children (in
eating area) and dogs (in bar), wheelchair
access, attractive sheltered garden, covered
area for smokers, open all day Sun with food
till 4pm. *(Bruce Horne)*

AYLBURTON
SO6101

Cross (01594) 842823

High Street; GL15 6DE Popular family-
run village pub, good choice of food from
sandwiches and sharing plates through pub
favourites to daily specials, changing ales
such as Bath, Butcombe and Wye Valley,
several wines by the glass and a dozen
whiskies, welcoming helpful staff, open-plan
layout with split-level flagstoned bar, beams,
modern furniture alongside high-backed
settles, old local photographs, woodburners
in large stone fireplaces, high-raftered
dining room; free wi-fi; children and dogs
welcome, wheelchair access from car park,
pleasant garden with play area, open all day
Fri-Sun. *(Lindy Andrews)*

BIBURY
SP1006

Catherine Wheel (01285) 740250

*Arlington; B4425 NE of Cirencester;
GL7 5ND* Bright cheerful dining pub,
enjoyable fresh food from sandwiches and
pizzas up, well kept Hook Norton, Sharps and
a guest, friendly attentive service, open-plan
main bar and smaller back rooms, low beams,
stripped stone, log fires, raftered dining
room; children and dogs welcome, picnic-sets
in front and in good-sized garden, famously
beautiful village, handy for country and
riverside walks, four bedrooms, open (and
food) all day. *(Jo Garnett)*

BISLEY
SO9006

Bear (01452) 770265

*Village signed off A419 E of Stroud;
GL6 7BD* New management for this
interesting 17th-c colonnaded inn (originally
a courthouse); L-shaped bar with low ceiling,
old oak settles, brass and copper implements
around extremely wide stone fireplace,
five well kept ales including Butcombe and
Charles Wells, enjoyable pubby food, friendly
staff, separate stripped-stone family area;
outside gents', ladies' upstairs; dogs welcome,
small flagstoned courtyard, stone mounting
blocks in garden across quiet road, one
bedroom, open all day Sun. *(Jo Garnett)*

BOURTON-ON-THE-WATER SP1621
Coach & Horses (01451) 798478
A429 Stow Road; GL54 2HN New management and refurbishment for this old roadside inn, ales such as Hook Norton Lion and Sharps Doom Bar in small convivial bar, enjoyable food and good friendly service, separate restaurant; TV; children and dogs (in bar) welcome, outside seating, five bedrooms in former stables, open all day. *(Peter and Jean Hoare)*

BRIMPSFIELD SO9413
★Golden Heart (01242) 870261
Nettleton Bottom (not shown on road maps, so instead we list the pub under the name of the nearby village); on A417 N of the Brimpsfield turning northbound; GL4 8LA Traditional old roadside inn with low-ceilinged bar divided into five cosy areas, log fire in huge inglenook, exposed stone walls and wood panelling, well worn built-in settles and other old-fashioned furnishings, brass items, typewriters and banknotes, parlour on right with decorative fireplace leading into further room, four well kept ales such as Brakspears, Cotswold Lion, Jennings and Ringwood, several wines by the glass, popular sensibly priced food from extensive blackboard menu including unusual choices like alpaca, kangaroo and buffalo, friendly staff; children and dogs welcome, seats and tables on suntrap terrace with pleasant valley views, nearby walks, two barn-conversion bedrooms, open all day weekends and school holidays. *(Guy Vowles, Gordon and Jenny Quick, Tom McLean, Ian Herdman, Richard Tilbrook, Giles and Annie Francis)*

BROAD CAMPDEN SP1537
★Bakers Arms (01386) 840515
Village signed from B4081 in Chipping Campden; GL55 6UR Friendly and relaxed 17th-c stone pub in delightful Cotswold village; tiny beamed character bar with stripped-stone walls and inglenook, ales such as North Cotswold, Stanway, Wickwar and Wye Valley, simply furnished beamed dining room with small open fire, popular pubby food (not Sun evening) plus blackboard specials; darts and board games; children (away from bar) and dogs (in bar) welcome, picnic-sets on terraces and in back garden, nearby walks, open all day Sat, till 7pm Sun, closed Mon. *(Edward May)*

BROADWELL SP2027
Fox (01451) 870909
Off A429, 2 miles N of Stow-on-the-Wold; GL56 0UF Family-run golden-stone pub above broad village green; traditional furnishings and flagstones in log-fire bar, stripped-stone walls, jugs hanging from beams, well kept Donnington BB and SBA, lots of rums, winter mulled wine, simple generously served food (not Sun evening),

efficient friendly staff, two carpeted dining areas; background music, darts, board games; children welcome, dogs in bar (theirs is Buster – also Molly the cat), picnic-sets on gravel in sizeable back garden, aunt sally, paddock with horse called Herman, camping. *(Clive and Fran Dutson)*

BROCKWEIR SO5301
Brockweir Inn (01291) 689548
Signed just off A466 Chepstow–Monmouth; NP16 7NG Welcoming country local near River Wye; beams and stripped stonework, quarry tiles, sturdy settles and woodburner, nice snug with parquet floor and open fire, four well kept ales including local Kingstone and Wye Valley, three ciders, enjoyable food (not Sun evening), small back dining area and room upstairs 'Devil's Pulpit' with games and books; children and dogs welcome, little walled garden with clay oven, good walks, open all day weekends. *(Bob and Margaret Holder)*

BUSSAGE SO8804
Ram (01453) 883163
At Eastcombe, take The Ridgeway and first right The Ridge; pub is 500 metres on left; GL6 8BB Tucked-away Cotswold-stone local with roomy opened-up interior, generous good value pub food (not Sun evening), four well kept ales such as Bath, Butcombe, Greene King and Thwaites, varied choice of wines, friendly welcoming staff; background and some live music; children welcome, a few picnic-sets outside, open all day weekends. *(Tom McLean)*

CAMP SO9111
★Fostons Ash (01452) 863262
B4070 Birdlip–Stroud, junction with Calf Way; GL6 7ES Popular open-plan dining pub (part of the small Cotswold Food Club group), light and airy, with good food from imaginative light dishes up, real ales such as Goffs, Greene King and Stroud, decent wines by the glass, welcoming helpful staff, one end with easy chairs and woodburner; background music, daily papers; children welcome, rustic tables in attractive garden with heated terrace and play area, good walks, open all day (food all day Sun). *(Belinda Stamp)*

CHACELEY SO8530
Yew Tree (01452) 780333
Stock Lane; GL19 4EQ Remote rambling country pub with spacious river-view dining room, generous helpings of enjoyable freshly made food, Prescott and a guest ale, good friendly service, bar in original 16th-c core with log fires, quarry tiles and stripped-stone walls, second bar with pool, skittle alley; children and dogs welcome, wheelchair access, terrace and attractive waterside lawns, own moorings, on Severn Way, closed Sun evening, Mon. *(Lindy Andrews)*

CHARLTON KINGS　　　SO9620
Royal　(01242) 228937
Horsefair, opposite church; GL53 8JH
Big 19th-c pub with clean modern décor, good
realistically priced food (not Sun evening) in
bar or dining conservatory, well kept real ales
and decent wines, prompt friendly service;
children and dogs welcome, picnic-sets in
garden overlooking church, open all day.
(Jo Garnett)

CHEDWORTH　　　SP0608
Hare & Hounds　(01285) 720288
*Fosse Cross – A429 N of Cirencester,
some way from village; GL54 4NN*
Rambling stone-built restauranty pub with
good interesting food, cheaper lunchtime set
menu and sandwiches too, well kept Arkells
and nice wines, efficient service, low beams
and wood floors, soft lighting, cosy corners
and little side rooms, two big log fires, small
conservatory; children (away from bar)
and dogs welcome, disabled facilities, ten
courtyard bedrooms. *(Dennis and Doreen
Haward)*

CHELTENHAM　　　SO9421
Jolly Brewmaster　(01242) 772261
Painswick Road; GL50 2EZ Popular
convivial local with open-plan linked areas
around big semicircular counter, fine range
of changing ales and ciders, friendly obliging
young staff, newspapers, log fire; quiz nights
Mon, Weds; dogs welcome, coachyard tables,
open from 2.30pm (midday Sat, Sun).
(Alison and Michael Harper)

CHELTENHAM　　　SO9624
★ **Plough**　(01242) 222180
Mill Street, Prestbury; GL52 3BG
Unspoilt convivial thatched village local
tucked away behind church; comfortable
front lounge, service from corner corridor
hatch in flagstoned back tap room,
grandfather clock and big log fire, up to four
well kept ales including a house beer from
Wickwar, proper ciders and good value home-
made food (not Sun evening, Mon), friendly
service; lovely big flower-filled back garden,
open all day in summer. *(Guy Vowles)*

CHELTENHAM　　　SO9321
Royal Union　(01242) 224686
Hatherley Street; GL50 2TT Backstreet
local with large bar and cosy snug up steps,
around eight well kept ales, reasonably
priced wines and good range of whiskies,
enjoyable reasonably priced food including
good steaks, Sun evening jazz and other live
music; well behaved children allowed (no
under-5s), courtyard behind, open all day.
(Guy Vowles)

CHELTENHAM　　　SO9522
Sandford Park　(01242) 571022
High Street; GL50 1DZ Recently
converted to a pub (was a nightclub), three

bar areas and upstairs function room,
up to eight real ales along with craft and
continental beers, several ciders, good value
home-cooked food from short menu (not Sun
evening, Mon lunchtime), friendly staff; bar
billiards, Sun quiz; large back garden, open
all day. *(Guy Vowles)*

CHIPPING CAMPDEN　　　SP1539
★ **Kings**　(01386) 840256
High Street; GL55 6AW Eclectic décor
in 18th-c hotel's bar-brasserie and separate
restaurant, cheery helpful service, good food
from lunchtime sandwiches and baguettes
to pubby dishes and more elaborate meals,
well kept Hook Norton Hooky and good
choice of wines by the glass, decent coffee,
daily papers and nice log fire; secluded back
garden with picnic-sets and terrace tables,
12 comfortable bedrooms, open all day.
(Lindy Andrews)

CHIPPING CAMPDEN　　　SP1539
Noel Arms　(01386) 840317
High Street; GL55 6AT Handsome 16th-c
inn with beamed and stripped-stone bar,
modern furniture, open fire, nice food from
sandwiches to steaks, some good curries too
from sri lankan chef, well kept Hook Norton
and local guests, good choice of wines by the
glass, coffee bar (from 9am), conservatory,
restaurant, friendly efficient staff; children
and dogs welcome, sunny courtyard tables,
28 well appointed bedrooms, good breakfast,
open all day. *(Anon)*

CHIPPING SODBURY　　　ST7381
Bell　(01454) 325582
Badminton Road (A432); BS37 6LL
Welcoming late 18th-c family-run inn, ales
such as Butcombe Gold, Sharps Doom Bar
and Wadworths 6X from ornate wooden
counter, three ciders and decent choice of
wines, good pub food including set lunch deal
Mon-Fri and other deals, friendly efficient
young staff, dining rooms either side of bar
area, some stripped stone and timbering,
sofas and open fires; background music, TV;
children welcome, four bedrooms, open all
day Thurs-Sun. *(Roger and Donna Huggins,
Paul and Sonia Broadgate, Stephen Woad)*

CIRENCESTER　　　SP0202
Corinium　(01285) 659711
Dollar Street/Gloucester Street; GL7 2DG
Civilised and comfortable Georgian-fronted
hotel (originally a 16th-c wool merchant's
house); bar with good mix of tables on wood
or flagstone floors, leather bucket seats by
woodburner in stone fireplace, enjoyable
fairly priced food from sandwiches to daily
specials, three well kept local ales and
decent wines, cheerful helpful young staff,
restaurant; entrance through charming
courtyard, wheelchair access with assistance,
picnic-sets in attractive walled garden,
15 bedrooms. *(Val and Alan Green)*

CIRENCESTER   SP0103

Drillmans Arms (01285) 653892
Gloucester Road, Stratton; GL7 2JY
Unpretentious two-room roadside local,
cheerful and welcoming, with well kept
Sharps Doom Bar and three quickly changing
guests, basic lunchtime food, low beams and
woodburner, skittle alley, darts and pool; dogs
welcome, tables out by small front car park,
open all day Sat. *(Richard Tilbrook)*

CIRENCESTER   SP0201

Marlborough Arms (01285) 651474
Sheep Street; GL7 1QW Renovated
bare-boards pub with eight well kept ales
including Box Steam and North Cotswold,
also good choice of proper ciders and
continental draught/bottled beers, friendly
landlord, good value traditional lunchtime
food (not Mon), brewery memorabilia,
pump clips and shelves of bottles, open
fire, live music and quiz nights; enclosed
back courtyard, open all day (till 10pm Sun,
Mon). *(Giles and Annie Francis, Tom McLean)*

COATES   SO9600

★Tunnel House (01285) 770280
*Follow Tarlton signs (right then left)
from village, pub up rough track on
right after railway bridge; OS Sheet 163
map reference 965005; GL7 6PW* Lively
bow-fronted stone house by entrance to
derelict canal tunnel; rambling character
rooms with beams, flagstones and good mix
of furnishings, plenty to look at including
enamel signs, racing tickets and air travel
labels, a stuffed boar's head and owl, even
an upside-down card table (complete with
cards and drinks) fixed to the ceiling, sofas
by log fire, Cotswold Lion, Prescott, Uley
and a guest, two farm ciders and 14 wines by
the glass, wide range of popular food, good
service, more conventional dining extension
and back conservatory; background music,
free wi-fi; children and dogs welcome, big
impressive views from front terrace, big
garden down to canal, good nearby walks,
open (and food) all day. *(Alan Bulley, Tom
and Ruth Rees, Sharon and John Hancock)*

COLD ASTON   SP1219

Plough (01451) 822602
*Aka Aston Blank; off A436 (B4068) or
A429 SW of Stow-on-the-Wold; GL54 3BN*
Attractive little 17th-c village pub
sympathetically restored and updated under
present owners; low beams, stone and wood
floors, inglenook woodburner, emphasis on
enjoyable freshly cooked food using local
suppliers from sandwiches and ciabattas to
charcoal-grilled steaks, regularly changing
beers such as Stanway tapped from the
cask; children and dogs welcome, smart
teak tables and chairs on new terraces,
three bedrooms, open all day Fri-Sun, closed
Mon lunchtime. *(Di and Mike Gillam, P and J
Shapley, Theocsbrian, Richard Tilbrook)*

COLEFORD   SO5813

Dog & Muffler (01594) 832444
*Joyford, best approached from
Christchurch 5-ways junction B4432/
B4428, by church – B4432 towards
Broadwell, then follow signpost; also
signposted from the Berry Hill post office
crossroads; beyond the hamlet itself,
bear right and keep your eyes skinned
for the pub sign, which may be obscured
by the hedge; OS Sheet 162 map reference
580134; GL16 7AS* Prettily located,
extended and modernised 17th-c country
dining pub, carpeted beamed bar with
woodburner in big fireplace, beamed back
part with dining conservatory, generous
helpings of enjoyable pubby food, Sharps
Doom Bar, Wye Valley Butty Bach and a guest,
good friendly service; children and dogs
welcome, lovely views from terrace, garden
with old cider press, nice walks, closed Mon.
(Edward May)

COLESBOURNE   SO9913

Colesbourne Inn (01242) 870376
*A435 Cirencester–Cheltenham;
GL53 9NP* Civilised 19th-c grey-stone
gabled coaching inn, good choice of enjoyable
home-made food from baguettes and wraps
up, friendly staff, well kept Wadworths ales
and lots of wines by the glass, linked partly
panelled rooms, log fires, soft lighting,
comfortable mix of settles, softly padded
seats and leather sofas, candlelit back dining
room; TV visible from fireplace; dogs welcome,
views from attractive back garden and
terrace, nine bedrooms in converted stable
block, good breakfast. *(Lindy Andrews)*

COMPTON ABDALE   SP0717

★Garniche at the Puesdown
(01451) 860262 *A40 outside village;
GL54 4DN* Spacious series of linked stylish
bars and eating areas, mainly stripped-stone
walls, rafter-effect or beamed ceilings,
rugs on bare boards, chesterfield sofas and
armchairs, high-backed dining chairs around
mix of tables, log fire and woodburner, a
couple of Hook Norton ales and Sharps
Doom Bar, pubby lunchtime food with more
elaborate evening choices, breakfast for
non-residents, morning coffee and afternoon
tea; gift shop; children welcome, dogs in bar,
tables in pretty back garden, comfortable
ground-floor bedrooms, closed Sun evening,
Mon, otherwise open all day. *(Jo Garnett)*

CRANHAM   SO8912

★Black Horse (01452) 812217
*Village signposted off A46 and B4070 N
of Stroud; GL4 8HP* Popular down-to-earth
17th-c local, cosy lounge, main bar with
traditional furniture, window seats and log
fire, well kept Otter, Sharps Doom Bar and
a guest, real ciders, good value home-made
blackboard food (not Sun evening when pub
opens at 8.30pm), two upstairs dining rooms

(one with log fire); well behaved children and dogs welcome, tables out in front and to the side, good country views and walks, closed Mon. *(Nick Sharpe)*

DIDMARTON   ST8187
Kings Arms (01454) 238245
A433 Tetbury road; GL9 1DT Welcoming beamed 17th-c coaching inn, dark colour scheme with flagstones and grey-painted half-panelling, armchairs by log fire, Bath, Otter and a guest, good food from sandwiches up, restaurant; soft background music; children welcome, pleasant back garden with pizza oven, bedrooms and self-catering cottages, handy for Westonbirt Arboretum, open all day (food all day weekends). *(Revd Michael Vockins)*

DOYNTON   ST7174
Cross House (0117) 937 4854
High Street; signed off A420 Bristol–Chippenham E of Wick; BS30 5TF New management and some refurbishment for this 18th-c village pub, real ales such as Bass, Bath Gem and Sharps Doom Bar, well priced pubby food cooked by landlady, fish Fri evening, carpeted bar with beams, some stripped stone, simple pub furniture and woodburner, cottagey dining room; children welcome, dogs in bar, picnic-sets out by the road, near fine walking country and Dyrham Park (NT), open all day Sun. *(Taff Thomas)*

DUNTISBOURNE ABBOTS   SO9709
⋆**Five Mile House** (01285) 821432
E of A417 on parallel old Main road; GL7 7JR 17th-c country pub continuing well under present management; pubby seats and tables in friendly drinking bar, flagstoned tap room with two ancient high-backed settles by stove, steps down to snug and down again to small cellar bar, front restaurant extension, well kept Hook Norton Hooky, Timothy Taylors Landlord and a summer guest, several wines by the glass, well liked food from father-and-son team; children welcome, dogs in bar, gardens with country views, smart smokers' shelter, open all day weekends, closed Mon. *(Giles and Annie Francis)*

DYMOCK   SO6931
Beauchamp Arms (01531) 890266
B4215; GL18 2AQ Friendly parish-owned pub with well kept ales and local ciders, popular good value pubby food (not Sun evening, Mon) including fresh fish Weds, cheerful helpful staff, three smallish rooms, log fire; children welcome, pleasant little garden with pond, local walks among daffodils and bluebells, church with corner devoted to the Dymock Poets, closed Mon lunchtime. *(Mike Swan)*

EASTLEACH TURVILLE   SP1905
⋆**Victoria** (01367) 850277
Off A361 S of Burford; GL7 3NQ Open-plan low-ceilinged rooms around central servery, attractive seats built in by log fire, unusual Queen Victoria pictures, well kept Arkells and several good value wines by the glass, shortish choice of sensibly priced pub food (not Sun evening), prompt friendly service; background music; children and dogs welcome, small pleasant front garden with picnic-sets overlooking picturesque village (famous for its spring daffodils), good walks, open all day Sat. *(Neil and Anita Christopher, R K Phillips)*

EBRINGTON   SP1839
⋆**Ebrington Arms** (01386) 593223
Off B4035 E of Chipping Campden or A429 N of Moreton-in-Marsh; GL55 6NH 17th-c Cotswold-stone pub in attractive village by green, character beamed bar with ladder-back chairs and cushioned settles on flagstones, some seats built into airy bow window, fine inglenook fireplace, half a dozen local ales including own Yubberton brews, nine wines by the glass, Weston's cider and a perry, similarly furnished dining room with another inglenook (original ironwork), interesting food including set lunch and early evening weekday deal; children and dogs (in bar) welcome, arched stone wall sheltering terrace picnic-sets, more on lawn, handy for Hidcote (NT) and Kiftsgate Court gardens, well equipped country-style bedrooms, open all day from 9am. *(K H Frostick, Clive and Fran Dutson, Guy Vowles, Michael Doswell, Sharon and John Hancock and others)*

EDGE   SO8409
⋆**Edgemoor** (01452) 813576
Gloucester Road (A4173); GL6 6ND Spacious modernised 19th-c dining pub with panoramic valley view across to Painswick from picture windows and pretty terrace, good food including deals, friendly efficient service, up to four well kept local ales, nice coffee, restaurant; no dogs inside; children welcome, good walks nearby, closed Sun evening in winter. *(Chris and Val Ramstedt)*

ELKSTONE   SO9610
⋆**Highwayman** (01285) 821221
Beechpike; A417 6 miles N of Cirencester; GL53 9PL Interesting rambling 16th-c building, low beams, stripped stone and log fires, cosy alcoves, antique settles among more modern furnishings, good value traditional home-made food from lunchtime sandwiches up, Arkells beers and good house wines, friendly service; free wi-fi; children and dogs welcome, disabled access, outside play area, bedrooms, closed Sun evening, Mon. *(Jo Garnett)*

FAIRFORD   SP1501
⋆**Bull** (01285) 712535
Market Place; GL7 4AA Civilised stone hotel with comfortably old-fashioned pubby furnishings in chatty main bar, beams, timbering and open fire, Arkells ales and decent fairly straightforward food, friendly

service, nice little residents' lounge with big stone fireplace; children and dogs (in bar) welcome, bedrooms, worth visiting the church which has Britain's only intact set of medieval stained-glass windows, open all day. *(Val and Alan Green)*

FORTHAMPTON   SO8731
Lower Lode Inn (01684) 293224
At the end of Bishop's Walk by river; GL19 4RE Brick-built 15th-c coaching inn with River Severn moorings and plenty of waterside tables (prone to winter flooding); beams, flagstones and traditional seating, woodburners, enjoyable pubby food including Sun carvery, half a dozen well kept interesting beers, friendly helpful staff, restaurant, back pool room; children and dogs welcome, disabled facilities, four bedrooms and campsite, open all day. *(Alison and Michael Harper)*

FOSSEBRIDGE   SP0711
★**Fossebridge Inn** (01285) 720721
A429 Cirencester to Stow-on-the-Wold; GL54 3JS New management for this 17th-c former coaching inn with four acres of attractive lawned riverside gardens; two original bar rooms with log fires and candlelight, beams, stripped-stone walls and flagstones, all sorts of chairs, stools and tables, copper implements, Wadworths 6X and a couple of guests, several wines by glass, popular traditional food, two other rather grand dining rooms; children, walkers and dogs welcome, nine bedrooms and two self-catering cottages, Chedworth Roman Villa (NT) nearby, open (and food) all day. *(Giles and Annie Francis, S F Parrinder, Guy Vowles, Dr A Y Drummond)*

FRAMPTON COTTERELL   ST6681
Globe (01454) 778286
Church Road; BS36 2AB Popular white-painted pub next to church, large knocked-through bar-dining area with black beams and some stripped stone, usual furniture on parquet or carpet, woodburner in old fireplace, six well kept ales including Butcombe, Fullers and St Austell, Ashton Press and Thatcher's ciders, well chosen wine list, enjoyable fairly priced pubby food from well filled panini up, attentive friendly staff; background music, Tues quiz; children and dogs welcome, wheelchair access via side door, disabled/baby changing facilities, big grassy garden with play area and smokers' gazebo, on Frome Valley Walkway, open all day. *(Roger and Donna Huggins, Chris and Angela Buckell)*

FRAMPTON MANSELL   SO9202
★**Crown** (01285) 760601
Brown sign to pub off A491 Cirencester–Stroud; GL6 8JG Welcoming 17th-c pub (a former cider house) with good choice of enjoyable hearty food including daily specials, well kept Butcombe Stroud, Uley

and a guest, friendly helpful young staff, heavy beams, stripped stone and rugs on bare boards, two log fires and woodburner, restaurant; children and dogs welcome, disabled access, picnic-sets in sunny front garden, pretty outlook, 12 bedrooms in separate block, open all day from midday. *(Anon)*

FRAMPTON-ON-SEVERN   SO7408
Bell (01452) 740346
The Green (B4071, handy for M5 junction 13, via A38); GL2 7EP Handsome brick-built Georgian inn (Quality Inns) with opened-up interior, enjoyable good value food including bargain weekday set lunch, extensive family dining area, proper locals' bar with quarry tiles and flagstones, well kept ales such as Butcombe, Exmoor, Moles and Sharps, real cider, steps up to restaurant, skittle alley; no dogs inside, plenty of seats outside (front and back), play area and children's farm, village cricket green opposite, bedrooms, open (and food) all day from 9pm for breakfast. *(Clive and Fran Dutson)*

FRAMPTON-ON-SEVERN   SO7407
Three Horseshoes (01452) 742100
The Green (B4071, handy for M5 junction 13, via A38); GL2 7DY Cheerfully unpretentious 18th-c pub by splendid green, welcoming staff and locals, well kept Sharps, Timothy Taylors and Uley from small counter, proper ciders/perry, good value home-made food including speciality pies, lived-in interior with parquet flooring, cushioned wall seats and open fire in large brick fireplace, quieter back lounge/dining room; folk nights, darts; children, walkers and dogs welcome, wheelchair access, picnic-sets out in front, garden behind with two boules pitches, views over Severn to Forest of Dean, parking can be tricky (narrow road), open all day weekends. *(Richard Tilbrook, Chris and Angela Buckell)*

GLASSHOUSE   SO7121
★**Glasshouse Inn** (01452) 830529
Off A40 just W of A4136; GL17 0NN Much extended beamed red-brick pub with series of small linked rooms, ochre walls and boarded ceilings, appealing old-fashioned and antique furnishings, hunting pictures and taxidermy, cavernous black hearth, well kept ales including cask-tapped Butcombe, Weston's cider, reasonably priced wines and some interesting malt whiskies, decent home-made food from sandwiches and basket meals up (no bookings except Sun lunch), good friendly service, big flagstoned conservatory; background music, no under-14s in bars; good disabled access, neat garden with rustic furniture, interesting topiary, flower-decked cider presses and lovely hanging baskets, nearby paths up wooded May Hill, closed Sun evening. *(Chris and Angela Buckell)*

GLOUCESTER — SO8318
Fountain (01452) 522562
Westgate Street; GL1 2NW Tucked-away 17th-c pub off pedestrianised street, well kept ales such as Butcombe, Fullers, Hook Norton, St Austell and Severn Vale, Weston's cider, reasonably priced pubby food from baguettes up, carpeted bar with handsome stone fireplace, some black beams and panelling, pubby furniture and built-in wall benches; background music; children welcome away from bar, disabled access, flower-filled courtyard, handy for cathedral and open all day. *(Chris and Angela Buckell, Theocsbrian)*

GLOUCESTER — SO8318
New Inn (01452) 522177
Northgate Street; GL1 1SF Lovely beamed medieval building with galleried courtyard, Butcombe, Sharps and up to eight guests including smaller local breweries, decent wines, bargain daily lunchtime carvery and other good value food, pleasant service, coffee shop, restaurant; soft background music (live Fri, disco Sat), sports TV, free wi-fi; children welcome, no dogs, wheelchair access to restaurant only, 33 affordably priced bedrooms, handy for cathedral, open all day. *(Val and Alan Green, Dave Braisted)*

GREAT BARRINGTON — SP2013
★ Fox (01451) 844385
Off A40 Burford–Northleach; pub towards Little Barrington; OX18 4TB Welcoming 17th-c inn with stripped stone, simple country furnishings and low ceiling, well kept Donnington BB and SBA, proper cider and good apple juice, decent choice of enjoyable quickly served food (all day weekends including good Sun carvery), big bare-boards river-view dining conservatory with riverbank mural, traditional games; background music, TV; children welcome and dogs (theirs is called Chester), two terraces by the Windrush (swans and private fishing), outside summer bar and barbecue, garden with orchard and ponds, seven bedrooms (four in separate building), open all day and can get very busy. *(Richard Tilbrook, Guy Vowles)*

GREAT RISSINGTON — SP1917
★ Lamb (01451) 820388
Turn off A40 W of Burford to the Barringtons; keep straight on past Great Barrington until Great Rissington is signed on left; GL54 2LN Cotswold-stone village pub with two-roomed bar, pubby furniture on red carpet, woodburner, chairs against counter serving Brakspears, Wychwood and a guest, decent wines by the glass and several malt whiskies, second woodburner in restaurant with agricultural tools on walls, well liked bar food; background music can be loud, large TV; seats in sheltered hillside garden where

Wellington bomber crashed in 1943 (see plaque and memorabilia), attractive circular walk, bedrooms. *(Bernard Stradling, Michael and Jenny Back)*

GUITING POWER — SP0924
★ Farmers Arms (01451) 850358
Fosseway (A429); GL54 5TZ Nicely old-fashioned with stripped stone, flagstones, lots of pictures and warm log fire, well kept cheap Donnington BB and SBA, wide blackboard choice of enjoyable honest food cooked by landlord including good rabbit pie and reasonably priced Sun roasts, welcoming prompt service, carpeted back dining part, games area with darts, dominoes, cribbage and pool, skittle alley; children welcome, garden with quoits, lovely village, good walks, bedrooms. *(Richard Tilbrook, Michael and Jenny Back)*

GUITING POWER — SP0924
Hollow Bottom (01451) 850392
Village signposted off B4068 SW of Stow-on-the-Wold (still called A436 on many maps); GL54 5UX Friendly bustle in this old stone cottage popular with racing fraternity; live horse racing on TV and associated memorabilia in beamed bar, log fire in unusual pillared stone fireplace, a beer named for the pub plus two changing guests, several wines by glass and a dozen malt whiskies, popular all-day food from good baguettes up, pleasant helpful service, public bar with flagstones and stripped stone, darts and board games; background music; children and dogs welcome, disabled access/facilities, country views from pleasant garden, nearby walks, bedrooms, car park down steep slope, open 9am-midnight. *(Michael Snelgrove, Michael Sargent, Michael and Jenny Back, D L Frostick and others)*

HAM — ST6898
Salutation (01453) 810284
On main road through village; GL13 9QH Unpretentious and welcoming three-room country local under enthusiastic landlord; brasses on beams, horse and hunt pictures on Artex walls, high-backed settles, bench seats and other pubby furniture, six well kept local ales including own-brew Tileys, nine real ciders/perries and good range of bottled beers, limited choice of simple low-priced lunchtime food (meat from own pigs), occasional live music including folk night last Sun of month, traditional games and skittle alley; free wi-fi; wheelchair access, beer garden with views over deer park, handy for Berkeley Castle, open all day weekends, closed Mon lunchtime. *(Chris and Angela Buckell)*

HANHAM — ST6470
Elm Tree (0117) 967 5193
Abbots Road; S, towards Willsbridge and Oldland Common; BS15 3NR Small stone

pub on fringe of Bristol; open-plan bar with carpeted dining area, woodburner in central fireplace, good fresh affordably priced food (not Sun evening) including OAP menu, friendly service, well kept Sharps Doom Bar and Wadworths 6X from brick-faced counter, decent wines by the glass; background music; level wheelchair access, picnic-sets in small enclosed back garden. *(Mike Swan)*

HARTPURY   SO7924
Royal Exchange (01452) 700273
A417 Gloucester–Ledbury; GL19 3BW Revamped 19th-c country pub with fresh modern interior, good food (not Sun evening) from sharing plates up including popular fish/ seafood night last Sat of month, Wye Valley ales and guests, local cider/perry, friendly young staff; occasional live music, sports TV; children and dogs (in bar) welcome, fine views from garden with terrace and covered deck, open all day Fri-Sun, closed Mon lunchtime. *(Anon)*

HAWKESBURY UPTON   ST7786
★Beaufort Arms (01454) 238217
High Street; GL9 1AU Unpretentious 17th-c pub in historic village, welcoming landlord and friendly chatty local atmosphere, up to five well kept changing local ales and good range of ciders, popular no-nonsense food (no starters, small helpings available), extended uncluttered dining lounge on right, darts in more spartan stripped-brick bare-boards bar, interesting local and brewery memorabilia, lots of pictures (some for sale), skittle alley; well behaved children allowed, dogs in bar, disabled access throughout and facilities, picnic-sets in smallish enclosed garden, on Cotswold Way and handy for Badminton Horse Trials, open all day. *(Chris and Angela Buckell, Martin and Margaret Thorpe)*

HILLESLEY   ST7689
Fleece (01453) 520003
Hawkesbury Road/Chapel Lane; GL12 7RD Comfortably updated old stone-roofed pub owned by the local community; four well kept changing local ales, Thatcher's cider, good wines by the glass and interesting malt whiskies, happy hour (3-7pm Mon-Fri), ample helpings of enjoyable good value pub food, friendly chatty staff, bar with coir matting and some polished boards, mix of pubby furniture, cushioned benches and wall seats, woodburner, steps down to dining room and snug; fortnightly quiz Sun and monthly acoustic music, darts, free wi-fi; children, dogs and walkers welcome, wheelchair access to main bar only, back garden with play area and smokers' shelter, small village in lovely countryside near

Cotswold Way, open all day. *(Alan Bulley, Chris and Angela Buckell)*

HINTON DYRHAM   ST7376
★Bull (0117) 937 2332
2.4 miles from M4 junction 18; A46 towards Bath, then first right (opposite the Crown); SN14 8HG 17th-c stone pub in nice setting, main bar with two huge fireplaces, low beams, oak settles and pews on ancient flagstones, horsebrasses, stripped-stone back area and simply furnished carpeted restaurant, food from pub standards to specials, well kept Wadworths ales; background music; children and dogs welcome, wheelchair accessible with help, seats on front balcony and in sizeable sheltered upper garden with play equipment, handy for Dyrham Park (NT), open all day weekends (food till 6pm Sun), closed Mon. *(Michael Doswell)*

KEMBLE   ST9899
★Thames Head (01285) 770259
A433 Cirencester–Tetbury; GL7 6NZ Stripped stone, timberwork, intriguing little front alcove, pews in cottagey back area with log-effect gas fire in big fireplace, country-look dining room with another fire, good generously served food from sandwiches and baked potatoes to steaks, good value wines and well kept Arkells, friendly obliging staff, skittle alley; TV; children welcome, tables in nice garden, four barn-conversion bedrooms, good breakfast, walk (crossing railway line) to nearby Thames source, open (and food) all day. *(Heulwen and Neville Pinfield, Dennis and Doreen Haward)*

KILKENNY   SP0118
Kilkeney Inn (01242) 820341
A436, 1 mile W of Andoversford; GL54 4LN Spacious interior (originally six stone cottages) with extended beamed bar, stripped-stone walls and white plasterwork, wheelbacks around tables on quarry tiles or carpet, various clocks dotted about (owner repairs them), open fire and woodburner, airy conservatory, Charles Wells beers, real cider and a dozen wines by the glass, enjoyable food including sandwiches and other bar snacks from shortish menu, pleasant young staff, restaurant; background music; children welcome, dogs in bar, lovely Cotswold views from tables out at front, white wicker furniture in back garden, bedrooms, open all day. *(Richard Tilbrook, Tom McLean)*

KINETON   SP0926
Halfway House (01451) 850344
Signed from B4068 and B4077 W of Stow-on-the-Wold; GL54 5UG Simple and welcoming 17th-c beamed village inn, big

---

Places with gardens or terraces usually let children sit there – we note in the text the very few exceptions that don't.

helpings of good reasonably priced pub food (not Sun evening) from lunchtime baguettes up, well kept Donnington BB and SBA, farm cider and decent wines, restaurant; log fire; pool and darts; children welcome, picnic-sets in sheltered back garden, good walks, bedrooms, open all day weekends. *(Richard Tilbrook)*

KINGSCOTE   ST8196
★**Hunters Hall** (01453) 860393
A4135 Dursley–Tetbury; GL8 8XZ Tudor beams, stripped stone, big log fires and plenty of character in individually furnished linked rooms, oak settles along with some sofas and easy chairs, wide choice of good home-made food at reasonable prices, well kept Greene King and Uley, friendly attentive service, flagstoned back bar with darts, pool and TV; children and dogs welcome, big garden with play area, 13 bedrooms, open all day. *(Emma Scofield)*

KNOCKDOWN   ST8388
Holford Arms (01454) 238669
A433; GL8 8QY Welcoming 16th-c beamed pub, stripped-stone walls, flagstone or wood floors, leather sofas, armchairs and cushioned wall/window seats, candles on old dining tables, woodburner in big stone fireplace, ales such as Bath, Box Steam and Stroud, local Sherston's cider and good well balanced wine list, enjoyable food from baguettes up including good value Sun lunch (own rare-breed pork); background and live music (bluegrass Fri), skittle alley; children and dogs welcome, disabled access, sets in side garden, camping, handy for Westonbirt Arboretum, open all day except Mon lunchtime. *(Chris and Angela Buckell)*

LECHLADE   SU2199
Swan (01367) 253571
Burford Street; GL7 3AP Welcoming refurbished 16th-c inn, Halfpenny and Old Forge beers (brewed at their sister pubs) and good choice of wines by the glass, sensibly priced bar food (not Sun evening) including generous sandwiches and range of burgers, good log fires, restaurant; four bedrooms, handy for Thames Path walkers, open all day. *(Dr A Y Drummond)*

LITTLE BARRINGTON   SP2012
★**Inn For All Seasons** (01451) 844324
A40 3 miles W of Burford; OX18 4TN Handsome old coaching inn with attractive comfortable lounge bar, low beams, stripped stone and flagstones, old prints, log fire, good food with an emphasis on fish, a couple of ales such as Otter and St Austell, lots of wines by the glass and malt whiskies, good courteous service, restaurant and conservatory, cookery school; background music, quiz nights; children and dogs (in bar) welcome, picnic-sets in garden with aunt sally, walks from door, ten bedrooms, open all day weekends. *(R K Phillips)*

LITTLETON-UPON-SEVERN   ST5989
★**White Hart** (01454) 412275
3.5 miles from M48 junction 1; BS35 1NR Former farmhouse with three main rooms, log fires and nice mix of country furnishings (some refurbishment planned), loveseat in inglenook, flagstones at front, huge tiles at back, fine old White Hart Inn Simonds Ale sign, family room and snug, Youngs ales and guests, good range of ciders (including their own) and of other drinks, well liked locally sourced food (all day Sun) cooked by landlord from traditional choices to more adventurous specials such as squirrel; dogs welcome, wheelchair access, tables on front lawn, more behind by orchard, vegetable patch and roaming poultry (eggs for sale), walks from the door, open all day. *(Chris and Angela Buckell)*

LONGBOROUGH   SP1729
Coach & Horses (01451) 830325
Ganborough Road; GL56 0QU Simple little 17th-c stone-built local, well kept/priced Donnington ales, Weston's cider and enjoyable wholesome food (not Sun evening, Mon), friendly staff, leather armchairs on flagstones, inglenook woodburner, darts, dominoes and cribbage; background music; children and dogs welcome, tables out at front looking down on stone cross and pretty village, two simple clean bedrooms, open all day weekends, closed Mon evening. *(Guy Vowles, Richard Tilbrook, Christian Mole)*

LOWER ODDINGTON   SP2326
★**Fox** (01451) 870862
Signed off A436; GL56 0UR Smart 16th-c creeper-covered inn with emphasis on good food (mix of modern and traditional), Hook Norton and Sharps Doom Bar, little country-style flagstoned rooms with assorted chairs around pine tables, hunting figures and pictures, inglenook fireplace, elegant restaurant; background music; children and dogs (in bar) welcome, white tables and chairs on heated terrace in cottagey garden, pretty village, three bedrooms. *(Richard Tilbrook, Bernard Stradling)*

MAISEMORE   SO8121
White Hart (01452) 500763
The Rudge, NW of Gloucester; GL2 8HY Flower-clad roadside village pub run by friendly nepalese family; black beams, pubby furniture on wood, tiled or carpeted floors, some dark wood dados, old local photos along with buddhist statues and masks, raised dining area and steps down to further room, ales such as Butcombe, St Austell and Sharps, Weston's cider, traditional lunchtime food, interesting evening nepalese menu, pleasant service; appropriate background music; children welcome, wheelchair access (low step) to main part, open all day. *(Chris and Angela Buckell)*

MARSHFIELD   ST7773

★ **Catherine Wheel** (01225) 892220
*High Street; signed off A420 Bristol–
Chippenham; SN14 8LR* Attractive
Georgian-fronted building in unspoilt village,
high-ceilinged bare-stone front part with
medley of settles, chairs and stripped tables,
charming dining room with open fire in
impressive fireplace, cottagey beamed back
area warmed by woodburners, well kept
Butcombe, Cotswold Spring and Sharps,
interesting wines and other drinks, enjoyable
sensibly priced food from pub favourites up
including set menus; darts and dominoes,
live music last Thurs of month; well behaved
children and dogs welcome, wheelchair
access with help, flower-decked backyard,
three bedrooms, open all day. *(Dr and
Mrs A K Clarke)*

MAYSHILL   ST6882

New Inn (01454) 773161
*Badminton Road (A432 Frampton
Cotterell–Yate); BS36 2NT* Popular largely
17th-c coaching inn with two comfortably
carpeted bar rooms leading to restaurant,
good choice of enjoyable generously served
food, friendly staff, three well kept changing
ales, Weston's cider and decent wines by the
glass, log fire; children and dogs welcome,
garden with play area, open all day Fri-Sun.
(Roger and Donna Huggins)

MEYSEY HAMPTON   SU1199

Masons Arms (01285) 850164
*Just off A417 Cirencester–Lechlade;
High Street; GL7 5JT* Welcoming 17th-c
village pub under new local ownership, good
attractively presented food at reasonable
prices, well kept Arkells, Weston's cider,
longish open-plan beamed bar with big
inglenook at one end, restaurant (expansion
planned); children and dogs (in bar)
welcome, tables out on green, six cosy
bedrooms, parking may be a problem, open
all day weekends (food all day Sun), from
8.30am weekdays with a break 3-5pm.
(Revd Michael Vockins)

MINCHINHAMPTON   SO8500

Old Lodge (01453) 832047
*Nailsworth–Brimscombe – on common,
fork left at pub's sign; OS Sheet 162 map
reference 853008; GL6 9AQ* Welcoming
dining pub (part of the Cotswold Food Club
group) with civilised bistro feel, wood floors,
stripped-stone walls, modern décor and
furnishings, good food from pub favourites
up, well kept beers and decent wines by the
glass; children welcome, tables on neat lawn
looking over NT common with grazing cows
and horses, six bedrooms, open all day (food
all day weekends). *(David and Stella Martin)*

MINSTERWORTH   SO7515

Severn Bore (01452) 750318
A48 2 miles SW; GL2 8JX In splendid
Severn-side position, open layout with central
fireplace, usual pubby furniture, Sharps
Doom Bar and a couple of local guests,
traditional cider, good choice of food (till
6pm Mon-Weds) including Sun carvery, skittle
alley with pool table and darts; children and
dogs welcome, wheelchair access (low step
into bar), big riverside garden with superb
views to the Cotswolds, play area, board
giving times/heights of Severn Bore, handy
for Westbury Court Gardens (NT), open all
day (till 8pm Sun) and for breakfast on
Bore days. *(Edward May)*

MISERDEN   SO9308

Carpenters Arms (01285) 821283
Off B4070 NE of Stroud; GL6 7JA
Welcoming country pub with open-plan
low-beamed bar, stripped-stone walls, log fire
and woodburner, Wye Valley and a guest ale,
good wine list, ample helpings of enjoyable
reasonably priced food using local and home-
grown produce, good vegetarian choices,
friendly staff and pub cat; charity quiz nights;
children and dogs welcome, garden tables,
popular with walkers and handy for Miserden
Park, open (and food) all day. *(Jo Garnett)*

MORETON-IN-MARSH   SP2032

Inn on the Marsh (01608) 650709
Stow Road next to duck pond; GL56 0DW
Interesting 19th-c beamed bar with
comfortable layout including curved sofa,
quite a dutch flavour to the bric-a-brac,
models, posters etc, inglenook woodburner,
dutch chef-landlady cooking good value
national specialities alongside pubby
favourites, well kept Marstons-related beers
and guests, cheerful welcoming staff, modern
conservatory restaurant; may be background
music; children and dogs welcome, seats at
front and in back garden, closed Sun and
Mon lunchtimes. *(Richard Tilbrook, Tony
Hobden)*

MORETON-IN-MARSH   SP2032

Redesdale Arms (01608) 650308
High Street; GL56 0AW Relaxed 17th-c
hotel (former coaching inn); alcoves and
big stone fireplace in comfortable solidly
furnished panelled bar on right, darts in
flagstoned public bar, Wickwar ales, decent
wines and coffee, enjoyable good value food
served by courteous helpful staff, spacious
child-friendly back brasserie and dining
conservatory; background music, TVs,
games machine; heated floodlit courtyard,
34 comfortable bedrooms (newer ones in
mews), open all day from 8am. *(Mike Swan)*

MORETON-IN-MARSH   SP2032

White Hart Royal (01608) 650731
High Street; GL56 0BA 17th-c coaching
inn with Charles I connection; cosy beamed
quarry-tiled bar with fine inglenook and nice
old furniture, adjacent smarter panelled
room with Georgian feel, separate lounge
and restaurant, Hook Norton and a guest ale,

good choice of wines, well priced enjoyable food from sandwiches and pub favourites to more inventive choices, friendly efficient service; background music; courtyard tables, bedrooms, good breakfast. *(Fiona Smith)*

NAILSWORTH   ST8499
Britannia (01453) 832501
Cossack Square; GL6 0DG Large open-plan pub (part of the small Cotswold Food Club chain) in former manor house; popular bistro food (best to book evenings) including bargain weekday lunch menu, takeaway pizzas, friendly service, well kept Greene King IPA and a couple of local beers, good choice of wines by the glass, big log fire; picnic-sets in front garden, open all day (food all day weekends). *(Tom and Ruth Rees)*

NAILSWORTH   ST8499
Egypt Mill (01453) 833449
Off A46; heading N towards Stroud, first right after roundabout, then left; GL6 0AE Converted 16th-c mill with working waterwheels; split-level bar with brick and stone floor, a dozen wines by the glass and well kept ales such as Wickwar and Wye Valley, stripped beams and some hefty ironwork in comfortable carpeted lounge, seating ranging from elegant wooden dining chairs to cushioned wall seats and sofas, generally well liked food at reasonable prices; background music, TV; children welcome, plenty of tables in floodlit garden overlooking millpond, nicely equipped bedrooms (some with fine beams and timbering), open (and food) all day. *(Dr and Mrs A K Clarke)*

NAUNTON   SP1123
★ **Black Horse** (01451) 850565
Off B4068 W of Stow-on-the-Wold; GL54 3AD Welcoming locals' pub with well kept/priced Donnington BB and SBA, Weston's cider and good food from traditional favourites to specials such as seasonal game, efficient service, black beams, stripped stone, flagstones and log fire, flowers on plain tables, dining room; background music, darts and dominoes; children and dogs welcome, small seating area outside, charming village and fine Cotswold walks (walking groups asked to pre-order food), open all day Fri-Sun. *(Richard Tilbrook, Barry Collett, Michael and Jenny Back and others)*

NIBLEY   ST6982
Swan (01454) 312290
Badminton Road; BS37 5JF Part of small local pub group, friendly and relaxed, with good food from snacks to daily specials, Bath, Butcombe and Cotswold Spring, real cider and over a dozen wines by the glass, good service, modernised interior with fireside leather sofas one side, dining tables the other, separate restaurant; background music; children and dogs (in bar welcome), garden picnic-sets, open all day in summer, all day Thurs-Sun winter. *(Roger and Donna Huggins)*

NORTH NIBLEY   ST7596
New Inn (01453) 543659
E of village itself; Waterley Bottom; GL11 6EF Former cider house in secluded rural setting popular with walkers, well kept Moles, Wickwar and a weekend guest from antique pumps, fine range of ciders and perries (more in bottles), enjoyable bar food from lunchtime sandwiches and good ploughman's up, lounge bar with cushioned windsor chairs and high-backed settles, partly stripped-stone walls, simple cosy public bar with darts (no children here after 6pm), cider festivals and other events; dogs welcome, hitching rail and trough for horses, picnic-sets and swings on lawn, covered decked area with pool table, two bedrooms, open all day weekends, closed Mon lunchtime (evening too in winter). *(Guy Vowles)*

OLD SODBURY   ST7581
★ **Dog** (01454) 312006
3 miles from M4 junction 18, via A46 and A432; The Hill (a busy road); BS37 6LZ Welcoming old pub with popular two-level bar, low beams, stripped stone and open fire, enjoyable food from sandwiches and baked potatoes to fresh fish and steaks, friendly young staff, well kept ales such as Wickwar, good wine and soft drinks choice; children and dogs welcome, big garden with barbecue and play area, bedrooms, open all day. *(Roger and Donna Huggins, Stephen Woad)*

PAINSWICK   SO8609
Falcon (01452) 814222
New Street; GL6 6UN Sizeable stone-built inn dating from the 16th c; sympathetically updated and comfortable open-plan layout with bar and two dining areas, popular food including daily specials, four well kept beers and good choice of wines by the glass, friendly young staff; Fri live music; children and dogs welcome, 12 bedrooms, opposite churchyard famous for its 99 yews. *(Emma Scofield)*

PARKEND   SO6107
Fountain (01594) 562189
Just off B4234; GL15 4JD Unpretentious 18th-c village inn by terminus of restored Lydney–Parkend steam railway; well kept Goffs, Sharps and Wye Valley, Weston's cider, wines in glass-sized bottles, enjoyable home-made traditional food including bargain OAP lunches and Sun carvery,

---

If you report on a pub that's not a featured entry, please tell us any lunchtimes or evenings when it doesn't serve bar food.

welcoming helpful staff, coal fire, assorted chairs and settles in two linked rooms, old tools, bric-a-brac, photographs and framed local history information; quiz and live music nights; children, walkers and dogs welcome, wheelchair access, side garden, eight bedrooms and bunkhouse, open all day Sat. *(Alison and Michael Harper)*

PARKEND　　　　　　　　　SO6308

Rising Sun (01594) 562008

Off B4431; GL15 4HN Perched on wooded hillside and approached by roughish single-track drive – popular with walkers and cyclists; open-plan carpeted bar with modern pub furniture, Butcombe and a guest, real ciders, straightforward generous food from sandwiches and baked potatoes up, friendly service, lounge/games area with pool and machines; children and dogs welcome, wheelchair access with help, balcony and terrace tables under umbrellas, big woodside garden with play area and duck pond, self-catering bedroom, open all day weekends in summer. *(Edward May)*

POULTON　　　　　　　　　SP1001

Falcon (01285) 850878

London Road; GL7 5HN Bistro feel with good food from landlord-chef including set lunch, well kept local ales and nice wines by the glass, friendly attentive service; well behaved children welcome, closed Sun evening, Mon. *(Tom and Ruth Rees)*

QUENINGTON　　　　　　　SP1404

Keepers Arms (01285) 750349

Church Road; GL7 5BL Community local in pretty Cotswold village, cosy and comfortable, with stripped stone, low beams and log fires, friendly landlord and staff, enjoyable fairly priced food in bar and restaurant from sandwiches to popular Sun lunch, good value steak night Weds, well kept changing local beers; dogs welcome, picnic-sets out in front, three bedrooms, closed Mon and Tues lunchtimes. *(Alan Bulley, Giles and Annie Francis)*

SALFORD HILL　　　　　　SP2629

Greedy Goose (01608) 646551

Junction A44/A436, near Chastleton; GL56 0SP Old roadside country dining pub with contemporary interior, enjoyable food from sandwiches and stone-baked pizzas up, three North Cotswolds ales, friendly staff; children and dogs welcome, seats out at front and in back decked/gravelled area, camping, open all day. *(Anon)*

SAPPERTON　　　　　　　　SO9403

Bell (01285) 760298

Village signposted from A419 Stroud–Cirencester; OS Sheet 163 map reference 948033; GL7 6LE Welcoming 250-year-old pub-restaurant, beams, flagstones and log fires, well kept ales such as Bath, Flying Monk, Hook Norton and Stroud, plenty

of wines by the glass including Bollinger, generally well liked food from sharing boards and pub favourites up, good service; children and dogs welcome, seats out in front and in back courtyard garden, plenty of surrounding walks, open all day (till 9pm Sun). *(Mike Swan)*

SAPPERTON　　　　　　　　SO9303

Daneway Inn (01285) 760297

Daneway; off A419 Stroud–Cirencester; GL7 6LN Quiet tucked-away relaxed local in charming wooded countryside, flagstones and bare boards, woodburner in amazing floor-to-ceiling carved oak dutch fireplace, sporting prints, well kept Wadworths ales, farm ciders and generous simple food from filled baps to good Sun lunch, amiable long-serving landlord and friendly staff, small family room, traditional games in inglenook public bar, folk night Tues; no dogs, tricky wheelchair access; terrace tables and lovely sloping lawn, camping possible, good walks by disused canal (some renovation) with tunnel to Coates. *(Giles and Annie Francis)*

SELSEY　　　　　　　　　　SO8303

Bell (01453) 753801

Bell Lane; GL5 5JY Attractively updated village inn with enjoyable home-made food (all day Sat, not Sun evening) using own farm produce and local game, ales including Wye Valley and decent wines by the glass, friendly relaxed service, open fire and woodburner, garden room dining extension; farm shop; children, walkers and dogs welcome, views from terrace tables, near Selsley Common and Cotswold Way, comfortable bedrooms, open all day (Sun till 9pm). *(Chris and Val Ramstedt)*

SHIPTON MOYNE　　　　　ST8989

Cat & Custard Pot (01666) 880249

Off B4040 Malmesbury–Bristol; The Street; GL8 8PN Popular chatty pub in picturesque village, several well kept ales such as Bath, Wadworths and Wickwar, decent wines, good pubby food promptly served by friendly staff, deceptively spacious inside with several dining areas, beams and bric-a-brac, hunting prints, cosy back snug, woodburner; children, walkers and dogs welcome, wheelchair access, tables out on lawn. *(Chris and Angela Buckell)*

SIDDINGTON　　　　　　　SU0399

Greyhound (01285) 653573

Ashton Road; village signed from A419 roundabout at Tesco; GL7 6HR Beamed village pub with linked rooms, flagstones and carpets, some bare stone walls, big log fires and woodburner, enjoyable good value food from sandwiches/baguettes up, smaller appetites catered for, well kept Wadworths ales and plenty of wines by the glass; background music; children welcome, garden tables, open all day weekends. *(Emma Scofield)*

SLAD   SO8707
Woolpack (01452) 813429
B4070 Stroud–Birdlip; GL6 7QA
Friendly old-fashioned hillside village pub
with lovely valley views, four little connecting
rooms, interesting photographs including
some of Laurie Lee (his books for sale), log
fire and nice tables, enjoyable food (not Sun
evening), well kept Uley ales and guests,
local farm ciders and perry, decent wines by
the glass; children and dogs welcome, nice
garden, open all day. *(Guy Vowles, Chris and
Val Ramstedt)*

SLIMBRIDGE   SO7204
Tudor Arms (01453) 890306
*Shepherds Patch; off A38 towards
Slimbridge Wetlands Centre; GL2 7BP*
Much extended red-brick pub just back from
canal swing bridge; welcoming and popular,
with several local ales, eight ciders/perries
and good wines by the glass, enjoyable food
(all day bar meals) from baguettes and
baked potatoes to daily specials, prompt
friendly service, linked areas with wood,
flagstone or carpeted floors, some leather
chairs and settles, comfortable dining
room, conservatory; darts, pool and skittle
alley; children and dogs welcome, disabled
facilities, picnic-sets outside (some on
covered terrace), boat trips, 12 annexe
bedrooms, caravan site off car park, open all
day. *(Chris and Angela Buckell, Theocsbrian)*

SNOWSHILL   SP0933
Snowshill Arms (01386) 852653
Opposite village green; WR12 7JU
Unpretentious country pub in honeypot
village (so no shortage of customers);
well kept Donnington ales and reasonably
priced straightforward (but tasty) food from
sandwiches up, prompt friendly service,
beams, log fire, stripped stone and neat array
of tables, charming village views from bow
windows, local photographs; skittle alley;
children welcome if eating, big back garden
with little stream and play area, handy for
Snowshill Manor (NT), lavender farm and
Cotswold Way walks. *(Edward May)*

SOMERFORD KEYNES   SU0195
Bakers Arms (01285) 861298
On main street through village; GL7 6DN
Pretty little 17th-c stone-built pub with
catslide roof, four real ales including
Butcombe, Sharps and Stroud, Addlestone's
cider, good house wines, generous helpings
of enjoyable traditional food, friendly service,
lots of pine tables in two linked areas, fire
in big stone fireplace; children and dogs
welcome, nice garden with play area, lovely
village, handy for Cotswold Water Park,
open (and food) all day except Sun when
shuts at 6pm. *(Lindy Andrews)*

ST BRIAVELS   SO5504
George (01594) 530228
High Street; GL15 6TA Old Wadworths
pub with their beers and a couple of guests,
enjoyable pubby food including OAP
deal (Mon-Fri lunchtimes) and good Sun
lunch, friendly helpful service, rambling
linked black-beamed rooms with attractive
old-fashioned décor, woodburner in big
stone fireplace, restaurant with another
woodburner; can get very busy weekends
(booking advised); children and dogs
welcome, flagstoned terrace over former
moat of neighbouring Norman fortress,
four refurbished bedrooms, open all day.
(Bob and Margaret Holder, Tom and Ruth Rees)

STAUNTON   SO5412
White Horse (01594) 834001
A4136; GL16 8PA Village pub on edge
of Forest of Dean close to the welsh border;
good freshly made food in bar or restaurant,
well kept local ales and ciders, friendly
service, two woodburners, café and small
shop; dogs and muddy boots welcome,
disabled access, picnic-sets in good-sized
garden, open all day weekends, closed Mon.
(Belinda Stamp)

STOW-ON-THE-WOLD   SP1925
★ **Bell** (01451) 870916
Park Street; A436 E of centre; GL54 1AJ
Creeper-clad dining pub with comfortable
homely décor, very good well presented
food from bar snacks to fish specials (best
to book), good service from friendly young
staff, nice wines (champagne happy hour
Friday evening), a couple of Youngs ales and
a guest, proper beamed and flagstoned bar
with woodburner; under-16s in dining part
only, dogs welcome, picnic-sets outside, five
bedrooms, open (and some food) all day.
(Richard Tilbrook)

STOW-ON-THE-WOLD   SP1925
Kings Arms (01451) 830364
The Square; GL54 1AF Revamped 16th-c
stone coaching inn, black-beamed bar with
wood floor, some blue-painted panelling
and stripped stone, woodburner, Greene
King including one named for the pub and
a guest, enjoyable food here or in upstairs
Chophouse restaurant with saggy oak floor,
leopard-skin bar stools and ink-spot tables,
friendly service; children and dogs welcome,
ten bedrooms including three courtyard
'cottages', open all day. *(George Atkinson)*

STOW-ON-THE-WOLD   SP1925
Queens Head (01451) 830563
The Square; GL54 1AB Old traditional
Donnington pub under newish management,
their good value beers kept well and decent
pubby food, stripped-stone front lounge,

If you know a pub is ever open all day, please tell us.

heavily beamed and flagstoned back bar with high-backed settles, coal-effect fire; background music; children and dogs welcome, tables in attractive sunny back courtyard, open all day. *(Richard Tilbrook)*

STROUD SO8505

Ale House (01453) 755447

John Street; GL5 2HA Fine range of well kept beers and ciders/perries (third-of-a-pint tasting glasses available), enjoyable food including signature curries and good value Sun lunch, main high-ceilinged part with sofa by big open fire, other rooms off; well behaved dogs welcome (resident irish wolfhound), small side courtyard, farmers' market Sat, open all day Fri-Sun.
(Guy Vowles)

SWINEFORD ST6969

Swan (0117) 932 3101

A431, right on the Somerset border; BS30 6LN Popular stone-built pub with well kept Bath Ales and a guest, decent ciders and carefully chosen range of other drinks including interesting wines, enjoyable food from bar snacks and pub favourites up, helpful friendly staff, plain furniture on bare boards or tiles, pastel paintwork and panelled dado, big open fire; children welcome, wheelchair access, large sunny garden with play area, open all day.
(Chris and Angela Buckell, Taff Thomas)

TETBURY ST8893

Priory (01666) 502251

London Road; GL8 8JJ Civilised restaurant-pub-hotel; central log fire in comfortable high-raftered stone-built former stables, enjoyable food (booking advised) with emphasis on interesting local produce, even a local slant to their good wood-fired pizzas, cheerful service, three well kept local ales including Uley, proper ciders and several wines by the glass, comfortable coffee lounge; children very welcome, dogs in bar, wheelchair access (staff helpful), roadside terrace picnic-sets, 14 bedrooms, open all day.
(Anon)

TETBURY ST8993

★Snooty Fox (01666) 502436

Market Place; GL8 8DD High-ceilinged stripped-stone hotel lounge (some recent refurbishment), four well kept local ales, a real cider and good house wines, enjoyable all-day bar food from sandwiches up, leather sofas and elegant fireplace, nice side room and anteroom, restaurant; background music; children and dogs welcome, a few sheltered tables out in front, 12 bedrooms.
(Taff Thomas)

TEWKESBURY SO8932

Nottingham Arms (01684) 276346

High Street; GL20 5JU Popular old black and white fronted bare-boards local, timbered bar with four well kept ales including St Austell and Sharps, Weston's cider, good home-made food at reasonable prices, back dining room, friendly efficient service; music and quiz nights; dogs welcome, open all day. *(Eddie Edwards, Dave Braisted)*

TEWKESBURY SO8932

Royal Hop Pole (01684) 274039

Church Street; GL20 5RT Wetherspoons conversion of old inn (some parts dating from the 15th c), their usual value-minded all-day food and drink, good service; free wi-fi; terrace seating and lovely garden leading down to river, 28 bedrooms, open from 7am.
(Theocsbrian, Roger and Donna Huggins, Dave Braisted)

TEWKESBURY SO8932

Theoc House (01684) 296562

Barton Street; GL20 5PY Old pub now more like a café/wine bar but with local ales, good range of food including tapas and vegetarian choices, reasonable prices, spacious split-level interior, books and board games; live jazz second and last Weds of month, free wi-fi; children and dogs welcome, open (and food) all day from 8.30am.
(Guy Vowles, Theocsbrian)

TODENHAM SP2436

★Farriers Arms (01608) 650901

Between A3400 and A429 N of Moreton-in-Marsh; GL56 9PF Unspoilt and welcoming old pub with exposed stone and plastered walls in bar, hop-hung beams, polished flagstones by counter, woodburner in big inglenook, cosy room off with old books and photos, neat restaurant; Hook Norton and a couple of guests, several wines by the glass, shortish choice of good value food from changing blackboard menu; background music, darts and board games; children and dogs (in bar) welcome, disabled access using ramp, country views from walled garden, terrace overlooking quiet village road and church, aunt sally, good surrounding walks.
(Dennis and Doreen Haward)

TOLLDOWN ST7577

Crown (01225) 891166

1 mile from M4 junction 18 – A46 towards Bath; SN14 8HZ Cosy heavy-beamed stone pub on crossroads; most here for the good food (all day Sun) from sandwiches and pub favourites to more upmarket choices, efficient chatty staff,

---

A star symbol before the name of a pub shows exceptional character and appeal. It doesn't mean extra comfort. Even quite a basic pub can win a star, if it's individual enough.

Wadworths ales, Thatcher's cider and plenty of wines by the glass, warm log fires, candles on pine tables, wood, coir and quarry-tiled floors, animal prints on green rough plaster walls, some bare stone; children and dogs (in bar) welcome, wheelchair access (no disabled loos), sunny beer garden, nine recently added bedrooms in separate building behind, handy for Dyrham Park (NT), open all day. *(Chris and Angela Buckell)*

ULEY   ST7998
Old Crown (01453) 860502
The Green; GL11 5SN Unspoilt 17th-c pub prettily set by village green just off Cotswold Way; long narrow room with settles and pews on bare boards, step up to partitioned-off lounge, six well kept local ales including Uley, decent wines by the glass and enjoyable reasonably priced pubby food from baguettes up, friendly service, open fire; children and dogs welcome, a few picnic-sets in front and attractive garden behind, four bedrooms, open all day. *(Guy Vowles)*

UPTON CHEYNEY   ST6969
Upton Inn (0117) 932 4489
Signed off A431 at Bitton; BS30 6LY Friendly 18th-c stone-built village pub, bar with old prints on stone and dark panelled walls, captain's chairs and old tables, step up to carpeted/bare-boards dining area with inglenook woodburner, decent choice of home-made pubby food from sandwiches up, good value lunchtime carvery (Sun, Weds), well kept Badger ales (happy hour Mon-Sat 4-6pm), Weston's Old Rosie cider, helpful service, opulent mock-Regency restaurant with pictures of Bath; background music; wheelchair access possible from car park using ramp, children and dogs welcome, terrace seating, picturesque spot with Avon Valley views, open all day. *(Chris and Angela Buckell, Taff Thomas, Tom and Ruth Rees)*

WESTONBIRT   ST8690
Hare & Hounds (01666) 881000
A433 SW of Tetbury; GL8 8QL Substantial roadside hotel with separate entrance for pub, good food from snacks up, Cotswold Spring and Wickwar, lots of wines by the glass, good selection of malts and other spirits, prompt cheery service, flagstoned bar with another panelled one to the left, series of interconnecting rooms with polished wood floors, woodburner in two-way fireplace, some leather sofas and banquettes, more formal restaurant; muddy boots and dogs welcome in bar, wheelchair access throughout, shaded tables out on front paved area, pleasant gardens, 42 bedrooms

including some in annexe, handy for Arboretum, open all day and gets very busy (especially weekend lunchtimes). *(Chris and Angela Buckell)*

WHITECROFT   SO6005
Miners Arms (01594) 562483
B4234 N of Lydney; GL15 4PE Friendly unpretentious local with up to five changing ales, farm ciders and perries, sensibly priced food from snacks up including some greek dishes (landlord is cypriot), attentive helpful service, two rooms on either side of bar, slate and parquet floors, pastel walls with old photographs, conservatory; background and some live music, skittle alley; children and dogs welcome, disabled access, nice gardens front and back, one with stream, good local walks, handy for steam railway, self-catering cottage, open all day. *(Edward Swan)*

WHITMINSTER   SO7607
Fromebridge Mill (01452) 741796
Fromebridge Lane (A38 near M5 junction 13); GL2 7PD Comfortable mill-based dining pub with interconnecting rooms, beams, bare brick walls, flagstone and carpeted floors, some tables overlooking river, well kept Greene King and guests, good choice of wines by the glass, popular food all day including lunchtime carvery (evenings too at weekends), helpful pleasant staff; can get very busy, no dogs inside; children welcome, wheelchair access throughout, picnic-sets in big garden with play area, pretty waterside setting, footbridge from car park. *(Chris and Angela Buckell)*

WILLERSEY   SP1039
★ Bell (01386) 858405
B4632 Cheltenham–Stratford, near Broadway; WR12 7PJ Well run neatly modernised stone-built pub, popular home-made food from sandwiches and baguettes up including weekday set lunch and daily specials, ales such as Pure UBU and Sharps Doom Bar, good friendly service; children and dogs welcome, overlooks village green and duck pond, lots of tables in big garden, five bedrooms in outbuildings, open all day weekends. *(Anon)*

WINCHCOMBE   SP0228
★ Lion (01242) 603300
North Street; GL54 5PS Stylish former coaching inn dating from the 15th c, plenty of rustic chic and appealing relaxed atmosphere, good (if not particularly cheap) food in bar or restaurant, well kept ales such as Prescott and Ringwood, nice

---

Post Office address codings confusingly give the impression that some pubs are in Gloucestershire, when they're really in Warwickshire (which is where we list them).

wines, smiling helpful service, newspapers, magazines and board games; background music; children welcome, dogs in bar and snug, tables in good-sized garden, seven bedrooms, open all day. *(Comus and Sarah Elliott, Richard Tilbrook, Guy Vowles)*

WINCHCOMBE   SP0228
Old Corner Cupboard

(01242) 602303 *Gloucester Street; GL54 5LX* Attractive old golden-stone pub with enjoyable food (all day weekends) including range of curries in back dining room, well kept ales such as Hook Norton and Wickwar, decent wines by the glass, good service, comfortable stripped-stone lounge bar with heavy-beamed Tudor core, traditional hatch-service lobby, small side room with woodburner in massive stone fireplace, traditional games; children welcome, tables in back garden, open all day. *(Guy Vowles, Steve Tilley, M G Hart)*

WINCHCOMBE   SP0228
Plaisterers Arms (01242) 602358

Abbey Terrace; GL54 5LL Traditional old split-level pub with beams and stripped stonework, well kept Timothy Taylors Landlord, Wye Valley and a guest, enjoyable pubby food served by friendly staff, two chatty front bars both with steps down to dimly lit lower back dining area, some stall tables, Hogarth prints, bric-a-brac and flame-effect fire; TV, darts and piano; children and dogs welcome, play area in long secluded back garden, five simple bedrooms (tricky stairs). *(Steve and Liz Tilley)*

WINCHCOMBE   SP0228
★White Hart (01242) 602359

High Street (B4632); GL54 5LJ Popular 16th-c inn with big windows looking out over village street, mix of chairs and small settles around pine tables, bare boards and grey-green paintwork, cricketing memorabilia, well kept Goffs and other ales such as Prescott, Wadworths and Wickwar, wine shop at back (corkage added if you buy to drink on premises), wide choice by the glass too, specialist sausage menu (including vegetarian) and other enjoyable food, good friendly service, separate restaurant, log

fire; sports TV; children and dogs (in bar and bedrooms) welcome, open all day from 9am (10am Sun). *(Steve Tilley, Dr Peter Crawshaw, Heulwen and Neville Pinfield, Steve and Liz Tilley, Guy Vowles)*

WITHINGTON   SP0315
Mill Inn (01242) 890204

Off A436 or A40; GL54 4BE Idyllic streamside setting for this mossy-roofed old stone inn, some refurbishment but keeping character with nice nooks and corners, beams, wood/flagstone floors, two inglenook log fires and a woodburner, Sam Smiths tapped from the cask, enjoyable reasonably priced food cooked by landlord, four dining rooms; children and dogs welcome, picnic-sets in big garden, splendid walks, open Fri-Sun. *(Guy Vowles)*

WOODCHESTER   SO8403
★Old Fleece (01453) 872582

Rooksmoor; A46 a mile S of Stroud; GL5 5NB Old wisteria-clad roadside pub, part of the small Cotswold Food Club chain; good choice of well presented interesting food, well kept mostly local beers and good wines by the glass, friendly accommodating staff, bar, dining room and snug, big windows, bare boards, panelling and stripped stone, modern paintings, large log fire; children welcome, wheelchair access (except dining area – you can also eat in bar), two front terraces, open (and food) all day. *(Alison and Michael Harper)*

WOODCHESTER   SO8302
Ram (01453) 873329

High Street, South Woodchester; off A46 S of Stroud; GL5 5EL Bustling country pub with up to half a dozen well priced changing ales and three ciders, enjoyable fairly standard home-made food including good value Sun lunch (they ask to keep a credit card while you eat), L-shaped beamed bar with bare boards and stripped stonework, nice mix of traditional furnishings including several cushioned antique panelled settles, open fires; children and dogs welcome, wheelchair access (steep incline from car park), terrace with lovely valley views, open all day. *(Tom and Ruth Rees)*

Hampshire

AMPORT SU2944 Map 2

Hawk Inn 🛏

(01264) 710371 – www.hawkinnamport.co.uk

Off A303 at Thruxton interchange; at Andover end of village just before Monxton;
SP11 8AE

Relaxed rambling old place with comfortable front bar, two dining areas, contemporary furnishings, helpful staff and well thought-of food; bedrooms

In warm weather, the sunny sandstone front terrace here is a much favoured spot, with picnic-sets looking across the lane to more seating on grass that leads down to Pill Hill brook. Inside, it's open-plan and contemporary with a comfortable front bar: brown leather armchairs and plush grey sofas by a low table with daily newspapers, a log fire in a brick fireplace and sisal matting on bare boards. To the left, a tucked-away snug room has horse-racing photographs, shelves of books and a TV. Two dining areas have smart window blinds, black leather cushioned wall seating and elegant wooden chairs (some carved) around pale tables, big oil paintings on pale walls above a grey dado, and a woodburning stove. Black-topped stools line the counter, where courteous staff serve Ramsbury Gold and Upham Tipster on handpump and quite a few wines by the glass. Bedrooms are up to date and comfortable, and the famous Hawk Conservancy Trust is in the village.

¶¶ Good all-day food (including breakfasts from 7.30am; 8.30am weekends) includes lunchtime sandwiches, crispy squid with aioli, chicken liver parfait with plum chutney, sharing plates, pork and leek sausages with mustard mash and shallot gravy, guinea fowl with sauté potatoes and bacon and leek jus, roasted artichoke pasta with wild mushrooms, leek and gorgonzola sauce, smoked haddock with herb mash and wholegrain mustard velouté, and puddings such as honeycomb parfait with passion-fruit syrup and chocolate brownie with salted caramel ice-cream. *Benchmark main dish: burger with toppings, relish and fries £13.95. Two-course evening meal £20.50.*

Free house ~ Licensee Rupert Fowler ~ Real ale ~ Open 10am-11pm (10.30 Sun) ~ Bar food 12-2.30, 6.30-9.30; 12-2.30, 6-9 Sun ~ Children welcome ~ Dogs allowed in bar ~ Wi-fi ~ Bedrooms: /£90 *Recommended by B J Harding, Katharine Cowherd, Emma Scofield, Gus Swan, Edward Mirzoeff*

BANK

Oak 🍺

SU2806 Map 2

(023) 8028 2350 – www.oakinnlyndhurst.co.uk

Signposted just off A35 SW of Lyndhurst; SO43 7FE

**New Forest pub with a good mix of customers, popular food
and interesting décor**

Given the peaceful and tucked-away location, it's quite a surprise how busy this pub always is. There's a warm welcome for all from the friendly staff, and the L-shaped bar has bay windows with built-in red-cushioned seats, and two or three little pine-panelled booths with small built-in tables and bench seats. The rest of the bare-boarded bar has low beams and joists, candles in brass holders on a row of stripped old and newer blond tables set against the wall and all manner of bric-a-brac: fishing rods, spears, a boomerang, old ski poles, brass platters, heavy knives and guns. There are cushioned milk churns along the bar counter and little red lanterns among hop bines above the bar. Fullers London Pride, Gales HSB and Seafarers and a changing guest on handpump and 14 wines by the glass; background music. The pleasant side garden has picnic-sets and long tables and benches by big yew trees.

Rewarding food includes lunchtime sandwiches, ham hock terrine with pineapple chutney, whole baked camembert with thyme and peach and maple syrup compote, sharing platters, a pie of the day, burger with onion marmalade and chips, spinach gnocchi filled with ricotta, pork belly braised in cider with apple compote, gravy and crackling, corn-fed chicken with carrot, pomegranate, radish and toasted pine nut salad, and puddings. *Benchmark main dish: scallops with king prawns, guacamole and mango salsa £20.00. Two-course evening meal £20.00.*

Fullers ~ Manager Carlos Dias ~ Real ale ~ Open 11.30-3, 5.30-11; 11.30-11 Sat; 12-10.30 Sun ~ Bar food 12-2.30, 6-9.30; all day weekends ~ Children welcome until 6pm; must be over 10 after 6pm ~ Dogs allowed in bar ~ Wi-fi *Recommended by Brian Glozier, Phil and Jane Villiers, Adrian Johnson, B R Merritt, Katharine Cowherd*

BAUGHURST

Wellington Arms 🎯 �peⁱ ☕

SU5860 Map 2

(0118) 982 0110 – www.thewellingtonarms.com

Baughurst Road, S of village; RG26 5LP

Hampshire Dining Pub of the Year

**Pretty small country pub-with-rooms, exceptional cooking and
a friendly welcome; bedrooms**

Most customers, of course, come to this charming little country inn for the excellent food or to stay in the delightful bedrooms, but they do keep a couple of ales such as Longdog Bunny Chaser and West Berkshire Good Old Boy on handpump, ten wines by the glass and a farm cider; background music. It's run with great care and enthusiasm by the friendly licensees and their courteous staff – and a genuine welcome is offered to all. The dining room is attractively decorated with an assortment of cushioned oak dining chairs around a mix of polished tables on terracotta tiles, pretty blinds, brass candlesticks and flowers and window sills stacked with cookery books. The garden has picnic-sets and herbaceous borders.

 Growing some of their own vegetables, rearing sheep and pigs and keeping bees and chickens, the very special food includes terrine of local rabbit, pigeon and pork with home-made apple chutney, creamy moules marinière, home-reared and cured tamworth ham and eggs, potato gnocchi in garlic and butter with butternut squash, walnuts, sage and parmesan, cod fillet with a preserved lemon and olive crust, samphire and crushed anya potatoes, roe deer, root vegetable and red wine pie, and puddings such as jelly of home-made elderflower cordial with rhubarb ripple ice-cream and chocolate squidgy pudding with stem ginger ice-cream; they also offer a two- and three-course set weekday lunch. *Benchmark main dish: twice-baked cheddar cheese soufflé on braised leeks with cream and parmesan £9.85. Two-course evening meal £22.00.*

Free house ~ Licensees Simon Page and Jason King ~ Real ale ~ Open 9-3, 6.30 (6 Sat)-11; 9-4 Sun ~ Bar food 12-1.30, 6.30-8.30 (9 Fri, Sat); 12-4 Sun ~ Children welcome but no high chairs ~ Dogs welcome ~ Wi-fi ~ Bedrooms: /£100 *Recommended by John T Ames, Mrs P Sumner, Ron Corbett*

BEAULIEU
SU3902 Map 2
Montagu Arms
(01590) 614986 – www.montaguarmshotel.co.uk
Almost opposite Palace House; SO42 7ZL

Separate Monty's Bar, open all day for both drinks and food

If you visit this picturesque village at the heart of the New Forest, do drop into Monty's Bar. It's attached to the solidly built and civilised Montagu Arms hotel (whose tucked-away back garden is quite charming in warm weather) but has its own entrance, atmosphere and customers. Usefully open all day, the simply furnished bar has panelling, bare floorboards, a couple of red leather chesterfield sofas facing each other in front of a log fire, a bow window set with armchairs and a table – and another big window with a large circular table surrounded by homely red-cushioned dining chairs; pool table, darts and TV. A few stools line the counter where they keep Ringwood Best and Fortyniner and a seasonal guest on handpump and several wines by the glass, served by cheerful, helpful bar staff. Across the entrance hall is a smarter panelled dining room.

Well liked food includes lunchtime sandwiches, home-made local pork scotch egg with a soft-boiled egg and spiced apple sauce, chicken liver parfait with red onion marmalade, local sausages with onion gravy, grilled halloumi with chargrilled vegetables, beer-battered haddock and chips, duck breast with pak choi, duck leg spring roll, ginger beer glaze and duck fat potatoes, grilled fresh fish of the day, and puddings; they also offer afternoon tea. *Benchmark main dish: burger with toppings, spiced tomato and red onion relish and fries £15.95. Two-course evening meal £14.00.*

Free house ~ Licensee Sunil Kanjanghat ~ Real ale ~ Open 11-11; 11-3, 6-11 in winter ~ Bar food 12-2.30 (3 weekends), 6.30-9.30 ~ Restaurant ~ Children welcome ~ Dogs allowed in bar ~ Wi-fi ~ Bedrooms: £169/£199 *Recommended by Isobel Mackinlay, Gavin and Helle May*

BENTWORTH
SU6740 Map 2
Sun ◀
(01420) 562338 – www.thesuninnbentworth.co.uk
Sun Hill; from the A339 coming from Alton, the first turning takes you there direct; or in village follow 'Shalden 2¼, Alton 4¼' signpost; GU34 5JT

Smashing choice of real ales in popular country pub; nearby walks

With an easy-going, chatty atmosphere and a fine choice of real ales, this tucked-away, 17th-c country tavern is run by a friendly, long-serving landlady and her helpful staff. The two little traditional communicating rooms have high-backed antique settles, pews and schoolroom chairs, olde-worlde prints and blacksmith's tools on the walls, and bare boards and scrubbed deal tables on the left; three big fireplaces with log fires make it especially snug in winter. An arch leads to a brick-floored room with another open fire. Kept well on handpump, the beers might include Black Sheep, Dartmoor Jail Ale, Flack Manor Double Drop, Itchen Valley Hampshire Rose, Ringwood Best, Sharps Doom Bar and Timothy Taylors Landlord. There are seats out in front and in the back garden; pleasant nearby walks.

Quite a choice of food includes prawns in filo pastry with sweet chilli dip, baked field mushrooms topped with stilton, chicken, ham and mushroom pie, half lamb shoulder in mint and honey, mushroom stroganoff, king prawn curry, calves liver and bacon, sticky honey and soy salmon, and puddings such as chocolate fudge cake and apple and raspberry crumble. *Benchmark main dish: beer-battered cod and chips £11.95. Two-course evening meal £19.00.*

Free house ~ Licensee Mary Holmes ~ Real ale ~ Open 12-3, 6-11; 12-10.30 Sun ~ Bar food 12-2, 7-9.30 ~ Children welcome ~ Dogs welcome ~ Wi-fi *Recommended by Isobel Mackinlay, Mike Swan, Tony and Wendy Hobden*

BIGHTON
SU6134 Map 2

English Partridge 🌟 ♟ ♈

(01962) 732859 – www.englishpartridge.co.uk
Bighton Dean Lane; village signed off B3046 N of Alresford; SO24 9RE

Charming country pub with a genuine welcome, much character in three bars, plenty to look at, good wines and beers and highly enjoyable food

You can be quite sure, whether a regular or a visitor, that you'll get a genuinely warm welcome from the chatty landlord and his young staff in this charming little country pub. At the front, a small simple room to the left of the door is just right for walkers and their dogs, with a warm open fire, a few chairs and tables and stools against the counter. The characterful main bar has a wonderful ancient parquet floor, a black dado with hunting prints, local shoot photographs and game bird pictures on the walls above, a stuffed pheasant in a glass cabinet, a woodburning stove in a brick inglenook and a fireplace filled with candles, and all sorts of dining chairs and tables. Flowerpots Bitter and Perridge Pale, Triple fff Alton Pride and Moondance and a guest beer on handpump, ten wines by the glass, eight gins, farm cider and Somerset cider brandy; darts, board games and maybe unobtrusive background music. Through an open doorway, the back dining room has long built-in wall seats with scatter cushions, similar chairs and tables (each set with a candle in a candlestick), a huge deer's head and a boar's head, antlers, shooting and hunting photographs and fish and bird prints. As we went to press they were landscaping the garden, but they did have a terrace with tables and chairs under parasols.

Rewarding food includes squid and chorizo salad, creamed mushrooms on toast with a poached egg, butternut squash risotto, steak pie, stuffed chicken leg with braised haricot beans, pulled pork with pan haggerty, cabbage and bacon and meat juices, stone bass fillet with sauté potatoes and caper and jus vinaigrette, and puddings such as sticky toffee pudding and maraschino cherry jelly with rum and raisin ice-cream. *Benchmark main dish: beer-battered fish and chips £10.00. Two-course evening meal £19.00.*

Free house ~ Licensee David Young ~ Real ale ~ Open 12-3, 5-11; 12-11 Sat; 12-8 Sun; closed Sun evening in winter ~ Bar food 12-2.30, 6.30-9.30; 12-4 Sun ~ Children welcome ~ Dogs welcome ~ Wi-fi *Recommended by Tony and Jill Radnor, Ann and Colin Hunt, M G Hart*

We say if we know a pub allows dogs.

BRANSGORE   SZ1997   Map 2

Three Tuns ★ ☐

(01425) 672232 – www.threetunsinn.com

Village signposted off A35 and off B3347 N of Christchurch; Ringwood Road, opposite church; BH23 8JH

Pretty thatched pub with proper old-fashioned bar and good beers, a civilised main dining area and inventive food

With five real ales and imaginative food, customers tend to return on a regular basis to this 17th-c thatched pub. The roomy low-ceilinged and carpeted main area has a fireside 'codgers' corner', as well as a good mix of comfortably cushioned low chairs around a variety of dining tables. On the right is a separate traditional regulars' bar that seems almost taller than it is wide, with an impressive log-effect stove in a stripped-brick hearth, some shiny black panelling and individualistic pubby furnishings. Otter Bitter and Ringwood Best and Fortyniner, plus guests such as St Austell Proper Job and Sharps Cornish Coaster on handpump, a dozen wines by the glass and farm cider; they hold a beer festival in September. The hanging baskets are lovely in summer and there are picnic-sets on an attractive, extensive, shrub-sheltered terrace with more tables on the grass looking over pony paddocks; pétanque. The Grade II listed barn is popular for parties – and they hold a civil ceremonies licence.

From an inventive menu (and usefully served all day at weekends), the interesting food includes sandwiches, snails from Dorset in garlic butter and gorgonzola, corned beef hash fritters with home-made brown sauce, moules marinière, venison pasty, lentil and bean fajitas with guacamole and sour cream, burger with toppings, onion relish, coleslaw and chips, goat curry, duck two-ways (pink breast and slow-cooked leg) with preserved cherries, turnip cream and potato balls, and puddings such as salted caramel and almond pie with pear 'bubble' and tropical 'egg and soldiers'. *Benchmark main dish: slow-roasted pork with apple, dauphinoise potatoes and mustard sauce £13.95. Two-course evening meal £19.50.*

Enterprise ~ Lease Nigel Glenister ~ Real ale ~ Open 11-11; 12-10.30 Sun ~ Bar food 12-2.15, 7-9; 12-9.15 weekends; all day bank holidays ~ Restaurant ~ Children welcome ~ Dogs allowed in bar ~ Wi-fi *Recommended by S Holder, Michael and Sheila Hawkins, Glenwys and Alan Lawrence*

DROXFORD   SU6018   Map 2

Bakers Arms ★ ☐

(01489) 877533 – www.thebakersarmsdroxford.com

High Street; A32 5 miles N of Wickham; SO32 3PA

Attractively opened-up and friendly pub with well kept beers, good, interesting cooking and cosy corners

With ale brewed just a mile away and tempting food cooked by the landlord, it's hardly surprising that this bustling pub is so popular. There's a friendly welcome for all and an easy-going atmosphere, and the place is attractively laid out with the central bar kept as the main focus: Bowman Swift One, Oakleaf Quercus Folium and Red Cat Best on handpump, local cider, and 15 wines by the glass from a short, carefully chosen list. Well spaced tables on carpet or neat bare boards are spread around the airy L-shaped open-plan bar, with low leather chesterfields and an assortment of comfortably cushioned chairs at one end; a dark panelled dado, dark beams and joists and a modicum of country oddments emphasise the freshness of the crisp white paintwork; good log fire and board games. To one side, with a separate entrance, is the village post office. There are picnic-sets outside.

 From a seasonal menu, the well presented food includes sandwiches, roasted duck breast and beetroot salad with orange dressing, game terrine with stewed plum and kaffir lime, a pie of the day, burger with toppings, spicy red pepper ketchup and fries, slow-cooked pork belly with pork and black pudding croquette, sour apple velouté and cider reduction, local trout with smoked fishcake and white wine butter sauce, and puddings such as rum baba (orange cake with rum and orange syrup) and peanut and caramel (salted caramel ice-cream, candied peanut dust and caramel peanut brittle with butterscotch sauce and chocolate shards); they also offer a two-course set menu (which includes a drink). *Benchmark main dish: confit duck leg with puy lentils and gravy £14.00. Two-course evening meal £20.00.*

Free house ~ Licensees Adam and Anna Cordery ~ Real ale ~ Open 11.45-3, 6-11; 12-3 Sun ~ Bar food 12-2.30, 6.30-9.30; 12-3 Sun ~ Well behaved children welcome ~ Dogs allowed in bar ~ Wi-fi *Recommended by Stephen and Jean Curtis, R Halliday*

FRITHAM
SU2314 Map 2

Royal Oak 🍺

(023) 8081 2606

Village signed from M27 junction 1; SO43 7HJ

Rural New Forest spot with traditional rooms, log fires, seven real ales and simple lunchtime food

'What a little gem' and 'a great favourite of ours' are just two comments from readers on this unspoilt and charming country pub. It's in a lovely spot right in the middle of the New Forest and part of a working farm, so there are ponies and pigs out on the green and plenty of livestock nearby. Three neatly kept black-beamed rooms are straightforward but full of proper traditional character, with prints and pictures involving local characters on the white walls, restored panelling, antique wheelback, spindleback and other old chairs and stools with colourful seats around solid tables on the oak floors, and two roaring log fires. The back bar has several books; darts and board games. Up to seven real ales are tapped from the cask including one named for the pub (from Bowman), Bowman Swift One, Flack Manor Double Drop, Hop Back Summer Lightning, Ringwood Best, Stonehenge Sign of Spring and a guest ale. Also, ten wines by the glass (mulled wine in winter), 14 country wines, local cider and a September beer festival; service remains friendly and efficient even when packed (which it often is). Summer barbecues may be held in the neatly kept big garden, which has a marquee for poor weather and a pétanque pitch. They now have three shepherd's huts to rent for overnight stays.

Good value, limited food – lunchtime only – consists of wholesome soup, a particularly good pork pie, quiche and sausages. *Benchmark main dish: ploughman's £8.50.*

Free house ~ Licensees Neil and Pauline McCulloch ~ Real ale ~ Open 11-11; 12-10.30 Sun; 11-3, 5.30-11 weekdays in winter ~ Bar food 12-2.30 (3 weekends) ~ Children welcome ~ Dogs welcome *Recommended by Ann and Colin Hunt, Sheila Topham, Adrian Johnson*

'Children welcome' means the pub says it lets children inside without any special restriction. If it allows them in, but to restricted areas such as an eating area or family room, we specify this. Some pubs may impose an evening time limit. We do not mention limits after 9pm as we assume children are home by then.

HIGHCLERE
Yew Tree ♀ ⇦

SU4358 Map 2

(01635) 253360 – www.theyewtree.co.uk

Hollington Cross; RG20 9SE

Friendly country inn with character rooms, a good choice of drinks, enjoyable food and seats in garden; bedrooms

Just a few minutes from Highclere Castle, this is a 17th-c country inn, popular with a wide mix of customers. The main door opens into a heavy-beamed character bar with leather tub chairs and a leather sofa facing one another across a low table in front of a two-way fireplace housing a chimenea stove, and stools and high chairs against the counter (church candles in chunky candlesticks to either side). Ringwood Best, Two Cocks 1643 Cavalier and Upham Punter on handpump and good wines by the glass, served by friendly, helpful staff. Leading off to the left is a room with antlers and stuffed squirrels on the mantelpiece above an inglenook fireplace, books piled on shelves, a pale button-back leather window seat, a mix of wooden and painted dining chairs around nice old tables on red and black tiles or carpet, and, at one end, a tartan and leather wall banquette; unobtrusive background music. Dining rooms to the left of the bar are divided by hefty timbers and have high-backed tartan seating creating booths and more wooden or painted chairs around a mix of tables on flagstones or sisal carpet. The atmosphere throughout is one of easy informality. Doors lead to the garden with an outside bar and a variety of elegant metal and teak seats and tables on gravel or a raised decked area. Well equipped and comfortable bedrooms are named after trees (two are on the ground floor); breakfasts good.

Highly enjoyable food includes sandwiches, woodcock and foie gras ballotine with apple chutney, devilled whitebait with lemon mayonnaise, honey-roast jerusalem artichoke with blue cheese and tarragon risotto, chicken caesar salad, burger with gherkins, tomato relish and fries, cod fillet with a tomato, mushroom and herb crust and grain mustard velouté, loin of local venison with steamed venison suet pudding and carrot and swede purée, and puddings such as vanilla panna cotta with raspberry crumb and black pepper sauce and dark chocolate and honeycomb pavlova. *Benchmark main dish: crispy pork belly £16.95. Two-course evening meal £23.00.*

Free house ~ Licensee Simon Davis and Tori Sambrook ~ Real ale ~ Open 9am-11pm ~ Bar food 12-2.30, 6.30-9.30 (7-8.30 Sun) ~ Children welcome ~ Dogs allowed in bar and bedrooms ~ Wi-fi ~ Bedrooms: /£95 *Recommended by Caroline Prescott, Emma Scofield*

HOOK
Hogget ◗

SU7153 Map 2

(01256) 763009 – www.thehogget.co.uk

1.1 miles from M3 junction 5; A287 N, at junction with A30 (car park just before traffic lights); RG27 9JJ

Well run and accommodating, a proper pub moving with the times and giving good value

As a break from either the A30 or the M3, this well run, bustling pub is just the ticket. There's a friendly atmosphere, a good mix of customers and rooms that ramble around the central servery so there's plenty of space for all. The wallpaper, lighting and carpet pattern, plus the leather sofas and tub chairs over on the right at the back, give an easy-going and homely feel – as does the way the layout provides several smallish distinct areas. Ringwood Best and Fortyniner and Wychwood Imperial Red on handpump, 11 wines by the glass and plenty of neatly dressed staff; daily papers, background music and books (often cookbooks) on shelves. A sizeable terrace had sturdy tables and chairs, including some in a heated covered area.

Ⅱ❘ Enjoyable food includes lunchtime sandwiches (not Sun), field mushrooms on toast topped with a poached egg, crispy calamari with garlic mayonnaise, chicken caesar salad, a vegetarian quiche of the day, chilli beef with melted cheese and nachos, sticky barbecue ribs with coleslaw and fries, bass with lemon and caper butter sauce, and puddings such as baked alaska with hot chocolate sauce and rhubarb and cranberry fool. *Benchmark main dish: burger with toppings and triple-cooked chips £11.00. Two-course evening meal £19.00.*

Marstons ~ Lease Tom and Laura Faulkner ~ Real ale ~ Open 12-3, 5.30-11; 12-11 Sat; 12-6 Sun ~ Bar food 12-2.30, 6.30-9; all day Sat; 12-6 Sun ~ Restaurant ~ Children welcome but not after 7pm Fri and Sat ~ Dogs allowed in bar ~ Wi-fi *Recommended by Caroline Prescott, Lindy Andrews, Mrs P Sumner*

HORDLE   SZ2996   Map 2

Mill at Gordleton 🏵 ⚲ 🛏

(01590) 682219 – www.themillatgordleton.co.uk

Silver Street; SO41 6DJ

Charming tucked-away country inn with friendly bar, exceptional food and drink and pretty waterside gardens; comfortable bedrooms

Our readers are delighted when they come across this rather special and gently civilised small hotel. The comfortable and individually furnished bedrooms make a perfect base for exploring the area, and as it's on the edge of the New Forest, there are plenty of nearby walks; breakfasts are excellent. The little panelled bar on the right is popular with locals (often with a dog) and has leather armchairs and Victorian-style mahogany dining chairs on parquet flooring, a feature stove, a pretty corner china cupboard, Ringwood Best and a guest beer on handpump, 18 good wines by the glass, 22 malt whiskies and a rack of daily papers. This overflows into a cosy lounge, and there's also a spacious second bar by the sizeable beamed restaurant extension, which is an attractive room with contemporary art and garden outlook. The gardens are really lovely, featuring an extensive series of interestingly planted areas looping about pools and a placid winding stream, dotted with intriguing art objects and with plenty of places to sit, from intimate pairs of seats to teak or wrought-iron tables on the main waterside terrace (which is beautifully lit up at night).

🌟 As well as value two- and three-course set menus and using the best local, organic produce, the excellent food includes sandwiches and toasties, twice-baked home-smoked haddock soufflé, game terrine with plum chutney, honey-glazed ham and free-range eggs, crab and gruyère tart, pork and apple meatballs with creamy mash and cider jus, spicy lamb and mango curry with almond and vegetable pilaf rice and pineapple relish, trio of fish (turbot, mussels, salmon with roasted shallot and fennel 'en papillote' and green peppercorn butter), and puddings such as white chocolate marquise with milk chocolate and honey ice-cream, mulled fruit and rich dark chocolate sauce and passion-fruit soufflé with kiwi and lime sorbet. *Benchmark main dish: rare-breed beef fillet with bacon, prune and potato rösti and madeira sauce £28.95. Two-course evening meal £35.00.*

Free house ~ Licensee Liz Cottingham ~ Real ale ~ Open 11-11; 12-10.30 Sun ~ Bar food 12-2.15, 7-9.15; 12-3, 7-9 Sun ~ Restaurant ~ Children welcome ~ Dogs allowed in bar ~ Wi-fi ~ Bedrooms: £135/£150 *Recommended by Michael Hill, Christopher and Elise Way, Gerry and Rosemary Dobson*

There are report forms at the back of the book.

HURSLEY   SU4225 Map 2

Kings Head ♀ ◖ ⇐

(01962) 775208 – www.kingsheadhursley.co.uk

A3090 Winchester–Romsey; SO21 2JW

Creeper-covered pub with an easy, friendly atmosphere, interestingly furnished rooms, well kept ales, good wines by the glass and enjoyable food; lovely bedrooms

A former coaching inn, this is a handsome brick building on the edge of a village and opposite the ancient church. The bar to the left has shutters by a cushioned window seat, high-backed plush green chairs and chunky leather stools around scrubbed tables on black floor slates, one high table with equally high chairs, a raised fireplace with church candles on the mantelpiece and stools against the S-shaped counter which is painted a contemporary grey. Bowman Swift One, Flack Manor Double Drop, Ringwood Best, Sharps Doom Bar and Upham Sprinter on handpump and 21 wines by the glass; background music, a piano, daily papers and board games. Staff are welcoming and helpful. A character lower room has a fine end brick wall, a woodburning stove and wall banquettes with leather, tartan and plush upholstery, and cushioned settles on floorboards. You can hire out the atmospheric downstairs skittle alley. As we went to press they were about to redo the garden. The bedrooms (named after previous owners of the Hursley Estate) have antiques and original fireplaces and are comfortable and thoughtfully equipped.

🍴 Imaginative food using local, seasonal and foraged produce includes lunchtime sandwiches, mussels in tomato and chilli sauce, pigs cheek and ham hock terrine with smoked bacon popcorn and pork scratching crumb, beer-battered fish and chips, a pie of the day, green pea, halloumi and pecorino risotto, burger with cheese, coleslaw and fries, spicy marinated chicken salad with candied pawpaw, mango, pineapple, mangetout and glass noodles, tiger prawn and caper beurre noisette and samphire, and puddings such as banana marshmallow, chocolate ice-cream and chocolate shavings and rhubarb and custard trifle. *Benchmark main dish: slow-roasted pork belly with dauphinoise potatoes and apple compote £16.95. Two-course evening meal £20.00.*

Free house ~ Licensees Mark and Penny Thornhill ~ Real ale ~ Open 11-11 ~ Bar food 12-3, 6-9; 12-9.30 Sat; 12-8 Sun ~ Restaurant ~ Children welcome ~ Dogs allowed in bar and bedrooms ~ Wi-fi ~ Bedrooms: £85/£100 *Recommended by Mrs Julie Thomas*

LISS   SU7826 Map 2

Jolly Drover ⇐

(01730) 893137 – www.thejollydrover.co.uk

London Road, Hill Brow; B2070 S of town, near B3006 junction; GU33 7QL

Friendly, comfortable pub with plenty of locals and visitors, real ales, popular food and seats outside; good bedrooms

A s a visitor, you'll feel genuinely welcomed in this bustling pub by both the long-serving, enthusiastic licensees and the cheerful, friendly locals. The neatly carpeted low-beamed bar has leather tub chairs and a couple of chesterfield sofas in front of the inglenook log fire, daily papers, board games and Bowman Wallops Wood, Sharps Doom Bar and Timothy Taylors Landlord on handpump and a dozen wines by the glass. The various areas, with understated décor mainly in muted terracotta or pale ochre, include two back dining sections, one of which opens on to a sheltered terrace with teak furniture, and a lawn with picnic-sets beyond. The neat bedrooms are in two barn conversions.

🍴 Good, honest food includes baps and sandwiches, chicken skewers with satay sauce, pork and mushroom pâté, tempura hake and chips, liver and bacon in onion gravy, walnut, cranberry and stilton flan, gammon with egg or pineapple, and puddings such as fruit crumble and banoffi pie. *Benchmark main dish: steak and kidney pie £12.00. Two-course evening meal £17.00.*

Enterprise ~ Lease Barry and Anne Coe ~ Real ale ~ Open 10.30-3, 5.30-11; 12-4 Sun ~ Bar food 12-2.15, 6-9.30; 12-3 Sun ~ Restaurant ~ Children welcome ~ Wi-fi ~ Bedrooms: £70/£90 *Recommended by Mr and Mrs J Watkins, Michael and Margaret Cross*

 LITTLETON   SU4532 Map 2
Running Horse 🛏
(01962) 880218 – www.runninghorseinn.co.uk
Main Road; village signed off B3049 NW of Winchester; SO22 6QS

Carefully renovated country pub with spreading dining areas, woodburning stove in the bar, enjoyable food and cabana in garden; pretty bedrooms

They usefully offer breakfasts to non-residents here from 7.30am during the week and 8am at weekends; the simply decorated bedrooms are pretty. Spreading dining areas are attractively furnished with an appealing variety of chairs and tables on big flagstones or bare boards, there are button-backed banquettes in a panelled alcove, a much prized cushioned seat in a bow window plus wooden armchairs around a table, and polo photographs on red walls. Also, unusual wine-bottle ceiling lights, old books on rustic bookshelves, antlers and big mirrors and a relaxed, friendly and chatty atmosphere. A brick fireplace holds a woodburning stove, and leather-topped stools line the counter where they serve Upham Tipster, Punter and Stakes on handpump, 14 wines by the glass and a farm cider. The front and back terraces have green metal tables and chairs, and there are picnic-sets on the back grass by a spreading sycamore and a popular cabana with cushioned seats. This is sister pub to the Thomas Lord in West Meon.

🍴 Tasty food includes sandwiches, pork pâté with macerated raisins and chive, shallot dressing, smoked haddock and mackerel fishcake with pickled lemon, kohlrabi rémoulade and crispy capers, butternut squash risotto with crispy sage, burnt butter and amaretti crumb, honey-roast ham with a duck egg, lamb rump with fondant potato, wild mushrooms and rosemary jus, and puddings such as mango panna cotta with coconut macaroon, burnt pineapple and green tea sorbet and toffee apple crumble with salted caramel ice-cream. *Benchmark main dish: beer-battered cod and triple-cooked chips £12.50. Two-course evening meal £20.50.*

Free house ~ Licensee Anita Peel ~ Real ale ~ Open 11-11 (10.30 Sun) ~ Bar food 12-2.30, 6.30-9.30; 12-3.30, 6.30-9 Sun ~ Restaurant ~ Children welcome ~ Dogs allowed in bar ~ Wi-fi ~ Bedrooms: /£105 *Recommended by Isobel Mackinlay, Mike Swan, Ian Herdman, M G Hart*

 LONGSTOCK   SU3537 Map 2
Peat Spade ♀
(01264) 810612 – www.peatspadeinn.co.uk
Off A30 on W edge of Stockbridge; SO20 6DR

Former coaching inn with boldly painted rooms, shooting and fishing themed décor, imaginative food and real ales; stylish bedrooms

Tired walkers on the Test Way are only too happy to rest with a pint and a meal here – it's popular with fishermen too, as the River Test (famous for fly fishing) is just 100 metres away. The bars have a sporting feel with stuffed fish, and lots of hunting pictures and prints on dark red or green walls. Both the bar and dining room have pretty windows, an interesting mix of dining chairs around miscellaneous tables on bare boards, standard lamps and candlelight; also, wine bottles, old stone bottles and soda siphons, a nice display of toby jugs and shelves of books. An upstairs room has comfortable sofas and armchairs. Upham Punter and Tipster and a weekly guest ale on handpump, 11 wines by the glass and 20 malt whiskies; background music. The terrace and garden have plenty of seats for warm weather and they've a little fishing shop. Bedrooms are stylish and contemporary.

Under the new licensee, the rewarding food includes lunchtime sandwiches, chicken liver parfait with pickles, venison carpaccio with celeriac, beetroot, horseradish and goats curd, sharing platters, cauliflower tart with onions and cheese, burger with toppings and fries, beer-battered hake and chips, guinea fowl with pumpkin, onion and quince, wild bass with barley, almonds, wild mushrooms and fennel, and puddings such as chocolate sponge tart with coffee and hazelnuts and meringue with lemon curd, honey granola and apricots; they also offer a two- and three-course set menu. *Benchmark main dish: local charcuterie board £17.00. Two-course evening meal £21.00.*

Free house ~ Licensee Nikki Swulinska ~ Real ale ~ Open 11-11 ~ Bar food 12-2.30, 6.30-9.30; 12-4, 6-9 Sun ~ Well behaved children welcome ~ Dogs allowed in bar and bedrooms ~ Wi-fi ~ Bedrooms: /$130 *Recommended by Mike Swan, Isobel Mackinlay, Richard Kennell, Ian Herdman, Mrs Julie Thomas*

LOWER FROYLE   SU 7643   Map 2
Anchor 🍴⭐ 🍷 🛏

(01420) 23261 – www.anchorinnatlowerfroyle.co.uk
Village signposted N of A31 W of Bentley; GU34 4NA

Civilised pub, lots to look at, real ales, good wines and imaginative bar food; comfortable bedrooms

This is a stylish and comfortable place to stay overnight and breakfasts are first class. The various bar rooms are civilised yet informal with log fires, candlelight, low beams and standing timbers, flagstones in the bar itself and wood stripped floors elsewhere, sofas and armchairs dotted here and there, and a mix of attractive tables and dining chairs. Throughout are all sorts of interesting knick-knacks, books, copper items, horsebrasses, and lots of pictures and prints on contemporary paintwork. High bar chairs line the counter where they keep Triple fff Moondance and guests such as Marstons Pedigree and Ringwood Fortyniner on handpump and nice wines by the glass.

Excellent food includes crab mayonnaise with chilli, lime and avocado and brown crab pâté on toast, jellied ham hock with piccalilli, pea and broad bean risotto with mint butter and parmesan, liver and bacon with red onion marmalade and gravy, stuffed free-range chicken leg with sun-blush tomato, cashew nut and bacon salad, lamb and rosemary pie, pork loin with pan haggerty, cabbage and bacon, pigs head ravioli and a medjool date and bacon sandwich and puddings such as apple crumble cheesecake with granny smith sorbet and salted caramel sauce and lardy cake with custard. *Benchmark main dish: beer-battered haddock and triple-cooked chips £13.00. Two-course evening meal £21.00.*

Free house ~ Licensee Alex Rooke ~ Real ale ~ Open 11-11 (10.30 Sun) ~ Bar food 12-2.30, 6.30-9.30; 12-4, 7-9 Sun ~ Restaurant ~ Children welcome ~ Dogs allowed in bar and bedrooms ~ Wi-fi ~ Bedrooms: /$120 *Recommended by Dr and Mrs P Truelove, Mrs P Sumner*

It's very helpful if you let us know up-to-date food prices when you report on pubs.

LOWER WIELD

SU6339 Map 2

Yew Tree ⭐ ☆ ♀ £

(01256) 389224 – www.the-yewtree.org.uk

Turn off A339 NW of Alton at 'Medstead, Bentworth 1' signpost, then follow village signposts; or off B3046 S of Basingstoke, signposted from Preston Candover; SO24 9RX

Bustling country pub with an enthusiastic landlord, relaxed atmosphere and super choice of wines and food; sizeable garden and nearby walks

Standards are as high as ever here and our readers love their visits. The hard-working, hands-on and charming landlord and his helpful staff make all their customers feel special – and prices are very fair to boot. A small flagstoned bar area on the left has pictures above a stripped-brick dado, a ticking clock and a log fire. There's carpet around to the right of the serving counter (with a couple of stylish wrought-iron bar chairs); throughout there is a mix of tables, including quite small ones for two, and miscellaneous chairs. Drinks include 13 wines by the glass from a well chosen list (with summer rosé and Louis Jadot burgundies), and a beer named for the pub (from Triple fff) and Bowman Yumi on handpump. Outside, there are solid tables and chunky seats on the front terrace, picnic-sets in a sizeable side garden, pleasant views and a cricket field across the quiet lane; nearby walks.

 Food is very good and reasonably priced: sandwiches, smoked haddock, spring onion and mozzarella fishcake with citrus tartare sauce, garlic and blue cheese mushrooms on toasted ciabatta, mushroom, courgette and leek stroganoff, local venison burger with bacon or cheese and chips, pork belly on mash with toffee apple cream sauce, cod loin with cumin crushed potatoes and lightly curried cream sauce, and puddings such as butterscotch and treacle sponge pudding and chocolate and apricot biscuit cake laced with amaretto. *Benchmark main dish: cheesy ham hock, leek and pea pie £9.95. Two-course evening meal £15.00.*

Free house ~ Licensee Tim Gray ~ Real ale ~ Open 12-3, 6-11; 12-10.30 Sun; closed Mon ~ Bar food 12-2, 6.30-9 (8.30 Sun) ~ Children welcome ~ Dogs allowed in bar ~ Wi-fi
Recommended by Ann and Colin Hunt, Tony and Jill Radnor, Martin and Karen Wake

LYMINGTON

SZ3295 Map 2

Angel & Blue Pig 🛏

(01590) 672050 – www.angel-lymington.com

High Street; SO41 9AP

Bustling, friendly inn with plenty of space in several connected rooms, four real ales, enjoyable food and helpful staff; bedrooms

Of course, being in the middle of a highly popular tourist town means this well run inn gets pretty busy – but if you can catch it during quieter periods, you can really appreciate its character. To the right of the door, the cosy front room has comfortable sofas and armchairs around a big chest, rugs on bare boards and an open fire; this leads into a pubby, flagstoned area with high tables and chairs and built-in leather wall seats. The two interconnected dining rooms to the left of the entrance – one carpeted, one with rugs on quarry tiles – have beams and timbers, dining chairs with zigzag backs and grey cushions around a variety of tables, an old range in a brick fireplace, a large boar's head, lots of books on shelves and a bookshelf mural; throughout are numerous hunting prints and porcine bits and pieces. At the back, overlooking the terrace where there are seats and tables under blue parasols, is yet another area with some nice old leather armchairs beside a woodburning stove and the serving counter where they keep Ringwood Best, Blonde Angel (named for the pub from Ringwood) and a couple of local guest ales on handpump, 16 wines by the glass and a choice of coffees; service is friendly and helpful. The stylish, modern bedrooms are comfortable and well equipped, and breakfasts are good.

Usefully served all day, the brasserie-style food includes their famous steaks as well as sandwiches and ciabattas, smoked haddock chowder with a poached egg, goats cheese panna cotta with beetroot purée, sharing platters, black treacle and ale braised beef short rib with horseradish mash, provençale fish stew with aioli, duo of pork (stuffed belly, slow-braised cheeks) with red wine jus and sweet potato mash, and puddings such as dark chocolate and praline pot and caramelised poached pear crème brûlée. *Benchmark main dish: half roast chicken with lemon and thyme butter, coleslaw and triple-cooked chips £10.95. Two-course evening meal £20.00.*

Free house ~ Licensee Matt England ~ Real ale ~ Open 10am-11pm (midnight Fri, Sat); 11-11 Sun ~ Bar food 12-10 (9 Sun) ~ Restaurant ~ Children welcome ~ Dogs allowed in bar ~ Wi-fi ~ Live music last Fri of month and first Sun afternoon of month ~ Bedrooms: £65/£95 *Recommended by J A Goulding, Phil and Jane Villiers*

NORTH WALTHAM   SU5645   Map 2
Fox £

(01256) 397288 – www.thefox.org
3 miles from M3 junction 7: A30 southwards, then turn right at second North Waltham turn, just after Wheatsheaf; pub also signed from village centre; RG25 2BE

Traditional flint country pub, very well run, with tasty food and drink and a nice garden

For travellers on the M3 and A30, this particularly well run country pub is a godsend, as it's within easy reach of both. The low-ceilinged bar on the left has Brakspears Bitter, Sharps Doom Bar, West Berkshire Good Old Boy and a guest beer on handpump, lots of bottled ciders plus Aspall's cider on draught; 13 wines by the glass, 22 malt whiskies and quite a collection of miniatures. The big woodburning stove, parquet floor, simple padded country kitchen chairs, and 'Beer is Best' and poultry prints above the dark dado – all give a comfortably old-fashioned feel, in which perhaps the vital ingredient is the polite and friendly efficiency of the hands-on landlord; background music, TV. The separate dining room, with high-backed leather chairs on a blue tartan carpet, is larger. The garden is colourful in summer with its pergola walkway from the gate on the lane and with immaculate flower boxes and baskets; it has picnic-sets under cocktail parasols in three separate areas. Walks include a pleasant one to Jane Austen's church at Steventon.

Popular food includes sandwiches, crispy duck cakes with mango and coriander salsa, deep-fried brie with redcurrant jelly, honey and mustard-baked ham and eggs, beer-battered haddock and chips, pork, smoked bacon and leek sausages with onion gravy, steak and venison pudding, lamb shank in red wine and rosemary, and puddings such as Mars Bar cheesecake and mixed berry pavlova; Monday is curry night, Tuesday is pie night and Thursday is steak night. *Benchmark main dish: venison haunch with creamed swede, glazed shallots and port glaze £16.50. Two-course evening meal £22.00.*

Free house ~ Licensees Rob and Izzy MacKenzie ~ Real ale ~ Open 11-11 (10 Sun); 10.30am-midnight Sat ~ Bar food 12-2.30, 6.30-9; 12-3, 6.30-8.30 Sun ~ Restaurant ~ Children welcome ~ Dogs allowed in bar ~ Wi-fi *Recommended by Jill Hurley, Glen Locke*

NORTH WARNBOROUGH
Mill House 🌟🍽 ♀ 🍺

SU7352   Map 2

(01256) 702953 – www.brunningandprice.co.uk/millhouse

A mile from M3 junction 5: A287 towards Farnham, then right (brown sign to pub) on to B3349 Hook Road; RG29 1ET

Converted mill with an attractive layout, inventive modern food, good choice of drinks and lovely waterside terraces

In warm weather, head for the extensive garden behind this raftered mill building where there are lots of solid tables and chairs on terraces, even more picnic-sets on grass and attractive landscaping around the sizeable millpond; there's a couple of swings too. Inside, several linked areas on the main upper floor have heavy beams, plenty of well spaced tables in a variety of sizes and styles, rugs on polished boards or beige carpet, coal-effect gas fires in pretty fireplaces, and a profusion of (often interesting) pictures. A section of floor is glazed to show the rushing water and mill wheel below, and a galleried section on the left looks down into a dining room, given a more formal feel by panelling. The well stocked bar has an interesting range of 50 malt whiskies, 18 wines by the glass and local farm cider, as well as Phoenix Brunning & Price Original, Andwell King John and Porter No 1, Hogs Back TEA, Triple fff Altons Pride and Weltons Pridenjoy on handpump. Service is courteous and efficient; background music and board games.

 Good, interesting food includes sandwiches, scallops wrapped in parma ham with red pesto and balsamic reduction, chicken liver pâté with apple and cider chutney, crab and dill quiche with cucumber and samphire salad, ricotta and pine nut stuffed aubergine with pomegranate and date salad and harissa ketchup, rabbit, ham, wild mushroom and lentil broth with herb dumplings, bass with provençale vegetables, basil mash and saffron vinaigrette, and puddings such as hot waffle with boozy cherries, vanilla ice-cream and cherry syrup and crème brûlée. *Benchmark main dish: braised lamb shoulder with rosemary gravy and minted potatoes £17.95. Two-course evening meal £19.00.*

Brunning & Price ~ Lease Ben Walton ~ Real ale ~ Open 11-11 ~ Bar food 12-10 (9.30 Sun) ~ Restaurant ~ Children welcome ~ Dogs allowed in bar ~ Wi-fi
Recommended by Edward Mirzoeff, B and M Kendall, Richard Dilnot, David Fowler

PETERSFIELD
Old Drum 🌟 ♀ 🍺

SU7423   Map 2

(01730) 300544 – www.theolddrum.co.uk

Chapel Street; GU32 3DP

Restored 16th-c inn with friendly staff and atmosphere in bars and dining room, interesting ales and food, and seats in back garden; bedrooms

By the time this book is published, there will be three more bedrooms, a much expanded garden and redecorated bars here. It's a friendly, bustling place and the airy L-shaped bar has all manner of antique dining chairs and tables on bare boards, with a comfortable chesterfield and armchair on a big rug by an open fire (there are three fires in all) and stools against the counter, where they keep Bowman Swift One and Wallops Wood, Dark Star American Red and Hophead and Suthwyk Liberation on handpump, 16 wines by the glass, ten malt whiskies and farm cider and perry; background jazz and board games. A cosy beamed dining room leads off, with more interesting old cushioned chairs and tables on rugs or floorboards; throughout there are prints and mirrors on pale paintwork or exposed bricks, modern lighting and fresh flowers.

Imaginative food includes lunchtime sandwiches, duck liver parfait with orange, sour cherry gel and savoury bakewell, venison scotch egg with black pudding purée and caramelised pear, toulouse sausage cassoulet, burger with toppings, beef-dripping chips and coleslaw, salmon with clams, sea lettuce and samphire, slow-cooked pork belly with bacon, lentils and pomegranate, and puddings such as banana brioche bread and butter pudding with banana ice-cream and peanut butter baked alaska, apple and salted caramel. *Benchmark main dish: fish dish of the day £13.15. Two-course evening meal £21.00.*

Free house ~ Licensee Dom Humphries ~ Real ale ~ Open 10am-11pm; 12-5 Sun ~ Bar food 10-9.30 ~ Restaurant ~ Children welcome until 8pm ~ Dogs allowed in bar ~ Wi-fi ~ Bedrooms: £70/£80 *Recommended by Val and Alan Green, Chris Nickson, Lindy Andrews*

PETERSFIELD SU7227 Map 2
Trooper 🏅 🍺 🛏

(01730) 827293 – www.trooperinn.com

From A32 (look for staggered crossroads) take turning to Froxfield and Steep; pub 3 miles down on left in big dip; GU32 1BD

Courteous landlord, popular food, decent drinks, persian knick-knacks and local artists' work; attractive bedrooms

This is a comfortable place to spend the weekend – the bedrooms are neatly kept and breakfasts good. It's a friendly place with a charming landlord, who with his attentive staff makes all customers feel genuinely welcome. The bar has all sorts of cushioned dining chairs around dark wooden tables, old film star photos, paintings by local artists (for sale), little persian knick-knacks here and there, several ogival mirrors, lit candles, fresh flowers and a log fire in a stone fireplace; there's also a sun room with lovely downland views, carefully chosen background music, board games, newspapers and magazines. Bowman Swift One, Ringwood Best and Triple fff Altons Pride and Moondance on handpump and several wines by the glass. The attractive raftered restaurant has french windows to a paved terrace with views across the open countryside, and there are lots of picnic-sets on an upper lawn. The horse rail in the car park is reserved 'for horses, camels and local livestock'. The inn backs on to Ashford Hangers nature reserve.

 Food is popular and very good: smoked duck breast with mulled plum compote, field mushrooms stuffed with red pepper and spinach and topped with goats cheese, wild mushroom and madeira baked risotto with basil oil, home-cooked ham with free-range eggs and bubble and squeak, burger with toppings, chutney and chips, sumac- and thyme-marinated free-range chicken with white wine and saffron cream sauce, individual beef wellington, and puddings such as sticky orange cake with orange syrup and sugared pistachios and chocolate torte. *Benchmark main dish: slow-roasted lamb shoulder with honey and mint gravy £17.50. Two-course evening meal £23.00.*

Free house ~ Licensee Hassan Matini ~ Real ale ~ Open 12-3, 6-11; 12-4 Sun; closed Sun and Mon evenings ~ Bar food 12-2, 6.30-9 (9.30 Sat); 12-2.30 Sun ~ Children welcome ~ Dogs allowed in bar ~ Wi-fi ~ Bedrooms: £69/£89 *Recommended by Mike Swan, Mike and Mary Carter, Katharine Cowherd, Christopher and Elise Way, Bede Feltham*

PETERSFIELD SU7129 Map 2
White Horse 🍺

(01420) 588387 – www.pubwithnoname.co.uk

Up on an old downs road about halfway between Steep and East Tisted, near Priors Dean – OS Sheet 186 or 197 map reference 715290; GU32 1DA

Much-loved old place with a great deal of simple character, friendly licensees and up to ten real ales

A fantastic choice of real ales in an unspoilt old pub keeps our readers and the loyal regulars very happy. The two parlour rooms remain charming and idiosyncratic: open fires, oak settles and a mix of dark wooden dining chairs, nice old tables (including some drop-leaf ones), various pictures, farm tools, rugs, a longcase clock, a couple of fireside rocking chairs and so forth. The beamed dining room is smarter with lots of pictures on the white or pink walls. Up to ten ales are kept on handpump: one or two named for the pub, plus Butcombe Bitter, Fullers London Pride, Ringwood Best, Boondoggle and Fortyniner and three quickly changing guests; lots of country wines. They hold a beer festival in June and a cider festival in September. There are some rustic seats outside and camping facilities.

As well as sandwiches and ciabattas, the tasty food includes interesting sausages with caramelised onions and gravy, vegetarian burger, home-cooked honey-glazed ham with free-range eggs and chips, smoked fish pie, burger with cheese, bacon and chips, salmon and prawn fishcakes with mustard cream sauce, and puddings such as sticky toffee pudding and fruit crumble. *Benchmark main dish: steak in ale pie £13.00. Two-course evening meal £20.00.*

Gales (Fullers) ~ Managers Georgie and Paul Stuart ~ Real ale ~ Open 12-midnight ~ Bar food 12-2.30, 6-9.30; all day weekends ~ Restaurant ~ Children welcome ~ Dogs allowed in bar *Recommended by Lindy Andrews, Isobel Mackinlay, Ann and Colin Hunt*

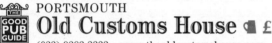

PORTSMOUTH   SZ6399   Map 2

Old Customs House £

(023) 9283 2333 – www.theoldcustomshouse.com

Vernon Buildings, Gunwharf Quays; follow brown signs to Gunwharf Quays car park; PO1 3TY

Well converted historic building in a prime waterfront development with real ales and popular bar food

Usefully open all day and just the place to head for after shopping in the extensive modern waterside complex (of which this fine Grade I listed building is part). It's a spacious, rambling pub with big-windowed high-ceilinged rooms, nautical prints and photographs on pastel walls, coal-effect gas fires, nice unobtrusive lighting and well padded chairs around sturdy tables of varying sizes on bare boards; the sunny entrance area has leather sofas. Broad stairs lead up to a carpeted restaurant with similar décor. Fullers ESB, HSB, London Pride and Seafarers and a couple of changing guests on handpump, a decent range of wines by the glass and good coffees and teas. Staff are efficient, the background music well reproduced and the games machines silenced. Picnic-sets out in front are just metres from the water; the bar has disabled access and facilities. The graceful Spinnaker Tower (170 metres tall with staggering views from its observation decks) is just around the corner. Good disabled access/facilities.

Starting with a fine choice of breakfasts (9am-midday daily), the well thought-of food includes lunchtime sandwiches and interesting salads, potted duck with spiced plum chutney, beer-battered cod cheeks with roasted pepper aioli, steak in ale pie, hake with lemon and garlic crust and leek and parsley sauce, boneless chicken thighs with sweet potato and chickpea salad and a tahini dressing, and puddings such as raspberry and white chocolate cheesecake and vintage ale and molasses sticky toffee pudding; they also offer a buffet menu Mon-Thurs. *Benchmark main dish: fishcakes £12.50. Two-course evening meal £19.00.*

Fullers ~ Manager Marc Duvauchelle ~ Real ale ~ Open 9.30am-11pm ~ Bar food 9.30am-11pm ~ Children welcome ~ Dogs allowed in bar ~ Wi-fi *Recommended by Brian and Anna Marsden, Ann and Colin Hunt, D J and P M Taylor, Stephen and Jean Curtis*

PRESTON CANDOVER
Purefoy Arms ★ ☆ ♀

SU6041   Map 2

(01256) 389777 – www.thepurefoyarms.co.uk

B3046 Basingstoke–Alresford; RG25 2EJ

First class food and wines in gently upmarket village pub

As well as running a fantastic pub, the hard-working licensees here somehow also find time to offer services such as cooking and serving a meal in your own home (and clearing up afterwards), baking and delivering delicious cakes and organising wedding packages; they also run a spanish tapas restaurant in nearby Alresford, Pulpo Negro. This is a smart and civilised place and the two pairs of smallish linked rooms have an easy-going country atmosphere. On the left, the airy front bar has chunky tables (including tall ones with bar stools) and a corner counter serving a fine changing choice of 15 wines by the glass, a farm cider and a beer named for the pub (from Upham), Itchen Valley QED, Palmers Copper and a guest beer from Flack Manor on handpump. This opens into a jute-floored back area with four dining tables and characterful mixed seats including old settles. The right-hand front room has red leather sofas and armchairs by a log fire, and leads back to a bare-boards area with three or four sturdy pale pine tables. The understated contemporary décor in grey and puce goes nicely with the informal friendliness of the service; maybe unobtrusive background music. Don't leave the pub empty-handed as there are chocolates made by the landlord's father and chutneys, ketchup and oils for sale. The sizeable sloping garden has well spaced picnic-sets, a wendy house and perhaps a big hammock slung between trees; there are teak tables on a sheltered terrace. This is an attractive village, with nearby snowdrop walks in February.

 Excellent food includes tapas-style dishes (such as manchego and quince, boquerones, spicy ibérico chorizo), as well as pork terrine with rhubarb and beetroot compote, cumin-cured salmon with pickled carrots, shallot bhaji and goats curd, clam, monkfish and mussel tagine with coriander and piquillo peppers, squash, ricotta and spinach rotolo pasta with cep sauce, pine nuts and sage, quail with braised chicory, walnuts and pomegranate, and puddings such as dark chocolate tart with mango salsa and coconut ice-cream and sicilian lemon cheesecake with stem ginger jelly, fennel pollen ice-cream and lemon granita. *Benchmark main dish: burifarra (catalan-style sausage) with parsnip purée and caramelised apples £14.00. Two-course evening meal £22.00.*

Free house ~ Licensees Andres and Marie-Louise Alemany ~ Real ale ~ Open 12-3, 6-11; 12-5 Sun; closed Sun evening, Mon ~ Bar food 12-3, 6-10; 12-4 Sun ~ Well behaved children welcome until 7pm ~ Dogs welcome ~ Wi-fi *Recommended by Isobel Mackinlay, Susan and John Douglas, Richard Skinner, John Evans*

ROCKBOURNE
Rose & Thistle ♀

SU1118   Map 2

(01725) 518236 – www.roseandthistle.co.uk

Signed off B3078 Fordingbridge–Cranborne; SP6 3NL

Pretty pub with hands-on landlord and friendly staff, informal bars, real ales and good food, and seats in garden

Even on the dreariest of days, you'll find this 16th-c thatched pub buzzing with customers – all welcomed by the new landlord. It's warm and cosy and the bar has homely dining chairs, stools and benches around a mix of old pubby tables, Butcombe Gold, Ringwood Boondoggle and Sharps Doom Bar on handpump, ten wines by the glass and three farm ciders; board games.

The restaurant has a log fire in each of its two rooms (one in a big brick inglenook), old engravings and cricket prints and an informal and relaxed atmosphere. There are benches and tables under pretty hanging baskets at the front of the building, with picnic-sets under parasols on grass; good nearby walks. This is a pretty village on the edge of the New Forest.

 Using local, seasonal produce, the tasty food includes lunchtime sandwiches, twice-baked cheese soufflé, mussels in shallots, garlic, wine and cream, chicken with smoked bacon, cheese and barbecue sauce, pasta with wild mushrooms, walnuts, stilton and cream, confit pork belly with parsnip and herb mash, crackling and gravy, venison with red wine and chocolate sauce, and puddings such as key lime cheesecake and chocolate brownie drizzled with salted caramel and amaretto ice-cream. *Benchmark main dish: steak and kidney pudding £14.50. Two-course evening meal £22.00.*

Free house ~ Licensee Chris Chester-Sterne ~ Real ale ~ Open 11-3, 6-11; 11-10.30 Sat; 12-8 Sun ~ Bar food 12-2.15, 7-9.15; 12-2.30 Sun ~ Restaurant ~ Children welcome ~ Dogs allowed in bar ~ Wi-fi *Recommended by Peter and Eleanor Kenyon, Fr Robert Marsh*

ROMSEY
SU3520 Map 2

Three Tuns 🍺

(01794) 512639 – www.the3tunsromsey.co.uk
Middlebridge Street (but car park signed straight off A27 bypass); SO51 8HL

Good food in cheerfully run village pub, four real ales and a fair choice of wines and friendly staff

While they do keep Andwell King John, Flack Manor Double Drop, Flowerpots Bitter and Upham Punter on handpump, 11 wines by the glass and local cider, there's no doubt that the food is the main star here. It's a 300-year-old inn just a few minutes' walk from the market square and the bar has a cushioned bow-window seat, red leather seating around dark wooden tables on flagstones, beer mats pinned to the walls and church candles in a fireplace. The two dining areas are on either side: one with a huge stuffed fish over a fireplace, the other with prints on yellow walls above a black dado. More dark furniture, a few rugs scattered around, heavy beams and antler chandeliers; background music and board games. There's a back terrace with picnic-sets under parasols and more at the front by the tiny street.

 Using the best local produce, the highly thought-of food includes lunchtime sandwiches, deep-fried breaded whitebait with devilled mayonnaise, smoked and poached salmon fishcakes with mango and chilli salsa, macaroni cheese with garlic focaccia, burger with cheese, mustard mayonnaise, slaw and fries, sea trout, chorizo and aubergine cannelloni with red pepper gazpacho, and puddings such as mango panna cotta with pineapple, mint sugar and vanilla ice-cream and chocolate and maple syrup cheesecake with key lime gel and lemon sorbet. *Benchmark main dish: beef and mushroom pie £12.95. Two-course evening meal £18.00.*

Enterprise ~ Lease Rob Price ~ Real ale ~ Open 11-11; 12-10.30 Sun ~ Bar food 12-2.30, 6-9.30; not Sun evening ~ Restaurant ~ Children welcome ~ Dogs welcome ~ Wi-fi
Recommended by Andrew Stone, John Harris

SPARSHOLT
SU4331 Map 2

Plough 🏵 ♀

(01962) 776353 – www.ploughinnsparsholt.co.uk
Village signposted off B3049 (Winchester–Stockbridge), a little W of Winchester; SO21 2NW

Neatly kept dining pub with interesting furnishings, an extensive wine list, highly rated bar food and big garden

Whatever time of day you choose, it's pretty essential to book a table in advance at this well run country pub. You'll get a proper welcome from the hospitable landlord and his friendly staff. The main bar has an interesting mix of wooden tables and farmhouse or upholstered chairs, plus farm tools, scythes and pitchforks attached to the ceiling; Wadworths 6X, Bishops Tipple, Horizon and IPA on handpump, and quite a few wines and champagne by the glass from an extensive list. The dining tables on the left look over fields and beyond to woodland. Outside, there are plenty of seats on the terrace and lawn and a children's play fort; disabled access and facilities.

 Good, popular food includes sandwiches, melon with parma ham, moules marinière, pork and chive sausages with parsley mash and red wine gravy, feta and spinach filo parcel with tomato and basil sauce, salmon and crab fishcakes with saffron sauce, beef and mushroom in ale pie, green thai chicken curry, venison steak with celeriac and potato purée and port sauce, duck breast with pak choi and plum and ginger jus, and puddings such as honey and thyme crème brûlée and chocolate brownie with vanilla ice-cream. *Benchmark main dish: burger with toppings and chips £13.95. Two-course evening meal £20.00.*

Wadworths ~ Tenant Richard Crawford ~ Real ale ~ Open 11-3, 6-11; 12-10.30 Sun ~ Bar food 12-2, 6-9 (8.30 Mon, 9.30 Fri, Sat); 12-2.30, 6-8.30 Sun ~ Children welcome ~ Dogs allowed in bar ~ Wi-fi *Recommended by Neil and Anita Christopher, R and S Bentley, Andrew Stone*

STEEP
SU7525 Map 2

Harrow 🍺 £

(01730) 262685 – www.harrow-inn.co.uk
Take Midhurst exit from Petersfield bypass, at exit roundabout take first left towards Midhurst, then first turning on left opposite garage, and left again at Sheet church; follow over dual carriageway bridge to pub; GU32 2DA

Unchanging, simple place with long-serving landladies, beers tapped from the cask, unfussy food and a big free-flowering garden; no children inside

Everything in this quite unspoilt and unchanging little country gem revolves around village chat and the friendly locals – who'll probably draw you into light-hearted conversation. It's been in the same family for 85 years and there's still no pandering to modern methods – no credit cards, no waitress service, no restaurant, no music and the rose-covered loos are outside. Adverts for logs sit next to calendars of local views (on sale in support of local charities) and news of various quirky competitions. The small public bar has hops and dried flowers (replaced every year) hanging from the beams, built-in wall benches on the tiled floor, stripped-pine wallboards, a good log fire in the big inglenook, and wild flowers on scrubbed deal tables; dominoes. Bowman Swift One, Dark Star Hophead, Flack Manor Double Drop, Hop Back Citra, Langham Hip Hop and Ringwood Best are tapped straight from casks behind the counter, and they have local wine and apple juice; staff are polite and friendly, even when under pressure. The big garden is left free-flowering so that goldfinches can collect thistle seeds from the grass, but there are some seats on paved areas. The Petersfield bypass doesn't intrude much on this idyll, though you'll need to follow the directions above to find the pub. No children inside and dogs must be on leads. They sell honesty-box flowers outside for Macmillan nurses.

🍴 The honest food includes hot scotch eggs, sandwiches, pea and ham soup, ploughman's, quiches, and puddings such as winter treacle tart and summer lemon crunch cheesecake. *Benchmark main dish: rare beef ploughman's £11.20. Two-course evening meal £16.70.*

Free house ~ Licensees Claire and Denise McCutcheon ~ Real ale ~ No credit cards ~ Open 12-2.30, 6-11; 11-3, 6-11 Sat; 12-3, 7-10.30 Sun; closed Sun evening in winter ~ Bar food 12-2, 7-9; not Sun evening ~ Dogs allowed in bar *Recommended by Tony and Jill Radnor, Edward May, Alfie Bayliss, Ann and Colin Hunt*

TOTFORD
SU5737   Map 2
Woolpack 🌟 ⌾ ♿

(01962) 734184 – www.thewoolpackinn.co.uk

B3046 Basingstoke–Alresford; SO24 9TJ

Charming country pub with carefully refurbished rooms, plenty of character, first class food and drink and seats outside; lovely bedrooms

Tucked away in Britain's smallest hamlet in the midst of the Candover Valley, you'll find the perfect retreat. You can have an excellent breakfast seven days a week from 9 to 10.30am (but why not stay in the deeply comfortable bedrooms beforehand?), delicious lunches and suppers, Sunday evening pizzas cooked in a wood-fired oven – and there's even a cake and cupcake-making service (given 72 hours' notice). A handsome flint and brick building, it has a gently civilised but easy-going atmosphere and a genuine welcome from courteous, friendly staff. The bar has wide floorboards, leather button-back armchairs, little stools and wooden chairs around a mix of tables, and high chairs against the counter where they offer Ramshead (a beer named for them from Marstons), Palmers Copper and a weekly changing guest beer on handpump, 15 wines by the glass and a rather special bloody mary. Leading off here a dining room has flagstones and carpet, a raised fireplace with guns, bellows and other country knick-knacks above it and chunky tables and chairs. Throughout the other rooms are rugs on flagstones, exposed brick and stone work, a few bits of timbering and beamery, church candles, lots of photographs, some cosy booth seating and high-back upholstered dining chairs and leather wall seats around a medley of tables. The pool table converts into a dining table when they're really busy. Outside, on the terrace, on gravel and on grass are teak tables and chairs and picnic-sets under parasols, and distant views.

🌟 Extremely good food includes crab cake with dill mayonnaise, shaved fennel and roast lemon dressing, free-range chicken and pistachio terrine with apple, walnuts and celery, field mushroom, spinach and wild garlic pasta, sausages with colcannon mash and shallot gravy, chalk-stream trout with dressed puy lentils, spring onions and herb dressing, liver and bacon with sage, greens and sherry vinegar sauce, slow-cooked lamb shoulder with rosemary, potato torte, carrot and kale, daily specials, and puddings such as dark chocolate tart with peanut butter parfait and key lime pie with coconut ice-ream. *Benchmark main dish: pie of the day £12.50. Two-course evening meal £20.50.*

Free house ~ Licensee Andrew Cooper ~ Real ale ~ Open 11-11; 11-12 Sat; 11-10.30 Sun ~ Bar food 12-2.30 (3 weekends), 6-9; 12-3, 5.30-8.30 Sun ~ Restaurant ~ Children welcome ~ Dogs allowed in bar and bedrooms ~ Wi-fi ~ Bedrooms: /£100
Recommended by Michael Cooper, Hilary and Neil Christopher

The star-on-a-plate award, 🌟, distinguishes pubs where the food is of exceptional quality. The knife-and-fork symbol just means the pub serves food.

WEST MEON   SU6424 Map 2

Thomas Lord

(01730) 829244 – www.thethomaslord.co.uk

High Street; GU32 1LN

Cricketing knick-knacks in character bar rooms, a smarter dining room, helpful staff, local beers, well thought-of food and pretty garden

As this pub is named after the founder of Lord's Cricket Ground, there's plenty of cricketing memorabilia: bats, gloves, balls, shoes, stumps, photographs and prints, and even stuffed squirrels playing the game in a display cabinet above the counter. And candles all over the place as well – in nice little teacups with saucers, in candlesticks, in silver glassware, in moroccan-style lanterns and in fireplaces. The relaxed, friendly bar has a leather chesterfield and armchairs beside a log fire, wooden chairs, animal hide stools and corner settles on parquet flooring, and Ringwood Best and Upham Punter, Stakes and Tipster on handpump, a dozen wines by the glass and seasonal cocktails, served by chatty, helpful staff. A small room leads off here with similar furnishings, plus a brace of pheasant in the fireplace and antlers above; background music and board games. The dining room is slightly more formal, with long wide tartan benches beside long tables, green cushioned chairs, a big clock above another fireplace and ruched curtains; another little room has a large button-back banquette, tables and a rustic mural. In the sizeable garden are picnic-sets, herbaceous borders, an outdoor pizza oven, a barbecue area, a chicken run and a kitchen garden. Sister pub is the Running Horse in Littleton.

Using home-grown produce and their own eggs, the ambitious food includes lunchtime sandwiches, white crab with brown crab custard, treacle bread and kohlrabi rémoulade, a sharing board of smoked and cured meats, artichokes, peppers and oven-dried tomatoes, beer-battered hake with caper mayonnaise and chips, wild mushroom and celeriac hotpot with soft cheese, shepherd's pie, chargrilled veal chops with pickled squash, rösti potato and mushroom and bone marrow consommé, and puddings such as honey and ginger panna cotta with liquorice jelly, candied almonds and gingerbread ice-cream and lardy cake with custard; they also offer a two- and three-course set menu (not Sun). *Benchmark main dish: dry-aged beef burger with smoked cheddar and truffle fries £11.50. Two-course evening meal £20.50.*

Free house ~ Licensee Clare Winterbottom ~ Real ale ~ Open 12-11 (midnight Sat, 10.30 Sun) ~ Bar food 12-2.30, 6-9.30 (10 Fri, Sat); 12-4, 6-9 Sun ~ Restaurant ~ Children welcome ~ Dogs allowed in bar ~ Wi-fi *Recommended by Isobel Mackinlay, Peter Brix*

WINCHESTER   SU4829 Map 2

Wykeham Arms 🏠 ♥ ♀

(01962) 853834 – www.wykehamarmswinchester.co.uk

Kingsgate Street (Kingsgate Arch and College Street are now closed to traffic; there is access via Canon Street); SO23 9PE

Tucked-away pub with lots to look at, several real ales, many wines by the glass and highly thought-of food; lovely bedrooms

As ever, we get nothing but praise from our readers for this particularly well run and characterful city pub. The series of bustling rooms have all sorts of interesting collections and three log fires – as well as 19th-c oak desks retired from Winchester College, kitchen chairs, candlelit deal tables and big windows with swagged curtains. A snug room at the back, known as the Jameson Room (after the late landlord Graeme Jameson), is decorated with a set of Ronald Searle 'Winespeak' prints. A second room is panelled. Fullers HSB, London Pride, Seafarers and a couple of guests such as Butcombe Rare Breed and Flowerpots Goodens Gold on handpump, 25 wines by the glass, 29 malt whiskies, a couple of farm ciders and quite a few ports and sherries; the tea list is pretty special. There are tables on a covered back terrace and in a small courtyard. This is a fine place to stay overnight and some of the individually styled bedrooms have four-posters; the two-level suite has its own sitting room.

Food is exceptional: lunchtime baguettes, seared scallops with hazelnuts, sesame purée and compressed apple, breast of quail with crispy leg, pear and red cabbage ketchup, beef burger with mature cheddar, coleslaw and frites, confit pork belly with chorizo hash and roasted swede, wild trout with sauté potatoes, pea shoots, clams and pea velouté, lamb rump with anchovies, faggot and dauphinoise potatoes, and puddings such as a crumble of the day and dark chocolate parfait with basil cake and lemon thyme ice-cream. *Benchmark main dish: pie of the day £10.00. Two-course evening meal £24.00.*

Fullers ~ Manager Jon Howard ~ Real ale ~ Open 11-11 (10.30) ~ Bar food 12-3 (2.30 Sat), 6-9.30; 12-3.30, 6.30-9 Sun ~ Restaurant ~ Dogs allowed in bar and bedrooms ~ Wi-fi ~ Bedrooms: £99/£156 *Recommended by B J Harding, Martin and Karen Wake, Hugh Roberts, Steve and Claire Harvey, Phil Bryant, Mrs Sally Scott, Stephen and Jean Curtis, Conor McGaughey*

Also Worth a Visit in Hampshire

Besides the fully inspected pubs, you might like to try these pubs that have been recommended to us and described by readers. Do tell us what you think of them: feedback@goodguides.com

ALRESFORD SU5832
Bell (01962) 732429
West Street; SO24 9AT Comfortable and welcoming Georgian coaching inn, good popular food including weekday fixed-price menu and plenty of daily specials, friendly attentive service, up to five well kept changing ales and good choice of reasonably priced wines, spic and span interior with bare boards, scrubbed tables and log fire, daily papers, smallish separate dining room, occasional live music (mainly jazz); dogs welcome in bar (resident spaniels Freddie and Teddy), attractive sunny back courtyard, six bedrooms, closed Sun evening, otherwise open all day (till 6pm Sun). *(Tony and Jill Radnor, Ann and Colin Hunt, David and Judy Robison, Tony and Wendy Hobden)*

ALRESFORD SU5831
Cricketers (01962) 732463
Jacklyns Lane; SO24 9LW Large welcoming pebble-dashed corner pub, cleanly refurbished inside, with good sensibly priced food including OAP lunch deal, well kept local beers and decent wines, pleasant attentive staff, separate dining area; monthly live music; children welcome, sizeable garden with covered terrace and good play area, open all day. *(Ann and Colin Hunt)*

ALRESFORD SU5832
Globe (01962) 733118
Bottom of Broad Street (B3046) where parking is limited; SO24 9DB Popular old tile-hung pub (sister to the Chestnut Horse at Easton), enjoyable food (all day Sun) including weekday lunchtime/early evening deal and Mon 'fizz & chips', Otter and a couple of guests; some live music – maybe Mon ukulele session; children and dogs welcome, nice garden overlooking Alresford Pond, good walks, open all day. *(Ann and Colin Hunt)*

AMPFIELD SU4023
★ White Horse (01794) 368356
A3090 Winchester–Romsey; SO51 9BQ Snug low-beamed front bar with candles and soft lighting, inglenook log fire and comfortable country furnishings, far-spreading beamed dining area behind, well kept Greene King ales and guests, good food including all-day snacks, several nice wines by the glass, efficient service, locals' bar with another inglenook; background music; children and dogs welcome, high-hedged garden with plenty of picnic-sets, cricket green beyond, good walks in Ampfield Woods and handy for Hillier Gardens, open all day. *(Andrew Stone)*

ARFORD SU8236
Crown (01428) 712150
Off B3002 W of Hindhead; GU35 8BT
Low-beamed pub with log fires in several
areas including local-feel bar and cosy
upper dining room, well kept changing ales
and decent wines by the glass, good food
from pub favourites to blackboard specials,
friendly staff; children welcome in eating
areas, picnic-sets in peaceful dell by little
stream across the road. *(Peter Brix)*

BARTON STACEY SU4341
Swan (01962) 760470
Village signed off A303; SO21 3RL
Welcoming atmosphere in this recently
refurbished beamed former coaching inn,
good affordably priced food from pubby
choices up, three changing ales, bar with
brick and timber walls, light wood floor
and inglenook, back restaurant; children
and dogs (in bar) welcome, picnic-sets
on front gravel, open all day Fri, Sat, till
10pm Sun. *(Mike Swan)*

BASING SU6653
Bartons Mill (Millstone)
(01256) 331153 *Bartons Lane, Old
Basing; follow brown signs to Basing
House; RG24 8AE* Busy pub in tucked-
away spot – lots of picnic-sets out by River
Loddon looking across to viaduct through
scrubland; Wadworths range kept well and
a guest, Kingston Press cider and several
wines by the glass, food (all day Sun) from
sandwiches and deli boards up; may be
background music, Thurs quiz, free wi-fi;
children and dogs welcome, by ruins of
Basing House, open all day.
(Anna McDermott)

BATTRAMSLEY SZ3098
Hobler (01590) 623944
*Southampton Road (A337 S of
Brockenhurst); SO41 8PT* Old roadside
pub with several rooms, modern furnishings
and décor contrasting ancient heavy beams,
wood and stone floors, log fire, good food
from sandwiches and sharing plates up using
fresh local ingredients, weekday set menu till
6pm, well kept Ringwood, Timothy Taylors
and decent choice of wines, friendly efficient
service; children welcome, nice garden with
some tables under cover, good New Forest
walks, open (and food) all day. *(Dennis and
Doreen Haward)*

BEAUWORTH SU5624
Milbury's (01962) 771248
*Off A272 Winchester–Petersfield;
SO24 0PB* Attractive old tile-hung country
pub, beams, panelling and stripped stone,
massive 17th-c treadmill for much older
incredibly deep well, galleried area, up
to five changing ales and straightforward
reasonably priced food, efficient service;
skittle alley; children in eating areas, garden

with fine downland views, good walks, two
bedrooms. *(Ann and Colin Hunt)*

BENTLEY SU7844
Star (01420) 23184
Centre of village on old A31; GU10 5LW
Small friendly village pub renovated
and doing well under local farmer, good
interesting reasonably priced food (not Sun
evening), Triple fff, Sharps Doom Bar and
a guest, decent wines, open fire, restaurant;
free wi-fi; children and dogs welcome,
garden with heated gazebos, open all day.
(Peter Brix)

BISHOP'S WALTHAM SU5517
Barleycorn (01489) 892712
Lower Basingwell Street; SO32 1AJ
Relaxed 18th-c two-bar village local, popular
generously served pub food at reasonable
prices, good friendly service, well kept
Greene King ales and a guest, decent wines,
spic and span interior with beams and some
low ceiling panelling, open fires; children
and dogs welcome, large garden with back
smokers' area, open all day. *(Ann and Colin
Hunt, Stephen and Jean Curtis)*

BISHOP'S WALTHAM SU5517
★ Bunch of Grapes (01489) 892935
*St Peter's Street – near entrance to
central car park; SO32 1AD* Neat civilised
little pub in quiet medieval street, smartly
furnished keeping individuality and unspoilt
feel (run by same family for a century), good
chatty landlord and regulars, Goddards and
guests tapped from the cask, own wines
from nearby vineyard, no food; charming
walled garden behind, opening times may
vary. *(Stephen and Jean Curtis, Phil and
Jane Villiers)*

BLACKNEST SU7941
Jolly Farmer (01420) 22244
Binsted Road/Blacknest Road; GU34 4QD
Bright and airy beamed dining pub with
pleasant relaxed atmosphere, good food from
lunchtime sandwiches and sharing boards up,
well kept Fullers beers, friendly staff, wood
and flagstone floors, sofas by log fire, function
room with skittle alley; children and dogs
welcome, picnic-sets in attractive fenced
garden, sheltered terrace and play area, open
all day. *(I D Barnett)*

BOLDRE SZ3198
★ Red Lion (01590) 673177
Off A337 N of Lymington; SO41 8NE
Licensees at this friendly pub on edge
of the New Forest retired as we went to
press – reports on new regime please; five
black-beamed rooms with heavy-horse
harness, gin traps, ferocious-looking man
traps, copper and brass pans and rural
landscapes, pews, sturdy cushioned dining
chairs and tapestried stools, three log fires,
old cooking range in cosy bar, Brakspears,
Ringwood and a guest, food has been popular;

opposite village green with seats out among flowering tubs and hanging baskets, more tables in back garden, has opened all day weekends. *(S Holder, Brian Glozier, Mike Swan, Phil and Jane Villiers, Michael and Jenny Back, Gavin and Helle May and others)*

BRAISHFIELD SU3724
Wheatsheaf (01794) 368652
Village signposted off A3090 on NW edge of Romsey; SO51 0QE Friendly beamed pub with tasty home-cooked food and four well kept beers, cosy log fire; background and some live music, sports TV and pool; children and dogs welcome, garden with nice views, woodland walks nearby, close to Hillier Gardens, open all day. *(Andrew Stone)*

BRAMBRIDGE SU4721
Dog & Crook (01962) 712129
Near M3 junction 12, via B3335; Church Lane; SO50 6HZ Cheerful bustling 18th-c pub with beamed bar and cosy dining room, enjoyable traditional food, Fullers, Ringwood and Sharps, several wines by the glass, friendly speedy service; background music, TV, regular events and summer music nights; children and dogs welcome, garden with decking and arbour, Itchen Way walks nearby, open all day weekends. *(Belinda Stamp)*

BRAMDEAN SU6127
Fox (01962) 771363
A272 Winchester–Petersfield; SO24 0LP Welcoming 17th-c part-weatherboarded pub doing well under newish owners; open-plan bar with black beams and log fires, well kept ales such as St Austell Tribute and Sharps Doom Bar, farmhouse ciders and several wines by the glass, good traditional home-made food served promptly by friendly staff; some live music; children and dogs welcome, walled-in terraced area and spacious lawn under fruit trees, good surrounding walks, open (and food) all day Fri-Sun. *(John Evans, Helen and Brian Edgeley, Richard Tilbrook)*

BREAMORE SU1517
Bat & Ball (01725) 512252
Salisbury Road; SP6 2EA Dutch-gabled red-brick roadside pub, enjoyable reasonably priced food including unusual choices such as kangaroo and crocodile, some south african influences too, well kept Ringwood ales, friendly service, two linked bar areas and restaurant; dogs welcome, pleasant side garden, bedrooms in two apartments, Avon fishing and walks (lovely ones up by church and stately Breamore House), open (and food) all day. *(Barrie and Mary Crees)*

BROCKENHURST SU3000
Filly (01590) 623449
Lymington Road (A337 Brockenhurst–Lymington); SO42 7UF Spotless roadside pub under new management, enjoyable well presented food (all day weekends) from varied menu including good steaks, friendly

welcoming staff, two changing local ales and decent selection of wines, bare-boards bar with oak beams, carriage-lamp lighting and attractive fireplace, two dining rooms; Sun afternoon jazz; children and dogs (in bar and garden room) welcome, sheltered tables outside, New Forest walks, five refurbished bedrooms, good breakfast, open all day. *(Guy and Caroline Howard)*

BROOK SU2714
Bell (023) 8081 2214
B3079/B3078, handy for M27 junction 1; SO43 7HE Really a hotel with golf club, but has neatly kept bar with lovely inglenook fire, well kept ales, good cider and plenty of wines by the glass, nice food too from sandwiches to blackboard specials, afternoon teas (perhaps with a glass of house champagne), helpful friendly uniformed staff; children and dogs welcome, big garden, delightful village, 27 comfortable bedrooms. *(Penny and Peter Keevil)*

BROOK SU2713
★Green Dragon (023) 8081 3359
B3078 NW of Cadnam, just off M27 junction 1; SO43 7HE Spic and span thatched New Forest dining pub dating from 15th c, welcoming helpful staff, good food (not Sun evening) including plenty of seasonal game and fish as well as pubby favourites, well kept Ringwood and a guest, decent wines, bright linked areas with stripped pine and other pubby furnishings, daily papers; children and dogs welcome (resident cat), disabled access from car park, attractive small terrace, garden with paddocks beyond, picturesque village, self-catering apartment. *(PL, Phil and Jane Villiers, David and Sally Frost, B R Merritt, Sir Michael and Lady Jackson)*

BROUGHTON SU3032
Tally Ho (01794) 301280
High Street, opposite church; signed off A30 Stockbridge–Salisbury; SO20 8AA Welcoming village pub with light airy bar and separate eating area, well kept ales such as Ringwood, Sharps and Timothy Taylors, good food from pub favourites up (more elaborate evening choice), friendly service; children welcome, charming secluded back garden, good walks, open all day (no food Sun evening). *(Ann and Colin Hunt)*

BUCKLERS HARD SU4000
Master Builders House
(01590) 616253 *M27 junction 2, follow signs to Beaulieu, turn left on to B3056, then left to Bucklers Hard; SO42 7XB* Sizeable hotel in lovely spot overlooking river; character main bar with heavy beams, log fire and simple furnishings, rugs on wooden floor, mullioned windows, interesting list of shipbuilders dating from 18th c, Ringwood Best and guests, stairs down to room with fireplace at each end, enjoyable

food (something available all day), afternoon teas, prompt friendly service; children welcome, small gate at bottom of garden for waterside walks, summer barbecues, 26 bedrooms. *(Mrs Sally Scott, Gerry and Rosemary Dobson)*

BURGHCLERE   SU4660
Carpenters Arms (01635) 278251
Harts Lane, off A34; RG20 9JY Small, unpretentious and well run village pub, enjoyable sensibly priced home-made food (not Sun evening) from sandwiches up, Arkells and an occasional guest, friendly helpful staff, good country views (Watership Down) from conservatory and terrace, log fire; background music; children, walkers and dogs welcome, tricky wheelchair access, handy for Sandham Memorial Chapel (NT) with its Stanley Spencer murals and Highclere Castle, six comfortable annexe bedrooms, open all day. *(Mrs P Sumner, Christine Newman, Mr and Mrs J Watkins)*

BURITON   SU7320
Five Bells (01730) 263584
Off A3 S of Petersfield; GU31 5RX Low-beamed 17th-c pub with big log fire and some ancient stripped masonry, popular food (not Sun evening) from sandwiches to daily specials, Badger ales and good wines by the glass; background music; children and dogs welcome, nice garden and sheltered terraces, pretty village with good local walks, self-catering in converted stables, open all day. *(Emma Scofield)*

BURLEY   SU2202
White Buck (01425) 402264
Bisterne Close; 0.7 miles E, OS Sheet 195 map reference 223028; BH24 4AZ Extensively refurbished 19th-c mock-Tudor hotel; well kept Fullers ales in long bar with two-way log fires each end, seats in big bow window, comfortable part-panelled shooting-theme snug with stag's head, spacious well divided dining area on different levels, good choice of enjoyable attractively presented food (not overly expensive) and nice wines, helpful personable staff; background music, free wi-fi; children and dogs welcome, terraces and spacious lawn, lovely New Forest setting with superb walks towards Burley itself and over Mill Lawn, good bedrooms, open all day. *(Sara Fulton, Roger Baker, Conor McGaughey, Glenwys and Alan Lawrence)*

BURSLEDON   SU4809
Fox & Hounds (023) 8040 2784
Hungerford Bottom; 2 miles from M27 junction 8; SO31 8DE Popular rambling 16th-c Chef & Brewer of unusual character, ancient beams, flagstones and big log fires,

linked by pleasant family conservatory area to ancient back barn, lantern-lit side stalls, lots of interesting farm equipment, well kept ales including Ringwood, good choice of wines and reasonably priced food; children allowed, tables outside. *(Edward May)*

BURSLEDON   SU4909
Jolly Sailor (023) 8040 5557
Off A27 towards Bursledon station, Lands End Road; handy for M27 junction 8; SO31 8DN Steps down to beamed Badger dining pub worth knowing for its prime location overlooking yachting inlet, their ales and decent wine choice, food cooked to order and can be good (may be a wait and not particularly cheap), log fires; dogs welcome, nice outside seating area, tidal moorings, open all day (food all day Fri-Sun). *(Peter Brix)*

CADNAM   SU3114
Compass (023) 8081 2237
Winsor Road, off Totton–Cadnam road at Bartley crossroads; OS Sheet 195 map ref 317143; SO40 2HE Popular 16th-c flower-decked local off the beaten track, friendly and chatty, with well kept ales and enjoyable traditional food including bargain lunchtime specials (Mon-Sat), brasses on beams, pubby furniture on bare boards, woodburner in brick fireplace; dogs very welcome (food for them), side garden with decorative arbour, open all day (food all day weekends). *(Phil and Jane Villiers)*

CADNAM   SU2913
Sir John Barleycorn
(023) 8081 2236 *Off Southampton Road; by M27 junction 1; SO40 2NP* Picturesque low-slung thatched dining pub extended from cosy beamed and timbered medieval core, decent choice of fairly standard food including good value weekday two-course menu (till 6pm), friendly if not always speedy service, well kept Fullers ales, two log fires, modern décor and stripped wood flooring; background music; children welcome, no dogs inside, suntrap benches in front and out in colourful garden, open (and food) all day. *(Brian Glozier)*

CHALTON   SU7316
★ Red Lion (023) 9259 2246
Off A3 Petersfield–Horndean; PO8 0BG Largely extended timber and thatch dining pub, interesting old core around inglenook (dates from the 12th c and has been a pub since the 15th c); wide range of popular food from sandwiches and sharing plates up, well kept Fullers/Gales ales and lots of country wines, friendly helpful service from smart young staff; children and dogs allowed, good disabled access and facilities, nice views

---

Pubs close to motorway junctions are listed at the back of the book.

from neat rows of picnic-sets on rectangular lawn by large car park, good walks, handy for Queen Elizabeth Country Park, open (and food) all day. *(Val and Alan Green, Tony and Wendy Hobden, R Halliday)*

CHAWTON   SU7037
Greyfriar (01420) 83841
Off A31/A32 S of Alton; Winchester Road; GU34 1SB Popular flower-decked beamed dining pub opposite Jane Austen's House; decent food (till 7pm Sun) from lunchtime sandwiches and bar snacks up, Fullers ales, welcoming relaxed atmosphere with comfortable seating and sturdy pine tables in neat linked areas, open fire in restaurant end; background music; children welcome till 9pm, dogs in bar, small garden with terrace, good nearby walks, open all day.
(B J Harding)

CHERITON   SU5828
★ Flower Pots (01962) 771318
Off B3046 towards Beauworth and Winchester; OS Sheet 185 map reference 581282; SO24 0QQ Unspoilt country local in same family for over 45 years; three or four good value own-brew beers tapped from the cask (brewery tours by arrangement), enjoyable reasonably priced home-made food (not Sun evening or bank holiday evenings, and possible restrictions during busy times) including range of casseroles and popular Weds curry night, cheerful welcoming staff, extended plain public bar with covered well, another straightforward but homely room with country pictures on striped wallpaper and ornaments over small log fire; no credit cards or children; dogs welcome, seats on pretty front and back lawns (some under apple trees), heated marquee, three bedrooms. *(Ann and Colin Hunt, Tony and Jill Radnor, David and Judy Robison)*

CHILWORTH   SU4118
Chilworth Arms (023) 8076 6247
Chilworth Road (A27 Southampton–Romsey); SO16 7JZ Modernised Mitchells & Butlers dining pub, popular food from sharing plates and home-made pizzas up including weekday fixed-price menu till 6pm, good wine choice, ales such as Robinsons and Sharps Doom Bar, cocktails, log fires, conservatory-style back restaurant; background music; children welcome, disabled access/facilities, large neat garden with terrace, open all day. *(John Jenkins)*

CHURCH CROOKHAM   SU8151
Tweseldown (01252) 613976
Beacon Hill Road; GU52 8DY Flower-decked 19th-c pub with lounge and public bars plus a sizeable split-level barn restaurant, Courage, Fullers, Triple fff and a guest, good choice of wines by the glass, enjoyable home-cooked food from standards to specials, cheerful service, horse-racing décor (Tweseldown Racecourse nearby), log

fires; pool, darts and fruit machine; children and dogs welcome, garden with heated smokers' shelter, open all day. *(Alfie Bayliss)*

COLDEN COMMON   SU4722
Rising Sun (01962) 711954
Spring Lane; SO21 1SB Refurbished 19th-c pub in residential street; reasonably priced tasty food including children's choices, up to four well kept ales, good friendly service, bare boards, half-panelling and painted ceiling joists, leather sofas by open fire; some live music; a few picnic-sets in front behind picket fence, more in garden beyond car park. *(Edward May)*

COPYTHORNE   SU3115
Empress of Blandings
(023) 8081 2321 *Copythorne Crescent, just off A31; SO40 2PE* Roomy pub-restaurant with PG Wodehouse/pig theme (note spelling on Hall & Woodhouse sign), enjoyable moderately priced food and some cosy corners, Badger ales, good friendly service; free wi-fi; children and dogs (in one area) welcome, picnic-sets in front and back gardens, open (and food) all day. *(Glenwys and Alan Lawrence)*

CRAWLEY   SU4234
★ Fox & Hounds (01962) 776006
Village signed from A272 and B3420 NW of Winchester; SO21 2PR Striking building in village of fine old houses; neatly linked rooms with brocaded and cushioned dining chairs, settles and wall seats around straightforward pubby tables on parquet or carpet, horse-racing prints, old jugs, plates and bowls on window sills, three open fires, Alfreds Saxon Bronze, Sharps Doom Bar, Wychwood Hobgoblin and a guest, 16 wines by the glass, a farm cider and wide choice of enjoyable food (not Sun evening); live music last Fri of month, free wi-fi; children and dogs (in bar) welcome, seats outside on grass, chalet-style bedrooms in converted stables, open all day in summer (all day Sat, till 8pm Sun in winter). *(Tom and Jill Jones, Phil Bryant, Laurie and Fiona Scott)*

CRONDALL   SU7948
Plume of Feathers (01252) 850245
The Borough; GU10 5NT Attractive 15th-c village pub popular for good range of generous home-made food from standards up, friendly helpful staff, well kept Greene King and some unusual guests, nice wines by the glass, beams and dark wood, red carpet, prints on cream walls, restaurant with log fire in big brick fireplace; soft background music, free wi-fi; children welcome, picturesque village, three bedrooms, open all day Sun. *(Caroline Prescott)*

CROOKHAM   SU7952
Exchequer (01252) 615336
Crondall Road; GU51 5SU Welcoming smartly done dining pub, popular

reliable home-made food from lunchtime sandwiches to blackboard specials in bar and restaurant, four local ales and good choice of wines by the glass, also cider and lager from local Hogs Back, daily papers, woodburner; terrace tables, near Basingstoke Canal, open (and food) all day Fri-Sun. *(Mike and Jayne Bastin)*

DENMEAD   SU6412
Fox & Hounds (023) 9225 5421
School Lane, Anthill Common; PO7 6NA
Village pub rescued from closure by the local community; modernised interior with comfortable log-fire bar and large back dining area, enjoyable food from shortish menu (order at the bar), four real ales, cheerful staff; open all day. *(Ann and Colin Hunt)*

DROXFORD   SU6118
Hurdles (01489) 877451
Brockbridge, just outside Soberton; from A32 just N of Droxford take B2150 towards Denmead; SO32 3QT
Modernised dining pub (former station hotel) with well liked food including early evening deal (Mon-Thurs); high ceilings and stripped floorboards, leather chesterfield and armchairs by log fire in one room, dining areas with eye-catching wallpaper and stripy chairs around shiny tables, well kept Bowmans and a guest, decent wines by the glass and good coffee, friendly service; background music; children and dogs (in bar) welcome, neat terraces (one covered and heated), flight of steps up to picnic-sets on sloping lawn by tall trees, open all day. *(John Evans, Tony and Wendy Hobden, Dave Braisted)*

DUMMER   SU5846
Queen (01256) 397367
Under a mile from M3 junction 7; take Dummer slip road; RG25 2AD
Comfortable beamed pub, well divided with lots of softly lit alcoves, Andwell, Otter and Sharps, decent choice of wines by the glass, popular food from lunchtime sandwiches and light dishes up, friendly service, big log fire, Queen and steeplechase prints; background music, free wi-fi; children welcome in restaurant, picnic-sets under parasols on terrace and in extended back garden, attractive village with ancient church. *(Edward May)*

DUNBRIDGE   SU3126
Mill Arms (01794) 340401
Barley Hill (B3084); SO51 0LF Much extended 18th-c coaching inn opposite station, welcoming informal atmosphere in spacious high-ceilinged rooms, scrubbed pine tables and farmhouse chairs on oak or flagstone floors, several sofas, two log fires, local ales such as Andwell and Flack Manor, enjoyable food including grills, dining conservatory, two skittle alleys; children

and dogs (in bar) welcome, big garden, plenty of walks in surrounding Test Valley, six comfortable bedrooms, open all day from 10am (till 5pm Sun). *(Belinda Stamp)*

DUNDRIDGE   SU5718
★ Hampshire Bowman (01489) 892940
Off B3035 towards Droxford, Swanmore, then right at Bishop's Waltham signpost; SO32 1GD Chatty mix of customers at this friendly relaxed country pub, five well kept local ales tapped from casks, summer farm cider and well liked good value food (all day Fri-Sun) from hearty pub dishes to specials using local produce, good cheerful service, stable bar and cosy unassuming original one; no mobile phones (£1 fine in charity box); children and dogs welcome, tables on heated terrace and peaceful lawn, play equipment, hitching post for horses, popular with walkers and cyclists, open all day.
(Ann and Colin Hunt)

DURLEY   SU5116
Farmers Home (01489) 860457
B3354 and B2177; Heathen Street/ Curdridge Road; SO32 2BT Comfortable red-brick beamed country pub, spacious but cosy, with two-bay dining area and restaurant, enjoyable food including good steaks and popular Sun lunch, friendly service, room for drinkers too with well kept Gales HSB, Ringwood and decent wines, woodburner; children and dogs (in bar) welcome, big garden with play area, nice walks, open (and food) all day. *(Ann and Colin Hunt, Gavin and Helle May)*

DURLEY   SU5217
★ Robin Hood (01489) 860229
Durley Street, just off B2177 Bishop's Waltham–Winchester – brown signs to pub; SO32 2AA Popular open-plan beamed pub with well prepared food from varied blackboard menu (order at bar), Greene King and a guest ale, nice wines, good informed service from friendly staff, log fire and leather sofas in bare-boards bar, dining area with stone floors and mix of old pine tables and chairs, bookcase door to loos; background music; children and dogs welcome, disabled facilities, decked terrace with barbecue, garden with play area and country views, open all day Sun. *(Gavin and Helle May, Phil and Jane Villiers, Roy and Gill Payne, Joy Griffiths)*

EAST BOLDRE   SU3700
Turf Cutters Arms (01590) 612331
Main Road; SO42 7WL Small dimly lit 18th-c New Forest local behind white picket fence, lots of beams and pictures, nicely worn-in furnishings on bare boards and flagstones, log fire, enjoyable home-made food (worth booking evenings/ weekends), well kept Ringwood ales and a guest, good friendly service and chatty relaxed atmosphere; children and dogs

welcome, picnic-sets in large back garden, good heathland walks, bedrooms in nearby converted barn, open all day. *(Peter Meister)*

EAST END SZ3696

★**East End Arms** (01590) 626223
Back road Lymington–Beaulieu, parallel to B3054; SO41 5SY Simple friendly pub (owned by former Dire Straits bass guitarist), determinedly unfussy bar with chatty locals and log fire, Ringwood Best or Fortyniner and several wines by the glass, enjoyable freshly made food (not Sun evening) served by cheerful helpful staff, attractive dining room; occasional live music, free wi-fi; children and dogs (in bar) welcome, picnic-sets in terraced garden, pretty cottagey bedrooms, open all day in summer (till 10pm Sun). *(Emma Scofield, Mike Swan)*

EAST MEON SU6822

★**Olde George** (01730) 823481
Church Street; signed off A272 W of Petersfield, and off A32 in West Meon; GU32 1NH Relaxing heavy-beamed village inn with well liked food from sandwiches and light lunches to more restauranty choices, Badger ales and decent selection of wines by the glass, good service from smartly dressed staff, cosy areas around central counter, inglenook log fires; children and dogs welcome, nice back terrace, five bedrooms, good breakfast, pretty village with fine church and surrounding walks, open all day Sun. *(Steve and Claire Harvey, Ann and Colin Hunt, Mrs Julie Thomas)*

EAST STRATTON SU5339

★**Northbrook Arms** (01962) 774150
Brown sign to pub off A33, 4 miles S of A303 junction; SO21 3DU New licensees and some redecoration for this attractive brick-built village pub; traditional tiled-floor beamed bar on right serving six mainly local ales such as Alfreds, Bowman, Flack Manor and Wild Weather, several wines by the glass, left-hand carpeted part and end dining room, food has been good, friendly helpful staff; background music, free wi-fi; children and dogs welcome, picnic-sets out on green across quiet road, more seats in pretty side garden, skittle alley in former stables, fine nearby walks, five bedrooms, open all day. *(Ann and Colin Hunt, Sara Fulton, Roger Baker, Office)*

EAST WORLDHAM SU7438

Three Horseshoes (01420) 83211
Cakers Lane (B3004 Alton–Kingsley); GU34 3AE Welcoming early 19th-c brick and stone roadside pub, comfortable and attractive, with good range of enjoyable reasonably priced food including daily specials, Fullers/Gales ales and one or two guests, good wines by the glass, friendly efficient staff, log fires; free wi-fi; children and dogs welcome, pleasant secluded garden with lots of picnic-sets, five well appointed

bedrooms, open all day weekends (till 6pm Sun). *(Susan Crabbe, Tony and Jill Radnor)*

EASTON SU5132

★**Chestnut Horse** (01962) 779257
3.6 miles from M3 junction 9: A33 towards Kings Worthy, then B3047 towards Itchen Abbas; Easton then signposted on right – bear left in village; SO21 1EG Smart and cosy 16th-c dining pub with welcoming hands-on landlady; open-plan interior with rustic feel in series of snug areas, black beams hung with mugs, jugs and chamber-pots, log fires in cottagey fireplaces, comfortable furnishings, candles and fresh flowers, Badger ales and a guest, a dozen wines by the glass and 20 malt whiskies, particularly good food (all day Sun) including two-course deal, efficient helpful staff; background music, free wi-fi; children and dogs (in bar) welcome, smallish sheltered deck with colourful tubs and baskets, picnic-sets out in front, pretty thatched village and good Itchen Valley walks, open all day Fri-Sun. *(Helen and Brian Edgeley, Richard Tilbrook, Mrs P Sumner, Katharine Cowherd and others)*

EASTON SU5132

Cricketers (01962) 791044
Off B3047; SO21 1EJ Light and airy traditional local in centre of village; enjoyable well priced home-made food in bar and smallish restaurant, three Marstons-related ales including Ringwood, friendly atmosphere, mix of wooden table and chairs on carpet, various odds and ends including cricketing and fishing memorabilia, bare-boards area with sports TV, open fire and small woodburner; background music, fortnightly Sun quiz; children and dogs welcome, front terrace with heated smokers' shelter, handy for Itchen Way walks, two bedrooms, open all day. *(Ann and Colin Hunt)*

ELLISFIELD SU6345

★**Fox** (01256) 381210
Green Lane; S of village off Northgate Lane; RG25 2QW Simple tucked-away country pub with friendly atmosphere; mixed collection of stripped tables, country chairs and cushioned wall benches on bare boards and old floor tiles, some exposed masonry, open fires in plain brick fireplaces, Sharps Doom Bar, Fullers London Pride and a guest or two, enjoyable sensibly priced home-made food; outside gents'; children and dogs welcome, picnic-sets in nice garden, good walking country near snowdrop and bluebell woods, open all day. *(Anon)*

EMERY DOWN SU2808

★**New Forest** (023) 8028 4690
Village signed off A35 just W of Lyndhurst; SO43 7DY Well run 18th-c weatherboarded village pub in one of the best parts of the Forest for walking; good honest home-made food including local

venison, popular Sun roasts (should book), friendly helpful uniformed staff, Ringwood and guest ales, real cider, good choice of wines by the glass, coffee and tea; attractive softly lit separate areas on varying levels, each with own character, hunting prints and two log fires; background music; children and dogs welcome, covered heated terrace and pleasant little garden on three-levels, clean bedrooms, open (and food) all day, can get very busy weekends. *(David and Sally Frost, Phil and Jane Villiers, Sara Fulton, Roger Baker)*

EMSWORTH   SU7405
Blue Bell (01243) 373394
South Street; PO10 7EG Friendly and relaxed little 1940s red-brick pub close to the quay, old-fashioned lived-in interior with lots of memorabilia, good choice of popular no-nonsense food including fresh fish, best to book weekends, bar nibbles Sun lunchtime, Sharps Doom Bar and well kept local guests, live music; dogs welcome, seats on small front terrace, Sun market in adjacent car park, open all day. *(Ann and Colin Hunt)*

EMSWORTH   SU7505
Lord Raglan (01243) 372587
Queen Street; PO10 7BJ Friendly 18th-c flint pub with wide choice of enjoyable home-made food and well kept Fullers/Gales beers, good service, log fire, restaurant; live music Sun evening, free wi-fi; pleasant waterside garden behind, open all day weekends. *(Ann and Colin Hunt)*

EVERSLEY   SU7861
Golden Pot (0118) 973 2104
B3272; RG27 0NB Mainly open-plan brick dining pub with restaurant at one end, sofas, cushioned settles and other traditional seating, two-sided woodburner, enjoyable blackboard food including speciality fish and steaks, changing local ales such as Andwell, Upham and Windsor & Eton, friendly efficient staff; background music (live Mon); children and dogs welcome, tables out in front and at back with view over fields, open all day. *(KC, John Pritchard)*

EVERSLEY CROSS   SU7861
Chequers (0118) 402 7065
Chequers Lane; RG27 0NS Attractively revamped Peach pub dating in part from the 14th c, well kept Sharps Doom Bar, Hogs Back and guests, carefully chosen wines and gins, good seasonal food from deli boards to daily specials, friendly service; children welcome, tables out at front under parasols, open all day from 9.30am for breakfast. *(Gus Swan)*

EVERTON   SZ2994
Crown (01590) 642655
Old Christchurch Road; pub signed just off A337 W of Lymington; SO41 0JJ Quietly set restaurant-pub on edge of New Forest, good food cooked by landlord-chef

including daily specials, friendly service, Ringwood and guests, decent wines, two attractive dining rooms off tiled-floor bar, log fires; children welcome, wheelchair access, picnic-sets on front terrace behind picket fence and in garden behind, closed Mon. *(John Harris)*

EXTON   SU6120
★ Shoe (01489) 877526
Village signposted from A32 NE of Bishop's Waltham; SO32 3NT Popular brick-built country pub on South Downs Way; three linked rooms with log fires, good well presented food from traditional favourites to more imaginative restaurant-style dishes using own produce, well kept Wadworths ales and a seasonal guest, good friendly service; children and dogs welcome, disabled facilities, seats under parasols at front, more in garden across lane overlooking River Meon. *(Annabel and James Bartle)*

FAREHAM   SU5806
Cams Mill (01329) 287506
Cams Hall Estate, off A27; PO16 8UP Large new Fullers waterside pub (oak-framed re-creation of former tidal mill); roomy interior including high-raftered and galleried eating area, good popular food, well kept ales and efficient friendly young staff, Fareham Creek views from big windows and terrace; free wi-fi; children and dogs welcome, nice circular creekside walk, open all day. *(Ann and Colin Hunt, David and Judy Robison)*

FAREHAM   SU5806
Cob & Pen (01329) 221624
Wallington Shore Road, not far from M27 junction 11; PO16 8SL Old roadside pub with well kept Otter, Ringwood and St Austell, decent choice of enjoyable fairly standard food (all day weekends), Sun carvery, reasonable prices and cheerful prompt service, homely inside with separate dining area and small games room; children welcome, large garden, open all day. *(Ann and Colin Hunt)*

FAREHAM   SU5806
Crown (01329) 241750
West Street; PO16 0JW Bustling Wetherspoons (their second in Fareham) in pedestrianised street and handy for shopping centre; attractive old building with proper pubby atmosphere, bits of local history on the walls, a couple of Greene King ales and three guests, usual well priced food, good friendly service; free wi-fi; children welcome, seats out on pavement, open all day from 7am. *(David M Smith)*

FAREHAM   SU5806
Golden Lion (01329) 234061
High Street; PO16 7AE Traditional 19th-c town local under newish management, well kept Fullers/Gales beers from dark wood servery, dining part to the right with

decent reasonably priced pubby food from sandwiches and baked potatoes up, friendly helpful staff; charity quiz Thurs, free wi-fi; children and dogs welcome, courtyard garden, open all day (till 6pm Sun). *(Val and Alan Green, Ann and Colin Hunt)*

FARNBOROUGH   SU8756
★ **Prince of Wales** (01252) 545578
Rectory Road, near station; GU14 8AL
Ten well kept ales including five quickly changing guests at this welcoming Victorian local, three small linked areas with exposed brickwork, carpet or wood floors, open fire and some antiquey touches, generous lunchtime pubby food, also Mon pie night and Fri evening fish and chips, good friendly service; terrace and smokers' gazebo, open all day Fri-Sun. *(Rob Anderson)*

FAWLEY   SU4603
Jolly Sailor (023) 8089 1305
Ashlett Creek, off B3053; SO45 1DT
Cottagey waterside pub near small boatyard and sailing club, straightforward good value bar food, Ringwood Best and a guest, cheerful service, mixed pubby furnishings on bare boards, raised log fire, second bar with darts and pool; children welcome, tables outside looking past creek's yachts and boats to busy shipping channel, good shore walks, handy for Rothschild rhododendron gardens at Exbury, open all day. *(Phil and Jane Villiers)*

FINCHDEAN   SU7312
George (023) 9241 2257
Centre of village; PO8 0AU Red-brick pub dating from the 18th c, beamed front bar, separate dining area with conservatory, enjoyable fairly priced food (all day weekends – till 8pm Sun) from bar snacks up, well kept mainstream ales such as Adnams, Fullers and Sharps, good friendly service, live music; children and dogs (in bar) welcome, picnic-sets out in front and in garden behind, good nearby walks, open all day till 10pm (midnight Fri, Sat). *(Val and Alan Green)*

FLEET   SU8053
Oatsheaf (01252) 819508
Crookham Road/Reading Road; GU51 5DR
Smartly updated Mitchells & Butlers dining pub with plenty of contemporary touches, usual good choice of enjoyable food including set deal (weekdays till 6pm), ales such as Timothy Taylors Landlord and several wines by the glass; children welcome, tables on front terrace, garden behind, open (and food) all day. *(Peter Brix)*

FROGHAM   SU1712
Foresters Arms (01425) 652294
Abbotswell Road; SP6 2JA Refurbished New Forest pub (part of the Little Pub Group); enjoyable good value food from lunchtime baguettes and bagels up, well kept Wadworths ales and a guest, friendly staff, cosy rustic-chic interior with rugs on light

wood floor, antlers above woodburner in brick fireplace, pale green panelling, mix of old and new furniture including settles and pews; children, walkers and dogs (in bar) welcome, front verandah and garden, maybe donkeys out at front, open all day Fri-Sun. *(Rob Anderson)*

GOODWORTH CLATFORD   SU3642
Royal Oak (01264) 324105
Longstock Road; SP11 7QY Comfortably modern L-shaped bar with welcoming staff, good carefully sourced food from pub staples up, Flack Manor and Ringwood ales, good choice of wines by the glass, Weds quiz night; children welcome, sheltered and very pretty dell-like garden, attractive Test Valley village and good River Anton walks, closed Sun evening. *(Edward May)*

GOSPORT   SU6101
Jolly Roger (023) 9258 2584
Priory Road, Hardway; PO12 4LQ
Popular extended waterfront pub with fine harbour views, traditional beamed bar with half a dozen well kept ales and decent house wines, good choice of home-made food from bar and restaurant menus, efficient friendly young staff, lots of bric-a-brac, log fire, attractive dining area with conservatory; children welcome, disabled access/facilities, seats outside, open all day. *(M G Hart, Ann and Colin Hunt, Val and Alan Green, Neil and Anita Christopher)*

GOSPORT   SZ6100
Queens (07974) 031671
Queens Road; PO12 1LG Classic bare-boards local with Oakleaf, Ringwood, Youngs and guests kept in top condition by long-serving landlady, popular Oct beer festival, three areas off bar with good log fire in interesting carved fireplace, sensibly placed darts; TV room (children welcome here daytime); closed lunchtimes Mon-Thurs, open all day Sat. *(Ann and Colin Hunt)*

GREYWELL   SU7151
Fox & Goose (01256) 702062
Near M3 junction 5; A287 towards Odiham, then first right to village; RG29 1BY Traditional two-bar village pub popular with locals and walkers, country kitchen furniture, open fire, enjoyable home-made pubby food from good lunchtime sandwiches up, Sun roast till 5pm, well kept ales including Sharps Doom Bar, friendly helpful service; children and dogs welcome, good-sized back garden and camping field, River Whitewater and Basingstoke Canal walks, open all day. *(Mike Swan)*

HAMBLE   SU4806
Bugle (023) 8045 3000
3 miles from M27 junction 8; SO31 4HA
Bustling little 16th-c village pub by River Hamble, beamed and timbered rooms with flagstones and polished boards, church

chairs, woodburner in fine brick fireplace, bar stools along herringbone-brick and timbered counter, Flack Manor Hedge Hop, Timothy Taylors Landlord and a beer named for the pub from Itchen Valley, popular food (all day Sun); background music, TV; children welcome, dogs in bar, seats on terrace with view of boats, open all day. *(Peter Brix)*

HAMBLE   SU4806
Olde Whyte Harte (023) 8045 2108
High Street; 3 miles from M27 junction 8; SO31 4JF Welcoming old-fashioned village pub, locally popular, with big inglenook log fire, flagstones and low dark 17th-c beams, small cottagey restaurant area, generous fresh pubby food all day along with specials, Fullers/Gales ales and a guest from stone-faced counter, good wines by the glass; background music; children and dogs welcome, small walled garden, handy for nature reserve, open all day. *(Anon)*

HAMBLEDON   SU6716
★ Bat & Ball (023) 9263 2692
Broadhalfpenny Down; about 2 miles E towards Clanfield; PO8 0UB Extended dining pub opposite historic cricket pitch and with plenty of cricketing memorabilia (the game's rules are said to have been written here), log fires and comfortable modern furnishings in three linked rooms, Fullers ales, enjoyable food from well priced snacks up, good friendly service, panelled restaurant; children and dogs welcome, tables on front terrace, garden behind with lovely downs views, good walks, open all day. *(Ann and Colin Hunt)*

HAMBLEDON   SU6414
Vine (023) 9263 2419
West Street; PO7 4RW Refurbished 400-year-old beamed village local, well kept Ringwood and enjoyable sensibly priced home-made food (not Sun-Tues evenings), friendly staff, internal well and two-way log fire; some live music; garden with small covered deck, good walks. *(Ann and Colin Hunt, Val and Alan Green)*

HAVANT   SU7206
Wheelwrights Arms (023) 9247 6502
Emsworth Road; PO9 2SN Sizeable red-brick Victorian pub recently revamped by Upham, their beers kept well and good range of popular food including OAP lunch deal Mon-Thurs, friendly service; children welcome, open all day. *(Rob Anderson)*

HAWKLEY   SU7429
Hawkley Inn (01730) 827205
Off B3006 near A3 junction; Pococks Lane; GU33 6NE Small traditional tile-hung village pub with half a dozen

well kept ales from central bar, real ciders too, enjoyable home-made food (not Sun evening), Mon steak night, open fires (large moose head above one), bare boards, flagstones and well used carpet, old pine tables and assorted chairs; children and dogs welcome, covered seating area at front, big back garden, useful for walkers on Hangers Way, four comfortable bedrooms, open all day weekends. *(Andrew Stone)*

HAYLING ISLAND   SU7201
Maypole (023) 924 63670
Havant Road; PO11 0PS Sizeable two-bar 1930s roadside local, family-run and friendly, with good reasonably priced home-made pub food including Fri fish night, well kept Fullers/Gales beers, parquet floors and polished panelling, plenty of good seating, open fires; Thurs quiz, darts; children and dogs welcome, garden picnic-sets and play equipment, closed Sun evening. *(Peter Brix)*

HECKFIELD   SU7260
New Inn (0118) 932 6374
B3349 Hook–Reading (former A32); RG27 0LE Rambling open-plan dining pub, good welcoming service, enjoyable pubby food (all day weekends) from sandwiches and baked potatoes up, well kept Badger ales and good choice of wines by the glass, attractive layout with some traditional furniture in original core, two log fires, restaurant; jazz first Thurs of month, quiz and curry last Thurs; children welcome, good-sized heated terrace, 16 comfortable bedrooms in extension, open all day. *(Darren and Jane Staniforth)*

HERRIARD   SS6744
Fur & Feathers (01256) 384170
Pub signed just off A339 Basingstoke–Alton; RG25 2PN Victorian country pub, clean, light and airy, with popular home-made blackboard food, four well kept ales including Sharps Doom Bar and good choice of wines, friendly staff, smallish bar with stools along counter, dining areas either side, pine furniture on stripped-wood flooring, painted half-panelling, old photographs and farm tools, two woodburners; background music; garden behind, open all day Fri and Sat, till 6pm Sun, closed Mon. *(Rob Anderson)*

HOUGHTON   SU3432
★ Boot (01794) 388310
Village signposted off A30 in Stockbridge; SO20 6LH Updated country pub with cheery log-fire bar and more formal dining room, well kept Ringwood and Sharps, Weston's cider, enjoyable bar and restaurant food (not Sun evening) including blackboard specials, friendly helpful staff; children and dogs welcome, picnic-sets out in front

We say if we know a pub has background music.

and in spacious tranquil garden by lovely (unfenced) stretch of River Test, outside summer grill, good walks, opposite Test Way cycle path, open all day Sun, closed Mon evening. *(Helen and Brian Edgeley)*

KEYHAVEN SZ3091
★ **Gun** (01590) 642391

Keyhaven Road; SO41 0TP Busy rambling 17th-c pub looking over boatyard and sea to Isle of Wight; low-beamed bar with nautical bric-a-brac and plenty of character (less in family rooms and conservatory), enjoyable fairly standard food including good local crab, well kept Ringwood, Sharps, Timothy Taylors and Charles Wells tapped from the cask, Weston's cider, lots of malt whiskies, helpful young staff, bar billiards; background music; tables out in front and in big back garden with swings and fish pond, you can stroll down to small harbour and walk to Hurst Castle, open all day Sat, closed Sun evening. *(Neil and Angela Huxter, M G Hart, David and Judy Robison)*

LANGSTONE SU7104
★ **Royal Oak** (023) 9248 3125

Off A3023 just before Hayling Island bridge; Langstone High Street; PO9 1RY Charmingly placed waterside dining pub overlooking tidal inlet and ancient wadeway to Hayling Island, boats at high tide, wading birds when it goes out; Greene King ales and good choice of wines by the glass, reasonably priced food with all-day sandwiches and snacks, spacious flagstoned bar and linked dining areas, log fire; nice garden and good coast paths nearby, open all day. *(John Harris)*

LINWOOD SU1910
High Corner (01425) 473973

Signed from A338 via Moyles Court, and from A31; BH24 3QY Big rambling pub in splendid New Forest position at end of track, with extensive neatly kept wooded garden and lots for children to do; popular and welcoming with some character in original upper log-fire bar, big back extensions for the summer crowds, nicely partitioned restaurant, verandah lounge and interesting family rooms, enjoyable generously served food, well kept Wadworths ales and Weston's Old Rosie cider; dogs welcome, horses too (stables and paddock available), seven bedrooms, open all day summer and weekends. *(Phil and Jane Villiers, Peter Meister)*

LITTLE LONDON SU6259
Plough (01256) 850628

Silchester Road, off A340 N of Basingstoke; RG26 5EP Tucked-away local, cosy and unspoilt, with log fires, low beams and mixed furnishings on brick and tiled floors (watch the step), well kept Palmers, Ringwood and interesting guests tapped from the cask, good value baguettes; bar billiards and darts; dogs welcome,

attractive garden, handy for Pamber Forest and Calleva Roman remains. *(Andrew Stone)*

LONG SUTTON SU7447
Four Horseshoes (01256) 862488

Signed off B3349 S of Hook; RG29 1TA Welcoming unpretentious country local; open plan with black beams and two log fires, long-serving landlord cooking uncomplicated bargain food such as lancashire hotpot and fish and chips, friendly landlady serving three changing ales such as Palmers, small glazed-in verandah; live jazz second and fourth Tues of month; children and dogs welcome, disabled access, lovely hanging baskets, picnic-sets on grass over road, play area, three good value bedrooms, closed Mon, Tues lunchtimes. *(Mike Swan)*

LONGPARISH SU4344
Cricketers (01264) 720335

B3048, off A303 just E of Andover; SP11 6PZ Friendly village local under new management; connecting rooms and cosy corners, beams, bare boards and flagstones, two woodburners (one double aspect), assorted cricketing memorabilia, enjoyable freshly made pubby food (not Sun evening, Mon), Wadworths ales; children and dogs welcome, sizeable back garden, open all day. *(Mel Spear)*

LONGPARISH SU4244
★ **Plough** (01264) 720358

B3048, off A303 just E of Andover; SP11 6PB Smart Victorian dining pub, original features mixing well with modern touches and furnishings, various neat rooms with beams, standing timbers, flagstone and oak floors, contemporary paintwork, high-backed dining chairs and pews, working fireplaces (one with woodburner), Ringwood Best, Sharps Doom Bar and Timothy Taylors Landlord, three ciders and several wines by the glass (there's a walk-in 'wine cellar'), enjoyable food from bar and restaurant menus, friendly staff; background music; children and dogs (in small bar area) welcome, garden with decking, handy for A303 and walking (Test Way passes through car park), open all day (Sun till 6pm). *(Richard and Patricia Jefferson, Stewart and Elizabeth Harvey, Hugh Roberts, B J Harding, Edward Mirzoeff)*

LYMINGTON SZ3295
Kings Head (01590) 672709

Quay Hill; SO41 3AR In steep cobbled lane of smart small shops, friendly dimly lit old pub with well kept Fullers London Pride, Ringwood, Timothy Taylors Landlord and a couple of guests, several wines by the glass, good choice of enjoyable home-made food from sandwiches to specials, pleasant helpful staff, nicely mixed old-fashioned furnishings in rambling beamed and bare-boarded rooms, log fire and woodburner, daily papers; background music, can get very busy and they may ask for a credit card if you run a tab; children and dogs welcome, nice little sunny courtyard behind, open all day. *(Tony and Wendy Hobden)*

LYNDHURST   SU2908
Waterloo Arms (023) 8028 2113
Pikes Hill, just off A337 N; SO43 7AS
Thatched 17th-c New Forest pub with low beams, stripped brick walls and log fire, two Ringwood beers and Sharps Doom Bar, pubby food including blackboard specials, friendly staff, comfortable bar and roomy back dining area, Tues quiz and Sun live music; children and dogs welcome, terrace and nice big garden, open (and food) all day. *(Anon)*

MAPLEDURWELL   SU6851
Gamekeepers (01256) 322038
Off A30, not far from M3 junction 6; RG25 2LU Dark-beamed dining pub with good upmarket food (not cheap and they add a service charge) from regularly changing blackboard menu, also some pubby choices and lunchtime baguettes, welcoming informal landlord and friendly staff, three well kept local ales including Andwells Resolute, good coffee, a few sofas by flagstoned and panelled core, well spaced tables in large dining room; background music, TV; children welcome, terrace and garden, lovely thatched village with duck pond, good walks, open all day weekends. *(John Harris)*

MARCHWOOD   SU3809
Pilgrim (023) 8086 7752
Hythe Road, off A326 at Twiggs Lane; SO40 4WU Popular picturesque thatched pub (originally three cottages), good choice of sensibly priced food from huge sandwiches up, well kept Fullers ales and decent wines, friendly helpful staff, open fires; dogs welcome, tree-lined garden with round picnic-sets, 14 stylish bedrooms in building across car park, open all day. *(Martin and Sue Radcliffe)*

MATTINGLEY   SU7357
Leather Bottle (0118) 932 6371
3 miles from M3 junction 5; in Hook, turn right-and-left on to B3349 Reading Road (former A32); RG27 8JU Old red-brick chain pub with good food from varied menu, three local ales including Andwell and plenty of wines by the glass, well spaced tables in linked areas, black beams, flagstones and bare boards, inglenook log fire, extension opening on to covered terrace; background music; children and dogs (in bar) welcome, disabled access/facilities, two garden areas, open (and food) all day. *(Anon)*

MEONSTOKE   SU6120
Bucks Head (01489) 877313
Village signed just off A32 N of Droxford; SO32 3NA Cleanly refurbished and opened up tile-hung pub in lovely village

setting with ducks on pretty little River Meon; stone floors and log fires, traditional food and well kept Greene King ales; children and dogs welcome, small walled gardens either side, one overlooking river, good walks, five bedrooms, open all day weekends (till 8pm Sun), closed Mon lunchtime. *(Ann and Colin Hunt)*

MICHELDEVER   SU5138
Half Moon & Spread Eagle
(01962) 774339 *Brown sign to pub off A33 N of Winchester; SO21 3DG* Simply furnished 18th-c beamed village local, bare-boards bar with woodburner, horsebrasses and old banknotes pinned overhead, five real ales, ample helpings of enjoyable well priced food in carpeted dining side, steps up to games area with pool and shelves of books; children and dogs welcome, sheltered back terrace and garden, pleasant walks nearby, open all day Sat, Sun till 8pm, closed Mon lunchtime. *(Jennifer Banks)*

MILFORD-ON-SEA   SZ2891
Beach House (01590) 643044
Park Lane; SO41 OPT Civilised well placed Victorian hotel-dining pub owned by Hall & Woodhouse; restored oak-panelled interior, entrance hall bar with Badger First Gold, Tanglefoot and a guest, enjoyable sensibly priced food from lunchtime baguettes and sharing boards up, friendly attentive service, magnificent views from dining room and terrace; children welcome, dogs in bar, grounds down to the Solent looking out to the Needles, 15 bedrooms, open (and food) all day. *(David and Sally Frost)*

MINLEY MANOR   SU8357
Crown & Cushion (01252) 545253
A327, just N of M3 junction 4A; GU17 9UA Attractive little pub dating from 1512, two well kept Shepherd Neame ales and good fairly priced food including a few far eastern choices, prompt cheerful service, Sun carvery in big separate raftered and flagstoned rustic 'meade hall' with huge log fire; children welcome, no dogs inside, heated terrace overlooking own cricket pitch, open (and food) all day. *(KC)*

MINSTEAD   SU2810
★ Trusty Servant (023) 8081 2137
Just off A31, not far from M27 junction 1; SO43 7FY Attractive 19th-c red-brick pub in pretty New Forest hamlet with interesting church (Sir Arthur Conan Doyle buried here), wandering cattle and ponies, plenty of easy walks; two-room bare-boards bar and big dining room, open fires, well kept local ales and good reasonably priced food from doorstep sandwiches to local game, welcoming efficient service even when busy; children and dogs welcome, terrace and big sloping garden, open all day (food all day Fri-Sun). *(Revd Michael Vockins, Wendy Breese, Tom and Jill Jones)*

MORTIMER WEST END   SU6364
Red Lion (0118) 970 0169
*Church Road; Silchester turn off
Mortimer–Aldermaston road; RG7 2HU*
Old country pub refurbished under new
management and specialising in enjoyable
well presented italian food, stripped
masonry, timbers and panelling, log fires;
pleasant garden and small front terrace,
handy for Roman Silchester. *(Malcolm and
Pauline Pellatt)*

NEW CHERITON   SU5827
★Hinton Arms (01962) 771252
A272 near B3046 junction; SO24 0NH
Neatly kept popular country pub with
cheerful accommodating landlord, three
or four real ales including Bowman
Wallops Wood and a house beer brewed by
Hampshire, decent wines by the glass, good
generous food from sandwiches to daily
specials, sporting pictures and memorabilia,
relaxing atmosphere and friendly staff; TV
lounge; well behaved children and dogs
welcome, terrace and big garden, very
handy for Hinton Ampner House (NT).
(Emma Scofield)

ODIHAM   SU7451
Water Witch (01256) 808778
*Colt Hill – quiet no-through road signed
off main street; RG29 1AL* Olde-worlde
décor in nicely kept Chef & Brewer by
picturesque stretch of Basingstoke Canal
(boat hire), big but cosily divided with more
formal dining area at back, wide choice of
food (can get busy and may be a wait), three
mainstream ales; children welcome, no dogs
inside, disabled access and parking, pretty
hanging baskets in front, terrace with awning
and garden down to the water, open all day.
(Barry Collett, Ann and Colin Hunt)

PETERSFIELD   SU7423
George (01730) 233343
The Square; GU32 3HH Old building
in square with café-style tables outside,
nicely updated interior (some recent
refurbishment), enjoyable food including
well filled sandwiches, sharing plates, home-
made burgers and Pieminister pies, three
well kept ales, good choice of wines by the
glass and decent coffee, friendly young staff;
some weekend live music; children welcome,
attractive courtyard garden with own bar,
open all day from 9am for breakfast.
(George Atkinson)

PETERSFIELD   SU7423
Good Intent (01730) 263838
College Street; GU31 4AF Homely 16th-c
coaching inn, friendly and chatty, with five
well kept Fullers/Gales beers and enjoyable
fresh pubby food (not Sun evening) including
range of O'Hagans sausages, low black
beams, pine tables and built-in upholstered
benches, separate large restaurant, log

fires; background and live music, quiz Mon;
children and dogs welcome, seats on front
terrace, narrow entrance to small back car
park, three bedrooms, open all day.
(John Harris)

PETERSFIELD   SU7423
Square Brewery (01730) 264291
The Square; GU32 3HJ Friendly town-
centre Fullers pub with five of their ales
kept well, small choice of enjoyable sensibly
priced breakfast/lunchtime food (also Weds,
Thurs evenings) from good ciabattas up,
live music Sat; free wi-fi; children and dogs
welcome, seats out in front and in courtyard
garden behind, open all day from 10am.
(Val and Alan Green)

PHOENIX GREEN   SU7555
Phoenix (01252) 842484
*London Road, A30 W of Hartley
Wintney; RG27 8RT* 18th-c pub with
lots of beams, timbers, rugs on bare
boards and big end inglenook, good freshly
made food from varied daily changing menu,
four well kept ales, a couple of good ciders
and 16 wines by the glass, friendly prompt
service, back dining room; pleasant outlook
from sunny garden (hats and sun cream
provided). *(Chris and Claire Taylor)*

PORTSMOUTH   SZ6399
Bridge Tavern (023) 9275 2992
East Street, Camber Dock; PO1 2JJ
Flagstones, bare boards and lots of dark
wood, comfortable furnishings, maritime
theme with good harbour views, Fullers
ales, sensibly priced food including plenty
of fish dishes; nice waterside terrace, open
all day. *(Ann and Colin Hunt)*

PORTSMOUTH   SZ6399
Dolphin (023) 9282 3595
*High Street, Old Portsmouth, opposite
cathedral; PO1 2LU* Spacious old beamed
pub – known as the country pub in town,
and furnished accordingly; half a dozen well
kept ales (some expensive), enjoyable food
including good vegetarian options, friendly
staff; children and dogs welcome, small
terrace behind. *(Ann and Colin Hunt)*

PORTSMOUTH   SU6706
George (023) 9222 1079
Portsdown Hill Road, Widley; PO6 1BE
Old-fashioned one-bar Georgian local
with village feel, seven well kept ales such
as Adnams, Flowers, Greene King and
Ringwood, simple lunchtime food including
good ploughman's, cheerful staff; live music
and quiz nights; dogs welcome, views of
Hayling Island, Portsmouth and Isle of Wight,
hill walks across the road, open all day.
(Val and Alan Green)

PORTSMOUTH   SU6501
George (023) 9275 3885
Queen Street, near dockyard entrance;

PO1 3HU Spotless old inn with two rooms, one set for dining, log fire, glass-covered well and maritime pictures, Hardys & Hansons Olde Trip, Sharps Atlantic and Doom Bar, well priced food (not Sun evening, Mon) from sandwiches up, friendly staff; eight bedrooms, handy for dockyard and HMS *Victory*, open all day. *(Ann and Colin Hunt)*

PORTSMOUTH SU6300
Lady Hamilton (023) 9287 0505
The Hard, near Gunwharf; PO1 3DT Small welcoming hotel with longish narrow bar, nautical theme including pictures of Nelson and Lady Hamilton, generous fairly priced food, real ales and decent coffee; clean bedrooms, open all day in summer. *(Ann and Colin Hunt)*

PORTSMOUTH SZ6399
Pembroke (023) 9282 3961
Pembroke Road; PO1 2NR Traditional well run corner local with good buoyant atmosphere, comfortable and unspoilt under long-serving licensees, Bass, Fullers London Pride and Greene King Abbot from L-shaped bar, fresh rolls, coal-effect gas fire; darts and weekend live music; open all day (break 4-7pm Sun). *(Ann and Colin Hunt)*

PORTSMOUTH SU6300
Ship Anson (023) 9282 4152
Victory Road, The Hard (opposite Esplanade station, Portsea); PO1 3DT No-frills mock-Tudor pub close to dockyard entrance, spacious and comfortable, with well kept Greene King ales and a guest, generous pub food at bargain prices, buoyant local atmosphere; fruit machines, sports TVs; children welcome, seats outside overlooking ferry port, very handy for HMS *Victory*, open all day. *(Richard Tilbrook)*

PORTSMOUTH SZ6299
Still & West (023) 9282 1567
Bath Square, Old Portsmouth; PO1 2JL Great location with superb views of narrow harbour mouth and across to Isle of Wight, especially from glazed-in panoramic upper family area and waterfront terrace; nautical bar with fireside sofas, Fullers ales and good choice of wines by the glass, enjoyable food from sandwiches and sharing plates to good fish dishes; background music, free wi-fi; handy for Historic Dockyard, nearby pay-and-display parking, open all day from 9am (11.30am Sun). *(Ann and Colin Hunt, Dr and Mrs J D Abell)*

PORTSMOUTH SZ6399
Wellington (023) 9281 8965
High Street, off Grand Parade, Old Portsmouth; PO1 2LY Smallish open-plan pub with large Georgian bay window, comfortable old-fashioned feel with drapes and red colour scheme, enjoyable reasonably priced food including fresh fish, three real ales, dining area at back, some live music;

children and dogs welcome, attractive little outside seating area, near seafront and historic square tower, open all day summer (all day Fri-Sun winter), closed Mon Jan-Mar. *(Ann and Colin Hunt)*

PORTSMOUTH SU6400
White Swan (023) 9289 1340
Guildhall Walk; PO1 2DD Refurbished mock-Tudor pub (Brewhouse & Kitchen) visibly brewing its own good beers, also decent choice of well priced food (all day Fri-Sun) from sandwiches and sharing boards up; live jazz Sun lunchtime; open all day. *(Ann and Colin Hunt)*

ROMSEY SU3523
Dukes Head (01794) 514450
A3057 out towards Stockbridge; SO51 0HB Attractive 16th-c roadside dining pub with warren of small comfortable linked rooms, big log fire, enjoyable generously served food including daily specials, big such as Flack Manor, Ringwood and Sharps, cheerful staff; children welcome, sheltered back terrace and pleasant garden, pretty hanging baskets, handy for Hillier Gardens, open all day weekends. *(Ann and Colin Hunt)*

ROMSEY SU3521
Old House at Home (01794) 513175
Love Lane; SO51 8DE Attractive 17th-c thatched pub surrounded by new development; friendly and bustling, with comfortable low-beamed interior, wide choice of freshly made sensibly priced bar food including popular Sun lunch, well kept Fullers/Gales ales and guests, Aspall's cider, cheerful efficient service; regular folk sessions; children and dogs (in bar) welcome, spilt-level back terrace, open all day (no food Sun evening). *(John Branston)*

ROTHERWICK SU7156
Coach & Horses (01256) 768976
Signed from B3349 N of Hook; also quite handy for M3 junction 5; RG27 9BG Friendly 17th-c pub with traditional beamed front rooms, good value locally sourced pubby food and well kept Badger ales, log fire and woodburners, newer back dining area; children, dogs and muddy boots welcome, tables out at front and on terrace behind overlooking fields, pretty flower tubs and baskets, good walks, open all day Sat, Sun till 6pm, closed Mon. *(Belinda Stamp)*

ROTHERWICK SU7156
Falcon (01256) 765422
Off B3349 N of Hook, not far from M3 junction 5; RG27 9BL Open-plan country pub with good freshly made food using local suppliers, friendly efficient service, well kept ales such as Otter and Ringwood, good selection of wines, rustic tables and comfy sofa in bare-boards bar, well laid flagstoned dining area, log fires; free wi-fi; children and dogs welcome, disabled access, tables

out in front and in back garden, open all day. *(Barbara Rothwell)*

ROWLAND'S CASTLE   SU7310
Robin Hood (023) 9241 2268
The Green; PO9 6AB Nicely refurbished inn overlooking village green, light and airy stone-tiled bar with log fire, decent choice of good value food, Badger ales and a guest, efficient service, restaurant; children and dogs welcome, disabled facilities, tables out on front terrace, six bedrooms, open all day. *(J A Snell)*

SHALDEN   SU7043
Golden Pot (01420) 80655
B3349 Odiham Road N of Alton; GU34 4DJ Airy light décor with timbered walls, bare boards and log fires, enjoyable food from baguettes up including themed nights, friendly service, a couple of ales such as Sharps Doom Bar and Triple fff Altons Pride, local artwork for sale in smallish restaurant; background music, quiz nights, skittle alley; children and dogs welcome, benches out in covered area at front, garden with play area, open all day. *(Tony and Jill Radnor)*

SHEDFIELD   SU5613
Samuels Rest (01329) 832213
Upper Church Road (signed off B2177); SO32 2JB Cosy unspoilt village local under welcoming licensees, good straightforward food and well kept Wadworths beers, nice eating area away from bar, conservatory; aviary with talking parrot; garden and terrace, lovely church. *(Ann and Colin Hunt)*

SHEDFIELD   SU5513
Wheatsheaf (01329) 833024
A334 Wickham–Botley; SO32 2JG Friendly no-fuss local with well kept Flowerpots and guests tapped from the cask, proper cider, short sensible choice of enjoyable bargain lunches (evening food Tues, Weds), good service, woodburner in public bar, smaller lounge; live music Sat; dogs welcome, garden, handy for Wickham Vineyard, open all day. *(Anon)*

SHERFIELD ENGLISH   SU3022
Hatchet (01794) 322487
Romsey Rd; SO51 6FP Beamed and panelled 18th-c pub, good choice of popular fairly priced food including two-for-one steak deal Tues and Thurs evenings, four well kept ales such as Dartmoor, St Austell, Sharps and Timothy Taylors, good wine choice, friendly hard-working staff, long bar with cosy area down steps, woodburner, more steps up to second bar with darts, TV and juke box; children and dogs welcome, outside

seating on two levels, play area, open all day weekends. *(Mike Swan)*

SHIPTON BELLINGER   SU2345
Boot (01980) 842279
High Street; SP9 7UF Village pub with vast range of enjoyable reasonably priced food including chinese, thai, italian and mexican as well as traditional english dishes, friendly staff; background music; children welcome, back garden with decked area, open all day Sun. *(Mrs Zara Elliott)*

SOPLEY   SZ1596
Woolpack (01425) 672252
B3347 N of Christchurch; BH23 7AX Pretty thatched 17th-c dining pub with rambling open-plan low-beamed bar (some refurbishment planned), enjoyable traditional food plus daily specials, Ringwood, Sharps Doom Bar and a guest, Thatcher's cider and good choice of wines by the glass, modern dining conservatory overlooking weir; children in eating areas, dogs in certain parts, terrace and charming garden with weeping willows, duck stream and footbridges, open (and food) all day. *(Edward May)*

SOUTHAMPTON   SU4111
★**Duke of Wellington** (023) 8033 9222
Bugle Street (or walk along city wall from Bar Gate); SO14 2AH Striking ancient timber-framed building dating from 14th c, cellars even older, heavy beams and great log fire, well kept Wadworths ales, good choice of wines by the glass and good value traditional pub food (not Sun evening), friendly helpful service; background music (live Fri); children welcome, sunny streetside picnic-sets, handy for Tudor House Museum, open all day. *(Nigel and Sue Foster)*

SOUTHAMPTON   SU4313
South Western Arms
(023) 8032 4542 *Adelaide Road, by St Denys station; SO17 2HW* Friendly backstreet local with ten well kept changing ales, also good choice of bottled beers and whiskies, friendly staff and easy-going atmosphere, bare boards and brickwork, lots of woodwork, toby jugs, pump clips and stag's head on beams, old range and earthenware, darts, pool and table football in upper gallery allowing children; some live music, beer festivals; dogs welcome on leads, picnic-sets in walled beer garden, open all day. *(Dr Martin Owton)*

SOUTHAMPTON   SU4213
White Star (023) 8082 1990
Oxford Street; SO14 3DJ Smart modern bar, banquettes and open fire, comfortable

---

Half pints: by law, a pub should not charge more for half a pint than half the price of a full pint, unless it shows that half-pint price on its price list.

sofas and armchairs in secluded alcoves by south-facing windows, bistro-style dining area serving good up-to-date food from interesting baguettes and light dishes up, efficient attentive service, Flack Manor and Itchen Valley ales, nice wines by the glass and lots of cocktails; they may ask to keep a credit card while you eat; sunny pavement tables on pedestrianised street, 13 boutique bedrooms, open all day. *(Peter Brix)*

SOUTHSEA SZ6699
Artillery Arms (023) 9273 3610
Hester Road; PO4 8HB Proper two-bar Victorian backstreet local, real ales including Bowman and Ringwood, decent food, friendly atmosphere; pool and darts; children welcome, garden with play equipment, open all day. *(Ann and Colin Hunt)*

SOUTHSEA SZ6698
Eastney Tavern (023) 9282 6246
Cromwell Road; PO4 9PN Bow-fronted corner pub just off the seafront, spacious well looked-after interior with various eating areas (plenty of room for drinkers too), good value popular food, three real ales and decent choice of wines by the glass, sporting memorabilia and sports TV, Tues quiz, Fri live music; children and dogs welcome, seats in courtyard garden, nearby parking difficult, closed Mon lunchtime, otherwise open all day. *(Ann and Colin Hunt)*

SOUTHSEA SZ6499
Eldon Arms (023) 9229 7963
Eldon Street/Norfolk Street; PO5 4BS Tile-fronted backstreet Victorian pub under welcoming newish management, Fullers London Pride, St Austell Tribute and guests, simple food, old pictures and advertisements, attractive mirrors, bric-a-brac and shelves of books; darts, bar billiards and pool; children welcome, tables in back garden, open all day. *(Ann and Colin Hunt)*

SOUTHSEA SZ6499
★ **Hole in the Wall** (023) 9229 8085
Great Southsea Street; PO5 3BY Friendly unspoilt little local in old part of town, excellent range of well kept/priced ales including cask-tapped Oakleaf Hole Hearted, Thatcher's cider, speciality local sausages, meat puddings and other simple good value food (evenings Tues-Sat, Fri lunchtime), nicely worn boards, dark pews and panelling, old photographs and prints, hundreds of pump clips on ceiling, little snug behind the bar, daily papers, quiz night Thurs, Oct beer festival; small outside area at front with benches, side garden, opens 4pm (noon Fri, 2pm Sun). *(Ann and Colin Hunt)*

SOUTHSEA SZ6499
King Street Tavern (023) 9287 3307
King Street; PO5 4EH Character corner pub in attractive conservation area, spectacular Victorian tiled façade, bare boards and original fittings, four well kept Wadworths ales and guests, Thatcher's cider, good value straightforward home-made food from short menu; background and live music including fortnightly Sat jazz; dogs welcome, courtyard tables, open all day Fri-Sun, closed Mon. *(Ann and Colin Hunt)*

SOUTHSEA SZ6598
Leopold (023) 9282 9748
Albert Road; PO4 0JT Traditional green-tiled corner local with ten well kept ales (tasters offered), good choice of ciders and over 100 bottled beers, bright interior with hundreds of pump clips on the walls and pictures of old Portsmouth, no food; unobtrusive TVs each end, games machines, darts, Mon quiz; walled beer garden behind, open all day. *(Ann and Colin Hunt)*

SOUTHSEA SZ6599
Northcote (023) 9278 9888
Francis Avenue; PO4 0HL Welcoming traditional Victorian backstreet pub, four well kept ales including Hop Back and Wadworths, cosy carpeted lounge with Sherlock Holmes memorabilia, public bar with pool and darts; terrace seating, open all day. *(Ann and Colin Hunt)*

SOUTHSEA SZ6698
Sir Loin of Beef (023) 9282 0115
Highland Road, Eastney; PO4 9NH Spic and span corner pub, at least eight well kept frequently changing ales (tasters offered), bottled beers, no food, helpful friendly staff and buoyant atmosphere, interesting submarine pictures and artefacts; bar billiards, juke box, monthly Sun jazz; open all day. *(Ann and Colin Hunt)*

SOUTHSEA SZ6499
Wine Vaults (023) 9286 4712
Albert Road, opposite King's Theatre; PO5 2SF Bustling Fullers pub with several chatty rooms on different floors, main panelled bar with long plain counter and pubby furniture, seven well kept ales and decent choice of food including pizzas and range of burgers, good service, separate restaurant; background music, sports TV; children welcome, dogs in bar, smokers' roof terrace, open (and food) all day. *(Ann and Colin Hunt)*

SOUTHWICK SU6208
Golden Lion (023) 9221 0437
High Street; just off B2177 on Portsdown Hill; PO17 6EB Friendly two-bar 16th-c beamed pub (where Eisenhower and Montgomery came before D-Day); up to six well kept local ales including two from Suthwyk using barley from surrounding fields, four ciders and a dozen wines by the glass, enjoyable locally sourced home-made food (not Sun or Mon evenings) from snacks up in bar and dining room, cosy lounge bar with sofas and log fire, live music including

Tues jazz; good outside loos; children and dogs welcome, picnic-sets on grass at side, picturesque Estate village with scenic walks, open all day Sat, till 7pm Sun. *(Ann and Colin Hunt)*

SOUTHWICK   SU6208
Red Lion (023) 9237 7223
High Street; PO17 6EF Neatly kept low-beamed village dining pub with good choice of well liked food (best to book), Fullers/Gales and a guest beer, several wines by the glass, efficient friendly staff even though busy; children welcome, nice walks, open all day weekends. *(Alfie Bayliss)*

ST MARY BOURNE   SU4250
Bourne Valley (01264) 738361
Upper Link (B3048); SP11 6BT Attractively updated old red-brick inn, bar with central servery and log fire, separate raftered restaurant, good food from lunchtime sandwiches and pubby choices to more upmarket dishes (service charge added), efficient service even at busy times, Upham Punter and three guests, lots of wines by the glass, deli counter; children and dogs welcome, terrace and nice garden backing on to stream, good walks, nine bedrooms, open all day. *(Mr and Mrs A H Young, Mrs Julie Thomas)*

STEEP   SU7325
Cricketers (01730) 261035
Church Road; GU32 2DW Light airy revamp under present owners; good modern pub food including pizzas from visible oven, welcoming helpful staff, ales such as Bowman, Flowerpots and Langhams, decent wines, log fires in brick fireplaces with old portraits above, stripped floorboards and green half-panelling, chandeliers, candelabra and some cricketing memorabilia, occasional live acoustic music; children welcome, painted picnic-sets on narrow front deck, clean comfortable bedrooms, closed Sun evening, otherwise open (and food) all day. *(David and Carole Kidd)*

STOCKBRIDGE   SU3535
Greyhound (01264) 810833
High Street; SO20 6EY Substantial inn reworked as civilised restaurant-pub, log fires each end of bow-windowed bar (restaurant to the right), scrubbed old tables on woodstrip floor, dark low beams, good range of well liked food especially fish, set menu and daily specials, three ales including a house beer from Ringwood, good wine and whisky choice, friendly efficient staff (service charge added to bills); tables in charming River Test-side garden behind, children and dogs allowed, bedrooms and fly fishing, open all day. *(John Evans, Mr and Mrs A Curry)*

STOCKBRIDGE   SU3535
★Three Cups (01264) 810527
High Street; SO20 6HB Lovely low-beamed building dating from 1500, spruced up and added to yet keeping country inn feel, some emphasis on dining with lots of smartly set pine tables, but also high-backed settles, rustic bric-a-brac and three well kept ales (two from local brewers), good interesting food along with more pubby choices, helpful amiable service, nice wines by the glass, extended 'orangery' restaurant; children and dogs welcome, vine-covered verandah and charming cottage garden with streamside terrace, eight bedrooms, open all day. *(Geoffrey Kemp, Val and Alan Green, Tony and Jill Radnor)*

STRATFIELD TURGIS   SU6960
Wellington Arms (01256) 882214
Off A33 Reading–Basingstoke; RG27 0AS Handsome old country hotel dating from the 17th c, restful and surprisingly pubby tall-windowed two-room bar, part flagstoned, part carpeted, with leather chesterfields by open fire, two well kept Badger ales, good food and service; children and dogs welcome, garden, 27 comfortable bedrooms, open all day. *(Jennifer Banks)*

STROUD   SU7223
Seven Stars (01730) 264122
Winchester Road; set back from A272 Petersfield–Winchester; GU32 3PG Extended and modernised open-plan flint and brick pub, panelling, beams, wood and flagstone floors, good log fires, separate counter for ordering wide choice of good value food including tasty home-made pies, fast friendly service, well kept Badger ales and good wine list, large restaurant; free wi-fi; children and dogs (in bar) welcome, outside tables, good if strenuous walking, open all day. *(Peter Brix)*

STUBBINGTON   SU5402
Crofton (01329) 314222
Crofton Lane; PO14 3QF Extended 1960s estate local with neat carpeted interior, half a dozen well kept ales including Sharps Doom Bar, good value wines and very popular food at reasonable prices, friendly smartly dressed staff; skittle alley, some live music; children and dogs welcome, open (and food) all day. *(David M Smith, Ann and Colin Hunt)*

SWANMORE   SU5716
Brickmakers (01489) 890954
Church Road; SO32 2PA Restyled 1920s pub with friendly relaxed atmosphere, four well kept ales including Bowman and Fullers, decent wines and good interesting food all day (till 6pm Sun) from landlord-chef, OAP

---

weekday lunch deal, leather sofas by log fire, dining area with local artwork; Tues quiz, some live music; children and dogs welcome (pub's dog is Rosie), garden with raised deck, open all day. *(Di Braund, Ann and Colin Hunt, Stephen and Jean Curtis)*

SWANMORE   SU5816
Hunters (01489) 877214
Hillgrove; SO32 2PZ Popular rambling old dining pub on edge of village, friendly long-serving licensees and nice staff, wide choice of good honest freshly made food including enjoyable Sun lunch, home-baked bread, well kept Bowman and a guest tapped from the cask, lots of wines by the glass, bank notes, carpentry and farm tools on the walls; background music; children and dogs welcome, big garden with play area, nice walks N of village, open all day weekends (can be very busy then). *(Val and Alan Green)*

SWANMORE   SU5815
★ Rising Sun (01489) 896663
Droxford Road; signed off A32 N of Wickham and B2177 S of Bishop's Waltham, at Hillpound E of village centre; SO32 2PS Former coaching inn with welcoming hands-on licensees and friendly staff; easy chairs and sofa by log fire in low-beamed carpeted bar, pleasant roomier dining area with brick barrel vaulting in one part, own-brewed beer along with Sharps Doom Bar and local guests, a dozen wines by the glass and reasonably priced fairly standard pub food; children and dogs (in bar) welcome, picnic-sets on side grass with a play area, Kings Way long-distance path nearby. *(Val and Alan Green, Ann and Colin Hunt, Jill Hurley)*

SWAY   SZ2898
Hare & Hounds (01590) 682404
Durns Town, just off B3055 SW of Brockenhurst; SO41 6AL Bright, airy and comfortable New Forest family dining pub, popular generously served food, well kept ales such as Itchen Valley, Ringwood, St Austell and Timothy Taylors, good friendly service, low beams and central log fire; background music; dogs welcome, picnic-sets and play frame in neatly kept garden, open all day. *(Alfie Bayliss)*

THRUXTON   SU2945
White Horse (01264) 772401
Mullens Pond, just off A303 eastbound; SP11 8EE Attractive old thatched pub tucked below A303 embankment, comfortably modernised, with emphasis on enjoyable fresh food, good friendly service, plenty of wines by the glass and well kept ales such as Greene King, spacious interior with very low beams, woodburner and separate dining area; good-sized garden and terrace, four bedrooms, closed Sun evening. *(Tony and Jill Radnor, B J Harding)*

TICHBORNE   SU5730
★ Tichborne Arms (01962) 733760
Signed off B3047; SO24 0NA Thatched pub (rebuilt in the 1930s) in rolling countryside; half-panelled bare-boards bar with interesting pictures and other odds and ends, candlelit pine tables and raised woodburner, Fullers and guests tapped from the cask, local cider, enjoyable home-made food from doorstep sandwiches up, locals' bar with piano, darts and open fire; children and dogs welcome, sheltered terrace, more seats in big garden growing own vegetables, Wayfarers Walk and Itchen Way pass close by, open all day Sat, till 7.30pm Sun. *(Tony and Jill Radnor)*

TIMSBURY   SU3325
Bear & Ragged Staff
(01794) 368602 *A3057 towards Stockbridge; pub marked on OS Sheet 185 map reference 334254; SO51 0LB* Roadside dining pub with good choice of popular food including blackboard specials, friendly service, lots of wines by the glass, three Fullers/Gales beers and a guest, good-sized beamed interior with log fire; children welcome in eating part, tables in extended garden with play area, handy for Mottisfont (NT), good walks, open all day. *(Anon)*

TITCHFIELD   SU5405
Wheatsheaf (01329) 842965
East Street; off A27 near Fareham; PO14 4AD Welcoming smartened-up old place with well kept ales such as Flowerpots and good popular food (all day Sun) including small plates menu and Tues steak night, bow-windowed front bar, back restaurant extension, log fires; background music; terrace, open all day. *(Ann and Colin Hunt)*

TWYFORD   SU4824
★ Bugle (01962) 714888
B3355/Park Lane; SO21 1QT Modern pub with good enterprising food (highish prices) from daily changing menu, also lunchtime sandwiches/snacks and Mon evening set deal, attentive friendly young staff, well kept ales from Bowman, Flowerpots and Upham, nice wines by the glass, woodburner; background music; attractive verandah seating area, good walks nearby, three newly refurbished bedrooms, good breakfast, open all day (no food Sun evening). *(Edward May)*

UPHAM   SU5320
★ Brushmakers Arms
(01489) 860231 *Shoe Lane; village signed from Winchester–Bishop's Waltham downs road, and from B2177; SO32 1JJ* Welcoming and popular low-beamed village pub (can get crowded, especially weekends); L-shaped bar divided by central woodburner, cushioned settles and chairs around mix of tables, lots of

brushes and related paraphernalia, little back snug, fairly straightforward home-made food including range of pies, Fullers, Ringwood, Upham and a guest, decent coffee, Sun bar nibbles; children and dogs welcome (pub cats are Luna and Baxter), big garden with picnic-sets on sheltered terrace and tree-shaded lawn, good walks nearby, open all day Sun. *(Ann and Colin Hunt, Phil and Jane Villiers)*

UPPER CLATFORD   SU3543
Crook & Shears (01264) 361543
Off A343 S of Andover, via Foundry Road; SP11 7QL Cosy 17th-c thatched pub, welcoming and relaxed, with well kept ales such as Otter, Ringwood and Sharps, Thatcher's cider, traditional reasonably priced food (not Sun evening) from good baguettes to enjoyable Sun roasts, also OAP weekday lunch deal and Tues steak night, friendly attentive service, open fires and woodburner, small dining room, back skittle alley with own bar; children and dogs welcome, pleasant secluded garden behind, closed Mon lunchtime. *(Penny Matthews)*

UPPER FARRINGDON   SU7135
Rose & Crown (01420) 588231
Off A32 S of Alton; Crows Lane – follow Church, Selborne, Liss signpost; GU34 3ED Airy 19th-c village pub under new hospitable licensees, L-shaped bar with bare boards and log fire, a couple of Triple fff ales along with Sharps Doom Bar and a guest, good reasonably priced home-cooked food (not Sun evening) including pizzas, friendly helpful staff, back dining room; children, walkers and dogs welcome, wide views from attractive garden, open all day weekends. *(N R White, Corinne Green)*

UPTON   SU3555
Crown (01264) 736638
N of Hurstbourne Tarrant, off A343; SP11 0JS Attractive old country pub with very welcoming helpful staff, good choice of enjoyable reasonably priced pubby food from baguettes to specials, OAP weekday lunch deal, well kept beers such as Andwell, Two Cocks and West Berkshire, good log fire, back conservatory extension, home-made jams and chutneys for sale; dogs welcome in main bar area, small garden and terrace, open all day. *(Michael and Jenny Back)*

UPTON GREY   SU6948
Hoddington Arms (01256) 862371
Signed off B3349 S of Hook; Bidden Road; RG25 2RL Nicely updated 18th-c beamed pub, good food from varied menu (sometimes themed), local ales such as Andwell along with a beer named for them (Hodd), a dozen wines by the glass, friendly staff, events including live music, movie nights and beer/cider festivals; children and dogs welcome, big enclosed garden with terrace, quiet pretty village with interesting

Gertrude Jekyll garden, good walking/cycling, open all day Fri-Sun. *(Rob Anderson)*

VERNHAM DEAN   SU3456
George (01264) 737279
Centre of village; SP11 0JY Rambling open-plan 17th-c beamed and timbered pub with notable eyebrow windows, some exposed brick and flint, inglenook log fire, well kept Flack Manor, Greene King, Hop Back and a guest such as local Betteridges, popular home-made pubby food, good friendly service; children and dogs welcome, pretty garden behind, lovely thatched village and fine walks, open all day (Sun till 5pm). *(David and Judy Robison)*

WALHAMPTON   SZ3396
Walhampton Arms (01590) 673113
B3054 NE of Lymington; aka Walhampton Inn; SO41 5RE Large comfortable Georgian-style family roadhouse handy for Isle of Wight ferry; popular well priced food including carvery in raftered former stables and two adjoining areas, pleasant lounge, Ringwood ales and traditional cider, cheerful helpful staff; attractive courtyard, good walks, open (and food) all day. *(John Harris)*

WALTHAM CHASE   SU5614
Black Dog (01329) 832316
Winchester Road; SO32 2LX Old brick-built pub with low-ceilinged carpeted front bar, three well kept Greene King ales and a guest, over a dozen wines by the glass, good well priced food (all day Sun) including weekday lunch deal, cheerful service, log fires, back restaurant; children and dogs welcome, colourful hanging baskets, tables in good-sized neatly kept garden with play area, open all day weekends. *(Ann and Colin Hunt)*

WELL   SU7646
★Chequers (01256) 862605
Off A287 via Crondall, or A31 via Froyle and Lower Froyle; RG29 1TL Appealing low-beamed country dining pub; very good restaurant-style food (some quite pricey) including fresh fish/seafood, also brasserie menu and lunchtime sandwiches, Badger ales and good choice of wines, friendly efficient service, wood floors, panelling and log fires; free wi-fi; bench seating on vine-covered front terrace, spacious back garden overlooking fields. *(F and N Hatch, Martin and Karen Wake, Tony and Jill Radnor)*

WEST TYTHERLEY   SU2730
Black Horse (01794) 340308
North Lane; SP5 1NF Compact unspoilt beamed village local, welcoming licensees and chatty regulars, traditional bar with a couple of long tables and woodburner in big fireplace, nicely set dining area off, four mainly local ales and a real cider, enjoyable reasonably priced food including popular Fri fish night and good Sun roasts; skittle alley,

quiz last Weds of month; children and dogs welcome (there are resident dogs), open all day Sun till 7.30pm, closed lunchtimes Mon-Weds (no evening food Mon, Tues). *(John Harris)*

WHERWELL   SU3839
Mayfly (01264) 860283
Testcombe (over by Fullerton, not in Wherwell itself); A3057 SE of Andover, between B3420 turn-off and Leckford where road crosses River Test; OS Sheet 185 map reference 382390; SO20 6AX Busy pub with decking and conservatory overlooking fast-flowing River Test; spacious beamed and carpeted bar with fishing paraphernalia, rustic pub furnishings and woodburner, Fullers ales and lots of wines by the glass, wide range of bar food (must book for a good table), prices generally on the high side and they add a surcharge if you pay by credit card; background music; well behaved children and dogs welcome, open (and food) all day. *(Helen and Brian Edgeley, Martin and Sue Day, R Halliday)*

WHERWELL   SU3840
White Lion (01264) 860317
B3420; SP11 7JF Early 17th-c multi-level beamed village inn, popular and friendly, with good choice of enjoyable food including speciality pies, well kept ales such as Flowerpots, Itchen Valley, Sharps and Timothy Taylors, several wines by the glass, cheery helpful staff, open fire, comfy leather sofas and armchairs, dining rooms either side of bar; background music; well behaved children welcome, dogs on leads, sunny courtyard with good quality furniture, Test Way walks, six bedrooms, open all day from 7.30am (breakfast for non-residents). *(Michael and Jenny Back, Dominic Riley, D J and P M Taylor)*

WICKHAM   SU5711
Greens (01329) 833197
The Square, at junction with A334; PO17 5JQ Civilised dining place with clean-cut modern décor, small bar with leather sofa and armchairs on light wood floor, wide wine choice and a couple of real ales such as Bowman, obliging young staff, step down to split-level balustraded dining areas, good if not always cheap food from typical bar lunches to imaginative specials, also weekday set lunch menu; background music; children welcome if eating, pleasant lawn overlooking water meadows, closed Sun evening, Mon. *(Val and Alan Green)*

WINCHESTER   SU4829
Bishop on the Bridge
(01962) 855111 *High Street/Bridge Street; SO23 9JX* Neat efficiently run red-brick Fullers pub, their well kept beers and decent food from sandwiches up, leather sofas, old local prints; free wi-fi; children and dogs welcome, nice back terrace overlooking River Itchen, open all day. *(Stephen and Jean Curtis, Gerry and Rosemary Dobson)*

WINCHESTER   SU4828
★ Black Boy (01962) 861754
B3403 off M3 junction 10 towards city, then left into Wharf Hill; no nearby daytime parking – 220 metres from car park on B3403; SO23 9NQ Splendidly eccentric décor at this chatty old-fashioned pub, floor-to-ceiling books, lots of big clocks, mobiles made of wine bottles or spectacles, stuffed animals including a baboon and dachshund, two log fires, orange-painted room with big oriental rugs on red floorboards, barn room with open hayloft, five local beers kept well, straightforward home-made food (not Sun evening, Mon, Tues lunchtime) including sandwiches; table football and board games; supervised children and dogs welcome, slate tables out in front and seats on attractive secluded terrace, ten bedrooms in adjoining building, open all day. *(Alfie Bayliss)*

WINCHESTER   SU4829
Eclipse (01962) 865676
The Square, between High Street and cathedral; SO23 9EX Picturesque unspoilt 16th-c local with massive beams and timbers in two small cheerful rooms, four well kept ales including Butcombe and Sharps, proper ciders and decent choice of wines by the glass, good value traditional lunchtime food including popular Sun roasts, oak settles and open fire; children in back area, seats outside, handy for cathedral, open all day. *(Val and Alan Green)*

WINCHESTER   SU4829
★ Old Vine (01962) 854616
Great Minster Street; SO23 9HA Lively big-windowed town bar with well kept ales such as Bowman, Flowerpots, Ringwood and St Austell, high beams, worn oak boards, smarter and larger dining side with good choice of up-to-date food plus sandwiches and pub staples, efficient service even though busy, modern conservatory; faint background music; by cathedral, with sheltered terrace, partly covered and heated, charming bedrooms, open all day. *(Val and Alan Green, Paul Humphreys, Helen and Brian Edgeley, Glenwys and Alan Lawrence)*

WOLVERTON   SU5658
George & Dragon (01635) 298292
Towns End; just N of A339 Newbury–Basingstoke; RG26 5ST Recently extended low-beamed and flagstoned 17th-c pub in remote rolling country, linked cosy areas, log fire, good choice of enjoyable unpretentious food from sandwiches up, beers such as Fullers, Greene King and Wadworths, decent wines, friendly attentive service; children and dogs welcome, big garden with terrace, ten bedrooms in separate block, good breakfast. *(J V Dadswell)*

Herefordshire

KEY ★ Star Pub 🔘 Top Quality Food 🍺 Great Beer

🍷 Good Wines £ Bargain Meals 🛏 Good Bedrooms 🍴 Serves Food

CAREY
SO5631 Map 4
Cottage of Content 🔘 🛏
(01432) 840242 – www.cottageofcontent.co.uk

Village signposted from good back road betweeen Ross-on-Wye and Hereford E of A49, through Hoarwithy; HR2 6NG

Country furnishings in a friendly rustic cottage with interesting food, real ales and seats on terraces; quiet bedrooms

---

Whether you're dropping in for a pint and a snack, a full meal or an overnight stay, this medieval cottage is rather special. It's tucked away in a tranquil spot near the River Wye and the friendly licensees offer a genuine welcome to both visitors and regulars (many with a dog in tow). The place has much character: a multitude of beams and country furnishings such as stripped-pine kitchen chairs, long pews beside one big table and various old-fashioned tables on flagstones or bare boards. Hobsons Best and Wye Valley Butty Bach on handpump and local cider during the summer; background music. There are picnic-sets on the flower-filled front terrace and in the rural-feeling garden at the back. The bedrooms are quiet and the breakfasts good.

🔘 Highly popular food includes rolls, smoked wild duck breast with pickled vegetables and an orange and toasted fennel seed dressing, potted pulled pork with jerk butter and crisp olive toasts, a pie of the day, aubergine and five-nut roast with grilled sweet potato and tomato and basil sauce, duck leg confit with rissole potatoes and rhubarb sauce, pot-roast lamb shoulder with balsamic redcurrant glaze, roasted roots and rosemary jus, a fish dish of the day, and puddings such as chocolate and peanut butter pie with praline ice-cream. *Benchmark main dish: sugar- and spice-cured pork belly, medallions, bacon-wrapped black pudding, apple and sage sauce £14.50. Two-course evening meal £22.00.*

Free house ~ Licensees Richard and Helen Moore ~ Real ale ~ Open 12-2.30 (3 weekends), 6.30-11; 12-2.30 Sun; closed Sun evening, Mon, winter Tues, one week Feb, one week Oct ~ Bar food 12-2, 6.30-9; 12-2 Sun ~ Restaurant ~ Children welcome ~ Dogs allowed in bar ~ Bedrooms: £65/£85 *Recommended by Michael and Mary Smith, Barry Collett, Derek Stafford*

EARDISLEY
SO3149 Map 6
Tram £
(01544) 327251 – www.thetraminn.co.uk

Corner of A4111 and Woodseaves Road; HR3 6PG

Character pub (the village itself is a big draw too) with welcoming licensees, a cheerful mix of customers and good food and beer

What shines through here is the genuine welcome from the friendly licensees and their smiling staff – it's what readers pick out first and foremost. There's a cheerful mix of both drinkers and diners, and the beamed bar on the left has warm local character, especially in the cosy back section behind sturdy standing timbers. Here, regulars congregate on the bare boards by the counter, which serves Hobsons Best, Ludlow Blonde and Wye Valley Butty Bach on handpump and three local organic ciders. Elsewhere, there are antique red and ochre floor tiles, a handful of nicely worn tables and chairs, a pair of long cushioned pews enclosing one much longer table, a high-backed settle, old country pictures and a couple of pictorial Wye maps. There's a small dining room on the right, a games room (with pool and darts) in a converted brewhouse and a covered terrace; background music. The outside gents' is one of the most stylish we've ever seen; the sizeable, neatly planted garden has picnic-sets on the lawn; pétanque.

Enjoyable food includes baguettes, spiced crispy whitebait with sweet chilli dip, quenelles of chicken and duck liver pâté with red onion marmalade, honey-roast ham and free-range eggs, all-day breakfast, mediterranean vegetable, spinach, butternut squash and mushroom lasagne, steak burger with toppings, coleslaw and chips, specials like asian-style beef skewers with noodle and crisp vegetable salad, and puddings such as chocolate and amaretto pot and Malteser cheesecake. *Benchmark main dish: steak in ale pie £9.50. Two-course evening meal £15.00.*

Free house ~ Licensees Mark and Kerry Vernon ~ Real ale ~ Open 12-3, 6-midnight; 12-4, 6-12.30 Sat; 12-4, 7-11 Sun; closed Mon except bank holidays ~ Bar food 12-3, 6-9; 12-3 Sun ~ Restaurant ~ Children welcome ~ Dogs allowed in bar ~ Wi-fi *Recommended by Miss B D Picton, Alan Bulley, R T and J C Moggridge, Darren and Jane Staniforth, Martin and Sue Day, David and Judy Robison, John and Jennifer Spinks*

KILPECK
SO4430   Map 6
Kilpeck Inn ♀
(01981) 570464 – www.kilpeckinn.com
Village and church signposted off A465 SW of Hereford; HR2 9DN

Imaginatively extended country inn in fascinating and peaceful village; bedrooms

If you stay in the eco-minded bedrooms here (there's a biomass boiler and rainwater recycling system), you can make the most of the interesting nearby castle ruins and the unique romanesque church. The beamed bar with dark slate flagstones rambles happily around to provide several tempting corners, with an antique high-backed settle in one and high stools around a matching chest-high table in another. This opens into three cosily linked dining rooms on the left, with high panelled wainscoting. Wye Valley Bitter, Butty Bach and HPA on handpump and several wines by the glass; background music, darts and TV. The neat back grass has picnic-sets.

Cooked by the landlord, the well liked food includes sandwiches, pigeon breast with mustard cream sauce, twice-baked cheese soufflé, mustard-roast ham and free-range eggs, mussels in cider and sage cream sauce, burger with toppings, gherkins and chips, local venison with parsnip mash, chestnuts and red wine, pheasant breast and confit leg with bread sauce and straw potatoes, Guinness-braised lamb with leek mash, and puddings such as rhubarb crème brûlée and chocolate fondant with pistachio ice-cream. *Benchmark main dish: duck breast, confit leg and orange stuffing with redcurrant jus £15.95. Two-course evening meal £18.00.*

Free house ~ Licensee Ross Williams ~ Real ale ~ Open 12-2.30, 5.30-11; 12-3 Sun ~ Bar food 12-2, 7-9; 12-2 Sun ~ Restaurant ~ Children welcome ~ Dogs allowed in bar ~ Wi-fi ~ Bedrooms: £70/£80 *Recommended by Miss B D Picton, Mike and Mary Carter, Robert Parker*

LEDBURY
Feathers 🌟 ♀ 🛏

SO7137   Map 4

(01531) 635266 – www.feathers-ledbury.co.uk

High Street (A417); HR8 1DS

Handsome old hotel with chatty relaxed bar, more decorous lounge, good food and friendly staff; comfortable bedrooms

For over 400 years, this strikingly timbered coaching inn has been the beating heart of the town. Today, it still welcomes travellers and although now more of a civilised hotel, it has kept a convivial back bar/brasserie with a chatty and cheerful mix of drinkers at one end. The long beams are a mass of hop bines, and prints and antique sale notices decorate the stripped panelling. Stools line the counter where they keep Fullers London Pride and a couple of guests such as Malvern Hills Black Pear and Sharps Doom Bar on handpump, good wines by the glass from an extensive list and 40 malt whiskies; staff are first class. In the main part, full of contented diners, there are cosy leather easy chairs and sofas by the fire, flowers and oil lamps on stripped kitchen and other tables, and comfortable bays of banquettes and other seats. The sedate lounge is just right for afternoon tea, with high-sided armchairs and sofas in front of a big log fire, and daily papers. In summer, the sheltered back terrace has seats and tables under parasols and abundant plant pots and hanging baskets. The bedrooms are individually furnished and comfortable.

 Attractively presented food using local, seasonal produce includes lunchtime sandwiches, moules marinière, twice-baked gruyère and dijon mustard soufflé, tuscan vegetable risotto with fresh basil oil, game pie, burger with toppings, spicy tomato salsa and fries, fishcakes with lemon and chervil mayonnaise, pork loin with dauphinoise potatoes and caramelised onion and red wine jus, and puddings. *Benchmark main dish: guinea fowl breast with parmentier potatoes and mushroom beurre blanc £17.75. Two-course evening meal £23.00.*

Free house ~ Licensee David Elliston ~ Real ale ~ Open 10am-11pm (10.30 Sun) ~ Bar food 12-2 (2.30 Fri, Sat), 6.30-9.30 (10 Fri-Sun) ~ Restaurant ~ Children welcome ~ Dogs allowed in bar and bedrooms ~ Wi-fi ~ Bedrooms: £95/£145 *Recommended by N R White, David Carr*

LITTLE COWARNE
Three Horseshoes ♀

SO6050   Map 4

(01885) 400276 – www.threehorseshoes.co.uk

Pub signposted off A465 SW of Bromyard; towards Ullingswick; HR7 4RQ

Long-serving licensees and friendly staff in bustling country pub with well liked food using home-grown produce; bedrooms

This is very much a family concern. Mr and Mrs Whittall have run this neatly kept inn for over 25 years and their son Philip is head chef. The L-shaped, quarry tiled middle bar has upholstered settles, wooden chairs and tables, old local photographs above the woodburning stove, hop-draped beams and local guidebooks. Opening off one side is the garden room, with wicker armchairs around tables, and views over the terraced seating area and well kept garden; leading off the other side is the games room, with pool, darts, juke box, games machine and cribbage. Wye Valley Bitter and Butty Bach and a guest such as Greene King Old Speckled Hen on handpump, local Oliver's cider and perry, a dozen wines by the glass and home-made elderflower cordial. A popular Sunday lunchtime carvery is offered in the stripped-stone, raftered and spacious restaurant extension. There are well sited tables and chairs on the terrace and on the neat, prettily planted garden. The bedrooms are accessed by outside stairs. Disabled access.

🍴 Using local suppliers and some home-grown summer produce (and making their own preserves and chutneys, which are sold at the bar), the popular food includes devilled kidneys on toast, prawn and haddock smokies, cheese, leek, celery, apple and walnut filo pastry, pheasant breast on parsnip mash with white wine and grape sauce, roasted bass fillets on creamed leeks, and puddings such as blackberry and apple pudding with custard and profiteroles filled with cherries and cream and home-made cherry vodka. *Benchmark main dish: steak in ale pie £13.50. Two-course evening meal £18.00.*

Free house ~ Licensees Norman and Janet Whittall ~ Real ale ~ Open 11-3, 6.30-11.30; 12-4, 7-9.30 Sun; closed Tues, winter Sun evening ~ Bar food 12-2.30, 6.30-9 (7-8.30 Sun in summer) ~ Restaurant ~ Children welcome ~ Wi-fi ~ Bedrooms: £40/£70
Recommended by Martin and Sue Day, Mr Brian Wells

ROSS-ON-WYE   SO5924   Map 6
Kings Head 🛏
(01989) 763174 – www.kingshead.co.uk
High Street (B4260); HR9 5HL

Welcoming bar in well run market-town hotel with real ales and tasty food; good bedrooms

'What a great place,' says one reader – a comment that sums up this friendly old hotel admirably. The little beamed and panelled bar on the right has traditional pub furnishings, including comfortably padded bar seats and an antique cushioned box settle, stripped floorboards and a couple of black leather armchairs by a log-effect fire. Wye Valley Bitter and Butty Bach and a guest beer such as Sharps Doom Bar on handpump, three farm ciders, and several wines by the glass at sensible prices. The beamed lounge bar on the left, also with bare boards, has some timbering, soft leather armchairs, padded bucket seats and shelves of books; unobtrusive background music. There's a big carpeted dining room and the sheltered back courtyard has contemporary tables and chairs. Bedrooms are comfortable and they do a good breakfast.

🍴 As well as a two- and three-course set lunch (not Sun), the rewarding food includes duck liver pâté with chutney, mussels in creamy white wine and garlic sauce, sharing boards, open lasagne of sweet potato, spinach, ricotta and basil velouté, chargrilled burger with toppings, battered onion rings and triple-cooked chips, chicken breast wrapped in parma ham with mushroom, baby onion and red wine jus, hake with chickpeas, chorizo, tomato and coriander, and puddings such as vanilla crème brûlée with candied ginger and dark chocolate truffle with marinated clementines. *Benchmark main dish: beer-battered fresh fish and chips £11.95. Two-course evening meal £18.00.*

Free house ~ Licensee James Vidler ~ Real ale ~ Open 11-11 (10.30 Sun) ~ Bar food 12-2.10 (3 Sun), 6.30-9 ~ Restaurant ~ Children welcome ~ Dogs allowed in bar and bedrooms ~ Wi-fi ~ Bedrooms: £60/£85 *Recommended by Mike and Mary Carter, Guy Vowles, Ann and Tony Bennett-Hughes, David Carr*

Real ale to us means beer that has matured naturally in its cask – not pressurised or filtered. We name all real ales stocked. We usually name ales preserved under a light blanket of carbon dioxide too, though purists – pointing out that this stops the natural yeasts developing – would disagree (most people, including us, can't tell the difference!)

SYMONDS YAT
Saracens Head 🍺 🛏️

SO5616 Map 4

(01600) 890435 – www.saracensheadinn.co.uk
Symonds Yat E; HR9 6JL

Lovely riverside spot with seats on waterside terraces, a fine range of drinks and interesting food; comfortable bedrooms

Even when really busy, the hands-on, friendly landlord is around to keep an eye on things in this 17th-c inn. There's a buoyant, welcoming atmosphere in the bustling, flagstoned bar and plenty of chatty customers – as well as cheerful staff who serve Sharps Doom Bar, Wye Valley Butty Bach and HPA and a couple of changing guest ales on handpump, 11 wines by the glass and a dozen malt whiskies. TV, background music and board games. There's also a cosy lounge and a modernised bare-boards dining room, as well as fine old photos of the area and fresh flowers in jugs. The terraces by the River Wye have plenty of seats, though you'll need to arrive early in fine weather to bag one. If you stay in the bedrooms in the main building, you'll have views over the water; there are two more contemporary rooms in the boathouse annexe. One way to reach the inn is on the little hand ferry (pulled by one of the staff). Disabled access to the bar and terrace.

Quite a choice of food includes lunchtime sandwiches and baguettes, sharing boards, moules marinière, smoked haddock and leek quiche with watercress mousse and pickled sweetcorn, a pie or sausages of the day, feta, pine nut and spinach in filo pastry with sweet red pepper syrup, burger with toppings and chips, chicken stuffed with maple-marinated goats cheese with potato and thyme crumble, pheasant on mushroom and butternut squash risotto with fig, apple and pumpkin chutney and cranberry jus, and puddings such as vanilla rice pudding with berry compote and baked vanilla and strawberry cheesecake with coconut sorbet. *Benchmark main dish: slow-braised lamb shoulder with sage and parsnip mash and honeyed carrots £15.95. Two-course evening meal £21.00.*

Free house ~ Licensees P K and C J Rollinson ~ Real ale ~ Open 10.30am-11pm ~ Bar food 12-2.30, 6.30-9 ~ Restaurant ~ Children welcome but must be over 7 in bedrooms ~ Dogs allowed in bar ~ Wi-fi ~ Bedrooms: £59/£89 *Recommended by Lois Dyer, John Ecklin, Steve Whalley, Chris and Angela Buckell*

TILLINGTON
Bell 🍺

SO4645 Map 6

(01432) 760395 – www.thebelltillington.com
Off A4110 NW of Hereford; HR4 8LE

Relaxed and friendly pub with a snug character bar opening into civilised dining areas – good value

Extremely popular locally, this busy pub also provides a warm welcome for visitors thanks to its friendly, hands-on landlord. The snug parquet-floored bar on the left has assorted bucket armchairs around low chunky mahogany-coloured tables, brightly cushioned wall benches, team photographs and shelves of books; the black beams are strung with dried hops. Otter Head, Wye Valley Bitter and a guest beer on handpump, cider made on site and locally produced spirits from Chase, all served by notably cheerful staff; daily papers, unobtrusive background music. The bar opens into a comfortable bare-boards dining lounge with stripy plush banquettes and a coal fire. Beyond that is a pitched-ceiling restaurant area with more banquettes and big country prints; through slatted blinds you can see a sunken terrace with contemporary tables, and a garden with teak tables, picnic-sets and a play area.

🍴 As well as baguettes and open sandwiches, the good quality food includes home-baked honey-roast ham and eggs, smoked haddock with chive mash, cheddar sauce and a poached egg, halloumi and chargrilled vegetables on five-bean and tomato cassoulet with sour cream, cottage pie, lambs liver with bacon and onion gravy, red snapper with provençale vegetables, clams and chargrilled fennel, and puddings such as fruit crumble and butterscotch tart. *Benchmark main dish: steak in ale pie £12.50. Two-course evening meal £19.00.*

Free house ~ Licensee Glenn Williams ~ Real ale ~ Open 11am-midnight; 11-11 Sun ~ Bar food 12-2.30, 6-9 ~ Restaurant ~ Children welcome ~ Dogs allowed in bar ~ Wi-fi
Recommended by Michael and Mary Smith, Paul and Sonia Broadgate, Lindy Andrews, Dave Braisted, John and Jennifer Spinks

TITLEY   SO3359   Map 6
Stagg ⭐ 🍷 🛏
(01544) 230221 – www.thestagg.co.uk
B4355 N of Kington; HR5 3RL

Herefordshire Dining Pub of the Year

Terrific food using tip top ingredients served in three dining rooms; real ales and a fine choice of other drinks, and seats in the two-acre garden; comfortable bedrooms

The civilised and comfortably hospitable little bar in this impressive dining pub remains the beating heart of the place, with chatty locals and a really interesting choice of drinks served by genuinely welcoming and courteous staff. There's Ludlow Gold, Mayfields Auntie Myrtle and Wye Valley Butty Bach and HPA on handpump, 11 house wines by the glass (plus a carefully chosen bin list), cocktails, local cider and perry, interesting local vodkas and gin from Chase, and quite a choice of other spirits too. Throughout, furnishings are simple: high-backed elegant wooden or leather dining chairs around a medley of tables on bare boards, candlelight and (in the bar) 200 jugs hanging from the ceiling. The two-acre garden has seats on a terrace and a croquet lawn. There are bedrooms above the pub and in a Georgian vicarage four minutes' walk away; super breakfasts. The inn is surrounded by good walking country and is handy for the Offa's Dyke Path.

🍴 The exceptional food uses some home-grown produce, their own eggs and the best local produce available: open sandwiches, scallops with celeriac and black pepper oil, steak tartare with truffle, spring vegetable pie, home-made sausages with onion rings and mash, crispy duck leg with cider, carrot and orange purée and dauphinoise potatoes, sea bass fillet with samphire, shrimps and parmentier potatoes, and puddings such as pedro ximénez cheesecake with prunes and coffee ice-cream and their famous bread and butter pudding. *Benchmark main dish: local rump steak with béarnaise sauce £16.90. Two-course evening meal £25.00.*

Free house ~ Licensees Steve and Nicola Reynolds ~ Real ale ~ Open 12-3, 6.30-11; 12-3, 7-10.30 Sun; closed Mon, Tues, one week Feb, two weeks Nov ~ Bar food 12-2, 6.30-9 (9.30 Sat); 12-3, 7-8.30 Sun ~ Restaurant ~ Children welcome ~ Dogs allowed in bar and bedrooms ~ Wi-fi ~ Bedrooms: £80/£100 *Recommended by Lindy Andrews, Harvey Brown*

UPPER COLWALL   SO7643   Map 4
Chase £
(01684) 540276 – www.thechaseinnuppercolwall.co.uk
Chase Road, brown sign to pub off B4218 Malvern–Colwall, first left after hilltop on bend going W; WR13 6DJ

Gorgeous sunset views from cheerful country tavern's garden, good drinks and cost-conscious food

Inside this friendly and nicely traditional pub, the atmosphere is chatty and companionable. There's an array of gilt cast-iron-framed and treadle sewing tables, a great variety of seats (from a wooden-legged tractor seat to a carved pew), an old black kitchen range and plenty of decorations – china mugs, blue glass flasks, lots of small pictures; bar billiards. Four well kept ales are tapped from the cask, such as Bathams Best, Ledbury Gold, Purity Mad Goose and Ringwood Fortyniner, and friendly staff also serve several wines by the glass. Tables on the steep series of small, pretty back terraces look across Herefordshire and, on a clear day, as far as the Black Mountains and even the Brecon Beacons. Plenty of good surrounding walks.

Fair value food, with some lunchtime main dishes costing under £10, includes sandwiches and rolls, grilled field mushroom topped with parmesan and herbs, smoked salmon with pink grapefruit and lemon and herb crème fraîche, vegetable risotto, honey-roasted ham and egg, a curry of the day, steak and kidney pie, chicken with smoked bacon and mozzarella and red pepper sauce, slow-braised pork belly with black pudding mash and port jus, and puddings. *Benchmark main dish: beer-battered cod and chips £10.50. Two-course evening meal £19.00.*

Free house ~ Licensee Robert Stirling ~ Real ale ~ Open 12-3, 5-11; 12-11 Sat; 12-10.30 Sun ~ Bar food 12-2 (2.30 Sun), 6.30-9 ~ Children welcome ~ Dogs allowed in bar ~ Wi-fi
Recommended by M G Hart

WALFORD   SO5820   Map 4

Mill Race 🏨⭐ ♟

(01989) 562891 – www.millrace.info
B4234 Ross-on-Wye to Lydney; HR9 5QS

Contemporary furnishings in uncluttered rooms, good quality food ingredients, real ales served by attentive staff, terrace tables and nearby walks

While there's quite an emphasis on dining in this pink-washed pub, drinkers are just as warmly welcomed – from the granite-topped modern bar counter, they serve Wye Valley Bitter and a changing guest ale on handpump, farm cider and 22 fairly priced wines by the glass. This is a stylish, civilised place with a row of strikingly high arched windows, comfortable leather armchairs and sofas on flagstones, and smaller chairs around broad pedestal tables. Photographs of the local countryside hang on the mainly cream or red walls and there's good unobtrusive lighting. One wall, stripped back to the stonework, contains a woodburning stove that's open to the comfortable, compact dining area on the other side; background music. After a walk (they have leaflets describing pleasant ones nearby), you can sit on the terrace and enjoy the view towards Goodrich Castle; the garden has plenty more seats and tables.

Much of the produce (cattle, rare-breed pigs, turkeys, geese, pheasant and ducks) comes from their nearby 1,000-acre farm and woodlands and they list other local suppliers on their website: sandwiches, gin-cured sea trout with earl grey smoked trout, egg mayonnaise, watercress purée and pickled cucumber, pigeon pasty with golden raisins, prunes, wild mushrooms and walnuts, home-made sausages with onion marmalade gravy, duck hash with duck liver pâté, a fried duck egg on brioche and truffle oil, pasta with local asparagus, roast garlic, butternut squash and dauphinoise sauce, battered fish of the day, and puddings such as sticky toffee pudding with toffee sauce, honeycomb ice-cream and cinder toffee and raisin and chocolate sponge with white chocolate mousse and white chocolate and chilli ice-cream. *Benchmark main dish: their own 12-hour braised beef with ravioli and creamed potatoes £19.50. Two-course evening meal £21.00.*

Free house ~ Licensee Luke Freeman ~ Real ale ~ Open 11-3, 5-11; 12-11 Sat; 12-10.30 Sun ~ Bar food 12-2 (4 Sun), 6-9 ~ Restaurant ~ Children welcome ~ Wi-fi
Recommended by Dr and Mrs A J Edwards, John Ecklin

WALTERSTONE   SO3424   Map 6

Carpenters Arms

(01873) 890353 – www.thecarpentersarmswalterstone.com
Follow Walterstone signs off A465; HR2 0DX

Unchanging country tavern in the same family for many years

On the edge of the Black Mountains, this unspoilt stone cottage has been run by the landlady, Vera Watkins, since she took over from her mother several years ago. The traditional rooms have remained unchanged: there are beams, broad polished flagstones, a roaring fire in a gleaming black range (complete with hot-water tap, bread oven and salt cupboard), and warming ancient settles against stripped-stone walls. Wadworths 6X and a guest such as Breconshire Brecon County tapped straight from the cask. The snug main dining room has mahogany tables and oak corner cupboards, and another little dining area has old oak tables and church pews on more flagstones. The outside lavatories are cold but in character.

Straightforward food includes sandwiches, a changing soup, pies such as salmon and leek or beef in Guinness, various curries, and puddings. *Benchmark main dish: local 10oz sirloin steak £15.95. Two-course evening meal £19.00.*

Free house ~ Licensee Vera Watkins ~ Real ale ~ No credit cards ~ Open 12-3, 7-11 ~ Bar food 12-3, 7-9 ~ Restaurant ~ Children welcome
Recommended by Toby Jones

WOOLHOPE   SO6135   Map 4

Butchers Arms 🏵 ☆ ⏸ 🍺

(01432) 860281 – www.butchersarmswoolhope.com
Off B4224 in Fownhope; HR1 4RF

Pleasant country inn in peaceful setting, with an inviting garden, interesting food and a fine choice of real ales

We've always enjoyed this pub and our readers feel the same. It's a friendly, half-timbered place set in lovely countryside with picnic-sets in a pretty, streamside garden. Inside, the bar has very low beams, built-in cushioned wall seats, farmhouse chairs and stools around a mix of old tables (some set for dining) on carpet, hunting and horse pictures on cream walls and an open fire in a big fireplace; there's also a little beamed dining room, similarly furnished. Wye Valley Bitter and Butty Bach and Ledbury Gold on handpump, six wines by the glass from a well annotated list, a dozen whiskies and a couple of farm ciders. To really appreciate the surroundings, turn left as you come out of the pub and take the tiny left-hand road at the end of the car park; this turns into a track and then a path, and the view from the top of the hill is quite something.

Cooked by the chef-patron, the good food includes sandwiches, twice-baked goats cheese soufflé, pigeon with black pudding, bacon and apple, thai green vegetable curry, lamb and beef meatballs in garlic, basil and tomato sauce on tagliatelle, grilled mackerel fillet with stewed rhubarb and parmentier potatoes, roast rump of lamb with redcurrant and thyme jus, and puddings such as dark chocolate cheesecake and cherry bakewell tart. *Benchmark main dish: rabbit, apple and cider pie £12.95. Two-course evening meal £20.00.*

Free house ~ Licensee Philip Vincent ~ Real ale ~ Open 12-3, 6-11; 12-3.30 Sun; closed Sun evening in winter, Mon except bank holidays ~ Bar food 12-2.30, 6-9 ~ Restaurant ~ Children welcome ~ Dogs welcome ~ Wi-fi *Recommended by Michael and Mary Smith, Martin and Sue Day, Des Mannion, Harvey Brown, David and Stella Martin*

WOOLHOPE
SO6135 Map 4

Crown

(01432) 860468 – www.crowninnwoolhope.co.uk
Village signposted off B4224 in Fownhope; HR1 4QP

Cheery village local with fine range of local ciders and perries, and popular food

In summer, there's a bar in the lovely big garden here, which also has a particularly comfortable smokers' shelter with cushions, darts and quoits, and marvellous views. It's a cheerful, busy pub and the refurbished bar has newly upholstered bench seats and dark wooden chairs and tables on floorboards, some standing timbers and both a woodburning stove and an open fire; background music, darts and board games. As well as Ledbury Bitter, Wye Valley HPA and a guest such as Malvern Hills Black Pear on handpump, the landlord makes four farm ciders and keeps 24 bottled ciders and perrys from within a 15-mile radius; they hold a May Bank Holiday festival. Disabled access.

The seasonal, honest food using local suppliers includes lunchtime baguettes, black pudding with sautéed baby potatoes, parmesan and a poached egg, twice-baked cheese soufflé, grilled goats cheese and field mushroom stack with red onion marmalade, poussin with wild mushrooms and black pudding, cider-braised ham with duck eggs, steak in ale pie, beer-battered haddock and chips, particularly good steaks, and puddings such as tonka bean crème brûlée and apple and blackberry crumble. *Benchmark main dish: slow-braised pork belly with shallot purée and crackling £13.50. Two-course evening meal £19.00.*

Free house ~ Licensees Matt and Annalisa Slocombe ~ Real ale ~ Open 12-3, 6-11; 12-midnight Sat; 12-11 Sun ~ Bar food 12-2 (2.30 Sat), 6-9 (9.30 Fri, Sat); 12-3, 6-8.30 Sun ~ Restaurant ~ Children welcome ~ Wi-fi *Recommended by Harvey Brown, Alfie Bayliss*

Also Worth a Visit in Herefordshire

Besides the fully inspected pubs, you might like to try these pubs that have been recommended to us and described by readers. Do tell us what you think of them: feedback@goodguides.com

ALLENSMORE SO4533
Three Horseshoes (01981) 570329
B4348; HR2 9AS Flower-decked 17th-c timbered dining pub, well kept Wye Valley and guests in cosy drinking area, enjoyable fairly pubby food from sandwiches and baked potatoes to grills, bargain OAP weekday lunch and early evening deal, friendly efficient service; children welcome, good walking country, three bedrooms, open (and food) all day. *(R T and J C Moggridge)*

ALMELEY SO3351
Bells (01544) 327216
Off A480, A4111 or A4112 S of Kington; HR3 6LF Welcoming old country local with original jug-and-bottle entry lobby and carpeted beamed bar with woodburner, second bar has been converted to village

If you know a pub is ever open all day, please tell us.

shop/deli, a couple of well kept ales such as Three Tuns and Woods, traditional cider, generous home-made food (not evenings) from sandwiches up; children and dogs welcome, garden with decked area and boules, open all day. *(Guy Vowles)*

AYMESTREY   SO4265

★ **Riverside Inn** (01568) 708440

A4110, at N end of village, W of Leominster; HR6 9ST Terrace and tree-sheltered garden making most of lovely waterside spot by ancient stone bridge over the Lugg; cosy rambling beamed interior with some antique furniture alongside stripped country kitchen tables, warm fires, well kept Hobsons, Wye Valley and a guest, local ciders, good lunchtime bar food and more expensive evening menu using rare-breed meat and own fruit and vegetables, warm friendly atmosphere with welcoming landlord and staff; quiet background music; children welcome, dogs in bar, bedrooms (fly fishing for residents), nice breakfast, closed Sun evening, Mon lunchtime (all day Mon in winter). *(Ann and David Packman, Mike and Mary Carter, Roy and Gill Payne)*

BISHOPS FROME   SO6648

Green Dragon (01885) 490607

Just off B4214 Bromyard–Ledbury; WR6 5BP Welcoming village pub with four linked rooms, unspoilt rustic feel, beams, flagstones and log fires (one in fine inglenook), half a dozen ales including Otter, Timothy Taylors and Wye Valley, real ciders, enjoyable traditional food Tues-Sat evenings and Sun lunchtime; children and dogs welcome, tiered garden with smokers' shelter, on Herefordshire Trail, closed weekday lunchtimes, open all day Sat. *(Harvey Brown)*

BODENHAM   SO5454

Englands Gate (01568) 797286

On A417 at Bodenham turn-off, about 6 miles S of Leominster; HR1 3HU Attractive black and white 16th-c coaching inn, rambling interior with beams and joists in low ceilings around a vast central stone chimneypiece, sturdy timber props, exposed stonework and well worn flagstones (one or two steps), Hobsons, Wye Valley and a guest, traditional cider, fairly pubby food from lunchtime baguettes up; background music; children welcome, dogs in bar, tables under parasols on terrace and in pleasant garden, modern bedrooms in converted coach house next door, open all day. *(Anon)*

BOSBURY   SO6943

Bell (01531) 640285

B4220 N of Ledbury; HR8 1PX Traditional village pub freshened up under new management; log fires in both bars, Otter, Wye Valley Butty Bach and a guest, three ciders and good choice of wines by the glass, dining area serving popular sensibly priced

traditional food (not Sun evening, Mon, Tues) including Sun carvery, friendly staff; darts in public bar; children and dogs welcome, large garden with covered terrace and play equipment, open all day weekends, closed Mon and Tues lunchtimes. *(John Evans)*

BRINGSTY COMMON   SO6954

★ **Live & Let Live** (01886) 821462

Off A44 Knightwick–Bromyard, 1.5 miles W of Whitbourne turn; take track southwards at Black Cat inn sign, bearing right at fork; WR6 5UW Bustling 17th-c timber and thatch cottage; cosy flagstoned bar with scrubbed or polished tables, cushioned chairs, long stripped pew and high-backed winged settle by log fire in cavernous stone fireplace, earthenware jugs hanging from low beams, old casks built into hop-hung bar counter, ales such as Ludlow, Malvern Hills and Wye Valley, local ciders and apple juice, well liked pubby food, two dining rooms upstairs under steep rafters; children and dogs welcome, glass-topped well and big wooden hogshead as terrace tables, peaceful views from picnic-sets in former orchard, handy for Brockhampton Estate (NT), closed Mon, otherwise open all day (Sun till 7pm). *(Alfie Bayliss)*

BROMYARD DOWNS   SO6755

★ **Royal Oak** (01885) 482585

Just NE of Bromyard; pub signed off A44; HR7 4QP Beautifully placed low-beamed 18th-c pub with wide views; open-plan carpeted and flagstoned bar, log fire and woodburner, dining room with huge bay window, well kept Malvern Hills, Purity and Woods, real cider, enjoyable food (special diets catered for), friendly service; background music, pool and darts; children, walkers and dogs welcome, picnic-sets on nice front terrace, swings, closed Sun evening, Mon (open all day bank holiday weekends). *(Dave Braisted, Neil and Anita Christopher)*

BUSH BANK   SO4551

Bush (01432) 830206

A4110, S of Knapton; HR4 8EH Welcoming country pub set back from the road, enjoyable good value home-cooked food including popular Sun lunch, well kept Sharps Doom Bar and Wye Valley HPA, good friendly service, comfortably modernised carpeted interior, some bare stone and timbering, old local photographs, copper and brass, woodburner; children welcome. *(Nigel and Sue Foster)*

CANON PYON   SO4648

Nags Head (01432) 830725

A4110; HR4 8NY Welcoming 17th-c timbered roadside pub, beamed log-fire bar, flagstoned restaurant and overspill/function room, popular pubby food (not Sun evening), well kept ales such as Otter and Wye Valley, friendly service; children welcome, extensive garden with play area, open all day Sun till 7pm, closed Mon, Tues lunchtimes. *(Toby Jones)*

CLIFFORD   SO2445
Castlefields (01497) 831554
B4350 N of Hay-on-Wye; HR3 5HB Rebuilt and enlarged family pub, some old features including a well, good popular fairly priced food, Sharps Doom Bar and Wye Valley Butty Bach, friendly helpful staff, red-carpeted floors, woodburner in two-way stone fireplace, restaurant; pool and darts; lovely country views, camping, closed Mon, otherwise open all day. *(Michael and Mary Smith)*

CLODOCK   SO3227
Cornewall Arms (01873) 860677
N of Walterstone; HR2 0PD Wonderfully old-fashioned and unchanging country local in remote hamlet by historic church and facing Black Mountains, stable-door bar with open fire each end, a few mats and comfortable armchairs on stone floor, lots of ornaments and knick-knacks, photos of past village events, books for sale, games including darts and 'devil among the tailors', bottled Wye Valley and cider, no food or credit cards; dogs welcome, erratic opening times. *(Belinda May)*

COLWALL   SO7440
Wellington (01684) 540269
A449 Malvern–Ledbury; WR13 6HW Welcoming landlord and friendly staff, very enjoyable sensibly priced food (special diets catered for) from standards up including good local beef and wild boar, well kept Goffs Tournament and a couple of guests, nice wines by the glass, comfortable lived-in two-level beamed bar with red patterned carpet and fire, spacious relaxed back dining area, newspapers and magazines, some live music; children and dogs welcome, picnic-sets on neat grass above car park, good local walks, closed Sun evening, Mon. *(Alison and Michael Harper)*

DORSTONE   SO3141
★ Pandy (01981) 550273
Pub signed off B4348 E of Hay-on-Wye; HR3 6AN Ancient timbered inn by village green, homely traditional rooms with low hop-strung beams, stout timbers, upright chairs on worn flagstones and in various alcoves, vast open fireplace, locals by bar with good range of beers including Wye Valley, summer farm cider, quite a few malts and irish whiskeys, enjoyable food from baguettes, pizzas and pubby choices up, friendly staff; background music, board games; children welcome, dogs in bar (their red setter is Apache), neat side garden with picnic-sets and play area, five good bedrooms in purpose-built timber lodge, open all day Sat, closed Mon lunchtime. *(Harvey Brown)*

EWYAS HAROLD   SO3828
Temple Bar (01981) 240423
Village centre signed from B4347; HR2 0EU Refurbished family-run village pub, friendly and welcoming, with good freshly made food from bar snacks to interesting well presented restaurant dishes, Wye Valley Butty Bach, HPA and a guest, local cider; three comfortable bedrooms, hearty breakfast, open all day weekends. *(Miss A M Kerruish)*

FOWNHOPE   SO5734
Green Man (01432) 860243
B4224; HR1 4PE Striking 15th-c black and white inn, wall settles, window seats and leather chairs in one beamed bar, standing timbers dividing another, warm woodburners in old fireplaces, good well presented imaginative food in bar and restaurant, friendly helpful service, three changing ales and Weston's cider, good wines, nice coffee; background music; children welcome, no dogs, attractive quiet garden, 11 bedrooms, open all day. *(Ruth May)*

FOWNHOPE   SO5734
New Inn (01432) 860350
B4224, centre of village; HR1 4PE Neat little local set back from the road, good pubby lunchtime food (not weekends) cooked by landlady, also Weds deal and evening food one day during the week, well kept Hobsons, Wye Valley and a guest, efficient friendly service, small dining area; children and walkers welcome, tables outside, picturesque village with unusual church and nice views, open all day weekends. *(R T and J C Moggridge)*

GARWAY   SO4622
Garway Moon (01600) 750270
Centre of village, opposite the green; HR2 8RQ Attractive 18th-c pub in pretty location overlooking common; good locally sourced food served by friendly staff, well kept ales including Butcombe, Kingstone and Wye Valley, local ciders, beams and exposed stonework, woodburner, restaurant; quiz last Sun of month; children, dogs and muddy boots welcome, garden with play area, three bedrooms, open all day weekends, closed lunchtimes Mon and Tues. *(Harvey Brown)*

GORSLEY   SO6726
★ Roadmaker (01989) 720352
0.5 miles from M50 junction 3; village signposted from exit – B4221; HR9 7SW Popular 19th-c village pub run well by group of retired Gurkhas; large carpeted lounge bar with central log fire, excellent good value nepalese food here and in evening restaurant, also Sun roasts and other english choices, well kept ales such as Brains and Butcombe, efficient courteous service; no dogs; children welcome, terrace with water feature, open all day. *(Alastair Cox)*

HAREWOOD END   SO5227

Harewood End Inn (01989) 730637

A49 Hereford to Ross-on-Wye; HR2 8JT
Interesting old inn with comfortable panelled
dining lounge with log fire and separate
restaurant, good choice of enjoyable home-
made food from lunchtime sandwiches
up, well kept ales such as Black Sheep
and Wychwood, decent wines, welcoming
attentive staff; area with pool, darts and TV,
free wi-fi; children and dogs welcome, nice
garden and walks, five bedrooms, closed
Mon. *(Alfie Bayliss)*

HEREFORD   SO5139

Barrels (01432) 274968

St Owen Street; HR1 2JQ Friendly 18th-c
coaching inn and former home to the Wye
Valley brewery, their very well kept keenly
priced ales from barrel-built counter (beer/
music festival end Aug), Thatcher's cider, no
food, cheerful efficient staff and good mix of
customers (very busy weekends); pool room,
big-screen sports TV, background and some
live music; partly covered courtyard behind,
open all day. *(Toby Jones)*

HEREFORD   SO5039

★ Lichfield Vaults (01432) 266821

Church Street; HR1 2LR A pub since
the 18th c (the Dog, then) in picturesque
pedestrianised area near cathedral; dark
panelling, some stripped brick and exposed
joists, impressive plasterwork in big-
windowed front room, traditionally furnished
with dark pews, padded pub chairs and a
couple of heavily padded benches, hot coal
stove, charming greek landlord and friendly
staff, five well kept ales such as Adnams,
Caledonian and Sharps, enjoyable food from
sandwiches up including greek dishes, good
Sun roasts, daily papers; faint background
music, live blues/rock last Sun of month,
TV projector for sports (particularly rugby),
games machines; children welcome, no dogs,
picnic-sets in pleasant back courtyard, open
all day. *(Richard Tilbrook, Robert Wivell)*

HOARWITHY   SO5429

New Harp (01432) 840900

*Off A49 Hereford to Ross-on-Wye;
HR2 6QH* Open-plan village dining pub
with cheerful bustling atmosphere, enjoyable
well presented local food from chef-landlord,
friendly helpful service, Wye Valley ales and
Weston's cider (maybe their own organic
cider in summer), pine tables on slate tiles,
two woodburners, darts; background and
some live music; children, walkers and dogs
welcome, pretty tree-sheltered garden with
stream, picnic-sets and decked area, little
shop and Mon morning post office, unusual

italianate Victorian church, open all day
Fri-Sun. *(Barry Collett)*

KENTCHURCH   SO4125

★ Bridge Inn (01981) 240408

B4347 Pontrilas–Grosmont; HR2 0BY
Ancient rustic pub bordering the River
Monnow (and Wales), welcoming staff and
warm local atmosphere, good reasonably
priced home-made food, well kept Otter and
a couple of guests, big log fire in bar, pretty
little back restaurant overlooking the river
(two miles of trout fishing); terrace and
waterside garden with pétanque, handy for
Herefordshire Trail, closed Sun evening,
Mon, Tues. *(Alex and Hazel Evans, Theocsbrian,
R T and J C Moggridge)*

KINGSLAND   SO4461

★ Corners (01568) 708385

*B4360 NW of Leominster, corner of
Lugg Green Road; HR6 9RY* Comfortably
updated, partly black and white 16th-c village
inn with snug nooks and corners, log fires,
low beams, dark red plasterwork and some
stripped brick, comfortable bow-window
seat, and group of dark leather armchairs
in softly lit carpeted bar, well kept Hobsons
Best and Wye Valley HPA, decent selection
of wines, airier big raftered side dining room
in converted hay loft with huge window,
enjoyable reasonably priced food from
pubby choices up, cheerful attentive service;
children welcome, no garden, comfortable
bedrooms in new block behind. *(Alison and
Michael Harper)*

KINGTON   SO3056

★ Olde Tavern (01544) 239033

*Victoria Road, just off A44 opposite
B4355 – follow sign to 'Town Centre,
Hospital, Cattle Market'; pub on
right opposite Elizabeth Road, no
inn sign but 'Estd 1767' notice; HR5
3BX* Gloriously old-fashioned with hatch-
served side room opening off small plain
parlour and public bar, plenty of dark brown
woodwork, big windows, settles and other
antique furniture on bare floors, gas fire,
old local pictures, china, pewter and curios,
well kept Hobsons, Ludlow, Wye Valley
and a guest, Weston's cider, beer festivals,
friendly atmosphere, no food; children
and dogs welcome, little yard at back,
open all day weekends, closed weekday
lunchtimes. *(Alison and Michael Harper)*

KINGTON   SO2956

Oxford Arms (01544) 230322

Duke Street; HR5 3DR Well worn-in
(not to everyone's taste) beamed inn with
woodburners in main bar on left and dining
area on right, smaller lounge with sofas and

If you report on a pub that's not a featured entry, please tell us any lunchtimes
or evenings when it doesn't serve bar food.

armchairs, Woods Shropshire Lad and a couple of guests, enjoyable reasonably priced food including Weds curry and Thurs steak night, good friendly service; some live music, pool; children and dogs welcome, terrace picnic-sets, bedrooms, open all day Fri-Sun, closed Mon, lunchtimes Tues-Thurs. *(Harvey Brown)*

KINGTON   SO2956
Royal Oak (01544) 230484
Church Street; HR5 3BE Cheerful and welcoming 17th-c two-bar pub, well kept Ringwood, Wye Valley and a guest, Somersby cider, enjoyable good value food including range of tapas-style dishes, two little open fires, bistro-style restaurant, darts and sports TV in public bar; children and dogs welcome, garden with terrace, handy for Offa's Dyke walkers, three neat simple bedrooms, open all day summer, closed Mon-Thurs lunchtimes in winter. *(Richard Tilbrook)*

LEDBURY   SO7137
★ Prince of Wales (01531) 632250
Church Lane; narrow passage from Town Hall; HR8 1DL Friendly old black and white local prettily tucked away down narrow cobbled alley, seven well kept ales, foreign draught/bottled beers and Weston's cider, knowledgeable staff, simple very good value home-made food from sandwiches up, low beams, nooks and crannies, shelves of books, long back room; faint background music (live folk Weds, blues bands Sun); a couple of tables in flower-filled backyard, open all day. *(N R White, Dave Braisted)*

LEDBURY   SO7137
Seven Stars (01531) 635800
Homend (High Street); HR8 1BN Convivial 16th-c beamed and timbered pub sympathetically restored after devastating 2001 fire; good well presented food from interesting sensibly short menu, three well kept ales, friendly helpful staff, bar area with comfortable seating and cosy open fire, dining room behind; free wi-fi; children and dogs welcome, walled terrace, three bedrooms. *(Toby Jones)*

LEDBURY   SO7137
Talbot (01531) 632963
New Street; HR8 2DX Comfortable 16th-c black and white fronted coaching inn; log-fire bar with Wadworths ales and guests, plenty of wines by the glass, good fairly traditional food from sharing boards and lunchtime sandwiches up, friendly efficient service, oak-panelled dining room; courtyard tables, six bedrooms, open all day. *(Anon)*

LEINTWARDINE   SO4073
Lion (01547) 540203
High Street; SY7 0JZ Restored inn beautifully situated by packhorse bridge over River Teme; helpful efficient staff and friendly atmosphere, good well presented

food from varied menu including some imaginative choices (can be pricey), Tues steak night, popular two-room restaurant, well kept beers such as Ludlow and Wye Valley; children welcome, safely fenced riverside garden with play area, eight attractive bedrooms, can arrange fishing trips, open all day (till 8pm Sun). *(Gordon and Margaret Ormondroyd)*

LEINTWARDINE   SO4073
★ Sun (01547) 540705
Rosemary Lane, just off A4113; SY7 0LP Fascinating 19th-c time warp; bare benches and farmhouse tables by coal fire in wallpapered brick-floored front bar (dogs welcome here), well kept Hobsons tapped from the cask and an occasional guest (Aug beer festival), another fire in snug carpeted parlour, pork pies and perhaps a lunchtime ploughman's (can bring food from adjacent fish and chip shop), friendly staff and cheery locals; open mike night last Fri of month; new pavilion-style building with bar and garden room, closed Mon lunchtime. *(Toby Jones)*

LEOMINSTER   SO4959
★ Grape Vaults (01568) 611404
Broad Street; HR6 8BS Compact two-room character pub, popular and friendly, with well kept ales including Ludlow, tasty good value pubby food (not Sun evening), coal fire, beams and stripped woodwork, original dark high-backed settles and round copper-topped tables on bare boards, old local prints and posters, bottle collection, shelves of books in snug; tiny gents'; dogs welcome, open all day. *(Richard Tilbrook)*

LINTON   SO6525
Alma (01989) 720355
On main road through village; HR9 7RY Cheerful unspoilt local in small village, up to six well kept/priced changing ales such as Butcombe, Ludlow and Malvern Hills, no food (may be free Sun nibbles), homely carpeted front room with sleepy cats by good fire, small back room with pool; three-day summer charity music festival; children very welcome, good-sized garden behind with nice view, closed weekday lunchtimes. *(Anon)*

MICHAELCHURCH
ESCLEY   SO3133
★ Bridge Inn (01981) 510646
Off back road SE of Hay-on-Wye, along Escley Brook valley; HR2 0JW Black-beamed riverside inn restored by current hard-working licences and delightfully tucked away in attractive valley; good home-made food including some unusual choices, well kept Wye Valley beers and local farm cider, friendly atmosphere; children welcome, seats out on waterside terrace, field for camping (also a yurt), bedrooms in nearby farmhouse, good walks, open all day Fri-Sun, closed Mon lunchtime. *(Alfie Bayliss)*

MUCH DEWCHURCH   SO4831
Black Swan (01981) 540295
*B4348 Ross-on-Wye to Hay-on-Wye;
HR2 8DJ* Roomy and attractive beamed
and timbered pub, partly 14th-c, with well
kept Timothy Taylors Landlord and three
local guests, decent wines and enjoyable
straightforward food (no credit cards),
log fires in cosy well worn bar and lounge
with eating area, welcoming long-serving
licensees, Thurs folk night; pool room
with darts, TV, juke box; children and dogs
welcome, seats on front terrace, open all
day Sun. *(Belinda May)*

MUCH MARCLE   SO6634
Royal Oak (01531) 660300
*On A449 Ross-on-Wye to Ledbury;
HR8 2ND* Roadside country pub with lovely
views, good reasonably priced food (Sun
till 6.30pm) using meat from local farms,
prompt friendly service, well kept Brakspears
and Marstons Pedigree, pleasant lounge
with open fire, library room and large back
dining area; skittle alley; children and dogs
welcome, garden and terrace seating, two
bedrooms. *(Harvey Brown)*

ORLETON   SO4967
★ Boot (01568) 780228
Off B4362 W of Woofferton; SY8 4HN
Popular pub with beams, timbering, even
some 16th-c wattle and daub, inglenook
fireplace in charming cosy traditional bar,
steps up to further bar area, good-sized
two-room dining part, varied choice of
interesting well presented food, friendly
quick service, Hobsons, Wye Valley and a
local guest (July beer/music festival), real
ciders; children and dogs welcome, seats
in garden under huge ash tree, fenced-in
play area, open all day weekends. *(Robert W
Buckle)*

PEMBRIDGE   SO3958
New Inn (01544) 388427
Market Square (A44); HR6 9DZ Timeless
ancient inn overlooking small black and
white town's church, unpretentious three-
room bar with antique settles, beams, worn
flagstones and impressive inglenook log
fire, well kept changing ales, farm cider and
generous helpings of popular good value
straightforward food, friendly service, quiet
little family dining room, traditional games;
downstairs lavatories; no dogs, simple
bedrooms. *(Belinda May)*

PRESTON   SO3841
Yew Tree (01981) 500359
Village W of Hereford; HR2 9JT Small
tucked-away pub handy for River Wye, simple
and welcoming, with two quickly changing
ales tapped from the cask and proper cider,

good value home-made food (not lunchtimes
Weds, Thurs), weekend live music; children
and dogs welcome, bunkhouse, closed
lunchtimes Mon, Tues. *(Darren and Jane
Staniforth)*

ROSS-ON-WYE   SO5924
Mail Rooms (01989) 760920
Gloucester Road; HR9 5BS Open modern
Wetherspoons conversion of former post
office, their usual well priced food and up
to five ales including Greene King, Weston's
cider and good choice of wines, friendly
service; silent TV; children welcome till
8pm, decked back terrace, open all day
from 8am. *(Mike and Mary Carter, David Carr)*

ROSS-ON-WYE   SO6024
White Lion (01989) 562785
Wilton Lane; HR9 6AQ Friendly riverside
pub dating from 1650, well kept Wye Valley
and a couple of guests, enjoyable traditional
food at reasonable prices, good service, big
fireplace in carpeted bar, stone-walled gaol
restaurant (building once a police station);
free wi-fi; children welcome, lots of tables in
garden and on terrace overlooking the Wye
and historic bridge, bedrooms and camping,
open all day. *(Alfie Bayliss)*

SELLACK   SO5526
Lough Pool (01989) 730888
Off A49; HR9 6LX Black and white
timbered cottage under new management,
simple bars with beams and standing
timbers, flagstones, rustic furniture, open fire
and woodburner, Wye Valley ales and a guest,
local farm ciders/perries and several wines
by the glass, food from traditional to more
upmarket choices cooked by landlord-chef,
back restaurant; children and dogs (in bar)
welcome, good surrounding walks, closed Sun
evening, Mon. *(Guy Vowles)*

STAPLOW   SO6941
Oak (01531) 640954
Bromyard Road (B4214); HR8 1NP
Popular roadside village pub, two snug
bar areas with beams, flagstones and
woodburners, open-kitchen restaurant
serving good (if not bargain) food from
lunchtime sandwiches up, Bathams, Ledbury,
Wye Valley and a guest, good choice of wines,
cheerful quick service; occasional acoustic
music; children and dogs welcome, garden
picnic-sets, four comfortable bedrooms, open
all day. *(Toby Jones)*

STIFFORDS BRIDGE   SO7348
Red Lion (01886) 880318
*A4103 3 miles W of Great Malvern;
WR13 5NN* Refurbished beamed roadside
pub; good choice of tasty well priced pubby
food (not Sun evening), Greene King,
Malvern Hills and Wye Valley, real ciders,

If we know a pub has an outdoor play area for children, we mention it.

friendly helpful staff; some live music; children and dogs welcome, tables in nicely kept garden, farmers' market first Sat of month, open all day Fri-Sun. *(Anon)*

STOCKTON CROSS   SO5161
★ **Stockton Cross Inn** (01568) 612509
Kimbolton; A4112, off A49 just N of Leominster; HR6 0HD Cosy half-timbered 16th-c drovers' inn, heavily beamed interior with huge log fire and woodburner, handsome antique settle, old leather chairs and brocaded stools, cast-iron-framed tables, well kept Wye Valley ales and guests, Robinson's cider, enjoyable food from pub favourites up, good friendly service; children and dogs welcome, pretty garden, handy for Berrington Hall (NT), open all day. *(Harvey Brown)*

SUTTON ST NICHOLAS   SO5345
Golden Cross (01432) 880274
Corner of Ridgeway Road; HR1 3AZ Thriving modernised pub with enjoyable food including deals, Wye Valley Butty Bach and two regularly changing guests from stone-fronted counter, good friendly service, clean décor, some breweriana, relaxed upstairs restaurant; live music Fri, pool and darts; children and dogs welcome, disabled facilities, pretty village and good walks. *(Anon)*

SYMONDS YAT   SO5515
Old Ferrie (01600) 890232
Ferrie Lane, Symonds Yat West; HR9 6BL Unpretentious old inn set in picturesque spot by River Wye with its own hand-pulled ferry; decent choice of enjoyable pubby food, Wye Valley ales and local cider, friendly helpful staff; games room; children welcome, waterside terrace, canoeing and good walks, bedrooms and two bunkhouses, open all day. *(Alfie Bayliss)*

TRUMPET   SO6639
Trumpet Inn (01531) 670277
Corner of A413 and A438; HR8 2RA Modernised black and white timbered pub dating from the 15th c, well kept Wadworths ales and plenty of wines by the glass, good food (all day Sat, till 7pm Sun) from sandwiches to specials, efficient service, carpeted interior with beams, stripped brickwork and log fires, restaurant; free wi-fi; children and dogs (in bar) welcome, tables in big garden behind, campsite with hard standings, open all day. *(Toby Jones)*

UPTON BISHOP   SO6326
Moody Cow (01989) 780470
B4221 E of Ross-on-Wye; HR9 7TT Refurbished dining pub, L-shaped bar with sandstone walls, slate floor and woodburner, biggish raftered restaurant and second more intimate eating area, good freshly made food, well kept ales and decent wines (including local ones), friendly efficient service; children, dogs and boots welcome, garden growing own fruit/vegetables, courtyard bedroom up spiral staircase, closed Sun evening, Mon. *(Alison and Michael Harper)*

WELLINGTON   SO4948
Wellington (01432) 830367
Village signed off A49 N of Hereford; HR4 8AT Red-brick Victorian pub-restaurant; bar with big high-backed settles, antique farm and garden tools, historical photographs of the village and woodburner in brick fireplace, Butcombe, Goffs, Wye Valley and a guest, enjoyable fairly traditional food (not Sun evening) cooked by landlord-chef, candlelit stable restaurant and conservatory; background music; children welcome, dogs in bar, nice back garden, closed Mon, and may shut early Sun if quiet. *(Harvey Brown)*

WELLINGTON HEATH   SO7140
Farmers Arms (01531) 634776
Off B4214 just N of Ledbury – pub signed right, from top of village; Horse Road; HR8 1LS Roomy open-plan beamed pub refurbished under present licensees, enjoyable food including daily specials, Otter, Wye Valley Butty Bach and a guest, friendly staff; free wi-fi; children and dogs welcome, picnic-sets on paved terrace, good walking country, open all day weekends, closed Mon. *(Belinda May)*

WEOBLEY   SO4051
Salutation (01544) 318443
Off A4112 SW of Leominster; HR4 8SJ Old beamed and timbered inn at top of delightful village green, enjoyable food cooked by chef-landlord from bar snacks up including set lunch/early evening deal, well kept ales such as Otter, Thwaites and Wye Valley, Robinson's cider, pleasant helpful service, two bars and restaurant, log fires; quiz/curry night first Weds of month; children welcome, sheltered back terrace, three bedrooms, good breakfast. *(Anon)*

WIGMORE   SO4168
Oak (01568) 770424
Ford Street; HR6 9UJ Recently restored 16th-c coaching inn mixing original features with contemporary styling, well liked interesting food from sensibly short menu including lunchtime sandwiches, Hobsons and guests such as Greene King, cheerful helpful service; children and dogs welcome, closed Tues. *(Alfie Bayliss)*

WINFORTON   SO2946
Sun (01544) 327677
A438; HR3 6EA Friendly unpretentious village pub with enjoyable freshly cooked food all sourced locally, Wye Valley Butty Bach, real ciders, country-style beamed areas either side of central servery, stripped stone and woodburners; background music; children and dogs welcome, garden picnic-sets, closed Sun evening, Mon (also Tues in winter). *(Harvey Brown)*

Hertfordshire

KEY ⭐ Star Pub   🍴 Top Quality Food   🍺 Great Beer

🍷 Good Wines   £ Bargain Meals   🛏 Good Bedrooms   🍽 Serves Food

---

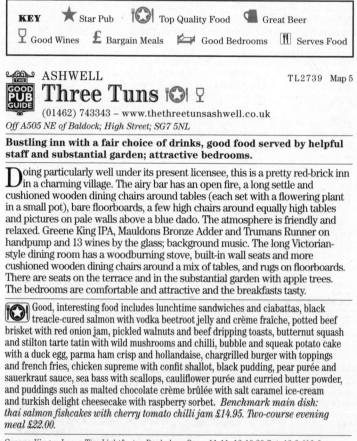

ASHWELL   TL2739   Map 5

Three Tuns 🍴 🍷

(01462) 743343 – www.thethreetunsashwell.co.uk
Off A505 NE of Baldock; High Street; SG7 5NL

Bustling inn with a fair choice of drinks, good food served by helpful staff and substantial garden; attractive bedrooms.

Doing particularly well under its present licensee, this is a pretty red-brick inn in a charming village. The airy bar has an open fire, a long settle and cushioned wooden dining chairs around tables (each set with a flowering plant in a small pot), bare floorboards, a few high chairs around equally high tables and pictures on pale walls above a blue dado. The atmosphere is friendly and relaxed. Greene King IPA, Mauldons Bronze Adder and Trumans Runner on handpump and 13 wines by the glass; background music. The long Victorian-style dining room has a woodburning stove, built-in wall seats and more cushioned wooden dining chairs around a mix of tables, and rugs on floorboards. There are seats on the terrace and in the substantial garden with apple trees. The bedrooms are comfortable and attractive and the breakfasts tasty.

🍴 Good, interesting food includes lunchtime sandwiches and ciabattas, black treacle-cured salmon with vodka beetroot jelly and crème fraîche, potted beef brisket with red onion jam, pickled walnuts and beef dripping toasts, butternut squash and stilton tarte tatin with wild mushrooms and chilli, bubble and squeak potato cake with a duck egg, parma ham crisp and hollandaise, chargrilled burger with toppings and french fries, chicken supreme with confit shallot, black pudding, pear purée and sauerkraut sauce, sea bass with scallops, cauliflower purée and curried butter powder, and puddings such as malted chocolate crème brûlée with salt caramel ice-cream and turkish delight cheesecake with raspberry sorbet. *Benchmark main dish: thai salmon fishcakes with cherry tomato chilli jam £14.95. Two-course evening meal £22.00.*

Greene King ~ Lease Tim Lightfoot ~ Real ale ~ Open 11-11; 12-10.30 Sat; 12-9 (12-6 winter) Sun ~ Bar food 12-3, 6-9.30; 12-4, 6-10 Sat; 12-4, 6-8 (12-5 winter) Sun ~ Restaurant ~ Children welcome ~ Dogs allowed in bar and bedrooms ~ Wi-fi ~ Bedrooms: /£100
Recommended by Martin and Alison Stainsby, Mrs Margo Finlay, Jörg Kasprowski

---

BARNET   TQ2599   Map 5

Duke of York 🍷

(020) 8449 0297 – www.brunningandprice.co.uk/dukeofyork
Barnet Road (A1000); EN5 4SG

Big place with reasonably priced bistro-style food and nice garden

Big windows and plenty of mirrors keep everything light and airy in this rather grand pub. The spreading rooms have been cleverly divided up using open doorways and stairs, but there are some cosy and intimate areas as well. The atmosphere is relaxed and friendly and there's an eclectic mix of furniture on tiled or wooden flooring, hundreds of prints and photos on cream walls, fireplaces and thoughtful touches such as table lamps, books, rugs, fresh flowers and pot plants. Stools line the impressive counter where friendly staff serve Phoenix Brunning & Price Original plus Adnams Lighthouse, Nethergate Growler, Oakham JHB and Trumans Swift on handpump, 20 wines by the glass, 70 whiskies and farm cider; background music. The garden is particularly attractive, with plenty of seats, tables and picnic-sets on a tree-surrounded terrace and lawn, and a tractor in the good play area.

Served all day, the rewarding food includes sandwiches, potted rabbit with radish salad and pear chutney, scallops with pickled salad, bacon crumb and pea jelly, crispy beef salad with sweet chilli sauce, honey-roast ham with free-range eggs, cauliflower and chickpea tagine with apricot and date couscous, steak burger with bacon, cheese, coleslaw and chips, salmon, smoked haddock and prawn pie, and puddings such as bread and butter pudding with apricot sauce and hot waffle with toffee apples, toffee sauce and honeycomb ice-cream. *Benchmark main dish: braised lamb shoulder with dauphinoise potatoes and gravy £16.95. Two-course evening meal £21.00.*

Brunning & Price ~ Manager Matthew Daniels ~ Real ale ~ Open 11-11; 12-10.30 Sun ~ Bar food 12-10 (9.30 Sun) ~ Children welcome ~ Dogs allowed in bar ~ Wi-fi
Recommended by Isobel Mackinlay, Edward May, Susan and John Douglas

EPPING GREEN   TL2906 Map 5
Beehive
(01707) 875959 – www.beehiveeppinggreen.co.uk
Off B158 SW of Hertford, via Little Berkhamsted; back road towards Newgate Street and Cheshunt; SG13 8NB

Cheerful bustling country pub, popular for its good value food

Many customers come to this weatherboarded country pub to enjoy the good, interesting fish dishes. The traditional, low-ceilinged bar has a friendly, informal atmosphere and a woodburning stove in a panelled corner, and serves Greene King Abbot, IPA and a changing guest on handpump alongside a good range of ten wines by the glass; background music. Between the low building and quiet country road is a neat lawn and decked area, with plenty of tables for enjoying the summer sunshine; good woodland walks nearby.

With daily deliveries from Billingsgate, you know the fish is as fresh as can be: scallops and chorizo salad, fresh crab and mango, fish pie, cod with bacon and mushroom sauce, tuna steak with chilli, lime and coriander; there are also sandwiches, baguettes and daily specials such as red onion and brie cannelloni in tomato sauce, steak and kidney pie and chicken bake with avocado salad. *Benchmark main dish: skate wing with caper butter £15.95. Two-course evening meal £16.50.*

Free house ~ Licensee Martin Squirrell ~ Real ale ~ Open 12-3, 5.30-11; 12-10.30 Sun ~ Bar food 12-2.30, 6-9.30; 12-4, 6-8.30 Sun ~ Children welcome *Recommended by Gordon Neighbour, Revd R P Tickle*

The details at the end of each featured entry start by saying whether the pub is a free house, or if it belongs to a brewery or pub group (which we name).

FLAUNDEN TL0101 Map 5

Bricklayers Arms ⭐ ♀

(01442) 833322 – www.bricklayersarms.com

4 miles from M25 junction 18; village signposted off A41 – from village centre follow Boxmoor, Bovingdon road and turn right at Belsize, Watford signpost into Hogpits Bottom; HP3 0PH

Hertfordshire Dining Pub of the Year

Cosy country restaurant with fairly elaborate food; very good wine list

In summer, the terrace and beautifully kept old-fashioned garden behind this civilised 18th-c pub really comes into its own; it's exceedingly peaceful. Stubs of knocked-through oak-timbered wall indicate the original room layout of the now fairly open-plan interior, and the nicely refurbished low-beamed bar is snug and comfortable, with a roaring log fire in winter. Stools line the brick counter where they keep Sharps Doom Bar and guests such as Haresfoot Lock Keepers, Rebellion Roasted Nuts and Tring Side Pocket for a Toad on handpump, and an extensive wine list with 25 by the glass; background music. Just up the Belsize road, a path on the left leads through delightful woods to a forested area around Hollow Hedge. The pub is just 15 minutes from the Warner Bros Studios where the Harry Potter films were made; you can tour the studios but must book in advance.

 Using home-smoked meat and fish, the imaginative food includes crab with home-smoked salmon, chive cream and blinis, shredded pork and golden beetroot piccalilli with red beetroot-crusted poached egg, lamb burger with home-pickled vegetables, crème fraîche and fries, sausages of the day with chive mash and red wine gravy, quail stuffed with mixed mushrooms with pheasant sausage, duck liver mousse and madeira jus, pork tenderloin wrapped in seaweed with parsnip and wasabi purée and sweet and sour jus, and puddings such as chocolate and honey fondant with pistachio ice-cream and sticky toffee pudding with date mascarpone. *Benchmark main dish: duck breast and duck leg confit with red apple and cider jus £17.95. Two-course evening meal £24.00.*

Free house ~ Licensee Alvin Michaels ~ Real ale ~ Open 12-11.30; 12-10.30 Sun ~ Bar food 12-2.30, 6.30-9.30; 12-3.30, 6.30-8.30 Sun ~ Restaurant ~ Children welcome ~ Dogs allowed in bar ~ Wi-fi *Recommended by Peter and Jan Humphreys, Alex and Hazel Evans, John and Penny Wheeler, Charles Hawkins*

FRITHSDEN TL0109 Map 5

Alford Arms ⭐ ♀

(01442) 864480 – www.alfordarmsfrithsden.co.uk

A4146 from Hemel Hempstead to Water End, then second left (after Red Lion) signed Frithsden, then left at T junction, then right after 0.25 miles; HP1 3DD

Thriving dining pub with a chic interior, good food from imaginative menu, and a thoughtful wine list

Despite the emphasis on dining in this pretty Victorian pub, they consider themselves a proper pub and you'll certainly find a few locals chatting at the bar. Sharps Doom Bar, a couple of guests such as Chiltern Beechwood and Tring Side Pocket for a Toad on handpump, plus 24 wines by the glass from a european list (quite a few sweet ones too) and a good choice of spirits; background jazz and darts. The elegant, understated interior has simple prints on pale cream walls, with blocks picked out in rich Victorian green or dark red, and an appealing mix of antique furniture (from Georgian chairs to old commode stands) on bare boards and patterned quarry tiles; it's all pulled together by luxuriously opulent curtains. There are plenty of tables outside and, as the pub is on the Ashridge Estate (National Trust), many customers combine a visit here with a walk.

Using local, seasonal and foraged produce, the tempting food includes cajun-spiced crispy squid with chorizo aïoli, free-range duck livers with cauliflower purée, salsify and balsamic jelly, butternut squash and sweet potato wellington with rosemary cream, free-range sausages of the day, free-range chicken with chickpea tagine and pumpkin seed pesto, salmon fillet with sweet potato gnocchi, clams, kale and lemon broth, and puddings such as dark chocolate truffle terrine with beetroot ice-cream and baked apple with hazelnut panna cotta. *Benchmark main dish: ale-braised shin of beef £15.50. Two-course evening meal £22.25.*

Salisbury Pubs ~ Lease Brandon Kirby ~ Real ale ~ Open 11-11; 12-10.30 Sun ~ Bar food 12-2.30 (3 Sat), 6.30-9.30 (10 Fri, Sat); 12-9 Sun ~ Restaurant ~ Children welcome ~ Dogs allowed in bar ~ Wi-fi *Recommended by Alex and Hazel Evans, Richard Kennell*

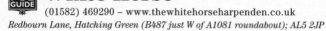

HARPENDEN
White Horse
TL1312   Map 5

(01582) 469290 – www.thewhitehorseharpenden.co.uk
Redbourn Lane, Hatching Green (B487 just W of A1081 roundabout); AL5 2JP

Smart up-to-date dining pub with civilised bar side

As this extended, white-weatherboarded pub is open all day from 9.30am, there's a steady stream of customers wanting breakfast, morning coffee and afternoon tea – as well as lunch and evening meals. The chatty bar is split-level (one part was once the stable) with prints on burnt orange-painted plank panelling, stools around tables, taller stools against the counter, and an open fire. Sharps Doom Bar and Tring Bring Me Sunshine and Side Pocket for a Toad on handpump and several wines by the glass, served by friendly, helpful staff; background music and board games. The airy, stylish dining room has tartan-upholstered dining chairs, cushioned wall seats and settles around pale wooden tables on floorboards, and black and white photographs on the walls. There's a huge sunny terrace and plenty of contemporary seats and tables under parasols.

They use a network of local suppliers for their highly rated food and there's a two- and three-course weekday set menu (12-6pm), as well as all-day sandwiches, duck terrine with orange compote, smoked haddock kedgeree with a free-range poached egg, various deli boards, steak burger with toppings, coleslaw and chips, chargrilled pork with sweet potato hash and apple and chilli ketchup, monkfish with curried clams, baby vegetables and confit lemon, award-winning steaks, and puddings such as Valrhona milk chocolate and orange panna cotta and steamed banoffi sponge with banana ice-cream. *Benchmark main dish: breaded cod scampi and skinny chips £12.50. Two-course evening meal £25.00.*

Peach Pub Company ~ Manager Samantha Aylard ~ Real ale ~ Open 9.30am-11pm (11.30 Sat, 10.30 Sun) ~ Bar food 12-9 ~ Restaurant ~ Children welcome ~ Dogs allowed in bar ~ Wi-fi *Recommended by Edward May, Isobel Mackinlay*

HERTFORD HEATH
College Arms
TL3510   Map 5

(01992) 558856 – www.thecollegearmshertfordheath.com
London Road (B1197); SG13 7PW

Light and airy rooms with contemporary furnishings, friendly service, good interesting food and real ales; seats outside

After a walk in the nearby woodlands, readers drop into this civilised and airy place for a drink and a meal. The bar has long cushioned wall seats and pale leather dining chairs around tables on rugs or wooden floorboards, and a modern bar counter where they serve Sharps Doom Bar and a changing guest on handpump and 22 wines by the glass; background jazz. Another area has more long wall seats and an open fireplace piled with logs. There's also a charming little room with brown leather armchairs, a couple of cushioned pews, a woodburning stove in an old brick fireplace, hunting-themed wallpaper and another rug on floorboards. The elegant, partly carpeted dining room contains a real mix of antique dining chairs and tables. The back terrace has tables, seats and a long wooden bench among flowering pots and a children's play house.

Enjoyable food includes sandwiches, salt and pepper squid with avocado purée and spicy pepper jam, sauté black pudding salad with new potatoes, crispy bacon and a poached egg, roasted vegetable wellington with wild mushroom sauce, sausage and mash with red wine jus, monkfish medallions on saffron risotto with fresh tomato salsa, duck breast with slow-braised cabbage, pancetta and red wine jus, 32-day-aged rib-eye steak with a choice of sauces and chips, and puddings such as chocolate fondant with burnt amaretto meringue and chocolate ice-cream and pecan pie with bourbon chantilly and sweet potato ice-cream. *Benchmark main dish: beer-battered fish and chips £12.50. Two-course evening meal £21.00.*

Punch ~ Lease Merissa Tharby ~ Real ale ~ Open 12-10 (11 Sat); 12-7 Sun ~ Bar food 12-3, 6-9 (9.30 Fri, Sat); 12-7 Sun ~ Restaurant ~ Children welcome ~ Dogs allowed in bar ~ Wi-fi ~ Quiz night every second Weds *Recommended by Mrs Margo Finlay, Jörg Kasprowski, David Hunt, David Jackson, Chris and Angela Buckell*

POTTERS CROUCH   TL1105   Map 5
Holly Bush 🍺 £

(01727) 851792 – www.thehollybushpub.co.uk
2.25 miles from M25 junction 21A: A405 towards St Albans, then first left, then after a mile turn left (ie away from Chiswell Green), then at T junction turn right into Blunts Lane; can also be reached fairly quickly, with a good map, from M1 exits 6 and 8; AL2 3NN

Well tended cottage with gleaming furniture, fresh flowers and china, well kept Fullers beers, good value food and an attractive garden

If you want to escape the dreary M25 for some peace and quiet, head for this neatly kept, popular pub – it's handy for St Albans too. It has highly polished dark wood furnishings, quite a few antique dressers (several filled with plates), a number of comfortably cushioned settles, a fox's mask, some antlers, a fine old clock with a lovely chime, daily papers and (on the right as you enter) a big fireplace. In the evening, neatly placed candles cast glimmering light over the varnished tables, all sporting fresh flowers. The long, stepped bar has particularly well kept Fullers ESB, London Pride, Seafarers and a Fullers seasonal beer on handpump, served by helpful staff who remain friendly even when pushed. The fenced-off back garden has plenty of sturdy picnic-sets on a lawn surrounded by handsome trees.

From a varied menu, the popular food includes lunchtime sandwiches and toasties, pâté with apple and ale chutney, caesar salad, deli platters, chilli con carne, beef or chicken burger with toppings and coleslaw, wild mushroom and asparagus in white wine and cream pie, lamb koftas with feta cheese salad, tzatziki and pitta bread, smoked haddock fishcakes with spinach and roasted vine tomatoes, and puddings such as belgian waffle with clotted cream ice-cream and maple syrup and sticky toffee pudding. *Benchmark main dish: steak in ale pie £12.50. Two-course evening meal £16.00.*

Fullers ~ Tenants Steven and Vanessa Williams ~ Real ale ~ Open 12-2.30, 6-11; 12-3,
7-10.30 Sun ~ Bar food 12-2, 6-9; 12-2.30 Sun; not Sun-Tues evenings ~ Children welcome
Recommended by Tina and David Woods-Taylor, Mrs Zara Elliott

PRESTON   TL1824   Map 5

Red Lion 🍺 £

(01462) 459585 – www.theredlionpreston.co.uk
Village signposted off B656 S of Hitchin; The Green; SG4 7UD

**Homely village local with changing beers, fair-priced food and neat
colourful garden**

In 1982, this became the first community-owned pub in the country and
it still offers a cheerful welcome to both locals and visitors. The main
room on the left, with grey wainscoting, has sturdy, well varnished furniture
including padded country kitchen chairs and cast-iron-framed tables on
patterned carpet, a generous window seat, a log fire in a brick fireplace and
fox hunting prints. The somewhat smaller room on the right has steeplechase
prints, varnished plank panelling and brocaded bar stools on flagstones
around the servery; darts and dominoes. Fullers London Pride and Youngs
Bitter on handpump with guests such as Dark Star Hophead and Titanic
Mild; also, four farm ciders, 11 wines by the glass (including an english house
wine), a perry and winter mulled wine. A few picnic-sets on the front grass
face lime trees on the peaceful village green, while the pergola-covered back
terrace and good-sized sheltered garden with its colourful herbaceous border
have seats and picnic-sets (some shade is provided by a tall ash tree).

 From a reasonably priced menu, there might be stilton-stuffed mushrooms,
garlic and chilli prawns, pumpkin and goats cheese tart, mussels and chips, liver
and bacon, lamb curry, rabbit and cider casserole, chicken, leek and mushroom pie,
pheasant in madeira sauce, and puddings such as chocolate fudge cake and bakewell
tart. *Benchmark main dish: fish pie £9.95. Two-course evening meal £14.00.*

Free house ~ Licensee Raymond Lambe ~ Real ale ~ Open 12-2.30, 5.30-11; 12-midnight Sat;
12-10.30 Sun ~ Bar food 12-2, 6.30-8.30; not Sun evening, Mon ~ Children welcome ~ Dogs
welcome ~ Wi-fi *Recommended by Lindy Andrews, Alfie Bayliss*

REDBOURN   TL1011   Map 5

Cricketers 🍺

(01582) 620612 – www.thecricketersofredbourn.co.uk
*3.2 miles from M1 junction 9; A5183 signed Redbourn/St Albans, at second
roundabout follow B487 for H Hempstead, first right into Chequer Lane,
then third right into East Common; AL3 7ND*

**Good food and beer in a nicely placed and attractively updated pub
with a bar and two restaurants**

After enjoying one of the numerous surrounding walking and cycling
routes, head to this friendly village pub for refreshment. The relaxed
front bar has country-style décor: comfortable tub chairs, cushioned bench
seating and high-backed bar stools on pale brown carpet, and a woodburning
stove. They serve five quickly changing ales on handpump such as Leighton
Buzzard Restoration Ale, Marstons Pedigree, Sharps Doom Bar and Tring
Brock Bitter and By George, 16 wines by the glass, farm cider, several malt
whiskies and good coffee; well reproduced background music. This bar
leads back into an attractive, comfortably refurbished and unusually shaped
modern restaurant; there's also an upstairs restaurant for private parties or
functions. The side garden has plenty of seating and summer barbecues; they
can help with information on the museum next door.

Good food includes lunchtime sandwiches, three-cheese soufflé, barbecue baby back ribs and slaw, various pizzas, beer-battered fish and chips, marinated chicken on skewers with mediterranean couscous and tzatziki, fillet steak strips with chilli, garlic, truffle oil and pecorino on linguine, calves liver and bacon with onion gravy, rolled pork belly with spring onion mash, apple velouté and jus, and puddings such as treacle and orange tart and white and dark chocolate mousse. *Benchmark main dish: crayfish and chilli risotto £12.90. Two-course evening meal £20.00.*

Free house ~ Licensees Colin and Debbie Baxter ~ Real ale ~ Open 12-11 (midnight Sat, 10.30 Sun) ~ Bar food 12-3, 6-9 (9.30 Sat); 12-4 Sun ~ Restaurant ~ Children welcome ~ Dogs allowed in bar ~ Wi-fi *Recommended by David Fowler, Mrs Margo Finlay, Jörg Kasprowski, Edward Mirzoeff*

SARRATT   TQ0498 Map 5
Cock
(01923) 282908 – www.cockinn.net
Church End: a very pretty approach is via North Hill, a lane N off A404, just under a mile W of A405; WD3 6HH

Plush pub with friendly staff and a wide choice of drinks and food – good for families outside on summer weekends

Picnic-sets at the front of this neat 17th-c pub look across a quiet lane towards a churchyard and the attractive, sheltered lawn and terrace have picnic-sets with open country views; there's a bouncy castle and play area for children. Inside, it's comfortably traditional and the latched back door opens straight into the homely tiled snug with its cluster of bar stools, vaulted ceiling and original bread oven. Through an archway, the partly oak-panelled, cream-walled lounge has a lovely log fire in an inglenook, pretty Liberty-style curtains, red plush chairs at oak tables, lots of interesting artefacts and several namesake pictures of cockerels. Badger First Call, Leaping Legend and Tanglefoot on handpump; background music. The restaurant is in an attractively converted barn.

 As well as an OAP three-course deal, the highly thought-of food includes sandwiches and paninis, moules marinière, a sharing platter, home-baked ham and eggs, pork and leek, wild boar and cumberland sausages with red wine and onion gravy, vegetable lasagne, a roast of the day, slow-roast pork belly with an oriental rub and stir-fried vegetables, beef goulash, and puddings such as chocolate roulade and fruit crumble and custard. *Benchmark main dish: steak in ale pie £13.25. Two-course evening meal £18.00.*

Badger ~ Tenants Brian and Marion Eccles ~ Real ale ~ Open 12-10.30 (11.30 Sat); 12-9 Sun ~ Bar food 12-2.30, 6-9; not Sun evening ~ Restaurant ~ Children welcome ~ Dogs allowed in bar ~ Wi-fi ~ Live music Sun afternoon *Recommended by Mrs P J Pearce, Roy Hoing, David Jackson, Tom and Ruth Rees*

SARRATT   TQ0499 Map 5
Cricketers
(01923) 270877 – www.brunningandprice.co.uk/cricketers
The Green; WD3 6AS

Plenty to look at in rambling rooms, up to six real ales, nice wines, enjoyable food and friendly staff; seats outside

You'll need to book a table in advance at peak times in this cleverly refurbished pub. It's made up of three charming old cottages and the interlinked rooms have numerous little snugs and alcoves – perfect for a quiet drink. There's all manner of antique dining chairs and tables on rugs or stripped floorboards, comfortable armchairs or tub seats, cushioned pews, wall seats and two open fires in raised fireplaces. Also, cricketing memorabilia, fresh flowers, large plants and church candles. Phoenix Brunning & Price Original and guests such as Haresfoot Sundial and Wild Boy, Timothy Taylors Boltmaker and Tring Side Pocket for a Toad on handpump, good wines by the glass and 50 malt whiskies; background music and board games. Several sets of french windows open on to the back terrace where there are tables and chairs, with picnic-sets on grass next to a colourfully painted tractor; seats at the front overlook the village green and duck pond.

Reliably good food from a varied menu includes sandwiches, king scallops with crispy pancetta, carrot purée and caper and herb dressing, char siu pork belly with pak choi and pickled ginger salad, squid and prawn linguine with chorizo, garlic and chilli, basil gnocchi with roasted red pepper coulis, cherry tomatoes and asparagus, steak burger with toppings, coleslaw and chips, duck with baby vegetables, peach purée and jus, and puddings such as lemon meringue pie with berry compote and chocolate brownie with dark chocolate sauce. *Benchmark main dish: beer-battered haddock and chips £12.75. Two-course evening meal £20.00.*

Brunning & Price ~ Licensee David Stowell ~ Real ale ~ Open 10am-11pm (10.30 Sun) ~ Bar food 12-10 (9.30 Sun) ~ Restaurant ~ Children welcome ~ Dogs allowed in bar ~ Wi-fi
Recommended by John Boothman, Barry Collett

WATTON-AT-STONE
Bull

TL3019 Map 5

(01920) 831032 – www.thebullwatton.co.uk
High Street; SG14 3SB

Bustling old pub with beamed rooms, candlelight and fresh flowers, real ales served by friendly staff and enjoyable food

At the heart of this 15th-c pub is a huge inglenook fireplace, which the customers who drop in and out all day (the place opens at 9.30am) tend to gravitate towards. There's a leather button-back chesterfield and armchairs on either side, a leather banquette beside a landscape-patterned wall, and solid dark wooden dining chairs and plush-topped stools around all sorts of tables on bare boards; fresh flowers. The atmosphere is relaxed and friendly, and hospitable staff serve Adnams Ghost Ship, Camerons Strongarm and Sharps Doom Bar on handpump and good wines by the glass; background music. Near the entrance are some high bar chairs along counters by the windows; from here, it's a step up to a charming little room with just four tables, wooden dining chairs, a wall banquette, decorative logs in a fireplace, books on shelves, board games and an old typewriter. At the other end of the building is an elegantly furnished dining room with carpet and a slate floor. Paintwork throughout is contemporary. Outside, there are church chairs and tables on a covered terrace, picnic-sets on grass, and a small, well equipped play area.

Rewarding all-day food includes breakfasts, morning coffee with pastries and a weekday £8 lunchtime deal; also, sandwiches, duo of chicken terrine with pickled mushrooms, prawn and crayfish cocktail, burger with toppings, onion rings and chips, vegetable tagine with halloumi, tzatziki and couscous, piri piri chicken with sweet potato chips, chilli jam and crème fraîche, cod with red wine reduction and dauphinoise potatoes, and puddings such as chocolate panna cotta with honeycomb, marshmallows and candied orange and sticky toffee pudding with butterscotch sauce. *Benchmark main dish: smoked pork belly and confit duck leg cassoulet £15.00. Two-course evening meal £19.00.*

Punch ~ Lease Alastair and Anna Bramley ~ Real ale ~ Open 9.30am-11pm; 12-6 Sun; closed Sun evening ~ Bar food 12-3, 6-10; 12-4, 6-10 Sat; 12-4 Sun ~ Restaurant ~ Children welcome ~ Dogs allowed in bar ~ Wi-fi *Recommended by Mrs Margo Finlay, Jörg Kasprowski*

Also Worth a Visit in Hertfordshire

Besides the fully inspected pubs, you might like to try these pubs that have been recommended to us and described by readers. Do tell us what you think of them: feedback@goodguides.com

ALDBURY   SP9612
★ **Greyhound** (01442) 851228
Stocks Road; village signed from A4251 Tring–Berkhamsted, and from B4506; HP23 5RT Picturesque village pub with some signs of real age inside; inglenook in cosy traditional beamed bar, more contemporary area with leather chairs, airy oak-floored back restaurant with wicker chairs at big new tables, Badger ales, traditional food (all day weekends) from lunchtime sandwiches and snacks up; children welcome, dogs in bar, front benches facing green with whipping post, stocks and duck pond, suntrap gravel courtyard, eight bedrooms (some in newer building behind), open all day. *(David Jackson, Conor McGaughey, Tracey and Stephen Groves)*

ALDBURY   SP9612
★ **Valiant Trooper** (01442) 851203
Trooper Road (towards Aldbury Common); off B4506 N of Berkhamsted; HP23 5RW Cheery traditional pub with appealing beamed bar, red and black floor tiles, built-in wall benches, a pew and small dining chairs around country tables, two further rooms (one with inglenook) and back barn restaurant, enjoyable generously served food (all day Sat, not Sun or Mon evenings), Chiltern, Fullers, Tring and a couple of guests, five ciders and several wines by the glass, friendly helpful staff; background music, free wi-fi; children and dogs (in bar) welcome, enclosed garden with wooden adventure playground, well placed for Ashridge Estate beechwoods, open all day. *(Ross Balaam, Tracey and Stephen Groves, Conor McGaughey, Richard Kennell)*

ALDENHAM   TQ1498
Round Bush (01923) 855532
Roundbush Lane; WD25 8BG Cheery and bustling village pub with plenty of atmosphere, two front rooms and back restaurant, popular generously served food from baguettes to specials, four well kept ales including St Austell, friendly efficient staff; quiz first Weds of month, live music, darts;

children and dogs welcome, big garden, good walks. *(Ross Balaam, Nigel and Sue Foster)*

AMWELL   TL1613
Elephant & Castle (01582) 832175
Amwell Lane; signed SW from Wheathampstead; AL4 8EA Low-beamed 18th-c country pub with two log fires (one in a great inglenook), panelling, quarry tiles and stripped brickwork, four well kept Greene King related ales, decent pub food (not Sun or Mon evenings), immensely deep covered well shaft in back room; children, walkers and dogs welcome, two gardens, open all day. *(Charlie May)*

ASHWELL   TL2639
Bushel & Strike (01462) 742394
Off A507 just E of A1(M) junction 10, N of Baldock, via Newnham; Mill Street opposite church, via Gardiners Lane (car park down Swan Lane); SG7 5LY Smartly modernised 19th-c village dining pub (originally a brewery), good food (Sun till 6pm) from chef-landlord, Charles Wells ales and good selection of wines by the glass, friendly service; picnic-sets on lawn and small terrace with view of church, closed Mon, otherwise open all day (till 10pm Sun). *(Martin and Alison Stainsby)*

AYOT GREEN   TL2213
Waggoners (01707) 324241
Off B197 S of Welwyn; AL6 9AA Former 17th-c coaching inn under french owners; good food from snacks and pubby choices in cosy low-beamed bar to more upmarket french cooking in comfortable restaurant extension, friendly attentive staff, good wine list, real ales; attractive and spacious suntrap back garden with sheltered terrace – some A1(M) noise, wooded walks nearby. *(Isobel Mackinlay)*

AYOT ST LAWRENCE   TL1916
Brocket Arms (01438) 820250
Off B651 N of St Albans; AL6 9BT Attractive 14th-c low-beamed inn with good interesting food (not Sun evening) in bar and restaurant, friendly helpful staff, six real

---

Places with gardens or terraces usually let children sit there – we note in the text the very few exceptions that don't.

ales including Greene King, Sharps and one badged for the pub from Nethergate, wide choice of wines by the glass, inglenook log fires; children welcome, dogs in bar, nice suntrap walled garden with play area, handy for George Bernard Shaw's house (Shaws Corner – NT), six comfortable bedrooms, open all day. *(Mike Swan)*

BALDOCK   TL2433
Orange Tree (01462) 892341
Norton Road; SG7 5AW
Welcoming old two-bar pub with up to 13 well kept ales including Buntingford and Greene King, local ciders such as Apple Cottage and large selection of whiskies, good value locally sourced home-made food (all day Sat, till 6pm Sun) including range of pies and blackboard specials, games room with bar billiards, quiz Tues, folk club Weds; children welcome and dogs (theirs is called Arthur), garden with play area and chickens, open all day Thurs-Sun. *(Stuart Gideon, Mrs Catherine Simmonds)*

BARKWAY   TL3834
★Tally Ho (01763) 848071
London Road (B1368); SG8 8EX Little village-edge pub refurbished under newish owners, clean modern décor with light wood flooring, log fire in central brick fireplace, well liked all-day food (not Sun evening) from interestingly varied menu including daily specials, changing ales and good range of other drinks, tea, coffee and freshly baked cakes, friendly helpful staff; children welcome, new decked seating area at front, picnic-sets and weeping willow in garden beyond car park, open all day from 7.30am (8am-7pm Sun). *(Edward May)*

BATCHWORTH HEATH   TQ1090
Olde Greene Manne (01923) 826433
London Road A404; WD3 1QB Pleasantly rambling beamed Vintage Inn, three well kept ales including Timothy Taylors Landlord, good choice of wines by the glass, popular fairly priced food including Weds pie day, prompt friendly service; children welcome, disabled access and facilities, spacious terrace, plenty of walks nearby, open all day. *(Ross Balaam)*

BATFORD   TL1415
★Gibraltar Castle (01582) 460005
Lower Luton Road; B653, S of B652 junction; AL5 5AH Traditional long carpeted bar with impressive military memorabilia – everything from rifles and swords to uniforms and medals (plenty of captions to read), also historical pictures of Gibraltar; area with low beams giving way to soaring rafters, comfortably cushioned wall benches, snug window alcoves and nice old fireplace, board games on piano, Fullers London Pride and ESB, popular home-made food (all day weekends), friendly service; background music; children and particularly

dogs welcome, seats on front terrace looking over road to nature reserve, more tables behind on large decked area with lots of flowers, open all day. *(AC)*

BENINGTON   TL3023
Bell (01438) 869827
Town Lane; just past post office, towards Stevenage; SG2 7LA Traditional 16th-c pub in very pretty village, local beers such as Buntingford and enjoyable caribbean food (new licensees are from trinidad), low beams, sloping walls and big inglenook, occasional folk and games evenings; big garden with country views, handy for Benington Lordship Gardens, open all day Sun (food till 6pm then), closed Mon. *(John and Mary Warner)*

BERKHAMSTED   SP9907
Rising Sun (01442) 864913
George Street; HP4 2EG Victorian canalside pub with five well kept ales including one badged for them by Tring, good range of ciders (three beer/cider festivals a year) and interesting range of spirits, two very small traditional rooms with a few basic chairs and tables, coal fire, snuff and cigars for sale, no food apart from ploughman's, friendly service; background music; children and dogs welcome, chairs out by canal and well worn seating in covered side beer garden, colourful hanging baskets, open all day in summer, closed winter lunchtimes Mon-Thurs. *(N R White)*

BISHOP'S STORTFORD   TL5021
Nags Head (01279) 654553
Dunmow Road; CM23 5HP Well restored 1930s art deco pub (Grade II listed), McMullens ales from island servery and plenty of wines by the glass, wide choice of enjoyable reasonably priced food, lots of smallish well spaced tables, good service; quiz last Weds of month, free wi-fi; children welcome, garden seating, open all day. *(Mrs K Hooker)*

BOURNE END   TL0206
★Three Horseshoes (01442) 862585
Winkwell; just off A4251 Hemel-Berkhamsted; HP1 2RZ 16th-c pub in charming setting by unusual swing bridge over Grand Union Canal, low-beamed three-room core with inglenooks, traditional furniture including settles, a few sofas, three well kept Charles Wells ales and enjoyable food from british tapas to good burgers, efficient staff (may ask to keep a credit card while you eat), bay-windowed extension overlooking canal; comedy and quiz nights; children welcome, picnic-sets out by the water, open (and food) all day. *(Ruth May)*

BRAUGHING   TL3925
Axe & Compass (01920) 821610
Just off B1368; The Street; SG11 2QR Nice country pub in pretty village with ford;

enjoyable freshly prepared food (till 6pm Sun) from varied menu, own-baked bread, well kept ales and several wines by the glass, friendly uniformed staff, mix of furnishings on wood floors in two roomy bars, lots of old local photographs, log fires, restaurant with little shop selling home-made produce; well behaved children and dogs welcome, garden overlooking playing field, outside bar. *(Anthony and Marie Lewis)*

BRAUGHING   TL3925
Golden Fleece (01920) 823555
Green End (B1368); SG11 2PE 17th-c dining pub with good freshly made food (special diets catered for) from chef-landlord including some imaginative choices, popular tapas night last Weds of month, Adnams Southwold and guests, plenty of wines by the glass, cheerful service, bare-boards bar and two dining rooms, beams and timbers, good log fire; quiz first Sun of month; children welcome, circular picnic-sets out in front, back garden with metal furniture on split-level paved terrace, play area, open all day weekends (food till 6pm Sun). *(Edward May)*

BUSHEY   TQ1394
Horse & Chains (020) 8421 9907
High Street; WD23 1BL Comfortably modernised dining pub with woodburner in big inglenook, good choice of wines by the glass, real ales and enjoyable bar food from sandwiches and sharing plates up, separate restaurant menu, kitchen view from compact dining room, good friendly service; children welcome, open (and food) all day. *(Jane Woodward)*

CHORLEYWOOD   TQ0395
★ Black Horse (01923) 282252
Dog Kennel Lane, The Common; WD3 5EG Welcoming old country pub popular for its good value generous food (smaller helpings available) from good sandwiches up, bargain OAP meals, well kept ales including Adnams, Wadworths and Charles Wells, decent wines, tea and coffee, good cheery service even when busy, low dark beams and two log fires in thoroughly traditional rambling bar, daily papers; big-screen TV; children, walkers and dogs welcome, picnic-sets overlooking common, open all day. *(Roy Hoing)*

CHORLEYWOOD   TQ0294
Land of Liberty Peace & Plenty (01923) 282226
Long Lane, Heronsgate, just off M25 junction 17; WD3 5BS Traditional 19th-c drinkers' pub in leafy outskirts, half a dozen well kept interesting ales and good choice of cider/perry, snacky food such as pasties, simple layout, darts, skittles and board games; background jazz, TV (on request), no mobile phones or children inside; dogs on leads welcome, garden with pavilion, open all day. *(Richard Kennell)*

CHORLEYWOOD   TQ0295
Stag (01923) 282090
Long Lane/Heronsgate Road; WD3 5BT Open-plan Edwardian dining pub with decent choice of enjoyable food from sandwiches and light meals up, weekday set lunch, McMullen ales and good choice of wines by the glass, friendly service, bar and eating areas extending into conservatory, woodburner in raised hearth; free wi-fi; children welcome, tables on back lawn, closed Mon, otherwise open all day from 9am (10am weekends), Sun till 7pm. *(Jean Plant, Richard Kennell)*

COLNEY HEATH   TL2007
Plough (01727) 823720
Sleapshyde; handy for A1(M) junction 3; A414 towards St Albans, double back at first roundabout then turn left; AL4 0SE Cosy 18th-c low-beamed thatched local, friendly chatty atmosphere, good value generous home-made food (not Sun-Tues evenings) from lunchtime baguettes and baked potatoes up, well kept Greene King, St Austell and a guest, friendly efficient staff, big log fire, small brighter back dining area; charity quiz first Sun of month, sports TV; children welcome, no dogs during food times, front and back terraces, picnic-sets on lawn overlooking fields, open all day weekends. *(Robert Turnham)*

COTTERED   TL3229
Bull (01763) 281243
A507 W of Buntingford; SG9 9QP Well run dining pub, popular and friendly, with airy low-beamed front lounge, good furniture on stripped wood floors, log fire, very well liked if not cheap food from sandwiches to speciality crab, Greene King ales and decent wines; unobtrusive background music; no prams, no under-5s Mon-Sat, big garden with tables beneath majestic old trees, open all day Sun. *(Gordon Neighbour, Alan and Angela Scouller)*

ESSENDON   TL2608
Candlestick (01707) 261322
West End Lane; AL9 6BA Peacefully located country pub under same ownership as the nearby Woodman at Wildhill; emphasis on dining but also well kept local beers and several wines by the glass, relaxed friendly atmosphere, good value freshly prepared bar and restaurant food, comfortable clean interior with faux black timbers, log fires; children and dogs welcome, plenty of seats outside, good walks, closed Mon, otherwise open all day (till 8pm Sun). *(Paul Humphreys, Peter and Jean Hoare)*

FLAUNDEN   TL0100
Green Dragon (01442) 832269
Flaunden Hill; HP3 0PP Comfortable and chatty 17th-c beamed pub with partly panelled extended lounge, back restaurant and traditional little tap bar, log fire,

popular good value food with emphasis on thai dishes, Fullers, St Austell and Charles Wells, friendly service, darts and other pub games; background music; children and dogs welcome, hitching rail for horses, well kept garden with smokers' shelter, pretty village, only a short diversion from Chess Valley Walk. *(Richard Kennell, N R White)*

GILSTON   TL4313
Plume of Feathers (01279) 424154
Pye Corner; CM20 2RD Old beamed corner pub with decent choice of well priced food (all day Fri-Sun) including cook your own meat on a volcanic rock, Courage Best, Adnams Broadside and local guests, Weston's cider and maybe a mulled winter one, good choice of wines by the glass, pleasant staff, carpeted interior with brass-hooded log fire; background music, free wi-fi; children welcome, seats on terrace and fenced grassy area with play equipment. *(Quentin and Carol Williamson)*

GREAT HORMEAD   TL4030
Three Tuns (01763) 289405
B1038/Horseshoe Hill; SG9 0NT Old thatched and timbered country pub in lovely surroundings, enjoyable home-made food including good fish and chips, three real ales such as Buntingford Twitchell, Greene King IPA and Sharps Doom Bar, good choice of wines by the glass, small linked areas redecorated under present friendly licensees, huge inglenook with another great hearth behind, back conservatory extension; free wi-fi; children and dogs welcome, nice secure garden, open all day Sun till 7pm. *(Mrs Zara Elliott)*

HATFIELD   TL2308
Eight Bells (01707) 272477
Park Street, Old Hatfield; AL9 5AX Attractive old beamed pub (two buildings knocked together) with Charles Dickens association; small rooms on different levels, wood floors and open fire, three well kept ales including Sharps Doom Bar and Charles Wells, good value food; background music (live Sat), games machine, free wi-fi; tables in back yard. *(Dr W I C Clark)*

HATFIELD   TL2308
Horse & Groom (01707) 264765
Park Street, Old Hatfield; AL9 5AT Friendly old town local with up to half a dozen well kept ales (beer festivals), good value pubby lunchtime food (free Tues and Sat nights if you buy a pint), dark beams and good winter fire, old local photographs, darts and dominoes; sports TV; dogs welcome, a few tables out behind, handy for Hatfield House, open all day. *(John and Mary Warner)*

HEMEL HEMPSTEAD   TL0411
Crown & Sceptre (01442) 234660
Bridens Camp; leaving on A4146, right at Flamstead/Markyate sign opposite

Red Lion; HP2 6EY Traditional rambling pub, welcoming and relaxed, with well kept Greene King ales and up to six guests, local cider, generous helpings of good reasonably priced pubby food (not Sun evening), cheerful efficient staff, dining room with woodburner; quiz nights (not in summer) and beer festivals; children allowed, outside bar/games room (dogs welcome here), picnic-sets out at front and in pleasant garden, good walks, open all day weekends. *(Peter and Jan Humphreys)*

HEMEL HEMPSTEAD   TL0604
Paper Mill (01442) 288800
Stationers Place, Apsley; HP3 9RH Recently built canalside pub on site of former paper mill; spacious open-plan interior with upstairs restaurant, Fullers ales and a couple of guests (usually local), food from sandwiches and sharing plates up, friendly staff, log fire; comedy, quiz and live music nights; children welcome, tables out on balcony and by the water, open all day. *(Ruth May)*

HIGH WYCH   TL4614
Rising Sun (01279) 724099
Signed off A1184 Harlow–Sawbridgeworth; CM21 0HZ Opened-up 19th-c red-brick village local, up to five well kept ales including Courage, Mighty Oak and Oakham tapped from the cask, friendly staff and regulars, woodburner, no food; walkers and dogs welcome, small side garden, closed Tues lunchtime. *(Isobel Mackinlay)*

HITCHIN   TL1828
Half Moon (01462) 452448
Queen Street; SG4 9TZ Tucked-away open-plan local, friendly and welcoming, with well kept Adnams, Charles Wells and half a dozen often local guests, real cider/perry and plenty of wines by the glass, good value traditional food (all day Fri, Sat) along with tapas, some themed nights, beer festivals Apr and Oct; open all day (till 1am Fri, Sat). *(Stuart Gideon, Mrs Catherine Simmonds, M and J White)*

HITCHIN   TL1929
Pitcher & Piano (01462) 434396
Market Place; SG5 1DY Light and spacious conversion of the old Corn Exchange, good variety of food and drinks, friendly attentive young staff; children welcome, open all day (till 1am Fri, Sat). *(David Hunt)*

HITCHIN   TL1929
Radcliffe Arms (01462) 456111
Walsworth Road; SG4 9ST Busy modernised Victorian pub-restaurant with good freshly made food (some quite pricey) from bar snacks up, local Buntingford ales, extensive wine list with many by the glass, decent coffee, friendly staff, bar area with central servery, conservatory; children welcome, terrace tables, open all day from 9am

for breakfast, closed Sun evening. *(Stuart Gideon, Mrs Catherine Simmonds)*

HITCHIN TL5122
Victoria (01462) 432682
Ickleford Road, at roundabout; SG5 1TJ Popular wedge-shaped Victorian corner local, Greene King ales and a couple of guests, Aspall's cider, enjoyable reasonably priced home-cooked food, events including live music and quiz nights, barn function room; children welcome, seats in sunny beer garden, open all day. *(Stuart Gideon, Mrs Catherine Simmonds)*

HUNSDON TL4114
Fox & Hounds (01279) 843999
High Street; SG12 8NJ Village dining pub with chef-landlord cooking good enterprising seasonal food (not cheap), weekday set menu, friendly efficient service, Adnams Southwold and a local guest, wide choice of wines by the glass, organic fruit juices, beams, panelling and fireside leather sofas, more formal restaurant with chandelier and period furniture, bookcase door to lavatories; children welcome, dogs in bar, heated covered terrace, closed Sun evening, Mon. *(Mrs Margo Finlay, Jörg Kasprowski)*

LEMSFORD TL2112
Crooked Chimney (01707) 397021
Cromer Hyde Lane (B653 towards Wheathampstead); AL8 7XE Substantial old building (originally a farmhouse) reworked as Vintage Inn dining pub, popular food including fixed-price menu (till 5pm Mon-Sat), friendly efficient service, three well kept mainstream ales and good choice of wines by the glass, beams and timbers, central feature fireplace and two further log fires; children welcome, pleasant garden by fields, play area, open all day. *(Ross Balaam)*

LEY GREEN TL1624
Plough (01438) 871394
Plough Lane, Kings Walden; SG4 8LA Small brick-built rural local, plain and old-fashioned, with two well kept Greene King ales and a guest, simple low-priced food, chatty regulars, folk session Tues (band second of month), more live music Sat; big informal garden with verandah, peaceful views, closed lunchtimes Mon and Tues, otherwise open all day. *(Conor McGaughey)*

LITTLE HADHAM TL4322
Nags Head (01279) 771555
Hadham Ford, towards Much Hadham; SG11 2AX Popular and welcoming 16th-c country dining pub with small linked heavily black-beamed rooms, enjoyable sensibly priced food from snacks up including good Sun roasts, close-set tables in small bar with three Greene King beers and decent wines, restaurant down a couple of steps; children in eating areas, tables in pleasant garden. *(Mrs Margo Finlay, Jörg Kasprowski)*

LONG MARSTON SP8915
Queens Head (01296) 668368
Tring Road; HP23 4QL Beamed village local under welcoming new management, well kept Fullers beers and enjoyable good value food from pub favourites up, helpful friendly service; children welcome, seats on terrace, good walks nearby, two bedrooms in separate annexe, open all day. *(Mike Swan)*

MUCH HADHAM TL4219
★ Bull (01279) 842668
High Street; SG10 6BU Neatly kept old dining pub with good home-made food from sandwiches to daily specials, nice choice of wines by the glass including champagne, well kept Brakspears and guests, cheerful efficient service even at busy times, inglenook log fire in unspoilt bar with locals and their dogs, roomy civilised dining lounge and back dining room; children welcome, good-sized garden, Henry Moore Foundation nearby, open all day weekends (food till 6.30 Sun). *(Rob Anderson)*

NORTHAW TL2702
Sun (01707) 655507
B156; on green opposite the church; EN6 4NL Appealing décor in 16th-c pub by village green; opened-up bar with curved counter and stained-glass gantry, some green-painted panelling and open fire, big boxes of vegetables dotted about (sounds odd but looks fun), ales such as Buntingford, Red Squirrel and Trumans on handpump, farm cider and 13 wines by the glass, enjoyable food from interestingly varied menu (highish prices), snug with another fireplace and two dining rooms with exposed brick walls and mix of old furniture; background music, free wi-fi; children and dogs (in bar) welcome, picnic-sets on back terrace, more on grass, open all day Sat, till 6pm Sun, closed Mon and 4-5pm Tues-Fri. *(David Jackson, Caroline Prescott)*

NUTHAMPSTEAD TL4134
★ Woodman (01763) 848328
Off B1368 S of Barkway; SG8 8NB Tucked-away thatched and weatherboarded village pub with comfortable unspoilt core, 17th-c low beams/timbers and nice inglenook log fire, plainer dining extension, enjoyable home-made food (not Sun evening, Mon) from traditional choices up, Buntingford, Greene King and Woodfordes tapped from the cask, friendly service, interesting USAF memorabilia and outside memorial (near World War II airfield); children and dogs (in bar) welcome, benches out overlooking tranquil lane, two comfortable bedrooms, open all day (Sun till 7pm, Mon 4-8pm). *(John and Mary Warner)*

PERRY GREEN TL4317
Hoops (01279) 843568
Off B1004 Widford–Much Hadham;

SG10 6EF Refurbished 19th-c pub-restaurant in grounds of the Henry Moore Foundation (the sculptor in evidence through posters, photographs, prints etc), airy open-plan interior with beams and standing timbers, spindleback chairs around rustic tables on tiled floor, green banquettes, inglenook woodburner, good reasonably priced locally sourced food from varied menu, Adnams Best; no dogs inside; children welcome, garden with large covered terrace, open all day Weds-Sat, till 6pm Sun, closed Mon, Tues. *(Grahame Brooks)*

REDBOURN   TL1011
Hollybush (01582) 792423
Church End; AL3 7DU Picturesque pub dating from the 16th c and under newish management, black-beamed lounge with big brick fireplace and heavy wooden doors, larger area with some built-in settles, well kept Brakspears and reasonably priced home-made food (not Sun-Tues evenings), good Thurs night folk club; children welcome, pleasant sunny garden (distant M1 noise) with play equipment, pretty spot near medieval church, open all day. *(Rob Anderson)*

RICKMANSWORTH   TQ0594
Feathers (01923) 770081
Church Street; WD3 1DJ Quietly set off the high street, beams, panelling and soft lighting, well kept Fullers London Pride, Tring and two guests, good wine list, varied choice of freshly prepared seasonal food (all day) from sandwiches up including lunchtime deal, good friendly young staff coping well when busy; children till 5pm, picnic-sets out behind. *(Brian Glozier)*

RIDGE   TL2100
Old Guinea (01707) 660894
Crossoaks Lane; EN6 3LH Welcoming modernised country pub with good pizzeria alongside traditional bar, St Austell Tribute, proper italian coffee, open fire; children welcome, dogs in bar, large garden with far-reaching views, open all day (food till 10pm). *(Anon)*

ROYSTON   TL3540
Old Bull (01763) 242003
High Street; SG8 9AW Chatty and relaxed coaching inn dating from the 16th c with bow-fronted Georgian façade; roomy high-beamed bar, exposed timbers and handsome fireplaces, wood flooring, easy chairs, papers and magazines, dining area with wall-sized photographs of old Royston, decent choice of food from ciabattas up, good value Sun carvery, Greene King ales and a guest, several wines by the glass, helpful pleasant service; background music and monthly live folk; children welcome, dogs in bar,

suntrap courtyard, 11 bedrooms, open all day from 8am. *(Mike Swan)*

SARRATT   TQ0499
★ Boot (01923) 262247
The Green; WD3 6BL Early 18th-c dining pub with good food (all day Sat, not Sun evening) from lunchtime sandwiches and sharing plates up, weekend breakfast from 9.30am, also tapas and pizzas Fri and Sat evenings, efficient service from friendly young staff, four well kept ales and good choice of wines by the glass, rambling bar with unusual inglenook, restaurant extension; children and (in some parts) dogs welcome, good-sized garden with polytunnel growing own produce, pleasant spot facing green, handy for Chess Valley walks, open all day. *(Ross Balaam, Tom and Ruth Rees)*

SAWBRIDGEWORTH   TL4814
Orange Tree (01279) 722485
West Road; CM21 0BP Refurbished dining pub on leafy outskirts, good freshly cooked food from interestingly varied menu including pub favourites, set lunch deal and daily specials, McMullens ales, friendly staff; children welcome, side garden, closed Mon. *(Mrs Margo Finlay, Jörg Kasprowski)*

ST ALBANS   TL1406
Fighting Cocks (01727) 869152
Abbey Mill Lane; through abbey gateway – you can drive down; AL3 4HE Ancient octagonal-shaped building (former dovecote) by River Ver; enjoyable food (not Sun evening) from enthusiastic landlord-chef including good Sun lunch, up to eight well kept changing ales such as Harviestoun, Leeds, Purity and Woodfordes, friendly helpful service, sunken Stuart cockfighting pit (now a dining area), low heavy beams and panelling, copper-canopied inglenook log fire; weekend live music, darts; children and dogs welcome, attractive public park beyond garden, open all day. *(Mrs Sally Scott)*

ST ALBANS   TL1406
Garibaldi (01727) 894745
Albert Street; left turn down Holywell Hill past White Hart – car park left at end; AL1 1RT Busy little Victorian backstreet local with well kept Fullers/Gales beers and a guest, good wines by the glass and reasonably priced tasty food (till 4.30pm Sun), friendly staff; live music, sports TV, free wi-fi; children and dogs welcome, garden tables, closed Mon lunchtime, otherwise open all day. *(Rob Anderson)*

ST ALBANS   TL1507
Mermaid (01727) 568912
Hatfield Road; AL1 3RL Bay-windowed pub with several seating areas (including

---

We include some hotels with a good bar that offers facilities comparable to those of a pub.

window seats) arranged around central servery, half a dozen well kept ales, a dozen ciders/perries and good selection of bottled beers, friendly knowledgeable staff, Pieminister pies; background and live music, sports TV, darts; beer garden behind, open all day. *(Anon)*

ST ALBANS TL1307

Six Bells (01727) 856945
St Michaels Street; AL3 4SH Rambling old pub with five well kept beers including Oakham, Timothy Taylors and Tring, reasonably priced home-made pubby food (not Sun evening) from lunchtime sandwiches up, cheerful helpful staff, low beams and timbers, log fire, quieter panelled dining room; some live music and quiz nights; children and dogs welcome, small back garden, handy for Verulamium Museum, open all day. *(Rob Anderson)*

ST ALBANS TL1406

White Hart Tap (01727) 860974
Keyfield, round corner from Garibaldi; AL1 1QJ Friendly 19th-c corner local with half a dozen well kept ales (beer festivals), decent choice of wines by the glass and reasonably priced fresh food (all day Sat, not Sun evening) including good fish and chips Fri; some live music, Weds quiz; tables outside, open all day. *(Stephen and Jean Curtis)*

TEWIN TL2715

Plume of Feathers (01438) 717265
Signed off B1000 NE of Welwyn; Upper Green Road, N end of village; AL6 0LX Nicely laid-out country pub with well kept Greene King ales, decent wines and popular food including pub favourites and grills, good friendly service; free wi-fi; children and dogs welcome, farmland views from garden tables, plenty of local walks, open all day. *(Ross Balaam)*

THERFIELD TL3337

Fox & Duck (01763) 287246
Signed off A10 S of Royston; The Green; SG8 9PN Open-plan 19th-c bay-windowed pub in peaceful village setting with picnic-sets on small front green, enjoyable food (not Sun evening) from pub favourites up, Greene King and a couple of guests, friendly helpful staff, country chairs and sturdy stripped-top tables on stone flooring, smaller boarded area on left with darts, carpeted back restaurant; children welcome, garden behind with gate to park (play equipment), pleasant walks nearby, open all day weekends, closed Mon. *(Mrs Margo Finlay, Jörg Kasprowski)*

TITMORE GREEN TL2126

Hermit of Redcoats (01438) 747333
Redcoats Green; SG4 7JR Large attractively updated red-brick Victorian pub, good food (not Sun evening) from light lunchtime choices up, Greene King ales,

plenty of wines by the glass and extensive range of gins, efficient friendly service; children, dogs and boots welcome, seats out in front behind picket fence, spacious garden, open all day. *(Paul Humphreys)*

TRING SP9211

Kings Arms (01442) 823318
King Street; by junction with Queen Street (which is off B4635 Western Road – continuation of High Street); HP23 6BE Cheerful backstreet pub under new family ownership; five well kept ales including Tring, real cider and decent choice of malt whiskies, good value food (not Sun evening) including specials and some unusual choices like 'Jack Daniels and Coke BBQ ribs with pork popcorn', stools around cast-iron tables, cushioned pews, some pine panelling and two warm coal fires; darts, free wi-fi; children till 8.30pm, no dogs inside, tables in side wagon yard, open all day weekends. *(Ruth May)*

TRING SP9211

★ **Robin Hood** (01442) 824912
Brook Street (B486); HP23 5ED Welcoming traditional local with good value pubby food (all day Sat, not Sun evening), half a dozen Fullers ales in good condition, homely atmosphere and genial service, several well cared for smallish linked areas, main bar has banquettes and standard pub chairs on bare boards or carpet, conservatory with vaulted ceiling and woodburner; background music, free wi-fi; children welcome, dogs in bar (resident yorkshire terrier and westie), small back terrace, public car park nearby, open all day Fri-Sun. *(Tony and Wendy Hobden)*

WARESIDE TL3915

Chequers (01920) 467010
B1004; SG12 7QY Proper old-fashioned country local with down-to-earth landlady, three well kept ales such as Buntingford, good straightforward home-made food at reasonable prices including vegetarian options, friendly staff, log fire; children, dogs and walkers welcome. *(Mike Swan)*

WELWYN TL2315

Steamer (01438) 715933
London Road; AL6 9DP Modernised pub with enjoyable reasonably priced food including breakfast from 9am, lunchtime burgers and full indian menu evenings and all day Sun, well kept McMullens ales, coffee and cocktails, efficient friendly service; free wi-fi; children and dogs welcome, open all day. *(Jason Hobbs)*

WHEATHAMPSTEAD TL1716

Cross Keys (01582) 832165
Off B651 at Gustard Wood 1.5 miles N; AL4 8LA Friendly 17th-c brick pub attractively placed in rolling wooded countryside, enjoyable reasonably priced

pubby food (not Sun-Tues evenings) in bar and beamed restaurant including good Sun roasts, four well kept ales, inglenook log fire; quiz second Mon of month; children, walkers and dogs welcome, picnic-sets in large garden with play area, three bedrooms, open all day weekends. *(Ron and June Buckler)*

WHEATHAMPSTEAD
TL1712
Wicked Lady
(01582) 832128
Nomansland Common; B651 0.5 miles S; AL4 8EL Chain dining pub with clean contemporary décor, wide range of food including weekday set menu till 6pm, well kept Adnams, Fullers and Timothy Taylors, plenty of wines by the glass, cocktails, friendly attentive young staff, various rooms and alcoves, low beams and log fires, conservatory; garden with pleasant terrace, open (and food) all day. *(John and Mary Warner)*

WIGGINTON
SP9310
Greyhound
(01442) 824631
Just S of Tring; HP23 6EH Friendly village pub with four well kept ales including Tring, enjoyable food from pubby choices to good daily specials, cheerful efficient service, restaurant; children and dogs welcome, back garden with fenced play area, handy for Ridgeway walks, three clean modern bedrooms, open all day, food all day too apart from Sun evening. *(Ross Balaam, Simon Le Fort, Roy Hoing)*

WILDHILL
TL2606
Woodman
(01707) 642618
Off B158 Brookmans Park–Essendon; AL9 6EA Simple tucked-away country local with friendly staff and regulars, well kept Greene King and four guests, open-plan bar with log fire, two smaller back rooms (one with TV), straightforward weekday bar lunches, darts; children and dogs welcome, plenty of seating in big garden. *(David Jackson)*

WILLIAN
TL2230
★ Fox
(01462) 480233
A1(M) junction 9; A6141 W towards Letchworth then first left; SG6 2AE Civilised contemporary dining pub, comfortable pale wood tables and chairs on stripped boards or big ceramic tiles, paintings by local artists, good inventive food along with more traditional choices, Adnams, Sharps, Woodfordes and a couple of guests, good wine list with 14 by the glass, attentive, friendly young staff; background music, TV; children and dogs (in bar) welcome, side terrace with smart tables under parasols, picnic-sets in good-sized back garden below handsome 14th-c church tower, open all day (no food Sun evening). *(Pat and Graham Williamson)*

WILLIAN
TL2230
Three Horseshoes
(01462) 685713
Baldock Lane, off Willian Road, handy for A1(M) junction 9; SG6 2AE Welcoming traditional village local, enjoyable home-made pubby food generously served and reasonably priced, well kept Greene King and guests, log fires; children and dogs welcome, lots of colourful hanging baskets, small sunny garden, open (and food) all day. *(Pat and Graham Williamson)*

WILSTONE
SP9014
Half Moon
(01442) 826410
Tring Road, off B489; HP23 4PD Traditional old village pub, clean and comfortable, with good value pubby food from sandwiches/panini up, three well kept ales including Sharps Doom Bar, friendly efficient staff, big log fire, low beams, old local pictures and lots of brasses; may be background radio; some seats out in front and in good-sized back garden, handy for Grand Union Canal walks. *(Ross Balaam, Conor McGaughey)*

Post Office address codings confusingly give the impression that some pubs are in Hertfordshire, when they're really in Bedfordshire, Buckinghamshire or Cambridgeshire (which is where we list them).

Isle of Wight

 BEMBRIDGE   SZ6587   Map 2

Crab & Lobster 🌟

(01983) 872244 – www.crabandlobsterinn.co.uk

Foreland Fields Road, off Howgate Road (which is off B3395 via Hillway Road);
PO35 5TR

Clifftop views from terrace and delicious seafood; bedrooms

In summer, the picnic-sets on the terrace here get bagged pretty quickly, so do arrive early. The wonderful view from this coastal bluff over the Solent is also enjoyed from window seats inside and from the bedrooms. The interior is roomier than you might expect and decorated in a parlour-like style, with lots of yachting memorabilia, old local photographs and a blazing winter fire; darts, dominoes and cribbage. Helpful, cheerful staff serve Goddards Fuggle-Dee-Dum, Greene King IPA and Sharps Doom Bar on handpump, a dozen wines by the glass, 16 malt whiskies and good coffee. The shore is just a stroll away.

As well as excellent seafood – crab and prawn cocktail, moules marinière, hot seafood platters, lobster salad and seafood pie – the good food includes lunchtime sandwiches and baguettes, roasted vegetable lasagne, burgers with toppings, onion rings, coleslaw and chips, cumberland sausage and mash with onion gravy, a pie of the day, barbecue chicken with pineapple, bacon, cheese and barbecue sauce, oriental duck stir-fry and puddings such as a cheesecake of the day and lemon posset. *Benchmark main dish: seafood mixed grill £17.50. Two-course evening meal £20.00.*

Enterprise ~ Lease Caroline and Ian Quekett ~ Real ale ~ Open 11-11; 12-10.30 Sun ~ Bar food 12-2.30, 6-9 (9.30 Fri, Sat); limited menu 2.30-5.30 weekends and holidays ~ Restaurant ~ Children welcome ~ Dogs allowed in bar ~ Wi-fi ~ Bedrooms: /$95
Recommended by Adrian Johnson, B J Harding, D J and P M Taylor

 FISHBOURNE   SZ5592   Map 2

Fishbourne Inn

(01983) 882823 – www.thefishbourne.co.uk

From Portsmouth car ferry turn left into Fishbourne Lane (no through road);
PO33 4EU

Attractively refurbished pub with a contemporary feel, real ales, plenty of wines by the glass and all-day food; bedrooms

Offering some sort of food all day, this attractive half-timbered pub is also handy for the Wightlink ferry terminal. The open-plan rooms are connected by knocked-through doorways and there's a mix of wooden and high-backed dining chairs around square tables on the slate floor, a red-painted area off the bar with a big model yacht and two leather sofas facing each other, and a woodburning stove in a brick fireplace with an ornate mirror above. The smart dining room has leather high-backed chairs around circular tables on wood flooring and another model yacht on the window sill; one comfortable room has huge brown leather sofas, and throughout there are country pictures on the partly panelled walls. Goddards Fuggle-Dee-Dum, Ringwood Best and Sharps Doom Bar on handpump and 11 wines by the glass from a good list; background music. This is sister pub to the Boathouse in Seaview and New Inn at Shalfleet.

As well as serving breakfasts (9-11am), the popular food includes lunchtime sandwiches and baguettes, an antipasti plate, half pint of shell-on prawns, pork and leek sausages with mash and gravy, a pie of the day, roasted vegetable couscous topped with goats cheese and red pepper dressing, chicken breast wrapped in parma ham with french-style peas, whole plaice with creamed leeks and spinach, and puddings such as vanilla and white chocolate cheesecake with berry compote and a crumble of the day. *Benchmark main dish: beer-battered fish and chips £10.95. Two-course evening meal £16.00.*

Enterprise ~ Lease Martin Bullock ~ Real ale ~ Open 9am-10.30pm (11 Fri, Sat) ~ Bar food 12-9.30; lighter menu 2.30-6 ~ Restaurant ~ Children welcome ~ Dogs allowed in bar ~ Wi-fi ~ Live music July, August ~ Bedrooms: £75/£120 *Recommended by Adrian Johnson, Ian Phillips, Mungo Shipley*

SEAVIEW
Boathouse 🛏

SZ5992   Map 2

(01983) 810616 – www.theboathouseiow.co.uk
On B3330 Ryde–Seaview; PO34 5BW

Contemporary décor in well run pub with real ales, quite a choice of food, a friendly welcome and seats outside; bedrooms

Just across the road from the beach, this extended blue-painted Victorian pub has a friendly, easy-going atmosphere. The interior is appealing: the bar has sturdy leather stools and tub-like chairs around circular wooden tables, a large model yacht on the mantelpiece above an open fire with a huge neat stack of logs beside it, fresh flowers and candles. Sharps Doom Bar and a summer guest from Goddards on handpump and 13 wines by the glass. In another room, a dinghy (complete with oars) leans against the wall. The dining room has elegant dining chairs, more wooden tables, portraits on pale blue walls and an ornate mirror over another open fire; background music. Throughout, the paintwork is light and fresh and there's a mix of polished bare boards, flagstones and carpet. Picnic-sets and tables and chairs, some under parasols, look out to sea and the comfortable bedrooms share the same view. This is sister pub to the Fishbourne Inn at Fishbourne and New Inn at Shalfleet.

As well as lunchtime sandwiches, the well liked food includes local lobster and crab, smoked mackerel pâté, local clams, local ham and eggs, wild mushrooms and roasted courgettes in truffle oil and cream on pasta, pork and leek sausages with red wine and onion gravy, beef in ale pie, beer-battered fish of the day with chips, local steaks, and puddings such as chocolate brownie with chocolate sauce. *Benchmark main dish: fish pie £10.95. Two-course evening meal £17.00.*

Punch ~ Tenant Martin Bullock ~ Real ale ~ Open 9am-10.30pm (11 Sat) ~ Bar food 12-9.30; lighter menu 2.30-6 ~ Children welcome ~ Dogs allowed in bar ~ Wi-fi ~ Bedrooms: £75/£125 *Recommended by John Jenkins*

SHALFLEET

SZ4089 Map 2

New Inn

(01983) 531314 – www.thenew-inn.co.uk
A3054 Newport–Yarmouth; PO30 4NS

• •

Isle of Wight Dining Pub of the Year

Popular pub with seafood specialities and good beers and wines

This former fishermen's pub is just a short stroll from the marshy inlets of the yacht-studded Newtown estuary. The rambling rooms have plenty of character, with warm fires, yachting photographs and pictures, boarded ceilings and scrubbed pine tables on flagstone, carpet and slate floors. Goddards Fuggle-Dee-Dum, Ringwood Best and Sharps Doom Bar on handpump, 11 wines by the glass and farm cider; background music. There may be double sittings in summer; dogs are only allowed in areas with stone floors. This is sister pub to the Fishbourne Inn at Fishbourne and Boathouse in Seaview.

Well thought-of all-day food includes lunchtime sandwiches and baguettes, local potted crab, shell-on prawns with garlic mayonnaise, local sausages of the day with wholegrain mustard mash and red wine sauce, honey-glazed local ham with fried eggs and chips, a pie of the day, chicken breast with wild mushroom and garlic sauce, skate wing with black olive tapenade and caper butter, wild mushroom and roasted chestnut risotto, local lobster salad and puddings such as lemon posset and dark chocolate and hazelnut brownie with toffee sauce. *Benchmark main dish: slow-cooked pork belly on cider creamed spinach and bacon £13.95. Two-course evening meal £16.00.*

Enterprise ~ Lease Martin Bullock ~ Real ale ~ Open 10am-10.30pm (11 Fri-Sun) ~ Bar food 12-9.30; lighter menu 2.30-6 ~ Children welcome ~ Dogs allowed in bar ~ Wi-fi ~ Live music July, August *Recommended by Penny and Peter Keevil, B J Harding*

SHORWELL

SZ4582 Map 2

Crown

(01983) 740293 – www.crowninnshorwell.co.uk
B3323 SW of Newport; PO30 3JZ

Popular pub with an appealing streamside garden and play area, pubby food and several real ales

On the pretty south-eastern side of the island, this friendly old place is in an attractive rural setting with a peaceful tree-sheltered garden; there's a little stream that broadens into a small trout-filled pool, plenty of closely spaced picnic-sets and white garden chairs and tables on grass, and a decent children's play area. Inside, four opened-up rooms spread around a central bar with carpet, tiles or flagstones, and there's a warm welcome for all. Adnams Broadside and Ghost Ship, Goddards Fuggle-Dee-Dum and Sharps Doom Bar on handpump, 11 wines by the glass and a farm cider. The beamed, knocked-through lounge has blue and white china on an attractive carved dresser, country prints on stripped-stone walls and a winter log fire with a fancy tilework surround. Black pews form bays around tables in a stripped-stone room off to the left, with another log fire; background music and board games.

As well as sandwiches, baguettes and paninis, food includes pâté, garlic mushrooms, vegetable chilli con carne, sharing platters, a choice of pizzas, ham and egg, burgers with toppings, relish and chips, a curry of the day, sausage and mash, fish pie, and puddings. *Benchmark main dish: beer-battered fish and chips £11.95. Two-course evening meal £18.50.*

Enterprise ~ Lease Nigel and Pam Wynn ~ Real ale ~ Open 10.30 (11.30 Sun)-11 ~ Bar food 12-9.30 ~ Children welcome ~ Dogs welcome ~ Wi-fi *Recommended by Toby Jones, Martin Jones*

Also Worth a Visit in Isle of Wight

Besides the fully inspected pubs, you might like to try these pubs that have been recommended to us and described by readers. Do tell us what you think of them: feedback@goodguides.com

ARRETON   SZ5386

★**White Lion** (01983) 528479
A3056 Newport–Sandown; PO30 3AA
Old white-painted village pub refurbished under present licensees; lightened-up beamed interior, bar with stripped-wood floor and comfortable seats by log fire, Sharps Doom Bar and Timothy Taylors Landlord, several wines by the glass and good choice of well liked fairly priced food, friendly helpful staff, restaurant; children and dogs welcome, pleasant garden, open (and food) all day. *(A N Bance)*

BEMBRIDGE   SZ6488

Pilot Boat (01983) 872077
Station Road/Kings Road; PO35 5NN
Welcoming little harbourside pub shaped like a boat – even has portholes; bare-boards interior with deep red walls and log fire, good food from sandwiches to local seafood, well kept Goddards and guests, friendly efficient service; children and dogs welcome, tables out overlooking water or in pleasant courtyard behind, well placed for coast walks, five bedrooms, open all day. *(A N Bance)*

BINSTEAD   SZ5792

Fleming Arms (01983) 563415
Binstead Road; PO33 3RD Spacious roadside pub with enjoyable reasonably priced home-cooked food including Sun carvery, Greene King Abbot and Sharps Doom Bar, friendly service, conservatory; quiz, bingo and karaoke nights, darts, shove-ha'penny and pool; children and dogs welcome (they have two mastiffs), disabled access/facilities, garden with macaws Bonnie and Charlie, pétanque, open all day. *(Toby Jones)*

BONCHURCH   SZ5778

★**Bonchurch Inn** (01983) 852611
Bonchurch Shute; from A3055 E of Ventnor turn down to Old Bonchurch; opposite Leconfield Hotel; PO38 1NU
Quirky former stables with restaurant run by welcoming italian family (here since 1984); congenial bar with narrow-planked ship's decking and old-fashioned steamer-style seats, Courage ales tapped from the cask,

bar food and good italian dishes, charming helpful service, fairly basic family room, darts, shove-ha'penny and other games; background music; dogs welcome, delightful continental-feel central courtyard (parking here can be tricky), holiday flat. *(Martin Jones)*

CARISBROOKE   SZ4687

★**Blacksmiths Arms** (01983) 529263
B3401 1.5 miles W; PO30 5SS Friendly family-run hillside pub, scrubbed tables in neat beamed and flagstoned front bars, superb Solent views from airy bare-boards family dining extension, ales such as Adnams, Island and Timothy Taylors, decent wines and cider, good food including fresh fish; children, dogs and walkers welcome (Tennyson Trail nearby), terrace tables and smallish back garden with same view, play area, open all day. *(Martin Jones, Toby Jones)*

COWES   SZ4995

Duke of York (01983) 295171
Mill Hill Road; PO31 7BT Welcoming inn with popular generously served pub food including good fish and chips, well kept ales such as Goddards, lots of nautical bits and pieces; free wi-fi; bedrooms. *(Anon)*

COWES   SZ5092

★**Folly** (01983) 297171
Folly Lane signed off A3021 just S of Whippingham; PO32 6NB Glorious Medina estuary views from bar and waterside terrace of this cheery laid-back place, timbered ship-like interior with simple wood furnishings, wide range of enjoyable sensibly priced food from breakfast on (may be queues at peak times but staff cope well), Greene King, Goddards and a guest; background and live music, TV, fruit machine; children and dogs welcome, weather forecasts, long-term parking and showers for sailors, water taxi, open (and food) all day. *(D J and P M Taylor, Richard Kennell)*

COWES   SZ4996

Union (01983) 293163
Watch House Lane, in pedestrian centre; PO31 7QH Old-town inn tucked back from seafront with good value freshly made food

and well kept Fullers/Gales beers, friendly helpful young staff, cosy areas around central bar, log fire, dining room and conservatory; children and dogs welcome, tables outside, six comfortable clean bedrooms. *(John Jenkins)*

FRESHWATER
SZ3487

Red Lion (01983) 754925

Church Place; from A3055 at E end of village by Freshwater Garage mini-roundabout follow Yarmouth signpost, then take first real right turn signed to Parish Church; PO40 9BP Bay-windowed red-brick pub on quiet village street, popular with locals and visitors; ales such as Goddards Fuggle-Dee-Dum, Sharps Doom Bar and West Berkshire Good Old Boy, 11 wines by the glass and well liked blackboard food, open-plan bar with country-style furnishings on flagstones or bare boards, woodburner; under-10s at landlord's discretion, dogs welcome, a couple of picnic-sets out at front with view of church, more tables in carefully tended back garden growing own herbs and vegetables, good walking on the nearby Freshwater Way. *(John Jenkins)*

GODSHILL
SZ5281

★ **Taverners** (01983) 840707

High Street (A3020); PO38 3HZ Welcoming 17th-c pub with good seasonal food from landlord-chef, emphasis on fresh local produce (some home-grown), booking advised weekends, well kept Fullers London Pride, a house beer from Yates and a guest, plenty of wines by the glass, good friendly service, spacious bar and two front dining areas, beams, bare boards and slate floors, woodburner; children and dogs welcome in certain parts, garden with terrace and play area, own shop, limited parking, handy for the Model Village, open all day, closed Sun evening (except bank/school summer holidays). *(B J Harding, D J and P M Taylor)*

GURNARD
SZ4796

Woodvale (01983) 292037

Princes Esplanade; PO31 8LE Large 1930s inn with splendid picture-window Solent views (great sunsets), good choice of food from sandwiches and baguettes to daily specials, Fullers London Pride, Ringwood Fortyniner and a couple of guests, plenty of wines by the glass, friendly staff; weekend live music, Mon quiz; children and dogs welcome, garden with terrace and summer barbecues, five bedrooms, open all day. *(Belinda Stamp)*

HAVENSTREET
SZ5590

White Hart (01983) 883485

Off A3054 Newport–Ryde; Main Road; PO33 4DP Old red-brick village pub with good choice of popular food (all day Sun) including daily specials, Ringwood and Goddards ales, cosy log-fire bar and carpeted dining area; children and dogs welcome,

tables in secluded garden behind, open all day. *(Toby Jones)*

HULVERSTONE
SZ3984

★ **Sun** (01983) 741124

B3399; PO30 4EH Pretty thatched pub with lovely views over the Channel and picnic-sets in secluded cottagey garden looking over the sea; low-ceilinged bar with nice mix of character furniture (including a lovely old settle) on flagstones and floorboards, brick and stone walls, horsebrasses and ironwork around a woodburning stove in a brick fireplace, Goddards Ale of Wight, Otter Ale, Sharps Doom Bar and Skinners Betty Stogs on handpump and several wines by the glass; background music; traditional carpeted dining room has large windows taking in the view; dog menu and treats. *(Guy and Caroline Howard, Mungo Shipley)*

NEWCHURCH
SZ5685

★ **Pointer** (01983) 865202

High Street; PO36 0NN Well run old two-room pub by Norman church, generous helpings of good fairly priced local food including blackboard specials (booking advised in season), well kept Fullers and a guest ale, friendly service; children and dogs welcome, views from pleasant back garden, boules, open (and food) all day. *(S Holder)*

NEWPORT
SZ5089

Bargemans Rest (01983) 525828

Little London; PO30 5BS Quayside pub with spreading bare-boards interior packed with nautical memorabilia, good choice of generous reasonably priced pubby food including vegetarian and gluten-free options, Goddards, Ringwood and four guests, frequent live music; free wi-fi; children (away from bar) and dogs welcome, part-covered terrace overlooking Medina river, handy for Quay Arts Centre, open (and food) all day. *(D J and P M Taylor)*

NINGWOOD
SZ3989

★ **Horse & Groom** (01983) 760672

A3054 Newport–Yarmouth, a mile W of Shalfleet; PO30 4NW Carefully extended roomy pub liked by families; comfortable leather sofas grouped around low tables on flagstones, sturdy tables and chairs well spaced for relaxed dining, winter log fire, Ringwood Best and a couple of guests, a dozen wines by the glass, popular fair value food served by friendly staff; background music, games machine, free wi-fi, board games; dogs allowed in bar, garden with bouncy castle, crazy golf and well equipped play area, nearby walks, open all day. *(Guy and Caroline Howard, Mrs J Ekins-Daukes)*

NITON
SZ5075

★ **Buddle** (01983) 730243

St Catherine's Road, Undercliff; off A3055 just S of village, towards

St Catherine's Point; PO38 2NE Stone pub surrounded by NT land with sea views from clifftop garden; traditional bar rooms with heavy black beams, captain's chairs and wheelbacks around solid wooden tables on big flagstones or carpet, some cushioned wall seating, open fire in broad stone fireplace with massive mantelbeam, ales such as Goddards, Island, Sharps, Yates and Youngs, traditional cider and several wines by the glass, food from sandwiches to daily specials; background and regular live music, free wi-fi; children and dogs welcome, picnic-sets on stone terraces and in neatly kept sloping garden, handy for coast path, open (and food) all day. *(Edward May, William Wright)*

NORTHWOOD   SZ4983
Travellers Joy (01983) 298024
Off B3325 S of Cowes; PO31 8LS Friendly pub refurbished under present licensees; up to eight well kept ales including Island Wight Gold and Goddards Wight Squirrel (tasters offered), enjoyable reasonably priced food from sandwiches and pubby choices to daily specials, long bar with log fire, dining conservatory, pool room, Sun quiz and some live music; children, walkers and dogs welcome, garden with pétanque and play area, open (and food) all day. *(Mungo Shipley)*

SEAVIEW   SZ6291
Seaview Hotel (01983) 612711
High Street; off B3330 Ryde–Bembridge; PO34 5EX Small gently civilised but relaxed hotel, traditional wood furnishings, seafaring paraphernalia and log fire in pubby bare-boards bar, comfortable more refined front bar, well kept Goddards, Yates and a guest, good wine list including some local ones, enjoyable pub food (smaller helpings available) and more elaborate restaurant menu using produce from their farm, pleasant staff (may ask for a credit card if you run a tab); background music, TV; children welcome, dogs in bar, sea glimpses from tables on tiny front terrace, 13 bedrooms (some with sea views, seven in modern back annexe), open all day. *(Martin Jones)*

SHANKLIN   SZ5881
★ Fishermans Cottage (01983) 863882
Bottom of Shanklin Chine; PO37 6BN Thatched cottage in terrific setting tucked into the cliffs on Appley beach, steep zigzag walk down beautiful chine; spotless little rooms with low-beams, flagstones and stripped-stone walls, old local pictures,

Island and Yates beers, good value pub food including plenty of fish; background and some live music; children and dogs welcome, sun-soaked terrace overlooking sea, lovely walk to Luccombe, open all day (closed weekdays end Oct to early March). *(Adrian Johnson, Mrs Sally Scott, Colin and Maggie Fancourt)*

SHANKLIN   SZ5881
Steamer (01983) 862641
Esplanade; PO37 6BS Busy nautical-theme bar, fun for holiday families, with good range of real ales and enjoyable well priced food including local seafood and imaginative specials, cheery on-the-ball staff, live music most weekends; fine sea views from covered floodlit terrace, eight bedrooms, open all day. *(A N Bance, Colin and Maggie Fancourt)*

ST HELENS   SZ6289
Vine (01983) 872337
Upper Green Road; PO33 1UJ Victorian pub overlooking cricket green, enjoyable home-cooked food (all day Sat, Sun) including stone-baked pizzas, ales such as Island and Ringwood, cheerful helpful staff; weekend live music, quiz Weds, pool, free wi-fi; children and dogs welcome, play area across road, openall day. *(Mungo Shipley)*

VENTNOR   SZ5677
Perks (01983) 857446
High Street; PO38 1LT Little bar packed with interesting memorabilia behind shop-window front, well kept ales including Bass, good range of wines, popular well priced home-made food from sandwiches and baked potatoes up, bargain OAP two-course lunch, fast friendly service. *(Anon)*

VENTNOR   SZ5677
★ Spyglass (01983) 855338
Esplanade, SW end; road down is very steep and twisty, and parking nearby can be difficult – best to use pay-and-display (free in winter) about 100 metres up the road; PO38 1JX Perched above the beach with a fascinating jumble of seafaring memorabilia in snug quarry-tiled interior, Ringwood ales and guests, popular food including fish dishes (well filled crab sandwiches), friendly helpful service; background music, live bands daily in summer (Weds-Sun winter); children welcome, dogs in bar, sea-wall terrace with lovely views, coast walk towards the Botanic Garden, heftier hikes on to St Boniface Down and towards the eerie shell of Appuldurcombe House,

---

'Children welcome' means the pub says it lets children inside without any special restriction. If it allows them in, but to restricted areas such as an eating area or family room, we specify this. Places with separate restaurants often let children use them, and hotels usually let children into public areas such as lounges. Some pubs impose an evening time limit – let us know if you find one earlier than 9pm.

bedrooms, open all day. *(Adrian Johnson, D J and P M Taylor, Colin and Maggie Fancourt)*

WHITWELL   SZ5277

White Horse (01983) 730375

High Street; PO38 2PY Popular extended old pub (dates from 1454) redecorated under new management, enjoyable good value food from pub staples to daily specials, well kept ales such as Goddards, Ringwood and Yates, good friendly service, carpeted beamed bar with exposed stonework, restaurant; Mon quiz, darts and pool; children and dogs welcome, picnic-sets among fruit trees in big garden with play area, open all day (food all day weekends). *(Guy and Caroline Howard)*

YARMOUTH   SZ3589

Bugle (01983) 760272

The Square; PO41 0NS Old coaching inn with long frontage, several linked areas including low-ceilinged panelled lounge and restaurant, generous helpings of enjoyable pub food (all day summer, all day weekends winter), ales such as Bass, Brakspears, Timothy Taylors and Wadworths, quick cheerful service, nautical-theme bar, conservatory; background and weekend live music; children and dogs welcome, courtyard garden with lots of hanging baskets, seven bedrooms, handy for ferry, open all day. *(Richard Kennell)*

YARMOUTH   SZ3589

Wheatsheaf (01983) 760456

Bridge Road, near ferry; PO41 0PH Modernised opened-up Victorian pub with good well priced food including nice burgers, cheerful service, Goddards, Ringwood and a guest, glazed extension; children and dogs welcome, handy for the harbour, open (and food) all day. *(Mungo Shipley)*

Kent

BIDBOROUGH
TQ5643 Map 3

Kentish Hare ♀

(01892) 525709 – www.thekentishhare.com

Bidborough Ridge; TN3 0XB

Plenty of drinking and dining space in well run pub with local ales, good wines, enjoyable food and attentive staff

We were delighted when this bustling pub reopened as it's not too far from our office. Smartened up both inside and out, it has plenty of room for drinkers and diners and an easy-going atmosphere. The main bar has leather armchairs grouped around an open fire with antlers above, some unusual stools made of corks, bookcase wallpaper and carved stools against the counter where they keep a beer named for them from Tonbridge, Harveys Best and a changing guest on handpump, 27 wines by the glass, cocktails and a farm cider; staff are friendly and efficient. A cosy middle room has a modern two-way woodburner at one end with leather sofas and armchairs beside it, old photographs of the pub, local people and the area, lamps made from fire extinguishers and wallpaper depicting old leather suitcases. On the other side of the woodburner is a second bar, with attractive chunky wooden chairs and cushioned settles around various tables on wide dark floorboards – some in small booths. The airy back restaurant is similarly furnished with industrial-style lights hanging from painted joists, pots of fresh flowers and candles, exposed brick walls and an open kitchen. A decked terrace with contemporary tables and chairs overlooks a lower terrace with picnic-sets.

As well as a two- and three-course set menu, the interesting food includes crispy pork fritters with goats cheese cream, scallops with pine nuts, golden raisins and curry oil, local sausages with onion gravy, steak burger with toppings, coleslaw and fries, beer-battered fish and chips, duck breast with orange and caramel glaze, turnips and pommes anna, guinea fowl with confit leg, girolles, braised lentils and cream sauce, and puddings such as vanilla cheesecake with gin and tonic sorbet and chocolate Rolo with caramel liquid centre, salted popcorn and milk sorbet. *Benchmark main dish: pork belly, braised cheek, cauliflower, pickled mushrooms and goats cheese fondue £17.95. Two-course evening meal £24.00.*

Free house ~ Licensees Chris and James Tanner ~ Real ale ~ Open 11-3, 5-11; 11-11 Sat; 11-4 Sun; closed Sun evening, Mon, first week Jan ~ Bar food 12-2.30, 6-9.30; 12-3 Sun ~ Restaurant ~ Children welcome ~ Dogs allowed in bar ~ Wi-fi *Recommended by Nigel and Jean Eames, Edward May*

BIDDENDEN
Three Chimneys

TQ8238 Map 3

(01580) 291472 – www.thethreechimneys.co.uk

Off A262 at pub sign, a mile W of village; TN27 8LW

Pubby beamed rooms of considerable individuality, log fires, imaginative food and big, pretty garden; bedrooms

---

This is a lovely old pub with a civilised but informal atmosphere and just the place for lunch after visiting nearby Sissinghurst gardens (National Trust). The small low-beamed rooms have plenty of character – they're simply done out with plain wooden furniture and old settles on flagstones and coir matting, some harness and sporting prints on the stripped-brick walls and good log fires. The public bar on the left is quite down to earth, with darts, dominoes and cribbage. Well trained, attentive staff serve Adnams Southwold, Old Dairy Blue Top, Harveys Best and a guest ale tapped from the cask, 15 wines by the glass, local Biddenden cider and 13 malt whiskies. A candlelit bare-boards restaurant has rustic décor and french windows that open into a conservatory; seats in the pretty garden. By the time this guide is published, there will be two new bedrooms in a separate building.

Using the best local, seasonal produce, the highly thought-of food includes ploughman's, salmon and smoked haddock fishcakes with tartare sauce, deep-fried brie with cumberland sauce, pork and sage sausages with mash and a port and red onion gravy, herb and pine nut pesto on potato wedge-topped couscous with grilled goats cheese, roasted vegetables and tomato sauce, rump of lamb with roasted butternut squash, dauphinoise potatoes and rich jus, sweet chilli-glazed salmon fillet with roasted sweet potatoes and spicy courgette and aubergine ragout, and puddings such as dark chocolate marquise with pistachio ice-cream and sticky toffee pudding. *Benchmark main dish: smoked haddock on creamed leeks with chive velouté £18.950. Two-course evening meal £20.00.*

Free house ~ Licensee Craig Smith ~ Real ale ~ Open 11.30-11; 12-11 Sun ~ Bar food 12-2.30, 6-9; 12-4, 6-9.30 weekends; lighter dishes all day ~ Restaurant ~ Children welcome ~ Dogs allowed in bar ~ Bedrooms: /£120 *Recommended by John Evans, Martin and Sue Day, S F Parrinder, Richard Kennell, Alan Cowell*

CHIDDINGSTONE CAUSEWAY
Little Brown Jug

TQ5146 Map 3

(01892) 870318 – www.thelittlebrownjug.co.uk

B2027; TN11 8JJ

Bustling pub with interconnected bar and dining rooms, lots to look at, open fires, five real ales and enjoyable food; seats outside

---

Handy for Penshurst station, this is a friendly pub in rolling countryside. The beamed front bar has rugs on wood or tiled floors, a roaring log fire, leather chesterfield sofas and chunky stools in one corner and high chairs against the carved counter where they keep Belhaven Grand Slam, Greene King Abbot, Larkins Traditional and Sharps Cornish Coaster on handpump and good wines by the glass; background music. Throughout, various dining areas merge together with open doorways and timbering, more open fires, hundreds of prints, framed old cigarette cards, maps and photos on painted walls, books on shelves, houseplants, old stone bottles and candles on window sills, big mirrors and all manner of cushioned wooden dining chairs, wall seats and settles with scatter cushions and polished dark wood or rustic tables. The garden has seats and tables on a terrace, picnic-sets on grass, several 'dining huts' (bookable in advance for £25) and a children's play area.

Quite a choice of good food includes sandwiches, devilled lamb kidneys and bacon, breaded camembert wedges with cumberland sauce, chicken caesar salad, ham and free-range eggs, butternut squash and sage risotto, chilli king prawn spaghetti, half shoulder of lamb in honey and mustard marinade with dauphinoise potatoes and rosemary and redcurrant sauce, beef stroganoff, and puddings such as chocolate brownie with chocolate sauce and sticky toffee pudding with honeycomb ice-cream. *Benchmark main dish: beer-battered fish and chips £12.95. Two-course evening meal £18.95.*

Whiting & Hammond ~ Lease Jan Webb ~ Real ale ~ Open 10am-11pm; 9am-midnight Fri, Sat; 9am-11pm Sun ~ Bar food 12 (9am Fri, Sat)-9.30pm; 9-9 Sun ~ Children welcome ~ Dogs allowed in bar ~ Wi-fi *Recommended by Mike Swan, Emma Scofield, Peter Meister*

CHIPSTEAD
TQ5056 Map 3

George & Dragon 🌟 💷 ♔

(01732) 779019 – www.georgeanddragonchipstead.com

Near M25 junction 5; TN13 2RW

Excellent food in popular village dining pub with three real ales, friendly, efficient service and seats in garden

There's always a good mix of both diners and drinkers in this particularly well run, 16th-c village pub and a warm welcome for all. The opened-up bar has heavy black beams and standing timbers, grey-green panelling, framed articles on the walls about their suppliers, and an easy-going, friendly atmosphere. In the centre, a comfortable sofa and table sit in front of a log fire, with a tiny alcove to one side housing a built-in wall seat and just one table and chair. Westerham Grasshopper and Georges Marvellous Medicine and a weekly changing guest beer on handpump and 21 wines by the glass. Up a step to each side are two small dining areas with more panelling, an attractive assortment of nice old chairs around various tables on bare floorboards and two more (unused) fireplaces. Upstairs is a sizeable timbered dining room with similar furnishings and a cosy room that's just right for a private party. The back garden has benches, modern chrome and wicker chairs and tables under parasols, and raised beds for flowers, herbs and vegetables.

 Taking great care with sourcing their produce, the highly rewarding food includes sandwiches, shredded beef and soft herb pastry roll with horseradish and crème fraîche, a changing terrine with fruit chutney, lunchtime deli boards, wild boar burger with smoked cheese and chips, sweet potato, chickpea and spinach curry with pomegranate and coriander quinoa, chicken suprême stuffed with gorgonzola and wrapped in bacon, chargrilled mackerel with mustard seed crushed new potatoes, venison haunch with celeriac and potato gratin, and puddings such as honey and walnut tart with clotted cream ice-cream and rosewater panna cotta with raspberry sorbet. *Benchmark main dish: slow-cooked pork belly with apple sauce £14.25. Two-course evening meal £20.00.*

Free house ~ Licensee Ben James ~ Real ale ~ Open 11-11 ~ Bar food 12-3 (4 weekends), 6-9.30 (8.30 Sun) ~ Restaurant ~ Children welcome ~ Dogs allowed in bar ~ Wi-fi *Recommended by Colin McLachlan, Gordon and Margaret Ormondroyd, Jörg Kasprowski, Tina and David Woods-Taylor, Mrs Margo Finlay, Dave Braisted*

GOUDHURST
TQ7037 Map 3

Green Cross

(01580) 211200 – www.greencrossinn.co.uk

East off A21 on to A262 (Station Road); TN17 1HA

Down-to-earth bar with real ales and more formal back restaurant

The marvellous fish and shellfish is what draws most customers to this bustling place, but the little two-roomed front bar is properly pubby and easy-going. There are stripped-wood floors, dark wood furnishings, wine bottles on window sills, hop-draped beams, brass jugs on the mantelshelf above the fire, and a few plush bar stools by the counter; background music. Harveys Best and half a dozen wines by the glass. Attractive in an old-fashioned sort of way, the back dining room is a little more formal with flowers on tables, dark beams in cream walls and country paintings for sale. You can sit out on a small terrace at the side of the pub.

Fine food includes potted brown shrimps, moules marinière, bass fillets with spring onion, ginger, soy sauce and white wine, cornish cock crab, skate wing with black butter and capers, and king scallops with creamy gratin sauce, mushrooms, shallots and white wine; non-fishy choices include filled baguettes, home-cooked ham and eggs, sausages and mash with onion gravy, rib-eye steak, and puddings such as chocolate tart with chocolate sauce and lemon chiffon. *Benchmark main dish: avocado and crab bake £9.05. Two-course evening meal £25.00.*

Free house ~ Licensees Lou and Caroline Lizzi ~ Real ale ~ Open 12-3, 6-11; closed Sun evening ~ Bar food 12-2.30, 7-9.30 ~ Restaurant ~ Children welcome ~ Wi-fi
Recommended by Harvey Brown, Emma Scofield

IVY HATCH   TQ5854   Map 3
Plough 🌟 ♀
(01732) 810100 – www.theploughivyhatch.co.uk
High Cross Road; village signed off A227 N of Tonbridge; TN15 0NL

Kent Dining Pub of the Year

Country pub with first class food, real ales and seats in landscaped garden

After a visit to nearby Ightham Mote (National Trust) this tile-hung village pub is the perfect place for lunch. The various rooms have light wooden floors, leather chesterfields grouped around an open fire, quite a mix of cushioned dining chairs around assorted tables, and high bar chairs by the wooden-topped bar counter where they keep Old Dairy Red Top, Tonbridge Blonde Ambition and Ringwood Best on handpump, 12 wines by the glass and farm cider. There's also a conservatory; background music and board games. Seats in the landscaped garden are surrounded by cob trees; pétanque. There are rewarding walks all around, through woodland and along the greensand escarpment near One Tree Hill.

As well as weekday breakfasts, the creative food cooked by the landlord and his team includes sandwiches, venison carpaccio with balsamic and parmesan, braised pig cheeks with parsnip purée and crispy bacon, confit duck salad with pomegranate, bulgar wheat and broccoli, rocket and orange, a charcuterie and a fish board, smoked haddock, salmon and grey mullet fish pie, wild boar and apple sausages with red onion marmalade, a mixed grill with bone marrow and red wine jus, and puddings such as tiramisu and chocolate fondant with vanilla yoghurt and chocolate sauce. *Benchmark main dish: burger in home-made brioche bun with coleslaw, barbecue sauce and rustic chips £10.00. Two-course evening meal £22.00.*

Free house ~ Licensee Miles Medes ~ Real ale ~ Open 9-3, 6-11; 10am-11pm Sat; 10-6 Sun ~ Bar food 12-2.45, 6-9.30; 12-5.30 Sun; breakfast 9-12 weekdays ~ Restaurant ~ Children welcome ~ Wi-fi *Recommended by Bob and Margaret Holder*

It's very helpful if you let us know up-to-date food prices when you report on pubs.

LANGTON GREEN TQ5439 Map 3

Hare ⭐ �

(01892) 862419 – www.brunningandprice.co.uk/hare
A264 W of Tunbridge Wells; TN3 0JA

**Interestingly decorated Edwardian pub with a fine choice of drinks
and imaginative, brasserie-style food**

Always deservedly busy, this is a well run mock-Tudor pub with a good
mix of cheerful customers. The high-ceilinged rooms are light and airy,
with dark dados below pale-painted walls covered in old photographs and
prints, 1930s-style oak furniture, light brown carpet and turkish-style rugs
on bare boards, old romantic pastels and a huge collection of chamber-pots
hanging from beams. Greene King Abbot, IPA and Morlands Old Speckled
Hen, Robinsons Trooper and Thornbridge Wild Swan on handpump, 30 wines
by the glass, 75 malt whiskies, 25 gins and a farm cider; background music
and board games. French windows open on to a big terrace with pleasant
views of the tree-ringed village green. Parking in front of the pub is limited
but you can park in the lane to one side.

Highly popular food includes sandwiches, crispy duck salad with hoisin,
watermelon and chilli, scallops with pea purée, crispy parmesan and caper and
herb dressing, platters, king prawn and chorizo linguine, thai green vegetable curry,
beer-battered haddock and chips, chicken, leek and ham pie, steak burger topped with
bacon and cheddar with coleslaw and chips, and puddings such as sticky toffee pudding
with toffee sauce and white chocolate and honeycomb cheesecake. *Benchmark main
dish: shoulder of lamb with dauphinoise potatoes and mint jus £16.95. Two-course
evening meal £21.00.*

Brunning & Price ~ Manager Tina Foster ~ Real ale ~ Open 11 (12 Mon)-11; 11am-midnight
Fri, Sat; 11-10.30 Sun ~ Bar food 12-9.30 (10 Fri, Sat, 9 Sun) ~ Restaurant ~ Children
welcome ~ Dogs allowed in bar ~ Wi-fi *Recommended by Gerry and Rosemary Dobson,
Mrs J Ekins-Dauke*

MATFIELD TQ6541 Map 3

Wheelwrights Arms ⭐ ♢ 🍺

(01892) 722129
The Green; TN12 7JX

**Cosy, character village pub with friendly staff, good food cooked
by the landlord, around seven real ales and decent wines and seats
on front terrace**

On our Sunday lunchtime visit, this attractive weatherboarded pub on
the edge of a village green and run by an enthusiastic, hard-working
young couple was buzzing. A group of cheerful locals had gathered at leather
armchairs in front of the woodburning stove, with more people around large
circular tables to one side. There are hop-strung beams, traditional dark
pubby tables and chairs on bare floorboards (one bench has a half wheel as
its back) and church candles. Brains Revd James, Larkins Traditional, Nelson
Friggin in the Riggin, Tonbridge Union Pale, Wells Bombardier Burning Gold,
Westerham British Bulldog BB and Summer Perle and Whitstable Oyster
Stout on handpump and a dozen good wines by the glass; helpful, courteous
service. The dining room leads off the bar with a decorative woodburner
in an inglenook fireplace, horse-tack, old soda siphons and other knick-
knacks dotted about, and some old photos of the pub and village along with
cricketing prints and cartoons on the walls. At the front are hanging baskets
and modern seats and tables.

Cooked by the landlord using the best local, seasonal produce and making their own bread, butter and preserves, the beautifully presented, rather special food includes lunchtime sandwiches, beetroot-cured salmon with roe, pickled cucumber, baby beetroots and rémoulade sauce, ballotine of chicken thigh with confit shank, seared breast, charred onion and crispy ratté potatoes, crumbed plaice with cockles, brown shrimps, chorizo and sea greens on linguine with paprika oil, and puddings such as rhubarb millefeuille with rhubarb and stem ginger ice-cream and ginger nut biscuit crumbs and dark chocolate brownie with salted caramel panna cotta, white chocolate parfait, milk sorbet and honeycomb. *Benchmark main dish: lamb three-ways with wild garlic, bombay potatoes, mint and chilli yoghurt £19.75. Two-course evening meal £22.00.*

Free house ~ Licensees Rob and Gem Marshall ~ Real ale ~ Open 12-11 (4-10 Mon); 12-9 Sun ~ Bar food 12-2.30, 6.30-9; 12-4 Sun; not Sun evening, Mon ~ Restaurant ~ Well behaved children welcome ~ Dogs allowed in bar ~ Wi-fi *Recommended by Sara Price, Mrs Ruth Lewis*

MEOPHAM   TQ6364 Map 3

Cricketers

(01474) 812163 – www.thecricketersinn.co.uk
Wrotham Road (A227); DA13 0QA

Popular village pub with friendly, chatty staff, plenty to look at in connected rooms, several real ales, good wines and well thought-of food

Cheerfully busy on our Sunday lunchtime visit, this is an attractively set country pub opposite the village green. Inside, the bar has cushioned wall settles, a medley of old-style wooden dining chairs and tables, a raised fireplace, newspapers to read and Bexley Bob, Sharps Doom Bar and a guest ale on handpump and around a dozen wines by the glass. Glass partitioning separates an end room with bookshelves either side of another fireplace, rugs on bare floorboards and big house plants. Down steps to one side of the bar is a sizeable dining room with another raised fireplace and similar chairs and tables on more rugs and boards. Throughout, there are frame-to-frame photos, prints and paintings on the walls, and church candles on each table; background music. A family room at the end has dark floor slates and doors that open to sizeable seating areas with contemporary black rattan-style seats under parasols overlooking a windmill; there are a few seats out in front too.

Tasty food includes sandwiches, mussels in cider and cream, tempura confit pork belly with quail egg, pickled cucumber and crackling, fried halloumi with tomatoes and caper and sage dressing, seafood tagliatelle, pork and leek sausages with mash and red wine and onion gravy, beer-battered cod and chips, calves liver with crispy pancetta and light mustard cream sauce, and puddings such as orange-scented honey cheesecake with vanilla syrup and strawberry millefeuille. *Benchmark main dish: half shoulder of lamb in honey and mustard marinade with rosemary and red wine sauce £18.95. Two-course evening meal £21.00.*

Whiting & Hammond ~ Manager Scott Hawkes ~ Real ale ~ Open 9am-11pm (midnight Fri, Sat) ~ Children welcome ~ Dogs allowed in bar ~ Wi-fi *Recommended by Tina and David Woods-Taylor, Gordon and Margaret Ormondroyd*

PENSHURST   TQ5142 Map 3

Bottle House

(01892) 870306 – www.thebottlehouseinnpenshurst.co.uk
Coldharbour Lane; leaving Penshurst SW on B2188 turn right at Smarts Hill signpost, then bear right towards Chiddingstone and Cowden; keep straight on; TN11 8ET

Country pub with friendly service, chatty atmosphere, real ales, decent wines, popular bar food and sunny terrace; nearby walks

The high standards here are held up year after year and our readers thoroughly enjoy their visits. It's a cottagey place with all sorts of joists and beams (a couple of particularly low ones are leather padded) and the open-plan rooms are split into cosy areas by numerous standing timbers. Pine wall boards and bar stools are ranged along the timber-clad copper-topped counter where they keep Harveys Best and Larkins Traditional on handpump and 19 wines by the glass from a good list. There's also a hotchpotch of wooden tables (fresh flowers and candles), fairly closely spaced chairs on dark boards or coir, a woodburning stove and photographs of the pub and local scenes; background music. Some of the walls are of stripped stone. The sunny, brick-paved terrace has teak chairs and tables under parasols, and olive trees in white pots; parking is limited. Good surrounding walks in this charming area of rolling country.

 Enjoyable food includes sandwiches, whitebait with smoked paprika and chive mayonnaise, fig, pear and blue cheese salad, chestnut and oyster mushroom carbonara, cottage pie topped with mustard mash, burger with toppings, chutney and skinny fries, smoked haddock florentine with a poached egg and cheese sauce, thai red monkfish, salmon and king prawn curry, pheasant breast in bacon en croûte with red wine and thyme reduction, and puddings such as pineapple and rum panna cotta and baked Nutella cheesecake with caramel sauce. *Benchmark main dish: pork belly with black pudding dauphinoise, creamed cabbage and bacon and pear cider sauce £15.50. Two-course evening meal £19.00.*

Free house ~ Licensee Paul Hammond ~ Real ale ~ Open 11-11; 12-10.30 Sun ~ Bar food 12-10 (9 Sun) ~ Restaurant ~ Children welcome ~ Dogs allowed in bar
Recommended by Christian Mole, Brian Dawes, Bob and Margaret Holder, Martin and Sue Day, Richard Kennell, Tina and David Woods-Taylor

PENSHURST
Leicester Arms 🛏

TQ5243 Map 3

(01892) 871617 – www.theleicesterarmshotel.com
High Street; TN11 8BT

Refurbished old inn in centre of lovely village with plenty of space in bars and dining rooms, local ales, good food and friendly staff; comfortable bedrooms

After visiting nearby Penshurst Place, this refurbished inn is just the place for lunch. The beamed and timbered bar rooms are to the right of the entrance hall; our favourite is the middle room. Here, there's a roaring fire in an open woodburner (two armchairs in front), an attractive mix of cushioned wooden dining chairs around dark tables, a lovely, wonky brick floor and, on the walls, a vast ornate gilt mirror and arty twisted vine stems (it sounds unusual but looks most attractive). From here steps lead up to an airy dining room with half panelling and contemporary paintwork, bookshelf wallpaper, similar tables and chairs on rugs and wooden flooring and big windows. The front bar has a second open woodburning stove (our dog was quick to plonk himself in front of it on a bitterly cold day), button-back wall seating and traditional seats and tables on wide floorboards, church candles and fresh flowers, lots of suspended saddles and horsey wallpaper; background pop music. Some bar chairs against the heavy wooden counter where they keep Harveys Best and local Larkins Traditional on handpump and several wines by the glass. To the left of the entrance hall is a purple-painted and panelled, more formal restaurant. The bedrooms are comfortable (some are four-poster) and some look over to the rather fine village church.

🍴 Good, popular food includes lunchtime sandwiches, scallops with boudin noir and apple and chive butter, chicken liver and foie gras parfait with orange brioche, butternut squash risotto with parmesan crisp, beer-battered fish and chips, pork fillet with pancetta, mushrooms, truffle mash and madeira cream, monkfish, crayfish and lobster ravioli with chervil cream, duck breast with red onion tart and kirsch cherries, and puddings such as sticky toffee pudding with cobnut ice-cream and crème brûlée with fruit compote. *Benchmark main dish: steak burger with tomato salsa, aioli and skinny chips £12.50. Two-course evening meal £20.00.*

Free house ~ Licensee Richard Barrett ~ Real ale ~ Open 9am-11pm (midnight Sat); 10am-10.30pm Sun ~ Bar food 12-3, 6.30-9.30; 12-4 Sun ~ Restaurant ~ Children welcome ~ Dogs allowed in bar and bedrooms ~ Wi-fi ~ Bedrooms: £75/£85 *Recommended by Isobel Mackinlay, Edward May*

PENSHURST   TQ5241 Map 3
Spotted Dog
(01892) 870253 – www.spotteddogpub.co.uk

Smarts Hill, off B2188 S; TN11 8EP

Charming old pub with character bars, four real ales, popular food and seats in front and back terraced gardens

In warm weather, the terraced seating areas on several levels to the front and at the back of this quaint old weatherboarded pub are much prized, so it's best to arrive early; the view from the back stretches over miles of lush countryside. First licensed in 1520, the pub has plenty of signs of age inside, with heavy low beams and timbers, attractive moulded panelling and a big inglenook fireplace, and throughout there are hops, horsebrasses, mirrors and lots of country pictures; furnishings are traditional and on bare boards or carpet. Harveys Best, Larkins Traditional, Tonbridge Blonde Ambition and Youngs Bitter on handpump and several wines by the glass.

🍴 Popular food includes sandwiches, tempura prawns with chilli dip, chicken liver parfait with plum sauce, sharing boards, home-cooked ham and free-range eggs, a curry and a pie of the day, wild mushroom stroganoff, burger with toppings, coleslaw and chips, chicken and chorizo tagliatelle, bass fillets in garlic butter with sauté potatoes, and puddings. *Benchmark main dish: local sausages with mash and onion gravy £10.95. Two-course evening meal £18.00.*

Free house ~ Licensees Louise and Nigel Hunt ~ Real ale ~ Open 11.30-11.30 (10 Sun) ~ Bar food 12-2.30 (3.30 weekends), 6-9; not Sun evening ~ Restaurant ~ Children welcome ~ Dogs allowed in bar ~ Wi-fi *Recommended by Mrs T A Bizat, Mrs J Ekins-Daukes*

PLUCKLEY   TQ9243 Map 3
Dering Arms 🍴★ ♀ ⇔
(01233) 840371 – www.deringarms.com

Pluckley station, which is signposted from B2077; or follow Station Road (left turn off Smarden Road in centre of Pluckley) for about 1.3 miles S, through Pluckley Thorne; TN27 0RR

Handsome building with stylish main bar, carefully chosen wines, three ales, good fish dishes and roaring log fire; comfortable bedrooms

Originally built as a hunting lodge on the Dering Estate, this is a striking building with an imposing frontage, mullioned arched windows and dutch gables. The high-ceilinged, stylishly plain main bar has a solid country feel with a variety of wooden furniture on the flagstones, a roaring log fire in a great fireplace, country prints and some fishing rods. The smaller half-panelled back bar has similar dark wood furnishings, plus an extension with a woodburning stove, comfortable armchairs, sofas and a grand piano; board games. Goachers Gold Star and a beer named for the pub from Goachers on handpump, 11 good wines by the glass from a fine list, 30 malt whiskies and 20 cognacs. Classic car meetings (the landlord James has a couple of classic motors) are held here on the second Sunday of the month. Readers very much enjoy staying here – and the breakfasts are good.

 Majoring on local fish and using home-grown herbs, the food includes oysters, provençale fish soup, skate wing with caper butter, lobster with garlic and cognac and a hot and cold fruit de mer platter; also, duck rillettes with orange vinaigrette, confit duck with bubble and squeak potato cake and wild mushroom sauce, venison steak with potato and celeriac purée and port sauce, and puddings such as banana and vanilla ice-cream pancake and tiramisu parfait with coffee sauce. *Benchmark main dish: monkfish, bacon and orange sauce £14.95. Two-course evening meal £27.00.*

Free house ~ Licensee James Buss ~ Real ale ~ Open 11.30 (11 Sat)-3.30, 6-11; 12-4 Sun ~ Bar food 12-2.30, 6.30-9; 12-4 Sun; not Sun evening, Mon ~ Restaurant ~ Children welcome ~ Dogs allowed in bar ~ Wi-fi ~ Bedrooms: £85/£95 *Recommended by Isobel Mackinlay*

SEVENOAKS
TQ5055 Map 3
Kings Head ♀
(01732) 452081 ~ www.kingsheadbesselsgreen.co.uk
Bessels Green; A25 W, just off A21; TN13 2QA

Bustling pub by village green, with open-plan character rooms, lots to look at, quite a choice of ales, good, popular food and seats in garden

Although most customers are here to enjoy the good food, this busy village-green pub does have a little bar with black and white floor tiles and stools against the counter (used by cheerful locals on our visit): Bombardier Burning Gold, Fullers London Pride, Larkins Traditional, Sharps Doom Bar and Tonbridge Coppernob on handpump and a dozen wines by the glass served by smiling, helpful young staff. An attractive small room with a two-way open fire leading off here is dog-friendly. Spreading dining areas fan out from the bar with a wide mix of cushioned dining chairs, button-back wall seats and settles with scatter cushions around rustic or dark wooden tables, bare board or tile floors, open fires, frame-to-frame prints, old photos and maps on painted walls, house plants, church candles and old bottles on window sills and bookshelves; background music. Teak tables and chairs on a terrace, picnic-sets on grass and one or two circular 'dining huts' (you can pre-book them for £25).

Rewarding food includes sandwiches, grilled sardines with tomato, black olive and onion salsa, whole baked camembert with confit garlic and rosemary and white onion and cranberry chutney, butternut squash risotto with parmesan, chicken burger with piri-piri sauce, mayonnaise and skinny fries, pork and chorizo, toulouse and merguez sausages in tomato, pasta with pancetta and basil sauce, beef stroganoff, and puddings such as triple chocolate brownie with chocolate sauce and a rocky road sharing board. *Benchmark main dish: half shoulder of lamb with rosemary and red wine sauce and dauphinoise potatoes £16.95. Two-course evening meal £21.00.*

Whiting & Hammond ~ Manager Paul Rosser ~ Real ale ~ Open 11-11 (midnight Sat); 11-10.30 Sun ~ Bar food 12-9.30 (9 Sun); 9-11.30am breakfast weekends ~ Children welcome ~ Dogs allowed in bar ~ Wi-fi *Recommended by Gordon and Margaret Ormondroyd*

All Guide inspections are anonymous. Anyone claiming to be a *Good Pub Guide* inspector is a fraud. Please let us know.

SEVENOAKS TQ5352 Map 3

White Hart 🍽 ♀

(01732) 452022 – www.brunningandprice.co.uk/whitehart
Tonbridge Road (A225 S, past Knole); TN13 1SG

**Well run and civilised coaching inn with many interesting rooms,
a thoughtful choice of drinks and food, and friendly, helpful staff**

There's plenty of character and an easy-going civilised feel to this carefully renovated coaching inn. Open doorways and steps connect the many rooms with open fires and woodburning stoves. All manner of nice wooden dining chairs around tables of every size sit on rugs or bare floorboards, cream walls are hung with lots of prints and old photographs (many of local scenes or schools) and there are fresh flowers and plants, daily papers, board games and plenty of chatty, cheerful customers. Phoenix Brunning & Price Original and Old Dairy Blue Top plus guests from breweries such as Empire, Harveys, Timothy Taylors, Tonbridge and Westerham on handpump, 20 good wines by the glass, 50 malt whiskies and a farm cider. At the front of the building there are picnic-sets under parasols, with wooden benches and chairs around tables under more parasols on the back terrace.

 The seasonal menu delivers good, modern pub dishes: cured salmon with wasabi cream, soy jelly and pickled ginger, pork, onion and sage terrine with sticky apple and crackling, bubble and squeak cake, home-baked beans and a fried duck egg, parmesan and pine nut gnocchi on mediterranean vegetables with basil pesto, rabbit and mixed mushroom stew with black pudding and olive oil mash, southern french bouillabaisse with chargrilled squid, chilli croutons and rouille, and puddings such as bread and butter pudding with apricot sauce and crème brûlée. *Benchmark main dish: lamb rump with white bean purée, tarragon rösti and tomato jus £18.95. Two-course evening meal £21.50.*

Brunning & Price ~ Manager Chris Little ~ Real ale ~ Open 12-11 (10.30 Sun) ~ Bar food 12-10 (9 Sun) ~ Children welcome away from bar until 7pm ~ Dogs allowed in bar ~ Wi-fi
Recommended by Gordon and Margaret Ormondroyd, Alan Cowell, Martin and Sue Day, Colin McLachlan, B J Harding, B and M Kendall

SHIPBOURNE TQ5952 Map 3

Chaser ♀

(01732) 810360 – www.thechaser.co.uk
Stumble Hill (A227 N of Tonbridge); TN11 9PE

**Busy country pub with lots to look at in rambling rooms, log fires,
good choice of drinks, enjoyable food and seats outside**

At weekends particularly, you need to book a table in advance in the comfortably opened-up and civilised bar and dining areas here; by 12.30 on our Sunday lunchtime visit, the place was packed to the gunnels – but the friendly young staff remained efficient and courteous. The rooms meander into one another with the serving counter at the centre: stripped wooden floors, frame-to-frame pictures, maps and old photos on the walls above pine wainscoting, house plants and antique glass bottles on window sills, several roaring log fires, shelves of books and an eclectic mix of solid wood tables (each set with a church candle) surrounded by prettily cushioned dining chairs. Butcombe Bitter, Larkins Traditional, Thornbridge Wild Swan, Thwaites Original and a couple of guest ales on handpump and good wines by the glass; background music. A striking, school chapel-like room at the back has wooden panelling and a high, timber-vaulted ceiling. French windows open on to an enclosed central courtyard with wicker-style tables and chairs on large flagstones and plants in wall pots; this has a woodburning stove and is covered in winter, creating extra family dining space. A side garden with hedges and shrubs has picnic-sets and is overlooked by the church. There's a small car park at the back or you can park in the lane opposite by the green-cum-common; local walks.

🍴 Very highly thought-of food includes sandwiches (until 6.30), pigeon breast with warm bacon, wild mushroom and pine nut salad and red wine vinaigrette, ham hock terrine with piccalilli, vegetable tagine with spicy couscous, beer-battered cod and chips, corned beef hash with sauté potatoes, grain mustard sauce and a duck egg, cajun chicken with coleslaw and sweet potato fries, cod with clam, prawn and pea risotto and lemon beurre blanc, and puddings such as banoffi pie with honeycomb and chocolate sauce and orange and Cointreau crème brûlée. *Benchmark main dish: shoulder of lamb with dauphinoise potatoes and rosemary and red wine sauce £19.95. Two-course evening meal £21.00.*

Whiting & Hammond ~ Manager Craig White ~ Real ale ~ Open 10.30am-11pm; 9am-midnight (10.30 Sun) Sat ~ Bar food 12-9.30 (9 Sun); 9-11.30am breakfast weekends ~ Children welcome ~ Dogs allowed in bar ~ Wi-fi *Recommended by Tina and David Woods-Taylor*

SISSINGHURST
Milk House 🏅 ⌂

TQ7937 Map 3

(01580) 720200 – www.themilkhouse.co.uk
The Street; TN17 2JG

Bustling village inn of character with well kept ales, enjoyable food and seats in big garden; restful bedrooms

From the notable entrance hall, turn right for the companiable bar which is relaxed and friendly with grey-painted beams, grey plush sofas facing one another across a simple table in front of a handsome Tudor fireplace and candles in hurricane jars; unusual touches include the book mural wallpaper, milk churns on window sills, wickerwork used on the bar counter and for lampshades, and a wire cow. Daily papers, board games and background music. Harveys Best, Old Dairy Red Top and a guest from Westerham on handpump, 15 wines by the glass and several malt whiskies, all served by friendly, helpful staff. The restaurant to the left is similarly furnished and there's also a small room leading off, just right for a private party. A large terrace outside the bar has sturdy tables and chairs under green parasols, there's an outdoor pizza and flatbread oven and picnic-sets and a children's play hut beside a fenced-in pond. The bedrooms are comfortable and well equipped and the breakfasts very good. Historic Sissinghurst Castle (National Trust) and its beautiful gardens are close by.

🏅 Well thought-of, interesting food includes smoked duck with potato galette, chicory and orange salad and mandarin oil, onion and shallot tart with a pine nut and parmesan crust, mixed cresses and walnut oil and chive dressing, beer-battered cod with lemon and thyme tartare sauce and fries, chicken and parmesan pasta with basil pesto pasta and red pepper and tomato coulis, kedgeree with a poached egg, rocket and parsley salad and turmeric and garam masala dressing, marmalade pork ribs with wild, red and brown rice salad and smoked tomato compote, and puddings such as rhubarb panna cotta with poached rhubarb and ginger syrup and pina colada baba with pineapple, mint, chilli and caramel salsa. *Benchmark main dish: local pork and herb sausages with wilted spinach mash, red onion marmalade and red wine jus £9.00. Two-course evening meal £21.00.*

Enterprise ~ Lease Dane and Sarah Allchorne ~ Real ale ~ Open 9am-11pm (midnight Sat) ~ Bar food 12-3, 6-9 ~ Restaurant ~ Children welcome ~ Dogs allowed in bar ~ Wi-fi ~ Bedrooms: /£100 *Recommended by Martin Jones, Toby Jones, Peter and Carole Jordan, Amy Dillman*

SPELDHURST
George & Dragon 🌠 ⚲

(01892) 863125 – www.speldhurst.com

Village signed from A264 W of Tunbridge Wells; TN3 0NN

Handsome old pub with beams, flagstones and huge fireplaces, local beers, good food and attractive outside seating areas

As one of the oldest pubs in the south of England, this fine half-timbered building is certainly worth wandering around. It's based around a 13th-c manorial hall and has a massive stone fireplace, heavy beams (installed during 'modernisation' in 1589 – until then, the room went up to the roof), and some of the biggest flagstones found anywhere; it's said that kentish archers returning from their victory at Agincourt rested on them in 1415. To the right of the rather splendid entrance hall a half-panelled room is set for dining, with a mix of old wheelback and other dining chairs and a cushioned wall pew around several tables, small pictures on the walls and horsebrasses on one huge beam. A doorway leads to another dining room with similar furnishings and a second big inglenook. Those wanting a drink and a chat tend to head to the room on the left of the entrance (you can eat in here too), where there's a woodburning stove in a small fireplace, high-winged cushioned settles and various wooden tables and dining chairs on a stripped-wood floor; background music. The restaurant is upstairs. The ales on handpump come from breweries such as Brakspears, Harveys and Larkins, there are 16 wines by the glass and a farm cider, served by friendly, efficient staff. Teak tables, chairs and benches sit on a nicely planted gravel terrace in front of the pub, while at the back is a covered area with big church candles on wooden tables and a lower terrace with seats around a 200-year-old olive tree; more attractive planting here and some modern garden design.

They take great care to source local produce and, as well as seasonal set menus, the rewarding food includes sandwiches, braised pork croquette with apple, celery and crackling, cornish mackerel with horseradish, new potatoes and soy dressing, burger with toppings, tomato salsa, aioli and chips, white onion and wild garlic risotto, chicken, olive and couscous salad with sunblush tomato and pesto dressing, lambs liver with maple-cured bacon and gravy, and puddings such as bakewell tart with plum compote and custard and chocolate délice with blood orange and kumquats. *Benchmark main dish: local sausages and mash with onion and cider gravy £14.50. Two-course evening meal £23.50.*

Free house ~ Licensee Julian Leefe-Griffiths ~ Real ale ~ Open 12-11 ~ Bar food 12-2.30, 7-9.30; 12-3, 6.30-9.30 Sat; 12-3.30 Sun ~ Restaurant ~ Children welcome ~ Dogs allowed in bar ~ Wi-fi *Recommended by Martin and Sue Day, Tracey and Stephen Groves, Hunter and Christine Wright*

STALISFIELD GREEN
Plough 🌠 🍺

(01795) 890256 – www.theploughinnstalisfield.co.uk

Off A252 in Charing; ME13 0HY

Ancient country pub with rambling rooms, open fires, interesting local ales and good bar food

The hop-draped rooms in this ancient country pub are liked by both diners and drinkers, and the atmosphere is relaxed and easy-going. They ramble around, up and down, with open fires in brick fireplaces, interesting pictures, books on shelves, farmhouse and other nice old dining chairs around a mix of pine or dark wood tables on bare boards, and the odd milk churn dotted about. Hopdaemon Incubus, Old Dairy Gold Top and Tonbridge Blonde Ambition on handpump, over a dozen wines by the glass and farm cider. The pub appears to perch on its own amid downland farmland, and picnic-sets on a simple terrace overlook the village green below.

 Cooked by the landlord, the imaginative food includes lunchtime sandwiches, scallops with pea panna cotta, local asparagus and wild garlic oil, chicken livers with black pudding and Jack Daniels cream sauce, roast beetroot and butternut squash salad with a goats curd and walnut dressing, chicken breast and confit leg with tarragon mash, wild mushrooms and hispi cabbage, local lamb rump with fennel purée and dauphinoise potatoes, skate wing with chorizo and buttered leeks, and puddings such as ginger parkin with toffee sauce and clotted cream ice-cream and rhubarb with rhubarb gel, mascarpone cream and meringues. *Benchmark main dish: pie of the day £13.50. Two-course evening meal £20.00.*

Free house ~ Licensees Richard and Marianne Baker ~ Real ale ~ Open 12-3, 6-11; 12-11.30 Sat; 12-6 Sun; closed Sun evening, Mon ~ Bar food 12-2 (3.30 Sat), 6-9; 12-4 Sun ~ Restaurant ~ Children welcome in designated areas ~ Dogs allowed in bar ~ Live music every two months *Recommended by Toby Jones, Martin Jones*

STODMARSH
TR2160   Map 3
Red Lion 🛏
(01227) 721339 – www.theredlionstodmarsh.com
High Street; off A257 just E of Canterbury; CT3 4BA

Interesting country pub with lots to look at, good choice of drinks and well liked food; bedrooms

With comfortable bedrooms and hearty breakfasts, this friendly country pub is handy for Stodmarsh National Nature Reserve. The hop-hung rooms have country kitchen chairs (some painted) and tables, books on window sills, shelves and the floor, tankards hanging from beams, various old stone bottles and lamps dotted about, full and empty wine bottles, a big log fire and plenty of candles and fresh flowers. Greene King IPA, Sharps Cornish Coaster and Wantsum Ravening Wolf tapped from the cask, eight wines by the glass and a farm cider; background music.

🍴 Popular food using local, seasonal produce includes sandwiches, duck hash cake topped with a fried free-range egg and bacon jam, sloe gin-cured salmon with pickled cucumber, breadcrumbed mozzarella and tomato risotto cakes with pesto cream, sausages with mash and onion gravy, a pie of the day, bass fillet with seaweed, samphire and lemon butter, venison with juniper, orange and redcurrant sauce, and puddings such as banoffi pie and bread and butter pudding; they also offer a two- and three-course set lunch. *Benchmark main dish: slow-roasted pork belly £14.00. Two-course evening meal £20.00.*

Free house ~ Licensees Richard and Carol Vale ~ Real ale ~ Open 11.30-11 (midnight Sat); 11.30-6 Sun ~ Bar food 12-2.15, 6.30-9.15; 12-3.30 Sun ~ Children welcome ~ Dogs allowed in bar ~ Wi-fi ~ Bedrooms: /£85 *Recommended by Pip White, Caroline Prescott*

STONE IN OXNEY
TQ9428   Map 3
Ferry
(01233) 758246 – www.oxneyferry.com
Appledore Road; N of Stone-cum-Ebony; TN30 7JY

Bustling small cottage with character rooms, candlelight, open fires, real ales and popular food

This is a pretty 17th-c cottage with an easy-going and chatty atmosphere. The main bar has hop-draped painted beams, a green dado and stools against the counter where they serve a beer named for the pub (from Westerham), Harveys Best, Isfield Bitter and Sharps Doom Bar on handpump, eight wines by the glass and farm ciders; they hold a festival in September with three days of live music, beers and ciders. To the right is a cosy eating area with wheelback chairs and a banquette around a few long tables, a log fire in an inglenook and candles in wall sconces on either side. To the left of the main door is a dining area with big blackboards on red walls, a woodburning stove beneath a large bressumer beam and high-backed light wooden dining chairs around assorted tables; up a couple of steps, a smarter dining area has modern chandeliers. Background music, TV, games machine, darts and pool in the games room. Throughout, there are wooden floors, all sorts of pictures and framed maps, a stuffed fish, beer flagons, an old musket and various brasses. In warm weather the tables and benches on the front terrace and seats in the back garden are much prized; a river runs along the bottom and sunsets can be lovely. Disabled access in the bar and on the terrace.

Highly thought-of food includes devilled lambs kidneys, moules marinière, sharing boards, wild mushroom and butternut squash risotto, turkey curry, battered cod and beef-dripping chips, rack of baby back pork ribs in sweet chilli and soy, seared tuna steak with rösti potatoes and peppercorn sauce, chicken breast stuffed with spinach and bacon with a creamed mushroom sauce, chargrilled king prawns with frites, and puddings. *Benchmark main dish: steak and chorizo burger with beef-dripping chips, coleslaw and barbecue-glazed corn salad £12.95. Two-course evening meal £19.00.*

Free house ~ Licensee Paul Withers Green ~ Real ale ~ Open 11-11; 12-10 Sun ~ Bar food 12-3, 6-9; 12-8 Sun ~ Restaurant ~ Children welcome ~ Dogs allowed in bar ~ Wi-fi
Recommended by Stuart Paulley, B and M Kendall

STOWTING
Tiger

TR1241 Map 3

(01303) 862130 ~ www.tigerinn.co.uk
3.7 miles from M20 junction 11; B2068 N, then left at Stowting signpost, straight across crossroads, then fork left after 0.25 miles and pub is on right; coming from N, follow Brabourne, Wye, Ashford signpost to right at fork, then turn left towards Posting and Lyminge at T junction; TN25 6BA

Peaceful pub with helpful staff, traditional furnishings, well liked food, several real ales and open fires; good walking country

Although this particularly well run and very popular pub is tucked away down narrow lanes, it's just a few minutes from junction 11 of the M20. The traditionally furnished bars, dating from the 17th c, have warming woodburning stoves and all sorts of wooden tables and chairs and built-in cushioned wall seats on floorboards. There's an unpretentious array of books, board games, candles in bottles, brewery memorabilia and paintings, lots of hops and some faded rugs on the stone floor towards the back of the pub. Shepherd Neame Master Brew and three or four guests from local brewers such as Harveys, Old Dairy and Tonbridge on handpump, plenty of malt whiskies, several wines by the glass, local Biddenden cider and local fruit juice. Staff are helpful with wheelchairs. On warmer days you can sit out on the front terrace, and there are plenty of nearby walks along the Wye Downs and North Downs Way.

Rewarding food includes baguettes, salt and pepper squid with chilli and mango dip, smoked fish and meat platter, burger with all the trimmings and chips, vintage parmesan soufflé with wild mushroom cream, steak and mushroom in ale pie, lamb hotpot, smoked haddock with a poached local duck egg, beef in red wine sauce, and puddings such as lemon cheesecake with strawberry coulis and banoffi pie. *Benchmark main dish: crackled pork belly £15.00. Two-course evening meal £20.00.*

Free house ~ Licensees Emma Oliver and Benn Jarvis ~ Real ale ~ Open 12-11 (10.30 Sun); closed Mon, Tues ~ Bar food 12-9.30 ~ Restaurant ~ Children welcome ~ Dogs allowed in bar ~ Wi-fi *Recommended by Alan Cowell, Richard Tilbrook, Ian Herdman, Chris and Jo Nicholls, Glenwys and Alan Lawrence, Malcolm Greening*

 TUNBRIDGE WELLS   TQ5839   Map 3
Black Pig
(01892) 523030 – www.theblackpig.net
Grove Hill Road; TN1 1RZ

Busy town pub with real ales in bar area, rewarding food in relaxed, informal dining room, friendly service and seats outside

With cheerful management and chatty customers, this is a bustling town-centre pub with good food and local ales. At one end of the long, narrow bar there's a woodburning stove in a brick fireplace with leather sofas to each side, bookshelves, a large antelope head and some unusual friesian cow wallpaper, and a few tables and chairs on bare boards; an overflow room up some steps to the right has wooden chairs around heavy, dark tables and more books on shelves. If dining, most customers head for the character room to the left of the bar: a mix of contemporary wallpaper and panelling, oriental paintings, large flower arrangements and candles, button-back wall banquettes and an assortment of wooden tables and chairs on more floorboards and an open kitchen. A back terrace has seats and tables set out on gravelling.

Using local, seasonal produce and making bread and chutneys in-house, the good, interesting food includes lunchtime open sandwiches, smoked salmon with avocado mousse, cockles, radish and beetroot, scotch egg with sweet mustard dressing, crispy leek and cauliflower, various boards, chicken caesar salad, curried and battered fish and chips, chicken breast with grilled hispi cabbage, cipollini onions and madeira cream, bass with saffron chickpeas, shallot confit and soft herb oil, and puddings. *Benchmark main dish: pork belly with parma ham, asparagus and brandy-caramelised pineapple £13.50. Two-course evening meal £21.00.*

Free house ~ Licensee Ajay Sandhu ~ Real ale ~ Open 12-11 (10 Sun) ~ Bar food 12-2.30, 7-9.30 (10 Fri); 12-3, 6-10 Sat; 12-9 Sun ~ Restaurant ~ Children welcome ~ Dogs allowed in bar ~ Wi-fi *Recommended by Edward May, Lindy Andrews*

TUNBRIDGE WELLS   TQ5839   Map 3
Sankeys
(01892) 511422 – www.sankeys.co.uk
Mount Ephraim (A26 just N of junction with A267); TN4 8AA

Pubby street-level bar, informal downstairs brasserie (wonderful fish and shellfish), real ales and good wines, a chatty atmosphere and seats on sunny back terrace

With 23 handpumps offering a constantly changing range of real ales, craft beers, fruit beers, lagers and ciders, this well run pub is always packed with cheerful customers. They always feature local Tonbridge Coppernob and a guest from breweries such as Dark Star, Larkins, Magic Rock and Thornbridge – and keep 16 wines by the glass and a wide choice of spirits.

The bar is light and airy with comfortably worn, informal leather sofas and pews around all sorts of tables on bare boards. There's also a fine collection of rare enamel signs and antique brewery mirrors, as well as old prints, framed cigarette cards and lots of old wine bottles and soda siphons; a big flat-screen TV (for rugby only) and background music. Downstairs is the informal fish restaurant with bistro-style décor; from here, french windows lead on to an inviting suntrap deck with wicker and chrome chairs around wooden tables.

Food in the upstairs bar includes sandwiches, baguettes and tortilla wraps, honey-roasted ham and free-range eggs, halloumi or thai beef salads, chilli con carne, local sausages and mash with onion gravy, smoked haddock and salmon fishcakes with garlic and spinach sauce, mussels done several ways and malaysian fish stew. The excellent à la carte fish and shellfish menu is only served downstairs – our Food Award is for this. *Benchmark main dish: burger with toppings and chips £8.00. Two-course evening meal £25.00.*

Free house ~ Licensee Matthew Sankey ~ Real ale ~ Open midday-1am (3am Sat); 12-11 Sun ~ Bar food 12-3, 6-10; 12-10 Sat; 12-8 Sun ~ Restaurant ~ Children welcome ~ Dogs allowed in bar ~ Wi-fi ~ Live music first Sun of month *Recommended by Edward May, Harvey Brown*

ULCOMBE   TQ8550 Map 3
Pepper Box
(01622) 842558 – www.thepepperboxinn.co.uk

Fairbourne Heath; signposted from A20 in Harrietsham, or follow Ulcombe signpost from A20, then turn left at crossroads with sign to pub, then right at next minor crossroads; ME17 1LP

Friendly country pub with lovely log fire, well liked food, fair choice of drinks, and seats in a pretty garden

Our readers enjoy their visits to this well run country pub very much. In summer, the hop-covered terrace and shrub-filled garden (looking out over a great plateau of rolling arable farmland) is just the place to relax after a walk along the nearby Greensand Way footpath. In winter, it's cosy and warm and hard to leave the two leather sofas by the splendid inglenook fireplace with its lovely log fire. The homely bar has standing timbers and a few low beams (some hung with hops), copper kettles and pans on window sills, and nice horsebrasses on the fireplace's bressumer beam. A side area, furnished more functionally for eating, extends into the opened-up beamed dining room with a range in another inglenook and more horsebrasses. Attentive and convivial licensees serve Shepherd Neame Master Brew and Spitfire and a seasonal beer on handpump and 15 wines by the glass; background music. The village church is worth a look.

Good, popular food includes lunchtime sandwiches, chilli and kaffir lime lamb skewers with minted yoghurt, chicken liver and brandy pâté with apricot chutney, aubergine, chickpea and lentil moussaka, local sausages with mash and onion gravy, beer-battered fresh cod and chips, chicken curry, bream in provençale sauce with sauté potatoes, and puddings such as crème brûlée of the day and salted caramel and chocolate tart with honeycomb ice-cream. *Benchmark main dish: steak in ale pie £9.00. Two-course evening meal £19.00.*

Shepherd Neame ~ Tenant Sarah Pemble ~ Real ale ~ Open 11-3, 6-11; 12-5 Sun ~ Bar food 12-2.15, 6.30-9.30; 12-3 Sun ~ Restaurant ~ Children over 7 only ~ Dogs allowed in bar
Recommended by Martin and Sue Day, Peter Meister, Tina and David Woods-Taylor

WHITSTABLE

TR1066 Map 3

Pearsons Arms ♀

(01227) 773133 – www.pearsonsarmsbyrichardphillips.co.uk

Sea Wall off Oxford Street after road splits into one-way system; public parking on left as road divides; CT5 1BT

Seaside pub with an emphasis on imaginative food, several local ales and good mix of customers

Whether it's a pint and a chat you're after or an interesting meal, there's space for both in this weatherboarded, beachside pub. The two front bars, divided by a central chimney, have cushioned settles, captain's chairs and leather armchairs on a stripped-wood floor, driftwood walls and big flower arrangements on the bar counter where they serve Nethergate Growler, Sharps Doom Bar, Timothy Taylors Landlord and Whitstable East India Pale Ale on handpump, 14 wines by the glass and an extensive choice of cocktails; background music. A cosy lower room has trompe l'oeil bookshelves, a couple of big chesterfields and dining chairs around plain tables on a stone floor. Up a couple of flights of stairs, the restaurant has sea views, mushroom-coloured paintwork, contemporary wallpaper, more driftwood and church chairs and pine tables on nice wide floorboards.

As well as a two- and three-course set lunch, the rewarding food includes lunchtime sandwiches, fried cod cheeks with crispy salt and pepper squid and a lemon and caper dressing, confit duck hash with a duck egg, pomegranate and radish salad and spicy sauce, sharing plates, burger with toppings, home-made brioche bun and chips, saddle of local venison with braised venison faggot, roasted celeriac, smoked pancetta and venison jus, and puddings such as treacle tart with lemon curd ice-cream and spiced apple cake with caramelised apple purée and spiced ice-cream. *Benchmark main dish: fish pie £14.75. Two-course evening meal £20.00.*

Enterprise ~ Lease Jake Alder ~ Real ale ~ Open 12-midnight (11 Sun) ~ Bar food 12-3, 6.30-9.30 ~ Restaurant ~ Children welcome ~ Dogs allowed in bar ~ Wi-fi ~ Live music Tues and Sun evenings *Recommended by Adrian Johnson, C and R Bromage, Eddie Edwards, Ian Herdman, Roy Hoing*

Also Worth a Visit in Kent

Besides the fully inspected pubs, you might like to try these pubs that have been recommended to us and described by readers. Do tell us what you think of them: feedback@goodguides.com

APPLEDORE   TQ9529

Black Lion (01233) 758206

The Street; TN26 2BU Compact 1930s village pub with bustling atmosphere, very welcoming helpful staff, good generous food all day from simple sandwiches to imaginative dishes, lamb from Romney Marsh and local fish, three or four well kept changing ales, Biddenden cider, partitioned back eating area, log fire; background music; tables out on green, attractive village and good Military Canal walks. *(Peter Meister)*

BADLESMERE   TR0154

Red Lion (01233) 740320

A251, S of M2 junction 6; ME13 0NX Spacious partly 16th-c roadside country pub

run by mother and daughter, friendly local atmosphere, Gadds and two or three guests from hop-strung bar (Easter and Aug bank holiday beer festivals), enjoyable well priced home-made food (not Sun evening) using local produce, weekday early-bird deals, beams, bare boards and stripped brickwork, books and board games; background music, monthly live music and quiz nights, free wi-fi; children and dogs welcome, large garden with paddock for camping, open all day (till 7pm Sun, 9pm Mon). *(Isobel Mackinlay)*

BARHAM   TR2050

Duke of Cumberland

(01227) 831396 *The Street; CT4 6NY* Open-plan pub close to village green, enjoyable home cooking including good

Sun roasts, well kept Harveys, Greene King, Timothy Taylors and a guest, friendly staff, plain tables and chairs on bare boards or flagstones, hops and log fire; live music, quiz nights, board games and darts; children welcome, dogs in bar, garden with boules and play area, three bedrooms, handy for A2, open all day, food all day weekends. *(Peter Smith and Judith Brown)*

BEARSTED   TQ7956
Bell (01622) 738021
Ware Street; by railway bridge, W of centre; ME14 4PA Welcoming old local under new management (some refurbishment planned); Greene King IPA, London Glory and a guest, ample helpings of enjoyable competitively priced home-cooked food, good friendly service; some live music; children and dogs welcome, garden and terrace, open all day. *(Mike Swan)*

BEARSTED   TQ8055
Oak on the Green (01622) 737976
The Street; ME14 4EJ Well run pub with bustling friendly atmosphere, two hop-festooned bar areas, bare boards and half-panelling, wide choice of home-made food including some mexican dishes, children's menu too, a house beer from 1648, Fullers London Pride and two local guests, restaurant (they also own the smaller fish restaurant next door); dogs allowed in bar, disabled access, seats out at front under big umbrellas, open (and food) all day. *(Conor McGaughey)*

BENENDEN   TQ8032
★ **Bull** (01580) 240054
The Street; by village green; TN17 4DE Relaxed informal atmosphere in bare-boards or dark terracotta-tiled rooms, pleasing mix of furniture, church candles on tables, hops, fire in brick inglenook, friendly hands-on licensees, ales such as Dark Star, Harveys, Larkins and Old Dairy from carved wooden counter, Biddenden cider, more formal dining room, tasty generously served food (not Sun evening) including speciality pies and popular Sun carvery, various offers; background music (live most Sun afternoons), quiz nights; children and dogs (in bar) welcome, picnic-sets out in front behind white picket fence, back garden, open all day. *(Mrs T A Bizat, Conrad Freezer)*

BETHERSDEN   TQ9240
George (01233) 820235
The Street; TN26 3AG Tile-hung village local with good buoyant atmosphere, well kept Brakspears, Harveys, Greene King Old Speckled Hen and a guest, generous sensibly priced food (not Sun evening, Mon lunchtime) including good value carvery (Sun, Weds), large public bar with open fire, smaller lounge next to dining area; pool, free wi-fi; children and dogs welcome, open all day. *(Tony and Wendy Hobden)*

BOTOLPHS BRIDGE   TR1233
Botolphs Bridge Inn
(01303) 267346 *W of Hythe; CT21 4NL* Edwardian red-brick country pub on edge of marshes; decent choice of good generous home-made food including fresh fish and Sun roasts, friendly service, well kept Greene King IPA, Sharps Doom Bar and a guest, airy and open-plan with tables laid for dining, carpets or bare boards, two log fires; background music, free wi-fi; children and dogs welcome, nice little garden with marshland view, open all day till 10pm (11pm Fri, Sat), closed Mon. *(Anon)*

BOUGH BEECH   TQ4846
★ **Wheatsheaf** (01732) 700100
B2027, S of reservoir; TN8 7NU Major refurbishment and new owners for this attractive 14th-c pub, emphasis on good freshly cooked food (not overly cheap) including children's meals, three Westerham ales along with Harveys and good choice of wines, friendly attentive service, beams, bare boards and log fires, high ceilinged dining room, more tables upstairs; dogs welcome, nice outside seating area, good walks including circular one around Bough Beech Reservoir, open all day (food till 6pm Sun). *(Mrs J Ekins-Daukes, Martin and Sue Day, B J Harding, Christian Mole)*

BOYDEN GATE   TR2265
★ **Gate Inn** (01227) 860498
Off A299 Herne Bay–Ramsgate – follow 'Chislet, Upstreet' sign opposite Roman Gallery; Chislet also signed off A28 Canterbury–Margate at Upstreet – after right turn into Chislet main street, keep right on to Boyden; CT3 4EB Rustic pub with unpretentious quarry-tiled bar rooms, cushioned pews around character tables, hop-strung beams, attractively etched windows and double aspect log fire, Shepherd Neame and occasional guests from tap room casks, popular sensibly priced pubby food including signature Gatewich sandwich, bare-boards restaurant in former bakery (original oven) with woodburner; Weds quiz and some live folk nights; children and dogs (in bar) welcome, sheltered garden bounded by two streams with ducks and chickens, open (and food) all day weekends. *(Toby Jones)*

BRABOURNE   TR1041
Five Bells (01303) 813334
East Brabourne; TN25 5LP Friendly 16th-c inn at foot of North Downs; opened-up interior with hop-draped beams, standing timbers and ancient brick walls, all manner of dining chairs and tables on stripped boards, wall seats here and there, two log fires, quirky decorations including candles in upturned bottles on the walls and a garland-draped mermaid figurehead, five changing local ales, Biddenden cider and selection of kentish wines, well liked food from varied

menu, shop selling local produce, monthly arts and crafts market; some live music, unisex loos; children and dogs welcome, comfortable if eccentric bedrooms, open all day from 9am for breakfast. *(Lindy Andrews)*

BRASTED   TQ4654
Stanhope Arms (01959) 561970
Church Road; TN16 1HZ Welcoming old village pub next to the church, Greene King ales and enjoyable pubby food (not Mon), cosy traditional bar with darts, restaurant; children and dogs welcome (resident labradors), back garden with summer barbecues and bat and trap, open all day. *(Edward May)*

BRENCHLEY   TQ6841
★ Halfway House (01892) 722526
Horsmonden Road; TN12 7AX Beamed 18th-c inn with attractive mix of rustic and traditional furnishings on bare boards, old farm tools and other bric-a-brac, two log fires, cheerful staff and particularly friendly landlord, up to a dozen well kept changing ales tapped from the cask, enjoyable traditional home-made food including popular Sun roasts, two eating areas; children and dogs welcome, picnic-sets and play area in big garden, summer barbecues and beer festivals, two bedrooms, open all day (no food Sun evening). *(Phil and Jane Hodson, Peter Meister)*

BROADSTAIRS   TR3967
Charles Dickens (01843) 600160
Victoria Parade; CT10 1QS Centrally placed with big busy bar, good choice of beers and wines, popular food including good local fish/seafood, weekend breakfast from 9am, friendly efficient service, upstairs restaurant with fine sea views, live music Fri, Sat; children welcome, tables out overlooking Viking Bay, almost next door to Dickens House Museum, open all day. *(John Wooll, Adrian Johnson)*

BROADSTAIRS   TR3868
Four Candles 07947 062063
Sowell Street; CT10 2AT Quirky one-room micropub in former shop, good selection of local beers chalked on blackboard including own brews, kentish wines, high tables and stools on sawdust floor, bucket lightshades and various odds and ends including pitchfork handles (Ronnie Barker's famous sketch was inspired by a Broadstairs ironmonger), local cheese and pork pies, friendly chatty service; closed weekday lunchtimes. *(Malcolm Greening)*

BROOKLAND   TQ9724
Woolpack (01797) 344321
On A259 from Rye, about a mile before Brookland, take the first right turn signposted Midley where the main road bends sharp left, just after the expanse of Walland Marsh; OS Sheet 189 map reference 977244; TN29 9TJ 15th-c cottage with lovely uneven brick floor in ancient entrance lobby, simple quarry-tiled main bar with low beams (thought to have come from local wrecks), long elm table with shove-ha'penny, local photographs and massive inglenook, traditional dining room, food has been popular (pub changing hands as we went to press), Shepherd Neame ales and several wines by the glass; may be background music; children and dogs welcome, picnic-sets under parasols in garden (nicely lit in the evening), has opened all day weekends. *(M and J White, DF and NF)*

BURMARSH   TR1032
Shepherd & Crook (01303) 872336
Shear Way, next to church; TN29 0JJ Traditional 16th-c local with smuggling history in marshside village; well kept Hop Fuzz, Old Dairy and maybe a guest, Weston's cider, good straightforward home-made food at low prices, prompt friendly service, interesting photographs and blow lamp collection, open fire; bar games; children and dogs welcome, seats on side terrace, closed Mon, Tues, otherwise open all day (Sun till 6pm). *(Edward May)*

CANTERBURY   TR1458
Dolphin (01227) 455963
St Radigunds Street; CT1 2AA Busy modernised dining pub with plenty of tables in spacious bar, enjoyable generous home-made pubby food from baguettes up, Sharps Doom Bar, Timothy Taylors Landlord and guests such as Gadds, nice wines including country ones, friendly staff, bric-a-brac on delft shelf, board games, flagstoned conservatory; pianist Sun evening, quiz first Mon of month, free wi-fi; children welcome, no dogs, disabled access, good-sized back garden with heaters, open all day. *(Ian Herdman, Peter Smith and Judith Brown)*

CANTERBURY   TR1457
Foundry (01227) 455899
White Horse Lane; CT1 2RU Pub in former 19th-c iron foundry, light and airy interior on two floors, six Canterbury Brewers beers from visible microbrewery plus local guests, craft lagers and kentish cider, enjoyable well presented pubby food till 6pm including good sandwiches, helpful cheerful staff; disabled access, small courtyard area, open all day (till late Fri, Sat). *(Peter Smith and Judith Brown)*

CANTERBURY   TR1458
Millers Arms (01227) 456057
St Radigunds Street/Mill Lane; CT1 2AA Shepherd Neame pub in quiet street near river, enjoyable well priced food from lunchtime sandwiches up and good wine choice, friendly helpful staff, flagstoned front bar, bare-boards back area, traditional solid furniture, newspapers and log fire, small conservatory; unobtrusive background

music; children and dogs welcome, good seating in attractive part-covered courtyard, 11 comfortable bedrooms, ample breakfast, handy for Marlowe Theatre and cathedral, open all day. *(Brian and Janet Ainscough)*

CANTERBURY   TR1457
Parrot (01227) 454170
Church Lane – the one off St Radigunds Street, 100 metres E of St Radigunds car park; CT1 2AG Ancient pub with heavy beams, wood and flagstone floors, stripped masonry, dark panelling and big open fire, Shepherd Neame ales and well liked food, friendly service, upstairs vaulted restaurant; nicely laid out courtyard with central woodburning barbecue, open all day. *(Edward May)*

CAPEL   TQ6444
Dovecote (01892) 835966
Alders Road; SE of Tonbridge; TN12 6SU Cosy beamed pub with some stripped brickwork and open fire, pitched-ceiling dining end, enjoyable well priced food (not Sun evening, Mon) from sandwiches to Sun roasts, up to six ales tapped from the cask including Harveys, Weston's cider, friendly helpful staff; well behaved children allowed, no dogs inside, lots of picnic-sets in back garden with terrace and play area, nice country surroundings, open all day Sun. *(Martin and Sue Day)*

CHARTHAM   TR1054
Artichoke (01227) 738316
Rottington Street; CT4 7JQ Attractive timbered pub dating from the 15th c, enjoyable reasonably priced home-made food from sandwiches and baked potatoes up, well kept Shepherd Neame ales, good service, carpeted log-fire bar, dining area with light wood tables (one built around a glass-topped well); darts and bat and trap; children welcome, picnic-sets in back garden, open all day. *(Peter Smith and Judith Brown)*

CHIDDINGSTONE   TQ5045
Castle Inn (01892) 870247
Off B2027 Tonbridge–Edenbridge; TN8 7AH Rambling traditional old pub in pretty NT village, handsome beamed bar with settles, sturdy wall benches and attractive mullioned window seat, woodburners, brick-floor snug, well kept Harveys and Larkins including winter Porter (brewed in the village), good choice of enjoyable food from sandwiches to blackboard specials, friendly helpful staff; children and dogs welcome, tables out at front and in nice secluded garden with own bar and summer barbecues, circular walks from village, handy for

Chiddingstone Castle, open all day. *(Brian Glozier, John Coatsworth, Mrs Sally Scott, Tina and David Woods-Taylor)*

CHIDDINGSTONE
CAUSEWAY   TQ5247
Greyhound (01892) 870275
Charcott, off back road to Weald; TN11 8LG Updated red-brick village local with good food cooked by landlord-chef from pub favourites up, well kept Harveys and a couple of guests such as Otter, friendly staff, log fire; children and dogs welcome, picnic-sets out in front and in garden, useful for walkers, open all day weekends. *(John Webb, Martin and Sue Day)*

CHILHAM   TR0653
★**White Horse** (01227) 730355
The Square; CT4 8BY 15th-c pub in picturesque village square; handsome ceiling beams and massive fireplace with lancastrian rose carved on mantel beam, chunky light oak furniture on pale wood flooring and more traditional pubby furniture on quarry tiles, four well kept ales including a house beer from Canterbury Brewers, enjoyable food (all day Sat, not Sun evening) with more adventurous evening choices, friendly helpful service; children welcome, dogs in bar (pub dog is Sean), handy for the castle, open all day. *(Mike Swan)*

CHILLENDEN   TR2653
★**Griffins Head** (01304) 840325
SE end of village; 2 miles E of Aylesham; CT3 1PS Attractive beamed and timbered 14th-c pub with two bar rooms and flagstoned back dining room, gently upscale local atmosphere, big log fire, full range of Shepherd Neame ales and decent choice of popular home-made food, good wine list, attentive service; no children, dogs welcome in some parts, pretty garden surrounded by wild roses, summer Sun barbecues, nice countryside, open all day. *(Emma Scofield)*

CHIPSTEAD   TQ4956
★**Bricklayers Arms** (01732) 743424
Chevening Road; TN13 2RZ Attractive popular place overlooking lake and green, wide choice of good fairly priced pub food (not Sun evening), well kept Harveys from casks behind long counter, efficient cheerful service and relaxed chatty atmosphere, heavily beamed bar with open fire and fine racehorse painting, larger back restaurant; various events including Tues quiz; children and dogs welcome, seats out in front, open all day. *(Alan Cowell, Nigel and Jean Eames, Martin and Sue Day, Tina and David Woods-Taylor, Mr and Mrs A Dempster)*

We mention bottled beers and spirits only if there is something unusual about them – imported belgian real ales, say, or dozens of malt whiskies; so do please let us know about them in your reports.

CONYER QUAY   TQ9664
Ship (01795) 520881
Conyer Road; ME9 9HR Well renovated
18th-c creekside pub owned by adjacent
Swale Marina; bare boards and open fires,
enjoyable home-cooked food including set
lunch (Mon-Sat), weekend breakfast from
10am, Adnams Southwold, Shepherd Neame
Master Brew and guests; live folk first and
third Tues of month, jazz dinner third Thurs;
children and dogs welcome, useful for
boaters, walkers (on Saxon Way) and birders,
open all day weekends (Sun till 9.30pm).
(Anon)

COWDEN   TQ4640
Fountain (01342) 850528
*Off A264 and B2026; High Street;
TN8 7JG* Good sensibly priced blackboard
food (not Sun evening) in attractive tile-
hung beamed village pub, steep steps up to
unpretentious dark-panelled corner bar, well
kept Harveys and decent wines by the glass,
friendly helpful staff, old photographs on
cream walls, good log fire, mix of tables in
adjoining room, woodburner in small back
dining area with one big table; background
music, Thurs quiz; children, walkers and dogs
welcome, picnic-sets on small terrace and
lawn, pretty village, open all day Sun.
(Graham and Carol Parker)

COWDEN   TQ4642
★Queens Arms
*Cowden Pound; junction B2026 with
Markbeech Road; TN8 5NP* Friendly
little Victorian time warp known as Elsie's
after previous long-serving landlady (same
family for 100 years) – new local owner
has, thankfully, kept things much the same;
two simple unpretentious rooms with open
fires, well kept/priced Larkins, no food,
darts and ring-throwing game, folk music,
morris dancers and Christmas mummers;
dogs welcome, limited often short opening
hours – closed Mon-Sat lunchtimes, Sun
evening. *(Toby Jones)*

CRANBROOK   TQ7736
George (01580) 713348
Stone Street; TN17 3HE Historic coaching
inn dating from the 14th c, main bar with
leather settees, armchairs and open fire,
beamed dining room with huge inglenook,
enjoyable food from pub favourites to
restaurant dishes, helpful friendly staff, well
kept Adnams and Harveys, smaller locals'
bar; suntrap terrace, a dozen character
bedrooms, good breakfast, open (and food)
all day. *(Emma Scofield)*

CROCKHAM HILL   TQ4450
Royal Oak (01732) 866335
Main Road; TN8 6RD Chatty old village
pub owned by Westerham brewery, their ales
kept well and good value fairly standard food
(till 7pm Sun) from sandwiches and sharing

plates up, friendly hard-working staff, mix
of furniture including comfy leather sofas
on stripped-wood floor, painted panelling,
original Tottering-by-Gently cartoons and
old local photographs, log fire in right-hand
bar; occasional live music, darts; children,
walkers and dogs welcome, small garden
behind car park, handy for Chartwell (NT),
open all day weekends. *(Tina and David
Woods-Taylor, Malcolm and Jane Levitt)*

CRUNDALE   TR0949
Compasses (01227) 700300
Sole Street; CT4 7ES Welcoming country
pub with really good imaginative food cooked
by landlord-chef using local ingredients,
well kept Shepherd Neame ales and maybe
a guest, traditional interior with hop-strung
beams and woodburner in brick inglenook;
children, walkers and dogs welcome, big
garden with play equipment, closed Mon
(including bank holidays), otherwise open
all day (till 6pm Sun). *(Roz and Richard
Goodenough)*

DARGATE   TR0761
Dove (01227) 751360
*Village signposted from A299;
ME13 9HB* Tucked-away 18th-c restaurary
pub with rambling rooms, good food (some
quite expensive), Shepherd Neame ales and
guests, nice wines by the glass, efficient
pleasant service, plenty of stripped-wood
tables, woodburner in brick and stone
fireplace, live music last Fri of month;
children, walkers and dogs welcome,
sheltered garden with bat and trap, summer
classic car meetings, open all day Fri, Sat.
(Anon)

DARTFORD   TQ5473
Malt Shovel (01322) 224381
Darenth Road; DA1 1LP Traditional
17th-c waney-boarded pub, well kept Youngs
and guests, good home-made food (not Tues,
or evenings Sun-Thurs), friendly helpful staff,
two bars and conservatory; children and dogs
welcome, tables on paved terrace, closed
Mon lunchtime, othewise open all day.
(Quentin and Carol Williamson)

DEAL   TR3751
Berry (01304) 362411
Canada Road; CT14 7EQ Small friendly
no-frills local opposite old Royal Marine
barracks, welcoming enthusiastic landlord,
fine selection of well kept ales including Dark
Star, Harveys and local Time & Tide (tasting
notes on slates, regular festivals), kentish
farm cider and perry, no food, L-shaped
carpeted bar with coal fire, newspapers, quiz
and darts teams, pool, some live music; dogs
welcome, small vine-covered back terrace,
open all day (from 2pm Tues). *(N R White)*

DEAL   TR3752
Bohemian (01304) 361939
Beach Street opposite pier; CT14 6HY

Refurbished seafront bar with five real ales, around 70 bottled beers and huge selection of spirits, popular traditional home-made food including Sun roasts, friendly helpful staff, L-shaped room with mismatched furniture (some découpage tables), polished wood floor, lots of pictures, mirrors, signs and other odds and ends (customers encouraged to donate items), sofas and weekend papers, similar décor in upstairs cocktail bar with good sea views; background music; children and dogs welcome, sunny split-level deck behind and heated smokers' gazebo, open all day (from 9am Sun) and can get very busy, particularly at weekends. *(N R White)*

DEAL TR3752

Just Reproach 07432 413226

King Street; CT14 6HX Popular and genuinely welcoming micropub in former corner shop; simple drinking room with sturdy tables on bare boards, stools and cushioned benches, friendly knowledgeable service from father and daughter team, three or four changing small brewery ales tapped from the cask, also real ciders and some organic wines, locally made cheese, friendly chatty atmosphere; no mobile phones; dogs welcome, closed Sun evening, Mon. *(N R White)*

DEAL TR3753

Prince Albert (01304) 375425

Middle Street; CT14 6LW Compact 19th-c corner pub in conservation area, bowed entrance doors, etched-glass windows and fairly ornate interior with assorted bric-a-brac, three changing local ales and popular food (not Mon, Tues) especially Sun carvery in back dining area, friendly staff; small garden behind, bedrooms, closed lunchtimes except Sun. *(Mike Swan)*

DEAL TR3753

Ship (01304) 372222

Middle Street; CT14 6JZ Dimly lit traditional two-room local in historic maritime quarter; five well kept ales including Caledonian Deuchars IPA, Dark Star and Gadds, friendly landlord, bare boards and lots of dark wood, stripped brick and local ship and wreck pictures, evening candles, cosy panelled back bar, piano, open fire and woodburner; no food; dogs welcome, small pretty walled garden, open all day. *(N R White)*

DOVER TR3241

Blakes (01304) 202194

Castle Street; CT16 1PJ Small flagstoned cellar bar down steep steps, brick and flint walls, dim lighting, woodburner, Adnams and six changing guests, farm ciders and perries, over 50 malt whiskies and several wines by the glass, decent lunchtime bar food from sandwiches up, panelled carpeted upstairs restaurant (food all day), friendly staff, daily papers; well behaved children welcome, dogs

in bar, side garden and suntrap back terrace, four bedrooms, open all day. *(N R White)*

DUNGENESS TR0916

Pilot (01797) 320314

Battery Road; TN29 9NJ Single-storey, mid 20th-c seaside café-bar by shingle beach, well kept Adnams, Courage, Harveys and a guest, decent choice of good value food from nice sandwiches to fish and chips, OAP lunch deal Mon (not bank holidays), open-plan interior divided into three areas, dark plank panelling including the slightly curved ceiling, lighter front part overlooking beach, prints and local memorabilia, books for sale (proceeds to Lifeboats Assoc), quick friendly service (even when packed); background music, free wi-fi; children welcome, picnic-sets in side garden, open all day till 10pm (9pm Sun). *(M and J White)*

DUNKS GREEN TQ6152

★ Kentish Rifleman (01732) 810727

Dunks Green Road; TN11 9RU Relaxing Tudor pub restored in modern rustic style, well kept ales such as Harveys and Westerham, Biddenden cider, good reasonably priced food (service charge added) from light meals to popular Sun roasts, friendly efficient staff, bar and two dining areas, rifles on low beams, cosy log fire; children and dogs welcome, tables in pretty garden with well, good walks from the door, open all day weekends (no food Sun evening). *(Bob and Margaret Holder, Christian Mole, Malcolm and Jane Levitt, B and M Kendall)*

EAST PECKHAM TQ6548

Man of Kent

Tonbridge Road; TN12 5LA Traditional tile-hung pub dating from the 16th c, low black beams, mix of pubby furniture on carpet or slate tiles, fresh flowers, big two-way woodburner in central fireplace, ales such as Harveys, Timothy Taylors, Tonbridge and Sharps, enjoyable well priced home-made food (all day Sat, not Sun evening) from sandwiches and pizzas up; children welcome, terrace seating by River Bourne, nearby walks, open all day. *(Phil and Jane Hodson)*

FAVERSHAM TR0161

Anchor (01795) 536471

Abbey Street; ME13 7BP Character beamed pub in attractive 17th-c street near historic quay; sensibly priced traditional food (not Sun or Mon evenings) from baguettes up, some meat from own farm, well kept Shepherd Neame range, friendly service, dimly lit bare-boards bar, frosted windows, panelling and woodburner, second room with wood and brick floors and good inglenook log fire, restaurant with white-painted floorboards and large anchor; background music (live Sun – fortnightly in winter); children and dogs welcome, tables in pretty enclosed back garden, open all day. *(N R White)*

FAVERSHAM
TR0161
Bear (01795) 532668
Market Place; ME13 7AG Traditional
late Victorian Shepherd Neame pub (back
part from 16th c), their ales kept well and
occasional guests, locals' front bar, snug
and back dining lounge all off side corridor,
pubby lunchtime food (evenings Tues-Thurs),
friendly service and relaxed atmosphere; quiz
nights second and last Mon of month, free
wi-fi; couple of pavement tables, open
all day. *(Conor McGaughey)*

FAVERSHAM
TR0160
Elephant (01795) 590157
The Mall; ME13 8JN Well run traditional
town pub, friendly and chatty, with four or
five good changing ales mainly from smaller
kent brewers, a local cider too, no food (can
bring your own), single bare-boards bar
with central log fire and cosy seating areas,
dim lighting; juke box and some live music,
games machine; children and dogs welcome,
peaceful suntrap back garden with pond,
open all day Sat, till 7pm Sun, from 3pm
weekdays, closed Mon. *(N R White)*

FAVERSHAM
TR0161
Phoenix (01795) 591462
Abbey Street; ME13 7BH Historic town
pub with heavy low beams and stripped stone
walls, six well kept beers including Harveys
and Timothy Taylors, food from pubby choices
up (all day Fri and Sat, not Sun evening),
friendly service, leather chesterfields by
inglenook log fire, restaurant, various events
including live music, charity quiz nights and
poetry reading; children and dogs welcome,
back garden, open all day. *(Conor McGaughey)*

FAVERSHAM
TR0161
Sun (01795) 535098
West Street; ME13 7JE Rambling old-world
15th-c pub in pedestrianised street, good
unpretentious atmosphere with small low-
ceilinged partly panelled rooms, scrubbed
tables and big inglenook, well kept Shepherd
Neame ales from nearby brewery, enjoyable
bar food, smart restaurant attached, friendly
efficient staff; unobtrusive background
music; wheelchair access possible (small
step), pleasant back courtyard, eight
bedrooms, open all day. *(Mike Swan)*

FINGLESHAM
TR3353
★ Crown (01304) 612555
*Just off A258 Sandwich–Deal; The
Street; CT14 0NA* Popular neatly kept
low-beamed country local dating from 16th c,
good value generous home-made food from
usual pub dishes to interesting specials,
friendly helpful service, well kept local ales
such as Ramsgate, Biddenden cider, softly lit

carpeted split-level bar with stripped stone
and inglenook log fire, two other attractive
dining rooms; children and dogs welcome,
lovely big garden with play area, bat and trap,
field for caravans, open all day Fri-Sun.
(N R White)

FRITTENDEN
TQ8141
Bell & Jorrocks (01580) 852415
*Corner of Biddenden Road/The Street;
TN17 2EJ* Welcoming simple 18th-c tile-
hung and beamed local, well kept Harveys,
Woodfordes and guests (Apr beer festival),
Weston's and Thatcher's ciders, good home-
made food (not Sun evening, Mon, Tues),
open fire with propeller from german bomber
above, hops over bar; live music and other
events, sports TV, kentish darts; children
and dogs welcome, farmers' market third
Sat of month (breakfast available then),
open all day. *(Toby Jones)*

GOODNESTONE
TR2554
★ Fitzwalter Arms (01304) 840303
*The Street; NB this is in E Kent not
the other Goodnestone; CT3 1PJ* Old
lattice-windowed beamed village pub, rustic
bar with wood floor and open fire, Shepherd
Neame ales and local wine, carpeted dining
room with another fire, enjoyable reasonably
priced home-made food (not Sun evening);
shove-ha'penny and bar billiards; well
behaved children and dogs welcome, terrace
with steps up to peaceful garden, lovely
church next door and close to Goodnestone
Park Gardens, open all day. *(Isobel Mackinlay)*

GOUDHURST
TQ7237
Star & Eagle (01580) 211512
High Street; TN17 1AL Steps up to
striking medieval building, now a small hotel,
next to the church; settles and Jacobean-
style seats in heavily beamed open-plan
carpeted areas, intriguing smuggling history,
log fires, good choice of enjoyable food
(some prices on the high side), well kept
Brakspears, Harveys and Wychwood, friendly
helpful staff, restaurant; children welcome,
no dogs inside, tables out at back with
lovely views, attractive village, 11 character
bedrooms, good breakfast, open all day.
(Dr and Mrs J D Abell)

GROOMBRIDGE
TQ5337
★ Crown (01892) 864742
B2110; TN3 9QH Charming tile-hung
wealden inn with snug low-beamed bar,
old tables on worn flagstones, panelling,
bric-a-brac, fire in sizeable brick inglenook,
well kept Harveys, Larkins and a guest,
enjoyable food (all day Sat, till 7pm Sun)
from traditional choices up including plenty
of gluten-free options, good service, separate
refurbished restaurant; free wi-fi; children

Virtually all pubs in this book sell wine by the glass.
We mention wines if they are a cut above the average.

and dogs (in bar) welcome, tables on narrow brick terrace overlooking steep green, more seats behind, four bedrooms, handy for Groombridge Place Gardens, open all day. *(Wendy Breese, Martin and Sue Day, D Marsh, Hunter and Christine Wright)*

HAWKHURST   TQ7529

★ **Black Pig** (01580) 752306

Moor Hill (A229); TN18 4PF Bustling pleasantly refurbished open-plan pub, L-shaped bar and eating areas on different levels, all manner of nice old dining chairs and tables, church candles, interesting old stove, lots of pictures on bare brick or painted walls, four well kept ales including Dark Star and Harveys, decent wines by the glass, good food from lunchtime sandwiches up, friendly attentive service; plenty of seats in surprisingly big back garden. *(Peter Meister)*

HAWKHURST   TQ7531

★ **Great House** (01580) 753119

Gills Green; pub signed off A229 N; TN18 5EJ Stylish white-weatherboarded restaurant pub (part of the Elite Pubs group), good variety of well liked if not always cheap food, ales such as Harveys, Old Dairy and Sharps from marble counter, polite efficient service, sofas, armchairs and bright scatter cushions in chatty bar, stools against counter used by locals, dark wood dining tables and smartly upholstered chairs on slate floor beside log fire, steps down to airy dining room with attractive tables and chairs, working Aga (they cook on it) and doors out to terrace with plenty of furniture; background music; children and dogs (in bar) welcome, open all day (food all day weekends). *(Nicci Carruthers)*

HEAVERHAM   TQ5758

Chequers (01732) 763968

Watery Lane; TN15 6NP Attractive 15th-c beamed country pub under new management; enjoyable traditional food (Sun evening by prior arrangement) including Fri fish night, well kept Shepherd Neame ales and a dozen wines by the glass, friendly helpful service, public bar with open fire, inglenook woodburner in dining area, raftered barn restaurant; quiz last Thurs of month, summer live music; children and dogs (in bar) welcome, big garden with play area and bat and trap, good North Downs walks, open all day Fri-Sun. *(Martin and Sue Day)*

HERNE   TR1865

Butchers Arms (01227) 371000

Herne Street (A291); CT6 7HL Britain's first micropub (converted from a butchers in 2005), up to half a dozen well kept changing ales (mainly local) tapped from backroom casks, friendly former motorcycle-racing landlord offers tasters, just a couple of benches and butcher's-block tables (seats about ten), lots of bric-a-brac, good local cheeses; dogs welcome, disabled access, tables out under awning, open 12-1.30pm, 6-9pm, closed Sun evening, Mon. *(Peter Meister)*

HERNE BAY   TR1768

Old Ship (01227) 366636

Central Parade; CT6 5HT Old weatherboarded pub with window tables looking across road to sea, well kept Otter, Sharps Doom Bar and a guest, popular pubby food, comfortable beamed and carpeted interior; children welcome till 6pm, sea-view deck, open all day. *(Anon)*

HERNHILL   TR0660

Red Lion (01227) 751207

Off A299 via Dargate, or A2 via Boughton Street and Staplestreet; ME13 9JR Pretty Tudor community pub by church and attractive village green, densely beamed and quite dark inside with pine tables and chairs on flagstones, log fires, generously served fairly traditional food at sensible prices, OAP lunch deal Weds, well kept Adnams Lighthouse, Sharps Doom Bar, Shepherd Neame Master Brew and guests, decent wines, friendly helpful staff, upstairs restaurant; soft background music; children and dogs welcome, seats in front and in big garden with play area, open all day. *(Edward May)*

HEVER   TQ4743

Greyhound (01732) 862221

Uckfield Lane; TN8 7LJ Welcoming and homely 19th-c country pub, beamed bar with log fire, good value generously served food and three well kept ales (usually one from Harveys), friendly accommodating staff, restaurant; no dogs inside; well behaved children allowed, tables on front decking and in garden behind, bedrooms, handy for Hever Castle, closed Sun evening (except run-up to Christmas). *(Mrs T A Bizat)*

HEVER   TQ4744

Henry VIII (01732) 862457

By gates of Hever Castle; TN8 7NH Predominantly 17th-c with some fine oak panelling, wide floorboards and heavy beams, inglenook fireplace, Henry VIII touches to décor, emphasis on enjoyable mainly traditional food from baguettes up, well kept Shepherd Neame ales, friendly efficient staff, restaurant; no dogs even in garden; outside covered area with a couple of leather sofas, steps down to deck and pondside lawn, bedrooms, open all day. *(B J Harding)*

HODSOLL STREET   TQ6263

★ **Green Man** (01732) 823575

Signed off A227 S of Meopham; turn right in village; TN15 7LE Bustling friendly village pub with neatly arranged traditional furnishings in big airy carpeted rooms, old photographs, plates and hops, log fire, Greene King, Harveys, Timothy Taylors and maybe a local guest, wide choice of enjoyable generously served food including good baguettes and popular two-course weekday lunch deal; background music – live Sun, quiz Mon; children and dogs welcome, tables and climbing frame on back lawn, also seats out at front overlooking green, open (and food) all day Fri-Sun. *(Mrs J Ekins-Daukes)*

HOLLINGBOURNE   TQ8455
Dirty Habit (01622) 880880
B2163, off A20; ME17 1UW Dimly lit ancient beamed pub in Elite Pubs group (Great House in Hawkhurst, Gun at Gun Hill in Sussex and others); ales including Harveys and Shepherd Neame, several wines by the glass, popular food (all day weekends) and friendly service, main bar area with armchairs and stools on slate floor, panelled end room with mix of tables and chairs, dining room under low beam, antlers here and there, further raftered eating area with brick floor and woodburner; children welcome, good outside shelter with armchairs and sofas, on North Downs Way (leaflets for walkers) and handy for Leeds Castle, open all day. *(Mike Swan)*

HOLLINGBOURNE   TQ8354
★Windmill (01622) 889000
M20 junction 8, A20 towards Lenham then left on to B2163 – Eyhorne Street; ME17 1TR Most people here for the impressive food but there is a small back bar serving Sharps Doom Bar, a guest beer and up to 15 wines by the glass; light and airy main room with white-painted beams, animal skins on bare boards and log fire in low inglenook, mix of furniture including armchairs, heavy settles with scatter cushions, red leather banquette and dark wood dining tables and chairs, two further dining rooms (steps up to one), candles and fresh flowers; background music (live Weds), free wi-fi; children and dogs (in bar) welcome, back terrace, summer barbecues, open all day. *(Christian Mole, Alan Cowell, Martin and Sue Day)*

ICKHAM   TR2258
★Duke William (01227) 721308
Off A257 E of Canterbury; The Street; CT3 1QP New management starting as we went to press; big spreading bar with huge oak beams and stripped joists, seats from settles to high-backed cushioned dining chairs around mix of tables on stripped-wood floor, log fire, Old Dairy, Sharps, Shepherd Neame and a guest from central counter, several wines by the glass, food (all day Sun) has been popular, low-ceilinged dining room, conservatory and separate snug with TV; background and monthly live music, daily papers; dogs welcome in bar, big terrace with

covered area to one side, more seats and play equipment on lawn, bedrooms, open all day. *(R and S Bentley, Glenwys and Alan Lawrence)*

IDE HILL   TQ4851
Cock (01732) 750310
Off B2042 SW of Sevenoaks; TN14 6JN Pretty village-green local dating from the 15th c, chatty and friendly, with two dimly lit bars (steps between), Greene King ales and enjoyable well priced traditional food (not Sun, Tues evenings), cosy in winter with good inglenook log fire; Mon quiz: well behaved children and dogs welcome, picnic-sets out at front, handy for Chartwell (NT) and nearby walks; was closed as we went to press due to planning dispute with the council, but we hope it will have reopened by the time you read this. *(Emma Scofield)*

IDEN GREEN   TQ7437
Peacock (01580) 211233
A262 E of Goudhurst; TN17 2PB Weatherboarded village local dating from the 14th c; blazing inglenook in low-beamed main bar, quarry tiles and old sepia photographs, well kept Shepherd Neame ales and enjoyable pubby food (all day Sat), helpful service, dining room and public bar with fire; well behaved children and dogs welcome, no muddy boots, attractive good-sized garden, closed Sun evening. *(Edward May)*

IDEN GREEN   TQ8031
★Woodcock (01580) 240009
Not the Iden Green near Goudhurst; village signed off A268 E of Hawkhurst and B2086 at W edge of Benenden; in village follow Standen Street sign, then fork left into Woodcock Lane; TN17 4HT Part weatherboarded 17th-c country pub in quiet spot with good surrounding walks; low-ceilinged bar with a couple of big standing timbers, stripped-brick walls hung with horse tack, inglenook woodburner, Greene King ales and a guest, seven wines by the glass, enjoyable food including blackboard specials, small panelled dining room; free wi-fi; children and dogs (in bar) welcome, pretty back garden, open all day, till 7pm Sun, closed Mon lunctime. *(M P Mackenzie, Conrad Freezer)*

IGHTHAM   TQ5956
★George & Dragon (01732) 882440
The Street, A227; TN15 9HH Ancient timbered pub with popular generously served food (not Sun evening) from snacks to daily specials, well kept Shepherd Neame ales and decent wines, friendly staff, sofas among other furnishings in long main bar, heavy-beamed end room, woodburner and open fires, restaurant; children and dogs welcome, back terrace, handy for Ightham Mote (NT),

good walks, open all day from 9am for breakfast. *(Bob and Margaret Holder)*

IGHTHAM COMMON   TQ5855
★ **Harrow** (01732) 885912
Signposted off A25 just W of Ightham; pub sign may be hard to spot; TN15 9EB
Smart yet comfortably genial with emphasis on good imaginative food from daily changing menu, also some traditional choices and Sunday roasts, relaxed cheerful bar area to the right with candles and fresh flowers, dining chairs on herringbone wood floor, winter fire, charming little antiquated conservatory and more formal dining room, ales such as Gravesend and Loddon; background music; children welcome (not in dining room on Sat evening), pretty little pergola-enclosed back terrace, handy for Ightham Mote (NT), closed Sun evening to Weds. *(Andrew Stone)*

IGHTHAM COMMON   TQ5955
Old House (01732) 886077
Redwell, S of village; OS Sheet 188 map reference 591559; TN15 9EE Basic two-room country local tucked down narrow lane, no inn sign, bare bricks and beams, huge inglenook, half a dozen interesting changing ales from tap room casks, no food; darts; dogs welcome, closed weekday lunchtimes, opens 7pm and may shut early if quiet. *(Mike Swan)*

KENNINGTON   TR0245
Old Mill (01223) 661000
Mill Lane; TN25 4DZ Updated and much extended dining pub dating from the early 19th c (same owners as the Oak on the Green at Bearsted); good choice of generously served food (some quite expensive), also lighter appetites menu Mon-Thurs till 5pm, a house beer from 1648, Fullers London Pride and local guests, good friendly service; children welcome, plenty of terrace and garden seating, open (and food) all day. *(Edward May)*

KILNDOWN   TQ7035
Globe & Rainbow (01892) 890803
Signed off A21 S of Lamberhurst; TN17 2SG Welcoming pub under friendly new management; small cheerful bar serving Harveys and guests, wines from well chosen list, bare-boards dining room with woodburner, well liked freshly made food from snacks up (not Sun, Mon evenings); children and dogs welcome, country views from decking out by cricket pitch, open all day (till 7pm Sun). *(Toby Jones)*

KINGSDOWN   TR3748
Kings Head (01304) 373915
Upper Street; CT14 8BJ Tucked-away split-level local with two cosy bars and L-shaped extension (children welcome here), black timbers, lots of old photographs on faded cream walls, a few vintage amusement machines, woodburner, Greene King IPA and two mainly local guests, popular reasonably priced food including blackboard specials, friendly landlord and staff; soft background music (occasional live), darts; dogs welcome, small side garden, skittle alley, open all day Sun, closed weekdays till 5pm. *(N R White)*

KINGSTON   TR2051
Black Robin (01227) 830230
Elham Valley Road, off A2 S of Canterbury at Barham signpost; CT4 6HS Recently refurbished 18th-c pub named after a notorious highwayman who was hanged nearby; kentish ales and good helpings of enjoyable home-made food from shortish menu (can eat in bar or back restaurant extension), friendly helpful staff; background and live music including some established folk artists, quiz nights; children and dogs welcome, disabled access, seats out on decking, open all day (till midnight Fri, Sat). *(Martin Jones)*

LADDINGFORD   TQ6848
Chequers (01622) 871266
The Street; ME18 6BP Friendly old beamed and weatherboarded village pub with good sensibly priced food from sandwiches and sharing boards up, well kept Adnams Southwold and three guests (Apr beer festival); children and dogs welcome, big garden with play area, shetland ponies in paddock, Medway walks nearby, one bedroom, open all day weekends. *(Lindy Andrews)*

LAMBERHURST   TQ6735
Vineyard (01892) 890222
Lamberhurst Down; S of village signed off A21; TN3 8EU Pretty dining pub by green and vineyards, same ownership as the Great House in Hawkhurst (Elite Pubs); main bar has most character with a few stools by counter serving Harveys, Sharps and a guest, log fire in brick fireplace with boar's head above, wall banquette draped with animal hide, cushioned leather armchairs and mix of dining furniture on flagstones or bare boards, enjoyable bistro-style food, long narrow room off with similar tables and chairs, equestrian pictures and antlers over fireplace, large ham for carving, sketched wallpaper of local landmarks, more formal panelled restaurant; seats and tables on terrace by car park, bedroom extension. *(Mike Swan)*

LINTON   TQ7550
Bull (01622) 743612
Linton Hill (A229 S of Maidstone); ME17 4AW Comfortably modernised 17th-c dining pub; good choice of food from sandwiches and light dishes to pub favourites and grills, popular carvery (Sun, Thurs evening), fine fireplace in nice old beamed bar, carpeted restaurant area, well kept Shepherd Neame ales, friendly efficient service; children welcome, dogs in bar,

side garden overlooking church, splendid far-reaching views from back decking, two gazebos, open all day. *(Edward May)*

LITTLE CHART   TQ9446
Swan (01233) 840702
The Street; TN27 0QB Attractive 15th-c beamed village pub with notable arched Dering windows, open fires in simple unspoilt front bar and good-sized dining area, enjoyable fairly traditional food (smaller appetites catered for), three well kept beers and decent wines, friendly staff; pool; children welcome, nice riverside garden, closed Mon and Tues, otherwise open all day till midnight (9pm Sun). *(Toby Jones, Martin Jones)*

LOWER HARDRES   TR1453
★**Granville** (01227) 700402
Faussett Hill, Street End; B2068 S of Canterbury; CT4 7AL Sister pub to the Sportsman at Seasalter; spacious and airy with contemporary furnishings in several linked areas, one with unusual central fire under large conical hood, also a proper public bar with farmhouse chairs, settles and woodburner, good food from simple bar lunches to more expensive restaurant-style dishes (not Sun evening, Mon – booking advised), fine choice of wines chalked on blackboard, Shepherd Neame Master Brew and a seasonal beer, efficient service, artwork for sale; background music, daily papers; children and dogs welcome, seats on small sunny terrace in and garden under large spreading tree, open all day Sun till 8pm, closed Mon evening. *(Alan Cowell)*

LUDDESDOWNE   TQ6667
★**Cock** (01474) 814208
Henley Street, N of village – OS Sheet 177 map reference 664672; off A227 in Meopham, or A228 in Cuxton; DA13 0XB Early 18th-c country pub with friendly long-serving no-nonsense landlord, at least six ales including Adnams, Goachers, Shepherd Neame and one brewed for the pub by local Musket, german beers too, good value straightforward food from large filled rolls and basket meals up, rugs on polished boards in pleasant bay-windowed lounge, beams and panelling, quarry-tiled locals' bar, woodburners, pews and other miscellaneous furnishings, aircraft pictures, masses of beer mats and bric-a-brac from stuffed animals to model cars, back dining conservatory; Tues quiz, bar billiards and darts; no children inside or on part-covered heated back terrace, dogs welcome, big secure garden, good walks, open all day. *(N R White)*

LYDDEN   TR2645
Bell (01304) 830296
Canterbury Road (B2060 NW of Dover); CT15 7EX Welcoming busy dining pub with good choice of well cooked interesting food along with pub favourites, meal deals

including popular Weds grill night (must book), well kept ales such as Sharps, friendly attentive staff, carpeted beamed bar with scrubbed pine tables, woodburner in large brick fireplace, restaurant; skittle alley; children welcome, picnic-sets in big sloping garden with play equipment, handy for A2, open (and food) all day Sun. *(David and Lesley Elliott, Peter Meister)*

MARDEN   TQ7547
Stile Bridge (01622) 831236
Staplehurst Road (A229); TN12 9BH Friendly roadside pub with five well kept ales and lots of bottled beers, proper ciders too, good traditional food (till 5pm Sun), events including beer festivals, live music and comedy nights; dogs welcome in bar, back garden, open all day (till 8pm Sun). *(Steve and Claire Harvey)*

MARGATE   TR3570
Lifeboat 07837 024259
Market Street; CT9 1EU Corner ale and cider house with cosy dimly lit front bar, barrel tables on sawdust floor, larger back room with open fire, up to six well kept local beers and excellent choice of kent ciders/perries, locally sourced cheeses, sausages, pies and seafood, friendly helpful service; regular live music, quiz Weds; handy for Turner Contemporary, open all day. *(Anon)*

MARTIN   TR3347
Old Lantern (01304) 852276
Off A258 Dover–Deal; The Street; CT15 5JL Pretty 17th-c pub (originally two farmworker's cottages), low beams, stripped brick and cosy corners in small neat bar with dining tables, well cooked food from traditional choices up, friendly quick service, Shepherd Neame ales and decent wines by the glass, soft lighting, open fire; quiet background music; children and dogs welcome, some tables out at front, more in good-sized back garden with big wendy house, beautiful setting, self-catering apartment, closed Sun evening, Mon and (apart from summer) Tues evening, no food Tues. *(Toby Jones)*

MATFIELD   TQ6642
Poet at Matfield (01892) 722416
Maidstone Road; TN12 7JH Attractively refurbished 17th-c beamed pub-restaurant named for Siegfried Sassoon who was born nearby; good well presented food from interesting varied menu (can be pricey and they add a service charge), ales such as Old Dairy and Tonbridge, nice wines and kentish gins, friendly efficient staff; open all day from 9.30am, closed Sun evening. *(Martin and Sue Day)*

MERSHAM   TR0438
Farriers Arms (01233) 720444
The Forstal/Flood Street; TN25 6NU Large opened-up beamed pub owned by

the local community, beers from own microbrewery including seasonal ones, enjoyable home made food from sandwiches to daily specials, children's menu, restaurant; live music and other events; pretty streamside garden behind, pleasant country views, open all day (till 1am Fri, Sat). *(Edward May)*

NEWENDEN   TQ8327
White Hart (01797) 252166
Rye Road (A268); TN18 5PN Popular 16th-c weatherboarded local; long low-beamed bar with big stone fireplace, dining areas off serving enjoyable good value pub food, well kept Harveys, Old Dairy, Rother Valley and guests, friendly helpful young staff; back games area with pool, sports TV, background music; children and dogs welcome, boules in large garden, near river (boat trips to NT's Bodiam Castle), six bedrooms, open all day. *(Belinda Stamp)*

NEWNHAM   TQ9557
★ George (01795) 890237
The Street; village signed from A2 W of Ospringe, outside Faversham; ME9 0LL Old-world pub with spreading open-plan rooms, hop-strung beams, stripped brickwork and polished floorboards, candles and lamps on handsome tables, two inglenooks (one with woodburner), generally well liked food, Shepherd Neame ales, real cider and ten wines by glass; monthly live music; children welcome, seats in spacious tree-sheltered garden, James Pimm (who devised the fruit cup Pimms) was born in the village, closed Sun evening. *(Dave Braisted, Gerald and Brenda Culliford, Roger and Anne Newbury)*

NONINGTON   TR2551
Royal Oak (01304) 841012
Holt Street; CT15 4HT Cleanly refurbished village pub-restaurant set up from the road, friendly welcoming staff, good pub food including range of burgers and daily specials, four well kept beers such as Fullers, Sharps, Wantsum and Whitstable; some live music; children and dogs welcome, picnic-sets on front deck looking over to village pond, more seats and play area in nice back garden, summer barbecues and outside bar, open all day, food all day Sat, till 5pm Sun. *(Luke Scotney)*

NORTHBOURNE   TR3352
Hare & Hounds (01304) 369188
Off A256 or A258 near Dover; The Street; CT14 0LG Chatty 17th-c village pub serving popular freshly made food (all day Sun till 6pm), well kept ales including Harveys and good choice of wines, friendly helpful service, clean interior with polished wood floors and exposed brickwork, log fire; quiz third Tues of month; children welcome, marquee and play area in garden, open all day. *(N R White)*

OARE   TR0163
★ Shipwrights Arms (01795) 590088
S shore of Oare Creek, E of village; signed from Oare Road/Ham Road junction in Faversham; ME13 7TU Remote and ancient marshland tavern with plenty of character, up to six kentish beers tapped from the cask (pewter tankards over counter), simple home-cooked food (not Sun evening or Mon), three dark simple little bars separated by standing timbers, wood partitions and narrow door arches, medley of seats from tapestry-cushioned stools to black panelled built-in settles forming booths, flags and boating pennants on ceiling, wind gauge above main door (takes reading from chimney); background local radio; children (away from bar area) and dogs welcome, large garden, path along Oare Creek to Swale estuary, lots of surrounding birdlife, closed Mon. *(N R White)*

OARE   TR0063
Three Mariners (01795) 533633
Church Road; ME13 0QA Comfortable simply restored 18th-c pub with good reputation for food including fresh fish, evening set menu option, Shepherd Neame ales and plenty of wines by the glass, local artwork on display, beams, bare-boards and log fire; attractive garden overlooking Faversham Creek, good walks, open all day. *(Colin McLachlan)*

OLD ROMNEY   TR0325
Rose & Crown (01797) 367500
Swamp Road off A259; TN29 9SQ Friendly bay-windowed pub with good value tasty food and well kept Greene King ales, Biddenden cider, helpful staff, dining conservatory; TV, pool and darts; children welcome, pretty garden with boules, chalet bedrooms, Romney Marsh view, closed Sun evening and Mon, otherwise open all day. *(Alan Cowell)*

OTFORD   TQ5259
Crown (01959) 522847
High Street, pond end; TN14 5PQ Well managed 16th-c local opposite village duck pond, pleasantly chatty beamed lounge with woodburner in old fireplace, unpretentious public bar, well kept ales such as Tonbridge and Westerham, friendly staff and forthright landlord (ex-army chef), popular food (not Sun-Tues evenings) including meal deals; monthly folk club and other live music, darts; dogs welcome, handy for walkers (North Downs Way passes the door), tree-shaded seats in back garden, open all day. *(Tina and David Woods-Taylor)*

PENSHURST   TQ4943
★ Rock (01892) 870296
Hoath Corner, Chiddingstone Hoath, on back road Chiddingstone–Cowden; OS Sheet 188 map reference 497431;

TN8 7BS Tiny welcoming cottage with undulating brick floor, simple furnishings and woodburner in fine brick inglenook, well kept Larkins and good home-made food from varied menu, large stuffed bull's head for ring the bull, up a step to smaller room with long wooden settle by nice table; walkers and dogs welcome, picnic-sets out in front and on back lawn. *(Martin and Sue Day)*

PETT BOTTOM   TR1652
Duck (01227) 830354
Off B2068 S of Canterbury, via Lower Hardres; CT4 5PB Popular tile-hung pub in attractive downland spot, long bare-boards bar with scrubbed tables, pine panelling and two log fires, very good freshly cooked food (not Sun evening) including weekday set lunch, friendly helpful service, two or three well kept beers such as Old Dairy and Tonbridge, Biddenden cider and good wine choice; children and dogs welcome, seats and old well out in front, garden behind where Ian Fleming was often to be found making notes for his James Bond books (see blue plaque), camping close by, shut Mon, otherwise open all day. *(Anon)*

PETTERIDGE   TQ6640
Hopbine (01892) 722561
Petteridge Lane; NE of village; TN12 7NE Unspoilt tiled and weatherboarded cottage in quiet hamlet, two small rooms with open fire between, traditional pubby furniture, hops and horsebrasses, three well kept local ales, enjoyable good value home-made food including wood-fired pizzas, friendly staff, steps up to simple back part with brick fireplace; outside gents'; terrace seating, open all day Fri-Sun. *(Lindy Andrews)*

PLAXTOL   TQ6054
★ Golding Hop (01732) 882150
Sheet Hill (0.5 miles S of Ightham, between A25 and A227); TN15 0PT Secluded old-fashioned country local with hands-on plain-talking landlord; simple dimly lit two-level bar, cask-tapped Adnams and guests kept well, local farm ciders (sometimes their own), short choice of basic good value bar food (not Mon or Tues evenings), old photographs of the pub, woodburners; bar billiards, portable TV for major sporting events; no children inside, suntrap streamside lawn and well fenced play area over lane, good walks; for sale as we went to press. *(Anon)*

PLUCKLEY   TQ9245
Black Horse (01233) 841948
The Street; TN27 0QS Attractive medieval pub behind Georgian façade (the Hare & Hounds in TV series *The Darling Buds of May*); five log fires including vast inglenook, bare boards, beams and flagstones, dark half-panelling and distinctive mullioned windows, ales such as Greene King, Harveys and

Shepherd Neame, enjoyable traditional food from baguettes to good Sun roasts, friendly attentive service, roomy carpeted dining areas, Gatling machine gun by the loos, assorted ghosts; background music; children and dogs welcome, spacious informal garden by tall sycamores, play area, good local walks, open all day. *(Peter Meister)*

PLUCKLEY   TQ9144
Rose & Crown (01233) 840048
Mundy Bois – spelled Monday Boys on some maps – off Smarden Road SW of village centre; TN27 0ST Popular 17th-c tile-hung pub with good food (all day Sun) from french chef, three well kept beers such as Hopdaemon, Shepherd Neame and Whitstable, friendly attentive service, main bar with massive inglenook, small snug and restaurant; background music; children and dogs welcome, pretty garden and terrace with views, play area, open all day. *(Caroline Prescott)*

RAMSGATE   TR3764
Conqueror 07890 203282
Grange Road/St Mildred's Road; CT11 9LR Cosy single-room micropub in former corner shop, welcoming enthusiastic landlord serving three changing ales straight from the cask, also local cider and apple juice, friendly chatty atmosphere, large windows (may steam up when busy) and old photos of the cross-channel paddle steamer the pub is named after; dogs welcome, closed Sun evening, Mon. *(Edward May)*

RAMSGATE   TR3765
Great Tree (01843) 590708
Margate Road; CT11 7SP Quirky relaxed place with four real ales and 20 or so proper ciders, interesting teas and good coffee too, various events including live jazz, opera (puerto rican landlady is an opera singer), film and poetry evenings, unusual café-bar décor with local artwork, various board games; children (away from the bar) and dogs welcome, closed weekday lunchtimes, open all day Sun. *(Simone Stream)*

RAMSGATE   TR3664
Sir Stanley Gray (01843) 599590
Pegwell Road; CT11 0NJ Over the road from the Pegwell Bay Hotel and connected by a tunnel; fine sea and coastline views from carpeted bar with plush seating and mock beams, open fire, wide choice of popular food all day, friendly service, ales including local Gadds; children welcome, terrace tables. *(Toby Jones)*

ROCHESTER   TQ7468
Coopers Arms (01634) 404298
St Margaret's Street; ME1 1TL Ancient jettied building behind cathedral, cosily unpretentious with two comfortable beamed bars, low-priced pub food and good range of well kept beers, list of landlords back

to 1543 and ghostly stories of a monk who was walled-up here (a mannequin marks the spot); live music (Sun) and quiz nights; tables in attractive courtyard, open all day. *(Mike Swan)*

ROCHESTER   TQ7467
Man of Kent 07772 214315
John Street; ME1 1YN Small basic backstreet corner pub with impressive range of well kept local ales including Goachers, Hopdaemon, Kent and Ramsgate, also draught and bottled continental beers, kentish wines and ciders, friendly knowledgeable staff, no-frills L-shaped bar with well worn seating, log fire, newspapers and board games; live music; decked back garden, open all day from 2pm weekdays (3pm Mon), noon Sat, Sun. *(Mike Swan)*

ROLVENDEN   TQ8431
Bull (01580) 241212
Regent Street; TN17 4PB Welcoming small tile-hung cottage with woodburner in fine brick inglenook, high-backed leather dining chairs around rustic tables on stripped boards, built-in panelled wall seats, fresh flowers, ales from Harveys and Old Dairy, enjoyable food (not Sun evening in winter) from favourites up, pale oak tables in dining room, friendly helpful service; soft background music; children welcome, dogs allowed in bar, a few picnic-sets in front, more seats in sizeable back garden, open all day. *(Caroline Prescott)*

ROLVENDEN LAYNE   TQ8530
Ewe & Lamb (01580) 241837
Maytham Road; TN17 4NP Beamed, bare-boards pub with well kept Adnams, Harveys and a guest ale, enjoyable home-made food including good value two-course lunch, friendly efficient service, back restaurant, log fires; children and dogs welcome, seats out at front behind white picket fence, open all day. *(V Brogden)*

SANDWICH   TR3358
★George & Dragon (01304) 613106
Fisher Street; CT13 9EJ Popular 15th-c backstreet dining pub run by two brothers (one cooks), very good often imaginative food from open kitchen, well kept Wantsum, Otter and a couple of guests, nice choice of wines by the glass, good friendly service, open-plan beamed interior with blazing fire; children and dogs (in bar) welcome, pretty back terrace, open all day Sat, closed Sun evening. *(Guy Vowles, Di and Mike Gillam)*

SARRE   TR2564
Crown (01843) 847808
Ramsgate Road (A253) off A28; CT7 0LF Historic 15th-c inn (Grade I listed) sandwiched between two main roads; front bar and other rambling rooms including restaurant, beams and log fires, well kept Shepherd Neame ales and decent wines,

own cherry brandy (the pub is known locally as the Cherry Brandy House), enjoyable locally sourced food from sandwiches up, good friendly service; children welcome, side garden (traffic noise), comfortable bedrooms, open all day. *(C and R Bromage)*

SEASALTER   TR0864
★Sportsman (01227) 273370
Faversham Road, off B2040; CT5 4BP Restaurant dining pub just inside seawall – rather unprepossessing from outside but surprisingly light and airy; imaginative contemporary cooking using plenty of seafood (not Sun evening, Mon, must book and not cheap), home-baked breads, good wine choice including english, a couple of well kept Shepherd Neame ales, knowledgeable landlord and friendly staff, two plain linked rooms and long conservatory, scrubbed pine tables, wheelback and basket-weave dining chairs on wood floor, local artwork; children welcome, plastic glasses for outside, wide views over marshland with grazing sheep and (from seawall) across to Sheppey, small caravan park one side, wood chalets the other, open all day Sun. *(Christian Mole, Martin and Sue Day)*

SELLING   TR0455
Rose & Crown (01227) 752214
Follow Perry Wood signs; ME13 9RY Tucked-away traditional 16th-c country pub with beams and two inglenooks, well kept Adnams, Harveys and a guest, pub food from sandwiches up, friendly service, games such as cribbage and shut the box; background music, quiz first Weds of month; children welcome, dogs on leads in bar, back garden with play area and bat and trap, nice walks (Pulpit viewing platform nearby), open all day Sun, closed Mon evening. *(Caroline Prescott)*

SEVENOAKS   TQ5354
Black Boy (01732) 452192
Bank Street; TN13 1UW Centrally placed Shepherd Neame pub in pedestrianised area, bare boards, open fire and some comfortable sofas, their well kept ales and decent wines by the glass, lunchtime pubby food from sandwiches up (just snacks in the evening), good friendly service, live acoustic music first Tues of month; free wi-fi; nice covered seating area outside, open all day (closed Sun in winter). *(David Hunt)*

SEVENOAKS   TQ5555
★Bucks Head (01732) 761330
Godden Green, just E; TN15 0JJ Welcoming and relaxed flower-decked pub with neatly kept bar and restaurant area, good freshly cooked blackboard food from sandwiches up, roast on Sun, well kept Shepherd Neame and a guest, beams, panelling and splendid inglenooks; children and dogs welcome, front terrace overlooking informal green and duck pond, pretty back

garden with mature trees, pergola and views over quiet country behind Knole (NT), popular with walkers. *(B J Harding)*

SEVENOAKS TQ5355
Halfway House (01732) 463667
*2.5 miles from M25 junction 5;
TN13 2JD* Nicely updated old roadside pub with friendly staff and regulars, good competitively priced food from sensibly short menu, three changing ales, upper bar with record deck and collection of LPs (can bring your own), some live music too; handy for the station, parking can be tricky, open all day (no food weekend evenings, Mon). *(Anon)*

SHOREHAM TQ5161
Two Brewers (01959) 522800
High Street; TN14 7TD Family-run village pub with two modernised beamed rooms, back part more restaurant, popular freshly made food and three well kept changing kentish ales, friendly helpful staff, snug areas with comfortable seating, two woodburners; some live music; handy for walkers, seats out in front behind picket fence, open all day Sat, till 6pm Sun, closed Mon, Tues. *(Martin and Sue Day)*

SNARGATE TQ9928
★**Red Lion** (01797) 344648
B2080 Appledore–Brenzett; TN29 9UQ Unchanging 16th-c pub in same family for over 100 years, simple old-fashioned charm in three timeless little rooms with original cream wall panelling, heavy beams in sagging ceilings, dark pine Victorian farmhouse chairs on bare boards, an old piano and coal fire, local cider and four or five ales including Goachers tapped from casks behind unusual free-standing marble-topped counter, no food, traditional games like toad in the hole, nine men's morris and table skittles; children in family room, dogs in bar, outdoor lavatories, cottage garden, closed Mon evening. *(Edward May)*

ST MARGARET'S BAY TR3744
★**Coastguard** (01304) 853176
Off A256 NE of Dover; keep on down through the village to the bottom of the bay, pub off on right by the beach; CT15 6DY At bottom of a steep windy road with lovely sea views (France visible on a clear day) from prettily planted balcony and beachside seating, nautical décor in carpeted wood-clad bar, four changing ales, bottled continentals, over 40 whiskies and a carefully chosen wine list (some kentish ones), popular fairly priced food from shortish menu, more fine views from restaurant with close-set tables on wood-strip floor; background music, free wi-fi (mobile phones pick up french signal); children and dogs allowed in certain areas, good walks, open all day. *(John Wooll, Peter Smith and Judith Brown, N R White)*

STAPLEHURST TQ7846
Lord Raglan (01622) 843747
About 1.5 miles from town centre towards Maidstone, turn right off A229 into Chart Hill Road opposite Chart Cars; OS Sheet 188 map reference 785472; TN12 0DE Country pub with cosy chatty area around narrow bar counter, hop-covered low beams, big log fire and woodburner, mix of comfortably worn dark wood furniture, good reasonably priced home-cooked food, Goachers, Harveys and a guest, farm cider and perry, good wine list; children and dogs welcome, reasonable wheelchair access, tables on terrace and in side orchard, Aug onion festival, closed Sun. *(Mike Swan)*

STONE IN OXNEY TQ9327
★**Crown** (01233) 758302
Off B2082 Iden–Tenterden; TN30 7JN Smart country dining pub with friendly landlord and staff, very good bistro-style food from landlady-chef, well kept Larkins tapped from the cask, light airy open feel with lots of wood, red walls and big inglenook log fire; no under-12s in the evening, rustic furniture on terrace, two bedrooms, open Thurs to Sun lunchtime. *(Stuart Paulley)*

TENTERDEN TQ8833
White Lion (01580) 765077
High Street; TN30 6BD Comfortably updated beamed and timbered 16th-c inn behind Georgian façade, enjoyable food including Josper grills and pizzas from open kitchen, mainly local ales such as Old Dairy and a beer badged for them, good choice of other drinks including cocktails, big log fire, friendly helpful staff; background music; heated terrace overlooking street, nicely refurbished bedrooms, good breakfast, open (and food) all day. *(Dave Braisted)*

THURNHAM TQ8057
★**Black Horse** (01622) 737185
Not far from M20 junction 7; off A249 at Detling; ME14 3LD Large busy dining pub with enjoyable food from good sandwiches up, children's menu, three well kept ales including Westerham, farm ciders and country wines, friendly efficient uniformed staff, alcove seating, timbers and hop-strung beams, bare boards and log fires, back restaurant area; dogs and walkers welcome, pleasant garden with partly covered terrace, nice views, by Pilgrims Way, comfortable modern bedroom block, hearty breakfast, open (and food) all day. *(Martin and Sue Day)*

TOYS HILL TQ4752
★**Fox & Hounds** (01732) 750328
Off A25 in Brasted, via Brasted Chart and The Chart; TN16 1QG Traditional country pub under newish management; bar area separated by two-way woodburner, plain tables and chairs on dark boards or stone

floor, hunting prints, old photographs, plates and copper jugs, modern carpeted dining extension with big windows overlooking tree-sheltered garden, enjoyable home-made pubby food (not Sun evening) from lunchtime sandwiches up, well kept Greene King ales and several wines by the glass, friendly efficient staff; background music, darts, free wi-fi; children and dogs (in bar) welcome, roadside verandah used by smokers, good local walks and views, handy for Chartwell and Emmetts Garden (both NT), open all day Fri-Sun. *(Brian Glozier)*

TUDELEY   TQ6145
Poacher & Partridge
(01732) 358934 *Hartlake Road; TN11 0PH* Newly refurbished in smart/country style by Elite Pubs (Great House in Hawkhurst, Dirty Habit at Hollingbourne and others), light modern interior with feature pizza oven, wide range of good food (all day weekends) including daily specials, ales such as Sharps Doom Bar and Timothy Taylors Landlord, good choice of wines by the glass, friendly attentive staff; children welcome, outside bar and grill, play area, near interesting church with Chagall stained glass (note roof paintings at pub's entrance), local walks (leaflets provided), open all day.
(Nigel and Jean Eames)

TUNBRIDGE WELLS   TQ5837
Bull (01892) 263489
Frant Road; TN2 5LH Friendly 19th-c pub towards the outskirts of town, two modernised linked areas with one or two quirky touches, chunky pine tables and kitchen chairs on stripped-wood floor, a couple of leather sofas by open fire, well kept Shepherd Neame ales, generous helpings of enjoyable home-cooked food from changing menu (not Sun evening, Mon); children (till 8.30pm) and dogs welcome, seats out on fenced roadside terrace, closed Mon lunchtime, otherwise open all day.
(Lindy Andrews)

TUNBRIDGE WELLS   TQ5838
Compasses (01892) 530744
Little Mount Sion; TN1 1YP Old pub tucked up from High Street and backing on to park, split-level beamed rooms around central bar, bare boards or carpet, log fires (one in large brick fireplace), some stained and frosted glass, six well kept ales including Greene King and a beer badged for the pub, well priced food from snacks up, proper coffee; background music, free wi-fi, bar billiards; children and dogs welcome, teak and rattan-style furniture on good-sized front terrace, open (and food) all day. *(Emma Scofield)*

TUNBRIDGE WELLS   TQ5839
Sussex Arms (01892) 549579
Nevill Street, off Frant Road; TN2 5TE Laid-back place hidden away behind the

---

Pantiles (if entering by side door, make sure you choose the right handle); opened-up areas around bar serving good selection of ales, craft beers and ciders, enjoyable lunchtime food (Thurs-Sun) from shortish menu, friendly staff and eclectic mix of customers, cellar bar for functions; live and background music (some from old vinyl), Thurs quiz, bar billiards; children and dogs welcome, seats on glass-covered terrace, open all day (till 1am Fri, Sat). *(Emma Scofield)*

UNDERRIVER   TQ5552
★White Rock (01732) 833112
SE of Sevenoaks, off B245; TN15 0SB Attractive village pub with good food from pubby choices up (all day weekends, best to book), well kept Harveys, Westerham and a guest, decent wines, friendly chatty staff and good mix of locals and visitors, beams, bare boards and stripped brickwork in cosy original part with adjacent dining area, another bar in modern extension with woodburner; background and some live music, pool; children welcome, dogs may be allowed (ask first), small front garden, back terrace and large lawn with boules and bat and trap, pretty churchyard and walks nearby, open all day summer, all day weekends winter. *(Martin and Sue Day, Tina and David Woods-Taylor)*

WEST MALLING   TQ6857
Bull (01732) 842753
High Street; ME19 6QH Friendly old pub with good selection of mainly local ales and reasonably priced traditional home-made food (not Sun-Weds evenings), hop-strung beams, bare boards and big log fire, refurbished restaurant; live music first Sat of month, Mon quiz; children and dogs welcome, open all day Fri-Sun. *(Mike Swan)*

WESTBERE   TR1862
Old Yew Tree (01227) 710501
Just off A18 Canterbury–Margate; CT2 0HH Heavily beamed 14th-c pub in pretty village, simply furnished bare-boards bar, inglenook log fire, good reasonably priced food from varied menu, Shepherd Neame Master Brew and a guest, friendly helpful staff, quiz first Weds of month; picnic-sets in garden behind, open all day weekends, closed Mon. *(Joan and Alec Lawrence)*

WESTERHAM   TQ4453
General Wolfe (01959) 562104
High Street, W side of village; TN16 1RQ Attractive 16th-c white weatherboarded pub, refurbished but keeping character, one long cottagey room with old beams and woodburner, also a snug, Greene King ales and a local guest, popular sensibly priced food (not Sun-Tues evenings) including one or two unusual dishes; dogs welcome, seats out on raised back deck, open all day. *(Anon)*

WESTERHAM   TQ4454
Grasshopper on the Green
(01959) 562926 *The Green; TN16 1AS*
Old black-beamed pub (small former
coaching house) facing village green, three
linked bar areas with log fire at back, well
kept ales including Westerham, popular
pubby food from sandwiches up, restaurant
upstairs; free wi-fi; children and dogs
welcome, seating out at front and in back
garden with play area, open all day. *(Martin
and Sue Day, Tony and Wendy Hobden)*

WESTGATE-ON-SEA   TR3270
Bake & Alehouse   07581 468797
*Off St Mildred's Road, down alley
by cinema; CT8 8RE* Former bakery
converted to micropub; simple little bare-
boards room with a few tables (expect to
share when busy), collages on walls, around
four well kept interesting cask-tapped ales,
real ciders – maybe a warm winter one
(Monks Delight), kentish wines, local cheese,
sausage rolls and pork pies, friendly chatty
atmosphere; closed Sun evening, Mon.
(Mike Swan)

WESTWELL   TQ9847
Wheel (01233) 712430
The Street; TN25 4LQ Traditional brick-
built village pub under welcoming new
management; popular fairly pubby food,
well kept Shepherd Neame ales and decent
choice of wines, dining areas around bar
with stripped-pine tables and chairs, cosy
atmosphere; children welcome, dogs in bar,
good-sized garden with metal furniture, close
to Pilgrims Way, open (and food) all day
weekends, closed Mon. *(Toby Jones)*

WHITSTABLE   TR1066
Black Dog
High Street; CT5 1BB Quirky micropub
(former deli) with five changing ales and
several artisan ciders tapped from back
room, friendly staff may offer tasters, snacky
food, narrow dimly lit Victorian-feel bar
with high tables and benches along two
sides, intriguing mix of pictures and other
bits and pieces on green walls, prominent
chandelier hanging from red ceiling; eclectic
background music and occasional folk
sessions; open all day. *(Dr Martin Owton)*

WHITSTABLE   TR1066
Old Neptune (01227) 272262
Marine Terrace; CT5 1EJ Great view
over Swale estuary from this popular

unpretentious weatherboarded pub set right
on the beach (rebuilt after being washed
away in 1897 storm); Harveys, Whitstable and
a guest, lunchtime food from shortish menu
including seafood specials, friendly young
staff; weekend live music; children and dogs
welcome, picnic-sets on the shingle (plastic
glasses out here and occasional barbecues),
fine sunsets, can get very busy in summer,
open all day. *(N R White, Adrian Johnson)*

WICKHAMBREAUX   TR2258
Rose (01227) 721763
The Green; CT3 1RQ Attractive 16th-c
and partly older pub with enjoyable home-
made food (more elaborate evening menu),
friendly helpful staff, Greene King IPA and
three guests (May/Aug beer festivals), real
ciders, small bare-boards bar with log fire in
big fireplace, dining area beyond standing
timbers with woodburner, hop-strung beams,
panelling and stripped brick, quiz second
Tues of month; children and dogs welcome,
enclosed side garden and small courtyard,
nice spot across green from church and
watermill, open all day, no food Sun evening.
(Toby Jones)

WILLESBOROUGH
STREET   TR0341
Blacksmiths Arms (01233) 623975
The Street; TN24 0NA Beamed village
pub dating in part from the 17th c, Fullers
London Pride and a couple of guests, good
home-cooked traditional food (not Sun
evening) from sandwiches and snacks
up, friendly service, open fires including
inglenook; children and dogs welcome,
picnic-sets in good-sized garden with play
area, handy for M20 (junction 10), open
all day. *(Tony and Vivien Smith)*

WORTH   TR3356
St Crispin (01304) 612081
*Signed off A258 S of Sandwich;
CT14 0DF* Dating from 15th c with
low beams, stripped brickwork and bare
boards, enjoyable traditional home-made
food including bargain OAP weekday
lunch in bar, carpeted restaurant or back
conservatory (dogs allowed here), four
real ales such as Black Sheep, Harveys,
Sharps and Timothy Taylors, central log
fire; children welcome away from bar, nice
big garden behind with terrace and play
area, seven bedrooms (three in motel-style
extension), lovely village position, closed
Mon, Tues; for sale last we heard, so things
may change. *(N R White)*

Real ale to us means beer that has matured naturally in its cask – not pressurised
or filtered. We name all real ales stocked. We usually name ales preserved under a
light blanket of carbon dioxide too, though purists – pointing out that this stops the
natural yeasts developing – would disagree (most people, including us,
can't tell the difference!)

WROTHAM
TQ6258

Moat (01732) 882263

London Road; TN15 7RR Extended Badger family dining pub, beams and stripped masonry, rugs on wood and stone floors, mix of furniture including leather sofas and country tables and chairs, wide range of good value plentiful food, their ales kept well, friendly efficient staff, medieval barn for functions; free wi-fi; garden tables and good play area, open (and food) all day. *(Gordon and Margaret Ormondroyd)*

WYE
TR0546

New Flying Horse (01233) 812297

Upper Bridge Street; TN25 5AN 17th-c Shepherd Neame inn with beams and inglenook, enjoyable food including fixed-price menu in bar and restaurant, friendly accommodating staff; Sun quiz, live music last Thurs of month; children welcome, good-sized pretty garden with play area and miniature thatched pub (former Chelsea Flower Show exhibit), nine bedrooms (some in converted stables), open all day. *(Peter Smith and Judith Brown)*

YALDING
TQ6950

★**Walnut Tree** (01622) 814266

B2010 SW of Maidstone; ME18 6JB Timbered village pub with split-level main bar, fine old settles, a long cushioned mahogany bench and mix of dining chairs on brick or carpeted floors, chunky wooden tables with church candles, interesting old photographs, big inglenook log fire, well kept Black Sheep, Harveys and Skinners, good bar food and more inventive restaurant menu, attractive raftered dining room with high-backed leather dining chairs on parquet flooring, lots of local events; background and occasional live music, TV; a few picnic-sets out by road. *(Steve and Claire Harvey)*

Lancashire

with Greater Manchester, Merseyside and Wirral

BARLEY SD8240 Map 7

Barley Mow 🛏

(01282) 690868 – www.seafoodpubcompany.com/barley-mow

Barley Lane; BB12 9JX

Interestingly furnished inn with interconnected bar and dining areas, woodburning stoves, rewarding food and ales and friendly staff; well equipped bedrooms

---

The attractively comfortable bedrooms here make the perfect base for exploring the lovely Pendle countryside and breakfasts are generous; they also have bike storage. Resembling a hunting lodge inside, the various bars and dining rooms have animal hide chairs and cushions, stuffed pheasant and fish, horns, antlers and a big boar's head – plus bellows, butterchurns and large stone bottles on the exposed-stone, cream-coloured or planked walls. There are woodburning stoves (one in a raised two-sided fireplace), all manner of mixed wooden and leather button-backed chairs and stools around tables of various sizes on carpet, bare boards and flagstones, long rustic wall seats with scatter cushions, armchairs and, against the counter, gold plush bar chairs. Moorhouses Pride of Pendle, Thwaites Wainwright and Timothy Taylors Landlord on handpump and eight wines by the glass; background music, TV and board games. It's all very relaxed and friendly; service is good. This is part of the Seafood Pub Company.

🍴 Good, hearty food includes breakfasts for non-residents (from 7.30am), sandwiches, whitebait with chilli and lime mayonnaise, meat and potato mini pasties with mustard sauce, chicken caesar salad, shepherd's pie with smoked cheese mash, cod and prawn fishcakes with tartare sauce, gammon and eggs, rack of baby back ribs with barbecue sauce and fries, mixed grill, and puddings such as apple crumble and jam roly-poly and custard. *Benchmark main dish: steak burger with toppings and fries £11.95. Two-course evening meal £19.00.*

Free house ~ Licensee Jocelyn Neve ~ Real ale ~ Open 7.30am-11pm; 8.30am-midnight (10 Sun) Sat ~ Bar food 12-8.30; 11.30-9.30 Fri, Sat; 11.30-8.30 Sun ~ Children welcome ~ Dogs allowed in bar ~ Wi-fi ~ Bedrooms: £75/£80 *Recommended by Caroline Prescott, Isobel Mackinlay*

BASHALL EAVES SD6943 Map 7

Red Pump 🛏

(01254) 826227 – www.theredpumpinn.co.uk

NW of Clitheroe, off B6478 or B6243; BB7 3DA

Beautifully placed country inn with a cosy bar, highly thought-of food in more contemporary dining rooms and changing beers; bedrooms

Full of character and interest, this is a former farmhouse in lovely Forest of Bowland countryside; there are splendid views from seats in the terraced gardens (where they grow their own herbs). Inside, there's a cheerful atmosphere, a chatty, helpful landlord, two pleasantly up-to-date dining rooms and a traditional, cosy central bar: bookshelves, cushioned settles, wheelbacks and other nice old chairs on flagstones and a log fire. The quickly changing range of three regional beers on handpump might include Bowland Hen Harrier, Ilkley Gold and Moorhouses Pendle Witches Brew and they also keep several wines by the glass and a good range of malt whiskies; board games. This is a comfortable place to stay (they were adding more bedrooms as we went to press), breakfasts are good and generous and residents can fish in the nearby river.

Well liked food includes lunchtime sandwiches, lamb kidneys with spinach and bacon on soda bread, home-cured salmon with caper and lemon dressing, mixed seafood or cured meat salads, sweet potato and goats cheese tart, beef in red wine with horseradish mash, chicken marinated in thyme and garlic with white wine, mushroom and cream sauce, slow-roast pork belly with bubble and squeak and sage and apple gravy, and puddings such as rhubarb and raspberry panna cotta and sticky toffee and date pudding with butterscotch sauce. *Benchmark main dish: rare-breed irish 25-day-aged sirloin steak £19.50. Two-course evening meal £20.00.*

Free house ~ Licensees Frances and Jonathan Gledhill ~ Real ale ~ Open 12-2, 5.30-11; 12-11 Sat; 12-10 Sun; closed Mon ~ Bar food 12-2, 6-9; 12-7.30 Sun ~ Restaurant ~ Children welcome ~ Dogs allowed in bar and bedrooms ~ Bedrooms: £75/£105
Recommended by Jo Garnett, Nick Sharpe

BISPHAM GREEN   SD4813 Map 7
Eagle & Child 🏅 ♟ 🍺
(01257) 462297 – www.ainscoughs.co.uk
Maltkiln Lane (Parbold–Croston road, off B5246); L40 3SG

Successful all-rounder with antiques in stylishly simple interior, enterprising food, an interesting range of beers and appealing rustic garden

As well as this bustling pub, there's a shop in a handsome side barn selling interesting wines and pottery, plus a proper butcher and a deli. The largely open-plan bar is carefully furnished with a mix of small old oak chairs, an attractive oak coffer, several handsomely carved antique oak settles (the finest made in part, it seems, from a 16th-c wedding bed-head), old hunting prints and engravings and hop-draped low beams. Also, red walls, coir matting, oriental rugs on ancient flagstones in front of a fine old stone fireplace and counter; the pub's dogs are called Betty and Doris. Friendly young staff serve Southport Golden Sands and Carousel, Thwaites Original and guests such as Butcombe Bitter, Cheddar Potholer, Cottage Lightning Ale and Lancaster Bomber on handpump, farm cider, decent wines and around 30 malt whiskies. A popular beer festival is usually held on the early May bank holiday weekend. The spacious, gently rustic garden has a well tended but unconventional bowling green; beyond is a wild area that's home to crested newts and moorhens. This is part of the Ainscoughs group.

The standard of food is high and includes sandwiches, twice-baked cheese soufflé with walnut, celery and apple salad, poached salmon and prawn cocktail, sausages and mash with onion gravy, beer-battered haddock with triple-cooked chips, sweet potato, feta and red pepper burger with mustard mayonnaise and spicy tomato salsa, monkfish wrapped in bacon with chorizo and butter bean cassoulet and garlic and tomato sauce, chicken with truffle gnocchi, baby vegetables and madeira sauce, and puddings such as peanut butter panna cotta with blackcurrant jelly and peanut brittle, and passion-fruit and mango eton mess. *Benchmark main dish: steak and mushroom in ale pie £12.75. Two-course evening meal £20.00.*

Free house ~ Licensee Peter Robinson ~ Real ale ~ Open 12-11 (10.30) ~ Bar food 12-2, 5.30-8.30 (9 Fri, Sat); 12-8.30 Sun ~ Children welcome ~ Dogs welcome
Recommended by Robert Wivell, Richard Kennell, Alison Ball, Ian Walton, Dr Kevan Tucker, R T and J C Moggridge

BLACKBURN   SD6525   Map 7
Oyster & Otter ★ ♀

(01254) 203200 – www.seafoodpubcompany.com/the-oyster-otter
1.8 miles from M65 junction 3: A674 towards Blackburn, turn right at Feniscowles mini-roundabout, signposted to Darwen and Tockholes, into Livesey Branch Road; BB2 5DQ

Contemporary informal bar-restaurant with good food, especially fresh fish and seafood

The modern layout in this distinctive clapboard and stone building perched above the road is very appealing and almost New England in style. Well cushioned dining booths line big windows on one side, while additional comfortable table seating is divided into cosy areas by shoulder-high walling and a big stone central hearth with a woodburning stove. If you just want a chat and a drink or coffee, there are high suede seats by a couple of tall tables, plaid bar stools by the serving counter, and an end area with squishy leather sofas, a plaid sofa and library chairs – with a view of the kitchen to tempt you to change your mind and have some food too. Thwaites Wainwright and a guest ale on handpump and ten wines by the glass. Helpful young staff wear neat black aprons, and the piped rock music suits the style of the place. There are teak tables on decking above the road. This is part of the Seafood Pub Company.

As well as particularly good fishy choices, such as vietnamese fishcakes with pineapple, chilli and mint dipping sauce, haddock with creamed spinach and lancashire cheese crumb, and hake with bacon and brioche crumb, red wine shallots and dauphinoise potatoes, the rewarding food includes interesting lunchtime rolls, baby back ribs with orange, rosemary and chilli, duck red curry with sweet potato, thai basil and coconut rice, slow-cooked shin of beef in ale with parsley mash, and puddings such as steamed syrup sponge with custard and caramel chocolate pot with salted peanut praline. *Benchmark main dish: beer-battered haddock and chips £10.50. Two-course evening meal £21.00.*

Free house ~ Licensee Joycelyn Neve ~ Real ale ~ Open 12-11 (midnight Fri, Sat) ~ Bar food 12-9 (10 Fri, Sat, 8.30 Sun) ~ Children welcome ~ Wi-fi ~ Live music third Fri of month *Recommended by W K Wood, Jo Garnett*

CLAUGHTON   SD5666   Map 7
Fenwick Arms

(01524) 221157 – www.seafoodpubcompany.com/the-fenwick
A683 Kirkby Lonsdale–Lancaster; LA2 9LA

Delicious fish (and non-fishy choices) in timbered refurbished pub with helpful, friendly staff, real ales and wines by the glass and seats outside

After a walk in the wonderful Lune Valley, this 250-year-old black and white pub is just the place to head for as their particularly good food – mainly seafood – is served all day. The atmosphere is warm and inviting and careful refurbishments include white-painted beams in wonky ceilings, open fires (one in a black range) and painted panelled walls. Smartly upholstered and antique-style dining chairs, stools and window seats with scatter cushions sit around all shapes of table on carpet or bare floorboards. Friendly, professional staff serve Thwaites Wainwright, Timothy Taylor Landlord and a guest beer on handpump, 14 wines by the glass and a good choice of spirits; background music. Outside on the front terrace are picnic-sets under parasols. This is part of the Seafood Pub Company.

Majoring on the freshest of fish, the particularly good choices include seaside fritto misto, smoked haddock with ale rarebit, goan spiced seafood kebab with minted yoghurt, regular or large fish and chips and a fish dish of the day. They also offer lunchtime sandwiches, twice-baked local cheese soufflé, chicken and ham pie, rack of baby back ribs with barbecue sauce, 28-day-aged steaks, and puddings such as caramel chocolate pot with salted peanut praline and lemon curd and gingernut cheesecake with poached blackberries; the set lunch menu includes a glass of wine or beer. *Benchmark main dish: peppered tuna steak with creamed spinach and parmesan fries £17.50. Two-course evening meal £20.00.*

Free house ~ Licensee Joycelyn Neve ~ Real ale ~ Open 12-10 (midnight Sat) ~ Bar food 12-9 (10 Fri, Sat, 8.30 Sun) ~ Restaurant ~ Children welcome ~ Dogs allowed in bar ~ Wi-fi
Recommended by Lindy Andrews, Dr Simon Innes, Ray and Winifred Halliday

DOWNHAM   SD7844   Map 7
Assheton Arms 🍴 ⌇

(01200) 441227 – www.seafoodpubcompany.com/the-assheton-arms
Off A59 NE of Clitheroe, via Chatburn; BB7 4BJ

Lancashire Dining Pub of the Year

Fine old inn with plenty of dining and drinking space, a friendly welcome, several real ales and creative food; bedrooms

If you dine in the two-level restaurant in this handsome stone pub, you'll have views over the picturesque village and Pendle Hill. There's an attractive assortment of dining chairs and tables on a wooden floor or carpeting, hunting prints on cream-painted walls, and two fireplaces with a woodburning stove in one and a lovely old black kitchen range in the other. It's a genuinely friendly place with helpful staff and an easy-going atmosphere. A small front bar, with a hatch to the kitchen, has tweed-upholstered armchairs and stools on big flagstones around a single table, a woodburning stove surrounded by logs, and drawings of dogs and hunting prints on grey-green walls. Off to the right, a wood-panelled partition creates a cosy area where there are similarly cushioned pews and nice old chairs around various tables on a rug-covered wooden floor, and a couple of window chairs. The main bar, up a couple of steps, has more tweed-upholstered seating and dark wooden tables and chairs, old photographs of the pub and the village on pale walls, and a marble bar counter where they serve Moorhouses Pride of Pendle, Thwaites Wainwright and Timothy Taylors Landlord on handpump, a dozen wines by the glass and farm cider; background music and board games. Outside at the front are picnic-sets and tables and chairs, and the setting at the top of a steep hill is very pretty; the church opposite is lovely. The newly opened bedrooms are in the former post office and two cottages. This is part of the Seafood Pub Company.

Delicious food using the finest ingredients includes lunchtime sandwiches, devilled crab, salmon and brown shrimp with sea salt croutes, lettuce rolls with wok-fried chicken and cashew nuts with ginger and chilli, grilled haddock with creamed spinach, cheese crumb and fries, slow-cooked beef and chorizo pie with manchego cheese and paprika fries, piggy grill (gammon with a duck egg, pork fillet wrapped in streaky bacon with pineapple and grain mustard ketchup, glazed pork belly and black pudding fritter), john dory with creamed white beans and wild mushrooms, and puddings such as steamed marmalade pudding with proper custard and After Eight chocolate ice-cream with chocolate mousse and chocolate crumble. *Benchmark main dish: goan king prawn curry with coconut rice £17.95. Two-course evening meal £22.00.*

Free house ~ Licensee Jocelyn Neve ~ Real ale ~ Open 12-11 (midnight Sat, 10.30 Sun)~ Bar food 12-9 (10 Fri, Sat, 8 Sun) ~ Restaurant ~ Children welcome ~ Dogs allowed in bar ~ Wi-fi *Recommended by Steve Whalley, Richard Cox*

FORMBY
SD3109   Map 7

Sparrowhawk ♀ ◖

(01704) 882350 – www.brunningandprice.co.uk/sparrowhawk
Southport Old Road; brown sign to pub just off A565 Formby bypass, S edge of Ainsdale; L37 0AB

Light and airy pub with plenty of drinking and dining space, interesting décor, good food and drinks choices and wooded grounds

At any time of day there's a good atmosphere at this bustling pub and a friendly welcome from helpful staff. The open-plan linked areas around the central bar have plenty of variation, from attractive prints on pastel walls, church candles and flowers, snug leather fireside armchairs in library corners, through tables with rugs on dark boards by big bow windows, and a comfortably carpeted conservatory dining room; daily papers. Throughout, there's a sense of contented well-being. The very wide choice of drinks includes 21 wines by the glass, 69 malt whiskies, Phoenix Brunning & Price Original, Bowland Hen Harrier and Sky Dancer, Hawkshead Windermere Pale and a couple of guest beers on handpump and farm cider. A flagstoned side terrace has sturdy tables, and several picnic-table sets are nicely spread on the woodside lawns by a set of swings and an old Fergie tractor (painted green instead of the usual grey). A walk from the pub to coastal nature reserves might just yield red squirrels, still hanging on in this area.

Highly rewarding food includes sandwiches, chicken liver pâté with plum and ginger chutney, sardines with sautéed potatoes and paprika mayonnaise, various platters, smoked salmon and asparagus quiche, rosemary and garlic chicken breast on pasta with wild mushrooms, bacon and spinach, steak in ale pie, cod loin with pancetta, broad beans, cockles, capers and crème fraîche, rosemary-crumbed lamb rump with pea purée and caper and mint jus, and puddings such as meringue with roasted plums and hazelnut cream and bread and butter pudding with apricot sauce. *Benchmark main dish: braised lamb shoulder with dauphinoise potatoes £16.96. Two-course evening meal £21.50.*

Brunning & Price ~ Manager Iain Hendry ~ Real ale ~ Open 10.30am-11pm; 10.30-10.30 Sun ~ Bar food 12-10 (9.30 Sun); 9-11.30am brunch weekends ~ Children welcome ~ Dogs allowed in bar ~ Wi-fi *Recommended by John and Hazel Sarkanen, Peter Pilbeam*

GREAT ECCLESTON
SD4240   Map 7

Farmers Arms ⍟ ♀

(01995) 672018 – www.seafoodpubcompany.com/farmers-arms
Halsall Square (just off A586); PR3 0YE

Smartly refurbished pub not far from the coast with smashing fish (and other) dishes and a good choice of drinks served by helpful staff; seats outside

Stylish, yet informally friendly, this attractively refurbished country pub is not far from the Fylde Coast and Blackpool. Of course, many customers are here to enjoy the top class fish (and other) dishes, but those in for a pint are just as welcome to sit with a newspaper in an armchair by the fire or at the high chairs on flagstones beside the counter: Thwaites Wainwright, Timothy Taylors Landlord and a guest ale on handpump and around 14 wines by the glass. The smart dining areas, on two floors, have painted panelled walls, woodburning stoves in stone fireplaces and an eclectic collection of cushioned settles and tartan and plush upholstered and wooden dining chairs around wooden tables on carpeting or polished floorboards. Outside, surrounded by lavender beds, the sheltered terrace has plenty of teak seats and tables. This is part of the Seafood Pub Company.

Using the freshest, seasonal fish, the interesting choices include devilled crab, salmon and brown shrimps, sesame king prawn soldiers with soy and citrus dipping sauce, smoked haddock with bubble and squeak, a poached egg and mustard butter sauce, and peppered tuna steak. Non-fishy choices include mushroom gnocchi with spinach, cream and breadcrumbs, steak burger with toppings and fries, free-range gammon steak with pineapple and sweet pepper salsa, satay chicken skewer with singapore fried rice, shrimp, shredded pork and peanut dressing, and puddings such as vanilla rice pudding with home-made raspberry jam and caramel chocolate pot with salted peanut praline. *Benchmark main dish: fritto misto £14.95. Two-course evening meal £20.00.*

Free house ~ Licensee Joycelyn Neve ~ Real ale ~ Open 12-11 (midnight Sat, 10.30 Sun) ~ Bar food 12-9 (10 Fri, Sat, 8.30 Sun) ~ Restaurant ~ Children welcome ~ Dogs allowed in bar ~ Wi-fi *Recommended by Lindy Andrews, Dr Simon Innes*

GREAT MITTON   SD7138 Map 7
Aspinall Arms 🍽️ ⏐ 🍺

(01254) 826555 – www.brunningandprice.co.uk/aspinallarms
B6246 NW of Whalley; BB7 9PQ

Cleverly refurbished and extended riverside pub with all manner of furnishings, cheerful friendly service and a fine choice of drinks and food

We've had nothing but warm reports from readers on this well run pub beside a great sweep of the River Ribble; picnic-sets overlook the water and there's a terrace with good quality seats and tables under parasols (also with lovely views). Inside, the various rambling rooms and snugger corners have a chatty, easy-going atmosphere with customers dropping in and out all day. Seating ranges from attractively cushioned old-style dining chairs through brass-studded leather ones to big armchairs and sofas around an assortment of dark tables. Floors are flagstoned, carpeted or wooden and topped with rugs, while the pale-painted or bare stone walls are hung with a big collection of prints and local photographs. Dotted about are large mirrors, house plants, stone bottles and bookshelves and there are both open fires and a woodburning stove. From the central servery young, friendly and helpful staff serve Phoenix Brunning & Price Original, Hawkshead Bitter, Hydes Spring Symphony, Lancaster Black, Moorhouses Aspinall Witch (named for the pub) and Phoenix Arizona on handpump, 15 wines by the glass, an amazing 150 malt whiskies, 20 gins and a farm cider; background music and board games.

A wide choice of interesting food includes sandwiches, scallops with cider-glazed bacon, shallot purée and perry jus, crispy duck salad with hoisin, watermelon and chilli cashews, smoked haddock and minted pea salad with a poached egg and wholegrain mustard sauce, steak and kidney pudding, cauliflower, sweet potato and chickpea tagine with couscous, barnsley lamb chop with salsa verde and sautéed rosemary potatoes, and puddings such as dark chocolate and peanut butter parfait with chocolate crumble and crème brûlée. *Benchmark main dish: fish pie with salmon, smoked haddock and prawns £13.95. Two-course evening meal £20.00.*

Brunning & Price ~ Manager Chris Humphries ~ Real ale ~ Open 10.30am-11pm; 10.30-10.30 Sun ~ Bar food 12-10 ~ Restaurant ~ Children welcome ~ Dogs allowed in bar ~ Wi-fi
Recommended by William Wright, Peter Pilbeam, Steve Whalley, W K Wood

 LATHOM   SD4510 Map 7

Ring o' Bells 🍺 £

(01704) 893157 – www.ainscoughs.co.uk
In Lathom, turn right into Ring o' Bells Lane; L40 5TE

Bustling, family-friendly canalside pub, interconnected rooms with antique furniture, six real ales, some sort of food all day and children's play areas inside and out

Set on the banks of the Leeds & Liverpool Canal, this red-brick Victorian pub is also handy as a break from the M6. Several interlinked rooms lead off from the handsome central bar counter with its pretty inlaid tiles: all manner of antique dining chairs and carved settles around lovely old tables, comfortable sofas, rugs on flagstones, lots of paintings and prints of the local area, sporting activities and plants, as well as large mirrors, brass lanterns and standard lamps; staffordshire dogs and decorative plates sit on mantelpieces above open fires. Cumberland Corby Blonde, Lancaster Amber, Moorhouses White Witch and Thwaites Nutty Black and Wainwright on handpump, good wines by the glass and over 25 whiskies; background music, TV, darts, board games. Downstairs is a more plainly furnished room and indoor and outdoor children's play areas. Plans for their four acres of land include a football pitch, vegetable garden and a cider orchard – and, of course, seats and tables by the canal. This is part of the Ainscoughs group.

Very well priced food includes breakfasts (9.30-11.30) as well as sandwiches, black pudding potato cake with an egg and caramelised red onion, prawn cocktail, cheese and onion pie, cumberland sausages and mash, burgers with toppings, relish and chips, lambs liver and bacon with onion gravy, beer-battered fish and chips, butterflied chicken topped with barbecue sauce, bacon and mozzarella, and puddings such as sticky toffee pudding with butterscotch sauce and apple crumble with custard. *Benchmark main dish: steak in ale pie £9.95. Two-course evening meal £15.00.*

Free house ~ Licensee Natalie Goldthorpe ~ Real ale ~ Open 11-11; 10am-midnight Sat; 10am-11pm Sun ~ Bar food 12-2.30, 5-9; 12-8 weekends ~ Children welcome ~ Dogs allowed in bar ~ Wi-fi ~ Live music last Fri of month *Recommended by Phil and Jane Hodson, Jo Garnett*

 LITTLE ECCLESTON   SD4240 Map 7

Cartford 🍴⭐ 🍺 🛏

(01995) 670166 – www.thecartfordinn.co.uk
Cartford Lane, off A586 Garstang–Blackpool, by toll bridge; PR3 0YP

Prettily placed 17th-c coaching inn on riverbank, attractively refurbished and with a thoughtful choice of drinks and food; waterside bedrooms

If you stay in the individually decorated bedrooms of this 17th-c coaching inn, you'll have tranquil views of the River Wyre on Lancashire's Fylde

Coast. Tables in the garden also overlook the river (crossed by a toll bridge), the Trough of Bowland and peaks of the Lake District. The unusual four-level layout blends both traditional and contemporary elements with an appealing mix of striking colours, natural wood and polished floors, while the log fire and eclectic choice of furniture create a comfortable and relaxed feel in the bar lounge; background music. Hawkshead Lakeland Gold, Moorhouses Black Cat and Pride of Pendle and a changing guest on handpump, alongside speciality bottled beers, ten wines by the glass and a dozen gins and a dozen malt whiskies. There's also another cosy lounge and a riverside restaurant.

Attractively presented and from a seasonal menu, the highly rewarding food includes lunchtime sandwiches, pigeon breast and blackberry salad with candied and golden beetroot, crispy pancetta and balsamic dressing, barbecued ribs, cumberland sausages with red onion gravy, wild mushroom stroganoff, moules frites, chicken breast with pancetta, cabbage and shallot and cider cream sauce, fish pie, braised beef cheeks with bourguignon sauce, and puddings such as a crème brûlée of the day and salted maple and pecan pie with ginger ice-cream. *Benchmark main dish: oxtail and beef in ale pudding £13.95. Two-course evening meal £21.00.*

Free house ~ Licensees Patrick and Julie Beaume ~ Real ale ~ Open 12-11 (midnight Sat, 10 Sun); closed Mon lunchtime ~ Bar food 12-2, 5.30-9 (10 Fri, Sat); 12-8.30 Sun ~ Restaurant ~ Children welcome until 9pm ~ Wi-fi ~ Bedrooms: £70/£120
Recommended by Peter Harrison, Caroline Prescott, Isobel Mackinlay

LONGRIDGE

SD6038 Map 7

Derby Arms

(01772) 782370 – www.seafoodpubcompany.com/derby-arms
Chipping Road, Thornley; 1.5 miles N of Longridge on back road to Chipping; PR3 2NB

Neatly kept, attractively refurbished dining pub with real ales and highly enjoyable food with an emphasis on seafood; comfortable bedrooms

As soon as this smartly refurbished pub opened, we started getting warmly enthusiastic reports from our readers. A creeper-clad building, it has good quality seats and tables on a front terrace behind neat picket fencing – and an open-plan interior. The bar and dining rooms are connected by wide doorways and the atmosphere throughout is one of friendly informality. There are wide floorboards and grey carpeting, a woodburning stove and an open fire, all manner of high-backed and attractively upholstered or leather and brass-studded chairs, settles with scatter cushions matching the tartan curtains, windsor chairs and armed wheelbacks, comfortable wall banquettes and leather-topped stools. Against the planked counter are some fat, squat chairs, with lots of church candles on the gantry above; Copper Dragon Golden Pippin, Thwaites Wainright and Timothy Taylors Boltmaker on handpump, served by cheerful, helpful staff. Bedrooms are comfortable, light and airy and breakfasts are good. This part of the Seafood Pub Company.

As well as breakfast (7.30-9.30, to non-residents too), there's quite an emphasis on daily fresh fish: coquille st jacques, devilled crab, salmon and brown shrimps, fish pie with cheese crumb, seafood linguine, and hake wrapped in prosciutto with olive crushed potatoes. Non-fishy items include lunchtime sandwiches, twice-baked local cheese soufflé, crispy duck and watermelon salad with spiced cashew and lemongrass dressing, lemon and rosemary chicken with salsa verde, double lamb cutlet and slow-cooked shoulder with button onions and gravy, and puddings. *Benchmark main dish: bass fillets on tomato and sweet peppers with king prawn koftas and couscous £17.50. Two-course evening meal £21.00.*

Free house ~ Licensee Jocelyn Neve ~ Real ale ~ Open 12-midnight ~ Bar food 12-9 (10 Fri, Sat, 8 Sun) ~ Restaurant ~ Children welcome ~ Dogs allowed in bar ~ Wi-fi ~ Bedrooms: /$95 *Recommended by Steve Whalley, Gilly and Frank Newman*

MANCHESTER SJ8297 Map 7
Wharf ♀ ◖

(0161) 220 2960 – www.brunningandprice.co.uk/thewharf
Blantyre Street/Slate Wharf; M15 4SW

Big wharf-like pub with large terrace overlooking canal basin, interesting furnishings, six real ales and a fine choice of other drinks, and good bistro-style food

With crowds of happy customers and a cheerful buzz in the main open-plan areas of this huge place, it's a marvel that the hard-pushed staff manage to remain so unfailingly helpful and friendly. On several levels – but with cosy alcoves and nooks despite its size; downstairs is more pubby and informal, with groups of high tables and chairs, while the restaurant upstairs has table service. Throughout there's an appealing variety of pre-war-style dining chairs around quite a choice of dark wooden tables on rugs and shiny floorboards, hundreds of interesting prints and posters on bare brick or painted walls, old stone bottles, church candles, house plants and fresh flowers on window sills and tables, bookshelves and armchairs here and there, and large mirrors over open fires. Phoenix Brunning & Price Original, Thwaites Wainwright and Weetwood Cheshire Cat plus seven quickly changing guest ales on handpump, 19 wines by the glass and lots of whiskies. The large front terrace has plenty of wood and chrome tables and chairs around a fountain, and picnic-sets overlooking the canal basin.

🍴 Enterprising food includes sandwiches, sticky walnut and pear salad with blue cheese and red onions, a charcuterie board, wild mushroom quiche with potato and spring onion salad, steak burger with toppings, coleslaw and chips, sticky braised beef with peanut sauce and asian salad, whole grilled lemon sole with caper butter and samphire, lamb shoulder with dauphinoise potatoes and red wine and rosemary sauce, and puddings such as white chocolate panna cotta with rhubarb broth and sticky toffee pudding with toffee sauce. *Benchmark main dish: beer-battered haddock and chips £12.75. Two-course evening meal £20.00.*

Brunning & Price ~ Manager Siobhan Youngs ~ Real ale ~ Open 11-11 (midnight Fri, Sat, 10.30 Sun) ~ Bar food 12-10 (9.30 Sun) ~ Restaurant ~ Children welcome ~ Dogs allowed in bar ~ Wi-fi ~ Live acoustic music Fri evening *Recommended by Ruth May, Edward May*

MELLOR SD6530 Map 7
Millstone ◖ ⌂

(01254) 813333 – www.millstonehotel.co.uk
The Mellor near Blackburn; Mellor Lane; BB2 7JR

Smart and popular dining pub run by an enthusiastic chef-patron, serving four real ales and rewarding hearty food; comfortable bedrooms

If you stay in this extended stone former coaching inn, the bedrooms (some in a separate block across the car park) are comfortable and well equipped, and the breakfasts good. On both sides of the central bar there's extensive panelling, and comfortable seats around polished tables in the dining rooms. At busy mealtimes, the whole space is opened into one big happy eating area around the bar itself, which has a handful of tables, settles, a housekeeper's chair and rugs on bare boards; log fires. Batemans XXXB, Thwaites Original and a guest beer on handpump and a dozen wines by the glass; service is informally friendly and helpful. Background music. There are seats and tables under parasols on a side terrace.

🍴 Cooked by the landlord from a seasonal menu, the highly thought-of food includes sandwiches (until 5pm, not Sunday), hand-made duck spring rolls with plum sauce and cucumber, tempura king prawn, squid and monkfish with thai dipping sauce, various boards, mushroom risotto with a soft poached egg and truffle oil, steak and kidney in ale pudding, aubergine, spinach and butter bean curry with mint yoghurt, a burger of the week with onion rings, coleslaw and chips, hake fillet with lemon hollandaise, and puddings such as apple charlotte and rhubarb compote. *Benchmark main dish: beer-battered haddock and chips £12.95. Two-course evening meal £18.00.*

Thwaites ~ Managers Anson and Sarah Bolton ~ Real ale ~ Open 12-11 ~ Bar food 12-9.30 (9 Sun) ~ Restaurant ~ Children welcome ~ Wi-fi ~ Bedrooms: £70/£80
Recommended by Steve Whalley, William and Ann Reid

SAWLEY
Spread Eagle 🛏️

SD7746 Map 7

(01200) 441202 – www.spreadeaglesawley.co.uk
Village signed just off A59 NE of Clitheroe; BB7 4NH

Nicely refurbished pub with quite a choice of food, riverside restaurant and four real ales; bedrooms

It makes sense to stay in the individually furnished and comfortable bedrooms here to explore the exhilarating walks in the Forest of Bowland and the nearby, substantial ruins of a 12th-c cistercian abbey. It's an attractive old coaching inn with a pleasing mix of nice old and quirky modern furniture – anything from an old settle and pine tables to new low chairs upholstered in animal print fabric, all set off well by the grey rustic stone floor. Low ceilings, cosy sectioning, a warming fire and cottagey windows keep it all feeling intimate. The dining areas are more formal, with modern stripes and (as a bit of a quip on the decorative trend for walls of unread books) a bookshelf mural; background music. A beer named for the pub (from Bowland), Dark Horse Hetton Pale Ale, Moorhouses Pride of Pendle and Thwaites Original on handpump and several wines by the glass. They have two porches for smokers.

🍴 Reliably good food includes sandwiches, duck liver pâté with piccalilli, crab, avocado and plum tomato cocktail, several platters, smoked haddock with grain mustard cream and poached free-range egg, a pie of the day, spiced cauliflower and chickpea tagine, steak burger with toppings, relish and chips, duck breast with roasted beetroot and black cherry sauce, and puddings such as chocolate cake with raspberry sorbet and raspberry curd and deep-fried churros with thick hot chocolate and cinnamon sugar; they also offer proper afternoon tea. *Benchmark main dish: rib-eye steak £19.50. Two-course evening meal £21.00.*

Individual Inns ~ Managers Greg and Natalie Barns ~ Real ale ~ Open 11-11 (10.30 Sun) ~ Bar food 12-2, 5.30-9; 12-2, 6-9.30 Sat; 12-7 Sun ~ Restaurant ~ Children welcome ~ Dogs allowed in bar ~ Wi-fi ~ Bedrooms: £92/£110 *Recommended by Steve Whalley, John and Sylvia Harrop, W K Wood, Brian and Janet Ainscough, Ann and Tony Bennett-Hughes*

Please tell us if the décor, atmosphere, food or drink at a pub is different from our description. We rely on readers' reports to keep us up to date: feedback@goodguides.com, or (no stamp needed) The Good Pub Guide, FREEPOST RTJR-ZCYZ-RJZT, Perrymans Lane, Etchingham TN19 7DN.

STALYBRIDGE   SJ9598   Map 7
Station Buffet ⌑ £
(0161) 303 0007 – www.stalybridgebuffetbar.co.uk
The Station, Rassbottom Street; SK15 1RF

Classic Victorian station buffet bar with eight quickly changing beers and tasty home-cooked meals

If only waiting for a train could always be as splendidly diverting as this unpretentious place – it remains a charming elaboration of a working station buffet. The bar has a welcoming fire below an etched-glass mirror, period advertisements, photographs of the station and other railway memorabilia on cosy wood-panelled and red walls, and there's a conservatory. A fine range of eight real ales might include Timothy Taylors Landlord and a beer from Millstone plus six quickly rotating guests from breweries such as Acorn, AllGates, Beartown, Bradfield, Magic Rock, Marble, Moorhouses, Thornbridge, Ticketybrew and Two Roses; also, seven wines by the glass, ten malt whiskies and a couple of farm ciders. An extension along the platform leads into what was the ladies' waiting room and part of the station-master's quarters, featuring original ornate ceilings and Victorian-style wallpaper.

Amazingly good value food includes hot and cold sandwiches, all-day breakfast, bubble and squeak with egg and beans, chicken, potato and mushroom masala, corned beef hash, swede and courgette cottage pie, cider sausages with mustard mash, and slow-cooked lamb and rosemary hotpot; spice night is on Wednesday and afternoon teas with home-made cakes on request. *Benchmark main dish: pie and gravy £4.25.*

Free house ~ Licensee Caroline Barnes ~ Real ale ~ No credit cards ~ Open 11-11; 12-10.30 Sun ~ Bar food 11-9 ~ Children welcome ~ Dogs welcome ~ Wi-fi ~ Live folk Sat evening
Recommended by John Fiander, P A Lord

THORNTON HOUGH   SJ2979   Map 7
Red Fox ♀ ⌑
(0151) 353 2920 – www.brunningandprice.co.uk/redfox
Liverpool Road; CH64 7TL

Big spreading pub with character rooms, a fine choice of beers, wines and whiskies, courteous staff serving enjoyable food and large back garden

This substantial brick and sandstone pub is on the edge of a village of striking mock-Elizabethan estate workers' houses, and is reached down its own drive. The main bar, up steps from the entrance, is big and spacious, with high stools and tables in the middle and plenty of dark wood tables and cushioned chairs divided up by large central pillars; to one side is a large old fireplace with fender seats and deep leather armchairs. This leads into a long, airy carpeted dining room with two rows of painted iron supports, hefty leather and wood chairs around highly polished tables and a raised fire pit; doors from here lead on to a terrace. Two additional dining rooms are similarly furnished, one with an elegant chandelier hanging from a fine moulded ceiling, the other with a huge metal elephant peeping through large house plants. Throughout there are photographs, prints and pictures covering the walls, big plants, stone bottles and shelves of books. Friendly, cheerful staff serve Phoenix Brunning & Price Original and Facers Sunny Bitter with guests such as Brimstage Scarecrow Bitter, Hobsons Town Crier, Peerless Crystal Maze, Phoenix Monkeytown Mild and Ticketybrew Table IPA on handpump, 21 wines by the glass, 147 malt whiskies and five farm ciders; background music. At the back, the terraces have good quality wooden chairs and tables under parasols with steps down to picnic-sets around a fountain on a spreading lawn, and country views.

🍴 Enterprising food includes sandwiches, cured salmon with wasabi cream, soy jelly and pickled ginger, chicken liver pâté with plum and ginger chutney, mussels in white wine, cream and garlic, whipped goats cheese, bulgar wheat and fig salad with sumac-toasted cauliflower and pomegranate, burger with toppings, coleslaw and chips, cumin and chilli chicken with roast sweet potato and tzatziki, duck breast with confit leg hash cake, carrot purée and cherry sauce, and puddings such as dark chocolate torte with pistachio praline and raspberry sorbet and crème brûlée. *Benchmark main dish: braised lamb shoulder with dauphinoise potatoes £16.95. Two-course evening meal £21.00.*

Brunning & Price ~ Manager David Green ~ Real ale ~ Open 10.30am-11pm (10.30 Sun) ~ Bar food 12-10 (9.30 Sun) ~ Restaurant ~ Children welcome ~ Dogs allowed in bar ~ Wi-fi
Recommended by Edward May, Isobel Mackinlay

UPPERMILL
SD0006 Map 7

Church Inn 🍺 £

(01457) 820902 – www.churchinnsaddleworth.co.uk
From the main street (A607), look out for the sign for Saddleworth Church, and turn off up this steep narrow lane – keep on up; OL3 6LW

Community pub with big range of own-brew beers at unbeatable bargain prices and tasty food; children very welcome

'A real gem' is a phrase used by several of our readers to describe this highly individual and cheerful local. And with very good value own-brewed beers and bargain-priced food, it's a winner. They keep up to 11 of their own Saddleworth beers – though, if the water levels from the spring aren't high enough for brewing, they bring in guests such as Black Sheep and Copper Dragon. Some of their own seasonal ales are named after the licensee's children, only appearing around their birthdays; two home-brewed lagers on tap too. The big unspoilt L-shaped main bar has high beams and some stripped stone, settles, pews, a good individual mix of chairs, lots of attractive prints, staffordshire and other china on a high delft shelf, jugs, brasses and so forth. TV (when there's sport on) and unobtrusive background music. A conservatory opens on to the terrace. The local bellringers arrive on Wednesdays to practise with a set of handbells kept here; anyone can join the morris dancing on Thursdays. Children enjoy all the animals, including rabbits, chickens, dogs, ducks, geese, alpacas, horses, 14 peacocks in the next-door field and some cats that live in an adjacent barn; dogs are made to feel very welcome. It's next to an isolated church, with fine views down the valley.

🍴 At very fair prices, the wide choice of honest food includes sandwiches, prawn cocktail, mushrooms in creamy garlic sauce, full english breakfasts, vegetable fajitas with guacamole, salsa and sour cream, beef chilli, lasagne, lamb shank in minted gravy, steak and kidney pudding, a roast of the day, and puddings such as jam roly-poly and a cheesecake of the day. *Benchmark main dish: jumbo cod and chips £9.95. Two-course evening meal £14.95.*

Own brew ~ Licensee Christine Taylor ~ Real ale ~ Open 12-12 (1am Sat) ~ Bar food 12-3, 5-9; 12-9 Fri-Sun and bank holidays ~ Restaurant ~ Children welcome ~ Dogs allowed in bar ~ Wi-fi *Recommended by Sharon Jacques, Andrew Laurence, John Fiander, Gordon and Margaret Ormondroyd*

Pubs close to motorway junctions are listed at the back of the book.

WADDINGTON
Lower Buck 🍺

SD7243 Map 7

(01200) 423342 – www.lowerbuck.co.uk

Edisford Road; BB7 3HU

Hospitable village pub with reasonably priced, tasty food and five real ales

A proper chatty local, this little stone building is tucked away behind the church. The several small, neatly kept cream-painted bars and dining rooms, each with a warming coal fire, have plenty of cheerful customers, good solid chairs and settles on carpet or stripped wooden floors and lots of paintings on the walls. Welcoming staff serve up to five real ales on handpump such as Bowland Hen Harrier and IPA, Lancaster Blonde, Moorhouses Premier Bitter and Timothy Taylors Landlord and ten wines by the glass; darts and pool. There are picnic-sets out on cobbles at the front and in the sunny back garden; good nearby Ribble Valley walks.

🍴 Well liked food includes lunchtime sandwiches, potted shrimps, creamy garlic mushrooms on a garlic crouton, various platters, steak and kidney pie, cauliflower cheese with a breadcrumb crust, lancashire hotpot, cumberland sausages with ale and onion gravy, grilled whole plaice with lemon and parsley, and puddings such as banoffi pie and sticky toffee pudding with toffee sauce. *Benchmark main dish: beer-battered haddock and chips £11.95. Two-course evening meal £19.50.*

Free house ~ Licensee Andrew Warburton ~ Real ale ~ Open 11-11; 11-midnight Fri, Sat ~ Bar food 12-2.30, 5-9; 12-9 Sat, Sun and bank holidays ~ Children welcome ~ Dogs allowed in bar ~ Wi-fi *Recommended by Caroline Prescott, Isobel Mackinlay*

WHITEWELL
Inn at Whitewell ★ 🍴⭐ 🍷 🍺 🛏

SD6546 Map 7

(01200) 448222 – www.innatwhitewell.com

Most easily reached by B6246 from Whalley; road through Dunsop Bridge from B6478 is also good; BB7 3AT

Fine manor house with smartly pubby atmosphere, top quality food, exceptional wine list, real ales and professional, friendly service; luxury bedrooms

Our readers love their visits to this elegant and civilised old manor house – for a drink after a glorious walk, for a rewarding meal or to stay overnight in the lovely bedrooms (several with open fires). There's a self-catering holiday house too, and they own several miles of trout, salmon and sea trout fishing on the Hodder; picnic hamper on request. Bar rooms have handsome old wood furnishings, including antique settles, oak gate-leg tables and sonorous clocks, set off beautifully against powder blue walls neatly hung with big appealing prints. The pubby main bar has roaring log fires in attractive stone fireplaces and heavy curtains on sturdy wooden rails; one area has a selection of newspapers and magazines, local maps and guidebooks. There's a piano for anyone who wants to play, and board games. The view from the riverside bar and adjacent terrace is idyllic. Early evening sees a cheerful bustle that later settles to a more tranquil and relaxing atmosphere. Drinks include a marvellous wine list of around 230 wines with 17 by the glass (reception has a good wine shop), 24 whiskies, eight gins, organic ginger beer, lemonade and fruit juices and Bowland Hen Harrier, Moorhouses Blond Witch, Timothy Taylors Landlord and a guest beer on handpump.

Using the best local, seasonal produce, the first class food includes lunchtime sandwiches, potted cornish crab with cucumber pickle and avocado purée, venison carpaccio with artichoke hearts and slow-roast tomatoes, cheese and onion pie, chicken thighs with chilli, lime, ginger, coriander and coconut milk, sweet potato wedges and spicy peanut sauce, beer-battered haddock and chips, slow-roast lamb shoulder with caramelised onions and hotpot potatoes, and puddings such as glazed lemon tart with berry compote and fruit coulis and chocolate and toffee cheesecake with apple purée and dark chocolate sauce. *Benchmark main dish: fish pie £11.25. Two-course evening meal £23.00.*

Free house ~ Licensee Charles Bowman ~ Real ale ~ Open 11am-midnight ~ Bar food 12-2, 7.30-9.30 ~ Restaurant ~ Children welcome ~ Dogs allowed in bar and bedrooms ~ Wi-fi ~ Bedrooms: £92/£128 *Recommended by John and Sylvia Harrop, Ian Herdman, Richard Cox, Steve Whalley*

WISWELL   SD7437 Map 7
Freemasons Arms 🏵 ♀ 🍷

(01254) 822218 – www.freemasonswiswell.co.uk

Village signposted off A671 and A59 NE of Whalley; pub on Vicarage Fold, a gravelled pedestrian passage between Pendleton Road and Old Back Lane in village centre (don't expect to park very close); BB7 9DF

Top drawer dining pub with exceptional food, fines wines and local ales, an informal yet civilised atmosphere and seats on heated terrace

Although this is a civilised dining place, it has the comfortingly informal feel of a smart pub – not to mention the thoroughly pubby advantage of well kept local ales on handpump, such as Bank Top Gold Digger, Lancaster Blonde, Reedley Hallows Filly Close Blonde and a changing guest. There are racks of well chosen wine bottles behind the tempting bar counter (with an excellent choice by the glass). Three rooms open together, with lots of antique, mainly sporting prints on cream or pastel walls, rugs on polished flagstones, carved oak settles and an attractive variety of chairs around handsome stripped or salvaged candlelit tables (all beautifully laid), and open fires, with a woodburning stove on the right. There are more rooms upstairs, including a comfortable one that's popular for pre-meal drinks, or good coffee afterwards. Service by neatly uniformed young staff is meticulous and courteous. The quiet flagstoned front terrace has teak seats and candlelit tables under an extendable awning, and heaters.

Highly accomplished, beautifully presented food includes foie gras (poached and roast) with rhubarb, smoked eel and beer vinegar, smoked salmon with sour cream and blinis, fish of the day with lemon and brown butter, leek fondue, potted shrimps and chips, suckling pig (maple-glazed belly and sausage) with kimchee, cheese potatoes and mead, roast venison saddle with loin tartare, apple, parsnip and stilton, and puddings such as lemon meringue pie with tropical fruits and rhubarb and vanilla millefeuille with honeycomb and cardamom ice-cream; they also offer a very fair value three-course set menu (not Sat evening or Sun). *Benchmark main dish: local lamb with haggis shepherd's pie, wild garlic, ewe's milk and black olives £24.95. Two-course evening meal £30.00.*

Free house ~ Licensee Steven Smith ~ Real ale ~ Open 12-2.30, 5.30-midnight; 12-midnight Sat; 12-11 Sun; closed Mon, Tues, first two weeks in Jan ~ Bar food 12-2.30, 5.30-9 Weds, Thurs; 12-2.30, 6-9.30 Fri, Sat; 12-7 Sun ~ Restaurant ~ Children welcome ~ Dogs allowed in bar *Recommended by Caroline Prescott, Emma Scofield*

There are report forms at the back of the book.

WORSLEY
SD7401   Map 7

Old Hall ♀

(0161) 703 8706 – www.brunningandprice.co.uk/worsleyoldhall

A mile from M60 junction 13: A575 Walkden Road, then after roundabout take first left into Worsley Park; M28 2QT

Very handsomely converted landmark building, now a welcoming pub scoring high on all counts

Careful restoration of this grand timbered mansion has made the most of some lovely architectural features: a gracefully arched inglenook and matching window alcove, handsome staircase and heavy beamery and glowing mahogany panelling. The relaxed and chatty main area spreads generously around the feature central bar, where exceptionally well trained staff serve 17 good wines by the glass, 123 malt whiskies, 38 gins and changing ales on handpump such as Phoenix Brunning & Price Original, Brightside Brindley Blonde and guests such as AllGates Pretoria, Blue Bee Bees Knees Bitter, Conwy Scrum Down and Timothy Taylors Dark Mild. There's also the usual abundance of well chosen prints, fireside armchairs and a wide collection of cushioned dining chairs and wooden tables, and rugs on oak parquet; daily papers, board games and unobtrusive background music. A big flagstoned terrace has heavy teak tables and a barbecue area, while the neat lawn beyond has a fountain among the picnic-table sets.

Some sort of creative food is served all day: sandwiches, beetroot-cured salmon with orange, fennel and horseradish, pigeon breast with apple, celery and candied walnuts, moules frites, sausages with mash and onion gravy, mushroom, ricotta and spinach wellington with roasted tomato sauce, steak burger with toppings, coleslaw and chips, cod loin with split pea risotto, asparagus and truffle oil, shredded roast rabbit with smoked almond and celery couscous and roasted plums, and puddings such as dark chocolate brownie with chocolate sauce and bread and butter pudding with apricot sauce. *Benchmark main dish: braised lamb shoulder with dauphinoise potatoes £16.95. Two-course evening meal £22.00.*

Brunning & Price ~ Manager David Green ~ Real ale ~ Open 10.30am-10.50pm ~ Bar food 12-10 (9.30 Sun) ~ Restaurant ~ Children welcome ~ Dogs allowed in bar ~ Wi-fi
Recommended by Peter Pilbeam, William Wright, Gerry and Rosemary Dobson, Michael Butler, Dr and Mrs A K Clarke

Also Worth a Visit in Lancashire

Besides the fully inspected pubs, you might like to try these pubs that have been recommended to us and described by readers. Do tell us what you think of them: feedback@goodguides.com

---

ARKHOLME   SD5872

★ **Redwell** (01524) 221240
B6254 Over Kellet–Arkholme; LA6 1BQ
Nicely renovated 17th-c country pub-restaurant, spacious interior with wooden tables and chairs on flagstones, also some easy chairs, woodburners, newspapers and magazines, very good individual cooking from landlord-chef including ingredients from next-door smokehouse, home-baked bread, well kept beers, friendly attentive service; background music; tables outside, closed Sun evening to Weds. *(Fay Craddock)*

BARLEY   SD8240

Pendle (01282) 614808
Barley Lane; BB12 9JX Friendly 1930s stone pub in shadow of Pendle Hill, three cosy rooms, two log fires, and six well kept regional ales including Moorhouses, simple substantial food (all day weekends) using local produce including good sandwiches, conservatory; garden, lovely village and good walking country, self-catering accommodation, open all day Fri-Sun.
(David Heath)

BARNSTON SJ2783

★ **Fox & Hounds** (0151) 648 7685
3 miles from M53 junction 3; A552 towards Woodchurch, then left on A551; CH61 1BW Well run and welcoming early 20th-c pub; local Brimstage, Theakstons and guests, 60 malt whiskies and good value traditional lunchtime food (evenings Tues-Fri), roomy carpeted bay-windowed lounge with built-in banquettes and plush-cushioned captain's chairs around solid tables, old local prints and collection of police and other headgear, charming quarry-tiled corner with antique range, copper kettles, built-in pine kitchen cupboards, enamel food bins and earthenware, small traditional locals' bar with collection of horsebrasses and metal ashtrays, snug where children allowed; dogs welcome in bar, picnic-sets at back among tubs and hanging baskets, open all day. *(Tony Tollitt, Ann and Tony Bennett-Hughes, Roger and Anne Newbury)*

BARTON SD5137

Sparling (01772) 860830
A6 N of Broughton; PR3 5AA Popular contemporary dining pub with some imaginative food including set deals, roomy bar with comfortable sofas and other seats, plenty of tables in linked areas off, wood and flagstone floors, real ales such as Thwaites Wainwright, good choice of wines by the glass, friendly efficient young staff; free wi-fi; children welcome, handy for M6. *(Peter Pilbeam)*

BAY HORSE SD4952

★ **Bay Horse** (01524) 791204
1.2 miles from M6 junction 33; A6 southwards, then off on left; LA2 0HR Civilised family-run country dining pub – a useful motorway stop; cosily pubby bar with cushioned wall banquettes and good log fire, ales such as Moorhouses, Thwaites and Timothy Taylors, 15 wines by the glass, smarter restaurant with cosy corners, another log fire and carefully presented innovative food (not Sun evening and not especially cheap), friendly efficient service; children welcome, garden tables, two bedrooms in converted barn over road, closed Mon, Tues. *(Edward May)*

BELMONT SD6715

Black Dog (01204) 811218
Church Street (A675); BL7 8AB Nicely set simple Holts pub with enjoyable food all day (till 6pm Sun), well kept beers and friendly service, cheery small-roomed traditional core, coal and gas fires, picture-window dining extension; children and dogs welcome, seats outside with moorland views above village, attractive part-covered smokers' area, good walks, three decent well priced bedrooms, open all day. *(Hilary Forrest)*

BLACKSTONE EDGE SD9617

★ **White House** (01706) 378456
A58 Ripponden–Littleborough, just W of B6138; OL15 0LG Beautifully placed moorland pub with remote views, emphasis on good value hearty food from sandwiches up (all day Sun), prompt friendly service and cheerful atmosphere, Black Sheep, Theakstons and a couple of regional guests, belgian bottled beers, carpeted main bar with fire, other areas off, most tables used for food; children welcome. *(Dr Simon Innes)*

BOLTON SD7112

Brewery Tap (01204) 302837
Belmont Road; BL1 7AN Two-room corner tap for Bank Top, their full range kept well and a guest, knowledgeable friendly staff, no food; dogs welcome, seats outside, open all day. *(Nick Sharpe)*

BOLTON SD6913

Wilton Arms (01204) 303307
Belmont Road, Horrocks Fold; BL1 7BT Friendly roadside pub on edge of West Pennine Moors, reasonably priced fresh food and three well kept regional ales including Bank Top Flat Cap, open fires, conservatory; children welcome, valley views and good walks, open (and food) all day. *(W K Wood)*

BRINDLE SD5924

★ **Cavendish Arms** (01254) 852912
3 miles from M6 junction 29, by A6 and B5256 (Sandy Lane); PR6 8NG Traditional village pub dating from the 15th c, welcoming and popular, with good inexpensive home-made food (all day weekends) from sandwiches up, Banks's, Marstons and two guest ales, beams, cosy snugs with open fires, stained-glass windows, carpets throughout; children welcome, dogs in tap room, heated canopied terrace with water feature, more tables in side garden, good walks, open all day. *(Gordon and Margaret Ormondroyd)*

BROUGHTON SD4838

Plough at Eaves (01772) 690233
A6 N through Broughton, first left into Station Lane under a mile after traffic lights, then left after 1.5 miles, Eaves Lane; PR4 0BJ Pleasantly unpretentious old country tavern with two beamed homely bars, well kept Thwaites ales, good choice of enjoyable food, friendly service, lattice windows and traditional furnishings, old guns over woodburner in one room, log fire in dining bar with conservatory; background music; children welcome, front terrace and spacious side/back garden, well equipped play area, open (and food) all day weekends. *(Edward May)*

BURNLEY SD8432

Bridge Bier Huis (01282) 411304
Bank Parade; BB11 1UH Open-plan pub

in town centre with five well kept/priced ales including Moorhouses, lots of foreign beers on tap and by the bottle, real cider, bargain straightforward food till 7pm (5pm Sun), friendly atmosphere; Weds quiz and some live music; open all day (till 1am Fri, Sat), closed Mon, Tues. *(Nick Sharpe)*

BURY   SD8313
Trackside (0161) 764 6461
East Lancashire Railway station,
Bolton Street; BL9 0EY Welcoming busy station bar by East Lancs steam railway, bright, airy and clean with nine changing ales, bottled imports, real ciders and great range of whiskies, enjoyable home-made food (not Mon, Tues), fine display of beer labels on ceiling; children welcome till 7.30pm, platform tables under canopy, open all day. *(P A Lord)*

CHATBURN   SD7644
Brown Cow (01200) 440736
Bridge Road; BB7 4AW Welcoming and relaxed village pub popular for its good value home-made food from sandwiches to blackboard specials, ales such as Bowland and Otter, good service; garden picnic-sets. *(Paul and Sue Merrick)*

CHEADLE HULME   SJ8785
Church Inn (0161) 485 1897
Ravenoak Road (A5149 SE); SK8 7EG
Popular old family-run pub with good food (Sun till 7.30pm) from varied menu including deals, well kept Robinsons beers and nice selection of wines by the glass, gleaming brass on panelled walls, warming coal fire, friendly staff and locals, back restaurant, live music most Sun evenings; children welcome, seats outside (some under cover), car park across road, open all day. *(Ruth May)*

CHIPPING   SD6141
★**Dog & Partridge** (01995) 61201
Hesketh Lane; crossroads Chipping–
Longridge with Inglewhite–Clitheroe;
PR3 2TH Comfortable old-fashioned and much altered 16th-c dining pub in grand countryside, enjoyable food (all day Sun) served by friendly staff, ales such as Thwaites and Tetleys, beams, exposed stone walls and good log fire, small armchairs around close-set tables in main lounge, restaurant; free wi-fi; children welcome, no dogs inside, open all day Sun, closed Mon, Tues evening. *(Jo Garnett)*

CHORLEY   SD5817
Yew Tree (01257) 480344
Dill Hall Brow, Heath Charnock – out
past Limbrick towards the reservoirs;
PR6 9HA Attractive tucked-away restauranty pub, modernised interior with open-view kitchen, good quality food from bar snacks and sharing plates up, Fri fish and chips deal, Blackedge ales including one badged for them, plenty of wines by the

glass, friendly helpful staff; background and some live music; children and dogs (in one part) welcome, picnic-sets out on decked area, open all day Sat, till 8.30pm Sun, closed Mon. *(Nick Sharpe)*

CHORLTON CUM HARDY   SJ8193
Horse & Jockey (0161) 860 7794
Chorlton Green; M21 9HS Comfortably refurbished pub with mock-Tudor façade, light and modern with several different seating areas around central bar, own-brewed Bootleg ales, Holts and guests, plenty of wines by the glass, knowledgeable chatty staff, good choice of food from sandwiches and deli boards through burgers and hotdogs up, further upstairs dining areas (evening/weekends); TV; children allowed till 9pm, dogs very welcome, plenty of tables on front terrace looking across to green, open (and food) all day. *(Pat and Graham Williamson)*

COLNE   SD8940
Black Lane Ends (01282) 863070
Skipton Old Road, Foulridge; BB8 7EP
Country pub tucked away in quiet lane, good sensibly priced food from large menu, well kept Copper Dragon and Timothy Taylors Landlord, cheerful attentive staff, two massive fires, small restaurant; children and dogs welcome, garden with play area, good Pennine views, handy for canal and reservoir walks. *(Peter Pilbeam)*

CONDER GREEN   SD4556
Stork (01524) 751234
Just off A588; LA2 0AN Fine spot where River Conder joins the Lune estuary among bleak marshes, two blazing log fires in rambling dark-panelled rooms, good reasonably priced food including some south african specialities, several well kept ales, friendly efficient staff; children, walkers and dogs welcome, beer garden, handy for Glasson Dock, seven bedrooms, open (and food) all day including breakfast for non-residents. *(Michael Butler)*

DENSHAW   SD9710
Printers Arms (01457) 874248
Oldham Road; OL3 5SN Above Oldham in shadow of Saddleworth Moor, modernised interior with small log-fire bar and three other rooms, popular good value food including bargain set menu (till 6.30pm, 4pm Sat, not Sun), Black Sheep and Timothy Taylors Golden Best, several wines by the glass, friendly efficient young staff; children welcome, lovely views from two-tier beer garden, open (and food) all day. *(Stuart Paulley)*

DENSHAW   SD9711
★**Rams Head** (01457) 874802
2 miles from M62 junction 22; A672
towards Oldham, pub N of village;
OL3 5UN Sweeping moorland views from this welcoming roadside dining pub (don't be

put off by the austere exterior); really good food (all day weekends) including seasonal game and seafood, well kept ales such as Marstons and Timothy Taylors, efficient friendly service, four thick-walled little rooms, beam-and-plank ceilings, panelling, oak settles and built-in benches, log fires, coffee shop and adjacent delicatessen selling local produce; soft background music; children welcome (not Sat evening), closed Mon except bank holidays. *(M C and S Jeanes, Michael Butler, Gordon and Margaret Ormondroyd)*

DENTON   SJ9395
Lowes Arms (0161) 336 3064
Hyde Road (A57); M34 3FF Thriving 19th-c family-run pub with up to four well kept ales such as local Hornbeam and Phoenix (the on-site brewery remains closed), jovial community-spirited landlord and helpful friendly staff, wide choice of good bargain food including daily specials, bar with pool and darts, restaurant; tables outside, smokers' shelter, open all day. *(Dennis Jones)*

DIGGLE   SE0007
Diggle (01457) 872741
Village signed off A670 just N of Dobcross; OL3 5JZ Sturdy four-square hillside inn overlooking west end of Standedge Canal tunnel; good value all-day food (till 7.30pm Sun) from snacks up, well kept ales such as Black Sheep, Copper Dragon, Millstone and Timothy Taylors, helpful staff; picnic-sets among trees, quiet spot just below the moors, four bedrooms, open (and food) all day. *(Tony Hobden)*

DOBCROSS   SD9906
Swan (01457) 873451
The Square; OL3 5AA Renovated low-beamed 18th-c pub, three areas off small central bar, all with open fires, flagstones and upholstered bench seating, five Marstons-related beers and enjoyable home-made food including specials, friendly atmosphere, folk, theatre and comedy evenings in upstairs function room; children and dogs welcome, tables out at front, attractive village below moors, open all day weekends, closed Mon lunchtime. *(Tricia Curley)*

DUNHAM TOWN   SJ7488
Axe & Cleaver (01619) 283391
School Lane; WA14 4SE Big 19th-c country house knocked into spacious open-plan Chef & Brewer (some recent refurbishment), good value popular food from light lunchtime choices and sharing plates up, friendly service; children welcome, garden picnic-sets, handy for nearby Dunham Massey Hall (NT), open (and food) all day. *(Hilary Forrest)*

ENTWISTLE   SD7217
Strawbury Duck (01204) 852013
Signed off Edgworth–Blackburn road;

by station; BL7 0LU Tucked-away beamed country pub, well kept ales such as Moorhouses, Sharps and Thwaites, good choice of popular home-made food (some from own farm), friendly efficient service, opened-up modernised areas around central bar, upholstered wall seats and open fires; background music, TV, daily papers; children, walkers and dogs welcome, tables outside, five bedrooms, open (and food) all day. *(Matthew Chapman, Steve Whalley)*

EUXTON   SD5318
Travellers Rest (01257) 451184
Dawbers Lane (A581 W); PR7 6EG Revamped 18th-c roadside dining pub with several connecting rooms (originally three cottages), good varied range of popular food (all day Sat, till 6pm Sun) including daily specials, organised friendly staff, well kept Black Sheep and four guests; Thurs quiz; children welcome, dogs allowed in part of back bar, nice side garden, open all day. *(Michael Butler)*

FENCE   SD8237
Fence Gate (01282) 618101
2.6 miles from M65 junction 13; Wheatley Lane Road, just off A6068 W; BB12 9EE Imposing 18th-c dining pub; good choice of enjoyable food, five real ales and several wines by the glass, refurbished panelled bar with pewter counter and woodburner in large stone fireplace, contemporary brasserie plus various function rooms, look out for their display of over 600 gins; background music and live music, DJ nights; children welcome, rattan-style furniture out at front, open all day. *(Nick Sharpe)*

FENCE   SD8237
White Swan (01282) 611773
Wheatley Lane; BB12 9QA Comfortably refurbished village pub, well kept Timothy Taylors, nice wines and very good attractively presented food from short daily changing menu, open fires; sports TV; heated outside seating areas on two levels, open all day, no food Mon. *(Dr Kevan Tucker)*

GARSTANG   SD4945
Th'Owd Tithebarn (01995) 604486
Off Church Street; PR3 1PA Creeper-clad tithe barn with big terrace overlooking Lancaster Canal marina and narrow boats; linked high-raftered rooms with red patterned carpet or flagstones, upholstered stools, armchairs and leather tub seats around assorted shiny tables, lots of cartwheels, rustic lamps, horse tack and a fine old kitchen range, four changing ales, fair value wines by the glass and well priced pubby food from hot and cold sandwiches to grills and specials, friendly staff; Tues quiz, TV, free wi-fi; children and dogs (in bar) welcome, open all day (food all day weekends). *(Caroline Prescott)*

GOOSNARGH   SD5738
★**Horns** (01772) 865230
*On junction of Horns Lane and
Inglewhite Road; pub signed off B5269,
towards Chipping; PR3 2FJ* Early
18th-c inn with neatly kept carpeted rooms
including a rare 'parlour' behind the servery,
popular food from pub standards to local
duck and game, own Goosnargh ales and an
occasional microbrewery guest, plenty of
wines by the glass and good choice of malts,
friendly helpful service, log fires; background
music; children welcome, dogs in garden
only, six bedrooms (some with road noise),
caravan park, not far from M6, open all
day Sun, closed Mon lunchtime. *(Ray and
Winifred Halliday)*

GREAT MITTON   SD7139
★**Three Fishes** (01254) 826888
*Mitton Road (B6246, off A59 NW
of Whalley); BB7 9PQ* Stylish and
contemporary with plenty of cosy corners;
areas by bar are elegantly traditional with
two big stone fireplaces and rugs on polished
floors, other individually furnished rooms
with some exposed stonework, very good
attractively presented food, Marstons,
Moorhouses, Reedley Hallows and Thwaites,
a dozen wines by the glass and 15 malt
whiskies, friendly smartly dressed young staff
and good chatty atmosphere; background
music, free wi-fi; children and dogs (in bar)
welcome, terrace and garden with fine Ribble
Valley views, open (and food) all day.
*(Ken Richards, Graham and Elizabeth Hargreaves,
Steve Whalley)*

GREENFIELD   SD9904
Railway Hotel (01457) 872307
*Shaw Hall Bank Road, opposite station;
OL3 7JZ* Friendly four-room stone pub with
half a dozen well kept mainly local ales, no
food, old local photographs and open fire; live
music Thurs, Fri and Sun, games bar with
darts and pool; on the Transpennine Rail Ale
Trail, open all day. *(Tony Hobden)*

HAWKSHAW   SD7515
Red Lion (01204) 856600
Ramsbottom Road; BL8 4JS
Pub-hotel owned by Lees, their well kept
ales and decent choice of enjoyable fairly
priced food including specials, good service;
children and dogs (in certain areas)
welcome, eight bedrooms, quiet spot by
River Irwell, open (and food) all day. *(Isobel
Mackinlay)*

HESKIN GREEN   SD5315
Farmers Arms (01257) 451276
*Wood Lane (B5250, N of M6 junction 27);
PR7 5NP* Popular country pub under long-
serving family, good choice of well priced
home-made food in two-level dining area,
ales such as Black Sheep, Jennings, Prospect
and Timothy Taylors, heavy black beams,

sparkling brasses, china and stuffed animals,
darts in public bar; background music, open
mike nights, Sky TV; children welcome, dogs
in bar/lounge, big colourful garden with play
area, more tables front and side, five good
value bedrooms, open all day. *(Jo Garnett)*

HEST BANK   SD4766
Hest Bank Inn (01524) 824339
*Hest Bank Lane; off A6 just N of
Lancaster; LA2 6DN* Good choice
of enjoyable food in picturesque three-
bar coaching inn, nice setting close to
Morecambe Bay, well kept ales such as Black
Sheep and Thwaites, decent wines, friendly
helpful young staff, separate restaurant
area with pleasant conservatory; children
welcome, plenty of tables out by Lancaster
Canal, open all day. *(Edward May)*

HORNBY   SD5868
Castle (01524) 221204
Main Street; LA2 8JT Sizeable Georgian
inn with interesting modernised interior, bar
with leather sofas and open fires, bistro and
restaurant, enjoyable food from sandwiches,
pub favourites and pizzas up, Black Sheep,
Bowland and guests, good selection of other
drinks, friendly helpful staff; courtyard
tables, six boutique bedrooms, open all day.
(Michael Butler)

HURST GREEN   SD6837
★**Shireburn Arms** (01254) 826678
*Whalley Road (B6243 Clitheroe–
Goosnargh); BB7 9QJ* Welcoming 17th-c
hotel; peaceful Ribble Valley views from big
airy restaurant and neatly kept garden with
attractive terrace, enjoyable food (all day
weekends) from sandwiches and traditional
dishes to daily specials, armchairs, sofas
and log fire in beamed and flagstoned lounge
bar with linked dining area, two well kept
ales such as Lancaster and Thwaites,
several wines by the glass, friendly helpful
service, daily papers; children and dogs
welcome, pretty Tolkien walk from here,
22 comfortable bedrooms, open all day
(from 9am for coffee). *(Steve Whalley)*

HYDE   SJ9495
Cheshire Ring 07917 055629
*Manchester Road (A57, between M67
junctions 2 and 3); SK14 2BJ* Welcoming
drinkers' pub tied to Beartown brewery,
their good value ales kept well along with
guests, also imports (draught and bottled),
traditional ciders/perries and good house
wines, Thurs curries; background music, quiz
Weds; open all day weekends, closed weekday
lunchtimes. *(Dennis Jones)*

HYDE   SJ9493
Joshua Bradley (0161) 406 6776
Stockport Road, Gee Cross; SK14 5EZ
Victorian mansion house handsomely
converted to pub-restaurant keeping
panelling, moulded ceilings and imposing

fireplaces, good range of well priced popular food, Hydes and a couple of guest beers in fine condition, friendly efficient staff, conservatory; children welcome, heated terrace, play area, open (and food) all day. *(Dennis Jones)*

HYDE   SJ9595
Sportsman (0161) 368 5000
Mottram Road; SK14 2NN Bright cheerful Victorian local, Rossendale ales and lots of changing guests (frequent beer festivals), welcoming licensees, bargain bar food, popular upstairs cuban restaurant, bare boards and open fires, pub games; children and dogs welcome, back terrace with heated smokers' shelter, open all day. *(Nick Sharpe)*

IRBY   SJ2586
★ Irby Mill (0151) 604 0194
Mill Lane, off Greasby Road; CH49 3NT Converted miller's sandstone cottage (original windmill demolished 1898), friendly and welcoming, with eight well kept ales including Caledonian Deuchars IPA, Greene King Abbot and Charles Wells Bombardier, good choice of wines by the glass, ample helpings of popular reasonably priced food from sandwiches up, efficient service, two low-beamed traditional flagstoned rooms and extended carpeted dining area, log fire, interesting old photographs and history; tables on terraces and revamped side area, good local walks, open (and food) all day, gets crowded evenings/weekends when parking limited. *(Paul Humphreys, Tony Tollitt, Clive Watkin)*

LANCASTER   SD4761
★ Borough (01524) 64170
Dalton Square; LA1 1PP Popular city-centre pub, stylish and civilised, with chandeliers, dark leather sofas and armchairs, lamps on antique tables, high stools and elbow tables, eight ales including their own from on-site microbrewery, lots of bottled beers, big dining room with central tables and booths along one side, enjoyable food with much emphasis on local suppliers, daily specials and meal deals, jams and local produce for sale, upstairs comedy night Sun; children and dogs welcome, lovely tree-sheltered garden, bedrooms, open (and food) all day from 8am for breakfast. *(Paul Humphreys)*

LANCASTER   SD4761
★ Sun (01524) 66006
Church Street; LA1 1ET Hotel's recently refurbished bar, ten well kept ales including five from Lancaster, plenty of continental beers and good choice of wines by the glass, popular food from deli boards and pub staples up, exposed stonework, panelling and several fireplaces, conservatory; background music, TV, Tues quiz; children welcome away from servery, tables on walled and paved terrace, 16 comfortable bedrooms, open all day. *(Dr Simon Innes)*

LANCASTER   SD4761
Water Witch (01524) 63828
Parking in Aldcliffe Road behind Royal Lancaster Infirmary, off A6; LA1 1SU Attractive conversion of 18th-c canalside barge-horse stabling, flagstones, stripped stone, rafters and pitch-pine panelling, seven well kept changing ales (taster glasses available) from mirrored bar, fairly traditional food from sandwiches and deli boards up including weekday lunch deal, upstairs restaurant; Thurs quiz, free wi-fi; children in eating areas, picnic-sets out by water, open (and food) all day. *(Dr Simon Innes)*

LANESHAW BRIDGE   SD9141
★ Alma (01282) 857830
Emmott Lane, off A6068 E of Colne; BB8 7EG Attractively renovated 18th-c inn with good popular food, several wines by the glass and four real ales including Moorhouses Pride of Pendle, friendly helpful service, flagstoned bar, part-panelled lounge with rugs on bare boards, open fires, large garden room extension; background music; well behaved children and dogs welcome, ten comfortable well appointed bedrooms, open (and food) all day, breakfast for non-residents. *(David Heath)*

LITTLEBOROUGH   SD9517
Moorcock (01706) 378156
Halifax Road (A58); OL15 0LD Long roadside inn high on the moors with far-reaching views, friendly and popular, with wide range of good value food (all day Fri-Sun) from sandwiches and pub favourites up in flagstoned bar or restaurant, four well kept beers; sports TV; terrace tables taking in the view, seven comfortable reasonably priced bedrooms, open all day. *(Simon Le Fort)*

LIVERPOOL   SJ3489
Baltic Fleet (0151) 709 3116
Wapping, near Albert Dock; L1 8DQ Unusual bow-fronted pub with six interesting beers including Wapping (brewed in the cellar), several wines by the glass, enjoyable straightforward well priced food (not Sat lunchtime) such as traditional scouse, weekend breakfasts, bare boards, big arched windows, simple mix of furnishings and nautical paraphernalia, upstairs lounge; background music, TV; children welcome in eating areas, dogs in bar, back terrace, open all day. *(Ruth May)*

LIVERPOOL   SJ3589
Belvedere (0151) 709 0303
Sugnall Street; L7 7EB Unspoilt 19th-c two-room pub with friendly chatty atmosphere, original fittings including etched glass, coal fires, four well kept ales such as Liverpool Craft and Liverpool Organic, good selection of bottled beers and

LIVERPOOL SJ3589

Cracke (0151) 709 4171

Rice Street; L1 9BB Friendly unsmart local with five well kept ales including Phoenix and Thwaites, traditional cider, no food, small unspoilt bar with bare boards and bench seats, snug and bigger back room with unusual Beatles diorama, local artwork and some photos of John Lennon who used to drink here; juke box, sports TV; picnic-sets in sizeable tree-shaded back garden, open all day. *(Claes Mauroy)*

LIVERPOOL SJ3590

Crown (0151) 707 6027

Lime Street; L1 1JQ Well preserved art nouveau showpiece with fine tiled fireplace and copper bar front, dark leather banquettes, splendid ceiling in airy corner bar, smaller back room with another good fireplace, impressive staircase sweeping up under splendid cupola to handsome area with ornate windows; good range of low-priced food and five real ales; sports TV; open all day from 8am for breakfast, very handy for the station. *(Claes Mauroy)*

LIVERPOOL SJ3589

Dispensary (0151) 709 2160

Renshaw Street; L1 2SP Small busy central pub worth knowing for its very well kept beers (up to ten), good choice of bottled imports too, no food, bare boards and polished panelling, wonderful etched windows, comfortable raised back bar with coal fire, Victorian medical artefacts; notices on house rules, service mostly friendly, background music, silent TVs; open all day. *(Ruth May)*

LIVERPOOL SJ3589

Fly in the Loaf (0151) 708 0817

Hardman Street; L1 9AS Former bakery with smart gleaming bar serving Okells and at least four guests, foreign beers too, enjoyable simple home-made food at low prices, friendly service, long refurbished room with panelling and some raised sections; background music, sports TV, upstairs lavatories; open all day, till midnight Fri, Sat. *(Nick Sharpe, Ruth May)*

LIVERPOOL SJ3590

Hole In Ye Wall (0151) 227 3809

Off Dale Street; L2 2AW Character 18th-c pub with thriving local atmosphere in high-beamed panelled bar, half a dozen changing ales fed by gravity from upstairs (no cellar as pub is on Quaker burial site), sandwiches and other simple low-priced food till 5pm, free chip butties Sun when there's a traditional sing-along, friendly staff, plenty of woodwork, stained glass and old Liverpool photographs, coal-effect gas fire in unusual brass-canopied fireplace; live music, sports

TV; children allowed till 5pm, no dogs, open all day. *(Claes Mauroy)*

LIVERPOOL SJ3490

Hub (0151) 709 2401

Hanover Street; L1 4AA Bar-bistro in bow-fronted corner building, light modern interior with wood flooring and big windows, decent choice of enjoyable food from sandwiches and stone-baked pizzas up, reasonably priced wines, five ales including Liverpool Organic, friendly staff; children welcome, open all day and can get very busy. *(David H Bennett)*

LIVERPOOL SJ3490

Lion (0151) 236 1734

Moorfields, off Tithebarn Street; L2 2BP Beautifully preserved ornate Victorian tavern, great changing beer choice and over 80 malt whiskies, good value simple lunchtime food including home-made pork pies, friendly staff, sparkling etched glass and serving hatches in central bar, unusual wallpaper and matching curtains, big mirrors, panelling and tilework, two small back lounges one with fine glass dome, coal fire; open all day. *(Claes Mauroy)*

LIVERPOOL SJ3590

Ma Egerton's Stage Door

(0151) 345 3525 *Pudsey Street, opposite side entrance to Lime Street station; L1 1JA* Victorian pub behind the Empire Theatre and named after a former long-serving landlady/theatrical agent; refurbished but keeping old-fashioned character with green leather button-back banquettes (note the bell pushes), swagged curtains, wood floors, panelling and small period fireplace, lots of celebrity pictures and other theatre memorabilia, a couple of changing ales and enjoyable food including sharing plates and pizzas, friendly staff; open all day. *(David H Bennett)*

LIVERPOOL SJ3489

Monro (0151) 707 9933

Duke Street; L1 5AG Stylish gastropub, popular, comfortable and well run, with interesting food including good value set menu (not after 5.30pm Fri, Sat or all day Sun), four well kept Marstons-related ales and several wines by the glass from small bar, good friendly service; children welcome, courtyard tables, open all day. *(Peter Pilbeam)*

LIVERPOOL SJ3589

Peter Kavanaghs (0151) 709 3443

Egerton Street, off Catherine Street; L8 7LY Shuttered Victorian pub with interesting décor in several small rooms including old-world murals, stained glass and all manner of bric-a-brac (lots hanging from ceiling), piano, wooden settles and real fires, well kept Greene King Abbot and guests, friendly licensees, popular with locals and students; open all day (till 1am Fri, Sat). *(Claes Mauroy)*

LIVERPOOL SJ3589
★ **Philharmonic Dining Rooms**
(0151) 707 2837 *36 Hope Street; corner of Hardman Street; L1 9BX* Beautifully preserved Victorian pub with wonderful period detail; centrepiece mosaic-faced counter, heavily carved and polished mahogany partitions radiating out under intricate plasterwork ceiling, main hall with stained glass of Boer War heroes Baden-Powell and Lord Roberts, rich panelling, mosaic floor and copper panels of musicians above fireplace, other areas including two side rooms called Brahms and Liszt, the original Adamant gents' is also worth a look, ten real ales, several wines by the glass and decent choice of malt whiskies, enjoyable fair-priced food, good service; background music and machines; children welcome till 7pm, open (and food) all day. *(Tom and Jill Jones, Kerry Law, David Field, Susan and John Douglas)*

LIVERPOOL SJ3490
Richmond (0151) 709 2614
Williamson Street; L1 1EB Popular little corner pub in pedestrianised area, well kept Bass and interesting guests from smaller brewers, over 50 malt whiskies; sports TVs; tables out in front, four bedrooms, open all day. *(Ruth May)*

LIVERPOOL SJ3589
Roscoe Head (0151) 709 4365
Roscoe Street; L1 2SX Unassuming old local with cosy bar, snug and two other spotless unspoilt little rooms, friendly long-serving landlady, well kept Jennings, Tetleys and four guests, inexpensive home-made lunches (not weekends), interesting memorabilia, traditional games including crib, quiz Tues and Thurs; open all day till midnight. *(Claes Mauroy)*

LIVERPOOL SJ3490
Ship & Mitre (0151) 236 0859
Dale Street; L2 2JH Friendly local with fine art deco exterior and ship-like interior, popular with university people, up to a dozen changing unusual ales (many beer festivals), real ciders and over 70 bottled beers, good value food (all day Fri-Sun) such as wraps and burgers, upstairs function room with original 1930s décor; well behaved children (till 7pm) and dogs welcome, open all day. *(Kerry Law)*

LIVERPOOL SJ3490
★ **Thomas Rigbys** (0151) 236 3269
Dale Street; L2 2EZ Spacious beamed and panelled Victorian pub, mosaic flooring, old tiles and etched glass, Okells and three changing guests from impressively long bar, also good range of imported draught and bottled beers, steps up to main area, table service from attentive staff, reasonably priced hearty home-made food till 7pm;

disabled access, seats in big courtyard, open all day. *(Claes Mauroy)*

LIVERPOOL SJ3490
White Star (0151) 231 6861
Rainford Gardens, off Matthew Street; L2 6PT Popular traditional local dating from the 18th c, cosy bar, lots of woodwork, boxing photographs, White Star shipping line and Beatles memorabilia (they used to rehearse in back room), well kept ales including Bowland and Draught Bass, basic snacky food, friendly staff; wheelchair access (ladies' is upstairs), open all day. *(Claes Mauroy)*

LONGRIDGE SD6037
New Drop (01254) 878338
Higher Road, Longridge Fell, parallel to B6243 Longridge–Clitheroe; PR3 2YX Modernised dining pub in lovely moors-edge country overlooking Ribble Valley, good choice of popular reasonably priced food, decent wines and three well kept ales (usually have Bowland Hen Harrier), friendly efficient service; children welcome, open all day Sun, closed Mon. *(David Heath)*

LYDGATE SD9704
★ **White Hart** (01457) 872566
Stockport Road; Lydgate not marked on some maps and not the one near Todmorden; take A669 Oldham–Saddleworth, right at brow of hill to A6050 after almost 2.5 miles; OL4 4JJ Smart up-to-date dining pub overlooking Pennine moors, mix of locals in bar or simpler end rooms and diners in elegant brasserie with smartly dressed staff, high quality food (not cheap), Lees, Timothy Taylors and a guest beer, 16 wines by the glass, old beams and exposed stonework contrasting with deep red or purple walls and modern artwork, open fires, newspapers; various events and a popular wedding/conference venue; children welcome, dogs in bar, picnic-sets on back lawn making most of position, 12 bedrooms, open all day. *(Nick Sharpe)*

LYTHAM SD3627
Queens (01253) 737316
A584/Bath Street; FY8 5LB Refurbished Victorian pub-restaurant-hotel with outdoor seating looking across green to sea and windmill, well kept ales including Theakstons Best, enjoyable food (all day Sun) from sandwiches to daily specials, friendly relaxed atmosphere; children and dogs welcome, ten bedrooms, open all day. *(Edward May)*

LYTHAM SD3627
★ **Taps** (01253) 736226
A584 S of Blackpool; Henry Street – in centre, one street in from West Beach; FY8 5LE Cheerful town pub a couple of minutes from the beach; around ten real ales (view-in cellar) including Greene King IPA,

proper cider, friendly knowledgeable staff, simple lunchtime food (not Sun); open-plan Victorian-style bar with bare boards and stripped-brick walls, nice old chairs in bays around sides, open fires and a coal-effect gas fire between built-in bookcases, plenty of stained glass; quiz Mon; children allowed till 7.30pm, heated canopied area outside, parking nearby difficult – best to use West Beach car park on seafront (free Sun), open all day. *(Steve Whalley)*

MANCHESTER　　　　　　SJ8498
Angel　(0161) 833 4786
Angel Street, off Rochdale Road; M4 4BR Friendly place on edge of the Northern Quarter, good value home-made food (not Sun evening), ten well kept ales including Bobs, bottled beers and a couple of ciders/perries, piano in bare-boards bar, smaller upstairs restaurant with two log fires and local artwork; live acoustic music Tues, free wi-fi; children and dogs welcome, back beer garden, open all day (till 2am Fri, Sat). *(The DIY School, P A Lord)*

MANCHESTER　　　　　　SJ8398
Ape & Apple　(0161) 839 9624
John Dalton Street; M2 6HQ Large open-plan pub with five well kept good value Holts beers plus guests, hearty traditional bar food including deals, comfortable seating, bare-boards, carpet and tiles, lots of old prints and posters, upstairs restaurant/function room, friendly atmosphere; Weds comedy night, juke box, games machines; heated central courtyard, open all day (till 9pm Sun). *(Jeremy King)*

MANCHESTER　　　　　　SJ8498
Bar Fringe　(0161) 835 3815
Swan Street; M4 5JN Long bare-boards bar specialising in continental beers, also five changing ales from smaller breweries and real cider, friendly staff, basic snacks till 4pm (no food weekends), daily papers, shelves of empty beer bottles, cartoons, posters, motorcycle hung above door; rock juke box; no children or dogs, tables out behind, open all day. *(Edward May)*

MANCHESTER　　　　　　SJ8397
★Britons Protection　(0161) 236 5895
Great Bridgewater Street, corner of Lower Mosley Street; M1 5LE Lively unpretentious pub with rambling rooms and notable tiled murals of 1819 Peterloo Massacre (took place nearby), plush little front bar with fine chequered tile floor, glossy brown and russet wall tiles, solid woodwork and elaborate plastering, two cosy inner lounges, both served by hatch, with attractive brass wall lamps and solidly comfortable furnishings, coal-effect gas fire in simple art nouveau fireplace, five ales including Jennings, Robinsons and a Thwaites beer named for the pub from massive counter with heated footrail, also some 330 malt

whiskies, straightforward lunchtime food Mon-Fri; occasional storytelling and live music; children till 5pm, tables in back garden, open all day (very busy lunchtime and weekends). *(Derek Wason)*

MANCHESTER　　　　　　SJ8498
Castle　(0161) 237 9485
Oldham Street, about 200 metres from Piccadilly, on right; M4 1LE Restored 18th-c pub well run by former *Coronation Street* actor; simple traditional front bar, small snug, Robinsons ales and guests from fine bank of handpumps, Weston's Old Rosie cider, back room for live music and other events, overspill upstairs room; nice tilework outside, open all day till late. *(Dr Simon Innes)*

MANCHESTER　　　　　　SJ8497
Circus　(0161) 236 5818
Portland Street; M1 4GX Traditional little two-room local with well kept Tetleys and Robinsons from tiny corridor bar (or may be table service), friendly staff, leatherette wall benches and panelling, back room has football memorabilia and period fireplace; sports TV; open all day and can get crowded. *(Dr Simon Innes)*

MANCHESTER　　　　　　SJ8398
City Arms　(0161) 236 4610
Kennedy Street, off St Peters Square; M2 4BQ Busy little pub with eight quickly changing real ales, belgian bottled beers and bargain bar lunches, friendly service, coal fires, bare boards and banquettes, prints, panelling and masses of pump clips, handsome tiled façade and corridor; background music, TV, games machine; wheelchair access but steps down to back lounge, open all day. *(P A Lord)*

MANCHESTER　　　　　　SJ8397
★Dukes 92　(0161) 839 8642
Castle Street, below the bottom end of Deansgate; M3 4LZ Converted former stables looking over canal basin, cheerful informal atmosphere, with old and modern furnishings including chaise longues and deep armchairs, whitewashed or red walls hung with photos and paintings, stylish gallery bar accessed by elegant spiral staircase, three real ales, decent wines and wide choice of spirits from handsome granite-topped counter, bar food including pizzas and deli boards, also a grill menu in one area; background music; children welcome, waterside tables on big terrace, open all day (till 1am Fri, Sat). *(Dr Simon Innes)*

MANCHESTER　　　　　　SJ8194
Font　(0161) 871 2022
Manchester Road, Chorlton; M21 9PG Relaxed split-level bar with regularly changing beers including eight real ales and 16 craft, also extensive bottled range and traditional ciders, cocktails too, eclectic

choice of enjoyable food (till 10pm) from deli boards to interesting salads and spicy african stews; weekend DJs, free wi-fi; children and dogs welcome, seats out at front behind railings, open all day (till 1am Fri, Sat). *(Mark and Sarah Bannister)*

MANCHESTER SJ8498

Hare & Hounds (0161) 832 4737

Shudehill, behind Arndale; M4 4AA
Old-fashioned 18th-c local with long narrow bar linking front snug and comfortable back lounge, notable tilework, panelling and stained glass, low-priced Holts beer, friendly staff; background music, TV; open all day. *(P A Lord)*

MANCHESTER SJ8397

Knott (0161) 839 9229

Deansgate; M3 4LY Friendly modern glass-fronted café-bar under railway arch by Castlefield heritage site; seven well kept ales including Castle Rock and Marble, also lots of craft beers and continental imports, enjoyable good value food; background music; upstairs smokers' balcony overlooking Rochdale Canal, open (and food) all day. *(Dr Simon Innes)*

MANCHESTER SJ8499

★Marble Arch (0161) 832 5914

Rochdale Road (A664), Ancoats; centre of Gould Street, just E of Victoria station; M4 4HY Cheery own-brew pub with fine listed Victorian interior; long narrow bar with wonderful gently barrel-vaulted high ceiling, extensive glazed brickwork, marble and tiling, sloping mosaic floor and frieze advertising various spirits and other drinks, their good Marble beers plus a couple of guests (brewery visible from windows in back dining room – tours by arrangement), well liked home-made food from varied menu; background music; children welcome, small garden, open all day (till midnight Fri, Sat). *(Nick Lawless)*

MANCHESTER SJ8398

Mark Addy (0161) 834 7271

Stanley Street, off New Bailey Street, Salford; M3 5EJ Stairs down to unusual converted waiting rooms for boat passengers, barrel-vaulted sandstone bays, cast-iron pillars and big windows overlooking river, five changing real ales; background music (live Sat), Fri DJ, comedy night last Weds of month, sports TVs, free wi-fi; long waterside terrace, open all day (till 2am Fri, Sat). *(Anon)*

MANCHESTER SJ8398

★Mr Thomas Chop House

(0161) 832 2245 *Cross Street; M2 7AR* Interesting late 19th-c pub, tall and narrow, with well preserved features; good generously served food including signature corned beef hash, friendly staff, ales such as Holts and Lees and decent wines by the glass, front bar

with panelling, original gas lamp fittings and framed cartoons, stools at wall and window shelves, back green-tiled eating areas with rows of tables on black and white Victorian tiles, archways and high ceilings; seats out at back, open all day. *(Jeremy King)*

MANCHESTER SJ8298

New Oxford (0161) 832 7082

Bexley Square, Salford; M3 6DB Red-brick Victorian corner pub with up to 18 well kept changing ales (chalked on blackboard), plus extensive range of draught and bottled continental beers, real ciders too, friendly staff, light airy feel in small front bar and back room, coal fire, low-priced basic food till 6pm; open mike and quiz nights, juke box, free wi-fi; café-style seating out in square, open all day. *(Dr Simon Innes)*

MANCHESTER SJ8398

Oast House (0161) 829 3830

Crown Square, Springfields; M3 3AY Quirky mock-up of kentish oast house surrounded by modern high-rises, rustic lofty interior with bare boards, timbers and plenty of tables, real ales and good selection of bottled beers and wines, enjoyable fairly priced food from deli boards to grills, friendly helpful young staff, busy lively atmosphere; prominent background music; children welcome, spacious outside seating area, open all day (till 2am Fri, Sat). *(John Wooll)*

MANCHESTER SJ8284

Parkfield (0161) 766 3923

Park Lane; M45 7GT Welcoming dining pub with good variety of food from sandwiches and pub staples to restauranty choices, all-day Sun roasts, three regional ales, freshly ground coffee, cocktails and good wine list; some live music; children and dogs welcome, garden behind, open all day. *(Anon)*

MANCHESTER SJ8397

★Peveril of the Peak (0161) 236 6364

Great Bridgewater Street; M1 5JQ Vivid art nouveau external tilework and three sturdily furnished old-fashioned bare-boards rooms, interesting pictures, lots of mahogany, mirrors and stained or frosted glass, log fire, four ales such as Black Sheep, Copper Dragon, Jennings and Skinners from central servery, cheap basic lunchtime food; table football, pool, background music, TV; children welcome, pavement tables, usually open all day. *(Ruth May)*

MANCHESTER SJ8498

Port Street Beer House

(0161) 237 9949 *Port Street; M1 2EQ* Fantastic range of beers from all over the world on draught and in bottles including well kept real ales, good service from knowledgeable staff, no food, can get very busy but more room upstairs, events such as 'meet the brewer' evenings; open all day weekends, from 2pm Fri, 4pm Tues-Thurs, closed Mon. *(Vikki and Matt Wharton)*

MANCHESTER   SJ8397
Rain Bar (0161) 235 6500
Great Bridgewater Street; M1 5JG
Bare boards and lots of woodwork in former umbrella works, well kept Lees ales and plenty of wines by the glass, enjoyable good value pubby food, friendly staff and relaxed atmosphere, nooks and corners, coal fire in small snug, large upstairs bar/function room; background music, Weds quiz; good back terrace overlooking spruced-up Rochdale Canal, handy for Bridgewater Hall, open (and food) all day. *(Peter Pilbeam)*

MANCHESTER   SJ8398
★**Sams Chop House** (0161) 834 3210
Back Pool Fold, Chapel Walks; M2 1HN
Thriving downstairs dining pub, offshoot from Mr Thomas Chop House, with original Victorian décor, generous helpings of good plain english food including weekend brunch, formal waiters, well kept beers and good wine choice, a former haunt of LS Lowry whose statue sits contemplatively at the bar, back restaurant with black and white tiled floor; background music, sports TV; some pavement tables, open all day. *(Jeremy King)*

MANCHESTER   SJ8398
★**Sinclairs** (0161) 834 0430
Cathedral Gates, off Exchange Square; M3 1SW Attractive low-beamed and timbered Sam Smiths pub (rebuilt here in redevelopment), all-day food including fresh oysters, brisk friendly service, bustling atmosphere, quieter upstairs bar with snugs and Jacobean fireplace; tables out in Shambles Square (plastic glasses), open all day. *(Anon)*

MARPLE   SJ9389
Hare & Hounds (0161) 427 0293
Dooley Lane (A627 W); SK6 7EJ Dining pub above River Goyt, modern layout and décor, enjoyable fairly traditional food at reasonable prices from sandwiches up, Hydes ales and a guest, friendly service; background music; well behaved children welcome, outside seating, open (and food) all day. *(Dennis Jones)*

MARPLE   SJ9588
Ring o' Bells (0161) 427 2300
Church Lane; by Macclesfield Canal, bridge 2; SK6 7AY Popular old-fashioned local with assorted memorabilia in four linked rooms, well kept Robinsons ales and decent food at reasonable prices; darts, quiz nights and some live music including brass bands in the waterside

garden, own narrowboat, one bedroom, open all day. *(Edward May)*

MARPLE BRIDGE   SJ9889
Hare & Hounds (0161) 427 4042
Mill Brow; from end of Town Street in centre turn left up Hollins Lane and keep on uphill; SK6 5LW Comfortable and civilised stone-built country pub in lovely spot, smallish and can get crowded, really good attractively presented food (not Mon, Tues) from short modern menu, well kept Robinsons ales and good wines, log fires; garden behind, open all day weekends, closed Mon-Thurs lunchtimes. *(Isobel Mackinlay)*

MELLOR   SJ9888
Devonshire Arms (0161) 427 2563
This is the Mellor near Marple, S of Manchester; heading out of Marple on the A626 towards Glossop, Mellor is the next road after the B6102, signposted off on the right at Marple Bridge; Longhurst Lane; SK6 5PP Front bar with old leather-seated settles and open fire, two small back rooms with Victorian fireplaces, well kept Robinsons and simple reasonably priced home-made food, friendly welcoming staff; quiz every other Tues, jazz on bank holidays; children and dogs welcome, garden with fish pond crossed by japanese bridge, large pergola, play area on small tree-sheltered lawn, open all day weekends. *(Hilary Forrest)*

MORECAMBE   SD4264
Midland Grand Plaza
(01524) 424000 *Marine Road W; LA4 4BZ* Classic art deco hotel in splendid seafront position, comfortable if unorthodox contemporary furnishings in spacious sea-view Rotunda Bar, rather pricey but enjoyable food from interesting lancashire tapas to restaurant meals, good service; children welcome, 44 bedrooms, open all day. *(J F M and M West)*

MORECAMBE   SD4364
Palatine (01524) 410503
The Crescent; LA4 5BZ Comfortable Edwardian seafront pub, enjoyable reasonably priced food including deli boards, pizzas and pub standards (good lancashire hotpot), four Lancaster ales and guests, good friendly staff, leather armchairs and some high tables with stools on wood floor, upstairs panelled sea-view dining lounge; seats out in front, open all day (till 1am Fri, Sat). *(Anon)*

NETHER BURROW   SD6175
★**Highwayman** (01524) 273338
A683 S of Kirkby Lonsdale; LA6 2RJ
Substantial skilfully reworked 17th-c stone

Half pints: by law, a pub should not charge more for half a pint than half the price of a full pint, unless it shows that half-pint price on its price list.

pub, well divided flagstoned interior with some intimate corners, informal wooden furnishings and a couple of big log fires, very good food, Thwaites ales, 14 wines by the glass and good range of other drinks, friendly efficient service; children and dogs (in bar) welcome, big terrace and lovely gardens, pretty Lune Valley countryside, open all day. *(Ray and Winifred Halliday, Caroline Prescott, Michael Doswell, Dr Kevan Tucker, Barbara and Peter Kelly)*

NEWTON   SD6950
★**Parkers Arms** (01200) 446236
B6478 7 miles N of Clitheroe; BB7 3DY Friendly welcome and very good locally sourced food from lunchtime sandwiches (home-baked bread) to imaginative specials, you can eat in the bar or restaurant, four real ales including Bowland, good range of wines, nice coffee and afternoon tea, log fires; children welcome, garden with lovely views, four bedrooms, pretty spot. *(Graham and Carol Parker, Ray and Winifred Halliday, Dr Peter Crawshaw)*

PARBOLD   SD4911
Windmill (01257) 462935
Mill Lane; WN8 7NW Nicely modernised and opened-up beamed pub, good coal fire, mix of furniture including settles and some interesting carved chairs, candles on tables laid for the popular well executed food (pub favourites to more adventurous specials), six well kept ales and eight wines by the glass, friendly service from young staff; downstairs gents'; seats out in front and behind, next to village windmill and facing Leeds & Liverpool Canal, good local walks, open all day (food all day Sun). *(Nick Sharpe)*

PLEASINGTON   SD6528
★**Clog & Billycock** (01254) 201163
Village signposted off A677 Preston New Road on W edge of Blackburn; Billinge End Road; BB2 6QB Attractive carefully modernised and extended old village pub, light and airy with flagstoned floors and high ceilings, cosier room with high-backed settles and fireplace at one end, well liked interesting food, small bar area serving Thwaites ales and several wines by the glass; background music, free wi-fi; seats outside in small garden, open (and food) all day, only light meals served weekday afternoons. *(W K Wood, Gordon and Margaret Ormondroyd)*

PRESTON   SD5329
Black Horse (01772) 204855
Friargate; PR1 2EJ Friendly pub in pedestrianised street with up to eight well kept Robinsons ales, unusual ornate curved and mosaic-tiled Victorian main bar, panelling, stained glass and old local photographs, two quiet cosy snugs, mirrored back area, open fires, upstairs bar serving inexpensive food (not evenings or Sun);

no children, open all day from 10.30am (midday Sun). *(Caroline Prescott)*

RABY   SJ3179
★**Wheatsheaf** (0151) 336 3416
Raby Mere Road, The Green; from A540 heading S from Heswall, turn left into Upper Raby Road, village about a mile further; CH63 4JH Up to nine well kept real ales in pretty thatched black and white pub, simply furnished rambling rooms with homely feel, cosy central bar and nice snug formed by antique settles around fine old fireplace, small coal fire in more spacious room, well liked reasonably priced bar food (not Sun or Mon evenings) including huge range of sandwiches, à la carte menu in large former cowshed restaurant (Tues-Sat evenings), good friendly service, conservatory; children welcome, dogs in bar, picnic-sets on terrace and in pleasant back garden, open all day and gets very busy at weekends. *(Roger and Anne Newbury)*

RAMSBOTTOM   SD8016
Eagle & Child (01706) 557181
Whalley Road (A56); BL0 0DL Friendly well run pub with good freshly made food (booking advised) using locally sourced produce including own vegetables, well kept Thwaites ales, real cider and decent choice of wines by the glass, good service; children welcome, interesting garden with valley views over roof tops to Holcombe Moor and Peel Tower, open all day Fri and Sat, till 7pm Sun. *(Glenasdias)*

RAMSBOTTOM   SD8017
★**Fishermans Retreat** (01706) 825314
Twine Valley Park/Fishery signed off A56 N of Bury at Shuttleworth; Bye Road; BL0 0HH Remote yet busy pub-restaurant, generous food (some quite pricey) using produce from surrounding Estate and trout lakes (they can arrange fishing), also have own land where they raise cattle; mountain lodge-feel bar with beams and bare stone walls, five well kept ales including Copper Dragon, Moorhouses, Timothy Taylors and Thwaites, over 500 malt whiskies (also sold in shop), good wine list, small family dining room and restaurant/function room extension, helpful friendly staff; a few picnic-sets with lovely valley views, closed Mon, otherwise open (and food) all day. *(Isobel Mackinlay)*

RAWTENSTALL   SD8213
Buffer Stops (0161) 764 7790
Bury Road; in East Lancashire Railway station; BB4 6EH Platform bar at Rawtenstall heritage station, five well kept changing ales, real cider/perry and selection of bottled beers, snacky food, popular with locals and railway enthusiasts; children welcome in former waiting room; open all day (till 9pm Mon, Tues). *(P A Lord)*

RILEY GREEN   SD6225
★ **Royal Oak** (01254) 201445
A675/A6061; PR5 0SL Cosy low-beamed
four-room pub (former coaching inn)
extended by present owners; good freshly
made food and friendly efficient service,
four Thwaites ales and maybe a guest from
long back bar, ancient stripped stone, open
fires, seats from high-backed settles to red
plush armchairs on carpet, lots of nooks and
crannies, soft lighting, impressive woodwork
and some bric-a-brac, comfortable dining
rooms; children and dogs welcome, picnic-
sets at front and in side beer garden, short
walk from Leeds & Liverpool Canal, footpath
to Hoghton Tower, open all day, food all day
weekends. *(W K Wood)*

ROCHDALE   SD8913
Baum (01706) 352186
*Toad Lane (off Hunters Lane) next to
the Rochdale Pioneers (Co-op) Museum;
OL12 0NU* In surviving cobbled street and
plenty of old-fashioned charm, seven well
kept changing ales and lots of bottled beers,
good value food all day (Sun till 6pm) from
sandwiches and tapas up including daily
roast, cheerful young staff, bare boards, old
advertising signs, conservatory; garden with
pétanque, open all day (till midnight Fri,
Sat). *(Nigel and Jean Eames, P A Lord)*

ROMILEY   SJ9390
Duke of York (0161) 406 9988
Stockport Road; SK6 3AN Popular former
coaching inn refurbished but keeping
character, four well kept beers including
Thwaites and Charles Wells Bombardier, good
reasonably priced food (not Sun evening,
Mon) in beamed bar or upstairs restaurant,
friendly efficient staff; seats out at front
behind white picket fence, open all day.
(Dennis Jones, Stuart Paulley)

ROMILEY   SJ9390
Platform 1 (0161) 406 8686
*Stockport Road next to the station;
SK6 4BN* Popular pub revamped in modern/
traditional style, open and airy with tiled
floor, some high tables and chairs, six mostly
local ales including a well priced house
beer, enjoyable good value pubby food from
sandwiches up, bargain OAP deal 12-5pm
weekdays, good friendly service, carpeted
upstairs restaurant called Platform 2; small
outside seating area, open (and food) all
day (last orders for food 6.45pm Sun).
(Dennis Jones)

ROUGHLEE   SD8440
Bay Horse (01282) 696558
*Blacko Bar Road; handy for M65
junction 13; BB9 6NP* Modern renovation
for this old village pub; slate floor bar/dining
area to the right, leather sofas and light
open feel, carpeted dining room to the left
with view in to back kitchen, good food (all

day weekends) including interesting daily
specials and good value lunchtime/early
evening set menu, short well priced wine
list, four local ales, friendly competent staff;
children welcome, pretty village in beautiful
valley near Pendle Hill, good walking
country. *(Dr Kevan Tucker)*

RUFFORD   SD4615
Hesketh Arms (01704) 821009
*Junction of Liverpool Road (A59) and
Holmeswood Road (B5246); L40 1SB*
Old beamed pub with modernised open-
plan interior arranged into distinct areas,
pictures and bric-a-brac, good choice of well
kept ales such as Moorhouses, Prospect,
Reedley Hallows and Tetleys, enjoyable fairly
traditional food along with some interesting
specials, early-bird deal (5-7pm Mon-Fri);
live music and quiz nights; short walk from
Leeds & Liverpool Canal, handy for Rufford
Old Hall (NT), open all day. *(Anon)*

SCARISBRICK   SD4011
Heatons Bridge Inn (01704) 840549
Heatons Bridge Road; L40 8JG Pretty
19th-c pub by bridge over Leeds & Liverpool
Canal (popular with boaters), good value
generous home-made food (till 6pm Sun,
not Mon, Tues), well kept Black Cat, Tetleys
and a guest, friendly welcoming staff, four
traditional cosy areas and dining room; free
wi-fi; children and dogs welcome, pretty
hanging baskets and garden with play area,
also World War II pillbox (the pub holds two
vintage military vehicle events during the
year), open all day. *(Dave Braisted)*

SCOUTHEAD   SD9605
Three Crowns (0161) 624 1766
Huddersfield Road; OL4 4AT Refurbished
dining pub with good food from sandwiches
to well presented imaginative dishes, good
value set menu too, cheerful efficient service,
well kept ales and decent choice of wines,
local artwork and photographs; children
welcome. *(Beverley Nicolaides)*

SLAIDBURN   SD7152
Hark to Bounty (01200) 446246
B6478 N of Clitheroe; BB7 3EP Attractive
old stone-built pub with homely linked
rooms, enjoyable fresh food (all day Sun)
from sandwiches and light dishes up,
friendly young staff, four real ales including
Theakstons, decent wines and whiskies,
comfortable chairs by open fire, games room
one end, restaurant the other; dogs welcome,
pleasant back garden, charming Forest
of Bowland village and good walks, nine
bedrooms, open all day. *(Ruth May)*

STOCKPORT   SJ8990
★ **Arden Arms** (0161) 480 2185
*Millgate Street/Corporation Street,
opposite pay car park; SK1 2LX*
Cheerful and thriving Victorian pub in
handsome dark-brick building, several well

preserved high-ceilinged rooms off island bar (one tiny old-fashioned snug accessed through servery), tiling, panelling and two coal fires, good sensibly priced food (not Mon or Tues evenings) from lunchtime sandwiches to interesting specials, half a dozen well kept Robinsons ales, friendly efficient service; background music; children welcome, tables in sheltered courtyard with much-used smokers' shelter, open all day. *(Dennis Jones, John Wooll)*

STOCKPORT   SJ8990
Crown (0161) 480 5850
Heaton Lane, Heaton Norris; SK4 1AR
Busy but welcoming partly open-plan Victorian pub popular for its well kept changing ales (up to 16), also bottled beers and real cider, three cosy lounge areas off bar, spotless stylish décor, wholesome bargain lunches; frequent live music, darts; tables in cobbled courtyard, huge viaduct soaring above, open all day. *(Dennis Jones)*

STOCKPORT   SJ8890
Magnet (0161) 429 6287
Wellington Road North; SK4 1HJ Busy pub with over half a dozen well kept ales including own Watts beers, pool and juke box in one of the five rooms; live acoustic music first Fri of month; open all day Fri-Sun, from 4pm other days. *(Dennis Jones)*

STOCKPORT   SJ8990
Railway (0161) 429 6062
Avenue Street (just off M63 junction 13, via A560); SK1 2BZ Bright and airy L-shaped corner bar with up to 15 ales (always a mild), lots of foreign beers and a real cider, friendly staff, no food, old Stockport and railway photographs, bar billiards; tables out behind, open all day. *(Jo Garnett)*

STOCKPORT   SJ8990
Red Bull (0161) 480 1286
Middle Hillgate; SK1 3AY Steps up to friendly well run pub, dimly lit beamed bar with dark panelling and wood and tile floor, various areas off, well kept Robinsons ales and good value home-cooked food; background and some live music; four bedrooms, open all day. *(Jo Garnett)*

STOCKPORT   SJ8990
Swan With Two Necks
(0161) 480 2341 *Princes Street; SK1 1RY* Traditional narrow pub with welcoming local atmosphere, front panelled bar, back room with button-back wall benches, stone fireplace and skylight, drinking corridor, well kept Robinsons ales and decent lunchtime food (not Sun, Mon) from sandwiches up;

small outside area, open all day Fri, Sat, other days till 7pm (6pm Sun). *(Jo Garnett)*

STRINES   SJ9686
Sportsmans Arms (0161) 427 2888
B6101 Marple–New Mills; SK6 7GE
Comfortable roadside local with panoramic Goyt Valley view from picture-window lounge bar, good changing ale range, enjoyable well priced home-made food including specials board, small separate bar, log fire folk night first Weds of month; children and dogs welcome, tables out on side decking, heated smokers' shelter, open all day weekends. *(Anon)*

TATHAM   SD6169
Tatham Bridge Inn (01524) 221326
B6480, off A683 Lancaster–Kirkby Lonsdale; LA2 8NL Popular old pub with cosy low-beamed bar, well kept ales such as Black Sheep, Tetleys and York, good range of enjoyable home-cooked food, friendly staff, dining rooms along corridor and upstairs; well behaved dogs welcome, bedrooms. *(Edward May)*

TOCKHOLES   SD6623
Black Bull (01254) 581381
Between Tockholes and Blackburn; BB3 0LL Welcoming tucked-away country pub home to the Three B's Brewery, their full range including Black Bull Bitter (tasting trays available), no food; seats outside with nice views, open all day weekends, from 4pm weekdays. *(Nige Collighan)*

TOCKHOLES   SD6621
Royal (01254) 705373
Signed off A6062 S of Blackburn, and off A675; Tockholes Road; BB3 0PA Friendly and unpretentious little rooms with big open fires, four well kept ales such as local Three B's from tiny back servery, well priced pubby food including some blackboard specials; children, walkers and dogs welcome, big garden with views from sheltered terrace, good walks including to Darwen Tower, closed Mon, otherwise open all day. *(Dr Kevan Tucker)*

TUNSTALL   SD6073
Lunesdale Arms (01524) 274203
A683 S of Kirkby Lonsdale; LA6 2QN Welcoming relaxed atmosphere at this attractive 18th-c dining pub; opened-up bare-boards interior with good mix of stripped tables and chairs, woodburner in solid stone fireplace, snugger little flagstoned back part and games area with pool, Black Sheep and a couple of guests, enjoyable sensibly priced food from weekly changing menu; children and dogs (in bar) welcome,

pretty Lune Valley village, church has Brontë associations, closed Mon. *(John Evans, John and Sylvia Harrop)*

WADDINGTON   SD7243
Higher Buck (01200) 423226
The Square; BB7 3HZ Welcoming pub in picturesque village; recently modernised open-plan interior with airy new england feel and good mix of seating, nice food (all day Sun till 8pm) from deli boards and pub favourites up, well kept Thwaites from smart pine servery, good friendly service; background music; children welcome, tables out on front cobbles and in small back courtyard, seven attractively refurbished bedrooms, open all day. *(Steve Whalley)*

WADDINGTON   SD7243
★Waddington Arms (01200) 423262
Clitheroe Road (B6478 N of Clitheroe); BB7 3HP. Character inn with friendly landlord and staff; four linked bars, left one snuggest with blazing woodburner in huge fireplace, other low-beamed rooms have lots to look at including antique and modern prints and vintage motor-racing posters, fine oak settles and chunky stripped-pine tables, generous helpings of popular tasty food, well kept Moorhouses and four guests, good choice of wines by the glass and a dozen malt whiskies; children and dogs welcome, wicker chairs on sunny front terrace looking over to village church, more seats on two-level back terrace and neat tree-sheltered lawn, comfortable bedrooms, good walks in nearby Forest of Bowland, open all day. *(John and Eleanor Holdsworth, David Jackman, Steve Whalley, Brian and Anna Marsden, Gordon and Margaret Ormondroyd and others)*

WALLASEY   SJ3094
Queens Royal (0151) 691 1010
Marine Promenade opposite the lake; CH45 2JT Welcoming double-fronted Victorian seafront hotel with airy modernised bar, six regional ales from island servery, enjoyable food including well priced early evening menu and Sun carvery, afternoon teas, good friendly service; children welcome, front terrace with striking sea views, comfortable bedrooms, open (and food) all day. *(Susan and John Douglas)*

WEETON   SD3834
Eagle & Child (01253) 836230
Singleton Road (B5260); PR4 3NB Rustic beamed dining pub with popular home-made food at fair prices including regular deals, well kept ales such as Caledonian, Theakstons, Thwaites and Timothy Taylors, good choice of wines by the

glass, efficient friendly service, log fires, low brick walls with old curved standing timbers, rugs on bare boards, mix of chairs around polished tables; Thurs quiz, TV; children welcome, seats out at front, garden to side and back, play area, open (and food) all day. *(Alan Eaves)*

WEST BRADFORD   SD7444
Three Millstones (01200) 443339
Waddington Road; BB7 4SX Attractive old building, but more restaurant than pub with all tables laid for dining; popular food from owner-chef including set deals and daily specials in four comfortable linked areas, beams, timbers and two grand fireplaces, ales such as Bowland and Moorhouses, good choice of wines, friendly efficient service; closed Sun evening, Mon, Tues. *(John and Eleanor Holdsworth, Steve Whalley)*

WEST KIRBY   SJ2186
White Lion (0151) 625 9037
Grange Road (A540); CH48 4EE Friendly proper pub in interesting 18th-c sandstone building, several small beamed areas on different levels, Black Sheep, Courage Director and a couple of quickly changing guests, good value simple bar lunches (not Sun), coal stove; no children, attractive secluded back garden up steep stone steps, fish pond, open all day. *(Tony Tollitt)*

WHALLEY   SD7336
★Swan (01254) 822195
King Street; BB7 9SN Popular 17th-c former coaching inn with friendly staff and good mix of customers in big bar, a couple of Bowland ales and Timothy Taylors Landlord, enjoyable food from fairly standard menu (Sun till 7pm), further room with leather sofas and armchairs on bare boards; background music, games machine; children and dogs (in bar) welcome, picnic-sets on back terrace and on grass strips by car park, six bedrooms named after nearby rivers and attractions, open all day. *(Steve Whalley, Brian and Anna Marsden)*

WHEATLEY LANE   SD8338
★Sparrowhawk (01282) 603034
Wheatley Lane Road; towards E end of village road, which runs N of and parallel to A6068; one way to reach it is to follow Fence signpost, then turn off at Barrowford signpost; BB12 9QG Comfortably civilised 1930s feel in imposing black and white pub, oak panelling, parquet flooring and leather tub chairs, unusual domed stained-glass skylight, six well kept ales including Reedley Hallows from

---

cushioned leatherette counter, nice wines by the glass and good food from sandwiches and light lunches up, friendly young staff; background and live music, comedy nights; children welcome, dogs in bar, heavy wooden tables on spacious front terrace with good views to the moors beyond Nelson and Colne, open (and food) all day. *(Jeremy King, Dr Kevan Tucker, Roger and Donna Huggins)*

WHEELTON · SD6021
★**Dressers Arms** (01254) 830041

Briers Brow; off A674, 2.1 miles from M61 junction 8; PR6 8HD Popular old stone-built pub fully restored after devastating 2014 fire; five well kept ales such as Black Sheep, Tetleys and Thwaites, good choice of enjoyable reasonably priced food including Sun carvery, friendly attentive service; Tues quiz; children and dogs welcome, open (and food) all day. *(Anon)*

WORSLEY · SD7201
Woodside (0161) 702 7246

Ellenbrook Road, just off A580; M28 1ES Victorian red-brick Vintage Inn with several eating areas around central bar, good choice of popular food including deals, up to five well kept ales such as Brakspears and Thwaites, decent wines by the glass, good friendly service, coal fires; children welcome, open (and food) all day. *(Gerry and Rosemary Dobson)*

WRIGHTINGTON · SD5011
Rigbye Arms (01257) 462354

3 miles from M6 junction 27; off A5209 via Robin Hood Lane and left into High Moor Lane; WN6 9QB 17th-c dining pub in attractive moorland setting, welcoming and relaxed, with wide choice of enjoyable sensibly priced food including a game menu, hot and cold sandwiches too, friendly prompt service even when busy, well kept Black Sheep, Tetleys and Timothy Taylors, decent wines, several carpeted rooms including cosy tap room, open fires, separate evening restaurant (Weds-Sat); free wi-fi; children welcome, garden, bowling green, regular car club meetings, open (and food) all day Sun. *(Ruth May)*

WRIGHTINGTON BAR · SD5313
Corner House (01257) 451400

B5250, N of M6 junction 27; WN6 9SE Opened-up 19th-c corner pub-restaurant, good food (all day weekends) from traditional to more upscale choices, meal deals and daily specials, real ales and good quality wines, plenty of tables in different modernised areas; children welcome, seats outside, open all day. *(Nick Sharpe)*

Leicestershire
and Rutland

KEY ★ Star Pub   ⭐ Top Quality Food   🍺 Great Beer

🍷 Good Wines   £ Bargain Meals   🛏 Good Bedrooms   🍴 Serves Food

---

BREEDON ON THE HILL   SK4022   Map 7

Three Horseshoes ⭐

(01332) 695129 – www.thehorseshoes.com

Main Street (A453); DE73 8AN

Comfortable pub with friendly licensees and emphasis on popular food

In the 18th c this started out as a farriers – today it's a carefully run dining pub with interesting food. The clean-cut central bar has a stylishly simple feel with heavy worn flagstones, green walls and ceilings, a log fire, pubby tables and a dark wood counter. Marstons Pedigree and Youngs Bitter on handpump and decent house wines served by chatty, helpful staff. Beyond the bar is a dining room with maroon walls, dark pews and tables, and a two-room dining area on the right has a comfortably civilised and chatty feel with big antique tables set quite closely together on seagrass matting, and colourful modern country prints and antique engravings on canary yellow walls. Even at lunchtime there are lit candles in elegant modern holders. The farm shop sells their own and other local produce: eggs, jams, meat, smoked foods and chocolates. Look out for the quaint conical village lock-up opposite.

⭐ The rewarding food includes sandwiches, fish and spinach pancake with cheese, grilled goats cheese with piccalilli, roast vegetable casserole, sausages with mash and onion gravy, chicken in stilton sauce with garlic mash, beef and mushroom casserole, blackened salmon with crème fraîche, fillet of beef with peppered sauce, and puddings such as treacle tart and chocolate whisky trifle. *Benchmark main dish: beer-battered cod and chips £10.75. Two-course evening meal £23.95.*

Free house ~ Licensees Ian Davison, Jennie Ison and Stuart Marson ~ Real ale ~ Open 11.30-2.30, 5.30-11; 12-3 Sun; closed Sun evening, Mon ~ Bar food 12-2, 5.30-9; 12-3 Sun ~ Restaurant ~ Children welcome ~ Dogs allowed in bar ~ Wi-fi *Recommended by Belinda Stamp, John Harris*

BUCKMINSTER   SK8822   Map 7

Tollemache Arms ⭐

(01476) 860477 – www.tollemache-arms.co.uk

B676 Colsterworth–Melton Mowbray; Main Street; NG33 5SA

Emphasis on good food in stylishly updated pub; bedrooms

Just a few minutes from the A1, this impressive 19th-c stone-built country pub is in a lovely village and offers a genuine welcome to all. Table and standard lamps, big bunches of flowers and the smell of baking bread from the kitchen create a homely feel, and there's plenty of wood throughout – floors, hand-made pews, chairs and tables, with leather armchairs beside an open fire in the bar. Next to the main restaurant is a library with books on shelves and leather sofas and armchairs; background music. Grainstore Red Kite and Rutland Panther, and Oakham JHB on handpump, a good choice of wines by the glass and several malt whiskies. There are plenty of teak tables and chairs in the garden. The recently renovated bedrooms are comfortable and well equipped and breakfasts are highly thought of.

 Enjoyable food includes lunchtime sandwiches, prawns in a sweet chilli and popcorn crumb on spiced slaw, smoked salmon roulade with lemon dressing, chicken in a basket, vegetable stacks topped with mozzarella and pesto dressing, mussels in chorizo, thyme and tomato sauce, fish pie, pork fillet with wholegrain mustard mash and shallot sauce, and puddings such as chocolate torte and honey parfait with a honeycomb and orange reduction. *Benchmark main dish: rack of lamb with dauphinoise potatoes and red wine jus £17.50. Two-course evening meal £21.00.*

Free house ~ Licensee Sarah Turner ~ Real ale ~ Open 10.30-3, 6-11; 11-11 Sat; 12-5 Sun; closed Sun evening, Mon ~ Bar food 12-3, 6-9; 12-9 Sat; 12-4 Sun ~ Restaurant ~ Children welcome ~ Dogs allowed in bar ~ Wi-fi ~ Bedrooms: /£75 *Recommended by Toby Jones, Barry Collett*

CLIPSHAM

SK9716 Map 8

Olive Branch ★

(01780) 410355 – www.theolivebranchpub.com

Take B668/Stretton exit off A1 N of Stamford; Clipsham signposted E from exit roundabout; LE15 7SH

An exceptional place for a drink, a meal or an overnight stay

As a civilised break from the A1, this rather special inn would be hard to beat. Once labourers'cottages, the various small and charmingly attractive rooms have a relaxed country cottage atmosphere, dark joists and beams, rustic furniture, an interesting mix of pictures (some by local artists), candles on tables, and a cosy log fire in a stone inglenook fireplace; background music. A carefully chosen range of drinks includes a beer named for the pub and a couple of guests from Grainstore or Timothy Taylors on handpump, an enticing wine list (with 17 by the glass), a thoughtful choice of spirits and cocktails (including winter sloe gin and damson vodka using berries from the local hedgerows) and several british and continental bottled beers. Outside, there are tables, chairs and big plant pots on a pretty little terrace, with seating on the neat lawn, sheltered in the crook of the two low buildings. The restful bedrooms (in a renovated Georgian house across the road) are extremely comfortable and the breakfasts are delicious. It can get pretty busy at peak times. The wine shop also sells their own jams and chutneys; you can order dishes to take away and they can even organise food for a dinner party at home. Sister pub is the Red Lion in Stathern.

 Cooked by one of the owners, the accomplished, beautifully presented food includes lunchtime sandwiches, ravioli of sweet potato, radicchio, sage and pine nut butter, ibérico ham croquettes with red pepper purée and blow-torched gem lettuce, wild mushroom risotto, smoked haddock rarebit with dill sauce and champ mash, guinea fowl with morteau sausage, pearl barley and glazed shallots, roast loin and braised shoulder of lamb with chorizo, hash browns and braised fennel, and puddings such as kaffir lime panna cotta with spiced pineapple and coconut sorbet and white forest gateau with cherry sorbet; they also offer two- and three-course set menus. *Benchmark main dish: a taste of pork (leg, belly, black pudding) with cider fondant and cabbage £17.75. Two-course evening meal £24.50.*

Free house ~ Licensees Sean Hope and Ben Jones ~ Real ale ~ Open 12-3, 6-11; 12-11 Sat; 12-10.30 Sun ~ Bar food 12-2 (2.30 Sat), 6.30-9.30; 12-3, 7-9 Sun ~ Restaurant ~ Children welcome ~ Dogs allowed in bar and bedrooms ~ Wi-fi ~ Bedrooms: £97.50/£115
Recommended by Derek and Sylvia Stephenson, P Dawn, Matt Gutteridge, Richard Kennell, Nick and Gillian Harrison, J F M and M West, Malcolm and Jane Levitt

GREETHAM
SK9314 Map 7

Wheatsheaf 🎯 ♀

(01572) 812325 – www.wheatsheaf-greetham.co.uk
B668 Stretton–Cottesmore; LE15 7NP

Warmly friendly stone pub with interesting food, real ales, a dozen wines and seats in front and back gardens

Always deservedly busy with both locals and visitors, this is a neatly kept and attractive shuttered stone pub that's very handy for the A1. The linked L-shaped rooms have both a log fire and a blazing open stove, traditional settles and cushioned captain's chairs around dark tables on blue patterned carpeting, and Brewsters Hophead, Greene King IPA and Nene Valley DXB on handpump and a dozen wines by the glass, served by genuinely welcoming and helpful licensees; background music. A games room has TV, darts, pool and board games. The pub dogs are a dachshund and a labradoodle, and visiting dogs are welcome in the bar. There are chunky picnic-sets on the front lawn and more seats on a back terrace by a pretty stream with a duck house; pétanque. They sell their own pickles, chutneys and chocolates; ramp for wheelchairs.

 Cooked by the landlady using local, seasonal produce, the tempting food includes sandwiches using home-baked bread, snails in their shells with garlic and parsley butter, chicken and bacon terrine with ale chutney, wild mushroom and leek lasagne with truffle oil, beef and mushroom in ale pie, tiger prawns with spinach, parsley, garlic and lemon, barbary duck breast with cauliflower purée, pickled beetroot and red wine sauce, slow-cooked oxtail with horseradish cream, and puddings such as drunken chocolate cake and rhubarb with orange, cardamom and rosewater ice-cream. *Benchmark main dish: chargrilled bavette steak with garlic and tarragon butter and chips £16.50. Two-course evening meal £21.00.*

Punch ~ Lease Scott and Carol Craddock ~ Real ale ~ Open 12-3, 6-11; 12-midnight Sat; 12-11 Sun; closed Mon except bank holidays, two weeks Jan ~ Bar food 12-2 (2.15 Sat), 6.30-9; 12-3 Sun ~ Restaurant ~ Children welcome ~ Dogs allowed in bar ~ Wi-fi
Recommended by Michael and Jenny Back, Colin McKerrow, Gordon and Margaret Ormondroyd

LYDDINGTON
SP8797 Map 4

Marquess of Exeter 🎯 ♀

(01572) 822477 – www.marquessexeter.co.uk
Main Street; LE15 9LT

Stone inn with contemporary décor, real ales and excellent food cooked by the landlord; bedrooms

You can be sure of a friendly welcome in this deservedly busy handsome pub – named after the Burghley family, which has long owned this charming village (Burghley House is about 15 miles away). The spacious open-plan areas have understated but stylish furnishings; the fine flagstone floors, thick walls, beams and exposed stonework are left to speak for themselves. There's a mix of old tables and chairs, smart fabrics, leather sofas, pine chests and old barrels that might always have been here. In winter, it's all warmed by several open fires – one a quite striking piece in dark iron. Ringwood Boondoggle and a beer named for the pub on handpump and around a dozen wines by the glass. Outside, a terrace has seats and picnic-sets, with more in the tree-sheltered gardens that seem to merge with the countryside beyond.

The landlord cooks the imaginative food: lunchtime sandwiches, mussels in cream, white wine and garlic, chicken liver parfait with fig chutney, tartlet of roasted tomatoes, mozzarella and basil, chicken caesar salad, crab, chilli and tomato with pasta, calves liver with crispy parma ham and onion dressing, lamb rack with spicy mint dressing, and puddings such as dark chocolate and beetroot cake with crème fraîche and crème brûlée; they also offer a two- and three-course set menu. *Benchmark main dish: grilled rib of beef for two with frites and béarnaise sauce £48.50. Two-course evening meal £20.00.*

Marstons ~ Lease Brian Baker ~ Real ale ~ Open 11-11 (midnight Sat); 12-10.30 Sun ~ Bar food 12-2.30, 6.30-9.30; 12-3.30, 6.30-9 Sun ~ Restaurant ~ Children welcome ~ Dogs allowed in bar and bedrooms ~ Wi-fi ~ Bedrooms: £79.50/£114.50
Recommended by Colin McLachlan, Alan Sutton

OADBY

SK6202 Map 4

Cow & Plough

(0116) 272 0852 – www.steamin-billy.co.uk
Gartree Road (B667 N of centre); LE2 2FB

Fantastic collection of brewery memorabilia, seven real ales and good bar food

With fair value food favourites and half a dozen real ales, these are interestingly converted farm buildings with a cheerful mix of customers. Two of the original dark back rooms, known as the Vaults, contain an extraordinary collection of brewery memorabilia (almost every piece has a story behind it): enamel signs and mirrors advertising long-forgotten brews, an aged brass cash register, and furnishings and fittings salvaged from pubs and even churches (there's some splendid stained glass behind the counter). As well as their own Steamin' Billy Bitter and Sky Diver on handpump, they keep guests such as Abbeydale Moonshine, Batemans Black & White, Fullers London Pride and Shipstones Bitter; also, a couple of farm ciders, 12 wines by the glass and a dozen malt whiskies. The long, light front extension has plenty of plants and fresh flowers, and a real mix of traditionally pubby tables and chairs, with lots of green leatherette sofas and small round cast-iron tables. The conservatory also has a fine collection of brewery and pub signs and the like, and a very eclectic mix of chairs and tables; TV, darts, board games and background music. There are picnic-sets outside in the old yard.

As well as favourites such as bubble and squeak with a poached egg and hollandaise sauce, beer-battered cod and chips, burgers with various toppings and lambs liver and bacon with wholegrain mash and peppercorn sauce, the good food includes lunchtime sandwiches, crab fritters with lemon mayonnaise, potted beef with pickles, smoked duck with asian salad, moroccan vegetable tagine with couscous, lemon and pepper chicken with garlic and thyme roasted potatoes, and puddings such as dark and white chocolate brownie and lemon tart with strawberry sorbet. Pie night is Thursday. *Benchmark main dish: steak in ale pie £10.00. Two-course evening meal £20.00.*

Free house ~ Licensee Christian Roberts ~ Real ale ~ Open 11-11 ~ Bar food 12-2.30 (4 Sat), 6-9; 12-4 Sun ~ Restaurant ~ Children welcome ~ Dogs welcome ~ Wi-fi ~ Live jazz Weds lunchtime *Recommended by Harvey Brown, Dr D J and Mrs S C Walker, Barry Collett*

OAKHAM

SK8509 Map 4

Grainstore ⬤ £

(01572) 770065 – www.grainstorebrewery.com

Station Road, off A606; LE15 6RE

Super own-brewed beers in a converted railway grain warehouse, cheerful customers and pubby food

You can book a brewery tour in this former Victorian grain store (though not on Friday or Saturday evenings) – tickets are available online. The ten own-brews are highly thought-of, and staff will usually offer a sample or two to help you decide. They are served traditionally at the left end of the bar counter and through swan necks with sparklers on the right. Following the traditional tower system of production, the beer is brewed on the upper floors of the building directly above the down-to-earth bar; during working hours, you'll hear the busy noises of the brewery rumbling overhead. They offer beer takeaways and hold a beer festival (with over 80 real ales and live music) on the August Bank Holiday weekend; there's also a farm cider, several wines by the glass and 15 malt whiskies. Décor is plain and functional, with well worn wide floorboards, bare ceiling boards above massive joists supported by red metal pillars, a long brick-built bar counter with cast-iron stools, tall cask tables and simple elm chairs; games machine, darts, board games, giant Jenga and bottle-walking. In summer, the huge glass doors are pulled back, opening on to a terrace with picnic-sets. Disabled access.

As well as weekend breakfasts (9-11am), the popular food includes sandwiches, baked whole camembert with spicy tomato salsa, prawn cocktail, grilled halloumi salad with garlic croutons, pork and ale sausages with a fried egg, chicken breast with cheese and ale sauce, lamb chops with minted gravy, and puddings such as chocolate brownie with raspberry coulis and lemon cheesecake with berry compote; curry night is Tuesday and pie and a pint evening is Wednesday. *Benchmark main dish: steak and ale burger with toppings and fries £9.00. Two-course evening meal £12.00.*

Own brew ~ Licensee Peter Atkinson ~ Real ale ~ Open 12-11 (midnight Fri); 9am-midnight Sat; 9am-11pm Sun ~ Bar food 12-3, 6-9; 9-3 weekends; no evening food Mon, Thurs, Fri, weekends ~ Children welcome ~ Dogs welcome ~ Wi-fi ~ Live music twice a month, comedy evening monthly *Recommended by P Dawn, Barry Collett, Anne and Ben Smith*

OAKHAM

SK8608 Map 4

Lord Nelson ★ ⚲ ⬤

(01572) 868340 – www.kneadpubs.co.uk

Market Place; LE15 6DT

Splendidly restored and full of interest, usefully open all day, real ales and ciders and enjoyable food

Under new management as we went to press, this is a carefully restored, handsome place with half a dozen rooms spread over two floors. You can choose from cushioned church pews, leather elbow chairs, long oak settles, sofas, armchairs – or, to watch the passing scene, a big bow-window seat; carpet, bare boards and ancient red and black tiles; paintwork in soft shades of ochre, canary yellow, sage or pink, and William Morris wallpaper. There's plenty to look at too, from intriguing antique *Police News* and other prints – plenty of Nelson, of course – to the collections of mullers, copper kettles and other homely bric-a-brac in the heavy-beamed former kitchen with its Aga. But the main thing is simply the easy-going, good-natured atmosphere. Castle Rock Harvest Pale, Fullers London Pride and guests such as Castle Rock Red

Riding Hood, Nene Valley NVB and Oakham Scarlet Macaw on handpump; also three farm ciders and 17 wines by the glass. Background music and TV.

 Tasty food includes sandwiches and wraps, nibbles (rosemary and garlic sauté potatoes, honey and smoked bacon doughballs, pigs in blankets with mustard mayonnaise), sharing antipasti plates, butter bean and squash crumble, roast baby chicken served in a box with stuffing, duck fat roasties, yorkshire pudding and gravy, shepherd's pie, steak burger with indian spices, sag aloo, sweet onion bhaji, lamb kofta and chickpea tagine, and puddings such as apple crumble and treacle tart with toffee ice-cream. *Benchmark main dish: stone-baked pizzas £10.00. Two-course evening meal £15.00.*

Knead Pubs ~ Managers Danielle Usher and Lee Jones ~ Real ale ~ Open 10am-11pm; 12-11 Sun ~ Bar food 12-2.30 (5 Sat), 6-9; 12-8 Sun ~ Children welcome ~ Dogs allowed in bar ~ Wi-fi *Recommended by J F M and M West, Barry Collett*

PEGGS GREEN
SK4117 Map 7

New Inn £
(01530) 222293 – www.thenewinnpeggsgreen.co.uk
Signposted off A512 Ashby–Shepshed at roundabout, then turn immediately left down Zion Hill towards Newbold; pub is 100 metres down on the right, with car park on opposite side of road; LE67 8JE

Intriguing bric-a-brac in unspoilt pub, friendly welcome, well liked food at fair prices and real ales; cottagey garden

The same family have run this cheerful pub for 38 years now and the diverting collection of old bric-a-brac that covers almost every inch of the walls and ceilings in the two cosy tiled front rooms is worth close inspection. The little room on the left, a bit like an old kitchen parlour (called the Cabin), has china on the mantelpiece, lots of prints and photographs, three old cast-iron tables, wooden stools and a small stripped kitchen table. The room to the right has attractive stripped panelling and more appealing bric-a-brac. The small back 'Best' room (good for private meetings) has a stripped-wood floor and a touching display of old local photographs including some colliery ones. Bass, Marstons Pedigree and a quickly changing guest beer on handpump; background music and board games. There are plenty of seats in front of the pub, with more in the peaceful back garden. Do check the unusual opening times carefully.

 Incredibly cheap food includes hot and cold cobs, chunky soup, faggots and peas, sausages in onion gravy, corned beef hash, ham and eggs, and smoked haddock; Monday is burger night, Tuesday is pie night and Wednesday nights are for pizzas. *Benchmark main dish: steak in ale pie £5.95.*

Enterprise ~ Lease Maria Christina Kell ~ Real ale ~ Open 12-2.30, 5.30-11; 12-3, 6.30-11 Sat; 12-3, 7-10.30 Sun; closed Tues-Thurs lunchtimes ~ Bar food 12-2, 6-8 Mon, 12-2 Fri, Sat; filled rolls might be available at other times ~ Well behaved children welcome ~ Dogs welcome ~ Wi-fi ~ Live folk club second Mon of month; quiz Thurs evening *Recommended by Adrian Johnson, Anne and Ben Smith*

SILEBY
SK6015 Map 7

White Swan £
(01509) 814832 – www.whiteswansileby.co.uk
Off A6 or A607 N of Leicester; in centre turn into King Street (opposite church), then after mini-roundabout turn right at Post Office signpost into Swan Street; LE12 7NW

Exemplary town local, a boon to its chatty regulars, with fair value home cooking and a friendly welcome

Walkers from Cossington Meadows and those moored at Sileby Marine are fond of this honest local – run for over 30 years by Mrs Miller – for the good value food and genuinely helpful, thoughtful service. It's got all the touches that marked the best of between-the-wars estate pub design, such as an art deco-tiled lobby, polychrome-tiled fireplaces, shiny red Anaglypta ceiling and a comfortable layout of linked but separate areas including a small restaurant (now lined with books). Packed with bric-a-brac from bizarre hats to decorative plates and lots of prints, it quickly draws you thanks to the genuinely bright and cheerful welcome. Bass and maybe a guest beer on handpump and six wines by the glass.

🍴 With around eight dishes costing £9.95 and exceptional value OAP Friday lunchtime deals, there might be prawn, chilli and ginger linguine, chicken in leek and stilton sauce, vegetable burger topped with caramelised onion chutney and cheese, braised lambs liver in onion gravy, beef and mushroom in ale pie, and puddings such as lemon tart and profiteroles with chocolate sauce. *Benchmark main dish: beef cobbler £13.50. Two-course evening meal £16.00.*

Free house ~ Licensee Theresa Miller ~ Real ale ~ Open 12-2 Tues-Thurs, Sat; 12-2, 6-11 Fri; 12-3 Sun; Bar food 12-2 (12-2, 6-8.30 Fri) ~ Children welcome ~ Wi-fi
Recommended by Harvey Brown, Emma Scofield

STATHERN
SK7731 Map 7
Red Lion 🏅 ⍔ 🍺
(01949) 860868 – www.theredlioninn.co.uk
Off A52 W of Grantham via the brown-signed Belvoir road (keep on towards Harby; Stathern is signposted on left); or off A606 Nottingham–Melton Mowbray via Long Clawson and Harby; LE14 4HS
••
Leicestershire Dining Pub of the Year

Country-style dining pub with fine range of drinks, imaginative food and lovely service; good garden with a play area

Everything here is first class – so, not surprisingly, the pub is thriving. There's a lovely welcoming and informal atmosphere created by impeccable staff and it's decorated in a charming rustic style. The yellow room on the right, with its collection of wooden spoons and lambing chairs, has a simple country-pub feel. The lounge bar has sofas, an open fire and a big table with books, newspapers and magazines; it leads to a smaller, more traditional flagstoned bar with terracotta walls, another fireplace and lots of beams and hops. A little room with tables set for eating connects to a long, narrow, main dining room and out to a nicely arranged suntrap lawn and terrace with good quality seats and tables; background music and TV. Red Lion Ale (from Grainstore) and guests such as Brewsters Aromantica and Fullers London Pride on handpump, with a lager from Brewsters, lots of bottled craft beers, cocktails and 12 wines by the glass. Behind the car park is an unusually big play area with swings and climbing frames. Sister pub is the first class Olive Branch in Clipsham.

🏅 Inventive and delicious, the food includes sandwiches, guinea fowl ballotine with haricot bean cassoulet and tomatoes, stilton panna cotta with cider caramel, walnuts and apple, saffron risotto with roast pepper and parmesan sausages with wholegrain mustard mash and cabbage, pork cheeks with white pudding terrine, chantenay carrot purée and cider sauce, duck breast with spiced puy lentils, braised chicory and turnip, pave of cod with sweetcorn and clam chowder broth, and puddings such as rocky road with toasted marshmallow, popcorn and caramel ice-cream and passion-fruit posset with granola. *Benchmark main dish: calves liver with parmentier potatoes and sage and onion juices £16.50. Two-course evening meal £20.00.*

Free house ~ Licensees Sean Hope and Ben Jones ~ Real ale ~ Open 12-3, 6-11; 12-11 Sat; 12-6 Sun ~ Bar food 12-2, 6.30 (6 Fri, Sat)-9; 12-5 Sun ~ Restaurant ~ Children welcome ~ Dogs allowed in bar ~ Wi-fi *Recommended by P Dawn, Comus and Sarah Elliott*

SUTTON CHENEY
Hercules Revived
SK4100 Map 4

(01455) 699336 – www.herculesrevived.co.uk
Off A447 3 miles S of Market Bosworth; CV13 0AG

18th-c inn with bustling bar and upstairs dining rooms, attractive furnishings, helpful staff, real ales and highly thought-of food

Carefully refurbished, this former coaching inn has plenty of room for both drinking and dining and the atmosphere is friendly and easy-going. The long bar has brown leather wall seating with attractive scatter cushions, upholstered brown and white checked or plain wooden church chairs around various tables, rugs on wooden flooring, fresh flowers, prints and ornamental plates on creamy yellow walls, and a big open fire. There are high leather chairs against the rough hewn counter, where they serve Battlefield Henry Tudor, Church End What the Foxs Hat and Tunnel Tradewinds IPA on handpump and 16 wines by the glass. Upstairs, each of the interlinked, grey carpeted dining rooms (one wall is a giant map of the area) have their own colour scheme and tartan dining chairs around dark wooden tables. There are picnic-sets under parasols on the little back terrace and views from the front end of the bar across a meadow to the church.

 Good, interesting food using fresh seasonal ingredients includes sandwiches and baguettes, prawn, avocado and tomato tian with cucumber and chive crème fraîche, goats cheese brûlée with plum tomato and endive balsamic salad, soda-battered haddock and chips, pork belly, faggot and mash with apple and ginseng sauce, corn-fed chicken with sage and prosciutto saltimbocca with warm potato salad, slow-braised beef with cheddar mash and hot pickled red cabbage and bacon, and puddings such as passion-fruit panna cotta with coconut macaroons and raspberry and lime jelly and dark chocolate brownie with white chocolate ice-cream and chocolate sauce. *Benchmark main dish: burger with blue cheese and chunky chips £11.25. Two-course evening meal £21.50.*

Free house ~ Licensee Oliver Warner ~ Real ale ~ Open 12-10.30; 12-9 Sun ~ Bar food 12-2.30, 6-9.30 (8 Sun) ~ Restaurant ~ Children welcome ~ Dogs allowed in bar
Recommended by Lindy Andrews, Alison and Michael Harper

SWITHLAND
Griffin
SK5512 Map 7

(01509) 890535 – www.oddjohn.co.uk/the-griffin-inn
Main Street; between A6 and B5330, between Loughborough and Leicester; LE12 8TJ

A good mix of cheerful customers and well liked food in a well run, busy pub

As we went to press, they were about to open a deli in this bustling country pub. It's a friendly place with a warm welcome for all, and the three beamed communicating rooms are cosy and traditional with some panelling, leather armchairs and sofas, cushioned wall seating, a woodburner and a nice mix of wooden tables and chairs. Stools line the counter where Adnams Southwold, Everards Original and Tiger and a guest such as Wadworths The Bishop's Tipple are well kept on handpump; also, a couple of farm ciders, several malt whiskies and wines by the glass from a good list; background music. The terrace, screened by plants, has wicker seats, and there are more seats in the streamside garden overlooking open fields, as well as painted picnic-sets outside the Old Stables. The pub is in a quiet tucked-away village in the heart of Charnwood Forest and is handy for Bradgate Country Park and walks in Swithland Woods. Good wheelchair access and disabled facilities.

Good food includes baguettes, crab and sweetcorn arancini with mustard dip, battered king prawns with sweet chilli, pork sausages with mash and gravy, ham and free-range eggs, wild mushroom and stilton risotto, moules frites, moroccan-style lamb tagine with couscous, bass fillets with seasonal vegetables and sauce vierge, chicken with sunblush tomato, basil and mozzarella sauce and spring onion mash, and puddings such as raspberry brûlée and chocolate orange tart with Cointreau cream. *Benchmark main dish: beer-battered fresh haddock and chips £11.95. Two-course evening meal £20.00.*

Everards ~ Tenant John Cooledge ~ Real ale ~ Open 9am-11pm (10.30 Sun) ~ Bar food 12-9 (8 Sun) ~ Restaurant ~ Children welcome ~ Wi-fi *Recommended by Robert Wivell*

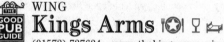

WING
Kings Arms 🌟 ♟ 🛏   SK8902 Map 4

(01572) 737634 – www.thekingsarms-wing.co.uk
Village signposted off A6003 S of Oakham; Top Street; LE15 8SE

Nicely kept old pub with big log fires, super choice of wines by the glass, and good modern cooking; bedrooms

Our readers enjoy their visits to this civilised former farmhouse very much, praising the first class food, comfortable bedrooms and excellent service. The attractive long bar is neatly kept and inviting, with two large log fires (one in a copper-canopied central hearth), various nooks and crannies, nice old low beams and stripped stone, and flagstone or wood-strip floors. Friendly, helpful staff serve almost three dozen wines by the glass, as well as Black Sheep, Grainstore Cooking and a couple of guest ales on handpump, farm ciders, ten home-made liqueurs and a dozen malt whiskies; dominoes. There are seats out in front, and more in the sunny yew-sheltered garden; the car park has plenty of space. You'll find a medieval turf maze just up the road and it's only a couple of miles to one of England's two osprey hotspots.

The excellent food uses produce from their own smokehouse, home-baked bread and home-made pickles, chutneys, preserves and so forth: lunchtime sandwiches, goose pithivier with wild mushrooms, a smokehouse platter, spicy vegetarian frittata, aged steak burger with toppings, their own sweet chilli ketchup and chips, turbot with wild garlic and parsley sauce, prawns, samphire and asparagus, stuffed pheasant with roasted root vegetables, mushrooms and madeira reduction, and puddings such as four-nut chocolate brownie with chocolate sauce and malted milk chocolate ice-cream and sticky toffee and ale pudding with butterscotch sauce and ale ice-cream. *Benchmark main dish: smoked venison fillet with beetroot, red cabbage and dauphinoise potatoes £17.50. Two-course evening meal £25.00.*

Free house ~ Licensee David Goss ~ Real ale ~ Open 12-3, 6.30-11; 12-midnight Sat; closed Mon lunchtime ~ Bar food 12-2, 6.30-8.30; 6.30-8 Mon; not Mon lunchtime, Sun evening ~ Restaurant ~ Children welcome ~ Dogs allowed in bar and bedrooms ~ Wi-fi ~ Bedrooms: £75/£100 *Recommended by Alan Johnson, R L Borthwick, Pat and Stewart Gordon, John Davis*

'Children welcome' means the pub says it lets children inside without any special restriction. If it allows them in, but to restricted areas such as an eating area or family room, we specify this. Some pubs may impose an evening time limit. We do not mention limits after 9pm as we assume children are home by then.

WOODHOUSE EAVES
SK5313 Map 7

Wheatsheaf 🛏

(01509) 890320 – www.wheatsheafinn.net

Brand Hill; turn right into Main Street, off B591 S of Loughborough; LE12 8SS

Bustling country pub with good bistro-type food and a fair choice of drinks; well equipped bedrooms

There's plenty to look at in this friendly pub and they've struck an easy balance between the chatty bar side and the interlinked dining rooms. The beamed bar areas are traditionally furnished (wheelback chairs, open fires, daily papers and the like) and full of interesting motor-racing and family RAF and flying memorabilia – a cosy dining area (called the Mess) even has an RAF Hurricane propeller. Other dining rooms have high-backed chairs around all sorts of tables and prints. It's all very cheerful and easy-going and the kind staff will help with wheelchair access. Adnams Broadside, Charnwood Vixen, Fullers Seafarers and Timothy Taylors Landlord on handpump and around 17 wines by the glass (including champagne) from a thoughtfully compiled list. Plenty of seating outside among bright window boxes and tubs, and the bedrooms are in a cottage annexe where there's a lounge/dining room for breakfast. There's a disabled parking space in the car park.

As well as sandwiches, the well liked food includes baked baby camembert with dipping bread, chicken liver pâté with red onion chutney, red lentil and sweet potato moussaka, three-fish pie, burger with toppings, coleslaw and fries, chicken and chorizo casserole, minty lamb chops with mediterranean vegetables, beef stroganoff, and puddings such as orange curd panna cotta with rosemary shortbread and hokey pokey (brandy snap basket with honeycomb ice-cream and hot chocolate sauce). *Benchmark main dish: their own smokies £13.00. Two-course evening meal £19.50.*

Free house ~ Licensees Richard and Bridget Dimblebee ~ Real ale ~ Open 12-3, 6-11; 12-11 Sat; 12-4 Sun ~ Bar food 12-2.30, 6-9; 12-3, 6-9.30 Sat; 12-4 Sun ~ Restaurant ~ Children welcome ~ Dogs allowed in bar ~ Wi-fi ~ Bedrooms: £70/£90
Recommended by Gordon and Jenny Quick, Ian Herdman, P and D Carpenter

WYMONDHAM
SK8518 Map 7

Berkeley Arms 🎖

(01572) 787587 – www.theberkeleyarms.co.uk

Main Street; LE14 2AG

Well run village pub with interesting food, interlinked beamed rooms, a relaxed atmosphere and sunny terrace

In a pretty village surrounded by walks, this is a friendly golden-stone inn with imaginative food cooked by the landlord. There's a welcoming, relaxed atmosphere, helped along by the landlady and her courteous staff, as well as knick-knacks, magazines, table lamps and cushions – and at one end (in front of a log fire), two wing chairs on patterned carpet beside a low coffee table. The red-tiled or wood-floored dining areas, dense with stripped beams and standing timbers, are furnished in a kitchen style with light wood tables and red-cushioned chunky chairs. Marstons Pedigree and guests such as Batemans XB, Castle Rock Harvest Pale and Grainstore Cooking on handpump, 11 wines by the glass and local cider. Outside, on small terraces to either side of the front entrance, picnic-sets get the sun nearly all day long.

 As well as a two- and three-course set evening menu, the highly rewarding food includes lunchtime sandwiches, rabbit and prune pâté with chutney, mussels in coconut milk, chilli, coriander and lemongrass, chicken breast with root vegetable gratin and wild mushrooms, lincolnshire sausages with bubble and squeak and sage and red onion gravy, sole roasted on the bone with cockles and clams, lamb rump with spicy tomato, aubergine and herb couscous, and puddings such as sticky toffee pudding with butterscotch sauce and passion-fruit cheesecake and passion-fruit sorbet. *Benchmark main dish: muntjac loin with fondant potato, red cabbage, red wine-poached pear and caramelised walnuts £18.00. Two-course evening meal £23.90.*

Free house ~ Licensee Louise Hitchen ~ Real ale ~ Open 12-3, 6-11; 12-5 Sun; closed Sun evening, Mon, first two weeks Jan, two weeks summer ~ Bar food 12-1.45, 6.30-9; 12-3 Sun ~ Restaurant ~ Children welcome ~ Dogs allowed in bar *Recommended by Neil Allen, John and Mary Warner*

Also Worth a Visit in Leicestershire

Besides the fully inspected pubs, you might like to try these pubs that have been recommended to us and described by readers. Do tell us what you think of them: feedback@goodguides.com

AB KETTLEBY   SK7519
Sugar Loaf   (01664) 822473
Nottingham Road (A606 NW of Melton); LE14 3JB Beamed pub under newish management, modern open-plan carpeted bar, bare-boards end with coal-effect gas fire, airy dining conservatory, enjoyable reasonably priced food including Sun carvery, four real ales, friendly attentive service; picnic-sets out by road and car park, open (and food) all day. *(Ryta Lyndley)*

BARKBY   SK6309
Malt Shovel   (0116) 269 2558
Main Street; LE7 3QG Popular and welcoming old village pub, enjoyable good value food (till 6pm Sun) including bargain offers, four well kept Thwaites ales and a couple of guests (beer festivals), good choice of wines by the glass, U-shaped carpeted bar with fire, small dining room (was the local jail); music quiz first Thurs of month; children and dogs welcome, garden with partly covered heated terrace, open all day weekends. *(Phil and Jane Hodson)*

BLABY   SP5697
Bakers Arms   (0116) 278 7253
Quite handy for M1 junction 21; The Green; LE8 4FQ Tucked-away thatched pub dating from 1485, lots of low beams, nooks and crannies in linked rooms, exposed brickwork and stone fireplaces, wide choice of good interesting food (not Sun evening) from sandwiches and bar snacks up, Everards ales, restored 19th-c bakery (the pub runs bread-making courses); children welcome, garden picnic-sets, open all day. *(John and Mary Warner)*

BOTCHESTON   SK4804
Greyhound   (01455) 822355
Main Street, off B5380 E of Desford; LE9 9FF Popular beamed village pub (originally three cottages) with wide range of good freshly cooked food at reasonable prices, Fri fish night, Marstons-related ales and decent choice of wines, friendly attentive service, pine tables in two light and airy dining rooms; children welcome, garden with play area, open all day weekends (till 9pm Sun). *(SAB and MJW)*

BRANSTON   SK8129
★ Wheel   (01476) 870376
Main Street near the church; NG32 1RU Beamed 18th-c stone-built village pub with stylishly simple open-plan décor, good country food cooked by chef-landlord, three well kept changing ales including Batemans from central servery (autumn beer festival), proper cider too, friendly smartly dressed staff, woodburner and open fires; background and occasional live music; children welcome, dogs in bar, attractive garden, splendid countryside near Belvoir Castle, closed Mon, otherwise open all day (till 9pm Sun). *(Phil and Jane Hodson, Comus and Sarah Elliott)*

BRAUNSTON   SK8306
Blue Ball   (01572) 722135
Off A606 in Oakham; Cedar Street; LE15 8QS Pretty thatched and beamed dining pub with good food (not Sun evening) including deals, well kept Marstons-related ales, decent wines, log fire, leather furniture and country pine in linked rooms, small conservatory, local art for sale; monthly jazz Sun lunchtime; free wi-fi; children welcome, painted furniture outside, attractive village, open all day Sat, till 8pm Sun. *(Barry Collett)*

BRAUNSTON   SK8306
Old Plough   (01572) 722714
Off A606 in Oakham; Church Street; LE15 8QT Comfortably opened-up black-beamed village local, well kept Fullers London Pride, Grainstore and a couple of guests, enjoyable good value pub food (not

Sun evening), pleasant attentive service, log fire, back dining conservatory; darts, free wi-fi; children, dogs and muddy boots welcome, tables in sheltered back garden with pétanque, five bedrooms, open all day weekends. *(Barry Collett, R L Borthwick)*

BRUNTINGTHORPE   SP6089

★ **Joiners Arms**   (0116) 247 8258

Off A5199 S of Leicester: Church Walk/ Cross Street; LE17 5QH More restaurant than pub with most of the two beamed rooms set for eating, drinkers have area by small light oak bar with open fire; civilised relaxed atmosphere, candles on tables, elegant dining chairs and big flower arrangements, first class imaginative food efficiently served by friendly staff, cheaper set lunch menu, plenty of wines by the glass including champagne, one mainstream ale such as Greene King or Sharps; picnic-sets in front, closed Sun evening, Mon. *(G Jennings, SAB and MJW)*

BURROUGH ON THE HILL   SK7510

Grants   (01664) 452141

Off B6047 S of Melton Mowbray; Main Street; LE14 2JQ Cosy old pub refurbished by present licensees, Parish ales brewed next door including the fearsomely strong Baz's Bonce Blower, well liked food served by smiley helpful staff, open fires, restaurant and games room; sports TV, free wi-fi; children and dogs welcome, garden, good walk to nearby Iron Age fort, open all day weekends, closed Mon lunchtime. *(Phil and Jane Hodson)*

BURTON OVERY   SP6797

Bell   (0116) 259 2365

Main Street; LE8 9DL Good interesting choice of well priced food (not Mon) from lunchtime sandwiches up in L-shaped open-plan and dining room (used mainly for larger parties), log fire, comfortable sofas, ales such as Langton and Timothy Taylors Landlord, pleasant unobtrusive service; children welcome, nice garden and lovely village, open all day weekends, closed Mon and Tues lunchtimes. *(SAB and MJW, R L Borthwick)*

CALDECOTT   SP8693

Plough   (01536) 770284

Main Street; LE16 8RS Welcoming pub in attractive ironstone village; carpeted bar with banquettes and small tables leading to spacious eating area, log fires, four well kept changing beers including a stout, wide range of popular inexpensive food (best to book) including blackboard specials, prompt service; children welcome, good-sized garden

at back, closed weekday lunchtimes, open all day weekends. *(Belinda Stamp)*

COLEORTON   SK4016

Angel   (01530) 834742

The Moor; LE67 8GB Friendly homely pub with good range of enjoyable reasonably priced food including Sun carvery, well kept beers such as Marstons Pedigree, hospitable attentive staff, beams and open fire; tables outside, open all day Sun. *(Paul and Karen Cornock)*

COLEORTON   SK4117

George   (01530) 834639

Loughborough Road (A512 E); LE67 8HF Attractive and homely with well divided beamed bar; dark panelled dado, scatter-cushioned pews, shelves of books and lots of local photographs, leather sofa and tub chairs by woodburner, Bass, Burton Bridge Bitter and Marstons Pedigree, bigger room on left with another woodburner and plenty to look at, enjoyable fair value food, friendly landlady and well trained young staff; background music, free wi-fi; supervised children welcome, dogs in bar, sturdy wooden furniture in spreading garden behind, play area, open all day Fri, Sat, closed Sun evening, Mon. *(Michael Butler, Comus and Sarah Elliott, Lesley and Peter Barrett)*

DADLINGTON   SP4097

Dog & Hedgehog   (01455) 213151

The Green, opposite church; CV13 6JB Popular red-brick village dining pub with good choice of well regarded food, friendly staff and hands-on character landlord, rebadged ales from brewers such as Quartz and Tunnel, nice wines, restaurant; children and dogs welcome, garden looking down to Ashby de la Zouch Canal, closed Sun evening, otherwise open all day. *(Gordon and Jenny Quick)*

DISEWORTH   SK4524

Plough   (01332) 810333

Near East Midlands Airport and M1 junction 23A; DE74 2QJ Extended and refurbished 16th-c beamed pub, well kept Bass, Greene King, Marstons and guests, low-priced traditional food (not Sun evening), friendly staff, bar and spacious well divided restaurant, log fires; dogs welcome, paved terrace with steps out to lawn, handy for Donington Park race track, open all day. *(Phil and Jane Hodson)*

EAST LANGTON   SP7292

★ **Bell**   (01858) 545278

Off B6047; Main Street; LE16 7TW Appealing creeper-clad beamed country inn

---

Please tell us if any pub deserves to be upgraded to a featured entry – and why: feedback@goodguides.com, or (no stamp needed) The Good Pub Guide, FREEPOST RTJR-ZCYZ-RJZT, Perrymans Lane, Etchingham TN19 7DN.

buzzing with locals and families (particularly at weekends), well kept Fullers, Greene King, Langton and a guest, nice wines, good well presented food including daily specials and popular Sun carvery, friendly efficient staff, long low-ceilinged stripped-stone bar, spacious restaurant, modern pine furniture, log fires; picnic-sets on sloping front lawn, bedrooms. *(Maurice and Janet Thorpe, Ron Corbett, Gerry and Rosemary Dobson)*

EXTON   SK9211
★**Fox & Hounds** (01572) 812403
The Green; signed off A606 Stamford–Oakham; LE15 8AP New landlady and major refurbishment for this handsome village inn as we went to press; high-ceilinged lounge with big stone fireplace, restaurant, has served Grainstore, Greene King and a guest; sheltered walled garden overlooking pretty paddocks, bedrooms, handy for Rutland Water and the gardens at Barnsdale; reports please. *(Colin McKerrow, Gordon and Margaret Ormondroyd, David and Shelagh Monks, Barry Collett, David Heath)*

FOXTON   SP6989
★**Foxton Locks** (0116) 279 1515
Foxton Locks, off A6 3 miles NW of Market Harborough (park by bridge 60/62 and walk); LE16 7RA Busy place in great canalside setting at foot of spectacular flight of locks; large comfortably reworked L-shaped bar, popular pubby food including Sun carvery, converted boathouse (not always open) for snacks, friendly service, well kept ales such as Greene King, Sharps and Theakstons; some live music, free wi-fi; children and dogs welcome, newly built glassed-in dining 'terrace' overlooking the water, steps down to fenced waterside lawn, good walks, open (and food) all day. *(G Jennings)*

GADDESBY   SK6813
Cheney Arms (01664) 840260
Rearsby Lane; LE7 4XE Red-brick country pub set back from the road; bar with bare-boards and terracotta-tiled floor, well kept Everards and a guest from brick-faced servery, open fires including inglenook in more formal dining room, big helpings of popular reasonably priced food (not Sun evening, Mon) from good lunchtime baguettes up, Weds pie night, Thurs steak night; sports TV, free wi-fi; children welcome, walled back garden with smokers' shelter, lovely medieval church nearby, four bedrooms, closed Mon lunchtime. *(Phil and Jane Hodson)*

GILMORTON   SP5787
Grey Goose (01455) 552555
Lutterworth Road; LE17 5PN Popular bar-restaurant with good range of enjoyable freshly made food from lunchtime sandwiches up, early-bird weekday deals and Sun carvery, ales such as Grainstore, several

wines by the glass including champagne, good friendly staff coping well at busy times, light contemporary décor, stylish wood and metal bar stools mixing with comfortable sofas and armchairs, woodburner in stripped-brick fireplace with logs stacked beside; modern furniture on terrace. *(R L Borthwick)*

GREAT BOWDEN   SP7488
Red Lion (01858) 463571
Off A6 N of Market Harborough; Main Street; LE16 7HB Attractively modernised place with good well presented food, carefully chosen wines and three real ales including a house beer from Langton, friendly competent service; background music; children welcome, tables in good-sized garden, open all day, no food Sun evening, Mon. *(Harvey Brown)*

GREETHAM   SK9214
Plough (01572) 813613
B668 Stretton–Cottesmore; LE15 7NJ Traditional village pub, comfortable and welcoming, with good home-made food including popular stone-baked pizzas and meal deals, Grainstore, Timothy Taylors and three guests, can eat in cosy lounge or fire-divided restaurant, helpful friendly service; children and dogs welcome, garden behind, good local walks and not far from Rutland Water, open all day Thurs-Sun. *(Martin and Alison Stainsby)*

GUMLEY   SP6890
Bell (0116) 279 0126
NW of Market Harborough; Main Street; LE16 7RU Friendly beamed village local, L-shaped bar with hunting prints and two open fires, Timothy Taylors Landlord and three guests, fair-priced home-cooked food including blackboard specials, weekday lunch deal and some themed nights; live music, sports TV; children welcome and dogs (theirs are Rhum and Islay), pond in terrace garden, local walks and cycle routes, open (and food) all day weekends. *(Toby Jones)*

HARBY   SK7531
Nags Head (01949) 869629
Main Street; LE14 4BN Popular old beamed pub with four comfortably refurbished linked rooms, good value pubby food (not Sun evening) including a burger menu, two Marstons-related ales and a guest, friendly service, real fires; live music first Fri of month, sports TV, free wi-fi; picnic-sets in large garden, interesting Vale of Belvoir village, open all day Fri-Sun, closed Mon lunchtime. *(Phil and Jane Hodson)*

HINCKLEY   SP4293
Railway (01455) 612399
Station Road; LE10 1AP Friendly chatty pub owned by the Steamin' Billy Brewing Company, their ales (contract-brewed nearby by Belvoir) and guests from seven pumps, also draught continentals and real cider,

sensibly priced food including Thurs steak night, friendly young staff, open fires, darts; dogs welcome, beer garden behind, handy for station. *(Phil and Jane Hodson)*

HOBY SK6717
Blue Bell (01664) 434247
Main Street; LE14 3DT Attractive well run thatched pub, good range of popular realistically priced food (smaller appetites catered for) including three-course deal Mon (best to book), friendly attentive uniformed staff, four well kept Everards ales, Adnams and a guest, good choice of wines by the glass, teas/coffees, open-plan and airy with beams, comfortable traditional furniture, old local photographs; background music; skittle alley and darts; children, walkers and dogs welcome, valley-view garden with picnic-sets and boules, open all day, food all day weekends. *(Phil and Jane Hodson, R L Borthwick)*

HOTON SK5722
Packe Arms (01509) 889106
A60; LE12 5SJ Spacious old Vintage Inn with sturdy beams and open fires, their usual choice of enjoyable good value food, up to three well kept changing ales and realistically priced wines, friendly service from uniformed staff; children welcome, tables outside, open (and food) all day. *(Anon)*

HOUGHTON ON THE HILL SK6703
Old Black Horse (0116) 241 3486
Main Street (just off A47 Leicester–Uppingham); LE7 9GD Welcoming village pub under new management, enjoyable home-made food (not Sun evening, Mon), well kept Everards ale and a guest and decent wines by the glass, opened up into distinct modernised areas, with mix of bare boards, tiles and carpet, some panelling; background music; children and dogs welcome, attractive big garden with boules, open all day Fri and Sun. *(Alison and Michael Harper)*

HUNGARTON SK6907
Black Boy (0116) 259 5410
Main Street; LE7 9JR Large open-plan partly divided restaurant bar with open fire, good well priced food cooked to order by landlord-chef (weekend booking advised), changing ales such as Greene King, Fullers and Charles Wells, cheerful welcoming staff; background music; picnic-sets out on deck, closed Sun evening, Mon lunchtime. *(Harvey Brown)*

ILLSTON ON THE HILL SP7099
★**Fox & Goose** (0116) 259 6340
Main Street, off B6047 Market Harborough–Melton Mowbray; LE7 9EG Individual little two-bar village local, simple, comfortable and friendly, with hunting pictures and assorted oddments including stuffed animals, woodburner and coal fire,

well kept Everards and a couple of guests, good choice of other drinks, enjoyable generously served home-made food (Thurs-Sat evenings only); children and dogs welcome, Sept onion growing competition, closed weekday lunchtimes, open all day weekends. *(Lindy Andrews)*

KIRBY MUXLOE SK5104
Royal Oak (0116) 239 3166
Main Street; LE9 2AN Refurbished modernish pub with good food from sandwiches and pub favourites to more inventive dishes, lunchtime/early evening set deal, Everards ales including one badged for the pub and a guest, good wine choice, sizeable restaurant; Mon quiz, some live jazz; children and dogs (in bar) welcome, disabled facilities, picnic-sets outside, 15th-c castle ruins nearby. *(Toby Jones)*

KNIPTON SK8231
Manners Arms (01476) 879222
Signed off A607 Grantham–Melton Mowbray; Croxton Road; NG32 1RH Handsome Georgian hunting lodge reworked as comfortable country inn, bare-boards bar with log fire, four well kept ales and nice choice of wines by the glass, good food here or in sizeable restaurant with attractive conservatory, friendly helpful staff; background music; terrace with ornamental pool, lovely views over pretty village, ten comfortable individually furnished bedrooms, open all day. *(Anon)*

KNOSSINGTON SK8008
Fox & Hounds (01664) 452129
Off A606 W of Oakham; Somerby Road; LE15 8LY Attractive 18th-c ivy-clad village dining pub, beamed bar with log fire and cosy eating areas, well liked food (best to book) from traditional choices to blackboard specials, Fullers London Pride, attentive friendly service; no under-8s, dogs welcome, big back garden, closed Sun evening, Mon, lunchtimes Tues-Thurs. *(Neil Allen)*

LEICESTER SK5804
Ale Wagon (0116) 262 3330
Rutland Street/Charles Street; LE1 1RE Basic 1930s two-room corner local with nine real ales including its own Hoskins Brothers beers, a traditional cider, no food except baps, coal fire, upstairs function room; background music; handy for Curve Theatre and station, open all day, closed Sun lunchtime. *(P Dawn)*

LEICESTER SK5804
Criterion (0116) 262 5418
Millstone Lane; LE1 5JN 1960s building with dark wood and carpeted main room, up to a dozen ales, 100 bottled beers and a couple of real ciders, good value stone-baked pizzas (not Sun) plus some other snacky food, room on left with games and old-fashioned juke box, regular live music and quiz nights,

annual comedy festival; picnic-sets outside, open all day. *(P Dawn)*

LEICESTER   SK5804
★ **Globe** (0116) 253 9492
Silver Street; LE1 5EU Refreshed but keeping original character, lots of woodwork in partitioned areas off central bar, bare boards and some Victorian mosaic floor tiles, mirrors and working gas lamps, four Everards ales along with three guests, two real ciders and over a dozen wines by the glass, friendly staff, enjoyable well priced food from bar snacks up, upstairs function room; background music (not in snug); children and dogs welcome, metal café-style tables out in front, open all day (Sun till 6pm).
(P Dawn)

LEICESTER   SK5803
Kings Head (0116) 254 8240
King Street; LE1 6RL Small drinkers' pub with good atmosphere and helpful friendly staff, three well kept Black Country ales and five regularly changing guests, craft beers and proper cider too, can bring your own food, log fire; sports TV; no children or dogs, raised back terrace, near rugby ground and busy on match days, open all day. *(John and Mary Warner)*

LEICESTER   SK5804
★ **Rutland & Derby Arms**
(0116) 262 3299 *Millstone Lane; nearby metered parking; LE1 5JN* Neatly kept modern town bar with open-plan interior; comfortable bar chairs by long counter, padded high seats including a banquette by chunky tall tables, some stripped brickwork and a few small prints of classic film posters, popular all-day food, Everards and guests, 20 wines by the glass and good range of malt whiskies and other drinks, helpful staff; background music, live acoustic session last Fri of month, free wi-fi; children welcome, sunny courtyard with tables under parasols, more seats on upper terrace, closed Sun, otherwise open all day (1am Fri, Sat).
(Emma Scofield)

LEICESTER   SK5803
Swan & Rushes (0116) 233 9167
Oxford Street/Infirmary Square; LE1 5WR Triangular-shaped pub with up to nine well kept ales including Batemans and Oakham, extensive range of bottled beers, real cider, welcoming staff and thriving local atmosphere in two rooms with big oak tables, low-priced home-made food (not Sun) including stone-baked pizzas; themed beer and cider festivals, Thurs quiz, maybe Sat live music, bar billiards and darts; dogs welcome,

sunny back terrace, open all day and very busy on match days. *(Anon)*

LONG WHATTON   SK4823
Royal Oak (01509) 843694
The Green; LE12 5DB Smartly updated dining pub with good well presented modern food along with pub favourites, early-bird menu 5.30-6.30pm, three well kept ales and decent choice of wines by the glass, friendly efficient staff; bedrooms in separate building, open all day. *(Ken and Lynda Taylor)*

LOUGHBOROUGH   SK5319
Swan in the Rushes (01509) 217014
The Rushes (A6); LE11 5BE Bare-boards town local with three smallish high-ceilinged rooms, good value Castle Rock and plenty of interesting changing guests, real cider and over 30 malt whiskies, well priced food (not Sun evenings) including Pieminister pies and vegetarian options, open fire and daily papers, good juke box, refurbished upstairs craft/world beer bar with roof terrace; some live music, free wi-fi; children welcome in eating areas, tables outside, open all day.
(P Dawn)

LOUGHBOROUGH   SK5319
Tap & Mallet (01509) 210028
Nottingham Road; LE11 1EU Basic friendly pub with well kept Abbeydale, Batemans, Salopian and interesting microbrew guests, also foreign beers and Weston's cider, coal fire, darts and pool, juke box; walled back garden with pets corner, open all day Sat, closed lunchtime other days. *(P Dawn)*

LYDDINGTON   SP8796
★ **Old White Hart** (01572) 821703
Village signed off A6003 N of Corby; LE15 9LR Popular welcoming old inn, softly lit front bar with heavy beams in low ceiling, just a few tables, glass-shielded log fire, Greene King IPA and a guest, good food (not Sun evening in winter) including own sausages and cured meats (landlord is a butcher), half-price offer Mon-Thurs, efficient obliging service, attractive restaurant, further tiled-floor room with rugs, lots of fine hunting prints and woodburner; children welcome, seats by heaters in pretty walled garden, eight floodlit boules pitches, handy for Bede House and good nearby walks, ten bedrooms, open all day (may be a break Sun afternoon). *(Lindy Andrews)*

MANTON   SK8704
Horse & Jockey (01572) 737335
St Mary's Road; LE15 8SU Welcoming stone pub from early 19th c with updated

---

A few pubs try to make you leave a credit card at the bar, as a sort of deposit if you order food. This is a bad practice, and the banks and credit card firms warn you not to let your card go like this.

low-beamed interior, modern furniture on wood or stone floors, woodburner, well kept ales such as Grainstore and Greene King plus a house beer (Fall at the First), decent fairly priced food from baguettes to blackboard specials, good cheery service; background music; children and dogs welcome, colourful tubs and hanging baskets, terrace picnic-sets, nice location, on Rutland Water cycle route (racks provided), open all day in summer (all day Fri, Sat, till 7pm Sun in winter). *(John and Sylvia Harrop, Barry Collett)*

MARKET HARBOROUGH   SP7387
Three Swans (01858) 466644
High Street; LE16 7NJ Recently revamped 16th-c coaching inn (Best Western), new bar areas and extended conservatory restaurant, good variety of enjoyable well presented food from sandwiches up, Langton Hop On, St Austell Tribute and a guest, several wines by the glass and cocktails, friendly staff, some original features including sturdy beams and inglenook, pricier more formal upstairs restaurant; background music; children welcome, attractive suntrap courtyard, useful parking, bedrooms, open all day from 9am. *(Gerry and Rosemary Dobson)*

MARKET OVERTON   SK8816
Black Bull (01572) 767677
Opposite the church; LE15 7PW Attractive thatch and stone low-beamed pub (dates from the 17th c) in pretty village well placed for Rutland Water, welcoming licensees and staff, good home-made food (booking advised) from pub staples up in long carpeted bar and two separate dining areas, well kept Black Sheep and a couple of guests, woodburner, banquettes and sofas, newspapers; some background and live music; children and dogs welcome, tables out in front by small carp pool, five bedrooms (the two in the pub are ensuite), open all day Sun till 6pm, closed Mon. *(Barry Collett)*

MEDBOURNE   SP7992
★ **Nevill Arms** (01858) 565288
B664 Market Harborough–Uppingham; LE16 8EE Handsome stone-built Victorian inn nicely located by stream and footbridge, wide range of good bar and restaurant food including vegetarian choices, pleasant helpful uniformed staff, well kept ales such as Bass, Adnams and Sharps, beams and mullion windows, log fires, modern artwork, stylish restaurant; no dogs, back terrace with stable-conversion café (8am-4pm), streamside picnic-sets, 11 refurbished bedrooms, good breakfast, open all day. *(Ian Herdman, Barry Collett)*

MELTON MOWBRAY   SK7519
Anne of Cleves (01664) 481336
Burton Street, by St Mary's Church; LE13 1AE Monks' chantry dating from the 14th c and gifted to Anne of Cleves by Henry VIII; chunky tables, character chairs and settles on flagstones, heavy beams and latticed mullioned windows, tapestries on burnt orange walls, well kept Everards and guests, decent wines and ample helpings of above average food, small end dining room; background music; tables in pretty little walled garden with flagstone terrace, open all day. *(P and D Carpenter)*

MELTON MOWBRAY   SK7518
Boat (01664) 500969
Burton Street; LE13 1AF Chatty and welcoming one-room local with four well kept ales and lots of malt whiskies, no food, panelling and open fire; darts; dogs welcome, open all day Thurs-Sun, closed Mon lunchtime. *(Phil and Jane Hodson)*

MOUNTSORREL   SK5715
Swan (0116) 230 2340
Loughborough Road, off A6; LE12 7AT Log fires, old flagstones and stripped stone, friendly staff and locals, enjoyable well priced often interesting food from baguettes up (best to book evenings), well kept ales including Theakstons, Weston's cider and good choice of wines, pine tables and gingham cloths in neat dining area and restaurant; dogs welcome in bar, pretty walled back garden down to canalised River Soar, open all day weekends. *(Harvey Brown)*

MOWSLEY   SP6488
Staff of Life (0116) 240 2359
Village signposted off A5199 S of Leicester; Main Street; LE17 6NT Gabled village pub with roomy fairly traditional bar, high-backed settles on flagstones, wicker chairs on shiny wood floor and stools around unusual circular counter, woodburner, Bass and Thwaites Wainwright, a dozen wines by the glass and decent whisky choice, well liked interesting mid-priced food (not Sun evening), set deal (Tues, Weds), good service; background music; well behaved children welcome (no under-12s Fri and Sat nights), no dogs, seats out in front and on nice leaf-shaded deck, open all day Sun, closed Mon and weekday lunchtimes. *(SAB and MJW)*

QUORNDON   SK5516
Manor House (01509) 413416
Woodhouse Road; LE12 8AL Sizeable late Victorian pub with good food (all day Sat, till 6pm Sun) from varied menu, also children's choices and set deals, six ales such as Bass, Belvoir, Theakstons and Timothy Taylors, friendly staff; free wi-fi; children welcome, good outside areas, next door to Quorn & Woodhouse heritage railway station, open all day. *(Mike and Mary Carter)*

REDMILE   SK7935
★ **Windmill** (01949) 842281
Off A52 Grantham–Nottingham; Main Street; NG13 0GA Snug low-beamed bar with sofas, easy chairs and log fire in large raised hearth, comfortable roomier dining

areas with woodburners, wide choice of good home-made food from sandwiches, burgers and stone baked pizzas up (maybe game from local Belvoir Estate), well kept ales such as Adnams, Newby Wyke and Oldershaws, nice wines by the glass; children welcome, sizeable well furnished front courtyard, open (and food) all day. *(Anon)*

ROTHLEY SK5912

Red Lion (0116) 230 2488

Loughborough Road; LE7 7NJ Comfortably refurbished chain dining pub, spacious open-plan interior, popular food including daily carvery and children's menu, real ales, friendly chatty staff; background music, sports TVs, free wi-fi; outside seating including covered area, open (and food) all day. *(Phil and Jane Hodson)*

ROTHLEY SK5812

Woodmans Stroke (0116) 230 2785

Church Street; LE7 7PD Family-run 18th-c thatched pub, good value weekday lunchtime bar food from sandwiches up, well kept changing ales and good wines by the glass including champagne, friendly service, beams and settles in front rooms, open fire, old local photographs plus rugby and cricket memorabilia; sports TV; pretty front hanging baskets, cast-iron tables in attractive garden with heaters, pétanque, open all day Sat. *(Gordon and Jenny Quick)*

RYHALL TF0310

Wicked Witch (01780) 763649

Bridge Street; PE9 4HH Refurbished dining pub under new ownership, good upmarket weekly changing set menus from chef-proprietor, Banks's Mansfield and an occasional guest, nice wines; children welcome till 7pm, tables in back garden, closed Sun evening, Mon. *(Toby Jones)*

SADDINGTON SP6591

Queens Head (0116) 240 2536

S of Leicester between A5199 (ex A50) and A6; Main Street; LE8 0QH Welcoming village pub with well kept Everards, nice wines and good attractively presented food (all day Sat, till 6pm Sun), cleanly updated interior on different levels, country and reservoir views from dining conservatory and sloping terrace; free wi-fi; children welcome, farm shop, open all day Weds-Sun. *(Veronica Brown)*

SEATON SP9098

George & Dragon (01572) 747773

Main Street; LE15 9HU Stone-built pub dating from the 17th c, two cosy split-level bars (one a former bakery) and separate restaurant, three real ales including Grainstore, good traditional home-made food (half-price mains Tues-Fri), attentive service and friendly local atmosphere; children welcome, outside tables, unspoilt hilltop village and good views of Harringworth

Viaduct, bedrooms, open all day Sat, Sun till 7pm, closed Mon lunchtime. *(Philip Meek)*

SHAWELL SP5480

White Swan (01788) 860357

Main Street; village signed down declassified road (ex A427) off A5/A426 roundabout – turn right in village; not far from M6 junction 1; LE17 6AG Attractive little beamed 17th-c dining pub given clean contemporary look by current owners; good interesting food all day (till 6pm Sun) from landlord-chef along with some pub staples, local Dow Bridge ales and guests, lots of wines by the glass, champagne breakfast Sat, restaurant; children welcome, open all day. *(Emma Scofield)*

SHEARSBY SP6290

Chandlers Arms (0116) 247 8384

Fenny Lane, off A50 Leicester–Northampton; LE17 6PL Comfortable old creeper-clad pub in attractive village, four well kept ales including Dow Bridge (tasting trays, July beer festival), Weston's cider, good value pubby food (not Sun evening) including vegetarian choices, wall seats and wheelback chairs, table skittles; background music, Weds quiz night (Sept-May); tables in secluded raised garden overlooking green, open all day Sun till 9pm, closed Mon. *(Harvey Brown)*

SILEBY SK6015

Horse & Trumpet (01509) 812549

Barrow Road, opposite church; LE12 7LP Friendly beamed village pub renovated by the Steamin' Billy group, their beers and guests kept well, real cider, fresh cobs; some live music including jazz second Mon of month, darts; well behaved dogs welcome, terrace picnic-sets, open all day. *(Anon)*

SOMERBY SK7710

★Stilton Cheese (01664) 454394

High Street; off A606 Oakham–Melton Mowbray, via Cold Overton, or Leesthorpe and Pickwell; LE14 2QB Good friendly staff in enjoyable ironstone pub with beamed bar/lounge, comfortable furnishings on red patterned carpets, country prints, plates and copper pots, stuffed badger and pike, Grainstore, Marstons, Tetleys and two guests, 30 malt whiskies, good reasonably priced pubby food along with daily specials, restaurant; children welcome, seats on terrace, peaceful setting on edge of pretty village. *(Alan Bulley)*

SOUTH CROXTON SK6810

Golden Fleece (01664) 840275

Main Street; LE7 3RL Restaurant more than pub; clean minimalist feel with comfortable modern furniture, good choice of popular food including cheaper weekday lunchtime/early evening set menu, Mon italian night and Sun carvery (till 7pm), friendly helpful service, ales such as Adnams and Charles Wells, good house wine, log fire; children welcome, lovely area. *(SAB and MJW)*

SOUTH LUFFENHAM   SK9401

★ **Coach House**   (01780) 720166
Stamford Road (A6121); LE15 8NT
Refurbished old inn with stripped-stone and flagstoned bar, scatter cushions on small pews, log fire, three real ales including Adnams and Greene King, decent wines by the glass, good well priced food served by friendly efficient staff, neat built-in seating in separate snug, smarter more modern-feeling back dining room; children welcome, dogs in bar, small deck behind, seven bedrooms, open all day Sat, till 5pm Sun, closed Mon lunchtime. *(Emma Scofield)*

SPROXTON   SK8524

Crown   (01476) 861608
Coston Road; LE14 4QB Friendly fairly compact 19th-c stone-built inn with spotless well laid-out interior, good reasonably priced food from bar snacks to restaurant dishes cooked by landlord-chef, three well kept changing ales, good wines and coffee, light airy bar with woodburner, lounge and restaurant with glassed-off wine store; children welcome, dogs in bar, lovely sunny courtyard, attractive village and nice local walks, three bedrooms, closed Mon. *(Phil and Jane Hodson and others)*

STRETTON   SK9415

★ **Jackson Stops**   (01780) 410237
Rookery Lane; a mile or less off A1, at B668 (Oakham) exit; follow village sign, turning off Clipsham Road into Manor Road, pub on left; LE15 7RA Attractive thatched former farmhouse with plenty of character; meandering rooms filled with period features, black-beamed country bar with wall timbering, coal fires and elderly settle on worn tile and brick floor, a couple of Grainstore ales, eight wines by the glass and ten malt whiskies, smarter airy room on right with mix of ancient and modern tables on dark blue carpet, corner fire, two dining rooms, one with stripped-stone walls and old open cooking range, well liked food including deals, warm friendly service; rare nurdling bench (a game involving old pennies), background music; children and dogs (in bar) welcome, closed Sun evening, Mon. *(Barry Collett, John and Sylvia Harrop)*

THORNTON   SK4607

Reservoir   (01530) 382433
Main Street; LE67 1AJ Busy pub with pleasant modern décor, popular home-made food from varied menu (not Sun evening)

including good value set lunch, chinese night Weds, Steamin' Billy ales, friendly efficient service; children welcome, dogs and muddy boots in bar, good circular walk around Thornton Reservoir. *(Hilary Edwards)*

THORPE LANGTON   SP7492

★ **Bakers Arms**   (01858) 545201
Off B6047 N of Market Harborough; LE16 7TS Civilised thatched restauranty pub with small bar; consistently good imaginative food (must book) from regularly changing menu including several seafood dishes, cottagey beamed linked areas and stylishly simple country décor, a well kept ale and good choice of wines by the glass, friendly efficient staff, maybe a pianist; no under-12s or dogs; picnic-sets in back garden with country views, closed weekday lunchtimes, Sun evening, Mon. *(R L Borthwick, SAB and MJW, Gerry and Rosemary Dobson)*

THRUSSINGTON   SK6415

Star   (01664) 424220
Village signposted off A46 N of Syston; The Green; LE7 4UH Neatly modernised 18th-c village inn, L-shaped bar with low stripped beams, broad floorboards and inglenook woodburner, unusual double-sided high-backed settle, Belvoir Star Bitter, Rugby Egg Chaser and Timothy Taylors Landlord, ten wines by the glass, steps up to skylit dining room, popular all-day food; background music, TV, free wi-fi; children and dogs (in bar) welcome, side garden and flagstoned terrace, bedrooms, open all day from 8am (9am Sun). *(Lindy Andrews)*

TUGBY   SK7600

Fox & Hounds   (0116) 259 8188
A47 6 miles W of Uppingham; LE7 9WB Attractively modernised village-green dining pub (reopened 2014), good well priced food (all day Sat, till 6pm Sun) from bar snacks up, efficient welcoming staff, ales such as Adnams, Grainstore and Greene King, compact open-plan interior with stripped beams and quarry tiles, dining part with light-wood furniture and woodburner; background music, TV; fenced terrace by car park, open all day Fri-Sun. *(R L Borthwick)*

UPPER HAMBLETON   SK8907

Finchs Arms   (01572) 756575
Off A606; Oakham Road; LE15 8TL Friendly 17th-c stone inn with outstanding views over Rutland Water, four log fires, beamed and flagstoned bar, Black Sheep, Timothy Taylors Landlord and a guest, several wines by the glass including champagne, elegant restaurant and second newly built dining room, well liked food

Post Office address codings confusingly give the impression that some pubs are in Leicestershire, when they're really in Cambridgeshire (which is where we list them).

including set menus, afternoon teas; children welcome, no dogs, suntrap hillside terrace making most of the view, good surrounding walks, ten bedrooms, open all day. *(Colin McLachlan)*

UPPINGHAM SP8699
Falcon (01572) 823535
High Street East; LE15 9PY Quietly refined old coaching inn, welcoming and relaxed, with oak-panelled bar, spacious nicely furnished lounge and restaurant, roaring fire and big windows overlooking market square, good food (not Sun evening) from bar snacks up, three Grainstore ales, efficient friendly service; children welcome, dogs in bar, back garden with terrace, bedrooms (some in converted stable block), open all day. *(Barry Collett, John and Sylvia Harrop)*

UPPINGHAM SP8699
Vaults (01572) 823259
Market Place; LE15 9QH Attractive comfortable old pub next to church, enjoyable reasonably priced traditional food served by friendly staff, four real ales including Adnams Broadside, Marstons Pedigree and a house beer from Grainstore, several wines by the glass, pleasant upstairs dining room; background music, sports TVs; children and dogs welcome, some tables out overlooking picturesque square, four bedrooms (booking from nearby Falcon Hotel), open all day. *(Barry Collett)*

WALTHAM ON THE WOLDS SK8024
Royal Horseshoes (01664) 464289
Melton Road (A607); LE14 4AJ Attractive smartly refurbished stone and thatch pub in centre of village, extensive choice of generous affordably priced food, ales such as Fullers and Greene King, over 20 gins, two main rooms with beams and open fires; no dogs, tables outside, good value annexe bedrooms. *(Adrian Johnson)*

WHITWICK SK4316
Three Horseshoes (01530) 837311
Leicester Road; LE67 5GN Unpretentious unchanging local with long quarry-tiled bar, old wooden benches and open fires, tiny snug to the right, well kept Bass and Marstons Pedigree, no food, piano, darts, dominoes and cards, daily newspapers; outside loos; no proper pub sign so easy to miss. *(Anon)*

WOODHOUSE EAVES SK5214
Curzon Arms (01509) 890377
Maplewell Road; LE12 8QZ Cheerful old beamed pub in pretty Charnwood Forest village; enjoyable food (not Sun evening) from lunchtime sandwiches and pub favourites up, also good value weekday set menu, ales such as Caledonian, Hook Norton, Sharps and Timothy Taylors, good friendly service, attractive up-to-date décor with interesting collection of wall clocks, carpeted dining room; background music, free wi-fi; children, walkers and dogs welcome, ramp for disabled access, good-sized front lawn and terrace, open all day weekends. *(R L Borthwick)*

WOODHOUSE EAVES SK5214
Old Bulls Head (01509) 890255
Main Street; LE12 8RZ Big contemporary open-plan Mitchells & Butlers dining pub, clean and tidy, with good choice of food including pizzas, pasta and grills, weekday set menu till 6pm, good wine list and well kept ales such as Brains Rev James, Marstons Pedigree and Sharps Doom Bar, friendly helpful staff; well behaved children welcome, outside tables, nice village setting and handy for Charnwood Forest and Bardon Hill, open (and food) all day. *(Graham H Ashworth)*

WYMESWOLD SK6023
Three Crowns (01509) 880153
Far Street (A6006) opposite church; LE12 6TZ Snug chatty 18th-c local in attractive village, good friendly staff, Adnams, Bass, Sharps and a guest, decent reasonably priced pubby food, pleasant character furnishings in beamed bar and lounge, open fire, lots of atmosphere; free wi-fi; children and dogs welcome, picnic-sets out on decking, open all day. *(Comus and Sarah Elliott)*

WYMESWOLD SK6023
Windmill (01509) 881313
Brook Street; LE12 6TT Bustling side-street village pub with enjoyable good value home-made food from lunchtime snacks up, three well kept rotating ales, good cheerful service even though busy; children welcome, dogs in bar, back garden with decked area, open all day Fri, Sat, till 9pm Sun. *(Mike and Mary Carter, Martin and Sue Day)*

Lincolnshire

BARNOLDBY LE BECK   TA2303   Map 8

Ship 🍴 🍷

(01472) 822308 – www.the-shipinn.com

Village signposted off A18 Louth–Grimsby; DN37 0BG

Tranquil refined dining pub with plenty to look at

The interesting collection of Edwardian and Victorian bric-a-brac in this delightful, neatly kept pub is really worth looking at: stand-up telephones, violins, a horn gramophone, a bowler and top hats, old racquets, riding crops and hockey sticks. Heavy dark-ringed drapes swathe the windows and the furnishings fit in well, with pretty cushions on comfortable dark green wall benches, heavily stuffed green plush Victorian-looking chairs on a green fleur de lys carpet and a warming winter coal fire. Batemans Yella Belly Gold, Black Sheep and Tom Woods Best Bitter on handpump, up to a dozen malt whiskies, wines by the glass from a good list and cocktails; background music. A fenced-off sunny area behind has hanging baskets and a few picnic-sets under parasols. This is a charming village.

🍴 Good, popular food includes smoked haddock scotch egg with hollandaise, crispy beef strips in hoisin, plum sauce and chilli, pesto spaghetti with courgette ribbons, sunblush tomatoes and parmesan, fish pie, duo of pork belly and tenderloin stuffed with apple and date with duxelle croquettes and cider jus, slow-roast lamb shank with redcurrant reduction, and puddings such as cheesecake with fresh fruit and sticky toffee pudding with crème anglaise. *Benchmark main dish: beer-battered haddock and chips £9.95. Two-course evening meal £18.00.*

Free house ~ Licensee Michele Hancock ~ Real ale ~ Open 12-2, 6-11; 12-5 Sun ~ Bar food 12-2, 7-9; 12-4 Sun ~ Restaurant ~ Children welcome ~ Wi-fi *Recommended by Paul Valentine, Michael Butler*

BASTON   TF1113   Map 8

White Horse 🍴 🍷 🍺

(01778) 560923 – www.thewhitehorsebaston.co.uk

Church Street; PE6 9PE

Blue-painted and refurbished village pub using reclaimed farm materials, four real ales, friendly staff and good, popular food

Saved from closure by a local farmer, this is a family run, 18th-c village pub with a warmly friendly atmosphere. Many elements from the farm have gone into the careful renovations: the bricks in the bay window, the boards in the ceiling, some of the beams and the huge piece of sycamore that acts as the counter in the snug bar. The main bar has built-in wall seats with scatter cushions, windsor and farmhouse chairs and stools around all sorts of tables on wooden flooring, a woodburning stove in a brick fireplace (with big logs piled into another) and horse-related items on pale paintwork; background music, TV, darts and board games. The dining area is similarly furnished. Stools line the blue-painted counter where they keep Abbeydale Absolution, Adnams Southwold, Oakham JHB and Star Winter Ale on handpump, a dozen wines by the glass and ten malt whiskies; the resident springer spaniel is called Audrey. There are seats and tables on a side terrace.

 Interesting food includes sandwiches, potted ham hock with pea and spring onion salad, rhubarb-cured sea trout with celeriac and apple salad, burger with bacon, cheese and chips, hand-made thai vegetable spring rolls with coconut rice and coconut sauce, five-spiced roasted pork belly with pak choi and pulled pork spring roll, chargrilled leg of lamb steak with ratatouille, basil confit potatoes and salsa verde, honey and mustard-marinated rump of beef with spring onion croquettes, and puddings such as chocolate Baileys brownie and pistachio ice-cream and banana tarte tatin with rum and raisin ice-cream. *Benchmark main dish: pork platter £14.50. Two-course evening meal £18.00.*

Free house ~ Licensees Ben and Germaine Larter ~ Real ale ~ Open 12-11 (midnight Fri, Sat); 4-11 Mon, Tues; 12-10.30 Sun ~ Bar food 12-2.30, 5.30-9; 5-8 Tues; 12-9 Sat; 12-6 Sun; not Mon ~ Restaurant ~ Children welcome until 9pm ~ Dogs allowed in bar ~ Wi-fi
Recommended by Elizabeth Tofts, Michael and Jenny Back, Chris and Val Ramstedt

DRY DODDINGTON   SK8546 Map 8
Wheatsheaf
(01400) 281458
Main Street; 1.5 miles off A1 N of Grantham; NG23 5HU

Friendly pub with popular food and drink

Handy for the A1, this is a friendly little pub. The front bar is basically two rooms with a woodburning stove, a variety of settles and chairs enlivened by bold patterned scatter cushions, and tables in the windows looking across to the green and the lovely 14th-c church with its crooked tower. The serving bar on the right has quickly changing ales such as Northumberland Sheep Dog and Poachers Hykeham Gold on handpump and decent wines by the glass. A slight slope leads down to the carpeted and comfortable extended dining room. Once a cow byre, this part is even more ancient than the rest of the building, perhaps dating from the 13th c; background music. The front terrace has neat tables under cocktail parasols among tubs of flowers; disabled access at the side.

Cooked by the landlady, the tasty food includes sandwiches, prawn cocktail, chicken liver pâté with onion marmalade, steak in Guinness or chicken and mushroom pies, beer-battered cod and triple-cooked chips, toad in the hole, vegetable lasagne, and puddings such as hot chocolate fondant and sticky toffee pudding with toffee sauce. *Benchmark main dish: lasagne £9.95. Two-course evening meal £17.00.*

Free house ~ Licensees Steven and Joanne McLeod ~ Real ale ~ Open 12-3, 5-11; 12-11 Sat, Sun; closed Mon, Tues lunchtime ~ Bar food 12-2, 6-9; 12-2.30, 6-9.30 Sat; 12-3 Sun ~ Restaurant ~ Children welcome ~ Dogs allowed in bar ~ Wi-fi *Recommended by T E Stone, Michael and Jenny Back, Gordon and Margaret Ormondroyd, Dr D J and Mrs S C Walker*

The ▧ symbol shows pubs that keep their beer unusually well,
have a particularly good range or brew their own.

GEDNEY DYKE
TF4125 Map 8
Chequers 🌟🍴 ♖
(01406) 366700 – www.the-chequers.co.uk
Off A17 Holbeach–Kings Lynn; PE12 0AJ

Smart dining pub with small bar, stylish restaurant rooms and imaginative food

Although many customers come to this stylish and friendly fenland village pub for the first class food, drinkers are made most welcome too. The beamed bar has seats against the counter where they serve Woodfordes Norfolk Nog and Wherry on handpump, 12 wines and champagne by the glass and a wide range of spirits. There are several high chairs around equally high tables and an open fire. The smart, interconnected, carpeted dining rooms and conservatory have high-backed cream or black dining chairs around white-clothed tables, and throughout there's bare brick here and there and good lighting; service is helpful and courteous. The back terrace and fenced-off garden have plenty of seats and tables.

 Tempting food includes pigeon and beetroot salad with pickled radish and jus, mackerel with waldorf salad, cumberland sausage with caramelised onion gravy, tomato, red onion and goats cheese tart, beer-battered cod and triple-cooked chips, pork fillet with cider jus and creamed cabbage, chicken breast with wild mushroom sauce and mash, stone bass fillet with pumpkin, parmesan and chorizo, and puddings such as iced peanut parfait with milk chocolate mousse and salted caramel and hot chocolate fondant with caramelised banana and banana sorbet; they also offer a two- and three-course set lunch (not Sunday). *Benchmark main dish: roast saddle of venison with onion tatin, pickled shimeji mushrooms and carrot and anise purée £22.00. Two-course evening meal £20.00.*

Free house ~ Licensee Gareth Franklin ~ Real ale ~ Open 11.30-3, 5-11.30 (midnight Sat); 12-5 Sun; closed Sun evening, Mon, Tues ~ Bar food 12-2.30, 6-9; 12-3 Sun ~ Restaurant ~ Children welcome ~ Dogs allowed in bar ~ Wi-fi *Recommended by Hilary and Neil Christopher, Carol and Barry Craddock*

HEIGHINGTON
TF0369 Map 8
Butcher & Beast 🍺 £
(01522) 790386 – www.butcherandbeast.co.uk
High Street; LN4 1JS

Traditional village pub with terrific range of drinks, pubby food and a pretty garden by stream

There's always something going on in this cheerful village pub – weekly themed food evenings, quizzes and beer festivals. The simply furnished bar has button-back wall banquettes, pubby furnishings and stools along the counter where the hard-working, hands-on licensees keep half a dozen ales such as Batemans XB, XXXB and a seasonal guest plus Bass and changing beers from Everards and Hop Back; also two farm ciders, eight wines by the glass, 30 gins and 20 malt whiskies; occasional TV. The Snug has red-cushioned wall settles and high-backed wooden dining chairs, and the beamed dining room is neatly set with proper tablecloths and napkins; throughout, the cream walls are hung with old village photos and country pictures. A lawn, with picnic-sets, runs down to a stream and the award-winning hanging baskets and tubs are very pretty in summer.

🍴 Fair priced food includes chicken goujons with sweet chilli sauce, whitebait, mushroom stir-fry, steak in ale pie, a pasta dish of the day, burgers with toppings and chips, lamb steak with mint gravy, salmon and prawn mornay, gammon with eggs and pineapple, and puddings. *Benchmark main dish: rump steak and chips with a choice of sauces £12.95. Two-course evening meal £16.50.*

Batemans ~ Tenants Mal and Diane Gray ~ Real ale ~ Open 12-11 (10.30 Sun) ~ Bar food 12-2.30, 5-8.30; 12-2.30, 6-8 Sun ~ Restaurant ~ Children welcome away from bar ~ Dogs allowed in bar ~ Wi-fi *Recommended by Chris Johnson*

HOUGH-ON-THE-HILL SK9246 Map 8

Brownlow Arms 🍽⭐ ♀ 🛏

(01400) 250234 – www.thebrownlowarms.com
High Road; NG32 2AZ

Lincolnshire Dining Pub of the Year

Refined country house with beamed bar, real ales, imaginative food and graceful terrace; bedrooms

'A total delight to stay here,' says one reader enthusiastically – and, indeed, the bedrooms in this smart old stone inn are well equipped and comfortable and the breakfasts very good. The comfortable, welcoming beamed bar has plenty of panelling, some exposed brickwork, local prints and scenes, a large mirror, and a pile of logs beside the big fireplace. Seating is on elegant, stylishly mismatched upholstered armchairs, and the carefully arranged furnishings give the impression of several separate and cosy areas. Served by impeccably polite staff, the ales on handpump are Timothy Taylors Landlord and Woodfordes Wherry, there are ten wines by the glass and up to 20 malt whiskies; easy-listening background music. Do check the limited opening times – and note that you'll probably need to book a table in advance.

 Accomplished cooking includes pork haslet (meatloaf) and confit duck rillettes with plum bread crisps, apricot purée and piccalilli, seared scallops with foie gras, chanterelle mushrooms and sauce bordelaise, pearl barley risotto with spring herbs, asparagus, a poached duck egg, truffle shavings and chive butter sauce, roast saddle of wild boar with parma ham potato gratin, caramel apple purée and calvados jus, roast poussin with fricassée of green and broad beans, peas, swede and smoked pancetta, stone bass fillet with crab-crushed potatoes, spinach and caviar beurre blanc, and puddings such as lemon and mascarpone crème brûlée with lemongrass-infused iced yoghurt and confit zest and rhubarb and rose jelly with stem ginger and orange parfait, poached rhubarb, warm gingerbread and a rhubarb crisp. *Benchmark main dish: rib-eye steak with pepper or smoked garlic and chive butter £24.95. Two-course evening meal £25.00.*

Free house ~ Licensee Paul L Willoughby ~ Real ale ~ Open 6-11; 12-3 Sun; closed Sun evening, Mon, lunchtimes Tues-Sat ~ Bar food 6.30-9 Tues-Sat; 12-3 Sun ~ Restaurant ~ Children over 8 allowed ~ Wi-fi ~ Bedrooms: £70/£110 *Recommended by Alan Clark, William and Ann Reid, Brian and Janet Ainscough, John Davis*

INGHAM SK9483 Map 8

Inn on the Green 🍽⭐

(01522) 730354 – www.innonthegreeningham.co.uk
The Green; LN1 2XT

Nicely modernised place serving thoughtfully prepared food; chatty atmosphere

With welcoming, caring staff and rewarding food, this friendly place is deservedly busy – it's best to book a table in advance. The locals' bar, with attractive views across the village green, has an informal, pubby feel and is liked by those just wanting a chat and a drink beside the log fire – though several tables are usually occupied by those enjoying the tasty food. The beamed and timbered dining room is spread over two floors, with lots of exposed brickwork, local prints and a warm winter fire. The lounge between these rooms has leather sofas and background music, and a bar counter where you can buy home-made jams, marmalade and chutney. Sharps Doom Bar and two guests such as Horncastle Angel of Light and Milestone Lock Keeper on handpump, ten wines by the glass, several malt whiskies and home-made cordials.

As well as a two- and three-course menu (12-2, 6-6.55), the rewarding food includes baguettes, tempura tiger prawns with confit tomato and harissa mayonnaise, pigeon pie with pistachio purée, apricot foam, honey glaze and granola, a seasonal risotto, vegetable lasagne, pulled pork burger with fries, coq au vin, fish stew with lemon beurre blanc, beef bourguignon, and puddings such as lemon and lavender meringue with lemon jelly, lavender marshmallow, lemon curd mousse and lavender brittle and black forest gateau (chocolate fondant, cherry sorbet, kirsch and cherry foam). *Benchmark main dish: lamb rump with mince croquette, saffron shallots and smoked potato purée £15.95. Two-course evening meal £22.50.*

Free house ~ Licensees Andrew Cafferkey and Sarah Sharpe ~ Real ale ~ Open 11.30-3, 6-11; 12-10.30 Sun; closed Mon ~ Bar food 12-2 (3.45 Sun), 6-9 ~ Restaurant ~ Children welcome ~ Wi-fi *Recommended by Stephen Woad, Richard Cole, Miss Barr*

KIRKBY LA THORPE   TF0945   Map 8
Queens Head 🏆 £

(01529) 305743 – www.thequeensheadinn.com
Village and pub signposted off A17, just E of Sleaford, then turn right into Boston Road cul-de-sac; NG34 9NU

Reliable dining pub very popular for its good food and helpful, efficient service

The top quality food cooked by one of the landlords continues to draw customers back on a regular basis. It's all neatly comfortable and gently traditional, with plenty of dark-waistcoated staff, open fires and elaborate flower arrangements. The carpeted bar has stools along the counter, button-back banquettes, sofas and captain's chairs around shiny dark tables. The smart, beamed restaurant has high-backed orange-upholstered dining chairs around linen-set tables on carpet, heavy drapes and a woodburning stove; there's also a popular dining conservatory. Nice decorative touches take in thoughtful lighting, big prints, china plates on delft shelves and handsome longcase clocks (it's quite something when they all chime at midday). Batemans XB and a guest such as Tom Woods Best Bitter on handpump; background music. Easy disabled access.

At lunchtime, the particularly good food includes several dishes at £8.95 (hence our Value Award): saddle of rabbit with juniper and merlot jus, camembert, baby spinach and wild mushroom pancake with creamy sherry sauce, whole plaice with brown shrimp and lemon butter, and venison pie with red wine gravy. Also, wild boar terrine with red onion chutney, salmon and coriander fishcakes with sweet chilli sauce, slow-braised lamb rump with smoked bacon and redcurrant and minted lamb jus, maple-glazed duck breast on a sweet potato galette with apricot, brandy and orange sauce, and puddings such as sticky ginger and date pudding with butterscotch sauce and toffee ice-cream and a plate of chocolate for two to share. *Benchmark main dish: steak in ale pie £8.95. Two-course evening meal £13.95.*

Free house ~ Licensee John Clark ~ Real ale ~ Open 12-3, 6-11; 12-10.30 Sun ~ Bar food 12-2.30, 6-9.30; 12-8.30 Sun ~ Restaurant ~ Children welcome until 7pm ~ Dogs allowed in bar ~ Wi-fi *Recommended by Phoebe Peacock, Andrew Stone*

STAMFORD   TF0306 Map 8

Bull & Swan ♀ 🛏

(01780) 766412 – www.thebullandswan.co.uk

High Street, St Martins; PE9 2LJ

Individually furnished bar and dining areas, open fires and beams, four real ales, enjoyable food and seats in back coachyard; comfortable bedrooms

A former staging post on the Great North Road, this is a handsome old place with nicely traditional rooms. Three connect together, with low beams, rugs on floorboards, portraits in gilt frames on painted or bare stone walls and several open fires. There are wheelback chairs, high-backed settles creating stalls, leather banquettes, bow window seats and carved wooden and button-back dining chairs around an eclectic mix of dark tables; background music. High chairs line the counter where they keep Adnams Southwold, Sharps Doom Bar and a couple of guests from Grainstore and Nene Valley on handpump, 20 wines by the glass and 30 malt whiskies; staff are helpful and friendly. The character bedrooms are named after animals. An arched passageway leads to a back coachyard with seats and tables.

Well liked food includes sandwiches and paninis, spiced crab cakes with fennel slaw and caperberry salad, duck liver and pistachio parfait with orange marmalade, sharing boards, chicken caesar salad, cheddar and chorizo beef burger with beer-battered onion rings, blue cheese and walnut soufflé, a pie of the day, cod fillet with minted pea purée and lemon dressing, rack of lamb with rosemary potatoes and port wine reduction, and puddings such as coffee crème brûlée and white and dark chocolate brownie with chocolate sauce. *Benchmark main dish: beer-battered fish and chips £12.95. Two-course evening meal £20.00.*

Free house ~ Licensee Paul Brown ~ Real ale ~ Open 7am-11pm; 8am-midnight Sat ~ Bar food 12-2.30, 6-9.30 ~ Children welcome ~ Dogs welcome ~ Wi-fi ~ Bedrooms: £90/£110
Recommended by John Harris, Andrew Stone

STAMFORD   TF0306 Map 8

George of Stamford ⭐ ♀ 🛏

(01780) 750750 – www.georgehotelofstamford.com

High Street, St Martins (B1081 S of centre, not the quite different central pedestrianised High Street); PE9 2LB

Handsome coaching inn with traditional bar, several dining areas and lounges, excellent staff and top class food and drink; lovely bedrooms

This is a special place and remains a favourite with many readers (and ourselves). It's exceptionally well run with professional and friendly staff, a civilised yet informal atmosphere and plenty of genuine character. The various areas are furnished with all manner of seats from leather, cane and antique wicker to soft sofas and easy chairs, and there's a room to suit all occasions. The central lounge is particularly striking with sturdy timbers, broad flagstones, heavy beams and massive stonework. The properly pubby little front York Bar has Adnams Broadside, Black Sheep and Grainstore Triple B on handpump alongside 20 wines from an exceptional list and 30 malt whiskies. There's an amazing oak-panelled restaurant (jacket or tie required) and a less formal Garden Room restaurant, which has well spaced furniture on herringbone glazed bricks around a central tropical planting. The seats in the charming cobbled courtyard are highly prized and the immaculately kept walled garden is beautifully planted; there are also sunken lawns – and croquet.

 Quality as high as this does come at a price; the simplest option is the York Bar snack menu with sandwiches (their toastie is especially good), a proper ploughman's and a plate of smoked salmon with capers. First class food in the restaurants includes prawn and crab cocktail, gruyère cheese fritters with thai jelly, burger with toppings, mango salsa and chips, half lobster with fine spaghetti with lobster oil and chilli, salt beef cooked in its own broth with root vegetables, cod with bombay potatoes, onion bhaji and mint yoghurt raita, and puddings. *Benchmark main dish: a taste of pork (slow-cooked pork belly, treacle-blackened loin, spiced collar paneer) £24.65. Two-course evening meal £24.00.*

Free house ~ Licensee Chris Pitman ~ Real ale ~ Open 11-11; 12-10.30 Sun ~ Bar food 12-2, 7-9 ~ Restaurant ~ Children must be over 8 in panelled dining room ~ Dogs allowed in bar and bedrooms ~ Wi-fi ~ Bedrooms: £100/£195 *Recommended by Barry Collett, Bill Oliver, Roy Hoing, Richard Tilbrook, Miss B D Picton*

STAMFORD
TF0307 Map 8
Tobie Norris
(01780) 753800 – www.kneadpubs.co.uk
St Pauls Street; PE9 2BE

A warren of ancient rooms, a good period atmosphere, a fine choice of drinks, enjoyable food and seats outside

Centuries old, beautifully restored and full of character, this lovely place is a charming series of little rooms. Add careful attention by friendly staff and five real ales, and you get an enjoyable, relaxed and easy-going atmosphere. The most has been made of the building's age – worn flagstones, meticulously stripped stonework, a huge hearth for one room's woodburning stove and steeply pitched rafters in one of the two upstairs rooms. There's a wide variety of furnishings from pews and wall settles to comfortable armchairs and a handsomely panelled shrine to Nelson and the Battle of Trafalgar. Adnams Southwold, Castle Rock Harvest Pale Ale and three quickly changing guests on handpump, farm cider and several wines by the glass. A snug end conservatory opens to a narrow but sunny two-level courtyard with seats and tables.

As well as lots of nibbles such as baked camembert with warm bread, pigs in blankets with duck-fat potatoes and honey and bacon doughballs, there might be sandwiches and wraps, antipasti platters, butter bean and squash crumble, cod and pancetta cassoulet, indian-style burger with sag aloo and sweet onion bhaji, chorizo and barbecue chicken lasagne, slow-cooked short rib of beef in rioja and shallots with horseradish butter, and puddings such as jam roly-poly and custard and millionaire's chocolate shortbread tart. *Benchmark main dish: home-made stone-baked pizzas with lots of toppings £8.95. Two-course evening meal £19.00.*

Free house ~ Licensees Tim Chantrell and Gemma Rogerson ~ Real ale ~ Open 11-11 ~ Bar food 12-2.30, 6-9; 12-5, 6-9 Sat ~ Children over 10 until 6pm only ~ Dogs welcome ~ Wi-fi *Recommended by Anne and Ben Smith, Andrew Stone*

WOOLSTHORPE
SK8334 Map 8
Chequers
(01476) 870701 – www.chequersinn.net
Woolsthorpe near Belvoir, signposted off A52 or A607 W of Grantham; NG32 1LU

Interesting food at comfortably relaxed inn with good drinks and appealing castle views from outside tables; bedrooms

If you want to explore the lovely Vale of Belvoir, it makes sense to stay in the comfortable bedrooms in the converted stables next door. A friendly former coaching inn, it has a heavy-beamed main bar with two big tables (one a massive oak construction), a comfortable mix of seating including some handsome leather chairs and banquettes, and a huge boar's head above a good log fire in the big brick fireplace. Among cartoons on the wall are some of the illustrated claret bottle labels from the series commissioned from famous artists. There are more leather seats in a dining area on the left, in what was once the village bakery. A corridor leads off to the light and airy main restaurant, decorated with contemporary pictures, and another bar; background music and board games. Grainstore Cooking, Wentworth Bumble Beer and White Horse Blowing Stone on handpump, around 30 wines by the glass, 50 malt whiskies, 20 gins, a seasonal cocktail list and a farm cider. There are good quality teak tables, chairs and benches outside and, beyond these, some picnic-sets on the edge of the pub's cricket field, with views of Belvoir Castle.

Enterprising food includes seared scallops with butternut squash purée, confit pork belly and maple compressed apple, stilton panna cotta with spiced braised figs and maple-glazed walnuts, mushroom and roquefort stuffed deep-fried risotto balls with wild mushroom fricassée, a pie of the day, local sausages with mash and onion gravy, paprika-spiced chicken breast with moroccan couscous and minted yoghurt, slow-braised lamb with haricot beans, bacon and cabbage, celeriac purée and dauphinoise potatoes, and puddings such as cherry bakewell tart with cinnamon ice-cream and chocolate fondant with salted caramel ice-cream. *Benchmark main dish: beer-battered fish and chips £11.95. Two-course evening meal £20.00.*

Free house ~ Licensee Justin Chad ~ Real ale ~ Open 12-11 (midnight Sat); 12-10.30 Sun ~ Bar food 12-2.30, 6-9.30; 12-4, 6-8.30 Sun ~ Restaurant ~ Children welcome ~ Dogs allowed in bar and bedrooms ~ Wi-fi ~ Bedrooms: £50/£70 *Recommended by Vikki and Matt Wharton, Ron Corbett, Ian Herdman, David Heath*

Also Worth a Visit in Lincolnshire

Besides the fully inspected pubs, you might like to try these pubs that have been recommended to us and described by readers. Do tell us what you think of them: feedback@goodguides.com

ALLINGTON   SK8540

★**Welby Arms** (01400) 281361
The Green; off A1 at N end of Grantham bypass; NG32 2EA Welcoming, well run and well liked inn with helpful friendly staff, large simply furnished bar divided by stone archway, beams and joists, log fires (one in an attractive arched brick fireplace), comfortable plush wall banquettes and stools, up to six changing ales, over 20 wines by the glass and plenty of malt whiskies, good popular food including blackboard specials, civilised back dining lounge; background music; children welcome, tables in walled courtyard with pretty flower baskets, picnic-sets on front lawn, comfortable bedrooms, open all day Sun. *(Michael and Jenny Back, Roger and Pauline Pearce, Gordon and Margaret Ormondroyd)*

BARHOLM   TF0810
Five Horseshoes (01778) 560238
W of Market Deeping; village signed from A15 Langtoft; PE9 4RA

Welcoming old-fashioned village local, cosy and comfortable, with beams, rustic bric-a-brac and log fire, well kept Adnams, Oakham and four guests, good range of wines, Fri pizza van; pool room with TV, some live music; children and dogs welcome, garden and shady arbour, play area, open all day weekends (from 1pm Sat), closed weekday lunchtimes. *(Ian and Tina Humphrey)*

BASSINGHAM   SK9160
Five Bells (01522) 788269
High Street; LN5 9JZ Cheerful old country pub with well liked food including good value set menu (booking advised), Greene King IPA and a couple of guests, several brandies, efficient friendly service, bare-boards interior with hop-strung beams and lots of brass and bric-a-brac, some quotations on the walls, cosy log fires, a well in one part; children and dogs (particularly) welcome, open all day (food till 7pm Sun). *(Ross Balaam, Tony and Maggie Harwood)*

BELCHFORD · TF2975

★ **Blue Bell** (01507) 533602 *Village signed off A153 Horncastle–Louth; LN9 6LQ* 18th-c dining pub with cosy comfortable bar, Batemans, Worthington and guests, Thatcher's cider, good traditional and modern food, efficient friendly service, restaurant; children and dogs welcome, picnic-sets in terraced back garden, good base for Wolds walks and Viking Way (remove muddy boots), open all day Sun, may close second and third weeks in Jan. *(Anne and Ben Smith)*

BILLINGBOROUGH · TF1134

★ **Fortescue Arms** (01529) 240228 *B1177, off A52 Grantham–Boston; NG34 0QB* Popular beamed country pub with old stonework, exposed brick, panelling and big see-through fireplace in carpeted rooms, well kept Greene King and guests, enjoyable pubby food including two-course deal (Mon-Thurs), good friendly service even at busy times, Victorian prints, brass and copper, a stuffed badger and pheasant, dining rooms at each end; children welcome, no dogs inside, picnic-sets and rattan-style furniture in sheltered courtyard with flowering tubs, open (and food) all day weekends. *(John Harris)*

BOSTON · TF3244

Mill (01205) 352874 *Spilsby Road (A16); PE21 9QN* Popular roadside pub with enjoyable reasonably priced food (not Tues) including some italian choices, Batemans XB and guest, friendly italian landlord and staff; children welcome, tables out in front. *(Carol and Barry Craddock)*

BURTON COGGLES · SK9725

Cholmeley Arms (01476) 550225 *Village Street; NG33 4JS* Well kept ales such as Fullers London Pride, Grainstore and Greene King Abbot in small beamed pubby bar with warm fire, generous helpings of good reasonably priced home-made food (not Sun evening), friendly efficient service, restaurant; farm shop, four bedrooms in separate building overlooking garden, handy for A1, open all day weekends, closed lunchtimes Mon, Tues. *(M and GR)*

CAYTHORPE · SK9348

Red Lion (01400) 272632 *Signed just off A607 N of Grantham; High Street; NG32 3DN* Popular village pub with good fairly traditional home-made food (booking advised) including early-bird deal (Weds-Fri 6-7pm), friendly helpful staff, well kept Adnams and Everards, good sensibly priced wine, bare-boards bar with light wood counter, black beams and roaring fire, modern restaurant; back terrace by car park. *(John Harris)*

CHAPEL ST LEONARDS · TF5672

Admiral Benbow (01754) 871847 *The Promenade; PE24 5BQ* Small beach bar serving three real ales and good choice of foreign bottled beers, ciders too, sandwiches and snacks, bare boards, cushioned bench seats and stools, barrel tables, lots of bric-a-brac and nautical memorabilia on planked walls and ceiling; children and dogs welcome, picnic-sets out on mock-up galleon, great sea views, open all day summer, all Fri-Sun winter. *(Adrian Johnson)*

CLAYPOLE · SK8449

Five Bells (01636) 626561 *Main Street; NG23 5BJ* Friendly brick-built village pub, good-sized beamed bar and smaller dining area beyond servery, well kept Greene King IPA and mainly local guests, a couple of ciders, good value home-made food including range of burgers and daily specials; pool and darts; children welcome, dogs in bar, grassy back garden with play area, four bedrooms, closed Mon lunchtime, otherwise open all day. *(Andrew Stone)*

CLEETHORPES · TA3009

No 2 Refreshment Room 07905 375587 *Station Approach; DN35 8AX* Small comfortable platform bar with well kept Hancocks HB, Rudgates Mild, Sharps Doom Bar and guests, real cider too, friendly staff, interesting old pictures of the station, historical books on trains and the local area, no food but free Sun night buffet; tables out under heaters, open all day from 7.30am. *(Caroline Prescott)*

CLEETHORPES · TA3108

★ **Willys** (01472) 602145 *Highcliff Road; south promenade; DN35 8RQ* Popular open-plan bistro-style seafront pub with panoramic Humber views, café tables, tiled floor and painted brick walls; visibly brews its own good ales, also changing guests and belgian beers, good home-made bar lunches (evening food Mon-Thurs), friendly fast service and good mix of customers; quiet juke box; a few tables out on the prom, open all day (till late Fri, Sat). *(Derek Wason)*

COLEBY · SK9760

Bell (01522) 813778 *Village signed off A607 S of Lincoln, turn right and right into Far Lane at church; LN5 0AH* Restauranty pub with wide variety of top notch food from owner-chef including set lunch and early-bird menus, welcoming cheerful staff, well kept Timothy Taylors and several wines by the glass (not cheap) including champagne, bar and three dining areas; children over 8 welcome, terrace tables, village on Viking Way with lovely fenland views, open evenings Weds-Sat and lunchtime Sun. *(David Hunt)*

CONINGSBY   TF2458
Leagate Inn (01526) 342370
Leagate Road (B1192 southwards, off A153 E); LN4 4RS Heavy-beamed 16th-c fenland pub with three cosy linked rooms, medley of furnishings including high-backed settles around the biggest of three log fires, dim lighting, ancient oak panelling, attractive dining room, even a priest hole, enjoyable well priced food (all day Sun) from extensive menu, Adnams, Batemans and Charles Wells ales, good friendly service; children welcome, dogs in bar, pleasant garden, site of old gallows at front, eight motel bedrooms, open all day Sun. *(Carol and Barry Craddock)*

FOSDYKE   TF3132
Ship (01205) 260764
Moulton Washway; A17; PE12 6LH Useful roadside pub with popular reasonably priced food from varied menu, Sun carvery, two Adnams beers and Batemans XB, friendly staff, simple pine and quarry tile decor, woodburner; children welcome, garden tables, open all day. *(Andrew Stone)*

FULBECK   SK9450
Hare & Hounds (01400) 272322
The Green (A607 Leadenham–Grantham); NG32 3JJ Converted 17th-c maltings overlooking attractive village green, modernised linked areas, log fire, highly regarded food from ciabattas and pub favourites up, friendly attentive service, well kept ales such as Brakspears and Marstons Pedigree, affordable wine list, raftered upstairs function room; terrace seating, eight bedrooms in adjacent barn conversion, closed Sun evening. *(David Hunt)*

GAINSBOROUGH   SK8189
Eight Jolly Brewers (01427) 611022
Ship Court, Silver Street; DN21 2DW Small drinkers' pub in former warehouse, eight interesting real ales, traditional cider and plenty of bottled beers, friendly staff and locals, bare brick, more room upstairs and live music Thurs; seats outside, open all day. *(Andrew Stone)*

GRANTHAM   SK9136
Blue Pig (01476) 563704
Vine Street; NG31 6RQ Cosy three-bar Tudor pub, well kept ales and decent reasonably priced pubby food, friendly staff, low beams, panelling, stripped stone and flagstones, open fire; dogs welcome; tables out behind, open all day. *(Carol and Barry Craddock)*

IRNHAM   TF0226
Griffin (01476) 550201
Bulby Road; NG33 4JG Welcoming old stone-built pub in nice village setting, generous home-made food (not Sun evening), ales such as Navigation and Oakham, three rooms (two for dining), log fires; background music; children welcome, no dogs inside (there's a resident bassett), classic car meet first Weds of month (spring/summer), four comfortable bedrooms, closed Mon, Tues. *(Ruth May)*

KIRKBY ON BAIN   TF2462
★Ebrington Arms (01526) 354560
Main Street; LN10 6YT Popular village pub with good value traditional food (booking advised), half a dozen well kept changing ales and friendly service, beer mats on low 16th-c beams, carpets and banquettes, open fire, restaurant behind; background music, darts; children and dogs welcome, wheelchair access, tables out in front by road, lawn to the side with play equipment, campsite next door, closed Mon lunchtime. *(Andrew Stone)*

LINCOLN   SK9871
Dog & Bone (01522) 522403
John Street; LN2 5BH Comfortable and welcoming backstreet local with well kept Batemans and guests, real cider, good value traditional food (evenings Thurs, Fri, lunchtimes Sat, first and third Sun of month), log fires, various things to look at including collection of valve radios, local artwork and exchange-library of recent fiction; background and live music; dogs welcome (theirs is called Blade), picnic-sets on back terrace, open all day Fri-Sun, from 4.30pm other days. *(Andrew Stone)*

LINCOLN   SK9771
Jolly Brewer (01522) 528583
Broadgate; LN2 5AQ Popular no-frills pub with art deco interior, good choice of well kept ales and ciders, no food; regular live music; back courtyard with covered area, open all day (till 8pm Sun). *(Andrew Stone)*

LINCOLN   SK9771
Strugglers (01522) 535023
Westgate; LN1 3BG Cosily worn-in beer lovers' haunt tucked beneath the castle walls, built in 1841 and once run by the local hangman (note the pub sign); half a dozen or more well kept ales including Bass and Timothy Taylors, bare boards throughout with lots of knick-knacks and pump clips, two open fires (one in back snug); some live acoustic music; no children inside, dogs welcome, steps down to sunny back courtyard with heated canopy, open all day (till 1am Fri, Sat). *(Richard Tilbrook)*

LINCOLN   SK9771
★Victoria (01522) 541000
Union Road; LN1 3BJ Just outside the castle gates, the main draw to this old-fashioned local are the real ales (including Batemans and Castle Rock), foreign draught and bottled beers and real cider; simply furnished tiled front lounge with pictures of Queen Victoria, coal fire, basic lunchtime food, friendly staff and good mix of customers (gets especially

busy lunchtime and later in evening); live music Sat; children and dogs welcome, seats on heated terrace, play area, good castle views, open all day till midnight (1am Fri, Sat). *(Chris Johnson)*

LINCOLN SK9771

Widow Cullens Well (01522) 523020

Steep Hill; just below cathedral; LN2 1LU
Ancient reworked building on two floors, cheap Sam Smiths beers and enjoyable food including children's choices, chatty mix of customers, good service, beams, stone walls and open fire, back extension with namesake well; terrace seating, open all day. *(Anon)*

LINCOLN SK9771

★ **Wig & Mitre** (01522) 535190

Steep Hill; just below cathedral; LN2 1LU
Civilised café-style dining pub with plenty of character and attractive period features over two floors; big-windowed downstairs bar, beams and exposed stone walls, pews and Gothic furniture on oak boards, comfortable sofas in carpeted back area, quieter upstairs dining room with views of castle walls and cathedral, antique prints and caricatures of lawyers/clerics, all-day food from breakfast on including good value set menus and some interesting seasonal dishes, extensive choice of wines by the glass from good list, well kept Everards Tiger and a couple of guests such as Black Sheep and Oakham, good service; children and dogs welcome, open 8am-midnight. *(Mrs Sally Scott, Philip Kingsbury)*

LONG BENNINGTON SK8344

★ **Reindeer** (01400) 281382

Just off A1 N of Grantham – S end of village, opposite school; NG23 5DJ
Intimate atmosphere in attractively traditional low-beamed pub with popular long-serving landlady, consistently good food (fair value considering the quality) from sandwiches up in bar and more formal restaurant, can get very busy so best to book, well kept John Smiths, Timothy Taylors Landlord and one or two guests, nice wines, good friendly service, coal-effect stove in stone fireplace; background music; picnic-sets under parasols in small front courtyard, closed Sun evening, Mon. *(Gordon and Margaret Ormondroyd, M and GR, Brian and Janet Ainscough)*

LONG BENNINGTON SK8344

Royal Oak (01400) 281332

Main Road; just off A1 N of Grantham; NG23 5DJ Popular local with good-sized bar serving well kept Marstons and Mansfield ales, several wines by the glass and good sensibly priced home-made food including

specials, friendly helpful staff; children welcome, seats out in front and in big back garden with play area, path for customers to river, open all day. *(Carol and Barry Craddock)*

LOUTH TF4083

Waggon & Horses (01507) 450364

A157; South Reston; LN11 8JQ
Welcoming roadside pub with good range of reasonably priced home-cooked food including daily specials and Sun carvery, bargain OAP lunch Weds, well kept Batemans and guests, decent wine list, friendly helpful service, comfortable panelled lounge bar with porcelain horse-and-cart models, brassware and collection of old photographs, open fire, well laid-out restaurant (children welcome here), conservatory; pool and darts; garden with play area, camping, open all day from 8.30am (afternoon break Sun). *(Roy and Lindsey Fentiman)*

LOUTH TF3287

Wheatsheaf (01507) 606262

Westgate, near St James Church; LN11 9YD Welcoming traditional 17th-c low-beamed pub, half a dozen well kept ales including Bass, Greene King and Tom Woods, real cider, enjoyable pubby food served by friendly helpful young staff, coal fires in all three bars, old photographs; children welcome, no dogs, tables outside, open all day and can get busy. *(Anne and Ben Smith)*

MARKET RASEN TF1089

Aston Arms (01673) 842313

Market Place; LN8 3HL Popular market-square pub serving generous helpings of inexpensive food, Theakstons, Charles Wells Bombardier and a guest, nice staff, beamed bar, lounge and games area; children and well behaved dogs welcome, side terrace, open all day. *(Phil and Jane Hodson)*

MINTING TF1873

Sebastopol (01507) 578577

Off A158 Lincoln–Horncastle; LN9 5RT
Updated 19th-c red-brick village pub; good attractively presented food from imaginative menu using Lincolnshire suppliers, well kept Batemans and a local guest, decent wines by the glass, friendly staff; charity quiz first Weds of month; children welcome, picnic-sets on front terrace, self-catering barn conversion, closed Sun evening, Mon. *(Anon)*

NORTON DISNEY SK8859

Green Man (01522) 789804

Main Street, off A46 Newark–Lincoln; LN6 9JU Old beamed pub-restaurant in village with opened-up modernised interior; enjoyable reasonably priced food

---

Real ale may be served from handpumps, electric pumps (not just the on-off switches used for keg beer) or – common in Scotland – tall taps called founts (pronounced 'fonts') where a separate pump pushes the beer up under air pressure.

from sandwiches and traditional dishes up
including some interesting specials, bargain
set deal Mon, three well kept changing
ales from central bar, friendly young
staff; fortnightly quiz Fri, TV; tables out
behind, open all day weekends, closed Mon
lunchtime. *(Tony and Maggie Harwood)*

SCAMPTON   SK9579
Dambusters (01522) 731333
High Street; LN1 2SD Welcoming pub
with several beamed rooms around central
bar, masses of interesting Dambusters and
other RAF memorabilia, generous helpings of
reasonably priced straightforward food (not
Sun evening), also home-made chutneys, pâté
and biscuits for sale, five interesting ales
including own microbrews (ceiling covered
in beer mats from past guests), short list of
well chosen wines, pews and chairs around
tables on wood floor, log fire in big two-way
brick fireplace, more formal seating at back;
children and dogs welcome (their black
labrador is Bomber), very near Red Arrows
runway viewpoint, open all day Fri, Sat, till
6pm Sun, closed Mon lunchtime. *(John and
Sylvia Harrop)*

SKILLINGTON   SK8925
Cross Swords (01476) 861132
The Square; NG33 5HB Traditional 19th-c
stone pub on crossroads in delightful village,
welcoming and homely, with good food
cooked by landlord-chef from bar snacks to
restaurant dishes, a couple of changing ales;
background music, no under-10s or dogs;
three annexe bedrooms, closed Sun evening,
Mon lunchtime. *(Andrew Stone)*

SLEAFORD   TF1131
Old Ship (01529) 241400
High Street, Pointon; NG34 0LX
Well looked-after village pub popular with
regulars and passers-by, good reasonably
priced freshly made food from baguettes,
pizzas and pub favourites to more
restauranty choices such as local game,
interesting home-made ice-creams too,
friendly attentive service, Greene King
Old Speckled Hen, restaurant; Weds quiz;
children welcome, dogs at certain times
(best to check), garden picnic-sets and play
area, closed Sun evening, Mon.
(Sam Armitage)

SOUTH RAUCEBY   TF0245
Bustard (01529) 488250
Main Street; NG34 8QG Modernised
19th-c stone-built pub with good food from
varied menu, three well kept ales including
one badged for them from Batemans, plenty
of wines by the glass, friendly efficient staff,
flagstoned bar with log fire, steps up to
bare-stone restaurant (former stables); quiz
second Weds of month, live jazz third and last
Weds; children welcome, attractive sheltered
garden, open all day Sat, closed Sun evening,
Mon. *(John Harris)*

SPALDING   TF2422
Priors Oven 07972 192750
Sheep Market; PE11 1BH Friendly
micropub in ancient building (former
bakery), small octagonal room with vaulted
ceiling, island bar serving up to six well kept
changing ales such as Austendyke, Oakham
and Tydd Steam, local ciders and maybe
english wines, no food, spiral stairs up to
comfortable lounge with period fireplace;
open all day. *(Anon)*

STAMFORD   TF0207
All Saints Brewery – Melbourn Brothers (01780) 7521865
All Saints Street; PE9 2PA Well reworked
old building (core is a medieval hall) with
warren of rooms on three floors; upstairs
bar serving bottled fruit beers from adjacent
early 19th-c brewery and low-priced Sam
Smiths on handpump, enjoyable food from
pub favourites up including set deals and
good vegetarian options, friendly staff,
ground-floor dining area with log fire and
woodburner, top floor with leather sofas and
wing chairs; children and dogs welcome,
picnic-sets in cobbled courtyard, brewery
tours, open all day. *(John Harris)*

STAMFORD   TF0207
★ Crown (01780) 763136
All Saints Place; PE9 2AG Substantial
well modernised stone-built hotel with
emphasis on good seasonal country cooking
using local produce (some from their own
farm), friendly helpful staff, well kept ales
such as Fullers London Pride, Oakham and
Timothy Taylors Landlord, lots of wines
by the glass and decent coffee, spacious
main bar with long leather-cushioned
counter, substantial pillars, step up to more
traditional flagstoned area with stripped
stone and armchairs, restaurant; background
music, free wi-fi; children and dogs welcome,
seats in back courtyard, 28 comfortable
bedrooms (some in separate townhouse),
good breakfast, open all day, food all day
weekends; ongoing refurbishment so may
be changes. *(John Harris, Andrew Stone)*

STAMFORD   TF0207
Jolly Brewer (01780) 755141
Foundry Road; PE9 2PP Welcoming
19th-c stone-built pub with half a dozen well
kept ales, traditional ciders/perries and wide
range of interesting whiskies (some from
india and japan), low-priced simple food,
regular beer festivals and quiz/curry nights,
nice open fire; sports TV, pool, darts and
other games; open all day. *(Andrew Stone)*

SURFLEET   TF2528
Mermaid (01775) 680275
*B1356 (Gosberton Road), just off A16
N of Spalding; PE11 4AB* Welcoming and
traditional with two high-ceilinged carpeted
rooms, huge sash windows, banquettes,

captain's chairs and spindlebacks, Adnams and a couple of guests, good choice of fairly standard popular food including a monthly themed night, friendly attentive service, restaurant; background music; pretty terraced garden with bar and seats under thatched parasols, children's play area walled from River Glen, moorings, four bedrooms, open all day Sat in summer, closed Sun evening. *(Michael and Jenny Back and others)*

TATTERSHALL THORPE   TF2159
Blue Bell   (01526) 342206
Thorpe Road; B1192 Coningsby–Woodhall Spa; LN4 4PE Ancient low-beamed pub (said to date from the 13th c) with friendly cosy atmosphere, RAF memorabilia including airmen's signatures on the ceiling (pub was used by the Dambusters), big open fire, three well kept ales such as local Horncastle, Thwaites Lancaster Bomber and Tom Woods Bomber County, some nice wines and enjoyable well priced pubby food, small dining room; garden tables, bedrooms, closed Sun evening (in winter), Mon. *(Barry Collett)*

TETFORD   TF3374
White Hart   (01507) 533255
East Road, off A158 E of Horncastle; LN9 6QQ Friendly bay-windowed village pub dating from the 16th c, Brains Rev James and a couple of guests, good value generous pubby food, pleasant inglenook bar with old-fashioned curved-back settles and slabby elm tables on red tiles, other areas including pool room; regular live music; children and dogs welcome, sheltered back lawn with guinea pigs and rabbits, pretty countryside, bedrooms, closed Mon. *(Anne and Ben Smith)*

THEDDLETHORPE ALL SAINTS   TF4787
★ Kings Head   (01507) 339798
Pub signposted off A1031 N of Maplethorpe; Mill Road; LN12 1PB Long 16th-c thatched pub with cheerful helpful landlord; carpeted two-room front lounge with very low ceiling, brass platters on timbered walls, antique dining chairs and tables, easy chairs by log fire, central bar (more low beams) with well kept ales such as Batemans and a local cider, coal fire with side oven, shelves of books, stuffed owls and country pictures, long dining room, good local food from sandwiches and sharing plates to steaks and fresh Grimsby fish, Sun carvery; one or two picnic-sets in front area, more on lawn, open all day Sat, closed Sun evening, Mon. *(Roy and Lindsey Fentiman)*

THREEKINGHAM   TF0836
Three Kings   (01529) 240249
Just off A52 12 miles E of Grantham; Saltersway; NG34 0AU Big entrance hall (former coaching inn), comfortable beamed lounge with fire and pubby furniture, panelled restaurant plus bigger dining/function room, good choice of enjoyable home-made food including Thurs steak night, Bass, Timothy Taylors Landlord and guests, friendly efficient staff; children and dogs (in bar) welcome, sunny paved terrace and small lawned area, various car club meetings, closed Mon. *(Anon)*

WAINFLEET   TF5058
★ Batemans Brewery   (01754) 882009
Mill Lane, off A52 via B1195; PE24 4JE Circular bar in brewery's ivy-covered windmill tower, Batemans ales in top condition, czech and belgian beers on tap too, ground-floor dining area with cheap food including baguettes and a few pubby dishes, plenty of old pub games (more outside), lots of brewery memorabilia and plenty for families to enjoy; no dogs inside, entertaining brewery tours and shop, tables on terrace and grass, open 11.30am-4pm (2.30pm in winter), closed Mon, Tues. *(Carol and Barry Craddock)*

WEST DEEPING   TF1009
Red Lion   (01778) 347190
King Street; PE6 9HP Welcoming stone-built pub under friendly family management; long low-beamed bar, four well kept usually local beers such as Hopshackle, popular freshly made food (not Sun evening) from baguettes up, weekday evening meal deal, back dining extension, stripped stone and open fire; some live music including monthly folk club, free wi-fi; children welcome, no dogs inside, tables in back garden with terrace and fenced play area, vintage car/motorcycle meetings, open all day Sat, till 4pm Sun, closed Mon. *(Howard and Margaret Buchanan)*

WITHAM ON THE HILL   TF0516
Six Bells   (01778) 590360
Village signed from A6121, SW of Bourne; PE10 0JH Well restored Edwardian stone inn, smart comfortable bar with woodburner, enjoyable food (not Sun evening) including wood-fired pizzas, well kept Bass and guests, good friendly service; children and dogs (in bar) welcome, picnic-sets on front terrace, nice village, three well appointed bedrooms, good breakfast, closed Sun evening, Mon. *(John Harris)*

WOODHALL SPA   TF1963
Village Limits   (01526) 353312
Stixwould Road; LN10 6UJ Modernised country pub with good local food cooked by landlord-chef, well kept ales such as Batemans and Tom Woods, friendly service, smallish beamed bar with banquettes, dining room, wood-strip floors and light wood furniture; children welcome, nine courtyard bedrooms, closed Mon lunchtime. *(David H Bennett)*

Norfolk

BAWBURGH

TG1508 Map 5

Kings Head 🍷🍺

(01603) 744977 – www.kingshead-bawburgh.co.uk

Harts Lane; A47 just W of Norwich then B1108; NR9 3LS

Busy, small-roomed pub with five real ales, good wines by the glass, interesting food and friendly service

Particularly well run by friendly, professional people and with a buoyant, cheerful atmosphere, this is a 17th-c pub that our readers enjoy unanimously. The small rooms have plenty of low beams and standing timbers, leather sofas and an attractive assortment of old dining chairs and tables on wood-strip floors; also, a knocked-through open fire and a couple of woodburning stoves in the restaurant areas. Adnams Bitter, Tring Moongazer and Woodfordes Wherry plus two guest beers on handpump, ten wines by the glass and 12 malt whiskies; service is friendly and helpful. Background music, TV and board games. There are seats in the garden and the pub is opposite a little green.

🍴 High quality food from an interesting menu includes sandwiches, pigeon breast with salted popcorn, sweetcorn purée, toasted seeds and young watercress, king scallops with pork belly, black pudding and apple purée, sharing platters, steak burger with skin-on chips and red cabbage coleslaw, crispy pork belly, pancetta and mixed bean broth with broccoli, smoked paprika and tomato ragoût, chicken with rösti potato, wild mushrooms, leeks and rosemary fricassée and truffle oil, and puddings such as hot banoffi fondant with caramel, caramelised banana and chocolate 'soil' and apple terrine with blackberry purée, cider jelly and vanilla cream. *Benchmark main dish: ham terrine with duck egg, pineapple relish and chips £11.00. Two-course evening meal £20.50.*

Free house ~ Licensee Anton Wimmer ~ Real ale ~ Open 11-11; 11-10.30 Sun; closed Sun evening in winter ~ Bar food 12-2, 5.30-9; 12-3, 6-9 Sun; no food Sun evenings Nov-Mar ~ Restaurant ~ Children welcome ~ Dogs allowed in bar ~ Wi-fi ~ Bedrooms: /£100
Recommended by David Jackman, Gordon and Margaret Ormondroyd, John Millwood, Tina and David Woods-Taylor

BURSTON

TM1383 Map 5

Crown 🍺

(01379) 741257 – www.burstoncrown.com

Village signposted off A140 N of Scole; Mill Road; IP22 5TW

Friendly, relaxed village pub usefully open all day, with a warm welcome, real ales and well liked bar food

'This is all that a good pub should be,' says one of our readers – and we agree. Locals tend to gather in an area by the bar counter where they serve Adnams Southwold and Ghost Ship and guests such as Green Jack Orange Wheat Beer and Greene King Suffolk Porter on handpump or tapped from the cask, a farm cider and eight wines by the glass. In cold weather, the best place to sit is the heavily beamed, quarry-tiled bar room with its comfortably cushioned sofas in front of a woodburning stove in a huge brick fireplace; there are also stools by a low chunky wooden table; newspapers and magazines. The public bar on the left has a nice long table and panelled settle on an old brick floor in one alcove, a pool table, and more tables and chairs towards the back near the dartboard. Both rooms are hung with paintings by local artists; background music and board games. The simply furnished, beamed dining room has another big brick fireplace. Outside, there's a smokers' shelter, seats and tables on a terrace and in the secluded garden where there's a play area for children.

Popular food includes sandwiches, chicken liver parfait with red onion marmalade, scallops with chorizo, lentil and chilli burger with spiced tomato relish, a platter of local meats and cheeses, ham and free-range eggs, beer-battered fish and chips, lasagne, diced chicken in peanut and pepper sauce, venison vindaloo, and puddings such as sticky toffee pudding with butterscotch sauce and plum tarte tatin. *Benchmark main dish: steak, mushroom and Guinness pie £12.50. Two-course evening meal £19.50.*

Free house ~ Licensees Bev and Steve Kembery ~ Real ale ~ Open 12-11; 12-10.30 Sun ~ Bar food 12 (10.30 Sat)-2, 6.30-9; 12-4 Sun; not Mon, evening Sun ~ Restaurant ~ Children welcome ~ Dogs allowed in bar ~ Wi-fi ~ Live music Thurs 8.30, every second Sun from 5 *Recommended by Philip and Susan Philcox, Ruth May*

CASTLE ACRE   TF8115 Map 8
Ostrich

(01760) 755398 – www.ostrichcastleacre.com
Stocks Green; PE32 2AE

Friendly old village pub with original features, fine old fireplaces, real ales and tasty food; bedrooms

If you're walking the ancient Peddars Way, why not stop at this characterful 16th-c inn for refreshment? The L-shaped, low-ceilinged front bar (on two levels) has a woodburning stove in a huge old fireplace, lots of wheelback chairs and cushioned pews around pubby tables on a wood-strip floor and gold patterned wallpaper; it's a step up to an area in front of the bar counter where there are similar seats and tables and a log fire in a brick fireplace. Do look out for the original masonry, beams and trusses. Greene King Abbot, IPA, Old Speckled Hen and a beer named for the pub on handpump, around a dozen wines by the glass and several malt whiskies. There's a separate dining room with another brick fireplace. The sheltered garden has picnic-sets under parasols and the inn faces the tree-lined village green; nearby are the remains of a Norman castle and a Cluniac monastery.

Tasty food includes lunchtime sandwiches, home-cured salmon gravadlax, pigeon with roasted beetroot, spinach, chopped hazelnuts and malbec jus, bubble and squeak with gruyère cheese, a free-range egg and parsley sauce, toad in the hole with gravy in a giant yorkshire pudding, steak burger with toppings and chips, beef in ale casserole, confit duck leg with parmentier potatoes, bass fillet on peppers and onions cooked in a rich stock, and puddings. *Benchmark main dish: steak burger with toppings and chips £13.95. Two-course evening meal £19.50.*

Greene King ~ Tenant Tiffany Turner ~ Real ale ~ Open 10am-11pm; 10am-midnight Sat ~ Bar food 12-3, 6-9 ~ Restaurant ~ Children welcome ~ Dogs allowed in bar ~ Wi-fi ~ Bedrooms: £75/£85 *Recommended by Graham and Elizabeth Hargreaves*

CLEY-NEXT-THE-SEA   TG0443 Map 8

George ♀ ⊨

(01263) 740652 – www.thegeorgehotelatcley.co.uk

Off A149 W of Sheringham; High Street; NR25 7RN

Pubby bar and two dining rooms in sizeable inn with real ales, good choice of wines and popular food; bedrooms

This is a warm and comfortable place to stay; some rooms overlook the salt marshes, and the bird-watching is very special. The little bar is the first point of call: a long leather settle and sturdy dark wooden chairs by a couple of green-topped tables on carpeting, photographs of Norfolk wherries and other local scenes on cream walls, a huge candle in a big glass jar on one window sill, a table of newspapers and a stained-glass window depicting St George and the dragon. Greene King Abbot, Woodfordes Wherry, Yetmans Red and a guest beer on handpump and 13 wines by the glass. The dining rooms are similarly furnished with pale wooden cushioned chairs and tables, and evening candlelight. Across a lane is a small garden with tables and seats. This is a charming, peaceful brick and flint village.

 As well as a brunch menu (11.30-5.30), food includes smoked haddock chowder, prawn cocktail with bloody mary sorbet, trio of sausages with mustard mash, onion rings and gravy, butternut squash, feta, almond and spinach filo strudel with herb butter sauce, burger with toppings, relish and fries, local plaice with smoked parsnip purée, apples, girolles and sage, venison casserole, and puddings such as dark chocolate and orange tart and sticky toffee pudding. *Benchmark main dish: beer-battered haddock and chips £12.95. Two-course evening meal £21.00.*

Free house ~ Licensee Stephen Cleeve ~ Real ale ~ Open 11-11 ~ Bar food 12-9; 12-2.30, 6-9 (8.30 Sun) in winter ~ Restaurant ~ Children welcome ~ Dogs allowed in bar and bedrooms ~ Wi-fi ~ Bedrooms: /£110 *Recommended by Tracey and Stephen Groves, Dennis and Doreen Haward*

EAST RUDHAM   TF8228 Map 8

Crown 🍽 ♀ ⊨

(01485) 528530 – www.crowninnnorfolk.co.uk

A148 W of Fakenham; The Green; PE31 8RD

Neat and smart with attractive open-plan seating areas, cosy back sitting room, very good food, real ales and friendly atmosphere; bedrooms

Open-plan and contemporary in design, this is a stylish place with several distinct, easy-going seating areas. One end of the main room has a log fire flanked by a grandfather clock and bookshelves, with wood and brown leather dining chairs around a mix of tables (including a huge round one) and rugs on stripped floorboards. The other end is slightly more informal, with another bookshelf beside a second fireplace, a pubby part with white-painted, cushioned built-in seats, and high chairs against the handsomely slate-topped counter where they keep Adnams Broadside, Black Sheep, Woodfordes Wherry and a changing guest on handpump and 20 wines by the glass. There's also a cosy lower area to the back of the building with comfortable leather sofas and armchairs and a flat-screen TV, as well as an upstairs dining room with a high-pitched ceiling and woodburning stove. The front gravelled terrace has seats under parasols. The bedrooms are airy and comfortable and the breakfasts hearty.

 Using local, seasonal produce, the highly rewarding food includes sandwiches, salt and pepper tempura squid, crispy ham hock with an egg, charred pineapple and merlot vinegar, burger with toppings, chunky chips and onion rings, wild mushroom linguine, prawn curry, chicken breast with sweetcorn velouté, crispy bacon and rainbow chard, bass niçoise with fennel cream, capers and olives, and puddings. *Benchmark main dish: roast monkfish with pea, broad bean and asparagus risotto £17.95. Two-course evening meal £21.00.*

Free house ~ Licensee Tristram McEwen ~ Real ale ~ Open 11-11; 11am-midnight Sat ~ Bar food 12-2.30, 6-9 (9.30 Sat); 12-8 Sun ~ Children welcome ~ Dogs welcome ~ Wi-fi ~ Bedrooms: /£90 *Recommended by Edward Mirzoeff, Tracey and Stephen Groves, Ruth May, Derek and Sylvia Stephenson*

GREAT BIRCHAM
Kings Head 🛏

TF7632   Map 8

(01485) 578265 – www.thekingsheadhotel.co.uk

B1155, S end of village (called and signed Bircham locally); PE31 6RJ

Cheerful little bar in relaxed hotel, comfortable seating areas, four real ales, enjoyable food and seats outside; bedrooms

The comfortable bedrooms in this handsome Edwardian hotel make a very good base for exploring the area, and the breakfasts are highly rated. The contemporary and attractive small bar is favoured by locals and those just wanting a chat and a pint; they keep up to four real ales on handpump: Adnams Broadside, Woodfordes Wherry and a couple of quickly changing guest beers. Also, 15 good wines by the glass, 18 malt whiskies and a fine choice of more than 50 gins. There are comfortable sofas and tub chairs, a few high chairs against the counter and a log fire, and also lounge areas and a light and airy modern restaurant. Staff are friendly and helpful. Tables and chairs outside, both front and back, have country views.

As well as serving breakfasts (7.30-10am; from 8am at weekends), the varied menu using local ingredients includes sandwiches, crab with caper and potato salad and lemon and chive mayonnaise, goats cheese salad with roasted beetroot and orange with citrus dressing, mushroom risotto, chicken breast with chicken mousse, oriental sesame beef broth, crisp vegetables and glass noodles, confit lamb with caramelised onions, glazed vegetables and rosemary lamb jus, black bream with spicy passata and sautéed potatoes, and puddings. *Benchmark main dish: beer-battered cod with chips and minted ham and pease pudding £11.25. Two-course evening meal £21.00.*

Free house ~ Licensee Craig Jackson ~ Real ale ~ Open 7am-11pm; 7am-midnight Sat ~ Bar food 12-2 (3 Sun), 6-9 ~ Restaurant ~ Children welcome ~ Dogs welcome ~ Wi-fi ~ Bedrooms: £105/£115 *Recommended by Derek Stafford, Mrs V Moody, Ruth May*

GREAT MASSINGHAM
Dabbling Duck 🍽⭐ 🍺

TF7922   Map 8

(01485) 520827 – www.thedabblingduck.co.uk

Off A148 King's Lynn–Fakenham; Abbey Road; PE32 2HN

Unassuming from the outside but with a friendly atmosphere, character bars and warm fires, real ales and interesting food; comfortable bedrooms

There's a good bustling atmosphere and quite a choice of drinks and imaginative food served by friendly staff in this attractively set pub. The relaxed bars have leather sofas and armchairs by woodburning stoves (three in all), a mix of antique wooden dining tables and chairs on flagstones or stripped wooden floors, a very high-backed settle, 18th- and 19th-c quirky prints and cartoons, and plenty of beams and standing timbers. At the back of the pub is the Blenheim room, just right for a private group, and there's also a candlelit dining room. Adnams Broadside, Beeston Worth the Wait, Woodfordes Wherry and a guest such as Belhaven Grand Slam on handpump and nine wines by the glass, served from a bar counter made of great slabs of polished tree trunk; background music, TV, darts and board games. Tables and chairs on a front terrace overlook the sizeable village green with its big duck ponds, and there are more seats and a play area in the enclosed back garden. The bedrooms are named after famous local sportsmen and airmen from the World War II air base in Massingham. Wheelchair access.

From a seasonal and interesting menu, the attractively presented food includes sandwiches, duck liver pâté with cranberries and pickled walnuts, local mussels with beer and crème fraîche, truffled macaroni with brie custard and tomato fondue, venison sausages with pickled blueberries and bitter chocolate, local quail with baby leeks, brown bread sauce and puffed rice, beer-cured sea trout with dill and crab sauce and sea vegetables, and puddings. *Benchmark main dish: beer-battered fish and chips £13.00. Two-course evening meal £20.00.*

Free house ~ Licensee Dominic Symington ~ Real ale ~ Open 12-11; 12-10.30 Sun ~ Bar food 12-2.30, 6.30-9 (9.30 Fri, Sat) ~ Restaurant ~ Children welcome ~ Dogs allowed in bar and bedrooms ~ Wi-fi ~ Bedrooms: £65/£90 *Recommended by Michael Sargent, Mike and Shelley Woodroffe, R T and J C Moggridge, M and GR, Simon and Mandy King*

HOLKHAM
Victoria ♀ ⇔
TF8943 Map 8

(01328) 711008 – www.victoriaatholkham.co.uk
A149 near Holkham Hall; NR23 1RG

Handsome, smart inn with pubby bar, plenty of character dining space, thoughtful choice of drinks, friendly staff and enjoyable food; bedrooms

In summer, if you're fresh off the beach (the vast stretch of Holkham Sands backed by pine woods is just minutes away), you could head here for the popular seafood shack and separate bar, both in an outside seating area. But in cooler weather too, this upmarket yet informal small hotel (owned by the Holkham Estate) is just as busy. The proper bare-boards bar to the left is popular with locals, while a spreading dining and sitting area has an appealing variety of antique-style dining chairs and tables on rugs and stripped floorboards, antlers and antique guns, and sofas by a big log fire. There's also a small drawing room to the right of the main entrance (for guests only) with homely furniture, an open fire and an honesty bar. Adnams Broadside and Ghost Ship and Woodfordes Wherry on handpump, 20 wines by the glass, good coffee and efficient, polite service. An airy conservatory dining room, decorated in pale beige, leads out to a back courtyard with green-painted furniture. Some of the stylish bedrooms have views of the sea and breakfasts are good and generous.

Using Estate and other local produce, the very good food is served all day from 8am for breakfast: ham hock terrine with chutney, lobster cocktail, risotto primavera (broad beans, peas, asparagus, parmesan), monkfish with parma ham, saffron potatoes and pepperonata, lambs liver, bacon and onions, pheasant breast with blackberries and fondant potato, bavette steak with caramelised shallots and chips, and puddings such as chocolate torte and pistachio praline and tarte au citron. *Benchmark main dish: Estate venison burger £12.75. Two-course evening meal £25.00.*

Free house ~ Licensee Lord Coke ~ Real ale ~ Open 8am-11pm; 8am-10.30pm Sun ~ Bar food 8am-9pm ~ Restaurant ~ Children welcome ~ Dogs welcome ~ Wi-fi ~ Bedrooms: £120/£180 *Recommended by Peter Sutton, Tracey and Stephen Groves*

KING'S LYNN   TF6119   Map 8

Bank House

(01553) 660492 – www.thebankhouse.co.uk

*Kings Staithe Square via Boat Street and along the quay in one-way system;
PE30 1RD*

**Georgian bar-brasserie with plenty of history and character, airy
rooms, real ales and imaginative food from breakfast onwards;
bedrooms**

Never people to rest on their laurels, the professional, friendly licensees here continue to add thoughtful changes to the stylish rooms. A log fire has been opened up (and fender seating installed) in the elegant bar with its sofas and armchairs – and a room they call the Boardroom has been redecorated. A new outside area has been created in the front courtyard, flanked by magnificent wrought-iron gates, with firepits for warmth on chillier evenings, and the riverside terrace (lovely sunsets) now has an open-air bar and smart new furniture. The restaurant has fine antique chairs and tables on bare boards, an airy brasserie has sofas and armchairs around low tables and a big brick fireplace, and two other areas (one with fine panelling, one with a half-size billiards table) have more open fires. The atmosphere throughout is bustling and welcoming, with customers popping in and out all day; service is helpful and courteous. Adnams Southwold, Sharps Doom Bar and Woodfordes Wherry on handpump, nine wines by the glass, farm cider and cocktails; background music. This is a splendid quayside spot and the Corn Exchange theatre and arts centre is just five minutes away. Sister pub is the Rose & Crown in Snettisham.

 Top quality food using the best local game, seafood and other produce includes sandwiches (not evenings), potted smoked salmon with melba toast, pear and walnut tart with blue cheese bonbon and pomegranate molasses dressing, sharing platters, arrabiata risotto with garlic bread, spicy lamb shank with aloo gobi and cashew and spring onion rice, monkfish wrapped in streaky bacon with red lentil and chorizo stew, and puddings such as baked vanilla cheesecake with apricot compote and white chocolate fondant with white chocolate ice-cream; they also offer Sunday brunch and a popular carve-your-own Sunday roast. *Benchmark main dish: steak burger with toppings, barbecue sauce and fries £11.50. Two-course evening meal £20.00.*

Free house ~ Licensee Anthony Goodrich ~ Real ale ~ Open 11-11; 11-midnight Fri, Sat; 11-10.30 Sun ~ Bar food 7.30am-9pm (9.30pm Fri, Sat) ~ Restaurant ~ Children welcome ~ Dogs allowed in bar ~ Wi-fi ~ Live jazz monthly Sun 4-7pm ~ Bedrooms: £90/£120
Recommended by John Wooll, R C Vincent

LARLING   TL9889   Map 5

Angel

(01953) 717963 – www.angel-larling.co.uk

*From A11 Thetford–Attleborough, take B1111 turn-off and follow pub signs;
NR16 2QU*

**Good-natured chatty atmosphere in busy pub with several real ales
and tasty bar food; bedrooms**

With lots of surrounding walks and good bird-watching, this 17th-c coaching inn is particularly busy in good weather. The comfortable 1930s-style lounge on the right has squared panelling, cushioned wheelback chairs, a nice long cushioned, panelled corner settle and some good solid tables for eating; plus, a collection of whisky-water jugs on a delft shelf over the big brick fireplace, a woodburning stove, a couple of copper kettles and some hunting prints. The same friendly family have run the inn since 1913 and they still have the original visitors' books from 1897 to 1909. Adnams Southwold and four guests such as Crouch Vale Brewers Gold, Elgoods Black Dog, Hop Back Summer Lightning and Orkney Raven Ale on handpump, 100 malt whiskies and ten wines by the glass; they hold an August beer festival with more than 100 real ales and ciders, live music and a barbecue. The quarry-tiled black-beamed public bar has a good local feel, with darts, juke box, games machine, board games and background music. There's a neat grass area behind the car park with picnic-sets around a big fairy-lit apple tree and a fenced play area. The four-acre meadow is a caravan and camping site from March to October.

Tasty food includes sandwiches and paninis, creamy mushroom pot, prawn cocktail, chicken caesar salad, burgers with toppings and chips, sausage, egg and chips, creamy salmon and prawn pasta, stilton and mushroom bake, barbecue rack of ribs, smoked haddock provençale, steaks with a choice of sauces, and puddings such as chocolate fudge cake and treacle and ginger sponge. *Benchmark main dish: steak and kidney pie £11.95. Two-course evening meal £16.00.*

Free house ~ Licensee Andrew Stammers ~ Real ale ~ Open 10am-11pm ~ Bar food 12-9.30 (10 Fri, Sat) ~ Restaurant ~ Children welcome ~ Wi-fi ~ Bedrooms: £50/£80
Recommended by Alex and Hazel Evans, Hilary and Neil Christopher, Andrew Stone

LETHERINGSETT
TG0638   Map 8

Kings Head 🛏

(01263) 712691 – www.kingsheadnorfolk.co.uk
A148 (Holt Road) W of Holt; NR25 7AR

Civilised manor house with character bars and dining areas, good choice of drinks, interesting food, friendly staff and seats in garden; bedrooms

There's plenty of character and a quietly civilised atmosphere in this country-house-style inn. The small bar to the right of the main door has dining chairs around scrubbed wooden tables, bookshelves beside a black fireplace and a flat-screen TV; the main bar, to the left, has leather armchairs and sofas, rugs on quarry tiles, hunting and coaching prints on mushroom-painted walls, daily papers and an open fire. Adnams Ghost Ship, Norfolk Brewhouse Moon Gazer Amber Ale and Woodfordes Wherry on handpump and plenty of wines by the glass served by friendly helpful young staff. The partly skylit, bare-boards dining room has scatter cushions on built-in wall seating, all manner of dining chairs around wooden tables, farm tools on cream-painted flint and cob walls and books on shelves. A back area, under a partly pitched ceiling with painted rafters, has more comfortable leather sofas and armchairs; background music. Outside at the front are picnic-sets under parasols with more on a side lawn. Bedrooms are up to date and comfortable.

Interesting food using local, seasonal ingredients includes lunchtime sandwiches, game terrine with sweet onion jam, fricassée of wild mushrooms and blue cheese, burger with toppings and chips, butternut squash pasta with parmesan cream sauce, beer-battered haddock and chips, chicken schnitzel with pink peppercorn sauce, and puddings such as white chocolate cheesecake with berry compote and sticky toffee pudding with butterscotch sauce. *Benchmark main dish: fish pie £13.95. Two-course evening meal £20.50.*

Free house ~ Licensee Phil Parker ~ Real ale ~ Open 11-11 ~ Bar food 12-2.30, 6.30-8.30 (9 Fri, Sat); 12-7.30 Sun; maybe all day during school holidays ~ Children welcome ~ Dogs welcome ~ Wi-fi ~ Bedrooms: /£110 *Recommended by Tracey and Stephen Groves, Dr Simon Innes, Anne and Ben Smith*

MORSTON
Anchor ⭐🍷
TG0043 Map 8

(01263) 741392 – www.morstonanchor.co.uk

A149 Salthouse–Stiffkey; The Street; NR2 7AA

Quite a choice of rooms filled with bric-a-brac and prints, real ales and some sort of food all day

Our readers thoroughly enjoy their visits to this bustling, friendly pub – all helped by the welcoming landlord and his young, enthusiastic staff. Three traditional rooms on the right have straightforward seats and tables on original wooden floors, coal fires, local 1950s beach photographs and lots of prints and bric-a-brac. Adnams Lighthouse, local Winters Golden and Woodfordes Wherry on handpump, 20 wines by the glass; background music, darts and board games. The contemporary airy extension on the left, with comfortable benches and tables, leads into the more formal restaurant where local art is displayed on the walls. You can sit outside at the front of the building. If parking is tricky at the pub, there's an overflow around the corner off-road and a National Trust car park five minutes' walk away. The surrounding area is wonderful for bird-watching and walking, and you can book seal-spotting trips here.

Using local produce, the very good food includes sandwiches, twice-baked cheese and spring onion soufflé with smoked haddock cream, scallops with celeriac and tonka bean purée, pancetta crisp and chive and garlic oil, angus rib burger with toppings, chilli and red onion jam, burger sauce and triple-cooked chips, mushrooms on toasted sourdough with hollandaise and a duck egg, fillet of line-caught pollock with lemon beurre blanc and pickled walnuts, and puddings such as hazelnut crème brûlée with cornflake ice-cream and sticky toffee pudding with salt caramel sauce and banoffi ice-cream; they usually offer a two-course set menu. *Benchmark main dish: beer-battered fresh fish of the day with triple-cooked chips £12.95. Two-course evening meal £18.00.*

Free house ~ Licensees Harry Farrow and Rowan Glennie ~ Real ale ~ Open 9am-11pm; 9am-10pm Sun; closed Sun evening Jan-Mar ~ Bar food 12-3, 6-9 ~ Restaurant ~ Children welcome ~ Dogs allowed in bar ~ Wi-fi *Recommended by David Carr, Roy Hoing, Peter Meister, Brian Glozier, Derek and Sylvia Stephenson*

NORTH CREAKE
Jolly Farmers
TF8538 Map 8

(01328) 738185 – www.jollyfarmersnorfolk.co.uk

Burnham Road; NR21 9JW

Friendly village local with three cosy rooms, open fires and woodburners, well liked food and several real ales

In a charming village, this well run former coaching inn is popular with both locals and visitors. Of the three cosy and relaxed rooms, the main bar has a large open fire in a brick fireplace, a mix of pine farmhouse and high-backed leather dining chairs around scrubbed pine tables on quarry tiles and pale yellow walls. Beside the wooden bar counter are some high bar chairs, and they keep Woodfordes Nelsons Revenge and Wherry tapped from the cask, ten wines by the glass and a dozen malt whiskies; service is helpful and friendly. There's also a cabinet of model cars. A smaller bar has pews and a woodburning stove, while the red-walled dining room has similar furniture to the bar and another woodburner. There are seats outside on the terrace.

Good food includes sandwiches, pear and stilton salad with caramelised walnuts, pigeon and bacon salad with a sweet dressing, home-roasted honey ham and eggs, moules frites, stilton macaroni with walnuts and tomato sauce, lambs liver and bacon in red wine gravy, prawn and coconut curry, local partridge filled with cranberry stuffing with gravy, and puddings such as dark chocolate, cherry and cherry wine tart and whisky and banana flummery. *Benchmark main dish: slow-braised lamb breast with mint and redcurrant glaze £13.50. Two-course evening meal £19.00.*

Free house ~ Licensees Adrian and Heather Sanders ~ Real ale ~ Open 12-2.30, 7-11; 12-7 Sun; closed Mon, Tues ~ Bar food 12-2, 7-9; 12-5.30 Sun ~ Children welcome ~ Dogs allowed in bar *Recommended by Linda Miller and Derek Greentree, Philip and Susan Philcox, Christopher and Elise Way*

NORWICH
TG2109   Map 5

Fat Cat 🍺

(01603) 624364 – www.fatcatpub.co.uk
West End Street; NR2 4NA

A place of pilgrimage for beer lovers and open all day; lunchtime rolls and pies

'Why oh why did I take the car?' asked one reader regretfully after a visit to this cheerful and lively pub. Offering an extraordinary range of up to 32 quickly changing ales, it's the sort of place you want to linger as the knowledgeable landlord and his helpful staff guide you through the choices. On handpump or tapped from the cask in a stillroom behind the bar – big windows reveal all – are their own beers (Fat Cat Bitter, Hell Cat, Honey Ale, Marmalade Cat and Wild Cat), as well as Crouch Vale Yakima Gold, Fullers ESB, Oakham Bishops Farewell, Timothy Taylors Landlord – and many more choices from across the country. You'll also find imported draught beers and lagers, over 50 bottled beers from around the world and 20 ciders and perries. The no-nonsense furnishings include plain scrubbed pine tables and simple solid seats, lots of brewery memorabilia, bric-a-brac and stained glass. There are tables outside.

🍴 Bar food consists of rolls and good pies at lunchtime (not Sunday).

Own brew ~ Licensee Colin Keatley ~ Real ale ~ No credit cards ~ Open 12-11 (midnight Fri); 11-midnight Sat ~ Bar food filled rolls available until sold out; not Sun ~ Children allowed until 6pm ~ Dogs allowed in bar ~ Wi-fi *Recommended by David Carr, Edward May, Mike Swan*

OXBOROUGH
TF7401   Map 5

Bedingfeld Arms 🛏

(01366) 328300 – www.bedingfeldarms.co.uk
Near church; PE33 9PS

Attractively furnished Georgian inn with restful rooms, thoughtful choice of drinks, enjoyable food and good service; lovely bedrooms

Peacefully set opposite Oxburgh Hall (National Trust), this is a late 18th-c coaching inn that's been comfortably refurbished by the owners. The relaxed, wood-floored bar has green leather chesterfields, leather tub chairs and window seats around tables of varying heights, an open fire in a marble fireplace with a large gilt mirror above, fresh flowers and candles, and high chairs against the long bar counter. The airy dining room, with more fresh flowers and candles, is furnished with high-backed wooden and cushioned chairs around antique tables, wall seating with scatter cushions, flower prints on pale grey walls and pretty window blinds. Adnams Broadside, Wolf Lupus Lupus and Woodfordes Wherry on handpump and ten wines by the glass served by courteous staff; TV for major sporting events, background music. The garden and terrace have plenty of picnic-sets under parasols. This is a lovely place to stay with four bedrooms in the inn and five in the coach house annexe; breakfasts are extremely good. The village green is opposite and there are good surrounding walks and cycling routes.

Using lamb and game from their farm, some home-grown vegetables and other local, seasonal produce, the highly thought-of food includes lunchtime sandwiches, duck spring roll with red thai dressing, mozzarella and ratatouille roulade with pesto dressing, beef or chicken burger with toppings, coleslaw and chips, chicken breast stuffed with mango and wrapped in filo pastry with caramelised apple sauce, and puddings such as dark chocolate brownie with peanut brittle and banana jam and treacle tart with orange sauce and clotted cream. *Benchmark main dish: king prawn, chilli garlic and spinach linguine £14.95. Two-course evening meal £18.00.*

Free house ~ Licensees Stephen and Catherine Parker ~ Real ale ~ Open 11-11; 11-midnight Fri, Sat ~ Bar food 12-3, 6-9 ~ Restaurant ~ Children welcome ~ Dogs allowed in bar and bedrooms ~ Wi-fi ~ Bedrooms: /£104 *Recommended by Mike Swan, John Harris*

SALTHOUSE   TG0743   Map 8
Dun Cow 🍴 🍺
(01263) 740467 – www.salthouseduncow.com
A149 Blakeney–Sheringham (Purdy Street, junction with Bard Hill); NR25 7XA

Relaxed seaside pub, a good all-rounder and with enterprising food

Even when really busy – which they deservedly often are – staff here remain helpful and friendly. It's a smashing pub: the flint-walled bar consists of a pair of high-raftered rooms opened up into one area, with stone tiles around the counter where regulars congregate, and a carpeted seating area with a fireplace at each end. Also, scrubbed tables, one very high-backed settle as well as country kitchen chairs and elegant little red-padded dining chairs, with big sailing ship and other prints. Adnams Ghost Ship, Woodfordes Wherry and changing guests such as Adnams Jester and Sharps Doom Bar on handpump, 19 wines by the glass, 14 malt whiskies and a good relaxed atmosphere. Picnic-sets on the front grass look across the bird-filled salt marshes towards the sea, and there are more tables in a sheltered back courtyard and an orchard garden beyond. The bedrooms are self-catering.

Using very local beef and mussels and helpfully served all day, the excellent food includes ciabatta sandwiches (until 5pm), herring roes on toast, lambs kidneys on toast with wholegrain mustard sauce, rare-breed burger with toppings, relish and fries, mediterranean vegetable and feta lasagne with greek salad, smoked haddock with poached egg and hollandaise sauce, steak and mushroom pie, 12-hour braised beef with root vegetable mash, and puddings such as crème brûlée and hot chocolate brownie with ice-cream. *Benchmark main dish: sticky baby back ribs with coleslaw and fries £13.00. Two-course evening meal £20.00.*

Punch ~ Lease Daniel Goff ~ Real ale ~ Open 11-11 ~ Bar food 12-9 ~ Children welcome ~ Dogs welcome ~ Wi-fi *Recommended by Brian Glozier, Philip and Susan Philcox, DF and NF, Mrs Margo Finlay, Jörg Kasprowski, Michael and Jenny Back, Neil and Angela Huxter,*

SNETTISHAM   TF6834   Map 8
Rose & Crown 🍴 ♀ 🛏
(01485) 541382 – www.roseandcrownsnettisham.co.uk
Village signposted from A149 King's Lynn–Hunstanton just N of Sandringham; coming in on the B1440 from the roundabout just N of village, take first left into Old Church Road; PE31 7LX

Particularly well run inn with log fires and interesting furnishings, imaginative food, a fine range of drinks and stylish seating on heated terrace; well equipped bedrooms

'We loved this pub', 'what a delightful place' and 'there's something for everyone here' are just a few of the enthusiastic comments from our readers on this first class pub. Standards remain high year after year, and Mr and Mrs Goodrich take great care not to rest on their laurels. The two main bars each have distinct character and simple charm, with an open fire and woodburning stove, old quarry tiles or coir flooring, cushioned wall seating and wooden tables and chairs, candles on mantelpieces and daily papers. There are stools against the bar where locals enjoy Adnams Southwold and Broadside, Fullers London Pride, Sharps Doom Bar and Woodfordes Wherry on handpump; also, 12 wines by the glass, eight malt whiskies and local cider and fruit juices served by neatly dressed, courteous staff. A small wooden-floored back room has old sports equipment, the landlord's sporting trophies, and photos of the pub's cricket team. The little, civilised restaurant has been redecorated in soft greys, cushions and picture mounts have splashes of bright green and flowers sit in an old galvanised watering can on the window sill. At the back of the building, the two rooms that make up the bustling Garden Room have sofas and big church candles in large lanterns, wooden farmhouse and white-painted dining chairs around a mix of tables, attractive striped blinds and doors that lead to the pretty walled garden. Here there are plenty of contemporary seats and tables under cream parasols, outdoor heaters, colourful herbaceous borders and a wooden galleon-shaped climbing fort for children. Bedrooms are spacious and well appointed and breakfasts very good. Disabled lavatories and wheelchair ramp. This is sister pub to the Bank House in King's Lynn.

Food is first class and uses the best local, seasonal produce: lunchtime sandwiches, lemongrass and chilli venison with pickled ginger and wasabi, moules marinière, wild boar sausages with braised red cabbage and sage liquor, wild mushroom and parmesan risotto, barbecue chicken and pulled pork burger with emmental cheese, onion rings and fries, guinea fowl breast with warm vegetable salad and tahini and maple dressing, beef goulash with sour cream and sweet paprika, and puddings such as white chocolate cheesecake with rhubarb and vanilla compote and lemon tart with tequila and lime sorbet. *Benchmark main dish: beer-battered fresh haddock and chips £12.75. Two-course evening meal £22.00.*

Free house ~ Licensee Anthony Goodrich ~ Real ale ~ Open 11-11; 11-10.30 Sun ~ Bar food 12-9 (9.30 weekends); 7.30-10 breakfast for non-residents ~ Restaurant ~ Children welcome ~ Dogs welcome ~ Wi-fi ~ Bedrooms: £105/£125 *Recommended by R C Vincent, Tom Carver, Dennis and Doreen Haward, John Wooll, DF and NF, Roy Hoing, Tracey and Stephen Groves*

STANHOE   TF8037   Map 8

Duck 🌟 ♥ 🛏

(01485) 518330 – www.duckinn.co.uk

B1155 Docking–Burnham Market; PE31 8QD

Smart candlelit country dining pub with popular food, real ales and appealing layout; bedrooms

There's plenty of room for both drinking and dining customers in this neatly kept place – and a welcome for all from the cheerful staff. The entrance bar has pale grey paintwork, cushioned edwardian-style chairs around wooden tables on dark floor slates, and stools against the panelled counter where they serve Elgoods Cambridge and Golden Newt on handpump from a fine slab-topped counter and 11 wines by the glass. A small wooden-floored area leads off, with a woodburning stove in an old brick fireplace and modern artwork, and this in turn opens into two dining rooms: cushioned chairs and farmhouse tables on more slates or coir carpeting, scatter cushions on wall seating and local seascapes on the walls. The small garden has picnic-sets under a fruit tree, and seats and tables in a garden room with fairy lights and candles; more seats and tables on the front gravel. The bedrooms are well appointed and comfortable.

Imaginative food includes lunchtime open sandwiches, confit smoked salmon with beetroot salad and horseradish, duck hearts with liver parfait, pickled cherries, celeriac and granary streusel, wild mushroom and truffle risotto with hazelnuts, free-range chicken kiev with macaroni cheese and mutton bacon, slow-cooked pork belly with braised cheek, crispy rillettes and celeriac, bass on the bone with cockle, lemon, caper and dill butter, and puddings such as triple chocolate brownie and apple and cinnamon crumble. *Benchmark main dish: beer-battered haddock and chips £12.95. Two-course evening meal £24.50.*

Elgoods ~ Tenants Sarah and Ben Handley ~ Real ale ~ Open 11-11; 12-10.30 Sun ~ Bar food 12-2.30, 6.30-9; 12-8 Sun ~ Restaurant ~ Children welcome ~ Dogs allowed in bar ~ Wi-fi ~ Bedrooms: £90/£135 *Recommended by R C Vincent, Edward Mirzoeff, Mrs J H Godding, Tracey and Stephen Groves, Simon and Mandy King, Christopher and Elise Way, R Halliday*

THORNHAM
Orange Tree 🎖️ ⬤ ▢ 🛏️

TF7343 Map 8

(01485) 512213 ~ www.theorangetreethornham.co.uk
Church Street/A149; PE36 6LY

Norfolk Dining Pub of the Year

Nice combination of friendly bar and good contemporary dining, plus suntrap garden; bedrooms

Come rain or shine, this place is packed – and deservedly so; you'll need to arrive early or book a table in advance. The sizeable bar is bustling and friendly, with red leather chesterfield sofas in front of a log fire, flowery upholstered or leather and wooden dining chairs and red or stripy plush wall seats around a mix of tables on wood or quarry-tiled floors, and white painted beams; background music, board games and flat-screen TV. Helpful, attentive staff serve Adnams Southwold, Woodfordes Wherry and a guest such as Bays Up and Under on handpump and 35 wines by the glass. A little dining room leads off here with silver décor, buddha heads and candles, and the two-part restaurant is simple and contemporary in style. In warm weather, the front garden is much in demand: lavender beds and climbing roses, lots of picnic-sets under parasols, outdoor heaters and a small smart corner pavilion. At the back of the building is a second outside area with children's play equipment. The bedrooms (our readers particularly recommend those in the Old Bakery) make a good base for this lovely stretch of the north Norfolk coast; breakfasts are good. They're kind to dogs and have a doggie menu plus snacks.

Exceptionally good and stylishly presented, the enticing food includes sandwiches (until 5pm), local brown shrimp, prawn and tiger prawn cocktail, tempura soft shell crab, pork belly carpaccio and seared king scallop with salt caramel and apple purée, salsa rossa and apple pearls, free-range chicken and wild mushroom pie with smoked pancetta mash, vegetable or black tiger prawn curry with raita, blade of rare-breed beef steak with potato and smoked bacon dauphinoise, parsley root purée, golden chanterelle and black trompette mushrooms and chasseur sauce, and puddings such as dark chocolate fondant with popcorn shake, popcorn panna cotta and chocolate and kumquat ice-cream and banana sticky toffee pudding with toffee sauce, vanilla parfait and banoffi ice-cream. *Benchmark main dish: duo of local pork (slow-roast belly, seared barbecue loin) with truffle jus £17.95. Two-course evening meal £23.00.*

Punch ~ Lease Mark Goode ~ Real ale ~ Open 11-11 (midnight Sat); 12-10.30 Sun ~ Bar food 12-9.30 ~ Restaurant ~ Children welcome ~ Dogs allowed in bar and bedrooms ~ Wi-fi ~ Bedrooms: £80/£89 *Recommended by Mr and Mrs P R Thomas, Tracey and Stephen Groves, David Carr, J R Wildon*

THORPE MARKET   TG2434 Map 8
Gunton Arms ♀
(01263) 832010 – www.theguntonarms.co.uk
Cromer Road; NR11 8TZ

Impressive place with an easy-going atmosphere, open fires and antiques in bar and dining rooms, real ales, interesting food and friendly staff; bedrooms

You certainly couldn't call this a straightforward pub, housed as it is in a grand country house and surrounded by a 1,000-acre deer park, but they do have a bar and a fine range of drinks – and it's fun. The large entrance hall sets the scene; throughout, the atmosphere is easy-going and friendly, but definitely gently upmarket. Simply furnished, the bar has dark pubby chairs and tables on a wooden floor, a log fire, a long settle beside a pool table, and high stools against the mahogany counter where they serve Adnams Southwold and Broadside, Humpty Dumpty Little Sharpie and Woodfordes Wherry on handpump, ten wines by the glass, 22 malt whiskies and two ciders; staff are chatty and helpful. Heavy curtains line an open doorway into a dining room, where vast antlers hang above a big log fire (they often cook over this) and there are straightforward chairs around scrubbed tables on stone tiles. There's also a lounge with comfortable old leather armchairs and a sofa on a fine rug in front of yet another log fire, some genuine antiques, big house plants and standard lamps, as well as a more formal restaurant with candles and napery, and two homely sitting rooms for hotel residents. Many of the walls are painted dark red and hung with assorted artwork and large mirrors; background music, darts, TV and board games. The bedrooms have many original fittings, but no TV or tea-making facilities.

Using Estate produce, the hearty rustic food includes sandwiches (until 5pm), local mussels in garlic, cream and parsley, lamb sweetbreads with spelt risotto, venison sausages with onion gravy, whipped squash with feta cheese and flatbread, chicken, bacon and leek pie, crisp pork belly with chorizo and beans, line-caught pollock with sea vegetables and mussels, braised ox cheek with parsley mash, and puddings such as boozy cherry cheesecake and iced Grand Marnier parfait with blood orange salad. *Benchmark main dish: loin of fallow deer with girolles £18.00. Two-course evening meal £24.00.*

Free house ~ Licensee Simone Baker ~ Real ale ~ Open 12-11; 12-10 Sun ~ Bar food 12-3, 6-10 (9 Sun) ~ Restaurant ~ Children welcome ~ Dogs allowed in bar and bedrooms ~ Wi-fi ~ Bedrooms: /£130 *Recommended by Paul Humphreys, N R White, David Carr, William and Megan, David Twitchett*

WARHAM   TF9441 Map 8
Three Horseshoes ★
(01328) 710547 – www.warhamhorseshoes.co.uk
Warham All Saints; village signed from A149 Wells-next-the-Sea to Blakeney, and from B1105 S of Wells; NR23 1NL

Interesting, simple furnishings in unchanging and unspoilt pub, pubby food, real ales and seats outside; bedrooms

Parts of this lovely old-fashioned pub date from 1720 and the gas-lit simple rooms look unchanged since the 1920s. There are stripped deal or mahogany tables (one marked for shove-ha'penny) on stone floors, red leatherette settles built around partly panelled walls in the public bar, royalist photographs, a longcase clock with a clear piping strike and open fires in Victorian fireplaces. The traditional local game of twister is nailed to the ceiling showing whose round it is. Norfolk Brewhouse Moon Gazer Dark Mild and two Norfolk guest ales on handpump or tapped from the cask and local cider served by friendly staff. There's a courtyard garden with flower tubs and a well. There are five basic bedrooms next door, in what used to be the post office.

Proper pubby food includes sandwiches, hearty soups, beans on toast, pies such as rabbit or mushroom and nut, pheasant or pigeon casserole, home-cooked gammon, and puddings such as crumbles and tarts with custard. *Benchmark main dish: steak in ale pie £10.80. Two-course evening meal £16.00.*

Free house ~ Licensee Iain Salmon ~ Real ale ~ Open 12-2.30 (3 weekends), 6-11 ~ Bar food 12-2, 6-8 (8.30 summer) ~ Children welcome away from bar area but not allowed in bedrooms ~ Dogs welcome ~ Wi-fi ~ Bedrooms: £40/£60 *Recommended by Derek and Sylvia Stephenson, Peter Meister, David Field, Roy Hoing*

WIVETON

Wiveton Bell 🏆 ⇌

TG0442 Map 8

(01263) 740101 – www.wivetonbell.co.uk

Blakeney Road; NR25 7TL

Busy, open-plan dining pub, drinkers welcomed too, local beers, consistently enjoyable food and seats outside; bedrooms

The comfortable, well equipped and character bedrooms here make a fine base for exploring the area; a continental breakfast hamper is delivered to your room each morning and three of the rooms have their own little terrace. There's also a self-catering cottage. Downstairs, it's mainly open-plan, with some fine old beams, an attractive mix of dining chairs around wooden tables on a stripped-wood floor, a log fire and prints on yellow walls. The sizeable conservatory has smart beige dining chairs around wooden tables on coir flooring. Friendly, attentive staff serve Humpty Dumpty Reedcutter, Norfolk Brewhouse Moon Gazer Amber Ale, Woodfordes Wherry and Yetmans Blue on handpump, and 13 wines by the glass. Picnic-sets on the front grass look across to the church; at the back, stylish wicker tables and chairs on several decked areas are set among decorative box hedging.

Enticing, well presented food includes bruschetta with several toppings, smoked mackerel rillette with chutney, pigs cheek terrine with grape chutney, salt marsh beef burger with smoked cheese, onion rings and chips, butternut squash, sage and chilli risotto, smoked haddock with parsley mash, free-ranged poached egg, wilted spinach and mustard cream sauce, chicken breast with sweetcorn velouté and honey and thyme-pickled prunes, and puddings such as warm chocolate brownie with blueberry ice-cream and raspberry and thyme crème brûlée. *Benchmark main dish: slow-roast pork belly with cider apple jus, champ mash and parsnip crisps £15.45. Two-course evening meal £21.00.*

Free house ~ Licensee Berni Morritt ~ Real ale ~ Open 12-11 (10.30 Sun) ~ Bar food 12-2.30, 6-8.30; 12-8.30 Sun ~ Children welcome ~ Dogs allowed in bar ~ Wi-fi ~ Bedrooms: /£130 *Recommended by John Millwood, John Wooll, David Carr, Stephen Burrows, Roy Hoing, Michael Sargent*

WOLTERTON   TG1732 Map 8
Saracens Head 🅾 ⇔
(01263) 768909 – www.saracenshead-norfolk.co.uk

Wolterton; Erpingham signed off A140 N of Aylsham, on through Calthorpe; NR11 7LZ

Remote inn with stylish bars and dining room and seats in courtyard; good bedrooms

Our readers continue to enjoy this civilised Georgian inn, and while it leans more towards dining, they do keep Woodfordes Wherry and a changing guest on handpump and several wines by the glass. The two-room bar is simple but stylish with high ceilings, light terracotta walls and tall windows with cream and gold curtains – all lend a feeling of space, though it's not large. There's a mix of seats from built-in wall settles to wicker fireside chairs, as well as log fires and flowers. The windows look on to a charming old-fashioned gravel stableyard with plenty of chairs, benches and tables. A pretty six-table parlour on the right has another big log fire. The bedrooms are comfortable and up to date.

 The exact mileage travelled by produce used in the highly thought-of cooking is listed on the menu: rabbit and pheasant terrine with elderberry chutney, king prawn and squid stir-fry with chilli, ginger and soy, roasted beetroot with thyme, braised puy lentils and grilled goats cheese, duck breast with blackberry and apple sauce and dauphinoise potatoes, venison loin with braised red cabbage, apple, parsnip crisps and red wine jus, and puddings such as chocolate nemesis with pistachio ice-cream and treacle tart; they often have a two- and three-course set lunch. *Benchmark main dish: slow-cooked pork belly with bubble and squeak and an apple fritter £14.50. Two-course evening meal £20.00.*

Free house ~ Licensees Tim and Janie Elwes ~ Real ale ~ Open 11-3, 6-11; closed Mon and Tues lunchtimes in winter ~ Bar food 12-2.30, 6.30-9; 12-2, 6.30-8.30 in winter ~ Restaurant ~ Children welcome ~ Dogs allowed in bar and bedrooms ~ Wi-fi ~ Bedrooms: £70/£100
Recommended by Paul Humphreys, Philip and Susan Philcox, John Wooll

WOODBASTWICK   TG3214 Map 8
Fur & Feather 🍺
(01603) 720003 – www.thefurandfeatherinn.co.uk

Off B1140 E of Norwich; NR13 6HQ

Full range of first class beers from next-door Woodfordes brewery, friendly service and popular bar food

This is a delightful pub in a lovely Estate village. Thatched and cottagey, it's next door to Woodfordes brewery so the ales tapped from the cask are in tip top condition: Bure Gold, Mardlers, Nelsons Revenge, Once Bittern, Sundew and Wherry. You can also visit the brewery shop. Efficient, helpful staff also serve a dozen wines by the glass and ten malt whiskies. The style and atmosphere are not what you'd expect of a brewery tap – it's set out more like a comfortable and roomy dining pub with wooden chairs and tables on tiles or carpeting, plus sofas and armchairs; background music. There are seats and tables in the pleasant garden.

🍴 Enjoyable food includes sandwiches and panini, slow-cooked ribs in beer and barbecue sauce, mushrooms with garlic and herbs on toast, venison and stilton or lamb and feta burgers with toppings, coleslaw and chips, local crab salad, steak in ale pie, chicken, chorizo and red peppers in creamy cheese sauce on pasta, skate wing with lemon and parsley butter, and puddings such as Malteser marshmallow sundae and raspberry sponge and custard. *Benchmark main dish: steak and kidney pudding £13.75. Two-course evening meal £19.50.*

Woodfordes ~ Tenant Tim Ridley ~ Real ale ~ Open 10-10 (9.30 Sun) ~ Bar food 10-9 ~ Restaurant ~ Children welcome ~ Wi-fi *Recommended by Stephen and Jean Curtis, Tracey and Stephen Groves, R C Vincent, Roy Hoing, David Carr*

Also Worth a Visit in Norfolk

Besides the fully inspected pubs, you might like to try these pubs that have been recommended to us and described by readers. Do tell us what you think of them: feedback@goodguides.com

AYLMERTON   TG1840
Roman Camp (01263) 838291
Holt Road (A148); NR11 8QD Large late 19th-c mock-Tudor roadside inn; comfortable panelled bar, cosy sitting room off with warm fire, and light airy dining room, decent choice of enjoyable sensibly priced food, well kept Adnams, Greene King and a guest, friendly helpful service from uniformed staff; children welcome, attractive sheltered garden behind with sunny terraces and pond, 15 bedrooms. *(John Wooll, David Carr)*

AYLSHAM   TG1926
★**Black Boys** (01263) 732122
Market Place; off B1145; NR11 6EH Small friendly hotel with imposing Georgian façade and informal open-plan beamed bar, popular generously served food from snacks up including good value Sun roasts, Adnams and guests, decent wines, comfortable seating and plenty of tables on carpet or bare boards, helpful young uniformed staff coping well at busy times; children and dogs welcome, seats in front by marketplace, more behind, bedrooms, big cooked breakfast, open (and food) all day. *(Alex and Hazel Evans, David Carr, John Wooll, John Evans)*

BANNINGHAM   TG2129
★**Crown** (01263) 733534
Colby Road; opposite church by village green; NR11 7DY Welcoming and popular 17th-c beamed pub in same family for 24 years (some recent refurbishment); good choice of enjoyable affordably priced food (they're helpful with gluten-free diets), well kept Greene King and local guests, decent wines, friendly well trained staff, log fires and woodburners; TV, free wi-fi; children and dogs welcome, disabled access, garden jazz festival Aug, open (and food) all day weekends. *(M J Bourke, R C Vincent, Brian Nicholson, David Twitchett)*

BARTON BENDISH   TF7105
Berney Arms (01366) 347995
Off A1122 W of Swaffham; Church Road; PE33 9GF Attractive dining pub in quiet village, good freshly made food from sandwiches and pub favourites to more inventive dishes, good value set menu too, service prompt and welcoming, Adnams beers and good choice of wines by the glass, afternoon teas, restaurant; children and dogs (in bar) welcome, pleasant garden, good bedrooms in converted stables and forge, open all day, food all day Sun. *(Mike Swan)*

BINHAM   TF9839
Chequers (01328) 830297
B1388 SW of Blakeney; NR21 0AL Long low-beamed 17th-c local away from the bustle of the coastal pubs; comfortable bar with coal fires at each end, Adnams Southwold, Norfolk Moongazer Golden and guests, enjoyable pub food at reasonable prices, friendly staff; various games; children and dogs welcome, picnic-sets in front and on back grass, interesting village with huge priory church, open all day weekends. *(Roy Hoing)*

BLAKENEY   TG0244
Blakeney Hotel (01263) 740376
The Quay; NR25 7ND Pleasant flint hotel nicely set near bird marshes, elegant harbour-view bar with good sensibly priced home-made food, friendly attentive staff, well kept Adnams and Woodfordes, restaurant, games room; 37 bedrooms. *(David Carr)*

BLAKENEY   TG0243
Kings Arms (01263) 740341
West Gate Street; NR25 7NQ A stroll from the harbour to this 18th-c pub, friendly and chatty, with Adnams, Greene King, Marstons and guests, generous wholesome food all day from breakfast on, three simple linked low-ceilinged rooms and airy garden room; children and dogs welcome, big garden, bedrooms, open from 9.30am (midday Sun). *(David Carr)*

BLAKENEY   TG0243
White Horse (01263) 740574
Off A149 W of Sheringham; High Street; NR25 7AL Friendly inn popular with both locals and holidaymakers, long split-level carpeted bar with fine-art equestrian prints and paintings, high-backed brown leather dining and other chairs around light oak tables, Adnams ales and a dozen wines by the glass, well liked food including local fish/shellfish; children and dogs welcome, wheelchair access to upper bar and dining conservatory only, seats in suntrap courtyard and pleasant paved garden, short stroll to harbour, bedrooms, open all day. *(David Carr, Simon and Mandy King)*

BLICKLING TG1728
Buckinghamshire Arms
(01263) 732133 *B1354 NW of Aylsham;
NR11 6NF* Handsome Jacobean inn well
placed by gates to Blickling Hall (NT);
small proper bar, lounge set for eating with
woodburner, smarter more formal dining
room with another fire, decent range of beers
including Woodfordes, several wines by the
glass and generally well liked food, friendly
attentive young staff; background music;
children and dogs welcome, tables out on
lawn, lovely walks nearby, three bedrooms,
open all day (food all day Sun). *(Dennis and
Doreen Haward, R C Vincent, David Twitchett)*

BODHAM STREET TG1240
Red Hart (01263) 588270
The Street; NR25 6AD Old family-run
village pub with well liked fairly traditional
home-cooked food, ales including Woodfordes
Wherry, efficient relaxed service; pool;
children and dogs welcome (menus for both),
open all day. *(R C Vincent)*

BRANCASTER TF7743
★Ship (01485) 210333
London Street (A149); PE31 8AP
Bustling roadside inn, part of the small
Flying Kiwi chain; compact bar with built-in
cushioned and planked wall seats, Jo C's
ales and guests, nice wines by the glass,
several dining areas with woodburner in one
and neatly log-piled fireplace in another,
contemporary paintwork throughout, pale
settles and nice mix of other furniture on
rugs and bare boards, bookcases, shipping
memorabilia and lots of prints, good modern
food, daily papers and friendly, helpful
service; background music, TV; children and
dogs welcome, gravelled seating area with
round picnic-sets out by car park, attractive
well equipped bedrooms, open all day.
(P and J Shapley, Tracey and Stephen Groves)

BRANCASTER STAITHE TF7944
★Jolly Sailors (01485) 210314
Main Road (A149); PE31 8BJ
Unpretentious pub set in prime bird-
watching territory on edge of NT dunes and
salt flats, chatty mix of locals and visitors
in simply furnished bars, wheelbacks,
settles and cushioned benches around
mix of tables on quarry tiles, photographs
and local maps on the walls, woodburner,
their own Brancaster ales (brewery not on
site) and guests, several wines by the glass,
sizeable back dining room with popular
food including pizzas; children and dogs
welcome, plenty of picnic-sets and play
equipment in peaceful back garden, ice-
cream hut in summer, vine-covered terrace,
open all day (food all day summer).
*(R C Vincent, Neil and Angela Huxter, Tracey
and Stephen Groves, Mrs V Moody, David Carr,
Simon and Mandy King and others)*

BRANCASTER STAITHE TF8044
★White Horse (01485) 210262
A149 E of Hunstanton; PE31 8BY
Popular restaurant place, but does have
proper informal front locals' bar; own good
Brancaster ales and guests, lots of wines by
the glass, log fire, pine furniture, historical
photographs and bar billiards, middle area
with comfortable sofas and newspapers, big
airy dining conservatory overlooking tidal
marshes, enjoyable bar and restaurant food
including 'tapas' and plenty of fish; they ask
for a credit card if you run a tab; children
welcome, dogs in bar, seats on sun deck
with fine views, more under cover on heated
terrace, nice bedrooms, coast path at bottom
of garden, open (and food) all day. *(Tracey
and Stephen Groves, John Wooll, DF and NF)*

BROOKE TM2899
Kings Head (01508) 550335
Norwich Road (B1332); NR15 1AB
Welcoming 17th-c village pub with popular
freshly cooked food from traditional choices
up, good friendly service, four real ales and
excellent choice of wines by the glass, maybe
a norfolk whisky, light and airy bare-boards
bar with log fire, eating area up a step;
quiz last Sun of month, free wi-fi; children
welcome, tables in sheltered garden,
open all day (from 9.30am weekends for
breakfast). *(Edward May)*

BROOME TM3591
Artichoke (01986) 893325
Yarmouth Road; NR35 2NZ
Unpretentious split-level roadside pub with
up to ten well kept ales (some from tap room
casks) including Adnams and Woodfordes,
belgian fruit beers and excellent selection
of whiskies too, good traditional home-made
food in bar or dining room, friendly helpful
staff, wood and flagstone floors, log fire in big
fireplace; dogs welcome, garden picnic-sets,
smokers' shelter, closed Mon otherwise
open all day (shuts weekday afternoons
in winter). *(John Harris)*

BURNHAM MARKET TF8342
Hoste (01328) 738777
The Green (B1155); PE31 8HD
Character front bar in smart hotel with
informal chatty feel, leather dining chairs,
settles and armchairs (note the glass-topped
suitcase table), wood-effect flooring, farming
tools and cartoons on walls, woodburner,
Greene King and Woodfordes, 19 wines by
the glass from extensive carefully chosen
list and several malt whiskies, good if not
cheap food including lunchtime sandwiches,
courteous service, elegant dining rooms, busy
conservatory and smart airy back restaurant,
art gallery upstairs; children and dogs (in
bar) welcome, attractive garden, luxurious
bedrooms, open all day from 9am. *(Tracey
and Stephen Groves, David Carr, Roy Hoing)*

BURNHAM MARKET   TF8342

Nelson (01328) 738321

Creake Road; PE31 8EN Dining pub with nice food from pizzas to more ambitious dishes in bar and restaurant, interesting vegetarian dishes and OAP lunch deal too, pleasant efficient uniformed staff, well kept Woodfordes Wherry and guests, extensive wine list, L-shaped bar with leather sofas and armchairs, local artwork for sale; children and dogs welcome, terrace picnic-sets under parasols, four bedrooms (two in converted outbuilding), open all day. *(Tracey and Stephen Groves)*

BURNHAM THORPE   TF8541

★ **Lord Nelson** (01328) 738241

Off B1155 or B1355, near Burnham Market; PE31 8HL Neatly kept 17th-c pub with lots of Nelson memorabilia (he was born in this sleepy village); antique high-backed settles on worn red tiles in small bar, smoke ovens in original fireplace, little snug leading off, two dining rooms one with flagstones and open fire, well liked sensibly priced bar food, Greene King, Woodfordes and a guest tapped from the cask, several wines by the glass, secret rum-based recipes (Nelson's Blood and Lady Hamilton's Nip); children and dogs welcome, good-sized play area and pétanque in long back garden, open all day in summer, closed Mon evening (except school/bank holidays). *(David Carr, R Halliday, Derek and Sylvia Stephenson)*

CHEDGRAVE   TM3699

White Horse (01508) 520250

Norwich Road; NR14 6ND Welcoming pub with Timothy Taylors Landlord and four other well kept ales, decent wines by the glass and good choice of enjoyable sensibly priced food from lunchtime baguettes up, friendly attentive young staff, log fire and sofas in bar, restaurant; regular events including live music, monthly quiz and beer festivals, pool and darts; children and dogs welcome, garden picnic-sets, open all day. *(Ruth May)*

CLEY-NEXT-THE-SEA   TG0443

★ **Three Swallows** (01263) 740526

Holt Road off A149; NR25 7TT Popular refurbished local, log fires in bar and dining room, stripped-pine tables, enjoyable reasonably priced pubby food (all day Sun) from sandwiches up, well kept Adnams, Greene King and Woodfordes from unusual richly carved bar, cheerfully busy staff; children and dogs welcome, disabled access, metal tables and chairs out at front facing green, big garden with surprisingly grandiose

fountain, aviary and heated smokers' shelter, four annexe bedrooms, good breakfast, handy for the salt marshes, open all day. *(M and GR, Simon Watkins)*

COCKLEY CLEY   TF7904

Twenty Churchwardens (01760) 721439 *Off A1065 S of Swaffham; PE37 8AN* Friendly informal pub in converted school next to church, three linked beamed rooms, good open fire, popular food including nice home-made pies, well kept Adnams Southwold; newspapers, second-hand books for sale, no credit cards; children and dogs welcome (there's a small pub dog), tiny unspoilt village. *(Hilary and Neil Christopher)*

COLTISHALL   TG2719

Kings Head (01603) 737426

Wroxham Road (B1354); NR12 7EA Popular dining pub close to River Bure and moorings, imaginative food from owner-chef (especially fish/seafood), also bar snacks, lunchtime set menu and children's choices, well kept Adnams and nice wines by the glass, good friendly service, open fire, fishing nets and stuffed fish including monster pike and bill from marlin caught by landlord, cookery school; background music; seats outside (noisy road), four bedrooms. *(Gilly and Frank Newman)*

CONGHAM   TF7123

Anvil (01485) 600625

St Andrews Lane; PE32 1DU Tucked-away modern country pub with welcoming licensees, wide choice of tasty generously served home-made food (smaller helpings available), good value Sun carvery, quick friendly service, three or more well kept ales (at least one local), reasonable prices; live music and quiz nights; children welcome, picnic-sets in small walled front garden, campsite, open all day weekends, closed Mon. *(R C Vincent)*

CROMER   TG2242

Red Lion (01263) 514964

Off A149; Tucker Street/Brook Street; NR27 9HD Substantial refurbished Victorian hotel with elevated sea views, original features including panelling and open fires, five well kept ales in bare-boards flint-walled bar, good food from sandwiches and platters up including daily specials, efficient friendly service, restaurant and conservatory; background music; children and dogs welcome, disabled facilities, tables in back courtyard, 14 bedrooms, open all day. *(David Carr, N R White, Revd R P Tickle, Tony and Maggie Harwood)*

A star symbol before the name of a pub shows exceptional character and appeal. It doesn't mean extra comfort. Even quite a basic pub can win a star, if it's individual enough.

DERSINGHAM
Feathers (01485) 540768
TF6930

B1440 towards Sandringham; Manor Road; PE31 6LN Refurbished Jacobean carrstone inn once part of the Sandringham Estate; two adjoining bars (main one with big open fire), well kept Adnams, Woodfordes and a guest, enjoyable food emphasising local produce and fish, OAP lunch deal Mon, Tues, friendly accommodating service, back dining room, function room in converted stables; background music; children and dogs welcome, large garden with play area, five bedrooms, open all day. *(Tracey and Stephen Groves, John Wooll)*

DOWNHAM MARKET
Railway Arms (01366) 386636
TF6003

At railway station, Railway Road; PE38 9EN Cosy station bar with tiny adjoining rooms, one with glowing coal fire, another with second-hand bookshop, real ales tapped from the cask and several good ciders, tea, coffee and some snacky food, friendly staff; board games; best to check opening times. *(Edward May)*

EAST WINCH
Carpenters Arms (01553) 841228
TF6916

A47 Lynn Road; PE32 1NP Useful roadside pub with good value home-made food including daily specials in bar or separate restaurant, several beers and ciders, friendly helpful service; children welcome, no dogs inside, open all day. *(R C Vincent)*

EDGEFIELD
★ **Pigs** (01263) 587634
TG0934

Norwich Road; B1149 S of Holt; NR24 2RL Friendly bustling pub with carpeted bar, Adnams, Greene King, Woodfordes and a house beer from Wolf tapped from casks, arches through to simply furnished area with mixed chairs and pews on broad pine boards, airy dining extension in similar style split into stalls by standing timbers and low brick walls, nice variety of good quality food (all day Sun) including Norfolk 'tapas', games room with bar billiards, also children's playroom; background music; dogs allowed in bar, good wheelchair access, rustic seats and tables on big covered front terrace, adventure playground, boules, ten bedrooms (seven with spa facilities including sauna and outside bath), open all day from 8am (breakfast for non-residents). *(Tracey and Stephen Groves, Roy Hoing, Peter Meister)*

ELSING
Mermaid (01362) 637640
TG0516

Church Road; NR20 3EA Welcoming 17th-c pub in quiet little village, L-shaped carpeted bar with woodburner, well kept Adnams, Woodfordes and guests tapped from the cask, enjoyable home-made food including range of pies and suet puddings (signature steak and kidney roly-poly), friendly helpful service; pool and other games such as dominoes and shut the box, free wi-fi; children and dogs welcome, handy for walkers on Wensum Valley Way, nice garden, 14th-c church opposite with interesting brasses, closed Mon lunchtime. *(Shaun Mahoney)*

GAYTON
Crown (01553) 636252
TF7219

Lynn Road (B1145/B1153); opposite church; PE32 1PA Low-beamed village pub with plenty of character, unusual old features and charming snug as well as three main areas, good value food including buffet lunch (Mon-Sat) and carvery (all day Sun, Tues-Fri evenings), well kept Greene King ales, friendly service, sofas and good log fire, games room; dogs welcome in bar, tables in attractive sheltered garden, four bedrooms, open (and food) all day. *(Paul Thompson, Tony Westhead)*

GELDESTON
★ **Locks**
TM3990

Off A143/A146 NW of Beccles; off Station Road S of village, obscurely signed down long rough track; NR34 0HW Remote candlelit pub at navigable head of River Waveney; ancient tiled-floor core with beams and big log fire, changing ales tapped from casks and decent food including burgers, vegetarian dishes and Fri curry night, large extension for summer crowds; regular live music, no credit cards; children welcome, riverside garden, moorings, open all day in summer (winter: all day Fri, Sat and till 7pm Sun, closed Mon-Weds and Thurs lunchtime). *(Mike Swan)*

GREAT CRESSINGHAM
★ **Windmill** (01760) 756232
TF8401

Village signed off A1065 S of Swaffham; Water End; IP25 6NN Interesting pictures and bric-a-brac in warren of rambling linked rooms, plenty of cosy corners, good value fresh bar food from baguettes to steak and Sun roasts, half a dozen ales including Adnams, Greene King and house beer called Windy Miller Quixote (brewed by Purity), decent wines, 60 malt whiskies and good coffee, cheery staff, pool room and other pub games; background music (live country & western Tues), big sports TV in side snug; children and dogs welcome, large garden with picnic-sets and good play area, caravan parking, bedroom extension, open all day. *(R C Vincent)*

Though we don't usually mention it in the text, most pubs will now make coffee or tea – it's always worth asking.

GREAT YARMOUTH   TG5207
Mariners   (01493) 332299
Howard Street S; NR30 1LN Dutch-gabled two-room pub popular for its excellent range of real ales and ciders (regular festivals), bargain food from sandwiches to specials, efficient staff; open all day. *(Dennis Jones)*

HARPLEY   TF7825
Rose & Crown   (01485) 521807
Off A148 Fakenham–King's Lynn; Nethergate Street; PE31 6TW Friendly old village pub competently run by welcoming licensees, nice range of good sensibly priced food, well kept Woodfordes Wherry and guests, Aspall's cider, modernised interior with open fires; children and dogs welcome, garden picnic-sets, closed Sun evening, all day Mon, Tues lunchtime. *(Derek and Sylvia Stephenson)*

HEYDON   TG1127
★ Earle Arms   (01263) 587376
Off B1149; NR11 6AD Popular old dutch-gabled pub overlooking green and church in delightfully unspoilt Estate village; well kept Adnams, Woodfordes and a guest, enjoyable food from varied if not extensive menu using local fish and meat (gluten-free choices marked), decent wine list, friendly efficient service, racing prints, some stuffed animals and good log fire in old-fashioned candlelit bar, more formal dining room; children and dogs welcome, picnic-sets in small cottagey back garden, open all day Sun (no evening food then), closed Mon. *(Philip and Susan Philcox, David Twitchett)*

HICKLING   TG4123
Greyhound   (01692) 598306
The Green; NR12 0YA Small busy pub with welcoming open fire, good choice of enjoyable food in bar and neat restaurant, well kept local ales and ciders, friendly long-serving landlord; well behaved children welcome, seats out at front and in pretty back garden with terrace, bedroom annexe. *(Roy Hoing)*

HINGHAM   TG0202
White Hart   (01953) 850214
Market Place, just off B1108 W of Norwich; NR9 4AF Flying Kiwi Inn with character rooms arranged over two floors, beams and standing timbers, stripped floorboards with oriental rugs, mix of furniture including comfortable sofas in quiet corners, lots of prints and photographs, woodburners, galleried long room up steps from main bar with egyptian frieze, own-brewed Jo C's plus Adnams, lots of wines by glass, food and service can be good; children and dogs (in bar) welcome, modern benches and seats in gravelled courtyard, pretty village with huge 14th-c church, open all day (food all day Sun till 8pm). *(Alcuin Bramerton)*

HOLME-NEXT-THE-SEA   TF7043
White Horse   (01485) 525512
Kirkgate Street; PE36 6LH Attractive old-fashioned place, cosy and rambling, with warm log fires, ample choice of food including local fish and specials, fair prices, friendly efficient service, Adnams, Greene King and decent wines, refurbished side extension; children and dogs welcome, small back garden, more seats out in front and on lawn opposite, play area. *(Richard and Liz Thorne)*

HOLT   TG0738
Feathers   (01263) 712318
Market Place; NR25 6BW Relaxed hotel with popular locals' bar comfortably extended around original panelled area, open fire, antiques in attractive entrance/reception area, good choice of enjoyable fairly priced food including blackboard specials, friendly helpful service, Greene King ales and decent wines, good coffee, restaurant and dining conservatory; background music, no dogs; children welcome, 13 comfortable bedrooms, open all day. *(John Evans, John Wooll, David Carr)*

HOLT   TG0738
Kings Head   (01263) 712543
High Street/Bull Street; NR25 6BN Bustling rustic public bar, two roomy back bars and conservatory, enjoyable reasonably priced food including charcoal-grilled steaks, prompt friendly service, Adnams, Greene King, Woodfordes and many guests, fair choice of wines; juke box (can be loud) and some live music, sports TV, pool; children and dogs welcome, back terrace with heated smokers' shelter, good-sized garden, three stylish bedrooms, open all day. *(Andrew Stone)*

HORSEY   TG4622
★ Nelson Head   (01493) 393378
Off B1159; The Street; NR29 4AD Nicely tucked-away (but popular) unspoilt red-brick country pub, impressive range of beers (some direct from the cask) as well as ciders, well liked sensibly priced bar food from sandwiches and snacks to daily specials, friendly chatty staff, good log fire and lots of interesting bric-a-brac including various guns, small side dining room; quiet background music; children and dogs welcome, outside seating including in field opposite, good coast walks (seals), open all day. *(Hilary and Neil Christopher)*

HORSTEAD   TG2619
Recruiting Sergeant   (01603) 737077
B1150 just S of Coltishall; NR12 7EE Light, airy and roomily set out roadside pub, enjoyable generously served food from fresh panini and wraps up including good fish choice, efficient friendly service even though busy, up to half a dozen changing ales such as Adnams, Greene King, Timothy Taylors

and Woodfordes, plenty of wines by the glass, big open fire; children welcome, terrace and garden tables, bedrooms, open all day. *(Alex and Hazel Evans)*

HUNSTANTON   TF6740
Waterside (01485) 535810
Beach Terrace Road; PE36 5BQ Former station buffet just above prom, now bar-restaurant with great sea views from popular conservatory (children welcome here), Adnams, Greene King and good value wines, straightforward inexpensive tasty food all day from sandwiches up, quick service by friendly uniformed staff, Fri quiz; dogs allowed if on the lead. *(John Wooll)*

HUNWORTH   TG0735
Hunny Bell (01263) 712300
Signed off B roads S of Holt; NR24 2AA Welcoming 18th-c beamed pub now owned by former manager; neat bar with cushioned country chairs around wooden tables including a couple of long slabby ones, stone floor and woodburner, cosy snug with homely furniture on old worn tiles and original stripped-brick walls, another woodburner in high-raftered bare-boards dining room, food from pub favourites up, ales such as Adnams, Greene King and Woodfordes, friendly helpful service; children welcome, wheelchair access, picnic-sets on terrace overlooking village green, more seats in garden among fruit trees, open all day Sun (no evening food then). *(Simon and Mandy King)*

INGHAM   TG3926
★ Swan (01692) 581099
Off A149 SE of North Walsham; signed from Stalham; NR12 9AB Smart 14th-c thatched dining pub nicely placed for Broads and coast; rustic main area divided by massive chimneybreast with woodburner on each side, low beams and hefty standing timbers, bare boards or parquet, some old farm tools, quieter small brick-floored part with leather sofas, good well presented restaurant-style food including set menu choices, home-baked bread, well kept Woodfordes, local cider and good selection of wines, friendly service; children welcome, picnic-sets on sunny back terrace, more at side, five comfortable bedrooms in converted stables, good breakfast. *(Revd R P Tickle, M and GR, Tom and Ruth Rees, Roy Hoing, Office)*

ITTERINGHAM   TG1430
★ Walpole Arms (01263) 587258
Village signposted off B1354 NW of Aylsham; NR11 7AR Beamed 18th-c pub close to Blickling Hall (NT); good modern cooking using fresh local ingredients (some from own farm) along with more traditional choices, efficient friendly service, well kept Adnams and Woodfordes, nice wines by the glass, sizeable open-plan bar with woodburner, stripped-brick walls and dark wood dining tables on red carpet, light

airy restaurant opening on to vine-covered terrace, Weds quiz; children welcome, dogs in bar, two-acre landscaped garden open all day Sat, closed Sun evening. *(Alan and Angela Scouller, Agnes Broda)*

KENNINGHALL   TM0485
Red Lion (01953) 887849
B1113 S of Norwich; East Church Street; NR16 2EP Stripped beams, bare boards and old floor tiles, cosy panelled snug, back stable-style restaurant, open fires and woodburners, enjoyable good value home-made food from baguettes and baked potatoes up, friendly helpful young staff, well kept Greene King IPA, Woodfordes Wherry and guests; regular live music; children (not in bar) and dogs welcome, tables out by back bowling green, bedrooms in former stable block, open all day Fri-Sun. *(John Harris)*

KING'S LYNN   TF6120
Crown & Mitre (01553) 774669
Ferry Street; PE30 1LJ Old-fashioned unchanging pub in great riverside spot, lots of interesting naval and nautical memorabilia, up to six well kept ales – the long-serving no-nonsense landlord is still hoping to brew his own beers, good value straightforward home-made food, river-view back conservatory; no credit cards; well behaved children and dogs welcome, quayside tables. *(Lawrence Pearse, John Wooll)*

KING'S LYNN   TF6120
Dukes Head (01553) 774996
Tuesday Market Place; PE30 1JS Imposing Georgian hotel overlooking market square; enjoyable food in comfortable modernised lounge bar, Adnams ales and nice selection of wines, elegant restaurant (quite pricey), cheerful attentive service; children welcome, good bedrooms (some in back extension), open all day. *(P and D Carpenter)*

KING'S LYNN   TF6220
Lattice House (01553) 769585
Corner of Market Lane, off Tuesday Market Place; PE30 1EG Old beamed and raftered Wetherspoons with good choice of ales, reasonably priced food and friendly service, several well divided areas including upstairs bar; children welcome, beer garden, open all day from 9am (till 1am Fri, Sat). *(Andrew Stone)*

KING'S LYNN   TF6119
Marriotts Warehouse
(01553) 818500 *South Quay; PE30 5DT* Bar-restaurant-café in converted 16th-c brick and stone warehouse; well liked/priced food from lunchtime sandwiches and light dishes up, wider evening choice, good range of wines, beers such as Sharps Doom Bar and Woodfordes Wherry, cocktails, small upstairs bar with river views; children welcome, quayside tables, open all day from 10am. *(John Wooll)*

LITTLE PLUMSTEAD TG3112
Brick Kilns (01603) 720043
Norwich Road (B1140); NR13 5JH
Pink-painted beamed country dining pub, wide choice of enjoyable fairly priced food including fish menu and plenty of vegetarian/vegan options, well kept Adnams and a guest, good friendly service, bare-boards bar area, carpeted restaurant and flagstoned conservatory overlooking paddock with horses, goats and donkeys; children welcome, three bedrooms, open all day. *(Alex and Hazel Evans)*

LYNG TG0617
Fox (01603) 872316
The Street; NR9 5AL Old beamed village pub with several newly refurbished linked areas and separate restaurant, ample helping of good inexpensive home-made food (notable fish and chips), ales such as Adnams and Woodfordes, friendly staff; pool and giant chessboard in one part; children and dogs (in front bar) welcome, enclosed garden with view of church, open (and food) all day. *(Richard Kennell)*

MARSHAM TG1924
Plough (01263) 735000
Old Norwich Road; NR10 5PS Welcoming 18th-c inn with split-level open-plan bar, enjoyable food using local produce including some interesting vegetarian choices, good value set lunch, Adnams Southwold and a couple of local guests, friendly helpful staff; free wi-fi; children welcome, dogs in garden only, comfortable bedrooms, open all day. *(Ruth May)*

MUNDFORD TL8093
Crown (01842) 878233
Off A1065 Thetford–Swaffham; Crown Road; IP26 5HQ Unassuming 17th-c pub, warmly welcoming, with heavy beams and huge fireplace, interesting local memorabilia, Courage Directors and one or two guests, over 50 malt whiskies, enjoyable generously served food at sensible prices, spiral iron stairs to two restaurant areas (larger one has separate entrance accessible to wheelchairs), locals' bar with sports TV; children and dogs welcome, back terrace and garden with wishing well, Harley-Davidson meeting first Sun of month, bedrooms (some in adjoining building), also self-catering accommodation, open all day. *(Mike Swan)*

NEW BUCKENHAM TM0890
Inn on the Green (01953) 860172
Chapel Street; NR16 2BB Swish modern renovation of late Victorian red-brick pub, good freshly prepared food from pub favourites to more restauranty dishes including blackboard specials, Adnams and Woodfordes, good selection of wines, pleasant efficient staff; quiz second Thurs of month; children (away from bar) and dogs (in bar) welcome, terrace tables, handy for Banham Zoo, closed Mon. *(Quentin and Carol Williamson)*

NORTH TUDDENHAM TG0413
Lodge (01362) 638466
Off A47; NR20 3DJ Modernised restaurant pub with enjoyable home-made food from traditional favourites up, local ales, friendly attentive service; children welcome, tables outside (some on decking), open all day, closed Sun evening, Mon. *(Ruth May)*

NORTHREPPS TG2439
Foundry Arms (01263) 579256
Church Street; NR27 0AA Welcoming village pub with good reasonably priced traditional food (not Sun evening, Mon), well kept Adnams and Woodfordes, decent choice of wines, woodburner, smallish restaurant; pool and darts in separate area; children and dogs welcome, picnic-sets in back garden, open all day. *(Mike Swan)*

NORWICH TG2309
★Adam & Eve (01603) 667423
Bishopgate; follow Palace Street from Tombland, N of cathedral; NR3 1RZ Ancient pub dating from at least 1240 when used by workmen building the cathedral, has Saxon well beneath the lower bar floor and striking dutch gables (added in 14th and 15th c); old-fashioned small bars with tiled or parquet floors, cushioned benches built into partly panelled walls and some antique high-backed settles, four ales including Adnams and Theakstons, Aspall's cider and around 40 malt whiskies, traditional pubby food (not Sun evening); background music; children allowed in snug till 7pm, no dogs inside, picnic-sets out among award-winning tubs and hanging baskets, open all day, closed 25, 26 Dec, 1 Jan. *(David Carr, Ian Phillips)*

NORWICH TG2408
Coach & Horses (01603) 477077
Thorpe Road; NR1 1BA Light and airy tap for Chalk Hill brewery (tours available), friendly staff, good value generous home-made food including all-day breakfast, L-shaped bare-boards bar with open fire, pleasant back dining area; sports TVs, gets very busy on home match days; disabled access possible (not to lavatories), front terrace, open all day. *(David Carr)*

NORWICH TG2210
Duke of Wellington (01603) 441182
Waterloo Road; NR3 1EG Friendly rambling local with up to 21 well kept quickly changing ales including Oakham and Wolf, many served from tap room casks, foreign bottled beers too, no food apart from sausage rolls and pies (can bring your own), real fire; traditional games, folk music Tues evening; well behaved dogs welcome, nice back terrace (Aug beer festival), open all day. *(David Carr)*

NORWICH TG2207
Eagle (01603) 624173
Newmarket Road (A11, between A140 and A147 ring roads); NR2 2HN
Sizeable red-brick Georgian pub; main bar with comfortable sofas and armchairs by open fire in ornate fireplace, white-painted chairs around pine tables on tiled or stripped-wood flooring, also cosy end room, low-ceilinged dining room and spiral staircase to further area, four ales including a house beer from Norfolk Brewhouse, decent wines and enjoyable food from sandwiches up; background music; children and dogs welcome, sunny terrace with picnic-sets and barbecue, more seats on grass, play area. *(David Carr)*

NORWICH TG2408
Fat Cat & Canary (01603) 436925
Thorpe Road; NR1 1TR Newest of this Norwich brewer's three pubs, their well kept beers and several guests, real ciders and good range of other drinks, some snacky food (burger van on busy match days), traditional interior with black and white floor tiles, friendly atmosphere; poker, quiz and music nights; sheltered seating area outside, open all day. *(Mike Swan)*

NORWICH TG2310
Fat Cat Tap (01603) 413153
Lawson Road; NR3 4LF This 1970s shed-like building is home to the Fat Cat brewery – and sister pub to the Fat Cat (see Main Entries) and Fat Cat & Canary; their beers and up to 12 guests along with draught continentals, lots of bottled beers and eight or more local ciders/perries, no food apart from rolls and pork pies; live music Fri night and Sun afternoon; children (till 6pm) and dogs welcome, seats out in front and behind, open all day. *(David Carr)*

NORWICH TG2309
★Kings Head (01603) 620468
Magdalen Street; NR3 1JE Traditional Victorian local with friendly licensees and good atmosphere in two simply furnished bare-boards bars, a dozen very well kept changing regional ales, good choice of imported beers and a local cider, no food except pork pies, bar billiards in bigger back bar; open all day. *(David Carr)*

NORWICH TG2208
Plough (01603) 661384
St Benedicts Street; NR2 4AR Friendly little city-centre pub owned by Grain, their ales and guests kept well, good wines, knowledgeable staff, food limited to sausage pie and summer barbecues, comfortable seating and open fire; good spacious beer garden behind, open all day. *(Mike Swan)*

NORWICH TG2308
Ribs of Beef (01603) 619517
Wensum Street, S side of Fye Bridge; NR3 1HY Welcoming and comfortable with nine real ales including Adnams, Wolf and Woodfordes, traditional cider and good wine choice, deep leather sofas and small tables upstairs, attractive smaller downstairs room with river view, generous well priced pubby food (till 5pm weekends), quick cheerful service; monthly quiz; children welcome, tables out on narrow waterside walkway, open all day. *(David Carr)*

NORWICH TG2308
Take Five (01603) 763099
Opposite cathedral gate; NR3 1HF Old black and white timber-fronted building, a mix of wine bar, pub and restaurant; four or five mainly local ales and decent wines, enjoyable well priced home-made food with good vegetarian choice, friendly efficient service, nice open fire; children welcome, closed Sun, otherwise open (and food) all day. *(Mike Swan)*

NORWICH TG2309
Wig & Pen (01603) 625891
St Martins Palace Plain; NR3 1RN Popular 17th-c beamed pub opposite cathedral close, lawyer and judge prints, woodburner, good value generous food with regularly changing specials, prompt friendly service, six ales including Adnams, Fullers, Oakham and Woodfordes, well priced wines; background music, sports TVs; tables out at front, open all day (till 6pm Sun). *(Revd R P Tickle)*

OLD BUCKENHAM TM0691
★Gamekeeper (01953) 860397
B1077 S of Attleborough; The Green; NR17 1RE Pretty 16th-c pub with civilised welcoming beamed bar, leather armchairs and sofa in front of big inglenook woodburner, nice mix of old wooden seats and tables on fine flagstones or wood floor, local watercolours and unusual interior bow window, well kept Adnams, Timothy Taylors and Woodfordes, Aspall's cider, quite a few wines by glass and several malt whiskies, good food from sandwiches and sharing plates to daily specials, comfortable main back dining area plus a small room for private dining; children welcome away from bar, dogs allowed,

sunny back garden with terrace, closed Sun evening. *(Sheila Topham)*

OVERSTRAND TG2440

Sea Marge (01263) 579579

High Street; NR27 0AB Substantial sea-view hotel (former Edwardian country house) with separate entrance to spacious bar area, enjoyable food from ciabattas up including good value weekday deal (till 7pm), restaurant; children welcome, five-acre grounds with terraced lawns down to coast path and beach, 25 comfortable bedrooms. *(David Carr)*

OVERSTRAND TG2440

White Horse (01263) 579237

High Street; NR27 0AB Comfortably modernised and stylish, with good choice of enjoyable food in bar, dining room or barn restaurant, at least three well kept local ales, friendly attentive staff, pool room; background music, silent sports TV; children and dogs welcome, picnic-sets in front, more in garden behind with play equipment, eight bedrooms, open all day from 8am. *(Hilary and Neil Christopher)*

RINGSTEAD TF7040

★ Gin Trap (01485) 525264

Village signed off A149 near Hunstanton; OS Sheet 132 map reference 707403; PE36 5JU Attractive 17th-c coaching inn refurbished under welcoming new management; two bar areas, original part with beams and woodburner, five well kept ales including Adnams, Greene King and Woodfordes, tasty home-made pubby food plus some blackboard specials, airy dining conservatory; children and dogs welcome, picnic-sets out in front and in walled back garden, play area, Peddars Way walks, three bedrooms, open all day. *(Tracey and Stephen Groves, Roy Hoing)*

ROYDON TF7022

Three Horseshoes (01485) 600666

The one near King's Lynn; Lynn Road; PE32 1AQ Refurbished brick and stone village pub now under same ownership as nearby Congham Hall Hotel; pleasant pastel décor with simple wood furniture, stone floor bar and split-level part-carpeted restaurant, woodburner in each, good uncomplicated food (all day Sun) from reasonably priced blackboard menu, weekday OAP lunch deal, three ales including Greene King and Woodfordes, friendly helpful staff; children and dogs (in bar) welcome, tables outside, closed Mon, Tues, otherwise open all day. *(John Wooll, R C Vincent)*

SCULTHORPE TF8930

Hourglass (01328) 856744

The Street; NR21 9QD Restaurant-y place with long open room combining light modern style with some dark beams, good choice of enjoyable fairly priced food including OAP lunch deal (Mon, Tues), Adnams Broadside and Woodfordes Wherry, quick friendly service. *(Edward May)*

SCULTHORPE TF8930

★ Sculthorpe Mill (01328) 856161

Inn signed off A148 W of Fakenham, opposite village; NR21 9QG Welcoming dining pub in rebuilt 18th-c mill, appealing riverside setting, seats out under weeping willows and in attractive garden behind; light, airy and relaxed with leather sofas and sturdy tables in bar/dining area, good reasonably priced food from sandwiches to daily specials, attentive service, Greene King ales and good house wines, upstairs restaurant; background music; six comfortable bedrooms, open all day in summer (all day weekends winter). *(George Atkinson, Roy Hoing, John Wooll)*

SEDGEFORD TF7036

King William IV (01485) 571765

B1454, off A149 King's Lynn–Hunstanton; PE36 5LU Homely inn handy for beaches and bird-watching; bar and dining areas decorated with paintings of north Norfolk coast and migrating birds, high-backed dark leather dining chairs around pine tables on slate tiles, log fires, Adnams, Greene King and Woodfordes, ten wines by the glass, straightforward food; children welcome (no under-4s in main restaurant after 6.30pm), dogs allowed in bar and a couple of the bedrooms, seats on terrace and under parasols on grass, also an attractive covered dining area surrounded by flowering tubs, closed Mon lunchtime, otherwise open all day. *(Roy Hoing)*

SHERINGHAM TG1543

Lobster (01263) 822716

High Street; NR26 8JP Almost on seafront and popular with locals and tourists, friendly panelled bar with log fire and seafaring décor, wide range of ales including Adnams, Greene King and Woodfordes, two or three ciders and decent wines by the glass, generous reasonably priced bar food, restaurant with seasonal seafood including lobster and crab, maybe live music Weds; children and dogs welcome, two courtyards, open all day. *(David Carr, N R White, Brian Glozier)*

SHERINGHAM TG1543

Two Lifeboats (01263) 823144

High Street/Promenade; NR26 8JR Cleanly refurbished open-plan seafront inn, enjoyable well priced pubby food from baguettes up, Adnams, Nethergate and Woodfordes, good choice of other drinks, friendly staff; background music; children welcome, no dogs in summer, picnic-sets on small terrace overlooking beach, six bedrooms (some with sea view), good breakfast, parking can be tricky. *(Dennis and Doreen Haward)*

SHOULDHAM   TF6708
Kings Arms (01366) 347410
The Green; PE33 0BY Prettily placed
community-owned pub, sympathetically
renovated (if a little sparse at present), with
well kept changing ales tapped from the cask
and generously served pubby food (not Sun
evening, Mon, Tues), pleasant staff, café;
some live music; children and dogs welcome,
classic car/motorcycle meetings first Sun
of month, open all day weekends, closed
lunchtimes Mon, Tues. *(Henry Fryer)*

SMALLBURGH   TG3324
Crown (01692) 536314
A149 Yarmouth Road; NR12 9AD
Character thatched and beamed village
inn dating from the 15th c, friendly
newish landlady from the ivory coast, well
kept Adnams, Fullers, Timothy Taylors,
Woodfordes and a guest, enjoyable home-
made food (english and african menus) in
log-fire bar and small dining room; darts,
monthly quiz; children and dogs welcome,
picnic-sets in pretty back garden, Aug anglo-
african festival, two bedrooms, open all day
(food all day summer). *(Philip and Susan
Philcox, Roy Hoing)*

SOUTH LOPHAM   TM0481
White Horse (01379) 688579
*A1066 Diss–Thetford; The Street;
IP22 2LH* Friendly beamed village pub, well
kept Adnams, Woodfordes and an occasional
guest, enjoyable home made food including
blackboard specials, log fires; live music and
quiz nights, TV; children welcome, big garden
with play area, handy for Bressingham
Gardens, open all day. *(John Harris)*

SOUTHREPPS   TG2536
★ Vernon Arms (01263) 833355
Church Street; NR11 8NP Popular
old-fashioned brick and cobble village pub,
welcoming and relaxed, with good home-
made food running up to steaks and well
priced crab (must book weekend evenings),
also good Sun roasts and takeaway fish and
chips (Tues-Sat evenings), friendly helpful
staff, well kept Adnams, Greene King,
Woodfordes and a guest, good choice of
wines and malt whiskies, big log fire; darts
and pool; tables outside, children, dogs and
muddy walkers welcome, open all day.
(Dr D J and Mrs S C Walker)

SPOONER ROW   TM0997
Boars (01953) 605851
*Just off A11 SW of Wymondham;
NR18 9LL* Interesting 1920s pub-restaurant
in tiny village, good variety of enjoyable
locally sourced food (not Mon evening)
from light meals to more expensive (though
not pretentious) choices including good
vegetarian options, well kept Adnams and
nice range of wines, friendly staff and pub
dog (others welcome in bar), amazing

collection of food/wine books; children
allowed, tables in well tended pretty garden.
(Ruth May)

SPORLE   TF8411
Peddars Inn (01760) 788101
The Street; PE32 2DR Refurbished
beamed pub with inglenook bar, dining room
and little conservatory, good sensibly priced
food from pub favourites to specials, well
kept Adnams and a couple of local guests,
Aspall's cider, friendly service, occasional live
music and charity quiz nights; children and
dogs welcome, a few seats outside on grass,
well placed for Peddars Way walkers, open
all day Sat, closed Sun evening, Mon and
lunchtime Tues. *(John Harris)*

STIFFKEY   TF9643
Red Lion (01328) 830552
A149 Wells–Blakeney; NR23 1AJ Popular
cheerful old pub, front bar with inglenook
fireplace, cushioned pews and other pubby
seats, local landscape photos, room off with
scatter cushions on settles, another room
with dark panelling and splendid winged
settle, Greene King and Woodfordes ales,
generally well liked food (all day Sun) from
pubby choices to local fish/shellfish (local
mussels a speciality), friendly service (may
slow at busy times), two back dining rooms,
one a flint-walled conservatory; children and
dogs welcome, big partly covered gravelled
courtyard, more tables on covered deck,
ten bedrooms in modern block with own
balconies or terraces, nearby coastal walks,
open all day. *(Alison Ball, Ian Walton,
Dr D J and Mrs S C Walker)*

STOKE HOLY CROSS   TG2302
Wildebeest Arms (01508) 492497
*Village signposted off A140 S of Norwich;
turn left in village; NR14 8QJ*
New licensees here and things may have
changed – reports please; long bar with
stools by sleek semicircular counter, one
changing real ale, décor has included an
understated african theme, carvings and
hangings on dark sandy walls and unusual
leather chairs grouped around striking
tables, generally well thought-of food (not
cheap) including fixed-price menus; subtly
lit front terrace sheltered from the road
by tall willow hurdling, open all day Sun.
(Belinda Stamp, Rob Anderson)

STOW BARDOLPH   TF6205
Hare Arms (01366) 382229
*Just off A10 N of Downham Market;
PE34 3HT* Cheerful bustling village pub
under long-serving licensees; bar with
traditional pub furnishings and interesting
bric-a-brac, log fire, Greene King ales and
a couple of guests, nine wines by glass and
several malt whiskies, well liked food (all day
Sun), refurbished dining room and family
conservatory, pub cats Otis and Martha;
plenty of seats in front and back gardens,

maybe wandering peacocks, Church Farm Rare Breeds Centre nearby. *(Denis and Margaret Kilner, Tracey and Stephen Groves)*

SWAFFHAM TF8109
Kings Arms (01760) 723244
Market Place; PE37 7LA Recently refurbished 17th-c coaching inn, enjoyable food from snacks and sharing boards up, good selection of drinks, restaurant and champagne/cocktail bar; children welcome, courtyard tables, closed Sun evening, Mon, Tues, otherwise open all day. *(Matt)*

SWANTON MORLEY TG0217
Darbys (01362) 637647
B1147 NE of Dereham; NR20 4NY Cosy unspoilt red-brick local (formerly two farm cottages), half a dozen ales tapped from the cask including Adnams, Beeston and Woodfordes, fair value pubby food, long bare-boards country-style bar with gin traps and farming memorabilia, log fire and bread oven, step up to attractive dining room with stripped-wood furniture, another small room with glassed-over well; background radio, TV, free wi-fi; children and dogs welcome, wheelchair access (easiest through french doors), back garden with picnic-sets and play area, campsite, open all day Fri-Sun. *(Peter Brix, Pip White, Simon and Mandy King, Shaun Mahoney)*

TACOLNESTON TM1495
★ Pelican (01508) 489521
Norwich Road (B1113 SW of city); NR16 1AL Former 17th-c coaching inn, chatty timbered bar with relaxed comfortable atmosphere, good log fire, sofas, armchairs and old stripped settle on quarry tiles, candles and flowers on tables, some booth seating, up to four well kept changing ales, Aspall's cider and 36 malt whiskies, restaurant area with high-backed leather chairs around oak tables, good choice of enjoyable food from pub favourites up, friendly service, shop selling local produce and bottled Norfolk/Suffolk ales; background music; children and dogs welcome, plenty of tables on decking behind, sheltered lawn beyond, bedrooms, open all day summer, closed weekday lunchtimes winter. *(Hilary and Neil Christopher)*

THOMPSON TL9296
Chequers (01953) 483360
Griston Road, off A1075 S of Watton; IP24 1PX Long, low and picturesque 16th-c thatched dining pub tucked away in attractive spot, enjoyable food including bargain weekday lunch offer, ales such as Greene King and Woodfordes, helpful staff and friendly atmosphere, series of quaint rooms with low beams, inglenooks and some stripped brickwork; children welcome, dogs allowed in bar, some seats out in front and in back garden with swing, bedroom block, open (and food) all day Sun. *(Andrew Stone)*

THORNHAM TF7343
★ Lifeboat (01485) 512236
A149 by Kings Head, then first left; PE36 6LT Sadly, this lovely pub went into administration as we went to press and future is unclear – news please; plenty of atmosphere in two pubby main bars, beams, lots of horse tack and farming implements, big lamps, brass measuring jugs, and chairs and settles around dark sturdy tables on quarry tiles, one bench has an antique penny-in-the-hole game, woodburners, cosy tap bar and spreading more formal restaurant, two-level conservatory with steps up to terrace garden, play area, more seats at the front, bedrooms, good nearby walks. *(Mr and Mrs P R Thomas, David and Ruth Hollands, John Wooll, Peter Sutton, David Carr, Derek and Sylvia Stephenson and others)*

WALSINGHAM TF9336
Bull (01328) 820333
Common Place/Shire Hall Plain; NR22 6BP Rather quirky pub in pilgrimage village; bar with various odds and ends including half-size statue of Charlie Chaplin, pictures of archbishops and clerical visiting cards, welcoming landlord and friendly efficient staff, tasty food (not Sat and Sun evenings) from shortish inexpensive menu, three well kept changing ales, log fire, typewriter in snug, old-fashioned cash register in gents'; free wi-fi; children welcome, courtyard and attractive flowery terrace by village square, dovecote stuffed with plastic lobsters and crabs, outside games room, bedrooms, snowdrop walk in nearby abbey garden, open all day. *(John Wooll)*

WEASENHAM ST PETER TF8522
Fox & Hounds (01328) 838868
A1065 Fakenham–Swaffham; The Green; PE32 2TD Traditional 18th-c beamed local with bar and two dining areas (one with inglenook woodburner), spotless and well run by friendly family, three changing ales, good reasonably priced home-made food (not Sun evening), pubby furniture and carpets throughout, brasses and lots of military prints; children welcome, big well kept garden and terrace, closed Mon. *(Edward May)*

WELLS-NEXT-THE-SEA TF9143
Albatros 07979 087228
The Quay; NR23 1AT Bar on 1899 quayside clipper, charts and other nautical memorabilia, Woodfordes beers served from the cask, dutch food including speciality pancakes, seats on deck with good views of harbour and tidal marshes, live weekend music; children and dogs welcome, not good for disabled, cabin accommodation with shared showers, open (and food) all day. *(Chris Johnson, John Wooll)*

WELLS-NEXT-THE-SEA   TF9143

Bowling Green (01328) 710100
Church Street; NR23 1JB Welcoming
17th-c pub, Greene King Abbot, Woodfordes
Wherry and a guest, generous helpings of
reasonably priced traditional food, L-shaped
bar with corner settles, flagstone and brick
floor, two woodburners, raised dining end;
children and dogs welcome, back terrace,
two bedrooms in converted barn, quiet spot
on outskirts. *(John Wooll)*

WELLS-NEXT-THE-SEA   TF9143

Crown (01328) 710209
The Buttlands; NR23 1EX Smart old
coaching inn (part of Flying Kiwi group)
overlooking tree-lined green; rambling bar
on several levels with beams and standing
timbers, grey-painted planked wall seats
and brown leather dining chairs on stripped
floorboards, Jo C's Norfolk Ale along with
Adnams and Woodfordes, several wines by
the glass, enjoyable modern food including
daily specials, friendly accommodating staff,
airy dining room and elegant more formal
restaurant; background music; children and
dogs (in bar) welcome, 12 bedrooms, open all
day from 8am for breakfast. *(David Carr)*

WELLS-NEXT-THE-SEA   TF9143

Edinburgh (01328) 710120
Station Road/Church Street; NR23 1AE
Traditional 19th-c pub near main shopping
area, enjoyable home-made food and three
well kept ales including Woodfordes, open
fire, sizeable restaurant, also 'lifeboat' dining
room decorated in RNLI colours; background
music, free wi-fi; children and dogs welcome,
disabled access, courtyard with heated
smokers' shelter, three bedrooms, open all day.
(David Carr, Brian and Jean Hepworth)

WELLS-NEXT-THE-SEA   TF9143

★ Globe (01328) 710206
The Buttlands; NR23 1EU Handsome
Georgian inn a short walk from the quay;
plenty of space and nice atmosphere in
opened-up contemporary rooms, tables on
oak boards, big bow windows, well kept
Adnams beers, thoughtful wine choice
and enjoyable seasonal food, good service;

background music, evening jazz third Sun of
month; children and dogs welcome, attractive
courtyard with pale flagstones, more seats
at front overlooking green, seven bedrooms
(more planned), open all day. *(Tracey and
Stephen Groves, David Carr, Brian and Jean
Hepworth, Derek and Sylvia Stephenson)*

WEST ACRE   TF7815

Stag (01760) 755395
Low Road; PE32 1TR Small family-run
local with three or more well kept changing
ales in appealing unpretentious bar, obliging
cheerful staff, good value home-made food,
neat dining room; quiz third Sun of month;
attractive spot in quiet village, closed Mon.
(Alan Weedon)

WEYBOURNE   TG1143

Ship (01263) 588721
*A149 W of Sheringham; The Street;
NR25 7SZ* Popular refurbished village
pub; well kept Woodfordes Wherry and two
local guests, good wine choice, big bar with
pubby furniture and woodburner, two dining
rooms, good reasonably priced home-made
food (not Mon, should book weekends)
from lunchtime sandwiches, through pub
favourites to local seafood, efficient friendly
young staff; background music, free wi-fi; well
behaved children welcome, dogs in bar, seats
out at front and in nice side garden handy for
Muckleburgh military vehicle museum, open
all day in season. *(S Holder, M and GR)*

WYMONDHAM   TG1001

★ Green Dragon (01953) 607907
Church Street; NR18 0PH Picturesque
heavily timbered medieval pub with plenty
of character, small beamed bar and snug,
bigger dining area, interesting pictures, log
fire under Tudor mantelpiece, four well kept
changing ales and over 50 whiskies, winter
mulled wine, plentiful helpings of popular
good value food including daily specials
(best to book), friendly helpful staff, upstairs
function room – open mike night third Sun
of month, ukulele group third Tues; children
and dogs welcome, garden behind with
raised deck, near glorious 12th-c abbey
church, open all day (food all day Fri-Sun).
(Hilary and Neil Christopher)

Post Office address codings confusingly give the impression that
a few pubs are in Norfolk, when they're really in Cambridgeshire or Suffolk
(which is where we list them).

Northamptonshire

ASHBY ST LEDGERS   SP5768   Map 4
Olde Coach House 🛏

(01788) 890349 – www.oldecoachhouse.co.uk

Main Street; 4 miles from M1 junction 18; A5 S to Kilsby, then A361 S towards
Daventry; village also signed off A5 N of Weedon; CV23 8UN

**Carefully modernised ex-farmhouse with original character,
real ales, good wines, friendly staff and plenty of outside seating;
well appointed bedrooms**

This is a lovely place to stay, with 11 of the well equipped, contemporary
bedrooms located in the converted stables; breakfasts are good. The
opened-up bar on the right, full of original charm, has stools against the
counter where they keep Everards Tiger, Wells Bombardier and Youngs Bitter
on handpump and eight wines by the glass, served by friendly staff. Several
dining areas, all very relaxed, take in paintwork ranging from white and light
beige to purple, and flooring that includes stripped wooden boards, original
red and white tiles and beige carpeting. All manner of pale wooden tables are
surrounded by assorted church chairs, high-backed leather dining chairs and
armchairs, with comfortable squashy leather sofas and pouffes in front of a
log fire. There are hunting pictures, large mirrors, an original old stove and
fresh flowers; background music and TV. The back garden has picnic-sets
among shrubs and trees, modern tables and chairs out in front under pretty
hanging baskets, and a dining courtyard. The nearby church is of interest.

🍴 As well as a two-course set menu (Mon-Thurs before 7.30pm, Fri lunchtime),
the good quality food includes sandwiches, chicken liver parfait with red onion
marmalade, fishcake with tartare sauce, a big choice of grazing boards, stone-fired
pizzas, burgers (chicken, pork and apple, steak and coriander) with toppings in a
toasted roll, beer-battered fish and chips, lambs liver and bacon with baby onions in
red wine, chicken and chorizo kebab with sweet chilli sauce, pork medallions with
wild mushroom sauce, and puddings such as vanilla crème brûlée and chocolate
brownie. *Benchmark main dish: steak in ale pie £12.95. Two-course evening
meal £19.00.*

Quicksilver Management ~ Lease Mark Butler ~ Real ale ~ Open 12-11 ~ Bar food 12-2.30,
6-9.30; 12-8 Sun ~ Restaurant ~ Children welcome ~ Dogs allowed in bar ~ Wi-fi ~
Bedrooms: /£75 *Recommended by George Atkinson, Mungo Shipley, Anne and Ben Smith*

Cribbage is a card game using a block of wood with holes for matchsticks or
special pins to score with; regulars in cribbage pubs are usually happy to teach
strangers how to play.

EASTON ON THE HILL   TF0104   Map 4

Exeter Arms

(01780) 756321 – www.theexeterarms.net

Stamford Road (A43); PE9 3NS

Carefully refurbished and opened-up inn, character rooms, real ales, quite a choice of popular food and seats outside; comfortable bedrooms

This 18th-c pub has been carefully and thoughtfully renovated to give plenty of space for both eating and drinking. The bar has a country feel with hops, cushioned captain's chairs, cushioned wall and window seats, copper pans on the wall above the woodburning stove and a couple of tractor seats by the counter where they serve Grainstore Triple B and Oakham JHB on handpump and several wines by the glass. There's a snug with smart high-backed beige chairs on carpet that leads into the restaurant (high-backed settles and an attractive medley of wooden tables and chairs) and an airy orangery (pretty wallpaper and rattan furniture) with doors opening on to a sunken terrace. Throughout, there are watering cans, stone jugs, fresh flowers, candlelight and even an old mangle. The atmosphere is friendly and easy-going. Dotted among geraniums in pots are picnic-sets on a lawn. The bedrooms are light and comfortable.

As well as lunchtime ciabattas, the enjoyable food includes crab ravioli with lemon and ginger butter sauce, twice-cooked cheese soufflé, roast shallot tarte tatin, lincolnshire sausages with mash and onion gravy, smoked lamb rump with orange-glazed carrots, parmentier potatoes and rosemary jus, pork tenderloin wrapped in parma ham with rhubarb purée, fondant potato and honey glaze, bass with spring onion purée, dauphinoise potatoes and herb oil, and puddings such as tonka bean and vanilla panna cotta and lemon curd tartlet with glazed meringues, praline and lemon sherbert. *Benchmark main dish: beer-battered fish and chips £12.95. Two-course evening meal £22.00.*

Free house ~ Licensee Sue Olver ~ Real ale ~ Open 9am-11pm; 9-9 Sun ~ Bar food 12-2.30, 6-9.30; 12-4 Sun ~ Restaurant ~ Children welcome ~ Dogs allowed in bar ~ Wi-fi ~ Bedrooms: $80/$100 *Recommended by Phoebe Peacock, Caroline Prescott*

FARTHINGSTONE   SP6155   Map 4

Kings Arms £

(01327) 361604

Off A5 SE of Daventry; village signed from Litchborough; NN12 8EZ

Individual place with cosy traditional interior, carefully prepared food and lovely garden

This is a cheerful little 18th-c traditional pub with plenty of chatty customers, and the cosy flagstoned bar has a huge log fire, comfortable homely sofas and armchairs near the entrance, whisky-water jugs hanging from oak beams, and lots of pictures and decorative plates on the walls. A games room at the far end has darts, dominoes, cribbage, table skittles and board games. Elgood Cambridge, St Austell Trelawney and Woodfordes Wherry on handpump and a short but decent wine list. Look out for the interesting newspaper-influenced décor in the outside gents'. The handsome gargoyled stone exterior is nicely weathered and very pretty in summer when the hanging baskets are at their best; there are seats on a tranquil terrace among plant-filled painted tractor tyres and recycled art. This is a picturesque village and good walks nearby include the Knightley Way. It's worth ringing ahead to check the opening and food times.

Using some home-grown produce, food – served weekend lunchtimes only – includes sandwiches, cheese, meat and fish platters, salmon with mustard and dill sauce, pork cassoulet, game casserole, and puddings such as gingerbread pudding and meringues. *Benchmark main dish: yorkshire pudding filled with steak, gammon and ale £8.45.*

Free house ~ Licensees Paul and Denise Egerton ~ Real ale ~ Open 7-11 Tues-Thurs; 6.30-midnight Fri; 12-midnight Sat; 12-6 (4.30 winter), 9-11 Sun; closed Mon, weekday lunchtimes ~ Bar food 12-2.30 weekends; phone for occasional evening food ~ Children welcome ~ Dogs allowed in bar ~ Wi-fi *Recommended by S F Parrinder, George Atkinson, Sharon and John Hancock*

FOTHERINGHAY
TL0593   Map 5

Falcon 🏮⭐ 🍷
(01832) 226254 – www.thefalcon-inn.co.uk
Village signposted off A605 on Peterborough side of Oundle; PE8 5HZ

Northamptonshire Dining Pub of the Year

Upmarket dining pub with good range of drinks and modern british food from snacks up, and attractive garden

Our readers very much enjoy their visits to this stylish and comfortably civilised pub, and it's certainly worth booking ahead to be sure of a table. There are winter log fires in stone fireplaces, fresh flowers, cushioned slatback armchairs, bucket chairs and comfortably cushioned window seats and bare floorboards. The Orangery restaurant opens on to a charming lavender-surrounded terrace with lovely views of the huge church behind and of the attractively planted garden; plenty of seats under parasols. Surprisingly, given the emphasis on dining, there's a thriving little locals' tap bar and a darts team, and a fine choice of drinks including Digfield Fool's Nook, Fullers London Pride and Greene King IPA on handpump, 16 good wines by the glass and several malt whiskies; board games. This is a lovely village (Richard III was born here) with plenty of moorings on the River Nene; the ruins of Fotheringhay Castle, where Mary Queen of Scots was executed, is nearby.

Highly enjoyable food includes open sandwiches, smoked ham hock and rabbit terrine with piccalilli, crispy duck salad with asian slaw and coriander dressing, asparagus, broad bean and spring risotto, corn-fed chicken with butternut squash purée and salsa verde, lamb three-ways (roast loin, confit shoulder, sweetbreads) with niçoise vegetables and red pepper purée, pork belly with cider fondant, cabbage and bacon, baby onions and gravy, and puddings such as seasonal fruit crumble and lemon curd tartlet with honey ice-cream; they also offer a two- and three-course set menu (not Sat evening or Sun lunchtime). *Benchmark main dish: salmon, crab and dill fishcakes with home-made tartare sauce £10.50. Two-course evening meal £19.50.*

Free house ~ Licensee Sally Facer ~ Real ale ~ Open 12-11; closed Sun evening Oct-Easter ~ Bar food 12-2, 6-9; 12-3 Sun ~ Restaurant ~ Children welcome ~ Dogs allowed in bar ~ Wi-fi *Recommended by Michael Sargent, Howard and Margaret Buchanan, Miss B D Picton, Ian Herdman*

GREAT BRINGTON
SP6664   Map 4

Althorp Coaching Inn 🍺
(01604) 770651 – www.althorp-coaching-inn.co.uk
Off A428 NW of Northampton, near Althorp Hall; until recently known as the Fox & Hounds; NN7 4JA

Friendly golden-stone thatched pub with a good choice of real ales, fine architectural features, tasty popular food and sheltered garden

Extremely and deservedly popular locally, this 16th-c coaching inn offers a genuine welcome to visitors too. They keep a fine range of real ales on handpump, such as Abbey Bellringer, Greene King IPA, Hook Norton Old Hooky, Phipps NBC India Pale Ale, St Austell Tribute and Tom Woods Mill Race; the extended dining area gives views of the 30 or so casks racked in the cellar. Also, eight wines by the glass and a dozen malt whiskies. The ancient bar has all the traditional features you'd wish for, from a dog or two sprawled by the huge log fire, to old beams, sagging joists and an appealing mix of country chairs and tables (maybe with fresh flowers) on broad flagstones and bare boards. There are snug alcoves, nooks and crannies with some stripped-pine shutters and panelling, two fine log fires and an eclectic medley of bric-a-brac from farming implements to an old clocking-in machine and country pictures. A function room in a converted stable block is next to the lovely cobbled and paved courtyard (also accessible by the old coaching entrance) with sheltered tables and tubs of flowers; more seating in the charming garden.

🍴 As well as sandwiches and baguettes (not Sunday lunchtime), the enjoyable food includes scallops with balsamic glaze and samphire, goats cheese, pear and walnut salad with honey and mustard dressing, wild mushroom and asparagus risotto, burger with toppings and chips, chicken and bacon pasta with smoked cheddar and leek sauce, lamb and mint sausages with onion gravy, pork fillet stuffed with apricot and sage with pear cider sauce, and puddings such as pineapple upside-down cake and chocolate brownie with ice-cream. *Benchmark main dish: pie of the day £9.95. Two-course evening meal £18.00.*

Free house ~ Licensee Michael Krempels ~ Real ale ~ Open 11am-midnight; 12-11 Sun ~ Bar food 12-3, 6.30-9.30 (10 Fri, Sat); 12-4.30, 5.30-8.30 Sun ~ Restaurant ~ Children welcome ~ Dogs allowed in bar ~ Wi-fi *Recommended by Gerry and Rosemary Dobson, George Atkinson*

 NETHER HEYFORD   SP6658   Map 4
Olde Sun 🍺 £
(01327) 340164 – www.theoldesun.co.uk
1.75 miles from M1 junction 16; village signposted left off A45 westbound; Middle Street; NN7 3LL

Unpretentious place with diverting bric-a-brac, reasonably priced pubby bar food and garden with play area

A perfect break from the M1, this is an honest, enjoyable pub with a good mix of both locals and visitors. The several small linked rooms have all manner of entertaining bric-a-brac hanging from the ceilings and packed into nooks and crannies. It includes brassware (one fireplace is a grotto of large brass animals), colourful relief plates, 1930s cigarette cards, railway memorabilia and advertising signs, World War II posters and rope fancywork. The nice old cash till on one of the two counters is wishfully stuck at one and a ha'penny: Banks's Bitter, Greene King IPA and Ruddles, Marstons Pedigree and a guest such as Green Jack Waxwing on handpump. Most of the furnishings are properly pubby, with the odd easy chair. There are beams and low ceilings (one painted with a fine sunburst), partly glazed dividing panels, steps between some areas, rugs on parquet, red tiles or flagstones, a big inglenook log fire and, up on the left, a room with full-sized hood skittles, a games machine, darts, cribbage and dominoes; background music. In the garden you'll find antiquated hand-operated farm machines, some with plants in their hoppers. The first thing that will catch your eye when you arrive will probably be a row of brightly coloured grain kibblers along the edge of the fairy-lit front terrace (with picnic-sets).

 Reasonably priced pubby food includes sandwiches, tempura mushrooms with garlic dip, farmhouse pâté with redcurrant sauce, vegetable curry, lasagne, cumberland sausage with onion gravy, steak pie, tuna steak with home-made salsa, and puddings such as jam sponge and apple pie, both with custard. *Benchmark main dish: home-cooked ham, free-range eggs and chips £7.95. Two-course evening meal £12.00.*

Free house ~ Licensees P Yates and Alan Ford ~ Real ale ~ Open 12-2.30, 5-11; 12-midnight Fri, Sat, Sun ~ Bar food 12-2, 6.30-9; 12-4 Sun ~ Restaurant ~ Children welcome ~ Dogs welcome *Recommended by Steve and Suzanne Griffiths, Phil and Jane Hodson, Gerry and Rosemary Dobson, Edward Mirzoeff, Martin and Sue Day, George Atkinson*

 NORTHAMPTON   SP7559 Map 4
Malt Shovel  £
(01604) 234212 – www.maltshoveltavern.com
Bridge Street (approach road from M1 junction 15); no parking in nearby street, best to park in Morrisons central car park, far end – passage past Europcar straight to back entrance; NN1 1QF

Friendly, well run real ale pub with bargain lunches and over a dozen varied beers

From a battery of handpumps lined up on the long counter in this cheerful tavern, they keep a fantastic choice of up to 13 real ales: Belhaven Grand Slam, Elgoods Black Dog, Exmoor Gold, Fullers London Pride, Hook Norton Cotswold Lion, Nobbys Best and T'owd Navigation, MerriMen Be Merri, Oakham Bishops Farewell and JHB, Phipps NBC India Pale Ale and Timothy Taylors Boltmaker. They also stock belgian draught and bottled beers, 50 malt whiskies, 17 rums, 17 vodkas and 17 gins, and Cheddar Valley farm cider; regular beer festivals. This is home to quite an extensive collection of carefully chosen brewing memoribilia – look out for the rare Northampton Brewery Company star, displayed outside the pub, and some high-mounted ancient beer engines. Staff are enthusiastic and helpful; darts, daily papers and background music. The secluded back yard has tables and chairs and a smokers' shelter; disabled facilities.

 Lunchtime-only food includes wraps and baguettes, three-cheese and broccoli bake, burger and chips, gammon and egg, lambs liver and bacon casserole, and pork belly with spring onion mash and red cabbage. *Benchmark main dish: fish pie £6.30.*

Free house ~ Licensee Mike Evans ~ Real ale ~ Open 11.30-3, 5-11; 11.30-11 Thurs-Sat; 12-10.30 Sun ~ Bar food 12-2; not Sun ~ Well behaved children welcome in bar ~ Dogs allowed in bar ~ Wi-fi ~ Blues Weds evening *Recommended by Dr J Barrie Jones, Richard Kennell, George Atkinson*

 OUNDLE   TL0388 Map 5
Ship  £
(01832) 273918 – www.theshipinn-oundle.co.uk
West Street; PE8 4EF

Bustling down-to-earth town pub with interesting beers and good value pubby food; bedrooms

In an elegant small town, this traditional local has an easy-going, companionable feel, chatty regulars and is run by two brothers. Off to the left of the central corridor, the heavily beamed lounge (refurbished in

2015) consists of cosy areas with a mix of leather and other seats, sturdy tables and a warming log fire in a stone inglenook. A charming little panelled snug at one end has button-back leather seats. The wood-floored public bar has poker evenings on Wednesdays, while the terrace bar has pool, darts, TV, board games and background music. Friendly staff serve Brewsters Hophead, Digfield Shacklebush, Nene Valley NVB Bitter and Sharps Doom Bar on handpump, eight wines by the glass and several malt whiskies. The wooden tables and chairs out on the series of small sunny, covered terraces are illuminated at night.

Good value food includes baguettes, breaded whitebait with home-made tartare sauce, house pâté, full english breakfast, chilli con carne, beer-battered haddock and chips, burger with toppings, coleslaw and fries, bangers and mash with onion gravy, and steaks. *Benchmark main dish: steak in ale pie £9.95. Two-course evening meal £14.00.*

Free house ~ Licensees Andrew and Robert Langridge ~ Real ale ~ Open 11am-11.30pm (midnight Sat); 12-11.30 Sun ~ Bar food 12-3, 6-9; 12-6 Sun ~ Children welcome ~ Dogs welcome ~ Wi-fi ~ Live bands last Sat of month, folk second Mon of month ~ Bedrooms: £39/£69 *Recommended by Phoebe Peacock, Andrew Stone*

SULGRAVE
SP5545 Map 4

Star

(01295) 760389 – www.thestarinnsulgrave.com

Manor Road; E of Banbury, signed off B4525; OX17 2SA

Handsome old inn with original features in character bars, good food, real ales and neat garden; bedrooms

This is a pretty, creeper-covered 300-year-old farmhouse just a stone's throw from the grounds of Sulgrave Manor (the ancestral home of George Washington). Original features are in keeping: working shutters, old doors and flagstones, brown-painted woodwork and moss or plum coloured walls. The furniture is a mix of antique, vintage and retro, and the filament-bulb lighting, candles and polished copper create an old-fashioned feel; a fine log fire burns in the inglenook fireplace. Hook Norton Cotswold Lion and Hooky and a couple of quickly changing guest craft ales from Hook Norton such as Oatmeal and Red Rye on handpump and seven wines by the glass. The original farmhouse kitchen (with its bread oven) is now called the Snug; the dining room has a working range cooker where cakes, bread and breakfasts are made. The neatly kept back garden has a vine-covered trellis and seats and tables.

Wholesome, enjoyable food includes baked camembert with garlic bread, seared pigeon breasts with spiced ale jus, beetroot and goats cheese tart, home-baked ham and free-range eggs, beer-battered cod and chips, cajun chicken with cream, steak burger with onions and melted cheese, tuna steak with olive oil, lemon and garlic, venison steak with red wine and mushroom gravy, and puddings such as winter steamed puddings and summer fruit pies; they hold regular themed food evenings. *Benchmark main dish: steak and onion pie £9.50. Two-course evening meal £16.00.*

Hook Norton ~ Tenant Sue Hilton ~ Real ale ~ Open 12-3, 6-11; 12-11 Sat; 12-9 (5 in winter) Sun; closed Mon ~ Bar food 12-3, 6-9; 12-9 Sat; 12-4 Sun ~ Restaurant ~ Children welcome ~ Dogs allowed in bar and bedrooms ~ Wi-fi ~ Bedrooms: /£69
Recommended by R L Borthwick, Andrew Stone

Also Worth a Visit in Northamptonshire

Besides the fully inspected pubs, you might like to try these pubs that have been recommended to us and described by readers. Do tell us what you think of them: feedback@goodguides.com

ABTHORPE SP6446
★ **New Inn** (01327) 857306
Signed from A43 at first roundabout S of A5; Silver Street; NN12 8QR
Traditional partly thatched country local run by cheery farming family, fairly basic rambling bar with dining area down a couple of steps, four well kept Hook Norton beers and Weston's cider, good pubby food (not Sun evening) using their own meat and home-grown herbs, beams, stripped stone and inglenook woodburner, darts and table skittles; quiz last Sun of month, occasional live music, free wi-fi; children, dogs and muddy boots welcome, garden tables, bedrooms in converted barn (short walk across fields), open all day Fri-Sun, closed Mon and Tues lunchtimes. *(Caroline Prescott)*

APETHORPE TL0295
Kings Head (01780) 470627
Kings Cliffe Road; PE8 5DG Roomy stone-built pub in conservation village, cosy right-hand bar with window seating, log fire in comfortable lounge to the left, Fullers London Pride and three local guests, sensibly short choice of enjoyable home-cooked food including bar snacks and daily specials, friendly efficient service, big dining area; TV; children, dogs and walkers welcome, some seats out at front and in nice sheltered courtyard behind, open all day Sat, till 7pm Sun. *(Andrew Stone)*

ARTHINGWORTH SP7581
Bulls Head (01858) 525637
Kelmarsh Road, just above A14 by A508 junction; pub signed from A14; LE16 8JZ Steps up to much extended black-beamed pub with various seating areas in L-shaped bar, pubby furniture and upholstered banquettes on patterned carpet, woodburner, fairly standard good value food including OAP weekday lunch deal, well kept Thwaites and a couple of guests, efficient cheery service, restaurant, darts and skittles; background music, TV, free wi-fi; disabled access (from back) and facilities, terrace picnic-sets, eight bedrooms in separate block, handy for Kelmarsh Hall, open all day weekends (food till 7.30pm Sun). *(Gerry and Rosemary Dobson)*

AYNHO SP5133
Cartwright (01869) 811885
Croughton Road (B4100); handy for M40 junction 10; OX17 3BE Spotless 16th-c coaching inn with linked areas, contemporary furniture on wood or tiled floors, some exposed stone walls, leather sofas by big log fire in small bar, ales such as Adnams and Hook Norton, nice wines and coffee, good well presented food including set deals, friendly efficient uniformed staff, daily papers; background music, TV, free wi-fi; children welcome, a few seats in pretty corner of former coachyard, 21 bedrooms, good breakfast, pleasant village with apricot trees growing against old cottage walls, open all day. *(George Atkinson)*

AYNHO SP4932
★ **Great Western Arms**
(01869) 338288 *On B4031 1.5 miles E of Deddington, 0.75 miles W of Aynho, adjacent to Oxford Canal and Old Aynho station; OX17 3BP* Attractive old pub with series of linked cosy rooms; fine solid country tables on broad flagstones, golden stripped-stone walls, warm cream and deep red plasterwork, fresh flowers and candles, log fires, well kept Hook Norton and guests, good wines by the glass and enjoyable fairly pubby food served by friendly attentive young staff, elegant dining area on right, extensive GWR collection including lots of steam locomotive photographs, daily papers and magazines; background music, skittle alley, pool; children and dogs welcome, white cast-iron furniture in back former stable courtyard, moorings on Oxford Canal and nearby marina, bedrooms (may ask for payment on arrival), open all day, food all day Sun. *(Michael Sargent, Phil and Jane Hodson)*

BADBY SP5659
Maltsters (01327) 702905
The Green; NN11 3AF Refurbished stone-built village pub, long beamed room with fire at each end, enjoyable home-cooked pubby food including deals and good value Sun roasts, Steak House restaurant, three well kept ales including Gun Dog, attentive friendly service; children welcome, pleasant side garden and courtyard, well placed for walks on nearby Knightley Way, five bedrooms, open (and food) all day, may not serve food some Sun evenings. *(Roy Shutz)*

BADBY SP5558
Windmill (01327) 311070
Village signposted off A361 Daventry-Banbury; NN11 3AN Attractive 17th-c thatched and beamed village pub, flagstoned bar area with woodburner in huge inglenook, up to five changing ales, good reasonably priced home-made food from lunchtime sandwiches up, welcoming helpful staff, restaurant extension; background and

occasional live music; children and dogs welcome, terrace out by pretty green, nice walks (Badby bluebell woods close by), eight good bedrooms, open all day. *(George Atkinson, Graham and Elizabeth Hargreaves)*

BRAUNSTON   SP5465
Admiral Nelson (01788) 891900
Dark Lane, Little Braunston, overlooking Lock 3 just N of Grand Union Canal tunnel; NN11 7HJ 18th-c ex-farmhouse in peaceful setting by canal and hump bridge, good range of generous home-made food (not Sun evening) from sandwiches and baguettes up, four changing ales, canal pictures, smallish log-fire bar, carpeted restaurant area with fairly modern pastel décor and brick pillars, games section with hood skittles and darts; some live music including Aug festival, free wi-fi; well behaved children and dogs welcome, lots of waterside picnic-sets, may close Mon lunchtime in winter, otherwise open all day. *(Richard Kennell)*

BRAYBROOKE   SP7684
Swan (01858) 462754
Griffin Road; LE16 8LH Nicely kept thatched pub with good drinks choice including Everards ales, popular sensibly priced food (not Sun evening) from sandwiches and pub favourites up, friendly attentive staff, fireside sofas, soft lighting, beams and some exposed brickwork, restaurant; quiet background music; children and dogs welcome, disabled facilities, pretty hedged garden with covered terrace, open all day Fri-Sun, closed Mon. *(Caroline Prescott)*

BRIXWORTH   SP7470
Coach & Horses (01604) 880329
Harborough Road, just off A508 N of Northampton; NN6 9BX Welcoming early 18th-c stone-built beamed pub, popular good value food from fairly straightforward menu plus more adventurous specials including seasonal game, lunchtime and early evening set deals, well kept Marstons-related ales, prompt friendly service, log-fire bar with small dining area off, back lounge; tables on gravelled terrace behind, bedrooms in converted outbuildings, charming village with famous Saxon church, open (and food) all day Sun. *(Gerry and Rosemary Dobson)*

BROUGHTON   SP8375
Red Lion (01536) 790239
High Street; NN14 1NF Large welcoming stone-built village local with half a dozen well kept ales, farm cider and good choice of wines by the glass from central bar, enjoyable competitively priced home-made food (not Sun evening), bargain OAP lunch Tues/Thurs and other deals, Sun carvery, good attentive service, comfortable lounge and dining room, plainer public bar with games, events including beer festivals, live music, poker and quiz nights; background music; children welcome, small pleasant garden with water

feature, open all day Fri-Sun, closed Mon lunchtime. *(Gerry and Rosemary Dobson)*

BUCKBY WHARF   SP6066
New Inn (01327) 844747
A5 N of Weedon; NN6 7PW Canalside pub with reasonably priced pubby food from baguettes and baked potatoes up, Marstons-related beers, quick cheerful service (may ask for a credit card if you run a tab), several rooms radiating from central servery including a small dining room with fire, games area with table skittles; children welcome, dogs outside only, plenty of picnic-sets by busy Grand Union Canal Lock 7, very popular with summer boaters, open all day. *(George Atkinson)*

BUGBROOKE   SP6756
Wharf Inn (01604) 832585
The Wharf, off A5 S of Weedon; NN7 3QB New owners for this well situated pub by Grand Union Canal; large beamed water-view restaurant, tiled and carpeted bar with small informal raised eating area, lots of stripped brickwork, enjoyable food from varied menu (till 7pm Sun), good friendly service, five changing ales and 24 wines by the glass; background music; children and dogs (in bar) welcome, disabled facilities, plenty of tables on big waterside lawn, moorings, open (and food) all day. *(Andrew Stone)*

BULWICK   SP9694
★Queens Head (01780) 450272 *Off A43 Kettering–Duddington; NN17 3DY* Relaxed 17th-c stone pub in lovely country spot; traditional beamed bar with exposed stone walls, contemporary paintwork and woodburner, another fireplace in dining room with high-backed chairs around light wood tables, Digfield, Oakham and guests, ten wines by the glass and several malt whiskies, well liked freshly cooked food, good friendly service; free wi-fi; children welcome, dogs in bar (theirs is Dewey), terrace with rattan furniture under pergola, outside pizza oven, closed Sun evening, Mon. *(Michael and Jenny Back, Colin McLachlan and others)*

CHACOMBE   SP4943
George & Dragon (01295) 711500
Handy for M40 junction 11, via A361; Silver Street; OX17 2JR Welcoming pub dating from the 17th c with beams, flagstones, panelling and bare stone walls, two inglenook woodburners and deep glass-covered well, good popular food (not Sun evening) in three dining areas from lunchtime sandwiches and traditional choices up, vegetarian options, good service, Everards and a couple of guests from brass-topped counter, several wines by the glass and decent coffee; background music (live last Fri of month), darts; children and dogs (in bar) welcome, picnic-sets on suntrap terrace, pretty village with interesting church, open all day. *(George Atkinson)*

CHAPEL BRAMPTON   SP7366
★ **Brampton Halt**   (01604) 842676
*Pitsford Road, off A5199 N of
Northampton; NN6 8BA* Popular well
laid out McManus pub on Northampton
& Lamport Railway (which is open some
weekends) in much-extended former station-
master's house, large restaurant, railway
memorabilia and train theme throughout,
wide choice of enjoyable generous food
(smaller helpings available) from sandwiches
to blackboard specials, meal deal Mon-Thurs,
good choice of well kept ales (beer festivals)
and several wines by the glass, cheerful
attentive service even when busy; TV in
bar, background music; children welcome,
lots of tables in big garden with awnings
and heaters, summer barbecues and maybe
marquee, pretty views over small lake,
Nene Way walks, open (and food) all day.
(Gerry and Rosemary Dobson)

CHAPEL BRAMPTON   SP7366
Spencer Arms   (01604) 842237
Northampton Road; NN6 8AE
Comfortable Chef & Brewer family dining
pub, plenty of tables in long timber-divided
L-shaped bar, good choice of sensibly
priced food including deals, well kept ales
such as Fullers, Sharps and Charles Wells,
several wines by the glass, friendly service,
beams, half-panelling and two log fires;
soft background music, free wi-fi; disabled
facilities, tables outside under parasols,
open (and food) all day. *(Gerry and Rosemary
Dobson)*

CHAPEL BRAMPTON   SP7266
Windhover   (01604) 847859
*Welford Road (A5199)/Pitsford Road;
NN6 8AA* Roomy Vintage Inn dining pub
with four well kept changing ales and good
choice of wines, their usual food including
competitively priced set menu (weekdays
till 5pm), friendly efficient service, open-
plan interior with nooks and crannies, log
fires; background music; children welcome,
disabled access and facilities, tables in
good-sized front garden with terrace and
old-fashioned lampposts, pleasant Brampton
Valley Way walks, open (and food) all day.
(Revd R P Tickle)

CLIPSTON   SP7181
Bulls Head   (01858) 525268
*B4036 S of Market Harborough;
LE16 9RT* Welcoming bustling village pub
with enjoyable good value food, Everards
ales and up to five guests, log fire and heavy
beams with coins in the cracks put there by
World War II airmen; background music, TV,
Tues quiz & curry night; children and dogs
welcome, terrace tables, three comfortable
bedrooms, open all day weekends. *(Anne and
Ben Smith)*

COLLINGTREE   SP7555
Wooden Walls of Old England
(01604) 760641   *1.2 miles from M1
junction 15; High Street; NN4 0NE*
Cosy thatch and stone village pub dating
from the 15th c and named as a tribute to
the navy; four well kept Marstons-related
ales and good choice of wines by the glass,
generous helpings of enjoyable home-made
food (not Sun evening), friendly staff, beams
and open fire; sports TV, table skittles, free
wi-fi; big back garden with terrace, open
all day Fri-Sun, closed Mon. *(Keith and Sue
Campbell)*

COLLYWESTON   SK9902
★ **Collyweston Slater**   (01780) 444288
The Drove (A43); PE9 3PQ Roomy 17th-c
main road inn with enjoyable generously
served pub food (all day Sun when can get
very busy), well kept Everards ales and
decent wines, friendly service, surprisingly
contemporary with brown leather easy
chairs and sofas, smart modern two-part
dining room (log fire) and two or three more
informal areas, one with a raised stove in
dividing wall, beams, stripped stone and mix
of dark flagstones, bare boards and carpeting;
background music, darts; children welcome,
teak seats on flagstoned terrace, boules,
three bedrooms, open all day. *(Terry Davis)*

CRICK   SP5872
★ **Red Lion**   (01788) 822342
*1 mile from M1 junction 18; in centre of
village off A428; NN6 7TX* Nicely worn-in
stone and thatch coaching inn run by same
family since 1979, traditional low-ceilinged
bar with lots of old horsebrasses (some
rare) and tiny log stove in big inglenook,
straightforward low-priced lunchtime
food, more elaborate evening menu (not
Sun) including popular steaks, plenty for
vegetarians too, Adnams Southwold, Greene
King Old Speckled Hen, Wells Bombardier
and a guest, good friendly service; free wi-fi;
children allowed (under-12s lunchtime only),
dogs welcome, picnic-sets on terrace and
in Perspex-covered coachyard with pretty
hanging baskets. *(Andrew Stone)*

DUDDINGTON   SK9800
Royal Oak   (01780) 444267
High Street, just off A43; PE9 3QE
Stone-built inn on edge of pretty village;
modern bar area with leather sofas and
chairs on flagstones, panelling and log fire,
three Grainstore ales from brick servery,
restaurant with stone walls, oak floor and

If you have to cancel a reservation for a bedroom or restaurant, please telephone
or write to warn them. You may lose your deposit if you've paid one.

light oak furniture, enjoyable food from pub favourites up including set lunch deal Mon-Fri; background music; children welcome, disabled facilities, tables on small grassy area at front, six bedrooms, open (and food) all day Fri-Sun. *(Ray and Winifred Halliday)*

EAST HADDON   SP6668
★**Red Lion** (01604) 770223
High Street; village signposted off A428 (turn right in village) and off A50 N of Northampton; NN6 8BU Substantial and elegant golden-stone thatched hotel with sizeable dining room, log-fire lounge and bar, emphasis on well presented imaginative food and most tables set for dining, but they do keep Charles Wells ales in good condition and offer over a dozen wines by the glass, efficient friendly service; background music; children welcome, attractive grounds including walled side garden, cookery school, seven comfortable bedrooms and two-bed cottage, good breakfast, closed Sun evening. *(Gerry and Rosemary Dobson)*

EASTON ON THE HILL   TF0104
Blue Bell (01780) 763003
High Street; PE9 3LR Welcoming stone-built village pub with strong italian influence to menu and staff, good food (not Sun evening, Mon), three changing ales and plenty of wines by the glass, pleasant atmosphere, restaurant, pool and TV in games area; children welcome, picnic-sets in good-sized sheltered garden behind, closed Mon lunchtime. *(Colin McLachlan)*

EYDON   SP5450
★**Royal Oak** (01327) 263167
Lime Avenue; village signed off A361 Daventry–Banbury, and from B4525; NN11 3PG Interestingly laid-out 300-year-old ironstone inn, some lovely period features including fine flagstone floors and leaded windows, cosy snug on right with cushioned benches built into alcoves, seats in bow window, cottagey pictures and inglenook log fire, long corridor-like central bar linking three other small characterful rooms, Fullers, Hook Norton, Timothy Taylors and a guest, good food (not Sun evening, takeaway only Mon evening), friendly staff and lively atmosphere, table skittles in old stable; background music, charity quiz first Sun of month; children, walkers and dogs welcome, terrace seating (some under cover), closed Mon lunchtime, otherwise open all day. *(Gene and Kitty Rankin)*

FARTHINGHOE   SP5339
★**Fox** (01295) 713965
Just off A422 Brackley–Banbury; Baker Street; NN13 5PH Carefully spruced-up golden-stone pub; pastel walls hung with small landscapes, old country photographs and framed period advertisements, seating from leather tub chairs, banquettes and

traditional wall seats to well cushioned ladder-backs in the eating area, dark-beamed front bar with log fire in big stripped-stone fireplace, Courage Directors and Youngs Bitter, nine good wines by the glass and cocktails, enjoyable food (not Sun evening) from lunchtime sandwiches up; background music, TV, free wi-fi; children and dogs (in bar) welcome, sheltered back terrace with neatly kept garden beyond, comfortable bedrooms in adjoining barn conversion, open all day Sat, till 9pm (6pm winter) Sun. *(JPC, George Atkinson)*

GRAFTON REGIS   SP7546
★**White Hart** (01908) 542123
A508 S of Northampton; NN12 7SR Thatched dining pub with several linked rooms, good pubby food (not Sun evening) including range of home-made soups and popular well priced Sun roasts (best to book) using local meat, Greene King ales and Aspall's cider, good wines by the glass, friendly helpful staff coping well when busy, african grey parrot (can be very vocal), restaurant with open fire and separate menu; background music; children and dogs welcome (they have a couple of boxers), terrace tables and gazebo in good-sized garden, closed Mon. *(George Atkinson)*

GREAT BILLING   SP8162
Elwes Arms (01604) 407521
High Street; NN3 9DT Thatched stone-built 16th-c village pub, two bars (steps between), wide choice of good value tasty food (all day weekends) including weekday lunchtime deal, Black Sheep, Wadworths 6X and Shepherd Neame Spitfire, friendly if not always speedy service, pleasant dining room (children allowed); background music, quiz Thurs and Sun, sports TV, darts, free wi-fi; no dogs, garden tables and nice covered decked terrace, play area, open all day Weds-Sun. *(Mungo Shipley)*

GREAT CRANSLEY   SP8276
Three Cranes (01536) 790287
Loddington Road; NN14 1PY Small stone-built village pub run by same family for over 26 years; small carpeted bar with dining area to right leading to little conservatory, well kept Banks's Bitter and Marstons Pedigree, enjoyable reasonably priced home-made food including monthly themed nights, prompt friendly service; free wi-fi; children welcome, dogs in garden only, closed Mon and weekday lunchtimes. *(Gerry and Rosemary Dobson)*

GREAT EVERDON   SP5957
Plough (01327) 361606
Next to church; NN11 3BL Small fairly simple bare-boards pub in tucked-away village; bar with a couple of steps down to lounge/dining area, open fire and woodburner, Greene King IPA, Gun Dog Jack's Spaniels and Sharps Doom Bar, decent wines, short choice of good reasonably

priced lunchtime food cooked by landlady (more substantial meals Fri evening and Sun lunchtime – must book), friendly obliging staff; fortnightly quiz Tues; dogs welcome, some seats out in front, more in spacious garden behind, shop (the Furrow) selling old furniture, collectables and plants, good walks nearby. *(George Atkinson)*

GREENS NORTON   SP6649
Butchers Arms (01327) 350488
High Street; NN12 8BA Comfortable family-run village pub with enjoyable straightforward food from sandwiches and pizzas up, lunchtime carvery Weds and Sun, reasonable prices, ales including St Austell and Timothy Taylors, pleasant chatty staff, bar and games room with pool, darts and skittles; background and some live music, fortnightly quiz Sun; children (till 9pm) and dogs allowed, disabled access, picnic-sets and play area outside, pretty village near Grafton Way walks, closed lunchtimes Mon, Tues. *(George Atkinson)*

GUILSBOROUGH   SP6772
Witch & Sow (01604) 743888
High Street; NN6 8PY Recently refurbished little 17th-c thatched and beamed pub in historic village, entrance lobby with frosted-glass panels, bar and lounge/dining area with open fire, Greene King IPA and three guests, well liked interesting food (not Sun evening) along with pub favourites, good friendly service; children and dogs welcome, tables on split-level back terrace, open all day Fri-Sun, closed Mon. *(Mungo Shipley)*

HACKLETON   SP8054
White Hart (01604) 870271
B526 SE of Northampton; NN7 2AD Comfortably traditional 18th-c country pub; wide choice of enjoyable food from sandwiches and baked potatoes up, friendly helpful staff, Fullers London Pride, Greene King IPA and a guest, decent choice of wines and other drinks, dining area up steps with flame-effect fire, beams, stripped stone and brickwork, illuminated well, split-level flagstoned bar with log fire; background music, TV, pool and hood skittles; supervised children and dogs welcome, disabled access, picnic-sets in sunny garden, open all day, no food Sun evening. *(W J Callis)*

HARRINGTON   SP7780
Tollemache Arms (01536) 710469
High Street; off A508 S of Market Harborough; NN6 9NU Pretty thatched Tudor pub in lovely quiet ironstone village; very low ceilings in compact bar with log fire and in pleasant partly stripped-stone dining room, enjoyable generous food from sandwiches up, well kept Charles Wells ales and a guest, friendly attentive staff, table skittles; children welcome, nice back garden with country views, handy

for Carpetbagger Aviation Museum, open all day in summer. *(George Atkinson)*

HARRINGWORTH   SP9197
White Swan (01572) 747035
Seaton Road; village SE of Uppingham, signed from A6003, A47 and A43; NN17 3AF Handsome former coaching inn with imposing central gable; woodburner dividing bar and two cosy dining areas, traditional furnishings and nice hand-crafted oak counter, three changing ales, enjoyable fairly traditional food (till 7pm Sun), friendly service; background music, TV, darts; children and dogs welcome, tables on paved terrace with pretty hanging baskets, not far from magnificent 82-arch viaduct spanning the Welland, eight bedrooms, good breakfast, open all day weekends, closed Mon lunchtime. *(Ross Balaam)*

HELLIDON   SP5158
Red Lion (01327) 261200
Stockwell Lane, off A425 W of Daventry; NN11 6LG Welcoming wisteria-clad inn on edge of village opposite small green; bar with woodburner, cosy lounge and softly lit low-ceilinged stripped-stone dining area, ample helpings of enjoyable home-made food served by helpful friendly staff, four changing ales, hood skittles and pool in back games room; children and dogs welcome, a few picnic-sets on front grass, windmill vineyard and pleasant walks nearby, open all day weekends. *(Anne and Ben Smith)*

HIGHAM FERRERS   SP9668
Griffin (01933) 312612
High Street; NN10 8BW 17th-c pub-restaurant (bigger than it looks) with good food including fresh fish and popular Sun carvery (till 5pm), five well kept rotating ales and good selection of wines and malt whiskies, comfortable front bar, large back restaurant and dining conservatory, friendly service; free wi-fi; tables on heated terrace, open all day Fri-Sun. *(Guy and Caroline Howard)*

HINTON-IN-THE-HEDGES   SP5536
Crewe Arms (01280) 705801
Off A43 W of Brackley; NN13 5NF Spruced-up 17th-c stone-built village pub, well kept ales including Hook Norton, enjoyable home-made food from bar snacks to specials, two-for-one deal Mon and Tues, good friendly service; background music; dogs welcome, two comfortable bothy bedrooms, open all day. *(Phoebe Peacock)*

KETTERING   SP8778
Alexandra Arms (01536) 522730
Victoria Street; NN16 0BU Backstreet real ale pub with up to 14 changing quickly, hundreds each year, knowledgeable landlord, basic opened-up bar with pump clips covering walls and ceiling, back games room with darts, hood skittles and TV, some snacky

food; a couple of picnic-sets out in front, small beer garden behind, open all day. *(George Atkinson)*

KILSBY   SP5671
★ **George** (01788) 822229
2.5 miles from M1 junction 18: A428 towards Daventry, left on to A5 – pub off on right at roundabout; CV23 8YE
Popular pub (handy for motorway) with cheerful obliging landlady, proper old-fashioned public bar, wood-panelled lounge with plush banquettes and coal-effect gas stove opening into smarter comfortably furnished area, well kept Adnams, Fullers, Timothy Taylors and a guest, fine range of malt whiskies, enjoyable good value home-made food including blackboard specials, friendly staff coping well at busy times; trad jazz first Sun of month, quiz nights, darts, free-play pool tables, TV; children welcome if dining, dogs in bar, garden picnic-sets, six bedrooms. *(Andrew Stone)*

KISLINGBURY   SP6959
Sun (01604) 833571
Off A45 W of Northampton; Mill Road; NN7 4BB Welcoming thatch and ironstone village pub; ales such as Greene King, Hoggleys, St Austell and Sharps, enjoyable fairly traditional food (not Sun evening) including pizza menu, popular with locals and visitors alike, L-shaped bar/lounge and small separate dining area; quiz last Sun of month, sports TV, free wi-fi; children and dogs welcome, disabled access, a few picnic-sets out in front, open all day Fri-Sun. *(George Atkinson)*

LITCHBOROUGH   SP6353
Old Red Lion (01327) 830064
Banbury Road, just off former B4525 Banbury–Northampton; opposite church; NN12 8JF Attractive beamed pub owned by local farming family and doubling as village shop; four rooms including cosy flagstoned bar with woodburner in big inglenook, ales such as Grainstore and Oakham, shortish choice of generously served food (not Sun evening) from sandwiches and baguettes up, friendly laid-back atmosphere, barn-conversion restaurant at back, skittles and pool; popular with walkers, terrace seating, open all day. *(George Atkinson)*

LITTLE BRINGTON   SP6663
★ **Saracens Head** (01604) 770640
4.5 miles from M1 junction 16, first right off A45 to Daventry; also signed off A428; Main Street; NN7 4HS Friendly old village pub with enjoyable fairly priced food (not Sun evening, Mon) from lunchtime sandwiches up, well kept Greene King IPA, Timothy Taylors Landlord and a guest, several wines by the glass, roomy U-shaped beamed lounge with woodburner, flagstones, bare boards and tiled floors, chesterfields and lots of old prints, book-lined dining room (proper

napkins); gentle background music; plenty of tables out on gravel/paved area with country views, walks nearby and handy for Althorp House and Holdenby House. *(Gerry and Rosemary Dobson, Dennis and Doreen Haward, George Atkinson)*

LITTLE HARROWDEN   SP8671
Lamb (01933) 673300
Orlingbury Road/Kings Lane – off A509 or A43 S of Kettering; NN9 5BH Popular pub in delightful village, split-level carpeted lounge with log fire and brasses on 17th-c beams, dining area, good promptly served food including bargain deals, Wells Eagle and a couple of guests, short sensibly priced wine list, good coffee, games bar with darts, hood skittles and machines, resident cocker spaniel called Rio; background music, free wi-fi; children welcome, small raised terrace and garden, open all day weekends. *(Caroline Prescott)*

LOWICK   SP9780
★ **Snooty Fox** (01832) 733434
Off A6116 Corby–Raunds; NN14 3BH Bustling 17th-c pub in peaceful village; spacious lounge bar with woodburner in sizeable fireplace, stripped stone and handsomely moulded dark oak beams, leather sofas, bucket armchairs and stools on big terracotta tiles, formidable carved counter serving ales such as Digfield and Nene Valley, real cider and 22 wines by the glass, well thought-of food in more formal dining rooms with chunky tables on pale wood floor, attentive helpful staff; background music, free wi-fi; children and dogs (in bar) welcome, picnic-sets under parasols on front grass, play area, open all day weekends, closed Mon. *(Pip White, Emma Scofield, Michael Sargent, George Atkinson, Clive and Fran Dutson)*

MAIDWELL   SP7477
Stags Head (01604) 686700
Harborough Road (A508 N of Northampton); a mile from A14 junction 2; NN6 9JA Comfortable dining pub with woodburner in pubby part by bar, extensive eating areas, fairly traditional fair-priced food including deals and children's menu, interesting range of well kept beers from small and large breweries, good choice of other drinks; background and some live music, quiz last Thurs of month, free wi-fi; disabled facilities, picnic-sets on back terrace (dogs on leads allowed here), good-sized sloping garden beyond, five bedrooms, not far from splendid Palladian Kelmarsh Hall and park, open all day Fri and Sun. *(Gerry and Rosemary Dobson)*

MOULTON   SP7866
Telegraph (01604) 648228
West Street; NN3 7SB Spacious old stone-built village pub, friendly and popular, with enjoyable promptly served

food (not Sun evening) from sandwiches and pizzas up, well kept Fullers, Sharps and a couple of guests, maybe an interesting craft keg, log fire in bar, back restaurant extension; children welcome, open all day Fri-Sun. *(Mr and Mrs D J Nash, Gerry and Rosemary Dobson, George Atkinson)*

NASSINGTON   TL0696
Queens Head (01780) 784006
Station Road; PE8 6QB Early 19th-c stone dining pub in delightful village; softly lit beamed bar with mix of old tables and chairs on bare boards, large oriental rug in front of roaring fire, good reasonably priced food from bar snacks to imaginative restaurant dishes using local ingredients, pleasant helpful uniformed staff, nice choice of wines by the glass, ales such as Greene King, Nene Valley and Oakham, good coffee, separate restaurant; children welcome, pretty garden by River Nene, narrow entrance to car park can be tricky, ten chalet bedrooms, open all day. *(Mungo Shipley)*

NORTHAMPTON   SP7261
Hopping Hare (01604) 580090
Harlestone Road (A428), New Duston; NN5 6DF Edwardian pub-restaurant-hotel on edge of housing estate; contemporary, stylish and comfortable, with good food from lunchtime sandwiches and pub favourites to sharing boards and up-to-date restaurantish dishes, Adnams, Black Sheep and a guest, good choice of wines by the glass including champagne, competent friendly service; background music, daily newspapers, free wi-fi, tables out on deck, 19 modern bedrooms, open all day, food all day weekends (and weekdays during school summer holidays). *(G Jennings)*

NORTHAMPTON   SP7560
Lamplighter (01604) 631125
Overstone Road; NN1 3JS Popular Victorian corner pub in the Mounts area, friendly and welcoming, with wide choice of draught and bottled beers and good value generously served food including range of burgers, regular live music, quiz Weds; children welcome if eating, picnic-sets in heated courtyard, open all day (till 1am Fri, Sat). *(Andrew Stone)*

NORTHAMPTON   SP7661
Olde England 07742 069768
Kettering Road, near the racecourse; NN1 4BP Quirky conversion of Victorian corner shop over three floors (steepish stairs to upper level and down to cellar bar), ground-floor room with assorted tables and chairs on bare boards, 20 well kept changing ales and similar number of ciders from hatch on stairs, lots of pictures with medieval or Arthurian themes, plus the odd banner, flag and suit of armour, bargain food including lunchtime set deal, more extensive choice evenings and weekends

when pub is at its busiest, friendly staff and broad mix of customers, cards and board games, folk music, quiz nights and poetry readings; children welcome, closed Mon lunchtime, otherwise open all day (no food Sun evening). *(George Atkinson)*

NORTHAMPTON   SP7560
Wig & Pen (01604) 622178
St Giles Street; NN1 1JA Long L-shaped beamed room with bar running most of its length, up to dozen well kept ales including Adnams, Fullers and Greene King, traditional ciders and good choice of bottled beers, enjoyable nicely presented food (not weekend evenings) from sandwiches and deli boards up, brunch from 10am, efficient friendly young staff; Tues jazz and other live music, sports TV; split-level walled garden, open all day (till 1.30am Fri, Sat). *(George Atkinson, Richard Tilbrook)*

OLD   SP7873
White Horse (01604) 781297
Walgrave Road, N of Northampton between A43 and A508; NN6 9QX Popular revamped village pub under welcoming newish management, good reasonably priced food from short menu supplemented by some interesting daily specials, three well kept changing local ales, proper ciders and decent wines by the glass, friendly efficient staff; quiz night first Thurs of month, live music last Fri, free wi-fi; well behaved children and dogs welcome, garden and deck overlooking 13th-c church, open all day Sat, till 7pm Sun, closed Mon. *(R L Borthwick, Gerry and Rosemary Dobson)*

OUNDLE   TL0388
Talbot (01832) 273621
New Street; PE8 4EA Handsome former merchant's house, now a hotel; various rooms including comfortably modernised bar, a couple of real ales such as Black Sheep and Digfield, enjoyable food from sandwiches and sharing plates up, good service, restaurant; children welcome, seats in courtyard and garden, 40 bedrooms, open all day. *(Ross Balaam)*

RAVENSTHORPE   SP6670
Chequers (01604) 770379
Chequers Lane; NN6 8ER Cosy old creeper-clad brick pub with L-shaped bar and restaurant, well kept ales including Oakham JHB, Sharps Doom Bar and Thwaites Original, good choice of generous sensibly priced food from light snacks to steaks and daily specials, friendly attentive staff, banquettes, cushioned pews and sturdy tables, coal-effect fire; children welcome, partly covered side terrace, play area and separate building for Northants skittles, handy for Ravensthorpe Reservoir and Coton Manor Gardens, open all day weekends. *(George Atkinson)*

RUSHDEN   SP9566
Station Bar (01933) 318988
Station Approach; NN10 0AW Not a pub,
part of station HQ of Rushden Historical
Transport Society (non-members can sign in
for £1); bar in former ladies' waiting room
with gas lighting, enamel signs and railway
memorabilia, seven well kept ales including
Oakham and Phipps, tea and coffee, filled
rolls and perhaps some hot food, friendly
staff; also museum and summer train rides,
table skittles in a Royal Mail carriage;
open all day weekends, closed weekday
lunchtimes. *(Andrew Stone)*

RUSHTON   SP8483
Thornhill Arms (01536) 710251
Station Road; NN14 1RL Rambling
family-run dining pub opposite lovely village's
cricket green, popular food including keenly
priced set menu (weekday evenings, Sat
lunchtime) and carvery (Sun, Mon evening),
prompt friendly service, usually three well
kept ales such as Fullers, Hook Norton and
Shepherd Neame, several neatly laid-out
dining areas including smart high-beamed
back restaurant, open fire; children welcome,
garden with decked area, open all day Sun.
(Mungo Shipley)

SLIPTON   SP9579
★Samuel Pepys (01832) 731739
*Off A6116 at first roundabout N of
A14 junction, towards Twywell and
Slipton; NN14 3AR* Old reworked stone
pub with long modernised bar, heavy low
beams, wood flooring, log fire and great
central pillar, up to five well kept ales
including local Digfield, decent choice of
ciders and wines by the glass, good variety
of popular food including daily specials and
weekday OAP lunch deal, friendly attentive
service, dining room extending into roomy
conservatory with country views; background
music; children and dogs (in bar) welcome,
wheelchair access from car park using ramp,
well laid-out sheltered garden with heated
terrace, open all day weekends (till 7pm
Sun in winter). *(Michael and Jenny Back
and others)*

SPRATTON   SP7170
Kings Head (01604) 847351
*Brixworth Road, off A5199 N of
Northampton; NN6 8HH* Enterprising
combination of pub, brasserie and coffee/
wine bar: pale flagstones and ancient
stripped stonework mixing well with
handsome new wood flooring and up-to-date
décor, leather chesterfield, antique settle and
café chairs around stripped brasserie-style
tables, ales such as Nobbys and Sharps, ten
wines by the glass and good interesting food
(best to book weekends), friendly service,
back cafeteria with tempting cake counter
and glass wall overlooking modern courtyard;
background music, free wi-fi, darts; children

and dogs (in bar) welcome, open all day
Fri-Sun, no food Sun evening. *(Gerry and
Rosemary Dobson, Paul Dickinson, Alan Sutton,
George Atkinson)*

STAVERTON   SP5461
Countryman (01327) 311815
Daventry Road (A425); NN11 6JH
Beamed and carpeted dining pub (some
recent refurbishment), popular food
including good value two-course menu
(weekday lunchtimes, early evening Mon-
Thurs), Wells Bombardier and a couple
of guests, good friendly service even when
busy, bar divided by brick pillars, restaurant;
background music; children and dogs (in
bar) welcome, disabled access, some tables
out at front and in small garden behind,
open all day Sun, closes for a week in Jan.
(George Atkinson)

STOKE BRUERNE   SP7449
Boat (01604) 862428
*3.5 miles from M1 junction 15 – A508
towards Stony Stratford, then signed on
right; Bridge Road; NN12 7SB* Old-world
flagstoned bar in picturesque canalside spot
by restored lock, more modern central-
pillared back bar and bistro, half a dozen
Marstons-related ales and maybe a local
guest, Thatcher's cider, enjoyable fairly
standard food from baguettes up including
deals, friendly if not always speedy service,
comfortable upstairs bookable restaurant
with more elaborate menu, shop for boaters
(nice ice-creams); background music, can
get busy in summer especially weekends
and parking nearby difficult; welcomes dogs
and children, disabled facilities, tables out
by towpath opposite canal museum, trips
on own narrowboat, open all day. *(George
Atkinson, Gerry and Rosemary Dobson)*

STOKE DOYLE   TL0286
★Shuckburgh Arms (01832) 272339
*Village signed (down Stoke Hill) from
SW edge of Oundle; PE8 5TG* Attractively
reworked relaxed 17th-c pub in quiet hamlet,
four traditional rooms with some modern
touches, low black beams in bowed ceilings,
pictures on pastel walls, lots of pale tables
on wood or carpeted floors, stylish art deco
seats and elegant dining chairs, inglenook
woodburner, ales such as Nene Valley and
Nobbys from granite-top bar, well selected
wines and good popular food including
two-course deal, helpful attentive staff; faint
background music; children welcome, garden
with decked area and play frame, bedrooms
in separate modern block, closed Sun
evening, Mon. *(Anne and Ben Smith)*

SUDBOROUGH   SP9682
Vane Arms (01832) 730033
Off A6116; Main Street; NN14 3BX
Thatched pub in pretty village, low beams,
stripped stonework and inglenook fires,
enjoyable freshly cooked food, well kept

Everards Tiger and guests, friendly staff,
restaurant; well behaved dogs welcome
in bar, terrace tables, three bedrooms in
nearby building, closed Sun evening.
(Caroline Prescott)

THORNBY   SP6675

★ **Red Lion** (01604) 740238

*Welford Road; A5199 Northampton–
Leicester; NN6 8SJ* Popular old country
pub with interesting choice of up to four well
kept/priced changing ales, good home-cooked
food (not Mon) from standards up including
popular steak and stilton pie, smaller
helpings available for some dishes, prompt
friendly service, beams and log fire, lots of
old local photos, back dining area; children
and dogs welcome, garden picnic-sets, open
all day weekends when can get very busy
(booking advised Sat night). *(Gerry and
Rosemary Dobson, George Atkinson)*

THORPE MANDEVILLE   SP5344

★ **Three Conies** (01295) 711025

Off B4525 E of Banbury; OX17 2EX
Attractive and welcoming 17th-c ironstone
pub, good choice of enjoyable food from
sandwiches up, well kept Hook Norton ales,
beamed bare-boards bar with some stripped
stone, mix of old tables and comfortable
seating, log fires, large dining room;
background and some live music, TV, hood
skittles; children and dogs welcome, disabled
facilities, tables out in front and behind on
decking and lawn, open all day (from 10am
for breakfast). *(Anne and Ben Smith)*

THRAPSTON   SP9978

Kings Arms (01832) 733911

High Street; NN14 4JJ Welcoming
traditional pub dating from the 18th c, mix of
furniture on wood or tiled floors in L-shaped
bar, three well kept ales such as local Nene
Valley, good affordably priced food (not
Sun evening, Mon) in bar or modernised
upstairs restaurant, prompt friendly service;
background music, sports TV; children
welcome, some seats outside, closed
Mon lunchtime, otherwise open all day.
(Dennis and Doreen Haward)

TOWCESTER   SP7047

Folly (01327) 354031

A5 S, opposite racecourse; NN12 6LB
Black-beamed early 18th-c thatched pub
opposite racecourse, enjoyable food from pub
favourites to more expensive restaurant-style
dishes, local ales and plenty of wines by the
glass, friendly helpful staff, steps up to dining
area; children welcome till 8pm, dogs in bar,
picnic-sets outside, open all day Sun till 9pm,
closed Mon. *(Darren and Jane Staniforth)*

TOWCESTER   SP6948

Towcester Mill (01327) 437060

Chantry Lane; NN12 6YY Old mill tucked
away behind market square and surrounded
by redevelopment; nice little beamed

bare-boards bar acting as tap for onsite
brewery (tours Mon and Tues evenings), six
ales including a couple of guests, also seven
real ciders and a dozen county wines, shop
selling their beers, June and Sept beer/music
festivals; walkers and dogs welcome, garden
behind with seats by mill-race and pond,
open all day summer (winter from
5pm Mon-Fri, all day Sat, till 5pm Sun).
(Andrew Stone)

TURWESTON   SP6037

Stratton Arms (01280) 704956

*E of crossroads in village; pub itself just
inside Buckinghamshire; NN13 5JX*
Friendly chatty local in picturesque village,
six well kept ales including Otter, Shepherd
Neame and Timothy Taylors, good choice
of other drinks, enjoyable reasonably
priced traditional food (Fri-Sun lunchtime
only), low ceilings and two log fires, small
restaurant; background music, sports TV;
children and dogs welcome, large pleasant
garden by Great Ouse with barbecue and play
area, camping, open all day. *(George Atkinson)*

TWYWELL   SP9578

Old Friar (01832) 732625

*Lower Street, off A14 W of Thrapston;
NN14 3AH* Well run popular pub with
enjoyable good value food including deals,
carvery all day Sun and Tues-Sat evenings,
Greene King and a couple of guests, cheerful
attentive service, modernised split-level
interior with beams and some exposed
stonework; children and dogs welcome,
garden with good play area, open all day
Fri-Sun, food all day weekends including
Sat breakfast. *(Mungo Shipley)*

UPPER BODDINGTON   SP4853

Plough (01327) 260364

Warwick Road; NN11 6DH Renovated
18th-thatched village inn keeping much
of its original character, small beamed and
flagstoned bar, lobby with old local photos,
Greene King IPA, Shepherd Neame Spitfire
and a guest, good value traditional food
(curry night Tues, fish Weds) in restaurant,
snug or intimate Doll's Parlour (named after
former veteran landlady), friendly service,
woodburners; quiz first Sun of month,
occasional live music and beer festivals,
free wi-fi; children and dogs welcome, five
bedrooms (some sharing bathroom), usually
closed weekday lunchtimes, open all day
weekends, no food Sun evening, Mon.
(R Anderson)

WADENHOE   TL0183

★ **Kings Head** (01832) 720024

*Church Street; village signposted
(in small print) off A605 S of Oundle;
PE8 5ST* Beautifully placed 17th-c country
pub with picnic-sets on sun terrace and
among trees on grassy stretch by River Nene
(moorings); uncluttered partly stripped-stone
bar with woodburner in fine inglenook, pale

pine furniture and a couple of cushioned wall seats, simple bare-boards public bar and attractive little beamed dining room with more pine furniture, three changing ales, several wines by the glass and good well presented food, friendly efficient service, games room with darts, dominoes and table skittles; children and dogs welcome, open all day in summer, all day Fri, Sat and till 6pm Sun in winter. *(Mungo Shipley)*

WALGRAVE   SP8072
Royal Oak (01604) 781248
Zion Hill, off A43 Northampton– Kettering; NN6 9PN Welcoming old stone-built village local, good choice of well presented food (best to book) including fish dishes, very popular two-for-one Tues evening deal on main courses, well kept Adnams, Greene King and three interesting guests, decent wines, friendly prompt service, long three-part carpeted beamed bar, small lounge, restaurant extension behind; children welcome, small garden with play area, open all day Sun. *(Gerry and Rosemary Dobson)*

WEEDON   SP6458
★Narrow Boat (01327) 340333
3.9 miles from M1 junction 16: A45 towards Daventry, left on to A5, pub then on left after canal, at Stowe Hill – junction Watling Street/Heyford Lane; NN7 4RZ Big draw for this neatly refurbished relaxed pub is its Grand Union Canal position – plenty of seats on covered deck and in garden sloping down to the water, summer bar out here and children's play trail; rambling bar with comfortable dark banquettes and padded chairs around neat tables, woodburner, a couple of Charles Wells ales and several wines by the glass, wide choice of generously served food (all day weekends), carpeted conservatory with heavy curtains for cooler nights; children and dogs (in bar) welcome, background music; disabled facilities, well equipped comfortable bedrooms in separate block, open all day. *(Michael Butler, Ian Herdman)*

WELFORD   SP6480
Wharf Inn (01858) 575075
Pub just over Leicestershire border; NN6 6JQ Spacious castellated Georgian folly in delightful setting by two Grand Union Canal marinas, Marstons, Oakham and three guests in unpretentious bar, popular straightforward pubby food at reasonable prices, good service, pleasant dining section; children and dogs welcome, big waterside garden, open all day. *(Dennis and Doreen Haward)*

WESTON BY WELLAND   SP7791
Wheel & Compass (01858) 565864
Valley Road; LE16 8HZ Old stone-built family-run country pub, wide range of enjoyable attractively priced food including Sun/Weds carvery, Black Sheep, Greene King, Marstons, Oakham, Sharps and a guest, good wine and soft drinks choice, friendly staff, comfortable bar, nice old-fashioned snug and plenty of dining space; children welcome, open (and food) all day. *(Howard and Margaret Buchanan)*

WHITTLEBURY   SP6943
Fox & Hounds (01327) 858048
High Street; NN12 8XJ Double-fronted 19th-c village bar-restaurant, smartly refurbished modern interior with wood flooring and comfy stylish seating, four ales such as Jennings and local Gun Dog, nice food from thick-cut sandwiches and sharing boards up, good friendly service; children and dogs welcome, picnic-sets on suntrap gravelled terrace, handy for Silverstone, open all day weekends, closed Mon. *(George Atkinson)*

YARDLEY HASTINGS   SP8656
★Rose & Crown (01604) 696276
Just off A428 Bedford–Northampton; NN7 1EX Spacious and popular 18th-c dining pub in pretty village; flagstones, beams, stripped stonework and quiet corners, step up to big comfortable dining room, flowers on tables, good well presented food from interesting daily changing menu along with bar snacks and pubby choices, good value set menu too, efficient friendly young staff, six real ales including a house beer from local Hart Family, four ciders and decent range of wines; background and occasional live music, daily newspapers; children welcome till 9pm, dogs in bar, tables under parasols in split-level garden, boules, open all day (from 5pm Mon). *(George Atkinson)*

Northumbria
(County Durham, Northumberland and Tyneside)

 ANICK   NY9565 Map 10

Rat 🍽️ 🍷 🍺

(01434) 602814 – www.theratinn.com

Village signposted NE of A69/A695 Hexham junction; NE46 4LN

Bustling pub with good views from garden and terrace, local real ales, lots of interesting knick-knacks and appealing food

Well kept ales, enjoyable food and a good mix of cheerful customers all come together in this hospitable country pub. The traditional bar is snug and welcoming with a coal fire in a blackened kitchen range, lots of cottagey knick-knacks from antique floral chamber-pots hanging from the beams to china and glassware on a delft shelf, and little curtained windows that allow in a soft and gentle light; background music, daily papers and magazines. The enthusiastic licensees keep Allendale Golden Plover, Blythe Bitter, Hexhamshire Shire Bitter, Tyne Bank Northern Porter, Timothy Taylors Landlord and Wylam Galaxia on handpump, a dozen wines by the glass (including champagne), a local gin and farm cider. The conservatory has pleasant views and the garden is quite charming with its dovecote, statues, pretty flower beds and North Tyne Valley views from seats on the terrace. Parking is limited, but you can park around the village green.

🍽️ As well as sandwiches, the highly popular food includes terrine of local game with fig chutney, kipper rillettes with potato and horseradish salad, pan haggerty of parsnips and wild mushrooms topped with cheese, local sausages with leek and potato cake and onion gravy, coley with creamed samphire, lemon and capers, confit duck leg with dauphinoise potatoes, rack of lamb with olives, rosemary and oven-dried tomatoes, and puddings such as apple and blueberry crème brûlée and chcolate and coconut bread and butter pudding. *Benchmark main dish: roast rib of beef for two people £49.50. Two-course evening meal £21.00.*

Free house ~ Licensees Phil Mason and Karen Errington ~ Real ale ~ Open 12-11 (10.30 Sun) ~ Bar food 12-2, 6-9; 12-3 Sun ~ Restaurant ~ Children welcome ~ Wi-fi ~ Live folk every two months *Recommended by Mike and Lynn Robinson, Dr Kevan Tucker, Comus and Sarah Elliott, GSB*

 **AYCLIFFE**   NZ2822 Map 10

County 🍽️ 🍺 🛏️

(01325) 312273 – www.thecountyaycliffevillage.com

The Green, Aycliffe; just off A1(M) junction 59, off A167 at West Terrace and then right to village green; DL5 6LX

Friendly, well run pub with four real ales, good wines and popular, interesting food; bedrooms

You can be sure of a genuinely warm welcome from the helpful landlady and her cheerful staff, and our readers very much enjoy staying in the individually designed and attractive bedrooms. More or less open-plan throughout, this smart inn is warmly decorated with red, green or cream paintwork, striped carpeting, contemporary lighting and candlelight. There are painted ceiling joists, a woodburner and open fires, an assortment of chairs from tartan banquettes and dining chairs to cushion-seated wooden ones around light or dark wood tables, and tartan curtains. Locals pop in for a chat and a pint and can usually be found at one of the high bar chairs by the counter where they keep Durham Evensong, Hawkshead Windermere Pale, Just a Minute About Time, Oakham Citra and Ossett Inception on handpump, 11 wines by the glass and eight malt whiskies. The wood-floored restaurant is minimalist with high-backed black leather dining chairs and dark window blinds. There are some metal tables and chairs out in front.

The highly rated and extremely good food includes sandwiches, ham hock terrine with pineapple pickle and fried quail egg, pigeon on a bed of greens with veal jus and berries, chestnut gnocchi with butternut squash, spinach and wild mushrooms, steak in ale pie, roast cod in serrano ham with chorizo and spinach potato cake and chive cream, calves liver with roast chicory, air-dried ham, green lentils and a rich jus, fillet steak with peppercorn sauce, and puddings such as elderflower and prosecco jelly with seasonal fruit and warm chocolate and walnut brownie with chocolate sauce and turkish delight ice-cream. *Benchmark main dish: chicken with cheese rösti and leeks in a cream chardonnay sauce £15.95. Two-course evening meal £21.00.*

Free house ~ Licensee Colette Farrell ~ Real ale ~ Open 11am–midnight ~ Bar food 12-2, 5.30-9; 12-9 Sun ~ Children welcome ~ Wi-fi ~ Bedrooms: £49/£70 *Recommended by Mike and Lynn Robinson, Alison Langton*

BLANCHLAND   NY£650   Map 10

Lord Crewe Arms ★ 🏅 ⍰ 🍴 🛏

(01434) 675469 – www.lordcrewearmsblanchland.co.uk
B6306 S of Hexham; DH8 9SP

Wonderful historic building with unique Crypt bar, cosy sitting rooms and spacious character restaurant; comfortable, well equipped bedrooms

In a lovely moorland village near Derwent Reservoir, this historic inn (built as a guest house in 1235 for the neighbouring Premonstratensian monastery) is popular with a good mix of people: locals, walkers and those enjoying the rather smart restaurant. The unique Crypt bar is a medieval vaulted room sculpted by thick stone walls, lit by candlelight and with family crests on the ceiling. There are high wooden stools by wall shelves and against the armour-plated counter, cushioned settles and plush stools around a few little tables, with Consett Ale Works Stout, Hadrian & Border Tyneside Blonde, Wylam Red Kite and a beer named for the inn (Lord Crewe Brew) on handpump, several wines by the glass, 30 malt whiskies and a farm cider; darts and board games. One character sitting area has a leather sofa and two big tartan armchairs on flagstones in front of a large open fire, while the grand yet informal restaurant features a fine old wooden floor, cushioned wall seating and leather-cushioned dining chairs around oak-topped tables, fresh flowers, antlers on the walls and a big central candelabra. The bedrooms are lovely.

First class food includes lunchtime 'on toast' choices (such as fried duck egg with spiced buttered shrimps or crab with brown crab mayonnaise), smoked salmon (from their own smokehouse), barbecue duck salad with sweet radish and pea shoots, fish fingers with chips, roasted chicken breast with st george's mushrooms, pork loin chop and cheek with roasted squash, roast rump of veal with sage butter, roasted fillet of haddock with Morecambe Bay shrimps, and puddings such as rum and nut tart with vanilla ice-cream and chocolate mousse. *Benchmark main dish: steak with herb baked bone marrow and green sauce £14.75. Two-course evening meal £20.00.*

Free house ~ Licensee Tommy Mark ~ Real ale ~ Open 11-11; 11-10.30 Sun ~ Bar food 12-2.30, 6-8.30 ~ Restaurant ~ Children welcome ~ Dogs allowed in bar and bedrooms ~ Wi-fi ~ Bedrooms: £90/£150 *Recommended by Martin Jones, Toby Jones, Michael Doswell, Dr Terry Murphy, Barry Collett*

CARTERWAY HEADS

NZ0452   Map 10

Manor House Inn

(01207) 255268 – www.themanorhouseinn.com
A68 just N of B6278, near Derwent Reservoir; DH8 9LX

Handy after a walk, with a traditional bar, comfortable lounge, bar food and five real ales; bedrooms

This is just the place to relax after walking around nearby Derwent Valley and Reservoir – there are stunning views over the water and beyond from picnic-sets on the terrace. Homely and old-fashioned, the locals' bar has an original boarded ceiling, pine tables, chairs and stools, old oak pews and a mahogany counter. The carpeted lounge bar (warmed by a woodburning stove) and restaurant are comfortably pubby with wheelback chairs, stripped-stone walls and picture windows that make the most of the lovely setting. Greene King Old Speckled Hen, Mordue Workie Ticket and Robinsons Dizzy Blonde on handpump, alongside ten wines by the glass, 20 malt whiskies and Weston's Old Rosie cider; darts, board games and background music. The comfortable bedrooms have fine views.

Some kind of good food is usefully served all day and includes seasonal game: sandwiches, a changing pâté with red onion marmalade, tempura prawns with sweet chilli dip, cumberland sausage and mash with onion gravy, venison burgers with toppings and chips, tandoori rabbit legs, beer-battered fish and chips, changing pies, steaks, daily specials and puddings. *Benchmark main dish: slow-roasted pork belly with clapshot (swede and potato), fondant carrot and apple purée £13.00. Two-course evening meal £19.00.*

Enterprise ~ Licensee Chris Baxter ~ Real ale ~ Open 12-11 (10.30 Sun) ~ Bar food 12-9; 12-8 Sun (7 in winter) ~ Restaurant ~ Children welcome ~ Dogs allowed in bar and bedrooms ~ Wi-fi ~ Bedrooms: £60/£85 *Recommended by Mike and Lynn Robinson, Michael Doswell, Adrian Johnson*

COTHERSTONE

NZ0119   Map 10

Fox & Hounds

(01833) 650241 – www.cotherstonefox.co.uk
B6277; DL12 9PF

Bustling inn with cheerful beamed bar, good bar food and quite a few wines by the glass; bedrooms

By an attractive stretch of the River Tees, this 18th-c country inn has hospitable licensees and makes a good base for exploring the area. The cheerful, simply furnished beamed bar has a partly wooden floor (elsewhere it's carpeted), a good winter log fire, thickly cushioned wall seats and local photographs and country pictures in its various alcoves and recesses. Bitter End Lakeland Best Gold, Black Sheep and a changing guest from Tirril on handpump alongside eight wines by the glass and around 15 malt whiskies from smaller distilleries. Don't be surprised by the unusual loo attendant – an african grey parrot called Reva. There are seats outside on a terrace and quoits.

🍴 Well liked food includes sandwiches, cheese and hazelnut pâté with caramelised onion relish, smoked salmon, prawn and melon platter, vegetable bake, beer-battered fresh haddock and chips, steak and black pudding in ale pie, smoked mackerel, prawn and salmon fishcake, lambs liver with bacon, mustard mash and rich gravy, steaks and puddings. *Benchmark main dish: cheese-filled chicken in creamy leek sauce £10.50. Two-course evening meal £16.00.*

Free house ~ Licensees Ian and Nichola Swinburn ~ Real ale ~ Open 12-3, 6-11 (10.30 Sun); closed Mon-Weds lunchtimes Nov-Easter ~ Bar food 12-2, 6-9 ~ Restaurant ~ Children welcome ~ Dogs allowed in bedrooms ~ Wi-fi ~ Bedrooms: £47.50/£75
Recommended by Isobel Mackinlay, WAH, Adrian Johnson

CRASTER
Jolly Fisherman

NU2519   Map 10

(01665) 576461 – www.thejollyfishermancraster.co.uk
Off B1339, NE of Alnwick; NE66 3TR

Stunning views, fine coastal walks and very good food attract lots of seasonal visitors to this carefully refurbished inn

The view through the big windows in the upstairs dining room is lovely, looking down on to the pretty harbour and out to sea – but you'll need to book a table in advance. The bustling bar, full of locals and ramblers, has a winter fire, leather button-back wall banquettes and upholstered and wooden dining chairs around hefty tables on bare boards, a few stools scattered here and there, and photographs and paintings in gilt-edged frames. Black Sheep, Mordue Workie Ticket, Timothy Taylors Landlord and a changing guest on handpump served by friendly staff. Seats and tables in the garden have the same outlook – and again, get snapped up pretty quickly. There's a stone fisherman's cottage for rent. You can walk along the cliff to Dunstanburgh Castle.

🍴 As well as their famous crab sandwiches and crab soup, the enjoyable food includes kipper pâté with toasted sourdough, a fish board, shetland mussels in wild garlic cream, a pie of the day, roast vegetable risotto with pesto, chicken in lemongrass and chilli with coconut rice, venison wellington with dauphinoise potatoes, pork three-ways (fillet, belly, spicy pork ball) on black pudding mash with wholegrain mustard and an apple pot, lamb cutlets with celeriac tart and rosemary reduction, and puddings. *Benchmark main dish: stone bass fillet with mango and sweet potato, crispy pancetta and lime mash £18.50. Two-course evening meal £22.00.*

Punch ~ Lease David Whitehead ~ Real ale ~ Open 11-11; 12-11 Sun; 11-3, 6-11 (10.30 Sun) in winter ~ Bar food 11-3, 5.30-9 ~ Restaurant ~ Children welcome ~ Dogs allowed in bar ~ Wi-fi *Recommended by Tony Baldwin, John and Sylvia Harrop, Comus and Sarah Elliott, Barry Collett*

DIPTONMILL
Dipton Mill Inn ♟ 🍺 £

NY9261   Map 10

(01434) 606577 – www.diptonmill.co.uk
S of Hexham; off B6306 at Slaley; NE46 1YA

Own-brew beers, good value bar food and waterside terrace

Everyone loves this quaint little country pub – locals and visitors alike. Now run by the son of Mr Brooker (the previous landlord), it's the home-brewed beers and very reasonably priced food that come in for much praise. The neatly kept snug bar has genuine character, dark ply panelling, low ceilings, red furnishings, a dark red carpet and two welcoming open fires. All six of the nicely named beers from the family-owned Hexhamshire Brewery are well kept on handpump: Blackhall English Stout, Devil's Elbow, Devil's Water, Old Humbug, Shire Bitter and Whapweasel. Also, 14 wines by the glass, more than 20 malt whiskies, Weston's Old Rosie and a guest cider. The garden is peaceful and pretty with its sunken crazy-paved terrace by a restored mill stream and attractive planting; Hexham Racecourse is not far away and there are nice woodland walks nearby.

Incredible value meals include lots of sandwiches, steak and kidney pie, tomato, bean and vegetable casserole, chicken breast in sherry sauce, duck with orange and cranberries, haddock with tomatoes and basil, beef braised in red wine, and puddings such as creamy lemon tart and fruit crumble. *Benchmark main dish: mince and dumplings £8.00. Two-course evening meal £14.00.*

Own brew ~ Licensee Mark Brooker ~ Real ale ~ No credit cards ~ Open 12-2.30, 6-11; 12-3 Sun ~ Bar food 12-2, 6.30-8.30; 12-2 Sun ~ Children welcome ~ Wi-fi
Recommended by Mike and Lynn Robinson, Comus and Sarah Elliott, Martinthehills

DURHAM
NZ2742   Map 10
Victoria
(0191) 386 5269 ~ www.victoriainn-durhamcity.co.uk
Hallgarth Street (A177, near Dunelm House); DH1 3AS

Unchanging and neatly kept Victorian pub with royal memorabilia, cheerful locals and well kept regional ales; bedrooms

For over 40 years, the same friendly family have been running this immaculately kept and delightfully unspoilt brick-built tavern. It's kept the original layout and Victorian décor with three little rooms leading off a central bar: mahogany, etched and cut glass and mirrors, colourful William Morris wallpaper over a high panelled dado, some maroon plush seats in little booths, leatherette wall seats and long narrow drinkers' tables. Also, coal fires in handsome iron and tile fireplaces, photographs and articles showing a real pride in the pub, lots of period prints and engravings of Queen Victoria, and staffordshire figurines of her and the Prince Consort. Coniston Bluebird Bitter, Big Lamp Bitter, Durham White Velvet, Hadrian & Border Stout and Saltaire Blonde on handpump, over 35 irish whiskeys, 50 scottish malts and cheap house wines; dominoes. Credit cards are accepted only for accommodation. No food.

Free house ~ Licensee Michael Webster ~ Real ale ~ No credit cards ~ Open 11.45-11; 12-2, 7-10.30 Sun ~ Children welcome ~ Dogs welcome ~ Bedrooms: £58/£80
Recommended by David Storey, Eric Larkham, Denis and Margaret Kilner

GILSLAND
NY6366   Map 10
Samson
(016977) 47880 ~ www.thesamson.co.uk
B6318, E end of village; CA8 7DR

Friendly village pub in wonderful countryside, cheerful atmosphere in cosy bar, local ales and enjoyable food; warm bedrooms

The warm, attractive bedrooms in this terraced Victorian pub make a good base for exploring nearby Hadrian's Wall – they're close to Hadrian's

Wall National Trail and Cycleway. The cosy bar has a chatty, easy-going atmosphere, red-patterned carpeting, swagged curtains, woodburning stoves, cushioned settles, traditional chairs and stools around sewing machine treadle and other pubby tables, and plush stools at the carved wooden counter. Allendale Pennine Pale and a guest from Pitstop on handpump and several wines by the glass, served by friendly staff; throughout the year they hold quiz nights, themed evenings and live music events. In the dining room are beige tartan-upholstered chairs around white-clothed tables on wide floorboards and prints on red or yellow walls. There are picnic-sets on the back lawn. They also run Willowford Farm B&B just outside the village.

Using their own lamb and other organic local produce, the rewarding food includes lunchtime ciabatta sandwiches, thai-spiced crab and prawn cakes with saffron and garlic mayonnaise, roast pear salad with stilton, caramelised walnuts and creamy chive dressing, beetroot risotto with minted feta and crispy onions, free-range chicken casserole in apple and cider, spicy lamb moussaka, peppered hake steak with mixed bean broth and rocket pesto, and puddings such as chocolate and cherry mousse with kirsch foam and chocolate shortbread and treacle tart with spiced pineapple and banana ice-cream; they may offer packed lunches on request. *Benchmark main dish: organic rare-breed burger £11.50. Two-course evening meal £18.00.*

Free house ~ Licensees Liam McNulty and Lauren Harrison ~ Real ale ~ Open 12-11 (11.30 Sat) ~ Bar food 12-2.30, 6-8.30 ~ Children welcome ~ Dogs allowed in bar ~ Wi-fi ~ Acoustic night second Sun of month ~ Bedrooms: £55/£75 *Recommended by Carol and Barry Craddock, Caroline Prescott, Michael Doswell*

HALTWHISTLE   NY7166 Map 10

Milecastle Inn £

(01434) 321372 – www.milecastle-inn.co.uk

Military Road; B6318 NE – OS Sheet 86 map reference 715660; NE49 9NN

Cosy little rooms warmed by winter log fires, real ales and straightforward bar food; fine views and walled garden

Despite the remote situation – on a moorland road running alongside Hadrian's Wall – this sturdy stone-built pub can get very busy at peak times. The snug little rooms of the beamed bar have two log fires and are decorated with brasses, horsey and local landscape prints and attractive fresh flowers; at lunchtime, the small comfortable restaurant is used as an overflow space. Big Lamp Bitter and Prince Bishop Ale on handpump, a few wines by the glass and a dozen malt whiskies. There are tables and benches in the big sheltered walled garden, with a dovecote and rather stunning views; two self-catering cottages and a large car park. No dogs inside.

Pubby food includes sandwiches, game pâté, prawn cocktail, lasagne, beer-battered haddock, gammon with egg and chips and steaks. *Benchmark main dish: wild boar and duckling pie £10.95. Two-course evening meal £16.00.*

Free house ~ Licensees Clare and Kevin Hind ~ Real ale ~ Open 12-3, 6-11; 12-11 Sat; 12-10.30 Sun; 12-3, 6-11 in winter ~ Bar food 12-2.30, 6-8.30 ~ Restaurant ~ Children welcome ~ Wi-fi *Recommended by Comus and Sarah Elliott*

'Children welcome' means the pub says it lets children inside without any special restriction. If it allows them in, but to restricted areas such as an eating area or family room, we specify this. Places with separate restaurants often let children use them, and hotels usually let children into public areas such as lounges. Some pubs impose an evening time limit – let us know if you find one earlier than 9pm.

HEDLEY ON THE HILL

Feathers ⭐ ♀ ◆

NZ0759 Map 10

(01661) 843607 – www.thefeathers.net

Village signposted from New Ridley, which is signposted from B6309 N of Consett; OS Sheet 88 map reference 078592; NE43 7SW

Northumbria Dining Pub of the Year

Imaginative food, interesting beers from small breweries and friendly welcome in quaint tavern

The friendly, hands-on licensees of this bustling hilltop tavern work very hard to make their pub an important part of the village, holding community events and regular folk music evenings and working closely with local farmers and producers. The three neat, homely bars are properly pubby, with open fires, tankard-hung beams, stripped stonework, solid furniture including settles, and old black and white photographs of local places and farm and country workers. Quickly changing beers include Consett Ale Works Red Dust, Cumberland Corby Noir, Hadrian & Border Gladiator Bitter, Mordue Workie Ticket, Northumberland Pit Pony and Wylam Northern Kite on handpump, as well as six farm ciders, 28 wines by the glass and 33 malt whiskies. They hold an Easter beer/food festival with over two dozen real ales, a barrel race on Easter Monday and other traditional events; darts and dominoes. The picnic-sets in front are a nice place to sit and watch the world drift by.

 Using the best, carefully sourced and local produce, the exceptional food includes sandwiches, roe deer haggis with bashed neeps and tatties, potted brown shrimps on toast, wild foraged mushroom risotto with cheese and truffle oil, beer-battered fish and chips, pot-roast wild duck with redcurrant jelly and game gravy, roast stuffed pork belly and cumberland sausage with cabbage and bacon and apple sauce, cod with sautéed chorizo, chickpeas and white wine and garlic sauce, and puddings such as marmalade bakewell tart and dark chocolate brownie with chestnut and vanilla cream. *Benchmark main dish: roe deer wellington £15.00. Two-course evening meal £20.00.*

Free house ~ Licensees Rhian Cradock and Helen Greer ~ Real ale ~ Open 12-11; 6-11 Mon; 12-10.30 Sun; closed Mon lunchtime except bank holidays, closed first two weeks Jan ~ Bar food 12-2 (2.30 Sat), 6-8.30; 12-4.30 Sun; not Sun evening, Mon ~ Children welcome ~ Wi-fi
Recommended by Mike and Lynn Robinson, Peter and Eleanor Kenyon, Dr Kevan Tucker

NEWTON

Duke of Wellington ♀ ◆ 🛏

NZ0364 Map 10

(01661) 844446 – www.thedukeofwellingtoninn.co.uk

Off A69 E of Corbridge; NE43 7UL

Big stone pub with modern and traditional furnishings, five real ales, good wines by the glass and highly thought-of food; bedrooms

Customers tend to come back to this warmly friendly and attractively refurbished inn on a regular basis; our readers enjoy their visits very much, and the well equipped and comfortable bedrooms make a good base for exploring the area. The bustling bar has leather chesterfields, built-in cushioned wall seats, farmhouse chairs and tables on honey-coloured flagstones, a woodburning stove with a shelf of books to one side, and rustic stools against the counter where they keep Hadrian & Border Tyneside Blonde, Timothy Taylors Landlord and three quickly changing local guests on handpump, a dozen wines by the glass and 12 malt whiskies; TV, darts, dominoes and daily papers. The L-shaped restaurant has elegant tartan and wood dining chairs around pale tables on bare boards, modern art on exposed stone walls, and french windows that lead out to the terrace. Paintwork throughout is contemporary. Seats on the back terrace have lovely views across the Tyne Valley. They hold regular wine tasting evenings and quiz and music nights.

As well as breakfasts for non-residents and afternoon teas, the rewarding all-day food includes sandwiches (until 5pm), prawn and pineapple cocktail, chicken liver parfait, tarragon gnocchi with smoked cream sauce, ballotine of chicken breast stuffed with wild mushroom duxelle, pork belly with glazed turnip and celeriac purée, braised lamb shank with red wine jus, and puddings such as rhubarb crème brûlée and chocolate brownie sundae. *Benchmark main dish: blade of beef with horseradish mash and pan jus £14.50. Two-course evening meal £20.00.*

Free house ~ Licensee Rob Harris ~ Real ale ~ Open 11-11 ~ Bar food 12-9 ~ Restaurant ~ Children welcome ~ Dogs allowed in bar ~ Wi-fi ~ Bedrooms: £95/£120
Recommended by Pat and Stewart Gordon, GSB, Dr Peter D Smart, Gerry and Rosemary Dobson

 NEWTON-BY-THE-SEA   NU2424 Map 10
Ship
(01665) 576262 – www.shipinnnewton.co.uk
Low Newton-by-the-Sea, signed off B1339 N of Alnwick; NE66 3EL

In a charming square of fishermen's cottages close to the beach, good simple food and own-brew beers

Even more special once the summer crowds have gone, this row of converted fishermen's cottages is the perfect place for a break while walking the lovely coastal path. Their own-brew ales on handpump remain a big draw; these usually include five at any one time from a choice of 20 – maybe Ship Inn Dolly Daydream, Hop Ale, Red Herring, Sandcastles at Dawn and Sea Coal. The plainly furnished but cosy bare-boards bar on the right has nautical charts on dark pink walls, while another simple room on the left has beams, hop bines, some bright modern pictures on stripped-stone walls and a woodburning stove in a stone fireplace; darts, dominoes. It can get extremely busy at peak times, so it's best to book in advance – and there might be a queue for the bar. Tables outside look across the sloping village green to the massive stretch of empty beautiful beach. No nearby parking from May to September, but there's a car park up the hill. Do check the opening hours in winter.

Good quality food based on first class local produce includes lunchtime sandwiches and toasties, grilled halloumi with roasted red peppers and tomatoes, kipper pâté, mushroom and feta tart with home-made piccalilli, lamb steaks in caraway marinade with crushed herby potatoes and mint sauce, pesto-stuffed whole mackerel with lemon mayonnaise, sirloin steak with onion marmalade, and puddings such as lemon tart and chocolate and butter pannetone. *Benchmark main dish: hand-picked local crab on herb, baby leaf and olive oil crouton salad £17.95. Two-course evening meal £19.00.*

Own brew ~ Licensee Christine Forsyth ~ Real ale ~ No credit cards ~ Open 11-11; 12-10 Sun; 11-4 Mon-Weds, 12-6 Sun in winter ~ Bar food 12-2.30, 7-8; not Sun-Tues evenings ~ Children welcome ~ Dogs welcome ~ Wi-fi ~ Live folk last Mon of month
Recommended by P Dawn, Mike and Lynn Robinson, Colin McLachlan, Comus and Sarah Elliott, Dr Kevan Tucker

We checked prices with the pubs as we went to press in summer 2015. They should hold until around spring 2016.

NORTH SHIELDS
Staith House ⭐

NZ3668   Map 10

(0191) 270 8441 – www.thestaithhouse.co.uk

Fish Quay/Union Road; NE30 1JA

Smashing food and real ales in refurbished dining pub, with friendly staff and seats outside

A former *MasterChef* finalist has refurbished and reopened what is now a relaxed and comfortable dining pub. The attractive interior blends stripped wood, brickwork and stone with upholstered armchairs and dining chairs, captain's chairs and tartan wall seating, a medley of wooden tables and slate flooring and bare boards; to one end are some high bar chairs around equally high tables. Above the white woodburning stove are candles on a big mantlebeam and a large, rustic mirror, while the walls have ships' lamps and old photographs of the Tyne. Caledonian Deuchars IPA, Greene King Old Speckled Hen and Robinsons Dizzy Blonde on handpump and six wines by the glass, served by enthusiastic staff. Outside are picnic-sets and solid benches and tables on side terraces, and hanging baskets that look pretty against the blue-painted pub walls.

 Cooked by the landlord with an interesting slant on familiar dishes, food includes sandwiches, potted pulled ham with fresh mint and pease pudding, king scallops with aioli and roast asparagus, corn-fed chicken pie with black pudding and charred sweetcorn salsa, Goosnargh duck breast with sauternes-soaked raisins, morels and duck fat potato cake, cod with chorizo, sauté potatoes, roast peppers, chilli and garlic butter, and puddings such as lemon and vanilla rice pudding with lemon curd, clotted cream and meringue and dark chocolate and peanut butter fondant with vanilla ice-cream. *Benchmark main dish: seared halibut with spelt and wild garlic risotto £16.00. Two-course evening meal £19.00.*

Free house ~ Licensee John Calton ~ Real ale ~ Open 12-10.30 (11.30 Sat) ~ Bar food 12-3, 6-9; 12-4, 6-9.30 Sat; 12-4 Sun ~ Children welcome until 7.30pm ~ Dogs allowed in bar ~ Wi-fi ~ Live music Sun 3pm   *Recommended by Michael Doswell, Comus and Sarah Elliott*

ROMALDKIRK
Rose & Crown ★ ⭐ ☖ 🛏

NY9922   Map 10

(01833) 650213 – www.rose-and-crown.co.uk

Just off B6277; DL12 9EB

A civilised base for the area, with accomplished cooking, attentive service and a fine choice of drinks; bedrooms

In a lovely Teesdale village opposite the green with its original stocks and water pump, this is a handsome 18th-c inn that makes a good base for exploring the area; the comfortable bedrooms are in the main building, the courtyard or Monk's Cottage, and breakfasts are highly rated. The cosily traditional beamed bar area has lots of brass and copper, old-fashioned seats facing a warming log fire, a Jacobean oak settle, a grandfather clock, and old farm tools and black and white pictures of Romaldkirk on the walls. Black Sheep and Thwaites Wainwright on handpump, ten wines by the glass and 15 malt whiskies. The hall has farm tools, wine maps and other interesting prints, along with a photograph (taken by a customer) of the Hale-Bopp comet over the interesting old village church. There's also a cosy little snug with sofas and armchairs by a woodburning stove, and an oak-panelled restaurant. There are seats outside. The exceptional Bowes Museum and High Force waterfall are nearby and the owners provide an in-house guide for days out in the area, and a *Walking in Teesdale* book.

Good, enjoyable food includes sandwiches, ham hock terrine with home-made pickles, burnt apple purée, hazelnuts, pork pie and parmesan, razor clams with mussels, shrimps, broad beans, peas and almonds, wild mushroom and leek wellington with blue cheese sauce, steak and mushroom pie with bubble and squeak, chicken with boulangère potatoes, spinach, pancetta and thyme-infused sauce, bass fillet with beer-battered king prawns, herb-crushed potatoes and fish velouté, and puddings such as lemon panna cotta with orange and pistachio and sticky toffee pudding with butterscotch sauce. *Benchmark main dish: local lamb loin, slow-cooked belly and lamb pastilla with mint jus and charred broccoli £21.00. Two-course evening meal £23.00.*

Free house ~ Licensee Cheryl Robinson ~ Real ale ~ Open 11-11 ~ Bar food 12-2.30, 6.30-9 ~ Restaurant ~ Children welcome but no under-7s after 8pm ~ Dogs allowed in bar and bedrooms ~ Wi-fi ~ Bedrooms: £95/£140 *Recommended by WAH, Gerry Price*

SEAHOUSES
Olde Ship ★ ◖ £ ⇱

NU2232 Map 10

(01665) 720200 – www.seahouses.co.uk
Just off B1340, towards harbour; NE68 7RD

Lots of atmosphere and maritime memorabilia in busy little inn; views across harbour to Farne Islands; bedrooms

The same friendly family have owned this harbourside stone inn since it was first licensed in 1812 and the old-fashioned bar has seen a rich assemblage of nautical bits and pieces growing ever since – even the floor is made of scrubbed ship's decking. As well as lots of shiny brass fittings, ship's instruments and equipment, and a knotted anchor made by local fishermen, there are sea pictures and model ships, including fine ones of the North Sunderland lifeboat and the Seahouses' Grace Darling lifeboat. There's also a model of the *Forfarshire*, the paddle steamer that local heroine Grace Darling went to rescue in 1838 (you can read more of the story in the pub), and even the ship's nameboard. An anemometer takes wind-speed readings from the top of the chimney. It's all gently lit by stained-glass sea-picture windows, lantern lights and a winter open fire. Simple furnishings include built-in leatherette pews around one end, stools and cast-iron tables. Black Sheep Best, Courage Directors, Greene King Old Speckled Hen and Hadrian & Border Farne Island on handpump (summer guests too), a good wine list and several malt whiskies; background music and TV. The battlemented side terrace (you'll also find fishing memorabilia out here) and one window in the sun lounge look across the harbour to the Farne Islands; if you find yourself here as dusk falls, the light of the Longstones lighthouse shining across the fading evening sky is a charming sight. It's not really suitable for children – though there is a little family room, and children are welcome (as are walkers) on the terrace. You can book boat trips to the Farne Islands at the harbour, and there are bracing coastal walks, notably to Bamburgh, Grace Darling's birthplace.

The sensibly short menu includes sandwiches and paninis, ham hock terrine with pease pudding, smoked salmon and crayfish cocktail, gammon with egg or pineapple, spinach and ricotta cannelloni, barbecue spare ribs with chips, chicken breast stuffed with apple, apricot and raisins, wrapped in bacon with

---

A star symbol after the name of a pub shows exceptional character and appeal. It doesn't mean extra comfort. And it's nothing to do with exceptional food quality, for which there's a separate star-on-a-plate symbol. Even quite a basic pub can win a star, if it's individual enough.

a creamy brandy sauce, seafood platter, and puddings such as banana and butterscotch pudding and lemon cheesecake. *Benchmark main dish: steak in ale pie £9.75. Two-course evening meal £15.50.*

Free house ~ Licensees Judith Glen and David Swan ~ Real ale ~ Open 11-11; 12-11 Sun ~ Bar food 12-2.30, 7-8.30; no evening food Dec-late Jan ~ Restaurant ~ Children allowed in lounge and dining room if eating, but must be over 10 if staying ~ Wi-fi ~ Bedrooms: £47/£94
Recommended by P Dawn, Mike and Lynn Robinson, Colin McLachlan, Dr Kevan Tucker, Peter Smith and Judith Brown

STANNERSBURN

NY7286 Map 10

Pheasant £ 🛏

(01434) 240382 – www.thepheasantinn.com
Kielder Water road signposted off B6320 in Bellingham; NE48 1DD

Friendly village inn with quite a mix of customers, homely bar food and streamside garden; bedrooms

Once settled in front of the fire with a pint of ale and good food, our readers find it hard to tear themselves away from this welcoming and family-run inn. Staying overnight in the comfortable bedrooms gives you time to explore the beautiful surrounding countryside; Kielder Water is nearby. It's cosy and traditional and the low-beamed lounge has ranks of old local photographs on stripped stone and panelling, brightly polished surfaces, shiny brasses, dark wooden pubby tables and chairs, and upholstered stools ranged along the counter; there are several open fires. The separate public bar is simpler and opens into another snug seating area with beams and panelling. The friendly licensees and courteous staff serve Timothy Taylors Landlord and a changing guest from Wylam on handpump, half a dozen wines by the glass and 34 malt whiskies. There are picnic-sets in the streamside garden, and a pony paddock too.

Popular food includes sandwiches, twice-baked cheese soufflé, chicken liver parfait with apple and ginger chutney, caramelised red onion and goats cheese tartlet, steak and kidney pie, lasagne, fresh dressed local crab, chicken breast filled with cream cheese and sun-dried tomatoes, salmon with lemon and dill mayonnaise, and puddings such as seasonal fruit crumble and chocolate pudding. *Benchmark main dish: slow-roasted local lamb with rosemary and redcurrant jus £11.50. Two-course evening meal £18.00.*

Free house ~ Licensees Walter and Robin Kershaw ~ Real ale ~ Open 12-3, 6-11; closed Mon, Tues Nov-Mar ~ Bar food 12-2.30, 6-8.30 ~ Restaurant ~ Children welcome ~ Dogs allowed in bedrooms ~ Bedrooms: £70/£99 *Recommended by Michael Doswell*

WARK

NY8676 Map 10

Battlesteads 🍺 🛏

(01434) 230209 – www.battlesteads.com
B6320 N of Hexham; NE48 3LS

Eco pub with good local ales, fair value interesting food and a relaxed atmosphere; comfortable bedrooms

Winning awards for their green credentials, the owners of this well run inn are extremely conscientious about the environment and gently weave their beliefs into every aspect of the business. They grow their own produce, have a charging point in the car park for electric cars and use a biomass boiler. The nicely restored carpeted bar has a woodburning stove with a traditional oak surround, low beams, comfortable seats including some deep leather sofas and easy chairs, and old *Punch* country life cartoons on the terracotta walls above a dark dado. As well as a dozen or so wines by the glass and a farm cider, they keep four good changing local ales such as Consett Ale Works Steel Town, Cullercoats Lovely Nelly, Durham Magus and Leamside Alexandrina on handpump at the heavily carved dark oak bar counter; service is excellent. Background music. There's also a restaurant, spacious conservatory and tables on the terrace. Some of the ground-floor bedrooms have disabled access, and they're licensed to hold civil marriages.

Using their own and other carefully sourced produce, the food includes sandwiches, organic duck liver parfait with own-made satsuma marmalade, a platter of their own smoked meat and fish, cumberland sausages with bubble and squeak, dry-cured gammon with free-range eggs, game pie, moroccan-style lamb tagine, coq au vin, and puddings such as a cheesecake of the day and sticky toffee pudding; there's a popular two- and three-course set menu. *Benchmark main dish: pheasant, rabbit and venison pie (part of a two-course menu) £23.50. Two-course evening meal £23.50.*

Free house ~ Licensees Richard and Dee Slade ~ Real ale ~ Open 11am-11.30pm ~ Bar food 12-3, 6.30-9 ~ Restaurant ~ Children welcome ~ Dogs allowed in bar and bedrooms ~ Wi-fi ~ Bedrooms: £70/£115 *Recommended by Mike and Lynn Robinson, John and Sylvia Harrop*

WINSTON
NZ1416   Map 10

Bridgewater Arms ⭐ ♀

(01325) 730302 – www.thebridgewaterarms.com
B6274, just off A67 Darlington–Barnard Castle; DL2 3RN

Carefully renovated former schoolhouse with quite a choice of appealing food, three real ales and seats outside

Just a stroll from a fine old bridge across the River Tees, this is a carefully converted Victorian schoolhouse with a good mix of both drinkers and diners. The high-ceilinged bar has an open log fire, cushioned settles and chairs, a wall lined with bookcases, and high chairs against the counter where they keep Jennings Cumberland, Timothy Taylors Landlord and Wensleydale Coverdale Gamekeeper on handpump, a dozen wines by the glass and 12 malt whiskies. The two rooms of the restaurant have high-backed black leather dining chairs around clothed tables on stripped wooden flooring or tartan carpet, wine bottles lining a delft shelf and various prints and pictures on pale yellow walls. There are some picnic-sets at the front.

With quite an emphasis on fish and shellfish, the menu includes king scallops and black pudding with sweet potato purée and oyster sauce, crab and samphire thermidor, monkfish wrapped in parma ham on curried prawn risotto and whole dover sole, as well as non-fishy dishes such as confit duck leg on garlic mash with red wine sauce, rack of lamb with leek and potato cake and rosemary gravy, and puddings such as ginger parkin with rhubarb and ginger ice-cream and jam roly-poly and custard. *Benchmark main dish: turbot fillet with scallop, wild garlic and lemon risotto £24.00. Two-course evening meal £34.00.*

Free house ~ Licensee Paul Grundy ~ Real ale ~ Open 12-3.30, 6-11; closed Sun, Mon ~ Bar food 12-2, 6-9 ~ Restaurant ~ Well behaved children welcome ~ Wi-fi
Recommended by Isobel Mackinlay, Edward May

Also Worth a Visit in Northumbria

Besides the fully inspected pubs, you might like to try these pubs that have been recommended to us and described by readers. Do tell us what you think of them: feedback@goodguides.com

ACOMB NY9366
Miners Arms (01434) 603909
Main Street; NE46 4PW Friendly little
18th-c village pub with three real ales
and good value traditional food (not Sun
evening, Mon) including popular Sun roasts,
comfortable settles in carpeted bar, huge
fire in stone fireplace, back dining area; folk
night first Mon of month, quiz last Thurs;
children and dogs welcome, a couple of
tables out in front, more in back courtyard,
open all day weekends, closed weekday
lunchtimes. *(Martin Jones)*

ALLENDALE NY8355
Golden Lion (01434) 683225
Market Place; NE47 9BD Friendly 18th-c
two-room pub with enjoyable good value
traditional food, well kept Wylam, Timothy
Taylors and three guests, games area with
pool and darts, upstairs weekend restaurant;
occasional live music; children and dogs
welcome, Allendale Fair first weekend June,
New Year's Eve flaming barrel procession,
open all day (till late Fri, Sat). *(Mike and
Lynn Robinson)*

ALNMOUTH NU2410
⋆ **Red Lion** (01665) 830584
Northumberland Street; NE66 2RJ
Friendly former coaching inn with seats in
peaceful sheltered garden and raised deck
giving views over Aln estuary; bar with heavy
black beams, classic leather wall banquettes
and window seats, old local photographs on
dark mahogany brown panelling, cheerful
fires and pleasant relaxed atmosphere,
ales such as Black Sheep, Roosters Yankee,
Tempest RyePA and Tyne Bank Silver Dollar,
half a dozen wines by the glass, popular often
interesting food in stripped-brick restaurant
with flagstones and woodburner; background
and monthly live music, free wi-fi; children
and dogs (in bar) welcome, comfortable
well equipped bedrooms, open all day from
9.30am. *(P Dawn, Mike and Lynn Robinson,
Alistair Forsyth, Barry Collett)*

ALNMOUTH NU2410
Sun (01665) 830983
Northumberland Street; NE66 2RA
Comfortable banquettes in long low-beamed
bar with open fire one end, woodburner
the other, carpet or bare boards, driftwood
decorations, small contemporary dining area,
well priced traditional food from sandwiches

and hot baguettes up, ales such as Black
Sheep and Mordue, good coffee, friendly
chatty staff; background music; children
welcome, attractive seaside village, four
bedrooms. *(Barry Collett)*

ALNWICK NU1911
Hogs Head (01665) 606576
*Hawfinch Drive; turn right at BP
petrol station; NE66 2BF* Newly built
pub-hotel just off the A1 south of Alnwick;
large open-plan high-ceilinged interior
with exposed brickwork and restful colours,
mix of dark wood tables and chairs on
light wood floor, some easy chairs and
banquettes, plants dotted about, enjoyable
fairly traditional food (all day from 7.30am)
including specials, children's menu and
Sun carvery, well kept local beers such as
Hadrian & Border, friendly helpful young
staff; spacious terrace with teak tables
under large white parasols, 53 bedrooms.
(Carol and Barry Craddock)

ALNWICK NU1813
John Bull (01665) 602055
Howick Street; NE66 1UY Popular chatty
drinkers' pub, essentially front room of early
19th-c terraced house, good selection of well
kept changing ales, real cider, extensive
choice of bottled belgian beers and well
over 100 malt whiskies; darts and dominoes;
closed weekday lunchtimes. *(Toby Jones)*

ALNWICK NU1813
Plough (01665) 602395
Bondgate Without; NE66 1PN Smart
contemporary pub-boutique hotel in
Victorian stone building (now under same
management as the Jolly Fisherman at
Craster – see Main Entries), well kept
Timothy Taylors Landlord and a guest
in lively front bar, several wines by the
glass, good food in bar, bistro or upstairs
restaurant, friendly helpful staff; pleasant
streetside raised terrace, seven bedrooms,
open all day. *(Barry Collett)*

ALNWICK NU1813
Tanners Arms (01665) 602553
Hotspur Place; NE66 1QF Welcoming
drinkers' pub with three well kept local ales
and a decent glass of wine, flagstones and
stripped stone, woodburner, plush stools and
wall benches, small tree in centre of room;
juke box, some live acoustic music, TV; dogs
welcome, closed lunchtime. *(Isobel Mackinlay)*

Tipping is not normal for bar meals, and not usually expected.

AMBLE
NU2604

Wellwood Arms (01665) 714646

High Street, off A1068; NE65 0LD
Open-plan dining pub with good value food
including pub favourites, evening carvery
(all day Sun) and indian menu, ales such
as Timothy Taylors Landlord, friendly staff;
children and dogs welcome, four bedrooms,
open all day. *(Toby Jones)*

BAMBURGH
NU1834

★**Castle** (01668) 214616

Front Street; NE69 7BW Clean
comfortably old-fashioned pub with
friendly welcoming staff, well kept ales
such as Alnwick and decent house wines,
wide choice of popular reasonably priced
food including good generously filled crab
sandwiches, expanded dining area to cope
with summer visitors, local artwork for
sale, open fires; children welcome, no dogs
inside, circular picnic-sets in nice beer
garden, open (and food) all day. *(Derek and
Sylvia Stephenson)*

BAMBURGH
NU1834

Lord Crewe Arms (01668) 214243

Front Street; NE69 7BL Small early 17th-c
hotel prettily set in charming coastal village
dominated by Norman castle; updated bar
and restaurant (Wynding Inn) with painted
joists and panelling, bare stone walls and
light wood floor, warm woodburner, beers
from Northumberland and Charles Wells,
good varied menu; sheltered garden with
castle view, short walk from splendid sandy
beach, 17 comfortable bedrooms. *(Mike and
Lynn Robinson)*

BARDON MILL
NY7566

Twice Brewed (01434) 344534

*Military Road (B6318 NE of Hexham);
NE47 7AN* Large busy inn well placed
for fell-walkers and major Hadrian's Wall
sites, half a dozen ales including local
microbrews and two badged for them by
Yates, over 50 rums, 20 malt whiskies and
seven reasonably priced wines by the glass,
good value hearty pub food from baguettes
to blackboard specials, quick cheerful
service, local photographs and art for sale;
quiet background music; children welcome,
no dogs, picnic-sets in back garden,
14 bedrooms, open all day. *(Mike and Lynn
Robinson, John and Sylvia Harrop)*

BARNARD CASTLE
NZ0516

Old Well (01833) 690130

The Bank; DL12 8PH Welcoming 17th-c
coaching inn with two busy bars, restaurant
and conservatory, enjoyable reasonably
priced food such as spiced mutton on
flatbread and rabbit and black pudding
casserole, friendly helpful staff, well kept
Courage Directors, Timothy Taylors Landlord
and three guests (beer festivals Easter and
end Oct), decent wines; Tues quiz, Thurs

acoustic night; children and dogs welcome,
secluded terrace over town walls, ten
bedrooms, useful for Bowes Museum, open
all day. *(Mrs D A Thatcher)*

BARRASFORD
NY9173

★**Barrasford Arms** (01434) 681237

*Village signposted off A6079 N of
Hexham; NE48 4AA* Bustling sandstone
inn with interesting highly regarded food
from owner-chef including good value
set lunch, friendly local atmosphere and
helpful obliging staff, traditional log-fire
bar with old photographs and bric-a-brac
from horsebrasses to antlers, up to three
ales such as Sharps and Wylam, two dining
rooms, one with wheelback chairs around
neat tables and stone chimneybreast
hung with guns and copper pans, the
other with comfortably upholstered dining
chairs; background music, TV, darts;
children welcome, plenty of nearby walks
and handy for Hadrian's Wall, 11 bedrooms
plus well equipped bunkhouse, open all
day weekends, closed Mon lunchtime
(no food Sun evening). *(Mike and Lynn
Robinson, Michael Doswell, John and
Sylvia Harrop)*

BEADNELL
NU2229

Beadnell Towers (01665) 721211

The Wynding, off B1340; NE67 5AY
Large slightly old-fashioned pub-hotel with
unusual mix of furnishings, good food in
log-fire bar or restaurant including local fish/
seafood, well kept ales such as Black Sheep,
Hadrian & Border and Jarrow, decent wines
from shortish list, pleasant staff, some live
music; can get busy with summer tourists
and booking advised; children welcome, seats
outside, ten bedrooms (a bit of a climb to
some), open all day weekends. *(Derek and
Sylvia Stephenson)*

BEADNELL
NU2229

Craster Arms (01665) 720272

The Wynding, off B1340; NE67 5AX
Roomy neatly kept old building with modern
fittings, wood floors, red banquettes,
stripped-brick and stone walls, popular pubby
food including fish/seafood specials, well
kept Black Sheep and a local guest, friendly
efficient staff, pictures for sale, July beer
and music festival; background music, TV;
children welcome, dogs in one area, picnic-
sets and decking in big enclosed garden,
three good bedrooms, open all day
in summer. *(Martin Jones)*

BEAMISH
NZ2154

Beamish Hall (01207) 233733

NE of Stanley, off A6076; DH9 0YB
Converted stone-built stables in courtyard
at back of hotel, popular and family friendly
(can get crowded), five or six beers from own
microbrewery, decent wines, enjoyable food
including some interesting choices and good
value Sun roast, uniformed staff; plenty of

seats outside, big play area, open (and food) all day. *(P Dawn, Peter Smith and Judith Brown)*

BEAMISH   NZ2055
Black Horse (01207) 232569
Red Row (off Beamishburn Road NW, near A6076); OS Sheet 88 map reference 205541; DH9 0RW Late 17th-c country pub reworked as stylish dining place, contemporary/rustic interior in heritage colours with beams, flagstones and some exposed stonework, enjoyable fairly traditional food (not Sun evening) including weekday set menu till 6pm, half a dozen well kept changing beers, nice wines, friendly attentive staff, cosy fire-warmed front room extending to light spacious dining area with central bar, another dining room upstairs, airy conservatory; children welcome, dogs in bar, restful views from big paved terrace, picnic-sets on grass, open all day, but may shut Mon if quiet. *(Peter Smith and Judith Brown)*

BEAMISH   NZ2154
Sun (0191) 370 2908
Far side of Beamish Open Air Museum – paid entry; DH9 0RG Edwardian pub moved from Bishop Auckland as part of the museum; small front bar with larger back seating area, authentic period décor and cheery costumed staff, Stables Beamish Hall Bitter and one or two guests such as Theakstons Old Peculier, pickled eggs and pork pies, big coal fires; children welcome, lavatories a few yards down the street, open till 5pm (4pm winter). *(Toby Jones)*

BERWICK-UPON-TWEED   NT9952
Barrels (01289) 308013
Bridge Street; TD15 1ES Small friendly pub with interesting collection of pop memorabilia and other bric-a-brac, eccentric furniture including barber's chair in bare-boards bar, red banquettes in back room, a house beer from Tyne Bank and five well kept changing guests, foreign bottled beers; live music (Fri) and DJs (Sat) in basement bar, good quality background music; open all day, from 2pm Jan, Feb. *(Mike and Lynn Robinson)*

CATTON   NY8257
★ Crown (01434) 618351
B6295, off A686 S of Haydon Bridge; NE47 9QS Welcoming 18th-c pub under newish management; inner bar with stripped-stone and bare boards, dark tables, mate's chairs and a traditional settle, good log fire, well kept Allendale beers and enjoyable home-cooked blackboard food, efficient staff, extension with folding glass doors opening on to small garden, lovely Allen Valley views; bar billiards, quiz Tues, folk night Thurs; children and dogs welcome, good walking country, open all day summer (all day weekends, from 4.30pm weekdays in winter). *(Carol and Barry Craddock)*

CHATTON   NU0528
Percy Arms (01668) 215244
B6348 E of Wooller; NE66 5PS Sympathetically refurbished stone-built country inn (same owners as the Northumberland Arms at Felton); good well presented food (not Mon, Tues) in flagstoned log-fire bar or light panelled dining room, well kept ales such as Allendale, Coquetdale and Hadrian & Border, good whisky choice, efficient friendly staff, open fire and woodburner; Weds quiz, darts; children and dogs (in bar) welcome, picnic-sets on small front lawn, five well appointed bedrooms, good breakfast, quiet vilage with sweeping views of the Cheviot Hills, closed Mon and Tues lunchtimes, otherwise open all day. *(Comus and Sarah Elliott, Michael Doswell)*

CHESTER-LE-STREET   NZ2753
Lambton Worm (0191) 387 1162
North Road; DH3 4AJ Interesting 1930s building on outskirts with striking union jack front door, spacious bare-boards bar with dark walls and heavily draped windows, comfortable button-back banquettes and some intimate candlelit booths, plenty to look at including pictures fixed to the ceiling and tale of the giant Lambton Worm that once terrorised the area, own Sonnet 43 beers, enjoyable well priced bar food along with à la carte choices, friendly service, large more formal back restaurant with dark half-panelling, ornate gilt ceiling and pictures of film stars and former prime ministers on red walls; live acoustic music Fri; children welcome, 14 refurbished bedrooms, open all day. *(Michael Doswell, Comus and Sarah Elliott)*

CORBRIDGE   NY9964
★ Angel (01434) 632119
Main Street; NE45 5LA Imposing coaching inn at end of broad street facing handsome Tyne bridge; sizeable modernised main bar with light wood tables and chairs, leather wall benches, blue-grey walls, up to six local ales including Wylam, Weston's cider, a dozen wines by the glass and 30 malts, popular all-day food (not Sun evening) including interesting specials and good value weekday set lunch, friendly efficient uniformed staff, separate oak-panelled lounge with button-back armchairs, sofa and big stone fireplace, daily papers, stripped masonry in raftered back restaurant; children welcome, seats on front cobbles below wall sundial, bedrooms, open all day from 7.30am (8.30am Sun) for breakfast. *(Mike and Lynn Robinson, Dr Kevan Tucker, Comus and Sarah Elliott, GSB, R Anderson and others)*

CORBRIDGE   NY9864
★ Black Bull (01434) 632261
Middle Street; NE45 5AT Rambling 18th-c beamed pub with four linked rooms, mix of traditional pub furniture including leather banquettes, wood, flagstone or carpeted

floors, log fires (one in open hearth with gleaming copper canopy), ceramic collection in front room and information about Hadrian's Wall, enjoyable pubby food, three Greene King ales and a guest such as Black Sheep, good choice of wines by the glass, efficient cheery service; children welcome, seats out on two-level terrace, open all day. *(Comus and Sarah Elliott, R Anderson, Ian Herdman)*

CORBRIDGE   NY9868
★ **Errington Arms** (01434) 672250
About 3 miles N of town; B6318, on A68 roundabout; NE45 5QB Busy 18th-c stone-built pub by Hadrian's Wall attracting good mix of diners and walkers, beamed bars with pine panelling, stone and burgundy walls, farmhouse and other chairs around pine tables on strip-wood flooring, log fire and woodburner, good choice of well liked fresh food from interesting sandwiches up, Jennings and Wylam ales, several wines by the glass, plenty of friendly helpful staff; background music; children welcome, a few picnic-sets out in front, closed Sun evening, Mon. *(Pat and Stewart Gordon)*

CORNHILL-ON-TWEED   NT8539
Collingwood Arms (01890) 882424
Main Street; TD12 4UH Restored and updated Georgian hotel with nice little bar, comfortable and relaxed, with a well kept local ale and around 25 malt whiskies, good food in adjoining dining room or more pricey restaurant, friendly helpful staff, open fires; children and dogs (in bar) welcome, tables out in lovely grounds, local fishing and shooting, 15 well appointed bedrooms (named after ships from the Battle of Trafalgar), good breakfast, open all day. *(Mrs Carolyn Dixon)*

CROOKHAM   NT9138
Blue Bell (01890) 820252
Pallinsburn; A697 Wooler–Cornhill; TD12 4SH Welcoming 18th-c roadside country pub with tasty freshly prepared food and well kept ales such as Fyne and Greene King, friendly attentive service; dogs welcome, comfortable clean bedrooms, good breakfast. *(Les and Sandra Brown)*

DARLINGTON   NZ2814
Number Twenty 2 (01325) 354590
Coniscliffe Road; DL3 7RG Long Victorian pub with high ceiling, wood and carpeted floors, exposed brickwork and striking red and gold wallpaper, up to 13 quickly changing ales including own Village Brewer range (supplied by Hambleton), draught continentals and decent wine

selection, snacky food till 7pm in back part, good friendly service; closed Sun, otherwise open all day. *(Rob Anderson)*

DINNINGTON   NZ2073
White Swan (01661) 872869
Prestwick Road; NE13 7AG Large open-plan pub-restaurant very popular for its wide range of competitively priced food including gluten-free menu, reasonably priced wines and a well kept changing ale, efficient friendly service even at very busy times; children welcome, no dogs inside, disabled facilities, new orangery and attractive back garden, handy for Newcastle Airport, open all day weekends. *(Michael Doswell)*

DUNSTAN   NU2419
Cottage (01665) 576658
Off B1339 Alnmouth–Embleton; NE66 3SZ Comfortable single-storey beamed inn, enjoyable reasonably priced food (smaller helpings available) from fairly standard menu, three well kept ales, restaurant and conservatory; live music and quiz nights, free wi-fi; children and dogs welcome (they have a jack russell), terrace tables and attractive garden with play area, ten bedrooms, open all day. *(Derek and Sylvia Stephenson)*

DURHAM   NZ2742
Court (0191) 384 7350
Court Lane; DH1 3AW Comfortable 19th-c town pub near law courts; wide range of good home-made food from baps and sharing plates up including local dishes such as panacalty and a lunchtime carvery, half a dozen changing ales, friendly helpful staff, extensive stripped-brick eating area with painted furniture on tartan carpet; background music; children and dogs welcome, seats outside, smokers' shelter, open (and food) all day. *(Peter Brix)*

DURHAM   NZ2742
Dun Cow (0191) 386 9219
Old Elvet; DH1 3HN Unchanging backstreet pub in pretty 16th-c black and white timbered cottage, tiny chatty front bar with wall benches, corridor to long narrow back lounge with banquettes, well kept ales such as Black Sheep, Camerons and Copper Dragon, good value simple food, friendly staff; background music; children and dogs welcome, open all day except Sun in winter. *(Rob Anderson)*

DURHAM
Head of Steam (0191) 386 6060
Reform Place, North Road; DH1 4RZ Hidden-away pub close to the river, modern

---

Anyone claiming to arrange, or prevent, inclusion of a pub in the *Guide* is a fraud. Pubs are included only if recommended by genuine readers and if our own anonymous inspection confirms that they are suitable.

open-plan interior, good range of well kept changing ales, real ciders and plenty of bottled continental beers, competitively priced till early evening (4pm Sun) including hot dogs and pizzas; background music (live upstairs); outside tables, open all day (till 1am Fri, Sat). *(Peter Smith and Judith Brown, Eric Larkham)*

DURHAM   NZ2742
Market Tavern (0191) 386 2069
Market Place; DH1 3NJ Welcoming Taylor Walker pub with decent choice of pubby food, six changing ales and a proper cider, friendly efficient service, popular with students (university run folk night Weds); looks out on marketplace at front and to indoor market at back, open (and food) all day. *(Dr J Barrie Jones)*

DURHAM   NZ2642
Old Elm Tree (0191) 386 4621
Crossgate; DH1 4PS Comfortable friendly old pub on steep hill across from castle, two-room main bar and small lounge, four well kept ales including Caledonian Deuchars IPA and Wychwood Hobgoblin (occasional beer festivals), reasonably priced home-made food, open fires, folk and quiz nights; dogs welcome, small back terrace, open all day. *(Peter Smith and Judith Brown)*

DURHAM   NZ2742
Swan & Three Cygnets
(0191) 384 0242 *Elvet Bridge; DH1 3AG* Victorian pub in good bridge-end spot high above river, city views from big windows and terrace, bargain lunchtime food and Sam Smiths ales, helpful friendly young staff, popular with locals and students; open all day. *(Mike and Lynn Robinson, Peter Smith and Judith Brown, Dr J Barrie Jones)*

EARSDON   NZ3273
Beehive (0191) 252 9352
Hartley Lane; NE25 0SZ Popular 18th-c beamed country pub, nicely renovated including one or two quirky touches, three well kept local ales (tasting tray available) and good fairly priced home-made food from sandwiches and sharing boards up (best to book weekends), friendly efficient staff; background and some live music; children welcome, dogs in certain areas, garden with summer bar, play area and pygmy goats, open (and food) all day, Sun till 6pm. *(Martinthehills)*

EGGLESCLIFFE   NZ4213
Pot & Glass (01642) 651009
Church Road; TS16 9DQ Friendly little 17th-c village pub; Bass, Black Sheep, Caledonian Deuchars IPA and three guests kept well by enthusiastic landlord, good value straightforward food; monthly folk club and quiz nights; picnic-sets on back terrace, lovely setting behind church, open all day Sun, closed Mon lunchtime. *(Rob Anderson)*

EGLINGHAM   NU1019
★Tankerville Arms (01665) 578444
B6346 Alnwick–Wooler; NE66 2TX Traditional pub with contemporary touches, cosy friendly atmosphere, beams, bare boards, some stripped stone, banquettes and warm fires, well kept Hadrian & Border with a guest such as Wylam, good wines, imaginative nicely presented food from shortish changing menu, raftered split-level restaurant; children and dogs welcome, country views from garden, attractive village, three bedrooms, closed lunchtimes Mon, Tues. *(Toby Jones)*

ELLINGHAM   NU1625
Pack Horse (01665) 589292
Signed off A1 N of Alnwick; NE67 5HA Nicely refurbished stone-built country inn under newish ownership, very good food (not Sun evening, Mon lunchtime) from fair-priced daily changing menu, Black Sheep and a local guest, masses of jugs hanging from beams in flagstoned bar with feature fireplace, bare-boards snug with deer's head above woodburner, high-backed leather dining chairs on tartan carpet in restauarant and conservatory; children and dogs welcome, enclosed garden growing own vegetables, five bedrooms, peaceful village. *(Comus and Sarah Elliott)*

EMBLETON   NU2322
Dunstanburgh Castle Hotel
(01665) 576111 *B1339; NE66 3UN* Comfortable hotel in attractive spot near magnificent coastline, good choice of enjoyable bar and restaurant food using local meat and fish, good for vegetarians too, efficient friendly service, local ales and nice wines (five by the glass), two lounges for coffee with open fires; children welcome, seats in nice garden, bedrooms and self-catering cottages, open all day. *(John and Sylvia Harrop)*

EMBLETON   NU2322
Greys (01665) 576983
Stanley Terrace off W T Stead Road, turn at the Blue Bell; NE66 3UY Welcoming pub with carpeted bar and cottagey back dining room, open fires, well priced home-made food (wider evening choice) including good crab sandwiches and local fish, interesting range of well kept regional beers; children and dogs welcome, small walled back garden, raised decking with village views, open all day. *(P Dawn, Derek and Sylvia Stephenson)*

ESH   NZ1944
Cross Keys (0191) 373 1279
Front Street; DH7 9QR Friendly 18th-c village local with hearty helpings of well liked good value food (not Sun evening), half a dozen ales such as Big Lamp, Black Sheep and Brains; children welcome, colourful

hanging baskets at front, good country views from behind, closed Mon, otherwise open all day. *(Michael Doswell)*

FELTON   NU1800

Northumberland Arms
(01670) 787370 *West Thirston; B6345, off A1 N of Morpeth; NE65 9EE* Stylish 19th-c inn across road from River Coquet (same owners as the Percy Arms at Chatton); beams, stripped stone/brickwork and woodburner in roomy open-plan lounge bar, flagstones and nice mix of furnishings including big sofas, restaurant with mix of light wood tables on bare boards, good sensibly priced food from bar snacks and standard dishes up (best to book), bread from their own bakery, three or four well kept mainly local beers and nice wines by the glass from short well chosen list, efficient friendly service; Thurs quiz, monthly folk night (fourth Tues); children welcome, dogs in bar, six good bedrooms, open (and food) all day. *(Comus and Sarah Elliott, Michael Doswell, GSB)*

FROSTERLEY   NZ0236

★ Black Bull (01388) 527784
Just off A689 W of centre; DL13 2SL Unique in having its own peal of bells (licensee is a campanologist); great atmosphere in three interesting traditional beamed and flagstoned rooms with coal fires, landlord's own fine photographs and three grandfather clocks, four well kept local ales, farm cider and perry, carefully chosen wines and malt whiskies, good food using local and organic ingredients (best to book evenings), popular Sun lunch; occasional acoustic live music; well behaved children and dogs welcome, attractive no-smoking terrace with wood-fired bread oven and old railway furnishings (opposite steam station), closed Sun evening to Weds, otherwise open all day. *(Peter Brix)*

GATESHEAD   NZ2563

Central (0191) 478 2543
Half Moon Lane; NE8 2AN Large well restored 19th-c wedge-shaped pub (Grade II listed), great choice of changing local ales, real ciders and lots of bottled beers, low-priced food including themed evenings, upstairs function rooms and roof terrace, live music; open all day (till 1am Fri, Sat). *(P Dawn, Peter Smith and Judith Brown, Eric Larkham)*

GREAT WHITTINGTON   NZ0070

Queens Head (01434) 672516
Village signed off A68 and B6018 N of Corbridge; NE19 2HP Handsome golden-stone village pub; dark leather chairs around sturdy tables, some stripped-stone walls and soft lighting, nice hunting mural above old fireplace in long narrow bar, Wylam ales, popular chinese restaurant at back with modern furnishings; background music;

children and dogs (in bar) welcome, picnic-sets under parasols on little front lawn, closed lunchtimes. *(Michael Doswell, Mike and Lynn Robinson, GSB)*

GRETA BRIDGE   NZ0813

★ Morritt (01833) 627232
Hotel signposted off A66 W of Scotch Corner; DL12 9SE Striking 17th-c country house hotel popular for weddings and the like; properly pubby bar with big windsor armchairs and sturdy oak settles around traditional cast-iron-framed tables, open fires and remarkable 1946 mural of Dickensian characters by JTY Gilroy (known for Guinness advertisements), big windows looking on to extensive lawn, Thwaites Major Morritt (named for them) and Timothy Taylors Landlord, 19 wines by the glass from extensive list, bar and restauarant food, friendly staff; background music; children and dogs (in bar and bedrooms) welcome, attractively laid-out split-level garden with teak tables and play area, open all day. *(S G N Bennett, WAH, Peter and Eleanor Kenyon, Peter Hacker, Comus and Sarah Elliott, Barry Collett and others)*

HART   NZ4634

White Hart (01429) 265468
Just off A179 W of Hartlepool; Front Street; TS27 3AW Welcoming end of terrace nautical-theme pub with old ship's figurehead outside, fires in both bars, wide choice of popular fairly traditional food cooked by pleasant landlady, ales such as Copper Dragon; children welcome, no dogs inside, open all day. *(Peter Hacker)*

HARTLEPOOL   NZ5132

Rat Race 07889 479378
Hartlepool station; TS24 7ED Micropub in former station newsagents, one small room (no bar), four well kept regularly changing ales, real cider and perry, you can bring your own food, newspapers; open all day Sat till 9pm, closed Sun, Mon. *(P Dawn)*

HAYDON BRIDGE   NY8364

★ General Havelock (01434) 684376
A69 Corbridge–Haltwhistle; NE47 6ER Old stone pub, a short stroll upstream from Haydon Bridge itself; best part of L-shaped bar is the back with interestingly shaped mahogany-topped tables, long pine benches with colourful cushions and pine chest of drawers topped with bric-a-brac, good wildlife photographs, ales such as Geltsdale and High House Farm, nine wines by the glass, well thought-of freshly made food (not Sun evening) from shortish menu including good steaks and daily specials, stripped-stone barn dining room and terrace with fine South Tyne river views; children welcome, dogs in bar, closed Mon. *(Geof Cox)*

HEBBURN

White Lead (0191) 489 4656

Blackett Street; NE31 1ST Revamped by Sonnet 43 (note the signature union jack doors), their beers and enjoyable food including good value set menu, friendly chatty staff; live music Sat; children welcome, outside seating on large deck, open all day. *(Gemma Malloy)*

HIGH HESLEDEN　　　　NZ4538

Ship (01429) 836453

Off A19 via B1281; TS27 4QD Popular Victorian inn with half a dozen well kept changing ales and good food cooked by landlady including some interesting restaurant dishes, friendly service and atmosphere, sailing ship models including big one hanging with lanterns from boarded ceiling, log fire; sea views over farmland from garden, six bedrooms in new block, open all day Sun, closed Mon and weekday lunchtimes. *(P Dawn)*

HOLWICK　　　　　　NY9126

Strathmore Arms (01833) 640362

Back road up Teesdale from Middleton; DL12 0NJ Attractive and welcoming old stone country pub in beautiful scenery just off Pennine Way, real ales including a house beer (Strathmore Gold) brewed by Allendale, low-priced traditional food all day, home-baked bread, beams, flagstones and open fire; live music Fri, quiz first Weds of month, pool, free wi-fi; well behaved dogs welcome, popular with walkers, four bedrooms and campsite, closed Tues. *(Rob Anderson)*

HOLY ISLAND　　　　　NU1241

Crown & Anchor (01289) 389215

Causeway passable only at low tide, check times (01289) 330733; TD15 2RX Comfortably unpretentious pub-restaurant by the priory, enjoyable traditional home-made food including specials (maybe local oysters), a couple of well kept Hadrian & Border ales, welcoming helpful staff, compact bar with open fire, roomy modern back dining room; children and dogs (in bar) welcome, garden with lovely views (may ask for a credit card if you eat out here), four bedrooms, open all day. *(Sheila Topham)*

HOLY ISLAND　　　　　NU1241

Ship (01289) 389311

Marygate; TD15 2SJ Nicely set pub (busy in season), beamed bar with wood floors, stone walls and maritime memorabilia, big stove, steps down to carpeted lounge/dining area, fairly pubby menu including fish/seafood, Hadrian & Border Holy Island Blessed Bitter badged for them plus one or two guests, 30 malt whiskies; background music; children welcome and usually dogs (but ask first), sheltered sunny garden, four bedrooms, may close at quiet times. *(Toby Jones)*

HORSLEY　　　　　　NZ0965

Lion & Lamb (01661) 852952

B6528, just off A69 Newcastle–Hexham; NE15 0NS 18th-c former coaching inn; main bar with scrubbed tables, stripped stone, flagstones and panelling, four changing ales and a real cider, decent choice of good food from sandwiches and hearty traditional choices up including summer seafood and winter game, also tapas, efficient service, bare-boards restaurant; children and dogs (not evenings) welcome, Tyne views from attractive garden with roomy terrace, play area, open all day. *(Michael Doswell)*

HURWORTH-ON-TEES　　NZ2814

★ Bay Horse (01325) 720663

Church Row; DL2 2AQ Popular dining pub (best to book, particularly weekends) with very good imaginative food, quite pricey but they do offer a fixed-price alternative (lunchtimes Mon-Sat, evenings Mon-Thurs), also vegetarian menu and children's meals, three well kept changing ales, smiling efficient young staff, sizeable bar with good open fire, restaurant; seats on back terrace and in well tended walled garden beyond, charming village by River Tees, open all day. *(Peter Hacker)*

HURWORTH-ON-TEES　　NZ3110

Otter & Fish (01325) 720019

Off A167 S of Darlington; Strait Lane; DL2 2AH Pleasant village setting across road from the River Tees; up-to-date open-plan layout with flagstones and stripped wood, open fires and church candles, nice mix of dining furniture, comfortable armchairs and sofas by bar, good well presented local food including set deals and decent vegetarian and children's choices (wise to book especially weekends), friendly helpful staff, ales such as Black Sheep and several wines by the glass; closed Sun evening. *(Comus and Sarah Elliott)*

KENTON BANKFOOT　　NZ2068

Twin Farms (0191) 286 1263

Main Road; NE13 8AB Roomy Fitzgerald pub in elegant period-rustic style, recycled stone, timbers etc, several pleasant softly lit areas off central bar, enjoyable reasonably priced food from sandwiches and sharing boards to imaginative specials, well kept changing ales (including local brews) and good selection of wines by the glass, friendly efficient service; background music; children welcome, disabled facilities, garden and terrace, handy for A1 and airport, open all day. *(Comus and Sarah Elliott, Eric Larkham, Peter and Eleanor Kenyon, R T and J C Moggridge)*

LANGDON BECK　　　　NY8531

Langdon Beck Hotel

(01833) 622267 *B6277 Middleton–Alston; DL12 0XP* Isolated unpretentious inn with two cosy bars and spacious lounge, well placed for walks including Pennine Way; good choice of enjoyable generous food using local Teesdale beef and lamb, Jarrow Rivet Catcher and Ringwood Best, friendly helpful staff, interesting rock collection in 'geology room'; events including Easter 'egg jarping', late May beer festival and Langdonbury music festival (July); wonderful fell views from garden, seven bedrooms (some sharing bathrooms), open all day, closed Mon in winter. *(Carol and Barry Craddock)*

LANGLEY ON TYNE NY8160
Carts Bog Inn (01434) 684338

A686 S, junction B6305; NE47 5NW Isolated 18th-c moorside pub with heavy beams and stripped-stone walls, old photographs, spindleback chairs around mix of tables on red carpet, nice open fire, good range of enjoyable generous food from sandwiches up including signature Bog Pie (steak and mushroom suet pudding) and popular Sun lunch (best to book), two or three well kept local ales, friendly efficient young staff, games room with pool and darts; children and dogs welcome, picnic-sets in big garden with views, quoits, open all day weekends, closed Mon (and Tues in winter). *(Rob Anderson)*

LESBURY NU2311
Coach (01665) 830865

B1339; NE66 3PP Picturesque stone pub at heart of pretty village; low-beamed rooms with pubby furniture on tartan carpet, dark leather stools by counter serving Black Sheep and Timothy Taylors Landlord, part off to left with sofas and armchairs, small dining room and a further seating area with woodburner and tub-like chairs, popular home-made food including daily specials, friendly staff; background music; children welcome, dogs in some parts, seats out in front and on terrace, pretty flowering tubs and baskets, handy for Alnwick Castle, open all day. *(Toby Jones)*

LONGFRAMLINGTON NU1301
Village Inn (01665) 570268

Just off A697; Front Street; NE65 8AD Friendly 18th-c stone inn arranged into three distinct areas; tasty freshly prepared pub food including good Sun carvery, own-brewed VIP beers along with local guests; some live music, Mon quiz, pool room; comfortable bedrooms and self-catering cabins (just outside the village), open all day. *(Cliff Sparkes)*

MICKLETON NY9724
★ Crown (01833) 640381

B6277; DL12 0JZ Cleanly refurbished buzzy bar with woodburner and view into kitchen, good varied choice of popular sensibly priced food from chef-landlord (smaller appetites catered for), up to four real ales, good wines by the glass and decent coffee, friendly young staff; children and dogs welcome, garden picnic-sets, self-catering accommodation and small campsite, good local walks, open (and food) all day. *(Gerry Price, Lesley and Peter Barrett)*

MIDDLETON NZ0685
Ox (01670) 772634

Village signed off B6343, W of Hartburn; NE61 4QZ Warmly welcoming Georgian country pub in small tucked-away village, a couple of local ales such as Acton and Wylam, tasty straightforward home-made food (not Sun evening); children and dogs welcome, seats outside, handy for Wallington (NT), open all day weekends, closed weekday lunchtimes. *(Rupert and Joey Stubbs)*

MILFIELD NT9333
Red Lion (01668) 216224

Main Road (A697 Wooler–Cornhill); NE71 6JD Comfortable 17th-c coaching inn with good fairly priced food including popular Sun carvery, OAP lunch Thurs, four well kept ales including Black Sheep, a dozen wines by the glass and decent coffee, friendly helpful service; Weds quiz; children welcome, pretty garden by car park at back, two bedrooms, good breakfast, closed Mon lunchtime. *(J F M and M West, John and Sylvia Harrop, Mrs Carolyn Dixon)*

MORPETH NZ1986
★ Tap & Spile (01670) 513894

Manchester Street; NE61 1BH Consistently welcoming, cosy and easy-going two-room pub; up to seven ales such as Caledonian, Everards, Hadrian & Border and Mordue, Weston's Old Rosie cider and country wines, short choice of good value lunchtime food Fri and Sat, traditional pub furniture and interesting old photographs, quieter back lounge (children allowed here) with coal-effect gas fire, board and other games; good local folk music Sun afternoon, quiz Mon, ukulele band Tues, unobtrusive background music, sports TV; dogs welcome in front bar, open all day Fri-Sun. *(Mike and Lynn Robinson)*

NETHERTON NT9807
Star (01669) 630238

Off B6341 at Thropton, or A697 via Whittingham; NE65 7HD Simple unchanging village local under charming long-serving landlady (licence has been in her family since 1917), friendly regulars, range of bottled beers (no real ale at present), large high-ceilinged room with wall benches, many original features; no food, music, children or dogs; open evenings only from 7.30pm, closed Mon and Thurs. *(P Dawn)*

NEW YORK NZ3269
★ Shiremoor Farm (0191) 257 6302

Middle Engine Lane; at W end of New York A191 bypass turn S into Norham Road, then first right (pub signed);

NE29 8DZ Large interesting dining pub cleverly converted from former derelict agricultural building, spacious well divided interior with beams and joists (the conical rafters of a former gin-gan in one part), broad flagstones, several kilims and mix of unusual furniture, farm tools, shields, swords, and country pictures, extremely popular fair-priced food, quieter bar with well kept mainly local ales, ten wines by the glass; children welcome, seats outside on covered heated terrace, open all day. *(Mike and Lynn Robinson, GSB, the Dutchman)*

NEWBIGGIN-BY-THE-SEA NZ3188
Queens Head (01670) 817293
High Street; NE64 6AT Popular down-to-earth Edwardian local with good friendly landlord, high-ceilinged opened-up rooms including cosy back snug, a couple of well kept low-priced ales (pump clips displayed from previous guests), original features including curved bar, mosaic floors and etched windows, lots of old local photographs, dominoes; dogs allowed in some parts, open all day. *(Martin Jones)*

NEWBROUGH NY8768
Red Lion (01283) 575785
Stanegate Road; NE47 5AR Light airy feel and buoyant atmosphere, log fire, flagstones and half-panelling, old local photographs plus some large paintings, good sensibly priced food (not Sun evening) in bar and two dining areas from well filled baguettes up (more elaborate evening menu), a couple of well kept local ales, efficient smiling service, games room with pool and darts; children and dogs (not at food times) welcome, garden behind with decking, good local walks and on NCN cycle route 72, five bedrooms, open all day. *(Michael Doswell)*

NEWBURN NZ1665
★ Keelman (0191) 267 0772
Grange Road: follow Riverside Country Park brown signs off A6085; NE15 8ND Former 19th-c pumping station with eight well kept Big Lamp beers (brewed on site), relaxed atmosphere and good mix of customers in airy high-ceilinged bar with lofty arched windows, well spaced tables and chairs, more seating in upper gallery, fair value traditional food served by friendly staff, modern dining conservatory; background music, free wi-fi; picnic-sets, tables and benches on spacious terraces among flower tubs and shrub beds, good play area, comfortable bedrooms in two separate buildings, open all day. *(P Dawn, Mike and Lynn Robinson, Peter Smith and Judith Brown)*

NEWCASTLE UPON TYNE NZ2464
★ Bacchus (0191) 261 1008
High Bridge E, between Pilgrim Street and Grey Street; NE1 6BX Smart, spacious and comfortable with ocean liner look, ship and shipbuilding photographs,

good value lunchtime food from sandwiches and panini to a few pubby main meals, Sun roasts, nine very well kept changing ales (beer festivals), plenty of bottled imports, farm cider and decent coffee, friendly helpful staff, can get very busy; background music; disabled facilities, handy for Theatre Royal, open all day. *(P Dawn, Mike and Lynn Robinson, Peter Smith and Judith Brown, Eric Larkham)*

NEWCASTLE UPON TYNE NZ2464
Bodega (0191) 221 1552
Westgate Road; NE1 4AG Majestic Edwardian drinking hall next to Tyne Theatre; Big Lamp, Durham and six guest ales, real cider and bottled beers, friendly service, snug front cubicles, spacious back area with two magnificent stained-glass cupolas; background music, Thurs quiz, big-screen TVs (very busy on match days), free wi-fi; open all day. *(P Dawn, Eric Larkham, Mike and Lynn Robinson, Roger and Donna Huggins)*

NEWCASTLE UPON TYNE NZ2563
Bridge (0191) 261 9966
Under the Tyne Bridge; NE1 3UF Conversion of the old Newcastle Arms; airy interior with brick walls and lots of wood, industrial-style ceiling, view into back microbrewery (joint venture with Wylam), ten ales including guests (sampling trays available), affordable all-day food (till 7pm Fri-Sun) from snacks and sharing boards up including some imaginative choices; background music; well behaved children and dogs welcome before 7pm, couple of outside seating areas, open all day (till 1am Fri, Sat). *(Michael Doswell, Comus and Sarah Elliott, Eric Larkham, GSB, Peter Smith and Judith Brown)*

NEWCASTLE UPON TYNE NZ2563
★ Bridge Hotel (0191) 232 6400
Castle Square, next to high-level bridge; NE1 1RQ Big, well divided, high-ceilinged bar around servery with replica slatted snob screens, Black Sheep, Caledonian Deuchars IPA and seven guests kept well, real cider, friendly staff, bargain generous lunchtime food (not weekends), magnificent fireplace, great river and bridge views from raised back area, live music upstairs including long-standing Mon folk club; background music, sports TV, games machines; flagstoned back terrace overlooking part of old town wall, open all day. *(P Dawn, Mike and Lynn Robinson, Peter Smith and Judith Brown, Roger and Donna Huggins, Eric Larkham)*

NEWCASTLE UPON TYNE NZ2563
Broad Chare (0191) 211 2144
Broad Chare, just off quayside opposite law courts; NE1 3DQ Traditional feel although only recently converted to a pub, british-leaning food from bar snacks such as crispy pigs ears and Lindisfarne oysters to

hearty main courses like steak and kidney pudding, four real ales including a house beer from Wylam (Writer's Block), good choice of bottled beers, wines and whiskies, bare-boards bar and snug, old local photographs, upstairs dining room; background music; children welcome till 7pm (later upstairs), no dogs, next door to the Live Theatre, open all day (no food Sun evening). *(Roger and Donna Huggins, Eric Larkham)*

NEWCASTLE UPON TYNE   NZ2464
Centurion   (0191) 261 6611
Central Station, Neville Street; NE1 5HL
Glorious high-ceilinged Victorian décor with tilework and columns in former first class waiting room, well restored with comfortable leather seats giving club-like feel, Black Sheep, Caledonian Deuchars IPA, Jarrow Rivet Catcher and a couple of guests, friendly staff; background music, big-screen sports TV; useful café-deli next door, open all day. *(Roger and Donna Huggins, Alan and Jane Shaw)*

NEWCASTLE UPON TYNE   NZ2664
Cluny   (0191) 230 4474
Lime Street; NE1 2PQ   Bar-café-music venue in interesting 19th-c mill/warehouse (part of the Head of Steam group); low-priced home-made food including various burgers and hot dogs, up to eight well kept ales, some exotic beers and rums, sofas in comfortable raised area with daily papers and art magazines, back gallery featuring local artists; background music and regular live bands (also in Cluny 2 next door); children welcome till 7pm, picnic-sets out on green, striking setting below Metro bridge, parking nearby can be difficult, open (and food) all day. *(Peter Brix)*

NEWCASTLE UPON TYNE   NZ2563
★**Crown Posada**   (0191) 232 1269
The Side; off Dean Street, between and below the two high central bridges (A6125 and A6127); NE1 3JE   City's oldest pub, just a few minutes' stroll from the castle; long narrow room with elaborate coffered ceiling, stained-glass counter screens and fine mirrors with tulip lamps on curly brass mounts (matching the great ceiling candelabra), long green built-in leather wall seat flanked by narrow tables, old photos of Newcastle and plenty of caricatures, Allendale, Hadrian & Border, Highland, Titanic and Wylam, may do sandwiches, heating from fat low-level pipes, music from vintage record player; no credit cards; well behaved children in front snug till 6pm, open all day (midnight Fri, Sat) and can get packed at peak times.
(P Dawn, Peter Smith and Judith Brown, Roger and Donna Huggins)

NEWCASTLE UPON TYNE   NZ2664
Cumberland Arms   (0191) 265 1725
James Place Street; NE6 1LD   Friendly,

unspoilt and traditional; half a dozen well kept mainly local ales along with a good range of craft beers and ciders/perries, two annual beer festivals, limited choice of good value snacky food, obliging staff, bare boards and open fires; events most nights including regular folk sessions, ukulele band Thurs; dogs welcome, tables out overlooking Ouseburn Valley, four bedrooms, open all day weekends, from 5pm Mon-Weds (3pm Thurs, Fri). *(Mike and Lynn Robinson)*

NEWCASTLE UPON TYNE   NZ2664
Free Trade   (0191) 265 5764
St Lawrence Road, off Walker Road (A186); NE6 1AP   Splendidly basic unpretentious pub with outstanding views up river from big windows, terrace tables and seats on grass, up to nine real ales, traditional ciders and plenty of bottled beers and whiskies, good sandwiches/pasties, original Formica tables and coal fire, free juke box, warm friendly atmosphere; steps down to back room and loos; open all day. *(Mike and Lynn Robinson, Peter Smith and Judith Brown, Roger and Donna Huggins, Comus and Sarah Elliott, Eric Larkham)*

NEWCASTLE UPON TYNE   NZ2266
Old George   (0191) 260 3035
Cloth Market, down alley past Pumphreys; NE1 1EZ   Attractive recently refurbished 16th-c pub (former coaching inn) in cobbled yard, beams and panelling, comfortable armchairs by open fire, five well kept/priced ales including Bass, good value food served by friendly staff; background music at one end, open mike Thurs and Sun, sports TV, free wi-fi; children welcome, open all day (till 2am Fri, Sat). *(Richard Tilbrook)*

NEWTON-ON-THE-MOOR   NU1705
Cook & Barker Arms
(01665) 575234   *Village signed from A1 Alnwick–Felton; NE65 9JY*   Traditional stone country inn; beamed bar with stripped-stone and partly panelled walls, broad-seated settles around oak-topped tables, horsebrasses, coal fires, Black Sheep, Timothy Taylors and a guest, extensive wine list, popular food using meat from own farm (set deals weekday lunchtimes and early evening Weds and Thurs), friendly staff, separate restaurant with french windows opening on to terrace; background music, TV; children welcome, no dogs, 18 comfortable bedrooms, Boxing Day hunt starts here, open all day. *(Martin Jones)*

NEWTON-BY-THE-SEA   NU2325
★**Joiners Arms**   (01665) 576112
High Newton-by-the-Sea, by turning to Linkhouse; NE66 3EA   Updated open-plan village pub-restaurant; flagstoned bar with big front windows and open fire, wood-clad dining area behind, good well presented food from interesting sandwiches and sharing plates up, four local ales including Anarchy,

carefully chosen wines and cocktails, cheerful helpful service from uniformed staff; background music; children and dogs welcome, picnic-sets out in front and behind, good coastal walks, five stylish bedrooms, open all day. *(Emma Beacham)*

NORTH SHIELDS   NZ3568
Quay Taphouse   (0191) 259 2023
Bell Street; NE30 1HF Clean and airy quayside pub with good value food including sharing platters and tapas, a couple of changing ales, several wines by the glass and decent coffee, quick friendly service; children welcome, open all day. *(Rob Anderson)*

PONTELAND   NZ1771
Badger   (01661) 867931
Street Houses; A696 SE, by garden centre; NE20 9BT Redecorated early 18th-c Vintage Inn with warren of rooms and alcoves, good log fire, well kept beers such as Bass, Black Sheep and Timothy Taylors, decent range of wines by the glass, their usual all-day food, helpful friendly service; background music; children welcome, handy for Newcastle Airport, open all day. *(Martin and Sue Day, Comus and Sarah Elliott)*

PONTELAND   NZ1773
Blackbird   (01661) 822684
North Road opposite church; NE20 9UH Imposing ancient stone pub under new management; open-plan interior with mix of furniture including several high tables, button-back banquettes, wood, slate and tartan-carpeted floors, striking old map of Northumberland and etching of Battle of Otterburn either side of fireplace, larger Tudor stone fireplace in unusual Tunnel Room, enjoyable food from bar snacks to restaurant dishes, six changing local ales and good selection of other draught beers, friendly service; background music, sports TV, free wi-fi; children and dogs welcome, picnic-sets out at front, more tables on back lawn, open all day, food till 6pm Sun. *(Michael Doswell, Mike and Lynn Robinson)*

RENNINGTON   NU2118
★ Horseshoes   (01665) 577665
B1340; NE66 3RS Comfortable and welcoming with nice local feel (may be horses in car park), well kept ales including Hadrian & Border and decent wines by the glass, ample helpings of enjoyable locally sourced food, friendly efficient service, simple neat bar with flagstones and woodburner, carpeted restaurant; children welcome, picnic-sets out on small front lawn, attractive quiet village near coast, Aug scarecrow competition, closed Mon. *(P Dawn)*

ROCHESTER   NY8497
Redesdale Arms   (01830) 520668
A68 3 miles W of Otterburn; NE19 1TA Isolated inn surrounded by unspoilt countryside, warm and cosy, with enjoyable food cooked by landlord, Allendale ales, friendly attentive staff; bedrooms, open (and food) all day. *(Comus and Sarah Elliott, Peter and Eleanor Kenyon)*

SEATON SLUICE   NZ3477
Kings Arms   (0191) 237 0275
West Terrace; NE26 4RD Friendly busy old pub in pleasant seaside location perched above tidal Seaton Sluice Harbour; good range of beers and enjoyable pubby food (not Sun evening) including gluten-free menu, beamed and carpeted bar with old photographs and woodburner at each end, restaurant; children welcome, a few picnic-sets on sunny front grass, more seats in enclosed beer garden behind, open all day. *(Mrs Carolyn Dixon, Eddie Edwards)*

SHINCLIFFE   NZ2940
Seven Stars   (0191) 384 8454
High Street N (A177 S of Durham); DH1 2NU Comfortable and welcoming 18th-c village inn, varied choice of good generous food from pub favourites up including deals, three well kept ales, coal-effect gas fire in lounge bar, panelled dining room; children in eating areas, dogs in bar, some picnic-sets outside, eight bedrooms, open all day. *(John and Sylvia Harrop)*

SLAGGYFORD   NY6754
Kirkstyle   (01434) 381559
Just N, signed off A689 at Knarsdale; CA8 7PB Welcoming 18th-c country pub in lovely spot looking over South Tyne Valley to hills beyond; good reasonably priced food (not Mon) including some interesting specials, well kept Yates and a summer guest, dining room, games area with darts and pool; dogs very welcome, quoits team, handy for Pennine Way, South Tyne Trail and South Tynedale Railway (Lintley terminus), closed Sun evening, Mon lunchtime (and Tues except school summer holidays), may shut from 9pm if quiet. *(Peter Brix)*

SLALEY   NY9757
Rose & Crown   (01434) 673996
Church Close; NE47 0AA Welcoming 17th-c pub owned by the village, local ales such as Allendale and enjoyable good value home-made food from sandwiches up, beams and log fires; Sun quiz; children and dogs welcome, garden with long country views, two bedrooms, open all day in summer, no food Sun evening, may be reduced choice Mon. *(Phil and Jane Hodson)*

SLALEY   NY9658
★ Travellers Rest   (01434) 673231
B6306 S of Hexham (and N of village); NE46 1TT Attractive stone-built country pub, spaciously opened up, with farmhouse-style décor, beams, flagstones and polished wood floors, huge fireplace, comfortable high-backed settles forming discrete areas,

friendly uniformed staff, popular good value food (not Sun evening) in bar or quieter dining room, good children's menu, real ales such as Allendale, Black Sheep and Caledonian; dogs welcome, tables outside with well equipped adventure play area on grass behind, three good value bedrooms, open all day. *(Comus and Sarah Elliott)*

SOUTH SHIELDS NZ3567
Alum Ale House (0191) 427 7245
Ferry Street (B1344); NE33 1JR
Welcoming 18th-c bow-windowed pub adjacent to North Shields ferry, a dozen well kept Marstons-related ales, open-plan bare-boards bar with fire in old range; music and quiz nights; seats out on front deck overlooking river, handy for marketplace, open all day. *(Toby Jones)*

SOUTH SHIELDS NZ3566
Steamboat (0191) 454 0134
Mill Dam/Coronation Street; NE33 1EQ
Friendly 19th-c corner pub with eight well kept changing ales, lots of nautical bric-a-brac, bar ceiling covered in flags, raised seating area and separate lounge; near river and marketplace, open all day. *(Toby Jones)*

STANNINGTON NZ2179
★ Ridley Arms (01670) 789216
Village signed off A1 S of Morpeth; NE61 6EL Extended village pub handy for A1; several separate areas, each with different mood and style, proper front bar with open fire and cushioned settles, stools along counter serving up to nine local ales including Alnwick and Hadrian & Border, a dozen wines by the glass and good coffee, decent choice of enjoyable reasonably priced food, pleasant helpful staff, several dining areas with comfortable upholstered bucket chairs around dark tables on bare boards or carpet, cartoons and portraits on cream, panelled or stripped-stone walls; background music, Tues quiz, free wi-fi; children welcome, good disabled access, picnic-sets in front and on back terrace, open (and food) all day. *(Peter and Eleanor Kenyon, Michael Doswell)*

STANNINGTON NZ1881
St Marys Inn (01670) 293293
Turn left in Stannington village and go past the church, follow Green Lane to St Marys Lane; NE61 6BL Major rework of gabled Edwardian building with clock tower (admin block for former asylum); series of rooms laid for dining, each with own character, contemporary décor mixing with more traditional elements, wood floors throughout, interesting artwork and several woodburners, well executed food from bar snacks and pub favourites up using local ingredients (some from own garden), prompt friendly service, a house beer from Wylam and a couple of guests, plenty of wines by the glass, nice coffee; children and dogs welcome, good comfortable

bedrooms, generous breakfast, handy for A1. *(Michael Doswell, Comus and Sarah Elliott)*

SUNDERLAND NZ4057
Ivy House (0191) 567 3399
Worcester Terrace; SR2 7AW Friendly Victorian corner pub off the beaten track, five well kept changing ales, interesting bottled beers and good range of spirits, popular food from open kitchen including burgers and pizzas; background and live music, Weds quiz, sports TV; open all day. *(Mikey)*

TYNEMOUTH NZ3669
Hugos at the Coast (0191) 257 8956
Front Street; NE30 4DZ Popular Sir John Fitzgerald pub with open-plan split-level interior, four changing ales and good choice of wines, bar food from sandwiches up, reasonable prices; TV, darts, Weds quiz; some pavement seats, open all day, food till 6pm (4pm Sun). *(Eric Larkham)*

WARENFORD NU1429
White Swan (01668) 213453
Off A1 S of Belford; NE70 7HY Simply decorated friendly bar with a couple of changing ales such as Greene King and Hadrian & Border, steps down to cosy restaurant with good carefully presented imaginative food, efficient helpful service, warm fires; children and dogs (in bar) welcome, open all day Sun. *(Carol and Barry Craddock)*

WELDON BRIDGE NZ1398
★ Anglers Arms (01665) 570271
B6344, just off A697; village signposted with Rothbury off A1 N of Morpeth; NE65 8AX Traditional coaching inn nicely located by bridge over River Coquet; two-part bar with cream walls or oak panelling, shiny black beams hung with copper pans, profusion of fishing memorabilia, taxidermy and a grandfather clock, some unexpectedly low tables with matching chairs, sofa by coal fire, Shepherd Neame Spitfire, Timothy Taylors Landlord and Youngs Bitter, around 36 malt whiskies and decent wines, well liked, generous food, friendly staff; background music; children and dogs (in bar) welcome, attractive garden and good play area with assault course, fishing rights, comfortable bedrooms, open (and food) all day. *(Mike and Lynn Robinson, Comus and Sarah Elliott, Ian Herdman)*

WEST BOLDON NZ3460
Red Lion (0191) 536 4197
Redcar Terrace; NE36 0PZ Bow-windowed, flower-decked family-run pub, hop-strung beamed bar with open fire, ales such as Black Sheep from ornate wood counter, separate snug and conservatory dining room, good choice of well priced pubby food, friendly smiling service; seats out on back decking, open all day. *(Roger and Donna Huggins)*

WEST WOODBURN
NY8986
Bay Horse (01434) 270218
A68; NE48 2RX Modernised 18th-c roadside inn with horse-theme décor, Belhaven and other Greene King ales, decent wines and good range of reasonably priced food including Sun carvery, friendly service, can eat in carpeted log fire-bar or separate restaurant; background music; children and dogs welcome, riverside garden, seven bedrooms. *(J V Dadswell)*

WHALTON
NZ1281
Beresford Arms (01670) 775273
B6524; NE61 3UZ Pub-restaurant in attractive village, popular reasonably priced home-made food (some dishes available in smaller sizes), Jarrow and a couple of local guests, friendly helpful staff, high-backed chairs at sturdy candlelit pine tables, tartan carpet, old photographs; darts and dominoes; children and dogs (in bar) welcome, disabled access, four comfortable bedrooms, open all day, food till 5pm Sun. *(Michael Doswell)*

WHITFIELD
NY7857
Elks Head (01434) 345282
Off A686 SW of Haydon Bridge; NE47 8HD Extended old stone pub attractively set in steep wooded valley, light and spacious, with bar and two dining areas, good value tasty food, Fullers London Pride and a couple of local guests, several wines by the glass, friendly helpful service; children and dogs (in bar) welcome, picnic-sets in small pretty front garden by little river, scenic area with good walks, ten bedrooms (some in adjacent cottage), open all day summer. *(Dr Kevan Tucker)*

WHITLEY BAY
NZ3572
King George (0191) 251 3877
North Parade; NE26 1PB Traditional pub connected to the trendier 42nd Street Bar; small old-world rooms from side-street entrance, at least one real ale, friendly service, piano; dogs welcome. *(Eddie Edwards)*

WHITLEY BAY
NZ3571
Rockliffe Arms (0191) 253 1299
Algernon Place; NE26 2DT Backstreet Sir John Fitzgerald pub with four well kept changing ales, a good refuge from busy town centre; sports TV, darts and dominoes; open all day. *(Eric Larkham)*

WHORLTON
NZ1014
Bridge Inn (01833) 627341
High Stakes, N of village green; DL12 8XD Comfortable old stone pub on green of nice village, log-fire bar and larger restaurant/tearoom, three well kept changing ales (often local Mithril), enjoyable reasonably priced food (more evening choice), friendly welcoming staff, grey-painted part panelled walls, wooden furniture and a few sofas on carpeted floors; free wi-fi; dogs welcome, near historic narrow suspension bridge over the Tees, closed lunchtimes Mon and Tues, all day Weds, otherwise open (and food) all day. *(GSB)*

WYLAM
NZ1164
★ Boathouse (01661) 853431
Station Road, handy for Newcastle–Carlisle railway line; across Tyne from village (and Stephenson's birthplace); NE41 8HR Convivial two-room pub with a dozen real ales, 14 ciders (some tapped from cellar) and good choice of malt whiskies, snacky food, friendly helpful young staff, light interior with one or two low beams, woodburner; fortnightly open mike night (Tues), juke box, sports TV; children and dogs welcome, seats outside, close to station and river, open all day (evenings can be very busy). *(Mike and Lynn Robinson, Comus and Sarah Elliott, Eric Larkham)*

Nottinghamshire

BLYTH   SK6287   Map 7

White Swan

(01909) 591222 – www.whiteswaninnblyth.co.uk

High Street; S81 8EQ

Bustling village pub popular with both locals and visitors, cosy rooms, real ales and well liked food

At the heart of the village community, this is an attractive pub with hands-on licensees and friendly staff who offer a warm welcome for all. There are beams, exposed brickwork, flagstones, carpeting and a mix of dining chairs and padded banquettes around an assortment of tables. Theakstons Black Bull and Wentworth New Zealand Pale Ale on handpump, seven wines by the glass and half a dozen malt whiskies. The live music events are extremely good and popular. The little back garden has seats and tables and the village green is opposite.

🍴 Quite a choice of food includes warm bacon and stilton salad with cider vinegar, mushrooms in peppercorn sauce with blue cheese, sharing boards, cajun chicken or steak burgers with chips, goats cheese tart with mediterranean vegetables, baby back barbecue pork ribs in barbecue sauce, 'hot rock' steaks with a choice of sauces, and puddings such as lemon meringue pie and strawberry and chocolate sundae. *Benchmark main dish: pie of the day £9.25. Two-course evening meal £16.00.*

Enterprise ~ Tenant Adam Kay ~ Real ale ~ Open 12-11 ~ Children welcome ~ Wi-fi ~ Live acoustic music Fri monthly, jazz Sun lunch monthly *Recommended by Caroline Prescott, Mike Swan*

CAYTHORPE   SK6845   Map 7

Black Horse 🍺 £

(0115) 966 3520 – www.caythorpebrewery.co.uk

Turn off A6097 0.25 miles SE of roundabout junction with A612, NE of Nottingham; into Gunthorpe Road, then right into Caythorpe Road and keep on; NG14 7ED

Quaintly old-fashioned little pub brewing its own beer, simple interior and enjoyable homely food; no children, no credit cards

Close to the River Trent where there are waterside walks, this 300-year-old country local has been run by the same friendly family for three generations. The uncluttered carpeted bar has just five tables, along with brocaded wall banquettes and settles, decorative plates on a delft shelf, a few horsebrasses attached to the ceiling joists, and a coal fire. Cheerful regulars might occupy the few bar stools to enjoy Caythorpe Bitter and a seasonal ale brewed in outbuildings here and served alongside a couple of guests such as Bass and Greene King Abbot on handpump; 11 wines by the glass too. Off the front corridor is an inner room, partly panelled with a wall bench running all the way round three unusual, long, copper-topped tables; there are several old local photographs, darts and board games. Down on the left, an end room has just one huge round table. There are seats outside.

Good value home-cooked food (you'll need to book a table in advance) includes sandwiches, omelettes, local sausages with onion gravy, grilled lamb chops, fresh fish, and puddings such as apple pie and sticky toffee pudding. *Benchmark main dish: fresh cod or haddock £11.00. Two-course evening meal £16.00.*

Own brew ~ Licensee Sharron Andrews ~ Real ale ~ No credit cards ~ Open 12-3, 5.30-11; 12-5, 8-11 Sun; closed Mon except bank holidays ~ Bar food 12-2, 6-8.30; not Sat evening, Sun ~ Dogs allowed in bar *Recommended by P Dawn, Peter and Jean Hoare, Dave Braisted*

COLSTON BASSETT   SK6933   Map 7
Martins Arms ✪ �

(01949) 81361 – www.themartinsarms.co.uk

Village signposted off A46 E of Nottingham; School Lane, near market cross in village centre; NG12 3FD

• •

Nottinghamshire Dining Pub of the Year

Smart dining pub with impressive food, good range of drinks including seven real ales and attractive grounds

A farmhouse in Elizabethan times, this is a civilised pub with first class food – most customers head for the elegant restaurant. There's a comfortably relaxed atmosphere, warm log fires in Jacobean fireplaces, fresh flowers and candlelight, and it's smartly decorated with period fabrics and colours, antique furniture and hunting prints. Neatly uniformed staff serve Bass, Belhaven Grand Slam, Black Sheep, Greene King IPA, Marstons Pedigree and Timothy Taylors Landlord on handpump, as well as 22 wines by the glass or carafe (including prosecco, champagne and sweet wines), Belvoir organic ginger beer and 17 malt whiskies. The lawned garden (summer croquet here) backs on to National Trust parkland. Readers recommend visiting the church opposite and Colston Bassett Dairy, which produces and sells its own stilton cheese, and is just outside the village.

Accomplished cooking includes lunchtime sandwiches, tempura scallops with pickled cockles, crispy bacon, black pudding and marie rose sauce, chicken liver parfait with foie gras cream and pear purée, roasted stuffed butternut squash with wild mushroom fricassée with gruyère herb crust, a pie of the day, bacon beef burger with stilton and triple-cooked chips, a fish dish of the day, local pheasant blanquette with crushed thyme potatoes, and puddings such as dark chocolate fondant with salted caramel bananas and vanilla bean ice-cream and roasted hazelnut cake with white chocolate and star anise sorbet and caramelised white chocolate. *Benchmark main dish: pork belly, black pudding and three-bean and mustard cassoulet £19.95. Two-course evening meal £26.00.*

Free house ~ Licensees Lynne Strafford Bryan and Salvatore Inguanta ~ Real ale ~ Open 12-3, 6-11; 12-3.30, 6.30-10.30 Sun ~ Bar food 12-2, 6-9; not Sun evening ~ Restaurant ~ Children welcome ~ Wi-fi ~ Local bands on bank holidays
Recommended by P Dawn, Ian Herdman, Caroline Prescott

> The star-on-a-plate award, ✪, distinguishes pubs where the food is of exceptional quality. The knife-and-fork symbol just means the pub serves food.

GRINGLEY ON THE HILL SK7390 Map 7

THE GOOD PUB GUIDE

Blue Bell

(01777) 816303 – www.bluebellinngringley.co.uk

High Street, just off A361 Bawtry–Gainsborough; DN10 4RF

Village pub with friendly owners, several refurbished bars, real ales and wines by the glass, highly thought-of food and seats in garden

This bustling village pub is run with care and enthusiasm by hard-working licensees and their friendly staff, who welcome visitors just as warmly as their regulars. The various interconnected rooms are on different levels with pale painted beams, bare boards and striped carpeting, carved wood and smart leather dining chairs around sturdy tables, mirrors and prints on wallpapered or painted walls, and open fires. Black Sheep, Tetleys Bitter and Theakstons Best on handpump, 30 whiskies and bourbons, a good choice of gins and wines by the glass; background music and TV. The back garden has picnic-sets under cocktail parasols, a children's play fort and summer marquee. The acoustic and jazz sessions are very popular.

A wide range of good, popular food includes thai-style fishcakes with sweet chilli sauce, creamy garlic mushrooms, sharing platters, burgers with lots of toppings and sauces, chickpea and date tagine with couscous, salmon fillet with dill and lemon sauce and creamy herb potatoes, black rock grills (steaks, wild boar, kangaroo and so forth cooked on volcanic rocks at your table), and puddings such as lemon crème brûlée cheesecake and sticky toffee pudding. *Benchmark main dish: beef and mushroom in ale pie with stilton pastry £9.95. Two-course evening meal £16.00.*

Enterprise ~ Tenants Adam and Louise Kay ~ Real ale ~ Open 12-11; 3-11 Mon ~ Bar food 12-2, 6-9; 12-9 Sat; 12-4 Sun; not Sun evening or Mon ~ Restaurant ~ Children welcome ~ Wi-fi ~ Live acoustic music Fri evening monthly, jazz Sat afternoon monthly
Recommended by Edward May, Jo Garnett

Also Worth a Visit in Nottinghamshire

Besides the fully inspected pubs, you might like to try these pubs that have been recommended to us and described by readers. Do tell us what you think of them: feedback@goodguides.com

AWSWORTH SK4844

Gate (0115) 932 9821

Main Street, via A6096 off A610 Nuthall–Eastwood bypass; NG16 2RN Friendly Victorian free house with good range of well kept ales including Burton Bridge, some snacky food, cosy bar, coal fire in lounge, small pool room and refurbished skittle alley; children welcome till 8pm, dogs in bar, disabled facilities, picnic-sets out in front, near site of once-famous railway viaduct, open all day. *(P Dawn)*

BAGTHORPE SK4751

Dixies Arms (01773) 810505

A608 towards Eastwood off M1 junction 27, right on B600 via Sandhill Road, left into School Road; Lower Bagthorpe; NG16 5HF Friendly unspoilt 18th-c brick local with D H Lawrence connections; beams and tiled floors, well kept Greene King Abbot, Theakstons Best and a guest, no food, entrance bar with tiny snug, good fire in small part-panelled parlour's fine fireplace, longer narrow room with toby jugs, darts and dominoes; live music Sat, quiz Sun, free wi-fi; children and dogs (on leads) welcome, picnic-sets out at front, big garden and play area behind, open all day. *(Mike Swan)*

BEESTON SK5236

Crown (0115) 925 4738

Church Street; NG9 1FY Restored Everards pub with 14 real ales including theirs and Browns, real ciders/perry and good choice of other drinks, no hot food but fresh cobs and snacks; front snug and bar with quarry-tiled floor, carpeted parlour with padded wall seats, Victorian décor and new polished bar in lounge, beams, panelling and bric-a-brac including an old red telephone box; regular quiz nights and beer festivals; terrace tables, open all day. *(P Dawn)*

BEESTON   SK5336

★**Victoria** (0115) 925 4049

*Dovecote Lane, backing on to railway
station; NG9 1JG* Genuine down-to-earth
all-rounder attracting good mix of customers,
up to 16 real ales (regular beer festivals),
two farm ciders, 120 malt whiskies and
30 wines by the glass, good value interesting
food (half the menu is vegetarian), friendly
efficient service, three fairly simple unfussy
rooms with original long narrow layout,
solid furnishings, bare boards and stripped
woodwork, stained-glass windows, open fires;
live music (Sun, Mon evening Oct-May),
newspapers and board games; children
welcome till 8pm, dogs in bar, seats out on
covered heated area overlooking platform
(trains pass just a few feet away), limited
parking, open all day. *(P Dawn)*

BINGHAM   SK7039

★**Horse & Plough** (01949) 839313

Off A52; Long Acre; NG13 8AF Former
1818 Methodist chapel with low beams,
flagstones and stripped brick, comfortable
open-plan seating including pews, prints
and old brewery memorabilia, well kept
Caledonian Deuchars IPA, Thwaites
Wainwright and four guests (tasters offered),
real cider, good wine choice, enjoyable
reasonably priced weekday bar food, popular
upstairs grill room (Tues-Sat evenings, all
day Sun) with polished boards, hand-painted
murals and open kitchen, good friendly
service; background music; children and dogs
welcome, disabled facilities, open all day.
(P Dawn)

BRAMCOTE   SK5037

White Lion (0115) 925 7841

*Just off A52 W of Nottingham; Town
Street; NG9 3HH* Small friendly 18th-c
village pub, well kept Greene King related
ales from bar serving two split-level adjoining
rooms, good choice of low-priced pubby food
(not Sun or Mon evenings) including Wed
curry and Thurs grill nights; events such as
quiz and poker evenings, live music last Sat
of month, darts; children and dogs welcome,
tables in garden behind, open all day.
(Jo Garnett)

BUNNY   SK5829

Rancliffe Arms (0115) 984 4727

*Loughborough Road (A60 S of
Nottingham); NG11 6QT* Substantial
early 18th-c former coaching inn with
linked dining areas, emphasis on good food
including popular carvery (Mon, Weds,
Sat and Sun) with excellent range of fresh
vegetables, friendly service, chunky country
chairs around mixed tables on flagstones or
carpet, well kept changing range of Marstons-
related ales in comfortable log-fire bar with
sofas and armchairs; background music;
children welcome, decking outside, open all
day Fri-Sun. *(Gerry and Rosemary Dobson)*

CAR COLSTON   SK7242

Royal Oak (01949) 20247

*The Green, off Tenman Lane (off A46
not far from A6097 junction);
NG13 8JE* Good well priced traditional
food (not Sun evening) in biggish 19th-c
pub opposite one of England's largest
village greens, four well kept Marstons-
related ales and decent choice of wines
by the glass, woodburner in lounge bar
with tables set for eating, public bar with
unusual barrel-vaulted brick ceiling,
spotless housekeeping; children welcome,
picnic-sets on spacious back lawn, heated
smokers' den, camping, open all day
Fri-Sun. *(P Dawn)*

CAUNTON   SK7459

★**Caunton Beck** (01636) 636793

Newark Road; NG23 6AE Reconstructed
low-beamed dining pub made to look old
using original timbers and reclaimed oak;
scrubbed pine tables and country-kitchen
chairs, open fire, three ales including
Oakham JHB and over two dozen wines
by the glass, well presented popular food
from breakfast on, decent coffee and daily
papers, relaxed atmosphere with cheerful
obliging staff; children welcome, dogs
in bar, seats on flowery terrace, open all
day from 8.30am, handy for A1. *(Ray and
Winifred Halliday)*

CLAYWORTH   SK7288

Blacksmiths Arms (01777) 818171

Town Street; DN22 9AD Individually
revamped village dining pub, good food
from lunchtime sandwiches and pub
favourites to inventive restaurant dishes
(not cheap), Timothy Taylors Landlord and
a guest, craft beers and good wine choice
including champagne by the glass, pleasant
well trained staff; children welcome, sunny
enclosed back garden, open till 8pm Sun
(no evening food then), closed Mon.
(Dan Thawley)

EAST MARKHAM   SK7473

Pheasantry Brewery

(01777) 870572 *Lincoln Road;
NG22 0SN* Microbrewery (tours available)
in converted farm buildings along with
modern raftered bar, restaurant and café;
four of their ales and good choice of food
from light bites and sandwiches up (booking
advised weekends), pleasant efficient young
staff, theme evenings and weekly events;
children welcome, tables outside, handy for
A1, closed all day Mon and evenings Tues,
Weds, Sun. *(David and Ruth Hollands)*

EDWINSTOWE   SK6266

Forest Lodge (01623) 824443

Church Street; NG21 9QA Friendly
18th-c inn with enjoyable home-made food
in pubby bar or restaurant, good service,
well kept Wells Bombardier and four

regularly changing guests (usually one from Welbeck Abbey), log fire; children welcome, 13 bedrooms, handy for Sherwood Forest. *(Derek and Sylvia Stephenson)*

FARNDON   SK7652
★ **Boathouse** (01636) 676578

Off A46 SW of Newark; keep on towards river – pub off Wyke Lane, just past the Riverside pub; NG24 3SX Big-windowed contemporary bar-restaurant overlooking the Trent, emphasis on food but Greene King IPA and a couple of guests from stylish counter, good choice of wines, main area indeed reminiscent of a boathouse with high ceiling trusses supporting bare ducting and scant modern decoration, second dining area broadly similar, modern cooking along with some pubby dishes, early-bird deal, neat young staff; background and live music (Sun), free wi-fi; children welcome, wicker chairs around teak tables on terrace, own moorings, open all day, food all day Sun. *(Mike Swan)*

GRANBY   SK7436
★ **Marquis of Granby** (01949) 859517

Off A52 E of Nottingham; Dragon Street; NG13 9PN Popular and friendly 18th-c pub in attractive Vale of Belvoir village, tap for Brewsters with their ales and interesting guests from chunky yew counter, no food apart from Fri evening fish and chips, two small comfortable rooms with broad flagstones, some low beams and striking wallpaper, open fire; children and dogs welcome, open all day weekends, from 4pm Mon-Fri. *(Peter Pilbeam)*

HALAM   SK6754
Waggon & Horses (01636) 813109

Off A612 in Southwell centre, via Halam Road; NG22 8AE Modernised and opened-up 17th-c beamed pub with several cosy areas, Thwaites beers and a couple of changing guests, Kingstone Press cider, enjoyable all-day food (till 5pm Sun) from lunchtime light bites to grills, friendly welcoming staff; children and dogs (in one area) allowed, terrace picnic-sets, open all day. *(Brian and Anna Marsden)*

HARBY   SK8870
Bottle & Glass (01522) 703438

High Street; village signed off A57 W of Lincoln; NG23 7EB Civilised dining pub with pair of bay-windowed front bars, attractive pubby furnishings, lots of bright cushions on built-in wall benches, arts and crafts chairs on dark flagstones, log fire, splendid range of wines (big vineyard map of Côte de Beaune in left-hand bar), Black Sheep and a couple of guests such as local Pheasantry, good food including set menu and blackboard specials, small area with squashy sofas and armchairs and more formal restaurant; children welcome, dogs in bar, modern wrought-iron

furniture on back terrace, picnic-sets on grass beyond, open all day. *(Mike Swan)*

HOCKERTON   SK7156
Spread Eagle (01636) 812019

A617 Newark–Mansfield; NG25 0PL Small village pub with linked rooms, well kept Timothy Taylors Landlord and three guests, nine wines by the glass and good pub food including a few daily specials, friendly efficient staff, log fire and woodburner; children welcome, open all day Fri, Sat, till 9pm Sun, closed Mon. *(John Wooll)*

HOVERINGHAM   SK6946
Reindeer (0115) 966 3629

Main Street; NG14 7GR Beamed village pub with intimate bar and busy restaurant (best to book), good home-made food from standards to more enterprising dishes, good value lunchtime set menu, Black Sheep, Castle Rock Harvest Pale and guests, good wines by the glass, log fire; children welcome, seats outside overlooking cricket pitch, closed Mon lunchtime, otherwise open all day, no evening food Sun, Weds, Thurs. *(P Dawn)*

KIMBERLEY   SK4944
★ **Nelson & Railway** (0115) 938 2177

Station Road; handy for M1 junction 26 via A610; NG16 2NR Victorian beamed pub in same family for over 40 years, popular and comfortable, with well kept Greene King ales and guests, good attractively priced home-made food including blackboard specials, mix of Edwardian-looking furniture, brewery prints (was tap for defunct Hardys & Hansons Brewery) and railway signs, dining extension; juke box, games machine, darts, free wi-fi; children and dogs allowed, nice front and back gardens, 11 good value bedrooms, open all day, food all day Sat, till 6pm Sun. *(Stephen Woad)*

KIMBERLEY   SK5044
Stag (0115) 938 3151

Nottingham Road; NG16 2NB Friendly 18th-c traditional local spotlessly kept by good landlady, two cosy rooms, small central counter and corridor, low beams, dark panelling and settles, table skittles and working vintage slot machines, old Shipstones Brewery photographs, well kept Adnams, Timothy Taylors Landlord and three guests (May beer festival), no food; children and dogs welcome, attractive back garden with play area, opens 5pm (1.30 Sat, 12 Sun). *(Peter Pilbeam)*

LAMBLEY   SK6345
Woodlark (0115) 931 2535

Church Street; NG4 4QB Welcoming and interestingly laid-out village local; neatly furnished bare-brick beamed bar, careful extension into next house giving comfortable lounge/dining area, popular good value freshly made food, downstairs steak bar

(Fri, Sat evenings), well kept Castle Rock, Sam Smiths, Timothy Taylors Landlord and a guest, open fire; children and dogs welcome, tables on side terrace, open all day. *(Dru and Louisa Marshall)*

LAXTON   SK7266
★**Dovecote** (01777) 871586
Off A6075 E of Ollerton; NG22 0NU Red-brick pub handy for A1; cosy country atmosphere in three traditionally furnished dining areas, well liked food including notable steak and ale pie and good value Sun lunch, well kept Castle Rock and guests, farm cider and several wines by the glass, friendly efficient staff; background music, free wi-fi; children welcome, no dogs inside, small front terrace and sloping garden with views towards church, interesting village that still uses the medieval 'strip farming' method, two bedrooms, open all day Sun. *(Pat and Stewart Gordon, Howard and Margaret Buchanan, Malcolm Phillips, Derek and Sylvia Stephenson)*

LOWDHAM   SK6646
Worlds End (0115) 966 3857
Plough Lane; NG14 7AT Small 18th-c village pub with long carpeted beamed bar/dining room, enjoyable traditional home-made food (all day Fri, Sat, not Sun evening), friendly service, three changing real ales from brick-faced counter, open fire; background music; children and dogs welcome, some covered seats out at front among colourful tubs and baskets, picnic-sets on lawned area, open all day. *(Richard Stanfield)*

MANSFIELD   SK5561
Il Rosso (01623) 623031
Nottingham Road (A60); NG18 4AF Restaurnty pub with good italian-influenced food including early-bird deal and fish Fri, three well kept ales, good service; regular live music, sports TV, free wi-fi; children welcome, no dogs inside, terraces front and back, open all day from 8.30am for breakfast. *(Derek and Sylvia Stephenson)*

MANSFIELD   SK5363
Railway Inn (01623) 623086
Station Street; best approached by viaduct from near Market Place; NG18 1EF Friendly traditional local with long-serving landlady, three changing ales, real cider and good bottled beer choice, bargain home-made food (till 5pm Sun), two little front rooms leading to main bar, another cosy room at back, laminate flooring throughout; some live music; children and dogs welcome, small courtyard and beer garden, handy for Robin Hood Line station, open all day. *(P Dawn)*

MAPLEBECK   SK7160
★**Beehive**
Signed down pretty country lanes from A616 Newark–Ollerton and from A617

Newark–Mansfield; NG22 0BS Unpretentious little beamed country tavern in nice spot, welcoming chatty landlady, tiny front bar with slightly bigger side room, traditional furnishings and antiques, open fire, a couple of well kept ales, no food; children and dogs welcome, tables on small terrace with flower tubs and grassy bank running down to stream, play area, may be closed weekday lunchtimes in winter, busy weekends and bank holidays. *(Anon)*

MORTON   SK7251
★**Full Moon** (01636) 830251
Pub and village signed off Bleasby–Fiskerton back road, SE of Southwell; NG25 OUT Attractive old brick pub tucked away in remote hamlet close to River Trent; modernised pale-beamed bar with two roaring fires, comfortable armchairs, eclectic mix of tables and other simple furnishings, Timothy Taylors Landlord and guests, nine wines by the glass, well thought-of food (not Sun evening) including good value lunchtime/early evening weekday set menu, separate carpeted restaurant; background music, board games, free wi-fi; children and dogs (in bar) welcome, picnic-sets out at front, more on a peaceful back terrace and sizeable lawn with sturdy play equipment, open all day weekends. *(P Dawn)*

NEWARK   SK7954
Castle (01636) 640733
Castle Gate; NG24 1AZ Old low-ceilinged pub (part of the Yard Glass group), half a dozen well kept ales including Sharps Doom Bar and a house brew from Oldershaw, bare-boards front room, long panelled and carpeted back one, old wooden furniture, lots of mirrors and prints, no food but can eat in next-door sister pub (the Mayze); background and regular live music, darts; no children, open all day. *(P Dawn)*

NEWARK   SK8053
Fox & Crown (01636) 605820
Appleton Gate; NG24 1JY Open-plan bare-boards Castle Rock pub with their well priced ales and guests from central servery, four ciders and dozens of whiskies, vodkas and other spirits, decent wines by the glass too, friendly obliging staff, inexpensive food from rolls and baked potatoes up, several side areas; background music (live Fri), free wi-fi; dogs welcome, children in dining room, good wheelchair access, open all day. *(P Dawn)*

NEWARK   SK7953
Just Beer 07983 993747
Swan & Salmon Yard, off Castle Gate (B6166); NG24 1BG Welcoming one-room micropub tucked down alley, four or five interesting quickly changing beers from brick bar, real cider/perry, limited range of other drinks, bright airy minimalist décor with some brewery memorabilia, half a dozen tables on stone floor, eclectic mix

of customers; darts, dominoes and board games; dogs welcome, open all day (from 1pm weekdays). *(P Dawn)*

NEWARK   SK7953

Prince Rupert   (01636) 918121

Stodman Street, off Castle Gate; NG24 1AW Ancient renovated timber-framed pub near market, several small rooms on two floors, beams, exposed brickwork and many original features, nice old furniture including high-backed settles, assorted bric-a-brac, mirrors and signs, conservatory, well kept Brains, Oakham and three guests, Weston's cider, blackboard choice of wines by the glass, pubby food plus speciality pizzas with some unusual toppings and other imaginative food, friendly staff, live music most weekends; dogs welcome, seats in small courtyard, open all day (till 1am Fri, Sat).
(P Dawn, Tony and Maggie Harwood)

NORMANTON ON
THE WOLDS   SK6232

Plough   (0115) 937 2401

Off A606 5 miles S of Nottingham; NG12 5NN Ivy-clad pub on edge of village, warm and welcoming, with good freshly made food from extensive menu including nice steaks, five real ales including Black Sheep, Fullers London Pride and Wells Bombardier, friendly uniformed staff, fires in bar and extended restaurant; soft background music; children welcome, big garden with play area and summer barbecues, open all day.
(Phil and Jane Hodson)

NOTTINGHAM   SK5739

★Bell   (0115) 947 5241

Angel Row; off Market Square; NG1 6HL Deceptively large pub with late Georgian frontage concealing two much older timber-framed buildings; front Tudor Bar with glass panels protecting patches of 300-year-old wallpaper, larger low-beamed Elizabethan Bar with half-panelled walls and maple parquet flooring, and upstairs Belfry with more heavy panelling and 15th-c crown post; up to a dozen real ales including Greene King and Nottingham from remarkable deep sandstone cellar (can arrange tours), ten wines by the glass, reasonably priced straightforward bar food; background and regular live music including trad jazz, TV, silent fruit machine; children welcome in some parts, pavement tables, open all day (till 1am Sat). *(P Dawn)*

NOTTINGHAM   SK5843

Bread & Bitter   (0115) 960 7541

Woodthorpe Drive; NG3 5JL In former suburban bakery still showing ovens, three bright and airy bare-boarded rooms, around a dozen well kept ales including Castle Rock, good range of bottled beers, traditional cider and decent wine choice, reasonably priced pub food from cobs to specials, friendly staff, defunct brewery memorabilia; music and

quiz nights; well behaved children and dogs welcome, open (and food) all day. *(P Dawn, Dru and Louisa Marshall)*

NOTTINGHAM   SK5739

Canalhouse   (0115) 955 5060

Canal Street; NG1 7EH Converted wharf building with bridge over indoors canal spur (complete with narrowboat), lots of bare brick and varnished wood, huge joists on steel beams, long bar serving Castle Rock and three guests, well over 100 bottled beers and good choice of wines, sensibly priced food from snacks up including range of burgers; background music (can be loud); masses of tables out on attractive waterside terrace, open all day (till 1am Fri, Sat), food till 7pm Sun. *(P Dawn)*

NOTTINGHAM   SK5739

★Cross Keys   (0115) 941 7898

Byard Lane; NG1 2GJ Restored Victorian city-centre pub on two levels, lower carpeted part with leather banquettes, panelling and chandeliers, upper area with old wooden tables and chairs and some bucket seats on bare boards, interesting pictures/prints and more pendant lighting, well kept Navigation ales and a couple of guests, good reasonably priced food from breakfast on, friendly service, upstairs function/dining room; sports TV; seats outside, open all day from 9am.
(P Dawn)

NOTTINGHAM   SK5739

Fellows Morton & Clayton

(0115) 950 6795 *Canal Street (part of inner ring road); NG1 7EH* Flower-decked former canal warehouse, up to nine well kept ales such as Black Sheep, Fullers, Nottingham, Sharps and Timothy Taylors, good value pubby food (not evenings Sun-Weds), softly lit downstairs bar with alcove seating, wood floors and lots of exposed brickwork, two raised areas, upstairs restaurant/function room; monthly quiz first Thurs, several sports TVs, free wi-fi; open all day, till midnight Fri, Sat.
(P Dawn, Tony Hobden)

NOTTINGHAM   SK5542

Fox & Crown   (0115) 942 2002

Church Street/Lincoln Street, Old Basford; NG6 0GA Range of good Alcazar beers brewed behind this open-plan pub (window shows the brewery – Sat tours), also guest ales, continentals and good choice of wines, restauarant area serving authentic thai food; background music, games machines and big-screen sports TV; disabled access, tables on back terrace, beer shop next door, open all day. *(P Dawn)*

NOTTINGHAM   SK5642

Gladstone   (0115) 912 9994

Loscoe Road, Carrington; NG5 2AW Welcoming mid-terrace backstreet local with half a dozen well kept ales such as Castle

Rock, Fullers, Oakham and Timothy Taylors, good range of malt whiskies, comfortable lounge with reading matter, basic bar with old sports memorabilia and darts, upstairs folk club Weds, quiz Thurs, monthly comedy night; background music and sports TV, free wi-fi; tables in back garden among colourful tubs and hanging baskets, closed weekday lunchtimes, open all day weekends. *(P Dawn, Jeremy King)*

NOTTINGHAM   SK5640
Hand & Heart (0115) 958 2456
Derby Road; NG1 5BA Unexceptional exterior but unusual inside with bar and dining areas cut deep into back sandstone, a house beer from Dancing Duck, Maypole and guests, two real ciders and good wine and whisky range, enjoyable fairly priced traditional food from sandwiches and snacks up, set lunch deal Mon-Sat, tasting menu first Mon of month, friendly helpful service, glassed-in upstairs room overlooking street; background and interesting live music Thurs; children welcome till 7pm if eating, dogs in bar, open all day (late licence Fri, Sat). *(P Dawn, Chris Johnson)*

NOTTINGHAM   SK5542
Horse & Groom (0115) 970 3777
Radford Road, New Basford; NG7 7EA Eight good changing ales and a real cider in popular open-plan local by former Shipstones Brewery, still with their name and memorabilia, good value fresh straightforward food from sandwiches up, snug with open fire; some live music; open all day (from 4pm Mon-Weds). *(P Dawn)*

NOTTINGHAM   SK5739
★Kean's Head (0115) 947 4052
St Mary's Gate; NG1 1QA Cheery pub in attractive Lace Market area; fairly functional single room with simple wooden café furnishings on wooden boards, some exposed brickwork and red tiling, low sofa by big windows overlooking street, stools by wood counter and small fireplace, Castle Rock and three guests, draught belgian and interesting bottled beers, 20 wines by the glass, around 60 malt whiskies and lots of teas/coffees, tasty fairly traditional food (not Sun evening), friendly service; background music, daily papers, free wi-fi; children welcome till 7pm, church next door worth a look, open all day. *(P Dawn)*

NOTTINGHAM   SK5539
King William IV (0115) 958 9864
Manvers Street/Eyre Street, Sneinton; NG2 4PB Two-room Victorian corner local with plenty of character, Oakham and

six guests from circular bar, Weston's Old Rosie cider, good fresh cobs and sausage rolls, friendly staff, fine tankard collection; regular folk music including irish session Thurs, silenced sports TV, pool upstairs; dogs welcome, heated smokers' shelter, handy for cricket, football and rugby grounds, open all day. *(P Dawn)*

NOTTINGHAM   SK5740
★Lincolnshire Poacher
(0115) 941 1584 *Mansfield Road; uphill from Victoria Centre; NG1 3FR* Impressive range of drinks at this popular down-to-earth pub (attracts younger evening crowd), 13 well kept ales including Castle Rock, lots of continental draught/bottled beers, half a dozen ciders and over 70 malt whiskies, shortish choice of reasonably priced uncomplicated food; big simple traditional front bar with wall settles, wooden tables and breweriana, plain but lively room on left and corridor to chatty panelled back snug with newspapers and board games, conservatory overlooking tables on large heated back area; live music Weds, Sun, free wi-fi; children (till 8pm) and dogs welcome, open all day (till midnight Thurs-Sat). *(P Dawn, David Hunt)*

NOTTINGHAM   SK5541
★Lion (0115) 970 3506
Lower Mosley Street, New Basford; NG7 7FQ Around ten real ales (tasters available) including Bass and Castle Rock from one of the city's deepest cellars (glass viewing panel – can be visited at quiet times), also plenty of craft beers and proper ciders, good well priced burger/hot dog menu; big open-plan room with feel of separate areas, bare bricks and polished dark oak boards, old brewery pictures and posters, open fires, daily papers; regular live music including popular Sun lunchtime jazz; children welcome till 6pm, no dogs, disabled facilities, garden with terrace and smokers' shelter, open all day. *(P Dawn, David Hunt)*

NOTTINGHAM   SK5739
Malt Cross (0115) 941 1048
St James's Street; NG1 6FG Refurbished former Victorian music hall with vaulted glass roof and gallery looking down on bar area, bare boards and ornate iron pillars, comfortable sofas, good selection of drinks including some interesting real ales, decent well priced food from shortish menu, teas, coffees and daily newspapers, quiz and music nights; cellars converted into art gallery/workshop areas, ancient caves (tours available); open all day (till 9pm Sun). *(Chris Johnson)*

Post Office address codings confusingly give the impression that a few pubs are in Nottinghamshire, when they're really in Derbyshire (which is where we list them).

NOTTINGHAM SK5739
News House (0115) 952 3061

Canal Street; NG1 7HB Friendly two-room 1950s Castle Rock pub with notable blue exterior tiling, their ales and half a dozen changing guests, belgian and czech imports, decent fresh lunchtime food (Mon-Sat), mix of bare boards and carpet, local newspaper/radio memorabilia, darts, table skittles and bar billiards; background music, Thurs quiz; big-screen sports TV; a few tables out at front, open all day. *(P Dawn)*

NOTTINGHAM SK5739
★ Olde Trip to Jerusalem

(0115) 947 3171 *Brewhouse Yard; from inner ring road follow 'The North, A6005 Long Eaton' signpost until in Castle Boulevard, then right into Castle Road; pub is on the left; NG1 6AD* Unusual rambling pub seemingly clinging to sandstone rock face, largely 17th c and a former brewhouse supplying the hilltop castle; downstairs bar carved into the stone with dark panelling and simple built-in seats, tables on flagstones, some rocky alcoves, Greene King IPA and H&H Olde Trip plus guests, good value food all day, efficient staff dealing well with busy mix of customers; popular little tourist shop with panelled walls soaring up into dark cavernous heights; children welcome, seats and ring the bull in snug courtyard, open all day (till midnight Fri, Sat). *(P Dawn, George Atkinson)*

NOTTINGHAM SK5640
Organ Grinder (0115) 970 0630

Alfreton Road; NG7 3JE Tap for Blue Monkey with up to nine well kept ales including guests, a couple of ciders and a perry, good local pork pies (some topped with stilton), open-plan interior with bare boards and woodburner; well behaved dogs welcome, outside seating, open all day. *(Chris Johnson)*

NOTTINGHAM SK5540
Plough (0115) 970 2615

St Peter's Street, Radford; NG7 3EN Friendly local with its own good value Nottingham ales brewed behind, also guest beers and traditional cider, weekday sandwiches, two bars (one carpeted, the other with terrazzo flooring), banquettes, old tables and chairs, bottles on delft shelving, coal fires; Thurs quiz with free food, TV, traditional games, skittle alley outside; dogs welcome (may get a treat), covered smokers' area, open all day. *(P Dawn)*

NOTTINGHAM SK5739
Salutation (0115) 947 6580

Hounds Gate/Maid Marian Way; NG1 7AA Proper pub, low beams, flagstones, ochre walls and cosy corners including two small quiet rooms in ancient lower back part, plusher modern front lounge, up to eight real ales and good choice of draught/bottled ciders, quickly served food till 8pm (6pm Sun), helpful friendly staff (ask them to show you the haunted caves below the pub); background music (live bands upstairs); open all day (till 3am Fri, Sat). *(P Dawn)*

NOTTINGHAM SK5640
Trent Bridge (0115) 977 8940

Radcliffe Road; NG2 6AA Good Wetherspoons in sizeable Victorian pub next to the cricket ground (busy on match days), comfortably refurbished linked rooms with panelling and cricketing memorabilia, a dozen well kept ales and decent good value food, efficient friendly staff; sports TVs, free wi-fi; children welcome, open all day from 8am. *(David Hunt)*

NOTTINGHAM SK5838
Trent Navigation (0115) 986 5658

Meadow Lane; NG2 3HS Welcoming tile-fronted Victorian pub close to canal and home to the Navigation Brewery, their beers and guests from half a dozen pumps along with ciders/perries, popular food including deals, regular live music (Fri blues) and well attended Sun quiz; sports TV (pub is next to Notts County FC); children welcome, brewery shop at back, open all day. *(P Dawn, Phil and Jane Hodson)*

NOTTINGHAM SK5739
★ Vat & Fiddle (0115) 985 0611

Queens Bridge Road; alongside Sheriffs Way (near multi-storey car park); NG2 1NB Open-plan 1930s brick pub – tap for next door Castle Rock Brewery; varnished pine tables, bentwood chairs and stools on parquet or terrazzo flooring, some brewery memorabilia and interesting photographs of demolished local pubs, a dozen real ales including guests, bottled continentals, traditional ciders and 60 malt whiskies, decent food including range of burgers and Thurs curry night, modern dining extension, visitors' centre with own bar; some live music; children and dogs welcome, picnic-sets out at front by road, open all day (till midnight Thurs-Sat). *(P Dawn)*

Please keep sending us reports. We rely on readers for news of new discoveries, and particularly for news of changes – however slight – at the fully described pubs: feedback@goodguides.com, or (no stamp needed) The Good Pub Guide, FREEPOST RTJR-ZCYZ-RJZT, Perrymans Lane, Etchingham TN19 7DN.

RADCLIFFE ON TRENT SK6439
Horse Chestnut (0115) 933 1994
Main Road; NG12 2BE Smart pub with plenty of Victorian/Edwardian features, well kept Castle Rock, Fullers, St Austell and three guests, decent wines by the glass and sensibly priced home-made food (not Sun evening) including some italian choices (good pizzas), friendly service, two-level main bar, parquet and mosaic floor, panelling, big mirrors and impressive lamps, handsome leather wall benches and period fireplaces; some live music; dogs welcome (theirs is Helmsley), disabled access, terrace seating, open all day, food all day Fri, Sat. *(Mike Swan)*

RAMPTON SK7978
Eyre Arms (01777) 248771
Main Street; DN22 0HR Shuttered red-brick village pub with enjoyable good value food from chef-owner including extensive specials and fish menu, well kept local ales, friendly helpful service, refurbished dining area overlooking pleasant garden, locals bar with pool; open all day. *(David and Ruth Hollands)*

RUDDINGTON SK5733
Three Crowns 07951 342201
Easthorpe Street; NG11 6LB Open-plan pub known locally as the Top House, well kept Fullers, Nottingham and three guests (beer festivals), good italian food in back Three Spices evening restaurant; open all day weekends, closed lunchtimes Mon and Tues. *(P Dawn)*

SELSTON SK4553
★ Horse & Jockey (01773) 781012
Handy for M1 junctions 27/28; Church Lane; NG16 6FB Interesting pub on different levels dating from the 17th c, low heavy beams, dark flagstones, individual furnishings and good log fire in cast-iron range, friendly staff, Greene King Abbot and Timothy Taylors Landlord poured from the jug and up to four guests, real cider, no food, games area with darts and pool; folk night Weds, quiz Sun; dogs welcome, terrace and smokers' shelter, pleasant rolling country. *(Derek and Sylvia Stephenson)*

SOUTHWELL SK7054
★ Final Whistle (01636) 814953
Station Road; NG25 0ET Popular railway-themed pub commemorating the long defunct Southwell line; ten well kept beers including Browns, Everards and Fullers (beer festivals), real ciders/perries, foreign bottled beers and good range of wines, cheeseboard and some other snacky food, traditional opened-up bar area with tiled or wood floor, settles and armchairs in quieter carpeted room, corridor drinking area, two open fires, panelling, lots of railway memorabilia and other odds and ends; quiz Tues and Sun, some live music; children and dogs welcome, back garden with wonderful mock-up of 1920s platform complete with track and buffers, on Robin Hood Way and Southwell Trail, open all day. *(Brian and Anna Marsden, P Dawn)*

THURGARTON SK6949
Red Lion (01636) 830351
Southwell Road (A612); NG14 7GP Cheery 16th-c pub with split-level beamed bars and restaurant, a couple of changing ales from dark-panelled bar, nice range of enjoyable reasonably priced food, good friendly service, comfortable banquettes and other seating on patterned carpets, lots of nooks and crannies, grandfather clock, open fires; children welcome, no dogs inside, attractive back garden on two levels, open (and food) all day weekends. *(Caroline Prescott)*

TUXFORD SK7471
Fountain (01777) 872854
Lincoln Road; NG22 0JQ Comfortably updated family dining pub with good range of affordably priced food from sandwiches/ciabattas through burgers and pizzas to grills and specials, food challenges including 72oz steak and the 'world's hottest curry' (free if you can finish them), local ales and ciders such as Welbeck Abbey and Scrumpy Wasp, friendly service; free wi-fi; picnic-sets out in fenced area, open all day. *(G L and V Bottomley)*

UNDERWOOD SK4751
Red Lion (01773) 810482
Off A608/B600, near M1 junction 27; Church Lane, nearly in Bagthorpe; NG16 5HD Welcoming 18th-c split-level beamed village pub, enjoyable sensibly priced food (all day Fri, Sat) including blackboard specials, OAP weekday lunch deal, Exmoor Gold, Marstons Pedigree, Sharps Doom Bar and a guest, open-plan quarry-tiled bar with dining area, some cushioned settles, coal-effect gas fire; background music, games machine in lobby; children and dogs (in bar) welcome, play area in big woodside garden with terrace, summer barbecues, good nearby walks, open all day. *(Peter Pilbeam)*

UPTON SK7354
★ Cross Keys (01636) 813269
Main Street (A612); NG23 5SY 17th-c pub in fine spot with rambling heavy-beamed bar, log fire in brick fireplace, own Mallard ales (brewed in Maythorne) and good home-made food (not Sun evening), friendly staff, back extension; seats on decked terrace, British Horological Institute opposite, open all day Fri-Sun, closed Mon and Tues lunchtimes. *(P Dawn)*

WEST BRIDGFORD SK5838
Larwood & Voce (0115) 981 9960
Fox Road; NG2 6AJ Well run open-plan dining pub (part of the small Moleface

group); good locally sourced home-made food in bar and restaurant area including some imaginative choices, plenty of wines by the glass, cocktail menu and three well kept ales, cheerful staff; sports TV; children welcome away from bar, seats out on raised deck with heaters, on the edge of the cricket ground and handy for Nottingham Forest FC, open all day, from 9am weekends for breakfast. *(P Dawn, David Hunt)*

WEST BRIDGFORD   SK5938
Poppy & Pint (0115) 981 9995
Pierrepont Road; NG2 5DX Converted former British Legion Club backing on to bowling green and tennis courts; large bar with raised section and family area, 12 real ales including Castle Rock, a couple of ciders, decent food; regular events such as dance classes and quiz nights; open all day from 9.30am for breakfast (10am Sun).
(R Galpin)

WEST BRIDGFORD   SK5837
★Stratford Haven (0115) 982 5981
Stratford Road, Trent Bridge; NG2 6BA Good Castle Rock pub; bare-boards front bar leading to linked areas including airy skylit back part with relaxed local atmosphere, their well kept ales and many guests (monthly brewery nights), exotic bottled beers, farm ciders and good wine and whisky choice, wide range of well priced home-made food, fast friendly service; some live music (nothing loud), Sun quiz, daily papers; dogs welcome, tables outside, handy for cricket ground and Nottingham Forest FC (busy on match days), open (and food) all day.
(P Dawn)

WEST STOCKWITH   SK7994
White Hart (01427) 892672
Main Street; DN10 4EY Small refurbished country pub at junction of Chesterfield Canal with River Trent, own good Idle beers from next-door brewery plus guests, enjoyable well priced traditional food, friendly atmosphere; live music Fri, quiz every other Tues, pool and sports TV; children and dogs welcome, garden overlooking the water, open all day. *(Anon)*

WYSALL   SK6027
Plough (01509) 880339
Keyworth Road; off A60 at Costock, or A6006 at Wymeswold; NG12 5QQ Attractive 17th-c beamed village local; popular good value lunchtime food from shortish menu, cheerful staff, Bass, Greene King Abbot, Timothy Taylors Landlord and three guests, rooms either side of bar with nice mix of furnishings, soft lighting, big log fire; Tues quiz, pool; french doors to pretty terrace with flower tubs and baskets, open all day. *(P Dawn)*

Oxfordshire

KEY ★ Star Pub ¶◯¶ Top Quality Food 🍺 Great Beer

🍷 Good Wines £ Bargain Meals 🛏 Good Bedrooms 🍴 Serves Food

 ASTHALL   SP2811 Map 4

Maytime ¶◯¶ 🛏

(01993) 822068 – www.themaytime.com

Off A40 at W end of Witney bypass, then first left; OX18 4HW

Carefully renovated Cotswold-stone inn with a cheerfully civilised feel, individually furnished bar and dining rooms, good food and drink and seats outside; smart bedrooms

This is a lovely place to stay, with stylish, smart and well equipped bedrooms and highly thought-of breakfasts; there are good walks from the door. It's a carefully refurbished 17th-c Cotswold-stone pub with a lofty bar: exposed roof trusses, flagstones, leather sofas, cushioned wall seats and stools against the counter where friendly staff serve Castle Rock Harvest Pale, Purple Moose Snowdonia Ale and a guest ale on handpump, good wines by the glass and a fine collection of 25 gins; background music. Several white-painted beamed rooms lead off on several levels, with cushioned window seats, a mix of tartan upholstered and traditional wooden chairs around tables of varying sizes on black slates or bare boards, and pictures on painted or stone walls; one room has a glass ceiling. The pub springer is called Alfie. Seats and tables sit under parasols on the back terrace where there's a herb garden and a view over watermeadows; there are also some picnic-sets out in front too.

¶◯¶ Enjoyable, interesting food includes sandwiches, red mullet with parsley purée and shallot rings, pigeon breast with blackberry, puy lentils and pancetta crisps, home-baked honey and mustard ham with free-range eggs, vegetable tagine with tabbouleh, sage and wild boar burger with onion rings and skinny chips, lamb rump with wild mushrooms, parmesan risotto and rosemary jus, fillet of bass with roast aubergine, sauté baby squid, saffron velouté and parmentier potatoes, and puddings such as cardamom panna cotta with tropical fruit coulis and ginger crumbs and assiette of apple with butterscotch sauce. *Benchmark main dish: lamb rump with rosemary and garlic jus £19.95. Two-course evening meal £22.00.*

Free house ~ Licensee Dominic Wood ~ Real ale ~ Open 11-11 ~ Bar food 12-2.30 (3 weekends), 6-9.30 ~ Restaurant ~ Children welcome ~ Dogs allowed in bar ~ Wi-fi ~ Bedrooms: £85/£95 *Recommended by Liz Bell, William and Megan*

BANBURY   SP4540 Map 4

Olde Reindeer 🍺 £

(01295) 264031 – www.yeoldereindeer.co.uk

Parsons Street, off Market Place; OX16 5NA

**Interesting town pub with a friendly welcome for both shoppers
and regulars, real ales and simple food**

Our readers very much enjoy their visits to this fine old pub, where
there are always plenty of cheerful customers. The front bar has a
good, bustling atmosphere, heavy 16th-c beams, very broad polished oak
floorboards, a magnificent carved overmantel for one of the two roaring log
fires and traditional solid furnishings; some interesting breweriana too. It's
worth looking at the handsomely proportioned Globe Room used by Oliver
Cromwell as his base during the Civil War. Quite a sight, it still has some
very fine 17th-c carved dark oak panelling. Hook Norton Hooky, Cotswold
Lion, Old Hooky, Hooky Mild and a couple of guest beers on handpump,
12 wines by the glass, fruit wines and several malt whiskies. The little back
courtyard has tables and benches under parasols, aunt sally and pretty
flowering baskets.

Good value, traditional food includes sandwiches, pâté with red onion chutney,
garlic mushroom medley on toast, a pie of the day, ham and eggs, venison burger
in a rosemary and sea salt focaccia bun, chicken kiev with coleslaw, braised lamb
shoulder with tomato and olive jus, sea bream fillet with ratatouille and gazpacho
sauce, and puddings. *Benchmark main dish: sausages and mash £10.00. Two-course
evening meal £18.00.*

Hook Norton ~ Tenant Jeremy Money ~ Real ale ~ Open 11-11 (midnight Sat); 12-10.30 Sun
~ Bar food 12-3, 6-9; 12-3 Sun ~ Children welcome until 8pm ~ Dogs allowed in bar ~ Live
music Sat from 9pm; poetry club second Thurs of month *Recommended by George Atkinson,
Barry Collett*

BESSELS LEIGH   SP4501   Map 4
Greyhound ♀ ☗
(01865) 862110 – www.brunningandprice.co.uk/greyhound
A420 Faringdon–Botley; OX13 5PX

**Handsome old pub with plenty of interest in rambling rooms,
up to half a dozen real ales, lots of wines by the glass and
enjoyable interesting food**

This is a handsome Cotswold-stone inn, dating back 400 years, with a
lot of character. The knocked-through rooms create plenty of space
and interest and the half-panelled walls are covered in all manner of old
photographs and pictures. Grouped on carpeting or rug-covered floorboards
are individually chosen cushioned dining chairs, leather-topped stools
and dark wooden tables, and there are books on shelves, glass and stone
bottles on window sills, big gilt mirrors, three fireplaces (one housing a
woodburning stove) and sizeable pot plants. Wooden bar stools sit against
the counter where they serve Phoenix Brunning & Price Original, Prescott
Summer Seasons Best, Ramsbury Deer Stalker, White Horse Village Idiot
and Wild Weather Black Night on handpump, 14 wines by the glass, 102 malt
whiskies and a farm cider. By the back dining extension is a white picket
fence-enclosed garden with picnic-sets under green parasols; the summer
window boxes and hanging baskets are very pretty.

High standards of modern cooking includes sandwiches, sardine fillets wrapped in
air-dried ham with spicy tomato salsa, crispy duck salad with hoisin, watermelon
and cashew nuts, spinach, ricotta and sun-dried tomato quiche, honey-roast ham with
free-range eggs, steak in ale pie, sicilian fish stew, steak burger with toppings, coleslaw
and chips, calves liver with carrot purée, crispy ham and madeira jus, and puddings such
as apple and rhubarb crumble and crème brûlée. *Benchmark main dish: slow-braised
lamb shoulder with dauphinoise potatoes and rosemary gravy £16.95. Two-course
evening meal £21.00.*

Brunning & Price ~ Manager Peter Palfi ~ Real ale ~ Open 11-11; 11.30-10.30 Sun ~
Bar food 12-10 (9.30 Sun) ~ Well behaved children welcome ~ Dogs allowed in bar ~ Wi-fi
Recommended by Taff Thomas, S F Parrinder, Neil and Angela Huxter, Tracey and Stephen Groves

BRIGHTWELL BALDWIN
Lord Nelson

SU6594   Map 4

(01491) 612497
Off B480 Chalgrove–Watlington, or B4009 Benson–Watlington; OX49 5NP

**Attractive inn with several character bars, real ales, good wines
by the glass and enjoyable well thought-of food; bedrooms**

Prettily placed on a quiet lane opposite a church, this is an extremely
popular 300-year-old inn. The bar has a good mix of both drinkers and
diners, an easy-going atmosphere, wheelback and other dining chairs around
assorted dark tables and a big brick inglenook fireplace; also, candles and
fresh flowers, wine bottles on window sills, horsebrasses on standing timbers
and lots of paintings on the white or red walls. One cosy room has cushions
on comfortable sofas, little lamps on dark furniture, ornate mirrors and
portraits in gilt frames; background music. Loose Cannon Abingdon Bridge
and Rebellion IPA on handpump, 20 wines (including champagne) by the
glass, a dozen malt whiskies and winter mulled wine. There are seats and
tables on the back terrace and in the willow-draped garden.

Assured cooking includes sandwiches, twice-baked cheese soufflé, tempura king
prawns with sweet chilli sauce, cauliflower and cheese bake, smoked haddock
on champ mash with grain mustard sauce and a free-range poached egg, pork fillet in
creamy wild mushroom sauce, venison medallions in blackberry sauce, chicken suprême
with chorizo and roast cherry tomatoes, and puddings; they also offer a two-course set
lunch (not weekends). *Benchmark main dish: beer-battered haddock and triple-
cooked chips £14.75. Two-course evening meal £23.00.*

Free house ~ Licensees Roger and Carole Shippey ~ Real ale ~ Open 12-3, 6-11; 12-11 Sun
(12-5 in winter) ~ Bar food 12-2, 6-10; ~ Restaurant ~ Children welcome ~ Dogs allowed
in bar ~ Wi-fi ~ Bedrooms: £75/£100 *Recommended by Colin McLachlan, Dr W I C Clark,
P and J Shapley, Roy Hoing*

BURFORD
Highway ♀ ⇆

SP2512   Map 4

(01993) 823661 – www.thehighwayinn.co.uk
High Street (A361); OX18 4RG

**Comfortable old inn overlooking this honeypot village's main street,
a good choice of wines and well liked bar food; comfortable bedrooms**

Readers enjoy staying in the country house-style, individually decorated
bedrooms in this 15th-c town inn; breakfasts are good. There are all
sorts of interesting touches in the bars, but the main feature is the pair of
big windows overlooking the bustle of the High Street; each consists of
several dozen panes of old float glass and has a long cushioned window
seat. Do notice the stag candlesticks for the rather close-set tables on well
worn floorboards, the neat modern dark leather chairs, the nice old station
clock above the big log fire in a pleasingly simple stone fireplace and the
careful balance of ancient stripped stone with filigree black and pale blue
wallpaper. A small corner counter has Hook Norton Hooky and Prescott Hill
Climb and Track Record on handpump, 20 wines (including champagne) by
the glass and 13 malt whiskies; they hold a beer festival and barbecue in the
second week of June. Background music, TV and board games. On the right,

a second bar room, with another big window seat, is carpeted but otherwise similar in style; there's also a downstairs cellar bar that's open for tapas at the weekend. A few front picnic-sets stand above the pavement.

As well as lunchtime sandwiches and omelettes, the interesting food includes calvados-braised ham hock terrine with red onion chutney, home-smoked salmon with buckwheat blini and chives, a vegetarian risotto, a pie of the day, chicken suprême with blackberries and potato galette, duck leg confit with white bean and chorizo cassoulet, pork belly with smoked pancetta, vine tomato confit and caramelised onion mash, and puddings. *Benchmark main dish: rack of barbecue baby back ribs with coleslaw and fries £15.00. Two-course evening meal £18.00.*

Free house ~ Licensees Dan, Jane and Michelle Arnell ~ Real ale ~ Open 12-11.30 (midnight weekends); closed first two weeks Jan ~ Bar food 12-2, 7-9 ~ Restaurant ~ Children welcome ~ Dogs allowed in bar and bedrooms ~ Wi-fi ~ Bedrooms: £90/£120
Recommended by George Atkinson, Ross Balaam, Ray and Janet Anstis, Roy Hoing

BURFORD
Lamb ⭐ ♀ 🍺 🛏

SP2412   Map 4

(01993) 823155 – www.cotswold-inns-hotels.co.uk/lamb
Village signposted off A40 W of Oxford; Sheep Street (B4425, off A361); OX18 4LR

Proper pubby bar in civilised inn, real ales and an extensive wine list, interesting bar and restaurant food, and pretty gardens; bedrooms

The cosy bar remains the heart of this lovely old inn with its restful, civilised atmosphere. This has cushioned settles and old chairs on flagstones in front of a log fire, china plates on shelves, Hook Norton Hooky and Wickwar Cotswold Way on handpump, an extensive wine list with 20 by the glass and 25 malt whiskies. The roomy beamed main lounge is charmingly traditional, with distinguished old seats including a chintzy high-winged settle, ancient cushioned wooden armchairs, and seats built into stone-mullioned windows; fresh flowers on polished oak and elm tables, rugs on wide flagstones and polished oak floorboards, a winter log fire under a fine mantelpiece and plenty of antiques and other decorations including a grandfather clock. A pretty terrace with teak furniture leads down to neatly kept lawns surrounded by flowers, shrubs and small trees. The garden, enclosed by the warm stone of the surrounding buildings, is a real suntrap. They're kind to dogs and even have a special menu for them.

Rewarding food includes lunchtime open sandwiches, scallops and black pudding, goats cheese panna cotta with sun-dried tomato and hazelnut salad and toasted home-made bread, quite a few deli boards, whole dressed crab with skinny chips, local sausages with mash and red onion confit, wagyu burger with blue cheese and chunky chips, crayfish and chive risotto, ten-hour confit duck with sauté potatoes, and puddings such as chocolate tart and peanut butter ice-cream and lemon posset with raspberry coulis. *Benchmark main dish: steak and mushroom in ale pie £13.95. Two-course evening meal £20.00.*

Cotswold Inns & Hotels ~ Manager Bill Ramsay ~ Real ale ~ Open 12-midnight ~ Bar food 12-9.30 ~ Restaurant ~ Children welcome ~ Dogs allowed in bar and bedrooms ~ Wi-fi ~ Bedrooms: £175/£185 *Recommended by Richard Stanfield, Richard Tilbrook, Michael Sargent, R K Phillips, Dr W I C Clark, Martin Cawley*

Please tell us if the décor, atmosphere, food or drink at a pub is different from our description. We rely on readers' reports to keep us up to date: feedback@goodguides.com, or (no stamp needed) The Good Pub Guide, FREEPOST RTJR-ZCYZ-RJZT, Perrymans Lane, Etchingham TN19 7DN.

CHURCHILL

SP2824 Map 4

Chequers 🍺

(01608) 659393 – www.thechequerschurchill.com

Church Road; B4450 Chipping Norton to Stow-on-the-Wold (and village signed off A361 Chipping Norton–Burford); OX7 6NJ

Bustling village pub with simple furnishings in spacious bars and dining rooms, a friendly relaxed atmosphere, good choice of beers and popular food

With interesting food and six real ales, this busy golden-stone inn draws in both regulars and visitors. The relaxed and friendly bar has an armchair and other comfortable chairs around an old trunk in front of an inglenook fireplace, some exposed stone walls, cushioned wall seats, a mix of wooden and antique leather chairs around nice old tables on bare floorboards, a few rugs here and there, and stools against the counter presided over by a big stag's head. Flying Monk Elmers, Hook Norton Hooky, Otter Bitter, Sharps Atlantic and Stroud Budding on handpump, 12 wines by the glass, 11 malt whiskies, mocktails and a farm cider; darts and background music. At the back is a large extension with soaring rafters, big lantern lights, long button-back leather banquettes and other seating, while upstairs is another similarly and simply furnished dining area and a room just right for a private party. The church opposite is impressive.

🍴 Interesting food includes devilled kidneys, crab linguine, asian-style duck salad, grilled leg of lamb for two with fennel, mint and salsa verde, whole lemon sole with brown butter, calves liver and bacon, slow-cooked rose veal with creamed asparagus, mushrooms and turnips, fillet of bass with cockles, bacon and seaweed, and puddings such as layered banoffi pot and elderflower, poached peach and raspberry eton mess. *Benchmark main dish: aberdeen angus steak with a choice of six sauces £17.00. Two-course evening meal £23.00.*

Free house ~ Licensee Peter Creed ~ Real ale ~ Open 11am-midnight ~ Bar food 12-3, 6-9.30 ~ Restaurant ~ Children welcome ~ Dogs welcome ~ Wi-fi ~ Live music monthly
Recommended by David Gunn, Bernard Stradling

EAST HENDRED

SU4588 Map 2

Eyston Arms 🎖️

(01235) 833320 – www.eystonarms.co.uk

Village signposted off A417 E of Wantage; High Street; OX12 8JY

Attractive bar areas with low beams, flagstones, log fires and candles, imaginative food and helpful service

Although most customers are here to eat the particularly good food, the atmosphere is always unpretentious and relaxed and the welcome genuinely warm and friendly. There are seats at the bar and they do keep a few tables free for drinkers keen to try the Hook Norton Hooky and Wadworths 6X on handpump, ten wines by the glass and 15 malt whiskies. Several separate-seeming candlelit areas have contemporary paintwork and modern country-style furnishings, low ceilings and beams, stripped timbers and the odd standing upright, nice tables and chairs on flagstones and carpet, some cushioned wall seats and an inglenook fireplace; background music. Picnic-sets outside overlook the pretty lane and there are seats in the courtyard garden at the back.

🎖️ Good, inventive food includes rillettes of confit duck with port and redcurrant jelly and pickled vegetables, gin-cured salmon with dill cream and baby fennel, pork and chorizo burger with smoked tomato chutney, melted gruyère and string chips, king prawn and smoked salmon linguine with tomatoes and chilli oil, corn-fed chicken breast salad with shaved beetroot, goats curd, poppyseed croutons and blackberry and rapeseed dressing, duck breast and confit croquette with squash purée and five-spice jus, and puddings such as rhubarb panna cotta with orange and rhubarb compote and blood orange sorbet and dark chocolate, espresso and pecan tart with clotted cream. *Benchmark main dish: fresh fish dish of the day £18.50. Two-course evening meal £22.00.*

Free house ~ Licensees George Dailey and Daisy Barton ~ Real ale ~ Open 11-11; 11-10 Sun ~ Bar food 12-2.30, 6-9; 12-9 Fri, Sat; 12-8 Sun ~ Restaurant ~ Children welcome ~ Dogs allowed in bar ~ Wi-fi *Recommended by John Oates, Fiona Smith, Nigel and Sue Foster*

 FILKINS   SP2304   Map 4

Five Alls

(01367) 860875 – www.thefiveallsfilkins.co.uk
Signed off A361 Lechlade–Burford; GL7 3JQ

Thoughtfully refurbished inn with creative food, quite a range of drinks, a friendly welcome and seats outside; bedrooms

There's plenty to do around this creeper-covered inn and the comfortable bedrooms make a good base for exploring; breakfasts are good. There's a cosy area in the beamed bar with three leather chesterfields grouped around a table by an open fire, an informal dining space with farmhouse chairs and cushioned pews around tables on bare boards and a nice little window seat for two. Stools line the bar where friendly staff serve a beer named for the pub (from Wychwood), Wychwood Hobgoblin and a couple of guests on handpump; a dozen wines by the glass, 12 malt whiskies and a cocktail of the day. The dining rooms are elegant and individually furnished – one has unusual postage stamp wallpaper – with an attractive mix of chairs and tables on rugs, floorboards and flagstones, plus chandeliers, church candles, fresh flowers and modern artwork on pale painted walls; background music. The back terrace has chunky tables and chairs under parasols and there are a few picnic-sets at the front.

Cooked by the landlord and his team using the best local produce, food is impressive: sandwiches, chicken and duck liver parfait with plum and apple chutney, tuna sashimi with soy, wasabi and pickled ginger, aubergine parmigiana, Guinness-roast gammon with free-range eggs, moroccan lamb stew with falafel, guacamole, yoghurt, flatbread and harissa, chargrilled calves liver with pancetta, bubble and squeak, pickled beetroot and mint and sage brown butter, steak, mushroom and kidney pie with caramelised root vegetables, and puddings such as chocolate fondant with Baileys ice-cream and baked alaska. *Benchmark main dish: grilled squid with sweet chilli jam and garlic roast potatoes £17.95. Two-course evening meal £25.00.*

Free house ~ Licensee Sebastian Snow ~ Real ale ~ Open 12-11; 12-9 Sun ~ Bar food 12-2.30, 6-9.30 (10 Fri, Sat); 12-3 Fri-Sun ~ Restaurant ~ Children welcome ~ Dogs allowed in bar ~ Wi-fi ~ Bedrooms: £90/£115 *Recommended by Mary Scott-Edeson, Dr and Mrs S G Barber, R K Phillips, Tracey and Stephen Groves, Liz Bell*

HEADINGTON   SP5407   Map 4

Black Boy

(01865) 741137 – www.theblackboy.uk.com
Old High Street/St Andrews Road; off A420 at traffic lights opposite B4495; OX3 9HT

Enterprising dining pub with good, enjoyable food and useful summer garden

This is a stylish place with a contemporary look: black leather seating on dark parquet, big mirrors, silvery patterned wallpaper, nightlights in fat opaque cylinders and glittering bottles behind the long bar counter. It's light and airy in feel, particularly at the two tables in the big bay window; just to the side are lower, softer seats beside an open fire. Crisp white tablecloths and bold black and white wallpaper lend the area on the left a touch of formality. Everards Beacon, White Horse Black Beauty and a guest from Everards on handpump, 20 wines by the glass, ten malt whiskies and several coffees and teas. Behind the building is an appealing terrace with picnic-sets under alternating black and white parasols on smart pale stone chippings, and a central seat encircling an ash tree.

Highly enjoyable food includes lunchtime sandwiches (not Sun), chicken liver parfait with seasonal chutney, salmon fishcakes with hollandaise sauce, lasagne of wild mushrooms and spinach with beurre blanc, burger with toppings and fries, chicken breast with braised leeks and sherry and wild mushroom sauce, slow-roast pork belly with garlic and thyme mash and cider jus, herb-crusted cod loin with wilted spinach, saffron and mussel sauce, and puddings such as iced white chocolate mousse with raspberry sorbet and sticky toffee pudding with caramel sauce and vanilla ice-cream. *Benchmark main dish: beer-battered fish and chips with mint purée £11.50. Two-course evening meal £20.50.*

Greene King ~ Lease Abi Rose and Chris Bentham ~ Real ale ~ Open 12-3, 5-11 ~ Bar food 12-2.45, 6-9.15 ~ Restaurant ~ Children welcome ~ Wi-fi
Recommended by Wilburoo, Neil Allen

HIGHMOOR
Rising Sun

SU6984 Map 2

(01491) 640856 – www.risingsunwitheridgehill.co.uk
Witheridge Hill, signposted off B481; OS Sheet 175 map reference 697841; RG9 5PF

Friendly country village pub with a welcoming landlord, character bars and eating areas, and good food and drink; seats in garden

At lunchtime, walkers from nearby Witheridge Hill drop by this charming 17th-c pub – but there are always locals and diners too, and all get a warm welcome from the friendly landlord. The cosy bar has beams, old red and white floor tiles, a comfortable sofa, lots of walking sticks in a pot by the woodburning stove, books on the window sill and leather stools against the counter where they serve Brakspears Bitter and Oxford Gold and Wychwood Hobgoblin on handpump and a dozen wines by the glass; background music. The three interlinked eating areas have rugs on bare boards, pictures on dark red walls and seating that includes captain's and farmhouse chairs, chunky benches and cushioned wall seats around an assortment of tables; one section has a log fire in a small brick fireplace. There are picnic-sets and white metal chairs and tables in the pleasant back garden.

As well as a good choice of sandwiches and little snacks, the enjoyable food includes chicken liver pâté with red onion chutney, black pudding, crispy bacon and egg on toast, spinach, pepper, harissa and cream cheese filo parcel with salsa verde, lamb and mint burger with spicy tomato salsa and sweet potato fries, chicken and leek pie, fish and chips with pea purée, sirloin steak with peppercorn sauce, and puddings. *Benchmark main dish: pork belly on black pudding mash £14.25. Two-course evening meal £19.00.*

Brakspears ~ Tenant Simon Duffy ~ Real ale ~ Open 12-3, 5-11; 12-11 Sat; 12-10 Sun ~ Bar food 12-2, 6-9; 12-2.30, 6-9.30 Sat; 12-3 Sun ~ Restaurant ~ Children welcome ~ Dogs allowed in bar ~ Wi-fi *Recommended by Bob and Margaret Holder, Alistair Forsyth, R K Phillips, Paul Humphreys, Roy Hoing*

KINGHAM   SP2624 Map 4

Plough 🏵 ♔ 🛏

(01608) 658327 – www.thekinghamplough.co.uk

Village signposted off B4450 E of Bledington; or turn S off A436 at staggered crossroads a mile SW of A44 junction – or take signed Daylesford turn off A436 and keep on; The Green; OX7 6YD

Oxfordshire Dining Pub of the Year

Friendly dining pub combining an informal pub atmosphere with creative food; bedrooms

There is a properly pubby bar in this dining pub-with-rooms with an interesting choice of drinks, but the inventive food cooked by chef-patron Emily Watkins is what most customers are here for. This bar has some nice old high-backed settles and brightly cushioned chapel chairs on broad dark boards, candles on stripped tables and cheerful farmyard animal and country prints; at one end is a big log fire, at the other a woodburning stove. A snug one-table area is opposite the servery where they keep Butcombe Bitter and Hook Norton Hooky on handpump, european wines by the glass, home-made cordials, local cider, some interesting liqueurs and a good choice of teas and coffees; board games. The fairly spacious and raftered two-part dining room is up a few steps. The bedrooms – refurbished in 2015 – are comfortable and pretty and the breakfasts very good.

 Exceptional food using the best local, seasonal produce includes nibbles (such as salt cod brandade with tartare sauce and home-made sausage roll with home-made ketchup), brill with mussel and seaweed butter and foraged sea vegetables, chicken suprême with devilled liver sauce, haddock and smoked haddock croquettes with charred leeks, chargrilled beef rump with bone marrow butter, onion rings and triple-cooked chips, and puddings such as blood orange tart with dark chocolate sorbet and baked custard with poached rhubarb and rhubarb granita. *Benchmark main dish: rabbit wellington with cauliflower, cavolo nero and confit potatoes £22.00. Two-course evening meal £30.00.*

Free house ~ Licensees Emily Watkins and Miles Lampson ~ Real ale ~ Open 12-11 (midnight Sat, 10 Sun) ~ Bar food 12-2 (2.30 Sat), 6.30-9; 12-3 Sun ~ Restaurant ~ Children welcome ~ Dogs allowed in bar ~ Wi-fi ~ Bedrooms: £110/£145
Recommended by Colin Flowers, Belinda May

KINGSTON LISLE   SU3287 Map 4

Blowing Stone 🏵 ♔ 🍺

(01367) 820288 – www.theblowingstone.co.uk

Village signposted off B4507 W of Wantage; OX12 9QL

Easy-going chatty country pub with up-to-date blend of simple comfort, good interesting food and drink

This is a deservedly busy pub and particularly popular at lunchtimes – although several separate areas radiate off, the heart of the place is the central bar. This is racehorse country, so there's the *Racing Post* alongside other daily papers, lots of photographs on the pale sage walls of racehorses (often spectacularly coming to grief over jumps) and broad tiles by the log fire which suit the muddy riding boots of the chatty young people in from nearby training stables. Most of the other rooms are on the small side, snug and carpeted, though the back dining conservatory is more spacious. Apart from a couple of high-backed winged settles, the furniture is mostly an unfussy mix of country dining tables, each with its own set of matching chairs, either padded or generously cushioned. Dark Star Hophead, Greene King Morland Original, Ramsbury Bitter and Sharps Atlantic on handpump, 13 decent wines by the glass, ten malt whiskies and two farm ciders; background music, TV and board games. There's a couple of picnic-sets under cocktail parasols on the pretty front terrace, with more on the back lawn by a rockery.

 As well as summer pizzas from the wood-fired oven in the garden (5.30-8.30 Sunday), the monthly changing menu (plus daily specials) includes sandwiches, scallop and king prawn ravioli with shellfish sauce, spicy lamb koftas with tzatziki, roasted squash, sweet potato and butter bean goulash, baby rack of barbecue ribs with coleslaw and fries, chicken kiev with greek salad, pork fillet with romesco sauce and mediterranean-style couscous, fresh tuna niçoise, and puddings such as cappuccino crème brûlée with toffee ice-cream and chocolate brownie with chocolate sauce. *Benchmark main dish: calves liver with crispy bacon and potatoes sautéed in sage butter £16.95. Two-course evening meal £20.00.*

Free house ~ Licensees Angus and Steph Tucker ~ Real ale ~ Open 12-11; 9.30am-midnight Sat ~ Bar food 12-2, 6.30-9 ~ Restaurant ~ Children welcome ~ Dogs allowed in bar ~ Wi-fi
Recommended by Katharine Cowherd, Neil and Angela Huxter, Tina and David Woods-Taylor

KIRTLINGTON
Oxford Arms

SP4919   Map 4

(01869) 350208 – www.oxford-arms.co.uk
Troy Lane, junction with A4095 W of Bicester; OX5 3HA

Civilised and friendly stripped-stone pub with enjoyable food using local produce and good wine choice

Next to the post office in a lovely village, this is a deservedly popular stone pub. The long line of linked rooms is divided by a central stone hearth with a great wood stove, and by the servery itself – where you'll find Black Sheep and Hook Norton Hooky on handpump, an interesting range of 16 wines by the glass, 13 malt whiskies, farm cider and organic soft drinks. Past the bar area with its cushioned wall pews, creaky beamed ceiling and age-darkened floor tiles, dining tables on parquet have neat red chairs; beyond that, leather sofas cluster round a log fire at the end. Also, church candles, fresh flowers and plenty of stripped stone. A sheltered back terrace has teak tables under giant parasols with heaters; further off are picnic-sets on gravel. The geranium-filled window boxes are pretty.

 Highly thought-of food includes sandwiches, potted shrimps on toast, a tart of the day, wild mushroom tagliatelle with truffle oil, salmon and prawn fishcakes with sweet chilli sauce, a risotto and pasta dish of the day, garlic and rosemary chicken with dauphinoise potatoes, wild bass with lemon oil, dry-aged sirloin steak with mustard and horseradish butter and triple-cooked chips, and puddings such as cognac prunes with vanilla ice-cream and bread and butter pudding. *Benchmark main dish: venison burger with triple-cooked chips £15.00. Two-course evening meal £20.00.*

Punch ~ Lease Bryn Jones ~ Real ale ~ Open 12-3, 6-11; 12-3 Sun ~ Bar food 12-2.30, 6.30-9.30; 12-3 Sun ~ Restaurant ~ Well behaved children welcome ~ Dogs welcome
Recommended by Robert Wivell, Brian and Anna Marsden, Simone Barratt, Steve and Liz Tilley, Elena Krasnova

---

'Children welcome' means the pub says it lets children inside without any special restriction. If it allows them in, but to restricted areas such as an eating area or family room, we specify this. Some pubs may impose an evening time limit. We do not mention limits after 9pm as we assume children are home by then.

LONGWORTH   SU3899 Map 4

Blue Boar ♀

(01865) 820494 – www.blueboarlongworth.co.uk

Tucks Lane; OX13 5ET

Smashing old pub with a friendly welcome for all, good wines and beer, and fairly priced reliable food; Thames-side walks nearby

From the outside this is pretty much the classic image of an english country pub – inside too, it's warmly traditional. The three low-beamed, characterful small rooms have a bustling but easy-going atmosphere, with brasses, hops and assorted knick-knacks (skis, an old clocking-in machine) on the walls and ceilings, scrubbed wooden tables and benches, faded rugs and floor tiles, fresh flowers on the bar and two blazing log fires (the one by the bar is noteworthy). The main eating area is the red-painted room at the end and there's a quieter restaurant extension too. Brakspears Bitter and Otter Ale on handpump, 20 malt whiskies and a dozen wines by the glass. There are tables in front and on the back terrace, and the Thames is a short walk away.

 The good, popular food includes salt and pepper squid with sweet chilli dipping sauce, duck liver pâté with chutney, stone-baked pizzas, burgers with toppings and chips, malaysian monkfish curry, duck breast with pak choi and citrus jus, spinach, butternut squash and wild mushroom cannelloni, sunblush tomato and pine nut-stuffed chicken with tabbouleh and pesto dressing, and puddings such as apple crumble with toffee apple ice-cream and chocolate mousse with salted pistachio caramel. *Benchmark main dish: beer-battered fish and chips £10.95. Two-course evening meal £21.00.*

Free house ~ Licensee Paul Dailey ~ Real ale ~ Open 12-11 (midnight Sat) ~ Bar food 12-2.30, 6.30-9.30 (10 Fri, Sat); 12-3, 6.30-9 Sun ~ Restaurant ~ Children welcome ~ Dogs allowed in bar ~ Wi-fi *Recommended by R K Phillips, Carol and Barry Craddock*

MINSTER LOVELL   SP3211 Map 4

Old Swan & Minster Mill ⚫ ♀ ⇌

(01993) 774441 – www.oldswanandminstermill.com

Just N of B4047 Witney–Burford; OX29 0RN

Carefully restored ancient inn with old-fashioned bar, real ales, a fine wine list, pubby and more elaborate food and acres of gardens and grounds; exceptional bedrooms

It's the unchanging, tranquil little bar in this rather lovely 15th-c Cotswold hotel that remains its beating heart. Here, you'll find stools at the wooden counter, Brakspears Oxford Gold, North Cotswold Windrush Ale and Wychwood Hobgoblin on handpump, good wines by the glass from a fine list, 23 malt whiskies and quite a choice of teas and coffees. Leading off are several attractive low-beamed rooms with big log fires in huge fireplaces, red and green leather tub chairs, all manner of comfortable armchairs, sofas, dining chairs and wooden tables, rugs on bare boards or ancient flagstones, antiques, prints, lots of horsebrasses, bed-warming pans, swords, hunting horns and even a suit of armour; also, fresh flowers everywhere, background music and board games. Seats are dotted around the 65 acres of grounds (the white metal ones beside the water are much prized) and they have fishing rights to a mile of the River Windrush, tennis courts, boules and croquet. The bedrooms have plenty of character; some are positively luxurious.

Food is excellent and uses produce from their own kitchen garden: sandwiches, free-range ham hock terrine with grape chutney, smoked salmon with citrus crème fraîche, horseradish purée and rye bread, beer-battered haddock and triple-cooked chips, braised ox cheek with champ mash, spiced chickpea and vegetable pie, guinea fowl with game jus, rack of lamb with redcurrant and rosemary sauce, sea bream with white wine and dill sauce, and puddings such as star anise crème brûlée and dark chocolate truffle torte. *Benchmark main dish: steak in ale pie £16.00. Two-course evening meal £30.00.*

Free house ~ Licensee Patrick Jones ~ Real ale ~ Open 12.30-3, 6.30-11 ~ Bar food 12.30-3, 6.30-9 (9.30 Fri, Sat) ~ Restaurant ~ Children welcome ~ Dogs allowed in bar and bedrooms ~ Wi-fi ~ Live jazz first Sun of month ~ Bedrooms: £149/£169 *Recommended by S F Parrinder, Neil Allen, Isobel Mackinlay*

 ## OXFORD

Bear

SP5106 Map 4

(01865) 728164 – www.bearoxford.co.uk

Alfred Street/Wheatsheaf Alley; OX1 4EH

Delightful pub with friendly staff, two cosy rooms, six real ales and well liked bar food

Tucked away off the tourist trail and the oldest pub in the city (dating from 1242), this little local is charming and easy-going. The two small low-ceilinged, beamed and partly panelled rooms – not over-smart and often packed with students – have a bustling chatty atmosphere, winter coal fires, thousands of vintage ties on the walls and up to six real ales from handpumps on the fine pewter bar counter: Fullers ESB, HSB, London Pride and Olivers Island, Gales Spring Sprinter and a guest from Prospect. Staff are friendly and helpful; board games. There are seats under parasols in the terraced back garden where summer barbecues are held.

Bar food includes sandwiches, goats cheese and mushroom parcels, whitebait with paprika mayonnaise, sharing platters, a quiche of the day, beef, chicken or vegetarian burgers with toppings and chips, winter home-made pies and stews, and puddings. *Benchmark main dish: beer-battered fish and chips £10.45. Two-course evening meal £16.00.*

Fullers ~ Manager James Vernede ~ Real ale ~ Open 11-11 (midnight Sat); 11.30-10.30 Sun ~ Bar food 12-4, 5-8 (8.30 Thurs, 9 Fri, Sat) ~ Children welcome ~ Dogs welcome ~ Wi-fi
Recommended by Gus Swan, Carol and Barry Craddock

OXFORD

Punter

SP5005 Map 4

(01865) 248832 – www.thepunteroxford.com

South Street, Osney (off A420 Botley Road via Bridge Street); OX2 0BE

Easy-going atmosphere in bustling pub overlooking the water, with plenty of character and enjoyable food

Actually on Osney Island and with views over the Thames, this is a cheerful place with an enthusiastic landlord and friendly staff. The lower area has attractive rugs on flagstones and an open fire, while the upper room has more rugs on bare boards and a single big table surrounded by oil paintings – just right for a private group. Throughout are all manner of nice old dining chairs around an interesting mix of tables, art for sale on whitewashed walls and a rather fine stained-glass window. Greene King Fireside, Morlands Original and Old Golden Hen on handpump from the tiled counter and several wines by the glass; board games.

Interesting contemporary food includes blue swimming crab and scallop mornay, baba ganoush with pomegranate, mushroom, pecorino and leek pie, toulouse sausages with beetroot and potato mash and gravy, prosciutto-wrapped cod loin with puy lentils and salsa verde, pork belly with cider-braised leeks, boulangère potatoes and gravy, and puddings. *Benchmark main dish: venison minute steak and frites £11.00. Two-course evening meal £17.00.*

Greene King ~ Lease Tom Rainey ~ Real ale ~ Open 12-midnight ~ Bar food 12-3, 6-10; all day weekends ~ Children welcome ~ Dogs welcome ~ Wi-fi *Recommended by Harvey Brown, Phoebe Peacock, Richard Tilbrook*

OXFORD
SP5107 Map 4

Rose & Crown ◗

(01865) 510551 – www.rose-n-crown.com

North Parade Avenue; very narrow, so best to park in a nearby street; OX2 6LX

Long-serving licensees at lively friendly local with a good mix of customers, fine choice of drinks and proper home cooking

The long-serving licensees give this bustling local a great deal of individuality. It's got a charming old-fashioned atmosphere and there's always a good mix of customers of all ages. The front door opens into a passage with a small counter and bookshelves of reference books for crossword buffs. This leads to two rooms: a cosy one at the front overlooking the street, and a panelled back room housing the main bar and traditional pub furnishings. Adnams Southwold, Box Clever Old Number 8, Hook Norton Old Hooky and Shotover Scholar on handpump, around 30 malt whiskies and a choice of wines by the glass (including champagne and sparkling wine). The pleasant walled and heated back courtyard can be covered with a huge awning; at the far end is a 12-seater dining/meeting room. The loos are basic.

Fairly priced and honest, the traditional food includes sandwiches and baguettes, potted shrimps, meatballs in salsa, ham and eggs, pies such as beef in ale or goats cheese, spinach, sweet potato and red onion, niçoise salad, omelettes, burger with toppings and chips, and puddings such as apple pie and chocolate cake. *Benchmark main dish: sausage and mash £8.95. Two-course evening meal £14.90.*

Free house ~ Licensees Andrew and Debbie Hall ~ Real ale ~ No credit cards ~ Open 10am-midnight (1am Sat); closed 2.30-5.30 Aug and Sept ~ Bar food 12-2.15, 6.30-9 ~ Well behaved and accompanied children may sit in courtyard until 5pm ~ Wi-fi ~ Occasional live music *Recommended by Tony and Jill Radnor*

RAMSDEN
SP3515 Map 4

Royal Oak ♀ ◗

(01993) 868213 – www.royaloakramsden.com

Village signposted off B4022 Witney–Charlbury; OX7 3AU

Busy pub with long-serving licensees, large helpings of varied food, carefully chosen wines and seats outside; bedrooms

The bedrooms in the converted coach house and stable block have been refurbished and in summer they now offer food service on the back terrace. The place has been under the same enthusiastic licensees for 28 years. The unpretentious rooms are relaxed and friendly with all manner of wooden tables, chairs and settles, cushioned window seats, exposed stone walls, bookcases with old and new copies of *Country Life* and, when the weather gets cold, a cheerful log fire. Flying Monk Elmers, Hook Norton Hooky and Wye Valley Ruby Ale on handpump, 40 wines by the glass from a carefully chosen list and three farm ciders. Folding doors from the restaurant give easy access to the terrace and there are some tables and chairs out in front. The village church is opposite.

Quite a choice of popular food includes sandwiches, smoked haddock cooked in whisky and cream and topped with cheese, devilled lambs kidneys in mustard sauce, meatballs in piquant tomato sauce on linguine, vegetable lasagne, a changing curry, a pie of the week, burger with toppings and french fries, poussin cooked with sweet peppers, chorizo and tomatoes, organic pork and black pudding with cider and calvados sauce, and puddings. *Benchmark main dish: steak and kidney pudding £15.50. Two-course evening meal £20.00.*

Free house ~ Licensee Jon Oldham ~ Real ale ~ Open 11.30-3, 6.30-11; 11.30-11 Sat; 12-10.30 Sun ~ Bar food 12-2.30, 7-10 ~ Restaurant ~ Children welcome ~ Dogs allowed in bar ~ Wi-fi ~ Bedrooms: £55/£85 *Recommended by Richard Stanfield, Lindy Andrews*

ROTHERFIELD GREYS
SU7282   Map 2

Maltsters Arms ♀

(01491) 628400 – www.maltsters.co.uk

Can be reached off A4155 in Henley, via Greys Road passing Southfields long-stay car park; or follow Greys Church signpost off B481 N of Sonning Common; RG9 4QD

Well run country pub in the Chilterns with well liked, fairly priced food, nice scenery and walks

In good walking country, this is a friendly, civilised place that our readers enjoy very much. The maroon-carpeted front room has comfortable wall banquettes and lots of horsebrasses on black beams, Brakspears Bitter and Oxford Gold and a guest beer on handpump and 12 wines by the glass; there's a warm open fire in winter and background music. Beyond the serving area, which have hop bines and pewter tankards hanging from its joists, a back room has cricketing prints on dark red walls over a shiny panelled dado, and a mix of furnishings from pink-cushioned pale wooden dining chairs to a pair of leatherette banquettes forming a corner booth. Terrace tables under a big heated canopy are set with linen for meals, and the grass behind has picnic-sets under green parasols, looking out over paddocks to rolling woodland. Greys Court (National Trust) is not far away.

Good, fairly priced food includes sandwiches, chicken liver and pork belly pâté, devilled lambs kidneys on toast, red pepper, tomato and pesto frittata, local pheasant and liver pâté wrapped in smoky bacon with a redcurrant glaze, chinese-style crispy chilli beef with spicy egg noodles, slow-roasted half shoulder of lamb with red wine jus, haddock on colcannon mash with spinach and béarnaise sauce, and puddings. *Benchmark main dish: chicken and mushroom pancake £9.95. Two-course evening meal £16.00.*

Brakspears ~ Tenants Peter and Helen Bland ~ Real ale ~ Open 11.45-3, 6-11; 11.45-midnight Sat; 11.45-9 Sun (11.45-6 in winter) ~ Bar food 12-2.15, 6.15-9.15; 12-2.30 Sun ~ Children welcome ~ Dogs allowed in bar ~ Wi-fi *Recommended by Cliff Sparkes, Roy Hoing, Penny and Peter Keevil*

SHILTON
SP2608   Map 4

Rose & Crown

(01993) 842280 – www.roseandcrownshilton.com

Just off B4020 SE of Burford; OX18 4AB

Simple and appealing little village pub, with a relaxed civilised atmosphere, real ales and good food

Even when this pretty, 17th-c stone pub is packed to the gunnels (it's best to book a table in advance), the friendly, hands-on licensee and his helpful staff make sure everything runs smoothly. The small front bar has an unassuming but civilised feel, low beams and timbers, exposed stone walls, a log fire in a big fireplace and half a dozen or so farmhouse chairs and tables on the red tiled floor. There are usually a few locals at the planked counter where they serve Butcombe Rare Breed, Hook Norton Cotswold Lion and Youngs Bitter on handpump, along with ten wines by the glass and six malt whiskies. A second room, similar but bigger, is used mainly for eating, with flowers on the tables and another fireplace. An attractive side garden has picnic-sets. This is a lovely village.

 The high quality food cooked by the landlord might include lunchtime ciabattas, game terrine with red onion marmalade, gravadlax with dill and mustard sauce, aubergine parmigiana, ham and egg, lambs liver and bacon, smoked haddock, salmon and prawn pie, pheasant with braised cabbage and bacon, venison with chestnut mash and cumberland sauce, and puddings such as spotted dick with custard and pear and almond tart. *Benchmark main dish: steak and mushroom in ale pie £13.50. Two-course evening meal £20.00.*

Free house ~ Licensee Martin Coldicott ~ Real ale ~ Open 11.30-3, 6-10.30; 11.30-11 Sat; 12-10 Sun ~ Bar food 12-2 (2.45 weekends and bank holidays), 7-9 ~ Children welcome lunchtime only ~ Dogs allowed in bar *Recommended by R K Phillips, Mrs V T Bone*

SHIPLAKE

SU7779 Map 2

Baskerville 🖂 ☆ ♟ 🍺 🛏

(0118) 940 3332 – www.thebaskerville.com
Station Road, Lower Shiplake (off A4155 just S of Henley); RG9 3NY

Emphasis on imaginative food but a proper public bar too, interesting sporting memorabilia and a pretty garden; bedrooms

Very much a family concern, this bustling and consistently well run pub remains as popular as ever with both regulars and visitors. Flowers and large house plants are dotted about, and the red walls are hung with a fair amount of sporting memorabilia and pictures (especially old rowing photos – Henley is very near) as well as signed rugby shirts and photos (the pub has its own rugby club) and maps of the Thames. Also, a few beams, red leather tub chairs, pale wood dining chairs and tables on floors of light wood or patterned carpet, plush red banquettes by the windows and a couple of log fires in brick fireplaces. Bar chairs line the light, modern counter where they keep Loddon Ferrymans Gold and Hoppit, Rebellion IPA and Sharps Doom Bar on handpump, 16 wines by the glass from a thoughtfully chosen list and 40 malt whiskies, all served by neat staff; they support WaterAid by charging 50p for a jug of iced water and at the time of writing have raised £5,000. Background music and TV. The whole place feels quite homely in a smart way, with chintzy touches such as a shelf of china cow jugs. There's a separate dining room and a small room for private parties. The pretty garden has a covered barbecue area, smart teak furniture under huge parasols, some rather fun statues cut from box hedging and a timber play frame. The bedrooms are well equipped and comfortable and the breakfasts extremely good.

 Enticing food using produce from the best local suppliers includes open sandwiches, pigeon breast with pancetta, sloe gin reduction, pickled wild mushrooms and cranberry compote, salt and pepper squid with saffron aioli, blue cheese and chestnut mushroom pasta, beer-battered cod and triple-cooked chips, seafood linguine, chicken with haggis, smoked bacon and whisky and mustard sauce, lamb rump with mint, cumin, potato cake and redcurrant jus, and puddings such as bitter chocolate tart with walnut ice-cream and cranberry and apple crumble with crème anglaise. *Benchmark main dish: steak in ale pie £14.00. Two-course evening meal £22.00.*

Free house ~ Licensee Allan Hannah ~ Real ale ~ Open 11-11; 12-10.30 Sun ~ Bar food 12-9 (10 Fri, Sat); 12-3.30 Sun ~ Restaurant ~ Children welcome but not in restaurant after 7pm Fri, Sat ~ Dogs allowed in bar and bedrooms ~ Wi-fi ~ Bedrooms: £95/£105
Recommended by John Pritchard, Simon Collett-Jones

SPARSHOLT   SU3487   Map 2
Star 🍽️⭐ 🛏️
(01235) 751873 – www.thestarsparsholt.co.uk
Watery Lane; OX12 9PL

Delicious food in refurbished inn, real ales and good wines by the glass, helpful friendly staff and seats in the garden; attractive bedrooms in converted barn

It's the first class food that draws most customers to this compact and inviting 16th-c dining pub. But they do have a simply furnished bar where they keep Purity Gold and Sharps Doom Bar on handpump and several wines by the glass, served by friendly, welcoming staff. The dining rooms have pale farmhouse chairs around chunky tables on floorboards or big flagstones, hops on beams, an open fire and old stone bottles and plants dotted about. The atmosphere is easy-going and informal. There are seats in the back garden and eight attractive, contemporary bedrooms in a smartly converted barn. You can enjoy walks along the Ridgeway and a carpet of spring snowdrops in the churchyard.

The beautifully presented, first class food includes lunchtime sandwiches, duck liver parfait with prune, port and soda bread, pigs cheek with hodge podge pudding and kohlrabi, chicken caesar salad with a soft poached egg, thyme and juniper polenta cake with goats cheese, red onion and white wine cream sauce, cottage pie, fillet of brill with lemon, haricot beans and wild nettles, lamb rump with sweetbreads and wild garlic, and puddings such as white chocolate crème brûlée with raspberry flavours and candied pistachio and stem ginger cheesecake with blueberry and lime. *Benchmark main dish: steak burger with toppings and fries £12.50. Two-course evening meal £20.50.*

Free house ~ Licensee Karen Williams ~ Real ale ~ Open 12-11 (midnight Fri, Sat, 9 Sun) ~ Bar food 12-2 (2.30 Sat), 6-9.30; 12-8 Sun ~ Restaurant ~ Children welcome ~ Dogs allowed in bar and bedrooms ~ Wi-fi ~ Bedrooms: /£105 *Recommended by John Harris, Neil Allen*

STANFORD IN THE VALE   SU3393   Map 4
Horse & Jockey ♀ £
(01367) 710302 – www.horseandjockey.org
A417 Faringdon–Wantage; Faringdon Road; SN7 8NN

Friendly traditional village local with real character, highly thought-of and good value food and well chosen wines

As this is racehorse training country (and given the pub's name) there are big Alfred Munnings racecourse prints, card collections of Grand National winners and other horse and jockey pictures on the walls. The place is split into two sections: a contemporary dining area and an older part with flagstones, wood flooring, low beams and raftered ceilings. There are old high-backed settles and leather armchairs, a woodburning stove in a big fireplace and an easy-going, friendly atmosphere. A beer named for the pub,

Tolly Cobbold Phoenix and Wolf Sirius Dog Star on handpump, carefully chosen wines by the glass and a dozen malt whiskies; background music. As well as tables under a heated courtyard canopy, there's a separate enclosed and informal garden. The recently refurbished bedrooms, housed in a separate building, are quiet and comfortable.

 Popular food includes lunchtime sandwiches, duck liver parfait with port and cranberry marmalade, salt and pepper chilli-battered calamari with sweet chilli sauce, fish and meat sharing boards, sticky pork barbecue ribs, seafood linguine, specials (Wednesday-Saturday evenings) such as hake fillet with chorizo crisps, guacamole and parmentier potatoes, beef and Guinness stew with dumplings, and chicken breast wrapped in parma ham with roast butternut squash and peppercorn sauce, and puddings that include 12 home-made ice-creams. *Benchmark main dish: steak in ale pie £11.95. Two-course evening meal £17.00.*

Greene King ~ Lease Charles and Anna Gaunt ~ Real ale ~ Open 11-3, 5-midnight; 11am-12.30am Sat; 11-11 Sun ~ Bar food 12-2.30, 6.30-9 (9.30 Fri, Sat) ~ Restaurant ~ Children welcome ~ Dogs allowed in bar ~ Wi-fi ~ Open mike first Weds of month ~ Bedrooms: £60/£70 *Recommended by Mrs V T Bone, R K Phillips*

STONESFIELD
SP3917   Map 4

White Horse

(01993) 891063 – www.whitehorsestonesfield.co.uk
Village signposted off B4437 Charlbury–Woodstock; Stonesfield Riding; OX29 8EA

Neatly kept little pub with a friendly, relaxed atmosphere and enjoyable food and beer

After a visit to the Roman villa at nearby North Leigh (English Heritage), come to this attractively upgraded small country pub for a weekend lunch – but do check the restricted opening hours. It's a friendly place with an uncluttered feel: just a few pieces of contemporary artwork and a fine old rug hung on green and cream paintwork. The cosy bar has a woodburning stove, country-style chairs and plush or leather stools around solid tables on bare boards, Ringwood Best Bitter on handpump and six wines by the glass; background music. There's an open fire in the pink-walled dining room and similar but more elegant furnishings; a nice touch is the inner room with just a pair of Sheraton-style chairs around a single mahogany table. Doors open on to a neat walled garden with picnic-sets and interesting plants in pots. There are good nearby walks as the pub is on the Oxfordshire Way.

 Using their own free-range eggs and home-grown produce, the well liked food includes sandwiches, smoked salmon pâté, courgette and tomato lasagne, burger with relish and french fries, pancetta-wrapped cod on garlic mash, slow-cooked pork belly with cider gravy and dauphinoise potatoes, and puddings such as double chocolate brownie and lemon and lime cheesecake. *Benchmark main dish: pie of the day £11.95. Two-course evening meal £17.00.*

Free house ~ Licensees John and Angela Lloyd ~ Real ale ~ Open 5-11; 12-3, 6-11 Sat; 12-3 Sun; closed Sun evening, Mon, lunchtimes Tues-Fri; first week Jan ~ Bar food 12-2, 7 (6.30 Fri, Sat)-9; 12-2.30 Sun ~ Restaurant ~ Children welcome ~ Dogs allowed in bar ~ Wi-fi *Recommended by Isobel Mackinlay, Gus Swan*

STONOR
SU7388   Map 2

Quince Tree ♀

(01491) 639039 – www.thequincetree.com
B480, off A4130 NW of Henley; RG9 6HE

Interesting pub with attached café and deli, plenty of dining space throughout, cosier bar and wide range of drinks and food

Built around the original pretty brick coaching inn is a smart new barn-like building housing a café on two floors and a farm shop-cum-deli (selling home-baked bread and pastries, chocolates, charcuterie, daily changing fruit and vegetables, bottled ales and ciders, wines, spirits and gifts). The bar in the pubby part is decorated in modern country style with upholstered wooden dining and red leather tub chairs around bleached wooden tables on floorboards, tartan scatter cushions on long wall banquettes, large windows with pretty blinds, and prints and photos on mushroom-coloured walls. The airy dining room is similar in style. Locals use the high bar stools against the pale counter where they keep Banks Sunbeam and a beer named for the pub (from Revisionist) on handpump and over 20 wines by the glass, served promptly by friendly staff; background music and daily papers. There are seats under parasols on the café terrace surrounded by a landscaped garden, plus more seats on the front pub terrace.

Inventive food includes lunchtime sandwiches, home-smoked duck with pecan brittle, watercress and blood orange, king prawn cocktail with bloody mary mayonnaise and horseradish cream, good sharing boards and salads, spinach, pea and wild garlic risotto, sea bream with olive oil mash and samphire, lamb rump with anchovy and rosemary dauphinoise potatoes, celeriac and beetroot, pork chop with crackling, apple and black pudding bonbon, and puddings; they also offer brunch and cream teas. *Benchmark main dish: wagyu beef pie with colcannon mash and leek and spinach gratin £13.00. Two-course evening meal £23.00.*

Free house ~ Licensee Jack Butler ~ Real ale ~ Open 11.30-5 Mon, Sun; 11.30-11 Tues-Sat ~ Bar food 12-9.30; 12-4.30 Mon, Sun ~ Restaurant ~ Children welcome ~ Dogs allowed in bar ~ Wi-fi *Recommended by Susan and John Douglas, Lindy Andrews*

SWERFORD SP3830 Map 4

Masons Arms ★ ♥

(01608) 683212 – www.masons-arms.com
A361 Banbury–Chipping Norton; OX7 4AP

Well liked food and fair choice of drinks in bustling dining pub with relaxed atmosphere and country views

In warm weather, head for the picnic-sets on grass in the neat back garden and enjoy the pretty views over the Oxfordshire countryside. The friendly bar is welcoming at any time of year with a big brown leather sofa facing a couple of armchairs in front of a log fire in a stone fireplace, rugs on pale wooden floors, Brakspears Bitter and Jennings Cumberland on handpump and 12 wines by the glass. The light and airy dining extension has pastel-painted dining chairs around nice old tables on beige carpet, and steps lead down to a cream-painted room with chunky tables and contemporary pictures. Around the other side of the bar is another spacious dining room with great views by day, candles at night and a civilised feel; background music.

Good, interesting food includes fish specials such as potted crab with brown shrimp butter, scallops with leeks, pancetta, butternut squash purée and langoustine tails in chorizo butter, and salmon on cream cheese and chive mash with lobster bisque. Non-fishy choices include sandwiches, ham hock terrine with red pepper salsa, local venison sausages on stilton mash with stout and onion jus, burgundy beef cobbler with horseradish dumplings, chicken roulade filled with mushroom and tarragon pâté and wrapped in smoked bacon with creamy smoked bacon sauce, and puddings such as a crumble of the day and dark chocolate and black cherry brownie with rum and raisin ice-cream. *Benchmark main dish: goan-style cod curry £14.95. Two-course evening meal £22.00.*

Free house ~ Licensee Louise Davies ~ Real ale ~ Open 11-3, 6-11; 11-6 Sun ~ Bar food 12-2.15, 6-9 (9.30 Sat); 12-6 Sun ~ Restaurant ~ Children welcome ~ Dogs allowed in bar ~ Wi-fi *Recommended by Mr and Mrs J Watkins, M J Winterton*

SWINBROOK
Swan

SP2812 Map 4

(01993) 823339 – www.theswanswinbrook.co.uk
Back road a mile N of A40, 2 miles E of Burford; OX18 4DY

Rather smart old pub with handsome oak garden rooms, antiques-filled bars, local beers and contemporary food; bedrooms

Our readers very much enjoy their visits to this civilised and particularly well run inn, with several calling it 'delightful'. It's owned by the Devonshire Estate and there are plenty of interesting Mitford family photographs blown up on the walls. The little bar has simple antique furnishings, settles and benches, an open fire and (in an alcove) a stuffed swan; locals drop in here for a pint and a chat. A small dining room leads off from the bar to the right of the entrance, and there are also two garden rooms with high-backed beige and green dining chairs around pale wood tables and views across the garden and orchard. Hook Norton Hooky Bitter and a couple of changing guests such as Butcombe Bitter and Flying Monk Elmers on handpump, ten wines by the glass and Weston's organic cider; background music. The elegant bedrooms are in a smartly converted stone barn beside the pub, with five beside the river. A fine time to visit is when the wisteria is in flower and the 400-year-old stone pub looks even prettier; seats and circular picnic-sets make the best of its position by a bridge over the River Windrush. The Kings Head in Bledington (Gloucestershire) is run by the same first class licensees.

Excellent food using the best seasonal produce includes sandwiches, home-cured bresaola with olive oil and parmesan, chicken liver parfait with onion marmalade, saffron risotto with sunblush tomatoes, grilled chorizo, sweetcorn pancake, tomatoes and a fried egg, corn-fed chicken breast with artichoke, olives, tomato and walnut pesto, shredded venison confit with haricot blanc, button onions, thyme and black pudding, fried herring roes, bacon, parsley and capers on toast with skinny chips, and puddings. *Benchmark main dish: grilled whole plaice with shrimp, dill and lemon butter £18.00. Two-course evening meal £26.00.*

Free house ~ Licensees Archie and Nicola Orr-Ewing ~ Real ale ~ Open 11.30-11; 12-10.30 Sun; 11-3, 6-11 in winter ~ Bar food 12-2, 7-9; 12-2.30, 6.30-9.30 Fri, Sat; 12-3, 6.30-8.30 Sun ~ Restaurant ~ Children welcome ~ Dogs allowed in bar ~ Wi-fi ~ Bedrooms: $100/$125 *Recommended by Lois Dyer, Richard Stanfield, Michael Sargent, Bernard Stradling, Tom McLean, Colin McLachlan, Edward Mirzoeff*

TADPOLE BRIDGE
Trout

SP3200 Map 4

(01367) 870382 – www.trout-inn.co.uk
Back road Bampton–Buckland, 4 miles NE of Faringdon; SN7 8RF

Busy country inn by the River Thames with a fine choice of drinks, popular modern food and seats in the waterside garden; bedrooms

This is a peaceful and picturesque spot by the Thames, so do arrive early in warm weather to bag one of the good quality teak chairs and tables under cream parasols in the pretty garden. You can hire punts with champagne hampers and there are moorings (book in advance) for six boats. It's a civilised inn with courteous, friendly staff. The L-shaped bar has attractive green and red checked chairs around a mix of nice wooden tables, rugs on flagstones, green paintwork behind a modern wooden bar counter, fresh flowers, two woodburning stoves and a large stuffed trout. The airy restaurant is appealingly candlelit in the evenings. Prescott Chequered Flag, Ramsbury Bitter, White Horse Wayland Smithy and a seasonal ale from Youngs on handpump, 12 wines by the glass from a wide-ranging, carefully chosen list, 14 malt whiskies and two farm ciders. The bedrooms are smart and well equipped.

With an emphasis on local suppliers, the highly popular food includes sandwiches, various tapas, scallops, chorizo, cauliflower purée and apple salad, smoked trout and spring onion risotto, butternut squash, blue cheese and spinach galette with rocket and pumpkin seed salad, a pie of the day, beer-battered haddock and chips, lamb rump with potato rösti, lamb sweetbreads, confit shallots and garlic basil jus, rib-eye steak with béarnaise sauce and skinny chips, and puddings such as passion-fruit crème brûlée and chocolate brownie with salted chocolate pot and white chocolate ice-cream. *Benchmark main dish: roulade of pork belly with pomme cocottes and cider jus £15.75. Two-course evening meal £20.00.*

Free house ~ Real ale ~ Open 11.30-11; 12-11 Sun; 11.30-3, 6-11 Mon-Thurs Oct-Apr ~ Bar food 12-2, 7-9 ~ Restaurant ~ Children welcome ~ Dogs welcome ~ Wi-fi ~ Bedrooms: £85/£130 *Recommended by Martin and Karen Wake, Mr and Mrs P R Thomas*

WOLVERCOTE
Jacobs Inn

SP4809   Map 4

(01865) 514333 – www.jacobs-inn.com
Godstow Road; OX2 8PG

Informal and friendly place with simple furnishings, some quirky touches, interesting cooking and seats in the garden

Brunch (9-5 daily) in this informally friendly, lively pub is proving a big hit with customers – as are their interesting nibbles. The simply furnished bar has leather armchairs and chesterfields, some plain tables and benches, wide floorboards, a small open fire and high chairs at the counter where they keep Brakspears Oxford Gold, Jennings Cumberland, Marstons EPA and Wychwood Hobgoblin on handpump, 13 wines by the glass and lots of teas and coffees. You can eat at plain wooden tables in a grey panelled area with an open fire or in the smarter knocked-through dining room. This has standing timbers in the middle, a fire at each end and shiny, dark wooden chairs and tables on floorboards; there are standard lamps, stags' heads, a reel-to-reel tape recorder, quite a few mirrors and deli items for sale – it's all quite quirky. Several seating areas outside have good quality tables and chairs under parasols, picnic-sets on decking, and deckchairs and more picnic-sets on grass.

Interesting food includes sandwiches, potted ham hock and ox tongue with pickled vegetables, mussels in white wine, garlic and cream, spicy home-reared chorizo with onion gravy, cheese tartiflette (french-style cheese and potato bake), braised rabbit and wild mushroom linguine with rosemary cream sauce, sea bream with celeriac and potato dauphinoise and sorrel sauce, braised ox cheek with crushed neeps and red wine and thyme sauce, and puddings such as rhubarb brûlée and chocolate pot with peanut crumble. *Benchmark main dish: slow-roast pork belly with creamed cabbage, smoked garlic mash and cider reduction £15.00. Two-course evening meal £20.00.*

Marstons ~ Lease Damion Farah and Johnny Pugsley ~ Real ale ~ Open 9am-11pm (midnight Sat) ~ Bar food 9am-10pm ~ Restaurant ~ Children welcome ~ Dogs allowed in bar ~ Wi-fi *Recommended by Phoebe Peacock, Harvey Brown*

WOODSTOCK   SP4416   Map 4

Kings Arms ⭐ £ 🛏

(01993) 813636 – www.kings-hotel-woodstock.co.uk
Market Street/Park Lane (A44); OX20 1SU

Stylish town-centre hotel with well liked food, a wide choice of drinks and an enjoyable atmosphere; comfortable bedrooms

A good mix of customers makes for a lively atmosphere in this stylish town-centre pub, which wins consistent high praise for both its choice of drinks and enjoyable food. The unfussy bar has an appealing variety of old and new furnishings including brown leather seats on the stripped-wood floor, smart blinds and black and white photographs; at the front is an old wooden settle and a modern woodburner. The neat restaurant has high-backed black leather dining chairs around a mix of tables on black and white floor tiles, and piles of neatly stacked logs on either side of another woodburning stove. Brakspears Bitter, Ringwood Fortyniner and a changing guest on handpump, 11 wines (plus champagne) by the glass and 35 malt whiskies. There are seats and tables on the street outside.

Rewarding food includes sandwiches (until 5pm), seared scallops with carrot purée, samphire and crispy bacon, poached duck egg with organic cheddar rarebit, beetroot and cheese tart with red onion salad, burger with toppings, horseradish coleslaw and chips, pine nut- and herb-crusted pollack with spinach cream, free-range chicken with vegetable and barley broth, lamb rump with apricot glaze and mint cracked wheat, and puddings such as custard tart with poached rhubarb and sticky coffee and date pudding with clotted cream; they also offer a two- and three-course set lunch (Mon-Thurs). *Benchmark main dish: slow-cooked duck leg with sherry cream sauce and raisins £15.75. Two-course evening meal £23.00.*

Free house ~ Licensees David and Sara Sykes ~ Real ale ~ Open 11-11 ~ Bar food 12-2.30, 6-9 (9.30 Fri, Sat) ~ Restaurant ~ Children welcome in bar and restaurant but no under-12s in bedrooms ~ Wi-fi ~ Bedrooms: £85/£150 *Recommended by Neil and Angela Huxter, Phil and Helen Holt, Richard Tilbrook*

Also Worth a Visit in Oxfordshire

Besides the fully inspected pubs, you might like to try these pubs that have been recommended to us and described by readers. Do tell us what you think of them: feedback@goodguides.com

ABINGDON   SU4997
Brewery Tap (01235) 521655
Ock Street; OX14 5BZ Former tap for defunct Morland Brewery but still serving Original along with changing guests, proper ciders and good choice of wines, enjoyable well priced food from bar snacks to popular Sun roasts, stone floors and panelled walls, two log fires; background and Sun live music, Tues quiz, darts, free wi-fi; children and dogs welcome, enclosed courtyard with aunt sally, three bedrooms, open all day (till 1am Fri, Sat). *(Harvey Brown)*

ADDERBURY   SP4735
★ **Red Lion** (01295) 810269
The Green; off A4260 S of Banbury; OX17 3NG Attractive 17th-c stone coaching inn with good choice of enjoyable well priced food (all day weekends) including deals, helpful friendly staff, Greene King ales, good wine range and coffee, linked bar rooms with high stripped beams, panelling and stonework, big inglenook log fire, old books and Victorian/Edwardian pictures, more modern restaurant extension; background music, games area, daily newspapers;

children (in eating areas) and dogs welcome, picnic-sets out on roadside terrace, 12 character bedrooms, good breakfast, open all day in summer. *(George Atkinson)*

ARDINGTON   SU4388
Boars Head (01235) 835466
Signed off A417 Didcot–Wantage; OX12 8QA Modernised 17th-c timber-framed pub with good value popular food from daily changing menu (more evening choice), friendly attentive staff, well kept ales including Loose Cannon, Fullers London Pride and one badged for them, low beams and log fires; background music (maybe live piano); children and dogs (in one area) welcome, terrace seating, peaceful attractive village. *(Helene Grygar)*

ARDLEY   SP5427
Fox & Hounds (01869) 346883
B430 (old A43), just SW of M40 junction 10; OX27 7PE Roadside pub dating from the early 19th c with later additions, long opened-up low-beamed dining lounge, big fireplaces each end, enjoyable home-made food from lunchtime snacks to daily specials, two changing ales and good wine choice, helpful friendly staff, another open fire in cosy carpeted bar; children welcome, no dogs inside, attractive beer garden, bedrooms, open (and food) all day weekends. *(Phil and Jane Hodson)*

ASCOTT UNDER
WYCHWOOD   SP2918
Swan (01993) 832332
Shipton Road; OX7 6AY Hospitable and comfortable 17th-c coaching inn, two Hook Norton ales and a guest, good home-cooked food (not Sun or Mon evenings) in bar or raftered restaurant; soft background jazz, folk club first and third Sat of month, Mon quiz (fish and chips from van); children and dogs welcome, six bedrooms, closed Mon lunchtime. *(Colin McKerrow)*

ASHBURY   SU2685
Rose & Crown (01793) 710222
B4507/B4000; High Street; SN6 8NA Friendly 16th-c coaching inn with roomy open-plan beamed bar, three well kept Arkells beers and decent range of wines by the glass, good food from 'grazing platters' and pub favourites up, polished woodwork, traditional pictures, chesterfields and pews, raised section with further oak tables and chairs, games room with table tennis, pool and darts, separate restaurant; background and occasional live music, quiz nights, sports TV; children and dogs welcome, disabled facilities, tables out at front and in garden behind, lovely view down pretty village street of thatched cottages, handy for Ridgeway walks, eight bedrooms, open all day summer. *(Phoebe Peacock)*

ASTON TIRROLD   SU5586
★**Sweet Olive** (01235) 851272
Aka Chequers; Fullers Road; village signed off A417 Streatley–Wantage; OX11 9EN Atmosphere of rustic french restaurant rather than village pub – but people do pop in just for a drink; main room with wall settles, mate's chairs, a few sturdy tables, matting over quarry tiles, small fireplace, very well liked if not cheap bistro-style food including daily specials, good french wines by the glass (wine box ends decorate back of servery), Brakspears and Fullers beers, friendly service, smaller room more formally set as restaurant; background music; children and dogs (in bar) welcome, picnic-sets under parasols in small cottagey garden, aunt sally, closed Sun evening, Weds and for three weeks Feb/Mar. *(Colin McLachlan)*

BANBURY   SP4540
Three Pigeons (01295) 275220
Southam Road; OX16 2ED Well renovated 17th-c coaching inn handy for town centre, several small rooms surrounding central bar, beams, flagstones, bare boards and woodburners, good friendly atmosphere, shortish choice of well prepared food from doorstep sandwiches to restaurant dishes, also set menu, three changing ales, decent selection of wines by the glass and around 30 malt whiskies, proper coffee too; children welcome, tables under parasols on paved terrace, three bedrooms, useful but limited parking, open all day. *(Roy Hoing, JHBS)*

BECKLEY   SP5611
★**Abingdon Arms** (01865) 351311
Signed off B4027; High Street; OX3 9UU Welcoming old dining pub in lovely unspoilt village; comfortably modernised simple lounge, smaller public bar with antique carved settles, open fires, well kept Brakspears and guests, fair range of good reasonably priced wines, enjoyable home-made food from smallish menu including good Sun roasts, friendly efficient service; background and some live music; children and dogs welcome, big garden dropping away from floodlit terrace to trees, summer house, superb views over RSPB Otmoor reserve and good walks, open all day weekends. *(Dennis and Doreen Haward)*

BEGBROKE   SP4713
Royal Sun (01865) 374718
A44 Oxford–Woodstock; OX5 1RZ Welcoming old stone pub with modernised

---

By law, pubs must show a price list of their drinks. Let us know if you're inconvenienced by any breach of this law.

bare-boards interior, wide choice of enjoyable good value food from snacks to Sun carvery, well kept Hook Norton and a guest, good friendly service; may be background music, big-screen sports TV, free wi-fi; children welcome, no dogs inside, tables on terrace and in small garden, open all day from 8.30am for breakfast. *(Carol and Barry Craddock)*

BLEWBURY   SU5385
Red Lion (01235) 850403
Nottingham Fee – narrow turning N from A417; OX11 9PQ Attractive red-brick downland village pub under good new management; enjoyable generously served home-made food with fresh fish a speciality, well kept Brakspears, good choice of wines and decent coffee, efficient friendly service, beams, tiled floor and big log fire, separate dining area; children and dogs (in bar) welcome, tables in peaceful enclosed back garden, pretty surroundings, two bedrooms. *(Harvey Brown)*

BLOXHAM   SP4235
★ Joiners Arms (01295) 720223
Old Bridge Road, off A361; OX15 4LY Golden-stone 16th-c inn with rambling rooms, white dining chairs around pale tables on wood floor, plenty of exposed stone, open fires, Marstons Burton and guests, enjoyable traditional food including deals (popular Tues steak night), old well in raftered room off bar; Weds quiz; children and dogs welcome, pretty window boxes, seats out under parasols on various levels – most popular down steps by stream (playhouse there too), open all day. *(Meg and Colin Hamilton)*

BRIGHTWELL   SU5890
Red Lion (01491) 837373
Signed off A4130 2 miles W of Wallingford; OX10 0RT Busy village local, four or five well kept ales with regulars Appleford, Loddon and West Berkshire, wines from nearby vineyard, enjoyable good value home-made food including proper pies, friendly efficient staff, two-part bar with snug seating by log fire, dining extension; dogs welcome, seats out at front and in back garden, open all day Sun till 9pm. *(John Pritchard)*

BRITWELL SALOME   SU6793
★ Red Lion (01491) 613140
B4009 Watlington–Benson; OX49 5LG Landlord's interesting (if not cheap) food is main draw to this brick and flint pub; friendly bar with comfortable sofas, pews and assorted tables and chairs, two red-walled dining rooms off, open fires and church candles, West Berkshire Mr Chubbs Lunchtime Bitter and Gun Dog Jack's Spaniels kept well, 13 wines by the glass and some unusual gins, good friendly service; children and dogs welcome, seats in

courtyard garden, closed Sun evening, Mon, Tues. *(C A Hall, Dennis and Doreen Haward)*

BROUGHTON   SP4238
★ Saye & Sele Arms (01295) 263348
B4035 SW of Banbury; OX15 5ED Attractive old stone house part of the Broughton Estate with castle just five minutes away; sizeable bar with polished flagstones, cushioned window seats and dark wooden furnishings, a few brasses, three real ales including Sharps Doom Bar and nine wines by the glass, good food cooked by landlord, friendly service, two carpeted dining rooms with exposed stone walls, open fires, over 240 ornate water jugs hanging from beams; children welcome, no dogs inside, picnic-sets and hanging baskets on terrace, neat lawn with tables under parasols, pergola and smokers' shelter, aunt sally, closed Sun evening. *(Isobel Mackinlay)*

BUCKLAND   SU3497
★ Lamb (01367) 870484
Off A420 NE of Faringdon; SN7 8QN 18th-c stone dining pub with good value interesting seasonal food in bar or restaurant, a couple of changing local ales and good choice of wines by the glass, friendly helpful staff; well behaved children and dogs welcome (resident cocker called Oats), pleasant tree-shaded garden, good walks nearby, three comfortable bedrooms, closed Sun evening and Mon. *(Harvey Brown)*

BURFORD   SP2512
Angel (01993) 822714
Witney Street; OX18 4SN Long heavy-beamed dining pub in interesting 16th-c building, warmly welcoming with roaring log fire, good popular food from sandwiches and pub favourites up, well chosen wines and Hook Norton ales; TV; children welcome, big secluded garden, three comfortable bedrooms, good english breakfast, open (and food) all day. *(Bernard Stradling)*

BURFORD   SP2512
Mermaid (01993) 822193
High Street; OX18 4QF Handsome old dining pub with beams, flagstones, panelling, stripped stone and nice log fire, decent food (all day weekends) at sensible prices including local free-range meat and fresh fish, friendly service, well kept Greene King ales and a guest, bay window seating at front, further airy back dining room and upstairs restaurant; background music, quiz first Mon of month, live music Fri, darts; children welcome, tables out at front and in courtyard behind, open all day. *(Paul and Sue Merrick)*

CAULCOTT   SP5024
★ Horse & Groom (01869) 343257
Lower Heyford Road (B4030); OX25 4ND Pretty 16th-c roadside thatched cottage, L-shaped red-carpeted room with log fire in big inglenook (brassware under

its long bressumer) and plush-cushioned settles, chairs and stools around a few dark tables at low-ceilinged bar end, White Horse Bitter and a couple of guests, decent house wines, good food (not Sun evening) cooked by french owner-chef, also O'Hagans sausage menu, dining room at far end with jugs hanging on black joists, decorative plates, watercolours and original drawings, small side sun lounge, shove-ha'penny and board games; well behaved over-5s welcome, picnic-sets in nice little front garden, no car park, closed Mon. *(Sue Callard, Colin McKerrow, George Atkinson)*

CHADLINGTON   SP3222
Tite (01608) 676910
Off A361 S of Chipping Norton; Mill End; OX7 3NY Friendly renovated 17th-c country pub; bar with eating areas either side, beams and stripped stone, pubby furniture including spindleback chairs and settles, flagstones and bare boards, woodburner in large fireplace, well kept Sharps Doom Bar and a couple of guests, a dozen wines by the glass, enjoyable fairly traditional home-cooked food (not Sun evening), good service; occasional live music, winter quiz nights; well behaved children and dogs welcome, split-level terrace and lovely shrub-filled garden, good walks nearby, open all day. *(Richard Stanfield, Colin McKerrow, Liz Bell)*

CHALGROVE   SU6397
Red Lion (01865) 890625
High Street (B480 Watlington–Stadhampton); OX44 7SS Attractive beamed village pub owned by local church trust since 1637; good home-made seasonal food (not Sun evening) from interesting menu, well kept Butcombe, Fullers London Pride, Rebellion Mild and two guests, friendly helpful staff, quarry-tiled bar with big open fire, separate carpeted restaurant; children and dogs welcome, nice front and back gardens, open all day Sun (and Sat if busy). *(Anon)*

CHARLTON-ON-OTMOOR   SP5615
Crown (01865) 331850
Signed off B4027 in Islip; High Street, opposite church; OX5 2UQ Refurbished 17th-c village local with welcoming relaxed atmosphere, bar and separate restaurant, good interesting food from landlord-chef, well kept Rebellion and a guest ale; children welcome. *(Tim Roberts)*

CHARNEY BASSETT   SU3794
Chequers (01235) 868642
Chapel Lane off Main Street; OX12 0EX Welcoming 18th-c village-green pub with spacious modernised interior, Brakspears and Wychwood ales, enjoyable fairly priced food from lunchtime sandwiches and baguettes to steaks (booking advised), log fire; children and dogs (in bar) welcome, picnic-sets in

small garden, three bedrooms, open all day. *(Carol and Barry Craddock)*

CHAZEY HEATH   SU6977
Pack Saddle (0118) 946 3000
A4074 Reading–Wallingford; RG4 7UD Renovated after fire; quite restauranty but retaining pub feel, panelled bar with steps down to dining area, ales such as Loddon, Fullers and Sharps, decent wines by the glass, good quality food from shortish menu, quick friendly service; children welcome, garden with covered terrace and play area, open (and food) all day. *(Anon)*

CHECKENDON   SU6684
★ Black Horse (01491) 680418
Village signed off A4074 Reading–Wallingford; RG8 0TE Charmingly old-fashioned country tavern (tucked into woodland away from main village) kept by same family for 110 years; relaxing and unchanging series of rooms, back one with West Berkshire and White Horse tapped from the cask, one with bar counter has some tent pegs above the fireplace (a reminder they used to be made here), homely side lounge with some splendidly unfashionable 1950s-style armchairs and another room beyond that, only baguettes and pickled eggs; no credit cards; children allowed but must be well behaved, dogs welcome, seats on verandah and in garden, popular with walkers and cyclists. *(Anon)*

CHILDREY   SU3687
Hatchet (01235) 751213
B4001/Stowhill; OX12 9UF Beamed village local, friendly and unpretentious, with Morland Original and a couple of guests, enjoyable straightforward food, games area with pool and darts; children and dogs welcome, a few picnic-sets out in front, garden play area, Ridgeway walks, closed lunchtimes Mon, Tues. *(Rob Anderson)*

CHIPPING NORTON   SP3127
Blue Boar (01608) 643525
High Street/Goddards Lane; OX7 5NP Spacious stone-built former coaching inn, ample helpings of enjoyable good value food (all day weekends), Marstons-related ales with guests such as local Cats, friendly helpful staff, raftered back restaurant and airy flagstoned garden room, woodburner in big stone fireplace; background music (live weekends), Thurs quiz, darts, sports TV, fruit machine; children welcome, open all day. *(George Atkinson)*

CHIPPING NORTON   SP3127
★ Chequers (01608) 644717
Goddards Lane; OX7 5NP Bustling traditional town pub with three softly lit beamed rooms, no frills but clean, comfortable and full of character, flagstones, low ochre ceilings and log fire, up to eight well kept ales (mainly Fullers), 15 wines by

the glass and good food (not Sun evening) from shortish menu, friendly helpful staff, airy conservatory restaurant behind; TV, free wi-fi; children and dogs (in bar) welcome, theatre next door, open all day. *(Richard Stanfield, Richard Tilbrook)*

CHIPPING NORTON SP3127
Crown & Cushion (01608) 642533
High Street; OX7 5AD Welcoming little bar at back of handsome old-fashioned 16th-c hotel, log fire, beams, some flagstones and stripped stone, well kept/priced Hook Norton Hooky, enjoyable good value bar food including OAP deal Tues, nice coffee, separate bistro restaurant; children welcome, tables in sheltered suntrap courtyard, 40 bedrooms, open all day. *(R C Vincent)*

CHISLEHAMPTON SU5998
Coach & Horses (01865) 890255
B480 Oxford–Watlington, opposite B4015 to Abingdon; OX44 7UX Extended 16th-c coaching inn with two homely and civilised beamed bars, big log fire, sizeable restaurant with polished oak tables and wall banquettes, good choice of popular reasonably priced food (not Sun evening), friendly obliging service, three well kept ales usually including Hook Norton; background music; neat terraced gardens overlooking fields by River Thame, some tables out in front, bedrooms in courtyard block, open all day (closed 3-7pm Sun). *(Roy Hoing, Mr and Mrs P R Thomas, Mike and Mary Carter)*

CHRISTMAS COMMON SU7193
Fox & Hounds (01491) 612599
Off B480/B481; OX49 5HL Welcoming old Chilterns pub (known locally as the Top Fox) in lovely countryside, some recent refurbishment in spacious front barn restaurant serving good value home-made food from open kitchen including set deal (Mon, Tues evenings), Brakspears and a guest, decent wines, two compact beamed rooms simply but comfortably furnished, bow windows, red and black floor tiles and big inglenook, snug little back room too; board games; children, walkers and dogs welcome, rustic benches and tables outside, open all day Weds-Sat, till 7pm Sun. *(Susan and John Douglas, Bill Gulliver and Harry Thomson)*

CHURCH ENSTONE SP3725
★ Crown (01608) 677262
Mill Lane; from A44 take B4030 turn-off at Enstone; OX7 4NN Pleasant bar in popular 17th-c beamed country pub, straightforward furniture, old local photographs on stone walls, some horsebrasses, log fire in large fireplace, well kept Hook Norton and guests, good food cooked by landlord from pub favourites

up, friendly efficient service, carpeted dining room with red walls, slate-floored conservatory; children welcome, dogs in bar, white metal furniture on front terrace overlooking lane, picnic-sets in sheltered back garden, closed Sun evening. *(Barry Collett)*

CLANFIELD SP2802
Plough (01367) 810222
Bourton Road; OX18 2RB Substantial old stone inn with lovely Elizabethan façade, civilised atmosphere, log fire in comfortable lounge bar, various dining areas, good food, particularly fish and seasonal game, well kept Hook Norton Hooky and a guest such as Prescott Hill Climb, good wine list and over 180 gins (can organise tasting sessions), attentive service; children and dogs welcome, attractive gardens with teak tables in nice front courtyard, 12 bedrooms, open all day. *(Wilburoo)*

COLESHILL SU2393
Radnor Arms (01793) 861575
B4019 Faringdon–Highworth; village signposted off A417 in Faringdon and A361 in Highworth; SN6 7PR Pub and village owned by NT; bar with cushioned settles, plush carver chairs and woodburner, back alcove with more tables, steps down to main dining area, once a blacksmiths' forge with lofty beamed ceiling, log fire, dozens of tools and smiths' gear on walls, Old Forge ales brewed on site (tasting trays available), well priced traditional food (not Sun evening); children, walkers and dogs welcome, garden with aunt sally and play area, open all day. *(Phil and Jane Villiers)*

CRAWLEY SP3412
Lamb (01993) 708792
Steep Hill; just NW of Witney; OX29 9TW 18th-c stone-built dining pub with good if not particularly cheap food from new owner-chef, Brakspears and Wychwood ales, friendly attentive staff, beamed bar with polished boards and lovely fireplace, steps up to dining room; dogs welcome in bar, views from tables on back terrace and lawn, summer barbecues and woodfired pizzas, pretty village, good walks (on Palladian Way), open all day Sat, closed Sun evening, Mon. *(Harvey Brown)*

CROWELL SU7499
Shepherds Crook (01844) 355266
B4009, 2 miles from M40 junction 6; OX39 4RR Continuing well under present management, beamed bar with stripped brick and flagstones, woodburner, high-raftered dining area, good varied choice of freshly prepared food (not Sun evening) including daily specials, up to half a dozen ales such as Adnams, Rebellion, St Austell and Timothy

---

There are report forms at the back of the book.

Taylors, extensive wine list with ten by the glass, 30 or so whiskies, 'jazz & dinner' evenings; children and dogs welcome, tables out on front terrace and village green, nice walks, open all day. *(Pheobe Peacock)*

CUMNOR SP4503
Bear & Ragged Staff
(01865) 862329 *Signed from A420; Appleton Road; OX2 9QH* Extensive restaurant-pub dating from 16th c, contemporary décor in linked rooms with wood floors and painted beams, good food from sandwiches and sharing plates (create your own) through pub favourites up, friendly efficient service, flagstoned bar with log fire, well kept Greene King ales and good wine choice, airy garden room; background music, TV, free wi-fi; children welcome, decked terrace and fenced play area, nine bedrooms, open (and food) all day. *(Anon)*

DEDDINGTON SP4631
★ Deddington Arms (01869) 338364
Off A4260 (B4031) Banbury–Oxford; Horse Fair; OX15 0SH Beamed and timbered hotel in charming village with lots of antiques shops and good farmers' market (last Sat of month); very well liked food including set lunch/evening menus in sizeable contemporary back dining room, comfortable more traditional bar with mullioned windows, flagstones and log fire, good food here too including sandwiches, Adnams, Black Sheep, Hook Norton and a guest, plenty of wines by the glass, attentive friendly service; unobtrusive background music, free wi-fi; children welcome, comfortable chalet bedrooms around courtyard, good breakfast, nice local walks, open all day. *(R C Vincent, George Atkinson, Gerry and Rosemary Dobson)*

DEDDINGTON SP4631
Unicorn (01869) 338838
Market Place; OX15 0SE Refurbished 17th-c inn continuing well under present management; beamed L-shaped bar, cosy snug with inglenook log fire, candlelit restaurant, good sensibly priced food (not Sun evening) combining traditional and modern cooking, three Charles Wells ales and good choice of wines by the glass, friendly service; background music (not in snug); well behaved children and dogs welcome, cobbled courtyard leading to long walled back garden, six bedrooms, open all day (all day weekends in winter) and from 9am for good farmers' market (last Sat of month). *(Carol and Barry Craddock)*

DENCHWORTH SU3891
Fox (01235) 868258
Off A338 or A417 N of Wantage; Hyde Road; OX12 0DX Comfortable 17th-c thatched and beamed pub in pretty village, good sensibly priced food from extensive menu including Sun carvery (best to book),

OAP lunch deal Mon-Thurs, friendly efficient staff, well kept Greene King ales, good choice of reasonably priced wines, two log fires and plush seats in low-ceilinged connecting areas, old prints and paintings, airy dining extension; children and dogs welcome, tables under umbrellas in pleasant sheltered garden with heated terrace and aunt sally. *(R K Phillips)*

DORCHESTER-ON-THAMES SU5794
Fleur de Lys (01865) 340502
Just off A4074 Maidenhead–Oxford; High Street; OX10 7HH Former 16th-c coaching inn opposite abbey, traditional split-level interior with interesting old photographs of the pub, plain wooden tables, open fire and woodburner, good imaginative evening set menu (not Sun), more straightforward lunchtime food, friendly efficient service, two changing ales; children (away from bar) and dogs welcome, picnic-sets on front terrace and in back garden with play area and aunt sally, five bedrooms, open all day weekends, closed Mon lunchtime. *(John Pritchard, Paul Humphreys)*

DORCHESTER-ON-THAMES SU5794
George (01865) 340404
Just off A4074 Maidenhead–Oxford; High Street; OX10 7HH Handsome 15th-c timbered hotel in lovely village, inglenook log fire in comfortably furnished beamed bar, enjoyable well presented food from baguettes up, three or four real ales such as Brakspears, Butcombe and Wadworths, cheerful efficient uniformed staff, restaurant; background music; children welcome, 17 bedrooms, open all day. *(Anon)*

DUCKLINGTON SP3507
Bell (01993) 700341
Off A415, a mile SE of Witney; Standlake Road; OX29 7UP Pretty thatched and beamed village local, good value home-made food including stone-baked pizzas, decent vegetarian options and Sun carvery, Greene King ales, friendly service, big stripped-stone and flagstoned bar with scrubbed tables, log fires, glass-covered well, old local photographs and farm tools, hatch-served public bar, roomy back restaurant, its beams festooned with bells; background music, sports TV, pool; children welcome, seats outside and play area, aunt sally, four bedrooms, open all day Fri-Sun, no food Sun evening or lunchtimes Mon, Tues. *(Dennis and Doreen Haward)*

EAST HENDRED SU4588
Plough (01235) 833213
Off A417 E of Wantage; Orchard Lane; OX12 8JW Timbered 16th-c village pub with good value traditional food (not Sun evening), Greene King-related ales and decent choice of wines by the glass, efficient

friendly service, lofty raftered main room with interesting farming memorabilia, side dining area; background music, sports TV, pool, machines; well behaved children and dogs allowed (pub labrador is Hugo), lovely enclosed back garden, attractive village, open all day weekends, closed Mon. *(Harvey Brown)*

EATON   SP4403
Eight Bells (01865) 862261
Signed off B4017 SW of Oxford; OX13 5PR Cosy unpretentious old pub with relaxed local atmosphere, two small low-beamed bars with open fires and a dining area, well kept Loose Cannon and guests, traditional low-priced food (not Sun evening) served by friendly helpful staff; pleasant garden with aunt sally, nice walks, open all day Fri-Sun, closed Mon. *(Lindy Andrews)*

EPWELL   SP3540
★Chandlers Arms (01295) 780153
Sibford Road, off B4035; OX15 6LH Welcoming little 16th-c stone pub renovated and doing well under award-winning licensees Peter and Assumpta Golding; high quality freshly made food (booking advised), well kept Hook Norton and a guest such as local Cats, proper coffee, bar with country-style furniture, two dining areas, good attentive service; occasional live music; pleasant garden with aunt sally, attractive out-of-the-way village near Macmillan Way long-distance path, open all day. *(Clive and Fran Dutson, P and J Shapley, Colin McKerrow, Bernard Stradling, Dennis and Doreen Haward)*

EWELME   SU6491
Shepherds Hut (01491) 836636
Off B4009 about 6 miles SW of M40 junction 6; High Street; OX10 6HQ Extended bay-windowed village pub, beams and bare boards, woodburner, enjoyable home-made food (not Sun evening) from good ciabattas up, Greene King ales and a guest, friendly helpful staff, back dining area; children, walkers and dogs welcome, terrace picnic-sets with steps up to lawn and play area, open all day. *(Paul Humphreys)*

EXLADE STREET   SU6582
★Highwayman (01491) 682020
Just off A4074 Reading–Wallingford; RG8 0UA Two beamed bar rooms, mainly 17th-c (parts older), with interesting rambling layout and mix of furniture, good food including set lunch, well kept beers and plenty of wines by the glass, friendly efficient service, airy conservatory dining room; soft background music; children and dogs welcome, terrace and garden with fine views, closed Sun evening, Mon. *(Harvey Brown)*

FERNHAM   SU2991
★Woodman (01367) 820643
A420 SW of Oxford, then left into B4508 after about 11 miles; village another 6 miles on; SN7 7NX Friendly 17th-c country pub under newish management; heavily beamed character main rooms, various odds and ends such as milkmaids' yokes, leather tack, coach horns and an old screw press, candlelit tables made from casks and a big open fire, also some comfortable newer areas, up to eight changing ales tapped from the cask, several malt whiskies and decent choice of wines by the glass, well thought-of food; background music; children and dogs (in bar) welcome, disabled facilities, terrace seats, good walks below the downs, open all day Fri-Sun. *(Anon)*

FIFIELD   SP2318
Merrymouth (01993) 831652
A424 Burford–Stow; OX7 6HR Simple but comfortable roadside inn dating from 13th c, L-shaped bar with bay-window seats, flagstones and low beams, some walls stripped back to old masonry, warm stove, quite dark in places, generous food cooked by landlord including blackboard fish specials, well kept ales such as Brakspears and Hook Norton, decent choice of wines, friendly staff; background music, free wi-fi; children and dogs welcome, tables on terrace and in back garden, nice views, nine stable-block bedrooms, good breakfast. *(Stanley and Annie Matthews, Richard Stanfield)*

FINSTOCK   SP3616
★Plough (01993) 868333
Just off B4022 N of Witney; High Street; OX7 3BY Thatched low-beamed village pub with long rambling bar, leather sofas by massive stone inglenook, pictures of local scenes and some historical documents connected with the pub, roomy dining room with candles on stripped-pine tables, popular home-made pubby food (best to book), two or three well kept ales including Adnams Broadside, traditional cider, several wines by the glass and decent choice of whiskies, friendly helpful staff; soft background music, bar billiards; children and dogs (in bar) welcome, seats in neatly kept garden with aunt sally, woodland walks and along River Evenlode, open all day Sat, closed Sun evening. *(Michèle Burton)*

FRINGFORD   SP6028
Butchers Arms (01869) 277363
Off A421 N of Bicester; Main Street; OX27 8EB Welcoming partly thatched creeper-clad local in Flora Thompson's 'Candleford' village; enjoyable traditional

---

We checked prices with the pubs as we went to press in summer 2015. They should hold until around spring 2016.

food including good Sun roasts (three sittings, best to book), well kept Brakspears, Hook Norton and Sharps, charming efficient service, unpretentious interior with L-shaped bar and back dining room; picnic-sets out at front beside cricket green. *(Anon)*

FYFIELD   SU4298
★ **White Hart** (01865) 390585

Main Road; off A420 8 miles SW of Oxford; OX13 5LW Grand medieval hall with soaring eaves, huge stone-flanked window embrasures and minstrels' gallery, contrasting cosy low-beamed side bar with large inglenook, fresh flowers and evening candles throughout, civilised friendly atmosphere and full of history; good imaginative modern food (best to book) cooked by licensee using home-grown produce, Hook Norton and a couple of guests (festivals May and Aug bank holidays), around 12 wines by the glass, several malt whiskies and maybe home-made summer elderflower pressé; background music; well behaved children welcome, elegant furniture under umbrellas on spacious heated terrace, lovely gardens, good Thames-side walks, open all day weekends, closed Mon. *(Rob Anderson)*

GALLOWSTREE COMMON   SU6980
Reformation (0118) 972 3126

Horsepond Road; RG4 9BP Friendly and welcoming black-beamed village local, enjoyable varied choice of home-made food, Brakspears and a couple of Marstons-related guests, plenty of wines by the glass, open fires, conservatory; some live music, other events such as tractor runs and log-splitting competitions; children and dogs welcome, garden with 'shipwreck' play area, closed Sun evening (and Mon in winter). *(Carol and Barry Craddock)*

GODSTOW   SP4809
★ **Trout** (01865) 510930

Off A40/A44 roundabout via Wolvercote; OX2 8PN Pretty 17th-c Mitchells & Butlers dining pub in lovely riverside location (gets packed in fine weather); good choice of food from varied menu including set weekday deal till 6pm (booking essential at busy times), four beamed linked rooms with contemporary furnishings, flagstones and bare boards, log fires in three huge hearths, Brakspears, Sharps and a guest, several wines by the glass; background music; children and dogs (in bar) welcome, plenty of terrace seats under big parasols, footbridge to island (may be closed), abbey ruins opposite, car park fee refunded at bar, open (and food) all day. *(Peter and DoDo Rawlings)*

GORING   SU5980
★ **Catherine Wheel** (01491) 872379

Station Road; RG8 9HB Friendly 18th-c village pub with two neat and cosily traditional bar areas, especially the more individual lower room with its dark beams

and inglenook log fire, popular home-made food (not Sun evening) from seasonal menu, well kept Brakspears and other Marstons-related ales, Thatcher's cider, back restaurant, notable doors to lavatories; monthly quiz, TV, free wi-fi; children and dogs welcome, sunny garden and gravel terrace, handy for Thames Path, open all day. *(Anon)*

GORING   SU5980
John Barleycorn (01491) 872509

Manor Road; RG8 9DP Friendly low-beamed cottagey local, cosy unpretentious lounge bar and adjoining dining room, popular good value pubby food (not Sun evening) from lunchtime sandwiches up, Brakspears, Ringwood Fortyniner and a guest, seven wines by the glass, cheerful swift service, public bar with log fire and bar billiards; children welcome, enclosed beer garden, short walk to the Thames, three bedrooms, open all day. *(Paul Humphreys)*

GOZZARD'S FORD   SU4698
Black Horse (01865) 390530

Off B4017 NW of Abingdon; N of A415 by Marcham–Cothill road; OX13 6JH Ancient pub in tiny hamlet, friendly new management and some refurbishment, enjoyable home-made food, well kept ales such as Loose Cannon and Morlands, comfortable beamed main bar partly divided by stout timbers and low steps, end woodburner, separate bare-boards public bar; weekend live music; children and dogs welcome, large garden, open all day. *(Harvey Brown)*

GREAT TEW   SP3929
★ **Falkland Arms** (01608) 683653

The Green; off B4022 about 5 miles E of Chipping Norton; OX7 4DB Part-thatched 16th-c golden-stone pub in lovely village, unspoilt partly panelled bar with high-backed settles, diversity of stools and plain tables on flagstones or bare boards, lots of mugs and jugs hanging from beam-and-boards ceiling, interesting brewerania, dim converted oil lamps, shutters for stone-mullioned latticed windows and open fire in fine inglenook, Wadworths and guests, Weston's cider, country wines and 30 malt whiskies, snuff for sale, locally sourced freshly made food, friendly service, separate dining room; live folk Sun evening; children and dogs welcome, tables out at front and under parasols in back garden, six bedrooms and cottage, open all day from 8am (breakfast for non-residents). *(Richard Stanfield, Mr and Mrs P R Thomas, Dr W I C Clark)*

HAILEY   SP3414
★ **Bird in Hand** (01993) 868321

Whiteoak Green; B4022 Witney–Charlbury; OX29 9XP Attractive 17th-c extended stone inn, good food including some welsh influences from owner-chef (best to book summer weekends), set lunch deal

Tues and Weds, helpful friendly service, well kept ales such as Brains and Hook Norton, several wines by the glass, beams, timbers and some stripped stone, comfortable armchairs on polished boards, large log fire, cosy corners in carpeted restaurant, witty references to Wales and rugby dotted about, lovely Cotswold views; parasol-shaded terrace tables, 16 bedrooms in modern block around grass quadrangle, good breakfast, open all day from 8am. *(Paul and Sue Merrick)*

HAILEY · SU6485
★**King William IV** (01491) 681845
The Hailey near Ipsden, off A4074 or A4130 SE of Wallingford; OX10 6AD Popular fine old pub in lovely countryside, beamed bar with good sturdy furniture on tiles in front of big log fire, three other cosy seating areas opening off, enjoyable freshly made food (not Sun evening) from baguettes to specials, Brakspears and guests tapped from the cask, helpful friendly staff; children and dogs welcome, terrace and large garden enjoying wide-ranging peaceful views, good walking (Chiltern Way and Ridgeway), leave muddy boots in porch, open all day weekends. *(Colin McLachlan, Bob and Margaret Holder)*

HAMPTON POYLE · SP5015
★**Bell** (01865) 376242
From A34 S, take Kidlington turn and village signed from roundabout; from A34 N, take Kidlington turn, then A4260 to roundabout, third turning signed for Superstore (Bicester Road); village signed from roundabout; OX5 2QD Front bar with three snug rooms, lots of big black and white photoprints, sturdy simple furnishings, scatter cushions and window seats, a stove flanked by bookshelves one end, large fireplace the other, open kitchen with feature pizza oven in biggish inner room, spreading restaurant with plenty of tables on pale limestone floor, inventive food, good choice of wines by the glass, ales such as Hook Norton and Wye Valley, efficient uniformed staff, cheerful buzzy atmosphere; background music; children and dogs (in bar) welcome, modern seats on sunny front terrace by quiet village lane, nine good bedrooms, open all day. *(Gerry Price)*

HANWELL · SP4343
Moon & Sixpence (01295) 730544
Main Street; OX17 1HN Refurbished stone-built pub in attractive village setting, good food cooked by owner-chef from pub favourites up including set menu choices, comfortable bar and dining areas with view into kitchen, friendly staff, well kept Charles Wells ales and several wines by the glass from good list; children welcome, disabled access, seats on back terrace, open till 6pm Sun. *(Gerry and Rosemary Dobson)*

HEADINGTON · SP5406
Butchers Arms (01865) 742470
Wilberforce Street; OX3 7AN Welcoming backstreet local with good mix of customers, refurbished bare-boards interior, well kept Fullers beers and good value tasty food (not Sun evening), roaring fire; children and dogs welcome, heated terrace with smokers' shelter, open all day Fri-Sun. *(Isobel Mackinlay)*

HENLEY · SU7682
Anchor (01491) 574753
Friday Street; RG9 1AH Refurbished beamed pub set just back from the river; uncluttered gently upmarket feel, wood and stone floors, tall tables, leather sofas and numbered dining tables with flowers, popular food from panini and sharing plates up, Brakspears Bitter and a guest, several wines by the glass; children welcome, smart sunny terrace at back, open all day. *(Paul Humphreys)*

HENLEY · SU7682
Angel on the Bridge (01491) 410678
Thames-side, by the bridge; RG9 1BH 17th-c and worth knowing for its prime Thames-side position (packed during the regatta); small front bar with log fire, downstairs back bar and adjacent restaurant, beams, uneven floors and dim lighting, Brakspears ales and maybe a guest such as Ringwood, good choice of wines by the glass, enjoyable food from sandwiches and pubby choices up, cheerful staff, newspapers; tables under parasols on popular waterside deck (plastic glasses here), moorings for two boats, open all day at least in summer. *(Ian Phillips)*

HENLEY · SU7582
★**Three Tuns** (01491) 410138
Market Place; RG9 2AA Small heavy-beamed front bar with fire, all tables set for eating (stools by counter for drinkers), Brakspears and guests such as Ringwood, good attractively presented food (not Sun evening) from imaginative menu, also good value set deal, nice wines, friendly helpful service, lighter panelled back dining area with painted timbers and wood floor; live music Sun, monthly comedy and cabaret nights; children welcome, tables in small attractive back courtyard, closed Mon, otherwise open all day. *(Paul Humphreys, Tracey and Stephen Groves)*

HOOK NORTON · SP3534
★**Gate Hangs High** (01608) 737387
N towards Sibford, at Banbury–Rollright crossroads; OX15 5DF Snug tucked-away old stone pub, low-ceilinged bar with traditional furniture on bare boards, attractive inglenook, good reasonably priced home-made food from bar snacks to daily specials, well kept Hook Norton ales

and a guest, decent wines, friendly helpful service, side dining extension; background music; children and dogs (in bar) welcome, pretty courtyard and country garden, four bedrooms, camping, quite near Rollright Stones (EH), open all day. *(Harvey Brown)*

HORNTON   SP3945
Dun Cow (01295) 670524
West End; OX15 6DA Traditional 17th-c thatch and ironstone village pub, friendly and relaxed, with sensibly short choice of good fresh food (not Sun or Mon evenings) from lunchtime sandwiches up using local suppliers, Hook Norton, St Austell and Wells Bombardier, a dozen wines by the glass; children and dogs welcome, appealing small garden behind, open all day weekends, closed lunchtimes Mon, Tues (in winter lunchtimes Mon-Thurs). *(Anon)*

KELMSCOTT   SU2499
★ **Plough** (01367) 253543
NW of Faringdon, off B4449 between A417 and A4095; GL7 3HG Popular 17th-c country pub with ancient flagstones, stripped stone and log fire, good food from light lunches to more restauranty evening choices, well kept beers such as Halfpenny, Hook Norton, Vale and Wye Valley, real cider, helpful friendly staff; children, dogs and boots welcome, tables out in covered area and garden, lovely spot near upper Thames (moorings a few minutes away), eight comfortable bedrooms, good breakfast, no car park, handy for Kelmscott Manor (open Weds and Sat Apr-Oct), pub open all day. *(R K Phillips, Phil and Jane Villiers)*

KIDMORE END   SU6979
New Inn (0118) 972 3115
Chalkhouse Green Road; signed from B481 in Sonning Common; RG4 9AU Extended black and white pub by village church; beams and big log fire, enjoyable freshly made food, well kept Brakspears ales and decent wines by the glass, pleasant restaurant; children welcome, tables in large sheltered garden with pond, six bedrooms, open all day Thurs-Sat, till 5pm Sun. *(Carol and Barry Craddock)*

KINGHAM   SP2523
★ **Wild Rabbit** (01608) 658389
Church Street; OX7 6YA Former 18th-c farmhouse owned by Lady Bamford; plenty of rustic chic with antique country furniture, limestone floors, bare stone walls, beams and huge fireplaces, contemporary artwork and fresh flowers, Hook Norton Hooky and a couple of guests, several wines by the glass including champagne, good food in bar or more upmarket choices (not cheap) in spacious brasserie-style restaurant with view into kitchen, pleasant young staff in jeans and check shirts; children welcome, dogs in bar, paved front terrace with topiary rabbits, 12 individual and sumptuously

appointed bedrooms, open all day. *(Liz Bell, Bernard Stradling)*

LANGFORD   SP2402
Bell (01367) 860249
Village signposted off A361 N of Lechlade, then pub signed; GL7 3LF New owners for this 17th-c pub set in charming village; cosy small bar with flagstones, larger one with open fire, three real ales including Brakspears Oxford Gold, decent wines by the glass and good selection of gins, two heavily beamed dining rooms with traditional tables and chairs on more flagstones, enjoyable food from bar snacks and deli boards up, friendly helpful staff; children and dogs welcome, small garden, open all day Fri-Sun, closed Mon. *(Mrs Julie Thomas, R K Phillips)*

LAUNTON   SP6022
Bull (01869) 248158
Just E of Bicester; Bicester Road; OX26 5DQ Cleanly modernised part-thatched 17th-c village pub, enjoyable good value food including OAP lunchtime deal (Mon-Fri) and Tues steak night, Greene King IPA and a couple of guests, friendly staff; background music, Sun quiz; children and dogs welcome, wheelchair access from car park, garden with terrace, open all day. *(Dennis and Doreen Haward)*

LEWKNOR   SU7197
★ **Olde Leathern Bottel**
(01844) 351482 *Under a mile from M40 junction 6; off B4009 towards Watlington; OX49 5TH* Popular and friendly family-run pub, two heavy-beamed bars with understated décor and rustic furnishings, open fires, well kept Brakspears and Marstons, several wines by the glass, tasty pub food and specials served quickly, family room separated by standing timbers; dogs welcome, splendid garden with plenty of picnic-sets under parasols, play area and boules, handy for walks on Chiltern escarpment. *(David Lamb)*

LONG HANBOROUGH   SP4214
★ **George & Dragon** (01993) 881362
A4095 Bladon–Witney; Main Road; OX29 8JX Substantial pub with original two-room bar (17th c or older), stripped stone, low beams and two woodburners, Charles Wells ales and decent range of wines, roomy thatched restaurant extension with comfortably padded dining chairs around sturdy tables on floorboards, plenty of pictures on plum walls, beams, wide choice of well liked food from lunchtime sandwiches and baked potatoes up, prompt friendly service; background music; children and dogs (in bar) welcome, large back garden with picnic-sets among shrubs, tables beneath canopy on separate sheltered terrace, summer barbecues, closed Sun evening. *(Dennis and Doreen Haward, Dave Braisted)*

LONG WITTENHAM   SU5493
Plough (01865) 407738
High Street; OX14 4QH Welcoming
17th-c local with low beams, inglenook fires
and lots of brass, two or three well kept
ales including Butcombe, good reasonably
priced home-cooked food (not Sun evening)
from sandwiches and traditional choices to
interesting specials, friendly helpful young
staff, dining room, games in public bar;
children welcome, Thames moorings
at bottom of long garden, open all day.
(David Lamb)

LONGCOT   SU2790
King & Queen (01793) 784348
Shrivenham Road, off B4508; SN7 7TL
Friendly beamed pub with good food cooked
by landlord-chef, three well kept ales
including Loose Cannon and Ramsbury,
proper ciders; occasional live music Fri, pool
and darts, free wi-fi; children and dogs (they
have a couple) welcome, terrace tables,
six bedrooms, closed Mon lunchtime.
(R K Phillips)

MAIDENSGROVE   SU7288
Five Horseshoes (01491) 641282
*Off B480 and B481, W of village;
RG9 6EX* Character 16th-c dining pub set
high in the Chilterns; rambling bar with
low ceiling and log fire, good food (not Sun
evening) from changing menu including
home-smoked salmon and seasonal game,
friendly service, well kept Brakspears and
good choice of wines by the glass, airy
conservatory restaurant; children and dogs
(in bar) welcome, plenty of tables in suntrap
garden with rolling countryside views,
wood-fired pizzas on summer weekends, good
walks, open all day Sat, Sun, closed Mon.
(Susan and John Douglas)

MARSH BALDON   SU5699
Seven Stars (01865) 343337
*The Baldons signed off A4074 N of
Dorchester; OX44 9LP* Enthusiastically
run, community-owned beamed pub on edge
of village green; refurbished bar areas, seats
by corner fire, good food all day including
plenty of gluten-free and vegetarian choices,
Fullers, Loose Cannon and a couple of local
guests, raftered barn restaurant; children,
dogs and muddy boots welcome, seats outside
overlooking fields and horses, open all day
(till midnight Fri, Sat). *(Jane Taylor and
David Dutton, Neil and Angela Huxter)*

MURCOTT   SP5815
★ Nut Tree (01865) 331253
*Off B4027 NE of Oxford, via Islip and
Charlton-on-Otmoor; OX5 2RE* Beamed
and thatched 15th-c dining pub, good
imaginative cooking (not cheap) using own
produce including home-reared pigs, neat
friendly young staff, Vale and two guests,
carefully chosen wines; background music;

children and dogs (in bar) welcome, terrace
and pretty garden, unusual gargoyles on front
wall (modelled loosely on local characters),
closed Sun evening, Mon. *(R A and E J
Harkness)*

NORTH MORETON   SU5689
Bear at Home (01235) 811311
*Off A4130 Didcot–Wallingford; High
Street; OX11 9AT* Dating from the 15th c
with traditional beamed bar, cosy fireside
areas and dining part with stripped-pine
furniture, friendly service from father and
daughter team, enjoyable sensibly priced
home-made food, Timothy Taylors, a beer for
the pub from West Berkshire and a couple
of local guests (July beer festival), Weston's
cider and a dozen wines by the glass; Mon
quiz; children and dogs welcome, nice back
garden overlooking cricket pitch, aunt sally,
pretty village, open all day Sat, closed Sun
evening. *(Eddie Edwards)*

NORTHMOOR   SP4202
Red Lion (01865) 300301
*B4449 SE of Stanton Harcourt;
OX29 5SX* Renovated 15th-c village pub
now owned by the local community, good
range of well presented freshly made food,
up to four ales such as Brakspears, Cotswold
Lion, Hook Norton and Wychwood, plenty
of wines by the glass, friendly young staff,
cosy atmosphere with heavy beams and
bare stone walls, scrubbed tables, open fire
one end, woodburner the other; free wi-fi;
children, walkers and dogs welcome, garden
tables, open all day Sat, closed Sun evening,
Mon. *(Helene Grygar)*

NUFFIELD   SU6787
Crown (01491) 641335
A4130/B481; RG9 5SJ Attractive little
brick and flint country pub with good home-
made food and well kept Brakspears ales,
efficient friendly service, beamed lounge
bar with bare boards and inglenook log fire;
children and dogs welcome in small garden
room, disabled access, tables out at front
and in enclosed back garden, good walks
(Ridgeway nearby), closed Sun evening, Mon.
(Bob and Margaret Holder)

OXFORD   SP5106
Chequers (01865) 727463
Off High Street; OX1 4DH Narrow 16th-c
courtyard pub tucked away down small
alleyway, several areas on three floors,
interesting architectural features, beams,
panelling and stained glass, eight or so
well kept ales and enjoyable good value
Nicholsons menu, friendly service; walled
garden, open (and food) all day. *(Anon)*

OXFORD   SP5106
★ Eagle & Child (01865) 302925
St Giles; OX1 3LU Long narrow
Nicholsons pub dating from the 16th c with
two charmingly old-fashioned panelled

front rooms, well kept Brakspears, Hook Norton and interesting guests, good choice of food from sandwiches to Sun roasts, friendly service and bustling atmosphere, stripped-brick back dining extension and conservatory, Tolkien and C S Lewis connections (the Inklings writers' group used to meet here); games machine; children allowed in back till 8pm, open (and food all day). *(John Pritchard, Mrs Sally Scott, Neil and Angela Huxter, Ian Herdman, Roger and Donna Huggins)*

OXFORD   SP5105

Head of the River (01865) 721600

Folly Bridge; between St Aldates and Christ Church Meadow; OX1 4LB Civilised well renovated pub by river, boats for hire and nearby walks; spacious split-level downstairs bar with dividing brick arches, flagstones and bare boards, well kept Fullers/Gales beers and good choice of wines by the glass, popular pubby food from sandwiches up, good service, daily papers; background music; tables on stepped heated waterside terrace, 12 bedrooms, open all day. *(Martin and Sue Day, Mrs Sally Scott)*

OXFORD   SP5203

Isis Farmhouse (01865) 243854

Off Donnington Bridge Road; no car access; OX4 4EL Charming waterside spot for early 19th-c former farmhouse (accessible only to walkers/cyclists), relaxed lived-in interior with two woodburners, short choice of enjoyable home-made food (sensible prices, no credit cards), Appleford and a guest such as Shotover, nice wines and interesting soft drinks, afternoon teas with wonderful home-baked cakes; some live music; children and dogs welcome, picnic-sets out on terrace and in garden, aunt sally by arrangement, canoe hire, short walk to Iffley Lock and nearby lavishly decorated early Norman church, open all day Thurs-Sat in summer (Fri-Sun in winter) and all bank holidays including Christmas. *(Isobel Mackinlay)*

OXFORD   SP5106

Kings Arms (01865) 242369

Holywell Street; OX1 3SP Relaxed place dating from the early 17th c and popular with locals and students, cosy rooms up and down steps, lots of panelling and pictures, well kept Youngs ales and guests, several wines by the glass, eating area with counter servery; free wi-fi; dogs welcome, a few tables outside, open from 10.30am. *(D J and P M Taylor)*

OXFORD   SP5006

Kite (01865) 248546

Mill Street; OX2 0AL Friendly refurbished Victorian pub run by Australian family, half

a dozen real ales and a couple of ciders on tap, tasty food including all day breakfast and good value two-for-one midweek deal; seven bedrooms (shared bathrooms), open all day. *(Richard Tilbrook)*

OXFORD   SP5106

Lamb & Flag (01865) 515787

St Giles/Banbury Road; OX1 3JS Old pub owned by nearby college, modern airy front room with light wood panelling and big windows over street, more atmosphere in back rooms with stripped stonework and low-boarded ceilings, a beer by Palmers for the pub (L&F Gold), Skinners Betty Stogs and guests, real cider/perry, some lunchtime food including sandwiches and home-made pies, Thomas Hardy's *Jude the Obscure* connection; open all day. *(Rob Anderson)*

OXFORD   SP5006

Old Bookbinders (01865) 553549

Victor Street; OX2 6BT Dark and mellow family-run local tucked away in the Jericho area; friendly and unpretentious, with old fittings and lots of interesting bric-a-brac, Greene King ales and three guests, decent choice of whiskies and other spirits, enjoyable french-leaning food including speciality crêpes and lunchtime/early evening set menu; board games and shove-ha'penny, Tues quiz, open mike night Sun; children, dogs and students welcome, entertaining features like multiple door handles to the gents', closed Mon and lunchtimes Tues, Weds, otherwise open all day. *(Josh Mullett)*

OXFORD   SP4907

Perch (01865) 728891

Binsey Lane, on right after river bridge leaving city on A420; OX2 0NG Beautifully set 17th-c thatched limestone dining pub in tiny riverside hamlet; good food from interesting varied menu, efficient friendly young staff, three well kept local ales including Hook Norton and plenty of wines by the glass from good list (some english ones), recent refurbishment blending well with old beams and flagstones, a couple of woodburners; June folk festival and other events recalling pub's connection with Lewis Carroll; children, walkers and dogs welcome, lovely garden running down to Thames Path, moorings, open (and food) all day. *(Neil and Angela Huxter, Colin McKerrow)*

OXFORD   SP5105

Royal Blenheim (01865) 242355

Ebbes Street; OX1 1PT Popular airy 19th-c corner pub, opened by Queen Victoria during her golden jubilee, and now the tap for the White Horse Brewery; their range and many interesting guests, good value straightforward

---

We accept no free drinks or meals and inspections are anonymous.

food (all day weekends) including some decent vegetarian options, friendly chatty staff, single room with original tiled floor, raised perimeter booth seating; big-screen sports TV, Weds quiz, Mon knitting club; open all day (till midnight Fri, Sat). *(Anon)*

OXFORD SP5106

Turf Tavern (01865) 243235

Bath Place; via St Helen's Passage, between Holywell Street and New College Lane; OX1 3SU Interesting character pub hidden away behind high walls, small dark-beamed bars with lots of snug areas, up to a dozen constantly changing ales including Greene King, Weston's cider and winter mulled wine, popular reasonably priced food from sandwiches up, pleasant helpful service; newspapers and free wi-fi; children and dogs welcome, three walled-in courtyards (one with own bar), open (and food) all day. *(John Pritchard, Roger and Donna Huggins)*

OXFORD SP5106

White Horse (01865) 204801

Broad Street; OX1 3BB Bustling and studenty, squeezed between parts of Blackwell's bookshop; small narrow bar with snug raised back alcove, low beams and timbers, beautiful view of the Clarendon Building and Sheldonian, half a dozen ales including Brakspears, Sharps, Shotover and a house beer from Marstons, enjoyable home-made food, friendly staff; open all day. *(Roger and Donna Huggins)*

PISHILL SU7190

★**Crown** (01491) 638364

B480 Nettlebed–Watlington; RG9 6HH 15th-c inn at heart of the Chilterns; beamed bars with old local photographs, prints and maps, some panelling and nice mix of wooden tables and chairs, Brakspears and Rebellion ales, seven wines by the glass and a dozen malt whiskies, decent food, knocked-through back area with standing timbers and three log fires (not always lit); priest hole is said to be one of the largest in the country; well behaved children welcome, dogs in bar, seats in pretty garden with thatched bar for functions, lots of nearby walks, self-catering cottage, closed Sun evening. *(Di and Mike Gillam)*

PLAY HATCH SU7477

Shoulder of Mutton (0118) 947 3908

W of Henley Road (A4155) roundabout; RG4 9QU Dining pub with low-ceilinged log-fire bar and large back conservatory restaurant, good food including signature mutton dishes, well kept Greene King and guests such as nearby Loddon, reasonably priced house wines, friendly attentive service; children welcome, picnic-sets in carefully tended walled garden with well, closed Sun evening. *(John Pritchard)*

ROKE SU6293

Home Sweet Home (01491) 838249

Off B4009 Benson–Watlington; OX10 6JD Wadworths country pub with two smallish bars, heavy stripped beams, big log fire and traditional furniture, carpeted room on right leading to restaurant area, good food served by friendly staff; background music, Rokefest music/beer festival late May Bank Holiday; children welcome and dogs, low-walled front garden, open all day Sun till 8pm (food till 3pm), closed Mon. *(Rob Peacock, Colin McLachlan)*

ROTHERFIELD PEPPARD SU7081

Unicorn (01491) 628674

Colmore Lane; RG9 5LX Attractive country pub in the Chilterns, run by same people as the Little Angel, Henley (see Berkshire) and Cherry Tree, Stoke Row (see below); bustling bar with open fire, Brakspears ales and good wines, dining room with high-backed chairs around mix of tables on stripped boards, well liked interesting food including lunchtime sandwiches and daily specials, friendly service; Thurs quiz and tapas night; seats out in front and in pretty back garden, open all day weekends. *(Phoebe Peacock)*

SHENINGTON SP3742

Bell (01295) 670274

Off A422 NW of Banbury; OX15 6NQ Popular home cooking in unpretentious 17th-c two-room pub, well kept Hook Norton Hooky and good range of wines by the glass, friendly service, heavy beams, some flagstones, stripped stone and pine panelling, two woodburners; children in eating areas and dogs in bar, picnic-sets out at front, charming quiet village with good walks, closed Sun evening, Mon. *(Anon)*

SHIPTON-UNDER-WYCHWOOD SP2717

★**Lamb** (01993) 830465

High Street; off A361 to Burford; OX7 6DQ Mother and son team at this handsome stone inn, beamed bar with oak-panelled settle, farmhouse chairs and polished tables on wood-block flooring, stripped-stone walls, church candles and log fire, Greene King IPA and a couple of guests, good wines (plenty by the glass) and well liked food including children's menu, pleasant friendly service, restaurant area; free wi-fi; dogs allowed in bar (they have their own), wheelchair access, garden with modern furniture on terrace, five themed bedrooms, open all day. *(R K Phillips)*

SHIPTON-UNDER-WYCHWOOD SP2717

Wychwood Inn (01993) 831185

High Street; OX7 6BA Refurbished and under same ownership as the Lamb in same village; contemporary décor in open-plan bar/dining area, more period character in flagstoned public bar with black beams and inglenook, up to eight real ales including one badged for them and plenty of wines by the glass, enjoyable food from wraps to grills, friendly young staff; sports TV, darts; children and dogs welcome, picnic-sets on small terrace, shop in glassed-in coach entrance, five bedrooms, open all day. *(Liz Bell)*

SHRIVENHAM   SU2488
Prince of Wales   (01793) 782268
High Street; off A420 or B4000 NE of Swindon; SN6 8AF 17th-c stone-built local continuing well under present landlord, good freshly cooked food from light meals to specials at fair prices, well kept Wadworths ales, pleasant helpful staff, low-beamed lounge with log fire, small dining area, side bar with darts; quiz nights and fortnightly jazz; children welcome, picnic-sets in secluded beer garden overlooking church. *(Dr John Clements, R K Phillips)*

SHUTFORD   SP3840
George & Dragon   (01295) 780320
Church Lane; OX15 6PG Ancient stone pub set down from the church; cosy L-shaped bar with flagstones and impressive fireplace, five well kept ales including Hook Norton, decent choice of wines by the glass, good locally sourced bar and restaurant food (not Sun evening, Mon), friendly service, dining room and separate room for sports TV, darts and dominoes; children and dogs (in bar) welcome, small garden overlooking village, aunt sally, closed lunchtimes Mon-Thurs, open all day weekends. *(Isobel Mackinlay)*

SIBFORD GOWER   SP3537
Wykham Arms   (01295) 788808
Signed off B4035 Banbury to Shipston-on-Stour; Temple Mill Road; OX15 5RX Cottagey 17th-c thatched and flagstoned dining pub, good food from light lunchtime menu up, friendly attentive staff, two well kept changing ales and 23 wines by the glass, comfortable open-plan interior with low beams and stripped stone, glass-covered well, inglenook; children and dogs welcome, country views from big garden, lovely manor house opposite and good walks nearby, open all day Sun, closed Mon. *(Lindy Andrews)*

SOULDERN   SP5231
Fox   (01869) 345284
Off B4100; Fox Lane; OX27 7JW Early 19th-c pub set in delightful village, open-plan beamed layout with woodburner in two-way fireplace, enjoyable fairly priced food, well kept ales including Hook Norton and several wines by the glass, friendly attentive service; terrace and walled garden, four bedrooms, open all day Sat, till 4pm Sun. *(Anon)*

SOUTH NEWINGTON   SP4033
Duck on the Pond   (01295) 721166
A361; OX15 4JE Refurbished roadside

dining pub with small flagstoned bar and linked carpeted eating areas up a step, well liked food from lunchtime ciabattas up including some good vegetarian choices and popular family Sun lunch, Hook Norton and a couple of guests, cheerful pleasant staff, woodburner; background music; no dogs, spacious grounds with tables on deck and lawn, aunt sally, pond with waterfowl, walk down to River Swere, open all day weekends, food till 7pm Sun. *(Harvey Brown)*

SOUTH STOKE   SU5983
Perch & Pike   (01491) 872415
Off B4009 2 miles N of Goring; RG8 0JS Brick and flint pub just a field away from the Thames, low-beamed flagstoned bar with open fire, well kept Brakspears and decent wines by the glass, enjoyable home-made food from varied changing menu, friendly helpful staff, sizeable restaurant in converted barn; children welcome, dogs in bar and snug, tables on terrace and flower-bordered lawn, four bedrooms, open all day Sat, till 6pm Sun. *(Dr and Mrs S G Barber)*

STANTON ST JOHN   SP5709
Talk House   (01865) 351654
Middle Road/Wheatley Road (B4027 just outside village); OX33 1EX Attractive part-thatched dining pub under new management; older part on left with steeply pitched rafters soaring above stripped-stone walls, mix of old dining chairs and big stripped tables, large rugs on flagstones; rest of building converted more recently but in similar style with massive beams, flagstones or stoneware tiles, and log fires below low mantelbeams, food from sandwiches up (not Sun), three Fullers ales and several wines by the glass; children welcome, inner courtyard with teak tables and chairs, a few picnic-sets on side grass, bedrooms, open all day except Sun evening. *(Carol and Barry Craddock)*

STEEPLE ASTON   SP4725
★ Red Lion   (01869) 340225
Off A4260 12 miles N of Oxford; OX25 4RY Cheerful village pub with neatly kept beamed and partly panelled bar, antique settle and other good furnishings, well kept Hook Norton ales and good choice of wines by the glass, enjoyable food from shortish menu including pizzas served by obliging young staff, back conservatory-style dining extension; well behaved children welcome lunchtime and until 7pm, dogs in bar, suntrap front garden with lovely flowers and shrubs, parking may be awkward, open all day Sat, till 5pm Sun. *(Robert Watt)*

STEVENTON   SU4691
North Star
Stocks Lane, The Causeway, central westward turn off B4017; OX13 6SG Very traditional little village pub through yew tree gateway; tiled entrance corridor, main area with ancient high-backed settles

forming booth in front of brick fireplace, well kept Morland Original and a couple of guests from side tap room, hatch service to another room with plain seating, a couple of tables and coal fire, simple lunchtime food, friendly staff; dogs welcome, tables on front grass, aunt sally, open all day weekends, closed Mon and weekday lunchtimes. *(Anon)*

STOKE LYNE   SP5628
Peyton Arms 07546 066160
From minor road off B4110 N of Bicester fork left into village; OX27 8SD
Beautifully situated and largely unspoilt one-room stone alehouse, character landlord (Mick the Hat) and loyal regulars, very well kept Hook Norton from casks behind small corner bar, no food apart from filled rolls, inglenook fire, tiled floor and lots of memorabilia, games area with darts and pool; no children or dogs; pleasant garden with aunt sally, open all day weekends till 7pm, closed weekday lunchtimes apart from Tues, and may shut early if quiet. *(Rob Anderson)*

STOKE ROW   SU6884
Cherry Tree (01491) 680430
Off B481 at Highmoor; RG9 5QA
Sympathetically modernised 18th-c pub-restaurant (originally three cottages), enjoyable often interesting food from sharing platters to daily specials, Brakspears ales and decent wines by the glass, helpful friendly staff, several small linked rooms mainly set for dining, heavy low beams, stripped boards and flagstones; background music, TV in bar; well behaved children and dogs welcome, lots of tables in attractive garden, nearby walks, four good bedrooms in converted barn, open all day (food all day Sun). *(Bob and Margaret Holder)*

STOKE ROW   SU6884
★Crooked Billet (01491) 681048
Nottwood Lane, off B491 N of Reading – OS Sheet 175 map reference 684844; RG9 5PU Lovely place, but more restaurant than pub; charming rustic layout with heavy beams, flagstones, antique pubby furnishings and great inglenook log fire, crimson Victorian-style dining room, very good interesting food (all day weekends) cooked by owner-chef using local ingredients, cheaper set lunches Mon-Fri, helpful friendly staff, Brakspears Oxford Gold tapped from the cask (no counter), good wines, relaxed homely atmosphere; weekly live music often including established artists; children very welcome, big garden by Chilterns beechwoods, open all day. *(Colin McLachlan)*

SUNNINGWELL   SP4900
Flowing Well (01865) 735846
Just N of Abingdon; OX13 6RB
Refurbished timbered pub (former 19th-c rectory); popular food including british tapas, range of burgers and other pub favourites, a couple of Greene King ales and a guest, good

choice of wines; children welcome, dogs in bar, large heated raised terrace, more seats in garden with small well, open (and food) all day. *(Harvey Brown)*

SWINFORD   SP4308
Talbot (01865) 881348
B4044 just S of Eynsham; OX29 4BT
Roomy and comfortable 17th-c beamed pub, well kept Arkells beers tapped from cooled casks, good choice of wines and soft drinks, enjoyable reasonably priced pubby food including OAP lunch deal and Sun carvery, friendly staff, long attractive flagstoned bar with some stripped stone, cheerful log-effect gas fire; charity quiz second Mon of month; children and dogs welcome, garden with decked area overlooking Wharf Stream, nice walk along lovely stretch of the Thames towpath, moorings quite nearby, 11 bedrooms, open all day. *(S F Parrinder)*

THAME   SP7105
Cross Keys (01844) 218202
Park Street/East Street; OX9 3HP
Friendly one-bar 19th-c corner local, eight well kept ales including own Thame beers (not always available) and half a dozen ciders, no food except scotch eggs but can bring your own; courtyard garden, open all day weekends. *(Gus Swan)*

THAME   SP7005
James Figg (01844) 260166
Cornmarket; OX9 2BL Friendly coaching inn, clean and well furnished, with four well kept ales including Purity and Vale, Addlestone's and Aspall's ciders, ten wines by the glass, enjoyable straightforward locally sourced food from sandwiches up, open fire in brick fireplace, portrait of eponymous James Figg (local 18th-c boxer) and photos of more recent sporting champions, converted stables with own bar for music/functions; gets busier and noisier in the evening; children and dogs welcome, back garden, open all day. *(Gus Swan)*

THAME   SP7006
★Thatch (01844) 214340
Lower High Street; OX9 2AA Characterful timbered and thatched 16th-c dining pub (part of the Peach group); good interesting food from deli boards to daily specials, well kept ales, nice wines and some interesting gins, friendly personable service, cosy bar and appealing collection of little higgledy-piggledy rooms, heavy beams, old quarry tiles, flagstones and double-sided inglenook, smart contemporary furnishings and bold paintwork; children welcome, prettily planted terraced garden with tables under parasols, open (and food) all day. *(Gus Swan)*

THRUPP   SP4815
★Boat (01865) 374279
Brown sign to pub off A4260 just N of Kidlington; OX5 1JY Attractive 16th-c

stone pub set back from the southern Oxford Canal (moorings), low ceilings, bare boards and some ancient floor tiles, log fires and old coal stove, enjoyable well priced home-made food including vegetarian options, specials and Sun carvery, friendly service, three Greene King ales and a guest, decent wines; gets busy in summer; children and dogs welcome, fenced garden behind with plenty of tables, open (and food) all day weekends. (S F Parrinder)

TOOT BALDON SP5600
★ Mole (01865) 340001
Between A4074 and B480 SE of Oxford; OX44 9NG Light open-plan restaurantsy dining pub with very good if not cheap food (booking advisable), friendly attentive service, nice wines by the glass, Hook Norton and a guest, leather sofas by bar, neat country furniture or more formal leather dining chairs in linked areas including conservatory, stripped 18th-c beams and big open fire; background music; children welcome, no dogs inside, lovely gardens, open all day. (Phoebe Peacock)

UFFINGTON SU3089
Fox & Hounds (01367) 820680)
High Street; SN7 7RP Traditional beamed village local with enjoyable fairly priced home-made food (not Sun evening) including one or two asian choices, three changing ales, friendly attentive staff; quiz fourth Mon of month, some live music; children and dogs welcome, garden picnic-sets, near Tom Brown's School Museum and handy for White Horse Hill, two ground-floor bedrooms, open all day. (Tina and David Woods-Taylor)

WALLINGFORD SU6089
George (01491) 836665
High Street; OX10 0BS Handsome extended 16th-c coaching inn, enjoyable food in bistro, restaurant or beamed bar with splendid fireplace, three Rebellion ales and good choice of other drinks, friendly helpful service; tables in spacious central courtyard, 39 bedrooms, good antiques centre close by. (George Atkinson)

WALLINGFORD SU6089
Partridge (01491) 839305
St Mary's Street; OX10 0ET More restaurant than pub; contemporary airy décor, bare boards and comfortably modern furnishings including bar stools, leather sofas and armchairs, open fires, good well presented food (not especially cheap) from sharing plates up, popular Sun roasts (should book), well chosen wines, neat helpful staff; children welcome, pleasant

back terrace, four bedrooms (three sharing bathroom), may be possible to park in St Leonard's Lane off Thames Street, closed weekday lunchtimes and Sun evening. (Colin McLachlan)

WANTAGE SU3987
King Alfreds Head (01235) 771595
Market Place; OX12 8AH Updated pub set back from market square, reasonable choice of enjoyable well priced food including one or two specials, Sun carvery, ales such as St Austell and plenty of wines by the glass, helpful friendly staff, linked areas, leather sofas by log fire; background music, sports TV, free wi-fi; children and dogs welcome, sizeable beer garden with summer barbecues and some live music, open all day. (R K Phillips)

WANTAGE SU3988
Lamb (01235) 766768
Mill Street, past square and Bell pub; downhill then bend to left; OX12 9AB Popular 17th-c thatched pub with low beams, log fire and cosy corners, well kept ales including Fullers London Pride from brick-faced bar, good straightforward food at fair prices; children welcome, disabled facilities, garden with play area, open all day. (Anon)

WANTAGE SU3987
★ Royal Oak (01235) 763129
Newbury Street; OX12 8DF Popular two-bar corner local with well kept West Berkshire ales (some named for the friendly knowledgeable landlord) along with Wadworths 6X and plenty of guests, excellent range of ciders and perries too, lots of decorative pump clips, old ship photographs, darts; closed weekday lunchtimes. (Gus Swan)

WARBOROUGH SU6093
★ Six Bells (01865) 858265
The Green S; just E of A329, 4 miles N of Wallingford; OX10 7DN Thatched 16th-c pub opposite village cricket green, well kept Brakspears and wide choice of good interesting food, friendly attentive staff, low beams and attractive country furnishings in small linked areas off bar, bare boards, stripped stone and big log fire; tables out in front and in pleasant orchard garden behind. (Colin McLachlan, John Pritchard, Roy Hoing)

WARDINGTON SP4946
Hare & Hounds (01295) 750645
A361 Banbury–Daventry; OX17 1SH Comfortable traditional village local with well kept Hook Norton and a friendly welcome, low-ceilinged bar leading to dining

---

The letters and figures after the name of each town are its Ordnance Survey map reference. *Using the Guide* at the beginning of the book explains how it helps you find a pub, in road atlases or large-scale maps as well as in our own maps.

area, woodburner, enjoyable home-made food; darts and dominoes; children and dogs welcome, garden with aunt sally, open all day Fri, Sat, till 8pm Sun. *(Harvey Brown)*

WESTON-ON-THE-GREEN SP5318
Chequers (01869) 351743
Handy for M40 junction 9 via A34; Northampton Road (B430); OX25 3QH
Extended thatched village pub with three areas off large semicircular raftered bar, enjoyable fair-priced food including good Sun lunch, well kept Fullers ales and decent wines by the glass, friendly unrushed service, log fires; children welcome, tables in pleasant garden, open all day Sat, till 6pm Sun. *(Paul Denny)*

WHITCHURCH SU6377
Ferry Boat (0118) 984 2161
High Street, near toll bridge; RG8 7DB
Welcoming comfortably updated 18th-c pub with airy log-fire bar and restaurant, good variety of enjoyable home-made food including stone-baked pizzas, friendly prompt service, real ales such as Black Sheep and Timothy Taylors Landlord, several wines by the glass; background music, free wi-fi; children (away from bar) and well behaved dogs welcome, café-style seating in courtyard garden, closed Sun evening, Mon. *(Paul Humphreys)*

WHITCHURCH SU6377
Greyhound (0118) 996 8947
High Street, just over toll bridge from Pangbourne; RG8 7EL Attractive former ferryman's cottage with small knocked-together rooms, low-beams and log fire, well kept Adnams Broadside, Black Sheep and Sharps Doom Bar, very good value tasty pub food (not Sun evening) from well filled baguettes up, friendly efficient staff; children and dogs welcome, small sheltered back garden, attractive village on Thames Path, open all day except Mon lunchtime.
(Paul Humphreys, John Pritchard)

WITNEY SP3509
Angel (01993) 703238
Market Square; OX28 6AL Wide choice of enjoyable well priced food from good sandwiches up in this unpretentious 17th-c town local, a house beer from Wychwood along with Hobgoblin, Brakspears, Marstons and occasional guest, quick friendly service even when packed, daily papers, hot coal fire; background music, sports TVs, pool; lovely hanging baskets, back terrace with smokers' shelter, parking nearby can be difficult, open all day. *(Phoebe Peacock)*

WITNEY SP3509
★**Fleece** (01993) 892270
Church Green; OX28 4AZ Smart civilised town pub (part of the Peach group), popular for its wide choice of good often imaginative food from sandwiches and deli boards up,

fixed-price lunchtime deal too, friendly helpful service, Greene King and a couple of guests, decent coffee, leather armchairs on wood floors, restaurant; background and occasional live music, daily papers; children welcome, café-style tables out at front overlooking green, ten affordable comfortable bedrooms, good breakfast, open (and food) all day from 9am.
(R K Phillips, Mrs B H Adams)

WITNEY SP3509
Hollybush (01993) 708073
Corn Street; OX28 6BT Popular recently refurbished 18th-c pub under same ownership as the Horseshoes across the road; front bar with woodburner in big fireplace, settles and window seats, various dining areas off, good food from sandwiches and deli boards up, three well kept ales including a house beer from Greene King, good wine selection, efficient friendly staff; background music, free wi-fi; children and dogs welcome, open (and food) all day. *(Anon)*

WITNEY SP3510
★**Horseshoes** (01993) 703086
Corn Street, junction with Holloway Road; OX28 6BS Attractive 16th-c stone pub, good freshly made food from pubby choices up, also a gluten-free menu and deli counter, three changing ales and decent wines by the glass, friendly accommodating staff, heavy beams, stripped-stone walls and log fires, separate back dining room; children and dogs welcome, tables on sunny terrace, open all day. *(Gus Swan)*

WOLVERCOTE SP4909
Plough (01865) 556969
First Turn/Wolvercote Green; OX2 8AH
Comfortably worn-in pubby linked areas, armchairs and Victorian-style carpeted bays in main lounge, well kept Greene King ales, farm cider and decent wines by the glass, friendly helpful staff and bustling atmosphere, enjoyable good value usual food in flagstoned former stables dining room and library (children allowed here), traditional snug, woodburner; dogs welcome in bar (there's a friendly dub dog), picnic-sets on part-decked terrace looking over rough meadow to canal and woods, open all day weekends. *(Harvey Brown)*

WOODSTOCK SP4417
Black Prince (01993) 811530
Manor Road (A44 N); OX20 1XJ
Old pub with one modernised low-ceilinged bar, timbers, stripped stone and log fire, suit of armour, good value home-made food from sandwiches to specials, well kept St Austell, Sharps and guests, friendly service, some live music; outside lavatories; children, walkers and dogs welcome, tables in pretty garden by small River Glyme, nearby right of way into Blenheim parkland, open all day.
(Malcolm Phillips)

WOODSTOCK   SP4416
Woodstock Arms (01993) 811251
Market Street; OX20 1SX Welcoming
16th-c heavy-beamed stripped-stone
pub, enjoyable home-made food (not Sun
evening), three well kept Greene King
ales and good wine choice, prompt helpful
service, log fire in splendid stone fireplace,
long narrow bar with end eating area
(refurbishment planned as we went to
press); background music; children and dogs
welcome, courtyard tables, open all day.
(Rob Anderson)

WOOLSTONE   SU2987
White Horse (01367) 820726
Off B4507; SN7 7QL Appealing partly
thatched pub with Victorian gables and
latticed windows, plush furnishings, spacious
beamed and part-panelled bar, two big open
fires, Arkells ales and enjoyable good value
food from lunchtime open sandwiches up,
wood-fired pizzas Thurs and Sun, restaurant;
free wi-fi; well behaved children and dogs
allowed, plenty of seats in front and back
gardens, secluded interesting village handy
for White Horse and Ridgeway, six bedrooms,
open all day. *(Anon)*

WOOTTON   SP4320
Killingworth Castle (01993) 811401
*Glympton Road; B4027 N of Woodstock;
OX20 1EJ* Under same ownership as
the Ebrington Arms in Ebrington (see
Gloucestershire); striking three-storey
17th-c coaching inn with simply furnished
candlelit rooms, built-in wall seats and mix
of chairs around farmhouse tables on bare
boards, woodburner in stone fireplace and
another fire, own Yubberton ales plus local
guests, cider and lager from Cotswold, good
range of spirits featuring smaller british
producers, popular interesting food
(themed evenings), friendly staff; garden
with circular picnic-sets under green
parasols, bedrooms, open all day from 9am.
(Gerry Price)

Post Office address codings confusingly give the impression that some pubs are in
Oxfordshire, when they're really in Berkshire, Buckinghamshire, Gloucestershire or
Warwickshire (which is where we list them).

Shropshire

 BRIDGNORTH   SO7192   Map 4

Old Castle £

(01746) 711420 – www.oldcastlebridgnorth.co.uk
West Castle Street; WV16 4AB

Traditional town pub, relaxed and friendly, with generous helpings of good value pubby food, well kept ales and good-sized suntrap terrace

Once two cottages, this is a cheerful town pub with plenty of customers. The low-beamed open-plan bar is properly pubby with some genuine character: you'll find tiles and bare boards, cushioned wall banquettes and settles around cast-iron-framed tables, and bar stools arranged along the counter where the friendly landlord and his staff serve Hobsons Town Crier, Sharps Doom Bar, Thwaites Lancaster Bomber and Wye Valley HPA on handpump. A back conservatory extension has darts and pool; background music and big-screen TV for sports events. A big plus is the sunny back terrace with picnic-sets, lovely hanging baskets, big pots of flowers, shrub borders, and decking at the far end that gives an elevated view over the west side of town; children's playthings. Do walk up the street to see the ruined castle – its 20-metre Norman tower tilts at such an extraordinary angle that it makes the leaning tower of Pisa look like a model of rectitude.

The reasonably priced, popular food includes sandwiches and baguettes, devilled whitebait, chicken dippers with barbecue sauce, vegetarian, beef and cajun chicken burgers with onion rings and chips, lasagne, beef curry, faggots in onion gravy, fish pie, minted lamb shank, a mixed grill, and puddings. *Benchmark main dish: steak in ale pie £9.00. Two-course evening meal £14.50.*

Punch ~ Tenant Bryn Charles Masterman ~ Real ale ~ Open 11.30-11 (11.30 Sat); 11.30-10 Sun ~ Bar food 12-3, 6.30-8.30 ~ Children welcome ~ Dogs welcome ~ Wi-fi
Recommended by R T and J C Moggridge, Robert Parker

 **CARDINGTON**   SO5095   Map 4

Royal Oak

(01694) 771266 – www.at-the-oak.com
Village signposted off B4371 Church Stretton–Much Wenlock, pub behind church; also reached via narrow lanes from A49; SY6 7JZ

Lovely country spot, heaps of character inside and seasonal bar food

Our readers enjoy their visits to this well run and friendly country pub very much – it's said to be Shropshire's oldest continuously licensed pub. The rambling low-beamed traditional bar has a roaring winter log fire, a cauldron, black kettle and pewter jugs in a vast inglenook fireplace, aged standing timbers from a knocked-through wall, and red and green tapestry seats solidly capped in elm; shove-ha'penny and dominoes. Big Shed Engineers Best, Ludlow Best, Sharps Doom Bar and Wye Valley Butty Bach on handpump, several wines by the glass and farm cider. A comfortable dining area has exposed old beams and studwork. This is glorious country for walks, such as the one to the summit of Caer Caradoc, a couple of miles to the west (ask for directions at the pub), and the front courtyard makes the most of its beautiful position.

Good, enjoyable food includes lunchtime baguettes, field mushroom stuffed with smoked bacon and topped with cheddar, smoked mackerel pâté, butternut squash lasagne, pork, black pudding, leek and chilli sausages with red wine gravy, steak and mushroom or fish pie, gammon with egg and pineapple, duck breast with plum, shallot and red wine sauce, mixed grill, and puddings. *Benchmark main dish: rump of lamb with rosemary, redcurrant and red wine jus £13.95. Two-course evening meal £17.00.*

Free house ~ Licensees Steve and Eira Oldham ~ Real ale ~ Open 12-2.30, 6-11; 12-11 Sat, Sun; 12-2.30, 6.30-11 in winter; closed winter Sun evening, Mon ~ Bar food 12-2.30, 6 (6.30 Jan-Mar)-9 ~ Restaurant ~ Children welcome ~ Dogs allowed in bar ~ Wi-fi
Recommended by Dr Peter Crawshaw, Tony Tollitt, Peter Meister, Dave Braisted

CHETWYND ASTON   SJ7517   Map 7

Fox 🏠 ▣ ♀ 🍺

(01952) 815940 – www.brunningandprice.co.uk/fox
Village signposted off A41 and A518 just S of Newport; TF10 9LQ

Civilised dining pub with generous helpings of well liked food and a fine array of drinks served by ever attentive staff

The spreading garden behind this neatly kept 1920s pub is quite lovely, with a sunny terrace, picnic-sets tucked into the shade of mature trees and extensive views across quiet country fields. Inside, it's a big place but there are cosy corners too, and the courteous staff cope well with the crowds. A series of linked areas, one with a broad arched ceiling, has plenty of tables in all shapes and sizes, some quite elegant, and a loosely matching diversity of comfortable chairs, all laid out in a way that's fine for eating but works equally well for just drinking and chatting. There are masses of attractive prints, three open fires and some oriental rugs on polished parquet, boards or attractive floor tiling; big windows and careful lighting contribute to the relaxed atmosphere; board games. The handsome bar counter, with a decent complement of bar stools, serves an excellent changing range of about 18 wines by the glass, 40 malt whiskies, 20 gins and Phoenix Brunning & Price Original, Three Tuns XXX, Woods Shropshire Lad and three quickly changing guests on handpump. Good disabled access.

Well executed food includes sandwiches, blue cheese beignets with smoked chilli jelly, a charcuterie plate for two to share, satay chicken with mango, cashew nut and noodle salad, spring onion and red pepper falafel with couscous, pomegranate and mint dressing, honey-glazed ham and free-range eggs, smoked haddock and salmon fishcakes, pork tenderloin with spring onion mash, rhubarb purée and sage crackling, and puddings such as cherry panna cotta with boozy cherries and chocolate brownie with chocolate fudge sauce. *Benchmark main dish: steak burger with toppings, coleslaw and chips £12.45. Two-course evening meal £20.00.*

Brunning & Price ~ Manager Samantha Forrest ~ Real ale ~ Open 11-11 ~ Bar food 12-10 (9.30 Sun) ~ Children welcome ~ Dogs allowed in bar ~ Wi-fi *Recommended by Ian Herdman, Phoebe Peacock*

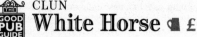

CLUN   SO3080   Map 6

White Horse ◨ £

(01588) 418139 – www.whi-clun.co.uk

The Square; SY7 8JA

Bustling local with own-brewed and guest ales and good value traditional food; bedrooms

If you stay here, the bedrooms are quiet and comfortable and you can make the most of their own-brewed Clun beers: Citadel Strong Ale, Loophole and Pale Ale, with guests such as Hobsons Best and Wye Valley Butty Bach, on handpump, served by attentive staff. They also keep five wines by the glass, a few malt whiskies and farm cider. There's always a friendly mix of both regulars and visitors. The low-beamed front bar is cosy and friendly and warmed in winter by an inglenook woodburning stove; from here, a door leads into a separate little dining room with a rare plank and munton screen. In the games room at the back you'll find a TV, games machine, darts, pool, juke box and board games; small garden.

 Fair value food includes sandwiches, home-breaded brie with redcurrant jelly, smoked salmon and prawn cocktail, mushroom stroganoff, liver and bacon casserole, sweet and sour battered chicken, pork sausages with egg and baked beans, beer-battered haddock and chips, lamb cutlets with redcurrant and rosemary gravy, and puddings such as hot chocolate fudge cake and pavlova with fruit and kirsch. *Benchmark main dish: salmon with green herb and mustard sauce £10.25. Two-course evening meal £16.00.*

Own brew ~ Licensee Jack Limond ~ Real ale ~ No credit cards ~ Open 12-midnight (1am Sat) ~ Bar food 12-2 (3 Sat), 6.30-8.30; 12.30-2.30, 6.30-8.30 Sun ~ Restaurant ~ Children welcome ~ Dogs allowed in bar and bedrooms ~ Wi-fi ~ Live music every second Fri, open mike every second Weds, comedy last Weds of month ~ Bedrooms: $42.50/$70
Recommended by Dr Peter Crawshaw, Mike and Jean Turner

COALPORT   SJ7002   Map 4

Woodbridge ♀ ◨

(01952) 882054 – www.brunningandprice.co.uk/woodbridge

Village signposted off A442 1.5 miles S of A4169 Telford roundabout; down in valley, turn left across narrow bridge into Coalport Road, pub immediately on left; TF8 7JF

Superb Ironbridge Gorge site for extensive handsomely reworked pub, an all-round success

In a smashing spot, this is a comfortable, civilised place with a wide choice of drinks and interesting food. There are log fires and Coalport-style stoves, rugs on broad boards as well as tiles or carpet, black beams in the central part, plenty of polished tables and cosy armchair corners – the atmosphere is relaxed and chatty. A mass of mainly 18th- and 19th-c prints decorates the spreading series of many linked rooms; the historic pictures, often of local scenes, are well worth a look. Phoenix Brunning & Price Original, Dickensian David Hopper Field Pale Ale Vol 2, Joules Blonde, Three Tuns XXX and Weetwood Mad Hatter on handpump, 16 wines by the glass, 45 malt whiskies and 15 gins; service is quick and friendly. Big windows look out on a lovely section of the wooded gorge, with the many tables and chairs on the big raised deck looking over the River Severn.

 Rewarding food includes sandwiches, scallops with ham fritters, pea purée and lemon dressing, spiced moroccan beef with tabbouleh and date purée, crab and leek quiche with crème fraîche potato salad, cumin- and chilli-spiced chicken with tzatziki and roast sweet potato, baked beetroot tart with peppered goats cheese, steak and kidney pudding, tandoori hake fillet with sag aloo potatoes and mint raita, venison haunch with blackberry jus and parsnips, and puddings such as dark chocolate and walnut brownie with chocolate fudge sauce and crème brûlée. *Benchmark main dish: braised lamb shoulder with rosemary and redcurrant jus and dauphinoise potatoes £17.25. Two-course evening meal £19.00.*

Brunning & Price ~ Manager Vrata Krist ~ Real ale ~ Open 11.30-11 (midnight Fri, Sat); 11.30-10.30 Sun ~ Bar food 12-10 (9.30 Sun) ~ Restaurant ~ Children welcome ~ Dogs allowed in bar ~ Wi-fi *Recommended by Dr Kevan Tucker, John Oates, Roger and Donna Huggins, R Anderson*

 IRONBRIDGE   SJ6703   Map 4

Golden Ball

(01952) 432179 – www.goldenballironbridge.co.uk
Brown sign to pub off Madeley Road (B4373) above village centre – pub behind Horse & Jockey, car park beyond on left; TF8 7BA

Low-beamed, partly Elizabethan pub with good value food and drink; bedrooms

Tucked away in a steep little hamlet of other ancient buildings, this is a friendly, unassuming inn. There are worn boards, red-cushioned pews, one or two black beams, a dresser of decorative china and a woodburning stove. Adnams Broadside, Black Sheep, St Austell Tribute, Salopian Golden Thread and a guest ale on handpump, six wines by the glass and a couple of farm ciders; background music and TV. A pretty fairy-lit pergola path leads to the door and a sheltered side courtyard has tables under cocktail parasols. This is a comfortable place to stay overnight and the breakfasts are good. You can walk down to the river, and beyond – but it's pretty steep getting back up.

Well thought-of food includes sandwiches, goats cheese and red onion marmalade tartlet, smoked salmon and prawn timbale, wild mushroom, spinach and ricotta filo parcel with tomato and basil sauce, steak in ale pie, salmon fillet with white wine and dill sauce, honey-roast duck breast with berry sauce, beef wellington, and puddings. *Benchmark main dish: chicken breast wrapped in bacon with stilton sauce £13.50. Two-course evening meal £17.00.*

Enterprise ~ Lease Helen Pickerill ~ Real ale ~ Open 12-3, 5-10.30 Mon-Weds; 12-11.30 Thurs-Sat; 12-10.30 Sun ~ Bar food 12-2.30, 6-8.30; 12-9 Sat; 12-7 Sun ~ Restaurant ~ Children welcome ~ Dogs allowed in bar and bedrooms ~ Wi-fi ~ Live band Fri monthly; open mike second Sun of month ~ Bedrooms: £55/£65 *Recommended by Roger and Donna Huggins*

 LUDLOW   SO5174   Map 6

Charlton Arms

(01584) 872813 – www.thecharltonarms.co.uk
Ludford Bridge, B4361 Overton Road; SY8 1PJ

Fine position for bustling pub near town centre, plenty of space for both drinking and dining, and extensive terraces overlooking the water; bedrooms

If you stay in the well equipped and cosy bedrooms here, you'll have a marvellous view over the River Teme; the two balconies with seats and tables share the same outlook over the water and down to the massive medieval bridge. The character bar has proper pubby tables and chairs on tiled and bricked floors, gluggle jugs along the gantry, a double-sided woodburning stove, and stools against the hop-hung counter where they keep Ludlow Gold and Stairway and Wye Valley Butty Bach on handpump, 11 wines by the glass and a farm cider. The two rooms of the lounge (sharing a two-way woodburning stove) are comfortable and chatty, with tub chairs and armchairs on pale wood flooring as well as high-backed black leather dining chairs around tables for eating, and pictures on pale yellow walls. The dining room, with high-backed striped chairs around attractive tables, looks over the fine bridge. Good, friendly service; background music and board games.

Food is carefully presented and good: sandwiches, crab and gruyère quiche with caramelised chicory, local rabbit and bacon pressé with rabbit liver mousse, apricots and pistachios, beer-battered cod with tempura langoustine, tagliatelle with wild mushrooms, mushroom velouté and parmesan, peppered saddle of roe deer with apples, celery, walnuts and celeriac purée, sea bream with white beans and bacon, and puddings such as almond milk panna cotta with figs and sticky toffee pudding with salted caramel and lime sorbet. *Benchmark main dish: burger with toppings, pickles and skinny fries £12.50. Two-course evening meal £22.00.*

Free house ~ Licensee Cedric Bosi ~ Real ale ~ Open 11-11 (midnight Sat); 12-10.30 Sun ~ Bar food 12-3, 6-9.15 (8.30 Sun) ~ Restaurant ~ Children welcome ~ Dogs allowed in bar and bedrooms ~ Wi-fi ~ Live music monthly (best to phone) ~ Bedrooms: £80/£100
Recommended by Robert W Buckle, Richard Tilbrook, Roy and Gill Payne, GSB

LUDLOW   SO5174   Map 4
Church Inn 🍺 £
(01584) 872174 – www.thechurchinn.com
Church Street, behind Butter Cross; SY8 1AW

Splendid range of real ales in characterful town-centre inn; bedrooms

Just up the road from the castle, this is a cheerful town-centre pub with a fine range of up to ten real ales on handpump. Regulars are Hobsons Town Crier and Mild, Ludlow Boiling Well and Gold, Wye Valley Bitter and HPA alongside four quickly changing guests; also, 30 malt whiskies, seven wines by the glass and a farm cider. The ground floor is divided into three appealingly decorated areas, with hops hanging from heavy beams, comfortable banquettes in cosy alcoves off the island counter (part of it is a pulpit), and pews and stripped stonework from the nearby church. There are displays of old photographic equipment, plants on window sills and church prints in the side room. A long central area has a fine stone fireplace and old black and white photos of the town; daily papers and background music. Upstairs, the civilised lounge bar (with good views of the church and surrounding countryside) has vaulted ceilings, a display case of glass, china and old bottles, and musical instruments on the walls. The bedrooms are simple but comfortable.

Good value food includes sandwiches, prawns and mushrooms in garlic butter, chicken liver pâté with onion marmalade, greek salad with feta cheese, creamy mushroom pasta, beer-battered cod and chips, faggots and mash, baked ham with parsley sauce, trio of local lamb chops with minted gravy, and puddings such as treacle and pecan pie and raspberry swirl cheesecake. *Benchmark main dish: pie of the day £6.95. Two-course evening meal £14.00.*

Free house ~ Licensee Graham Willson-Lloyd ~ Real ale ~ Open 10am-midnight (1am Fri, Sat); 11am-midnight Sun ~ Bar food 12-9 (8.30 Sun) ~ Restaurant ~ Children welcome ~ Dogs allowed in bar and bedrooms ~ Wi-fi ~ Bedrooms: £50/£80
Recommended by Dr Kevan Tucker, David Buffham, Ken Richards, Richard Tilbrook

MAESBURY MARSH
Navigation

SJ3125   Map 6

(01691) 672958 – www.thenavigation.co.uk

Follow Maesbury Road off A483 S of Oswestry; by canal bridge; SY10 8JB

Versatile and friendly canalside pub with cosy bar and local seasonal produce in a choice of dining areas

An old wharf building on the banks of the Montgomery Canal, this is run by friendly, hands-on licensees. As well as being a traditional pub, they have a book exchange, a shop where you can buy fresh local produce (including fish and shellfish) and a two-pint takeaway service. The quarry-tiled bar on the left has squishy brown leather sofas by a traditional black range blazing in a big red fireplace, little upholstered cask seats around three small tables, and dozens of wrist- and pocket-watches hanging from the beams. A couple of steps lead up to a carpeted area beyond a balustrade, with armchairs and sofas around low tables, and a piano; off to the left is a dining area with cheerful prints. The main beamed dining room, with some stripped stone, is beyond another small bar (they serve cocktails here) with a coal-effect gas fire – and an amazing row of cushioned carved choir stalls complete with misericord seats. Six Bells Cloud Nine and Stonehouse Cambrian Gold on handpump, 11 wines by the glass and eight malt whiskies (one from Wales); quiet background music and board games. Picnic-sets are safely fenced off from the water.

Using only carefully sourced local produce, the range of tasty food includes sandwiches, panko breadcrumbed fishcake with sweet chilli sauce, chicken and charred baby leek terrine with spiced rhubarb compote, spinach, red onion and potato frittata, free-range pork faggots with wholegrain mustard mash and Bovril gravy, baked ham (from outdoor reared pigs) with sauté potatoes and parsley sauce, macaroni cheese, a roast of the day, and puddings such as vanilla crème brûlée and peanut butter and chocolate brownie; they also offer two- and three-course set menus, including lunch (Weds-Sat) and early-bird (Tues-Fri evenings). *Benchmark main dish: burger with home-made brioche bun and chips £9.50. Two-course evening meal £18.00.*

Free house ~ Licensees Brent Ellis and Mark Baggett ~ Real ale ~ Open 12-2, 6-11 (midnight Sat); 12-6 Sun; closed Sun evening, all day Mon, lunchtime Tue, first two weeks Jan ~ Bar food 12-1.45, 6-8.30; 12-1.45 Sun ~ Restaurant ~ Children welcome ~ Dogs allowed in bar ~ Wi-fi ~ Folk music last Weds of month *Recommended by Steve Whalley, Clive and Fran Dutson*

NORTON
Hundred House ♀ ⌂

SJ7200   Map 4

(01952) 730353 – www.hundredhouse.co.uk

A442 Telford–Bridgnorth; TF11 9EE

Family-run inn with rambling rooms, open fires and quite a choice of drinks and good food; comfortable large bedrooms

The lovely garden behind this carefully kept, family-run inn has old-fashioned roses, herbaceous plants and a big working herb garden (with around 50 varieties); there are two rescue donkeys too. The rambling bar rooms have log fires in handsome fireplaces (one has a great Jacobean arch with fine old black cooking pots) and a variety of interesting chairs and settles with long colourful patchwork leather cushions around sewing machine tables. Hops and huge bunches of dried flowers and herbs hang from beams, and bunches of fresh flowers brighten the tables and counter in the neatly kept bar. Steps lead up past a little balustrade to a partly panelled eating area, where the stripped brickwork looks older than it does elsewhere. A guest from Heritage and Three Tuns Mild, Rantipole and Stout on handpump, 12 wines by the glass, a dozen malt whiskies and a farm cider; background music. The bedrooms have antique four-posters or half-testers, Victorian-style baths and rain showers, and their trademark velvet-cushioned swing.

Using local beef and game from the Apley Estate, the popular food includes sandwiches, chicken liver pâté with onion chutney, black pudding, apple and chorizo stack with smoked cheese sauce and crispy onion rings, chicken three-ways (breast, chicken, bacon and mushroom pie, crispy wing) with rösti potato and savoury jus, roulade of squash with chickpea and herb salad, red pepper coulis and aioli, monkfish with garlic prawns and bisque sauce, venison steak with suet pudding and juniper sauce, and puddings such as lemon tart with raspberry coulis and apple pie with custard. *Benchmark main dish: 10oz sirloin steak with chips and herb-grilled tomato £19.95. Two-course evening meal £24.00.*

Free house ~ Licensees Henry, Stuart and David Phillips ~ Real ale ~ Open 11-11 (11.30 Sat); 11-10.30 Sun ~ Bar food 12-2.30, 6-9.30; 12-9 Sun ~ Restaurant ~ Children welcome ~ Dogs allowed in bar and bedrooms ~ Wi-fi ~ Bedrooms: £75/£79
Recommended by Alfie Bayliss, Charlie May

SHIPLEY   SO8095   Map 4
Inn at Shipley ♀ ◖
(01902) 701639 – www.brunningandprice.co.uk/innatshipley
Bridgnorth Road; A454 W of Wolverhampton; WV6 7EQ

Light and airy country pub – a good all-rounder

A rather fine Georgian building that's well preserved, gently civilised and popular with a wide mix of customers. Rambling around the central bar are several woodburning stoves and log fires: one in a big inglenook in a cosy, traditionally tiled black-beamed end room, another by a welcoming set of wing and other leather armchairs. All sorts of dining chairs are grouped around a variety of well buffed tables, rugs sit on polished boards, attractive pictures are hung frame to frame, and big windows let in plenty of daylight; church candles, careful spotlighting and chandeliers add atmosphere. The various areas are interconnected but manage to also feel distinct and individual; upstairs is a separate private dining room. Phoenix Brunning & Price Original, Longden The Golden Arrow and Salopian Oracle with three quickly changing guests on handpump, 17 wines by the glass, 82 malt whiskies and a farm cider; good neatly dressed staff, piped music, daily papers, board games. There are plenty of sturdy tables outside, some on a sizeable terrace with a side awning, others by weeping willows on the main lawn behind the car park, more on smaller lawns around the building.

Contemporary brasserie-style dishes include sandwiches, crispy duck salad with hoisin, watermelon and chilli cashews, orange- and tarragon-cured salmon with pickled fennel and tarragon cream, ricotta- and pear-filled pasta with broad beans, asparagus and pea velouté, chicken, ham hock and leek pie, tandoori-roasted cod with crab spring roll and cucumber and fennel salad, braised lamb shoulder with dauphinoise potatoes and rosemary gravy, and puddings such as bread and butter pudding with apricot sauce and meringue with lemon curd cream, raspberries and blackberries. *Benchmark main dish: beer-battered haddock and chips £12.75. Two-course evening meal £20.00.*

Brunning & Price ~ Manager Marc Eeley ~ Real ale ~ Open 10.30am-11pm ~ Bar food 12-10 (9.30 Sun) ~ Restaurant ~ Children welcome ~ Dogs allowed in bar ~ Wi-fi
Recommended by Isobel Mackinlay

SHREWSBURY

Armoury 🍴⭐ ♀ 🍺

SJ4812   Map 6

(01743) 340525 – www.armoury-shrewsbury.co.uk

Victoria Quay, Victoria Avenue; SY1 1HH

Vibrant atmosphere in interestingly converted riverside warehouse, with enthusiastic young staff, tempting all-day food and excellent choice of drinks

An 18th-c former warehouse, this lively place makes quite an impression as you arrive, especially in summer when the hanging baskets are in full bloom. The spacious open-plan interior has long runs of big arched windows with views across the broad River Severn – but despite its size it also has a personal feel, helped by the eclectic décor, furniture layout and cheerful bustle. A mix of wooden tables and chairs are grouped on stripped-wood floors, the huge brick walls display floor-to-ceiling books or masses of old prints mounted edge to edge, and there's a grand stone fireplace at one end. Colonial-style fans whirr away on the ceilings, which are supported by green-painted columns, and small wall-mounted glass cabinets display smokers' pipes. The long bar counter has a terrific choice of drinks including Phoenix Brunning & Price Original, Longden The Golden Arrow, Salopian Oracle, Woods Shropshire Lad and a couple of guest beers on handpump, 17 wines by the glass, 100 malt whiskies, a dozen gins, lots of rums and vodkas, a variety of brandies and a farm cider. The pub doesn't have its own car park, but there are plenty of parking places nearby.

Enjoyable food includes sandwiches, ham, apricot and pistachio terrine with gooseberry chutney, goats cheese and chive panna cotta with tomato and red pepper jam, king prawn and chorizo risotto, chestnut mushroom, courgette and smoked tomato ragoût with herb puy lentils, indonesian-style beef curry with pak choi, moroccan-style chicken with couscous, burger with toppings, coleslaw and chips, and puddings such as sticky toffee pudding with toffee sauce and raspberry crème brûlée. *Benchmark main dish: beer-battered haddock and chips £12.75. Two-course evening meal £20.00.*

Brunning & Price ~ Manager Emily Waring ~ Real ale ~ Open 12-11 (10.30 Sun) ~ Bar food 12-10 (9.30 Sun) ~ Children welcome ~ Dogs allowed in bar ~ Wi-fi
Recommended by Brian and Anna Marsden

SHREWSBURY

Lion & Pheasant 🍴⭐ ♀ 🛏

SJ4912   Map 6

(01743) 770345 – www.lionandpheasant.co.uk

Follow City Centre signposts across the English Bridge; SY1 1XJ

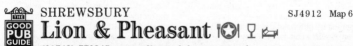

Shropshire Dining Pub of the Year

Civilised bar and upstairs restaurant in comfortable, neatly updated and well placed inn; bedrooms

Built in the 16th c, this appealing, carefully run inn has a thoughtful mix of original features blending seamlessly with more contemporary touches. The big-windowed bar is made up of three linked levels, the lowest of which has armchairs on dark flagstones by a big inglenook; elsewhere there's a cushioned settee, but most of the seats are at sturdy stripped tables on dark floorboards. A few modern paintings, plentiful flowers and church candles brighten up the restrained cream and grey décor, as do the friendly staff and background music. Salopian Oracle and Shropshire Gold, Three Tuns XXX and Woods Shropshire Lad on handpump and 14 wines by the glass.

Off quite a warren of corridors, the restaurant (you can eat from its menu in the bar too) is in the older back part of the building with beams and timbering. Outside, there are seats and tables under parasols with olive trees and flowering pots dotted about. Some of the bedrooms provide glimpses of the River Severn below the nearby English Bridge; breakfasts are good.

Imaginative food includes sandwiches, cured salmon gravadlax with pickled shallots, capers and wasabi cream cheese, duck rillette with parma ham, golden raisin and juniper oil, tagliatelle with roasted red pepper, spinach and slow-cooked egg, beer-battered haddock with triple-cooked chips, beef tasting plate with chive mash, honeyed baby parsnips and burnt onion, bass with scallops, tomato and chorizo risotto, and puddings such as dark chocolate fondant and passion-fruit tart with caribbean salad. *Benchmark main dish: thyme-roast chicken with butternut squash, chanterelles and crispy skin £17.50. Two-course evening meal £25.00.*

Free house ~ Licensee Jim Littler ~ Real ale ~ Open 11-11 (midnight Sat); 11-10.30 Sun ~ Bar food 12-2.30 (3 Sun), 6-9 ~ Restaurant ~ Children welcome ~ Wi-fi ~ Bedrooms: £99/£119 *Recommended by Isobel Mackinlay, Edward May*

Also Worth a Visit in Shropshire

Besides the fully inspected pubs, you might like to try these pubs that have been recommended to us and described by readers. Do tell us what you think of them: feedback@goodguides.com

ADMASTON   SJ6313

Pheasant (01952) 251989
Shawbirch Road; TF5 0AD Red-brick Victorian pub with good locally sourced food (all day Sat, till 7pm Sun), three or four well kept ales including Salopian and Woods, pleasant staff; Thurs quiz; garden with play area, open all day. *(Mrs Sally Evans)*

ALBRIGHTON   SJ8104

Shrewsbury Arms (01902) 373003
High Street; WV7 3LA Refurbished brick and timber dining pub, good home-cooked food from light dishes and sharing plates up, deals including weekday two-course lunch, Sharps Doom Bar and up to three local guests, friendly helpful staff; live music Fri, Sat; children and dogs welcome, open (and food) all day. *(John Oates, Mrs B H Adams)*

ASTON MUNSLOW   SO5187

Swan (01584) 841415
Off B4368, in lane NW of village; SY7 9ER Former 14th-c coaching inn improved under new welcoming family, bar and two dining areas, black beams and open fires, enjoyable good value traditional food, well kept ales such as Hobsons, Ludlow and Wye Valley, chatty helpful service; pool room; children welcome, garden with shady areas, open all day weekends, closed Mon lunchtime. *(Steve and Jane Payne)*

BISHOP'S CASTLE   SO3288

Boars Head (01588) 638521
Church Street; SY9 5AE Comfortable beamed and stripped-stone bar with mix of furniture including pews and settles on bare boards, woodburner in big inglenook, welcoming efficient young staff, three well kept changing ales and enjoyable fairly priced pub food including good shropshire hotpot, family room with TV and another inglenook, some live music; free wi-fi; no dogs inside; picnic-sets on back terrace, three roomy high-raftered bedrooms in converted barn, open (and food) all day. *(Phoebe Peacock)*

BISHOP'S CASTLE   SO3288

★**Castle Hotel** (01588) 638403
Market Square, just off B4385; SY9 5BN Substantial coaching inn at top of lovely market town, clubby little beamed and panelled bar with log fire, larger rooms off with big Victorian engravings and another fire, well kept Clun, Hobsons, Six Bells and Three Tuns, local cider, ten wines by the glass (maybe one from nearby vineyard) and 30 malt whiskies, popular food served by friendly staff, handsome panelled dining room; background music, darts and board games; children and dogs welcome, pretty hanging baskets at front, garden behind with terrace seating, pergolas and climbing plants, surrounding walks, nice spacious bedrooms, good breakfast, open all day. *(Mike and Eleanor Anderson, A N Bance, Paul and Kate O'Donnell, Richard Tilbrook, David Field)*

BISHOP'S CASTLE   SO3288

★**Six Bells** (01588) 630144
Church Street; SY9 5AA Friendly 17th-c pub with character landlord and own-brew beers (brewery tours available); smallish

no-frills bar with mix of well worn furniture, old local photographs and prints, bigger room with stripped-stone walls, benches around plain tables on bare boards and inglenook woodburner, country wines and summer cider, July beer festival, good value straightforward home-made food (not Mon or evenings Tues, Sun); no credit cards; well behaved children and dogs welcome, open all Sat, closed Mon lunchtime. *(Charlie May)*

BISHOP'S CASTLE   SO3288
★ **Three Tuns** (01588) 638797

Salop Street; SY9 5BW Extended old pub adjacent to unique four-storey Victorian brewhouse (a brewery said to have existed here since 1642), busy chatty atmosphere in public, lounge and snug bars, Three Tuns beers (including 1642) from old-fashioned handpumps (cheaper 5-7pm Fri), several wines by the glass, tasty good value food (not Sun evening) from sandwiches up, friendly young staff, modernised dining room done out in smart oak and glass; lots going on including film club, music nights, July beer festival and maybe morris men or a brass band in the garden; children and dogs welcome, open all day. *(Kerry Law, Mike and Eleanor Anderson, Dr Peter Crawshaw, Lois Dyer)*

BRIDGES   SO3996
★ **Bridges** (01588) 650260

Bridges, W of Ratlinghope; SY5 0ST Old renovated beamed country pub, now the Three Tuns tap with their full range in excellent condition, bare-boards bar to right, large dining room to left, woodburner, fairly traditional home-made food (not Sun evening, winter Mon), helpful staff; regular live music; children welcome, dogs in room off bar, tables out by the little River Onny (some on raised deck), bedrooms, also camping and youth hostel nearby, great walking country, open all day. *(Dr Kevan Tucker, D W Stokes, Dr Peter Crawshaw)*

BRIDGNORTH   SO6890
★ **Down** (01746) 789539

The Down; B4364 Ludlow Road 3 miles S; WV16 6UA Good value roadside dining pub overlooking rolling countryside, enjoyable food including popular daily carvery, efficient service, a house beer (Down & Out) from Three Tuns and a couple of local guests; background music; children welcome, nine comfortable bedrooms, open all day. *(Anon)*

BRIDGNORTH   SO7193
Kings Head (01746) 762141

Whitburn Street; WV16 4QN 17th-c timbered coaching inn with high-raftered back stable bar, good food here from 5pm (all day weekends) or in all-day restaurant with separate menu, friendly staff, Hobsons and a couple of guests, winter mulled wine, log fires, beams and flagstones, pretty leaded windows; children and dogs welcome, courtyard tables, open all day. *(Alfie Bayliss)*

BRIDGNORTH   SO7192
★ **Railwaymans Arms** (01746) 764361

Severn Valley Station, Hollybush Road (off A458 towards Stourbridge); WV16 5DT Bathams, Hobsons and plenty of other well kept ales in chatty old-fashioned converted waiting room at Severn Valley steam railway terminus, bustling on summer days; old station signs and train nameplates, superb mirror over fireplace, may be simple summer snacks, Sept beer festival; children welcome, wheelchair access with help, tables out on platform – the train to Kidderminster (station bar there too) has an all-day bar and bookable Sun lunches, open all day. *(Phoebe Peacock)*

BROMFIELD   SO4877
★ **Clive** (01584) 856565

A49, 2 miles NW of Ludlow; SY8 2JR Sophisticated minimalist bar-restaurant taking its name from Clive of India who once lived here; emphasis mainly on the imaginative well presented food but also Hobsons and Ludlow ales, several wines by the glass and a bar menu, welcoming well trained staff, dining room with light wood tables, door to sparsely furnished bar with metal chairs, glass-topped tables and sleek counter, step down to room with soaring beams and rafters, exposed stonework and woodburner in huge fireplace; background music, free wi-fi; children welcome, tables under parasols on secluded terrace, fish pond, 15 stylish bedrooms, good breakfast, open all day. *(Gordon and Margaret Ormondroyd, Mike and Mary Carter)*

BUCKNELL   SO3574
Baron (01547) 530549

Chapel Lawn Road; just off B4367 Knighton Road; SY7 0AH Modernised family-owned country inn, friendly and efficiently run, with enjoyable home-made food from panini and pizzas up, well kept Ludlow and Wye Valley, log fire in carpeted front bar, back dining room with old cider press and grindstone, conservatory; free wi-fi; children welcome, lovely views from big garden, five bedrooms, camping field, open all day Sat, closed Sun evening and lunchtimes Mon-Thurs. *(Malcolm and Pauline Pellatt)*

BURLTON   SJ4526
Burlton Inn (01939) 270284

A528 Shrewsbury–Ellesmere, near B4397 junction; SY4 5TB Welcoming attractively updated 18th-c pub with enjoyable good value food, Robinsons ales and a guest, friendly helpful staff, beams, timbers and log fires, comfortable snug, restaurant with garden room; children and dogs welcome (there are two pub dogs), disabled facilities, teak furniture on pleasant terrace, comfortable well equipped bedrooms, good breakfast. *(Alfie Bayliss)*

BURWARTON
SO6185

★ **Boyne Arms** (01746) 787214
B4364 Bridgnorth–Ludlow; WV16 6QH
Handsome Georgian coaching inn with
welcoming cheerful staff, enjoyable generous
food (not Sun evening, Mon) including
good value deals, up to three real ales such
as Battlefield, Otter and Timothy Taylors,
Robinson's and Thatcher's cider, decent
coffee, separate restaurant and public bar
(dogs allowed here), function room with
pool and other games; children welcome,
good timber adventure playground in pretty
garden, hitching rail for horses, open all day
weekends, closed Mon lunchtime. *(Anon)*

CHURCH STRETTON
SO4593

Bucks Head (01694) 722898
High Street; SY6 6BX Old town pub
with several good-sized modernised areas
including restaurant, up to four well kept
Marstons ales, decent good value pubby food
plus vegetarian options, friendly attentive
staff, black beams and timbers, mixed dark
wood tables and chairs; four bedrooms, open
all day. *(Anon)*

CHURCH STRETTON
SO4593

Housmans (01694) 724441
High Street; SY6 6BX Buzzing and
welcoming restaurant-bar with two well
kept ales from Three Tuns and good wine
and cocktail lists, food mainly tapas-style
sharing plates but also good value two-course
weekday lunch deal, local art on walls;
occasional live jazz and other acoustic
music; children welcome, open all day
weekends. *(Alfie Bayliss)*

CLAVERLEY
SO8095

Woodman (01746) 710553
B4176/Danford Lane; WV5 7DG Rural
19th-c red-brick dining pub refurbished
under newish management; contemporary
beamed interior arranged around central bar,
good popular food (must book) using local
produce – some from farm opposite, well
kept Black Sheep and Enville, lots of wines
by the glass and interesting range of gins,
good well organised service; terrace
and garden tables, closed Sun evening.
(Paul Humphreys, Paul and Sue Merrick)

CLUN
SO3080

Sun (01588) 640559
High Street; SY7 8JB Beamed and
timbered 15th-c pub with traditional
flagstoned public bar, woodburner in
inglenook, larger carpeted lounge bar,
enjoyable home-made food (not Sun evening)
from lunchtime sandwiches up, four well
kept Three Tuns ales, friendly helpful staff;
children and dogs welcome, paved back
terrace, peaceful village and lovely rolling
countryside, bedrooms (some in converted
outbuildings), closed Mon lunchtime,
otherwise open all day. *(Charlie May)*

CLUNTON
SO3381

Crown (01588) 660265
B4368; SY7 0HU Cosy old country local,
welcoming and friendly, with three well kept
ales including Hobsons and Stonehouse,
enjoyable generously served food (Thurs-Sat
evenings), also Weds fish and chips and good
value Sun lunch, log fire in small flagstoned
bar, dining room, games room with TV; folk
night third Weds of month; open all day
Fri-Sun, closed lunchtimes other days.
(Phoebe Peacock)

COALPORT
SJ6903

Half Moon (01952) 884443
Off Salthouse Road; TF8 7LP Renovated
pub in lovely Severn-side position, three
local ales and good choice of fairly priced
food from sandwiches and home-made
pizzas to grills and daily specials, prompt
friendly service; some live music; children
welcome, picnic-sets out overlooking river,
four bedrooms, open (and food) all day
summer. *(Adrian Johnson)*

COALPORT
SJ6902

Shakespeare (01952) 580675
High Street; TF8 7HT Welcoming early
19th-c inn by pretty Severn gorge park,
timbering, bare stone walls and tiled floors,
well kept Everards, Hobsons, Ludlow and
a guest, good value generously served food
from sandwiches through pub standards
to mexican specialities; children welcome,
picnic-sets in tiered garden with play area,
handy for China Museum, four bedrooms,
open all day weekends, closed weekdays
till 5pm. *(Andrew Stone)*

CORFTON
SO4985

Sun (01584) 861239
*B4368 Much Wenlock–Craven Arms;
SY7 9DF* Lived-in unchanging three-
room country local, own good Corvedale
ales (including an unfined beer), friendly
long-serving landlord (often busy in back
brewery), decent pubby food from baguettes
to steaks, lots of breweriana, basic quarry-
tiled public bar with darts, pool and juke box,
quieter carpeted lounge, dining room with
covered well, tourist information; children
welcome, dogs in bar, good wheelchair
access throughout and disabled loos, tables
on terrace and in large garden with good
play area. *(Robert W Buckle)*

CRAVEN ARMS
SO5485

Tally Ho (01584) 841811
Bouldon; SY7 9DP Welcoming tucked-
away pub owned by group of villagers;
good local beers such as Hobsons and big
helpings of enjoyable freshly made pub food
at very reasonable prices, service with a
smile; dogs welcome, country views from
nice garden. *(Brian and Jacky Wilson,
David Buffham, Paul Sayers)*

GRINDLEY BROOK SJ5242

Horse & Jockey (01948) 662723

A41; SY13 4QJ Extended 19th-c pub with enjoyable good value food from varied menu, friendly helpful service, eight well kept ales including a house beer from Phoenix named after resident chocolate labrador Blaze, teas and coffees, well divided open-plan interior with mix of furniture on wood or carpeted floors, some interesting bits and pieces, woodburners; sports TV, pool; children, dogs and muddy boots welcome, big play area, handy for Sandstone Trail and Llangollen Canal, open all day, food all day weekends. *(Robert W Buckle)*

GRINSHILL SJ5223

★**Inn at Grinshill** (01939) 220410

Off A49 N of Shrewsbury; SY4 3BL Civilised early Georgian country inn; comfortable 19th-c panelled bar with log fire in raised two-way hearth, Greene King and a couple of local guests, spacious modern restaurant with view into kitchen, good food and friendly competent service; background music, TV; children and dogs welcome, pleasant back garden with plenty of tables and chairs, comfortable clean bedrooms, closed Sun evening, Mon, Tues. *(Andrew Stone)*

HIGHLEY SO7483

Ship (01746) 861219

Severnside; WV16 6NU Refurbished 18th-c inn in lovely riverside location, enjoyable pubby food including bargain OAP weekday lunch and early-bird deal, Sun carvery, five real ales; children welcome, tables on raised front deck, handy for Severn Way walks (and Severn Valley Railway), fishing rights, bedrooms, open all day. *(Phoebe Peacock)*

HODNET SJ6128

★**Bear** (01630) 685214

Drayton Road (A53); TF9 3NH Old village inn with very good affordably priced food (all day Fri, Sat, till 4pm Sun, booking advised) from well executed pub favourites to more creative restaurant dishes, four well kept changing ales and 14 wines by the glass, friendly helpful staff, rambling open-plan main area, snug end alcoves with heavy 16th-c beams and timbers, small beamed quarry-tiled bar, woodburners; charity quiz second Mon of month, some live music; children welcome, dogs in one area (resident jack russells are Jack and Russell), picnic-sets in garden with play area, seven bedrooms (two more in annexe), opposite Hodnet Hall Gardens and handy for Hawkstone Park, open all day (till 8pm Sun). *(James Austin, Jo Weller)*

HOPE SJ3401

Stables (01743) 891344

Just off A488 3 miles S of Minsterley; SY5 0EP Hidden-away little 17th-c beamed country pub (former drovers' inn), friendly

and welcoming, with nice home-made food and a couple of well kept ales such as Wye Valley Butty Bach, newspapers, log fires; dogs welcome (their irish wolfhound is Murphy) fine views from garden, two bedrooms and a 'shepherd's hut' for the glamping enthusiast, closed weekday lunchtimes. *(Anon)*

HOPTON WAFERS SO6376

Crown (01299) 270372

A4117; DY14 0NB Attractive 16th-c creeper-clad inn, light comfortable décor and furnishings, beams and big inglenook, good food (all day Sun) in three separate dining areas, weekday set deal lunchtime/early evening, ales such as Ludlow and Wye Valley, good choice of wines and decent coffee, cheerful helpful staff, relaxed atmosphere; children and dogs welcome, inviting garden with terraces, duck pond and stream, 18 bedrooms (11 in new adjoining building), open all day. *(Ryta Lyndley, Robert Parker, Ross Balaam)*

IRONBRIDGE SJ6603

★**Malthouse** (01952) 433712

The Wharfage (bottom road alongside Severn); TF8 7NH Converted 18th-c malthouse wonderfully located in historic gorge, spacious bar with iron pillars supporting heavy pine beams, lounge/dining area, up to three well kept changing ales and good reasonably priced food from baguettes up, friendly attentive staff; live music Fri, Sat; children and dogs welcome, terrace tables, 11 individually styled bedrooms and self-catering cottage, open (and food) all day. *(Isobel Mackinlay)*

KNOCKIN SJ3322

Bradford Arms (01691) 682358

B4396 NW of Shrewsbury; SY10 8HJ Sizeable neatly kept village local with notable three-faced roof clock, enjoyable good value pub food and well kept Marstons-related beers, friendly welcoming staff, games rooms; TV, free wi-fi; children and dogs welcome, garden behind by car park, open (and food) all day. *(Anon)*

KNOWBURY SO5874

Bennetts End (01584) 890220

Hope Bagot Lane; SY8 3LL Extended 17th-c country pub with very well liked freshly made food including good value early evening set menu, well kept local ales, real cider and decent wines, friendly enthusiastic staff, cosy rooms with log fires, restaurant; dogs welcome, garden overlooking farmland and 18th-c aqueduct, good local walks, open all day Sat, closed Sun evening and weekday lunchtimes. *(Paul Sayers)*

LEEBOTWOOD SO4798

★**Pound** (01694) 751477

A49 Church Stretton–Shrewsbury; SY6 6ND Thatched cruck-framed building dating from 1458 – thought to be oldest in the village; stylishly modern bar rooms with minimalist fixtures and wooden furnishings, good interesting food cooked by chef-owner from light meals up, also pub favourites, a couple of real ales and nice wines by the glass, friendly efficient service; background music; seats on flagstoned terrace; disabled parking (level access to bar), closed Sun evening, Mon. *(Charlie May)*

LEIGHTON   SJ6105
Kynnersley Arms (01952) 510233
B4380; SY5 6RN Victorian building built on remains of an ancient corn mill; coal fire and woodburner in main opened-up area, armchairs and sofas in back part with stairs to lower level containing mill machinery (there's also a 17th-c blast furnace), five well kept mainly local ales including Salopian Shropshire Gold and a house beer (Next of Kyn) from Woods, traditional food along with pizzas and pasta dishes, Sun carvery, friendly helpful staff; background and occasional live music, sports TV, pool; children and dogs welcome, good walks nearby, open all day. *(John Oates)*

LEINTWARDINE   SO4175
★ Jolly Frog (01547) 540298
A4113 Ludlow–Knighton, E edge of village; The Toddings; SY7 0LX Cheerful well run bar-bistro in glorious countryside; front bar with just a few tables on light oak boards, check tablecloths and red leatherette dining chairs, woodburner at each end and frenchified décor (kepis and other hats hanging from stripped beams, Paris street signs and a Metro map), similarly furnished dining room up a few steps, ales such as Otter and Three Tuns, good wines by the glass and well liked food from wood-fired pizzas to fresh fish/seafood, friendly professional staff; background music, free wi-fi; children welcome, inner courtyard with tables under sail canopy, more seating on upper deck with wide pastoral views, closed Mon. *(W M Lien, Gordon and Margaret Ormondroyd, Dave Braisted, Steve Whalley, Clive Watkin)*

LITTLE STRETTON   SO4491
Green Dragon (01694) 722925
Village well signed off A49 S of Church Stretton; Ludlow Road; SY6 6RE Cleanly refurbished village pub at foot of Long Mynd; popular good value food in bar or adjacent dining area (well behaved children allowed here), well kept Wye Valley beers and guests, a proper cider, friendly efficient young staff, warm woodburner; stone-floored area for booted walkers, tables outside and play area, handy for Cardingmill Valley (NT), open (and food) all day. *(D W Stokes, Robert W Buckle, Peter Meister)*

LITTLE STRETTON   SO4492
★ Ragleth (01694) 722711
Village well signed off A49 S of Church Stretton; Ludlow Road; SY6 6RB

Characterful opened-up 17th-c dining pub; light and airy bay-windowed front bar with eclectic mix of old tables and chairs, some exposed brick and timber work, huge inglenook in heavily beamed brick and tile-floored public bar, four mainly local beers such as Hobsons, very good food with plenty of fish dishes, cheerful attentive owners and staff; background music, TV, darts and board games; children welcome, dogs in bar, lovely garden with tulip tree-shaded lawn and good play area, thatched and timbered church and fine hill walks nearby, open all day Sat (summer) and Sun. *(Patrick and Daphne Darley, John Oates, Ray and Winifred Halliday)*

LITTLE WENLOCK   SJ6507
Huntsman (01952) 503300
Wellington Road; TF6 5BH Welcoming modernised village pub, good food (till 7pm Sun) from lunchtime ciabattas and pub standards up, Fri fish night, four well kept changing ales and good selection of wines, black beamed bar with stone floor and central log fire, carpeted restaurant with high-backed upholstered chairs at light wood tables and woodburner in big fireplace; children and dogs (in bar) welcome, terrace seating, bedrooms, handy for Wrekin walks, open (and food) all day. *(John Oates, S Holder)*

LUDLOW   SO5174
Queens (01584) 879177
Lower Galdeford; SY8 1RU Welcoming and popular 19th-c family-run pub, good reasonably priced food with emphasis on fresh local produce, four well kept ales including Hobsons, Ludlow and Wye Valley, long narrow oak-floor bar, steps down to vaulted-ceiling dining area, good friendly service; some live music; children welcome (not in bar after 6pm), dogs allowed in one area, modern seating on enclosed deck, courtyard accommodation, open all day. *(Roy and Gill Payne)*

LUDLOW   SO5174
Rose & Crown (01584) 872098
Off Church Street, behind Buttercross; SY8 1AP Small unpretentious pub with 13th-c origins, owned by Joules with their beers and guests, real cider and traditional food including range of pies, friendly staff, comfortably lived-in L-shaped bar with hops and mugs hanging from black beams, open brick fireplace, separate dining area; outside loos; children and dogs welcome, approached through passageway with a few courtyard seats at front, pretty spot, three bedrooms, open all day. *(Dr Kevan Tucker, Stanley and Annie Matthews, Roy and Gill Payne)*

LUDLOW   SO5175
Unicorn (01584) 873555
Corve Street, bottom end; SY8 1DU Small half-timbered 17th-c coaching inn, character bar with hop-festooned beams and part panelled walls, enjoyable fairly traditional

food from good sharing boards up, well kept ales such as Ludlow, friendly service from hands-on landlady, back dining room; live folk first Fri of the month, charity quiz first Sun; children welcome, terrace among willows by river, open (and food) all day. *(Richard Tilbrook, Paul Sayers)*

MAESBURY   SJ3026
Original Ball (01691) 654880
Maesbury Road; SY10 8HB Refurbished old brick-built pub, hefty beams, woodburner in central fireplace, Marstons Pedigree and Stonehouse Station Bitter, decent wines and enjoyable reasonably priced pub food including Sun carvery, friendly helpful staff; some live music, TV, pool; children and dogs welcome, open all day weekends, from 4pm other days. *(Jill Sparrow)*

MARKET DRAYTON   SJ6734
Red Lion (01630) 652602
Great Hales Street; TF9 1JP Extended 17th-c coaching inn now tap for Joules Brewery; back entrance into attractive modern bar with light wood floor and substantial oak timbers, traditional dark-beamed part to the right, updated but keeping original features, with pubby furniture on flagstones, brewery mirrors and signs, woodburner, more breweriana in dining/function room to left featuring 'Mousey' Thompson carved oak panelling and fireplace; Joules Pale Ale, Blonde, Slumbering Monk and a seasonal beer (tasting trays available), good selection of wines, fairly straightforward food including range of pies and Sun carvery till 4pm, some live music; picnic-sets outside, brewery tours first Weds of the month, open all day. *(Barry Collett)*

MARTON   SJ2802
★Sun (01938) 561211
B4386 NE of Chirbury; SY21 8JP Welcoming family-run dining pub, clean and neatly kept, with high standard of cooking including seasonal game and good fresh fish, light and airy black-beamed bar with comfortable sofa and traditional furnishings, woodburner in big stone fireplace, Hobsons Best and several wines by the glass, chunky pale tables and ladder-back chairs in restaurant; children welcome, dogs in bar (but ask first), front terrace, closed Sun evening, Mon and lunchtime Tues. *(Roger and Anne Newbury)*

MUCH WENLOCK   SO6299
Gaskell Arms (01952) 727212
High Street (A458); TF13 6AQ 17th-c coaching inn with comfortable old-fashioned lounge divided by brass-canopied log fire, enjoyable straightforward bar food at fair prices, friendly attentive service, three well kept ales such as Ludlow, Salopian and Wye Valley, brasses and prints, civilised beamed restaurant, locals' public bar; background music; well behaved children allowed, no

dogs, disabled facilities, roomy neat back garden with terrace, 16 bedrooms, open all day. *(Charlie May)*

MUCH WENLOCK   SO6299
★George & Dragon (01952) 727312
High Street (A458); TF13 6AA Friendly town pub filled with fascinating collection of pub paraphernalia – old brewery and cigarette advertisements, bottle labels, beer trays and George and the Dragon pictures, also 200 jugs hanging from beams; main quarry-tiled room with antique settles and open fires in two attractive Victorian fireplaces, timbered back dining room, Greene King, Hobsons, St Austell, Shepherd Neame and Thwaites, enjoyable good value food (not Weds or Sun evenings); background and some live music; children and dogs (in bar) welcome, pay-and-display car park behind, open all day. *(Patrick and Daphne Darley, Dr Kevan Tucker, Robert Parker, Di and Mike Gillam)*

MUNSLOW   SO5287
★Crown (01584) 841205
B4368 Much Wenlock–Craven Arms; SY7 9ET Former courthouse with imposing exterior and pretty back façade showing Tudor origins; lots of nooks and crannies, split-level lounge bar with old-fashioned mix of furnishings on broad flagstones, old bottles, country pictures, bread oven by log fire, traditional snug with another fire, eating area with tables around central oven chimney, more beams, flagstones and stripped stone, good restauranty food (local suppliers listed) including popular Sun lunch, steak night Tues, Weds, ales such as Otter, Three Tuns and Wye Valley, local bottled cider, nice wines, helpful efficient staff and friendly bustling atmosphere; background music; children welcome, level wheelchair access to bar only, bedrooms, closed Sun evening, Mon. *(Glenwys and Alan Lawrence, Dr Peter Crawshaw)*

NEENTON   SO6387
Pheasant (01746) 787955
B4364 Bridgnorth–Ludlow; WV16 6RJ Refurbished village pub owned by the local community, three or four well kept ales including Hobsons and over a dozen wines by the glass, good fairly priced home-made food from shortish menu, friendly young staff, comfortable seating by inglenook woodburner, oak-framed dining extension; free wi-fi; children and dogs (in bar) welcome, tables in orchard garden, three bedrooms, open all day weekends, closed Mon. *(Lynda and Trevor Smith, John and Jennifer Spinks)*

NESSCLIFFE   SJ3819
Old Three Pigeons (01743) 741279
Off A5 Shrewsbury–Oswestry (now bypassed); SY4 1DB Friendly 16th-c pub with two bar areas and restaurant, good

fairly priced food including fresh fish and plenty of daily specials, Thurs spanish night, three well kept local ales, nice wines by the glass, black beams, wood floors and warm log fires; children and dogs welcome, picnic-sets in garden with fountain and covered area, opposite Kynaston's Cave, good cliff walks, open all day Sun, closed Mon lunchtime. *(Alfie Bayliss)*

PICKLESCOTT   SO4399
Bottle & Glass (01694) 751252
Off A49 N of Church Stretton; SY6 6NR
Remote 17th-c rambling country pub with friendly landlord; plenty of character in quarry-tiled bar and lounge/dining areas, low black beams, oak panelling and log fires, assortment of old tables and chairs, enjoyable traditional home-made food (not Sun evening) from baps up, well kept ales such as Hobsons and Woods; TV; children welcome, dogs in bar, seats out on raised front area, good walks, three bedrooms, open till 7pm Sun, closed Mon lunchtime (and evening winter). *(Gordon and Margaret Ormondroyd)*

PORTH-Y-WAEN   SJ2623
Lime Kiln (01691) 839599
A495, between village and junction with A483, S of Oswestry; SY10 8LX
Popular beamed roadside pub with very good affordably priced food (not Sun evening) cooked by owner-chef, welcoming efficient service, dining area and small quarry-tiled bar with cushioned wall benches and sofa by open fire, well kept beers, organic cider and a local lager, nice wines too; children welcome, closed Mon, lunchtime Tues. *(Jill Sparrow)*

RODINGTON   SJ5914
Bulls Head (01952) 770219
Almost opposite the church; SY4 4QS
Recently refurbished beamed village pub, good range of enjoyable well priced home-made food including speciality steaks, set menu and two-for-one lunchtime deal Mon-Fri, a couple of well kept ales such as local Rowtons and Theakstons, friendly staff; well behaved children and dogs welcome, open (and food) all day. *(Isobel Mackinlay)*

SHAWBURY   SJ5621
Fox & Hounds (01939) 250600
Wytheford Road; SY4 4JG Light and spacious 1960s pub, various opened-up areas including book-lined dining room with woodburner, rugs and assorted dark furniture on wood floors, cream-painted dados and lots of pictures, good fairly priced food from light lunches and sharing boards to daily specials, four or five well kept ales and good choice of wines, efficient helpful service; children welcome, picnic-sets on terrace and lawn, open (and food) all day. *(Mr and Mrs David Horton)*

SHIFNAL   SJ74508
White Hart (01952) 461161
High Street; TF11 8BH Eight well kept interesting ales in chatty 17th-c timbered pub, quaint and old-fashioned with separate bar and lounge, good home-made lunchtime food (not Sun), several wines by the glass, friendly welcoming staff; couple of steep steps at front door, back terrace and beer garden, open all day. *(Anon)*

SHREWSBURY   SJ4912
Admiral Benbow (01743) 244423
Swan Hill; SY1 1NF Great choice of regional ales, also ciders and bottled belgian beers, friendly staff; darts; no children, beer garden behind, closed lunchtimes except Sat. *(Andrew Stone)*

SHREWSBURY   SJ4812
Boat House Inn (01743) 231658
New Street/Quarry Park; leaving centre via Welsh Bridge/A488 turn into Port Hill Road; SY3 8JQ Refurbished pub in lovely position by footbridge to Severn park, river views from long bar and terrace tables; pastel blue panelling, painted tables and chairs on bare boards, some beams and timbering, log fire, well kept regional ales and enjoyable food from wraps to grills, friendly staff; background music, TV; children welcome, no dogs inside, outside summer bar, open all day. *(Brian Glozier)*

SHREWSBURY   SO4912
Coach & Horses (01743) 365661
Swan Hill/Cross Hill; SY1 1NF Friendly and relaxed beamed corner local; panelled main bar, cosy little side room and back dining lounge, good freshly made food, well kept Salopian, Stonehouse and guests, real cider, happy hour (5-7pm Mon-Fri, 7-10pm Sun), friendly helpful staff dressed in black, interesting Guinness prints; background music (maybe live Sun); children allowed in dining room, dogs in bar, disabled facilities (other lavatories up spiral staircase), smokers' roof terrace, open all day. *(Brian and Anna Marsden)*

SHREWSBURY   SJ4913
Dolphin (01743) 247005
A49 0.5 mile N of station; SY1 2EZ Traditionally refurbished little 19th-c pub with good mix of regulars and visitors, friendly welcoming staff, well kept Joules beers and a couple of guests, short choice of good bar snacks and simple meals, reasonable prices, original features including gas lighting, log fires; music and charity quiz nights, darts; seats on sunny back deck, open all day. *(Keith Fawcett, Robert W Buckle)*

SHREWSBURY   SJ4912
Loggerheads (01743) 360275
Church Street; SY1 1UG Chatty old-fashioned local with panelled back room,

flagstones, scrubbed-top tables, high-backed settles and coal fire, three other rooms with lots of prints, bare boards and more flagstones, quaint linking corridor and hatch service of five Marstons-related ales, short choice of bargain pub food, friendly prompt service; live folk Thurs and Sun; open all day. *(Andrew Stone)*

SHREWSBURY   SJ4912
Nags Head (01743) 362455
Wyle Cop; SY1 1XB Attractive old two-room pub, small, unpretentious and welcoming, with good range of well kept beers, no food; TV, juke box; remains of ancient timbered building (used as a smokers' shelter) and garden behind, open all day (till 1am Fri, Sat). *(Andrew Stone)*

SHREWSBURY   SJ4911
Prince of Wales (01743) 343301
Bynner Street; SY3 7NZ Traditional backstreet pub popular for its good range of well kept ales, friendly atmosphere, lunchtime food Fri and Sun, Shrewsbury Town FC memorabilia, darts; children and dogs welcome, sunny back deck overlooking own bowling green, open all day Fri-Sun, from 5pm other days. *(Andrew Stone)*

SHREWSBURY   SJ4912
Salopian Bar (01743) 351505
Smithfield Road; SY1 1PW Modernised pub facing river; eight well kept ales including Salopian and Stonehouse, good choice of foreign beers and real ciders (regular beer/cider festivals), cheap sandwiches and pies, friendly staff; open mike and quiz nights, sports TV, fruit machine; open all day. *(Andrew Stone)*

SHREWSBURY   SJ4912
★ **Three Fishes** (01743) 455229
Fish Street; SY1 1UR Well run timbered and heavily beamed 16th-c pub in quiet cobbled street, small tables around three sides of central bar, flagstones, old pictures, half a dozen well kept beers from mainstream and smaller brewers, good value wines and enjoyable fairly priced food (not Sun) from baguettes to blackboard specials ordered from separate servery, good friendly service even when busy; no mobile phones; open all day Fri-Sun. *(A N Bance)*

STIPERSTONES   SJ3600
★ **Stiperstones Inn** (01743) 791327
Village signed off A488 S of Minsterley; SY5 0LZ Cosy traditional pub useful for a post-walk drink – some stunning hikes on Long Mynd or up dramatic quartzite ridge of the Stiperstones; small carpeted lounge with comfortable leatherette wall banquettes and lots of brassware on ply-panelled walls, plainer public bar with chairs, TV and fruit machine, a couple of real ales such as Hobsons and Three Tuns, good value bar food usefully served all day, also afternoon teas with freshly baked

cakes and home-made jams, friendly helpful service; background music; children and dogs welcome, two comfortable bedrooms, open all day. *(Alfie Bayliss)*

STOTTESDON   SO6782
Fighting Cocks (01746) 718270
High Street; DY14 8TZ Welcoming old half-timbered community pub in unspoilt countryside, carpeted split-level interior with low ceilings and log fire, good hearty home-made food using local produce, well kept Hobsons and a couple of guests; live music and occasional quiz nights; small shop behind; nice views from garden and good walks, open all day weekends, closed weekday lunchtimes (possibly not in summer); for sale last we heard so things may change. *(Charlie May)*

TELFORD   SJ6910
Crown (01952) 610888
Market Street, Oakengates (off A442, handy for M54 junction 5); TF2 6EA Bright 19th-c local (list of licensees to 1835), Hobsons, Joules and many changing guests (May and Oct beer festivals with up to 60 ales), draught continentals and lots of foreign bottled beers, a real cider or perry, friendly knowledgeable staff, simple snacky food (can bring your own), bustling front bar with light oak flooring and woodburner, small skylit side room and quarry-tiled back room; regular live music, quiz and comedy nights; suntrap courtyard, handy for station, open all day. *(Anon)*

UPTON MAGNA   SJ5512
Haughmond (01743) 709918
Pelham Road; SY4 4TZ Welcoming village pub refurbished under newish owners; log-fire bar with painted beams, oak-strip flooring and carpet, a house beer (Antler) brewed by Marstons and two local guests from brick servery, good food in brasserie and more upmarket and expensive restaurant (open evenings Thurs-Sat), village shop; children welcome, dogs in bar, great view to the Wrekin from attractive back garden, handy for Haughmond Hill walks and Attingham Park (NT), five bedrooms, open all day weekends. *(Robert W Buckle)*

WALL UNDER HEYWOOD   SO5092
Plough (01694) 771833
B4371; SY6 7DS Welcoming country pub with good generously served food including Sun carvery, five well kept ales such as Big Shed, Greene King and Hobsons, log fire and various odds and ends in small front bar, snug with darts, comfortable 'piano' lounge and dining conservatory; some live jazz; children and dogs welcome, tables in back garden, good local walks, open all day. *(Paul Bright)*

WELLINGTON   SJ6511
Cock (01952) 244954
Holyhead Road (B5061 – former A5); TF1 2DL 18th-c coaching inn popular for

its friendly real ale bar, Hobsons and five well kept quickly changing guests usually from small breweries, handpulled cider, separate bar specialising in belgian beers, friendly knowledgeable staff, big fireplace; beer garden with covered area, bedrooms, closed lunchtime Mon-Weds, open all day Thurs-Sat. *(Charlie May)*

WELLINGTON SJ6410
Old Orleton (01952) 255011
Holyhead Road (B5061, off M54 junction 7); TF1 2HA Modernised 17th-c red-brick coaching inn with restaurant and bar, well presented food from good varied menu including vegetarian options, a couple of Hobsons beers and Weston's cider, welcoming helpful staff; nice view of the Wrekin, ten bedrooms, good breakfast. *(Isobel Mackinlay)*

WELLINGTON SJ6411
Pheasant (01952) 260683
Market Street; TF1 1DT Recently renovated town-centre pub with microbrewery (can arrange tours), own Wrekin beers alongside guests including Everards (eight in total), a real cider, enjoyable good value lunchtime food, friendly staff; disabled access and facilities, beer garden, open all day. *(Bill Jones, Brian Banks)*

WELLINGTON SJ6511
William Withering (01952) 642800
New Street; TF1 1LU Comfortable and reliable open-plan Wetherspoons named after 18th-c local physician, ten real ales including Salopian and other local brews, usual good value food till 10pm, friendly staff, interesting pictures of historic Wellington; free wi-fi; handy for station, open all day from 8am. *(Mrs Sally Evans, Bill Jones)*

WELSHAMPTON SJ4335
Sun (01948) 710847
A495 Ellesmere–Whitchurch; SY12 0PH Friendly refurbished village pub with good choice of enjoyable reasonably priced food (order at bar), real ales such as Stonehouse; children and dogs welcome, big back garden, 15-minute walk to Llangollen/Shropshire Union Canal, three bedrooms, open (and food) all day. *(Anon)*

WHITCHURCH SJ5441
Anchor (01948) 663806
Pepper Street; SY13 1BG Renovated 17th-c pub tucked down small side street, spic and span bare-boards bar and flagstoned restaurant, well kept Sharps Doom Bar and three guests, enjoyable reasonably priced food including imaginative vegetarian choices, courteous attentive staff; free wi-fi; children welcome, tables in small courtyard, six comfortable bedrooms, open all day. *(Jennifer Banks, Robert W Buckle)*

WHITCHURCH SJ5441
Black Bear (01948) 663800
High Street/Bargates; SY13 1AZ Black and white building opposite church (a pub since 1667), six well kept interesting beers including Phoenix, enjoyable home-made food from open sandwiches up, characterful interior and good atmosphere; live acoustic music second Tues of the month; children and dogs (in bar) welcome, beer garden behind, open all day weekends. *(John and Hazel Sarkanen)*

WHITCHURCH SJ5441
Old Town Hall Vaults
(01948) 662251 *St Mary's Street; SY13 1QU* Red-brick 19th-c Joules local (birthplace of composer Sir Edward German), four of their ales and a guest, good value straightforward food from snacks up, main room divided into distinct areas with bar in one corner, oak panelling, stained glass, mirrors and signs, sturdy furniture including bench seating and cast-iron-framed tables, log fires, further room with glazed ceiling; outside listed gents'; dogs welcome, partly covered yard with barrel tables, open all day. *(Clive and Fran Dutson)*

WHITCHURCH SJ5345
Willey Moor Lock (01948) 663274
Tarporley Road; signed off A49 just under 2 miles N; SY13 4HF Large opened-up pub in picturesque spot by Llangollen Canal; two log fires, low beams and countless teapots and toby jugs, cheerful chatty atmosphere, half a dozen changing local ales and around 30 malt whiskies, good value quickly served pub food from sandwiches up; background music, games machine, no credit cards (debit cards accepted); children welcome away from bar, no dogs inside, terrace tables, secure garden with big play area. *(Charlie May)*

WISTANSTOW SO4385
Plough (01588) 673251
Off A49 and A489 N of Craven Arms; SY7 8DG Welcoming village pub adjoining the Woods brewery, their beers in peak condition and enjoyable home-made food including daily specials, friendly efficient service, smallish bar, airy high-ceilinged modern restaurant, games part with darts, dominoes and pool; background music, sports TV, free wi-fi; children and dogs welcome, some tables outside, open all day Fri-Sun, closed Tues. *(Patrick and Daphne Darley, Glenwys and Alan Lawrence, Ken Richards)*

WOORE SJ7342
Swan (01630) 647220
Nantwich Road (A51); CW3 9SA Handsome recently refurbished 19th-c pub, popular well kept ales and over 40 gins, friendly service, spacious interior with mix of bare boards, quarry tiles and carpet, some booth seating, panelling and pretty tiled fireplaces; background music; open all day. *(Anon)*

Somerset

 **ASHCOTT**   ST4337 Map 1
Ring o' Bells ◖
(01458) 210232 – www.ringobells.com
High Street; pub well signed off A39 W of Street; TA7 9PZ

Friendly village pub with homely décor in several bars, separate restaurant, tasty bar food and changing local ales

The same friendly family have run this traditional 18th-c pub for many years and a lot of their customers are loyal regulars. The three main bars, on different levels, are all comfortable: maroon plush-topped stools, cushioned mate's chairs and dark wooden pubby tables on patterned carpet, horsebrasses along the bressumer beam above the big stone fireplace and a growing collection of hand bells; background music. Bude Haven and RCH PG Steam on handpump, eight wines by the glass and local farm cider. There's also a separate restaurant, a skittle alley/function room, and plenty of picnic-sets out on the terrace and in the garden. The RSPB reserve Ham Wall is nearby.

Well thought-of food includes sandwiches, brie fritters with cranberry sauce, fresh grilled sardines, celery, almond and cashew nut roast with cheese sauce, a pie of the day, pork sausages with mustard mash and onion gravy, gammon with free-range egg or pineapple, wild bass fillet with roasted mediterranean vegetables, slow-cooked pork belly with spicy asian sauce, and puddings such as blueberry cheesecake and toffee apple pudding with custard. *Benchmark main dish: local smoked chicken with bacon and mushrooms au gratin £10.95. Two-course evening meal £20.00.*

Free house ~ Licensees John and Elaine Foreman and John Sharman ~ Real ale ~ Open 12-3, 7-11 (10.30 Sun) ~ Bar food 12-2, 7-10 ~ Restaurant ~ Children welcome ~ Dogs allowed in bar ~ Wi-fi *Recommended by Belinda Stamp, Martin Jones, Patrick and Daphne Darley*

 **BABCARY**   ST5628 Map 2
Red Lion ⭐ Y ⇌
(01458) 223230 – www.redlionbabcary.co.uk
Off A37 S of Shepton Mallett; about 2 miles N of roundabout where A37 meets A303 and A372; TA11 7ED

Thatched pub with comfortable rambling rooms, interesting daily changing food and local beers; good bedrooms

There's plenty of room in this bustling thatched inn for both drinkers and diners and the courteous staff make everyone welcome. Several distinct areas work their way around the bar; to the left is a longish room with dark red walls, a squashy leather sofa and two housekeeper's chairs around a low table by a woodburning stove, and a few well spaced tables and captain's chairs. There are elegant rustic wall lights, clay pipes in a cabinet, local papers or magazines to read and board games. A more dimly lit public bar with lovely dark flagstones has a high-backed old settle and other more straightforward chairs; table skittles and background music. In the good-sized dining room there's a large stone lion's head on a plinth above an open fire, and tables and chairs on a big rug and polished boards. Otter Ale and Teignworthy Reel Ale on handpump, a dozen wines by the glass and two farm ciders. The Den, in the pretty courtyard, has light modern furnishings, a summer wood-fired pizza oven and a brasserie-style menu, and doubles as a party, wedding and conference venue. There are picnic-sets and a play area in the long informal garden. The bedrooms are comfortable and well equipped and the pub is handy for the Fleet Air Arm Museum at Yeovilton, the Haynes Motor Museum in Sparkford and for shopping at Clarks Village in Street. Wheelchair access.

 Rewarding food includes sandwiches, duck liver parfait, devilled lambs kidneys with bacon, onions and toasted milk loaf, home-cooked honey-glazed ham and free-range eggs, a pie of the day, twice-baked cheese soufflé with cheese fondue, burger with toppings, pickles and triple-cooked chips, crispy confit duck leg with roasted beetroots and pearl barley, cod fillet with chorizo, butter beans, clams and white wine butter sauce, and puddings such as dark chocolate fondant with berries and apple and pear crumble with crème anglaise. *Benchmark main dish: slow-roast pork belly with mustard mash, braised red cabbage and red wine jus £15.50. Two-course evening meal £20.00.*

Free house ~ Licensee Charles Garrard ~ Real ale ~ Open 12-3, 6-midnight ~ Bar food 12-2.30 (3 weekends), 6.30-9.30 (9 Sun) ~ Restaurant ~ Children welcome ~ Dogs allowed in bar ~ Wi-fi ~ Live music Fri monthly ~ Bedrooms: £90/£110 *Recommended by Bob and Margaret Holder, Mike and Mary Carter, Helen and Brian Edgeley*

BATH
ST7465   Map 2
Chequers
(01225) 360017 – www.thechequersbath.com
Rivers Street; BA1 2QA

City-centre pub with friendly staff, pretty upstairs restaurant and enjoyable food and beers

Since 1776, this bustling pub has been offering refreshment to both locals and visitors. Being so central it's a popular spot; the two bar rooms have tartan-cushioned wall pews, chapel, farmhouse and kitchen chairs around all sorts of tables (each set with flowers) on parquet flooring, wedgwood blue paintwork and some fine plasterwork and a coal fire in a white-painted fireplace. Bath Gem and Butcombe Bitter on handpump and several wines by the glass. The attractive little restaurant upstairs has high-backed pale lilac suede dining chairs around candlelit tables, a wooden floor, a large wall mirror and a huge window into the kitchen. In warm weather there are picnic-sets under awning on the pavement.

Good, interesting food includes salt and pepper squid with aioli, chicken, leek and mushroom terrine with pickled mushrooms, artichoke and hazelnuts, burger with toppings, coleslaw and fries, gnocchi with seasonal vegetables and cheese, game pie with duck fat chips, teriyaki salmon salad with crab spring roll, seaweed, peanuts and coriander, and puddings such as dark chocolate fondant and burnt passion-fruit custard with mango and coconut. *Benchmark main dish: beer-battered haddock and chips £13.50. Two-course evening meal £22.30.*

Bath Pub Company ~ Lease Joe Cussens ~ Real ale ~ No credit cards ~ Open 12-11 ~
Bar food 6-9.30 Mon-Fri; 12-2.30, 6-10 Sat; 12-8 Sun ~ Restaurant ~ Children welcome ~
Dogs allowed in bar ~ Wi-fi *Recommended by Mr and Mrs A H Young, Dr Simon Innes*

BATH   ST7467 Map 2

Hare & Hounds

(01225) 482682 – www.hareandhoundsbath.com

Lansdown Road, Lansdown Hill; BA1 5TJ

Lovely views from back terrace with plenty of seating, relaxed bar areas, real ales, nice food and helpful staff

From windows in the bar and from seats and tables on the decked back terrace you can look down across villages and fields for miles. The atmosphere in the single long bar is relaxed and friendly, helped along by cheerful staff. There are chapel chairs and long cushioned wall settles around pale wood-topped tables on bare boards, minimal decoration on pale walls above a blue-grey dado and an attractively carved counter where they serve a beer named for the pub (from Caledonian) and St Austell Tribute on handpump and several wines by the glass; background music. There's a bronze hare and hound at one end of the mantelpiece above a log fire, and a big mirror above. A little side conservatory is similarly furnished, with dark slate flagstones. The neat small garden has seats beneath a gazebo.

As well as breakfasts (8.30-11.30am), the highly thought-of food includes sandwiches, sharing platters, gammon with bubble and squeak and a fried egg, wild mushroom and cherry vine tomato ragout with rosemary and garlic-infused polenta cake, a pie of the day, herb-crusted cod fillet with bacon, chorizo, spinach and bean cassoulet, and puddings such as dark chocolate and Cointreau brownie with chocolate orange sauce and apple and blackberry crumble; they also offer a two- and three-course set lunch. *Benchmark main dish: burger with toppings, coleslaw and fries £12.00. Two-course evening meal £21.20.*

Bath Pub Company ~ Lease Joe Cussens ~ Real ale ~ Open 8.30am-11pm (10.30 Sun) ~
Bar food 8.30-3, 5.30-9 (9.30 Fri, Sat); 8.30-4, 6-8 Sun ~ Children welcome ~ Dogs welcome
~ Wi-fi *Recommended by Richard Mason, Mr and Mrs A H Young, Dr and Mrs A K Clarke*

BATH   ST7465 Map 2

Marlborough

(01225) 423731 – www.marlborough-tavern.com

35 Marlborough Buildings/Weston Road; BA1 2LY

Open all day and with plenty of customers; candles, fresh flowers, cheerful staff and good food

The U-shaped bar here is busy throughout the day and the cheerful staff keep the atmosphere easy-going and friendly. There are bare boards throughout, church candles in sizeable jars on window sills and on the mantelpiece above a fireplace strung with fairy lights, and plenty of nightlights; each table has a single flower in a vase. Seating ranges from hefty button-back wall seats to chapel, kitchen and high-backed cushioned dining chairs. Above the green-grey dado on wallpaper or pale-painted walls are some cow and parrot paintings; background music. Chunky bar stools line the counter, where they serve Butcombe Bitter and guests such as Box Steam Piston Broke and Twisted Conscript on handpump and several wines by the glass. The little courtyard side garden is a suntrap in summer and there are benches and chairs around tables among the various plantings.

The reliably good food includes lemon vodka-cured salmon, hot smoked mackerel and pickled cockles with horseradish crème fraîche and beetroot and grapefruit salad, pigeon with black pudding, blue cheese and quince purée, butternut squash and chestnut mushroom risotto, burger with toppings, coleslaw and fries, five-spice duck breast with confit leg, carrot purée and soy and sesame dressing, and puddings such as lemon possett with orange purée, candied orange and almond crumble and buttermilk panna cotta with rhubarb and ginger cake; they also offer a two- and three-course set weekday lunch. *Benchmark main dish: smoked beef with garlic mash, braised leeks and red wine jus £20.50. Two-course evening meal £22.00.*

Free house ~ Licensees Joe Cussens and Justin Sleath ~ Real ale ~ Open 8am (9am weekends)-11pm (10.30 Sun) ~ Bar food 12-2.30, 6-9.30; 12-3, 6-10 Sat; 12-8 Sun ~ Children welcome ~ Dogs welcome ~ Wi-fi *Recommended by N R White*

 BATH　　　　　　　　　　　　　　　　　　　　　　　ST7564　Map 2

Old Green Tree 🍺

(01225) 448259

Green Street; BA1 2JZ

Tiny, unspoilt local with six real ales and lots of cheerful customers

As unchanging and unspoilt as ever, this tiny 18th-c tavern offering half a dozen beers remains a favourite with many (including us). The three small rooms – with oak panelling and low ceilings of wood and plaster – include a comfortable lounge on the left as you go in, its walls decorated with wartime aircraft pictures (in winter) and local artists' work (in spring and summer). There's also a back bar; the big skylight lightens things attractively. Green Tree Bitter (named for the pub by Blindmans Brewery), Butcombe Bitter and RCH Pitchfork, with guests such as Cotswold Spring Old Sodbury Mild, Cottage Iron Duke and Sarah Hughes Dark Ruby Mild on handpump, seven wines by the glass from a nice little list with helpful notes, 36 malt whiskies and a farm cider. The gents' is basic and down steep steps. No children.

 Lunchtime-only food includes sandwiches, soup, pâté, sausages with ale and onion gravy, vegetable curry, steak in ale pie and chicken korma. *Benchmark main dish: rare roast beef platter £9.00.*

Free house ~ Licensees Nick Luke and Tim Bethune ~ Real ale ~ No credit cards ~ Open 11-11; 12-6.30 Sun ~ Bar food 12-4.30; not evenings or Mon
Recommended by Dr J Barrie Jones, Roger and Donna Huggins, N R White

 BATH　　　　　　　　　　　　　　　　　　　　　　　ST7565　Map 2

Star 🍺

(01225) 425072 – www.abbeyales.co.uk/www.star-inn-bath.co.uk

Vineyards; The Paragon (A4), junction with Guinea Lane; BA1 5NA

Quietly chatty and unchanging old town local, the brewery tap for Abbey Ales

You get a real sense of the past in the four small linked rooms of this charming and unspoilt pub, and there's always a good mix of both locals and visitors. The many original features include traditional wall benches (one is known as Death Row), panelling, dim lighting and open fires. Abbey Bellringer plus guests such as Acorn Darkness, Bass, Coach House Cheshire Gold and Cross Bay Zenith on handpump, several wines by the glass, 30 malt whiskies and Cheddar Valley cider; darts, shove ha'penny, board games – and complimentary snuff. It gets particularly busy at weekends and is a bit of a walk from the city centre.

🍴 Food consists of filled rolls.

Punch ~ Lease Paul Waters and Alan Morgan ~ Real ale ~ Open 12-2.30, 5.30-midnight;
noon-1am Fri, Sat; 12-midnight Sun ~ Children welcome ~ Dogs welcome ~ Wi-fi
Recommended by Taff Thomas, Dr J Barrie Jones, N R White

BISHOPSWOOD
ST2512 Map 1

Candlelight 🌟| 🍺

(01460) 234476 – www.candlelight-inn.co.uk

Off A303/B3170 S of Taunton; TA20 3RS

**Friendly, hard-working licensees in neat dining pub with real ales
and farm cider, enjoyable imaginative food and seats in the garden**

For a friendly and gently civilised break from the A303, this extremely
well run pub is just the ticket. The neatly kept, more or less open-plan
rooms are separated into different areas by standing stone pillars and open
doorways. The beamed bar has high chairs by the counter where they serve
a fine range of drinks: Bass and Otter Bitter with guests such as Glastonbury
Lady of the Lake and Teignworthy Gun Dog tapped from the cask, nice wines
by the glass, a couple of farm ciders and winter drinks such as hot Pimms,
whisky toddies and hot chocolate. Also, captain's chairs, pews and cushioned
window seats around a mix of wooden tables on sanded boards, and a small
ornate fireplace. To the left is a comfortable area with a button-back sofa
beside a big woodburner, wheelback chairs and cushioned settles around
wooden tables set for dining, with country pictures, photos, a hunting horn
and bugles on the granite walls; background music and shove-ha'penny.
On the other side of the bar is a similarly furnished dining room. Outside,
a decked area has picnic-sets and a neatly landscaped garden has a paved
path winding through low walls set with plants.

🌟 Imaginative food (using their own vegetables) includes sandwiches, twice-baked
montgomery cheddar soufflé with red onion marmalade, scallops with pea and
mint purée and basil dressing, three-bean stew with tomato, rosemary, paprika and
garlic croutons, pork loin with sauté potatoes, chorizo, peppers and salsa verde, sea
bream with wild mushroom risotto, bordelaise sauce and beurre blanc, and puddings
such as chocolate meringues with chocolate mousse and raspberry coulis and vanilla
crème brûlée; they also offer a two- and three-course set lunch. *Benchmark main dish:
duck breast with dauphinoise potatoes, savoy and red cabbage and redcurrant jus
£17.00. Two-course evening meal £21.00.*

Free house ~ Licensees Tom Warren and Debbie Lush ~ Real ale ~ Open 12-2.30 (3 Sat),
6-11; 12-11 Sun; closed Mon, first week Nov ~ Bar food 12-2 (2.30 weekends), 7-9 (9.30 Fri,
Sat) ~ Well behaved children welcome away from bar area ~ Dogs allowed in bar ~ Wi-fi
Recommended by Michael and Diana Clatworthy, Patrick and Daphne Darley

BRISTOL
ST5873 Map 2

Highbury Vaults 🍺 £

(0117) 973 3203 – www.highburyvaults.co.uk

St Michael's Hill, Cotham; BS2 8DE

**Cheerful town pub with up to eight real ales, good value tasty
bar food and friendly atmosphere**

As ever, this unpretentious, friendly pub is full of customers keen to try
the fine range of regularly changing real ales on handpump. There might
be Youngs Bitter and London Gold plus guests such as Bath Gem, Cotswold

Spring Stunner, Flying Monk Elmers, St Austell Tribute and Towles Old Smiler; six wines by the glass and eight malt whiskies too. The little front bar, with a corridor beside it, leads through to a series of small rooms: wooden floors, green and cream paintwork and old-fashioned furniture and prints (including plenty of royal family period engravings and lithographs in the front room). A model railway runs on a shelf the full length of the pub, with tunnels through the walls; bar billiards, TV and board games. The attractive back terrace has tables built into a partly covered flowery arbour; disabled access to main bar (but not the loos).

Good value food includes filled rolls, lasagne, fish pie, burgers with toppings and coleslaw, meat or vegetarian chilli, and puddings such as chocolate brownie and sticky toffee pudding. *Benchmark main dish: chilli con carne £6.75. Two-course evening meal £15.00.*

Youngs ~ Manager Bradd Francis ~ Real ale ~ No credit cards ~ Open 12-midnight (11 Sun) ~ Bar food 12-2, 5.30-8.30; 12-3 Sun ~ Children welcome ~ Dogs allowed in bar ~ Wi-fi
Recommended by Carol and Barry Craddock, Lindy Andrews

CHARLTON HORETHORNE
Kings Arms 🌟 ⇔   ST6623   Map 2
(01963) 220281 – www.thekingsarms.co.uk
B3145 Wincanton–Sherborne; DT9 4NL

Bustling inn with relaxed bars and more formal restaurant, good ales and wines and enjoyable food; bedrooms

Many customers are here to enjoy the rewarding food but the enthusiastic, hands-on licensee also offers a warm welcome to those who might want just a pint and a chat. It's a smart place and the main bar has an appealing assortment of local art (all for sale) on dark mulberry or cream walls, nice old carved wooden dining chairs and pine pews around a mix of tables, a slate floor and a woodburning stove. Leading off is a cosy room with sofas, and newspapers on low tables. Butcombe Bitter, Wadworths 6X and a guest beer on handpump are served from the rather fine granite bar counter; they also keep 14 wines by the glass, nine malt whiskies and local farm cider. To the left of the main door is an informal dining room with Jacobean-style chairs and tables on a pale wooden floor and more local artwork. The back restaurant (past the open kitchen which is fun to peek into) has decorative wood and glass mirrors, wicker or black leather high-backed dining chairs around chunky, polished, pale wooden tables on coir carpeting, and handsome striped curtains. The attractive courtyard at the back of the inn has chrome and wicker chairs around teak tables under green parasols; a smokers' shelter overlooks a croquet lawn. The comfortable bedrooms are well equipped and contemporary.

The enterprising food, using home-made pasta, bread and ice-cream, includes twice-baked cheese soufflé with cranberry sauce, home-smoked pheasant with pancetta crisp and braised lentils, steak burger with stilton, red onion marmalade and chips, jerusalem artichoke and goats cheese risotto, hake with pea purée, fennel, mooli and rocket salad and caper and parsley butter, venison suet pudding with pancetta and baby onion jus, and puddings such as bakewell tart and Valrhona chocolate fondant with cherry sorbet. *Benchmark main dish: mozzarella-stuffed chicken breast wrapped in parma ham with mediterranean vegetables £16.95. Two-course evening meal £23.50.*

Free house ~ Licensee Tony Lethbridge ~ Real ale ~ Open 10am-11pm; 10.30-10.30 Sun ~ Bar food 12-2.30, 7-9.30 (10 Fri, Sat); 12-2.30, 7-9 Sun ~ Restaurant ~ Children welcome ~ Dogs allowed in bar ~ Wi-fi ~ Bedrooms: /£135 *Recommended by Mike and Mary Carter, John Chambers, Chris and Angela Buckell, Bob West, Michael Hill*

CHURCHILL

ST4459 Map 1

Crown 🍺 £

(01934) 852995 –

The Batch; in village, turn off A368 into Skinners Lane at Nelson Arms; BS25 5PP

Unspoilt and unchanging small cottage with friendly customers and staff, super range of real ales and homely lunchtime food

Tapped from the cask, the eight real ales here might be Bath Gem, Butcombe Bitter, Otter Bitter, Palmers IPA, RCH IPA, St Austell Tribute and two quickly changing guests; several wines by the glass and local ciders too. It's an untouched simple old pub; the small and rather local-feeling stone-floored and cross-beamed room on the right has a wooden window seat, an unusually sturdy settle, built-in wall benches, a log fire and chatty, friendly customers. The left-hand room has a slate floor, and steps that lead past the big log fire in its large stone fireplace to another sitting area. There's no noise from music or games (except perhaps dominoes). The outside lavatories are basic. There are garden tables at the front, more seats on the back lawn and hill views; the Mendip morris men visit in summer and some of the best walking on the Mendips is nearby. There isn't a pub sign outside, but no one seems to have a problem finding it.

🍴 The fair-priced traditional food – served at lunchtime only – includes sandwiches (the rare roast beef is popular), beef casserole, cauliflower cheese, lasagne, and puddings such as spotted dick with custard and chocolate pudding. *Benchmark main dish: chilli beef £6.40.*

Free house ~ Licensee Brian Clements ~ Real ale ~ No credit cards ~ Open 11 (12 Sun)-11 ~ Bar food 12-2.30 ~ Children welcome away from bar ~ Dogs allowed in bar ~ Wi-fi
Recommended by Taff Thomas, Hugh Roberts

CLAPTON-IN-GORDANO

ST4773 Map 1

Black Horse 🍺 £

(01275) 842105 – www.thekicker.co.uk

4 miles from M5 junction 19; A369 towards Portishead, then B3124 towards Clevedon; in North Weston opposite school, turn left signposted Clapton, then in village take second right, may be signed 'Clevedon, Clapton Wick'; BS20 7RH

Unpretentious old pub with lots of cheerful customers, friendly service, real ales, cider and simple lunchtime food; pretty garden

Thankfully, things don't change here: it remains an old-fashioned and unspoilt 14th-c local that appeals to customers of all ages. The partly flagstoned, partly red-tiled main room has winged settles and built-in wall benches around narrow, dark wooden tables, window seats, a big log fire with stirrups and bits on the mantelbeam, and amusing cartoons and photographs of the pub. A window in an inner snug retains metal bars from the days when this room was the petty sessions gaol; also, high-backed settles – one with a marvellous carved and canopied creature, another with an art nouveau copper insert reading 'East, West, Hame's Best' – lots of mugs hanging from black beams and numerous small prints and photographs. A simply furnished room is the only place families are allowed; background music. Bath Gem, Butcombe Bitter, Courage Best, Otter Ale and St Austell Proper Job on handpump or tapped from the cask, six wines by the glass and three farm ciders. There are old rustic tables and benches in the garden, with more to one side of the car park – the summer flowers are quite a sight. Paths from the pub lead up Naish Hill or to Cadbury Camp (National Trust) and there's access to local cycle routes.

Straightforward lunchtime food includes baguettes and baps with lots of hot and cold fillings and daily specials such as lasagne, pork in cider, beef goulash and paprika chicken. *Benchmark main dish: slow-cooked lamb casserole £8.50.*

Enterprise ~ Lease Nicholas Evans ~ Real ale ~ Open 11-11; 12-10 Sun ~ Bar food 12-2.30; not evenings or Sun ~ Children in family room only ~ Dogs allowed in bar ~ Wi-fi
Recommended by Taff Thomas, Comus and Sarah Elliott, Chris and Angela Buckell, Roy Hoing, John Pritchard

COMBE HAY
ST7359 Map 2
Wheatsheaf ★ ☆ 🍷 🛏
(01225) 833504 – www.wheatsheafcombehay.co.uk
Village signposted off A367 or B3110 S of Bath; BA2 7EG

Smart and cheerful country dining pub with first class food using locally foraged produce; attractive bedrooms

Much of the space in this 16th-c pub is given over to diners enjoying the delicious food, but drinkers can sit in a central area by a big fireplace, with sofas on dark flagstones and daily papers and current issues of *The Field* and *Country Life* on a low table. Friendly staff serve Butcombe Bitter and Otter Bitter on handpump, 16 wines by the glass from a very good list, 15 malt whiskies and a farm cider. Other areas have stylish high-backed grey wicker dining chairs around chunky modern dining tables, on parquet or coir matting. It's fresh and bright, with block-mounted photo-prints, contemporary artwork and mirrors with colourful ceramic mosaic frames (many for sale) on white-painted stonework or robin's-egg blue plaster walls. The sills of the many shuttered windows house anything from old soda siphons to a stuffed kingfisher and a Great Lakes model tugboat. Glinting glass wall chandeliers and nightlights in entertaining holders supplement the ceiling spotlights; background music and a cheerful cocker spaniel. The two-level front garden has picnic-sets and a fine view over the church and valley, and the bedrooms are stylishly simple and spacious; surrounding walks.

 The impressive food (they keep chickens, ducks and bees and grow their own produce) includes sandwiches, lamb terrine with minted beetroot ketchup, scallops with fish soup and rouille, burger with cheese and chips, venison cottage pie with griottine cherries, duck breast with confit leg, Cointreau and cranberry jus, gloucester old spot pork with parma ham, black pudding and sage and onion croquettes, rib-eye steak with bone marrow butter and skinny chips, and puddings such as treacle tart with lemon curd ice-cream and dark chocolate fondant with morello cherry sorbet; they also offer a two- and three-course set menu (Tues-Fri). *Benchmark main dish: daily fresh fish dish £16.50. Two-course evening meal £25.00.*

Free house ~ Licensee Ian Barton ~ Real ale ~ Open 10-3, 6-11; 10-3 Sun; closed Sun evening, Mon (except bank holidays), first week Jan ~ Bar food 12-2, 6.30-9; 12-2.30 Sun ~ Restaurant ~ Children welcome ~ Dogs welcome ~ Wi-fi ~ Bedrooms: /£120
Recommended by Mrs Julie Thomas, Nick Lawless

COMPTON MARTIN
ST5457 Map 2
Ring o' Bells
(01761) 221284 – www.ringobellscomptonmartin.co.uk
A368 Bath–Weston; BS40 6JE

Seats in country garden, traditional bar rooms and a friendly atmosphere; bedrooms

This bustling country pub is in an attractive spot overlooked by the Mendip Hills and the big garden has seats and tables and a children's play area.

The traditional flagstoned front bar has a big inglenook log fire, traditional seats on flagstones and steps that lead up to a spacious back area with oak boards, stripped-stone walls, various odds and ends, gold discs and signed celebrity photos. Friendly staff serve Butcombe Bitter and a changing guest on handpump and several wines by the glass; board games and background music. The two spacious bedrooms are comfortable.

As well as lunchtime sandwiches, the popular food includes salt and pepper squid, scallops with pancetta and maple syrup, braised ham hock with poached eggs, triple-cheese macaroni, venison sausages with cannelloni beans and redcurrant jelly, aged rib-eye steak with chips and salsa verde, grilled mackerel with bulgar wheat, plums and cream, duck breast with parsnip fondant, leeks, capers and brown butter, and puddings such as lemon meringue cream and dark chocolate brownie with peanut butter ice-cream and mixed fruit jam. *Benchmark main dish: beef in ale pie £10.00. Two-course evening meal £19.00.*

Free house ~ Licensees Jo and Ian Bennett ~ Real ale ~ Open 12-3, 6-11; 12-11 Thurs-Sun ~ Bar food 12-2.45, 6-8.45; 12-5 Sun ~ Restaurant ~ Children allowed until 8.30 ~ Dogs allowed in bar ~ Wi-fi ~ Weekly live music Fri or Sat *Recommended by Gus Swan, Neil Allen*

CORTON DENHAM

Queens Arms ⭐ ♀ 🍺 🛏

ST6322   Map 2

(01963) 220317 – www.thequeensarms.com
Village signposted off B3145 N of Sherborne; DT9 4LR

Civilised stone inn with super choice of drinks, interesting food and a sunny garden; comfortable, stylish bedrooms

With lots to do in the surrounding area, it makes sense to stay overnight in the comfortable bedrooms here (they have lovely country views) and enjoy the particularly good breakfasts (available to non-residents too). The bustling, high-beamed bar has rugs on flagstones and two big armchairs in front of an open fire, some old pews, barrel seats and a sofa, church candles and big bowls of flowers. There's also a couple of separate restaurants – one with cushioned wall seating and chunky leather chairs around dark wooden tables, mirrors down one side and a drop-down cinema screen (screenings are held twice a month). Exmoor Ale, Gyle 59 Toujours, Otter Bitter and Teignworthy Reel Ale on handpump, 22 wines (including champagne) by the glass from a carefully chosen list, 57 malt whiskies, 18 gins, six ciders, unusual bottled beers from Belgium, Germany and the US, and four local apple juices. A south-facing back terrace has teak tables and chairs under parasols (or heaters, if it's cool) and colourful flower tubs. Good walks.

Using produce from their own farm, the imaginative food includes tapas (such as whitebait with bloody mary mayo, and treacle and stout pork cheek nuggets) as well as sandwiches, guinea fowl with ragu, pasta, yorkshire toast and truffle breadcrumbs, a fish plate to share, rib burger, smoked chicken thigh, home-cured bacon and fennel pollen-chicken drumstick with chips, hazelnut, taleggio and spinach tortellini with rocket pesto and fennel salad, mutton and celeriac pie with slow-roasted lamb rump, roasted carrots and chanterelle mushroom jus, and puddings such as saffron and cider-poached pear tarte tatin with lemon curd mousse and caramel panna cotta with parkin, burnt orange sorbet and chocolate soil. *Benchmark main dish: honey-and sesame-glazed duck breast with compressed pear and artichokes and charred liver jus £18.95. Two-course evening meal £25.00.*

Free house ~ Licensees Jeanette and Gordon Reid ~ Real ale ~ Open 8am-11.30pm (midnight Sat); 8am-11pm Sun ~ Bar food 12-3, 6-10 (9 Sun) ~ Restaurant ~ Children welcome ~ Dogs allowed in bar and bedrooms ~ Bedrooms: £85/£110
Recommended by Mike and Mary Carter

CROSCOMBE

ST5844 Map 2

George 🍺 🛏

(01749) 342306 – www.thegeorgeinn.co.uk

Long Street (A371 Wells–Shepton Mallet); BA5 3QH

Warmly welcoming and family-run coaching inn with informative canadian landlord, enjoyable food, good local beers and attractive garden; bedrooms

'A first class pub in all aspects,' says a reader about this particularly well run and genuinely friendly inn – and we'd second that opinion. The main bar has a good mix of locals and visitors, stripped stone, dark wooden tables and chairs and more comfortable seats, a settle by one of the log fires in inglenook fireplaces, and the family's grandfather clock; a snug area has a woodburning stove. The attractive dining room has more stripped stone, local artwork and family photographs on burgundy walls and high-backed cushioned dining chairs around a mix of tables. The back bar has canadian timber and a pew reclaimed from the local church, and there's a family room with games and books for children. King George the Thirst (from Blindmans), Abbey Bellringer, Cheddar Potholer and Twisted Gaucho on handpump or tapped from the cask, four farm ciders, ten wines by the glass and home-made elderflower cordial. Darts, a skittle alley, board games, shove-ha'penny and a canadian wooden table game called crokinole. The attractive, sizeable garden has seats on a heated and covered terrace, flower borders, a grassed area, a wood-fired pizza oven (used on Fridays) and chickens; children's swings.

The highly thought-of food, using their own and other local produce, includes lunchtime baguettes, smoked mackerel pâté, prawn cocktail, home-cooked ham and eggs, lasagne, vegetable curry, steak in ale pie, coconut and lime chicken with spicy chickpeas and onion and mint salad, scallops in garlic butter with balsamic reduction, and puddings such as apple and blackberry crumble and crème brûlée; Wednesday is steak and chips night. *Benchmark main dish: smoked haddock with sauté mushrooms, greens and poached egg £15.00. Two-course evening meal £20.00.*

Free house ~ Licensees Peter and Veryan Graham ~ Real ale ~ Open 10-3, 6-11; 10-11 Sat, Sun ~ Bar food 12-2.30, 6-9; 12-8 Sun ~ Restaurant ~ Children welcome ~ Dogs allowed in bar ~ Wi-fi ~ Bedrooms: £50/£80 *Recommended by Dr J Barrie Jones, Taff Thomas, Ann and Colin Hunt*

DULVERTON

SS9127 Map 1

Woods ★ 🌟 ♀

(01398) 324007 – www.woodsdulverton.co.uk

Bank Square; TA22 9BU

Smartly informal place with exceptional wines, real ales, first rate food and a good mix of customers

A stunning wine list and excellent food continue to draw enthusiastic praise from our readers – but this is a proper pub too, with locals (and maybe their dogs) crowding around the bar and enjoying the well kept St Austell Cornish Best, HSD and Proper Job tapped from the cask. The genuinely friendly staff also serve farm cider, many sherries, some unusual spirits and they will open any of their 400 wines from an extraordinarily good list for just a glass; there's also an unlisted collection of about 500 well aged new world wines that the landlord will happily chat about. The pub is on the edge of Exmoor, and there are plenty of good sporting prints on the salmon pink walls, antlers and other hunting trophies, stuffed birds and a couple of salmon rods. There are bare boards on the left by the bar counter, daily papers, tables partly separated by stable-style timbering and masonry dividers, and a carpeted area on the right with a woodburning stove in a big fireplace; there may be unobjectionable background music. Big windows look on to the quiet town centre (there's also a couple of metal tables on the pavement) and a small suntrap back courtyard has a few picnic-sets.

Using their own farm produce and other west country ingredients, the first class food includes lunchtime baguettes, chicken liver and foie gras parfait with pickled wild mushrooms, quail egg and port wine syrup, gravadlax, smoked salmon tartare and lightly cured trout fillet with horseradish and almond sauce, wild mushroom linguine with truffle oil, corn-fed organic chicken on puy lentils with roasted garlic and shallots and madeira sauce, bass fillet, razor clam and scallop with creamed leeks, celeriac and sauce vierge, lamb rump, grilled chop and black pudding with caramelised onion and thyme sauce, and puddings such as coconut panna cotta with iced pineapple parfait and hot dark chocolate fondant with vanilla ice-cream. *Benchmark main dish: seared steak salad £10.50. Two-course evening meal £18.00.*

Free house ~ Licensee Patrick Groves ~ Real ale ~ Open 12-3, 6-11 ~ Bar food 12-2, 7-9.30 ~ Restaurant ~ Children welcome ~ Dogs welcome ~ Wi-fi *Recommended by Matias Ramon Mendiola, Richard and Penny Gibbs, Keith Stevens, Lynda and Trevor Smith, Sheila Topham, Richard and Patricia Jefferson, M G Hart*

DUNSTER
Luttrell Arms ⭐ ♀ 🛏

SS9943 Map 1

(01643) 821555 – www.luttrellarms.co.uk
High Street; A396; TA24 6SG

Character bars and dining areas in lovely hotel, antiques and fresh flowers, a thoughtful choice of drinks, enjoyable food and seats in courtyard and garden; luxurious bedrooms

There are some fine medieval features in this civilised and rather special hotel. The Old Kitchen Bar has the workings of the former kitchen with meat hooks on the beamed ceiling and a huge log fire and bread oven. The main bar – popular locally – has swords and guns on the wall above a huge fireplace, cushions on antique chairs, horsebrasses, copper kettles, plates and warming pans, animal furs dotted here and there, a stag's head and an antler chandelier, and various country knick-knacks. Exmoor Ale, Otter Amber and Quantock Wills Neck on handpump, 16 good wines by the glass, a dozen malt whiskies and farm cider; staff are courteous and helpful. There's also the Boot Bar with a lovely panelled wall seat and rugs on quarry tiles, a small snug and a deeply comfortable sitting room with one beautiful panelled wall, a woodburning stove and plenty of armchairs, sofas and window seats. The lovely garden is on several levels with seats on lawns or terraces and haunting castle views; a little galleried courtyard has metalwork chairs and tables. Some of the bedrooms are opulent with four-posters, antiques and carved fireplaces; breakfasts are first class. The town, on the edge of Exmoor National Park, is pretty and full of interest.

A wide choice of interesting food includes sandwiches and ciabattas, beetroot and vodka-cured salmon with home-made fennel bread and lemon mayonnaise, chicken and mushroom terrine with piccalilli, blue cheese and plum tomato tart with pear chutney, green vegetable risotto with a poached egg, a curry of the week, venison sausages with champ potato and caramelised onion gravy, a pie of the week, pork cutlet with black pudding mash, sauté hispi cabbage, apple purée and tarragon jus, a fish dish of the day with brown shrimp butter, and puddings such as dark and white chocolate mousse and date and walnut pudding with butterscotch sauce and jaffa cake ice-cream. *Benchmark main dish: beer-battered fish and chips £11.95. Two-course evening meal £20.00.*

Free house ~ Licensee Tim Waldren ~ Real ale ~ Open 11-11; 12-11 Sun ~ Bar food 9.30-9.30 ~ Restaurant ~ Children welcome ~ Dogs allowed in bar and bedrooms ~ Wi-fi ~ Bedrooms: £100/£140 *Recommended by Richard and Penny Gibbs, Martin Jones, Isobel Mackinlay*

EXFORD

SS8538 Map 1

Crown 🛏

(01643) 831554 – www.crownhotelexmoor.co.uk

The Green (B3224); TA24 7PP

17th-c coaching inn in pretty moorland village, with friendly character bar with hunting-theme decor, real ales, enjoyable food and big back garden; comfortable bedrooms

The two-room bar in this family-run Exmoor inn has an easy-going atmosphere and is very much the hub of village life. It has a log fire in a big stone fireplace, plenty of stuffed animal heads and hunting prints on cream walls, some hunting-themed plates and old photographs of the area, cushioned benches and other traditional pubby tables and chairs on bare boards. There are stools against the counter where they serve Exmoor Ale and Gold and St Austell Trelawny on handpump, a dozen wines by the glass, 15 malt whiskies and three farm ciders; TV and board games. The dining room is rather smart. At the front of the building are some tables and chairs with more on a back terrace – as well as a stream threading its way past gently sloping lawns in the three-acre garden. The bedrooms are warm and comfortable, they're very dog friendly, have stabling for horses and can arrange riding, fishing, shooting, hunting, wildlife-watching, cycling and trekking.

Rewarding food using organic produce includes baguettes, mussels in cider, onion and garlic, ham hock and guinea fowl terrine wrapped in parma ham with chutney, wild boar and apple sausages with wholegrain mustard potatoes and caramelised onion sauce, wild mushroom risotto with truffle oil, beer-battered cod and triple-cooked chips, braised lamb shoulder with cauliflower purée and dauphinoise potatoes, and puddings such as chocolate tart with raspberry coulis and pistachio ice-cream and blackcurrant soufflé with liquorice ice-cream. *Benchmark main dish: beef in ale pie £13.95. Two-course evening meal £19.50.*

Free house ~ Licensees Sara and Dan Whittaker ~ Real ale ~ Open 12-11 ~ Bar food 12-2.30, 6-9.30 ~ Restaurant ~ Children in eating area of bar and restaurant ~ Dogs welcome ~ Wi-fi ~ Bedrooms: £69/£125 *Recommended by Emma Scofield, Martin Jones*

HINTON ST GEORGE

ST4212 Map 1

Lord Poulett Arms 🎯 🍷 🛏

(01460) 73149 – www.lordpoulettarms.com

Off A30 W of Crewkerne and off Merriott road (declassified – former A356, off B3165) N of Crewkerne; TA17 8SE

Somerset Dining Pub of the Year

Thatched 17th-c stone inn with antiques-filled rooms, top class food using home-grown vegetables, good choice of drinks and a pretty garden; attractive bedrooms

Our readers love this particularly well run and civilised inn, with many praising the pretty bedrooms and splendid breakfasts. Several attractive and cosy linked bar areas have hop-draped beams, walls of honey-coloured stone or painted in bold Farrow & Ball colours, rugs on bare boards or flagstones, open fires (one in an inglenook, another in a raised fireplace that separates two rooms), antique brass candelabra, fresh flowers and candles, and some lovely old farmhouse, windsor and ladderback chairs around fine oak or elm tables. Branscombe Vale Bitter and Branoc and Otter Ale on handpump, 11 wines by the glass, jugs of Pimms and home-made cordial, some interesting whiskies and local bottled cider and perry; board games. The pub cat is called Honey. Outside, beneath a wisteria-clad pergola, are white metalwork tables and chairs in a mediterranean-style lavender-edged gravelled area, and picnic-sets in a wild flower meadow; boules. This is a peaceful and attractive village with nice surrounding walks.

Exceptional food using home-grown and other local, organic produce includes sandwiches, bass tataki with ginger, lime, sesame, chilli, coriander and soy sauce, duck ravioli with jerusalem artichoke purée, duck ham, orange coulis and truffled honey, beetroot risotto with goats cheese and basil, burger with black pudding, pickled cucumber, fried egg, aioli and triple-cooked chips, tandoori chicken with lentil salad, tomato and onion achar (indian-style pickle) and mint yoghurt, and puddings such as praline fondant with coffee ice-cream and walnut 'snow' and eton mess with mango, passion fruit and lime; they also offer a two- and three-course set menu. *Benchmark main dish: smoked lamb rump with aubergine caviar, red pepper and balsamic jus £20.00. Two-course evening meal £21.00.*

Free house ~ Licensees Steve Hill and Michelle Paynton ~ Real ale ~ Open 12-11 ~ Bar food 12-2.30, 6-9.15; 12-3.15 Sun ~ Children welcome ~ Dogs allowed in bar ~ Wi-fi ~ Live music summer Sun afternoons ~ Bedrooms: £60/£85 *Recommended by Gene and Tony Freemantle, Bob and Margaret Holder, John Chambers, Patrick and Daphne Darley*

HOLCOMBE
Holcombe Inn 🎔 🛏

ST6649   Map 2

(01761) 232478 – www.holcombeinn.co.uk
Off A367; Stratton Road; BA3 5EB

Charming inn with far-reaching views, cosy bars, open woodburners, a wide choice of drinks and good food; lovely bedrooms

With a really friendly welcome, enjoyable food and stylish bedrooms, this country inn is a winner with our readers. The cosy room to the right of the main entrance has sofas around a central table and an open woodburning stove. To the left is the bar: fine old flagstones, window seats and chunky captain's chairs around pine-topped tables, and a carved wooden counter where they serve Bath Gem and Butcombe Bitter on handpump, 21 wines and champagne by the glass, 25 malt whiskies, cocktails and a thoughtful choice of local drinks (cider, vodka, sloe gin, various juices); board games and background music. A two-way woodburning stove also warms the dining room, which is partly carpeted and partly flagstoned, and has partitioning creating snug seating areas, a mix of high-backed patterned or leather and brass-studded dining chairs around all sorts of tables; daily newspapers. A little sitting area leads off here and serves specialist teas and coffees. The bedrooms are well equipped and some have views over peaceful farmland to Downside Abbey's school; there are picnic-sets on a terrace and side lawn, and the sunsets can be stunning.

The highly rated food includes lunchtime sandwiches, salt and pepper squid with garlic aioli, seared pigeon breast with parsnip purée and red wine jus, roasted butternut squash cannelloni in rich cheese sauce, lager-battered cod and chips, trio of local sausages with crispy pancetta and red onion gravy, rack of local lamb with home-made faggot, dauphinoise potatoes and rosemary jus, pork medallion with slow-roasted belly, braised cheek, morcilla ball and apple and cider jus, and puddings. *Benchmark main dish: pie of the day £13.95. Two-course evening meal £22.00.*

Free house ~ Licensee Julie Berry ~ Real ale ~ Open 12-11 ~ Bar food 12-2.30, 6-9; 12-9 Fri-Sun ~ Restaurant ~ Children welcome ~ Dogs allowed in bar and bedrooms ~ Wi-fi ~ Bedrooms: £75/£120 *Recommended by Tony Tollitt*

HUISH EPISCOPI   ST4326 Map 1
Rose & Crown 🍺 £
(01458) 250494
Off A372 E of Langport; TA10 9QT

17th-c pub in the same family for almost 150 years, local cider and real ales, simple food and a friendly welcome

This unspoilt thatched inn is known locally as 'Eli's' after the friendly licensees' grandfather, and it's been in the same family for well over 145 years. There's no bar as such, just a central flagstoned still room where drinks are served: Teignworthy Reel Ale and a couple of guests such as Glastonbury Mystery Tor and Hop Back Crop Circle, local farm cider and Somerset cider brandy. The casual little front parlours, with their unusual pointed-arch windows, have family photographs, books, cribbage, dominoes, shove-ha'penny, bagatelle and attract a good mix of both locals and visitors. A much more orthodox big back extension has pool, a games machine and a juke box. There are plenty of seats and tables in the big outdoor area and two lawns – one is enclosed and has a children's play area; you can camp on the adjoining paddock. There's also a separate skittle alley, a big car park, morris men (in summer) and fine nearby river walks; the site of the Battle of Langport (1645) is close by.

 Reasonably priced food includes sandwiches, good soups, chicken in creamy tarragon and white wine sauce, cottage pie, broccoli and stilton tart, pork, apple and cider cobbler, and puddings such as sticky toffee pudding and apple crumble. *Benchmark main dish: steak in ale pie £8.45. Two-course evening meal £12.50.*

Free house ~ Licensees Maureen Pittard, Stephen Pittard and Patricia O'Malley ~ Real ale ~ No credit cards ~ Open 11.30-2.30, 5.15-11; 11.30-11.30 Fri, Sat; 12-10.30 Sun ~ Bar food 12-2, 5.30-7.30; not Sun evening ~ Children welcome ~ Dogs allowed in bar ~ Wi-fi ~ Live music last Thurs of month, storytelling second Sun of month, folk May-Sept third Sat of month *Recommended by Peter Meister, Kevin Chamberlain, Robert Colledge*

KINGSDON   ST5126 Map 2
Kingsdon Inn 🍷
(01935) 840543 – www.kingsdoninn.co.uk
Off B3151; TA11 7LG

Charming old cottage with low-ceilinged rooms, west country beers, friendly staff and well thought-of food; bedrooms

This former cider house looks rather like a private cottage from the outside, but it's just the place to escape the A303 for a lunchtime stop. The main bar has a woodburning stove, built-in wooden and cushioned wall seats with pretty scatter cushions, farmhouse and wheelback chairs around scrubbed kitchen tables set with candles and fresh flowers, and red quarry tiles; background classical music. Some steps lead up to a carpeted dining area with a few low sagging beams, half-panelled walls and similar furnishings; one table is snugly set into a former inglenook fireplace. Stools on pale tiles against the counter are popular with locals, and friendly, helpful staff serve Butcombe Bitter and St Austell Tribute on handpump and 18 wines by the glass. There's a second dining area plus an attractive separate restaurant with another woodburning stove. The garden has picnic-sets on grass and a small path leading to the front door. The pub is handy for the Fleet Air Arm Museum.

Good food includes wild rabbit and pistachio terrine with apple chutney, hand-picked crab meat with fennel and orange salad, smoked haddock with bubble and squeak, a poached egg and wholegrain mustard velouté, sausages with roasted red onion gravy, chicken with honey-glazed root vegetables and red wine jus, cottage pie, and puddings such as sticky toffee pudding with butterscotch sauce and home-made ginger ice-cream and vanilla crème brûlée with roasted plums; they also offer a two- and three-course set lunch. *Benchmark main dish: caremelised free-range duck breast with potato terrine, truffled leeks and manuka honey caramel £16.00. Two-course evening meal £21.50.*

Game Bird Inns ~ Managers Adam Cain and Cinzia Iezzi ~ Real ale ~ Open 12-3, 6-11 (7-10.30 Sun) ~ Bar food 12-2, 6.30-9; 12-3, 7-9 Sun ~ Children welcome ~ Dogs allowed in bar ~ Wi-fi ~ Bedrooms: £65/£95 *Recommended by Alfie Bayliss, Dr Simon Innes*

MELLS
Talbot 🌟 ⍾ 🛏
ST7249 Map 2

(01373) 812254 – www.talbotinn.com

W of Frome, off A362 or A361; BA11 3PN

Carefully refurbished and interesting old coaching inn, real ales and good wines, inventive food and seats in courtyard; lovely bedrooms

The countryside surrounding this handsome former coaching inn is stunning and the eight smart and stylish bedrooms make a good base for exploring the area; breakfasts are especially good. The bustling candlelit bar is nicely informal with various wooden tables and chairs on big quarry tiles, a woodburning stove in a stone fireplace, and stools (much used by locals) against the counter where friendly, helpful staff serve a beer named for the pub (from Keystone), Butcombe Bitter and a couple of guests such as Butcombe Big IPA and Hop Back Citra on handpump, several good wines by the glass and a farm cider. The two linked dining rooms have brass-studded leather chairs around wooden tables, a log fire with candles in fine clay cups on the mantelpiece above and lots of coaching prints on the walls; quiet background music and board games. The courtyard, with its pale green metalwork chairs and tables, has a mediterranean feel. Off here, in separate buildings, are the enjoyable, rustic-feeling sitting room with sofas, chairs and tables, smart magazines, a huge mural and vast glass bottles (free films or popular TV programmes are shown here on Sunday evenings); and the grill room, where food is cooked simply on a big open fire and served at shared refectory tables overlooked by 18th-c portraits. Until the dissolution of the monasteries in the early 16th c, this village was owned by Glastonbury Abbey – do visit the lovely church where Siegfried Sassoon is buried; the walled gardens opposite the inn are very pretty. This is sister pub to the Beckford Arms at Fonthill Gifford (Wiltshire).

Impressive food includes lunchtime sandwiches, mackerel tartare with cauliflower kimchi, sesame and radish salad and soya mayonnaise, goats curd with carrots, fermented elderberries, hazelnuts and linseeds, burger with toppings, coleslaw and chips, fennel seed-grilled pork neck with charred onions and wild garlic, red deer steak with parsley root purée, pearl barley, beetroots and nuts, cod with beans, fennel, smoked paprika and crab mayonnaise, and puddings such as white chocolate cheesecake with artichoke fudge and clotted cream ice-cream and lemon parfait with lemon curd, meringue and lime granita. *Benchmark main dish: 42-day-aged sirloin steak with chips and wild garlic butter £21.00. Two-course evening meal £23.00.*

Free house ~ Licensee Matt Greenlees ~ Real ale ~ Open 8am-11pm (10.30 Sun) ~ Bar food 12-3, 6-9.30 (9 Sun); breakfasts 8-10am ~ Restaurant ~ Children welcome ~ Dogs welcome ~ Wi-fi ~ Bedrooms: /£95 *Recommended by B and F A Hannam, S G N Bennett, Miss B D Picton, Heulwen and Neville Pinfield, Ann and Colin Hunt, David and Judy Robison*

MIDFORD
ST7660   Map 2

Hope & Anchor

(01225) 832296 – www.hopeandanchormidford.co.uk
Bath Road (B3110); BA2 7DD

Welcoming, partly 17th-c pub with popular food and several real ales

Friendly, long-serving licensees run this neat, open-plan dining pub that's just ten minutes from Bath. There's a civilised bar plus a heavy-beamed restaurant with a long cushioned settle against red-patterned wallpaper, a mix of dark wooden dining chairs and tables on flagstones and a woodburning stove. The back conservatory is modern, stylish and popular with families. Box Steam Tunnel Vision, Otter Amber, Sharps Doom Bar and a guest or two on handpump, 11 wines by the glass and a farm cider served by courteous staff. Outside, there are seats on the sheltered back terrace with an upper tier. The pub is on the Colliers Way cycle/walking path and near walks on the disused Somerset and Dorset railway.

The well thought-of food comes in generous helpings and includes deep-fried camembert with onion marmalade, pork and sage dumpling parcels with onions, bacon and sour cream, steak and mushroom in ale pie, salmon fillet and prawns in creamy chilli sauce, rosemary and garlic marinated venison with sloe gin and blueberry sauce, duck with stir-fried vegetables and plum sauce on chinese noodles, and puddings such as chocolate brownie with white chocolate sauce and eton mess with strawberry coulis. *Benchmark main dish: chicken satay with green peppercorn cream sauce and cucumber and yoghurt salad £12.50. Two-course evening meal £21.00.*

Free house ~ Licensee Richard Smolarek ~ Real ale ~ Open 11.30-3, 6-11; 11.30-11 Sat, Sun ~ Bar food 12-2 (3 weekends), 6-9.30 ~ Restaurant ~ Children welcome ~ Wi-fi
Recommended by M G Hart

MILVERTON
ST1225   Map 0

Globe 🏆

(01823) 400534 – www.theglobemilverton.co.uk
Fore Street; TA4 1JX

Bustling and friendly inn with a welcome for all, good ales, quite a choice of tasty food and seats outside; bedrooms

There's no doubt that many of the customers at this handsome former coaching inn are here for the particularly good food – but they do keep local ales on handpump, served by cheerful, helpful staff. The opened-up rooms have solid, rustic tables surrounded by an attractive mix of wooden or high-backed black leather chairs, local artwork (for sale) on pale-painted walls above a red dado, and a big gilt-edged mirror above the woodburning stove in an ornate fireplace. Bar chairs line the counter where they keep Butcombe Bitter, Cotleigh Commando Hoofing and Otter Bitter on handpump, nine wines by the glass and local farm cider; there's a friendly pub labrador. The sheltered outside terrace has raffia-style chairs and tables and cushioned wall seating under parasols. The two bedrooms are comfortable and breakfasts are continental.

Using the best local produce, the highly thought-of seasonal food includes sandwiches, cave-aged cheddar and chive soufflé with home-made walnut bread, lamb kofta with roasted vegetable couscous and harissa yoghurt, butternut squash stuffed with leeks, walnuts, garlic and brie with redcurrant sauce, free-range chicken breast with bubble and squeak and garlic and chive butter, grilled red mullet with pea pesto and onion confit, duck with port, plum and orange sauce and crispy cabbage, and puddings such as chocolate brownie with chocolate sauce and white chocolate ice-cream and poached pear with flapjack and cinnamon ice-cream. *Benchmark main dish: slow-roast honey-glazed pork belly £14.95. Two-course evening meal £21.00.*

Free house ~ Licensees Mark and Adele Tarry ~ Real ale ~ Open 12-3, 6-11; 12-3 Sun; closed Sunday evening, Mon lunchtime ~ Bar food ~ Restaurant ~ Children welcome ~ Dogs allowed in bar ~ Wi-fi ~ Bedrooms: £55/£60 *Recommended by Patrick and Daphne Darley*

MONKSILVER
Notley Arms ⭐ ♟ 🛏

ST0737 Map 1

(01984) 656095 – www.notleyarmsinn.co.uk

B3188; TA4 4JB

Bustling friendly pub with a good mix of regulars and visitors, enjoyable food and drink and seats in streamside garden; comfortable bedrooms

This is an enjoyable place to stay with attractive and comfortable bedrooms in the former coach house; one is suitable for disabled customers. The open-plan bar rooms each have their own atmosphere. There are two open fires plus two woodburning stoves (the one in the lounge is fronted by chesterfield sofas), cushioned window seats and settles, an appealing collection of old dining chairs around mixed wooden tables on slate tiles or flagstones, original paintings on cream walls and panelling, and fresh flowers, church candles and big stone bottles; background music. Tractor seats line the bar where they keep Exmoor Ale, St Austell Tribute and Pleasant Pheasant (named for the pub from St Austell) on handpump, 22 wines by the glass, over 20 malt whiskies and farm cider; staff are courteous and helpful. At the bottom of the neat garden is a clear-running stream and plenty of picnic-sets on grass; a heated, circular wooden pavilion is just right for a party of 12. The pub is on the edge of Exmoor National Park in a lovely village.

Well liked food includes free-range scotch egg with sweet chilli sauce, whipped goats cheese mousse with beetroot and celery salad and candied walnuts, rare-breed local sausages with onion gravy, smoked salmon linguine with lemon cream sauce, venison burger with coleslaw and triple-cooked chips, a pie of the day, fillet of bream on crab and prawn cannelloni with butternut squash, and puddings such as chocolate marquise with mango sorbet and lemon curd and banana parfait and raspberry coulis. *Benchmark main dish: lamb rump with feta, confit tomatoes, broad beans and pea purée £18.00. Two-course evening meal £21.00.*

Free house ~ Licensees Simon and Caroline Murphy ~ Real ale ~ Open 8am-11pm ~ Bar food 12-2.30, 6-9.30 ~ Restaurant ~ Children welcome ~ Dogs welcome ~ Wi-fi ~ Bedrooms: /£75 *Recommended by Richard and Penny Gibbs, Mike and Lynne Steane, Bob and Margaret Holder*

You can send reports directly to us at feedback@goodguides.com

MONKTON COMBE   ST7761 Map 2

Wheelwrights Arms 🛏

(01225) 722287 – www.wheelwrightsarms.co.uk

Just off A36 S of Bath; Church Cottages; BA2 7HB

Relaxed and friendly bar-dining room in 18th-c stone pub, cheerful mix of customers, helpful landlord and staff, good food and seats outside; quiet, comfortable bedrooms

---

The bar-dining room here is bustling and friendly (you must book to be sure of a table); at one end there's an open fire in a raised fireplace with logs piled on either side, cushioned and wood-planked built-in wall seats, rush-seated or cushioned high-backed dining chairs around tables (each set with a small lamp), parquet flooring or carpet, and old photographs and oil paintings (the one above the fireplace of the dog is particularly nice). The middle room has some pretty frieze work, a high shelf of wooden wader birds, and stools against the green-painted counter where they keep Butcombe Bitter and Otter Bitter on handpump, 11 wines by the glass and farm cider; background jazz and board games. A small end room is just right for a group. The gravelled terraces have wood and metal tables and chairs and picnic-sets. This is an enjoyable place to stay and the bedrooms, in a restored annexe, are quiet, well equipped and comfortable. The peaceful village is surrounded by picturesque hills and valleys, and Bath is nearby.

Rewarding food includes lunchtime sandwiches, mussels in white wine and cream, whole baked camembert with honey, garlic and herbs, broccoli and chilli tagliatelle with capers and cream, home-made sausages with mash and red onion gravy, coriander and mustard burger with toppings, coleslaw and chips, steaks with garlic butter and field mushrooms, beetroot-cured salmon fillet with pickled and roasted beetroot and salsify velouté, and puddings such as orange cream doughnuts with rhubarb sorbet, braised rhubarb and rhubarb jam and candied lemon and honey sponge with lemon and crème fraîche sorbet. *Benchmark main dish: beer-battered fish and chips £13.00. Two-course evening meal £21.00.*

Free house ~ Licensee David Munn ~ Real ale ~ Open 11-11 (10 Sun) ~ Bar food 12-2 (3 weekends), 6-9.30 ~ Children welcome ~ Wi-fi ~ Bedrooms: £85/£150
Recommended by Dr Simon Innes, Carol and Barry Craddock

ODCOMBE   ST5015 Map 2

Masons Arms 🍺 🛏

(01935) 862591 – www.masonsarmsodcombe.co.uk

Off A3088 or A30 just W of Yeovil; Lower Odcombe; BA22 8TX

Own-brew beers and tasty food in pretty thatched cottage; bedrooms

---

Even when busy – which they usually are – staff remain helpful and friendly; it's best to book a table in advance. The simple little bar has joists and a couple of standing timbers, a mix of cushioned dining chairs around all sorts of tables on cream and blue patterned carpet, and a couple of tub chairs and a table in the former inglenook fireplace. Up one step is a similar area, while more steps lead down to a dining room with a squashy brown sofa and a couple of cushioned dining chairs in front of a woodburning stove; the sandstone walls are hung with black and white local photographs and country prints. Their own-brewed Odcombe No.1, Roly Poly and seasonal beers are kept on handpump, they make their own sloe and elderflower cordials, have 11 wines by the glass and serve farm cider. There's a thatched smokers' shelter and picnic-sets in the garden, plus a vegetable patch and chicken coop. Bedrooms are well equipped and comfortable, and the breakfasts good and hearty; there's also a campsite.

Using home-grown and other local produce, the good food includes brunch (8am-2pm), lunchtime sandwiches and panini, pork and apple pâté, asian-style bass with baby vegetables, ham and duck eggs, vegetable and cashew nut stir-fry with satay sauce, corn-fed chicken with chorizo and roasted shallots, barbecue ribs with sweet potato and parsnip slaw, and puddings such as peanut butter and banana croissant bread and butter pudding with crème anglaise and dark chocolate and salted caramel mousse cake. *Benchmark main dish: lambs liver, bacon, onion rings and gravy £14.75. Two-course evening meal £21.00.*

Own brew ~ Licensees Drew Read and Paula Tennyson ~ Real ale ~ Open 8am-3.30pm, 6-midnight ~ Bar food 12-2, 6.30-9.30; breakfast for non-residents 8-11am ~ Children welcome ~ Dogs welcome ~ Wi-fi ~ Bedrooms: £55/£85 *Recommended by Michael Doswell, Mike and Mary Carter, Mr and Mrs P R Thomas, S G N Bennett*

PITNEY
ST4527 Map 1

Halfway House 🍺 £

(01458) 252513 ~ www.thehalfwayhouse.co.uk
Just off B3153 W of Somerton; TA10 9AB

Bustling, friendly local with nine real ales, local ciders and good simple food

The fine range of up to ten regularly changing beers draws in a good cross-section of cheerful customers to this reliably idiosyncratic and unpretentious village local. The atmosphere is chatty and easy-going, and the three old-fashioned rooms have communal tables, roaring log fires and a homely feel underlined by a profusion of books, maps and newspapers. Tapped from the cask, the ales might include Bath Golden Hare, Butcombe Rare Breed, Dark Star American Pale Ale, Glastonbury Thriller, Hop Back Summer Lightning, Otter Bitter and Bright, Teignworthy Reel Ale and Whitstable East India Pale Ale; also, four farm ciders, a dozen malt whiskies and several wines by the glass; board games. There are tables outside.

Generous helpings of simple food includes lunchtime sandwiches, soup of the day, sausage and mash with onion gravy, beef in ale casserole, venison burger, lots of curries, chilli con carne and pork steak in cider sauce. *Benchmark main dish: beer-battered fish and chips £9.50. Two-course evening meal £13.50.*

Free house ~ Licensee Mark Phillips ~ Real ale ~ Open 11.30-3, 4.30-11 (midnight Sat); 12-11 Sun ~ Bar food 12-2.30, 7-9.30; 1-5 Sun ~ Children welcome ~ Dogs welcome ~ Wi-fi *Recommended by Bob and Margaret Holder, S G N Bennett, Mr Yeldahn, Richard and Penny Gibbs*

PRIDDY
ST5250 Map 2

Queen Victoria £

(01749) 676385 ~ www.queenvictoria.butcombe.com
Village signed off B3135; Pelting Drove; BA5 3BA

Stone-built country pub with interconnecting rooms, open fires and woodburners, friendly atmosphere, real ales and honest food; seats outside

This creeper-clad pub is just the place to head for after a walk (dogs are very welcome); the various dimly lit rooms and alcoves have a lot of character and plenty of original features, and customers are chatty and cheerful. One room leading off the main bar has a log fire in a big old stone fireplace with a huge cauldron to one side. There are flagstoned or slate floors, bare stone walls (the smarter dining room is half panelled and half painted), horse tack, farm tools and photos of Queen Victoria. Furniture is traditional: cushioned wall settles, farmhouse and other solid chairs around all manner of wooden tables, a nice old pew beside a screen settle making a cosy alcove, and high chairs next to the bar counter where they serve Butcombe Bitter and a seasonal guest and Fullers London Pride on handpump, two farm ciders, 15 malt whiskies and nine wines by the glass; shove-ha'penny. There are seats in the front courtyard and more across the lane where there's also a children's playground. Wheelchair access and disabled loos.

Traditional food includes sandwiches, chicken liver and bacon pâté, deep-fried brie wedges with plum sauce, ham and eggs, a curry of the day, fish pie, vegetarian quiche, lamb and mint burger with mint jelly and chips, chicken and mushroom stroganoff, rump steak with onion rings and chips, and puddings such as chocolate fudge cake and treacle sponge with custard. *Benchmark main dish: beef in ale pie £9.95. Two-course evening meal £14.00.*

Butcombe ~ Manager Mark Walton ~ Real ale ~ Open 12-11 (10.30 Sun) ~ Bar food 12-2, 6-9; 12-8 Sat (9 Sun) ~ Children welcome ~ Dogs welcome ~ Wi-fi ~ Live folk second Mon of month; folk festival early July *Recommended by Chris and Angela Buckell, Mr and Mrs P R Thomas*

SOMERTON
White Hart ♀ ⇐

ST4828 Map 2

(01458) 272273 – www.whitehartsomerton.com
Market Place; TA11 7LX

Attractive old place in lovely village, several bars with open fires, simple dining room and enjoyable food; comfortable bedrooms

---

Located in the market square and serving some sort of food all day, this handsome stone inn has customers dropping in and out at all hours. The main bar has long wall seats with attractive scatter cushions, stools around small tables, big mirrors on the wall, Bath Gem, Cheddar Potholer and guests such as Box Steam Golden Bolt and Otter Amber on handpump, farm ciders and 14 wines by the glass, served by friendly staff. A doorway leads to a cosy room with a leather sofa, armchairs, a chest table and an open fire. Another snug bar has comfortable sofas and armchairs, a cushioned window seat and more chest tables, while a simpler room has straightforward wooden dining chairs and tables, a little brick fireplace and some stained glass. Throughout, there are rugs on parquet flooring (some plain bare boards too), church candles, contemporary paintwork and interesting lighting – look out for the antler 'chandelier' with its pretty hanging lampshades; background music and board games. Outside, the flower-filled terrace has tables and chairs under parasols with more on grass. Some of the airy, well equipped bedrooms overlook the square and church.

As well as breakfasts (served 9-11am), the assured food (much of which is wood-roasted) includes smoked ham hock terrine with rosemary and garlic crispbread and home-made piccalilli, crab cakes with tomato, chilli and lime salsa, spiced beetroot and chickpea burger with tarragon mayonnaise and beetroot salsa, whole sole with chive and caper butter, chicken bruschetta with chargrilled baby gem and madeira sauce, rare-breed steak with a choice of sauces, and puddings such as chocolate terrine with strawberry sorbet and caramel popcorn and rhubarb eton mess with rosewater and chocolate marshmallow. *Benchmark main dish: wood-roasted pork belly stuffed with chilli, sage and onion with dauphinoise potatoes and cider sauce £17.00. Two-course evening meal £21.00.*

Free house ~ Licensee Natalie Patrick ~ Real ale ~ Open 9am-11pm (10 Sun) ~ Bar food
12-3, 6-10; 12-9 Sun ~ Children welcome ~ Dogs allowed in bar and bedrooms ~ Wi-fi ~
Bedrooms: /£85 *Recommended by Martin Jones, Isobel Mackinlay, Hugh Roberts*

STANTON WICK
Carpenters Arms 🏮 ⌐ 🛏

ST6162 Map 2

(01761) 490202 – www.the-carpenters-arms.co.uk
Village signposted off A368, just W of junction with A37 S of Bristol; BS39 4BX

**Bustling, friendly dining pub in country setting with enjoyable food,
helpful staff and fine choice of drinks; comfortable bedrooms**

Once again, warm praise from our readers on the quiet and comfortable
bedrooms here and the warmth of the welcome from the landlord and
his attentive staff. Coopers Parlour on the right has a couple of beams,
seats around heavy tables on a tartan carpet and attractive curtains; in the
angle between here and the bar area is a wide woodburning stove in an
opened-through fireplace. The bar has wall settles with cushions, stripped-
stone walls and a big log fire in an inglenook. There's also a snug inner
room (brightened by mirrors in arched recesses) and a restaurant with
leather sofas, easy chairs and a lounge area at one end. Butcombe Bitter and
Sharps Atlantic and Doom Bar on handpump, ten wines by the glass (and
some interesting bin ends) and several malt whiskies; TV in the snug. There
are picnic-sets on the front terrace along with pretty flower beds, hanging
baskets and tubs. Nearby walks.

🍴 The highly thought-of food includes duck liver and port pâté with spicy tomato and
caramelised onion chutney, salmon fishcake with saffron and garlic mayonnaise,
ham and free-range eggs, wild and field mushrooms in puff pastry with leeks, red onions
and a chive cream sauce, bass fillet on stir-fried vegetables with noodles and honey,
soy, chilli and spring onion dressing, slow-braised beef with onion and thyme sauce,
and puddings such as lime and lemon cheesecake with lemon drizzle and crushed
meringues and chocolate and hazelnut brownie with banana and salted caramel ice-
cream. *Benchmark main dish: chicken with leeks, bacon and sauté potatoes with
mushroom and tarragon sauce £14.95. Two-course evening meal £21.00.*

Buccaneer Holdings ~ Manager Simon Pledge ~ Real ale ~ Open 11-11; 12-10.30 Sun ~
Bar food 12-2.30, 6-9.30 (10 Fri, Sat); 12-9 Sun ~ Restaurant ~ Children welcome ~
Dogs allowed in bar ~ Wi-fi ~ Bedrooms: £75/£110 *Recommended by Phil and Helen Holt,
Taff Thomas, Mr and Mrs J Watkins, William and Ann Reid, Dr and Mrs A K Clarke*

WATERROW
Rock 🏮 🛏

ST0525 Map 1

(01984) 623293 – www.rockinnwaterrow.co.uk
B3227 Wiveliscombe–Bampton; TA4 2AX

**Handsome inn with local ales, interesting food and a nice mix
of customers; comfortable bedrooms**

The good, interesting food cooked by the landlord continues to draw both
locals and visitors to this striking timbered inn built into the rock face on
the edge of Exmoor National Park. The relaxed and informal bar area has
dining chairs and cushioned window seats around scrubbed kitchen tables
on tartan carpet, sympathetic lighting and a log fire in a stone fireplace. High
black leather bar chairs line the copper-topped bar counter where they serve
Quantock Wills Neck and St Austell Tribute on handpump, several wines by
the glass and farm cider. The elegant restaurant is up some steps from the bar
with pale grey-painted panelled walls, and there's also a snug with a big leather

sofa and leather armchairs. The pretty, cottagey bedrooms are comfortable and breakfasts good. There are seats under umbrellas out in front.

From a seasonal menu, the high quality food includes wild boar pâté with pickled quail eggs and shallot marmalade, mussels in cider and shallot broth, beetroot gnocchi with creamed jerusalem artichoke, roasted vegetables and parmesan, beer-battered fish and chips, free-range duck breast with truffle dauphinoise potatoes and sherry shallot sauce, chicken curry, haunch of fallow deer with red wine sauce, horseradish mash and fried brussels sprouts, and puddings. *Benchmark main dish: slow-cooked short rib of beef with black treacle sauce and smoked cheddar mash £15.95. Two-course evening meal £21.50.*

Free house ~ Licensees Daren and Ruth Barclay ~ Real ale ~ Open 12-3, 6-11; closed Sun evening, all day Mon, Tues lunchtime ~ Bar food 12-2, 6.30-9 ~ Restaurant ~ Children welcome ~ Dogs allowed in bar and bedrooms ~ Wi-fi ~ Bedrooms: £65/£85
Recommended by Bob and Margaret Holder, Paul Fitzpatrick

WEDMORE   ST4348   Map 1

Swan ⭐ ♀ 🍺

(01934) 710337 ~ www.theswanwedmore.com
Cheddar Road, opposite Church Street; BS28 4EQ

Bustling place with a friendly, informal atmosphere, lots of customers, efficient service and enjoyable all-day food and drinks

The good food here starts with breakfast (9-11am) through home-made cakes and brownies with morning coffee and afternoon tea and, of course, lunch and supper; bar snacks are served throughout the day and customers are always dropping in and out, which creates a lively, buoyant atmosphere. The layout is open-plan, with mirrors giving the feeling of even more space. The main bar has all sorts of wooden tables and chairs on polished floorboards, a wall seat with attractive scatter cushions, a woodburning stove, suede stools against the panelled counter and a rustic central table with daily papers. Bath Gem, Cheddar Potholer, Otter Bitter and a guest such as Cottage Lightning Ale on handpump and nine good wines by the glass are served by quick, friendly staff. At one end of the room, a step leads down to an area with rugs on huge flagstones, a leather chesterfield, armchairs and brass-studded leather chairs, then down another step to more sofas and armchairs. The airy dining room has attractive high-backed chairs, tables set with candles in glass jars and another woodburner, and off here is the former skittle alley. There are plenty of seats and tables on the terrace and lawn, and the metal furniture among flowering tubs at the front of the building gives a continental feel. The contemporary bedrooms are well equipped and comfortable.

Creative food using the best local produce includes sandwiches on home-made bread, crab cakes with lime, chilli and tomato salsa, rare roast beef and baby gem salad with crispy anchovies and caesar dressing, dry-cured gammon and eggs, spinach gnocchi with slow-roasted tomatoes, cheese and pine nuts, whole plaice and clams steamed with nettles, chilli and garlic, herb-crusted lamb rump with chargrilled spring onions, radishes, fregola and crème fraîche, chargrilled dry-aged steak with parsley and garlic butter and chips, and puddings such as strawberry trifle with local cider brandy and chocolate mousse with hazelnut crumb. *Benchmark main dish: slow-cooked pork belly stuffed with wild garlic, chilli, mozzarella and herbs £16.50. Two-course evening meal £21.00.*

Free house ~ Licensee Natalie Zvonek-Little ~ Real ale ~ Open 9am-11pm (10.30 Sun) ~ Bar food 9am-10pm; snacks in afternoon ~ Restaurant ~ Children welcome ~ Dogs allowed in bar ~ Wi-fi ~ Live events; phone for details ~ Bedrooms: /£100 *Recommended by Taff Thomas*

WRAXALL
ST4971   Map 2

Battleaxes 🛏

(01275) 857473 – www.flatcappers.co.uk

Bristol Road B3130, E of Nailsea; BS48 1LQ

Bustling pub with relaxed drinking and dining areas, helpful staff and enjoyable food; big bedrooms with contemporary bathrooms

Handy for Tyntesfield (National Trust), this is an interesting stone-built Victorian pub with a friendly landlady. The spacious interior is split into separate areas with polished floorboards or flagstones, portraits and pictures on walls above painted, panelled dados, mirrors on boldly patterned wallpaper, fresh flowers and house plants, books on window sills and church candles. The bar has leather-topped stools against the counter where they keep Butcombe Bitter and a beer named for the pub on handpump and several wines by the glass; background music. Throughout, there are long pews with scatter cushions, church chairs and a medley of other wooden dining chairs around chunky tables and groups of leather armchairs; it's all very easy-going. There are picnic-sets outside and some of the spacious bedrooms have country views. Wheelchair access using ramps.

Interesting food includes sandwiches (until 5pm), spiced crispy whitebait with aioli, chicken liver parfait with red onion marmalade, sharing boards, chicken caesar salad, a pie of the day, beef, chicken or vegetable burgers with toppings and chips, calves liver, bubble and squeak and bacon jus, smoked haddock and salmon fishcake with buttered spinach, a poached egg and hollandaise, and puddings such as chocolate and orange mousse with chantilly cream and lemon tart with clotted cream. *Benchmark main dish: pork tenderloin with mustard mash and jus £11.95. Two-course evening meal £19.00.*

Flatcappers ~ Manager Sarah Davidson ~ Real ale ~ Open 10am-11pm ~
Bar food 8am-10pm ~ Children welcome ~ Dogs allowed in bar ~ Wi-fi ~ Bedrooms: /£80
Recommended by Dr Simon Innes, Gus Swan

WRINGTON
ST4762   Map 2

Plough

(01934) 862871 – www.theploughatwrington.co.uk

2.5 miles off A370 Bristol–Weston, from bottom of Rhodiate Hill; BS40 5QA

Welcoming, popular pub with bustling bar and two dining rooms, good food using local produce and well kept beer, and seats outside

Handy for both Cheddar Gorge and Bristol Airport, this is a neatly kept and well run village pub. It's extremely popular (best to book a table in advance) and there's a chatty bar with stools against the counter where they serve Butcombe Bitter (the brewery is in the village), St Austell Tribute and Youngs Special on handpump and 18 wines by the glass. Staff are friendly and efficient. The two dining rooms (the one at the back has plenty of big windows overlooking the gazebo and garden) have open doorways and throughout you'll find (three) winter fires, slate or wooden floors, beams and standing timbers, plenty of pictures on the planked, red or yellow walls and all manner of high-backed leather or wooden dining or farmhouse chairs around tables of many sizes. Also, fresh flowers, table skittles and a chest of games. There are picnic-sets at the front and on the back grass; boules. They hold a farmers' market on the second Friday of the month. This is sister pub of the Rattlebone at Sherston (Wiltshire). Disabled access.

🍴 Popular pub food plus more inventive dishes includes lunchtime sandwiches and ciabattas, seared tuna with asian salad and lime and sesame dressing, wild mushroom arancini with truffle oil, mixed charcuterie sharing board, home-cooked ham and free-range eggs, moroccan-spiced chickpea stew, goan fish curry, pork tenderloin with carrot purée and black pudding sauce, sea trout fillet with mussel broth, celeriac purée and apples, and puddings such as white chocolate and orange crème brûlée and dark chocolate délice with bourbon crumbs and salted caramel sauce. *Benchmark main dish: lamb rump and braised shoulder with onion purée and red wine jus £16.75. Two-course evening meal £21.00.*

Youngs ~ Tenant Jason Read ~ Real ale ~ Open 12-3, 5-11; 12-midnight Fri, Sat; 12-11 Sun ~ Bar food 12-2.30, 6-9.30; 12-9 Sun ~ Restaurant ~ Children welcome ~ Dogs allowed in bar ~ Wi-fi *Recommended by Hugh Roberts, Bob and Margaret Holder, Chris and Angela Buckell, Dr and Mrs A K Clarke*

Also Worth a Visit in Somerset

Besides the fully inspected pubs, you might like to try these pubs that have been recommended to us and described by readers. Do tell us what you think of them: feedback@goodguides.com

APPLEY ST0721
Globe (01823) 672327
Hamlet signposted from the network of back roads between A361 and A38, W of B3187 and W of Milverton and Wellington; OS Sheet 181 map reference 072215; TA21 0HJ Welcoming 15th-c pub under new management; entrance corridor with serving hatch, simple pubby furnishings in beamed front room, another with 1930s railway posters and GWR bench, further room with easy chairs, three local ales and traditional cider, sensibly priced home-made food (not Sun evening) including specials, friendly service; skittle alley; children, walkers and dogs welcome, picnic-sets in garden with play area, path opposite leading to River Tone, open all day. *(R T and J C Moggridge)*

ASHILL ST3116
Square & Compass (01823) 480467
Windmill Hill; off A358 between Ilminster and Taunton; up Wood Road for a mile behind Stewley Cross service station; OS Sheet 193 map reference 310166; TA19 9NX Simple pub in the Blackdown Hills with long-serving owners; log fire in small beamed bar, heavy furniture and upholstered window seats taking in the country view, Exmoor and St Austell ales, several wines by the glass, farm cider, fair-priced traditional food served by friendly staff; background music and regular live music in separate sound-proofed barn; garden with picnic-sets and large glass-covered walled terrace, eight bedrooms in new stable block, also camping, closed lunchtimes Tues-Thurs. *(Gene and Tony Freemantle)*

AXBRIDGE ST4354
Lamb (01934) 732253
The Square; off A371 Cheddar–Winscombe; BS26 2AP Big rambling carpeted pub with heavy 15th-c beams and timbers, stone and roughcast walls, large stone fireplaces, old settles, unusual bar front with bottles set in plaster, Butcombe and a guest, well chosen wine and good coffee, generous food (all day Sat, till 6pm Sun) from sandwiches and baked potatoes up, lunch deal (Tues, Thurs), they may ask for a credit card if you run a tab, board games, table skittles and alley; sports TV; children and dogs allowed, small sheltered back garden, medieval King John's Hunting Lodge (NT) opposite, open all day. *(Ann and Colin Hunt, Roger and Donna Huggins)*

BACKWELL ST4969
George (01275) 462770
Farleigh Road; A370 W of Bristol; BS48 3PG Modernised and extended main road dining pub (former coaching inn), popular food in bar and restaurant from sandwiches and sharing boards up, two-for-one pizzas before 6pm Mon-Sat, well kept Bath, Butcombe, St Austell and a guest, good choice of wines; background music in some areas; children and dogs welcome, gravel terrace and lawn behind, seven bedrooms, open all day. *(Taff Thomas, Richard and Judy Winn)*

BARROW GURNEY ST5367
Princes Motto (01275) 472282
B3130, just off A370/A38; BS48 3RY Cosy and welcoming, with unpretentious local feel in traditional tap room, long lounge/dining area up behind, four Wadworths ales with Butcombe as guest,

modestly priced simple lunchtime food (all day Fri, breakfast available Sat), log fire, some panelling, cricket team photographs, jugs and china; dogs welcome, pleasant garden with terrace, open all day. *(Comus and Sarah Elliott, Taff Thomas)*

BATCOMBE ST6839

★**Three Horseshoes** (01749) 850359
Village signposted off A359 Bruton–Frome; BA4 6HE Handsome honey-coloured stone inn with long narrow main room, beams, local pictures, built-in cushioned window seats and nice mix of tables, woodburner one end, open fire the other, Butcombe, Wild Beer and a couple of guests, around a dozen wines by the glass and several malt whiskies, very good food (best to book, especially weekends), efficient service, attractive stripped-stone dining room; open mike night last Thurs of month; children and dogs welcome, three simple but pretty bedrooms, lovely church next door, open all day weekends. *(Steve and Irene Homer, Steve and Liz Tilley, Ann and Colin Hunt)*

BATH ST7464

Bath Brew House (01225) 805609
James Street West; BA1 2BX Interesting spaciously converted pub visibly brewing its own James Street beers, also guest ales and craft beers, food including spit-roasts from open kitchen, sports TV and various events such as comedy nights in upstairs room with own bar; well behaved children and dogs allowed in some areas, sizeable split-level beer garden with covered eating area, summer barbecues, open (and food) all day. *(Taff Thomas, Dr and Mrs A K Clarke)*

BATH ST7565

Bell (01225) 460426
Walcot Street; BA1 5BW Long narrow split-level pub owned by the local community; nine real ales and traditional cider, some basic good value food, lots of pump clips and gig notices, a couple of fires (one gas), bar billiards and table football; packed and lively in the evenings with regular live music and DJ sets, free wi-fi; canopied garden, even has its own laundrette, open all day. *(Emma Scofield)*

BATH ST7564

Boater (01225) 464211
Argyle Street, by Pulteney Bridge; BA2 4BQ Refurbished Fullers pub in good spot near river, fairly traditional bare-boards bar with at least five well kept ales, fine range of draught/bottled craft beers and good choice of wines by the glass, popular fairly priced food from lunchtime sandwiches and pub favourites up, quick friendly service, upstairs restaurant with nice view of weir,

cosy cellar bar; children and dogs welcome, sizeable back terrace on two levels, open all day (till 1am Fri, Sat). *(Martin Jones)*

BATH ST7165

Boathouse (01225) 482584
Newbridge Road; BA1 3NB Large light and airy pub in fine riverside spot near Kennet & Avon marina; food from club sandwiches and sharing boards up, efficient courteous young staff, well kept Brains and guests along with a beer named for them, decent house wines, lower level conservatory, newspapers; free wi-fi; children very welcome, boat views from garden tables and raised deck, nine bedrooms some with balconies overlooking the river, open all day. *(Steve and Liz Tilley, Adrian Johnson)*

BATH ST7564

★**Coeur de Lion** (01225) 463568
Northumberland Place, off High Street by W H Smith; BA1 5AR Tiny stained-glass-fronted single-room pub, simple, cosy and friendly, with candles and log-effect gas fire, well kept Abbey ales and guests, good well priced traditional food from snacks and baguettes up (vegetarian options), Christmas mulled wine, more room and loos upstairs; may be background music; tables out in charming flower-filled flagstoned pedestrian alley, open all day, food till 6pm. *(N R White)*

BATH ST7564

★**Crystal Palace** (01225) 482666
Abbey Green; BA1 1NW Spacious two-room Fullers pub, rugs on wood floors and comfortable mix of seating, panelled walls and groups of pictures, popular sensibly priced food from lunchtime sandwiches up, Somerset cheese and port menu, speedy friendly service, four well kept ales from plank-faced bar, log fire, garden room opening on to nice sheltered courtyard; background music, sports TV, free wi-fi; children welcome, handy for Roman Baths and main shopping areas, open (and food) all day. *(Roger and Donna Huggins, Martin Cawley, Roger and Anne Newbury)*

BATH ST7464

★**Garricks Head** (01225) 318368
St Johns Place/Westgate, beside Theatre Royal; BA1 1ET Civilised and relaxed place with high-windowed bar, armchairs by gas-effect coal fire, church candles on mantelpiece and fine silver meat domes on wall above, wheelback and other dining chairs around wooden tables on bare boards, a couple of sizeable brass chandeliers, four interesting regional ales, real ciders and decent wines by the glass, proper cocktails, good food including pre-theatre menu, separate smartly set dining room; may be

---

We include some hotels with a good bar that offers facilities comparable to those of a pub.

soft background jazz; children welcome, dogs in bar, pavement tables, open all day. *(Belinda Stamp)*

BATH   ST7766
George (01225) 425079
Bathampton, E of Bath centre, off A36 or (via toll bridge) off A4; Mill Lane; BA2 6TR Beautifully placed old canalside Chef & Brewer, busy and buzzy, with popular reasonably priced food including deals, well kept Bath, Charles Wells and three guests, good choice of wines by the glass, young well organised staff, spacious bar opening into cosy beamed rooms with three log fires, contemporary décor and furnishings; background music; children welcome, no dogs inside, wheelchair access, enclosed suntrap terrace and waterside tables, interesting church opposite with Australian links (the first governor is buried here), open (and food) all day. *(Giles and Annie Francis, Dr and Mrs A K Clarke)*

BATH   ST7564
Graze (01225) 429392
Behind Bath Spa station; BA1 1SX Spacious Bath Ales bar-restaurant (part of the city's Vaults development) arranged over upper floor and served by lift; modern steel and glass construction with leather chairs and benches on wood-strip flooring, slatted ceiling with exposed ducting and pendant lighting, good selection of beers (some from on-site microbrewery, can be pricey), extensive range of wines and spirits, enjoyable food cooked in open kitchen from light dishes to dry-aged steaks, good value weekday set lunch, helpful cheery staff coping well at busy times; children welcome, disabled facilities, two sizeable terraces overlooking Bath one side, the station the other, life-size models of cows, pigs and chickens, open all day from 8am (9am Sun) for breakfast. *(Roger and Donna Huggins, Chris and Angela Buckell)*

BATH   ST7465
Hall & Woodhouse (01225) 469259
Old King Street; BA1 2JW Conversion of stone-fronted warehouse/auction rooms; big open-plan interior on two floors, steel girders and glass, palms and chandeliers, mix of modern and traditional furniture including old-fashioned iron-framed tables with large candles and some simple bench seating, parquet and slate floors, Badger ales from full-length servery on the right, sweeping stairs up to another bar and eating area (disabled access via lift), roof terrace, decent choice of food from pub favourites to specials, helpful chatty staff; gets very busy

with after-work drinkers when standing room only, open (and food) all day from 8am (9am weekends). *(Dr and Mrs A K Clarke)*

BATH   ST7465
★ Hop Pole (01225) 446327
Albion Buildings, Upper Bristol Road; BA1 3AR Bustling family-friendly Bath Ales pub, their ales and guests kept well, decent wines by the glass and good choice of whiskies and other spirits, nice food (not Sun evening, Mon lunchtime) from traditional favourites up in bar and former skittle alley restaurant, efficient friendly staff, settles and other pub furniture on bare boards in four linked areas, lots of black woodwork, ochre walls, some bric-a-brac; background music, Mon quiz, discreet sports TV; wheelchair access to main bar area only, pleasant two-level back courtyard with boules, fairy-lit vine arbour and heated summerhouses, opposite Victoria Park (great kids' play area), open all day. *(Roger and Donna Huggins, Chris and Angela Buckell)*

BATH   ST7565
King William (01225) 428096
Thomas Street/A4 London Road; BA1 5NN Small corner dining pub with well cooked food from short daily changing menu, four local ales and good choice of wines by the glass, chunky old tables on bare boards, steep stairs up to simple attractive dining room; background music; children and dogs welcome, open all day weekends. *(Dr and Mrs A K Clarke)*

BATH   ST7565
Pig & Fiddle (01225) 460868
Saracen Street; BA1 5BR Lively place (particularly weekends) with half a dozen well kept ales and fairly simple food including range of burgers, reasonable prices and friendly staff, two big open fires, bare boards and collection of sporting memorabilia, steps up to bustling servery and little dining area, games part; live music and DJ nights, several TVs for sport; picnic-sets on big heated terrace, open all day, food till early evening. *(Martin Cawley)*

BATH   ST7565
Pulteney Arms (01225) 463923
Daniel Street/Sutton Street; BA2 6ND Cosy, cheerful and largely unspoilt 18th-c pub, Fullers London Pride, Otter, Timothy Taylors Landlord and guests, Thatcher's cider, enjoyable well priced fresh food including Fri fish night, lots of Bath RFC memorabilia, traditional furniture on wooden floors, old gas lamps, woodburner; background music, sports TV; pavement

---

tables and small back terrace, handy for Sydney Gardens and Holburne Museum, open all day Fri-Sun. *(Giles and Annie Francis, Taff Thomas, Dr and Mrs A K Clarke)*

BATH ST7464

Raven (01225) 425045

Queen Street; BA1 1HE Small buoyant 18th-c city-centre free house, two well kept ales for the pub from Blindmans and four guests, craft beers and a changing cider, decent wines by the glass too, limited choice of food (good Pieminister pies), quick friendly service, bare boards, some stripped stone and an open fire, newspapers, quieter upstairs bar; storytelling evenings and monthly talks on science and the arts; no under-14s or dogs; open all day. *(N R White, Comus and Sarah Elliott)*

BATH ST7466

Richmond Arms (01225) 316725

Richmond Place, off Lansdown Road; BA1 5PZ Small 18th-c bow-windowed pub (under new ownership) in quiet setting off the tourist track; enjoyable sensibly priced home-made food (not Sun evening, Mon) including daily specials, Butcombe, Sharps Doom Bar and a guest, ciders from Symond's and Thatcher's, lots of wines by the glass, friendly service, mix of tables and chairs on bare boards, local artwork for sale; monthly quiz; children and dogs welcome, enclosed pretty front garden, summer barbecues, open all day. *(Richard Mason, Dr and Mrs A K Clarke)*

BATH ST7364

Royal Oak (01225) 481409

Lower Bristol Road; near Oldfield Park station; BA2 3BW Friendly roadside pub with Butts ales and four regularly changing guests, good range of ciders/perries and bottled beers too, no food, regular live music including Weds folk night; dogs welcome (they have two), side beer garden, open all day Fri-Sun, from 4pm other days. *(Taff Thomas)*

BATH ST7564

Royal Oak (01225) 335220

A36 Pulteney Road; BA2 4HN Bare-boards community pub popular with Bath RFC supporters and busy on match days, Bath Gem, Exmoor Gold, Sharps Doom Bar and guests, Thatcher's cider, reasonably priced tasty pub food; big-screen TVs for sport, free wi-fi; outside seating, open all day Fri, Sat and till 7pm Sun, closed lunchtimes Mon-Thurs. *(Taff Thomas)*

BATH ST7464

Salamander (01225) 428889

John Street; BA1 2JL Busy city local tied to Bath Ales, their full range and a guest kept well, good choice of wines by the glass, bare boards, black woodwork and ochre walls, popular food from sandwiches up (more choice evenings/weekends), friendly helpful

young staff, upstairs restaurant with open kitchen; background music, daily papers; children till 8pm, no dogs, open all day (till 1am Fri, Sat). *(Roger and Donna Huggins, Steve and Liz Tilley, N R White, Comus and Sarah Elliott)*

BATH ST7564

Sam Weller (01225) 474910

Upper Borough Walls; BA1 1RH Fairly simple pub with ales such as Abbey Bellringer, Sharps Doom Bar and Timothy Taylors Landlord, decent choice of wines by the glass and sensibly priced tasty food, friendly service, small and cosy with big window to watch the world go by; open all day (may shut early Sun if quiet). *(Neil Allen)*

BATH ST7564

Volunteer Riflemans Arms (01225) 425210 *New Bond Street Place; BA1 1BH* Friendly little city-centre pub-café with leather sofas and just four close-set tables, wartime/military posters, open fire, well kept ales including a beer named for them from Moles, a couple of draught ciders, good value tasty food, upstairs restaurant and roof terrace; background music; pavement tables, open all day. *(Roger and Donna Huggins, N R White)*

BATH ST7564

White Hart (01225) 338053

Widcombe Hill; BA2 6AA Bistro-style pub with scrubbed pine tables on bare boards, candles and fresh flowers, good imaginative if not cheap food, well kept Butcombe from traditional panelled counter, proper cider and plenty of wines by the glass, quick friendly service; background music; children and dogs welcome, pretty beer garden, bedrooms (some sharing bathroom), open all day (Sun till 5pm). *(Gus Swan)*

BATHFORD ST7866

Crown (01225) 852426

Bathford Hill, towards Bradford-on-Avon, by Batheaston roundabout and bridge; BA1 7SL Welcoming bistro pub with good blackboard food including weekday set deals, ales such as Bath and Timothy Taylors Landlord, nice wines, charming french landlady; children and dogs welcome, tables out in front and in back garden with pétanque, open all day. *(Taff Thomas, Dr and Mrs A K Clarke)*

BECKINGTON ST8051

Woolpack (01373) 831244

Warminster Road, off A36 bypass; BA11 6SP Old village inn with welcoming helpful staff, enjoyable home-made food from sandwiches to steaks, meal deals including OAP menu and Weds curry night, Greene King ales and a guest, real cider and decent wines, big log fire and chunky candlelit tables in flagstoned bar, attractive oak-panelled dining room, conservatory; children and dogs welcome, terrace tables, 12 bedrooms, open (and food) all day. *(Neil Allen)*

BICKNOLLER   ST1139
Bicknoller Inn (01984) 656234
Church Lane; TA4 4EW Old thatched pub nestling below the Quantocks, traditional flagstoned front bar with woodburner, side room and large back restaurant with open kitchen, good food from pub favourites up, Sun carvery, well kept Palmers ales, skittle alley; children and dogs (in bar) welcome, courtyard and good sized garden, boules, attractive village, open till 6pm Sun, closed Mon lunchtime. *(Emma Scofield)*

BLAGDON   ST5058
New Inn (01761) 462475
Signed off A368; Park Lane/Church Street; BS40 7SB Lovely view over Blagdon Lake from seats in front; well kept Wadworths and guests, decent wines and reasonably priced food, bustling bars with two inglenook log fires, heavy beams hung with horsebrasses and tankards, comfortable antique settles and mate's chairs among more modern furnishings, old prints and photographs, plainer side bar; no under-10s, dogs welcome, wheelchair access best from front. *(Anon)*

BLAGDON HILL   ST2118
Blagdon Inn (01823) 421296
4 miles S of Taunton; TA3 7SG Refurbished village pub with several linked bar and dining areas (one room upstairs), mix of elegant and traditional furnishings, flagstones and carpet, local artwork for sale, inglenook log fire, imaginative well presented food from co-owner/chef using local and own produce, good wine list, ales such as Butcombe; children and dogs welcome, picnic-sets out in front, more seats on terrace leading from upper dining room, adjoining fields with pigs, sheep and chickens, open all day Sat, closed Sun evening, Mon. *(Patrick and Daphne Darley)*

BLAGDON HILL   ST2118
Lamb & Flag (01823) 421736
4 miles S of Taunton; TA3 7SL Atmospheric country pub (some recent refurbishment) with 16th-c beams, mixed traditional furniture and woodburner in double-sided fireplace, four well kept west country ales, traditional food (not Mon lunchtime) with smaller helpings available, friendly service, games room/skittle alley, occasional live music; children and dogs welcome, picnic-sets in nice garden with Taunton Vale views, shop and post office, open all day Fri, Sat, till 6pm Sun (10.30pm summer). *(William Ruxton)*

BLEADON   ST3457
★ Queens Arms (01934) 812080
Just off A370 S of Weston; Celtic Way; BS24 0NF Popular 16th-c beamed village

pub with informal chatty atmosphere in carefully divided areas, generous reasonably priced food (not Sun evening) from lunchtime baguettes to steaks, friendly service, well kept Butcombe and guests tapped from the cask, local cider and decent wines by the glass, flagstoned restaurant and stripped-stone back bar with woodburner, sturdy tables and winged settles, old hunting prints; children (away from bar) and dogs (not in restaurant) welcome, partial wheelchair access, picnic-sets on pretty heated terrace, open all day. *(Chris and Angela Buckell)*

BRISTOL   ST5773
Alma (0117) 973 5171
Alma Vale Road, Clifton; BS8 2HY Two-bar pub with good range of beers, proper cider and several wines by the glass, very well liked imaginative food along with more traditional choices including good Sun roasts, friendly helpful service, sofas and armchairs as well as plain tables and chairs, local art displayed in back room, thriving upstairs theatre (10% food discount for ticket holders); background music, jazz pianist Sun; easy wheelchair access, small terrace behind (not late evening), open all day. *(Chris and Angela Buckell, Clive Watkin)*

BRISTOL   ST5873
Bank (0117) 930 4691
John Street; BS1 2HR Small proper single-bar pub, centrally placed (but off the beaten track) and popular with office workers; four changing local ales (may include a porter), real ciders, enjoyable well priced food till 4pm including sandwiches, burgers and one or two unusual choices, comfortable bench seats, newspapers, books on shelf above fireplace, blackboard for quirky facts (not all verified); background and regular live music, quiz nights, free wi-fi; dogs welcome, wheelchair access, tables under umbrellas in paved courtyard, open all day (till 1am Thurs-Sat). *(Taff Thomas)*

BRISTOL   ST5972
Barley Mow (0117) 930 4709
Barton Road; The Dings; BS2 0LF Late 19th-c Bristol Beer Factory pub in old industrial area close to floating harbour; their well kept ales and guests, excellent selection of craft kegs and bottled beers, proper cider and decent choice of wines by the glass, enjoyable good value food (not Sun evening) from shortish but well thought-out menu, cheerful chatty staff, simply refurbished interior with wood floors, off-white walls and painted panelled dados, cushioned wall seats and pubby furniture, various odds and ends dotted about, open fire in brick fireplace; Mon quiz, free wi-fi; disabled access, open all day (till 10pm Sun). *(Mike and Eleanor Anderson, Taff Thomas)*

BRISTOL ST5872
Beer Emporium (0117) 379 0333
King Street; BS1 4EF Cellar bar-restaurant with two vaulted rooms; long stone-faced counter under stained-glass skylight, 12 regularly changing ales/craft beers (tasters offered) plus over 150 in bottles from around the world, good selection of malt whiskies and other spirits, interesting wine list, coffees and teas, food from british tapas to steaks, cheerful chatty staff; some live music; disabled facilities and access via lift, opposite the Old Vic (pre-theatre menu), open all day till 2am (midnight Sun), can get crowded. *(Roger and Donna Huggins, Chris and Angela Buckell, Taff Thomas)*

BRISTOL ST5774
Blackboy (0117) 973 5233
Whiteladies Road; BS8 2RY Refurbished dining pub with good uncomplicated food from chef-owner, relaxed friendly atmosphere, back eating area with light wood furniture, small front bar with sewing-machine tables, armchairs and open fire, Butcome Bitter, St Austell Tribute and Timothy Taylors Landlord, several draught continental lagers; open all day. *(Gus Swan)*

BRISTOL ST5872
BrewDog (0117) 927 9258
Baldwin Street, opposite church; BS1 1QW Corner bar serving own BrewDog beers and guests from other craft breweries (draught and bottled), knowledgeable young staff offer tasters, limited but interesting selection of substantial bar snacks, starkly modern feel with exposed brick, stainless-steel furniture and granite surfaces; can get noisily busy; wheelchair access, open all day till midnight. *(Gus Swan)*

BRISTOL ST5873
Colston Yard (0117) 376 3232
Upper Maudlin Street/Colston Street; BS1 5BD Popular Butcombe pub (the Yard) on site of the old Smiles Brewery, their ales and guests kept well, interesting bottled beers and good choice of wines and whiskies, bare-boards front bar split into two, leather stools and banquettes, brewery mirrors, newspapers and board games, larger dining room, good quality pub food all day from lunchtime sandwiches to grills and evening restaurant menu, friendly staff; background music, sports TV; children welcome, disabled access/facilities (other lavatories downstairs), a few pavement tables, open all day (till 8pm Sun). *(Chris and Angela Buckell, Taff Thomas, Bob and Margaret Holder)*

BRISTOL ST5872
Commercial Rooms (0117) 927 9681
Corn Street; BS1 1HT Spacious colonnaded Wetherspoons (former early 19th-c merchants' club) in good location, main part with lofty stained-glass domed ceiling, gas lighting, comfortable quieter back room with ornate balcony; good changing choice of real ales and nice chatty bustle (busiest weekend evenings), their usual food all day, low prices; ladies' with chesterfields and open fire; children welcome, no dogs, side wheelchair access and disabled facilities, open all day from 8am and till late Fri-Sun. *(Roger and Donna Huggins, Taff Thomas, D J and P M Taylor)*

BRISTOL ST5872
Cornubia (0117) 925 4415
Temple Street; BS1 6EN Tucked-away 18th-c real ale pub with up to 12 including a seasonal house beer from Arbor, interesting bottled beers, farm ciders and perry, snacky food such as pasties and pork pies, friendly service, walls and ceilings covered in pump clips, live music including Thurs blues night; can be crowded evenings, not for wheelchairs; dogs welcome, picnic-sets in secluded front beer garden (summer barbecues), boules pitch, closed Sun and bank holidays, otherwise open all day. *(Taff Thomas)*

BRISTOL ST5772
Cottage (0117) 921 5256
Baltic Wharf, Cumberland Road; BS1 6XG Converted stone-built harbour master's office on wharf near Maritime Heritage Centre, comfortable and roomy with fine views of Georgian landmarks and Clifton suspension bridge, popular generous pub food from sandwiches up at reasonable prices, well kept Butcombe ales and a guest, real cider and nice wines, good service even when busy; background music; children welcome, portable ramps for wheelchairs, waterside terrace tables, access through sailing club, on foot along waterfront or by round-harbour ferry, open all day. *(Taff Thomas)*

BRISTOL ST5773
Eldon House (0117) 922 1271
Lower Clifton Hill, Clifton; BS8 1BT Extended terrace-end pub, bare boards and mix of wooden tables and chairs, round stone-walled dining area with glazed roof, snug with original stained glass and half-door servery, well kept Bath Ales and a couple of guests, several wines by the glass, decent good value food (not Sun evening) including blackboard specials, friendly staff; background music (live Sun), Mon quiz, free wi-fi; children till 8pm, open all day Fri-Sun, closed lunchtimes Mon-Weds. *(Taff Thomas)*

BRISTOL ST5872
Golden Guinea (0117) 987 2034
Guinea Street; BS1 6SX Steps up to cosy backstreet pub, well kept changing ales and real ciders, simple bargain home-made food, friendly staff, pews, wing armchairs and farmhouse tables on bare boards, some flock wallpaper and contemporary street art; live

music, comedy and quiz nights; seats out front and back, closed lunchtimes Mon and Tues, otherwise open all day. *(Taff Thomas)*

BRISTOL ST5772
Grain Barge (0117) 929 9347
Hotwell Road; BS8 4RU Converted 100-ft barge owned by Bristol Beer Factory, their ales kept well and fair priced food including good sandwiches, burgers and Sun roasts, great harbour views from seats out on top deck, tables and sofas in wood floor bar below, also a 'hold bar' for functions and Fri live music, art exhibitions; popular with younger crowd; open all day. *(Taff Thomas, Steve and Liz Tilley)*

BRISTOL ST5872
Gryphon
Colston Road; BS1 5AP Wedge-shaped heavy metal/real ale pub with loyal following, half a dozen well kept quickly changing beers served by friendly staff, background music from the likes of Iron Maiden, Metallica and Napalm Death, live bands upstairs; handy for Colston Hall, open till late Fri, Sat. *(Taff Thomas)*

BRISTOL ST5772
★Hope & Anchor (0117) 929 2987
Jacobs Wells Road, Clifton; BS8 1DR Welcoming 18th-c pub opposite 11th-century Jacobs Well, half a dozen changing ales from central bar, nice wines and good choice of malt whiskies, tables of various sizes (some shaped to fit corners) on bare boards, darker back area, enjoyable food including home-made pizzas, friendly staff; background and occasional live music; children welcome, disabled access, attractive tiered back garden, parking nearby can be tricky, open (and food) all day. *(Taff Thomas)*

BRISTOL ST5873
Horts City Tavern (0117) 925 2520
Broad Street; BS1 2EJ Open-plan 18th-c Youngs pub, their well kept ales and Bath Gem, good fairly priced food including burgers and pizzas, big windows overlooking street, 26-seat cinema at back (free entry if you have a meal); background music, sports TV; tables in cobbled courtyard, open (and food) all day. *(Roger and Donna Huggins)*

BRISTOL ST5874
Kensington Arms (0117) 944 6444
Stanley Road; BS6 6NP Dining pub in the centre of Redland (some restoration after recent fire); good interesting food from light lunches up, well kept Greene King and guests, plenty of wines by the glass, cheerful accommodating staff and nice buoyant atmosphere; may be background music; children and dogs welcome, disabled facilities (no wheelchair access to dining room, but can eat in bar), heated terrace, open all day. *(Chris and Val Ramstedt)*

BRISTOL ST5972
★Kings Head (0117) 929 2338
Victoria Street; BS1 6DE Welcoming and relaxed 17th-c pub, big front window and splendid mirrored bar-back, corridor to cosy panelled snug with serving hatch, four well kept ales including Butcombe and Sharps Doom Bar, toby jugs on joists, old-fashioned local prints and photographs, good value pub food weekday lunchtimes (get there early for a seat); background music, no credit cards; pavement tables, open all day (closed Sun afternoon). *(Taff Thomas, D J and P M Taylor)*

BRISTOL ST5276
Lamplighters (0117) 279 3754
End of Station Road, Shirehampton; BS11 9XA Popular 18th-c riverside pub recently reopened after four-year closure; well kept Bath Ales and a guest, Thatcher's ciders, teas and coffees, competitively priced traditional food including children's choices, modern bar furniture on carpet or bare boards, some faux leather sofas and armchairs, pastel walls with darker greeny-blue dados, bold patterned wallpaper here and there, mezzanine dining area and cellar bar (not always open); disabled access/facilities, picnic-sets on paved front terrace, limited parking nearby (beware the high spring tides), riverside walks, open all day. *(Chris and Angela Buckell)*

BRISTOL ST5673
Mall (0117) 974 5318
The Mall, Clifton; BS8 4JG Relaxed corner pub with well kept changing ales, interesting continental beers and lots of wines by the glass, enjoyable modern pub food, tall windows ornate ceiling, some panelling and mix of old furniture on wood floors, downstairs bar; Thurs quiz, free wi-fi; small garden behind, open all day till midnight. *(Taff Thomas)*

BRISTOL ST5772
Nova Scotia (0117) 929 7994
Baltic Wharf, Cumberland Basin; BS1 6XJ Old local on S side of floating harbour with views to Clifton and Avon Gorge; Courage Best and guests, a real cider and generous helpings of enjoyable pub food, four linked areas, snob screen, mahogany and mirrors, nautical charts as wallpaper, welcoming atmosphere and friendly regulars; wheelchair access with help through snug's door, plenty of tables out by water, bedrooms sharing bathroom. *(Taff Thomas)*

BRISTOL ST5872
Old Duke (0117) 927 7137
King Street; BS1 4ER Named after Duke Ellington and festooned with jazz posters, plus one or two instruments, good bands nightly and Sun lunchtime, usual pub furnishings, real ales and simple food; in interesting cobbled area between docks and

Bristol Old Vic, gets packed evenings, open all day (till 1am Fri, Sat). *(Taff Thomas)*

BRISTOL ST5872
Old Fish Market (0117) 921 1515
Baldwin Street; BS1 1QZ Imposing brick-built former fish market, some recent refurbishment and relaxed friendly atmosphere, well kept Fullers/Gales beers from handsome wooden counter, fine range of gins, food from pizzas up (no longer does thai); background music, Thurs comedy/theatre night, sports TVs, free wi-fi; open all day (food all day weekends). *(Taff Thomas)*

BRISTOL ST5772
Orchard
Hanover Place, Spike Island; BS1 6XT Friendly unpretentious corner local with up to eight well kept ales from stillage behind bar and great range of ciders, food from bar snacks up in bar or upstairs dining room, woodburner; live music including Mon blues jam and Tues jazz, quiz Thurs, sports TV – pub gets busy on match days; tables out in front, handy for SS *Great Britain*, open all day (from 9am weekends for breakfast). *(Gus Swan)*

BRISTOL ST5672
Portcullis (0117) 908 5536
Wellington Terrace; BS8 4LE Compact two-storey pub in Georgian building close to Clifton bridge, well kept Dawkins and several changing guests, farm ciders, fine range of wines by the glass and spirits, tapas-style food, good friendly staff, flame-effect gas fire, dark wood and usual pubby furniture; free wi-fi; dogs welcome, tricky wheelchair access, garden behind on upper level, closed weekday lunchtimes, open all day weekends. *(Roger and Donna Huggins, Trevor Graveson)*

BRISTOL ST5772
Pump House (0117) 927 2229
Merchants Road; BS8 4PZ Spacious nicely converted dockside building (former 19th-c pumping station); charcoal grey brickwork, tiled floors and high ceilings, good food in bar and smart candlelit mezzanine restaurant, ales such as Bath, Butcombe and St Austell, decent wines from comprehensive list and huge choice of gins, friendly staff, cheerful atmosphere; waterside tables. *(Taff Thomas)*

BRISTOL ST5872
Royal Naval Volunteer
(0117) 316 9237 *King Street; BS1 4EF* Modernised 17th-c pub in cobbled street, wide range of draught and bottled british beers, ciders/perries and a dozen wines by the glass, friendly knowledgeable staff, good interesting food in back restaurant; weekend live music, sports TV; dogs welcome, terrace seating. *(Taff Thomas)*

BRISTOL ST5972
Seven Stars (0117) 927 2845
Thomas Lane; BS1 6JG Unpretentious one-room real ale pub near harbour (and associated with Thomas Clarkson and slave trade abolition), popular with students and local office workers, eight well kept changing ales (20 from a featured county on first Mon-Thurs of the month), some interesting malts and bourbons, dark wood and bare boards, old local prints and photographs, no food – can bring in takeaways; weekend folk music, juke box, pool, games machine; disabled access (but narrow alley with uneven cobbles and cast-iron kerbs), open all day. *(Chris and Angela Buckell, Taff Thomas)*

BRISTOL ST5872
Three Tuns (0117) 907 0689
St George's Road; BS1 5UR Under new ownership and some refurbishment; seven real ales including local Arbor, craft kegs and interesting selection of bottled beers, several ciders too, simple food such as baguettes, wraps and burgers, bar area with pine tables on bare boards, a couple of small leather sofas in alcoves, open fire; regular events including art exhibitions, music, quiz and magic nights; covered and heated terrace, near cathedral, open all day. *(Taff Thomas)*

BRISTOL ST5773
Victoria (0117) 974 5675
Southleigh Road, Clifton; BS8 2BH Modest little two-room pub, popular and can get crowded, with half a dozen or more changing small brewery ales including a couple from Dawkins, interesting bottled belgian beers, local cider and good selection of malt whiskies and wines by the glass, cheerful knowledgeable staff, basic snacks such as pies and sausage rolls, big mirrors and open fire, cards and board games, old silent movies some winter evenings; free wi-fi; dogs welcome, disabled access (a few low kerbs/steps), open all day weekends, from 4pm Mon-Fri. *(Chris and Angela Buckell)*

BRISTOL ST5773
W G Grace (0117) 946 9780
Whiteladies Road; BS8 2NT Popular Wetherspoons with rather austere dark frontage – tables and chairs on front terrace; small lounge areas either side of entrance with upholstered chairs, sofas and low tables, grey stone tiles in bar area, wood elsewhere, some alcove seating, Greene King and four local guests from long chrome-topped servery, usual food and value, bare-brick and mock-stone walls in much higher ceilinged eating area at back, history of W G Grace, old Bristol photos and mirrored Betjeman poems on walls; sports TVs, fruit machines, free wi-fi; wheelchair access throughout, open all day from 8am. *(Chris and Angela Buckell)*

BRISTOL   ST5976
Wellington (0117) 951 3022
Gloucester Road, Horfield (A38);
BS7 8UR Lively and roomy 1920s red-
brick pub refitted in traditional style, well
kept Bath Ales and guests, good choice of
bottled beers and other drinks, enjoyable
food till 10pm, pleasant efficient service,
large horseshoe bar, sofas and low tables in
extended lounge with dining area overlooking
sunny terrace; very busy on Bristol RFC
or Rovers match days; children welcome,
disabled access/facilities, refurbished
boutique bedrooms (best to book early),
open all day, from 9am weekends for
breakfast. *(Chris and Angela Buckell)*

BRISTOL   ST5873
White Lion (0117) 927 7744
Quay Head, Colston Avenue; BS1 1EB
Small friendly city-centre pub with simple
bare-boards bar, four Wickwar ales and a
guest, range of Pieminister pies, good coffee,
daily newspapers and free wi-fi; spiral stairs
down to lavatories; café-style pavement
tables under awning. *(Taff Thomas)*

BROADWAY   ST3215
Bell (01460) 52343
Broadway Lane; TA19 9RG Welcoming
village pub attracting good mix of locals
and visitors, flagstones and open fires,
comfortable leather sofas and armchairs,
innovative well priced food (not Sun evening)
along with more traditional choices and
bargain OAP lunch, Charles Wells ales, skittle
alley; quiz second Tues of month; children
and dogs welcome, seats out in front and on
back terrace, good value bedrooms, open all
day Fri-Sun. *(Martin and Alison Stainsby)*

CHEDDAR   ST4653
White Hart (01934) 741261
The Bays; BS27 3QN Welcoming village
local with well kept beers, traditional ciders
and enjoyable fairly priced home-made food
from good ploughman's to Sun carvery, log
fire; live music and quiz nights, free wi-fi;
children welcome, picnic-sets out in front
and in back garden with play area, open
(and food) all day. *(Eddie Edwards)*

CHEW MAGNA   ST5763
Pelican (01275) 331777
South Parade; BS40 8SL Friendly buoyant
atmosphere at this welcoming village pub;
opened-up modern interior with polished
wood flooring, candles on chunky tables,
some old pew chairs and high-backed settles,
leather armchairs by woodburners in stone
fireplaces, well kept changing ales such as
Butcombe, Otter and St Austell, plenty of
wines by the glass and good fairly priced food
including daily specials, efficient service;
children and dogs welcome, wheelchair
access from back courtyard, grassy beer
garden, open all day (Sun till 6pm).

(Taff Thomas, Comus and Sarah Elliott, Chris and
Angela Buckell, Hugh Roberts and others)

CHEW MAGNA   ST5861
★ Pony & Trap (01275) 332627
Knowle Hill, New Town; from B3130
in village, follow Bishop Sutton, Bath
signpost; BS40 8TQ Michelin-starred
dining pub in nice rural spot near Chew
Valley Lake; really good imaginative food
from sandwiches through to beautifully
presented restaurant dishes (must book),
good friendly service, Butcombe ales and a
guest, front bar with cushioned wall seats
and built-in benches on parquet, old range
in snug area on left, dark plank panelling
and housekeeper's chair in corner, lovely
pasture views from two-level back dining
area with white tables on slate flagstones;
children welcome, dogs in bar, modern
furniture on back terrace, picnic-sets on
grass with chickens in runs below, front
smokers' shelter, good walks. *(Comus and*
Sarah Elliott, Michael Doswell, Taff Thomas,
Steve and Liz Tilley,)

CHILCOMPTON   ST6451
Somerset Wagon (01761) 232732
B3139; Broadway; BA3 4JW Cosy and
welcoming 19th-c pub (former railway inn),
well liked good value food, Wadworths ales
with Butcombe as a guest, Thatcher's and
Weston's ciders, decent wines, good service
even when packed, pleasant olde-worlde
areas off central bar, lots of settles, log fire;
some live music; children welcome, small
front garden, open all day Sun. *(Ian Phillips)*

COMPTON DANDO   ST6464
Compton Inn (01761) 490321
Court Hill; BS39 4JZ Welcoming stone-
built village pub in lovely setting; enjoyable
home-made food (not Sun evening), well kept
Butcombe, Sharps and a guest, wood-floored
bar with dining area at each end (one down
a couple of steps), two-way woodburner
in stone fireplace; charity quiz first Mon
of month, TV; children, walkers and dogs
welcome, picnic-sets out in front, garden
behind with boules, open all day.
(Taff Thomas)

CONGRESBURY   ST4363
Plough (01934) 877402
High Street (B3133); BS49 5JA Popular
old-fashioned character local – a pub since
the 1800s; half a dozen well kept changing
west country ales such as Butcombe, St
Austell and Twisted Oak, ciders from Moles
and Thatcher's, quick smiling service,
generous helpings of well cooked food
(not Sun evening) including daily specials,
several small interconnecting rooms off
flagstoned main bar, mix of furniture old and
new, built-in pine wall benches, old prints,
photos, farm tools and some morris dancing
memorabilia, log fires; Sun quiz; no children
inside, dogs welcome, wheelchair access from

car park, garden with rustic furniture and boules. *(Chris and Angela Buckell, Hugh Roberts)*

CORFE   ST2319
White Hart (01823) 421388
B3170 S of Taunton; TA3 7BU Friendly 17th-c village pub, enjoyable sensibly priced pubby food (not Tues) including some vegetarian options, well kept ales, hot woodburner and open fire; bar billiards, skittle alley; dogs welcome, open all day Sat, closed Tues lunchtime. *(Bob and Margaret Holder)*

CROSS   ST4254
New Inn (01934) 732455
A38 Bristol–Bridgwater, junction A371; BS26 2EE Steps up to friendly roadside pub with five well kept ales (discount Thurs evening), good choice of enjoyable fairly traditional food from baguettes and baked potatoes up; children and dogs welcome, nice hillside garden with play area, open (and food) all day. *(Hugh Roberts)*

CULBONE HILL   SS8247
Culbone (01643) 862259
Culbone Hill; A39 W of Porlock, opposite Porlock Weir Toll Road; TA24 8JW Set high on Exmoor and perhaps more restaurant-with-rooms than pub; good food including themed nights, up to three well kept local ales and decent choice of malt whiskies, good friendly service; children welcome, terrace with wonderful views over Lorna Doone valley, five well appointed bedrooms, open all day, food all day weekends and in high season. *(Neil Allen)*

DINNINGTON   ST4013
Dinnington Docks (01460) 52397
NE of village; Fosse Way; TA17 8SX Good cheery atmosphere in large old-fashioned rural local, unspoilt and unfussy, with good choice of inexpensive genuine home cooking including fresh fish Fri, well kept Butcombe and guests, farm ciders, friendly attentive staff, memorabilia to bolster myth that there was once a railway line and dock here, log fire, family room; some live music, skittle alley in adjoining building; large garden behind, good walks, open all day Fri-Mon. *(S Holder)*

DITCHEAT   ST6236
★ **Manor House** (01749) 860276
Signed off A37 and A371 S of Shepton Mallet; BA4 6RB Pretty 17th-c red-brick village inn, buoyant atmosphere and popular with jockeys from nearby stables, enjoyable home-made food from sandwiches and pubby bar meals to more sophisticated choices, well kept Butcombe and guests, friendly helpful staff, unusual arched doorways linking big flagstoned bar to comfortable lounge and restaurant, open fires, skittle alley; children welcome, tables on back grass, handy for Royal Bath & West

showground, three mews bedrooms, good breakfast, open all day. *(Carey Smith)*

DOWLISH WAKE   ST3712
New Inn (01460) 52413
Off A3037 S of Ilminster, via Kingstone; TA19 0NZ Comfortable and welcoming dark-beamed village pub, enjoyable home-made food including blackboard specials, well kept Butcombe and Otter, local cider, friendly helpful staff, woodburners in stone inglenooks, pleasant dining room; dogs welcome, attractive garden and village, Perry's cider mill and shop nearby, four bedrooms in separate annexe. *(Emma Scofield)*

DULVERTON   SS9127
Bridge Inn (01398) 324130
Bridge Street; TA22 9HJ Welcoming unpretentious little pub next to River Barle; reasonably priced food using local suppliers, up to four well kept ales including Exmoor, some unusual imported beers, Addlestone's cider and 30 malt whiskies, comfortable sofas, woodburner; folk night third Sat of month, fortnightly quiz Sun; children and dogs welcome, two terraces, open all day summer (all day Fri-Sun, closed Mon evening winter). *(Richard and Penny Gibbs, Eddie Edwards)*

DUNDRY   ST5666
Carpenters (0117) 964 6423
Wells Road; BS41 8NE Renovated village pub continuing well under present management, well kept ales such as Bath and Butcombe, Thatcher's cider, enjoyable fairly priced traditional food including specials, helpful friendly staff; quiz third Weds of the month; children welcome, picnic-sets on lawn, open all day Fri, Sat, till 6pm Sun. *(Comus and Sarah Elliott, David and Jill Wyatt, Taff Thomas and others)*

DUNDRY   ST5566
Dundry Inn (0177) 964 1722
Church Road, off A38 SW of Bristol; BS41 8LH Renovated roomy village pub, half-panelled bar with cushioned window seats and comfy armchairs on oak floor, steps up to stone-tiled dining area with open fire, Bath, Butcombe and Sharps, enjoyable imaginative food along with pubby choices; well behaved children welcome, no wheelchair access, picnic-sets in enclosed church-side garden with outstanding views over Bristol and beyond, two bedrooms, handy for airport, closed Sun evening, Mon. *(Comus and Sarah Elliott)*

DUNSTER   SS9843
★ **Stags Head** (01643) 821229
West Street (A396); TA24 6SN Friendly helpful staff in unassuming 16th-c roadside inn, enjoyable good value food including daily specials, Exmoor and a guest ale, candles, beams, timbers and inglenook log fire, steps up to small back dining room; dogs

welcome in bar area, comfortable simple bedrooms, good breakfast, closed Weds lunchtime. *(John Chambers)*

EAST HARPTREE   ST5453
Castle of Comfort (01761) 221321
B3134, SW on Old Bristol Road; BS40 6DD Welcoming family-managed former coaching inn set high in the Mendips (last stop before the gallows for some past visitors); hefty timbers and exposed stonework, cushioned settles and other pubby furniture on carpet, log fires, Butcombe, Sharps and a guest, ample helpings of reasonably priced traditional food including good steaks, friendly staff; children (away from bar) and dogs welcome, wheelchair access, big garden with raised deck and play area, fine walks nearby. *(Taff Thomas)*

EAST LAMBROOK   ST4218
Rose & Crown (01460) 240433
Silver Street; TA13 5HF Stone-built dining pub spreading extensively from compact 17th-c core with inglenook log fire, friendly staff and relaxed atmosphere, decent choice of freshly made food using local supplies, Palmers ales and nine wines by the glass, restaurant extension with old glass-covered well, skittle alley; quiz and curry night third Thurs of month; children and dogs (in bar) welcome, picnic-sets on neat lawn, opposite East Lambrook Manor Garden, closed Sun evening, Mon. *(Neil Allen)*

EAST WOODLANDS   ST7944
★ Horse & Groom (01373) 462802
Off A361/B3092 junction; BA11 5LY Small pretty pub (aka the Jockey) tucked away down country lanes, friendly and relaxed, with good choice of enjoyable well priced food (not Sun evening) including some real bargains, quickly changing ales and real ciders, pews and settles in flagstoned bar, woodburner in comfortable lounge, big dining conservatory, traditional games; children welcome in eating areas, dogs in bar, disabled access, tables out in nice front garden with more seats behind, handy for Longleat. *(Belinda Stamp)*

EVERCREECH   ST6336
Natterjack (01749) 860253
A371 Shepton Mallet–Castle Cary; BA4 6NA Former Victorian station hotel (line closed 1966), good choice of popular generous food at reasonable prices, Butcombe and a couple of guests, real cider and good range of wines, welcoming landlord and cheerful efficient staff, long bar with eating areas off; lots of tables under parasols in big neatly kept garden, five bedrooms in restored cider house. *(Anon)*

EXEBRIDGE   SS9324
Anchor (01398) 323433
B3222 S of Dulverton; pub itself actually over the river, in Devon; TA22 9AZ Idyllically placed Exmoor-edge inn with good food using local suppliers, some emphasis on fresh fish/shellfish, Sun carvery, Exmoor, Greene King and guests, Thatcher's cider and seven wines by the glass, friendly staff, simply furnished bar with woodburner, light spacious river-view restaurant; children welcome, dogs in bar, nice big riverside garden with plenty of tables, six bedrooms (fishing rights for residents), open (and food) all day weekends. *(Taff Thomas, M G Hart)*

EXFORD   SS8538
★ White Horse (01643) 831229
B3224; TA24 7PY Popular and welcoming three-storey creeper-clad inn, more or less open-plan bar, high-backed antique settle among more conventional seats, scrubbed deal tables, hunting prints and local photographs, good log fire, Exmoor ales and Sharps Doom Bar, over 100 malt whiskies, Thatcher's cider, enjoyable hearty food from sandwiches to good value Sun carvery; children and dogs welcome, tables outside and play area, pretty village, Land Rover Exmoor safaris, comfortable bedrooms, open all day from 8am. *(Lynda and Trevor Smith)*

FAULKLAND   ST7555
★ Tuckers Grave (01373) 834230
A366 E of village; BA3 5XF Tiny cider house, unspoilt and unchanging, with chatty locals and warm friendly atmosphere; flagstoned entrance opening into simple room with casks of Butcombe and Thatcher's Cheddar Valley cider in alcove on left, perhaps lunchtime sandwiches, two high-backed settles facing each other across a single table on right, side room with shove-ha'penny, open fires, skittle alley; children welcome in one area, lots of tables and chairs on attractive back lawn, good views, closed Mon lunchtime (except bank holidays). *(Roger and Donna Huggins)*

FRESHFORD   ST7960
Inn at Freshford (01225) 722250
Off A36 or B3108; BA2 7WG Roomy old stone-built village pub in lovely spot near river, enjoyable locally sourced food (not Sun evening) from lunchtime baguettes and pub favourites to more adventurous choices, well kept Box Steam and guests, local ciders/perries, good wine list, decent gins and nice coffee, helpful chatty young staff; children and dogs welcome, wheelchair access from car park, pretty hillside garden overlooking valley, good waterside walks. *(Taff Thomas, Nick Lawless, Chris and Angela Buckell)*

FROME   ST7748
Griffin (01373) 467766
Milk Street; BA11 3DB Unpretentious bare-boards bar with etched glass and open fires, long counter serving good Milk Street beers brewed here by friendly landlord, hot food Weds and Sun, easy-going mixed crowd;

regular quiz and music nights; small garden, open till 1am Fri, Sat, closed lunchtimes except Sun. *(Neil Allen)*

GLASTONBURY ST4938
George & Pilgrim (01458) 831146
High Street; BA6 9DP Comfortable 15th-c inn with magnificent carved stone façade and some interesting features, carpeted bar with handsome stone fireplace, moulded beams, oak panelling and traceried stained-glass bay window, St Austell and guests, restaurant; 14 bedrooms, open all day. *(Ann and Colin Hunt)*

GLASTONBURY ST5039
Who'd A Thought It (01458) 834460
Northload Street; BA6 9JJ Interesting pub filled with oddments and memorabilia – red phone box (complete with mannequin), bicycle chained to the ceiling, lots of enamel signs and old photographs, coal fire in old range, beams, flagstones, stripped brick and pine panelling, well kept Palmers ales and decent wines by the glass, enjoyable freshly cooked food; free wi-fi; children and dogs welcome, terrace picnic-sets, five comfortable bedrooms, open all day. *(Chris and Angela Buckell)*

HALLATROW ST6357
★ Old Station (01761) 452228
A39 S of Bristol; BS39 6EN Former 1920s station hotel with extraordinary collection of bric-a-brac including railway memorabilia, musical instruments, china cows, post boxes, even half an old Citroën, wide mix of furnishings, Brains Rev James, Butcombe Bitter and a guest, several wines by the glass, popular varied choice of food cooked by landlord, pullman carriage restaurant; children and dogs (in bar) welcome, café-style furniture on decking, picnic-sets on grass, also crazy golf, football pitch and polytunnel growing own vegetables, five bedrooms in converted outbuilding (no breakfast), open all day Fri-Sun. *(Emma Scofield)*

HARDWAY ST7234
★ Bull (01749) 812200
Off B3081 Bruton–Wincanton at brown sign for Stourhead and King Alfred's Tower; Hardway; BA10 0LN Charming beamed 17th-c country dining pub, good popular food (not Sun evening, Mon) in comfortable bar and character dining rooms, well kept Butcombe and Otter, farm cider and reasonably priced wines by the glass, friendly long-serving landlord and good informal service, log fire; unobtrusive background music; tables and barbecues in lovely garden behind, more seats in pretty rose garden over road, closed Sun evening in winter. *(Michael Hill)*

HILLFARANCE ST1624
Anchor (01823) 461334
Oake; pub signed off Bradford-on-Tone to Oake road; TA4 1AW Comfortable village pub with dining area off attractive two-part bar, good choice of enjoyable food including Sun carvery, nice atmosphere, three local ales; children welcome, garden with play area, bedrooms and holiday apartments. *(Bob and Margaret Holder)*

HINTON BLEWETT ST5956
★ Ring o' Bells (01761) 452239
Signed off A37 in Clutton; BS39 5AN Charming low-beamed stone country local opposite village green, old-fashioned bar with solid furniture including pews, log fire, good value food (not Sun evening) cooked by landlady, obliging service, Butcombe, Fullers and guests, good wines by the glass, dining room; children, walkers and dogs welcome, good view from tables in sheltered front yard, open all day in summer. *(Taff Thomas)*

HINTON CHARTERHOUSE ST7758
★ Rose & Crown (01225) 722153
B3110 about 4 miles S of Bath; BA2 7SN Friendly 18th-c village pub with partly divided bar, fine panelling, cushioned wall seats and bar stools, farmhouse chairs around chunky tables on red carpeting, woodburner in ornate carved stone fireplace (smaller brick one on other side), Butcombe, Fullers and a seasonal guest, several wines by glass, tasty good value food from baguettes to grills, long dining room and steps to lower area with unusual beamed ceiling; background music, TV; children and dogs welcome, picnic-sets under parasols in terraced garden, pretty window boxes, monthly summer live music and barbecue, bedrooms, open all day Weds-Sun. *(David and Stella Martin, Mark Sykes)*

HOLCOMBE ST6648
Duke of Cumberland
(01761) 233731 *Edford Hill; BA3 5HQ* Popular modernised riverside pub with good competitively priced food including home-made pizzas, Butcombe, Fullers, Sharps and Woodfordes, ciders from Long Ashton and Thatcher's, friendly helpful staff, log fires, skittle alley; background and some live music, sports TV; children and dogs welcome, small waterside garden, open all day from 10am. *(Ian Phillips)*

HOLTON ST6826
Old Inn (01963) 32002
Off A303 W of Wincanton; BA9 8AR Modernised and extended 16th-c dining pub with enjoyable food from tapas up, well kept beers such as Butcombe, local cider, painted beams, ancient flagstones and big woodburner, lots of button-back leather banquettes, raftered restaurant with pale green and cherry pink walls; children and dogs welcome, picnic-sets in front, sheltered garden up steps, open all day Sun. *(Gus Swan)*

HORTON   ST3214
★ **Five Dials** (01460) 55359
Hanning Road; off A303; TA19 9QH
Cleanly updated village pub run by friendly
helpful couple, popular reasonably priced
home-made food including good steaks and
fish, Otter, Sharps Doom Bar and a guest,
local ciders and good choice of wines by the
glass, restaurant; children and dogs welcome,
six comfortable bedrooms, open all day
Fri-Sun, closed Mon. *(Evelyn and Derek Walter)*

KELSTON   ST7067
Old Crown (01225) 423032
Bitton Road; A431 W of Bath; BA1 9AQ
17th-c creeper-clad inn with four small
traditional rooms, beams and polished
flagstones, carved settles and cask tables,
logs burning in ancient open range, two more
coal-effect fires, well kept Butcombe ales and
real cider, enjoyable fairly priced food in bar
and small restaurant, good value lunchtime
set menu and other deals; children and
dogs welcome, wheelchair access with help,
picnic-sets under apple trees in sheltered
sunny back garden, play area, four bedrooms
in converted outbuildings, open all day.
(M G Hart, Taff Thomas)

KEYNSHAM   ST6669
★ **Lock-Keeper** (0117) 986 2383
*Keynsham Road (A4175 NE of town);
BS31 2DD* Friendly riverside pub with
plenty of character, bare boards and relaxed
worn-in feel, simple left-hand bar with big
painted settle, cushioned wall benches,
trophy cabinet and old local photographs, two
more little rooms with assorted cushioned
dining chairs, more photographs and rustic
prints, Charles Wells ales and guests, good
quality wines, whiskies and gins, nice coffee
too, popular well priced bar food served by
cheerful helpful young staff, light modern
conservatory (quite different in style); live
music Fri, Sat; children welcome, dogs in bar,
disabled access/facilities, teak furniture and
giant parasols on big heated deck overlooking
water, steps down to picnic-sets on grass,
outside bar and barbecue, pétanque, open
all day. *(Chris and Angela Buckell, Taff Thomas,
Dr and Mrs A K Clarke and others)*

KINGSTON ST MARY   ST2229
Swan (01823) 451383
*Lodes Lane, in centre of village;
TA2 8HW* Cosy 17th-c roadside village
pub, neat and tidy, with long knocked-
through panelled bar, modern furniture on
carpets, black-painted beams and rough
plastered walls with signed cricket bats,
big stone fireplaces, popular home-made
mostly pubby food (not Sun evening), well
kept ales such as Dartmoor, Exmoor and
Sharps, Thatcher's cider, pleasant helpful
staff; background music; children welcome,
no dogs inside, front wheelchair access,
garden with play area, skittle alley, handy

for Hestercombe Gardens. *(Chris and
Angela Buckell, Bob and Margaret Holder)*

KNAPP   ST3025
Rising Sun (01823) 491027
*Village W of North Curry (pub signed
from here); TA3 6BG* Tucked-away 15th-c
longhouse surrounded by lovely countryside;
handsome beams, flagstones and two
inglenooks with woodburners, Exmoor and
Sharps Doom Bar, proper cider, good food
with emphasis on fish/seafood, seasonal game
too, friendly helpful staff; children and dogs
welcome, sunny little front terrace, open all
day Sat, closed Sun evening (except first Sun
of month when there's a quiz), Mon, Tues
lunchtime. *(Mr Yeldahn)*

KNOLE   ST4825
Lime Kiln (01458) 241242
A372 E of Langport; TA10 9JH Creeper-
clad beamed 17th-c country pub set back
from the road, good range of well priced
traditional food including children's menu,
ales such as Butcombe, Otter and Ringwood,
Thatcher's Cheddar Valley cider, friendly
attentive staff, flagstoned bar and large
carpeted dining room, inglenook log fire;
pleasant garden with southerly views, open
all day weekends. *(Helen and Brian Edgeley)*

LANGFORD BUDVILLE   ST1122
★ **Martlet** (01823) 400262
Off B3187 NW of Wellington; TA21 0QZ
Cosy, comfortable and cottagey with friendly
landlady and staff, good generously served
food (becomes more restauranty in evenings
with fewer drinkers), popular OAP lunch
deal Weds-Fri, well kept/priced local ales
including Exmoor, inglenook, beams and
flagstones, central woodburner, steps up
to dining room, conservatory; children
welcome, terrace picnic-sets, closed Mon
and lunchtime Tues; for sale so things may
change. *(Patrick and Daphne Darley,
S G N Bennett)*

LANGLEY MARSH   ST0729
Three Horseshoes (01984) 623763
Just N of Wiveliscombe; TA4 2UL
Traditional red-sandstone pub with well kept
beers tapped from the cask and enjoyable
pubby food in bar and dining area, plenty of
cheerful staff, low modern settles in back
bar, stone fireplace; background music;
seats on verandah and in sloping back
garden, monthly vintage car meetings, good
walks nearby, closed Sun evening, Mon and
lunchtimes except Sun. *(Gus Swan)*

LANGPORT   ST4625
★ **Devonshire Arms** (01458) 241271
*B3165 Somerton–Martock, off A372
E of Langport; TA10 9LP* Handsome
gabled inn (former hunting lodge); simple
flagstoned bar with high-backed chairs
around dark tables, up to three west country
ales tapped from the cask, several wines

by the glass and local cider brandy, stylish main room with comfortable leather sofas and glass-topped log table by fire, scatter cushions on long wall bench, church candles, elegant dining room with wicker chairs and pale wood tables on broad boards, good interesting food from lunchtime sandwiches up (local suppliers listed), charming efficient service, evening pianist; wheelchair access from car park, teak furniture out at front, pretty box-enclosed courtyard with water-ball feature, more seats on raised terraces, nice bedrooms, good breakfast. *(Hugh Roberts, B and F A Hannam)*

LONG ASHTON ST5370
Bird in Hand (01275) 395222
Weston Road; BS41 9LA Stone-built dining pub with good locally sourced food from bar meals to imaginative restaurant dishes, well kept Bath Gem, St Austell Tribute and two guests, Ashton Press cider, nice wines, friendly welcoming young staff, spindleback chairs and blue-painted pine tables on wood floors, open fire and woodburner; children and dogs welcome, side terrace, parking can be tricky, open all day. *(Roger and Anne Newbury)*

LONG ASHTON ST5370
Miners Rest (01275) 393449
Providence Lane; BS41 9DJ Welcoming three-room country pub, comfortable and unpretentious, with well kept Butcombe and an occasional guest such as Sharps Doom Bar tapped from the cask, five good traditional ciders, generous helpings of simple inexpensive lunchtime food, cheerful prompt service, local mining memorabilia, log fire, darts; no credit cards; well behaved children and dogs welcome, wheelchair access with some heroics, vine-covered verandah and suntrap terrace, open all day. *(Chris and Angela Buckell)*

LOVINGTON ST5831
★ **Pilgrims** (01963) 240600
B3153 Castle Cary–Keinton Mandeville; BA7 7PT More of a restaurant but does have a pubby corner serving Bath Ales Gem, Orchard Pig cider and plenty of wines by the glass, good imaginative food (not cheap) using local produce, efficient friendly service, cosy flagstoned inner area with modern prints, bookshelves, china and some sofas by big fireplace, compact eating area with candles on tables and more formal carpeted dining room; children welcome, dogs in bar, decked terrace in enclosed garden, car park exit with own traffic lights, five bedrooms (no children), open evenings Tues-Sat, lunchtimes Fri and Sat. *(Emma Scofield)*

LOWER GODNEY ST4742
Sheppey Inn (01458) 831594
Tilleys Drove; BA5 1RZ Revamped character pub attracting good mix of customers; at least six local ciders tapped from the barrel along with local ales and craft beers, imaginative choice of well liked food, some cooked in charcoal oven, plain furniture on bare boards, black beams, stripped-stone walls and open fire, stuffed animals, old local photographs and modern artwork, long simply furnished dining area with pitched ceiling; regular live music; children welcome, seats on deck overlooking small river. *(Peter Meister)*

LUXBOROUGH SS9837
Royal Oak (01984) 641498
Kingsbridge; S of Dunster on minor roads into Brendon Hills; TA23 0SH Friendly new landlord and refurbishment for this atmospheric old inn set deep in Exmoor National Park; compact beamed bar with ancient flagstones, several rather fine settles, scrubbed kitchen tables and huge brick inglenook, back bar with cobbled floor, some quarry tiles and stone fireplace, cosy side room set for eating plus two further dining rooms, Exmoor and a couple of guests, generous food from pub favourites to more upmarket choices including seasonal game; pool, shove-ha'penny and board games in back room, also a radiogram with stack of old LPs; children and dogs welcome, seats in lovely sunny back courtyard, eight revamped bedrooms, good walks nearby including Coleridge Way, open all day weekends (no food Sun evening), closed Mon and weekday lunchtimes. *(Bob and Margaret Holder, Richard and Penny Gibbs)*

MARK ST3747
Pack Horse (01278) 641209
B3139 Wedmore–Highbridge; Church Street; TA9 4NF Attractive traditional 16th-c village pub run by welcoming greek-cypriot family, good choice of enjoyable home-made food including Sun roasts and fresh Brixham fish (prices can be on the high side), well kept Butcombe and guests, good friendly service, log fire; children welcome. *(Neil Allen)*

MINEHEAD SS9646
Duke of Wellington (01643) 701910
Wellington Square; TA24 5LJ Wetherspoons conversion of 19th-c coaching inn, usual good value, friendly efficient staff; children welcome, disabled access and facilities, bedrooms, open all day from 7am. *(S Holder)*

MONTACUTE ST4917
Kings Arms (01935) 822255
Bishopston; TA15 6UU Extended 17th-c inn under newish management; stripped-stone bar with comfortable seating and log fire, contemporary restaurant, three real ales including Greene King, enjoyable food from bar snacks to restaurant dishes, friendly staff; pleasant garden behind, 15 bedrooms (most ensuite), handy for Montacute House (NT). *(A H Baker)*

NAILSEA   ST4469
Blue Flame (01275) 856910
Netherton Wood Lane, West End;
BS48 4DE Small friendly 19th-c farmers'
local with two unchanging lived-in rooms,
coal fire, well kept ales from casks behind
bar, traditional ciders, fresh rolls and pork
pies, pub games; outside lavatories including
roofless gents', limited parking (may be filled
with Land Rovers and tractors); children's
room, sizeable informal garden, open all day
weekends, closed lunchtimes Mon, Tues.
(Taff Thomas)

NEWTON ST LOE   ST7065
Globe (01225) 872891
A4/A36 roundabout; BA2 9BB Popular
17th-c Vintage Inn, large and rambling, with
pleasant décor and dark wood partitions,
pillars and timbers giving secluded feel, log
fire, their usual food including set deals,
well kept Butcombe, St Austell Tribute
and a guest, prompt friendly service from
uniformed staff, good atmosphere; children
welcome, nice back terrace, open (and food)
all day. *(Taff Thomas)*

NORTH CURRY   ST3125
Bird in Hand (01823) 490248
Queens Square; off A378 (or A358)
E of Taunton; TA3 6LT Friendly village
pub with cosy main bar, old pews, settles,
benches and yew tables on flagstones, some
original beams and timbers, good inglenook
log fire, well kept ales and decent wines by
the glass, enjoyable food in separate dining
part; background music; children, dogs and
muddy boots welcome, open all day Sun.
(Bob and Margaret Holder)

NORTON ST PHILIP   ST7755
★ George (01373) 834224
A366; BA2 7LH Wonderful building full
of history and interest – an inn for over 700
years; heavy beams, timbering, stonework
and panelling, vast open fires, distinctive
furnishings, plenty of 18th-c pictures, fine
pewter and heraldic shields, Wadworths ales
and enjoyable food from varied menu, good
friendly service; children and particularly
dogs welcome, appealing galleried courtyard,
atmospheric bedrooms (some reached by
Norman turret), worth strolling over meadow
to attractive churchyard, open all day.
(John Coatsworth, Roger and Donna Huggins,
Taff Thomas, R K Phillips, Mark Sykes)

NUNNEY   ST7345
George (01373) 836458
Church Street; signed off A361 Shepton
Mallet–Frome; BA11 4LW Smart 17th-c
coaching inn set in quaint village with ruined
castle; comfortably modern open-plan lounge
with beams, stripped stone and woodburner
in big fireplace, good food from sharing
plates, pizzas and burgers up, Wadworths
ales and a guest, nice wines by the glass and

good coffee, separate restaurant; children
and dogs (in bar) welcome, attractive split-
level walled garden, rare 'gallows' inn-sign
spanning road, nine bedrooms, open all day.
(Heulwen and Neville Pinfield, Ian Phillips, Ann
and Colin Hunt)

OAKHILL   ST6347
Oakhill Inn (01749) 840442
A367 Shepton Mallet–Radstock; BA3 5HU
Dining pub with sofas and easy chairs
among candlelit tables around bar, friendly
welcoming atmosphere, enjoyable food
including pizzas and chargrills, up to four
real ales such as Abbey, Bath and Butcombe,
dining extension in former skittle alley,
rugs on bare boards, wall of clocks, log fires;
background music; nice views from garden,
five bedrooms, open all day weekends.
(Dr Simon Innes)

OVER STRATTON   ST4315
★ Royal Oak (01460) 240906
Off A303 via Ilminster turn at
S Petherton roundabout; TA13 5LQ
Friendly thatched family dining pub,
enjoyable reasonably priced food including
bargain two-course lunch (Tues-Sat),
well kept Badger ales, linked rooms with
attractive rustic décor, flagstones, thick stone
walls and prettily stencilled beams, scrubbed
kitchen tables, pews and settles, log fires;
tables outside, secure play area, closed Mon.
(Bob and Margaret Holder)

PITMINSTER   ST2219
Queens Arms (01823) 421529
Off B3170 S of Taunton (or reached
direct); near church; TA3 7AZ Popular
village pub-restaurant with competitively
priced good food from varied menu (best
to book), also set deal Tues-Sat, well
kept west country ales and decent wines;
downstairs skittle alley; closed Sun evening,
Mon. *(Patrick and Daphne Darley, Bob and*
Margaret Holder)

PORLOCK   SS8846
★ Ship (01643) 862507
High Street; TA24 8QD Picturesque old
thatched pub with beams, flagstones and
big inglenook log fire, popular reasonably
priced food from sandwiches up, well kept
ales such as Cotleigh, Exmoor, Otter and St
Austell, friendly service, back dining room,
small locals' front bar with games; children
welcome, attractive split-level sunny garden
with decking and play area, nearby nature
trail to Dunkery Beacon, five bedrooms,
open all day; known as the Top Ship to
distinguish it from the Ship at Porlock Weir.
(Tom McLean)

PORLOCK WEIR   SS8846
★ Ship (01643) 863288
Porlock Hill (A39); TA24 8PB
Unpretentious thatched pub in wonderful
spot by peaceful harbour – can get packed;

long and narrow with dark low beams, flagstones and stripped stone, simple pub furniture, woodburner, west country ales including Exmoor, real ciders and a perry, good whisky and soft drinks choice, enjoyable pubby food served promptly by friendly staff, games rooms across small backyard, tea room; background music and big-screen TV; children and dogs welcome, sturdy picnic-sets in front and at side, good coast walks, three decent bedrooms, limited free parking but pay and display opposite; calls itself the Bottom Ship to avoid confusion with the Ship at Porlock. *(Mr and Mrs D J Nash)*

PORTBURY ST4975
★ **Priory** (01275) 376307
Station Road, 0.5 miles from A369 (just S of M5 junction 19); BS20 7TN
Spreading early 19th-c Vintage Inn, lots of linked beamed areas, appealing mix of comfortable furnishings in alcoves, tartan carpets, log fire, popular sensibly priced food including deals, well kept Butcombe, St Austell and a guest, good range of wines by the glass, friendly efficient young staff; background music; children welcome, no dogs inside, pleasant front and back gardens, open (and food) all day. *(Steve and Claire Harvey, Michael Doswell, Bob and Margaret Holder)*

PORTISHEAD ST4576
★ **Windmill** (01275) 818483
M5 junction 19; A369 into town, then follow Sea Front sign and into Nore Road; BS20 6JZ Busy dining pub making most of terrific panorama over Bristol Channel; curving glass frontage rising two storeys (adjacent windmill remains untouched), contemporary furnishings, four Fullers ales and a couple of guests, plenty of wines by the glass, decent range of enjoyable food from sandwiches and baked potatoes to daily specials, early-bird deal 3-7pm Mon-Fri (6pm Sat), efficient friendly staff; children welcome, dogs allowed in bar, disabled access including lift, picnic-sets on tiered lantern-lit terraces and decking, open (and food) all day. *(P and J Shapley, John Pritchard, Steve and Claire Harvey)*

PRIDDY ST5450
★ **Hunters Lodge** (01749) 672275
From Wells on A39 pass hill with TV mast on left, then next left; BA5 3AR
Welcoming and unchanging farmers', walkers' and potholers' pub above Ice Age cavern, in same family for generations, well kept local beers tapped from casks behind bar, Thatcher's and Wilkin's ciders, simple cheap food, log fires in huge fireplaces, low beams, flagstones and panelling, old lead mining photographs, perhaps live folk music; no mobiles or credit cards; children and dogs in family room, wheelchair access, garden picnic-sets. *(Taff Thomas, M G Hart)*

PRISTON ST6960
Ring o' Bells (01761) 471467
Village SW of Bath; BA2 9EE
Unpretentious old stone pub with large knocked-through bar, good reasonably priced traditional food cooked by licensees using nearby farm produce, real ales from small local brewers including a house beer from Blindmans, quick friendly service, flagstones, beams and good open fire; skittle alley; children, dogs and muddy boots welcome, benches out at front overlooking little village green (maypole here on May Day), good walks, two bedrooms, closed Mon lunchtime. *(Taff Thomas)*

PURITON ST3141
Puriton Inn (01278) 683464
Just off M5 junction 23; Puriton Hill; TA7 8AF Traditional pub well screened from motorway, clean and tidy, with ample straightforward food and well kept ales, warmly welcoming service even when busy; pool, free wi-fi; children allowed, good disabled access, front terrace and back garden with play area, open (and food) all day. *(Carol and Barry Craddock)*

RICKFORD ST4859
Plume of Feathers (01761) 462682
Very sharp turn off A368; BS40 7AH
Cottagey 17th-c local with enjoyable reasonably priced home-made food in bar and dining room, friendly service, well kept Butcombe and guests, local cider and good choice of wines, black beams and half-panelling, mix of furniture including cast-iron tables and settles, log fires; table skittles, darts and pool; well behaved children and dogs welcome, rustic tables on narrow front terrace, pretty streamside hamlet, bedrooms, open all day. *(Dr and Mrs A K Clarke)*

RIMPTON ST6021
White Post Inn (01935) 851525
Rimpton Hill, B3148; BA22 8AR Small pub straddling Dorset border (boundary actually runs through the bar) and refurbished by newish chef-owner; good well presented imaginative food from reworked pub favourites up, local ales and ciders, friendly helpful staff, cosy bar with sofas and woodburner, fine country views from restaurant and back terrace; children welcome, three bedrooms, open all day Sat, closed Sun evening. *(Neil Allen)*

RODE ST8053
Bell (01373) 830356
Frome Road (A361); BA11 6PW
New family owners and bright airy refurbishment for this roadside pub, good food from pub favourites up (more evening choice), ales such as Bath, Hook Norton and Sharps, friendly helpful service; children welcome, garden, open all day. *(Taff Thomas)*

SALTFORD ST6968
Jolly Sailor (01225) 873002
Off A4 Bath–Keynsham; Mead Lane; BS31 3ER Worth knowing for its great River Avon setting by lock and weir; good range of food from bar snacks and pub favourites to more imaginative choices, Wadworths ales and guests, flagstones, low beams and two log fires, daily papers, conservatory dining room overlooking the water; background music; children and dogs (in bar) allowed, disabled access/facilities, paved lockside terrace, open (and food) all day. *(Chris and Angela Buckell, Dr and Mrs A K Clarke)*

SHEPTON MONTAGUE ST6731
★Montague Inn (01749) 813213
Village signed off A359 Bruton–Castle Cary; BA9 8JW Simply but tastefully furnished dining pub with welcoming licensees, popular for a civilised meal or just a drink, stripped-wood tables and kitchen chairs, inglenook log fire, nicely presented often interesting food including daily specials, well kept ales such as Bath, Cottage and Wadworths tapped from the cask, farm ciders, good wine and whisky choice, friendly well informed young staff, bright spacious restaurant extension behind; children and dogs (in bar) welcome, garden and big terrace with teak furniture, maybe summer Sun jazz, peaceful farmland views, closed Sun evening. *(Edward Mirzoeff, Hugh Roberts)*

SIMONSBATH SS7739
★Exmoor Forest Inn (01643) 831341
B3223/B3358; TA24 7SH Friendly family-run inn beautifully placed in remote countryside; split-level bar with circular tables by counter, larger area with cushioned settles, upholstered stools and mate's chairs around mix of tables, hunting trophies, antlers and horse tack, woodburner, good reasonably priced traditional food alongside more imaginative choices including local game, well kept ales such as Clearwater, Exmoor and Otter, real cider, good range of wines and malt whiskies, residents' lounge, airy dining room; children and dogs welcome, seats in front garden, fine walks along River Barle, own trout and salmon fishing, ten comfortable bedrooms, open all day in high season. *(Bob and Margaret Holder, Sheila Topham)*

SOMERTON ST4928
Globe (01458) 272474
Market Place; TA11 7LX Old stone-built local with good reasonably priced food and friendly attentive staff, well kept Butcombe, Sharps Doom Bar and a couple of guests, two spacious lived-in bars with flagstones and bare boards, inglenook log fire, dining conservatory, pool in back games room, skittle alley; children welcome, garden with summer marquee, open all day. *(Bob and Margaret Holder)*

SPAXTON ST2336
Lamb (01278) 671350
Barford Road, Four Forks; TA5 1AD Welcoming simply furnished little pub at foot of the Quantocks, open-plan beamed bar with woodburner, well kept beers and enjoyable good value food (not Sun evening) cooked by landlady including notable local steaks (booking advised); quiz last Sun of month; tables on lawn behind, closed all day Mon and lunchtimes apart from Sun. *(PLC)*

STANTON DREW ST5963
Druids Arms (01275) 332230
Off B3130; BS39 4EJ Refurbished pub in stone-circle village (there are some standing stones in the garden); linked flagstoned rooms with low black beams, bare stone walls and green dados, cushioned window seats and pubby furniture, candles here and there, open fires, tractor-seat stools by pale wood bar serving Butcombe and Sharps Doom Bar, Thatcher's cider and modest wine list, enjoyable often creative food (not Sun evening) from bar snacks up; children welcome, front wheelchair access using portable ramp, picnic-sets out by lane and in garden backing on to 14th-c church, open all day. *(Taff Thomas, Chris and Angela Buckell)*

STAPLE FITZPAINE ST2618
Greyhound (01823) 480227
Off A358 or B3170 S of Taunton; TA3 5SP Rambling country pub with generally good food from varied menu (best to book evenings), well kept Badger ales and good wines by the glass, welcoming helpful staff, flagstones and inglenooks, nice mix of settles and chairs, olde-worlde pictures, farm tools and so forth; children and dogs welcome, comfortable well equipped bedrooms, good breakfast, open all day. *(Guy Vowles, Sara Fulton, Roger Baker)*

STOGUMBER ST0937
White Horse (01984) 656277
Off A358 at Crowcombe; TA4 3TA Friendly old village local with well kept ever-changing west country ales, real ciders and decent home-made food, carpeted beamed bar with raised end section, old local photographs, log fire, separate restaurant, games room with pool; quiet back terrace, two bedrooms accessed by external staircase, open all day (and may be discounted drinks weekday afternoons). *(Bob and Margaret Holder)*

STOKE ST GREGORY ST3527
★Rose & Crown (01823) 490296
Woodhill; follow North Curry signpost off A378 by junction with A358 – keep on to Stoke, bearing right in centre, passing church and follow lane for 0.5 miles; TA3 6EW Popular previous Main Entry under long-serving family, but for sale as we went to press – reports please;

more or less open-plan, stools by curved brick and wood counter serving Exmoor, Otter and a guest, local cider, long airy dining room with high-raftered ceiling, two further beamed dining areas, one with glass-covered well, food has been good; seats on sheltered front terrace, three bedrooms. *(Stan Lea, Alistair Forsyth)*

TARR SS8632

★ **Tarr Farm** (01643) 851507

Tarr Steps – narrow road off B3223 N of Dulverton; deep ford if you approach from the W (inn is on E bank); TA22 9PY Fine Exmoor position for this 16th-c inn above River Barle's medieval clapper bridge; compact unpretentious bar rooms with good views, stall seating, wall seats and leather chairs around slabby rustic tables, game bird pictures on wood-clad walls, three woodburners, well kept Exmoor ales and several wines by the glass, good food using local produce, residents' end with smart evening restaurant, friendly helpful service, pleasant log-fire lounge with dark leather armchairs and sofas; children and dogs welcome, slate-topped stone tables outside making most of setting, extensive grounds, good bedrooms (no under-10s), open all day but closed 1-10 Feb. *(Bob and Margaret Holder, Lynda and Trevor Smith, M G Hart)*

TAUNTON ST2525

★ **Hankridge Arms** (01823) 444405

Hankridge Way, Deane Gate (near Sainsbury's); just off M5 junction 25 – A358 towards city, then right at roundabout, right at next roundabout; TA1 2LR Interesting nicely restored Badger dining pub based on 16th-c former farmhouse – quite a contrast to the modern shopping complex surrounding it; different-sized linked areas, big log fire, popular generous food from interesting sandwiches through pubby choices to restaurant dishes, set lunch deal, well kept ales and decent wines by the glass, quick friendly young staff; background music; dogs welcome, plenty of tables in pleasant outside area. *(Taff Thomas, Bob and Margaret Holder, R T and J C Moggridge, Dr and Mrs A K Clarke)*

TAUNTON ST2225

Plough (01823) 324404

Station Road; TA1 1PB Popular little pub with three or four local ales including Otter tapped from cooled casks, up to ten racked ciders with more on draught, also Otter Tarka lager and seven wines by the glass, simple food all day till 10pm including range of pies, bare boards, panelling, candles on tables, cosy nooks and open fire, hidden

door to lavatories; background music (live weekends), popular quiz Tues; dogs welcome, handy for station, open all day (till 2am Fri, Sat). *(Phil and Jane Hodson)*

TAUNTON ST2223

Vivary Arms (01823) 272563

Wilton Street; across Vivary Park from centre; TA1 3JR Popular low-beamed 18th-c local (Taunton's oldest), good value fresh food from light lunches up in snug plush lounge and small dining room, friendly helpful young staff, well kept ales including Butcombe, decent wines, interesting collection of drink-related items; pool and darts; lovely hanging baskets and flowers. *(Bob and Margaret Holder, Alistair Forsyth)*

TINTINHULL ST5019

★ **Crown & Victoria** (01935) 823341

Farm Street, village signed off A303; BA22 8PZ Handsome golden-stone inn, carpeted throughout, with high bar chairs by new oak counter, well kept Butcombe, Cheddar, Sharps and Yeovil, farmhouse furniture and big woodburner, good popular food using free range/organic ingredients (maybe home-reared pork), efficient friendly service, dining room with more pine tables and chairs, former skittle alley also used for dining, end conservatory; children welcome, disabled facilities, big garden with play area, five bedrooms, convenient for Tintinhull Garden (NT). *(Patrick and Daphne Darley, Simon Whitaker)*

TRISCOMBE ST1535

Blue Ball (01984) 618242

Village signed off A358 Crowcombe– Bagborough; turn off opposite sign to youth hostel; OS Sheet 181 map reference 155355; TA4 3HE Smartly revamped old thatched inn tucked beneath the Quantocks; all on first floor of original stables sloping down gently on three levels, each with own fire and divided by hand-cut beech partitions, local ales and ciders, several wines by the glass and interesting food; background music; children and dogs welcome, chair lift for disabled customers, decking at top of woodside terraced garden making most of views, two cottage bedrooms, closed Sun evening, otherwise open all day. *(Bob and Margaret Holder, Richard and Patricia Jefferson, Martin and Sue Day)*

TRULL ST2122

Winchester Arms (01823) 284723

Church Road; TA3 7LG Cosy streamside village pub with good value generous food including blackboard specials and popular Sun lunch, west country ales and ciders, friendly helpful service, small dining room,

---

All *Guide* inspections are anonymous. Anyone claiming to be a *Good Pub Guide* inspector is a fraud. Please let us know.

skittle alley; garden with decked area, summer barbecues, six bedrooms. *(Carol and Barry Craddock)*

UPTON   ST0129
Lowtrow Cross Inn (01398) 371220
A3190 E of Upton; TA4 2DB Welcoming old pub with character low-beamed bar, log fire and woodburner, bare boards and flagstones, two carpeted country-kitchen dining areas, one with enormous inglenook, generous helpings of tasty home-made food (not Mon, lunchtime Tues), Cotleigh and a couple of guests, good mix of locals and diners; children and dogs welcome, lovely surroundings, camping nearby, closed Mon lunchtime. *(Dr Simon Innes)*

VOBSTER   ST7049
★Vobster Inn (01373) 812920
Lower Vobster; BA3 5RJ Roomy old stone-built dining pub with popular reasonably priced food including fresh fish, good friendly service, Butcombe, Ashton Press cider and nice wines by the glass, three comfortable open-plan areas with antique furniture, plenty of room for just a drink; children and dogs (in bar) welcome, seats on lawn, boules, four bedrooms, closed Sun evening, Mon. *(M G Hart)*

WAMBROOK   ST2907
Cotley Inn (01460) 62348
Off A30 W of Chard; don't follow the small signs to Cotley itself; TA20 3EN Refurbished old stone pub under welcoming licensees; light and airy beamed bar with flagstones and double-sided woodburner, carpeted dining areas off, two further fires, well kept Otter ales and a guest tapped from the cask, enjoyable reasonably priced traditional food, friendly attentive service, skittle alley; background music; children and dogs welcome, lovely view from terrace tables, nice garden below, quiet spot with plenty of surrounding walks, tethering for horses, closed Sun evening, Mon lunchtime. *(Gerry Price, Bob and Margaret Holder)*

WANSTROW   ST7141
Pub at Wanstrow (01749) 850455
A359 Frome–Bruton; BA4 4SZ Friendly village local with four well kept beers including Bass and Blindmans, proper cider, no food unless pre-booked, flagstone bar with open fire, dining room, bar billiards and other traditional games; closed weekday lunchtimes. *(Dr and Mrs A K Clarke)*

WASHFORD   ST0440
White Horse (01984) 640415
Abbey Road/Torre Rocks; TA23 0JZ Welcoming and popular old local, good selection of well kept ales and enjoyable reasonably priced pubby food including specials and deals, can eat in bar or separate restaurant, log fires; large smokers' pavilion over road next to trout stream,

field with interesting collection of fowl and goats, bedrooms, good traditional breakfast. *(Richard and Penny Gibbs)*

WATCHET   ST0743
Pebbles (01984) 634737
Market Street; TA23 0AN Popular, welcoming and relaxed little bar in former shop, extensive range of regional ciders, also cask-tapped ales such as Exmoor, Moles and Otter and good choice of whiskies, cider brandies and other drinks, friendly helpful staff, no food but can bring your own (plates and cutlery supplied); regular live music (some impromptu) including folk and jazz, sea shanty and poetry evenings, free wi-fi; dogs on leads welcome, open all day (from 3pm Weds). *(Richard and Penny Gibbs)*

WATCHET   ST0643
Star (01984) 631367
Mill Lane (B3191); TA23 0BZ Late 18th-c beamed pub at end of lane just off Watchet harbour; main flagstoned bar with other low-ceilinged side rooms, some exposed stonework and rough wood partitioning, mix of traditional furniture including oak settles, window seats, local artwork for sale, woodburner in ornate fireplace, good selection of pubby food mostly sourced locally including fresh fish, four well kept ales such as Butcombe, Otter, Quantock and Ringwood, Sheppy's cider and a few malt whiskies, cheerful efficient staff; background music; children and dogs welcome, wheelchair access, picnic-sets out in front and in sloping beer garden behind, handy for marina and West Somerset Railway. *(Eddie Edwards, Chris and Angela Buckell)*

WELLOW   ST7358
Fox & Badger (01225) 832293
Signed off A367 SW of Bath; BA2 8QG Opened-up village pub with good mix of customers, flagstones one end, bare boards the other, some snug corners, woodburner in massive hearth, Butcombe, Fullers, Greene King and Sharps, four ciders including Thatcher's, wide range of enjoyable bar food from doorstep sandwiches and generous ploughman's up, good Sun lunch, friendly accommodating service; children and dogs welcome, picnic-sets in covered courtyard, open all day Fri, Sat. *(Nigel Long, Taff Thomas)*

WELLS   ST5445
★City Arms (01749) 673916
High Street; BA5 2AG Bustling town-centre pub with up to seven well kept ales, three ciders and enjoyable reasonably priced food from varied menu including themed nights (may include sushi), modernised main bar and restaurant areas; background music; children and dogs welcome, cobbled courtyard and some reminders that the building was once a jail, first-floor terrace, four bedrooms, open (and food) all day. *(Dr J Barrie Jones, R K Phillips)*

WELLS ST5445
Crown (01749) 673457
Market Place; BA5 2RF Former 15th-c coaching inn overlooked by cathedral, various bustling areas with light wooden flooring, plenty of matching chairs and cushioned wall benches, Butcombe and Sharps Doom Bar, popular good value food from sandwiches up in bar and bistro including set deal (weekday lunchtimes and early evenings), cheerful helpful staff; background music, TV and games machine; children until 8pm, no dogs, small heated courtyard, 15 bedrooms, open all day. *(Stan Lea, Ann and Colin Hunt, Richard Tilbrook)*

WELLS ST5546
★ Fountain (01749) 672317
St Thomas Street; BA5 2UU Restaurant-y place with big comfortable bar, interesting décor and large open fire, quite a choice of popular food here or in upstairs dining room (booking advised weekends), Mon steak night, Tues OAP lunch, ales such as Bath, Butcombe and Sharps, several wines by the glass, courteous helpful staff; unobtrusive background music; children welcome, pretty in summer with window boxes and blue shutters, handy for cathedral and moated Bishop's Palace, closed Sun evening, Mon lunchtime. *(R K Phillips, Hugh Roberts, Ann and Mike Bolton, Ian Phillips and others)*

WEST BAGBOROUGH ST1733
★ Rising Sun (01823) 432575
Village signed off A358 NW of Taunton; TA4 3EF Charming village pub lit up with evening candles; small flagstoned bar to right of massive main door with settles and carved dining chairs around polished tables, daily papers on old-fashioned child's desk, fresh flowers and some quirky ornaments dotted about, well kept west country ales, good if not cheap food including daily specials, friendly service, smart cosy dining room with attractive mix of chippendale and other chairs around a few dark wood tables, big modern photographs and coal-effect gas fire in pleasant back snug, upstairs room with trusses in high pitched ceiling, refectory tables and oriental rug on wood floor, large prints of cathedral cities; children and dogs welcome, teak seats outside by lane, two bedrooms, no car park, closed Sun evening (and Mon in winter). *(Bob and Margaret Holder)*

WEST HATCH ST2719
Farmers Arms (01823) 480980
Slough Green, W of village; TA3 5RS Welcoming tucked-away pub (former farmhouse) doing well under present owners;

four linked rooms with beams, stripped boards and some exposed stonework, country pine and leather sofas, woodburner, four well kept west country ales and plenty of wines by the glass, good popular home-made food from bar and restaurant menus, afternoon teas, cheerful helpful service; Tues quiz, monthly live music; children welcome, terrace and small lawn, good local walks, five bedrooms. *(John Chambers, Richard and Patricia Jefferson, Hugh Roberts, Bob and Margaret Holder)*

WEST HUNTSPILL ST3145
Crossways (01278) 783756
A38, between M5 junctions 22 and 23; TA9 3RA Rambling 17th-c tile-hung pub with six well kept mostly local ales (tasting trays available), good choice of enjoyable generously served food at reasonable prices, cheerful efficient staff (they ask for a credit card if you run a tab), split-level carpeted areas with beams and log fires, skittle alley; pool, TV; children and dogs welcome, disabled facilities, garden with play area and heated smokers' shelter, seven bedrooms, open all day. *(Brian and Anna Marsden, R K Phillips)*

WEST MONKTON ST2628
★ Monkton (01823) 412414
Blundells Lane; signed from A3259; TA2 8NP Popular and welcoming village dining pub with good choice of freshly made food including some south african influences (best to book weekends), bare-boards bar with central woodburner and snug off, separate carpeted restaurant, Exmoor, Otter and Sharps Doom Bar, Aspall's and Thatcher's ciders, several wines by the glass, good service; children and dogs welcome, wheelchair access from car park, lots of tables in big garden bounded by stream, play area. *(Bob and Margaret Holder)*

WEST PENNARD ST5438
Lion (01458) 832941
A361 E of Glastonbury; Newtown; BA6 8NH Traditional stone-built 16th-c village inn; bar and dining areas off small flagstoned black-beamed core, enjoyable pubby food plus daily specials, Sun carvery, Butcombe, Otter and Sharps Doom Bar, inglenook woodburner and open fires; background music; children and dogs welcome, tables on big forecourt, good nearby walks, seven refurbished bedrooms in converted side barn. *(Dr Simon Innes)*

WINCANTON ST7028
Nog Inn (01963) 32998
South Street; BA9 9DL Welcoming old split-level pub with Otter, Sharps and

---

If you have to cancel a reservation for a bedroom or restaurant, please telephone or write to warn them. You may lose your deposit if you've paid one.

a couple of guests, real cider and continental beers, good reasonably priced traditional food including Sun carvery (not summer) and blackboard specials, bare boards, carpet and flagstones, pump clips on ceiling, log fires; background and some live music, comedy nights, charity quiz (last Thurs of month), darts; well behaved children and dogs welcome, pleasant back garden with heated smokers' shelter, open (and food) all day. *(Neil Allen)*

WINFORD   ST5262
Crown (01275) 472388
Crown Hill, off Regil Road; BS40 8AY Popular old pub in deep country with linked beamed rooms, mix of pubby furniture including settles on flagstones or quarry tiles, old pictures and photographs on rough walls, copper and brass, leather sofas in front of big open fire, enjoyable generous home-made food (all day Sun) at very reasonable prices, Butcombe, Wadworths 6X and a guest, good choice of wines by the glass, friendly attentive landlord and staff; table skittles and skittle alley; children and dogs welcome, wheelchair access with help, tables out in front and in back garden, closed Mon lunchtime, otherwise open all day. *(Taff Thomas)*

WINSFORD   SS9034
★ Royal Oak (01643) 851455
Off A396 about 10 miles S of Dunster; TA24 7JE Prettily placed thatched and beamed Exmoor inn, good choice of enjoyable local food including daily specials, Exmoor ales and west country ciders, friendly helpful staff, carpeted bar with woodburner in big stone fireplace, large bay window seat looking across towards village green and foot and packhorse bridges over River Winn, restaurant and other lounge areas; children and dogs (in bar) welcome, disabled facilities, eight good bedrooms some with four-posters. *(Bob and Margaret Holder, Phil Bartley)*

WITHAM FRIARY   ST7440
★ Seymour Arms (01749) 850742
Signed from B3092 S of Frome; BA11 5HF Well worn-in unchanging flagstoned country tavern, in same friendly family since 1952; two simple rooms off 19th-c hatch-service lobby, one with darts and bar billiards, other with central table skittles, well kept Cheddar Potholer and an occasional guest, Rich's local cider tapped from back room, low prices, open fires, panelled benches, cards and dominoes, no food (can bring your own); children and dogs welcome, garden by main rail line, cricket pitch over the road, open all day. *(Gus Swan)*

WITHYPOOL   SS8435
★ Royal Oak (01643) 831506
Village signed off B3233; TA24 7QP Prettily placed country inn – where author

R D Blackmore stayed while writing *Lorna Doone*; lounge with raised working fireplace, comfortably cushioned wall seats and slat-backed chairs, sporting trophies, paintings and copper/brass ornaments, enjoyable food here and in restaurant, well kept Exmoor ales, friendly helpful service, character locals' bar; walkers and dogs welcome (leave muddy boots in porch), children in eating areas, wooden benches on terrace, attractive riverside village with lovely walks, grand views from Winsford Hill just up the road, eight bedrooms (twisting staircase to top floor), open all day, but may close for a week in Feb. *(Lynda and Trevor Smith, Sheila Topham)*

WOOKEY   ST5245
★ Burcott (01749) 673874
B3139 W of Wells; BA5 1NJ Beamed roadside pub with two simply furnished old-fashioned front bar rooms, flagstones, some exposed stonework and half-panelling, lantern wall lights, old prints, woodburner, a couple of real ales such as Hop Back Summer Lightning and a proper cider, enjoyable food (not Mon evening, or Tues evening in winter) from snacks up in bar and restaurant (children allowed here), good service, small games room with built-in wall seats; soft background music, no dogs; wheelchair access, front window boxes and tubs, picnic-sets in sizeable garden with Mendip Hills views, four self-catering units in converted stables, closed Sun evening, also Mon lunchtime in winter. *(Taff Thomas)*

WOOKEY HOLE   ST5347
Wookey Hole Inn (01749) 676677
High Street; BA5 1BP Usefully placed open-plan family dining pub, welcoming and relaxed, with idiosyncratic contemporary décor, two eating areas and bar, wood floors and good log fire, three local ales such as Cottage, Glastonbury and Quantock, several belgian beers, ciders and perry, good food from pub favourites to daily specials, tables with paper cloths for drawing on (crayons provided), efficient friendly staff; background music; dogs allowed in bar, pleasant garden with various sculptures, five individually styled bedrooms, open all day except Sun evening. *(Ann and Colin Hunt)*

WOOLVERTON   ST7954
Red Lion (01373) 830350
Set back from A36 N of village; BA2 7QS Roomy refurbished and extended pub, beams, panelling and lots of stripped wood, candles and log-effect fire, well kept Wadworths, decent wines by the glass, good choice of enjoyable food from baguettes up including children's meals, friendly quick service, locals' bar with fire (dogs allowed here); background music, free wi-fi; plenty of tables outside, play area, open all day Fri, Sat, till 9pm Sun. *(Dave Braisted)*

WRAXALL   ST4971

★ **Old Barn** (01275) 819011
Just off Bristol Road (B3130) in
grounds of Wraxall House; BS48 1LQ
Idiosyncratic gabled barn conversion,
scrubbed tables, school benches and soft
sofas under oak rafters, stripped boards
and flagstones, various pictures and odds
and ends, welcoming atmosphere and
friendly service, five well kept ales including
Butcombe, Fullers and Palmers tapped from
the cask, farm ciders, good wines by the
glass, simple sandwiches, unusual board
games; occasional background music and
sports TV; dogs welcome, nice garden with
terrace barbecue (bring your own meat) and
smokers' shelter, open all day. *(Taff Thomas,*
Steve and Liz Tilley)

YARLINGTON   ST6529

Stags Head (01963) 440393
Pound Lane; BA9 8DG Old low-ceilinged
and flagstoned country pub tucked away
in rustic hamlet; well kept Bass, Greene
King and Otter from small central bar,
woodburner, chapel chairs and mixed pine
tables on left, carpeted dining area on right
with big log fire, modern landscape prints
and feature cider-press table, second dining
room with doors on to terrace, enjoyable food
from traditional choices up including bargain
OAP lunch (Mon-Sat), good friendly service;
background music; well behaved children
welcome, dogs in bar, picnic-sets in sheltered
back garden with small stream, maybe
summer morris men, three bedrooms, closed
Sun evening. *(Stan Lea, Robert Watt)*

Real ale may be served from handpumps, electric pumps (not just the on-off switches
used for keg beer) or – common in Scotland – tall taps called founts (pronounced
'fonts') where a separate pump pushes the beer up under air pressure.

Staffordshire

CAULDON

SK0749   Map 7

Yew Tree ★★ £

(01538) 309876 – www.yewtreeinncauldon.co.uk

Village signposted from A523 and A52 about 8 miles W of Ashbourne; ST10 3EJ

Treasure trove of fascinating antiques and dusty bric-a-brac, simple good value snacks and bargain beer; very eccentric

Don't let the unassuming exterior put you off this extraordinary roadside local. It's still run with warmth and friendliness (as it has been for over 50 years) by the jovial Alan East – helped now by his stepson Dan. The curiosities are extraordinary, with the most impressive pieces being the working polyphons and symphonions – 19th-c developments of the musical box, some taller than a person, each with quite a repertoire of tunes and elaborate sound effects. There are also two pairs of Queen Victoria's stockings, an amazing collection of ceramics and pottery including a Grecian urn dating back almost 3,000 years, penny-farthing and boneshaker bicycles and the infamous Acme Dog Carrier. Soggily sprung sofas mingle with 18th-c settles, plenty of little wooden tables and a four-person oak church choir seat with carved heads that came from St Mary's church in Stafford. As well as all this, there's an array of musical instruments ranging from a one-string violin (phonofiddle) through pianos and sousaphones to the aptly named serpent. Drinks are very reasonably priced, so it's no wonder the place is popular with locals. You'll find Burton Bridge Bitter, Rudgate Ruby Mild and a guest or two on handpump, ten interesting malt whiskies, eight wines by the glass and farm cider; darts, table skittles, dominoes and cribbage. There are seats outside the front door and in the cobbled stable yard, and they hold vintage car and motorcyle meetings. There's a basic campsite for pub customers and a small caravan for hire. The pub is tucked unpromisingly between enormous cement works and quarries and almost hidden by a towering yew tree.

The modest menu offers hearty choices such as sandwiches, pork pies and locally produced pies with mash and gravy. *Benchmark main dish: pie with peas and gravy £7.20. Two-course evening meal £10.00.*

Free house ~ Licensee Alan East ~ Real ale ~ Open 12-3, 6-11; 12-midnight Sat; 12-11 Sun; closed winter weekday lunchtimes ~ Bar food 12-3, 6-9; 12-9 weekends ~ Children allowed in polyphon room ~ Dogs allowed in bar ~ Wi-fi ~ Live folk music first Tues of month
Recommended by Dr Simon Innes, Mungo Shipley

Cribbage is a card game using a block of wood with holes for matchsticks or special pins to score with; regulars in cribbage pubs are usually happy to teach strangers how to play.

CHEADLE   SK0342   Map 7

Queens at Freehay

(01538) 722383 – www.queensatfreehay.co.uk

A mile SE of Cheadle; take Rakeway Road off A522 (via Park Avenue or Mills Road), then after 1 mile turn into Counslow Road; ST10 1RF

Friendly dining pub with three real ales and attractive garden

In warm weather, the attractive and immaculately kept little garden behind this 18th-c pub is a fine place to sit, with its picnic-sets among mature shrubs and flowering tubs. It's a friendly place with a welcoming landlord and the neat rooms have some cottagey touches that blend in well with the modern refurbishments; the atmosphere is relaxed and gently civilised. The comfortable lounge bar has pale wood tables on stripped wood floors, small country pictures and curtains with matching cushions, and opens via an arch into a simple, light, airy dining area with elegant chairs and tables on tartan carpeting. Helpful staff serve Peakstones Rock Alton Abbey and a couple of guest beers on handpump and nine wines by the glass; some seating is set aside for those who want just a drink and a chat.

Good, enjoyable food includes moules marinière, creamy garlic mushrooms, leek, bacon and cheese oatcakes, sausage and eggs, beer-battered fish and chips, burger with toppings, crispy onions and chips, chicken filled with stilton wrapped in crispy smoked bacon with wholegrain mustard sauce, slow-roast lamb shank with Guinness gravy and spring onion mash, and puddings such as passion-fruit and peach cheesecake and caramel waffle with toffee sauce; steak nights are Monday and Wednesday. *Benchmark main dish: beef in red wine pie £12.95. Two-course evening meal £18.00.*

Free house ~ Licensee Adrian Rock ~ Real ale ~ Open 12-3, 6-11; 12-3, 6.30-10.30 Sun ~ Bar food 12-2, 6-9.30; 12-2.30, 6.30-9.30 Sun ~ Restaurant ~ Children welcome ~ Wi-fi
Recommended by Mr and Mrs J Morris, R L Borthwick, Dr Simon Innes

ELLASTONE   SK1143   Map 7

Duncombe Arms 🍴 ♀

(01335) 324275 – www.duncombearms.co.uk

Main Road; DE6 2GZ

• •
Staffordshire Dining Pub of the Year

Interesting seating areas, nooks and crannies, a thoughtful choice of drinks, friendly staff and lovely food; seats outside

Whatever your mood, you'll find somewhere interesting to sit in this stylishly refurbished village pub. There are beams here and there, painted, bare brick and exposed stone walls, open fires and woodburners, horse prints and photos, big bold paintings of pigs, sheep, cows and chickens, large clocks and fresh flowers, church candles on mantelpieces, in big glass jars and on tables – and flooring that ranges from carpet to flagstones to bare floorboards and brick. Furnishings are just as eclectic: long leather button-back and cushioned wall seats, armchairs, all manner of wooden or upholstered dining chairs and tables made from mahogany, pine and even driftwood. Marstons Pedigree, Timothy Taylors Landlord and a beer named for the pub on handpump, an extraordinary 46 wines by the glass from a fine list and 20 malt whiskies; background music and TV. An attractive terrace has wooden or rush seats around tables under parasols, braziers for cooler evenings and a view down over the garden to Worthy Island Wood.

As well as a two- and three-course set lunch (not Sun), the rewarding food includes lunchtime ciabatta sandwiches, beetroot-cured salmon with horseradish and potato mousse, beef carpaccio with pea panna cotta and crispy shin, ricotta and basil dumplings with tomato and black bean stew, beer-battered fish with triple-cooked chips, burger with toppings and fries, stone bass with patatas bravas and chorizo, barbecue-glazed pork cutlet with mustard mash and roast apple, and puddings such as rhubarb cheesecake with gingerbread ice-cream and lemon curd tart with lemon meringue and blackberry sorbet. *Benchmark main dish: rib-eye steak with triple-cooked chips £19.00. Two-course evening meal £22.00.*

Free house ~ Licensees Johnny and Laura Greenall ~ Real ale ~ Open 12-11 (10.30 Sun) ~ Bar food 12-2.30, 6-9; 12-2.30, 5.30-10 Fri, Sat; 12-8 Sun ~ Restaurant ~ Children welcome ~ Dogs allowed in bar ~ Wi-fi *Recommended by Mr and Mrs S Hollaway*

LONGDON GREEN   SK0813 Map 7
Red Lion ♀ ◖

(01543) 490410 – www.brunningandprice.co.uk/redlion
Hay Lane; WS15 4QF

Large, well run pub by village green with interesting furnishings, a fine range of drinks, enjoyable food and spreading garden

Extended and thoughtfully opened-up inside, this handsome pub sits opposite the village green where summer cricket matches are held. The large garden has a suntrap terrace with wooden tables and chairs; beyond is a gazebo, picnic-sets on grass, and swings and a play tractor for children. The bar is at the heart of the building with spreading rooms and nooks and crannies leading off. One dining room has skylights, rugs on nice old bricks, house plants lining the window sill, an elegant metal chandelier and a miscellany of cushioned dining chairs around dark wooden tables. Similar furnishings fill the other rooms, and the walls are covered with old photos, pictures and prints relating to the local area and big gilt-edged mirrors. Open fires include a raised central fire pit. Phoenix Brunning & Price Original, Derby Pennys Porter, Purple Moose Ysgawen, Salopian Shropshire Gold and Timothy Taylors Boltmaker, 25 wines by the glass, 40 malt whiskies and two farm ciders. Staff are friendly, courteous and helpful.

Rewarding, brasserie-style food includes sandwiches, seared scallops with black pudding on pea purée with pancetta wafer and green apple reduction, wild mushrooms on toast with béarnaise sauce, poached egg and truffle oil, smoked salmon pasta with tarragon velouté, jerk-spiced chicken with fresh mango and chilli salsa, steak burger with toppings, coleslaw and chips, venison rump with duck and cherry faggot, parsnip rösti and game jus, and puddings such as eton mess with roasted rhubarb and sticky toffee pudding with toffee sauce and amaretti ice-cream. *Benchmark main dish: steak and kidney pudding with grain mustard mash £13.95. Two-course evening meal £20.00.*

Brunning & Price ~ Manager Chloe Turner ~ Real ale ~ Open 10.30am-11pm; 10.30-10.30 Sun ~ Bar food 12-10 (9.30 Sun) ~ Restaurant ~ Children welcome ~ Dogs allowed in bar ~ Wi-fi *Recommended by Belinda May, Peter Brix*

SALT   SJ9527 Map 7
Holly Bush £

(01889) 508234 – www.hollybushinn.co.uk
Village signposted off A51 S of Stone (and A518 NE of Stafford); ST18 0BX

Delightful medieval pub with all-day food

A charming thatched pub in a pretty village that draws in both locals and visitors – all are welcomed by the friendly staff. Several cosy areas spread out from the standing-only serving section, with high-backed cushioned pews, old tables and more conventional seats. The oldest part has a heavy-beamed and planked ceiling (some of the beams are attractively carved), a woodburning stove and a salt cupboard built into a big inglenook, with other nice old-fashioned touches including copper utensils, horsebrasses and an ancient pair of riding boots on the mantelpiece. A modern back extension, with beams, stripped brickwork and a small coal fire, blends in well. Adnams Bitter, Marstons Pedigree and a guest ale on handpump, alongside ten wines by the glass. They operate a secure locker system for credit cards, which they'll ask to keep if you run a tab. Outside, the back is beautifully tended and filled with flowers, with rustic picnic-sets on a big lawn.

Reasonably priced and hearty, the food includes sandwiches, baked camembert topped with apricot preserve, prawn cocktail, a daily vegetarian dish, burgers with toppings and chips, venison casserole, chicken breast stuffed with spiced pork and wrapped in smoked bacon with rich Guinness gravy, mixed grill, and puddings. *Benchmark main dish: steak in ale pie £10.45. Two-course evening meal £15.00.*

Admiral Taverns ~ Licensees Geoffrey and Joseph Holland ~ Real ale ~ Open 12-11 (10.30 Sun) ~ Bar food 12-9.30 (9 Sun) ~ Children welcome ~ Wi-fi *Recommended by Brian and Anna Marsden, Stephen Shepherd, Dave Braisted, Steve and Liz Tilley*

WRINEHILL
Hand & Trumpet 🏅 ♀ ⬛

SJ7547 Map 7

(01270) 820048 – www.brunningandprice.co.uk/hand
A531 Newcastle–Nantwich; CW3 9BJ

All-day food in big attractive dining pub with a good choice of ales and wines by the glass, served by courteous staff

Just the place for a relaxing meal, this is a substantial and stylish dining pub – though there's still an intimate feel to the linked, open-plan areas. These, working their way around the long, solidly built counter, have a mix of dining chairs and sturdy tables on polished tiles or stripped-oak boards, with several warming oriental rugs that soften the acoustics. There are nicely lit prints and mirrors on cream walls between a mainly dark dado, plenty of house plants, open fires and deep red ceilings. Original bow windows and a large skylight keep the place light and airy, and french windows open on to a spacious balustraded deck with teak tables and chairs, with a view down to ducks swimming on a big pond in the sizeable garden. Friendly attentive staff serve Phoenix Brunning & Price Original, Salopian Oracle and Timothy Taylors Boltmaker with guests such as Black Sheep Golden Sheep, Hawkshead Windermere Pale and Tatton Gold on handpump, as well as 16 wines by the glass and about 70 whiskies; good disabled access and facilities; board games.

Interesting food includes sandwiches, home-cured duck rillettes with blood orange jelly and kumquat and berry dressing, venison tortellini with capers, wilted spinach and lemon, crab and asparagus quiche, smoked haddock and salmon fishcakes, steak burger with toppings, coleslaw and chips, thai chicken salad with pak choi, pineapple salsa and coconut and lime dressing, braised lamb shoulder with red wine and redcurrant gravy and roast potatoes, slow-roast pork belly with girolle mushrooms, artichoke and glazed apples, and puddings such as bread and butter pudding with apricot compote and gin and tonic jelly with cucumber sorbet.

Benchmark main dish: half shoulder of lamb with dauphinoise potatoes and redcurrant and red wine gravy £17.25. Two-course evening meal £21.00.

Brunning & Price ~ Manager John Unsworth ~ Real ale ~ Open 11.30-11 (10.30 Sun) ~ Bar food 12-10 ~ Children welcome ~ Dogs allowed in bar ~ Wi-fi
Recommended by Dr and Mrs A K Clarke

Also Worth a Visit in Staffordshire

Besides the fully inspected pubs, you might like to try these pubs that have been recommended to us and described by readers. Do tell us what you think of them: feedback@goodguides.com

ABBOTS BROMLEY   SK0824
Coach & Horses (01283) 840256
High Street; WS15 3BN Modernised hospitable 18th-c village pub with good choice of well liked home-made food from baguettes and pizzas up, beamed bar with stone floor, carpeted restaurant, log fire, three well kept ales such as St Austell and Marstons and several wines by the glass, friendly helpful staff; children and dogs (in bar) welcome, pleasant garden with circular picnic-sets, open all day Sun (food till 5pm), closed Mon. *(Dr Simon Innes)*

ABBOTS BROMLEY   SK0824
★Goats Head (01283) 840254
Market Place; WS15 3BP Beamed and timbered 16th-c village pub with friendly local atmosphere, half a dozen well kept ales including St Austell, Sharps and Timothy Taylors (May beer festival), lots of wines by the glass, enjoyable home-made food (not Sun evening) served by attentive helpful staff, opened-up cream-painted interior, unpretentious but comfortable, with oak floors, traditional furnishings and fire in big inglenook; juke box and TV; children and dogs welcome, teak furniture on deck and sheltered lawn looking up to church tower, open all day. *(Clifford Blakemore)*

ALSAGERS BANK   SJ8048
Gresley Arms (01782) 722469
High Street; ST7 8BQ At the top of Alsagers Bank with wonderful far-reaching views; eight or more interesting ales from smaller breweries and several real ciders, good value pubby food (not lunchtimes apart from Sun), bargain Thurs steak night, traditional slate-floor bar with beams and open fire, comfortable lounge, picture-window dining room taking in the view, and a lower family room; monthly folk night, beer festivals; walkers and dogs welcome, garden picnic-sets, open all day Thurs-Sun, from 3pm other days. *(Mungo Shipley)*

ALSTONEFIELD   SK1355
★George (01335) 310205
Village signed from A515 Ashbourne–Buxton; DE6 2FX Welcoming stone

pub overlooking small village green, straightforward bar with low beams, old Peak District photographs and pictures, warming fire, well kept Marstons-related beers from copper-topped counter, a dozen wines by the glass, farmhouse furniture and woodburner in neat dining room, good freshly made often inventive food from shortish menu (some prices on the high side) using local ingredients including own herbs and vegetables; children welcome, dogs in bar, seats out in front or in big sheltered back stableyard, open all day Fri-Sun. *(Jill and Julian Tasker, Joy Griffiths)*

ALSTONEFIELD   SK1255
Watts Russell Arms (01335) 310126
Hopedale; DE6 2GD Nicely placed 18th-c stone-built beamed pub, three well kept Thornbridge ales, Ashover's cider, fairly short menu including lunchtime wraps and perhaps lobby (a local stew), tapas-style food Fri evening, two lived-in carpeted rooms with pubby furniture and banquettes, stone fireplace; children and dogs welcome (Hector is the large pub dog), picnic-sets on sheltered tiered terrace and in garden, open all day, closed Mon evening. *(Belinda May)*

BLACKBROOK   SJ7638
Swan with Two Necks
(01782) 680343 *Nantwich Road (A51); ST5 5EH* Country pub-restaurant with smart contemporary décor in civilised open-plan dining areas, good well presented food (booking advised) from sharing boards up, Salopian, Sharps, Shepherd Neame and Timothy Taylors, nice wines by the glass including champagne, efficient friendly service (they may ask to keep a credit card while running a tab); background music; children welcome, comfortable tables out on decking, open (and food) all day. *(Anon)*

BLITHBURY   SK0819
Bull & Spectacles (01889) 504201
Uttoxeter Road (B5014 S of Abbots Bromley); WS15 3HY Friendly 17th-c pub with good choice of enjoyable freshly served food including bargain lunchtime Hot Table (half a dozen or so generous main dishes with help-yourself vegetables, and

some puddings), also good value steak night (Mon, Thurs), a couple of changing ales such as Hook Norton Lion and Wells Bombardier; children and dogs welcome, next door to reindeer farm, open all day Sun. *(Mungo Shipley)*

BREWOOD   SJ8808
Swan (01902) 850330
Market Place; ST19 9BS Former coaching inn with two low-beamed bars, Caledonian, Courage Theakstons and some more local beers, good selection of whiskies, no food apart from lunchtime baguettes, inglenook log fire, upstairs skittle alley; open all day. *(Belinda May)*

BURSLEM   SJ8649
Leopard (01782) 819644
Market Place; ST6 3AA Traditional Victorian city-centre pub with three rooms including a snug, good choice of enjoyable home-made food (Tues-Sun lunchtimes, Fri and Sat evenings), Bass and up to five changing guests, well priced wines, friendly helpful service; live music, ghost tours in derelict hotel part; open all day. *(Jeremy King)*

BURTON UPON TRENT   SK2523
★Burton Bridge Inn (01283) 536596
Bridge Street (A50); DE14 1SY Genuinely friendly down-to-earth local with good Burton Bridge ales from brewery across old-fashioned brick yard; simple little front area leading into adjacent bar with pews, plain walls hung with notices, awards and brewery memorabilia, 20 malt whiskies and lots of country wines, small beamed and oak-panelled lounge with simple furniture and flame-effect fire, panelled upstairs dining room, short choice of low-priced lunchtime food Weds-Sat, skittle alley; no credit cards; children welcome, dogs in bar, open all day Fri, Sat. *(Dr Simon Innes)*

BURTON UPON TRENT   SK2423
★Coopers Tavern (01283) 532551
Cross Street; DE14 1EG Old-fashioned 19th-c backstreet local tied to Joules – was tap for the Bass brewery and still has some glorious ephemera including mirrors and glazed adverts; homely and warm with coal fire, straightforward front parlour, back bar doubling as tap room with up to half a dozen guest beers including Bass and good selection of ciders/perries, friendly landlady, pork pies only but can bring your own food (or take beer to next-door curry house); live music including Tues folk night; children and dogs welcome, small back garden, open all day Thurs-Sun, from 5pm Mon, 3pm Tues and Weds. *(Dr Simon Innes)*

BURTON UPON TRENT   SK2423
Old Cottage Tavern (01283) 511615
Rangemoor Street/Byrkley Street; DE14 2EG Friendly corner local acting as tap for Burton Old Cottage, their ales in top condition and three guests, bars front and back and a snug, upstairs games room with skittle alley; folk nights; bedrooms, open all day. *(Dr Simon Innes)*

CANNOCK WOOD   SK0412
Park Gate (01543) 682223
Park Gate Road, S side of Cannock Chase; WS15 4RN Large red-brick dining pub with popular food including various deals and children's menu, ales such as Holdens, St Austell and Sharps, rustic feel bar with woodburner, other comfortably modernised areas and conservatory; background music; dogs allowed in bar, nice secluded back garden with plenty of picnic-sets and play area, by Castle Ring Iron Age fort, good Cannock Chase walks, open all day. *(Brian and Anna Marsden)*

CHEDDLETON   SJ9752
Black Lion (01538) 360620
Leek Road, by the church; ST13 7HP Refurbished 19th-c village local, well kept Bass, Welbeck Abbey and two guests, freshly made traditional lunchtime food (snacks such as local pork pies in the evening), woodburner; some live music, pool and darts; dogs welcome, seats out in front and in fenced back garden. *(Mungo Shipley)*

CODSALL   SJ8603
Codsall Station (01902) 847061
Chapel Lane/Station Road; WV8 1BY Converted vintage waiting room and ticket office of working station, comfortable and welcoming, with well kept Holdens ales and a couple of guests, good value food (sandwiches only Sun) including blackboard specials, lots of railway memorabilia, open fire, conservatory; terrace seating, open all day Fri-Sun. *(Belinda May)*

CONSALL   SK0049
★Black Lion (01782) 550294
Consall Forge, OS Sheet 118 map reference 000491; best approach from Nature Park, off A522, using car park 0.5 miles past Nature Centre; ST9 0AJ Traditional take-us-as-you-find-us place tucked away in rustic canalside spot by restored steam railway station; generous helpings of enjoyable pub food, five well kept ales including Peakstones Rock and several ciders, flagstones and good coal fire; background music; children and dogs welcome, seats out overlooking canal, area for campers and shop for boaters, good walks, open (and food) all day, can get very busy weekend lunchtimes. *(Anon)*

COPMERE END   SJ8029
Star (01785) 850279
W of Eccleshall; ST21 6EW Friendly two-room 19th-c country local with well kept Bass, Titanic, Wells Bombardier and a couple of guests, good variety of reasonably

priced food from sandwiches up, open fire and woodburner, piano; children and dogs welcome, tables and play area in back garden overlooking mere, good walks, open all day weekends, closed Mon. *(Margaret and Peter Staples)*

DENSTONE SK0940
Tavern (01889) 590847
College Road; ST14 5HR Welcoming 17th-c stone-built village pub, comfortable lounge with antiques, good food (not Mon) including freshly made pizzas (Fri, Sat evenings), well kept Marstons ales and good choice of wines by the glass, pleasant service, dining conservatory; children welcome, picnic-sets out at front among tubs and hanging baskets, lovely church and well stocked farm shop, open all day Fri-Sun, closed Mon lunchtime. *(Brian and Jacky Wilson)*

DUSTON SP7262
Hopping Hare (01604) 580090
Hopping Hill Gardens; NN5 6PF Imposing red-brick former manor surrounded by housing; largish bar adjacent to entrance, log fires and lots of different dining areas, well kept Adnams, Black Sheep and a guest, good range of wines by the glass and nicely presented food from good varied menu, attentive friendly service; children welcome, seats out on decking, 19 bedrooms, open all day, food all day weekends. *(Gerry and Rosemary Dobson)*

ECCLESHALL SJ8329
Old Smithy (01785) 850564
Castle Street; ST21 6DF Pub-restaurant with comfortable clean modern décor, popular freshly made food (all day Sun) at fair prices including decent vegetarian options, four mostly mainstream ales and good choice of other drinks, friendly helpful staff, maybe Mon evening pianist; children welcome, open all day. *(Mr and Mrs J Morris)*

ECCLESHALL SJ8329
Royal Oak (01785) 859065
High Street; ST21 6BW Old colonnaded coaching inn restored by Joules Brewery and run by father and son team; their well kept ales and enjoyable locally sourced food including Mon and Tues bargains, welcoming chatty staff; beer garden, open all day. *(Kerry Law, Robert W Buckle)*

FLASH SK0267
Travellers Rest/Knights Table
(01298) 236695 *A53 Buxton–Leek; SK17 0SN* Isolated main-road pub and one of the highest in Britain, clean and friendly, with good reasonably priced traditional food (not Sun evening), four well kept ales and good selection of wines, beams, bare stone walls and open fires, medieval knights theme; free wi-fi; children welcome, great Peak District views from back terrace, classic car meeting last Thurs

of month, bedrooms, closed Mon, otherwise open all day. *(John Wooll)*

FRADLEY SK1414
White Swan (01283) 790330
Fradley Junction; DE13 7DN Good canalside location at Trent & Mersey and Coventry junction, well kept Black Sheep, Greene King Abbot, Marstons Pedigree and three guests, cheery traditional public bar with two fires, quieter plusher lounge and lower vaulted room (former stable), decent reasonably priced food including pizzas and Sun carvery; Thurs folk night, open mike Sun; children (not in bar) and dogs welcome, waterside tables, classic car/motorbike meetings, open all day. *(Anon)*

GNOSALL SJ8220
Boat (01785) 822208
Gnosall Heath, by Shropshire Union Canal Bridge 34; ST20 0DA Popular little canalside pub run by friendly family, comfortable first-floor bar with curved window seat overlooking narrowboats, decent choice of reasonably priced pub food (not Sun evening, Mon), Marstons-related ales, open fire; children and dogs welcome, tables out by canal, moorings and nice walks, open all day weekends, closed Mon lunchtime. *(Dr Simon Innes)*

HANLEY SJ8847
Coachmakers Arms (01782) 262158
Lichfield Street; ST1 3EA Chatty traditional 19th-c town local with four small rooms and drinking corridor, five well kept ales including Bass, darts, cards and dominoes, original seating and local tilework, open fires; children and dogs welcome, open all day (remains under threat of demolition). *(Belinda May)*

HAUGHTON SJ8620
Bell (01785) 780301
A518 Stafford–Newport; ST18 9EX Recently refurbished 19th-c village pub with good value popular food (not Sun or Mon evenings, best to book), lunchtime deal Mon-Sat, five well kept ales including Marstons, Timothy Taylors and a house beer from Jennings, friendly attentive service even when busy, restaurant behind; children welcome, no dogs inside, picnic-sets in back garden, open all day Fri-Sun. *(Anon)*

HIGH OFFLEY SJ7725
Anchor (01785) 284569
Off A519 Eccleshall–Newport; towards High Lea, by Shropshire Union Canal Bridge 42; Peggs Lane; ST20 0NG Built around 1830 to serve the Shropshire Union Canal and little changed in the century or more this family has run it; two small simple front rooms, one with a couple of fine high-backed settles on quarry tiles, Wadworths 6X and Weston's cider, sandwiches on request, owners' sitting room behind bar, occasional

weekend sing-alongs; outbuilding with semi-open lavatories (swallows may fly through); no children inside, lovely garden with hanging baskets and notable topiary anchor, small shop, moorings (near Bridge 42), caravan/campsite, closed Mon-Thurs in winter. *(Mungo Shipley)*

HIMLEY   SO8990

★**Crooked House** (01384) 238583
Signed down long lane from B4176 Gornalwood–Himley, OS Sheet 139 map reference 896908; DY3 4DA Extraordinary sight, building thrown wildly out of kilter by mining subsidence, one side 4 ft lower than the other and slopes so weird that things appear to roll up them; public bar (dogs allowed here) with grandfather clock and hatch serving Banks's and other Marstons-related ales, lounge bar, good food from bar snacks and pub standards to more unusual creative choices, cheery service, some local antiques in level extension, conservatory; children welcome in eating areas, big outside terrace, closed Mon, otherwise open all day (till 8pm Sun). *(Dave Braisted)*

KIDSGROVE   SJ8354

★**Blue Bell** (01782) 774052
Hardingswood; off A50 NW edge of town; ST7 1EG Simple friendly pub (looks more like a house) with half a dozen thoughtfully chosen and constantly changing ales from smaller breweries, around 30 bottled continentals, up to three draught farm ciders and a perry, filled rolls weekends only; four small, carpeted rooms, unfussy and straightforward, with blue upholstered benches and basic pub furniture, gas-effect coal fire; may be background music and the occasional folk session, no credit cards; dogs and well behaved children welcome, tables in front and on little back lawn, close to Trent & Mersey and Macclesfield Canal junction, open all day Sun, closed Mon and weekday lunchtimes. *(Belinda May)*

KNIGHTON   SJ7240

White Lion (01630) 647300
B5415 Woore–Market Drayton; TF9 4HJ Recently refurbished roadside pub with enjoyable food (not Mon) including tapas, three Theakstons ales, friendly attentive service, open fires, dining conservatory; background music; children welcome but no dogs inside, small outside seating area, open all day. *(Dr Simon Innes)*

LEEK   SJ9856

Den Engel (01538) 373751
Stanley Street; ST13 5HG Relaxed belgian-style bar in high-ceilinged Jacobean building, great selection of bottled and draught continental beers, three dozen

genevers, plus four changing real ales (always one from Titanic), knowledgeable landlord, enjoyable food (not Mon, Tues) in upstairs restaurant such as moules frites; background classical music, can get packed weekends; dogs welcome, tables on back terrace, closed lunchtimes, open all day weekends, from 4pm other days. *(Anon)*

LEEK   SJ9856

★**Wilkes Head**
St Edward Street; ST13 5DS Friendly three-room local dating from the 18th c (still has back coaching stables), owned by Whim with their ales and interesting guests, real ciders and good choice of whiskies, filled rolls, gas fire and lots of pump clips, pub games, juke box in back room, regular live music (landlord is a musician); children allowed in one room (not really a family pub), dogs welcome but ask first, fair disabled access, garden with stage, open all day except Mon lunchtime. *(Rob Anderson)*

LICHFIELD   SK0705

★**Boat** (01543) 361692
From A5 at Muckley Corner, take A461 signed Walsall; pub is on right just before M6 toll; WS14 0BU Popular efficiently run dining pub – handy break for a meal off M6 toll; most emphasis on food with huge floor-to-ceiling menu boards, views into kitchen and dishes ranging from lunchtime sandwiches through light snacks to interesting main choices; entrance part with leather club chairs and sofas around coffee tables and potted palms, split-level bar/dining areas with sturdy modern pine furniture on carpet, views of canal (currently being restored), three well kept changing ales and a dozen wines by the glass; background music; children and dogs (in bar) welcome, wheelchair access, garden with seats on raised deck, open (and food) all day Sun. *(Richard Kennell, Phil and Jane Hodson)*

LICHFIELD   SK1109

Duke of York (01543) 300386
Greenhill/Church Street; WS13 6DY Old beamed pub with split-level front bar, cosy carpeted lounge and converted back stables bar, inglenook woodburners, well kept Joules ales and guests, simple lunchtime food (not Sun), pleasant staff; no children but dogs allowed, terrace picnic-sets behind and own bowling green, open all day. *(George Atkinson)*

LICHFIELD   SK1308

★**Horse & Jockey** (01543) 262924
Tamworth Road (A51 Lichfield–Tamworth); WS14 9JE Cosy old-fashioned pub with wide range of popular freshly

---

You can send reports directly to us at feedback@goodguides.com

prepared food including good home-made pies and fish specials (booking advisable), ales such as Castle Rock, Marstons and Sharps good friendly service, open fire; darts; children welcome if eating, no dogs, open all day Sun. *(Dr Simon Innes)*

LITTLE BRIDGEFORD   SJ8727
Mill (01785) 282710
Worston Lane; near M6 junction 14; turn right off A5013 at Little Bridgeford; ST18 9QA Useful sensibly priced dining pub in attractive 1814 watermill, enjoyable food in bar and restaurant including children's menu and Sun carvery, ales such as Greene King and Marstons, good friendly service, Thurs quiz; pleasant grounds with adventure playground and nature trail (lakes, islands etc); open all day. *(Rob Anderson)*

LONGNOR   SK0965
Old Cheshire Cheese (01298) 83218
High Street; SK17 0NS Welcoming and relaxed 17th-c village pub, three well kept Robinsons ales and decent good value food including blackboard specials and Weds steak night, open fire, bric-a-brac and pictures in traditional main bar, two dining rooms, pool and TV in separate rooms; free wi-fi; children, walkers and dogs welcome, tables out in front and on back grass, four bedrooms in converted stables over road, closed Mon, otherwise open all day. *(Brian and Anna Marsden)*

MARCHINGTON   SK1330
Dog & Partridge (01283) 820394
Church Lane; ST14 8LJ Flower-decked 18th-c village pub with various beamed and tile-floored rooms, Bass and three changing guests, good food (not Sun evening) including themed nights and bargain two-course lunch deal, good value wines, attentive friendly staff, real fires, some interesting bits and pieces on the walls, *Beano* wallpaper in the gents; background music, free wi-fi; children and dogs (in bar) welcome, paved back terrace by car park, open all day Sun with live music from 5pm. *(Paul Humphreys)*

MEERBROOK   SJ9960
Lazy Trout (01538) 300385
Centre of village; ST13 8SN Popular country dining pub with good imaginative food and friendly attentive staff, bar area with well kept Banks's, Marstons Pedigree and a couple of guests from curved stone counter, comfortable dining lounge to the right with log fire, second quarry-tiled dining room to the left with pine furniture and cooking range; juke box; children welcome, dogs and muddy boots in some parts, seats out at front by quiet lane and in appealing garden behind with splendid views to the Roaches and Hen Cloud, good walks, open (and food) all day. *(Brian and Anna Marsden)*

ONECOTE   SK0455
Jervis Arms (01538) 304206
B5053; ST13 7RU Popular country pub with own Mixon Grange beers and a guest, enjoyable reasonably priced home-cooked food, black-beamed main bar with inglenook woodburner, separate dining and family rooms; live country/blues first Fri of month, folk club second Sun; dogs welcome in some parts, attractive streamside (River Hamps) garden with footbridge to car park, play area, open all day Sun. *(Anon)*

PENKRIDGE   SJ9214
Littleton Arms (01785) 716300
St Michael's Square/A449 – M6 detour between junctions 12 and 13; ST19 5AL Cheerfully busy dining pub-hotel (former coaching inn) with contemporary open-plan layout, varied choice of enjoyable well presented food from sandwiches and sharing boards to popular Sun lunch, good wines by the glass and five well kept changing ales from island servery, friendly accommodating staff; background music; children and dogs (in bar area) welcome, ten bedrooms, open all day. *(Stuart Paulley)*

SEIGHFORD   SJ8725
Hollybush (01785) 281644
3 miles from M6 junction 14 via A5013/ B5405; ST18 9PQ Modernised and extended beamed pub owned by the village and leased to Titanic, their ales and guests, good value locally sourced pubby food (all day Fri and Sat, till 7pm Sun) from lunchtime sandwiches and light choices up; monthly charity quiz, portable skittle alley; children and dogs welcome, beer garden, open all day Fri-Sun. *(Rob Anderson)*

SHEEN   SK1160
Staffordshire Knot (01298) 84329
Off B5054 at Hulme End; SK17 0ET Welcoming traditional 17th-c stone-built village pub, nice mix of old furniture on flagstones or red and black tiles, stag's head and hunting prints, two log fires in hefty stone fireplaces, good interesting food cooked by landlady, well kept local Whim Hartington and reasonably priced wines, friendly helpful staff; closed Mon. *(Belinda May)*

STAFFORD   SJ9323
Swan (01785) 258142
Greengate Street; ST16 2JA Modernised 18th-c coaching inn with two bars, well kept Marstons-related ales and guests, good sensibly priced bar and brasserie food

---

Post Office address codings confusingly give the impression that some pubs are in Staffordshire, when they're really in Cheshire or Derbyshire (which is where we list them).

including themed evenings (Tues vegetarian/vegan, Weds steak, Thurs fish), coffee shop, friendly helpful staff; courtyard with rattan-style furniture, 31 bedrooms, open (and food) all day. *(Robert W Buckle)*

STOKE-ON-TRENT   SJ8649
Bulls Head (01782) 834153
St John's Square, Burslem; ST6 3AJ
Old-fashioned two-room tap for Titanic with up to ten ales (including guests) from horseshoe bar, also good selection of belgian beers, ciders and wines, well cared-for interior with varnished tables on wood or carpeted floors, coal fire; bar billiards, table skittles and good juke box; drinking area outside (may be barbecue if Port Vale are at home), open all day Fri-Sun, closed till 3pm Mon, Tues. *(Jeremy King)*

STOKE-ON-TRENT   SJ8745
Glebe (01782) 860670
35 Glebe Street, by the Civic Centre; ST4 1HG Well restored 19th-c Joules corner pub, their ales, real cider and good reasonably priced wines from central mahogany counter, William Morris leaded windows, bare boards and panelling, some civic portraits and big fireplace with coat of arms above, wholesome bar food (not Sun, Mon evening), friendly staff; quite handy for station, open all day. *(Dr J Barrie Jones)*

STONE   SJ8933
Wayfarer (01785) 811023
The Fillybrooks (A34 just N); ST15 0NB Sizeable 1930s pub beside dual-carriageway, contemporary décor and same owners as the Swan with Two Necks at Blackbrook; good food from varied menu including sharing plates and stone-baked pizzas, beers such as Fullers, Sharps and Timothy Taylors, lots of wines by the glass including champagne, friendly attentive staff; terrace seating, open all day. *(Anon)*

STOWE   SK0027
★Cock (01889) 270237
Off A518 Stafford–Uttoxeter; ST18 0LF Popular bistro-style conversion of old beamed village pub (calls itself Bistro le Coq), good competently cooked french food (not Mon) from sensibly short set menus, well chosen affordably priced wines, small bar area serving real ale, friendly efficient service; well behaved children welcome, closed Sun evening, Mon lunchtime. *(Dr Simon Innes)*

TRYSULL   SO8594
Bell (01902) 892871
Bell Road; WV5 7JB Extended 18th-c red-brick village pub next to church, cosy bar, inglenook lounge and large high-ceilinged back dining area, well kept Holdens, Bathams and a guest, reasonably priced wines and popular good value food, friendly helpful service; children and dogs (in bar) welcome, paved front terrace, open all day weekends. *(Robert Parker, Paul Humphreys)*

WETTON   SK1055
Olde Royal Oak (01335) 310287
Village signed off Hulme End–Alstonefield road, between B5054 and A515; DE6 2AF Welcoming new management for this old stone-built pub in lovely NT countryside – a popular stop for walkers; traditional bar with white ceiling boards above black beams, small dining chairs around rustic tables, open fire in stone fireplace, carpeted sun lounge, four changing ales and good selection of malt whiskies, enjoyable good value home-made food; background and live music, darts, dominoes and shove-ha'penny; children and dogs welcome, picnic-sets in shaded garden, closed Mon, otherwise open (and food) all day. *(Mungo Shipley)*

WHITTINGTON   SK1608
Dog (01543) 432601
The one near Lichfield; Main Street; WS14 9JU Beamed 18th-c village inn with good freshly made food (not Sun evening, Mon) from sensibly short menu including lunchtime deal, well kept Bass, Black Sheep and Greene King, decent choice of wines by the glass, pleasant efficient service; children welcome, no dogs inside, seats on small terrace, bedrooms, open all day Fri-Sun, closed Mon lunchtime. *(Dr Simon Innes)*

YOXALL   SK1418
Golden Cup (01543) 472295
Main Street (A515); DE13 8NQ Well run village inn dating from the early 18th c, reasonably priced traditional home-made food from sandwiches to good value three-course Sun lunch, well kept Marstons Pedigree and a guest, lounge bar, games and sports TV in public bar; cheery window boxes and hanging baskets, lovely garden down to small river, reasonably priced bedrooms, camping, open all day Fri-Sun. *(Belinda May)*

Suffolk

ALDEBURGH   TM4656 Map 5
Cross Keys

(01728) 452637 – www.aldeburgh-crosskeys.co.uk

Crabbe Street; IP15 5BN

16th-c pub with seats outside near the beach, chatty atmosphere, friendly licensee and local beers; bedrooms

Dating from 1540, this is a traditional pub with a fine seafront position. In warm weather it's best to get here early as seats on the sheltered back terrace with views across the promenade and shingle to the water are quickly snapped up. Inside, the cheery bustling atmosphere is helped along by the obliging licensee and his staff. The low-ceilinged interconnecting bars have antique and other pubby furniture, miscellaneous paintings on the walls and log fires in two inglenook fireplaces. Adnams Southwold, Broadside and Ghost Ship on handpump, decent wines by the glass and several malt whiskies; background music and games machine. The bedrooms are attractively furnished.

🍴 Well liked food includes sandwiches, local sprats, smoked mackerel pâté, goats cheese tart, ham and egg, steak and kidney pudding, rib-eye steak and chips, fresh fish dishes such as mussels, whole plaice, hake and skate wing with brown butter, and puddings such as sticky toffee pudding and apple tart. *Benchmark main dish: beer-battered fresh cod and chips £10.50. Two-course evening meal £20.50.*

Adnams ~ Tenants Mike and Janet Clement ~ Real ale ~ Open 11am (12 Sun)-midnight ~ Bar food 12-2 (3 weekends), 6.30-9; no food Sun evening ~ Children welcome ~ Dogs allowed in bar and bedrooms ~ Wi-fi ~ Bedrooms: /$89.50 *Recommended by Pat and Graham Williamson, MDN, N R White, Nick Sharpe, Peter Pilbeam*

BOXFORD   TL9640 Map 5
Fleece 🍺

(01787) 211183 – www.boxfordfleece.com

Broad Street (A1071 Sudbury–Ipswich); CO10 5DX

Attractively restored, partly 15th-c pub flourishing under current ownership

There's a great deal of character in this companionable pub – and genuinely welcoming licensees. Head first to the Corder Room: beautifully done out, it has dark panelled wainscoting, handsome William Morris wallpaper under a high delft shelf, sweeping heavy red curtains and a handful of attractive period dining tables with good chairs and a built-in wall settle. The beamed bar on the left has a woodburning stove in the terracotta-tiled front part, a big fireplace beneath a wallhanging at the back with a couple of rugs on boards, and a mix of pews, a winged settle and other seats around old stripped tables. The key attraction is the serving counter, with local farm cider and changing ales on handpump: Adnams Southwold and Ghost Ship and Sharps Doom Bar; also, 11 wines by the glass, several malt whiskies and their own cider.

 Enjoyable food includes sandwiches and baguettes, prawn cocktail, deep-fried breaded brie with redcurrant jelly, mushroom and pepper stroganoff, burgers with toppings, coleslaw and chips, steak in ale pie, chicken in creamy leek and bacon sauce, chilli con carne, salmon, asparagus and cream cheese tagliatelle, and puddings such as crème brûlée and apple crumble. *Benchmark main dish: beer-battered cod and chips £9.25. Two-course evening meal £15.00.*

Free house ~ Licensees Judith and John Stevenson ~ Real ale ~ Open 12-3, 5-11; 12-midnight Fri, Sat; 12-11 Sun ~ Bar food 12-2.30, 6-9; 12-4 Sun, not Sun evening or Mon ~ Restaurant ~ Children welcome away from bar ~ Dogs allowed in bar ~ Wi-fi
Recommended by Giles and Annie Francis, Peter Pilbeam

BURY ST EDMUNDS
Old Cannon 🍺 🛏

TL8564   Map 5

(01284) 768769 – www.oldcannonbrewery.co.uk
Cannon Street, just off A134/A1101 roundabout at N end of town; IP33 1JR

Busy own-brew town pub with local drinks and interesting bar food; bedrooms

The own-brewed and guest beers here make this stylish townhouse pub well worth seeking out. The brewery is actually in the bar: there are two huge gleaming stainless-steel brewing vessels and views up to a steel-balustraded open-plan malt floor above the counter: Old Cannon Best and Gunner's Daughter and seasonal ales such as Black Pig, Brass Monkey and Hornblower, plus Adnams Southwold and a couple of guests on handpump. Also ten wines by the glass and carefully chosen spirits. A row of chunky old bar stools line the ochre-painted counter, and there's an appealing assortment of old and new chairs and tables and upholstered banquettes on well worn bare boards; background music. The comfortable bedrooms are in the old brewhouse across the courtyard. Behind, through the old coach arch, is a good-sized cobbled courtyard with hanging baskets and stylish metal tables and chairs.

 Popular food includes baguettes, moules marinière, asparagus topped with a crispy duck egg and chorizo and sorrel butter, thai green vegetable curry, smoked haddock and cockles in creamy herb sauce, lamb cutlets with roasted sweet potatoes, pak choi and spicy vietnamese sauce, chicken stuffed with goats cheese and tomatoes with red pepper coulis, and puddings such as a cheesecake of the day and Grand Marnier dark chocolate pot. *Benchmark main dish: local sausages with colcannon mash, beer-batter pudding and onion gravy £12.25. Two-course evening meal £19.00.*

Own brew ~ Licensee Garry Clark ~ Real ale ~ Open 12-11 (10.30 Sun) ~ Bar food 12-9; 12-3 Sun ~ Restaurant ~ Children must be over 10 ~ Wi-fi ~ Bedrooms: £95/£130
Recommended by Barry Collett

CHELMONDISTON
Butt & Oyster

TM2037   Map 5

(01473) 780764 – www.debeninns.co.uk/buttandoyster
Pin Mill – signposted from B1456 SE of Ipswich; continue to bottom of road; IP9 1JW

Chatty old riverside pub with pleasant views, good food and drink and seats on the terrace

Popular with the boating fraternity, this simple old bargeman's pub has fine views over the River Orwell from seats on the terrace or by the windows in the bar. The half-panelled little smoke room is pleasantly worn and unfussy with high-backed and other old-fashioned settles on a tiled floor. There's also a two-level dining room with country kitchen furniture on bare boards, and pictures and boat-related artefacts on the walls above the dado. Adnams Southwold and Ghost Ship and a couple of guests tapped from the cask by friendly, efficient staff, several wines by the glass and local cider; board games. The annual Thames Barge Race (end June/early July) is fun. The car park can fill up pretty quickly.

The menu is strong on fish such as scallops and chorizo salad, crispy squid with sweet chilli dip, seafood risotto, fish stew and fritto misto; they also offer sandwiches, burgers with toppings and chips, vegetable stir-fry, sausages with mash and gravy, chicken in rosemary and garlic, pulled pork shoulder with coleslaw, and puddings such as lemon tart and triple-chocolate brownie. *Benchmark main dish: beer-battered fish and chips £10.95. Two-course evening meal £15.00.*

Adnams ~ Lease Steve Lomas ~ Real ale ~ Open 9am-11pm ~ Bar food 9am-9.30pm ~ Restaurant ~ Children welcome ~ Dogs allowed in bar ~ Wi-fi *Recommended by Steve and Irene Homer, Pat and Tony Martin, Dennis and Doreen Haward, Mrs Margo Finlay, Jörg Kasprowski*

DUNWICH
TM4770 Map 5

Ship 🍺 🛏

(01728) 648219 – www.shipatdunwich.co.uk
St James Street; IP17 3DT

Friendly, well run and pleasantly traditional pub in a coastal village, tasty bar food and local ales; bedrooms

In what is left of a charming village (coastal erosion has put most of it under the sea), this is a delightful old pub with a warmly welcoming licensee and friendly staff. The traditionally furnished main bar has benches, pews, captain's chairs and wooden tables on a tiled floor, a woodburning stove (left open in cold weather) and lots of sea prints. Adnams Bitter and a couple of changing guests are served from antique handpumps at the handsomely panelled bar counter, as well as several wines by the glass; board games. A simple conservatory looks on to a back terrace, and the large garden is very pleasant, with well spaced picnic-sets, two large anchors and an enormous fig tree. The comfortable bedrooms make a good base for exploring the area and breakfasts are hearty. The RSPB reserve at Minsmere and nearby Dunwich Museum are worth visiting and there are good walks in Dunwich Forest.

The high quality food includes potted duck leg with apple, pear and date chutney, goats cheese croquettes with herb mayonnaise, chicken kiev with oven-dried tomatoes, butternut squash, red onion and sage risotto, honey-baked glazed ham with free-range eggs, pineapple relish and chips, salt cod and salmon fishcake with a poached free-range egg, brown shrimps and shellfish sauce, and puddings such as spiced chocolate mousse and white chocolate rice pudding with home-made damson jam. *Benchmark main dish: aromatic confit pork belly with caraway carrots, seasonal greens and pan gravy £14.95. Two-course evening meal £21.00.*

Free house ~ Licensee Matt Goodwin ~ Real ale ~ Open 12-11; 12-10.30 Sun ~ Bar food 12-3, 6-9; 12-9 Fri-Sun; all day in school holidays ~ Restaurant evening only ~ Children welcome ~ Dogs allowed in bar and bedrooms ~ Wi-fi ~ Live music last Thurs of month ~ Bedrooms: £85/£112.50 *Recommended by Tracey and Stephen Groves, Barry Collett, Denis and Margaret Kilner*

EASTBRIDGE
TM4566 Map 5

Eels Foot 🛏

(01728) 830154 – www.theeelsfootinn.co.uk

Off B1122 N of Leiston; IP16 4SN

Country local with hospitable atmosphere, fair value food and Thursday evening folk sessions; bedrooms

This is a popular spot with bird-watchers, cyclists and walkers; the inn borders the freshwater marshes, a footpath leads directly to the sea and RSPB Minsmere is nearby. It's a friendly, simple place with light modern furnishings on stripped-wood floors in the upper and lower parts of the bar, a warming fire, Adnams Southwold, Broadside, Ghost Ship and Jester on handpump, 11 wines by the glass, several malt whiskies and a farm cider; darts in a side area, board games, cribbage and a neat back dining room. There are seats on the terrace and benches in the lovely big back garden. Our readers enjoy staying in the comfortable, attractive and quiet bedrooms in a separate building (one room has wheelchair access) and breakfasts are good. They are now a certified Caravan Club site and can provide electric hook-ups.

🍴 Tasty food includes sandwiches, baguettes, ham and eggs, meat or vegetarian lasagne, various pies, winter casseroles, beer-battered line-caught fish and chips, steaks, and puddings such as crumble and sticky toffee pudding. *Benchmark main dish: welsh rarebit with Adnams Blackshore Stout, smoked haddock, poached egg and chips £9.75. Two-course evening meal £16.00.*

Adnams ~ Tenant Julian Wallis ~ Real ale ~ Open 12-3, 6-11; 12-11 Fri; 11.30-11 Sat; 12-11.30 Sun ~ Bar food 12-2.30, 6.30-9 ~ Children welcome ~ Dogs welcome ~ Wi-fi ~ Live folk music Thurs and last Sun of month ~ Bedrooms: £80/£99 *Recommended by Peter Meister, Pat and Alan Timmon, Giles and Annie Francis, Roy Hoing*

IPSWICH
TM1844 Map 5

Fat Cat 🍺

(01473) 726524 – www.fatcatipswich.co.uk

Spring Road, opposite junction with Nelson Road (best bet for parking is up there); IP4 5NL

Fantastic range of changing real ales in a well run town pub; garden

Sourced from across the country, the fantastic range of up to 21 real ales on handpump or tapped from the cask in this warmly friendly and cheerful town pub continues to draw crowds. There might be Brains Rev James, Brandon Rusty Bucket, Colchester Mild Ale, Crouch Vale Brewers Gold and Yakima Gold, Earl Soham Victoria Bitter, Everards Tiger, Fullers London Pride, Green Jack Trawlerboys Best, Hop Back Summer Lightning, Marble Dobber, Nethergate Old Growler, Rudgate Dark Cherry Mild, Sharps Doom Bar, Thwaites Magic Sponge and Woodfordes Wherry. They also stock quite a few belgian bottled beers, farm cider and seven wines by the glass. The bars have a mix of café chairs and stools, unpadded wall benches and cushioned seats around cast-iron and wooden pub tables, bare floorboards, with lots of enamel brewery signs and posters on canary-yellow walls; board games and shove-ha'penny. There's also a spacious back conservatory and several picnic-sets on the terrace and lawn. Very little nearby parking. Well behaved dogs are welcome but must be kept on a lead.

They keep a supply of baguettes, spicy scotch eggs and pasties made in their small kitchen and are happy for you to bring in takeaway food (not Friday or Saturday).

Free house ~ Licensees John and Ann Keatley ~ Real ale ~ No credit cards ~ Open 12-11; 12-midnight Sat; 12-10.30 Sun ~ Bar food all day while it lasts ~ Wi-fi
Recommended by Richard Kramer, Edward May, Mike Swan, Peter Brix

 LINDSEY TYE   TL9846   Map 5
Red Rose ♀
(01449) 741424 – www.thelindseyrose.co.uk
Village signposted off A1141 NW of Hadleigh; IP7 6PP

15th-c hall house with a couple of neat bars, enjoyable popular food, real ales and plenty of outside seating

Our readers very much enjoy their visits to this handsome and consistently well run hall house. The neatly kept main bar has low beams, some standing timbers and an assortment of wooden tables and chairs. In front of a splendid log fire in an old brick fireplace are a couple of squashy red leather sofas, a low table and some brass measuring jugs. A second room is furnished in a similar way and also has a big brick fireplace, but is much simpler in feel and perhaps quieter. Adnams Southwold and Ghost Ship and Mauldons Bitter on handpump and 11 wines by the glass. There are flowering tubs and a few picnic-sets in front, with more picnic-sets at the back – where there's also a children's play area and a football pitch.

 The thoughtful choice of food includes chicken liver parfait with red onion marmalade, crispy haggis scotch egg with swede and potato purée, tomato tarte tatin with pesto and mozzarella, creamy pasta carbonara, salmon, caper and lemon fishcake with a poached egg and hollandaise sauce, thai chicken curry, pork belly and tenderloin with colcannon mash, crackling and cider jus, and puddings such as apple and cinnamon crumble and creamy lemon posset. *Benchmark main dish: rare-breed burger with toppings and chips £12.50. Two-course evening meal £19.00.*

Free house ~ Licensee Peter Miller ~ Real ale ~ Open 11-3, 5-11; 11-11 Sat; 11-10.30 Sun; 11-3, 5-11 weekends in winter ~ Bar food 12-2.30, 6-9; 12-3 Sun (12-4 in winter) ~ Children welcome ~ Dogs welcome ~ Wi-fi *Recommended by Mrs Carolyn Dixon, Mrs Margo Finlay, Jörg Kasprowski*

 LONG MELFORD   TL8646   Map 5
Black Lion 🌟 ♀ 🛏
(01787) 312356 – www.blacklionhotel.net
Church Walk; CO10 9DN

Well appointed hotel with relaxed and comfortable bar, modern bar food, attentive staff and seats in pretty garden; bedrooms

The individually decorated bedrooms in this comfortable and civilised hotel are attractive and well equipped and make a fine base for exploring the area; breakfasts are particularly good. The back bar, where locals drop in for a drink and a chat, has two comfortable sofas, leather winged armchairs, an open fire and Adnams Southwold on handpump and 18 wines by the glass; background music. The red-walled dining room has attractive chairs around handsome candlelit tables on tartan carpet, another open fire and heavy swagged curtains; the windows overlook the village green. In warm weather you can take afternoon tea in the appealing Victorian walled garden.

Good, interesting food includes chargrilled squid stuffed with chorizo, lemon and fennel, devilled lambs kidneys on sourdough toast with mustard sauce, pumpkin gnocchi with sage pesto and toasted pine nuts, oriental-style pork belly with apple gel, gressingham duck, faggots and walnut praline, sea trout with seaweed, clams and crab arancini, and puddings such as dark chocolate terrine with griottine cherries and fruit crumble with crème anglaise; they also offer cream teas and two- and three-course set menus. *Benchmark main dish: beer-battered cod and chips £13.95. Two-course evening meal £16.95.*

Ravenwood Group ~ Licensee Craig Jarvis ~ Real ale ~ Open 7.30am (8.30 weekends)-11pm ~ Bar food 12-2, 7-9.30; breakfasts for non-residents 7.30-9.30 weekdays, 8.30-10 weekends ~ Restaurant ~ Children welcome ~ Dogs allowed in bar and bedrooms ~ Wi-fi ~ Bedrooms: £102/£125 *Recommended by Mrs Margo Finlay, Jörg Kasprowski, Bill Adie*

 ## MIDDLETON
Bell  £   TM4267 Map 5
(01728) 648286

Off A12 in Yoxford via B1122 towards Leiston; also signposted off B1125 Leiston–Westleton; The Street; IP17 3NN

Thatch and low beams, friendly chef-landlord, good beer and popular good value food – a peaceful spot

In a quiet village location overlooked by the church's grand flint tower, this is a cheerful, bustling pub with a warm welcome from the character landlord. On the left, the traditional bar has a log fire in a big hearth, old local photographs, a low plank-panelled ceiling, bar stools and pew seating, with Adnams Southwold, Broadside and Ghost Ship tapped from the cask and nine wines by the glass. On the right, an informal two-room carpeted lounge/dining area has padded mate's and library chairs around dark tables under low black beams, with pews by a big woodburning stove and modern seaside brewery prints. Dogs are welcomed with treats and a bowl of water. It's a pretty cream-washed building, with picnic-sets under cocktail parasols out in front, and camping available in the broad meadow behind. RSPB Minsmere is nearby, as are walks along the coast.

Generous helpings of good value food include lunchtime sandwiches, a trio of cured fish, smoked mackerel pâté with chutney, sausages and mash, ham and egg, liver and bacon, baked and stuffed field mushroom with vegetable couscous and goats cheese fritter, lamb steak with mint and redcurrant dressing, whole lemon sole with white wine and grapes, and puddings such as double-chocolate cheesecake and sticky toffee pudding. *Benchmark main dish: beer-battered fish and chips £9.50. Two-course evening meal £15.00.*

Adnams ~ Tenants Nicholas and Trish Musgrove ~ Real ale ~ Open 12-3, 6-11 (midnight Fri); 12-midnight Sat; 12-10.30 Sun; closed Mon ~ Bar food 12-2.15, 6-9.15; 12-5 Sun ~ Restaurant ~ Well behaved children allowed away from bar ~ Dogs allowed in bar *Recommended by Peter Meister, Peter Smith and Judith Brown*

 ## PETTISTREE
Greyhound   TM2954 Map 5
(01728) 746451 – www.greyhoundinnpettistree.co.uk

The Street; brown sign to pub off B1438 S of Wickham Market, 0.5 miles N of A12; IP13 0HP

Neatly kept village pub with enjoyable food and drink

If you can't find this cheerful pub, just look for the next door church. It's basically just two smallish rooms with open fires, some rather low beams, chunky farmhouse chairs and cushioned settles around dark wooden tables on bare floorboards and candlelight. The hard-working, friendly licensees keep Earl Soham Victoria Bitter and guests such as Adnams Ghost Ship and Shortts Farm Blondie on handpump, several wines by the glass and quite a few malt whiskies; it's best to book in advance to be sure of a table. The well kept side garden has picnic-sets under parasols, with more beside the gravelled front car park.

🍴 Local produce is at the heart of the highly thought-of food cooked by the landlady: ciabatta sandwiches, duo of salmon (beetroot-cured and whisky-cured) with dill mayonnaise, pheasant and black pudding terrine with apple chutney, crab, garlic and chilli tagliatelle, gammon with a poached egg and chunky chips, basil gnocchi with sun-dried tomato pesto and roasted peppers, chicken breast stuffed with mushrooms and wrapped in bacon with herb butter, confit duck leg with red onion jam and dauphinoise potatoes, and puddings such as elderflower panna cotta and chocolate brownie with pistachio ice-cream. *Benchmark main dish: slow-cooked lamb shoulder in red wine with dauphinoise potatoes and mint salsa £15.95. Two-course evening meal £19.00.*

Free house ~ Licensees Stewart and Louise McKenzie ~ Real ale ~ Open 12-3, 6-11; 12-4, 7-10.30 Sun; closed Mon, two weeks Jan ~ Bar food 12-3, 6-9; 12-3 Sun ~ Restaurant ~ Children welcome ~ Dogs allowed in bar *Recommended by Paul Whayman, Richard Kevern, Peter Brix*

REDE
Plough
(01284) 789208
Village signposted off A143 Bury St Edmunds–Haverhill; IP29 4BE

TL8055 Map 5

Well liked and promptly served food in a 16th-c pub, with several wines by the glass and friendly service

A cheerful, friendly landlord runs this quaint, partly thatched and pink-washed pub. The pretty bar is traditional with low beams, comfortable seating and a solid-fuel stove in a brick fireplace, and they keep changing ales from breweries such as Nethergate, Ringwood and Sharps on handpump and several wines by the glass; background music. There are picnic-sets in the sheltered cottagey garden and at the front near the village green.

🍴 Well liked food includes a changing scallop dish and a pâté of the day, ham, egg and chips, honey-roast vegetables with puy lentil casserole, chicken and porcini mushrooms with pasta, rabbit with leeks and spring onion, calves liver and bacon, moroccan-spiced lamb tagine, oxtail casserole, and puddings such as Tia Maria cheesecake and louisiana bread and butter pudding. *Benchmark main dish: slow-cooked rioja lamb with chorizo and vegetables £13.95. Two-course evening meal £19.00.*

Admiral Taverns ~ Tenant Brian Desborough ~ Real ale ~ Open 11-3, 6.30-11.30; 12-3, 7-11 Sun ~ Bar food 12-2, 7-9; 12-2 Sun ~ Restaurant ~ Children welcome until 8pm ~ Wi-fi
Recommended by Mike and Lynne Steane, R A P Cross, Lindy Andrews

SIBTON
White Horse 🍽⭐ ♀ 🛏
(01728) 660337 – www.sibtonwhitehorseinn.co.uk
Halesworth Road/Hubbard's Hill, N of Peasenhall; IP17 2JJ

TM3570 Map 5

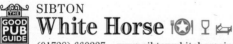

Suffolk Dining Pub of the Year

Particularly well run inn with nicely old-fashioned bar, good mix of customers, real ales and imaginative food; comfortable bedrooms

This bustling village inn is an enjoyable place to stay in warm, contemporary and well equipped bedrooms in a separate building next door. It's run by hard-working, hands-on licensees who take great care of their customers and their pub – you can be sure of a genuine welcome. The appealing bar has a roaring log fire in a large inglenook fireplace, horsebrasses and tack on the walls, old settles and pews, and they serve Adnams Southwold, Shortts Farm Strummer and Woodfordes Bure Gold on handpump, nine wines by the glass and 15 malt whiskies from an old oak-panelled counter. Beer festivals are held in June and August and a viewing panel reveals the working cellar and its ancient floor. Steps lead up past an old, partly knocked-through timbered wall into a carpeted gallery, and there's also a smart dining room and a secluded (and popular) dining terrace. The big garden has plenty of seats.

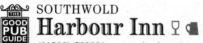 Using local produce (some of it home-grown, and their own eggs), the rewarding seasonal food includes sandwiches, confit duck leg terrine with spiced plum, hoisin and sesame dressing, grilled goats cheese with beetroot and walnut salad, hazelnuts and basil pesto, beer-battered fresh cod with triple-cooked chips, chicken breast with wilted pak choi, sun-blush tomato and madeira cream, smoked haddock with bubble and squeak cake, a poached free-range egg and chive and tomato cream, lamb belly stuffed with lamb mince and apricot with crushed swede and mint gravy, and puddings such as white chocolate cheesecake with cranberry ice-cream and pistachio frangipane tart with tonka bean ice-cream and textures of cherry. *Benchmark main dish: cod loin with pea purée £12.25. Two-course evening meal £20.00.*

Free house ~ Licensees Neil and Gill Mason ~ Real ale ~ Open 12-2.30, 6.30-11; 12-3.30, 7-10.30 Sun; closed Mon lunchtime, one week Jan ~ Bar food 12-2, 6.30-9; 12-2.30, 7-8.30 Sun ~ Restaurant ~ Well behaved children welcome but must be over 7 in evening; not in bedrooms ~ Dogs allowed in bar ~ Wi-fi ~ Music and beer festival in summer, barbecue Fri weekly in summer ~ Bedrooms: £80/£95 *Recommended by M and J White, Simon Rodway, David Jackman, Robert Turnham, Lindy Andrews, Isobel Mackinlay*

SOUTHWOLD   TM4975 Map 5
Harbour Inn ♀ ◧
(01502) 722381 – www.harbourinnsouthwold.co.uk
Blackshore, by the boats; from A1095, turn right at the Kings Head and keep on past the golf course and water tower; IP18 6TA

Great spot down by the boats, with lots of outside tables and interesting interior; popular food with emphasis on local seafood

Picnic-sets on the terrace in front of this old fisherman's pub look over the boats on the Blyth estuary; there are also seats and tables behind the pub, which overlook the marshy commons to the town. The back bar is nicely nautical, with dark panelling and built-in wall seats around scrubbed tables; the low ceiling is draped with ensigns, signal flags, pennants and a line strung with ancient dried fish, and there's a quaint old stove, rope fancywork, local fishing photographs and even portholes with water bubbling behind them. Cheerful staff serve 16 wines by the glass, along with Adnams Southwold, Broadside and Ghost Ship on handpump. They have their own weather station for walkers and sailors. The lower front bar, with tiled floor and panelling, is broadly similar, while the large, elevated dining room has panoramic views of the harbour, lighthouse, brewery and churches beyond the marshes. You can walk from here along the estuary to Walberswick (where the Bell is under the same good management as this pub) via a footbridge and return by the one-man ferry.

As well as numerous tapas-style dishes (such as smoked sprats, thai-style whelk salad and sticky chinese-style ribs), the popular food includes sandwiches, vegetarian moussaka, cumberland sausages with free-range eggs, steak and mushroom in ale pudding, grilled chicken with coleslaw and chips, local crab salad with lemon mayonnaise, moroccan-style lamb curry, clam, king prawn and smoked haddock chowder, and puddings such as bakewell tart and knickerbocker glory. *Benchmark main dish: beer-battered fish and chips £11.00. Two-course evening meal £18.00.*

Adnams ~ Tenant Nick Attfield ~ Real ale ~ Open 11-11 ~ Bar food 12-9 ~ Children welcome away from top bar ~ Dogs allowed in bar ~ Folk singers Thurs and Sun evenings *Recommended by Rita Scarratt, Peter Meister, Pat and Tony Martin, Ian Herdman, Phoebe Peacock, Barry Collett*

SOUTHWOLD
Lord Nelson 🍺 £

TM5076 Map 5

(01502) 722079 – www.thelordnelsonsouthwold.co.uk
East Street, off High Street (A1095); IP18 6EJ

Bow-windowed town pub with long-serving owners, well liked pubby food and a good choice of drinks; seats outside

Just a few steps from the seafront, this bustling local is popular with both regulars and visitors and all are made welcome by the efficient staff. The partly panelled traditional bar and its two small side rooms are kept spotless and have some interesting Nelson memorabilia, including attractive nautical prints and a fine model of HMS *Victory*, good lighting, a small but extremely hot coal fire, light wood furniture on a tiled floor, and lamps in nice nooks and corners. They serve Adnams Southwold, Broadside and Ghost Ship alongside two seasonal beers on handpump, 12 wines by the glass and several malt whiskies; board games. There are seats out in front with a sidelong view of the sea and more in a sheltered (and heated) back garden, with the Adnams brewery in sight (and often the appetising fragrance of brewing in progress). Disabled access is not perfect but is possible.

Well liked food at reasonable prices includes sandwiches, chicken liver pâté with redcurrant jam, king scallops with chorizo, tempura king prawns and squid ink mash, ham with pineapple and chips, rump burger topped with bacon and cheese, thai green vegetable curry, local pheasant breast with confit leg, bacon and red wine jus, and puddings such as apple crumble and treacle tart. *Benchmark main dish: beer-battered cod and chips £10.50. Two-course evening meal £17.00.*

Adnams ~ Tenants David and Gemma Sanchez ~ Real ale ~ Open 10.30am-11pm; 12-10.30 Sun ~ Bar food 12-2, 6.30-9 ~ Children welcome in snug and family room ~ Dogs welcome ~ Wi-fi *Recommended by Rita Scarratt, Sheila Topham, Pat and Tony Martin, Tracey and Stephen Groves, MDN, David Jackman, David Carr, Ian Herdman, Barry Collett, N R White, Giles and Annie Francis*

STOKE-BY-NAYLAND
Crown ★ 🍴 ♀ 🛏

TL9836 Map 5

(01206) 262001 – www.crowninn.net
Park Street (B1068); CO6 4SE

Smart dining pub with attractive modern furnishings, imaginative food using local produce, real ales and a great wine choice; good bedrooms

Our readers return to this civilised and relaxed inn on a regular basis – to stay overnight in the well equipped and comfortable bedrooms or for an enjoyable meal. The extensive open-plan dining bar is well laid out to give several distinct-feeling areas: a sofa and easy chairs on flagstones near the serving counter, a couple of armchairs under heavy beams by the big woodburning stove, one sizeable table tucked nicely into a three-sided built-in seat and a lower side room with more beams and cheerful floral wallpaper. Tables are mostly stripped veterans, with high-backed dining chairs, but there are more modern chunky pine tables at the back; contemporary artwork (mostly for sale) and daily papers. Friendly and informally dressed staff bustle happily about. They keep Adnams Southwold, Crouch Vale Brewers Gold, Woodfordes Wherry and a changing guest such as Wolf Lupus Lupus on handpump and Aspall's cider. Wine is a key feature, with 30 by the glass and hundreds more from the glass-walled 'cellar shop' in one corner – you can buy there to take away too. The sheltered flagstoned back terrace has comfortable teak furniture, with heaters, big terracotta-coloured parasols and a peaceful view over rolling, lightly wooded countryside; good disabled access. This pretty village is worth exploring and there are plenty of well-marked surrounding footpaths.

Imaginative food includes seared hare loin with blood orange, toasted pistachio, broad beans and watercress salad, tiger prawns with garlic, chilli, tamarind and a peanut and spring onion salad, grilled mackerel fillets with roasted beetroot purée, pickled fennel and apple salad and wasabi yoghurt, butternut squash with red kidney and cannellini beans, red peppers, chilli, sour cream and home-made cajun flatbread, steak and kidney pudding, chicken escalope with purple sprouting broccoli pesto and lemon and caper mash, and puddings such as apple parfait with apple purée and chocolate brownie and espresso custard tart with sugar-dipped pistachios and chocolate sauce. *Benchmark main dish: beer-battered haddock and chips £13.95. Two-course evening meal £22.00.*

Free house ~ Licensee Richard Sunderland ~ Real ale ~ Open 11-11; 12-10.30 Sun ~ Bar food 12-2.30, 6-9.30 (10 Fri, Sat); all day Sun ~ Children welcome ~ Dogs allowed in bar ~ Wi-fi ~ Bedrooms: £95/£135 *Recommended by Mrs Margo Finlay, Jörg Kasprowski, Jocelyn Matheson, MDN, N R White, Christopher and Elise Way, Mrs Carolyn Dixon*

STRATFORD ST MARY   TM0434 Map 5
Swan

(01206) 321244 – www.stratfordswan.com
Lower Street; CO7 6JR

Excellent food and a fine choice of interesting drinks in 16th-c coaching inn; riverside seats

Although much emphasis in this handsome, 16th-c timbered coaching inn is on the excellent food, this is no straightforward dining pub. As well as having Green Jack Trawlerboys Best, Oakham JHB and Timothy Taylors Landlord on handpump, several craft ales, 100 bottled beers, 38 wines by the glass, five ciders and a fine choice of spirits, they've planted 100 dwarf hop varieties which they'll be testing in their microbrewery; beer festivals are held twice a year. There's a log fire in a Tudor brick fireplace in one of the two beamed bars and a coal fire in the other, and an eclectic mix of old furniture on parquet or brick floors; the compact and timbered back restaurant is rather elegant; board games. Outside is a sun terrace with teak tables and chairs under parasols, as well as a big lawn and, across the road, more seats under willow trees by the banks of River Stour (where there's a landing stage).

Using the best seasonal produce (and their charcoal oven), each of the dishes on the creative menu is paired with a wine or beer: pickled mackerel with dill mayonnaise and salted cucumber, antipasti platter, wild mushroom tart with watercress, a poached egg and truffle oil, confit duck leg with mash and kale, skate wing with anchovy butter, pork platter (home-made sausages, confit pork belly, pigs head croquette), and puddings such as rhubarb and ginger tart with salted caramel ice-cream and passion-fruit parfait with meringue. *Benchmark main dish: rare-breed meat platter (rump steak, venison chop, lambs kidneys, home-made sausage) £25.50. Two-course evening meal £22.00.*

Free house ~ Licensee Jane Dorber ~ Real ale ~ Open 11 (10.30 Sat)-11; 11-10.20 Sun; closed Mon (except bank holidays), Tues ~ Bar food 12 (10.30 weekends)-3, 6-9 ~ Restaurant ~ Children welcome ~ Dogs allowed in bar ~ Wi-fi ~ Regular live music *Recommended by Gus Swan, Charlie May, Phoebe Peacock*

WALBERSWICK

TM4974   Map 5

Anchor ♀ ⇌

(01502) 722112 – www.anchoratwalberswick.com
The Street (B1387); village signed off A12; IP18 6UA

Friendly, bustling pub with plenty of space for both drinking and dining, particularly good food and thoughtful choice of drinks; bedrooms

The six spacious chalet-style rooms in the garden here have views of either the sea or beach huts and sand dunes, while from the bedrooms in the main house you can hear the sea just a few hundred yards away; dogs are allowed in some rooms. The simply furnished front bar, divided into snug halves by a two-way open fire, has big windows, heavy stripped tables on original oak flooring, sturdy built-in green leather wall seats and nicely framed black and white photographs of fishermen displayed on colour-washed panelling; daily papers and board games. Helpful, friendly staff serve Adnams Southwold, Broadside and Ghost Ship on handpump, 50 bottled beers and around 20 wines by the glass. The extensive dining area stretches back from a small more modern-feeling lounge. There are plenty of seats in the attractive garden, and an outdoor bar and wood-fired pizza oven serving the flagstoned terraces. As well as the coast path, there's a pleasant walk to Southwold.

Using local seasonal produce, the enterprising food includes sprats with red pepper aioli, duck liver parfait with brûlée topping and apple chutney, tempura mushroom with teriyaki glaze and calabrese and chilli salad, mussels with garlic, cream and wine, duck confit with spicy red cabbage, lamb noisette with mediterranean vegetable stew, and puddings such as chocolate fondant with salted caramel ice-cream and vanilla and cardamom panna cotta with pistachio syrup. *Benchmark main dish: beer-battered cod and chips £13.75. Two-course evening meal £19.75.*

Boudica Inns ~ Lease Mark and Sophie Dorber ~ Real ale ~ Open 11-11 ~ Bar food 12-3, 6-9 ~ Restaurant ~ Children welcome ~ Dogs allowed in bar and bedrooms ~ Wi-fi ~ Bedrooms: £120/£145 *Recommended by John Warbey, Tracey and Stephen Groves, Denis and Margaret Kilner*

WALBERSWICK

TM4974   Map 5

Bell ⬤ ♀ ⬤ ⇌

(01502) 723109 – www.bellinnwalberswick.co.uk
Just off B1387; IP18 6TN

Interesting and thriving 16th-c inn with good food and drinks choice, friendly atmosphere and nice garden; cosy bedrooms

The rambling bar in this well run inn is charming and has a lovely, chatty atmosphere and plenty of customers: antique curved settles, cushioned pews and window seats, scrubbed tables and two huge fireplaces (one with an elderly woodburning stove watched over by a pair of staffordshire china dogs). The fine old flooring encompasses sagging ancient bricks, broad boards, flagstones and black and red tiles. Friendly staff serve 16 good wines by the glass, several malt whiskies and Adnams Southwold, Broadside and Ghost Ship on handpump; background music. Don't miss the classic *New Yorker* wine cartoons in the lavatories. The Barn Café is open during the school holidays for light snacks, cakes, teas and so forth. A big, neatly planted sheltered garden behind has smart oak tables and chairs under blue parasols and a view over the dunes to the sea; pétanque. The rowing-boat ferry to Southwold is nearby (there's a footbridge a bit further away). Bedrooms, some with sea or harbour views, are attractively decorated, and breakfasts are good. This is sister pub to the Harbour Inn in Southwold.

The particularly good and highly popular food using top local produce includes sandwiches, suffolk smokies (flaked smoked haddock in cheese sauce) on granary toast, sticky barbecue pork ribs with sour cream and chive dip, spinach, mushroom and ricotta lasagne, home-baked honey and mustard ham and a free-range egg, a curry and a pie of the week, gloucester old spot pork belly with black pudding faggot, bubble and squeak and cider gravy, moussaka with green salad, and puddings such as chocolate and walnut brownie with cinnamon ice-cream and bread and butter pudding. *Benchmark main dish: fish pie £12.00. Two-course evening meal £18.00.*

Adnams ~ Tenant Nick Attfield ~ Real ale ~ Open 11-11 ~ Bar food 12-2.30, 6-9 ~ Children welcome away from bar ~ Dogs allowed in bar and bedrooms ~ Wi-fi ~ Bedrooms: £80/£95
Recommended by Tracey and Stephen Groves, N R White, Peter Pilbeam, Giles and Annie Francis

WALDRINGFIELD
Maybush
TM2844   Map 5

(01473) 736215 – www.debeninns.co.uk/maybush
Off A12 S of Martlesham; The Quay, Cliff Road; IP12 4QL

Busy pub with tables outside by the riverbank; nautical décor and a fair choice of drinks and good value food

Do arrive early on a fine day as the picnic-sets overlooking the River Deben get snapped up pretty quickly; some of the tables by the windows have the same view. This spot is a haven for bird-watchers and ramblers and river cruises are available nearby (though you have to pre-book). The spacious knocked-through bar is divided into separate areas by fireplaces or steps. There's a nautical theme, with an elaborate ship's model in a glass case and a few more in a light, high-ceilinged extension – as well as lots of old lanterns, pistols and aerial photographs; background music and board games. Adnams Southwold, Broadside and Ghost Ship on handpump and a fair choice of wines by the glass; board games.

The well thought-of food includes sandwiches, prawn and crayfish cocktail, baked baby camembert with tomato chutney, sharing platters, barbecue chicken with crispy bacon, smoked cheese and chips, veggie burger with caramelised red onion hummus, sausages with mash and cider gravy, cold or hot seafood boards, braised lamb shank with balsamic and red wine jus, and puddings such as chocolate brownie and blackberry panna cotta. *Benchmark main dish: beer-battered fish and chips £10.95. Two-course evening meal £17.00.*

Adnams ~ Lease Steve and Louise Lomas ~ Real ale ~ Open 9am-11pm ~ Bar food 9am-9.30pm ~ Restaurant ~ Children welcome ~ Dogs allowed in bar ~ Wi-fi
Recommended by Margaret and Peter Staples

The details at the end of each featured entry start by saying whether the pub is a free house, or if it belongs to a brewery or pub group (which we name).

WESTLETON
TM4469   Map 5

Crown 🕙 ⚲ 🛏

(01728) 648777 – www.westletoncrown.co.uk

B1125 Blythburgh–Leiston; IP17 3AD

Bustling old inn with a cosy chatty bar, plenty of dining areas, carefully chosen drinks and interesting food; comfortable modern bedrooms

Our readers enjoy staying in this stylish old coaching inn – the bedrooms are comfortable and spotlessly kept (some are in the main inn, others in converted stables and cottages); breakfasts are excellent. The heart of the place remains the attractive little bar with a lovely log fire and plenty of original features. Locals drop in here for a pint and a chat which keeps the atmosphere informal and relaxed, and they serve Adnams Southwold and Woodfordes Once Bittern with a couple of guests from breweries such as Green Jack and Nethergate on handpump, 13 wines by the glass from a thoughtful list and ten malt whiskies; background music and board games. There's also a parlour, a dining room and a conservatory, all manner of wooden dining chairs and tables and historic photographs on some fine old bare-brick walls. The charming terraced garden has plenty of seats and tables.

As well as breakfast for non-residents, the imaginative food includes lunchtime sandwiches, mussels with tomatoes, chilli and vodka, chicken, leek and black pudding terrine, gammon with bubble and squeak, fried egg and mustard sauce, smoked haddock and spring onion fishcake with watercress, lemon and chive butter sauce, jasmine tea-smoked duck with asian-spiced duck bun, stir-fried greens and duck and shiitake mushroom broth, roast lamb loin with seared kidney, red wine sauce and olive mash, and puddings such as rhubarb, elderflower and pink champagne jelly with lemon curd ice cream and dark chocolate ganache tart with raspberry compote and raspberry sorbet; they also offer a two- and three-course set lunch. *Benchmark main dish: beer-battered fish and chips £14.25. Two-course evening meal £23.00.*

Free house ~ Licensee Gareth Clarke ~ Real ale ~ Open 7am (7.30 Sun)-11pm ~ Bar food 12-2.30, 6.30-9.30 ~ Restaurant ~ Children welcome ~ Dogs allowed in bar and bedrooms ~ Wi-fi ~ Bedrooms: £90/£95 *Recommended by Tracey and Stephen Groves, Roy Hoing, Peter Smith and Judith Brown*

WHEPSTEAD
TL8258   Map 5

White Horse 🕙 ⚲

(01284) 735760 – www.whitehorsewhepstead.co.uk

Off B1066 S of Bury; Rede Road; IP29 4SS

Charmingly reworked country pub with attractively furnished rooms and well liked food and drink

There are plenty of areas for a drink or a meal in the several Victorian additions to what was originally a 17th-c building. The dark-beamed bar has a woodburning stove in a low fireplace, stools around pubby tables on a tiled floor, and boards listing the menu. Linked rooms have sturdy, country kitchen tables and chairs on striped carpeting or antique floor tiles, with some nicely cushioned traditional wall seats and some rather fine old farmhouse chairs. Oil paintings of food by a local artist (for sale) and old prints decorate walls painted in Farrow & Ball lichen green; the bookshelves have books that are actually worth reading. Adnams Southwold and Broadside on handpump and eight wines by the glass, served by attentive, friendly staff; the resident westie is called Skye. A tuck shop sells sweets, chocolates and ice-creams. The neat sheltered back terrace is brightened up by colourful oilcloth tablecloths, and birdsong, heard at the picnic-sets on the grass, emphasises what a peaceful spot this is.

Highly popular food includes ham hock terrine with home-made piccalilli, salmon gravadlax with sweet dill dressing, local sausages with paprika and tomato, chargrilled chicken caesar salad, madras-style fish curry, steak burger with spicy tomato jam and chips, grilled salmon on braised leeks with saffron and cream sauce, venison ragoût with juniper berries and dark chocolate, and puddings such as spotted dick with golden syrup and crème anglaise and chocolate brownie. *Benchmark main dish: smoked haddock with spinach and cream £13.95. Two-course evening meal £18.50.*

Free house ~ Licensees Gary and Di Kingshott ~ Real ale ~ Open 12-3, 7-11; 12-3 Sun ~ Bar food 12-2, 7-9 ~ Children welcome ~ Dogs welcome *Recommended by Mike and Mary Carter, Peter Pilbeam, Lindy Andrews*

Also Worth a Visit in Suffolk

Besides the fully inspected pubs, you might like to try these pubs that have been recommended to us and described by readers. Do tell us what you think of them: feedback@goodguides.com

ALDEBURGH   TM4656
White Hart (01728) 453205
High Street; IP15 5AJ Friendly one-room local in former reading room, panelling, stained-glass windows and high ceiling, Adnams ales and guests, decent wines by the glass, summer pizzas in back courtyard, open fire; no children inside, dogs welcome, open all day. *(Giles and Annie Francis)*

ALDRINGHAM   TM4461
Parrot & Punchbowl
(01728) 830221 *B1122/B1353 S of Leiston; IP16 4PY* Welcoming 17th-c beamed country pub, good fairly priced traditional food, well kept Adnams Southwold, Woodfordes Wherry and a guest, two-level restaurant; live music third Weds of month; children and dogs (in bar) welcome, nice sheltered garden, also family garden with adventure play area, closed Sun evening. *(Gus Swan)*

BADINGHAM   TM3068
White Horse (01728) 638280
A1120 S of village; IP13 8JR Welcoming 16th-c low-beamed pub refurbished under present owners; generous helpings of well liked food including themed nights, OAP lunch Mon-Thurs, Earl Soham and three guests, Aspall's and Weston's ciders, inglenook log fire and a couple of woodburners; charity quiz first Tues of month, local band last Tues; children, dogs and muddy boots welcome, neat bowling green and nice rambling garden, open all day Sun. *(Peter Pilbeam)*

BARHAM   TM1251
Sorrel Horse (01473) 830327
Old Norwich Road; IP6 0PG Friendly

open-plan beamed and timbered country inn with good log fire in central chimneybreast, well kept ales including Greene King, popular pubby food (all day weekends); free wi-fi; children and dogs welcome, disabled facilities, picnic-sets on side grass with big play area, bedrooms in converted barn, open all day Weds-Sun. *(Charlie May)*

BARTON MILLS   TL7217 3
Olde Bull (01638) 711001
Just S of Mildenhall; The Street; IP28 6AA Revamped former coaching inn with good food (not particularly cheap) from lunchtime sandwiches and pubby dishes to interesting restaurant choices, Adnams Broadside and a couple of guests, decent wine list and coffee, friendly staff; background and some live music; well behaved children welcome, no dogs inside, 15 individually styled bedrooms with plenty of quirky touches, open (and food) all day. *(D and M T Ayres-Regan)*

BILDESTON   TL9949
Crown (01449) 740510
B1115 SW of Stowmarket; IP7 7EB Picturesque and impressively refurbished 15th-c timbered country inn, smart beamed main bar with leather armchairs and inglenook log fire, more intimate back area with contemporary art, ales such as Greene King and nice choice of wines by the glass, good food from reworked pub favourites to upmarket choices including tasting menu in more formal dining room; children welcome, disabled access and parking, tables laid for eating in appealing central courtyard, more in large beautifully kept garden with decking, quiet comfortable bedrooms. *(Mrs Carolyn Dixon)*

BILDESTON   TL9949
Kings Head (01449) 741434
High Street; IP7 7ED Small beamed
16th-c village pub brewing its own good beers
(brewery tours), also local microbrewery
guests, well priced home-made food (Fri
evening, Sat, Sun lunchtime), pleasant
chatty staff, wood floor bar with inglenook
woodburner, darts; children welcome, back
garden with terrace and play equipment,
open all day weekends, closed Mon, Tues and
lunchtimes Weds-Fri. *(Peter Pilbeam)*

BLAXHALL   TM3656
Ship (01728) 688316
*Off B1069 S of Snape; can be reached
from A12 via Little Glemham; IP12 2DY*
Charming country setting for this popular
and friendly low-beamed 18th-c pub; good
reasonably priced traditional food in bar and
restaurant, well kept Adnams Southwold,
Woodfordes Wherry and guests, some live
music including folk in side room with piano;
children in eating areas, dogs in bar, eight
chalet bedrooms, good breakfast, open all day
weekends. *(Pat and Alan Timmon)*

BRAMFIELD   TM3973
★ Queens Head (01986) 784214
*The Street; A144 S of Halesworth;
IP19 9HT* Village pub next to interesting
church; various rooms with heavy beams,
timbering and exposed brickwork, country
kitchen-style furniture on carpet, local
artwork on walls, high-raftered lounge with
log fire in impressive fireplace, separate
bar also with open fires, Adnams ales and
enjoyable home-made food (not Sun evening
in winter) from ciabattas up, good friendly
service; regular live music; children away
from main bar area and dogs welcome,
picnic-sets in tiered garden; up for sale last
we heard, so may be changes. *(Caroline
Prescott, Gavin and Helle May, Simon Rodway,
Peter Smith and Judith Brown, Peter Meister)*

BRENT ELEIGH   TL9348
★ Cock (01787) 247371
A1141 SE of Lavenham; CO10 9PB
Timeless and friendly thatched country pub,
Adnams, Greene King Abbot and a guest,
organic farm cider, enjoyable traditional food
cooked by landlady, cosy ochre-walled snug
and second small room, antique floor tiles,
lovely coal fire, old photographs of village
(church well worth a look), darts, shove-
ha'penny and toad in the hole; well behaved
children and dogs welcome, picnic-sets up
on side grass with summer hatch service,
one bedroom, open all day Fri-Sun.
(Mrs Carolyn Dixon)

BROCKLEY GREEN   TL7247
★ Plough (01440) 786789
Hundon Road; CO10 8DT Friendly neatly
kept knocked-through bar, beams, timbers
and stripped brick, scrubbed tables and open

fire, good food from lunchtime sandwiches
and deli boards up, cheerful efficient staff,
three changing ales and good choice of
wines by the glass, several malt whiskies
too, restaurant; children and dogs welcome,
attractive grounds with peaceful country
views, comfortable bedrooms, open all day
weekends. *(Adele Summers, Alan Black)*

BUNGAY   TM3389
Castle (01986) 892283
Earsham Street; NR35 1AF Pleasantly
informal 16th-c dining inn with good
interesting food from chef-owner; opened-up
beamed interior with restaurant part at front,
two open fires, friendly efficient staff, Earl
Soham Victoria and a guest, Aspall's cider,
nice choice of wines by the glass, afternoon
teas, french windows to pretty courtyard
garden; children welcome, dogs in bar area,
four comfortable bedrooms, open all day
(till 4pm Sun) in summer. *(Gus Swan)*

BURY ST EDMUNDS   TL8463
Dove (01284) 702787
Hospital Road; IP33 3JU Friendly 19th-c
alehouse with rustic bare-boards bar and
separate parlour, half a dozen well kept beers
and some real ciders; quiz and folk nights,
maybe a local morris troupe; closed weekday
lunchtimes. *(Lindy Andrews)*

BURY ST EDMUNDS   TL8564
★ Nutshell (01284) 764867
*The Traverse, central pedestrian link
off Abbeygate Street; IP33 1BJ* Tiny
simple local with timeless interior (can be
a crush at busy times), lots of interest such
as a mummified cat (found walled up here)
hanging from dark brown ceiling along with
companion rat, bits of a skeleton, vintage
bank notes, cigarette packets, military and
other badges, spears and a great metal
halberd, one short wooden bench along
shopfront corner windows, a cut-down
sewing-machine table and an elbow rest
running along a rather battered counter,
Greene King ales, no food; background
music, steep narrow stairs up to lavatories;
children (till 7pm) and dogs welcome, open
all day. *(Barry Collett)*

BURY ST EDMUNDS   TL8564
One Bull (01284) 848220
Angel Hill; IP33 1UZ Smartly refurbished
pub with own Brewshed beers and local
guests, extensive choice of wines by the glass
and good food from sandwiches and sharing
boards up, friendly helpful staff; free wi-fi;
children till 6pm in bar (8pm restaurant),
closed Sun evening, otherwise open all day.
(Jeremy King)

BURY ST EDMUNDS   TL8563
★ Rose & Crown (01284) 755934
Whiting Street; IP33 1NP Cheerful
black-beamed corner local with long-serving
affable licensees, bargain simple lunchtime

home cooking (not Sun), particularly well kept Greene King ales (including XX Mild) and guests, pleasant lounge with lots of piggy pictures and bric-a-brac, good games-oriented public bar, rare separate off-sales counter; background radio, no credit cards or under-14s; pretty back courtyard, open all day weekdays. *(Lindy Andrews)*

BUXHALL   TM9957
★**Crown** (01449) 736521

Off B1115 W of Stowmarket; Mill Road; IP14 3DW A pub of two halves; steps down to cosy low-beamed bar on left with woodburner in brick inglenook, timbered dining area beyond, well kept Adnams Broadside, Earl Soham Victoria and nice choice of wines by the glass, light airy dining room to the right with its own bar and another woodburner, good interesting attractively presented food (not particularly cheap), friendly service; children and dogs welcome, plenty of tables on terrace with views over open country (ignore the pylons), herb garden, closed Sun evening, Mon. *(R A P Cross, Jeremy King)*

CAVENDISH   TL8046
Bull (01787) 280245

A1092 Long Melford–Clare; CO10 8AX New management and some refurbishment for this traditional old pub; heavy beams, timbers and fine fireplaces, Nethergate Suffolk County and up to four guests, a real cider on handpump too, enjoyable reasonably priced pub food (not Sun evening), good friendly service; charity quiz first Sun of month; children in eating areas, no dogs inside, paved back terrace with steps up to car park (useful in this picturesque honeypot village), open all day weekends, closed Tues. *(Gus Swan)*

CAVENDISH   TL8046
★**George** (01787) 280248

A1092; The Green; CO10 8BA Restauaranty 16th-c inn with contemporary feel in two bow-windowed front areas, beams and timbers, big woodburner in stripped-brick fireplace, very well liked food from interesting varied menu including set deals, two Nethergate ales and plenty of wines by the glass, Aspall's cider, back servery and further eating area, charming young staff, daily newspapers; children and well behaved dogs welcome, stylish furniture on sheltered back terrace, tree-shaded garden with lovely village church behind, five bedrooms up rather steep staircase, good breakfast, open all day except Sun evening. *(Robert and Sarah Milne, Marianne and Peter Stevens)*

CHELSWORTH   TL9848
Peacock (01449) 740758

B1115 Sudbury–Needham Market; IP7 7HU Prettily set old dining pub with lots of Tudor brickwork and exposed beams, separate pubby bar with big inglenook,

local ales and fairly standard food (not Sun evening), friendly service; dogs welcome (resident greyhounds), four bedrooms, attractive small garden and village. *(Edward May)*

CHILLESFORD   TM3852
★**Froize** (01394) 450282

B1084 E of Woodbridge; IP12 3PU Restaurant rather than pub (open only when they serve food, so not Mon or evenings Sun-Weds), pleasant bar and restaurant, reliably good if not cheap buffet-style food from owner-chef using carefully sourced local produce including game, nice wines by the glass and well kept Adnams, warmly welcoming service, little deli next to bar; no dogs inside. *(Gus Swan)*

CREETING ST MARY   TM1155
Highwayman (01449) 760369

A140, just N of junction with A14; IP6 8PD Attractively modernised 17th-c pub with two bars and pleasant galleried barn extension, welcoming landlord and friendly relaxed atmosphere, good freshly cooked food from landlady-chef, well kept H&H Olde Trip and Woodfordes Wherry, decent wines; unobtrusive background music; children welcome, no dogs inside, tables on gravel terrace and back lawn with pretty pond, closed Sun evening, Mon. *(David Twitchett)*

CRETINGHAM   TM2260
Bell (01728) 685419

The Street; IP13 7BJ Attractive old pub refurbished by current friendly owners; good home-made food and well kept ales such as Adnams and Earl Soham, nice wines by the glass, bare-boards bar, dining tables in tiled second room, beams and timbers, leather sofa and armchairs by woodburner; dogs welcome in snug, garden picnic-sets. *(J F M and M West)*

DENNINGTON   TM2867
★**Queen** (01728) 638241

A1120; The Square; IP13 8AB Beamed and timbered Tudor pub-restaurant prettily placed by church, L-shaped main bar with log fire, Adnams and maybe a guest, Aspall's cider, good food (best to book weekends) including some interesting specials, friendly welcoming staff; background music, daily papers; children in family room, side lawn by noble lime trees, decking and carp pond behind, backs on to Dennington Park with swings etc. *(Edward May)*

EARL SOHAM   TM2263
Victoria (01728) 685758

A1120 Yoxford–Stowmarket; IP13 7RL Simple two-bar pub serving Earl Soham beers from nearby brewery, kitchen chairs and pews, scrubbed country tables, tiled or bare board floors, panelling and open fire, reasonably priced unfussy home-cooked food; outside gents'; children and dogs welcome, seats out in front and on raised back lawn, handy for working windmill at Saxted. *(Sheila Topham, Pat and Tony Martin, J F M and M West)*

EAST BERGHOLT   TM0734
Kings Head (01206) 298190
Burnt Oak, towards Flatford Mill; CO7 6TL Refurbished 17th-c village dining pub, good freshly made food including lunchtime set offer, Adnams, Crouch Vale and guests, good choice of wines, pleasant staff; live music first Sun of month; children and dogs welcome, side garden and terrace, handy for Flatford Mill (NT), closed Mon lunchtime, otherwise open all day, from 9.30am weekends for breakfast.
(Carolyn Dixon)

EASTON   TM2858
★ White Horse (01728) 746456
N of Wickham Market on back road to Earl Soham and Framlingham; IP13 0ED Attractive early 18th-c pub with three smart but simple rooms, farmhouse tables, country kitchen chairs, pews and settles, open fires, Adnams Southwold and two local guests, ten wines by the glass, good locally sourced food including blackboard specials, friendly staff, restaurant; background music; children and dogs welcome, seats out at front and in back garden, good local walks, open (and food) all day weekends. *(Ian Phillips, J F M and M West)*

EDWARDSTONE   TL9542
★ White Horse (01787) 211211
Mill Green, just E; village signed off A1071 in Boxford; CO10 5PX Unpretentious pub with own good Mill Green beers and guests, various sized bars with lots of beer mats, rustic prints and photos on walls, second-hand tables and chairs including an old steamer bench and panelled settle on bare boards, woodburner and open fire, well liked food (booking advised); bar billiards, darts, ring the bull and other games, regular beer/music festivals; children and dogs welcome, end terrace with sturdy teak furniture, attractive smokers' shelter, makeshift picnic-sets on grass, two scandinavian-style self-catering 'cottages' plus campsite with shower block, open (and food) all day in summer. *(Giles and Annie Francis, Mrs Margo Finlay, Jörg Kasprowski, Jeremy King)*

EYE   TM1473
Queens Head (01379) 870153
Cross Street; IP23 7AB Three-room beamed pub under newish management; Adnams and local guests tapped from the cask, 11 wines by the glass and good fairly priced food (not Sun evening) cooked by landlord including fish specials, friendly accommodating staff; background music; children and dogs (theirs is Franco) welcome, garden with play area, open all day (Sun till 9pm), breakfast from 8.30am.
(Bev Page)

FELIXSTOWE   TM2734
Fludyers Arms (01394) 691929
Undercliff Road E; IP11 4SH Restored and extended Edwardian pub-hotel on seafront, opened-up bare boards bar, several dining areas including panelled restaurant, Adnams, Woodfordes and guests, popular food from bar snacks up including set menu, good friendly service; events such as live jazz; children welcome, sea views from heated front terrace, 12 bedrooms and mews apartment, open (and food) all day.
(Mrs M S Forbes)

FELIXSTOWE FERRY   TM3237
Ferry Boat (01394) 284203
Off Ferry Road, on the green; IP11 9RZ Much-modernised 17th-c pub tucked between golf links and dunes near harbour, martello tower and summer rowing-boat ferry; enjoyable fair value pub food including good fish dishes, friendly efficient staff (may ask for a credit card while you eat), well kept Adnams Southwold, Woodfordes Wherry and a guest, decent coffee, warm log fire; background music; children and dogs welcome, tables out in front, on green opposite and in fenced garden, good coast walks, open all day weekends and busy in the summer. *(J F M and M West)*

FRAMLINGHAM   TM2863
Crown (01728) 723521
Market Hill; IP13 9AP Stylishly updated 16th-c beamed coaching inn, good food from lunchtime sandwiches and pizzas up, Greene King and guests, several wines by the glass, friendly helpful staff, open fires; background and some live acoustic music, free wi-fi; children and dogs welcome, tables in back courtyard, 14 bedrooms, open all day.
(Peter Pilbeam)

FRAMLINGHAM   TM2862
Station Hotel (01728) 723455
Station Road (B1116 S); IP13 9EE Simple high-ceilinged big-windowed bar with scrubbed tables on stripped boards, candles in bottles, well kept Earl Soham ales and good choice of house wines, popular freshly cooked food from interesting menu, wood-fired pizzas too, friendly staff and relaxed atmosphere, back snug with tiled floor;

A star symbol before the name of a pub shows exceptional character and appeal. It doesn't mean extra comfort. Even quite a basic pub can win a star, if it's individual enough.

children and dogs welcome, picnic-sets in pleasant garden. *(J F M and M West)*

FRESSINGFIELD TM2677
★**Fox & Goose** (01379) 586247
Church Street; B1116 N of Framlingham; IP21 5PB Relaxed dining pub in beautifully timbered 16th-c building next to church, very good food in cosy informal heavy-beamed rooms with log fire, upstairs restaurant, friendly efficient service, good wines by the glass, Adnams and a guest tapped from the cask in side bar; faint background music; children welcome, downstairs disabled facilities, tables out by duck pond, closed Mon. *(W K Wood)*

GREAT BRICETT TM0450
Red Lion (01473) 657799
B1078, E of Bildeston; IP7 7DD Old extended beamed pub serving very good interesting vegetarian and vegan food at competitive prices (nothing for meat eaters), children's menu and takeaways too; dogs welcome in bar, garden with deck and play equipment, closed Mon. *(Mrs Carolyn Dixon)*

GREAT GLEMHAM TM3461
Crown (01728) 663693
Between A12 Wickham Market–Saxmundham and B1119 Saxmundham–Framlingham; IP17 2DA Early 19th-c red-brick village pub again under new management; traditionally restored interior with some nice old suffolk furniture on wood and quarry-tiled floors, two big fireplaces, good range of mostly local beers from old brass handpumps, enjoyable food (not Sun evening, Tues) including pub favourites, back coffee lounge with freshly baked cakes, friendly helpful staff; some acoustic music, monthly quiz, darts, table skittles, free wi-fi; well behaved children and dogs welcome, disabled facilities, cast-iron furniture on back lawn, self-catering cottage, open all day weekends, closed Tues lunchtime. *(Charlie May)*

GREAT WRATTING TL6848
Red Lion (01440) 783237
School Road; CB9 7HA Popular country pub with a couple of ancient whale bones flanking the entrance; well kept Adnams in log-fire bar with lots of copper and brass, ample helpings of enjoyable pub food, friendly welcoming staff, restaurant; children allowed – big garden for them to play in, open all day Sat. *(Adele Summers, Alan Black)*

GRUNDISBURGH TM2250
★**Dog** (01473) 735267
The Green; off A12 via B1079 from Woodbridge bypass; IP13 6TA Friendly pink-washed pub with villagey public bar, log fire, settles and dark wooden carvers around pubby tables on tiles, Adnams, Earl Soham, Woodfordes and a guest, half a dozen wines by the glass, well liked good value

food including daily specials, set lunch deal Tues-Sat, relaxing carpeted lounge linking to bare-boards dining room; children and dogs (in bar) welcome, picnic-sets out in front by flowering tubs, more seats in wicker-fenced mediterranean-feel back garden, play area, open all day Fri-Sun, closed Mon. *(Pat and Alan Timmon, J F M and M West)*

HADLEIGH TM0242
Kings Head (01473) 828855
High Street; IP7 5EF Modernised old pub with popular food from daily changing menu, also good wood-fired pizzas, Adnams, Greene King, Crouch Vale and guests, Aspall's cider, friendly staff; open all day (Sun till 5pm). *(Mrs Carolyn Dixon)*

HADLEIGH TM0242
Ram (01473) 822880
Market Place; IP7 5DL Popular smartly refurbished bar-restaurant (sister to the Swan at Long Melford and Greyhound at Lavenham) facing Georgian corn exchange; good well presented food (not Sun evening) including fixed-price menu, brunch from 10am, plenty of wines by the glass from extensive list, cocktails and Greene King IPA, efficient service; children welcome, small courtyard garden behind, open all day (Sun till 7pm). *(Mrs Carolyn Dixon)*

HAWKEDON TL7953
★**Queens Head** (01284) 789218
Off A143 at Wickham Street, NE of Haverhill; and off B1066; IP29 4NN Flint Tudor pub in pretty setting looking down broad peaceful green to interesting largely Norman village church; quarry-tiled bar with dark beams and ochre walls, plenty of pews and chapel chairs around scrubbed tables, elderly armchairs by antique woodburner in huge fireplace, cheerful helpful staff, Adnams, Woodfordes and guests, proper cider/perry and nice choice of wines, good popular food (not Mon, Tues) using home-reared meat, dining area stretching back with country prints and a couple of tusky boars' heads; some live music; picnic-sets out in front, more on back terrace overlooking rolling country, little shop (Fri and Sat mornings) selling their own bacon, pies, casseroles etc, open all day Fri-Sun, closed lunchtimes Mon-Thurs. *(R A P Cross)*

HITCHAM TL9851
White Horse (01449) 740981
The Street (B1115 Sudbury–Stowmarket); IP7 7NQ Welcoming 16th-c village pub – former staging post for travellers between London and Norfolk; two beamed and timbered bars, a couple of local ales such as Adnams and Earl Soham, enjoyable fairly pubby food at reasonable prices, dark wood chairs around clothed tables in restaurant; children and dogs welcome, three bedrooms in separate block. *(Iain Lister)*

HOLBROOK   TM1636
Compasses (01473) 328332
Ipswich Road; IP9 2QR Roomy simple
village pub with enjoyable straightforward
food including children's, prompt friendly
service, well kept Adnams and Sharps Doom
Bar, Aspall's cider, big log fire, restaurant;
seats out at front under cover, garden with
play area, good walks nearby. *(David and
Judy Robison)*

IPSWICH   TM1644
Dove Street (01473) 211270
St Helen's Street; IP4 2LA Over 20 well
kept quickly changing ales including their
own brews (regular beer festivals), farm
ciders, bottled beers and good selection
of whiskies, low priced simple pub food
including substantial pork pies, hot drinks,
bare-boards bar, carpeted snug and back
conservatory; dogs welcome, children till
7pm, seats on heated covered terrace, two
bedrooms and brewery shop across the
road, open (and food) all day.
(Tony Hobden)

IPSWICH   TM1645
Greyhound (01473) 252862
Henley Road/Anglesea Road; IP1 3SE
Popular 19th-c pub close to Christchurch
Park; cosy front bar, corridor to larger
lounge/dining area, five well kept Adnams
ales and a couple of guests, good home
cooking including bargain weekday lunch
and daily specials, quick friendly service;
Sun quiz, sports TV, free wi-fi; children
welcome, picnic-sets under parasols on back
terrace, open all day Fri-Sun (breakfast Sun
from 10am). *(Lindy Andrews)*

IPSWICH   TM1747
Railway Inn (01473) 252337
Westerfield Road; IP6 9AA Refurbished
pub popular locally for its good reasonably
priced food (all day weekends) including set
menus and daily specials, three well kept ales
from Adnams and several wines by the glass,
pleasant attentive service; children and dogs
(in bar area) welcome, four new bedrooms,
tables outside, open all day Fri-Sun.
(J F M and M West)

IPSWICH   TM1744
Woolpack (01473) 215862
Tuddenham Road; IP4 2SH Welcoming
traditional red-brick pub dating from the
1600s, Adnams and four other well kept ales,
several wines by the glass and good coffee,
popular fairly priced home-cooked food
including blackboard specials, two bars, snug
and back dining area, corner with piano and
board games; live music and quiz nights;
dogs welcome, seats on heated front terrace,
opposite Christchurch Park, open all day
from 9.30am for breakfast. *(Gus Swan)*

KERSEY   TM0044
Bell (01473) 823229
*Signed off A1141 N of Hadleigh;
The Street; IP7 6DY* Ancient black and
white pub in notably picturesque village;
good value traditional home-made food (not
Mon evening), Adnams Broadside, Greene
King IPA and a guest, friendly helpful service,
low-beamed log-fire bar with dining area,
restaurant; children and dogs (in bar)
welcome, sheltered back terrace, open
all day. *(Paul and Marion Watts)*

KESGRAVE   TM2346
Kesgrave Hall (01473) 333741
Hall Road; IP5 2PU Country hotel with
comfortably contemporary bare-boards bar,
Adnams and a couple of guests from granite-
topped servery, several wines by the glass and
cocktails, popular often imaginative food in
open-kitchen brasserie (no booking so best
to arrive early), efficient young staff; children
and dogs welcome, attractive heated terrace
with huge retractable awning, 23 stylish
bedrooms, open (and food) all day.
(J F M and M West)

LAVENHAM   TL9149
★ Angel (01787) 247388
Market Place; CO10 9QZ Handsome Tudor
building under new management (Cozy Pubs
Co); long bar with inglenook log fire and
some fine 16th-c ceiling plasterwork, relaxed
feel with chesterfield sofas and armchairs,
further dining areas and more heavy beams
and panelling, good freshly made seasonal
food from interesting sandwiches, deli boards
and pub favourites up, well kept ales such as
Adnams and Woodfordes, Aspall's cider and
good range of wines, efficient friendly staff;
children and dogs (in bar) welcome, sizeable
back garden, eight refurbished bedrooms,
delightful small town, open all day from
8am (10am Sun). *(Toby Jones, Emma Scofield,
Bill Adie, Mrs Carolyn Dixon)*

LAVENHAM   TL9149
Greyhound (01787) 249553
High Street; CO10 9PZ Refurbished
14th-c pub under same management as the
Swan at Long Melford and Ram at Hadleigh;
Greene King IPA and four guests, a dozen
wines by the glass, good food from varied
menu including some thoughtful vegetarian
choices, brunch from 10am, friendly service,
opened-up beamed interior with inglenook
woodburner; children and dogs (in bar)
welcome, back terrace, open all day.
(Mrs Carolyn Dixon)

We include some hotels with a good bar that offers facilities
comparable to those of a pub.

LAVENHAM
TL9149

Swan (01787) 247477

High Street; CO10 9QA Smart hotel incorporating handsome medieval buildings, appealing network of beamed and timbered alcoves and more open areas, tiled-floor inner bar with memorabilia from its days as the local for US 48th Bomber Group, well kept Adnams and a guest, wide choice of good food in informal brasserie or lavishly timbered restaurant, efficient young staff; children and dogs welcome, sheltered courtyard garden, 45 bedrooms, open all day. *(Ian and Rose Lock, Mrs Carolyn Dixon, Bill Adie)*

LAXFIELD
TM2972

★ Kings Head (01986) 798395

Gorams Mill Lane, behind church; IP13 8DW Unspoilt thatched pub with no bar counter – Adnams ales and a guest poured in tap room; interesting little chequer-tiled front room dominated by three-sided booth of high-backed settles in front of old range fire, two other rooms with pews, old seats and scrubbed deal tables, well liked tasty food including good home-made pies, friendly helpful staff; children and dogs welcome, neatly kept garden with arbour and small pavilion for cooler evenings, boules, two bedrooms, open all day (till 7pm Sun). *(Peter Brix)*

LAXFIELD
TM2972

Royal Oak (01986) 798666

High Street; IP13 8DH Extended Tudor pub next to 14th-c church; beams, old quarry tiles and inglenook, half a dozen well kept ales including Adnams and Woodfordes, good value food (not Sun evening) served by friendly staff; quiz and music nights; children and dogs welcome, tables out in front, open all day. *(Rita Scarratt)*

LEVINGTON
TM2339

Ship (01473) 659573

Gun Hill; from A14/A12 Bucklesham roundabout take A1156 exit, then first sharp left into Felixstowe Road, after nearly a mile, the village and pub are signed to right; IP10 0LQ Charming old part-thatched village pub under new management; beams, timber dividers and some nautical trappings, settles and built-in wall benches, inglenook woodburner, Adnams ales and good locally sourced food cooked by landlord, friendly attentive staff, restaurant; children and dogs welcome, beside little lime-washed church and has views (if a little obscured) over River Orwell estuary, good circular walk, open all day. *(Mrs Carolyn Dixon)*

LONG MELFORD
TL8645

Bull (01787) 378494

Hall Street (B1064); CO10 9JG Small 15th-c hotel in good location and full of character; old-fashioned timbered front lounge with beautifully carved beams,

antique furnishings, log fire in huge fireplace, more spacious back bar with sporting prints, well kept Greene King ales and a guest, Aspall's cider, decent wines, reasonably priced standard Old English Inns menu, good service, restaurant; children welcome, tables in attractive courtyard, comfortable bedrooms and substantial breakfast, open all day weekends. *(Anon)*

LONG MELFORD
TL8645

Crown (01787) 377666

Hall Street; CO10 9JL Partly 17th-c inn with four well kept ales including Adnams and Greene King, central servery with unusual bar chairs, log fire, some stripped brickwork and tartan carpet, oak-floored restaurant with high-backed chairs and vibrant red walls, good locally sourced food (all day Sun) from bar snacks up, friendly helpful service; tables under parasols on attractive split-level terrace, 12 well equipped bedrooms, open all day. *(Alan Thwaite)*

LONG MELFORD
TL8645

Swan (01787) 464545

Hall Street; CO10 9JQ Well run beamed dining pub (same group as Greyhound at Lavenham and Ram at Hadleigh); good up-to-date food (best to book) from daily changing menu, set choices weekday lunchtimes and Mon-Thurs evenings, well selected wines, cocktails and a couple of real ales, obliging service, pastel grey-green décor with high-backed dining chairs on bare boards, modern artwork; unobtrusive background music; tables outside, open all day (till 7pm Sun). *(Alan Thwaite)*

LOWESTOFT
TM5593

Triangle (01502) 582711

St Peter's Street; NR32 1QA Popular two-bar tap for Green Jack ales, guest beers too and real cider, regular beer festivals, breweriana, open fire; pool and TV in back bar, live music Fri; open all day (till 1am Fri, Sat). *(Gus Swan)*

MELTON
TM2850

Olde Coach & Horses

(01394) 384851 *Melton Road; IP12 1PD* Attractively modernised beamed former staging inn, good choice of enjoyable fairly priced food from sandwiches, snacks and sharing plates up (special diets catered for), Adnams and decent wines by the glass, good friendly service; free wi-fi; children welcome, dogs in wood-floored area, tables outside under parasols, colourful hanging baskets and planters, open all day from 9am for breakfast. *(Nick and Gillian Harrison)*

MONKS ELEIGH
TL9647

Swan (01449) 763163

A1141 NW of Hadleigh; IP7 7AU Refurbished thatched and beamed pub overlooking small village green (same owners as Anchor at Nayland and Angel at Stoke-by-Nayland), good food (not Mon) from bar snacks to interesting restaurant dishes, Fri night tapas, Adnams Southwold and a guest, plenty of wines by the glass including champagne, friendly accommodating staff; quiz second Sun of month; children welcome, dogs in bar, open all day Fri-Sun. *(Mrs Carolyn Dixon)*

MOULTON   TL6964
Packhorse (01638) 751818
Bridge Street; CB8 8SP Stylishly revamped and more restaurant-with-rooms than pub; good popular (if pricey) food from owner-chef including some inventive choices (must book), carve your own Sun roast at the table, well kept Adnams Ghost Ship, Woodfordes Wherry and a guest, good wines by the glass, pleasant attentive service; dogs welcome, adjacent to delightful 15th-c bridge across the Kennett, handy for Newmarket races, four bedrooms, open all day. *(J F M and M West, John and Enid, Caroline Prescott)*

NAYLAND   TL9734
★Anchor (01206) 262313
Court Street; just off A134 – turn-off S of signposted B1087 main village turn; CO6 4JL Friendly pub by River Stour under same ownership as the Angel at Stoke-by-Nayland and Swan at Monks Eleigh; bare-boards bar with assorted wooden dining chairs and tables, big gilt mirror on silvery wallpaper one end, another mirror above pretty fireplace at the other, five changing ales and several wines by the glass, interesting food (some home-smoked) along with more standard dishes, Fri evening tapas, two other rooms behind and steep stairs up to cosy restaurant; quiz last Sun of month; children welcome, dogs in bar, terrace tables overlooking river, open all day. *(Peter Brix)*

NEWBOURNE   TM2743
★Fox (01473) 736307
Off A12 at roundabout 1.7 miles N of A14 junction; The Street; IP12 4NY Pink-washed 16th-c pub decked with summer flowers, low-beamed bar with slabby elm and other dark tables on tiled floor, stuffed fox in inglenook, comfortable carpeted dining room with various mirrors, Adnams Southwold and guests, decent wines by the glass, good variety of well liked food including reasonably priced Sun roasts, good service; background music, free wi-fi; children and dogs (in bar) welcome, wheelchair access, attractive grounds with rose garden and pond, open (and food) all day. *(Lindy Andrews)*

ORFORD   TM4249
★Jolly Sailor (01394) 450243
Quay Street; IP12 2NU Welcoming old pub under mother and daughter team; several

snug rooms with exposed brickwork, boating pictures and other nautical memorabilia, four well kept Adnams beers and popular sensibly priced food from lunchtime sandwiches up, friendly efficient service, unusual spiral staircase in corner of flagstoned main bar by brick inglenook, horsebrasses and local photographs, two cushioned pews and long antique stripped-deal table, maybe local sea shanty group; free wi-fi; children and dogs welcome, tables on back terrace and lawn with views over marshes, popular with walkers and bird-watchers, bedrooms, open all day weekends. *(Brian Glozier, Roger and Pauline Pearce, Penny Lang)*

POLSTEAD   TL9938
Cock (01206) 263150
Signed off B1068 and A1071 E of Sudbury, then pub signed; Polstead Green; CO6 5AL Welcoming 16th-c beamed and timbered village local; bar with woodburner, Greene King IPA and two guests, good choice of wines and enjoyable reasonably priced home-made food from lunchtime sandwiches up, helpful friendly staff, light and airy barn restaurant; background music; children and dogs welcome, disabled facilities, picnic-sets overlooking small green, open all day Sat, closed Sun evening. *(Carol and Luke Wilson)*

RAMSHOLT   TM3041
Ramsholt Arms (01394) 411209
Signed off B1083; Dock Road; IP12 3AB Lovely isolated spot overlooking River Deben and under same management as the Crown at Ufford; modernised open-plan bar busy on summer weekends and handy for bird walks and Sutton Hoo (NT), enjoyable food from lunchtime sandwiches up, Adnams and a couple of guests, decent wines by the glass, log fire; children and dogs welcome, plenty of tables outside taking in the view, open all day in high summer, best to check other times (may close Jan). *(Nick and Gillian Harrison, N R White)*

REYDON   TM4977
★Randolph (01502) 723603
Wangford Road (B1126 just NW of Southwold); IP18 6PZ Stylish inn with quite an emphasis on dining and bedroom side; bar with high-backed leather dining chairs around chunky wooden tables on parquet floor, sofa and a couple of comfortable armchairs, prints of pub from 1910 and photographs of Southwold beach, Adnams beers, dining room with more high-backed chairs on red carpet, pretty little Victorian fireplace filled with candles, nicely varied menu including children's choices, pleasant staff; background music, TV, games machine; dogs welcome in small back bar, wheelchair access, picnic-sets on decked area and grass, ten bedrooms, good breakfast, open all day. *(N R White)*

ROUGHAM   TL9063

★ **Ravenwood Hall** (01359) 270345
Off A14 E of Bury St Edmunds;
IP30 9JA Country-house hotel with two
compact bar rooms, tall ceilings, patterned
wallpaper and big heavily draped windows
overlooking sweeping lawn with stately cedar,
back area set for eating with upholstered
settles and dining chairs, sporting prints and
log fire, very good well presented food (own
smoked meats and fish), well kept Adnams,
good choice of wines and malt whiskies,
pleasant attentive staff, comfortable lounge
area with horse pictures, a few moulded
beams and early Tudor wall decoration
above big inglenook, separate more formal
restaurant; background music; children and
dogs welcome, teak furniture in garden,
swimming pool and croquet, geese, pygmy
goats and shetland ponies in big enclosures,
14 bedrooms, open 9am-midnight.
(J F M and M West)

SAXTEAD GREEN   TM2564
Old Mill House (01728) 685064
B1119; The Green; IP13 9QE Roomy
dining pub across green from windmill,
beamed carpeted bar, neat country-look
flagstoned restaurant extension, wooden
tables and chairs, good choice of generous
well priced fresh food (all day Sun) including
daily carvery, good friendly service, well kept
Greene King ales and decent wines; discreet
background music; children very welcome,
attractive garden with terrace and good play
area, open all day Sun. *(J F M and M West)*

SHOTTISHAM   TM3244
Sorrel Horse (01394) 411617
Hollesley Road; IP12 3HD Charming
15th-c thatched community-owned local;
well kept Adnams, Earl Soham, Woodfordes
and guests tapped from casks, decent choice
of home-made traditional food including
deals, attentive helpful young staff, good
log fire in tiled-floor bar with games area
(bar billiards), woodburner in attractive
dining room, fortnightly quiz Weds, free
wi-fi; children and dogs welcome, tables out
on sloping front lawn and in small garden
behind, open all day weekends. *(Peter Brix)*

SNAPE   TM3958
★ **Crown** (01728) 688324
Bridge Road (B1069); IP17 1SL Small
well laid-out 15th-c beamed pub with brick
floors, inglenook log fire and fine double
suffolk settle, well kept Adnams ales, good
fresh food using local ingredients including
own meat (reared behind the pub), reasonable
prices, efficient friendly young staff; folk
night last Thurs of month, darts, free wi-fi;
children and dogs welcome, garden, two
bedrooms. *(Pat and Alan Timmon)*

SNAPE   TM4058
★ **Golden Key** (01728) 688510
Priory Lane; IP17 1SA Traditionally
furnished village pub with low-beamed
lounge, old-fashioned settle and
straightforward tables and chairs on
chequerboard tiled floor, log fire, small snug
and two dining rooms, well kept Adnams ales,
local cider and a dozen wines by the glass,
enjoyable food from monthly changing menu,
friendly attentive staff; children and dogs
welcome, two terraces with pretty hanging
baskets and seats under large parasols,
handy for the Maltings, three comfortable
bedrooms, open all day weekends. *(Tracey
and Stephen Groves, Susan and Jeremy Arthern,
Peter Smith and Judith Brown)*

SNAPE   TM3957
★ **Plough & Sail** (01728) 688413
The Maltings, Snape Bridge (B1069 S);
IP17 1SR Nicely placed dining pub (part
of the Maltings complex) airily extended
around original 16th-c core, mostly open-plan
with good blend of traditional and modern
furnishings, Adnams Bitter, Woodfordes
Wherry and guests, a dozen wines by the
glass including champagne, good bistro-style
food (pre- and post-concert menus), spacious
dining room and upstairs restaurant, efficient
well organised service; background music;
children and dogs (in bar) welcome, teak
furniture on flower-filled terrace, picnic-sets
at front, open all day. *(Edward Mirzoeff,
N R White, Tracey and Stephen Groves)*

SOUTHWOLD   TM5076
★ **Crown** (01502) 722275
High Street; IP18 6DP Civilised hotel with
popular oak-panelled back locals' bar (dogs
allowed here), red leatherette wall benches
on red carpet, three Adnams ales and
14 wines by the glass from good list, elegant
beamed front bar with settles and fine carved
fireplace, first rate imaginative food, friendly
courteous staff; children welcome, seats
outside in sunny sheltered corner, smart
comfortable bedrooms, good breakfast, open
all day from 8am. *(Sheila Topham, M and GR,
David Carr, Ian Herdman, Colin McLachlan,
John and Enid)*

SOUTHWOLD   TM5076
★ **Red Lion** (01502) 722385
South Green; IP18 6ET Cheerful pubby
front bar with big windows looking over green
towards the sea, sturdy wall benches and
bar stools on flagstones, well kept Adnams
including seasonals, quieter back room with
mate's chairs, cushioned pews and polished
dark tables on pale woodstrip flooring,
seaside cartoons by Giles, Mac and the like,
good range of popular reasonably priced food
served by friendly neatly dressed staff, three

We say if we know a pub allows dogs.

linked dining rooms; background music (live Sun afternoon); tables out in front and in small sheltered back courtyard, right by the Adnams retail shop. *(Peter Pilbeam)*

SOUTHWOLD   TM5076

Sole Bay (01502) 723736

East Green; IP18 6JN Busy pub near Adnams Brewery, their full range kept well and good wine choice, cheerful efficient staff, enjoyable reasonably priced simple food (not Sun evening) including good fish and chips, airy interior with well spaced tables, conservatory; sports TV; children and dogs welcome, disabled facilities, picnic-sets outside, moments from sea and lighthouse, open all day. *(David Carr, N R White)*

SOUTHWOLD   TM5076

★ **Swan** (01502) 722186

Market Place; IP18 6EG Relaxed comfortable back bar in smart Adnams-owned hotel, their full range kept well and bottled beers, good wines and malt whiskies, enjoyable bar food including lunchtime set menu (Mon-Sat), cheerful competent staff, coffee and teas in luxurious chintzy front lounge, restaurant; nice garden, 42 bedrooms – some in separate block where (by arrangement) dogs can stay too, good breakfast. *(M and GR, David Carr, Ian Herdman)*

STANSFIELD   TL7851

Compasses (01284) 789263

High Street; CO10 8LN Simple little country pub with good often interesting food (some from next door farm) cooked by character landlord, own-brewed beers and local guests, beams, bare boards and large woodburner, walkers and dogs welcome, outside tables with lovely rural views, good walks, open all day weekends, closed Mon, Tues. *(Anon)*

STOKE ASH   TM1170

White Horse (01379) 678222

A140/Workhouse Road; IP23 7ET Sizeable 17th-c roadside coaching inn, beams and inglenook fireplaces, generous helpings of good reasonably priced pub food all day from 8am, well kept Adnams, Greene King and Woodfordes, local Calvors lager and Aspall's cider, prompt friendly service from young staff; children welcome, bedrooms in modern annexe. *(Robert and Sarah Milne)*

STOKE-BY-NAYLAND   TL9836

★ **Angel** (01206) 263245

B1068 Sudbury–East Bergholt; CO6 4SA Elegant and comfortable 17th-c inn; lounge with handsome beams, timbers and stripped brickwork, leather chesterfields and wing armchairs around low tables, pictures of local scenes, more formal room with deep glass-covered well, chatty bar with straightforward furniture on red tiles, well kept Banks's Mansfield and a guest, ten wines by the

glass, wide range of enterprising food (all day weekends) served promptly by friendly uniformed staff; children and dogs (in bar) welcome, seats on sheltered terrace, six individually styled bedrooms, open all day from 8am (midday Sun). *(N R White, MDN, Mrs Carolyn Dixon)*

STOWMARKET   TW0558

Kings Arms (01449) 675232

Station Road East; IP14 1RQ Friendly double-fronted Victorian pub with three rooms, half a dozen mainly local ales including Woodfordes Wherry, Weston's cider, straightforward food; pool, TV; dogs welcome when not too busy, back terrace and a room for occasional live music, also beer festivals and barbecues, open all day and handy for station. *(Tony and Wendy Hobden)*

STOWMARKET   TM0457

Magpie (01449) 612727

Combs Ford; IP14 2AP Friendly beamed local with enjoyable home-made food including good value Sun carvery, Greene King IPA, Sharps Doom Bar and four or five guests, pleasant conservatory; weekend live music, darts, pool, sports TV, fruit machine; closed Tues lunchtime, otherwise open all day. *(John Middlemiss)*

STUTTON   TM1434

Gardeners Arms (01473) 328868

Manningtree Road, Upper Street (B1080); IP9 2TG Cottagey roadside pub on edge of small village, well kept Adnams Southwold and guests, enjoyable home-made food including daily specials and OAP meals, friendly helpful service, cosy L-shaped bar with log fire, side dining room and larger area stretching to the back, lots of bric-a-brac, film posters and musical instruments; children and dogs (on leads) welcome, two-tier back garden with pond, open all day Sun, closed Mon. *(N R White)*

SUDBURY   TL8741

Brewery Tap (01787) 370876

East Street; CO10 2TP Corner tap for Mauldons Brewery, their range and guests kept well, good choice of malt whiskies, bare boards and scrubbed tables, some food (can bring your own); darts, cribbage and bar billiards, live music and quiz nights; dogs welcome, open all day. *(Lindy Andrews)*

SWILLAND   TM1852

Moon & Mushroom (01473) 785320

Off B1078; IP6 9LR Popular 16th-c country local serving East Anglian beers from racked casks behind long counter, old tables and chairs on quarry tiles, log fire, enjoyable good value home-made food such as venison and ale steamed pudding; quiz first Weds of month; children and dogs welcome, heated terrace with grapevines and roses, closed Sun evening, Mon. *(Peter Pilbeam)*

THORNDON
TM1469

Black Horse (01379) 678523

*Off A140 or B1077, S of Eye; The Street;
IP23 7JR* Friendly 17th-c village pub
with enjoyable food including good value
lunchtime carvery, three well kept local
ales, beams, lots of timbering, stripped brick
and big fireplaces; well behaved children
welcome, tables on lawn, country views
behind, open all day Sun till 9pm.
(Malcolm Greening)

THORNHAM MAGNA
TM1070

Four Horseshoes (01379) 678777

*Off A140 S of Diss; Wickham Road;
IP23 8HD* Extensive thatched dining pub
dating from 12th c, dimly lit rambling well
divided carpeted bar, Greene King ales
and good choice of wines and whiskies,
enjoyable reasonably priced food with main
courses available in two sizes, popular
Sun carvery, friendly helpful staff, very low
heavy black beams, country pictures and
brass, big log fireplaces, illuminated interior
well; background music; children and
dogs welcome, disabled access, handy for
Thornham Walks and interesting thatched
church, picnic-sets on big sheltered lawn,
seven comfortable bedrooms, open all day.
(Charlie May)

THORPENESS
TM4759

★ **Dolphin** (01728) 454994

*Just off B1353; Old Homes Road; village
signposted from Aldeburgh; IP16 4FE*
Neatly kept extended dining pub in
interesting seaside village (all built in the
early 1900s); main bar with scandinavian
feel, pale wooden tables and assortment of
old chairs on broad modern quarry tiles, log
fire, Adnams, Woodfordes and a guest, several
wines by the glass, more traditional public
bar with pubby furniture on stripped-wood
floor, built-in cushioned wall seats and old
local photographs, airy dining room with
country kitchen-style furniture, good food
and friendly service; background music, TV,
free wi-fi; children and dogs welcome, good
sized garden with terrace, bedrooms, open
all day weekends in summer. *(David Jackman,
Peter Meister)*

THURSTON
TL9165

Fox & Hounds (01359) 232228

Barton Road; IP31 3QT Quite an imposing
building, welcoming inside, with well kept
Adnams, Greene King and guests, pubby
furnishings in neatly kept carpeted lounge
(back part set for dining), lots of pump
clips, ceiling fans, big helpings of reasonably
priced pubby food (not Sun evening or Mon),
bare-boards public bar with pool, darts
and machines; background and some live
music, quiz nights; dogs welcome, picnic-sets
on grassed area by car park and on small
covered side terrace, pretty village, two
bedrooms, open all day Fri-Sun. *(Jeremy King)*

TUDDENHAM
TM1948

★ **Fountain** (01473) 785377

*The Street; village signed off B1077 N of
Ipswich; IP6 9BT* Popular well run dining
pub in nice village, several linked café-style
rooms (minimal décor) with heavy beams
and timbering, stripped floors, wooden dining
chairs around light tables, open fire, lots of
prints (some by cartoonist Giles who spent
time here after World War II), wide choice
of well cooked food (all day Sun till 7pm)
including set menus, Adnams Bitter and good
selection of wines by the glass, decent coffee,
pleasant helpful service; background music;
no under-10s in bar after 6.30pm, wicker
and metal chairs on covered heated terrace,
rows of picnic-style tables under parasols on
sizeable lawn, closed first week Jan.
(J F M and M West, Ryta Lyndley)

UFFORD
TM2952

★ **Crown** (01394) 461030

High Street; IP13 6EL Welcoming family-
run pub-restaurant, Adnams and a seasonal
guest, Aspall's cider and a dozen wines by the
glass, good well presented food from varied
menu (changes daily), attentive friendly
service, newspapers; children welcome,
garden picnic-sets and play area, open all
day weekends (till 9pm Sun), closed Tues.
*(Pat and Graham Williamson, Nick and Gillian
Harrison)*

UFFORD
TM2952

White Lion (01394) 460770

*Lower Street (off B1438, towards Eyke);
IP13 6DW* 16th-c village pub near quiet
stretch of River Deben; home to the Uffa
Brewery with their beers and guests tapped
from the cask, enjoyable generous home-
made food (own pigs, free-range hens and
bees), raised woodburner in large central
fireplace, captain's chairs and spindlebacks
around simple tables, shop/deli; regular
events including quiz nights, beer festivals
and vintage car rallies; nice views from
outside tables, summer barbecues, closed
Sun evening, Mon lunchtime. *(Pat and
Graham Williamson)*

WANGFORD
TM4679

Angel (01502) 578636

*Signed just off A12 by B1126 junction;
High Street; NR34 8RL* Handsome old
village coaching inn with airy beamed and
carpeted bar, enjoyable good value food from
sandwiches up, pleasant efficient service,
Adnams, Brakspears, Greene King and up to
two guests, decent wines, family dining room;
dogs welcome, seven comfortable bedrooms
(the church clock sounds on the quarter),
good breakfast, open all day Sun (and other
days if busy). *(Anon)*

WENHASTON
TM4274

Star (01502) 478240

Hall Road; IP19 9HF Friendly well run

19th-c country pub, Adnams Southwold and guests, good wine choice and wide range of enjoyable inexpensive home-made food; children, dogs and muddy boots welcome, sizeable lawn with boules, nice views, open all day Sun. *(David Field)*

WESTLETON   TM4469
White Horse (01728) 648222
Darsham Road, off B1125 Blythburgh–Leiston; IP17 3AH Friendly and relaxed traditional pub with good home-cooked food from blackboard menu including specials, four well kept Adnams ales, unassuming high-ceilinged bar with central fire, steps down to stone-floored back dining room; children welcome, picnic-sets in cottagey garden with climbing frame, more out by village duck pond, four bedrooms, good breakfast, open (and food) all day Fri-Sun. *(Peter Meister)*

WOODBRIDGE   TM2648
Cherry Tree (01394) 384627
Opposite Notcutts Nursery, off A12; Cumberland Street; IP12 4AG Opened-up 17th-c pub (bigger than it looks) with well kept Adnams and guests, good wines by the glass and ample helpings of reasonably priced tasty food including specials, friendly service, beams and two log fires, mix of pine furniture, old local photographs; children and dogs (in bar) welcome, garden with play area, three bedrooms in converted barn, good breakfast (for non-residents too), open all day. *(Nick and Gillian Harrison, MDN, Peter Smith and Judith Brown)*

WOODBRIDGE   TM2748
Crown (01394) 384242
Thoroughfare/Quay Street; IP12 1AD Stylish 17th-c dining inn, well kept ales such as Adnams from glass-roofed bar (boat suspended above counter), lots of wines by the glass, good imaginative food including fixed-price menu (Mon-Thurs), also brunch and afternoon teas, pleasant young staff, various eating areas with contemporary

furnishings; live jazz last Thurs of month; children and dogs (in bar) welcome, courtyard tables, ten well appointed bedrooms, open all day. *(Gus Swan)*

WOODBRIDGE   TM2749
Kings Head (01394) 387750
Market Hill; IP12 4LP Handsome Elizabethan beams in opened-up town bar, log fire in massive central chimneybreast, good home-made food from crab sandwiches up in bar and dining room down a couple of steps, Adnams ales, some nice local pictures; background music; dogs welcome (menu for them) and well behaved children, disabled facilities, tables on heated terrace. *(Pat and Tony Martin)*

WOODBRIDGE   TM2749
Olde Bell & Steelyard
(01394) 382933 *New Street, off Market Square; IP12 1DZ* Ancient and unpretentious timber-framed pub with two smallish beamed bars and compact dining room, lots of brassware, log fire, Greene King ales and guests from canopied servery, real ciders, enjoyable home-made food served by friendly staff, traditional games including bar billiards, live music; children and dogs welcome, back terrace, steelyard still overhanging street, open till late Fri and Sat. *(Peter Smith and Judith Brown, Simon Tucker)*

WOOLPIT   TL9762
Swan (01359) 240482
The Street; IP30 9QN Welcoming old coaching house pleasantly situated in village square, heavy beams and painted panelling, mixed tables and chairs on carpet, roaring log fire one end, good inventive food from daily changing blackboard menu, prompt friendly service, well kept Adnams from slate-top counter and lots of wines by the glass; soft background music; walled garden behind, four bedrooms in converted stables, closed Mon lunchtime. *(Jeremy King)*

Post Office address codings confusingly give the impression that some pubs are in Suffolk, when they're really in Cambridgeshire, Essex or Norfolk (which is where we list them).

Surrey

BRAMLEY
Jolly Farmer 🍷 🍺
TQ0044 Map 3

(01483) 893355 – www.jollyfarmer.co.uk
High Street; GU5 0HB

Relaxed village inn near Surrey hills with great selection of beers

With up to eight real ales and a friendly welcome, it's not surprising this family-run pub is so popular. On handpump there might be Bowmans Swift One and Youngs Original plus guests such as Black Country Pig on the Wall, Firebird Heritage XX, Goffs Tournament, Irving Type 42 and Pilgrim Surrey Bitter. Also, 14 wines by the glass, nine malt whiskies and two farm ciders. The traditional interior is filled with a homely miscellany of wooden tables and chairs, with collections of plates, enamel advertising signs, sewing machines, antique bottles, prints and old tools filling the walls and surfaces. Timbered semi-partitions, a mix of brick and timbering and an open fireplace give the place a snug, cosy feel; background music and board games. There are tables out by the car park, and the village is handy for Winkworth Arboretum (National Trust) and walks up St Martha's Hill.

🍽 Quite a choice of food includes sandwiches, salt and pepper squid with chilli sauce, wild mushrooms in tarragon butter on a crouton, vegetable risotto with parmesan, assorted pizzas, local pork sausages with wholegrain mustard mash and onion gravy, burgers with lots of toppings and chips, honey and mustard home-cooked ham and eggs, rack of barbecue pork ribs with fries, sirloin steak teriyaki stir-fry with japanese udon noodles, and puddings such as crème brûlée and eton mess. *Benchmark main dish: chilli chicken in sweet red pepper and creamy cheese sauce £12.50. Two-course evening meal £18.00.*

Free house ~ Licensees Steve and Chris Hardstone ~ Real ale ~ Open 11-11; 12-11 Sun ~ Bar food 12-2.30, 7-9.30 ~ Restaurant ~ Children welcome ~ Dogs allowed in bar ~ Wi-fi ~ Bedrooms: £60/£70 *Recommended by Patrick Hamblin, John Thompson, TomH, Tom and Ruth Rees,*

CHIPSTEAD
White Hart 🍴⭐ 🍷
TQ2757 Map 3

(01737) 554455 – www.brunningandprice.co.uk/whitehartchipstead
Hazelwood Lane; CR5 3QW

Plenty to look at in open-plan rooms, thoughtful choice of drinks, interesting food and friendly staff

The open-plan rooms in this bustling pub have an informal, friendly atmosphere and there's a lot to look at. A raftered dining room to the right has elegant metal chandeliers, rough-plastered walls, an open fire in a brick fireplace and a couple of carved metal standing uprights. The central bar has stools at the panelled counter where helpful staff serve Phoenix Brunning & Price Original, Pilgrim Surrey Bitter, Sharps Doom Bar, Surrey Hills Shere Drop and Twickenham Sundancer on handpump, 14 wines by the glass and up to 60 malt whiskies; background music and board games. The long room to the left is light and airy, with wall panelling at one end, a woodburning stove and numerous windows overlooking the seats on the terrace. Throughout, there's a fine mix of antique dining chairs and settles around all sorts of tables (each set with a church candle), rugs on bare boards or flagstones, hundreds of interesting cartoons, country pictures, cricketing prints and rugby team photographs, large, ornate mirrors and, on the window sills and mantelpieces, old glass and stone bottles, clocks, books and plants.

A thoughtful choice of food includes sandwiches, scallops with wasabi cream, soy jelly and pickled ginger, a charcuterie platter for two people, crab and asparagus quiche, breaded pork escalope with tagliatelle in a creamy lemon sauce, spatchcock baby chicken with crispy serrano ham, fries and garlic mayonnaise, beer-battered haddock and chips, duck breast with root vegetable terrine, roast onion purée and juniper and thyme jus, and puddings such as lemon drizzle cake with candied kumquats and dark chocolate and hazelnut torte with sour cherry sorbet. *Benchmark main dish: fish pie £13.95. Two-course evening meal £21.00.*

Brunning & Price ~ Manager Damian Mann ~ Real ale ~ Open 11.30-11; 12-10.30 Sun ~ Bar food 12-10 (9.30 Sun) ~ Restaurant ~ Children welcome ~ Dogs allowed in bar ~ Wi-fi
Recommended by John Branston, Fr Robert Marsh

CHOBHAM
White Hart ♀ ◀

SU9761   Map 2

(01276) 857580 – www.brunningandprice.co.uk/whitehartchobham
4 miles from M3 junction 3; High Street; GU24 8AA

Handsome brick-built village inn with a bustling atmosphere, a thoughtful choice of food and drink and plenty of cheerful customers

This venerable inn with its attractive brickwork is one of the oldest properties in the village, dating from the early 16th c. The opened-up bar has white-painted beams, standing pillars, rugs on parquet or wide boards, an assortment of dark wooden dining chairs and tables, and armchairs beside two fireplaces. High chairs line the counter where cheerful, well trained staff serve Phoenix Brunning Price Original, Thurstons Horsell Gold, Tillingbourne Hop Troll IPA, Twickenham Naked Ladies and XT 4 Mellow Amber on handpump, and a fine choice of wines and whiskies. An L-shaped dining room has a leather wall banquette and leather and brass-studded dining chairs around a mix of tables and lots of old photos and prints on exposed brick or painted walls. There's also a carpeted, comfortable dining room with similar furniture and a big elegant metal chandelier. The little side garden has seats under parasols.

As well as serving weekend brunches, the extremely good food includes sandwiches, rabbit, ham hock and tarragon croquettes with piccalilli, basil panna cotta with heritage tomato salad and black olive tapenade, fried mackerel with crab fritter and crunchy asian salad, steak burger with toppings, coleslaw and chips, duck breast with duck hash cake and black cherry sauce, bass with tagliatelle, baby leeks, mussels and saffron sauce, and puddings such as hot waffle with caramelised banana, toffee sauce and vanilla ice-cream and white and dark chocolate truffle torte with sour cherry and amaretto sorbet. *Benchmark main dish: pork loin and confit belly with bubble and squeak, fennel croquette and pickled apple puree £16.95. Two-course evening meal £21.00.*

Brunning & Price ~ Manager Nikki Szabo ~ Real ale ~ Open 11-11; 9am-11pm Sat; 9am-10.30pm Sun ~ Bar food 12-10; 9-10 Sat; 9-9.30 Sun ~ Restaurant ~ Children welcome ~ Dogs allowed in bar ~ Wi-fi *Recommended by Ian Phillips, Dr Simon Innes*

CRANLEIGH   TQ0539 Map 3
Richard Onslow 🍺 🛏
(01483) 274922 – www.therichardonslow.co.uk
High Street; GU6 8AU

Busy pub with a good mix of customers in several bar rooms, four real ales and interesting all-day food; smart bedrooms

Customers drop in and out of this bustling town-centre pub all day – starting with breakfasts at 7am. The cheerful little public bar has stools by the counter, leather tub chairs and a built-in sofa, and a slate-floored drinking area where they keep Adnams Ghost Ship, Firebird Heritage XX, Sharps Doom Bar and Surrey Hills Shere Drop on handpump, ten wines by the glass, a few malt whiskies and a farm cider. Two dining rooms have a mix of tartan tub chairs around wooden tables, a rather fine long leather-cushioned church pew, local photographs on mainly pale paintwork and a couple of open fires, one in a nice brick fireplace. The sizeable restaurant, with pale tables and chairs on the wooden floor and modern flowery wallpaper, has big windows overlooking the street; background music and board games. There are a few tables and chairs in the terraced back garden and on the front pavement. The bedrooms are smart and well equipped.

The good and extremely popular food includes honey and thyme roasted quail with salt-baked beetroot and port sauce, crab cocktail with avocado salad, several platters, vegetable risotto with parmesan crisp, maple-cured free-range gammon with a poached egg, free-range duck and crunchy vegetable salad with toasted cashews and oriental dressing, rack of lamb with ratatouille and olive oil mash, and puddings such as raspberry and white chocolate cheesecake and iced lemon meringue parfait with toasted marshmallows and balsamic syrup. *Benchmark main dish: 28-day dry-aged steak with chips and a choice of sauces £19.75. Two-course evening meal £20.00.*

Peach Pub Company ~ Manager John Taylor ~ Real ale ~ Open 7am-midnight ~ Bar food 7.30am-10pm ~ Restaurant ~ Children welcome ~ Dogs allowed in bar and bedrooms ~ Wi-fi ~ Bedrooms: /£90 *Recommended by David Jackman, Christopher and Elise Way*

ESHER   TQ1566 Map 3
Marneys
(020) 8398 4444 – www.marneys.com
Alma Road (one-way), Weston Green; heading N on A309 from A307 roundabout, after Lamb & Star pub turn left into Lime Tree Avenue (signposted to All Saints Parish Church), then left at T junction into Chestnut Avenue; KT10 8JN

Country-feeling pub with good value traditional food and attractive garden

A good local following enjoys the chatty low-beamed bar in this charming small pub – and it's handy for Hampton Court Palace. Fullers London Pride, Sharps Doom Bar and Youngs Original on handpump, 16 wines by the glass, ten malt whiskies and perhaps horse-racing on the unobtrusive corner

TV. To the left, past a little cast-iron woodburning stove, the dining area has big pine tables, pews, pale country kitchen chairs and cottagey blue-curtained windows; background music. There are seats and wooden tables on the front terrace, which has views over the wooded common, village church and duck pond, and more seats on the decked area in the pleasantly planted sheltered garden.

At fair prices for the area, the well liked food includes box-baked camembert with chutney, pint of prawns with aioli, beetroot and goats cheese salad with sun-dried tomatoes and pine nuts, lamb and rosemary or beef burgers with toppings and chips, thai-style salmon fishcakes with sweet chilli sauce, minute steak topped with garlic butter with fries, and puddings such as crème brûlée and sticky toffee pudding. *Benchmark main dish: steak in ale pie £11.95. Two-course evening meal £20.00.*

Free house ~ Licensee Thomas Duxberry ~ Real ale ~ Open 11-11; 12-10.30 Sun ~ Bar food 12-2.30, 6-9; 12-4 Sun; not Fri-Sun evenings ~ Restaurant ~ Children welcome away from bar ~ Dogs allowed in bar ~ Wi-fi *Recommended by Simon Rodway, Belinda May*

MICKLEHAM

TQ1753   Map 3

Running Horses ♀ ⇔

(01372) 372279 – www.therunninghorses.co.uk
Old London Road (B2209); RH5 6DU

Refurbished country pub with plenty of customers in bar and dining rooms, enjoyable food and drink and seats on big front terrace; bedrooms

After a refurbishment, this gently civilised pub is as busy as ever. The stylish and spacious bar has cushioned wall settles and other dining chairs around straightforward tables on new parquet flooring, racing cartoons and Hogarth prints on the walls, lots of race tickets hanging from a beam and a log fire in an inglenook fireplace. Stools line the counter where friendly, helpful staff serve a beer named for the pub (from Banks's), Brakspears Bitter and Oxford Gold, Fullers London Pride and Ringwood Best on handpump, alongside 21 good wines by the glass; background music. New character booths with wood panelling and red leather banquettes have been added. The restaurant, also panelled, has an attractive mix of upholstered and wooden dining chairs around a medley of tables on tartan carpet. Parking is in a narrow lane (or park on the main road). The front terrace is a fine place to sit on a warm day among lovely flowering tubs and hanging baskets, and there's a peaceful view of the old church with its strange stubby steeple. A notice by the door asks walkers to remove or cover their boots.

Particularly good food includes sandwiches, smoked mackerel and chilli fishcake with sweetcorn velouté, twice-baked cheddar soufflé, toasted brioche with wild mushrooms, spinach, a poached egg and hollandaise sauce, chicken with porcini mushrooms, roasted shallots and tarragon, calves liver with pancetta, caramelised onions and red wine jus, grilled salmon with sauce vierge, and puddings such as chocolate sauce with chantilly cream and rapsberry and white chocolate bread and butter pudding with raspberry sorbet. *Benchmark main dish: crisp roast pork belly with champ mash, braised red cabbage and cider jus £16.00. Two-course evening meal £22.00.*

Brakspears ~ Manager Melanie Gowers ~ Real ale ~ Open 12-11; 12-10.30 Sun ~ Bar food 12-3, 6-10; 12-10 Sat; 12-6 Sun ~ Restaurant ~ Children welcome but must be over 10 in bar area ~ Dogs allowed in bar ~ Wi-fi ~ Bedrooms: /£135
Recommended by John Evans, Conor McGaughey, Sheila Topham, Tony Scott

MILFORD

SU9542   Map 2

Refectory ♀ ◀

(01483) 413820 – www.brunningandprice.co.uk/refectory

Portsmouth Road; GU8 5HJ

Lovely pub with plenty of interest in beamed and timbered rooms, six real ales and other thoughtful drinks and well liked food

Friendly, courteous staff in this handsome place create an easy-going atmosphere that our readers enjoy very much. The L-shaped, mainly open-plan rooms are spacious and extremely interesting: there are strikingly heavy beams, exposed stone walls, stalling and standing timbers creating separate seating areas, and a couple of big log fires in handsome stone fireplaces. A two-tiered and balconied part at one end has a wall covered with huge brass platters; elsewhere there are nice old photographs and a variety of paintings. Dining chairs and dark wooden tables are grouped on wooden, quarry-tiled or carpeted flooring, and there are also rugs, bookshelves, big pot plants, stone bottles on window sills and fresh flowers. High wooden bar stools line the long counter where they serve Phoenix Brunning & Price Original, Hogs Back TEA, Dark Star Hophead and guests such as Surrey Hills Ranmore Ale, Tillingbourne Falls Gold and Twickenham Redhead on handpump, a dozen wines by the glass, around 80 malt whiskies and two farm ciders. There are teak tables and chairs in the back courtyard adjacent to the characterful pigeonry. Facilities for wheelchair users are outstandingly good and there are disabled parking spaces.

Enterprising food includes sandwiches, seared scallops with black pudding, cauliflower purée and apple dressing, rabbit rillettes salad with pear jelly, pickled vegetables and crispy croûtes, king prawn and chorizo linguine with oven-dried cherry tomatoes and capers, rosemary and garlic chicken with pasta, wild mushrooms, bacon and spinach, thai green sweet potato and spinach curry with coconut flatbread, honey-spiced duck breast salad with pak choi, beansprouts, cashews and pomegranate dressing, and puddings such as sticky toffee pudding with toffee sauce and chocolate brownie with boozy dark cherry compote. *Benchmark main dish: beef and mushroom in ale pie £14.95. Two-course evening meal £21.00.*

Brunning & Price ~ Manager Lee Parry ~ Real ale ~ Open 12-11; 12-10.30 Sun ~ Bar food 12-10 (9.30 Sun) ~ Restaurant ~ Children welcome ~ Dogs allowed in bar ~ Wi-fi
Recommended by Phil Bryant, Martin and Alison Stainsby, Mrs Sally Scott, Ron Corbett, Tony Scott

SHAMLEY GREEN

TQ0343   Map 3

Red Lion

(01483) 892202 – www.redlionshamleygreen.com

The Green; GU5 0UB

Pleasant dining pub with popular tasty food and nice gardens

The friendly, helpful staff here come in for warm praise from our readers – and the food is highly rated too. It's a well run pub next to the village green and the two connected bars are fairly traditional with a mix of new and old wooden tables, chairs and cushioned settles on bare boards and red carpet, stripped standing timbers, fresh white walls, deep red ceilings and open fires; background music. Youngs IPA and a couple of guests such as Hogs Back TEA and Sharps Doom Bar on handpump, and 11 wines by the glass. There are plenty of hand-made rustic tables and benches outside, both at the front and at the back – which is more secluded and has seats on a heated, covered terrace and grassed dining areas.

🍴 Good, enjoyable food includes sandwiches, crispy duck salad with oranges, watercress and hoisin dressing, grilled goats cheese with pesto, greek-style spinach and feta pie, chilli con carne, chicken curry, lambs liver and bacon with red wine gravy, veal schnitzel in lemon and garlic butter topped with an egg, steaks with a choice of sauces, and puddings. *Benchmark main dish: steak in ale pie £12.50. Two-course evening meal £17.50.*

Punch ~ Lease Debbie Ersser ~ Real ale ~ Open 11.30-11; 12-10 Sun (12-8 in winter) ~ Bar food 12-2.30 (3 weekends), 6.30-9.30; 12-3, 6.30-8.30 Sun; no food winter Sun evening ~ Restaurant ~ Children welcome ~ Dogs allowed in bar ~ Wi-fi *Recommended by Tony and Rachel Schendel, C Merritt*

 SUNBURY   TQ1068   Map 3

Flower Pot 🛏

(01932) 780741 – www.theflowerpothotel.co.uk

1.6 miles from M3 junction 1; follow Lower Sunbury sign from exit roundabout, then at Thames Street turn right; pub on next corner, with Green Street; TW16 6AA

Former coaching inn with appealing, contemporary bar and dining room, real ales and all-day food; bedrooms

Attractively refurbished, this is a handsome, neatly kept pub with elegant wrought-iron balconies and pretty summer hanging baskets. The airy bar has leather tub chairs around copper-topped tables, high chairs upholstered in brown and beige tartan around equally high tables in pale wood, attractive flagstones, contemporary paintwork and stools against the counter; there's also a couple of comfortably plush burgundy armchairs. The bar leads into the dining area, which has duck egg blue-painted and dark wooden cushioned dining chairs around an assortment of partly painted tables on wooden flooring, all manner of artworks on wallpapered walls and a large gilt-edged mirror over an open fireplace; candles in glass jars, fresh flowers, background music and newspapers. Brakspears Bitter and Oxford Gold and a guest beer such as Wychwood Hobgoblin on handpump and 15 wines by the glass. A side terrace has wood and metal tables and chairs. The bedrooms are smart and comfortable.

🍴 Quite a choice of food includes sandwiches, prawns in chilli and tarragon butter, baked camembert with garlic and rosemary, sharing boards, slow-braised ham hock and broad bean salad with crispy bacon, boiled egg, sauté potatoes and wholegrain mustard and honey dressing, sausages with bubble and squeak and home-made boston beans, cod loin wrapped in parma ham with capers and tomato sauce, 28-day-aged steak with a choice of sauces, and puddings. *Benchmark main dish: pie of the day £13.50. Two-course evening meal £20.00.*

Brakspears ~ Tenant Simon Bailey ~ Real ale ~ Open 7am-11pm; 8am-midnight Sat; 8am-11pm Sun ~ Bar food 7-3, 6-9 (10 Fri, Sat); 8am-9pm Sun ~ Restaurant ~ Children welcome ~ Dogs allowed in bar ~ Wi-fi ~ Bedrooms: /£99
Recommended by Martin Jones, Isobel Mackinlay, Ron Corbett

 THAMES DITTON   TQ1667   Map 12

Olde Swan 🍺

(020) 8398 1814 – www.yeoldeswan-thames-ditton.co.uk

Summer Road; KT7 0QQ

Fine spot by the Thames with terraced seating outside, character bars, several ales and tasty pubby food

It's best to arrive early at this partly 13th-c inn – particularly if you want to bag one of the smart wooden tables and chairs under blue parasols overlooking a quiet Thames backwater and across to Ditton Island. The long bar area has wood and flagstone flooring, dark farmhouse and other dining chairs around all sorts of tables, and comfortable leather sofas in front of a big brick fireplace with an open log fire. Greene King IPA and Abbot with guests such as Ascot On the Rails, Cottage Goldrush, Hogs Back Surrey Nirvana and Twickenham Naked Ladies on handpump, 18 wines by the glass and ten malt whiskies. The carpeted dining rooms are similarly furnished and have more open fires (one in a Tudor fireplace), standing timbers, bare brick or interestingly wallpapered walls, and various prints and paintings; TV for major sports events.

A wide choice of tasty food includes sandwiches, breaded garlic mushrooms with mayonnaise, prawn cocktail, aubergine and beetroot curry, beef in ale pie, chicken with cheese, bacon and barbecue sauce, lasagne, confit duck leg with cherry and red wine sauce, slow-cooked lamb shank, and puddings such as ginger, pear and caramel crumble tart with maple and walnut ice-cream and fruit compote-based crème brûlée; Wednesday is curry night and they offer a set menu with two main courses for £10.99 (not weekends). *Benchmark main dish: beer-battered fish and chips £10.00. Two-course evening meal £16.00.*

Greene King ~ Manager Mike Dandy ~ Real ale ~ Open 11-11; 12-10.30 Sun ~ Bar food 11-10; 12-9 Sun ~ Restaurant ~ Children welcome ~ Dogs allowed in bar ~ Wi-fi ~ Live jazz third Sun afternoon of month, disco last Fri of month
Recommended by Tony Scott, Dr Simon Innes

WEST END   SU9461   Map 2
The Inn West End 🌟 ♀ 🛏
(01276) 858652 – www.the-inn.co.uk
Just under 2.5 miles from M3 junction 3; A322 S, on right; GU24 9PW

Surrey Dining Pub of the Year

Beautifully refurbished from top to toe with plenty of dining and drinking room, excellent wines and inventive food; lovely bedrooms

Although big changes have taken place here – it's much more open and airy – the atmosphere remains easy-going and friendly, and the hard-working licensees are as enthusiastic as ever. The bar has been moved into what was the restaurant: it has white-painted beams, slatted and cushioned wooden benches and elegant chairs around a mix of tables on bare floorboards, pretty curtains, a big central barrel and chairs against the counter where they keep Fullers London Pride and Seafarers and Thurstons Horsell Gold on handpump, 20 wines by the glass from a fantastic list of around 500 (iberia is the speciality) and several sherries, sweet wines and port. Do ask about the unusual clock. The extended restaurant occupies what was the garden room, and between these two rooms is a lounge with books on shelves, daily papers and an open fire; Sunny and Teddy are the pub dogs. The pretty garden and terrace have plenty of seats for warm weather. Newly opened, the bedrooms are extremely well equipped and comfortable – two allow dogs and one has disabled facilities. No children.

 Serving breakfasts, morning coffee and afternoon tea, the particularly good, interesting food includes sandwiches, smoked salmon, spinach, a duck egg and brioche, chicken liver pâté with plum and raspberry jam, cumberland sausages with caramelised onion jus, smoked haddock kedgeree with a soft poached egg, wild mushroom, chestnut and spinach risotto with truffle oil, fillets of gurnard with mussels and saffron sauce, lamb rump with gratin potatoes and mint jus, and puddings such as vanilla crème brûlée and plum pudding with crème anglaise and boozy cherries.

Benchmark main dish: wild venison with braised red cabbage and thyme jus £20.00. Two-course evening meal £25.00.

Free house ~ Licensees Gerry and Ann Price ~ Real ale ~ Open 9am-11pm; 12-10.30 Sun ~ Bar food 12-3, 6-9.30; some kind of food all day ~ Restaurant ~ Dogs allowed in bedrooms ~ Wi-fi ~ Bedrooms: /£90 *Recommended by, Edward Mirzoeff, Susan and John Douglas, S F Parrinder*

Also Worth a Visit in Surrey

Besides the fully inspected pubs, you might like to try these pubs that have been recommended to us and described by readers. Do tell us what you think of them: feedback@goodguides.com

ABINGER COMMON   TQ1146
Abinger Hatch (01306) 730737
Off A25 W of Dorking, towards Abinger Hammer; RH5 6HZ Modernised dining pub in beautiful woodland spot, spacious interior with heavy beams and log fires, enjoyable food from sharing plates up, plenty of wines by the glass, Ringwood Best and guests; children and dogs (in one area) welcome, some disabled access, picnic-sets in side garden with boules, summer barbecues, near pretty church and pond, open (and food) all day. *(Martin Jones)*

ALBURY   TQ0447
★ **Drummond Arms** (01483) 202039
Off A248 SE of Guildford; The Street; GU5 9AG Modernised 19th-c pub in pretty village; ales such as Adnams, Courage, Sharps and Hogs Back, good choice of wines, food from sandwiches and light dishes up, cheerful courteous service, opened-up bar with leather chesterfields, log fire and newspapers, parquet-floored dining room, conservatory; good-sized pretty back garden by little River Tillingbourne, duck island, summer barbecues and hog roasts, pleasant walks nearby, nine bedrooms, open all day (food all day weekends). *(John Branston, Nigel and Sue Foster)*

ALFOLD   TQ0435
Alfold Barn (01403) 752288
Horsham Road, A281; GU6 8JE Beautifully preserved 16th-c building with bar and restaurant, good locally sourced home-made food from daily changing menu including weekday lunch deal, friendly attentive service, up to three well kept ales from nearby breweries, beams and rafters, mixed furniture on flagstones or carpet, warming log fires; children welcome, garden with play area and animals including Rosie the goat, closed Sun evening, Mon. *(Dr Simon Innes)*

ALFOLD   TQ0334
Three Compasses (01483) 275729
Dunsfold Road; GU6 8HY Reworked 400-year-old pub with interesting 1940s theme (plenty to look at); well kept Otter, Sharps Doom Bar and a guest, enjoyable freshly made food (not Sun evening, Mon) in bar and restaurant area, games room with darts, table skittles and bar billiards; Mon swing/jive classes; children and dogs welcome, good-sized garden with play area, on back lane to former Dunsfold Aerodrome (now Dunsfold Park with little museum), Wey & Arun Canal nearby, open all day in summer, may close Sun evening, Mon in winter. *(Tony and Wendy Hobden)*

BANSTEAD   TQ2559
Woolpack (01737) 354560
High Street; SM7 2NZ Open-plan pub with well kept Shepherd Neame ales and a couple of interesting guests, enjoyable home-made food from standard dishes up (some available in smaller helpings), friendly helpful service, restaurant; Mon quiz, live music including afternoon trad jazz (first Tues of month), TVs, buoyant local atmosphere evenings; plenty of seats in big garden, open all day. *(Sue and Mike Todd, Conor McGaughey, Ross Balaam)*

BATTS CORNER   SU8140
Blue Bell (01252) 792801
Batts Corner; GU10 4EX Tucked-away country pub with linked stone-floor rooms, light fresh décor and mix of furniture, sofas by log fire, Hogs Back TEA, Triple fff Moondance and guests such as Frensham, good home-made food from sensibly short menu including popular Sun lunch (must book), friendly attentive staff; children and dogs on leads welcome, attractive spacious garden with rolling views, summer barbecues and good play area, handy for Alice Holt Forest, open all day Sat, till 7pm Sun. *(Tony and Jill Radnor)*

BETCHWORTH   TQ2149
Dolphin (01737) 842288
Off A25 W of Reigate; The Street; RH3 7DW Cosy 16th-c beamed local in picturesque village on Greensand Way, neat front bar with inglenook log fire and plain tables on ancient flagstones, snug and another panelled bar with chiming grandfather clock, nice old local

photographs, well kept Charles Wells ales and guests, decent choice of wines and enjoyable fair-priced traditional food (all day weekends) including daily specials, friendly efficient young staff, restaurant; children, walkers and dogs welcome, front and side terraces, back garden, fine Pre-Raphaelite pulpit in church opposite, open all day. *(John Evans and others)*

BLETCHINGLEY   TQ3250
Red Lion (01883) 743342
Castle Street (A25), Redhill side; RH1 4NU Modernised well looked-after beamed village dining pub, good reasonably priced home-made food such as rabbit and venison pie, friendly staff, well kept Greene King ales and good choice of wines by the glass; children welcome (under-10s till 7pm), heated part-covered terrace, secret garden, summer barbecues, open all day. *(Geoffrey Kemp)*

BLETCHINGLEY   TQ3250
Whyte Harte (01883) 743231
2.5 miles from M25 junction 6, via A22 then A25 towards Redhill; RH1 4PB Low-beamed Tudor inn with good well presented food served by friendly staff, three changing ales and plenty of wines by the glass, big inglenook log fire in extensive open-plan bar, separate dining area; background music; dogs welcome, lovely beer garden, eight bedrooms, good breakfast, attractive village street (shame about the traffic), open all day. *(Nick Lawless, Fiona Smith)*

BLINDLEY HEATH   TQ3645
Red Barn (01342) 830820
Tandridge Lane, just off B2029, which is off A22; RH7 6LL Splendid farmhouse/barn conversion; contemporary furnishings mixing with 17th-c beams and timbers, central glass-sided woodburner (its flue soaring into the roof), large model plane hanging from rafters, one wall with shelves of books, another hung with antlers, clever partitioning creating cosier areas too; red cooking range and big wooden tables in farmhouse-style room, adjacent bar with sofas by large fireplace, one or two real ales and good wine list, generally well liked food; background and some live music, bar billiards; children and dogs (in bar) welcome, solid granite tables on lawn, farmers' market first Sat of month, open all day. *(Mrs Sally Scott, Tony Scott)*

BROCKHAM   TQ1949
Inn on the Green (01737) 845101
Brockham Green; RH3 7JS Restaurant pub facing village green (part of the small Grumpy Mole group), enjoyable food from traditional choices up including cook-your-own steaks on a hot stone, well kept Fullers London Pride and Surrey Hills Shere Drop, several wines by the glass, afternoon teas, conservatory; children welcome, picnic-sets

out at front, garden behind, open all day, food all day weekends. *(Dr Simon Innes)*

BROCKHAM   TQ1949
Royal Oak (01737) 843241
Brockham Green; RH3 7JS Nice spot on charming village green below North Downs; bare-boards bar and light airy dining area, well kept Sharps and Charles Wells, enjoyable freshly cooked pub food at reasonable prices, good service from warmly welcoming staff; children and dogs allowed, tables out in front looking across to fine church, more seats in back garden, handy for Greensand Way. *(Peter Hailey, C and R Bromage, Conor McGaughey)*

BROOK   SU9238
Dog & Pheasant (01428) 682763
Haslemere Road (A286); GU8 5UJ Popular pub looking across busy road to cricket green, friendly landlord, long bar divided up by standing timbers, heavy beams, open fire in brick fireplace, cushioned wall settles, four well kept ales including Ringwood and Sharps from nice linenfold counter, dining area on right, room to left with big inglenook log fire and pubby furniture, well liked food including Weds grill night; children welcome, picnic-sets on back decking and grass, play equipment, open all day, no food Sun evening (and may shut early then if quiet). *(Belinda May)*

BUCKLAND   TQ2250
★ **Jolly Farmers** (01737) 221355
Reigate Road (A25 W of Reigate); RH3 7BG Unusual pub-eatery-cum-farm shop; informal beamed and flagstoned bar with two changing local ales, small brick fireplace separating wood-floored dining room, enjoyable food from sandwiches and sharing plates up, friendly helpful staff, three-room shop selling deli produce, cakes and own preserves; free wi-fi; children and dogs (in bar) welcome, tables on back terrace, play area, open (and food) all day, breakfast from 8am (9am weekends). *(Richard Tilbrook, Ian Herdman, Mrs Margo Finlay, Jörg Kasprowski, Roger and Anne Newbury)*

BURROWHILL   SU9763
Four Horseshoes (01276) 857581
B383 N of Chobham; GU24 8QP Busy recently refurbished pub attractively set by village green, beams and log fires, three well kept ales including one badged for them, popular food served by cheerful staff, modern dining extension; children, dogs and muddy boots welcome, tables out at front (some under ancient yew), open all day (Sun till 7pm). *(Martin Jones)*

CARSHALTON   TQ2764
Hope (020) 8240 1255
West Street; SM5 2PR Chatty male-dominated pub owned by local consortium;

Downton, Windsor & Eton and five guests, also craft beers, real cider/perry and over 50 bottled beers, generous low-priced pubby food (limited evening choice), 1950s feel with a room either side of bar, lots of pump clips on walls, open fire, larger back room with bar billiards, acoustic music second Weds of month, regular beer and cider festivals; garden, open all day. *(Conor McGaughey)*

CATERHAM   TQ3254
Harrow (01883) 343260
Stanstead Road, Whitehill; CR3 6AJ
Simple beamed 16th-c pub high up in open country by North Downs Way; L-shaped bare-boards bar and carpeted back dining area, several real ales (sometimes straight from the cask), enjoyable food (not Sun evening) including daily specials, good local atmosphere and friendly service; children and dogs welcome, garden picnic-sets, popular with walkers and cyclists, open all day. *(Belinda May)*

CHARLESHILL   SU8844
Donkey (01252) 702124
B3001 Milford–Farnham near Tilford; coming from Elstead, turn left as soon as you see pub sign; GU10 2AU
Old-fashioned beamed dining pub with enjoyable home-made food including set menus and other deals, up to three well kept changing ales and good choice of wines by the glass, prompt friendly service, conservatory restaurant, traditional games; children and dogs welcome, attractive garden with wendy house, much-loved donkeys Pip and Dusty in paddock, good walks, open all day weekends. *(Martin Jones)*

CHERTSEY   TQ0466
Thyme at the Tavern
(01932) 429667 *London Street; KT16 8AA* Busy pub with well kept Courage Best, St Austell Tribute and two local guests (beer festivals), well priced pubby food (not Mon, Sat or evenings Fri, Sun) including popular Sun lunch (must book); live music Fri; dogs welcome, four bedrooms, open all day (from 5pm Mon). *(Hunter and Christine Wright)*

CHIDDINGFOLD   SU9635
★ ## Crown (01428) 682255
The Green (A283); GU8 4TX Lovely 700-year-old timbered building with strong sense of history; bar and connected dining rooms with massive beams (some over 2-ft thick), oak panelling, fine stained-glass windows and magnificently carved fireplace, mate's and other pubby chairs, cushioned wall seats and some nice antique tables, lots

of portraits, simple split-level back public bar with open fire, up to five changing ales and several wines by the glass, enjoyable often interesting food (all day Fri-Sun); children (there's a playroom) and dogs welcome in some areas, seats outside looking across village green to interesting church, more tables in sheltered central courtyard, character bedrooms, open all day from 7am (8am Sun) for breakfast. *(Dr Simon Innes)*

CHIDDINGFOLD   SU9635
Swan (01428) 682073
Petworth Road (A283 S); GU8 4TY
Stylishly updated boutique hotel/dining pub, good well presented modern food together with pub favourites, friendly attentive service, bar with polished wood floor and brick inglenook, local ales such as Surrey Hills, restaurant; children welcome, attractive three-tier back terrace, ten bedrooms, open all day. *(Belinda May)*

CHILWORTH   TQ0347
Percy Arms (01483) 561765
Dorking Road; GU4 8NP Partly 18th-c inn with south african influences in décor and food, good choice of wines by the glass, four real ales including Greene King and one named for the pub, front bar and lounge with steps down to dining area, efficient service despite being busy; newspapers and background jazz; children welcome, garden tables with pretty views over Vale of Chilworth to St Martha's Hill, good walks, five bedrooms, open all day, food all day weekends. *(Anne and Ben Smith)*

CHIPSTEAD   TQ2757
Ramblers Rest (01737) 552661
Outwood Lane (B2032); CR5 3NP
Mitchells & Butlers country dining pub with contemporary furnishings in partly 14th-c rambling building, low beams (old and new), flagstones, panelling and log fires, enjoyable up-to-date and more traditional food including popular Sun lunch, Adnams Broadside, Sharps Doom Bar and interesting continental beers, Meantime lager and Aspall's cider, good value wines by the glass, young friendly staff (can get distracted at times), dining extension; children and dogs welcome, disabled access (from front) and facilities, big pleasant garden with terrace, attractive views, good walks, open (and food) all day. *(Sheila Topham)*

CHIPSTEAD   TQ2555
Well House (01737) 830640
Chipstead signed with Mugswell off A217, N of M25 junction 8; CR5 3SQ
Originally three 16th-c cottages (converted

'Children welcome' means the pub says it lets children inside without any special restriction; some may impose an evening time limit earlier than 9pm – please tell us if you find this.

from tearooms to pub in 1955); log fires in all three rooms, low beams and rustic décor, bric-a-brac and pewter tankards hanging from ceiling, well kept Adnams, Fullers, Surrey Hills and local guests, Millwhite's cider, food from baguettes up (not Sun evening), friendly staff, small conservatory, resident ghost called Harry the Monk; dogs allowed (they have cats), large pleasing hillside garden with ancient well (reputed to be mentioned in the Domesday Book), delightful country setting, open all day. *(Conor McGaughey)*

CHURT   SU8538
Crossways (01428) 714323
Corner of A287 and Hale House Lane; GU10 2JE Friendly down-to-earth local, quarry-tiled public bar and carpeted saloon with panelling and plush banquettes, busy evenings for good changing beer range at reasonable prices, also four or more real ciders, enjoyable well priced home-made pub lunches (not Sun) including nice pies, evening food Weds only, cheerful young staff; TVs and machines; dogs welcome, garden, open all day Fri-Sun. *(Tony and Jill Radnor)*

CLAYGATE   TQ1563
★Foley (01372) 462021
Hare Lane; KT10 0LZ Beautifully restored 19th-c Youngs pub; pubby part at front with wooden tables and chairs on bare boards, leather armchairs and sofas by Victorian fireplace, lots of interconnected sitting and dining areas leading off, their well kept ales and a guest, 30 wines by the glass, interesting spirits and good range of coffees and teas, highly thought-of food from open kitchen; background music, daily papers and free wi-fi; children and dogs (in bar) welcome, seats on two-level terrace, well equipped, modern bedrooms, open (and food) all day including breakfast from 7.30am (8.30am Sun). *(Martin Jones, Caroline Prescott)*

CLAYGATE   TQ1563
Hare & Hounds (01372) 465149
The Green; KT10 0JL Renovated flower-decked Victorian/Edwardian village pub with small restaurant, good sensibly priced french food along with some pub favourites and Thurs curry night, nice wines and well kept changing ales, competent friendly service; Sun quiz, free wi-fi; children and dogs welcome, outside seating at front and in small back garden with play area, open all day. *(Geoffrey Kemp)*

COBHAM   TQ1159
Running Mare (01932) 862007
Tilt Road; KT11 3EZ Attractive old flower-decked pub overlooking green (can get very busy); well kept Fullers, Hogs Back and Youngs, good food including popular Sun lunch, efficient friendly service, two timbered bars and restaurant; children very welcome,

a few tables out at front and on rose-covered back terrace, open all day. *(Geoffrey Kemp, C and R Bromage)*

COLDHARBOUR   TQ1544
Plough (01306) 711793
Village signposted in the network of small roads around Leith Hill; RH5 6HD Cosy two-bar pub with own-brewed Leith Hill ales and guests, proper cider and several wines by the glass, open fires, light beams and timbering, food in bar or restaurant (not always open) including range of home-made burgers, pleasant service, snug games room with darts, board games and cards; background music, Thurs quiz, TV; children (if eating) and dogs welcome, front terrace and quiet back garden overlooking fields, five bedrooms (ones above bar can be noisy), open all day. *(Richard Stanfield)*

COMPTON   SU9646
★Withies (01483) 421158
Withies Lane; pub signed from B3000; GU3 1JA Carefully altered 16th-c pub, charmingly civilised and gently old-fashioned, with low-beamed bar, some 17th-c carved panels between windows, splendid art nouveau settle among old sewing-machine tables, log fire in massive inglenook, well kept Adnams, Greene King, Hogs Back and Sharps, popular (not cheap) bar food served by efficient bow-tied staff; children welcome, seats on terrace, under apple trees and creeper-hung arbour, flower-edged neat front lawn, on edge of Loseley Park and close to Watts Gallery, closed Sun evening. *(Colin McKerrow, Helen and Brian Edgeley, Geoffrey Kemp)*

DORKING   TQ1649
Cricketers (01306) 889938
South Street; RH4 2JU Chatty and relaxed little Fullers local, well kept Chiswick, London Pride, ESB and a guest, simple lunchtime food (not weekends), solidly comfortable furniture, cricketing memorabilia on stripped-brick walls, friendly service, events including beer festivals, a Scalextric championship and onion growing competition; darts, sports TV, free wi-fi; nice split-level back terrace, open all day. *(Conor McGaughey)*

DORMANSLAND   TQ4042
Old House At Home (01342) 836828
West Street; RH7 6QP Friendly 19th-c village pub, beamed bar with open fire and traditional furniture on parquet floor, horsebrasses above unusual barrel-fronted counter serving Shepherd Neame ales, enjoyable well priced food (not Sun evening) including fresh pizzas, carpeted restaurant and plainer room with darts and TV; some live music; children and dogs (in bar) welcome, a few picnic-sets in front, beer garden behind, closed Mon lunchtime, otherwise open all day. *(Tony Scott)*

DORMANSLAND TQ4042
Plough (01342) 832933
Plough Road, off B2028 NE; RH7 6PS
Friendly traditional old pub in quiet village, well kept Fullers, Harveys and Sharps, Weston's cider, decent wines, good choice of enjoyable bar food including specials board, thai restaurant (Mon-Sat), log fires and original features; children welcome, disabled facilities, good-sized garden. *(R and S Bentley, David Jackman, Tony Scott)*

DUNSFOLD TQ0036
Sun (01483) 200242
Off B2130 S of Godalming; GU8 4LE
Old double-fronted pub with four rooms (brighter at the front), beams and some exposed brickwork, scrubbed pine furniture and two massive log fires, ales such as Adnams, Harveys and Sharps, decent wines, enjoyable home-made pub food at reasonable prices including popular Sun lunch (best to book), good friendly service; Sun quiz, darts; children and dogs welcome, seats on terrace and common opposite, good walks. *(Ian Phillips)*

EASHING SU9543
★Stag (01483) 421568
Lower Eashing, just off A3 southbound; GU7 2QG Civilised, gently upmarket riverside inn with Georgian façade masking much older interior; attractively opened-up rooms including charming old-fashioned locals' bar with armchairs on red and black quarry tiles, cosy log-fire snug beyond, Hogs Back TEA, one or two Marstons-related ales and a beer badged for the pub, Hazy Hog cider, plenty of emphasis on food with several linked dining areas including river room up a couple of steps, attentive courteous staff; children welcome, dogs in bar, extensive terrace with wicker or wooden furniture under parasols (some by weir), picnic-sets on grass, seven bedrooms, open all day. *(Anne and Ben Smith)*

EAST CLANDON TQ0551
★Queens Head (01483) 222332
Just off A246 Guildford–Leatherhead; The Street; GU4 7RY Busy dining pub in same small group as Duke of Cambridge at Tilford, Stag at Eashing and Wheatsheaf in Farnham, well liked food (best to book) from light dishes to good daily specials, set lunch deal (Mon-Thurs), a beer badged for them and changing guests such as Ringwood and Surrey Hills from fine elm-topped counter, also Hazy Hog cider and nice wines by the glass, good friendly service, comfortable linked rooms, log fire in big inglenook; daily newspapers and free wi-fi, silent TV in bar; children welcome, tables out in front and

on side terrace, handy for Hatchlands (NT), open all day Fri and Sat, till 9pm Sun. *(John Wooll, John Evans, Ian Phillips and others)*

EAST MOLESEY TQ1568
Albion (020) 8783 9342
Bridge Road; KT8 9HA Comfortable open-plan Ember Inn near the river, drinking area to the left with window seating, dining area to the right, well kept Brakspears, Fullers, Windsor & Eton and four guests (reduced prices Mon), Weston's Old Rosie cider and several wines by the glass, decent good value food including deals; background music, free wi-fi; children welcome, handy for Hampton Court, open all day (food till 10pm). *(Tony Hobden)*

EAST MOLESEY TQ1267
Bell (020) 8941 0400
Bell Road; KT8 0SS Tucked-away 15th-c gabled pub (aka the Crooked House) recently refurbished by Spirit Pub Co; opened-up interior with plenty of nooks and crannies, beams and open fires, half a dozen real ales, good value food from sandwiches and baked potatoes up, lunchtime set deal Mon-Fri, friendly staff; sports TV and darts in one part; children welcome, big garden, open all day. *(Dr Simon Innes)*

EFFINGHAM TQ1153
★Plough (01372) 458121
Orestan Lane; KT24 5SW Popular refurbished Youngs pub with well kept ales and enjoyable home-made food including good Sun roasts and proper children's menu, plenty of wines by the glass, friendly efficient staff, open interior around central bar, grey painted beams, delft shelving and half-panelling, wood floors, two coal-effect gas fires; plenty of tables on forecourt and in pretty garden with fruit trees, disabled access and parking, handy for Polesden Lacey (NT), closed Sun evening. *(Simon and Mandy King)*

ELSTEAD SU9044
Mill at Elstead (01252) 703333
Farnham Road (B3001 just W of village, which is itself between Farnham and Milford); GU8 6LE Fascinating sensitively converted 18th-c watermill in pretty setting above River Wey; rambling linked bar areas on spacious ground floor, Fullers/Gales beers and good range of wines by the glass, reliably good food, upstairs restaurant with leather armchairs and neat modern furniture on dark woodstrip flooring, also big country tables on broad ceramic tiles, iron pillars, stripped masonry and log fire in huge inglenook; background music, free wi-fi; children welcome, dogs in bar, picnic-sets by the water with its lovely millpond, swans and

---

If you know a pub is ever open all day, please tell us.

weeping willows, charmingly floodlit at night, open (and food) all day. *(Peter Chapman, Christopher and Elise Way)*

ELSTEAD   SU9043
Woolpack (01252) 703106
B3001 Milford–Farnham; GU8 6HD Comfortably modernised tile-hung dining pub under italian owners, enjoyable home-cooked food including stone-baked pizzas, Thurs italian night, Sat fish night and Sun carvery, cask tapped ales and decent wines by the glass, friendly efficient staff, long main bar, restaurant, open fires; children welcome, garden with picnic-sets, open all day Sun. *(D J and P M Taylor)*

EPSOM   TQ2160
Rising Sun (01372) 740809
Heathcote Road; KT18 5DX Friendly well restored Victorian backstreet pub, open-plan but with well defined cosy front bar, St Austell, Youngs and a couple of guests, several wines by the glass, enjoyable home-made food with some imaginative additions to traditional menu, efficient courteous service, open fire; Sun quiz; disabled access and facilities, nice garden with covered area, barbecues, open all day. *(Simon and Mandy King)*

EPSOM   TQ2158
Rubbing House (01372) 745050
Langley Vale Road (on Epsom Downs Racecourse); KT18 5LJ Restaurant dining pub popular for its fantastic racecourse views – can get very busy but staff cope well; attractive modern décor, good value promptly served food including children's menu, tables perhaps a little close together, Greene King and Sharps ales, serious wine list, upper balcony for Derby days; background music; seats out by the course, open all day. *(N R White)*

FARNHAM   SU8346
Wheatsheaf (01252) 717135
West Street; GU9 7DR Stylishly refurbished old pub in same group as the Queens Head at East Clandon, Stag at Eashing and Duke of Cambridge at Tilford; good food (all day Fri-Sun) from open kitchen including weekday set menu, gluten-free diets catered for, well kept local ales such as Hogs Back, craft beers and good choice of wines and whiskies, friendly helpful staff; free wi-fi; children welcome, seats in back courtyard, open all day (from 9am weekends for breakfast), no nearby parking. *(Belinda May)*

FICKLESHOLE   TQ3960
White Bear (01959) 573166
Featherbed Lane/Fairchildes Lane; off A2022 just S of A212 roundabout; CR6 9PH Long 16th-c country dining pub with lots of small rooms, beams, flagstones and open fires, popular good value food, orders taken from the bar (they may ask for

a credit card if you run a tab), Brakspears, Pilgrim and a couple of guests; children and well behaved dogs welcome, picnic-sets and stone bear on front terrace, sizeable back garden with pond and summer 'kitchen', open all day (till 9.30pm Sun). *(Alec and Joan Laurence, David Jackman)*

FOREST GREEN   TQ1241
Parrot (01306) 621339
B2127 just W of junction with B2126, SW of Dorking; RH5 5RZ Old tile-hung village pub, heavy beams, timbers, flagstones and nooks and crannies, inglenook log fire, popular food (not Sun evening) using produce from own farm, five well kept changing ales including Ringwood, 16 wines by the glass, local fruit juices; shop selling own meat, cheeses, cured hams, pies and so forth; dogs welcome in bar, disabled facilities, attractive gardens with lovely country views, good walks nearby, open all day (till midnight Sat). *(Richard Stanfield, Guy Vowles, P and J Shapley)*

GODALMING   SU9643
Star (01483) 417717
Church Street; GU7 1EL Friendly 17th-c local in cobbled pedestrian street, cosy low-beamed and panelled L-shaped bar, up to eight well kept changing ales (four tapped from the cask) including Greene King, five proper ciders/perries, lunchtime bar food, more modern back room; Mon folk night, Sun quiz; no dogs, heated back terrace, open all day. *(Anne and Ben Smith)*

GOMSHALL   TQ0847
Compasses (01483) 202506
Station Road (A25); GU5 9LA Popular village pub with plain bar and much bigger comfortable dining room, also café and post office, good value home-made food, well kept Surrey Hills and decent wines by the glass, friendly helpful service; background music (live Fri), also Aug 'Gomstock' festival; children and dogs welcome, pretty garden sloping down to roadside mill stream, two bedrooms, open (and food) all day, closes around 8pm Sun. *(Belinda May)*

GRAYSWOOD   SU9134
Wheatsheaf (01428) 644440
Grayswood Road (A286 NE of Haslemere); GU27 2DE Welcoming family-run dining pub with light airy décor, enjoyable freshly made food in bar and restaurant, good range of well kept beers, friendly helpful staff; front verandah, side terrace, seven bedrooms in extension, good breakfast. *(Anon)*

GUILDFORD   SU9949
Kings Head (01483) 575004
Quarry Street; GU1 3XQ Dating from the 16th c with lots of beams and stripped brickwork, cosy corners with armchairs, stylish oval tables, inglenook log fire, well

kept Hogs Back and guests, decent wines, enjoyable reasonably priced food (not Sun evening) including variety of burgers and pizzas, quiz-and-curry night Mon, friendly young staff; background music (live Sun), fruit machine, sports TV; no dogs inside, picnic-sets in pleasant back courtyard with roof terrace giving castle views, open all day (till 2.30am Fri, Sat). *(Phil and Jane Villiers, Tony Scott)*

GUILDFORD   SU9948

Olde Ship   (01483) 575731

Portsmouth Road (St Catherine's, A3100 S); GU2 4EB Three cosy areas around central bar, ancient beams, bare boards and flagstones, roaring log fire in big fireplace, woodburner the other end, comfortable mix of furniture, enjoyable food including good wood-fired pizzas, well kept Greene King ales and a guest, Hogs Back Hazy Hog cider, decent wines, friendly staff and locals; dogs welcome, open all day weekends. *(Belinda May)*

GUILDFORD   SU9949

Weyside   (01483) 568024

Shalford Road, Millbrook; across car park from Yvonne Arnaud Theatre, beyond boatyard; GU1 3XJ Big riverside pub (former Boatman) refurbished by Youngs, their ales and enjoyable food from sharing dishes and pub favourites up, friendly service, large split-level bar dropping down to back dining conservatory, also barn-room restaurant; children and dogs welcome, terrace overlooking River Wey, open all day. *(Martin Jones)*

GUILDFORD   SU9949

White House   (01483) 302006

High Street; GU2 4AJ Refurbished Fullers pub in pretty waterside setting, their ales and good range of wines, enjoyable food from small plates up, sizeable bar with conservatory, upstairs rooms and roof terrace; children welcome, a few picnic-sets by River Wey, open (and food) all day. *(Tony Scott)*

HAMBLEDON   SU9639

Merry Harriers   (01428) 682883

Off A283; just N of village; GU8 4DR Beamed 16th-c country local with huge inglenook log fire and pine tables on bare boards, five well kept ales including Pilgrim, Surrey Hills and Tillingbourne, local cider and lots of wines by the glass, generally well liked home-cooked food, friendly staff; monthly live music and quiz nights; children welcome, seats out in front and in big garden

with boules, llamas in adjacent fields, good walking country near Greensand Way, three bedrooms in converted barn, campsite, open all day weekends in summer. *(Anon)*

HOLMBURY ST MARY   TQ1144

Kings Head   (01306) 730282

Pitland Street; RH5 6NP Welcoming bare-boards pub in walking country, some refurbishment under newish owners, good home-made food and well kept ales such as Dark Star Hophead, Otter and Surrey Hills Shere Drop, log fires; background and occasional live music, darts; children and dogs welcome, pretty spot with seats out facing green, more in big sloping back garden, may close Mon lunchtime. *(Belinda May)*

HORLEY   TQ2742

Olde Six Bells   (01293) 825028

Quite handy for M23 junction 9, off Horley turn from A23; Church Road – head for the church spire; RH6 8AD Ancient stone-roofed Vintage Inn – part of heavy-beamed open-plan bar was probably a medieval chapel and some masonry may date from the 9th c; their usual good value food, Fullers London Pride, Sharps Doom Bar and a guest, log fires, upstairs overflow raftered dining room, conservatory; children welcome, tables out by bend in River Mole, open all day. *(Tony Scott)*

HORSELL   SU9859

Cricketers   (01483) 762363

Horsell Birch; GU21 4XB Country pub popular for its good sensibly priced food including set deals and Sun carvery, cheerful efficient service, Shepherd Neame ales and plenty of wines by the glass, quietly comfortable sections and extended back eating area, log fires, newspapers; live jazz Mon, quiz every other Tues; no dogs inside; children welcome, wheelchair access, picnic-sets out at front overlooking Horsell Common, big back garden with barbecue and good play area, open all day. *(Anne and Ben Smith)*

HORSELL   SU9959

Plough   (01483) 714105

Off South Road; Cheapside; GU21 4JL Small friendly local overlooking wooded heath, relaxed atmosphere, well kept Dartmoor, Sharps and a guest, reasonably priced home-made food (not Sun or Mon evenings) including daily specials and weekday set menu, L-shaped bar with woodburner; Weds quiz; families and dogs welcome (theirs is Buddy), tables in pretty

---

We mention bottled beers and spirits only if there is something unusual about them – imported belgian real ales, say, or dozens of malt whiskies; so do please let us know about them in your reports.

garden with play area, open all day.
(Dr Simon Innes)

HORSELL   SU9959
★ **Red Lion** (01483) 768497
High Street; GU21 4SS Large and very
popular with light airy feel, split-level bar
with comfortable sofas and easy chairs,
clusters of pictures on cream-painted walls,
Fullers London Pride, St Austell Tribute
and a guest from long wooden servery, a
dozen wines by the glass, back dining room
with exposed brick walls, old pews and
blackboards listing the good bistro-style
food, efficient service; children allowed till
early evening, ivy-clad passage to garden and
comfortable tree-sheltered terrace, good
walks, open all day. *(Ian Phillips, Phil Bryant)*

HORSELL COMMON   TQ0160
★ **Sands at Bleak House**
(01483) 756988 *Chertsey Road, The
Anthonys; A320 Woking–Ottershaw;
GU21 5NL* Smart contemporary pub-
restaurant on edge of Horsell Common; grey
sandstone for floor and face of bar counter,
brown leather sofas and cushioned stools,
two dining rooms with dark wood furniture,
woodburners, good if not cheap food,
Andwell, Hogs Back and Sharps; background music,
TV, free wi-fi; children welcome, courtyard
with picnic-sets and smokers' shelter, good
shortish walk to sandpits that inspired
H G Wells's *The War of the Worlds*, seven
bedrooms, open all day, till 6pm Sun. *(Anon)*

IRONSBOTTOM   TQ2546
Three Horseshoes (01293) 862315
Sidlow Bridge, off A217; RH2 8PT
Welcoming roadside pub with good
reasonably priced home-made food (not Sun
evening) from pub favourites up, well kept
Fullers, Harveys, Youngs and three guests,
several wines by the glass, quick friendly
service, traditional furnishings including
upholstered banquettes, dark wood and red
patterned carpet, some barrel tables; darts;
tables outside, summer barbecues, handy
for Gatwick airport, open all day (till 8pm
Sun). *(Martin Jones)*

LALEHAM   TQ0568
★ **Three Horseshoes** (01784) 455014
Shepperton Road (B376); TW18 1SE
Bustling dining pub near pleasant stretch
of the Thames; bar with white walls and
contrasting deep blue woodwork, easy-going
mix of tables and chairs on bare boards, log
fire fronted by armchairs and squashy sofa,
well kept Fullers/Gales beers and plenty of
wines by the glass, popular sensibly priced
food including blackboard specials (booking
advised), efficient friendly staff, dining areas
with assorted tables and chairs, pictures and
mirrors on grey walls; soft background music,
free wi-fi; children welcome till 7.30pm,
attractive flagstoned terrace, picnic-sets on

grass, open (and food) all day. *(Hunter and
Christine Wright, Eddie Edwards, Geoffrey Kemp,
Simon Collett-Jones and others)*

LEATHERHEAD   TQ1656
Running Horse (01372) 372081
Bridge Street; KT22 8BZ Split-level
Shepherd Neame pub dating from the early
15th c, their beers along with Surrey Hills
Ranmore, good value traditional food, beams,
timbers and half-panelling, pubby furniture
on patterned carpet, log fire; quiz nights
and monthly live music, TV, pool and darts;
children (till 8pm) and dogs welcome, beer
garden, close to River Mole, open all day.
(Conor McGaughey)

LEIGH   TQ2147
★ **Seven Stars** (01306) 611254
*Dawes Green, south of A25 Dorking–
Reigate; RH2 8NP* Attractive tile-hung
country dining pub, comfortable beamed and
flagstoned bar with traditional furnishings
and inglenook, Fullers, Sharps, Youngs
and a guest from glowing copper counter,
several wines by the glass, popular food all
day (till 6pm Sun), plainer public bar and
sympathetic restaurant extension where
children allowed; dogs welcome in bars,
plenty of outside seating, open all day.
(Anon)

LIMPSFIELD CHART   TQ4251
Carpenters Arms (01883) 722209
Tally Road; RH8 0TG Friendly open-plan
pub owned by Westerham, their full range
kept well (tasting trays available), popular
home-made food (not Sun evening) from light
lunches up, friendly helpful staff, garden
room; free wi-fi; tables on terrace and lawn,
delightful setting by village common, lovely
walks and handy for Chartwell (NT), open all
day weekends. *(Nick Lawless, B J Harding)*

LINGFIELD   TQ3844
Hare Bar & Grill (01342) 832351
*Turn off B2029 N at Crowhurst/
Edenbridge signpost; RH7 6BZ* Recently
refurbished open-plan dining pub, good
attractively presented food from french
chef-owner including charcoal grills, good
wines by the glass and well kept ales such
as Harveys and Sharps; background music;
children and dogs welcome, tables in
pleasant split-level garden with decking
and pizza oven, nice walking country, open
all day, closed Sun evening. *(Anne and
Ben Smith)*

MICKLEHAM   TQ1753
King William IV (01372) 372590
*Just off A24 Leatherhead–Dorking;
Byttom Hill; RH5 6EL* Steps up to small
nicely placed country pub, well kept Hogs
Back TEA, Surrey Hills Shere Drop and
a guest, enjoyable food from lunchtime
sandwiches to blackboard specials, friendly
attentive service, pleasant outlook from snug

plank-panelled front bar, carpeted dining area with grandfather clock and log fire; background music, live jazz Sun evening; children and dogs welcome, plenty of tables (some in heated open-sided timber shelters) in pretty terraced garden, lovely valley views, open (and food) all day. *(Martin Jones)*

MOGADOR   TQ2453

Sportsman (01737) 246655

From M25 up A217 past second roundabout, then Mogador signed; KT20 7ES Modernised and extended low-ceilinged pub on edge of Walton Heath (originally 16th-c royal hunting lodge), well kept ales including Sharps and Charles Wells, good food from varied interesting menu, friendly attentive service, restaurant with raised section, Mon quiz; children welcome (no pushchairs), dogs in bar, picnic-sets out on common and on back lawn, more seats on front verandah, popular with walkers and riders, open all day. *(Brian Glozier)*

NUTFIELD   TQ3050

Queens Head (01737) 823619

A25 E of Redhill; RH1 4HH Welcoming three-room beamed pub with good locally sourced food (not Sun evening) including themed nights, well kept ales such as Harveys, Pilgrim, Sharps and Surrey Hills, plenty of wines by the glass; regular live music, Sun quiz, darts; picnic-sets on side lawn, summer barbecues, open all day. *(David and Sally Cullen, Caroline Hoyle, Mrs S Slater)*

OCKLEY   TQ1337

★ Punchbowl (01306) 627249

Oakwood Hill, signed off A29 S; RH5 5PU Attractive 16th-c tile-hung country pub with Horsham slab roof; friendly landlord and welcoming relaxed atmosphere, wide choice of good value generously served food (not Sun evening), Badger ales, central bar with huge inglenook, polished flagstones and low beams, collections of brass spiles, horsebrasses and cigarette lighters, restaurant area to left and another bar to right with sofas, armchairs and TV, daily papers; children welcome and dogs (water bowl and biscuits), picnic-sets in pretty garden, smokers' awning, quiet spot with good walks including Sussex Border Path, open all day. *(Belinda May)*

OUTWOOD   TQ3246

★ Bell (01342) 842989

Outwood Common, just E of village; off A23 S of Redhill; RH1 5PN Attractive 17th-c extended dining pub; smartly rustic beamed bar with oak and elm furniture (some Jacobean in style), soft lighting, low beams and vast stone inglenook, Fullers London Pride, ESB and a guest, 20 wines by the glass and wide range of spirits, popular food from pub standards up (best to book, especially evenings when drinking-only space limited); background music, free wi-fi; children and dogs (in bar) welcome, well maintained garden looking out past pine trees to rolling fields, open all day, food all day weekends. *(John Branston, Tony Scott)*

OUTWOOD   TQ3146

Dog & Duck (01342) 842964

Prince of Wales Road; turn off A23 at station sign in Salfords, S of Redhill – OS Sheet 187 map reference 312460; RH1 5QU Unhurried beamed country pub with fairly priced home-made food in bar or restaurant, friendly service, well kept Badger ales from brick-faced bar, decent wines, warm winter fires; monthly quiz and live music nights; children welcome, garden with duck pond and play area. *(Mrs Sally Scott, Tony Scott)*

OXTED   TQ4048

Royal Oak (01883) 722207

Caterfield Lane, Staffhurst Wood, S of town; RH8 0RR Popular country pub, cheerful and comfortable, with ales such as Adnams, Larkins and Sharps, also good range of ciders including Biddenden and Weston's, enjoyable locally sourced home-made food (not Sun or Mon evenings), back dining room, open fire; children and dogs welcome, nice garden with lovely views across fields, open all day Fri-Sun. *(Simon Rodway, R and S Bentley)*

PUTTENHAM   SU9347

Good Intent (01483) 810387

Signed off B3000 just S of A31 junction; The Street/Seale Lane; GU3 1AR Well worn-in convivial beamed village local, Otter, Sharps, Timothy Taylors and three guests, popular reasonably priced traditional food (not Sun, Mon evenings), log fire in cosy front bar with alcove seating, some old photographs of the pub, simple dining area; well behaved children and dogs welcome, small sunny garden, good walks, open all day weekends. *(Alan and Shirley Sawden)*

PYRFORD LOCK   TQ0559

Anchor (01932) 342507

3 miles from M25 junction 10 – S on A3, then take Wisley slip road and go on past RHS Wisley garden; GU23 6QW Light and airy waterside dining pub (can get

---

Please tell us if the décor, atmosphere, food or drink at a pub is different from our description. We rely on readers' reports to keep us up to date: feedback@goodguides.com, or (no stamp needed) The Good Pub Guide, FREEPOST RTJR-ZCYZ-RJZT, Perrymans Lane, Etchingham TN19 7DN.

very busy and may be queues), enjoyable
food from sandwiches up, Badger ales and
several wines by the glass, simple tables
on bare boards, quieter more comfortable
panelled back area, narrowboat memorabilia,
pleasant oak-framed conservatory with raised
woodburner, daily papers; children welcome,
dogs in some areas, splendid terrace by
bridge and locks on River Wey Navigation,
moorings, large car park across road, handy
for RHS Wisley, open (and food) all day.
(Katharine Cowherd, Colin McKerrow)

REDHILL   TQ2750
Garland (01737) 764612
Brighton Road; RH1 6PP Friendly 19th-c
Harveys corner local under new management,
their full range including seasonals, well
priced traditional lunchtime food (also
Fri evening, Sun till 4pm), darts and bar
billiards; live music Sat, free wi-fi; children
(till 7.30pm) and well behaved dogs welcome,
picnic-sets in back garden, open all day.
(Tony Hobden, Tony Scott)

REDHILL   TQ2850
Home Cottage (01737) 762771
Redstone Hill; RH1 4AW Stylishly updated
19th-c Youngs pub with their ales and guests,
several wines by the glass (can be pricey)
and good variety of enjoyable food in bar and
restaurant; seats outside including covered
terrace, open (and food) all day. *(PL)*

REDHILL   TQ2749
Plough (01737) 766686
Church Road, St John's; RH1 6QE
Friendly early 17th-c beamed pub, lots of bits
and pieces to look at including copper and
brass hanging from ceiling, Fullers, Youngs
and a couple of guests, enjoyable sensibly
priced blackboard food (not Sun evening),
open fire; Weds quiz; no under-10s inside,
dogs welcome, back garden with terrace,
open all day. *(Tony Scott)*

REIGATE HEATH   TQ2349
Skimmington Castle (01737) 243100
*Off A25 Reigate–Dorking via Flanchford
Road and Bonny's Road; RH2 8RL* Nicely
located small country pub with emphasis
on enjoyable home-made food (can get very
busy, best to book), Harveys, St Austell and
a couple of guests, friendly helpful service,
panelled beamed rooms, big working
fireplace; children, dogs and muddy boots
welcome, open all day, food till 7pm Sun.
*(C and R Bromage, Brian Glozier, Mrs Sally Scott,
Tony Scott)*

RIPLEY   TQ0556
Anchor (01483) 211866
High Street; GU23 6AE Refurbished
former 16th-c almshouse, clean modern
décor in low-ceilinged linked areas,
reminders here and there of Ripley's cycling
heritage, good interesting food from bar
snacks up, quite pricey but they do offer

a lunchtime set menu (not Sun), Timothy
Taylors Landlord and local guests, several
wines by the glass including champagne;
children welcome, rattan-style furniture in
sunny decked courtyard, closed Sun evening,
Mon, otherwise open all day. *(Gerry Price,
Christopher and Elise Way, Geoffrey Kemp)*

RIPLEY   TQ0456
Seven Stars (01483) 225128
Newark Lane (B367); GU23 6DL Neat
and comfortable 1930s pub, enjoyable food
from extensive menu, Brakspears, Fullers,
Sharps and Shepherd Neame, good wines
and coffee, snug areas, red patterned carpet,
gleaming brasses and open fire; quiet
background music; picnic-sets and heated
wooden booths in tidy garden, river and
canalside walks, closed Sun evening.
(Tom and Ruth Rees)

SEND   TQ0156
New Inn (01483) 762736
Send Road, Cartbridge; GU23 7EN
Well placed old pub by River Wey Navigation,
long bar and dining room, Adnams, Fullers,
Greene King, Sharps and a guest, good
choice of nicely presented food (something
available all day) from sandwiches, through
grills to blackboard specials, friendly service,
beams and log-effect gas fires; children and
dogs welcome, large waterside garden with
moorings. *(Anne and Ben Smith)*

SHALFORD   SU9946
Parrot (01483) 561400
Broadford Road; GU4 8DW Big welcoming
inn with wide range of popular freshly made
food, Fullers London Pride, Sharps Doom Bar
and Surrey Hills Shere Drop, good friendly
service, rows of neat pine dining tables,
some easy chairs around low tables, pleasant
conservatory; free wi-fi; children welcome till
8pm, attractive garden, four bedrooms, handy
for Loseley Park. *(David M Smith)*

SHALFORD   TQ0047
Seahorse (01483) 514351
*A281 S of Guildford; The Street;
GU4 8BU* Gently upmarket Mitchells &
Butlers dining pub with wide range of food
including popular set menu (weekdays till
6pm), friendly young staff, Adnams and
Sharps Doom Bar, good choice of wines and
other drinks, contemporary furniture and
artwork, two-way log fire, smart dining room,
comfortable part near entrance with sofas
and huge window; picnic-sets in big lawned
garden, covered terrace, handy for Shalford
Mill (NT), open all day. *(Richard Tilbrook)*

SHAMLEY GREEN   TQ0343
Bricklayers Arms (01483) 898377
Guildford Road, S of the green; GU5 0UA
Red-brick village pub with five well kept
ales such as Exmoor, Hogs Back and Surrey
Hills, enjoyable pubby food (not Sun evening)
including fish and steak specials (Fri, Sat),

U-shaped layout with bare boards, carpets and flagstones, exposed brick and stripped wood, old local photographs, sofas by woodburner, games area with pool, darts and machines; quiz and poker nights, TV; children welcome, couple of picnic-sets out in front, more seats behind, open all day. *(Ian Phillips)*

SHERE   TQ0747
White Horse (01483) 202518
Shere Lane; signed off A25 3 miles E of Guildford; GU5 9HS Splendid Chef & Brewer with uneven floors, massive beams and timbers, Tudor stonework, oak wall seats and two log fires (one in huge inglenook), several rooms off small bar, good range of enjoyable food including deals, ales such as Sharps, Surrey Hills and Tillingbourne, Weston's Old Rosie cider and plenty of wines by the glass, good service; children welcome, seats out at front and in big garden behind, beautiful film-set village, open (and food) all day. *(Ian Phillips, Tony Scott)*

SHERE   TQ0747
William Bray (01483) 202044
Shere Lane; GU5 9HS Emphasis on well presented locally sourced food (not particularly cheap), ales such as Surrey Hills and decent choice of wines and whiskies, roomy contemporary bar with stone floor and woodburner, more formal airy restaurant with comfortable leather chairs and large F1 racing photographs (owner was driver for Tyrell and Lotus); background music; dogs welcome, tables on front split-level terrace, pretty landscaped garden, useful car park, open all day. *(Anon)*

STAINES   TQ0371
Bells (01784) 454240
Church Street; TW18 4ZB Comfortable and sociable Youngs pub in old part of town, their well kept ales and a guest, decent choice of wines and good promptly served fresh food (special diets catered for), central fireplace; dogs allowed in bar, tables in nice back garden with heated terrace, limited roadside parking, open all day weekends (no food Sun evening). *(Belinda May)*

STAINES   TQ0371
Swan (01784) 452494
The Hythe; south bank, over Staines Bridge; TW18 3JB Sizeable unchanging old pub-hotel in splendid Thames-side setting with verandah and terrace overlooking the water, big conservatory, several distinctly different areas including river-view upstairs restaurant, well kept Fullers ales, food can be good; children welcome, 11 comfortable bedrooms, moorings, open all day and gets busy Sun lunchtime and summer evenings, parking may be difficult. *(Richard Stanfield)*

STOKE D'ABERNON   TQ1259
★ **Old Plough** (01932) 862244
Station Road, off A245; KT11 3BN Popular nicely updated 300-year-old pub in same group as the Onslow Arms at West Clandon, Red Lion at Horsell and Three Horseshoes in Laleham; good freshly made food including daily specials, Fullers and a guest such as Surrey Hills, plenty of wines by the glass, competent friendly staff, restaurant with various knick-knacks; newspapers and free wi-fi; children welcome in restaurant till 7.30pm, dogs in bar, seats out under pergola and in attractive garden, open (and food) all day. *(C and R Bromage)*

SUNBURY   TQ1068
Magpie (01932) 782024
Thames Street; TW16 6AF Multi-room pub on two levels with lovely Thames views from upper bar/dining area and small heated terrace; popular food from bar snacks up, friendly staff, Greene King IPA, a beer badged for the pub and four fairly local ales, decent wines; children welcome, steps down to moorings, open (and food) all day. *(Ian Phillips)*

SUTTON ABINGER   TQ1045
Volunteer (01306) 730985
Water Lane; just off B2126 via Raikes Lane, 1.5 miles S of Abinger Hammer; RH5 6PR Picturesque family-run pub in delightful setting above clear stream, low-ceilinged linked rooms, log fires, enjoyable traditional food from sandwiches up, Badger ales and several wines by the glass, good friendly service, restaurant; children and dogs welcome, terrace and sun-trap lawns stepped up behind, nice local walks, open all day Sat, Sun till 5pm. *(Dr Simon Innes)*

SUTTON GREEN   TQ0054
★ **Olive Tree** (01483) 729999
Sutton Green Road; GU4 7QD Big rambling dining pub in quiet countryside; bar area with leather sofas by open fire, Sharps Doom Bar and Timothy Taylors Landlord, good range of wines by the glass and seasonal home-made drinks such as elderflower cordial, highly regarded food including plenty of fish dishes, spreading dining room with clean-cut modern décor; children and dogs (in bar) welcome, tables under parasols on back terrace, closed Sun and Mon evenings; change of management expected as we went to press – reports please. *(Peter Sutton, Peter Brix, David Jackman)*

TADWORTH   TQ2355
★ **Dukes Head** (01737) 812173
Dorking Road (B2032 opposite common and woods); KT20 5SL Roomy and

---

We say if we know a pub has background music.

comfortably modernised 19th-c pub, popular for its good varied choice of well priced food (all day except Sun evening, booking advised), five well kept ales including a house beer (KT20) brewed by Morlands, Aspall's cider, good choice of wines by the glass, helpful cheery staff, three dining areas and two big inglenook log fires; background music, Weds quiz; lots of hanging baskets and plenty of tables in well tended back garden, open all day (till 8pm Sun). *(C and R Bromage)*

THAMES DITTON — TQ1567
Albany (020) 8972 9163
Queens Road, signed off Summer Road; KT7 0QY Mitchells & Butlers bar-with-restaurant in lovely Thames-side position, light airy modern feel, with good variety of food from sharing plates and pizzas to more upscale dishes, weekday lunchtime and early evening fixed-price menu, good choice of wines by the glass, cocktails and a couple of ales such as Sharps and Timothy Taylors, cheerful service, log fire, river pictures, daily papers; nice balconies and river-view terrace, moorings, open all day. *(John Branston, Tony Scott)*

THAMES DITTON — TQ1667
Red Lion (020) 8398 8662
High Street; KT7 0SF Revamped and extended pub with enjoyable home-made food from regularly changing menu, decent wines and coffee, ales such as Surrey Hills and Twickenham from servery clad in reclaimed doors, cheerful young staff, mismatched furniture in bare-boards bar, back conservatory; children welcome, seats on split-level enclosed terrace with Lego wall, open (and food) all day. *(Tom and Ruth Rees)*

THURSLEY — SU9039
★ Three Horseshoes (01252) 703268
Dye House Road, just off A3 SW of Godalming; GU8 6QD Pretty tile-hung pub owned by village consortium; convivial beamed front bar with log fire, well kept Hogs Back TEA and guests, 18 wines by the glass, good popular food (not Sun evening) served by friendly competent staff, dining room with paintings for sale; background music; well behaved children welcome, dogs in bar, attractive two-acre garden with pleasant views over common and Saxon church, play fort, open all day Sat, till 8pm Sun. *(Hunter and Christine Wright, Martin and Karen Wake, Tony and Jill Radnor, Christopher and Elise Way and others)*

TILFORD — SU8742
Duke of Cambridge (01252) 792236
Tilford Road; GU10 2DD Civilised dining pub in same small local group as Queens Head at East Clandon, Stag at Eashing and Wheatsheaf at Farnham; enjoyable food with emphasis on local ingredients from interesting menu, children's meals too, good

choice of wines, ales such as Hogs Back TEA and Surrey Hills Shere Drop, helpful service; May charity music festival; children and dogs welcome, part-covered terrace and garden with outside bar/grill, good play area, open all day. *(Martin Jones)*

TONGHAM — SU8848
White Hart (01252) 782419
The Street; GU10 1DH Large welcoming corner pub very popular locally; bar, dining lounge and back games room with pool and darts, carpets and faux beams, good choice of beers including Hogs Back (brewery nearby), enjoyable straightforward food (not Sun evening, Mon) at reasonable prices, good friendly service; Tues quiz, music nights, sports TV; children and dogs welcome, outside seating front and back including raised deck, open all day. *(Tony Hobden)*

VIRGINIA WATER — SU9968
Rose & Olive Branch
(01344) 843713 *Callow Hill; GU25 4LH* Small unpretentious red-brick pub, with good choice of popular food including speciality pies, gluten-free and children's choices too, two Greene King ales and a guest, decent wines, friendly busy staff; background music; tables on front terrace and in garden behind, good walks, open (and food) all day Sun. *(D J and P M Taylor)*

WALLISWOOD — TQ1138
Scarlett Arms (01306) 627243
Signed from Ewhurst–Rowhook back road, or off A29 S of Ockley; RH5 5RD Cottagey 16th-c village pub with low beams and flagstones, simple furniture and two log fires (one in big inglenook), Badger ales, well priced traditional food (not Sun evening) including malaysian and indian evenings, friendly helpful staff, dining room behind; background music; children and dogs welcome, tables out at front and in garden under parasols, good walks, open all day Fri, Sat, till 9.30pm Sun, closed Mon lunchtime. *(Anon)*

WALTON-ON-THAMES — TQ1068
Weir (01932) 784530
Towpath, Waterside Drive, off Sunbury Lane; KT12 2JB Edwardian pub in nice Thames-side spot with big terrace overlooking river, weir and steel walkway, decent choice of food all day (till 7.30pm Sun) from snacks up, Greene King, Sharps and a couple of guests, traditional décor, river pictures, newspapers; children and dogs welcome, lovely towpath walks, six bedrooms. *(Anne and Ben Smith)*

WEST CLANDON — TQ0451
★ Bulls Head (01483) 222444
A247 SE of Woking; GU4 7ST Comfortable unchanging pub based on 1540s timbered hall house, popular especially with older diners at lunchtime for its good value

straightforward food (not Sun evening) including proper home-made pies, friendly helpful staff, ales from Sharps, Surrey Hills and Youngs, good coffee, small lantern-lit beamed front bar with open fire and some stripped brick, old local prints, bric-a-brac and hops, simple raised back inglenook dining area, games room with darts and pool; children and dogs welcome, disabled access from car park, good play area in neat little garden, nice walks. *(Ian Phillips)*

WEST CLANDON   TQ0452

★**Onslow Arms** (01483) 222447

A247 SE of Woking; GU4 7TE Busy pub with heavily beamed rambling rooms leading away from central bar; wooden dining chairs and tables on wide floorboards, built-in cushioned window seats, all sorts of copper implements, hunting horns and china in cabinets, leather sofas by woodburner, ales including Sharps, Surrey Hills and a house beer from Caledonian, good popular food from traditional choices up, efficient friendly staff, big back restaurant with rugs on bare boards and chesterfields in front of open fire; live music Weds, free wi-fi; children (till early evening) and dogs welcome, courtyard garden with tables under parasols, pretty pots and huge stone dog, open (and food) all day. *(Christopher and Elise Way, Gordon and Margaret Ormondroyd)*

WEST HORSLEY   TQ0853

★**Barley Mow** (01483) 282693

Off A246 Leatherhead–Guildford at Bell & Colvill garage roundabout; The Street; KT24 6HR Welcoming tree-shaded traditional pub, low beams, mix of flagstones, bare boards and carpet, two log fires, well kept ales such as Fullers, Surrey Hills and Youngs, decent wines, good thai food (not Sun) along with traditional lunchtime menu, barn function room; background music; children welcome, dogs on leads, picnic-sets in good-sized garden, open all day. *(Martin Jones)*

WEST HORSLEY   TQ0752

King William IV (01483) 282318

The Street; KT24 6BG Comfortable and welcoming early 19th-c village pub, low entrance door to front and side bars, beams, flagstones and log fire, back conservatory restaurant, good variety of enjoyable food (not Sun evening), gluten-free menu, four real ales including Courage and Surrey Hills, decent choice of wines by the glass and good coffee; background and live music, quiz nights, free wi-fi; children and dogs welcome, disabled access, small sunny garden with deck and play area, open all day. *(Richard Stanfield, Ian Phillips)*

WEYBRIDGE   TQ0765

Minnow (01932) 831672

Thames Street/Walton Lane; KT13 8NG Busy bay-windowed Mitchells & Butlers

dining pub; contemporary pastel décor and unusual decorative panels, chunky tables and chairs on gleaming flagstones, some sofas and armchairs, two-way log fire in raised hearth, popular food including fixed-price weekday menu till 6pm, ales such as Fullers, Timothy Taylors and Youngs, good wines by the glass, friendly staff; children welcome, big front terrace with heaters, open all day. *(Katharine Cowherd)*

WEYBRIDGE   TQ0765

★**Old Crown** (01932) 842844

Thames Street; KT13 8LP Comfortably old-fashioned three-bar pub dating from the 16th c, good value traditional food (not Sun-Tues evenings) from sandwiches to fresh fish, Courage, Youngs and a guest kept well (not cheap), good choice of wines by the glass, friendly efficient service, family lounge and conservatory, coal-effect gas fire; may be sports TV in back bar with Lions RFC photographs, silent fruit machine; secluded terrace and smokers' shelter, steps down to suntrap garden overlooking Wey/Thames confluence, mooring for small boats, open all day. *(Anon)*

WEYBRIDGE   TQ0664

Queens Head (01932) 839820

Bridge Road; KT13 8XS 18th-c pub owned by Raymond Blanc's White Brasserie Company, emphasis on dining but also a proper bar serving Fullers, Sharps and a couple of guests, plenty of wines by the glass including champagne, friendly staff, newspapers; soft background music; children welcome, a couple of picnic-sets outside, open (and food) all day. *(Ian Phillips)*

WINDLESHAM   SU9464

Brickmakers (01276) 472267

Chertsey Road (B386, W of B383 roundabout); GU20 6HT Airy red-brick country dining pub, updated linked areas in pastel shades or vibrant reds, light wood furniture on flagstone and wood floors, two-way woodburner, good freshly prepared food (all day Fri-Sun when best to book) using local suppliers, Courage Best, Fullers London Pride and Sharps Doom Bar, good choice of wines by the glass and decent coffee, efficient friendly service, conservatory; well behaved children allowed, appealing garden with pergola, open all day from 9am for breakfast. *(Geoffrey Kemp, D J and P M Taylor, Phil Bryant, Gerry Price)*

WITLEY   SU9439

White Hart (01428) 683695

Petworth Road; GU8 5PH Picture-book beamed Tudor pub, well kept St Austell, Charles Wells and a guest, plenty of wines by the glass and extensive range of whiskies, good food including signature home-smoked/chargrilled meats, friendly helpful staff, log fire in cosy panelled inglenook snug where George Eliot drank, bar and restaurant;

children and dogs welcome, tables on cobbled terrace and in garden, nice walks nearby, open all day Tues-Sat, till 6pm Sun, closed Mon lunchtime. *(Anon)*

WOKING   TQ0058
Herbert Wells (01483) 722818
Chertsey Road; GU21 5AJ Corner Wetherspoons named after H G Wells, busy with shoppers yet with lots of cosy areas and side snugs, eight or so well kept ales, similar number of ciders and their usual competitively priced all-day food including Tues steak night, friendly helpful staff, daily papers, old local pictures; free wi-fi; pavement tables, open from 8am.
(Ian Phillips, Tony Hobden)

WOOD STREET   SU9550
Royal Oak (01483) 235137
Oak Hill; GU3 3DA Popular 1920s village local with half a dozen well kept ales including Ringwood, good value traditional home-cooked food (not Mon), bargain OAP lunch Thurs, friendly staff; music and quiz nights, free wi-fi; dogs welcome, good-sized garden. *(Alan and Shirley Sawden)*

WORPLESDON   SU9854
Jolly Farmer (01483) 234658
Burdenshott Road, off A320 Guildford–Woking, not in village; GU3 3RN Cosy old Fullers pub in pleasant country setting, their well kept ales in dark-beamed bar with small log fire, enjoyable traditional food from

lunchtime sandwiches up (they may ask to swipe your credit card if running a tab), bare boards dining extension; background music, free wi-fi; children and dogs welcome, garden tables under parasols and pergola, open all day. *(Edward and Jill Wilson)*

WRECCLESHAM   SU8344
Bat & Ball (01252) 792108
Bat & Ball Lane, South Farnham; approach from Sandrock Hill and Upper Bourne Lane, then narrow steep lane to pub; GU10 4SA Fairly traditional pub tucked away in hidden valley, decent range of food (all day weekends) from pubby choices up including good puddings display, six well kept local ales (June beer and music festival), plenty of wines by the glass, friendly efficient staff; Tues quiz, open mike night last Thurs of month; children and dogs welcome, disabled facilities, tables out on attractive heated terrace with vine arbour and in garden with substantial play fort, open all day. *(Dr Simon Innes)*

WRECCLESHAM   SU8244
Royal Oak (01252) 728319
The Street; GU10 4QS Bustling 17th-c black-beamed village local, enjoyable good value home-made food (smaller helpings available), Greene King IPA and a couple of guests, friendly helpful staff, log fire; Sun quiz, sports TV; children and dogs welcome, big garden with play area, open all day. *(Tony and Jill Radnor)*

Post Office address codings confusingly give the impression that some pubs are in Surrey when they're really in Hampshire or London (which is where we list them). And there's further confusion from the way the Post Office still talks about Middlesex – which disappeared in local government reorganisation nearly 50 years ago.

Sussex

ALFRISTON   TQ5203   Map 3

George 🍷

(01323) 870319 ~ www.thegeorge-alfriston.com

High Street; BN26 5SY

Venerable 14th-c timbered inn in lovely village with comfortable, heavily beamed bars, good wines and several real ales; charming bedrooms

Highly popular and very well run, this fine old place has plenty of character. The long bar, dominated by a huge stone inglenook fireplace with a winter log fire (or summer flower arrangement), has massive hop-hung low beams, soft lighting, lots of copper and brass, and settles and chairs around sturdy stripped tables. Greene King Abbot and Old Speckled Hen, Dark Star Hophead and Hardys & Hansons Olde Trip on handpump, 14 wines by the glass (including champagne and a pudding wine), ten gins, board games and background music; good service. The lounge has comfortable sofas, standing timbers and rugs on the wooden floor, and the restaurant is cosy and candlelit. There are seats in the spacious flint-walled garden, and the beamed bedrooms are comfortable; there's no car park but you can park a couple of minutes away. This is a lovely village to wander around and two long-distance paths (the South Downs Way and Vanguard Way) cross here; the quietly beautiful Cuckmere Haven is nearby.

🍴 Helpfully served all day, the popular food includes sandwiches and toasties (until 6pm), chicken liver parfait with apple chutney, thai-spiced prawn and salmon fishcakes, rustic sharing boards, ham and free-range eggs, filo parcel filled with aubergine, feta, spinach and pine nuts with spiced chickpeas, chicken breast stuffed with tomato and basil wrapped in parma ham with dauphinoise potatoes, sea bream fillets with hollandaise sauce, and puddings such as banoffi pie and chocolate cheesecake with passion-fruit coulis. *Benchmark main dish: king prawn and chorizo linguine with spinach, chilli and garlic £14.50. Two-course evening meal £20.00.*

Greene King ~ Lease Roland and Cate Couch ~ Real ale ~ Open 11 (12 weekends)-11 ~ Bar food 12-9 ~ Restaurant ~ Children welcome ~ Dogs welcome ~ Wi-fi ~ Bedrooms: $75/$120
Recommended by Fr Robert Marsh, Tony and Wendy Hobden, Mr and Mrs P R Thomas

---

Real ale to us means beer that has matured naturally in its cask – not pressurised or filtered. We name all real ales stocked. We usually name ales preserved under a light blanket of carbon dioxide too, though purists – pointing out that this stops the natural yeasts developing – would disagree (most people, including us, can't tell the difference!)

BRIGHTON
Jolly Poacher ⭐❢ ♀

TQ3105   Map 3

(01273) 683967 – www.thejollypoacher.com

Ditchling Road; BN1 4SG

Rustic, friendly bar with easy-going atmosphere, a good choice of drinks, particularly good food and seats outside

---

There's plenty of rustic character in the U-shaped bar-cum-dining room with high-backed cushioned wooden chairs around a mix of tables on wide floorboards. Most emphasis is on the imaginative food cooked by the chef-patron, but they keep a couple of real ales on handpump and customers do drop in for a drink and a chat. There's modern artwork on pale paintwork above a grey-green dado, a couple of fireplaces, contemporary steel lights hanging from the high ceiling and an open kitchen. Friendly, helpful staff serve Harveys Best and Long Man American Pale Ale, 11 good wines by the glass and cocktails (chalked on a blackboard – two-for-one after 4pm on Sundays); background music. A narrow terrace runs along the outside of the building with a few metal chairs and tables.

As well as a popular weekend brunch menu and some all-day snacks, the interesting food includes crispy thai-spiced crab fritters and chilli salt squid with nam jim dressing, goose liver parfait with onion marmalade, beer-battered cod with triple-cooked chips, vegetable and portobello mushroom arancini with root vegetable and butter bean cassoulet, ox cheek with battered oysters and black cabbage, sea bream with braised fennel, spinach and salsa verde, and puddings; they also offer a two-course set menu. *Benchmark main dish: roast fennel seed pork belly with roast beetroot and quince aioli £15.00. Two-course evening meal £22.00.*

Enterprise ~ Lease Kirsten Wass ~ Real ale ~ Open 12 (10 Sat)-11; 10-10 Sun; closed Mon ~ Bar food 12-2.30, 6-9.30 (10 Fri); 10-3, 6-10 Sat; 10-3 Sun ~ Restaurant ~ Children welcome ~ Dogs welcome ~ Wi-fi *Recommended by Lindy Andrews, Harvey Brown*

BRIGHTON
Stanmer House ♀

TQ3309   Map 3

(01273) 680400 – www.stanmerhouse.co.uk

Stanmer Park; BN1 9QA

Stately home-like mansion in parkland with fine rooms, an informal, friendly atmosphere, real ales, enjoyable food and seats in garden

---

This is a rather extraordinary place. Just north of Brighton, it's a grand, Grade I listed 18th-c mansion opposite a flint church and surrounded by 5,000 acres of lovely parkland. On our sunny Sunday visit there were dog walkers, cyclists, families enjoying brunch, friends meeting for coffee and cake in the back café and couples sizing up the rooms for forthcoming weddings. Three impressive front rooms are the most informal: button-back leather chesterfields and armchairs on bare boards or marble flagstones, ornate fireplaces, gilt-edged mirrors, shelves of books and stone bottles, old photographs of the building, the area and Brighton, stone lions or metal sculptures in wall recesses, heavy curtains lining tall windows and chandeliers in high ceilings. The enthusiastic, friendly barman keeps Park Life (brewed for them by Turners) and a changing guest from a brewery such as Arundel on handpump and 16 wines by the glass; they usually hold a doggy brunch on the last Sunday of the month (best to phone). To the left, three fine dining rooms are furnished with Victorian and Edwardian-style chairs around heavy dark tables on rugs and more bare boards; big portraits, paintings, mirrors and photographs cover the walls, church candles and opulent flower arrangements are dotted here and there and each room has at least one fireplace. The terrace and garden have lots of rustic chairs and tables around a pond, and at the front are some contemporary seats on flagstones.

¶| Interesting food includes prawn cocktail, welsh rarebit with crispy bacon on toast, shallot and butternut squash salad with toasted walnuts and marinated feta, steak burger with toppings, blue cheese mayonnaise and skinny fries, confit duck leg with lentils, pancetta and rich jus, rabbit ragoût with chestnuts and pasta, bass fillets on curried risotto with lemon balm, and puddings such as dark chocolate brownie with chocolate ice-cream and tiramisu. *Benchmark main dish: slow-cooked lamb shoulder with dauphinoise potatoes £17.95. Two-course evening meal £21.00.*

Whiting & Hammond ~ Manager Mark Barrett ~ Real ale ~ Open 9am-11pm ~ Bar food 9-9; reduced menu 3-6 ~ Restaurant ~ Children welcome ~ Dogs welcome ~ Wi-fi
Recommended by Mungo Shipley, John Harris

CHARLTON
SU8812   Map 2

Fox Goes Free ♀

(01243) 811461 – www.thefoxgoesfree.com
Village signposted off A286 Chichester–Midhurst in Singleton, also from Chichester–Petworth via East Dean; PO18 0HU

Comfortable old pub with beamed bars, popular food and drink, and big garden; bedrooms

Being handy for Goodwood, this friendly pub is always busy – but the courteous and efficient staff cope well with the crowds. The bar, the first of several cosy separate rooms, has old irish settles, tables and chapel chairs and an open fire. Standing timbers divide up a larger beamed bar, which has a huge brick fireplace and old local photographs on the walls. A dining area overlooks the garden. The family extension is a clever conversion from horseboxes and the stables where the 1926 Goodwood winner was once housed; darts and background music. A beer named for the pub (from Arundel), Arundel Sussex Gold, Shepherd Neame Spitfire and a guest from breweries such as Dark Star or Harveys on handpump, 15 wines by the glass and Addlestone's cider. The attractive back garden has the Downs as a backdrop and is just the spot to while away a warm lunchtime; there are also rustic benches and tables on the gravelled front terrace. You can walk up to Levin Down nature reserve, or stroll around the Iron Age hill fort on the Trundle, with huge views to the Isle of Wight; the Weald & Downland Open Air Museum and West Dean Gardens are nearby too.

¶| Making their own bread, ice-cream and chips, the very good, seasonal food includes lunchtime ciabattas (not Sunday), home-cured tarragon and dill salmon gravadlax with mustard mayonnaise, tuna niçoise salad, a vegetarian risotto of the day, cumberland sausages with red onion marmalade, fillet of pork with butternut squash, leek bubble and squeak and apple and cider cream sauce, chicken wrapped in parma ham with wholegrain mustard jus, and puddings such as mint panna cotta with mixed berry compote and sticky toffee pudding. *Benchmark main dish: fish pie £13.50. Two-course evening meal £22.00.*

Free house ~ Licensee David Coxon ~ Real ale ~ Open 11-11 (midnight Sat); 12-10.30 Sun ~ Bar food 12-2.30, 6.15-10; 12-10 weekends ~ Restaurant ~ Children welcome ~ Dogs allowed in bar ~ Wi-fi ~ Live music Weds monthly ~ Bedrooms: £70/£95 *Recommended by J A Snell, Richard Tilbrook, Roy Hoing, Tracey and Stephen Groves, Richard and Judy Winn*

Children – if the details at the end of a featured entry don't mention them, you should assume that the pub does not allow them inside.

CHILGROVE

SU8116 Map 2

Royal Oak £

(01243) 535257 – www.royaloakhooksway.co.uk

Off B2141 Petersfield–Chichester, signed Hooksway; PO18 9JZ

Unchanging and peaceful country pub with welcoming licensees, honest food and big pretty garden

Happily, nothing much changes in this tucked-away country pub; as it's close to the South Downs Way, many customers are ramblers – often with their dogs. The two simple, cosy bars have huge log fires, plain country kitchen tables and chairs and cottagey knick-knacks, and Arundel Castle, Exmoor Beast and Fullers HSB and Seafarers on handpump. There's also a homely dining room with a woodburning stove and a plainer family room; background music, cribbage, dominoes and shut the box. Twiglet and Amber are the pub staffies and the parrot is called Gilbert. The big, pretty garden has picnic-sets under parasols.

 Simple food includes lunchtime rolls, deep-fried whitebait, duck and orange pâté, vegetable lasagne, burger of the day with coleslaw and fries, tuna pasta bake, spicy jerk chicken with fries, pork schnitzel with creamy dill sauce, a curry of the day, and puddings. *Benchmark main dish: venison pie £10.95. Two-course evening meal £17.00.*

Free house ~ Licensee Dave Jeffery ~ Real ale ~ Open 11.30-2.30 (3 Sat), 6-11; 12-3 Sun; closed Sun evening, Mon and Nov ~ Bar food 12-2, 7-9 ~ Restaurant ~ Children in family room ~ Dogs allowed in bar ~ Wi-fi ~ Live music last Fri evening of month
Recommended by Peter Brix, Martin Jones

CHILGROVE

SU8214 Map 2

White Horse 🍴⭐ ☆ 🛏

(01243) 519444 – www.thewhitehorse.co.uk

B2141 Petersfield–Chichester; PO18 9HX

18th-c whitewashed inn with original features, a thoughtful choice of drinks, first class food and plenty of outside seating; well appointed bedrooms

In a lovely downland valley with lots of fine walks nearby, this is a handsome former coaching inn with a gently civilised atmosphere and a lot of character. The bar area has leather armchairs in front of a woodburning stove, and daily papers on the light oak counter. Just off here, a room with leather button-back wall seats and mate's and other dark wooden dining chairs has all sorts of country knick-knacks: stuffed animals, china plates, riding boots, flower paintings, dog drawings, stone bottles and books on shelves. The dining room to the other side of the bar has a huge painting of a galloping white horse, a long suede wall banquette, high-backed settles creating stalls, elegant chairs, lots of mirrors and big metal chandeliers. Throughout, there are fat candles in lanterns, flagstones and coir carpet, beams and timbering, and animal skin throws. Friendly staff serve Arundel Castle, Ballards Best Bitter, Langham Hip Hop and Wychwood Hobgoblin on handpump and 23 good wines by the glass; board games. A two-level terrace has dark grey rattan-style seats around glass-topped tables under parasols among pretty flowering tubs; an area up steps has rustic benches and tables and there are picnic-sets on grass at the front. Each of the comfortable, contemporary and light bedrooms has a little private courtyard (two have a hot tub).

Using the best local suppliers and game caught nearby, the highly rewarding food includes sandwiches, mussels in cider, pancetta and leeks, duck egg with wilted spinach and wild mushroom butter on toasted brioche, a risotto of the day, guinea fowl breast with caesar salad, roast rack of lamb with lamb hotpot and rosemary jus, sea bream fillet with lemon and olive crushed potatoes, samphire and salsa verde, and puddings such as chocolate truffle torte with caramel sauce and stem ginger panna cotta with rhubarb and grenadine syrup. *Benchmark main dish: pie of the day £14.95. Two-course evening meal £22.00.*

Free house ~ Licensee Niki Burr ~ Real ale ~ Open 12-11; 12-10.30 Sun ~ Bar food 12-3, 6-9; 12-9.30 Sat; 12-8.30 Sun ~ Restaurant ~ Children welcome ~ Dogs allowed in bar and bedrooms ~ Wi-fi ~ Live jazz Sun 2.30 ~ Bedrooms: £60/£90 *Recommended by Mungo Shipley, Nick Sharpe*

COOLHAM   TQ1423 Map 3
George & Dragon
(01403) 741320 – www.thegeorgeanddragon.co
Dragons Green, Dragons Lane; pub signed off A272; RH13 8GE

Delightful small pub in a fine walking area, heavily beamed bar and dining room, friendly staff and seats in pretty garden; bedrooms

This tile-hung cottage in a little hamlet surrounded by lovely countryside is especially charming in warm weather, when you can sit in the pretty garden with a drink or meal. Inside, the chatty, cosy bar has heavily timbered walls, unusually low and massive black beams (see if you can decide whether the date cut into one is 1677 or 1577), traditional seats and tables and a big inglenook fireplace. Dark Star Hophead, Harveys Sussex Best Bitter, Skinners Betty Stogs and a guest beer on handpump and decent wines by the glass. The dining room has pale farmhouse chairs around rustic tables on a wooden floor. There are two attractive double bedrooms in a converted outbuilding.

 Good food includes sandwiches, salmon gravadlax, pork terrine with sweet chutney, wild boar sausages with onion gravy, chilli burger with chips, lamb shank with mint gravy, bass stuffed with herbs, and puddings such as banoffi pie and raspberry and white chocolate cheesecake. *Benchmark main dish: local sirloin steak with peppercorn sauce £13.95. Two-course evening meal £20.00.*

Free house ~ Licensees John Ewers, Simon Corby ~ Real ale ~ Open 12-3, 6-11; 12-11 Fri, Sat; 12-10.30 Sun ~ Bar food 12-3, 6-9; 12-4 Sun; not Sun, Mon or Tues evenings ~ Restaurant ~ Children welcome ~ Dogs allowed in bar *Recommended by Mungo Shipley, Nick Sharpe*

COPTHORNE   TQ3240 Map 3
Old House ♀ 🛏
(01342) 718529 – www.theoldhouseinn.co.uk
B2037 NE of village; RH10 3JB

Charming old place with interconnected rooms, nooks and crannies, plenty of character, real ales, enjoyable food and attentive staff; attractive bedrooms

Inside this black and white, higgledy-piggledy place is a lovely old inn with warmly friendly, chatty staff and an easy-going atmosphere. The immediately welcoming little bar has a brown leather chesterfield and a mix of armchairs and carved wooden chairs around all sorts of tables, a big sisal mat on flagstones, a decorative fireplace and lots of nightlights dotted about. Ringwood Best, Sharps Doom Bar and a guest from Copthorne on handpump, several good wines by the glass and a couple of huge glass flagons holding Sipsmith vodka and gin. Off to the left is a charming small room with a woodburning stove in an inglenook fireplace and two leather armchairs in front, white-painted beams in a low ceiling (this is the oldest part, dating from the 16th c), cushioned settles and pre-war-style cushioned dining chairs around varying tables. A teeny back room, like something you'd find on an old galleon, has button-back wall seating up to the roof, a few chairs and heavy ropework. The dining rooms are beamed (some painted) and timbered with parquet or sisal flooring and quarry tiles, high-backed leather and other dining chairs, more wall seating and mixed tables and fresh flowers and candles; background music and TV. A converted barn houses smartly comfortable bedrooms (named after local woods) that overlook the terraced garden with its heavy rustic tables and benches. Gatwick airport is close by.

Rewarding food from a seasonal menu includes crab cannelloni with pickled mushrooms and shiso cress, chicken and foie gras parfait with pistachio butter, risotto with fine herbs and soft cheese, burger with bacon, toppings and fries, skate wing with grain mustard gnocchi and black olive oil with seasonal greens, rump of rose veal with tonnato dressing and curly endive, and puddings such as flaming crème brûlée and lemon posset; they also offer a two- and three-course set lunch (not Sunday). *Benchmark main dish: beer-battered fish and chips £12.50. Two-course evening meal £22.00.*

Free house ~ Licensee Stephen Godsave ~ Real ale ~ Open 11-11; 11-9 Sun ~ Bar food 12-3, 6-9 (9.30 Fri, Sat); 12-4, 6-8 Sun ~ Restaurant ~ Children welcome ~ Dogs allowed in bar ~ Wi-fi ~ Bedrooms: /£90 *Recommended by Isobel Mackinlay*

DANEHILL
Coach & Horses 🏮 ♟

TQ4128 Map 3

(01825) 740369 – www.coachandhorses.co
Off A275, via School Lane towards Chelwood Common; RH17 7JF

Well run dining pub with bustling bars, welcoming staff, very good food and ales and a big garden

'This has everything you could want in a proper country pub,' says one reader with enthusiasm. The little bar to the right has half-panelled walls, simple furniture on polished floorboards, a small woodburner in a brick fireplace and a big hatch to the bar counter: Harveys Best and a guest such as Dark Star Best on handpump, local Black Pig farmhouse cider and a dozen wines by the glass including prosecco and Bluebell sparkling wine from Sussex. A couple of steps lead down to a half-panelled area with a mix of dining chairs around characterful wooden tables (set with flowers and candles) on a fine brick floor, and changing artwork on the walls; cribbage, dominoes and cards. Down another step is a dining area with stone walls, beams, flagstones and a woodburning stove. There's an adults-only terrace beneath a huge maple tree, and picnic-sets and a children's play area in the big garden which has fine views of the South Downs.

The good, imaginative food includes lunchtime baguettes, cured salmon with fennel jam and lemon and mustard seed bruschetta, game faggots with parsnip purée and parsnip crisps, moules frites, cauliflower bhaji with lentil dhal and spiced parmentier potatoes, confit duck leg with green peppercorn sauce, bass fillet with black cabbage, clams and white wine sauce, guinea fowl with pancetta, jerusalem artichoke and pickled walnut vinaigrette, and puddings. *Benchmark main dish: crisp roast pork belly with bubble and squeak £14.00. Two-course evening meal £20.00.*

Free house ~ Licensee Ian Philpots ~ Real ale ~ Open 12-3, 5.30-11; 12-11 Sat; 12-10.30 Sun ~ Bar food 12-2, 6.30-9; 12-2.30, 6.30-9.30 Sat; 12-3 Sun ~ Restaurant ~ Well behaved children welcome but not on adult terrace ~ Dogs allowed in bar ~ Wi-fi *Recommended by R and S Bentley, Alan Cowell, Martin and Karen Wake, Duane Lawrence, Nick Lawless*

DIAL POST
TQ1519 Map 3

Crown

(01403) 710902 – www.crowninndialpost.co.uk
Worthing Road (off A24 S of Horsham); RH13 8NH

Tile-hung village pub with interesting food and a good mix of drinkers and diners; bedrooms

Our readers thoroughly enjoy their visits to this bustling village pub, with several giving top marks to the service from the helpful young staff. The beamed bar has a couple of standing timbers, brown squashy sofas, pine tables and chairs on the stone floor, a small woodburning stove in a brick fireplace, and Harveys Best and a guest from Kissingate on handpump served from the attractive herringbone brick counter; eight wines by the glass plus prosecco and a pudding wine. To the right of the bar, the restaurant (with more beams) has an ornamental woodburner in a brick fireplace, a few photographs, chunky pine tables, chairs, a couple of cushioned pews and a shelf of books; steps lead down to an additional dining room; board games. The pub dog is called Chops. The straightforwardly furnished dining conservatory, facing the village green, is light and airy. There are picnic-sets in the garden behind the pub.

Rewarding food using local produce includes lunchtime sandwiches (not Sunday), duck rillettes with orange coulis, goats cheese panna cotta with poached pear, endive and honey-toasted walnuts, various grazing boards, chicken and mushroom pie, three-cheese and onion tart with coleslaw, steak burger with toppings and chips, mutton curry with onion bhaji and poppadums, and puddings such as a chocolate pudding of the day and sticky toffee pudding with toffee sauce and home-made ice-cream. *Benchmark main dish: beer-battered fish and chips £12.00. Two-course evening meal £18.00.*

Free house ~ Licensees James and Penny Middleton-Burn ~ Real ale ~ Open 12-3, 6-11; 12-3 Sun ~ Bar food 12-2.15, 6-9 (9.30 Fri, Sat); 12-3 Sun ~ Children welcome but must be dining after 7pm ~ Dogs welcome ~ Wi-fi ~ Bedrooms: £51/£75 *Recommended by Martin Stafford, Tony and Wendy Hobden, Richard Tilbrook*

DITCHLING
TQ3215 Map 3

Bull 🍴🏵 ♀ 🍺 🛏

(01273) 843147 – www.thebullditchling.com
High Street (B2112); BN6 8TA

Ancient local in centre of village with three bars and dining rooms, a good choice of ales and popular food; bedrooms

Dating back 500 years and a busy coaching inn on the London–Brighton route in the 19th c, this character place is just as welcoming today. The beamed main room on the right is a cosy haven in winter with a log fire in a sizeable inglenook fireplace, and friendly, helpful young staff who greet you at the bar counter where they serve Bedlam Best, Timothy Taylors Landlord and three changing guest beers on handpump, 22 wines by the glass and a large choice of spirits. There are benches, scrubbed wooden tables and leather chesterfields on bare boards, modern artwork and historic photos of the village on the walls; daily papers and background music. Two other rooms lead off to the left from the main entrance. You can sit in the garden at benches around wooden tables under apple trees or on a terrace; a kitchen garden has been added with fruit, vegetables and herbs. The comfortable bedrooms are well equipped and recently refurbished.

 As well as super weekend breakfasts (8.30-10.30am), the tempting food using some home-grown and other local produce includes ham hock terrine with piccalilli, salsify, pancetta and an egg with truffle dressing, wild boar burger with cheese, cranberry and chips, pumpkin, spinach, pine nut and feta filo parcel with sage beurre noisette, confit pork belly with butter beans, chorizo and black pudding, seared bass with hispi cabbage, cauliflower and almonds, and puddings such as poached rhubarb, orange curd and coconut sorbet and sticky toffee pudding with butterscotch sauce. *Benchmark main dish: duck breast with potato rösti and griottine cherry sauce £18.00. Two-course evening meal £23.00.*

Free house ~ Licensee Dominic Worrall ~ Real ale ~ Open 11 (7.30am weekends)-11 (10.30 Sun) ~ Bar food 12-2.30, 6 (5 Fri)-9.30; 12-9.30 Sat; 12-9 Sun ~ Restaurant ~ Children welcome ~ Dogs allowed in bar ~ Wi-fi ~ Bedrooms: /£120
Recommended by Harvey Brown, Tony Scott, Nick Sharpe

DUNCTON
Cricketers

SU9517 Map 3

(01798) 342473 – www.thecricketersduncton.co.uk
Set back from A285; GU28 0LB

Charming old coaching inn with friendly licensees, real ales, popular food and suntrap back garden

Visitors to this bustling inn are given a genuine welcome from the friendly landlord and his regulars, and the place makes the best of its position in the Goodwood Hills. The traditional bar has a display of cricketing memorabilia, a few standing timbers, simple seating and an open woodburning stove in an inglenook fireplace. Steps lead down to a dining room with farmhouse chairs around wooden tables. Dark Star Partridge, Triple fff Moondance and a guest ale on handpump, nine wines by the glass and two farm ciders. There are picnic-sets out in front beneath the flowering window boxes and more on decked areas and under parasols on the grass in the picturesque back garden.

Using local suppliers, the tasty food includes lunchtime sandwiches, sticky duck salad, duo of mackerel, chicken caesar salad, wild mushroom, spinach and goats cheese risotto, burger with toppings and chips, steak and mushroom in ale pie, beer-battered fresh haddock and chips, sizzling pork, pear and parsnip skillet and puddings. *Benchmark main dish: steak in ale pie £11.95. Two-course evening meal £20.00.*

Inn Company ~ Manager Martin Boult ~ Real ale ~ Open 11-11; 12-10.30 Sun ~ Bar food 12-2.30, 6-9; 12-9 Sat, Sun; brunch 11-midday, hot snacks 3-6 ~ Children welcome ~ Dogs allowed in bar *Recommended by Colin McKerrow, David Jackman*

EARTHAM
George ♀ ◖

SU9309 Map 2

(01243) 814340 ~ www.thegeorgeeartham.com
Signed off A285 Chichester–Petworth, from Fontwell off A27, from Slindon off A29; PO18 0LT

170-year-old pub in tucked-away village with country furnishings and contemporary touches, local ales and enjoyable food

There's a cheerful mix of customers and a warm welcome for all from the friendly landlord in this well run village pub. The light and airy bar is prettily decorated with scatter cushions on a long wall pew, painted dining chairs around wood-topped tables (each set with fresh flowers and candles) and parquet flooring. There are sofas, armchairs, a dresser with country knick-knacks, beams, timbering, paintings on cream-painted walls above a grey planked dado, stone bottles and books and three open fires; background music and board games. A beer named for the pub (from Otter) and guests such as Goldmark Liquid Gold, Hammerpot HPA and Langham Hip Hop on handpump, 13 wines by the glass and a decent choice of spirits. The large garden has picnic-sets on grass and seats and tables under a gazebo. The pub is surrounded by the rolling Downs, with some lovely walks and cycle routes nearby. Easy disabled access.

Interesting food includes sandwiches, ham hock terrine with piccalilli, 'popcorn' cockles with halloumi fritters and chilli mayonnaise, a pie of the day, vegetable, coconut, ginger and cardamom curry, chicken breast with turnip and potato dauphinoise and mushroom and tarragon sauce, confit duck with bubble and squeak and plum and star anise sauce, halibut fillet with celeriac fondant and beetroot purée, and puddings such as a fruit crumble of the day and walnut panna cotta with walnut praline and sugar-coated walnuts. *Benchmark main dish: burger with toppings, relish and skinny fries £12.50. Two-course evening meal £21.00.*

Free house ~ Licensees James and Anita Thompson ~ Real ale ~ Open 11.30-11; 12-7 Sun (12-6 in winter); closed Mon ~ Bar food 12-3, 6-9 (9.30 Fri, Sat); 12-4 Sun ~ Restaurant ~ Children welcome ~ Dogs allowed in bar *Recommended by Mrs T A Bizat, Nick Sharpe*

EAST DEAN   TV5597   Map 3

Tiger 🍷 🛏

(01323) 423209 – www.beachyhead.org.uk

Off A259 Eastbourne–Seaford; BN20 0DA

Pretty old pub with two little bars and a dining room, an informal and friendly atmosphere, own-brewed beers and tasty food; bedrooms

The delightful cottage-lined green makes a perfect setting for this long low tiled pub; the green acts as an overflow area when the pub is busy – which it often is. You need to arrive early to be sure of a seat and they only take table reservations from October to March. The focal point of the little beamed main bar is the open woodburning stove in a brick inglenook, surrounded by polished horsebrasses; there are just a few rustic tables with benches, simple wooden chairs, a window seat and a long cushioned wall bench. The walls are hung with fish prints and a stuffed tiger's head, and a couple of hunting horns hang above the long bar counter. Friendly, attentive staff serve Harveys Best, their own-brewed Beachy Head Legless Rambler (brewery tours available on request) and a guest beer on handpump, and nine wines by the glass. Down a step on the right is a small room with an exceptionally fine high-backed curved settle, a couple of other old settles and nice old chairs and wooden tables on coir carpeting; on the walls there's an ancient map of Eastbourne and Beachy Head and photographs of the pub. The dining room to the left of the main bar has a cream woodburner and hunting prints. There are picnic-sets on the terrace among window boxes and flowering climbers. Bedrooms are comfortable and breakfasts good. The pub is well positioned for walks to the coast and along the clifftops of the Seven Sisters and up to Belle Tout Lighthouse and Beachy Head.

Breakfasts are usefully served to non-residents from 8am. Other food includes pâté of the day with home-made chutney, sausages with mustard mash and sweet red onion gravy, a seasonal risotto of the day, beer-battered cod and chips, gammon and eggs, duck breast with rhubarb and ginger sauce, pork loin with champ mash, caramelised apples and cider and mustard sauce, and puddings such as a cheesecake and a steamed pudding of the day. *Benchmark main dish: burger with bacon, cheese and chips £10.95. Two-course evening meal £22.00.*

Free house ~ Licensee Janice Avis ~ Real ale ~ Open 8am-11pm ~ Bar food 12-3, 6-9 ~ Restaurant ~ Children welcome ~ Dogs allowed in bar ~ Wi-fi ~ Bedrooms: /£130
Recommended by Simon Rodway, Emma Scofield, Mrs Sally Scott, Phil and Jane Villiers

ERIDGE GREEN
TQ5535 Map 3

Nevill Crest & Gun ♀ ◖

(01892) 864209 – www.brunningandprice.co.uk/nevillcrestandgun
A26 Tunbridge Wells–Crowborough; TN3 9JR

Handsome old building with lots of character, plenty to look at, six real ales and enjoyable modern food

The bustling, informal feel here is aided by the wide mix of customers – all welcomed by the courteous and helpful staff. The 500-year-old former farmhouse has been cleverly and carefully opened up inside, with standing timbers and doorways keeping some sense of separate rooms. Throughout, there are heavy beams (some carved), panelling, rugs on wooden floors and woodburning stoves and open fires in three fireplaces (the linenfold carved bressumer above one is worth seeking out). Also, all manner of individual dining chairs around dark wood or copper-topped tables, lots of pictures, maps and photographs relating to the local area, and window sills crammed with toby jugs, stone and glass bottles and plants. Phoenix Brunning & Price Original, Adnams Southwold, Arundel Sussex Gold, Harveys Sussex Best Bitter, Long Man American Pale Ale, Tonbridge Coppernob and Youngs Original on handpump, a farm cider, 15 wines by the glass and 100 malt whiskies; daily papers, board games and background music. There are a few picnic-sets in front of the building and teak furniture on the back terrace, next to the newer dining extension with its large windows, light oak rafters, beams and coir flooring.

As well as sandwiches, the interesting menu includes ham hock and tarragon croquettes with piccalilli, crispy duck salad with chilli, watermelon and cashew nuts, courgette and red onion quiche with potato salad, pork and leek sausages with red wine and onion gravy, moroccan-style chicken with fig and pomegranate salad and harissa dressing, bass with tagliatelle, spinach, baby leeks, mussels and saffron sauce, braised lamb shoulder with rosemary gravy, and puddings such as dark chocolate crumble tart with salted caramel ice-cream and bread and butter pudding with apricot sauce and clotted cream. *Benchmark main dish: malaysian chicken curry £13.95. Two-course evening meal £21.00.*

Brunning & Price ~ Manager Adam Holland ~ Real ale ~ Open 12-11 (10.30 Sun) ~ Bar food 12-9.30 (10 Fri, Sat) ~ Children welcome ~ Dogs allowed in bar ~ Wi-fi
Recommended by Edward May, Hilary and Neil Christopher

EWHURST GREEN
TQ7924 Map 3

White Dog

(01580) 830264 – www.thewhitedogewhurst.co.uk
Turn off A21 to Bodiam at S end of Hurst Green, cross B2244, pass Bodiam Castle, cross river then bear left uphill at Ewhurst Green sign; TN32 5TD

Welcoming village pub with a nice little bar, several real ales and popular food; bedrooms

On a warm day you can sit in the back garden at seats and tables and marvel at the stunning view over Bodiam Castle (National Trust). But this family-run inn is appealing in colder weather too, with its roaring log fire in an inglenook fireplace, hop-draped beams, wood panelling, farm implements, horsebrasses and mix of chairs and tables on old brick or flagstoned floors. There's also a high-backed cushioned settle by the counter where they keep four real ales from breweries such as Harveys, Old Dairy, Pig & Porter and Tonbridge on handpump and 20 wines by the glass. A dining room has sturdy wooden tables and chairs on more flagstones and the games room has darts and pool; background music. The light and airy bedrooms have been recently decorated.

As well as summer pizzas from their wood-fired oven, the seasonally changing food includes sandwiches, whole baked camembert with garlic and rosemary, smoked haddock fishcakes with creamy leek sauce, filo parcels filled with sweet potato, goats cheese and garlic topped with red pepper and tomato sauce, locally caught mackerel with sweet chilli sauce, pork belly with red wine jus and red cabbage, and puddings. *Benchmark main dish: fresh fish dish of the day £13.95. Two-course evening meal £20.00.*

Free house ~ Licensees Harriet and Dale Skinner ~ Real ale ~ Open 12-11.30 (midnight weekends); 12-3, 6-11 in winter ~ Bar food 12-2 (2.30 weekends), 6.30-9 (9.30 weekends) ~ Restaurant ~ Children welcome ~ Dogs allowed in bar ~ Wi-fi ~ Occasional live music ~ Bedrooms: /£95 *Recommended by Roger White, Kevin Streeter, John Wideman, Paul Austin, David Jackman*

FIRLE
Ram

TQ4607 Map 3

(01273) 858222 – www.raminn.co.uk
Village signed off A27 Lewes–Polegate; BN8 6NS

Bustling country pub with three open fires, character rooms, good food and drink and seats in garden; comfortable bedrooms

With a good mix of chatty regulars and visitors, this friendly old place is always deservedly busy. The main bar has a log fire, captain's and mate's chairs and a couple of gingham armchairs around dark pubby tables on bare boards or quarry tiles, gilt-edged paintings on dark brown walls, Burning Sky Aurora, Harveys Sussex Best Bitter, Isfield Straw Blond, and Long Man Copper Hop on handpump, 21 wines by the glass and eight malt whiskies; service is welcoming and helpful. A cosy bar leads off here with another log fire, olive green built-in planked and cushioned wall seats and more dark chairs and tables on parquet flooring. Throughout, there are various ceramic ram's heads or skulls, black and white photos of the local area, candles in hurricane jars and daily papers; darts and board games. The back dining room is up some steps and overlooks the garden where there are tables and chairs on a terrace and picnic-sets on grass; more picnic-sets under parasols at the front. The bedrooms are comfortable and the breakfasts feature local bacon, eggs and sausages.

Using local produce, the enjoyable food includes lunchtime sandwiches, local scallops with chorizo aioli and fennel tarte tatin, ham hock, pea and cheese croquette with wholegrain mustard sauce, various sharing boards, rabbit gnocchi with rum and raisin braising juices, carrot, celeriac and beetroot gratin, free-range chicken with white onion and tarragon cream, venison loin with peas, smoked pancetta and red wine jus, and puddings such as dark chocolate, orange and cardamom torte with Cointreau brûlée and crème fraîche and coconut panna cotta with caramelised pineapple and mango coulis. *Benchmark main dish: pork belly £14.00. Two-course evening meal £22.00.*

Free house ~ Licensee Hayley Bayes ~ Real ale ~ Open 9am-11pm ~ Bar food 9am-9.30pm ~
Children welcome away from bar ~ Dogs welcome ~ Folk music first Mon of month
Recommended by Alfie Bayliss, Harvey Brown

FLETCHING TQ4223 Map 3
Griffin 🍴 ⚲ 🛏

(01825) 722890 – www.thegriffininn.co.uk
Village signposted off A272 W of Uckfield; TN22 3SS

**Busy, gently upmarket inn with a fine wine list, real ales, bistro-style
bar food and a big garden; pretty bedrooms**

At the bottom of the two-acre garden behind this civilised inn is an outside
bar and wood oven (where they hold smashing barbecues), tables
and chairs under parasols and a stunning view over Sheffield Park – it's
pretty special on a warm evening. There are more seats on the sandstone
terrace. Inside, the beamed and quaintly panelled bar rooms have blazing
log fires, old photographs and hunting prints, straightforward close-set
furniture including some captain's chairs, and china on a delft shelf. A small
bare-boarded serving area is off to one side and there's a cosy separate bar
with sofas and a TV. The place gets pretty packed at weekends. Burning
Sky Plateau, Gun American Pale Ale, Harveys Sussex Best Bitter and Long
Man Best Bitter on handpump, plus 20 wines by the glass from a good list
(including champagne and pudding wine); they hold a monthly wine club
(on a Thursday evening) with supper. The bright and pretty bedrooms are
comfortable and the breakfasts good. There are ramps for wheelchairs.

🏅 Excellent food using local and organic produce includes tempura monkfish
with red pepper and chilli jam, pork rillettes with apple sauce and a deep-fried
egg, burger with manchego, roasted red pepper and plum relish and chips, chargrilled
courgette with lemon and mint pasta with parmesan, duck breast with parmentier
potatoes, chorizo and a light orange jus, wild bass with sea spinach and verjus beurre
blanc, and puddings such as chocolate and hazelnut cheesecake with pistachio
praline and mango and redcurrant bombe with caramelised lime syrup and crushed
meringue. *Benchmark main dish: fresh crab linguine with chilli and samphire
£14.00. Two-course evening meal £23.00.*

Free house ~ Licensees James Pullan and Samantha Barlow ~ Real ale ~ Open 11am-1am ~
Bar food 12-3, 7-9.30 ~ Restaurant ~ Children welcome ~ Dogs allowed in bar ~ Wi-fi ~
Live jazz Fri evening, Sun lunch ~ Bedrooms: £70/£100 *Recommended by Sheila Topham,
John Ralph, Christopher and Elise Way, Alan Cowell*

FRIDAY STREET TV6203 Map 3
Farm at Friday Street 🍺

(01323) 766049 – www.farmfridaystreet.com
B2104, Langney; BN23 8AP

**Handsome 17th-c house with lots to look at, plenty of dining and
drinking space, and efficient staff serving popular food and drink**

This is a former farmhouse (although houses have replaced the fields that
once surrounded it), with a very easy-going atmosphere and friendly,
efficient young staff who keep things buzzing along nicely. The old core has
many newer extensions but it's been done well, and the open-plan rooms are
split by brick pillars into cosier areas with sofas, stools and all manner of
wooden dining chairs and tables on bare boards, creamy coloured flagstones,
coir and carpet. Throughout, there are open fires, big house plants, stubby
church candles, frame-to-frame prints and pictures and farming implements.

Old Dairy Blue Top, Sharps Doom Bar, Timothy Taylors Landlord and a guest from St Austell on handpump and 14 wines by the glass. The dining room is on two levels with timbered walls, glass partitions, a raised conical roof and an open kitchen. The front lawn has plenty of picnic-sets.

 Rewarding food includes sandwiches, cured venison with celeriac rémoulade and beetroot, baked boxed camembert with garlic and rosemary and cranberry compote, three-cheese macaroni, beef and bacon burger with toppings and fries, pork and leek sausages with onion gravy, poached haddock with niçoise salad and a poached egg, lamb kofta with sweet potato fries and garlic mayonnaise, duck breast with grilled artichokes, baby spinach and balsamic syrup, and puddings such as sticky toffee pudding with butterscotch sauce and espresso panna cotta with hazelnut praline. *Benchmark main dish: braised half shoulder of lamb with dauphinoise potatoes and rosemary sauce £17.95. Two-course evening meal £21.00.*

Whiting & Hammond ~ Manager Paul Worman ~ Real ale ~ Open 11-11 ~ Bar food 12-9.30 (9 Sun) ~ Restaurant ~ Children welcome ~ Dogs allowed in bar ~ Wi-fi
Recommended by John Harris, Anne and Ben Smith

HEATHFIELD TQ5920 Map 3

Star

(01435) 863570 – www.starinnoldheathfield.co.uk
Church Street, Old Heathfield, off A265/B2096 E; TN21 9AH

Pleasant old pub with bustling, friendly atmosphere, well liked food, a decent choice of drinks and seats in lovely garden

Turner thought this 14th-c inn fine enough to paint and it's certainly pretty, tucked beneath the ancient tower of the church next door. There are ancient heavy beams, built-in wall settles and window seats, panelling, inglenook fireplaces and a roaring winter log fire; a doorway leads to a similarly decorated room set up more for eating with wooden tables and chairs (one table has high-backed white leather dining chairs) and a woodburning stove. An upstairs dining room has a striking barrel-vaulted ceiling (it was originally a dormitory for masons working on the reconstruction of the church after a fire in 1348). Harveys Sussex Best Bitter and guests from breweries such as St Austell and Shepherd Neame on handpump, and an extensive wine list with 11 by the glass; background music. The very prettily planted garden has rustic furniture under smart umbrellas and lovely views of rolling pasture dotted with sheep and lined with oak trees.

 Popular food using local, seasonal produce includes chicken liver parfait, devilled whitebait with tartare sauce, pea, leek and four-cheese tart with sweet potato chips, free-range pork and ale sausages with balsamic onion gravy, goat curry with onion bhaji and chana dhal, plaice fillets with vegetable nage and saffron potatoes, free-range local chicken stuffed with mushroom duxelle and gorgonzola wrapped in parma ham with a tomato and pesto dressing, and puddings such as plum and almond tart and tequila, lime and mint panna cotta with balsamic strawberries. *Benchmark main dish: crab and crayfish tian wrapped in cucumber with watermelon and feta salad £13.50. Two-course evening meal £20.00.*

Free house ~ Licensees Mike and Sue Chappell ~ Real ale ~ Open 11-11; 12-10 Sun ~ Bar food 12-2.30, 6.30-9; 12-3, 6-8.30 Sun ~ Restaurant ~ Children welcome ~ Dogs allowed in bar ~ Wi-fi *Recommended by Martin Day*

The symbol shows pubs that keep their beer unusually well,
have a particularly good range or brew their own.

HENLEY   SU8925 Map 2

Duke of Cumberland Arms 🌟 ♟

(01428) 652280 – www.dukeofcumberland.com

Off A286 S of Fernhurst; GU27 3HQ

Charming country pub with two character rooms, an airy dining room, local beers and enjoyable food

In fine weather, this wisteria-covered 16th-c stone pub is a lovely place to be thanks to the beautiful hill views from seats and picnic-sets on decking and in the charming big sloping garden; the many ponds contain trout. Inside, the two small rooms have big scrubbed oak tables on brick or flagstoned floors, low ceilings and rustic decorations. A woodburning stove surrounded by sofas is just the place to sit on a cold night. Harveys Sussex Best Bitter, Langham Hip Hop and Sadlers English Pride on handpump and several wines by the glass. A dining extension has a light and more modern feel.

 Reliably good, interesting food includes lunchtime baguettes, five-spice crispy pork pancake with hoisin sauce, salt and pepper squid with pickled samphire, saffron mayonnaise and wasabi nut crumble, pea, prawn and crayfish risotto, sausages and mash with red onion gravy, chargrilled chicken with chorizo, avocado, mozzarella and sunblush tomato salad with harissa mascarpone, braised lamb shank with roast garlic mash and mint jus, and puddings such as chocolate bread and butter pudding with Baileys crème anglaise and apple and pear crumble. *Benchmark main dish: confit free-range pork belly with calvados glaze, creamed cabbage and thyme jus £17.95. Two-course evening meal £29.00.*

Free house ~ Licensee Simon Goodman ~ Real ale ~ Open 11.30-11.30; 12-10.30 Sun ~ Bar food 12-2, 7-9; not Sun or Mon evenings ~ Restaurant ~ Children welcome ~ Dogs allowed in bar ~ Wi-fi *Recommended by Christopher and Elise Way, John Evans*

HIGH HURSTWOOD   TQ4925 Map 3

Hurstwood 🌟 ♟

(01825) 732257 – www.thehurstwood.com

Hurstwood Road off A272; TN22 4AH

Friendly, bustling dining pub with chatty bar area, real ales and good wines by the glass, excellent food and seats in the garden

Locals drop into this bustling, friendly pub for a drink and a chat but most customers are here to enjoy the excellent food. The U-shaped and beamed open-plan interior has high spindleback chairs against the counter, and an area beside the log fire in the tiled Victorian fireplace with a couple of leather sofas, armchairs and two tables. Attentive young staff serve Harveys Sussex Best Bitter and a local guest on handpump, ten good wines by the glass, a fair choice of spirits and cocktails; good coffees. The dining areas have tables set with red gingham napkins, little plants and church candles in rustic ironwork candlesticks, chairs that range from farmhouse to captain's to cushioned dining ones on bare boards, hunting prints and other artwork on pale painted walls above a grey dado, various lamps and lanterns, and a piano (which does get used). French windows at one end open out to decking with seats and tables, which leads down to a grassed area with more seats.

Creative food using local produce where possible includes open sandwiches, pigeon breast with puy lentils, swede purée, wild mushroom sauce and game chips, curried feta, date and sweetcorn fritters with greek yoghurt, sesame seed-coated teriyaki salmon with sautéed pak choi, ginger, mangetout and sweet potato wedges, pork escalopes with grilled sage polenta and caper and tomato sauce, duck breast with potato gratin, grilled cherry tomatoes and red wine jus, and puddings such as orange polenta cake with orange syrup and mascarpone and basil panna cotta with berry compote. *Benchmark main dish: crab linguine £14.95. Two-course evening meal £22.00.*

Free house ~ Licensees Martin and Lenka Spanek ~ Real ale ~ Open 11.30-11; 12-5.30 Sun; closed Sun evening except bank holiday weekends ~ Bar food 12-2.30, 6.30-9.30; 12-3 Sun; snacks all day ~ Children welcome ~ Dogs allowed in bar ~ Wi-fi *Recommended by John Harris, Nick Sharpe*

HORSHAM TQ1730 Map 3

Black Jug

(01403) 253526 – www.brunningandprice.co.uk/blackjug

North Street; RH12 1RJ

Lively town pub with wide choice of drinks, efficient staff and rewarding food

With interesting food and a fine range of drinks, this friendly town pub is always deservedly busy. The single, large, early 20th-c room has a long central bar, a nice collection of sizeable dark wood tables and comfortable chairs on a stripped-wood floor, bookcases and interesting old prints and photographs above a dark wood-panelled dado on cream walls; board games. A spacious, bright conservatory has similar furniture and lots of hanging baskets. Caledonian Deuchars IPA and Harveys Sussex Best Bitter with guests such as Adnams Old Ale, Brains SA Gold and Wells Bombardier Reserve The Colonels Choice on handpump, 19 wines by the glass, over 100 malt whiskies, 40 bourbons and farm cider. The pretty, flower-filled back terrace has plenty of garden furniture; parking is in the council car park next door, as the small one by the pub is for staff and deliveries only.

Well executed food includes sandwiches, vegetable spring roll with asian slaw and sweet chilli sauce, ham hock and mozzarella arancini with roasted tomato coulis, pork sausages with onion gravy, thai chicken salad with pak choi, mango and coconut and lime dressing, steak and kidney pie, cod loin with fennel croquette and Pernod cream sauce, venison casserole with horseradish mash, and puddings such as hot waffle with caramelised banana and toffee sauce and apple and blackberry crumble with crème anglaise. *Benchmark main dish: steak burger with toppings, coleslaw and fries £12.45. Two-course evening meal £21.00.*

Brunning & Price ~ Tenant Alastair Craig ~ Real ale ~ Open 11.30am-11pm; 12-10.30 Sun ~ Bar food 12-10 ~ Children welcome till 5pm ~ Dogs allowed in bar ~ Wi-fi
Recommended by Nick Sharpe, Tony Scott, Elliot Baker

LURGASHALL SU9327 Map 2

Noahs Ark

(01428) 707346 – www.noahsarkinn.co.uk

Off A283 N of Petworth; GU28 9ET

Busy old pub in nice spot with neatly kept rooms, real ales and pleasing food using local produce

Picnic-sets in front of this well run pub make the most of the view of the village green and cricket pitch; there are more tables in a large side garden. Inside, there's a bustling atmosphere and the simple, traditional bar, popular with locals, has leather-topped bar stools by the counter where they serve Greene King IPA and Abbot and a guest such as Skinners Splendid

Tackle on handpump, eight wines by the glass and local sparkling cider. There are also beams, a mix of wooden chairs and tables, parquet flooring and an inglenook fireplace. Open to the top of the rafters, the dining room is spacious and airy with church candles and fresh flowers on light wood tables; a couple of comfortable sofas face each other in front of an open woodburning stove; background music. The pub's border terrier is called Gillie and visiting dogs may get a dog biscuit.

Good food using local produce includes sandwiches, kipper pâté with horseradish crème fraîche, prawn cocktail with bloody mary mayonnaise, cheddar-smoked macaroni with mushrooms and spinach, free-range chicken with chilli pumpkin hummus and watercress, beer-battered haddock and chips, rib-eye steak with chips, and puddings such as crème brûlée and chocolate brownie with chocolate sauce. *Benchmark main dish: burger with toppings, slaw and chips £12.50. Two-course evening meal £20.00.*

Greene King ~ Lease Henry Coghlan and Amy Whitmore ~ Real ale ~ Open 11am-midnight; 12-9 Sun ~ Bar food 12-2.30, 7-9.30; 12-3.30 Sun ~ Restaurant ~ Children welcome ~ Dogs allowed in bar ~ Wi-fi *Recommended by Ian Phillips, John Millwood, Colin McKerrow*

MARK CROSS   TQ5831   Map 3
Mark Cross Inn ♀
(01892) 852423 – www.themarkcross.co.uk
A267 N of Mayfield; TN6 3NP

Sizeable pub with interconnected rooms, candlelight and fresh flowers, several real ales and popular food, and good views from seats in the garden

Usefully serving food all day, this is a big spreading pub with linked areas on several levels. It's kept cosy with church candles and open fires, shelves lined with books and stone bottles, gilt-edged mirrors, big clocks, large house plants and fresh flowers. There's all manner of seating from farmhouse, mate's and cushioned dining chairs to settles and stools grouped around dark shiny tables on rugs and bare boards, and the walls are lined almost frame-to-frame with photographs, prints, paintings and old newspaper cuttings. Helpful staff serve Fullers London Pride, Longman Best, St Austell Tribute and Sharps Doom Bar on handpump and good wines by the glass; daily papers and background music. The far-reaching views can be enjoyed from benches and tables on a terrace and picnic-sets on grass at the back of the building; there's a children's play fort.

Quite a choice of food includes sandwiches, spicy chicken wings with watermelon, radish and peanut salad, mediterranean vegetable tian with rocket dressing, corned beef hash with beer mustard sauce, sauté potatoes and a fried egg, steak and bacon burger with toppings, relish and skinny fries, grilled local plaice with lemon and parsley beurre noisette, roasted lamb rump with peppered goats cheese, confit potato and red wine jus, and puddings such as eton mess and sticky toffee pudding with toffee sauce. *Benchmark main dish: fish pie £12.95. Two-course evening meal £20.00.*

Whiting & Hammond ~ Manager Kiran Shukla ~ Real ale ~ Open 9am-11pm (midnight Fri, Sat); 9-10.30 Sun ~ Bar food 12-9.30 (9 Sun); 9-11am weekend brunch ~ Restaurant ~ Children welcome ~ Dogs allowed in bar ~ Wi-fi· *Recommended by Nigel and Jean Eames*

Bedroom prices are for high summer. Even then you may get reductions for more than one night, or (outside tourist areas) weekends. Winter special rates are common, and many inns cut bedroom prices if you have a full evening meal.

OVING
Gribble Inn ◀
(01243) 786893 – www.gribbleinn.co.uk
Between A27 and A259 E of Chichester; PO20 2BP

SU9005   Map 2

Own-brewed beers in bustling 16th-c thatched pub with well liked bar food and pretty garden

---

Newly thatched and pretty, this village pub offers ales that have been brewed here for over 30 years. On handpump, these might include Fuzzy Duck, Gribble Ale, Pig's Ear, Plucking Pheasant, Reg's Tipple and three seasonal ales, such as Sussex Quad Hopper or strong Wobbler Ale. The chatty bar features a lot of heavy beams and timbering while the other various linked rooms have a cottagey feel and sofas around two roaring log fires; board games. The barn now houses a venue for parties. There are seats outside in a covered area and more chairs and tables in the pretty garden with its apple and pear trees.

Making their own ice-cream, chips and bread, the tasty food includes sandwiches, breaded whitebait with tartare sauce, a cured meat platter, home-cooked ham and free-range eggs, sausages with rich onion gravy, steak, ale and stilton pie, beer-battered haddock and chips, rabbit in creamy grain mustard sauce, confit duck leg with caraway and orange-scented carrots, and puddings such as sticky toffee pudding with ale ice-cream and chocolate marquise with coffee sauce. *Benchmark main dish: pork belly in cider with mash, creamed cabbage and bacon £14.95. Two-course evening meal £19.00.*

Badger ~ Licensees Simon Wood and Nicola Tester ~ Real ale ~ Open 10am-11pm; 12-10 Sun ~ Bar food 12-2.30, 6-9; 12-3 Sun ~ Restaurant ~ Children welcome away from bar ~ Dogs allowed in bar ~ Wi-fi *Recommended by Tony Hobden*

 PETWORTH
Angel ◉ ♀ ⇌
(01798) 342153 – www.angelinnpetworth.co.uk
Angel Street; GU28 0BG

SU9721   Map 2

Medieval building with an 18th-c façade, chatty atmosphere in beamed bars, friendly service and good, interesting food; bedrooms

---

Our readers particularly enjoy the very good food, ales and wine in this bustling and carefully renovated inn – and the courteous staff come in for warm praise too. The interconnected rooms have kept many of their original features. The front bar has beams, a log fire in an inglenook fireplace and an appealing variety of old wooden and cushioned dining chairs and tables on wide floorboards. It leads through to the main room with high chairs by the counter where they keep a beer named for the pub (from Langham) plus a guest such as Dorking Smokestack Lightnin' on handpump, 22 wines by the glass from an extensive list and a good range of malt whiskies and gins; board games. There are also high-backed brown leather and antique chairs and tables on pale wooden flooring, the odd milk churn and french windows to a three-level terrace garden. The cosy and popular back bar is similarly furnished, with a second log fire. The bedrooms are comfortable and breakfasts good.

Accomplished and extremely good, the food includes sandwiches, smoked haddock on hash browns with spinach and a poached egg, seared cured beef carpaccio with mustard mayonnaise, spinach crêpes with a parmesan and nutmeg cream, miso-glazed salmon fillet with sesame asparagus, rum-glazed pork skewers with coconut rice, pot-roast venison with shrewsbury sauce, and puddings such as chocolate and Baileys cheesecake with blood orange sorbet and chocolate sauce and baked alaska. *Benchmark main dish: steak and kidney pudding £13.25. Two-course evening meal £18.50.*

Free house ~ Licensee Murray Inglis ~ Real ale ~ Open 10.30am-11pm; 11.30-10.30 Sun ~ Bar food 12-2.30, 6.30-9.30; 12-3, 6-9 Sun ~ Children welcome ~ Dogs allowed in bar and bedrooms ~ Wi-fi ~ Live jazz summer Sun 4pm ~ Bedrooms: $90/$100
Recommended by Tony and Wendy Hobden, Michael and Sheila Hawkins, David Jackman, Mr and Mrs P R Thomas

RINGMER
TQ4313   Map 3
Cock £
(01273) 812040 – www.cockpub.co.uk
Uckfield Road – blocked-off section of road off A26 N of village turn-off; BN8 5RX

16th-c country pub with a wide choice of popular bar food, real ales in character bar, and plenty of seats in the garden

The friendly licensees greet all their customers, whether regulars or visitors, personally – it's something our readers always note. A 16th-c former coaching inn, it has an unspoilt bar with traditional pubby furniture on flagstones, heavy beams, a log fire in an inglenook fireplace, Harveys Sussex Best Bitter and a couple of guests from local breweries on handpump, 12 wines by the glass and a dozen malt whiskies; good service. There are also three dining areas; background music. Outside, on the terrace and in the garden, are lots of picnic-sets with views across open fields to the South Downs. The owners' dogs are called Bailey and Tally, and visiting dogs are offered a bowl of water and a chew. This is sister pub to the Highlands at Uckfield.

A huge choice of top quality food includes sandwiches, deep-fried camembert with cranberry sauce, prawn cocktail, local venison sausages with mash and onion gravy, mixed nut roast with tomato, mushroom and red wine sauce, chicken curry, salmon fillet with cream and watercress sauce, lamb chops with garlic and rosemary, and puddings such as jam roly-poly with custard and a seasonal crumble. *Benchmark main dish: steak in ale pie £11.25. Two-course evening meal £16.75.*

Free house ~ Licensees Ian, Val, Nick and Matt Ridley ~ Real ale ~ Open 11-3, 6-11.30; 11-11.30 Sun ~ Bar food 12-2.15 (2.30 Sat), 6-9.30; 12-9.30 Sun ~ Restaurant ~ Well behaved children welcome (no toddlers) ~ Dogs allowed in bar ~ Wi-fi *Recommended by Ann and Colin Hunt, Tony and Wendy Hobden*

ROBERTSBRIDGE
TQ7323   Map 3
George
(01580) 880315 – www.thegeorgerobertsbridge.co.uk
High Street; TN32 5AW

Former coaching inn with good food and ales and seats in courtyard garden; comfortable bedrooms

In the centre of a bustling village, this is a handsome old inn with friendly, hands-on licensees. There's a log fire in a brick inglenook fireplace with a leather sofa and a couple of armchairs in front – just the place for a quiet pint and a chat – plus high bar stools by the counter where they serve Harveys Sussex Best Bitter, Sharps Doom Bar and a guest such as Franklins English Garden on handpump, good wines by the glass and a farm cider. Off from here is a dining area with elegant high-backed beige tartan or leather chairs around a mix of tables (each with fresh flowers and a tea-light) on stripped floorboards and more tea-lights in a small fireplace; background music. In warm weather there are plenty of seats and tables on the outside back terrace. The bedrooms are comfortable and the breakfasts good.

 Enjoyable food includes hot and cold lunchtime baguettes, mackerel fillet with rhubarb jam, chicken satay with peanut dipping sauce, several platters, burger with toppings and chips, calves liver with smoked bacon, onion and herb-stuffed baked potato and gravy, moroccan-marinated lamb chop with couscous and minty yoghurt dip, and puddings. *Benchmark main dish: tempura-battered cod and chips £11.00. Two-course evening meal £19.50.*

Free house ~ Licensees John and Jane Turner ~ Real ale ~ Open 11-11; 12-8 Sun; closed Mon ~ Bar food 12-2.30, 6.30-9, 12-3 Sun ~ Children welcome but must be accompanied by adult at all times ~ Dogs allowed in bar ~ Wi-fi *Recommended by Tom and Jill Jones, David Jackman, Peter Meister*

RYE
Ship

TQ9120 Map 3

(01797) 222233 – www.theshipinnrye.co.uk
The Strand, at the foot of Mermaid Street; TN31 7DB

Informal and prettily set old inn with unusual furnishings, local ales and tasty food; bedrooms

The décor in this 16th-c inn is an unusual blend of quirkiness and comfort. The ground floor is opened up, from the sunny big-windowed front part to a snugger section at the back, with a log fire in the stripped-brick fireplace below a stuffed boar's head. Flooring varies from one area to the next: composition, stripped boards, flagstones, a bit of carpet in the armchair corner. There are beams and timbers, a mixed bag of rather second-hand-feeling furnishings – a cosy group of overstuffed leather armchairs and sofa, random stripped or Formica-topped tables and various café chairs – that suit it nicely, as do the utilitarian bulkhead wall lamps. Long Man Best Bitter, Old Dairy Gold Top and Rother Valley Boadicea on handpump and several wines by the glass; board games. In addition to the simply furnished but comfortable bedrooms, the pub rents a 300-year-old single-storey cottage and 500-year-old house. There are picnic-sets and a couple of cheerful oilcloth-covered tables out by the quiet lane.

 Popular food includes sandwiches, mackerel pâté with radish and caper salad, an antipasti plate, southern-style chicken with ranch dressing and fries, burger with toppings and chipotle mayonnaise, roast garlic gnocchi with wild mushroom ragoût, barbecue ribs with matchstick potatoes and coleslaw, and puddings. *Benchmark main dish: local fish pie £13.00. Two-course evening meal £19.00.*

Enterprise ~ Lease Karen Northcote ~ Real ale ~ Open 8am-11pm (10.30 Sun) ~ Bar food 12-3 (4 weekends), 6-10; breakfast 8-11.30am ~ Children welcome ~ Dogs allowed in bar and bedrooms ~ Wi-fi ~ Bedrooms: £90/£110 *Recommended by Simon Rodway, Mike and Eleanor Anderson, Anthony Barnes, David Jackman*

RYE
Ypres Castle

TQ9220 Map 3

(01797) 223248 – www.yprescastleinn.co.uk
Gun Garden; steps up from A259, or down past Ypres Tower; TN31 7HH

Traditional pub with several real ales, quite a choice of bar food and seats in sheltered garden

In warm weather the sheltered garden here is very tempting, with views over the River Rother and Romney Marsh. Inside, it's unpretentious and traditional: the main bar has wall banquettes with pale blue cushions, an open fire in a stone fireplace with a mirror above and easy chairs in front, assorted chairs and tables (each set with a modern oil lamp) and local artwork. Stools line the blue-panelled counter where they keep five real ales from breweries such as Harveys, Larkins, Long Man, Old Dairy and Westerham on handpump, eight wines by the glass and farm cider; background music and board games. The back dining room has paintings and pictures of Rye and similar furnishings to the bar; there's another dining room at the front.

The highly thought-of food includes sandwiches, crab and avocado salad, leek and blue cheese tartlet, mustard and honey ham and egg, vegetarian chilli, burger with toppings, egg and chips, fish pie, slow-roasted lamb shank with minted mash, and puddings such as apple crumble and spotted dick with custard. *Benchmark main dish: beer-battered fish and chips £11.00. Two-course evening meal £20.00.*

Free house ~ Licensee Garry Dowling ~ Real ale ~ Open 12-11 (10.30 Sun); closed Mon Nov-late Mar ~ Bar food 12-3, 6-9 (8 Fri); 12-3 Sun ~ Children welcome ~ Dogs welcome ~ Wi-fi ~ Live music Fri and Sun evenings *Recommended by Bill Adie, Peter Smith and Judith Brown, Peter Meister, Anthony Barnes, M and J White*

SALEHURST

TQ7424 Map 3

Salehurst Halt £ 🍺

(01580) 880620 – www.salehursthalt.co.uk

Village signposted from Robertsbridge bypass on A21 Tunbridge Wells–Battle; Church Lane; TN32 5PH

Bustling local in quiet hamlet with chatty atmosphere, real ales, well liked bar food and seats in pretty back garden

This is a smashing little country pub with particularly helpful staff who offer just as warm a welcome to visitors as they do to their loyal regulars. To the right of the door is a small stone-floored area with a couple of tables, a settle, a TV and an open fire. Furniture includes a nice long scrubbed pine table, a couple of sofas and a mix of more ordinary pubby tables and wheelback and mate's chairs on the wood-strip floor; occasional background music, board games and books on shelves. Dark Star American Pale Ale, Harveys Sussex Best Bitter, Isfield Flapjack and Old Dairy Red Top on handpump, farm cider, several malt whiskies and eight wines by the glass. The cottagey and charming back garden has views over the Rother Valley and the summer barbecues and pizzas from the wood-fired oven are extremely popular; there's also a terrace with metal chairs and tiled tables, and outdoor table tennis as well as other garden games.

Extremely popular food includes sandwiches, a daily changing pâté, vegetarian indian meze plate, chicken caesar salad, german sausages with sauerkraut, baked bass on roasted vegetables, game pie, beer-battered local fish and chips, and puddings such as raspberry cheesecake and chocolate and cherry torte. *Benchmark main dish: curried fish stew £11.50. Two-course evening meal £16.50.*

Free house ~ Licensee Andrew Augarde ~ Real ale ~ Open 12-11 (10.30 Sun); closed Mon, may close 9.30 Sun in winter ~ Bar food 12-2.30, 7-9.30; 12.30-3 Sun ~ Children welcome ~ Dogs welcome ~ Wi-fi ~ Live music second Sun of month *Recommended by Peter Meister*

If we know a featured-entry pub does sandwiches, we always say so – if they're not mentioned, you'll have to assume you can't get one.

TICEHURST

Bell 🛏

TQ6830 Map 3

(01580) 200234 – www.thebellinticehurst.com

High Street; TN5 7AS

Carefully restored inn with heavily beamed rooms, real ales and good wines by the glass, popular food and friendly service; interesting, well equipped bedrooms

As well as comfortable and very individually decorated bedrooms in the coaching inn, there are new separate lodges each with their own little garden built around a firepit. The main back garden has been extended, with seats and tables on the lower part and built-in cushioned seating up steps on the terrace. The heavily beamed bar has an inglenook fireplace, tables surrounded by a mix of cushioned wooden dining chairs on bare boards, some quirky decorations such as a squirrel in a rocking chair, and stools by the counter where cheerful staff serve Harveys Sussex Best Bitter and Tonbridge Rustic on handpump, around 16 wines by the glass and a dozen malt whiskies. The dining room continues from the bar and is similarly furnished, with the addition of cushioned wall settles and an eclectic choice of paintings on the red walls; background music. A separate room has comfortable sofas grouped around a low table in front of another open fire, interesting wallpaper, a large globe, an ancient typewriter and various books and pieces of china. What was the carriage room holds a long sunken table with benches on either side (perfect for an informal party) and there's an upstairs function room too.

Rewarding food includes lunchtime sandwiches, smoked duck breast with shaved fennel and avocado purée, smoked mackerel pâté, wild mushroom and butternut squash open ravioli, burger with barbecue sauce and triple-cooked chips, trio of guinea fowl with boulangère potatoes, carrot purée and rich jus, smoked salmon fishcake with sea spinach and tartare sauce, and puddings such as dark chocolate fondant with pistachio ice-cream and crème brûlée. *Benchmark main dish: local rump steak with garlic or peppercorn sauce and triple-cooked chips £17.50. Two-course evening meal £21.00.*

Free house ~ Licensee Kit Smith ~ Real ale ~ Open 9am-11 (10.30 Sun) ~ Bar food 12-3, 6-9.30 (9 Sun) ~ Restaurant ~ Children welcome ~ Dogs allowed in bar and bedrooms ~ Wi-fi ~ Bedrooms: /£145 *Recommended by Peter Meister, David Jackman, Martin Day, Roger and Anne Newbury*

TILLINGTON

Horse Guards 🍴 ☆ � 🛏

SU9621 Map 2

(01798) 342332 – www.thehorseguardsinn.co.uk

Off A272 Midhurst–Petworth; GU28 9AF

Sussex Dining Pub of the Year

300-year-old inn with beams, panelling and open fires in rambling rooms, inventive food and charming garden; cottagey bedrooms

An all-round favourite with many of our readers, this 300-year-old inn offers delicious food, a careful choice of drinks and a genuine welcome from thoughtful staff. With a gently civilised atmosphere, the neatly kept, beamed front bar has some good country furniture on bare boards, a chesterfield in one corner and a lovely view beyond the village to the Rother Valley from a seat in the big panelled bow window. High bar chairs line the counter where they keep Harveys Sussex Best Bitter, Long Man Long Blonde and Otter Bitter on handpump, 15 wines by the glass, home-made sloe gin and local farm juices. Other rambling beamed rooms have similar furniture on brick floors, rugs and original panelling and there are fresh flowers throughout. In warm weather the leafy, lush and sheltered garden has picnic-sets, day beds, deck chairs and even a hammock, and there's also a charming terrace. The cosy country bedrooms are comfortable and breakfasts are good. The medieval church with its unusual spire was painted by Constable and Turner; Petworth House (National Trust) is nearby.

 Food is exceptionally good and includes lunchtime only dishes (such as black treacle-cured bacon and duck egg and barbecue pulled pork bap with celeriac coleslaw and fries) as well as game terrine with apple chutney, oak-smoked prawn bisque with chilli sherry, pigeon breasts with braised puy lentils, confit root vegetables and red wine gravy, bhel puri (indian puffed rice, pomegranate, chickpeas, potato, tamarind, coriander relish and yoghurt), slow-cooked pork belly with moroccan spices, prunes, apricots, couscous, skate wing with bouillabaisse and saffron cream, and puddings such as dark chocolate and cashew nut tart, cocoa nibs, blood orange and soft whipped cream and iced bramley apple parfait, pecan and oat crumb and stem ginger syrup. *Benchmark main dish: venison haunch £16.50. Two-course evening meal £22.00.*

Enterprise ~ Lease Sam Beard ~ Real ale ~ Open 12-midnight ~ Bar food 12-2.30 (3 Sat), 6.30-9 (9.30 Fri, Sat); 12-3.30, 6.30-9 Sun ~ Children welcome ~ Dogs welcome ~ Wi-fi ~ Bedrooms: £95/£100 *Recommended by Sheila Topham, Christopher and Elise Way, John Evans, Tracey and Stephen Groves, Richard Tilbrook, Ron and June Buckler, Richard Dilnot, Ann and Colin Hunt*

UCKFIELD
Highlands

TQ4720 Map 3

(01825) 762989 – www.highlandsinn.co.uk
Eastbourne Road/Lewes Road; TN22 5SP

Busy, well run pub with plenty of space, real ales and well thought-of food, good service, seats and a children's play area outside

---

On our Sunday lunchtime visit, the large, spreading restaurant (on the right) was full of cheerful local families and friends all enjoying a choice of three roasts. There's a dividing wall (with bookcase wallpaper) splitting the room in two, painted rafters in high ceilings, big glass lamps and local photographs and animal pictures on the walls. Also, all manner of cushioned dining and painted farmhouse chairs, long chesterfield sofas, upholstered banquettes and scatter cushions on settles around wooden tables on the part carpeted, part wooden and part ceramic flooring; background music. Our favourite spot is around the bar counter where it's quieter, with customers reading newspapers with a pint or a glass of wine: high tartan benches, high leather chairs around equally high tables and armchairs here and there. Harveys Sussex Best Bitter and a couple of local guests on handpump, 11 wines by the glass and a dozen malt whiskies. Service from friendly, helpful young staff is good. The bar at the end of the building has more long chesterfields and armchairs, a pool area, TV, fruit machine and an open fire. Outside, there's a decked smoking shelter, a children's play area and picnic-sets on a terrace and on grass. This is sister pub to the Cock at Ringmer.

A wide choice of popular food includes sandwiches, tiger prawns in garlic and herb butter, mushrooms in creamy stilton sauce, sharing platters, a pie of the day, mixed bean chilli, home-cooked ham and eggs, chicken with bacon, cheese and barbecue cream sauce, haddock topped with welsh rarebit with spinach mash and chive cream sauce, braised lamb shank with red wine gravy and dauphinoise potatoes, and puddings such as crème brûlée and a crumble of the day. *Benchmark main dish: burger with toppings and fries £10.95. Two-course evening meal £18.00.*

Ridley Inns ~ Managers Ian, Val, Nick and Matt Ridley ~ Real ale ~ Open 11-11 (midnight Sat); 12-10.30 Sun ~ Bar food 12-2.30, 6-9.30 (all day Sat); 12-6 Sun ~ Restaurant ~ Children welcome ~ Dogs allowed in bar ~ Wi-fi *Recommended by Mike and Eleanor Anderson*

WARNINGLID
TQ2425 Map 3

Half Moon

(01444) 461227 – www.thehalfmoonwarninglid.co.uk
B2115 off A23 S of Handcross or off B2110 Handcross–Lower Beeding; RH17 5TR

Good modern cooking in simply furnished pub with real ales, lots of wines by the glass and seats in sizeable garden; bedrooms

Three contemporary and comfortable bedrooms have been opened in this friendly pub and breakfasts are highly regarded. It has a proper pubby atmosphere and the lively locals' bar has straightforward wooden furniture on bare boards and a small Victorian fireplace; a room just off here has oak beams and flagstones. A couple of steps lead down to the dining areas with a mix of wooden chairs, cushioned wall settles and nice old tables on floorboards, plank panelling and bare brick, and old village photographs; there's also another open fire and a glass-covered well. Adnams Broadside, Harveys Sussex Best Bitter and Hurst Founder's Best Bitter on handpump, around 18 wines by the glass, several malt whiskies and a farm cider. There are quite a few picnic-sets on the lawn in the sheltered, sizeable garden, which has a most spectacular avenue of trees, with uplighters that glow at night-time.

Interesting and very good, the seasonal food includes wild sea trout and dill tartlet with spinach and crayfish cream, chilli beef spring roll with arrabiata sauce, star anise drizzle and pickled cucumber and coriander salad, local sausages with mash and onion gravy, chargrilled halloumi with crispy lemon polenta, ratatouille and black olive tapenade, beer-battered cod, pea purée and chips, venison burger with horseradish mayonnaise, toppings and chips, duck breast with potato and orange croquettes and beetroot purée and jus, and puddings such as double chocolate brownie with white chocolate ice-cream and vanilla and cardamom panna cotta with blood orange syrup and sorbet and roasted pine nuts. *Benchmark main dish: venison fillet and pie with redcurrant jus £18.00. Two-course evening meal £22.00.*

Free house ~ Licensee James Amico ~ Real ale ~ Open 11.30-3, 5.30-11; 11.30-11 Sat; 12-9 Sun ~ Bar food 12-2, 6-9.30; 12-3 Sun ~ Restaurant ~ Children welcome ~ Dogs allowed in bar ~ Wi-fi ~ Bedrooms: /£120 *Recommended by John Harris, Belinda May*

WEST HOATHLY
TQ3632 Map 3

Cat 🌟 ♀ 🛏

(01342) 810369 – www.catinn.co.uk
Village signposted from A22 and B2028 S of East Grinstead; North Lane; RH19 4PP

Popular 16th-c inn with old-fashioned bar, airy dining rooms, local real ales, tempting food and seats outside; lovely bedrooms

Kept spruced up by the friendly, hands-on landlord, this bustling old inn is as popular as ever. The lovely old bar has beams, proper pubby tables and chairs on an old wooden floor, and a fine log fire in an inglenook fireplace. There's a focus on local breweries, with Harveys Sussex Best Bitter and Old Ale, Larkins Traditional and Long Man American Pale Ale available on handpump, as well as local cider and apple juice and 17 wines by the glass (plus five locally made sparkling ones); look out for the glass cover over the 75-ft well. The light, airy dining rooms have a nice mix of wooden dining chairs and tables on pale wood-strip flooring, and throughout there are hops, china platters, brass and copper ornaments and a gently upmarket atmosphere. The contemporary-style garden room has glass doors that open on to a terrace with teak furniture. The cocker spaniel is called Harvey. Bedrooms are comfortable, very pretty and well equipped and breakfasts are highly thought of. Steam train enthusiasts can visit the Bluebell Railway, and the Priest House in the village is a fascinating museum in a cottage endowed with an extraordinary array of ancient anti-witch symbols. Parking is limited.

Appealing food using local, organic produce includes lunchtime sandwiches, potted crab, pickled fennel and brown crab sablé biscuit, a charcuterie board, spinach and ricotta cannelloni with tomato and basil, beer-battered fish and chips, guinea fowl with pancetta and braised lentils and jus, beef bourguignon, hake with chorizo, haricot beans and red pepper cassoulet, and puddings such as Valrhona chocolate brownie with malt ice-cream and caramelised lime tart with blueberry sorbet. *Benchmark main dish: steak and mushroom in ale pie £14.75. Two-course evening meal £21.00.*

Free house ~ Licensee Andrew Russell ~ Real ale ~ Open 12-11; 12-3.30 Sun ~ Bar food 12-2, 6-9; 12-2.30, 6-9.30 Fri, Sat; 12-2.30 Sun ~ Children welcome ~ Dogs allowed in bar and bedrooms ~ Wi-fi ~ Pianist last Fri evening of month and every other Sun lunch ~ Bedrooms: £85/£120 *Recommended by J A Snell, Hunter and Christine Wright, Wendy Breese, Mrs Sally Scott, Sheila Topham, Nick Lawless, S G N Bennett, Martin Day*

Also Worth a Visit in Sussex

Besides the fully inspected pubs, you might like to try these pubs that have been recommended to us and described by readers. Do tell us what you think of them: feedback@goodguides.com

ALBOURNE   TQ2514
Ginger Fox   (01273) 857888
Take B2117 W from A23; pub at junction with A281; BN6 9EA Thatched country dining pub with simple rustic interior, emphasis on restaurant side (there is a small bar area serving local ales such as Harveys), highly regarded modern cooking, not cheap but they also do a good value two-course lunch/early evening menu (Mon-Fri), lots of wines by the glass from a good list, friendly professional service; children welcome, attractive garden with Downs views, play area, open all day. *(John Evans)*

ALCISTON   TQ5005
Rose Cottage   (01323) 870377
Village signposted off A27 Polegate–Lewes; BN26 6UW As we went to press the long-serving landlord at this old-fashioned cottage (a former Main Entry) was preparing to move on, taking Jasper the talkative parrot with him; has had simple furnishings, log fires and interesting country bric-a-brac, good food and ales such as Burning Sky and Harveys; you can walk straight to the South Downs from here; news please. *(Tom and Jill Jones, R and S Bentley, Alan Cowell, Phil and Jane Villiers, Stuart and Diana Hughes)*

ALFOLD BARS   TQ0333
Sir Roger Tichborne
(01403) 751873 *B2133 N of Loxwood; RH14 0QS* Renovated and extended beamed country pub keeping original nooks and crannies, good well presented food (not Sun evening) from varied reasonably priced menu, friendly prompt service, five well kept ales including one for the pub from local Firebird, flagstones and log fires; children and dogs welcome, back terrace and sloping lawn with lovely rural views, good walks, open all day. *(Emma Scofield)*

ALFRISTON   TQ5203
Olde Smugglers   (01323) 870241
Waterloo Square; BN26 5UE Low-beamed 14th-c village inn, brick floor, panelling and various nooks and crannies, sofas by huge inglenook, well kept Harveys and a couple of guests, Weston's Old Rosie cider and several wines by the glass, reasonably priced bar food from sandwiches to daily specials; background music; children in eating area and conservatory, dogs welcome, tables on well planted back suntrap terrace and lawn, four bedrooms, open (and food) all day. *(Tony Scott)*

ALFRISTON   TQ5203
Star (01323) 870495
High Street; BN26 5TA Fair-sized hotel
with fine painted medieval carvings outside,
heavy-beamed old-fashioned bar with some
interesting features including a sanctuary
post, antique furnishings and big log fire in
Tudor fireplace, comfortable lounge with
easy chairs, more space behind for eating,
enjoyable bar food (pricier restaurant
menu), ales such as Beachy Head and Long
Man; background music, monthly quiz;
children and dogs (in bar) welcome, lovely
village on South Downs Way, 37 bedrooms
(most in 1960s part behind), open all day in
summer. *(Tom and Jill Jones, John Beeken)*

AMBERLEY   TQ0211
Bridge (01798) 831619
Houghton Bridge, off B2139; BN18 9LR
Popular and welcoming open-plan dining
pub, comfortable and relaxed, with pleasant
bar and two-room dining area, candles on
tables, log fire, wide range of reasonably
priced generous food (not Sun evening) from
good sandwiches up, well kept ales including
Harveys, cheerful efficient young service;
children and dogs welcome, seats out in
front, more tables in enclosed side garden,
handy for station, open all day. *(Martin Jones)*

AMBERLEY   TQ0313
Sportsmans (01798) 831787
*Crossgates; Rackham Road, off B2139;
BN18 9NR* Popular 17th-c pub with
enjoyable fairly priced food and three
well kept ales including Harveys, friendly
efficient young staff, three bars including
brick-floored one with darts, great views over
Amberley Wildbrooks nature reserve from
pretty back conservatory restaurant and
tables outside; dogs welcome, good walks,
five neat bedrooms, open all day. *(Tony Scott)*

ANGMERING   TQ0604
Lamb (01903) 774300
The Square; BN16 4EQ Airy updated
village coaching inn, enjoyable food (not Sun
evening) from varied menu including good
value two-course lunch, ales such as Fullers
and Harveys from light wood servery, good
choice of wines by the glass, friendly service,
painted half-panelling and wood-strip
floors, inglenook log fire in bar, woodburner
on raised plinth in restaurant; children
welcome, refurbished bedrooms, open all day.
(Tom and Ruth Rees)

ANGMERING   TQ0704
Spotted Cow (01903) 783919
High Street; BN16 4AW Up to six well kept
ales including Harveys, Sharps and Timothy
Taylors, decent wines by the glass and good
choice of popular food from traditional
choices up, efficient friendly service, smallish
bar to the left, long dining extension with
large conservatory on right, two fires,

sporting caricatures, smuggling history;
occasional live music and quiz nights, free
wi-fi; children and dogs (in bar) welcome,
disabled access (outside gents'), hedged
garden with lovely flower borders, also lower
garden with country views, boules and play
area, nice walk to Highdown Hill fort, open
all day Fri-Sun. *(John Beeken, Tony and Wendy
Hobden)*

ARDINGLY   TQ3430
★**Gardeners Arms** (01444) 892328
B2028 2 miles N; RH17 6TJ Well liked
food from sandwiches and pub favourites up
in old linked rooms, Badger beers, pleasant
efficient service, standing timbers and
inglenooks, scrubbed pine on flagstones and
broad boards, old local photographs, mural in
back part, lighted candles and nice relaxed
atmosphere; children and dogs welcome,
disabled facilities, café-style furniture on
pretty terrace and in side garden, opposite
South of England showground and handy
for Borde Hill Garden and Wakehurst Place
(NT), open all day. *(Anne and Ben Smith)*

ARLINGTON   TQ5507
Old Oak (01323) 482072
*Caneheath; off A22 or A27 NW of
Polegate; BN26 6SJ* 17th-c former
almshouse with open-plan L-shaped bar,
beams, log fires and comfortable seating, well
kept Harveys and a guest tapped from the
cask, traditional bar food (all day weekends)
from sandwiches and baked potatoes up;
background music, toad in the hole played
here; children and dogs welcome, round
picnic-sets out in front and in quiet garden,
play area, walks in nearby Abbots Wood, open
all day. *(Belinda May)*

ARLINGTON   TQ5407
Yew Tree (01323) 870590
*Off A22 near Hailsham, or A27 W of
Polegate; BN26 6RX* Neatly modernised
Victorian village pub popular for its good
value generous home-made food (booking
advised), well kept Harveys and Long Man,
decent wines, prompt friendly service even
when busy, log fires, hop-covered beams
and old local photographs, darts in thriving
bare-boards bar, plush lounge, comfortable
conservatory; children welcome, nice big
garden with play area, paddock with farm
animals, good local walks. *(John Beeken)*

ARUNDEL   TQ0208
★**Black Rabbit** (01903) 882828
*Mill Road, Offham; keep on and don't
give up; BN18 9PB* Refurbished riverside
pub in lovely spot near wildfowl reserve with
timeless views of water meadows and castle
– well organised for families and can get very
busy; long bar with eating areas at either end,
good choice of enjoyable reasonably priced
food from baguettes and sharing boards up,
well kept Badger ales and decent wines by
the glass, good service, log fires, newspapers;

background music, Tues quiz; dogs welcome, covered tables and pretty hanging baskets out at front, extensive terrace across road overlooking river, play area, boat trips and good walks, open (and food) all day. *(John Beeken, Tony Scott)*

ARUNDEL   TQ0107
Swan (01903) 882314
High Street; BN18 9AG Georgian inn's comfortably relaxed L-shaped bar, well kept Fullers/Gales beers and occasional guests, popular fairly priced food including deals, friendly efficient young staff, wood flooring, sporting memorabilia and old photographs, open fire, connecting restaurant; 14 bedrooms, no car park (pay and display opposite), open all day. *(Anon)*

ASHURST   TQ1816
★ ## Fountain (01403) 710219
B2135 S of Partridge Green; BN44 3AP Attractive 16th-c pub with plenty of character; rustic tap room on right with log fire in brick inglenook, country dining chairs around polished tables on flagstones, opened-up snug with heavy beams and another inglenook, Harveys Best and guests, several wines by the glass, generally well liked home-cooked food (all day weekends) from varied menu, skittle alley/function room; children (not in front bar) and dogs welcome, seats on front brick terrace, pretty garden with raised herb beds, orchard and duck pond, summer barbecues, open (and food) all day. *(Tom and Jill Jones, Nick Lawless, Tony Scott)*

BALCOMBE   TQ3033
Cowdray Arms (01444) 811280
London Road (B2036/B2110 N of village); RH17 6QD Refurbished 1930s roadside pub with good food including bargain fixed-price deals, friendly helpful staff, Greene King and guests; children (till 9pm), dogs welcome, garden tables. *(Mrs P R Sykes)*

BALCOMBE   TQ3033
Half Moon (01444) 811582
Haywards Heath Road; RH17 6PA Cheerful village local with welcoming hard-working landlady, beams and wood floors, some comfy leather sofas, candles on tables, antlers over log fire, three real ales and enjoyable well priced food; regular live music and quiz nights; children and dogs welcome, a few seats outside and pretty hanging baskets, good walking area, closed Mon. *(Mrs P R Sykes)*

BALLS CROSS   SU9826
★ ## Stag (01403) 820241
Village signed off A283 at N edge of Petworth; GU28 9JP Cheery unspoilt 17th-c country pub, fishing rods, country knick-knacks and old photographs, tiny flagstoned bar with log fire in huge

inglenook, a few seats and bar stools, Badger beers and several wines by the glass, second tiny room and appealing old-fashioned bare-boards restaurant, enjoyable pubby food (not Sun evening), good service; bar skittles, darts and board games in separate room, outside loos; well behaved children allowed away from main bar, dogs welcome, seats out in front and in pretty back garden, open all day weekends. *(Colin McKerrow)*

BARCOMBE   TQ4416
Anchor (01273) 400414
Barcombe Mills; BN8 5BS Late 18th-c pub with lots of tables out by winding River Ouse (boat hire), well kept ales including Harveys and reasonably priced pubby food, friendly smartly dressed staff, two beamed bars, restaurant and small front conservatory; children and dogs welcome, self-catering chalet, open all day. *(Mrs Sally Scott)*

BARCOMBE CROSS   TQ4212
Royal Oak (01273) 400418
Off A275 N of Lewes; BN8 5BA Welcoming family-run village pub with good mix of locals and visitors, up to five well kept Harveys ales and reasonably priced wines, enjoyable generously served food from bar snacks up, friendly helpful service, long bar with restaurant attached, beams, bare boards and open fire, local art for sale; skittle alley; a few tables out in front and in small tree-shaded garden, open all day. *(John Beeken)*

BARNS GREEN   TQ1227
Queens Head (01403) 730436
Chapel Road; RH13 0PS Welcoming traditional village pub, blackboard choice of good generous home-made food (not Sun evening), three well kept ales including Fullers London Pride and Long Man Best, ciders such as local Hairy Pig and Weston's; live music, quiz nights; children and dogs welcome, tables out at front and in back garden with play area, open all day weekends. *(Emma Scofield)*

BECKLEY   TQ8423
Rose & Crown (01797) 252161
Northiam Road (B2088); TN31 6SE Popular friendly village local with five or so well kept ales including Harveys, generous pub food from baguettes up, cosy lower eating area with log fire; children welcome, views from pleasant garden. *(Conrad Freezer)*

BERWICK   TQ5105
★ ## Cricketers Arms (01323) 870469
Lower Road, S of A27; BN26 6SP Charming flint local with three small unpretentious bars, huge supporting beam in each low ceiling, simple country furnishings on quarry tiles, cricketing pictures and bats, two log fires, friendly staff, four Harveys ales tapped from the cask, country wines and good coffee, well cooked uncomplicated food, old Sussex coin game toad in the hole;

children in family room only, dogs welcome, delightful cottagey front garden with picnic-sets among small brick paths, more seats behind, Bloomsbury Group wall paintings in nearby church, good South Downs walks, open all day summer, closed weekday afternoons winter. *(Mrs Sally Scott, Tony Scott, Alan Cowell)*

BILLINGSHURST TQ0830
Blue Ship (01403) 822709
The Haven; hamlet signposted off A29 just N of junction with A264, then follow signpost left towards Garlands and Okehurst; RH14 9BS Unspoilt pub in quiet country spot, beamed and brick-floored front bar, scrubbed tables and wall benches, inglenook woodburner, Badger ales tapped from the cask and served from hatch, good home-made food from pub favourites up, two small carpeted back rooms; darts, bar billiards, shove-ha'penny, cribbage and dominoes; children and dogs welcome, tables out at front and in side garden with play area, camping, closed Sun evening, Mon. *(Ian Phillips, Mrs Sally Scott, Tony Scott)*

BILLINGSHURST TQ0725
Limeburners (01403) 782311
Lordings Road, Newbridge (B2133/A272 W); RH14 9JA Friendly characterful pub in converted row of cottages, three Fullers ales and enjoyable fairly priced food (not Sun evening) from snacks up, good friendly service, open fires; quiz nights; children welcome, pleasant front garden, play area behind. *(Tony and Wendy Hobden)*

BLACKBOYS TQ5220
★**Blackboys Inn** (01825) 890283
B2192, S edge of village; TN22 5LG Old weatherboarded inn set back from road; main bar to the right with beams, timbers, dark wooden furniture and log fire, locals' bar to left with lots of bric-a-brac, Harveys ales including seasonals, several wines by the glass and wide choice of enjoyable food (all day Sat, till 7pm Sun), panelled dining areas; background and some live music; children and dogs (in bar) welcome, sizeable garden with seats under trees, on terrace and under cover by duck pond, good walks (Vanguard Way passes the pub, Wealdway close by), open all day. *(Edward May)*

BOGNOR REGIS SZ9201
Royal Oak (01243) 821002
A259 Chichester Road, North Bersted; PO21 5JF Old-fashioned two-bar beamed local (aka the Pink Pub), well kept Long Man, shortish choice of popular reasonably priced food till 6.30pm (not Sun evening),

friendly service; bar billiards, darts, sports TV; children and dogs welcome (pub boxer is Alfie). *(Anon)*

BOLNEY TQ2623
Bolney Stage (01444) 881200
London Road, off old A23 just N of A272; RH17 5RL Sizeable 16th-c black and white dining pub, good varied choice of popular food, four changing ales (blackboard descriptions) and good selection of wines by the glass, friendly prompt service, low beams and polished flagstones, nice mix of old furniture, woodburner and big two-way log fire; children and dogs (in main bar) welcome, disabled facilities, tables on terrace and lawn, play area, handy for Sheffield Park (NT), Bluebell Railway and a useful M23/A23 stop, open (and food) all day. *(David Jackman, Tony and Wendy Hobden, Tony Scott)*

BOLNEY TQ2622
Eight Bells (01444) 881396
The Street; RH17 5QW Popular village pub with wide choice of good sensibly priced food from baguettes up, bargain OAP lunch Tues, Weds, efficient friendly young staff, well kept Harveys and a couple of guests, decent choice of wines including some from local vineyard, brick-floored bar with eight handbells suspended above servery, second flagstoned bar set for eating, open fires, timbered dining extension; bar billiards, pool and darts; children welcome, disabled facilities, tables out on deck under huge canopy, outside bar and play area, annual pram race (Easter Mon), three bedrooms in separate beamed cottage. *(John Beeken, Ross Balaam, Tony Scott)*

BOSHAM SU8003
★**Anchor Bleu** (01243) 573956
High Street; PO18 8LS Waterside inn overlooking Chichester Harbour; two simple bars with low ochre ceilings, worn flagstones and exposed timbered brickwork, lots of nautical bric-a-brac, robust furniture (some tables close together), up to six real ales and popular sensibly priced bar food, efficient friendly staff (they may ask for a credit card if you run a tab), upstairs dining room; children and dogs welcome, seats on front terrace and raised back one (access through massive wheel-operated bulkhead door), lovely views over sheltered inlet, can park by water but note tide times, church up lane figures in Bayeux Tapestry, village and shore worth exploring, open all day in summer and can get very crowded. *(B and M Kendall, Dr and Mrs J D Abell, Mrs Sally Scott, J A Snell, Roy Hoing and others)*

A few pubs try to make you leave a credit card at the bar, as a sort of deposit if you order food. This is a bad practice, and the banks and credit card firms warn you not to let your card go like this.

BOSHAM
SU8105

White Swan (01243) 696465
*A259 roundabout; Station Road;
PO18 8NG* Refurbished 18th-c dining pub
with enjoyable sensibly priced food (not
Sun evening), well kept Dark Star, Hop Back
and a couple of guests, good sized bar area
with bucket chairs on flagstones, restaurant
beyond with old bread oven, darts in snug;
children and dogs welcome in certain areas,
open all day. *(Edward May)*

BREDE
TQ8218

Red Lion (01424) 882188
A28 opposite church; TN31 6EJ Popular
beamed village pub with plain tables and
chairs on bare boards, candles and inglenook
log fire, good reasonably priced food (should
book) including local fish and Sun carvery,
well kept Harveys, Sharps, Charles Wells and
guests, short good value wine list, friendly
swift service even when busy, back dining
area decorated with sheet music and musical
instruments; children and dogs welcome, a
few picnic-sets out at front, garden behind
with roaming chickens (eggs for sale),
narrow entrance to car park, open all day
Fri-Sun. *(Peter Meister, Alec and Joan Laurence,
Conrad Freezer, V Brogden)*

BRIGHTON
TQ3104

★ Basketmakers Arms
(01273) 689006 *Gloucester Road – the
E end, near Cheltenham Place; off
Marlborough Place (A23) via Gloucester
Street; BN1 4AD* Cheerful bustling
backstreet local with eight pumps serving
Fullers/Gales beers and guests, decent
wines by the glass, over 100 malt whiskies
and good choice of other spirits, enjoyable
very well priced bar food all day (till 6pm
weekends), two small low-ceilinged rooms,
lots of interesting old tins, enamel signs,
photographs and posters; background music;
children welcome till 8pm, dogs on leads,
a few pavement tables, open all day (till
midnight Fri, Sat). *(Emma Scofield)*

BRIGHTON
TQ3004

Brighton Beer Dispensary
(01273) 205797 *Dean Street; BN1 3EG*
Popular little terraced pub jointly owned
by Brighton Bier and Late Knights Brewery,
their ales along with many guests, craft
beers and an extensive bottled range,
four hand-pulled ciders too, well informed
friendly staff, bar snacks and burgers, small
back conservatory; quiz nights and perhaps
storytelling evenings; open all day and can
get packed. *(Anon)*

BRIGHTON
TQ3005

Chimney House (01273) 556708
Upper Hamilton Road; BN1 5DF
Revamped red-brick corner pub in
residential area, good innovative food using
locally sourced ingredients (some foraged)

from open kitchen, four real ales including
Harveys, home-made jams, chutney and
bread for sale; folk night Sun; children and
dogs welcome, closed Mon, otherwise open
all day (till 9pm Sun). *(Robert MacGregor)*

BRIGHTON
TQ3104

Colonnade (01273) 328728
*New Road, off North Street; by Theatre
Royal; BN1 1UF* Small richly restored
theatre bar with ornate frontage – note
Willie the 19th-c automaton in small bay
window; shining brass and mahogany, plush
banquettes, velvet swags and gleaming
mirrors, interesting pre-war playbills and
signed theatrical photographs, three well
kept ales including Fullers London Pride,
good range of wines and interesting gins;
downstairs lavatories; pavement seats
overlooking Pavilion gardens, open all day.
(Anne and Ben Smith)

BRIGHTON
TQ3004

Craft Beer Company
Upper North Street; BN1 3FG Busy corner
pub with fine selection of interesting draught
and bottled beers from UK and international
brewers, friendly knowledgeable staff,
snacky food such as pork pies and scotch
eggs, simple L-shaped bar with raised back
section; open all day. *(N R White)*

BRIGHTON
TQ3104

Cricketers (01273) 329472
Black Lion Street; BN1 1ND Darkly
Victorian pub with some interesting bits
and pieces including pictures fastened to
the ceiling, Fullers London Pride and four
guests, well priced home-cooked food, tables
in covered former stables courtyard, upstairs
bar with Jack the Ripper and Graham Greene
memorabilia (pub features in Greene's novel
Brighton Rock); background and live music;
children allowed till 8pm, tables out in front,
open all day. *(N R White)*

BRIGHTON
TQ3004

★ Evening Star (01273) 328931
Surrey Street; BN1 3PB Popular chatty
drinkers' pub with good mix of customers,
simple pale wood furniture on bare boards,
up to four well kept Dark Star ales (originally
brewed here) and lots of changing guest
beers including continentals (in bottles too),
traditional ciders/perries and country wines,
lunchtime baguettes, friendly staff coping
well when busy; background and some live
music; pavement tables, open all day.
(Peter Meister, N R White)

BRIGHTON
TQ2804

Foragers (01273) 733134
3 Stirling Place, Hove; BN3 3YU Relaxed
Victorian corner pub, good food (not Sun
evening) from varied menu including some
unusual choices (emphasis on organic
sustainable produce – some foraged), well
kept Harveys and interesting range of wines

and spirits, friendly service; children welcome, picnic-sets out at front, garden behind, open all day. *(Mr and Mrs A Dempster)*

BRIGHTON   TQ2804
★**Ginger Pig** (01273) 736123
Hove Street; BN3 2TR Bustling place just minutes from the beach; informal bare-boards bar area with plush stools and simple wooden dining chairs around mixed tables, armchairs and sofas here and there, Harveys Best and a guest, nice wines by the glass and interesting local spirits and soft drinks, raised restaurant part with long button-back wall seating and more wooden tables and chairs, contemporary cow paintings, enterprising modern food served by friendly competent staff; background jazz; children welcome, open all day. *(Val and Alan Green, Martin Day)*

BRIGHTON   TQ3103
Hand in Hand (01273) 699595
Upper St James's Street, Kemptown; BN2 1JN Brighton's smallest pub, but its canary yellow exterior makes it hard to miss; own-brewed ales along with five well kept changing guests, plenty of bottled beers and a real cider, dimly lit bar with a few tables and benches, tie collection and lots of newspaper cuttings on the walls, photographs including Victorian nudes on the ceiling, food limited to local sausage rolls, cheerful service and colourful mix of customers; interesting background music (live jazz Sun), veteran fruit machine; dogs welcome, open all day and can get crowded. *(Peter Meister)*

BRIGHTON   TQ3104
Prince George (01273) 681055
Trafalgar Street; BN1 4EQ Quirky décor in various linked rooms, mix of furnishings on stripped floor, some bare brick walls and several big mirrors, six well kept changing local ales, craft beers and lots of wines by the glass, good inexpensive vegetarian/vegan food, friendly helpful staff; children (till 7pm) and dogs welcome, chunky tables in small heated back courtyard, open (and food) all day. *(John Harris)*

BRIGHTON   TQ3004
Pub du Vin (01273) 718588
Ship Street; BN1 1AD Next to Hotel du Vin; long narrow stripped-boards bar with comfortable wall seating one end, bay window the other, soft lighting and local photographs, five well kept ales including Arundel and Dark Star from ornate pewter counter, good choice of wines by the glass, enjoyable pubby food served by friendly staff, modern leather-seated bar chairs and light oak tables, flame-effect fire, small cosy coir-carpeted room opposite with squashy

black armchairs and sofas; splendid gents' with original marble fittings; 11 comfortable bedrooms, open all day. *(John Harris)*

BROWNBREAD STREET   TQ6714
Ash Tree (01424) 892104
Off A271 (was B2204) W of Battle; 1st northward road W of Ashburnham Place, then 1st fork left, then bear right into Brownbread Street; TN33 9NX Tranquil 17th-c country local tucked away in isolated hamlet, enjoyable affordably priced home-made food including specials, good choice of wines and well kept ales such as Harveys Best, cheerful service, cosy beamed bars with nice old settles and chairs, stripped brickwork, interesting dining areas with timbered dividers, good inglenook log fires; quiz first Tues of month; children (in eating area) and dogs welcome, pretty garden, open all day. *(Belinda May)*

BURPHAM   TQ0308
★**George** (01903) 883131
Off A27 near Warningcamp; BN18 9RR Busy 17th-c beamed pub succeeding well under community ownership; Greene King, Harveys and a house beer (By George) from Arundel, wide range of wines by the glass including champagne and local fizz, cocktails and decent coffee, interesting choice of good freshly made food from sensibly short menu, efficient courteous service, attractive simple décor; drop-down sports TV, free wi-fi; children and dogs welcome, picnic-sets out in front, hilltop village with splendid views down to Arundel Castle and river, open all day Sat, till 7pm Sun. *(John Davis, Mike and Marion Higgins, Celia Caulkin)*

BURWASH   TQ6724
Rose & Crown (01435) 882600
Inn sign on A265; TN19 7ER Old tile-hung local tucked down lane in pretty village, well kept Harveys, decent wines and enjoyable food, very low ceilings with banknotes stuck to beams near servery, pubby furniture on patterned carpet, inglenook log fire, separate restaurant with another inglenook, glass-covered well just inside front door; children and dogs welcome, small side garden and pleasant back terrace, bedrooms, open all day weekends. *(Martin Day, Tony Scott)*

BURY   TQ0013
Squire & Horse (01798) 831343
Bury Common; A29 Fontwell–Pulborough; RH20 1NS Smart roadside dining pub with good imaginative food from australian chef, friendly service, well kept Harveys and a guest, good choice of wines, several attractive partly divided beamed areas, plush wall seats, hunting prints and

---

It's very helpful if you let us know up-to-date food prices when you report on pubs.

ornaments, log fire; children welcome, no dogs inside, pleasant garden and pretty terrace (some road noise), open all day Sun. *(Michael and Sheila Hawkins, Paul Lucas)*

BYWORTH   SU9821

★ **Black Horse**   (01798) 342424
Off A283; GU28 0HL Popular and chatty country pub with smart simply furnished bar, pews and scrubbed tables on bare boards, pictures and old photographs, daily papers and open fires, four ales including Flowerpots and Fullers, Weston's Old Rosie cider, decent food (not Sun evening) from light lunchtime dishes up, children's menu, nooks and crannies in back restaurant with old range, spiral staircase to heavily beamed function/dining room, games room with pool and darts; dogs allowed in bar, attractive garden with tables on steep grassy terraces, lovely Downs views, new stable-block bedrooms, open all day. *(John Davis, Ann and Colin Hunt)*

CHAILEY   TQ3919

Five Bells   (01825) 722259
A275, 9 miles N of Lewes; BN8 4DA Attractive rambling roadside pub with good food (not Sun or Mon evenings) from sharing plates up, well kept Harveys and a guest, decent wine choice, friendly helpful staff, lots of different rooms and alcoves leading from low-beamed central bar, inglenook; children and dogs welcome, pretty garden front and side with picnic-sets, open all day. *(Martin Jones)*

CHAILEY   TQ3919

Horns Lodge   (01273) 400422
A275; BN8 4BD Traditional former coaching inn, heavily timbered inside, with settles, horsebrasses and local prints, fireplaces at each end of longish front bar, well kept Dark Star, Harveys and two guests (tasters offered), real cider, good range of fairly priced bar food (not Tues) from sandwiches up, obliging efficient staff, brick-floored restaurant, games area with bar billiards, darts and old Sussex coin game toad in the hole, cribbage, dominoes and board games too; background music; children and dogs welcome, tables in garden with sandpit, open all day weekends; still for sale, but business as usual. *(Paul Lucas, John Beeken, Tony and Wendy Hobden)*

CHALVINGTON   TQ5209

Yew Tree Inn   (01323) 811326
Chalvington Road, between Chalvington and Golden Cross; BN27 3TB Isolated low-beamed 17th-c country pub, flagstones, stripped brickwork, and inglenook, enjoyable well priced home-made food (not Sun evening) from lunchtime baguettes up, well kept Harveys and guests, conservatory; children and dogs welcome, good-sized terrace, extensive grounds with play area, own cricket pitch and camping, good walks, open all day (till 6pm Sun). *(Emma Scofield)*

CHICHESTER   SU8605

Chichester Inn   (01243) 783185
West Street; PO19 1RP Georgian pub (quieter than the city-centre ones) with half a dozen local ales such as Dark Star, Harveys and Langhams, good value pubby food from snacks up, friendly service, smallish front lounge with plain wooden tables and chairs, sofas by open fire, larger back public bar; live music Weds, Fri and Sat, sports TV, pool; courtyard garden with smokers' shelter, two bedrooms, open all day summer, all day Fri-Sun winter. *(B and M Kendall, Tony and Wendy Hobden)*

CHICHESTER   SU8604

Eastgate   (01243) 774877
The Hornet (A286); PO19 7JG Welcoming opened-up town pub with light airy interior extending back, three Fullers ales and a guest, well cooked affordably priced traditional food, cheerful prompt service, woodburner; background and weekend live music, darts, pool and cribbage; children and dogs welcome, small heated back terrace, open all day. *(Tony and Wendy Hobden)*

CHICHESTER   SU8605

Park Tavern   (01243) 785057
Priory Road, opposite Jubilee Park; PO19 1NS Friendly lively pub in pleasant spot opposite Priory Park, good choice of Fullers/Gales beers and enjoyable reasonably priced home-made food, smallish front bar and extensive back eating area; quiz Tues, live music Sun; dogs welcome (they have two), open all day. *(Phil and Jane Villiers)*

CHIDDINGLY   TQ5414

★ **Six Bells**   (01825) 872227
Village signed off A22 Uckfield–Hailsham; BN8 6HE Lively unpretentious village local run well by hard-working hands-on landlord; small linked bars with interesting bric-a-brac, local pictures and posters, old furniture, cushioned window seats and log fires, family extension giving much-needed extra space, well kept Courage Directors, Harveys Best and a guest, decent wines by the glass and a farm cider, bargain food; good weekend live music, free wi-fi; dogs welcome in bar, seats at the back by big raised goldfish pond, boules, monthly vintage and kit-car meetings, church opposite with interesting Jefferay Monument, open (and food) all day Fri-Sun. *(Tom and Jill Jones)*

CHIDHAM   SU7804

Old House At Home   (01243) 572477
Off A259 at Barleycorn pub in Nutbourne; Cot Lane; PO18 8SU Neat cottagey pub in remote unspoilt farm-hamlet; good choice of popular food including fish specials, friendly efficient service, five real ales and decent wines, low beams and timbering, log fire; children allowed in eating areas, tables in nice garden, nearby walks by

Chichester Harbour, open all day. *(Tony and Jill Radnor, Michael and Sheila Hawkins)*

CLAPHAM   TQ1105
Coach & Horses (01903) 694721
Arundel Road (A27 Worthing–Arundel); BN13 3UA Friendly 18th-c former coaching inn (beside dual carriageway) once again under new management; well liked food including blackboard specials and set-menu choices, four changing ales (always one from Arundel), local gins and vodka, refurbished interior with comfortable seating by open fire, flagstoned dining area to left of bar; background music, quiz last Weds of month; children and dogs welcome, tables on back terrace, play area, open all day, food all day Sun. *(Tony and Wendy Hobden)*

COCKING CAUSEWAY   SU8819
Greyhound (01730) 814425
A286 Cocking–Midhurst; GU29 9QH Pretty 18th-c tile-hung pub, enjoyable good value home-made food (should book weekends), three or four changing ales such as Long Man, Shepherd Neame and Sharps, open-plan but cosy beamed and panelled bar with alcoves, log fire, pine furniture in big new dining conservatory; children welcome, grassed area at front with picnic-sets and huge eucalyptus, sizeable garden and play area behind, open all day Sun. *(John Beeken)*

COLEMANS HATCH   TQ4533
★ Hatch (01342) 822363
Signed off B2026, or off B2110 opposite church; TN7 4EJ Quaint and appealing little weatherboarded Ashdown Forest pub dating from 1430, big log fire in quickly filling beamed bar, small back dining room with another fire, good generous home-made food, well kept Harveys, Larkins and one or two guest beers, quick service from friendly young staff, good mix of customers including families and dogs; not much parking so arrive early; picnic-sets on front terrace and in beautifully kept big garden, open all day Sun, and Sat in summer. *(Tony Scott)*

COMPTON   SU7714
Coach & Horses (02392) 631228
B2146 S of Petersfield; PO18 9HA Welcoming 17th-c two-bar local in charming downland village, not far from Uppark (NT), beams, panelling, shuttered windows and log fires, up to five changing ales including a house beer from Ballards, good food cooked by landlord-chef; bar billiards; dogs welcome, tables out by village square, nice surrounding walks, closed Mon. *(Edward May)*

COOKSBRIDGE   TQ4014
Rainbow (01273) 400334
Junction A275 with Cooksbridge and Newick Road; BN8 4SS Attractive 18th-c flint dining pub (same owners as the Fountain at Ashurst and Royal Oak in Poynings), good locally sourced food from sandwiches to specials, helpful friendly service, nice choice of wines and three well kept ales, small bar area with open fire, restaurant; children welcome, large garden with terrace, open (and food) all day. *(John Beeken)*

COUSLEY WOOD   TQ6533
★ Old Vine (01892) 782271
B2100 Wadhurst–Lamberhurst; TN5 6ER Popular 16th-c weatherboarded pub with linked, uncluttered rooms, heavy beams and open timbering, candles on attractive old pine tables surrounded by farmhouse chairs, several settles (one by big log fire has an especially high back), wood or brick flooring (restaurant area is carpeted), well kept Harveys Best and a guest from attractively painted servery, several good wines by the glass, tasty food served by friendly helpful staff; occasional live jazz; dogs welcome, picnic-sets on front terrace, three bedrooms, open all day weekends (food till 6.30pm Sun). *(Nigel and Jean Eames)*

COWBEECH   TQ6114
★ Merrie Harriers (01323) 833108
Off A271; BN27 4JQ White clapboarded 16th-c village local, beamed public bar with inglenook log fire, high-backed settle and mixed tables and chairs, old local photographs, step up to carpeted dining lounge with small open fire, well kept Harveys Best, winter mulled wine and good food from bar snacks up, friendly service, brick-walled back restaurant; occasional background music; rustic seats in terraced garden with country views, open all day Fri-Sun. *(Conor McGaughey)*

COWFOLD   TQ2122
Hare & Hounds (01403) 865354
Henfield Road (A281 S); RH13 8DR Small friendly village pub with well kept Dark Star, Harveys and a guest, good value traditional home-made food including Thurs OAP lunch, flagstoned bar with log fire, little room off to the right, carpeted dining room to the left; children and dogs welcome, a couple of picnic-sets out in front, back terrace, open all day weekends. *(Tony and Wendy Hobden)*

CRAWLEY DOWN   TQ3437
Dukes Head (01342) 712431
A264/A2028 by roundabout; RH10 4HH Big refurbished dining pub with large lounge bar and three differently styled eating areas, log fires, good range of generally well liked food including weekday fixed-price menu (till 6pm), a couple of real ales, lots of wines by the glass including champagne, cocktails, friendly if not always speedy service; can get very busy weekends; children welcome, lots of space outside, handy for Gatwick airport, open (and food) all day. *(Judy and Paul Cove, Tony Scott)*

CUCKFIELD   TQ3025
Rose & Crown (01444) 414217
London Road; RH17 5BS Popular 17th-c
former coaching inn recently refurbished by
father and son team, good if pricey food from
interesting weekly changing menu, well kept
Harveys and guests, local Hepworth's lagers
and good choice of wines, friendly staff;
children and dogs welcome, tables out in
front and in nice garden behind, closed Mon,
otherwise open all day (Sun till 9pm).
(Phil and Jane Hodson)

CUCKFIELD   TQ3024
Talbot (01444) 455898
High Street; RH17 5JX Recently
refurbished dining pub; imaginative food in
bar and upstairs restaurant, real ales, good
service; open all day. *(John Harris)*

DALLINGTON   TQ6619
★ Swan (01424) 838242
Woods Corner, B2096 E; TN21 9LB
Popular old local with cheerful chatty
atmosphere, well kept Harveys and a guest,
decent wines by the glass and enjoyable
blackboard food, efficient friendly service,
bare-boards bar divided by standing timbers,
mixed furniture including cushioned settle
and high-backed pew, candles in bottles and
fresh flowers, big woodburner, simple back
restaurant with far-reaching views to the
coast; occasional background music; children
and dogs welcome, tables down to lavatories
and garden. *(Edward May)*

DELL QUAY   SU8302
Crown & Anchor (01243) 781712
*Off A286 S of Chichester – look out for
small sign; PO20 7EE* 19th/20th-c beamed
pub (some refurbishment by present owners)
in splendid spot overlooking Chichester
Harbour – best at high tide and quiet times
(can be packed on sunny days and parking
difficult); comfortable bow-windowed lounge
bar, panelled public bar (dogs welcome), two
log fires, well kept Charles Wells ales and
a guest, lots of wines by the glass including
champagne, enjoyable food from pub
favourites to specials, friendly staff; children
and dogs welcome, views from large terrace,
nice walks, open (and food) all day.
(Ian Phillips)

DENTON   TQ4502
Flying Fish (01273) 515440
Denton Road; BN9 0QB Welcoming
17th-c flint village pub, enjoyable food from
baguettes up, well kept Shepherd Neame ales
and guests including Harveys, friendly helpful
staff; picnic-sets out by road and on back
deck looking up to sloping garden, handy for
South Downs Way, open all day. *(John Harris)*

DONNINGTON   SU8501
Blacksmiths (01243) 785578
B2201 S of Chichester; PO20 7PR Small
roadside pub renovated by present owners;
fresh modern décor with white walls and
light wood floors, one or two beams, modern
artwork and some quirky touches, interesting
food from sensibly short menu, local ales and
mainly organic wines, open fire; children
welcome, big back garden with terrace, herb
garden and chickens, three bedrooms, open
all day, till 6pm Sun. *(Belinda May)*

EAST ASHLING   SU8207
★ Horse & Groom (01243) 575339
B2178; PO18 9AX Busy country pub with
five well kept ales including Dark Star, Hop
Back, Sharps and Charles Wells, decent
choice of wines by the glass, good food from
sandwiches and baguettes up, reasonable
prices and efficient friendly service,
unchanging front drinkers' bar with old pale
flagstones and inglenook range, carpeted
area with scrubbed trestle tables, fresh and
airy extension with solid pale country kitchen
furniture on neat bare boards; children and
dogs allowed in some parts, garden picnic-
sets under umbrellas, 11 bedrooms (some
in barn conversion), open all day Sat, closed
Sun evening. *(J A Snell, Ross Balaam)*

EAST CHILTINGTON   TQ3715
★ Jolly Sportsman (01273) 890400
*2 miles N of B2116; Chapel Lane – follow
sign to 13th-c church; BN7 3BA* Inventive
modern food cooked by landlord in this
civilised place; small character log-fire
bar for drinkers, Dark Star and Harveys
tapped from the cask, excellent range of
malt whiskies, cognacs and armagnacs and
a remarkably good wine list, smart but cosy
restaurant with contemporary light wood
furniture and modern landscapes, garden
room; free wi-fi; children and dogs (in bar)
welcome, cottagey front garden with rustic
tables under gnarled trees, more seats on
big back lawn with views towards the Downs,
open all day Sat, till 4pm Sun, closed Mon.
(Nick Sharpe, Isobel Mackinlay)

EAST DEAN   SU9012
Star & Garter (01243) 811318
*Village signed with Charlton off A286
in Singleton; also signed off A285;
PO18 0JG* Airy dining pub in peaceful
village-green setting; pleasant bar and
restaurant with exposed brickwork, panelling
and oak floors, furnishings from sturdy
stripped tables and country kitchen chairs
through chunky modern to antique carved
settles, Arundel ales tapped from the cask
and several wines by the glass, good food
including local fish/seafood, friendly service;

Virtually all pubs in this book sell wine by the glass. We mention wines
if they are a cut above the average.

background music; children and dogs (in bar) welcome, teak furniture on heated terrace, smokers' shelter, steps down to walled lawn with picnic-sets, near South Downs Way, bedrooms, open (and food) all day weekends. *(Lindy Andrews)*

EAST HOATHLY   TQ5116
Foresters Arms (01825) 840208
Off A22 Hailsham–Uckfield; South Street; BN8 6DS Friendly village pub with enjoyable freshly made food from pub favourites up (not Sun evening or Mon), four well kept Harveys ales and several wines by the glass; darts; children and dogs welcome, disabled facilities, garden with picnic-sets and play area, open all day weekends, closed lunchtimes Mon, Tues. *(Conrad Freezer)*

EAST HOATHLY   TQ5216
Kings Head (01825) 840238
High Street/Mill Lane; BN8 6DR Creeper-clad 17th-c pub on crossroads (was the village school), own 1648 ales (brewed next door) plus Harveys Best, long open-plan room with wood floor, brick walls and log fire, pubby furniture including upholstered settles, enjoyable reasonably priced traditional food, friendly staff and good mix of locals and visitors, function room; TV, free wi-fi; dogs welcome in bar area, steps up to walled back garden, safe for children, open all day. *(John Beeken)*

EAST LAVANT   SU8608
★**Royal Oak** (01243) 527434
Pook Lane, off A286; PO18 0AX Pretty dining pub with low beams, crooked timbers and exposed brickwork in open-plan rooms, log fires and church candles, drinking part at front with wall seats and sofas, Long Man and Sharps tapped from the cask, many wines by the glass and some 20 malt whiskies, dining area with leather chairs and scrubbed pine tables, imaginative food including specials, good friendly service; background music, free wi-fi; children and dogs (in bar) welcome, flagstoned front terrace with far-reaching views to the Downs, more seats to the side and back, stylish bedrooms and self-catering cottages, car park across the road, handy for Goodwood, open 7.30am-10.30pm.
(John Evans, Tracey and Stephen Groves, Christopher and Elise Way and others)

EASTBOURNE   TV6098
Bibendum (01323) 735363
Grange Road/South Street opposite Town Hall; BN21 4EU Roomy 19th-c corner place with bit of a wine bar feel, good choice of beers and decent food, friendly helpful staff, restaurant; seats out in front, open (and food) all day. *(Tom and Jill Jones)*

EASTBOURNE   TV6199
Marine (01323) 720464
Seaside Road (A259); BN22 7NE Spacious comfortable pub near seafront

run by welcoming long-serving licensees, panelled bar, lounge with sofas and tub chairs, log fire, three well kept ales and good choice of wines, whiskies and brandies, generous helpings of good freshly made food, back conservatory; children welcome, terrace and covered smokers' area, open (and food) all day Sun. *(Alan Johnson)*

EASTBOURNE   TV6097
Pilot (01323) 723440
Holywell Road, Meads; just off front below approach from Beachy Head; BN20 7RW Busy renovated corner inn with good fairly priced home-cooked food from lunchtime sandwiches up, well kept Harveys Best, Sharps Doom Bar and a guest, good selection of wines by the glass, friendly staff; free wi-fi; children welcome, dogs in bar, seats out in front and in nice split-level beer garden behind, three updated bedrooms, open all day. *(Mr and Mrs A Dempster)*

EASTERGATE   SU9405
Wilkes Head (01243) 543380
Just off A29 Fontwell–Bognor; Church Lane; PO20 3UT Small friendly red-brick local with two traditional bars and back dining extension, beams, flagstones and inglenook log fire, enjoyable reasonably priced blackboard food from sandwiches up, Adnams and guests such as Ballards, Bowman and St Austell, proper cider; darts; children welcome, tables in big garden with play area, open all day weekends. *(John Beeken, Tony and Wendy Hobden)*

ELSTED   SU8320
Elsted Inn (01730) 813662
Elsted Marsh; GU29 0JT Attractive and welcoming Victorian country pub, enjoyable reasonably priced food (not Sun evening, Mon) from shortish menu, three or four changing ales and decent wines by the glass, friendly accommodating service, two log fires, nice country furniture on bare boards, old Goodwood racing photos (horses and cars), dining area at back; children and dogs (in bar) welcome, plenty of seating in lovely enclosed Downs-view garden with big terrace, four bedrooms, open all day weekends. *(Emma Scofield)*

ELSTED   SU8119
★**Three Horseshoes** (01730) 825746
Village signed from B2141 Chichester–Petersfield; from A272 about 2 miles W of Midhurst, turn left heading W; GU29 0JY A congenial bustle at this pretty white-painted old pub, beamed rooms, log fires and candlelight, ancient flooring, antique furnishings and interesting prints and photographs, up to five ales tapped from the cask such as Bowman, Flowerpots, Langhams and Youngs, summer cider, well liked food from blackboard menu, good friendly service; children allowed, dogs in bar, two delightful connecting gardens with plenty of seats,

lovely roses and fine Downs views, good surrounding walks. *(Mrs K Hooker, Christopher and Elise Way, Tony and Jill Radnor, John Evans, Miss A E Dare)*

ERIDGE STATION   TQ5434
★**Huntsman** (01892) 864258
Signed off A26 S of Eridge Green; TN3 9LE Country local with two opened-up rooms, pubby furniture on bare boards, some tables with carved/painted board games including own 'Eridgeopoly', hunting pictures, three Badger ales and over a dozen wines by the glass, popular bar food (not Sun evening, Mon) including fresh fish, seasonal game and home-grown produce, friendly staff; children and dogs welcome, picnic-sets and heaters on decking, outside bar, more seats on lawn among weeping willows, open all day weekends, closed Mon lunchtime. *(John Harris)*

FERRING   TQ0903
Henty Arms (01903) 241254
Ferring Lane; BN12 6QY Six well kept changing ales and generous well priced food (can get busy so best to book), breakfast from 9am Tues-Fri, friendly staff, opened-up lounge/dining area, log fire, separate bar with games and TV; garden tables. *(Tony and Wendy Hobden)*

FINDON   TQ1208
Gun (01903) 873206
High Street; BN14 0TA Low-beamed pub with opened-up bar area and restaurant, enjoyable food including good value french night (Tues) and popular Sun lunch, four well kept Marstons-related beers, friendly staff, log fire; free wi-fi; children and dogs (in bar) welcome, sheltered garden, pretty village below Cissbury Ring (NT), Sept sheep fair, open all day, no food Sun evening. *(Tony and Wendy Hobden)*

FISHBOURNE   SU8304
Bulls Head (01243) 839895
Fishbourne Road (A259 Chichester–Emsworth); PO19 3JP Former 17th-c farmhouse with traditional interior, copper pans on black beams, some stripped brick and panelling, good log fire, well kept Fullers/Gales beers and popular home-made food; background music; children welcome, tables on heated covered deck, four bedrooms in former skittle alley, handy for Fishbourne Roman villa, open all day weekends. *(Emma Scofield)*

FITTLEWORTH   TQ0118
Swan (01798) 865429
Lower Street (B2138), off A283 W of Pulborough); RH20 1EL Pretty tile-hung dining inn with beamed main bar, mix of furniture including windsor chairs, high-backed stools and button-backed banquettes on wood flooring, wall of pictures and old pub sign one end, big inglenook log

fire the other, Harveys, Sharps Doom Bar and a guest, several wines by the glass and traditional cider, good food from pubby choices up in bar and separate panelled restaurant, set lunch deal Mon-Fri, efficient friendly staff; background music, free wi-fi, children and dogs welcome, big back lawn with plenty of tables, good walks nearby, 14 comfortable well priced bedrooms, open all day weekends. *(Chris Wall, John Davis, Colin McKerrow)*

FULKING   TQ2411
Shepherd & Dog (01273) 857382
Off A281 N of Brighton, via Poynings; BN5 9LU 17th-c bay-windowed pub in beautiful spot below the Downs; low beams, panelling and inglenook, good range of real ales and craft beers including Downland (brewed a couple of miles away), lots of wines by the glass, enjoyable food from summer tapas up, friendly efficient service; beer, cider and gin & jazz festivals; children and dogs welcome, terrace and pretty streamside garden with own bar, straightforward climb to Devil's Dyke, open all day, food till 6pm Sun. *(Keith Stevens)*

FUNTINGTON   SU7908
★**Fox & Hounds** (01243) 575246
Common Road (B2146); PO18 9LL Bustling old bay-windowed pub with updated beamed rooms in grey/green shades, welcoming log fires, good food from open sandwiches and snacks to daily specials and popular Sun carvery (booking advised weekends), well kept Dark Star, Timothy Taylors and guests, lots of wines by the glass and good coffee, friendly service, comfortable spacious dining extension; free wi-fi; children and dogs welcome, tables out in front and in walled back garden, pair of inn signs – one a pack of hounds, the other a family of foxes, open (and food) all day, from 9am weekends for breakfast. *(David Jackman, I Short)*

GLYNDE   TQ4508
Trevor Arms (01273) 858208
Over railway bridge, S of village; BN8 6SS Fine downland views from character brick and flint village pub (same management as the Ram at Firle – see Main Entries); main opened-up bar with two boar's heads, piano and large woodburner, church pews and wheelbacks around dark tables on bare boards, daily papers, trivia machine, well kept Harveys Best and local guests, small simply furnished tap bar with chatty regulars, dining area with mix of high-backed settles, pews and cushioned chairs around assorted tables, toad in the hole and darts, old local photos including Harveys brewery, popular fairly traditional home-made food (all day weekends); children and dogs welcome, big back garden with wendy house, swings and picnic-sets (more in front), popular with walkers, station next door, open all day. *(John Beeken, Tony Scott)*

GRAFFHAM   SU9218
Foresters Arms (01798) 867202
Village off A285; GU28 0QA Popular
16th-c pub renovated under new owners;
main bar with heavy beams and log fire in
huge brick fireplace, two other connecting
rooms, ales such as Arundel, Firebird, Hogs
Back and Langhams, good food including
italian specials from neapolitan chef, friendly
attentive service; jazz and other live music;
children and dogs welcome, attractive sunny
back garden and good local walks, three
refurbished bedrooms. *(Colin McKerrow)*

GUN HILL   TQ5614
★Gun (01825) 872361
*Off A22 NW of Hailsham, or off A267;
TN21 0JU* Big 15th-c country dining pub
with good popular bistro-style food and
efficient friendly service; large central bar
with nice old brick floor, stools against
counter, Aga in corner, small grey-panelled
room off with rugs on bare boards, animal
skins on cushioned wall benches and mix
of scrubbed and dark tables, logs piled into
tall fireplace, well kept Harveys and Timothy
Taylors, decent wines by the glass, close-set
tables in two-room cottagey restaurant,
beams and open fires, old bottles and glasses
along gantry, gun prints and country pictures;
background music; children welcome,
picnic-sets in garden and on lantern-lit front
terrace, Wealdway walks, open all day Sun.
(Tom and Jill Jones)

HALNAKER   SU9008
★Anglesey Arms (01243) 773474
A285 Chichester–Petworth; PO18 0NQ
Georgian pub belonging to the Goodwood
Estate; bare boards, settles and log fire, well
kept Otter, Youngs and a couple of guests,
decent wines, good varied if not particularly
cheap food including local organic produce
and Selsey fish, friendly accommodating
service, simple but smart L-shaped dining
room (children allowed) with woodburners,
stripped pine and some flagstones;
traditional games; dogs welcome in bar,
tables in big tree-lined garden, good nearby
walks, open all day Fri-Sun. *(Harvey Brown)*

HAMMERPOT   TQ0605
★Woodman Arms (01903) 871240
On N (eastbound) side of A27; BN16 4EU
Pretty thatched pub with beams, timbers
and inglenook woodburner, good choice of
well liked reasonably priced food (smaller
helpings available) including popular Sun
lunch, three or four Fullers/Gales beers and
nice wines by the glass, attentive thoughtful
service from friendly staff, comfortable bar
with snug to the left, restaurant to the right;
occasional live music; children welcome if
eating, no dogs inside, tables in nice garden,
open all day Sat, till 5pm Sun. *(David Holmes,
Tony and Wendy Hobden, PL)*

HANDCROSS   TQ2529
Royal Oak (01444) 401406
*Horsham Road (A279, off A23);
RH17 6DJ* Traditional comfortably
refurbished tile-hung village pub, well kept
Fullers, Harveys and a guest, good choice of
enjoyable food (not Mon evening), friendly
helpful staff; fortnightly quiz Tues, free wi-fi;
children and dogs welcome, seats out at front
and on small terrace overlooking fields and
woods, handy for Nymans (NT), open all day
Fri-Sun. *(Mrs P R Sykes)*

HANDCROSS   TQ2328
Wheatsheaf (01444) 400472
B2110 W; RH13 6NZ Welcoming country
pub with good range of generous home-
made food using local produce, Badger ales,
efficient staff (they ask to swipe a card if
running a tab), two simply furnished bars
with lots of horse tack and farm tools, log
fires, caged parrot; children welcome, garden
with covered terrace and play area, near
Nymans (NT), open all day (till 7pm Sun).
(Tony and Wendy Hobden)

HASTINGS   TQ8109
Crown (01424) 465100
All Saints Street, Old Town; TN34 3BN
Revamped cosy corner pub, good range
of well kept local beers and other drinks,
enjoyable food including seafood and
charcuterie boards, friendly staff and buzzy
atmosphere with good mix of customers,
interesting artwork on the walls, open fire in
main bar, board games; children welcome,
open all day. *(Alfie Bayliss)*

HASTINGS   TQ8209
First In Last Out (01424) 425079
High Street, Old Town; TN34 3EY
Congenial and chatty pub serving its own
FILO beers (brewed close by) and a guest
ale, good food (not Sun, lunchtime Mon) from
varied menu including evening tapas (Mon)
and indian thali (Thurs), friendly helpful
staff, open-plan carpeted bar with 1970s
Artex walls, dark wood booths and feature
central raised log fire, lighter dining room;
regular live music, quiz first Sun of month;
open all day. *(Mike and Eleanor Anderson,
Dave and Jan Pilgrim)*

HERMITAGE   SU7505
★Sussex Brewery (01243) 371533
A259 just W of Emsworth; PO10 8AU
Bustling little 18th-c pub on the West Sussex/
Hampshire border, small bare-boards bar
with good fire in brick inglenook, simple
furniture, flagstoned snug, well kept Youngs
ales and guests, ten wines by the glass, hearty
food including speciality sausages (even
vegetarian ones), small upstairs restaurant;
children and dogs welcome, picnic-sets in
back courtyard, open all day. *(Edward May)*

HOOE   TQ6910
Red Lion (01424) 892371
Denbigh Road; TN33 9EW Attractive old
local behind screen of pollarded lime trees,
plenty of original features including two big
inglenooks (some refurbishment by new
owners), enjoyable home-cooked food from
shortish menu, well kept Harveys and a guest,
good friendly service, main bar and back
snug, overflow function room and further
eating space upstairs; children and dogs
welcome, seats out at front and in garden
behind, open all day. *(Paul Lucas)*

HOUGHTON   TQ0111
★George & Dragon (01798) 831559
B2139 W of Storrington; BN18 9LW
13th-c beams and timbers in attractive spic
and span bar rambling up and down steps,
note the elephant photograph above the
fireplace, good Arun Valley views from back
extension, well liked reasonably priced food,
Marstons-related ales and decent wines by
the glass, good friendly service; background
music; children and dogs welcome, seats on
decked terrace taking in the views and in
charming sloping garden, good walks, open
all day Fri and Sat, till 9pm Sun. *(Tony Scott)*

HUNSTON   SU8601
Spotted Cow (01243) 786718
B2145 S of Chichester; PO20 1PD
Friendly modernised village pub with beams,
flagstone floors and big log fires, good choice
of enjoyable food (not Sun, Mon evenings)
including specials, Fullers/Gales beers,
small front bar, roomier side lounge with
armchairs, sofas and low tables, airy high-
ceilinged restaurant; may be background
music; children (if eating) and dogs welcome,
good disabled access, pretty garden, handy
for towpath walkers, open all day.
(John Harris)

HURSTPIERPOINT   TQ2816
New Inn (01273) 834608
High Street; BN6 9RQ Popular 16th-c
beamed village pub, Harveys and a couple of
guests, good wines by the glass and enjoyable
food from bar snacks up, friendly staff,
linked areas including oak-panelled back
bar with sofas and log fire and more formal
dining room; quiz and music nights, sports
TV; children and dogs welcome, good sized
garden with play area, open all day, food
all day Fri-Sun. *(Alfie Bayliss)*

ICKLESHAM   TQ8716
★Queens Head (01424) 814552
Off A259 Rye–Hastings; TN36 4BL
Friendly well run country pub, extremely
popular locally (and at weekends with
cyclists and walkers), open-plan areas around
big counter, high timbered walls, vaulted
roof, shelves of bottles, plenty of farming
implements and animal traps, pubby furniture
on brown pattered carpet, other areas with
inglenooks and a back room with old bicycle
memorabilia, up to eight well kept ales
including Greene King and Harveys, local
cider, several wines by the glass, good choice
of reasonably priced home-made food (all
day weekends); background jazz and blues
(live 4-6pm Sun); well behaved children till
8.30pm, dogs welcome, picnic-sets, boules
and play area in peaceful garden with fine Brede
Valley views, you can walk to Winchelsea,
open all day. *(Mrs Sally Scott, Tony Scott,
Tom and Jill Jones, Tony and Wendy Hobden)*

ICKLESHAM   TQ8716
★Robin Hood (01424) 814277
Main Road; TN36 4BD Friendly family-
run beamed pub with great local atmosphere,
good value unpretentious home-made food
(all day Sun, not Tues evening) including
blackboard specials, up to seven well kept
changing ales (always have Greene King IPA)
and three proper ciders, hops overhead, lots
of copper bric-a-brac, log fire, games area
with pool, back dining conservatory; free
wi-fi; children and dogs (in bar) welcome,
big garden with new play area and boules,
fine Brede Valley views, open all day
Fri-Sun. *(Emma Scofield)*

ISFIELD   TQ4417
Laughing Fish (01825) 750349
Station Road; TN22 5XB Opened-up
Victorian local with affable landlord and
cheerful staff, good value home-made bar
food (not Sun evening) including specials
board and some good vegetarian options,
well kept Greene King ales with three local
guests (always one from Isfield), open fire,
bar billiards and other traditional games,
various events including entertaining beer
race Easter Mon; children and dogs welcome,
disabled access, small pleasantly shaded
walled garden with enclosed play area, field
for camping, right by Lavender Line railway
(pub was station hotel), open all day.
(Ann and Colin Hunt, John Beeken)

KINGSTON   TQ3908
★Juggs (01273) 472523
*Village signed off A27 by roundabout
W of Lewes; BN7 3NT* Popular tile-hung
village pub with heavy 15th-c beams and
very low front door, lots of neatly stripped
masonry, sturdy wooden furniture on bare
boards and stone slabs, log fires, smaller
eating areas including a family room, variety
of enjoyable reasonably priced food from
sandwiches and pub standards up (some
interesting choices), well kept Harveys and
Shepherd Neame, good wines and coffee,
friendly helpful young staff; background
music, fortnightly quiz; dogs welcome,
disabled access/facilities, outside tables
including covered area with heaters (they
ask to swipe a credit card if you eat here),
lots of tubs and hanging baskets, play area,
nice walks, open all day. *(Keith Stevens,
Mrs Sally Scott, John Beeken, Paul Lucas)*

LANCING
TQ1704

Crabtree
(01903) 755514

Crabtree Lane; BN15 9NQ Friendly 1930s pub with Fullers London Pride and three changing guests, bargain lunches including Sun carvery, comfortable lounge with wood floor, unusual domed ceiling and art deco lights, games area in large public bar; quiz nights; children and dogs welcome, garden with Downs views and play area, open all day. *(Tony and Wendy Hobden)*

LEWES
TQ4110

Black Horse
(01273) 473653

Western Road; BN7 1RS Bow-windowed Greene King 'Local Heroes' pub, knocked-through bar keeping traditional feel with two log fires, wood floor, panelling and lots of old pictures, half a dozen ales mainly from smaller local brewers and some interesting gins, enjoyable home-made food, friendly service; quiz nights, sports TV, bar billiards and toad in the hole; children welcome, beer garden, open all day. *(Tony Scott)*

LEWES
TQ4210

Gardeners Arms
(01273) 474808

Cliffe High Street; BN7 2AN Unpretentious little bare-boards local opposite brewery shop, lots of beer mats on gantry, homely stools, built-in wall seats and plain scrubbed tables around three narrow sides of bar, dog water bowl by blocked-up fireplace, Harveys and five interesting changing guests, farm ciders, some lunchtime food including sandwiches, pasties and pies, bar nibbles on Sun, photos of Lewes bonfire night; background music, TV, darts; no children; open all day. *(John Harris)*

LEWES
TQ4210

★ John Harvey
(01273) 479880

Bear Yard, just off Cliffe High Street; BN7 2AN Bustling tap for nearby Harveys brewery, four of their beers including seasonals kept in top condition, some cask tapped, good well priced food (not Sun evening) from lunchtime sandwiches, baked potatoes and ciabattas up, friendly efficient young staff, flagstoned bar with one great vat halved to make two towering 'snugs' for several people, lighter room on left, woodburner, upstairs restaurant/function room; live music including Tues folk and Weds jazz; a few tables outside, open all day. *(Tony and Wendy Hobden, Phil and Jane Villiers, Peter Meister, Tony Scott)*

LEWES
TQ4110

★ Lewes Arms
(01273) 473152

Castle Ditch Lane/Mount Place – tucked behind castle ruins; BN7 1YH Cheerful unpretentious little local with five well kept Fullers ales and two guests, 30 malt whiskies and plenty of wines by the glass, good reasonably priced generous bar food, tiny front bar on right with stools along nicely curved counter and bench window seats, two other simple rooms hung with photographs and information about the famous Lewes bonfire night, beer mats pinned over doorways, poetry and folk evenings and more obscure events like pea throwing and dwyle flunking; background music; children away from front bar and dogs welcome (there are two pub dogs), picnic-sets on attractive split-level back terrace, open all day (till midnight Fri, Sat). *(Tony Scott, Tony and Wendy Hobden, Conor McGaughey, J A Snell, Ann and Colin Hunt)*

LEWES
TQ4110

★ Pelham Arms
(01273) 476149

At top of High Street; BN7 1XL Popular 17th-c beamed pub, good well presented food (booking advised) including some interesting vegetarian choices, friendly staff, three Badger ales, character rambling interior with inglenook; vintage swing night first Thurs of month; children till 8pm, dogs in bar areas, small courtyard garden, open all day. *(John Harris)*

LEWES
TQ4110

Rights of Man
(01273) 486894

High Street; BN7 1YE Newish Harveys pub close to the law courts, five of their ales kept well and enjoyable food including tapas, spruced-up Victorian-style décor with a series of booths, legal-theme pictures, another bar at the back and roof terrace; background music, free wi-fi; open all day. *(Tony and Wendy Hobden)*

LEWES
TQ4210

★ Snowdrop
(01273) 471018

South Street; BN7 2BU Welcoming pub tucked below the chalk cliffs; narrowboat theme with brightly painted servery and colourful jugs, kettles, lanterns etc hanging from curved planked ceiling, wide mix of simple furniture on parquet flooring, old sewing machines and huge stone jars, slightly bohemian atmosphere; well kept range of ales including Dark Star and Harveys, a couple of ciders, hearty helpings of enjoyable good value local food including good vegetarian choice, nice coffee, cheerful efficient staff (may ask for a credit card if running a tab), more tables in upstairs room (spiral stairs) with bar billiards and darts; background music – live jazz Mon; dogs very welcome (menu for them), outside seating on both sides with pretty hanging baskets, open all day. *(Ann and Colin Hunt, Peter Meister, Robert W Buckle)*

LINDFIELD
TQ3425

Bent Arms
(01444) 483146

High Street; RH16 2HP Refurbished 16th-c village coaching inn, surprisingly spacious inside with most tables laid for dining, low black beams, timbers and some stained glass, popular affordably priced home-made food including lunchtime sandwiches using own bread, evening set menu, three well kept Badger ales, friendly service; children welcome, sizeable back garden with covered area, nine bedrooms and cottage. *(Tony and Wendy Hobden, Tony Scott, Mrs P R Sykes)*

LITLINGTON TQ5201
Plough & Harrow (01323) 870632
Between A27 Lewes–Polegate and A259 E of Seaford; BN26 5RE Neatly extended 17th-c flint village pub, large beamed bar with smaller rooms off, half a dozen well kept ales including at least three from Long Man, decent wines by the glass and good selection of food from lunchtime pub staples to more enterprising dishes using local ingredients, friendly attentive service; children and dogs welcome, attractive back garden, good walks (on South Downs Way), open all day, food all day weekends. *(John Beeken)*

LITTLEHAMPTON TQ0202
★Arun View (01903) 722335
Wharf Road; W towards Chichester; BN17 5DD In lovely harbour spot with busy waterway directly below windows, popular food (all day Sun) from sandwiches to good fresh fish, well kept Arundel, Fullers and Ringwood, several wines by the glass, cheerful helpful staff, flagstoned and panelled back bar with banquettes and dark wood tables, large conservatory; background and some live music, TVs, pool; children welcome, disabled facilities, flower-filled terrace, interesting waterside walkway to coast, four bedrooms, open all day. *(Tony and Wendy Hobden)*

LITTLEHAMPTON TQ0202
Steam Packet (01903) 715994
River Road; BN17 5BZ Renovated corner pub just across from the Arun View; open-plan interior providing several separate seating areas, well kept Caledonian Deuchars IPA, Courage Directors and a guest, shortish menu of snacks and light meals plus good specials board; quiz Thurs; seats out in small area facing river, raised back garden, open all day, no food Sun evening. *(Tony Scott, Tony and Wendy Hobden)*

LODSWORTH SU9321
Halfway Bridge Inn (01798) 861281
Just before village, on A272 Midhurst–Petworth; GU28 9BP Restauranty 17th-c coaching inn, various character rooms with good oak chairs and individual mix of tables, log fires (one in polished kitchen range), interconnecting restaurant areas with beams and wooden floors, well liked food (all day weekends), Langhams, Long Man and Sharps Doom Bar, wide range of wines by the glass; background music, free wi-fi, daily newspapers; children and dogs (in bar) welcome, small back terrace, seven bedrooms in former stable yard, open all day. *(Anon)*

LODSWORTH SU9223
Hollist Arms (01798) 861310
Off A272 Midhurst–Petworth; GU28 9BZ In lovely spot by village green and under friendly new management; small snug room on right with open fire, public bar on left serving local Langhams, two guest beers and a dozen wines by the glass, enjoyable fairly traditional food (not Sun evening) including some european influences, L-shaped dining room with wood-strip floor, inglenook and comfortable seating area, interesting prints and paintings (some by the chef); children and dogs welcome, steps up to cottagey back garden, picnic-sets on terrace or you can sit under a huge horse chestnut on the green, good walks nearby, open all day. *(Lindy Andrews)*

LOWER BEEDING TQ2225
Crabtree (01403) 892666
Brighton Road; RH13 6PT Family-run pub with Victorian façade but much older inside with Tudor beams and huge inglenook (dated 1537), simple light modern décor, dining room in converted barn, good interesting food (not Sun evening) using local seasonal produce, friendly service, well kept Badger beers and good selection of wines by the glass including english fizz; children welcome, dogs in bar, landscaped garden, with fine country views, handy for Nymans (NT), open all day. *(Anne and Ben Smith)*

LOXWOOD TQ0331
Onslow Arms (01403) 752452
B2133 NW of Billingshurst; RH14 0RD Comfortable and welcoming 17th-c pub sandwiched between Wey & Arun Canal and river, popular well priced food from snacks to daily specials, afternoon cream teas, three Badger ales and decent wines by the glass, beams and log fires; free wi-fi; children and dogs welcome, two gardens, one with play area, the other overlooking canal, good walks and boat trips, open (and food) all day. *(Tony and Wendy Hobden)*

LYMINSTER TQ0204
Six Bells (01903) 713639
Lyminster Road (A284), Wick; BN17 7PS Unassuming 18th-c flint pub with open bar area and separate dining room, well kept Fullers London Pride and Sharps Doom Bar, good house wine, generous helpings of enjoyable food cooked by landlord (best to book weekends), friendly efficient staff, low black beams, wood floor and big inglenook with horsebrasses, pubby furnishings; background music, free wi-fi; children and dogs (in one area) welcome, terrace and garden seating. *(John Beeken, Tony and Wendy Hobden)*

MAYFIELD TQ5826
Middle House (01435) 872146
High Street; TN20 6AB Handsome 16th-c timbered inn, L-shaped beamed bar with

massive fireplace, several well kept ales including Harveys, local cider and decent wines, quiet lounge area with leather chesterfields around log fire in ornate carved fireplace, good choice of enjoyable food, friendly staff coping well at busy times, attractive panelled restaurant; background music; children welcome, terraced back garden with lovely views, five bedrooms, open all day. *(Martin and Alison Stainsby, Tony Scott, R and S Bentley)*

MAYFIELD   TQ5927
★ **Rose & Crown** (01435) 872200
Fletching Street; TN20 6TE Pretty 16th-c weatherboarded pub set down lane from village centre; two cosy front character rooms with coins stuck to low ceiling boards, bench seats built into partly panelled walls and simple furniture on floorboards, inglenook log fire, tankards above bar serving Harveys and a guest, several wines by the glass, decent all-day food (till 7pm Sun), further small room behind servery and larger carpeted one down steps; live music Sat, free wi-fi; children (till 8.30pm) and dogs welcome, raised front terrace, decked back garden, open all day (till midnight Fri, Sat). *(Lindy Andrews)*

MID LAVANT   SU8508
Earl of March (01243) 533993
A286 Lavant Road; PO18 0BQ Updated and extended with emphasis on eating, but seats for drinkers in flagstoned log-fire bar, well kept ales such as Harveys, Hop Back and Timothy Taylors, nice wines by the glass including champagne and english fizz, good if pricey food with much sourced locally, plush dining area and conservatory with seafood bar, pleasant staff; free wi-fi; children and dogs welcome, delightful location with view up to Goodwood from neatly kept garden, local walks, open all day. *(Tracey and Stephen Groves, Miss A E Dare)*

MILLAND   SU8328
Rising Sun (01428) 741347
Iping Road junction with main road through village; GU30 7NA 20th-c red-brick Fullers pub, three of their ales and varied choice of fresh well presented food including specials and weekday lunchtime/early evening offers, friendly helpful staff, three linked rooms including cheery log-fire bar and bare-boards restaurant; live music first Fri of month, free wi-fi; children welcome (popular with families at weekends), extensive lawns attractively divided by tall yew hedge, canopied heated terrace and smokers' gazebo, good walking area, open all day weekends. *(Emma Scofield)*

MILTON STREET   TQ5304
★ **Sussex Ox** (01323) 870840
Off A27 just under a mile E of Alfriston roundabout; BN26 5RL Extended country pub (originally a 1900s slaughterhouse) with

magnificent Downs views; bar area with a couple of high tables and chairs on bare boards, old local photographs, three real ales including Harveys and good choice of wines by the glass, lower brick-floored room with farmhouse furniture and woodburner, similarly furnished dining room (children allowed here), further two-room front eating area with high-backed rush-seated chairs, popular food from traditional choices up, friendly service; dogs welcome in bar, teak seating on raised back deck taking in the view, picnic-sets in garden below and more under parasols at front, open all day weekends. *(Tom and Jill Jones, Tony Scott, Dr Nigel Bowles)*

NETHERFIELD   TQ7118
Netherfield Arms (01424) 838282
Just off B2096 Heathfield–Battle; TN33 9QD Low-ceilinged 18th-c country dining pub with wide choice of enjoyable food including good specials, friendly attentive service, decent wines and a well kept ale such as Long Man, inglenook log fire, cosy restaurant; lovely back garden, far reaching views from front, closed Sun evening, Mon. *(Mr and Mrs J Mandeville)*

NEWHAVEN   TQ4500
Hope (01273) 515389
Follow West Beach signs from A259 westbound; BN9 9DN Big-windowed pub overlooking busy harbour entrance, long bar with raised area, open fires and comfy sofas, upstairs dining conservatory and breezy balcony tables with even better views towards Seaford Head, well kept ales such as Dark Star and Harveys, good choice of generous realistically priced food, friendly staff; tables on grassed waterside area. *(John Beeken)*

NUTBOURNE   TQ0718
Rising Sun (01798) 812191
Off A283 E of Pulborough; The Street; RH20 2HE Unspoilt creeper-clad village pub dating partly from the 16th c, beams, exposed brickwork, bare boards and scrubbed tables, friendly helpful licensees (same family ownership for over 30 years), well kept Fullers London Pride and guests, good home-made food including some unusual choices, big log fire, daily papers, enamel signs and 1920s fashion and dance posters, cosy snug, attractive back family room; live music last Tues of month; dogs welcome, garden with small back terrace under apple tree, smokers' shelter, listed outside lavatory, closed Sun evening. *(Tony and Wendy Hobden, Richard Tilbrook)*

NUTHURST   TQ1926
Black Horse (01403) 891272
Off A281 SE of Horsham; RH13 6LH Welcoming 17th-c country pub under newish management; low black beams, flagstones/bare boards, inglenook log fire and plenty of character in its several small

rooms, enjoyable good value food served by friendly attentive staff, four real ales including Fullers London Pride; charity quiz Weds; children and dogs welcome, pretty streamside back garden, more seats on front terrace, open all day Sat, till 8pm Sun. *(Ian Phillips)*

NYETIMBER   SZ8998

Inglenook (01243) 262495

Pagham Road; PO21 3QB Substantial 16th-c hotel run by same family for 40 years; warren of rooms including carpeted beamed bar with two big fireplaces and a caged parrot, well kept Fullers London Pride, Youngs Special and guests, good range of enjoyable food including Sun carvery, restaurant with pitched roof section, garden room, friendly staff and locals; children welcome, attractive gardens behind, comfortable bedrooms, open all day.
(Tony and Wendy Hobden)

OFFHAM   TQ3912

Blacksmiths Arms (01273) 472971

A275 N of Lewes; BN7 3QD Civilised open-plan dining pub with some recent refurbishment (changed hands 2014), good food from fairly pubby menu, well kept Goldstone, Harveys and Hurst, efficient friendly service, huge end inglenook; children and dogs (in bar) welcome, french windows to terrace, four bedrooms (steep stairs), open all day. *(PL)*

OFFHAM   TQ4011

⋆**Chalk Pit** (01273) 471124

Offham Road (A275 N of Lewes); BN7 3QF Former late 18th-c chalk pit building on three levels, well kept Harveys and a guest, decent wines by the glass, wide choice of popular generously served home-made food including OAP bargains, attentive cheerful staff, neat restaurant extension, skittle alley, toad in the hole played Mon nights; children welcome, garden with terrace seating, smokers' shelter with pool table, three bedrooms, open (and usually food) all day Fri-Sun. *(Ann and Colin Hunt, John Beeken)*

PARTRIDGE GREEN   TQ1819

⋆**Green Man** (01403) 710250

Off A24 just under a mile S of A272 junction – take B2135 at West Grinstead signpost; pub at Jolesfield, N of Partridge Green; RH13 8JT Relaxed gently upmarket dining pub with popular enterprising food, well chosen wines by the glass including champagne, Dark Star and Harveys, excellent service; unassuming front area by counter with bentwood bar seats, stools and library chairs around one or two low tables, old curved high-back settle, main eating area widening into back part with pretty enamelled stove and pitched ceiling on left, more self-contained room on right with stag's head, minimal decoration but plenty of

atmosphere; cast-iron seats and picnic-sets under parasols in neat back garden, closed Sun evening. *(Anon)*

PARTRIDGE GREEN   TQ1819

Partridge (01403) 710391

Church Road/High Street; RH13 8JS Spacious 19th-c village pub (former station hotel) now tap for Dark Star, their full range and maybe a guest, real cider, enjoyable sensibly priced home-made food (not Sun, Mon evenings) including blackboard specials and deals, friendly relaxed atmosphere; darts and pool; children and dogs welcome, garden with play equipment and large terrace, open all day. *(Tony and Wendy Hobden)*

PATCHING   TQ0705

Fox (01903) 871299

Arundel Road; signed off A27 eastbound just W of Worthing; BN13 3UJ Generous good value home-made food including popular Sun roasts (best to book), quick friendly service even at busy times, two or three well kept local ales, large dining area off roomy panelled bar, dark pubby furniture on patterned carpet, hunting pictures; quiet background music; children and dogs welcome, disabled access, colourful hanging baskets and good-sized tree-shaded garden with well laid-out seating, heaters and play area, open all day Sun till 9pm. *(Tony and Wendy Hobden, David Jackman)*

PETT   TQ8713

Royal Oak (01424) 812515

Pett Road; TN35 4HG Light and airy pub under same ownership as the Queens Head at Icklesham; roomy main bar with big open fire, well kept Harveys and a couple of changing guests, good popular home-made food (not Sun evening) including plenty of fish and decent vegetarian options, two dining areas, efficient friendly service, monthly live music and quiz nights; dogs welcome (maybe a biscuit), small garden behind, open all day. *(Peter Meister)*

PETT   TQ8613

Two Sawyers (01424) 812255

Pett Road, off A259; TN35 4HB Meandering low-beamed rooms including bare-boards bar with stripped tables, tiny snug, passage sloping down to restaurant allowing children, popular good value freshly made food, friendly helpful service, well kept Harveys and guests, local cider/perry and wide range of wines; background music; dogs allowed in bar, suntrap front courtyard, back garden with shady trees and well spaced tables, three bedrooms, open all day.
(Alfie Bayliss)

PETWORTH   SU9719

Badgers (01798) 342651

Station Road (A285 1.5 miles S); GU28 0JF Restauranty dining pub with good up-to-date food including tapas, seasonal game and seafood, can eat in bar areas or restaurant, friendly accommodating staff, a couple of changing ales and good choice of wines, cosy fireside area with sofas; free wi-fi; over-5s allowed in bar's eating area, stylish tables and seats on terrace by water lily pool, summer barbecues, three well appointed bedrooms, good breakfast, closed winter Sun evening. *(Colin McKerrow)*

PETWORTH   SU9721
Star (01798) 342569
Market Square; GU28 0AH Airy open-plan pub in centre with seats out in front, well kept Fullers ales and decent wines, enjoyable fairly priced food (not Sun evening), good coffee, leather armchairs and sofa by open fire, friendly atmosphere; free wi-fi; open all day. *(Edward May)*

PETWORTH   SU9722
Stonemasons (01798) 342510
North Street; GU28 9NL Attractive low-beamed 17th-c inn refurbished under present owners; enjoyable freshly made food at fair prices, two or three ales including Skinners Betty Stogs, helpful efficient staff, opened-up areas in former adjoining cottages, inglenook log fires (not always lit); children and dogs welcome, picnic-sets in pleasant sheltered back garden, five bedrooms, opposite Petworth House (NT) so can get busy, open all day. *(Ian Phillips, Tony and Wendy Hobden)*

PLAYDEN   TQ9121
Playden Oasts (01797) 223502
Rye Road; TN31 7UL Converted three-roundel oast with comfortable bar and restaurant, enjoyable food (all day Sun evening) from fairly pubby menu, Harveys Best, friendly homely atmosphere; children and dogs welcome, eight bedrooms, open all day. *(Nick Sharpe)*

PLUMPTON   TQ3613
★Half Moon (01273) 890253
Ditchling Road (B2116); BN7 3AF Enlarged beamed and timbered dining pub with good locally sourced food from pub favourites up, children's menu, local ales and plenty of wines by the glass, good friendly service, log fire with unusual flint chimneybreast; background music; dogs welcome in bar, tables in wisteria-clad front courtyard and on back terrace, big Downs-view garden with picnic area, summer family days with face painting and bouncy castle (last Sun of July and Aug), good walks, open all day (till 6pm Sun). *(Edward May)*

POYNINGS   TQ2611
Royal Oak (01273) 857389
The Street; BN45 7AQ Well run 19th-c pub with large beamed bar, good food from

sandwiches and sharing plates up, friendly attentive service, real ales including Harveys from three-sided servery, leather sofas and traditional furnishing, woodburner; children and dogs welcome, attractive big garden with country/Downs views. *(Mr and Mrs J Watkins)*

RINGMER   TQ4512
Green Man (01273) 812422
Lewes Road; BN8 5NA Welcoming 1930s roadside pub with busy mix of locals and visitors, five real ales from brick-faced counter including Greene King, wide choice of generous good value food, log fire, restaurant; children and dogs welcome, terrace tables, more on lawn under trees, play area, open (and food) all day. *(John Beeken)*

ROWHOOK   TQ1234
★Chequers (01403) 790480
Off A29 NW of Horsham; RH12 3PY Attractive 15th-c country pub, beamed and flagstoned front bar with portraits and inglenook log fire, step up to low-ceilinged lounge, well kept Harveys and guests, decent wines by the glass and good food from chef-landlord using local ingredients including home-grown vegetables, separate restaurant; background music; children and dogs welcome, tables out on front terraces and in pretty garden behind, good play area, closed Sun evening. *(Belinda May)*

RUSHLAKE GREEN   TQ6218
Horse & Groom (01435) 830320
Off B2096 Heathfield–Battle; TN21 9QE Pretty little village green pub refreshed under welcoming new dutch licensees; L-shaped low-beamed bar with brick fireplace, small room down a step and restaurant, good interesting food (more pubby at lunchtime) including some dutch dishes, Harveys, Shepherd Neame and decent wines by the glass; children and dogs welcome, cottagey garden with country views, nice walks, closed Sun evening, Mon, otherwise open all day. *(Nick Sharpe)*

RUSPER   TQ1836
★Royal Oak (01293) 871393
Friday Street, towards Warnham – back road N of Horsham, E of A24 (OS Sheet 187 map reference 185369); RH12 4QA Old-fashioned and well worn-in tile-hung pub in very rural spot on Sussex Border Path, small carpeted top bar with leather sofas and armchairs, log fire, steps down to long beamed main bar with plush wall seats, pine tables and chairs and homely knick-knacks, well kept Surrey Hills Ranmore and six changing guests, farm ciders and perries, short choice of enjoyable low-priced lunchtime food (evenings and Sun lunch by

---

If we know a pub has an outdoor play area for children, we mention it.

pre-arrangement), plain games room with darts; no children inside, a few picnic-sets on grass by road and in streamside garden beyond car park, roaming chickens (eggs for sale), bedrooms, closes at 9pm (4pm Sun). *(Tony Scott)*

RUSPER TQ2037
Star (01293) 871264
Off A264 S of Crawley; RH12 4RA Several linked rooms in rambling 15th-c beamed coaching inn, friendly staff and cosy atmosphere, well kept Fullers London Pride, Greene King Abbot and Sharps Doom Bar, good choice of popular food from sandwiches and light meals up including some greek choices, wood floors, old tools on walls, fine brick inglenook; dogs welcome, small back terrace. *(Ian Phillips)*

RYE TQ9220
★**George** (01797) 222114
High Street; TN31 7JT Sizeable hotel with popular beamed bar, mix of furniture including settles on bare boards, log fire, ales such as Dark Star, Franklins, Harveys and Old Dairy, continental beers on tap too, good friendly service from neat young staff, interesting bistro-style food, big spreading restaurant to right of main door; may be background jazz; children and dogs welcome, attractive bedrooms, open all day. *(Caroline Prescott)*

RYE TQ9220
★**Globe** (01797) 225220
Military Road; TN31 7NX Small weatherboarded pub under same owners as Five Bells at Brabourne (Kent), revamped interior full of quirky touches such as corrugated iron-clad walls, hanging lobster pot lights and eclectic range of furniture from school chairs to a table made from part of an old fishing boat, even hay bale seats in one part, scatter cushions, fresh flowers, candles and paraffin lamps, two log fires, good locally sourced food from open kitchen with wood-fired oven, interesting local ales and ciders (no bar as such), also some wines from nearby Chapel Down, shelves of home-made preserves for sale, quick cheerful service; unisex loos; children and dogs welcome, seats on side decking, open all day. *(Peter Meister, Mike and Eleanor Anderson, Tracy Collins)*

RYE TQ9220
★**Mermaid** (01797) 223065
Mermaid Street; TN31 7EY Lovely old timbered inn on famous cobbled street (cellars date from 12th c, although pub was rebuilt in 1420); civilised antiques-filled bar, Victorian gothick carved chairs, older but plainer oak seats, huge working inglenook with massive bressumer, Fullers, Greene King and Harveys, good selection of wines and malt whiskies, well liked food in bar (not Sat evening) or restaurant with more elaborate

and expensive evening choices, efficient friendly service, reputedly haunted by five ghosts; background music; children welcome, seats on small back terrace, bedrooms (most with four-posters), open all day. *(DF and NF)*

RYE HARBOUR TQ9419
Inkerman Arms (01797) 222464
Rye Harbour Road; TN31 7TQ Friendly 19th-c end of terrace pub near nature reserve, enjoyable food including good fish and chips, Old Dairy Red Top, Gold Top and an occasional guest; children and dogs welcome, picnic-sets in sheltered back terrace with pond, open all day Fri-Sun. *(Emma Scofield)*

SEDLESCOMBE TQ7817
Queens Head (01424) 870228
The Green; TN33 0QA Attractive tile-hung village-green pub; beamed main bar on right with mixed tables and wheelback chairs on wood floor, church candles and fresh flowers, a huge cartwheel and some farming odds and ends, Harveys and Sharps Doom Bar from plank-fronted servery, side room laid for dining with brick fireplace, sofas in back lounge, another dining room to left of entrance with sisal flooring and huge working inglenook, good popular food (best to book) from shortish menu; quiet background music; children and dogs welcome, garden picnic-sets. *(Caroline Prescott)*

SHOREHAM-BY-SEA TQ2105
Red Lion (01273) 453171
Upper Shoreham Road; BN43 5TE Dimly lit low-beamed and timbered 16th-c pub with settles in snug alcoves, well kept Harveys and changing guests (Easter beer festival), traditional summer ciders and decent wines, pubby food from sandwiches up, log fire in unusual fireplace, another open fire in dining room, further bar with covered terrace; dogs welcome, pretty sheltered garden behind, old bridge and lovely Norman church opposite, good Downs views, popular with walkers and cyclists (on Downs Link trail), open all day. *(Tony and Wendy Hobden)*

SHORTBRIDGE TQ4521
★**Peacock** (01825) 762463
Piltdown; OS Sheet 198 map reference 450215; TN22 3XA Civilised and welcoming old country dining pub with two fine yew trees flanking entrance, dark beams, timbers and big inglenook, some nice old furniture on parquet floors, good freshly made food from light dishes up (not Sun night), two or three well kept ales and nice wines by the glass, friendly attentive staff, restaurant; children welcome, back garden and terrace. *(Mrs Sally Scott, Tony Scott)*

SIDLESHAM SZ8697
★**Crab & Lobster** (01243) 641233
Mill Lane; off B2145 S of Chichester; PO20 7NB Restaurant-with-rooms rather

than pub but walkers and bird-watchers welcome in small flagstoned bar for light meals, Harveys and Sharps, 17 wines by the glass including champagne, stylish, upmarket restaurant with good imaginative (and pricey) food including excellent local fish, competent friendly young staff; background music; children welcome, tables on back terrace overlooking marshes, smart bedrooms, self-catering cottage, open all day (food all day weekends). *(Paddy and Annabelle Cribb, John Wooll, Tracey and Stephen Groves, Richard Tilbrook)*

SINGLETON   SU8713
Partridge (01243) 811251
Just off A286 Midhurst–Chichester; PO18 0EY Pretty 16th-c pub in attractive village setting; all sorts of light and dark wood tables and dining chairs on polished wooden floors, flagstones or carpet, some country knick-knacks, open fires and woodburner, well kept Fullers London Pride, Harveys Best and a summer guest, several wines by the glass, generally well liked food from lunchtime sandwiches up, efficient service, daily papers and board games, maybe summer table tennis; background music; children welcome, plenty of seats under parasols on terrace and in walled garden, handy for Weald & Downland Open Air Museum. *(Nigel and Sue Foster, Robert Wivell)*

SLINDON   SU9708
Spur (01243) 814216
Slindon Common; A29 towards Bognor; BN18 0NE Roomy 17th-c pub with wide choice of popular food from bar snacks to more upmarket (but good value) restaurant dishes, Courage Directors and Sharps Doom Bar, friendly staff, pine tables and two big log fires, large panelled restaurant with linen tablecloths, games room with darts and pool, skittle alley; children welcome, dogs in bar, pretty garden (traffic noise), good local walks, open all day Sun. *(Tony and Wendy Hobden)*

SOMPTING   TQ1605
Gardeners Arms (01903) 233666
West Street; BN15 0AR 19th-c pub run by friendly licensees, just off main coast road (the famous Saxon church is unfortunately on the far side of the dual carriageway), generous helpings of tasty low-priced pub food including some real bargains (railway carriage restaurant no longer in use), Bass, Harveys, Sharps Doom Bar and a guest, log fire; background music, Tues quiz; children and dogs welcome, seats on raised terrace, open all day. *(Tony and Wendy Hobden)*

SOUTH HARTING   SU7819
White Hart (01730) 825124
B2146 SE of Petersfield; GU31 5QB Welcoming sympathetically renovated old beamed pub; well kept Upham ales and good interesting food from sourdough baguettes and sharing plates up, pub favourites too, split-level bare-boards interior, inglenook log fires; children, dogs and walkers welcome, terrace and garden with spectacular Downs views, one bedroom (can sleep four), handy for Uppark (NT), open all day. *(Val and Alan Green)*

SOUTHWATER   TQ1528
Bax Castle (01403) 730369
Two Mile Ash, a mile or so NW; RH13 0LA Early 19th-c country pub with well liked traditional home-made food and wood-fired pizzas, three Marstons-related ales, friendly staff, sofas next to big log fire, barn restaurant; background music; children and dogs welcome, pleasant garden with play area, near Downs Link path on former railway track, open all day (till 9pm Sun). *(Mrs Sally Scott, Tony Scott)*

STAPLEFIELD   TQ2728
Victory (01444) 400463
Warninglid Road; RH17 6EU Pretty little shuttered dining pub overlooking cricket green (and London to Brighton veteran car run, first Sun in Nov), friendly welcoming staff, good choice of popular home-made food, smaller helpings for children, well kept Harveys Best from zinc-topped counter, local cider and decent wines, beams and woodburner; dogs welcome, nice tree-shaded garden with play area. *(C and R Bromage)*

STEDHAM   SU8522
Hamilton Arms (01730) 812555
School Lane (off A272); GU29 0NZ Village local run by friendly thai family, standard pub food as well as good thai bar snacks and restaurant dishes (you can buy ingredients in their little shop), good value Sun buffet, reasonably priced wines and four or more well kept ales, games room; unobtrusive background music, muted TV; pretty hanging baskets on front terrace overlooking small green, good nearby walks, closed Mon, otherwise open all day. *(Anon)*

STOPHAM   TQ0318
★ **White Hart** (01798) 874903
Off A283 E of village, W of Pulborough; RH20 1DS Fine old beamed pub by medieval River Arun bridge, new owners and refurbishment since 2014 floods, well kept Harveys, Langhams and Sharps, good food from ciabattas, sharing plates and stone-baked pizzas up, friendly efficient service; summer Sun afternoon jazz; children and dogs (in bar) welcome, waterside tables, open all day, food all day Sat, till 6pm Sun. *(Nick Sharpe)*

STOUGHTON   SU8011
Hare & Hounds (02392) 631433
Signed off B2146 Petersfield–Emsworth; PO18 9JQ Airy pine-clad country dining pub with good reasonably priced fresh food from sandwiches to Sun roasts, up to six

well kept ales and Weston's cider, cheerful service, flagstones and big open fires, locals' bar with darts, quiz nights; children in eating areas, dogs welcome, tables on pretty front terrace and grass behind, lovely setting near Saxon church, good walks, open all day Fri-Sun. *(Ann and Colin Hunt)*

SUTTON   SU9715

★**White Horse** (01798) 869221

The Street; RH20 1PS Cleanly modernised country inn close to Bignor Roman Villa; bar with an open brick fireplace at each end, tea-lights on mantelpieces, cushioned high bar chairs, three well kept ales and good wines by the glass, two-room barrel-vaulted dining area with minimalist décor and another little fire, good value well thought-of food from sandwiches up, friendly helpful young staff; children welcome, dogs in bar, steps up to lawn with plenty of picnic-sets, more seats in front, good surrounding walks, bedrooms, closed Sun evening, Mon. *(Martin and Karen Wake)*

THAKEHAM   TQ1017

White Lion (01798) 813141

Off B2139 N of Storrington; The Street; RH20 3EP Steps up to 16th-c pub in pretty village (level access from back car park); heavy beams, panelling, bare boards and traditional furnishings, four changing ales and decent wines by the glass, well liked food (not Sun evening) including good selection of blackboard specials, efficient service, pleasant dining room with inglenook; children and dogs welcome, nice sunny terrace and small enclosed lawn, open all day. *(Celia Caulkin)*

TICEHURST   TQ6831

Bull (01580) 200586

Three Legged Cross; off B2099 towards Wadhurst; TN5 7HH Attractive 14th-c pub with big log fires in two heavy-beamed old-fashioned bars, well kept Harveys and a couple of guests, contemporary furnishings and flooring in light airy dining extension serving good food (not Sun evening); children and dogs welcome, charming front garden (busy in summer), bigger back one with play area, four bedrooms, open all day. *(John Harris)*

TURNERS HILL   TQ3435

Crown (01342) 715218

East Street; RH10 4PT Refurbished village pub dating from the 16th c, low-beamed bar with sofas by big log fire, steps down to high-raftered dining area with parquet floor and another fire, decent food from sandwiches and pubby choices up, well kept ales including Harveys and St Austell, good service; children welcome, picnic-sets out in front, sheltered back garden with paved terrace and valley views, open all day. *(C and R Bromage)*

TURNERS HILL   TQ3435

★**Red Lion** (01342) 715416

Lion Lane, just off B2028; RH10 4NU Old-fashioned, unpretentious and welcoming country local, snug parquet-floored bar with plush wall benches and small open fire, steps up to carpeted dining area with inglenook log fire, cushioned pews and settles, old photos and brewery memorabilia, well kept Harveys ales and good home-made food (lunchtime only – must book Sun); live music and quiz nights; children (away from bar) and dogs welcome, picnic-sets on side grass overlooking village, open all day weekends. *(Tony and Wendy Hobden, Mrs P R Sykes, Nick Lawless, Tony Scott)*

UDIMORE   TQ8818

Plough (01797) 223381

Cock Marling (B2089 W of Rye); TN31 6AL Popular recently refurbished and extended 17th-c roadside pub; enjoyable freshly made food including tapas, bargain main course deal Weds evening, well kept Harveys, a house beer brewed by Old Dairy and a guest, good choice of wines by the glass, weekday happy hour (5.30-7pm), friendly service, L-shaped main bar with wood floor, separate back dining room, two woodburners; children and dogs welcome, tables on good-sized sunny back terrace, Brede Valley views, closed Sun evening. *(Peter Meister)*

UPPER DICKER   TQ5409

Plough (01323) 844859

Coldharbour Road; BN27 3QJ Extended 17th-c pub improved and continuing well under current licensees; small central beamed bar with seats by inglenook, two dining areas off to left and step up to larger dining bar on right with raised area, well kept Shepherd Neame with Harveys as guest, good choice of enjoyable food (some quite pricey); background music, Tues quiz; children and dogs welcome, good-sized garden with elevated deck and play area, open (and food) all day. *(Fr Robert Marsh, Mike and Shelley Woodroffe, Nigel and Jean Eames, Paul A Moore)*

WADHURST   TQ6431

White Hart (01892) 782850

High Street; TN5 6AP Refurbished late 19th-c village-centre pub (part of Greene King 'Local Heroes' scheme); L-shaped bar with squashy sofa at one end, old local photos on grey-green paintwork above a darker dado, wooden and cushioned dining chairs around tables of varying sizes on stripped wood flooring, large map of the area covering one wall, gilt-edged mirror above open fireplace, up to six well kept predominantly local ales such as Larkins, Long Man and Old Dairy, decent wines by the glass, good choice of food (not Sun evening) including tapas and pizzas, friendly staff; background music;

chunky picnic-sets out in front, more in neat crazy-paved little back garden, open all day. *(Edward May)*

WALDERTON   SU7910
Barley Mow (02392) 631321
Stoughton Road, just off B2146 Chichester–Petersfield; PO18 9ED
Popular country pub under new management; well liked food including Sun carvery, ales such as Adnams, Ringwood and Sharps, friendly service, two log fires in U-shaped bar with roomy dining areas, skittle alley; children welcome, big streamside back garden, good walks (Kingley Vale nearby), handy for Stansted Park, open all day, food till 6pm Sun. *(Alfie Bayliss)*

WALDRON   TQ5419
★ Star (01435) 812495
Blackboys–Horam side road; TN21 0RA
Pretty pub in quiet village, beamed main bar with settle next to good log fire in brick inglenook, wheelbacks around pubby tables on old quarry tiles, several built-in cushioned wall and window seats, old local pictures and photographs, high stools by central counter serving a couple of well kept Harveys ales and a guest, maybe own apple juice, good food including lunchtime sandwiches and platters, pubby dishes and specials, dining areas with painted chairs around pine-topped tables on parquet or bare boards, bookshelf wallpaper, chatty local atmosphere and friendly staff; music and quiz nights; picnic-sets in pleasant back garden, wassailing on Twelfth Night, small café and shop next door. *(Paul Lucas, Mike and Eleanor Anderson)*

WARBLETON   TQ6018
★ Black Duck (01435) 830636
S of B2096 SE of Heathfield; TN21 9BD
Friendly licensees at this small renovated pub tucked down from church; L-shaped main room with pale oak flooring, cushioned leather sofas in front of roaring inglenook, beams and walls hung with horsebrasses, tankards, musical instruments, farm tools, even an old typewriter, high-backed dining chairs around mix of tables, popular pubby food including daily specials, bar area up a step with stools along counter, Harveys, Sharps Doom Bar and nice wines by the glass, cabinet of books and board games, perky pub dog; background music; picnic-sets in back garden with sweeping valley views, more on front grass. *(Lindy Andrews)*

WARTLING   TQ6509
★ Lamb (01323) 832116
Village signed with Herstmonceux Castle off A271 Herstmonceux–Battle; BN27 1RY Popular family-owned country pub; small entrance bar with open fireplace, ales such as Harveys, Old Dairy and Pig & Porter, several wines by the glass, two-level beamed and timbered dining room to the left with inglenook woodburner, bigger back

bar and restaurant, well liked food including blackboard specials, friendly service; children and dogs welcome, steps up to garden with chunky seats, bedrooms, closed Sun evening, otherwise open all day. *(Steve and Liz Tilley)*

WEST ASHLING   SU8007
Richmond Arms (01243) 572046
Just off B2146; Mill Road; PO18 8EA
Village dining pub in quiet pretty setting near big millpond with ducks and geese, good interesting food (quite pricey, best to book), also wood-fired pizzas cooked in a vintage van (Fri, Sat evenings), Harveys ales and plenty of wines by the glass, competent friendly staff; children welcome, no dogs, two nice bedrooms, closed Sun evening, Mon and Tues. *(Ann and Colin Hunt)*

WEST WITTERING   SZ8099
Lamb (01243) 511105
Chichester Road; B2179/A286 towards Birdham; PO20 8QA Modernised 18th-c tile-hung country pub, three Badger ales and enjoyable home-cooked food, friendly staff coping well during busy summer months, bar with painted beams and timbers, assorted furniture on wood floor including kitchen chairs and scrubbed pine tables, woodburner in brick fireplace, two bare-boards dining rooms off with some interesting artwork; background music; children and dogs welcome, tables out in front and in small sheltered back garden, open all day Sat, closed Sun evening. *(Emma Scofield)*

WILMINGTON   TQ5404
★ Giants Rest (01323) 870207
Just off A27; BN26 5SQ Busy country pub with long wood-floored bar, adjacent open areas with simple furniture, rural pictures and pot plants, log fire, well kept/priced Long Man range and maybe a cider from the village, enjoyable well presented food cooked by french chef-landlord including specials and gluten-free options, friendly helpful staff; children and dogs welcome, lots of seats in front garden, surrounded by South Downs walks and village famous for chalk-carved Long Man, two comfortable bedrooms up narrow stairs sharing bathroom, open all day weekends (food all day Sun). *(John Beeken, Fr Robert Marsh, Tom and Jill Jones, Paul A Moore and others)*

WINCHELSEA   TQ9017
New Inn (01797) 226252
German Street; just off A259; TN36 4EN
Attractive 18th-c pub with L-shaped front bar mainly laid for dining, good fair-value food from sandwiches to local fish, well kept Greene King and guests, friendly helpful staff, some slate flagstones, blackened beams and log fire, separate back bar with darts and TV; background music; children welcome, pleasant tree-shaded walled garden, delightful setting opposite church

where Spike Milligan is buried, comfortable bedrooms, good breakfast. *(Peter Meister, John Beeken, Peter Smith and Judith Brown)*

WINEHAM   TQ2320
★ **Royal Oak** (01444) 881252
Village signposted from A272 and B2116; BN5 9AY Splendidly old-fashioned local with log fire in enormous inglenook, Harveys Best and guests tapped from casks in still room, enjoyable seasonal food (not Sun evening), jugs and ancient corkscrews on very low beams, collection of cigarette boxes, a stuffed stoat and crocodile, more bric-a-brac in back parlour with views of quiet countryside; children away from bar and dogs welcome (they have a staffie called Ace), picnic-sets outside, closed evenings 25 and 26 Dec, 1 Jan. *(Tony Scott)*

WISBOROUGH GREEN   TQ0526
Cricketers Arms (01403) 700369
Loxwood Road, just off A272 Billingshurst–Petworth; RH14 0DG Attractive old pub with four or five well kept ales such as Dark Star, Fullers, Harveys and St Austell, good choice of food including specials, cheerful staff, open-plan with two big woodburners, pleasing mix of country furniture, stripped-brick dining area on left; some weekend live music; tables out on terrace, across lane from green, open all day. *(Tony Scott, John Davis)*

WISBOROUGH GREEN   TQ0525
Three Crowns (0333) 700 7333
Billingshurst Road (A272); RH14 0DX Well looked-after beamed pub with enjoyable freshly made food (not Sun evening) from sharing boards and pub favourites up, prompt friendly service, well kept Harveys and a couple of guests, extensive choice of wines by the glass including champagne and good range of gins; live music and monthly quiz; children welcome, sizeable tree-shaded back garden, open all day. *(Val and Alan Green)*

WITHYHAM   TQ4935
★ **Dorset Arms** (01892) 770278
B2110; TN7 4BD Nicely refurbished late 16th-c pub back under ownership of the Buckhurst Estate (had been Harveys since 1986); light fresh décor but keeping cosy pub feel with beams and large inglenook, well liked locally sourced food (not Sun evening) including seasonal game and other meat from the Estate, ales such as Harveys, Larkins and Hepworths, friendly helpful staff, restaurant; children and dogs welcome, handy for Forest Way walks, open all day. *(John Harris)*

WOODMANCOTE   SU7707
Woodmancote (01243) 371019
The one near Emsworth; Woodmancote Lane; PO10 8RD Well run village pub with interesting contemporary décor – plenty of quirky touches; good popular food from sandwiches and sharing boards up (best to book), ales such as Brains, Courage and Hogs Back, several wines by the glass, restaurant; dogs welcome in bar, seats out under cover, open all day. *(Wendda and John Knapp)*

WORTHING   TQ1502
Selden Arms
Lyndhurst Road, between Waitrose and hospital; BN11 2DB Friendly unchanging 19th-c backstreet local opposite the gasworks, welcoming long-serving licensees, six well kept ales (Jan beer festival), craft kegs and continental draught/bottled beers, bargain lunchtime food (not Sun) including doorstep sandwiches, Fri curry night, comfortably worn interior with photographs of old Worthing pubs, pump clips on ceiling, log fire; occasional live music, quiz last Weds of month, darts; dogs welcome, open all day. *(Tony and Wendy Hobden)*

WORTHING   TQ1502
Swan (01903) 232923
High Street; BN11 1DN Villagey atmosphere with good mix of customers in U-shaped bar, four well kept ales such as Arundel, Harveys, Hogs Back and Otter, reasonably priced pubby lunchtime food (also Fri, Sat evenings), friendly welcoming staff, old-fashioned carpeted interior with lots of odds and ends hanging from beams, some stained glass; regular live music, Tues quiz night, bar billiards; children welcome, small back terrace used by smokers, open all day. *(Tony and Wendy Hobden)*

Anyone claiming to arrange, or prevent, inclusion of a pub in the *Guide* is a fraud. Pubs are included only if recommended by genuine readers and if our own anonymous inspection confirms that they are suitable.

Warwickshire

with Birmingham and West Midlands

KEY ★ Star Pub 🍽️ Top Quality Food 🍺 Great Beer

🍷 Good Wines £ Bargain Meals 🛏️ Good Bedrooms 🍴 Serves Food

ALDERMINSTER
SP2348 Map 4

Bell 🍽️ 🍷 🛏️

(01789) 450414 – www.thebellald.co.uk
A3400 Oxford–Stratford; CV37 8NY

Fine old inn with a smart feel, real ales, a good choice of wines, excellent modern cooking and helpful service; comfortable bedrooms

Part of the Alscot Estate, this is a civilised Georgian coaching inn with a friendly, easy-going atmosphere. The open-plan rooms cleverly manage to create a contemporary feel that goes well with the many original features: beams, standing timbers, flagstoned or wooden floors, fresh flowers and candles. A small, bustling bar serves Alscot Ale (named for the pub from North Cotswold), North Cotswold Windrush Ale, Purity Lawless and a guest from Stratford upon Avon on handpump, a dozen wines by the glass and proper cocktails (including a special bloody mary). It's furnished with comfortable brown leather armchairs in front of an open fire, high bar chairs by the blue-painted counter and daily papers; background music. The restaurant has an eclectic mix of furniture including painted dining chairs and tables, and leads into the conservatory, which shares the same Stour Valley views as the appealing courtyard with its modern chairs and tables. The boutique-style bedrooms are individually decorated and comfortable.

 Using produce from the Estate, the imaginative food includes lunchtime sandwiches, pressed ham hock with piccalilli purée and pickled vegetables, venison carpaccio with shallots, capers and parmesan, grazing boards, chicken caesar salad, twice-baked cheddar soufflé with sweet potato bubble and squeak and tomato coulis, seared hake with crayfish risotto, trio of lamb (leg, shoulder and loin) with mint jus, and puddings such as glazed lemon tart with italian meringue and lemon sorbet and dark chocolate and rosemary fondant with raspberry textures; they also offer a smaller sized two-course set menu. *Benchmark main dish: burger with toppings and chips £12.95. Two-course evening meal £17.00.*

Free house ~ Licensee Emma Holman-West ~ Real ale ~ Open 9am-11pm; 11-10 Sun ~ Bar food 12-2.30, 6.30-9.30; 12-3, 6.30-8.30 Sun ~ Restaurant ~ Children welcome ~ Dogs allowed in bar ~ Wi-fi ~ Bedrooms: $70/$110 *Recommended by P and J Shapley, John Harris*

ARMSCOTE
SP2444 Map 4

Fuzzy Duck 🍽️ 🍷 🛏️

(01608) 682635 – www.fuzzyduckarmscote.com
Off A3400 Stratford–Shipston; CV37 8DD

Interestingly refurbished former coaching inn with real ales, a good wine list, imaginative food and seats outside; lovely bedrooms

The family behind the Baylis & Harding beauty products company have stylishly reworked this former 18th-coaching inn and their luxury products can be found in the deeply comfortable, thoughtfully equipped and pretty bedrooms – each named after a species of duck. The bar has high, chunky leather chairs around equally high metal tables on flagstones, an open fire and more leather chairs against the counter where friendly staff serve Everards Tiger and Purity Mad Goose on handpump, 12 wines by the glass, a dozen malt whiskies and farm cider; a wall of glass-faced boxes holds bottles of spirits belonging to regular customers. Three interconnected dining rooms have a mix of dark wooden tables surrounded by leather and other elegant chairs on pale floorboards, a sofa here and there and a two-way woodburning stove in an open fireplace. Throughout, cartoons and arty photographs hang on pale or dark grey walls and flowers are arranged in big vases; background music. At the back is another dining room (also used for private parties) that leads to a decked terrace with basket-weave armchairs, cushioned sofas and little modern metal chairs and tables under big parasols, and there's a small lawn with fruit trees. Plenty of walks in surrounding rolling countryside and Stratford-upon-Avon is close by.

 Creative, seasonal food includes sandwiches, crab on toast with hazelnut dukkah, duck liver parfait with orange marmalade, sharing platters, free-range sausage and mash with onion gravy, blue cheese arancini with wild nettle purée and tomato salsa, free-range duck breast with smoked bacon and potato terrine, a fresh fish dish of the day, free-range pork three-ways (loin, belly, ham hock pâté) with salsa verde, and puddings such as banoffi tart with ginger ice-cream and dark chocolate fondant with raspberries and white chocolate ice-cream; they also offer a two- and three-course set lunch. *Benchmark main dish: beer-battered cod and chips £14.25. Two-course evening meal £23.00.*

Free house ~ Licensee Solanche Craven ~ Real ale ~ Open 12-11; 12-5 Sun; closed Sun evening, Mon, first week Jan ~ Bar food 12-2.30, 6.30-9 (9.30 Fri, Sat); 12-4 Sun ~ Children welcome ~ Dogs welcome ~ Wi-fi ~ Bedrooms: /£110 *Recommended by Ian Herdman*

BARSTON SP1978 Map 4
Malt Shovel 🍴⭐ 🍷
(01675) 443223 – www.themaltshovelatbarston.com
3 miles from M42 junction 5; A4141 towards Knowle, then first left into Jacobean Lane/Barston Lane; B92 0JP

Well run country dining pub full of happy customers, with an attractive layout, good service and seats in sheltered garden

Once you've found this particularly well run pub, you'll be drawn back to it on a regular basis. Everything is just right: the atmosphere, service, food and drink and the genuine mix of both diners and drinkers. The light, airy, newly refurbished bar rambles extensively around the zinc-topped central counter; it has big terracotta floor tiles neatly offset by dark grouting, and paintwork that's now cream, tan and blue. Black Sheep, St Austell Trelawny and Sharps Doom Bar on handpump and 18 wines served by the glass. Furnishings are comfortable, with informal dining chairs and scatter-cushioned pews around stripped-top tables of varying types and sizes. Cheerful fruit and vegetable paintings hang on the walls and there are french café-style shutters; efficient service by neat young staff. The sheltered back garden with its weeping willow has picnic-sets, and the terrace and verandah tables have cushions on the teak seats in summer.

Excellent food includes pigeon breast with pear and vanilla purée, harissa and honey-marinated chicken with slaw and coriander, open camembert wellington with artichoke, fire-roasted peppers and courgettes, steak in ale pudding, cocoa-marinated venison with sour cherries, cabbage, bacon and fondant potato, halibut with elderflower-roasted parsnips, parma ham and rocket, and puddings such as pecan treacle tart with hazelnut chocolate cream and ginger sponge with rum-marinated pineapple, coconut ice-cream and lime. *Benchmark main dish: salmon fishcakes with spinach, poached eggs and tarragon hollandaise £13.95. Two-course evening meal £21.25.*

Free house ~ Licensee Helen Somerfield ~ Real ale ~ Open 12-12; 12-7 Sun ~ Bar food 12-2.30, 6-9.30; 12-4 Sun ~ Restaurant ~ Children welcome ~ Dogs allowed in bar
Recommended by Roy Shutz, Mike and Mary Carter, Di and Mike Gillam, Susan and John Douglas, Ian Herdman, Peter J and Avril Hanson

 BIRMINGHAM   SP0686   Map 4
Old Joint Stock ◖ £
(0121) 200 1892 – www.oldjointstocktheatre.co.uk
Temple Row West; B2 5NY

Big bustling Fullers pie-and-ale pub with impressive Victorian façade and interior, and a small back terrace

To find this extraordinary place, just head for the cathedral – the pub is opposite. The interior is impressively flamboyant: chandeliers hang from the soaring pink and gilt ceiling, gently illuminated busts line the top of the ornately plastered walls and there's a splendid cupola above the centre of the room. Photographs of the historic building's past line the walls; there's also a big dining balcony reached up a grand sweeping staircase. As well as Fullers ESB, London Pride, Chiswick and Seafarers on handpump, they keep local microbrewery guests and a beer named for the pub (from Silhill); background music. Most nights see something on in the smart purpose-built little theatre on the first floor. The small back terrace has cast-iron tables and chairs and wall-mounted heaters.

Popular food includes sandwiches (until 5pm), smoked salmon with bubble and squeak potato cake, a poached egg and chive cream sauce, soup of the day, wild mushroom ravioli with tarragon butter and tomatoes, cumberland sausages with mustard and ale chutney, pies such as spiced mutton, black pudding and plum, beer-battered cod and chips, and puddings such as vintage ale and molasses sticky toffee pudding with toffee sauce and apple and blackberry crumble. *Benchmark main dish: steak in ale pie £12.75. Two-course evening meal £16.00.*

Fullers ~ Manager Paul Bancroft ~ Real ale ~ Open 10am-11pm; 12-5 Sun ~ Bar food 12-10; 12-4 Sun ~ Restaurant ~ Children welcome in dining area only ~ Wi-fi ~ Regular live entertainment in theatre *Recommended by Mrs Julie Thomas, Theocsbrian, Barry Collett, Ross Balaam, Alan Johnson, Sharon and John Hancock*

 GAYDON   SP3654   Map 4
Malt Shovel ◖
(01926) 641221 – www.maltshovelgaydon.co.uk
Under a mile from M40 junction 12; B4451 into village, then over roundabout and across B4100; Church Road; CV35 0ET

Bustling pub in a quiet village with a nice mix of pubby bar and smarter restaurant

A perfect break from the M40, this is a cheerful village pub with a bustling atmosphere and plenty of customers. Mahogany-varnished boards through to bright carpeting link the entrance and the bar counter to the right, with a woodburning stove on the left. The central area has a high-pitched ceiling, milk churns and earthenware containers in a loft above the bar and three steps that lead up to a space with comfortable sofas overlooked by a big stained-glass window; reproductions of classic posters line the walls. Brains SA and Rev James, Fullers London Pride and Sharps Doom Bar on handpump, with 11 wines by the glass and two farm ciders. A busy eating area has fresh flowers on a mix of kitchen, pub and dining tables; background music, darts. The pub's jack russell is called Mollie.

The well liked food, cooked by the landlord, includes lunchtime sandwiches, baguettes and paninis, smoked haddock welsh rarebit, grilled goats cheese and beetroot toasts, a big breakfast, three-cheese vegetarian lasagne, gammon with tomatoes, mushrooms and eggs, steak and kidney pudding, wild boar and apple sausages braised in cider and calvados on mustard mash, and puddings such as lemon cheesecake and chocolate, cherry and brandy fudge slice. *Benchmark main dish: pie of the day £10.95. Two-course evening meal £15.00.*

Enterprise ~ Lease Richard and Debi Morisot ~ Real ale ~ Open 11-3, 5-11; 11-11 Fri, Sat; 12-10.30 Sun ~ Bar food 12-2, 6.30-9 ~ Restaurant ~ Children welcome ~ Dogs allowed in bar ~ Wi-fi *Recommended by Dave Braisted, David and Shelagh Monks, Joy Griffiths, Steve Whalley*

HAMPTON-IN-ARDEN
White Lion 🍺

SP2080 Map 4

(01675) 442833 – www.thewhitelioninn.com
High Street; handy for M42 junction 6; B92 0AA

Popular village local with a good choice of ales; bedrooms

In an attractive village and handy for the NEC, this former farmhouse has a good choice of ales. The carpeted bar is nice and relaxed, with a mix of furniture trimly laid out, neatly curtained small windows, low-beamed ceilings and some local memorabilia on the fresh cream walls. Castle Rock Harvest Pale, Hobsons Best, M&B Brew XI, St Austell Proper Job, Sharps Doom Bar and Wychwood Hobgoblin Gold on handpump from the timber-planked bar; background music, TV and board games. The modern dining areas are fresh and airy with light wood and cane chairs on stripped floorboards. The bedrooms are quiet and comfortable. The church opposite is mentioned in the Domesday Book.

Traditional food includes a wide choice of sandwiches, whitebait with dijon mustard mayonnaise, smoked haddock fishcake with spinach, a poached egg and white wine sauce, sharing boards, a quiche and a risotto of the day, burger with coleslaw and chips, beef bourguignon, salmon and creamy leek parcel, mixed grill, and puddings. *Benchmark main dish: pork fillet and belly with black pudding, colcannon mash and red wine and apple sauce £12.95. Two-course evening meal £20.50.*

Free house ~ Licensee Chris Roach ~ Real ale ~ Open 12-11 (midnight Sat); 12-10.30 Sun ~ Bar food 12-2.30, 6-9.30; 12-4 Sun ~ Restaurant ~ Children welcome ~ Dogs welcome ~ Wi-fi ~ Bedrooms: £75/£85 *Recommended by Malcolm Phillips*

HUNNINGHAM
Red Lion

SP3768   Map 4

(01926) 632715 – www.redlionhunningham.co.uk

Village signposted off B4453 Leamington–Rugby just E of Weston, and off B4455
Fosse Way 2.5 miles SW of A423 junction; CV33 9DY

Fine riverside spot for civilised but friendly pub, good range of drinks and well liked food

The garden of this friendly pub looks across to the charmingly arched 14th-c bridge over the River Leam; there are plenty of picnic-sets here and at the front, and they have a basket of rugs for customers to take outside – a lovely idea for a warm day. The interior is light and open-plan – yet cleverly sectioned – and appealingly furnished: pews with scatter cushions, an assortment of antique dining chairs and stools around nice polished tables on bare boards (a few big rugs here and there), contemporary paintwork and walls hung with film and rock star photographs (one long wall is a papered mural of bookshelves). A cosy room has tub armchairs around an open coal fire. Greene King IPA, Morlands Old Golden Hen and guests such as Hardys & Hansons Olde Trip and Warwickshire Best Bitter on handpump, ten wines by the glass and 40 malt whiskies; background music.

High quality food includes baked crab and leek gratin, chicken liver pâté with apricot chutney, cumberland sausages with onion gravy, steak and kidney pie, chicken breast with black cabbage, wild mushrooms and madeira jus, stone bass with sweet potato saag aloo and onion bhaji, and puddings such as lemon curd and blueberry mess and sticky toffee pudding with butterscotch sauce. *Benchmark main dish: rare-breed burger with smoked cheese and chips £12.50. Two-course evening meal £19.00.*

Greene King ~ Lease Richard Merand ~ Real ale ~ Open 11-11 ~ Bar food 12-9 ~ Restaurant ~ Children welcome ~ Dogs allowed in bar ~ Wi-fi *Recommended by Dru and Louisa Marshall, George Atkinson*

LONG COMPTON
Red Lion

SP2832   Map 4

(01608) 684221 – www.redlion-longcompton.co.uk

A3400 S of Shipston-on-Stour; CV36 5JS

Traditional character and contemporary touches in comfortably furnished coaching inn; good bedrooms

We get warm praise year after year for this lovely old coaching inn – about all aspects. The roomy, charmingly furnished lounge bar has some exposed stone and beams and nice rambling corners with cushioned settles among pleasantly assorted and comfortable seats and leather armchairs; there are tables on flagstones and carpets, animal prints on warm paintwork and both an open fire and a woodburning stove. Hook Norton Hooky and a couple of guests such as Caledonian 80/- and Wickwar Cotswold Way on handpump and a dozen wines by the glass; the chocolate labrador is called Cocoa. The simple public bar has darts, pool, a juke box and a TV; background music. There are tables out in the big back garden, with a play area. This is a charming place to stay in pretty bedrooms.

Rewarding food from a seasonal menu includes sandwiches, grilled mackerel with sweet potatoes, onions and horseradish dressing, smoked duck with watermelon and feta salad and raspberry vinaigrette, steak in ale pie, wild mushroom, leek and stilton vol-au-vent with mustard cream sauce, pancetta-wrapped guinea fowl suprême with garlic and thyme jus, bass fillets with ratatouille and salsa verde, and puddings such as chocolate, morello cherry and kirsch trifle and white chocolate and orange cheesecake with orange and cranberry compote; they also offer a two- and three-course set menu at lunch and until 7pm (not weekends). *Benchmark main dish: beer-battered cod and chips £14.00. Two-course evening meal £22.00.*

Cropthorne Inns ~ Manager Lisa Phipps ~ Real ale ~ Open 10-2.30, 6-11; 10am-11pm Fri-Sun ~ Bar food 12-2.30, 6-9; 12-9.30 Fri, Sat; 12-9 Sun ~ Restaurant ~ Children welcome ~ Dogs welcome ~ Wi-fi ~ Bedrooms: £60/£90 *Recommended by Clive and Fran Dutson, Lesley Finch, Martin Cawley, P and J Shapley, Sarah Williamson, Alun and Jennifer Evans, David Jackman*

LOWER BRAILES   SP3139   Map 4
George 🍺
(01608) 685788 – www.georgeinnbrailes.com
B4035 Shipston–Banbury; OX15 5HN

Handsome stone inn dating from the 14th c, cheerful landlord and customers and well liked food; bedrooms

There's a friendly welcome for all in this ancient place – dogs included. The back bar is beamed and panelled and has a cheerful atmosphere helped along by chatty locals. There's also a roomy front bar with dark oak chairs and tables on flagstones and an inglenook fireplace, and a separate restaurant. Hook Norton Hooky, Old Hooky and Lion and a guest on handpump, nine wines by the glass and farm cider; background music, TV, games machine, darts, pool, juke box and board games. Aunt sally and picnic-sets (some blue-painted) in the sizeable and sheltered back garden and on the terrace; a few tables and chairs out in front. The comfortable bedrooms are fair value. Good nearby walks.

Tasty food includes lunchtime sandwiches, chicken liver pâté, smoked fish platter with cucumber and lime dressing, a pie of the day, a changing vegetarian choice, lambs liver and bacon on bubble and squeak, honey-glazed confit duck leg with marmalade sautéed potatoes, beer-battered haddock and chips, and puddings such as hot chocolate fondant and lemon posset. *Benchmark main dish: slow-cooked lamb shoulder £12.95. Two-course evening meal £17.00.*

Free house ~ Licensee Baggy Saunders ~ Real ale ~ Open 12-11 (midnight Fri); 5-11 Mon; 11am-midnight Sat; 12-11 Sun ~ Bar food 12-2.30, 6-9; 12-3.30 Sun; not Sun evening or Mon ~ Restaurant ~ Children welcome but not in bar after 8pm Fri, Sat ~ Dogs allowed in bar and bedrooms ~ Wi-fi ~ Bedrooms: £40/£60 *Recommended by Phoebe Peacock, Peter Brix, JHBS*

PRESTON BAGOT   SP1765   Map 4
Crabmill 🍽️ ♀
(01926) 843342 – www.thecrabmill.co.uk
A4189 Henley-in-Arden to Warwick; B95 5EE

Comfortable décor, open fires and particularly good food and drink in converted mill

Offering impressive food served by courteous staff and a good choice of drinks, this is a rambling old cider mill with a gently civilised atmosphere. It's attractively decorated throughout, with contemporary furnishings and warm colour combinations. The smart two-level lounge has comfortable sofas and chairs, low tables, big table lamps and a couple of rugs on bare boards. The elegant, low-beamed dining area is roomy with caramel leather banquettes and chairs at pine tables, while the beamed and flagstoned bar area has stripped-pine country tables and chairs and snug corners; open fires. From the gleaming metal bar counter they serve Purity Gold and Sharps Atlantic and Doom Bar on handpump and nine wines by the glass; background music. There are plenty of tables (some under cover) in the large, attractive, decked garden.

 Good and highly enjoyable, the food includes crab and prawns with guacamole, tomato, bloody mary mayonnaise and melba toast, lambs kidneys in devilled sauce with bacon and scorched onions, sharing plates, free-range chicken with a carolina-style rub, sweetcorn and sweet potato ragu and pickled red onion, duck breast with ratte potatoes, white beetroot, figs and parsnip and vanilla purée, seared tuna with sicilian caponata, toasted home-made sourdough and balsamic gel, and puddings such as caramel and peanut torte and iced raspberry pavlova. *Benchmark main dish: whole plaice with samphire and hollandaise £15.95. Two-course evening meal £21.00.*

Free house ~ Licensee Sally Coll ~ Real ale ~ Open 11-11; 12-6 Sun ~ Bar food 12-2.30 (3 Fri, Sat), 6.30-9.30; 12-4 Sun ~ Restaurant ~ Children welcome ~ Dogs allowed in bar ~ Wi-fi *Recommended by Mrs Blethyn Elliott, Ian Herdman, Clive and Fran Dutson*

SHIPSTON-ON-STOUR   SP2540   Map 4
Black Horse 🍺
(01608) 238489 – www.blackhorseshipston.com
Station Road (off A3400); CV36 4BT

Character bars in thatched pub with simple country furnishings, well kept ales, an extensive choice of thai food and seats outside

Chocolate-box pretty with flowering baskets and tubs under a heavy thatched roof, this ancient stone tavern has held a pub licence since 1540. Low-beamed, character bars lead off a central entrance passage, with some fine old flagstones and floor tiles, two open fires (one an inglenook), wheelbacks, stools, rustic seats and tables and built-in wall benches, half-panelled or exposed stone walls, and plenty of copper kettles, pans and bed warmers, horse tack and toby jugs. Friendly staff serve Prescott Hill Climb, Purity UBU and Wye Valley Dorothy Goodbody's Golden Ale on handpump and several wines by the glass; TV, darts. The little dining room has pale wooden tables and chairs on bare boards. There are a couple of benches on the front cobbles, contemporary seats and tables on a partly covered raised decked area at the back and picnic-sets on grass.

 The popular food is thai: tom yum soups, steamed dumplings, chicken satay, spicy salads such as seafood, lots of curries, chicken, duck and pork in tamarind, sweet soy and plum sauces, stir-fries and a big choice of dishes with noodles and rice. *Benchmark main dish: thai green curry £7.99. Two-course evening meal £16.50.*

Free house ~ Licensee Gabe Saunders ~ Real ale ~ Open 12-3, 6-11; 6-11 Mon; 12-11 Thurs-Sun ~ Bar food ~ Restaurant ~ Children welcome ~ Dogs allowed in bar ~ Wi-fi *Recommended by Charlie May, Peter Brix*

WELFORD-ON-AVON   SP1452   Map 4
Bell 🎯 🍷 🍺
(01789) 750353 – www.thebellwelford.co.uk
Off B439 W of Stratford; High Street; CV37 8EB

Warwickshire Dining Pub of the Year

Enjoyably civilised pub with appealing ancient interior, good carefully sourced food, a great range of drinks and a pretty garden with table service

This is a special place and our readers love it. The food is excellent, the choice of drinks is thoughtful and the service is first class. The attractive interior – with plenty of signs of the building's venerable age – is divided into five comfortable areas, each with its own character, from the cosy terracotta-painted bar to a light and airy gallery room with antique wood panelling, solid oak floor and contemporary Lloyd Loom chairs. Flagstone floors, stripped or well polished antique or period-style furniture and three good fires (one in an inglenook) add warmth and cosiness. Hobsons Best, Purity Pure Gold and UBU and a guest on handpump and 18 wines (including prosecco and champagne) by the glass. In summer, the virginia creeper-covered exterior is festooned with colourful hanging baskets. The lovely garden has solid teak furniture, a vine-covered terrace, water features and gentle lighting. This riverside village has a handsome church and pretty thatched black and white cottages and is certainly worth exploring.

Using the best local, seasonal produce, the highly enjoyable food includes sandwiches, duck terrine with orange jelly, devilled crab and avocado tian, roasted red onion and goats cheese tart with sweet grape dressing, duck breast with fondant potato and apple marmalade sauce, smoked haddock and chive fishcakes on creamed leeks, guinea fowl with ginger and thyme stuffing, dauphinoise potatoes, redcurrant and port jus and spiced apple chutney, and puddings such as double chocolate, brandy and orange truffle tart and sticky toffee pudding. *Benchmark main dish: rack of lamb with dauphinoise potatoes and red wine jus £17.95. Two-course evening meal £22.00.*

Laurel (Enterprise) ~ Lease Colin and Teresa Ombler ~ Real ale ~ Open 11.30-3, 6-11; 11.30-11.30 Sat; 11.45-10.30 Sun ~ Bar food 11.45-2.30, 6.15-9.30; 11.45-10 Sat; 12-9.30 Sun ~ Children welcome *Recommended by Kim Andrews, Peter Elliott, Ron Corbett, Susan and John Douglas, Hugh Roberts, Joan Cole, Sharon and John Hancock, M G Hart*

Also Worth a Visit in Warwickshire

Besides the fully inspected pubs, you might like to try these pubs that have been recommended to us and described by readers. Do tell us what you think of them: feedback@goodguides.com

ALCESTER   SP0957
Holly Bush (01789) 507370
Henley Street (continuation of High Street towards B4089; not much nearby parking); B49 5QX
Refurbished 17th-c pub now owned by Everards, four of their well kept beers and a couple of guests, two real ciders, enjoyable good value food from sandwiches and platters up, six smallish rooms with simple furniture including pews and wall benches, bare boards, flagstones and carpet, some dark board panelling, log fires; seats outside, closed Mon lunchtime, otherwise open all day (till 9pm Sun). *(Roger and Donna Huggins)*

ALCESTER   SP0857
Turks Head (01789) 765948
High Street, across from church; B49 5AD Nicely updated old town pub with small front room and another off corridor, well kept Wye Valley and three guests, several bottled beers and good choice of wines, enjoyable food (not Sun evening) from

sharing plates and pizzas up including good fish and chips, Sat brunch; free wi-fi; children welcome, tables in walled garden behind, open all day. *(Theocsbrian)*

ALDRIDGE   SK0900
Old Irish Harp (01922) 455968
Chester Road, Little Aston (A452 over Staffordshire border); WS9 0LP Popular modernised pub with good choice of enjoyable food including speciality rotisserie chicken, meal deal Mon-Fri, Banks's Bitter, Jennings Cumberland and Marstons Pedigree, extensive dining area; free wi-fi; children welcome, plenty of seats outside, open all day. *(Clifford Blakemore)*

ALVESTON   SP2356
Ferry (01789) 269883
Ferry Lane; end of village, off B4086 Stratford–Wellesbourne; CV37 7QX Comfortable and stylish beamed dining pub, good imaginative food along with pub favourites and sandwiches, reasonable prices, ales such as Hook Norton, Sharps and Youngs,

friendly staff; nice spot with seats out in front, open all day Sat, closed Sun evening and first Mon of month. *(Mr and Mrs J Watkins)*

ARDENS GRAFTON   SP1153
★**Golden Cross** (01789) 772420
Off A46 or B439 W of Stratford, corner of Wixford Road/Grafton Lane; B50 4LG
Bustling 18th-c stone pub with friendly relaxed beamed bar, rugs on dark flagstones, mix of furniture including chapel chairs around kitchen tables, modern local photos, woodburner in big old fireplace, Purity, Charles Wells and a guest, ten wines by the glass, enjoyable food (some served on boards and slates), attractive dining room with unusual coffered ceiling and big mullioned bay window; background and live acoustic music (Thurs), free wi-fi; children and dogs (in bar) welcome, picnic-sets in good-sized, neatly planted back garden with heated terrace, nice views, open (and food) all day weekends. *(R T and J C Moggridge, Michael Butler, Stanley and Annie Matthews, Sharon and John Hancock)*

BARFORD   SP2660
★**Granville** (01926) 624236
1.7 miles from M40 junction 15; A429 S (Wellesbourne Road); CV35 8DS
Friendly village pub with good mix of diners and drinkers; attractively decorated with sage green paintwork, pale wooden tables and chairs on floorboards, comfortable leather sofas by open fire, more formal raftered and stripped-brick restaurant, well kept Fullers, Hook Norton and Purity, 13 wines by the glass, good food (not Sun evening); free wi-fi; children and dogs welcome, floodlit back terrace with tables under big retractable awnings, disabled parking (wheelchair access from side entrance), open all day weekends. *(Simon and Mandy King, Dennis and Doreen Haward, Dr and Mrs A K Clarke, Brian Glozier)*

BARSTON   SP2078
★**Bulls Head** (01675) 442830
From M42 junction 5, A4141 towards Warwick, first left, then signed down Barston Lane; B92 0JU Unassuming and unspoilt partly Tudor village pub, four well kept ales such as Adnams, Purity, Woodfordes and Wye Valley, popular traditional home-made food from sandwiches to specials, friendly helpful staff, log fires, comfortable lounge with pictures and plates, oak-beamed bar and separate dining room; children and dogs allowed, good-sized secluded garden alongside pub and barn, open all day Fri-Sun, no food Sun evening. *(Clive and Fran Dutson)*

BINLEY WOODS   SP3977
Roseycombe (024) 7654 1022
Rugby Road; CV3 2AY Warm and friendly 1930s pub with wide choice of bargain home-made food, Bass and Theakstons; Weds quiz night, some live music; children

welcome, large garden. *(Alan Johnson, Roger and Donna Huggins)*

BIRMINGHAM   SP0788
★**Bartons Arms** (0121) 333 5988
High Street, Aston (A34); B6 4UP
Magnificent Edwardian landmark, an oasis in a rather daunting area, impressive linked richly decorated rooms from the palatial to the snug, original tilework murals, stained glass and mahogany, decorative fireplaces, sweeping stairs to handsome upstairs rooms, well kept Oakham ales and a guest from ornate island bar with snob screens in one section, interesting imported bottled beers and frequent mini beer festivals, nice choice of well priced thai food, good young staff; open all day. *(Charlie May)*

BIRMINGHAM   SP0688
Lord Clifden (0121) 523 7515
Great Hampton Street (Jewellery Quarter); B18 6AA Fairly traditional with leather banquettes and padded stools around dimpled copper-top tables, bustling atmosphere, wide choice of good value generous food from sandwiches to daily specials, Wye Valley and guests, continental beers, prompt friendly service, interesting collection of street art including Banksy's, darts in front bare-boards section; sports TVs (outside too), Thurs quiz night and weekend DJs; plenty of seats in enclosed part-covered beer garden with table tennis and table football, open all day (till late Fri, Sat). *(John Harris)*

BIRMINGHAM   SP0786
Old Contemptibles (0121) 236 5264
Edmund Street; B3 2HB Spacious well restored Edwardian corner pub with lofty ceiling and lots of woodwork, decent choice of real ales (customers vote for guest beers), enjoyable well priced food including range of sausages and pies, friendly efficient young staff; upstairs lavatories; no children, handy central location, popular at lunchtime with office workers, open all day (till 6pm Sun). *(Alan Johnson)*

BIRMINGHAM   SP0784
Old Moseley Arms (0121) 440 1954
Tindal Street; B12 9QU Tucked-away Victorian pub with four well kept ales including Enville and Wye Valley (regular festivals), keenly priced indian snacks and full meals (all day Sun); sports TV, juke box, live music Sun; outside seating area, handy for Edgbaston cricket ground, open all day. *(Chris and Angela Buckell)*

BIRMINGHAM   SP0686
Pennyblacks (0121) 632 1460
Mailbox shopping mall, Wharfside Street; B1 1RQ Contemporary bar in good canalside spot; spacious well divided interior including some booth seating, wall paintings and neon, three real ales, plenty of wines

and cocktails, enjoyable food; DJ nights, Sky Sports, free wi-fi; seats out by water, open all day till late. *(Phoebe Peacock)*

BIRMINGHAM   SP0686
Post Office Vaults (0121) 643 7354
New Street/Pinfold Street; B2 4BA
Two entrances to this simple downstairs bar with 13 interesting ciders/perries, eight real ales including Hobsons and Salopian and over 300 international bottled beers, friendly knowledgeable staff, no food but can bring your own (plates and cutlery supplied); handy for New Street station, open all day. *(Mike and Eleanor Anderson, Tony and Wendy Hobden)*

BIRMINGHAM   SP0687
Rose Villa (0121) 236 7910
By clock in Jewellery Quarter (Warstone Lane/Vyse Street); B18 6JW Listed 1920s building with panelled front saloon leading through to small but magnificent bar, floor-to-ceiling green tiles and massive tiled arch over fireplace, original parquet flooring and impressive stained glass, quirky touches such as antler chandeliers and a red phone box, four or five well kept ales including Sharps Doom Bar, cocktails, reasonably priced food from american diner menu; live music and DJs Fri, Sat till late – can get very busy; open all day, from 11am weekends for brunch. *(John Harris)*

BIRMINGHAM   SP0686
★ Wellington (0121) 200 3115
Bennetts Hill; B2 5SN Old-fashioned high-ceilinged pub with superb range of changing beers (listed on TV screens – order by number), most from small breweries and always one from Black Country Ales, also farm ciders, experienced landlord, friendly staff and nice pub cat, no food but plates and cutlery if you bring your own, regular beer festivals and quiz nights, can get very busy; tables out behind, open all day. *(Alan Johnson, Tony and Wendy Hobden)*

BRIERLEY HILL   SO9286
★ Vine (01384) 78293
B4172 between A461 and (nearer) A4100; immediately after the turn into Delph Road; DY5 2TN Popular Black Country pub (aka the Bull & Bladder) offering a true taste of the West Midlands; down-to-earth welcome and friendly chatty locals in meandering series of rooms, each different in character, traditional front bar with wall benches, comfortable extended snug with solidly built red plush seats, tartan-decorated back bar, well kept and priced Bathams from brewery next door, a couple of simple very cheap lunchtime dishes (no

credit cards); TV, games machine, darts and dominoes; children and dogs welcome, tables in backyard, open all day. *(Charlie May)*

BROOM   SP0853
Broom Tavern (01789) 773666
High Street; off B439 in Bidford; B50 4HL Spacious 16th-c brick and timber village pub, relaxed and welcoming, with good interesting food from chef-owners, four well kept ales such as North Cotswold, Purity, Sharps and Wye Valley, well balanced wine list with several by the glass, good attentive (but not intrusive) service, main room divided into two parts, one with cottage-style tables and chairs, the other with oak furniture, black beams and log fire, also a snug perfect for a group of diners; Mon quiz; children welcome, tables out on grass either side, handy for Ragley Hall, open all day weekends. *(Clive and Fran Dutson, Stanley and Annie Matthews)*

CLAVERDON   SP2064
★ Red Lion (01926) 842291
Station Road; B4095 towards Warwick; CV35 8PE Popular beamed Tudor dining pub with good food (all day Sun) from pub favourites up, friendly attentive service, decent wines and well kept Hook Norton Lion, log fires, linked rooms including back dining area with country views over sheltered heated deck and gardens; open all day. *(Peter Brix)*

COVENTRY   SP3279
Old Windmill (024) 7625 1717
Spon Street; CV1 3BA Friendly 15th-c pub with lots of tiny rooms (known locally as Ma Brown's), exposed beams in uneven ceilings, inglenook woodburner, half a dozen well kept ales including Theakstons, Timothy Taylors and Wychwood, good local pork pies; live music, juke box and games machines, darts; closed Mon lunchtime, otherwise open all day (till 1am Fri, Sat), busy at weekends. *(Charlie May)*

COVENTRY   SP3379
Town Wall (024) 7622 0963
Bond Street, among car parks behind Belgrade Theatre; CV1 4AH Busy Victorian city-centre local with half a dozen well kept ales including Adnams and Bass, Weston's cider, enjoyable food (not Sun evening, Mon) from lunchtime sandwiches to hearty dishes such as rabbit pie, unspoilt basic front bar and tiny snug, engraved windows, bigger back lounge with actor/playwright photographs and pictures of old Coventry, open fires; big-screen sports TV; no children, open all day. *(Ian Barritt, Alan Johnson)*

Places with gardens or terraces usually let children sit there – we note in the text the very few exceptions that don't.

COVENTRY SP3378
Whitefriars (024) 7625 1655
Gosford Street; CV1 5DL Pair of well
preserved medieval townhouses, three
old-fashioned rooms on both floors, lots
of ancient beams, timbers and furniture,
flagstones, cobbles and coal fire, five
well kept changing ales, bar lunches (not
weekends); some live music; no children
inside unless eating, smokers' shelter on
good-sized back terrace, open all day
(1am Fri, Sat). *(Alan Johnson)*

DUDLEY SO9591
Bottle & Glass
*Black Country Museum, Tipton Road;
DY1 4SQ* Reconstructed alehouse moved
here as were other buildings in this extensive
open-air working museum (well worth a visit
for its re-created period village complete
with shops, fairground, school, barge wharf
and tram system); friendly staff in costume,
three well kept local beers, chunky filled
rolls, front parlour and back room with
piano, wall benches, sawdust on old boards,
two fires. *(Peter Brix)*

DUNCHURCH SP4871
Green Man (01788) 810210
Daventry Road; CV22 6NS Small beamed
village local with enjoyable home-made food
at reasonable prices, four well kept beers
such as Greene King, St Austell, Timothy
Taylors and Charles Wells, decent wines by
the glass, good friendly service, open fire,
pool; children welcome, picnic-sets and
play area on back lawn, bedrooms.
(Phoebe Peacock)

EASENHALL SP4679
★Golden Lion (01788) 833577
Main Street; CV23 0JA Spotless bar
in 16th-c part of busy comfortable hotel,
white-painted beams, half-panelling and
log fire, some original wattle and daub and
fine 17th-c carved bench depicting the 12
apostles, up to four well kept changing ales
(usually one from Charles Wells), enjoyable
bar food including good Sun carvery, friendly
helpful service, more formal restaurant;
background music; children and small dogs
welcome, disabled access/loos, tables on
side terrace and spacious lawn, 20 well
equipped bedrooms (some with four posters),
attractive village, open all day, food all day
weekends. *(Gerry and Rosemary Dobson,
M J Winterton, Simon Le Fort)*

EDGE HILL SP3747
★Castle (01295) 670255
Off A422; OX15 6DJ Curious crenellated
octagonal tower built 1742 as gothic folly
(marks where Charles I raised his standard
at start of Battle of Edgehill); major revamp
creating bar and four dining areas, plenty
of original features including arched
windows and doorways, beams and stone
fireplaces, fantastic views (some floor-
to-ceiling windows), good food (not Sun
evening), deli bar for sandwiches, coffee and
afternoon teas, well kept Hook Norton ales,
friendly enthusiastic young staff; downstairs
lavatories; children welcome, seats in lovely
big garden with more outstanding views,
beautiful Compton Wynyates nearby, four
refurbished tower bedrooms, open all day
Sat, till 7pm Sun. *(Susan and John Douglas,
G Jennings)*

ETTINGTON SP2748
★Chequers (01789) 740387
Banbury Road (A422); CV37 7SR
Good enterprising food is the main draw
here, but they do keep Butcombe, Greene
King, Purity and a decent range of wines
by the glass; bar and restaurant areas with
variety of comfortable and rather elegant
dining chairs, big mirrors, a piano and
richly figured velvet curtains and wall
hangings, good service and relaxed friendly
atmosphere; background music, free
wi-fi; children and dogs (in bar) welcome,
sheltered back garden with picnic-sets on
lawn and stylish furniture on terrace, open
all day Sat, till 6pm Sun, closed Mon.
*(Emma Scofield, Caroline Prescott, K H Frostick,
Dr and Mrs A K Clarke)*

FARNBOROUGH SP4349
★Inn at Farnborough (01295) 690615
Off A423 N of Banbury; OX17 1DZ
Golden-stone dining pub in NT village; cosy
right-hand bar with beams, flagstones and
stripped stone walls, bucket armchairs with
scatter cushions, window seats, log fire,
Purity Gold and UBU, good wines by the
glass, well liked food from interesting if not
particularly cheap menu, compact two-room
dining area divided by double aspect
fireplace, book wallpaper and mix of tables
and chairs; background music, free wi-fi;
children and dogs (in bar) welcome, neat
sloping garden with blue picnic-sets and
canopied decked area, local walks, not much
parking nearby, open all day weekends,
closed Tues-Thurs lunchtime. *(R Anderson,
Geoff and Linda Payne)*

FENNY COMPTON SP4152
Merrie Lion (01295) 771134
Brook Street; CV47 2YH Spotless early
18th-c beamed village pub; three well kept
beers including one badged for them, decent
range of wines and good freshly made food
from pubby choices up, friendly welcoming
atmosphere; tables outside, handy for Burton
Dassett Hills Country Park, open all day
weekends. *(Sharon and John Hancock)*

FILLONGLEY SP2787
Cottage (01676) 540599
Black Hall Lane; CV7 8EG Popular
country dining pub on village outskirts,
good value fairly traditional food including
early bird and OAP deals, beers such as

Marstons, St Austell and Timothy Taylors, friendly caring service; back terrace and lawn overlooking fields, closes Sun evening at 6pm. *(Graham and Elizabeth Hargreaves)*

FIVE WAYS   SP2270
⭐**Case is Altered** (01926) 484206
Follow Rowington signs at junction roundabout off A4177/A4141 N of Warwick, then right into Case Lane; CV35 7JD Convivial unspoilt old cottage licensed for over three centuries; Old Pie Factory, Wye Valley and three guests served by friendly long-serving landlady, no food, simple small main bar with fine old poster of Lucas, Blackwell & Arkwright Brewery (now flats), clock with hours spelling out Thornleys Ale (another defunct brewery), and just a few sturdy old-fashioned tables and couple of stout leather-covered settles facing each other over spotless tiles, modest little back room with old bar billiards table (it takes sixpences); no children, dogs or mobiles; full disabled access, stone table on little brick courtyard, open all day Sun till 7.30pm. *(Kerry Law)*

FLECKNOE   SP5163
Old Olive Bush (01788) 891134
Off A425 W of Daventry; CV23 8AT Unspoilt little Edwardian pub in quiet photogenic village, friendly chatty atmosphere, enjoyable traditional food cooked by landlady, well kept changing ales and decent wines, open fire in bar with stripped-wood floor, steps up to games room with table skittles, small dining room with etched-glass windows and another fire; Thurs quiz; children welcome, pretty garden, closed Mon, weekday lunchtimes. *(Peter Brix)*

FRANKTON   SP4270
Friendly (01926) 632430
Just over a mile S of B4453 Leamington Spa–Rugby; Main Street; CV23 9NY Popular 16th-c village pub living up to its name, four well kept ales and good traditional home-made food, two low-ceilinged rooms, open fire; quiz last Thurs of month; open all day weekends, closed Mon lunchtime. *(Charlie May)*

GREAT WOLFORD   SP2434
⭐**Fox & Hounds** (01608) 674220
Village signed on right on A3400, 3 miles S of Shipston-on-Stour; CV36 5NQ This delightful unspoilt 16th-c inn was about to reopen under new owners as we went to press – reports please; inglenook log fire with bread oven, low beams and appealing collection of old furniture including tall pews on flagstones, has served Hook Norton, Purity and a guest from old-fashioned tap room,

food has also been good; outside lavatories; terrace with solid wooden furniture and well. *(Clive and Fran Dutson)*

HALFORD   SP2645
Halford (01789) 748217
A429 Fosse Way; CV36 5BN Cotswold-stone inn handy if walking Fosse Way; pastel-walled bar on right of cobbled entry with lattice-decorated dining chairs around chunky tables, bay window seats and leather sofa by woodburner, Hook Norton Old Hooky and St Austell Tribute, well liked generously served food, unusual rustic benches and table in back room, partly flagstoned restaurant on left with dark wooden tables and chairs and another fire; background music; teak furniture in spacious old coachyard, water feature and contemporary ironwork, 11 comfortable modern bedrooms, open all day. *(K H Frostick)*

HARBORNE   SP0384
Plough (0121) 427 3678
High Street; B17 9NT Popular quirky place with enjoyable range of food including stone-baked pizzas and chargrilled burgers, regular offers, well kept Purity, Wye Valley and a guest, plenty of wines by the glass and some 50 whiskies, good coffee too; background music; well behaved children welcome, garden with covered area, open all day from 8am (9am weekends) for breakfast. *(John Harris)*

HARBOROUGH MAGNA   SP4779
Old Lion (01788) 833238
3 miles from M6 junction 1; B4112 Pailton Road; CV23 0HQ Welcoming stylishly updated village pub, emphasis on enjoyable home-cooked food from pub favourites and stone-baked pizzas to steaks, friendly attentive staff, Greene King ales and nice choice of wines; children welcome, closed Mon lunchtime, otherwise open all day. *(Peter Brix)*

HARBURY   SP3759
Gamecock (01926) 258859
Chapel Street; CV33 9HT Revamped village pub with well kept Brakspears and a couple of guests, Symond's and Thatcher's ciders and excellent choice of wines by the glass, good traditional food but also deli boards/tapas, friendly helpful staff; children welcome, garden, open all day weekends, closed weekday lunchtimes. *(Sharon and John Hancock)*

HATTON   SP2367
⭐**Falcon** (01926) 484281
Birmingham Road, Haseley (A4177, not far from M40 junction 15); CV35 7HA

If you report on a pub that's not a featured entry, please tell us any lunchtimes or evenings when it doesn't serve bar food.

Smartly updated dining pub with relaxing rooms around island bar, lots of stripped brickwork and low beams, tiled and oak-planked floors, good moderately priced food (not Sun evening) from sandwiches and pub favourites up, lunchtime/early evening deal Mon-Fri, friendly service, nice choice of wines by the glass, well kept Marstons-related ales, barn-style back restaurant; children welcome, disabled facilities, garden (dogs allowed here) with heated covered terrace, eight bedrooms in converted barn, open all day. *(John Harris)*

HENLEY-IN-ARDEN   SP1566
★ **Bluebell** (01564) 793049
High Street (A3400, off M40 junction 16); B95 5AT Impressive timber-framed dining pub with fine coach entrance, well liked imaginative food (not Sun evening) served by cheerful helpful staff, rambling old beamed and flagstoned interior with contemporary furnishings creating a stylish but relaxed atmosphere, big fireplace, well kept ales such as Church End and Purity, 20 wines by the glass, good coffee and afternoon teas, daily papers; may be background music; children welcome if eating, dogs allowed, tables on back decking, open till 7.30pm Sun, closed Mon, otherwise open all day. *(Ian Herdman)*

HIMLEY   SO8791
Himley House (01902) 892468
Stourbridge Road (A449); DY3 4LD Big Chef & Brewer in handsome Georgian building (former lodge for Himley Hall), wide choice of popular well cooked food including deals, up to four real ales such as Enville and Hobsons Town Crier, nice dining area opening on to lawned garden; children welcome, bedrooms (some with four-posters), open (and food) all day. *(Paul and Sue Merrick)*

ILMINGTON   SP2143
★ **Howard Arms** (01608) 682226
Village signed with Wimpstone off A3400 S of Stratford; CV36 4LT Golden-stone inn by village green, several beamed rooms with nice mix of furniture from pews and rustic stools to leather dining chairs around all sorts of tables, fine old flagstones, bare boards and rugs, prints on gold-painted walls, shelves of books, candles, log fire in big inglenook, Hook Norton, North Cotswold, Timothy Taylors and Wye Valley beers, 30 wines by the glass and a dozen malt whiskies, good imaginative freshly made food (all day Sun till 8pm), friendly attentive service; background music, free wi-fi; children and dogs (in bar) welcome, picnic-sets under parasols and colourful herbaceous border

in big back garden, nearby hill walks, comfortable bedrooms, open all day. *(Mr and Mrs A H Young, Susan and John Douglas, Alan Clark, Bernard Stradling)*

ILMINGTON   SP2143
Red Lion (01608) 682366
Front Street; CV36 4LX Popular stone-built village pub, flagstoned bar with fire on one side of central servery, dining room the other, well kept Hook Norton and good nicely presented food cooked by landlady; secluded garden. *(K H Frostick)*

KENILWORTH   SP2872
Clarendon Arms (01926) 852017
Castle Hill; CV8 1NB Busy pub opposite castle and under same ownership as next-door Harringtons restaurant; well kept Hook Norton, Sharps, Wye Valley and a local guest, tasty reasonably priced pub food, several rooms off long bare-boards bustling bar, largish peaceful upstairs dining room, cheerful young staff; children welcome, dogs in bar, metal tables on small raised terrace, daytime car park fee deducted from food bill, open all day Fri-Sun. *(Alan Johnson, Tony and Wendy Hobden)*

KENILWORTH   SP2872
Cross (01926) 853840
New Street; CV8 2EZ Smart 19th-c Michelin-starred restaurant-pub with skilfully cooked classy food (not cheap), set lunch Tues-Sat, 18 wines by the glass and a couple of ales including Charles Wells Bombardier, open-plan split-level interior with view into kitchen, front bar for drinkers; terrace and small garden, closed Mon, otherwise open all day, no food Sun evening. *(Clive and Fran Dutson)*

KENILWORTH   SP2871
Queen & Castle (01926) 852661
Castle Green; CV8 1ND Modernised beamed Mitchells & Butlers dining pub opposite castle, good range of enjoyable food including weekday set menu (till 6pm), plenty of wines by the glass; children welcome, open all day. *(Christopher and Elise Way)*

KENILWORTH   SP2872
★ **Virgins & Castle** (01926) 853737
High Street; CV8 1LY Maze of intimate rooms off inner servery, small snugs by entrance corridor, flagstones, heavy beams, lots of woodwork including booth seating, coal fire, four well kept Everards ales and a couple of guests, good food at reasonable prices, friendly service, restaurant, games bar upstairs; children in eating areas, disabled

---

The letters and figures after the name of each town are its Ordnance Survey map reference. *Using the Guide* at the beginning of the book explains how it helps you find a pub, in road atlases or large-scale maps as well as in our own maps.

facilities, tables in sheltered garden, parking can be a problem, open all day. *(Dr D J and Mrs S C Walker, Dr and Mrs A K Clarke)*

LADBROKE   SP4158
Bell (01926) 811224

Signed off A423 S of Southam; CV47 2BY Refurbished beamed country pub set back from the road, smallish bar with tub chairs by log fire, snug off with library wallpaper and another fire in little brick fireplace, three ales including Ringwood and plenty of wines by the glass, enjoyable food from pub favourites and grills up, weekday set menu, airy restaurant with light oak flooring, good friendly service; background music, free wi-fi; children and dogs (in bar) welcome, a few picnic-sets out in front and on side grass, pleasant surroundings, closed Sun evening, Mon. *(John Marshall)*

LAPWORTH   SP1871
★ **Boot** (01564) 782464

Old Warwick Road; B4439 Hockley Heath–Warwick – 2.8 miles from M40 junction 1, but from southbound carriageway only, and return only to northbound; B94 6JU Popular upmarket dining pub near Stratford Canal, good range of food from interesting menu including weekday fixed-price offer, efficient cheerful young staff, upscale wines, Purity UBU and St Austell Tribute, stripped beams and dark panelling, big antique hunting prints, cushioned pews and bucket chairs on ancient quarry tiles and bare boards, warm fire, charming low-raftered upstairs dining room; background music; children and good-natured dogs welcome, teak tables, some under extendable canopy on side terrace, and picnic-sets on grass beyond, nice walks, open all day. *(R L Borthwick)*

LAPWORTH   SP1970
Navigation (01564) 783337

Old Warwick Road (B4439 SE); B94 6NA Renovated beamed pub by the Grand Union Canal; slate-floor bar with woodburner, bare-boards snug and restaurant, well kept ales such as Byatts, Purity, Timothy Taylors, Thwaites and Wadworths, unusually Guinness also on handpump, decent wines and reasonably priced food (all day Fri-Sun) from sandwiches and other bar choices up, friendly hard-working staff; children welcome, dogs in bar, covered terrace and waterside garden, handy for Packwood House and Baddesley Clinton (both NT), open all day. *(W M Lien, Clive and Fran Dutson)*

LAPWORTH   SP1872
Punch Bowl (01564) 784564

Not far from M42 junction 4, off old Warwick–Hockley Heath Road; B94 6HR Completely reconstructed using old beams etc, main emphasis on dining with good range of well presented interesting food from lunchtime sandwiches/panini and light

---

dishes up, stools along bar for drinkers, Greene King IPA and Wells Bombardier, friendly efficient staff; garden picnic-sets, open all day. *(John Harris)*

LEAMINGTON SPA   SP3165
Cricketers Arms (01926) 881293

Archery Road; CV31 3PT Friendly town local opposite bowling greens; enjoyable fairly priced food using meat from good local butcher, popular Sun roasts (till 6pm), also nice home-made sausage rolls and scotch eggs, well kept Slaughterhouse and a couple of guests such as Timothy Taylors from central bar, Weston's cider, comfortable banquettes, some panelling and cricketing memorabilia, open fires; darts, sports TV, fortnightly quiz Mon; children and dogs welcome, heated back terrace, open all day. *(Tony and Wendy Hobden)*

LEEK WOOTTON   SP2868
Anchor (01926) 853355

Warwick Road; CV35 7QX Neat and well run dining lounge popular for its good fresh food including fish specials, well kept Hook Norton, Purity and two guests, good selection of affordably priced wines and soft drinks, attentive friendly service, lots of close-set tables, smaller overflow dining area; background music, sports TV; children welcome, no dogs inside, long garden behind with play area, open all day Sun. *(Ian Herdman)*

LIGHTHORNE   SP3455
Antelope (01926) 651188

Old School Lane, Bishops Hill; a mile SW of B4100 N of Banbury; CV35 0AU Attractive early 18th-c stone pub in pretty village setting, two neatly kept comfortable bars (one old, one newer), separate dining area, beams, flagstones and big open fire, well kept Greene King IPA , Sharps Doom Bar and a couple of guests, enjoyable food from good sandwiches up, friendly effective service; children welcome, picnic-sets out by well and on small grassy area, open all day Fri-Sun. *(Clive and Fran Dutson)*

LITTLE COMPTON   SP2530
★ **Red Lion** (01608) 674397

Off A44 Moreton-in-Marsh to Chipping Norton; GL56 0RT Thriving low-beamed 16th-c Cotswold-stone inn, enjoyable good value food cooked by landlady from pubby choices up, Donnington ales and good choice of wines by the glass, snug alcoves, inglenook woodburner; darts and pool in public bar; well behaved children and dogs welcome, pretty side garden with aunt sally, two nice bedrooms. *(K H Frostick)*

LONG ITCHINGTON   SP4165
Buck & Bell (01926) 811177

A423 N of Southam; The Green; CV47 9PH Attractively laid-out dining pub with plenty of character in several linked rambling areas, good choice of food including lunchtime set menu, decent wines by the glass and well kept Banks's, Marstons, Sharps and a guest, efficient staff, big log fireplaces, hunting prints and interesting variety of seating around cast-iron-framed tables, elegantly furnished flagstoned restaurant, stairs up to carpeted gallery; background music; tables on back verandah, more in front looking across village green and rookery, open all day. *(Clive and Fran Dutson, Dru and Louisa Marshall, George Atkinson)*

LOWER GORNAL
SO9191
Fountain (01384) 242777
Temple Street; DY3 2PE Lively two-room local with eight well kept ales including Greene King, Hobsons and RCH, draught continentals, real ciders and country wines, enjoyable inexpensive food (not Sun evening), back dining area; background music; garden behind, open all day. *(Charlie May)*

LOWSONFORD
SP1868
Fleur de Lys (01564) 782431
Off B4439 Hockley Heath–Warwick; Lapworth Street; B95 5HJ Prettily placed by Stratford Canal, linked beamed rooms of different sizes, log fires, good fairly priced food including range of pies, Greene King Abbot, IPA and a guest, plenty of wines by the glass, cocktails, friendly helpful staff; children welcome, large waterside garden, open (and food) all day. *(Chris Sallnow)*

LYE
SO9284
★Windsor Castle (01384) 897809
Stourbridge Road (corner A458/A4036; car park in Pedmore Road just above traffic lights – don't be tempted to use the next-door restaurant's parking!); DY9 7DG Interesting well kept beers from impressive row of handpumps including own Sadlers ales (brewery tours available); central flagstoned part with bar stools by counter and window shelf overlooking road, several snugger rooms off, some brewing memorabilia, enjoyable home-cooked food (not Sun evening) from deli boards up, friendly service; children and dogs welcome, disabled facilities, terrace and verandah seating, four bedrooms, handy for Lye station, open all day. *(Peter Brix)*

MONKS KIRBY
SP4682
Bell (01788) 832352
Just off B4027 W of Pailton; CV23 0QY Popular pub run by hospitable long-serving spanish landlord; lived-in interior with dark beams, timber dividers, flagstones and cobbles, wide choice of good spanish food including starters doubling as tapas, fine range of spanish wines and plenty of malt whiskies and brandies, two well kept Greene King ales, relaxed informal service;

appropriate background music; children and dogs welcome, streamside back terrace with country view, closed Mon. *(Susan and John Douglas)*

NAPTON
SP4560
Folly (01926) 815185
Off A425 towards Priors Hardwick; Folly Lane, by locks; CV47 8NZ Popular beamed red-brick pub in lovely spot on Oxford Canal by Napton Locks and Folly Bridge (113): three bars on different levels, mix of furnishings and two big fireplaces (one with woodburner), lots of interesting bric-a-brac, pictures and old framed photographs, good straightforward home-made food (not Sun evening), well kept ales including Hook Norton, friendly efficient staff; children and dogs welcome. *(Clive and Fran Dutson, Adrian Johnson)*

NETHER WHITACRE
SP2292
Gate (01675) 481292
Gate Lane; B46 2DS Welcoming traditional community pub, seven well kept Marstons-related ales and good honest local food, different rooms reflecting generations of expansion and change, conservatory, games room with pool; children and dogs (in bar) welcome, garden picnic-sets, open all day. *(Dave Bell)*

NETHERTON
SO9488
★Old Swan (01384) 253075
Halesowen Road (A459 just S of centre); DY2 9PY Victorian tavern full of traditional character and known locally as Ma Pardoe's after a former long-serving landlady; wonderfully unspoilt front bar with big swan centrepiece in patterned enamel ceiling, engraved mirrors, traditional furnishings and old-fashioned cylinder stove, other rooms including cosy back snug and more modern lounge, good value own-brewed ales, wholesome bar food, upstairs restaurant; no under-16s, dogs allowed in bar, open all day. *(Phoebe Peacock)*

NEWBOLD ON STOUR
SP2446
White Hart (01789) 450205
A3400 S of Stratford; CV37 8TS Welcoming dining pub in same family for many years, proper pubby atmosphere, with enjoyable varied home-made food (not always Sun evening) including specials board, Adnams Southwold and Purity Mad Goose, nice wines, long airy beamed bar with good log fire in large stone fireplace, flagstones and big bay windows, back bar and separate dining room; pool, darts and ring the bull; children and dogs welcome, picnic-sets out at front and on back lawned area, open all day weekends. *(Lois Dyer)*

OFFCHURCH
SP3665
★Stag (01926) 425801
N of Welsh Road, off A425 at Radford Semele; CV33 9AQ Popular 16th-c

thatched and beamed village pub, oak-floored bar with log fires, ales such as Purity and Warwickshire, a dozen wines by the glass, good interesting food served by friendly efficient young staff, more formal cosy restaurant areas with bold wallpaper, striking fabrics, animal heads and big mirrors; children welcome, dogs in bar, nice garden with rattan-style furniture on terrace, open all day. *(Roy Shutz)*

OLD HILL   SO9686
Waterfall (0121) 561 3499
Waterfall Lane; B64 6RG Friendly unpretentious two-room local, well kept Bathams, Holdens and several guests, straightforward low-priced home-made food, tankards and jugs hanging from boarded ceiling; dogs welcome, seats on small raised front area and in back garden, open all day. *(Dave Braisted)*

OXHILL   SP3149
★Peacock (01295) 688060
Off A422 Stratford–Banbury; CV35 0QU Popular pleasantly upgraded stone-built country pub, good varied menu including blackboard specials and gluten-free choices, friendly attentive young staff, house beer from Wychwood and a couple of guests, good selection of wines by the glass, cosy beamed bar with big solid tables and woodburner, half-panelled bare-boards dining room; light background music; children and dogs (in bar) welcome, nice back garden, pretty village, open all day. *(George Atkinson, Clive and Fran Dutson)*

PRINCETHORPE   SP4070
Three Horseshoes (01926) 632345
High Town; junction A423/B4453; CV23 9PR Friendly old beamed village pub with Marstons EPA and Pedigree and Charles Wells Bombardier, enjoyable traditional food including children's choices, good service, decorative plates, pictures, comfortable settles and chairs, two restaurant areas; free wi-fi; big garden with terrace and play area, five bedrooms, open all day Fri-Sun. *(Alan Johnson, Shaun Mahoney)*

PRIORS MARSTON   SP4857
Holly Bush (01327) 260934
Off A361 S of Daventry; Holly Bush Lane; CV47 7RW 16th-c pub with beams, flagstones and lots of stripped stone in rambling linked rooms, log fire and woodburners, enjoyable well presented food (not Sun evening) including pizzas and popular Tues steak night, St Austell Tribute, Sharps Doom Bar and a couple of guests, friendly if not always speedy service; darts, free wi-fi; children welcome, dogs in

bar, terrace and sheltered garden (summer barbecues), June beer and music festival, open all day Sun till 8pm, closed Mon. *(Alan Johnson)*

RATLEY   SP3847
Rose & Crown (01295) 678148
Off A422 NW of Banbury; OX15 6DS Ancient golden-stone village pub, charming and cosy, with five well kept changing ales (St Austell Tribute and Charles Wells Bombardier feature regularly), enjoyable good value food from ciabattas up, friendly staff, carpeted black-beamed bar with woodburner each end, traditional furniture and window seats, cosy snug; background and some live music, darts; children, walkers and dogs welcome, tables on sunny split-level terrace, aunt sally, near lovely church in sleepy village, handy for Upton House (NT), closed Mon lunchtime. *(JHBS, John Allman)*

ROWINGTON   SP1969
Tom o' the Wood (01564) 782252
Off B4439 N of Rowington, following Lowsonford sign; Finwood Road; CV35 7DH Spaciously modernised and extended canalside pub, good home-cooked food (not Sun evening) from sharing baskets and stone-baked pizzas up, well kept Greene King IPA and a guest, Weston's Rosie's Pig cider, friendly staff and pub labrador (Boris), conservatory; live music Fri; children and dogs welcome, tables on terrace and side lawn, open all day (Sun till 8pm). *(Nigel and Sue Foster)*

RUGBY   SP5075
Merchants (01788) 571119
Little Church Street; CV21 3AN Open-plan pub tucked away near main shopping area, cheerfully busy, with nine quickly changing ales (some unusual for the area), real ciders and huge selection of belgian and other bottled imports, regular beer/cider festivals, shortish choice of low-priced food including speciality fish and chips, quite dark inside with beams, bare boards and mat-covered flagstones, lots of interesting breweriana; background music (live Tues), quiz late Mon of month, sports TVs; open all day, till 1am Fri, Sat. *(George Atkinson)*

RUGBY   SP5075
Seven Stars (01788) 546611
Albert Square; CV21 2SH Traditionally refurbished 19th-c red-brick local with great choice of ales including B&T and Everards, personable landlord and friendly staff, main bar, lounge, snug and conservatory; some outside seating, open all day. *(John Harris)*

Ring the bull is an ancient pub game – you try to lob a ring on a piece of string over a hook (occasionally a bull's horn) on a wall or ceiling.

RUSHALL   SK03001
Manor Arms (01922) 642333
Park Road, off A461; WS4 1LG
Interesting low-beamed 18th-c pub (on much
older foundations) by Rushall Canal, three
rooms in contrasting styles, one with big
inglenook, good value simple food including
generous sandwiches, friendly staff, well
kept Banks's ales from pumps fixed to
the wall (there's no counter); waterside
garden, moorings, by Park Lime Pits nature
reserve. *(James Simister)*

SAMBOURNE   SP0561
Green Dragon (01527) 892465
Village signed off A448; B96 6NU
Early 18th-c pub opposite village green, low-
beamed rooms with flagstones and open fires,
enjoyable fairly straightforward food (not Sun
evening) including deals, well kept Hobsons,
Purity and a guest; children welcome, seats
in courtyard, six bedrooms, closed Sun
evening. *(Peter Brix)*

SEDGLEY   SO9293
★Beacon (01902) 883380
*Bilston Street; A463, off A4123
Wolverhampton–Dudley; DY3 1JE* Plain
old brick pub with own good Sarah Hughes
ales from traditional Victorian tower brewery
behind; cheery locals in simple quarry-tiled
drinking corridor, little snug on left with wall
settles, imposing green-tiled marble fireplace
and glazed serving hatch, old-fashioned
furnishings such as velvet and net curtains,
mahogany tables on patterned carpet, small
landscape prints, sparse tap room on right
with blackened range, dark-panelled lounge
with sturdy red leather wall settles and big
dramatic sea prints, plant-filled conservatory
(no seats), little food apart from cobs; no
credit cards; children allowed in some parts
including garden with play area.
(John Harris)

SHIPSTON-ON-STOUR   SP2540
★Horseshoe (01608) 662190
Church Street; CV36 4AP Pretty 17th-c
timbered coaching inn, friendly and relaxed,
with open-plan carpeted bar, big fireplace,
refurbished restaurant, three ales such as
Sharps, Thwaites and Wye Valley, Hogan's
cider, good reasonably priced food (not Sun
evening); live folk second Tues of month, quiz
third Tues, pub games including aunt sally,
free wi-fi; children and dogs welcome, sunny
back terrace with heated smokers' shelter,
open all day. *(Anon)*

SHIPSTON-ON-STOUR   SP2540
White Bear (01608) 661558
High Street; CV36 4AJ Georgian coaching

inn improved under new family management;
three Donnington ales, decent wines and
well cooked food including good steaks, two
bars (sports TV in one), restaurant; free
wi-fi; garden behind with aunt sally, nine
refurbished bedrooms, open all day. *(JHBS)*

SHUSTOKE   SP2290
★Griffin (01675) 481205
*Church End, a mile E of village; 5 miles
from M6 junction 4; A446 towards
Tamworth, then right on to B4114
straight through Coleshill; B46 2LB*
Unpretentious country local with a dozen
changing ales including own Griffin (brewed
in next-door barn), farm cider and country
wines, may be winter mulled wine, standard
lunchtime bar food (not Sun); cheery
low-beamed L-shaped bar with log fires in
two stone fireplaces (one a big inglenook),
fairly simple décor including cushioned café
seats, elm-topped sewing trestles and a nice
old-fashioned settle, beer mats on ceiling,
conservatory (children allowed here); games
machine; dogs welcome, old-fashioned
seats on back grass with distant views of
Birmingham, large terrace, play area and
summer marquee (live music), camping field,
open all day Sun. *(Anon)*

SHUSTOKE   SP2290
Plough (01675) 481557
B4114 Nuneaton–Coleshill; B46 2AN
Old-fashioned feel with a number of rooms
around the bar, well kept Bass, Black Sheep,
Everards and a guest, good choice of fairly
straightforward food served by friendly
helpful staff, separate dining room, black
beams, open fire and gleaming brass; pool
and darts; seats out at back along with
caged rabbits and exotic birds, open all day
weekends. *(Clive and Fran Dutson)*

STOURBRIDGE   SO9084
Duke William (01384) 440202
Coventry Street; DY8 1EP Friendly
Edwardian corner pub in semi-pedestrianised
area, own Craddocks beers from on-site
microbrewery (tour available) plus guests
and draught/bottled imports, good pie, mash
and peas menu, plenty of events including
music, quiz and film nights (some in upstairs
function room), traditional old black country
atmosphere with long corridor, open fire in
bar and cosy snug; no children, beer garden,
open all day. *(Dave Braisted)*

STOURBRIDGE   SO8983
Plough & Harrow (01384) 397218
Worcester Street; DY8 1AX Friendly
little bay-windowed end of terrace local
(sister to the nearby Duke William), well
kept Craddocks ales and guests, snacky

By law, pubs must show a price list of their drinks. Let us know if you're
inconvenienced by any breach of this law.

food (nothing hot), cosy horseshoe bar with log fires and piano; dogs welcome, partly covered beer garden with woodburner, close to Mary Stevens Park, open all day. *(Dave Braisted)*

STRATFORD-UPON-AVON SP2055
★**Bear** (01789) 265540
Swans Nest Hotel, just off A3400 Banbury Road, by bridge; CV37 7LT Part of the Swans Nest Hotel complex; bar with eight real ales from pewter-topped counter including a house beer brewed by North Cotswold, 26 wines by the glass and several malt whiskies, good value popular food (all day weekends), professional service, two traditional linked rooms with china and other bric-a-brac on delft shelf above panelling, a couple of wing armchairs by fire and variety of other seating including sofas, scatter-cushioned banquettes, a character settle and splendid long bench with baluster legs, river views from big windows; free wi-fi; children and dogs welcome, tables on waterside lawn (beyond service road), open all day. *(Val and Alan Green, Clive and Fran Dutson)*

STRATFORD-UPON-AVON SP2054
★**Encore** (01789) 269462
Bridge Street; CV37 6AB More modern bar than traditional pub; main beamed area with big windows, well spaced cast-iron tables, bucket armchairs and square stools on broad oak boards or pale flagstones, large charcoal sketches of local scenes, softly lit dark-walled back area with barrel and other rustic tables, stairs up to long comfortable dining room with river views, log fire, Purity, Robinsons and Sharps, plenty of wines by the glass and good coffee, popular food including weekday set menu; background music; children welcome, dogs in bar, open (and food) all day from 9.30am, can get very busy weekends. *(Hugh Roberts, Mitchell Cregor)*

STRATFORD-UPON-AVON SP2054
★**Garrick** (01789) 292186
High Street; CV37 6AU Ancient bustling pub with heavy beams and timbers in irregularly shaped rooms, simple furnishings on bare boards or flagstones, enjoyable fairly priced food from sandwiches and light dishes up, well kept Greene King ales and decent wines by the glass, friendly helpful staff, small air-conditioned back dining area; background music, TV, games machine; children welcome, open (and food) all day. *(Alan Johnson)*

STRATFORD-UPON-AVON SP1955
Old Thatch (01789) 295216
Rother Street/Greenhill Street; CV37 6LE Cosy and welcoming thatched pub dating from the 15th c on corner of market square, well kept Fullers ales, nice wines, popular fairly priced food including Sun carvery,

rustic décor, beams, slate or wood floors, sofas and log fire, back dining area; children welcome, covered tables outside, open all day (Sun till 6pm). *(Alan Johnson)*

STRATFORD-UPON-AVON SP2055
Old Tramway (01789) 297593
Shipston Road; CV37 7LW Mid 19th-c red-brick pub backing on to the old Moreton-in-Marsh horse-drawn tramway (now an embankment footpath); cosy fairly traditional interior with log fire, three real ales and good choice of popular reasonably priced pub food, friendly staff; sports TV, free wi-fi; children and dogs welcome, small front garden, partly covered heated terrace behind with summer bar, open (and food) all day. *(B and F A Hannam)*

STRATFORD-UPON-AVON SP1954
Windmill (01789) 297687
Church Street; CV37 6HB Ancient pub (with town's oldest licence) beyond the striking Guild Chapel, very low beams, panelling, mainly stone floors, big fireplace (gas fire), Greene King, Purity UBU and guests, good value food including deals, friendly efficient staff; background music, sports TV, games machines; courtyard tables, open all day. *(Charlie May)*

STRETTON-ON-FOSSE SP2238
★**Plough** (01608) 661053
Just off A429; GL56 9QX Popular little 17th-c village local under friendly newish ownership; central servery separating small bar and snug dining area, four changing mainly local ales, enjoyable home-cooked food (not Sun evening) including blackboard specials, stripped brick/stone walls and some flagstones, low oak beams, inglenook log fire; dominoes and cribbage, free wi-fi; children welcome, no dogs, a few tables outside, open all day. *(K H Frostick)*

TANWORTH-IN-ARDEN SP1071
Warwickshire Lad (01564) 742346
Broad Lane/Wood End Lane, Wood End; B94 5DP Beamed country pub with enjoyable reasonably priced traditional food, good value weekday set menu till 6pm, four well kept ales including Wye Valley and St Austell, quick helpful service; popular with walkers (bridleway opposite), open (and food) all day and fairly convenient for M42 (junction 3). *(Clive and Fran Dutson)*

TEMPLE GRAFTON SP1355
Blue Boar (01789) 750010
A mile E, towards Binton; off A422 W of Stratford; B49 6NR Welcoming stone-built dining pub with good choice of enjoyable food from bar snacks up, four well kept ales, afternoon teas, beams, stripped stonework and log fires, glass-covered well with goldfish, smarter dining room up a couple of steps; big-screen TVs; children and dogs welcome, picnic-sets outside, bedrooms. *(Anon)*

TIPTON
SO9492

Pie Factory (0121) 557 1402
Hurst Lane, Dudley Road towards Wednesbury; A457/A4037; DY4 9AB
Eccentric décor and quirky food – the mixed grill comes on a shovel, and you're awarded a certificate if you finish their massive Desperate Dan Cow Pie (comes with pastry horns) – other pies and good value food including Sun carvery, well kept Lump Hammer house ales brewed by Enville plus a guest; background music (live weekends), TV; children welcome, bedrooms.
(Phoebe Peacock)

UPPER BRAILES
SP3039

Gate (01608) 685212
B4035 Shipston-on-Stour to Banbury; OX15 5AX Traditional low-beamed village local, well kept Hook Norton and a guest, Weston's cider and enjoyable reasonably priced food (not Sun evening, Mon) including good fish and chips, efficient friendly service, coal fire; TV, darts; children welcome, tables in extensive back garden with play area and aunt sally, pretty hillside spot with lovely walks, two comfortable bedrooms, good breakfast, closed Mon lunchtime. *(JHBS)*

UPPER GORNAL
SO9292

★**Britannia** (01902) 883253
Kent Street (A459); DY3 1UX Popular old-fashioned 19th-c local with friendly chatty atmosphere (known locally as Sally's after former landlady), particularly well kept/priced Bathams, coal fires in front bar and time-trapped little back room with its wonderful wall-mounted handpumps, some bar snacks including good local pork pies; sports TV; dogs welcome, nice flower-filled backyard, open all day. *(John Harris)*

WALSALL
SP0198

Black Country Arms
(01922) 640588 *High Street; WS1 1QW*
Imposing old town pub on three levels, a dozen well kept ales including Black Country, real ciders and decent home-made pubby food at bargain prices (till 4pm Sun, Mon), good friendly service; background and live music, quiz nights, sports TV; no dogs, small side terrace, open all day (till midnight Fri, Sat). *(Pat and Tony Martin, Theocsbrian)*

WARMINGTON
SP4147

Plough (01295) 690666
Just off B4100 N of Banbury; OX17 1BX
Attractive and welcoming old stone pub under brother and sister team, some refurbishment but keeping character and good local atmosphere, low heavy beams and exposed stone walls, comfortable chairs by inglenook woodburner, well kept Greene

King ales and Sharps Doom Bar, enjoyable traditional home-made food (not Mon), extended dining room; children welcome, tables on back terrace, delightful village with pond and interesting church, closed Sun evening. *(Nigel and Sue Foster, Clive and Fran Dutson)*

WARWICK
SP2864

★**Rose & Crown** (01926) 411117
Market Place; CV34 4SH Friendly bustling inn with uncluttered up-to-date décor, big leather sofas and low tables by open fire, dining area with large modern photographs, good choice of interesting sensibly priced food, well kept Purity and Sharps Doom Bar, plenty of fancy keg dispensers, good wines and coffee, cheerful efficient service, newspapers; background music; tables out under parasols, comfortable good-sized bedrooms, open (and food) all day from 8am for breakfast. *(Alan Johnson, Christopher and Elise Way)*

WARWICK
SP2967

★**Saxon Mill** (01926) 492255
Guys Cliffe, A429 just N; CV34 5YN
Mitchells & Butlers dining pub in charmingly set converted mill; beams and log fire, smart contemporary chairs and tables on polished boards and flagstones, cosy corners with leather armchairs and big rugs, mill race and turning wheel behind glass, enjoyable food in bar and (best to book) upstairs family restaurant including good value two-course lunch, local beers and several wines by the glass, friendly service; background music; tables out on terraces by broad willow-flanked river, more over bridge, delightful views across to Guys Cliffe House ruins, open all day. *(Adrian Johnson)*

WHICHFORD
SP3134

Norman Knight (01608) 684621
Ascott Road, opposite village green; CV36 5PE Sympathetically extended beamed and flagstoned pub under new ownership; own Stratford upon Avon beers and enjoyable home-made food, friendly service; live music including monthly folk club; children and dogs welcome, tables out by lovely village green, aunt sally, site at back for five caravans, good walks, open all day Fri, Sat, till 6pm Sun, closed Mon lunchtime. *(Anon)*

WILLEY
SP4885

Wood Farm (01788) 833469
Coalpit Lane; CV23 0SL Modern visitor centre attached to (and with view into) Wood Farm Brewery, up to eight of their ales and occasional guests, substantial helpings of reasonably priced food including Sun carvery, cheerful service, upstairs galleried function/ overflow room; children welcome, no dogs,

---

There are report forms at the back of the book.

picnic-sets outside with country views, camping, brewery tours (must pre-book, not Sun), open all day (till 6pm Sun). *(Alan Johnson, George Atkinson)*

WILLOUGHBY   SP5267

Rose (01788) 891180

Just off A45 E of Dunchurch; Main Street; CV23 8BH Neatly decorated old thatched dining pub; low beamed and planked ceiling, wood or tiled floors, some panelling and inglenook woodburner, good range of food cooked well by italian chef-landlord including pizzas, weekday set italian menu, tapas night last Thurs of month, well kept Hook Norton and Sharps Doom Bar, reasonably priced house wines, friendly attentive young staff; children and dogs welcome, disabled facilities, seating in side garden with gate to park and play area, closed Sun evening, Mon. *(M C and S Jeanes, George Atkinson, Clive and Fran Dutson)*

WIXFORD   SP0854

Fish (01789) 778593

B4085 Alcester–Bidford; B49 6DA Old pub by pretty brick bridge over the River Arrow, enjoyable reasonably priced food including bargain weekday set menu, three real ales, friendly attentive staff, contemporary bare-boards interior with plenty of quirky touches, log fire; children and dogs welcome, big riverside garden, open (and food) all day. *(B and F A Hannam)*

WOLVERHAMPTON   SO9298

★**Great Western** (01902) 351090

Corn Hill/Sun Street, behind railway

station; WV10 0DG Cheerful pub hidden away in cobbled lane down from mainline station; Holdens and guest beers kept well, real cider, bargain home-made food (not Sun), helpful friendly staff, traditional front bar, other rooms including neat dining conservatory, interesting railway memorabilia, open fires; background radio, TV; children and dogs welcome, maybe summer barbecues in yard, open all day and busy with Wolves fans on match days. *(John Harris)*

WOLVERHAMPTON   SO8698

Mermaid (01902) 764896

Bridgnorth Road (A454 W); WV6 8BN Comfortable 18th-c roadside Vintage Inn, good choice of popular well priced food (best to book weekends), two changing real ales, helpful friendly service; children welcome, next to Wightwick Manor (NT), open all day. *(Paul and Sue Merrick)*

WOOTTON WAWEN   SP1563

Bulls Head (01564) 795803

Stratford Road, just off A3400; B95 6BD Attractive 17th-c black and white building, more restaurant than pub but does serve a couple of Marstons-related ales; good well presented food from snacks and light dishes up, extensive wine list, friendly helpful staff, Elizabethan beams and timbers, stone and quarry-tiled floors, log fires; children welcome, dogs in snug, outside tables front and back, handy for one of England's finest churches and Stratford Canal walks, open all day Fri, Sat and till 6pm Sun. *(Mrs B H Adams)*

A star symbol before the name of a pub shows exceptional character and appeal. It doesn't mean extra comfort. Even quite a basic pub can win a star, if it's individual enough.

Wiltshire

 ALDBOURNE   SU2675   Map 2

Blue Boar 🍺 £

(01672) 540237 – www.theblueboarpub.co.uk

The Green (off B4192 in centre); SN8 2EN

Busy local with simple pubby furnishings in bar, cottagey restaurant and seats outside

Very much a local but with a genuinely warm welcome for visitors too, this has a good, bustling atmosphere and is in a pretty village-green setting. The heavily beamed bar has built-in wooden window seats, tall farmhouse chairs and other red-cushioned pubby chairs on flagstones or bare boards, a woodburning stove in an inglenook fireplace with a stuffed boar's head and large clock above it, horsebrasses on the bressumer beam, and a noticeboard with news of beer festivals and live music events. There are stools by the counter where they keep Wadworths IPA and 6X plus guests such as Hydes Nelson and a seasonal ale from Wadworths on handpump, eight wines by the glass, 17 malt whiskies and a farm cider. The back restaurant is beamed and cottagey with standing timbers, dark wooden chairs and tables on floorboards and rugs, and plates on a dresser. Picnic-sets in front make the most of the charming location and the window boxes are lovely.

🍽 Fairly priced tasty food includes lunchtime sandwiches and baguettes, deep-fried whitebait with tartare sauce, smoked mackerel pâté, sausages and mash with onion gravy, pumpkin and parmesan ravioli with pesto, chicken breast with white wine and tarragon sauce, salmon fillet with lemon and parsley butter, and puddings such as Baileys and dark chocolate cheesecake and lemon tart. *Benchmark main dish: steak and kidney pie £9.50. Two-course evening meal £16.00.*

Wadworths ~ Tenants Michael and Joanne Hehir ~ Real ale ~ Open 11.30-3, 5.30-11.30; 11.30am-midnight Fri, Sat; 12-11 Sun ~ Bar food 12-2 (2.30 Fri, Sat), 6.30-9; 12-4 Sun ~ Restaurant ~ Children welcome ~ Dogs allowed in bar ~ Wi-fi ~ Live music regularly; phone to check *Recommended by Hilary and Neil Christopher*

 BRADFORD-ON-AVON   ST8261   Map 2

Castle 🍺

(01225) 865657 – www.flatcappers.co.uk

Mount Pleasant, by junction with A363, N edge of town; extremely limited pub parking but spaces in nearby streets; BA15 1SJ

Substantial stone inn with local ales, popular food, plenty of character and fine views; bedrooms

The seats at the front of this handsome stone building offer sweeping town views, while in the back garden you look across lovely countryside. Inside, the unspoilt bar has a lot of individual character, a wide range of seats (church chairs, leather armchairs, cushioned wall seating and brass and leather studded dining chairs) around chunky pine tables on dark flagstones, church candles, fringed lamps and a good log fire; daily papers, background music and board games. A bare-boards snug on the right is similar in style. Cheerful staff serve two beers named for the pub (from Three Castles Brewery), Box Steam Golden Bolt, Otter Bright, Plain Innocence, Three Castles Saxon Archer and Three Daggers Daggers Ale on handpump and several wines by the glass; they hold a beer and music festival twice a year. The boldly decorated bedrooms are comfortable with spacious bathrooms.

As well as sandwiches, the good food includes a choice of breakfasts (8.30-midday), sharing boards, chicken with roasted artichoke, butternut purée and olive tapenade, sausages of the week, cottage pie, beer-battered cod and chips, slow-roasted pork belly with poached pear and cider sauce, duck confit cassoulet with sausage, smoked bacon, butter beans and tomatoes, and puddings such as chocolate and hazelnut brownie with chocolate sauce and a crumble of the day. *Benchmark main dish: burger in a sourdough bun with toppings and red cabbage slaw £8.95. Two-course evening meal £15.00.*

Free house ~ Licensee Ben Paxton ~ Real ale ~ Open 9am-11pm ~ Bar food 8am-10pm; 8.30am-9.30pm Sun ~ Children welcome but must be seated from 7.30pm ~ Wi-fi ~ Bedrooms: £90/£100 *Recommended by Hugh Roberts, Chris and Angela Buckell*

BROUGHTON GIFFORD
ST8763 Map 2

Fox 🌟 ♀

(01225) 782949 ~ www.thefox-broughtongifford.co.uk
Village signposted off A365 to B3107 W of Melksham; The Street; SN12 8PN

Comfortably stylish pub with good interesting food, real ales and several wines by the glass, and a pleasant garden; bedrooms

'A thoroughly nice village pub with enthusiastic staff to boot,' says one reader happy after his regular visit to this civilised and friendly pub. Each of the interconnected areas has a chatty atmosphere, and the big bird and plant prints, attractive table lamps and white-painted beams contrast attractively with the broad dark flagstones. You can sink into sofas or armchairs by a table of daily papers (another has magazines and board games), take one of the padded stools by the pink-painted bar counter, or go for the mix of gently old-fashioned dining chairs around the unmatched stripped dining tables adorned with candles in brass candlesticks. There's also a warm log fire in a stone fireplace. Courteous, helpful staff serve Bath Gem and Butcombe Bitter on handpump, a dozen wines by the glass and a dozen each of malt whiskies and gin; background music. The terrace behind has picnic-sets, and leads on to a good-sized sheltered lawn.

 Rearing their own livestock and growing vegetables for use in the seasonal menus, the rewarding food includes sandwiches, confit chicken, pistachio and leek terrine with piccalilli, smoked haddock scotch egg with truffled creamy leeks, tagliatelle with pea, asparagus and wild garlic, own-made sausages with mash, chicken breast with potato rösti, sautéed chard and béarnaise sauce, fresh fish of the day with sauce vierge, and puddings such as treacle tart with clotted cream and irish coffee brûlée with a pistachio biscotti; they also offer a two- and three-course set lunch. *Benchmark main dish: fillet of beef with boulangère potatoes and garlic and shallot purée £26.95. Two-course evening meal £29.00.*

Free house ~ Licensee Alex Geneen ~ Real ale ~ Open 12-11; 9am-midnight Sat; 12-10 Sun; closed Mon ~ Bar food 12-2.30, 6-9.30; not Sun evening ~ Children welcome ~ Dogs welcome ~ Bedrooms: /£150 *Recommended by Mr and Mrs P R Thomas, Mr and Mrs A H Young, Michael Doswell*

CHICKSGROVE

ST9729 Map 2

Compasses ★ ⊕ ♀ ⇌

(01722) 714318 – www.thecompassesinn.com

From A30 5.5 miles W of B3089 junction, take lane on N side signposted 'Sutton Mandeville, Sutton Row', then first left fork (small signs point the way to the pub; in Lower Chicksgrove; look out for the car park); can also be reached off B3089 W of Dinton, passing the glorious spire of Teffont Evias church; SP3 6NB

Excellent all-rounder with enjoyable food, a genuine welcome, four real ales and seats in the quiet garden; attractive bedrooms

After enjoying one of the surrounding walks, this thatched 14th-c inn is the ideal place to retire to for a rewarding pint. The unchanging bar has plenty of real character: old bottles and jugs hanging from beams above the roughly timbered counter, farm tools and traps on the part-stripped stone walls, high-backed wooden settles forming snug booths around tables on the mostly flagstoned floor, and a log fire. Butcombe Bitter, Keystone Large One and Waylands Sixpenny 6d Gold on handpump, nine wines by the glass and nine malt whiskies. The quiet garden behind has seating on terraces and in a flagstoned courtyard. Bedrooms are comfortable and popular.

 Reliably high quality and innovative food includes grey mullet with rice noodles, chilli and mushroom broth, chicken ballotine stuffed with tomato and parsley mousse with potato rösti and sweetcorn purée, roasted vegetable and mozzarella tian with tomato dressing, calves liver with bacon and red onion gravy, monkfish with smoked mackerel dauphinoise and hot tartare sauce, slow-roast pork belly with bubble and squeak, celeriac and blue cheese purée and cider jus, and puddings such as chocolate brownie with marshmallow ice-cream and banana and toffee popcorn parfait with peanut butter ice-cream. *Benchmark main dish: shoulder of lamb with mini shepherd's pie and dauphinoise potatoes £15.50. Two-course evening meal £21.50.*

Free house ~ Licensee Alan Stoneham ~ Real ale ~ Open 12-3, 6-11; 12-3, 7-10.30 Sun; closed Mon lunch Jan-Easter ~ Bar food 12-2, 7-9 ~ Children welcome ~ Dogs welcome ~ Wi-fi ~ Bedrooms: £65/£85 *Recommended by Phil and Jane Hodson, Tony and Rachel Schendel, Wendy Breese, Ian Herdman, Howard and Margaret Buchanan*

COMPTON BASSETT

SU0372 Map 2

White Horse ⊕ ♀ ⇌

(01249) 813118 – www.whitehorse-comptonbassett.co.uk

At N end of village; SN11 8RG

Bustling, refurbished village pub with four ales, good wines by the glass, inventive food and seats in big garden; pretty bedrooms

Our readers enjoy staying in the attractive and well equipped bedrooms here (in a separate building and overlooking the grounds) and breakfasts are highly regarded. The friendly, simply furnished, bustling bar has some homely upholstered chairs and a nice carved settle around assorted tables on parquet flooring, a woodburning stove, and bar stools against the counter where they keep Bath Gem, Ramsbury Gold, Sharps Doom Bar and Wadworths 6X on handpump, 15 wines (including champagne) by the glass, 20 malt whiskies, a good range of spirits and farm cider. Staff are lovely. The dining room has red walls and carpet at one end and bare floorboards and pale paintwork at the other; throughout there are beams and joists and miscellaneous antique tables and chairs, and another woodburning stove. Background music and board games. The large, neatly kept garden has picnic-sets and other seats and a boules pitch, while the paddock holds pigs, sheep and geese; good walking nearby.

Making their own pasta and sausages and using local, seasonal game, the imaginative food includes lunchtime sandwiches, seared king scallop with cauliflower beignet and spinach and red pepper sauce, scotch egg (guinea fowl egg wrapped in venison) with duck and rabbit sausage and wasabi sauce, steak and kidney pudding, hake fillet with risotto nero, roasted peppers and parsley sauce, duck breast with creamed savoy cabbage, roast beetroot and raspberry jus, and puddings such as pecan tart with vanilla ice-cream and dark chocolate and griottine cherry torte with cherry mousse. *Benchmark main dish: rack of lamb with belly crisp, wilted leaves and a rich lamb jus £21.15. Two-course evening meal £22.00.*

Free house ~ Licensees Danny and Tara Adams ~ Real ale ~ Open 12-11 (9 Sun, 10 Mon) ~ Bar food 12-9 (6.30 Sun, 8 Mon) ~ Restaurant ~ Children welcome ~ Dogs allowed in bar ~ Wi-fi ~ Bedrooms: £85/£95 *Recommended by Michael Doswell, S G N Bennett*

CORSHAM ST8670 Map 2
Methuen Arms 🎯 🛏
(01249) 717060 – www.themethuenarms.com
High Street; SN13 0HB

● ●
Wiltshire Dining Pub of the Year

Bustling hotel with character bars, friendly staff, imaginative food, good wines and ales, and seats outside; comfortable bedrooms

Although many customers come to this civilised inn for a first class meal or to stay in the well equipped and comfortable bedrooms, it retains a proper little front bar for those just wanting a chat and a pint. Snug in the evening with candlelight, it has a log fire, a big old clock under a sizeable mirror, an assortment of antique dining chairs and tables, rugs on elm floorboards, Bath SPA, Otter Amber and Moles Landlords Choice on handpump, 12 wines by the glass and ten malt whiskies. Across the green-painted bar counter is a second small bar, with similar furnishings, bare boards and rugs and a couple of armchairs. The dining room has settles (carved and plain), high-backed dining chairs with wooden arms around old sewing-machine tables, an open fire with tea-lights, fine black and white photographs of large local houses on sage green paintwork and swagged curtains. Another room leads off here, and there's also a back restaurant. The garden to the side of the handsome Georgian building has seats and tables.

Faultless food from an imaginative menu includes lunchtime sandwiches, thin-sliced rare roast venison with grilled fennel, pickled mushrooms and ewes curd, prawns with chilli, garlic and parsley butter on sourdough bruschetta, spinach and ricotta pancake with wild garlic, pesto and tomato, burger with toppings, chilli relish and chips, monkfish wrapped in parma ham and sage with olive oil mash and black olive dressing, and puddings such as Valrhona dark chocolate mousse cake with amaretto and brown bread ice-cream, smoked salt and chocolate tuille and baked lemon cheesecake with blood oranges in caramel and Cointreau; they also offer a two- and three-course set weekday menu. *Benchmark main dish: roasted cod with marsh samphire £18.50. Two-course evening meal £22.50.*

Free house ~ Licensees Martin and Debbie Still ~ Real ale ~ Open 12-11 (10.30 Sun) ~ Bar food 12-3, 6-10 ~ Restaurant ~ Children welcome ~ Dogs allowed in bar ~ Wi-fi ~ Bedrooms: £90/£140 *Recommended by Mr and Mrs P R Thomas, Roger and Donna Huggins, Michael Doswell*

CRICKLADE
SU1093   Map 4

Red Lion 🍺 ⌂
(01793) 750776 – www.theredlioncricklade.co.uk
Off A419 Swindon–Cirencester; High Street; SN6 6DD

16th-c inn with well liked food in two dining rooms, ten real ales, friendly, relaxed atmosphere and big garden; bedrooms

A fine range of drinks in this very well run coaching inn includes around ten real ales on handpump, 60 bottled beers, up to eight farm ciders, ten wines by the glass, 20 malt whiskies and 20 gins (gin hour is 5.30-6.30). The changing ales served by friendly staff might be their own-brewed Hop Kettle North Wall, Pale By Comparison and Tricerahops, plus guests such as Arbor Half-day IPA, Burning Sky Porter and Rebellion Seven Seas. The bar has a good community atmosphere, stools by the nice old counter, wheelbacks and other chairs around dark wooden tables on red patterned carpet, an open fire and all sorts of bric-a-brac on the stone walls including stuffed fish and animal heads and old street signs. You can eat here or in the slightly more formal dining room, furnished with pale wooden farmhouse chairs and tables, beige carpeting and a woodburning stove in a brick fireplace. There are plenty of picnic-sets in the big back garden. Bedrooms are comfortable and breakfasts good. You can walk along the nearby Thames Path or through the pretty, historic town.

Quite a choice of tasty food includes lunchtime sandwiches (not Sunday), potted brown shrimps on toast, quail with pearl barley risotto, beetroot, jerusalem artichoke crisps and cumberland jelly, home-cooked honey and mustard ham with free-range eggs, stilton, cauliflower and broccoli cheese, local sausages with mash and onion gravy, blade of rare-breed beef with black pudding bonbon, truffle mash and baby turnips, wild bass fillet with king prawn and mussel bouillabaisse, and puddings such as dark chocolate brownie with chocolate sauce and tonka bean crème brûlée. *Benchmark main dish: burger with toppings, chilli jam and triple-cooked chips £11.95. Two-course evening meal £20.00.*

Free house ~ Licensee Tom Gee ~ Real ale ~ Open 12-11 (midnight Sat); 12-10.30 Sun ~ Bar food 12-2.30 (3 Sun), 6.30-9 (9.30 Sat) ~ Restaurant ~ Children welcome ~ Dogs welcome ~ Wi-fi ~ Bedrooms: /£85 *Recommended by Guy Vowles, Phil and Jane Villiers, Rob Henderson, Tracey and Stephen Groves, DF and NF*

CRUDWELL
ST9592   Map 4

Potting Shed 🏅 ♟ 🍺
(01666) 577833 – www.thepottingshedpub.com
A429 N of Malmesbury; The Street; SN16 9EW

Civilised but relaxed dining pub with low-beamed rooms, friendly, helpful staff, an interesting range of drinks and creative cooking; seats in the big garden

'We braved floods and a blizzard to get here – and it really was worth it!' High praise indeed from an enthusiastic reader. Low-beamed rooms rambling around the bar have two woodburning stoves (one in a big worn stone fireplace), mixed plain tables and chairs on pale flagstones, some homely armchairs in one corner – and daily papers. Four steps take you up into a high-raftered area with wood flooring, and there's another smaller separate room that's ideal for a lunch or dinner party. The quirky, rustic decorations are not overdone: a garden fork door handle, garden tool beer pumps, rather witty big black and white photographs. A fine range of drinks includes Bath Gem, Flying Monk Elmers, Timothy Taylors Landlord and a guest ale from Prescott on handpump, as well as 24 wines and champagne by the glass, three farm ciders, home-made seasonal cocktails using local or home-grown fruit, local fruit liqueurs, good coffees and popular winter mulled cider; well chosen background music and board games. Barney, Rubble and Tilly are the pub dogs. There are sturdy teak seats around cask tables as well as picnic-sets out on the side grass among weeping willows. The pub's two acres of gardens supply many of the ingredients used in the food; they've also developed ten raised beds and donated them to local villagers – these are pleasant to wander through. Good access for those in need of extra assistance. They also own the hotel across the road.

The delicious, creative food using home-grown and other local produce includes lunchtime sandwiches, miso-cured trout and salt and pepper squid with coriander salad and shiso dressing, pigeon breast, leg and apple terrine with pistachio purée, breaded chicken fillet burger with grilled chorizo, garlic mayonnaise and triple-cooked chips, truffled macaroni cheese with chanterelle mushrooms and confit tomatoes, local fallow deer with game sausage toad in the hole and red cabbage, and puddings such as bitter orange, polenta and olive oil cake with vanilla corn ice-cream and chocolate, sloe gin and juniper pudding with plum ice-cream. *Benchmark main dish: burger with tomato chutney and triple-cooked chips £15.75. Two-course evening meal £21.00.*

Enterprise ~ Lease Jonathan Barry and Julian Muggridge ~ Real ale ~ Open 11-11 ~ Bar food 12-2.30, 7-9.30 (9 Sun) ~ Restaurant ~ Children welcome ~ Dogs welcome ~ Wi-fi
Recommended by Maureen Wood, M G Hart, Di and Mike Gillam, Phil and Jane Villiers, Michael Sargent, Dr W I C Clark, Taff Thomas

EAST CHISENBURY   SU1352   Map 2
Red Lion ⭐ ♟ 🛏

(01980) 671124 – www.redlionfreehouse.com
At S end of village; SN9 6AQ

Country inn in peaceful village run by hard-working chef-owners, contemporary décor, an informal atmosphere and excellent food; bedrooms

This thatched inn is a special place with exceptional food cooked by the owners, Mr and Mrs Manning, who are both top chefs. Most customers are here to dine – but they do keep a fine range of drinks and locals congregate at high chairs by the counter for a pint and a chat: beers from Otter and Stonehenge breweries on handpump, 25 wines by the glass, home-made cordial and quite a range of gins and malt whiskies. One long room is split into different areas by brick and green-planked uprights. A big woodburner sits in a brick inglenook fireplace at one end; at the other is a comfortable black leather sofa and armchairs, and in between are high-backed and farmhouse wooden dining chairs around various tables on bare boards or stone tiles, with pretty flowers and church candles dotted about. There's an additional dining room too; background music. Outside, the terrace and grassed area above have picnic-sets and tables and chairs. The very well equipped, boutique-style bedrooms are in a separate building with private decks just a few metres from the River Avon; breakfasts are delicious and the bloody marys and bucks fizz are complimentary. They can organise a packed lunch for walkers and make their own dog treats.

They name their suppliers, grow their own produce and rear pigs and chicken. The seriously good, confident food includes sandwiches, chicken liver pâté with madeira jelly, brill goujons with tartare sauce, risotto primavera with glazed vegetables, home-grown herbs and goats cheese, roast wild sea trout with samphire, ratte potatoes, brown shrimps and sauce vierge, smoked pork belly with braised octopus, grilled potatoes, peppers, olives and romesco sauce, and puddings such as passion-fruit baked alaska with macadamia nuts and ginger, and german chocolate cake with toasted coconut, pecans and cherry ice-cream. *Benchmark main dish: rib-eye steak for two with chips and béarnaise sauce £60.00. Two-course evening meal £28.00.*

Free house ~ Licensees Britt and Guy Manning ~ Real ale ~ Open 12-11 (10 Sun) ~ Bar food 12-2.15, 6-8.30 (8 Sun) ~ Children welcome ~ Dogs allowed in bar and bedrooms ~ Wi-fi ~ Bedrooms: /£150 *Recommended by Val and Alan Green, Mrs Zara Elliott, Wilburoo, Ian Herdman, R T and J C Moggridge*

 EAST KNOYLE   ST8731   Map 2

Fox & Hounds ♀

(01747) 830573 – www.foxandhounds-eastknoyle.co.uk

Village signposted off A350 S of A303; The Green (named on some road atlases), a mile NW at OS Sheet 183 map reference 872313; or follow signpost off B3089, about 0.5 miles E of A303 junction near Little Chef; SP3 6BN

Pretty thatched village pub with splendid views, welcoming service, good beers and popular enjoyable food

It's well worth the effort negotiating the little lanes to reach this ancient pretty pub, especially on a clear day when you can enjoy the marvellous views over into Somerset and Dorset from picnic-sets facing the green. Inside, the three linked areas – on different levels around the central horseshoe-shaped servery – have big log fires, plentiful oak woodwork and flagstones, comfortably padded dining chairs around big scrubbed tables, and a couple of leather sofas; the furnishings are all very individual and uncluttered. There's also a small light-painted conservatory restaurant. Hop Back Summer Lightning, Otter Amber and Palmers Copper Ale on handpump, ten wines by the glass and Thatcher's farm cider; background music. The nearby woods are good for a stroll and the Wiltshire Cycleway passes through the village.

From a varied menu, the good quality food includes deep-fried rosemary and garlic-crusted brie wedges with cranberry jelly, lamb samosa with mango chutney, spinach and ricotta cannelloni, pizzas cooked in their clay oven, bacon-wrapped chicken with pesto cream sauce, steak and kidney pudding, duck breast with port and redcurrant sauce, slow-roast lamb shank in red wine, and puddings such as pear and almond tart and lemon posset. *Benchmark main dish: beer-battered fish and chips £12.00. Two-course evening meal £20.00.*

Free house ~ Licensee Murray Seator ~ Real ale ~ Open 11.30-3, 5.30-11 (10 Sun) ~ Bar food 12-2.30, 6.30-9 ~ Children welcome ~ Dogs welcome ~ Wi-fi *Recommended by Martin and Karen Wake, Paul Goldman, Roy Hoing*

 EDINGTON   ST9353   Map 2

Three Daggers 🍺

(01380) 830940 – www.threedaggers.co.uk

Westbury Road (B3098); BA13 4PG

Rejuvenated village pub, open fires, beams and candlelight, modern conservatory, helpful staff, enjoyable food and own-brew beers; bedrooms

This appealing brick pub is heavily beamed and open-plan with a friendly, easy-going atmosphere. There are leather sofas and armchairs at one end in front of a woodburning stove, kitchen and chapel chairs and built-in planked wall seats with scatter cushions, leather-topped stools against the counter, and a cosy nook with just one table. A two-way fireplace opens into the candlelit restaurant, which has similar tables and chairs on a dark slate floor, and lots of photos of local people and views; stairs lead up to another dining room with beams in a high roof and some unusual large wooden chandeliers. Their own hand-pumped beers, Daggers Ale, Black, Blonde and Edge, are brewed in the farm shop building and they also have 14 wines by the glass, ten malt whiskies and a couple of farm ciders; background music, darts, TV and board games. The airy conservatory has tea-lights or church candles on scrubbed kitchen tables and wooden dining chairs. Just beyond this are picnic-sets on grass plus a fenced-off, well equipped children's play area. The three bedrooms are pretty. Do visit their farm shop opposite.

As well as breakfasts (from 8am), the enjoyable food includes sandwiches, bubble and squeak with streaky bacon, poached egg and hollandaise sauce, beef carpaccio with blue cheese and rocket, sharing boards, mushroom and cheese quiche, a pie of the day, spatchcock chicken with coleslaw, paprika mayonnaise and chips, a fish dish of the day, sirloin steak with béarnaise or peppercorn sauce, and puddings such as rhubarb tart and chocolate torte. *Benchmark main dish: cheese burger with gherkins and skinny chips £11.75. Two-course evening meal £22.00.*

Free house ~ Licensee Robin Brown ~ Real ale ~ Open 8am-11pm ~ Bar food 12-2.30, 6-9 (9.30 Fri, Sat); 12-10.30 Sun; breakfasts 8.30-11am ~ Restaurant ~ Children welcome ~ Dogs allowed in bar ~ Wi-fi ~ Bedrooms: £85/£95 *Recommended by John Matthews, Hilary and Neil Christopher*

FONTHILL GIFFORD
Beckford Arms ⍟ ♙ ⇧

ST9231 Map 2

(01747) 870385 – www.beckfordarms.com

Off B3089 W at Fonthill Bishop; SP3 6PX

18th-c coaching inn with character bar and restaurant, unfailingly good food, thoughtful choice of drinks and an easy-going atmosphere; individually decorated bedrooms

Glorious countryside surrounds this golden-stone Georgian coaching inn and the well equipped and comfortable bedrooms make a good base; breakfasts are good and generous. There's almost a country-house hotel feel to the place with its civilised but informal atmosphere and charming, attentive service – but the bar has plenty of chatty locals and they keep an interesting range of drinks: Butcombe Bitter, Keystone Phoenix (brewed especially for them) and Otter Bitter on handpump, 15 wines by the glass, 20 malt whiskies, winter mulled wine and cider, and cocktails such as a bellini using locally produced peach liqueur and a bloody mary using home-grown horseradish. The main bar has a huge fireplace, bar stools beside the counter and various old wooden dining chairs and tables on parquet flooring. The cosy sitting room is stylish with comfortable sofas facing one another across a low table of newspapers, a nice built-in window seat among other chairs and tables, and an open fire in a stone fireplace with candles in brass candlesticks and fresh flowers on the mantelpiece. There's also a separate restaurant and private dining room. Much of the artwork on the walls is by local artists. They host film nights on occasional Sundays and will provide water and bones for dogs (the pub dog is called Elsa). The mature rambling garden has seats on a brick terrace, hammocks under trees, games for children, a dog bath and boules.

From an imaginative menu and using the best seasonal and local produce (some home-grown), the accomplished food includes sandwiches, pigeon with charred leeks and parsley root purée, smoked chalk-stream trout with pickled radish, marinated celery and lemon mayonnaise, gammon with a duck egg and chips, smoked butter beans with garlic puy lentils, chard, parsnip crisps, sorrel oil and smoked almonds, hake and mussels with samphire and cider cream sauce, and puddings such as chocolate and Cointreau délice with blood orange, honeycomb and orange sorbet and blueberry and almond tart with cinnamon cream. *Benchmark main dish: burger with toppings, pickle and chips £11.50. Two-course evening meal £23.50.*

Free house ~ Licensees Dan Brod and Charlie Luxton ~ Real ale ~ Open 7am-11pm ~ Bar food 12-3, 6-9 ~ Children welcome ~ Dogs welcome ~ Wi-fi ~ Bedrooms: /£95
Recommended by Gerry Price, Ian Herdman, Michael Sargent, Michael Doswell

GREAT BEDWYN   SU2764   Map 2
Three Tuns 🏵 ♀

(01672) 870280 – www.threetunsbedwyn.co.uk
Village signposted off A338 S of Hungerford, or off A4 W of Hungerford via Little Bedwyn; High Street; SN8 3NU

Carefully refurbished village pub with a friendly welcome, real ales and highly rated food

Once the village bakery (and still with its original bread oven), this is a neatly kept 18th-c village pub run with enthusiasm by the chef-owner and his wife. The beamed front bar is traditional and simply furnished with pubby stools and chairs on bare floorboards, and has an open fire, artwork by local artists on the walls and plenty of original features. Butcombe Bitter, Otter Amber, Ramsbury Gold and a guest or two on handpump, eight wines by the glass, several malt whiskies and farm cider. French windows in the back dining room lead into the garden (which has undergone a lot of work) where there are new tables and chairs and a new outdoor grill. The pub is on the edge of the Savernake Forest and there are lovely walks nearby.

🏵 Cooked by the landlord using seasonal produce, the interesting food includes morcilla (spanish sausage) scotch egg with celeriac rémoulade, half a pint of prawns with aioli, fettucine with broccoli, roasted garlic, confit tomatoes and aged parmesan, muntjac ragoût with rosemary and truffle oil, pollack with carrot risotto, merlot-braised ox cheek and cavolo nero, duck breast with roasted shallot purée, sticky red cabbage and boudin noir, and puddings such as peanut butter and dulce de leche chocolate cup with shaved Snickers and rhubarb and vanilla crème brûlée. *Benchmark main dish: crispy pig's head £16.00. Two-course evening meal £22.00.*

Free house ~ Licensees James and Ashley Wilsey ~ Real ale ~ Open 10am-midnight; 12-6 Sun; closed Sun evening, Mon, first week Jan ~ Bar food 12.30-2.30, 6-9.30; 12.30-9.30 Fri, Sat; 12-3 Sun ~ Restaurant ~ Children welcome ~ Dogs welcome ~ Wi-fi ~ Live jazz Sun in summer   *Recommended by Caroline Prescott, Alfie Bayliss*

HOLT   ST8561   Map 2
Toll Gate 🛏

(01225) 782326 – www.tollgateinn.co.uk
Ham Green; B3107 W of Melksham; BA14 6PX

Friendly former weavers' shed with cheerful staff, woodburning stoves in bars, real ales and popular food; pretty bedrooms

The friendly licensees and their staff welcome all their customers – regulars and visitors – into their 16th-c pub. The relaxed bar has real character with seats by one woodburner, a mix of tables and chairs on pale floorboards and plenty of paintings by local artists for sale. Box Steam Half Sovereign and Tunnel Vision (the brewery is in the village), Butcombe Bitter and Fullers London Pride on handpump, 16 wines by the glass and three farm ciders; background music and board games. The dining room leads off the bar with high-backed leather and other cushioned chairs, a second woodburner, fresh flowers and cream window blinds. Up a few steps, the high-raftered restaurant is similarly furnished with white deer heads on a dark blue wall and church windows (this used to be a workers' chapel). The back terrace has seats and tables, and there's a new boules pitch. Bedrooms have open fires.

Using local, seasonal produce, the highly thought-of food includes lunchtime sandwiches (not Sunday), pickled salmon tartare en croûte with herb pesto and horseradish crème fraîche, pulled ham and black pudding fritter with apple and fennel salad, a meze board, beer-battered fish and chips with pea purée, a risotto and a pie of the day, pork tenderloin wrapped in streaky bacon with date and walnut reduction, and puddings such as millefeuille of berry and almond parfait with raspberry jelly and berry coulis and chocolate and hazelnut brownie with hot chocolate sauce. *Benchmark main dish: stuffed chicken breast and duck leg rillette with chestnut sausage meat and gravy £14.95. Two-course evening meal £19.00.*

Free house ~ Licensees Laura Boulton and Mark Hodges ~ Real ale ~ Open 10am-11.30pm (midnight Sat); 10-4 Sun ~ Bar food 12-2, 6.30-9; 12-2.30 Sun ~ Restaurant ~ Children welcome ~ Wi-fi ~ Live music outside in summer ~ Bedrooms: /£70
Recommended by Pip White, Toby Jones, Comus and Sarah Elliott

 LOWER CHUTE   SU3153 Map 2

Hatchet

(01264) 730229 – www.thehatchetinn.com
The Chutes well signposted via Appleshaw off A342, 2.5 miles W of Andover; SP11 9DX

**Neatly kept old country inn with a friendly welcome for all,
four beers and enjoyable food; comfortable bedrooms**

There can't be many other pubs in Wiltshire that can match this cottagey place for sheer rural charm, and the convivial landlord offers a warm welcome to all. The very low-beamed bar has a peaceful local feel plus a splendid 16th-c fireback in a huge fireplace (and a roaring winter log fire) and various comfortable seats around oak tables; there's also an extensive restaurant. Exmoor Ale, Otter Bitter, Timothy Taylors Landlord and a guest from breweries such as Hook Norton and Stonehenge on handpump, eight wines by the glass, 20 malt whiskies and several farm ciders; board games. There are seats out on a terrace and the side grass and a safe play area for children. The snug bedrooms make this a fine place to stay (dogs are welcome in one room) and breakfasts are hearty.

The highly rated food includes sandwiches, tempura prawns with garlic bread, chicken liver pâté with apricot chutney, ham and eggs, spinach and red pepper lasagne, steak in ale pie, liver and bacon, scampi and chips, lamb shank with red wine, redcurrant and rosemary sauce, and puddings. *Benchmark main dish: fish pie £12.95. Two-course evening meal £19.50.*

Free house ~ Licensee Jeremy McKay ~ Real ale ~ Open 11.30-3, 6-11; 12-4, 7-10.30 Sun ~ Bar food 12-2.15, 6.30-9.45; 12-3, 7.30-9.30 Sun ~ Restaurant ~ Children welcome ~ Dogs welcome ~ Wi-fi ~ Open mike nights first Fri of month, quiz Tues evening ~ Bedrooms: £70/£80 *Recommended by Pip White, Hilary and Neil Christopher*

The star-on-a-plate award, |❂|, distinguishes pubs where the food is of exceptional quality. The knife-and-fork symbol just means the pub serves food.

MANTON

SU1768   Map 2

Outside Chance ♀

(01672) 512352 – www.theoutsidechance.co.uk

Village (and pub) signposted off A4 just W of Marlborough; High Street; SN8 4HW

Popular dining pub, civilised and traditional, nicely reworked with sporting theme; interesting modern food

A very enjoyable and well kept little pub, this is comfortable, cosy and set in a pretty village; it's also co-owned by 20-times champion jump jockey A P McCoy. The three small linked rooms have hops on beams, flagstones or bare boards, and mainly plain pub furnishings such as chapel chairs and a long-cushioned pew; one room has a more cosseted feel, with panelling and a comfortable banquette. The décor celebrates unlikely horse-racing winners Caughoo, Foinavon, Mr Spooner's Only Dreams (a 100-1 winner at Leicester in 2007) and the odd-gaited little Seabiscuit, who cheered many thousands of americans with his dogged pursuit of victory during the Depression. There's a splendid log fire in the big main fireplace and maybe fresh flowers and candlelight; background music and board games. Wadworths IPA, 6X and a guest from Wadworths on handpump, eight good wines by the glass and lovely coffee served by neatly dressed young staff; background music, board games and TV. A suntrap side terrace has contemporary tables with metal frames and granite tops, while the good-sized garden has sturdy rustic tables and benches under ash trees; they have private access to the local playing fields and children's play area. There are plenty of walks and things to see and do nearby.

A wide choice of good food might include panko-breaded langoustine tails with pea purée, herbed scotch egg with pork crackling and curried mayonnaise, pea, goats curd and pea shoot risotto, home-baked ham eggs benedict, beer-battered haddock with triple-cooked chips, a tart of the day, cajun chicken with potato, green bean and shallot salad, rib-eye steak with green peppercorn sauce, and puddings such as chocolate brownie with warm chocolate sauce and sticky toffee pudding with toffee sauce. *Benchmark main dish: burger with toppings, red onion jam, coleslaw and frites £13.95. Two-course evening meal £21.00.*

Wadworths ~ Tenant Howard Spooner ~ Real ale ~ Open 12-11 ~ Bar food 12-2, 6.30-9; 12-4, 6.30-9 Sun ~ Children welcome ~ Dogs welcome ~ Wi-fi *Recommended by Edward May, Toby Jones, Michael Doswell, Wilburoo, Tina and David Woods-Taylor*

MARLBOROUGH

SU1869   Map 2

Lamb 🍺

(01672) 512668 – www.thelambinnmarlborough.com

The Parade; SN8 1NE

Friendly former coaching inn with big helpings of popular food, real ales, plenty of customers and traditional pubby furnishings; comfortable bedrooms

Our readers enjoy very much their visits to this family-run local – tucked away in a side street – and there's always a good bustling atmosphere. The L-shaped bar has lots of hop bines, wall banquettes, wheelback chairs around wooden tables on parquet flooring, Cecil Aldin prints on red walls, candles in bottles and a two-way woodburning stove; the easy-going bulldog may be poddling about. Wadworths IPA, 6X, Horizon and Swordfish tapped from the cask, ten wines by the glass and 15 malt whiskies; games machine, juke box, darts and TV. There are picnic-sets and modern alloy and wicker seats and tables in the attractive back courtyard. The bedrooms are light and cottagey (some are in a former stable block) and breakfasts hearty. In summer, the window boxes are very pretty.

Generous helpings of fair priced food includes sandwiches, prawn cocktail, black pudding, sauté potatoes and a poached egg, rare-breed sausages with onion gravy, steak and kidney in Guinness pie, butternut squash and chickpea tagine with pistachio rice, burger with toppings, onion rings and fries, herb-battered cod and chips, daily specials such as red thai king prawn curry and cottage pie cooked by the landlady, and puddings. *Benchmark main dish: Sunday roast with ten different vegetables £10.00. Two-course evening meal £18.00.*

Wadworths ~ Tenant Vyv Scott ~ Real ale ~ Open 11-11 (11.30 Fri, Sat); 12-10.30 Sun ~ Bar food 12-2.30, 6.30-9; not Fri-Sun evenings ~ Children welcome until 8pm ~ Dogs allowed in bar and bedrooms ~ Wi-fi ~ Bedrooms: $55/$85 *Recommended by Tony Baldwin, Sheila and Robert Robinson*

MARSTON MEYSEY   SU 1297   Map 4
Old Spotted Cow 🏵 ♀

(01285) 810264 ~ www.theoldspottedcow.co.uk
Off A419 Swindon–Cirencester; SN6 6LQ

An easy-going atmosphere in cottagey bar rooms, friendly young staff, lots to look at, well kept ales and enjoyable food

There are indeed cows of some sort all around this friendly, charming pub (and some actually are spotted): paintings, drawings, postcards, all manner and colour of china objects and embroidery and toy ones too. The main bar has high-backed cushioned dining chairs around chunky pine tables on wooden floorboards or parquet, a few rugs here and there, an open fire at each end of the room (with comfortable sofas in front of one), fresh flowers and brass candlesticks with candles, and beer mats and bank notes pinned to beams. Butcombe Gold, Otter Ale and Wadworths 6X on handpump, a dozen wines by the glass, farm cider, a proper bloody mary and home-made cordials served by helpful staff. Two cottagey dining rooms lead off here with similar tables and chairs, a couple of long pews and a big bookshelf. There are seats and picnic-sets on the front grass and a children's play area beyond a big willow tree. A classic car show is held here on the first May bank holiday.

Consistently good and interesting, the food includes sandwiches, citrus and vodka-cured salmon with sour cream and bloody mary sauce, shish and kofta kebabs with pickled red cabbage, sweet chilli sauce and tzatziki, bubble and squeak with bacon, a poached egg and mustard cream sauce, macaroni cheese with white truffle crumb and garlic and parmesan toast, lamb and harissa burger with sweet potato chips, beer-battered haddock and chips, venison goulash, and puddings such as grilled pears in honey with local blue brie and welsh cakes and sticky toffee pudding with toffee sauce. *Benchmark main dish: scallops with roasted beetroot, caramelised apple, black pudding and crispy parma ham £13.00. Two-course evening meal £10.00.*

Free house ~ Licensee Anna Langley-Poole ~ Real ale ~ Open 11-11; 11-9 Sun ~ Bar food 12-2, 7-9; 12-3 Sun ~ Restaurant ~ Children welcome but must be over 10 in bar ~ Dogs allowed in bar ~ Wi-fi *Recommended by Gavin and Helle May, Isobel Mackinlay, David Fowler, Mr and Mrs John and Anne Selby*

Please keep sending us reports. We rely on readers for news of new discoveries, and particularly for news of changes – however slight – at the fully described pubs: feedback@goodguides.com, or (no stamp needed) The Good Pub Guide, FREEPOST RTJR-ZCYZ-RJZT, Perrymans Lane, Etchingham TN19 7DN.

MONKTON FARLEIGH
Muddy Duck 🏠

ST8065   Map 2

(01225) 858705 – www.themuddyduckbath.co.uk
Signed off A363 Bradford-on-Avon to Bath BA15 2QH

Grand stone building in pretty village with character bar and dining room, open fire, real ales, enjoyable food and seats at the front and back; bedrooms

With Bath nearby and some lovely surrounding walks, this imposing 17th-c stone inn makes a good base for exploring the area: three of the five individually decorated bedrooms have woodburning stoves, and two are separate from the main building and have their own little courtyards. The bar and dining room are similarly furnished with wooden and upholstered chairs around tables of all shapes on bare boards or parquet flooring, sofas in front of an open fire, cushioned pews, the odd duck ornament, beams, half-panelled walls and low-hanging lamps. High red leather chairs line the counter where friendly staff serve Box Steam Funnel Blower, Butcombe Bitter and St Austell Proper Job on handpump and good wines by the glass; background music and board games. In front of the building there's an impressive wisteria and picnic-sets under parasols; at the back, colourful tables and chairs sit in a fairy-lit, gravelled courtyard with views over open country. This is a pretty village.

🍽 Using ingredients from small local producers, the rewarding food includes sandwiches, confit chicken terrine and pâté with frozen grapes, crab tortellini and velouté with orange dressing, tomato and ricotta tart with crispy courgettes, beer-battered haddock and triple-cooked chips, slow-cooked pork belly with seared scallops, braised fennel and maple glaze, rump and slow-roast shoulder of lamb and braised baby gem, fish stew with clams and prawns, croutes and aioli, and puddings. *Benchmark main dish: fresh fish of the day £15.00. Two-course evening meal £25.00.*

Punch ~ Lease Joe Holden ~ Real ale ~ Open 12-11; 12-9 Sun ~ Bar food 12-2.30, 6-9; 12-3, 6-9.30 Sat; 12-4 Sun ~ Restaurant ~ Children welcome ~ Dogs allowed in bar ~ Wi-fi
Recommended by Taff Thomas

NEWTON TONY
Malet Arms 🍽 🍺

SU2140   Map 2

(01980) 629279 – www.maletarms.com
Village signposted off A338 Swindon–Salisbury; SP4 0HF

Smashing village pub with no pretensions, a good choice of local beers and highly thought-of food

Thanks to plenty of genuine, unspoilt character and a charming, enthusiastic landlord, our readers continue to enjoy their visits here. The low-beamed interconnecting rooms have nice furnishings, including a mix of tables of different sizes with high-winged wall settles, carved pews, chapel and carver chairs, and lots of pictures of local scenes and from imperial days. The main front windows are said to be made from the stern of a ship, and there's a log and coal fire in a huge fireplace. The snug is noteworthy for its fantastic collection of photographs and prints celebrating the local aviation history of Boscombe Down, alongside archive photographs of Stonehenge festivals of the 1970s and '80s. At the back is a homely, red-painted dining room. Four real ales on handpump come from breweries such as Butcombe, Flack Manor, Fullers, Itchen Valley, Ramsbury, Stonehenge and Triple fff and they also keep 40 malt whiskies, eight wines by the glass and Weston's Old Rosie cider. There are seats on the small front terrace with more on grass and in the back garden. The road to the pub goes through a ford, and it may be best to use an alternative route in winter, as the water can be quite deep. There's an all-weather cricket pitch on the village green.

 Using seasonal game from local shoots (some bagged by the landlord), lamb raised in the surrounding fields and free-range local pork, the country cooking includes venison liver pâté with spicy home-made plum chutney, smokey devil rarebit (fjordling with smoked cheddar, horseradish, rosemary and tabasco on toast), millionaire's fish pie (scallops, prawns, pollack and smoked salmon), haunch of venison with sweet potato ribbons and port jus, beef braised in rioja with tomatoes and herbs, and puddings such as spiced pear crumble cake and custard and fudge cheesecake. *Benchmark main dish: burger with toppings and chips £9.95. Two-course evening meal £18.00.*

Free house ~ Licensees Noel and Annie Cardew ~ Real ale ~ Open 11-3, 6-11; 12-3 (4 in winter), 7-10.30 Sun; closed Sun evening in winter ~ Bar food 12-2.30, 6.30-9.30; 12-3, 6-9 Sun ~ Restaurant ~ Children allowed only in restaurant or snug ~ Dogs allowed in bar *Recommended by Pat and Tony Martin, David Silk, John Allman*

PITTON
Silver Plough ♀ ⇤
SU2131 Map 2

(01722) 712266 – www.silverplough-pitton.co.uk
Village signed from A30 E of Salisbury (follow brown signs); SP5 1DU

Bustling country dining pub with popular, reasonably priced bar food, good drinks and nearby walks; bedrooms

We always get warm praise from our readers for this particularly well run pub, where there's a cheerful mix of both locals and visitors – all are welcomed by the friendly landlord, and dogs might get a free biscuit. The comfortable, nicely kept front bar has plenty to look at: black beams strung with hundreds of antique boot warmers and stretchers, pewter and china tankards, copper kettles, toby jugs, earthenware and glass rolling pins, and so forth. Seats include half a dozen cushioned antique oak settles (one elaborately carved, next to a very fine reproduction of an Elizabethan oak table) around rustic pine tables. They keep Badger Bitter, Sussex and Tanglefoot on handpump and 13 wines by the glass served from a bar made from a hand-carved Elizabethan overmantel. The back bar is simpler, but still has a big winged high-backed settle, cases of antique swords and some substantial pictures, and there are two woodburning stoves for winter warmth; background music. The skittle alley is for private use only. The quiet south-facing lawn has picnic-sets and other tables beneath parasols and there are more seats on the heated terrace; occasional barbecues. If you stay overnight and don't have breakfast, prices are cheaper than those given below. There are plenty of walks in the surrounding woodland and on downland paths.

Good, popular food includes lunchtime sandwiches, duck liver parfait with kumquat marmalade, whole baked camembert infused with garlic porcini mushrooms, vegetable chilli with sour cream, chicken with spinach bubble and squeak, roast beetroot and mushroom and brandy sauce, bass fillet with sauté samphire, banana shallots and shellfish bisque, trio of lamb (chargrilled chop, rump, breaded slow-roasted), minted butter beans and matchstick potatoes, and puddings such as passion-fruit and white chocolate mousse and cheesecake of the day. *Benchmark main dish: slow-cooked cider pork belly with boulangère potatoes and apple and sage sauce £13.95. Two-course evening meal £18.00.*

Badger ~ Tenants Katie Hunter and Mike Reeves ~ Real ale ~ Open 12-3, 6-11; 12-9 Sun ~ Bar food 12-2, 6-9; 12-8 Sun ~ Restaurant ~ Children welcome ~ Dogs allowed in bar ~ Wi-fi

~ Bedrooms: £50/£60 *Recommended by Fr Robert Marsh, Helen and Brian Edgeley, Norman Patterson, Peter Andrews, Peter Meister, Tom and Ruth Rees, I D Barnett, David and Judy Robison*

 POULSHOT   ST9760   Map 2

Raven 🍺

(01380) 828271 – www.ravenpoulshot.co.uk

Off A361; SN10 1RW

Pretty village pub with friendly licensees, enjoyable beer and food (cooked by the landlord) and seats in a walled back garden

You can be sure of a friendly welcome from the professional licensees of this pretty half-timbered pub – and it's just the place for refreshment after enjoying a nearby walk. The two cosy, black-beamed rooms are spotlessly kept with comfortable banquettes, pubby chairs and tables and an open fire. Wadworths IPA and 6X plus a guest such as Wadworths Waterloo tapped from the cask and 13 wines by the glass; background music in the dining room only. The jack russell is called Faith and the doberman Harvey. There are picnic-sets under parasols in the walled back garden and the pub is just across from the village green.

 Cooked by the landlord, the well liked food includes baguettes, chicken liver pâté with redcurrant jelly, crab bruschetta, asian chicken salad with fresh chilli, pickled ginger, peanuts, coriander and crispy onion, butternut squash, chestnut mushroom and spinach lasagne, steak and kidney pie, beer-battered haddock with home-made tartare sauce, liver and bacon with red wine gravy, free-range pork belly with cider and cranberry gravy, and puddings such as spotted dick with custard and rhubarb eton mess. *Benchmark main dish: fish crumble £11.95. Two-course evening meal £18.00.*

Wadworths ~ Tenants Jeremy and Nathalie Edwards ~ Real ale ~ Open 11.30-3, 6.30-11; 12-3.30, 7-10.30 Sun; closed Sun evening Oct-Easter, Mon except bank holidays ~ Bar food 12-2 (2.30 Sun), 6.30-9 ~ Restaurant ~ Children welcome ~ Dogs allowed in bar ~ Wi-fi
Recommended by Toby Jones, Charlie May

RAMSBURY   SU2771   Map 2

Bell 🍽 🛏

(01672) 520230 – www.thebellramsbury.com

Off B4192 NW of Hungerford, or A4 W; SN8 2PE

Lovely old inn with a civilised and relaxed atmosphere, character rooms with beams, timbering and contemporary furnishings, and a thoughtful choice of both drinks and food; spotless bedrooms

A lot of care and thought went into the refurbishment of this handsome and civilised 300-year-old former coaching inn, with original features and contemporary paintwork and furnishings blending well together. Attracting a cheerful mix of customers, the two rooms of the bar have a woodburning stove, tartan-cushioned wall seats and pale wooden dining chairs around assorted tables, country and wildlife paintings, interesting stained-glass windows and stools against the counter where efficient black-clothed staff keep Ramsbury Bitter, Gold and Sunsplash and a guest from Downton on handpump, a dozen wines by the glass and 20 malt whiskies. A cosy room between the bar and restaurant has much-prized armchairs and sofas before an open fire, a table of magazines and papers, a couple of portraits, stuffed birds and a squirrel, books on shelves and patterned wallpaper. The restaurant, smart but relaxed, is similarly furnished to the bar with white-clothed tables on bare boards or rugs, oil paintings and winter-scene photographs on beige walls; fresh flowers decorate each table.

A nice surprise is the charming back café with white-painted farmhouse, tub and wicker chairs on floorboards, where they offer toasties, buns, cakes and so forth – it's very popular for morning coffee and afternoon tea. The garden has picnic-sets on a lower terrace and raised lawn, with more on a little terrace towards the front. The restful, well equipped bedrooms are named after game birds or fish.

 Using produce (often organic) from their own kitchen garden and other local suppliers, the first class food includes potted salmon with tomato jelly and sorbet and crème fraîche, bacon, black pudding and soft-boiled egg salad with walnuts, blue cheese and beer dressing, burger with toppings, caramelised onion mayonnaise and triple-cooked chips, a pie of the day, free-range duck breast with spiced leg bonbon, roasted tomato couscous and roasting juices, and puddings such as frozen strawberry and mint parfait with Pimms gel, cucumber sorbet and candied cucumber and an ice-cream trio (ale cake, brownie and flapjack). *Benchmark main dish: beer-battered fish of the day and triple-cooked chips £12.00. Two-course evening meal £24.00.*

Free house ~ Licensee Alistair Ewing ~ Real ale ~ Open 12-11 (10 Sun) ~ Bar food 12-2.30, 6-9; 12-3, 6-8 Sun ~ Restaurant ~ Children welcome ~ Dogs allowed in bar ~ Wi-fi ~ Bedrooms: /£110 *Recommended by Alfie Bayliss, Jo Garnett, Richard Tilbrook*

SHERSTON
Rattlebone ♀

ST8585 Map 2

(01666) 840871 – www.therattlebone.co.uk
Church Street; B4040 Malmesbury–Chipping Sodbury; SN16 0LR

Village pub with rambling rooms, real ales and good bar food using local and free-range produce; friendly staff

They balance the pub and restaurant elements in this 17th-c village pub very well and our readers thoroughly enjoy their visits. The softly lit rambling rooms have a lot of character and a bustling atmosphere; there's a public bar as well as a long back dining room. Throughout, you'll find beams, standing timbers and flagstones, pews, settles and country kitchen chairs around an assortment of tables, and armchairs and sofas by roaring fires. Flying Monk Elmers, St Austell Tribute and Youngs Special on handpump, 16 wines by the glass from a thoughtful list, local cider and home-made lemonade; background music, board games, TV and games machine. Outside is a skittle alley and three boules pitches, often in use by one of the many pub teams; a boules festival is held in July, as well as mangold hurling (similar to boules, but using cattle-feed turnips) and other events. The two pretty gardens include an extended terrace where they hold barbecues and spit roasts. Wheelchair access.

As well as generous sandwiches, the enjoyable food includes lunchtime sandwiches, chicken liver parfait with spiced pear chutney, smoked salmon and crayfish roulade with cream cheese and tarragon, sharing boards, spicy pumpkin and coconut curry, burger with toppings, onion rings and skinny fries, a pie of the day, honey and lemon-glazed duck breast with roast shallots and dauphinoise potatoes, rack of lamb with lamb shoulder croquette, celeriac purée and red wine jus, and puddings such as toffee profiteroles and chantilly cream and lemon crème brûlée. *Benchmark main dish: pork tenderloin with sage mash, creamed leeks, blue cheese sauce and toasted cashews £14.50. Two-course evening meal £20.00.*

Youngs ~ Tenant Jason Read ~ Real ale ~ Open 12-3, 5-11 (midnight Fri); 12-midnight Sat; 12-11 Sun ~ Bar food 12-2.30, 6-9.30; 12-3, 6-8.30 Sun ~ Restaurant ~ Children welcome ~ Dogs allowed in bar ~ Wi-fi ~ Live music last weekend of month *Recommended by Chris and Angela Buckell, R T and J C Moggridge*

SOUTH WRAXALL ST8364 Map 2

Longs Arms 🍽️✪

(01225) 864450 – www.thelongsarms.com

Upper S Wraxall, off B3109 N of Bradford-on-Avon; BA15 2SB

Friendly licensees for well run old stone inn with plenty of character, real ales and first class food

Many of our readers come back to this handsome stone inn on a regular basis and feel it's really quite special on all counts – of course, having such an affable and enthusiastic landlord is paramount. The bar has windsor and other pubby chairs around wooden tables on flagstones, a fireplace with a woodburning stove, and high chairs by the counter where they keep Wadworths IPA and 6X on handpump and ten wines by the glass. Another room has cushioned and other dining chairs, a nice old settle and a wall banquette around a mix of tables on carpeting, fresh flowers and lots of prints and paintings; board games and skittle alley. There are tables and chairs in the pretty walled back garden, which also has raised beds and a greenhouse for salad leaves and herbs. Dog biscuits are kept behind the bar.

 The good, interesting food is cooked by the landlord: sandwiches, lambs kidneys with black pudding, chicken liver pâté with medlar jelly, rare-breed pork sausages with mash and gravy, twice-baked cheese soufflé, chicken and leek pie, line-caught bass with Morecambe Bay shrimps, crispy gnocchi and lobster sauce, organic lamb shoulder with champ, red cabbage and hazelnuts, and puddings such as Valrhona chocolate fondant with salted peanut caramel and malted milk ice-cream and vanilla and ginger nut cheesecake with rhubarb and honeycomb. *Benchmark main dish: duck breast with duck scratchings, beetroot and sauté potatoes £17.00. Two-course evening meal £20.00.*

Wadworths ~ Tenants Rob and Liz Allcock ~ Real ale ~ Open 12-3.30, 5.30-11.30; 12-11.30 Sat, Sun; closed Mon, three weeks Jan ~ Bar food 12-2.30, 5.30-9.30; 12-9.30 Fri, Sat; 12-5 Sun ~ Children welcome ~ Dogs allowed in bar ~ Wi-fi *Recommended by David and Jill Wyatt, Michael Doswell, Taff Thomas, Mr and Mrs A H Young, Mr and Mrs P R Thomas*

SWINDON SU1384 Map 2

Weighbridge Brewhouse 🍺

(01793) 881500 – www.weighbridgebrewhouse.co.uk

Penzance Drive; SN5 7JL

Stunning building with stylish modern décor, own microbrewery ales, a huge wine list, a big range of popular food and helpful staff

Although much emphasis is placed on the highly popular food, this huge place is a brewhouse and you can peak through a glass viewing panel to see the brewing equipment. They keep six of their own ales at any one time, such as Weighbridge American Pale Ale, Best, Brinkworth Village, English Ale, Headbanger and Pooley's Golden; also, 23 wines by the glass, 25 malt whiskies and a cocktail menu. The bar area has comfortable brown leather chesterfields and wood and leather armchairs around a few tables on dark flagstones, much-used blue bar chairs against the long dimpled and polished steel counter and a sizeable carved wooden eagle on a stand. The fantastic-looking, stylishly modern, open-plan dining room has a steel-tensioned high-raftered roof (the big central skylight adds even more light), attractive high-backed striped chairs and long wall banquettes, bare brick walls, candles in red glass jars on window sills and a glass cabinet at the end displaying about 1,000 bottled beers from around the world. Metal stairs lead up to an area overlooking the dining room below, with big sofas and chairs beside a glass piano; another room on the same level is used for cosier dining occasions. There are seats on an outside terrace.

🍴 The wide choice of highly popular food includes lunch dishes (all priced at £12.50) such as home-made faggots with onion gravy and dauphinoise potatoes, local trout en papillote with white wine, dill, tarragon and concasse tomato sauce, seafood tagliatelle, steak and kidney pie, bone-in pork chop with cider, chorizo, mushroom and cream sauce and veal stroganoff. Also, pricier items such as beef and black pudding stack with shiitake mushrooms in creamy marsala sauce, indian-style lamb shank, rabbit and pork pudding in cider gravy, and puddings such as banoffi pie with toffee sauce and mixed berry brûlée. *Benchmark main dish: half a crispy duck with strawberry sauce £25.00. Two-course evening meal £35.00.*

Free house ~ Licensees Anthony and Allyson Windle ~ Real ale ~ Open 11.30-11.30; 12-10 Sun ~ Restaurant ~ Children welcome before 7.30pm ~ Dogs allowed in bar ~ Live music Thurs-Sat evenings *Recommended by Pat and Tony Martin, Roger and Donna Huggins*

TOLLARD ROYAL   ST9317   Map 2
King John 🏵 ⇌
(01725) 516207 – www.kingjohninn.co.uk
B3081 Shaftesbury–Sixpenny Handley; SP5 5PS

Pleasing contemporary furnishings in carefully opened-up pub, courteous, helpful service, a good choice of drinks and excellent food; pretty bedrooms

Locals do drop in for a pint of Flack Manor Double Drop, Ringwood Best and Waylands Sixpenny 6d Gold on handpump or a glass of wine from a good list – but most customers come to this civilised pub to enjoy the particularly good, inventive food. The L-shaped, open-plan bar has a relaxed atmosphere, a log fire, nice little touches such as a rosemary plant and tiny metal buckets of salt and pepper on scrubbed kitchen tables, dog-motif cushions, a screen made up of the sides of wine boxes, and candles in big glass jars. An attractive mix of seats takes in spindlebacks, captain's and chapel chairs (some built into the bay windows) plus the odd cushioned settle, and there are big terracotta floor tiles, lantern-style wall lights, hound, hunting and other photographs, and prints of early 19th-c scientists. A second log fire has fender seats on each side and leather chesterfields in front, and there's also a stuffed heron and grouse and daily papers. Outside at the front are seats and tables beneath parasols, with more up steps in the raised garden where there's also an outdoor kitchen pavilion. The bedrooms are comfortable and pretty and there's a self-catering cottage opposite.

🏵 Using the best local, seasonal produce, the interesting food includes pigeon and bacon salad with croutons, house-smoked trout with a crispy egg and gherkins, twice-baked cheddar cheese soufflé, line-caught fish and chips with tartare sauce, roast duck legs with chilli duck noodle soup, rose veal chop with béarnaise sauce, and puddings such as chocolate fondant and sticky toffee pudding, both with ice-cream. *Benchmark main dish: venison haunch with beetroot pearl barley, greens and red wine reduction £17.95. Two-course evening meal £22.00.*

Free house ~ Licensee Adam Wilson ~ Real ale ~ Open 11-midnight ~ Bar food 12-2.30, 7-9.30; 12-3, 7-9 Sun ~ Restaurant ~ Children welcome ~ Dogs welcome ~ Wi-fi ~ Bedrooms: £95/£140 *Recommended by Mr and Mrs J J A Davis, Peter and Eleanor Kenyon, Michael Doswell, Michael Hill*

The details at the end of each featured entry start by saying whether the pub is a free house, or if it belongs to a brewery or pub group (which we name).

UPTON LOVELL
ST9441 Map 2
Prince Leopold
(01985) 850460 – www.princeleopoldinn.co.uk
Up Street, village signed from A36; BA12 0JP

Snug little rooms, a friendly atmosphere, welcoming licensees and enjoyable food and drink; bedrooms

Run by charming licensees and their friendly staff, this is a prettily tucked-away and neatly modernised Victorian pub. The simply furnished bar – busy with chatty locals – has two farmhouse tables with sturdy chairs and stools against the hand-crafted elm counter where they serve Butcombe Bitter and Plain Sheep Dip and Innspiration on handpump, 16 wines by the glass and interesting spirits. Off the bar is a cosy little snug with an open fire and a book-lined wall, tapestry cushions on comfortable sofas and a table with daily papers; two other linked rooms have scrubbed tables and wooden dining chairs, rugs on bare boards and some country prints on pale green walls. The back restaurant is light and airy and overlooks the River Wylye – as do some outdoor balcony tables. The garden has its own charming bar and seats and tables by the river. The cottagey bedrooms are comfortable and well equipped.

 The reliably good food includes sandwiches, salt and pepper squid with sweet chilli dip, tian of crayfish and prawns with lemon and pickled ginger, pork sausages with mash and onion gravy, cajun chicken burger with chilli mayonnaise and skinny fries, fillet of black bream with creamy white wine sauce and spring greens, confit duck leg with blackcurrant jus and dauphinoise potatoes, and puddings such as vanilla crème brûlée and chocolate and hazelnut brownie with white chocolate ice-cream. *Benchmark main dish: cannon of lamb and confit lamb shoulder with broccoli purée and romanesco and red wine jus £21.50. Two-course evening meal £22.00.*

Free house ~ Licensee Liza Kearney ~ Real ale ~ Open 12-3 (3.30 in winter), 6-11; 12-11 Sat; 12-9.30 (12-4 in winter) Sun ~ Bar food 12-2.30, 6-8.30 (9 Sat, 8 Sun in summer) ~ Restaurant ~ Children welcome ~ Dogs allowed in bar and bedrooms ~ Wi-fi ~ Bedrooms: £60/£75 *Recommended by Hugh Roberts, Steve and Liz Tilley*

UPTON SCUDAMORE
ST8647 Map 2
Angel
(01985) 213225 – www.theangelinn.co.uk
Off A350 N of Warminster; BA12 0AG

Bustling bar and dining rooms where old and new features blend together, real ales, good wines, well thought-of food and seats in garden; attractive bedrooms

Recently refurbished, this 16th-c coaching inn makes a good base for exploring the area – Longleat House and Safari Park are close by. The bedrooms are comfortable and contemporary and breakfasts good. The spreading bar and lounge area has big leather sofas by an open fire, house plants and candles in lanterns, and stools against the counter where they serve Butcombe Bitter and Wadworths 6X on handpump and good wines by the glass; service is friendly and helpful. Steps lead up to an informal dining room with farmhouse and wheelback chairs around rustic tables on bare boards, and there's also a restaurant with a pitched ceiling, elegant antique-style chairs and tables on tartan carpet and hanging lamps. Throughout there are big paintings, prints and ornate mirrors on bold paintwork and pretty flower arrangements. The flower-filled, terraced back garden has modern chairs and tables under parasols.

❚❙ Good food with modern touches includes sandwiches, ham hock terrine with pea panna cotta, baked goats cheese with honey, pine nuts and compressed pear, ham and eggs with triple-cooked chips, a pie of the day, wild mushroom risotto, pork tenderloin with cider and butter fondant potato and confit of tomato and jus, swordfish steak with sauté potatoes and Pernod cream, and puddings such as vanilla cheesecake with blackcurrant sorbet and lemon posset. *Benchmark main dish: tiger prawns with garlic, shallots and sweet chilli cream and chips £17.00. Two-course evening meal £18.00.*

Free house ~ Licensee Sharon Cornelius ~ Real ale ~ Open 11.30-3, 6-11; 11.30-4, 5.30-10 Sun; see website for opening times in winter ~ Bar food 12-2, 6.30-9; 12-3, 6.30-8 Sun ~ Restaurant ~ Children welcome ~ Dogs allowed in bar ~ Wi-fi ~ Bedrooms: £90/£100
Recommended by Neil Allen, John Harris

WEST LAVINGTON
SU0052 Map 2

Bridge Inn ⭐️

(01380) 813213 – www.the-bridge-inn.co.uk
Church Street (A360); SN10 4LD

Friendly dining pub with good bar food cooked by the landlord, real ales and a light, comfortable bar

The comfortable, spacious bar in this quietly civilised village pub mixes contemporary elements with firmly traditional fixtures such as the enormous brick inglenook with its roaring log fire; at the opposite end (in an area set mostly for dining) is a smaller modern fireplace. Cream-painted or exposed brick walls are hung with local pictures of the Lavingtons, there are fresh flowers, evening candlelight and an easy-going atmosphere; timbers and the occasional step divide the various areas. Sharps Doom Bar and Wadworths IPA on handpump, ten wines by the glass and half a dozen malt whiskies; background music and board games. The raised lawn at the back is a pleasant place to spend a summer's afternoon, and there are large vegetable patches for home-grown produce and chickens; boules.

⭐️ Rewarding food cooked by the landlord includes lunchtime sandwiches, seared scallops with onion purée, chorizo, capers and sultana jus, crispy pig's head with black pudding, apple sauce and crackling, potato gnocchi with spicy tomato sauce and parmesan, beer-battered fish and chips, bass fillet with spring onion mash, pak choi, soy dressing and crispy ginger, and puddings such as double chocolate brownie with cherry ripple ice-cream and bread and butter pudding. *Benchmark main dish: haunch of venison, mini venison pie, potato rösti and red wine jus £16.50. Two-course evening meal £20.00.*

Enterprise ~ Lease Emily Robinson and James Stewart ~ Real ale ~ Open 12-3, 6-10 (12-11 Sat in summer); 12-5 Sun; closed Sun evening, Mon ~ Bar food 12-2.30, 6.30-9; 12-3 Sun ~ Restaurant ~ Children welcome ~ Dogs welcome ~ Wi-fi *Recommended by Belinda Stamp, Jo Garnett*

'Children welcome' means the pub says it lets children inside without any special restriction. If it allows them in, but to restricted areas such as an eating area or family room, we specify this. Places with separate restaurants often let children use them, and hotels usually let children into public areas such as lounges. Some pubs impose an evening time limit – let us know if you find one earlier than 9pm.

Also Worth a Visit in Wiltshire

Besides the fully inspected pubs, you might like to try these pubs that have been recommended to us and described by readers. Do tell us what you think of them: feedback@goodguides.com

ALDBOURNE   SU2675
Crown (01672) 540214
The Square; SN8 2DU Old local overlooking pretty village's pond, good value enjoyable food including pizzas and Sun carvery, Sharps Doom Bar, Shepherd Neame Spitfire and guests, friendly helpful staff, comfortable two-part beamed lounge with sofas by log fire in huge brick inglenook linking to public bar, old tables and bare boards, small nicely laid out dining room; background and some live music, Mon movie night, Tues quiz; children and dogs welcome, courtyard tables, Early English church nearby, four bedrooms, open (and food) all day. *(John Harris)*

ALVEDISTON   ST9723
Crown (01722) 780335
Off A30 W of Salisbury; SP5 5JY Cosy 15th-c thatched inn with three very low-beamed, partly panelled rooms, two inglenooks, good choice of enjoyable fairly priced home-made food, four well kept ales including Sixpenny, Wessex cider, pleasant service; children and dogs welcome, pretty views from attractive garden with terrace, good local walks, three bedrooms, open all day Sat, till 9pm Sun. *(David and Judy Robison)*

BADBURY   SU1980
★ Plough (01793) 740342
A346 (Marlborough Road) just S of M4 junction 15; SN4 0EP Busy country pub well placed for M4 with wide choice of good fairly priced food, friendly efficient service, well kept Arkells and decent wines, large rambling bar with log fire, light airy dining room; background music; children and dogs welcome, tree-shaded garden with Downs views, open all day from 9am for breakfast, food all day Sun till 8pm. *(Giles and Annie Francis, R T and J C Moggridge, R K Phillips, Richard and Judy Winn)*

BARFORD ST MARTIN   SU0531
★ Barford Inn (01722) 742242
B3089 W of Salisbury (Grovely Road), just off A30; SP3 4AB Welcoming 16th-c coaching inn, dark panelled front bar with big log fire, other interlinking rooms, old utensils and farming tools, beamed bare-brick restaurant, wide choice of enjoyable reasonably priced food including deals, prompt friendly service, well kept Badger ales and decent wines by the glass; children welcome, dogs in bar, disabled access (not to bar) and loos, terrace tables, more tables in back garden, four comfortable annexe bedrooms, good walks, open all day. *(Wendy Breese, Michael Hill)*

BECKHAMPTON   SU0868
★ Waggon & Horses (01672) 539418
A4 Marlborough–Calne; SN8 1QJ Handsome stone and thatch former coaching inn; generous fairly priced food cooked to order from varied menu in open-plan beamed bar or separate dining area, well kept Wadworths ales, good cheerful service; background music; children and dogs welcome, pleasant raised garden with play area, handy for Avebury (NT and EH), open all day Fri-Sun. *(Sheila and Robert Robinson)*

BERWICK ST JAMES   SU0739
★ Boot (01722) 790243
High Street (B3083); SP3 4TN Welcoming flint and stone pub not far from Stonehenge; good locally sourced food from daily changing blackboard menu including some unusual bar snacks, friendly efficient staff, well kept Wadworths ales and a guest, huge log fire in inglenook at one end, sporting prints over brick fireplace the other, lit candles, small back dining room with collection of celebrity boots; children and dogs welcome, sheltered side lawn. *(Dennis and Doreen Haward)*

BERWICK ST JOHN   ST9422
★ Talbot (01747) 828222
Village signed from A30 E of Shaftesbury; SP7 0HA Unspoilt 17th-c pub in attractive village, simple furnishings and big inglenook in heavily beamed bar, Ringwood Best, Wadworths 6X and a guest, several wines by the glass, good choice of popular home-made food including decent vegetarian options, friendly service, restaurant, darts; free wi-fi; children welcome and dogs (pub has its own), seats outside, good local walks, closed Sun evening, Mon. *(Pip White, Toby Jones, Helen and Brian Edgeley)*

BIDDESTONE   ST8673
★ Biddestone Arms (01249) 714377
Off A420 W of Chippenham; The Green; SN14 7DG Spacious white-painted stone pub mostly set out for its very popular food from standards to specials, good vegetarian options, gluten-free choices and Sun carvery too, friendly efficient service despite being busy, well kept Sharps, Wadworths and guests, nice open fire; children and dogs (in front bar) welcome, pretty back garden, attractive village with lovely pond. *(Mr and Mrs A H Young, R K Phillips, Roger and Donna Huggins)*

BOX   ST8168
Northey Arms (01225) 742333
A4, Bath side; SN13 8AE Stone-built
19th-c dining pub with good choice of
enjoyable food, Wadworths ales and decent
wines by the glass, fresh contemporary décor
with chunky modern tables and high-backed
rattan chairs; background music; children
welcome, garden tables, five bedrooms, open
(and food) all day from 8am. *(Taff Thomas)*

BOX   ST8369
★ Quarrymans Arms (01225) 743569
*On A4 (London Road) from Bath, right
into Beech Road, keep left then right into
Bargates Hill; from Corsham, left after
Rudloe Park Hotel into Beech Road, then
third left on to Barnetts Hill; OS Sheet
173 map reference 834694; SN13 8HN*
Enjoyable unpretentious pub with friendly
staff and informal relaxed atmosphere,
plenty of mining-related photographs and
memorabilia (once a local for Bath-stone
miners – you can hire a key to visit the
extensive mines or take a guided tour),
well kept Butcombe, Moles, Wadworths and
guests, 60 malt whiskies and several wines
by the glass, decent choice of enjoyable fairly
priced food (all day Sun) including daily
specials; children and dogs welcome, picnic-
sets on terrace with sweeping views, popular
with walkers and potholers, four bedrooms,
open all day. *(Roger and Donna Huggins,
Alan and Jane Shaw, Taff Thomas)*

BRADFORD-ON-AVON   ST8260
Barge (01225) 863403
Frome Road; BA15 2EA Large modernised
stone inn set down from canal, well kept
ales such as Brakspears, Fullers, Marstons
and Ringwood, nice wines by the glass and
enjoyable pub food including children's
choices, good friendly staff and atmosphere,
open-plan interior with stripped stone,
flagstones and solid furniture, woodburners;
wheelchair access, garden with smokers'
pavilion, steps up to canalside picnic-sets,
moorings, five bedrooms. *(John Coatsworth,
Taff Thomas, Giles and Annie Francis)*

BRADFORD-ON-AVON   ST8060
Cross Guns (01225) 862335
*Avoncliff, 2 miles W; OS Sheet 173 map
reference 805600; BA15 2HB* Congenial
bustle on summer days with swarms of
people in partly concreted areas steeply
terraced above the bridges, aqueducts and
river; appealingly quaint at quieter times,
with stripped-stone low-beamed bar, 16th-c
inglenook, full Box Steam range kept well
and a guest, several ciders, lots of malt
whiskies and interesting wines by the glass
including country ones, decent choice of
sensibly priced food from baguettes and light
meals up, good friendly service, upstairs
river-view restaurant; children and dogs
welcome, wheelchair accessible, bedrooms,

self-catering cottage and canal moorings,
open (and food) all day. *(Nick Lawless,
Giles and Annie Francis)*

BRADFORD-ON-AVON   ST8161
Dog & Fox (01225) 862137
Ashley Road; BA15 1RT Welcoming
new owners for this unpretentious little
two-room pub on country outskirts, beams
and painted half-panelling, well kept Bath
Gem, Courage Best and Sharps Doom, four
draught ciders, enjoyable affordably priced
traditional food, right-hand part with
little serving hatch and comfy seating by
woodburner, carpeted dining area behind,
small bare-boards bar to the left with darts;
children and dogs welcome, picnic-sets and
play area in lawned garden, open all day
Fri-Sun. *(Taff Thomas)*

BRADFORD-ON-AVON   ST8260
Swan (01225) 868686
*Church Street; car park off A363
Trowbridge Road, beside central bridge;
BA15 1LN* Don't be put off by the rather
unprepossessing approach from the car
park at the back of this old inn, the interior
is nicely decorated and the young staff
cheerful and welcoming, Greene King Old
Speckled Hen and a guest or two, decent
cider and enjoyable food from pub favourites
to authentic thai dishes, can eat in bar or
restaurant; some live music including Tues
folk club; terrace tables, bedrooms.
(Tom and Jill Jones)

BRINKWORTH   SU0184
★ Three Crowns (01666) 510366
*The Street; B4042 Wootton Bassett–
Malmesbury; SN15 5AF* Most pubby part
is the chatty locals' bar, beams, partitioning,
cushioned wall settles and sturdy mate's
chairs around shiny tables on patterned
carpet, horsebrasses, jugs and mugs,
fireplace at each end, Fullers London Pride,
Sharps Doom Bar and a guest, real cider
and 18 wines by the glass, conservatory-style
restaurant with flagstones and ceiling fans,
other spreading dining areas with hunting
horns, shelves of bottles, shells in hanging
nets and a giant pair of bellows, well liked
food including set menu choices; background
music, TV, free wi-fi; children and dogs
welcome, tables under parasols on terrace,
more seats in garden overlooking church
and farmland, open all day (food all day Sun
till 8pm). *(Anon)*

BROAD HINTON   SU1176
★ Barbury (01793) 731510
*On A4361 Swindon–Devizes, E of
village; SN4 9PF* Roadside sister pub
to the Vine Tree in Norton; long bar with
woodburner at each end, a few wicker
armchairs and tables on bare boards,
hunting and shooting prints, Regency-striped
modern armchairs around counter serving
St Austell and a guest, 30 wines by the glass,

steps up to carpeted dining room, enjoyable often interesting food (not Sun evening); background music, daily newspapers, free wi-fi; children and dogs welcome, seats and tables on partly covered back terrace, open all day. *(Isobel Mackinlay, Martin Jones, Tony Baldwin, Hilary and Neil Christopher)*

BROMHAM   ST9665
Greyhound (01380) 850241
Off A342; High Street; SN15 2HA
Popular old beamed dining pub with light modern décor, comfortable sofas and log fires, walk-across well in back bar, wide choice of good reasonably priced home-made food including weekday set lunch, efficient friendly service, well kept Wadworths ales and wide choice of wines, upstairs skittle alley/restaurant; background music; children welcome, no dogs inside, pretty hanging baskets in front, big enclosed garden with decking and boules, open (and food) all day. *(Mr and Mrs P R Thomas)*

BULKINGTON   ST9458
Well (01380) 828287
High Street; SN10 1SJ Popular dining pub with modernised open-plan interior, good food from traditional favourites up, theme night first Mon of month, efficient friendly service, ales such as Butcombe, Sharps, Timothy Taylors and Wadworths, well priced wines; background music; closed Mon lunchtime. *(Hilary and Neil Chrisopher)*

BURCOMBE   SU0631
★ Ship (01722) 744879
Burcombe Lane; brown sign to pub off A30 W of Salisbury, then turn right; SP2 0EJ Busy pub under welcoming new ownership (some refurbishment); most customers here for the enjoyable fairly traditional pub food including good dry-aged steaks; section by entrance with log fire, beams and leather-cushioned wall and window seats on slate tiles, steps up to spreading area of pale wood dining chairs around bleached tables, more beams (one supporting splendid chandelier), three changing local ales, Thatcher's heritage cider, nice wines by the glass and good range of gins and whiskies; background music, free wi-fi; children, dogs and muddy boots welcome, picnic-sets in informal back garden sloping down to willows by fenced-off River Nadder, open (and food) all day weekends. *(Jo Garnett)*

CASTLE COMBE   ST8477
Castle Inn (01249) 783030
Off A420; SN14 7HN Handsome inn centrally placed in this remarkably preserved Cotswold village; beamed bar with big inglenook, padded bar stools and fine old settle, hunting and vintage motor-racing pictures, Butcombe and Castle Combe, decent wines by the glass, well liked bar food and more restaurary evening menu, friendly

attentive service, two snug lounges, formal dining rooms and big upstairs eating area opening on to charming little roof terrace; children welcome, no dogs inside, tables out at front looking down idyllic main street, fascinating medieval church clock, 11 bedrooms, limited parking, open all day from 9.30am. *(Mr and Mrs A H Young)*

CASTLE COMBE   ST8477
White Hart (01249) 782295
Signed off B4039 Chippenham–Chipping Sodbury; SN14 7HS Attractive 14th-c Wadworths pub in centre of this popular honeypot village, beams, panelling, flagstones and log fires, seats in stone-mullioned window, lots of old local photographs, good choice of enjoyable generously served food from doorstep sandwiches up, modern restaurant on left; children, dogs and walkers welcome (handy for Macmillan Way and new Palladian Way), tables on pavement and in sheltered courtyard, open all day. *(Roger and Donna Huggins)*

CHILMARK   ST9732
Black Dog (01722) 716344
B3089 Salisbury–Hindon; SP3 5AH Cosy 15th-c beamed village pub with several linked areas, cushioned window seats, inglenook woodburner, a suit of armour in one part, black and white film star pictures in another, enjoyable home-made food from lunchtime sandwiches and pizzas up, Wadworths ales, friendly service; free wi-fi; children and dogs welcome, disabled access, good-sized garden fenced from road, closed Sun evening, also Tues Oct-Mar. *(Helen and Brian Edgeley)*

CORSHAM   ST8670
Hare & Hounds (01249) 701106
Pickwick (A4 E); SN13 0HY Friendly old pub by mini roundabout, popular well priced food (smaller helpings available), well kept ales such as Bath Gem and Caledonian Deuchars IPA, plenty of wines by the glass, log fire; Tues quiz; children (if eating) and dogs welcome, picnic-sets on strip of lawn between car park and road, open (and food) all day. *(Roger and Donna Huggins, Alan and Jane Shaw, Dr and Mrs A K Clarke)*

CORSHAM   ST8670
★ Two Pigs (01249) 712515
Pickwick (A4); SN13 0HY Friendly and cheerfully eccentric little beer lovers' pub run by character landlord – most lively on Mon evenings when there's live blues/rock; collection of bric-a-brac in narrow dimly lit flagstoned bar, enamel signs on wood-clad walls, pig-theme ornaments and old radios, Stonehenge ales including Pigswill and a couple of guests; background blues, no food or under-21s; covered yard outside called the Sty, closed lunchtimes except Sun. *(Roger and Donna Huggins, Alan and Jane Shaw)*

CORTON   ST9340

★**Dove** (01985) 850109

*Off A36 at Upton Lovell, SE of
Warminster; BA12 0SZ* On edge of small
Wylye Valley village not far from the A303;
popular well prepared food from baguettes
and pub favourites to more enterprising
dishes, good service, at least three well kept
ales such as Otter and Sharps, nice wines by
the glass and good choice of malt whiskies,
opened-up rooms with flagstones, oak boards,
magnolia walls and pale green dados, lots
of animal pictures/figurines, photographs
of horse racing and other sporting events,
flowers on good quality dining tables,
newspapers and woodburner in bar, sunny
conservatory; can get very busy; children
and dogs welcome, wheelchair access/loos,
rustic furniture in garden, five comfortable
bedrooms in courtyard annexe, open all day.
(Chris and Angela Buckell)

CROCKERTON   ST8642

★**Bath Arms** (01985) 212262

*Off A350 Warminster–Blandford;
BA12 8AJ* Welcoming old dining pub (some
recent refurbishment), bar with plush
banquettes and matching chairs, well spaced
tables on parquet, beams in whitewashed
ceiling, woodburner, two Wessex ales and a
weekend guest, real cider and several wines
by the glass, good food from interesting
changing menu (booking advised), cheerful
staff, two restaurant areas and a garden
room; background music, free wi-fi; children
and dogs (in bar) welcome, plenty of picnic-
sets in well divided garden, gets crowded
during school holidays (Longleat close by),
two bedrooms, open all day (till 6pm Sun in
winter). *(Mr and Mrs A H Young)*

DEVIZES   SU0061

Bear (01380) 722444

Market Place; SN10 1HS Ancient coaching
inn with big carpeted main bar, log fires,
winged wall settles and upholstered bucket
armchairs, steps up to room named after
portrait painter Thomas Lawrence with
oak-panelled walls and large open fireplace,
well kept Wadworths, a couple of decent
ciders and extensive choice of wines by
the glass, good food from sandwiches and
light dishes up, Bear Grills bistro, cellar bar
with live music (Fri) and comedy night first
Thurs of month; children welcome, dogs in
front bar, wheelchair access throughout,
mediterranean-style courtyard, 25 bedrooms,
open all day. *(Tom and Jill Jones)*

DEVIZES   SU0061

British Lion (01380) 720665

A361 Swindon roundabout; SN10 1LQ
Chatty little beer lovers' pub with four well
kept quickly changing ales, bare-boards bar
with brewery mirrors, gas fire, back part with
pool and darts, no food; garden behind, open
all day. *(Belinda Stamp)*

DONHEAD ST ANDREW   ST9124

★**Forester** (01747) 828038

*Village signposted off A30 E of
Shaftesbury, just E of Ludwell; Lower
Street; SP7 9EE* Attractive 14th-c thatched
restaurant-pub in charming village; relaxed
atmosphere in nice bar, stripped tables on
wood floors, log fire in inglenook, alcove
with sofa and magazines, Butcombe Bitter
and a guest, 15 wines by the glass including
champagne, very good well presented food
from bar tapas up with much emphasis on
fresh fish/seafood, good service, comfortable
main dining room with well spaced country
kitchen tables, second cosier dining room;
children and dogs welcome, seats outside
on good-sized terrace with country views,
can walk up White Sheet Hill and past the
old and 'new' Wardour castles, closed Sun
evening, Mon. *(David and Judy Robison,
Edward Mirzoeff)*

EBBESBOURNE WAKE   ST9924

★**Horseshoe** (01722) 780474

*On A354 S of Salisbury, right at
signpost at Coombe Bissett; village about
8 miles further; SP5 5JF* Unspoilt country
pub in pretty village with plenty of regular
customers, welcoming long-serving landlord
and friendly staff, well kept Bowman, Otter,
Palmers and guests tapped from the cask,
farm cider, good traditional food (not Mon)
with lots of accompanying vegetables,
neatly kept and comfortable character bar,
collection of farm tools and bric-a-brac on
beams, conservatory extension and small
restaurant; children (away from bar) and
dogs welcome, seats in pretty little garden
with views over Ebble Valley, play area,
chickens and a goat in paddock, good nearby
walks, one bedroom, closed Sun evening,
Mon lunchtime. *(Michael and Mary Smith,
Michael Hill)*

ENFORD   SU14351

Swan (01980) 670338

Long Street, off A345; SN9 6DD
Attractive thatched village pub under
welcoming newish management, comfortable
beamed interior with log fire in large
fireplace, Marstons-related beers with local
guests such as Stonehenge, enjoyable home-
made food from lunchtime sandwiches up;
children and dogs welcome (pub dogs are
Digger and Pickle), seats out on small front
terrace, 'gallows' style pub sign spanning
the road, may open all day in summer.
(Hugh Roberts, Mrs Zara Elliott)

FORD   ST8474

White Hart (01249) 782213

*Off A420 Chippenham–Bristol;
SN14 8RP* Handsome 16th-c Marstons-
managed country inn; beamed bars with bare
boards or quarry tiles, lots of prints on bold
paintwork, dining and tub chairs, cushioned
wall seats, leather-padded benches and

button-back sofas, log fire and woodburner, a house beer from Ringwood with guests such as Bath, Box Steam and Brakspears, 22 wines by the glass and a dozen malt whiskies, popular food specialising in steaks; free wi-fi; children and dogs (in bar) welcome, front courtyard and terrace, trout stream by small stone bridge, comfortable modern bedrooms, open (and food) all day. *(Mr and Mrs D J Nash, Roger and Donna Huggins, Sara Fulton, Roger Baker, David Jackman)*

FOXHAM   ST9777
Foxham Inn (01249) 740665
NE of Chippenham; SN15 4NQ Small remote country dining pub with simple traditional décor, enterprising food strong on local produce along with more straightforward bar meals, some themed evenings, well kept ales such as Butcombe and Sharps, good choice of wines by the glass and nice coffee, woodburner, more contemporary back restaurant, own bread, chutneys, jams etc for sale; children and dogs welcome, disabled access and facilities, terrace with pergola, extensive views from front, two bedrooms, closed Mon. *(Mr and Mrs A H Young)*

FROXFIELD   SU2968
Pelican (01488) 682479
Off A4; SN8 3JY Modernised 17th-c coaching inn, good choice of enjoyable home-made food served by helpful friendly young staff, local ales, comfortable relaxed atmosphere; pleasant streamside garden with terrace and duck pond, Kennet & Avon Canal walks, bedrooms, open all day. *(Tony Hobden)*

GRITTLETON   ST8680
★ ## Neeld Arms (01249) 782470
From M4 junction 17, follow A429 to Cirencester and immediately left, signed Stanton St Quinton and Grittleton; SN14 6AP Popular and welcoming 17th-c village pub, pleasantly updated open-plan rooms with stone walls and painted panelling, nice mix of furniture, woodburner in little brick fireplace, inglenook on the right, ales such as Castle Combe, Flying Monk and Wadworths from pale oak-topped counter, good blackboard food from pub favourites up, back dining area with another inglenook; free wi-fi; children and dogs welcome, terrace with pergola, comfortable character bedrooms. *(David and Sue Medcalf, Sara Fulton, Simon and Mandy King, Roger Baker)*

HAMPTWORTH   SU2419
Cuckoo (01794) 390302
Hamptworth Road; SP5 2DU 17th-c thatched New Forest pub owned by the Hamptworth Estate and freshened up under friendly new landlady; peaceful and unspoilt, with friendly mix of customers from farmers to families in four compact rooms around tiny servery, ales such as Bowman, Hop Back and Ringwood tapped from the cask, real ciders/perry, simple food including sandwiches, ploughman's and pies, basic wooden furniture (some new tables being made using Estate trees), open fire and woodburner; occasional live music; children (till 9pm) and dogs welcome, big garden with view of golf course, open all day Fri-Sun. *(Jo Garnett)*

HANNINGTON   SU1793
Jolly Tar (01793) 762245
Off B4019 W of Highworth; Queens Road; SN6 7RP Old painted stone pub in pretty village, relaxing beamed bar with big log fire, steps up to flagstoned and stripped-stone dining area, good reasonably priced home-made food including popular Sun lunch (should book), well kept Arkells ales, friendly helpful service; children welcome, dogs in bar, picnic-sets on front terrace and in big garden with play area, four comfortable bedrooms, good breakfast, closed Mon lunchtime, no food Sun evening. *(Alfie Bayliss)*

HEDDINGTON   ST9966
Ivy (01380) 859652
Off A3102 S of Calne; SN11 0PL Picturesque thatched 15th-c village local under newish licensees; good inglenook log fire in L-shaped bar, heavy low beams, timbered walls, assorted furnishings on parquet floor, cask-tapped Wadworths ales, good value pubby food including Sun carvery, back dining room; children and dogs welcome, disabled access, picnic-sets in small side garden, open all day Sat, till 8pm Sun, closed Mon. *(John Harris)*

HEYTESBURY   ST9242
Angel (01985) 840330
Just off A36 E of Warminster; High Street; BA12 0ED Beamed 16th-c coaching inn in quiet village just below Salisbury Plain, spacious and comfortably modernised, with good popular food (not Sun evening, must book weekends), friendly helpful staff, Greene King ales, log fire; children and dogs (in bar) welcome, bedrooms, open all day (till 8pm Sun). *(Ann and Colin Hunt, Hugh Roberts)*

HINDON   ST9032
Angel (01747) 820696
B3089 Wilton–Mere; SP3 6DJ Village dining pub with big log fire, flagstones and other coaching-inn survivals, good food from

---

We include some hotels with a good bar that offers facilities comparable to those of a pub.

pub favourites through grills to specials, friendly efficient service, nice choice of wines, Timothy Taylors and guests, daily newspapers, restaurant; children and dogs (in bar) welcome, courtyard tables, nine comfortable bedrooms (named after game birds), open all day. *(Edward Mirzoeff)*

HINDON ST9132
Lamb (01747) 820573
B3089 Wilton–Mere; SP3 6DP Attractive recently refurbished old hotel; long roomy log-fire bar, two flagstoned lower sections with very long polished table, high-backed pews and settles, up steps to a third, bigger area, well kept Youngs, Wells Bombardier and a guest such as local Keystone, several wines by the glass and around 25 malt whiskies, cocktails and cuban cigars, enjoyable bar and restaurant food (service charge added), friendly helpful staff; can get very busy; children and dogs welcome, tables on roadside terrace and in garden across road with boules, 19 bedrooms, good breakfast, open all day from 7.30am for breakfast. *(Hilary and Neil Christopher)*

HONEYSTREET SU1061
Barge (01672) 851705
Off A345 W of Pewsey; SN9 5PS Quirky early 19th-c stone pub in nice setting by Kennet & Avon Canal, open-plan bar with wood floor and dark walls, some unusual furnishings, good Honeystreet beers (brewed by Stonehenge) including 1810, Croppie and Alien Abduction, traditional cider, tasty reasonably priced traditional food, friendly service, pool room with painted ceiling of the surrounding area, local photographs for sale; live music Sat, occasional magic shows; children, dogs, crop-circle and UFO enthusiasts welcome, waterside picnic-sets, camping field, good walks, open all day summer. *(Giles and Annie Francis)*

HORNINGSHAM ST8041
Bath Arms (01985) 844308
By tradesmen's entrance to Longleat House; BA12 7LY Handsome old stone-built inn on pretty village's sloping green, stylishly opened up as welcoming dining pub with several linked areas including a proper bar, polished wood floors and open fires, enjoyable food from bar snacks up, well kept Wessex ales and a guest such as Sharps Doom Bar, Weston's cider, good choice of wines and other drinks, charming efficient staff, side restaurant and conservatory; can get very busy; wheelchair access to bars via side door, attractive garden with neat terraces, smokers' gazebo, 15 bedrooms, open all day. *(Chris and Angela Buckell)*

HORTON SU0363
Bridge Inn (01380) 860273
Horton Road; village signed off A361 London Road, NE of Devizes; SN10 2JS Former flour mill and bakery by Kennet

& Avon Canal, carpeted log-fire area on left with tables set for dining, more pubby part to right of bar with some stripped brickwork and country kitchen furniture on reconstituted flagstones, old bargee photographs and rural pictures, Wadworths ales tapped from the cask, good value food including Weds curry buffet and Sun carvery, friendly service; background music, TV; well behaved children welcome, dogs in bar, disabled facilities, safely fenced garden with picnic-sets, original grinding wheel, canal walks and moorings, bedrooms, closed Mon. *(Giles and Annie Francis)*

KILMINGTON ST7835
Red Lion (01985) 844263
B3092 Mere–Frome, 2.5 miles S of Maiden Bradley; 3 miles from A303 Mere turn-off; BA12 6RP NT-owned country pub under welcoming new management; low-beamed flagstoned bar with cushioned wall and window seats, curved high-backed settle, woodburners in big fireplaces at either end, well kept ales such as Butcombe and Wessex, traditional ciders, enjoyable straightforward home-made food (more evening choice), newer big-windowed back dining area; children and dogs (in bar) welcome, picnic-sets in large attractive garden with fine views, White Sheet Hill (hang-gliding) and Stourhead gardens (NT) nearby, no evening food Sun, Mon. *(Edward Mirzoeff)*

KINGTON ST MICHAEL ST9077
Jolly Huntsman (01249) 750305
Handy for M4 junction 17; SN14 6JB Roomy welcoming stone-built pub dating from the 18th c, Moles Tap, Wadworths 6X and a couple of guests, good home-made food from pub standards to unusual things like kangaroo, carpeted interior with some scrubbed tables, comfortable sofas and good log fire; children and dogs (in bar) welcome, nine bedrooms in separate block. *(Roger and Donna Huggins)*

LACOCK ST9268
Bell (01249) 730308
E of village; SN15 2PJ Extended cottagey pub with warm welcome, local beers including a house brew from Bath Ales (beer festivals), traditional ciders, decent wines by the glass and good selection of malt whiskies and gins, well liked food from lunchtime platters through pub favourites and grills up, linked rooms off bar including pretty restaurant and conservatory; children welcome away from bar, disabled access from car park, sheltered well tended garden with smokers' shelter and play area, open (and food) all day weekends. *(Chris and Angela Buckell)*

LACOCK ST9168
George (01249) 730263
West Street; village signed off A350 S of Chippenham; SN15 2LH Rambling

inn at centre of busy NT tourist village; low-beamed bar with upright timbers creating cosy corners, armchairs and windsor chairs around close-set tables, seats in stone-mullioned windows, some flagstones, dog treadwheel in outer breast of central fireplace, lots of old pictures and bric-a-brac, souvenirs from filming *Cranford* and *Harry Potter* in the village, Wadworths beers and Weston's cider, bar food from snacks up; background music; children and dogs welcome, tricky wheelchair access, picnic-sets on grass and in attractive courtyard with pillory and well, open all day in summer. *(Roger and Donna Huggins, Alan and Jane Shaw, Adrian Johnson)*

LACOCK   ST9168
★ **Red Lion** (01249) 730456
High Street; SN15 2LQ Popular NT-owned Georgian inn, sizeable opened-up interior with log fire in big stone fireplace, bare boards and flagstones, roughly carved screens here and there and some cosy alcoves, well kept Wadworths ales, Thatcher's and Weston's ciders, enjoyable food from sandwiches and sharing plates up, good friendly service even when busy; background music; children and dogs welcome, wheelchair access to main bar area only, picnic-sets out on gravel, four modern bedrooms, open (and food) all day. *(Dave Braisted)*

LACOCK   ST9367
★ **Rising Sun** (01249) 730363
Bewley Common, Bowden Hill – out towards Sandy Lane, up hill past abbey; OS Sheet 173 map reference 935679; SN15 2PP Unassuming stone pub with three knocked-together simply furnished rooms, open fire, Moles ales, real cider and enjoyable fairly priced traditional food (not Sun evening), friendly attentive service; background music, free wi-fi; well behaved children welcome, dogs in bar, tricky disabled access, wonderful views across Avon Valley from conservatory and two-level terrace, open all day (till 10pm Sun). *(Charlie May)*

LIDDINGTON   SU2081
Village Inn (01793) 790314
Handy for M4 junction 15, via A419 and B4192; Bell Lane; SN4 0HE Comfortable and welcoming with enjoyable good value food from varied menu including early-bird bargains and daily specials, well kept Arkells beers, pleasant helpful staff, linked bar areas, stripped-stone and raftered back dining extension, conservatory, log fire in splendid fireplace; well behaved children over 8 allowed in restaurant area, no under-14s in bar, disabled facilities, terrace tables, village shop in car park selling basics. *(R K Phillips, KC)*

LITTLE SOMERFORD   ST9784
Somerford Arms (01666) 826535
Signed off B4042 Malmesbury–Brinkworth; SN15 5JP Popular (can be noisy) modernised village pub, easy chairs in front of bar's woodburner, green-painted half-panelling and stone flooring, linked restaurant with enjoyable home-made food from varied menu, well kept changing ales and lots of wines by the glass, friendly service; children, dogs (pub boxer is Nutmeg) and muddy boots welcome, open all day. *(Anon)*

LONGBRIDGE DEVERILL   ST8640
George (01985) 840396
A350/B3095; BA12 7DG Popular refurbished and extended roadside inn owned by Upham, their beers kept well and generous helpings of enjoyable freshly made food, Sun carvery, friendly enthusiastic staff, conservatory; children welcome, big riverside garden with play area and maybe summer marquee, 12 bedrooms, handy for Longleat, open all day (breakfast from 8am). *(Edward Mirzoeff, Comus and Sarah Elliott)*

LOWER WOODFORD   SU1235
★ **Wheatsheaf** (01722) 782203
Signed off A360 just N of Salisbury; SP4 6NQ Updated and extended 18th-c Badger dining pub, open airy feel, with good choice of fairly priced traditional food from sharing boards up (booking advised weekends), well kept beers, good wines and coffee, well trained genial staff, beams, panelling and exposed brickwork, mix of old furniture, log fire and woodburner; background music, free wi-fi; children welcome, dogs in bar, disabled access and parking, tree-lined fenced garden with play area, pretty setting, open (and food) all day. *(Robert Watt, Mrs Zara Elliott)*

LUCKINGTON   ST8384
★ **Old Royal Ship** (01666) 840222
Off B4040 SW of Malmesbury; SN14 6PA Friendly pub by village green, opened up inside with one long bar divided into three areas, Bass, Stonehenge, Wadworths and Wickwar from central servery, also farm cider and several wines by the glass, good range of well liked food including vegetarian, decent coffee, pompt service, neat tables, spindleback chairs and small cushioned settles on dark boards, some stripped masonry and small open fire, skittle alley; background music – live jazz second Weds of

---

month, games machine; children welcome, garden (beyond car park) with boules, play area and plenty of seats, Badminton House close by, open all day weekends. *(Guy Vowles)*

MARDEN   SU0857
Millstream (01380) 848490
Village signposted off A342 SE of Devizes; SN10 3RH Wadworths red-brick country dining pub, much-liked food cooked by landlady-chef including plenty of fish/seafood specials and good value Sun lunch (best to book), appealing layout of linked cosy areas, beams and log fires, red-cushioned dark pews and small padded dining chairs around sturdy oak and other good tables, friendly attentive service; free wi-fi; children and dogs welcome (resident pointers are Sophie and Francesca), disabled access/loos, garden down to tree-lined stream, 12th-c church worth a visit, closed Sun and Mon evenings. *(Alan and Audrey Moulds)*

MARLBOROUGH   SU1869
Castle & Ball (01672) 515201
High Street; SN8 1LZ Popular coaching inn dating from the 15th c (Old English Inns); spacious interior with lounge bar and restaurant, wide choice of enjoyable food including deals, Thurs curry night, Greene King ales and nice range of well listed wines by the glass, good attentive service; background music, free wi-fi; children and dogs (in bar) welcome, seats out under projecting colonnade and in back walled garden, 37 bedrooms, open all day. *(Alfie Bayliss)*

NETHERHAMPTON   SU1129
★Victoria & Albert (01722) 743174
Just off A3094 W of Salisbury; SP2 8PU Cosy black-beamed bar in simple thatched cottage, good generous food from sandwiches up, sensible prices and local supplies, three well kept changing ales, farm cider and decent wines, welcoming helpful staff, old-fashioned traditional wall settles on ancient floor tiles, log fire, restaurant; children and dogs welcome, hatch service for sizeable terrace and garden behind, handy for Wilton House and Nadder Valley walks. *(Charlie May)*

NORTON   ST8884
★Vine Tree (01666) 837654
4 miles from M4 junction 17; A429 towards Malmesbury, then left at Hullavington, Sherston signpost, then follow Norton signposts; in village turn right at Foxley signpost, which takes you into Honey Lane; SN16 0JP Civilised dining pub (sister to the Barbury in Broad Hinton), three neat small rooms, beams, old settles and unvarnished wooden tables on flagstones, sporting prints and church candles, large fireplace in central bar, woodburner in restaurant, St Austell Tribute

and a guest, 40 wines by the glass and several malt whiskies, well liked imaginative food (not Sun evening); children and dogs welcome, picnic-sets and play area in two-acre garden, suntrap terrace. *(Edward May, Mike and Mary Carter)*

OGBOURNE ST ANDREW   SU1871
Silks on the Downs (01672) 841229
A345 N of Marlborough; SN8 1RZ Popular civilised restauranty pub with horse-racing theme, good variety of enjoyable food (best to book), ales such as Adnams, Ramsbury and Wadworths, decent wines by the glass, good friendly service, stylish décor with mix of dining tables on polished wood floors, some good prints and photographs as well as framed racing silks; well behaved children allowed, small decked area and garden, closed Sun evening. *(John Harris)*

PEWSEY   SU1561
Waterfront (01672) 564020
Pewsey Wharf (A345 just N); SN9 5NU Bar-bistro in converted wharf building next to Kennet & Avon Canal, good reasonably priced food including daily specials, three well kept changing ales tapped from the cask in upstairs bar (can eat here too), efficient friendly staff; children and dogs (in bar) welcome, waterside picnic-sets, open all day Fri-Sun. *(Giles and Annie Francis)*

REDLYNCH   SU2021
Kings Head (01725) 510420
Off A338 via B3080; The Row; SP5 2JT Early 18th-c pub on edge of New Forest; three or four well kept ales including Hop Back Summer Lightning and Ringwood Best, decent house wines and coffee, good value home-made food including OAP weekday lunch deal for two, beamed and flagstoned main bar with woodburner in large brick fireplace, small conservatory; free wi-fi; children, dogs and muddy boots welcome, picnic-sets out in front and in side garden, nice Pepperbox Hill (NT) walks nearby, shuts 3-6pm. *(Toby Jones)*

ROWDE   ST9762
★George & Dragon (01380) 723053
A342 Devizes–Chippenham; SN10 2PN Lots of character in this welcoming and well run 16th-c coaching inn, two low-beamed rooms with large open fireplaces, wooden dining chairs around candlelit tables, antique rugs and walls covered with old pictures and portraits, Butcombe and guests, good food including plenty of fresh fish/seafood; background music; children and dogs welcome, seats in pretty back garden, Kennet & Avon Canal nearby, three bedrooms, closed Sun evening. *(Mr and Mrs A H Young)*

SALISBURY   SU1430
Avon Brewery (01722) 416184
Castle Street; SP1 3SP Long narrow city bar with frosted and engraved bow window,

dark mahogany and two open fires, friendly staff and regulars, well kept Ringwood Best and a Marstons-related guest, good portuguese food in back restaurant, also pub favourites; sheltered courtyard garden overlooking river, open all day. *(John Harris)*

SALISBURY   SU1429
★ **Haunch of Venison** (01722) 411313
Minster Street, opposite Market Cross; SP1 1TB New licensees taking over as we went to press – reports please; ancient pub oozing history with tiny downstairs rooms dating from 1320, massive beams, stout oak benches built into timbered walls, open fire, tiny snug liked by locals with unique pewter counter and rare set of antique taps for gravity-fed spirits; halfway upstairs is panelled room with splendid fireplace and (behind glass) the mummified hand of an 18th-c card sharp still clutching his cards; has opened all day. *(Tony and Rachel Schendel, Mrs Sally Scott, Ann and Colin Hunt)*

SALISBURY   SU1429
Kings Head (01722) 342050
Bridge Street; SP1 2ND Corner Wetherspoons in nice spot by river (site of former hotel), variety of seating in large relaxed bar with separate TV area, upstairs gallery, two Greene King ales and four quickly changing guests, low-priced menu including breakfast, log fire; good value bedrooms, open all day from 7am (till 1am Thurs-Sat). *(Ann and Colin Hunt)*

SALISBURY   SU1429
New Inn (01722) 326662
New Street; SP1 2PH Much-extended old building with massive beams and timbers, good choice of enjoyable home-made food from pub staples up, well kept Badger ales and decent house wines, cheerful service, flagstones, floorboards and carpet, quiet cosy alcoves, inglenook log fire; children welcome, pretty walled garden with striking view of nearby cathedral spire, three bedrooms, open all day. *(Michael and Mary Smith)*

SALISBURY   SU1429
Village (01722) 329707
Wilton Road; SP2 7EF Friendly corner pub popular for its interesting range of real ales including Downton, railway memorabilia (near the station); sports TV, free wi-fi; open all day (from 4pm Mon-Thurs). *(Phil and Jane Villiers)*

SALISBURY   SU1430
Wyndham Arms (01722) 331026
Estcourt Road; SP1 3AS Corner local with unpretentious modern décor, popular and friendly, with full Hop Back range (brewery was originally based here) and a guest such

as Downton, bottled beers and country wines, no food, small front and side rooms, longer main bar; darts and board games; children and dogs welcome, open all day Thurs-Sun, from 4.30pm other days. *(Tony and Rachel Schendel, Phil and Jane Villiers)*

SANDY LANE   ST9668
★ **George** (01380) 850403
A342 Devizes–Chippenham; SN15 2PX Handsome family-run Georgian pub with neat cosy bar, straightforward seats and tables on wooden flooring, open fire, Wadworths and a guest, plenty of wines by the glass, popular home-made food including some italian influences, back dining room and wood-framed conservatory; children and dogs (in bar) welcome, terrace with rattan furniture, more seats on lawn, charming thatched village, Bowood Estate walks, may close Sun evening, Mon. *(Caroline Prescott)*

SEEND   ST9361
Barge (01380) 828230
Seend Cleeve; signed off A361 Devizes–Trowbridge; SN12 6QB Busy waterside pub with plenty of seats in garden making most of boating activity on Kennet & Avon Canal (moorings), some unusual seating in bar including painted milk churns, pretty Victorian fireplace, Wadworths ales and extensive range of wines by the glass, decent choice of enjoyable well priced food, efficient service; background music, free wi-fi; children and dogs welcome, summer barbecues, open all day. *(Giles and Annie Francis)*

SEEND   ST9562
Three Magpies (01380) 828389
Sells Green – A365 towards Melksham; SN12 6RN Traditional partly 18th-c roadside pub with well kept Wadworths and decent choice of wines by the glass, enjoyable home-made pubby food at reasonable prices, good friendly service, two warm fires; free wi-fi; children welcome, dogs allowed in bar, big garden with play area, campsite next door, Kennet & Avon Canal close by, open all day. *(John Allman, Giles and Annie Francis)*

SEMINGTON   ST9259
Lamb (01380) 870263
The Strand; A361 Devizes–Trowbridge; BA14 6LL Refurbished dining pub with various eating areas including bar with wood-strip floor and log fire, enjoyable food from pub favourites to specials, a couple of Box Steam ales, friendly staff; background music; children and dogs welcome, pleasant garden with views to the Bowood Estate, play area, two self-catering cottages, open all day weekends. *(Belinda Stamp)*

Virtually all pubs in this book sell wine by the glass. We mention wines if they are a cut above the average.

SHALBOURNE SU3162
Plough (01672) 870295
Off A338; SN8 3QF Low-beamed
traditional village pub on green, good
variety of enjoyable fairly priced food
cooked by landlord including vegetarian
options, Butcombe and Wadworths, friendly
helpful landlady and staff, open fire in neat
bar, separate carpeted restaurant with
central woodburner; free wi-fi; children
and dogs welcome, disabled access, small
garden with play area, closed Mon.
(Charlie May)

SHAW ST8765
Golden Fleece (01225) 702050
*Folly Lane (A365 towards Atworth);
SN12 8HB* Attractive former coaching inn
with low-ceilinged L-shaped bar and long
front dining extension, good reasonably
priced food including blackboard specials,
early evening deal Tues and Weds, ales such
as Bath, Dartmoor and St Austell, pleasant
welcoming staff; background music, quiz
nights; children allowed, back terrace with
steps up to lawn, open all day Sun, closed Mon.
(Neil Allen)

SOUTH MARSTON SU1987
Carpenters Arms (01793) 822997
Just off A420 E of Swindon; SN3 4ST
Roomy old Arkells local with warm friendly
atmosphere, good choice of enjoyable
well priced food (not Sun evening, Mon
lunchtime), beamed bar with open fire,
separate carpeted restaurant, pool room;
background music; children and dogs
welcome, big back garden with terrace and
play area, nine motel bedrooms (some train
noise), caravan parking, open all day.
(Charlie May)

STEEPLE ASHTON ST9056
Longs Arms (01380) 870245
High Street; BA14 6EU Spotless 17th-c
coaching inn with friendly local atmosphere,
well kept Sharps and Wadworths, plenty
of wines by the glass, good choice of fresh
locally sourced food including lunchtime
sandwiches, bar with lots of pictures and old
photos, adjacent dining area, woodburner;
free wi-fi; children and dogs welcome, big
garden with play area, adjoining self-catering
cottage, delightful village, open all day
weekends if busy. *(Michael Doswell)*

STIBB GREEN SU2262
Three Horseshoes (01672) 810324
Just N of Burbage; SN8 3AE Welcoming
thatched village pub with enjoyable
affordably priced food and well kept
Wadworths ales, inglenook log fire in
comfortable beamed front bar, railway
memorabilia, small dining room; dogs
welcome, seats in nice garden, closed Mon.
(Neil Allen)

STOURTON ST7733
★**Spread Eagle** (01747) 840587
*Church Lawn; follow Stourhead brown
signs off B3092, N of junction with
A303 W of Mere; BA12 6QE* Busy
Georgian inn at entrance to Stourhead
Estate; old-fashioned, rather civilised interior
with antique panelback settles, solid tables
and chairs, sporting prints and log fires in
handsome fireplaces, room by entrance with
armchairs, longcase clock and corner china
cupboard, well kept Butcombe and Wessex,
interesting wines by the glass and popular
home-made food served by efficient helpful
staff, cream teas, restaurant; background
music; children welcome, wheelchair
access (step down to dining areas), smart
back courtyard with round picnic-sets, five
bedrooms (guests can wander freely around
famous NT gardens outside normal hours),
open all day. *(Dave Braisted, Sheila Topham)*

SUTTON BENGER ST9478
Wellesley Arms (01249) 721721
*Handy for M4 junction 17, via B4122
and B4069; High Street; SN15 4RD*
Beamed 15th-c Cotswold-stone pub with
pleasant bar areas and restaurant, good
pubby food including lunchtime set menu
(Tues-Fri) and very popular Sun lunch,
well kept Wadworths ales, efficient friendly
service; background music, TV; children
and dogs welcome, garden with play area,
paddock, open all day weekends (no food Sun
night), closed Mon lunchtime. *(David Crook)*

SUTTON VENY ST8941
Woolpack (01985) 840834
High Street; BA12 7AW Small well run
1920s village local, good blackboard food
including some inventive dishes cooked by
landlord-chef (best to book), home-made
chutneys, pickles etc for sale, Marstons
and Ringwood ales, sensibly priced wines
by the glass, charming service, modernised
interior with compact side dining area
screened from bare-boards bar, woodburner;
background music; closed Sun evening, Mon
lunchtime. *(John Harris)*

TISBURY ST9429
Boot (01747) 870363
High Street; SP3 6PS Ancient
unpretentious village local with long-serving
and welcoming licensees, three well kept
changing ales tapped from the cask, cider/
perry, range of pizzas and reasonably priced
pubby food, notable fireplace; dogs welcome,
tables in good-sized back garden, closed Sun
evening and lunchtimes Mon, Tues.
(Charlie May)

UPAVON SU1355
Ship (01980) 630313
High Street; SN9 6EA Large thatched
pub with welcoming local atmosphere,
good choice of enjoyable home-made food

including wood-fired pizzas (Thurs-Sat. evenings), friendly helpful service, well kept changing ales, a couple of traditional ciders and decent range of wines and whiskies, some interesting nautical memorabilia; occasional live acoustic music; dogs welcome, picnic-sets in front and on small side terrace, parking can be tricky. *(Phil and Jane Villiers)*

WARMINSTER   ST8644
Fox & Hounds (01985) 216711
Deverill Road; BA12 9QP Friendly two-bar community local, Wessex beers and at least one guest, half a dozen ciders; skittle alley; sports TV, pool; open all day. *(Dr and Mrs A K Clarke)*

WARMINSTER   ST8745
Organ (01985) 211777
49 High Street; BA12 9AQ Sympathetic restoration of former 18th-c inn (reopened 2006 after 93 years as a shop), front bar, snug and traditional games room, welcoming owners and chatty regulars, four regional beers including one named for them, real ciders/perries, good cheap lunchtime cheeseboard, skittle alley, local art in upstairs gallery; no under-21s, open 4pm-midnight, all day Sat. *(Alfie Bayliss)*

WARMINSTER   ST8745
★**Weymouth Arms** (01985) 216995
Emwell Street; BA12 8JA Charming backstreet pub with snug panelled entrance bar, log fire in fine stone fireplace, ancient books on mantelpiece, leather tub chairs around walnut and satinwood table, more seats against the walls, daily papers, Butcombe and Wadworths 6X, nice wines by the glass, second heavily panelled room with wide floorboards and smaller fireplace, candles in brass sticks, split-level dining room stretching back to open kitchen, good interesting food, friendly attentive service; children welcome, dogs in bar, seats in flower-filled back courtyard, six well equipped comfortable bedrooms, closed Mon lunchtime. *(S G N Bennett, Edward Mirzoeff)*

WEST OVERTON   SU1368
Bell (01672) 861099
A4 Marlborough–Calne; SN8 1QD Early 19th-c coaching inn with good imaginative cooking from owner-chef using fresh local ingredients, bar with woodburner, spacious restaurant beyond, well kept Wadworths and other local beers such as Moles, attentive friendly uniformed staff; background music; disabled access, nice secluded back garden

with terrace and own bar, country views, good walks nearby, closed Sun evening, Mon. *(Mr and Mrs P R Thomas, Mr and Mrs A H Young, Michael Doswell, Tina and David Woods-Taylor)*

WESTWOOD   ST8159
★**New Inn** (01225) 863123
Off B3109 S of Bradford-on-Avon; BA15 2AE Traditional 18th-c country pub with several linked rooms, beams and stripped stone, scrubbed tables on slate floor, lots of pictures, imaginative good value food (not Sun evening) cooked by chef-owner together with pub staples, generous Sun lunch and some themed nights, well kept Wadworths, cheerful buzzy atmosphere; children and dogs welcome, tables in paved garden behind, pretty village with good surrounding walks, Westwood Manor (NT) opposite. *(Hilary and Neil Christopher)*

WHITEPARISH   SU2423
Fountain (01794) 884266
The Street; SP5 2SG Friendly little green-shuttered 17th-c beamed inn, enjoyable well priced traditional food in log-fire bar or restaurant, Sharps Atlantic and Doom Bar plus a guest; free wi-fi; a few seats out at back, six bedrooms, open all day Fri and Sat, till 6pm Sun, closed lunchtimes Mon-Weds. *(Colin McKerrow)*

WILTON   SU2661
★**Swan** (01672) 870274
The village S of Great Bedwyn; SN8 3SS Popular light and airy 1930s pub, good well presented seasonal food (not Sun evening) including daily specials, two Ramsbury ales and a local guest, farm ciders and good value wines from extensive list, friendly efficient staff, stripped pine tables, high-backed settles and pews on bare boards, woodburner; children and dogs welcome, disabled access, front garden with picnic-sets, picturesque village with windmill, open all day weekends. *(JPC, Alan and Audrey Moulds, Tony Hobden)*

WINGFIELD   ST8256
★**Poplars** (01225) 752426
B3109 S of Bradford-on-Avon (Shop Lane); BA14 9LN Appealing country pub with beams and log fires, very popular (especially with older people at lunchtime) for its sensibly priced food from pub staples to interesting specials, Wadworths ales (including seasonal) and Weston's cider, friendly fast service even when busy, warm atmosphere, light and airy family dining extension; quiz second Sun of month; nice garden, own cricket pitch. *(Taff Thomas)*

A star symbol before the name of a pub shows exceptional character and appeal. It doesn't mean extra comfort. And it's nothing to do with exceptional food quality, for which there's a separate star-on-a-plate symbol. Even quite a basic pub can win a star, if it's individual enough.

WINSLEY   ST7960
★**Seven Stars** (01225) 722204
*Off B3108 bypass W of Bradford-on-
Avon (pub just over Wiltshire border);
BA15 2LQ* Handsome bustling inn with low-
beamed linked areas, light pastel paintwork
and stripped-stone walls, farmhouse chairs
around candlelit tables on flagstones or coir,
woodburner, very good freshly made food
using local suppliers, friendly helpful service,
changing west country ales, Thatcher's and
Weston's ciders, nice wines by the glass;
background music; children and dogs (in
bar) welcome, disabled access with ramp,
tables under parasols on terrace and neat
grassy surrounds, bowling green opposite,
closed Sun evening. *(Dr Matt Burleigh,
Chris and Angela Buckell, Howard and Margaret
Buchanan, Michael Doswell, B and F A Hannam)*

WINTERBOURNE
BASSETT   SU1075
White Horse (01793) 731257
Off A4361 S of Swindon; SN4 9QB
Roadside dining pub with gently old-
fashioned feel, carpeted bar with plenty of
wood, wrought-iron plush-topped stools and
cushioned dining chairs, Wadworths ales
and quite a few wines by the glass, enjoyable
home-made food including daily specials

(seasonal game), dining rooms with country
kitchen furniture on light wood floors, old
prints and paintings, woodburner in little
brick fireplace, conservatory; background
music; children welcome, dogs in bar, tables
on good-sized lawn, closed Sun evening, Mon
lunchtime. *(Charlie May)*

WOOTTON RIVERS   SU1963
Royal Oak (01672) 810322
Off A346, A345 or B3087; SN8 4NQ
Cosy 16th-c beamed and thatched pub, ales
such as Ramsbury and Wadworths 6X, plenty
of wines by the glass and enjoyable food
from lunchtime sandwiches to fish dishes,
comfortable L-shaped dining lounge with
woodburner, timbered bar and small games
area; free wi-fi; children and dogs welcome,
tables out in yard, pleasant village, bedrooms
in adjoining building, open (and food)
all day Sun. *(Guy Vowles)*

ZEALS   ST7831
Bell & Crown (01747) 840404
A303; BA12 6NJ Nicely laid out beamed
dining pub, warm and friendly, with good
food cooked by chef-landlord, efficient
service, ales such as Butcombe, Palmers and
Wadworths, nice wines by the glass, big log
fire in flagstoned bar, restaurant; closed Sun
evening. *(Neil Allen)*

Worcestershire

BRANSFORD
SO8052 Map 4

Bear & Ragged Staff 🍽 🍷

(01886) 833399 – www.bearatbransford.co.uk

Off A4103 SW of Worcester; Station Road; WR6 5JH

Cheerfully run dining pub with pleasant places to sit both inside and out and well liked food and drink

'A lovely pub run by first class, genuinely welcoming licensees,' says one reader with enthusiasm. This is a civilised dining pub but there's a relaxing bar as well: Hobsons Twisted Spire and Sharps Doom Bar on handpump, ten wines by the glass, several malt whiskies and quite a few brandies and liqueurs. The restaurant is more formal with upholstered dining chairs, proper tablecloths and linen napkins. These interconnecting rooms give fine views of attractive rolling country (as do the pretty garden and terrace). In winter, there's a warming open fire; background music. Good disabled access and facilities.

🍽 Using carefully sourced local produce, growing some fruit, vegetables and salads themselves and making everything in-house, the impressive food includes lunchtime sandwiches, confit duck roulade with chargrilled polenta and balsamic vinegar jam, ham hock and root vegetable terrine with crispy quail egg and piccalilli, a curry of the day, provençale vegetable risotto with charred red pepper purée, pork belly in five spice with carrot and ginger purée, sweet potato fondant and pak choi stir-fry, corn-fed chicken breast with confit leg parcel, haricot beans and braised vegetables, and puddings such as dark chocolate fondant with honeycomb ice-cream and vanilla panna cotta with rhubarb jelly, rhubarb crisp and rhubarb sorbet. *Benchmark main dish: roast cod with salt cod fishcakes, braised greens, mushrooms and tarragon cream sauce £16.95. Two-course evening meal £21.00.*

Free house ~ Licensee Lynda Williams ~ Real ale ~ Open 11.30-2.30, 6-11; 12-2.30 Sun ~ Bar food 11.30-2, 6.30-9; 12-2.30 Sun ~ Restaurant ~ Children welcome ~ Dogs allowed in bar ~ Wi-fi *Recommended by Mike and Mary Carter, Brian Parry*

BRETFORTON
SP0943 Map 4

Fleece ★ 🍺 £

(01386) 831173 – www.thefleeceinn.co.uk

B4035 E of Evesham: turn S off this road into village; pub is in central square by church; there's a sizeable car park at one side of the church; WR11 7JE

Marvellously unspoilt medieval pub owned by the National Trust; bedrooms

When the last member of the family that owned this marvellous old farm for around 500 years bequeathed it to the National Trust in 1977, she ensured that it would become a piece of living history. Its fine country rooms remain filled with original antique furnishings, many of them heirlooms: a great oak dresser holds a priceless 48-piece set of Stuart pewter, there are two fine grandfather clocks, ancient kitchen chairs, curved high-backed settles, a rocking chair and a rack of heavy pointed iron shafts, probably for spit roasting in one of the huge inglenook fireplaces; two other log fires. There are massive beams and exposed timbers, worn and crazed flagstones (scored with marks to keep out demons) and plenty of oddities such as a great cheese-press and set of cheese moulds and a rare dough-proving table; a leaflet details the more bizarre items. Uley Pigs Ear, Wye Valley Bitter and a guest or two on handpump, 20 wines by the glass, a similar number of malt whiskies and four farm ciders; board games. They hold an asparagus auction at the end of May, as part of the Vale of Evesham Asparagus Festival, and also host the village fête on August Bank Holiday Monday. The calendar of events also includes morris dancing and the village silver band plays here regularly. The lawn, with fruit trees around a beautifully restored thatched and timbered barn, is a lovely place to sit, and there are more picnic-sets and a stone pump-trough in the front courtyard. If you're visiting to enjoy the famous historic interior, best to go midweek as it can get very busy at weekends.

🍴 Bar food includes sandwiches, chicken liver pâté with Cointreau marmalade, smoked salmon and prawn fishcake with horseradish crème fraîche, a pie of the day, beer-battered cod with triple-cooked chips, lambs liver with bacon, mustard mash and onion gravy, wild mushroom, brie and thyme tart with red pepper coulis, chicken with garlic and black pudding hash, and puddings such as apple and date crumble and mocha brûlée. *Benchmark main dish: local pork sausages with red onion marmalade £8.95. Two-course evening meal £15.00.*

Free house ~ Licensee Nigel Smith ~ Real ale ~ Open 10am-11pm (10.30 Sun) ~ Bar food 12-2.30, 6.30-9 ~ Restaurant ~ Children welcome ~ Dogs allowed in bar ~ Wi-fi ~ Live music monthly ~ Bedrooms: /£97.50 *Recommended by K H Frostick, Philip Meek, Stanley and Annie Matthews, David Carr, Steve Whalley*

BROADWAY
Crown & Trumpet 🍺 £

SP0937 Map 4

(01386) 853202 – www.cotswoldholidays.co.uk
Church Street; WR12 7AE

Honest local with good real ale and decent food; bedrooms

'A real gem' and 'so friendly and chatty' are two warm comments from our reporters. It's old-fashioned and unpretentious and both regulars and visitors love it. The bustling beamed and timbered bar has a cheerful, easy-going feel, antique dark high-backed settles, large solid tables and a blazing log fire. You'll find Stanway Artists Ale, Stroud Tom Long and Timothy Taylors Landlord on handpump, alongside four local farm ciders, nine wines by the glass, ten malt whiskies, hot toddies, mulled wine and a good range of soft drinks. There's an assortment of pub games, including darts, cribbage, shut the box, dominoes, bar skittles and ring the bull, as well as a games machine, TV and background music. The hardwood tables and chairs outside, among flowers on a slightly raised front terrace, are popular with walkers.

🍴 Very good value food includes lunchtime baguettes and paninis, devilled whitebait with cayenne, various omelettes, lasagne, venison sausages with onion gravy, steak and kidney pie, battered haddock and chips, chicken and chorizo with sauté potatoes, and puddings such as rhubarb and ginger crumble and treacle tart and custard; they also offer an early evening menu (6-7pm). *Benchmark main dish: pie of the day £8.95. Two-course evening meal £12.00.*

Laurel (Enterprise) ~ Lease Andrew Scott ~ Real ale ~ Open 11-11 (midnight Sat); 12-11 Sun ~ Bar food 12-2.30, 5.45-9.30; 12-9.30 Fri-Sun ~ Children welcome ~ Dogs allowed in bar ~ Wi-fi ~ Live jazz/blues Thurs evening, 1960s-'80s music Sat evening ~ Bedrooms: /£68
Recommended by Mark Delap, Dave Braisted, Theocsbrian, Guy Vowles, M G Hart, David Carr

CHILDSWICKHAM
SP0738 Map 4

Childswickham Inn

(01386) 852461 – www.childswickhaminn.co.uk
Off A44 NW of Broadway; WR12 7HP

Bustling dining pub with highly regarded food, good drinks choice, attentive staff and seats in neat garden

This is a popular place in a peaceful village, and most customers are here to enjoy the interesting food. But the locals' lounge bar is full of chatty regulars (dogs are allowed here too) and there are leather sofas and armchairs and Hook Norton Old Hooky, Sharps Doom Bar and Timothy Taylors Landlord on handpump, several wines by the glass, malt whiskies and farm cider; background music. There are two dining areas, one with high-backed dark leather chairs on terracotta tiles, the other with country kitchen chairs on bare floorboards; both have contemporary artwork on part-timbered walls painted cream or pale violet; an open fire and woodburning stove. Outside, the neat garden has rush-seated chairs and tables on decking and also separate areas under parasols. Disabled facilities.

Well thought-of food includes ham hock and black pudding terrine with potato rösti and crispy egg, potted smoked mackerel with pickled cucumber, ham and free-range eggs, a pie of the day, a changing curry, chicken wrapped in parma ham with dauphinoise potatoes and thyme jus, caribbean-style fishcake with mango and pomegranate slaw and garlic mayonnaise, and puddings such as plum and cinnamon tart with vanilla and nutmeg panna cotta and sticky date pudding with butterscotch sauce. *Benchmark main dish: gressingham duck breast with pancetta sauerkraut and cherry and vanilla jus £16.25. Two-course evening meal £20.00.*

Punch ~ Tenant Carol Marshall ~ Real ale ~ Open 12-3, 5.30-11; 12-11.30 Sat; 12-10.30 Sun ~ Bar food 12-2, 6-9; 12-8 Sun ~ Restaurant (not Sun evening or Mon lunch) ~ Children welcome ~ Dogs allowed in bar ~ Wi-fi *Recommended by Roy and Gill Payne*

CLENT
SO9279 Map 4

Fountain 🏮 ♀

(01562) 883286 – www.thefountainatclent.co.uk
Adams Hill/Odnall Lane; off A491 at Holy Cross/Clent exit roundabout, via Violet Lane, then right at T junction; DY9 9PU

Restauranty pub often packed to overflowing, with imaginative dishes and good choice of drinks

The friendly licensees and their helpful staff keep this bustling pub spotless – and the four real ales and consistently tasty food draw in plenty of customers. The long carpeted dining bar (consisting of three knocked-together areas) is fairly traditional, with teak chairs and pedestal tables and some comfortably cushioned brocaded wall seats. There are nicely framed local photographs on the rag-rolled pinkish walls above a dark panelled dado, pretty wall lights and candles on the tables (flowers in summer). The changing real ales on handpump include Jennings Bitter, Marstons Burton Bitter and EPA, and Milestone New World Bitter, and most of their wines are available by the glass; also speciality teas and good coffees. Background music and skittle alley. There are tables outside on a decked area.

Particularly good food includes open and grilled sandwiches, tiger prawns with garlic butter, baked goats cheese with piperade, barbecue pork belly, couscous-stuffed aubergine with spicy tomato sauce, chicken with asparagus, mushrooms and creamy white wine and tarragon sauce, scallops with noodles and thai salad, steaks with lots of sauces, and puddings such as banana fritter with whisky and butterscotch sauce and lemon curd meringue; they also offer a two- and three-course menu (not Friday or Saturday evenings or Sunday). *Benchmark main dish: lamb pot roast £15.95. Two-course evening meal £25.00.*

Marstons ~ Lease Richard and Jacque Macey ~ Real ale ~ Open 11-11; 12-9.30 Sun ~ Bar food 12-2, 6-9 (9.30 Fri, Sat); 12-6 Sun ~ Children welcome ~ Wi-fi
Recommended by Ian Herdman, S Holder

CUTNALL GREEN   SO8868 Map 4
Chequers 🌟 ♀
(01299) 851292 – www.chequerscutnallgreen.co.uk
Kidderminster Road; WR9 0PJ

Bustling roadside pub with plenty of drinking and dining space in interesting rooms and rewarding food

A lot of careful work has gone into revamping the pretty garden here. There are three 'beach huts' to hire, chairs with barrel tables and sofas and the terrace now has heated parasols. Many customers are here for the very good food cooked by the former England football team chef Roger Narbett. It's an interesting pub, built some 90 years ago on the site of an old coaching inn, and is a clever mix of ancient and modern: red-painted walls between beams and timbering, broad floorboards and weathered quarry tiles, and warm winter fires. There are leather sofas and tub chairs, high-backed purple and red or ladderback dining chairs around all sorts of tables, plenty of mirrors giving the impression of even more space, brass plates and mugs, candles and fresh flowers. Sharps Doom Bar, Wye Valley HPA and a guest ale on handpump and a dozen wines by the glass. One elegant but cosy room, known as the Players Lounge, has photographs of Mr Narbett's football chef days. This is sister pub to the Bell & Cross at Holy Cross.

A wide choice of interesting food includes baps, various platters, smoked salmon with guacamole, sour cream and crayfish, lamb koftas with tzatziki, flatbread and pomegranate and cashew nut salad, various stone-baked pizzas, a pie of the day, burger with toppings, relish and skinny fries, malaysian chicken curry, vegetarian moussaka, barbecue duck leg with wok-fried greens and chow mein noodle salad, and puddings such as chocolate fudge brownie cookies with white chocolate ice-cream and coconut and pineapple tart with lime drizzle and coconut ice-cream; they also offer a two- and three-course set menu (not Friday evenings or weekends). *Benchmark main dish: slow-cooked lamb shoulder with sweet potato dauphinoise and pea and mint purée £16.75. Two-course evening meal £17.00.*

Free house ~ Licensees Roger and Jo Narbett ~ Real ale ~ Open 12-11 (10.30 Sun) ~ Bar food 12-9 (9.30 Fri, Sat, 8.30 Sun) ~ Restaurant ~ Children welcome ~ Dogs allowed in bar ~ Wi-fi *Recommended by Phil and Helen Holt, Fiona Thomas, Dave Braisted, Dr and Mrs A K Clarke*

HOLY CROSS
SO9278 Map 4

Bell & Cross ★ ⭐️ 🍷

(01562) 730319 – www.bellandcrossclent.co.uk

4 miles from M5 junction 4: A491 towards Stourbridge, then follow Clent signpost off on left; DY9 9QL

● ●

Worcestershire Dining Pub of the Year

A delightful old interior, particularly good food, staff with a can-do attitude and a pretty garden

Of course, many customers are here to enjoy the imaginative food, but there are always some chatty locals in the cosy bar where neatly dressed, courteous staff serve Enville Ale, Marstons Burton Bitter, Purity Pure Gold and Timothy Taylors Landlord on handpump and 12 wines by the glass. Four attractively decorated dining rooms (with a choice of carpet, bare boards, lino or nice old quarry tiles) have a variety of moods, from snug and chatty to bright and airy. Décor includes theatrical engravings on red walls, nice sporting prints on pale green walls, and racing and gundog pictures above a black panelled dado; most rooms have coal fires. The lovely garden has a spacious lawn, and the terrace offers pleasant views. This is sister pub to the Chequers at Cutnall Green.

 Tempting food from a well judged menu includes baps, confit duck rillettes with port and cranberry chutney, whiskey-cured salmon gravadlax with pickled shallots, cucumber ribbons, blinis and crème fraîche, burger with toppings, chilli jam and skinny fries, vegetable and feta moussaka with giant bean stew and flatbread, a pie of the day, slow-cooked shoulder of lamb with baby onions, mushrooms, bacon and peppered swede, and puddings such as crème brûlée banana daiquiri with toffee ripple and honeycomb crisp and chocolate and salted peanut tart with caramel ice-cream; they also offer a two- and three-course set menu (not Friday evenings or weekends). *Benchmark main dish: chicken escalope with parma ham, macaroni cheese, vine tomatoes and basil £14.95. Two-course evening meal £20.00.*

Enterprise ~ Lease Roger and Jo Narbett ~ Real ale ~ Open 12-3, 6-11; 12-10.30 Sun ~ Bar food 12-2, 6-9 (9.30 Sat); 12-7 Sun ~ Restaurant ~ Children welcome ~ Dogs allowed in bar ~ Wi-fi *Recommended by Dr D J and Mrs S C Walker, Roger and Donna Huggins, R T and J C Moggridge, Dr and Mrs A K Clarke, Steve Whalley*

KNIGHTWICK
SO7355 Map 4

Talbot ⭐️ 🍷 🍺 🛏️

(01886) 821235 – www.the-talbot.co.uk

Knightsford Bridge; B4197 just off A44 Worcester–Bromyard; WR6 5PH

Interesting old coaching inn with good own-brewed beer and riverside garden; comfortable bedrooms

The own-brew beers and impressive food continue to draw in customers to this rambling country hotel. The heavily beamed and extended traditional lounge bar has a warm winter log fire, a variety of seats from small carved or leatherette armchairs to winged settles by the windows, and a vast stove in a big central stone hearth. The bar opens into a light and airy garden room. The well furnished back public bar has pool on a raised side area, TV, darts, a juke box and cribbage. In contrast, the dining room is a sedate place for a quiet meal. Their Teme Valley microbrewery uses locally grown hops to produce That, This, T'Other and a seasonal ale that are served alongside Hobsons Best and a changing guest on handpump, a dozen wines by the glass and 16 malt whiskies; they hold regular beer festivals. A farmers' market takes place here on the second Sunday of the month. In warm weather, it's lovely to use the tables on the lawn beside the River Teme (it's across the lane but they serve out here too) or you can sit in front of the building on old-fashioned seats.

 They grow their own produce, forage for wild food and make the preserves, bread, raised pies and black pudding in-house for the enjoyable food, which includes sandwiches, pork, orange and cognac pâté, fishcakes with garlic mayonnaise, cottage pie, roast sweet potato and leek crumble, lamb tagine, slow-roast pork with griddled black pudding and apple fritters, fresh cod with a cheese, herb and breadcrumb topping and rich tomato sauce, venison casserole, and puddings such as chocolate truffle cake and lemon meringue roulade; they also offer a two- and three-course set lunch. *Benchmark main dish: cold raised pork and game pie £14.00. Two-course evening meal £20.00.*

Own brew ~ Licensee Annie Clift ~ Real ale ~ Open 8am-11pm ~ Bar food 8am-9pm ~ Restaurant ~ Children welcome ~ Dogs welcome ~ Wi-fi ~ Bedrooms: £60/£100
Recommended by Patrick and Daphne Darley, Pat and Tony Martin, Tony and Wendy Hobden, Alan and Angela Scouller

MALVERN
SO7845 Map 4
Nags Head
(01684) 574373 – www.nagsheadmalvern.co.uk
Bottom end of Bank Street, steep turn down off A449; WR14 2JG

A delightfully eclectic layout and décor, remarkable choice of ales, tasty lunchtime bar food and warmly welcoming atmosphere

Always deservedly packed out with customers keen to enjoy the fine range of ales and the cheerful, chatty atmosphere, this remains a favourite with many. A series of snug, individually decorated rooms, separated by a couple of steps and with two open fires, have all sorts of chairs including leather armchairs, pews sometimes arranged as booths and a mix of tables (including sturdy ones stained different colours). There are bare boards here, flagstones there, carpet elsewhere, plenty of interesting pictures and homely touches such as house plants, shelves of well thumbed books and daily papers; board games. If you struggle to choose from the 15 or so beers on handpump, you'll be offered a taster by the professional, friendly staff: Banks's Bitter, Bathams Best Bitter, Courage Directors, Lymestone Stone The Crows, Marstons Pedigree New World, Otter Bitter, Ramsbury Flint Knapper, St Georges Charger, Dragon's Blood, Dreamweaver and Friar Tuck, Ringwood Fortyniner and Woods Shropshire Lad plus changing guests. Also, two farm ciders, 30 malt whiskies, ten gins, ten bottled craft ales/lagers and ten wines by the glass including pudding ones. The front terrace and garden have picnic-sets, benches and rustic tables as well as parasols and heaters.

Tasty lunchtime food includes sandwiches, various platters, home-cooked ham and eggs, steak and mushroom in ale pie, mixed bean and chickpea chilli with sour cream and beer-battered cod and chips, with evening meals (served in the barn extension dining room only) such as honey and ginger chicken wings with chilli and pepper salsa, smoked salmon and crayfish arancini, pulled chicken stroganoff with herb butter and noodles and monkfish with roast fennel and courgette with rosemary butter. *Benchmark main dish: smoked rump burger with caramelised red onion, maple-cured bacon and chips £14.90. Two-course evening meal £20.00.*

Free house ~ Licensees Clare Keane and Alex Whistance ~ Real ale ~ Open 11am-11.15pm (11.30 Fri, Sat); 12-11 Sun ~ Bar food 12-2.30, 6.30-8.30; 12-2.30, 7-8.30 Sun ~ Restaurant ~ Children welcome ~ Dogs welcome ~ Wi-fi *Recommended by Pat and Tony Martin, Chris and Angela Buckell, Barry Collett*

NEWLAND

SO7948 Map 4

Swan ◖

(01886) 832224 – www.theswaninnmalvern.co.uk

Worcester Road (set well back from A449 just NW of Malvern); WR13 5AY

Popular, interesting pub with six real ales and seats in the big garden

The dimly lit dark-beamed bar at this attractive old place is quite traditional, with a forest canopy of hops, whisky-water jugs, beakers and tankards. Several of the comfortable and clearly individually chosen seats are worth a close look for their carving, and the wall tapestries are interesting. The carved counter has Exmoor Gold, Purity Mad Goose, St Georges Dragon's Blood and Friar Tuck, Ringwood Fortyniner and a changing guest on handpump, plus several wines, malt whiskies and four farm ciders. On the right is a broadly similar red-carpeted dining room and beyond it, in complete contrast, an ultra-modern glass garden room; background music and board games. The garden itself is as individual as the pub, with a cluster of huge casks topped with flowers, even a piano doing flower-tub duty – and a set of stocks on the pretty front terrace.

 As well as sandwiches and hot baguettes, the interesting food includes cod and crab lemongrass shish kebab, deep-fried breaded blue cheese with chilli jam, black treacle ham hock with potato hash, pearl barley risotto with grilled halloumi and roasted squash, beer-battered fresh cod and chips, game pie in red wine and rosemary sauce, chicken and mango curry, mustard-crusted lamb breast with root vegetable broth, and puddings. *Benchmark main dish: beer-battered cod and chips £12.50. Two-course evening meal £21.00.*

Free house ~ Licensee Nick Taylor ~ Real ale ~ Open 12-11.30 ~ Bar food 12-2.30, 6-9; 12-3, 7-9 Sun ~ Restaurant ~ Children welcome but not in one bar after 8pm ~ Dogs allowed in bar *Recommended by P and J Shapley, M G Hart*

TENBURY WELLS   SO6468   Map 4

Talbot ♀ ⇆

(01584) 781941 – www.talbotinnnewnhambridge.co.uk

Newnham Bridge; A456; WR15 8JF

Carefully refurbished coaching inn with character bar and dining rooms and highly rated food; bedrooms

The thoughtfully decorated and well equipped bedrooms in this 19th-c coaching inn make a good base for exploring the lovely Teme Valley and nearby towns. It's a friendly, gently civilised place with nice old red and black and original quarry tiles, bare floorboards, open fires and candlelight, with the bar and dining rooms being quite different in style: an assortment of dark pubby, high-backed painted wooden and comfortably upholstered dining chairs around a variety of tables, leather tub chairs and sofas here and there, bookshelves, old photographs of the local area, table lights and standard lamps, some elegant antiques dotted about and pretty arrangements of fresh flowers. It gets pretty busy at the weekend, when you'll need to book a table in advance. Hobsons Best Bitter and Twisted Spire and Wye Valley HPA on handpump, local cider and nine wines by the glass from a good list.

 Enjoyable food includes smoked trout pâté with pickled pear, lemon confit and fennel, corned beef hash with a poached duck egg and sweetcorn fritter, gnocchi with wild mushrooms, walnuts and white truffle oil, beef in stilton pie, beer-battered cod and chips, chicken with creamed leeks, pancetta and dauphinoise potatoes, bass with white bean cassoulet and greens, and puddings such as honeycomb toffee cheesecake with glazed banana and toffee sauce and fruit crumble with cinnamon ice-cream. *Benchmark main dish: slow-cooked lamb with croquette shoulder and minted pea purée £17.00. Two-course evening meal £20.00.*

Free house ~ Licensee Ian Dowling ~ Real ale ~ Open 10am-11pm (11.30 Sat); 10-9 Sun ~ Bar food 12-2.30, 6-9; 12-5 Sun ~ Restaurant ~ Children welcome ~ Dogs allowed in bar ~ Wi-fi ~ Bedrooms: £75/£85 *Recommended by Gavin and Helle May, Isobel Mackinlay*

WELLAND   SO8039 Map 4
Inn at Welland ⭐ 🍷
(01684) 592317 – www.theinnatwelland.co.uk
Drake Street; A4104 W of Upton upon Severn; WR13 6LN

Stylish contemporary country dining bar with good food and wines and nice tables outside

This is a thoroughly enjoyable pub; our readers agree with warm and enthusiastic reports. With a gently civilised atmosphere and a feel of unobtrusive good taste, it has cool grey paintwork, a few carefully chosen modern prints and attractive seat fabrics, with beige flagstones in the central area, wood flooring to the sides and a woodburning stove at one end. The lively buzz of conversation is gently underscored by barely perceptible background music. There's Malvern Hills Black Pear, Otter Bitter and Wye Valley Butty Bach on handpump, 18 wines by the glass including an unusually wide range of pudding wines, and two farm ciders; plenty of efficient neatly dressed staff. The good-sized neat garden, offering tranquil views of the Malvern Hills, has tables with comfortable teak or wicker chairs, some on a biggish sheltered deck, others on individual separate terraces set into lawn. The pub is handy for the Three Counties Showground.

Using the best local, seasonal produce and making everything in-house, the imaginative food includes lunchtime sandwiches, pigeon breast with maple-glazed bacon, chicory and frisée salad and red wine dressing, seared scallops with burnt apple, pulled pork and crackling, corned beef hash with black pudding and a free-range egg, a pie of the day, thai-style vegetable and coconut milk curry, hake fillet with pea and pancetta risotto, pea shoot and herb oil, free-range chicken with charred leeks, braised gem lettuce and madeira 'café au lait' sauce, and puddings such as white chocolate cheesecake with Malteser ice-cream and apple tarte tatin with caramel sauce. *Benchmark main dish: aberdeen angus burger with toppings, truffled mayonnaise and french fries £12.90. Two-course evening meal £20.00.*

Free house ~ Licensees David and Gillian Pinchbeck ~ Real ale ~ Open 12-3.30, 6-11; 12-4 Sun; closed Sun evening, Mon ~ Bar food 12-2.30, 6-9.30; 12-3 Sun ~ Children welcome ~ Wi-fi *Recommended by Alfie Bayliss, Caroline Prescott, Richard Kennell, R T and J C Moggridge, Dave Braisted, Chris and Val Ramstedt, Bernard Stradling*

Also Worth a Visit in Worcestershire

Besides the fully inspected pubs, you might like to try these pubs that have been recommended to us and described by readers. Do tell us what you think of them: feedback@goodguides.com

ABBERLEY   SO7567
Manor Arms (01299) 890300
Netherton Lane; WR6 6BN
Refurbished country inn tucked away in quiet village backwater opposite fine Norman church; changing ales and good selection of wines, enjoyable food from pub favourites up, friendly service; two-level deck with lovely valley views, good walks (on Worcestershire Way), six bedrooms, open all day. *(Pip White)*

ALVECHURCH SP0172

Weighbridge (0121) 445 5111

Scarfield Wharf; B48 7SQ Converted little house by Worcester & Birmingham Canal marina, bar and a couple of small rooms, five well kept ales such as Kinver Bargee Bitter and Weatheroaks Tillerman's Tipple, simple low-priced food (not Tues, Weds); tables outside. *(Alfie Bayliss)*

ASHTON UNDER HILL SO9938

Star (01386) 881325

Elmley Road; WR11 7SN Smallish pub perched above road in quiet village at foot of Bredon Hill; linked beamed rooms around bar, one with flagstones and log fire, steps up to pitch-roofed dining room with woodburner, good choice of well liked food (not Sun or Mon evenings) from fresh baguettes to specials, real ales such as Black Sheep and Greene King IPA, friendly staff; background music, TV and games machine; children and dogs welcome, picnic-sets in pleasant garden, good walks, open all day. *(Dave Braisted)*

ASTON FIELDS SO9669

Ladybird Inn (01527) 878014

Finstall Road (B184 just S of Bromsgrove); B60 2DZ Light and airy red-brick Edwardian local adjoining hotel (next to station), panelled bar and comfortable lounge, reasonably priced pub food along with separate italian restaurant, own Birds ales and guests such as Bathams and Wye Valley, good service (may ask for a credit card if running a tab); children welcome, open all day. *(Caroline Prescott)*

BARNARDS GREEN SO7945

Bluebell (01684) 575031

Junction B4211 to Rhydd Green with B4208 to Three Counties Showground; WR14 3QP Chain dining pub nicely set back from the road, comfortable and reliable, with good choice of enjoyable well priced food including deals, four Marstons-related ales, friendly staff coping well at busy times; quiz first Thurs of month; free wi-fi; children welcome, dogs in one part of bar, disabled facilities, nice outside seating areas, open (and food) all day. *(S F Parrinder)*

BAUGHTON SO8742

Jockey (01684) 592153

4 miles from M50 junction 1; A38 northwards, then right on to A4104 Upton–Pershore; WR8 9DQ Well refurbished and extended dining pub reopened after long closure; spacious open-plan interior with slate-floored beamed bar and various eating areas off, good choice of well liked food including lunchtime set menu, three Wye Valley ales, Sharps Doom Bar and 19 wines by the glass, cocktails, friendly proficient service; children welcome, no dogs inside, tables in paved back courtyard, open all day (till 6pm Sun). *(Mrs Zara Elliott)*

BECKFORD SO9835

Beckford Inn (01386) 881532

A435; GL20 7AN Sizeable 18th-c roadside inn recently acquired by Wadworths and undergoing major refurbishment as we went to press – reports please. *(Roger and Donna Huggins)*

BELBROUGHTON SO9177

Queens (01562) 730276

Queens Hill (B4188 E of Kidderminster); DY9 0DU Old refurbished red-brick pub by Belne Brook, several linked areas including beamed slate-floor bar, good modern food alongside pub standards, also set menu choices, three well kept beers and nice selection of wines, friendly staff coping well at busy times; disabled facilities, small roadside terrace, pleasant village and handy for M5 (junction 4), open all day weekends. *(Neil Allen)*

BELBROUGHTON SO9277

Talbot (01562) 730249

Off A491; DY9 9TG Popular village pub with enjoyable good value food in bar and restaurant, set deal Mon-Weds, well kept Jennings Cocker Hoop and guests, friendly staff; garden with covered terrace, open (and food) all day. *(Dave Braisted)*

BERROW SO7835

Duke of York (01684) 833449

Junction A438/B4208; WR13 6JQ Bustling old country pub with two spic and span linked rooms, beams, nooks and crannies and log fire, welcoming friendly staff, good food from baguettes up including daily fresh fish, well kept Wye Valley and a guest ale, restaurant; big garden behind, handy for Malvern Hills. *(Theocsbrian)*

BERROW GREEN SO7458

★Admiral Rodney (01886) 821375

B4197, off A44 W of Worcester; WR6 6PL Light and roomy high-beamed 17th-c dining pub, big stripped kitchen tables and two woodburners, popular reasonably priced food from varied menu (should book Fri, Sat evenings), friendly fast service, well kept Birds, Wye Valley and guests, real cider/perry, charming split-level restaurant in rebuilt barn; folk music third Weds of month, skittle alley; well behaved children and dogs welcome, disabled facilities, tables outside with pretty view and heated covered terrace, good walks, three bedrooms, closed Mon lunchtime, open all day weekends. *(John and Jennifer Spinks)*

BEWDLEY SO7775

Hop Pole (01299) 401295

Hop Pole Lane; DY12 2QH Friendly modernised family-run pub, good choice of enjoyable food (booking advised) from pub classics up including set lunch menu, three or four well kept Marstons-related ales and several wines by the glass, walls decorated with old tools etc, cast-iron range in dining area; live music Weds, free wi-fi; children and dogs (not during food times) welcome, front garden with scarecrow and vegetable patch, open all day (afternoon break Mon). *(Ron and Sue Gilbert)*

BEWDLEY   SO7875
★ **Little Pack Horse**   (01299) 403762
High Street; no nearby parking – best to use main car park, then cross B4190 (Cleobury Road) and keep walking on down narrowing High Street; DY12 2DH
Friendly town pub tucked away in side street with nicely timbered rooms, reclaimed oak panelling and floorboards, woodburner, tasty food including good pies and suet puddings, Bewdley and a couple of guest ales, selection of bottled ciders and perries and good wine choice, cheerful helpful service, restaurant; background music, TV; children and dogs (in bar) welcome, heated outside area, open all day weekends, closed Mon-Thurs. *(Mike Tippins)*

BEWDLEY   SO7875
Mug House   (01299) 402543
Severn Side North; DY12 2EE 18th-c bay-windowed pub in charming spot by River Severn, good food from traditional choices up including set menus, five well kept ales such as Bewdley, Timothy Taylors and Wye Valley, log fire, restaurant with lobster tank; children (till 8pm) and dogs welcome, disabled access, glass-covered terrace behind, seven river-view bedrooms, open all day. *(Caroline Prescott)*

BISHAMPTON   SO9445
Dolphin   (01386) 462343
Main Street; WR10 2LX Comfortably updated village pub with good reasonably priced food (not Sun evening, Mon) cooked by landlord-chef including daily specials, Tues curry and Weds steak night, beers such as Hook Norton and Sharps, well chosen wines by the glass, efficient friendly young staff; children and dogs welcome, seats on paved terrace and small raised deck, open all day Sat, till 9pm Sun, closed Mon lunchtime. *(Anon)*

BREDON   SO9236
★ **Fox & Hounds**   (01684) 772377
4.5 miles from M5 junction 9; A438 to Northway, left at B4079, in Bredon follow sign to church; GL20 7LA Cottagey 16th-c thatched pub with open-plan carpeted bar, low beams, stone pillars and stripped timbers, central woodburner, traditional furnishings including upholstered settles, a variety of wheelback, tub and kitchen chairs around handsome mahogany and cast-iron-framed tables, elegant wall lamps, smaller side bar, Butcombe and a guest, nice wines by the glass, wide choice of food including specials, fast friendly service; background

music; children and dogs (in bar) welcome, outside picnic-sets (some under cover), open every other Sun evening for quiz. *(Dr D J and Mrs S C Walker)*

BROADWAS-ON-TEME   SO7555
Royal Oak   (01886) 821353
A44; WR6 5NE Red-brick roadside pub with various areas including unusual lofty-raftered medieval-style dining hall, good value daily carvery and other popular food, well kept ales and decent wines by the glass, friendly helpful service; free wi-fi; children welcome, disabled access, garden with play area, open all day weekends. *(Alfie Bayliss)*

CALLOW END   SO8349
Blue Bell   (01905) 830261
Upton Road; WR2 4TY Popular Marstons local with two bars and dining area, wide variety of enjoyable food including lots of specials (some good vegetarian choices), well kept beers and friendly welcoming staff, open fire; children allowed, dogs in garden only, open all day weekends. *(Dave Braisted)*

CALLOW HILL   SO7473
Royal Forester   (01299) 266286
Near Wyre Forest visitor centre; DY14 9XW Dining pub dating in part from the 15th c, good food and friendly helpful service, relaxed lounge bar with well kept Wye Valley HPA and a guest, Robinson's cider, restaurant; children and dogs welcome, seats outside, seven contemporary bedrooms, open all day. *(Pip White)*

CAUNSALL   SO8480
Anchor   (01562) 850254
Caunsall Road, off A449; DY11 5YL Traditional unchanging two-room pub (in same family since 1927), friendly atmosphere and can get busy, half a dozen well kept ales including Hobsons and Wye Valley, traditional ciders and generously filled cobs, friendly efficient service; dogs welcome, tables outside, near canal. *(Andrew Stone)*

CLAINES   SO8558
Mug House   (01905) 456649
Claines Lane, off A449 3 miles W of M5 junction 3; WR3 7RN Fine views from ancient country tavern in unique churchyard setting by fields below the Malvern Hills; several small rooms around central bar, low doorways and heavy oak beams, well kept Banks's and other Marstons-related beers, simple lunchtime pub food (not Sun); no credit cards, outside lavatories; children allowed away from servery, open all day weekends. *(Anon)*

CROWLE   SO9256
Old Chequers   (01905) 381275
Crowle Green, not far from M5 junction 6; WR7 4AA Civilised 17th-c dining pub mixing traditional and contemporary décor; oak beams and log fires,

leather sofas, modern tables and chairs in bar and restaurant, friendly prompt service, good variety of enjoyable home-made food from pub favourites up including two-course weekday lunch deal, three real ales and nice choice of wines by the glass, baby grand piano, some live jazz; children and dogs (in bar) welcome, disabled facilities, picnic-sets in garden behind, open all day, closed Sun evening. *(Alan Weedon, Dave Braisted)*

DEFFORD   SO9042
★ **Monkey House** (01386) 750234
A4104, after passing Oak pub on right, it's the last of a small group of cottages; WR8 9BW Tiny black and white thatched cider house, a wonderful time warp and in the same family for over 150 years; drinks limited to cider and a perry tapped from barrels into pottery mugs and served by landlady from a hatch, no food (can bring your own); children welcome, no dogs (resident rottweilers), garden with caravans, sheds and Mandy the horse, small spartan outbuilding with a couple of plain tables, settle and fireplace, open Fri and Sun lunchtimes, Weds and Sat evenings.
(Caroline Prescott)

DEFFORD   SO9042
Oak (01386) 750327
Woodmancote (A4104); WR8 9BW Modernised 17th-c beamed country pub with two front bars and back restaurant, well kept Sharps Doom Bar and Wye Valley ales, Thatcher's cider, good fairly priced food including deals and themed nights, friendly staff; children and dogs welcome, vine-covered front pergola, garden with chickens and orchard, open all day, from 9am weekends for breakfast. *(Pip White)*

DROITWICH   SO8963
Gardeners Arms (01905) 772936
Vines Lane; WR9 8LU Individual place on the edge of town; cosy traditional bar to the right, bistro-style restaurant to the left with red gingham tablecloths and lots of pictures (mostly for sale), four Marstons-related ales, well priced food from varied menu including range of good local sausages, friendly attentive service, live music and quiz nights, also themed food evenings, whisky tastings and a cigar club; children and dogs welcome, outside seating areas on different levels below railway embankment with quirky mix of furniture, play area, camping, close to Droitwich Canal, open all day. *(Clive and Fran Dutson, Dave Braisted, John and Hazel Sarkanen)*

DROITWICH   SO9063
Hop Pole (01905) 770155
Friar Street; WR9 8ED Heavy-beamed local with panelled rooms on different levels,

friendly staff, well kept Enville, Malvern Hills, Wye Valley and a guest, bargain home-made lunchtime food including doorstep sandwiches, dominoes, darts and pool, live music first Sun of month; children welcome, partly canopied back garden, open all day. *(Dave Braisted, Tony and Wendy Hobden, Alan Weedon)*

ELDERSFIELD   SO8131
★ **Butchers Arms** (01452) 840381
Village signposted from B4211; Lime Street (coming from A417, go past the Eldersfield turn and take the next one), OS Sheet 150 map reference 815314; also signposted from B4208 N of Staunton; GL19 4NX Pretty cottage with deliberately simple unspoilt little locals' bar, ales such as St Austell, Wickwar and Wye Valley tapped from the cask, a farm cider and short but well chosen wine list, just a dozen seats in candlelit dining room and booking essential for owner-chef's highly regarded imaginative food (not cheap); no under-10s, garden picnic-sets, nice surroundings, closed Sun evening, Mon, ten days in Jan and the latter part of Aug, food served lunchtime Fri-Sun, evening Tues-Sat. *(Alfie Bayliss)*

EVESHAM   SP0344
Evesham Hotel (01386) 765566
Coopers Lane; WR11 1DA Idiosyncratic hotel's busy bar with amazing range of malt whiskies and spirits, a beer from Teme Valley and good if quirky wine list, interesting menu including good value lunchtime buffet (no tips or service charge), elegant dining room; remarkable lavatories with talking mirrors; children welcome (toys for them), indoor swimming pool, 39 comfortable bedrooms, open all day. *(Miss B D Picton)*

EVESHAM   SP0344
Old Red Horse (01386) 442784
Vine Street; WR11 4RE Attractive black and white former coaching inn, three real ales and enjoyable straightforward food at reasonable prices, good cheerful service, two bars with bare boards, beams and open fires; TV and machines; nice covered inner courtyard with small pond, five bedrooms, open all day. *(George Atkinson)*

FECKENHAM   SP0061
Forest (01527) 894422
B4090 Droitwich–Alcester; B96 6JE Contemporary décor and good interesting food at this village dining pub from lunchtime sandwiches and sharing boards up, well kept Hook Norton and Timothy Taylors, efficient friendly service, oak-floored bar with light-wood stools at high tables and some other more comfortable seating, panels of bookshelf wallpaper dotted about,

It's very helpful if you let us know up-to-date food prices when you report on pubs.

woodburner, adjoining restaurant with upholstered booth seats, conservatory; children welcome, disabled access/facilities, rattan furniture on block-paved terrace with big outdoor fireplace, more tables on raised lawn, open all day. *(Dave Braisted, Mike and Mary Carter)*

FLADBURY SO9946

Chequers (01386) 861854

Chequers Lane; WR10 2PZ Refurbished old pub in peaceful village; long beamed bar with log fire in old-fashioned range, ales such as Sharps Doom Bar and Wye Valley, Aspall's and Weston's ciders, enjoyable sensibly priced home-made food including Mon steak night, timbered back restaurant with conservatory; background music, free wi-fi; children welcome, steps up to walled terrace, play area on lawn with country views, eight bedrooms in extension, open all day Fri-Sun, closed Mon lunchtime. *(Rob Anderson)*

GRIMLEY SO8359

Camp House (01905) 640288

A443 5 miles N from Worcester, right to Grimley, right at village T junction; WR2 6LX Simple unspoilt old pub in same family since 1939, appealing Severn-side setting (prone to flooding) with own landing stage, generous home-made food at bargain prices, well kept Bathams and guests, Thatcher's and Robinson's ciders, friendly laid-back atmosphere; no credit cards; children and well behaved dogs welcome, attractive lawns (maybe wandering peacocks), small campsite, open all day. *(Caroline Prescott)*

HADLEY SO8662

Bowling Green (01905) 620294

Hadley Heath; off A4133 Droitwich–Ombersley; WR9 0AR Friendly 16th-c inn with beams and big log fire, sofas in back lounge, well kept Wadworths range and decent wines by the glass, good food (all day Sun) from sandwiches, deli boards and pizzas up, restaurant; children welcome, tables out overlooking own bowling green (UK's oldest), eight comfortable bedrooms, nice walks (footpath starts from car park), open all day. *(M C and S Jeanes)*

HALLOW SO8258

Crown (01905) 640408

Main Road; WR2 6LB Large low-beamed 17th-c pub with good food including set menu choices, Sat steak night, St Austell, Herefordshire and Sharps, friendly helpful staff; children welcome, tables on terrace and grassed area, open all day, food till 6pm Sun. *(Dave Braisted)*

HANBURY SO9662

Vernon (01527) 821236

Droitwich Road (B4090); B60 4DB 18th-c former coaching inn, contemporary refurbishment and much emphasis on food, but still serves real ales such as Wye Valley and Sharps in beamed bar with woodburner, nice food from light choices to more enterprising restaurant-style dishes, set lunch menu too, good friendly service; children welcome, modern terrace seating, five boutique-style bedrooms, open all day from 9.30am. *(Alfie Bayliss)*

HANLEY CASTLE SO8342

★Three Kings (01684) 592686

Church End, off B4211 N of Upton upon Severn; WR8 0BL Timeless, hospitable and by no means smart – in same family for over 100 years and a favourite with those who put unspoilt character and individuality first; cheerful, homely tiled-floor tap room separated from entrance corridor by monumental built-in settle, equally vast inglenook fireplace, room on left with darts and board games, separate entrance to timbered lounge with second inglenook and neatly blacked kitchen range, leatherette armchairs, spindleback chairs and antique winged settle, well kept Butcombe, Hobsons and three guests from smaller brewers, Weston's cider and around 75 malt whiskies, simple snacks; live music; old-fashioned wood and iron seats on front terrace looking across to great cedar shading tiny green. *(M G Hart, Barry Collett)*

HARTLEBURY SO8470

Tap House (01299) 253275

Station Road; DY11 7YJ Converted station buildings with bar and restaurant, enjoyable bargain food and keenly priced Worcestershire ales from adjacent brewery; background music, TV, free wi-fi; terrace table with valley views, open all day. *(Dave Braisted)*

HIMBLETON SO9458

Galton Arms (01905) 391672

Harrow Lane; WR9 7LQ Friendly old black and white bay-windowed country pub, enjoyable food including daily specials in split-level beamed bar or restaurant, well kept Banks's, Bathams, Wye Valley and a guest, woodburner; sports TV; children and dogs welcome, picnic-sets in small part-paved garden, own pigs and chickens, local walks, open all day Sun, closed Mon lunchtime. *(Dave Braisted)*

KIDDERMINSTER SO8376

King & Castle (01562) 747505

Railway Station, Comberton Hill; DY10 1QX Neatly re-created Edwardian refreshment room in Severn Valley Railway terminus, steam trains outside and railway memorabilia and photographs inside, simple furnishings, half a dozen ales including Bathams, reasonably priced straightforward food in adjacent dining room 9am-4pm (6pm weekends); little museum close by, open all day and busy bank holidays/railway gala days. *(Roger and Donna Huggins, Dave Braisted)*

KINGTON   SO9855

Red Hart (01386) 792559

Cockshot Lane; WR7 4DD Modernised and extended old pub with enjoyable home-made food (not Mon) including specials, Marstons-related ales, friendly attentive young staff, restaurant; closed Mon lunchtime, otherwise open all day. *(Paul Humphreys)*

LONGDON   SO8434

Hunters Inn (01684) 833388

B4211 S, towards Tewkesbury; GL20 6AR Country pub with beams, flagstones, timbers, some stripped brick and log fires, good locally sourced food including aberdeen angus beef from own farm, Sun carvery, real ales such as Donnington and Otter, local ciders and decent wines by the glass, friendly smiling service, raftered dining area with linen tablecloths, good views; children welcome, extensive well tended garden, open all day Sun. *(Alfie Bayliss)*

MALVERN   SO7746

Foley Arms (01684) 573397

Worcester Road; WR14 4QS Substantial Georgian hotel owned by Wetherspoons (former coaching inn), friendly staff and usual good value; children welcome, splendid views from sunny terrace and back bedrooms, open all day from 7am. *(Alan Weedon, David Carr)*

MALVERN   SO7640

Malvern Hills Hotel (01684) 540690

Opposite British Camp car park, Wynds Point; junction A449/B4232 S; WR13 6DW Big comfortable dark-panelled lounge bar, very popular weekends, enjoyable food from baguettes up, well kept changing ales such as local Malvern Hills and Wye Valley, quite a few malt whiskies and good coffee, friendly service, woodburner, downstairs pool room, smart more expensive restaurant; background music; dogs welcome, great views from terrace, bedrooms small but comfortable, open all day. *(David Edwards)*

MALVERN   SO7746

Red Lion (01684) 564787

St Ann's Road; WR14 4RG Enjoyable food (all day weekends) from substantial sandwiches and baguettes up, also good adjacent thai restaurant, well kept Marstons-related ales, cheerful prompt service, airy modern décor with stripped pine, bare boards, flagstones and pastel colours; background and live music; attractive partly covered front terrace, well placed for walks, open all day weekends, closed Mon-Thurs lunchtimes. *(Pip White)*

MALVERN   SO7643

Wyche (01684) 575396

Wyche Road; WR14 4EQ Comfortable busy pub near top of Malvern Hills, splendid views and popular with walkers, five local ales and affordable pubby food; children and dogs welcome, four bedrooms, open all day. *(Guy Vowles)*

OMBERSLEY   SO8463

★ Cross Keys (01905) 620588

Just off A449; Main Road (A4133, Kidderminster end); WR9 0DS Carpeted bar with easy-going atmosphere, archways opening into several separate areas – nicest on left with attractive Bob Lofthouse animal etchings, hop-strung beams and some horse tack on dark varnished country panelling, Timothy Taylors Landlord, Wye Valley HPA and maybe a guest, several wines by the glass and decent coffee, comfortable back room with softly upholstered sofas and armchairs leading to dining conservatory, plenty of emphasis on their well liked food from baguettes to enterprising daily specials (good fish choice), lunchtime set deal, friendly helpful service; unobtrusive background music; children welcome if eating, no dogs, terrace with alloy furniture under big heated canopy, open all day Sun. *(David Edwards, Robert W Buckle)*

OMBERSLEY   SO8463

★ Kings Arms (01905) 620142

Main Road (A4133); WR9 0EW Imposing beamed and timbered Tudor pub, spotless rambling rooms with nooks and crannies, three splendid fireplaces, low-ceilinged quarry-tiled bar with dark wood pew and stools around cast-iron tables, three dining areas, one room with Charles II coat of arms decorating the ceiling, Marstons-related ales, good food popular with older diners; background music; children and dogs welcome, seats on tree-sheltered courtyard, colourful hanging baskets and tubs, open all day, food all day weekends. *(Richard and Penny Gibbs, David and Stella Martin)*

PENSAX   SO7368

★ Bell (01299) 896677

B4202 Abberley–Clows Top, Snead Common part of village; WR6 6AE Mock-Tudor roadside pub with good local atmosphere and friendly staff, half a dozen changing ales such as Hobsons (festival last weekend of June), also cider and perry, well liked good value pubby food (not Sun evening) from sandwiches up, L-shaped main bar with traditional décor, cushioned pews and pubby tables on bare boards, vintage beer ads and wartime front pages, two open fires and woodburner, dining room with french windows opening on to deck; children welcome, dogs in bar, country-view garden, open all day summer weekends, closed Mon. *(Lynda and Trevor Smith)*

PEOPLETON   SO9350

Crown (01905) 840222

Village and pub signed off A44 at Allens Hill; WR10 2EE Cosy village pub with welcoming owners and friendly mix of drinkers and diners, beamed bar with big inglenook, well laid-out eating area, good food (must book) from sandwiches and pub favourites up including lunchtime set deal, Fullers, Sharps and Wye Valley, nice wines by the glass, efficient pleasant service; surcharge added if paying by credit card; children and dogs (in bar) welcome, flower-filled back garden, open all day, no food Sun evening. *(A Phelps)*

PERSHORE   SO9545

Angel (01386) 552046

High Street; WR10 1AF Comfortably renovated old bow-windowed coaching inn, various well cared-for areas including flagstoned bar, beams, panelling and original fireplaces, Hook Norton, Sharps and a guest, decent wines and popular good value food from baguettes up, good friendly service; background music, TV; grounds at back, 15 bedrooms, open all day. *(Stanley and Annie Matthews)*

PERSHORE   SO9545

★ **Brandy Cask** (01386) 552602

Bridge Street; WR10 1AJ Plain high-ceilinged bow-windowed bar, own good ales from courtyard brewery and guests, friendly helpful service, coal fire, reasonably priced generous food from sandwiches to steaks, dining room; well behaved children allowed, no dogs inside, terrace and koi pond in long attractive garden down to river. *(Caroline Prescott)*

SEVERN STOKE   SO8544

Rose & Crown (01905) 371249

A38 S of Worcester; WR8 9JQ Attractive 16th-c black and white pub, low beams, knick-knacks and good fire in character bar, some cushioned wall seats and high-backed settles among more modern pub furniture, well kept Marstons-related ales, decent choice of enjoyable sensibly priced food, good friendly service, carpeted back restaurant; fortnightly quiz Weds, monthly folk night; dogs welcome, wheelchair access with help, picnic-sets in big garden with play area, Malvern Hills views and good walks, open (and food) all day. *(Pip White)*

SHATTERFORD   SO7981

Bellmans Cross (01299) 861322

Bridgnorth Road (A442); DY12 1RN Welcoming 19th-c mock-Tudor dining pub with good well presented food cooked by french chef-landlord, restaurant with kitchen view, Enville and a couple of guests from neat timber-effect bar, good choice of wines, teas and coffees; children welcome, picnic-sets outside, handy for Severn Woods walks, open (and food) all day weekends. *(Alfie Bayliss)*

STANFORD BRIDGE   SO7165

Bridge (01886) 812771

Signed from B4203; WR6 6RU Large rambling mock-Tudor fronted pub set back

from the River Teme, half a dozen well kept ales such as Hobsons, Otter, Popes and Wye Valley (regular beer festivals), local ciders/perries and enjoyable well priced food (not Sun evening) including some unusual specials, restaurant, games room with pool; quiz last Weds of month, live music; children and dogs welcome, seats outside, charity plastic duck race Aug, open all day (till 1am Fri, Sat). *(Dave Braisted)*

STOKE POUND   SO9667

Queens Head (01527) 557007

Sugarbrook Lane, by Bridge 48, Worcester & Birmingham Canal; B60 3AU Smartly refurbished by the small Lovely Pubs group; fairly large pub with comfortable seating area, dedicated dining part beyond, good choice of enjoyable food including sharing plates, wood-fired pizzas and charcoal spit-roasts, early evening discount Mon-Fri, well kept ales such as Greene King, Purity and Wye Valley, large selection of wines from glass-fronted store, helpful pleasant young staff; children welcome, waterside garden with tepee, moorings, good walk up the 36 locks of the Tardebigge Steps, quite handy for Avoncroft Museum, open all day. *(Clive and Fran Dutson, Helene Grygar, Dave Braisted)*

STOKE WORKS   SO9365

Bowling Green (01527) 861291

A mile from M5 junction 5, via Stoke Lane; handy for Worcester & Birmingham Canal; B60 4BH Friendly comfortable pub with enjoyable straightforward food at bargain prices (particularly good faggots), Banks's and a Marstons guest, wall chart showing cost of a pint over the years; children welcome, big garden with play area and neat bowling green, open all day, no food Sun. *(Dave Braisted)*

TIBBERTON   SO9057

Bridge Inn (01905) 345874

Plough Road; WR9 7NQ By Bridge 25, Worcester & Birmingham Canal; two comfortable dining sections with central fireplace, separate public bar, enjoyable reasonably priced traditional food, Banks's ales and a guest from Marstons, friendly staff; some live music; children, dogs and muddy boots welcome, picnic-sets by water and in garden with secure play area, moorings, open all day. *(Andrew Stone)*

UPHAMPTON   SO8464

Fruiterers Arms (01905) 620305

Off A449 N of Ombersley; WR9 0JW Homely country local (looks like a private house, and has been in the same family for over 160 years), good value Cannon Royall ales brewed at the back of the pub and guest beers, farm cider and perry, simple rustic Jacobean panelled bar and lounge with comfortable armchairs, beams and log fire, lots of photographs and memorabilia, no food except filled rolls Fri-Sun; children till 9pm, dogs welcome in one area, back terrace and some seats out in front, open all day. *(Caroline Prescott)*

WEATHEROAK HILL   SP0574
★ **Coach & Horses** (01564) 823386
Icknield Street – coming S on A435 from Wythall roundabout, filter right off dual carriageway a mile S, then in village turn left towards Alvechurch; not far from M42 junction 3; B48 7EA
Roomy country pub (in same family since 1968) brewing its own good Weatheroak Hill beers, well kept guests too and farm ciders, enjoyable choice of fairly priced home-cooked food (not Sun evening); proper old-fashioned tiled-floor bar with log fire (dogs allowed here), lounge bar with steps up to comfortably furnished high-raftered room with another fire, modern barn-style restaurant; children welcome, plenty of seats out on lawns and terrace, open all day. *(Pip White)*

WEST MALVERN   SO7645
★ **Brewers Arms** (01684) 568147
The Dingle, signed off B4232; WR14 4BQ
Attractive and friendly little two-bar beamed country local down steep path, Malvern Hills, Marstons, Wye Valley and up to five guests, good value home-made food (not Sun evening), neat airy dining room; children, walkers and dogs welcome, glorious view from small garden, smokers' folly, open all day Fri-Sun (may be under new ownership by the time you read this). *(Anon)*

WILDMOOR   SO9675
Wildmoor Oak (0121) 453 2696
A mile from M5 junction 4 – first left off A491 towards Stourbridge; Top Road; B61 0RB Busy country local with good choice of enjoyable food including caribbean dishes cooked by landlord, changing real ales, ciders and perries, friendly atmosphere; live jazz last Sun of month, soul disco first Fri, free wi-fi; small sloping terrace and garden, closed Mon lunchtime, otherwise open all day (winter hours may differ). *(Sarah Rees)*

WILLERSEY   SP1039
New Inn (01386) 853226
Main Street; WR12 7PJ Friendly old stone-built local in lovely village, generous good value pub food (not Sun evening) from sandwiches up, prompt service, well kept Donnington ales, flagstoned bar with raised quarry-tiled end section, some black beams, games room with pool and darts, separate

skittle alley; background music, TV; rattan-style tables and chairs outside, good local walks, open all day. *(Guy Vowles)*

WITHYBED GREEN   SP0172
Crown (0121) 445 2300
Near Bridge 61, Worcester & Birmingham Canal; B48 7PN Tucked-away pub in row of former canal workers' cottages overlooking fields, Greene King Abbot and a couple of guests, simple low-priced food (not Sun), series of small rooms with two open fires; children and dogs welcome, picnic-sets out in front and on terrace, open all day. *(Dave Braisted)*

WOLVERLEY   SO8379
Lock (01562) 850581
Wolverley Road (B4189 N of Kidderminster, by Staffordshire & Worcestershire Canal); DY10 3RN Roadside pub next to narrow lock on canal; pleasant and comfortable, with enjoyable good value food (all day weekends) including range of burgers and grills, Banks's and a couple of Marstons-related guests, cheerful staff, separate tea room; children and dogs welcome, waterside picnic-sets, handy for Kingsford Country Park, open all day. *(Dave Braisted)*

WORCESTER   SO8554
Cardinals Hat (01905) 724006
Friar Street; just off A44 near cathedral; WR1 2NA Dating from the 14th c with three small character rooms (one with fine oak panelling), half a dozen changing ales, real ciders and plenty of bottled beers, friendly well informed staff, good bar snacks and cheese/meat platters; free wi-fi; children welcome, pleasant little brick-paved terrace behind, closed Mon lunchtime, otherwise open all day. *(Lesley and Brian Lynn)*

WORCESTER   SO8455
Dragon (01905) 25845
The Tything (A38); WR1 1JT Simply furnished open-plan alehouse with six well kept interesting beers from smaller brewers including own Little Ale Cart (brewed in Sheffield), bottled belgians and Thatcher's cider too, friendly staff; dogs welcome, partly covered back terrace, open all day Fri and Sat (lunchtime food then, roasts on Sun), closed Mon and Tues lunchtimes. *(Pip White)*

WORCESTER   SO8454
Farriers Arms (01905) 27569
Fish Street; WR1 2HN Welcoming and relaxed old timbered pub rambling through pleasant lounge/dining area and public bar, enjoyable inexpensive food, well kept ales

Post Office address codings confusingly give the impression that some pubs are in Worcestershire, when they're really in Gloucestershire, Herefordshire, Shropshire or Warwickshire (which is where we list them).

such as Wells Bombardier and decent house wines, good cheerful service; TV, pool, darts; beer garden, handy for cathedral, open all day. *(George Atkinson)*

WORCESTER   SO8554
King Charles II (01905) 726100
New Street; WR1 2DP Small jettied Tudor building, heavy beams, fine panelling and woodburners in carved fireplaces, settles and pews on bare boards, well kept Craddocks and associated Bridgnorth and Two Thirsty Brewers, traditional ciders, enjoyable range of pies served with different types of mash, upstairs area with bench seating, old tapestry and some leather easy chairs; ask about the skeleton under the back floor hatch; open all day (food all day weekends). *(Dave Braisted)*

WORCESTER   SO8455
★ **Marwood** (01905) 330460
The Tything (A38); some nearby parking; WR1 1JL Easy to miss this old building, quirky and civilised with a long narrow series of small linked areas, dark flagstones and broad floorboards, stripped or cast-iron-framed tables, the odd chandelier, a few italian deco posters, open fires, upstairs room looking across to law courts, four well kept changing ales, enjoyable food (not Sun evening) from sandwiches and tapas up, friendly service; background music; children (in bar till 7.30pm) and dogs welcome, sunny flagstoned courtyard, open all day (till late Sat). *(David Carr)*

WORCESTER   SO8555
Plough (01905) 21381
Fish Street; WR1 2HN Traditional corner pub with two simple rooms off entrance lobby, six interesting ales including Hobsons and Malvern Hills, farm cider and perry, good whisky choice, coal-effect gas fire; outside lavatories; small back terrace with cathedral view, open all day. *(Alfie Bayliss)*

WORCESTER   SO8455
Postal Order (01905) 22373
Foregate Street; WR1 1DN Popular Wetherspoons in former sorting office, wide range of well kept beers, Weston's cider and their usual good value food; open all day from 8am. *(David Carr)*

WORCESTER   SO8554
Swan With Two Nicks
(01905) 28190 *New Street/Friar Street; WR1 2DP* Rambling early 16th-c backstreet pub, plenty of character in bare-boards low-ceilinged front rooms, four changing local ales and some interesting bottled ciders, decent whisky and rum choice too, well priced food including good pies, friendly atmosphere, upstairs cocktail bar (Fri, Sat evenings), another part for Fri live music and comedy nights; open all day. *(Dave Braisted, Phil and Jane Hodson)*

WYRE PIDDLE   SO9647
Anchor (01386) 641510
Off A4538 NW of Evesham; WR10 2JB Great position by River Avon with moorings, decking on three levels, floodlit lawn and view from airy back dining room; enjoyable well priced home-made food (not Tues, Weds) from baguettes up, beers such as Wye Valley in beamed and flagstoned bar with inglenook stove, good friendly service; children welcome, open all Fri, Sat, till 6pm Sun, closed Mon. *(Andrew Stone)*

Yorkshire

KEY ★ Star Pub 🌟 Top Quality Food 🍺 Great Beer

🍷 Good Wines £ Bargain Meals 🛏 Good Bedrooms 🍴 Serves Food

 ADDINGHAM   SE0749 Map 7

Fleece 🌟 🍷

(01943) 830491 – www.fleeceinnaddingham.co.uk

Main Street (B6160, off A65); LS29 0LY

Enterprising management with strong sense of style; good food cooked by the landlord and his team using local produce

---

Extremely popular with our readers, this is a well run pub with caring staff and delicious food. The smart bar on the right has a cool décor of dark flagstones, polished floorboards, crisp cream paintwork and wallpaper based on antique fish prints above a charcoal-grey high dado. A pair of grey plaid tub armchairs stand by a great arched stone fireplace, and down a few steps is the civilised dining room. The interesting black-beamed village bar on the left has a roaring log fire in its high-mantel fireplace, broad floorboards, comfortably worn easy chairs as well as cushioned wall benches and window seats, and some very unusual substantial tables. Nicely framed local photographs include a series devoted to former landlord 'Heapy', heroic survivor of a 1944 torpedoing. A good range of carefully chosen drinks includes Black Sheep Best, Saltaire Blonde, Timothy Taylors Landlord and a guest beer on handpump, ten wines (including champagne and rosé) by the glass and a dozen malt whiskies; background music and board games. In warm weather, you can sit beneath giant parasols on the flagstoned front terrace; another dining terrace looks out over the garden. They have a deli next door serving sandwiches, bagels and salads all day as well as home-made pâté, chutney and cakes. This is sister pub to the Craven Heifer in Addingham

---

🌟 Using the best local, seasonal ingredients and listing their producers on a board, the imaginative modern food includes southern-fried rabbit leg with slaw, tempura king prawns with sweet chilli dip, pork and sage scotch egg with piccalilli, smoked haddock and leek risotto with a poached free-range egg, sweet potato, chickpea and spinach curry with coconut rice, pancetta-wrapped chicken with baby vegetables and barley in lemon and thyme broth, calves liver with caramelised onion gravy, and puddings such as chocolate brownie with vanilla ice-cream and strawberry eton mess; they also offer a set menu (12-3, 6-7; not weekends). *Benchmark main dish: pig on a plate (slow-cooked belly and cheek, parma ham-wrapped loin, red wine jus) £19.00. Two-course evening meal £24.00.*

Punch ~ Lease Craig Minto ~ Real ale ~ Open 12-11 (midnight Sat); 12-10.30 Sun ~ Bar food 12-2, 6-9; 12-7 Sun ~ Restaurant ~ Children welcome ~ Dogs allowed in bar ~ Wi-fi

Recommended by Gordon and Margaret Ormondroyd, Walter and Susan Rinaldi-Butcher

ASENBY
Crab & Lobster ★ ♀ ⌂

SE3975 Map 7

(01845) 577286 – www.crabandlobster.co.uk

Dishforth Road; village signed off A168 – handy for A1; YO7 3QL

Interesting furnishings and décor in rambling bar, inventive restaurant food, good drinks choice and seats on attractive terrace; smart bedrooms

This isn't a straightforward pub, of course: the main emphasis is on the hotel and restaurant side, but the rambling L-shaped bar in this smart, handsome building attracts customers dropping in for a drink and a chat and they keep Copper Dragon Best and Golden Pippin on handpump. This bustling bar has an interesting jumble of seats, from antique high-backed and other settles through sofas and wing armchairs heaped with cushions to tall and rather theatrical corner seats; the tables are almost as much of a mix. The walls and available surfaces are a jungle of bric-a-brac including lots of race tickets, while standard and table lamps and candles keep the lighting pleasantly informal. There's also a cosy main restaurant and a dining pavilion with big tropical plants, nautical bits and pieces and Edwardian sofas; background music. The gardens have bamboo and palm trees lining the path, which lead to a gazebo; there are seats on a mediterranean-style terrace. The opulent bedrooms (based on famous hotels around the world) are in nearby Crab Manor, which has seven acres of mature gardens and a 180-metre golf hole with full practice facilities.

Good and interesting – if not cheap – food includes mussels with cider, smoked bacon, cabbage and cream, sticky orange spare ribs with five spice, Jack Daniels, treacle and chilli, queenie scallops with shallots, garlic butter, gruyère, cheddar and breadcrumbs, tart of local goats cheese with red onion confit, beetroot and dijon and honey ice-cream, free-range chicken with ham, cheese, herb breadcrumbs and cream on pasta, almond-crusted venison loin with red cabbage and spiced sultanas and game parcel, and puddings such as dark chocolate tart with orange and mango salad and knickerbocker glory; they also offer a two- and three-course set lunch. *Benchmark main dish: half lobster thermidor £24.00. Two-course evening meal £28.00.*

Vimac Leisure ~ Licensee Mark Spenceley ~ Real ale ~ Open 11am-11.30pm ~ Bar food 12-2.30, 7-9; 12-2.30, 6.30-9.30 Sat ~ Restaurant ~ Children welcome ~ Wi-fi ~ Live jazz Weds evening ~ Bedrooms: /£170 *Recommended by Henry Curran, Pat and Graham Williamson, J R Wildon*

BECK HOLE
Birch Hall

NZ8202 Map 10

(01947) 896245 – www.beckhole.info/bhi.htm

Off A169 SW of Whitby, from top of Sleights Moor; YO22 5LE

Extraordinary place in lovely valley with friendly landlady, real ales and simple snacks

The surroundings are stunning, so it makes sense that this tiny pub-cum-village shop is resolutely walker- and dog-friendly. The two unchanging rooms have simple furnishings, built-in cushioned wall seats, wooden tables (one embedded with 136 pennies), flagstones or composition flooring, unusual items such as a tube of toothpaste priced 1/-3d, and a model train running around a head-height shelf. North Yorkshire Beckwatter, Spitting Feathers Thirst Quencher and a guest ale on handpump and several malt whiskies and wines by the glass. The shop sells postcards, sweets and ice-creams. There are benches outside in a streamside garden and one of the wonderful nearby walks is along a disused railway. They have a self-catering cottage for hire.

 Bar snacks only, such as local pork pie, butties, scones and their famous beer cake.

Free house ~ Licensee Glenys Crampton ~ Real ale ~ No credit cards ~ Open 11-11; 11-3, 7.30-11 Weds-Sun in winter; closed Mon evening in winter, all day Tues Nov-Apr ~ Bar food available during opening hours ~ Children in small family room ~ Dogs welcome
Recommended by William Wright, Toby Jones

BLAKEY RIDGE

SE6799   Map 10

Lion 🍺 🛏

(01751) 417320 – www.lionblakey.co.uk
From A171 Guisborough–Whitby follow 'Castleton, Hutton-le-Hole' signposts; from A170 Kirkby Moorside–Pickering follow 'Keldholm, Hutton-le-Hole, Castleton' signposts; OS Sheet 100 map reference 679996; YO62 7LQ

Extended pub in fine scenery and open all day; popular food; bedrooms

If you wish to stay here, you'll need to book well in advance as it's a popular base for walkers – there are numerous surrounding hikes and the Coast to Coast path is nearby; the views over the valleys of Rosedale and Farndale are breathtaking. The low-beamed rambling bars have open fires, a few big high-backed rustic settles around cast-iron-framed tables, lots of small dining chairs, a nice leather sofa and stone walls hung with old engravings and photographs of the pub under snow (it can easily get cut off in winter – 40 days is the record so far). The fine choice of beers on handpump might include Black Sheep Best, Copper Dragon Golden Pippin, Theakstons Best, Double Cross IPA and Old Peculier, Thwaites Wainwright and York Guzzler, and they have 13 wines by the glass and several malt whiskies; background music and games machine.

 Well liked food includes sandwiches, prawn cocktail, breaded mushrooms with garlic dip, home-cooked ham with an egg or pineapple, steak and mushroom pie, roasted vegetable lasagne, beef curry, chicken breast in creamy mushroom sauce, beer-battered haddock and chips, daily specials, and puddings such as hot chocolate fudge cake and a cheesecake of the day. *Benchmark main dish: steak and mushroom pie £11.50. Two-course evening meal £15.75.*

Free house ~ Licensees Barry, Diana, Paul and David Crossland ~ Real ale ~ Open 10am-11pm (midnight Sat) ~ Bar food 12-10 ~ Restaurant ~ Children welcome ~ Dogs allowed in bar and bedrooms ~ Wi-fi ~ Bedrooms: £42.50/£84 *Recommended by WAH, Richard Cole, Dr J Barrie Jones, Tina and David Woods-Taylor, Walter and Susan Rinaldi-Butcher*

BOROUGHBRIDGE

SE3966   Map 7

Black Bull £

(01423) 322413 – www.blackbullboroughbridge.co.uk
St James Square; B6265, just off A1(M); YO51 9AR

Bustling town pub with real ales, several wines by the glass and traditional bar food; bedrooms

With good value bar food and a warm welcome, this ancient and attractive inn makes an invaluable break from the busy A1. There are lots of separate drinking and eating areas where cheerful regulars drop in for a pint and a chat. The main bar area has a big stone fireplace and comfortable seats and is served through an old-fashioned hatch; there's also a cosy snug with traditional wall settles, and a tap room, lounge bar and restaurant. John Smiths Cask, Rudgate Battle Axe and a changing guest from Timothy Taylors on handpump, six wines by the glass and 19 malt whiskies; dominoes. The borzoi dog is called Spot and the two cats Kia and Mershka. The hanging baskets are lovely.

Fairly priced bar snacks (the Value Award is for these dishes) include hot and cold sandwiches, chicken liver pâté with cumberland sauce, crispy duck salad with hoisin sauce, pork sausages with onion gravy, fishcakes with chips and salad, pork tenderloin in creamy pink-peppercorn sauce, salmon with noodles and thai sweet and sour sauce, thick pork chop with chips, and puddings such as chocolate fudge cake and jam sponge with custard. *Benchmark main dish: pie of the day £9.95. Two-course evening meal £15.00.*

Free house ~ Licensee Anthony Burgess ~ Real ale ~ Open 11-11 (midnight Fri, Sat); 11.30-11.30 Sun ~ Bar food 12-2, 6-9 (9.30 Fri, Sat) ~ Restaurant ~ Children welcome ~ Dogs welcome ~ Wi-fi ~ Bedrooms: £50/£75 *Recommended by John and Eleanor Holdsworth, Denis and Margaret Kilner*

BRADFIELD   SK2290   Map 7
Strines Inn £ 🛏

(0114) 285 1247 – www.thestrinesinn.webs.com

From A57 heading E of junction with A6013 (Ladybower Reservoir), take first left turn (signposted with Bradfield) then bear left; with a map can also be reached more circuitously from Strines signpost on A616 at head of Underbank Reservoir, W of Stocksbridge; S6 6JE

Surrounded by fine scenery, with quite a mix of customers and traditional beer and bar food; bedrooms

Our readers enjoy staying in this former manor house where the bedrooms have four-poster beds and a dining table (they serve breakfast in your room); the front room overlooks Strines Reservoir. The main bar has a coal fire in a rather grand stone fireplace, black beams liberally decked with copper kettles and so forth, quite a menagerie of stuffed animals, and homely red plush-cushioned traditional wooden wall benches and small chairs. Two other rooms, to the right and left, are similarly furnished. Acorn Yorkshire Pride, Jennings Cocker Hoop, Marstons Pedigree and Wychwood Hobgoblin on handpump and nine wines by the glass. There are plenty of picnic-sets outside, as well as swings, a play area, and peacocks, geese and chickens. The Peak District National Park is on the doorstep and the surrounding scenery is superb.

Honest pubby food includes sandwiches and paninis, giant yorkshire pudding with onion gravy, game pâté, butter bean stew with garlic bread, burgers with chips, liver and onions with gravy, a daily fresh fish dish, gammon with eggs or pineapple, a huge mixed grill, and puddings such as caramel apple pie and treacle sponge. *Benchmark main dish: steak in ale pie £9.75. Two-course evening meal £14.00.*

Free house ~ Licensee Bruce Howarth ~ Real ale ~ Open 10.30am-11pm ~ Bar food 12-9; 12-2.30, 5.30-8.30 weekdays in winter ~ Children welcome ~ Dogs welcome ~ Bedrooms: £65/£85 *Recommended by Mr and Mrs N Davies, Robert Parker*

Please let us know what you think of a pub's bedrooms: feedback@goodguides.com or (no stamp needed) The Good Pub Guide, FREEPOST RTJR-ZCYZ-RJZT, Perrymans Lane, Etchingham TN19 7DN.

CONSTABLE BURTON
SE1690 Map 10

Wyvill Arms 🌟 ♀ 🍺 🛏

(01677) 450581 – www.thewyvillarms.co.uk

A684 E of Leyburn; DL8 5LH

Well run, friendly dining pub with interesting food, a dozen wines by the glass, real ales and efficient helpful service; bedrooms

A lovely base for exploring the Dales, this is a stylish inn opposite Constable Burton Hall. The small bar area has a finely worked plaster ceiling with the Wyvill family's coat of arms, a mix of seating and an elaborate stone fireplace with a warm winter fire. The second bar has a lower ceiling with fans, leather seating, old oak tables, various alcoves and a model train on a railway track running around the room; the reception area includes a huge leather sofa that can seat up to eight people, another carved stone fireplace and an old leaded stained-glass church window partition. Both rooms are hung with pictures of local scenes. The three real ales on handpump are Theakstons Best, Wensleydale Coverdale Gamekeeper and a guest beer from Rudgate, plus nine wines by the glass and nine malt whiskies; chess, backgammon and dominoes. There are several large wooden benches under sizeable white parasols for outdoor dining and picnic-sets by a well. The bedrooms are comfortable and the generous breakfasts very good (you can buy their home-made marmalade).

 Using home-grown and other top quality local produce, the highly enjoyable food includes lunchtime baps, duck liver pâté, battered king prawns with onions and dip, wild mushroom risotto, salmon on steamed leeks with grain mustard sauce, battered fresh fish and chips, steak and onion pie, half a crispy duck confit with black cherry sauce, steaks with a choice of sauces, and puddings such as sticky toffee pudding with toffee sauce and vanilla panna cotta with strawberry sauce. *Benchmark main dish: breaded chicken stuffed with mozzarella with smoked bacon on creamed leeks and stilton sauce £14.50. Two-course evening meal £19.50.*

Free house ~ Licensee Nigel Stevens ~ Real ale ~ Open 11-3, 5.30 (6 Sun)-11; closed Mon ~ Bar food 12-2.15, 5.30-9 ~ Restaurant ~ Children welcome until 8.30 ~ Dogs allowed in bar ~ Wi-fi ~ Bedrooms: £65/£85 *Recommended by Michael Doswell*

CRAYKE
SE5670 Map 7

Durham Ox 🌟 ♀ 🛏

(01347) 821506 – www.thedurhamox.com

Off B1363 at Brandsby, towards Easingwold; West Way; YO61 4TE

Friendly, well run inn with interesting décor in old-fashioned rooms, fine drinks and smashing food; lovely views and comfortable bedrooms

There's always a good mix of both locals and visitors in this particularly well run and civilised inn – all are welcomed by the courteous staff. The old-fashioned lounge bar has venerable tables, antique seats and settles on flagstones, pictures and photographs on dark red walls, interesting satirical carvings in the panelling (Victorian copies of medieval pew ends), polished copper and brass and an enormous inglenook fireplace. In the bottom bar is a framed illustrated account of local history (some of it gruesome) dating back to the 12th c, and a large framed print of the famous Durham Ox, which weighed 171 stone. The Burns Bar has a woodburning stove, exposed brickwork and large french windows that open on to a balcony. Black Sheep Best, Timothy Taylors Boltmaker, York Guzzler and a changing guest on handpump, 20 wines by the glass, a dozen malt whiskies and interesting spirits; background music and board games. There are seats in the courtyard garden and fantastic views over the Vale of York on three sides; on the fourth is a charming view to the medieval church on the hill – supposedly the very hill up which the Grand Old Duke of York marched his men. The bedrooms, in the main building or in renovated farm cottages (dogs allowed here), are well equipped, spacious and comfortable; breakfasts are very good. The nearby A19 leads straight to a park & ride for York. The pub belongs to Provenance Inns.

Using their own-made bread and petits fours and top quality local, seasonal produce, the impressive food includes sandwiches, twice-baked cheese soufflé with parmesan cream, baked queen scallops with gruyère, cheddar and garlic butter, spatchcock poussin with piri-piri, aioli and skinny fries, moroccan vegetable tagine, barbecue sticky pork rib platter, beer-battered fish and chips, venison haunch steak with creamy savoy cabbage and bitter chocolate sauce, and puddings such as apple tarte tatin and poached pears in red wine with pear sorbet; they still offer seven dishes at £7 each before 7pm (not Saturday) and a two- and three-course set lunch. *Benchmark main dish: rib-eye steak and frites £24.95. Two-course evening meal £23.95.*

Free house ~ Licensee Michael Ibbotson ~ Real ale ~ Open 12-11.30; 12-midnight Sat; 12-10.30 Sun ~ Bar food 12-2.30, 5.30-9.30; 12-3, 5.30-8.30 Sun ~ Restaurant ~ Children welcome ~ Dogs allowed in bar and bedrooms ~ Wi-fi ~ Bedrooms: £100/£120
Recommended by Gordon and Margaret Ormondroyd, Christopher and Elise Way, Walter and Susan Rinaldi-Butcher

DOWNHOLME
SE1197 Map 10

Bolton Arms

(01748) 823716 – www.boltonarmsdownholme.com
Village signposted just off A6108 Leyburn–Richmond; DL11 6AE

Tasty food and ales in stone-built country pub; bedrooms

The views are magnificent from both the conservatory dining room and seats in the neat garden; there are also picnic-sets and benches on a lower level terrace and very pretty summer hanging baskets. The simply furnished, carpeted bar is down a few steps and has two smallish linked areas off the servery where they keep Timothy Taylors Landlord and Wensleydale Bitter on handpump, ten wines by the glass and ten malt whiskies. There are comfortable plush wall banquettes, a log fire in a neat fireplace, quite a collection of gleaming brass, a few small country pictures and drink advertisements on pinkish rough-plastered walls; background music and dominoes.

Popular food includes lunchtime sandwiches and baguettes, black pudding stack with cheese and bacon, prawn cocktail, chicken caesar salad, various omelettes, spinach and ricotta pancakes, steak and mushroom pie, fresh seafood tagliatelle, lambs liver and bacon, guinea fowl stuffed with black pudding with mushroom and shallot sauce, beef stroganoff, and puddings such as apple pie and hot chocolate fudge cake; they also offer a two- and three-course early-bird set menu (6-7pm Monday-Thursday). *Benchmark main dish: kleftico (a slow-roast cypriot lamb dish) £15.50. Two-course evening meal £20.00.*

Free house ~ Licensees Steve and Nicola Ross ~ Real ale ~ Open 11-3, 6-11.30 (midnight weekends); closed Tues lunchtime ~ Bar food 12-2, 6-9 ~ Restaurant ~ Children welcome ~ Wi-fi ~ Bedrooms: £45/£70   *Recommended by David Bird, Mungo Shipley*

People named as recommenders after the full entries have told us that the pub should be included. But they have not written the report – we have, after anonymous on-the-spot inspection.

EAST WITTON

SE1486   Map 10

Blue Lion ⭐ ⬤ ▯ 🛏

(01969) 624273 – www.thebluelion.co.uk

A6108 Leyburn–Ripon; DL8 4SN

Civilised dining pub with a proper bar, real ales and daily papers, delicious food, and courteous service; comfortable bedrooms

'**O**utstanding' and 'superb in every way' are just two recent comments from readers about this 18th-c coaching inn. You can drop in for a drink beside the log fire or stay longer for an excellent meal – you'll be warmly welcomed by the courteous staff whichever you choose; they're kind to dogs too. The big squarish bar is civilised but informal with soft lighting, high-backed antique settles and old windsor chairs on turkish rugs and flagstones, ham hooks in the high ceiling decorated with dried wheat, teazles and so forth, a delft shelf filled with appropriate bric-a-brac, plus several prints, sporting caricatures and other pictures; daily papers. Black Sheep Best and Golden Sheep and Theakstons Best on handpump, an impressive wine list including a dozen (plus champagne) by the glass and 17 malt whiskies. The candlelit, high-ceilinged and elegant dining room has another open fire. Picnic-sets on the gravel outside look beyond the stone houses on the far side of the village green to Witton Fell, and there's a big attractive back garden. The comfortable bedrooms with pretty country furnishings are located in the main house and in converted stables across the courtyard (where dogs are welcome).

⭐ The exceptional food using the best local produce includes goose rillettes with red onion marmalade, smoked salmon and celeriac rémoulade with crispy capers and lemon oil, wild mushroom and chestnut cottage pie, local beef in ale pudding, fillet of sea trout with warm potato salad and sauce vierge, chicken breast with lyonnaise potatoes, sautéed wild mushrooms and cep sauce, venison haunch with shallot and thyme potatoes and redcurrant jus, and puddings such as dark chocolate and strawberry mousse with white chocolate ice-cream and yoghurt and honey cheesecake with confit fig; they also offer a two- and three-course set lunch. *Benchmark main dish: slow-cooked pork belly with pickled apple purée, black pudding scotch egg and cider reduction £19.95. Two-course evening meal £25.00.*

Free house ~ Licensee Paul Klein ~ Real ale ~ Open 11-11 ~ Bar food 12-2, 7-9; 12-9 Sun ~ Restaurant ~ Children welcome ~ Dogs allowed in bar and bedrooms ~ Wi-fi ~ Bedrooms: £84/£109 *Recommended by Michael Doswell, Neil and Angela Huxter, Tracey and Stephen Groves, Gordon and Margaret Ormondroyd, Simon Cleasby*

ELSLACK

SD9249   Map 7

Tempest Arms ⭐ ⬤ ▯ 🍺 🛏

(01282) 842450 – www.tempestarms.co.uk

Just off A56 Earby–Skipton; BD23 3AY

Friendly inn with three log fires in stylish rooms, six real ales, good wines and popular food; bedrooms

As ever, this consistently well run 18th-c stone inn continues to draw warmly enthusiastic praise from our readers. It's stylish but understated and cosy with a happy mix of customers and plenty of character in the bar and surrounding dining areas: cushioned armchairs, built-in wall seats with comfortable cushions, stools, plenty of tables and three log fires – one greets you at the entrance and divides the bar and restaurant. There's quite a bit of exposed stonework, amusing prints on cream walls, half a dozen real ales such as Dark Horse Hetton Pale Ale,

Ilkley Black, Naylors Brew 1641, Thwaites Wainwright, Theakstons Best and a guest on handpump, 12 wines by the glass, 30 malt whiskies and 20 gins; background music and board games. The tables outside are largely screened from the road by a raised bank. The bedrooms are comfortable and well equipped and make a perfect base for exploring the beautiful scenery and walks of the Yorkshire Dales.

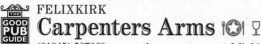 Inventive and first class food includes sandwiches, baked brie with apple, mango and honey sauce, button mushrooms in cream, ale and stilton sauce, sharing boards, cheese and onion pie with home-made baked beans, steak burger with toppings, coleslaw and chips, thai red prawn curry, chicken stuffed with sun-dried tomato, basil and mozzarella with herby wine sauce, venison, wild mushroom and chestnut casserole, salmon on crab and prawn risotto with crispy pancetta and pesto dressing, and puddings such as a giant meringue with strawberries and fruit sauce and jam roly-poly with custard. *Benchmark main dish: slow-cooked lamb shoulder with minty jus and roasted root vegetables £15.50. Two-course evening meal £20.00.*

Individual Inns ~ Managers Martin and Veronica Clarkson ~ Real ale ~ Open 11-11 (10.30 Sun) ~ Bar food 12-2.30, 6-9 (9.30 Fri, Sat); 12-7.30 Sun ~ Restaurant ~ Children welcome ~ Dogs allowed in bar ~ Wi-fi ~ Bedrooms: £75/£100 *Recommended by Gordon and Margaret Ormondroyd, Hilary Forrest, Claes Mauroy, John and Sylvia Harrop, S Holder*

FELIXKIRK   SE4684   Map 10
Carpenters Arms ⭐ ♀

(01845) 537369 – www.thecarpentersarmsfelixkirk.com
Village signed off A170 E of Thirsk; YO7 2DP

Stylishly refurbished village pub with opened-up rooms, friendly service, real ales and highly regarded food; lodge-style bedrooms

With a warm welcome for both drinkers and diners, this friendly pub has something for everyone. The opened-up bars are spacious and relaxed with dark beams and joists, candlelight and fresh flowers, stools against the panelled counter where they keep Black Sheep Best, Timothy Taylors Boltmaker and a changing guest from Theakstons on handpump, 19 wines by the glass and 18 malt whiskies, and a mix of chairs and tables on big flagstones or carpet. There's also a snug seating area with tartan armchairs in front of a double-sided woodburning stove. The red-walled dining room has a mix of antique and country kitchen chairs around scrubbed tables, and the walls throughout are hung with traditional prints, local pictures and maps; background music and board games. There are seats and tables on a raised decked area overlooking the landscaped garden and picnic-sets at the front. The ultra-modern, well equipped bedrooms come with a drying wardrobe for wet days and a log-effect gas fire – they make a good base for both short walks and long-distance hikes (the Cleveland Way is in the locality); dogs are welcome. This is part of the Provenance Inns group.

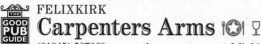 Good, inventive food using much local produce includes chicken liver and mushroom parfait with caramelised red onions, chilli and lime chicken with candied peanuts, lentil and sweet potato curry, barbecue sticky pork ribs platter, confit duck leg with crispy kale, braised red cabbage and cherry sauce, halibut fillet with lemon and parsley crust, shellfish broth and saffron potatoes, slow-cooked pork belly with black pudding, crushed swede and carrot, and puddings such as sticky toffee pudding with toffee sauce and apple and frangipane tart with ice-cream; they also offer seven dishes at £7 each before 7pm (not Saturday). *Benchmark main dish: charcoal-grilled steaks with various sauces and chips £17.95. Two-course evening meal £21.00.*

Free house ~ Licensee Michael Ibbotson ~ Real ale ~ Open 12-11 ~ Bar food 12-2.30, 5.30-9.30; 12-3, 5.30-8.30 Sun ~ Children welcome ~ Dogs allowed in bar and bedrooms ~

Wi-fi ~ Live music monthly Sun evening ~ Bedrooms: /£165 *Recommended by Harvey Brown, Dr Simon Innes*

GRANTLEY   SE2369 Map 7

Grantley Arms 🍽️ ♀

(01765) 620227 – www.grantleyarms.com

Village signposted off B6265 W of Ripon; HG4 3PJ

Relaxed and interesting dining pub with good food

One of our readers regularly travels over 40 miles to visit this creeper-clad 17th-c country inn run by affable and hands-on licensees – he says it's always 'highly enjoyable all round'. The front bar has a huge fireplace built of massive stone blocks and housing a woodburning stove, brown beams supporting shiny cream ceiling planks, and traditional furnishings: flowery carpet, green wall banquettes, comfortable dining chairs, tea-lights on polished tables (some with cast-iron frames), and some of the landlady's own paintings of ponies and dogs above the green dado. The back dining room has crisp linen tablecloths, decorative plates and more paintings, mainly landscapes. Great Yorkshire Yorkshire Classic and Theakstons Best on handpump, nine wines by the glass, eight malt whiskies, a farm cider and attentive friendly service. Teak tables and chairs on the flagstoned front terrace have a pleasant outlook, and Fountains Abbey and Studley Royal Water Garden (National Trust) is nearby.

 Using home-made bread and chutneys, the rewarding food includes open sandwiches, prawn cocktail, scotch egg with black pudding sausage meat, mustard mayonnaise and piccalilli, lager-battered haddock and chips, potato gnocchi with spinach, root vegetables and parmesan and cheddar cheese sauce, a pie of the week, pheasant breast with chestnut and thyme stuffing, bacon and red wine and redcurrant sauce, and puddings such as caramelised lemon tart and apple pie with home-made custard; they also have a coffee morning menu (from 9am) and a two- and three-course set lunch (Tuesday-Friday). *Benchmark main dish: fish pie £13.95. Two-course evening meal £19.00.*

Free house ~ Licensees Valerie Sails and Eric Broadwith ~ Real ale ~ Open 12-3, 5.30-10.30; 12-3, 5.30-11 Fri, Sat; 12-10.30 Sun; closed Mon except bank holidays ~ Bar food 12-2, 5.30-9 (9.30 Sat); 12-3.30, 5.30-8 Sun ~ Restaurant ~ Well behaved children welcome ~ Wi-fi
Recommended by Gordon and Margaret Ormondroyd

GRINTON   SE0498 Map 10

Bridge Inn 🍺 🛏️

(01748) 884224 – www.bridgeinn-grinton.co.uk

B6270 W of Richmond; DL11 6HH

Bustling pub with traditional, comfortable bars, log fires, several real ales and malt whiskies, and tasty bar food; neat bedrooms

This is a godsend for thirsty walkers and cyclists (the pub is in the centre of the Yorkshire Dales National Park) – and you can be sure of a warm welcome from the friendly landlord. There's a relaxing, comfortable atmosphere, bow-window seats and a pair of stripped traditional settles among more usual pub seats (all well cushioned), a good log fire, and Brakspears Oxford Gold, Jennings Cumberland, Marstons Revisionist Dark IPA and a guest ale on handpump; also, eight wines by the glass, 20 malt whiskies and ten gins. On the right, a few steps lead down into a room with darts and ring the bull. On the left, past leather armchairs and a sofa next to a second log fire (and a glass chess set), is an extensive two-part dining room with décor in cream and shades of brown, and a modicum of fishing memorabilia. The bedrooms are neat, simple and comfortable, and breakfasts good. There are picnic-sets outside and the lovely church opposite is known as the Cathedral of the Dales.

Using game shot by the landlord and other local produce, some sort of popular food is served all day: sandwiches, duck liver parfait with pickled carrot ribbons, goats cheese en croûte with sticky shredded beetroot and raspberry coulis, pea and sun-blush tomato risotto, cajun chicken burger with toppings and barbecue sauce, cod in ale and dill batter with chips, pheasant breast with bacon-wrapped leg and red wine jus, pork medallions with bubble and squeak, black pudding and wholegrain mustard sauce, and puddings such as almond and apricot treacle tart and ginger sponge with sticky toffee sauce. *Benchmark main dish: steak in ale pie £10.95. Two-course evening meal £17.00.*

Jennings (Marstons) ~ Lease Andrew Atkin ~ Real ale ~ Open 12-11 (midnight Sat) ~ Bar food 12-9 ~ Restaurant ~ Children welcome ~ Dogs allowed in bar and bedrooms ~ Wi-fi ~ Bedrooms: £51/£82 *Recommended by Duncan, Carol and Alistair Hallows, Geoff and Linda Payne, Tracey and Stephen Groves*

HALIFAX
Shibden Mill 🏅 ♀ 🍺

SE1027   Map 7

(01422) 365840 – www.shibdenmillinn.com
Off A58 into Kell Lane at Stump Cross Inn, near A6036 junction; keep on, pub signposted from Kell Lane on left; HX3 7UL

300-year-old interesting pub with a cosy rambling bar, four real ales and inventive, top class bar food; luxury bedrooms

Maintaining its consistently high standards, this tucked-away restored mill remains as popular as ever with readers. The rambling bar is full of nooks and crannies and the bustling atmosphere is helped along by a good mix of locals and visitors. Some cosy side areas have banquettes heaped with cushions and rugs, well spaced attractive old tables and chairs, and candles in elegant iron holders giving a feeling of real intimacy; also, old hunting prints, country landscapes and a couple of big log fires. A beer named for them (from Moorhouses) plus ales from Black Sheep, Copper Dragon and Little Valley on handpump and 21 wines by the glass from a wide list. There's also an upstairs restaurant; background music and TV. Outside on the pleasant heated terrace are plenty of seats and tables, and the building is prettily floodlit at night. The bedrooms are stylish and well equipped, and there are lovely walks nearby.

Enticing food using top quality local produce includes sandwiches, scallops and treacle-cured salmon with pickled clams and passion fruit, partridge and chestnut pie with cherry purée and grape chutney, rare-breed pork and apple sausages with bourguignon sauce, burger with toppings, crispy onion rings, home-made ketchup and fries, mackerel and brown crab strudel with fennel, citrus butter and sweet potato purée, chicken with boulangère potatoes and wild mushroom, leek and sweetcorn velouté, and puddings such as caramelised lemon tart with mango and coconut parfait and rhubarb panna cotta crumble with rhubarb schnapps; they also offer a two- and three-course set menu at lunchtime (not Sunday) and Monday-Thursday evenings (5.30-7pm). *Benchmark main dish: potato gnocchi with feta and honey-roast beetroot, pickled courgettes and crispy barley £13.00. Two-course evening meal £19.00.*

Free house ~ Licensee Glen Pearson ~ Real ale ~ Open 12-11 (10.30 Sun) ~ Bar food 12-2, 5.30-9; 12-2.30, 5.30-9.30 Fri, Sat; 12-7.30 Sun ~ Restaurant ~ Children welcome ~ Dogs allowed in bar ~ Wi-fi ~ Bedrooms: £100/£125 *Recommended by Dr Kevan Tucker, Gordon and Margaret Ormondroyd*

HARTSHEAD

SE1822 Map 7

Gray Ox ⭐ ♀

(01274) 872845 – www.grayoxinn.co.uk

3.5 miles from M62 junction 25; A644 towards Dewsbury, left on to A62, next left on to B6119, first left into Fall Lane, left into Hartshead Lane – pub on right; WF15 8AL

Handsome dining pub with cosy beamed bars, inventive cooking, real ales, several wines by the glass and fine views

Although this well run, smart dining pub is in the middle of nowhere, it's always packed with cheerful customers – even at 4.30pm on a Sunday. The main bar has a roaring log fire, beams and flagstones, bentwood chairs and leather stools around stripped-pine tables; leading off from here, the comfortable carpeted dining areas have bold paintwork and leather dining chairs around polished tables. The hunting-theme wallpaper is interesting and unusual. There's also a private dining room. A beer named for the pub (from Jennings) and Jennings Cumberland and Cocker Hoop on handpump, 15 wines by the glass and a cocktail menu; background music. There are picnic-sets outside, and fine views through the latticed pub windows across the Calder Valley to the distant outskirts of Huddersfield – the lights are pretty at night.

 Extremely popular food – they list their 'food heroes' on a board – includes blue cheese and pear tartlet with hazelnut dressing, smoked haddock croquettes with pea and mint purée, butternut squash gnocchi with toasted pine nuts and pesto dressing, chicken with leek and potato rösti, goats cheese and red onion spring roll and wholegrain mustard cream, trio of lamb (cutlet, slow-braised shoulder, seared liver) with shallot purée and pea and butter sauce, a daily fresh fish dish, and puddings such as dark chocolate torte with milk sorbet and lemon brûlée tart with berry sorbet; they also offer an early-bird menu (12-2, 6-7, not weekends). *Benchmark main dish: monkfish with king prawn skewer, crispy cod cheeks, potato rösti and a lightly curried cream £18.00. Two-course evening meal £21.00.*

Banks's (Marstons) ~ Lease Bernadette McCarron ~ Real ale ~ Open 12-3, 6-midnight; 12-midnight Sat; 12-11 Sun ~ Bar food 12-2, 6-9 (9.30 Sat); 12-7 Sun ~ Restaurant ~ Children welcome ~ Wi-fi *Recommended by Gordon and Margaret Ormondroyd, Brian and Anna Marsden, John and Eleanor Holdsworth, Michael Butler*

HELPERBY

SE4370 Map 7

Oak Tree ⭐ ♀ 🛏

(01423) 789189 – www.theoaktreehelperby.com

Raskelf Road; YO61 2PH

Attractive pub with real ales in friendly bar, fine food in elegant dining rooms, bold paintwork and seats on terrace; comfortable bedrooms

Carefully renovated and pretty, this village pub is liked by both drinkers and diners. The informal bar has church chairs and elegant wooden dining chairs around a mix of wooden tables on old quarry tiles, flagstones and oak floorboards, prints and paintings on bold red walls, and open fires; background music. Stools line the counter where they keep Black Sheep Best, John Smiths and a guest or two such as Rudgate Hop & Glory and York Guzzler on handpump and a dozen wines by the glass. The main dining room has a large woodburner in a huge brick fireplace, a big central flower arrangement, high-backed burgundy and graceful wooden chairs around nice old tables on oak flooring, ornate mirrors and some striking artwork on the turquoise or exposed brick walls. French windows lead out to the terrace where there are plenty of seats and tables for summer dining. Upstairs, a private dining room has a two-way woodburner, a sitting room and doors to a terrace. The bedrooms are comfortable and well equipped. The pub is part of Provenance Inns.

 As well as breakfasts for non-residents (from 8am), the good modern food includes sandwiches, deep-fried brie with cranberry sauce, arancini risotto balls with smoked mozzarella, basil and tomato, spicy burger with chilli cheddar and skinny fries, half roast charcoal-grilled chicken with piri-piri sauce, beer-battered fish and chips, barbecue rack of baby back ribs, and puddings such as sunken chocolate cake with vanilla ice-cream and iced Nutella cheesecake; they also offer a menu of seven dishes at £7 each before 7pm (not Saturday). *Benchmark main dish: steak with a choice of potatoes and sauces £15.00. Two-course evening meal £21.00.*

Free house ~ Licensee Michael Ibbotson ~ Real ale ~ Open 11-11 ~ Bar food 12-2.30, 5.30-9.30; 12-3, 5.30-8.30 Sun ~ Restaurant ~ Children welcome ~ Dogs allowed in bar and bedrooms ~ Wi-fi ~ Bedrooms: /£140 *Recommended by Michael Butler, Michael Doswell, John and Eleanor Holdsworth, Comus and Sarah Elliott*

HETTON
SD9658 Map 7

Angel 🌟 ♀ 🛏

(01756) 730263 – www.angelhetton.co.uk

Off B6265 Skipton–Grassington; BD23 6LT

Creeper-covered inn with timbers and beams, real ales and an excellent wine list, good service and delicious food; comfortable, smart bedrooms

This mainly 18th-c former drovers' inn (some parts are even older) is a lovely place to stay, with individually styled bedrooms and suites in a converted barn or the more modern Sycamore Bank opposite; breakfasts are excellent. Other guests are mainly here to enjoy the first class food but if it's just a pint and a chat you're after, you'll be made most welcome in the bar-brasserie. This is a fine, panelled and beamed room with standing timbers, a working Victorian farmhouse range set in a big stone fireplace, copper kettles, bed warmers, horsebrasses and the odd gun or two on red-painted walls, and farmhouse and wheelback chairs around wooden tables on carpeting. Black Sheep, Dark Horse Hetton Pale Ale and Naylors Pinnacle Blonde on handpump, an award-winning wine list with 20 by the glass and a large choice of malt whiskies. The two smart restaurant rooms, also beamed and with some timbering, have high-backed and plush tub dining chairs around white-clothed tables, with paintings and photographs on gold-leaf wallpapered walls. Tables and chairs on the front terrace are under retractable awnings. The surrounding countryside is glorious.

 Beautifully presented food using the best local produce includes sandwiches, pressing of chicken and black pudding with chicken liver parfait and piccalilli, roasted shallot tarte tatin with sprouting broccoli tempura and celeriac and potato gratin, venison haunch with celeriac timbale, beetroot purée, honey parsnips and dark chocolate and red wine sauce, specials such as hake fillet with lime and honey-glazed salsify, sesame cabbage, queenie scallops and thai foam, and puddings such as lemon meringue pie with lime sorbet and lemon custard and chocolate textures with 'soil', mousse, coconut sorbet and toffee; the english cheeseboard is good and comes with quince paste and their own Guinness and walnut cake. *Benchmark main dish: seafood 'moneybags' (seafood baked in crispy pastry, served with lobster sauce) £7.25. Two-course evening meal £23.00.*

Free house ~ Licensee Juliet Watkins ~ Real ale ~ Open 12-11 (11.30 Sat); 12-10.30 Sun; closed 1 week Jan ~ Bar food 12-2.15, 6-9.30 (10 Sat); 12-2.30, 6-8.30 Sun ~ Restaurant ~

Children welcome ~ Wi-fi ~ Bedrooms: £135/£150 *Recommended by W K Wood, Peter Smith and Judith Brown, Ray and Winifred Halliday, Clive Watkin*

ILKLEY
SE1347   Map 7
Wheatley Arms ♀ 🍺 🛏
(01943) 816496 – www.wheatleyarms.co.uk
Wheatley Lane, Ben Rhydding; LS29 8PP

Smart stone inn with plenty of room in boldly decorated dining rooms, cosy bar, professional service and good food and drink; comfortable bedrooms

With very good food, polished service and a fine range of ales, this substantial stone inn is always full of customers. The interconnected dining rooms have all manner of nice antique and upholstered chairs and stools and prettily cushioned wooden or rush-seated settles around assorted tables, rugs on bare boards, some bold wallpaper, various prints and two log fires; our readers like the smart garden room. One half of the locals' bar has tub armchairs and other comfortable seats, the other has tartan-cushioned wall seats and mate's chairs, with classic wooden stools against the counter where they keep Ilkley Mary Jane, Thwaites Original and Wharfedale Black and a couple of guests on handpump. Also, 23 wines by the glass (including prosecco and champagne), a dozen malt whiskies and a farm cider; background music and TV. There are seats and tables on the terrace. Bedrooms are individually decorated, well equipped and comfortable (some have a private roof terrace), and breakfasts are good.

🍴 Reliably good food from a wide menu includes breakfasts (also available to non-residents until 10am), sandwiches (until 5.30), crab cakes with tarragon mayonnaise, poached pear, stilton and chicory salad with hazelnut dressing, sharing boards, slow-roast pork belly with black pudding croquette, golden beetroot and prune sauce, pies such as steak and mushroom or fish and shellfish with herb topping, pressed ham hock with a free-range egg, chicken with sweetcorn and coriander risotto, and puddings. *Benchmark main dish: monkfish scampi and chips £12.00. Two-course evening meal £20.00.*

Free house ~ Licensee Steve Benson ~ Real ale ~ Open 6am-11pm (midnight Fri, Sat); 11-10.30 Sun ~ Bar food 12-2, 5.30-9 (9.30 Sat); 12-7.30 Sun ~ Restaurant ~ Children welcome ~ Dogs allowed in bar ~ Wi-fi ~ Live jazz lunch first Sun of month ~ Bedrooms: £89.99/£100 *Recommended by Gordon and Margaret Ormondroyd*

KIRKBY FLEETHAM
SE2894   Map 10
Black Horse ♀ 🍺 🛏
(01609) 749011 – www.blackhorsekirkbyfleetham.com
Village signposted off A1 S of Catterick; Lumley Lane; DL7 0SH

Attractively reworked country inn with well liked food, a good choice of drinks and a cheerful atmosphere; bedrooms are stylish and comfortable

The long softly lit beamed bar on the right as you enter this carefully run village pub has flagstones, cushioned wall seats, some little settles and high-backed dining chairs by the log fire at one end (blazing even for breakfast) and, at the other, wrought-iron chairs that are a good deal more comfortable than they look. The cosy snug has darts. As well as 11 wines by the glass, there's Black Sheep Best, Timothy Taylors Landlord and York Guzzler on handpump. The dining room towards the back is light and open, with big bow windows on either side and a casual contemporary look thanks to loose-covered dining chairs or pastel garden settles with scatter cushions around tables painted pale green. There's also a dark and intimate private dining room; maybe background pop music. The neat sheltered back lawn and flagstoned side terrace have teak seats and tables and there are picnic-sets at the front; quoits. The attractive, comfortable bedrooms have a lot of antique charm and the breakfasts are good – though they don't start till 9am (if you can't wait, you can get continental hampers).

Quite a choice of popular food includes sandwiches, ham hock terrine with pineapple pickle and a quail egg, prawn and crayfish cocktail with bloody mary dressing, steak in ale pie, leek and goats cheese en croûte with vegetable fricassée and grain mustard velouté, burger with toppings, dill pickle and toasted muffin, thai green chicken curry, local lamb rump with red lentil dhal, onion bhaji and raita, monkfish with prosciutto, herb-crushed potatoes and French-style peas, and puddings such as pistachio cake with elderflower jelly and apricot syrup and lemon curd and passion-fruit posset with pineapple and mango salsa and coconut tuille. *Benchmark main dish: confit pork belly with home-made black pudding and apple hash £16.95. Two-course evening meal £21.50.*

Free house ~ Licensee Jacque Gardner ~ Real ale ~ Open 12-11.30 (midnight Sat, 10.30 Sun) ~ Bar food 12-2.30, 6-9 (9.30 Fri, Sat); 12-8 Sun ~ Restaurant ~ Children welcome ~ Dogs allowed in bar and bedrooms ~ Wi-fi ~ Bedrooms: /£120 *Recommended by Toby Jones, Martin Jones*

LEDSHAM
SE4529 Map 7
Chequers ⭐ ♀
(01977) 683135 – www.thechequersinn.com
1.5 miles from A1(M) junction 42: follow Leeds signs, then Ledsham signposted; Claypit Lane; LS25 5LP

Friendly village pub with hands-on landlord, log fires in several beamed rooms, real ales and interesting, very popular food; pretty back terrace

'As good as ever' is how many readers describe this neatly kept and very well run village pub; as it's handy for the A1, it's best to book a table in advance. The several small, individually decorated rooms have plenty of character, with low beams, log fires, lots of cosy alcoves, toby jugs and all sorts of knick-knacks on the walls and ceilings (cricket fans will be interested to see a large photo in one room of four yorkshire heroes). From the little old-fashioned, panelled-in, central servery they offer Brown Cow Sessions Pale Ale, Leeds Best, Theakstons Best, Timothy Taylors Landlord and a guest beer on handpump and eight wines by the glass. The lovely sheltered two-level terrace at the back has plenty of tables among roses, and the hanging baskets and flowers are very pretty. RSPB Fairburn Ings reserve is not far and the ancient village church is worth a visit.

Reliably good traditional food with some modern touches includes sandwiches, seared scallops and crab with apple salad, duck liver pâté with beetroot chutney, corned beef hash layered with potatoes and caramelised onions, wild boar sausage with apple-ribboned mash and onion gravy, wild mushroom and asparagus risotto, confit duck leg with celeriac mash and flageolet bean ragoût, venison shank with braised and spiced red cabbage and shallot and madeira sauce, tuna loin with mango and red pepper salsa, and puddings such as chocolate sponge with hot chocolate sauce and crème brûlée. *Benchmark main dish: steak and mushroom pie £13.45. Two-course evening meal £21.00.*

Free house ~ Licensee Chris Wraith ~ Real ale ~ Open 11-11; 12-6 Sun ~ Bar food 12-9; 12-5 Sun ~ Restaurant ~ Children until 8pm ~ Dogs allowed in bar ~ Wi-fi

*Recommended by B and M Kendall, Alistair Forsyth, Gordon and Margaret Ormondroyd,
Richard Cole, Denis and Margaret Kilner*

LEVISHAM
Horseshoe

SE8390 Map 10

(01751) 460240 – www.horseshoelevisham.co.uk
Off A169 N of Pickering; YO18 7NL

**Friendly village pub run by two brothers (one cooks the good,
popular food), neat rooms, real ales and seats on the village green;
bedrooms**

As this warmly friendly and traditional family-run inn is so popular, it's
best to book a table in advance. The bustling bars have beams, blue
banquettes, wheelback and captain's chairs around a variety of tables on
polished wooden floors, vibrant landscapes by a local artist on the walls and
a log fire in the stone fireplace; an adjoining snug has a woodburning stove,
comfortable leather sofas and old photographs of the pub and the lovely
village. Served by the courteous landlord and his helpful staff are Black
Sheep Best and guests such as Box Steam Tunnel Vision, Cropton Yorkshire
Moors and Wold Top Spring Fling on handpump, half a dozen wines by
the glass and 15 malt whiskies; background music. There are seats on the
attractive green, with more in the back garden. Four new bedrooms have
been added and this makes a good base for exploring the North York Moors
National Park; breakfasts are hearty. The historic church is worth a visit.
This is sister pub to the Fox & Rabbit in Lockton.

Cooked by one of the landlords and served in generous helpings, the very good
food includes sandwiches, smoked salmon and orange salad, grilled black
pudding wrapped in bacon with apple sauce, mushroom risotto, sausage and mash with
onion gravy, beef stroganoff, chicken breast wrapped in bacon on creamed leeks, deep-
fried haddock and chips, and puddings. *Benchmark main dish: venison pie £10.95.
Two-course evening meal £17.00.*

Free house ~ Licensees Toby and Charles Wood ~ Real ale ~ Open 11-11 (10.30 Sun) ~
Bar food 12-2, 6-8.30 ~ Children welcome ~ Dogs allowed in bar ~ Wi-fi ~ Bedrooms: £45/£80
Recommended by David Heath, Sara Fulton, Roger Baker, Stanley and Annie Matthews

LEYBURN
Sandpiper

SE1190 Map 10

(01969) 622206 – www.sandpiperinn.co.uk
Just off Market Place; DL8 5AT

**Appealing food and cosy bar for drinkers in 17th-c cottage,
real ales and impressive choice of whisky; bedrooms**

With lovely food, a genuine welcome from courteous staff (for both
customers and their canine friends) and comfortable, well equipped
bedrooms – it's hard to fault this attractive 17th-c inn. The cosy bar has
a couple of black beams in the low ceiling, a log fire and wooden or
cushioned built-in wall seats around a few tables. The back snug, up three
steps, features lovely Dales photographs – get here early if you want a seat.
There are photographs and a woodburning stove in a stone fireplace by the
linenfold panelled bar counter; to the left is the attractive restaurant, with
dark wooden tables and chairs on bare boards and fresh flowers. Black
Sheep Best and a guest from breweries such as Rudgate and Wensleydale
on handpump, up to 75 malt whiskies and a decent wine list with ten by
the glass; background music and dominoes. In good weather, you can

enjoy a drink on the front terrace among the pretty hanging baskets and flowering climbers.

 Excellent food cooked by the chef-patron includes sandwiches, chicken and venison terrine with cumberland jelly, seared scallops with pork belly, celeriac and apple, chicken caesar salad, twice-baked cheese soufflé with roast pear and butternut squash, omelette arnold bennett (smoked haddock and potato omelette glazed with cheese), steak burger with toppings and brioche bun, crispy duck leg with braised red cabbage and sauté potatoes, fish pie with cheddar crust, and puddings such as dark chocolate marquise with cappuccino sauce and toffee popcorn and apple and plum crumble with vanilla custard. *Benchmark main dish: pressed lamb with dauphinoise potatoes and cranberry and mint sauce £18.00. Two-course evening meal £25.00.*

Free house ~ Licensee Jonathan Harrison ~ Real ale ~ Open 11.30-3, 6.30 (6 Sat)-11; 11.30-3, 6-10 Sun; closed Mon, some winter Tues, two weeks early Jan ~ Bar food 12-2.30, 6.30-9 (9.30 Sat, 8 Sun) ~ Restaurant ~ Children welcome ~ Dogs allowed in bar and bedrooms ~ Bedrooms: £80/£90 *Recommended by WAH, Lynda and Trevor Smith, Pat and Graham Williamson, Geoff and Linda Payne, John and Enid, Michael Butler*

LINTON IN CRAVEN
Fountaine ◀

SD9962   Map 7

(01756) 752210 – www.fountaineinnatlinton.co.uk
Off B6265 Skipton–Grassington; BD23 5HJ

Neatly kept pub in charming village with attractive furnishings, open fires, five real ales and popular food; bedrooms

Even on a miserable, cold and wet midweek day, you'll find this civilised and friendly inn packed out with customers keen to enjoy the well kept beers and highly thought-of food. There are beams and white-painted joists in the low ceilings, log fires (one in a beautifully carved heavy wooden fireplace), attractive built-in cushioned wall benches and stools around a mix of copper-topped tables, little wall lamps and quite a few prints on the pale walls. John Smiths, Tetleys Cask, Thwaites Original and guests such as Dark Horse Hetton Pale Ale and Wharfedale Blonde on handpump, 17 wines by the glass and a dozen malt whiskies served by efficient staff; background music, darts and board games. The terrace, looking across the road to the duck pond, has teak benches and tables under green parasols, and the hanging baskets are most appealing. The well equipped bedrooms are in a converted barn behind the pub. This is a pretty hamlet with fine walks in the beautiful Dales countryside.

From a thoughtful menu, the reliably good food includes sandwiches, ham hock terrine with a soft poached egg and piccalilli, black pudding and local cheese stack with golden beetroot chutney, sharing plates, cumberland sausage on savoy cabbage and bacon with rich gravy, steak pie, gammon and eggs, half a roast duck in ginger, spring onion and honey sauce, slow-braised lamb shank in redcurrant and mint sauce, and puddings such as chocolate fudge brownie and white chocolate cheesecake. *Benchmark main dish: mixed fish stew in rich tomato sauce £11.50. Two-course evening meal £20.00.*

Individual Inns ~ Manager Christopher Gregson ~ Real ale ~ Open 11-11; 12-10.30 Sun ~ Bar food 12-9 ~ Restaurant ~ Children welcome ~ Dogs allowed in bar ~ Wi-fi ~ Bedrooms: £75/£99 *Recommended by Lynda and Trevor Smith, Peter Smith and Judith Brown, John and Sylvia Harrop, Hilary Forrest*

We say if we know a pub allows dogs.

LOCKTON

SE8488   Map 10

Fox & Rabbit

(01751) 460213 – www.foxandrabbit.co.uk

A169 N of Pickering; YO18 7NQ

**Neatly kept pub with fine views, a friendly atmosphere in bars
and restaurant and real ales and highly regarded food**

'This is spot-on in every way,' enthuses one reader – and the two brothers running this attractive pub work hard to make sure this remains the case. The interconnected rooms have beams, panelling and some exposed stonework, wall settles and banquettes, dark pubby chairs and tables on tartan carpet, a log fire and a warm inviting atmosphere; fresh flowers, brasses, china plates, prints and old local photographs too. The locals' bar is busy and cheerful and there are panoramic views from the comfortable restaurant– it's worth arriving early to bag a window seat. Black Sheep, Theakstons Lightfoot Bitter and Yorkshire Moors on handpump, a dozen wines by the glass, 12 malt whiskies and home-made elderflower cordial; background music, games machine, pool, juke box and board games. Outside are seats under parasols and some picnic sets. The inn is in the North York Moors National Park, so there are plenty of surrounding walks. They have a caravan site. This is sister pub to the Horseshoe in Levisham.

From a seasonal menu, the hearty food includes sandwiches with chips and coleslaw, chicken liver pâté with red onion marmalade, prawn cocktail, lasagne, deep-fried Whitby haddock with chips, local sausages with onion gravy, gammon with eggs and pineapple, spinach and ricotta cannelloni in tomato sauce, slow-braised lamb shank with parsley mash, and puddings such as lemon tart and crème brûlée. *Benchmark main dish: steak in ale pie £11.95. Two-course evening meal £19.00.*

Free house ~ Licensees Toby and Charles Wood ~ Real ale ~ Open 10am-11.30pm ~ Bar food 12-4 (2 in winter), 5-8.30; 12-8.30 Sun ~ Restaurant ~ Children welcome ~ Dogs allowed in bar ~ Wi-fi *Recommended by Stanley and Annie Matthews, Sara Fulton, Roger Baker, Michael Butler*

LOW CATTON

SE7053   Map 7

Gold Cup

(01759) 371354 – www.goldcuplowcatton.com

*Village signposted with High Catton off A166 in Stamford Bridge or A1079
at Kexby Bridge; YO41 1EA*

**Friendly, pleasant pub with attractive bars, real ales, decent
dependable food, seats in garden and ponies in paddock**

The neatly kept bar in this comfortable white-rendered house is very much a village affair, but both locals and visitors are warmly welcomed by the long-serving and amiable licensees. There's a bustling atmosphere, plenty of smart tables and chairs on the stripped wooden floors, quite a few pictures, an open fire at one end opposite a gas-effect stove and coach lights on the rustic-looking walls. The spacious restaurant, with solid wooden pews and tables (said to be made from a single oak tree), has pleasant views of the surrounding fields. Theakstons Black Bull on handpump; background music and pool. There's a grassed area in the garden for children and the back paddock houses three ponies: Cinderella, Dobbin and Polly. The pub has fishing rights on the adjacent River Derwent.

Usefully served all day at weekends, the popular food includes lunchtime sandwiches, beer-battered mushrooms with garlic mayonnaise, prawn and crayfish cocktail in a filo basket, chicken curry, wild mushroom stroganoff, home-baked ham with creamy stilton sauce, steak in ale pie, bass fillet on sweet potato mash with lemon sauce, a roast of the day, and puddings; they also offer a two- and three-course candlelit supper menu on weekday evenings. *Benchmark main dish: spicy cajun chicken with minted yoghurt £10.50. Two-course evening meal £15.00.*

Free house ~ Licensees Pat and Ray Hales ~ Real ale ~ Open 12-2.30, 6-11; 12-11 Sat; 12-10.30 Sun; closed Mon lunchtime ~ Bar food 12-2, 6-9; 12-9 Sat; 12-8 Sun ~ Restaurant ~ Children welcome ~ Dogs allowed in bar ~ Wi-fi *Recommended by David and Carole Newton, Gordon and Margaret Ormondroyd*

MALHAM   SD9062   Map 7

Lister Arms

(01729) 830330 – www.listerarms.co.uk
Off A65 NW of Skipton; BD23 4DB

Friendly inn in fine countryside with cosy bars and dining room, Thwaites ales, enjoyable food and seats outside; comfortable bedrooms with views

The surrounding fells are a dream for walkers, while the comfortable bedrooms in this handsome, creeper-covered inn are warm and comfortable with views over the charming village green or the Yorkshire Dales National Park; breakfasts are generous and good. One bar has a medley of cushioned dining chairs and leather or upholstered armchairs around antique wooden tables on slate flooring, with a big deer's head above the inglenook fireplace. A second bar has a small brick fireplace with logs piled to each side, rustic slab tables, cushioned wheelback chairs and comfortable wall seats. Thwaites Original Bitter, Lancaster Bomber, Nutty Black, Wainwright and seasonal ales plus guests such as Dark Horse Hetton Pale Ale and Settle Signal Main Line on handpump, 20 wines by the glass and Weston's farm cider. A woodburning stove stands in the fireplace of the dining room where there are swagged curtains and smartly upholstered high-backed and pale wooden farmhouse chairs around rustic tables on bare floorboards. The flagstoned and gravelled courtyard has seats and benches around tables under parasols; some overlook the small green at the front.

As well as hot and cold sandwiches, the rewarding food includes salt and pepper crispy squid with garlic mayonnaise, black pudding fritters with sweet chilli jam, sharing platters, oak-smoked chicken caesar salad, burgers with toppings and fries, seafood linguine, roasted seasonal vegetables with chargrilled polenta and rocket pesto, steaks with various sauces and chips, and puddings such as rhubarb and custard crème brûlée and chocolate and hazelnut brownie with chocolate sauce. *Benchmark main dish: pie of the day £10.95. Two-course evening meal £21.00.*

Thwaites ~ Manager Darren Dunn ~ Real ale ~ Open 8am-11pm ~ Bar food 12-9.30 (10 Fri, Sat) ~ Restaurant ~ Children welcome ~ Dogs allowed in bar and bedrooms ~ Wi-fi ~ Bedrooms: £83/£89 *Recommended by Dr Simon Innes, Lindy Andrews*

MARTON-CUM-GRAFTON   SE4263   Map 7

Punch Bowl

(01423) 322519 – www.thepunchbowlmartoncumgrafton.com
Signed off A1 3 miles N of A59; YO51 9QY

Refurbished old inn in lovely village, with character bar and dining rooms, real ales, interesting food using seasonal local produce and seats outside

'A lovely place to enjoy some excellent food efficiently served by friendly staff' – we agree wholeheartedly with our reader's comments. This is a particularly well run handsome old inn with many original features: the main bar is beamed and timbered with a built-in window seat at one end, lots of red leather-topped stools, and cushioned settles and church chairs around pubby tables on flagstones or bare floorboards. Black Sheep Best, Tetleys Cask Bitter, Timothy Taylors Landlord and a guest from Roosters on handpump, 23 wines by the glass and a dozen malt whiskies. Open doorways lead to five separate dining areas, each with an open fire, heavy beams and an attractive mix of cushioned wall seats and wooden or high-backed red dining chairs around antique tables on oak floors; the red walls are covered with photographs of vintage motor races and racing drivers, the pub and the village plus sporting-themed cartoons. Up a swirling staircase is a coffee loft and a private dining room. There are seats and tables in the back courtyard where they hold summer barbecues. The pub belongs to the Provenance Inns group.

Carefully presented and using the best local produce, the very good food includes sandwiches, duck ballotine with truffle croutes, baked camembert with garlic and rosemary, queen scallops with cheddar and gruyère crust, garlic and parsley butter and skinny fries, spicy harissa chicken with flatbread, minted yoghurt and garlic aioli, pea and shallot tortellini, beer-battered fish and chips, burgers with toppings and battered onion rings, halibut fillet with vegetable niçoise and quail eggs, and puddings such as seville orange and Cointreau parfait with caramel sauce and treacle tart with berries; they also offer seven dishes for £7 each before 7pm (not Saturday). *Benchmark main dish: herb-crusted lamb rump with dauphinoise potatoes and pea and mint dressing £16.95. Two-course evening meal £22.50.*

Free house ~ Licensee Michael Ibbotson ~ Real ale ~ Open 12-3, 5-11; 12-11.30 Sat; 12-10.30 Sun ~ Bar food 12-2.30, 5.30-9.30; 12-3, 5.30-8.30 Sun ~ Children welcome ~ Dogs allowed in bar ~ Live music evening weekly (best to phone) *Recommended by Peter and Anne Hollindale, Michael Doswell*

MASHAM
SE2281 Map 10
Black Sheep Brewery

(01765) 680100 – www.blacksheepbrewery.co.uk
Brewery signed off Leyburn Road (A6108); HG4 4EN

Lively place with friendly staff, quite a mix of customers, unusual décor in big warehouse room, well kept beers and popular food

The tours of this sizeable brewery are interesting and a glass wall reveals the brewing exhibition centre; there's also a shop selling beers and beer-related items from pub games and T-shirts to pottery and fudge. In general, it's more of a bistro than a pub, though a huge upper warehouse room has a bar serving Black Sheep Best, Ale, Golden Sheep and Riggwelter plus a couple of changing guests on handpump, several wines by the glass and a fair choice of soft drinks. Most of the good-sized tables have cheery gingham tablecloths and brightly cushioned green café chairs, and there are some modern pubbier tables near the bar. The space is partly divided by free-standing partitions and there's a good deal of bare woodwork, with cream-painted rough stonework and green-painted steel girders and pillars; background music and friendly service. Picnic-sets out on the grass.

Popular food includes sandwiches, queenie scallops and prawns in smoked bacon and cheese sauce, chicken liver parfait with ale chutney, beer-battered fresh haddock and chips, roasted vegetable lasagne, pork and ale sausages with onion gravy, gammon with a duck egg and fresh pineapple, lambs liver with sage mash, black pudding and bacon, corn-fed chicken on pearl barley risotto with ceps, walnuts and tarragon oil, and puddings. *Benchmark main dish: burger with toppings, battered onion rings and skinny fries £10.50. Two-course evening meal £17.00.*

Free house ~ Licensee Paul Casterton ~ Real ale ~ Open 10-5 Mon-Weds, Sun; 10am-11pm Sat ~ Bar food 12-2.30 Sun-Weds; 12-2.30, 6-8.30 Thurs-Sat ~ Children welcome ~ Wi-fi
Recommended by Gavin and Helle May, Isobel Mackinlay, Janet and Peter Race

---

MOULTON
NZ2303 Map 10

Black Bull 🍴⭐ ♀

(01325) 377556 – www.theblackbullmoulton.com
Just E of A1, a mile E of Scotch Corner; DL10 6QJ

Carefully refurbished character pub with bar and dining areas, good choice of drinks, high quality food and courteous efficient service

---

Handy for Scotch Corner, this substantial place has been completely refurbished by Provenance Inns. The friendly bar has a convivial feel, with deep pink walls hung with all sorts of pictures and prints, and high chairs against the counter where they serve Black Sheep and Golden Sheep and a guest beer on handpump, 20 wines by the glass and over 20 malt whiskies. There's also some original panelling and leather wall seating topped with scatter cushions. A dining area has cushioned wooden chairs around a mix of tables on pale flagstones, a couple of leather armchairs in front of a woodburner in a brick fireplace, some horsetack, and stone bottles, wooden pails and copper items on window sills. The new dining extension – with tall windows and wooden floor – has attractive brown-orange high-backed dining chairs or cushioned settles and a rather nice wire bull; background music and board games. Doors from here lead out to a neat terrace with modern seats and tables among pots of rosemary or tall bay trees. Bedrooms are planned.

🍴 From a well judged menu, the rewarding food includes sandwiches, queenie scallops with thermidor sauce and gruyère crust, ham hock terrine with caramelised onion, a seafood sharing platter, burger with toppings, onion rings and chips, steak in ale pie, charcoal-grilled barbecue baby back ribs, chicken with pancetta, warm vegetable salad and madeira jus, local lamb with crispy goats cheese and tarragon jus, moules marinière with frites, and puddings such as dark chocolate and praline mousse with raspberry sorbet and sticky toffee and date pudding with butterscotch sauce; they also offer seven dishes at £7 each before 7pm (not Saturday). *Benchmark main dish: beer-battered fresh fish and chips £12.95. Two-course evening meal £20.00.*

Free house ~ Licensee Michael Ibbotson ~ Real ale ~ Open 12-3, 5-11; 12-midnight Sat; 12-11 Sun ~ Bar food 12-2.30, 5.30-9.30; 12-3, 6-9.30 Sun ~ Restaurant ~ Children welcome ~ Dogs allowed in bar ~ Wi-fi *Recommended by Michael Doswell*

RIPPONDEN
SE0419 Map 7

Old Bridge ♀

(01422) 822595 – www.theoldbridgeinn.co.uk
From A58, best approach is Elland Road (opposite the Golden Lion); park opposite the church in pub's car park and walk back over ancient hump-back bridge; HX6 4DF

Pleasant old pub by medieval bridge with relaxed communicating rooms and well liked food

---

This notably welcoming 14th-c inn, in a lovely spot, continues to effortlessly be both a local pub and a dining pub; the third generation of the family running it work hard to keep the atmosphere informal and bustling. The three communicating rooms, each on a slightly different level, have oak settles built into window recesses in the thick stone walls, antique oak tables, rush-seated chairs and comfortably cushioned free-standing settles, a few well chosen pictures and prints on the panelled or painted walls and a big woodburning stove. Timothy Taylors Best, Dark Mild, Golden Best and Landlord and a couple of guests such as Church End Blue Norther, Oates Wild Oates and Phoenix Navvy on handpump, quite a few foreign bottled beers, a dozen wines by the glass, 30 malt whiskies and farm cider; quick, efficient service. The pub is next to a beautiful medieval packhorse bridge over the little River Ryburn and seats in the pub garden overlook the water. If you have trouble finding the pub (there's no traditional pub sign outside), just head for the church.

 The ever popular weekday lunchtime cold meat and salad buffet has been running since 1963 (they also offer soup and sandwiches at lunch). Evening and weekend choices include sandwiches, thai-spiced tiger prawns with mango and mixed leaves, game terrine with date and apple relish, black pudding, bacon and poached egg with mustard and honey, a vegetarian dish of the day, lamb burger with red pepper and tomato chutney, raita and dripping chips, beer-battered haddock and chips, beef goulash with herb dumpling and sour cream, and puddings. *Benchmark main dish: smoked haddock and spinach pancakes £10.25. Two-course evening meal £20.00.*

Free house ~ Licensees Tim and Lindsay Eaton Walker ~ Real ale ~ Open 12-3, 5.30-11; 12-11 Fri-Sun ~ Bar food 12-2, 6.30-9.30; 12-4 Sun ~ Children allowed until 8pm but must be seated away from bar ~ Wi-fi *Recommended by Dr Kevan Tucker, Richard Kennell, Brian and Anna Marsden*

ROBIN HOOD'S BAY
Laurel

NZ9505 Map 10

(01947) 880400

Bay Bank; village signed off A171 S of Whitby; YO22 4SE

Delightful little pub in unspoilt fishing village with neat friendly bar and real ales; no food

In one of the prettiest and most unspoilt fishing villages on the north-east coast, this little local pub is at the bottom of a row of fishermen's cottages. It remains quite unchanged and the charming landlord is welcoming to all. The neatly kept beamed main bar has an open fire and is decorated with old local photographs, Victorian prints and brasses and lager bottles from across the world. There's Adnams Southwold and Theakstons Best and Old Peculier on handpump; darts, board games and background music. In summer, the hanging baskets and window boxes are lovely. They rent out a self-contained apartment for two people. There's no food but you can bring in sandwiches from the tea shop next door and eat them in the pub.

Free house ~ Licensee Brian Catling ~ Real ale ~ No credit cards ~ Open 12-11 (10.30 Sun); 3-11 Mon-Thurs in winter ~ Children in snug bar only ~ Dogs welcome
Recommended by Harvey Brown, Toby Jones, David Carr

ROECLIFFE
Crown

SE3765 Map 7

(01423) 322300 – www.crowninnroecliffe.com

Off A168 just W of Boroughbridge; handy for A1(M) junction 48; YO51 9LY

Smartly updated and attractively placed pub with a civilised bar, first class enterprising food and a fine choice of drinks; charming bedrooms

'As good as it gets – excellent food, lovely beer and faultless service.' Who could disagree with this reader? The hard-working Mainey family continue to welcome the cheerful crowd of locals and visitors who fill their lovely inn, whether for a drink and a chat, a fine meal or an overnight stay. The bar has a contemporary colour scheme of dark reds and off-whites with pleasant prints carefully grouped and lit; one area has chunky pine tables on flagstones, while another, with a log fire, has dark tables on plaid carpet. Theakstons Best, Timothy Taylors Landlord and a couple of guests such as Rudgate Jorvik Blonde and Yorkshire Heart Silverheart IPA on handpump, 30 wines by the glass and 15 malt whiskies. For meals, you can choose between a small candlelit olive-green bistro with nice tables, a longcase clock and a couple of paintings, and a more formal restaurant. The garden has been smartened up this year with rattan sofas and tables on new decking. This is a very nice place to stay, with cosy, country-style bedrooms. The village green is opposite.

Using their own smokehouse and making everything in-house (including bread daily), the excellent food includes sandwiches, mini rabbit pie over cranberry and oranges, smoked and poached salmon terrine with pickled quail eggs and cucumber salad, steak burger with toppings and relish, cumberland sausage with red onion and thyme mash and roast shallot gravy, bass fillet with crab risotto, sweet baby peppers and chorizo dressing, eight-hour-cooked ox cheeks with bacon and charred baby cabbage, and puddings such as lemon and honey panna cotta with fresh orange, ginger and vanilla syrup and belgian chocolate tart with lime zest and vanilla ice-cream and edible 24-carat gold leaf. *Benchmark main dish: steak in ale pie £13.85. Two-course evening meal £20.00.*

Free house ~ Licensee Karl Mainey ~ Real ale ~ Open 12-11; 12-7 Sun ~ Bar food 12-2.15, 6-9.15; 12-7 Sun ~ Restaurant ~ Children welcome ~ Dogs allowed in bar and bedrooms ~ Wi-fi ~ Bedrooms: £80/£100 *Recommended by C A Hall, Nick and Gillian Harrison, Alistair Forsyth, David and Carole Newton, Derek and Sylvia Stephenson, Lesley and Peter Barrett, Tracey and Stephen Groves, Janet and Peter Race, S Holder, Simon Cleasby, Les and Sandra Brown*

SANCTON

SE9039 Map 7

Star

(01430) 827269 – www.thestaratsancton.co.uk
King Street (A1034 S of Market Weighton); YO43 4QP

Cheerful bar with four real ales, more formal dining rooms with accomplished food, and a friendly, easy-going atmosphere

This carefully extended old pub is at the foot of the Yorkshire Wolds Railway, so many walkers and cyclists use it as a base for both a pint and a chat and a good meal. There's a bar with a woodburning stove, traditional red plush stools around a mix of tables, and a cheerful atmosphere helped along by the enthusiastic, hard-working licensees. Ales from breweries such as Black Sheep, Copper Dragon, Great Newsome and Wold Top are served on handpump from the brick counter and they keep 18 wines by the glass including prosecco and champagne and over 20 malt whiskies. The more formal (though still relaxed) dining rooms have comfortable high-backed dark leather dining chairs around wooden tables on carpeting, and prints on red- or cream-painted walls; background music. There are picnic-sets outside at the back.

Using home-grown ingredients and produce from village allotments, the delicious food includes sandwiches, chicken liver and foie gras parfait with onion and chorizo loaf, white crab bake and brown crab 'scottie' with samphire, aioli, fennel and pickled cauliflower, deep-fried goats cheese and candied walnuts with roast squash and beetroot and port reduction, lemon sole with roast salsify, winter greens, beurre noisette and hazelnuts, braised lamb shank with red onion tarte tatin, soubise sauce and rosemary lamb jus, venison loin with juniper sausage roll, beetroot fondant, jerusalem artichoke with truffle and game juices, and puddings such as vanilla and clementine cheesecake with pomegranate jelly and clementine sorbet and vanilla crème brûlée with berry compote. *Benchmark main dish: steak in ale pie £13.95. Two-course evening meal £27.00.*

Free house ~ Licensees Ben and Lindsey Cox ~ Real ale ~ Open 12-3, 6-11; 12-11 Sun; closed Mon ~ Bar food 12-2, 6-9.30; 12-3, 6-8 Sun ~ Restaurant ~ Children welcome
Recommended by John and Eleanor Holdsworth, Michael Butler

SANDHUTTON
Kings Arms ◖
SE3882 Map 10

(01845) 587887 – www.thekingsarmssandhutton.co.uk
A167, 1 mile N of A61 Thirsk–Ripon; YO7 4RW

Cheerful pub with friendly service, interesting food and beer, and comfortable furnishings; bedrooms

While there's quite a focus on food in this charming village inn, the friendly son and father licensees remain committed to providing a traditional pubby atmosphere. The bar has an unusual circular woodburner in one corner, a high central table with four equally high stools, modern ladder-back wooden dining chairs around light pine tables, a couple of cushioned wicker armchairs, some attractive modern bar stools and photographs of the pub in years gone by. Black Sheep Best, Rudgate Viking, Theakstons Best and Village Brewer White Boar Bitter on handpump, nine wines by the glass and efficient, friendly service. The two connecting dining rooms have similar furnishings to the bar (plus some high-backed brown leather dining chairs), arty flower photographs on cream walls and a small woodburning stove; background music, darts, board games and TV. They have a shop selling their own ready meals as well as sausages, pies and sandwiches. Only one dog at a time is allowed inside, so it's first come, first served.

Good, popular food includes lunchtime sandwiches, king scallops with braised pig cheeks and honey drizzle, twice-cooked cheddar soufflé with carrot, orange and toasted pine nut salad, chilli con carne, their own-cured ham with free-range eggs, salmon, prawn and cod fishcake with sweet chilli sauce, a pie of the day, mediterranean vegetable and goats cheese pancake topped with gruyère, burger with toppings and chips, monkfish wrapped in parma ham with pea and mint sauce, and puddings. *Benchmark main dish: home-made scampi and chips £11.25. Two-course evening meal £19.00.*

Free house ~ Licensees Raymond and Alexander Boynton ~ Real ale ~ Open 11-11 (midnight Sat); 11-10 Sun ~ Bar food 12-2.30, 5.30-9; 12-7 (5 in winter) Sun ~ Restaurant ~ Children welcome ~ Dogs allowed in bar ~ Wi-fi ~ Bedrooms: $45/$70
Recommended by Brian and Jean Hepworth

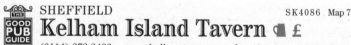
SHEFFIELD
Kelham Island Tavern ◖ £
SK4086 Map 7

(0114) 272 2482 – www.kelhamtavern.co.uk
Kelham Island; S3 8RY

Busy little local with 13 changing real ales, basic but decent lunchtime pub food, a friendly welcome and pretty back garden

Although major upcoming refurbishments will alter the inside and outside, the wonderful range of ales in this busy tavern remains unchanged. There's usually up to 13 interesting brews on handpump (always a mild and a stout or porter), served by well organised, knowledgeable and friendly staff. Their regulars are Abbeydale Deception, Acorn Barnsley Bitter and Bradfield Farmers Blonde with guests from breweries such as BAD, Dark Star, Hop Studio, North Riding, Rudgate, Thwaites, Wold Top and Yorkshire Dales; also, 40 malt whiskies and farm cider and perry. It's a busy backstreet local with a wide array of cheerful customers and pubby furnishings; dominoes and board games. The unusual, flower-filled back courtyard garden has plenty of seats and tables and a woodburning stove for chilly evenings. The front window boxes regularly win awards.

Tasty and very good value pubby food includes sandwiches and locally made pork pies (always available), plus lunchtime-only hot dishes such as burgers with chips, liver and onions, chilli prawns, mushroom and red pepper stroganoff and lamb curry. *Benchmark main dish: steak in ale pie £5.50.*

Free house ~ Licensee Trevor Wraith ~ Real ale ~ Open 12-midnight ~ Bar food 12-3; not Sun (no hot food but sandwiches available) ~ Children allowed in back room ~ Dogs welcome ~ Live folk Sun evening *Recommended by Toby Jones, Edward May, Sharon and John Hancock, Pat and Tony Martin*

SOUTH DALTON
Pipe & Glass 🏅 ♀ 🛏

SE9645 Map 8

(01430) 810246 – www.pipeandglass.co.uk
West End; brown sign to pub off B1248 NW of Beverley; HU17 7PN

Yorkshire Dining Pub of the Year

Attractive dining pub with a proper bar area, real ales, interesting modern cooking, good service, garden and front terrace; stylish bedrooms

Three new luxury suites are to be added to this attractive whitewashed dining pub – the two stylish rooms already in use have their own little terrace and views over Dalton Park. The exceptional food continues to draw high praise from our readers, but the proper bar has a chatty atmosphere plus Black Sheep Best, Two Chefs (named for them from Great Yorkshire) and a couple of guests from Scarborough and Wold Top on handpump, 15 wines by the glass, 40 malt whiskies and a farm cider. Service is prompt and friendly. The beamed and bow-windowed bar has copper pans hanging above the log fire in the sizeable fireplace, cushioned window seats and high-backed wooden dining chairs around a mix of tables (each set with a church candle) and some old prints. Beyond, all is airy and comfortably contemporary, angling around some chunky button-back leather chesterfields into a light restaurant area overlooking the park, with similar tables and chairs on bare boards; background music. There are tables on the garden's peaceful lawn and picnic-sets on the front terrace; the yew tree is said to be 500 years old. The village is charming and its elegant Victorian church spire, 62 metres tall, is visible for miles around.

Cooked by the landlord, this is accomplished, beautifully presented food at its very best: lunchtime sandwiches, spiced ale-cured salmon with pickled cucumber, oyster fritter, oyster mayonnaise and coriander, Gloucester old spot potted pork with sticky apple and crackling salad and warm spelt toast, guinea fowl breast with a crispy leg meat parcel, devils on horseback, burnt onion purée and kale and sherry cream, pork sausages with bubble and squeak and ale, sage and onion gravy, blue cheese croquettes with cauliflower champ, baby leeks, hazelnuts, milk and hyssop, beef fillet with ox cheek fritter, watercress and pickled red onion salad, horseradish hollandaise and chips, and puddings such as hot dark chocolate, juniper and sloe gin pudding with hazelnut ice-cream and a trio of apples (apple and bramble crumble, sticky apple sponge, apple sorbet). *Benchmark main dish: roast partridge with black pudding, parsnips and burnt apple purée £24.00. Two-course evening meal £30.00.*

Free house ~ Licensees Kate and James Mackenzie ~ Real ale ~ Open 12-11 (10.30 Sun); closed Mon except bank holidays ~ Bar food 12-9.30; 12-4 Sun ~ Restaurant ~ Children welcome ~ Wi-fi ~ Bedrooms: /£170 *Recommended by Mary Kirkwood, Emma Scofield, John Harris*

THORNTON WATLASS

Buck

SE2385 Map 10

(01677) 422461 – www.buckwatlass.co.uk
Village signposted off B6268 Bedale–Masham; HG4 4AH

Honest village pub with five real ales, traditional bars, well liked food and popular Sunday jazz; bedrooms

With clean, comfortable bedrooms and tasty breakfasts, our readers enjoy staying here. A recently refurbished, bustling village pub, it's been run by the hands-on licensees for 29 years, and the pleasantly traditional bar on the right has upholstered wall settles on carpet, a fine mahogany bar counter, local artwork on the walls and a brick fireplace. The Long Room (overlooking the cricket green) has photos, prints and other memorabilia from Thornton Watlass cricket teams past and present, and is the venue for the Sunday afternoon jazz sessions. Black Sheep Bitter, Theakstons Best, Walls Gun Dog Bitter and a couple of guests from local breweries on handpump, seven wines by the glass, 20 interesting malt whiskies; darts. The sheltered garden has a well equipped children's play area and two quoits pitches (games take place on summer Wednesday evenings).

Popular food includes lunchtime sandwiches, ciabattas and baguettes, creamy garlic mushrooms, prawn cocktail, rarebit with home-made chutney, lasagne, wild mushroom stroganoff, cajun chicken with spicy tomato relish, burgers with toppings and chips, seafood linguine, oriental pork stir-fry, lamb shank with minted gravy, and puddings such as bakewell tart with custard and chocolate cheesecake. *Benchmark main dish: beer-battered fish and chips £9.95. Two-course evening meal £14.00.*

Free house ~ Licensees Victoria and Tony Jowett ~ Real ale ~ Open 12-11 (10.30 Sun) ~ Bar food 12-2, 6-9; 12-3, 6-8.30 Sun ~ Restaurant ~ Children welcome ~ Dogs allowed in bar and bedrooms ~ Wi-fi ~ Live trad jazz some Sun lunchtimes (best to phone) ~ Bedrooms: £55/£85 *Recommended by Belinda Stamp, Dave Braisted*

WASS

Wombwell Arms

SE5579 Map 7

(01347) 868280 – www.wombwellarms.co.uk
Back road W of Ampleforth; or follow brown sign for Byland Abbey off A170 Thirsk–Helmsley; YO61 4BE

Consistently enjoyable village pub with a friendly atmosphere, good mix of locals and visitors, interesting bar food and real ales; bedrooms

With Byland Abbey (English Heritage) nearby, it's best to book ahead if you want a table at lunchtime. The two bustling bars are carefully looked after, with simple character, pine farmhouse chairs and tables, some exposed stone walls and log fires; the walls of the Poacher's Bar (dogs are welcome here) are hung with brewery memorabilia. From the panelled bar counter, friendly staff serve Black Sheep, Great Newsome Marvellously Poetic Porter and Wold Top Wold Gold on handpump, nine wines by the glass (quite a few from Mrs Walker's native South Africa) and ten malt whiskies; darts and board games. The two restaurants are incorporated into a former granary and there are seats outside. This is a pretty village below the Hambleton Hills with fine surrounding walks.

Cooked by the landlady and with some south african touches, the good food includes sandwiches, oak-smoked snoek (a south african fish) pâté, pork belly lollipops with apple in breadcrumbs, rooibos tea-smoked chicken and chorizo omelette, burger with toppings and chips, king prawn paella, bobotie (a fruity mince curry), vegetable pie, chicken ballotine stuffed with smoked cheese and apricots and wrapped in streaky bacon with creamy sauce, pork medallions with mushrooms and baby onions in brandy and mustard sauce, and puddings such as chocolate mousse cake with chocolate sauce and tipsy tart with brandy toffee sauce and toffee fudge ice-cream. *Benchmark main dish: steak in Guinness pie £12.95. Two-course evening meal £18.00.*

Free house ~ Licensees Ian and Eunice Walker ~ Real ale ~ Open 12-3, 6-11; 12-11 Sat; 12-10.30 Sun ~ Bar food 12-2 (2.30 Sat), 6-8.30 (9 Fri, Sat); 12-3, 6-8 Sun ~ Restaurant ~ Children welcome ~ Dogs allowed in bar ~ Wi-fi ~ Bedrooms: £75/£99
Recommended by Dr Peter Crawshaw, Mike Swan

WELBURN
Crown & Cushion 🍺 ♈

SE7168   Map 7

(01653) 618777 – www.thecrownandcushionwelburn.com
Off A64; YO60 7DZ

Carefully refurbished and extended old pub, plenty of dining and drinking space, real ales and particularly good food and seats outside

In an area popular with walkers and bird-watchers and handy for Castle Howard, this is a carefully refurbished and extended 18th-c inn. There's a little tap room with rustic tables and chairs on wide floorboards, high stools around an equally high central table, beams and timbering, and Black Sheep, Brass Castle Best Bitter, York Guzzler and a guest beer on handpump and 22 wines by the glass served by friendly, helpful staff. The other attractively refurbished, interconnecting rooms are for dining and on different levels: smart high-backed chairs mix with wooden ones and an assortment of cushioned settles and wall seats around various tables on flagstones or red and black floor tiles. There are open fires and a woodburning stove, old prints of the pub and local scenes on painted or exposed stone walls and lots of horsebrasses, copper pans and kettles and old stone bottles. Contemporary tables and chairs sit on a terrace with picnic-sets below and a long-reaching view across to the Howardian Hills. This is part of the Provenance Inns group.

Using some of their own-grown produce and plenty of local ingredients, the reliably good, interesting food includes lunchtime sandwiches, queenie scallops topped with garlic, butter and cheese, game terrine with pear purée, burgers with various toppings and chips, candied butternut squash tortellini with crème fraîche, fish pie, maple-cured bacon loin with a crispy free-range egg and caper butter, lamb rump with dauphinoise potatoes, pancetta and basil jus, and puddings such as eton mess and lemon and thyme panna cotta; they also offer seven dishes for £7 each before 7pm (not Saturday). *Benchmark main dish: rib-eye steak with onion rings and chips £23.95. Two-course evening meal £21.00.*

Free house ~ Licensee Michael Ibbotson ~ Real ale ~ Open 12-3, 5.30-11; 12-11 Fri-Sun ~
Bar food 12-3, 5.30-9 (9.30 Fri, Sat); 12-8 Sun ~ Restaurant ~ Children welcome ~
Dogs allowed in bar *Recommended by Dr and Mrs J D Abell, Caroline Prescott, Belinda Stamp*

WIDDOP   SD9531   Map 7
Pack Horse ◀ £
(01422) 842803 – www.thepackhorse.org

*The Ridge; from A646 on W side of Hebden Bridge, turn off at Heptonstall signpost
(as it's a sharp turn, coming out of Hebden Bridge the road signs direct you around
a turning circle), then follow Slack and Widdop signposts; can also be reached from
Nelson and Colne, on high, pretty road; OS Sheet 103 map reference 952317; HX7 7AT*

**Friendly pub up on the moors and liked by walkers for generous,
tasty honest food, four real ales and lots of malt whiskies**

After a wet moorland walk, this isolated traditional pub is a cosy haven.
The bar has welcoming winter fires, window seats cut into the partly
panelled stripped-stone walls (from where you can take in the beautiful
views), sturdy furnishings and horsey mementoes. Black Sheep and Thwaites
Wainwright plus guests such as Cottage Comet and Greyhawk Blonde
Obsession on handpump, over 100 single malt whiskies and some irish ones,
and 11 wines by the glass. The friendly golden retrievers are called Padge and
Purdey, the alsatian is Holly. There are seats outside in the cobblestoned beer
garden and pretty summer hanging baskets. They have a smart self-catering
apartment for rent.

Hearty food plus daily specials includes sandwiches, garlic mushrooms with stilton,
devilled kidneys, vegetable gratin, cottage hotpot, gammon and eggs, half a roast
pheasant with cranberry sauce and gravy, haddock, salmon and smoked haddock pie,
duck breast with honey-roast parsnips, leeks and orange jus, cod fillet with parsley
mash and prawn butter sauce, and puddings such as sticky toffee and bread and butter
puddings. *Benchmark main dish: rack of lamb with red wine jus £14.95. Two-course
evening meal £20.00.*

Free house ~ Licensee Andrew Hollinrake ~ Real ale ~ Open 12-3, 5.30-11; 12-10 Sun;
closed Mon except bank holidays, Tues Jan, Feb, lunchtimes Mon-Thurs Oct-Apr ~
Bar food 12-2, 5.30-9; 12-7 Sun ~ Well behaved children allowed until 8.30 ~ Dogs welcome
Recommended by Emma Scofield, Toby Jones

YORK   SE5951   Map 7
Maltings ◀ £
(01904) 655387 – www.maltings.co.uk

Tanners Moat/Wellington Row, below Lendal Bridge; YO1 6HU

**Bustling, friendly city pub with cheerful landlord, interesting real ales
and other drinks plus good value standard food**

A fine choice of drinks served by the jovial landlord draws in customers
from far and wide. The atmosphere is bustling and cheerful and the
eight real ales on handpump include Black Sheep Bitter and Golden Sheep,
one each from Roosters and York and four that change daily. They also
keep six continental beers on tap, two craft beers, lots of bottled beers, four
farm ciders, 15 country wines and 25 whiskies from all over the world. The
tricksy décor is strong on salvaged, somewhat quirky junk: old doors for the
bar front and much of the ceiling, a marvellous collection of railway signs
and amusing notices, an old chocolate dispensing machine, cigarette and
tobacco advertisements alongside cough and chest remedies, what looks like
a suburban front door for the entrance to the ladies', partly stripped orange

brick walls and even a lavatory pan in one corner; games machine. The day's papers are framed in the gents'. Nearby parking is difficult; the pub is very handy for the National Railway Museum and the station. Please note that dogs are allowed only after food service has finished.

🍴 Incredibly good value pubby food includes sandwiches and toasties, baked potatoes, beef in ale pie, ham and egg, sausage with beans and chips, beer-battered haddock and chips, and mushroom and spinach lasagne. *Benchmark main dish: cheesy chips £4.30.*

Free house ~ Licensee Shaun Collinge ~ Real ale ~ No credit cards ~ Open 11am-11.30pm; 12-10.30 Sun ~ Bar food 12-2 weekdays; 12-4 weekends ~ Children allowed only during meal times ~ Dogs allowed in bar ~ Wi-fi ~ Live music Mon and Tues evenings
Recommended by Pat and Graham Williamson, Phil Bryant, Dr J Barrie Jones, Eddie Edwards

Also Worth a Visit in Yorkshire

Besides the fully inspected pubs, you might like to try these pubs that have been recommended to us and described by readers. Do tell us what you think of them: feedback@goodguides.com

ADDINGHAM   SE0749
Craven Heifer (01943) 830106
Main Street; LS29 0PL Sister inn to the Fleece at other end of village – see Main Entries; very good food (not Sun evening, Mon) from bar snacks to upmarket restaurant choices including a seven-course tasting menu, friendly efficient service, four well kept ales such as Black Sheep and Saltaire, pebble-floored bar with restaurant areas off, open fires; a few tables out in front, seven individually styled bedrooms, open all day (Mon till 6pm). *(Emma Scofield)*

AINDERBY STEEPLE   SE3392
Wellington Heifer (01609) 775718
A684, 3 miles from A1; opposite church; DL7 9PU Nicely refurbished late 18th-c pub with four connecting rooms, flagstone floors and log fires, comfortable scatter-cushion bench seating and sturdy tables, good range of beers and wines from carved counter, enjoyable food including good value lunchtime/early evening set menu, restaurant at end of corridor; children welcome, two well appointed bedrooms, open all day (food all day Sun till 7pm). *(Peter Hacker, Michael Doswell)*

AINTHORPE   NZ7007
Fox & Hounds (01287) 660218
Brook Lane; YO21 2LD Traditional beamed moorland inn dating from the 16th c, tranquil setting with sheep grazing freely and wonderful views; nice open fire in unusual stone fireplace, comfortable seating, well kept Theakstons ales and good choice of wines by the glass, generous fairly priced food including daily specials, friendly staff, restaurant, games room; free wi-fi; dogs welcome, great walks from the door, seven bedrooms and attached self-

catering cottage in 18th-c buildings, open all day. *(Rod Lambert)*

ALDBOROUGH   SE4166
Ship (01423) 322749
Off B6265 just S of Boroughbridge, close to A1; YO51 9ER Attractive 14th-c beamed village dining pub adjacent to medieval church, good home-made food from sandwiches and pub standards to seafood, cheerful helpful service, well kept ales including Theakstons, extensive affordably priced wine list, some old-fashioned seats around cast-iron-framed tables, lots of copper and brass, inglenook fire, candlelit back restaurant; children and dogs welcome, a few picnic-sets outside, handy for Roman remains and museum, bedrooms, open all day Sun, closed Mon lunchtime. *(Peter Hacker)*

AMPLEFORTH   SE5878
★**White Swan** (01439) 788239
Off A170 W of Helmsley; East End; YO62 4DA Popular village pub with plum-coloured beamed lounge, slate or carpeted floors, sporting prints and two-way woodburner, locals' bar with beams and standing timbers, patterned wall seating and log fire, more formal dining area has plush furnishings and linen-clothed tables, good food from traditional choices up, Black Sheep and Theakstons, decent wines by the glass and ten malt whiskies, friendly service; background music, pool, darts and dominoes; children welcome, back terrace overlooking valley, open all day weekends. *(Debi Henson)*

APPLETON-LE-MOORS   SE7388
★**Moors** (01751) 417435
N of A170, just under 1.5 miles E of Kirkby Moorside; YO62 6TF Traditional stone-built village pub, beamed bar with built-in high-backed settle next to

old kitchen fireplace, plenty of other seating, some sparse decorations (a few copper pans, earthenware mugs, country ironwork), three changing regional ales and over 50 malt whiskies, popular good value home-made food (something all day) using vegetables from own allotment, friendly helpful staff; background music, darts; children and dogs welcome, tables in lovely walled garden with quiet country views, walks to Rosedale Abbey or Hartoft End, seven good bedrooms, open all day. (T E Stone, Ann and Tony Bennett-Hughes)

APPLETON-LE-STREET　　SE7373
Cresswell Arms　(01653) 693647
B1257/Appleton Lane; YO17 6PG Modernised stone country inn dating from the 1800s, pleasant carpeted bar with log fire, good-sized bare-boards restaurant with pine furniture and fittings, well kept Wold Top and enjoyable pubby food (all day Sun) from sandwiches up; children welcome, ten bedrooms, closed Mon and Tues lunchtimes in winter. *(Michael Butler)*

APPLETREEWICK　　SE0560
Craven Arms　(01756) 720270
Off B6160 Burnsall–Bolton Abbey; BD23 6DA Character creeper-clad 16th-c beamed pub, cushioned settles and rugs on flagstones, fire in old range, gas lighting and some interesting pictures and bric-a-brac, up to eight well kept ales including a house beer from Dark Horse, several wines by the glass, home-made food from baguettes up, friendly helpful service, small dining room and splendid thatched and raftered cruck barn with gallery; free wi-fi; children, dogs and muddy boots welcome (plenty of surrounding walks), wheelchair access, nice country views from front picnic-sets, more seats in back garden, open all day. *(Lynda and Trevor Smith, Pat and Graham Williamson, Hilary Forrest, Gordon and Margaret Ormondroyd)*

ARNCLIFFE　　SD9371
★Falcon　(01756) 770205
Off B6160 N of Grassington; BD23 5QE Basic no-frills country tavern in lovely setting on village green, coal fire in small bar with elderly furnishings, well kept Timothy Taylors Landlord and a guest either from handpump or tapped from cask to stoneware jugs in central hatch-style servery, inexpensive simple lunchtime food, friendly service, attractive watercolours, sepia photographs and humorous sporting prints, back sun room overlooking pleasant garden; children till 9pm and dogs welcome, four miles of trout fishing, nice walks, five bedrooms (two with own bathroom), breakfast and evening meal for residents. *(B and M Kendall, Claes Mauroy)*

ASKRIGG　　SD9491
Crown　(01969) 650387
Main Street; DL8 3HQ Friendly open-plan local in James Herriot village, three areas off

main bar, open fires including old-fashioned range, buzzy atmosphere, enjoyable simple pub food at reasonable prices, Black Sheep, Theakstons and a guest; children, walkers and dogs welcome, tables outside, open all day. *(Geoff and Linda Payne)*

ASKRIGG　　SD9491
Kings Arms　(01969) 650113
Signed from A684 Leyburn–Sedbergh in Bainbridge; DL8 3HQ Popular 18th-c coaching inn (the Drovers in TV's *All Creatures Great and Small*) and under same ownership as the Charles Bathurst at Langthwaite; flagstoned high-ceilinged main bar with good log fire, traditional furnishings and décor, a couple of well kept house beers from nearby Yorkshire Dales plus Black Sheep, Theakstons and a guest, 13 wines by the glass, enjoyable reasonably priced food including evening offers (Mon, Tues), friendly efficient service, more modern restaurant with inglenook, games room in former barrel-vaulted beer cellar; background music, TV; children welcome, side courtyard, bedrooms run separately as part of Holiday Property Bond complex behind, open all day. *(Comus and Sarah Elliott, Mrs Carolyn Dixon, Tracey and Stephen Groves, John and Enid)*

AUSTWICK　　SD7668
★Game Cock　(01524) 251226
Just off A65 Settle–Kirkby Lonsdale; LA2 8BB Quaint civilised place in pretty spot below Three Peaks; good log fire in old-fashioned beamed bare-boards back bar, cheerful efficient staff and friendly locals, well kept Thwaites and a guest, winter mulled wine and nice coffee, most space devoted to the food side, with good fairly priced choice from french chef-landlord, pizzas and children's meals as well, two dining rooms and modern conservatory-type extension at front; walkers and dogs welcome, garden with play equipment, four neat bedrooms, closed Mon, otherwise open all day (till 1am if busy). *(M and GR)*

AYSGARTH　　SE0188
Aysgarth Falls　(01969) 663775
A684; DL8 3SR Creeper-clad moorland hotel refurbished under present licensees, comfortable eating areas, some interesting ancient masonry at the back recalling its days as a pilgrims' inn, good food and welcoming accommodating service, ales such as Black Sheep, Theakstons and Wensleydale in log-fire bar where dogs welcome; great scenery near broad waterfalls, 11 bedrooms, camping (adults only). *(Lynda and Trevor Smith, John Gosling)*

AYSGARTH　　SE0088
★George & Dragon　(01969) 663358
Just off A684; DL8 3AD Welcoming 17th-c posting inn with emphasis on good food from sandwiches to dishes such as venison wellington, two big dining areas,

small beamed and panelled bar with log fire, well kept ales including Black Sheep Bitter, Theakstons Best and a house beer from Yorkshire Dales, good choice of wines by the glass, friendly helpful staff; may be background music; children and dogs (in bar) welcome, nice paved garden, lovely scenery and walks, handy for Aysgarth Falls, seven bedrooms, open all day. *(Geoff and Linda Payne, Stuart Paulley, Malcolm and Jane Levitt)*

BARKISLAND   SE0419
★**Fleece** (01422) 820687
B6113 towards Ripponden; HX4 0DJ
Well renovated and extended 18th-c beamed moorland dining pub, very good food (all day from breakfast on, till 7pm Sun) including weekday set menu, efficient friendly uniformed staff, well kept Timothy Taylors Landlord and a couple of guests; background music, popular monthly comedy club; children welcome, lovely Pennine views from first-floor terrace and garden, five bedrooms, handy for M62, open all day from 9am. *(Gordon and Margaret Ormondroyd, Pat and Tony Martin, John and Eleanor Holdsworth)*

BARMBY-ON-THE-MARSH   SE6828
Kings Head (01757) 630705
High Street; DN14 7HT Renovated and extended early 19th-c beamed village pub, good locally sourced food including some imaginative choices, Yorkshire 'tapas', Sun lunchtime carvery, four well kept local ales, bar, lounge and restaurant, deli (home-baked bread to order); children welcome, disabled facilities, open all day weekends, closed Mon and Tues lunchtimes. *(Toby Jones)*

BARNSLEY   SE3203
Strafford Arms (01226) 287488
Near Northern College, about 2.5 miles NW of M1 junction 36; S75 3EW Pretty stone-built village pub owned by Fine & Country Inns, decent food (some cooked in Josper grill), Timothy Taylors ales and good range of wines, open fires including one in big Yorkshire range; free wi-fi; children, dogs and muddy boots welcome, on Trans Pennine Trail and by entrance to Wentworth Castle, open (and food) all day. *(Dr Simon Innes)*

BEDALE   SE2688
Old Black Swan (01677) 422973
Market Place; DL8 1ED Thriving old pub with attractive façade, generous helpings of good value popular food, friendly efficient staff, well kept ales including Theakstons, log fire, darts, pool; sports TV; children welcome, disabled facilities, small covered back terrace, Tues market, open all day. *(Emma Scofield)*

BEVERLEY   TA0339
White Horse (01482) 861973
Hengate, off North Bar; HU17 8BN
Known locally as Nellie's and a carefully preserved Victorian interior with basic little rooms huddled around central bar, brown leatherette seats (high-backed settles in one little snug) and plain chairs and benches on bare boards, antique cartoons and sentimental engravings, gas-lit chandelier, open fires, games room, upstairs family room, bargain Sam Smiths and guest beers, basic food; children till 7pm, no dogs, open all day. *(Belinda May)*

BEVERLEY   TA0239
Woolpack (01482) 867095
Westwood Road, W of centre; HU17 8EN
Small proper pub in pair of 19th-c cottages kept spotless by welcoming landlady, good traditional food at reasonable prices including Tues pie-and-pint night, seven well kept Marstons-related beers, cosy snug, open fires, simple furnishings, brasses, knick-knacks and prints; Thurs quiz; beer garden, open all day weekends, closed Mon lunchtime. *(C A Hall)*

BILTON   SE4750
Chequers (01423) 359637
Pub signed just off B1224; YO26 7NN
Quietly placed cream-washed inn, Black Sheep, Timothy Taylors and a summer guest, hearty helpings of good freshly made and often interesting food from hot and cold lunchtime sandwiches up, afternoon teas, linked areas with comfortable seating including leather armchairs and banquettes, woodburner, some open shelving separating part-panelled dining room; picnic-sets in small garden with extensive country views, three bedrooms, open all day (food all day Sun). *(Michael Doswell)*

BINGLEY   SE1242
Dick Hudsons (01274) 552121
Otley Road, High Eldwick; BD16 3BA
Well run Vintage Inn family dining pub, Black Sheep, Marstons and Timothy Taylors, lots of wines by the glass, their usual food served quickly by pleasant staff; tables out by cricket field, great views, open all day. *(Pat and Graham Williamson, Gordon and Margaret Ormondroyd)*

BIRSTWITH   SE2459
★**Station Hotel** (01423) 770254
Off B6165 W of Ripley; HG3 3AG
Welcoming immaculately kept stone-built Dales pub; bar, log-fire restaurant and garden room, good sensibly priced home-made food from extensive menu including lunchtime/

Half pints: by law, a pub should not charge more for half a pint than half the price of a full pint, unless it shows that half-pint price on its price list.

early evening set deal, four local ales and 14 wines by the glass, friendly efficient staff; open mike and quiz nights; tables in landscaped garden with heated smokers' shelter, picturesque valley, five bedrooms, open (and food) all day. *(M S Catling, Gordon and Jenny Quick, John and Eleanor Holdsworth)*

BOLTON ABBEY   SE0754
Devonshire Arms (01756) 710441
B6160; BD23 6AJ Comfortable and elegant 18th-c hotel in wonderful position on edge of Bolton Abbey Estate; good if pricey food from light meals up in bright modern brasserie-bar, good service, contemporary paintings (some for sale) on roughcast walls, colourful armchairs around cast-iron-framed tables on pale wood floor, four well kept Copper Dragon ales and good wines by the glass, afternoon teas, more formal restaurant; tables in spacious courtyard with extensive views, Estate and Strid river valley walks, bedrooms in old and new wings. *(Richard Kennell)*

BRADFIELD   SK2692
Old Horns (0114) 285 1207
High Bradfield; S6 6LG Welcoming old stone pub in hill village with stunning views; good hearty food including bargain weekday lunchtime deal and Sun carvery, can eat in partly flagstoned bar or carpeted pitch-roofed dining room, half a dozen predominantly Thwaites beers, friendly helpful staff; Tues quiz, background music and TV; children welcome, raised terrace taking in the view, picnic-sets and play area in garden, next to interesting 14th-c church, good walks, open all day. *(Roger and Pauline Pearce)*

BRADFORD   SE1533
Fighting Cock (01274) 726907
Preston Street (off B6145); BD7 1JE Busy bare-boards traditional alehouse by industrial estate, a dozen well kept changing ales, foreign draught/bottled beers and real ciders, friendly staff and lively atmosphere, all-day sandwiches plus good simple lunchtime hot dishes (not Sun), may be free bread and dripping on the bar, low prices, coal fires; open all day. *(Harvey Brown)*

BRADFORD   SE1533
New Beehive (01274) 721784
Westgate; BD1 3AA Robustly old-fashioned five-room Edwardian inn, plenty of period features including gas lighting, big mirrors, interesting paintings and coal fires, changing ales (mostly from smaller brewers) along with continental bottled beers, welcoming staff and friendly atmosphere, pool room, weekend live music in cellar bar; children welcome, nice back courtyard, 17 simple bedrooms, open all day (till 1am Fri, Sat), from 6pm Sun. *(Harvey Brown)*

BRADFORD   SE1633
Sparrow Bier Café (01677) 470411
North Parade; BD1 3HZ Bare-boards bar with great selection of bottled beers, draught continentals and local real ales, friendly knowledgeable staff, good deli platters and pies, local artwork, more tables in cellar bar; background music; open all day. *(Pat and Tony Martin)*

BRADFORD   SE1938
Stansfield Arms (0113) 250 2659
Apperley Lane, Apperley Bridge; off A658 NE; BD10 0NP Popular ivy-clad pub dating from the 16th c, enjoyable food including early-bird and other deals, well kept Black Sheep, Timothy Taylors Landlord and a guest, beams, friendly helpful service, stripped stone and dark panelling, restaurant; children welcome, tables out on front decking, pleasant setting, open all day till midnight (2am Fri, Sat) and can get very busy. *(John and Eleanor Holdsworth)*

BRAMHAM   SE4242
Swan (01937) 843570
Just off A1 2 miles N of A64; LS23 6QA Unspoilt and unchanging little local up steep hill from village square – also known as the 'Top Pub'; friendly atmosphere and good mix of customers, well kept Black Sheep, Hambleton and Leeds Pale, no food, two coal fires; open all day. *(Les and Sandra Brown, Michael Butler)*

BRANDESBURTON   TA1147
Dacre Arms (01964) 542392
Signed off A165 N of Beverley and Hornsea turn-offs; YO25 8RL Modernised old pub popular for its good value generously served food from lunchtime sandwiches to grills, also bargain OAP two-course deal and children's meals, friendly young staff, well kept ales such as John Smiths, Theakstons and Wold Top, restaurant; picnic-sets out in small fenced area, open (and food) all day Fri-Sun. *(C A Hall)*

BREARTON   SE3260
★ Malt Shovel (01423) 862929
Village signposted off A61 N of Harrogate; HG3 3BX Welcoming 15th-c dining pub continuing well under present owners; heavily beamed rooms with two open fires and woodburner, attractive mix of tables and chairs on wood or slate floors, some partitioning separating several eating areas, good food from light lunches up, helpful friendly staff, well kept Black Sheep, Timothy Taylors Landlord and a guest from linenfold oak counter, plenty of wines by the glass, airy conservatory; children welcome, tables under parasols in garden and pretty summer hanging baskets, circular walks from the pub, closed Sun evening, Mon. *(Derek and Sylvia Stephenson, Mr and Mrs D Hammond)*

BRIDGE HEWICK   SE3370
Black-a-moor (01765) 603511
Boroughbridge Road (B6265 E of Ripon); HG4 5AA Roomy family-run dining

pub with wide choice of popular home-cooked food including good value early-bird deal (lunchtime and evening), well kept local beers and good selection of wines, friendly young staff, sofas and woodburner in bar area; free wi-fi; children welcome, comfortable bedrooms. *(Duncan, Carol and Alistair Hallows, Janet and Peter Race)*

BROUGHTON   SD9450
★**Bull** (01756) 792065
A59; BD23 3AE Handsome carefully refurbished old inn, flagstones, exposed stone walls and lots of pale oak, built-in wall seats and mix of dining chairs around polished tables, open fires, good brasserie-style food including set menu (Mon-Thurs), Dark Horse, Moorhouses and Thwaites, a couple of proper ciders, ten wines by the glass and several malt whiskies, friendly service; children and dogs (in bar) welcome, rattan furniture on attractive front terrace, can walk through Broughton Estate's 3,000 acres of lovely parkland, open all day, food all day weekends. *(Dr Kevan Tucker)*

BUCKDEN   SD9477
Buck (01756) 761401
B6160; BD23 5JA Steps up to large creeper-clad stone pub-hotel; modernised and extended open-plan bar, log fire (stag's head above) and flagstones in original core, restaurant with high-backed chairs at linen-clothed tables, ample helpings of enjoyable food including specials, well kept Theakstons and guests, friendly helpful staff; children and dogs welcome, terrace with good surrounding moorland views, popular walking spot, 12 bedrooms, good breakfast, open (and food) all day. *(Peter Smith and Judith Brown)*

BURN   SE5928
★**Wheatsheaf** (01757) 270614
Main Road (A19 Selby–Doncaster); YO8 8LJ Welcoming busy mock-Tudor roadside pub, comfortable seats and tables in partly divided open-plan bar with masses to look at: air force wartime memorabilia, gleaming copper kettles, black dagging shears, polished buffalo horns, cases of model vans and lorries, decorative mugs above one bow-window seat, a drying rack over the log fire; John Smiths, Timothy Taylors and guests, 20 malt whiskies, straightforward food (not Sun-Weds evenings), roast only on Sun; pool table, games machine, TV and may be unobtrusive background music; children and dogs welcome, picnic-sets on heated terrace in small back garden, open all day till midnight. *(Emma Scofield)*

BURNSALL   SE0361
★**Red Lion** (01756) 720204
B6160 S of Grassington; BD23 6BU Family-run 16th-c inn in lovely spot by River Wharfe, attractively panelled, sturdily furnished front dining rooms with log fire, more basic back public bar, good imaginative

food, well kept ales such as Copper Dragon and Timothy Taylors, nice wines, efficient friendly service, conservatory; children welcome, tables out on front cobbles and on big back terrace, views across to Burnsall Fell, comfortable bedrooms (dogs allowed in some of these and in bar), fishing permits available, open all day, food all day weekends. *(Dr Simon Innes)*

BURTON LEONARD   SE3263
★**Hare & Hounds** (01765) 677355
Off A61 Ripon–Harrogate, handy for A1(M) junction 48; HG3 3SG Civilised and welcoming 19th-c village dining pub; good popular food from lunchtime sandwiches up using fresh local ingredients, set menu choices, well kept ales such as Black Sheep and Timothy Taylors, nice wines by the glass and decent coffee, efficient friendly service, cosy carpeted bar with woodburner, large dining area beyond; children in eating areas, pretty little back garden, closed Mon. *(Michael Butler, Peter Hacker)*

CARLTON   SE0684
Foresters Arms (01969) 640272
Off A684 W of Leyburn; DL8 4BB Old stone pub owned by local co-operative; log fire bar with dark low beams and flagstones, four well kept local ales and good range of popular affordably priced food, carpeted restaurant, events such as book club, children's cookery classes and fortnightly Tues quiz; disabled access, a few picnic-sets out at front, pretty village in heart of Yorkshire Dales National Park, lovely views, three bedrooms, open all day weekends, closed Mon lunchtime. *(Dr Peter Crawshaw, Gordon and Jenny Quick)*

CARLTON HUSTHWAITE   SE4976
Carlton Inn (01845) 501265
Butt Lane; YO7 2BW Cosy modernised beamed dining pub; good fairly priced food cooked by landlady including daily specials and lunchtime/early evening set menu, cheerful helpful service, John Smiths and Theakstons, local cider, mix of country furniture including some old settles, open fire; children welcome, dogs in back bar area, garden picnic-sets, open all day Sun, closed Mon. *(Walter and Susan Rinaldi-Butcher, Dr Peter Crawshaw)*

CARTHORPE   SE3083
★**Fox & Hounds** (01845) 567433
Village signed from A1 N of Ripon, via B6285; DL8 2LG Long-serving owners for neatly kept dining pub with emphasis on good well presented food, attractive high-raftered restaurant with lots of farm and smithy tools, Black Sheep and Worthington in L-shaped bar with two log fires, plush seating, plates on stripped beams and evocative Victorian photographs of Whitby, some theatrical memorabilia in corridors,

good friendly service; background classical music; children welcome, handy for A1, closed Mon and first week Jan. *(Janet and Peter Race)*

CATTAL SE4455
Victoria (01423) 330249
Station Road; YO26 8EB Bustling Victorian-themed dining pub, good nicely presented food (should book) from extensive menu including specials, charming attentive service, well kept ales with one from local Rudgate named for the landlord, good value wines; children welcome, picnic-sets in gravelled back garden, closed lunchtime (except Sun) and all day Mon, handy for station. *(Brian and Janet Ainscough, Les and Sandra Brown)*

CAWOOD SE5737
Ferry (01757) 268515
King Street (B1222 NW of Selby), by Ouse swing bridge; YO8 3TL Interesting 16th-c inn with several comfortable areas, enjoyable unpretentious food including good Sunday roasts, well kept ales, log fire in massive inglenook, low beams, stripped brickwork and bare boards; nice flagstone terrace and lawn down to river, bedrooms, open all day (from 3pm Mon). *(Pat and Graham Williamson)*

CHAPEL-LE-DALE SD7477
★ Old Hill Inn (01524) 241256
B6255 Ingleton–Hawes, 3 miles N of Ingleton; LA6 3AR Welcoming former farmhouse with fantastic views to Ingleborough and Whernside, a haven for weary walkers (wonderful remote surrounding walks); clean rustic interior with beams, log fires and bare-stone recesses, straightforward furniture on stripped-wood floors, nice pictures and some interesting local artefacts, Black Sheep, Dent and a guest, good wholesome food (not that cheap) including lovely puddings (look out for the landlord's sugar sculptures), separate dining room and sun lounge, relaxed chatty atmosphere; children welcome, dogs in bar, two bedrooms and space for five caravans, open all day Sat, closed Mon. *(Lynda and Trevor Smith)*

CLAPHAM SD7469
New Inn (01524) 251203
Off A65 N of Settle; LA2 8HH Stylishly renovated 18th-c riverside inn in famously pretty village, good well presented food in bar or restaurant including some interesting vegetarian options, local ales such as Copper Dragon, friendly staff; children and dogs welcome, tables outside, handy for walk to Ingleborough Cave or

more adventurous hikes, 20 refurbished bedrooms. *(Michael Butler)*

CLIFTON SE1622
★ Black Horse (01484) 713862
Westgate/Coalpit Lane; signed off Brighouse Road from M62 junction 25; HD6 4HJ Friendly 17th-c inn-restaurant, pleasant décor, front dining rooms with good interesting food including a few pubby dishes, can be pricey, efficient uniformed service, open fire in back bar with beam-and-plank ceiling, well kept Timothy Taylors Landlord and a house beer brewed by Brass Monkey, decent wines; nice courtyard, 21 comfortable bedrooms, pleasant village, open all day. *(Michael Butler)*

CLOUGHTON SE9798
Falcon (01723) 870717
Pub signed just off A171 out towards Whitby; YO13 0DY Big 19th-c country inn set in five-acre grounds, well divided opened-up interior including log-fire lounge and dining conservatory, enjoyable freshly made pubby food from sandwiches to daily specials, Theakstons and a guest, good choice of wines, distant sea view from end windows; background music; children welcome, picnic-sets in neat walled garden, good walks (leave muddy boots by the door), eight bedrooms and 11 camping pods, closed Mon, Tues in winter. *(Ian and Jane Irving)*

CLOUGHTON NEWLANDS TA0195
Bryherstones (01723) 870744
Newlands Road, off A171 in Cloughton; YO13 0AR Traditional stone pub with several interconnecting rooms including dining room up on right and flagstoned stable-theme bar on left, lighter bare-boards back room with open fire, extremely good food using locally sourced meat, Timothy Taylors and a house beer from Wold Top, good friendly service, games room (pool and darts); children and dogs welcome, picnic-sets and play area in sheltered back garden, closed lunchtimes Mon-Weds. *(Emma Scofield)*

COLTON SE5444
★ Old Sun (01904) 744261
Off A64 York–Tadcaster; LS24 8EP Top notch cooking at this extended 18th-c beamed dining pub, good wine list with plenty available by the glass, well kept Black Sheep and local guests (proper bar area), friendly competent staff; cookery demonstrations and little shop selling home-made and local produce; children welcome, seats out on sunny front terrace, bedrooms in separate building, open all day Sun (food till 7pm then). *(David and Carole Newton, Christian Mole, John and Eleanor Holdsworth)*

The letters and figures after the name of each town are its Ordnance Survey map reference. *Using the Guide* at the beginning of the book explains how it helps you find a pub, in road atlases or large-scale maps as well as in our own maps.

CONEYTHORPE   SE3958

★**Tiger** (01423) 863632
2.3 miles from A1(M) junction 47; A59
towards York, then village signposted
(and brown sign to Tiger Inn); bear left
at brown sign in Flaxby; HG5 0RY
Spreading red-carpeted bar with hundreds
of pewter tankards hanging from ochre-
painted joists, olde-worlde prints, china
figurines in one arched alcove, padded grey
wall seats, pews and settles around sturdy
scrubbed tables, open fire, more formal
back dining area, tasty sensibly priced food
from lunchtime sandwiches through pub
favourites, also set deals, well kept Black
Sheep, Copper Dragon and Timothy Taylors
Landlord, nice wines, friendly helpful staff;
nostalgic background music; picnic-sets
on front gravel terrace and on small green
opposite, open all day. *(Pat and Graham*
Williamson, Margaret and Peter Staples)

COXWOLD   SE5377

Fauconberg Arms (01347) 868214
Off A170 Thirsk–Helmsley, via Kilburn
or Wass; easily found off A19 too;
YO61 4AD 17th-c village pub under new
management; heavily beamed flagstoned
bar, log fires in both linked areas (one in
an unusual arched fireplace in a broad low
inglenook), some attractive oak chairs made
by local craftsmen alongside more usual
pub furnishings, old local photographs and
copper implements, Theakstons and a couple
of guests, proper cider and good range of
malt whiskies, enjoyable traditional home-
cooked food, friendly staff, elegant, gently
upmarket dining room; live music some
weekends, pool, free wi-fi; children welcome,
dogs in bar, views from terrace look across
fields to Byland Abbey (EH) ruins, picnic-sets
on front cobbles, eight bedrooms, open all
day. *(Duncan, Carol and Alistair Hallows, David*
and Carole Newton, John Harris, Gus Swan)

CROPTON   SE7588

New Inn (01751) 417330
Village signposted off A170 W of
Pickering; YO18 8HH Modernised
village pub with own Great Yorkshire beers
and guests (can tour brewery for £7.50 –
includes free pint); public bar with plush
seating, panelling and small fire, downstairs
conservatory (doubles as visitor centre at
busy times) and elegant restaurant with local
artwork, straightforward food; background
music, TV, games machine, darts and
pool; well behaved children and dogs (in
bar) welcome, garden and brewery shop,
bedrooms, open all day. *(P Dawn)*

DACRE BANKS   SE1961

★**Royal Oak** (01423) 780200
B6451 S of Pateley Bridge; HG3 4EN
Popular solidly comfortable 18th-c pub with
Nidderdale views, good traditional food
(not Sun evening) along with daily specials

and events such as summer crab festival,
attentive friendly staff, well kept Greene King
ales and good choice of wines by the glass,
interesting selection of gins too, beams and
panelling, log-fire dining room, games room
with darts, dominoes and pool; background
music, TV; children welcome in eating areas,
terrace and informal back garden, three
bedrooms, big breakfast, open all day.
(Dr Simon Innes)

DANBY   NZ7008

Duke of Wellington (01287) 660351
West Lane; YO21 2LY 18th-c creeper-clad
inn overlooking village green, usually four
Yorkshire ales such as Copper Dragon and
Daleside, enjoyable home-made food; clean,
tidy bedrooms. *(JHBS)*

DARLEY   SE1961

Wellington Arms (01423) 780362
B6451; Darley Head; HG3 2QQ Roadside
stone inn with fine Nidderdale views, beams
and big open fire, good freshly made food
(same menu lunchtime and evening), well
kept Black Sheep, Copper Dragon, Timothy
Taylors and Tetleys, helpful friendly staff;
dogs and children welcome, seats on large
grassed area, refurbished bedrooms, good
breakfast, open all day. *(Stanley and Annie*
Matthews)

DEWSBURY   SE2622

Huntsman (01924) 275700
Walker Cottages, Chidswell Lane, Shaw
Cross – pub signed; WF12 7SW Cosy
low-beamed converted cottages alongside
urban-fringe farm, lots of agricultural
bric-a-brac and blazing log fire, small front
extension, Timothy Taylors Landlord and
three guests, well priced home-made food
(lunchtimes Tues-Sat, evenings Thurs, Fri till
7.30pm), quiet relaxed atmosphere; open all
day weekends, closed Mon. *(Michael Butler)*

DEWSBURY   SE2421

★**West Riding Licensed**
Refreshment Rooms (01924) 459193
Station, Wellington Road; WF13 1HF
Convivial three-room early Victorian station
bar, eight well kept changing ales such as
Black Sheep, Oakham, Timothy Taylors and
Sportsman (brewed at their sister pub, the
Sportsman in Huddersfield), foreign bottled
beers and farm ciders, bargain generous
lunchtime food on scrubbed tables, popular
pie night Tues, world food night Thurs, good
Saturday breakfast too, friendly staff, lots
of steam memorabilia including paintings
by local artists, coal fire, daily papers,
impressive juke box and some live music;
children till 6pm in two end rooms, disabled
access, open all day. *(Jim and Sheila Wilson)*

DONCASTER   SE5702

Corner Pin (01302) 340670
St Sepulchre Gate West, Cleveland Street;
DN1 3AH Plush beamed lounge with old

local pub prints, welsh dresser and china, York Guzzler and interesting guests kept well (beer festivals), good value traditional home-made food including popular Sun lunch, friendly landlady, cheery public bar with darts, games machine and TV; back decking, open all day. *(P Dawn)*

DUNNINGTON   SE6751
Windmill (01904) 481898
Hull Road (A1079); YO19 5LP Welcoming dining pub, large and fairly modern, with generous helpings of popular home-made food served by friendly staff, good range of beers, back conservatory, quieter small raised dining area; ten bedrooms, open all day Sun. *(Harvey Brown)*

EASINGWOLD   SE5270
★George (01347) 821698
Market Place; YO61 3AD Neat, bright and airy market town hotel (former 18th-c coaching inn), quiet corners even when busy, helpful cheerful service, well kept Black Sheep, Moorhouses and a guest, good sensibly priced food in bar and restaurant, beams, horsebrasses and warm log fires, slightly old-fashioned feel and popular with older customers; pleasant bedrooms, good breakfast. *(Belinda Stamp)*

EAST MARTON   SD9050
Cross Keys (01282) 844326
A59 Gisburn–Skipton; BD23 3LP Comfortable and welcoming 18th-c pub behind small green looking down on Leeds & Liverpool Canal; heavy beams and big open fire, patterned carpets and bare boards, good freshly cooked food (Sun till 7pm) from shortish menu supplemented by interesting blackboard specials, well kept Copper Dragon and a guest like Theakstons, friendly service, more restauranty dining room; background music, daily newspapers, pool; children and dogs welcome, tables on front deck, near Pennine Way, open (and food) all day summer, food all day weekends in winter; refurbishment planned as we went to press. *(Chilliski, John and Sylvia Harrop)*

EAST MORTON   SE0941
Busfeild Arms (01274) 563169
Main Road; BD20 5SP Attractive 19th-c stone-built village pub (originally a school); traditionally furnished beamed and flagstoned bar with woodburner, Saltaire, Timothy Taylors, Tetleys and a guest, good range of enjoyable well priced food including gluten-free menu, weekday early-bird deal (5.30-6.30pm), efficient cheerful service, restaurant; Thurs quiz, live music Sat, sports TV; children welcome, picnic-sets on front terrace, three bedrooms, open all day, food

till 6pm Sun. *(John and Eleanor Holdsworth, Gordon and Margaret Ormondroyd)*

EAST WITTON   SE1487
★Cover Bridge Inn (01969) 623250
A6108 out towards Middleham; DL8 4SQ Cosy and welcoming 16th-c flagstoned country local, good choice of well kept Yorkshire-brewed ales and guest, generously served pub food at sensible prices, small restaurant, roaring fires; children and dogs welcome, riverside garden with play area, three bedrooms, open all day. *(Dr Simon Innes)*

EGTON   NZ8006
★Wheatsheaf (01947) 895271
Village centre; YO21 1TZ 19th-c village pub of real character, interesting pictures and collectables in small bare-boards bar with fire in old range, very good generously served food including fresh fish and seasonal game, friendly service, Black Sheep, Timothy Taylors Landlord and a summer guest, several wines by the glass, restaurant; four bedrooms in adjacent cottage, open all day weekends, closed Mon. *(P Dawn)*

EGTON BRIDGE   NZ8005
Horseshoe (01947) 895245
Village signed off A171 W of Whitby; YO21 1XE Attractively placed 18th-c stone inn with open fire, high-backed built-in winged settles, wall seats and spindleback chairs, various odds and ends including a big stuffed trout (caught nearby in 1913), Theakstons Best and a couple of guests, decent, traditional food; background music; children welcome, dogs in side bar during mealtimes, seats on quiet terrace in nice mature garden by small River Esk, good walks (on Coast to Coast path), six bedrooms, open all day weekends. *(P Dawn, Vikki and Matt Wharton)*

EGTON BRIDGE   NZ8005
★Postgate (01947) 895241
Village signed off A171 W of Whitby; YO21 1UX Moorland village pub next to station; good imaginative food at fair prices including fresh local fish, friendly staff, well kept Black Sheep and a guest, traditional quarry-tiled bar with beams, panelled dado and coal fire in antique range, elegant restaurant; children and dogs welcome, walled front garden with picnic-sets either side of brick path, three nice, clean bedrooms. *(Tina and David Woods-Taylor, P Dawn)*

ELLAND   SE1021
Barge & Barrel (01422) 371770
Quite handy for M62 junction 24;

We include some hotels with a good bar that offers facilities comparable to those of a pub.

Park Road (A6025, via A629 and B6114); HX5 9HP Large roadside pub by Calder & Hebble Navigation, own-brew beers along with plenty of guests including regulars Abbeydale, Black Sheep, Milltown and Timothy Taylors, pubby food, lounge bar, snug with open fire and games room; Thurs quiz and occasional live music; children welcome, waterside seats and moorings, limited parking, open all day. *(Tony Hobden)*

EMBSAY   SE0053

Elm Tree (01756) 790717

Elm Tree Square; BD23 6RB Popular open-plan beamed village pub, hearty helpings of good value food (different lunchtime and evening menus), four well kept ales such as Tetleys and Thwaites, cheerful young staff; comfortable bedrooms, handy for steam railway. *(Martin Denbigh)*

ETTON   SE9743

Light Dragoon (01430) 810282

3.5 miles N of Beverley, off B1248; Main Street; HU17 7PQ Roomy country local continuing well under present landlord, enjoyable good value food, two real ales and several wines by the glass, cheerful helpful staff, inglenook fireplace; children and muddy walkers welcome, small back garden with swings and slide, nice village on Wolds cycle route, open all day Sun, closed Mon. *(C A Hall)*

FERRENSBY   SE3660

★**General Tarleton** (01423) 340284

A655 N of Knaresborough; HG5 0PZ Carefully renovated 18th-c coaching inn, more restaurant-with-rooms than pub, but there's an informal bar with sofas and woodburner serving Black Sheep, Timothy Taylors Landlord and a dozen wines by the glass; other open-plan rooms with low beams, brick pillars creating alcoves, exposed stonework and dark leather high-backed dining chairs around wooden tables, first class modern cooking from owner-chef along with more traditional food and children's menu, good well trained staff; seats in covered courtyard and tree-lined garden, pretty country views, 13 stylish bedrooms, good breakfast. *(Dr P Brown, Richard Cole, Pat and Graham Williamson)*

FILEY   TA1180

Bonhommes (01723) 514054

The Crescent; YO14 9JH Friendly bustling bar with several well kept ales including one badged for them, popular food including Sunday lunch, live music and quiz nights; children and dogs welcome, open all day till late. *(Edward May)*

FINGHALL   SE1889

★**Queens Head** (01677) 450259

Off A684 E of Leyburn; DL8 5ND Welcoming comfortable dining pub, log fires either end of low-beamed bar with stone archway, settles making stalls around big tables, Theakstons and guests, good food from sandwiches, deli boards and traditional favourites up, midweek deals and Sat brunch, extended back dining room with Wensleydale view; children welcome, no dogs inside, disabled facilities, back garden with decking sharing same view, three bedrooms, open all day weekends in summer. *(Belinda Stamp)*

FIXBY   SE1119

Nags Head (01727) 871100

New Hey Road, by M62 junction 24 south side, past Hilton; HD2 2EA Spacious ivy-covered chain dining pub, appealing outside and comfortable in, pubby bar with four well kept ales, enjoyable fairly priced food including carvery and OAP deals, friendly helpful service, linked areas with wood and slate floors, restaurant on two levels; garden tables, bedrooms in adjoining Premier Inn, open all day. *(Gordon and Margaret Ormondroyd)*

GARGRAVE   SD9253

Masons Arms (01756) 749510

Church Street/Marton Road (off A65 NW of Skipton); BD23 3NL Welcoming beamed pub with friendly local atmosphere, open interior divided into bar, lounge and restaurant, log fire, ample helpings of enjoyable home-made food at very fair prices, well kept ales such as Black Sheep, Copper Dragon, Tetleys and Timothy Taylors from ornate counter; live acoustic music first Fri of month in winter, darts; children and dogs welcome, tables out behind overlooking own bowling green, charming village on Pennine Way and not far from Leeds & Liverpool Canal, six bedrooms in converted barn, open (and food) all day. *(Michael Butler)*

GIGGLESWICK   SD8164

★**Black Horse** (01729) 822506

Church Street – take care with the car park; BD24 0BE Hospitable licensees in 17th-c village pub prettily set by church; cosy bar with gleaming brass, copper and bric-a-brac, coal-effect fire, good value generous food, well kept Timothy Taylors, Tetleys and guests, intimate dining room, good service; piano (often played), monthly quiz; children welcome till 9pm, no dogs, sheltered heated back terrace, smokers' shelter, three reasonably priced comfortable bedrooms and good breakfast, open all day weekends; for sale as we went to press, but business as usual. *(M and GR)*

GIGGLESWICK   SD8164

Harts Head (01729) 822086

Belle Hill; BD24 0BA Cheerful bustling 18th-c village inn, comfortable carpeted bar/lounge with well kept Caledonian, Kirkby Lonsdale, Tetleys and three guests, good choice of enjoyable reasonably priced food, restaurant, residents' snooker room; sports TV; picnic-sets on sloping lawn, ten bedrooms, open all day Fri-Sun, closed lunchtimes Tues, Thurs. *(Toby Jones)*

GILLAMOOR SE6890
★ **Royal Oak** (01751) 431414
Off A170 in Kirkbymoorside; YO62 7HX
Stone-built 18th-c dining pub with interesting locally sourced food at sensible prices including specials, friendly staff, ales such as Black Sheep and Copper Dragon, reasonably priced wines, roomy bar with heavy dark beams, log fires in two tall stone fireplaces (one with old kitchen range), overspill dining room (dogs allowed here); children welcome, eight comfortable modern bedrooms, good breakfast, attractive village handy for Barnsdale Moor walks. *(Stanley and Annie Matthews)*

GILLING EAST SE6176
★ **Fairfax Arms** (01439) 788212
Main Street (B1363, off A170 via Oswaldkirk); YO62 4JH Smart country inn, beamed bar with bare boards by handsome oak counter, carpeted area with woodburner, Black Sheep, Tetleys and some interesting wines by the glass, daily newspapers, two-part carpeted dining room with big hunting prints on red walls, nicely old-fashioned floral curtains and some padded oak settles, modern food plus pubby choices, neat black-aproned staff; picnic-sets out in front by floodlit roadside stream, pleasant village well placed for Howardian Hills and North York Moors, comfortable up-to-date bedrooms, good breakfast, open all day weekends. *(Mungo Shipley)*

GLUSBURN SD9944
Dog & Gun (01535) 633855
Colne Road (A6068 W); BD20 8DS
Sizeable stone pub, attractive inside and out, and very popular for its wide choice of enjoyable good value food, quick cheerful service, well kept Timothy Taylors ales; children welcome, tables out in front and on small roof terrace, open (and food) all day. *(Gordon and Margaret Ormondroyd)*

GOATHLAND NZ8200
Mallyan Spout Hotel
(01947) 896486 *Opposite church; YO22 5AN* Old creeper-clad stone hotel with three spacious lounges and traditional bar, open fires and fine views, fairly priced bar food and Sun lunchtime carvery, three real ales, good malt whiskies and wines, friendly helpful staff, smart restaurant; well behaved children in eating areas, handy for namesake waterfall, comfortable bedrooms and good buffet breakfast, open all day. *(Emma Scofield)*

GOODMANHAM SE8943
Goodmanham Arms (01430) 873849
Main Street; YO43 3JA Unpretentious little red-brick country pub (not to everyone's taste) with three traditional linked areas,

beam-and-plank ceilings, some red and black floor tiles, mix of furniture and plenty of interesting odds and ends, even a Harley-Davidson, seven real ales – three from on-site All Hallows microbrewery, unfussy food from italian chef-owner (no starters) including a winter casserole cooked over the open fire, evening meals served 5-7pm Mon and Fri only, occasional acoustic music; outside gents'; children and dogs welcome, good walks (on Wolds Way), open all day.
(P Dawn, R Anderson)

GRANGE MOOR SE2215
Kaye Arms (01924) 840228
Wakefield Road (A642); WF4 4BG
Smartly refurbished dining pub divided into three distinct areas, very popular good value food including deals, well kept ales and plenty of wines by the glass, efficient friendly service; handy for National Coal Mining Museum, open all day weekends. *(Gordon and Margaret Ormondroyd, Michael Butler and others)*

GRASSINGTON SE0064
★ **Devonshire** (01756) 752525
The Square; BD23 5AD Handsome old stone hotel, reliably run, with cheerful bustling atmosphere, good window seats and tables outside overlooking sloping village square, enjoyable generously served pubby food from sandwiches up, Fri fish night, well kept Black Sheep, Copper Dragon, Moorhouses and Tetleys, plenty of wines by the glass, bar, snug and spacious restaurant, interesting pictures and ornaments, beams and open fires; children and dogs (in bar) welcome, seven comfortable bedrooms, open (and food) all day. *(Dr Kevan Tucker)*

GRASSINGTON SE0064
Foresters Arms (01756) 752349
Main Street; BD23 5AA Comfortable opened-up old coaching inn with friendly bustling atmosphere, good reasonably priced hearty food, well kept ales including Black Sheep, cheerful helpful service, log fires, dining room off on right, pool and sports TV on left; popular Mon quiz; children welcome, tables outside, 14 affordable bedrooms (ones over bar noisy), good breakfast, fine walking country, open all day. *(Anon)*

GREAT AYTON NZ5610
Royal Oak (01642) 200283
Off A173 – follow village signs; High Green; TS9 6BW Popular 18th-c village inn with good promptly served traditional food including deals, well kept Caledonian Deuchars IPA and Theakstons, convivial bar with log fire, beam-and-plank ceiling and bulgy old partly panelled stone walls, traditional furnishings including antique settles, pleasant views of elegant green from bay windows, two linked dining rooms, back one appealingly old-fashioned and catering for tour groups; children welcome, dogs in

bar, four comfortable bedrooms, handy for Cleveland Way, open (and food) all day. *(WAH)*

GREAT BROUGHTON   NZ5405
Bay Horse (01642) 712319
High Street; TS9 7HA Big creeper-clad dining pub in attractive village, wide choice of food including blackboard specials and good value set lunch, friendly attentive service, real ales such as Camerons and Jennings, restaurant; children welcome, seats outside, open (and food) all day weekends. *(Belinda Stamp)*

GREAT HABTON   SE7576
★**Grapes** (01653) 669166
Corner of Habton Lane and Kirby Misperton Lane; YO17 6TU Traditionally refurbished and genuinely friendly beamed dining pub in small village, homely and cosy, with good cooking including fresh local fish and game, home-baked bread, Marstons-related ales, open fire, small public bar with darts and TV; background music; a few roadside picnic-sets (water for dogs), nice walks, open all day Sun, closed Mon, lunchtime Tues. *(Dr Simon Innes)*

GUISELEY   SE1941
Coopers (01943) 878835
Otley Road; LS20 8AH Small, cosy conversion of former Co-operative store, open-plan bare-boards bar with good range of food from lunchtime sandwiches up, eight real ales including Black Sheep and Timothy Taylors, music nights in upstairs function/dining room; open all day. *(Harvey Brown)*

HALIFAX   SE0924
Three Pigeons (01422) 347001
Sun Fold, South Parade; off Church Street; HX1 2LX Carefully restored, four-room 1930s pub (Grade II listed), art deco fittings, ceiling painting in octagonal main area, original flooring, panelling and tiled fireplaces with log fires, at least five Ossett ales along with Fernandes, Rat and sometimes Fullers, good Robinson's pies, friendly chatty staff; tables outside, handy for Eureka! museum and Shay Stadium (pub very busy on match days), open all day Fri-Sun, from 4pm other days. *(Eric Larkham, Pat and Tony Martin)*

HARDEN   SE0838
Malt (01535) 272357
Wilsden Road, off B6429; BD16 1BG Handsome recently refurbished dark stone pub (part of the small Pickles group), neat beamed rooms with flagstones and painted panelling, log fires, decent choice of popular sensibly priced food from hot or cold sandwiches and deli platters to specials, Theakstons ales, pleasant staff, sizeable new dining conservatory with raised woodburner; background music, Mon quiz; children and dogs welcome, picnic-sets in fenced garden,

lovely streamside spot, open all day (food all day Sun till 6pm). *(John and Eleanor Holdsworth)*

HARDRAW   SD8691
★**Green Dragon** (01969) 667392
Village signed off A684; DL8 3LZ Friendly traditional Dales pub dating from 13th c and full of character; stripped stone, antique settles on flagstones, lots of bric-a-brac, low-beamed snug with fire in old iron range, another in big main bar, five well kept ales including one badged for them from Yorkshire Dales, generously served food, small restaurant; annual brass band competition and other live music; children and dogs welcome, ten bedrooms, bunkhouse and camping, next to Hardraw Force (England's highest single-drop waterfall). *(J R Wildon, Eddie Edwards, Tracey and Stephen Groves)*

HAROME   SE6482
★**Star** (01439) 770397
High Street; village signed S of A170, E of Helmsley; YO62 5JE Restaurant-with-rooms in pretty 14th-c thatched building, but bar does have informal feel; bowed beam-and-plank ceiling, plenty of bric-a-brac, interesting furniture including 'Mousey' Thompson pieces, log fire and well polished tiled kitchen range, inventive ambitious cooking from chef-owner (not cheap), three changing ales and plenty of wines by the glass, home-made fruit liqueurs, snacks served in cocktail bar, coffee loft in the eaves, well trained helpful staff; background music; children welcome, seats on sheltered front terrace, more in garden, open all day Sun, closed Mon lunchtime. *(B R Merritt, Geoff and Linda Payne, J F M and M West)*

HARPHAM   TA0961
St Quintin Arms (01262) 490329
Main Street; YO25 4QY Comfortable old village pub with enjoyable reasonably priced home-made food (not Sun evening) including plenty of specials, well kept Tetleys and Wold Top, friendly landlord and staff, wide mix of customers in small dining room; sheltered garden with pond, on National Cycle Route 1, three bedrooms, open all day Sun, closed lunchtimes Mon and Tues. *(Dr Simon Innes)*

HARROGATE   SE3155
Coach & Horses (01423) 561802
West Park; HG1 1BJ Very friendly bustling pub with half a dozen good Yorkshire brewed ales, over 30 gins and 80 malt whiskies, enjoyable lunchtime food at bargain prices, obliging service, nice interior with booth seating; no children, dogs allowed after 4pm, open all day. *(Emma Scofield)*

HARROGATE   SE2955
★**Hales** (01423) 725570
Crescent Road; HG1 2RS Classic Victorian décor in 18th-c gas-lit local close to Pump

Rooms, leather seats in alcoves, stuffed birds, comfortable saloon and tiny snug, half a dozen ales including Daleside, simple good value lunchtime food, friendly helpful staff; can get lively weekend evenings, open all day. *(Emma Scofield)*

HARROGATE   SE2955
★ **Old Bell** (01423) 507930
Royal Parade; HG1 2SZ Thriving Market Town Tavern with eight mainly local beers from handsome counter, lots of bottled continentals and impressive choice of wines by the glass, friendly helpful staff, traditional lunchtime snacks including sandwiches, more elaborate evening meals upstairs, bare boards and panelling, old sweet shop ads and breweriana, daily newspapers; no children; dogs welcome, open all day. *(Michael Butler, Steve Ickringill)*

HARROGATE   SE3055
Swan on the Stray (01423) 524587
Corner of Devonshire Place and A59; HG1 4AA Market Town Tavern with enjoyable fairly priced food from shortish menu plus a few specials, eight mostly local ales, good range of imported beers and several ciders, cheerful efficient service, daily newspapers; dogs welcome, open all day (food till 6pm Sun). *(Brian and Janet Ainscough, Steve Ickringill)*

HARROGATE   SE3155
Winter Gardens (01423) 877010
Royal Baths, Crescent Road; HG1 2RR Interesting Wetherspoons transformation of former ballroom in landmark building, well kept ales, generous usual good value food, many original features, comfortable sofas in lofty hall, upper gallery; very busy late evening; attractive terrace, open all day. *(Emma Scofield)*

HAWES   SD8789
Crown (01969) 667212
Market Place; DL8 3RD Traditional market town local divided into four areas, hearty helpings of good value pub food, four well kept Theakstons ales and a couple of guests, polite efficient service, open fires/woodburners, interesting old photos; free wi-fi; children, walkers and dogs welcome, seats out on cobbled front forecourt and in back split-level beer garden with lovely Wensleydale views, three bedrooms. *(Eddie Edwards)*

HAWES   SD8789
Old Board (01969) 667223
Market Place; DL8 3RD Traditional single-bar pub, Black Sheep, Timothy Taylors, Theakstons and a couple of guests, generous reasonably priced home-made food, friendly helpful staff, popular with locals in the evening; children and dogs welcome, seats out in front, bedrooms, good breakfast, open all day. *(Eddie Edwards)*

HAWES   SD8789
White Hart (01969) 667214
Main Street; DL8 3QL Friendly recently renovated coaching inn, emphasis on good fairly priced food, bar with fire in antique range, restaurant; children and dogs welcome, five bedrooms, open (and food) all day. *(Eddie Edwards)*

HAWNBY   SE5489
Inn at Hawnby (01439) 798202
Aka Hawnby Hotel; off B1257 NW of Helmsley; YO62 5QS Pleasantly situated inn with good local food including some interesting choices, helpful welcoming service, Black Sheep, Great Newsome and Timothy Taylors, good choice of wines by the glass; children and dogs (in bar) welcome, lovely views from restaurant and garden tables, pretty village in walking country (packed lunches available), nine quiet bedrooms (three in converted stables over road), open all day Fri-Sun. *(Edward May)*

HEADINGLEY   SE2736
Arcadia (0113) 274 5599
Arndale Centre; LS6 2UE Small Market Town Tavern in former bank, good choice of changing regional ales, lots of continental bottled beers and good range of wines, knowledgeable staff, bar food (Thurs-Sun), stairs to mezzanine; no children; open all day. *(Peter Smith and Judith Brown)*

HEATH   SE3520
Kings Arms (01924) 377527
Village signposted from A655 Wakefield-Normanton – or, more directly, turn off to the left opposite Horse & Groom; WF1 5SL Old-fashioned gas-lit pub with genuine character, fire in black range (long row of smoothing irons on the mantelpiece), plain elm stools, built-in oak settles and dark panelling, well kept Ossett and several guests, standard food (all day Fri and Sat, till 7pm Sun), more comfortable extension preserving the original style, two other small flagstoned rooms and a conservatory; summer folk events, Tues quiz; children and dogs (in bar) welcome, benches out at front facing village green (surrounded by fine 19th-c stone merchants' houses), picnic-sets on side lawn and in nice walled garden, open all day (may shut early if quiet). *(C A Hall)*

HEBDEN   SE0263
Clarendon (01756) 752446
B6265; BD23 5DE Pleasant well cared-for pub under new licensees and newly refurbished; surrounded by wonderful moorland walking country; bar, snug and dining area, open fire, Thwaites and good variety of interesting and enjoyable food including blackboard choices, cheerful relaxed atmosphere; children welcome,

farm shop, three bedrooms, open all day weekends (food all day Sun). *(B and M Kendall)*

HEBDEN BRIDGE SD9922

Hinchcliffe Arms (01422) 883256

Off B6138; HX7 5TA Friendly stone-built pub in great walking country on the Calderdale Way and near Stoodley Pike; open-plan with bar area to the left and slightly smarter restaurant to the right, coal fire, four real ales and enjoyable food from pub favourites up, good informal service; children and dogs (in bar) welcome, a few seats out at front, close to stream and Victorian church, open all day weekends, closed Mon, lunchtime Tues. *(Dr Kevan Tucker)*

HEBDEN BRIDGE SD9927

Old Gate (01422) 843993 *Oldgate; HX7 8JP* Bar-restaurant with buzzy atmosphere, wide choice of good value all-day food (till 7pm Sun), nine well kept ales and plenty of bottled beers, lots of wines by glass including champagne, bar popular with young people, upstairs room for comedy club and other events; children welcome, tables outside, open all day. *(Jim and Sheila Wilson)*

HEBDEN BRIDGE SD9827

Stubbings Wharf (01422) 844107

About a mile W; HX7 6LU Friendly pub in good spot by Rochdale Canal with adjacent moorings, popular good value food (all day weekends, booking advised) from sandwiches and light meals up, half a dozen well kept regional ales, proper ciders; children and dogs welcome, boat trips, open all day. *(Jim and Sheila Wilson)*

HELMSLEY SE6183

Feathers (01439) 770275

Market Place; YO62 5BH Substantial stone inn with sensibly priced generous food from sandwiches to popular Sun carvery, well kept Black Sheep, Tetleys and a guest, good friendly service, several rooms with comfortable seats, oak and walnut tables (some by Robert 'Mouseman' Thompson – as is the bar counter), flagstones or tartan carpet, heavy medieval beams and huge inglenook log fire, panelled corridors; children welcome in eating area, tables out in front, 22 comfortable bedrooms, open all day. *(Chris Willers)*

HELWITH BRIDGE SD8169

Helwith Bridge Inn

Off B6479 N of Stainforth; BD24 0EH Friendly unpretentious village local popular with walkers, up to eight well kept ales in flagstoned bar, enjoyable reasonably priced pub food (all day weekends), dining room with light wood furniture on bare boards; children welcome, camping and basic bunkhouse, by River Ribble and Settle–Carlisle railway, open all day. *(Mike Swan)*

HEPWORTH SE1606

Butchers Arms (01484) 687147

Village signposted off A616 SE of Holmfirth; Towngate; HD9 1TE Old country dining pub with enjoyable french-influenced food (till 7pm Sun, not Mon evening) including good value set menu, three well kept Yorkshire ales and decent wines by the glass, friendly staff, flagstones by counter, bare boards elsewhere, log fire, low beams (handsomely carved in room on right – a particularly nice beam-and-plank ceiling); children, walkers and dogs welcome, terrace seating, open all day. *(Karen Percival)*

HOLMFIRTH SD1408

Nook (01484) 681568

Victoria Square/South Lane; HD9 2DN Friendly tucked-away 18th-c stone local (aka Rose & Crown) with own-brew beers and guests, no-frills bar areas with flagstones and quarry tiles, big open fire, low-priced home-made pubby food including good burgers, adjoining tapas bar; juke box and some live music, pool; heated streamside terrace, bedrooms, open (and food) all day. *(Belinda Stamp)*

HORBURY SE2918

Boons (01924) 277267

Queen Street; WF4 6LP Lively, chatty and comfortably unpretentious flagstoned local, Clarkes, John Smiths, Timothy Taylors Landlord and up to four quickly changing guests, pleasant young staff, no food, rugby league memorabilia, warm fire, back tap room with pool and TV; no children, courtyard tables, open all day Fri-Sun. *(Michael Butler)*

HORBURY SE2917

Bulls Head (01924) 265526

Southfield Lane; WF4 5AR Large open-plan dining pub popular locally for its food (particularly Sun lunch), smart attentive staff, Black Sheep and Tetleys, lots of wines by the glass; front picnic-sets. *(Michael Butler)*

HORBURY SE2918

Cricketers (01924) 267032

Cluntergate; WF4 5AG Welcoming refurbished Edwardian pub, Bosuns, Timothy Taylors and six local guests including Sportsman (brewed at their sister pub in Huddersfield), also craft beers such as BrewDog, real cider and good selection of spirits, reasonably priced cheeseboards and meze platters; Weds quiz, monthly acoustic night and regular beer festivals; open all day Fri-Sun, from 4pm other days. *(Michael Butler)*

HORSFORTH SE2438

Town Street Tavern (0113) 281 9996

Town Street; LS18 4RJ Market Town Tavern with eight well kept ales and lots of draught/bottled continental beers, good generous food in small bare-boards bar and upstairs evening bistro (closed Sun), good service; children and dogs welcome, small terrace, open all day. *(Dr Simon Innes)*

HUBBERHOLME   SD9278

★**George** (01756) 760223

Dubbs Lane; BD23 5JE Ancient little Dales inn, beautifully placed and run by friendly licensees; heavy beams, flagstones and stripped stone, enjoyable fairly priced home-made food including good steak and ale pie (booking advised evenings), Black Sheep and three guests, open fire, perpetual candle on bar; outside lavatories; children allowed in dining area, dogs usually welcome (but ask first), terrace seating, River Wharfe fishing rights, six comfortable clean bedrooms (three in annexe), good breakfast, closed Mon lunchtime, Tues, otherwise open all day. *(Steve Lumb, Claes Mauroy)*

HUDDERSFIELD   SE1416

Grove (01484) 430113

Spring Grove Street; HD1 4BP Friendly two-bar pub with huge selection of bottled beers, 18 well kept/priced ales including Magic Rock, Timothy Taylors and Thornbridge, 120 malt whiskies and 60 vodkas, also real cider, knowledgeable staff, no food but choice of snacks from dried crickets to biltong, regular live music (Tues and Thurs evenings), art gallery; children and dogs welcome, back terrace, open all day. *(Harvey Brown)*

HUDDERSFIELD   SE1416

Head of Steam (01484) 454533

St Georges Square, part of the station (direct access to platform 1); HD1 1JF Railway memorabilia and old advertising signs, model trains, cars, buses and planes for sale, long bar with up to ten changing ales, lots of bottled beers, farm ciders and perry, good choice of enjoyable well priced food, black leather easy chairs and sofas, hot coal fire, back buffet, some live jazz and blues nights in lounge; unobtrusive background music, can be very busy; open all day. *(Jim and Sheila Wilson)*

HUDDERSFIELD   SE1416

Kings Head (01484) 511058

Station, St Georges Square; HD1 1JF Victorian station building housing friendly well run pub (perhaps more utilitarian than the alternative Head of Steam); large open-plan room with original tiled floor, two smaller rooms off, ten well kept beers, good sandwiches and cobs, some live afternoon/evening music, Jimi Hendrix pub sign; disabled access via platform 1, open all day. *(Harvey Brown)*

HUDDERSFIELD   SE1416

Rat & Ratchet (01484) 542400

Chapel Hill; HD1 3EB Split-level flagstone and bare-boards local with its own-brew

beers and several guests such as Fullers, Pictish and Ossett, good range of farm ciders/perries too, pork pies and sausage rolls, friendly staff, some brewery memorabilia and music posters, pinball machine; open all day Fri-Sun, from 3pm other days. *(Harvey Brown)*

HUDDERSFIELD   SE1417

Slubbers Arms (01484) 429032

Halifax Old Road; HD1 6HW Friendly V-shaped traditional three-room pub, good range of beers including Timothy Taylors from horseshoe bar, pie-and-peas menu, black and white photographs and old wartime posters, warm fire, games room; well behaved dogs welcome, terrace for smokers, open all day and busy on match days. *(Harvey Brown)*

HUDDERSFIELD   SE1417

Sportsman 07766 131123

St Johns Road; HD1 5AY Same owners as the West Riding Licensed Refreshment Rooms at Dewsbury; eight real ales including Black Sheep, Timothy Taylors and their own beers (brewed in the cellar), regular beer festivals, good value food such as meat and cheese boards, hot lunchtime food Fri-Sun (bargain roast), comfortable lounge and two cosy side rooms; handy for station, open all day. *(Tony Hobden)*

HUDDERSFIELD   SE1415

Star (01484) 545443

Albert Street, Lockwood; HD1 3PJ Unpretentious friendly local with excellent range of competitively priced ales kept well by enthusiastic landlady, continental beers and farm cider, beer festivals in back marquee, open fire; open all day weekends, closed Mon and lunchtimes Tues-Fri. *(Edward May)*

HUDSWELL   NZ1400

George & Dragon (01748) 518373

Hudswell Lane; DL11 6BL Popular community-owned village pub under newish landlord, enjoyable reasonably priced home-made food including daily specials, well kept ales such as Copper Dragon, Daleside and Rudgates, various craft beers like BrewDog and Revisionist, friendly atmosphere; small shop and library, free wi-fi; children and dogs welcome, panoramic Swaledale views from back terrace, open all day weekends (food all day Sun till 6pm). *(Ms S Young)*

HULL   TA1028

★**Olde White Harte** (01482) 326363

Passage off Silver Street; HU1 1JG Ancient pub with Civil War history, carved heavy beams, attractive stained glass and two big inglenooks with frieze of delft tiles, well kept Caledonian, Theakstons and guests from copper-topped counter, 80 or so malt whiskies; old skull displayed in a Perspex case (found here in the 19th c); children welcome, dogs in bar, heated courtyard, open all day. *(Belinda Stamp)*

HULL   TA0929
Whalebone (01482) 226648
Wincolmlee; HU2 0PA Friendly local brewing its own good value ales such as Neck Oil, also Copper Dragon, Tetley, Timothy Taylors Landlord and other guests, real ciders and perry, no food, old-fashioned décor and plenty of memorabilia including Hull City AFC and black and white photos of closed local pubs; open all day. *(Mungo Shipley)*

HUTTON-LE-HOLE   SE7089
Crown (01751) 417343
The Green; YO62 6UA Overlooking pretty village green with wandering sheep in classic coach-trip country; enjoyable home-made pubby food (not Sun evening), Black Sheep, Tetleys and a guest, decent wines by the glass, cheerful efficient service, opened-up bar with varnished woodwork, dining area; quiz first Sun of month; children and clean dogs welcome, small site available for caravans behind, Ryedale Folk Museum next door and handy for Farndale walks, open all day Sun till 6pm, closed winter Mon, Tues. *(Belinda Stamp)*

ILKLEY   SE1147
Bar t'at (01943) 608888
Cunliffe Road; LS29 9DZ Extended Market Town Tavern pub, eight mainly Yorkshire ales kept well, good wine and bottled beer choice, enjoyable well priced pubby food from sandwiches and snacks up, candlelit cellar dining area, friendly service; upstairs loos; dogs welcome, back terrace with heated canopy, open all day, food all day Fri and Sat, till 6pm Sun. *(Steve Ickringill, Pat and Tony Martin)*

ILKLEY   SE1147
Ilkley Moor Vaults (01943) 607012
Stockeld Road/Stourton Road, off A65 Leeds–Skipton; LS29 9HD Atmospheric flagstoned pub with good home-made food including own-smoked fish and meats, Sunday roasts and summer barbecues, well kept Caledonian Deuchars IPA, Theakstons Black Bull, Timothy Taylors Landlord and a guest, decent wines by the glass, friendly helpful service, log fire; children welcome, open all day weekends, closed Mon. *(John and Eleanor Holdsworth)*

KEIGHLEY   SE0641
Boltmakers Arms (01535) 661936
East Parade; BD21 5HX Small open-plan split-level character local, friendly and bustling, with full Timothy Taylors range and a guest kept well, malt whiskies and farm cider, keen prices, limited food, lots to look at including brewing pictures and celebrity photos, coal fire; Tues quiz, some live music, sports TV; short walk from Keighley & Worth Valley Railway, open all day. *(Martin Jones)*

KELD   NY8900
Keld Lodge (01748) 886259
Butthouse Rigg (B6270); DL11 6LL Remote former youth hostel now serving as village inn, three well kept Black Sheep ales and tasty sensibly priced food, good service, various rooms including conservatory-style restaurant with superb Swaledale views; children and dogs welcome, well liked by Coast to Coast walkers, 11 popular bedrooms, open all day. *(Harvey Brown)*

KETTLESING   SE2257
★ Queens Head (01423) 770263
Village signposted off A59 W of Harrogate; HG3 2LB Popular stone pub with very good well priced traditional food, L-shaped carpeted main bar with lots of close-set cushioned dining chairs and tables, open fires, little heraldic shields on walls, 19th-c song sheet covers and lithographs of Queen Victoria, delft shelf of blue and white china, smaller bar on left with built-in red banquettes and cricketing prints, life-size portrait of Elizabeth I in lobby, well kept Black Sheep, Roosters and Theakstons, efficient friendly service; background radio; children welcome, seats in neatly kept suntrap back garden, benches in front by lane, eight bedrooms, open all day Sun. *(Margaret and Peter Staples, John and Eleanor Holdsworth, Robert Wivell)*

KETTLEWELL   SD9672
Blue Bell (01756) 760230
Middle Lane; BD23 5QX Roomy knocked-through 17th-c coaching inn with friendly, cheerful landlord, Copper Dragon ales kept well and enjoyable home-made food using local ingredients, low beams and snug simple furnishings, old country photographs, daily newspapers, woodburner, restaurant; Sun quiz, TV and free wi-fi; children welcome, shaded picnic-sets on cobbles facing bridge over the Wharfe, six annexe bedrooms, open (and food) all day. *(Emma Scofield)*

KETTLEWELL   SD9772
★ Kings Head (01756) 761600
The Green; BD23 5RD Refurbished old pub tucked away near church, flagstoned main bar with log fire in big stone inglenook, three local ales and well chosen wines, good affordably priced food (all day Sun till 7pm) cooked by chef-landlord from pub favourites to imaginative restaurant dishes, efficient friendly service; children welcome, no dogs inside, six renovated bedrooms named after kings, attractive village and good surrounding walks, closed Mon, otherwise open all day. *(B and M Kendall)*

KETTLEWELL   SD9672
★ Racehorses (01756) 760233
B6160 N of Skipton; BD23 5QZ Comfortable, civilised and friendly two-bar inn with dining area, enjoyable sensibly

priced food, three well kept Timothy Taylors ales, good log fire; children welcome, dogs in bar areas, front and back terrace seating, pretty village well placed for Wharfedale walks, parking can be difficult, 13 good bedrooms, open all day. *(Jeremy King)*

KILBURN SE5179
Forresters Arms (01347) 868386
Between A170 and A19 SW of Thirsk; YO61 4AH Welcoming beamed inn next to Robert Thompson furniture workshops (early examples of his work in both bars); roaring fires, well kept local ales and good choice of food including home-made ice-cream and cakes, lounge and restaurant; background music, TV; children welcome, dogs in some areas, suntrap seats out in front, smokers' shelter at back, ten decent bedrooms, open all day. *(Emma Scofield)*

KIRBY HILL NZ1406
Shoulder of Mutton (01748) 822772
Off A66 NW of Scotch Corner, via Ravensworth; DL11 7JH Welcoming bustle and character landlady at this 18th-c ivy-clad village inn, good freshly made pub food (not Mon, Tues), friendly accommodating staff, Daleside and up to four guests, front bar areas linking to long back restaurant, open fires; children and dogs (in bar) welcome, fine Holmedale views from picnic-sets behind and from bedrooms (you do hear the tuneful church bell), closed Mon and Tues lunchtimes. *(Gerry Price)*

KIRKBY OVERBLOW SE3249
Shoulder of Mutton (01423) 871205
Main Street; HG3 1HD Creeper-clad 19th-c village pub with three linked areas, bare boards or flagstones, comfortable banquettes, open fire and woodburner, well kept ales such as Black Sheep and Timothy Taylors Landlord and plenty of wines by the glass, good freshly prepared food (all day Sun till 7pm) including early-bird menu, friendly attentive service; quiz second Sun of month; picnic-sets in back garden, closed Mon. *(Margaret and Peter Staples, John and Eleanor Holdsworth)*

KIRKBYMOORSIDE SE6986
George & Dragon (01751) 433334
Market Place; YO62 6AA Family-run 17th-c coaching inn, front bar with beams and panelling, tub seats around wooden tables on carpet or stripped wood, log fire, good choice of well kept ales and several malt whiskies, enjoyable generous bar food, afternoon teas, good service; also a snug, bistro and more formal restaurant; background music; children welcome, seats and heaters on front and back terraces, Weds market day, open all day. *(Peter Smith and Judith Brown, Chris Willers)*

KIRKHAM SE7365
Stone Trough (01653) 618713
Kirkham Abbey; YO60 7JS Beamed country pub in beautiful setting with several cosy log-fire rooms, enjoyable food and three well kept ales such as Tetleys, Tom Woods and York, afternoon teas, restaurant; children welcome, seats outside with lovely views over Kirkham Priory (EH), good walks, Castle Howard nearby, open all day. *(Stanley and Annie Matthews)*

KNARESBOROUGH SE3556
Blind Jacks (01423) 869148
Market Place; HG5 8AL Simply done multi-floor tavern in 18th-c building (pub since 1990s), old-fashioned traditional character with low beams, bare brick and floorboards, cast-iron-framed tables, pews and stools, brewery mirrors etc, good range of real ales and craft kegs including own Bad beers (no longer brewed on-site), friendly helpful staff, limited food (cheese and pâté), two small downstairs rooms, quieter upstairs; well behaved children allowed away from bar, dogs welcome, open all day weekends, from 4pm other days. *(Harvey Brown)*

KNARESBOROUGH SE3457
Mitre (01423) 868948
Station Road; HG5 9AA Red-brick 1920s Market Town Tavern by the station, clean fresh décor and friendly staff, up to eight regional ales including Black Sheep, Hawkshead and Roosters, interesting continental beers, enjoyable sensibly priced food (not Sun evening) in side dining room and evening brasserie (Fri, Sat), live music Sun evening; children and dogs welcome, terrace tables under parasols, four bedrooms, open all day. *(Roger and Donna Huggins)*

KNAYTON SE4388
Dog & Gun (01845) 537368
Moor Road, off A19; YO7 4AZ Attractive well cared-for family-run pub, cosy and comfortable, with roaring fire at one end, tables laid for the very popular traditional home-made food (best to book) including blackboard specials, Black Sheep and Copper Dragon, good friendly service; children and dogs welcome, heated outside seating area, open all day weekends (food till 7pm Sun), closed Mon and lunchtimes Tues-Fri. *(Michael Doswell)*

LANGTHWAITE NY0002
★Charles Bathurst (01748) 884567
Arkengarthdale, a mile N towards Tan Hill; DL11 6EN Welcoming busy 18th-c country inn (worth checking no corporate events/weddings on your visit) with strong emphasis on dining and bedrooms, but pubby feel in long bar; scrubbed pine tables and country chairs on stripped floors, snug alcoves, open fire, Black Sheep, Caledonian

Deuchars IPA and a local guest, several wines by the glass and good choice of popular interesting food, cheerful helpful staff, dining room with views of Scar House, Robert 'Mousey' Thompson furniture, several other eating areas; background music, TV, pool and darts; children welcome, dogs in bar, lovely walks from the door and views over village and Arkengarthdale, 19 smart bedrooms (best not above dining room), open all day. *(Walter and Susan Rinaldi-Butcher)*

LANGTHWAITE NZ0002
★ **Red Lion** (01748) 884218
Just off Arkengarthdale Road, Reeth–Brough; DL11 6RE Proper pub dating from 17th c, homely and relaxing, in beguiling Dales village with ancient bridge; friendly and welcoming with character landlady, lunchtime sandwiches, pasties and sausage rolls, a couple of well kept Black Sheep ales, Thatcher's cider, country wines, tea and coffee, well behaved children allowed lunchtime in low-ceilinged side snug, newspapers and postcards; the ladies' is a genuine bathroom; no dogs inside, good walks including circular ones from the pub – maps and guides for sale. *(Dr Simon Innes)*

LASTINGHAM SE7290
★ **Blacksmiths Arms** (01751) 417247
Off A170 W of Pickering; YO62 6TL Popular old beamed pub opposite beautiful Saxon church in charming village, log fire in open range, traditional furnishings, Theakstons and other regional ales, several wines by the glass, good generously served home-made food (not Sun evening), friendly prompt service, darts, board games; background music; children and walkers welcome, seats in back garden, three bedrooms, open all day. *(Toby Jones)*

LEALHOLM NZ7607
★ **Board** (01947) 897279
Off A171 W of Whitby; YO21 2AJ In wonderful moorland village spot by wide pool of River Esk; homely bare-boards bar on right with squishy old sofa and armchairs by big black stove, local landscape photographs on stripped-stone or maroon walls, china cabinet and piano, left-hand bar with another fire, traditional pub furniture, darts and a stuffed otter, carpeted dining room, four well kept changing ales, five ciders (maybe a raspberry one) and dozens of whiskies, good seasonal food using meat from own farm and other local produce, friendly helpful landlady; children, dogs and muddy boots welcome, secluded waterside garden with decking, bedrooms (good breakfast) and self-catering cottage, open all day. *(Vikki and Matt Wharton)*

LEAVENING SE7863
Jolly Farmers (01653) 658276
Main Street; YO17 9SA Bustling village local, friendly and welcoming, with four

changing ales and popular good value traditional food (not Mon, Tues), front bar with eating area behind, separate dining room; some live music; open all day weekends, closed weekday lunchtimes. *(Mike Swan)*

LEEDS SE2932
Cross Keys (0113) 243 3711
Water Lane, Holbeck; LS11 5WD Welcoming early 19th-c pub; flagstones and bare boards, stripped brick, original tiling and timbers, old prints and photographs, a collection of clocks in one part, three or four interesting Yorkshire ales plus imported bottled beers, shortish choice of good well prepared food (not Sun evening), winding stairs up to function/dining room, newspapers and board games; children welcome, tables under big parasols in sheltered back courtyard, open all day. *(Jeremy King, Nigel and Sue Foster)*

LEEDS SE3131
Garden Gate (0113) 277 7705
Whitfield Place, Hunslet; LS10 2QB Impressive Edwardian pub (Grade II★ listed) owned by Leeds Brewery with their well kept ales from rare curved ceramic counter, a wealth of other period features in rooms off central drinking corridor including intricate glass and woodwork, art nouveau tiling, moulded ceilings and mosaic floors; tables out in front. *(Dr Simon Innes)*

LEEDS SE2932
★ **Grove** (0113) 243 9254
Back Row, Holbeck; LS11 5PL Unspoilt and lived-in 1930s-feel local overshadowed by towering office blocks, tables and stools in main bar with marble floor, panelling and original fireplace, large back room and snug off drinking corridor, good choice of well kept ales including Daleside and Moorhouses, Weston's cider, lunchtime food (not Sat), friendly staff, live music most evenings; open all day. *(Mike Swan)*

LEEDS SE2932
Midnight Bell (0113) 244 5044
Water Lane, Holbeck; LS11 5QN Leeds Brewery pub on two floors in Holbeck Urban Village, three of their ales and guests kept well, enjoyable home-made food (all day weekends including good Sun lunch), friendly staff, light contemporary décor mixing with original beams and stripped brickwork; families welcome, courtyard beer garden, open all day. *(Jeremy King)*

LEEDS SE3037
Mustard Pot (0113) 269 5699
Strainbeck Lane, Chapel Allerton; LS7 3QY Friendly management in relaxed easy-going dining pub, enjoyable food (all day Sun) from lunchtime sandwiches to daily specials, Marstons-related ales, decent wines

by the glass, mix of furniture from farmhouse tables and chairs to comfortable banquettes and leather chesterfields, half-panelling and open fire; background music; children welcome, pleasant front garden with heaters, open all day. *(Mike Swan)*

LEEDS   SE2236
Palace (0113) 244 5882
Kirkgate; LS2 7DJ Traditional Nicholsons pub, some recent redecoration, with stripped boards and polished panelling, friendly staff, good choice of reasonably priced food, Bass, Fullers, Tetleys and six guests; no dogs inside, tables out in front and in small back courtyard, open (and food) all day from 10am.
(Mike Swan)

LEEDS   SE2933
Pour House 07816 481492
Canal Wharf, Holbeck; LS11 5PS
Canalside pub in old granary building, good value food from sandwiches and sharing plates up, friendly service, two Wharfe Bank ales and good choice of bottled beers and other drinks, seating on two levels; Mon quiz; open (and food) all day. *(Harvey Brown)*

LEEDS   SE3033
Victoria (0113) 245 1386
Great George Street; LS1 3DL
Opulent early Victorian pub with grand cut and etched mirrors, impressive globe lamps extending from majestic bar, carved beams, leather-seat booths with working snob screens, smaller rooms off, eight real ales and standard Nicholsons food in separate room with serving hatch, friendly efficient service; live jazz first Thurs of month; open all day. *(Peter Smith and Judith Brown)*

LEEDS   SE3033
★**Whitelocks** (0113) 245 3950
Turks Head Yard, off Briggate; LS1 6HB
Classic Victorian pub, a little worn around the edges but full of character; long narrow bar with tiled counter, grand mirrors, mahogany and glass screens, heavy copper-topped tables and red leather, well kept Theakstons ales and enjoyable generous food, friendly hard-working young staff; crowded at lunchtime; children welcome, tables in narrow courtyard, open (and food) all day. *(Kay and Alistair Butler)*

LEYBURN   SE1190
Black Swan (01969) 623131
Market Place; DL8 5AS Attractive old creeper-clad hotel with chatty locals and character landlord in cheerful open-plan bar, decent range of food including popular Sun carvery, quick service, well kept Black Sheep, Timothy Taylors, Theakstons and a guest, good wines by the glass; no credit cards; children welcome, dogs allowed before 6pm, disabled access, tables on cobbled terrace, seven bedrooms, open all day.
(Toby Jones)

LEYBURN   SE1190
Bolton Arms (01969) 623327
Market Place; DL8 5BW Substantial 18th-c stone-built inn at top of marketplace, well priced basic pub food including popular Sun carvery, Black Sheep, Richmond and Wensleydale, good mix of customers; sports TV; seats outside, four bedrooms. *(Gus Swan)*

LINTHWAITE   SE1014
★**Sair** (01484) 842370
Lane Top, Hoyle Ing, off A62; HD7 5SG
Old-fashioned four-room pub brewing its own good value Linfit beers, pews and chairs on rough flagstones or wood floors, log-burning ranges, dominoes, cribbage and shove-ha'penny, piano and vintage rock juke box; no food or credit cards; dogs welcome, children till 8pm, plenty of tables out in front with fine Colne Valley views, restored Huddersfield Narrow Canal nearby, open all day weekends, from 5pm weekdays. *(Tony Hobden)*

LINTON   SE3846
★**Windmill** (01937) 582209
Off A661 W of Wetherby; LS22 4HT
Welcoming upmarket 16th-c inn on different levels, beams and stripped stone, antique settles around copper-topped tables, log fires, good reasonably priced food (greater evening choice), Theakstons Best and guests, several wines by the glass, prompt cheerful service, restaurant and conservatory; background music; children and dogs (in bar) welcome, sunny back terrace and sheltered garden with pear tree raised from seed brought back from Napoleonic Wars, two bedrooms in annexe, open all day Fri-Sun (food all day Sat, till 6pm Sun). *(Margaret Tait, Ray and Winifred Halliday, Robert Watt, Michael Butler)*

LITTON   SD9074
Queens Arms (01756) 770096
Off B6160 N of Grassington; BD23 5QJ
Beautifully placed 17th-c Dales pub; main bar with stone floor and beam-and-plank ceiling, old photographs on rough stone walls, coal fire, plainer carpeted dining room with woodburner and pictures of local scenes, Black Sheep, Goose Eye and Thwaites, enjoyable freshly made food, friendly staff; children and dogs welcome, plenty of seats in two-tier garden, country views and good surrounding walks, six bedrooms, open all day Sat, till 5pm Sun, closed Mon; new management as we went to press, so may be changes. *(Michael Doswell, Claes Mauroy)*

LOFTHOUSE   SE1073
Crown (01423) 755206
Pub signed from main road; Nidderdale; HG3 5RZ Prettily placed Dales pub, friendly and relaxed, with hearty simple food from sandwiches up, well kept Black Sheep and Theakstons, small public bar, comfortable dining extension where children allowed; no credit cards, outside gents'; dogs welcome,

good walks from the door, bedrooms.
(Claes Mauroy, B and M Kendall)

LOW BRADFIELD SK2691
Plough (0114) 285 1280
Village signposted off B6077 and B6076
NW of Sheffield; New Road; S6 6HW
Traditionally refurbished pub ideally placed
for some of South Yorkshire's finest scenery;
L-shaped bar with stone walls, comfortable
wall banquettes and captain's chairs, big
arched inglenook log fire, well kept Bradfield,
Thwaites and a guest, good value food from
sandwiches and baked potatoes to grills, two-
for-one deals weekday lunchtimes and Sun
carvery; background music, sports TV, Weds
quiz; children and dogs welcome, seats on
back verandah, terrace and lawn, good walks,
Damflask and Agden Reservoirs close by,
open (and food) all day. *(Emma Scofield)*

LOW ROW SD9898
★ **Punch Bowl** (01748) 886233
B6270 Reeth–Muker; DL11 6PF
17th-c country inn under same ownership
as the Charles Bathurst at Langthwaite;
long bare-boards bar with peaceful view
over Swaledale, stripped kitchen tables and
a variety of seats, armchairs and sofa by
woodburner at one end, pastel walls, good
food (menu on huge mirror) including some
interesting choices, nice wines by the glass,
well kept Black Sheep ales and a guest,
cheerful efficient staff, separate dining room
similar in style; wide views from terrace set
above road, comfortable bedrooms, good
breakfast, open all day. *(Michael Doswell)*

LUND SE9748
★ **Wellington** (01377) 217294
Off B1248 SW of Driffield; YO25 9TE
Smart busy pub with cosy Farmers Bar,
beams, well polished wooden banquettes and
square tables, quirky fireplace, plainer side
room with flagstones and wine-theme décor,
Yorkstone walkway to room with village's
Britain in Bloom awards, highly rated well
presented food (not Sun evening and not
cheap) in restaurant and bistro dining area,
well kept ales including Timothy Taylors and
Theakstons, good wine list, 25 malt whiskies,
friendly efficient staff; background music,
TV; children welcome, benches in pretty
back courtyard, open all day Sun, closed Mon
lunchtime. *(P Dawn, Pat and Stewart Gordon,
Michael Butler)*

MANFIELD NZ2213
Crown (01325) 374243
Vicars Lane; DL2 2RF Traditional
unpretentious village local, friendly and
welcoming, with eight interesting regularly
changing ales including own Village Brewer
beers (brewed by Hambleton), enjoyable
simple home-made food, two bars and games
room with pool; dogs welcome, garden, good
walks nearby, open all day weekends, closed
weekday lunchtimes. *(Belinda May)*

MARSDEN SE0411
Riverhead Brewery Tap
(01484) 841270 Peel Street, next to
Co-op; just off A62 Huddersfield–
Oldham; HD7 6BR Owned by Ossett with
up to ten well kept ales including Riverhead
range (microbrewery visible from bare-
boards bar), bustling friendly atmosphere,
airy upstairs beamed restaurant with
stripped tables (moors view from some) and
open kitchen, good choice of enjoyable food
(not Mon) including OAP weekday lunch
deal; background and some live music, Tues
quiz; dogs welcome, wheelchair access, some
riverside tables, open all day. *(Tony Hobden)*

MASHAM SE2280
Kings Head (01765) 689295
Market Place; HG4 4EF Handsome 18th-c
stone inn (Chef & Brewer), two modernised
linked bars with stone fireplaces, well kept
Black Sheep and Theakstons, nice choice of
wines, good food served by friendly helpful
staff, part-panelled restaurant; background
music, TV; children welcome, tables out at
front and in sunny back courtyard,
27 bedrooms, open all day. *(Mike Swan)*

MASHAM SE2281
White Bear (01765) 689227
Wellgarth, Crosshills; signed off A6108
opposite turn into town; HG4 4EN
Comfortably updated stone-built beamed inn,
small public bar with full range of Theakstons
ales kept well, larger lounge with welcoming
coal fire, big helpings of popular food from
sandwiches up (not Sun evening), decent
wines by the glass, friendly efficient staff,
restaurant extension; background music;
children and dogs welcome, terrace tables,
14 bedrooms, open all day. *(Mike Swan)*

MAUNBY SE3586
★ **Buck** (01845) 587777
Off A167 S of Northallerton; YO7 4HD
Warmly welcoming dining pub in quiet
out-of-the-way village by River Swale,
interesting highly regarded food (not Sun
evening, Mon) cooked by owner-chef, also
traditional choices and good value set menu,
ales such as Rudgate and Theakstons, nice
wines from good list, friendly on-the-ball
service, carpeted beamed bar with comfy
leather sofa and captain's chest in front of
inviting fire, more contemporary restaurant
(flowers and candles) and conservatory
with one huge table; children welcome, dogs
in bar. *(John and Eleanor Holdsworth,
Michael Doswell)*

MENSTON SE1744
Fox (01943) 873024
Bradford Road (A65/A6038); LS29 6EB
Contemporary Mitchells & Butlers dining
pub in former coaching inn on busy junction,
decent fairly priced food, efficient friendly
staff, Black Sheep, Timothy Taylors Landlord

and a guest, Aspall's cider, big fireplace, flagstones and polished boards in one part; background music; two terraces looking beyond car park to cricket field, open all day. *(Gordon and Margaret Ormondroyd)*

MIDDLEHAM SE1288
Richard III (01969) 623240
Market Place; DL8 4NP Traditional 17th-c beamed inn with friendly landlady and locals, cosy front bar, Black Sheep, John Smiths and Theakstons, good range of food cooked by landlord, back bar and restaurant, lots of racehorse pictures; tables out by square, six bedrooms, open all day, food all day Fri-Sun. *(Michael Butler)*

MIDDLEHAM SE1287
★White Swan (01969) 622093
Market Place; DL8 4PE Extended coaching inn opposite cobbled market town square, beamed and flagstoned entrance bar with built-in window pew and pubby furniture, log fire, well kept Theakstons ales, several wines by the glass and malt whiskies, enjoyable bistro-style food (all day Sun), friendly efficient staff, modern brasserie with large fireplace, more dining space in back room; background music; children welcome, 17 comfortable bedrooms, hearty breakfast. *(WAH, Michael Butler)*

MIDDLESMOOR SE0974
Crown (01423) 755204
Top of Nidderdale Road from Pateley Bridge; HG3 5ST Remote unpretentious family-run inn with beautiful view over stone-built hamlet high in upper Nidderdale, warmly welcoming character landlord and good local atmosphere, well kept Black Sheep and guests, several whiskies, simple wholesome food, blazing fires in cosy spotless rooms full of photographs, bric-a-brac and awards, homely dining room; children and dogs welcome, small garden, good value bedrooms, camping and self-catering cottage, open all day weekends. *(Claes Mauroy)*

MIDDLETON TYAS NZ2205
Shoulder of Mutton (01325) 377271
Just E of A1 Scotch Corner roundabout; DL10 6QX Welcoming old pub with three softly lit low-ceilinged rooms on different levels, good freshly made food from snacks to appealing specials, well kept Adnams, Black Sheep and a guest, prompt friendly service; a useful A1/A66 stop. *(Michael Doswell)*

MILLINGTON SE8351
Gait (01759) 302045
Main Street; YO42 1TX Honest, friendly 16th-c beamed local, well kept ales such as Haworth Steam, Titanic and Wold Top, enjoyable straightforward home-made food (maybe beef from own herd), nice mix of old and newer furnishings, large map of Yorkshire on the ceiling, big inglenook log fire, live music or quiz Weds; children and

dogs welcome, garden picnic-sets, appealing village in good Wolds walking country, closed Mon and lunchtimes Tues-Thurs. *(Robert Wivell)*

MOORSHOLM NZ6912
Jolly Sailor (01287) 660270
A171 nearly a mile E; TS12 3LN Remotely placed dining pub with good cross-section of enjoyable food, well kept Black Sheep and a guest, friendly staff, long beamed and stripped-stone bar, restaurant; children and dogs welcome, tables looking out to the surrounding moors, open all day. *(WAH)*

MUKER SD9097
★Farmers Arms (01748) 886297
B6270 W of Reeth; DL11 6QG Small unpretentious walkers' pub in beautiful valley village, four well kept local ales, wines, teas and coffees, enjoyable good value straightforward food, warm fire, simple modern pine furniture, flagstones and panelling; soft background music, darts and dominoes; children and dogs welcome, hill views from terrace tables, stream across road, open all day. *(John and Enid)*

MYTHOLMROYD SD9922
Hinchcliffe Arms (01422) 883256
Off B6138 S at Cragg Vale; HX7 5TA Tucked-away old stone-built pub with well liked food, four well kept ales including a house beer from Ilkley, friendly staff, open fires; well behaved dogs allowed in bar, lovely setting near village church on road leading only to reservoir, popular with walkers, open all day weekends (Sun till 9pm), closed Mon and lunchtime Tues. *(Belinda May)*

MYTHOLMROYD SE0125
Shoulder of Mutton (01422) 883165
New Road (B6138); HX7 5DZ Comfortable fairly basic local with popular low-priced home cooking, friendly efficient service, family dining areas and cosy child- and food-free parts, well kept Black Sheep, Copper Dragon, Timothy Taylors and guests, toby jugs and other china; sports TV; streamside back terrace, open all day weekends. *(Tony Hobden)*

NEWTON-ON-OUSE SE5160
★Dawnay Arms (01347) 848345
Off A19 N of York; YO30 2BR 18th-c pub with two bars and airy river-view dining room, low beams, stripped masonry, open fire and inglenook woodburner, chunky pine tables and old pews on bare boards and flagstones, fishing memorabilia, highly regarded original food (till 6pm Sun), also good lunchtime sandwiches (home-baked bread), interesting vegetarian menu and children's choices, ales such as Tetleys and Timothy Taylors, good range of wines by the glass, friendly efficient service; terrace tables, lawn running down to Ouse moorings, handy for Beningbrough

Hall (NT), open all day Sun till 6pm, closed Mon. *(Pat and Graham Williamson)*

NORLAND   SE0521
Moorcock   (01422) 832103
Moor Bottom Lane; HX6 3RP Modernised old building with fairly simple L-shaped bar and beamed restaurant, enjoyable fair priced food including set menus, friendly service, well kept Timothy Taylors and Thwaites; children welcome, fine valley views from village, popular scarecrow festival early Sept, open all day Fri-Sun, closed Mon and lunchtimes Tues-Thurs. *(Toby Jones)*

NORTH DALTON   SE9352
Star   (01377) 217688
B1246 Pocklington–Driffield; YO25 9UX Picturesque 18th-c inn next to village pond, good range of changing ales and man-sized helpings of well cooked food including blackboard specials and tasty Sunday lunch, open fire in pubby bar, restaurant; children welcome, bedrooms. *(C A Hall)*

NORTH RIGTON   SE2749
Square & Compass   (01423) 733031
Hall Green Lane/Rigton Hill; LS17 0DJ Substantial stone building with beamed bar, Copper Dragon, Leeds and Theakstons, plenty of wines by the glass, good choice of food from sandwiches and sharing boards up, pleasant service by aproned staff, restaurant; well behaved children and dogs (in bar) welcome, tables on tiered terrace, peaceful village, open all day from 9am. *(Revd R P Tickle)*

NORTHALLERTON   SE3794
Tithe Bar   (01609) 778482
Friarage Street; DL6 1DP Market Town Tavern with seven good mainly local ales along with plenty of continental beers, tasty well priced food including specials, friendly young staff, modernised bar split into three areas, upstairs evening brasserie; children and dogs welcome, open all day. *(Richard Tilbrook)*

NUN MONKTON   SE5057
Alice Hawthorn   (01423) 330303
Off A59 York–Harrogate; The Green; YO26 8EW Refurbished beamed dining pub in picturesque location on broad village green with pond and lovely avenue to church and Rivers Nidd and Ouse – maybe cows grazing peacefully; good imaginative well presented food (can be pricey), local ales, bar with big brick inglenook, restaurant; open all day Sat, closed Sun evening to Tues lunchtime. *(John and Eleanor Holdsworth)*

NUNNINGTON   SE6679
Royal Oak   (01439) 748271
Church Street; at back of village, which is signposted from A170 and B1257; YO62 5US Welcoming old pub neatly refurbished by present owners, bar with high beams and some farming memorabilia on bare-stone wall, nice mix of furniture, dining area linked by double-sided woodburner, good food with tuscan influences, Theakstons, York and a guest such as Timothy Taylors, nice wines and italian coffee; bar billiards; children and dogs welcome, terrace seating, handy for Nunnington Hall (NT), open all day Sun (no evening food), closed Mon, Tues. *(Emma Scofield)*

OAKWORTH   SE0138
Grouse   (01535) 643073
Harehills, Oldfield; 2 miles towards Colne; BD22 0RX Comfortable old pub with enjoyable food from light lunches to good steaks and daily specials, well kept Timothy Taylors ales, friendly service; children and dogs (in snug) welcome, undisturbed hamlet in fine moorland surroundings, picnic-sets on terrace with lovely Pennine views, open (and food) all day. *(Toby Jones)*

OLDSTEAD   SE5380
★Black Swan   (01347) 868387
Village signed off Thirsk Bank, W of Coxwold; YO61 4BL Tucked-away 16th-c restaurant with rooms in beautiful surroundings; bar with beams, flagstones and 'Mousey' Thompson furniture, log fire, lots of wines by the glass and well kept Black Sheep, attractive back dining rooms serving first class food (Michelin starred and not cheap), good friendly service; children welcome, picnic-sets out in front, four comfortable well equipped bedrooms with own terrace, good breakfast, fine surrounding walks, closed weekday lunchtimes and two weeks in Jan. *(Hunter and Christine Wright)*

OSMOTHERLEY   SE4597
★Golden Lion   (01609) 883526
The Green, West End; off A19 N of Thirsk; DL6 3AA Attractive busy old stone pub with friendly welcome, Timothy Taylors and guests, around 50 malt whiskies, roomy beamed bar on left with old pews and a few decorations, similarly unpretentious well worn-in eating area on right, weekend dining room, well liked pubby food and good service; background music; children welcome, dogs in bar, seats in covered courtyard, benches out at front overlooking village green, 44-mile Lyke Wake Walk starts here and Coast to Coast one nearby, comfortable bedrooms, closed Mon and Tues lunchtimes, otherwise open all day. *(WAH, Walter and Susan Rinaldi-Butcher)*

OSSETT   SE2719
★Brewers Pride   (01924) 273865
Low Mill Road/Healey Lane (long cul-de-sac by railway sidings, off B6128); WF5 8ND Friendly local with Bobs White Lion (brewed at back of pub), Rudgate Ruby Mild and seven guests, cosy front rooms and flagstoned bar, open fires, brewery

memorabilia, good well priced food (not Sun evening) including Tues night tapas, modern back dining extension (Millers Restaurant); live music first Sun of month, quiz Mon; well behaved children and dogs welcome, big back garden, near Calder & Hebble Navigation, open all day. *(Michael Butler)*

OSSETT   SE2820
Old Vic (01924) 273516
Manor Road, just off Horbury Road; WF5 0AU Friendly four-room roadside pub with well kept Ossett ales and a guest such as Fullers London Pride, competitively priced home-cooked food (not Sun evening, Mon), traditional décor with old local photographs, shelves of bottles and antique range, pool room; children and dogs welcome, open all day Fri-Sun, closed lunchtime other days. *(Michael Butler)*

OSSETT   SE2719
Tap (01924) 272215
The Green; WF5 8JS Tap for the Ossett Brewery; simple traditional décor with flagstones, bare boards and woodburner, mix of seating including upholstered banquettes and padded stools, photos of other Ossett pubs, their ales and guests (usually Fullers London Pride), decent wines by the glass, friendly relaxed atmosphere; small car park (parking elsewhere nearby can be difficult), open all day Thurs-Sun, from 3pm other days. *(Michael Butler)*

OSWALDKIRK   SE6278
Malt Shovel (01439) 788461
Signed off B1363/B1257 S of Helmsley; YO62 5XT Attractive former small 17th-c manor house under welcoming new licensees, two cosy bars and dining room, well kept/priced Sam Smiths OBB and enjoyable good value food, huge log fires, heavy beams and flagstones; views from garden. *(Caroline Prescott)*

OTLEY   SE1945
Fleece (01943) 465034
Westgate (A659); LS21 3DT Refurbished stone-built pub keeping original layout, full range of Wharfe Bank ales and three changing guests, good food (all day weekends) including early-bird deal Mon-Fri, dining room at back with fine views over narrow River Wharfe, open fires; free wi-fi; children and dogs (in snug) welcome, front disabled access, garden sloping down to the river, open all day. *(Gordon and Margaret Ormondroyd)*

OTLEY   SE2045
Horse & Farrier (01943) 468400
Bridge Street; LS21 1BQ Nicely updated Market Town Tavern, five real ales and good

reasonably priced food (all day weekends) from pie and peas to well liked fish, most main courses available in smaller helpings, friendly helpful young staff; disabled facilities, four bedrooms, tables in small courtyard. *(Pat and Tony Martin, D W Stokes)*

OTLEY   SE2045
Old Cock (01943) 464424
Crossgate; LS21 1AA Traditional two-room drinkers' pub with nine mainly local ales and a couple of ciders, also foreign imports and range of gluten-free bottled beers, no cooked food but good pies and sausage sandwiches, more room upstairs; no under-18s, dogs welcome, open all day. *(Pat and Tony Martin)*

OTLEY   SE2047
Roebuck (01943) 463063
Roebuck Terrace; LS21 2EY Low-beamed pub refurbished to a high standard, highly thought-of food from sandwiches and sharing plates up including range of hearty pies, Black Sheep, Saltaire, Tetleys and a guest, plenty of wines by the glass, good helpful service, log fire; children welcome, wheelchair access, tables out in neat garden, open all day weekends. *(John and Eleanor Holdsworth)*

OXENHOPE   SE0434
★ Dog & Gun (01535) 643159
Off B6141 towards Denholme; BD22 9SN Beautifully placed roomy 17th-c moorland pub, smartly extended, comfortable and can be busy, wide choice of good generously served food from sandwiches to daily specials, attentive friendly staff and ebullient landlord, full Timothy Taylors range kept well, good selection of malts, beamery, copper, brasses, plates and jugs, big log fire each end, padded settles and stools, glass-covered well in one dining area, wonderful views; five bedrooms in adjoining hotel, open all day weekends. *(John and Eleanor Holdsworth, Gordon and Margaret Ormondroyd and others)*

PICKERING   SE7984
White Swan (01751) 472288
Market Place, just off A170; YO18 7AA Civilised and welcoming 16th-c coaching inn run by the same family for 30 years; cosy properly pubby bar, sofas and a few tables, panelling and log fire, Black Sheep, Timothy Taylors Landlord and a dozen wines by the glass, second bare-boards room with big bow window and handsome art nouveau iron fireplace, good food in flagstoned restaurant and next-door deli, efficient friendly staff, residents' lounge in converted beamed barn; children and dogs (in bar) welcome, bedrooms, open all day from 7.30am. *(Pat and Graham Williamson, John Evans)*

Pubs close to motorway junctions are listed at the back of the book.

PICKHILL SE3483

★**Nags Head** (01845) 567391

A1 junction 50 (northbound) or junction 51 (southbound), village signed off A6055, Street Lane; YO7 4JG
Welcoming dining inn with many tables set for eating, but bustling tap room on left (lots of ties, jugs, coach horns and ale-yards) serves Black Sheep, Rudgate, Theakstons and a guest, along with 30 malt whiskies, vintage Armagnacs and rare wines by the glass, smarter lounge bar with deep green plush banquettes, pictures for sale and open fire, library-themed restaurant, good choice of enjoyable food from bar snacks up; background music, TV, free wi-fi; well behaved children welcome till 7.30pm (after that in dining room only), dogs in bar, front verandah, boules/quoits pitch and nine-hole putting green, comfortable bedrooms, buffet-style breakfast, open all day.
(Michael Doswell, Pat and Tony Martin, David and Ruth Hollands, Ian Malone)

POOL SE2445

White Hart (0113) 203 7862

Just off A658 S of Harrogate, A659 E of Otley; LS21 1LH Light and airy Mitchells & Butlers dining pub (bigger inside than it looks), well liked food from sharing plates and pizzas to more restaurant dishes, set menu too, good service from friendly young staff, nice choice of wines by the glass, Leeds, Timothy Taylors and a guest, stylishly simple bistro eating areas, armchairs and sofas on bar's flagstones and bare boards; plenty of tables outside, open (and food) all day.
(Michael Butler)

POTTO NZ4703

Dog & Gun (01642) 700232

Cooper Lane; DL6 3HQ Tucked-away modern bar-restaurant-hotel, clean contemporary décor, well liked food from varied menu, a house beer brewed by local Wainstones, Black Sheep and a guest, good choice of wines, friendly attentive service; tables under parasols on front decking, five bedrooms, closed lunchtimes Mon and Tues, otherwise open (and food) all day.
(Emma Scofield)

REDMIRE SE0491

Bolton Arms (01969) 624336

Hargill Lane; DL8 4EA Welcoming village dining pub (former 17th-c farmhouse) with good value fairly traditional food, well kept Black Sheep, Theakstons, Thwaites and a guest, efficient friendly service even at busy times, woodburner in comfortable carpeted bar, attractive dining room; free wi-fi; children welcome, disabled facilities, picnic-sets in small part-paved garden, handy for Wensleydale Railway and Bolton Castle, good walks, three bedrooms (two with views from shared balcony, others in converted outbuilding), open all day. *(WAH, Tracey and Stephen Groves)*

REETH SE0499

Buck (01748) 884210

Arkengarthdale Road/Silver Street; DL11 6SW Newish owners for beamed 18th-c coaching inn by village green, Black Sheep, Caledonian, Copper Dragon, Timothy Taylors and a guest, decent food, regular live music including name bands; free wi-fi; children welcome, dogs in bar, a few tables out in front, also a secret walled garden, good walking country, ten bedrooms, open all day.
(Toby Jones)

RIPLEY SE2860

Boars Head (01423) 771888

Off A61 Harrogate–Ripon; HG3 3AY Old hotel with informal relaxed atmosphere, long bar-bistro with nice mix of dining chairs and tables, walls hung with golf clubs, cricket bats, some jolly cricketing/hunting drawings, a boar's head and interesting religious carving, Black Sheep, Daleside and Theakstons, 20 wines by the glass and several malt whiskies, food can be good and includes produce from the Estate (the Ingilby family have lived in next-door Ripley Castle for over 650 years), separate restaurant; children welcome, dogs in bar and bedrooms, pleasant little garden, open all day summer.
(Mr and Mrs P R Thomas)

RIPON SE3171

★**One-Eyed Rat** (01765) 607704

Allhallowgate; HG4 1LQ Little bare-boards pub with numerous well kept ales (occasional festivals), farm cider, draught continentals and lots of bottled beers, country wines too, long narrow bar with roaring fire, cigarette cards, framed beer mats, bank notes and old pictures, no food but may be free black pudding, pool; children welcome, nice outside seating area, open all day Sat, closed weekday lunchtimes.
(Paul Humphreys, Paul Bromley)

RIPON SE3171

Royal Oak (01765) 602284

Kirkgate; HG4 1PB Centrally placed, well run 18th-c coaching inn on pedestrianised street; smart modern refurbishment by Timothy Taylors with their ales and guests kept well and good choice of wines, dining area on two levels and much emphasis on good food (all day weekends) from sandwiches and pub staples to more enterprising dishes, lunchtime and early evening deals, good service; background music; children welcome, no dogs inside, teak furniture on courtyard terrace, six updated bedrooms, open all day.
(Paul Humphreys, Brian and Anna Marsden)

RIPON SE3170

Water Rat (01765) 602251

Bondgate Green, off B6265; HG4 1QW Small pub on two levels, prettily set by footbridge over River Skell and near restored canal basin; well kept ales such as Black Sheep, a real cider and keenly priced wines, enjoyable straightforward food including notable steak and kidney pie, good friendly service, conservatory; charming view of cathedral, ducks and weir from riverside terrace. *(Paul Humphreys, Pat and Graham Williamson)*

RIPPONDEN   SE0319
Fox (01422) 825880
Oldham Road; just off M62 junction 22; HX6 4DP Modern timber-fronted pub-restaurant with wide choice of food cooked by landlord-chef including fresh fish/seafood and picnic bench afternoon tea, efficient service, well kept Copper Dragon Golden Pippin and Thwaites Wainwright, live acoustic music last Thurs of month; children welcome, seats outside, open (and food) all day weekends, closed Mon-Thurs lunchtimes. *(Gus Swan)*

RISHWORTH   SE0316
Booth Wood (01422) 825600
Oldham Road (A672); HX6 4QU Welcoming beamed and flagstoned country dining pub, smartened-up but keeping cosy atmosphere; good range of enjoyable well priced food from sandwiches to blackboard specials, lunchtime/early evening bargains, local Oates beers and guests, friendly staff, some leather sofas and wing-back chairs, two blazing woodburners; live music including folk nights; children welcome, open all day (from 9.30 Sun for breakfast). *(Gordon and Margaret Ormondroyd, Stuart Paulley)*

RISHWORTH   SE0216
Turnpike (01422) 822789
Opposite Booth Wood Reservoir, near M62 junction 22; HX6 4RH Revamped 19th-c country dining inn, spacious modern interior keeping some original features, large dining extension, good value food from sandwiches and sharing boards up, Lees ales, friendly uniformed service; children welcome, tables outside overlooking reservoir, surrounding moorland and motorway, six bedrooms, open all day. *(Gordon and Margaret Ormondroyd, Michael Butler)*

ROBIN HOOD'S BAY   NZ9504
Bay Hotel (01947) 880278
The Dock, Bay Town; YO22 4SJ Friendly old village inn at end of the 191-mile Coast to Coast path – so popular with walkers; fine sea views from cosy picture-window upstairs bar (Wainwright bar downstairs open too if busy), ales including Caledonian Deuchars IPA and Theakstons, reasonably priced home-made food in bar and separate dining area from sandwiches up, young staff coping well, log fires; background music; dogs welcome, lots of tables outside, bedrooms, steep road down and no parking at bottom, open all day. *(Caroline Prescott)*

ROBIN HOOD'S BAY   NZ9505
Victoria (01947) 880205
Station Road; YO22 4RL Clifftop Victorian hotel with great bay views, good choice of beers from curved counter in traditional carpeted bar, enjoyable fresh food here, in restaurant or large family room, also a coffee shop/tearoom; dogs welcome, useful car park, play area in big garden overlooking sea and village, comfortable bedrooms, good breakfast. *(Mike Swan)*

SANDSEND   NZ8612
Hart (01947) 893304
East Row; YO21 3SU Shoreside pub with good choice of generously served traditional food including fish/seafood (best to book a table), well kept ales such as Black Sheep, prompt friendly service, log fire in beamed and flagstoned bar, upstairs dining room; dogs welcome, picnic-sets on small side terrace, open all day (till 6pm Sun). *(Stephen Woad)*

SAWDON   TA9484
★ **Anvil** (01723) 859896
Main Street; YO13 9DY Attractive high-raftered former smithy with emphasis on chef-landlord's good locally sourced food (best to book), well kept ales including Black Sheep and nice range of wines, friendly attentive service from smart staff, feature smith's hearth, anvil and old tools, hops, scrubbed pine tables and good woodburner, lower-ceilinged second bar leading to small neat dining room; dogs allowed in some areas, terrace seating, two self-catering cottages, closed Mon, Tues. *(Garth and Lyn Lewis, Sara Fulton, Roger Baker)*

SAWLEY   SE2467
Sawley Arms (01765) 620642
Village signposted off B6265 W of Ripon; HG4 3EQ Renovated village dining pub with well liked food from sandwiches and light meals up, ales such as Timothy Taylors and good choice of wines by the glass, friendly helpful staff, conservatory; seats on terrace and in attractive garden, close to Fountains Abbey (NT), open (and food) all day. *(John and Eleanor Holdsworth)*

SCARBOROUGH   TA0588
Golden Ball (01723) 353899
Sandside, opposite harbour; YO11 1PG Mock-Tudor seafront pub with good harbour and bay views from highly prized window seats (busy in summer); panelled bar with some nautical memorabilia, well kept low-priced Sam Smiths; family lounge upstairs, tables out in yard, open all day. *(David Carr)*

SCARBOROUGH   TA0387
Valley (01723) 372593
Valley Road; YO11 2LX Family-run Victorian pub with basement bar, up to six well kept changing ales and eight ciders/

perries, excellent choice of bottled belgian beers too, friendly staff, no food, more seats upstairs and pool room; bedrooms, open all day. *(Toby Jones)*

SCAWTON   SE5483
★ **Hare** (01845) 597769
Off A170 Thirsk–Helmsley; YO7 2HG
Attractive quietly placed dining pub with really good imaginative food (not cheap) cooked by chef-owner, nice wines by the glass and well kept ales such as Black Sheep in small bar area, stripped-pine tables, heavy beams and some flagstones, open fire and woodburner, pub ghost called Bob; children and dogs (in bar) welcome, garden tables, closed Sun evening, Mon, Tues. *(Mungo Shipley)*

SCORTON   NZ2500
Farmers Arms (01748) 812533
Northside; DL10 6DW Comfortably refurbished little pub in terrace of old cottages overlooking green, well kept Black Sheep, Copper Dragon and Courage Directors, decent wines and enjoyable food including good rabbit pie, fresh Whitby fish and popular Sun lunch (till 3pm), friendly accommodating staff, bar with open fire, darts and dominoes, restaurant; background music, fortnightly quiz; children and dogs welcome, open all day Fri-Sun, closed Mon lunchtime. *(Pat and Stewart Gordon)*

SCOTTON   SE3259
Guy Fawkes Arms (01423) 862598
Main Street; HG5 9HU Hospitable neatly refurbished village pub run by two local families, much-liked food (must book) including plenty of fish and good value set lunch, well kept Black Sheep, Copper Dragon and three local guests, charming staff; Mon quiz; children and dogs (not at food times) welcome, open all day (food all day Sat, till 7pm Sun). *(Margaret and Peter Staples, Michael Doswell)*

SETTLE   SD8163
Lion (01729) 822203
B6480 (main road through town), off A65 bypass; BD24 0HB Market-town inn with grand staircase sweeping down into baronial-style high-beamed hall bar, lovely log fire, second bar with bare boards and dark half-panelling, lots of old local photographs and another open fire, enjoyable good value food including deli boards and specials, well kept Thwaites and occasional guests, decent wines by the glass, helpful welcoming staff, restaurant; Tues jazz, monthly quiz, silent TV and games machine; children and dogs welcome, courtyard tables, 14 bedrooms, open (and food) all day. *(Michael Butler)*

SHAROW   SE3371
Half Moon (01765) 278524
Sharow Lane; HG4 5BP Nice little village pub recently reopened and sympathetically refurbished; well kept Theakstons ales, tasty home-made food such as steak and Old Peculier pie and venison bourguignon from sensibly short blackboard menu, early-bird deal Tues-Thurs (5.30-7pm), Victorian pictures and ornate gilded mirror on grey/green walls, lots of pine furniture, sofa and easy chairs one end, cosy dining room the other with open fire, small gift shop; children welcome, dogs in bar area, open all day Sun till 7.45pm, closed Mon. *(Michael Doswell)*

SHEFFIELD   SK3487
Bath (0114) 249 5151
Victoria Street, off Glossop Road; S3 7QL
Victorian corner pub with well restored 1930s interior, two rooms and a drinking corridor, friendly staff, well kept Thornbridge and guests, simple lunchtime bar food (sandwiches only Sat), live music Sun and Weds with some emphasis on jazz/blues; open all day (from 4pm Sun). *(Martin Day, David Carr)*

SHEFFIELD   SK3687
★ **Fat Cat** (0114) 249 4801
23 Alma Street; S3 8SA Busy little local with up to 13 interesting brews on handpump (always a mild and a stout or porter) served by knowledgeable and friendly staff: regulars are Abbeydale Deception, Acorn Barnsley Bitter, Bradfield Farmers Blonde and Pictish Brewers Gold with guests from breweries such as North Riding, Rudgate, Thwaites, Wentworth, Wold Top and Yorkshire Dales; also, 40 malt whiskies and farm cider; good value pubby food, cheerful customers and pubby furnishings; flower-filled and unusual back courtyard garden with woodburning stove for chilly evenings; award-winning front window boxes. *(David Carr)*

SHEFFIELD   SK3687
Gardeners Rest (0114) 272 4978
Neepsend Lane; S3 8AT Welcoming beer-enthusiast landlord serving his own good Sheffield ales from light wood counter, also several changing guests tapped from the cask, farm cider and continental beers, no food, old brewery memorabilia and changing local artwork, daily papers, games including bar billiards, live music and popular Sun quiz; well behaved children (till 9pm) and dogs welcome, disabled facilities, back conservatory and tables out overlooking River Don, open all day Thurs-Sun, from 3pm other days. *(Harvey Brown)*

SHEFFIELD   SK3588
Harlequin (0114) 275 8195
Nursery Street; S3 8GG Welcoming open-plan corner pub owned by nearby Brew Company, their well kept ales and great selection of changing guests, also bottled imports and real ciders/perries, straightforward cheap lunchtime food including Sun roasts, beer festivals, weekend

live music, Weds quiz; children till 7pm and dogs welcome, outside seating, open all day. *(Harvey Brown)*

SHEFFIELD   SK3687
★**Hillsborough** (0114) 232 2100
Langsett Road/Wood Street; by Primrose View tram stop; S6 2UB Chatty and friendly pub-in-hotel, own microbrews (brewed in cellar) along with four quickly changing guests, good choice of wines and soft drinks, generous well priced food including Sun roasts, daily papers, open fire, bare-boards bar, lounge, views to ski slope from attractive back conservatory and terrace tables; silent TV; children and dogs welcome, six good value bedrooms, covered parking, open all day. *(Mike Swan)*

SHEFFIELD   SK3290
★**New Barrack** (0114) 234 9148
601 Penistone Road, Hillsborough; S6 2GA Friendly lively pub with nine ales including Castle Rock and lots of bottled belgian beers, good choice of whiskies too, tasty good value bar food (Fri, Sat light suppers till midnight), Sun carvery, comfortable front lounge with log fire and upholstered seats on old pine floors, tap room with another fire, back room for small functions, daily papers, bar billiards, regular events including chess club, live music and comedy nights; TV; children (till 9pm) and dogs welcome, attractive little walled garden, difficult local parking, closed lunchtimes Mon and Tues, otherwise open all day. *(Anon)*

SHEFFIELD   SK3186
Ranmoor (0114) 230 1325
Fulwood Road (across from church); S10 3GD Comfortable and neat open-plan Victorian local, five well kept ales including Abbeydale, Bradfield and Timothy Taylors, good value food including some tapas (not Sun, Mon), leather sofas by etched bay windows, big mirrors and period fireplaces, well varnished tables, china display cabinet, piano (often played), newspapers; dogs welcome, two outside seating areas, open all day. *(Jeremy King)*

SHEFFIELD   SK3185
Rising Sun (0114) 230 3855
Fulwood Road; S10 3QA Friendly drinkers' pub with 13 ales including seven from Abbeydale (July beer festival), plenty of bottled beers too, two rooms, one with raised back area, some leather sofas and other well worn furniture, prints and black and white photos, shelves of books, simple lunchtime food; soft background music (live Mon), quiz Weds and Sun; dogs welcome, a few

tables out in front, more on back terrace, open all day. *(Jeremy King)*

SHEFFIELD   SK3586
Sheffield Tap (0114) 273 7558
Station, platform 1B; S1 2BP Busy station bar in restored Edwardian refreshment room, popular for its huge choice of world beers on draught and in bottles, also own Tapped ales from visible microbrewery and plenty of guests including Thornbridge, knowledgeable helpful staff, snacky food, tiled interior with vaulted roof; open all day. *(David Carr)*

SHEFFIELD   SK3687
★**Wellington** (0114) 249 2295
Henry Street; by Shalesmoor tram stop; S3 7EQ Unpretentious relaxed corner pub with up to ten changing beers including own bargain Little Ale Cart brews, bottled imports, real cider, coal fire in lounge, photographs of old Sheffield, daily papers and pub games, friendly staff; tables out behind, open all day with afternoon break on Sun. *(Mike Swan)*

SHELLEY   SE2112
★**Three Acres** (01484) 602606
Roydhouse (not signed); from B6116 towards Skelmanthorpe, turn left in Shelley (signposted 'Flockton, Elmley, Elmley Moor'), go up lane for 2 miles towards radio mast; HD8 8LR Civilised former coaching inn with emphasis on hotel and dining side; roomy lounge with leather chesterfields, old prints and so forth, tankards hanging from main beam, well kept Copper Dragon, 40 malt whiskies and up to 17 wines by the glass from serious (not cheap) list, several formal dining rooms, wide choice of good if expensive food from lunchtime sandwiches up, competent friendly service; conferences, weddings and events; children welcome, fine moorland setting and lovely views, smart well equipped bedrooms. *(Michael Butler)*

SHEPLEY   SE1809
Farmers Boy (01484) 605355
Marsh Lane, W of village – off A629 at Black Bull (leads on past pub to A635); HD8 8AP Smart stone-built dining pub, small traditional beamed public bar on right, Black Sheep, Bradfield and Copper Dragon, bare-boards area on left with coal fire and sturdy country tables, carpeted part rambling back through plenty of neat linen-set dining tables, barn restaurant with own terrace, popular often imaginative food, not cheap but good value set menu (weekday lunchtime, Mon-Thurs 6-7pm), friendly service; unobtrusive background music; picnic-sets out in front, open all day. *(Anon)*

All *Guide* inspections are anonymous. Anyone claiming to be a *Good Pub Guide* inspector is a fraud. Please let us know.

SHIPLEY   SE1437

Fannys Ale House (01274) 591419

Saltaire Road; BD18 3JN Cosy and
friendly bare-boards alehouse on two floors,
gas lighting, log fire and woodburner, brewery
memorabilia, up to ten real ales including
Timothy Taylors and Theakstons in top
condition, bottled beers and farm ciders,
back extension; can be crowded weekend
evenings; dogs welcome, open all day, closed
Mon lunchtime. *(Toby Jones)*

SHIPLEY   SE1337

Hop (01274) 582111

Bingley Road; BD18 4DH Roomy open-
plan tramshed conversion, full Ossett range
and guests from curved counter, good choice
of enjoyable food including sandwiches,
sharing boards and wood-fired pizzas,
friendly helpful service; regular live music,
quiz night Thurs; no under-18s after 8pm, on
edge of Saltaire World Heritage Site, open all
day (food all day Fri, Sat and till 7pm Sun).
(Pat and Tony Martin)

SINNINGTON   SE7485

★ **Fox & Hounds** (01751) 431577

Off A170 W of Pickering; YO62 6SQ
Pretty village's popular 18th-c coaching
inn, carpeted beamed bar with two-way
woodburner, comfortable seating, various
pictures and old artefacts, imaginative
attractively presented food served by
friendly helpful staff, well kept ales such
as Black Sheep, Copper Dragon and Wold
Top, several wines by the glass and some
rare whiskies, lounge and smart separate
restaurant; background music, free wi-fi;
children and dogs welcome, picnic-sets
out at front and in garden, ten good
comfortable bedrooms. *(Ralph Beaumont,
Pat and Stewart Gordon)*

SKIPTON   SD9851

★ **Narrow Boat** (01756) 797922

*Victoria Street; pub signed down alley
off Coach Street; BD23 1JE* Lively
extended pub down cobbled alley, eight well
kept ales, draught and bottled continental
beers, farm cider and perry, dining chairs,
pews and stools around wooden tables on
bare boards, various breweriana, upstairs
galleried area with interesting canal mural,
fair-priced food (not Sun evening), folk club
Mon evening, quiz Weds; children allowed if
eating, dogs welcome, picnic-sets under front
colonnade, Leeds & Liverpool Canal nearby,
open all day. *(Dr Kevan Tucker)*

SKIPTON   SD9851

Woolly Sheep (01756) 700966

Sheep Street; BD23 1HY Bustling
refurbished narrow pub with full Timothy
Taylors range kept well and a guest,
prompt friendly enthusiastic service,
two beamed bars off flagstoned passage,
exposed brickwork, stone fireplace, lots of

sheep prints and bric-a-brac, daily papers,
attractive and comfortable lunchtime
dining area at back, good value and variety
of enjoyable food (plenty for children);
wheelchair access with help, covered decked
terrace behind, good breakfast, open all day. *(M and J White,
Dr Kevan Tucker, JHBS)*

SLAITHWAITE   SE0813

Commercial (01484) 846258

Carr Lane; HD7 5AN Centrally placed
busy corner pub with eight real ales including
two low-priced ones from local Empire, farm
cider, some snacky food; dogs welcome, near
the station and on the Transpennine Real Ale
Trail, open all day. *(Tony Hobden)*

SLEDMERE   SE9364

★ **Triton** (01377) 236078

*B1252/B1253 junction, NW of Great
Driffield; YO25 3XQ* Handsome old inn
by Sledmere House, open-plan bar with
old-fashioned atmosphere, dark wooden
furniture on red patterned carpet, 15 clocks
ranging from grandfather to cuckoo, lots of
willow pattern plates, all manner of paintings
and pictures, open fire, Greene King, Timothy
Taylors, Tetleys and Wold Top, 50 different
gins, well liked freshly cooked food (only
take bookings in separate restaurant),
friendly helpful staff; children welcome till
8pm, five good bedrooms, massive breakfast,
open all day Sun till 9pm, closed winter Mon
lunchtime. *(Dennis Jones)*

SLINGSBY   SE6975

Grapes (01653) 628076

*Off B1257 Malton–Hovingham; Railway
Street; YO62 4AL* Stone-built 18th-c
village pub, good sensibly priced food (not
Sun evening) from traditional menu, Black
Sheep, Copper Dragon, Timothy Taylors and
Theakstons, cheerful staff, bare boards,
flagstones and painted beams, nice mix of
old furniture and some interesting bits and
pieces including a tusky boar's head above
one of the woodburners, games area with
bar billiards; tables out behind, open all day
Fri-Sun, closed Mon. *(Belinda Stamp)*

SNAINTON   TA9182

Coachman (01723) 859231

Pickering Road W (A170); YO13 9PL
Ongoing refurbishment and perhaps more
restaurant-with-rooms, but does have a small
lively log-fire bar serving local ales, good well
presented food in smart linen-clothed dining
room, friendly service; well tended gardens,
three bedrooms, good breakfast. *(Sara Fulton,
Roger Baker)*

SNAITH   SE6422

Brewers Arms (01405) 862404

Pontefract Road; DN14 9JS Georgian
inn tied to local Old Mill Brewery, their
distinctive range from brick and timber-
fronted servery, decent home-made food

including fresh fish/seafood and decent quality Sun lunch, friendly helpful staff, open-plan carpeted interior, old well complete with skeleton; children welcome in eating areas, attractive, good quality bedrooms. *(Toby Jones)*

SNAPE SE2684
★ Castle Arms (01677) 470270
Off B6268 Masham–Bedale; DL8 2TB Welcoming homely pub in pretty village, flagstoned bar with open fire, horsebrasses on beams, straightforward pubby furniture, Banks's, Jennings and Marstons, enjoyable food, dining room (also flagstoned) with dark tables and chairs and another fire; children and dogs welcome, picnic-sets out at front and in courtyard, fine walks in Yorkshire Dales and on North York Moors, nine good bedrooms. *(Mike Swan)*

SOUTH KILVINGTON SE4284
Old Oak Tree (01845) 523276
Stockton Road (A61); YO7 2NL Spacious low-ceilinged pub with three linked rooms and long back conservatory, good honest food and well kept beers served by friendly staff; tables on sloping lawn. *(Tina and David Woods-Taylor)*

SOWERBY BRIDGE SE0623
Shepherds Rest (01422) 831937
On A58 Halifax–Sowerby Bridge; HX6 2BD Friendly two-room Ossett pub, their full range and guests such as Fernandes and Rat, no food; suntrap back terrace, open all day Fri-Sun, from 3pm other days. *(Pat and Tony Martin)*

SOWERBY BRIDGE SE0523
Works (01422) 834821
Hollins Mill Lane, off A58; HX6 2QG Large airy bare-boards pub in converted joinery workshop by Rochdale Canal, seating from pews to comfortable sofas, at least eight well kept ales including Timothy Taylors Landlord and Golden Best, a couple of ciders, good bargain home-made food from sandwiches and pub favourites to vegetarian choices and specials, Weds curry night, Sun brunch, comedy and music nights in big upstairs room; children and dogs welcome, backyard (covered in poor weather), disabled facilities, open (and food) all day. *(Pat and Tony Martin)*

STAMFORD BRIDGE SE7055
★ Three Cups (01759) 377381
A166 W of town; YO41 1AX Good Vintage Inn family dining pub with popular food including meal deals, plenty of wines by the glass and three well kept beers, friendly helpful staff, pleasant rustic décor with two blazing fires, glass-topped well in bar; disabled access, play area behind, river walks nearby, open (and food) all day. *(Pat and Graham Williamson)*

STANBURY SE0037
Old Silent (01535) 647437
Hob Lane; BD22 0HW Friendly moorland dining pub with genuine welcome, enjoyable reasonably priced home-made food, Timothy Taylors Landlord, Theakstons Old Peculier and guests, attentive helpful service, character linked rooms with beams, flagstones, mullioned windows and open fires, restaurant and conservatory; free wi-fi; children and dogs welcome, bedrooms, open all day till 9pm (8pm Sun). *(Belinda Stamp)*

STAVELEY SE3662
Royal Oak (01423) 340267
Signed off A6055 Knaresborough–Boroughbridge; HG5 9LD Popular welcoming pub in village conservation area; beams and panelling, open fires, broad bow window overlooking front lawn, well kept Black Sheep, Timothy Taylors and a guest, several wines by the glass, good choice of enjoyable food in bar and restaurant. *(Mike Swan)*

STILLINGTON SE5867
Bay Tree (01347) 811394
Main Street; leave York on outer ring road (A1237) to Scarborough, first exit on left signposted B1363 to Helmsley; YO61 1JU Cottagey pub-restaurant in pretty village's main street, contemporary bar areas with civilised chatty atmosphere, comfortable cushioned wall seats and leather/bamboo tub chairs around mix of tables, church candles and lanterns, central gas-effect coal fire, real ales such as Black Sheep, several wines by the glass and enjoyable bistro-style food including blackboard specials, steps up to cosy dining area, larger conservatory-style back restaurant; background music; seats in garden and a couple of picnic-sets at front, closed Mon. *(Anon)*

SUTTON UPON DERWENT SE7047
★ St Vincent Arms (01904) 608349
Main Street (B1228 SE of York); YO41 4BN Enjoyable cheerful pub with Fullers and up to seven guests, lots of wines by the glass, good popular bar food (more elaborate evening meals – need to book weekends), bustling parlour-style front bar with panelling, traditional high-backed settles, windsor chairs, cushioned bow-window seat and gas-effect coal fire, another lounge and separate dining room open off here; children welcome, dogs in bar, garden tables, handy for Yorkshire Air Museum. *(Kay and Alistair Butler)*

SUTTON-UNDER-WHITESTONECLIFFE SE4983
Whitestonecliffe Inn
(01845) 597271 *A170 E of Thirsk; YO7 2PR* Well located 18th-c beamed roadside pub, enjoyable fairly priced food

from traditional menu along with blackboard specials, three well kept ales including Black Sheep, friendly staff, log fire and some exposed stonework in bar, separate restaurant, games room with pool and darts; quiz last Fri of month; children and dogs welcome, six self-catering cottages, open all day weekends, closed Mon lunchtime. *(Helen and Brian Edgeley, Chris Willers)*

TAN HILL   NY8906
★ **Tan Hill Inn** (01833) 628246
Arkengarthdale Road, Reeth–Brough, at junction Keld/West Stonesdale Road; DL11 6ED Basic old pub (Britain's highest) in wonderful bleak setting on Pennine Way, full of bric-a-brac and interesting photographs, simple sturdy furniture, flagstones, ever-burning big log fire (with prized stone side seats), chatty atmosphere, five well kept ales including one badged for them from Dent, good cheap pubby food, family room, live weekend music; can get overcrowded, often snowbound; children and dogs welcome, seven bedrooms, bunk rooms and camping, ducks and chickens, Swaledale sheep show here last Thurs in May, open all day. *(Emma Scofield)*

THIRSK   SE4282
Golden Fleece (01845) 523108
Market Place; YO7 1LL Comfortable bustling old coaching inn with enjoyable bar food and afternoon tea, Black Sheep ales and good friendly service, restaurant, view across marketplace from bay windows; dogs welcome, 23 bedrooms, good breakfast. *(Mike Swan)*

THIXENDALE   SE8461
Cross Keys (01377) 288272
Off A166 3 miles N of Fridaythorpe; YO17 9TG Unspoilt country pub in deep valley below the rolling Wolds and popular with walkers; cosy and relaxed L-shaped bar with fitted wall seats, well kept Tetleys and a couple of guests, generous uncomplicated blackboard food; no children inside, big garden behind with views, handy for Wharram Percy earthworks, comfortable bedrooms in converted stables, good breakfast, closed Mon lunchtime (Mon-Thurs luchtimes winter). *(Anon)*

THOLTHORPE   SE4766
New Inn (01347) 838329
Flawith Road; YO61 1SL Cleanly updated beamed village-green pub with log-fire bar and candlelit restaurant, good, highly regarded, locally sourced food (not Tues lunchtime) including early-bird deal, allergies catered for, John Smiths and a local guest; children welcome, closed Mon. *(John and Eleanor Holdsworth)*

THORNTON   SE0933
Ring o' Bells (01274) 832296
Hill Top Road, W of village, and N of

B6145; BD13 3QL Hilltop dining pub under long-serving owners, cosy series of linked rooms with dark beams and panelling, plush seating for glass-topped tables on red carpeting, old local photographs at one end, more modern restaurant the other, Black Sheep Best, Copper Dragon Golden Pippin and Saltaire Blonde, nine wines by the glass and 20 malt whiskies, quite a range of food from pubby dishes up; background music; high position gives long views towards Shipley and Bingley. *(Toby Jones)*

THORNTON   SE0832
White Horse (01274) 834268
Well Heads; BD13 3SJ Deceptively large country pub popular for its wide choice of good food including early-bird menu, five well kept Timothy Taylors ales, pleasant helpful staff, four separate areas, two with log fires; children welcome, upstairs lavatories (disabled ones on ground level), also disabled parking, open all day, food all day weekends (till 7.45pm Sun). *(Gordon and Margaret Ormondroyd, John and Eleanor Holdsworth and others)*

THORNTON DALE   SE8383
New Inn (01751) 474226
The Square; YO18 7LF Friendly early 18th-c beamed coaching inn doing well under newish young couple – packed weekend evenings; well kept ales and good traditional food cooked by landlord; dogs welcome in bar, courtyard tables, bedrooms, pretty village in walking area. *(Sara Fulton, Roger Baker)*

THORNTON-LE-CLAY   SE6865
White Swan (01653) 618286
Off A64 SW of Malton, via Foston; Low Street; YO60 7TG 19th-c family-run village pub; Black Sheep, Moorhouses and a beer named for the pub, nice wines by the glass and highly enjoyable well priced home-made food including daily specials, friendly helpful young staff, some local chutneys, preserves etc for sale; children welcome, large garden (maybe summer bouncy castle), attractive countryside nearby and Castle Howard, closed Mon, Tues, open all day weekends. *(Mike Swan)*

THORP ARCH   SE4346
Pax (01937) 843183
The Village; LS23 7AR Welcoming 19th-c village pub, enjoyable home-made food (notable steak and ale pie) at sensible prices, ales such as Abbeydale, Moorhouses and Roosters, friendly helpful service, two bar areas, open fire, back dining area; children and dogs welcome, useful stop for A1, open all day weekends, closed Mon. *(Les and Sandra Brown)*

THRESHFIELD   SD9863
Old Hall Inn (01756) 752441
B6160/B6265 just outside Grassington; BD23 5HB Old creeper-clad village inn set

back from the road, enjoyable food served by attentive friendly staff, good choice of beers and wines, flagstoned bar with dining rooms either side, open fires (one in fine blacked kitchen range), high beam-and-plank ceiling, cushioned wall pews; neat garden and pretty hanging baskets, seven comfortable bedrooms, self-catering cottage, open (and food) all day. *(T Peter Wall, Gordon and Margaret Ormondroyd)*

TIMBLE   SE1852
★ **Timble Inn** (01943) 880530
Off Otley–Blubberhouses moors road; LS21 2NN Smartly restored 18th-c inn tucked away in quiet farmland hamlet, good food from pub favourites up including well aged Nidderdale beef (booking advised), ales such as Copper Dragon, Ilkley and Theakstons; children welcome, no dogs at food times, good walks from the door, seven well appointed bedrooms, closed Sun evening to Weds lunchtime. *(Mungo Shipley)*

TOCKWITH   SE4652
Spotted Ox (01423) 358387
Westfield Road, off B1224; YO26 7PY Traditional beamed village local, friendly and relaxed, with well served ales including Tetleys, good choice of enjoyable sensibly priced home-made food, attentive staff, three areas off central bar, interesting local history; open all day Fri-Sun. *(Les and Sandra Brown)*

TONG   SE2230
Greyhound (0113) 285 2427
Tong Lane; BD4 0RR Traditional low-beamed and flagstoned local by village cricket field, distinctive areas including cosy dining room, generous helpings of enjoyable good value food, ales such as Black Sheep, Leeds, Timothy Taylors and Tetleys, several wines by the glass, good friendly service; tables outside, open all day (food till 5.45pm Sun). *(Gordon and Margaret Ormondroyd, Michael Butler)*

TOPCLIFFE   SE4076
Angel (01845) 578000
Off A1, take A168 to Thirsk, after 3 miles follow signs for Topcliffe; Long Street; YO7 3RW Part of the West Park Inns group; softly lit bare-boards bar with log fire, real ales and good choice of wines by the glass, enjoyable food in carpeted grill restaurant, weekday early-bird deal (5-6pm), cheerful helpful service; background music, comedy night (usually first Tues of month); children welcome, nice garden, 16 bedrooms, open all day (food all day Sun till 7pm). *(John and Eleanor Holdsworth, Michael Doswell)*

TOTLEY   SK3080
Cricket (0114) 236 5256
Signed from A621; Penny Lane; S17 3AZ Tucked-away 19th-c stone-built pub (part of the BrewKitchen group) beside rustic cricket field, much focus on dining but still

a friendly local atmosphere, pews, mixed chairs and pine tables on bare boards and flagstones, log fires, good quality blackboard food from sandwiches and pub staples to more unusual choices including portuguese dishes and own-smoked fish/meats, cheaper lunchtime/early evening set menu (Mon-Fri), Thornbridge ales and good choice of wines from extensive list, friendly service; children and dogs welcome, outside tables and summer barbecues, Peak District views, open (and food) all day. *(Mrs Jo Rees, David Carr)*

TOWTON   SE4839
Rockingham Arms (01937) 530948
A162 Tadcaster–Ferrybridge; LS24 9PB Comfortably refurbished roadside village pub, enjoyable home-made food including early-bird menu (5-7pm Tues-Thurs), friendly attentive service, ales such as Black Sheep and Theakstons, back conservatory; garden tables, handy for Towton Battlefield, closed Sun evening, Mon, otherwise open all day. *(Revd R P Tickle)*

WAINSTALLS   SE0428
Cat i' th' Well (01422) 244841
From Halifax, turn left at the Crossroads pub in Wainstalls, follow narrow road downhill, pub is on left after steep bend over little bridge; HX2 7TR Picturesque country pub in fine hidden-away spot towards the windy top of Luddenden Dean; dining area on the left, larger flagstoned bar with attractive fireplace on right, some 19th-c reclaimed panelling, well kept Timothy Taylors ales and a guest, decent home-made food (not Mon-Weds, till 6pm Sun) from lunchtime sandwiches up, friendly service; children and walkers welcome, no dogs inside, tables outside (some under cover), handy for Calderdale Way, open all day Fri-Sun. *(Gordon and Margaret Ormondroyd)*

WAKEFIELD   SE3320
Bull & Fairhouse (01924) 362930
George Street; WF1 1DL Welcoming chatty 19th-c pub, well kept Bobs White Lion, Great Heck Golden Bull and four other changing ales (beer festivals), bare-boards bar with comfortable rooms off, open fire, no food, live music weekends, quiz Thurs; children welcome till 8pm, dogs on leads, open all day Fri-Sun, from 4pm other days. *(Harvey Brown)*

WAKEFIELD   SE3417
Castle (01924) 256981
Barnsley Road, Sandal; WF2 6AS Popular dining pub with good affordably priced food cooked to order, well kept beers such as York, friendly staff and pleasant relaxed atmosphere; unobtrusive background music. *(Toby Jones)*

WAKEFIELD   SE3320
Fernandes Brewery Tap (01924) 386348 *Avison Yard, Kirkgate;*

WF1 1UA Owned by Ossett but still brewing Fernandes ales in cellar, interesting guest beers, bottled imports and traditional ciders, ground-floor bar with flagstones, bare brick and panelling, original raftered top-floor bar with unusual breweriana; dogs welcome, open all day Fri-Sun (when some lunchtime food available), from 4pm other days. *(Anon)*

WAKEFIELD SE3220
Harrys Bar (01924) 373773
Westgate; WF1 1EL Cheery little one-room local with friendly staff serving well kept Leeds, Ossett and guests, stripped-brick walls, open fire, live music Weds; small back garden, open all day Sun, closed lunchtime other days. *(Mike Swan)*

WALKINGTON SE9937
Dog & Duck (01482) 423026
B1230, East End; HU17 8RX Comfortably modernised pub with enjoyable generously served food including blackboard specials and Sun lunch, four well kept Marstons-related beers, friendly helpful service; sports TV; children welcome, garden and terrace with pizza oven and barbecue, charming village, open (and food) all day. *(Belinda May)*

WALKINGTON SE9937
Ferguson-Fawsitt Arms
(01482) 882665 *East End; B1230 W of Beverley; HU17 8RX* Named after two important local families and known as the 'Fergie'; new manager is friendly and service is good, wide choice of popular reasonably priced food including carvery (all day Sun), real ales and decent wines, interesting mock-Tudor bars; children welcome, tables out on terrace, ten good value bedrooms in modern annexe, delightful village. *(Harvey Brown)*

WALTON SE4447
Fox & Hounds (01937) 842192
Hall Park Road, off back road Wetherby–Tadcaster; LS23 7DQ Newish owners for busy dining pub with good reasonably priced food from sandwiches to specials (should book Sun lunch), well kept Black Sheep, John Smiths and a guest, friendly thriving atmosphere; children welcome, handy A1 stop. *(Malcolm and Pauline Pellatt)*

WALTON SE3517
New Inn (01924) 255447
Shay Lane; WF2 6LA Open-plan village pub with several well kept beers including Ossett, Theakstons and Timothy Taylors, good helpings of tasty well priced food, friendly staff and buoyant atmosphere, split-level back dining extension; quiz and music nights; garden with play area; children welcome, dogs in bar, open (and food) all day. *(Michael Butler)*

WARLEY TOWN SE0524
Maypole (01422) 835861
Signed off A646 just W of Halifax; HX2 7RZ Friendly open-plan village dining pub, enjoyable good value food from fairly traditional menu including lunchtime/early evening set deal, well kept ales such as Black Sheep, pleasant young staff, two-way woodburner; children welcome, open all day Fri-Sun, closed Mon lunchtime. *(John and Eleanor Holdsworth, Pat and Tony Martin)*

WATH SE3277
George (01765) 641324
Main Street; village N of Ripon; HG4 5EN Friendly refurbished village pub with good range of enjoyable traditional food (not Sun evening), Rudgate, Theakstons and a guest, decent choice of wines; five comfortable bedrooms, open all day weekends closed lunchtimes Mon, Tues. *(Toby Jones)*

WATH-IN-NIDDERDALE SE1467
★Sportsmans Arms (01423) 711306
Nidderdale road off B6265 in Pateley Bridge; village and pub signposted over hump-back bridge, on right after a couple of miles; HG3 5PP Civilised, beautifully located restaurant with rooms run by long-serving owner; although most emphasis on the excellent food and bedrooms, it does have a proper welcoming bar with open fire (a highly rated ploughman's here), Black Sheep and Timothy Taylors Landlord, Thatcher's cider, 20 wines by the glass from extensive list and 40 malt whiskies, helpful hospitable staff; background music; children welcome, dogs in bar, benches and tables outside, pretty garden with croquet, own fishing on River Nidd. *(Hunter and Christine Wright, Gordon and Margaret Ormondroyd, Lynda and Trevor Smith, Stephen Woad)*

WEAVERTHORPE SE9670
Blue Bell (01944) 738204
Main Road; YO17 8EX Upscale country dining pub, quite ornate in parts, with good attractively presented food and fine choice of wines (many by the glass including champagne), well kept Tetleys and Timothy Taylors Landlord, cosy cheerful bar with unusual collection of bottles and packaging, open fire, intimate back restaurant, friendly attentive staff; 12 bedrooms (six in annexe), interesting village, closed Sun evening, Mon. *(Dr Simon Innes)*

WENSLEY SE0989
Three Horseshoes (01969) 622327
A684; DL8 4HJ Simple little beamed and flagstoned country pub, friendly staff and

---

There are report forms at the back of the book.

regulars, warm woodburner, good selection
of local ales and tasty straightforward food;
outside lavatories; dogs welcome, lovely
views from garden, popular with walkers,
open all day. *(Caroline Prescott)*

WENTWORTH   SK3898
Rockingham Arms (01226) 742075
*3 miles from M1 junction 36; B6090,
signed off A6135; Main Street; S62 7TL*
Welcoming 19th-c ivy-clad inn (John Barras),
comfortable traditional furnishings, stripped
stone and open fires, bar with two snug
rooms off, more formal dining room, several
ales including Theakstons and good choice
of wines by the glass, well priced traditional
food; background music, TV; dogs allowed in
part, attractive garden with bowling green,
11 bedrooms, open (and food) all day.
(Michael Butler)

WEST TANFIELD   SE2678
Bruce Arms (01677) 470325
Main Street (A6108 N of Ripon); HG4 5JJ
Doing well under new management with
good food (nice Sun lunch) in comfortable,
welcoming rooms, well kept Black Sheep
and Copper Dragon, nice wines, flagstones
and log fires; two bedrooms, good
breakfast. *(Harvey Brown)*

WEST TANFIELD   SE2678
Bull (01677) 470678
*Church Street (A6108 N of Ripon);
HG4 5JQ* New owners for busy inn with
open-plan rooms, slightly raised dining
area to the left and flagstoned bar on right,
popular fairly standard food (all day Sat, not
Sun evening), well kept Black Sheep and
Theakstons, pleasant service; background
and occasional live music; children (away
from bar) and dogs welcome, tables on
terraces in attractive garden sloping steeply
to River Ure and its old bridge, five bedrooms,
open all day weekends, closed Tues.
(Belinda Stamp)

WEST WITTON   SE0588
Wensleydale Heifer (01969) 622322
A684 W of Leyburn; DL8 4LS Stylish
restaurant-with-rooms rather than pub, but
can pop in just for a drink; excellent food
with emphasis on fish/seafood and grills (not
cheap), also good value set menu (lunchtime/
early evening), good wines, cosy informal
upmarket food bar with Black Sheep and a
house beer brewed by Yorkshire, extensive
main formal restaurant, attentive helpful
service; saucy seaside postcards in gents';
13 good bedrooms (back ones quietest),
big breakfast, open all day. *(Geoff and Linda
Payne, Comus and Sarah Elliott)*

WESTOW   SE7565
Blacksmiths Arms (01653) 619606
*Off A64 York–Malton; Main Street;
YO60 7NE* 18th-c pub with attractive
beamed bar, woodburner in brick inglenook,

original bread oven, beers such as Copper
Dragon, Tetleys and Thwaites, enjoyable
home-made food from sandwiches and pub
favourites up, restaurant; picnic-sets on side
terrace, closed Mon, otherwise open all day.
(Emma Scofield)

WETHERBY   SE4048
Swan & Talbot (01937) 582040
Handy for A1; North Street; LS22 6NN
Comfortable traditional town pub (former
posting inn) with large bar area and
restaurant, good generous food including
deals, nice Sunday lunch and daily specials,
well kept ales such as Black Sheep, Fullers
and John Smiths, busy friendly staff;
children welcome, courtyard tables, open
all day. *(Gordon and Jenny Quick)*

WHITBY   NZ9011
Black Horse (01947) 602906
Church Street; YO22 4BH Small
traditional two-room pub, much older than
its Victorian frontage, and previously a
funeral parlour and brothel; friendly and
down to earth with Adnams, Black Dog,
Timothy Taylors and a couple of guests,
Yorkshire 'tapas', tins of snuff for sale;
dogs welcome, four cosy bedrooms, open
all day. *(David Carr)*

WHITBY   NZ9011
Board (01947) 602884
Church Street; YO22 4DE Busy pub in
good spot opposite fish quay, faux-beamed
bar with nice old range in one part,
banquettes and other pubby furniture on
patterned carpet, modern dining room
downstairs with fine harbour view from big
windows, well kept Caledonian Deuchars IPA
and Theakstons, good value pub food, friendly
staff; background and live music, Weds quiz,
TV and games machine; bedrooms. *(Stanley
and Annie Matthews)*

WHITBY   NZ9011
Dolphin (01947) 602197
*Bridge Street, just over bridge to E/Old
Whitby; YO22 4BG* Well positioned inn
with good harbour views, enjoyable home-
made food from lunchtime sandwiches up,
friendly service, ales such as Black Sheep,
Copper Dragon and Timothy Taylors, various
linked areas on different levels; TV, games
machine, darts; children and dogs welcome,
seats out in front by swing bridge, six
bedrooms (five with views). *(David Carr)*

WHITBY   NZ9011
★ Duke of York (01947) 600324
*Church Street, Harbour East Side;
YO22 4DE* Busy pub in fine harbourside
position, good views and handy for the
famous 199 steps leading up to abbey;
comfortable beamed lounge bar with fishing
memorabilia, Black Sheep, Caledonian and
three guests, decent wines and several malt
whiskies, enjoyable straightforward bar

food at reasonable prices, attentive service; background music, TV, games machine; children welcome, bedrooms overlooking water, no nearby parking, open (and food) all day. *(Pat and Graham Williamson, David Carr, Ian and Jane Irving)*

WHITBY NZ8911
Station Inn (01947) 603937
New Quay Road; YO21 1DH Friendly three-room bare-boards drinkers' pub across from the station and harbour, clean and comfortable, with good mix of customers, seven well kept ales including a house beer brewed by Whitby, Weston's cider and good wines by the glass, traditional games; background music and regular live music; dogs welcome, open all day. *(Dr Simon Innes)*

WIGGLESWORTH SD8056
Plough (01729) 840243
B6478, off A65 S of Settle; BD23 4RJ Light, airy and comfortable old inn with good elegantly presented modern food (all day Sun till 7pm), friendly efficient service, local ales and decent wines by the glass, cosy log fire, panoramic Dales views; quiet bedrooms. *(Mike Swan)*

WIGHILL SE4746
White Swan (01937) 832217
Main Street; LS24 8BQ Updated fairly modern village pub with two cosy front rooms and larger side extension, genuinely friendly staff, enjoyable traditional home-cooked food, well kept Black Sheep, a house brew from Moorhouses and a guest, tea room; children welcome, no dogs inside, wheelchair access with help (steps down to lavatories), picnic-sets on side lawn, closed Mon, Tues lunchtime. *(Emma Scofield)*

WOMBLETON SE6683
Plough (01751) 431356
Main Street; YO62 7RW Welcoming village local with good home-made food including highly thought-of blackboard specials, ales such as Black Sheep, John Smiths, Tetleys and Theakstons, bar eating area and restaurant; tables outside. *(Stanley and Annie Matthews)*

WORTLEY SK3099
Wortley Arms (0114) 288 8749
A629 N of Sheffield; S35 7DB 18th-c stone-built coaching inn with several comfortably furnished rooms, beams, panelling and large inglenook, good food (all day Sat) and five well kept ales including Timothy Taylors and Wentworth; children and dogs (in bar) welcome, nice village about ten minutes from M1, open all day (till 8.30pm Sun). *(Fiona Thomas, Michael Butler)*

YORK SE6051
Black Swan (01904) 686910
Peaseholme Green (inner ring road); YO1 7PR Striking timbered and jettied Tudor building, compact panelled front bar, crooked-floored central hall with fine period staircase, vast inglenook in black-beamed back bar, good choice of real ales, decent wines and reasonably priced generous helpings of pubby food from sandwiches up; background music; children welcome, useful car park behind, bedrooms, open all day. *(Dr Simon Innes)*

YORK SE6051
★**Blue Bell** (01904) 654904
Fossgate; YO1 9TF Delightfully old-fashioned little Edwardian pub, very friendly and chatty, with well kept Bradfield, Rudgate, Timothy Taylors Landlord and three guests (a dark mild always available), good value lunchtime sandwiches (not Sun), daily papers, tiny tiled-floor front bar with roaring fire, panelled ceiling and stained glass, corridor to small back room with hatch service, lamps and candles, pub games; soft background music; no children, dogs welcome, open all day (but maybe just for locals on busy nights). *(Toby Jones)*

YORK SE5951
★**Brigantes** (01904) 675355
Micklegate; YO1 6JX Refurbished Market Town Tavern bar-bistro with shop-style frontage, wooden table and chairs on bare boards, blue-painted half-panelling and screens forming booths, ten well kept mainly Yorkshire ales (York Brewery is in street behind), good range of bottled beers, Broadoak's cider, decent wines and coffee, good food from fairly priced varied menu, quick cheerful service, upstairs function room; children and dogs welcome, open all day, food all day weekends. *(Brian and Janet Ainscough, GSB, Pat and Tony Martin)*

YORK SE6051
Golden Ball (01904) 652211
Cromwell Road/Victor Street; YO1 6DU Friendly and busy well preserved four-room Edwardian corner pub owned by local co-operative, five well kept changing ales, no food apart from bar snacks, bar billiards, cards and dominoes, live music Thurs; TV; lovely small walled garden, open all day weekends, closed weekday lunchtimes. *(Toby Jones)*

YORK SE6051
Golden Fleece (01904) 625171
Pavement; YO1 9UP Popular little city-centre pub with good value generously served food, well kept beers from Copper Dragon, Timothy Taylors, Theakstons and Wychwood, long corridor from bar to comfortable back dining room (sloping floors – it dates from 1503), interesting décor with quite a library, lots of pictures and ghost stories; background music and occasional folk evenings; children allowed if eating, no dogs, four bedrooms, open all day. *(Dr Simon Innes)*

YORK   SE6052
Golden Slipper (01904) 651235
Goodramgate; YO1 7LG Dating from
15th c with unpretentious bar and three
comfortably old-fashioned small rooms, one
lined with books, cheerful efficient licensees,
simple but popular low-priced lunchtime food
(till 6pm Thurs-Sun) from sandwiches up,
five changing ales, Weds quiz, Sun live music;
TV, free wi-fi; children welcome, tables in
back courtyard. *(Anon, Toby Jones)*

YORK   SE6052
Guy Fawkes (01904) 466674
High Petergate; YO1 7HP Friendly pub
in splendid spot next to the Minster, dark
panelled interior with small bar to the left,
half a dozen real ales including a house
beer from Great Heck, enjoyable sensibly
priced food (not Sun evening) from shortish
menu plus blackboard specials, good helpful
service, dining rooms lit by gas wall-lights
and candles, open fires; courtyard tables,
13 bedrooms, open all day. *(Paul Humphreys,
Phil Bryant)*

YORK   SE6051
Harkers (01904) 672795
St Helens Square; YO1 8QN Handsome
late Georgian building (basement has part
of Roman gateway) converted by Nicholsons,
spacious split-level bar with high ceilings and
columns, a couple of smaller rooms off, half
a dozen ales including Rudgate, John Smiths
and York from long counter, their usual good
value food; open all day. *(Theocsbrian)*

YORK   SE6052
House of Trembling Madness
(01904) 640000 *Stonegate; YO1 8AS*
Unusual place above own off-licence;
impressive high-raftered medieval room
with collection of stuffed animal heads from
moles to lions, eclectic mix of furniture
including cask seats and pews on bare
boards, lovely old brick fireplace, real ales
and craft beers from pulpit servery, also huge
selection of bottled beers (all available to
buy downstairs), good knowledgeable staff,
hearty reasonably priced food including
various platters; two self-catering apartments
in ancient courtyard behind, open (and food)
all day. *(Eric Larkham)*

YORK   SE6052
Lamb & Lion (01904) 612078
High Petergate; YO1 7EH Sparse
furnishings and low lighting including
candles giving a spartan Georgian feel,
four well kept ales including Black Sheep
and a locally brewed house beer, enjoyable
simple bar food plus more elaborate evening
set menu (Tues-Sat), no food Sun evening,
compact rooms off dark corridors; steep steps
up to small attractive garden below city wall
and looking up to the Minster, 12 bedrooms,
open all day. *(Paul Humphreys, John T Ames)*

YORK   SE6051
Lendal Cellars (01904) 623121
Lendal; YO1 8AA Split-level ale house
in broad-vaulted 17th-c cellars, stripped
brickwork, stone floor, linked rooms and
alcoves, good choice of changing ales and
wines by the glass, foreign bottled beers,
farm cider and decent coffee, good value
popular pubby food, friendly helpful staff;
background music; children allowed if
eating, no dogs, open (and food) all day.
(Dr Simon Innes)

YORK   SE6052
Old White Swan (01904) 540911
Goodramgate; YO1 7LF Bustling spacious
Nicholsons pub with Victorian, Georgian
and Tudor-themed bars, popular good value
food, eight well kept ales and good whisky
choice, central glass-covered courtyard (dogs
allowed here); background and monthly live
music, big-screen sports TV, games machines;
children welcome (till 9pm if eating), open
all day. *(Phil Bryant)*

YORK   SE6051
Phoenix (01904) 656401
George Street; YO1 9PT Friendly little
pub next to city walls, proper front public
bar and comfortable back horseshoe-
shaped lounge, five well kept ales for
Yorkshire brewers, decent wines and
simple food, live jazz two or three times
a week, bar billiards; beer garden, handy
for Barbican, open all day Sat, closed
lunchtimes other days. *(Anon)*

YORK
Pivni (01904) 635464
Patrick Pool; YO1 8BB Old black and
white pub close to the Shambles, extensive
range of foreign draught and bottled beers
(some unusual choices), also good selection
of local ales, friendly knowledgeable staff,
small narrow bar, more seats upstairs,
snacky food and good coffee; open all day.
(Phil Bryant)

YORK   SE6051
Punch Bowl (01904) 655147
Stonegate; YO1 8AN Bustling 17th-c
black and white fronted pub with small
panelled rooms off corridor, good choice
of well kept ales, decent wines and sensibly
priced Nicholsons menu, efficient friendly
service, dining room at back with fireplace;
background music; a couple of tables out
by pavement, open (and food) all day.
(Eddie Edwards)

YORK   SE6052
Snickleway (01904) 656138
Goodramgate; YO1 7LS Interesting little
open-plan pub behind big shop-front window,
lots of antiques, copper and brass, cosy fires,
five well kept ales, some lunchtime food (not
Sun) including good sandwiches, cheery

landlord and prompt friendly service, Tues quiz, various ghosts including Mrs Tulliver and her cat; open all day. *(Paul Humphreys)*

YORK   SE6052
Star Inn the City (01904) 619208
Museum Street; YO1 7DR Restaurant y place (sister to the Star at Harome) in wonderful central riverside setting – a former 19th-c pumping station with modern glass extension; very good but not cheap food (they also do a weekday set menu till early evening), beers including a house brew (Two Chefs) from Great Yorkshire, good range of wines by the glass and cocktails, friendly service; open all day from 8am (9am Sun) for breakfast. *(Richard Tilbrook)*

YORK   SE6051
Swan (01904) 634968
Bishopgate Street, Clementhorpe; YO23 1JH Unspoilt 1930s pub (Grade II listed), hatch service to lobby for two small rooms off main bar, several changing ales and ciders, friendly knowledgeable staff may offer tasters; small pleasant walled garden, near city walls, open all day weekends, closed weekday lunchtimes. *(Dr Simon Innes)*

YORK   SE6052
★Three Legged Mare (01904) 638246
High Petergate; YO1 7EN Bustling light and airy modern café-bar with York Brewery's full range and guests kept well (12 handpumps), plenty of belgian beers too, quick friendly young staff, interesting sandwiches and some basic lunchtime hot food, back conservatory; no children; disabled facilities (other lavatories down spiral stairs), back garden with replica gallows after which pub is named, open all day till midnight (11pm Sun). *(Theocsbrian)*

YORK   SE5951
Whippet (01904) 500660
Opposite Park Inn Hotel, North Street; YO1 6JD Steak and ale house in street set back from the river, good popular food including dry-aged chargrilled steaks, small bar area with four well kept ales from Yorkshire brewers, lots of wines by the glass, interesting cocktails and excellent range of gins, friendly well informed staff; no children, open all day. *(Pat and Graham Williamson)*

YORK   SE5951
York Tap (01904) 659009
Station Road; YO24 1AB Restored Edwardian bar at York station, high ceiling with feature stained-glass dome, columns and iron fretwork, bentwood chairs and stools on terrazzo floor, button-back banquettes, period fireplaces, great selection of real ales from circular counter with brass footrail, also bottled beers listed on blackboard, good pork pies (three types); open all day from 10am. *(Dave Braisted)*

YORK   SE6052
Yorkshire Terrier (01904) 621162
Stonegate; YO1 8AS Unpretentious little pub tucked behind the York Brewery shop (enter by side door): their full range and guests (tasting trays available), interesting bottled beers, friendly helpful staff, good value simple lunchtime food such as pie and peas, small conservatory, upstairs room with stair lift; weekend live music; children and dogs welcome, handy for the Minster, open all day. *(Pat and Tony Martin, Eddie Edwards)*

London

KEY	⭐ Star Pub	🏅 Top Quality Food	🍺 Great Beer
	🍷 Good Wines	£ Bargain Meals	🛏 Good Bedrooms	🍴 Serves Food

CENTRAL LONDON   Map 13

Admiral Codrington 🍷

(020) 7581 0005 – www.theadmiralcodrington.co.uk
Mossop Street; ⊖ South Kensington; SW3 2LY

Long-standing Chelsea landmark with easy-going bar and pretty restaurant, popular food and seats outside

Tucked away down a small street in Chelsea, this is a well run, bustling place with a civilised but informal air. A central dark-panelled bar has high red chairs beside the counter with more around equally high tables on either side of the log-effect gas fire, button-back wall banquettes with cream and red patterned seats, little stools and plain wooden chairs around a medley of tables on black-painted boards, patterned wallpaper above a dado and a shelf with daily papers. There are also ornate flower arrangements, a big portrait above the fire, several naval prints and quiet background music. The friendly, helpful staff serve Marstons Pedigree New World and Upham Punter and Tipster on handpump, good wines by the glass and, of course, their famous bloody mary. The recently refurbished light and airy restaurant area is a total contrast: high-backed pretty wall seats and green plush dining chairs around light tables, an open kitchen, fish prints on pale green paintwork, a second fireplace and an impressive retractable skylight. The back garden has chunky benches and tables under a summer awning.

🍴 Enjoyable food includes salt and pepper squid with chilli, ham hock terrine with prune and brandy purée, asparagus and pine nut risotto, crab linguine, fresh battered haddock with triple-cooked chips, confit duck leg with red wine jus and crushed swede, 35-day-aged rare breed steak with fries and a choice of sauces, and puddings such as sticky toffee pudding and rhubarb and plum crumble; they also serve a two- and three-course set weekday menu. *Benchmark main dish: rare-breed burger with toppings, coleslaw and chips £14.50. Two-course evening meal £22.00.*

Free house ~ Lease Siobhain Mosley ~ Real ale ~ Open 11.30-11 (midnight Weds, Thurs, 1am Fri, Sat); 12-10.30 Sun; closed 24-26 Dec ~ Bar food 12-3, 6-10 (11 Thurs, Fri); 12-4, 7-11 Sat; 12-9 Sun ~ Restaurant ~ Children welcome ~ Dogs allowed in bar ~ Wi-fi
Recommended by Edward May, Isobel Mackinlay

CENTRAL LONDON   Map 13

Bountiful Cow

(020) 7404 0200 – www.thebountifulcow.co.uk
Eagle Street; ⊖ Holborn; WC1R 4AP

Bustling and informal place that's popular with meat lovers

Most customers are here to enjoy the excellent burgers and steaks, but there are chrome and beige leatherette bar stools against the counter (grabbed quickly by those wanting a chat and a pint) and they keep Adnams Broadside, Southwold and Ghost Ship on handpump and around ten wines by the glass. The informal street-level bar has a raised area by the windows with booth seating and a smallish upper room with red wicker dining chairs around oak tables on oak floorboards, with beef-related prints and posters on the painted brick walls; piped jazz. There's also a larger downstairs dining room decorated with cow prints. This is sister pub to the Seven Stars, also in Holborn.

As well as big steaks and burgers, the food includes duck rillettes with toast, octopus salad, napoli sausages with mash, beef hash with a fried egg, bruschetta with guacamole, tomato and artichoke hearts, bass fillets with crushed fennel seeds, lamb rump with sauté potatoes, and puddings such as crème brûlée and belgian apple tart. *Benchmark main dish: burger in a bun with toppings £10.50. Two-course evening meal £21.00.*

Free house ~ Licensee Cveta Dukovska ~ Real ale ~ Open 11-11; 12-11 Sat; closed Sun ~ Bar food 12-10.30 ~ Children welcome ~ Wi-fi *Recommended by Hilary and Neil Christopher, Belinda May*

CENTRAL LONDON   TQ2781   Map 13
Grazing Goat ♀ ⇐

(020) 7724 7243 – www.thegrazinggoat.co.uk
New Quebec Street; ⊖ Marble Arch; W1H 7RQ

A good mixed crowd of customers, restful pale décor, a thoughtful choice of drinks and good interesting food; bedrooms

It's hard to believe that goats used to graze on this land, tucked away as it is behind busy Oxford Street. A stylish pub with a rustic feel, it has a big gilt-edged mirror above an open fire and plenty of spreading dining space with white cushioned and beige dining chairs around pale tables on bare boards, sage green or light oak-panelled walls, hanging lamps and lanterns and some goat memorabilia dotted about. Efficient, friendly staff serve Florence A Head in a Hat Topee and Capper on handpump, over 20 wines by the glass and plenty of cocktails. The upstairs restaurant is more formal. Glass doors open on to the street where there are a few wooden-slatted chairs and tables. The bedrooms are modern and well equipped, with good bathrooms.

Imaginative food includes chilli squid with greengage and lime dressing, potted pork with apricot chutney and cider brandy, corn-fed chicken, red quinoa, courgette, beetroot and yorkshire fettle salad with citrus and herb dressing, spiced aubergine, goats cheese and onion tart with nasturtiums, beer-battered fish and chips, short rib and applewood cheddar pie with runner bean salad, treacle beef rump with braised ox cheek, smoked fennel, beluga lentils and goats curd, and puddings such as pistachio brûlée with sour cherry shortbread and lemon curd swiss roll with passion-fruit mousse and tea parfait. *Benchmark main dish: Sunday roast £19.50. Two-course evening meal £22.00.*

Free house ~ Real ale ~ Open 7.30am-11pm (10.30 Sun) ~ Bar food 7.30am-10pm (9.30 Sun) ~ Restaurant ~ Children welcome ~ Dogs allowed in bar ~ Wi-fi ~ Bedrooms: £210/£250 *Recommended by Mike Swan, Emma Scofield*

CENTRAL LONDON
Harp ◀

Map 13

(020) 7836 0291 – www.harpcoventgarden.com

47 Chandos Place; ⊖ ⇌ *Charing Cross* ⊖ *Leicester Square; WC2N 4HS*

Ten real ales and lots of ciders and perries in bustling narrow pub; pretty summer hanging baskets

Under the new landlady, this much-loved pub is as busy as ever – it does get packed as it's so central and handy for the theatres; at peak times, customers are happy to spill out on to the pavement or the back alley. It pretty much consists of one long narrow, very traditional bar, with lots of high bar stools along the wall counter and around elbow tables, big mirrors on the red walls, some lovely stained glass and loads of interesting, quirkily executed celebrity portraits. If you're very lucky, you may be able to snare one of the prized seats by the front windows. A little room upstairs is much quieter, with comfortable furniture and a window overlooking the road below. The ten real ales on handpump are particularly well kept and quickly changing: usually three from Dark Star, one from Harveys, two from Sambrooks and one or two widely sourced guests – maybe from Ascot, Burton Bridge, Redemption, Red Squirrel, Twickenham and Windsor & Eton; up to nine farm ciders and three perries and quite a few malt whiskies.

Food – served at lunchtime only – consists of sandwiches, sausage rolls and pork pies.

Free house ~ Licensee Sarah Bird ~ Real ale ~ Open 10.30am-11.30pm; 12-10.30 Sun ~ Bar food 12-3 ~ Wi-fi *Recommended by N R White, Taff Thomas, Tony Scott*

CENTRAL LONDON
Lamb & Flag ◀ £

Map 13

(020) 7497 9504 – www.lambandflagcoventgarden.co.uk

Rose Street, off Garrick Street; ⊖ *Covent Garden, Leicester Square; WC2E 9EB*

Historic yet unpretentious, full of character and atmosphere and with eight real ales and pubby food

This is the most characterful pub in Covent Garden, so you'll never have it to yourself – but customers spill out on to the pavement, even in winter. It's an unspoilt and, in places, rather basic old tavern: the more spartan front room leads into a cosy, atmospheric, low-ceilinged back bar with high-backed black settles and an open fire. The pub is owned by Fullers, so they keep around half a dozen of their beers plus guests such as Adnams Ghost Ship and Butcombe Bitter on handpump, as well as 12 wines by the glass and 25 malt whiskies. The pub cat is called Beautiful. The upstairs Dryden Room is often less crowded and has more seats (though fewer beers). There's a lively and well documented history: Dryden was nearly beaten to death by hired thugs outside, and Dickens made fun of the Middle Temple lawyers who frequented it when he was working in nearby Catherine Street.

Tasty bar food, served upstairs, includes sandwiches, chicken caesar salad, a pie of the day, honey-mustard ham and egg, burger with gherkins and relish, beer-battered cod and chips, marinated half chicken with coleslaw and chips, and puddings such as chocolate brownie and eton mess. *Benchmark main dish: sausages, mash and gravy £9.50. Two-course evening meal £15.00.*

Fullers ~ Manager Christopher Buckley ~ Real ale ~ Open 11-11; 12-10.30 Sun ~ Bar food 12-8 (5 Fri, Sat); 12-9 Sun ~ Restaurant ~ Children in upstairs dining room only ~ Dogs allowed in bar ~ Wi-fi ~ Live jazz first Sun evening of month *Recommended by Tony Scott, Sharon and John Hancock, Brian and Anna Marsden*

CENTRAL LONDON   Map 13

Old Bank of England 🍷 🍺

(020) 7430 2255 – www.oldbankofengland.co.uk

Fleet Street; ⊖ Chancery Lane (not Sundays), Temple (not Sundays)
⊖ ⇌ Blackfriars; EC4A 2LT

**Dramatically converted former bank building, with gleaming
chandeliers in impressive, soaring bar, well kept Fullers beers
and good pies**

Once a subsidiary branch of the Bank of England, this has a quite
astounding interior. It's a Grade I listed Italianate building and the
soaring spacious bar has three gleaming chandeliers hanging from an
exquisitely plastered ceiling that's high above an unusually tall island bar
counter crowned with a clock. The end wall has huge paintings and murals
that look like 18th-c depictions of Justice, but, in fact, feature members of
the Fuller, Smith and Turner families, who set up the brewery that owns
the pub. There are well polished dark wooden furnishings, luxurious
curtains swagging massive windows, plenty of framed prints and, despite
the grandeur, some surprisingly cosy corners, with screens between tables
creating an unexpectedly intimate feel. The quieter galleried section upstairs
offers a bird's-eye view of the action; some smaller rooms (used mainly for
functions) open off. Seven Fullers beers are on handpump alongside a good
choice of malt whiskies and a dozen wines by the glass. At lunchtime, the
background music is generally classical or easy listening; it's louder and
livelier in the evening. There's also a garden with seats (one of the few pubs
in the area to have one).

 Pies have a long if rather dubious pedigree in this area: it was in the vaults and
tunnels below the Old Bank and the surrounding buildings that Sweeney Todd
butchered the clients destined to provide the fillings at his mistress Mrs Lovett's nearby
pie shop. Somehow or other, good home-made pies have become a speciality on the
menu here too: sweet potato, spinach and goats cheese, lamb with red wine, rosemary
and mint and traditional fish. Also, sandwiches, ham hock terrine with piccalilli, beer-
battered cod and chips, feta and rocket pesto on linguine, beer-marinated chicken with
bacon and beer and mustard sauce, burger with toppings, relish and chips, and puddings
such as chocolate brownie and raspberry and vanilla cheesecake. *Benchmark main
dish: steak in ale pie £12.75. Two-course evening meal £16.00.*

Fullers ~ Manager Jo Farquhar ~ Real ale ~ Open 11-11; closed weekends and bank
holidays ~ Bar food 12-9 Mon-Fri ~ Children welcome until 5pm ~ Wi-fi
*Recommended by Taff Thomas, Dr and Mrs A K Clarke, Simon Collett-Jones, Richard Kennell,
Barry Collett, Tony Scott*

CENTRAL LONDON   Map 13

Olde Mitre 🍺 £

(020) 7405 4751 – www.yeoldemitreholburn.co.uk

*Ely Place; the easiest way to find it is from the narrow passageway beside
8 Hatton Garden; ⊖ Chancery Lane (not Sundays); EC1N 6SJ*

**Hard to find but well worth it – an unspoilt old pub with lovely
atmosphere, unusual guest beers and bargain toasted sandwiches**

Although the current building dates from 1782, there's actually been a
tavern here since 1546 – it's hard to believe you're so close to Holborn
and the edge of the City. The cosy small rooms have lots of dark panelling
as well as antique settles and – particularly in the popular back room, where
there are more seats – old local pictures and so forth. It gets good-naturedly

packed with the City suited-and-booted between 12.30pm and 2.15pm, filling up again in the early evening, but in the early afternoons and by around 8pm is a good deal more tranquil. An upstairs room, mainly used for functions, may double as an overflow area at peak periods. The new licensee keeps Fullers London Pride and Seafarer and four quickly changing guests on handpump, and they hold three beer festivals a year; farm cider and several wines by the glass. No music, TV or machines – the only games here are cribbage and dominoes. There's some space for outside drinking by the pot plants and jasmine in the narrow yard between the pub and St Ethelreda's Church (which is worth a look). Note the pub doesn't open on weekends or bank holidays. The iron gates that guard one entrance to Ely Place are a reminder of the days when the law in this district was administered by the Bishops of Ely. The best approach is from Hatton Garden, walking up the right-hand side away from Chancery Lane; an easily missed sign on a lamp-post points the way down a narrow alley. No children.

Served all day, bar snacks are limited to scotch eggs, pork pies and sausage rolls, and really good value toasties.

Fullers ~ Manager Judith Norman ~ Real ale ~ Open 11-11; closed weekends and bank holidays ~ Bar food 11.30-9.30 ~ Wi-fi *Recommended by Mrs Sally Scott, Conor McGaughey, Tony Scott, N R White*

CENTRAL LONDON   Map 13

Orange 🏵️ 🍷 🛏️

(020) 7881 9844 – www.theorange.co.uk

Pimlico Road; ⊖ *Sloane Square; SW1W 8NE*

Carefully restored pub with simply decorated rooms, thoughtful choice of drinks and good modern cooking; bedrooms

With an easy-going, gently civilised feel and courteous, friendly staff, this restored Georgian inn is usefully placed right in the heart of Pimlico. The two floors of the pub itself have huge sash windows on all sides making the interconnected rooms light and airy; throughout, the décor is shabby chic and simple and the atmosphere easy-going and chatty. The high-ceilinged downstairs bar has wooden dining chairs around pale tables on bare boards, an open fire at one end and a big carved counter where they keep Adnams Lighthouse and Florence A Head in a Hat Topee and Capper on handpump, 18 wines by the glass and a lengthy cocktail list. The dining room to the right, usually packed with cheerful customers, is decorated with prints, glass bottles and soda siphons, big house plants and a few rustic knick-knacks. Upstairs, the linked restaurant rooms are similarly furnished with old french travel posters and circus prints on cream walls, more open fireplaces, big glass ceiling lights and chandeliers and quiet background jazz. This is a comfortable place to stay in well equipped bedrooms; breakfasts are first class.

As well as wood-fired pizzas, the good modern food includes breakfasts (for non-residents too, until 11.30am), pigeon breast with pearl barley, girolles, cherry and dark chocolate jus, smoked trout pâté with beetroot and orange relish, avocado and black garlic aioli, chicken caesar salad, globe artichokes with goats cheese, spring greens, smoked tomato and rocket pesto, rabbit saddle with confit leg, pancetta, spring onions and mustard frites, yellowfin tuna with samphire, smoked yoghurt and tomato and fennel ragoût, and puddings such as orange and almond cake with pomegranate and chocolate and peanut brownie with popcorn custard and malt ice-cream. *Benchmark main dish: Sunday roast £19.50. Two-course evening meal £20.00.*

Free house ~ Real ale ~ Open 8am-11.30pm (midnight Sat); 8am-10.30pm Sun ~ Bar food 8am-10pm (10.30 Sat, 9 Sun) ~ Restaurant ~ Children welcome ~ Dogs allowed in bar ~ Wi-fi ~ Bedrooms: £210/£250 *Recommended by Peter Sutton, Charlie May, Nick Sharpe*

CENTRAL LONDON
Map 13

Pantechnicon 🍴⭐ ♀

(020) 7730 6074 – www.thepantechnicon.com

Motcomb Street; ⊖ *Knightsbridge; SW1X 8LA*

Bustling and civilised with good drinks choice, rewarding food and friendly, helpful service

Located in a quiet residential area, this civilised place is named after the 1830s landmark building just up the road. It s all very relaxed, with customers drinking and chatting, working at laptops or enjoying the interesting, good quality food. Apart from one table surrounded by stools beside the bar counter, there are high-backed upholstered dining chairs around wooden tables on parquet flooring, comfortable leather wall seats and eclectic décor that ranges from 19th-c postcards to portraits of nobility, and envelopes displayed address-side out to Edward Lear illustrations and World War II prints – plus antique books on window sills. Friendly, helpful staff serve Florence A Head in a Hat Topee on handpump, cocktails and quite a few wines by the glass. The upstairs restaurant has leather chairs and wooden tables on more parquet and a huge mirror above an open fire. Above that is a room for private hire, while up again is a cosy loft used for monthly events such as cheese tastings. The front pavement has tables and chairs beneath a striped awning.

🍴⭐ Rewarding food includes salt and chilli squid with smoked chilli and lime dressing, smoked ham hock and pork shoulder terrine with piccalilli, grilled artichokes with quinoa, goats cheese, asparagus and merlot dressing, rare-breed burger with caramelised onions, tomato relish and smoked aioli, yellowfin tuna cooked rare with asparagus, pickled vegetables and pomegranate dressing, outdoor-reared pork chop with plum chutney with a choice of potato, and puddings such as treacle tart with lemon curd ice-cream and white chocolate and passion-fruit cheesecake with banana yoghurt sorbet. *Benchmark main dish: fresh fish of the day £16.50. Two-course evening meal £24.00.*

Free house ~ Real ale ~ Open 12-11; 9am-11pm Sat; 9am-10.30pm Sun ~ Bar food 12-10; 9-4 weekend brunch ~ Children welcome ~ Dogs allowed in bar *Recommended by Toby Jones, Caroline Prescott*

CENTRAL LONDON
Map 13

Punchbowl ♀

(020) 7493 6841 – www.punchbowllondon.com

Farm Street; ⊖ *Green Park; W1J 5RP*

Bustling, rather civilised pub with good wines and ales, enjoyable food and helpful service

Tucked away in a side street, this characterful Mayfair pub was once a magistrate's court – look for the 18th-c wig enclosed in a glass container built into one wall. The nicest part is at the back where several panelled booths have suede bench seating, animal scatter cushions, some etched glasswork and church candles on tables. Elegant spoked chairs are grouped around dark tables on worn floorboards, a couple of long elbow shelves are lined with high chairs and one fireplace has a coal fire while the other is piled with logs. At the front it's simpler, with cushioned bench seating and pubby tables and chairs on floor tiles. All sorts of artwork from cartoons to oil paintings line the walls and the ceiling has interesting old hand-drawn street maps; background music. Caledonian Deuchars IPA and Edinburgh Castle 80/- and Theakstons Best Bitter on handpump, good wines by the glass and professional, friendly service. The smart restaurant upstairs has plush furnishings, large artworks and a huge gilt mirror above an open fire; there are private dining facilities too.

 Good food includes sandwiches, mackerel on toast with a spicy tomato dressing, steak tartare with quail egg yolk, a pie of the day, roasted vegetable hotpot with cheddar mash, salmon and haddock fishcakes with creamed spinach, a poached egg and lemon butter sauce, battered fish of the day with triple-cooked chips, roast venison with duck fat roast potatoes, yorkshire pudding and red wine gravy, and puddings such as plum tart and dark chocolate and orange slice. *Benchmark main dish: beer-battered fish and chips £14.50. Two-course evening meal £25.00.*

Free house ~ Real ale ~ Open 12-11 (10.30 Sun) ~ Children welcome if seated and dining ~ Dogs allowed in bar ~ Wi-fi *Recommended by Edward May, Belinda Stamp*

CENTRAL LONDON
Seven Stars ◖

Map 13

(020) 7242 8521 – www.thesevenstars1602.co.uk

Carey Street; ⊖ Temple (not Sundays), Chancery Lane (not Sundays), Holborn; WC2A 2JB

Quirky pub with cheerful staff, an interesting mix of customers and a good choice of drinks and food

Numerous caricatures of barristers and judges line the red-painted walls of the two main rooms in this unchanging little pub – which is appropriate since the place is a favourite with lawyers, Church of England music directors and choir singers. There are also posters of legal-themed british films, big ceiling fans, checked tablecloths that add a quirky, almost continental touch, and a relaxed, intimate atmosphere. A third area, in what was formerly a legal wig shop next door, still retains its original frontage, with a neat display of wigs in the window. It's worth arriving early as they don't take bookings and tables get snapped up quickly. Adnams Broadside and guests from breweries such as Hop Back, Sambrooks and Sharps on handpump and six wines by the glass (they import wine from France); they do a particularly good dry martini. On busy evenings, customers overflow on to the quiet road in front; things generally quieten down after 8pm and there can be a nice, sleepy atmosphere some afternoons. The Elizabethan stairs up to the loos are rather steep, but there's a good strong handrail. The pub cat, who wears a ruff, is called Ray Brown. The licensees also run the Bountiful Cow on Eagle Street, near Holborn tube station. No children.

 Cooked according to the landlady's fancy, the good, interesting food includes pork and leek pearl barley orzotto, a proper meatloaf, duck hash, rabbit stew and nasi goreng shrimp omelette. *Benchmark main dish: pie of the day £11.00. Two-course evening meal £15.00.*

Free house ~ Licensee Roxy Beaujolais ~ Real ale ~ Open 11 (12 Sat)-11; 12-10.30 Sun; closed some bank holidays ~ Bar food 1-9.30 ~ Wi-fi *Recommended by N R White, Brian and Anna Marsden, Dr and Mrs A K Clarke, Dr J Barrie Jones*

CENTRAL LONDON
Star ◖

Map 13

(020) 7235 3019 – www.star-tavern-belgravia.co.uk

Belgrave Mews West, behind the German Embassy, off Belgrave Square; ⊖ Knightsbridge, Hyde Park Corner; SW1X 8HT

Bustling local with restful bar, upstairs dining room, Fullers ales, well liked bar food and colourful hanging baskets

Although packed out at peak times, outside these hours there's a restful, local feel to this tucked-away pub in a cobbled mews. The small bar is pleasant, with sash windows, a wooden floor, stools by the counter, an open winter fire and Fullers ESB, London Pride and Seafarers plus a guest beer on handpump, nine wines by the glass and a few malt whiskies. An arch leads to the main seating area with well polished tables and chairs and good lighting; there's also an upstairs dining room. In summer, the front of the building is covered with an astonishing array of hanging baskets and flowering tubs. It's said that this is where the Great Train Robbery was planned.

Tasty food includes lunchtime sandwiches, ham hock and mustard terrine, smoked trout salad with radish, fennel, grapefruit and dill, sharing plates, burger with toppings and chips, a pasta dish of the day, smoked salmon niçoise salad with a soft boiled egg, chicken breast with peas, pancetta and tarragon pesto, cod with olives, capers, pepperonata, samphire and parsley butter, rib-eye steak with chilli and tarragon butter and chips, and puddings such as apple and rhubarb crumble with cinnamon ice-cream and chocolate fudge cake. *Benchmark main dish: beer-battered fish and chips £12.00. Two-course evening meal £17.00.*

Fullers ~ Manager Marta Lemieszewska ~ Real ale ~ Open 11 (12 Sat)-11; 12-10.30 Sun ~ Bar food 12-3, 5-9; 12-4, 5-9 Sun ~ Restaurant ~ Children welcome ~ Dogs welcome ~ Wi-fi
Recommended by Mike and Jayne Bastin, Michael Butler

CENTRAL LONDON

Map 13

Thomas Cubitt ★ ♀

(020) 7730 6060 – www.thethomascubitt.co.uk
Elizabeth Street; ⊖ Sloane Square ⊖ ⇌ Victoria; SW1W 9PA

Belgravia pub with a civilised but friendly atmosphere and enjoyable food and drink

Named after the legendary builder and located in well heeled Elizabeth Street, this bustling place has a bar with miscellaneous Edwardian-style dining chairs around wooden tables on stripped parquet flooring, and architectural prints and antlers on panelled or painted walls; open fires and lovely flower arrangements. Attentive staff serve Florence A Head in a Hat Topee and Capper on handpump, cocktails and quite a few wines by the glass. The more formal dining room upstairs has smart upholstered wooden chairs around white-clothed tables, candles in wall holders, a few prints, house plants and window blinds. In warm weather, the floor-to-ceiling glass doors are pulled back to the street where there are cordoned-off tables and chairs on the pavement.

Enterprising food includes scallops with peas, lemon mayonnaise and black olives, smoked quail with baby beetroots, scotch egg and charred endive, salt-baked golden beetroot with pickled peach, goats cheese and almonds, slow-cooked chicken with peas, broad beans and truffle jus, dry-aged beef fillet with braised brisket, bone marrow mash and nasturtiums, halibut with smoked brown shrimps and chive cream sauce, and puddings such as strawberry cheesecake with hibiscus parfait and wild strawberries and lemon polenta cake with blueberries and frozen yoghurt. *Benchmark main dish: Sunday roast £19.50. Two-course evening meal £22.00.*

Free house ~ Real ale ~ Open 12-11 (10.30 Sun) ~ Bar food 12-10.30 (9.30 Sun) ~ Restaurant ~ Children welcome ~ Dogs allowed in bar *Recommended by Peter Loader, Tracey and Stephen Groves*

The ◖ symbol shows pubs that keep their beer unusually well, have a particularly good range or brew their own.

NORTH LONDON
Map 13
Drapers Arms ⭐ ♀

(020) 7619 0348 – www.thedrapersarms.com

Far west end of Barnsbury Street; ⊖ ⇄ *Highbury & Islington; N1 1ER*

A thoughtful choice of drinks and imaginative modern food in charming pub, and seats in attractive back garden

With a friendly landlord and courteous staff, this simply furnished Georgian townhouse is popular with both locals and visitors – always a good sign. The spreading bar has a mix of elegant dark wooden tables and dining chairs on bare boards, an arresting bright green-painted counter that contrasts with soft duck-egg blue walls, gilt mirrors over smart fireplaces, a sofa and some comfortable chairs. Harveys Sussex, Otley Thai Bo and Sambrooks Wandle on handpump, 17 carefully chosen wines by the glass and british draught lagers. Upstairs, the stylish dining room has similar tables and chairs on a striking chequerboard-painted wooden floor; background music and board games. In good weather, the lovely back terrace is a real bonus, with white or green benches and chairs around zinc-topped tables – each set with a church candle in a hurricane lamp – flagstones and large parasols.

First class modern food includes smoked sprats with cucumber and sour cream, deep-fried quail with aioli and pickled chillies, pork belly with roasted fennel and gooseberries, calves liver with roasted red onion and gravy, oxtail with roast courgettes and mint and garlic yoghurt, sea trout with tartare potatoes and brown butter, and puddings such as chocolate and caramel pot and gingerbread pudding with whipped cream. *Benchmark main dish: a pie of the day £13.50. Two-course evening meal £22.00.*

Free house ~ Licensee Nick Gibson ~ Real ale ~ Open 12-11 ~ Bar food 12-3, 6-10.30; 12-4, 7-10.30 Sat; 12-8.30 Sun ~ Restaurant ~ Children welcome but must be seated and dining after 6pm ~ Dogs allowed in bar ~ Wi-fi *Recommended by Paul A Moore, Belinda May*

NORTH LONDON
Map 12
Holly Bush ♀

(020) 7435 2892 – www.hollybushhampstead.co.uk

Holly Mount; ⊖ *Hampstead; NW3 6SG*

Unique village local, with good food and drinks and lovely unspoilt feel

This timeless old favourite, originally a stable block, is tucked away among some of Hampstead's most villagey streets. The old-fashioned front bar has a dark sagging ceiling, brown and cream panelled walls (decorated with old advertisements and a few hanging plates), open fires, bare boards and secretive bays formed by partly glazed partitions. The slightly more intimate back room, named after the painter George Romney, has an embossed red ceiling, panelled and etched glass alcoves, and ochre-painted brick walls covered with small prints; lots of board and card games. Fullers London Pride and Oliver's Island on handpump, as well as 15 malt whiskies and 14 wines by the glass from a good wine list. The upstairs dining room has table service at the weekend, as does the rest of the pub on Sundays. There are benches on the pavement outside.

Interesting food includes lunchtime sandwiches, pulled pork rillettes with pickles, veal carpaccio with tuna dressing and onion bread, cauliflower pakora with squash fritters and green pepper and coconut dhal, hot smoked salmon salad with jersey royals, beetroot, quail eggs and dill crème fraîche, guinea fowl two-ways with pancetta and parmentier potatoes, veal T-bone with gnocchi, lemon and caper sauce, octopus with cod, asparagus, barley and romesco dressing, and puddings such as rhubarb and apple crumble with ginger ice-cream and caramel chocolate mousse with salted peanut caramel. *Benchmark main dish: beer-battered fish and chips £14.50. Two-course evening meal £20.50.*

Fullers ~ Manager Ben Ralph ~ Real ale ~ Open 12-11 (10.30 Sun) ~ Bar food 12-3 (4 Sat), 6-10; 12-8 Sun ~ Restaurant ~ Children welcome ~ Dogs welcome ~ Wi-fi *Recommended by Di and Mike Gillam, Dave Braisted, Tony Scott*

NORTH LONDON   Map 12
Princess of Wales
(020) 7722 0354 – www.lovetheprincess.com
Fitzroy Road/Chalcot Road; ⊖ Chalk Farm via Regents Park Road and footbridge; NW1 8LL

Friendly, buzzy place with three different seating areas, enjoyable food, wide choice of drinks and funky garden

Some kind of food is served all day at weekends here – starting with breakfast. The place is spread over three floors; the main bar, at ground level, is open-plan and light with big windows looking out to the street, wooden tables and chairs on bare boards and plenty of high chairs against the counter: By the Horns The Mayor of Garratt and a couple of quickly changing guests on handpump, 16 wines by the glass, 11 malt whiskies and good cocktails. Upstairs, the smarter dining room has beige- and white-painted chairs, leather sofas and stools around wooden tables on more bare boards, big gilt-edged mirrors and chandeliers; two TVs. Orange and green plush banquettes create a diner-like feel in the colourful Garden Room downstairs, and doors lead out to the suntrap garden with its Bansky-style mural, framed wall mirrors and picnic-sets (some painted pink and purple) under parasols.

Good food includes a highly rated weekend breakfast, lunchtime sandwiches, smoked mackerel pâté, parma ham with roasted figs, baby buffalo mozzarella and aged balsamic reduction, spicy thai beef salad with mixed leaves, crushed chilli and sesame seeds, beer-battered fish and chips, a pie of the day, rare-breed sausages with mash and onion gravy, sea bream with baby aubergine, artichoke and spinach, and puddings such as double chocolate and peanut brownie with salted caramel ice-cream and banoffi pie. *Benchmark main dish: burger with toppings, onion rings and chips £12.50. Two-course evening meal £20.00.*

Free house ~ Licensee Lawrence Santi ~ Real ale ~ Open 11am-midnight; 9am-midnight Sat; 9am-11.30pm Sun ~ Bar food 12-3.30, 6-10; 9am-10pm Sat; 9am-9.30pm Sun ~ Restaurant ~ Children welcome ~ Dogs allowed in bar ~ Wi-fi *Recommended by Edward May, Harvey Brown*

SOUTH LONDON   Map 12
Earl Spencer 🍺
(020) 8870 9244 – www.theearlspencer.co.uk
Merton Road; ⊖ Southfields; SW18 5JL

Good, interesting food and six real ales in busy but friendly pub

Particularly well run and with a cheerful, chatty atmosphere, this is a sizeable Edwardian pub with plenty of customers. There are cushioned wooden, farmhouse and leather dining tables around all sorts of tables on bare boards, standard lamps, modern art on the walls and an open fire; the back bar has long tables, pews and benches. Stools line the U-shaped counter where efficient, friendly staff serve six ales on handpump: Adnams Lighthouse, Black Sheep, Hop Back Summer Lightning, Otter Amber, Sambrooks Wandle and Timothy Taylors Landlord. Also, 20 wines by the glass and 20 malt whiskies; they also sell 23 kinds of cigar. There are picnic-sets out on the front terrace.

 Popular food includes daily home-baked bread, half pint of home-smoked prawns with aioli, ham hock and parsley terrine with piccalilli, polenta, jerusalem artichokes, red onion marmalade, rocket and parmesan, braised ox cheeks with parsnip mash, skate wing with caper and tomato dressing and sauté potatoes, guinea fowl breast with herb risotto cake and truffle jus, and puddings such as sticky ginger pudding with toffee sauce and chocolate and hazelnut terrine with chantilly cream and frangelico syrup. *Benchmark main dish: bavette steak with parsley and garlic butter and chips £16.50. Two-course evening meal £20.50.*

Enterprise ~ Lease Michael Mann ~ Real ale ~ Open 4-11 Mon-Thurs; 11am-midnight Fri, Sat; 12-10.30 Sun ~ Bar food 7-10 Mon-Thurs; 12.30-3.30, 7-10 Fri, Sat; 12.30-4, 7-9.30 Sun ~ Children welcome ~ Dogs allowed in bar ~ Wi-fi *Recommended by Mrs G Marlow, Belinda May*

SOUTH LONDON — Map 13
Royal Oak

(020) 7357 7173 – www.harveys.org.uk

Tabard Street/Nebraska Street; ⊖ Borough ⊖⇄ London Bridge; SE1 4JU

Old-fashioned corner house with particularly well kept beers and honest food

Painstakingly transformed by Sussex brewery Harveys, this has the look and feel of a traditional London alehouse – you'd never imagine it had been any different. The place is always packed with customers of varying ages, all keen to enjoy the full range of Harveys ales on handpump and Thatcher's cider. The two little L-shaped rooms (the front bar is larger and brighter, the back room cosier with dimmer lighting) meander around the central wooden servery, which has a fine old clock in the middle. The rooms are done out with patterned rugs on wooden floors, plates running along a delft shelf, black and white scenes or period sheet music on red-painted walls, and an assortment of wooden tables and chairs. There's disabled access at the Nebraska Street entrance.

 Tasty food includes sandwiches, deep-fried whitebait, duck liver pâté, salmon fishcakes, rabbit in mustard sauce, game pie, goats cheese and beetroot salad, and puddings such as treacle tart and sherry trifle. *Benchmark main dish: bubble and squeak with black pudding, bacon and duck egg £9.25. Two-course evening meal £16.50.*

Harveys ~ Tenants John Porteous and Frank Taylor ~ Real ale ~ Open 11-11; 12-9 Sun ~ Bar food 12-2.45, 5-9.15; 12-8 Sun ~ Children welcome until 9pm ~ Dogs welcome *Recommended by B and M Kendall, Phil Bryant, N R White, Tony Scott*

SOUTH LONDON — Map 12
Victoria

(020) 8876 4238 – www.thevictoria.net

West Temple Sheen; ⇄ Mortlake; SW14 7RT

Excellent food in attractive inn, airy conservatory, cosy bar and seats in pretty garden; comfortable bedrooms

The emphasis here, unsurprisingly, is on the light and airy back conservatory restaurant with its dark chunky furniture and doors that open out into a pretty garden; there are plenty of seats and tables under a huge parasol and an outside bar. The bar has leather sofas facing each other beside a fireplace, wooden seats and tables in a bow window with more on bare boards around the counter. Fullers London Pride, Timothy Taylors Landlord and a guest beer on handpump, 25 wines by the glass from a good list and home-made elderflower cordial; friendly service and background music. The stylish modern bedrooms are comfortable and breakfasts are good. The inn is just a few minutes' walk from Richmond Park.

 Imaginative food includes lunchtime sandwiches, duck confit terrine with dried cranberries and red onion jam, salmon sashimi with shallot and chilli crunch, ketjap manis (Indonesian soy sauce) and pickled cucumber, chargrilled rare-breed hot dog with sauerkraut and american yellow mustard, spinach, mushroom and ricotta wellington with root vegetable purée and honey and thyme roast potatoes, yoghurt-spiced chicken with bhel puri salad and chilli, mint and pomegranate, rainbow trout with cockles, bacon, monks beard and cider jus, and puddings such as lemon posset with lemon thyme and pistachio croquant and dark chocolate shortbread with milk chocolate mousse and peanut butter ice-cream; they also offer Saturday brunch. *Benchmark main dish: burger with toppings and triple-cooked chips £12.00. Two-course evening meal £25.00.*

Enterprise ~ Lease Greg Bellamy ~ Real ale ~ Open 11-11; 12-10 Sun ~ Bar food 12-2.30, 6-10; 11-3, 6-10 Sat; 12-4 Sun ~ Restaurant ~ Children welcome ~ Dogs allowed in bar ~ Wi-fi ~ Live music every second Sun evening 5-8pm ~ Bedrooms: £125/£135
Recommended by Simon Rodway, Colin McLachlan

WEST LONDON TQ1370 Map 12
Bell
(020) 8941 9799 ~ www.thebellinnhampton.co.uk
Thames Street, Hampton; ⇒ *Hampton; TW12 2EA*

Bustling pub by the Thames with seats outside, real ales, a good choice of food and friendly service

From the long panelled bar counter here, friendly staff serve Hogs Back TEA, Sambrooks Wandle and Sharps Doom Bar on handpump, 20 wines by the glass and speciality teas and coffees. The interconnected rooms have wooden dining and tub chairs around copper-topped or chunky wooden tables, comfortably upholstered wall seats with scatter cushions, various mirrors, old photographs and lots of church candles. There are plenty of contemporary seats and tables in the garden, which has heaters, lighting and booth seating; summer barbecues.

Quite a choice of food includes sandwiches, chicken liver, orange and Cointreau pâté with chutney, paprika and tarragon chicken 'lollipops' with mustard and honey mayonnaise, sharing boards, beer-battered hake and chips, spatchcock free-range chicken piri-piri with shoestring fries and coleslaw, slow-braised lamb shoulder with mint and rosemary broth, pulled crispy duck burger with hoisin sauce and spring onion and cucumber salad, and puddings such as a seasonal crumble and warm chocolate fudge cake. *Benchmark main dish: burger with toppings, relish, coleslaw and chips £11.50. Two-course evening meal £18.00.*

Authentic Inns ~ Lease Simon Bailey ~ Real ale ~ Open 11-11 (midnight Fri, Sat) ~ Bar food 12-3, 6-10; 12-10 Sat; 12-9 Sun ~ Restaurant ~ Children welcome ~ Dogs allowed in bar ~ Wi-fi ~ Live music Sat evening *Recommended by Emma Scofield, Caroline Prescott*

We say if we know a pub allows dogs.

WEST LONDON
Map 12
Crown & Sceptre
(020) 7603 2007 – www.crownandsceptrepub.com

Holland Road; ⊖ Earl's Court (weekends only) ⇌ Kensington (Olympia); W14 8BA

Friendly corner pub with an easy-going atmosphere, attentive staff and a pleasing selection of both food and drinks

With a light and airy interior, this is a civilised Victorian corner pub with a friendly welcome for all. There are sofas, antique-style dining chairs and leather cube stools around wooden tables, rugs on bare boards, an open gas fire, fresh flowers and papers to read. Courage Directors, Youngs London Gold and a guest beer on handpump, 20 wines by the glass, 25 gins and 30 malt whiskies; background music, TV and board games. There's also a cosy cellar bar with banquette seating, big prints on rough wood walls, some leather cube stools, candles in bottles and a roulette wheel carved into one large table. On the pavement outside are a few tables and chairs. The bedrooms are up to date and comfortable.

Good food includes lunchtime sandwiches, rabbit and chicken terrine with sweet shallot jelly and confit onion and raisin salad, thai mussels in ginger, chilli and coconut milk, cheeseburger with toppings, coleslaw and fries, cumberland sausages with caramelised onion gravy, wild mushroom pasta with white wine and truffle sauce, pork belly skewers marinated in orange zest, ginger, garlic and soy with basmati rice, bass with sweet potatoes, courgette 'spaghetti' and cauliflower purée, and puddings such as white chocolate and raspberry cheesecake with berry coulis and sticky date pudding with toffee sauce. *Benchmark main dish: rotisserie chicken and roasted mediterranean vegetables £13.95. Two-course evening meal £25.00.*

Free house ~ Licensee Freddie Van Hagen ~ Real ale ~ Open 7.30am-11pm (10.30 Sun) ~ Bar food 12-3, 6-9.30; 12-7 Sun ~ Restaurant ~ Children welcome ~ Dogs allowed in bar ~ Wi-fi ~ Bedrooms: £90/$100 *Recommended by Ian Phillips, Edward May*

WEST LONDON
Map 12
Dove ♀
(020) 8748 9474 – www.dovehammersmith.co.uk

Upper Mall; ⊖ Ravenscourt Park; W6 9TA

One of London's best known pubs, with a lovely riverside terrace, cosily traditional front bar and an interesting history

With a great deal of charm and a very special position, this bustling place remains as much loved as ever. The front snug is in the Guinness World Records for having the smallest bar room (a mere 1.3 metres by 2.4 metres) and is cosy, traditional and unchanging, with black panelling and red leatherette cushioned built-in wall settles and stools around assorted tables. It leads to a bigger, similarly furnished back room that's more geared to eating, which in turn leads to a conservatory. Fullers ESB, HSB and London Pride plus a guest or two on handpump and 19 wines by the glass including champagne and sparkling wine. Head down steps at the back to reach the verandah with its highly prized tables looking over a low river wall to the Thames Reach just above Hammersmith Bridge; a tiny exclusive area, reached up a spiral staircase, is a prime spot for watching rowers on the water. The pub has played host to many writers, actors and artists over the years (there's a fascinating framed list on a wall); it's said to be where 'Rule Britannia' was composed and was a favourite with Turner, who painted the view of the Thames from the delightful back terrace, and with Graham Greene. The street itself is associated with the foundation of the arts and crafts movement – William Morris's old residence, Kelmscott House (open certain afternoons), is nearby.

 Well thought-of food includes rabbit terrine with piccalilli, beetroot-cured salmon with lemon and dill cream, sharing boards, olive, tomato, feta and wild garlic pesto linguine, burger with toppings, relish and rustic chips, mussels with chilli, chorizo and coriander and skinny fries, chargrilled rib-eye steak with green peppercorn sauce, and puddings such as tiramisu roulade with brandy butter ice-cream and chocolate brownie with peanut brittle. *Benchmark main dish: beer-battered cod and chips £12.95. Two-course evening meal £21.00.*

Fullers ~ Manager Rob Collett ~ Real ale ~ Open 11-11; 12-10.30 Sun ~ Bar food 12-10; 12-9 (8 in winter) Sun ~ Children welcome ~ Dogs welcome ~ Wi-fi *Recommended by Hunter and Christine Wright, Taff Thomas, Tony Scott*

WEST LONDON
Duke of Sussex

Map 12

(020) 8742 8801 ~ www.thedukeofsussex.co.uk
South Parade; ⊖ Chiswick Park ⇌ South Acton; W4 5LF

Attractively restored Victorian local with interesting bar food, a good choice of drinks and a lovely big garden

The unexpectedly big garden behind this well run pub is a real treat on a warm day – there are seats and tables under parasols, nicely laid out plants, carefully positioned lighting and (if it gets cooler in the evening) heaters. The classy, simply furnished bar has some original etched glass, chapel and farmhouse chairs around scrubbed pine and dark wood tables, and huge windows overlooking Acton Green. The big horseshoe-shaped counter, lined with high bar stools, is where they serve Itchen Valley Hampshire Rose, St Austells Proper Job, Trumans Lazarus, Twickenham Daisy Cutter and Windsor & Eton Guardsman on handpump, 30 wines by the glass and 15 malt whiskies. Off here is a dining room, again with simple wooden furnishings on parquet, but also six-seater booths, chandeliers, antique lamps, a splendid skylight framed by colourfully painted cherubs, and a couple of big mirrors, one above a small tiled fireplace.

The interesting and highly regarded food includes tapas such as chipirones (deep-fried squid), pinchos morunos (spicy marinated beef skewers) and various tortillas, plus game liver pâté, chilli and garlic prawns, braised rabbit leg with ham, chickpeas and rosemary, steak in ale pie for two to share, wild boar chop with cep gravy, beer-battered fish and chips, skirt steak with aioli, and puddings such as pear and chocolate tart and mango and raspberry pavlova. *Benchmark main dish: seafood paella £14.50. Two-course evening meal £21.00.*

Greene King ~ Manager Matt Mullett ~ Real ale ~ Open 12-11 (11.30 Fri, Sat); 12-10.30 Sun ~ Bar food 12-10 (10.30 Fri, Sat); 12-9 Sun ~ Restaurant ~ Children welcome ~ Dogs allowed in bar ~ Wi-fi *Recommended by Simon Rodway, Keith Mantle*

WEST LONDON
Mute Swan

TQ1568 Map 12

(020) 8941 5959 ~ www.brunningandprice.co.uk/muteswan
Palace Gate, Hampton Court Road; ⇌ Hampton Court; KT8 9BN

Handsome pub close to the Thames with sunny seats outside, relaxed bar, upstairs dining room and imaginative food and drinks choice

Always bustling and friendly, this well run pub is just yards from the River Thames (though there's no view). The light and airy bar has four big leather armchairs grouped around a low table in the centre, while the rest of the room has brown leather wall seats, high-backed Edwardian-style cushioned dining chairs around dark tables and rugs on bare boards. The walls are covered in interesting photographs, maps, prints and posters and there are sizeable house plants, glass and stone bottles on the window sills and a woodburning stove; the atmosphere is informal and relaxed. Brunning & Price Phoenix Original, Oakham Scarlet Macaw, Sambrooks Wandle, Slaters Queen Bee and XT 4 Mellow Amber and XT 13 Pacific Red Ale on handpump, a carefully chosen wine list with 19 by the glass, farm cider and 75 malt whiskies; staff are efficient and helpful. A metal spiral staircase – presided over by an elegant metal chandelier – leads up to the dining area where there are caramel leather brass-studded chairs around well spaced tables on bare boards or carpeting, and numerous photographs and prints. The tables and chairs on the front terrace get snapped up quickly and the pub is opposite the gates to Hampton Court Palace. There are a few parking spaces in front, but you'll probably have to park elsewhere.

Enjoyable food includes sandwiches, crab and cheddar arancini with wild garlic mayonnaise, basil panna cotta with tomato salad and black olive tapenade, scallops with saffron and pea risotto and tempura samphire, burger with toppings, coleslaw and chips, slow-cooked rabbit ragoût with tagliatelle, beetroot and goats cheese salad with yoghurt and chilli and honey walnuts, braised lamb shoulder with dauphinoise potatoes and red wine and rosemary sauce, and puddings such as rhubarb and ginger cheesecake with stem ginger ice-cream and bread and butter pudding with apricot sauce. *Benchmark main dish: duck trio (breast, croquette, leg) with spinach and rosemary jus £17.95. Two-course evening meal £21.00.*

Brunning & Price ~ Manager Sal Morgan ~ Real ale ~ Open 9am-11pm (midnight Fri, Sat); 11-9.30 Sun ~ Bar food 9am-10pm ~ Children welcome in upstairs restaurant only ~ Dogs welcome ~ Wi-fi *Recommended by Harvey Brown, Toby Jones*

WEST LONDON   Map 3
Old Orchard ⭐ ♀
(01895) 822631 – www.brunningandprice.co.uk/oldorchard
Off Park Lane; Harefield; ⇌ *Denham (some distance away); UB9 6HJ*

Wonderful views from the front garden, a good choice of drinks and interesting brasserie-style food

The splendid view from tables on the front terrace (and in the garden) looks down to the narrowboats on the canal and across to the lakes that are part of the conservation area known as the Colne Valley Regional Park – a haven for wildlife. Inside, the open-plan rooms have an attractive mix of cushioned dining chairs around all sizes and shapes of dark wooden tables, lots of prints, maps and pictures covering the walls, books on shelves, old glass bottles on window sills and rugs on wood or parquet flooring. One room is hung with a sizeable rug and some tapestry. There are daily papers to read, three cosy coal fires, big pot plants and fresh flowers. Half a dozen real ales on handpump served by friendly, efficient staff include Phoenix Brunning & Price Original, Mighty Oak Oscar Wilde and Tring Side Pocket for a Toad alongside guests such as Dark Star Festival, Haresfoot Lock Keeper and Twickenham Winter Cheer; also, 17 wines by the glass, 140 malt whiskies and two farm ciders. The atmosphere is civilised and easy-going.

Rewarding food includes sandwiches, chicken liver and madeira parfait with peach and chilli chutney, a charcuterie platter, caramelised onion, tomato and mozzarella quiche, chicken, ham hock and leek pie, honey-roast ham and free-range eggs, charred pork cutlets with chilled soba noodles and sherry tarragon dressing, beer-battered haddock and chips, crispy beef salad with sweet chilli sauce and peanuts, and puddings such as crème brûlée and hot waffle with caramelised banana, toffee sauce and honeycomb ice-cream. *Benchmark main dish: lamb shoulder with sweet potato dauphinoise and crispy kale £17.45. Two-course evening meal £20.00.*

Brunning & Price ~ Manager Dan Redfern ~ Real ale ~ Open 11.30-11; 12-10.30 Sun ~ Bar food 12-10 (9.30 Sun) ~ Children welcome ~ Dogs welcome ~ Wi-fi
Recommended by Brian Glozier, Patrick and Daphne Darley, Richard Elliott

WEST LONDON   Map 12

Portobello Gold 🏅 ♀

(020) 7460 4910 ~ www.portobellogold.com
Portobello Road, opposite Denbigh Terrace; ⊖ *Notting Hill Gate; W11 2QB*

Engaging combination of pub, hotel and restaurant with a relaxed atmosphere and enjoyable food and drink; bedrooms

Right in the heart of Notting Hill, this enterprising and rather bohemian place holds a monthly art or photography exhibition, regular live music and offers breakfast, morning coffee with pastries and newspapers. Our favourite part is the tropical conservatory restaurant with palms and banana trees (which sometimes bear fruit), where you can snack on sashimi in one of the 'hippy decks' set high up among the vegetation or dine in one of the booths. A cage of vocal canaries and a tropical fish tank add to the outdoor effect and in summer they open the sliding roof. The smaller front bar has a nice old fireplace and cushioned banquettes, and there's an oyster bar. It's very relaxed, cheerful and informal, but can get a bit rushed when busy in the evening. Harveys Best on handpump plus an interesting range of bottled beers, 18 wines by the glass from a thoughtfully chosen list, 'as many quality tequilas as are imported into the UK' and classic cocktails; an eclectic choice of background music, TV, chess and backgammon. There are tables and chairs outside on the mainly pedestrianised street. Some bedrooms are small, but all are ensuite with 'smart' TVs. There's a four-poster suite and rooftop apartment with a sunny garden and putting green. Although parking nearby is restricted, you can usually find a space (except on Saturdays).

 The particularly good food includes toasties, oysters, roasted squash salad with prosciutto and parmesan, seafood linguine, vegetarian or meat fajitas, wild boar and apple sausages on parsley mash with gravy, butterflied cajun jumbo shrimps with salsa, duck breast on teriyaki stir-fry, harissa-marinated chicken on spinach fettucine, trout with sautéed mediterranean vegetables, and puddings such as eton mess. *Benchmark main dish: burgers with toppings and chips £12.50. Two-course evening meal £21.00.*

Enterprise ~ Lease Michael Bell and Linda Johnson-Bell ~ Real ale ~ Open 10am-midnight; 9am-12.30am Sat; 10am-11.30pm Sun ~ Bar food 10-10; 10-5, 7-10 Sat; 10-9 Sun ~ Restaurant ~ Children welcome ~ Dogs allowed in bar ~ Wi-fi ~ Live music Sun evening ~ Bedrooms: /£80 *Recommended by Martin Jones, Harvey Brown*

WEST LONDON   Map 12

Princess Victoria 🏅 ♀

(020) 8749 5886 – www.princessvictoria.co.uk
Uxbridge Road; ⊖ *Shepherd's Bush Market; W12 9DH*

London Dining Pub of the Year

A fine choice of drinks, enterprising food and friendly welcome in handsome former gin palace; seats in garden

At this imposing gin palace of a Victorian pub there are 20 gins (and several gin cocktails) on offer. Also, a fantastic wine list (they have a shop where you can browse and buy wines to take away) and Hackney New Zealand Pale Ale, Sambrooks Wandle and a couple of daily changing guests on handpump served by helpful, friendly staff. The rather grand bar – carefully restored – has oil paintings on slate-coloured walls, a couple of stuffed animal heads, comfortable leather wall seats, parquet flooring and a small fireplace. A large dining room has plenty of original features, more paintings and cuban cigars. On the pretty terrace are white wrought-iron tables and chairs; there's a popular artisan market on Saturdays at the front.

 As well as nibbles such as quail eggs with celery salt, and tempura soft shell crab with cucumber pickle and wasabi mayonnaise, the imaginative food (they cure their own fish, make sausages and bake bread daily) includes ham and parsley terrine, citrus salmon ceviche with lime and coriander crème fraîche, truffled macaroni cheese, cottage pie, roast rack and braised shoulder of lamb with mergeuz sausage and new potatoes for two to share, sea trout with pak choi, brown shrimps, beansprouts and spring onion crab broth, and puddings such as plum frangipane tart with burnt milk ice-cream and sticky toffee pudding with toffee and pecan sauce; they also offer a two-course set lunch. *Benchmark main dish: Sunday roast £15.50. Two-course evening meal £26.00.*

Enterprise ~ Lease James McLean ~ Real ale ~ Open 11.30-11 (midnight Fri, Sat); 11.30-10.30 Sun ~ Bar food 12-3 (4.30 Sun), 6.30-10.30 (9.30 Sun) ~ Children welcome ~ Dogs allowed in bar ~ Wi-fi *Recommended by Hilary and Neil Christopher, Nick Sharpe*

WEST LONDON

Map 12

Truscott Arms ♀ ◖

(020) 7266 9198 – www.thetruscottarms.com

Shirland Road; ⊖ Warwick Avenue; W9 2JD

Carefully renovated sizeable pub with lots of space for eating and drinking, a fine range of drinks and enjoyable food

This five-storey Victorian pub has been restored to its former glory, with original tiles, cornices, ceiling roses and wooden flooring but adding a modern twist to things. The various bars and dining rooms have contemporary seats and tables mixed with traditional wooden ones; one cosy room has a clubby feel with upholstered tub chairs and dark wooden tables, while the airy restaurant has huge windows and simple furnishings. It's all very easy-going, and staff are helpful and friendly. Moncada Notting Hill Blonde, Redemption Big Chief, Sambrooks Wandle and Twickenham Grandstand Bitter on handpump, 34 wines by the glass, cocktails and a wide choice of spirits; background music. The garden has colourful tables and chairs among tubs of plants.

As well as breakfasts (until 2pm), the imaginative food includes pulled lamb sandwich with mint pesto, fishcake with red cabbage slaw, cornish crab with cucumber, radishes and borage, veal sweetbreads with lavender honey, hazelnuts and endive, sharing boards, grilled mackerel with purple potatoes, pickled cucumber, pea shoots and lemon and chervil dressing, sausages and mash with onion gravy, roasted squash and pumpkin salad with spelt, goats curd, honey and truffle dressing, halibut with smoked clams, salsify, pink onions, sea beet and cider sauce, and puddings such as rhubarb crumble and chocolate mousse with honeycomb and yoghurt ice-cream. *Benchmark main dish: slow-braised beef shin and chips £17.00. Two-course evening meal £32.00.*

~ Licensee Andrew and Mary Jane Fishwick ~ Real ale ~ Open 10am-11.30pm (midnight Sat); 10am-10.30pm Sun ~ Bar food 10am-10pm ~ Restaurant ~ Children welcome ~ Dogs allowed in bar ~ Wi-fi *Recommended by Nick Sharpe, Belinda May*

WEST LONDON
Map 12

White Horse 🏅 🍷 🍺

(020) 7736 2115 – www.whitehorsesw6.com

Parsons Green; ⊖ Parsons Green; SW6 4UL

Cheerfully relaxed local with big terrace, excellent range of carefully sourced drinks and imaginative food

---

On summer evenings and weekends, the front terrace – overlooking Parsons Green itself – has something of a continental feel with its many seats and tables; there are barbecues most sunny evenings. Inside, the stylishly modernised U-shaped bar has a gently upmarket and chatty atmosphere, plenty of leather chesterfield sofas and wooden tables, huge windows with slatted wooden blinds, flagstone and wood floors, and winter coal and log fires (one in an elegant marble fireplace). There's also an upstairs dining room with its own bar. The impressive range of drinks takes in real ales such as Adnams Broadside, Harveys Sussex, Milk Street Ra, Timothy Taylors Landlord, West Berkshire Maggs Mild and three guest beers on handpump, imported keg beers from overseas (usually belgian and german but occasionally from further afield), six of the seven trappist beers, around 135 other foreign bottled beers, several malt whiskies and 20 good wines by the glass. They hold quarterly beer festivals, often spotlighting regional breweries.

 As well as breakfast, the highly enjoyable food includes sandwiches, salt and pepper squid with spicy mayonnaise, smoked chicken and duck rillettes with apricot and apple chutney, quinoa, couscous and lentil salad with almonds, radish, asparagus, carrots and seeds, smoked chicken caesar salad, fresh cod in cider and tarragon batter with chips, free-range sausages with beer mustard mash and red wine gravy, burger with toppings, bacon jam and fries, 28-day-aged rib-eye steak with a choice of sauces, and puddings such as dark chocolate brownie with vanilla pod ice-cream and blood orange cheesecake with strawberry compote. *Benchmark main dish: slow-roast pork belly, braised onion, pearl barley and chorizo with red wine sauce £15.50. Two-course evening meal £23.00.*

Mitchells & Butlers ~ Manager Jez Manterfield ~ Real ale ~ Open 9.30am-11.30pm (midnight Thurs-Sat) ~ Bar food 12-10.30 ~ Restaurant ~ Children welcome ~ Dogs allowed in bar ~ Wi-fi *Recommended by Tony Scott, Edward May*

WEST LONDON
Map 12

Windsor Castle 🍺

(020) 7243 8797 – www.thewindsorcastlekensington.co.uk

Campden Hill Road; ⊖ Notting Hill Gate; W8 7AR

Genuinely unspoilt, with lots of atmosphere in tiny, dark rooms and lovely summer garden

---

There's a great deal of character and genuine old-fashioned charm here, with a wealth of dark oak furnishings, sturdy high-backed built-in elm benches, time-smoked ceilings, soft lighting and a coal-effect fire. Three of the tiny unspoilt rooms have their own entrance from the street, but it's much more fun trying to navigate through the minuscule doors between them inside. Usually fairly quiet at lunchtime, it tends to be packed most evenings. The panelled and wood-floored dining room at the back overlooks the garden. Brains Rev James, Hop Back Summer Lightning, Robinsons Trooper, Timothy Taylors Landlord and Boltmaker and Windsor & Eton Knight of the Garter on handpump, decent house wines, farm ciders, malt whiskies and jugs of Pimms. The garden, on several levels, has tables and chairs on flagstones and feels secluded thanks to the high ivy-covered walls; heaters for cooler evenings.

🍴 Good, popular food includes sandwiches, crumbed pig cheek with celeriac remoulade and cucumber, tomato and mint dressing, smoked chicken and duck rillettes with apricot and apple chutney, free-range sausages with beer mustard mash and onion gravy, chicken, leek and ham hock pie, kale, cauliflower and cheddar tart, burger with toppings, bacon jam and fries, salmon fillet with asparagus and wild garlic pesto, and puddings such as chocolate praline profiteroles with salted caramel ice-cream and caramel sauce and blackcurrant curd eton mess. *Benchmark main dish: fresh cod in tarragon and cider batter with chips £14.00. Two-course evening meal £23.00.*

Mitchells & Butlers ~ Manager Nicola Smith ~ Real ale ~ Open 12-11 (10.30 Sun) ~ Bar food 12-10 (9 Sun) ~ Restaurant ~ Children welcome till 7pm ~ Dogs welcome ~ Wi-fi
Recommended by Hilary and Neil Christopher, Harvey Brown

Also Worth a Visit in London

Besides the fully inspected pubs, you might like to try these pubs that have been recommended to us and described by readers. Do tell us what you think of them: feedback@goodguides.com

CENTRAL LONDON
EC1

Bishops Finger (020) 7248 2341
West Smithfield; EC1A 9JR Welcoming little pub close to Smithfield Market, Shepherd Neame ales including seasonal brews, good range of sausages and other food in bar or upstairs room; children welcome, seats out in front, closed weekends and bank holidays, otherwise open all day and can get crowded. *(N R White, Tony Scott)*

Butchers Hook & Cleaver
(020) 7600 9181 *West Smithfield; EC1A 9DY* Fullers conversion of bank and adjoining butcher's, their full range kept well and enjoyable pubby food including various pies, efficient service, spiral stairs to mezzanine; background music, free wi-fi; closed weekends, otherwise open (and food) all day, gets busy with after-work drinkers. *(N R White)*

Craft Beer Company
Leather Lane; EC1N 7TR Corner drinkers' pub with excellent selection of real ales and craft beers plus an extensive bottled range, good choice of wines and spirits too, high stools and tables on bare boards, big chandelier hanging from mirrored ceiling, can get very busy but service remains efficient and friendly, food limited to snacks, upstairs room; open all day. *(N R White, Conor McGaughey)*

Dovetail (020) 7490 7321
Jerusalem Passage; EC1V 4JP Fairly small and can get very busy with drinkers spilling into alleyway, specialises in draught/bottled belgian beers and serves popular food including some belgian dishes, efficient staff cope well at busy times; open all day (from 2pm Sun). *(N R White)*

Fox & Anchor (020) 7250 1300
Charterhouse Street; EC1M 6AA Beautifully restored late Victorian pub by Smithfield Market (note the art nouveau façade); long slender bar with unusual pewter-topped counter, lots of mahogany, green leather and etched glass, small back snugs, Youngs ales and guests, oyster bar and decent choice of other freshly cooked food, friendly efficient staff; six individual well appointed bedrooms, open all day from 7am (8am weekends). *(N R White)*

★Hand & Shears (020) 7600 0257
Middle Street; EC1A 7JA Traditional panelled Smithfield pub with three basic bright rooms and small snug off central servery, a couple of gas fires, bustling at lunchtime and early evening, up to six changing ales, friendly service, interesting prints and old photographs; open all day, closed weekends. *(N R White)*

★Jerusalem Tavern (020) 7490 4281
Britton Street; EC1M 5UQ Atmospheric re-creation of a dark 18th-c tavern (1720 merchant's house with shopfront added 1810), tiny dimly lit bar, simple wood furnishings on bare boards, some remarkable old wall tiles, coal fires and candlelight, stairs to a precarious-feeling (though perfectly secure) balcony, plainer back room, St Peters beers tapped from the cask and in bottles, short choice of lunchtime food including good sandwiches, friendly attentive young staff; can get very crowded at peak times; no children, dogs welcome, seats out on pavement (plastic glasses if you drink

out here), open all day weekdays, closed weekends, bank holidays and 24 Dec-2 Jan. *(N R White, Conor McGaughey)*

Old Fountain (020) 7253 2970

Baldwin Street; EC1V 9NU Popular traditional old pub in same family since 1964; long bar serving two rooms, up to eight real ales chalked up on board including Fullers London Pride, interesting craft beers too, pubby food from sandwiches up (not Sat lunchtime), main carpeted part with wooden tables and chairs, padded stools and fish tank, darts, roof terrace and function room for live music; open all day. *(Nick Sharpe)*

Old Red Cow (020) 7726 2595

Long Lane; EC1A 9EJ Cheerful little corner pub close to the Barbican and within sight of Smithfield Market, fine changing selection of cask, craft and bottled beers, tasters offered by friendly knowledgeable staff, well liked if not particularly cheap food from sharing boards and home-made pies to good Sun roasts, modern interior with larger room upstairs; open all day and popular with after-work drinkers, no food Sun evening. *(N R White, Tony Scott)*

EC2

★ **Dirty Dicks** (020) 7283 5888

Bishopsgate; EC2M 4NR Olde-worlde re-creation of traditional City tavern, busy and fun for foreign visitors, booths, barrel tables, exposed brick and low beams, interesting old prints, Charles Wells ales and a guest such as Sambrooks, good variety of enjoyable well priced food from sandwiches up, pleasant service, cellar bar with wine racks overhead in brick barrel-vaulted ceiling (some live music and comedy nights), further upstairs area too; background music, games machines and TV; closed weekends. *(N R White, Tony Scott)*

Hamilton Hall (020) 7247 3579

Bishopsgate; also entrance from Liverpool Street station; EC2M 7PY Showpiece Wetherspoons with flamboyant Victorian baroque décor, plaster nudes and fruit mouldings, chandeliers, mirrors, good-sized comfortable mezzanine, lots of real ales including interesting guests, decent wines and coffee, their usual food and competitive pricing, friendly staff doing their best at busy times; silenced machines, free wi-fi, TVs showing train times; good disabled access, café-style furniture out in front, open all day from 7am, can get very crowded after work. *(Claes Mauroy, Tony and Wendy Hobden)*

Lord Aberconway (020) 7929 1743

Old Broad Street; EC2M 1QT Victorian feel with high moulded ceiling, dark panelling, some red leather bench seating and drinking booths, six well kept ales such as Fullers, Sharps and Trumans, reasonably priced Nicholsons menu from sandwiches

up, upper dining gallery with wrought-iron rail; silent fruit machine; handy for Liverpool Street station, gets busy with after-work drinkers, open till 9.30pm Sat, closed Sun, otherwise open all day. *(N R White)*

EC3

East India Arms (020) 7265 5121

Fenchurch Street; EC3M 4BR Standing-room 19th-c corner pub popular with City workers, well kept Shepherd Neame ales, good service, small single room with wood floor, panelling, old local photographs and brewery mirrors; tables outside, closed weekends and may shut by 9pm weekdays. *(Taff Thomas, N R White)*

Hoop & Grapes (020) 7481 4583

Aldgate High Street; EC3N 1AL Originally 17th-c (dismantled and rebuilt 1983) and much bigger inside than it looks; long partitioned bare-boards bar with beams, timbers and panelling, furniture more modern including sofas, seven real ales and standard Nicholsons menu (very popular at lunchtime), friendly efficient service; a few seats in front, closed Sun, otherwise open (and food) all day. *(N R White, Tony Scott)*

Jamaica Wine House

(020) 7929 6972 *St Michael's Alley, Cornhill; EC3V 9DS* 19th-c pub on the site of London's first coffee house, in a warren of small alleys; traditional Victorian décor with ornate ceilings, oak-panelled bar, booths and bare boards, Shepherd Neame ales and wide choice of wines, food in downstairs lunchtime dining area, friendly helpful service, bustling atmosphere (quietens after 8pm); closed weekends. *(N R White, Tony Scott)*

Lamb (020) 7626 2454

Leadenhall Market; EC3V 1LR Well run stand-up bar with friendly staff coping admirably with hordes of after-work drinkers, Youngs ales and good choice of wines by the glass, dark panelling, engraved glass, plenty of ledges and shelves, spiral stairs up to tables and seating in small light and airy carpeted gallery overlooking market's central crossing, corner servery for lunchtime carvery and other food, separate stairs to nice bright dining room (not cheap), also basement bar with shiny wall tiling and own entrance; tables out under splendid Victorian market roof – crowds here in warmer months, open all day, closed weekends. *(N R White, Tony Scott)*

Ship (020) 7702 4422

Hart Street; EC3R 7NB Tiny one-room 19th-c City pub with ornate flower-decked façade; Caledonian ales and two well kept guests, some food including sandwiches and burgers, friendly staff, limited seating, upstairs function room; spiral stairs down to lavatories; closed weekends. *(Taff Thomas, N R White)*

Ship (020) 7929 3903
Talbot Court, off Eastcheap; EC3V 0BP
Interesting pub tucked down alleyway;
busy bare-boards bar with soft lighting and
ornate décor, candles in galleried dining
area, friendly efficient staff, several well kept
ales including a house beer from St Austell,
good value Nicholsons menu; open all day
weekdays, closed weekends. *(N R White,
Tony Scott)*

Simpsons Tavern (020) 7626 9985
Just off Cornhill; EC3V 9DR Pleasingly
old-fashioned place founded in 1757; rather
clubby small panelled bar serving five real
ales including a guest, stairs down to another
bar with snacks, traditional chophouse with
upright stall seating (expect to share a table)
and similar upstairs restaurant, good value
straightforward food from sandwiches and
snacks up; open weekday lunchtimes and
from 8am Tues-Fri for breakfast.
(Belinda May)

Swan (020) 7929 6550
*Ship Tavern Passage, off Gracechurch
Street; EC3V 1LY* Traditional Fullers
pub with bustling narrow flagstoned bar,
their ales kept well, generous lunchtime
sandwiches and snacks, friendly efficient
service, neatly kept Victorian panelled décor,
low lighting, larger more ordinary carpeted
bar upstairs; silent corner TV; covered alley
used by smokers, open all day Mon-Fri (may
be closed by 8.30pm), shut at weekends.
(N R White)

EC4
★**Black Friar** (020) 7236 5474
Queen Victoria Street; EC4V 4EG
An architectural gem (some of the best
Edwardian bronze and marble art nouveau
work to be found anywhere) and built on
site of 13th-c Dominican priory; inner back
room (the Grotto) with low vaulted mosaic
ceiling, big bas-relief friezes of jolly monks
set into richly coloured florentine marble
walls, gleaming mirrors, seats built into
golden marble recesses and an opulent
pillared inglenook, tongue-in-cheek verbal
embellishments such as Silence is Golden
and Finery is Foolish, and opium-smoking
hints modelled into the front room's
fireplace; six ales including Fullers, Sharps
and St Austell Nicholsons, plenty of wines
by the glass, sound traditional all-day food
(speciality pies); children welcome if quiet,
plenty of room on wide forecourt, handy for
new Blackfriars station. *(Sue and Mike Todd,
N R White, Barry Collett)*

Castle (020) 7405 5470
Castle Street/Furnival Street; EC4A 1JS
A pub has existed here since the 16th c

– although present building dates from
1901; traditional bare-boards bar with dark
panelling, mirrors and minimal furnishings
(window ledges and stools), eight ales
including house Red Car with many from
smaller breweries, several wines by the glass,
limited lunchtime bar food such as steak
and stilton pie and a daily roast, friendly
staff, upstairs dining area; background
music, TV; open all day weekdays, closed
weekends. *(Phil Bryant)*

Centre Page (020) 7236 3614
*Aka the Horn; Knightrider Street near
Millennium Bridge; EC4V 5BH*
Modernised pub with window booths or
'traps' in narrow entrance room, more space
beyond, traditional style with panelling
and subdued lighting, chatty atmosphere,
mix of after-work drinkers and tourists,
friendly efficient young staff, simple
reasonably priced bar menu (from 9am for
breakfast), downstairs dining room, well
kept Fullers ales, tea and coffee; background
music; tables outside with good view of St
Paul's. *(John Jenkins, David Jackman)*

Cockpit (020) 7248 7315
*St Andrew's Hill/Ireland Place, off
Queen Victoria Street; EC4V 5BY* Plenty
of atmosphere in this little corner pub
near St Paul's; as name suggests, a former
cockfighting venue with surviving spectators'
gallery; good selection of ales such as
Adnams, Black Sheep, Dartmoor and Timothy
Taylors, lunchtime food. *(Richard Tilbrook)*

Old Bell (020) 7583 0216
*Fleet Street, near Ludgate Circus;
EC4Y 1DH* Dimly lit 17th-c tavern backing
on to St Bride's church; stained-glass bow
window, heavy black beams, bare boards
and flagstones, half a dozen or more well
kept changing ales from island servery (can
try before you buy, tasting trays available),
usual Nicholsons food, friendly helpful
young staff and cheery atmosphere, various
seating nooks, brass-topped tables, coal
fire; background music; covered and heated
outside area, open all day (may close early
weekend evenings). *(N R White)*

★**Olde Cheshire Cheese**
(020) 7353 6170 *Wine Office Court,
off 145 Fleet Street; EC4A 2BU* Best to
visit this 17th-c former chophouse outside
peak times when it can be packed (early
evening especially); soaked in history with
warren of old-fashioned unpretentious
rooms, high beams, bare boards, old built-in
black benches, Victorian paintings on dark
brown walls, big open fires, tiny snug and
steep stone steps down to unexpected series
of cosy areas and secluded alcoves, Sam

Smiths, all-day pubby food; look out for the famous parrot (now stuffed) that entertained princes and other distinguished guests for over 40 years; children allowed in eating area lunchtime only, closed Sun evening. *(N R White, Tony Scott)*

Olde Watling (020) 7248 8935

Watling Street; EC4M 9BR Heavy-beamed and timbered post-blitz replica of pub built by Wren in 1668; interesting choice of well kept beers, standard Nicholsons menu, good service, quieter back bar and upstairs dining room; open all day. *(Anon)*

SW1

Albert (020) 7222 5577

Victoria Street; SW1H 0NP Busy open-plan airy bar with cut and etched windows, gleaming mahogany, ornate ceiling and solid comfortable furnishings, enjoyable pubby food all day from sandwiches up, well kept Fullers London Pride, Charles Wells Bombardier and guests, 24 wines by the glass, efficient cheerful service, handsome staircase lined with portraits of prime ministers leading up to carvery/dining room; background music, games machine, lavatories down steep stairs; children welcome if eating, open all day from 8am (breakfast till noon). *(Tony Scott)*

Antelope (020) 7824 8512

Eaton Terrace; SW1W 8EZ Pretty little flower-decked Belgravia local, traditional interior with snug seating areas, bare boards and panelling, mix of old and new furniture including leather bucket chairs, interesting prints, gas-effect coal fire in tiled Victorian fireplace, Fullers ales from central servery and decent house wines, upstairs dining room (children allowed) serving reasonably priced pubby food; TVs, free wi-fi, daily papers; dogs welcome, open all day and can get crowded in the evening. *(Anthony and Marie Lewis)*

Buckingham Arms (020) 7222 3386

Petty France; SW1H 9EU Welcoming and relaxed bow-windowed early 19th-c local, Youngs ales and a guest from long curved bar, good range of wines by the glass, reasonably priced pubby food from back open kitchen, elegant mirrors and dark woodwork, stained-glass screens, stools at modern high tables, some armchairs and upholstered banquettes, unusual side corridor with elbow ledge for drinkers; background music, TV; dogs welcome, handy for Buckingham Palace, Westminster Abbey and St James's Park, open all day, till 6pm weekends. *(Nick Sharpe)*

Cask & Glass (020) 7834 7630

Palace Street; SW1E 5HN Snug one-room traditional pub with good range of Shepherd Neame ales, friendly staff and atmosphere, good value lunchtime sandwiches, old prints and shiny black panelling; quiet corner TV;

hanging baskets and a few tables outside, handy for Queen's Gallery, open all day, till 8pm Sat, closed Sun. *(Belinda Stamp)*

Cask Pub & Kitchen

(020) 7630 7225 *Charlwood Street/ Tachbrook Street; SW1V 2EE* Modern and spacious with simple furnishings, excellent choice of real ales and craft beers, also over 500 in bottles, decent range of wines too, friendly knowledgeable staff, good burgers and other good food (roasts on Sun), chatty atmosphere – can get packed evenings and noisy, regular beer-related events such as 'Meet the Brewer'; downstairs gents'; some outside seating, open all day. *(Richard Tilbrook, N R White)*

Clarence (020) 7930 4808

Whitehall; SW1A 2HP Civilised beamed corner pub (Geronimo Inn), Youngs and guests, decent wines by the glass and popular food from snacks up, friendly chatty staff, well spaced tables and varied seating including tub chairs and banquettes, upstairs dining area; pavement tables, open (and food) all day. *(John Harris)*

★ Fox & Hounds (020) 7730 6367

Passmore Street/Graham Terrace; SW1W 8HR Small convivial Youngs local, warm red décor with big hunting prints, old sepia photographs and toby jugs, wall benches and sofas, book-lined back room, hanging plants under attractive skylight, coal-effect gas fire, some low-priced pubby food; can get crowded with after-work drinkers. *(Anon)*

★ Grenadier (020) 7235 3074

Wilton Row; the turning off Wilton Crescent looks prohibitive, but the barrier and watchman are there to keep out cars; SW1X 7NR Steps up to cosy old mews pub with lots of character and military history, but not much space (avoid 5-7pm); simple unfussy panelled bar, stools and wooden benches on bare boards, changing ales such as Fullers, Timothy Taylors, Woodfordes and Youngs from rare pewter-topped counter, famous bloody marys, bar food on blackboard, intimate back restaurant; no mobiles or photography; children over 8 and dogs allowed, hanging baskets, sentry box and single table outside, open all day. *(Richard Tilbrook)*

Jugged Hare (020) 7828 1543

Vauxhall Bridge Road/Rochester Row; SW1V 1DX Popular Fullers Ale & Pie pub in former colonnaded bank; pillars, dark wood, balustraded balcony, large chandelier, busts and sepia London photographs, smaller back dining room, six well kept ales, reasonably priced food from sandwiches up including pie range, good friendly service; background music, TVs, silent fruit machine; open all day. *(Peter Pilbeam)*

★Lord Moon of the Mall

(020) 7839 7701 *Whitehall; SW1A 2DY*
Popular Wetherspoons bank conversion with
elegant main room, big arched windows
looking over Whitehall, old prints and a
large painting of Tim Martin (founder of the
chain), through an arch the style is more
recognisably Wetherspoons with neatly tiled
areas, bookshelves opposite long bar, up to
nine real ales and their good value food
(from breakfasts up); silent fruit machines,
cash machine; children allowed if eating,
dogs welcome, open all day from 8am
(till midnight Fri, Sat). *(Tina and David
Woods-Taylor)*

Morpeth Arms (020) 7834 6442

Millbank; SW1P 4RW Victorian pub
facing Thames, roomy and comfortable,
with view across river to MI6 headquarters
from upstairs Spy Room, some etched and
cut glass, lots of mirrors, paintings, prints
and old photographs (some of british spies),
well kept Charles Wells and a guest, decent
choice of wines, fair value food served all day,
welcoming helpful staff, reputedly haunted
(built on site of Millbank Prison, some cells
remain below); background music; seats
outside (a lot of traffic), handy for Tate
Britain and Thames Path walkers.
(Robert Lester)

★Red Lion (020) 7321 0782

Duke of York Street; SW1Y 6JP Pretty
little Victorian pub, remarkably preserved
and packed with customers often spilling
out on to pavement by mass of foliage and
flowers; series of small rooms with lots of
polished mahogany, a gleaming profusion
of mirrors, cut/etched windows and
chandeliers, striking ornamental plaster
ceiling, Fullers/Gales beers, traditional food
(all day weekdays, snacks evening, diners
have priority over a few of the front tables);
no children; dogs welcome, closed Sun and
bank holidays, otherwise open all day.
(Belinda May)

Red Lion (020) 7930 4141

*Crown Passage, behind St James's
Street; SW1Y 6PP* Cheerful traditional
little pub tucked down narrow passage near
St James's Palace, dark panelling, settles
and leaded lights, lots of prints, decorative
plates and horsebrasses, well kept Adnams
and St Austell, friendly service, lunchtime
sandwiches (no hot food), narrow overflow
room upstairs; sports TV in one corner;
colourful hanging baskets, closed Sun,
otherwise open all day. *(Michael Butler,
Tony Scott)*

Red Lion (020) 7930 5826

Parliament Street; SW1A 2NH Victorian
pub by Houses of Parliament, used by Foreign
Office staff and MPs, divided bare-boards
bar with showy chandeliers suspended from
fine moulded ceiling, parliamentary cartoons
and prints, Fullers/Gales beers and decent
wines from long counter, good range of food,
efficient staff, also clubby cellar bar and
upstairs panelled dining room; free wi-fi;
children welcome, outside bench seating,
open all day (till 9pm Sun). *(Nick Sharpe)*

Speaker (020) 7222 1749

Great Peter Street; SW1P 2HA Bustling
chatty atmosphere in unpretentious
smallish corner pub (can get packed at
peak times), well kept Timothy Taylors,
Youngs and guests, lots of whiskies, limited simple but well
liked food all day, friendly staff, panelling,
political cartoons and prints, no mobiles or
background music; open all day weekdays,
closed Sat, Sun. *(Peter Pilbeam)*

★St Stephens Tavern (020) 7925 2286

Parliament Street; SW1A 2JR Victorian
pub opposite Houses of Parliament and
Big Ben (so quite touristy), lofty ceilings
with brass chandeliers, tall windows with
etched glass and swagged curtains, gleaming
mahogany, charming upper gallery bar
(may be reserved for functions), four well
kept Badger ales from handsome counter
with pedestal lamps, friendly efficient staff,
enjoyable good value all day food from
sandwiches up, division bell for MPs and lots
of parliamentary memorabilia; open all day.
(Paul Humphreys)

Wetherspoons (020) 7931 0445

Victoria station; SW1V 1JT Modern
pub up escalators on mezzanine with glass
wall overlooking main concourse and
platform indicators, good selection of well
priced changing ales, plenty of wines by the
glass and a couple of real ciders, decent
reasonably priced food, quick service; free
wi-fi; children welcome, some tables outside,
open all day from 7am. *(Tony and Wendy
Hobden, George Atkinson)*

White Swan (020) 7821 8568

Vauxhall Bridge Road; SW1V 2SA Roomy
corner pub handy for Tate Britain, lots of
dark dining tables on three levels in long
room, well cooked reasonably priced pubby
food, six or more ales including Adnams,
Fullers, St Austell and Youngs, decent wines
by the glass, quick helpful uniformed staff;
background music, can get very busy at peak
times; open all day. *(Dr and Mrs J D Abell)*

SW3

★Coopers Arms (020) 7376 3120

Flood Street; SW3 5TB Useful bolthole
for King's Road shoppers (so can get busy);
comfortable dark-walled open-plan bar with
mix of good-sized tables on floorboards,
pre-war sideboard and dresser, railway
clock and moose head, Youngs and guests,
good all-day bar food; well behaved children
till 7pm, dogs allowed in bar, courtyard
garden. *(Anon)*

Cross Keys (020) 7351 0686
Lawrence Street; SW3 5NB Recently reopened under same owners as the Brown Cow and Sands End (both SW6); open-plan bare-boards interior with skylit back dining area, exposed brick walls and some recycled wood panelling, Greene King IPA and three guests from central servery, good food (not cheap) including all-day bar snacks, attentive friendly service, home-made jams, chutneys etc for sale. *(Richard and Penny Gibbs)*

Pigs Ear (020) 7352 2908
Old Church Street; SW3 5BS Civilised L-shaped corner pub, friendly and relaxed, with short interesting choice of bar food and more elaborate evening menu, lots of wines by the glass including champagne and good Ridgeview english sparkling wine, three changing ales such as Caledonian Deuchars IPA , Uley Pigs Ear and Wandle, good coffee and service, tables and benches on wood floors, butterflies and 1960s posters on grey/green panelling, large mirrors and huge windows, open fire, upstairs restaurant; background music; children and dogs (in bar) welcome, open all day and food all day weekends. *(Belinda May)*

Surprise (020) 7351 6954
Christchurch Terrace; SW3 4AJ Late Victorian Chelsea pub revamped by Geronimo Inns and popular with well heeled locals, Sharps, Youngs and a house beer (HMS Surprise) from light wood servery, champagne and plenty of other wines by the glass, interesting food including british tapas-style choices, canapé boards and set menu, friendly service, soft grey décor and comfortable furnishings with floral sofas and armchairs on sturdy floorboards, stained-glass partitioning, upstairs dining room, daily papers; open all day. *(Nick Sharpe)*

W1

★**Argyll Arms** (020) 7734 6117
Argyll Street; W1F 7TP Popular and unexpectedly individual pub with three interesting little front cubicle rooms (essentially unchanged since 1860s), wooden partitions and impressive frosted and engraved glass, mirrored corridor to spacious back room, good choice of beers including Brains, Nicholsons, Fullers and Sharps, well liked reasonably priced food in bar or upstairs dining room overlooking pedestrianised street, teas and coffees, theatrical photographs; background music, fruit machine; children welcome till 8pm, open (and food) all day. *(Ian Phillips, Tracey and Stephen Groves, Dr Kevan Tucker, Barry Collett, Tony Scott)*

★**Audley** (020) 7499 1843
Mount Street; W1K 2RX Classic late Victorian Mayfair pub, opulent red plush, mahogany panelling and engraved glass, chandeliers and clock in extravagantly carved bracket hanging from ornately corniced ceiling, Fullers London Pride, Sharps Doom Bar, Taylor Walker 1730 and guests from long polished bar, good choice of pub food (reasonably priced for the area), friendly efficient service, upstairs panelled dining room, wine bar in cellar; quiet background music, TV, pool; children till 6pm, pavement tables, open (and food) all day. *(Tony Scott)*

Crown & Two Chairmen
(020) 7437 8192 *Bateman Street/Dean Street; W1D 3SB* Large main room with smaller area off to the right, different height tables on bare boards, Sharps, Windsor & Eton and three guests, also craft beers such as Camden Town, decent food from bar snacks up including set menu and Sun roasts, upstairs dining room, good mix of customers (gets busy with after-work drinkers); free wi-fi; open (and food) all day. *(Jeremy King)*

★**Dog & Duck** (020) 7494 0697
Bateman Street/Frith Street; W1D 3AJ Bags of character in this tiny Soho pub – best enjoyed in the afternoon when not so packed; unusual old tiles and mosaics (the dog with tongue hanging out in hot pursuit of a duck is notable), heavy old advertising mirrors and open fire, Fullers London Pride and guests from unusual little counter and quite a few wines by the glass, enjoyable well priced food in cosy upstairs dining room where children welcome; background music; dogs allowed in bar, open (and food) all day. *(Jeremy King, David Jackman, Dr and Mrs A K Clarke)*

French House (020) 7437 2477
Dean Street; W1D 5BG Small character Soho pub with impressive range of wines and bottled beers, other unusual drinks, some draught beers (no real ales or pint glasses), lively chatty atmosphere – mainly standing room, theatre memorabilia, shortish choice of reasonably priced food (Mon-Fri till 4pm) in bar or upstairs restaurant, efficient staff; no music or mobile phones, can get very busy evenings with customers spilling on to the street, open all day. *(Jeremy King)*

★**Grapes** (020) 7493 4216
Shepherd Market; W1J 7QQ Genuinely old-fashioned pub with dimly lit bar, plenty of well worn plush red furnishings, stuffed birds and fish in display cases, wood floors, panelling, coal fire and snug back alcove, six ales including Fullers, Sharps and a house beer from Brains, good choice of authentic thai food (not Sun evening), english food too, lots of customers (especially early evening) spilling out on to square; children till 6pm weekdays (anytime weekends), open all day. *(Ian Phillips, Dr W I C Clark, Tony Scott)*

★**Guinea** (020) 7409 1728
Bruton Place; W1J 6NL Lovely hanging baskets and chatty customers outside this tiny 17th-c mews pub, standing room only at

peak times, a few cushioned wooden seats and tables on tartan carpet, side elbow shelf and snug back area, old-fashioned prints, planked ceiling, Youngs and a guest from striking counter, famous steak and kidney pie, grills and some sandwiches (no food weekends), smart Guinea Grill restaurant; no children; closed Sat lunchtime, Sun and bank holidays. *(Hilary and Neil Christopher)*

Old Coffee House   (020) 7437 2197
Beak Street; W1F 9SF Long, thin and unsmart corner pub with stools around bar serving Brodies ales, rugs on wood floors, old signs, advertising mirrors, musical instruments and other bric-a-brac; background music, games machine, sports TV; children allowed in upstairs dining room, open all day. *(Jeremy King)*

Prince Regent   (020) 7486 7395
Marylebone High Street; W1U 5JN Victorian corner pub in Marleybone village, flamboyant (if slightly worn) bare-boards interior with richly coloured furnishings, large gilt mirrors and opulent chandeliers, four changing ales, sensibly priced home-made food including good value weekday set menu and Sun roast, upstairs 'Opium Room'; free wi-fi; open all day. *(John Voos)*

Running Horse   (020) 7493 1275
Davies Street/Davies Mews; W1K 5JE Refurbished 18th-c pub with open-plan bare-boards bar, appealing collection of dining chairs and cushioned settles around mix of tables, tartan armchairs in front of green-tiled fireplace, Rebellion and Wye Valley, lots of wines by the glass and imaginative food, horse-racing prints on plain or navy-painted panelling, projector showing live televised racing, upstairs more Mayfair than pubby, with button-back club chairs, brass chandeliers and more horsey prints on racing colours wallpaper; free wi-fi; children and dogs welcome, contemporary wicker seats and tables on the pavement outside, closed Sun evening, otherwise open all day.
(Stuart Gideon, Mrs Catherine Simmonds)

Shakespeares Head
(020) 7734 2911 *Great Marlborough Street; W1F 7HZ* Taylor Walker corner pub dating from the early 18th c (though largely rebuilt in the 1920s), dark beams, panelling and soft lighting, well kept ales including Fullers and Sharps, enjoyable pubby food from sandwiches and baked potatoes up, friendly staff, upstairs dining room overlooking Carnaby Street; open (and food) all day. *(Anon)*

Three Tuns   (020) 7408 0330
Portman Mews S; W1H 6HP Large bare-boards front bar and sizeable lounge/dining area with beams and nooks and crannies, Fullers, Timothy Taylors and guests, enjoyable reasonably priced pubby food,

good friendly staff and vibrant atmosphere; street benches. *(Peter Pilbeam)*

Tottenham   (020) 7636 8324
Oxford Street, near junction with Tottenham Court Road; W1D 1AN Ornate late Victorian pub with long narrow bar, old tiling, mirrors, mahogany fittings and so forth, also three notable murals behind glass of voluptuous nymphs, dark floorboards and leather banquettes, extensive range of reasonably priced beers, enjoyable all-day food from Nicholsons menu, friendly service, dining room downstairs; background music and fruit machine; can get very busy at lunchtime. *(John Harris)*

W2   TQ2680
Leinster Arms   (020) 7402 4670
Leinster Terrace; W2 3EU Flower-decked Bayswater pub close to Hyde Park, friendly and busy, with good range of beers and highly rated food; sports TV, free wi-fi; children and dogs welcome, open (and food) all day. *(Dr and Mrs A K Clarke)*

Mad Bishop & Bear
(020) 7402 2441 *Paddington station; W2 1HB* Up escalators from concourse, full Fullers range kept well and a guest beer, good wine choice, reasonably priced standard food quickly served including breakfast from 8am (10am Sun), ornate plasterwork, etched mirrors and fancy lamps, parquet, tiles and carpet, booths with leather banquettes, lots of wood and prints, train departures screen; background music, TVs, games machine; tables out overlooking station, open all day till 11pm (10.30pm Sun). *(Dr and Mrs A K Clarke, Roger and Donna Huggins)*

★Victoria   (020) 7724 1191
Strathearn Place; W2 2NH Well run bare-boards pub with lots of Victorian pictures and memorabilia, cast-iron fireplaces, gilded mirrors and mahogany panelling, brass mock-gas lamps above attractive horseshoe bar serving Fullers ales and guests from smaller breweries, several wines by the glass and reasonably priced popular food, friendly service and chatty relaxed atmosphere; upstairs has small library/snug and replica of Gaiety Theatre bar (mostly for private functions now); quiet background music, TV; pavement tables, open all day.
(Hilary and Neil Christopher)

WC1
Calthorpe Arms   (020) 7278 4732
Grays Inn Road; WC1X 8JR Friendly early well run Victorian corner local with good Youngs ales and guests, enjoyable low-priced pub food including good Sun roasts, free bar nibbles too on Sun, carpeted bar with plush wall seats, upstairs overspill dining/function room; sports TV; dogs welcome, pavement tables, open all day. *(John Harris)*

★**Cittie of Yorke** (020) 7242 7670
High Holborn; WC1V 6BN Splendid
back bar rather like a baronial hall with
extraordinarily extended bar counter, 1,000-
gallon wine vats resting above gantry, big
bulbous lights hanging from soaring raftered
roof, intimate ornately carved booths,
triangular fireplace with grates on all three
sides, smaller comfortable panelled room
with lots of little prints of York, cheap Sam
Smiths beers and reasonably priced bar food,
lots of students, lawyers and City types but
plenty of space to absorb crowds; children
welcome, open all day, closed Sun. *(Phil
Bryant, Mrs Sally Scott, Barry Collett, Tony Scott)*

Lady Ottoline (020) 7831 0008
Northington Street; WC1N 2JF Well
restored 19th-c Bloomsbury pub; original
fitted benches and some utilitarian 1940s
furniture on bare boards, modern artwork
including portrait of Lady Ottoline Morrell
who had associations with the Bloomsbury
Set, enjoyable food from short menu, four
real ales and good wines, friendly service,
staircase with risqué Victorian photographs
up to dining rooms; children (till 6pm) and
dogs allowed, peaceful atmosphere despite
TV, open all day. *(Susan and John Douglas)*

★**Lamb** (020) 7405 0713
Lamb's Conduit Street; WC1N 3LZ
Famously unspoilt Victorian pub with bank
of cut-glass swivelling snob screens around
U-shaped counter, sepia photographs
of 1890s actresses on ochre panelled
walls, traditional cast-iron-framed tables,
snug little back room, Charles Wells and
guests, good choice of malt whiskies,
straightforward pubby food from baguettes
up; children welcome till 5pm, slatted
wooden seats out in front, more in small
courtyard, Foundling Museum nearby, open
all day (till midnight Thurs-Sat) and can
get very busy. *(Roy Hoing, Tracey and Stephen
Groves, Brian and Anna Marsden)*

Museum Tavern (020) 7242 8987
*Museum Street/Great Russell Street;
WC1B 3BA* Traditional high-ceilinged
ornate Victorian pub facing British Museum,
busy lunchtime and early evening, but
can be quite peaceful other times, half a
dozen ales and several wines by the glass,
straightforward Taylor Walker menu, friendly
helpful staff; one or two tables out under gas
lamps, open all day. *(Eric Larkham)*

Norfolk Arms (020) 7388 3937
Leigh Street; WC1H 9EP Atmospheric
tile-fronted pub with ornate ceiling and other
high Victorian features, very good tapas, a
couple of well kept changing ales and nice
wines, close-set tables in bustling U-shaped

bar, friendly efficient service; handy for
British Museum. *(Tracey and Stephen Groves,
Richard Tilbrook)*

Penderels Oak (020) 7242 5669
High Holborn; WC1V 7HJ Vast
Wetherspoons with attractive décor and
woodwork, lots of books, pew seating around
central tables, their well priced food and
fine choice of good value real ales, efficient
friendly staff, cellar bar; pavement seating,
open all day from 8am. *(John Harris)*

★**Princess Louise** (020) 7405 8816
High Holborn; WC1V 7EP Splendid
Victorian gin palace with extravagant décor
– even the gents' has its own preservation
order; gloriously opulent main bar with wood
and glass partitions, fine etched and gilt
mirrors, brightly coloured and fruit-shaped
tiles, slender Portland stone columns soaring
towards the lofty and deeply moulded plaster
ceiling, open fire, cheap Sam Smiths from
long counter, competitively priced pubby food
(not Fri-Sun) in quieter upstairs room; gets
crowded early weekday evenings, no children;
open all day. *(Ian Phillips, Barry Collett)*

Queens Larder (020) 7837 5627
Queen Square; WC1N 3AR Small
character pub on corner of traffic-free square
and cobbled Cosmo Place, also known as
Queen Charlotte (where she stored food
for her mad husband George III who was
being cared for nearby); circular cast-iron
tables, wall benches and stools around
attractive U-shaped bar, theatre posters
on dark panelled walls, Greene King ales,
decent pubby food, upstairs function room;
background jazz; dogs welcome, picnic-sets
and heater outside. *(John Harris)*

Skinners Arms (020) 7837 5621
Judd Street; WC1N 9NT Richly decorated,
with glorious woodwork, marble pillars,
high ceilings and ornate windows, lots of
London prints on busy wallpaper, interesting
layout including comfortable back seating
area, Greene King Abbot and guests from
attractive long bar, decent home-made food
(very popular burgers and fish and chips);
unobtrusive background music, muted
corner TV; pavement picnic-sets, handy for
British Library, open all day, closed Sun.
(Roger and Donna Huggins)

WC2

Angel (020) 7240 2876
St Giles High Street; WC2H 8LE
Interesting Victorian pub with warren of
little rooms including comfortable upstairs
sitting area, cheap Sam Smiths Old
Brewery tapped from the cask, welcoming
landlord. *(Richard Tilbrook)*

We say if we know a pub has background music.

Bear & Staff (020) 7930 5261

Bear Street; WC2H 7AX Traditional Nicholsons corner pub with six well kept changing ales, standard pubby food from sandwiches and sharing platters up, upstairs dining room named after Charlie Chaplin who used the pub; open all day. *(Nick Sharpe)*

Chandos (020) 7836 1401

St Martin's Lane; WC2N 4ER Busy bare-boards bar (can get packed early evening) with snug cubicles, lots of theatre memorabilia on stairs up to more comfortable split-level lounge with opera photographs, low wooden tables, panelling, leather sofas and stained-glass windows, cheap Sam Smiths and reasonably priced food; background music and games machines; children upstairs till 6pm, note the automaton on the roof (working 10am-2pm, 4-9pm), open all day from 9am (for breakfast). *(Peter Smith and Judith Brown)*

Cheshire Cheese (020) 7836 2347

Little Essex Street/Milford Lane; WC2R 3LD Small cosy 1920s corner pub, leaded bow windows, beams and panelling, cushioned oak settles and assorted bric-a-brac, well kept St Austell Tribute, Sharps Doom Bar and guests, good value wines and pubby food, friendly staff, games room with bar billiards, darts and table skittles, upstairs dining/function room; background music, sports TV; closed Sun, otherwise open all day. *(Tony and Wendy Hobden, David and Sally Frost)*

Coal Hole (020) 7379 9883

Strand; WC2R 0DW Well preserved Edwardian pub adjacent to the Savoy; original leaded windows, classical wall reliefs, mock-baronial high ceiling and raised back gallery, ten changing ales from central servery, standard Nicholsons menu, wine bar downstairs; sports TV; open all day. *(N R White, Tony Scott)*

★Cross Keys (020) 7836 5185

Endell Street/Betterton Street; WC2H 9EB Foliage-covered Covent Garden pub with fascinating interior, masses of photographs, pictures and posters including Beatles memorabilia, all kinds of brassware and bric-a-brac from stuffed fish to musical instruments, three well kept Brodies ales and couple of guests (usually smaller London brewers), decent wines by the glass, good lunchtime sandwiches and a few bargain hot dishes; fruit machine, gents' downstairs; sheltered outside cobbled area with flower tubs, open all day. *(Hilary and Neil Christopher)*

Edgar Wallace (020) 7353 3120

Essex Street; WC2R 3JE Simple spacious open-plan pub dating from 18th c, eight well kept ales including some unusual ones and a beer badged for them from Nethergate, enjoyable good value food all

day from sandwiches up, friendly efficient service, half-panelled walls and red ceilings, interesting Edgar Wallace memorabilia (pub renamed in 1975 to mark his centenary) and lots of old beer and cigarette adverts, upstairs dining room; a few high tables in side alleyway, closed weekends. *(N R White)*

George (020) 7353 9638

Strand; WC2R 1AP Timbered pub near the law courts, long narrow bare-boards bar, nine real ales and a dozen wines by the glass, lunchtime food from sandwiches up, also upstairs bar/restaurant, pre-theatre meal discount till 7pm; open all day. *(N R White, Tony Scott)*

Knights Templar (020) 7831 2660

Chancery Lane; WC2A 1DT Good Wetherspoons in big-windowed former bank, marble pillars, handsome fittings and plasterwork, bustling atmosphere on two levels, some interesting real ales at bargain prices, good wine choice and enjoyable well priced food, friendly staff; remarkably handsome lavatories, free wi-fi; open all day Mon-Fri, till 5pm Sat, closed Sun. *(Taff Thomas, Ian Herdman)*

Porterhouse (020) 7379 7917

Maiden Lane; WC2E 7NA Good daytime pub (can be packed evenings), London outpost of Dublin's Porterhouse microbrewery, their interesting beers along with guests and lots of bottled imports, good choice of wines by the glass, pubby food, shiny three-level labyrinth of stairs (lifts for disabled), galleries and copper ducting and piping, some nice design touches, sonorous open-work clock, neatly cased bottled beer displays; background and live music, sports TV (repeated in gents'); tables on front terrace, open all day. *(Peter Pilbeam)*

Salisbury (020) 7836 5863

St Martin's Lane; WC2N 4AP Gleaming Victorian pub in the heart of the West End, a wealth of cut-glass and mahogany, curved upholstered wall seat creating impression of several distinct areas, wonderfully ornate bronze light fittings, lots of mirrors, back room popular with diners (can be closed for private functions) and separate small side room, some interesting photographs including Dylan Thomas enjoying a drink here in 1941, lots of theatre posters, up to six well kept ales, bar food (from sharing platters up) all day, coffees and cheerful staff; steep stairs down to lavatories; children allowed till 5pm, fine details on building exterior, seats in pedestrianised side alley, open till midnight Fri, Sat. *(Hilary and Neil Christopher)*

Ship (020) 7405 1992

Gate Street; WC2A 3HP Tucked-away bare-boards pub with roomy minimally furnished bar, some booth seating, chesterfields by open fire, quite dark with leaded lights, panelling and plaster relief ceiling, six well kept changing ales, enjoyable bar food, upstairs restaurant with separate menu, friendly service; background music; open (and food) all day. *(John Evans)*

★**Ship & Shovell** (020) 7839 1311
Craven Passage, off Craven Street; WC2N 5PH Unusually split between two facing buildings; well kept Badger ales and a guest, decent reasonably priced food including wide range of baguettes, bar snacks and pubby choices, good friendly service; one side brightly lit with dark wood, etched mirrors and interesting mainly naval pictures, plenty of tables, some stall seating and open fire; other side (across 'Underneath the Arches' alley) has a cosily partitioned bar; open all day, closed Sun. *(Tony Scott)*

Temple Brew House
(020) 7936 2536 *Essex Street; WC2R 3JF* Refurbished basement bar under new management; fine range of beers including some from on-site microbrewery, lots of wines by the glass and well liked food from sandwiches, small plates and burgers up (own smokehouse), friendly service from enthusiastic knowledgeable young staff; open (and food) all day. *(Nick Sharpe)*

Wellington (020) 7836 2789
Strand/Wellington Street; WC2R 0HS Long narrow traditional corner pub next to the Lyceum; Adnams, Fullers, Timothy Taylors and plenty of guests, several wines by the glass, usual Nicholsons menu, friendly staff, quieter upstairs bar/restaurant; tables outside, open all day from 9am. *(Tony Scott, Dr Kevan Tucker)*

EAST LONDON

E1

★**Prospect of Whitby** (020) 3603 4041
Wapping Wall; E1W 3SH Claims to be oldest pub on the Thames dating from 1520 (although largely rebuilt after much later fire), was known as the Devil's Tavern and has a colourful history (Pepys and Dickens used it regularly and Turner came for weeks at a time to study the river views) – tourists love it; L-shaped bare-boards bar with plenty of beams, flagstones and panelling, five changing ales served from fine pewter counter, good choice of wines by the glass, bar food and more formal restaurant upstairs; children welcome (only if eating after 5.30pm), unbeatable views towards Docklands from tables on waterfront courtyard, open all day. *(Taff Thomas, Mrs Sally Scott)*

Town of Ramsgate (020) 7481 8000
Wapping High Street; E1W 2PN Interesting olde-London Thames-side setting

affording a restricted but evocative river view from small back floodlit terrace with mock gallows (hanging dock was nearby), long narrow chatty bar with squared oak panelling, Fullers London and Youngs, friendly helpful service, good choice of generous standard food and daily specials, various deals; background music, Mon quiz; open all day. *(N R White)*

Water Poet (020) 7426 0495
Folgate Street; E1 6BX Big rambling Spitalfields pub with bohemian feel and ornate touches, enjoyable food in bar and dining room including popular Sun roasts, good selection of real ales and craft beers, decent wines, friendly staff and nice mix of customers, comfortable leather sofas and armchairs on wood floor, basement bar/function room, comedy club, separate pool room with two tables; sports TV; large enclosed outside area with 'barn' room and barbecue, open all day. *(John Harris)*

Williams (020) 7247 5163
Artillery Lane; E1 7LS Busy pub with wide range of real ales including Greene King and several from smaller London brewers, proper ciders too, comfortable interior with several seating areas including some leather sofas, pictures of old London breweries on the walls; weekend live music; closed Sun, otherwise open (and food) all day. *(Tony and Wendy Hobden)*

E2

Carpenters Arms (020) 7739 6342
Cheshire Street; E2 6EG Welcoming neatly kept little corner pub just off Brick Lane and once owned by the Kray twins, enjoyable blackboard food and well kept beers including Timothy Taylors Landlord; beer garden at back, closed lunchtime Mon-Weds, otherwise open all day. *(Neil Hosland-Round)*

Sun (020) 7739 4097
Bethnal Green Road; E2 0AN Revamped 19th-c bar with good choice of local beers and other drinks including cocktails, friendly helpful service, padded stools around copper-topped counter with lanterns above, bare boards, exposed brickwork and some leather banquettes, bar snacks; open all day. *(Belinda Stamp)*

E3

★**Crown** (020) 8880 7261
Grove Road/Old Ford Road; E3 5SN Dining pub (part of the Geronimo Inns group) with relaxed welcoming bar, faux animal hide stools and chunky pine tables on polished boards, big bay window with comfortable scatter cushion seating area, books etc on open shelves, well kept Youngs and guests, good choice of wines by the glass, three individually decorated upstairs dining areas overlooking Victoria Park, imaginative food (all day Sun); background music;

children and dogs welcome, open all day.
(Hilary and Neil Christopher)

Palm Tree (020) 8980 2918

Haverfield Road; E3 5BH Lone survivor of blitzed East End terrace tucked away in Mile End Park by Regent's Canal; two Edwardian bars around oval servery, old-fashioned and unchanging under long-serving licensees, a couple of well kept ales, lunchtime sandwiches, good local atmosphere with popular weekend jazz; no credit cards; open all day (till late Sat). *(John Harris)*

E10

King William IV (020) 8556 2460

High Road Leyton; E10 6AE Imposing flower-decked Victorian building, home to Brodies brewery; up to 20 well kept low-priced ales including guests, beer festivals, enjoyable food, darts and bar billiards; big-screen sports TV; six bedrooms.
(Edward May)

E14

★Grapes (020) 7987 4396

Narrow Street; E14 8BP Relatively unchanged since Charles Dickens used it as a model for his Six Jolly Fellowship Porters in *Our Mutual Friend*; a proper traditional tavern with friendly atmosphere and good mix of customers, partly panelled bar with prints of actors, old local maps and the pub itself, elaborately etched windows, plates along a shelf, larger back area leading to small deck with views over river towards Canary Wharf, Adnams, Marstons, Timothy Taylors and a guest, good value tasty bar food, upstairs restaurant with fine views; no children, dogs on the lead welcome, can catch Canary Wharf ferry and enter pub via steps from foreshore, open all day.
(Phil Bryant, N R White, Claes Mauroy)

★Gun (020) 7515 5222

Coldharbour; E14 9NS Dining pub with great views from riverside terrace of the O2 centre; smart front restaurant and two character bars – busy flagstoned drinkers' one with antique guns and log fire, cosy red-painted next-door room with leather sofas and armchairs, stuffed boar's head and modern prints, Adnams Bitter and guests, several wines by the glass and very well liked contemporary food (not cheap), efficient service from friendly staff; background music; children welcome till 8pm, open all day (may close for weddings and other events – best to check website). *(Taff Thomas)*

Narrow (020) 7592 7950

Narrow Street; E14 8DJ Popular stylish dining pub (owned by Gordon Ramsay) with great Thames views from window seats and covered terrace, simple but smart bar with white walls and blue woodwork, mosaic-tiled fireplaces and colourful striped armchairs, Adnams, Greene King and a guest, good

wines, food from bar snacks to pricier restaurant meals, dining room also white with matching furnishings, local maps, prints and a suspended boat; background music (live Weds); children welcome, open all day.
(N R White)

E17

Queens Arms (020) 8520 9184

Orford Road; E17 9NJ Recently refurbished 19th-c corner pub in Walthamstow village, spacious and comfortable, with well kept ales such as Sharps Doom Bar and numerous wines by the glass, nice food from interesting changing menu, friendly service and good buoyant atmosphere; children welcome, seats outside. *(Michael Butler)*

NORTH LONDON

N1

Albion (020) 7607 7450

Thornhill Road; N1 1HW Charming wisteria-clad Georgian building in Islington conservation area; attractive bare-boards interior with minimalist front bar and spacious back lounge/dining room, interesting choice of good mid-priced home-made food, a couple of well kept ales such as Caledonian Deuchars IPA and Ringwood Best, helpful cheerful service; tables out at front and in impressive walled back garden with pergola, open all day. *(Hilary and Neil Christopher)*

Charles Lamb (020) 7837 5040

Elia Street; N1 8DE Small friendly backstreet corner pub, four well kept ales such as Dark Star and Windsor & Eton, interesting bottled beers and decent choice of wines by the glass including own-label, good blackboard food (brunch Sat from 11am), big windows, polished boards and simple traditional furniture; background jazz; pavement tables, closed Mon and Tues lunchtimes, otherwise open all day.
(N R White)

Craft Beer Company

(020) 7278 4560 *White Lion Street; N1 9PP* Flower-decked Islington pub with extensive choice of interesting draught and bottled beers, good range of wines and spirits too, cosy and softly lit with dark green walls, wood-strip or red carpeted floors, a couple of ornate Victorian pillars, leather armchairs under a portrait of Churchill, high tables in main bar, low ones in adjacent areas, good mix of customers; occasional live acoustic music; small side garden, open all day Fri-Sun, from 4pm other days. *(John Harris)*

Duke of Cambridge (020) 7359 3066

St Peter's Street; N1 8JT Well established as London's first organic pub, simply decorated busy main room with chunky wooden tables, pews and benches on bare boards, corridor past open kitchen to more formal dining room and conservatory, ales such as Little Valley, Pitfield and St Peters, also organic draught lagers, ciders, spirits and wines, interesting bar food using seasonal produce but not cheap and they add a service charge, teas and coffees; children welcome, dogs in bar, open all day. *(Peter Pilbeam)*

Earl of Essex (020) 7424 5828
Danbury Street; N1 8LE One-room Islington pub brewing its own Earl ales, great choice of other beers too on draught and in bottles, straightforward but decent home-made food with beer recommendations listed on menu; back walled garden, open all day. *(Anon)*

Hemingford Arms (020) 7607 3303
Hemingford Road; N1 1DF Ivy-clad Metropolitan (formerly Capital) pub filled with bric-a-brac, good choice of real ales from central servery, traditional food alongside thai restaurant and popular Sunday roasts, open fire, upstairs bar, live music and Weds quiz night; sports TV, machines; picnic-sets outside. *(Belinda May)*

Marquess Tavern (020) 7359 4615
Canonbury Street/Marquess Road; N1 2TB Imposing refurbished Victorian pub, bare boards and a mix of furniture including sofas around big horseshoe servery, a couple of fireplaces and lots of prints (some recalling George Orwell who used to drink here), Youngs beers and good selection of wines, traditional and more adventurous food in bar or back skylit room with classical wall columns, big mirrors and modern lights dangling from the high ceiling; background music, TV; children and dogs welcome, a few seats out behind front railings, open (and food) all day. *(Emma Scofield)*

★Parcel Yard (020) 7713 7258
King's Cross station, N end of new concourse, up stairs (or lift); N1C 4AH Impressive restoration of listed Victorian parcel sorting office, lots of interesting bare-boards rooms off corridors around airy central atrium, pleasing old-fashioned feel with exposed pipework and ducting adding to the effect, back bar serving full range of well kept Fullers beers plus guests from long modern counter, plenty of wines by the glass, similar upstairs area with old and new furniture including comfortable sofas, railway memorabilia and some nice touches like Victorian envelope wallpaper, good bistro-pub food from bar snacks up, breakfast till 11.45am, attentive smiling service,

power points to recharge phones/laptops, platform views; open all day from 8am (9am Sun). *(Roger and Donna Huggins, Eric Larkham, Susan and John Douglas, Peter Smith and Judith Brown, John Oates, Dr Kevan Tucker)*

Wenlock Arms (020) 7608 3406
Wenlock Road; N1 7TA Corner local with friendly service and excellent choice of real ales and craft beers, half a dozen ciders and foreign bottled beers too from central servery, simple food, alcove seating, coal fires, darts; open all day. *(Edward May)*

N6

★Flask (020) 8348 7346
Highgate West Hill; N6 6BU Comfortable traditional Georgian pub owned by Fullers; intriguing up-and-down layout, sash-windowed bar hatch, panelling and high-backed carved settle in snug lower area with log fire, wide choice of food; picnic-sets out in front courtyard, handy for strolls around Highgate village or Hampstead Heath, open all day. *(Edward May)*

Prince of Wales (020) 8340 0445
Highgate High Street; N6 5JX Small unpretentious bare-boards local with bench seats, stools and old wooden tables, two coal-effect gas fires, well kept Butcombe and up to three guests from horseshoe bar, decent choice of blackboard wines, food from thai dishes to Sun roasts, friendly prompt service; background music, TV, Tues quiz; tables on small terrace behind, open all day. *(John Harris)*

Victoria (020) 8341 3290
North Hill; N6 4QA Tucked-away traditional Victorian pub in tree-lined street, beers such as Long Man, Sharps, Trumans and Westerham, good food including popular Sun lunch, themed nights, Mon quiz; children and dogs welcome. *(John Harris)*

N8

Kings Head (020) 8340 1028
Crouch End Hill/Broadway; N8 8AA Victorian corner pub with open-plan bar, cushioned window seats, leather banquettes, high stools and elbow tables on bare boards, well kept ales such as Sambrooks and Sharps, good choice of other drinks, enjoyable food including set menu, friendly helpful staff, downstairs comedy club (Thurs, Sat, Sun); background music, TV; open all day (till 2am Fri, Sat). *(Edward May)*

NW1

Albert (020) 7722 1886
Princess Road; NW1 8JR Welcoming split-level Victorian corner pub tucked

---

If you report on a pub that's not a featured entry, please tell us any lunchtimes or evenings when it doesn't serve bar food.

away in residential street; partly green-tiled exterior, roomy U-shaped bar with corniced ceiling, bare boards and cast-iron fireplace (new licensees plan some refurbishment), good choice of decent food, well kept Greene King and Timothy Taylors Landlord, obliging friendly staff, conservatory, live music and quiz nights; children welcome, attractive back garden. *(Peter Pilbeam)*

Bree Louise (020) 7681 4930

Cobourg Street/Euston Street; NW1 2HH Determinedly no-frills corner pub with wide selection of real ales on handpump and gravity, good choice of ciders too, food emphasising pies (Mon-Thurs bargains), basic décor and well worn furnishings; can get very busy early evening; pavement tables, handy for Euston station, open all day. *(Richard Tilbrook, Eric Larkham, Tony Scott)*

★Chapel (020) 7402 9220

Chapel Street; NW1 5DP Busy and noisy in the evening (quieter during the day), corner dining pub attracting an equal share of drinkers; spacious rooms dominated by open kitchen, smart but simple furnishings, sofas at lounge end by big fireplace, a couple of real ales such as Adnams and Black Sheep, good choice of wines by the glass, several coffees and teas, good food from daily changing blackboard menu, brisk friendly service; children and dogs welcome, picnic-sets in sizeable back garden, more seats on decking under heated parasols, covered smokers' area, open all day. *(Tracey and Stephen Groves)*

Constitution (020) 7380 0767

St Pancras Way; NW1 0QT Traditional standalone 19th-c pub close to Camden Lock and a quieter alternative to the busy market area; three local beers and good selection of wines by the glass, pubby lunchtime food Mon-Fri, friendly staff and nice atmosphere; pool, darts and juke box, cellar bar for live music; barbecues in lovely sunny garden overlooking canal, open all day. *(John Harris)*

★Doric Arch (020) 7388 2221

Eversholt Street; NW1 2DN Virtually part of Euston station, up stairs from bus terminus with raised back section overlooking it – a haven of peace away from the concourse says one reader; well kept Fullers ales and guests, enjoyable well priced pubby food from snacks and sharing plates to specials, friendly prompt service, pleasantly nostalgic atmosphere and some quiet corners, intriguing train and other transport memorabilia; discreet sports TV; open (and food) all day. *(Eric Larkham, Dave Braisted)*

Euston Flyer (020) 7383 0856

Euston Road, opposite British Library; NW1 2RA Big welcoming open-plan pub, Fullers/Gales beers and enjoyable fairly standard food including Weds curry night, relaxed lunchtime atmosphere (can get packed evenings), plenty of light wood, mix of furniture on carpet or boarded floors, mirrors, photographs of old London, smaller raised areas and private corners, big doors open to street in warm weather; background music, Sky TV, silent games machine; open (and food) all day. *(Eric Larkham)*

Euston Tap (020) 3137 8837

Euston Road; NW1 2EF Small 19th-c neoclassical lodge in front of Euston station, good selection of ever-changing real ales and imported beers including huge bottled range, friendly knowledgeable staff, evening pizzas Tues-Sat, limited seating but more space and lavatory up spiral staircase; outside tables, open all day from noon; identical building opposite dedicated to ciders/perries (open from 3.30pm, closed Sun). *(Eric Larkham, N R White, Claes Mauroy, Tracey and Stephen Groves)*

Metropolitan (020) 7486 3489

Baker Street station, Marylebone Road; NW1 5LA Flight of steps up to Wetherspoons in impressively ornate pillared hall (designed by Metropolitan Railway architect Charles W Clarke), lots of tables on one side, very long bar the other, leather sofas and some elbow tables, ten or more real ales, good coffee and their usual inexpensive food; games machines, free wi-fi; family area, open all day from 8am (10am Sun). *(Tony Hobden)*

Tapping the Admiral

(020) 7267 6118 *Castle Road; NW1 8SU* Friendly local with fine range of well kept ales mainly from London brewers, fairly priced home-made food including range of pies; quiz Weds, Irish music Thurs; beer garden, open all day. *(Anon)*

NW3

★Flask (020) 7435 4580

Flask Walk; NW3 1HE Bustling local with two traditional front bars divided by unique Victorian screen, smart banquettes, panelling and lots of little prints, attractive fireplace, Youngs and a guest, plenty of wines by the glass and maybe winter mulled wine, popular all-day food, good friendly service, dining conservatory; background music, TV; children (till 8pm) and dogs welcome, seats and tables in alley, open (and food) all day. *(Roger and Donna Huggins)*

★Spaniards Inn (020) 8731 8406

Spaniards Lane; NW3 7JJ Busy 16th-c pub next to Hampstead Heath with charming garden – flagstoned walk among roses, side arbour with climbing plants and plenty of seats on crazy-paved terrace (arrive early weekends as popular with dog walkers and families); attractive and characterful low-ceilinged rooms with oak panelling, antique winged settles, snug alcoves and open fires, up to five real ales, continental draught beers and several wines by glass, popular pubby food including range of burgers, upstairs dining room; car park fills fast and nearby parking difficult, open (and food) all day. *(Belinda May)*

Stag (020) 7722 2646
Fleet Road; NW3 2QU Handy for Royal Free Hospital with button-back leather wall banquettes and little stools around a mix of tables on bare boards, Thornbridge Jaipur and Timothy Taylors Boltmaker, craft (such as Meantime) and bottled beers, cocktails, 17 wines by the glass and good, contemporary food, upstairs party floor and roof terrace; big back garden with a cabana and lots of picnic-sets, open (and food) all day. *(Anon)*

NW5   TQ2886

★Bull & Last (020) 7267 3641
Highgate Road; NW5 1QS Traditional décor with a stylish twist in this Victorian corner dining pub; single room with big windows, colonial-style fans in planked ceiling, bulls' heads and other stuffed animals, stone fireplace one end along with collection of tankards and big faded map of London, much emphasis on the good imaginative food (not cheap), takeaway tubs of home-made ice-cream and picnic hampers for Hampstead Heath, well kept changing ales and a house craft beer (So Solid Brew from Five Points), good selection of wines, whiskies and gins, friendly staff, upstairs restaurant; children (away from bar) and dogs welcome, hanging baskets and picnic-sets by street, open all day. *(Lois Dyer)*

Junction Tavern (020) 7485 9400
Fortess Road; NW5 1AG Victorian corner pub with good, interesting food, dining room and back conservatory, modern décor, St Austell, Sambrooks, Shepherd Neame and Thwaites (beer festivals), good choice of wines by the glass, friendly, helpful staff; background music; no children after 7pm, picnic-sets in back garden, shut Mon lunchtime. *(John Harris)*

Southampton Arms 07958 780073
Highgate Road; NW5 1LE Simply furnished drinkers' pub with wall seats and stools around tables on bare boards, 11 beers from breweries such as Crouch Vale, Meantime, Oakham, Slaters, Otley and Twickenham, eight ciders, bar snacks; live piano Tues, Weds and Sun evenings, Mon quiz; open all day. *(Nick Sharpe)*

SOUTH LONDON

SE1

Anchor (020) 7407 1577
Bankside; SE1 9EF In great Thames-side spot with river views from upper floors and roof terrace, beams, stripped brickwork

and old-world corners, well kept Adnams, St Austell and Sharps, good choice of wines by the glass, popular fish and chip bar (takeaways available) and other good value all-day food, breakfast/tea room, can get very busy; background music; provision for children, disabled access, more tables under big parasols on raised riverside terrace, bedrooms in Premier Inn behind. *(Mrs Sally Scott)*

Anchor & Hope (020) 7928 9898
The Cut; SE1 8LP Informal bare-boards gastropub, food from changing menu can be good (and prices can be high), well kept Charles Wells and guests, sensibly priced wines by tumbler or carafe, plain bar with big windows and mix of furniture including elbow tables, curtained-off dining part with small open kitchen, tight-packed scrubbed tables and contemporary art; children and dogs welcome, on same street as Young and Old Vics, closed Sun evening and Mon lunchtime, otherwise open all day. *(Peter Smith and Judith Brown)*

Dean Swift (020) 7357 0748
Gainsford Street; SE1 2NE Well run and enjoyable one-room pub tucked away behind Tower Bridge, good selection of cask and craft beers such as Moor, London Fields, Kernel, Magic Rock and Redwell, several wines by the glass, friendly well informed staff, great food from bar snacks to Sun roasts; sports TV, Sun quiz; open (and food) all day. *(Stuart Warmsley)*

★Founders Arms (020) 7928 1899
Hopton Street; SE1 9JH Modern glass-walled building in superb location – outstanding terrace views along Thames and handy for South Bank attractions; plenty of customers (City types, tourists, theatre- and gallery-goers) spilling on to pavement and river walls, Charles Wells and a guest, lots of wines by the glass, extensive choice of well priced bar food all day (weekend breakfasts from 9am), tea and coffee from separate servery, cheerful service; background music; children welcome away from bar, open till midnight Fri, Sat. *(Jeremy King, Ian Phillips, Phil and Jane Villiers)*

Garrison (020) 7089 9355
Bermondsey Street; SE1 3XB Interesting tile-fronted corner dining pub with idiosyncratic mix of styling, popular modern food including breakfast from 8am (9am weekends), a real ale or two but perhaps more emphasis on wine than beer, buzzy atmosphere, cinema/ function room downstairs; open all day. *(Nick Sharpe)*

★George (020) 7407 2056
Off 77 Borough High Street; SE1 1NH Tucked-away 16th-c coaching inn (mentioned in *Little Dorrit*), owned by the National Trust

and beautifully preserved; lots of tables in bustling cobbled courtyard with views of the tiered exterior galleries, series of no-frills ground-floor rooms with black beams, square-latticed windows and some panelling, plain oak or elm tables on bare boards, old-fashioned built-in settles, dimpled glass lanterns and a 1797 Act of Parliament clock, impressive central staircase up to a series of dining rooms and balcony, well kept Greene King ales and a beer badged for the pub, good value traditional food all day (not Sun evening), friendly staff; children welcome away from bar, open all day. *(Roger and Donna Huggins, N R White, Tony Scott)*

★ **Kings Arms** (020) 7207 0784
Roupell Street; SE1 8TB Proper corner local tucked away amid terrace houses, bustling and friendly, with curved servery dividing traditional bar and lounge, bare boards, open fire and various bits and pieces including local road signs on the walls, nine well kept changing ales, good wine and malt whisky choice, welcoming efficient staff, enjoyable food from thai dishes to Sun roasts, big back extension with conservatory/courtyard dining area; background music; open all day. *(B and M Kendall)*

★ **Market Porter** (020) 7407 2495
Stoney Street; SE1 9AA Properly pubby no-frills place opening at 6am weekdays for workers at neighbouring Borough Market, up to ten unusual real ales (over 60 guests a week) often from far-flung brewers and in top condition, particularly helpful friendly service, bare boards and open fire, beams with barrels balanced on them, simple furnishings, food in bar and upstairs lunchtime restaurant with view over market; background music; children allowed weekends till 7pm, dogs welcome, gets very busy with drinkers spilling on to the street, open all day. *(Jeremy King, B and M Kendall, Phil and Jane Villiers, Tony Scott)*

Rake (020) 7407 0557
Winchester Walk; SE1 9AG Tiny discreetly modern Borough Market bar with amazing bottled beer range in wall-wide cooler, also half a dozen continental lagers on tap and three real ales, good friendly service; fair-sized covered and heated outside area. *(Jeremy King)*

Roebuck (020) 7357 7324
Great Dover Street; SE1 4YG Victorian pub with open-plan bar, big windows and high ceilings, a mix of wooden chairs and tables and leather chesterfields on bare boards, ales from Meantime, Sambrooks and Trumans, farm cider and several wines by the glass, good pubby food (all day Sun); upstairs lounge with own bar (Charlie Chaplin is said to have performed here as a boy), Tues rock quiz, Thurs poetry readings; picnic-sets outside, open all day. *(Anon)*

Sheaf (020) 7407 9934
Southwark Street; SE1 1TY In cellars beneath the Hop Exchange, brick vaulted ceilings and iron pillars, high stools around elbow tables, traditional wooden tables and chairs, ten real ales, decent pubby food; sports TV; open all day. *(Gus Swan)*

Wheatsheaf (020) 7940 3880
Stoney Street; opposite Borough Market main entrance under new railway bridge; SE1 9AA Youngs pub with comfortably refurbished interior, three of their well kept beers and a guest, 'street food with style' from side campervan kitchen, heated back garden; open all day from 9am (12 Sun). *(Harvey Brown)*

White Hart (020) 7928 9190
Cornwall Road/Whittlesey Street; SE1 8TJ Backstreet corner local near Waterloo station; friendly community bustle, comfortable sofas, stripped boards and so forth, real ales, craft beers and artisan spirits, lots of bottled beers, good range of ciders and wines, sensibly priced up-to-date blackboard food as well as pub standards, Sunday bloody marys and newspapers, helpful efficient staff; background music; open all day. *(Ian Phillips)*

SE5

★ **Crooked Well** (020) 7252 7798
Grove Lane; SE5 8SY Popular early 19th-c restaurant pub with really good imaginative food including two-course lunch deal (Tues-Fri), nice wines and cocktails, Sharps Doom Bar, welcoming helpful staff; seats outside, closed Mon lunchtime, otherwise open all day. *(John Harris)*

SE8

Dog & Bell (020) 8692 5664
Prince Street; SE8 3JD Friendly old-fashioned local tucked away on Thames Path, wood benches around bright cheerfully decorated L-shaped bar, open fire, up to half a dozen well kept ales including Fullers, bottled belgians, prompt friendly service, reasonably priced pub food from good sandwiches up, dining room, bar billiards; TV; tables in yard, open all day. *(Gus Swan)*

SE9

Park Tavern (020) 8850 8919
Passey Place; SE9 5DA Traditional Victorian corner pub off Eltham High Street, half a dozen well kept changing ales and 14 wines by the glass, log fire, friendly easy-going atmosphere; soft background music; pleasant little garden behind, open all day. *(Taff Thomas)*

SE10

Cutty Sark (020) 8858 3146
Ballast Quay, off Lassell Street; SE10 9PD Great Thames views from this early 19th-c Greenwich tavern, genuinely

unspoilt old-fashioned bar, dark flagstones, simple furnishings including barrel seats, open fires, narrow openings to tiny side snugs, upstairs room (reached by winding staircase) with ship deck-feel and prized seat in big bow window, up to five well kept changing ales, organic wines, malt whiskies and enjoyable all-day bar food; background music; children and dogs welcome, busy riverside terrace across narrow cobbled lane, limited but free parking if you get a space. *(Taff Thomas)*

★ **Greenwich Union** (020) 8692 6258
Royal Hill; SE10 8RT Feels more like a bar than a pub with full Meantime craft range, 150 bottled beers, unusual spirits and interesting choice of teas and coffees, good food too from varied menu, friendly brisk service; long narrow stone-flagged room with simple front area, wooden furniture, stove and daily papers, comfortable part with sofas and cushioned pews, end conservatory with booth seating; free wi-fi; well behaved children and dogs welcome, appealing terrace with green picnic-sets, old-fashioned lamp posts and end fence painted as a poppy field, open (and food) all day. *(John Fiander, Taff Thomas, Tracey and Stephen Groves)*

Old Brewery (020) 3327 1280
Pepys Building, Old Royal Naval College; SE10 9LW Modernised 19th-c building in grounds of Old Royal Naval College and a stone's throw from the *Cutty Sark*; front bar with Meantime beers (some brewed here) and guests plus many more in bottles, gleaming brewery equipment in separate back hall acting as café/evening restaurant; nice courtyard garden, open (and food) all day. *(Belinda May)*

Pilot (020) 8858 5910
River Way, Blackwall Lane; SE10 0BE Refurbished early 19th-c pub surviving amid O2 development; opened-up interior on three levels with roof terrace overlooking park, well kept Fullers/Gales beers, good choice of food (all day Fri, Sat, till 6pm Sun) from pubby choices and charcoal grills to daily specials; background music, newspapers and free wi-fi; dogs welcome, picnic-sets in front, more seating in enclosed back garden with paving, lawn and covered area, ten well equipped boutique bedrooms, open all day. *(Taff Thomas)*

Richard I (020) 8692 2996
Royal Hill; SE10 8RT Friendly recently modernised two-bar Youngs pub (next to the Greenwich Union), their well kept ales and guests plus one or two craft kegs, lots of wines by the glass, popular food from lunchtime sandwiches up, good service, dining room and new conservatory; children welcome, seats out at front and in nice paved garden behind, open all day. *(Taff Thomas)*

Trafalgar (020) 8858 2909
Park Row; SE10 9NW Substantial 18th-c building with splendid river views from big windows directly above water in four elegant high-ceilinged rooms, oak panelling and good maritime and local prints, three real ales and decent house wines, enjoyable if pricey food (not Sun evening) including signature whitebait and massive ciabattas; background music; children welcome, tables out by Nelson statue, handy for Maritime Museum, open all day (can get packed Fri, Sat evenings). *(Paul Humphreys, Tracey and Stephen Groves)*

Yacht (020) 7858 0175
Crane Street; SE10 9NP Neatly modernised with great river views from spacious room up a few steps from bar, four well kept ales and wide choice of reasonably priced food, friendly attentive staff, cosy banquettes, light wood panelling, portholes and yacht pictures; children welcome, cheerful hanging baskets in front, open (and food) all day. *(Mrs Sally Scott, Tony Scott)*

SE11
Prince of Wales (020) 7735 9916
Cleaver Square; SE11 4EA Comfortably traditional little Edwardian pub in smart quiet Georgian square near the Oval, well kept Shepherd Neame ales, bar food from filling sandwiches up, warm friendly atmosphere; pavement seats, boules available to play in the square, open all day. *(David M Smith)*

SE12 TQ3974
Lord Northbrook (020) 8318 1127
Burnt Ash Road; SE12 8PU Opened-up Victorian corner pub with armchairs, wooden dining tables and chairs on bare boards, contemporary paintwork, friendly staff, decent food from sharing plates up (all day weekends), five interesting ales; tables and chairs in back garden; open all day. *(Hilary and Neil Christopher)*

SE15 TQ3575
Ivy House (020) 7277 8233
Stuart Road; SE15 3BE Co-operatively owned pub with excellent range of changing ales and craft beers, well priced food including burgers and hot dogs, old-fashioned panelled interior, stage in back room for live music, comedy and theatre nights; children (till 8pm) and dogs welcome, rack for cyclists, open all day. *(Gus Swan)*

Old Nuns Head (020) 7639 4007
Nunhead Green; SE15 3QQ Open-plan 1930s brick and timber pub on edge of small green, popular locally, four well kept changing ales and enjoyable food (especially the burgers) from standards up including some interesting choices, roasts only on Sun, cheerful efficient staff, Thurs quiz; children

welcome, back garden and a few seats out in front, handy for the fascinating Nunhead Cemetery. *(Edward May)*

SE16

★ **Mayflower** (020) 7237 4088

Rotherhithe Street; SE16 4NF Unchanging cosy old riverside pub in unusual street with lovely early 18th-c church; good generous bar food including more upmarket daily specials, well kept Greene King and guests such as Dark Star and Purity, good value wines and decent coffee, friendly young staff, black beams, panelling, nautical bric-a-brac, high-backed settles and coal fires, good Thames views from upstairs evening restaurant; background music; children welcome, fun jetty/terrace over water (barbecues), handy for Brunel Museum, open all day.
(Jeremy King)

SE19   TQ3370

Westow House (020) 8670 0654

Westow Hill; SE19 1TX Character local with six well kept beers and interesting modern all-day cooking, chesterfield sofas, cushioned wall seating and a mix of wooden dining chairs and tables, artwork on walls, lots of books on shelves, busy convivial atmosphere, table football and pinball, regular live music Thurs evenings, open all day. *(Nick Sharpe)*

SE22

Clockhouse (020) 8693 2901

Peckham Rye/Barry Road; SE22 9QA Light and airy restyled Victorian pub, well kept Charles Wells and guests, decent wines and cocktail list, enjoyable fairly priced home-cooked food, busy hard-working staff, front bar with dining area behind, upstairs function room; background music, Tues quiz; children (till 7pm) and dogs welcome, tables on front terrace looking across to Peckham Rye, open (and food) all day.
(Paul Humphreys, John Wooll)

SW4

Bobbin (020) 7738 8953

Lillieshall Road; SW4 0LN Tucked-away 19th-c pub in Clapham Old Town, unpretentious opened-up front bar with blue walls and blue-painted chairs on bare boards, upholstered wall benches, ales such as Harveys and Sambrooks, enjoyable reasonably priced food including Sun lunch, flagstoned back conservatory; background music, darts and board games; sunny walled beer garden, open all day Fri-Sun, from 5pm other days. *(John Harris)*

Windmill (020) 8673 4578

Clapham Common South Side; SW4 9DE Big bustling pub by the common, modern front bar, quite a few original Victorian features, pillared dining room leading through to conservatory-style eating area, popular, varied choice of food all day (good breakfasts, too), Wells Bombardier and Youngs Bitter ales and decent wines by the glass, background music, Sun quiz; children welcome, bar, tables under red umbrellas along front, also seats in side garden area, good bedrooms, open all day. *(Gus Swan)*

SW11

Eagle Ale House (020) 7228 2328

Chatham Road; SW11 6HG Attractive unpretentious backstreet local, seven changing ales including southern brewers like Harveys, Surrey Hills and Westerham, welcoming efficient service, worn leather chesterfield in fireside corner of L-shaped bar; big-screen sports TV; dogs welcome, back terrace with heated marquee, small front terrace too, open all day weekends, from 4pm other days. *(Edward May)*

Falcon (020) 7228 2076

St John's Hill; SW11 1RU Lively Victorian pub with ten well kept beers from remarkably long light oak counter, period partitions, cut-glass and mirrors, subdued lighting, quieter back dining area serving good value pub food, friendly service; TV; handy for Clapham Junction station, open all day. *(Ross Balaam)*

Fox & Hounds (020) 7924 5483

Latchmere Road; SW11 2JU Victorian pub with good mediterranean food (all day Sun, not Mon-Thurs lunchtimes), four real ales and several wines by glass, spacious straightforward bar with big windows overlooking street, bare boards, mismatched tables and chairs, photographs on walls, fresh flowers, daily papers, view of kitchen behind; background music, TV; children (till 7pm) and dogs welcome, garden seats under big parasols, open all day Fri-Sun, closed Mon lunchtime. *(Hilary and Neil Christopher)*

Prince Albert (020) 7228 0923

Albert Bridge Road; SW11 4PF Large modernised Victorian pub (Geronimo Inn) popular with young professionals, raised dining area, mix of wooden dining and armchairs around pale wooden tables, plenty of space, open fire, good range of beers, quite a choice of popular food and efficient friendly staff; regular backgammon tournaments; seats and heaters out in front overlooking Battersea Park, garden behind; dogs welcome. *(Gus Swan)*

Westbridge (020) 7228 6482

Battersea Bridge Road; SW11 3AG Interesting ever-changing choice of real ales, craft beers and ciders, good food from open

---

There are report forms at the back of the book.

kitchen particularly hotdogs and steaks, can eat in bar or back restaurant, friendly staff; background music may be loud, popular with art students early evening; seats for smokers out at front and back, open all day. *(Pip White)*

Woodman (020) 7228 2968
Battersea High Street; SW11 3HX Sensitively refurbished by welcoming young couple (he's the chef), good seasonal food from bar snacks and sharing platters up, Badger ales, Weston's cider and several wines by the glass, good friendly service, has village-local feel and can get very busy (particularly in summer); dogs welcome, garden. *(Belinda May)*

SW12
Avalon (020) 8675 8613
Balham Hill; SW12 9EB Part of the Renaissance group, popular often interesting food including weekend brunch, well kept changing ales and good choice of wines by the glass, plenty of room in split-level bar and back dining area, big murals, stuffed animals and coal fires; sports TV; children welcome, front terrace and nice sunny large garden behind, open all day (till 1am Fri, Sat). *(Hilary and Neil Christopher)*

★ Nightingale (020) 8673 1637
Nightingale Lane; SW12 8NX Recently refurbished early Victorian local, cosy and civilised, with small front bar opening into larger back area and attractive family conservatory, well kept Charles Wells ales with guests such as Sambrooks and Sharps, enjoyable sensibly priced bar food, friendly service, open fire; nice secluded back beer garden with summer barbecues, open all day. *(Hilary and Neil Christopher)*

SW13
Bulls Head (020) 8876 5241
Lonsdale Road; SW13 9PY Imposing Victorian pub by the river in Barnes, popular and welcoming, with good live jazz (nightly and Sun afternoon) in back music room; comfortable open-plan areas refurbished by Geronimo Inns in their usual colourful, quirky modern style, good food and service, three real ales including Sharps and Youngs from central servery, upstairs balconied restaurant; children welcome, open (and food) all day. *(Edward Mirzoeff)*

Idle Hour (020) 8878 5555
Railway Side (off White Hart Lane between Mortlake High Street and Upper Richmond Road); SW13 0PQ Tucked-away organic dining pub, chatty and relaxed, with good interesting food including Weds curry night, organic soft drinks, wines and beers, also cocktails (good bloody mary) and fine range of gins, nice chunky old tables on bare boards, a profusion of wall clocks on different times, comfortable sofa by small fireplace; background music, daily

papers and magazines; no children, tables with candles in small pretty yard behind, if driving, park at end of Railway Side and walk (road gets too narrow for cars), closed weekday lunchtimes. *(Edward Mirzoeff)*

White Hart (020) 8876 5177
The Terrace; SW13 0NR Revamped open-plan Barnes dining pub with fine river views, well kept Charles Wells ales along with craft beers such as Camden Town and Meantime from island servery, good selection of wines by the glass, popular food in bar or upstairs restaurant with open kitchen and balcony; seats outside, open (and food) all day. *(Edward Mirzoeff)*

SW15
Bricklayers Arms (020) 8789 3932
Down cul-de-sac off Lower Richmond Road near Putney Bridge; SW15 1DD Welcoming tucked-away little 19th-c local, up to ten well kept changing ales, proper cider/perry and good selection of english wines, efficient friendly young staff, no food, long L-shaped room with pitched-roof section, pine tables on bare boards, lots of pictures on painted panelling, log fire; background music, sports TV; paved side terrace, open all day. *(Dr Kevan Tucker)*

Half Moon (020) 8780 9383
Lower Richmond Road; SW15 1EU Good long-standing music venue restyled by Geronimo Inns, Charles Wells and a couple of guests from elegant curved counter, food from burgers and hot dogs to more elaborate choices, free lunchtime jazz, nightly gigs in back music room; open all day (till 1am Fri, Sat). *(David M Smith)*

Jolly Gardeners (020) 8789 2539
Lacy Road; SW15 1NT Revamped bare-boards pub in residential Putney; gardening theme with trowels and watering cans on walls, potted flowers and botanical prints, a reclining gnome, row of colourful heated sheds in the back garden; four changing ales and several other draught beers, good selection of wines, enjoyable pubby food including good value set menu and weekend brunch; board games, newspapers and free wi-fi; front fairy-lit terrace, open (and food) all day. *(Gus Swan)*

★ Telegraph (020) 8788 2011
Telegraph Road; SW15 3TU Big pub on Putney Heath, two attractively modernised rooms with bold décor, leather armchairs and sofas, rugs on polished wood, grand dining table, eight real ales including house Semaphore brewed by Weltons, bistro-style food all day, newspapers and board games; background music and live blues/jazz nights, sports TV, occasional quiz; children and dogs welcome, great garden with rural feel, busy outside with families and dogs in summer. *(Colin McKerrow)*

SW16

Earl Ferrers (020) 8835 8333

Ellora Road; SW16 6JF Opened-up Streatham corner local, Sambrooks and several other well kept ales (tasters offered), interesting food along with pub standards, good friendly service, mixed tables and chairs, sofas, old photographs; pool and darts, music Mon and Thurs, quiz Weds plus other events such as book and knitting clubs; children welcome, some tables outside with tractor-seat stools, open all day weekends, from 5pm weekdays. *(Edward May)*

Railway (020) 8769 9448

Greyhound Lane, Streatham; SW16 5SD Busy Streatham corner local with two big rooms (back one for families), rotating ales from London brewers such as Meantime, Redemption, Sambrooks and Trumans, enjoyable freshly made food, friendly staff, events including Tues quiz and monthly farmers' market; walled back garden, open all day (till 1am Fri, Sat). *(John Harris)*

SW18

Alma (020) 8870 2537

York Road, opposite Wandsworth Town station; SW18 1TF Corner Victorian pub-hotel with well kept Charles Wells ales and good choice of wines from island bar, sofas and informal mix of tables and chairs on wood floor, mosaic plaques and painted mirrors, wide range of good food from bar snacks up, back restaurant, friendly helpful staff; 23 bedrooms, open all day. *(Mrs G Marlow)*

Cats Back (020) 8617 3448

Point Pleasant; SW18 1NN Traditionally refurbished 19th-c corner pub, Harveys first in SW London, four of their ales along with bottled beers, enjoyable food including Sun roasts, friendly staff, regular blues bands; partially covered beer garden with heaters, open all day weekends. *(Gus Swan)*

Ship (020) 8870 9667

Jews Row; SW18 1TB Popular riverside pub by Wandsworth Bridge; light and airy conservatory-style décor, mix of furnishings on bare boards, church candles on tables, basic public bar, well kept Charles Wells, Sambrooks and a guest, freshly cooked interesting bistro food (not particularly cheap) in extended restaurant with own garden; children and dogs welcome, good-sized terrace with barbecue and outside bar, open all day. *(Pip White)*

SW19

Alexandra (020) 8947 7691

Wimbledon Hill Road; SW19 7NE Busy Youngs pub with their well kept beers and guests from central bar, good wine choice, enjoyable food from sandwiches to good Sun roasts, friendly alert service, comfortably up-to-date décor in linked rooms; sports TVs; tables out in mews and on attractive roof terrace. *(Colin McKerrow)*

Crooked Billet (020) 8946 4942

Wimbledon Common; SW19 4RQ Busy 18th-c pub popular for its position by common (almost next door to the Hand in Hand); Youngs ales and guests, good choice of wines and enjoyable food in bar or dining room, friendly helpful staff, clean traditional interior with high-backed settles and scrubbed pine tables on oak boards, some interesting old prints, winter fire, board games and Mon quiz; children (away from bar) and dogs welcome, plastic glasses for outside, open (and food) all day. *(Tony Swindells)*

Fox & Grapes (020) 8619 1300

Camp Road; SW19 4UN Popular 18th-c dining pub by Wimbledon Common; modern bistro feel but keeping some original features in the two linked areas (step between), some adventurous cooking from french chef-owner alongside more traditional dishes (not cheap and they add a service charge), view into kitchen from high-ceilinged upper room with its unusual chandeliers, well chosen wines by the glass, Sharps Doom Bar and guest from central servery, pleasant relaxed atmosphere; children and dogs welcome, three bedrooms, open all day, food all day Sun. *(Susan and John Douglas, Peter Sutton)*

Hand in Hand (020) 8946 5720

Crooked Billet; SW19 4RQ Friendly Youngs local on edge of Wimbledon Common, their ales and guests kept well, enjoyable home-made pubby food, several areas off central bar including family room with games, log fire; front courtyard, benches out by common, open all day. *(Tony Swindells)*

Sultan (020) 8544 9323

Norman Road; SW19 1BN Red-brick 1930s drinkers' pub owned by Hop Back and hidden in a tangle of suburban roads; their ales and maybe a guest in top condition (carry-outs available), friendly locals, big scrubbed tables, darts in public bar; nice walled beer garden with summer barbecues, open all day. *(Nick Sharpe)*

WEST LONDON

SW6

★ Atlas (020) 7385 9129

Seagrave Road; SW6 1RX Busy tucked-away pub with long simple bar, plenty of panelling and dark wall benches, mix of old tables and chairs, brick fireplaces, good enjoyable food (all day Sun), well kept Fullers, St Austell, Sharps and a guest, lots of wines by the glass and decent coffee, friendly service; background music; children (till 7pm) and dogs welcome, seats under awning on heated and attractively planted side terrace, open all day. *(Hilary and Neil Christopher)*

Brown Cow (020) 7384 9559

Fulham Road; SW6 5SA Popular rustic-style dining pub (same owner as nearby Sands End), assortment of old furniture on bare boards including butcher's block table, pendant lighting, Victorian prints of prize cows, one wall clad in distressed mirrored glass, enjoyable if not particularly cheap modern pub food from bar snacks to Sunday roasts, ales such as Greene King and Trumans, 'larder shop' selling home-made jams etc; dogs welcome, benches and milk churns outside, open all day. *(Susan and John Douglas)*

Eight Bells (020) 7736 6307

Fulham High Street/Ranelagh Gardens; SW6 3JS Friendly traditional local tucked away near Putney Bridge, Fullers London Pride, Sharps Doom Bar and a guest, good value standard pub menu; sports TV; dogs welcome, seats outside under awning, close to Bishop's Park and church used in horror film *The Omen*, open all day and busy with away supporters on Fulham match days. *(Dr Kevan Tucker)*

Harwood Arms (020) 7386 1847

Walham Grove; SW6 1QP Bare-boards Fulham gastropub with good food from bar snacks to enterprising pricey full meals, extensive wine list, a couple of well kept changing ales, bar area with leather sofas, young lively atmosphere; closed Mon lunchtime, otherwise open all day. *(Edward May)*

Malt House (020) 7084 6888

Vanston Place; SW6 1AY Large refurbished corner pub with U-shaped bar, high ceilings and big windows, contemporary dark wooden dining chairs and a long wall banquette, pale-topped tables and groups of sofas/armchairs on wood floors, planked walls hung with watercolours, Brakspears, Marstons and several wines by the glass, popular interesting food; background music; children and dogs welcome, small paved garden behind with pretty hanging baskets and fairy-lit gazebo, airy bedrooms, good breakfast, open all day. *(Richard Tilbrook, Mike Swan)*

Sands End (020) 7731 7823

Stephendale Road; SW6 2PR Fulham dining pub with mix of wooden dining chairs around medley of tables on bare boards, open fire, good modern british food including weekend brunch, plenty of wines by the glass, Greene King IPA, Otter Amber and a couple of guests, home-made jams, chutneys etc for sale; attracts upmarket crowd and can be very busy, open (and food) all day. *(Richard Kennell)*

SW7

★Anglesea Arms (020) 7373 7960

Selwood Terrace; SW7 3QG Very busy Victorian pub, well run and friendly, with mix of cast-iron tables on wood-strip floor, central elbow tables, panelling and heavy portraits, large brass chandeliers hanging from dark ceilings, big windows with swagged curtains, several booths at one end with partly glazed screens, half a dozen ales including Adnams, Fullers London Pride and Sambrooks, around 20 malt whiskies and 30 wines by the glass, interesting bar food, steps down to refurbished dining room; children welcome, dogs in bar, heated front terrace, open all day. *(Peter Sutton)*

Queens Arms (020) 7823 9293

Queen's Gate Mews; SW7 5QL Popular Victorian corner pub with open-plan bare-boards bar, generous helpings of enjoyable good value home-made food, decent wines by the glass and good selection of beers, friendly helpful service; TV; children welcome, disabled facilities, handy for Royal Albert Hall, open all day. *(N R White)*

SW10

Chelsea Ram (020) 7351 4008

Burnaby Street; SW10 0PL Corner Geronimo Inn, mix of furniture on bare boards or stripy carpet including farmhouse tables, padded stools around an old workbench, cushioned wall seats, shelves of books and some striking artwork, tiled Victorian fireplace, Youngs and guests, good food including daily specials and popular Sun roasts, friendly service, board games; pavement picnic-sets, open all day. *(John Harris)*

W4

★Bell & Crown (020) 8994 4164

Strand on the Green; W4 3PF Fullers local with great Thames views from back bar and conservatory, standard food and good friendly staff, panelling and log fire, lots of atmosphere and can get very busy weekends; dogs welcome, terrace and towpath area, good walks, open all day. *(N R White)*

★Bulls Head (020) 8994 1204

Strand on the Green; W4 3PQ Refurbished old Thames-side pub (served as Cromwell's HQ during Civil War), seats by windows overlooking the water in beamed rooms, steps up and down, ales such as St Austell and Sharps, several wines by the glass, decent all-day pubby food served by friendly helpful staff; background music; seats out by river, pretty hanging baskets, part of Chef & Brewer chain. *(Nick Sharpe)*

City Barge (020) 8994 2148

Strand on the Green; W4 3PH Extensive refurbishment for this old riverside pub; light modern split-level interior keeping a few original features such as Victorian panelling and open fires, good choice of ales/craft beers and wines by the glass (prosecco on tap), interesting food from open kitchen including good fish choice, weekend brunch, friendly young staff; background music, Weds quiz; children and dogs welcome, waterside picnic-sets facing Oliver's Island, deck-chairs on grass and more formal terrace, open all day. *(Gordon and Jenny Quick)*

Roebuck (020) 8995 4392

Chiswick High Road; W4 1PU Popular relaxed Victorian dining pub with high ceilings and bare boards, front bar and roomy back dining area opening on to delightful paved garden, enjoyable well presented food (all day Sun) from open kitchen, daily changing menu, four real ales and good choice of wines by the glass; dogs welcome, open all day. *(Simon Rodway)*

Swan (020) 8994 8262

Evershed Walk, Acton Lane; W4 5HH Cosy well supported 19th-c local with good mix of customers and convivial atmosphere, nice food (not weekday lunchtimes, all day Sun) including some interesting choices, friendly staff, a dozen or so wines by the glass, St Austell, Sambrook and Twickenham, two bars with wood floors and panelling, leather chesterfields by open fire; dogs very welcome, children till 7.30pm, picnic-sets on good spacious terrace, open all day weekends, from 5pm other days. *(Simon Rodway)*

Tabard (020) 8994 3492

Bath Road; W4 1LW Roomy Chiswick pub built in 1880, pleasant chatty atmosphere, up to ten changing ales, decent choice of wines and all-day pubby food, friendly efficient staff, arts and crafts interior with lots of nooks and corners, period mirrors and high frieze of William de Morgan tiles; fringe theatre upstairs; well behaved children welcome, disabled access, terrace tables by busy road, open all day. *(John Harris)*

W6

★Anglesea Arms (020) 8749 1291

Wingate Road; W6 0UR Bustling Victorian corner pub now under same ownership as the Atlas in Fulham and Swan in Chiswick; good food from interesting modern menu, four changing ales and plenty of wines by the glass, friendly staff, roaring fire in bare-boards panelled bar, close-set tables in sky-lit bare-brick dining room; children and dogs welcome, tables out by quiet street, open all day Fri-Sun, closed lunchtimes other days. *(Anon)*

Black Lion (020) 8748 2639

South Black Lion Lane; W6 9TJ Welcoming old pub set back from the river; helpful friendly staff, up to half a dozen well kept ales such as Fullers, Butcombe and

St Austell, good choice of wines by the glass and nice coffee, enjoyable food including New Zealand influences and tapas, L-shaped interior with bare boards, half-panelling and some high tables and stools, comfortable armchairs too; back skittle alley; children and dogs welcome, tables on heated terrace with table tennis, garden, open all day. *(Simon Rodway)*

Blue Anchor (020) 8748 5774

Lower Mall; W6 9DJ Right on the Thames a short walk from Hammersmith Bridge; two traditional linked areas with oak floors and panelling, mirrors one end with oars above, a house beer from Nelsons and three well kept guests from smaller London brewers, enjoyable food from light meals up, pleasant river-view dining room upstairs with balcony; TV; disabled facilities, waterside pavement tables, open all day (food all day weekends). *(N R White)*

Blue Boat (020) 3092 2090

Thames Path, off Chancellors Road; W6 9GD Newly built Fullers riverside pub with views over to Hammersmith Bridge and the Harrods Depository building; wide (not very deep) interior with long bar serving their full range, lively chatty atmosphere, well divided areas including cosy part to the left with library of local interest books, assortment of old and new furniture, some booth seating, rough wood cladding, reclaimed metal pillars and exposed ceiling ducting, popular food from open kitchen served by friendly staff, underfloor heating, on warm days french windows open out to terrace with cushioned chairs, parasols and an old rowing boat; open (and food) all day from 10am for brunch. *(Susan and John Douglas)*

Carpenters Arms (020) 8741 8386

Black Lion Lane; W6 9BG Good imaginative cooking at this relaxed corner dining pub, fine for just a drink too with plenty of wines by the glass and Adnams Bitter, friendly staff, wide mix of customers, simple bare-boards interior with open fire; dogs welcome, attractive garden, open all day. *(Simon Rodway)*

Hampshire Hog (020) 8748 3391

King Street; W6 9JT Run by former long-serving team from the Engineer in Primrose Hill, and described as an oasis in Hammersmith by one reader; light, airy and spacious with plenty of emphasis on food from interesting varied menu, charming if not always speedy service, good choice of wines including 50cl carafes, cocktails; unobtrusive background music; nice big garden with some seats under cover, open (and food) all day from 10am. *(Simon Rodway, Edward Mirzoeff)*

Latymers (020) 8748 3446

Hammersmith Road; W6 7JP Big lively bar with mirrored ceiling in 1980s corner building, well kept Fullers ales, friendly staff and good reasonably priced thai food in spacious back restaurant; sports TVs, free wi-fi; children and dogs welcome, pavement seating, open all day. *(Susan and John Douglas)*

Pear Tree (020) 7381 1787

Margravine Road; W6 8HJ Arts and crafts building with plenty of original features tucked away behind Charing Cross Hospital; cleanly kept cosily lived-in interior with heavy curtains, drapes on doors and cushions on well worn seating, soft lighting and candlelight, fresh flowers and crisp white evening tablecloths, open fires, good modern pub food from bar snacks up, popular Mon half-price deal, well kept beers and good range of wines by the glass, efficient service; background music including jazz; dogs welcome, seats in small garden, open (and food) all day Fri-Sun, closed Mon-Thurs lunchtimes. *(Susan and John Douglas)*

Queens Head (020) 7603 3174

Brook Green; W6 7BL Big Fullers pub dating from early 18th c with cosy linked rooms, beams, open fires, country furniture and pictures in keeping with period, good menu from sandwiches up, four well kept beers and nice wines, attentive service; tables out in front overlooking green with tennis courts, pleasant garden behind. *(Nick Sharpe)*

W7

Fox (020) 8567 4021

Green Lane; W7 2PJ Friendly open-plan 19th-c local in quiet cul-de-sac near Grand Union Canal, several real ales including Fullers London Pride, Sharps Cornish Coaster and Timothy Taylors Landlord, decent wines by the glass and well priced food including popular Sun lunch, panelling and stained glass, farm tools hung from ceiling; children and dogs welcome, small side garden, horse and donkey in pub's field across road, food/crafts market last Sat of month, towpath walks, open all day. *(Pip White)*

W8

Britannia (020) 7937 6905

Allen Street, off Kensington High Street; W8 6UX Recently refurbished Youngs pub; decent-sized traditional front bar with pastel shades contrasting dark panelling, patterned rugs on bare boards, banquettes, leather tub chairs and sofas, steps down to back area with wall-sized photograph of the old Britannia Brewery (now demolished), dining conservatory beyond, enjoyable freshly

prepared food including pub staples, spiral staircase up to overflow/function room; background music, Tues quiz, sports TV; children welcome, open (and food) all day. *(John Harris)*

★ Churchill Arms (020) 7727 4242

Kensington Church Street; W8 7LN Character long-serving irish landlord as the bustling old pub, eclectic interior dense with bric-a-brac – prints and books of butterflies, countless lamps, miners' lights, horse tack, bedpans and brasses hanging from the ceiling, prints of american presidents and lots of Churchill memorabilia, a couple of interesting carved figures and statuettes behind central counter, well kept Fullers ales, 18 wines by the glass and good value thai food, spacious rather smart plant-filled dining conservatory; free wi-fi; children and dogs welcome, some chrome tables and chairs outside, stunning display of window boxes and hanging baskets, open (and food) all day. *(Edward Mirzoeff, Tony Scott)*

Scarsdale (020) 7937 1811

Edwardes Square; W8 6HE Busy Georgian pub in leafy square with easy-going feel, scrubbed pine tables, simple cushioned dining chairs, pews and built-in wall seats on bare boards, oil paintings in fancy gilt frames and old local photographs, heavily swagged curtains, coal-effect gas fires, Adnams, Fullers and a guest, 16 wines by the glass and a dozen malt whiskies, well liked food; free wi-fi; children (in dining area) and dogs welcome, seats and tables under parasols on attractive front terrace, open (and food) all day. *(Emma Scofield, Mike Swan, Tony Scott)*

W9

Prince Alfred (020) 7286 3287

Formosa Street; W9 1EE Well preserved austerely ornate Victorian pub (some recent refurbishment) with five separate bars (lots of mahogany), snob screens and duck-through doors, beautiful etched-glass bow window, Youngs ales, enjoyable all-day food including some imaginative choices in airy modern dining room with large centre skylight, cellar function rooms; background music; open all day. *(Edward May)*

Warwick Castle (020) 7266 0921

Warwick Place; W9 2PX Popular character pub in narrow street near Little Venice, open-fronted with a few pavement tables, unspoilt rooms with comfortable lived-in atmosphere, etched windows, panelling, open fires and some striking light fittings, friendly landlady and staff, real ales such as Greene King and guests, blackboard food

---

A star symbol before the name of a pub shows exceptional character and appeal. It doesn't mean extra comfort. Even quite a basic pub can win a star, if it's individual enough.

from sandwiches and pub standards up.
(Phil Bryant, Susan and John Douglas)

W13

Duke of Kent (020) 8991 7820

Scotch Common; W13 8DL Large refurbished open-plan pub with lots of interesting discrete areas, coal fires, several Fullers ales and guests, good food from pub standards up, friendly staff; live music Sun, free wi-fi; children welcome, big garden with partly covered terrace and play area, open all day. *(Revd R P Tickle, Susan and John Douglas)*

W14　　　　　　　　　　　　　　TQ2477

★Colton Arms (020) 7385 6956

Greyhound Road; W14 9SD Unspoilt little gem, like an old-fashioned country tavern and in same family for over 40 years; main U-shaped front bar with log fire, polished brasses, fox mask, hunting crops and hunting-scene plates, fine collection of handsomely carved antique oak furniture, two tiny back rooms with own serving counters (ring bell for service), Fullers London Pride, Sharps Doom Bar and a guest, old-fashioned brass till; no food or credit cards; children (over 4) till 7pm, dogs allowed in bar, charming back terrace with neat rose arbour, next to the Queen's Club tennis courts and gardens. *(Belinda May)*

★Havelock Tavern (020) 7603 5374

Masbro Road; W14 0LS Busy pub in former shop premises, light airy L-shaped bar with plain unfussy décor, second small room with pews, reasonable choice of often good food, Sambrooks Wandle, Sharps Doom Bar and guests, wide variety of interesting wines by the glass, efficient friendly service; free wi-fi; children and dogs welcome, picnic-sets on small paved terrace, open all day. *(Gus Swan)*

OUTER LONDON

BARNET EN5　　　　　　　　　　TQ2496

Black Horse (020) 8449 2230

Wood Street/Union Street; EN5 4HY Modernised homely 19th-c pub with eight real ales including own Barnet beers from back microbrewery, good range of enjoyable food, friendly staff; live music Sat: children and dogs (in bar) welcome, terrace seating, open all day (food all day weekends).
(Nigel and Sue Foster)

Gate (020) 8449 7292

Barnet Road (A411, near Hendon Wood Lane); EN5 3LA Modernised country pub feel with comfortably opened-up areas, beams and log fires, good choice of enjoyable home-made food from lunchtime sandwiches/ciabattas up, well kept Greene King, Sharps and a guest, friendly staff and atmosphere; children welcome, open (and food) all day.
(Nigel and Sue Foster)

BECKENHAM BR3　　　　　　　TQ3769

George (020) 8663 3468

High Street; BR3 1AG Busy weatherboarded pub with friendly efficient staff, half a dozen real ales and good value food including deals; children welcome, side garden with terrace, open all day.
(Eddie Edwards)

Jolly Woodman (020) 8663 1031

Chancery Lane; BR3 6NR Welcoming old-fashioned local in conservation area, cosy chatty atmosphere in L-shaped bar with woodburner, five or so well kept changing ales such as Harveys and Timothy Taylors Landlord, good choice of whiskies, reasonably priced home-made food (weekday lunchtimes only) including sandwiches; dogs welcome, pavement tables and sunny flower-filled back courtyard, open all day (from 4pm Mon).
(N R White, B J Harding)

BEXLEY DA5　　　　　　　　　　TQ4973

Kings Head (01322) 553137

Bexley High Street; DA5 1AA Dating from 14th c, linked rooms with low beams and brasses, open fires, well kept Greene King ales and enjoyable pub food including all-day breakfast, friendly staff. *(Ross Balaam)*

BEXLEYHEATH DA6　　　　　　TQ4875

Robin Hood & Little John

(020) 8303 1128　*Lion Road; DA6 8PF* Small 19th-c family-run local in residential area, welcoming and spotless, with eight well kept ales such as Adnams, Brains, Fullers, Harveys and Sharps, popular bargain pubby lunchtime food (not Sun); well behaved children allowed away from the bar till 8.30pm, garden. *(John Harris)*

BIGGIN HILL TN16　　　　　　TQ4359

★Old Jail (01959) 572979

Jail Lane; (E off A233 S of airport and industrial estate, towards Berry's Hill and Cudham); TN16 3AX Big family garden with picnic-sets, substantial trees and good play area for this popular country pub (on fringe of London); traditional beamed and low-ceilinged rooms with RAF memorabilia, two cosy small areas to right divided by timbers, one with big inglenook, other with cabinet of Battle of Britain plates, ales such as Harveys, Long Man and Sharps, good choice of enjoyable reasonably priced food (not Sun evening) from sandwiches up, friendly attentive service, step up to dining room with small open fire; background music; dogs welcome, open all day (food all day Thurs-Sat). *(Alan Weedon, David Jackman, David Greene, B and M Kendall)*

BOTANY BAY EN2　　　　　　　TQ2999

Robin Hood (020) 8363 3781

2 miles from M25 junction 24; Ridgeway (A1005 Enfield Road); EN2 8AP Busy open-plan Edwardian roadhouse, enjoyable home-made pub food including daily specials, well kept McMullens and decent wines, friendly uniformed staff; free wi-fi; good-sized garden with roses and weeping willow, open all day. *(Nigel and Sue Foster, Conrad Freezer)*

BROMLEY BR1   TQ4069
Red Lion   (020) 8460 2691
North Road; BR1 3LG Chatty well managed backstreet local in conservation area, traditional dimly lit interior with wood floor, tiling, green velvet drapes and shelves of books, well kept Greene King, Harveys and guests, lunchtime food, good friendly service; tables out in front, open all day. *(N R White)*

BROMLEY BR2   TQ4265
Two Doves   (020) 8462 1627
Oakley Road (A233); BR2 8HD Popular Victorian local, comfortable and unpretentious, with cheerful staff and regulars, well kept St Austell Tribute, Charles Wells and a guest, snacky food such as rolls and baked potatoes, modern back conservatory and lovely garden; open all day Fri-Sun. *(B and M Kendall)*

CHELSFIELD BR6   TQ4864
Five Bells   (01689) 821044
Church Road; just off A224 Orpington bypass; BR6 7RE Chatty low-ceilinged white weatherboarded village local, two separate bars and dining area, settle by inglenook, friendly staff, well kept Courage, Harveys and guests, reasonably priced food from snacks up (evening food Thurs-Sat only), live music including jazz, Tues quiz; sports TV; children welcome, picnic-sets among flowers out in front, open all day. *(Pip White)*

CHISLEHURST BR7   TQ4469
Crown   (020) 8467 7326
School Road; BR7 5PQ Imposing Victorian pub overlooking common, simple attractive interior with flagstoned bar and several dining areas, well kept Shepherd Neame ales and good quality food with dishes such as sea bream and guinea fowl, friendly helpful service; terrace tables, pétanque, seven bedrooms, open all day. *(B and M Kendall)*

Sydney Arms   (020) 8467 3025
Old Perry Street; BR7 6PL Friendly pub in residential road almost opposite entrance to Scadbury Park; four mainstream beers along with a smaller brewery guest, enjoyable inexpensive pub food, two bars, dining room and big conservatory; children and dogs (in bars) welcome, pleasant garden, open all day (food all day weekends). *(B J Harding)*

EASTCOTE HA5   TQ1089
Case Is Altered   (020) 8866 0476
High Road/Southill Lane; HA5 2EW Attractive 17th-c pub in quiet setting adjacent to cricket ground; main bar, flagstoned snug and barn dining area, Sharps Doom Bar and three guests such as

---

Rebellion, good choice of tasty generously served food all day (Sun till 6pm), lunchtime deal Mon-Thurs, friendly efficient staff; children and dogs welcome, nice front garden (very popular in fine weather), handy for Eastcote House Gardens. *(Brian Glozier)*

HAMPTON TW12   TQ1469
Jolly Coopers   (020) 8979 3384
High Street; TW12 2SJ Friendly end of terrace Georgian local with four or five well kept ales including Caledonian Deuchars IPA, Courage Best and Hop Back Summer Lightning, good choice of wines, well liked freshly cooked food in back restaurant extension including some tapas; quiz last Tues of month; terrace with climbing plants and summer barbecues, open all day. *(Simon and Mandy King)*

HAMPTON COURT KT8   TQ1668
★ ## Kings Arms   (020) 8977 1729
Hampton Court Road, by Lion Gate; KT8 9DD Civilised well run pub by Hampton Court itself (so popular with tourists), comfortable furnishings including sofas in back area, attractive Farrow & Ball colours, good open fires, lots of oak panelling, beams and some stained glass, well kept Badger beers, good choice of wines by the glass, friendly service, enjoyable food from sandwiches up, restaurant too (food all day weekends); background music; children and dogs welcome, picnic-sets on roadside front terrace, limited parking, 13 bedrooms, open all day. *(Hilary and Neil Christopher)*

HARROW HA1   TQ1587
Castle   (020) 8422 3155
West Street; HA1 3EF Edwardian Fullers pub in picturesque part, their ales and guests kept very well, decent food from lunchtime sandwiches to full meals, several rooms around central servery, open fires, rugs on bare boards and lots of panelling, collection of clocks in cheery front bar, more sedate back lounge; children welcome, steps up from street, nice garden behind, open (and food) all day. *(Brian Glozier)*

ISLEWORTH TW7   TQ1675
London Apprentice   (020) 8560 1915
Church Street; TW7 6BG Large Thames-side Taylor Walker pub, reasonably priced food from sandwiches up, well kept ales such as Adnams, Fullers and guests, good wine choice, log fire, pleasant friendly service; upstairs river-view restaurant; may be background music; children welcome, attractive riverside terrace with good quality benches, chairs and tables under parasols, open all day. *(Edward May)*

KEW TW9   TQ1977
Coach & Horses   (020) 8940 1208
Kew Green; TW9 3BH Attractive coaching inn overlooking green, Youngs ales and a guest, enjoyable food from sandwiches and

traditional choices up, friendly young staff, relaxed open-plan interior with armchairs, sofas and log fire, shelves of books, restaurant with kitchen view; background music, sports TV; children and dogs welcome, teak tables on front terrace, secret garden behind with chickens, nice setting handy for Kew Gardens and National Archive (beware of parking restrictions), 31 good bedrooms, buffet breakfast, open all day. *(N R White, Susan and John Douglas)*

KINGSTON KT2   TQ1869
Boaters (020) 8541 4672
Canbury Gardens (park in Lower Ham Road if you can); KT2 5AU Family-friendly pub by the Thames in small park, half a dozen ales such as Hogs Back, Twickenham and Sambrooks, decent wines from reasonably priced list, food can be good (service charge added to bill), comfortable banquettes in split-level wood-floored bar; Sun evening jazz; smart riverside terrace and balcony, parking nearby can be difficult, open all day, food all day weekends. *(Tom and Ruth Rees)*

Canbury Arms (020) 8255 9129
Canbury Park Road; KT2 6LQ Popular open-plan pub with simple contemporary décor, bare boards and big windows, relaxed friendly atmosphere, good up-to-date food including breakfast from 9am (not Sun), helpful young staff, five well kept ales and good wine choice, nice coffee, stone-floor side conservatory; regular events such as quiz and music nights, wine tasting and camera club; children and dogs welcome, tables out at front under parasols, open all day. *(David and Sally Frost)*

ORPINGTON BR6   TQ4963
★ Bo-Peep (01959) 534457
Hewitts Road, Chelsfield; 1.7 miles from M25 junction 4; BR6 7QL Useful M25 country-feel dining pub, old low beams and enormous inglenook in carpeted bar, two cosy candlelit dining rooms, airy side room overlooking lane and fields, well kept Sharps Doom Bar, Charles Wells Bombardier and a changing beer from Westerham, cheerful efficient staff, good helpings of enjoyable food (all day Sat, not Sun evening) from traditional choices up; background music; children welcome, dogs in bar, picnic-sets on big brick terrace, open all day. *(Alan Cowell, B and M Kendall)*

PETTS WOOD BR5   TQ4467
Sovereign of the Seas
(01689) 891606 *Queensway; BR5 1DG* Popular roomy Wetherspoons with a dozen well kept ales including Greene King and

decent good value food; children welcome, on London Loop walk and handy for station, open all day from 9am. *(Ross Balaam)*

PINNER HA5   TQ1289
Queens Head (020) 8868 4607
High Street; HA5 5PJ Traditional beamed and panelled local dating from the 16th c, welcoming bustle and interesting décor, seven well kept ales from breweries such as Adnams, Greene King, Rebellion and Sharps, simple good value lunchtime bar food; no children inside; dogs welcome (not during lunch), small back terrace for evening sun, open all day. *(Brian Glozier)*

RICHMOND UPON THAMES TW9   TQ1774
Princes Head (020) 8940 1572
The Green; TW9 1LX Large open-plan pub overlooking cricket green near theatre, clean and well run, with low-ceilinged panelled areas off big island bar, well kept Fullers ales, popular sensibly priced pub food from sandwiches up, friendly young staff and chatty locals, coal-effect fire; over-21s only, dogs welcome, circular picnic-sets outside, open all day. *(Belinda May)*

Watermans Arms (020) 8940 2893
Water Lane; TW9 1TJ Friendly old-fashioned Youngs local with their well kept ales and a couple of guests from Twickenham, enjoyable thai food, traditional layout with open fire, red banquettes and model of a Thames barge, upstairs restaurant; handy for the river. *(Ian Phillips)*

★ White Cross (020) 8940 6844
Water Lane; TW9 1TH Lovely garden with terrific Thames views, seats on paved area, outside bar and boats to Kingston and Hampton Court; two chatty main rooms with local prints and photographs, three log fires (one unusually below a window), well kept Youngs and guests from old-fashioned island servery, a dozen wines by the glass, decent bar food all day, bright and airy upstairs room (children welcome here till 6pm) with pretty cast-iron balcony for splendid river view, good mix of customers; background music, TV; dogs welcome, tides can reach the pub entrance (wellies provided). *(Gordon and Jenny Quick, Tom and Ruth Rees, N R White, Ian Phillips)*

White Swan (020) 8940 0959
Old Palace Lane; TW9 1PG Small 18th-c cottagey pub, civilised and relaxed, with rustic dark-beamed open-plan bar, well kept Otter, St Austell, Sharps and Timothy Taylors, popular freshly made food, coal-effect fires, back dining conservatory and upstairs restaurant; soft background music; children

---

Though we don't usually mention it in the text, most pubs will now make coffee or tea – it's always worth asking.

allowed until 6.30, some seats on narrow paved area at front, more in pretty walled back terrace below railway, open all day. *(Ian Phillips)*

RICHMOND UPON THAMES TW10   TQ1874

White Horse   (020) 8940 2418

Worple Way, off Sheen Road; TW10 6DF Large open-plan Fullers pub, their ales and good choice of wines from long aluminium counter, airy interior with pastel shades, exposed brickwork and mix of old and new furniture on bare boards including some easy chairs, enjoyable food from traditional favourites up, friendly helpful service; free wi-fi; children welcome (playground next door), two-level back terrace, open all day. *(Phil Bryant)* ·

ROMFORD RM1   TQ5188

Golden Lion   (01708) 740081

High Street; RM1 1HR Popular former coaching inn (one of the town's oldest buildings) with spacious beamed interior, four or five well kept ales, good value pubby food including some bargains, friendly staff and good mix of customers; weekend live music, sports TV, free wi-fi; open (and food) all day. *(Robert Lester, Richard Tilbrook)*

ROMFORD RM2   TQ5188

Ship   (01708) 741571

Main Road; RM2 5EL 17th-c black and white pub, panelling, low beams and woodburner in fine brick fireplace, Adnams, Courage, Fullers, Sharps and guests, all-day food from sandwiches and sharing boards up (till 5pm Fri-Sun), live weekend music; children and dogs welcome, picnic-sets in back garden under parasols. *(Robert Lester)*

TWICKENHAM TW1

Crown   (020) 8892 5896

Richmond Road, St Margarets; TW1 2NH Refurbished Georgian pub with emphasis on good food from sandwiches and sharing plates to restauranty choices, several large dining areas including splendid Victorian back hall, also well kept ales, nice wines by the glass and decent coffee, friendly efficient staff; newspapers and free wi-fi; children welcome, picnic-sets in sunny courtyard garden, open (and food) all day. *(Hunter and Christine Wright)*

White Swan   (020) 8892 2166

Riverside; TW1 3DN Refurbished 17th-c Thames-side pub up steep anti-flood steps; bare-boards L-shaped bar with cosy log fire, river views from prized bay window, Fullers, Sharps and guests such as Twickenham, enjoyable fairly priced food (all day Sat, Sun till 6pm), friendly local atmosphere, board games; live acoustic music and quiz nights; children and dogs welcome, tranquil setting opposite Eel Pie Island with well used balcony and waterside terrace (liable to flooding) across quiet lane, open all day. *(Edward Mirzoeff, Ian Phillips)*

TWICKENHAM TW2   TQ1572

Sussex Arms   (020) 8894 7468

Staines Road; TW2 5BG Traditional bare-boards pub with 18 handpumps plus ciders and perries from long counter, plenty in bottles too, simple food including good home-made pies, friendly staff, walls and ceilings covered in beer mats and pump clips, open fire, some live acoustic music; large back garden with boules, open all day. *(Gus Swan)*

UXBRIDGE UB8   TQ0582

Malt Shovel   (01895) 812797

Iver Lane, Cowley (B470); UB8 2JE Vintage Inn by Grand Union Canal, their usual fair-priced food including set deal, ales such as Caledonian, Fullers and Greene King served by pleasant staff; children welcome, seats outside, open (and food) all day. *(Barrie and Mary Crees)*

SCOTLAND

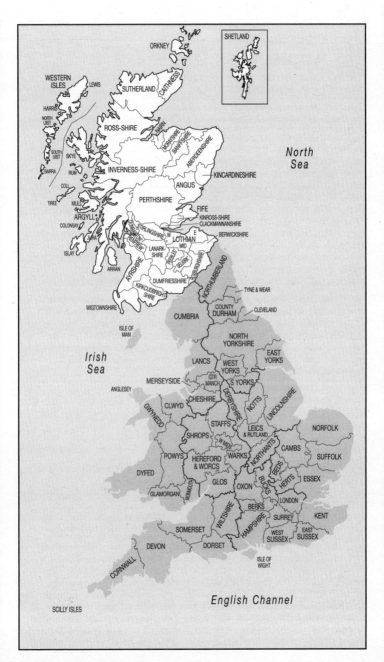

SHETLAND

ORKNEY

WESTERN
ISLES
LEWIS

SUTHERLAND

CAITHNESS

HARRIS

NORTH
UIST

ROSS-SHIRE

NAIRN

SOUTH
UIST

SKYE

BARRA

MORAYSHIRE

BANFFSHIRE

ABERDEENSHIRE

North
Sea

COLL

INVERNESS-SHIRE

KINCARDINESHIRE

TIREE

MULL

PERTHSHIRE

ANGUS

ARGYLL

FIFE

COLONSAY

STIRLINGSHIRE

KINROSS-SHIRE

CLACKMANNANSHIRE

W

JURA

DUNBARTON

E

RENFREW

LOTHIAN

MID

BERWICKSHIRE

ISLAY

LANARK-
SHIRE

PEEBLES

SELKIRK

ROXBURGHSHIRE

AYRSHIRE

ARRAN

DUMFRIESSHIRE

NORTHUMBERLAND

KIRKCUDBRIGHT
SHIRE

TYNE & WEAR

WIGTOWNSHIRE

CUMBRIA

COUNTY
DURHAM

CLEVELAND

ISLE OF
MAN

NORTH
YORKSHIRE

Irish
Sea

LANCS

WEST
YORKS

EAST
YORKS

MERSEYSIDE

GTR
MANCH

S YORKS

ANGLESEY

CHESHIRE

DERBYSHIRE

NOTTS

LINCOLNSHIRE

CLWYD

GWYNEDD

STAFFS

LEICS
& RUTLAND

NORFOLK

SHROPS

W MIDS

WARKS

NORTHANTS

CAMBS

SUFFOLK

POWYS

HEREFORD
& WORCS

BEDS

DYFED

BUCKS

HERTS

ESSEX

GLOS

OXON

LONDON

GLAMORGAN

MONMOUTH

BERKS

SURREY

KENT

WILTSHIRE

HAMPSHIRE

SOMERSET

WEST
SUSSEX

EAST
SUSSEX

DEVON

DORSET

ISLE OF
WIGHT

CORNWALL

English Channel

SCILLY ISLES

KEY ★ Star Pub   🏆 Top Quality Food   🍺 Great Beer

♀ Good Wines   £ Bargain Meals   🛏 Good Bedrooms   🍴 Serves Food

---

APPLECROSS
NG7144   Map 11

Applecross Inn ★ 🛏

(01520) 744262 – www.applecross.uk.com

Off A896 S of Shieldaig; IV54 8LR

Wonderfully remote pub on famously scenic route on west coast; particularly friendly welcome, real ales and good seafood; bedrooms

'Superb as usual – we cannot keep away,' says one reader with enthusiasm, and, considering that getting here is quite an experience, there are always plenty of customers. Reached by driving through miles of spectacularly wild, unpopulated scenery and over the famous Pass of the Cattle (Bealach na Bà), it looks across the water to the Cuillin Hills on Skye. The no-nonsense, welcoming bar has a woodburning stove, exposed stone walls, upholstered pine furnishings and a stone floor; An Teallach Ale and Isle of Skye Red on handpump, over 50 malt whiskies and a good, varied wine list; pool (winter only), TV and board games. The tables in the shoreside garden enjoy magnificent views. If you wish to stay here, you must book some months ahead. The alternative route, along the single-track lane winding around the coast from just south of Shieldaig, has equally glorious sea loch (and then sea) views nearly all the way. Some disabled facilities.

🍴 Emphasis is on the top quality local fish and seafood dishes – squat lobsters, oysters, fresh haddock, a seafood platter, king scallops and dressed crab with smoked salmon – but they also serve haggis in Drambuie with cream, gammon and eggs, chicken green thai curry, local venison casserole, sirloin steak with pepper sauce and chips, and puddings such as hot chocolate fudge cake and raspberry cranachan. *Benchmark main dish: local langoustines in garlic butter £18.50. Two-course evening meal £25.00.*

Free house ~ Licensee Judith Fish ~ Real ale ~ Open 11am-11.30pm (midnight Sat); 12-11 Sun ~ Bar food 12-9 ~ Children welcome till 8.30pm ~ Dogs welcome ~ Wi-fi ~ Bedrooms: £65/£130 *Recommended by John and Pauline Cope, Ken Richards, Edna Jones, Barry Collett, Roy and Gill Payne, the Dutchman, M J Winterton, John and Enid*

DALKEITH
NR3264   Map 11

Sun 🏆 ♀ 🛏

(0131) 663 2456 – www.thesuninnedinburgh.co.uk

A7 S; EH22 4TR

Family-run inn with charming bar and restaurant, open fires, leafy garden, local ale and delicious food; comfortable, airy bedrooms

With Edinburgh just 20 minutes away, this family-run former coaching inn is the perfect country retreat after a day in the city. Bedrooms are thoughtfully equipped and comfortable and breakfasts highly rated. Seats on the covered courtyard overlook the garden where they hold popular summer barbecues, and it's surrounded by five acres of wooded grounds. The bars have been carefully renovated with walls stripped back to the original stone (or with hunting-theme wallpaper), bare floorboards and refurbished fireplaces. There are cushioned built-in settles, all sorts of wooden dining chairs around an appealing collection of tables, gilt-edged mirrors, and high stools against the counter where friendly staff serve Alechemy Rhapsody and a guest beer on handpump and good wines by the glass; background music.

 Cooked by the landlord and his son, the good, interesting food includes moules marinière, rump of beef and asian salad with soy, star anise and honey dressing, burger with toppings, skinny fries and burnt onion ketchup, smoked haddock and leek risotto with a soft poached egg, free-range chicken with onion bhajis and onion cream, beef bourguignon with horseradish mash, monkfish wrapped in pancetta with clams, chorizo and broad bean salad and chorizo oil dressing, and puddings such as poached peach with passion-fruit jelly, candied walnut crumb and mango sorbet and sticky toffee pudding with butterscotch sauce; they also offer an early-bird weekday two- and three-course menu. *Benchmark main dish: 10oz rib-eye steak with crispy onion rings, chips and green peppercorn sauce £22.00. Two-course evening meal £21.00.*

Free house ~ Licensee Bernadette McCarron ~ Real ale ~ Open 12-11 ~ Bar food 12-9; 12-2, 6-9 Sat; 12-3.30, 5-7 Sun ~ Children welcome ~ Wi-fi ~ Bedrooms: £75/£95
Recommended by Edward May, Isobel Mackinlay

EDINBURGH
Abbotsford ■ £

NT2574 Map 11

(0131) 225 5276
Rose Street; E end, beside South St David Street; EH2 2PR

Busy city pub with period features, changing beers, and bar and restaurant food

A s always, the fine choice of real ales here draws in plenty of customers. Served from the hefty Victorian island bar (ornately carved from dark spanish mahogany and highly polished), these might come from breweries such as Atlas, Caledonian, Fyne Ales, Harviestoun, Orkney and Stewart; also, a selection of bottled american craft beers and around 70 malt whiskies. It's a handsome place with a lively atmosphere and an unchanging feel, and you'll usually find an eclectic mix of business people and locals occupying stools around the bar at lunchtime. Long wooden tables and leatherette benches run the length of the high-panelled dark wood walls, while high above is a rather handsome green and gold plaster-moulded ceiling. The smarter upstairs restaurant, with white tablecloths, black walls and high ornate white ceiling, looks impressive too.

 Bar food includes sharing platters, haggis, neeps and tatties, beef in ale pie, mississippi chicken burger with toppings, coleslaw and chips, roast vegetable risotto, grilled bass with fennel, pomegranate and orange salsa, and puddings such as lemon posset and sticky toffee pudding. *Benchmark main dish: breaded fish and chips £9.95. Two-course evening meal £15.00.*

Stewart ~ Licensee Daniel Jackson ~ Real ale ~ Open 11-11 (midnight Sat) ~ Bar food 12-3, 5.30-10; 12-10 Fri, Sat ~ Restaurant 12-2.15, 5.30-9.30 ~ Children over 5 allowed in restaurant *Recommended by the Dutchman, Eric Larkham*

EDINBURGH
Bow Bar ■

NT2574 Map 11

(0131) 226 7667
West Bow; EH1 2HH

Cosy, enjoyably unpretentious backstreet pub with an excellent choice of well kept beers

T his cheerfully traditional alehouse is a haven of old-fashioned drinking with a splendid range of real ales. The rectangular bar has an impressive carved mahogany gantry, and from the tall 1920s founts on the bar counter knowledgeable staff dispense eight well kept real ales, such as Alechemy Bowhemia Pale, Arbor Smokescreen, Cromarty Happy Chappy, Dark Star Espresso Stout, Fyne Ales Jarl, Highland The Duke, Stewart Edinburgh Number 3 and Tempest Elemental Porter; regular beer festivals. Also on offer are some 290 malts, including five 'malts of the moment', a good choice of rums, 50 international bottled beers and 20 gins. The walls are covered with a fine collection of enamel advertising signs and handsome antique brewery mirrors, and there are sturdy leatherette wall seats and café-style bar seats around heavy narrow tables on the wooden floor. No children allowed. Food is limited to pies.

Free house ~ Licensee Mike Smith ~ Real ale ~ Open 12-midnight; 12.30-11.30 Sun ~ Bar food 12 (12.30 Sun)-3 ~ Dogs welcome ~ Wi-fi *Recommended by R T and J C Moggridge, Eric Larkham, Dr Matt Burleigh*

EDINBURGH
Guildford Arms ◀ £

NT2574 Map 11

(0131) 556 4312 – www.guildfordarms.com
West Register Street; EH2 2AA

Busy and friendly, with spectacular Victorian décor, a marvellous range of real ales and good food

The chief glory here is the splendid Victorian décor. Opulently excessive, this features ornate painted plasterwork on the lofty ceiling, heavy swagged velvet curtains, dark mahogany fittings and a busy patterned carpet. Tables and stools are lined up along the towering arched windows opposite the bar, where knowledgeable, efficient staff may offer a taste of the ten, quickly changing ales before you select what you want: Belhaven IPA, Fyne Ales Jarl, Knops East Coast, Oakham Bishops Farewell, Orkney Dark Island, Mordue IPA, Stewart Pentland IPA and guests from breweries such as Alechemy, Fallen and Highland. Also, ten wines by the glass, about 50 malt whiskies, a dozen rums and a dozen gins; TV and background music. The snug little upstairs gallery restaurant, with strongly contrasting modern décor, gives a fine dress-circle view of the main bar (on the way up, notice the lovely old mirror decorated with two tigers).

🍽 Tasty food includes sandwiches, mussels in creamy garlic and white wine, hot smoked salmon with tomato salsa, mushroom, spinach and hazelnut wellington, haggis, neeps and tatties, breaded haddock and chips, burgers with toppings and fries, fillet steak in wild mushroom, sherry and crème fraîche sauce, and puddings; they also offer weekend breakfasts (10am-midday). *Benchmark main dish: steak in ale pie £9.95. Two-course evening meal £18.00.*

Stewart ~ Lease Steve Jackson ~ Real ale ~ Open 11-11 (midnight Thurs, Fri); 10am-midnight Sat; 10am-11pm Sun ~ Bar food 12-2.30 (3 Sun), 5.30-9.30; 12-10 Sat; snacks throughout afternoon except Fri, Sat ~ Restaurant ~ Children welcome in upstairs gallery if dining and over 5 ~ Dogs allowed in bar ~ Wi-fi ~ Live music during Edinburgh Festival *Recommended by Comus and Sarah Elliott, Eric Larkham, Brian and Anna Marsden, Dr J Barrie Jones, Dr Matt Burleigh, Barry Collett*

'Children welcome' means the pub says it lets children inside without any special restriction. If it allows them in, but to restricted areas such as an eating area or family room, we specify this. Places with separate restaurants often let children use them, and hotels usually let children into public areas such as lounges. Some pubs impose an evening time limit – let us know if you find one earlier than 9pm.

EDINBURGH
NT2574   Map 11

Kays Bar ◆ £

(0131) 225 1858 – www.kaysbar.co.uk

Jamaica Street West; off India Street; EH3 6HF

Cosy, enjoyably chatty backstreet pub with good value lunchtime food and an excellent choice of well kept beers

'A must whenever we visit the city' is a phrase used by several readers about this convivial little backstreet pub. With an enjoyable local feel and an eclectic mix of customers, it has long curving well worn red-plush wall banquettes and stools around cast-iron tables on red carpet, and red pillars supporting a red ceiling. Décor is simple with big casks and vats arranged along the walls, old wine and spirits merchant notices and gas-type lamps. A quiet panelled back room (a bit like a library) leads off, with a narrow plank-panelled pitched ceiling and a collection of books ranging from dictionaries to ancient steam-train books for boys; there's a lovely warming coal fire in winter. Seven real ales on handpump might include Caledonian Deuchars IPA and Theakstons Best, plus guests such as Belhaven Golden Bay, Greene King Old Speckled Hen, Knops East Coast and Timothy Taylors Landlord; they also stock more than 70 malt whiskies aged from eight to 50 years old, and ten blended whiskies; board games. In days past, the pub was owned by John Kay, a whisky and wine merchant; wine barrels were hoisted up to the first floor and dispensed through pipes attached to nipples that are still visible around the ceiling light rose. Dogs are allowed but not during food service times.

 Very reasonably priced lunchtime-only food includes pâté, an antipasti platter, baked potatoes, haggis, neeps and tatties, and chicken or beef curry. *Benchmark main dish: chilli beef £4.95.*

Free house ~ Licensee Fraser Gillespie ~ Real ale ~ Open 11am-midnight (1am Fri, Sat); 12.30-11 Sun ~ Bar food 12-2.30; not Sun ~ Wi-fi *Recommended by Mary Kirkwood*

GLASGOW
NS5965   Map 11

Babbity Bowster ♀

(0141) 552 5055 – www.babbitybowster.com

Blackfriars Street; G1 1PE

A lively mix of traditional and modern with a continental feel too; bedrooms

This 18th-c former tobacco merchant's house remains very much a Glasgow institution, with a thoroughly convivial atmosphere and a good mix of locals and visitors. The simply decorated, light-filled interior has fine tall windows, plush stools and cushioned ladder-back chairs around a mix of dark tables on bare boards, some wall bench seating, open fires and attractive plant prints on light paintwork. The bar opens on to a pleasant terrace with picnic-sets under parasols and there's another back terrace too. High chairs line the counter where they keep Caledonian Deuchars IPA and a couple of guests such as Fyne Ales Jarl and Williams Brothers May Bee on air-pressure tall fount, and a remarkably sound collection of wines and malt whiskies; good tea and coffee too. On Saturday evenings, the pub has live traditional scottish music, while at other times you may find games of boules in progress outside. Note the bedroom price is for the room only.

A short choice of enjoyable food includes sandwiches, mackerel pâté with toast, haggis, neeps and tatties, butternut squash risotto, a pie of the day and daily specials, while the upstairs restaurant might have cullen skink, mussels in creamy saffron sauce, gressingham duck breast with mandarin orange sauce, and puddings such as caramelised lemon tart and clootie dumpling with toffee sauce; they also offer a three-course set menu. *Benchmark main dish: haunch of venison £15.25. Two-course evening meal £20.00.*

Free house ~ Licensee Fraser Laurie ~ Real ale ~ Open 11am-midnight; 12.30-midnight Sun ~ Bar food 12-10 ~ Restaurant ~ Children welcome if eating ~ Wi-fi ~ Live traditional music Weds afternoon, Sat early evening ~ Bedrooms: $50/$65 *Recommended by Isobel Mackinlay, Mungo Shipley*

GLASGOW NS5965 Map 11
Bon Accord ◖ ▮ £
(0141) 248 4427 – www.bonaccordweb.co.uk
North Street; G3 7DA

Remarkable choice of drinks including an impressive range of whiskies and real ales, a good welcome and bargain food

Alongside Caledonian Deuchars, this cheerful alehouse keeps nine daily changing guests sourced from breweries around Britain and served from swan-necked handpumps. Also, continental bottled beers, a farm cider and, in a remarkable display behind the counter, 380 malt whiskies and lots of gins, vodkas and rums. Staff are knowledgeable, so do ask for help if you need it. The several linked traditional bars are warmly understated with cream or terracotta walls, a mix of chairs and tables, a leather sofa and plenty of bar stools on polished bare boards or carpeting; TV, background music and board games. There are circular picnic-sets on a small terrace, and modern tables and chairs out in front.

 Quite a choice of incredibly cheap food includes baguettes, french fries topped with cheese and bacon, filled yorkshire pudding, scottish breakfast, battered fresh haddock and chips, chicken curry, burgers with various toppings, gammon and egg, and puddings such as clootie dumpling or apple pie and custard. *Benchmark main dish: steak pie £5.95. Two-course evening meal £.9.50*

Free house ~ Licensee Paul McDonagh ~ Real ale ~ Open 11am-midnight; 12.30-midnight Sun ~ Bar food 11 (12.30 Sun)-8 ~ Children welcome until 8pm ~ Wi-fi ~ Live band Sat evening *Recommended by Mary Kirkwood, Neil Allen*

GLENCOE NN1058 Map 11
Clachaig ◖
(01855) 811252 – www.clachaig.com
Old Glencoe Road, behind NTS Visitor Centre; PH49 4HX

Climbers' and walkers' haunt with a huge selection of scottish beers, malts, gins and other artisan spirits, and well liked food; bedrooms in adjoining hotel

As this 300-year-old inn is surrounded by the majestic mountain scenery of Glencoe, many of the customers are walkers, climbers and mountain bikers who gather beside the log fire in the Boots Bar and swap stories. They're also here to try the fantastic choice of 14 scottish real ales on handpump: from a quickly changing choice there might be beers from An Teallach, Cairngorm, Caledonian, Houston, Isle of Skye, Loch Lomond, Orkney, River Leven and Williams. For something a little stronger, there's a choice of some 300 malts, and an increasing range of artisan gins, vodkas and rums from across Scotland. Bands play here on Saturday nights. There's also a whisky barrel-panelled, slate-floored snug with a fire, and a lounge with a mix of tables and booths, its walls hung with photos signed by famous climbers and artwork from local artists. Background music and pool. This makes a useful and comfortable base to stay overnight and they also run self-catering properties in the area.

 Hearty food includes venison pastrami, Stornoway black pudding with local bacon and apple and plum chutney, haggis with neeps and tatties, breadcrumbed and oatmeal haddock with pea and potato mash, pork and chorizo chilli angus burger with cheese, and puddings such as ecclefechan tart, made with mixed fruits and nuts. *Benchmark main dish: venison pie £11.95. Two-course evening meal £18.00.*

Free house ~ Licensees Guy and Edward Daynes ~ Real ale ~ Open 11-11 (midnight Fri); 11-11.30 Sat ~ Bar food 12-9 ~ Children allowed in lounge ~ Dogs welcome ~ Wi-fi ~ Live music Sat night ~ Bedrooms: £52/£104 *Recommended by Isobel Mackinlay*

ISLE OF WHITHORN NX4736 Map 9
Steam Packet ♀ ⇔
(01988) 500334 – www.thesteampacketinn.biz
Harbour Row; DG8 8LL

Waterside views from friendly, family-run inn with six real ales and tasty pubby food; bedrooms

This is a friendly, family-run inn right by the picturesque working harbour with big picture windows overlooking the bustle of yachts and inshore fishing boats; some bedrooms have the same outlook. The comfortable low-ceilinged bar is split into two: on the right, plush button-back banquettes and boat pictures, and on the left, stools around cast-iron-framed tables on big stone tiles and a woodburning stove in the bare stone wall. There's a lower beamed dining room with high-backed leather dining chairs around square tables on wooden flooring plus another woodburner, a small eating area off the lounge bar, and an airy conservatory leading into the garden. Belhaven IPA, Fyne Ales Jarl, Timothy Taylors Landlord and guest beers from brewers such as Kelburn and Orkney on handpump, quite a few malt whiskies and 11 wines by the glass; TV, dominoes and pool. You can walk from here up to the remains of St Ninian's kirk, on a headland behind the village.

 Quite a choice of food – with an emphasis on fish and seafood – includes baguettes and ciabattas, tempura squid with sweet chilli dip, ham hock and pigeon terrine with pickled beetroot, vegetable curry, seafood linguine, slow-braised pork belly with egg noodle stir-fry, burgers with toppings, onion rings and chips, chicken stuffed with sunblush tomato mousse on caramelised shallot risotto with creamy white wine sauce, and puddings such as trio of chocolate and Drambuie crème brûlée. *Benchmark main dish: beer-battered haddock and chips £10.95. Two-course evening meal £15.00.*

Free house ~ Licensee Alastair Scoular ~ Real ale ~ Open 11-11 (midnight Sat); 12-11 Sun; 11-2.30, 6-11 Tues-Fri in winter ~ Bar food 12-2, 6.30-9; snacks 2-6pm ~ Restaurant ~ Children welcome except in public bar ~ Dogs allowed in bar and bedrooms ~ Wi-fi ~ Folk music third Sun of month ~ Bedrooms: £30/£60 *Recommended by Isobel Mackinlay, the Dutchman*

KIPPEN NS6594 Map 11
Cross Keys ⇔
(01786) 870293 – www.kippencrosskeys.com
Main Street; village signposted off A811 W of Stirling; FK8 3DN

Cosy 18th-c inn with obliging staff, real ales, tasty food and views of the Trossachs; bedrooms

In a small village just a few minutes from Stirling, this is a comfortable and unpretentious early 18th-c inn. There's always a good mix of both locals and visitors and the kindly staff offer a warm welcome to all. The two bars have log fires, bare boards or carpeting, cushioned and panelled built-in wall seating, wooden dining chairs and bar stools against the counter, and some bare stone walls. Fallen 1703 (named Archie's Amber here) and a guest such as Belhaven Best on handpump, 20 malt whiskies, a dozen wines by the glass and a farm cider; background music. Tables in the garden look across to the Ochil Hills. The bedrooms are comfortable and the breakfasts generous.

Enjoyable food includes lunchtime sandwiches, game terrine with chutney, cullen skink with black pudding crumble, burger with toppings, relish and chips, braised ox cheek with horseradish mash and honeyed carrots, bangers and mash with caramelised onion gravy, venison and beetroot stew with herb dumplings, squash, spinach and chickpea curry with almond rice, and puddings such as chocolate and orange parfait with fruit coulis and lime and lemon crème brûlée. *Benchmark main dish: moroccan lamb with bulgar wheat and flatbread £14.00. Two-course evening meal £17.00.*

Free house ~ Licensees Debby McGregor and Brian Horsburgh ~ Real ale ~ Open 12-3, 5-midnight (1am Fri); 12-1am Sat; 12-midnight Sun ~ Bar food 12-2.30, 5-9; 12-9 Sat; 12-8 Sun ~ Children welcome until 9pm ~ Dogs welcome ~ Wi-fi ~ Folk music first and third Sun of month ~ Bedrooms: £55/£80 *Recommended by Lindy Andrews, Sally Anne and Peter Goodale*

MEIKLEOUR
Meikleour Arms 🛏

NO1539 Map 11

(01250) 883206 – www.meikleourarms.co.uk
A984 W of Coupar Angus; PH2 6EB

Traditional 19th-c inn and part of the Meikleour Estate; a welcoming and well run base for the area; bedrooms

This country inn makes a very good base for exploring rural Perthshire, with lots to do and see nearby – including one of the best salmon beats in Scotland; the pretty bedrooms are comfortable, warm and well appointed and breakfasts are good. The main lounge bar is basically two rooms (one carpeted, the other with a stone floor) with comfortable seating, some angling equipment and fishing/shooting pictures and open wood fires. There's a beer named for the pub (from Inveralmond), Orkney Dark Island and Strathbraan Due South on handpump, 50 malt whiskies and nine wines by the glass, served by attentive, friendly staff; background music. The panelled and tartan-carpeted dining room is elegant and more formal. The garden has seats on a small colonnaded verandah, and a sloping lawn with distant Highland views. Do visit the spectacular beech hedge just 300 metres away which was planted over 250 years ago – it's the tallest in the world.

Using Estate produce and some from their own walled garden, the interesting food includes smoked trout pâté with dill, horseradish and pickled cucumber, ham hock terrine with piccalilli, shrimp, scallop and calamari salad with avocado, tomatoes and lemon vinaigrette, leek and asparagus quiche, chicken escalope with lemon, rosemary and sage crumb, pork fillet filled with spinach, ricotta and apricots with a grainy mustard sauce, rib-eye steak with chips and a choice of sauces, and puddings such as salted caramel profiteroles filled with chantilly cream and baked alaska. *Benchmark main dish: beer-battered haddock and chips £11.95. Two-course evening meal £18.00.*

Free house ~ Licensee Greg Burgess ~ Real ale ~ Open 11-11 (midnight Sat) ~ Bar food 12-9 ~ Restaurant ~ Children welcome ~ Dogs allowed in bar and bedrooms ~ Wi-fi ~ Bedrooms: £90/£110 *Recommended by Mr and Mrs J Watkins, Les and Sandra Brown*

MELROSE

NT5433   Map 9

Burts Hotel ★♨ 🛏

(01896) 822285 – www.burtshotel.co.uk

B6374, Market Square; TD6 9PL

Scotland Dining Pub of the Year

Comfortable town-centre hotel with imaginative food and a fine array of malt whiskies; bedrooms

'**S**plendid in every respect' and 'a wonderful hotel' are just two examples of praise from our readers. A smart place run by the same family for many years, it's in the middle of a beautifully unspoilt small town; the abbey ruins are just a few steps away. Neat public areas are maintained with attention to detail. The welcoming red-carpeted bar has tidy pub tables between cushioned wall seats and windsor armchairs, a warming fire, scottish prints on pale green walls and a long dark wood counter serving Scottish Borders Game Bird, Thwaites Lancaster Bomber and Timothy Taylors Landlord on handpump, 12 wines by the glass from a good wine list, a farm cider and around 70 malt whiskies. The elegant restaurant with its swagged curtains, dark blue wallpaper and tables laid with white linen offers a smarter dining experience; background music. Service here is helpful and polite and the licensees are very hands-on. The bedrooms, though quite small, are immaculate and comfortably decorated and the breakfasts are well regarded. In summer you can sit out in the well tended garden.

Top quality food includes sandwiches, guinea fowl, chicken liver and smoked bacon terrine with orange and pineapple compote, crab salad with quail eggs, salmon parfait and herb crostini, artichoke and wild mushroom open lasagne, smoked haddock and spring onion risotto with a soft poached egg, duck breast with pak choi, caramelised water chestnuts and sesame and honey noodles, salmon with tiger prawn mousse, almond crust and sauce vierge, pork belly roulade with black pudding bonbons, date purée and five-spice jus, and puddings such as white chocolate soup with chocolate brownie and chocolate mousse and orange panna cotta with mango and mint salsa; they also offer a two- and three-course set menu. *Benchmark main dish: harissa-marinated local lamb rump, spiced couscous and yoghurt £15.95. Two-course evening meal £22.50.*

Free house ~ Licensees Graham and Nick Henderson ~ Real ale ~ Open 11-2.30, 5-11; 12-2.30, 6-11 Sun; closed 1 week Jan ~ Bar food 12-2, 6-9.30 (10 Fri, Sat) ~ Restaurant ~ Children welcome ~ Dogs allowed in bar and bedrooms ~ Wi-fi ~ Bedrooms: £76/£140
Recommended by Comus and Sarah Elliott, William and Ann Reid, Roy and Gill Payne, Ian Herdman, Martin Day

PLOCKTON

NG8033   Map 11

Plockton Hotel ★ ♨ 🛏

(01599) 544274 – www.plocktonhotel.co.uk

Village signposted from A87 near Kyle of Lochalsh; IV52 8TN

Lovely views from this family-run loch-side hotel; very good food with emphasis on local seafood and real ales; bedrooms

The setting here is very special. In a lovely village owned by the National Trust for Scotland, this family-run hotel is right by the loch. Half the comfortable bedrooms have extraordinary water views while the others, some with balconies, look over the hillside garden; breakfasts are good. The welcoming, comfortably furnished lounge bar has window seats with views of the harbour boats, as well as antiqued dark red leather seating around neat Regency-style tables on a tartan carpet, three model ships set into the woodwork and partly panelled stone walls. The separate public bar has pool, board games, TV, a games machine, juke box and background music. Cromarty Kowabunga, Highland Island Hopping and a couple of guest ales on handpump, 30 malt whiskies and several wines by the glass. Tables in the front garden look out past the village's trademark palm trees and shore lined with colourful flowering shrubs, across the sheltered anchorage, to the rugged mountainous surrounds of Loch Carron; a stream runs down the hill into a pond in the attractive back garden. There's a hotel nearby called the Plockton, so don't get the two confused.

Good, popular food includes lunchtime sandwiches, creamy smoked fish soup, smoked mackerel layered with cream, cheese and tomatoes with a crisp topping, breadcrumbed fish and chips, haggis, neeps and tatties, venison casserole, king prawn tails in garlic butter, chicken stuffed with smoked ham and cheese in a sun-dried tomato, garlic and basil sauce, local seafood platter, whisky and cream fillet steak strips, and puddings. *Benchmark main dish: salmon with chilli, lime and spring onion £12.95. Two-course evening meal £20.00.*

Free house ~ Licensee Alan Pearson ~ Real ale ~ Open 11-midnight (11.30 Sat); 12-11 Sun ~ Bar food 12-2.15, 6-9 ~ Restaurant ~ Children welcome ~ Live music Weds evening ~ Bedrooms: £60/£140 *Recommended by Ken Richards, Les and Sandra Brown, Barry Collett, M J Winterton*

RATHO
NT1470   Map 11

Bridge 🍷 🍺

(0131) 333 1320 – www.bridgeinn.com
Baird Road; EH28 8RA

Canalside inn with cosy bar and airy restaurant, a thoughtful wine list, real ales, enjoyable food and barge restaurant; attractive bedrooms

A unique part of the friendly licensees' business here is their summer restaurant barge, which travels from the inn down the Union Canal to the Almondell Aqueduct over the River Almond; there's a full kitchen team on board and you can have lunch, afternoon tea or supper. The inn is also a charming place to stay with individually decorated and well equipped bedrooms with water views; lovely breakfasts. The cosy bar has an open fire with leather armchairs to either side and a larger area with a two-way fireplace and upholstered tub and cushioned wooden chairs on pale boards around a mix of tables; a contemporary and elegant dining room leads off. Alechemy Stella Burst, Cairngorm Trade Winds, Orkney Raven Ale and a guest on handpump, 36 wines by the glass and 50 malt whiskies. The main restaurant is light and airy with up-to-date pale oak settles, antique-style chairs and big windows overlooking the water. Seats on the terrace share the same canal view.

Growing produce in their walled garden and raising pigs and sheep for their highly thought-of food, the menu includes sandwiches (until 5.30pm), pork and apple terrine with parsley dressing and pickled vegetables, pigeon breast with truffled white polenta and red wine jus, sharing platters, chickpea curry with naan bread and chutney, burger with toppings and skinny fries, salmon and fennel risotto with prosciutto crisp, pork sausages with black pudding, crackling and gravy, trio of lamb (rump, rack and shank) with mint sauce, and puddings such as cinnamon crème brûlée and dark chocolate brownie with vanilla ice-cream. *Benchmark main dish: pie of the day £12.95. Two-course evening meal £24.00.*

Free house ~ Licensees Graham and Rachel Bucknall ~ Real ale ~ Open 9am-11pm; 11am-midnight Sat; 11-11 Sun ~ Bar food 12-3, 5-30-9; 12-9 Sat; 12-8 Sun ~ Restaurant ~ Children welcome but not in bar after 8pm ~ Dogs allowed in bar ~ Wi-fi ~ Live music monthly (best to phone) ~ Bedrooms: £75/£90 *Recommended by Pat and Stewart Gordon*

SCALASAIG

NR3893 Map 11

Colonsay 🛏

(01951) 200316 – www.colonsayholidays.co.uk

W on B8086; PA61 7YP

Extended hotel with a good mix of customers in cheerful bar, enjoyable food and drink and friendly atmosphere; comfortable bedrooms

This is a stylish 18th-c hotel and a haven for ramblers and birders. The chatty bar is the hub of the island and full of both locals and visitors and they keep Colonsay IPA on handpump, several wines by the glass and interesting malt whiskies; board games, TV and background music. There are comfortable sofas and armchairs, log fires, pastel walls hung with interesting old islander pictures and polished painted boards. The relaxed and informal restaurant overlooks the harbour and has a woodburning stove with neatly piled logs to each side. From seats in the gardens there are pleasant views. The bedrooms are comfortable and pretty.

 They grow their own organic produce and have an oyster farm for the enjoyable food, which includes lunchtime sandwiches, oysters, ham hock terrine with chutney, langoustines with mayonnaise, burger with coleslaw and chips, pasta with goats curd, wild garlic and thyme, steak in ale pie, scallops with cauliflower purée and black pudding, lamb shank with red wine and cannellini beans, and puddings such as pink rhubarb fool and raspberry cranachan; they offer morning coffee, afternoon tea and have a pre-ferry two-course set menu. *Benchmark main dish: aberdeen angus rib-eye steak with chips £21.00. Two-course evening meal £22.00.*

Free house ~ Licensee Jane Howard ~ Real ale ~ Open 12-11 (1am Sat); closed Nov-Feb except Christmas and New Year ~ Bar food 12-2.30, 6-9 ~ Restaurant ~ Children welcome ~ Dogs allowed in bar and bedrooms ~ Wi-fi ~ Bedrooms: £75/£90
Recommended by Mary Kirkwood, Neil Allen

SHIELDAIG

NG8153 Map 11

Tigh an Eilean Hotel 🛏

(01520) 755251 – www.tighaneilean.co.uk

Village signposted just off A896 Lochcarron–Gairloch; IV54 8XN

Separate, contemporary hotel bar memorably placed beneath formidable peaks, with real ales and enjoyable food; tranquil bedrooms

For lovers of wildlife, this friendly hotel makes a fine base – if you're lucky you might see otters, sea eagles, seals and even the rare pine marten. To preserve the peace and quiet, the comfortable bedrooms have no televisions and no telephones, though each has its own sitting area. The setting is stunning, looking over forested Shieldaig Island to Loch Torridon and then the sea beyond. Separate from the hotel, the bright, attractive bar is on two storeys with an open staircase; dining is on the first floor and a decked balcony has a magnificent loch and village view. The place is gently contemporary and nicely relaxed with timbered floors, timber-boarded walls, shiny bolts through exposed timber roof beams and an open kitchen. A couple of changing ales from An Teallach on handpump (although sometimes in January there may be no real ale on offer) and up to a dozen wines by the glass. Tables outside in a sheltered little courtyard are well placed to enjoy the gorgeous position.

🍴 Enjoyable food using the best local produce includes sandwiches, gratin of crab with pink grapefruit, wild mushroom tortellini with pea and herb velouté and a parmesan wafer, pizzas from their wood-fired oven, crab and salmon cakes with home-made lemon mayonnaise, haggis, neeps and tatties, fish stew in crab bisque, duck breast with fresh mango, honey and soy sauce, bream in fennel, leek and saffron broth with steamed mussels and grilled scallop, and puddings such as roasted plums with brioche doughnuts and brandy anglaise and vanilla crème brûlée with a date and walnut base and tropical fruit salad. *Benchmark main dish: local langoustines with garlic butter £16.99. Two-course evening meal £23.00.*

Free house ~ Licensee Cathryn Field ~ Real ale ~ Open 11-11 (1am Fri, Sat) ~ Bar food 12-9; 12-2.30, 6.30-9 in winter ~ Restaurant ~ Children welcome till 10pm ~ Dogs allowed in bar and bedrooms ~ Wi-fi ~ Traditional live folk music in summer ~ Bedrooms: $80/$160 *Recommended by the Dutchman, John and Enid*

SLIGACHAN
Sligachan Hotel 🍺 🛏

NG4930   Map 11

(01478) 650204 – www.sligachan.co.uk
A87 Broadford–Portree, junction with A863; IV47 8SW

Spectacularly set mountain hotel with walkers' bar and plusher side, all-day food and impressive range of whiskies

The huge, modern pine-clad main bar in this stunningly set hotel falls somewhere between a basic climbers' bar and the plusher, more sedate hotel side. It's spaciously open to the ceiling rafters and has geometrically laid-out dark tables and chairs on neat carpets; pool, TV, darts, games machine and board games. As well as their own Cuillin Black Face, Pinnacle and Skye, they keep a guest on handpump plus an incredible display of over 400 malt whiskies at one end of the counter. It can get quite lively in here some nights, but there's a more sedate lounge bar with leather bucket armchairs on plush carpets and a coal fire; background highland and islands music. The separate restaurant is in the hotel itself. The interesting little museum, well worth a visit, charts the history of the hotel and its famous climbers, with photographs and climbing and angling records. There are tables out in the garden and a big play area for children, which can be seen from the bar. The bedrooms are comfortable, bright and modern, they offer self-catering and have a campsite with caravan hook-ups. Dogs are allowed only in the main bar and not in the hotel's cocktail bar – but may stay in some bedrooms. Some of the most testing walks in Britain are right on the doorstep of the hotel.

🍴 Food of some sort is usefully served all day: paninis (until 5pm), haggis bonbons with clapshot and whisky jus, mussels in cider, leek and tarragon broth, bean, venison or beef burgers with curly fries, goats cheese and aubergine lasagne, venison in port wine and juniper with sticky red cabbage, chicken with haggis and whisky and pink-peppercorn sauce, megrim with rosemary potatoes and lemon butter sauce, and puddings such as iced cranachan parfait with coulis and chocolate tart with chantilly cream. *Benchmark main dish: venison casserole £12.95. Two-course evening meal £14.00.*

Own brew ~ Licensee Sandy Coghill ~ Real ale ~ Open 9am-midnight; 11am-midnight Sun; closed Nov-Feb (hotel), phone for bar times ~ Bar food 7.30am-9.30pm ~ Restaurant ~ Children welcome ~ Dogs allowed in bar and bedrooms ~ Wi-fi ~ Live music every second Sat of month ~ Bedrooms: $50/$100 *Recommended by Caroline Prescott, Anne and Ben Smith*

The details at the end of each featured entry start by saying whether the pub is a free house, or if it belongs to a brewery or pub group (which we name).

STEIN

NG2656 Map 11

Stein Inn 🛏

(01470) 592362 – www.steininn.co.uk

End of B886 N of Dunvegan in Waternish, off A850 Dunvegan–Portree; OS Sheet 23 map reference 263564; IV55 8GA

Lovely setting on Skye's northern corner for this welcoming 18th-c inn with good, simple food and lots of whiskies; a rewarding place to stay

All the bedrooms in this old inn of great character have stunning views across Loch Bay; it's worth pre-ordering the smoked kippers as part of the tasty breakfasts. The unpretentious original public bar makes a particularly inviting retreat from the elements, with sturdy country furnishings, flagstones, beam-and-plank ceiling, partly panelled stripped-stone walls and a warming double-sided stove between the two rooms. Caledonian Deuchars IPA and a couple of local guests such as Cairngorm Trade Winds and Orkney Dark Island on handpump, eight wines by the glass and over 135 malt whiskies. Good service from smartly uniformed staff. Pool, darts, board games, dominoes and cribbage in the games area, and maybe background music. There's a lively indoor play area for children and showers for yachtsmen. Benches outside look over the water.

🍴 Using local fish and highland meat, the popular food at sensible prices includes sandwiches, black pudding with a whisky and mustard dressing, deep-fried whitebait, macaroni cheese, venison burger with cranberry sauce, beef braised in ale, double pork loin steak with mustard cream sauce, sirloin steak with onions and peppercorn sauce, and puddings such as white chocolate cheesecake and apple and blueberry crumble. *Benchmark main dish: beer-battered haddock and chips £10.25. Two-course evening meal £18.00.*

Free house ~ Licensees Angus and Teresa Mcghie ~ Real ale ~ Open 11am-midnight; 11.30-11 Sun; 12-11 in winter ~ Bar food 12-4, 6-9.30; 1.30-4, 6-9 Sun ~ Children welcome ~ Dogs allowed in bar and bedrooms ~ Wi-fi ~ Bedrooms: £45/£77 *Recommended by Edna Jones*

STONEHAVEN

NO8595 Map 11

Lairhillock

(01569) 730001 – www.lairhillock.co.uk

Netherley; 6 miles N of Stonehaven, 6 miles S of Aberdeen, take the Durris turn-off from the A90; AB39 3QS

Bustling, family-run inn with fine views, a thoughtful choice of drinks, good food and kind service

This smartly extended country pub is very much a family business and you can be sure of a genuine welcome for all. The cheerful beamed bar has a traditional feel with panelled wall benches and an attractive mix of old seats, dark woodwork, lots of brass and copper items and a good open fire. The spacious lounge has an unusual central fire. At the back, the conservatory has rattan furniture with scatter cushions and fine panoramic views. Stools line the counter where they keep Timothy Taylors Landlord and guests such as Strathaven Clydesdale and Windswept Aurora on handpump, several wines by the glass and good malt whiskies.

🍴 As well as baguettes and ciabattas, the interesting food includes their own-smoked salmon and arbroath smokie roulade with horseradish mayonnaise, smoked duck breast with crispy pancetta and black pudding, feta cheese and baby leek cannelloni with sunblush tomato and herb crouton, lasagne, a pie of the day, chicken breast stuffed with sage and onion, wrapped in prosciutto with juniper-infused red wine jus, herb-crusted venison fillet on carrot and potato rösti with blackberry jus, and puddings such as peach crumble and sticky toffee pudding with toffee sauce and toffee ice-cream. *Benchmark main dish: prawns in chilli, lime and coconut £13.95. Two-course evening meal £25.00.*

Free house ~ Licensee Donald Law ~ Real ale ~ Open 11-11 ~ Bar food 12-2, 6-9.15; 12-2, 5-8.45 Sun ~ Restaurant ~ Children welcome ~ Dogs allowed in bar
Recommended by Gus Swan, Neil Allen

SWINTON
NT8347 Map 10

Wheatsheaf 🅧 ♀ 🛏

(01890) 860257 – www.wheatsheaf-swinton.co.uk

A6112 N of Coldstream; TD11 3JJ

Civilised place with small bar for drinkers, comfortable lounges, quite a choice of food and drinks and professional service; appealing bedrooms

Most customers are here to enjoy the particularly good food and accommodation (it's more a restaurant-with-rooms than a straightforward pub) but the friendly, attentive staff welcome customers in the little bar and informal lounges. Here they keep Belhaven IPA on handpump alongside 50 malt whiskies and 18 wines by the glass. There are comfortable plush armchairs, several nice old oak settles with cushions, a little open fire, sporting prints and china plates on the bottle-green walls in the bar and small agricultural prints and a fishing-theme décor on the painted or bare stone walls in the lounges. The dining room and front conservatory with its vaulted pine ceiling have high-backed slate-grey chairs around pale wood tables set with fresh flowers, and carpet, while the more formal restaurant has black leather high-backed dining chairs around clothed tables; background music. The well equipped, comfortable bedrooms have been refurbished in Farrow & Ball colours and the scottish breakfasts are good. This is a pretty village surrounded by rolling countryside and only a few miles from the River Tweed.

Creative food under the new chef includes bar staples (such as gammon and egg, corn-fed chicken with walnut and baby gem salad with raspberry dressing, and cottage pie), with more imaginative choices such as smoked haddock, salmon and trout scotch egg with curry mayonnaise, air-dried smoked juniper mutton with pine nut cream and parmesan crisp, pea and mint risotto with rosemary and soft cheese, stuffed rabbit loin with crispy bacon and kidney, carrot and cumin mousse, apple purée and fondant potato, fillet of sea trout with saffron and mussel velouté, confit golden beetroots and spinach purée, and puddings such as egg custard tart with apple and ginger purée and nutmeg ice-cream and dark chocolate and cherry tobacco pave with caramel ice-cream. *Benchmark main dish: roast loin of organic pork with asian dressing, tempura courgette and caramelised cashews £19.50. Two-course evening meal £20.00.*

Free house ~ Licensees Chris and Jan Winson ~ Real ale ~ Open 11-11 (midnight Sat); 11-10 Sun ~ Bar food 12-2, 6-9 ~ Restaurant ~ Children welcome but under-10s only in restaurant 6-7pm ~ Dogs allowed in bar and bedrooms ~ Wi-fi ~ Bedrooms: £89/£119
Recommended by Belinda May, Nick Sharpe

Please keep sending us reports. We rely on readers for news of new discoveries, and particularly for news of changes - however slight - at the fully described pubs: feedback@goodguides.com, or (no stamp needed) The Good Pub Guide, FREEPOST RTJR-ZCYZ-RJZT, Perrymans Lane, Etchingham TN19 7DN.

THORNHILL
NS6699 Map 11

Lion & Unicorn

(01786) 850204 – www.lion-unicorn.co.uk

Main Street (A873); FK8 3PJ

Busy, interesting pub with emphasis on its home-made food; friendly staff and bedrooms

Traditionally furnished and friendly, this is a neatly kept inn with attentive licensees. There's a back bar with pubby character, some exposed stone walls, wooden flooring and stools lined along the counter where they keep An Teallach Ale and Greene King Ruddles Best on handpump and several wines by the glass; log fires. This opens to a games room with a pool table, juke box, fruit machine, darts, TV and board games. The more restauranty-feeling carpeted front room has pub furniture, usually set for dining, a beamed ceiling and – as evidence of the building's 17th-c past – an original massive fireplace with a log fire in a high brazier, almost big enough to drive a car into; background music. Outside, there are benches in a gravelled garden and a lawn with a play area.

Well liked food includes sandwiches, haggis fritters with whisky, honey and grain mustard dip, prawn cocktail, chicken, leek and mushroom pie, steak burger with toppings and chips, leek, field mushroom and parsnip crumble, chicken fillet topped with haggis, wrapped in bacon with whisky cream sauce, steaks with beer-battered onion rings and chips, and puddings such as sticky toffee pudding. *Benchmark main dish: breaded fresh haddock and chips £10.25. Two-course evening meal £19.00.*

Free house ~ Licensee Fiona Stevenson ~ Real ale ~ Open 12-midnight (1am Fri, Sat) ~ Bar food 12-9 ~ Restaurant ~ Children welcome ~ Dogs allowed in bar ~ Wi-fi ~ Bedrooms: £55/£75 *Recommended by Lindy Andrews, Anne and Ben Smith*

WEEM
NN8449 Map 11

Ailean Chraggan ♀

(01887) 820346 – www.aileanchraggan.co.uk

B846; PH15 2LD

Changing range of seasonal food in family-run hotel

The bedrooms are warm and spacious and the breakfasts very tasty in this friendly small hotel with its good mix of customers. The busy bar has a chatty feel, Inveralmond Ossian on handpump and over 100 malt whiskies; winter darts. There's also an adjoining neatly old-fashioned dining room and a comfortable carpeted modern lounge. The flower-filled covered terrace and the garden offer great views to the mountains beyond the Tay up to Ben Lawers (the highest peak in this part of Scotland); the owners can arrange fishing nearby.

Featuring local seafood and game, the rewarding food includes sandwiches, duck liver pâté with port jelly, salmon and smoked haddock fishcake with sweet chilli sauce, roast butternut squash puff pastry with asparagus and spiced tomato sauce, scallops with white wine sauce and potato gratin, bacon-wrapped pork fillet with potato rösti and meat jus, seared goose breast with rich jus, haunch of venison with poached pear and chocolate raspberry sauce, and puddings such as lavender crème brûlée and coconut panna cotta with pineapple carpaccio. *Benchmark main dish: seafood platter (not Mon or Tues) £24.00. Two-course evening meal £20.00.*

Free house ~ Licensee Alastair Gillespie ~ Real ale ~ Open 11-11 ~ Bar food 12-2, 5.30-8.30 (9 Sat) ~ Restaurant ~ Children welcome ~ Dogs allowed in bar and bedrooms ~ Wi-fi ~ Bedrooms: £55/£110 *Recommended by Isobel Mackinlay, Neil and Angela Huxter*

Also Worth a Visit in Scotland

Besides the fully inspected pubs, you might like to try these pubs that have been recommended to us and described by readers. Do tell us what you think of them: feedback@goodguides.com

ABERDEENSHIRE

ABERDEEN NJ9406
BrewDog (01224) 631223
Gallowgate; AB25 1EB The original BrewDog outlet (opened 2010), and pivotal in the craft beer revolution, their range and several guests, enthusiastic knowledgeable staff; open all day (till 1am Fri, Sat).
(Neil Allen)

ABERDEEN NJ9305
Grill (01224) 573530
Union Street; AB11 6BA Don't be put off by the outside of this 19th-c granite building – the remodelled 1920s interior is well worth a look; long wood-floored bar with fine moulded ceiling, mahogany panelling and original button-back leather wall benches, ornate servery with glazed cabinets housing some of the 500 or so whiskies (including a few distilled in the 1930s, and 60 from around the world), five well kept ales including Caledonian 80/- and Harviestoun Bitter & Twisted, basic snacks; no children or dogs; open all day (till 1am Fri, Sat). *(Mungo Shipley)*

ABERDEEN NJ9406
★**Prince of Wales** (01224) 640597
St Nicholas Lane; AB10 1HF Individual and convivial old tavern with eight changing ales from very long counter, bargain hearty food, painted floorboards, flagstones or carpet, pews and screened booths, original tiled spittoon running length of bar; games machines; live acoustic music Sun evening; children over 5 welcome if eating, open all day from 10am (11am Sun). *(Belinda May)*

ABOYNE NO5298
★**Boat** (01339) 886137
Charlestown Road (B968, just off A93); AB34 5EL Friendly country inn with fine views across River Dee, partly carpeted bar with model train chugging its way around just below ceiling height, scottish pictures, brasses and woodburner in stone fireplace, games in public bar end, spiral stairs up to roomy additional dining area, three well kept ales, decent wines and some 30 malts, tasty bar food from sandwiches up, more elaborate seasonal evening menu; background music, games machine; children welcome, dogs in bar, six comfortable well equipped bedrooms, open all day. *(Robert Watt)*

ALFORD NJ5617
Forbes Arms (01975) 562108
A944; by the bridge; AB33 8QJ Small riverside hotel with good value pub food including high teas, a changing scottish ale, two bars (one with projector screen for sports events), restaurant and conservatory extension; seats in garden sloping down to River Don (fishing permits available), nine comfortable bedrooms, closed Mon, Tues lunchtimes, otherwise open all day.
(David and Betty Gittins)

BALMEDIE NJ9619
Cock & Bull (01358) 743249
A90 N of Balmedie; AB23 8XY Pleasant atmosphere and interesting décor in this food-led country pub, a well kept ale such as Burnside and good locally sourced food, obliging attentive service, beamed log-fire lounge, restaurant and conservatory; children and dogs (in bar) welcome, four bedrooms in converted cottage, open (and food) all day.
(Mandy Davidson)

OLDMELDRUM NJ8127
Redgarth (01651) 872353
Kirk Brae, off A957; AB51 0DJ Good-sized comfortable lounge with traditional décor and subdued lighting, two or three well kept ales and good range of malt whiskies, popular reasonably priced food, friendly attentive service, restaurant; children welcome, lovely views to Bennachie, bedrooms (get booked quickly). *(David and Betty Gittins)*

PENNAN NJ8465
Pennan Inn (01346) 561201
Just off B9031 Banff–Fraserburgh; AB43 6JB Whitewashed building in long row of old fishermen's cottages, wonderful spot right by the sea – scenes from film *Local Hero* (1983) shot here; small bar with simple furniture and exposed stone walls, separate restaurant (more spacious in feel) with wooden tables and upholstered high-backed chairs, pictures on plain painted walls, enjoyable sensibly priced food from shortish menu including some thai dishes, at least one real ale, friendly service; five bedrooms, at foot of steep winding road and parking along front limited, closed Mon, shut out of season. *(GSB)*

ANGUS

BROUGHTY FERRY NO4630
★**Fishermans Tavern** (01382) 775941
Fort Street; turning off shore road; DD5 2AD Once a row of fishermen's cottages, this friendly pub is just steps from the beach, up to eight well kept changing ales (May beer festival) and good range of

malt whiskies, secluded lounge area with coal fire, small carpeted snug with basket-weave wall panels, another fire in back bar popular with diners for the wide choice of fair priced pubby food (offers available), fiddle music Thurs night, quiz every other Mon; TV, fruit machine; children and dogs welcome, disabled facilities, tables on front pavement, more in secluded little walled garden, 12 bedrooms, open all day (till 1am Thurs-Sat). *(Neil Allen)*

ARGYLL

BRIDGE OF ORCHY   NN2939

★ **Bridge of Orchy Hotel**
(01838) 400208 *A82 Tyndrum–Glencoe; PA36 4AB* Spectacular spot on West Highland Way, very welcoming with good fairly priced all-day food in bar, lounge and smarter restaurant, decent choice of well kept ales, house wines and malt whiskies, interesting mountain photographs; ten good bedrooms (refurbished recently), more in airy riverside annexe. *(Lindy Andrews)*

CAIRNDOW   NN1811

★ **Cairndow Stagecoach Inn**
(01499) 600286 *Village and pub signed off A83; PA26 8BN* Refurbished 17th-c coaching inn in wonderful position on edge of Loch Fyne, good sensibly priced food including local venison and fresh fish, ales from nearby Fyne and over 40 malt whiskies, friendly accommodating staff; children and dogs welcome, lovely peaceful lochside garden, 13 comfortable bedrooms, six more in modern annexe with balconies overlooking the water, good breakfast, open (and food) all day. *(Pat and Stewart Gordon, Roy and Lindsey Fentiman)*

CONNEL   NM9034

Oyster (01631) 710666
A85, W of Connel Bridge; PA37 1PJ 18th-c pub opposite former ferry slipway, lovely view across the water (especially at sunset), decent-sized bar with friendly highland atmosphere, log fire in stone fireplace, café with cakes, ice-cream and coffees, enjoyable food including delicious local seafood, Caledonian Deuchars IPA, good range of wines and malts, attentive service; sports TV, pool and darts; modern hotel part with 16 attractive bedrooms next door with separate evening restaurant. *(Mungo Shipley)*

INVERARAY   NN0908

★ **George** (01499) 302111
Main Street East; PA32 8TT Very popular Georgian hotel (packed during holiday times) at hub of this appealing small town; bustling pubby bar with exposed joists, bare stone walls, old tiles and big flagstones, antique settles, carved wooden benches and cushioned stone slabs along the walls, four log fires, a couple of real ales and 100 malt whiskies, good food in bar and smarter restaurant, live entertainment Fri, Sat; children and dogs welcome, well laid-out terraces with plenty of seats, bedrooms, Inveraray Castle and walks close by, open all day till 1am. *(Anon)*

LOCH ECK   NS1491

Coylet (01369) 840426
A815, E shore; PA23 8SG Former coaching inn in beautiful lochside setting, simply furnished bar with big stag's head above fireplace, good pubby food, Fyne Highlander on draught; four bedrooms, sells fishing permits and can arrange boat trips. *(Belinda May)*

OBAN   NM8530

Cuan Mor (01631) 565078
George Street; PA34 5SD Contemporary quayside bar-restaurant with lots of kitchen-style chairs and tables on bare boards, snug bar with open fire, over 100 malts and their own-brewed real ales, wide choice of competitively priced food all day, friendly service; children welcome, some seats outside. *(Gus Swan)*

OBAN   NM8529

Lorne (01631) 570020
Stevenson Street; PA34 5NA Victorian décor including tiles and island bar with ornate brasswork, well kept Oban Bay ales, reasonably priced food from ciabattas and wraps through pizzas to local fish, good service; live music and DJs at weekends; children welcome, sheltered beer garden, open all day till late. *(Jim and Sheila Wilson)*

OTTER FERRY   NR9384

Oystercatcher (01700) 821229
B8000, by the water; PA21 2DH Friendly family-run pub-restaurant in old building in outstanding spot overlooking Loch Fyne, good food using local fish and shellfish, well kept ales including Fyne from pine-clad bar, decent wine list, friendly staff and pub dog; lots of tables out on spit, free moorings, open all day. *(Darren and Jane Staniforth)*

TARBERT   NR8365

West Loch Hotel (01880) 820283
A83, a mile S; PA29 6YF Friendly 18th-c family-run inn overlooking sea loch, comfortably updated with exposed stone walls, pale-topped tables and high-backed dark dining chairs, relaxing lounges with fine views or open fire, enjoyable food using local produce (try the Iron Bru ice-cream), Belhaven and good selection of whiskies and gins, helpful cheerful service; children and dogs welcome, eight bedrooms (some with loch views), handy for ferry terminal. *(M J Winterton)*

TAYVALLICH   NR7487

Tayvallich Inn (01546) 870282
B8025; PA31 8PL Small single-storey conversion by Loch Sween specialising in

good local seafood; pale pine furnishings on quarry tiles, local nautical charts, good range of whiskies and usually a couple of beers from Loch Ness, friendly atmosphere; background music (live first Fri of month); children and dogs welcome, a few picnic-sets on front deck with lovely views over yacht anchorage, open all day weekends, closed Mon. *(Jim and Sheila Wilson)*

AYRSHIRE

AYR   NS3321
West Kirk (01292) 880416
Sandgate; KA7 1BX Wetherspoons conversion of 19th-c church keeping original stained glass, pulpit, balconies, doors and so forth, seven real ales and their usual food; TVs, free wi-fi; open all day from 8am. *(Dr Peter Crawshaw)*

DUNURE   NS2515
Dunure (01292) 500549
Just off A719 SW of Ayr; KA7 4LN Welcoming place attractively set by harbourside ruined castle; updated bar, lounge and restaurant, varied food including fresh fish/seafood, nice wines; no real ales; courtyard tables, bedrooms and two cottages, not far from Culzean Castle (NTS). *(Isobel Mackinlay)*

SYMINGTON   NS3831
Wheatsheaf (01563) 830307
Just off A77 Ayr–Kilmarnock; Main Street; KA1 5QB Single-storey former 17th-c posting inn, charming and cosy, with first class food (must book weekends) including lunchtime/early evening set menu, efficient friendly service, log fire; children welcome, tables outside, quiet pretty village, open (and food) all day. *(Barry Collett)*

BERWICKSHIRE

ALLANTON   NT8654
★ Allanton Inn (01890) 818260
B6347 S of Chirnside; TD11 3JZ Well run 18th-c stone-built village inn with attractive open-plan interior, very good fairly priced food with emphasis on fresh fish/seafood from daily changing menu, well kept ales such as Scottish Borders and Timothy Taylors, good wine list and speciality gins, friendly efficient service, cosy bare boards bar with scatter cushions on bench seats, immaculate dining areas, log fire; background music; children welcome, picnic-sets in sheltered garden behind, nice views, seven bedrooms, open all day. *(John and Sylvia Harrop, Dr Peter Crawshaw, Michael Doswell)*

AUCHENCROW   NT8560
Craw (01890) 761253
B6438 NE of Duns; pub signed off A1; TD14 5LS Delightful little 18th-c village pub in row of cream-washed slate-roofed

cottages, friendly and welcoming, with enjoyable well presented food including fresh fish and seafood, changing ales from smaller brewers (Aug, Nov beer festivals), good wine list, beams decorated with hundreds of pump clips, pictures on panelled walls, woodburner, more formal back restaurant; children welcome, tables on decking behind and out on village green, three bedrooms and self-catering apartment, open all day weekends. *(Alistair Forsyth)*

LAUDER   NT5347
Black Bull (01578) 722208
Market Place; TD2 6SR Comfortable white-painted 18th-c inn festooned with cheerful window boxes and hanging baskets, cosy rustic-feel bar with country scenes on panelled walls, quieter room off and restaurant, well kept Stewart Edinburgh Gold and a local guest, enjoyable food including deals, friendly service; background music, sports TV, free wi-fi; children and dogs (in bar) welcome, eight bedrooms, open (and food) all day. *(Phil and Jane Hodson)*

CAITHNESS

MEY   ND2872
Castle Arms (01847) 851244
A836; KW14 8XH 19th-c former coaching inn, enjoyable home-made food (restaurant shut winter lunchtimes) including takeaway fish and chips Weds and Fri from 4.30, friendly helpful service, plenty of malt whiskies, views of Dunnet Head and across Pentland Firth to the Orkneys; pool; seven comfortable bedrooms and two suites in back extension, well placed for N coast of Caithness, Gills Bay ferry and Castle of Mey. *(Belinda May)*

DUMFRIESSHIRE

BARGRENNAN   NX3576
House O' Hill (01671) 840243
Off A714, road opposite church; DG8 6RN Small pub on edge of Galloway Forest (good mountain biking) with enthusiastic owners, interesting well cooked/priced food using local seasonal produce (best to book), a couple of real ales and good wine list, friendly helpful staff; two comfortable bedrooms (good breakfast) and self-catering cottage, open all day. *(Mike Swan)*

BEATTOCK   NT0702
Old Stables (01683) 300134
Smith Way; ¼ mile from M74 junction 15; DG10 9QX Turreted 19th-c pub on edge of village, bargain home-cooked food served by friendly staff, Belhaven beers, restaurant with gingham-clothed tables and railway memorabilia (the old Beattock line was famous for its steep gradients); pool, darts, big-screen TVs and fruit machine; covered outside seating area, three bedrooms and

parking for campervans, open all day.
(Phil and Jane Hodson)

DUMFRIES   NX9776
★ **Cavens Arms** (01387) 252896
Buccleuch Street; DG1 2AH Good
generously served home-made food (not
Mon) from pubby standards up, seven well
kept interesting ales, Aspall's and Weston's
cider, fine choice of malts, friendly landlord
and good helpful staff, civilised front part
with lots of wood, drinkers' area at back with
bar stools, banquettes and traditional cast-
iron tables, recently added lounge/restaurant
areas; can get very busy, discreet TV, no dogs
or children; disabled facilities, small terrace
at back, open all day. *(Dr J Barrie Jones)*

DUMFRIES   NX9775
Globe (01387) 252335
High Street; DG1 2JA Proper town pub
with strong Burns connections, especially
in old-fashioned dark-panelled 17th-century
snug and little museum of a room beyond;
main part more modern in feel, ales such
as Caledonian and Sulwath, plenty of
whiskies, good value pubby food (evening by
arrangement), friendly service; live music
Mon evening, children welcome in eating
areas, terrace seating, open all day.
(Mike Swan)

MOFFAT   NT0805
Black Bull (01683) 220206
Churchgate; DG10 9EG Attractive small
hotel (former coaching inn), comfortable
dimly lit bar with Burns memorabilia, well
kept Caledonian Deuchars IPA and several
dozen malts, enjoyable food including steaks
and grills, simply furnished carpeted dining
room, friendly public bar across courtyard
with railway memorabilia, pool, darts and
big-screen sports TV; background and live
acoustic music; children welcome, tables in
courtyard, eight small bedrooms in annexe
(dogs welcome), hearty breakfast, no car
park, open all day. *(Johnston and Maureen
Anderson)*

MOFFAT   NT0805
Buccleuch Arms (01683) 220003
High Street; DG10 9ET Friendly rather
old-fashioned Georgian coaching inn with
roomy carpeted bar and lounge areas, open
fire, good popular food using local produce
(suppliers listed) from sandwiches and
toasties up, informal upstairs restaurant,
polite quick service, interesting wines by
the glass, over 70 malts and bottled beers,
cocktails; soft background music, Sky TV
(in public bar next door); dogs welcome,
garden (bike storage), 16 bedrooms, open
all day. *(Jo Garnett)*

MOFFAT   NT0905
Star (01683) 220156
High Street; DG10 9EF Amazingly narrow
building (in the Guinness World Records)

yet has two surprisingly capacious bars
including comfortable, relaxing lounge, warm
friendly atmosphere, generous helpings
of popular reasonably priced pubby food,
well kept ales such as Greene King IPA and
Sulwath, moderately priced wine by the
bottle, restaurant; sports TV, free wi-fi; dogs
welcome, bedrooms, open (and food) all day.
*(Johnston and Maureen Anderson, David and
Betty Gittins)*

DUNBARTONSHIRE

ARROCHAR   NN2903
Village Inn (01301) 702279
*A814, just off A83 W of Loch Lomond;
G83 7AX* Friendly cosy and interesting
with well kept ales such as Caledonian and
Fyne, good hearty home-made food in simple
all-day dining area (gets booked up) with
heavy beams, bare boards, some panelling
and roaring fire, steps down to unpretentious
bar, several dozen malts, good coffee, fine
sea and hill views; background music, juke
box; children welcome in eating areas till
8pm, no dogs, tables out on deck and lawn,
comfortable bedrooms including spacious
ones in former back barn, good breakfast,
open all day. *(Gus Swan)*

EAST LOTHIAN

ABERLADY   NT4679
Old Aberlady (01875) 870503
Main Street; EH32 0NF In pretty coastal
village and much improved/modernised
under new management; good varied choice
of food, Caledonian Deuchars IPA and a
guest, good wine and whisky selection,
friendly staff; children and dogs welcome,
six bedrooms, open all day.
(Alistair Forsyth)

GULLANE   NT4882
★ **Old Clubhouse** (01620) 842008
East Links Road; EH31 2AF Single-storey
building in nice position overlooking Gullane
Links, cosy bar and more formal dining
room, seating from wooden dining chairs and
banquettes to big squashy leather armchairs
and sofas, Victorian pictures and cartoons,
stuffed birds, sheet music covers, golfing and
other memorabilia, open fires, good choice
of food plus specials, four ales including
Belhaven and Caledonian, nice house wines,
fast friendly service; children and dogs
welcome, plenty of seats out at front, open
all day. *(Alistair Forsyth)*

HADDINGTON   NT5173
Victoria (01620) 823332
Court Street; EH41 3JD Popular bar-
restaurant with a mix of cushioned dining
chairs and wall banquettes on wooden
flooring or carpets, woodburning stove, good
imaginative local food cooked by chef-
landlord, a couple of changing real ales,
short but decent wine list, efficient friendly

service; five bedrooms, open all day.
(Comus and Sarah Elliott)

HADDINGTON NT5173

Waterside (01620) 825674

Waterside; just off A6093, over pedestrian bridge at E end of town; EH41 4AT Attractively set riverside dining pub next to historic bridge, spacious but cosy modernised interior with some stylish touches, enjoyable bistro-style food, three changing ales from smaller brewers, good wine choice, pleasant friendly staff; children welcome (family room with toys), picnic-sets out overlooking the River Tyne. *(Comus and Sarah Elliott)*

FIFE

CULROSS NS9885

Red Lion (01383) 880225

Low Causeway; KY12 8HN Popular old pub in pretty NTS village, good value food, a beer from Inveralmond and several wines by the glass, beams and amazing painted ceilings; seats outside, open (and food) all day. *(Brian and Anna Marsden)*

CUPAR NO3714

Boudingait (01334) 654681

Bonnygate; KY15 4BU Bustling bar with high-backed, captain's and cushion-seated chairs around dark tables on wood flooring, open fire, high chairs against counter serving Caledonian Deuchars IPA, good variety of well liked reasonably priced home-made food (something available all day), friendly attentive staff; live folk and quiz nights; children welcome. *(Anne and Ben Smith)*

ELIE NO4999

Ship (01333) 330246

The Toft, off A917 (High Street) towards harbour; KY9 1DT Recently refurbished and in great position for enjoying a drink overlooking the sandy bay; bar and two restaurants (one upstairs), generally well liked food, friendly service; seats on terrace (own bar) looking out to stone granary and pier, maybe back cricket, six boutique-style bedrooms, open all day. *(Brian and Anna Marsden)*

ST ANDREWS NO5116

Central (01334) 478296

Market Street; KY16 9NU Traditional Victorian town-centre pub (Taylor Walker) with good choice of english and scottish beers from island servery, knowledgeable friendly staff, fair-priced pubby food from sandwiches up, busy mix of customers; pavement tables, open all day. *(Anon)*

INVERNESS-SHIRE

ARDGOUR NN0163

Inn at Ardgour (01855) 841225

From A82 follow signs for Strontian A861 and take Corran Ferry across loch to the inn – ferry does not sail over Christmas period; PH33 7AA Traditional fairly remote roadside inn by Corran Ferry slipway; enjoyable food and decent beer and whisky choice, friendly accommodating staff, restaurant; children welcome, a few tables outside, fine Loch Linnhe views, clean bedrooms, open all day. *(Eddie Edwards)*

AVIEMORE NH8612

Cairngorm (01479) 810233

Grampian Road (A9); PH22 1PE Large flagstoned bar in traditional hotel, lively and friendly, with prompt helpful service, good value food all day from wide-ranging menu using local produce, Cairngorm ales and good choice of other drinks, tartan-walled and carpeted restaurant with skulls and antlers; live music, sports TV; children welcome, comfortable smart bedrooms (some with stunning views). *(Isobel Mackinlay)*

CARRBRIDGE NH9022

Cairn (01479) 841212

Main Road; PH23 3AS Welcoming tartan-carpeted, traditionally furnished hotel bar, enjoyable pubby food using local produce, well kept ales such as Black Isle, Cairngorm and Highland, old local pictures, warm coal fire, separate more formal dining room; pool and sports TV; children and dogs welcome, white metal seats and tables out in front, seven comfortable bedrooms, open all day. *(Neil Allen)*

DORES NH5934

★ Dores (01463) 751203

B852 SW of Inverness; IV2 6TR Traditional country pub with exposed stone walls and low ceilings in delightful spot on the shore of Loch Ness; small attractive bar on right with two or three well kept changing scottish ales, daily newspapers, good interesting food (pub favourites too) at affordable prices in two-part dining area to the left, friendly staff; children and dogs welcome, sheltered front garden, more tables out behind taking in the spectacular view, open (and food) all day. *(the Dutchman)*

FORT WILLIAM NN1274

Ben Nevis Inn (01397) 701227

N off A82: Achintee; PH33 6TE Roomy, well converted, raftered stone barn in stunning spot by path up to Ben Nevis, good

---

We mention bottled beers and spirits only if there is something unusual about them – imported belgian real ales, say, or dozens of malt whiskies; so do please let us know about them in your reports.

mainly straightforward food (lots of walkers so best to book), ales such as Cairngorm and Isle of Skye, prompt cheery service, bare-boards dining area with steps up to bar; live music (Tues in summer, first and third Thurs in winter); children welcome, no dogs, seats out at front and back, bunkhouse below, open all day Apr-Oct, otherwise closed Mon-Weds. *(Anon)*

GLEN SHIEL   NH0711
★ **Cluanie Inn** (01320) 340238
A87 Invergarry–Kyle of Lochalsh, on Loch Cluanie; IV63 7YW Welcoming inn in lovely isolated setting by Loch Cluanie, stunning views, friendly table service for drinks including well kept Isle of Skye, fine malt range, big helpings of enjoyable food (good local game and salmon) in three knocked-together rooms with dining chairs around polished tables, overspill into restaurant, warm log fire, chatty parrots in lobby – watch your fingers; children allowed, dogs too (owners have several of their own), big comfortable pine-furnished modern bedrooms, self-catering club house, great breakfasts (non-residents welcome), open all day. *(Neil Allen)*

GLENFINNAN   NM9080
Glenfinnan House (01397) 722235
Take A830 off A32 to Glenfinnan, turn left after Glenfinnan Monument Visitors' Centre; PH37 4LT Beautifully placed 18th-c hotel by Loch Shiel, traditional bar with well kept ales and over 50 whiskies, good well presented food including fish/seafood dishes and local venison, restaurant, some live folk music; lawns down to the water, comfortable bedrooms, may be closed in winter. *(M J Winterton)*

GLENUIG   NM6576
Glenuig Inn (01687) 470219
A861 SW of Lochailort, off A830 Fort William–Mallaig; PH38 4NG Friendly refurbished bar on picturesque bay, enjoyable locally sourced all-day food including some from next-door smokery, well kept Cairngorm ales and a scottish cider on tap, lots of bottled beers and good range of whiskies, woodburner in dining room; dogs welcome, bedrooms in adjoining block, also bunkhouse popular with walkers and divers, moorings for visiting yachts, open all day. *(Nick Sharpe)*

INVERIE   NG7500
★ **Old Forge** (01687) 462267
Park in Mallaig for ferry; PH41 4PL Utterly remote waterside stone pub with stunning views across Loch Nevis; comfortable mix of old furnishings, lots of charts and sailing prints, open fire, buoyant atmosphere, good reasonably priced bar food including fresh seafood and good venison burgers, two well kept changing ales in season such as local Glenfinnan, lots of whiskies and good wine choice, restaurant

extension, occasional live music and ceilidhs (instruments provided), the snag is getting there – boat (jetty moorings and new pier), Mallaig foot ferry six times a day (four in winter), or 15-mile walk through Knoydart from nearest road; children and dogs welcome, two bedrooms (get booked early), open all day summer. *(David Crook, R Anderson)*

INVERMORISTON   NH4216
Glenmoriston Arms (01320) 351206
A82/A887; IV63 7YA Small civilised hotel dating in part from 1740 when it was a drovers' inn, tartan-carpeted bar with open fire and big old stag's head, neatly laid out restaurant with antique rifles, well kept beer and over 100 malt whiskies, enjoyable food from lunchtime sandwiches up, friendly staff; handy for Loch Ness, ten bedrooms (three in converted outbuilding). *(Nick Sharpe)*

INVERNESS   NH6645
Kings Highway (01463) 251830
Church Street; IV1 1EN A Wetherspoons Lodge in former 19th-c hotel; plenty of seating in comfortable open-plan interior, up to ten real ales and their usual well priced food including good fish and chips; TVs, free wi-fi; children welcome, 27 refurbished bedrooms, open all day from 7am for breakfast, handy for station. *(Edna Jones)*

INVERNESS   NH6645
Number 27 (01463) 241999
Castle Street; IV2 3DU Busy pub opposite the castle, cheery welcoming staff, plenty of draught and bottled beers, good choice of well prepared food at reasonable prices, restaurant at back; open all day. *(The Dutchman)*

INVERNESS   NH6645
Phoenix Ale House (01463) 240300
Academy Street; IV1 1LX Bare-boards 1890s bar refurbished under new owners but keeping the fine oval servery with its spittoon, up to ten real ales and enjoyable well priced food, adjoining dining room; sports TV; open (and food) all day. *(Pat and Stewart Gordon)*

MALLAIG   NM6796
Steam (01687) 462002
Davies Brae; PH41 4PU Refurbished Victorian inn run by mother and daughter, good choice of food including freshly landed fish (takeaway menu too), speedy service, bar with open fire and pool, split-level restaurant with high-backed dark leather chairs around pale tables on floorboards; live music; children and dogs welcome (not in bedrooms), tables in back garden, five bedrooms. *(Isobel Mackinlay)*

ONICH   NN0263
Four Seasons (01855) 821393
Off A82, signed for Inchree, N of village; PH33 6SE Wooden building

– part of Inchree holiday complex; bare-boards bar with cushioned wall benches, dining area with unusual central log fire, up to three scottish ales and decent choice of whiskies, generous varied evening food at reasonable prices, friendly helpful staff, local maps and guidebooks for sale, daily weather forecast and free wi-fi; children (till 8.30pm) and dogs welcome, hostel, lodge and chalet accommodation, handy for Corran Ferry, open all day in season (when can be very busy), check winter opening. *(Eddie Edwards)*

KINCARDINESHIRE

FETTERCAIRN   NO6573

Ramsay Arms (01561) 340334
Burnside Road; AB30 1XX Hotel with decent food under newish chef in tartan-carpeted bar and smart oak-panelled restaurant, friendly service, well kept ales and several malts including the local Fettercairn; children welcome, picnic-sets in garden, attractive village (liked by Queen Victoria who stayed at the hotel), 12 comfortable bedrooms, good breakfast. *(Anne and Ben Smith)*

STONEHAVEN   NO8785

Marine Hotel (01569) 762155
Shore Head; AB39 2JY Popular harbourside pub with six well kept ales including own Dunnottar brews, over 170 bottled belgian beers and plenty of whiskies, good food especially local fish/seafood, efficient service, large stripped-stone bar with log fire in cosy side room, upstairs sea-view restaurant; live acoustic music last Thurs of month; children welcome, pavement tables, bedrooms, open all day (till 1am Fri, Sat). *(Robert Watt)*

KINROSS-SHIRE

KINNESSWOOD   NO1801

Well Country Inn (01592) 840444
A911; Scotlandwell; KY13 9JA Old pub in centre of village, comfortable and welcoming, with good selection of scottish ales, decent wines and enjoyable food served by pleasant helpful staff, main bar with areas off, small restaurant; children welcome, nine bedrooms (six in separate annexe). *(J V Dadswell)*

KIRKCUDBRIGHTSHIRE

GATEHOUSE OF FLEET   NX6056

Masonic Arms (01557) 814335
Ann Street; off B727; DG7 2HU Spacious dining pub with comfortable two-room pubby bar, traditional seating, pictures on timbered walls, plates on delft shelf, stuffed fish above brick fireplace, a couple of real ales and good choice of malts, enjoyable food in bar and contemporary restaurant, tapas night Tues, spanish set menu Fri, attractive terracotta-tiled conservatory with cane furniture;

background music (live Thurs), quiz Weds, free wi-fi; children and dogs welcome, picnic-sets under parasols in neatly kept sheltered garden, more seats in front, open all day. *(Anne and Ben Smith)*

GATEHOUSE OF FLEET   NX5956

Ship (01557) 814217
Fleet Street; DG7 2JT Late Victorian village inn on the banks of the River Fleet, popular food, Belhaven beers and good choice of malt whiskies, neatly kept refurbished interior with woodburner, pleasant service, restaurant with chairs and wall banquettes around wooden tables; waterside garden, comfortable bedrooms and tasty breakfasts; Dorothy Sayers wrote *Five Red Herrings* while staying here in the 1930s. *(Neil Allen)*

HAUGH OF URR   NX8066

★ Laurie Arms (01556) 660246
B794 N of Dalbeattie; Main Street; DG7 3YA Neatly kept and attractively decorated 19th-c pub with good local atmosphere, traditional furnishings in log-fire bar with steps up to similar area, restaurant with napery, tasty food from bar snacks to steaks, good changing real ales and decent wines by the glass, welcoming attentive service, games room with darts, pool and juke box, splendid Bamforth comic postcards in the gents'; tables out at front and picnic-sets on sheltered terrace behind, open all day (and for food) weekends; up for sale as we went to press. *(Anon)*

KIRKCUDBRIGHT   NX6850

Selkirk Arms (01557) 330402
High Street; DG6 4JG Comfortable well run 18th-c hotel in pleasant spot by mouth of the Dee, simple locals' front bar (own street entrance), partitioned high-ceilinged and tartan-carpeted lounge with upholstered armchairs, wall banquettes and paintings for sale, ales including a house beer from local Sulwath, enjoyable food in bistro and restaurant from pub standards up, efficient service; background music, TV; children (not in bar) and dogs welcome, smart wooden furniture under blue parasols in neat garden with 15th-c font, 16 comfortable bedrooms, open all day. *(R A and E J Harkness)*

LANARKSHIRE

BALMAHA   NS4290

Oak Tree (01360) 870357
B837; G63 0JQ Family-run slate-clad inn on Loch Lomond's quiet side, beams, timbers and panelling, pubby bar with lots of old photographs, farm tools and collection of grandfather clocks, log fire, good choice of enjoyable food from sandwiches and snacks up, scottish ales (own brew-house being built), good whisky selection, restaurant and new coffee shop and ice-cream parlour; children welcome, plenty of tables out

around ancient oak tree, popular with West Highland Way walkers, seven attractive bedrooms, two bunkhouses and four cottages. *(Mungo Shipley)*

BIGGAR   NT0437
Crown (01899) 220116
High Street (A702); ML12 6DL Friendly old pub with enjoyable food all day including home-made burgers and pizzas, Sun carvery, two well kept changing ales, open fire in beamed front bar, panelled lounge with old pictures, restaurant; fortnightly acoustic music, Thurs poker night; children welcome, open (and food) all day. *(David and Betty Gittins)*

GLASGOW   NS5767
Belle (0141) 339 2299
Great Western Road; G12 8HX Busy pub with wide mix of customers; leather-topped stools, modern and traditional chairs around all sorts of tables on polished wood floor, stags' heads and unusual mirrors on painted or exposed stone walls, open fire, american craft beers and european lagers; dogs welcome, tables and chairs on pavement and in tiny leafy back garden. *(Belinda May)*

GLASGOW   NS5965
Counting House (0141) 225 0160
St Vincent Place/George Square; G1 2DH Impressive Wetherspoons bank conversion, imposing interior rising into lofty richly decorated coffered ceiling culminating in great central dome, big windows, decorative glasswork, wall-safes, several areas with solidly comfortable seating, smaller rooms (former managers' offices) around perimeter, one like a well stocked library, a few themed with pictures and prints of historical characters, real ales from far and wide, bottled beers, and lots of malt whiskies, usual good value food all day; children welcome if eating, open 8am-midnight. *(Gus Swan)*

GLASGOW   NS5865
Drum & Monkey (0141) 221 6636
St Vincent Street; G2 5TF Lively and busy Nicholsons bank conversion with ornate ceiling, granite pillars and lots of carved mahogany, Caledonian and other beers from island bar, decent range of wines and good value food, pleasant staff, quieter back area; open all day. *(Gus Swan)*

GLASGOW   NS5865
Pot Still (0141) 333 0980
Hope Street; G2 2TH Comfortable and welcoming little pub with hundreds of malt whiskies (good value whisky of the month), traditional bare-boards interior with raised back area, button-back leather bench

seats, dark panelling, etched and stained glass, columns up to ornately corniced ceiling, four changing ales and interesting bottled beers from nice old-fashioned servery, knowledgeable friendly staff; silent fruit machine; open all day and can get packed. *(Frank Murphy, Dr J Barrie Jones)*

GLASGOW   NS5965
★ Sloans (0141) 221 8886
Argyle Arcade; G2 8BG Restored Grade A listed building over three floors, many original features including a fine mahogany staircase, etched glass, ornate woodwork and moulded ceilings, Caledonian Deuchars IPA and Kelburn, enjoyable food from sandwiches up in ground-floor bar-bistro and upstairs restaurant, friendly staff, events in impressive barrel-vaulted parquet-floored ballroom; children welcome, tables in courtyard, weekend market, open all day (till late Fri, Sat). *(Gus Swan)*

GLASGOW   NS5865
State (0141) 332 2159
Holland Street; G2 4NG High-ceilinged bar with marble pillars, lots of carved wood including handsome oak island servery, half a dozen or so well kept changing ales, bargain basic lunchtime food from sandwiches up (not weekends), some areas set for dining, good atmosphere and friendly staff, armchairs among other comfortable seats, coal-effect gas fire in big wooden fireplace, old prints and theatrical posters; background music (live weekends and comedy nights), silent sports TVs, games machine; open all day. *(Neil Allen)*

GLASGOW   NS5666
Tennents (0141) 339 7203
Byres Road; G12 8TN Big busy high-ceilinged Victorian corner pub near university, ornate plasterwork, panelling and paintings, traditional tables and chairs, stools and wall seating, a dozen well kept ales and keenly priced wines, wide range of good value food from sandwiches and baked potatoes up including bargain offers and Sunday breakfast, basement bar for weekend DJs and Mon quiz; sports TVs; open all day. *(Dr J Barrie Jones)*

GLASGOW   NS5666
Three Judges (0141) 337 3055
Dumbarton Road, opposite Byres Road; G11 6PR Traditional corner bar with up to nine quickly changing ales from small breweries far and wide (they get through several hundred a year), farm cider, pump clips on walls, friendly staff and locals, no food; live jazz Sun afternoons; dogs welcome, open all day. *(Neil Allen)*

We include some hotels with a good bar that offers facilities comparable to those of a pub.

MIDLOTHIAN

EDINBURGH   NT2473
Blue Blazer (0131) 229 5030
Spittal Street/Bread Street; EH3 9DX
Traditional two-room drinkers' pub with
up to eight interesting scottish ales, good
selection of rums, whiskies and gins too,
helpful knowledgeable staff, bare boards
and high ceilings, lots of black and white
photos, cartoons and drawings on the walls,
open fire; background and some live acoustic
music, TV; dogs welcome, open all day.
(Eric Larkham, Jeremy King)

EDINBURGH   NT2574
★Café Royal (0131) 556 1884
West Register Street; EH2 2AA Opulent
building's dazzling Victorian baroque
interior – a must for anyone visiting the
city says one reader; floors and stairway
laid with marble, chandeliers hanging
from magnificent plasterwork ceilings,
superb series of Doulton tilework portraits
of historical innovators (Watt, Faraday,
Stephenson, Caxton, Benjamin Franklin and
Robert Peel), substantial island bar serving
well kept Broughton Coulsons EPA and seven
guests, several wines by the glass and 40
malts, very well liked food with emphasis
on fresh seafood, good friendly service, the
restaurant's stained glass is also worth a look
(children welcome here); background music
and games machine; open all day (till 1am
Fri, Sat); can get very busy. *(Jeremy King, Pat
and Stewart Gordon, the Dutchman, Ken Richards,
Eric Larkham, Barry Collett)*

EDINBURGH   NT2471
★Canny Man's (0131) 447 1484
*Morningside Road; aka Volunteer
Arms; EH10 4QU* Utterly individual and
distinctive, and always busy; saloon, lounge
and snug with fascinating bric-a-brac, ceiling
papered with sheet music, huge range of
appetising open sandwiches, lots of whiskies,
good wines and well kept ales such as
Caledonian and Timothy Taylors Landlord,
efficient friendly service; no credit cards,
mobile phones or backpackers; children
welcome, courtyard tables. *(Pat and Stewart
Gordon, Ken Richards)*

EDINBURGH   NT2573
Deacon Brodies (0131) 225 6531
Lawnmarket; EH1 2NT Commemorating
the notorious highwayman town councillor
who was eventually hanged on the scaffold
he'd designed; very busy, ornately high-
ceilinged city bar, well kept Belhaven and
Caledonian from long counter, decent whisky
selection, good choice of reasonably priced
food in upstairs dining lounge; background
music, TV; pavement seating. *(Anon)*

EDINBURGH   NT2573
Doric (0131) 225 1084
Market Street; EH1 1DE Welcoming 17th-c
pub-restaurant with plenty of atmosphere,
simple furnishings in small bar with wood
floor and lots of pictures, good range of
changing ales and bottled beers, 50 single
malts, friendly young staff, popular food
(must book) in upstairs wine bar (children
welcome) and bistro; handy for Waverley
station, open all day. *(Dr Peter D Smart)*

EDINBURGH   NT2573
Ensign Ewart (0131) 225 7440
*Lawnmarket, Royal Mile; last pub on
right before castle; EH1 2PE* Charming
dimly lit old-world pub handy for castle (so
gets busy), beams peppered with brasses,
huge painting of Ewart at Waterloo capturing
french standard, assorted furniture including
elbow tables, well kept Caledonian ales and
plenty of whiskies, straightforward bar food;
background music, games machine, keypad
entry to lavatories, live music five nights a
week; open all day. *(Gus Swan)*

EDINBURGH   NT2573
★Halfway House (0131) 225 7101
*Fleshmarket Close (steps between
Cockburn Street and Market Street,
opposite Waverley station); EH1 1BX*
Tiny one-room pub off steep steps, part
carpeted, part tiled, with a few small tables
and high-backed settles, lots of prints
(some golf and railway themes), four well
kept scottish ales (third-of-a-pint glasses
available), good range of malt whiskies,
short choice of decent cheap, friendly staff;
dogs welcome, open (and food) all day.
(Comus and Sarah Elliott, Dr J Barrie Jones)

EDINBURGH   NT2473
Hanging Bat (0131) 229 0759
Lothian Road; EH3 9AB Modern bar on
three levels with own microbrewery, fine
selection of craft beers and real ales, over
100 bottled beers and good range of wines
and gins, barbecue-style food; dogs welcome,
children till 8pm, open (and food) all day.
(Eric Larkham)

EDINBURGH   NT2573
Inn on the Mile (0131) 556 9940
High Street; EH1 1LL Centrally placed
pub-restaurant-boutique hotel in former
bank, long high-ceilinged bar with booth
seating, good selection of beers such as
BrewDog, Caledonian, Harviestoun and Innis
& Gunn, also a house beer (Mile Ale), plenty
of wines, whiskies and cocktails, well priced
food from panini to hearty helpings of pubby
food, good friendly service; live music and
quiz nights, big screens for sport, free wi-fi;
children welcome, a few seats outside, nine

If we know a pub has an outdoor play area for children, we mention it.

bedrooms, open all day (till 1am Fri, Sat when it can be lively). *(Nigel and Jean Eames)*

EDINBURGH   NT2573
Jolly Judge (0131) 225 2669
James Court, by 495 Lawnmarket; EH1 2PB Small comfortable basement of 16th-c tenement with interesting fruit- and flower-painted wooden ceiling, welcoming relaxed atmosphere, two changing ales and good range of malts, lunchtime bar meals, log fire; no children, open all day. *(Giles and Annie Francis)*

EDINBURGH   NT2676
Kings Wark (0131) 554 9260
The Shore, Leith; EH6 6QU Enjoyable old bare-boards pub on Leith's restored waterfront; plenty of atmosphere in stripped-stone candlelit interior, good selection of well kept ales, interesting modern cooking including popular Sunday breakfasts, good value wines; seats outside, open all day. *(Neil Allen)*

EDINBURGH   NT1968
Kinleith Arms (0131) 453 3214
Lanark Road (A70); EH14 5EN Friendly traditional local with well kept Caledonian ales and enjoyable good value pub food (seafood chowder recommended) and weekday early-bird menu; sports TV, darts; suntrap back garden; open all day. *(R T and J C Moggridge)*

EDINBURGH   NT2573
Sandy Bells (0131) 225 1156
Forrest Road; EH1 2QH Small unpretentious place popular for its nightly live folk music, eight scottish ales and wide choice of whiskies (including whisky of the month), simple food, good mix of customers and friendly atmosphere; open all day. *(Giles and Annie Francis)*

EDINBURGH   NT2374
Scran & Scallie (0131) 332 6281
Comely Bank Road; EH4 1DT Very good food here but also a proper bar serving scottish ales such as Fyne and Harviestoun, impressive range of whiskies and inventive house cocktails; simple modern furnishings with tweed and tartan fabrics, the odd fur throw and pale floorboards, sizeable dining area (and smaller room off) with mismatched wooden chairs around medley of tables, bare and painted brick walls, contemporary wallpaper and cream-coloured woodburner, staff are interested and helpful; children and dogs welcome, open all day weekends. *(Anne and Ben Smith)*

EDINBURGH   NT2872
Sheep Heid (0131) 661 7974
The Causeway, Duddingston; EH15 3QA Comfortably updated former coaching inn (part of the Village Pub & Kitchen chain) in lovely spot near King Arthur's Seat, long

history and some famous guests such as Mary, Queen of Scots, fine rounded servery in main room, well kept beers and good, enterprising food including children's menu, friendly young staff, attractive dining rooms, skittle alley; courtyard tables, open (and food) all day. *(Adrian Johnson)*

EDINBURGH   NT2574
Standing Order (0131) 225 4460
George Street; EH2 2LR Grand Wetherspoons bank conversion in three elegant Georgian houses, imposing columns, enormous main room with elaborate colourful ceiling, lots of tables, smaller side booths, other rooms including two with floor-to-ceiling bookshelves, comfortable clubby seats, Adam fireplace and portraits, wide range of real ales from long counter, bar food, gets very busy (particularly Sat night) but obliging staff cope well; weekend live music, sports TV, free wi-fi; children welcome, disabled facilities, open 8am-1am. *(R T and J C Moggridge)*

EDINBURGH   NT2574
★ Starbank (0131) 552 4141
Laverockbank Road, off Starbank Road, just off A901 Granton–Leith; EH5 3BZ Cheerful pub in a fine spot with terrific views over the Firth of Forth, long airy bare-boards bar with leather bench and tub seats, up to eight well kept ales and good choice of malt whiskies, interesting food (and set menus) in conservatory restaurant; background and some live music, sports TV, fruit machine; children welcome till 9pm if dining, dogs on leads, sheltered back terrace, parking on adjacent hilly street, open all day. *(Gus Swan)*

MORAYSHIRE
FINDHORN   NJ0464
Crown & Anchor (01309) 690243
Off A96; IV36 3YF Nice village setting adjacent to small sheltered harbour, enjoyable food including good fish/seafood specials, a couple of real ales and plenty of whiskies, woodburner in cosy bar; sports TV; children welcome (under-14s in conservatory and restaurant till 8pm), outside seating and smokers' shelter 'the Smokooterie', seven bedrooms, sand dune walks and good boating in Findhorn Bay, open all day. *(Martin and Alison Stainsby)*

PEEBLESSHIRE
INNERLEITHEN   NT3336
★ Traquair Arms (01896) 830229
B709, just off A72 Peebles–Galashiels; follow signs for Traquair House; EH44 6PD Modernised inn at heart of pretty borders village, one of the few places serving Traquair ale (produced in original oak vessels in 18th-c brewhouse at nearby Traquair House), also Caledonian Deuchars IPA and Timothy Taylors Landlord, 40 malt

whiskies, enjoyable italian-influenced food (all day weekends), main bar with warm open fire, another in relaxed bistro-style restaurant, good mix of customers; background music, TV; children welcome, dogs in bar, picnic-sets on neat back lawn, 14 bedrooms and six self-catering cottages, open all day. *(Isobel Mackinlay)*

PERTHSHIRE

BANKFOOT   NO0635
Bankfoot (01738) 787243
Main Street; PH1 4AB Traditional coaching inn dating from 1760, two bars and restaurant, well kept local ales and enjoyable food cooked by landlady, friendly helpful staff, open fires; live folk night Weds; dogs welcome, comfortable bedrooms, open all day weekends, closed lunchtimes Mon, Tues. *(Neil Allen)*

BLAIR ATHOLL   NN8765
★ Atholl Arms (01796) 481205
B8079; PH18 5SG Sizeable hotel with two cosy bar rooms (one beamed and tartan-carpeted), open fires, armchairs, sofas and traditional tables, chairs and benches, grand dining room with suit of armour and stag's head, four local Moulin ales, good well priced food all day using local salmon and meat, quick friendly service; 31 good value bedrooms, lovely setting near the castle *(Mungo Shipley)*

BRIG O' TURK   NN5306
★ Byre (01877) 376292
A821 Callander–Trossachs, just outside village; FK17 8HT Beautifully placed byre conversion with slate-floored log-fire bar and roomier high-raftered restaurant, popular food (best to book) including local game and fish, some imaginative dishes and Sun roasts, friendly helpful staff; picnic-sets out on gravel in front and at the back, boules piste, good walks, open all day, closed Jan. *(Mungo Shipley)*

DUNBLANE   NN7801
Tappit Hen (01786) 825226
Kirk Street; FK15 0AL Across close from cathedral, small drinkers' pub with five changing ales and good range of other drinks, friendly busy atmosphere; traditional music Tues; open all day (till 1am Fri, Sat). *(Les and Sandra Brown)*

DUNKELD   NO0243
Atholl Arms (01350) 727219
Atholl Street (A923); PH8 0AQ Sizeable Victorian hotel with comfortably furnished smallish bar and lounge, open fires, good choice of well kept ales such as Inveralmond, enjoyable food from varied menu including cullen skink and beef stovies, pleasant service; 17 bedrooms (some with views of River Tay). *(Anon)*

DUNNING   NO0114
Kirkstyle (01764) 684248
B9141, off A9 S of Perth; Kirkstyle Square; PH2 0RR Unpretentious 18th-c streamside pub with chatty regulars, log fire in snug bar, up to three real ales from across Britain and good choice of whiskies, enjoyable good value home-made food including some interesting specials (book in season), attentive friendly service, split-level stripped-stone back restaurant; background music; children welcome, dogs allowed in garden only, open all day weekends, closed Mon and Tues lunchtimes. *(Mungo Shipley)*

KENMORE   NN7745
★ Kenmore Hotel (01887) 830205
A827 W of Aberfeldy; PH15 2NU Civilised small hotel dating from the 16th c in pretty Loch Tay village; comfortable traditional front lounge with warm log fire and poem pencilled by Burns himself on the chimney breast, dozens of malts helpfully arranged alphabetically, polite uniformed staff, modern restaurant with balcony; back public bar and terrace overlooking River Tay with enjoyable food from lunchtime soup and sandwiches up (especially good grills), Inveralmond Ossian, decent wines by the glass; pool and winter darts, juke box, TV, fruit machine; children and dogs welcome, 40 good bedrooms plus luxury lodges, open all day. *(Belinda May)*

KILMAHOG   NN6008
★ Lade (01877) 330152
A84 just NW of Callander, by A821 junction; FK17 8HD Lively place with a strong scottish theme – traditional weekend music, real ale shop with over 190 bottled beers from regional microbreweries and their own-brewed WayLade ales; plenty of character in several cosy beamed areas with panelling and stripped stone, highland prints and works by local artists, 40 malt whiskies, enjoyable home-made food from bar snacks up, big-windowed restaurant, friendly staff; background music; children and dogs (in bar) welcome, terrace tables, pleasant garden with fish ponds, open all day (till 1am Fri, Sat). *(Pat and Stewart Gordon)*

PERTH   NO1223
Greyfriars (01738) 633036
South Street; PH2 8PG Small comfortable local in old part of town, a couple of well kept changing ales and good whisky/gin range, enjoyable lunchtime food (not Sun) in bar or little upstairs dining room, friendly welcoming staff; live music Weds (open mike) and Sat; open all day. *(Tony Scott)*

PITLOCHRY   NN9163
★ Killiecrankie Hotel (01796) 473220
Killiecrankie, off A9 N; PH16 5LG Comfortable splendidly placed country hotel with attractive panelled bar and airy conservatory, imaginative food, friendly

efficient service, well kept ales, fine range of malts and good choice of wines, restaurant; children in eating areas, extensive peaceful grounds with dramatic views, ten pretty bedrooms. *(Mr and Mrs J Watkins)*

PITLOCHRY NN9459
★**Moulin** (01796) 472196
Kirkmichael Road, Moulin; A924 NE of Pitlochry centre; PH16 5EH Attractive much-extended inn brewing its own good beers in stables across the street, decent wines by the glass and 45 malt whiskies, lively down-to-earth bar in oldest part with traditional character, smaller bare-boards room and bigger carpeted area with cushioned booths divided by stained-glass country scenes, well liked food, separate restaurant; bar billiards and a 1960s one-arm bandit; children and dogs (in bar) welcome, picnic-sets on gravel looking across to village kirk, good nearby walks, 15 comfortable bedrooms and two self-catering cottages, open all day. *(Johnston and Maureen Anderson, Barry Collett, Mr and Mrs J Watkins, Adrian Johnson)*

PITLOCHRY NN9358
Old Mill (01796) 474020
Mill Lane; PH16 5BH Welcoming family-run inn (former 19th-c watermill), enjoyable food from sandwiches and sharing plates up, four real ales including Strathbraan and good wine and whisky choice, friendly staff; regular live music, free wi-fi; courtyard tables by Moulin Burn, comfortable bedrooms, open (and food) all day. *(Susan Ingram)*

ROSS-SHIRE

BADACHRO NG7873
★**Badachro Inn** (01445) 741255
2.5 miles S of Gairloch village turn off A832 on to B8056, then after another 3.25 miles turn right in Badachro to the quay and inn; IV21 2AA Superbly positioned by Loch Gairloch with terrific views from decking down to water's edge, popular (especially summer) with mix of sailing visitors (free moorings) and chatty locals; welcoming bar with interesting photographs, An Teallach, Caledonian and a guest ale, about 30 malt whiskies and eight wines by the glass, quieter eating area with big log fire, dining conservatory overlooking bay, good reasonably priced food including locally smoked fish and seafood; background music; children and dogs welcome, one bedroom, open all day. *(The Dutchman, Edna Jones)*

FORTROSE NH7256
★**Anderson** (01381) 620236
Union Street, off A832; IV10 8TD Friendly enthusiastic american licensees at this seaside hotel with vast selection of international beers (one of the largest collections of bottled belgians in the

UK), also four well kept changing ales, Addlestone's cider and 250 malt whiskies, quite a few wines too, good food in homely bar and light airy dining room with open fire, board and puzzle-type games; background and live traditional music (every other Sun), knitting club and monthly quiz; children welcome, dogs in bar (resident dog and cat), seats out behind on gravel, nine bedrooms, open from 4pm (3pm Sun). *(Dr Peter Crawshaw)*

GAIRLOCH NG8075
Old Inn (01445) 712006
Just off A832/B8021; IV21 2BD Quietly positioned old drovers' inn by stream, own-brew beers and guests, decent wines by the glass and 20 malt whiskies, food (not Sun evening) including local fish and game, own smokery, relaxed locals' bar with traditional décor and woodburner, bistro/restaurant; background music (live Fri), TV, fruit machine; children and dogs welcome, picnic-sets out by trees, bedrooms, open all day till 1am (11pm Sun). *(Neil Allen)*

PLOCKTON NG8033
★**Plockton Inn** (01599) 544222
Innes Street; unconnected to Plockton Hotel; IV52 8TW Close to the harbour in this lovely village, congenial bustling atmosphere even in winter, good well priced food with emphasis on local fish/seafood (some from own back smokery), friendly efficient service, well kept changing beers and good range of malts, lively public bar with traditional music Thurs (also Tues in summer); seats out on decking, 14 bedrooms (seven in annexe over road), good breakfast. *(Neil Allen)*

SHIEL BRIDGE NG9319
Kintail Lodge (01599) 511275
A87, N of Shiel Bridge; IV40 8HL Lots of varnished wood in large plain bar adjoining hotel, convivial bustle in season, Isle of Skye Red and plenty of malt whiskies, particularly good food (making the most of top quality local produce) from same kitchen as attractive restaurant and conservatory with magnificent view down Loch Duich to Skye, friendly efficient service; 12 comfortable bedrooms, bunkhouse, good breakfast, dogs welcome. *(Anon)*

ULLAPOOL NH1293
★**Ceilidh Place** (01854) 612103
West Argyle Street; IV26 2TY Pretty white house and more arty café-bar than pub with gallery, bookshop and coffee shop; conservatory-style main area with mix of dining chairs around dark wood tables, cosy bar and other rooms filled with armchairs, sofas and scatter-cushioned wall seats, rugs on floors, woodburner, a beer from An Teallach, lots of wines by the glass and 75 malt whiskies, tasty food (something available all day); regular jazz, folk and

classical music; children welcome (but must leave bar by 7pm), tables on front terrace looking over houses to distant hills beyond natural harbour, comfortable bedrooms, open all day, closed Jan. *(Isobel Mackinlay, Mary Kirkwood)*

ULLAPOOL NH1294
Morefield Motel (01854) 612161
A835 N edge of town; IV26 2TQ Modern family-run place, clean and bright, with cheerful L-shaped lounge bar, reliably good food including local fish and seafood, well kept changing ales, decent wines and over 50 malt whiskies, large conservatory; background music, pool and darts; children welcome, terrace tables, bedrooms, open all day. *(Anon)*

ROXBURGHSHIRE

KELSO NT7234
Cobbles (01573) 223548
Bowmont Street; TD5 7JH Small comfortably refurbished 19th-c dining pub just off the main square, friendly and well run with good range of food from pub standards to more enterprising dishes, brewery tap for local Tempest ales, decent wines and malts from end bar, open fire and pubby furnishings in bar, elegantly furnished dining room with overspill room upstairs; folk music Fri evening; children welcome, disabled facilities, open all day. *(Neil Allen)*

KIRK YETHOLM NT8328
Border (01573) 420237
Village signposted off B6352/B6401 crossroads, SE of Kelso; The Green; TD5 8PQ Welcoming comfortable hotel facing village green, unpretentious bar with beams, flagstones and log fire, snug side rooms, two or three changing scottish ales and numerous whiskies, good fairly priced home-made food from snacks up, spacious dining room with fishing theme, lounge with another fire and neat conservatory; background music; children welcome, dogs in bar, sheltered back terrace, five bedrooms, open all day. *(John and Sylvia Harrop)*

ST BOSWELLS NT5930
Buccleuch Arms (01835) 822243
A68 just S of Newtown St Boswells; TD6 0EW Civilised 19th-c sandstone hotel opposite village green; bar, comfortable lounge and bistro, good popular food promptly served by friendly staff, two or three changing real ales, open fires; children and dogs welcome, tables in attractive garden behind, 19 bedrooms, open (and food) all day. *(Pat and Stewart Gordon, Martin Day)*

SELKIRKSHIRE

MOUNTBENGER NT3324
Gordon Arms (01750) 82261
A708/B709; TD7 5LE Nice old pub under

enthusiastic licensees – an oasis in these empty moorlands; simply furnished public bar and lounge area, woodburner, Scottish Borders Game Bird and a guest ale, enjoyable reasonably priced pubby food cooked by landlord, good regular traditional music including open sessions (there's a recording studio on site); free wi-fi; children and dogs welcome, six comfortable bedrooms, good walking country, open all day in summer (shuts Mon-Weds winter). *(Charles Mason)*

STIRLINGSHIRE

DRYMEN NS4788
Winnock (01360) 660245
Just off A811; The Square; G63 0BL Best Western's big modern split-level stripped-stone and beamed lounge bar, blazing log fires, leather sofas and easy chairs, well kept Caledonian Deuchars IPA and good choice of malt whiskies, wide choice of well thought-of food, quick service from neat helpful young staff, steps down to restaurant area, airy conservatory; background music; large garden, 73 comfortable bedrooms. *(Nick Sharpe)*

STRATHCLYDE

CAIRNDOW NN1810
Stagecoach (01499) 600286
Just off and signed from A83; PA26 8BN Modernised old inn run by same family for over 40 years and in lovely setting overlooking Loch Fyne; good local fish and seasonal produce in bar and restaurant, Fyne ales and plenty of whiskies, efficient friendly service; live music and quiz nights; children welcome, garden picnic-sets, 19 bedrooms (some in separate building with balconies taking in the view), open (and food) all day. *(Darren and Jane Staniforth)*

SUTHERLAND

KYLESKU NC2333
★ Kylesku Hotel (01971) 502231
A894, S side of former ferry crossing; IV27 4HW Remote NW hotel on shores of Loch Glendhu, pleasant tartan-carpeted bar facing glorious mountain and loch view, with seals and red-throated divers often in sight (tables outside too); wonderfully fresh seafood along with other locally sourced food, friendly accommodating staff, well kept ales such as An Teallach, good wines by the glass and numerous malt whiskies, more expensive loch-view bedroom extension; children welcome, eight comfortable bedrooms, good boat trips from hotel slipway, closed in the winter. *(Neil and Angela Huxter)*

LAIRG NC5224
★ Crask Inn (01549) 411241
A836 13 miles N towards Altnaharra; IV27 4AB Remote homely inn on single-track road through peaceful moorland, good

simple food cooked by landlady including own lamb (the friendly hard-working licensees keep sheep on this working croft), comfortably basic bar with large peat stove to dry the sheepdogs (other dogs welcome), a summer real ale, Black Isle bottled beers in winter, interesting books, piano, pleasant separate dining room; three bedrooms (lights out when generator goes off), simple nearby bunkhouse. *(Dr Peter Crawshaw)*

LOCHINVER   NC0922
Caberfeidh (01571) 844321
Culag Road (A837); IV27 4JY Delightful lochside position and lovely views; cosy bar, conservatory and more formal restaurant, shortish menu with emphasis on local seafood (tapas too), well kept beers including Caledonian, charming landlord; dogs welcome, small harbourside garden, open all day (shut Mon). *(Anne and Ben Smith)*

WEST LOTHIAN
BO'NESS   NS9981
Corbie (01506) 825307
A904 Corbiehall; EH51 0AS Refurbished pub with up to six well kept local ales including own Kinneil brewed behind, 70 malt whiskies (tasting evenings) and enjoyable uncomplicated food at very reasonable prices, friendly staff; children welcome, garden with play area, open (and food) all day. *(John Grace)*

LINLITHGOW   NS0077
★ Four Marys (01506) 842171
High Street; 2 miles from M9 junction 3 (and little further from junction 4) – town signposted; EH49 7ED Evocative 16th-c place – named after Mary, Queen of Scots' four ladies-in-waiting – and filled with mementoes of the ill-fated queen including pictures and written records, pieces of bed curtain and clothing, even a facsimile of her death-mask; neatly kept L-shaped room with mahogany dining chairs around stripped period and antique tables, attractive old corner cupboards, elaborate Victorian dresser serving as part of the bar, mainly stripped-stone walls with some remarkable masonry in the inner area, up to nine well kept ales (third-of-a-pint taster glasses, May, Oct festivals), good range of malt whiskies, fair value food including good cullen skink, cheery landlord and courteous staff; background music; children in dining area until 9.30pm, heated outdoor smoking area, difficult parking, open all day (till 1am Fri, Sat). *(Giles and Annie Francis)*

QUEENSFERRY   NT1378
Hawes (031) 331 1990
Newhalls Road; EH30 9TA Vintage Inn renovation featured famously in Robert Louis Stevenson's *Kidnapped*, a great spot for tourists with fine views of the Forth bridges (one rail bridge support in the car

park); wide choice of enjoyable food in roomy separate dining areas, friendly efficient staff, plenty of wines by the glass, Caledonian Deuchars IPA and two other ales; children welcome, tables on back lawn with play area, 14 bedrooms, open (and food) all day. *(Barry Collett, Adrian Johnson)*

WIGTOWNSHIRE
BLADNOCH   NX4254
Bladnoch Inn (01988) 402200
Corner of A714 and B7005; DG8 9AB Cheerful bar, neat and bright, with eating area, enjoyable well priced pubby food from sandwiches up, Sun carvery, a beer such as Belhaven, friendly obliging service, restaurant; background music; children and dogs welcome, picturesque riverside setting across from Bladnoch distillery (tours), four good value bedrooms, open all day. *(Pat and Stewart Gordon)*

PORTPATRICK   NW9954
Crown (01776) 810261
North Crescent; DG9 8SX Popular seafront hotel in delightful harbourside village, enjoyable reasonably priced food all day including notable seafood, friendly prompt service, several dozen malts, decent wines by the glass, warm fire in rambling traditional bar with cosy corners, sewing machine tables, old photographs and posters, attractively decorated early 20th-c dining room opening through conservatory into sheltered back garden; background music, TV; children and dogs welcome, tables out in front. *(Belinda May)*

STRANRAER   NX0660
Grapes (01776) 703386
Bridge Street; DG9 7HY Popular and welcoming 19th-c local, simple and old-fashioned with 1940s feel, a couple of well kept ales and over 60 malts, regular traditional music in bar or upstairs room; dogs welcome, courtyard seating, open all day. *(Gus Swan)*

Scottish Islands
ARRAN
CATACOL   NR9049
Catacol Bay (01770) 830231
A841; KA27 8HN Unpretentious hotel rather than pub run by same family for 30 years and in wonderful setting yards from the sea (own mooring) with bay window looking across to Kintyre – cosy when gales blow; simple bar with woodburning stove, ales from Belhaven, Houston and Timothy Taylors, pool, all-day food (Sunday buffet until 4pm) and hearty breakfasts; tables outside and children's area, six simple bedrooms with washbasins – the ones at the front have the view. *(Anne and Ben Smith)*

BARRA

CASTLEBAY   NL6698
Castlebay Hotel (01871) 810223
*By aeroplane from Glasgow or ferry
from Oban; HS9 5XD* Cheerful bar – once
popular with those in the herring trade –
next to hotel, popular meeting place, regular
local musicians and comedians, comfortable
seating, two-level restaurant (carpeted or
with wooden flooring) with great harbour
view, popular food, pleasant young staff;
decent bedrooms (dogs allowed). *(Anon)*

BUTE

PORT BANNATYNE   NS0767
Port Royal (01700) 505073
Marine Road; PA20 0LW Cheerful
stone-built place (more restaurant than
pub) looking across sea to Argyll, interior
reworked as pre-revolution russian tavern
with bare boards, painted timbers and
tapestries, food including russian dishes
and good seafood, choice of russian beers
and vodkas too, open fire, candles and wild
flowers; two annexe bedrooms, substantial
breakfast, closed lunchtimes and all day Tues.
(Mungo Shipley)

ROTHESAY   NS0864
Black Bull (01700) 502366
W Princes Street; PA20 9AF Traditional
comfortably furnished pub with enjoyable
reasonably priced food and two well kept
ales, good attentive service, fine display of
old Clyde steamers; opposite pier with its
wonderfully restored Victorian gents', open
all day. *(Dennis Jones)*

CUMBRAE

MILLPORT   NS1554
Frasers (01475) 530518
Cardiff Street; KA28 0AS Small pub set
just back from the harbour, bar and lounge
with old paddle steamer pictures, open fire,
enjoyable very reasonably priced pubby food,
a couple of beers from Houston, friendly staff;
children welcome, no dogs, tables in yard
behind, open all day. *(Dave Braisted)*

HARRIS

TARBERT   NB1500
★ Harris Hotel (01859) 502154
Scott Road; HS3 3DL Large hotel in same
family for over a century, nice small panelled
bar with welcoming feel, local Hebridean
ales, rare malt whiskies, interesting food
with modern touches using best local meat

and shellfish and ranging from lunchtime
baguettes through afternoon teas and
up, smart but relaxed airy restaurant; 23
comfortable bedrooms (some up narrow
stairs) with sea views. *(Anne and Ben Smith)*

ISLAY

BOWMORE   NR3159
★ Harbour Inn (01496) 810330
The Square; PA43 7JR Fine inn with
traditional local bar and plenty of regulars,
lovely harbour and loch views from attractive
dining room, good local fish and seafood,
proper afternoon teas, pleasant service,
nice choice of wines and Islay malts
including attractively priced rarities, warmly
welcoming service; good value bedrooms with
views. *(Anon)*

PORT ASKAIG   NR4369
Port Askaig (01496) 840245
A846, by port; PA46 7RD Family-run inn
on shores of Sound of Islay overlooking ferry
pier; snug, tartan-carpeted original bar with
good range of malt whiskies, local bottled
ales, popular all-day bar food, neat bistro
restaurant with view of the sea and ferries,
traditional residents' lounge; dogs welcome
in bar, plenty of picnic-sets on grass, eight
clean, neat bedrooms plus apartment, open
all day. *(Neil Allen)*

PORT CHARLOTTE   NR2558
★ Port Charlotte Hotel
(01496) 850360 *Main Street; PA48 7TU*
Most beautiful of Islay's Georgian villages
and in lovely position with sweeping views
over Loch Indaal, exceptional collection of
about 150 Islay malts including rare ones,
two changing local ales, decent wines by the
glass, good food using local meat, game and
seafood, civilised bare-boards pubby bar with
padded wall seats, open fire and modern
art, comfortable back bar, neatly kept
separate restaurant and roomy conservatory
(overlooking beach); regular traditional live
music; children welcome, garden tables, near
sandy beach, ten attractive bedrooms (nine
with sea view), open all day till 1am.
(Anne and Ben Smith, Neil Allen)

PORTNAHAVEN   NN1652
An Tighe Seinnse (01496) 860224
Queen Street; PA47 7SJ Friendly little end
of terrace harbourside pub tucked away in
this remote attractive fishing village, cosy bar
with room off, open fire, fair-priced tasty food
including local seafood, Belhaven keg beer
and bottled Islay ales, good choice of malts;
sports TV and occasional live music; can get
crowded, open all day. *(Neil Allen)*

Please tell us if any pub deserves to be upgraded to a featured entry – and why:
feedback@goodguides.com, or (no stamp needed) The Good Pub Guide,
FREEPOST RTJR-ZCYZ-RJZT, Perrymans Lane, Etchingham TN19 7DN.

JURA

CRAIGHOUSE   NR5266
Jura Hotel (01496) 820243
A846, opposite distillery; PA60 7XU
Family-run and in superb setting with view
over the Small Isles to the mainland, bar, two
lounges and restaurant and good, tasty food;
garden down to water's edge, 17 bedrooms,
most with sea view; camping by water's
edge. *(Anon)*

MULL

DERVAIG   NM4251
★ **Bellachroy** (01688) 400314
B8073; PA75 6QW Island's oldest inn
dating from 1608, pub and restaurant food
including local seafood, afternoon teas,
local ales, good choice of whiskies and wine,
traditional bar with darts, attractive dining
area, comfortable residents' lounge with
games and TV; children and dogs welcome,
covered outside area plus plenty of picnic-
sets, nice spot in sleepy lochside village,
six comfortable bedrooms, open all year.
(Chris Grant)

TOBERMORY   NM5055
Macdonald Arms (01688) 302011
Main Street; PA75 6NT Seafront hotel
very popular for its tasty low-priced food,
well kept Belhaven Best, basic décor and
furnishings and winter fire. *(Chris Grant)*

TOBERMORY   NM5055
Mishnish (01688) 302500
*Main Street – the yellow building;
PA75 6NU* Popular and lively place right
on the bay, dimly lit two-room bar with cask
tables, old photographs and nautical/fishing
bric-a-brac, woodburner, little snugs, well
kept Belhaven and Isle of Mull, enjoyable
bar food, can also eat in next-door Mishdish
restaurant or new italian restaurant upstairs;
background and live music, pool; beer garden
behind, 14 refurbished bedrooms (some with
sea view), good breakfast, open all day till late.
(Pat and Stewart Gordon)

ORKNEY

DOUNBY   HY3001
Merkister (01856) 771366
*Russland Road, by Harray Loch;
KW17 2LF* Fishing hotel in great location
on the loch shore, bar dominated by prize
catches, good food here and in evening
restaurant including hand-dived scallops and
local aberdeen angus steaks, local bottled
beers, good friendly service; 16 bedrooms,
open all day. *(Neil Allen)*

ST MARY'S   HY4700
Commodore (01856) 781788
A961; KW17 2RU Modern single-storey
building with stunning views over Scapa

Flow, bar with well kept Orkney beers, pool
and darts, highly enjoyable food using local
produce (takeaway dishes Fri, Sat evenings)
in contemporary restaurant with high-backed
dark leather dining chairs around wood block
tables on pale wooden flooring; open all day.
(Neil Allen)

WESTRAY   HY4348
Pierowall Hotel (01857) 677472
*Centre of Pierowall village, B9066;
KW17 2BZ* Comfortable pub-hotel near
ferry, friendly main bar largely given over
to eating, from sandwiches and light snacks
up including good freshly landed fish,
bottled Orkney beers and good choice of
malts,lounge bar with TV, pool room and
separate dining area; six bedrooms with bay
or hill views. *(Anon)*

SKYE

ARDVASAR   NG6303
Ardvasar Hotel (01471) 844223
*A851 at S of island, near Armadale pier;
IV45 8RS* Wonderful sea and mountain
views from this comfortable peacefully
placed white stone inn, charming owner
(will pick you up from the ferry) and friendly
efficient staff, good home-made food using
local fish and meat, lots of malt whiskies,
real ales including Isle of Skye, two bars
and games room; background music, TV;
children welcome in eating areas, tables
outside, lovely walks, ten bedrooms (front
ones overlook the sound), open all day.
(Dave Braisted)

CARBOST   NG3731
★ **Old Inn** (01478) 640205
B8009; IV47 8SR Little-changed
unpretentious waterside pub with stunning
views, well positioned for walkers and
climbers; simply furnished chatty bar with
exposed stone walls, bare-board or tiled
floors, open fire, Cuillin Pinnacle, Skye Ale
and a guest, traditional cider and quite a few
malt whiskies, tasty fair priced food using
local fish and highland meat; background
music (live Fri), darts and pool; children and
dogs welcome, picnic-sets on terrace by the
water, bedrooms and bunkhouse taking in
the views, Talisker distillery nearby, closed
afternoons in winter, otherwise open (and
food) all day. *(Isobel Mackinlay)*

DUNVEGAN   NG2547
Dunvegan (01470) 521497
A850/A863; IV55 8WA Early 19th-c inn
on the Duirnish peninsula; plenty of tables
in airy lounge bar, good enjoyable food from
baguettes up including local seafood, evening
restaurant (open Easter-Oct), conservatory
with superb loch and mountain views, warmly
friendly and helpful service, live music in
cellar bar (Thurs and Sat evenings) with
pool and snooker; waterfront garden, six
bedrooms and bunkhouse. *(Chris Grant)*

EDINBAINE   NG3451

Edinbaine (01470) 582414

*Just off A850, signed for Meadhan
a Bhaile; IV51 9PW* Friendly former
farmhouse with open fire and stove, exposed
stone walls, simply furnished bar with local
ales, airy dining room, attractively presented
good food including local fish and seafood;
regular live music; children and dogs
welcome. *(James Darkins)*

ISLE ORNSAY   NG7012

★ Eilean Iarmain (01471) 833332

*Off A851 Broadford–Armadale;
IV43 8QR* Small traditional bar at
smartly old-fashioned hotel in beautiful
location, friendly locals and staff, good
bar food using local produce and served
most of the day from same kitchen as
charming sea-view restaurant, Isle of Skye
real ale, good choice of vatted (blended)
malt whiskies including their own Gaelic
Whisky Collection, banquettes, open fire;
traditional background music; children
welcome, outside tables with spectacular
views, 16 very comfortable bedrooms, open
all day. *(Anne and Ben Smith)*

SOUTH UIST

LOCH CARNAN   NF8144

Orasay Inn (01870) 610298

*Signed off A865 S of Creagorry;
HS8 5PD* Lovely remote spot overlooking
sea, wonderful sunsets, friendly service,
tempting local fish/seafood and beef from
own herd in comfortable modern lounge
and conservatory-style restaurant, pleasant
public bar, straightforward furnishings
and décor; seats outside on raised decked
area, compact comfortable bedrooms – two
with own terrace, open all day at least in
summer. *(Anon)*

WALES

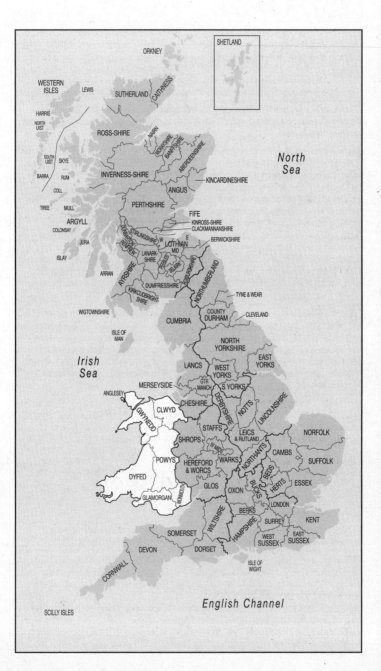

ORKNEY

SHETLAND

WESTERN ISLES

LEWIS

SUTHERLAND

CAITHNESS

HARRIS

NORTH UIST

ROSS-SHIRE

NAIRN

MORAYSHIRE

BANFFSHIRE

ABERDEENSHIRE

North Sea

SOUTH UIST

SKYE

BARRA

RUM

INVERNESS-SHIRE

COLL

KINCARDINESHIRE

TIREE

MULL

ANGUS

ARGYLL

PERTHSHIRE

FIFE

COLONSAY

KINROSS-SHIRE

CLACKMANNANSHIRE

JURA

STIRLINGSHIRE

DUNBARTON

W

LOTHIAN

BERWICKSHIRE

ISLAY

RENFREW

LANARK-SHIRE

MID

E

PEEBLES

SELKIRK

ARRAN

AYRSHIRE

ROXBURGHSHIRE

DUMFRIESSHIRE

NORTHUMBERLAND

KIRKCUDBRIGHT-SHIRE

TYNE & WEAR

WIGTOWNSHIRE

COUNTY DURHAM

CLEVELAND

ISLE OF MAN

CUMBRIA

Irish Sea

NORTH YORKSHIRE

LANCS

WEST YORKS

EAST YORKS

MERSEYSIDE

GTR MANCH

S YORKS

ANGLESEY

CHESHIRE

DERBYSHIRE

NOTTS

LINCOLNSHIRE

GWYNEDD

CLWYD

STAFFS

LEICS & RUTLAND

NORFOLK

SHROPS

W MIDS

NORTHANTS

CAMBS

POWYS

HEREFORD & WORCS

WARKS

SUFFOLK

DYFED

GLOS

OXON

BEDS

HERTS

ESSEX

GLAMORGAN

MONMOUTH

BUCKS

LONDON

WILTSHIRE

BERKS

SURREY

KENT

HAMPSHIRE

SOMERSET

WEST SUSSEX

EAST SUSSEX

DEVON

DORSET

ISLE OF WIGHT

CORNWALL

English Channel

SCILLY ISLES

KEY ★ Star Pub   🌟 Top Quality Food   🍺 Great Beer

🍷 Good Wines   £ Bargain Meals   🛏 Good Bedrooms   🍴 Serves Food

---

ANGLE   SM8703   Map 6

Old Point House £

(01646) 641205

Signed off B4320 in village, along long rough waterside track; SA71 5AS

Thoroughly unpretentious, welcoming seafarers' pub on the Pembrokeshire Coast Path, with quite a choice of food and waterside tables; bedrooms

In a picturesque spot, this quaint, simple place – known as the 'lifeboatman's local' – is run by a friendly landlord and his welcoming staff. The rooms have stacks of seafaring character, with numerous photographs and charts and some of the little windows and picnic-sets on the big gravelled terrace give charming views across the water. Until the 1980s the tiny spartan snug bar was the only public room: it has a small length of bar in one corner serving Evan Evans Cwrw and Felinfoel Dragons Heart on handpump, farm cider and several wines by the glass; also, two simple wood settles and a warming fire in a lovely old fireplace. There's also a lounge bar and a separate dining room; outside lavatories. Walks nearby are splendid; you can walk west from here around the peninsula to the beach at West Angle Bay. Do note that the road from Angle is unmade and gets cut off by spring tides about four times a year for a couple of hours.

🍴 As well as an excellent fish chowder, the popular pubby food includes sandwiches and baguettes, prawn cocktail, a curry of the day, vegetable stir-fry, barbecue spare ribs with their own special sauce, a daily pasta dish, chicken breast with ham and mushrooms in cream sauce, local rib-eye steak with tarragon butter and chips, and puddings such as banana bread and butter pudding with strawberries and apple crumble. *Benchmark main dish: beer-battered fish and chips £9.80. Two-course evening meal £17.00.*

Free house ~ Licensee Robert Noble ~ Real ale ~ Open 12-10 (11 Sat); 12-3, 6-10 Weds-Sun in winter; closed Mon and Tues in winter ~ Bar food 12.30-2.30, 6.30-8.30; no food except for residents Mon-Thurs Nov-Feb ~ Restaurant ~ Children welcome ~ Dogs allowed in bar and bedrooms ~ Wi-fi ~ Bedrooms: /£90 *Recommended by Stephen and Jean Curtis*

BEAUMARIS   SH6076   Map 6

Olde Bulls Head 🌟 🍷 🛏

(01248) 810329 ~ www.bullsheadinn.co.uk

Castle Street; LL58 8AP

Interesting historic inn of many faces including a rambling bar, stylish brasserie and restaurant; well equipped bedrooms

This roomy 15th-c inn has a delightful beamed bar that can't have changed much since Charles Dickens popped in for a drink in 1859. It's a rambling place with comfortable low-seated settles, leather-cushioned window seats and a good log fire and there are plenty of interesting reminders of the town's past such as a rare 17th-c brass water clock, a bloodthirsty crew of cutlasses and even an oak ducking stool tucked among the snug alcove; lots of copper and china jugs too. Kindly staff serve Bass, Hancocks HB and a guest such as AllGates Admiral on handpump. In contrast, the busy brasserie behind is lively and stylishly modern with around 14 wines by the glass, while the exceptionally good upstairs restaurant is an elegantly smart choice for a more formal meal and has a wine list that runs to 120 bottles. The entrance to the pretty courtyard is closed by a huge simple-hinged door that's an astonishing 3.3 metres wide and 4 metres high. The bedrooms in the inn are named after characters in Dickens's novels and are very well equipped; some are traditional, others more contemporary in style. They also have bedrooms in the Townhouse, an adjacent property with disabled access.

Enterprising modern food includes lunchtime sandwiches, hotpot of smoked haddock with tomatoes, cream and parmesan, blow-torched pork belly with garlic cream, blanched leeks and gin-soaked raisins, beer-battered and fennel seed hake with chips, cauliflower, butter bean and root vegetable fricassée with laverbread and smoked cheese scone, fillet of sea trout with fennel risotto, kohlrabi, confit lemon and ginger velouté, canon of lamb with salt-baked shoulder, goose fat potatoes and onion textures, and puddings such as apple and lime cheesecake with dehydrated apple sponge and basil ice-cream and treacle tart with glazed banana, clotted cream and walnut milk. *Benchmark main dish: slow-cooked lamb shank with rosemary mash £15.00. Two-course evening meal £22.00.*

Free house ~ Licensee David Robertson ~ Real ale ~ Open 11-11; 12-10.30 Sun ~ Bar food 12-2 (3 Sun), 6-9; Loft restaurant 12-2, 7 (6.30 Fri, Sat)-9.30 ~ Restaurant ~ Children welcome in China Bar only till 9pm ~ Dogs allowed in bar and bedrooms ~ Wi-fi ~ Bedrooms: $82.50/$105 *Recommended by Martin Jones, Toby Jones, Chris and Val Ramstedt*

COLWYN BAY

Pen-y-Bryn 🌟 ♀ 🍺

SH8478 Map 6

(01492) 533360 – www.brunningandprice.co.uk/penybryn
B5113 Llanwrst Road, on southern outskirts; when you see the pub, turn off into Wentworth Avenue for the car park; LL29 6DD

Spacious open-plan modern bungalow overlooking the bay, with reliable food all day, good range of drinks and obliging staff

Although the pub describes itself as looking rather like a medical centre from the front, the award-winning flowering tubs and hanging baskets are lovely and, inside, it's delightful. Extending around the three long sides of the bar counter, you'll find welcoming coal fires, oriental rugs on pale stripped boards, a mix of seating and well spaced tables, shelves of books, a profusion of pictures, big pot plants, careful lighting and dark green old-fashioned school radiators. A fine choice of drinks served by knowledgeable, perky young staff includes Phoenix Brunning & Price Original, Phoenix Tennis Elbow, Purple Moose Snowdonia Ale and three quickly changing guests on handpump, well chosen good value wines including 19 by the glass and 65 malt whiskies; board games and background music. The big windows at the back look over seats and tables on the terraces and in the sizeable garden and then out to sea and the Great Orme.

From a well judged menu, the contemporary dishes include sandwiches, peppered mackerel fillet with crème fraîche and apple and beetroot purée, home-made crabsticks with lemon gel and radish salad, king prawn linguine with spicy tomato and chorizo sauce, pea risotto with roasted asparagus, dried vine tomatoes and parmesan crisp, honey-roasted ham and free-range eggs, chargrilled chicken with feta and basil couscous, mediterranean vegetables and orange and chilli glaze, and puddings such as rhubarb panna cotta with stem ginger ice-cream and crumble and lemon meringue roulade with raspberry coulis and lemon sorbet. *Benchmark main dish: slow-braised lamb shoulder with dauphinoise potatoes and red wine sauce £16.95. Two-course evening meal £21.00.*

Brunning & Price ~ Manager Andrew Grant ~ Real ale ~ Open 11.30-11; 12-10.30 Sun ~
Bar food 12-9.30 (9 Sun) ~ Children welcome ~ Dogs allowed in bar ~ Wi-fi
Recommended by Chris and Val Ramstedt, W K Wood

CRICKHOWELL
SO2118 Map 6
Bear ★ ♀ ⌂
(01873) 810408 – www.bearhotel.co.uk
Brecon Road; A40; NP8 1BW

**Convivial and interesting inn, a splendid, old-fashioned bar area
warmed by a log fire and rewarding food; comfortable bedrooms**

Happily, everything about this delightful old inn is as good as ever and our
readers love the place. You can be sure of a genuinely warm welcome
from the friendly family who run it, the atmosphere is bustling and chatty
and both the food and drink are highly enjoyable. The heavily beamed lounge
has lots of little plush-seated bentwood armchairs and handsome cushioned
antique settles, fresh flowers on tables, and a window seat that looks down on
the market square. Next to the great roaring log fire are a big sofa and leather
easy chairs, on oak parquet flooring with rugs. Other antiques include a fine
oak dresser filled with pewter mugs and brassware, a longcase clock and
interesting prints. Brains Rev James, Wye Valley Butty Bach, Sharps Doom Bar
and a frequently changing guest on handpump, alongside 50 malt whiskies,
local ciders, vintage and late-bottled ports and unusual wines (with several by
the glass); disabled lavatories. This is a particularly appealing place to stay: the
older bedrooms in the main building have antiques; some of the refurbished
ones are in a country style and the luxury ones have hot tubs and four-poster
beds; breakfasts are excellent. Reception rooms, ably hosted by patient staff,
are comfortably furnished, and there are seats in the small garden.

From a seasonally changing menu, the good, popular food includes sandwiches and
baguettes, duck liver and Armagnac parfait with red onion marmalade, chicken
satay with peanut sauce, cumberland sausage ring with mash and gravy, cauliflower,
cheese and potato cake with red pepper and tomato sauce, jamaican-style flat rib of
beef with sweet potato fries, seared salmon with salsa verde, and puddings such as apple
and whimberry crumble and triple chocolate and pistachio brownie with chocolate
sauce. *Benchmark main dish: chicken with wild mushroom, marsala and peppercorn
sauce and sautéed potatoes £14.50. Two-course evening meal £20.00.*

Free house ~ Licensee Judy Hindmarsh ~ Real ale ~ Open 10am-11pm; 12-10.30 Sun ~
Bar food 12-9.30 ~ Restaurant ~ Children welcome but no under-6s in restaurant areas ~
Dogs allowed in bar and bedrooms ~ Wi-fi ~ Bedrooms: /$110 *Recommended by S Holder,
Mike and Mary Carter, Tom and Ruth Rees, B and M Kendall, Mike Beach*

DALE
SM8105 Map 6
Griffin
(01646) 636227 – www.griffininndale.co.uk
B4327, by sea on one-way system; SA62 3RB

**Friendly waterside pub with fresh fish and shellfish, local ales
and two attractive rooms**

A warmly friendly couple run this old pub right by the water; picnic-sets
on the front terrace make the most of the lovely estuary view, and
there's a pontoon, a sea wall and lovely coastal walks to either side. The two
imaginatively decorated rooms have open fires, wood panelling, traditional
red quarry tiles, an easy-going atmosphere and Brains Rev James, Buckleys
Best and Cwrw lâl Hâf Gwyn on handpump, six wines by the glass and malt
whiskies – including a welsh one; background music and board games.

The pub co-owns a local fishing boat, so the menu majors on fresh fish and shellfish: razor clams, scallops, calamari, prawns, bass, hake, john dory, pollock, haddock and cod. They also offer lunchtime baguettes, mackerel pâté, goats cheese tartlet, lasagne, burger with onion rings and relish, beef in ale pie, local gammon with free-range egg, and puddings such as fruit crumble and triple chocolate neapolitan. *Benchmark main dish: hake fillet with red pepper and chorizo sauce £19.95. Two-course evening meal £22.00.*

Free house ~ Licensees Sian Mathias and Simon Vickers ~ Real ale ~ Open 12-11; check website for times in winter ~ Bar food 12-3, 6-8.30; 12-3, 5-9 Aug ~ Restaurant ~ Children welcome ~ Wi-fi *Recommended by John and Enid, Harvey Brown*

EAST ABERTHAW
Blue Anchor 🍺

ST0366 Map 6

(01446) 750329 – www.blueanchoraberthaw.com
Village signed off B4265; CF62 3DD

Thatched character pub with cosy range of low-beamed little rooms, making a memorable spot for a drink

This is one of the oldest pubs in Wales, dating from 1380. It's an attractive, massive-walled building with a warren of low-beamed character rooms that lead off from the central servery: there are tiny doorways, open fires (including one in an inglenook with antique oak seats built into the stripped stonework) and other seats and tables worked into a series of chatty little alcoves. The more open front bar still has an ancient lime-ash floor and keeps Brains Bitter, Theakstons Old Peculier, Wadworths 6X and Wye Valley HPA on handpump, as well as farm cider and eight wines by the glass. Rustic seats shelter peacefully among tubs and troughs of flowers outside, with stone tables on a newer terrace. The pub can get very full in the evenings and on summer weekends. A path from here leads to the shingle flats of the estuary.

 Good, consistently popular food includes lunchtime baguettes, serrano ham-wrapped chicken and pistachio terrine with butternut squash and ginger salad, home-cured treacle-marinated salmon with pepper chutney, spinach and sun-dried tomato cheesecake with red pepper pesto, thai green chicken curry, gammon with fresh pineapple and a fried egg, venison sausages with cinnamon and red wine on creamy mash, duck breast with roasted garlic and parsley mash and red wine-poached pears, and puddings such as vanilla and honeycomb cheesecake with salted caramel sauce and sticky toffee pudding with toffee sauce. *Benchmark main dish: roast local venison with sweet potato mash, roasted beetroot and red wine jus £12.95. Two-course evening meal £18.00.*

Free house ~ Licensee Jeremy Coleman ~ Real ale ~ Open 11-11; 12-10.30 Sun ~ Bar food 12-2, 6-9; 12-3 Sun ~ Restaurant ~ Children welcome ~ Dogs allowed in bar ~ Wi-fi *Recommended by Alfie Bayliss, Harvey Brown*

FELINFACH
Griffin ⭐ 🍷 🍺 🛏

SO0933 Map 6

(01874) 620111 – www.eatdrinksleep.ltd.uk
A470 NE of Brecon; LD3 0UB

Highly thought-of dining pub with excellent food, a fine range of drinks and upbeat rustic décor; inviting bedrooms

Our readers love all aspects of this particularly well run place, from the genuinely friendly welcome, through the thoughtful choice of drinks to the exceptional modern cooking. It makes a fine base for exploring the area too, with comfortable, tastefully decorated bedrooms and hearty breakfasts that are nicely informal – you make your own toast and help yourself to home-made marmalade and jam. The back bar is quite pubby in an up-to-date way, with four leather sofas around a low table on pitted quarry tiles by a high slate hearth with a log fire. Behind them are mixed stripped seats around scrubbed kitchen tables on bare boards, and a bright blue and ochre colour scheme with some modern prints. The acoustics are pretty lively, due to so much bare flooring and uncurtained windows; background music, board games and plenty of books. Efficient staff serve interesting drinks, many from smaller independent suppliers, including well chosen wines (18 by the glass and carafe and they have a wine shop too), welsh spirits, cocktails, local bottled cider, locally sourced apple juice, non-alcoholic cocktails made with produce from their garden, unusual continental and local bottled beers and a range of sherries. There's Kite Cwrw Gorslas, Montys Pale Ale and Wye Valley Butty Bach on handpump. The two smallish front dining rooms that link to the back bar are attractive. On the left: mixed dining chairs around mainly stripped tables on flagstones and white-painted rough stone walls, with a cream-coloured Aga in a big stripped-stone embrasure. On the right: similar furniture on bare boards, big modern prints on terracotta walls and smart dark curtains. Children can play with the landlady's dog and visit the chickens in the henhouse. Dogs may sit with owners at certain tables while dining. Seats and tables outside; good wheelchair access.

Using home-grown organic and other local, seasonal produce, the delicious modern food from sensibly shortish menus includes pork, apple and black pudding terrine with piccalilli, baba ganoush, imam bayildi and goats curd with buttermilk cracker, seafood stew, slow-cooked chicken leg with pomme purée, artichoke, pancetta and stilton, venison haunch with red cabbage and parsnips, pork belly with hash browns, pumpkin and garlic clams, and puddings such as pear and almond tart with amaretti cream and chocolate brownie with peanut crunch and chocolate ice-cream; they also offer a two- and three-course set menu. *Benchmark main dish: rump of local beef with garlic pomme purée, trompette mushrooms and truffle £19.50. Two-course evening meal £25.00.*

Free house ~ Licensees Charles and Edmund Inkin and Julie Bell ~ Real ale ~ Open 11-11 ~ Bar food 12-2.30, 6-9 (9.30 Fri, Sat) ~ Restaurant ~ Children welcome ~ Dogs allowed in bar and bedrooms ~ Acoustic singer first Sun lunch of month ~ Bedrooms: £107/£130
Recommended by Alex and Hazel Evans, R T and J C Moggridge, Taff Thomas, Ian and Rose Lock, John Jenkins, Mrs A W Johns, Miss B D Picton

GRESFORD
SJ3453 Map 6

Pant-yr-Ochain ⭐ ♀ ◖

(01978) 853525 – www.brunningandprice.co.uk/pantyrochain
Off A483 on N edge of Wrexham: at roundabout take A5156 (A534) towards Nantwich, then first left towards the Flash; LL12 8TY

Thoughtfully run and extremely popular dining pub with good food all day, a very wide range of drinks and pretty lakeside garden

Surrounded by attractive grounds and reached down a long, sweeping drive, this elaborately gabled 16th-c place has the feel of an elegant country house. There are good quality seats and tables on the front terrace surrounded by herbaceous borders, with more furniture under parasols overlooking a lake with waterfowl. Inside, the light and airy rooms are stylishly decorated, with a wide range of interesting prints and bric-a-brac, and a good mix of individually chosen country furnishings, including comfortable seats for relaxing as well as more upright ones for eating. One area is set out as a library, with floor-to-ceiling bookshelves, there's a good open fire and a popular dining conservatory overlooking the garden; board games. The impressive line-up of drinks served by exemplary staff includes Phoenix Brunning & Price Original, Derby Penny's Porter, Joules Slumbering Monk, Purple Moose Snowdonia Ale and Weetwood Eastgate Ale on handpump, a farm cider, 17 wines by the glass, around 80 malt whiskies and a good choice of gins and vodkas. Good disabled access.

The particularly good, interesting food includes sandwiches, chilli tiger prawns with chorizo and tomato dressing, sesame pork belly with ginger and orange dressing, smoked haddock, leek and rarebit quiche, cauliflower, chickpea and almond tagine with apricot and date couscous, steak and kidney pudding, thyme-roast chicken with bacon and red wine jus, sea trout with mussel and cockle saffron stew and crisp samphire, and puddings such as apple and blackberry crumble and dark chocolate torte with pistachio praline and raspberry sorbet. *Benchmark main dish: steak burger with toppings, coleslaw and chips £12.45. Two-course evening meal £18.40.*

Brunning & Price ~ Licensee James Meakin ~ Real ale ~ Open 11-11; 12-10.30 Sun ~ Bar food 12-9.30 (9 Sun) ~ Children welcome ~ Dogs allowed in bar ~ Wi-fi
Recommended by R T and J C Moggridge, Brian and Anna Marsden, Clive Watkin

LLANARMON DYFFRYN CEIRIOG   SJ1532 Map 6

Hand

THE GOOD PUB GUIDE

(01691) 600666 ~ www.thehandhotel.co.uk
B4500 from Chirk; LL20 7LD

16th-c country inn with easy-going atmosphere in bar and dining room, friendly owners and enjoyable food and drinks; bedrooms

You can walk for hours from this comfortable and welcoming former drovers' inn as it's at the heart of the Upper Ceiriog Valley and backdropped by the Berwyn Mountains; the well equipped and spacious bedrooms make the perfect base for exploring, and breakfasts are splendid. A low-beamed bar has an inglenook log fire, sturdy tables and a mix of seating including settles, wheelbacks and mate's chairs on carpet, old prints on the walls and stools along the counter where they keep Big Hand Bastion and Weetwood Cheshire Cat Blonde Ale on handpump, seven wines by the glass and several malt whiskies. The largely stripped-stone dining room has a woodburning stove, and there's a quiet sitting room (ideal for planning excursions); the games room has darts and pool. Picnic-tables sit on the crazy-paved front terrace and the garden has more seats and tables. Dogs are allowed in some bedrooms – best to ring in advance.

From a seasonal menu, the popular food includes ham and apple pakoras with sweet and sour sauce, chicken liver pâté with fruit chutney, gammon and free-range eggs, baked peppers with goats cheese, rice and broccoli fritters, a pie of the day, a plate of pork (ham, faggot, black pudding and pork belly) with mustard mash and apple and cider sauce, Whitby scampi and chips, local lamb rump with manchego cheese and cauliflower purée, and puddings such as sticky toffee pudding with caramel sauce and Valrhona dark chocolate brownie. *Benchmark main dish: local lamb rump with redcurrant and mint jus £16.50. Two-course evening meal £21.00.*

Free house ~ Licensees Jonathan and Jackie Greatorex ~ Open 11-11 (12.30am Fri, Sat) ~ Bar food 12.15-2.30, 6-8.15 ~ Restaurant ~ Children welcome but not after 8pm in bar ~ Dogs allowed in bar and bedrooms ~ Wi-fi ~ Bedrooms: £55/£107.50
Recommended by Simon and Mandy King, Vikki and Matt Wharton, Clive Watkin

It's very helpful if you let us know up-to-date food prices when you report on pubs.

LLANARMON DYFFRYN CEIRIOG

SJ1532 Map 6

West Arms 🍴 ⚡ 🛏

(01691) 600665 – www.thewestarms.co.uk

End of B4500 W of Chirk; LL20 7LD

Former drovers' inn in lovely surroundings with public bar, lounge and separate restaurant, excellent food and pretty gardens; bedrooms

With a pretty lawn running down to River Ceiriog (fishing for residents) and good surrounding walks, this 16th-c inn is a lovely place to stay; the character bedrooms are in the main building with contemporary ones at the back, and all are well equipped and comfortable. As well as a small back public bar, there's a beamed and timbered smarter lounge with antique settles, sofas and even an elaborately carved confessional stall. The old-fashioned entrance hall has more sofas, and there are several log fires, horsebrasses and copper and brass items and an attractive, slightly more formal restaurant. Black Sheep, Stonehouse Station Bitter and Timothy Taylors Landlord on handpump served by friendly staff, six wines by the glass and six malt whiskies; background music.

 Extremely good, interesting food that's strong on local produce includes lunchtime baguettes, italian seafood brodo, spiced cured beef with watercress and parmesan salad, wild mushroom and spinach parcels in cheese sauce with tempura vegetables, Whitby scampi with chips, game pie, red mullet marinated in lemongrass, lime and coriander with prawn risotto, fillet of local beef with champ and curly kale, and puddings such as orange butterscotch cheesecake with chantilly cream and ricotta doughnuts with vanilla pastry cream and raspberry curd. *Benchmark main dish: loin of local lamb wrapped in herbs and leeks, with butternut purée, rösti potato and red wine sauce £17.00. Two-course evening meal £22.00.*

Free house ~ Licensees Geoff and Gill Leigh Ford ~ Real ale ~ Open 8am-11pm ~ Bar food 12-2.30, 6.30-9; 12-9 Sun ~ Restaurant ~ Children welcome ~ Dogs allowed in bar and bedrooms ~ Wi-fi ~ Bedrooms: £65/£115 *Recommended by Isobel Mackinlay, Belinda May*

LLANBERIS

SH6655 Map 6

Pen-y-Gwryd 🛏

(01286) 870211 – www.pyg.co.uk

Nant Gwynant; at junction of A498 and A4086, ie across mountains from Llanberis – OS Sheet 115 map reference 660558; LL55 4NT

Atmospheric and cheerfully unchanged mountaineers' haunt in the wilds of Snowdonia, run by the same family since 1947; bedrooms

Thankfully, this family-run mountain inn has changed remarkably little over many years. Memorably placed beneath Snowdon and the Glyders, it's packed with items left by the climbing fraternity. You can still make out the fading signatures scrawled on the ceiling by the 1953 Everest team, who used this as a training base, and on display is the very rope that connected Hillary and Tenzing on top of the mountain. One snug little room in the homely, slate-floored log cabin bar has built-in wall benches and sturdy country chairs. From here you can look out to precipitous Moel Siabod beyond the lake opposite. A smaller room has a worthy collection of illustrious boots from famous climbs, while a cosy panelled smoke room has more fascinating climbing mementoes and equipment; darts, pool, board games, skittles, bar billiards and table tennis. Purple Moose Glaslyn and Madogs are on handpump and they have several malts. Staying in the comfortable but basic bedrooms can be quite an experience, and the excellent traditional breakfast is served between 8.30 and 9am (they may serve earlier); dogs £5 a night. The inn has its own chapel (built for the millennium and dedicated by the Archbishop of Wales), sauna and outdoor natural pool, and the garden overlooks a lake.

 Ordered through a hatch, the short choice of simple, good-value lunchtime food includes rolls, ploughman's, pies, salads and quiche of the day, as well as daily specials such as roast beef. The hearty three- or five-course set meal in the evening restaurant is signalled by a gong at 7.30pm (if you're late, you'll miss it): maybe chicken liver pâté or smoked salmon salad followed by loin of pork with leeks, cannellini beans and cream, beef and Guinness pie or salmon fillet with hollandaise, and puddings such as chocolate bread and butter pudding and banoffi pie. *Benchmark main dish: roast lamb with redcurrant gravy £10.00. Evening meal £30.00.*

Free house ~ Licensee Nicholas Pullee ~ Real ale ~ Open 11-11; closed Jan, Feb ~ Bar food 12-2; evening meal 7.30pm ~ Restaurant ~ Children welcome ~ Dogs allowed in bar and bedrooms ~ Wi-fi ~ Bedrooms: £43/£104 *Recommended by Alison and Michael Harper, Isobel Mackinlay*

LLANDUDNO JUNCTION
SH8180 Map 6
Queens Head 🏵 ♀
(01492) 546570 – www.queensheadglanwydden.co.uk
Glanwydden; heading towards Llandudno on B5115 from Colwyn Bay, turn left into Llanrhos Road at roundabout as you enter the Penrhyn Bay speed limit; Glanwydden is signed as the first left turn; LL31 9JP

Consistently good food served all day at comfortably modern dining pub

As the very good food at this modest-looking village pub draws in so many customers, it's best to book a table in advance. The spacious modern lounge bar – partly divided by a white wall of broad arches – has beams, beige plush wall banquettes, rush-seated wooden and high-backed black leather dining chairs around neat black tables on tartan carpeting, an open woodburning stove and fresh flowers. The little public bar keeps Adnams Best, Great Orme IPA and a guest beer on handpump, 12 decent wines by the glass, several malt whiskies and good coffee; unobtrusive background music. There's a pleasing mix of seats and tables under parasols outside. Northern Snowdonia is within easy reach, and the pretty stone cottage (which sleeps two) across the road is for rent.

 Highly enjoyable food includes lunchtime ciabattas, confit duck leg with sticky red onion marmalade, deep-fried local brie with home-made cranberry chutney, portobello mushroom burger with toppings and chips, steak and mushroom in ale pie, seared king scallops with crispy pork belly, pea purée and roasted vine tomatoes, calves liver and crispy bacon with onion rings, monkfish and king prawn curry, and puddings such as baked chocolate pot and brioche bread and butter pudding. *Benchmark main dish: bass with prawns and almonds £14.25. Two-course evening meal £20.50.*

Free house ~ Licensees Robert and Sally Cureton ~ Real ale ~ Open 11.30-10.30 ~ Bar food 12-9 ~ Restaurant ~ Children welcome ~ Wi-fi *Recommended by Mike and Mary Carter*

LLANELIAN-YN-RHOS
SH8676 Map 6
White Lion
(01492) 515807 – www.whitelioninn.co.uk
Signed off A5830 (shown as B5383 on some maps) and B5381, S of Colwyn Bay; LL29 8YA

Bustling village local with bar and spacious dining areas, tasty food, real ales and helpful staff

Each of the two distinct parts of this bustling village local, linked by a broad flight of steps, has its own cheery personality. Up at the top is a very spacious and neat dining area, while at the other end is a traditional old bar with antique high-backed settles fitting snugly around a big fireplace, and flagstones by the counter; parts of the building are said to date back 1,200 years. Marstons Burton Bitter and Pedigree and a guest such as Heavy Industry Electric Mountain on handpump, 12 wines by the glass and several malt whiskies are served by helpful staff. Off to the left is another dining room with jugs hanging from beams and teapots above the windows; background music. There are tables in an attractive courtyard (also used for parking) next to the church. The pub is tucked away in a knot of lanes in rolling country above Colwyn Bay.

Hearty, well liked food includes lunchtime sandwiches and baguettes, black pudding and smoked bacon salad with honey and wholegrain mustard sauce, prawn cocktail, goats cheese, mushroom and leek tart with red onion chutney, steak and kidney pie, barbecued spare ribs with chips, chicken curry, sirloin steak with a choice of sauces, and puddings such as chocolate fudge cake and apple pie; they also offer a two-course set lunch (Tuesday-Friday). *Benchmark main dish: chicken topped with smoked bacon, cheese and mushrooms in cider, rosemary and sage sauce £12.95. Two-course evening meal £16.00.*

Free house ~ Licensee Simon Cole ~ Real ale ~ Open 12-3.30, 6 (5 Sat)-11; 12-10.30 Sun; closed Mon except school and bank holidays ~ Bar food 12-2, 6 (5 Fri, Sat)-9; 12-9 Sun ~ Restaurant ~ Children welcome ~ Wi-fi ~ Live jazz Tues evening, sing-along first Sun of month *Recommended by Rob Anderson, Alison and Michael Harper*

LLANFAETHLU

SH3286 Map 6

Black Lion 🌟 ☞

(01407) 730718 – www.blacklionanglesey.com
A5025; LL65 4NL

Carefully renovated inn with enjoyable food and drink, a friendly welcome and fine views from terrace; comfortable bedrooms

An enthusiastic and hard-working local couple have renovated this 18th-c inn – it had been derelict for seven years. It's been done with elegant simplicity and contemporary paintwork and the atmosphere throughout is easy-going and friendly. There's a cosy bar with a woodburning stove, wooden tables and chairs on black slates and a few high-backed stools at the oak-topped counter where they keep Marstons Pedigree and Purple Moose Snowdonia Ale on handpump, seven wines by the glass and welsh whisky and gin; background music. A high-raftered and similarly furnished dining room with another woodburner has french doors to the terrace, where there are seats that look across the countryside to the magnificent Snowdonia mountains. The two spacious bedrooms are well appointed.

Using meat from the family farm and other local and foraged produce, the highly regarded food includes sandwiches, scallops with pancetta, pea purée and black pudding bonbons, creamy white wine and garlic mussels, grilled fish of the day with vegetable 'spaghetti' and lemon butter sauce, garlic mushroom and herb linguine, seared chicken with tomato salsa, hasselback potatoes and balsamic reduction, duck two-ways (confit leg, roasted breast) with redcurrant reduction and parsnip crisps, and puddings such as glazed citrus crème brûlée with lemon thyme shortbread and chocolate cheesecake with white chocolate sauce. *Benchmark main dish: pressed pork belly with black pudding, apple purée, anise, crackling and port reduction £15.95. Two-course evening meal £23.50.*

Free house ~ Licensees Leigh and Mari Faulkner ~ Real ale ~ Open 12-2.30, 6-11;
12-11 Sat, Sun; closed lunchtimes Mon-Weds in winter, 2nd and 3rd weeks Jan; check
website for winter hours ~ Bar food 12-2.30, 6-8 (9 Fri, Sat); 12-3 Sun ~ Children welcome
~ Dogs welcome ~ Wi-fi ~ Bedrooms: £90/£115 *Recommended by Rob Anderson, Alison and
Michael Harper, Pip White*

LLANFIHANGEL-Y-CREUDDYN SN6676 Map 6
Y Ffarmers ⭐

(01974) 261275 – www.yffarmers.co.uk
Village signed off A4120 W of Pisgah; SY23 4LA

**Welsh- and English-speaking pub with traditional furnishings in bar
and dining areas, local ales and good food**

Opposite the 13th-c church and right on the village square, this bilingual
country pub is the hub of the community. It's been carefully and simply
refurbished by the chef-landlord and his wife to attract both drinkers and
diners, with high chairs and stools against the green-painted counter where
they keep local ales on handpump such as Evan Evans Cwrw, Mantle Moho
and a guest from Evan Evans, farm ciders and six wines by the glass;
background music, TV and darts. There's a woodburning stove in a little
fireplace, cushioned armed wheelback chairs, mate's chairs and a box settle
around dark tables (each set with fresh flowers), wooden floors and walls
painted white or red. As well as a sunken terrace with seats, there's a lawn
with picnic-sets under parasols.

 Cooked by the landlord using local produce, the tempting food includes cockle
and treacle bacon cakes with laverbread sauce, spiced lamb and pine nuts in
filo pastry with mint and cucumber dip, beer-battered haddock and chips, a pie of
the day, sausages and mash with onion gravy, free-range chicken breast with bacon,
cheese and warm green bean salad, wild bass fillet and cockle linguine, lamb shank
in red wine with creamy mash, and puddings such as lemon cheesecake with lemon
meringue ice-cream and chocolate brownie with salt caramel ice-cream; they also offer
takeaways. *Benchmark main dish: local lamb tagine £14.00. Two-course evening
meal £18.50.*

Free house ~ Licensees Esther Prytherch and Rhodri Edwards ~ Real ale ~ Open 12-2,
6-11 (midnight Sat); 12-2, 7-11 Sun; closed Mon, first week Jan ~ Bar food 12-2, 6-9;
not Sun evening, Mon, Tues lunchtime ~ Restaurant ~ Children welcome ~ Dogs allowed
in bar ~ Wi-fi *Recommended by Andrew Stone, Toby Jones*

LLANGOLLEN SJ2142 Map 6
Corn Mill ⭐ 🍷 🍺

(01978) 869555 – www.brunningandprice.co.uk/cornmill
*Dee Lane, very narrow lane off Castle Street (A539) just S of bridge; nearby parking
can be tricky, may be best to use public park on Parade Street/East Street and walk;
LL20 8PN*

**Excellent on all counts, with personable young staff, super food all
day and good beers in a fascinating riverside building with fine views**

On a warm day, customers are quick to bag seats on the raised deck in
front of this cleverly restored watermill to look over the rushing mill race
and rapids below; you can also watch steam trains arriving and leaving the
station on the opposite riverbank. Inside, the interior has been interestingly
refitted with pale pine flooring on stout beams, a striking open stairway
with gleaming timber and tensioned steel rails, and mainly stripped-stone
walls. Quite a lot of the old machinery is still in place, including the huge

waterwheel (often turning) and there are good-sized dining tables, big rugs, thoughtfully chosen pictures (many to do with water) and several pot plants. One of the two serving bars, away from the water, has a much more local feel with regulars sitting on bar stools, pews on dark slate flagstones and daily papers. Helpful young staff serve Phoenix Brunning & Price Original and Facers DHB on handpump, with three guests such as Brimstage Sandpiper Pale, Derby Dark Delight and Pixie Spring Golden Pixie; also, farm cider, around 50 sensibly priced malt whiskies and a decent wine choice with around a dozen by the glass.

 From an imaginative menu, the well presented food includes sandwiches, scallops with black pudding, cauliflower purée and rhubarb dressing, air-dried beef with pickled vegetables, crab linguine with ginger, chilli and coriander, spinach and ricotta tortellini with butternut squash and sunblush tomato dressing, steak in ale pie, sea trout with pea and smoked bacon croquettes and sauce vierge, duck breast with duck hash cake and blackberry sauce, and puddings such as chocolate torte with amaretto ice-cream and raspberry and almond bakewell tart. *Benchmark main dish: braised shoulder of lamb with dauphinoise potatoes and red wine and rosemary gravy £17.95. Two-course evening meal £21.00.*

Brunning & Price ~ Manager Andrew Barker ~ Real ale ~ Open 12-11 (10.30 Sun) ~ Bar food 12-9.30 (9 Sun) ~ Restaurant ~ Children welcome ~ Dogs allowed in bar
Recommended by JPC, Clive and Fran Dutson, Clive Watkin, John and Enid, Mike and Mary Carter

LLANMADOC
Britannia

SS4493   Map 6

(01792) 386624 – www.britanniainngower.co.uk
The Gower, near Whiteford Burrows (NT); SA3 1DB

Fine views from seats behind this popular pub with more in the big garden, well liked food and ales and friendly staff

The picnic-sets on the raised decked area behind this dining pub are snapped up quickly in warm weather as the views over the Loughor estuary are lovely; there are also tables out in front and in the big garden and they have a rabbit hutch and an aviary with budgies, cockatiels, quails and a parrot. Inside, the beamed bar has a warm stove, traditional mate's chairs and plush stools around dark tables on a patterned carpet, brass and copper items and Fullers London Pride, Gower Gold and Marstons Pedigree on handpump and several wines by the glass; darts and TV. The beamed restaurant has attractive modern wooden tables and chairs on a striped carpet and paintings on bare stone walls. Lovely nearby walks.

The high quality food includes baguettes, chicken liver parfait with onion chutney, local mussels in white wine, chilli and confit tomato broth, steak in ale pie, thai vegetable curry, lamb tagine, slow-braised barbecue spare ribs, ballotine of free-range chicken with crispy wings, sauté vegetables and port jus, trio of lamb (shoulder, loin, chops) with truffled celeriac purée and dauphinoise potatoes, and puddings such as profiteroles filled with white chocolate mousse with hot chocolate sauce and elderflower poached rhubarb crumble with thyme ice-cream; they also offer a two- and three-course set menu. *Benchmark main dish: bass with gnocchi and local cockle and crab velouté £22.00. Two-course evening meal £25.00.*

Enterprise ~ Tenants Martin and Lindsey Davies ~ Real ale ~ Open 12-11; 12-3, 5-11 in winter ~ Bar food 12-3, 6.30-8.30 ~ Restaurant ~ Children welcome ~ Dogs allowed in bar ~ Wi-fi *Recommended by Hugh Roberts, Canon Michael Bourdeaux, R T and J C Moggridge*

We accept no free drinks or meals and inspections are anonymous.

MOLD
Glasfryn 🖈🏵 ♀ 🍴

(01352) 750500 – www.brunningandprice.co.uk/glasfryn

N of the centre on Raikes Lane (parallel to the A5119), just past the well signposted Theatr Clwyd; CH7 6LR

Lively open-plan bistro-style pub with inventive all-day food, nice décor and wide choice of drinks

A former judges' residence and farm, this neat, rather unassuming-looking pub is lively and cheerful inside with a wide mix of customers. The open-plan interior is cleverly laid out to create plenty of nice quiet corners with a mix of informal, attractive country furnishings, turkey-style rugs on bare boards, deep red ceilings (some high), a warming fire and plenty of close-hung homely pictures; background music. Phoenix Brunning & Price Original, Facers Flintshire and Purple Moose Snowdonia Ale on handpump alongside up to seven several swiftly changing guests, 22 wines by the glass, local apple juice, farm cider and 40 malt whiskies. On warm days, the wooden tables on the large front terrace are a restful place to sit, providing sweeping views of the Clwydian Hills. Theatre Clwyd is just over the road.

 The modern, high quality food includes sandwiches, smoked salmon blinis with pickled radishes and horseradish and lemon crème fraîche, beetroot and goats cheese croquettes with pickled beetroot salad, crispy duck salad with watermelon, cashews and pomegranate soy dressing, pork and leek sausages with onion gravy, beef curry with onion bhaji, chicken breast saltimbocca with lemon and caper crushed potatoes, pork belly with black pudding, boulangère potatoes and roast tomato jus, and puddings such as chocolate brownie with dark chocolate sauce and vanilla cheesecake with roasted pineapple and passion-fruit coulis. *Benchmark main dish: beer-battered haddock and chips £12.75. Two-course evening meal £20.00.*

Brunning & Price ~ Manager Graham Arathoon ~ Real ale ~ Open 11.30-11; 12-10.30 Sun ~ Bar food 12-9.30 (9 Sun) ~ Children welcome ~ Dogs allowed in bar ~ Wi-fi
Recommended by Gerry and Rosemary Dobson, Clive Watkin, Mike and Mary Carter, Stuart Paulley

MONKNASH
Plough & Harrow 🍴 £

(01656) 890209 – www.ploughandharrow.org

Signposted 'Marcross, Broughton' off B4265 St Brides Major–Llantwit Major – turn left at end of Water Street; OS Sheet 170 map reference 920706; CF71 7QQ

Old building full of history and character, with a huge log fire and a good choice of real ales

If you're visiting the spectacular stretch of coastal cliffs nearby, this historic pub makes an ideal stopping point. Part of the building dates back 900 years and formed part of a monastic grange – the ruins can be seen in adjacent fields. The unspoilt main bar with its massively thick stone walls used to be the scriptures room and mortuary; it has ancient ham hooks in the heavily beamed ceiling, an intriguing arched doorway at the back, broad flagstones and a comfortably informal mix of furnishings that includes three fine stripped-pine settles. There's a log fire in a huge fireplace with a side bread oven large enough to feed a village; background music in the left-hand room. The eight real ales on handpump or tapped from the cask might include Bass, Hancocks HB, Wye Valley HPA and four changing guests such as Brains Rev James, Otley O-Mai, Skinners Pennycomequick and Timothy Taylors Landlord; they usually hold beer festivals in June and September. Also, a good range of local farm cider and welsh and scottish malt whiskies.

The front garden has some picnic-sets. Dogs are welcome in the bar, but not while food is being served.

🍽 From a daily changing menu, the well liked food includes sandwiches, chicken liver pâté with chutney, deep-fried whitebait, field mushroom stuffed with beetroot and goats cheese, burger with toppings and chips, barbecued pulled pork with onion rings and chips, cajun chicken with sauté potatoes, and puddings such as apple and mixed berry crumble and sticky date pudding with caramel sauce. *Benchmark main dish: steak in ale pie £8.95. Two-course evening meal £16.00.*

Free house ~ Licensee Paula Jones ~ Real ale ~ Open 12-11 (10.30 Sun) ~ Bar food 12-2.30 (5 weekends), 6-9; not Sun evening ~ Restaurant ~ Children welcome ~ Dogs allowed in bar ~ Live music Sat evening *Recommended by Martin Jones, Andrew Stone*

NEWPORT
SN0539   Map 6
Golden Lion 🛏
(01239) 820321 – www.goldenlionpembrokeshire.co.uk
East Street (A487); SA42 0SY

Nicely redone and friendly local, with tasty food and pleasant staff; well appointed bedrooms

They cleverly manage to combine a lively local with an incredibly popular restaurant here – and offer comfortable, fair value bedrooms too. We hear nothing but praise from our readers. As well as a genuinely pubby bar, there's a cosy series of beamed rooms with distinctive old settles, Bluestone Rockhopper Pale Bitter and a guest or two on handpump, as well as several malt whiskies, wines by the glass and Gwynt y Ddraig cider; pool, juke box, darts, board games, dominoes and games machine. The dining room has elegant blond oak furniture, whitewashed walls and potted plants; service is efficient and friendly. There are tables outside at the front and in a side garden; good disabled access and facilities.

🍽 Enjoyable and consistently good, the food includes sandwiches, a meat or vegetable antipasti plate, creamy garlic mushrooms on toasted brioche, mediterranean vegetable lasagne, thai green free-range chicken curry, burger with toppings, mustard mayonnaise and chips, local lamb chops with fresh mint and rosemary, rib-eye steak with a choice of sauces, and puddings such as tiramisu and fruit crumble with a coconut and almond topping. *Benchmark main dish: beer-battered cod and chips £11.95. Two-course evening meal £19.00.*

Free house ~ Licensee Daron Paish ~ Real ale ~ Open 12pm-2am ~ Bar food 12-2.30, 6.30-9 ~ Restaurant ~ Children welcome ~ Dogs allowed in bar and bedrooms ~ Wi-fi ~ Live music Sat evenings Oct-Mar ~ Bedrooms: £70/£90 *Recommended by J A Snell, Ron Corbett, R T and J C Moggridge*

OLD RADNOR
SO2459   Map 6
Harp 🎖 🛏
(01544) 350655 – www.harpinnradnor.co.uk
Village signposted off A44 Kington–New Radnor in Walton; LD8 2RH

Charming inn in beautiful spot, with cottagey bar, tasty food and well kept ales; comfortable bedrooms

This is a delightful place and our readers very much enjoy staying in the spic and span rooms (no door keys) which have the most lovely views; enjoyable breakfasts too. All are welcomed by the hands-on landlord and landlady, and the characterful public bar has high-backed settles, an antique reader's chair and other venerable chairs around a log fire; board games, cribbage, darts and quoits. The snug slate-floored bar contains a handsome curved antique settle, a log fire in a fine inglenook and lots of local books and guides for residents; a quieter dining area off to the right extends into another dining room with a woodburning stove. There are a couple of changing real ales from breweries such as Ludlow, Salopian, Three Tuns and Wye Valley on handpump, as well as five wines by the glass, Dunkerton's cider and perry, local cassis and several malt whiskies. Tables outside make the most of the view overlooking the heights of Radnor Forest. The impressive village church is worth a look for its early organ case (Britain's oldest), fine rood screen and ancient font.

Good, interesting food includes salt and pepper squid with noodles and sweet chilli sauce, pigeon breast with roast garlic mash and raspberry vinegar dressing, ham and eggs, goats cheese and mediterranean vegetable tian with cherry tomato pickle, beer-battered cod and chips, venison burger with blue cheese and raspberry vinegar dressing, lamb rump with dauphinoise potatoes, carrot purée and madeira jus, and puddings such as ginger cake with butterscotch sauce and rum and raisin crème brûlée with coconut ice-cream. *Benchmark main dish: local rump steak with a choice of sauces and chips £15.00. Two-course evening meal £20.00.*

Free house ~ Licensees Chris and Angela Ireland ~ Real ale ~ Open 6-11; 12-3, 6-11 Fri, Sat; 12-3, 6-10.30 Sun; closed Mon, Tues, lunchtimes Weds and Thurs ~ Bar food 12-2.30 Fri-Sun, 6-9 Weds-Sat ~ Children welcome ~ Dogs allowed in bar and bedrooms ~ Wi-fi ~ Bedrooms: £75/£100 *Recommended by Dr Kevan Tucker, Sara Fulton, Roger Baker*

OVERTON BRIDGE
Cross Foxes 🍽 ♀

SJ3542   Map 6

(01978) 780380 – www.brunningandprice.co.uk/crossfoxes
A539 W of Overton, near Erbistock; LL13 0DR

Terrific river views from well run 18th-c coaching inn with tasty bar food and an extensive range of drinks

The raised terrace with oak chairs and tables has fine views over the River Dee below this substantial 18th-c coaching inn, while picnic-sets down on a lawn are even closer to the water. Inside, the ancient low-beamed bar, with its red tiled floor, dark timbers, warm fire in the big inglenook and built-in old pews, is more traditional than most pubs in the Brunning & Price group, though the characteristic turkey rugs, big pot plants and frame-to-frame pictures are present, as they are in the dining areas; board games and newspapers. Big windows all round the airy dining conservatory also overlook the river. Friendly, competent staff serve Phoenix Brunning & Price Original, Brakspears Bitter, Jennings Cumberland and a couple of guests such as Marstons EPA and Ringwood Fortyniner on handpump, a farm cider, 40 malts, an excellent range of 30 Armagnacs, 28 gins and around 40 wines by the glass.

Highly competent modern cooking includes dishes such as sandwiches, tiger prawns with garlic and sweet peppers on bruschetta, ham hock and tarragon croquettes with piccalilli, feta fritters with saffron and lemon couscous, roast mediterranean vegetables and pesto dressing, rosemary and garlic chicken with wild mushrooms, bacon and spinach linguine, smoked haddock and salmon fishcakes with tartare sauce, sesame pork belly with pak choi, pickled ginger and watermelon salad with mirin and chilli dressing, and puddings such as meringue with toffee cream and mulled fruits and chocolate brownie with chocolate sauce. *Benchmark main dish: braised shoulder of lamb with dauphinoise potatoes and rosemary gravy £16.95. Two-course evening meal £21.00.*

Brunning & Price ~ Manager Ian Pritchard-Jones ~ Real ale ~ Open 11-11 (10.30 Sun) ~ Bar food 12-9.30 (9 Sun) ~ Children welcome ~ Dogs allowed in bar ~ Wi-fi
Recommended by Mike and Mary Carter, Peter and Josie Fawcett, Roger and Anne Newbury

PANTYGELLI
SO3017 Map 6

Crown

(01873) 853314 – www.thecrownatpantygelli.com

Old Hereford Road N of Abergavenny; off A40 by war memorial via Pen Y Pound,
passing leisure centre; Pantygelli also signposted from A465; NP7 7HR

Country pub in the Brecon Beacons National Park, attractive inside and out, with good food and drinks

With rewarding food and a genuine welcome from the friendly licensees, this attractively placed pub is just the place to head for after a walk up the Sugar Loaf. Wrought-iron and wicker chairs on the flower-filled front terrace look up from this lush valley to the hills and there's also a smaller back terrace surrounded by lavender. Inside, the dark flagstoned bar, with sturdy timber props and beams, has a log fire in a stone fireplace, a piano at the back with darts opposite, Bass, Rhymney Best, Wye Valley HPA and a local guest on handpump from the slate-roofed counter, Gwatkin's farm cider, seven good wines by the glass, local organic apple juice and good coffees. On the left are four smallish, linked, carpeted dining rooms, the front pair separated by a massive stone chimneybreast; thoughtfully chosen individual furnishings and lots of attractive prints by local artists make it all thoroughly civilised. Also, background music, darts and board games.

Using the best local produce, the reliably good food includes king prawn, herring and locally smoked salmon salad, pâté with home-made chutney, venison sausages with red wine gravy, goats cheese, cherry tomatoes and red onion puff with balsamic dressing, beef braised in stout with chips, a spicy dish of the day, chicken breast with ham-wrapped baby gem lettuce, sticky red cabbage and red wine and thyme sauce, and puddings such as elderflower jelly with lemon sorbet and raspberry crème brûlée and strawberry eton mess. *Benchmark main dish: cold rare roast beef with bubble and squeak £11.00. Two-course evening meal £17.00.*

Free house ~ Licensees Steve and Cherrie Chadwick ~ Real ale ~ Open 12-2.30 (3 Sat), 6-11; 12-3, 6-10.30 Sun; closed Mon lunchtime ~ Bar food 12-2, 7-9; not Sun evening or Mon ~ Restaurant ~ Children welcome ~ Dogs allowed in bar ~ Wi-fi
Recommended by Heulwen and Neville Pinfield, John Jenkins

PENNAL
SH6900 Map 6

Riverside

(01654) 791285 – www.riversidehotel-pennal.co.uk

A493; opposite church; SY20 9DW

Carefully refurbished pub with tasty food and local beers, and efficient young staff; bedrooms

Most customers are here to enjoy the highly thought-of food – often after a walk in the surrounding Dyfi Valley. There's always a wide mix of customers, children and dogs included, and the neatly furnished rooms have green and white walls, slate tiles on the floor, a woodburning stove, modern light wood dining furniture and some funky fabrics. High-backed stools are lined up along the stone-fronted counter where they serve four changing beers on handpump such as Purple Moose Madogs Ale and Snowdonia Ale and guests such as Salopian Golden Thread and Thornbridge Jaipur, 30 malt whiskies, 25 gins, ten wines by the glass and farm cider; dominoes. There are seats and tables in the garden, and they also run a Georgian guesthouse in the pretty village.

From a thoughtful menu, the wide choice of food includes lunchtime rolls and sharing boards, monkfish with crispy black pudding and pea purée, duck confit with moroccan-style couscous and chutney, wild mushroom and chestnut cottage pie, steak burger with toppings, onion rings and skinny fries, prawn and chorizo linguine with chilli, lime and ginger, pork schnitzel with parsnip mash and cider and sage sauce, venison loin with bubble and squeak and red wine and thyme sauce, and puddings such as crème brûlée and chocolate and Cointreau cheesecake with raspberry coulis. *Benchmark main dish: spiced mediterranean fish stew £14.00. Two-course evening meal £18.00.*

Free house ~ Licensees Glyn and Corina Davies ~ Real ale ~ Open 12-11 (midnight Sat); closed Mon lunchtime except bank holidays, and all day Mon in winter ~ Bar food 12-2 (2.30 Sun), 6-9 ~ Restaurant ~ Children welcome ~ Dogs allowed in bar and bedrooms ~ Wi-fi ~ Live music monthly (check website) ~ Bedrooms: £55/£75
Recommended by Mike and Mary Carter, John Evans, Michael Butler

 PENTYRCH   ST1081   Map 6

Kings Arms

(029) 2089 0202 – www.kingsarmspentyrch.co.uk
Church Road; CF15 9QF

Village pub very much part of the community with a perky bar, civilised lounge and top class food in a bustling dining room

The delicious food in this 16th-c longhouse is so popular that it's best to book a table in advance. But this is not a straightforward dining place, it's very much a proper pub with plenty of local customers – the cosy bar has a cheerful atmosphere, an open log fire in a sizeable brick fireplace and a mix of seats on flagstones. There's Brains Bitter and SA, Caledonian Deuchars IPA and guests such as Otley O3 Boss and Tiny Rebel Fubar on handpump, 14 wines by the glass and up to ten malt whiskies, all served by helpful, friendly staff. There's also a comfortable lounge and a cosy restaurant. Plenty of seats on a terrace and picnic-sets under parasols in the garden. Their deli and greengrocers is next door.

Cooked by the chef-patron, the enticing food includes lunchtime baguettes, salt-cured salmon pastrami with salmon crackling and lemon crème fraîche, hickory smoked duck with honeyed figs and walnuts and local sea salt croutons, merguez lamb sausage and mash with rosemary jus, duck breast with roasted celeriac, beetroot, kale and pine nuts, fried cod with laverbread and bacon hash, local mussels and garlic cream, chicken breast with leek and thyme orzotto and gremolata, and puddings such as warm chocolate brownie with chocolate sauce and sticky toffee pudding with toffee sauce; they also offer a two- and three-course set menu (weekday lunchtimes and Monday-Wednesday supper). *Benchmark main dish: beer-battered fish and chips £10.50. Two-course evening meal £18.00.*

Free house ~ Licensee Andrew Aston ~ Real ale ~ Open 12-11 (midnight Sat); 12-8 Sun ~ Bar food 12-3, 5.30-9.30; 12-9.30 Sat; 12-4 Sun ~ Restaurant ~ Children welcome ~ Dogs allowed in bar ~ Wi-fi *Recommended by Martin Jones, Toby Jones, Patrick and Daphne Darley*

PONTYPRIDD   ST0790   Map 6

Bunch of Grapes

(01443) 402934 – www.bunchofgrapes.org.uk
Off A4054; Ynysangharad Road; CF37 4DA

Wales Dining Pub of the Year

Bustling pub with a fine choice of drinks in friendly, relaxed bar, delicious inventive food and a warm welcome for all

'This place just gets better and better,' says one reader who visits this 18th-c pub regularly. As well as creative food, there's a fantastic range of drinks served by knowledgeable, friendly and efficient staff: their own Otley O2 Croeso and three Otley guests plus another four quickly changing guests from other breweries such as Dark Star, Oakham, Saltaire and Tiny Rebel on handpump. They hold around six beer and music festivals each year, and also keep continental and american ales on draught or in bottles, a couple of local ciders or perrys, eight wines by the glass and good coffee. The cosy bar has an informal, relaxed atmosphere, comfortable leather sofas, wooden chairs and tables, a roaring log fire, newspapers to read and background music. There's also a restaurant with elegant high-backed wooden dining chairs around a mix of tables and black and white local photo-prints taken by the landlord (an ex-professional photographer). A deli offers home-baked bread and chutneys, home-cooked ham, local eggs and quite a choice of welsh cheeses and so forth; they hold regular themed cookery evenings. There are seats outside on decking.

The imaginative, daily changing food might include lunchtime sandwiches and burgers with toppings, coleslaw and chips plus poached crayfish and chive mousse with anchovy aioli and caperberries, pork, apple and cider terrine with white onion and szechuan pepper chutney, lasagne of beetroot, chives and smoked tomato sauce with melted cheese, kohlrabi salsa and garlic bread, sauerkraut of pheasant, pigeon breast, streaky bacon and white pudding, caramelised apple sauce and juniper berries, slow-braised venison haunch with burnt onion purée, pommes gaufrettes, jerusalem artichokes and stout braising jus, and puddings such as coffee and whisky cheesecake with whisky syrup and toasted marshmallow and dark chocolate fondant with milk chocolate ganache, white chocolate sauce, hazelnut and almond crumble and lemon ice-cream. *Benchmark main dish: 12-hour braised beef with parsnip purée, sun-dried tomato and spring onion mash, red onion jus £15.50. Two-course evening meal £21.50.*

Free house ~ Licensee Nick Otley ~ Real ale ~ Open 11am-11.30pm; 12-11 Sun ~ Bar food 12-8.30 (7 Fri, Sat); 12-3.30 Sun ~ Restaurant ~ Children welcome ~ Dogs allowed in bar ~ Wi-fi *Recommended by Taff Thomas, R T and J C Moggridge, John Jenkins*

RAGLAN
Clytha Arms 🏵 🍷 🍺 🛏

SO3609 Map 6

(01873) 840206 – www.clytha-arms.com
Clytha, off Abergavenny road – former A40, now declassified; NP7 9BW

Fine setting in spacious grounds, a relaxing spot for enjoying good food and impressive range of drinks; comfortable bedrooms

They cleverly manage to appeal to a wide mix of customers at this gracious old country inn from walkers with their dogs, locals in for a pint and chat and those keen to dine in the smart restaurant. With long heated verandahs and diamond-paned windows, the bar and lounge are comfortable, light and airy, with a good mix of old country furniture, pine settles, window seats with big cushions, scrubbed wood floors and a couple of open log fires; the contemporary restaurant is linen-set. The notable array of drinks includes Brecon Three Beacons, Untapped Sundown (from a little brewery just down the road) and Wye Valley Bitter and three swiftly changing guests on handpump, an extensive wine list with 13 by the glass, 20 malt whiskies, three farm ciders, their own perry and various continental beers; they hold a cider and beer festival over the late May Bank Holiday weekend. Darts, bar skittles, boules, board games and large-screen TV for rugby matches. The bedrooms are comfortable and the welsh breakfasts are good. The inn is attractively set in spacious grounds on the edge of Clytha Park and a short stroll from the riverside path by the Usk. Dogs are welcome – the pub has its own labrador and collie.

Making impressive use of local ingredients the interesting food includes tapas (such as black pudding with fried apple, potted crab and laverbead, and beer-battered calamari with aioli), plus sandwiches, shellfish bourride, pork and wild mushroom faggots with black pudding mash, a pie of the day, rabbit leg in cider with bacon and herb dumplings, chicken curry, wild boar bratwurst and silesian sausages with potato pancakes, ham with parsley sauce and bubble and squeak, and puddings such as a trio of chocolate and treacle pudding with custard. *Benchmark main dish: duck and wild boar cassoulet £14.50. Two-course evening meal £23.00.*

Free house ~ Licensees Andrew and Beverley Canning ~ Real ale ~ Open 12-3, 6-midnight; 12-midnight Fri, Sat; 12-10.30 Sun; closed Mon lunchtime ~ Bar food 12.30-2.15, 7-9.30; not Sun evening ~ Restaurant ~ Children welcome ~ Dogs allowed in bar and bedrooms ~ Wi-fi ~ Bedrooms: £60/£90 *Recommended by N R White, Andrew Stone*

SKENFRITH
Bell 🍴 ♟ 🛏

SO4520   Map 6

(01600) 750235 – www.skenfrith.co.uk
Just off B4521, NE of Abergavenny and N of Monmouth; NP7 8UH

Elegant but relaxed inn much praised for classy food and thoughtful choice of drinks; excellent bedrooms

The individually decorated bedrooms in this civilised, smart country inn – a fine base for exploring the area – are named after brown trout fishing flies; dogs are welcome in some rooms. The flagstoned bar at the back is neat, light and airy with dark wooden country kitchen and rush-seated dining chairs, church candles and fresh flowers on dark tables, canary yellow walls and brocaded curtains. The flagstone bar on the left is similarly decorated, with old local and school photographs, a couple of pews and sofas, dining tables and café chairs, and board games. From the bleached oak counter they serve Bespoke Saved by the Bell, Wickwar BOB and Wye Valley Butty Bach and Hereford Pale Ale on handpump, plus bottled local cider and perry, 12 wines by the glass from an impressive list, local sparkling wine, early-landed cognacs and a good range of malt whiskies. The lounge bar on the right, opening into the dining area, has an impressive Jacobean-style carved settle and a housekeeper's chair by a log fire in the big fireplace; there's also a sitting room with comfortable sofas, daily papers and magazines and a log fire. The terrace has good solid tables under parasols, with steps leading up to a sloping lawn and an orchard area (ideal for families); the kitchen garden is immaculate. The inn is close to the impressive ruin of Skenfrith Castle (National Trust) and a pretty bridge over the River Monnow, and they have leaflets for six circular walks. Good disabled access.

Using home-grown and other local, seasonal produce, the tempting food includes sandwiches, pigeon breast with chestnut mushroom tart and nettle purée, calves tongue fritters with black pudding, a fried quail egg and brown sauce, sharing boards, cheeseburger with dijon mustard and chips, twice-baked three-cheese soufflé with wild mushroom cream, slow-cooked pork belly with pine nut and sultana jus, rib-eye steak with béarnaise sauce, and puddings such as glazed lemon tart with blackcurrant sorbet and hot chocolate fondant with pistachio ice-cream and white chocolate sauce. *Benchmark main dish: beef wellington £23.00. Two-course evening meal £25.00.*

Free house ~ Licensee Richard Ireton ~ Real ale ~ Open 9am-11pm ~ Bar food 12-2.30, 6.30-9; 12-8 Sun; 9-10am breakfast ~ Restaurant ~ Well behaved children welcome but not in dining room after 6.30pm ~ Dogs allowed in bar and bedrooms ~ Wi-fi ~ Bedrooms: /£160 *Recommended by Dr Peter Crawshaw, Miss B D Picton*

ST GEORGE
SH9775 Map 6

Kinmel Arms 🍴⭐ 🛏

(01745) 832207 – www.thekinmelarms.co.uk

Off A547 or B5381 SE of Abergele; LL22 9BP

Stylish food in handsome inn, a wide choice of drinks, courteous staff and lovely surrounding countryside; bedrooms

With good walks from the door and comfortable modern suites (each with their own decked area), this 17th-c sandstone inn with mullioned windows and carriage-lamps makes a fine base for exploring the stunning nearby countryside. There's a bar with sofas on either side of a woodburning stove, an attractive mix of nice old wooden chairs and tables on the wooden floor and seats against the counter (with stained glass above) where they keep Facers Clwyd Gold and Flintshire Bitter on handpump, 21 wines by the glass and farm cider; service is helpful and friendly. The restaurant, with rattan chairs around marble-topped tables, has big house plants, contemporary art painted by Tim Watson (one of the owners) and evening candles and twinkling lights. There are picnic-sets out in front.

 Appealing, brasserie-style food using the best local produce includes mussels in creamy thai sauce, eggs benedict, partridge breast and crispy leg with pickled pear, alsace cabbage and caramelised walnuts, burger with sticky red onions, cheese, gherkins and chips, pie of the day, bass with salt-baked kohlrabi, celeriac purée, burnt leeks, vanilla gel and roasted fish stock cream, slow-cooked roe deer haunch with port-braised red cabbage, chestnut, pancetta and sprouts, fondant potato and juniper jus, and puddings such as panna cotta with poached rhubarb, parkin and star anise ice-cream and passion-fruit soufflé. *Benchmark main dish: slow-cooked venison £22.00. Two-course evening meal £25.00.*

Free house ~ Licensees Lynn Cunnah-Watson and Tim Watson ~ Real ale ~ Open 12-3, 5.45-11.30; closed Sun and Mon ~ Bar food 12-2, 6-9 (9.30 Fri, Sat) ~ Restaurant ~ Children welcome but not in bedrooms ~ Dogs allowed in bar ~ Wi-fi ~ Bedrooms: £115/£135
Recommended by Pip White, Alison and Michael Harper

STACKPOLE
SR9896 Map 6

Stackpole Inn 🍴⭐ 🛏

(01646) 672324 – www.stackpoleinn.co.uk

Village signed off B4319 S of Pembroke; SA71 5DF

Busy pub, a good base for the area, with enjoyable food and friendly service; comfortable bedrooms

Within walking distance of the Pembrokeshire Coast Path and the Bosherston Lily Ponds, this is a highly popular pub on the National Trust's Stackpole Estate. The attractive gardens feature colourful flowerbeds and mature trees and there are plenty of picnic-sets at the front. An area around the bar has pine tables and chairs, but most of the pub, L-shaped on four different levels, is given over to diners, with neat light oak furnishings, ash beams and low ceilings to match; background music and board games. Brains Rev James, Evan Evans Cwrw, Felinfoel Best Bitter and Mantle Rock Steady on handpump, 14 wines by the glass, 15 malt whiskies and two farm ciders. The bedrooms are spotless and the breakfasts enjoyable.

🍴⭐ As well as a walker's lunch (12-2pm) and rustic rolls, the highly rated food includes pork and thyme terrine with piccalilli, beetroot-marinated gravadlax with sour cream, celeriac and mustard seeds, risotto verde with asparagus and peas, honey- and mustard-glazed sausages with spring onion mash and rich cider gravy, chicken, courgette and tomato tagliatelle with mature local cheese, lamb rump on potato rösti with pea purée and minted jus, and puddings such as rosemary and vanilla panna cotta with apple crisp and poached rhubarb and almond slice with orange and lemon parfait and toffee orange sauce. *Benchmark main dish: grilled haddock topped with welsh rarebit £14.00. Two-course evening meal £20.00.*

Free house ~ Licensees Gary and Becky Evans ~ Real ale ~ Open 12-3, 6-11; 12-11 Sat, Sun ~ Bar food 12-2, 6.30-9 ~ Restaurant ~ Children welcome ~ Dogs allowed in bar ~ Wi-fi ~ Bedrooms: £60/£90 *Recommended by M G Hart*

 TY'N-Y-GROES   SH7773 Map 6

Groes 🌟 🛏

(01492) 650545 – www.groesinn.com

B5106 N of village; LL32 8TN

Stacks of character in gracious, antiques-filled 15th-c Snowdonia hotel with local beer and lovely garden

With a fine setting overlooking the Vale of Conwy and the peaks of Snowdonia, this efficiently run hotel has been welcoming visitors since well before 1573. Customers are still more than happy to stay here: the bedrooms are now well equipped suites (some with terraces or balconies) and have gorgeous views; they also rent out a well appointed wooden cabin and a cottage in the historic centre of Conwy. Past the hot woodburning stove in the entrance area, the rambling, low-beamed and thick-walled rooms are nicely decorated with antique settles and an old sofa, with old clocks, portraits, hats and tins hanging from the walls and fresh flowers. Built into one wall is a fine antique fireback – perhaps originally from the formidable fireplace in the back bar, which houses a collection of stone cats as well as cheerful winter log fires; background music. You might find a harpist playing here on certain days. They keep Groes Ale (named for the pub) from the family's own Great Orme brewery a couple of miles away, alongside a guest such as Sharps Doom Bar, on handpump, several bottled Great Orme beers, 20 wines by the glass and 20 malt whiskies. Several options for dining include an airy conservatory and a smart restaurant set with white linen. The idyllic back garden has flower-filled hayracks and a verdant outlook, and there are more seats on a narrow flower-decked roadside terrace.

Using local, seasonal produce, the hearty food includes lunchtime sandwiches, mussel popcorn with sweet chilli dip, confit duck leg with plum sauce, mushroom and herb pancake with creamy cheese sauce, chicken curry with naan and poppadums, burger with toppings, onion rings and chips, bass with scallops and cauliflower purée, steak and kidney pudding, pigeon with cider apple confit and roast potatoes, and puddings such as chocolate and amaretto mousse and elderflower and lime jelly with chantilly cream. *Benchmark main dish: local lamb cutlets with redcurrant and rosemary gravy £16.75. Two-course evening meal £20.00.*

Free house ~ Licensee Dawn Humphreys ~ Real ale ~ Open 12-3, 6-11 (10.30 Sun) ~ Bar food 12-2, 6.30-9; 12-3, 6-8 Sun ~ Restaurant ~ Children welcome ~ Dogs allowed in bar and bedrooms ~ Wi-fi ~ Bedrooms: £100/£125 *Recommended by Paul and Sonia Broadgate, Derek Stafford*

 USK   SO3700 Map 6

Nags Head ♀

(01291) 672820

The Square; NP15 1BH

Spotlessly kept and traditional in style with a hearty welcome and good food and drinks

For 48 years, this handsome coaching inn has been run by the friendly and enthusiastic Key family. The traditional main bar is cheerily chatty and cosy, with lots of well polished tables and chairs packed under its beams (some with farming tools, lanterns or horsebrasses and harness attached), as well as leatherette wall benches and various sets of sporting prints and local pictures – look out for the original deeds to the pub. Tucked away at the front is an intimate little corner with some african masks, while on the other side of the room a passageway leads to a dining area; background music. There may be prints for sale, and perhaps a group of sociable locals. They offer a dozen wines by the glass, along with Brains Rev James and SA, and a guest such as Sharps Doom Bar on handpump. The church is well worth a look. The pub has no parking and nearby street parking can be limited.

Generous helpings of well liked food include sandwiches, leek and welsh cheddar soup, faggots and gravy, steak pie, sausages and mash, pheasant in port, half a duck in Cointreau, and puddings such as treacle and walnut tart and sticky toffee pudding. *Benchmark main dish: rabbit pie £10.00. Two-course evening meal £15.00.*

Free house ~ Licensee Key family ~ Real ale ~ Open 10.30-3, 5-11 ~ Bar food 11.30-2, 5.30-9.30 ~ Restaurant ~ Children welcome ~ Dogs welcome ~ Wi-fi
Recommended by Phil and Jane Hodson

Also Worth a Visit in Wales

Besides the fully inspected pubs, you might like to try these pubs that have been recommended to us and described by readers. Do tell us what you think of them: feedback@goodguides.com

ANGLESEY

ABERFFRAW   SH3568
Crown (01407) 840222
Bodorgan Square; LL63 5BX Refurbished pub in small village set back from the coast, well kept Sharps Doom Bar and two local beers, enjoyable competitively priced home-made food, quick friendly service; sports TV; well behaved children and dogs welcome, suntrap beer garden with sturdy furniture and views towards the dunes, closed Mon, Tues, otherwise open all day (Sun till 8pm). *(Michael Butler)*

MENAI BRIDGE   SH5773
Gazelle (01248) 713364
Glyngarth; A545, halfway towards Beaumaris; LL59 5PD Hotel and restaurant rather than pub in outstanding waterside position looking across to Snowdonia, main bar with smaller rooms off, up to three Robinsons ales kept well and seven wines by the glass, good reasonably priced food from bar snacks up; children and dogs (in bar) welcome, steep garden behind (and walk down from car park), 11 bedrooms, slipway and mooring for visiting boats, open all day summer, all day Fri-Sun winter. *(Paul and Karen Cornock)*

RED WHARF BAY   SH5281
Ship (01248) 852568
Village signed off A5025 N of Pentraeth; LL75 8RJ Whitewashed 18th-c pub worth visiting for position right on Anglesey's east coast (arrive early for a seat with fantastic views of miles of tidal sands); big old-fashioned rooms either side of bar counter, nautical bric-a-brac, long varnished wall pews, cast-iron-framed tables and open fires, three well kept ales including Adnams, 50 malt whiskies and decent choice of wines, enjoyable food; if you run a tab they lock your card in a numbered box and hand you the key, background music in lounge; children welcome in room on left, dogs in bar, limited disabled access, numerous outside tables, open all day. *(Michael Butler)*

RHOSCOLYN   SH2675
★**White Eagle** (01407) 860267
Off B4545 S of Holyhead; LL65 2NJ Remote place rebuilt almost from scratch on site of an old pub; airy modern feel in neatly kept rooms, relaxed atmosphere and nice winter fire, Marstons, Weetwood and three guests from smart oak counter, several wines by the glass, extensive choice of good locally sourced food (all day weekends and school holidays, best to book), friendly helpful

---

Pubs close to motorway junctions are listed at the back of the book.

service, restaurant; children welcome, dogs in bar (biscuits for them), terrific sea views from decking and picnic-sets in good-sized garden, lane down to beach, open all day. *(Michael Butler, Roy and Gill Payne, Chris and Val Ramstedt)*

RHOSNEIGR   SH3272
Oystercatcher (01407) 812829
A4080; LL64 5JP Modern glass-fronted Huf Haus set in dunes close to the sea – same owners as the White Eagle at Rhoscolyn but not really a pub (created as a restaurant/chefs' academy); great views from upstairs restaurant and bar with good range of enjoyable food, a house beer from Marstons and a couple of guests such as Conwy, decent choice of wines by the glass, ground-floor coffee/wine bar serving lighter meals till 6pm; children welcome, upper terrace with rattan sofas and colourful reproduction beach huts, full wheelchair access, open all day. *(Simon and Mandy King, Chris and Val Ramstedt)*

CLWYD

CAERWYS   SJ1373
Piccadilly (01352) 720284
North Street; CH7 5AW Pleasantly modernised pub-restaurant under newish management, high-ceilinged bare-boards bar with raised central woodburner, dining room across corridor with white-painted beams and tartan carpet, spacious slate-floor restaurant behind, banquettes and light wood furniture, stairs up to further eating area, good choice of enjoyable food from sandwiches, sharing boards and pub favourites up, Weds burger night, three real ales, good smiling service; background music, daily papers; children welcome, partly covered side terrace, open (and food) all day, till 7.30pm Sun. *(Robert Wivell)*

CARROG   SJ1143
Grouse (01490) 430272
B5436, signed off A5 Llangollen–Corwen; LL21 9AT Small unpretentious pub with superb views over River Dee and beyond from bay window and balcony, Lees ales, decent food all day from sandwiches up, reasonable prices, friendly helpful staff, local pictures, pool in games room; background music; children welcome, wheelchair access (side door a bit tight), tables in pretty walled garden, covered terrace for smokers, narrow turn into car park, handy for Llangollen steam railway. *(Alison and Michael Harper)*

GRAIG FECHAN   SJ1454
Three Pigeons (01824) 703178
Signed off B5429 S of Ruthin; LL15 2EU Extended largely 18th-c pub with enjoyable inexpensive food from sandwiches up (all day Sun), friendly licensees, good range of real

ales and plenty of wines by the glass, various nooks and corners, interesting mix of furniture and some old signs on the walls, great country views from restaurant; children allowed if eating, big garden with terrace and same views, two self-catering apartments, closed Mon, good walks. *(Rob Anderson)*

HAWARDEN   SJ3266
Glynne Arms (01244) 569988
Glynne Way; CH5 3NS Nicely renovated early 19th-c stone coaching inn, generally well liked food (prices can be on the high side) in bar and bistro-style restaurant using own locally farmed produce (they also have a farm shop nearby), four welsh ales; children welcome, dogs in bar, open (and food) all day. *(Andrew Stone)*

LLANFERRES   SJ1860
Druid (01352) 810225
A494 Mold–Ruthin; CH7 5SN Extended 17th-c whitewashed inn set in fine walking country along the Alyn Valley towards Loggerheads Country Park, or up Offa's Dyke Path to Moel Famau; views from broad bay window in civilised plush lounge and from bigger beamed back bar with two handsome antique oak settles, pleasant mix of more modern furnishings and quarry-tiled area by log fire. Marstons-related ales, 30 malt whiskies, reasonably priced traditional food plus specials, games room with darts and pool, board games; background music, TV; children welcome, dogs in bar and bedroom, stables outside at the front, open all day Fri, Sat, till 10pm Sun. *(Pip White)*

MINERA   SJ2651
Tyn-y-Capel (01978) 269347
Church Road; LL11 3DA Community-owned pub run mainly by volunteers, good locally sourced food (not Sun evening) including ramblers' menu, half a dozen changing ales (one badged for them from Big Hand), local cider; Sun quiz, also traditional music first Sun afternoon of the month; children and dogs (in bar) welcome, lovely hill views from terrace, park opposite with play area, closed Mon, Tues, lunchtime Weds, otherwise open all day. *(Helen Eustace, Dr David and Mrs Clare Gidlow)*

RUABON   SJ3043
Bridge End (01978) 810881
Bridge Street; LL14 6DA Proper old-fashioned pub owned by McGivern, their ales (brewed here) and several guests, local ciders, friendly staff and cheerful atmosphere, snacky food (can bring takeaways from next-door chinese restauarant), black beams and open fires; Tues quiz; children and dogs welcome, garden, open all day weekends and from 5pm weekdays (4pm Fri). *(Alison and Michael Harper)*

DYFED

ABERAERON   SN4562
Cadwgan (01545) 570149
Market Street; SA46 0AU Small late 18th-c
pub opposite harbour, basic with friendly
regulars, well kept Hancocks HB and a guest,
some nautical memorabilia and interesting
old photographs, open fire, no food; sports TV;
children and dogs welcome, pavement seats
and little garden behind, closed Sun evening,
Mon lunchtime, otherwise open all day.
(Andrew Stone)

ABERAERON   SN4562
Castle (01545) 570205
Market Street; SA46 0AU Red-painted
early 19th-c corner building with popular
boldly decorated café-bar and elegant
wood-floored restaurant upstairs, friendly
efficient service, good freshly cooked food
and sensibly priced wine list (prosecco on
tap), Evan Evans or Sharps Doom Bar, welsh
whisky; background music, sports TV; six
comfortable bedrooms and self-catering
apartment, open all day. *(Francis)*

ABERAERON   SN4562
★Harbourmaster (01545) 570755
Harbour Lane; SA46 0BA Handsome,
well run and welcoming small hotel in
prime spot by yacht-filled harbour; bar
with assortment of leather sofas, zinc-clad
counter and stuffed albatross (reputed to
have collided with a ship belonging to the
owner's great-grandfather), two ales from
Purple Moose including one for the pub, a
guest beer, traditional cider and 14 good
wines by the glass, big minimalist dining area
with modern light wood furniture on pale
floorboards, good interesting food, there's
also a four-seater cwtch (or snug) in former
porch; TV for rugby, free wi-fi; children over
5 welcome if staying, disabled access, can sit
on outside bench and take in the view, most
bedrooms also overlook the harbour, good
breakfast, self-catering cottage, open all day
from 8am. *(Lois Dyer, Dr Kevan Tucker,
Mr and Mrs P R Thomas and others)*

ABERCYCH   SN2539
★Nags Head (01239) 841200
Off B4332 Cenarth–Boncath; SA37 0HJ
Friendly tucked-away riverside pub with
dimly lit beamed and flagstoned bar, stripped
wood tables and woodburner in big fireplace,
hundreds of beer bottles, clocks showing
time around the world, photographs of locals
on brick and stone walls, a coracle hanging
from the ceiling in one part, even a large
stuffed rat, Mantle Cwrw Teifi and two guests,
pubby food and specials in two sizeable
dining areas; background music, piano;
children and dogs welcome (pub yorkie is
Scrappy), benches in garden overlooking
river (fishing rights), play area with wooden
castle, barbecues, three bedrooms, open all

day Fri-Sun, closed Mon lunchtime.
(R T and J C Moggridge, John and Enid)

ABERGORLECH   SN5833
★Black Lion (01558) 685271
B4310; SA32 7SN Friendly old pub in
fine rural position, traditional stripped-
stone beamed bar, oak furniture and
black settles on flagstones, old jugs and
other bits and pieces on shelves, local
paintings, woodburner, Rhymney and a
guest beer, proper ciders, good varied
choice of inexpensive home-cooked food,
dining extension with another woodburner;
background music, free wi-fi; children and
dogs welcome, lovely views of Cothi Valley
from riverside garden, two self-catering
cottages, good nearby mountain biking, open
all day weekends, closed Mon. *(Rob Anderson)*

BOSHERSTON   SR9694
St Govans Country Inn
(01646) 661311 *Off B4319 S of
Pembroke; SA71 5DN* Busy pub with
big modernised open-plan bar, cheery and
simple, with several changing ales and
enjoyable well priced pub food, good climbing
photographs and murals of local beauty spots,
log fire in large stone fireplace, dominoes,
board games, pool (winter only); background
music, TV, games machine; children and dogs
welcome, picnic-sets on small front terrace,
four good value bedrooms (car park if you
stay), handy for water-lily lakes, beach and
cliff walks, open all day in season (all day
weekends at other times). *(Ian and Jane
Irving)*

BROAD HAVEN   SM8614
★Druidstone Hotel (01437) 781221
*N on coast road, bear left for about 1.5
miles then follow sign left to Druidstone
Haven; SA62 3NE* Cheerfully informal
country house in grand spot above the sea,
individual, relaxed and with terrific views,
inventive cooking using fresh often organic
ingredients (best to book) including good
value themed 'feast evening' Tues, helpful
efficient service, cellar bar with local ale
tapped from the cask, country wines and
other drinks, ceilidhs and folk events,
friendly pub dogs (others welcome), all
sorts of sporting activities from boules to
sand-yachting; attractive high-walled garden,
spacious homely bedrooms and self-catering
cottages, closed Jan, Nov, restaurant closed
Sun evening. *(Richard and Judy Winn, John
and Enid)*

BURRY PORT   SN4400
Cornish Arms (01554) 833224
Gors Road; SA16 0EL Nothing special
from the outside but worth knowing for
its good fresh fish (plenty of blackboard
specials) and four well kept welsh ales,
cheerful helpful service, large back
restaurant; children welcome, handy for the
station, open all day. *(Carol and Luke Wilson)*

CAIO   SN6739
Brunant Arms (01558) 650483
Off A482 Llanwrda–Lampeter;
SA19 8RD Unpretentious and interestingly
furnished village pub, comfortable and
friendly with helpful staff, beams and nice
log fire, a couple of ales such as Evan Evans,
enjoyable regularly changing home-made
food from baguettes up, stripped-stone public
bar with games including pool; some live
music, sports TV; children and dogs welcome,
small Perspex-roofed verandah and lower
terrace, handy for Dolaucothi Gold Mines
(NT), open all day. *(Andrew Stone)*

CAREW   SN0403
★Carew Inn (01646) 651267
A4075 off A477; SA70 8SL Stone-built
pub with appealing cottagey atmosphere,
unpretentious small panelled public bar,
nice old bentwood stools and mix of tables
and chairs on bare boards, small dining
area, lounge bar with low tables, warm open
fires, Brains, Sharps, Worthington and a
guest, enjoyable generously served food, two
upstairs dining rooms with black leather
chairs at black tables; background music,
darts; children and dogs (in bar) welcome,
enclosed back garden with play equipment,
view of imposing Carew Castle ruins and
remarkable 9th-c celtic cross, open all day.
(N R White)

CILYCWM   SN7540
Neuadd Fawr Arms (01550) 721644
By church entrance; SA20 0ST Restored
18th-c drovers' inn with eclectic mix of
old furniture on huge slate flagstones,
woodburners, good seasonal food with
interesting specials in bar or smaller dining
room, one or two changing local ales,
friendly helpful service; children and dogs
welcome, good spot by churchyard above
River Gwenlais, among lanes to Llyn Brianne,
open all day weekends, may close weekday
lunchtimes in winter. *(Rob Anderson)*

COSHESTON   SN0003
Brewery Inn (01646) 686678
Signed E from village crossroads;
SA72 4UD Welcoming 17th-c village pub
under new ownership, good fairly priced food
from shortish menu, a locally brewed house
beer and a guest, helpful friendly service;
children and dogs welcome, closed Sun
evening, Mon. *(Alison and Michael Harper)*

CRESSWELL QUAY   SN0506
★Cresselly Arms (01646) 651210
Village signed from A4075; SA68 0TE
Simple unchanging alehouse overlooking
tidal creek; plenty of local customers in two
old-fashioned linked rooms, built-in wall
benches, kitchen chairs and plain tables on
red and black tiles, open fire in one room,
Aga in the other with lots of pictorial china
hanging from high beam-and-plank ceiling,

a third more conventionally furnished
red-carpeted room, a house beer from Caffle
along with Sharps, Worthington and a guest
served from glass jugs; no children or dogs,
seats outside making most of view, you can
arrive by boat if tide is right, open all day in
summer. *(Giles and Annie Francis)*

CWM GWAUN   SN0333
★Dyffryn Arms (01348) 881305
Cwm Gwaun and Pontfaen signed off
B4313 E of Fishguard; SA65 9SE Classic
rural time warp, virtually the social centre
for this lush green valley, very relaxed, basic
and idiosyncratic, with much-loved veteran
landlady (her farming family have run it
since 1840 and she's been in charge for well
over a third of that time); 1920s front parlour
with plain deal furniture and draughts boards
inlaid into tables, red and black quarry tiles,
woodburner, well kept Bass served by jug
through sliding hatch, low prices, World War
I prints and posters, a young portrait of the
Queen and large collection of banknotes,
darts; may be duck eggs for sale; lovely
outside view and walks in nearby Preseli
Hills, open more or less all day (may close
if no customers). *(Giles and Annie Francis,
Dr Kevan Tucker)*

DINAS   SN0139
Old Sailors (01348) 811491
Pwllgwaelod; from A487 in Dinas Cross
follow Bryn-henllan signpost; SA42 0SE
Shack-like building in superb position,
snugged down into the sand by isolated cove
below Dinas Head with its bracing walks;
specialising in fresh local seafood (usually
have crab and lobster), also good snacks,
coffee and summer cream teas, well kept
Felinfoel Double Dragon and decent wine,
maritime bric-a-brac; children welcome, no
dogs inside, picnic-sets on grass overlooking
beach with views across to Fishguard, closed
Mon, open all day rest of week (Tues till 6pm
if quiet), shut Jan. *(Dr Kevan Tucker)*

FISHGUARD   SM9537
★Fishguard Arms (01348) 872763
Main Street (A487); SA65 9HJ Tiny
unspoilt bay-windowed terrace pub with
friendly community atmosphere and
character landlord, front bar with unusually
high counter serving well kept/priced Bass
direct from the cask, rugby photographs
and open fire, back snug with woodburner,
traditional games and sports TV, no food;
smokers' area out behind, open all day,
closed Weds evening. *(Giles and Annie Francis)*

FISHGUARD   SM9637
Ship (01348) 874033
Newport Road, Lower Town; SA65 9ND
Cheerful atmosphere and charming landlord
in softly lit 18th-c pub near old harbour,
well kept Felinfoel Double Dragon and
Theakstons tapped from the cask, coal fire,
lots of boat pictures, model ships and photos

of actors such as Richard Burton and Peter O'Toole who drank here while filming locally, no food, piano and occasional live music; TV for rugby; children welcome (toys provided), dogs on leads, open all day weekends, closed Mon (also Tues in winter) and weekday lunchtimes. *(Giles and Annie Francis)*

HERMON   SN2031
Lamb (01239) 831864
Taylors Row; SA36 0DS Friendly family-run pub dating from the 17th c, homely and comfortable, with generously served food cooked by landlady; well behaved dogs welcome, three good value bedrooms, caravan pitches. *(Ron Corbett)*

JAMESTON   SS0699
Tudor Lodge (01834) 871212
A4139, E of Jameston; SA70 7SS Friendly family-run inn close to the coast, two character bars with open fire and woodburner, Sharps Doom Bar and several wines by the glass, airy carpeted dining room with pale beams and high-backed chairs around sturdy tables, second dining room with modern art, well liked food including Tues curries and Thurs steak night; children welcome, play area and plenty of picnic-sets outside, stylishly comfortable bedrooms, good breakfast, open all day weekends, from 4pm weekdays. *(M G Hart)*

LITTLE HAVEN   SM8512
★**Castle Inn** (01437) 781445
Grove Place; SA62 3UF Welcoming pub well placed by green looking over sandy bay (lovely sunsets), popular generously served food including pizzas and good local fish, Marstons-related ales, decent choice of wines by the glass, tea and cafetière coffee, bare-boards bar and carpeted dining area with big oak tables, beams, some stripped stone, castle prints, pool in back area; children and dogs welcome, picnic-sets out in front, New Year's Day charity swim, open all day. *(Norman Jones, John and Enid)*

LITTLE HAVEN   SM8512
St Brides Inn (01437) 781266
St Brides Road; SA62 3UN Just 20 metres from Pembrokeshire Coast Path; neat stripped-stone bar and linked carpeted dining area, traditional furnishings, log fire, interesting well in back corner grotto thought to be partly Roman, Banks's, Marstons and a guest, enjoyable bar food; background music and TV; children welcome, dogs in bar, seats in sheltered suntrap terrace garden across road, two bedrooms, open all day in summer. *(Rob Anderson)*

LLANDDAROG   SN5016
★**Butchers Arms** (01267) 275330
On back road by church; SA32 8NS Ancient heavily black-beamed local with three intimate eating areas off small central bar, welcoming young staff, good generously served popular food, cask-tapped Felinfoel ales and nice wines by the glass, conventional pub furniture, gleaming brass, candles in bottles, open woodburner in biggish fireplace; background music; children welcome, tables outside and pretty window boxes, bedroom in converted stables, closed Sun and Mon. *(Pip White)*

LLANDDAROG   SN5016
White Hart (01267) 275395
Aka Yr Hydd Gwyn; off A48 E of Carmarthen, via B4310; SA32 8NT Ancient thatched pub with own-brew beers using water from 90-metre borehole, also own ciders; comfortable lived-in beamed rooms with lots of engaging bric-a-brac and antiques including a suit of armour, 17th-c carved settles by huge log fire, interestingly furnished high-raftered dining room, fish tank and parrot in one part, generous if not cheap food, home-made jams, chutneys and honey for sale; cash or debit cards only, background music; children welcome, no dogs inside, disabled access (ramps provided), picnic-sets on front terrace and in back garden with play area, small farmyard, closed Weds. *(Mike and Mary Carter)*

LLANDOVERY   SN7634
Castle (01550) 720343
Kings Road; SA20 0AP Popular and welcoming hotel next to castle ruins, good attractively presented food from sandwiches and deli boards to charcoal grills and fresh fish specials, courteous efficient service, well kept Gower Gold and a couple of guests; children and dogs welcome, picnic-sets out in front under parasols, comfortable bedrooms, open all day. *(R T and J C Moggridge)*

LLANDOVERY   SN7634
Kings Head (01550) 720393
Market Square; SA20 0AB Early 18th-c beamed coaching inn, pattern-carpeted bar with exposed stonework and large woodburner, enjoyable food from snacks and bar meals up, three well kept ales including Evan Evans, friendly service; children and dogs welcome, nine bedrooms, open all day. *(R T and J C Moggridge)*

LLANFALLTEG   SN1519
Plash (01437) 563472
Village NE of Whitland; SA34 0UN Small mid-terrace village local with a warm welcome from enthusiastic licensees, beamed bar with piano and open fire, well kept ales such as Purple Moose, Salopian, Three Tuns and Wye Valley, Stowford Press cider, some low-priced bar food along with pizzas; children and dogs welcome, garden tables, self-catering cottage, open all day (no food Mon). *(Andrew Stone)*

LLANGRANNOG   SN3154
Pentre Arms (01239) 654345
On the front; SA44 6SP Friendly old

seafront pub beautifully placed in this pretty coastal village, magnificent sunset sea-views from bar's picture window, well kept Gales, St Austell and a guest, standard food including good steaks and often fresh fish, separate restaurant, pool room with games machines and TV; live music Sat; children and dogs (in bar) welcome, seven bedrooms (some directly overlooking the small bay), staff will advise on dolphin watching, handy for coast path, open all day. *(Mike and Eleanor Anderson)*

LLANGRANOG   SN3154
Ship (01239) 654510
Near the front, by car park entrance; SA44 6SL Just back from the bay with tables out by beachside car park; good generous food including local fish/seafood (booking advised weekends), friendly accommodating staff, well kept ales such as Mantle and good selection of gins, refurbished bare-boards bar with burnt-orange walls and big woodburner, further spacious upstairs eating area, local artwork for sale, games room with pool; weekend live music; children and dogs welcome, can get busy summer, car parking charge refunded against food, open all day. *(Mike and Eleanor Anderson)*

MARLOES   SM7908
Lobster Pot (01646) 636233
Gay Lane; SA62 3AZ Village local handy for lovely beach and coast walk; friendly staff, enjoyable reasonably priced food from well filled baguettes up, Felinfoel Double Dragon and Sharps Doom Bar, games area with darts; background music; children welcome, no dogs inside, tables out in front and in back garden with play area, open all day. *(Mike and Jayne Bastin)*

NEWCHAPEL   SN2239
Ffynnone Arms (01239) 841800
B4332; SA37 0EH Welcoming 18th-c beamed pub with enjoyable traditional food including Sun carvery, special diets catered for and some produce home-grown, a couple of changing ales, local cider and afternoon teas in season, two woodburners; darts, pool and table skittles; disabled facilities, picnic-sets in small garden, open all day weekends (from 2pm Sat), closed weekday lunchtimes, food served Wed evening to Sun lunchtime. *(Alison and Michael Harper)*

NEWPORT   SN0539
Castle (01239) 820742
Bridge Street; SA42 0TB Welcoming old pub with bar, lounge and restaurant, enjoyable reasonably priced home-made food including Sun carvery, ales from Mantle and Wye Valley, pleasant service; some live music, quiz night Thurs; children and dogs welcome, three bedrooms, handy for Parrog estuary walk (especially for bird-watchers), open all day. *(Pip White)*

PEMBROKE DOCK   SM9603
Shipwright (01646) 682090
Front Street; SA72 6JX Little blue-painted end of terrace pub on waterfront overlooking estuary, enjoyable home-made food and well kept Sharps Doom Bar, friendly efficient staff, bare-boards interior with nautical and other memorabilia, some booth seating; children welcome, five minutes from Ireland ferry terminal. *(R T and J C Moggridge, D and M T Ayres-Regan)*

PENRHIWLLAN   SN3641
Daffodil (01559) 370343
A475 Newcastle Emlyn–Lampeter; SA44 5NG Contemporary open-plan dining pub with comfortable welcoming bar (though most there to eat), sofas and leather tub chairs on pale limestone floor, woodburner, Greene King Abbot and guests from granite-panelled counter, two lower-ceilinged end rooms with big oriental rugs, steps down to a couple of airy dining rooms, one with picture windows by open kitchen, well liked food including daily specials and two-course lunch menu; background music; children welcome, nicely furnished decked area outside with valley views. *(Andrew Stone)*

PONTRHYDFENDIGAID   SN7366
Black Lion (01974) 831624
Off B4343 Tregaron–Devils Bridge; SY25 6BE Relaxed country inn under friendly landlord, smallish main bar with dark beams and floorboards, lots of stripped stone, old country furniture, woodburner and big pot-irons in vast fireplace, copper, brass and so forth on mantelpiece, historical photographs, Felinfoel Double Dragon and a local guest, seven wines by the glass, enjoyable good value home-cooked food including vegetarian/vegan options, quarry-tiled back dining room, small games room with pool and darts; background music; children and dogs (away from diners) welcome, back courtyard and tree-shaded garden, seven bedrooms (five in converted stables), good walking/cycling country and not far from Strata Florida Abbey, open all day. *(Taff Thomas, B and M Kendall)*

PORTHGAIN   SM8132
★ Sloop (01348) 831449
Off A487 St Davids–Fishguard; SA62 5BN Busy tavern (especially holiday times) snuggled down in cove wedged tightly between headlands on Pembrokeshire Coast Path – fine walks in either direction; plank-ceilinged bar with lots of lobster pots and fishing nets, ship clocks, lanterns and some relics from local wrecks, decent-sized eating area with simple furnishings and freezer for kid's ice-creams, well liked bar food from sandwiches to good steaks and fresh fish (own fishing business), Brains, Felinfoel and Greene King, separate games room with juke box; seats on heated terrace overlooking

harbour, self-catering cottage in village, open all day from 9.30am for breakfast, till 1am Fri, Sat. *(Simon Watkins)*

PUMSAINT SN6540

Dolaucothi Arms (01558) 650237

A482 Lampeter–Llandovery; SA19 8UW Welcoming NT-owned pub (part of the Dolaucothi Estate), local beers and hearty home-made food (not Sun evening), flagstoned bar with two woodburners; muddy walkers and dogs welcome, garden overlooking Cothi River – pub has 4 miles of fishing rights, two bedrooms, closed Mon and lunchtime Tues, otherwise open all day. *(Andrew Stone)*

RHANDIRMWYN SN7843

Royal Oak (01550) 760201

7 miles N of Llandovery; SA20 0NY Friendly 17th-c stone inn set in remote and peaceful walking country, comfortable traditional bar with log fire, four well kept local ales, ciders and perries, good variety of popular sensibly priced food sourced locally, big dining area, pool room; children and dogs welcome, hill views from garden and cottagey bedrooms, handy for Brecon Beacons. *(Anon)*

ROSEBUSH SN0729

★Tafarn Sinc (01437) 532214

B4329 Haverfordwest–Cardigan; SA66 7QU Former Victorian hotel on long-defunct railway (once served the nearby abandoned slate quarries); extraordinary maroon-painted corrugated structure; the halt itself has been more or less re-created, even down to life-size dummy passengers on the platform, the sizeable garden is periodically enlivened by sounds of chuffing steam trains (actually broadcast from a replica signal box); interior reminiscent of a local history museum with sawdust floors, hams, washing and goodness knows what else hanging from the ceiling, bar has plank panelling, informal mix of old chairs and pews and a woodburner, Cwrw Tafarn Sinc (brewed locally for them) and Sharps Doom Bar, simple food, buoyant atmosphere with Welsh spoken; background music, darts, games machine, board games and TV; children welcome, closed Mon (except Aug and bank holidays), otherwise open all day. *(Dr Kevan Tucker, Simon Watkins, John and Enid)*

ST DAVIDS SM7525

Farmers Arms (01437) 721666

Goat Street; SA62 6RF Bustling old-fashioned low-ceilinged pub by cathedral gate, cheerful and unpretentiously pubby, mainly drinking on the left and eating on the right, central servery with three well kept ales including Felinfoel Double Dragon, tasty good value food from snacks up (not during the winter), friendly staff and atmosphere; TV for rugby, pool, free wi-fi; children and

dogs welcome, cathedral view from large tables on big back suntrap terrace, open all day in summer, closed weekday lunchtimes winter. *(B and M Kendall)*

ST DOGMAELS SN1646

Ferry (01239) 615172

B4546; SA43 3LF Old stone building with spectacular views of Teifi estuary and hills from picture-window dining extension, popular freshly made food, character bar with pine tables and interesting old photographs, Brains and summer guest ales, several wines by the glass, pleasant attentive staff; background music, monthly quiz; children and dogs welcome, plenty of room outside on linked decked areas, open all day. *(Alison and Michael Harper)*

TENBY SN1300

Buccaneer (01834) 842273

St Julian's Street; SA70 7AS Popular place with generous helpings of enjoyable affordably priced food, well kept ales and friendly efficient service; live music Weds and Fri; children welcome, sunny beer garden, open (and food) all day. *(Mike and Mary Carter)*

TRESAITH SN2751

★Ship (01239) 811816

Off A487 E of Cardigan; bear right in village and keep on down – pub car park fills quickly; SA43 2JL Recent refurbishment and in excellent position beside broad sandy surfing beach (maybe dolphins), seats under canopy on heated deck and picnic-sets on two-level terrace; front dining area with same view, room behind with winter log fire and two further back rooms – one with stove, Brains Rev James and SA, food can be good; children and dogs welcome, four sea-view bedrooms and lovely coastal walks from this steep little village, open all day. *(Simon Rodway, Lois Dyer, Kay and Alistair Butler)*

GLAMORGAN

BISHOPSTON SS5789

Joiners Arms (01792) 232658

Bishopston Road, just off B4436 SW of Swansea; SA3 3EJ Thriving local brewing its own good value Swansea ales along with well kept guests such as Courage Best, ample helpings of enjoyable freshly made pub food (not Sun evening, Mon), friendly staff, unpretentious quarry-tiled bar with massive solid-fuel stove, comfortable lounge; TV for rugby; children welcome, open all day. *(M G Hart)*

CARDIFF ST1876

City Arms (029) 2064 1913

Quay Street; CF10 1EA City-centre alehouse with four Brains beers and ten regularly changing guests (some cask-tapped), tasting trays available, also plenty of draught/bottled continentals and real cider, friendly knowledgeable staff, no food; some live music, free wi-fi; open all day (till 2am Fri, Sat). *(Pip White)*

CARDIFF ST1876
Cottage (029) 2033 7195
St Mary Street, near Howells; CF10 1AA
Traditional 18th-c Brains pub with their full range kept well, long neat bar with narrow frontage and back eating area, lots of polished wood, glass and mirrors, pictures on papered walls, brasserie-style food including sharing platters, good cheerful service and relaxed friendly atmosphere even Fri and Sat when crowded (gets packed on rugby international days); open all day. *(Pip White)*

CARDIFF ST1776
Cricketers (029) 2034 5102
Cathedral Road; CF11 9LL Victorian townhouse in quiet residential area backing on to Glamorgan CC, well kept Evan Evans ales and enjoyably freshly made food (not Sun evening), Thurs jazz supper; children welcome, sunny back garden, open all day. *(Michael Butler)*

CARDIFF ST1876
Goat Major (029) 2033 7161
High Street, opposite castle; CF10 1PU Named for Royal Welsh Regiment mascot (plenty of pictures), Victorian-style décor with dark panelling and green leatherette wall seats, shiny floor tiles around bar, carpets beyond, Brains beers kept well, pie-based menu till 6pm (4pm Sun), friendly young staff; background music, silent TVs showing subtitled news; children welcome, open all day. *(Jeremy King, Dave Braisted)*

CARDIFF ST1876
Zero Degrees (029) 2022 9494
Westgate Street; CF10 1DD Lively contemporary place on two levels visibly brewing its own interesting beers, good selection of other drinks including cocktails and 'beertails', enjoyable italian-leaning food (popular pizzas) and mussel dishes, friendly staff; background music, sports TVs, free wi-fi; open all day. *(Berwyn Owen)*

COWBRIDGE SS9974
★ Bear (01446) 774814
High Street, with car park behind off North Street; signed off A48; CF71 7AF Busy Georgian coaching inn in smart village, well kept Brains, Hancocks and guests, decent house wines, enjoyable usual food from good sandwiches and wraps up, friendly helpful service, three attractively furnished bars with flagstones, bare boards or carpet, some stripped stone and panelling, big hot open fires, barrel-vaulted cellar restaurant; children and dogs (in one bar) welcome, courtyard tables, comfortable quiet bedrooms, disabled parking, open all day. *(Alison and Michael Harper)*

GWAELOD-Y-GARTH ST1183
Gwaelod y Garth Inn
(029) 2081 0408 *Main Road; CF15 9HH* Meaning 'foot of the mountain', this stone-built village pub has wonderful valley views and is popular with walkers on the Taff Ely Ridgeway Path; highly thought-of well presented food (all day Fri and Sat, not Sun evening), friendly efficient service, own-brew beer along with Wye Valley and guests from pine-clad bar, log fires, upstairs restaurant (disabled access from back car park); table skittles, pool, juke box; children and dogs welcome, three bedrooms, open all day. *(Rob Anderson)*

KENFIG SS8081
★ Prince of Wales (01656) 740356
2.2 miles from M4 junction 37; A4229 towards Porthcawl, then right when dual carriageway narrows on bend, signed 'Maudlam, Kenfig'; CF33 4PR Ancient local with plenty of individuality by historic sand dunes, cheerful welcoming landlord, well kept ales tapped from the cask, decent wines and good choice of malts, enjoyable straightforward generous food at fair prices (not Mon), chatty panelled room off main bar (dogs allowed here), log fires, stripped stone and lots of wreck pictures, restaurant with upstairs overspill room, several ghosts; TV for special rugby events; children till 9pm, handy for nature reserve (June orchids), open all day. *(Alison and Michael Harper)*

LISVANE ST1883
Ty Mawr Arms (01222) 754456
From B4562 on E edge turn N into Church Road, bear left into Llwyn y Pia Road, keep on along Graig Road; CF14 0UF Large welcoming country pub with good choice of popular food, well kept Brains and guest ales, decent wines by the glass, teas and coffees, friendly service, great views over Cardiff from spacious bay-windowed dining area off traditional log-fire bar; children welcome, disabled access with help to main bar area, attractive big garden with pond, open all day. *(Roger and Donna Huggins)*

LLANBLETHIAN SS9873
Cross (01446) 772995
Church Road; CF71 7JF Welcoming former staging inn, enjoyable freshly made food from pubby choices up in bar or airy split-level restaurant, reasonable prices and various deals, well kept Wye Valley and guests, good choice of wines, woodburner and open fire; children welcome, dogs in bar, tables out on decking, open all day. *(Ruth May)*

LLANCARFAN ST0570
Fox & Hounds (01446) 781287
Signed off A4226; can also be reached from A48 from Bonvilston or B4265 via Llancadle; CF62 3AD Good attractively

presented food using local ingredients in neat comfortably modernised village pub, Brains beers kept well and nice choice of wines, friendly staff; unobtrusive background music; tables on covered terrace, charming streamside setting by interesting church, eight comfortable and pretty bedrooms, good breakfast, closed Sun evening. *(Anon)*

LLANGENNITH SS4291
Kings Head (01792) 386212
Clos St Cenydd, opposite church; SA3 1HX Extended 17th-c stone inn with wide choice of popular food including good curries, own Gower brews and guests kept well, over 100 malt whiskies, friendly staff; pool and juke box in lively public bar – back bar quieter with dining areas; children and dogs welcome, large terrace with village views, good walks, not far from great surfing beach and large campsite, in separate buildings to the side and rear, open (and food) all day. *(Canon Michael Bourdeaux, David and Judy Robison)*

MUMBLES SS6287
Pilot 07897 895511
Mumbles Road; SA3 4EL Friendly 19th-c seafront local with half a dozen well kept ales including some from own back microbrewery, slate-floored bar with boat suspended from planked ceiling, no food; daily newspapers, TV, free wi-fi; dogs welcome, open all day. *(Chris Marsh)*

OLDWALLS SS4891
Greyhound (01792) 391027
W of Llanrhidian; SA3 1HA 19th-c pub with spacious beamed and dark-panelled carpeted lounge bar, well kept ales including own Gower brews, decent wine and coffee, wide choice of popular food from sandwiches and wraps up, friendly staff, hot coal fires, back dining room and upstairs overspill/function room; children and dogs welcome, picnic-sets in big garden with terrace, play area and good views, open all day. *(Rob Anderson)*

PENARTH ST1771
Pilot (029) 2071 0615
Queens Road; CF64 1DJ Clean fresh refurbishment for this end of terrace pub set high in residential area overlooking Cardiff Bay; good often interesting food from changing menu, four well kept ales, friendly welcoming staff; children and dogs allowed, tables out in narrow front area, open all day. *(John Jenkins)*

PONTNEDDFECHAN SN8907
Angel (01639) 722013
Just off A465; Pontneathvaughan Road; SA11 5NR Comfortably opened-up 16th-c pub with friendly staff and atmosphere, well kept ales such as Neath and Rhymney, enjoyable fairly priced pub food (good lamb cawl), masses of jugs on beams, ancient

houseware and old kitchen range, separate flagstoned bar; children welcome, terrace tables, good walks including the waterfalls, open all day in summer. *(Andrew Stone)*

REYNOLDSTON SS4889
★ ### King Arthur (01792) 390775
Higher Green, off A4118; SA3 1AD Cheerful pub-hotel with timbered main bar and hall, country-style restaurant, family summer dining area (games room with pool in winter), good fairly priced food, friendly staff coping well when busy, Felinfoel and guests kept well, country house bric-a-brac, log fire, lively local atmosphere evenings; background music; tables out on green, play area, 19 bedrooms and self-catering cottage, open (and food) all day. *(M G Hart)*

ST HILARY ST0173
Bush (01446) 776888
Off A48 E of Cowbridge; CF71 7DP Cosily restored 16th-c thatched and beamed pub, flagstoned main bar with inglenook, bare-boards lounge and snug, nice mix of old furniture, Bass, Greene King, Hancocks and a guest, Weston's cider and good wines by the glass, enjoyable food including home-made pies, gluten-free choices too, friendly service, restaurant; children and dogs (in bar) welcome, some picnic benches out at front, garden behind, open all day Fri-Sun. *(Andrew Stone)*

SWANSEA SS6492
Brunswick (01792) 465676
Duke Street; SA1 4HS Large rambling local with traditional pubby furnishings, lots of knick-knacks, artwork and prints for sale, bargain popular weekday food till 7.30pm (also Sun lunch), six well kept ales including Brains, Caledonian, Courage and Greene King, friendly helpful service, regular live music, quiz night Mon; no dogs, open all day. *(Anon)*

TAFFS WELL ST1283
Fagins (029) 2081 1800
Cardiff Road, Glan-y-Llyn; CF15 7QD Terrace-row pub with well kept Dark Star Hophead and interesting range of cask-tapped guests, friendly olde-worlde atmosphere, benches, pine tables and other pubby furniture on flagstones, faux black beams, woodburner, good value straightforward food (not Sun evening, Mon) from filling lunchtime baguettes up, restaurant; live music, sports TV; children and dogs welcome, open all day. *(R T and J C Moggridge)*

GWENT

ABERGAVENNY SO2914
Angel (01873) 857121
Cross Street, by town hall; NP7 5EN Comfortable late Georgian coaching inn; good local atmosphere in two-level bar,

rugs on flagstones, big sofas, armchairs and settles, some lovely bevelled glass behind counter serving Evan Evans, Hereford, Rhymney and Wye Valley, 11 wines by the glass, 15 malt whiskies and proper cider, well liked food, friendly helpful staff, attractive lounge (popular afternoon tea) and smart dining room; free wi-fi; children welcome, dogs in bar, pretty candlelit courtyard, 35 bedrooms (some in other buildings), open all day. *(Toby Jones)*

ABERGAVENNY   SO3111

★ **Hardwick** (01873) 854220
Hardwick; B4598 SE, off A40 at A465/ A4042 exit – coming from E on A40, go right round the exit system, as B4598 is final road out; NP7 9AA Restaurant-with-rooms – you'll need to book for owner-chef's highly regarded imaginative food; drinkers welcome in simple bar with spindleback chairs around pub tables, stripped brickwork by fireplace and small corner counter serving Rhymney and Wye Valley, local perry and a dozen wines by the glass, two dining rooms, one with beams, bare boards and huge fireplace, the other in lighter carpeted extension, friendly service; background music; no under-8s in restaurant after 8pm, teak tables and chairs under umbrellas by car park, neat garden, bedrooms, open all day (till 10pm Sun), closed winter Mon and second week Jan. *(John Jenkins)*

CAERLEON   ST3490

★ **Bell** (01633) 420613
Bulmore Road; off M4 junction 24 via B4237 and B4236; NP18 1QQ Nicely furnished linked beamed areas in old stone coaching inn, good popular (often imaginative) food using local ingredients (should book weekends), lunchtime two-course deal, well kept Sharps Atlantic and a couple of guests, over 20 welsh ciders and perries, big open fireplace; unobtrusive background music (live Sun afternoon); children welcome, pretty back terrace with koi tank, open all day. *(Martin Jones)*

CHEPSTOW   ST5394

Three Tuns (01291) 645797
Bridge Street; NP16 5EY Early 17th-c and a pub for much of that time; refurbished bare-boards interior with painted farmhouse pine furniture, couple of mismatched sofas by woodburner, dresser with china plates, local ales and ciders from nice wooden counter at unusual angle, very reasonably priced home-made bar food (not Mon or Tues), friendly staff; background music (live Sat); dogs welcome, pretty bedrooms, open all day; disabled access (one bedroom suitable). *(Alison and Michael Harper)*

GROSMONT   SO4024

Angel (01981) 240646
Corner of B4347 and Poorscript Lane; NP7 8EP Small welcoming 17th-c local

under new ownership; rustic interior with simple wooden furniture, Wye Valley Butty Bach, a couple of guests and local cider, reasonably priced traditional food (not Sun, Mon or Weds), pool room with darts; live music (instruments provided including piano), TV for rugby, no lavatories – public ones close by; dogs welcome, seats out by ancient market cross on attractive steep single street in sight of castle, back garden with boules, good local walks, two bedrooms planned, open all day Sat, closed Sun evening and lunchtimes Mon-Weds. *(Martin Jones)*

LLANDENNY   SO4103

★ **Raglan Arms** (01291) 690800
Centre of village; NP15 1DL Some redecoration under new owners for this well run dining pub; interesting freshly cooked food (not Sun evening), Wye Valley Butty Bach and good selection of wines, friendly welcoming young staff, big pine tables and a couple of leather sofas in linked dining rooms leading to conservatory, log fire in flagstoned bar's handsome stone fireplace, relaxed informal atmosphere; children welcome, garden tables, closed Mon. *(Rob Anderson)*

LLANGATTOCK LINGOED   SO3620

Hunters Moon (01873) 821499
Off B4521 just E of Llanvetherine; NP7 8RR Attractive tucked-away pub dating from 13th c, beams, dark stripped stone and flagstones, woodburner, friendly licensees and locals, welsh ales tapped from the cask, separate dining room, enjoyable straightforward all-day food; children welcome, tables out on deck and in charming dell with ducks, waterfall, four comfortable bedrooms, glorious country on Offa's Dyke Path, open all day. *(Anon)*

LLANGYBI   ST3797

White Hart (01633) 450258
On main road; NP15 1NP Friendly village dining pub in delightful 12th-c monastery building (part of Jane Seymour's dowry); pubby bar with roaring log fire, steps up to pleasant light restaurant, good if not particularly cheap food, afternoon tea, breakfasts Sat morning, several well kept mainly welsh ales and good choice of wines by the glass; children welcome, two nice bedrooms, open all day, closed Sun evening, Mon. *(Rob Anderson)*

LLANOVER   SO2907

★ **Goose & Cuckoo** (01873) 880277
Upper Llanover signed up track off A4042 S of Abergavenny; after 0.5 miles take first left; NP7 9ER Remote pub looking over picturesque valley just inside Brecon Beacons National Park; essentially one small rustically furnished room with woodburner in arched stone fireplace, small picture-window extension makes most of the view, well kept ales such as Rhymney, 80 whiskies and generous helpings of simple

tasty food, daily papers, board games, cribbage and darts; no credit cards; children and dogs welcome, picnic-sets out on gravel below, they keep sheep, geese and chickens and may have honey for sale, bedrooms, open all day weekends, closed Mon. *(Guy Vowles)*

LLANTHONY   SO2827
★ **Priory Hotel** (01873) 890487
Aka Abbey Hotel, Llanthony Priory; off A465, back road Llanvihangel Crucorney–Hay; NP7 7NN Magical setting for plain bar in dimly lit vaulted crypt of graceful ruined Norman abbey, lovely in summer, with lawns around and the peaceful border hills beyond; well kept ales such as Brains, Felinfoel and Newmans, summer farm cider, good coffee, simple lunchtime bar food (can be long queue on fine summer days, but number system works well), evening restaurant, occasional live music; no dogs, children welcome but not in hotel area (four bedrooms in restored parts of abbey walls), open all day Sat, summer Sun, closed winter Mon-Thurs, Sun evening. *(Taff Thomas)*

LLANTRISANT FAWR   ST3997
Greyhound (01291) 672505
Off A449 near Usk; NP15 1LE Prettily set 17th-c country inn with relaxed homely feel in three linked beamed rooms, steps between two, nice mix of furnishings and rustic decorations, enjoyable home cooking at sensible prices, efficient service, two or more well kept ales, decent wines by the glass, log fires, pleasant panelled dining room; muddy boots/dogs welcome in stable bar, attractive garden with big fountain, hill views, comfortable bedrooms in converted stable block, closed Sun evening. *(Alison and Michael Harper)*

MAMHILAD   SO3004
Horseshoe (01873) 880542
Old Abergavenny Road; NP4 8QZ New owners for this old beamed country pub, slate-floor bar with traditional pubby furniture, a couple of unusual posts acting as elbow tables, original Hancocks pub sign, ornate woodburner in stone fireplace, tasty fairly priced food (good pies) from lunchtime baguettes up, Sharps Doom Bar and a local guest, Blaengawney cider; children welcome, dogs away from dining area, lovely views particularly from tables by car park over road, open all day Fri-Sun. *(Martin Jones)*

PENALLT   SO5209
★ **Inn at Penallt** (01600) 772765
Village signed off B4293; at crossroads in village turn left; NP25 4SE 17th-c stone inn with good imaginative food using local produce including set lunch, also local ales and cider, well priced wine list, courteous efficient service, roaring woodburner in airy slate-floored bar, restaurant and small back conservatory with fine Forest of Dean views; children and

dogs welcome, big garden with terrace and play area, four bedrooms, closed Sun evening, Mon, Tues lunchtime (also Weds lunchtime in winter), otherwise open all day. *(Mr Jim Allen)*

RAGLAN   SO4107
Beaufort Arms (01291) 690412
High Street; NP15 2DY Pub-hotel (former 16th-c coaching inn) with two character beamed bars, one with big stone fireplace and comfortable seats on slate floor, well kept Fullers London Pride and Wye Valley Butty Bach, good varied range of locally sourced food (own-grown produce) including set lunch/early evening menu, light airy brasserie, friendly attentive service; background music; children welcome, terrace tables, 17 good bedrooms, open all day. *(Alison and Michael Harper)*

REDBROOK   SO5309
★ **Boat** (01600) 712615
Car park signed on A466 Chepstow–Monmouth, then 30-metre footbridge over Wye; or very narrow steep car access from Penallt in Wales; NP25 4AJ Beautifully set riverside pub with well kept Wye Valley and guests tapped from the cask, lots of ciders, perries and country wines, enjoyable good value food from baguettes and baked potatoes up (nothing fried) including signature pan haggerty, helpful staff, unchanging interior with stripped-stone walls, flagstones and roaring woodburner; live bands Thurs evening, children and dogs welcome, rough home-built seats in informal tiered suntrap garden with stream spilling down into duck pond, open all day (till 9pm Mon), no food Sun evening. *(Pip White)*

TALYCOED   SO4115
Warwicks (01600) 780227
B4233 Monmouth–Abergavenny; though its postal address is Llantilio Crossenny, the inn is actually in Talycoed, a mile or two E; NP7 8TL Pretty wisteria-clad 17th-c beamed pub under welcoming new management; softly lit snug bar with good log fire in stone fireplace, settles and mix of other old furniture, horsebrasses and assorted memorabilia, well kept Wye Valley, good food including tapas and daily specials, cosy little dining room; quiz last Weds of month; seats on front terrace and in neat garden, lovely countryside and surrounding walks, open all day Fri-Sun, closed Mon-Weds lunchtime. *(Derek Stafford)*

TINTERN   SO5300
★ **Anchor** (01291) 689582
Off A466 at brown Abbey sign; NP16 6TE Medieval building next to the magnificent abbey ruins; bar was originally the abbey's cider mill with beams, flagstones and bare stone walls, Bath Ales, Otter, Wye Valley and a guest, wide range of farm and local bottled ciders plus several wines by the

glass and Penderyn whisky/gin, airy garden room with brightly painted chairs around wooden tables, picture windows making most of the view (abbey floodlit at night), restaurant in former ferryman's cottage, good range of interesting food, friendly hard-working staff; children and dogs welcome, wheelchair access to bar only, terrace and lawn with picnic-sets, River Wye just behind and lots of surrounding walks, open all day from 9am. *(Neil and Anita Christopher, Ian and Rose Lock, Chris and Angela Buckell, Harvey Brown)*

TRELLECK   SO5005

Lion (01600) 860322

B4293 6 miles S of Monmouth; NP25 4PA Open-plan bar with one or two low black beams, nice mix of old furniture, two log fires, ales such as Butcombe, Felinfoel and Wye Valley, wide range of fair-priced traditional food with specials such as ostrich and kangaroo, takeaway pizzas, games such as shove-ha'penny, ring the bull and table skittles; background music; children and dogs welcome, picnic-sets on grass, side courtyard overlooking church, self-catering cottage, open all day, closed Sun evening. *(Rob Anderson)*

TRELLECK GRANGE   SO5001

Fountain (01291) 689303

Minor road Tintern–Llanishen, SE of village; NP16 6QW Traditional 17th-c country pub under friendly family management, enjoyable local food from pub favourites to game specials, three well kept welsh ales, farm cider and perry, roomy low-beamed flagstoned bar with log fire; dogs welcome, small walled garden, peaceful spot on small winding road, comfortable bedrooms (no children), camping, closed Mon and lunchtime Tues, otherwise open all day (till 9pm Tues, Sun). *(Anon)*

USK   SO3700

Kings Head (01291) 672963

Old Market Street; NP15 1AL 16th-c family-run inn with chatty relaxed atmosphere, very popular, generously served traditional food and well kept beers, friendly efficient staff, huge log fire in superb fireplace; sports TV; bedrooms, open all day. *(Martin Jones)*

GWYNEDD

ABERDOVEY   SN6196

Britannia (01654) 767426

Sea View Terrace; LL35 0EF Friendly bustling harbourside inn; great estuary

and distant mountain views from upstairs restaurant with balcony, good range of enjoyable well priced food including fresh crab and summer afternoon teas with home-made cakes, locals' bar downstairs with five real ales, darts and TV, woodburner in cosy back snug; children welcome (not in bar), three bedrooms, open all day. *(Rob Anderson)*

ABERDOVEY   SN6196

★**Penhelig Arms** (01654) 767215

Opposite Penhelig station; LL35 0LT Fine harbourside location for this popular 18th-c hotel; traditional bar with warm fire in central stone fireplace, some panelling, Brains ales and a guest, good choice of wines and malt whiskies, enjoyable food including good fish and chips; children welcome, dogs allowed in bar and comfortable bedrooms (some have balconies overlooking estuary, ones nearest road can be noisy), open all day. *(Pip White)*

BETWS-Y-COED   SH7955

★**Ty Gwyn** (01690) 710383

A5 just S of bridge to village; LL24 0SG Family-run restaurant-with-rooms rather than pub (you must eat or stay overnight to be served alcohol), but pubby feel in character beamed lounge bar with ancient cooking range, easy chairs, antiques, silver, cut-glass, old prints and bric-a-brac, really good interesting food using local produce including own fruit and vegetables, beers such as Brains and Great Orme, friendly professional service; background music; children welcome, 12 comfortable bedrooms and holiday cottage, closed Mon-Weds in Jan. *(Mike and Mary Carter)*

BLAENAU FFESTINIOG   SH7041

Pengwern Arms (01766) 762200

Church Square, Ffestiniog; LL41 4PB Co-operative-owned village square pub (being restored in stages) with welcoming enthusiastic staff; panelled bar with well kept/priced Cwrw Llyn or Purple Moose and a guest, dining area serving standard weekend food including bargain Sun lunch, friendly local atmosphere; Mon quiz; fine views from back garden, bedrooms. *(Harvey Brown)*

CAERNARFON   SH4762

★**Black Boy** (01286) 673604

Northgate Street; LL55 1RW Busy traditional 16th-c inn with cosy beamed lounge bar, sumptuously furnished and packed with tables, additional dining room across corridor and dimly lit atmospheric public bar with well kept Bass, Cwrw Llyn, Purple Moose and two guests, enjoyable

---

Please tell us if the décor, atmosphere, food or drink at a pub is different from our description. We rely on readers' reports to keep us up to date: feedback@goodguides.com, or (no stamp needed) The Good Pub Guide, FREEPOST RTJR-ZCYZ-RJZT, Perrymans Lane, Etchingham TN19 7DN.

generous food from sandwiches up (try the traditional 'lobsgows' stew), lunchtime set deal, good friendly service and lots of welsh chat; soft 1970s background music, TV, free wi-fi; disabled access (ramps) and facilities, a few pavement tables, 26 bedrooms, more in separate townhouse, open (and food) all day. *(Simon and Mandy King)*

CAPEL CURIG SH7257
★ **Bryn Tyrch** (01690) 720223
A5 E; LL24 0EL Family-owned roadside inn perfectly placed for mountains of Snowdonia; bare-stone walkers' bar with big communal tables and amazing picture-windows views, Conwy Welsh Pride and a guest, quite a few malt whiskies, comprehensive choice of good well presented food including packed lunches and hampers; second bar with big menu boards, leather sofas and mix of tables on floorboards, coal fire; children and dogs welcome, steep little side garden, more seats on terrace and across road by stream, 11 bedrooms including two bunk rooms, open all day weekends, from 4.30pm weekdays (midday during holidays). *(Harvey Brown)*

CAPEL CURIG SH7357
Tyn y Coed (01690) 720331
A5 SE of village; LL24 0EE Bustling inn across road from River Llugwy with stage coach at entrance; enjoyable good value home-made food using local produce, well kept Purple Moose and three guests, pleasant quick service, log fires, pool room with juke box; nice side terrace, good surrounding walks, comfortable bedrooms, cycle storage and drying room, closed weekday lunchtimes out of season, otherwise open all day. *(Anon)*

CONWY SH7777
Albion (01492) 582484
Uppergate Street; LL32 8RF Sensitively restored 1920s pub thriving under the collective ownership of four welsh brewers – Bragd'yr Nant, Great Orme, Nant and Purple Moose, their beers and guests kept well, interesting building with plenty of well preserved features including stained glass and huge baronial fireplace, quieter back room with serving hatch; open all day. *(Ruth May)*

LLANDUDNO SH7882
Cottage Loaf (01492) 870762
Market Street; LL30 2SR Friendly former bakery with woodburning stoves, flagstones, rugs on bare boards and salvaged ship's timbers, mix of individual tables, benches, cushioned settles and attractive dining chairs, enjoyable brasserie-style food, well kept Conwy, Courage, Brains and a couple of guests (often from local microbreweries), big garden room extension; children welcome, open (and food) all day. *(Harvey Brown)*

LLANDUDNO SH7882
Queen Victoria (01492) 860952
Church Walks; LL30 2HD Traditional Victorian pub away from the high-street bustle, well kept Banks's, Marstons Pedigree and guests, good choice of affordable pubby food in bar or upstairs restaurant, congenial atmosphere and good service; children and dogs welcome, a few seats out in front, not far from the Great Orme Tramway, open (and food) all day. *(Adrian Johnson)*

LLANFROTHEN SH6141
Brondanw Arms (01766) 770555
Aka Y Ring; A4085 just N of B4410; LL48 6AQ Welsh-speaking village pub at end of short whitewashed terrace, main bar with slate floor and woodburner in large fireplace, pews and window benches, old farm tools on the ceiling, snug with panelled booths and potbelly stove, long spacious dining room behind with contrasting red walls, good home-cooked food (all day Sun), Robinsons ales, friendly helpful staff; free wi-fi; children welcome, wheelchair access (two long shallow steps at front), Snowdonia views from garden with play area, camping and good walks, handy for Plas Brondanw Gardens. *(Simon and Mandy King)*

LLANUWCHLLYN SH8730
Eagles (01678) 540278
Aka Eryrod; A494/B4403; LL23 7UB Family-run and welcoming with good reasonably priced food (not Mon lunchtime) using own farm produce, ales such as Purple Moose, limited wine choice in small bottles, opened-up slate-floor bar with log fire, beams and stripped stone, back picture-window view of mountains with Lake Bala in distance; sports TV; children welcome, metal tables and chairs on flower-filled back terrace, open all day summer (afternoon break Mon). *(Mike and Mary Carter)*

MAENTWROG SH6640
Grapes (01766) 590365
A496; village signed from A470; LL41 4HN Handsome refurbished 17th-c inn, three bars and good-sized conservatory with views of steam trains on Ffestiniog Railway, enjoyable food from traditional favourites up, Evan Evans and a seasonal guest, smiling helpful staff; children and dogs welcome, seats on pleasant terrace, boutique-style bedrooms, open all day. *(Rob Anderson)*

PORTH DINLLAEN SH2741
★ **Ty Coch** (01758) 720498
Beach car park signed from Morfa Nefyn, then 15-minute walk; LL53 6DB Former 19th-c vicarage in idyllic location right on beach with great view along coast to mountains, far from roads and only reached on foot; bar crammed with nautical paraphernalia, pewter, old miners' and

railway lamps, RNLI memorabilia etc, simple furnishings and coal fire, up to three real ales and a craft beer (served in plastic as worried about glass on beach), short lunchtime bar menu; children and dogs welcome, open all day in season and school holidays (till 5pm Sun), 12-4pm weekends only during the winter. (Alison and Michael Harper)

PORTHMADOG   SH5738
Spooners (01766) 516032
Harbour station; LL49 9NF Platform café-bar at steam line terminus, lots of railway memorabilia including a former working engine in one corner, Marstons-related ales and welsh guests such as Purple Moose, good value pub food including popular Sun lunch, evening meals Tues-Sat (all week in high season); children welcome, platform tables, open all day. (Brian and Anna Marsden)

RHYD DDU   SH5652
Cwellyn Arms (01766) 890321
A4085 N of Beddgelert; LL54 6TL Simple 18th-c Snowdon pub not far below Welsh Highland Railway top terminus, up to nine real ales and good choice of popular well presented food from home-baked rolls to blackboard specials, friendly helpful staff, two cosy bars and restaurant, log fires; children, walkers and dogs welcome, spectacular Snowdon views from garden tables, babbling stream just over wall, campsite, bedrooms and bunkhouses, open all day. (Paul Collins)

TREFRIW   SH7863
Old Ship (01492) 640013
B5106; LL27 0JH Well run old pub with nice staff and cheerful local atmosphere, good home-made food from daily changing blackboard menu, particularly well kept Marstons-related beers and local guests, good selection of wines/malt whiskies, log fire and inglenook woodburner; garden with picnic-sets by stream, children welcome, open all day weekends, closed Mon except bank holidays. (Martin Cawley)

TREMADOG   SH5640
Union (01766) 512748
Market Square; LL49 9RB Traditional early 19th-c stone-built pub in terrace overlooking square, cosy and comfortable, with quiet panelled lounge on left, carpeted public bar to the right with bare stone walls and woodburner, well kept ales such as Great Orme and Purple Moose, enjoyable pubby food including an authentic daily curry, friendly staff, back restaurant; darts and TV; children welcome, paved terrace behind. (Simon and Mandy King)

TUDWEILIOG   SH2336
Lion (01758) 659724
Nefyn Road (B4417), Llyn Peninsula; LL53 8ND Cheerful village inn with

enjoyable sensibly priced food from baguettes to blackboard specials, homely furnishings in lounge bar and two dining rooms (one for families, other with woodburner), quick friendly service, real ales such as Purple Moose (up to three in summer), dozens of malt whiskies, decent wines, pool table and board games in public bar; pleasant front garden, four bedrooms, open all day in season. (Rob Anderson)

POWYS

BLEDDFA   SO2068
Hundred House (01547) 550441
A488 Knighton–Penybont; LD7 1PA 16th-c pub (former courthouse) opposite village green, friendly licensees, carpeted lounge bar with woodburner in big inglenook, L-shaped room with lower flagstoned bar, another big fireplace in cosy dining room, much-liked traditional food, Radnorshire ales; background music; children welcome, tables in side garden with play area, lovely countryside, closed Mon, otherwise open all day. (Andrew Stone)

CRICKHOWELL   SO2118
Dragon (01873) 810362
High Street; NP8 1BE Welcoming old family-owned inn, more hotel-restaurant than pub, but with small bar serving Rhymney, flagstone, slate and wood floors, sofas and armchairs by open fire, enjoyable traditional food including welsh choices, good friendly service; 15 bedrooms. (Martin Jones)

CRICKHOWELL   SO1919
★ Nantyffin Cider Mill
(01873) 810775 *A40/A479 NW; NP8 1SG* Former 16th-c drovers' inn facing River Usk in lovely Black Mountains countryside – charming views from tables on lawn; bar with solid tables and chairs on tiles or carpet, woodburner in broad fireplace, Felinfoel Double Dragon, proper ciders and several wines by the glass, open-plan main area with beams, standing timbers and open fire in grey stonework wall, striking high-raftered restaurant with old cider press, good often interesting food from shortish menu including chargrills; background music; children and dogs (in bar) welcome, bedrooms, handy for Tretower Court and Castle, open all day Sat, closed Mon, Tues and winter Sun evening. (B and M Kendall, Mike and Mary Carter, Taff Thomas)

DERWENLAS   SN7299
★ Black Lion (01654) 703913
A487 just S of Machynlleth; SY20 8TN Cosy 16th-c country pub with extensive range of good well priced food including children's menu and daily specials, friendly staff coping well at busy times, Wye Valley Butty Bach and a guest, decent wines, heavy black beams, thick walls and black timbering, attractive pictures, brasses and lion models, tartan

carpet over big slate flagstones, good log fire; background music; garden behind with play area and steps up into woods, limited parking, bedrooms, closed Mon. *(B and M Kendall, Lois Dyer, John Evans)*

DINAS MAWDDWY   SH8514
Red Lion (01650) 531247
Dyfi Road; off A470 (N of A458 junction); SY20 9JA Two small traditional front bars and more modern back extension, changing ales including some from small local brewers, decent food, friendly efficient service, open fire, beams and lots of brass; children welcome, simple bedrooms, pub named in welsh (Llew Coch). *(Andrew Stone)*

GLADESTRY   SO2355
Royal Oak (01544) 370669
B4594; HR5 3NR Old-fashioned village pub on Offa's Dyke Path with friendly licensees, simple stripped-stone slate-floored walkers' bar, beams hung with tankards and lanterns, piano, darts, carpeted lounge, open fires, ales from Golden Valley and Wye Valley, uncomplicated home-made food; no credit cards; children welcome, dogs in bar (and bedrooms by arrangement), sheltered back garden, camping, closed Sun evening, all day Mon and Tues. *(Belinda May)*

GLASBURY   SO1839
Harp (01497) 847373
B4350 towards Hay, just N of A438; HR3 5NR Homely old place, welcoming and relaxed, with good value pubby food (not Mon) cooked by landlady including proper pies and take-away pizzas, log-fire lounge with eating areas, airy bar, well kept local ales, picture windows over wooded garden sloping to River Wye; some live music, darts; river views from picnic-sets on terrace and back bedrooms, good breakfast. *(Andrew Stone)*

HAY-ON-WYE   SO2242
★ Blue Boar (01497) 820884
Castle Street/Oxford Road; HR3 5DF Medieval bar in character pub, cosy corners, dark panelling, pews and country chairs, open fire in Edwardian fireplace, four well kept local ales including a house beer from Hydes, organic bottled cider and several wines by the glass, enjoyable food (from breakfast on) in quite different long open café/dining room, bright light décor, local artwork for sale and another open fire, friendly efficient service; background music; children and dogs welcome, tables in tree-shaded garden, open all day from 9am. *(John and Bryony Coles, Ian and Rose Lock)*

HAY-ON-WYE   SO2242
★ Three Tuns (01497) 821855
Broad Street; HR3 5DB Sizeable old pub with low beams, exposed stone walls and inglenook woodburners, lighter sofa area, ancient stairs to raftered restaurant, well kept ales and good wine choice, popular

freshly prepared food (all day Sat) from ciabattas, pizzas and pubby choices to pricier upscale dishes, prompt helpful service (they ask for a credit card if you run a tab); children welcome till 7pm, no dogs, disabled facilities, seats under big parasols in sheltered courtyard, open all day weekends, may close Mon and Tues out of season. *(Anon)*

KNIGHTON   SO2872
Horse & Jockey (01547) 520062
Wylcwm Place; LD7 1AE Popular old family-run pub with several cosy areas, one with log fire, enjoyable good value food from traditional choices and pizzas up in bar and adjoining restaurant, cheerful service, well kept beers; tables in pleasant medieval courtyard, six bedrooms, handy for Offa's Dyke Path. *(Lois Dyer)*

LLANBEDR   SO2320
Red Lion (01873) 810754
Off A40 at Crickhowell; NP8 1SR Quaint old local in pretty village set in dell, heavy beams, antique settles in lounge and snug, log fires, well kept Rhymney, Wye Valley and a guest ale, front dining area with fair value home-made food; good walking country (porch for muddy boots), closed weekday lunchtime (except 2-5pm Weds), open all day weekends. *(Guy Vowles)*

LLANFIHANGEL-NANT-MELAN   SO1958
Red Lion (01544) 350220
A44 10 miles W of Kington; LD8 2TN Enjoyable stripped-stone and beamed 16th-c roadside dining pub, roomy main bar with flagstones and woodburner, carpeted restaurant, front sun porch, good reasonably priced home-made food from shortish interesting menu, Brains and changing guests, friendly service, back bar with woodburner; pool and darts; children and dogs welcome, country views from pleasant garden, seven bedrooms (three in annexe), handy for Radnor Forest walks and near impressive waterfall, open all day Sun till 9pm, closed Tues. *(Dave Braisted)*

LLANFRYNACH   SO0725
White Swan (01874) 665277
Village signposted from B4558, off A40 E of Brecon – take second turn to village, which is also signed to pub; LD3 7BZ Comfortably upmarket country dining pub under new management; original part with stripped stone and flagstones, sturdy oak tables and woodburner, enjoyable fairly traditional food served by friendly efficient staff, Brains, Sharps and a guest, decent wines and coffee, modern high-ceilinged bare-boards bar extension; background music; children and dogs (in bar) welcome, charming back terrace attractively divided by low privet hedges, towpath walks along canal, open all day, closed Mon winter. *(Anon)*

LLANGEDWYN   SJ1924
Green Inn (01691) 828234
B4396 E of village; SY10 9JW Old country
dining pub refurbished under new owners;
various snug alcoves, nooks and crannies,
good mix of furnishings including oak settles
and leather sofas, woodburner, Stonehouse,
Sharps Doom Bar and a guest, enjoyable food
served by friendly helpful staff; children and
dogs welcome, attractive garden over road
running down towards River Tanat, closed
Mon, otherwise open all day. *(Alison and
Michael Harper)*

LLANGURIG   SN9079
Blue Bell (01686) 440254
A44 opposite church; SY18 6SG Friendly
old-fashioned village inn with well kept
Brains Rev James and Wye Valley Butty
Bach, Thatcher's cider, ample helpings of
enjoyable good value pubby food, comfortable
flagstoned bar, games room with darts,
dominoes and pool, small dining room;
background music; children welcome, no
dogs, nine simple inexpensive bedrooms,
open all day. *(Lois Dyer, Kay and Alistair Butler)*

LLANIDLOES   SN9584
Crown & Anchor (01686) 412398
Long Bridge Street; SY18 6EF Friendly
unspoilt town-centre pub known locally
as Rubys after landlady who has run it for
50 years, well kept Brains Rev James and
Worthington Bitter, chatty locals' bar, lounge,
snug and two other rooms, one with pool and
games machine separated by central hallway;
open all day. *(Rob Anderson)*

LLANWRTYD WELLS   SN8746
Neuadd Arms (01591) 610236
The Square; LD5 4RB Sizeable 19th-c
hotel (friendly and by no means upmarket)
brewing its own good value Heart of Wales
beers in back stable block, enjoyable
straightforward home-made food, log fires in
lounge and small tiled public bar still with
old service bells, restaurant, games room;
lots of outdoor events in village (some rather
outré such as bogsnorkelling and man v
horse); well behaved dogs welcome in bars,
a few tables out in front, 21 bedrooms
(front ones can be noisy), engaging very
small town in good walking area, open all day.
(Taff Thomas)

MALLWYD   SH8612
Brigands (01650) 511999
*A470 by roundabout in village;
SY20 9HJ* Sizeable 15th-c beamed
coaching inn refurbished a couple of years
ago, good food from reasonably priced

bar snacks up, lunchtime two-course deal
Mon-Fri, local Cader and Sharps Doom Bar,
friendly efficient staff; children and dogs
welcome, extensive lawns with lovely views,
can arrange fishing on River Dovey, nine
bedrooms, open (and some food) all day.
(Mike and Mary Carter)

PAINSCASTLE   SO1646
★ Roast Ox (01497) 851398
*Off A470 Brecon–Builth Wells, or from
A438 at Clyro; LD2 3JL* Well restored
pub with beams, flagstones, stripped
stone, appropriate simple furnishings
and some rustic bric-a-brac, huge antlers
above open fire, ales tapped from the cask
and good range of ciders, popular freshly
made food, friendly quick service; children
and dogs welcome, picnic-sets outside,
attractive hill country, ten comfortable neat
bedrooms. *(Taff Thomas)*

PENCELLI   SO0925
Royal Oak (01874) 665396
B4558 SE of Brecon; LD3 7LX
Unpretentious and friendly with two small
bars, low beams, assorted pine furniture on
polished flagstones, autographed sporting
memorabilia, log fires, well kept Brains Rev
James and a guest, small blackboard choice
of enjoyable home-made food (standard
times in summer, Thurs-Sat evenings and
weekend lunchtimes in winter), may be just
soup and sandwiches lunchtime, simple
modern candlelit dining room; children
welcome, terraces backing on to Monmouth
& Brecon Canal (nearby moorings), lovely
canalside walks and handy for Taff Trail,
closed Mon-Weds out of season. *(Martin
Jones)*

PENYCAE   SN8313
Ancient Briton (01639) 730273
Brecon Road (A4067); SA9 1YY Friendly
opened-up roadside pub, seven or more well
kept ales from far and wide, local cider,
enjoyable reasonably priced home-made food;
children and dogs welcome, seats outside
and play area, four bedrooms, campsite (good
facilities), handy for Dan-yr-Ogof caves,
Henrhyd Waterfall and Carig-y-Nos Country
Park, open all day. *(Harvey Brown)*

RHAYADER   SN9768
Lamb & Flag (01597) 810819
North Street; LD6 5BU Welcoming large
L-shaped bar with simple pubby furniture
and good open fire in big stone fireplace,
well kept Hancocks and Sharps, enjoyable
generously served pub food, separate
overspill dining room; good value clean
bedrooms, open all day. *(Taff Thomas)*

A star symbol before the name of a pub shows exceptional character and appeal.
It doesn't mean extra comfort. Even quite a basic pub can win a star,
if it's individual enough.

RHAYADER   SN9668

★**Triangle** (01597) 810537
*Cwmdauddwr; B4518 by bridge over
River Wye, SW of centre; LD6 5AR*
Interesting mainly 16th-c pub, small and
spotless, with buoyant local atmosphere and
welcoming helpful staff, shortish choice of
good value home-made pubby food (best
to book evenings), well kept Brains Rev
James and Hancocks HB, small selection of
reasonably priced wines, dining area with
nice view over park to Wye, darts and quiz
nights; three tables on small front terrace,
parking can be difficult. *(Taff Thomas,
Lois Dyer)*

TALYBONT-ON-USK   SO1122

★**Star** (01874) 676635
B4558; LD3 7YX Old-fashioned canalside
inn with several plainly furnished pubby
rooms, open fires (one in splendid stone
fireplace), five good changing ales (regular
beer festivals) served by enthusiastic
landlord, real cider, enjoyable fairly priced
bar food (more interesting evening choice),
good mix of customers including walkers
with dogs; sports TV, juke box, live music
last Fri of month, Weds quiz, free wi-fi;
children welcome, picnic sets in sizeable
tree-ringed garden with path leading to river,
lovely village surrounded by Brecon Beacons
National Park, two bedrooms, open all day
summer (all day Fri-Sun winter), no food Sun
evening. *(Guy Vowles)*

A little further afield

CHANNEL ISLANDS

GUERNSEY

FOREST
Deerhound (01481) 238585
Le Bourg; GY8 0AN Spacious roadside
dining pub with modern interior, popular well
priced food including summer seafood menu,
Liberation ales, friendly helpful service; free
wi-fi; children welcome, sunny, sheltered
terrace with parasols, handy for the airport,
open all day. *(Peter Brix)*

KING'S MILLS
★**Fleur du Jardin** (01481) 257996
King's Mills Road; GY5 7JT Lovely 15th-c
country hotel in attractive walled garden
with solar-heated swimming pool, relaxing
low-beamed flagstoned bar with good log
fire, old prints and subdued lighting, good
food strong on local produce and seafood,
afternoon tea, friendly helpful service,
Liberation ales plus guests, good choice of
wines by the glass, local cider, restaurant;
background music; children and small dogs
welcome, plenty of tables on back terrace,
15 clean comfortable bedrooms, open all day.
(Gus Swan, Andrew Stone)

ST PETER PORT
Ship & Crown (01481) 728994
*Opposite Crown Pier, Esplanade;
GY1 2NB* Bustling town pub with bay
windows overlooking harbour, very popular
with yachting people and smarter locals;
interesting photographs (especially of World
War II occupation, also boats and local
shipwrecks), decent all-day bar food from
sandwiches up, three changing ales and a
proper cider, welcoming prompt service even
when busy, more modern-feel Crow's Nest
brasserie upstairs with fine views; sports TVs
in bar; open all day from 10am till late.
(Stephen and Jean Curtis)

VALE
Houmet (01481) 242214
Grande Havre; GY6 8JR Modern building
overlooking Grande Havre Bay, front
restaurant/bar with conservatory, good
choice of reasonably priced popular food
(best to book) including fresh local fish and
seafood, friendly service, a couple of real ales
and several wines by the glass, back public
bar with pool, darts and big-screen sports
TV (dogs allowed here); children welcome,
tables out on decking, open all day (not Sun
evening). *(Gus Swan)*

JERSEY

GRÈVE DE LECQ
★**Moulin de Lecq** (01534) 482818
Mont de la Grève de Lecq; JE3 2DT
Cheerful family-friendly converted mill
dating from 12th c with massive waterwheel
dominating the softly lit beamed bar, good
pubby food, four changing ales and a couple
of real ciders, prompt friendly service, lots of
board games, pool in upstairs games room,
restaurant extension; dogs welcome in bar;
terrace picnic-sets and good adventure
playground, quiet streamside spot with nice
walks, open all day in summer. *(Peter Brix)*

ST AUBIN
Boat House (01534) 747141
North Quay; JE3 8BS Modern steel
and timber-clad harbourside building with
great views (window tables for diners),
bar serving well kept local ales and several
wines by the glass, good food ranging from
tapas to Josper-grilled steaks, airy upstairs
restaurant; balcony and decked terrace, open
all day. *(Edward May)*

ST AUBIN
★**Old Court House Inn**
(01534) 746433 *Harbour Boulevard;
JE3 8AB* Pubby low-beamed downstairs bar
with bustling atmosphere, open fire, other
rambling areas including bistro, appetising
food from pubby snacks to lots of good fresh
fish, well kept real ales and nice wines by the
glass, handsome upstairs restaurant, glorious
views across harbour to St Helier; children
welcome, front deck overlooking harbour,
more seats in floral courtyard behind, ten
comfortable bedrooms, open all day (food all
day in summer). *(Paul and Sue Merrick)*

ST AUBIN
Tenby (01534) 741224
*Le Boulevard, towards St Helier;
JE3 8AB* Randalls pub overlooking harbour
with seats on decked area and small terrace;

wide choice of food including plenty of fish dishes, a couple of real ales such as Skinners and helpful service; open (and food) all day. *(Paul and Sue Merrick)*

ST BRELADE
Old Smugglers (01534) 741510
Ouaisne Bay; OS map reference 595476; JE3 8AW Happily unpretentious black-beamed pub just above Ouaisne beach, up to four well kept ales including Bass, farm cider, enjoyable reasonably priced pubby food (good steaks), friendly service, log fires, traditional built-in settles, darts, cribbage and dominoes, restaurant; occasional live music, sports TV; children and dogs welcome, sun porch with interesting coast views, open all day in summer. *(Gus Swan)*

ST HELIER
Cock & Bottle (01534) 722184
Royal Square; JE2 4WA Big lively outside eating area in Royal Square with lovely hanging baskets, rattan tables and chairs under parasols, heaters and blankets for cooler evenings; cosy inside with tartan-upholstered settles and small stools in front of large fireplace, wide choice of good food from sandwiches and baguettes through pubby and french choices to summer seafood menu, local ales; open all day, no food Sat or Sun evenings. *(Paul and Sue Merrick)*

ST HELIER
Halkett (01534) 732769
Halkett Place; JE2 4WG Modern pub-bar close to tree-lined square, mix of traditional and contemporary décor and furnishings, Liberation ale, 17 wines by the glass and wide choice of food from pubby and brasserie dishes to summer seafood menu; very busy with visitors and locals; free live entertainment Thurs-Sat evenings; open all day, no food Sun evening. *(Paul and Sue Merrick)*

ST HELIER
★ Lamplighter (01534) 723119
Mulcaster Street; JE2 3NJ Small friendly pub with up to eight well kept ales including Liberation, local cider, around 160 whiskies, bargain simple food such as crab sandwiches, heavy timbers, rough panelling and scrubbed pine tables; sports TV, can get very busy; interesting patriotic façade (the only union flag visible during Nazi occupation), open all day. *(Paul and Sue Merrick, David Carr)*

ST HELIER
Post Horn (01534) 872853
Hue Street; JE2 3RE Popular centrally located pub with cosy corners and traditional furnishings, more airy dining room, Liberation ales and eight wines by the glass, fair value pubby food, upstairs function room; seats outside, open all day, no food Sun. *(Paul and Sue Merrick)*

ST MARY
St Marys (01534) 482897
La Rue des Buttes; JE3 3DF Friendly old inn opposite attractive church, modern interior with bar and spacious dining area, good choice of popular reasonably priced food from lunchtime sandwiches up, Liberation and guest beers, plenty of wines by the glass; pool, darts free wi-fi; children welcome, seats in front garden and back courtyard, bedrooms, open all day. *(Peter Brix)*

ISLE OF MAN

BALDRINE	SC4180

Liverpool Arms (01624) 674787
Main Road; IM4 6AE Former coaching inn with enjoyable choice of reasonably priced pub food (all day Fri-Sun), Okells and guests, friendly welcoming staff, open fires; sports TV, pool and darts; children allowed, open all day. *(Anne and Ben Smith)*

LAXEY	SC4382

Shore (01624) 861509
Old Laxey Hill; IM4 7DA Friendly nautically themed village pub brewing its own Old Laxey Bosun Bitter, good value wines by the glass and enjoyable pubby lunchtime food (also Tues curry and Thurs steak nights); children welcome till 9pm, picnic-sets out by lovely stream, nice walk to Laxey waterwheel, open all day. *(Belinda May)*

PEEL	SC2484

Creek (01624) 842216
Station Place/North Quay; IM5 1AT In lovely setting on the ancient quayside opposite Manannan Heritage Centre, welcoming relaxed atmosphere, wide choice of highly thought-of food including fish, crab and lobsters fresh from the boats, good local kippers too, well kept Okells and nine guest ales, nautical theme lounge bar with etched mirrors and mainly old woodwork, public bar with TVs and weekend live music; children welcome, tables outside overlooking harbour, open (and food) all day. *(Isobel Mackinlay)*

PORT ERIN	SC1969

Falcons Nest (01624) 834077
Station Road; IM9 6AF Friendly family-run hotel overlooking the bay, food including local fish/seafood and Sun carvery, five well kept ales (May beer festival) and some 70 malt whiskies, two bars, one with open fire, conservatory and restaurant; children welcome, 39 bedrooms many with sea view, also eight self-catering apartments, handy for steam rail terminus, open all day. *(Neil Allen, Belinda May)*

Pubs that serve food all day

We list here all the pubs (in the Main Entries) that have told us they plan to serve food all day, even if it's only one day of the week. The individual entries for the pubs themselves show the actual details.

Bedfordshire

Ireland, Black Horse

Oakley, Bedford Arms

Berkshire

Cookham Dean, Chequers

Kintbury, Dundas Arms

Peasemore, Fox

Sonning, Bull

White Waltham, Beehive

Buckinghamshire

Coleshill, Harte & Magpies

Forty Green, Royal Standard of England

Stoke Mandeville, Bell

Wooburn Common, Chequers

Cambridgeshire

Cambridge, Punter

Peterborough, Brewery Tap

Stilton, Bell

Cheshire

Aldford, Grosvenor Arms

Allostock, Three Greyhounds Inn

Astbury, Egerton Arms

Aston, Bhurtpore

Bostock Green, Hayhurst Arms

Bunbury, Dysart Arms

Burleydam, Combermere Arms

Burwardsley, Pheasant

Chester, Architect

Chester, Mill

Chester, Old Harkers Arms

Cholmondeley, Cholmondeley Arms

Cotebrook, Fox & Barrel

Delamere, Fishpool

Eaton, Plough

Lach Dennis, Duke of Portland

Lower Withington, Black Swan

Macclesfield, Sutton Hall

Marton, Davenport Arms

Mobberley, Bulls Head

Mobberley, Church Inn

Mottram St Andrew, Bulls Head

Nether Alderley, Wizard

Spurstow, Yew Tree

Thelwall, Little Manor

Warmingham, Bears Paw

Cornwall

Morwenstow, Bush

Mylor Bridge, Pandora

Porthtowan, Blue

Cumbria

Cartmel Fell, Masons Arms
Crosthwaite, Punch Bowl
Elterwater, Britannia
Ings, Watermill
Levens, Strickland Arms
Lupton, Plough
Ravenstonedale, Black Swan

Derbyshire

Chelmorton, Church Inn
Fenny Bentley, Coach & Horses
Hathersage, Plough
Hayfield, Lantern Pike
Hayfield, Royal
Ladybower Reservoir, Ladybower Inn
Ladybower Reservoir, Yorkshire Bridge

Devon

Avonwick, Turtley Corn Mill
Cockwood, Anchor
Iddesleigh, Duke of York
Postbridge, Warren House
Sidbury, Hare & Hounds
Topsham, Globe

Dorset

Tarrant Monkton, Langton Arms
Weymouth, Red Lion
Worth Matravers, Square & Compass

Essex

Aythorpe Roding, Axe & Compasses
Feering, Sun
Fyfield, Queens Head
Little Walden, Crown
Little Waltham, White Hart
South Hanningfield, Old Windmill

Gloucestershire

Ford, Plough
Nailsworth, Weighbridge
Sheepscombe, Butchers Arms

Hampshire

Bransgore, Three Tuns
Littleton, Running Horse
Portsmouth, Old Customs House

Hertfordshire

Ashwell, Three Tuns
Barnet, Duke of York
Harpenden, White Horse

Isle of Wight

Fishbourne, Fishbourne Inn
Seaview, Boathouse
Shorwell, Crown

Kent

Chiddingstone Causeway, Little Brown Jug
Langton Green, Hare
Penshurst, Bottle House
Sevenoaks, White Hart
Shipbourne, Chaser
Stalisfield Green, Plough
Stowting, Tiger

Lancashire

Barley, Barley Mow
Bashall Eaves, Red Pump
Bispham Green, Eagle & Child
Blackburn, Oyster & Otter
Formby, Sparrowhawk
Great Mitton, Aspinall Arms

Longridge, Derby Arms
Manchester, Wharf
Stalybridge, Station Buffet
Uppermill, Church Inn
Waddington, Lower Buck

Leicestershire

Lyddington, Marquess of Exeter
Swithland, Griffin
Woodhouse Eaves, Wheatsheaf

Lincolnshire

Kirkby la Thorpe, Queens Head
Stamford, George of Stamford

Norfolk

King's Lynn, Bank House
Larling, Angel
Morston, Anchor
Salthouse, Dun Cow
Thorpe Market, Gunton Arms
Woodbastwick, Fur & Feather

Northamptonshire

Ashby St Ledgers, Olde Coach House
Oundle, Ship

Northumbria

Aycliffe, County
Blanchland, Lord Crewe Arms
Carterway Heads, Manor House Inn
Newton, Duke of Wellington

Oxfordshire

Kingham, Plough
Oxford, Bear
Oxford, Punter
Wolvercote, Jacobs Inn

Shropshire

Chetwynd Aston, Fox
Shipley, Inn at Shipley
Shrewsbury, Armoury

Somerset

Bath, Marlborough
Dunster, Luttrell Arms
Hinton St George, Lord Poulett Arms
Stanton Wick, Carpenters Arms
Wedmore, Swan

Staffordshire

Longdon Green, Red Lion
Salt, Holly Bush
Wrinehill, Hand & Trumpet

Suffolk

Chelmondiston, Butt & Oyster
Southwold, Harbour Inn
Stoke-by-Nayland, Crown
Waldringfield, Maybush

Surrey

Chobham, White Hart
Milford, Refectory

Sussex

Alfriston, George
Charlton, Fox Goes Free
Eridge Green, Nevill Crest & Gun
Friday Street, Farm at Friday Street
Horsham, Black Jug
Ringmer, Cock

Warwickshire

Birmingham, Old Joint Stock
Hunningham, Red Lion
Long Compton, Red Lion

Shipston-on-Stour, Black Horse

Welford-on-Avon, Bell

Wiltshire

Bradford-on-Avon, Castle

Yorkshire

Beck Hole, Birch Hall

Blakey Ridge, Lion

Bradfield, Strines Inn

Elslack, Tempest Arms

Grinton, Bridge Inn

Halifax, Shibden Mill

Hartshead, Gray Ox

Hetton, Angel

Ledsham, Chequers

Linton in Craven, Fountaine

Welburn, Crown & Cushion

Widdop, Pack Horse

London

Central London, Bountiful Cow, Old Bank of England, Olde Mitre, Seven Stars, Thomas Cubitt

North London, Holly Bush

South London, Victoria

West London, Dove, Duke of Sussex, Old Orchard, Portobello Gold, White Horse, Windsor Castle

Outer London (Hampton Court), Mute Swan

Scotland

Applecross, Applecross Inn

Edinburgh, Abbotsford

Glasgow, Babbity Bowster

Glasgow, Bon Accord

Glencoe, Clachaig

Kippen, Cross Keys

Shieldaig, Tigh an Eilean Hotel

Sligachan, Sligachan Hotel

Thornhill, Lion & Unicorn

Wales

Colwyn Bay, Pen-y-Bryn

Gresford, Pant-yr-Ochain

Llandudno Junction, Queens Head

Llanelian-yn-Rhos, White Lion

Llangollen, Corn Mill

Mold, Glasfryn

Overton Bridge, Cross Foxes

Pontypridd, Bunch of Grapes

Pubs near motorway junctions

The number at the start of each line is the junction number.

Detailed directions are given in the main entry for each pub. In this section, to help you find the pubs quickly before you're past the junction, we give the name of the chapter where you'll find the text.

M1

9: Redbourn, Cricketers (Hertfordshire) 3.2 miles

13: Woburn, Birch (Bedfordshire) 3.5 miles

16: Nether Heyford, Olde Sun (Northamptonshire) 1.75 miles

18: Ashby St Ledgers, Olde Coach House (Northamptonshire) 4 miles

M3

1: Sunbury, Flower Pot (Surrey) 1.6 miles

3: West End, The Inn West End (Surrey) 2.4 miles; Chobham, White Hart (Surrey) 4 miles

5: North Warnborough, Mill House (Hampshire) 1 mile; Hook, Hogget (Hampshire) 1.1 miles

7: North Waltham, Fox (Hampshire) 3 miles

M4

9: Bray, Crown (Berkshire) 1.75 miles; Bray, Hinds Head (Berkshire) 1.75 miles

13: Chieveley, Crab & Boar (Berkshire) 3.5 miles; Peasemore, Fox (Berkshire) 4 miles

14: Shefford Woodlands, Pheasant (Berkshire) 0.3 miles

M5

4: Holy Cross, Bell & Cross (Worcestershire) 4 miles

10: Coombe Hill, Gloucester Old Spot (Gloucestershire) 1 mile

13: Eastington, Old Badger (Gloucestershire) 1 mile

19: Clapton-in-Gordano, Black Horse (Somerset) 4 miles

30: Topsham, Globe (Devon) 2 miles; Woodbury Salterton, Diggers Rest (Devon) 3.5 miles

M6

16: Barthomley, White Lion (Cheshire) 1 mile

17: Sandbach, Old Hall (Cheshire) 1.2 miles

18: Allostock, Three Greyhounds Inn (Cheshire) 4.7 miles

19: Mobberley, Bulls Head (Cheshire) 4 miles

36: Lupton, Plough (Cumbria) 2 miles; Levens, Strickland Arms (Cumbria) 4 miles

40: Yanwath, Gate Inn (Cumbria) 2.25 miles; Clifton, George & Dragon (Cumbria) 3 miles; Tirril, Queens Head (Cumbria) 3.5 miles

M11

9: Hinxton, Red Lion (Cambridgeshire) 2 miles

10: Duxford, John Barleycorn (Cambridgeshire) 1.8 miles; Whittlesford, Tickell Arms (Cambridgeshire) 2.4 miles

M20

11: Stowting, Tiger (Kent) 3.7 miles

M25

5: Chipstead, George & Dragon (Kent) 1.25 miles

16: Denham, Swan (Buckinghamshire) 0.75 miles

18: Flaunden, Bricklayers Arms (Hertfordshire) 4 miles

21A: Potters Crouch, Holly Bush (Hertfordshire) 2.25 miles

M27

1: Fritham, Royal Oak (Hampshire) 4 miles

M40

2: Hedgerley, White Horse (Buckinghamshire) 2.4 miles; Forty Green, Royal Standard of England (Buckinghamshire) 3.5 miles

12: Gaydon, Malt Shovel (Warwickshire) 0.9 miles

M42

5: Barston, Malt Shovel (Warwickshire) 3 miles

6: Hampton-in-Arden, White Lion (Warwickshire) 1.25 miles

M50

3: Kilcot, Kilcot Inn (Gloucestershire) 2.3 miles

M60

13: Worsley, Old Hall (Lancashire) 1 mile

M62

25: Hartshead, Gray Ox (Yorkshire) 3.5 miles

M65

3: Blackburn, Oyster & Otter (Lancashire) 1.8 miles

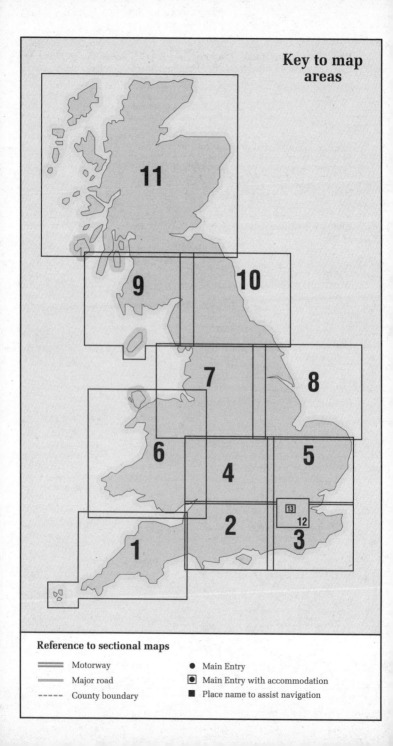

Key to map areas

11

9

10

7

8

6

4

5

13

2

12

3

1

Reference to sectional maps

☰ Motorway	●	Main Entry
Major road	◉	Main Entry with accommodation
--- County boundary	■	Place name to assist navigation

MAPS

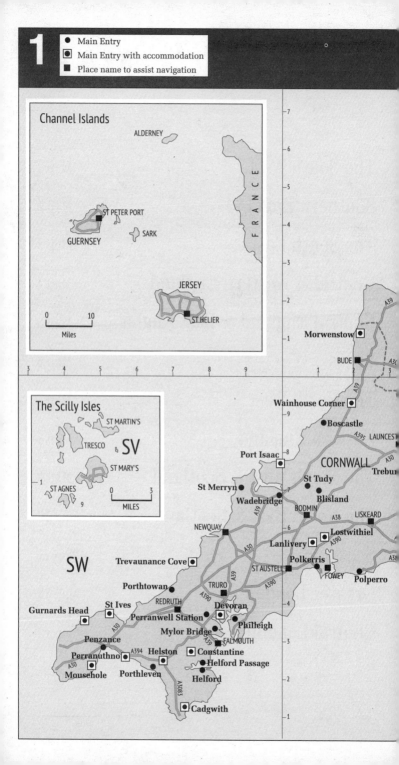

1

- ● Main Entry
- ◉ Main Entry with accommodation
- ■ Place name to assist navigation

Channel Islands

ALDERNEY

FRANCE

ST PETER PORT ■

GUERNSEY

SARK

JERSEY

ST HELIER ■

0   10
Miles

The Scilly Isles

ST MARTIN'S

TRESCO

SV

ST MARY'S

ST AGNES

0   3
MILES

Morwenstow ◉

BUDE ■

Wainhouse Corner ◉

● Boscastle

LAUNCEST

CORNWALL

Port Isaac ◉

St Tudy ●

Trebur

Wadebridge ■

St Merryn ●

BODMIN

● Blisland

LISKEARD

NEWQUAY ■

● Lostwithiel

Lanlivery ◉

● Polkerris

Trevaunance Cove ◉

ST AUSTELL ■

SW

TRURO ■

FOWEY

Polperro ●

Porthtowan ●

REDRUTH

Devoran ◉

Gurnards Head ◉

St Ives ◉

Perranwell Station ●

Philleigh ■

Penzance ■

Mylor Bridge ■

FALMOUTH

Perranuthno ◉

A394   Helston ◉

◉ Constantine

Mousehole ◉

Porthleven ●

● Helford Passage

Helford ■

Cadgwith ◉

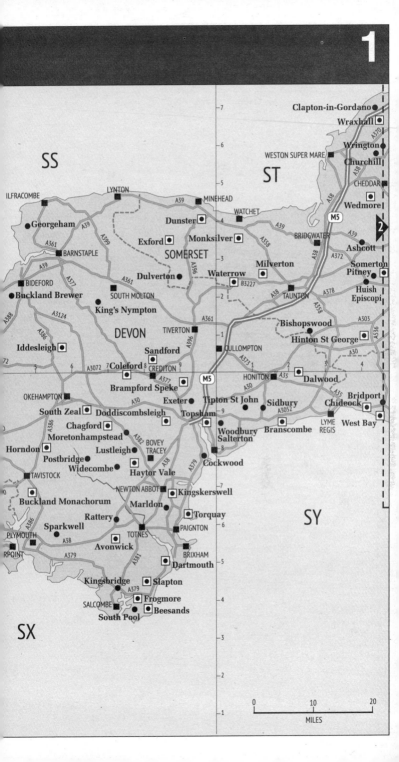

SS

ST

SY

SX

Clapton-in-Gordano
Wraxhall
Wrington
Churchill
CHEDDAR
Wedmore
Ashcott
Somerton
Pitney
Huish
Episcopi

WESTON SUPER MARE

MINEHEAD
WATCHET
Dunster
Monksilver
BRIDGWATER
Exford
Milverton
Waterrow
B3227
TAUNTON
Bishopswood
Hinton St George
Dalwood
Bridport
Chideock
West Bay

ILFRACOMBE
LYNTON
Georgeham
BARNSTAPLE
BIDEFORD
Buckland Brewer
SOUTH MOLTON
Dulverton
King's Nympton
DEVON
TIVERTON
Iddesleigh
Sandford
Coleford
CREDITON
Brampford Speke
CULLOMPTON
HONITON
OKEHAMPTON
South Zeal
Doddiscombsleigh
Exeter
Tipton St John
Sidbury
Chagford
Moretonhampstead
BOVEY TRACEY
Topsham
Woodbury
Salterton
Branscombe
LYME
REGIS
Horndon
Lustleigh
Postbridge
Widecombe
Haytor Vale
Cockwood
TAVISTOCK
NEWTON ABBOT
Kingskerswell
Buckland Monachorum
Marldon
Torquay
Rattery
PAIGNTON
PLYMOUTH
Sparkwell
TOTNES
BRIXHAM
Avonwick
Dartmouth
Kingsbridge
Slapton
Frogmore
SALCOMBE
Beesands
South Pool

M5

SOMERSET

MILES

0   10   20

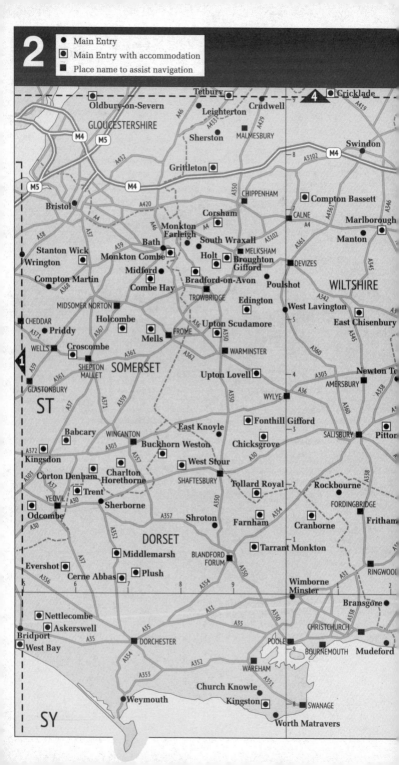

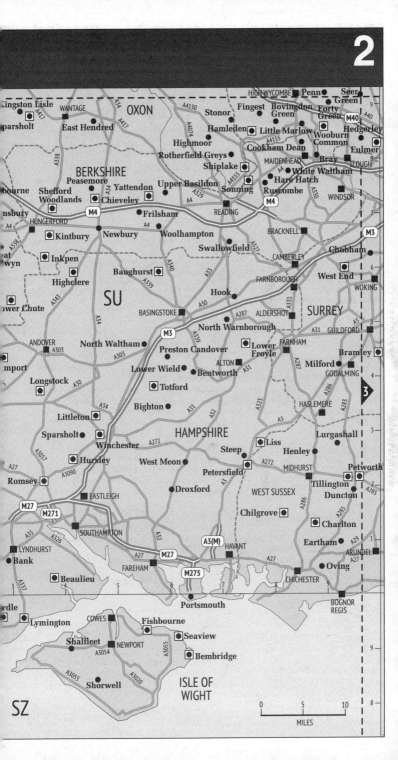

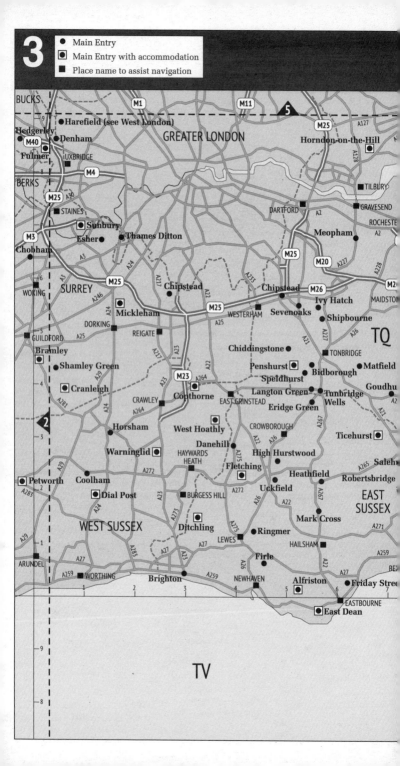

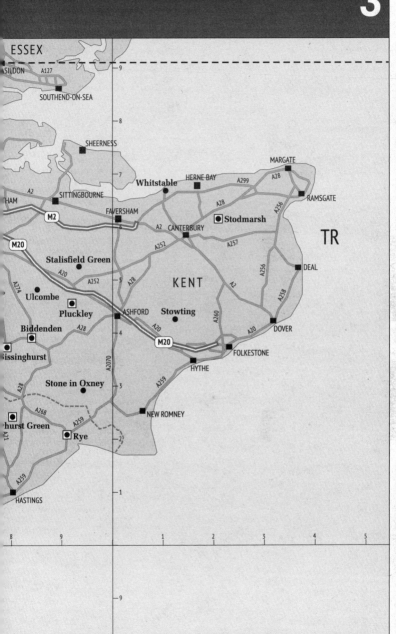

ESSEX

SILDON A127

SOUTHEND-ON-SEA

SHEERNESS

HAM A2 SITTINGBOURNE

M2

M20

FAVERSHAM

Whitstable HERNE BAY A299 MARGATE A28

RAMSGATE A256

A28

A2 CANTERBURY ● **Stodmarsh**

A252 A257 TR

Stalisfield Green

A20 A252 5 A28 **KENT** A256 ● DEAL

Ulcombe A274

Pluckley ASHFORD ● **Stowting** A2 A258

Biddenden A28 4 A260 DOVER

sissinghurst **M20** A20 A20 FOLKESTONE

Stone in Oxney A2070 HYTHE

A28 3 A359

hurst Green A268 A359 NEW ROMNEY

● **Rye** 2

A359

■ HASTINGS 1

8 9 1 2 3 4 5

9

8

0 5 10

MILES

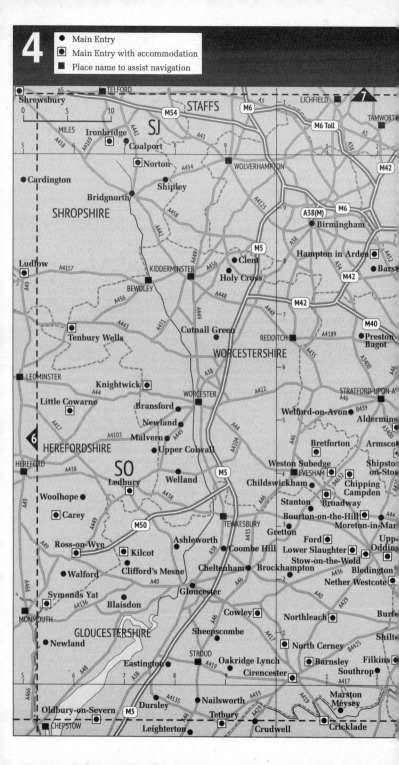

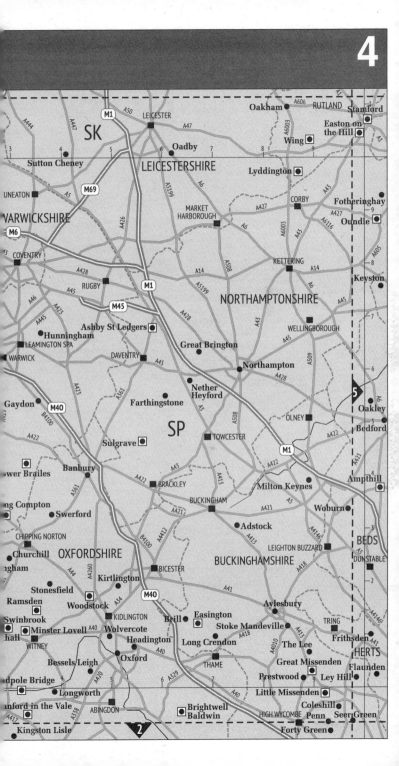

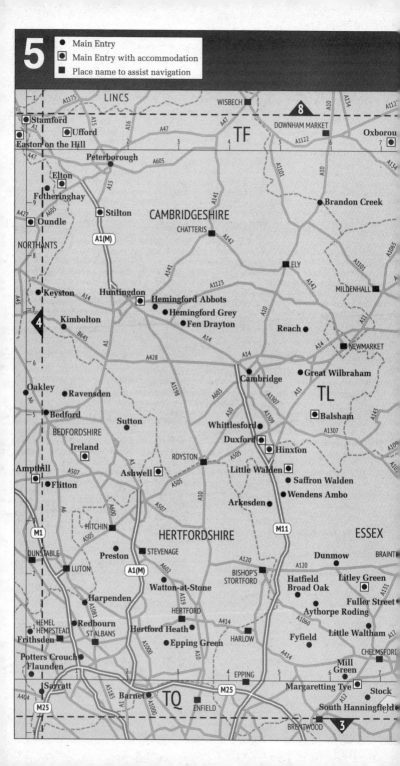

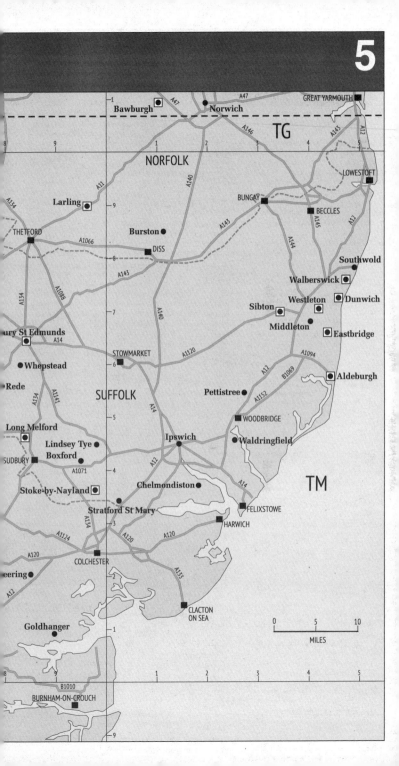

5

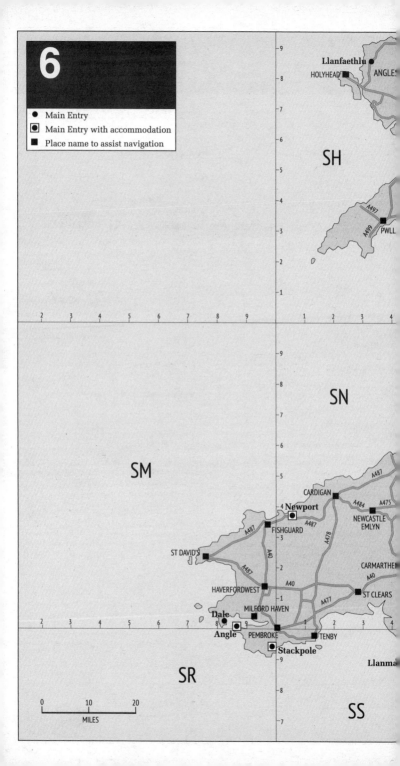

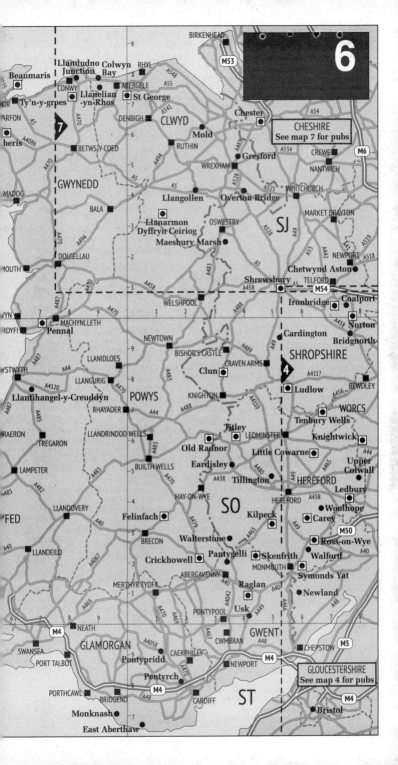

NORTH
SD
YORKSHIRE

Masham
Wass
Coxwold
A61
A168
Asenby
A169
A6108
Crayke
Grantley
RIPON
A1(M)
Helperby
Welburn
Roecliffe
Boroughbridge
A64
Marton cum Grafton
A19
A166
Malham
Linton in Craven
HARROGATE
A59
A59
York
Low Catton
EAST
YORKSHIRE
Hetton
A661
A1079
A614
SKIPTON
WETHERBY
A64
A65
Timble
SE
MARKET WEIGHTON
Elslack
Addingham
A638
A65
OTLEY
A1(M)
A19
A613
Sancton
KEIGHLEY
Ilkley
A61
A1034
NELSON
A650
M1
A63
WEST YORKSHIRE
LEEDS
SELBY
A64A
M62
Widdop
BRADFORD
Ledsham
A19
Halifax
Hartshead
M62
8
Ripponden
WAKEFIELD
PONTEFRACT
SCUNTHORPE
HDALE
A638
A638
HUDDERSFIELD
A1
M62
M62
A62
A646
BARNSLEY
M18
M180
OLDHAM
Uppermill
A628
SOUTH YORKSHIRE
DONCASTER
A169
60
Stalybridge
M1
A1(M)
BAWTRY
LINCS
Manchester
A616
Bradfield
ROTHERHAM
A631
Gringley on the Hill
A631
OCKPORT
Ladybower
A638
GAINSBOROUGH
Hayfield
Reservoir
Sheffield
Blyth
A156
Ingham
Mottram
Bradwell
Chinley
Hathersage
A57
A1500
Andrew
A623
Bretton
A635
WORKSOP
Whiteley Green
Great
A61
Kettleshulme
Longstone
Baslow
CHESTERFIELD
SK
her
Macclesfield
BUXTON
erley
Hassop
A619
Chelmorton
A515
Marton
Over
Ashover
MANSFIELD
Eaton
Hurdlow
Haddon
Stanton
A46
CONGLETON
in Peak
Woolley Moor
A133
Astbury
A52
NOTTS
NEWARK
SGROVE
LEEK
A520
A523
M1
A614
ON TRENT
A53
Fenny Bentley
Kirk Ireton
A38
Hough-on-
Cauldon
A517
the-Hill
Ellastone
ASHBOURNE
A52
Caythorpe
A46
OKE
A52
A6
A38
Dry Doddington
GRANTHAM
Cheadle
A515
NOTTINGHAM
A52
Woolsthorpe
SJ
A50
DERBYSHIRE
A60
Colston Bassett
A607
UTTOXETER
A518
DERBY
A606
Stathern
Buckminster
M6
A50
Ingleby
Wymondham
Salt
A515
Breedon on the Hill
MELTON
LEICS
Greetham
STAFFORD
BURTON UPON TRENT
Peggs Green
LOUGHBOROUGH
MOWBRAY
A607
Clipsham
AFFS
A38
A512
Sileby
RUGELEY
Longdon Green
Woodhouse Eaves
A511
Swithland
Oakham
A5
A34
LICHFIELD
A444
4

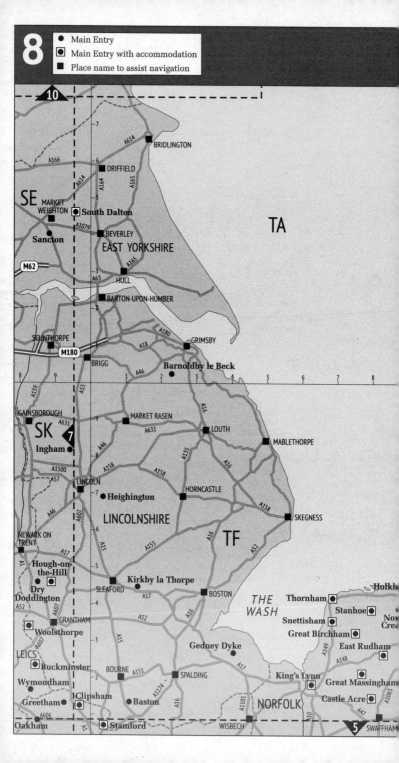

8

- ● Main Entry
- ◉ Main Entry with accommodation
- ■ Place name to assist navigation

10

BRIDLINGTON

DRIFFIELD

SE

MARKET WEIGHTON

◉ South Dalton

BEVERLEY

EAST YORKSHIRE

Sancton

M62

HULL

BARTON-UPON-HUMBER

TA

SCUNTHORPE

M180

GRIMSBY

BRIGG

● Barnoldby le Beck

GAINSBOROUGH

SK

7

Ingham

MARKET RASEN

LOUTH

MABLETHORPE

LINCOLN

● Heighington

HORNCASTLE

SKEGNESS

LINCOLNSHIRE

TF

NEWARK ON TRENT

◉ Hough-on-the-Hill

Dry Doddington

● Kirkby la Thorpe

SLEAFORD

BOSTON

THE WASH

Thornham ◉

Holkh

Stanhoe ◉

Nor Crea

GRANTHAM

◉ Woolsthorpe

Snettisham ◉

Great Birchham ◉

East Rudham ◉

LEICS

◉ Buckminster

Wymondham

Gedney Dyke ●

BOURNE

SPALDING

King's Lynn ◉

Great Massingham

◉ Clipsham

● Baston

NORFOLK

Castle Acre ◉

Greetham ●

Oakham

◉ Stamford

WISBECH

5

SWAFFHAM

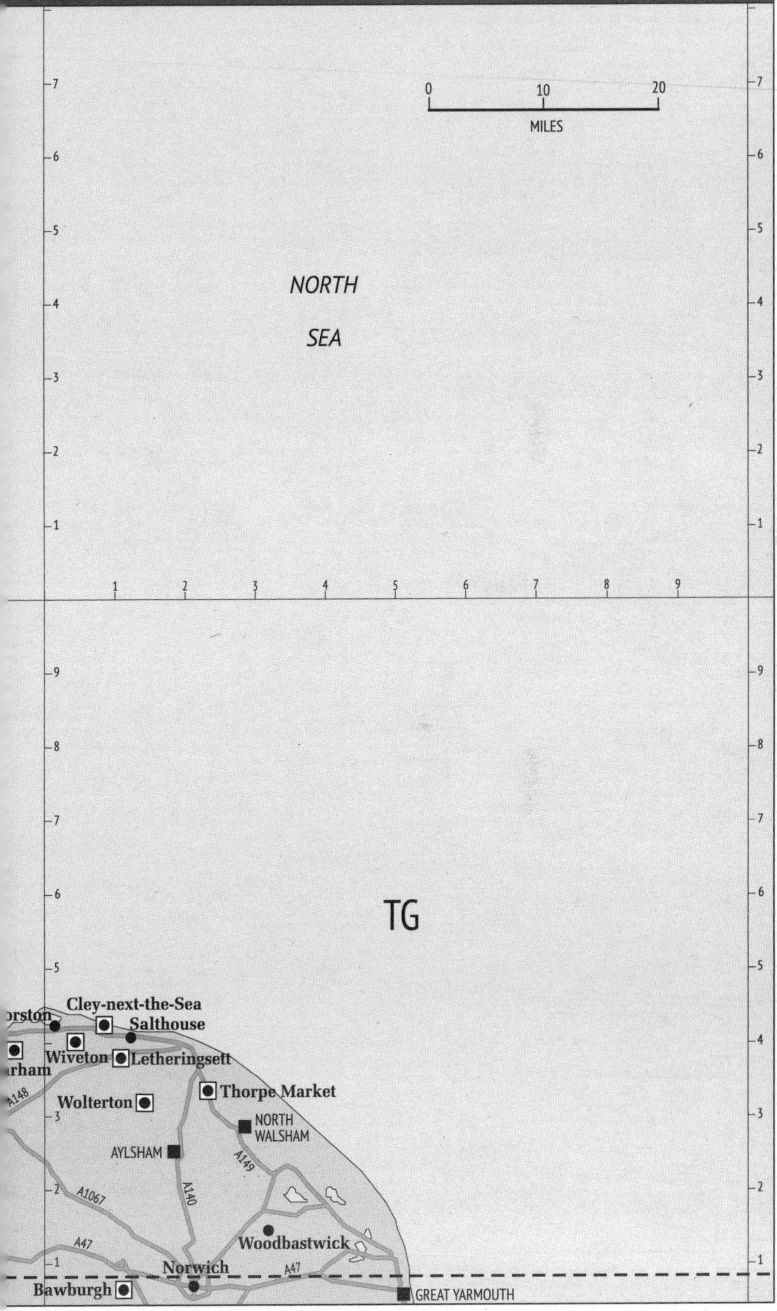

0   10   20

MILES

NORTH

SEA

TG

orston

Cley-next-the-Sea

Salthouse

Wiveton **Letheringsett**

rham

Wolterton   **Thorpe Market**

A148

NORTH
WALSHAM

AYLSHAM

A149

A1067

A140

A47

Woodbastwick

Bawburgh

Norwich   A47

GREAT YARMOUTH

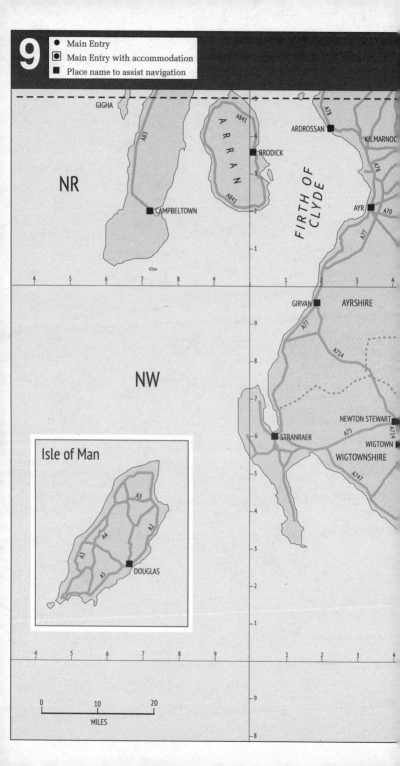

● Main Entry
◉ Main Entry with accommodation
■ Place name to assist navigation

GIGHA

A841

ARRAN

A83

A841

A841

BRODICK

ARDROSSAN

A78

KILMARNOC

NR

FIRTH OF CLYDE

CAMPBELTOWN

AYR

A70

A77

A78

GIRVAN

AYRSHIRE

A77

A714

NW

NEWTON STEWART

A714

A75

STRANRAER

WIGTOWN

Isle of Man

WIGTOWNSHIRE

A747

A3

A4

A2

A3

A5

DOUGLAS

0   10   20
MILES

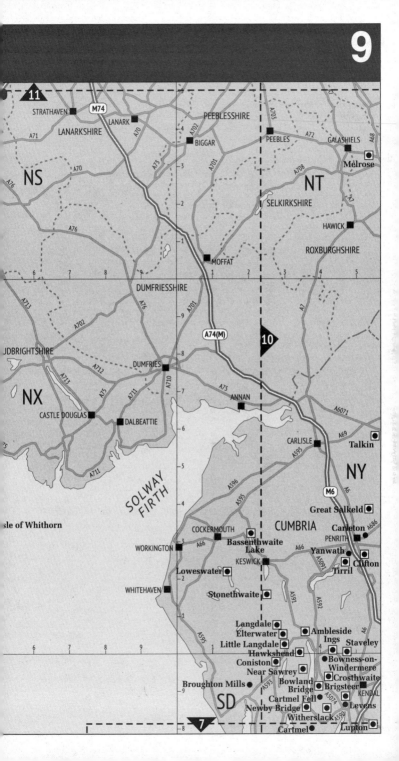

11

STRATHAVEN
M74
LANARK
A71
LANARKSHIRE
A70
A70
A76
NS
A76

PEEBLESSHIRE
A703
A702
BIGGAR
A701
PEEBLES
A72
GALASHIELS
A68
Melrose
A708
NT
SELKIRKSHIRE
A7
MOFFAT
1
2
HAWICK
3
4
5
ROXBURGHSHIRE

6
7
8
9

DUMFRIESSHIRE
A701
9
A7
A113
A702
A76
A76
A74(M)
10
JDBRIGHTSHIRE
8
DUMFRIES
A710
A75
A711
A712
A75
ANNAN
A6071
NX
CASTLE DOUGLAS
DALBEATTIE
7
6
A711
A596
CARLISLE
A595
A69
Talkin
NY
5
M6
A6
SOLWAY
FIRTH
Great Salkeld
sle of Whithorn
COCKERMOUTH
CUMBRIA
Carleton
A686
PENRITH
WORKINGTON
3
A66
Bassenthwaite
Lake
A66
Yanwath
A6091
Clifton
KESWICK
Tirril
Loweswater
2
WHITEHAVEN
Stonethwaite
1
A591
A592
A595
Langdale
Elterwater
Ambleside
Little Langdale
Ings
Staveley
A6
Hawkshead
4
Coniston
Bowness-on-
Near Sawrey
Windermere
A593
Bowland
Crosthwaite
Broughton Mills
Bridge
Brigsteer
Cartmel Fell
A5074
KENDAL
9
SD
Newby Bridge
Levens
Witherslack
A590
Cartmel
Lupton
8
7

6
7
8
9

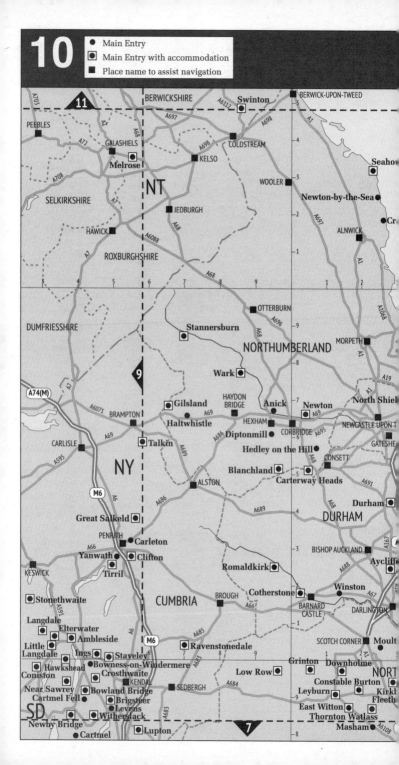

- ● Main Entry
- ◉ Main Entry with accommodation
- ■ Place name to assist navigation

▲ 11

BERWICKSHIRE

Swinton

BERWICK-UPON-TWEED

A6112

A705

PEEBLES

A72

A3

A697

A698

COLDSTREAM

A1

GALASHIELS

A68

A698

KELSO

◉ Melrose

WOOLER

Seaho◉

SELKIRKSHIRE

A708

A7

A7

NT

JEDBURGH

Newton-by-the-Sea ●

A697

Cr●

HAWICK ■

A6088

A68

ROXBURGHSHIRE

ALNWICK ◉

A1

A68

DUMFRIESSHIRE

OTTERBURN ■

A1068

Stannersburn ◉

A696

A68

NORTHUMBERLAND

MORPETH

A74(M)

9

Wark ◉

A1

A6071

BRAMPTON ■

Gilsland ◉

HAYDON BRIDGE

Anick ◉ Newton ◉

North Shiel●

A69

Haltwhistle ●

A69

CARLISLE ■

A69

Talkin ◉

HEXHAM ■

Diptonmill ●

CORBRIDGE

A695

NEWCASTLE UPON T

A595

A6

NY

A689

A686

Hedley on the Hill ●

A68

CONSETT ■

GATESHE

ALSTON ■

Blanchland ◉

Carterway Heads ◉

A691

A689

Great Salkeld ◉

A686

DURHAM

Durham ◉

PENRITH

Carleton ●

A66

BISHOP AUCKLAND ■

A167

Yanwath ●

Clifton ◉

Romaldkirk ◉

A688

Aycliff●

KESWICK

Tirril ◉

◉ Stonethwaite

A591

CUMBRIA

BROUGH

Cotherstone ◉

Winston ●

A67

DARLINGTON

Langdale ◉

A6

BARNARD CASTLE

Elterwater ◉ Ambleside ◉

A685

Ravenstonedale ◉

A683

SCOTCH CORNER

Moult●

Little Langdale ◉

Ings ◉ Staveley ◉

M6

Grinton ◉ Downholme ◉

NORT

Hawkshead ◉ Bowness-on-Windermere ●

Low Row ●

Coniston ◉ Crosthwaite ◉

Constable Burton ◉

Near Sawrey ◉ KENDAL ■ Bowland Bridge ◉

A684

SEDBERGH ■

Leyburn ◉

Kirkl●

Fleeth●

Cartmel Fell ◉ Brigsteer ◉

A683

East Witton ◉

SD

Levens ◉

Thornton Watlass●

Newby Bridge ● Witherslack ◉

Masham ●

A6108

Cartmel ● ◉ Lupton

▼ 7

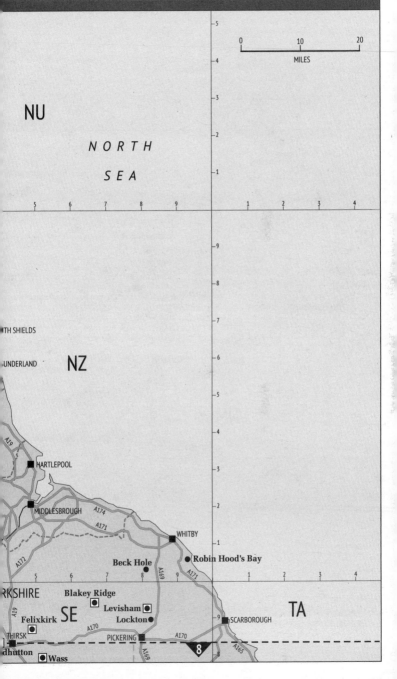

NU

N O R T H

S E A

0   10   20

MILES

TH SHIELDS

UNDERLAND

NZ

■ HARTLEPOOL

A19

■ MIDDLESBROUGH   A174

A171

A172

■ WHITBY

Beck Hole ●   ● Robin Hood's Bay

A169   A171

RKSHIRE   Blakey Ridge

A19   SE   ◉ Levisham ◉

Felixkirk ◉   Lockton ●

THIRSK ■   A170   ◉ SCARBOROUGH

dhutton   PICKERING ■   A170   TA

◉ Wass   A169   A165

◆ **8**

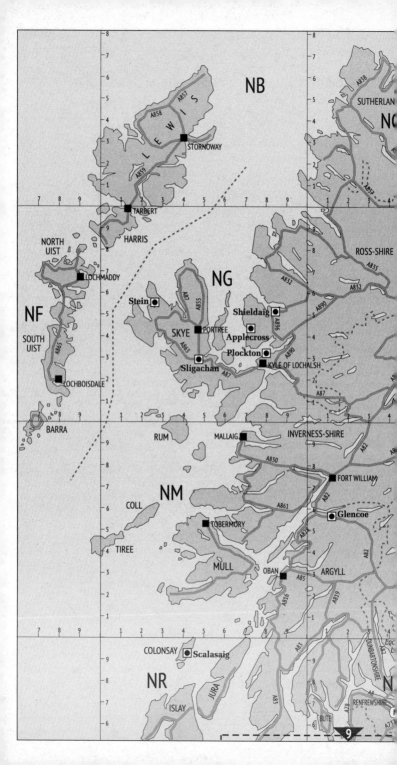

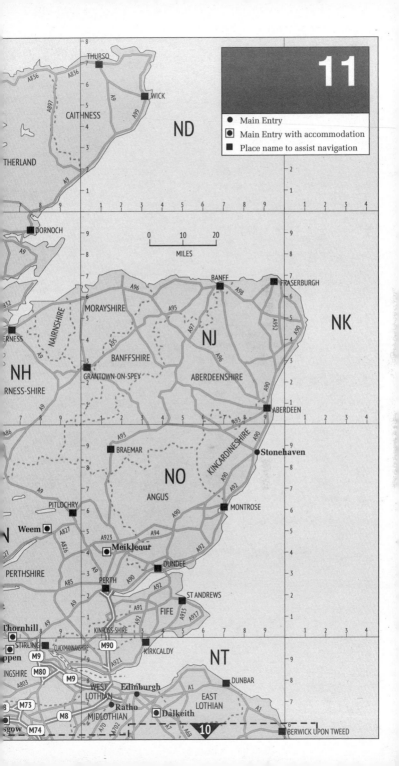

- Main Entry
- Main Entry with accommodation
- Place name to assist navigation

THURSO

WICK

CAITHNESS

ND

A836 A836

A897 A9 A9

THERLAND

DORNOCH

0   10   20
MILES

NAIRNSHIRE

MORAYSHIRE

BANFF

FRASERBURGH

A96

A95

A98

A952

A90

NJ

NK

852

A95

A97

A96

RNESS

A95

BANFFSHIRE

NH

ABERDEENSHIRE

RNESS-SHIRE

GRANTOWN-ON-SPEY

A90

A86

A93

A93

ABERDEEN

A9

A9

BRAEMAR

Stonehaven

KINCARDINESHIRE

NO

A90

A92

A9

ANGUS

PITLOCHRY

MONTROSE

Weem

A827

A826

A923

A94

A92

Meikleour

A9

DUNDEE

PERTHSHIRE

A85

PERTH

A90

A92

ST ANDREWS

A9

FIFE

A915

A917

A91

KINROSS-SHIRE

Thornhill

A9

STIRLING

CLACKMANNANSHIRE

M90

ppen

M9

KIRKCALDY

NT

INGSHIRE

M80

A971

M9

A803

WEST

DUNBAR

M73

M8

LOTHIAN

Edinburgh

A1

EAST

LOTHIAN

Ratho

Dalkeith

A1

gow

M74

MIDLOTHIAN

A68

A7

10

BERWICK UPON TWEED

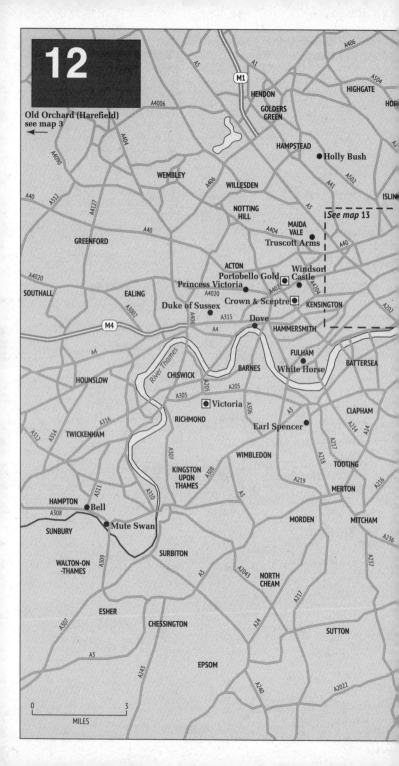

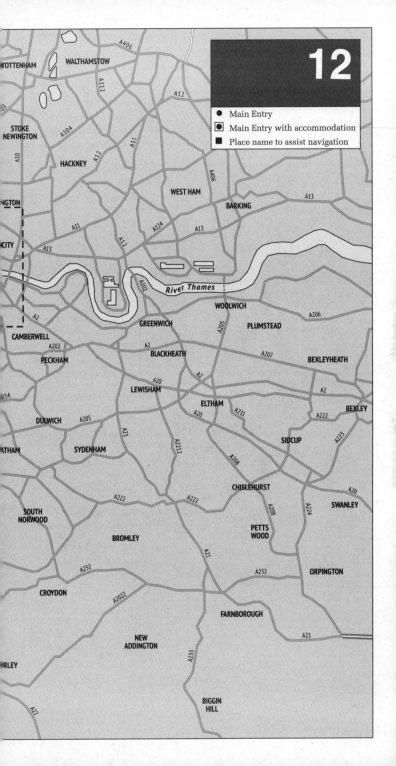

12

- ● Main Entry
- ◉ Main Entry with accommodation
- ■ Place name to assist navigation

TOTTENHAM
WALTHAMSTOW
A406
A112
A12

STOKE
NEWINGTON
A104
A11
A12
A11
HACKNEY
A12

A406

WEST HAM
A13

BARKING
A13

NGTON
A11
A124
A13
CITY
A13
A12

River Thames
A102

WOOLWICH
A2
A206
CAMBERWELL
A202
GREENWICH
A205
PLUMSTEAD

PECKHAM
A2
BLACKHEATH
A207
BEXLEYHEATH

214
A20
LEWISHAM
A2
A2

DULWICH
A205
ELTHAM
A211
A222
BEXLEY
A21
A20
A223
THAM
SYDENHAM
A212
SIDCUP
A208

CHISLEHURST
A20
SOUTH
NORWOOD
A222
A222
A208
SWANLEY
PETTS
WOOD
A224
BROMLEY
A21

A232
A232
ORPINGTON
CROYDON
A2022

FARNBOROUGH

NEW
ADDINGTON
A233
A21

RLEY

A22

BIGGIN
HILL

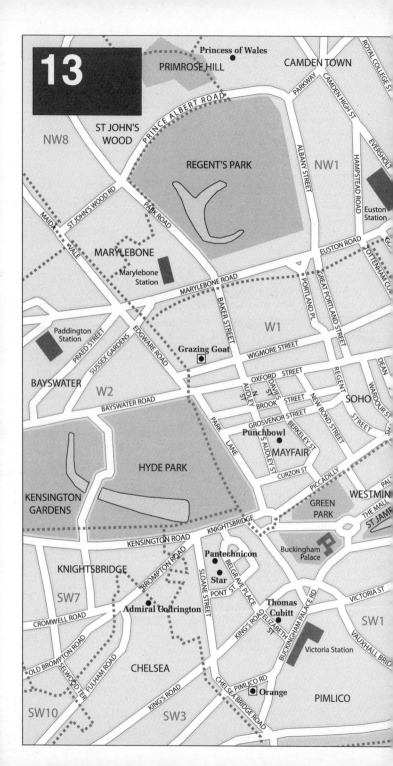

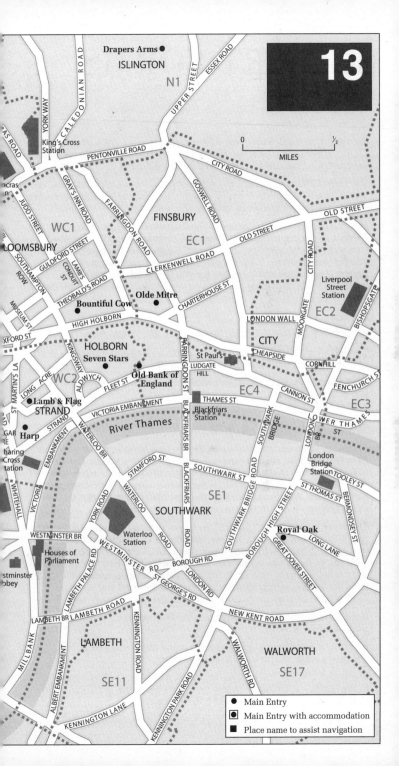

13

ISLINGTON
Drapers Arms ●
N1

King's Cross Station

PENTONVILLE ROAD

CITY ROAD

FINSBURY
EC1

OLD STREET
OLD STREET

Liverpool Street Station
EC2

WC1

BLOOMSBURY

Olde Mitre ●
Bountiful Cow ●

CHARTERHOUSE ST

LONDON WALL

CITY

CHEAPSIDE

CORNHILL

HIGH HOLBORN

HOLBORN
Seven Stars ●

St Paul's
LUDGATE HILL

EC4

FENCHURCH ST

EC3

WC2

Old Bank of England ●

FLEET ST

CANNON ST

LOWER THAMES ST

Lamb & Flag ●
STRAND

VICTORIA EMBANKMENT

THAMES ST
Blackfriars Station

LONDON BR

Harp ●

River Thames

London Bridge Station

TOOLEY ST

Charing Cross Station

STAMFORD ST

SOUTHWARK ST

ST THOMAS ST

SE1

SOUTHWARK

WESTMINSTER BR

Waterloo Station

Royal Oak ●

Houses of Parliament

WESTMINSTER RD

BOROUGH RD

LONG LANE

Westminster Abbey

LAMBETH BR LAMBETH ROAD

ST GEORGE'S RD

NEW KENT ROAD

LAMBETH

WALWORTH
SE17

SE11

KENNINGTON LANE

● Main Entry
◉ Main Entry with accommodation
■ Place name to assist navigation

0 — ½ MILES

REPORT FORMS

We would very much appreciate hearing about your visits to pubs in this *Guide*, whether you have found them as described and recommend them for continued inclusion or noticed a fall in standards.

We'd also be glad to hear of any new pubs that you think we should know about. Readers' reports are very valuable to us, and sometimes pubs are dropped simply because we have had no up-to-date news on them.

You can use the tear-out forms on the following pages, email us at feedback@goodguides.co.uk or send us comments via our website (www.thegoodpubguide.co.uk) or app. We include two types of forms: one for you to simply list pubs you have visited and confirm that our review is accurate, and the other for you to give us more detailed information on individual pubs. If you would like more forms, please write to us at:

The Good Pub Guide

FREEPOST RTJR-ZCYZ-RJZT, Perrymans Lane, Etchingham TN19 7DN

Though we try to answer all letters, please understand if there's a delay (particularly in summer, our busiest period).

We'll assume we can print your name or initials as a recommender unless you tell us otherwise.

MAIN ENTRY OR 'ALSO WORTH A VISIT'?

Please try to gauge whether a pub should be a Main Entry or go in the Also Worth a Visit section (and tick the relevant box). Main Entries need to have qualities that would make it worth other readers' while to travel some distance to them. If a pub is an entirely new recommendation, the Also Worth a Visit section may be the best place for it to start its career in the *Guide* – to encourage other readers to report on it.

The more detail you can put into your description of a pub, the better. Any information on how good the landlord or landlady is, what it looks like inside, what you like about the atmosphere and character, the quality and type of food, which real ales are available and whether they're well kept, whether bedrooms are available, and how big/attractive the garden is. Other helpful information includes prices for food and bedrooms, food service and opening hours, and if children or dogs are welcome.

If the food or accommodation is outstanding, tick the FOOD AWARD or the STAY AWARD box.

If you're in a position to gauge a pub's suitability or otherwise for disabled people, do please tell us about that.

If you can, give the full address or directions for any pub not currently in the *Guide* – most of all, please give us its postcode. If we can't find a pub's postcode, we don't include it in the *Guide*.

I have been to the following pubs in *The Good Pub Guide 2016* in the last few months, found them as described, and confirm that they deserve continued inclusion:

continued overleaf

PLEASE GIVE YOUR NAME AND ADDRESS ON THE BACK OF THIS FORM

Pubs visited continued..........

Your own name and address *(block capitals please)*

....

....

....

Postcode...

Please return to

The Good Pub Guide
FREEPOST RTJR-ZCYZ-RJZT,
Perrymans Lane,
Etchingham
TN19 7DN

IF YOU PREFER, YOU CAN SEND
US REPORTS BY EMAIL:

feedback@goodguides.com

I have been to the following pubs in *The Good Pub Guide 2016* in the last few months, found them as described, and confirm that they deserve continued inclusion:

continued overleaf

PLEASE GIVE YOUR NAME AND ADDRESS ON THE BACK OF THIS FORM

Pubs visited continued..........

Your own name and address *(block capitals please)*

....

....

....

Postcode...

Please return to

The Good Pub Guide
FREEPOST RTJR-ZCYZ-RJZT,
Perrymans Lane,
Etchingham
TN19 7DN

IF YOU PREFER, YOU CAN SEND
US REPORTS BY EMAIL:

feedback@goodguides.com

I have been to the following pubs in *The Good Pub Guide 2016* in the last few months, found them as described, and confirm that they deserve continued inclusion:

continued overleaf

Pubs visited continued..........

Your own name and address *(block capitals please)*

....

....

....

Postcode...

Please return to

The Good Pub Guide
FREEPOST RTJR-ZCYZ-RJZT,
Perrymans Lane,
Etchingham
TN19 7DN

IF YOU PREFER, YOU CAN SEND
US REPORTS BY EMAIL:

feedback@goodguides.com

I have been to the following pubs in *The Good Pub Guide 2016* in the last few months, found them as described, and confirm that they deserve continued inclusion:

continued overleaf

PLEASE GIVE YOUR NAME AND ADDRESS ON THE BACK OF THIS FORM

Pubs visited continued..........

Your own name and address *(block capitals please)*

....

....

....

Postcode..

Please return to

The Good Pub Guide
FREEPOST RTJR-ZCYZ-RJZT,
Perrymans Lane,
Etchingham
TN19 7DN

IF YOU PREFER, YOU CAN SEND
US REPORTS BY EMAIL:

feedback@goodguides.com

I have been to the following pubs in *The Good Pub Guide 2016* in the last few months, found them as described, and confirm that they deserve continued inclusion:

continued overleaf

Pubs visited continued..........

Your own name and address *(block capitals please)*

....

....

....

Postcode...

Please return to

The Good Pub Guide
FREEPOST RTJR-ZCYZ-RJZT,
Perrymans Lane,
Etchingham
TN19 7DN

IF YOU PREFER, YOU CAN SEND
US REPORTS BY EMAIL:

feedback@goodguides.com

I have been to the following pubs in *The Good Pub Guide 2016* in the last few months, found them as described, and confirm that they deserve continued inclusion:

continued overleaf

PLEASE GIVE YOUR NAME AND ADDRESS ON THE BACK OF THIS FORM

Pubs visited continued..........

Your own name and address *(block capitals please)*

....

....

....

Postcode..

Please return to

The Good Pub Guide
FREEPOST RTJR-ZCYZ-RJZT,
Perrymans Lane,
Etchingham
TN19 7DN

IF YOU PREFER, YOU CAN SEND
US REPORTS BY EMAIL:

feedback@goodguides.com

I have been to the following pubs in *The Good Pub Guide 2016* in the last few months, found them as described, and confirm that they deserve continued inclusion:

continued overleaf

PLEASE GIVE YOUR NAME AND ADDRESS ON THE BACK OF THIS FORM

Pubs visited continued..........

Your own name and address *(block capitals please)*

....

....

....

Postcode..

Please return to

The Good Pub Guide
FREEPOST RTJR-ZCYZ-RJZT,
Perrymans Lane,
Etchingham
TN19 7DN

IF YOU PREFER, YOU CAN SEND
US REPORTS BY EMAIL:

feedback@goodguides.com

I have been to the following pubs in *The Good Pub Guide 2016* in the last few months, found them as described, and confirm that they deserve continued inclusion:

continued overleaf

PLEASE GIVE YOUR NAME AND ADDRESS ON THE BACK OF THIS FORM

Pubs visited continued..........

Your own name and address *(block capitals please)*

....

....

....

Postcode..

Please return to

The Good Pub Guide
FREEPOST RTJR-ZCYZ-RJZT,
Perrymans Lane,
Etchingham
TN19 7DN

IF YOU PREFER, YOU CAN SEND
US REPORTS BY EMAIL:

feedback@goodguides.com

I have been to the following pubs in *The Good Pub Guide 2016* in the last few months, found them as described, and confirm that they deserve continued inclusion:

continued overleaf

PLEASE GIVE YOUR NAME AND ADDRESS ON THE BACK OF THIS FORM

Pubs visited continued..........

Your own name and address *(block capitals please)*

....

....

....

Postcode...

Please return to

The Good Pub Guide
FREEPOST RTJR-ZCYZ-RJZT,
Perrymans Lane,
Etchingham
TN19 7DN

IF YOU PREFER, YOU CAN SEND
US REPORTS BY EMAIL:

feedback@goodguides.com

Report on (pub's name)

....

Pub's address

....

☐ YES MAIN ENTRY ☐ YES WORTH A VISIT ☐ NO don't include

Please tick one of these boxes to show your verdict, and give reasons, descriptive comments, prices and the date of your visit

☐ Deserves **FOOD Award** ☐ Deserves **STAY Award** 2016: 1

PLEASE GIVE YOUR NAME AND ADDRESS ON THE BACK OF THIS FORM

✂ ....

Report on (pub's name)

....

Pub's address

....

☐ YES MAIN ENTRY ☐ YES WORTH A VISIT ☐ NO don't include

Please tick one of these boxes to show your verdict, and give reasons, descriptive comments, prices and the date of your visit

☐ Deserves **FOOD Award** ☐ Deserves **STAY Award** 2016: 2

PLEASE GIVE YOUR NAME AND ADDRESS ON THE BACK OF THIS FORM

Your own name and address *(block capitals please)*

In returning this form I confirm my agreement that the information I provide may be used by The Random House Group Ltd, its assignees and/or licensees in any media or medium whatsoever.

DO NOT USE THIS SIDE OF THE PAGE FOR WRITING ABOUT PUBS

✂ ....

Your own name and address *(block capitals please)*

In returning this form I confirm my agreement that the information I provide may be used by The Random House Group Ltd, its assignees and/or licensees in any media or medium whatsoever.

DO NOT USE THIS SIDE OF THE PAGE FOR WRITING ABOUT PUBS

By returning this form, you consent to the collection, recording and use of the information you submit, by The Random House Group Ltd. Any personal details which you provide from which we can identify you are held and processed in accordance with the Data Protection Act 1998 and will not be passed on to any third parties. The Random House Group Ltd may wish to send you further information on their associated products. Please tick box if you do not wish to receive any such information.

Report on   (pub's name)

....

Pub's address

....

☐ YES MAIN ENTRY   ☐ YES WORTH A VISIT   ☐ NO don't include

Please tick one of these boxes to show your verdict, and give reasons,
descriptive comments, prices and the date of your visit

☐ Deserves **FOOD Award**   ☐ Deserves **STAY Award**   2016: 3

PLEASE GIVE YOUR NAME AND ADDRESS ON THE BACK OF THIS FORM

✂ ....

Report on   (pub's name)

....

Pub's address

....

☐ YES MAIN ENTRY   ☐ YES WORTH A VISIT   ☐ NO don't include

Please tick one of these boxes to show your verdict, and give reasons,
descriptive comments, prices and the date of your visit

☐ Deserves **FOOD Award**   ☐ Deserves **STAY Award**   2016: 4

PLEASE GIVE YOUR NAME AND ADDRESS ON THE BACK OF THIS FORM

Your own name and address *(block capitals please)*

In returning this form I confirm my agreement that the information I provide may be used by The Random House Group Ltd, its assignees and/or licensees in any media or medium whatsoever.

DO NOT USE THIS SIDE OF THE PAGE FOR WRITING ABOUT PUBS

By returning this form, you consent to the collection, recording and use of the information you submit, by The Random House Group Ltd. Any personal details which you provide from which we can identify you are held and processed in accordance with the Data Protection Act 1998 and will not be passed on to any third parties. The Random House Group Ltd may wish to send you further information on their associated products. Please tick box if you do not wish to receive any such information. ☐

✂ ....

Your own name and address *(block capitals please)*

In returning this form I confirm my agreement that the information I provide may be used by The Random House Group Ltd, its assignees and/or licensees in any media or medium whatsoever.

DO NOT USE THIS SIDE OF THE PAGE FOR WRITING ABOUT PUBS

By returning this form, you consent to the collection, recording and use of the information you submit, by The Random House Group Ltd. Any personal details which you provide from which we can identify you are held and processed in accordance with the Data Protection Act 1998 and will not be passed on to any third parties. The Random House Group Ltd may wish to send you further information on their associated products. Please tick box if you do not wish to receive any such information. ☐

Report on (pub's name)

....

Pub's address

....

☐ YES MAIN ENTRY ☐ YES WORTH A VISIT ☐ NO don't include

Please tick one of these boxes to show your verdict, and give reasons, descriptive comments, prices and the date of your visit

☐ Deserves **FOOD Award** ☐ Deserves **STAY Award** 2016: 5

PLEASE GIVE YOUR NAME AND ADDRESS ON THE BACK OF THIS FORM

✂ ....

Report on (pub's name)

....

Pub's address

....

☐ YES MAIN ENTRY ☐ YES WORTH A VISIT ☐ NO don't include

Please tick one of these boxes to show your verdict, and give reasons, descriptive comments, prices and the date of your visit

☐ Deserves **FOOD Award** ☐ Deserves **STAY Award** 2016: 6

PLEASE GIVE YOUR NAME AND ADDRESS ON THE BACK OF THIS FORM

Your own name and address *(block capitals please)*

In returning this form I confirm my agreement that the information I provide may be used by The Random House Group Ltd, its assignees and/or licensees in any media or medium whatsoever.

DO NOT USE THIS SIDE OF THE PAGE FOR WRITING ABOUT PUBS

✂ ....

Your own name and address *(block capitals please)*

In returning this form I confirm my agreement that the information I provide may be used by The Random House Group Ltd, its assignees and/or licensees in any media or medium whatsoever.

DO NOT USE THIS SIDE OF THE PAGE FOR WRITING ABOUT PUBS

Report on (pub's name)

....

Pub's address

....

☐ YES MAIN ENTRY ☐ YES WORTH A VISIT ☐ NO don't include

Please tick one of these boxes to show your verdict, and give reasons,
descriptive comments, prices and the date of your visit

☐ Deserves **FOOD Award** ☐ Deserves **STAY Award** 2016: 7
PLEASE GIVE YOUR NAME AND ADDRESS ON THE BACK OF THIS FORM

✂ ....

Report on (pub's name)

....

Pub's address

....

☐ YES MAIN ENTRY ☐ YES WORTH A VISIT ☐ NO don't include

Please tick one of these boxes to show your verdict, and give reasons,
descriptive comments, prices and the date of your visit

☐ Deserves **FOOD Award** ☐ Deserves **STAY Award** 2016: 8
PLEASE GIVE YOUR NAME AND ADDRESS ON THE BACK OF THIS FORM

Your own name and address *(block capitals please)*

In returning this form I confirm my agreement that the information I provide may be used by The Random House Group Ltd, its assignees and/or licensees in any media or medium whatsoever.

DO NOT USE THIS SIDE OF THE PAGE FOR WRITING ABOUT PUBS

✂ ....

Your own name and address *(block capitals please)*

In returning this form I confirm my agreement that the information I provide may be used by The Random House Group Ltd, its assignees and/or licensees in any media or medium whatsoever.

DO NOT USE THIS SIDE OF THE PAGE FOR WRITING ABOUT PUBS

By returning this form, you consent to the collection, recording and use of the information you submit, by The Random House Group Ltd. Any personal details which you provide from which we can identify you are held and processed in accordance with the Data Protection Act 1998 and will not be passed on to any third parties. The Random House Group Ltd may wish to send you further information on their associated products. Please tick box if you do not wish to receive any such information.

Report on (pub's name)

....

Pub's address

....

☐ YES MAIN ENTRY ☐ YES WORTH A VISIT ☐ NO don't include

Please tick one of these boxes to show your verdict, and give reasons,
descriptive comments, prices and the date of your visit

☐ Deserves **FOOD Award** ☐ Deserves **STAY Award** 2016: 9

PLEASE GIVE YOUR NAME AND ADDRESS ON THE BACK OF THIS FORM

✂ ....

Report on (pub's name)

....

Pub's address

....

☐ YES MAIN ENTRY ☐ YES WORTH A VISIT ☐ NO don't include

Please tick one of these boxes to show your verdict, and give reasons,
descriptive comments, prices and the date of your visit

☐ Deserves **FOOD Award** ☐ Deserves **STAY Award** 2016: 10

PLEASE GIVE YOUR NAME AND ADDRESS ON THE BACK OF THIS FORM

Your own name and address *(block capitals please)*

In returning this form I confirm my agreement that the information I provide may be used by The Random House Group Ltd, its assignees and/or licensees in any media or medium whatsoever.

DO NOT USE THIS SIDE OF THE PAGE FOR WRITING ABOUT PUBS

✂ . . . .

Your own name and address *(block capitals please)*

In returning this form I confirm my agreement that the information I provide may be used by The Random House Group Ltd, its assignees and/or licensees in any media or medium whatsoever.

DO NOT USE THIS SIDE OF THE PAGE FOR WRITING ABOUT PUBS

Report on (pub's name)

....

Pub's address

....

☐ YES MAIN ENTRY   ☐ YES WORTH A VISIT   ☐ NO don't include

Please tick one of these boxes to show your verdict, and give reasons, descriptive comments, prices and the date of your visit

☐ Deserves **FOOD Award**   ☐ Deserves **STAY Award**   2016: 11

PLEASE GIVE YOUR NAME AND ADDRESS ON THE BACK OF THIS FORM

✂ ....

Report on (pub's name)

....

Pub's address

....

☐ YES MAIN ENTRY   ☐ YES WORTH A VISIT   ☐ NO don't include

Please tick one of these boxes to show your verdict, and give reasons, descriptive comments, prices and the date of your visit

☐ Deserves **FOOD Award**   ☐ Deserves **STAY Award**   2016: 12

PLEASE GIVE YOUR NAME AND ADDRESS ON THE BACK OF THIS FORM

Your own name and address *(block capitals please)*

In returning this form I confirm my agreement that the information I provide may be used by The Random House Group Ltd, its assignees and/or licensees in any media or medium whatsoever.

DO NOT USE THIS SIDE OF THE PAGE FOR WRITING ABOUT PUBS

By returning this form, you consent to the collection, recording and use of the information you submit, by The Random House Group Ltd. Any personal details which you provide from which we can identify you are held and processed in accordance with the Data Protection Act 1998 and will not be passed on to any third parties. The Random House Group Ltd may wish to send you further information on their associated products. Please tick box if you do not wish to receive any such information.

✂ ....

Your own name and address *(block capitals please)*

In returning this form I confirm my agreement that the information I provide may be used by The Random House Group Ltd, its assignees and/or licensees in any media or medium whatsoever.

DO NOT USE THIS SIDE OF THE PAGE FOR WRITING ABOUT PUBS

By returning this form, you consent to the collection, recording and use of the information you submit, by The Random House Group Ltd. Any personal details which you provide from which we can identify you are held and processed in accordance with the Data Protection Act 1998 and will not be passed on to any third parties. The Random House Group Ltd may wish to send you further information on their associated products. Please tick box if you do not wish to receive any such information.

Report on (pub's name)

....

Pub's address

....

☐ YES MAIN ENTRY ☐ YES WORTH A VISIT ☐ NO don't include

Please tick one of these boxes to show your verdict, and give reasons, descriptive comments, prices and the date of your visit

☐ Deserves **FOOD Award** ☐ Deserves **STAY Award** 2016: 13

PLEASE GIVE YOUR NAME AND ADDRESS ON THE BACK OF THIS FORM

✂ ....

Report on (pub's name)

....

Pub's address

....

☐ YES MAIN ENTRY ☐ YES WORTH A VISIT ☐ NO don't include

Please tick one of these boxes to show your verdict, and give reasons, descriptive comments, prices and the date of your visit

☐ Deserves **FOOD Award** ☐ Deserves **STAY Award** 2016: 14

PLEASE GIVE YOUR NAME AND ADDRESS ON THE BACK OF THIS FORM

Your own name and address *(block capitals please)*

In returning this form I confirm my agreement that the information I provide may be used by The Random House Group Ltd, its assignees and/or licensees in any media or medium whatsoever.

DO NOT USE THIS SIDE OF THE PAGE FOR WRITING ABOUT PUBS

✂ ....

Your own name and address *(block capitals please)*

In returning this form I confirm my agreement that the information I provide may be used by The Random House Group Ltd, its assignees and/or licensees in any media or medium whatsoever.

DO NOT USE THIS SIDE OF THE PAGE FOR WRITING ABOUT PUBS